TITLE 33—NAVIGATION AND NAVIGABLE WATERS

CHAPTER 1—NAVIGABLE WATERS GENERALLY

SUBCHAPTER I—GENERAL PROVISIONS

SUBCHAPTER II—WATERS DECLARED NONNAVIGABLE: CHANGE OF NAME

SUBCHAPTER I—GENERAL PROVISIONS

§1. Regulations by Secretary of the Army for navigation of waters generally

It shall be the duty of the Secretary of the Army to prescribe such regulations for the use, administration, and navigation of the navigable waters of the United States as in his judgment the public necessity may require for the protection of life and property, or of operations of the United States in channel improvement, covering all matters not specifically delegated by law to some other executive department. Such regulations shall be posted, in conspicuous and appropriate places, for the information of the public; and every person and every corporation which shall violate such regulations shall be deemed guilty of a misdemeanor and, on conviction thereof in any district court of the United States within whose territorial jurisdiction such offense may have been committed, shall be punished by a fine not exceeding $500, or by imprisonment (in the case of a natural person) not exceeding six months, in the discretion of the court.

Any regulations prescribed by the Secretary of the Army in pursuance of this section may be enforced as provided in section 413 of this title, the provisions whereof are made applicable to the said regulations.

(Aug. 18, 1894, ch. 299, §4, 28 Stat. 362; June 13, 1902, ch. 1079, §§6, 11, 32 Stat. 374; Aug. 8, 1917, ch. 49, §7, 40 Stat. 266; July 26, 1947, ch. 343, title II, §205(a), 61 Stat. 501.)

CODIFICATION

The first paragraph of this section is from section 4 of act Aug. 18, 1894, popularly known as the "River and Harbor Act of 1894", as amended.

As originally enacted, said section 4 made it the duty of the Secretary of War to prescribe rules and regulations for the use, administration, and navigation of any or all canals and similar works of navigation owned, operated, or maintained by the United States, and provided for the posting of such regulations and the punishment of violations thereof.

Said section 4 was amended by section 11 of act June 13, 1902, principally by adding to the original section provisions authorizing the Secretary also to prescribe regulations to govern the speed and movement of vessels and other water craft in any public navigable channel which had been improved under authority of Congress, whenever in his judgment such regulations were necessary to protect such improved channel from injury or to prevent interference with the operations of the United States in improving navigable waters or injury to any plant that might be employed in such operations.

Section 4 was also amended by section 7 of act Aug. 8, 1917, to read as set forth in the first paragraph hereof.

The last paragraph of this section is from section 6 of act June 13, 1902. Said section 6 is also the source of the last proviso in section 499 of this title.

CHANGE OF NAME

Department of War designated Department of the Army and title of Secretary of War changed to Secretary of the Army by section 205(a) of act July 26, 1947, ch. 343, title II, 61 Stat. 501. Section 205(a) of act July 26, 1947, was repealed by section 53 of act Aug. 10, 1956, ch. 1041, 70A Stat. 641. Section 1 of act Aug. 10, 1956, enacted "Title 10, Armed Forces" which in sections 3010 to 3013 continued Department of the Army under administrative supervision of Secretary of the Army.

RULES AND REGULATIONS

Administrative provisions covering definitions which the Coast Guard uses to examine waters to determine whether the Coast Guard has jurisdiction on those waters under particular laws of the United States are set out in chapter I, subchapter A, part 2, of Title 33, Navigation and Navigable Waters, in the Code of Federal Regulations. Such part 2, consisting of sections 2.01–1 to 2.10–10, sets out definitions of jurisdictional terms and provides for the availability of jurisdictional decisions.

§2. Regulations for navigation of South and Southwest Passes of Mississippi River; penalties

The Secretary of the Army is authorized to make such rules and regulations for the navigation of the South and Southwest Passes of the Mississippi River as to him shall seem necessary or expedient for the purpose of preventing any obstruction to the channels through said South and Southwest Passes and any injury to the works therein constructed. The term "South and Southwest Passes", as employed in this section, shall be construed as embracing the entire extent of channel in each case, between the upper ends of the works at the head of the pass and the outer or sea ends of the jetties at the entrance from the Gulf of Mexico; and any willful violation of any rule or regulation made by the Secretary of the Army in pursuance of this section shall be deemed a misdemeanor, for which the owner or owners, agent or agents, master or pilot of the vessel so offending shall be separately or collectively responsible, and on conviction thereof shall be punished by a fine of not less than $100, nor exceeding $500, or by imprisonment for not exceeding three months, or by both fine and imprisonment, at the discretion of the court.

(Mar. 3, 1909, ch. 264, §5, 35 Stat. 818; July 26, 1947, ch. 343, title II, §205(a), 61 Stat. 501.)

CODIFICATION

These provisions were part of section 5 of act Mar. 3, 1909, popularly known as the "River and Harbor Appropriation Act of 1909".

These provisions superseded previous similar provisions relating to the navigation of the South Pass only, contained in act Aug. 11, 1888, ch. 860, §5, 25 Stat. 424, amended by act Sept. 19, 1890, ch. 907, §3, 26 Stat. 452.

CHANGE OF NAME

Department of War designated Department of the Army and title of Secretary of War changed to Secretary of the Army by section 205(a) of act July 26, 1947, ch. 343, title II, 61 Stat. 501. Section 205(a) of act July 26, 1947, was repealed by section 53 of act Aug. 10, 1956, ch. 1041, 70A Stat. 641. Section 1 of act Aug. 10, 1956, enacted "Title 10, Armed Forces" which in sections 3010 to 3013 continued Department of the Army under administrative supervision of Secretary of the Army.

§3. Regulations to prevent injuries from target practice

Authority to adopt regulations—In the interest of the national defense, and for the better protection of life and property on the navigable waters of the United States, the Secretary of the Army is authorized and empowered to prescribe such regulations as he may deem best for the use and navigation of any portion or area of the navigable waters of the United States or waters under the jurisdiction of the United States endangered or likely to be endangered by Artillery fire in target practice or otherwise, or by the proving operations of the Government ordnance proving grounds at Sandy Hook, New Jersey, or at any Government ordnance proving ground that may be established elsewhere on or near such waters, and of any portion or area of said waters occupied by submarine mines, mine fields, submarine cables, or other material and accessories pertaining to seacoast fortifications, or by any plant or facility engaged in the execution of any public project of river and harbor improvement; and the said Secretary shall have like power to regulate the transportation of explosives upon any of said waters: *Provided*, That the authority conferred shall be so exercised as not unreasonably to interfere with or restrict the food fishing industry, and the regulations prescribed in pursuance hereof shall provide for the use of such waters by food fishermen operating under permits granted by the Department of the Army.

Detail of vessels to enforce regulations—To enforce the regulations prescribed pursuant to this section, the Secretary of the Army, may detail any public vessel in the service of the Department of the Army, or, upon the request of the Secretary of the Army, the head of any other department may enforce, and the head of any such department is authorized to enforce, such regulations by means of any public vessel of such department.

Posting and violation of regulations—The regulations made by the Secretary of the Army pursuant to this section shall be posted in conspicuous and appropriate places, designated by him, for the information of the public; and every person who and every corporation which shall willfully violate any regulations made by the said Secretary pursuant to this section shall be deemed guilty of a misdemeanor, and upon conviction thereof in any court of competent jurisdiction shall be punished by a fine not exceeding $500, or by imprisonment (in the case of a natural person) not exceeding six months, in the discretion of the court.

Venue and jurisdiction of offenses; procedure—Offenses against the provisions of this section, or any regulation made pursuant thereto, committed in any Territory or other place subject to the jurisdiction of the United States where there is no court having general jurisdiction of crimes against the United States, shall be cognizable in any court of such place or Territory having original jurisdiction of criminal cases in the place or Territory in which the offense has been committed, with the same right of appeal in all cases as is given in other criminal cases where imprisonment not exceeding six months forms a part of the penalty, and jurisdiction is conferred upon such courts and such courts shall exercise the same for such purposes; and in case any such offense be committed beyond the territorial jurisdiction of any court having jurisdiction thereof, the offense shall be deemed and held to have been committed within the jurisdiction in which the offender may be found or into which he is first brought, and shall be tried by the court having jurisdiction thereof.

(July 9, 1918, ch. 143, subch. XIX, §§1–4, 40 Stat. 892, 893; July 26, 1947, ch. 343, title II, §205(a), 61 Stat. 501.)

CODIFICATION

Undesignated pars. 1 to 4 of this section are from sections 1 to 4, respectively, of act July 9, 1918, popularly known as the "Army Appropriation Act of 1919".

Undesignated pars. 1 and 2 of this section superseded similar provisions of act Aug. 8, 1917, ch. 49, §8, 40 Stat. 266.

CHANGE OF NAME

Department of War designated Department of the Army and title of Secretary of War changed to Secretary of the Army by section 205(a) of act July 26, 1947, ch. 343, title II, 61 Stat. 501. Section 205(a) of act July 26, 1947, was repealed by section 53 of act Aug. 10, 1956, ch. 1041, 70A Stat. 641. Section 1 of act Aug. 10, 1956, enacted "Title 10, Armed Forces" which in sections 3010 to 3013 continued Department of the Army under administrative supervision of Secretary of the Army.

Coast Artillery changed to Artillery under authority of section 306(a) of act June 28, 1950, ch. 383, title III, 64 Stat. 269. Section 306(a) of act June 28, 1950 was repealed by section 53 of act Aug. 10, 1956, ch. 1041, 70A Stat. 641. Section 1 of act Aug. 10, 1956, enacted "Title 10, Armed Forces" which in section 3063 continued the Artillery as a basic branch of the Army.

TRANSFER OF FUNCTIONS

For transfer of certain functions insofar as they pertain to Air Force, and to extent that they were not previously transferred to Secretary of the Air Force and Department of the Air Force from Secretary of the Army and Department of the Army, see Secretary of Defense Transfer Order No. 40 [App. A(55)], July 22, 1949.

§4. Water gauges on Mississippi River and tributaries

The Secretary of the Army is authorized and directed to have water gauges established, and daily observations made of the rise and fall of the Mississippi River and its tributaries.

For the purpose of securing the uninterrupted gauging of the waters of the Mississippi River and its tributaries, as provided for in this section, upon the application of the Chief of Engineers, the Secretary of the Army is authorized to draw his warrant or requisition, from time to time, upon the Secretary of the Treasury for such sums as may be necessary to do such work, not to exceed in the aggregate for each year the sum of $9,600.

(R.S. §5252; Aug. 11, 1888, ch. 860, §6, 25 Stat. 424; June 13, 1902, ch. 1079, §9, 32 Stat. 374; July 26, 1947, ch. 343, title II, §205(a), 61 Stat. 501; Aug. 30, 1954, ch. 1076, §1(15), 68 Stat. 967.)

CODIFICATION

R.S. §5252 derived from Res. Feb. 21, 1871, No. 40, 16 Stat. 598.

The first paragraph of this section is from R.S. §5252, which, as enacted, authorized and directed the establishment of water gauges and the making of daily observations at or in the vicinity of certain enumerated places, and at such other places as the Secretary of War might deem advisable. It further provided that the expenditure should be made from the appropriation for the improvement of rivers and harbors and that the annual cost of the observations should not exceed $5,000. These latter provisions were apparently modified by section 6 of act Aug. 11, 1888, as amended by section 9 of act June 13, 1902, which was substantially the second paragraph of this section. As originally enacted, section 6 of act Aug. 11, 1888, provided for the gauging of the waters of the Lower Mississippi and tributaries, and limited the cost for each year to the amount appropriated in the act for such purpose.

AMENDMENTS

1954—Act Aug. 30, 1954, repealed proviso requiring that an itemized statement of expenses incurred in gauging waters of the Mississippi River and its tributaries, as provided in this section, should accompany the annual report of the Chief of Engineers.

CHANGE OF NAME

Department of War designated Department of the Army and title of Secretary of War changed to Secretary of the Army by section 205(a) of act July 26, 1947, ch. 343, title II, 61 Stat. 501. Section 205(a) of act July 26, 1947, was repealed by section 53 of act Aug. 10, 1956, ch. 1041, 70A Stat. 641. Section 1 of act Aug. 10, 1956, enacted "Title 10, Armed Forces" which in sections 3010 to 3013 continued Department of the Army under administrative supervision of Secretary of the Army.

APPROPRIATIONS

Section 2 of act June 26, 1934, ch. 756, 48 Stat. 1225, which was classified to section 725a of former Title 31,

Money and Finance, repealed the permanent appropriation under the title "Gauging waters of the Mississippi and its tributaries (fiscal year) (8–961.54)" effective July 1, 1935, and provided that such portions of any Acts as make permanent appropriations to be expended under such account are amended so as to authorize, in lieu thereof, annual appropriations from the general fund of the Treasury in identical terms and in such amounts as now provided by the laws providing such permanent appropriations.

§5. Abolition of tolls on Government canals, canalized rivers, etc.; expense of operation, repairs to and reconstruction of canals, etc.; Panama Canal excepted; levies by non-Federal interest

(a) No tolls or operating charges whatever shall be levied upon or collected from any vessel, dredge, or other water craft for passing through any lock, canal, canalized river, or other work for the use and benefit of navigation, now belonging to the United States or that may be hereafter acquired or constructed; and for the purpose of preserving and continuing the use and navigation of said canals and other public works without interruption, the Secretary of the Army, upon the recommendation of the Chief of Engineers, United States Army, is authorized to draw his warrant or requisition, from time to time, upon the Secretary of the Treasury to pay the actual expenses of operating, maintaining, and keeping said works in repair, which warrants or requisitions shall be paid by the Secretary of the Treasury out of any money in the Treasury not otherwise appropriated: *Provided*, That whenever, in the judgment of the Secretary of the Army, the condition of any of the aforesaid works is such that its entire reconstruction is absolutely essential to its efficient and economical maintenance and operation as herein provided for, the reconstruction thereof may include such modifications in plan and location as may be necessary to provide adequate facilities for existing navigation: *Provided further*, That the modifications are necessary to make the reconstructed work conform to similar works previously authorized by Congress and forming a part of the same improvement, and that such modifications shall be considered and approved by the Board of Engineers for Rivers and Harbors and be recommended by the Chief of Engineers before the work of reconstruction is commenced: *And provided further*, That nothing contained in this section shall be held to apply to the Panama Canal.

(b) No taxes, tolls, operating charges, fees, or any other impositions whatever shall be levied upon or collected from any vessel or other water craft, or from its passengers or crew, by any non-Federal interest, if the vessel or water craft is operating on any navigable waters subject to the authority of the United States, or under the right to freedom of navigation on those waters, except for—

(1) fees charged under section 2236 of this title;

(2) reasonable fees charged on a fair and equitable basis that—

(A) are used solely to pay the cost of a service to the vessel or water craft;

(B) enhance the safety and efficiency of interstate and foreign commerce; and

(C) do not impose more than a small burden on interstate or foreign commerce; or

(3) property taxes on vessels or watercraft, other than vessels or watercraft that are primarily engaged in foreign commerce if those taxes are permissible under the United States Constitution.

(July 5, 1884, ch. 229, §4, 23 Stat. 147; Mar. 3, 1909, ch. 264, §6, 35 Stat. 818; July 26, 1947, ch. 343, title II, §205(a), 61 Stat. 501; Aug. 30, 1954, ch. 1076, §1(15), 68 Stat. 967; Pub. L. 107–295, title IV, §445, Nov. 25, 2002, 116 Stat. 2133; Pub. L. 108–176, title VIII, §829(a), Dec. 12, 2003, 117 Stat. 2597.)

Codification

Section is from act July 5, 1884, popularly known as the "Rivers and Harbors Appropriation Act of 1884".

The section, as originally enacted, was as follows:

"No tolls or operating charges whatsoever shall be levied or collected upon any vessel or vessels, dredges, or other passing water-craft through any canal or other work for the improvement of navigation belonging to the United States; and for the purpose of preserving and continuing the use and navigation of said canals, rivers, and other public works without interruption, the Secretary of War, upon the application of the chief engineer in charge of said works, is hereby authorized to draw his warrant or requisition from time to time upon the Secretary of the Treasury to pay the actual expenses of operating and keeping said works in repair, which warrants or requisitions shall be paid by the Secretary of the Treasury, out of any money in the Treasury not otherwise appropriated: *Provided, however*, That an itemized statement of said expenses shall accompany the annual report of the chief of engineers."

It was amended by act March 3, 1909, to read substantially as set forth above.

Amendments

2003—Subsec. (b)(3). Pub. L. 108–176 added par. (3).

2002—Pub. L. 107–295 designated existing provisions as subsec. (a) and added subsec. (b).

1954—Act Aug. 30, 1954, repealed last proviso requiring that an itemized statement of expenses incurred in operating, maintaining, keeping in repair, and reconstructing locks, canals, etc., other than the Panama Canal, as provided in this section, should accompany the annual report of the Chief of Engineers.

Change of Name

Department of War designated Department of the Army and title of Secretary of War changed to Secretary of the Army by section 205(a) of act July 26, 1947, ch. 343, title II, 61 Stat. 501. Section 205(a) of act July 26, 1947, was repealed by section 53 of act Aug. 10, 1956, ch. 1041, 70A Stat. 641. Section 1 of act Aug. 10, 1956, enacted "Title 10, Armed Forces" which in sections 3010 to 3013 continued Department of the Army under administrative supervision of Secretary of the Army.

Effective Date of 2003 Amendment

Pub. L. 108–176, title VIII, §829(b), Dec. 12, 2003, 117 Stat. 2597, provided that: "The amendment made by subsection (a) [amending this section] is effective on and after November 25, 2002."

Termination of Board of Engineers for Rivers and Harbors and Reassignment of Duties and Responsibilities

For termination of Board of Engineers for Rivers and Harbors 180 days after Oct. 31, 1992, and reassignment of duties and responsibilities by Secretary of Army, see section 223 of Pub. L. 102–580, set out as a note under section 541 of this title.

Appropriations

Section 2 of act June 26, 1934, ch. 756, 48 Stat. 1225, which was classified to section 725a of former Title 31,

Money and Finance, repealed the permanent appropriation under the title "Operating and care of canals and other works of navigation (8x881)" effective July 1, 1935, and provided that such portions of any Acts as make permanent appropriations to be expended under such account are amended so as to authorize, in lieu thereof, annual appropriations from the general fund of the Treasury in identical terms and in such amounts as now provided by the laws providing such permanent appropriations.

§ 6. Free passage to harbor of Michigan City, Indiana

The passage of vessels to and from the harbor of Michigan City, in Indiana, shall be free and not subject to toll or charge.

(R.S. § 5247.)

CODIFICATION

R.S. § 5247 derived from acts June 23, 1866, ch. 138, § 1, 14 Stat. 73; Mar. 2, 1867, ch. 144, § 2, 14 Stat. 421.

§ 7. Use of Government iron pier in Delaware Bay

The Government iron pier in Delaware Bay near Lewes, Delaware, shall be open to public use under regulations to be prescribed by the Secretary of the Army.

(July 27, 1916, ch. 260, § 1, 39 Stat. 394; July 26, 1947, ch. 343, title II, § 205(a), 61 Stat. 501.)

CODIFICATION

Section is from act July 27, 1916, popularly known as the "Rivers and Harbors Appropriation Act of 1916".

A further provision of act July 27, 1916, repealed act Mar. 3, 1891, ch. 542, 26 Stat. 969, which authorized a transfer of the iron pier to the Treasury Department.

CHANGE OF NAME

Department of War designated Department of the Army and title of Secretary of War changed to Secretary of the Army by section 205(a) of act July 26, 1947, ch. 343, title II, 61 Stat. 501. Section 205(a) of act July 26, 1947, was repealed by section 53 of act Aug. 10, 1956, ch. 1041, 70A Stat. 641. Section 1 of act Aug. 10, 1956, enacted "Title 10, Armed Forces" which in sections 3010 to 3013 continued Department of the Army under administrative supervision of Secretary of the Army.

§ 8. Toll free rivers in Alabama

The Tennessee, Coosa, Cahawba, and Black Warrior Rivers, within the State of Alabama, shall be forever free from toll for all property belonging to the United States, and for all persons in their service, and for all citizens of the United States, except as to such tolls as may be allowed by Act of Congress.

(R.S. § 5244.)

CODIFICATION

R.S. § 5244 derived from act May 23, 1828, ch. 75, § 7, 4 Stat. 290.

Another R.S. 5244 is classified to section 43 of Title 12, Banks and Banking.

§ 9. Des Moines River as toll free

The Des Moines River shall forever remain free from any toll, or other charge whatever, for any property of the United States, or persons in their service, passing along the same.

(R.S. § 5246.)

CODIFICATION

R.S. § 5246 derived from acts Aug. 8, 1846, ch. 103, § 3, 9 Stat. 78; Jan. 20, 1870, ch. 7, 16 Stat. 61.

§ 10. Waters in Louisiana Purchase as public highways

All the navigable rivers and waters in the former Territories of Orleans and Louisiana shall be and forever remain public highways.

(R.S. § 5251.)

CODIFICATION

R.S. § 5251 derived from act Mar. 3, 1811, ch. 46, § 12, 2 Stat. 606.

§ 11. Authority for compact between Middle Northwest States as to jurisdiction of offenses committed on boundary waters

The consent of the Congress is given to the States of North Dakota, South Dakota, Minnesota, Wisconsin, Iowa, and Nebraska, or any two or more of them, by such agreement or compact as they may deem desirable or necessary, or as may be evidenced by legislative acts enacted by any two or more of said States, not in conflict with the Constitution of the United States or any law thereof, to determine and settle the jurisdiction to be exercised by said States, respectively, over offenses arising out of the violation of the laws of any of said States upon any of the waters forming the boundary lines between any two or more of said States, or waters through which such boundary line extends, and that the consent of the Congress be, and the same is, given to the concurrent jurisdiction agreed to by the States of Minnesota and South Dakota, as evidenced by the act of the Legislature of the State of Minnesota approved April 20, 1917, and the act of the Legislature of the State of South Dakota approved February 13, 1917.

(Mar. 4, 1921, ch. 176, 41 Stat. 1447.)

CODIFICATION

This section is from a resolution entitled a "Joint Resolution giving consent of the Congress of the United States to the States of North Dakota, South Dakota, Minnesota, Wisconsin, Iowa, and Nebraska, or any two or more of said States, to agree upon the jurisdiction to be exercised by said States over boundary waters between any two or more of said States".

§ 12. Port Arthur Ship Canal

After there shall be conveyed to the United States, free of cost, a valid title to the line of water communication between Taylors Bayou and Sabine Pass, in the State of Texas, known as the Port Arthur Ship Canal, together with a valid title to the turning basin as existing June 19, 1906, and to the artificial slip on which the lumber dock of the Port Arthur Canal and Dock Company is built, the said waterways shall thereupon become free public waters of the United States, and be subject to the laws enacted by Congress for the maintenance, preservation, protection, and regulation of navigable waters: *Provided*, That the company or corporation conveying title to said canal as aforesaid shall also convey to the United States, free of cost, the fee to a strip of land one hundred and fifty feet wide along the westerly margin of the canal, except that where the right of way of the Southern Pacific Railroad Company prevents the transfer of such strip of land along the westerly margin of said canal there shall be conveyed such strip on the easterly margin thereof as may be necessary to make up such one hundred and fifty feet of width, with the reservation that until Congress shall have authorized and provided for the enlargement and widening of said canal the said company or corporation, its successors or assigns, shall have the right to control, occupy, and use the said strip of land and every part thereof in the same manner and to the same extent as before the execution and delivery of the conveyance, and also the right to transfer, lease, sell, quitclaim, or otherwise dispose of said property and every part thereof, subject to the grant made to the United States. The charges for the use of said docks and wharves shall be just and reasonable and shall not be greater than charges for similar services at other ports of the United States on the Gulf of Mexico.

(June 19, 1906, ch. 3436, §1, 34 Stat. 302.)

CODIFICATION

This section is from a proviso following provisions establishing an additional collection district in the State of Texas to be known as the district of Sabine; the establishment of the said district being conditioned on the making of the conveyance referred to in this section.

Further provisions of the said proviso authorizing the Secretary of War to accept the said waterways as the property of the United States, and directing that the Act take effect only when the requirements of the section be fully complied with to the satisfaction of the Secretary of War, have been omitted as executed and obsolete.

SUBCHAPTER II—WATERS DECLARED NONNAVIGABLE: CHANGE OF NAME

§21. Bayou Cocodrie, Louisiana

Bayou Cocodrie, from its source to its junction with Bayou Chicot, in the State of Louisiana, is declared to be not a navigable water of the United States within the meaning of the laws enacted by the Congress for the preservation and protection of such waters.

The right to alter, amend, or repeal this section is expressly reserved.

(Feb. 25, 1921, ch. 71, §§1, 2, 41 Stat. 1145.)

CODIFICATION

The first sentence hereof is section 1 and the second sentence section 2 of act Feb. 25, 1921, entitled "An Act to declare Bayou Cocodrie nonnavigable from its source to its junction with Bayou Chicot".

§22. Bayou Meto, Arkansas

The Bayou Meto, in the State of Arkansas, is declared to be a nonnavigable stream within the meaning of the Constitution and laws of the United States.

(Aug. 8, 1917, ch. 49, §16, 40 Stat. 268.)

§23. Bear Creek, Mississippi

Bear Creek in Humphreys, Leflore, and Sunflower Counties, in the State of Mississippi, is declared to be a nonnavigable stream within the meaning of the Constitution and the laws of the United States.

The right of Congress to alter, amend, or repeal this section is expressly reserved.

(Mar. 3, 1923, ch. 229, §§1, 2, 42 Stat. 1442.)

CODIFICATION

The first sentence hereof is section 1 and the last sentence section 2 of act Mar. 3, 1923, entitled "An Act declaring Bear Creek in Humphreys, Leflore, and Sunflower counties, Mississippi, to be a nonnavigable stream".

§24. Big Tarkio River, Missouri

The Big Tarkio River, in the counties of Holt and Atchison, in the State of Missouri, is declared to be not a navigable water of the United States within the meaning of the laws enacted by Congress for the preservation and protection of such waters.

The right to alter, amend, or repeal this section is expressly reserved.

(Feb. 15, 1910, ch. 33, §§1, 2, 36 Stat. 194.)

CODIFICATION

The first sentence hereof is section 1 and the last sentence section 2 of act Feb. 15, 1910, entitled "An Act to declare Big Tarkio River, in Holt and Atchison counties, Missouri, nonnavigable".

§25. Cache River, Arkansas

The Cache River in the State of Arkansas is declared to be a nonnavigable stream within the meaning of the Constitution and laws of the United States. This provision shall become void after one year from July 27, 1916, unless within said period the Legislature of Arkansas shall pass an act expressly approving this declaration. The right of the Congress to alter, amend, or repeal this section is expressly reserved.

(July 27, 1916, ch. 260, §1, 39 Stat. 399.)

CODIFICATION

Section was a provision of section 1 of act July 27, 1916, popularly known as the "Rivers and Harbors Appropriation Act of 1916".

APPROVAL OF DECLARATION

See Arkansas Laws 1917, ch. 2, act 406.

§26. Calumet River, Cook County, Illinois, old channel

The portion of the old channel of the Calumet River in the northwest quarter of section thirty, township thirty-seven north, range fifteen east, of the third principal meridian, in Cook County, Illinois, which lies outside of the new channel lines as established by the United States and shown on "Map of the Calumet River, Illinois, from Lake Michigan to Calumet Lake, to accompany report of W. G. Ewing, United States attorney to the Attorney-General, respecting cession of right of way for improvement of said river under Act of Congress approved July fifth, eighteen hundred and eighty-four," is hereby abandoned as navigable water from and after the time that a navigable channel shall be cut through said quarter section within the new channel lines of the river as shown on the said map.

The portion of the old channel of the Calumet River in the north quarter of fractional section 7, township 37 north, range 15 east, of the third principal meridian, south of the Indian boundary line, in Cook County, Illinois, which lies outside of the new channel lines as established by the United States and shown on "map of the Calumet River, Illinois, from Lake Michigan to Calumet Lake, to accompany report of W. G. Ewing, United States attorney, to the Attorney General, respecting cession of right of way for improvement of said river, under Act of Congress approved July 5, 1884", is abandoned as navigable water.

(Apr. 21, 1904, ch. 1409, 33 Stat. 239, 240; Feb. 27, 1915, ch. 68, 38 Stat. 817.)

REFERENCES IN TEXT

Act of Congress approved July 5, 1884, referred to in text, is act July 5, 1884, ch. 229, 23 Stat. 143, which provided in part for the appropriation of $50,000 for the continuing improvement of the Calumet River, provided that no part of such appropriation be expended until the right of way should have been conveyed to the United States, free from expense, and the United States released from liability to adjacent property owners, to the satisfaction of the Secretary of War.

§26a. Additional portion of Calumet River, old channel, abandoned as navigable water

The portion of the old channel of the Calumet River in sections eighteen and nineteen, township thirty-seven north, range fifteen east, of the third principal meridian, in Cook County, Illinois, which lies outside of the new channel lines established by the United States and shown on the map referred to in section 26 of this title, and which lies outside of the exterior limits of the turning basin to be established on said Calumet River in said sections, is abandoned as navigable water of the United States from and after the time when the United States shall have secured title to the land necessary for the establishment of the turning basin at some point, to be approved by the Chief of Engineers, between One hundred and thirteenth Street and One hundred and seventeenth Street in the city of Chicago.

(Mar. 4, 1913, ch. 144, §1, 37 Stat. 816.)

§26b. Portion of Calumet River, Chicago, as nonnavigable stream

The portion of the Calumet River, in the city of Chicago, county of Cook, State of Illinois, lying between the intersections of this river with the two lines described below, is a nonnavigable stream within the meaning of the Constitution and laws of the United States:

Beginning at a point on the south line of the north half of section 36, township 37 north, range 14 east, of the third principal meridian, one thousand eight hundred and seventy-three and seven-hundredths feet west of the east line of said section; thence northwesterly on a straight line to a point three thousand two hundred and eighty feet west of the east line and seven hundred and eighty-five feet south of the north line of said section; and

Beginning at a point five hundred and eighty-five feet east of the west line and seven hundred and thirty-two feet north of the south line of section 31, township 37 north, range 15 east, of the third principal meridian; thence north forty-six degrees and thirty minutes east along a straight line to the easterly water's edge of said river.

The right to alter, amend, or repeal this section is expressly reserved.

(June 14, 1937, ch. 338, §§2, 3, 50 Stat. 258, 259.)

§27. Chicago River at Chicago, Illinois

All of that portion of the West Fork of the South Branch of the Chicago River in the county of Cook and State of Illinois, extending west from the west line of the collateral channel of the sanitary district of Chicago, in the northwest quarter of section 36, township 39 north, range 13 east, of the third principal meridian, is declared to be a nonnavigable stream within the meaning of the Constitution and laws of the United States. The right of Congress to alter, amend, or repeal this provision is expressly reserved.

The provisions of sections 401 and 403 of this title shall not apply to that portion of the west arm of the South Fork of the South Branch of the Chicago River, lying between the east line of Ashland Avenue and the north line of Thirty-ninth Street, in the city of Chicago, Illinois, as the same now exists or may hereafter be extended. All rights, authority, or control over that part of the Chicago River possessed or assumed by the United States are relinquished and abandoned, and all rights, authority, or control over the same that were possessed by the State of Illinois are fully restored to said State.

As soon as the city of Chicago, or any other governmental agency or any corporation thereunto duly authorized by the Secretary of the Army, shall have constructed, after June 7, 1924, a new channel for the South Branch of the Chicago River between West Polk Street and West Nineteenth Street in said city of Chicago, then, and in that event, so much of the channel of the South Branch of the Chicago River as shall be superseded and replaced by said new channel in accordance with the permit of the Secretary of the Army shall be discontinued and abandoned.

(Jan. 24, 1923, ch. 33, §§1, 2, 42 Stat. 1171; Feb. 27, 1923, ch. 142, 42 Stat. 1323; June 7, 1924, ch. 337, 43 Stat. 646; July 26, 1947, ch. 343, title II, §205(a), 61 Stat. 501.)

CODIFICATION

The two sentences comprising the first paragraph of this section are, respectively, sections 1 and 2 of act Jan. 24, 1923.

The second paragraph of this section is from act Feb. 27, 1923.

The last paragraph of this section is from act June 7, 1924.

CHANGE OF NAME

Department of War designated Department of the Army and title of Secretary of War changed to Secretary of the Army by section 205(a) of act July 26, 1947, ch. 343, title II, 61 Stat. 501. Section 205(a) of act July 26, 1947, was repealed by section 53 of act Aug. 10, 1956, ch. 1041, 70A Stat. 641. Section 1 of act Aug. 10, 1956, enacted "Title 10, Armed Forces" which in sections 3010 to 3013 continued Department of the Army under administrative supervision of Secretary of the Army.

§27a. Chicago River, West Fork of South Branch

That portion of the West Fork of the South Branch of the Chicago River in Cook County, Illinois, lying between the west line (produced north) of the Collateral Channel of the Sanitary District of Chicago, in the northwest quarter of section 36, township 39 north, range 13 east, third principal meridian, and a line one thousand three hundred feet east of and parallel to the west line of section 30 (section line in South Western Avenue), township 39 north, range 13 east, third principal meridian, in the city of Chicago, Illinois, as the same now exists or may hereafter be extended, is declared to be a nonnavigable stream within the meaning of the Constitution and laws of the United States.

The right to alter, amend, or repeal this section is expressly reserved.

(Aug. 30, 1935, ch. 831, §10, 49 Stat. 1048.)

§27b. Chicago River, West arm of South Fork of South Branch

The portion of the west arm of the South Fork of the South Branch of the Chicago River, as established by the ordinance of the city of Chicago on July 17, 1911, in the southwest quarter of section 32, township 39 north, range 14 east of the third principal meridian, in the city of Chicago, county of Cook, State of Illinois, lying westerly of a straight line drawn from a point in south dock line of the said west arm 203.94 feet westerly of the point of intersection of the south dock line of the said west arm with the west dock line of the east arm of the South Fork of the South Branch of the Chicago River as established by said city of Chicago ordinance of July 17, 1911, measured along the south dock line of said west arm, thence to a point in the north dock line of the said west arm said point being 278 feet westerly of the intersection of the north dock line of the said west arm with the west dock line of the South Fork of the South Branch of the Chicago River as established by said city of Chicago ordinance of July 17, 1911, measured along the north dock line of said west arm of the South Fork of the South Branch of the Chicago River, is declared to be and is on and after September 1, 1959 to be regarded as a nonnavigable water of the United States within the meaning of the Constitution and laws of the United States: *Provided*, That plans for a suitable bulkhead to retain any fill to be placed in the waterway shall be submitted to and approved by the Corps of Engineers, United States Army, prior to the placing of such fill.

(Pub. L. 86–218, Sept. 1, 1959, 73 Stat. 448.)

§28. Crum River; old channel at mouth, Delaware Bay

After the channel of the Crum River where the same empties into the Delaware River has been changed, diverted, and straightened under the authority given to Alba B. Johnson and Samuel M. Vauclain and the Baldwin Locomotive Works by Act July 27, 1916, chapter 260, the said Crum River, as so straightened, shall be a public navigable stream, and the course and channel of the said river, as it existed July 27, 1916, from the right-of-way of the Philadelphia and Reading Railway Company to the low-water line in the Delaware River shall be abandoned and vacated when the above-mentioned new channel shall have been completed to a depth of four feet at mean low water, with a bottom width of sixty-two feet and width of one hundred feet at mean low-water level: *Provided*, That the Government shall have such right, title, and interest in and to the bed of said new channel as will assure the public the right to the perpetual use of said channel for all the purposes of navigation and commerce.

(July 27, 1916, ch. 260, §1, 39 Stat. 393.)

References in Text

Act July 27, 1916, chapter 260, referred to in text, is act July 27, 1916, ch. 260, 39 Stat. 393, which is classified to sections 7, 25, 28, 38, 424, and 648 to 650 of this title. For complete classification of this Act to the Code, see Tables.

Codification

Section is from a provision of section 1 of act July 27, 1916, popularly known as the "Rivers and Harbors Appropriation Act of 1916".

The portion of that section authorizing the changing, diverting, and straightening of the channel of the river has been omitted as temporary and executed.

§29. Cuivre River, Missouri

Cuivre River, in the counties of Lincoln and Saint Charles, in the State of Missouri, being the dividing line, is declared not to be a navigable stream, and shall be so treated by the Secretary of the Army and all other authorities.

(Mar. 23, 1900, ch. 88, 31 Stat. 50; July 26, 1947, ch. 343, title II, §205(a), 61 Stat. 501.)

Change of Name

Department of War designated Department of the Army and title of Secretary of War changed to Secretary of the Army by section 205(a) of act July 26, 1947, ch. 343, title II, 61 Stat. 501. Section 205(a) of act July 26, 1947, was repealed by section 53 of act Aug. 10, 1956, ch. 1041, 70A Stat. 641. Section 1 of act Aug. 10, 1956, enacted "Title 10, Armed Forces" which in sections 3010 to 3013 continued Department of the Army under administrative supervision of Secretary of the Army.

§29a. East River, Wisconsin

All of that portion of the East River, in the county of Brown, State of Wisconsin, extending from Baird Street, in the city of Green Bay, east and south is declared to be a nonnavigable stream within the meaning of the Constitution and Laws of the United States of America.

The right of Congress to alter, amend or repeal this section is expressly reserved.

(Aug. 30, 1935, ch. 831, §9, 49 Stat. 1048.)

§30. Grand River, Missouri, above Brunswick

Grand River in the State of Missouri above the city of Brunswick, in the county of Chariton in said State, is declared to be not a navigable stream and shall be so treated by the Secretary of the Army and by all other authorities.

(Feb. 15, 1905, ch. 574, 33 Stat. 715; July 26, 1947, ch. 343, title II, §205(a), 61 Stat. 501.)

Change of Name

Department of War designated Department of the Army and title of Secretary of War changed to Secretary of the Army by section 205(a) of act July 26, 1947, ch. 343, title II, 61 Stat. 501. Section 205(a) of act July 26, 1947, was repealed by section 53 of act Aug. 10, 1956, ch. 1041, 70A Stat. 641. Section 1 of act Aug. 10, 1956, enacted "Title 10, Armed Forces" which in sections 3010 to 3013 continued Department of the Army under administrative supervision of Secretary of the Army.

§31. Iowa River, Iowa, above Toolsboro

So much of the Iowa River within the State of Iowa, as lies north of the town of Wapello, and so much of the said river within the State of Iowa, as lies between the town of Toolsboro and the town of Wapello, in the county of Louisa, shall not be deemed a navigable river or public highway, but dams and bridges may be constructed across it.

(R.S. §5248; Aug. 18, 1894, ch. 299, §1, 28 Stat. 356.)

CODIFICATION

R.S. §5248 derived from Res. July 13, 1868, No. 55, 15 Stat. 257; act May 6, 1870, ch. 92, 16 Stat. 121.

The portion of this section relating to the Iowa river north of the town of Wapello is from R.S. §5248.

The remainder the section, relating to so much of the river as lies between Toolsboro and Wapello, is from act Aug. 18, 1894.

§32. Lake George, Mississippi

Lake George, in Yazoo County, in the State of Mississippi, is declared to be not a navigable water of the United States within the meaning of the laws enacted by the Congress for the preservation and protection of such waters.

The right of Congress to alter, amend, or repeal this section is expressly reserved.

(May 24, 1922, ch. 198, §§1, 2, 42 Stat. 552.)

CODIFICATION

The two sentences comprising this section are respectively sections 1 and 2 of act May 24, 1922, entitled "An act declaring Lake George, Yazoo County, Mississippi, to be a nonnavigable stream".

§33. Little River, Arkansas, from Big Lake to Marked Tree

Little River, from Big Lake in Mississippi County to Marked Tree in Poinsett County, Arkansas, is declared to be not a navigable waterway of the United States within the meaning of the laws enacted by Congress for the protection of such waterways.

(Mar. 2, 1919, ch. 95, §4, 40 Stat. 1287.)

CODIFICATION

Section is from section 4 of act Mar. 2, 1919, popularly known as the "Rivers and Harbors Appropriation Act of 1919".

§34. Mill Slough, Oregon

Mill Slough, a tidal tributary of Coos Bay, lying within the limits of the city of Marshfield, State of Oregon, is declared to be not a navigable waterway of the United States, within the meaning of the laws enacted by Congress for the preservation and protection of such waterways, and the consent of Congress is given to the filling in of said slough by the said city of Marshfield.

(Oct. 23, 1913, ch. 33, 38 Stat. 233.)

§35. Mississippi River, West Channel, opposite La Crosse, Wisconsin

The branch of the Mississippi River flowing between Grand Island and the mainland opposite the city of La Crosse, State of Wisconsin, and known as the West Channel, is declared unnavigable, and the said city of La Crosse is relieved of the necessity of maintaining a draw or pontoon bridge over said West Channel.

(Feb. 23, 1901, ch. 470, 31 Stat. 804.)

§36. Mosquito Creek, South Carolina

Mosquito Creek, in Colleton County, South Carolina, is declared to be a nonnavigable stream within the meaning of the Constitution and laws of the United States.

(Aug. 8, 1917, ch. 49, §15, 40 Stat. 268.)

§37. Nodaway River, Missouri

Nodaway River, in the counties of Andrew, Holt, and Nodaway, in the State of Missouri, is declared to be not a navigable water of the United States within the meaning of the laws enacted by Congress for the preservation and protection of such waters.

The right to alter, amend, or repeal this section is expressly reserved.

(Feb. 15, 1910, ch. 32, §§1, 2, 36 Stat. 194.)

§38. Oklawaha River, Florida; Kyle and Young Canal and "Morrison Landing extension" substituted

Upon the conveyance to the United States, free of cost, title to the land occupied by what is known as the "Kyle and Young Canal" and the "Morrison Landing extension" of the same, on the Oklawaha River, in the State of Florida, together with title to a strip of land on the east side of said canal of such width as in the judgment of the Secretary of the Army may be required for the future widening of said canal and extension by the United States, the said canal and extension shall become a free public waterway of the United States in place of the natural bed of the river.

(July 27, 1916, ch. 260, §1, 39 Stat. 396; July 26, 1947, ch. 343, title II, §205(a), 61 Stat. 501.)

CHANGE OF NAME

Department of War designated Department of the Army and title of Secretary of War changed to Secretary of the Army by section 205(a) of act July 26, 1947, ch. 343, title II, 61 Stat. 501. Section 205(a) of act July 26, 1947, was repealed by section 53 of act Aug. 10, 1956, ch. 1041, 70A Stat. 641. Section 1 of act Aug. 10, 1956, enacted "Title 10, Armed Forces" which in sections 3010 to 3013 continued Department of the Army under administrative supervision of Secretary of the Army.

§39. Ollala Slough, Oregon

All of that portion of Ollala Slough in Lincoln County, Oregon, above a point where a line that is one hundred and twenty rods south and running east and west and parallel with the section line between sections 8 and 17 in township 11 south, range 10 west of the Willamette meridian, crosses said stream, is declared to be a nonnavigable stream.

(Feb. 26, 1917, ch. 119, 39 Stat. 937.)

§40. One Hundred and Two River, Missouri

One Hundred and Two River south of the north boundary line of Andrew County, Missouri, as now located, is declared to be not a navigable water of the United States within the meaning of the laws enacted by Congress for the preservation and protection of such waters.

The right to alter, amend, or repeal this section is expressly reserved.

(Feb. 15, 1910, ch. 31, §§1, 2, 36 Stat. 194.)

§41. Osage River, Missouri

The Osage River in the State of Missouri above the point where the south line of sections 15 and 16 in township 40 north, of range 22 west, of the fifth principal meridian, and in the county of Benton, State of Missouri, crosses said river, is declared not to be a navigable stream, and shall be so treated by the Secretary of the Army and by all other authorities.

(Mar. 4, 1904, ch. 393, 33 Stat. 58; July 26, 1947, ch. 343, title II, §205(a), 61 Stat. 501.)

Codification

This section superseded act June 24, 1902, ch. 1154, 32 Stat. 398, which declared that the Osage River above the point where the dividing line between the counties of Benton and Saint Clair crosses the river should not be a navigable stream.

Change of Name

Department of War designated Department of the Army and title of Secretary of War changed to Secretary of the Army by section 205(a) of act July 26, 1947, ch. 343, title II, 61 Stat. 501. Section 205(a) of act July 26, 1947, was repealed by section 53 of act Aug. 10, 1956, ch. 1041, 70A Stat. 641. Section 1 of act Aug. 10, 1956, enacted "Title 10, Armed Forces" which in sections 3010 to 3013 continued Department of the Army under administrative supervision of Secretary of the Army.

§42. Platte River, Missouri

The Platte River in the State of Missouri is declared to be a nonnavigable stream within the meaning of the Constitution and laws of the United States, and jurisdiction over said river is declared to be vested in the State of Missouri.

The right of Congress to alter, amend, or repeal this section is expressly reserved.

(Feb. 16, 1921, ch. 62, §§1, 2, 41 Stat. 1105.)

Codification

The two sentences of this section are, respectively, from sections 1 and 2 of act Feb. 16, 1921, entitled "An Act declaring the Platte River to be a nonnavigable stream".

§43. Saint Marys River, Ohio and Indiana

Saint Marys River, Ohio and Indiana, is declared to be a nonnavigable stream within the meaning of the Constitution and laws of the United States.

(Aug. 8, 1917, ch. 49, §17, 40 Stat. 268.)

§44. Sturgeon Bay, Illinois

So much of the west fork of Sturgeon Bay within the county of Mercer and State of Illinois as lies west of the line between the east half and the west half of the east half of section 25, in township 14 north, range 6 west of the fourth principal meridian, and so much of the east fork of said Sturgeon Bay as lies north of the north line of section 30, in township 14 north, range 5 west of the fourth principal meridian, shall not be deemed navigable waters of the United States.

(Feb. 7, 1907, No. 13, 34 Stat. 1421.)

§45. Swan Creek, Toledo, Ohio

Swan Creek, a stream lying within the limits of the city of Toledo, State of Ohio, is declared to be not a navigable waterway of the United States within the meaning of the laws enacted by Congress for the preservation and protection of such waterways, and the consent of Congress is given for the filling in of said creek by the local authorities.

(Mar. 4, 1915, ch. 142, §13, 38 Stat. 1055.)

Codification

Section is from act Mar. 4, 1915, popularly known as the "Rivers and Harbors Appropriation Act of 1915".

§46. Tchula Lake, Mississippi

Tchula Lake, in Holmes County, in the State of Mississippi, is declared to be a nonnavigable stream within the meaning of the Constitution and laws of the United States.

The right of Congress to alter, amend, or repeal this section is expressly reserved.

(July 1, 1922, ch. 266, §§1, 2, 42 Stat. 816.)

Codification

The two sentences comprising this section are, respectively, sections 1 and 2 of act July 1, 1922, entitled "An act declaring Tchula Lake, Holmes County, Mississippi, to be a nonnavigable stream".

§47. Eagle Lake, Louisiana-Mississippi

Eagle Lake, which lies partly within the limits of the State of Mississippi, in Warren County, and partly within the limits of the State of Louisiana, in Madison Parish, is declared to be a nonnavigable stream within the meaning of the Constitution and laws of the United States.

The right to alter, amend, or repeal this section is expressly reserved.

(June 2, 1926, ch. 445, §§1, 2, 44 Stat. 681.)

§48. Noxubee River, Mississippi

That portion of the Noxubee River in Noxubee County, in the State of Mississippi is declared to be a nonnavigable stream within the meaning of the Constitution and laws of the United States.

The right of Congress to amend or repeal this section is expressly reserved.

(Feb. 24, 1934, ch. 25, §§1, 2, 48 Stat. 356.)

§49. Bayou Saint John in New Orleans

Bayou Saint John, in the city of New Orleans, Louisiana, is declared to be not a navigable water of the United States within the meaning of the laws enacted by Congress for the preservation and protection of such waters.

The right to alter, amend, or repeal this section is expressly reserved.

(June 5, 1936, ch. 530, §§1, 2, 49 Stat. 1484.)

§50. Turtle Bay and Turtle Bayou, Texas

Turtle Bay and Turtle Bayou, in Chambers County, in the State of Texas, are declared to be nonnavigable waterways within the meaning of the Constitution and laws of the United States of America.

The existing project for Turtle Bayou, Texas, authorized by the Rivers and Harbors Act approved June 25, 1910 (Act June 25, 1910, ch. 382, 36 Stat. 630), is abandoned.

The right of Congress to alter, amend, or repeal this section is expressly reserved.

(Mar. 10, 1937, ch. 36, §§ 1–3, 50 Stat. 28.)

REFERENCES IN TEXT

The Rivers and Harbors Act approved June 25, 1910, referred to in text, is act June 25, 1910, ch. 382, 36 Stat. 630, as amended, which is classified to sections 546, 564, and 643 of this title. For complete classification of this Act to the Code, see Tables.

§ 51. Scajaquada Creek, New York

Scajaquada Creek, Erie County, New York, is declared to be nonnavigable east of a line one hundred and thirty feet west of the west line of Niagara Street, city of Buffalo, county of Erie, New York, within the meaning of the Constitution and laws of the United States.

The right to alter, amend, or repeal this section is expressly reserved.

(May 14, 1937, ch. 183, §§ 1, 2, 50 Stat. 165.)

§ 52. Park River, Connecticut

The Park River, a minor tributary of the Connecticut River, located in Hartford County, Connecticut, is declared to be a nonnavigable waterway within the meaning of the Constitution and laws of the United States of America.

The right of Congress to alter, amend, or repeal this section is expressly reserved.

(May 24, 1937, ch. 246, §§ 1, 2, 50 Stat. 201.)

§ 53. Benton Harbor Canal, Michigan

The Benton Harbor Canal at and above the west line of Ninth Street, in the city of Benton Harbor and State of Michigan, is declared to be not a navigable water of the United States within the meaning of the Constitution and laws of the United States.

The right to alter, amend, or repeal this section is expressly reserved.

(June 2, 1937, ch. 288, §§ 1–3, 50 Stat. 243.)

§ 53a. Additional portion of Benton Harbor Canal, abandoned as navigable water

The Benton Harbor Canal, from the west line of Ninth Street extended northerly to the west line of Riverview Drive extended northerly in the city of Benton Harbor and State of Michigan, be, and the same is hereby, declared to be not a navigable water of the United States within the meaning of the Constitution and laws of the United States.

(Pub. L. 88–88, § 1, Aug. 5, 1963, 77 Stat. 118.)

§ 54. Burr Creek, Bridgeport, Connecticut

That portion of Burr Creek in the city of Bridgeport, Connecticut, lying north of a line across the creek beginning at the point of intersection of the south side of Yacht Street extended and the west harbor line of the harbor lines established by the Secretary of War December 9, 1924, thence south eighty-five degrees forty-six minutes seventeen seconds east to the east harbor line of said creek, is declared to be not a navigable water of the United States within the meaning of the Constitution and laws of the United States.

Any project heretofore authorized by any Act of Congress, insofar as such project relates to the above described portion of Burr Creek in the city of Bridgeport, Connecticut, is abandoned.

The right to alter, amend, or repeal this section is expressly reserved.

(Aug. 12, 1937, ch. 607, 50 Stat. 632; July 26, 1947, ch. 343, title II, § 205(a), 61 Stat. 501.)

CHANGE OF NAME

Department of War designated Department of the Army and title of Secretary of War changed to Secretary of the Army by section 205(a) of act July 26, 1947, ch. 343, title II, 61 Stat. 501. Section 205(a) of act July 26, 1947, was repealed by section 53 of act Aug. 10, 1956, ch. 1041, 70A Stat. 641. Section 1 of act Aug. 10, 1956, enacted "Title 10, Armed Forces" which in sections 3010 to 3013 continued Department of the Army under administrative supervision of Secretary of the Army.

§ 55. Bayou Savage (or Chantilly) in New Orleans

Bayou Savage, also styled Bayou Chantilly, in the city of New Orleans, Louisiana, is declared to be a nonnavigable waterway within the meaning of the Constitution and laws of the United States.

The right to alter, amend, or repeal this section is expressly reserved.

(Aug. 16, 1937, ch. 650, 50 Stat. 649.)

§ 56. Fort Point Channel and South Bay, Boston, Massachusetts

The portion of the tidewaters in the waterway in which is located Fort Point Channel and South Bay in the city of Boston, Massachusetts, lying above the easterly side of the highway bridge over Fort Point Channel at Dorchester Avenue in the city of Boston is declared to be a nonnavigable water of the United States within the meaning of the Constitution and laws of the United States.

The right to alter, amend, or repeal this section is expressly reserved.

(May 13, 1955, ch. 37, 69 Stat. 48.)

§ 57. Pike Creek, Wisconsin

Pike Creek, in the State of Wisconsin, above the easterly side of the highway bridge at Sixth Avenue in the city of Kenosha is declared to be a nonnavigable stream within the meaning of the Constitution and laws of the United States.

The right to alter, amend, or repeal this section is expressly reserved.

(July 26, 1955, ch. 377, 69 Stat. 373.)

§ 58. Acushnet River section of New Bedford and Fairhaven Harbor, Massachusetts

The portion of the waterway in the city of New Bedford and the towns of Fairhaven and Acushnet lying north of the Coggeshall Street Bridge (north 41 degrees 31 minutes 00 seconds), is declared to be a nonnavigable water of the

United States within the meaning of the Constitution and laws of the United States. Any project heretofore authorized by any Act of Congress, insofar as such project relates to the above-described portions of the Acushnet River section of New Bedford and Fairhaven Harbor, is hereby abandoned.

The right to alter, amend, or repeal this section is expressly reserved.

(Aug. 3, 1955, ch. 495, 69 Stat. 443.)

§ 59. West River in West Haven, Connecticut

The portion of the waterway in which is located the West River in the town of West Haven, Connecticut, and the city of New Haven, Connecticut, lying northerly of a line extending north 85 degrees 54 minutes 43.5 seconds east, from a point (1,158.535 feet from the most westerly corner of the existing bulkhead and pier line) whose coordinates in the Corps of Engineers Harbor Line System are north 4,616.76 and west 9,450.80, is declared to be a nonnavigable water of the United States within the meaning of the Constitution and laws of the United States.

The line hereinbefore described shall be established as a combined pierhead and bulkhead line of the West River.

Any project heretofore authorized by an Act of Congress, insofar as such project relates to the above-described portion of the West River, is hereby abandoned.

The right to alter, amend, or repeal this section is expressly reserved.

(Aug. 9, 1955, ch. 649, 69 Stat. 576.)

§ 59a. Back Cove, Portland, Maine

(a) Portion declared nonnavigable

That portion of Back Cove at Portland, Maine, lying southerly of a line across the twelve-foot Federal project channel in Back Cove twenty-five hundred feet upstream from the Tukey Bridge, to the head of Back Cove, is declared to be a nonnavigable water of the United States within the meaning of the Constitution and laws of the United States.

(b) Portion abandoned

That portion of the twelve-foot Federal project channel in Back Cove lying southerly of a line across the channel twenty-five hundred feet upstream from the Tukey Bridge, to the head of Back Cove, a distance of approximately thirty-five hundred feet, is abandoned.

(c) Preservation of right to alter, amend or repeal section

The right to alter, amend, or repeal this section is expressly reserved.

(Pub. L. 85–126, Aug. 13, 1957, 71 Stat. 344.)

§ 59b. Bayous Terrebonne and LeCarpe, Louisiana

Bayou Terrebonne west of Barrow Street and Bayou LeCarpe west of the Intracoastal Waterway in the city of Houma, State of Louisiana, are declared to be not navigable waters of the United States within the meaning of the Constitution and laws of the United States.

The right to alter, amend, or repeal this section is expressly reserved.

(Pub. L. 86–226, §§ 2, 3, Sept. 8, 1959, 73 Stat. 455.)

§ 59c. East River, New York

That portion of the East River, in New York County, State of New York, lying between the south line of East Seventeenth Street, extended eastwardly, the United States pierhead line as it existed on July 1, 1965, and the south line of East Thirtieth Street, extended eastwardly, is hereby declared to be not a navigable water of the United States within the meaning of the Constitution and the laws of the United States.

(Pub. L. 89–298, title III, § 307, Oct. 27, 1965, 79 Stat. 1094.)

§ 59c–1. East and Hudson Rivers, New York

Those portions of the East and Hudson Rivers in New York County, State of New York, lying shoreward of a line within the United States Pierhead Line as it exists on August 13, 1968, and bounded on the north by the north side of Spring Street extended westerly and the south side of Robert F. Wagner, Senior Place extended eastwardly, are hereby declared to be nonnavigable waters of the United States within the meaning of the laws of the United States. This declaration shall apply only to portions of the above-described area which are bulkheaded and filled. Plans for bulkheading and filling shall be approved by the Secretary of the Army, acting through the Chief of Engineers, on the basis of engineering studies to determine the location and structural stability of the bulkheading and filling in order to preserve and maintain the remaining navigable waterway. Local interests shall reimburse the Federal Government for any engineering costs incurred under this section.

(Pub. L. 90–483, title I, § 113, Aug. 13, 1968, 82 Stat. 736.)

§ 59c–2. East River, New York

If the Secretary of the Army, acting through the Chief of Engineers, finds that the proposed project to be erected at the location to be declared non-navigable under this section is in the public interest, on the basis of engineering studies to determine the location and structural stability of the bulkheading and filling and permanent pile-supported structures in order to preserve and maintain the remaining navigable waterway and on the basis of environmental studies conducted pursuant to the National Environmental Policy Act of 1969 [42 U.S.C. 4321 et seq.], then those portions of the East River in New York County, State of New York, bounded and described as follows are hereby declared to be not navigable waters of the United States within the meaning of the laws of the United States, and the consent of Congress is hereby given to the filling in of all or any part thereof or the erection of permanent pile-supported structures thereon: That portion of the East River in New York County, State of New York, lying shoreward of a line with the United States pierhead line as it exists on March 7, 1974, bounded on the north by the south side of Rutgers Slip extended easterly, and bounded on the south by the southeasterly border of Battery Park at a point adjacent to the westerly end of South Street extended south by southwest, is hereby declared to be non-navigable waters of the United States. This declaration shall apply only to portions of the above-described area which are bulkheaded and filled or occupied by permanent pile-supported structures. Plans for bulkheading and filling and permanent pile-supported structures shall be approved by the Secretary of the Army, acting through the Chief of Engineers. Local interests shall reimburse the Federal Government for engineering and all other costs incurred under this section.

(Pub. L. 93–251, title I, §51, Mar. 7, 1974, 88 Stat. 26.)

REFERENCES IN TEXT

The National Environmental Policy Act of 1969, referred to in text, is Pub. L. 91–190, Jan. 1, 1970, 83 Stat. 852, as amended, which is classified generally to chapter 55 (§4321 et seq.) of Title 42, The Public Health and Welfare. For complete classification of this Act to the Code, see Short Title note set out under section 4321 of Title 42 and Tables.

§ 59c–3. Queens County, New York

(a) Description of nonnavigable area

Subject to subsections (b) and (c) of this section, the area of Long Island City, Queens County, New York, that—

(1) is not submerged;

(2) as of October 12, 1996, lies between the southerly high water line of Anable Basin (also known as the "11th Street Basin") and the northerly high water line of Newtown Creek; and

(3) extends from the high water line (as of October 12, 1996) of the East River to the original high water line of the East River;

is declared to be nonnavigable waters of the United States.

(b) Requirement that area be improved

(1) In general

The declaration of nonnavigability under subsection (a) of this section shall apply only to those portions of the area described in subsection (a) of this section that are, or will be, bulkheaded, filled, or otherwise occupied by permanent structures or other permanent physical improvements (including parkland).

(2) Applicability of Federal law

Improvements described in paragraph (1) shall be subject to applicable Federal laws, including—

(A) sections 401 and 403 of this title;

(B) section 1344 of this title;

(C) the National Environmental Policy Act of 1969 (42 U.S.C. 4321 et seq.).

(c) Expiration date

The declaration of nonnavigability under subsection (a) of this section shall expire with respect to a portion of the area described in subsection (a) of this section, if the portion—

(1) is not bulkheaded, filled, or otherwise occupied by a permanent structure or other permanent physical improvement (including parkland) in accordance with subsection (b) of this section by the date that is 20 years after October 12, 1996; or

(2) requires an improvement described in subsection (b)(2) of this section that is subject to a permit under an applicable Federal law, and the improvement is not commenced by the date that is 5 years after the date of issuance of the permit.

(Pub. L. 104–303, title V, §556, Oct. 12, 1996, 110 Stat. 3782.)

REFERENCES IN TEXT

The National Environmental Policy Act of 1969, referred to in subsec. (b)(2)(C), is Pub. L. 91–190, Jan. 1, 1970, 83 Stat. 852, as amended, which is classified generally to chapter 55 (§4321 et seq.) of Title 42, The Public Health and Welfare. For complete classification of this Act to the Code, see Short Title note set out under section 4321 of Title 42 and Tables.

§ 59d. River Raisin, Michigan

The old channel of the River Raisin in Monroe County, Michigan, lying between the Monroe Harbor range front light and Raisin Point, its entrance into Lake Erie, is declared to be not a navigable stream of the United States within the meaning of the Constitution and the laws of the United States, and the consent of Congress is hereby given for the filling in of the old channel by the riparian owners on such channel.

(Pub. L. 89–298, title III, §308, Oct. 27, 1965, 79 Stat. 1094.)

§ 59e. Bayou Lafourche, Louisiana

Bayou Lafourche, in the State of Louisiana, between Canal Boulevard, city of Thibodaux, Parish of Lafourche, State of Louisiana, and the head of the bayou at its junction with the Mississippi River levee at the city of Donaldsonville, Parish of Ascension, State of Louisiana, is hereby declared to be a nonnavigable waterway of the United States within the meaning of the laws of the United States. The existing project for Bayou Lafourche, Louisiana, authorized by the Acts of August 30, 1935 (49 Stat. 1028) and July 14, 1960 (74 Stat. 480) is hereby deauthorized in the reach of Bayou Lafourche herein declared nonnavigable.

The right to alter, amend, or repeal this section is hereby expressly reserved.

(Pub. L. 90–149, Nov. 22, 1967, 81 Stat. 507.)

REFERENCES IN TEXT

The provisions of the Acts of August 30, 1935 (49 Stat. 1028) and July 14, 1960 (74 Stat. 480), referred to in text, authorizing the Bayou Lafourche, Louisiana, project, are not classified to the Code.

PORTION OF BAYOU LAFOURCHE DECLARED TO BE NAVIGABLE WATERWAY

Pub. L. 101–595, title III, §314, Nov. 16, 1990, 104 Stat. 2987, provided that: "Bayou Lafourche, in the State of Louisiana, between the Percy Brown Road (Hwy 648), city of Thibodaux, parish of Lafourche, and the Southern Pacific Railroad bridge crossing the bayou, city of Thibodaux, parish of Lafourche, is declared to be navigable waterway of the United States under chapter 11 of title 33, United States Code."

§ 59e–1. Additional portion of Bayou Lafourche, Louisiana

Bayou Lafourche, in the State of Louisiana, between Canal Boulevard, city of Thibodaux, parish of Lafourche and the Southern Pacific Railroad bridge crossing the bayou, city of Thibodaux, parish of Lafourche, is hereby declared to be a nonnavigable waterway of the United States within the meaning of the General Bridge Act of 1946 (33 U.S.C. 525 et seq.).

(Pub. L. 99–307, §5, May 19, 1986, 100 Stat. 447.)

REFERENCES IN TEXT

The General Bridge Act of 1946, referred to in text, is title V of act Aug. 2, 1946, ch. 753, 60 Stat. 847, as amended, which is classified generally to subchapter III (§525 et seq.) of chapter 11 of this title. For complete classification of this Act to the Code, see Short Title note set out under section 525 of this title and Tables.

§59f. Boston Inner Harbor and Fort Point Channel, Massachusetts

That portion of Boston Inner Harbor and Fort Point Channel in Suffolk County, Commonwealth of Massachusetts, lying within the following described area is hereby declared to be not a navigable water of the United States within the meaning of the laws of the United States: Beginning at the intersection of the northeasterly sideline of Northern Avenue and the westerly United States Pierhead Line of the Fort Point Channel and running northwesterly by the northwesterly sideline of Northern Avenue to the westerly sideline of Atlantic Avenue: thence turning and running northerly and northwesterly by the westerly sideline of Atlantic Avenue and of Commercial Street to the southeasterly sideline of Hanover Street; thence turning and running northeasterly by the southeasterly sideline of Hanover Street to the southwesterly property line of the United States Coast Guard Base; thence turning and running southeasterly by the southwesterly property line of the United States Coast Guard Base to the southeasterly property line of the United States Coast Guard Base; thence turning and running northeasterly by the southeasterly property line of the United States Coast Guard Base extended to the United States Pierhead Line; thence turning and running southeasterly, southerly and southwesterly by the United States Pierhead Line, to the point of beginning.

(Pub. L. 90–312, May 18, 1968, 82 Stat. 125.)

§59g. Steele and Washington Bayous, and Lake Washington, Mississippi

Steele Bayou, in Warren, Issaquena, Sharkey, and Washington Counties, Mississippi, Washington Bayou, in Issaquena and Washington Counties, Mississippi, and Lake Washington, in Washington County, Mississippi, are hereby declared to be nonnavigable within the meaning of the laws of the United States.

(Pub. L. 90–483, title I, §108(a), Aug. 13, 1968, 82 Stat. 735.)

§59h. Northern Embarcadero area, San Francisco, California

That portion of the Northern Embarcadero area, beginning at the intersection of the northwesterly line of Bryant Street with the southwesterly line of Spear Street, which intersection lies on the line of jurisdiction of the San Francisco Port Authority; following thence westerly and northerly along said line of jurisdiction as described in the State of California Harbor and Navigation Code Section 1770, as amended in 1961, to its intersection with the easterly line of Van Ness Avenue produced northerly; thence northerly along said easterly line of Van Ness Avenue produced to its intersection with the United States Government pier-head line; thence following said pier-head line easterly and southerly to its intersection with the northwesterly line of Bryant Street produced northeasterly; thence southwesterly along said northwesterly line of Bryant Street produced to the point of beginning, is hereby declared to be nonnavigable waters within the meaning of the laws of the United States, and the consent of Congress is hereby given for the filling in of all or any part of the described area. This declaration shall apply only to portions of the above-described area which are bulkheaded and filled or are occupied by permanent pile-supported structures. Plans for bulkheading and filling and permanent pile-supported structures shall be approved by the Secretary of the Army, acting through the Chief of Engineers, on the basis of engineering studies to determine the location and structural stability of the bulkheading and filling and permanent pile-supported structures in order to preserve and maintain the remaining navigable waterway. Local interests shall reimburse the Federal Government for any engineering costs incurred under this section.

(Pub. L. 90–483, title I, §114, Aug. 13, 1968, 82 Stat. 736.)

REFERENCES IN TEXT

Section 1770 of the State of California Harbor and Navigation Code was repealed by Cal. Stats. 1970, ch. 385, p. 799, §2.

§59h–1. San Francisco, California, waterfront area

(a) Area to be declared nonnavigable; public interest

Unless the Secretary finds, after consultation with local and regional public officials (including local and regional public planning organizations), that the proposed projects to be undertaken within the boundaries of the portion of the San Francisco, California, waterfront area described in subsection (b) are not in the public interest, such portion is declared to be nonnavigable waters of the United States.

(b) Northern embarcadero south of Bryant Street

The portion of the San Francisco, California, waterfront area referred to in subsection (a) is as follows: Beginning at the intersection of the northeasterly prolongation of that portion of the northwesterly line of Bryant Street lying between Beale Street and Main Street with the southwesterly line of Spear Street, which intersection lies on the line of jurisdiction of the San Francisco Port Commission; following thence southerly along said line of jurisdiction as described in the State of California Harbor and Navigation Code Section 1770, as amended in 1961, to its intersection with the southeasterly line of Townsend Street; thence northeasterly along said southeasterly line of Townsend

Street, to its intersection with a line that is parallel and distant 10 feet southerly from the existing southern boundary of Pier 40 produced; thence easterly along said parallel line, to its point of intersection with the United States Government Pierhead line; thence northerly along said Pierhead line to its intersection with a line parallel with, and distant 10 feet easterly from, the existing easterly boundary line of Pier 30–32; thence northerly along said parallel line and its northerly prolongation, to a point of intersection with a line parallel with, and distant 10 feet northerly from, the existing northerly boundary of Pier 30–32; thence westerly along last said parallel line to its intersection with the United States Government Pierhead line; thence northerly along said Pierhead line, to its intersection aforementioned northwesterly line of Bryant Street produced northeasterly; thence southwesterly along said northwesterly line of Bryant Street produced to the point of beginning.

(c) Requirement that area be improved

The declaration of nonnavigability under subsection (a) applies only to those parts of the area described in subsection (b) that are or will be bulkheaded, filled, or otherwise occupied by permanent structures and does not affect the applicability of any Federal statute or regulation applicable to such parts the day before November 8, 2007, including sections 401 and 403 of this title, section 1344 of this title, and the National Environmental Policy Act of 1969 (42 U.S.C. 4321 et seq.).

(d) Expiration date

If, 20 years from November 8, 2007, any area or part thereof described in subsection (b) is not bulkheaded or filled or occupied by permanent structures, including marina facilities, in accordance with the requirements set out in subsection (c), or if work in connection with any activity permitted in subsection (c) is not commenced within 5 years after issuance of such permits, then the declaration of nonnavigability for such area or part thereof shall expire.

(Pub. L. 110–114, title V, § 5052, Nov. 8, 2007, 121 Stat. 1211.)

REFERENCES IN TEXT

The National Environmental Policy Act of 1969, referred to in subsec. (c), is Pub. L. 91–190, Jan. 1, 1970, 83 Stat. 852, which is classified generally to chapter 55 (§ 4321 et seq.) of Title 42, The Public Health and Welfare. For complete classification of this Act to the Code, see Short Title note set out under section 4321 of Title 42 and Tables.

"SECRETARY" DEFINED

Secretary means the Secretary of the Army, see section 2 of Pub. L. 110–114, set out as a note under section 2201 of this title.

§ 59i. Patapsco River, Maryland

That portion of the Northwest Branch of the Patapsco River located generally south of Pratt Street, east of Light Street, north of Key Highway, in the city of Baltimore, State of Maryland, and being more particularly described as all of that portion of the Northwest Branch of the Patapsco River lying west of a series of lines beginning at the point formed by the intersection of the south side of Pratt Street, as now laid out, and the west side of Pier 3 and running thence binding on the west side of Pier 3, south 04 degrees 19 minutes 47 seconds east 726.59 feet to the southwest corner of Pier 3; thence crossing the Northwest Branch of the Patapsco River, south 23 degrees 01 minutes 15 seconds west 855.36 feet to the point formed by the intersection of the existing pierhead and bulkhead line and the east side of Battery Avenue, last said point of intersection being the end of the first line of the fourth parcel of land conveyed by J. and F. Realty, Incorporated to Allegheny Pepsi-Cola Bottling Company by deed dated December 22, 1965, and recorded among the Land Record of Baltimore City in Liber J. F. C. numbered 2006 folio 345, the location of said pierhead and bulkhead line is based upon the Corps of Engineers, Baltimore District, Baltimore, Maryland, coordinate value for station LIV of said pierhead and bulkhead line, the coordinate value as referred to the Lambert grid plane coordinate system for the State of Maryland of said station LIV being east 2,111,161.40, north 527,709.27 and thence binding on the east side of Battery Avenue, south 03 degrees 09 minutes 07 seconds east 568 feet, more or less, to intersect the north side of Key Highway as now laid out and located is hereby declared to be not a navigable stream of the United States within the meaning of the laws of the United States, and the consent of Congress is hereby given for the filling in of all or any part of the described area.

(Pub. L. 90–483, title I, § 115, Aug. 13, 1968, 82 Stat. 736.)

§ 59j. Delaware River, Philadelphia County, Pennsylvania; permanent structures

That portion of the Delaware River in Philadelphia County, Commonwealth of Pennsylvania, lying between all that certain lot or piece of ground situate in the second and fifth wards of the city of Philadelphia described as follows:

Beginning at a point on the easterly side of Delaware Avenue (variable width) said side being the bulkhead line of the Delaware River (approved by the Secretary of War on September 10, 1940), at the distance of 1,833.652 feet from an angle point on the easterly side of said Delaware Avenue south of Washington Avenue;

thence extending along the easterly side of said Delaware Avenue the following courses and distances, (1) north 0 degree 45 minutes 33.2 seconds west 2,524.698 feet to a point; (2) north 9 degrees 36 minutes 25 seconds east, 2,168.160 feet to a point; (3) north 13 degrees 26 minutes 45.8 seconds east, 2,039.270 feet to a point; (4) north 20 degrees 12 minutes 52.4 seconds east, 35.180 feet to an angle point in Delaware Avenue; thence continuing north 20 degrees 12 minutes 52.4 seconds east along the said bulkhead line, the distance of 574.970 feet to a point on the south house line of Callowhill Street produced;

thence extending along the south house line of Callowhill Street produced south 80 degrees 47 minutes 30.6 seconds east, the distance of 523.908 feet to a point on the pierhead line of the Delaware River (approved by the Secretary of War on September 10, 1940);

thence extending along the said pierhead line the following courses and distances, (1) south 17 degrees 52 minutes 48.5 seconds west, 605.262 feet to a point; (2) south 14 degrees 14 minutes 14.7 seconds west, 1,372.530 feet to a point; (3) south 10 degrees 37 minutes 35.3 seconds west, 1,252.160 feet to a point; (4) south 8 degrees 23 minutes 50.4 seconds west, 1,450.250 feet to a point; (5) south 2 degrees 22 minutes 45.9 seconds west, 1,221.670 feet to a point; (6) south 1 degree 4 minutes 36 seconds east, 1,468.775 feet to a point on the north house line of Catherine Street extended, thence extending north 76 degrees 56 minutes 29.2 seconds west, the distance of 555.911 feet to the first mentioned point and place of beginning is hereby declared not to be a navigable water of the United States within the meaning of the Constitution and laws of the United States, and the Consent of Congress is hereby given, for the filling or erection of permanent structures in all or any part of the described area.

(Pub. L. 92–605, §1, Oct. 31, 1972, 86 Stat. 1493.)

CHANGE OF NAME

Department of War designated Department of the Army and title of Secretary of War changed to Secretary of the Army by section 205(a) of act July 26, 1947, ch. 343, title II, 61 Stat. 501. Section 205(a) of act July 26, 1947, was repealed by section 53 of act Aug. 10, 1956, ch. 1041, 70A Stat. 641. Section 1 of act Aug. 10, 1956, enacted "Title 10, Armed Forces" which in sections 3010 to 3013 continued Department of the Army under administrative supervision of Secretary of the Army.

PERMANENT STRUCTURES IN ABOVE-DESCRIBED AREA; APPROVAL OF PLANS

Section 2 of Pub. L. 92–605 provided that: "This declaration [this section] shall apply only to portions of the above-described area which are filled or occupied by permanent structures. No such filling or erection of structures in the above-described area shall be commenced until the plans therefor have been approved by the Secretary of the Army who shall, prior to granting such approval, give consideration to all factors affecting the general public interest and the impact of the proposed work on the environment."

§59j–1. Declaration of nonnavigability for portions of the Delaware River

(a) Area to be declared non-navigable; public interest

Unless the Secretary finds, after consultation with local and regional public officials (including local and regional public planning organizations), that the proposed projects in Philadelphia, Pennsylvania, to be undertaken within the boundaries described below, are not in the public interest then, subject to subsections (b) and (c) of this section, those portions of the Delaware River, bounded and described as follows, are declared to be non-navigable waters of the United States:

(1) LIBERTY LANDING. [Omitted]

(2) MARINA TOWERS AND WORLD TRADE CENTER—PIER 25 NORTH. [Omitted]

(3) MARINE TRADE CENTER—PIER 24 NORTH. [Omitted]

(4) NATIONAL SUGAR COMPANY "SUGAR HOUSE". [Omitted]

(5) RIVERCENTER. [Omitted]

(b) Limits on applicability; regulatory requirements

The declaration under subsection (a) of this section shall apply only to those parts of the areas described in subsection (a) of this section which are or will be bulkheaded and filled or otherwise occupied by permanent structures, including marina facilities. All such work is subject to all applicable Federal statutes and regulations, including, but not necessarily limited to, sections 401 and 403 of this title, section 1344 of this title, and the National Environmental Policy Act of 1969 [42 U.S.C. 4321 et seq.].

(c) Expiration date

If, 20 years from November 17, 1988, any area or part thereof described in subsection (a) (except 30 years from November 17, 1988, in the case of the area or any part thereof described in subsection (a)(5)) is not bulkheaded or filled or occupied by permanent structures, including marina facilities, in accordance with the requirements set out in subsection (b) of this section, or if work in connection with any activity permitted in subsection (b) of this section is not commenced within 5 years after issuance of such permits, then the declaration of non-navigability for such area or part thereof shall expire.

(Pub. L. 100–676, §38, Nov. 17, 1988, 102 Stat. 4032; Pub. L. 110–114, title III, §3181(g), Nov. 8, 2007, 121 Stat. 1162.)

REFERENCES IN TEXT

The National Environmental Policy Act of 1969, referred to in subsec. (b), is Pub. L. 91–190, Jan. 1, 1970, 83 Stat. 852, as amended, which is classified generally to chapter 55 (§4321 et seq.) of Title 42, The Public Health and Welfare. For complete classification of this Act to the Code, see Short Title note set out under section 4321 of Title 42 and Tables.

CODIFICATION

The text of the boundary descriptions contained in pars. (1) to (5) of subsec. (a), which is not set out in the Code, appears at 102 Stat. 4032 to 4038.

AMENDMENTS

2007—Subsec. (c). Pub. L. 110–114 substituted "subsection (a) (except 30 years from November 17, 1988, in the case of the area or any part thereof described in subsection (a)(5))" for "subsection (a) of this section".

"SECRETARY" DEFINED

Secretary means the Secretary of the Army, see section 2 of Pub. L. 100–676, set out as a note under section 2201 of this title.

§59k. Wicomico River, Maryland

(a) If the Secretary of the Army acting through the Chief of Engineers, finds that the proposed project in Salisbury, Maryland, to be undertaken at the locations to be declared nonnavigable under this section is in the public interest, on the basis of engineering studies to determine the location and structural stability of any bulkheading and filling and permanent pile-supported structures, in order to preserve and maintain the remaining navigable waterway and on the basis of environmental studies conducted pursuant to the National Environmental Policy Act of 1969 [42 U.S.C. 4321 et seq.], then those portions of the South Prong of the Wicomico

River in Wicomico County, State of Maryland, bounded and described as follows, are declared to be not a navigable water of the United States within the meaning of the laws of the United States, and the consent of Congress is hereby given, consistent with subsection (b) of this section, to the filling in of a part thereof or the erection of permanent pile-supported structures thereon: That portion of the South Prong of the Wicomico River in Salisbury, Maryland, bounded on the east by the west side of United States Route 13; on the west by the west side of the Mill Street Bridge; on the south by a line five feet landward from the present water's edge at high tide extending the entire length of the South Prong from the east boundary at United States Route 13 to the west boundary at the Mill Street Bridge; and on the north by a line five feet landward from the present water's edge at high tide extending the entire length of the South Prong from the east boundary at United States Route 13 to the west boundary at the Mill Street Bridge.

(b) This declaration shall apply only to the portions of the areas described in subsection (a) of this section which are bulkheaded and filled or occupied by permanent pile-supported structures. Plans for bulkheading and filling and permanent pile-supported structures shall be approved by the Secretary of the Army, acting through the Chief of Engineers. Such bulkheaded and filled areas or areas occupied by permanent pile-supported structures shall not reduce the existing width of the Wicomico River to less than sixty feet and a minimum depth of five feet shall be maintained within such sixty-foot width of the Wicomico River. Local interests shall reimburse the Federal Government for engineering and all other costs incurred under this section.

(Pub. L. 93–251, title I, §97, Mar. 7, 1974, 88 Stat. 40.)

REFERENCES IN TEXT

The National Environmental Policy Act of 1969, referred to in text, is Pub. L. 91–190, Jan. 1, 1970, 83 Stat. 852, as amended, which is classified generally to chapter 55 (§4321 et seq.) of Title 42, The Public Health and Welfare. For complete classification of this Act to the Code, see Short Title note set out under section 4321 of Title 42 and Tables.

§ 59*l*. Nonapplicability of prohibitions and provisions for review and approval concerning wharves and piers

The prohibitions and provisions for review and approval concerning wharves and piers in waters of the United States as set forth in sections 403 and 565 of this title shall not apply to any body of water located entirely within one State which is, or could be, considered to be a navigable body of water of the United States solely on the basis of historical use in interstate commerce.

(Pub. L. 94–587, §154, Oct. 22, 1976, 90 Stat. 2932.)

§ 59m. Lake Oswego, Oregon; Lake Coeur d'Alene, Idaho; and Lake George, New York

For the purposes of section 403 of this title the following bodies of water are declared nonnavigable: Lake Oswego, Oregon; Lake Coeur d'Alene, Idaho; and Lake George, New York.

(Pub. L. 94–587, §162, Oct. 22, 1976, 90 Stat. 2934.)

CODIFICATION

"Section 403 of this title" substituted in text for "section 10 of the Act of March 3, 1899 (30 Stat. 1151) (33 U.S.C. 401)" as the probable intent of Congress in that section 10 of said act is set out as section 403 of this title while section 401 of this title is based on section 9 of the act of Mar. 3, 1899.

§ 59n. Hudson River, Hudson County, New Jersey

(a) If the Secretary of the Army, acting through the Chief of Engineers, finds that the proposed project to be erected at the location to be declared nonnavigable under this section is in the public interest, on the basis of engineering studies to determine the location and structural stability of any bulkheading and filling and permanent pile-supported structure, in order to preserve and maintain the remaining navigable waterway and on the basis of environmental studies conducted pursuant to the National Environmental Policy Act of 1969 [42 U.S.C. 4321 et seq.], then that portion of the Hudson River in Hudson County, State of New Jersey, bounded and described as follows is hereby declared to be nonnavigable water of the United States within the meaning of the laws of the United States, and the consent of Congress is hereby given to the filling in of all or any part thereof and the erection of permanent pile-supported structures thereon:

Such portion is in the township of North Bergen in the county of Hudson and State of New Jersey, and is more particularly described as follows: At a point in the easterly right-of-way of New Jersey Shore Line Railroad (formerly New Jersey Junction Railroad) said point being located northerly, measured along said easterly right-of-way, 81.93 feet from Station 54+42.4 as shown on construction drawing dated May 23, 1931, of River Road, filed in the Office of the Hudson County Engineer, Jersey City, New Jersey:

thence (1) northerly and along said easterly right-of-way on a bearing of north 12 degrees 11 minutes 14 seconds east, a distance of 280 feet to a point;

thence (2) south 75 degrees 28 minutes 24 seconds east, a distance of 310 feet to a point;

thence (3) south 17 degrees 15 minutes 41 seconds east, a distance of 101.70 feet to a point;

thence (4) south 62 degrees 18 minutes 12 seconds east a distance of 355.64 feet to a point in the exterior solid fill line of April 7, 1903, and the bulkhead line of April 28, 1904, on the Hudson River;

thence (5) along said exterior solid fill and bulkhead lines south 28 degrees 55 minutes 51 seconds west, a distance of 523 feet to a point in the northerly line of lands now or formerly of New York State Realty and Terminal Company;

thence (6) north 61 degrees 34 minutes 29 seconds west, and along said northerly line of the New York State Realty and Terminal Company, a distance of 590.08 feet to a point in the aforementioned easterly right-of-way of the New Jersey Shore Line Railroad;

thence (7) northerly and along said easterly right-of-way of the New Jersey Shore Line

Railroad on a curve to the left a radius of 995.09 feet, an arc length of 170.96 feet to a point therein;

thence (8) northerly, still along the same, on a bearing of north 12 degrees 11 minutes 14 seconds east, a distance of 81.93 feet to the point and place of beginning.

Said parcel containing 8 acres being the same more or less.

(b) The declaration in subsection (a) of this section shall apply only to portions of the above-described area which are either bulkheaded and filled or occupied by permanent pile-supported structures. Plans for bulkheading and filling and permanent pile-supported structures shall be approved by the Secretary of the Army, acting through the Chief of Engineers. Local interests shall reimburse the Federal Government for engineering and all other costs incurred under this section.

(Pub. L. 94–587, § 178, Oct. 22, 1976, 90 Stat. 2937.)

REFERENCES IN TEXT

The National Environmental Policy Act of 1969, referred to in subsec. (a), is Pub. L. 91–190, Jan. 1, 1970, 83 Stat. 852, as amended, which is classified generally to chapter 55 (§ 4321 et seq.) of Title 42, The Public Health and Welfare. For complete classification of this Act to the Code, see Short Title note set out under section 4321 of Title 42 and Tables.

§ 59n–1. Caven Point, New Jersey

That portion of the Hudson River in the New York Bay consisting of—

(1) all that piece or parcel of land, containing 120.54 acres, situate, lying and being in the city of Jersey City, Hudson County, State of New Jersey, upon or around that certain lot or piece of land known as the Caven Point Area; and

(2) all that piece or parcel of land, containing 18 acres more or less, situate on the northwesterly side of New Jersey State Highway Route 185,

more particularly described in the Congressional Record dated March 11, 1986, pages S2446–2447, is hereby declared to be not a navigable water of the United States within the meaning of the Constitution and the laws of the United States, except for the purposes of the Federal Water Pollution Control Act [33 U.S.C. 1251 et seq.].

(Pub. L. 99–662, title XI, § 1118, Nov. 17, 1986, 100 Stat. 4237.)

REFERENCES IN TEXT

The Federal Water Pollution Control Act, referred to in text, is act June 30, 1948, ch. 758, as amended generally by Pub. L. 92–500, § 2, Oct. 18, 1972, 86 Stat. 816, which is classified generally to chapter 26 (§ 1251 et seq.) of this title. For complete classification of this Act to the Code, see Short Title note set out under section 1251 of this title and Tables.

§ 59*o*. Hackensack River, Hudson County, New Jersey

(a) If the Secretary of the Army, acting through the Chief of Engineers finds that the proposed project to be erected at the location to be declared nonnavigable under this section is in the public interest, on the basis of engineering studies to determine the location and structural stability of any bulkheading and filling and permanent pile-supported structure, in order to preserve and maintain the remaining navigable waterway, and on the basis of environmental studies conducted pursuant to the National Environmental Policy Act of 1969 [42 U.S.C. 4321 et seq.], then those portions of the Hackensack River in Hudson County, State of New Jersey, bounded and described as follows are hereby declared to be nonnavigable waters of the United States within the meaning of the laws of the United States, and the consent of Congress is hereby given to the filling in of all or any part thereof and the erection of permanent pile-supported structures thereon:

Beginning at a point where the southeasterly shoreline (mean high water line) of the Hackensack River intersects the easterly line of the Erie Railroad said point property being 2,015.38 feet northerly along said railroad property from where it intersects the northerly line of the Meadowlands Parkway (100 feet wide) and running from:

thence north 19 degrees 20 minutes 54 seconds west 50.00 feet;

thence north 37 degrees 30 minutes 08 seconds east 615.38 feet;

thence north 03 degrees 02 minutes 56 seconds east, 2,087 feet;

thence north 31 degrees 11 minutes 06 seconds east 577 feet;

thence north 74 degrees 29 minutes 18 seconds east 541.25 feet;

thence south 62 degrees 01 minutes 31 seconds east 400 feet;

thence south 55 degrees 46 minutes 27 seconds east 612.52 feet;

thence south 34 degrees 13 minutes 33 seconds west 517.79 feet;

thence south 55 degrees 46 minutes 27 seconds east 158.81 feet;

thence south 34 degrees 13 minutes 33 seconds west 310 feet;

thence north 55 degrees 26 minutes 27 seconds north 15 feet;

thence south 34 degrees 13 minutes 33 seconds west 592 feet;

thence running in a southwesterly direction along the shoreline (mean high water line) of the Hackensack River, a distance of 2,360 feet being the same more or less to the easterly property line of the Erie Railroad and the point or place of beginning.

Said parcel containing 67.6 acres being the same more or less.

(b) The declaration in subsection (a) of this section shall apply only to portions of the described area which are either bulkheaded and filled or occupied by permanent pile-supported structures. Plans for bulkheading and filling and permanent pile-supported structures shall be approved by the Secretary of the Army, acting through the Chief of Engineers. Local interests shall reimburse the Federal Government for engineering and all other costs incurred under this section.

(Pub. L. 94–587, § 179, Oct. 22, 1976, 90 Stat. 2938.)

REFERENCES IN TEXT

The National Environmental Policy Act of 1969, referred to in subsec. (a), is Pub. L. 91–190, Jan. 1, 1970, 83

Stat. 852, as amended, which is classified generally to chapter 55 (§4321 et seq.) of Title 42, The Public Health and Welfare. For complete classification of this Act to the Code, see Short Title note set out under section 4321 of Title 42 and Tables.

§59p. Kenduskeag Stream, Penobscot County, Maine

The Kenduskeag Stream, a minor tributary of the Penobscot River, located in Penobscot County, in the State of Maine, be, and the same is hereby, declared to be a nonnavigable waterway within the meaning of the Constitution and laws of the United States of America.

(July 11, 1947, ch. 236, §1, 61 Stat. 316.)

§59q. Erie Basin, Buffalo Harbor, New York

That portion of the Erie Basin in the Buffalo Harbor lying within the following described area is hereby declared to be not a navigable water of the United States within the meaning of the Constitution and the laws of the United States.

(Pub. L. 96–520, §1, Dec. 12, 1980, 94 Stat. 3033.)

References in Text

The following described area, referred to in text, refers to the metes and bounds description of that portion of the Erie Basin in the Buffalo Harbor set out in the second paragraph of section 1 of Pub. L. 96–520, Dec. 12, 1980, 94 Stat. 3033–3035, which is not classified to the Code.

§59q–1. Union Canal, Outer Buffalo Harbor, New York

The portion of the Union Canal, also known as the Union Ship Canal, an appendage of the Buffalo Outer Harbor, located in the City of Buffalo, State of New York, is declared to be a nonnavigable waterway of the United States within the meaning of the General Bridge Act of 1946 (33 U.S.C. 525, et seq.) from a point two hundred feet west of Fuhrmann Boulevard east to its terminus.

(Pub. L. 100–202, §101(*l*) [title III, §332], Dec. 22, 1987, 101 Stat. 1329–358, 1329–384.)

References in Text

The General Bridge Act of 1946, referred to in text, is title V of act Aug. 2, 1946, ch. 753, 60 Stat. 847, as amended, which is classified generally to subchapter III (§525 et seq.) of chapter 11 of this title. For complete classification of this Act to the Code, see Short Title note set out under section 525 of this title and Tables.

§59r. Trent River, Craven County, North Carolina

Those portions of the Trent River in the city of New Bern, county of Craven, State of North Carolina, bounded and described in Committee Print 95–56 of the Committee on Public Works and Transportation of the House of Representatives are hereby declared to be nonnavigable waters of the United States within the meaning of the laws of the United States.

(Pub. L. 96–520, §3, Dec. 12, 1980, 94 Stat. 3036.)

Change of Name

Committee on Public Works and Transportation of House of Representatives treated as referring to Committee on Transportation and Infrastructure of House of Representatives by section 1(a) of Pub. L. 104–14, set out as a note preceding section 21 of Title 2, The Congress.

§59s. Green River, Washington

For the purposes of section 401 of this title, the portion of the Green River in the State of Washington lying upstream from that State Highway 516 bridge which is in existence on October 26, 1981, is hereby declared to be not a navigable waterway.

(Pub. L. 97–68, §2(b), Oct. 26, 1981, 95 Stat. 1040.)

§59t. Burnham Canal, Milwaukee, Wisconsin

The portion of the Burnham Canal, in Milwaukee, Wisconsin, which is underneath and west of a point one hundred feet east of South Eleventh Street is declared to be not a navigable water of the United States within the meaning of the Constitution and laws of the United States. The right to alter, amend, or repeal this section is hereby expressly reserved.

(Pub. L. 97–468, title V, §503, Jan. 14, 1983, 96 Stat. 2552.)

§59u. Lawyer's Ditch, Essex County, New Jersey

The body of water known as Lawyer's Ditch located at block 5,000 in the city of Newark, county of Essex, New Jersey, is declared to be a nonnavigable waterway of the United States within the meaning of the General Bridge Act of 1946 (33 U.S.C. 525 et seq.).

(Pub. L. 99–307, §3, May 19, 1986, 100 Stat. 446.)

References in Text

The General Bridge Act of 1946, referred to in text, is title V of act Aug. 2, 1946, ch. 753, 60 Stat. 847, as amended, which is classified generally to subchapter III (§525 et seq.) of chapter 11 of this title. For complete classification of this Act to the Code, see Short Title note set out under section 525 of this title and Tables.

§59v. Middle River, Maryland

(a) Description

That portion of the waterway in which is located Dark Head Creek in the community of Middle River, Baltimore County, Maryland, lying northwest of a line extending south 68 degrees 37 minutes 56 seconds west from a point (227.50 feet from the northeast corner of the existing bulkhead and pier line) whose coordinates in the Maryland State Coordinate System are north 544967.24 and east 962701.05 (latitude north 39 degrees 19 minutes 42 seconds and longitude west 76 degrees 25 minutes 29.5 seconds) and thence south 44 degrees 48 minutes 20 seconds west, 350.12 feet to a point (at the southwest corner of the existing bulkhead and pier line) whose coordinates in the Maryland State Coordinate System are north 544635.94 and east 962242.46 (latitude north 39 degrees 19 minutes 39 seconds and longitude west 76 degrees 25 minutes 35.4 seconds), is declared to be a nonnavigable water of the United States for purposes of the navigation servitude.

(b) Pierhead and bulkhead line of Dark Head Creek

The line described in subsection (a) of this section shall be established as a combined pierhead and bulkhead line of Dark Head Creek.

(c) Previously authorized projects

Any project heretofore authorized by any Act of Congress, insofar as such project is within the boundaries of Dark Head Creek as described in subsection (a) of this section, is not authorized after November 17, 1986.

(d) Reservation of rights

The right to alter, amend, or repeal this section is hereby expressly reserved.

(Pub. L. 99–662, title XI, § 1160, Nov. 17, 1986, 100 Stat. 4257.)

§ 59w. Norton Basin and Jamaica Bay, New York

The two portions of Norton Basin and Jamaica Bay, New York, that are particularly described in Committee Print 99–58 of the Committee on Public Works and Transportation of the House of Representatives are hereby declared to be nonnavigable waters of the United States for purposes of the navigation servitude.

(Pub. L. 99–662, title XI, § 1168, Nov. 17, 1986, 100 Stat. 4259.)

CHANGE OF NAME

Committee on Public Works and Transportation of House of Representatives treated as referring to Committee on Transportation and Infrastructure of House of Representatives by section 1(a) of Pub. L. 104–14, set out as a note preceding section 21 of Title 2, The Congress.

§ 59x. Exemption from General Bridge Act of 1946

(a) Waters declared nonnavigable

The waters described in subsection (b) of this section are declared to be nonnavigable waters of the United States for purposes of the General Bridge Act of 1946 (33 U.S.C. 525 et seq.).

(b) Waters described

The waters referred to in subsection (a) of this section are a drainage canal which—

(1) is an unnamed tributary of the creek known as Newton Creek, located at block 641 (formerly designated as block 860) in the city of Camden, New Jersey;

(2) originates at the north bank of Newton Creek approximately 1,200 feet east of the confluence of Newton Creek and the Delaware River; and

(3) terminates at drainage culverts on the west side of Interstate Highway 676.

(Pub. L. 100–448, § 16, Sept. 28, 1988, 102 Stat. 1845; Pub. L. 100–457, title III, § 325, Sept. 30, 1988, 102 Stat. 2150.)

REFERENCES IN TEXT

The General Bridge Act of 1946, referred to in subsec. (a), is title V of act Aug. 2, 1946, ch. 753, 60 Stat. 847, as amended, which is classified generally to subchapter III (§ 525 et seq.) of chapter 11 of this title. For complete classification of this Act to the Code, see Short Title note set out under section 525 of this title and Tables.

CODIFICATION

Pub. L. 100–448 and Pub. L. 100–457 enacted identical sections.

§ 59y. Declaration of nonnavigability for portions of Coney Island Creek and Gravesend Bay, New York

(a) Area to be declared non-navigable; public interest

Unless the Secretary finds, after consultation with local and regional public officials (including local and regional public planning organizations), that the proposed projects to be undertaken within the boundaries in the portions of Coney Island Creek and Gravesend Bay, New York, described below, are not in the public interest then, subject to subsections (b) and (c) of this section, those portions of such Creek and Bay, bounded and described as follows, are declared to be non-navigable waters of the United States:

Beginning at the corner formed by the intersection of the Westerly Line of Cropsey Avenue, and the Northernmost United States Pierhead Line of Coney Island Creek.

Running thence south 12 degrees 41 minutes 03 seconds E and along the westerly line of Cropsey Avenue, 98.72 feet to the northerly channel line as shown on Corps of Engineers Map Numbered F. 150 and on Survey by Rogers and Giollorenzo Numbered 13959 dated October 31, 1986.

Running thence in a westerly direction and along the said northerly channel line the following bearings and distances:

South 48 degrees 59 minutes 27 seconds west, 118.77 feet; south 37 degrees 07 minutes 01 seconds west, 232.00 feet; south 23 degrees 17 minutes 10 seconds west, 430.03 feet; south 31 degrees 25 minutes 46 seconds west, 210.95 feet; south 79 degrees 22 minutes 49 seconds west, 244.18 feet; north 55 degrees 00 minutes 29 seconds west, 183.10 feet; north 41 degrees 47 minutes 04 seconds west, 315.16 feet;

North 41 degrees 17 minutes 43 seconds west, 492.47 feet to the said Pierhead Line; thence north 73 degrees 58 minutes 40 seconds west and along said pierhead line, 2,665.25 feet to the intersection of the United States bulkhead line;

Thence north 0 degree 19 minutes 35 seconds west and along the United States Bulkhead line 1,138.50 feet to the intersection of the westerly prolongation of the center line of 26th Avenue,

Thence north 58 degrees 25 minutes 06 seconds east and along the center line of said 26th Avenue, 2,320.85 feet to the westerly line of Cropsey Avenue, then southeasterly and along the southerly line of Cropsey Avenue the following bearings and distances:

South 31 degrees 34 minutes 54 seconds east, 4,124.59 feet; and

South 12 degrees 41 minutes 03 seconds east, 710.74 feet to the point or place of beginning.

Coordinates and bearings are in the system as established by the United States Coast and Geodetic Survey for the Borough of Brooklyn. The Secretary shall make the public interest determination separately for each proposed project, using reasonable discretion, within 150 days after submission of appropriate plans for each proposed project.

(b) Limits on applicability; regulatory requirements

The declaration under subsection (a) of this section shall apply only to those parts of the areas described in subsection (a) of this section which are or will be bulkheaded and filled or otherwise occupied by permanent structures, including marina facilities. All such work is subject to all applicable Federal statutes and regulations, including, but not necessarily limited to, sections 401 and 403 of this title, section 1344 of this title, and the National Environmental Policy Act of 1969 [42 U.S.C. 4321 et seq.].

(c) Expiration date

If, 20 years from November 17, 1988, any area or part thereof described in subsection (a) of this section is not bulkheaded or filled or occupied by permanent structures, including marina facilities, in accordance with the requirements set out in subsection (b) of this section, or if work in connection with any activity permitted in subsection (b) of this section is not commenced within 5 years after issuance of such permits, then the declaration of non-navigability for such area or part thereof shall expire.

(Pub. L. 100–676, § 39, Nov. 17, 1988, 102 Stat. 4039.)

REFERENCES IN TEXT

The National Environmental Policy Act of 1969, referred to in subsec. (b), is Pub. L. 91–190, Jan. 1, 1970, 83 Stat. 852, as amended, which is classified generally to chapter 55 (§ 4321 et seq.) of Title 42, The Public Health and Welfare. For complete classification of this Act to the Code, see Short Title note set out under section 4321 of Title 42 and Tables.

"SECRETARY" DEFINED

Secretary means the Secretary of the Army, see section 2 of Pub. L. 100–676, set out as a note under section 2201 of this title.

§ 59z. Declaration of nonnavigability of bodies of water in Ridgefield, New Jersey

The three bodies of water located at block 4004, lots 1 and 2, and block 4003, lot 1, in the Borough of Ridgefield, County of Bergen, New Jersey, which have their mouths at the Hackensack River at 40 degrees 49 minutes 58 seconds north latitude and 74 degrees 01 minute 46 seconds west longitude, 40 degrees 49 minutes 46 seconds north latitude and 74 degrees 01 minute 55 seconds west longitude, and 40 degrees 49 minutes 35 seconds north latitude and 74 degrees 02 minutes 04 seconds west longitude, respectively, and the body of water located at block 4006, lot 1, in the Borough of Ridgefield, County of Bergen, New Jersey, which has its mouth at the Hackensack River at 40 degrees 49 minutes 15 seconds north latitude and 74 degrees 01 minute 52 seconds west longitude, are declared to be nonnavigable waterways of the United States within the meaning of the General Bridge Act of 1946 (33 U.S.C. 525 et seq.) and section 401 of this title.

(Pub. L. 100–676, § 54, Nov. 17, 1988, 102 Stat. 4046.)

REFERENCES IN TEXT

The General Bridge Act of 1946, referred to in text, is title V of act Aug. 2, 1946, ch. 753, 60 Stat. 847, as amended, which is classified generally to subchapter III (§ 525 et seq.) of chapter 11 of this title. For complete classification of this Act to the Code, see Short Title note set out under section 525 of this title and Tables.

§ 59aa. Nonnavigability of Wisconsin River

The portion of the Wisconsin River above the hydroelectric dam at Prairie du Sac, Wisconsin, is hereby declared to be a nonnavigable waterway of the United States for purposes of title 46, including but not limited to the provisions of such title relating to vessel inspection and vessel licensure, and the other maritime laws of the United States.

(Pub. L. 101–595, title III, § 318, Nov. 16, 1990, 104 Stat. 2988.)

§ 59bb. Declaration of nonnavigability for portions of Lake Erie

(a) Area to be declared nonnavigable; public interest

Unless the Secretary finds, after consultation with local and regional public officials (including local and regional public planning organizations), that the proposed projects to be undertaken within the boundaries of Lake Erie described in Committee Print 101–48 of the Committee on Public Works and Transportation of the House of Representatives, dated July 1990, are not in the public interest then, subject to subsections (b) and (c) of this section, those portions of Lake Erie, bounded and described in such Committee print, are declared to be nonnavigable waters of the United States.

(b) Limits on applicability; regulatory requirements

The declaration under subsection (a) of this section shall apply only to those parts of the areas described in the Committee print referred to in subsection (a) of this section which are or will be bulkheaded and filled or otherwise occupied by permanent structures, including marina facilities. All such work is subject to all applicable Federal statutes and regulations including, but not limited to, sections 401 and 403 of this title, section 1344 of this title, and the National Environmental Policy Act of 1969 [42 U.S.C. 4321 et seq.].

(c) Expiration date

If, 20 years from November 28, 1990, any area or part thereof described in the Committee print referred to in subsection (a) of this section is not bulkheaded or filled or occupied by permanent structures, including marina facilities, in accordance with the requirements set out in subsection (b) of this section, or if work in connection with any activity permitting[1] in subsection (b) of this section is not commenced within 5 years after issuance of such permits, then the declaration of nonnavigability for such area or part thereof shall expire.

(Pub. L. 101–640, title IV, § 408, Nov. 28, 1990, 104 Stat. 4647.)

REFERENCES IN TEXT

The National Environmental Policy Act of 1969, referred to in subsec. (b), is Pub. L. 91–190, Jan. 1, 1970, 83

[1] So in original. Probably should be "permitted".

Stat. 852, as amended, which is classified generally to chapter 55 (§ 4321 et seq.) of Title 42, The Public Health and Welfare. For complete classification of this Act to the Code, see Short Title note set out under section 4321 of Title 42 and Tables.

CHANGE OF NAME

Committee on Public Works and Transportation of House of Representatives treated as referring to Committee on Transportation and Infrastructure of House of Representatives by section 1(a) of Pub. L. 104–14, set out as a note preceding section 21 of Title 2, The Congress.

"SECRETARY" DEFINED

Secretary means the Secretary of the Army, see section 2 of Pub. L. 101–640, set out as a note under section 2201 of this title.

§ 59bb–1. Declaration of nonnavigability for Lake Erie, New York

(a) Area to be declared nonnavigable; public interest

Unless the Secretary finds, after consultation with local and regional public officials (including local and regional public planning organizations), that the proposed projects to be undertaken within the boundaries in the portion of Erie County, New York, described in subsection (b) of this section, are not in the public interest then, subject to subsection (c) of this section, those portions of such county that were once part of Lake Erie and are now filled are declared to be nonnavigable waters of the United States.

(b) Boundaries

The portion of Erie County, New York, referred to in subsection (a) of this section is all that tract or parcel of land, situated in the town of Hamburg and the city of Lackawanna, Erie County, New York, being part of Lots 12, 13, 14, 15, 16, 17, 18, 19, 20, 21, 22, 23, 24, and 25 of the Ogden Gore Tract and part of Lots 23, 24, and 36 of the Buffalo Creek Reservation, Township 10, Range 8 of the Holland Land Company's Survey and more particularly bounded and described as follows:

[Omitted.]

(c) Limits on applicability; regulatory requirements

The declaration under subsection (a) of this section shall apply to those parts of the areas described in subsection (b) of this section that are filled portions of Lake Erie. Any work on these filled portions shall be subject to all applicable Federal statutes and regulations, including sections 401 and 403 of this title, section 1344 of this title, and the National Environmental Policy Act of 1969 (42 U.S.C. 4321 et seq.).

(d) Expiration date

If, 20 years from December 11, 2000, any area or part thereof described in subsection (a) of this section is not occupied by permanent structures in accordance with the requirements set out in subsection (c) of this section, or if work in connection with any activity permitted in subsection (c) of this section is not commenced within 5 years after issuance of such permits, then the declaration of nonnavigability for such area or part thereof shall expire.

(Pub. L. 106–541, title III, §346, Dec. 11, 2000, 114 Stat. 2614.)

REFERENCES IN TEXT

The National Environmental Policy Act of 1969, referred to in subsec. (c), is Pub. L. 91–190, Jan. 1, 1970, 83 Stat. 852, as amended, which is classified generally to chapter 55 (§ 4321 et seq.) of Title 42, The Public Health and Welfare. For complete classification of this Act to the Code, see Short Title note set out under section 4321 of Title 42 and Tables.

CODIFICATION

The provisions of subsec. (b) of this section, which contain the text of the boundary descriptions, have been omitted. Such provisions appear at 114 Stat. 2614 to 2618.

"SECRETARY" DEFINED

Secretary means the Secretary of the Army, see section 2 of Pub. L. 106–541, set out as a note under section 2201 of this title.

§ 59cc. Declaration of nonnavigability of portion of Hudson River, New York

(a) Declaration of nonnavigability

Subject to subsections (c), (d), and (e) of this section, the area described in subsection (b) of this section is declared to be nonnavigable waters of the United States.

(b) Area subject to declaration

The area described in this subsection is the portion of the Hudson River, New York, described as follows (according to coordinates and bearings in the system used on the Borough Survey, Borough President's Office, New York, New York):

Beginning at a point in the United States Bulkhead Line approved by the Secretary of War, July 31, 1941, having a coordinate of north 1918.003 west 9806.753;

Running thence easterly, on the arc of a circle curving to the left, whose radial line bears north 3°–44′–20″ east, having a radius of 390.00 feet and a central angle of 22°–05′–50″, 150.41 feet to a point of tangency;

Thence north 71°–38′–30″ east, 42.70 feet;

Thence south 11°–05′–40″ east, 33.46 feet;

Thence south 78°–54′–20″ west, 0.50 feet;

Thence south 11°–05′–40″ east, 2.50 feet;

Thence north 78°–54′–20″ east, 0.50 feet;

Thence south 11°–05′–40″ east, 42.40 feet to a point of curvature;

Thence southerly, on the arc of a circle curving to the right, having a radius of 220.00 feet and a central angle of 16°–37′–40″, 63.85 feet to a point of compound curvature;

Thence still southerly, on the arc of a circle curving to the right, having a radius of 150.00 feet and a central angle of 38°–39′–00″, 101.19 feet to another point of compound curvature;

Thence westerly, on the arc of a circle curving to the right, having a radius of 172.05 feet and a central angle of 32°–32′–03″, 97.69 feet to a point of curve intersection;

Thence south 13°–16′–57″ east, 50.86 feet to a point of curve intersection;

Thence westerly, on the arc of a circle curving to the left, whose radial bears north 13°–16′–57″ west, having a radius of 6.00 feet and a central angle of 180°–32′–31″, 18.91 feet to a point of curve intersection;

Thence southerly, on the arc of a circle curving to the left, whose radial line bears north 75°–37′–11″ east, having a radius of 313.40 feet and a central angle of 4°–55′–26″, 26.93 feet to a point of curve intersection;

Thence south 70°–41′–45″ west, 36.60 feet;

Thence north 13°–45′–00″ west, 42.87 feet;

Thence south 76°–15′–00″ west, 15.00 feet;

Thence south 13°–45′–00″ east, 44.33 feet;

Thence south 70°–41′–45″ west, 128.09 feet to a point in the United States Pierhead Line approved by the Secretary of War, 1936;

Thence north 63°–08′–48″ west, along the United States Pierhead Line approved by the Secretary of War, 1936, 114.45 feet to an angle point therein;

Thence north 61°–08′–00″ west, still along the United States Pierhead Line approved by the Secretary of War, 1936, 202.53 feet;

The following three courses being along the lines of George Soilan Park as shown on map prepared by The City of New York, adopted by the Board of Estimate, November 13, 1981, Acc. N° 30071 and lines of property leased to Battery Park City Authority and B. P. C. Development Corp;

Thence north 77°–35′–20″ east, 231.35 feet;

Thence north 12°–24′–40″ west, 33.92 feet;

Thence north 54°–49′–00″ east, 171.52 feet to a point in the United States Bulkhead Line approved by the Secretary of War, July 31, 1941;

Thence north 12°–24′–40″ west, along the United States Bulkhead Line approved by the Secretary of War, July 31, 1941, 62.26 feet to the point or place of beginning; [1]

(c) Determination of public interest

The declaration made in subsection (a) of this section shall not take effect if the Secretary of the Army (acting through the Chief of Engineers), using reasonable discretion, finds that the proposed project is not in the public interest—

(1) before the date which is 120 days after the date of the submission to the Secretary of appropriate plans for the proposed project; and

(2) after consultation with local and regional public officials (including local and regional public planning organizations).

(d) Limitation on applicability of declaration

(1) Affected area

The declaration made in subsection (a) of this section shall apply only to those portions of the area described in subsection (b) of this section which are or will be occupied by permanent structures (including docking facilities) comprising the proposed project.

(2) Application of other laws

Notwithstanding subsection (a) of this section, all activities conducted in the area described in subsection (b) of this section are subject to all Federal laws which apply to such activities, including—

(A) sections 401 and 403 of this title;

(B) section 1344 of this title; and

(C) the National Environmental Policy Act of 1969 (42 U.S.C. 4321 et seq.).

(e) Expiration date

The declaration made in subsection (a) of this section shall expire—

(1) on the date which is 6 years after December 18, 1991, if work on the proposed project to be performed in the area described in subsection (b) of this section is not commenced before such date; or

(2) on the date which is 20 years after December 18, 1991, for any portion of the area described in subsection (b) of this section which on such date is not bulkheaded, filled, or occupied by a permanent structure (including docking facilities).

(f) "Proposed project" defined

For the purposes of this section, the term "proposed project" means any project for the rehabilitation and development of—

(1) the structure located in the area described in subsection (b) of this section, commonly referred to as Pier A; and

(2) the area surrounding such structure.

(Pub. L. 102–240, title I, § 1078, Dec. 18, 1991, 105 Stat. 2015.)

References in Text

The National Environmental Policy Act of 1969, referred to in subsec. (d)(2)(C), is Pub. L. 91–190, Jan. 1, 1970, 83 Stat. 852, as amended, which is classified generally to chapter 55 (§ 4321 et seq.) of Title 42, The Public Health and Welfare. For complete classification of this Act to the Code, see Short Title note set out under section 4321 of Title 42 and Tables.

§ 59dd. Declaration of nonnavigability of portions of Cleveland Harbor, Ohio

(a) to (c) Omitted

(d) Area to be declared nonnavigable; public interest

Unless the Secretary of the Army finds, after consultation with local and regional public officials (including local and regional public planning organizations), that the proposed projects to be undertaken within the boundaries in the portions of Cleveland Harbor, Ohio, described below, are not in the public interest then, subject to subsections (e) and (f) of this section, those portions of such Harbor, bounded and described as follows, are declared to be nonnavigable waters of the United States:

Situated in the City of Cleveland, Cuyahoga County and State of Ohio, T7N, R13W and being more fully described as follows:

Beginning at an iron pin monument at the intersection of the centerline of East 9th Street (99 feet wide) with the centerline of relocated Erieside Avenue, N.E., (70 feet wide) at Cleveland Regional Geodetic Survey Grid System, (CRGS) coordinates N92,679.734, E86,085.955;

Thence south 56°–06′–52″ west on the centerline of relocated Erieside Avenue, N.E., a distance of 89.50 feet to a drill hole set.

Thence north 33°–53′–08″ west a distance of 35.00 feet to a drill hole set on the northwesterly right-of-way line of relocated Erieside Avenue, N.E., said point being the true place of beginning of the parcel herein described.

Thence south 56°–06′–52″ west on the northwesterly right-of-way line of relocated Erieside Avenue, N.E., a distance of 23.39 feet to a ⅝ inch re-bar set;

[1] So in original. The semicolon probably should be a period.

Thence southwesterly on the northwesterly right-of-way line of relocated Erieside Avenue, N.E., along the arc of a curve to the left with a radius of 335.00 feet, and whose chord bears south 42°–36′–52″ west 156.41 feet, an arc distance of 157.87 feet to a ⅝ inch re-bar set;

Thence south 29°–06′–52″ west on the northwesterly right-of-way line of relocated Erieside Avenue, N.E., a distance of 119.39 feet to a ⅝ inch re-bar set;

Thence southwesterly on the northwesterly right-of-way of relocated Erieside Avenue, N.E., along the arc of a curve to the right with a radius of 665.00 feet, and whose chord bears south 32°–22′–08″ west 75.50 feet, an arc distance of 75.54 feet to a ⅝ inch re-bar set;

Thence north 33°–53′–08″ west a distance of 279.31 feet to a drill hole set;

Thence south 56°–06′–52″ west a distance of 37.89 feet to a drill hole set;

Thence north 33°–53′–08″ west a distance of 127.28 feet to a point;

Thence north 11°–06′–52″ east a distance of 225.00 feet to a point;

Thence south 78°–53′–08″ east a distance of 150.00 feet to a drill hole set;

Thence north 11°–06′–52″ east a distance of 32.99 feet to a drill hole set;

Thence north 33°–53′–08″ east a distance of 46.96 feet to a drill hole set;

Thence north 56°–06′–52″ east a distance of 140.36 feet to a drill hole set on the southwesterly right-of-way line of East 9th Street;

Thence south 33°–53′–08″ east on the southwesterly right-of-way line of East 9th Street a distance of 368.79 feet to a drill hole set;

Thence southwesterly along the arc of a curve to the right with a radius of 40.00 feet, and whose chord bears south 11°–06′–52″ west 56.57 feet, an arc distance of 62.83 feet to the true place of beginning containing 174,764 square feet (4.012 acres) more or less.

(e) Limits on applicability; regulatory requirements

The declaration under subsection (d) of this section shall apply only to those parts of the areas described in subsection (d) of this section which are or will be bulkheaded and filled or otherwise occupied by permanent structures, including marina facilities. All such work is subject to all applicable Federal statutes and regulations, including sections 401 and 403 of this title, section 1344 of this title, and the National Environmental Policy Act of 1969 [42 U.S.C. 4321 et seq.].

(f) Expiration date

If, 20 years from December 18, 1991, any area or part thereof described in subsection (d) of this section is not bulkheaded or filled or occupied by permanent structures, including marina facilities, in accordance with the requirements set out in subsection (e) of this section, or if work in connection with any activity permitted in subsection (e) of this section is not commenced within 5 years after issuance of such permit, then the declaration of nonnavigability for such area or part thereof shall expire.

(Pub. L. 102–240, title I, §1079, Dec. 18, 1991, 105 Stat. 2017.)

References in Text

The National Environmental Policy Act of 1969, referred to in subsec. (e), is Pub. L. 91–190, Jan. 1, 1970, 83 Stat. 852, as amended, which is classified generally to chapter 55 (§4321 et seq.) of Title 42, The Public Health and Welfare. For complete classification of this Act to the Code, see Short Title note set out under section 4321 of Title 42 and Tables.

Codification

Section is comprised of section 1079 of Pub. L. 102–240. Subsections (a), (b), and (c) of section 1079 of Pub. L. 102–240 provided for deauthorization of a portion of a project for harbor modification of Cleveland Harbor which was authorized by section 202(a) of the Water Resources Development Act of 1986, Pub. L. 99–662, title II, Nov. 17, 1986, 100 Stat. 4095, which is not classified to the Code.

§59ee. Portion of Sacramento River Barge Canal declared to not be navigable waters of United States

For purposes of bridge administration, the Sacramento River Barge Canal, which connects the Sacramento Deep Water Ship Channel with the Sacramento River in West Sacramento, Yolo County, California, is declared to not be navigable waters of the United States for purposes of the General Bridge Act of 1946 (33 U.S.C. 525 et seq.) from the eastern boundary of the Port of Sacramento to a point 1,200 feet east of the William G. Stone Lock.

(Pub. L. 102–241, §34, Dec. 19, 1991, 105 Stat. 2223.)

References in Text

The General Bridge Act of 1946, referred to in text, is title V of act Aug. 2, 1946, ch. 753, 60 Stat. 847, as amended, which is classified generally to subchapter III (§525 et seq.) of chapter 11 of this title. For complete classification of this Act to the Code, see Short Title note set out under section 525 of this title and Tables.

§59ee–1. Declaration of nonnavigability for portion of Sacramento Deep Water Ship Channel

All waters within such portion of the project are declared to be nonnavigable waters of the United States solely for the purposes of the General Bridge Act of 1946 (33 U.S.C. 525 et seq.) and section 401 of this title.

(Pub. L. 106–541, title III, §347(a)(2), Dec. 11, 2000, 114 Stat. 2618.)

References in Text

"Such portion of the project", referred to in text, means "The portion of the project for navigation, Sacramento Deep Water Ship Channel, California, authorized by section 202(a) of the Water Resources Development Act of 1986 (100 Stat. 4092), beginning from the confluence of the Sacramento River and the Barge Canal to a point 3,300 feet west of the William G. Stone Lock western gate (including the William G. Stone Lock and the Bascule Bridge and Barge Canal)." See first sentence of section 347(a)(2) of Pub. L. 106–541, Dec. 11, 2000, 114 Stat. 2618.

The General Bridge Act of 1946, referred to in text, is title V of act Aug. 2, 1946, ch. 753, 60 Stat. 847, as amended, which is classified generally to subchapter III (§525 et seq.) of chapter 11 of this title. For complete classification of this Act to the Code, see Short Title note set out under section 525 of this title and Tables.

Codification

Section is comprised of the last sentence of section 347(a)(2) of Pub. L. 106–541.

§ 59ff. Declaration of nonnavigability for portions of Pelican Island, Texas

(a) Descriptions of nonnavigable areas

Subject to the provisions of subsections (b), (c), and (d) of this section, those portions of Pelican Island, Texas, which are not submerged and which are within the following property descriptions, are declared to be nonnavigable waters of the United States:

(1) to (5) Omitted.

(b) Exceptions

Notwithstanding the declaration under subsection (a) of this section, the following portions of Pelican Island, Texas, within those lands described in subsection (a) of this section shall remain navigable waters of the United States:

(1) to (3) Omitted.

(c) Requirement that areas be improved

The declaration under subsection (a) of this section shall apply only to those parts of the areas described in subsection (a) of this section and not described in subsection (b) of this section which are or will be bulkheaded and filled or otherwise occupied by permanent structures or other permanent physical improvements, including marina facilities. All such work is subject to applicable Federal statutes and regulations, including sections 401 and 403 of this title, section 1344 of this title and the National Environmental Policy Act of 1969 [42 U.S.C. 4321 et seq.].

(d) Expiration

If, 20 years from December 19, 1991, any area or part thereof described in subsection (a) of this section and not described in subsection (b) of this section is not bulkheaded or filled or occupied by permanent structures or other permanent physical improvements, including marina facilities, in accordance with the requirements set out in subsection (c) of this section, or if work is not commenced within five years after issuance of any permits required to be obtained under subsection (c) of this section, then the declaration of nonnavigability for such area or part thereof shall expire.

(Pub. L. 102–241, § 52, Dec. 19, 1991, 105 Stat. 2228.)

REFERENCES IN TEXT

The National Environmental Policy Act of 1969, referred to in subsec. (c), is Pub. L. 91–190, Jan. 1, 1970, 83 Stat. 852, as amended, which is classified generally to chapter 55 (§ 4321 et seq.) of Title 42, The Public Health and Welfare. For complete classification of this Act to the Code, see Short Title note set out under section 4321 of Title 42 and Tables.

CODIFICATION

The text of the boundary descriptions contained in pars. (1) to (5) of subsec. (a) and pars. (1) to (3) of subsec. (b), which is not set out in the Code, appears at 105 Stat. 2228 to 2231.

§ 59gg. Declaration of nonnavigability for portions of Cuyahoga County, Ohio

(a) Area to be declared nonnavigable; public interest

Unless the Secretary finds, after consultation with local and regional public officials (including local and regional public planning organizations), that the proposed projects to be undertaken within the boundaries in the portions of the county of Cuyahoga, Ohio, described as follows, are not in the public interest then, subject to subsections (b) and (c) of this section, those portions of such county, bounded and described as follows, are declared to be nonnavigable waters of the United States:

Situated in the city of Cleveland, county of Cuyahoga, and State of Ohio, T7N, R13W, and known as being a part of original two acre lots numbers 16, 17, 18, 19, and 20 and the northerly extensions thereof, and being more fully described as follows:

Beginning at the intersection of the centerline of East 9th Street (99 feet wide) with the centerline of Relocated Erieside Avenue, N.E. (70 feet wide); thence south 56 degrees 06 minutes 52 seconds west on the centerline of Relocated Erieside Avenue, N.E., a distance of 112.89 feet to a point; thence north 33 degrees 53 minutes 08 seconds west a distance of 35.00 feet to a ⅝-inch rebar on the northwesterly right-of-way line of Relocated Erieside Avenue, N.E.; thence southwesterly on the northwesterly right-of-way line of Relocated Erieside Avenue, N.E., along the arc of a curve to the left, with a radius of 335.00 feet and whose chord bears south 42 degrees 36 minutes 52 seconds west 156.41 feet, an arc distance of 157.87 feet to a ⅝-inch rebar; thence south 29 degrees 06 minutes 52 seconds west on the northwesterly right-of-way line of Relocated Erieside Avenue, N.E., a distance of 119.39 feet to a ⅝-inch rebar; thence southwesterly on the northwesterly right-of-way line of Relocated Erieside Avenue, N.E., along the arc of a curve to the right, with a radius of 665.00 feet and whose chord bears south 39 degrees, 49 minutes 33 seconds west 247.19 feet, an arc distance of 248.64 feet to a ⅝-inch rebar and the true place of beginning of the parcel herein described; thence southwesterly on the northwesterly right-of-way line of Relocated Erieside Avenue, N.E., along the arc of a curve to the right, with a radius of 665.00 feet and whose chord bears south 53 degrees, 17 minutes 33 seconds west 64.05 feet, an arc distance of 64.08 feet to a ⅝-rebar set; thence south 56 degrees 03 minutes 30 seconds west on the northwesterly right-of-way line of Relocated Erieside Avenue, N.E., a distance of 248.38 feet to a ⅝-rebar set; thence northwesterly on the northeasterly right-of-way line of Relocated Erieside Avenue, N.E., along the arc of a curve to the right, with a radius of 265.00 feet and whose chord bears north 79 degrees 02 minutes 42 seconds west 374.09 feet, an arc distance of 415.31 feet to a drill hole set; thence north 34 degrees 08 minutes 55 seconds west on the northeasterly right-of-way line of Relocated Erieside Avenue, N.E., a distance of 505.30 feet to a ⅝-inch rebar set; thence northwesterly on the northeasterly right-of-way line of Relocated Erieside Avenue, N.E., along the arc of a curve to the left, with a radius of 112.00 feet and whose chord bears north 40 degrees 32 minutes 41 seconds west 24.95 feet, an arc distance of 25.01 feet to a drill hole set on the southerly right-of-way line of former Erieside Avenue, as vacated by city of Cleveland Ordinance No. 1100–87, passed June 16, 1987; thence northeasterly on the former right-of-way line along the arc of a curve to the right, with a radius of 515.00 feet and whose chord bears north 75 degrees 36 minutes 18 seconds east 136.45 feet, an arc distance of 136.85 feet to a ⅝-inch rebar set; thence north 86 degrees 13 minutes 04 seconds east on said former right-of-way line a distance of 294.57 feet to a ⅝-inch rebar set; thence north 52 degrees 57 minutes 23 seconds east on said former right-of-way line a distance of 56.98 feet to a ⅝-inch rebar set; thence south 33 degrees 53 minutes 08 seconds east a distance of 244.65 feet to a ⅝-inch rebar set; thence south 78 degrees 53 minutes 08 seconds east a distance of 105.04 feet to a ⅝-inch rebar set; thence north 56 degrees 06 minutes 52 seconds east a distance of 70.75 feet to a ⅝-inch rebar set; thence south 33 degrees 53 minutes 08 seconds east a distance of 274.74 feet to the true place of beginning containing 325,706 square feet (7.477 acres) more or less.

(b) Limits on applicability; regulatory requirements

The declaration under subsection (a) of this section shall apply to those parts of the areas described in subsection (a) of this section which are or will be bulkheaded and filled or otherwise occupied by permanent structures, including marina facilities. All such work is subject to all applicable Federal statutes and regulations, including sections 401 and 403 of this title, section 1344 of this title, and the National Environmental Policy Act of 1969 [42 U.S.C. 4321 et seq.].

(c) Expiration date

If, 20 years from October 31, 1992, any area or part thereof described in subsection (a) of this section is not bulkheaded or filled or occupied by permanent structures, including marina facilities, in accordance with the requirements set forth in subsection (b) of this section, or if work in connection with any activity permitted in subsection (b) of this section is not commenced within 5 years after issuance of such permits, then the declaration of nonnavigability for such area or part thereof shall expire.

(Pub. L. 102–580, title III, §335, Oct. 31, 1992, 106 Stat. 4853.)

References in Text

The National Environmental Policy Act of 1969, referred to in subsec. (b), is Pub. L. 91–190, Jan. 1, 1970, 83 Stat. 852, as amended, which is classified generally to chapter 55 (§4321 et seq.) of Title 42, The Public Health and Welfare. For complete classification of this Act to the Code, see Short Title note set out under section 4321 of Title 42 and Tables.

"Secretary" Defined

Secretary means the Secretary of the Army, see section 3 of Pub. L. 102–580, set out as a note under section 2201 of this title.

§59hh. Declaration of nonnavigability for portion of Pelican Island, Texas

(a) In general

The Secretary of the Army is authorized to convey to the City[1] of Galveston, Texas, fee simple absolute title to all or any part of a parcel of land containing approximately 605 acres known as the San Jacinto Disposal Area located on the east end of Galveston Island, Texas, in the W.A.A. Wallace Survey, A–647 and A–648, City[1] of Galveston, Galveston County, Texas, being part of the old Fort San Jacinto site, at the fair market value of such parcel to be determined in accordance with the provisions of subsection (d) of this section. Such conveyance shall only be made by the Secretary of the Army upon the agreement of the Secretary and the City[1] as to all compensation due herein.

(b) Compensation for conveyance

(1) In general

Upon receipt of compensation from the city of Galveston, the Secretary shall convey the parcel, or any part of the parcel, as described in subsection (a) of this section.

(2) Full parcel

If the full 605-acre parcel is conveyed, the compensation shall be—

(A) conveyance to the Department of the Army of fee simple absolute title to a parcel of land containing approximately 564 acres on Pelican Island, Texas, in the Eneas Smith Survey, A–190, Pelican Island, city of Galveston, Galveston County, Texas, adjacent to property currently owned by the United States, with the fair market value of the parcel being determined in accordance with subsection (d) of this section; and

(B) payment to the United States of an amount equal to the difference between the fair market value of the parcel to be conveyed under subsection (a) of this section and the fair market value of the parcel to be conveyed under subparagraph (A).

(3) Partial parcel

If the conveyance is 125 acres or less, compensation shall be an amount equal to the fair market value of the parcel to be conveyed, with the fair market value of the parcel being determined in accordance with subsection (d) of this section.

(c) Disposition of spoil

Costs of maintaining the Galveston Harbor and Channel will continue to be governed by the Local Cooperation Agreement (LCA) between the United States of America and the City[1] of Galveston dated October 18, 1973, as amended. Upon conveyance of the parcel, or any part of the parcel, described in subsection (a) of this section, the Department of the Army shall be compensated directly for the present value of the total costs to the Department for disposal of dredge material and site preparation pursuant to the LCA, if any,,[2] in excess of the present value of the total costs that would have been incurred if this conveyance had not been made.

(d) Determination of fair market value

The fair market value of the land to be conveyed pursuant to subsections (a) and (b) of this section shall be determined by independent appraisers using the market value method.

[1] So in original. Probably should not be capitalized.

[2] So in original.

(e) Navigational servitude

(1) Declaration of nonnavigability; public interest

Unless the Secretary finds, after consultation with local and regional public officials (including local and regional public planning organizations), that the proposed projects to be undertaken within the parcel described in subsection (a) of this section are not in the public interest then, subject to paragraphs (2) and (3), such parcel is declared to be nonnavigable waters of the United States.

(2) Limits on applicability; regulatory requirements

The declaration under paragraph (1) shall apply only to those parts of the parcel described in subsection (a) of this section which are or will be bulkheaded and filled or otherwise occupied by permanent structures, including marina facilities. All such work is subject to all applicable Federal statutes and regulations including, but not limited to, sections 401 and 403 of this title, section 1344 of this title, and the National Environmental Policy Act of 1969 [42 U.S.C. 4321 et seq.].

(3) Expiration date

If, 20 years after October 28, 1993, any area or part thereof described in subsection (a) of this section is not bulkheaded or filled or occupied by permanent structures, including marina facilities, in accordance with the requirements set out in paragraph (2), or if work in connection with any activity permitted in paragraph (2) is not commenced within 5 years after issuance of such permits, then the declaration of nonnavigability for such area or part thereof shall expire.

(f) Survey and study

The 605-acre parcel and the 564-acre parcel shall be surveyed and further legally described prior to conveyance. Not later than 60 days following October 28, 1993, if he deems it necessary, the Secretary of the Army shall complete a review of the applicability of section 1344 of this title to the said parcels.

(Pub. L. 103–126, title I, §108, Oct. 28, 1993, 107 Stat. 1320; Pub. L. 106–53, title V, §585, Aug. 17, 1999, 113 Stat. 377.)

REFERENCES IN TEXT

The National Environmental Policy Act of 1969, referred to in subsec. (e)(2), is Pub. L. 91–190, Jan. 1, 1970, 83 Stat. 852, as amended, which is classified generally to chapter 55 (§4321 et seq.) of Title 42, The Public Health and Welfare. For complete classification of this Act to the Code, see Short Title note set out under section 4321 of Title 42 and Tables.

AMENDMENTS

1999—Subsec. (a). Pub. L. 106–53, §585(1), inserted "all or any part of" after "absolute title to" in first sentence.

Subsec. (b). Pub. L. 106–53, §585(2), amended heading and text of subsec. (b) generally. Prior to amendment, text read as follows: "Upon receipt of compensation from the City of Galveston, the Secretary shall convey the parcel as described in subsection (a) of this section. Such compensation shall include—

"(1) conveyance to the Department of the Army of fee simple absolute title to a parcel of land containing approximately 564 acres on Pelican Island, Texas, in the Eneas Smith Survey, A–190, Pelican Island, City of Galveston, Galveston County, Texas, adjacent to property currently owned by the United States. The fair market value of such parcel will be determined in accordance with the provision of subsection (d) of this section; and

"(2) payment to the United States of an amount equal to the difference of the fair market value of the parcel to be conveyed pursuant to subsection (a) of this section and the fair market value of the parcel to be conveyed pursuant to paragraph (1) of this subsection."

Subsec. (c). Pub. L. 106–53, §585(3), in second sentence, inserted ", or any part of the parcel," after "parcel" and ", if any," after "LCA".

§59ii. Declaration of nonnavigability of a portion of the canal known as the James River and Kanawha Canal in Richmond, Virginia

(a) Canal declared nonnavigable

The portion of the canal known as the James River and Kanawha Canal in Richmond, Virginia, located between the Great Ship Lock on the east and the limits of the City of Richmond on the west is hereby declared to be a nonnavigable waterway of the United States for purposes of subtitle II of title 46.

(b) Ensuring public safety

The Secretary of Transportation shall provide such technical advice, information, and assistance as the City of Richmond, Virginia, or its designee may request to insure that the vessels operating on the waters declared nonnavigable by subsection (a) of this section are built, maintained, and operated in a manner consistent with protecting public safety.

(c) Termination of declaration

(1) In general

The Secretary of Transportation may terminate the effectiveness of the declaration made by subsection (a) of this section by publishing a determination that vessels operating on the waters declared nonnavigable by subsection (a) of this section have not been built, maintained, and operated in a manner consistent with protecting public safety.

(2) Public input

Before making a determination under this subsection, the Secretary of Transportation shall—

(A) consult with appropriate State and local government officials regarding whether such a determination is necessary to protect public safety and will serve the public interest; and

(B) provide to persons who might be adversely affected by the determination the opportunity for comment and a hearing on whether such action is necessary to protect public safety and will serve the public interest.

(Pub. L. 106–32, §2, June 1, 1999, 113 Stat. 115.)

FINDINGS

Pub. L. 106–32, §1, June 1, 1999, 113 Stat. 115, provided that: "The Congress finds the following:

"(1) The canal known as the James River and Kanawha Canal played an important part in the economic development of the Commonwealth of Virginia and the City of Richmond.

"(2) The canal ceased to operate as a functioning waterway in the conduct of commerce in the late 1800s.

"(3) Portions of the canal have been found by a Federal district court to be nonnavigable.

"(4) The restored portion of the canal will be utilized to provide entertainment and education to visitors and will play an important part in the economic development of downtown Richmond.

"(5) The restored portion of the canal will not be utilized for general public boating, and will be restricted to activities similar to those conducted on similar waters in San Antonio, Texas.

"(6) The continued classification of the canal as a navigable waterway based upon historic usage that ceased more than 100 years ago does not serve the public interest and is unnecessary to protect public safety.

"(7) Congressional action is required to clarify that the canal is no longer to be considered a navigable waterway for purposes of subtitle II of title 46, United States Code."

§ 59jj. Designation of nonnavigability for portions of Gloucester County, New Jersey

(a) Designation

(1) In general

The Secretary of the Army (referred to in section[1] as the "Secretary") shall designate as nonnavigable the areas described in paragraph (3)[2] unless the Secretary, after consultation with local and regional public officials (including local and regional planning organizations), makes a determination that 1 or more projects proposed to be carried out in 1 or more areas described in paragraph (2) are not in the public interest.

(2) Description of areas

The areas referred to in paragraph (1) are certain parcels of property situated in the West Deptford Township, Gloucester County, New Jersey, as depicted on Tax Assessment Map #26, Block #328, Lots #1, 1.03, 1.08, and 1.09, more fully described as follows:

(A) Beginning at the point in the easterly line of Church Street (49.50 feet wide), said beginning point being the following 2 courses from the intersection of the centerline of Church Street with the curved northerly right-of-way line of Pennsylvania-Reading Seashore Lines Railroad (66.00 feet wide)—

(i) along said centerline of Church Street N. 11°28′50″ E. 38.56 feet; thence

(ii) along the same N. 61°28′35″ E. 32.31 feet to the point of beginning.

(B) Said beginning point also being the end of the thirteenth course and from said beginning point runs; thence, along the aformentioned[3] Easterly line of Church Street—

(i) N. 11°28′50″ E. 1052.14 feet; thence

(ii) crossing Church Street, N. 34°19′51″ W. 1590.16 feet; thence

(iii) N. 27°56′37″ W. 3674.36 feet; thence

(iv) N. 35°33′54″ W. 975.59 feet; thence

(v) N. 57°04′39″ W. 481.04 feet; thence

(vi) N. 36°22′55″ W. 870.00 feet to a point in the Pierhead and Bulkhead Line along the Southeasterly shore of the Delaware River; thence

(vii) along the same line N. 53°37′05″ E. 1256.19 feet; thence

(viii) still along the same, N. 86°10′29″ E. 1692.61 feet; thence, still along the same the following thirteenth courses

(ix) S. 67°44′20″ E. 1090.00 feet to a point in the Pierhead and Bulkhead Line along the Southwesterly shore of Woodbury Creek; thence

(x) S. 39°44′20″ E. 507.10 feet; thence

(xi) S. 31°01′38″ E. 1062.95 feet; thence

(xii) S. 34°34′20″ E. 475.00 feet; thence

(xiii) S. 32°20′28″ E. 254.18 feet; thence

(xiv) S. 52°55′49″ E. 964.95 feet; thence

(xv) S. 56°24′40″ E. 366.60 feet; thence

(xvi) S. 80°31′50″ E. 100.51 feet; thence

(xvii) N. 75°30′00″ E. 120.00 feet; thence

(xviii) N. 53°09′00″ E. 486.50 feet; thence

(xix) N. 81°18′00″ E. 132.00 feet; thence

(xx) S. 56°35′00″ E. 115.11 feet; thence

(xxi) S. 42°00′00″ E. 271.00 feet; thence

(xxii) S. 48°30′00″ E. 287.13 feet to a point in the Northwesterly line of Grove Avenue (59.75 feet wide); thence

(xxiii) S. 23°09′50″ W. 4120.49 feet; thence

(xxiv) N. 66°50′10″ W. 251.78 feet; thence

(xxv) S. 36°05′20″ E. 228.64 feet; thence

(xxvi) S. 58°53′00″ W. 1158.36 feet to a point in the Southwesterly line of said River Lane; thence

(xxvii) S. 41°31′35″ E. 113.50 feet; thence

(xxviii) S. 61°28′35″ W. 863.52 feet to the point of beginning.

(C)(i) Except as provided in clause (ii), beginning at a point in the centerline of Church Street (49.50 feet wide) where the same is intersected by the curved northerly line of Pennsylvania-Reading Seashore Lines Railroad right-of-way (66.00 feet wide), along that Railroad, on a curve to the left, having a radius of 1465.69 feet, an arc distance of 1132.14 feet—

(I) N. 88°45′47″ W. 1104.21 feet; thence

(II) S. 69°06′30″ W. 1758.95 feet; thence

(III) N. 23°04′43″ W. 600.19 feet; thence

(IV) N. 19°15′32″ W. 3004.57 feet; thence

(V) N. 44°52′41″ W. 897.74 feet; thence

(VI) N. 32°26′05″ W. 2765.99 feet to a point in the Pierhead and Bulkhead Line along the Southeasterly shore of the Delaware River; thence

(VII) N. 53°37′05″ E. 2770.00 feet; thence

(VIII) S. 36°22′55″ E. 870.00 feet; thence

(IX) S. 57°04′39″ E. 481.04 feet; thence

(X) S. 35°33′54″ E. 975.59 feet; thence

(XI) S. 27°56′37″ E. 3674.36 feet; thence

(XII) crossing Church Street, S. 34°19′51″ E. 1590.16 feet to a point in the easterly line of Church Street; thence

(XIII) S. 11°28′50″ W. 1052.14 feet; thence

(XIV) S. 61°28′35″ W. 32.31 feet; thence

(XV) S. 11°28′50″ W. 38.56 feet to the point of beginning.

(ii) The parcel described in clause (i) does not include the parcel beginning at the point in the centerline of Church Street (49.50 feet

[1] So in original. Probably should be preceded by "this".

[2] So in original. Probably should be paragraph "(2)".

[3] So in original. Probably should be "aforementioned".

wide), that point being N. 11°28′50″ E. 796.36 feet, measured along the centerline, from its intersection with the curved northerly right-of-way line of Pennsylvania-Reading Seashore Lines Railroad (66.00 feet wide)—

(I) N. 78°27′40″ W. 118.47 feet; thence

(II) N. 15°48′40″ W. 120.51 feet; thence

(III) N. 77°53′00″ E 189.58 feet to a point in the centerline of Church Street; thence

(IV) S. 11°28′50″ W. 183.10 feet to the point of beginning.

(b) Limits on applicability; regulatory requirements

(1) In general

The designation under subsection (a)(1) of this section shall apply to those parts of the areas described in subsection (a) of this section that are or will be bulkheaded and filled or otherwise occupied by permanent structures, including marina facilities.

(2) Applicable law

All activities described in paragraph (1) shall be subject to all applicable Federal law, including—

(A) the Act of March 3, 1899 (30 Stat. 1121, chapter 425);

(B) section 1344 of this title; and

(C) the National Environmental Policy Act of 1969 (42 U.S.C. 4321 et seq.).

(c) Termination of designation

If, on the date that is 20 years after November 12, 2001, any area or portion of an area described in subsection (a)(3)[4] of this section is not bulkheaded, filled, or otherwise occupied by permanent structures (including marina facilities) in accordance with subsection (b) of this section, or if work in connection with any activity authorized under subsection (b) of this section is not commenced by the date that is 5 years after the date on which permits for the work are issued, the designation of nonnavigability under subsection (a)(1) of this section for that area or portion of an area shall terminate.

(Pub. L. 107–66, title I, §107, Nov. 12, 2001, 115 Stat. 494.)

REFERENCES IN TEXT

Act of March 3, 1899, referred to in subsec. (b)(2)(A), is act Mar. 3, 1899, ch. 425, 30 Stat. 1121, as amended, which enacted sections 401, 403, 404, 406, 407, 408, 409, 411 to 416, 418, 502, 549, and 687 of this title and amended section 686 of this title. For complete classification of this Act to the Code, see Tables.

The National Environmental Policy Act of 1969, referred to in subsec. (b)(2)(C), is Pub. L. 91–190, Jan. 1, 1970, 83 Stat. 852, as amended, which is classified generally to chapter 55 (§4321 et seq.) of Title 42, The Public Health and Welfare. For complete classification of this Act to the Code, see Short Title note set out under section 4321 of Title 42 and Tables.

§ 59kk. Wateree River

For purposes of bridge administration, the portion of the Wateree River in the State of South Carolina, from a point 100 feet upstream of the railroad bridge located at approximately mile marker 10.0 to a point 100 feet downstream of such bridge, is declared to not be navigable waters of the United States for purposes of the General Bridge Act of 1946 (33 U.S.C. 525 et seq.).

(Pub. L. 108–293, title VI, §610, Aug. 9, 2004, 118 Stat. 1058.)

REFERENCES IN TEXT

The General Bridge Act of 1946, referred to in text, is title V of act Aug. 2, 1946, ch. 753, 60 Stat. 847, as amended, which is classified generally to subchapter III (§525 et seq.) of chapter 11 of this title. For complete classification of this Act to the Code, see Short Title note set out under section 525 of this title and Tables.

CHAPTER 2—INTERNATIONAL RULES FOR NAVIGATION AT SEA

§§ 61 to 63. Repealed. Oct. 11, 1951, ch. 495, § 5, 65 Stat. 407

Section 61, acts Aug. 19, 1890, ch. 802, §1, 26 Stat. 320; Feb. 19, 1895, ch. 102, §1, 28 Stat. 672; June 7, 1897, ch. 4, §1, 30 Stat. 96, related to adoption of rules for navigation on high seas. See section 1602 of this title.

Section 62, act Aug. 19, 1890, ch. 802, §1, 26 Stat. 320, 321, defined "sailing vessel", "steam vessel", and "under way". See section 1601 of this title.

Section 63, act Aug. 19, 1890, ch. 802, §1, 26 Stat. 321, defined "visible".

EFFECTIVE DATE OF REPEAL

Section 5 of act Oct. 11, 1951, provided that the repeal of these sections is effective upon the taking effect of regulations proclaimed under section 1 of act Oct. 11, 1951. Such regulations were proclaimed by Proc. No. 3030 of Aug. 1, 1953, 18 F.R. 4983, and were to be effective Jan. 1, 1954.

§§ 71 to 84. Repealed. Oct. 11, 1951, ch. 495, § 5, 65 Stat. 407

Section 71, act Aug. 19, 1890, ch. 802, §1, 26 Stat. 321, provided that rules concerning lights be complied with from sunset to sunrise.

Section 72, act Aug. 19, 1890, ch. 802, §1, 26 Stat. 321, related to lights of steam vessel under way.

Section 73, act Aug. 19, 1890, ch. 802, §1, 26 Stat. 321, related to lights of vessel towing another vessel or vessels.

Section 74, act Aug. 19, 1890, ch. 802, §1, 26 Stat. 322, related to lights and day signals of vessel not under control and of telegraph cable vessel.

Section 75, act Aug. 19, 1890, ch. 802, §1, 26 Stat. 322, related to lights of sailing vessel under way and of vessel in tow.

Section 76, act Aug. 19, 1890, ch. 802, §1, 26 Stat. 322, related to lights of small vessel under way in bad weather.

Section 77, acts Aug. 19, 1890, ch. 802, §1, 26 Stat. 322; May 28, 1894, ch. 83, 28 Stat. 82, related to substitute lights for small vessel and rowing boats.

Section 78, acts Aug. 19, 1890, ch. 802, §1, 26 Stat. 323; Feb. 19, 1900, ch. 22, §1, 31 Stat. 30, related to lights of pilot vessel on and off duty, and steam pilot vessel.

Section 79, acts Aug. 19, 1890, ch. 802, §1, 26 Stat. 323; May 28, 1894, ch. 83, 28 Stat. 82; Jan. 19, 1907, ch. 300, §1, 34 Stat. 850, related to lights and day signals of fishing vessels and boats.

Section 80, act Aug. 19, 1890, ch. 802, §1, 26 Stat. 324, related to lights on overtaken vessel.

Section 81, act Aug. 19, 1890, ch. 802, §1, 26 Stat. 324, related to lights on vessel at anchor or aground.

Section 82, act Aug. 19, 1890, ch. 802, §1, 26 Stat. 325, authorized additional lights and signals when necessary.

Section 83, act Aug. 19, 1890, ch. 802, §1, 26 Stat. 325, related to special lights for ships of war and recognition signals.

[4] So in original. Probably should be "subsection (a)(2)".

Section 84, act Aug. 19, 1890, ch. 802, §1, 26 Stat. 325, related to day signal of steam vessel under sail.

EFFECTIVE DATE OF REPEAL

Repeal effective Jan. 1, 1954, see note set out under sections 61 to 63 of this title.

§§ 91, 92. Repealed. Oct. 11, 1951, ch. 495, § 5, 65 Stat. 407

Section 91, acts Aug. 19, 1890, ch. 802, §1, 26 Stat. 325; June 10, 1896, ch. 401, §1, 29 Stat. 381, related to sound signals for fog.

Section 92, act Aug. 19, 1890, ch. 802, §1, 26 Stat. 325, related to speed in fog.

EFFECTIVE DATE OF REPEAL

Repeal effective Jan. 1, 1954, see note set out under sections 61 to 63 of this title.

§§ 101 to 113. Repealed. Oct. 11, 1951, ch. 495, § 5, 65 Stat. 407

Section 101, act Aug. 19, 1890, ch. 802, §1, 26 Stat. 326, provided suggestion for ascertainment of risk of collision.

Section 102, act Aug. 19, 1890, ch. 802, §1, 26 Stat. 326, related to sailing vessels approaching one another.

Section 103, act Aug. 19, 1890, ch. 802, §1, 26 Stat. 326, related to steam vessels meeting end on.

Section 104, act Aug. 19, 1890, ch. 802, §1, 26 Stat. 327, related to steam vessels crossing.

Section 105, act Aug. 19, 1890, ch. 802, §1, 26 Stat. 327, related to steam and sailing vessels meeting.

Section 106, acts Aug. 19, 1890, ch. 802, §1, 26 Stat. 327; May 28, 1894, ch. 83, 28 Stat. 83, provided that vessel having the right-of-way keep course.

Section 107, act Aug. 19, 1890, ch. 802, §1, 26 Stat. 327, related to crossing ahead of vessel having right-of-way.

Section 108, act Aug. 19, 1890, ch. 802, §1, 26 Stat. 327, related to duty of steam vessel to slacken speed.

Section 109, act Aug. 19, 1890, ch. 802, §1, 26 Stat. 327, provided that overtaking vessel keep out of the way of the overtaken vessel, defined "overtaken vessel".

Section 110, act Aug. 19, 1890, ch. 802, §1, 26 Stat. 327, related to steam vessel in narrow channel.

Section 111, act Aug. 19, 1890, ch. 802, §1, 26 Stat. 327, related to right of way of fishing vessels or boats, and obstruction of fairways.

Section 112, act Aug. 19, 1890, ch. 802, §1, 26 Stat. 327, related to special circumstances requiring departure from rules.

Section 113, act Aug. 19, 1890, ch. 802, §1, 26 Stat. 328, related to sound signals of steam vessel indicating course.

EFFECTIVE DATE OF REPEAL

Repeal effective Jan. 1, 1954, see note set out under sections 61 to 63 of this title.

§ 121. Repealed. Oct. 11, 1951, ch. 495, § 5, 65 Stat. 407

Section, act Aug. 19, 1890, ch. 802, §1, 26 Stat. 328, related to additional precautions.

EFFECTIVE DATE OF REPEAL

Repeal effective Jan. 1, 1954, see note set out under sections 61 to 63 of this title.

§ 131. Repealed. Oct. 11, 1951, ch. 495, § 5, 65 Stat. 407

Section, act Aug. 19, 1890, ch. 802, §1, 26 Stat. 328, related to local rules for harbors and inland waters.

EFFECTIVE DATE OF REPEAL

Repeal effective Jan. 1, 1954, see note set out under sections 61 to 63 of this title.

§ 141. Repealed. Oct. 11, 1951, ch. 495, § 5, 65 Stat. 407

Section, acts Aug. 19, 1890, ch. 802, §1, 26 Stat. 328; May 28, 1894, ch. 83, 28 Stat. 83, related to distress signals.

EFFECTIVE DATE OF REPEAL

Repeal effective Jan. 1, 1954, see note set out under sections 61 to 63 of this title.

§ 142. Repealed. Oct. 11, 1951, ch. 495, § 5, 65 Stat. 407

Section, act Aug. 19, 1890, ch. 802, §1, as added Aug. 21, 1935, ch. 595, §1, 49 Stat. 668, related to orders to helmsmen.

EFFECTIVE DATE OF REPEAL

Repeal effective Jan. 1, 1954, see note set out under sections 61 to 63 of this title.

§§ 143 to 143b. Repealed. Pub. L. 88–131, § 3, Sept. 24, 1963, 77 Stat. 194

Section 143, act Oct. 11, 1951, ch. 495, §1, 65 Stat. 406, related to adoption of rules for prevention of collisions on the high seas, and to their geographical applicability.

Section 143a, act Oct. 11, 1951, ch. 495, §2, 65 Stat. 407, provided that Navy and Coast Guard be exempt from the requirements of the rules.

Section 143b, act Oct. 11, 1951, ch. 495, §6, 65 Stat. 408, related to identity of regulations authorized to be proclaimed.

EFFECTIVE DATE OF REPEAL

Repeal effective Sept. 1, 1965, see Proc. No. 3632, Dec. 29, 1964, 29 F.R. 19167, and section 3 of Pub. L. 88–131, both set out as notes under section 1051 of this title.

PROCLAMATION NO. 3030

Proc. No. 3030, Aug. 19, 1953, 18 F.R. 4983, which was the enabling proclamation for adopting Regulations for Preventing Collisions at Sea, 1948, under act Oct. 11, 1951, ch. 495, §1, 65 Stat. 406, was superseded by Proc. No. 3632, Dec. 29, 1964, 29 F.R. 19167, set out as a note under former section 1051 of this title.

EXECUTIVE ORDER NO. 10402

Ex. Ord. No. 10402, Oct. 30, 1952, 17 F.R. 9917, which enforced the Convention for the Safety of Life at Sea, 1948, was revoked by Ex. Ord. No. 12234, Sept. 3, 1980, 45 F.R. 58801, set out as a note under section 1602 of this title.

§ 144. Repealed. Pub. L. 88–131, § 3, Sept. 4, 1963, 77 Stat. 194

Section, act Oct. 11, 1951, ch. 495, §6, Pt. A, 65 Stat. 408, related to applicability of sections 144 to 147d of this title, provided that rules concerning lights be complied with from sunset to sunrise, and defined terms used in sections 145 to 147d of this title.

EFFECTIVE DATE OF REPEAL

Repeal effective Sept. 1, 1965, see Proc. No. 3632, Dec. 29, 1964, 29 F.R. 19167, and section 3 of Pub. L. 88–131, both set out as notes under section 1051 of this title.

§§ 145 to 145n. Repealed. Pub. L. 88–131, § 3, Sept. 24, 1963, 77 Stat. 194

Section 145, act Oct. 11, 1951, ch. 495, §6, Pt. B, 65 Stat. 408, related to lights of power-driven vessels under way and of seaplanes under way on the water.

Section 145a, act Oct. 11, 1951, ch. 495, §6, Pt. B, 65 Stat. 410, related to lights of vessel or seaplane towing or pushing other vessels or seaplanes.

Section 145b, act Oct. 11, 1951, ch. 495, §6, Pt. B, 65 Stat. 410, related to lights and day signals of vessel not under command and of vessels engaged in specified operations.

Section 145c, act Oct. 11, 1951, ch. 495, §6, Pt. B, 65 Stat. 411, related to lights of sailing vessel under way and of vessel or seaplane in tow and of vessels being pushed ahead.

Section 145d, act Oct. 11, 1951, ch. 495, §6, Pt. B, 65 Stat. 411, related to lights of small vessel in bad weather.

Section 145e, act Oct. 11, 1951, ch. 495, §6, Pt. B, 65 Stat. 411, related to substitute lights for small vessel and rowing boats.

Section 145f, act Oct. 11, 1951, ch. 495, §6, Pt. B, 65 Stat. 412, related to lights of pilot vessel on and off duty.

Section 145g, acts Oct. 11, 1951, ch. 495, §6, Pt. B, 65 Stat. 413; June 26, 1953, ch. 155, §1, 67 Stat. 83, related to lights and day signals of fishing vessels.

Section 145h, acts Oct. 11, 1951, ch. 495, §6, Pt. B, 65 Stat. 414, related to stern and tail lights.

Section 145i, acts Oct. 11, 1951, ch. 495, §6, Pt. B, 65 Stat. 414; June 26, 1953, ch. 155, §2, 67 Stat. 83, related to lights on vessels or seaplanes at anchor or aground.

Section 145j, act Oct. 11, 1951, ch. 495, §6, Pt. B, 65 Stat. 415, related to additional lights and signals when necessary.

Section 145k, act Oct. 11, 1951, ch. 495, §6, Pt. B, 65 Stat. 415, related to special lights for ships of war, for vessels sailing under convoy and for seaplanes on the water, recognition signals adopted by shipowners, and lights of naval and military vessels and seaplanes of special construction.

Section 145*l*, act Oct. 11, 1951, ch. 495, §6, Pt. B, 65 Stat. 415, related to day signal of steam vessel under sail.

Section 145m, act Oct. 11, 1951, ch. 495, §6, Pt. B, 65 Stat. 415, related to sound signals under conditions of restricted visibility.

Section 145n, act Oct. 11, 1951, ch. 495, §6, Pt. B, 65 Stat. 417, related to speed in weather restricting visibility.

EFFECTIVE DATE OF REPEAL

Repeal effective Sept. 1, 1965, see Proc. No. 3632, Dec. 29, 1964, 29 F.R. 19167, and section 3 of Pub. L. 88–131, both set out as notes under section 1051 of this title.

§§ 146 to 146k. Repealed. Pub. L. 88–131, § 3, Sept. 24, 1963, 77 Stat. 194

Section 146, act Oct. 11, 1951, ch. 495, §6, Pt. C, 65 Stat. 417, provided methods of obeying and construing sections 146 to 146k, suggestion for ascertainment of risk of collision, and advice concerning the operation of seaplanes.

Section 146a, act Oct. 11, 1951, ch. 495, §6, Pt. C, 65 Stat. 417, related to sailing vessels approaching one another.

Section 146b, act Oct. 11, 1951, ch. 495, §6, Pt. C, 65 Stat. 417, related to power-driven vessels meeting end on.

Section 146c, act Oct. 11, 1951, ch. 495, §6, Pt. C, 65 Stat. 418, related to power-driven vessels crossing.

Section 146d, act Oct. 11, 1951, ch. 495, §6, Pt. C, 65 Stat. 418, related to vessels or seaplanes meeting.

Section 146e, act Oct. 11, 1951, ch. 495, §6, Pt. C, 65 Stat. 418, related to the course of vessels having the right of way, and the duty in aiding to avert collision.

Section 146f, act Oct. 11, 1951, ch. 495, §6, Pt. C, 65 Stat. 418, related to crossing ahead of vessel having right of way.

Section 146g, act Oct. 11, 1951, ch. 495, §6, Pt. C, 65 Stat. 418, related to duty of power-driven vessel to slacken speed.

Section 146h, act Oct. 11, 1951, ch. 495, §6, Pt. C, 65 Stat. 418, provided that overtaking vessel keep out of the way of the overtaken vessel, defined "overtaken vessel".

Section 146i, act Oct. 11, 1951, ch. 495, §6, Pt. C, 65 Stat. 419, related to power-driven vessels in narrow channels and in nearing bends in a channel.

Section 146j, act Oct. 11, 1951, ch. 495, §6, Pt. C, 65 Stat. 419, related to right of way of fishing vessels, and obstruction of fairways.

Section 146k, act Oct. 11, 1951, ch. 495, §6, Pt. C, 65 Stat. 419, related to special circumstances requiring departure from rules.

EFFECTIVE DATE OF REPEAL

Repeal effective Sept. 1, 1965, see Proc. No. 3632, Dec. 29, 1964, 29 F.R. 19167, and section 3 of Pub. L. 88–131, both set out as notes under section 1051 of this title.

§§ 147 to 147d. Repealed. Pub. L. 88–131, § 3, Sept. 24, 1963, 77 Stat. 194

Section 147, act Oct. 11, 1951, ch. 495, §6, Pt. D, 65 Stat. 419, related to sound signals of vessels indicating course.

Section 147a, act Oct. 11, 1951, ch. 495, §6, Pt. D, 65 Stat. 419, related to additional precautions.

Section 147b, act Oct. 11, 1951, ch. 495, §6, Pt. D, 65 Stat. 420, related to local rules for harbors and inland waters.

Section 147c, act Oct. 11, 1951, ch. 495, §6, Pt. D, 65 Stat. 420, related to distress signals.

Section 147d, act Oct. 11, 1951, ch. 495, §6, Pt. D, 65 Stat. 420, related to orders to helmsmen, and has been omitted.

EFFECTIVE DATE OF REPEAL

Repeal effective Sept. 1, 1963, see Proc. No. 3632, Dec. 29, 1964, 29 F.R. 19167, and section 3 of Pub. L. 88–131, both set out as notes under section 1051 of this title.

CHAPTER 3—NAVIGATION RULES FOR HARBORS, RIVERS, AND INLAND WATERS GENERALLY

SUBCHAPTER I—PRELIMINARY

§ 151. High seas and inland waters demarcation lines

(a) Establishment and purpose

The Secretary of the department in which the Coast Guard is operating shall establish appropriate identifiable demarcation lines dividing the high seas from harbors, rivers, and other inland waters of the United States, for the purpose of determining the applicability of special navigational rules in lieu of the International Regulations for Preventing Collisions at Sea.

(b) Applicability of other statutes; limitation; position

The Secretary shall also establish appropriate identifiable lines dividing inland waters of the United States from the high seas for the purpose of determining the applicability of each statute that refers to this section or this section, as amended. These lines may not be located more than twelve nautical miles seaward of the base line from which the territorial sea is measured. These lines may differ in position for the purposes of different statutes.

(c) "United States" defined

For the purposes of this section, the term "United States" includes the several States of the United States, the District of Columbia, the Commonwealth of Puerto Rico, Guam, American Samoa, the United States Virgin Islands, the Commonwealth of the Northern Mariana Islands, the Trust Territory of the Pacific Islands, and any other Commonwealth, territory, or possession of the United States.

(Feb. 19, 1895, ch. 102, §2, 28 Stat. 672; Pub. L. 96–324, §1, Aug. 8, 1980, 94 Stat. 1020; Pub. L. 96–376, §13, Oct. 3, 1980, 94 Stat. 1511; Pub. L. 96–591, §9, Dec. 24, 1980, 94 Stat. 3436.)

REFERENCES IN TEXT

The International Regulations for Preventing Collisions at Sea, referred to in subsec. (a), are maintained and published by the United States Coast Guard, U.S. Department of Homeland Security, in the publication *Navigation Rules*, which is available for sale by the Superintendent of Documents, U.S. Government Printing Office, Washington, D.C. 20402. See International Regulations for Preventing Collisions at Sea, 1972 note under section 1602 of this title.

CODIFICATION

Section was not enacted as part of act June 7, 1897, ch. 4, 30 Stat. 96, which comprises a major part of this chapter.

AMENDMENTS

1980—Subsec. (a). Pub. L. 96–324 designated existing provisions as subsec. (a), substituted provision authorizing the Secretary of the Department in which the Coast Guard is operating to establish demarcation lines for provision authorizing the Secretary of the Treasury to establish demarcation lines, and inserted provision specifying the purpose of establishing demarcation lines as determining the applicability of special navigational rules in lieu of the International Regulations for Preventing Collisions at Sea.

Subsec. (b). Pub. L. 96–324 added subsec. (b).

Subsec. (c). Pub. L. 96–591 and Pub. L. 96–376 made identical amendments by striking out reference to the Canal Zone.

Pub. L. 96–324 added subsec. (c).

TRANSFER OF FUNCTIONS

For transfer of authorities, functions, personnel, and assets of the Coast Guard, including the authorities and functions of the Secretary of Transportation relating thereto, to the Department of Homeland Security, and for treatment of related references, see sections 468(b), 551(d), 552(d), and 557 of Title 6, Domestic Security, and the Department of Homeland Security Reorganization Plan of November 25, 2002, as modified, set out as a note under section 542 of Title 6.

TERMINATION OF TRUST TERRITORY OF THE PACIFIC ISLANDS

For termination of Trust Territory of the Pacific Islands, see note set out preceding section 1681 of Title 48, Territories and Insular Possessions.

TERRITORIAL SEA OF UNITED STATES

For extension of territorial sea of United States, see Proc. No. 5928, set out as a note under section 1331 of Title 43, Public Lands.

§152. Regulation of length of towlines

The Commandant of the Coast Guard shall prepare regulations limiting the length of hawsers between towing vessels and seagoing barges in tow and the length of such tows within any of the inland waters of the United States designated and defined from time to time pursuant to section 151 of this title, and such regulations shall have the force of law.

(May 28, 1908, ch. 212, §14, 35 Stat. 428; June 17, 1910, ch. 301, §§4, 6, 36 Stat. 537, 538; Mar. 4, 1913, ch. 141, §1, 37 Stat. 736; June 30, 1932, ch. 314, §§501, 502, 47 Stat. 415; May 27, 1936, ch. 463, §1, 49 Stat. 1380; 1939 Reorg. Plan No. II, §2(a), eff. July 1, 1939, 4 F.R. 2731, 53 Stat. 1432; 1946 Reorg. Plan No. 3, §§101–104, eff. July 16, 1946, 11 F.R. 7875, 60 Stat. 1097; Aug. 4, 1949, ch. 393, §§1, 20, 63 Stat. 496, 561.)

CODIFICATION

Section was not enacted as part of act June 7, 1897, ch. 4, 30 Stat. 96, which comprises a major part of this chapter.

TRANSFER OF FUNCTIONS

"Commandant of the Coast Guard" substituted in text for provision that the Chairman of the Light House Board, the Supervising Inspector General of the Steamboat Inspection Service and the Commissioner of Navigation shall convene as a board to prepare regulations, and for approval of the regulations by the Secretary of Commerce and Labor.

Secretary of Commerce and Labor designated Secretary of Commerce by act Mar. 4, 1913, which created Department of Labor.

Sections 4 and 6 of act June 17, 1910, established in Department of Commerce and Labor a Bureau of Lighthouses with a Commissioner of Lighthouses as its head, and transferred duties of Light House Board to such Commissioner. Said sections 4 and 6 were repealed by section 20 of act Aug. 4, 1949, section 1 of which reestablished Coast Guard by enacting Title 14, Coast Guard. Section 2(a) of Reorg. Plan No. II, of 1939, set out in the Appendix to Title 5, Government Organization and Employees, consolidated Bureau of Lighthouses with Coast Guard, the Chief of which is Commandant of the Coast Guard.

Supervising Inspector General of the Steamboat Inspection Service and Commissioner of Navigation of Bureau of Navigation were affected by Secretary's authority to retain or dismiss officers and employees upon consolidation of bureaus under section 502(b) of act June 30, 1932.

Steamboat Inspection Service and Bureau of Navigation consolidated into Bureau of Navigation and Steamboat Inspection to be under direction of a chief of bureau by section 501 of act June 30, 1932.

Director of the Bureau of Navigation and Steamboat Inspection was designation given to chief of such Bureau by Secretary of Commerce under section 502(b) of act June 30, 1932.

Bureau of Marine Inspection and Navigation was designation given to Bureau of Navigation and Steamboat Inspection by act May 27, 1936.

Functions of Secretary of Commerce and Director of Bureau of Marine Inspection and Navigation under this section transferred to Commandant of the Coast Guard by Reorg. Plan No. 3, of 1946, §§101 to 104, set out in the Appendix to Title 5.

For transfer of authorities, functions, personnel, and assets of the Coast Guard, including the authorities and functions of the Secretary of Transportation relating thereto, to the Department of Homeland Security, and for treatment of related references, see sections 468(b), 551(d), 552(d), and 557 of Title 6, Domestic Security, and the Department of Homeland Security Reorganization Plan of November 25, 2002, as modified, set out as a note under section 542 of Title 6.

Coast Guard transferred to Department of Transportation, and functions, powers, and duties relating to Coast Guard of Secretary of the Treasury and of other officers and offices of Department of the Treasury transferred to Secretary of Transportation by Pub. L. 89–670, §6(b)(1), Oct. 15, 1966, 80 Stat. 938. Section 6(b)(2) of Pub. L. 89–670, however, provided that notwithstanding such transfer of functions, Coast Guard shall operate as part of Navy in time of war or when President directs as provided in section 3 of Title 14, Coast Guard. See section 108 of Title 49, Transportation.

For transfer of functions of other officers, employees, and agencies of Department of the Treasury, with certain exceptions, to Secretary of the Treasury with power to delegate, see Reorg. Plan No. 26 of 1950, §§1, 2, eff. July 31, 1950, 15 F.R. 4935, 64 Stat. 1280, 1281, set out in the Appendix to Title 5. Functions of Coast Guard, and Commandant of the Coast Guard, excepted from transfer when Coast Guard is operating as part of Navy under sections 1 and 3 of Title 14, Coast Guard.

§153. Penalty for use of unlawful towline

The master of the towing vessel shall be liable to the suspension or revocation of his license for any willful violation of regulations issued pursuant to section 152 of this title in the manner prescribed for incompetency, misconduct, or unskillfulness.

(May 28, 1908, ch. 212, §15, 35 Stat. 429.)

CODIFICATION

Section was not enacted as part of act June 7, 1897, ch. 4, 30 Stat. 96, which comprises a major part of this chapter.

§154. Repealed. Pub. L. 96–591, §8(a), Dec. 24, 1980, 94 Stat. 3435

Section, acts June 7, 1897, ch. 4, §1, 30 Stat. 96; May 21, 1948, ch. 328, §1, 62 Stat. 249; Aug. 8, 1953, ch. 386, §1, 67 Stat. 497, provided for adoption of rules of navigation of harbors, rivers, and inland waters. See section 2001 of this title.

Prior rules for preventing collision prescribed by R.S. §4233 to be followed by vessels of the Navy and mercantile marine of the United States, applicable originally to all waters, were superseded as to navigation on the high seas and waters connected therewith by the International Rules (act Aug. 19, 1890, ch. 802 [sec. 61 et seq. of this title]) were superseded as to navigation on the Great Lakes and their connecting and tributary waters as far east as Montreal, by act Feb. 8, 1895, ch. 64 (section 241 et seq. of this title); were adopted as special rules for the navigation of harbors, rivers, and inland waters of the United States, except the Great Lakes and their connecting and tributary waters as far east as Montreal by act of Feb. 19, 1895, ch. 102 (see section 301 et seq. of this title); and were superseded by act June 7, 1897, ch. 4, as to navigation of all harbors, rivers, and inland waters of the United States except as specified in this paragraph, leaving them applicable solely to the Red River of the North and the rivers emptying into the Gulf of Mexico and their tributaries (see section 2001 et seq. of this title).

EFFECTIVE DATE OF REPEAL

Repeal effective Dec. 24, 1981, see section 7 of Pub. L. 96–591, set out as an Effective Date note under section 2001 of this title.

§§155 to 159. Repealed. Pub. L. 96–591, §8(a), Dec. 24, 1980, 94 Stat. 3435

Section 155, act June 7, 1897, ch. 4, §1, 30 Stat. 96, defined "sailing vessel", "steam vessel", and "under way". See section 2003 of this title.

Section 156, act June 7, 1897, ch. 4, §1, 30 Stat. 96, defined "visible". See section 2003 of this title.

Section 157, acts June 7, 1897, ch. 4, §2, 30 Stat. 102; May 25, 1914, ch. 98, 38 Stat. 381; June 30, 1932, ch. 314, §§501, 502(b), 47 Stat. 415; May 27, 1936, ch. 463, §1, 49 Stat. 1380; 1946 Reorg. Plan No. 3, §§101–104, eff. July 16, 1946, 11 F.R. 7875, 60 Stat 1097; May 21, 1948, ch. 328, §3, 62 Stat. 249; Aug. 14, 1958, Pub. L. 85–656, §1, 72 Stat. 612, provided for promulgation of special rules by the Secretary of the department in which the Coast Guard is operating, and covered publication of rules and hearings in connection therewith. See section 2071 of this title.

Section 157a, Pub. L. 88–163, Oct. 30, 1963, 77 Stat. 281, provided for regulations for navigation or operation under bridges over navigable waters. See section 2001 et seq. of this title.

Section 158, acts June 7, 1897, ch. 4, §3, 30 Stat. 102; May 21, 1948, ch. 328, §3, 62 Stat. 249; Aug. 14, 1958, Pub. L. 85–656, §1, 72 Stat. 612, set out penalties for violations by pilots, engineers, mates, or masters. See section 2072 of this title.

Section 159, acts June 7, 1897, ch. 4, §4, 30 Stat. 103; May 21, 1948, ch. 328, §3, 62 Stat. 249; Aug. 14, 1958, Pub. L. 85–656, §1, 72 Stat. 612, provided for a penalty for violations by vessels. See section 2072 of this title.

EFFECTIVE DATE OF REPEAL

Repeal effective Dec. 24, 1981, see section 7 of Pub. L. 96–591, set out as an Effective Date note under section 2001 of this title.

SUBCHAPTER II—RULES CONCERNING LIGHTS, ETC.

§§171 to 183. Repealed. Pub. L. 96–591, §8(a), Dec. 24, 1980, 94 Stat. 3435

Section 171, act June 7, 1897, ch. 4, §1, 30 Stat. 96, made general provision for the application of rules regarding lights. See section 2020 of this title.

Section 172, act June 7, 1897, ch. 4, §1, 30 Stat. 96, related to lights of steam vessels underway. See section 2023 of this title.

Section 173, acts June 7, 1897, ch. 4, §1, 30 Stat. 97; May 20, 1936, ch. 433, 49 Stat. 1367; May 21, 1948, ch. 328, §2, 62 Stat. 249; Aug. 14, 1958, Pub. L. 85–635, §1, 72 Stat. 590, related to lights of vessels towing or pushing another vessel. See section 2024 of this title.

Section 174, acts June 7, 1897, ch. 4, §1, 30 Stat. 97; Mar. 1, 1933, ch. 157, 47 Stat. 1417, related to lights of sailing vessels underway and vessels being towed. See sections 2024 and 2025 of this title.

Section 175, act June 7, 1897, ch. 4, §1, 30 Stat. 97, related to lights of small vessels underway in bad weather. See section 2023 of this title.

Section 176, act June 7, 1897, ch. 4, §1, 30 Stat. 98, related to lights of rowboats. See section 2025 of this title.

Section 177, acts June 7, 1897, ch. 4, §1, 30 Stat. 98; Feb. 19, 1900, ch. 22, §1, 31 Stat. 30, related to lights of pilot vessels on and off duty. See section 2029 of this title.

Section 178, act June 7, 1897, ch. 4, §1, 30 Stat. 98; 1946 Reorg. Plan No. 3, §§101–104, eff. July 16, 1946, 11 F.R.

7875, 60 Stat. 1097, related to lights of fishing vessels. See section 2026 of this title.

Section 179, acts June 7, 1897, ch. 4, §1, 30 Stat. 98; Aug. 14, 1958, Pub. L. 85–635, §2, 72 Stat. 590, related to lights of overtaken vessels. See section 2022 of this title.

Section 180, acts June 7, 1897, ch. 4, §1, 30 Stat. 98; Apr. 22, 1940, ch. 128, §1, 54 Stat. 150; Aug. 5, 1963, Pub. L. 88–84, §1, 77 Stat. 116; Oct. 15, 1966, Pub. L. 89–670, §6, 80 Stat. 937, related to lights of vessels at anchor. See section 2030 of this title.

Section 181, act June 7, 1897, ch. 4, §1, 30 Stat. 99, related to additional lights when necessary. See section 2022 of this title.

Section 182, act June 7, 1897, ch. 4, §1, 30 Stat. 99, related to special lights for ships of war and convoy. See section 2071 of this title.

Section 183, act June 7, 1897, ch. 4, §1, 30 Stat. 99, related to day signal of vessels under sail. See section 2025 of this title.

EFFECTIVE DATE OF REPEAL

Repeal effective Dec. 24, 1981, see section 7 of Pub. L. 96–591, set out as an Effective Date note under section 2001 of this title.

SUBCHAPTER III—SOUND SIGNALS FOR FOG, ETC.; SPEED

§§191, 192. Repealed. Pub. L. 96–591, §8(a), Dec. 24, 1980, 94 Stat. 3435

Section 191, acts June 7, 1897, ch. 4, §1, 30 Stat. 99; Aug. 5, 1963, Pub. L. 88–84, §2, 77 Stat. 116, made general provision for sound signals for fog, etc. See section 2035 of this title.

Section 192, act June 7, 1897, ch. 4, §1, 30 Stat. 99, related to speed of vessels in fog, etc. See section 2006 of this title.

EFFECTIVE DATE OF REPEAL

Repeal effective Dec. 24, 1981, see section 7 of Pub. L. 96–591, set out as an Effective Date note under section 2001 of this title.

SUBCHAPTER IV—STEERING AND SAILING RULES AND SIGNALS

§§201 to 213. Repealed. Pub. L. 96–591, §8(a), Dec. 24, 1980, 94 Stat. 3435

Section 201, act June 7, 1897, ch. 4, §1, 30 Stat. 100, related to ascertainment of risk of collision. See section 2007 of this title.

Section 202, act June 7, 1897, ch. 4, §1, 30 Stat. 100, related to sailing vessels approaching one another. See section 2012 of this title.

Section 203, acts June 7, 1897, ch. 4, §1, 30 Stat. 100; Aug. 21, 1935, ch. 595, §2, 49 Stat. 669, related to steam vessels approaching, meeting, or passing one another. See section 2013 et seq. of this title.

Section 204, act June 7, 1897, ch. 4, §1, 30 Stat. 101, related to steam vessels crossing. See section 2015 of this title.

Section 205, acts June 7, 1897, ch. 4, §1, 30 Stat. 101; Nov. 5, 1966, Pub. L. 89–764, §1, 80 Stat. 1313, related to steam and sailing vessels meeting. See section 2018 of this title.

Section 206, act June 7, 1897, ch. 4, §1, 30 Stat. 101, provided that vessel having the right of way was to keep course. See section 2017 of this title.

Section 207, act June 7, 1897, ch. 4, §1, 30 Stat. 101, related to situation when a vessel crosses ahead of a vessel having the right-of-way. See section 2015 of this title.

Section 208, act June 7, 1897, ch. 4, §1, 30 Stat. 101, related to duty of steam vessels to slacken speed. See section 2006 of this title.

Section 209, act June 7, 1897, ch. 4, §1, 30 Stat. 101, provided that an overtaking vessel keep out of the way and defined the term "overtaking vessel". See section 2013 of this title.

Section 210, acts June 7, 1897, ch. 4, §1, 30 Stat. 101; Nov. 5, 1966, Pub. L. 89–764, §2, 80 Stat. 1313, related to operation of steam vessels in a narrow channel. See section 2009 of this title.

Section 211, act June 7, 1897, ch. 4, §1, 30 Stat. 102, related to right of way of fishing vessels or boats. See section 2018 of this title.

Section 212, act June 7, 1897, ch. 4, §1, 30 Stat. 102, provided for departure from the rules in special circumstances. See section 2002 of this title.

Section 213, act June 7, 1897, ch. 4, §1, 30 Stat. 102, related to signal to be given that a vessel's engines are going at full speed astern. See section 2034 of this title.

EFFECTIVE DATE OF REPEAL

Repeal effective Dec. 24, 1981, see section 7 of Pub. L. 96–591, set out as an Effective Date note under section 2001 of this title.

SUBCHAPTER V—NO VESSEL UNDER ANY CIRCUMSTANCES TO NEGLECT PROPER PRECAUTIONS

§§221, 222. Repealed. Pub. L. 96–591, §8(a), Dec. 24, 1980, 94 Stat. 3435

Section 221, act June 7, 1897, ch. 4, §1, 30 Stat. 102, related to usual additional precautions generally required. See section 2002 of this title.

Section 222, act June 7, 1897, ch. 4, §1, 30 Stat. 102, related to suspension of rules regarding the exhibition of lights on vessels of war or of the Coast Guard. See section 2001 of this title.

EFFECTIVE DATE OF REPEAL

Repeal effective Dec. 24, 1981, see section 7 of Pub. L. 96–591, set out as an Effective Date note under section 2001 of this title.

SUBCHAPTER VI—DISTRESS SIGNALS

§231. Repealed. Pub. L. 96–591, §8(a), Dec. 24, 1980, 94 Stat. 3435

Section, act June 7, 1897, ch. 4, §1, 30 Stat. 102, related to distress signals. See section 2037 of this title.

EFFECTIVE DATE OF REPEAL

Repeal effective Dec. 24, 1981, see section 7 of Pub. L. 96–591, set out as an Effective Date note under section 2001 of this title.

SUBCHAPTER VII—ORDERS

§232. Repealed. Pub. L. 96–591, §8(a), Dec. 24, 1980, 94 Stat. 3435

Section, act June 7, 1897, ch. 4, §1, as added Aug. 21, 1935, ch. 595, §2, 49 Stat. 669, related to orders to helmsmen.

EFFECTIVE DATE OF REPEAL

Repeal effective Dec. 24, 1981, see section 7 of Pub. L. 96–591, set out as an Effective Date note under section 2001 of this title.

CHAPTER 4—NAVIGATION RULES FOR GREAT LAKES AND THEIR CONNECTING AND TRIBUTARY WATERS

Prior rules for preventing collision prescribed by R.S. §4233 to be followed by vessels of the Navy and mercantile marine of the United States, applicable originally to all waters, were superseded as to navigation on the high seas and waters connected therewith by the International Rules (act Aug. 19, 1890, ch. 802 [sec. 61 et seq. of this title]) were superseded as to navigation on the Great Lakes and their connecting and tributary waters as far east as Montreal, by act Feb. 8, 1895, ch. 64 (section 241 et seq. of this title); were adopted as special rules for the navigation of harbors, rivers, and inland waters of the United States, except the Great Lakes and their connecting and tributary waters as far east as Montreal by act of Feb. 19, 1895, ch. 102 (see section 301 et seq. of this title); and were superseded as to navigation of all harbors, rivers, and inland waters of the United States, except the Great Lakes and their connecting and tributary waters as far east as Montreal and the Red River of the North and rivers emptying into the Gulf of Mexico and their tributaries by act June 7, 1897, ch. 4, § 1, 30 Stat. 96 (section 151 et seq. of this title), leaving them applicable solely to the Red River of the North and rivers emptying into the Gulf of Mexico. See section 2001 et seq. of this title.

SUBCHAPTER I—PRELIMINARY

§§ 241 to 244. Repealed. Pub. L. 96–591, § 8(b), Dec. 24, 1980, 94 Stat. 3435

Section 241, acts Feb. 8, 1895, ch. 64, § 1, 28 Stat. 645; Mar. 28, 1958, Pub. L. 85–350, § 1, 72 Stat. 49, required adoption of rules for navigation of Great Lakes and connecting and tributary waters. See section 2001 of this title.

Section 242, acts Feb. 8, 1895, ch. 64, § 1, 28 Stat. 645, defined "sailing vessel", "steam vessel" and "under way". See section 2003 of this title.

Section 243, acts Feb. 8, 1895, ch. 64, § 3, 28 Stat. 649; Feb. 14, 1903, ch. 552, § 10, 32 Stat. 829; Mar. 4, 1913, ch. 141, § 1, 37 Stat. 736; 1946 Reorg. Plan No. 3, §§ 101–104, eff. July 16, 1946, 11 F.R. 7875, 60 Stat. 1097, related to authority of Commandant of the Coast Guard to establish necessary regulations. See section 2071 of this title.

Section 244, acts Feb. 8, 1895, ch. 64, § 2, 28 Stat. 649; Mar. 28, 1958, Pub. L. 85–350, § 2, 72 Stat. 49, related to liability of persons and private vessels for violation of provisions. See section 2072 of this title.

Effective Date of Repeal

Repeal effective Mar. 1, 1983, pursuant to 47 F.R. 15135, Apr. 8, 1982, see section 7 of Pub. L. 96–591, set out as an Effective Date note under section 2001 of this title.

SUBCHAPTER II—RULES CONCERNING LIGHTS, ETC.

§§ 251 to 262. Repealed. Pub. L. 96–591, § 8(b), Dec. 24, 1980, 94 Stat. 3435

Section 251, acts Feb. 8, 1895, ch. 64, § 1, 28 Stat. 645; May 17, 1928, ch. 600, 45 Stat. 592, related to time for lights and exclusivity of prescribed lights, and defined "visible". See section 2020 of this title.

Section 252, acts Feb. 8, 1895, ch. 64, § 1, 28 Stat. 645; May 17, 1928, ch. 600, 45 Stat. 592; Feb. 28, 1929, ch. 370, 45 Stat. 1405; May 9, 1932, ch. 175, § 1, 47 Stat. 152; Mar. 18, 1948, ch. 138, §§ 1–3, 62 Stat. 82, related to lights of steam vessels under way. See section 2023 of this title.

Section 253, act Feb. 8, 1895, ch. 64, § 1, 28 Stat. 646, related to lights of steam vessels having a tow other than a raft. See section 2024 of this title.

Section 254, act Feb. 8, 1895, ch. 64, § 1, 28 Stat. 646, related to lights of steam vessels having a raft in tow. See section 2024 of this title.

Section 255, act Feb. 8, 1895, ch. 64, § 1, 28 Stat. 646, related to lights of sailing vessels under way and vessels in tow. See sections 2024 and 2025 of this title.

Section 256, acts Feb. 8, 1895, ch. 64, § 1, 28 Stat. 646; May 17, 1928, ch. 601, § 1, 45 Stat. 593; 1946 Reorg. Plan No. 3, §§ 101–104, eff. July 16, 1946, 11 F.R. 7875, 60 Stat. 1097, related to lights of small tugs, boats on River St. Lawrence, ferryboats, rafts and canal boats.

Section 257, act Feb. 8, 1895, ch. 64, § 1, 28 Stat. 646, related to lights of small vessels under way in bad weather.

Section 258, acts Feb. 8, 1895, ch. 64, § 1, 28 Stat. 647; May 17, 1928, ch. 600, 45 Stat. 592; Apr. 22, 1940, ch. 128, § 2, 54 Stat. 150; Jan. 12, 1983, Pub. L. 97–449, § 2(d)(1), 96 Stat. 2440, related to lights of vessels at anchor. See section 2030 of this title.

Section 259, acts Feb. 8, 1895, ch. 64, § 1, 28 Stat. 647; 1946 Reorg. Plan No. 3, §§ 101–104, eff. July 16, 1946, 11 F.R. 7875, 60 Stat. 1097, related to lights of produce boats, canal boats, etc., navigating by hand or horsepower or by sail or by current, or at anchor.

Section 260, act Feb. 8, 1895, ch. 64, § 1, 28 Stat. 647, related to lights of open boats.

Section 261, act Feb. 8, 1895, ch. 64, § 1, 28 Stat. 647, related to use of torch by sailing vessels on approach of steamer.

Section 262, act Feb. 8, 1895, ch. 64, § 1, 28 Stat. 647, related to suspension of lights by vessels of war or Coast Guard vessels. See section 2001 of this title.

Effective Date of Repeal

Repeal effective Mar. 1, 1983, pursuant to 47 F.R. 15135, Apr. 8, 1982, see section 7 of Pub. L. 96–591, set out as an Effective Date note under section 2001 of this title.

SUBCHAPTER III—SOUND SIGNALS FOR FOG, ETC.; SPEED

§§ 271, 272. Repealed. Pub. L. 96–591, § 8(b), Dec. 24, 1980, 94 Stat. 3435

Section 271, acts Feb. 8, 1895, ch. 64, § 1, 28 Stat. 647; 1946 Reorg. Plan No. 3, §§ 101–104, eff. July 16, 1946, 11 F.R. 7875, 60 Stat. 1097; Mar. 18, 1948, ch. 138, § 4, 62 Stat. 82, related to sound signals in fog, etc., of steam and sailing vessels under way, at anchor or aground. See section 2032 et seq. of this title.

Section 272, act Feb. 8, 1895, ch. 64, § 1, 28 Stat. 648, related to speed in fog, etc. See sections 2019 and 2035 of this title.

Effective Date of Repeal

Repeal effective Mar. 1, 1983, pursuant to 47 F.R. 15135, Apr. 8, 1982, see section 7 of Pub. L. 96–591, set out as an Effective Date note under section 2001 of this title.

SUBCHAPTER IV—STEERING AND SAILING RULES

§§ 281 to 293. Repealed. Pub. L. 96–591, § 8(b), Dec. 24, 1980, 94 Stat. 3435

Section 281, act Feb. 8, 1895, ch. 64, § 1, 28 Stat. 648, related to steering and sailing rules for sailing vessels approaching one another. See section 2012 of this title.

Section 282, act Feb. 8, 1895, ch. 64, § 1, 28 Stat. 648, related to steam vessels meeting end on. See section 2014 of this title.

Section 283, act Feb. 8, 1895, ch. 64, § 1, 28 Stat. 648, related to steam vessels crossing. See section 2015 of this title.

Section 284, acts Feb. 8, 1895, ch. 64, § 1, 28 Stat. 648; Nov. 5, 1966, Pub. L. 89–764, § 3, 80 Stat. 1313, related to steam and sailing vessels meeting. See section 2018 of this title.

Section 285, act Feb. 8, 1895, ch. 64, § 1, 28 Stat. 649, related to maintenance of course and speed by vessel having right-of-way. See section 2017 of this title.

Section 286, act Feb. 8, 1895, ch. 64, § 1, 28 Stat. 649, related to duty of steam vessel to slacken speed. See section 2017 of this title.

Section 287, act Feb. 8, 1895, ch. 64, § 1, 28 Stat. 649, related to duty of overtaking vessel to keep out of the way. See section 2013 of this title.

Section 288, act Feb. 8, 1895, ch. 64, § 1, 28 Stat. 649, related to whistle signals of steam vessels to indicate course. See section 2034 of this title.

Section 289, acts Feb. 8, 1895, ch. 64, § 1, 28 Stat. 649; Nov. 5, 1966, Pub. L. 89–764, § 4, 80 Stat. 1313, related to right-of-way when steam vessels meet in narrow channels having current and certain rivers, etc. See section 2009 of this title.

Section 290, act Feb. 8, 1895, ch. 64, § 1, 28 Stat. 649, related to steam vessels passing in narrow channels and slackening speed when meeting in narrow channels. See section 2008 of this title.

Section 291, act Feb. 8, 1895, ch. 64, § 1, 28 Stat. 649, related to dissent to or misunderstanding of signal given and duty to reduce speed. See section 2034 of this title.

Section 292, act Feb. 8, 1895, ch. 64, § 1, 28 Stat. 649, related to departure from rules to avert immediate danger. See section 2002 of this title.

Section 293, act Feb. 8, 1895, ch. 64, § 1, 28 Stat. 649, related to usual additional precautions generally required. See section 2002 of this title.

EFFECTIVE DATE OF REPEAL

Repeal effective Mar. 1, 1983, pursuant to 47 F.R. 15135, Apr. 8, 1982, see section 7 of Pub. L. 96–591, set out as an Effective Date note under section 2001 of this title.

SUBCHAPTER V—ORDERS

§ 294. Repealed. Pub. L. 96–591, § 8(b), Dec. 24, 1980, 94 Stat. 3435

Section, act Feb. 8, 1895, ch. 64, § 1, as added Aug. 21, 1935, ch. 595, § 3, 49 Stat. 669, related to orders to helmsmen.

EFFECTIVE DATE OF REPEAL

Repeal effective Mar. 1, 1983, pursuant to 47 F.R. 15135, Apr. 8, 1982, see section 7 of Pub. L. 96–591, set out as an Effective Date note under section 2001 of this title.

SUBCHAPTER VI—VESSELS NOT UNDER WAY

§ 295. Repealed. Pub. L. 96–591, § 8(b), Dec. 24, 1980, 94 Stat. 3435

Section, act Feb. 8, 1895, ch. 64, § 1, as added Mar. 18, 1948, ch. 138, § 5, 62 Stat. 82, related to day and night signals for vessels anchored, not under command, or aground. See section 2035 of this title.

EFFECTIVE DATE OF REPEAL

Repeal effective Mar. 1, 1983, pursuant to 47 F.R. 15135, Apr. 8, 1982, see section 7 of Pub. L. 96–591, set out as an Effective Date note under section 2001 of this title.

CHAPTER 5—NAVIGATION RULES FOR RED RIVER OF THE NORTH AND RIVERS EMPTYING INTO GULF OF MEXICO AND TRIBUTARIES

The rules for preventing collisions prescribed by R.S. § 4233, as amended, formed the basis of this chapter. Those rules as enacted were not limited in application to the navigation of any waters. But they were superseded as to navigation on the high seas and in all coast waters of the United States, except such as were otherwise provided for, by the adoption of "Revised International Regulations" by act Mar. 3, 1885, ch. 354, 23 Stat. 438; and these regulations were superseded by the adoption of the subsequent regulations of act Aug. 19, 1890, set out as section 61 et seq. and section 1051 et seq. of this title. The rules prescribed by R.S. § 4233 were further superseded, as to navigation on the Great Lakes and their connecting and tributary waters as far east as Montreal, by the rules applying to such navigation prescribed by act Feb. 8, 1895 (section 241 et seq. of this title). The provisions of R.S. §§ 4233, 4412, and 4413 and regulations pursuant thereto were adopted as special rules for the navigation of harbors, rivers, and inland waters of the United States (except the Great Lakes and their connecting and tributary waters as far east as Montreal) by act Feb. 19, 1895. R.S. §§ 4412 and 4413 were classified to section 381 of former Title 46, Shipping. But thereafter the rules prescribed by R.S. § 4233, were further superseded as to navigation of all harbors, rivers, and inland waters except the Red River of the North and rivers emptying into the Gulf of Mexico and their tributaries, by the rules applying to all such waters other than the specific exceptions, of act June 7, 1897 (section 151 et seq. of this title). The rules prescribed by R.S. § 4233, therefore, remained in force only as to the navigation of the Red River of the North and rivers emptying into the Gulf of Mexico and their tributaries. See section 2001 et seq. of this title.

SUBCHAPTER I—PRELIMINARY

§§ 301 to 303. Repealed. Pub. L. 96–591, § 8(a), Dec. 24, 1980, 94 Stat. 3435

Section 301, R.S. § 4233; Aug. 19, 1890, ch. 802, 26 Stat. 320; Feb. 8, 1895, ch. 64, § 1, 28 Stat. 645; Feb. 19, 1895, ch. 102, § 1, 28 Stat. 672; June 7, 1897, ch. 4, 30 Stat. 96; May 21, 1948, ch. 328, § 4, 62 Stat. 250; Aug. 8, 1953, ch. 386, § 2, 67 Stat. 497, made provision for the adoption of rules for navigation on the Red River of the North and rivers emptying into the Gulf of Mexico and tributaries. See section 2001 et seq. of this title.

Section 302, R.S. § 4233; Feb. 19, 1895, ch. 102, § 1, 28 Stat. 672; Mar. 3, 1905, ch. 1457, § 10, 33 Stat. 1032; May 21, 1948, ch. 328, § 4, 62 Stat. 250, defined the terms "steam vessel", "under way", "visible", and "distinct blast". See section 2003 of this title.

Section 303, act Feb. 19, 1895, ch. 102, § 3, 28 Stat. 672, set penalties for violation by vessels. See section 2072 of this title.

EFFECTIVE DATE OF REPEAL

Repeal effective Dec. 24, 1981, see section 7 of Pub. L. 96–591, set out as an Effective Date note under section 2001 of this title.

SUBCHAPTER II—RULES CONCERNING LIGHTS

§§ 311 to 323. Repealed. Pub. L. 96–591, § 8(a), Dec. 24, 1980, 94 Stat. 3435

Section 311, R.S. § 4233; Feb. 19, 1895, ch. 102, § 1, 28 Stat. 672; May 21, 1948, ch. 328, § 4, 62 Stat. 250, related generally to the times during which rules for the display of lights were to be followed. See section 2020 of this title.

Section 312, R.S. § 4233; Feb. 19, 1895, ch. 102, § 1, 28 Stat. 672; May 21, 1948, ch. 328, § 4, 62 Stat. 250; Aug. 14, 1958, Pub. L. 85–635, § 3, 72 Stat. 590, set out requirements for lights on vessels towing alongside or pushing a vessel or vessels. See section 2024 of this title.

Section 313, R.S. § 4233; Feb. 19, 1895, ch. 102, § 1, 28 Stat. 672; May 21, 1948, ch. 328, § 4, 62 Stat. 251, related to lights of vessels towing a vessel or vessels astern. See section 2024 of this title.

Section 314, R.S. § 4233; Feb. 19, 1895, ch. 102, § 1, 28 Stat. 672; May 21, 1948, ch. 328, § 4, 62 Stat. 251, related to lights of seagoing steam vessels under way. See section 2023 of this title.

Section 315, R.S. § 4233; Feb. 19, 1895, ch. 102, § 1, 28 Stat. 672; May 21, 1948, ch. 328, § 4, 62 Stat. 251, related to lights of river steamers. See section 2023 of this title.

Section 316, R.S. § 4233; Mar. 3, 1893, ch. 202, 27 Stat. 557; Feb. 19, 1895, ch. 102, § 1, 28 Stat. 672; 1946 Reorg. Plan No. 3, §§ 101–104, eff. July 16, 1946, 11 F.R. 7875, 60 Stat. 1097; May 21, 1948, ch. 328, § 4, 62 Stat. 251, related to requirements of additional lights and to requirements of lights on steam vessels not otherwise provided for. See section 2023 of this title.

Section 317, R.S. § 4233; Feb. 19, 1895, ch. 102, § 1, 28 Stat. 672; May 21, 1948, ch. 328, § 4, 62 Stat. 251, related to lights of sailing vessels under way and vessels being towed. See sections 2024 and 2025 of this title.

Section 318, R.S. § 4233; Feb. 19, 1895, ch. 102, § 1, 28 Stat. 672; May 21, 1948, ch. 328, § 4, 62 Stat. 251, related to lights of small vessels in bad weather. See sections 2020 and 2022 of this title.

Section 319, R.S. § 4233; Feb. 19, 1895, ch. 102, § 1, 28 Stat. 672; Apr. 22, 1940, ch. 128, § 3, 54 Stat. 151; May 21, 1948, ch. 328, § 4, 62 Stat. 252; Aug. 14, 1958, Pub. L. 85–635, § 4, 72 Stat. 591, related to lights of overtaken vessels. See section 2022 of this title.

Section 320, R.S. § 4233; Feb. 19, 1895, ch. 102, § 1, 28 Stat. 672; Mar. 3, 1897, ch. 389, § 5, 29 Stat. 689; May 21, 1948, ch. 328, § 4, 62 Stat. 252, related to lights of sailing and steam pilot vessels. See sections 2025 and 2029 of this title.

Section 321, R.S. § 4233; Feb. 19, 1895, ch. 102, § 1, 28 Stat. 672; May 21, 1948, ch. 328, § 4, 62 Stat. 252, related to lights on motorboats. See section 2023 of this title.

Section 322, R.S. § 4233; Feb. 19, 1895, ch. 102, § 1, 28 Stat. 672; May 21, 1948, ch. 328, § 4, 62 Stat. 252; Aug. 5, 1963, Pub. L. 88–84, § 3, 77 Stat. 116; Oct. 15, 1966, Pub. L. 89–670, § 6(g)(1)(D), 80 Stat. 941, related to lights of vessels at anchor. See section 2030 of this title.

Section 323, R.S. § 4233; Feb. 19, 1895, ch. 102, § 1, 28 Stat. 672; Mar. 3, 1897, ch. 389, § 12, 29 Stat. 690; May 21, 1948, ch. 328, § 4, 62 Stat. 253, related to lights on warships and Coast Guard cutters. See section 2001 of this title.

EFFECTIVE DATE OF REPEAL

Repeal effective Dec. 24, 1981, see section 7 of Pub. L. 96–591, set out as an Effective Date note under section 2001 of this title.

SUBCHAPTER III—SOUND SIGNALS FOR FOG, ETC.

§ 331. Repealed. Pub. L. 96–591, § 8(a), Dec. 24, 1980, 94 Stat. 3435

Section, R.S. § 4233; Feb. 19, 1895, ch. 102, § 1, 28 Stat. 672; Mar. 3, 1897, ch. 389, § 12, 29 Stat. 690; May 21, 1948, ch. 328, § 4, 62 Stat. 253; Aug. 5, 1963, Pub. L. 88–84, § 4, 77 Stat. 117, related to manner of giving signals for vessels under way, in fog or bad weather, or at anchor. See section 2035 of this title.

EFFECTIVE DATE OF REPEAL

Repeal effective Dec. 24, 1981, see section 7 of Pub. L. 96–591, set out as an Effective Date note under section 2001 of this title.

SUBCHAPTER IV—STEERING AND SAILING RULES

§§ 341 to 351. Repealed. Pub. L. 96–591, § 8(a), Dec. 24, 1980, 94 Stat. 3435

Section 341, R.S. § 4233; Feb. 19, 1895, ch. 102, § 1, 28 Stat. 672; Mar. 3, 1897, ch. 389, § 12, 29 Stat. 690; May 21, 1948, ch. 328, § 4, 62 Stat. 253, related to rate of speed in fog or bad weather conditions. See sections 2006 and 2019 of this title.

Section 341a, R.S. § 4233; May 21, 1948, ch. 328, § 4, 62 Stat. 254, related to ascertainment of risk of collision. See section 2007 of this title.

Section 342, R.S. § 4233; Feb. 19, 1895, ch. 102, § 1, 26 Stat. 672; Mar. 3, 1897, ch. 389, § 12, 29 Stat. 690; May 21, 1948, ch. 328, § 4, 62 Stat. 253, related to situation in which sailing vessels were approaching one another. See section 2012 of this title.

Section 343, R.S. § 4233; Feb. 19, 1895, ch. 102, § 1, 28 Stat. 672; May 21, 1948, ch. 328, § 4, 62 Stat. 254, related to steam vessels meeting end on. See section 2014 of this title.

Section 344, R.S. § 4233; Feb. 19, 1895, ch. 102, § 1, 28 Stat. 672; May 21, 1948, ch. 328, § 4, 62 Stat. 254, related to signals to be given in the situation where steam vessels are crossing. See sections 2015 and 2034 of this title.

Section 345, R.S. § 4233; Feb. 19, 1895, ch. 102, § 1, 28 Stat. 672; May 21, 1948, ch. 328, § 4, 62 Stat. 255; Nov. 5, 1966, Pub. L. 89–764, § 5, 80 Stat. 1313, related to steam vessels and sailing vessels meeting. See section 2018 of this title.

Section 346, R.S. § 4233; Feb. 19, 1895, ch. 102, § 1, 28 Stat. 672; May 21, 1948, ch. 328, § 4, 62 Stat. 255, related to duty of steam vessels to slacken speed. See sections 2006, 2017 of this title.

Section 347, R.S. § 4233; Feb. 19, 1895, ch. 102, § 1, 28 Stat. 672; May 21, 1948, ch. 328, § 4, 62 Stat. 255, related to duty of an overtaking vessel to keep out of the way. See section 2013 of this title.

Section 348, R.S. § 4233; Feb. 19, 1895, ch. 102, 28 Stat. 672; May 21, 1948, ch. 328, § 4, 62 Stat. 255, set out rule that a vessel having the right of way was to keep course. See section 2017 of this title.

Section 348a, R.S. § 4233, Rule 23(A), as added Pub. L. 89–764, § 6, Nov. 5, 1966, 80 Stat. 1313, related to rule that a steam vessel could not hamper safe passage of a large vessel or vessel in tow. See section 2018 of this title.

Section 349, R.S. § 4233; Feb. 19, 1895, ch. 102, § 1, 28 Stat. 672; May 21, 1948, ch. 328, § 4, 62 Stat. 255, related to danger signals, responding signals, and additional signals. See section 2032 et seq. of this title.

Section 350, R.S. § 4233; Feb. 19, 1895, ch. 102, § 1, 28 Stat. 672; Mar. 3, 1897, ch. 389, § 13, 29 Stat 690; May 21 1948, ch. 328, § 4, 62 Stat. 256, related to departures from the rules to avoid collision. See sections 2008 and 2017 of this title.

Section 351, R.S. § 4233; Feb. 19, 1895, ch. 102, § 1, 28 Stat. 672; Mar. 3, 1897, ch. 389, § 13, 29 Stat. 690; May 21, 1948, ch. 328, § 4, 62 Stat. 256, related to usual additional precautions required. See section 2002 of this title.

EFFECTIVE DATE OF REPEAL

Repeal effective Dec. 24, 1981, see section 7 of Pub. L. 96–591, set out as an Effective Date note under section 2001 of this title.

SUBCHAPTER V—ORDERS

§ 352. Repealed. Pub. L. 96–591, § 8(a), Dec. 24, 1980, 94 Stat. 3435

Section, R.S. § 4233; Feb. 19, 1895, ch. 102, § 1, 28 Stat. 672; Aug. 21, 1935, ch. 595, § 4, 49 Stat. 669; May 21, 1948, ch. 328, § 4, 62 Stat. 256, related to orders given to helmsmen.

EFFECTIVE DATE OF REPEAL

Repeal effective Dec. 24, 1981, see section 7 of Pub. L. 96–591, set out as an Effective Date note under section 2001 of this title.

SUBCHAPTER VI—MISCELLANEOUS PROVISIONS

§§ 353 to 356. Repealed. Pub. L. 96–591, § 8(a), Dec. 24, 1980, 94 Stat. 3435

Section 353, R.S. § 4233A, as added May 21, 1948, ch. 328, § 4, 62 Stat. 256; amended Aug. 14, 1958, Pub. L. 85–656, § 2, 72 Stat. 612, related to establishment of special rules. See section 2001 of this title.

Section 354, R.S. § 4233B, as added May 21, 1948, ch. 328, § 4, 62 Stat. 256, related to penalties for violations by pilots, engineers, mates, or masters. See section 2072 of this title.

Section 355, R.S. § 4233C, as added May 21, 1948, ch. 328, § 4, 62 Stat. 257, related to penalties for violation of the rules by a vessel. See sections 2002 and 2072 of this title.

Section 356, acts May 21, 1948, ch. 328, § 5, 62 Stat. 257; Oct. 15, 1966, Pub. L. 89–670, § 6(b)(1), 80 Stat. 938, related to exempted status of Navy and Coast Guard vessels from complying with International Rules of the Road. See section 2001 of this title.

EFFECTIVE DATE OF REPEAL

Repeal effective Dec. 24, 1981, see section 7 of Pub. L. 96–591, set out as an Effective Date note under section 2001 of this title.

CHAPTER 5A—EXEMPTION OF NAVY OR COAST GUARD VESSELS FROM CERTAIN NAVIGATION RULES

§§360, 360a. Repealed. Pub. L. 96–591, §8(a), Dec. 24, 1980, 94 Stat. 3435

Section 360, acts Dec. 3, 1945, ch. 511, §1, 59 Stat. 590; Oct. 15, 1966, Pub. L. 89–670, §6(b)(1), 80 Stat. 938, provided that vessels of special construction be exempted from requirements with regard to number and position of lights. See section 2001 of this title.

Section 360a, acts Dec. 3, 1945, ch. 511, §2, 59 Stat. 591; Oct. 15, 1966, Pub. L. 89–670, §6(b)(1), 80 Stat. 938, related to publication of notice when the Secretary of the department in which the Coast Guard was operating made findings or certifications described in section 360 of this title.

EFFECTIVE DATE OF REPEAL

Repeal effective Dec. 24, 1981, see section 7 of Pub. L. 96–591, set out as an Effective Date note under section 2001 of this title.

CHAPTER 6—GENERAL DUTIES OF SHIP OFFICERS AND OWNERS AFTER COLLISION OR OTHER ACCIDENT

§§361 to 368. Repealed. Pub. L. 98–89, §4(b), Aug. 26, 1983, 97 Stat. 599

Section 361, act June 20, 1874, ch. 344, §10, 18 Stat. 128; 1946 Reorg. Plan. No. 3, §§101–104, eff. July 16, 1946, 11 F.R. 7875, 60 Stat. 1097, required filing of reports to Coast Guard on accidents involving United States vessels and provided penalty for failure to comply. See sections 6101, 6103 of Title 46, Shipping.

Section 362, act June 20, 1874, ch. 344, §11, 18 Stat. 128; 1946 Reorg. Plan No. 3, §§101–104, eff. July 16, 1946, 11 F.R. 7875, 60 Stat. 1097, required reporting of probable loss of vessels and provided penalty for failure to comply. See sections 6101, 6103 of Title 46.

Section 363, acts June 20, 1874, ch. 344, §12, 18 Stat. 128; Feb. 14, 1903, ch. 552, §10, 32 Stat. 829; Mar. 4, 1913, ch. 141, §1, 37 Stat. 736; 1946 Reorg. Plan No. 3, §§101–104, eff. July 16, 1946, 11 F.R. 7875, 60 Stat. 1097, related to transmission of reports by Coast Guard officials to Commandant of Coast Guard.

Section 364, acts June 20, 1874, ch. 344, §13, 18 Stat. 128; Mar. 3, 1897, ch. 389, §11, 29 Stat. 689; Feb. 14, 1903, ch. 552, §10, 32 Stat. 829; Mar. 4, 1913, ch. 141, §1, 37 Stat. 736; 1946 Reorg. Plan No. 3, §§101–104, eff. July 16, 1946, 11 F.R. 7875, 60 Stat. 1097, related to remission and recovery of penalties. See section 2107 of Title 46.

Section 365, act Mar. 4, 1915, ch. 153, §15, 38 Stat. 1184; 1946 Reorg. Plan No. 3, §§101–104, eff. July 16, 1946, 11 F.R. 7875, 60 Stat. 1097, related to reports by owners of barges in tow. See section 6101 of Title 46.

Section 366, act Mar. 4, 1915, ch. 153, §15, 38 Stat. 1184; 1946 Reorg. Plan No. 3, §§101–104, eff. July 16, 1946, 11 F.R. 7875, 60 Stat. 1097, required Commandant of Coast Guard to transmit annually to Congress a summary of reports transmitted to him by Coast Guard officials as required under sections 361 to 365 of this title. See section 6307 of Title 46.

Section 367, act Sept. 4, 1890, ch. 875, §1, 26 Stat. 425, related to duty of master of a vessel in collision to give aid, and to give name of his vessel together with other information about his vessel. See sections 2303, 2304 of Title 46.

Section 368, act Sept. 4, 1890, ch. 875, §2, 26 Stat. 425, set out penalties for failure to give aid as required by section 367 of this title. See sections 2303, 2304 of Title 46.

Act Sept. 4, 1890, ch. 875, §3, 26 Stat. 425, which provided that sections 367 and 368 of this title were to take effect at a time to be fixed by President by proclamation (effective Dec. 15, 1890, by Presidential Proclamation of Nov. 18, 1890, 26 Stat. 1561), was repealed by Pub. L. 98–89, §4(b), 97 Stat. 599.

CHAPTER 7—REGULATIONS FOR THE SUPPRESSION OF PIRACY

§381. Use of public vessels to suppress piracy

The President is authorized to employ so many of the public armed vessels as in his judgment the service may require, with suitable instructions to the commanders thereof, in protecting the merchant vessels of the United States and their crews from piratical aggressions and depredations.

(R.S. §4293.)

CODIFICATION

R.S. §4293 derived from acts Mar. 3, 1819, ch. 77, §1, 3 Stat. 510; Jan. 30, 1823, ch. 7, 3 Stat. 721.

§382. Seizure of piratical vessels generally

The President is authorized to instruct the commanders of the public armed vessels of the United States to subdue, seize, take, and send into any port of the United States, any armed vessel or boat, or any vessel or boat, the crew whereof shall be armed, and which shall have attempted or committed any piratical aggression, search, restraint, depredation, or seizure, upon any vessel of the United States, or of the citizens thereof, or upon any other vessel; and also to retake any vessel of the United States, or its citizens, which may have been unlawfully captured upon the high seas.

(R.S. §4294.)

CODIFICATION

R.S. §4294 derived from acts Mar. 3, 1819, ch. 77, §2, 3 Stat. 512; Jan. 30, 1823, ch. 7, 3 Stat. 721.

§383. Resistance of pirates by merchant vessels

The commander and crew of any merchant vessel of the United States, owned wholly, or in part, by a citizen thereof, may oppose and defend against any aggression, search, restraint, depredation, or seizure, which shall be attempted upon such vessel, or upon any other vessel so owned, by the commander or crew of any armed vessel whatsoever, not being a public armed vessel of some nation in amity with the United States, and may subdue and capture the same; and may also retake any vessel so owned which may have been captured by the commander or crew of any such armed vessel, and send the same into any port of the United States.

(R.S. §4295.)

CODIFICATION

R.S. §4295 derived from acts Mar. 3, 1819, ch. 77, §3, 3 Stat. 513; Jan. 30, 1823, ch. 7, 3 Stat. 721.

§ 384. Condemnation of piratical vessels

Whenever any vessel, which shall have been built, purchased, fitted out in whole or in part, or held for the purpose of being employed in the commission of any piratical aggression, search, restraint, depredation, or seizure, or in the commission of any other act of piracy as defined by the law of nations, or from which any piratical aggression, search, restraint, depredation, or seizure shall have been first attempted or made, is captured and brought into or captured in any port of the United States, the same shall be adjudged and condemned to their use, and that of the captors after due process and trial in any court having admiralty jurisdiction, and which shall be holden for the district into which such captured vessel shall be brought; and the same court shall thereupon order a sale and distribution thereof accordingly, and at its discretion.

(R.S. § 4296.)

CODIFICATION

R.S. § 4296 derived from acts Mar. 3, 1819, ch. 77, § 4, 3 Stat. 513; Jan. 30, 1823, ch. 7, 3 Stat. 721; Aug. 5, 1861, ch. 48, § 1, 12 Stat. 314.

§ 385. Seizure and condemnation of vessels fitted out for piracy

Any vessel built, purchased, fitted out in whole or in part, or held for the purpose of being employed in the commission of any piratical aggression, search, restraint, depredation, or seizure, or in the commission of any other act of piracy, as defined by the law of nations, shall be liable to be captured and brought into any port of the United States if found upon the high seas, or to be seized if found in any port or place within the United States, whether the same shall have actually sailed upon any piratical expedition or not, and whether any act of piracy shall have been committed or attempted upon or from such vessel or not; and any such vessel may be adjudged and condemned, if captured by a vessel authorized as mentioned in section 386 of this title to the use of the United States, and to that of the captors, and if seized by a collector, surveyor, or marshal, then to the use of the United States.

(R.S. § 4297.)

REFERENCES IN TEXT

Surveyor, referred to in text, is probably an obsolete office in view of act July 5, 1932, ch. 430, title I, § 1, 47 Stat. 584, which abolished the offices of surveyors of customs, except at the Port of New York. Ports of delivery, except those which were made ports of entry, were abolished and the use of the term "port of delivery" was discontinued under the President's plan of reorganization of the customs service communicated to Congress by message dated Mar. 3, 1913.

CODIFICATION

R.S. § 4297 derived from act Aug. 5, 1861, ch. 48, § 1, 12 Stat. 314.

TRANSFER OF FUNCTIONS

All offices of collector of customs, comptroller of customs, surveyor of customs, and appraiser of merchandise in Bureau of Customs of Department of the Treasury to which appointments were required to be made by President with advice and consent of Senate ordered abolished with such offices to be terminated not later than December 31, 1966, by Reorg. Plan No. 1 of 1965, eff. May 25, 1965, 30 F.R. 7035, 79 Stat. 1317, set out in the Appendix to Title 5, Government Organization and Employees. All functions of offices eliminated were already vested in Secretary of the Treasury by Reorg. Plan No. 26 of 1950, eff. July 31, 1950, 15 F.R. 4935, 64 Stat. 1280, set out in the Appendix to Title 5.

§ 386. Commissioning private vessels for seizure of piratical vessels

The President is authorized to instruct the commanders of the public-armed vessels of the United States, and to authorize the commanders of any other armed vessels sailing under the authority of any letters of marque and reprisal granted by Congress, or the commanders of any other suitable vessels, to subdue, seize, take, and, if on the high seas, to send into any port of the United States, any vessel or boat built, purchased, fitted out, or held as mentioned in section 385 of this title.

(R.S. § 4298.)

CODIFICATION

R.S. § 4298 derived from act Aug. 5, 1861, ch. 48, § 2, 12 Stat. 315.

§ 387. Duties of officers of customs and marshals as to seizure

The collectors of the several ports of entry, the surveyors of the several ports of delivery, and the marshals of the several judicial districts within the United States, shall seize any vessel or boat built, purchased, fitted out, or held as mentioned in section 385 of this title, which may be found within their respective ports or districts, and to cause the same to be proceeded against and disposed of as provided by that section.

(R.S. § 4299.)

REFERENCES IN TEXT

Surveyors of the several ports of delivery, referred to in text, are probably obsolete offices in view of act July 5, 1932, ch. 430, title I, § 1, 47 Stat. 584, which abolished the offices of surveyors of customs, except at the Port of New York. Ports of delivery, except those which were made ports of entry, were abolished and the use of the term "port of delivery" was discontinued under the President's plan of reorganization of the customs service communicated to Congress by message dated Mar. 3, 1913.

CODIFICATION

R.S. § 4299 derived from act Aug. 5, 1861, ch. 48, § 3, 12 Stat. 315.

TRANSFER OF FUNCTIONS

All offices of collector of customs, comptroller of customs, surveyor of customs, and appraiser of merchandise in Bureau of Customs of Department of the Treasury to which appointments were required to be made by President with advice and consent of Senate ordered abolished, with such offices to be terminated not later than December 31, 1966, by Reorg. Plan No. 1, of 1965, eff. May 25, 1965, 30 F.R. 7035, 79 Stat. 1317, set out in the Appendix to Title 5, Government Organization and Employees. All functions of offices eliminated were already vested in Secretary of the Treasury by Reorg. Plan No. 26 of 1950, eff. July 31, 1950, 15 F.R. 4935, 64 Stat. 1280, set out in the Appendix to Title 5.

CHAPTER 8—SUMMARY TRIALS FOR CERTAIN OFFENSES AGAINST NAVIGATION LAWS

§ 391. Summary trials authorized

Whenever a complaint shall be made against any master, officer, or seaman of any vessel belonging, in whole or in part, to any citizen of the United States, of the commission of any offense, not capital or otherwise infamous, against any law of the United States made for the protection of persons or property engaged in commerce or navigation, it shall be the duty of the United States attorney to investigate the same, and the general nature thereof, and if, in his opinion, the case is such as should be summarily tried, he shall report the same to the district judge, and the judge shall forthwith, or as soon as the ordinary business of the court will permit, proceed to try the cause, and for that purpose may, if necessary, hold a special session of the court, either in term time or vacation.

(R.S. § 4300; June 25, 1948, ch. 646, § 1, 62 Stat. 909.)

CODIFICATION

R.S. § 4300 derived from act June 11, 1864, ch. 121, § 2, 13 Stat. 124.

CHANGE OF NAME

Act June 25, 1948, eff. Sept. 1, 1948, substituted "United States attorney" for "district attorney". See section 541 of Title 28, Judiciary and Judicial Procedure, and Historical and Revision Notes set out thereunder.

§ 392. Complaint and answer; jury trial

At the summary trial of offenses against the laws for the protection of persons or property engaged in commerce or navigation, it shall not be necessary that the accused shall have been previously indicted, but a statement of complaint, verified by oath in writing, shall be presented to the court, setting out the offense in such manner as clearly to apprise the accused of the character of the offense complained of, and to enable him to answer the complaint. The complaint or statement shall be read to the accused, who may plead to or answer the same, or make a counterstatement. The trial shall thereupon be proceeded with in a summary manner, and the case shall be decided by the court, unless, at the time for pleading or answering, the accused shall demand a jury, in which case the trial shall be upon the complaint and plea of not guilty.

(R.S. § 4301.)

CODIFICATION

R.S. § 4301 derived from act June 11, 1864, ch. 121, §§ 3, 4, 13 Stat. 125.

§ 393. Amendments of complaint and adjournments

It shall be lawful for the court to allow the United States attorney to amend his statement of complaint at any stage of the proceedings, before verdict, if, in the opinion of the court, such amendment will work no injustice to the accused; and if it appears to the court that the accused is unprepared to meet the charge as amended, and that an adjournment of the cause will promote the ends of justice, such adjournment shall be made, until a further day, to be fixed by the court.

(R.S. § 4302; June 25, 1948, ch. 646, § 1, 62 Stat. 909.)

CODIFICATION

R.S. § 4302 derived from act June 11, 1864, ch. 121, § 6, 13 Stat. 125.

CHANGE OF NAME

Act June 25, 1948, eff. Sept. 1, 1948, substituted "United States attorney" for "district attorney". See section 541 of Title 28, Judiciary and Judicial Procedure, and Historical and Revision Notes set out thereunder.

§ 394. Challenge to jurors

At the trial in summary cases, if by jury, the United States and the accused shall each be entitled to three peremptory challenges. Challenges for cause, in such cases, shall be tried by the court without the aid of triers.

(R.S. § 4303.)

CODIFICATION

R.S. § 4303 derived from act June 11, 1864, ch. 121, § 7, 13 Stat. 125.

§ 395. Limit of sentence

It shall not be lawful for the court to sentence any person convicted in such trial to any greater punishment than imprisonment in jail for one year, or to a fine exceeding $500, or both, in its discretion, in those cases where the laws of the United States authorize such imprisonment and fine.

(R.S. § 4304.)

CODIFICATION

R.S. § 4304 derived from act June 11, 1864, ch. 121, § 5, 13 Stat. 125.

§ 396. Recovery of penalties and forfeitures generally

All the penalties and forfeitures which may be incurred for offenses against title 48 of the Revised Statutes may be sued for, prosecuted, and recovered in such court, and be disposed of in such manner, as any penalties and forfeitures which may be incurred for offenses against the laws relating to the collection of duties, except when otherwise expressly prescribed.

(R.S. § 4305.)

REFERENCES IN TEXT

Title 48 of the Revised Statutes, referred to in text, was in the original "this Title", meaning title 48 of the Revised Statutes, consisting of R.S. §§ 4131 to 4305. For complete classification of R.S. §§ 4131 to 4305 to the Code, see Tables.

CODIFICATION

R.S. § 4305 derived from act Dec. 31, 1792, ch. 1, § 29, 1 Stat. 298.

CHAPTER 9—PROTECTION OF NAVIGABLE WATERS AND OF HARBOR AND RIVER IMPROVEMENTS GENERALLY

SUBCHAPTER I—IN GENERAL

SUBCHAPTER II—OIL POLLUTION OF COASTAL WATERS

SUBCHAPTER III—NEW YORK HARBOR, HARBOR OF HAMPTON ROADS, AND HARBOR OF BALTIMORE

SUBCHAPTER IV—POTOMAC RIVER AND TRIBUTARIES IN DISTRICT OF COLUMBIA

SUBCHAPTER V—NAVIGABLE WATERS OF MARYLAND

SUBCHAPTER VI—WATER POLLUTION CONTROL

SUBCHAPTER I—IN GENERAL

§401. Construction of bridges, causeways, dams or dikes generally; exemptions

It shall not be lawful to construct or commence the construction of any bridge, causeway, dam, or dike over or in any port, roadstead, haven, harbor, canal, navigable river, or other navigable water of the United States until the consent of Congress to the building of such structures shall have been obtained and until the plans for (1) the bridge or causeway shall have been submitted to and approved by the Secretary of Transportation, or (2) the dam or dike shall have been submitted to and approved by the Chief of Engineers and Secretary of the Army. However, such structures may be built under authority of the legislature of a State across rivers and other waterways the navigable portions of which lie wholly within the limits of a single State, provided the location and plans thereof are submitted to and approved by the Secretary of Transportation or by the Chief of Engineers and Secretary of the Army before construction is commenced. When plans for any bridge or other structure have been approved by the Secretary of Transportation or by the Chief of Engineers and Secretary of the Army, it shall not be lawful to deviate from such plans either before or after completion of the structure unless modification of said plans has previously been submitted to and received the approval of the Secretary of Transportation or the Chief of Engineers and the Secretary of the Army. The approval required by this section of the location and plans or any modification of plans of any bridge or causeway does not apply to any bridge or causeway over waters that are not subject to the ebb and flow of the tide and that are not used and are not susceptible to use in their natural condition or by reasonable improvement as a means to transport interstate or foreign commerce.

(Mar. 3, 1899, ch. 425, §9, 30 Stat. 1151; Pub. L. 97–322, title I, §107(b), Oct. 15, 1982, 96 Stat. 1582; Pub. L. 97–449, §2(f), Jan. 12, 1983, 96 Stat. 2440.)

CODIFICATION

Section is from act Mar. 3, 1899, popularly known as the "Rivers and Harbors Appropriation Act of 1899", and together with section 403 of this title superseded act Sept. 19, 1890, ch. 907, §7, 26 Stat. 454, as amended by act July 13, 1892, ch. 158, §3, 27 Stat. 88, which prohibited the erection of obstructions to navigation, and prohibited the erection of bridges over navigable waters under State legislation before the approval of the plans by the Secretary of War, and prohibited the alteration of channels unless authorized by that Secretary.

AMENDMENTS

1983—Pub. L. 97–449 amended section generally to reflect transfer of certain functions, powers, and duties of Secretary of the Army under this section to Secretary of Transportation. See Transfer of Functions note below.

1982—Pub. L. 97–322 inserted sentence at end relating to exemption.

TRANSFER OF FUNCTIONS

Enforcement functions of Secretary or other official in Department of Transportation related to compliance with permits for bridges across navigable waters issued under this section with respect to pre-construction, construction, and initial operation of transportation system for Canadian and Alaskan natural gas were transferred to the Federal Inspector, Office of Federal Inspector for the Alaska Natural Gas Transportation System, until the first anniversary of date of initial operation of the Alaska Natural Gas Transportation System, see Reorg. Plan No. 1 of 1979, §§102(c), 203(a), 44 F.R. 33663, 33666, 93 Stat. 1373, 1376, effective July 1, 1979, set out in the Appendix to Title 5, Government Organization and Employees. Office of Federal Inspector for the Alaska Natural Gas Transportation System abolished and functions and authority vested in Inspector transferred to Secretary of Energy by section 3012(b) of Pub. L. 102–486, set out as an Abolition of Office of Federal Inspector note under section 719e of Title 15, Commerce and Trade. Functions and authority vested in Secretary of Energy subsequently transferred to Federal Coordinator for Alaska Natural Gas Transportation Projects by section 720d(f) of Title 15.

Functions, powers, and duties of Secretary of the Army [formerly War] and other offices and officers of Department of the Army [formerly War] under this section to extent that they relate generally to location and clearances of bridges and causeways in navigable waters of United States transferred to and vested in Secretary of Transportation by Pub. L. 89–670, §6(g)(6)(A), Oct. 15, 1966, 80 Stat. 941. Pub. L. 97–449 amended this section to reflect transfer made by section 6(g)(6)(A) of Pub. L. 89–670, and repealed section 6(g)(6)(A).

§402. Construction of bridges, etc., over Illinois and Mississippi Canal

The provisions of section 401 of this title are made applicable alike to the completed and uncompleted portions of the Illinois and Mississippi Canal. Whenever the Secretary of the Army shall approve plans for a bridge to be built across said canal he may, in his discretion, and subject to such terms and conditions as in his judgment are equitable, expedient, and just to the public, grant to the person or corporation building and owning such bridge a right of way across the lands of the United States on either side of and adjacent to the said canal; also the privilege of occupying so much of said lands as may be necessary for the piers, abutments, and other portions of the bridge structure and approaches.

(June 13, 1902, ch. 1079, §10, 32 Stat. 374; July 26, 1947, ch. 343, title II, §205(a), 61 Stat. 501.)

CODIFICATION

Section is from part of act June 13, 1902, popularly known as the "Rivers and Harbors Appropriation Act of 1902".

CHANGE OF NAME

Department of War designated Department of the Army and title of Secretary of War changed to Secretary of the Army by section 205(a) of act July 26, 1947, ch. 343, title II, 61 Stat. 501. Section 205(a) of act July 26, 1947, was repealed by section 53 of act Aug. 10, 1956, ch. 1041, 70A Stat. 641. Section 1 of act Aug. 10, 1956, enacted "Title 10, Armed Forces" which in sections 3010 to 3013 continued Department of the Army under administrative supervision of Secretary of the Army.

TRANSFER OF FUNCTIONS

Functions, powers, and duties of Secretary of the Army and other offices and officers of Department of the Army under section 401 of this title to extent that they relate generally to location and clearances of bridges and causeways in navigable waters of United States transferred to and vested in Secretary of Transportation by Pub. L. 89–670, § 6(g)(6)(A), Oct. 15, 1966, 80 Stat. 941. Pub. L. 97–449 amended section 401 of this title to reflect transfer made by section 6(g)(6)(A) of Pub. L. 89–670, and repealed section 6(g)(6)(A).

§ 403. Obstruction of navigable waters generally; wharves; piers, etc.; excavations and filling in

The creation of any obstruction not affirmatively authorized by Congress, to the navigable capacity of any of the waters of the United States is prohibited; and it shall not be lawful to build or commence the building of any wharf, pier, dolphin, boom, weir, breakwater, bulkhead, jetty, or other structures in any port, roadstead, haven, harbor, canal, navigable river, or other water of the United States, outside established harbor lines, or where no harbor lines have been established, except on plans recommended by the Chief of Engineers and authorized by the Secretary of the Army; and it shall not be lawful to excavate or fill, or in any manner to alter or modify the course, location, condition, or capacity of, any port, roadstead, haven, harbor, canal, lake, harbor or refuge, or inclosure within the limits of any breakwater, or of the channel of any navigable water of the United States, unless the work has been recommended by the Chief of Engineers and authorized by the Secretary of the Army prior to beginning the same.

(Mar. 3, 1899, ch. 425, § 10, 30 Stat. 1151; July 26, 1947, ch. 343, title II, § 205(a), 61 Stat. 501.)

CODIFICATION

Section is from act Mar. 3, 1899, popularly known as the "Rivers and Harbors Appropriation Act of 1899".

PRIOR PROVISIONS

This section and section 9 of act Mar. 3, 1899 (section 401 of this title), superseded provisions of act Sept. 19, 1890, ch. 907, § 7, 26 Stat. 454, as amended by act July 13, 1892, ch. 158, § 3, 27 Stat. 110, which prohibited the erection of obstructions to navigation, and prohibited the erection of bridges over navigable waters under State legislation before the approval of the plans by the Secretary of War, and prohibited the alteration of channels unless authorized by said Secretary.

CHANGE OF NAME

Department of War designated Department of the Army and title of Secretary of War changed to Secretary of the Army by section 205(a) of act July 26, 1947, ch. 343, title II, 61 Stat. 501. Section 205(a) of act July 26, 1947, was repealed by section 53 of act Aug. 10, 1956, ch. 1041, 70A Stat. 641. Section 1 of act Aug. 10, 1956, enacted "Title 10, Armed Forces" which in sections 3010 to 3013 continued Department of the Army under administrative supervision of Secretary of the Army.

TRANSFER OF FUNCTIONS

Enforcement functions of Secretary of the Army, Chief of Engineers, or other official in Corps of Engineers of the United States Army related to compliance with permits for structures in navigable waters issued under this section with respect to pre-construction, construction, and initial operation of transportation system for Canadian and Alaskan natural gas were transferred to the Federal Inspector, Office of Federal Inspector for the Alaska Natural Gas Transportation System, until the first anniversary of date of initial operation of the Alaska Natural Gas Transportation System, see Reorg. Plan No. 1 of 1979, §§ 102(b), 203(a), 44 F.R. 33663, 33666, 93 Stat. 1373, 1376, effective July 1, 1979, set out in the Appendix to Title 5, Government Organization and Employees. Office of Federal Inspector for the Alaska Natural Gas Transportation System abolished and functions and authority vested in Inspector transferred to Secretary of Energy by section 3012(b) of Pub. L. 102–486, set out as an Abolition of Office of Federal Inspector note under section 719e of Title 15, Commerce and Trade. Functions and authority vested in Secretary of Energy subsequently transferred to Federal Coordinator for Alaska Natural Gas Transportation Projects by section 720d(f) of Title 15.

Functions, powers, and duties of Secretary of the Army and other offices and officers of Department of the Army under section 401 of this title to extent that they relate generally to location and clearances of bridges and causeways in navigable waters of United States transferred to and vested in Secretary of Transportation by Pub. L. 89–670 § 6(g)(6)(A), Oct. 15, 1966, 80 Stat. 941. Pub. L. 97–449 amended section 401 of this title to reflect transfer made by section 6(g)(6)(A) of Pub. L. 89–670, and repealed section 6(g)(6)(A).

§ 403a. Creation or continuance of obstruction of navigable waters

The creation of any obstruction, not affirmatively authorized by law, to the navigable capacity of any waters, in respect of which the United States has jurisdiction, is hereby prohibited. The continuance of any such obstruction, except bridges, piers, docks, and wharves, and similar structures erected for business purposes, whether heretofore or hereafter created, shall constitute an offense and each week's continuance of any such obstruction shall be deemed a separate offense. Every person and every corporation which shall be guilty of creating or continuing any such unlawful obstruction in this act mentioned, or who shall violate the provisions of the last four preceding sections of this act, shall be deemed guilty of a misdemeanor, and on conviction thereof shall be punished by a fine not exceeding five thousand dollars, or by imprisonment (in the case of a natural person) not exceeding one year, or by both such punishments, in the discretion of the court, the creating or continuing of any unlawful obstruction in this act mentioned may be prevented and such obstruction may be caused to be removed by the injunction of any district court exercising jurisdiction in any district in which such obstruction may be threatened or may exist; and proper proceedings in equity to this end may be instituted under the direction of the Attorney-General of the United States.

(Sept. 19, 1890, ch. 907, §10, 26 Stat. 454; Mar. 3, 1911, ch. 231, §291, 36 Stat. 1167.)

REFERENCES IN TEXT

This act, referred to in text, is act Sept. 19, 1890, ch. 907, 26 Stat. 426. Sections 6 to 9 of the Act are not classified to the Code. For complete classification of this act to the Code, see Tables.

CODIFICATION

Text of section, which was previously omitted from the Code, was restored in view of conflicting court decisions as to whether or not section had been repealed or superseded. See eg. United States v. Wishkah Boom Co., 136 F. 42 (9th Cir. 1905), (appeal dismissed [1906] 202 U.S. 613); United States v. Wilson, 235 F.2d 251 (2d Cir. 1956).

§403b. Lighting at docks and boat launching facilities

Whenever the Secretary considers a permit application for a dock or a boat launching facility under section 403 of this title, the Secretary shall consider the needs of such facility for lighting from sunset to sunrise to make such facility's presence known within a reasonable distance.

(Pub. L. 99–662, title IX, §946, Nov. 17, 1986, 100 Stat. 4200.)

"SECRETARY" DEFINED

Secretary means the Secretary of the Army, see section 2201 of this title.

§404. Establishment of harbor lines; conditions to grants for extension of piers, etc.

Where it is made manifest to the Secretary of the Army that the establishment of harbor lines is essential to the preservation and protection of harbors he may, and is, authorized to cause such lines to be established, beyond which no piers, wharves, bulkheads, or other works shall be extended or deposits made, except under such regulations as may be prescribed from time to time by him: *Provided*, That, whenever the Secretary of the Army grants to any person or persons permission to extend piers, wharves, bulkheads, or other works, or to make deposits in any tidal harbor or river of the United States beyond any harbor lines established under authority of the United States, he shall cause to be ascertained the amount of tidewater displaced by any such structure or by any such deposits, and he shall, if he deem it necessary, require the parties to whom the permission is given to make compensation for such displacement either by excavating in some part of the harbor, including tidewater channels between high and low water mark, to such an extent as to create a basin for as much tidewater as may be displaced by such structure or by such deposits, or in any other mode that may be satisfactory to him.

(Mar. 3, 1899, ch. 425, §11, 30 Stat. 1151; July 26, 1947, ch. 343, title II, §205(a), 61 Stat. 501.)

CODIFICATION

Section is from act Mar. 3, 1899, popularly known as the "Rivers and Harbors Appropriation Act of 1899".

PRIOR PROVISIONS

This section and section 406 of this title, superseded act Aug. 11, 1888, ch. 860, §12, 25 Stat. 425, as amended by act Sept. 19, 1890, ch. 907, §12, 26 Stat. 455, which authorized the establishment of harbor lines, and prescribed a penalty for a violation of the section or any rule made in pursuance of it.

Section also superseded act Aug. 18, 1894, ch. 299, §9, 28 Stat. 364, which contained provisions for compensation for tide water displaced similar to the proviso in this section.

Act Aug. 5, 1886, ch. 929, §2, 24 Stat. 329, which was probably omitted from the Code as superseded by this section, provided that: "In places where harbor-lines have not been established, and where deposits of débris of mines or stamp works can be made without injury to navigation, within lines to be established by the Secretary of War, said officer may, and is hereby authorized to, cause such lines to be established; and within such lines such deposits may be made, under regulations to be from time to time prescribed by him."

CHANGE OF NAME

Department of War designated Department of the Army and title of Secretary of War changed to Secretary of the Army by section 205(a) of act July 26, 1947, ch. 343, title II, 61 Stat. 501. Section 205(a) of act July 26, 1947, was repealed by section 53 of act Aug. 10, 1956, ch. 1041, 70A Stat. 641. Section 1 of act Aug. 10, 1956, enacted "Title 10, Armed Forces" which in sections 3010 to 3013 continued Department of the Army under administrative supervision of Secretary of the Army.

TRANSFER OF FUNCTIONS

Functions, powers, and duties of Secretary of the Army and other offices and officers of Department of the Army under section 401 of this title to extent that they relate generally to location and clearances of bridges and causeways in navigable waters of United States transferred to and vested in Secretary of Transportation by Pub. L. 89–670, §6(g)(6)(A), Oct. 15, 1966, 80 Stat. 941. Pub. L. 97–449 amended section 401 of this title to reflect transfer made by section 6(g)(6)(A) of Pub. L. 89–670, and repealed section 6(g)(6)(A).

§405. Establishment and modification of harbor lines on Potomac and Anacostia Rivers

The provisions of section 404 of this title are made applicable to the Potomac and Anacostia Rivers, and after July 25, 1912, harbor lines in the District of Columbia, or elsewhere on said rivers, shall be established or modified as therein provided.

(July 25, 1912, ch. 253, §1, 37 Stat. 206.)

CODIFICATION

Section is from part of section 1 of act July 25, 1912, popularly known as the "Rivers and Harbors Appropriation Act of 1912".

§406. Penalty for wrongful construction of bridges, piers, etc.; removal of structures

Every person and every corporation that shall violate any of the provisions of sections 401, 403, and 404 of this title or any rule or regulation made by the Secretary of the Army in pursuance of the provisions of section 404 of this title shall be deemed guilty of a misdemeanor, and on conviction thereof shall be punished by a fine not exceeding $2,500 nor less than $500, or by imprisonment (in the case of a natural person) not exceeding one year, or by both such punishments, in the discretion of the court. And further, the removal of any structures or parts of structures erected in violation of the provisions of the said sections may be enforced by the injunction of any district court exercising jurisdiction in any district in which such structures may exist, and proper proceedings to this end may be instituted under the direction of the Attorney General of the United States.

(Mar. 3, 1899, ch. 425, § 12, 30 Stat. 1151; Feb. 20, 1900, ch. 23, § 2, 31 Stat. 32; Mar. 3, 1911, ch. 231, § 291, 36 Stat. 1167; July 26, 1947, ch. 343, title II, § 205(a), 61 Stat. 501.)

CODIFICATION

Section is from act Mar. 3, 1899, popularly known as the "Rivers and Harbors Appropriation Act of 1899".

AMENDMENTS

1911—Act Mar. 3, 1911, transferred to the District Courts the enforcement powers formerly lodged in the Circuit Courts.

1900—Act Feb. 20, 1900, substituted "section eleven" for "section fourteen" where first appearing, which for codification purposes, was translated as "section 404 of this title".

CHANGE OF NAME

Department of War designated Department of the Army and title of Secretary of War changed to Secretary of the Army by section 205(a) of act July 26, 1947, ch. 343, title II, 61 Stat. 501. Section 205(a) of act July 26, 1947, was repealed by section 53 of act Aug. 10, 1956, ch. 1041, 70A Stat. 641. Section 1 of act Aug. 10, 1956, enacted "Title 10, Armed Forces" which in sections 3010 to 3013 continued Department of the Army under administrative supervision of Secretary of the Army.

TRANSFER OF FUNCTIONS

Functions, powers, and duties of Secretary of the Army and other offices and officers of Department of the Army under section 401 of this title to extent that they relate generally to location and clearances of bridges and causeways in navigable waters of United States transferred to and vested in Secretary of Transportation by Pub. L. 89–670, § 6(g)(6)(A), Oct. 15, 1966, 80 Stat. 941, which created Department of Transportation. Pub. L. 97–449 amended section 401 of this title to reflect transfer made by section 6(g)(6)(A) of Pub. L. 89–670, and repealed section 6(g)(6)(A).

§ 407. Deposit of refuse in navigable waters generally

It shall not be lawful to throw, discharge, or deposit, or cause, suffer, or procure to be thrown, discharged, or deposited either from or out of any ship, barge, or other floating craft of any kind, or from the shore, wharf, manufacturing establishment, or mill of any kind, any refuse matter of any kind or description whatever other than that flowing from streets and sewers and passing therefrom in a liquid state, into any navigable water of the United States, or into any tributary of any navigable water from which the same shall float or be washed into such navigable water; and it shall not be lawful to deposit, or cause, suffer, or procure to be deposited material of any kind in any place on the bank of any navigable water, or on the bank of any tributary of any navigable water, where the same shall be liable to be washed into such navigable water, either by ordinary or high tides, or by storms or floods, or otherwise, whereby navigation shall or may be impeded or obstructed: *Provided*, That nothing herein contained shall extend to, apply to, or prohibit the operations in connection with the improvement of navigable waters or construction of public works, considered necessary and proper by the United States officers supervising such improvement or public work: *And provided further*, That the Secretary of the Army, whenever in the judgment of the Chief of Engineers anchorage and navigation will not be injured thereby, may permit the deposit of any material above mentioned in navigable waters, within limits to be defined and under conditions to be prescribed by him, provided application is made to him prior to depositing such material; and whenever any permit is so granted the conditions thereof shall be strictly complied with, and any violation thereof shall be unlawful.

(Mar. 3, 1899, ch. 425, § 13, 30 Stat. 1152; July 26, 1947, ch. 343, title II, § 205(a), 61 Stat. 501.)

CODIFICATION

Section is from act Mar. 3, 1899, popularly known as the "Rivers and Harbors Appropriation Act of 1899".

PRIOR PROVISIONS

This section and sections 408, 411, and 412 of this title, superseded act Aug. 18, 1894, ch. 299, §§ 6, 7, 8, 28 Stat. 363, which prohibited the depositing of refuse in navigable waters for the improvement of which money had been appropriated, and the injury to sea walls and other works built by the Government, and prescribed penalties for violations, including penalties against masters, etc., and vessels.

Section also superseded act Sept. 19, 1890, ch. 907, § 6, 26 Stat. 453, which prohibited obstructing navigation by deposits of refuse, etc., in navigable waters.

CHANGE OF NAME

Department of War designated Department of the Army and title of Secretary of War changed to Secretary of the Army by section 205(a) of act July 26, 1947, ch. 343, title II, 61 Stat. 501. Section 205(a) of act July 26, 1947, was repealed by section 53 of act Aug. 10, 1956, ch. 1041, 70A Stat. 641. Section 1 of act Aug. 10, 1956, enacted "Title 10, Armed Forces" which in sections 3010 to 3013 continued Department of the Army under administrative supervision of Secretary of the Army.

SHORT TITLE

This section is popularly known as the "Refuse Act of 1899".

TRANSFER OF FUNCTIONS

Functions, powers, and duties of Secretary of the Army and other offices and officers of Department of the Army under section 401 of this title to extent that they relate generally to location and clearances of bridges and causeways in navigable waters of United States transferred to and vested in Secretary of Transportation by Pub. L. 89–670, § 6(g)(6)(A), Oct. 15, 1966, 80 Stat. 941, which created Department of Transportation. Pub. L. 97–449 amended section 401 of this title to reflect transfer made by section 6(g)(6)(A) of Pub. L. 89–670, and repealed section 6(g)(6)(A).

TERMINATION OF DISCHARGE PERMIT PROGRAM

No permits for discharges into navigable waters to be issued under this section after Oct. 18, 1972, and the discharge permit program to be carried out instead under section 1342 of this title, with applications under this section pending on Oct. 18, 1972, to be deemed applications for permits under section 1342, see section 1342 of this title.

EXECUTIVE ORDER NO. 11574

Ex. Ord. No. 11574, Dec. 23, 1970, 35 F.R. 19627, which provided for administration of a permit program to regulate discharge of pollutants and other refuse matter into navigable waters or their tributaries and placement of such matter on their banks, was revoked by Ex. Ord. No. 12553, Feb. 25, 1986, 51 F.R. 7237.

§407a. Deposit of debris of mines and stamp works

In places where harbor-lines have not been established, and where deposits of debris of mines or stamp works can be made without injury to navigation, within lines to be established by the Secretary of the Army, said officer may, and is authorized to, cause such lines to be established; and within such lines such deposits may be made, under regulations to be from time to time prescribed by him.

(Aug. 5, 1886, ch. 929, §2, 24 Stat. 329; July 26, 1947, ch. 343, title II, §205(a), 61 Stat. 501.)

CHANGE OF NAME

Department of War designated Department of the Army and title of Secretary of War changed to Secretary of the Army by section 205(a) of act July 26, 1947, ch. 343, title II, 61 Stat. 501. Section 205(a) of act July 26, 1947, was repealed by section 53 of act Aug. 10, 1956, ch. 1041, 70A Stat. 641. Section 1 of act Aug. 10, 1956, enacted "Title 10, Armed Forces" which in sections 3010 to 3013 continued Department of the Army under administrative supervision of Secretary of the Army.

TRANSFER OF FUNCTIONS

Functions, powers, and duties of Secretary of the Army and other offices and officers of Department of the Army under section 401 of this title to extent that they relate generally to location and clearances of bridges and causeways in navigable waters of United States transferred to and vested in Secretary of Transportation by Pub. L. 89–670, §6(g)(6)(A), Oct. 15, 1966, 80 Stat. 941, which created Department of Transportation. Pub. L. 97–449 amended section 401 of this title to reflect transfer made by section 6(g)(6)(A) of Pub. L. 89–670, and repealed section 6(g)(6)(A).

§408. Taking possession of, use of, or injury to harbor or river improvements

It shall not be lawful for any person or persons to take possession of or make use of for any purpose, or build upon, alter, deface, destroy, move, injure, obstruct by fastening vessels thereto or otherwise, or in any manner whatever impair the usefulness of any sea wall, bulkhead, jetty, dike, levee, wharf, pier, or other work built by the United States, or any piece of plant, floating or otherwise, used in the construction of such work under the control of the United States, in whole or in part, for the preservation and improvement of any of its navigable waters or to prevent floods, or as boundary marks, tide gauges, surveying stations, buoys, or other established marks, nor remove for ballast or other purposes any stone or other material composing such works: *Provided*, That the Secretary of the Army may, on the recommendation of the Chief of Engineers, grant permission for the temporary occupation or use of any of the aforementioned public works when in his judgment such occupation or use will not be injurious to the public interest: *Provided further*, That the Secretary may, on the recommendation of the Chief of Engineers, grant permission for the alteration or permanent occupation or use of any of the aforementioned public works when in the judgment of the Secretary such occupation or use will not be injurious to the public interest and will not impair the usefulness of such work.

(Mar. 3, 1899, ch. 425, §14, 30 Stat. 1152; July 26, 1947, ch. 343, title II, §205(a), 61 Stat. 501; Pub. L. 99–88, title I, §100, Aug. 15, 1985, 99 Stat. 315.)

CODIFICATION

Section is from act Mar. 3, 1899, popularly known as the "Rivers and Harbors Appropriation Act of 1899".

PRIOR PROVISIONS

Section superseded act Sept. 19, 1890, ch. 907, §9, 26 Stat. 426, which prohibited persons taking possession of or using or injuring government works in navigable waters.

Act Aug. 14, 1876, ch. 267, §3, 19 Stat. 139, penalizing persons injuring any pier breakwater, or other work of the United States for the improvement of rivers or harbors or navigation, was probably omitted from the Code as superseded by this section.

AMENDMENTS

1985—Pub. L. 99–88 inserted further proviso empowering Secretary, on recommendation of Chief of Engineers, to grant permission for alteration or permanent occupation or use of any of public works mentioned in this section when in judgment of Secretary such occupation or use will not be injurious to public interest and will not impair usefulness of such work.

CHANGE OF NAME

Department of War designated Department of the Army and title of Secretary of War changed to Secretary of the Army by section 205(a) of act July 26, 1947, ch. 343, title II, 61 Stat. 501. Section 205(a) of act July 26, 1947, was repealed by section 53 of act Aug. 10, 1956, ch. 1041, 70A Stat. 641. Section 1 of act Aug. 10, 1956, enacted "Title 10, Armed Forces" which in sections 3010 to 3013 continued Department of the Army under administrative supervision of Secretary of the Army.

TRANSFER OF FUNCTIONS

Functions, powers, and duties of Secretary of the Army and other offices and officers of Department of the Army under section 401 of this title to extent that they relate generally to location and clearances of bridges and causeways in navigable waters of United States transferred to and vested in Secretary of Transportation by Pub. L. 89–670, §6(g)(6)(A), Oct. 15, 1966, 80 Stat. 941, which created Department of Transportation. Pub. L. 97–449 amended section 401 of this title to reflect transfer made by section 6(g)(6)(A) of Pub. L. 89–670, and repealed section 6(g)(6)(A).

§409. Obstruction of navigable waters by vessels; floating timber; marking and removal of sunken vessels

It shall not be lawful to tie up or anchor vessels or other craft in navigable channels in such a manner as to prevent or obstruct the passage of other vessels or craft; or to sink, or permit or cause to be sunk, vessels or other craft in navigable channels; or to float loose timber and logs, or to float what is known as "sack rafts of timber and logs" in streams or channels actually navigated by steamboats in such manner as to obstruct, impede, or endanger navigation. And whenever a vessel, raft or other craft is wrecked and sunk in a navigable channel, it shall be the duty of the owner, lessee, or operator of such sunken craft to immediately mark it with a buoy or beacon during the day and, unless otherwise granted a waiver by the Commandant of the Coast Guard, a light at night, and to maintain such marks until the sunken craft is removed or abandoned, and the neglect or failure of the said owner, lessee, or operator so to do shall be unlawful; and it shall be the duty of the owner, lessee, or operator of such sunken craft to commence the immediate removal of the same, and prosecute such removal diligently, and failure to do so shall be considered as an abandonment of such craft, and subject the same to removal by the United States as provided for in sections 411 to 416, 418, and 502 of this title. The Commandant of the Coast Guard may waive the requirement to mark a wrecked vessel, raft, or other craft with a light at night if the Commandant determines that placing a light would be impractical and granting such a waiver would not create an undue hazard to navigation.

(Mar. 3, 1899, ch. 425, §15, 30 Stat. 1152; Pub. L. 99–662, title IX, §939(a), Nov. 17, 1986, 100 Stat. 4199; Pub. L. 108–293, title III, §301, Aug. 9, 2004, 118 Stat. 1041.)

CODIFICATION

Section is from act Mar. 3, 1899, popularly known as the "Rivers and Harbors Appropriation Act of 1899".

AMENDMENTS

2004—Pub. L. 108–293 substituted "day and, unless otherwise granted a waiver by the Commandant of the Coast Guard, a light" for "day and a lighted lantern" in second sentence and inserted at end "The Commandant of the Coast Guard may waive the requirement to mark a wrecked vessel, raft, or other craft with a light at night if the Commandant determines that placing a light would be impractical and granting such a waiver would not create an undue hazard to navigation."

1986—Pub. L. 99–662 substituted "or to sink" for "or to voluntarily or carelessly sink", struck out "accidentally or otherwise," after "navigable channel,", and inserted ", lessee, or operator" after "owner" in three places.

§410. Exception as to floating loose timber, sack rafts, etc.; violation of regulations; penalty

The prohibition contained in section 409 of this title against floating loose timber and logs, or sack rafts, so called, of timber and logs in streams or channels actually navigated by steamboats, shall not apply to any navigable river or waterway of the United States or any part thereof whereon the floating of loose timber and logs and sack rafts of timber and logs is the principal method of navigation. But such method of navigation on such river or waterway or part thereof shall be subject to the rules and regulations prescribed by the Secretary of the Army as provided in this section.

The Secretary of the Army shall have power, and he is authorized and directed to prescribe rules and regulations, which he may at any time modify, to govern and regulate the floating of loose timber and logs, and sack rafts, (so called) of timber and logs and other methods of navigation on the streams and waterways, or any thereof, of the character, as to navigation, heretofore in this section described. The said rules and regulations shall be so framed as to equitably adjust conflicting interests between the different methods or forms of navigation; and the said rules and regulations shall be published at least once in such newspaper or newspapers of general circulation as in the opinion of the Secretary of the Army shall be best adapted to give notice of said rules and regulations to persons affected thereby and locally interested therein. And all modifications of said rules and regulations shall be similarly published. And such rules and regulations when so prescribed and published as to any such stream or waterway shall have the force of law, and any violation thereof shall be a misdemeanor, and every person convicted of such violation shall be punished by a fine of not exceeding $2,500 nor less than $500, or by imprisonment (in case of a natural person) for not less than thirty days nor more than one year, or by both such fine and imprisonment, in the discretion of the court: *Provided*, That the proper action to enforce the provisions of this section may be commenced before any magistrate judge, judge, or court of the United States, and such magistrate judge, judge, or court shall proceed in respect thereto as authorized by law in the case of crimes or misdemeanors committed against the United States.

The right to alter, amend, or repeal this section at any time is reserved.

(May 9, 1900, ch. 387, §§1–3, 31 Stat. 172; July 26, 1947, ch. 343, title II, §205(a), 61 Stat. 501; Pub. L. 90–578, title IV, §402(b)(2), Oct. 17, 1968, 82 Stat. 1118; Pub. L. 101–650, title III, §321, Dec. 1, 1990, 104 Stat. 5117.)

CHANGE OF NAME

Department of War designated Department of the Army and title of Secretary of War changed to Secretary of the Army by section 205(a) of act July 26, 1947, ch. 343, title II, 61 Stat. 501. Section 205(a) of act July 26, 1947, was repealed by section 53 of act Aug. 10, 1956, ch. 1041, 70A Stat. 641. Section 1 of act Aug. 10, 1956, enacted "Title 10, Armed Forces" which in sections 3010 to 3013 continued Department of the Army under administrative supervision of Secretary of the Army.

"Magistrate judge" substituted in text for "magistrate" pursuant to section 321 of Pub. L. 101–650, set out as a note under section 631 of Title 28, Judiciary and Judicial Procedure. Previously, "magistrate" was substituted for "commissioner" pursuant to Pub. L. 90–578. See chapter 43 (§631 et seq.) of Title 28.

TRANSFER OF FUNCTIONS

Functions, powers, and duties of Secretary of the Army and other offices and officers of Department of the Army under section 401 of this title to extent that they relate generally to location and clearances of bridges and causeways in navigable waters of United States transferred to and vested in Secretary of Transportation by Pub. L. 89–670, §6(g)(6)(A), Oct. 15, 1966, 80 Stat. 941, which created Department of Transportation. Pub. L. 97–449 amended section 401 of this title to reflect transfer made by section 6(g)(6)(A) of Pub. L. 89–670, and repealed section 6(g)(6)(A).

§411. Penalty for wrongful deposit of refuse; use of or injury to harbor improvements, and obstruction of navigable waters generally

Every person and every corporation that shall violate, or that shall knowingly aid, abet, authorize, or instigate a violation of the provisions of sections 407, 408, 409, 414, and 415 of this title shall be guilty of a misdemeanor, and on conviction thereof shall be punished by a fine of up to $25,000 per day, or by imprisonment (in the case of a natural person) for not less than thirty days nor more than one year, or by both such fine and imprisonment, in the discretion of the court, one-half of said fine to be paid to the person or persons giving information which shall lead to conviction.

(Mar. 3, 1899, ch. 425, §16, 30 Stat. 1153; Pub. L. 104–303, title II, §218(a), Oct. 12, 1996, 110 Stat. 3696.)

CODIFICATION

Section is from part of section 16 of act Mar. 3, 1899, popularly known as the "Rivers and Harbors Appropriation Act of 1899". The balance of such section, relating to liability of masters, pilots, and so forth and of vessels engaged in violations, is classified to section 412 of this title.

AMENDMENTS

1996—Pub. L. 104–303 substituted "407, 408, 409, 414, and 415" for "407, 408, and 409" and "of up to $25,000 per day" for "not exceeding twenty-five hundred dollars nor less than five hundred dollars".

§412. Liability of masters, pilots, etc., and of vessels engaged in violations

Any and every master, pilot, and engineer, or person or persons acting in such capacity, respectively, on board of any boat or vessel who shall knowingly engage in towing any scow, boat, or vessel loaded with any material specified in section 407 of this title to any point or place of deposit or discharge in any harbor or navigable water, elsewhere than within the limits defined and permitted by the Secretary of the Army, or who shall willfully injure or destroy any work of the United States contemplated in section 408 of this title, or who shall willfully obstruct the channel of any waterway in the manner contemplated in section 409 of this title, shall be deemed guilty of a violation of this Act, and shall upon conviction be punished as provided in section 411 of this title, and shall also have his license revoked or suspended for a term to be fixed by the judge before whom tried and convicted. And any boat, vessel, scow, raft, or other craft used or employed in violating any of the provisions of sections 407, 408, 409, 414, and 415 of this title shall be liable for the pecuniary penalties specified in section 411 of this title, and in addition thereto for the amount of the damages done by said boat, vessel, scow, raft, or other craft, which latter sum shall be placed to the credit of the appropriation for the improvement of the harbor or waterway in which the damage occurred, and said boat, vessel, scow, raft, or other craft may be proceeded against summarily by way of libel in any district court of the United States having jurisdiction thereof.

(Mar. 3, 1899, ch. 425, §16, 30 Stat. 1153; July 26, 1947, ch. 343, title II, §205(a), 61 Stat. 501; Pub. L. 104–303, title II, §218(a)(1), Oct. 12, 1996, 110 Stat. 3696.)

REFERENCES IN TEXT

This Act, referred to in text, is act Mar. 3, 1899, ch. 425, 30 Stat. 1148, as amended, popularly known as the Rivers and Harbors Appropriation Act of 1899, which enacted sections 401, 403, 404, 406, 407, 408, 409, 411 to 416, 418, 502, 549, and 687 of this title, and amended section 686 of this title. For complete classification of this Act to the Code, see Tables.

CODIFICATION

Section is from part of section 16 of act Mar. 3, 1899, popularly known as the "Rivers and Harbors Appropriation Act of 1899". The balance of such section, relating to penalties for the wrongful deposit of refuse, is classified to section 411 of this title.

AMENDMENTS

1996—Pub. L. 104–303 substituted "407, 408, 409, 414, and 415 of this title" for "407, 408, and 409 of this title".

CHANGE OF NAME

Department of War designated Department of the Army and title of Secretary of War changed to Secretary of the Army by section 205(a) of act July 26, 1947, ch. 343, title II, 61 Stat. 501. Section 205(a) of act July 26, 1947, was repealed by section 53 of act Aug. 10, 1956, ch. 1041, 70A Stat. 641. Section 1 of act Aug. 10, 1956, enacted "Title 10, Armed Forces" which in sections 3010 to 3013 continued Department of the Army under administrative supervision of Secretary of the Army.

TRANSFER OF FUNCTIONS

Functions, powers, and duties of Secretary of the Army and other offices and officers of Department of the Army under section 401 of this title to extent that they relate generally to location and clearances of bridges and causeways in navigable waters of United States transferred to and vested in Secretary of Transportation by Pub. L. 89–670, §6(g)(6)(A), Oct. 15, 1966, 80 Stat. 941, which created Department of Transportation. Pub. L. 97–449 amended section 401 of this title to reflect transfer made by section 6(g)(6)(A) of Pub. L. 89–670, and repealed section 6(g)(6)(A).

§413. Duty of United States attorneys and other Federal officers in enforcement of provisions; arrest of offenders

The Department of Justice shall conduct the legal proceedings necessary to enforce the provisions of sections 401, 403, 404, 406, 407, 408, 409, 411, and 412 of this title; and it shall be the duty of United States attorneys to vigorously prosecute all offenders against the same whenever requested to do so by the Secretary of the Army or by any of the officials hereinafter designated, and it shall furthermore be the duty of said United States attorneys to report to the Attorney General of the United States the action taken by him against offenders so reported, and a transcript of such reports shall be transmitted to the Secretary of the Army by the Attorney General; and for the better enforcement of the said provisions and to facilitate the detection and bringing to punishment of such offenders, the officers and agents of the United States in charge of river and harbor improvements, and the assistant engineers and inspectors employed under them by authority of the Secretary of the Army, and the United States collectors of customs and other revenue officers shall have power and authority to swear out process, and to arrest and take into custody, with or without process, any person or persons who may commit any of the acts or offenses prohibited by the said sections, or who may violate any of the provisions of the same: *Provided*, That no person shall be arrested without process for any offense not committed in the presence of some one of the aforesaid officials: *And provided further*, That whenever any arrest is made under such sections, the person so arrested shall be brought forthwith before a magistrate judge, judge, or court of the United States for examination of the offenses alleged against him; and such magistrate judge, judge, or court shall proceed in respect thereto as authorized by law in case of crimes against the United States.

(Mar. 3, 1899, ch. 425, §17, 30 Stat. 1153; July 26, 1947, ch. 343, title II, §205(a), 61 Stat. 501; June 25, 1948, ch. 646, §1, 62 Stat. 909; Pub. L. 90–578, title IV, §402(b)(2), Oct. 17, 1968, 82 Stat. 1118; Pub. L. 101–650, title III, §321, Dec. 1, 1990, 104 Stat. 5117.)

CODIFICATION

Section is from act Mar. 3, 1899, popularly known as the "Rivers and Harbors Appropriation Act of 1899".

PRIOR PROVISIONS

Act Sept. 19, 1890, ch. 907, §11, 26 Stat. 455, was probably omitted from the Code as superseded by this section, or as rendered obsolete by act March 3, 1899, different sections of which superseded provisions of the act of 1890, the enforcement of which was provided for by section 11. It read as follows: "It shall be the duty of officers and agents having the supervision, on the part of the United States, of the works in progress for the preservation and improvement of said navigable waters, and, in their absence, of the United States collectors of customs and other revenue officers to enforce the provisions of this act by giving information to the district attorney of the United States for the district in which any violation of any provision of this act shall have been committed: *Provided*, That the provisions of this act shall not apply to Torch Lake, Houghton County, Michigan."

CHANGE OF NAME

Act June 25, 1948, eff. Sept. 1, 1948, substituted "United States attorneys" for "district attorneys of the United States" and "district attorneys". See section 541 of Title 28, Judiciary and Judicial Procedure, and Historical and Revision Notes set out thereunder.

Department of War designated Department of the Army and title of Secretary of War changed to Secretary of the Army by section 205(a) of act July 26, 1947, ch. 343, title II, 61 Stat. 501. Section 205(a) of act July 26, 1947, was repealed by section 53 of act Aug. 10, 1956, ch. 1041, 70A Stat. 641. Section 1 of act Aug. 10, 1956, enacted "Title 10, Armed Forces" which in sections 3010 to 3013 continued Department of the Army under administrative supervision of Secretary of the Army.

"Magistrate judge" substituted in text for "magistrate" pursuant to section 321 of Pub. L. 101–650, set out as a note under section 631 of Title 28, Judiciary and Judicial Procedure. Previously, "magistrate" was substituted for "commissioner" pursuant to Pub. L. 90–578. See chapter 43 (§631 et seq.) of Title 28.

TRANSFER OF FUNCTIONS

Functions, powers, and duties of Secretary of the Army and other offices and officers of Department of the Army under section 401 of this title to extent that they relate generally to location and clearances of bridges and causeways in navigable waters of United States transferred to and vested in Secretary of Transportation by Pub. L. 89–670, §6(g)(6)(A), Oct. 15, 1966, 80 Stat. 941, which created Department of Transportation. Pub. L. 97–449 amended section 401 of this title to reflect transfer made by section 6(g)(6)(A) of Pub. L. 89–670, and repealed section 6(g)(6)(A).

All offices of collector of customs, comptroller of customs, surveyor of customs, and appraiser of merchandise in Bureau of Customs of Department of the Treasury to which appointments required to be made by President with advice and consent of Senate were ordered abolished with such offices to be terminated not later than Dec. 31, 1966, by Reorg. Plan No. 1 of 1965, eff. May 25, 1965, 30 F.R. 7035, 79 Stat. 1317, set out in the Appendix to Title 5, Government Organization and Employees. All functions of the offices eliminated were already vested in Secretary of the Treasury by Reorg. Plan No. 26 of 1950, eff. July 31, 1950, 15 F.R. 4935, 64 Stat. 1280, set out in the Appendix to Title 5.

§414. Removal by Secretary of the Army of sunken water craft generally; liability of owner, lessee, or operator

(a) Whenever the navigation of any river, lake, harbor, sound, bay, canal, or other navigable waters of the United States shall be obstructed or endangered by any sunken vessel, boat, water craft, raft, or other similar obstruction, and such obstruction has existed for a longer period than thirty days, or whenever the abandonment of such obstruction can be legally established in a less space of time, the sunken vessel, boat, water craft, raft, or other obstruction shall be subject to be broken up, removed, sold, or otherwise disposed of by the Secretary of the Army at his discretion, without liability for any damage to the owners of the same: *Provided*, That in his discretion, the Secretary of the Army may cause reasonable notice of such obstruction of not less than thirty days, unless the legal abandonment of the obstruction can be established in a less time, to be given by publication, addressed "To whom it may concern," in a newspaper published nearest to the locality of the obstruction, requiring the removal thereof: *And provided also*, That the Secretary of the Army may, in his discretion, at or after the time of giving such notice, cause sealed proposals to be solicited by public advertisement, giving reasonable notice of not less than ten days, for the removal of such obstruction as soon as possible after the expiration of the above specified thirty days' notice, in case it has not in the meantime been so removed, these proposals and contracts, at his discretion, to be conditioned that such vessel, boat, water craft, raft, or other obstruction, and all cargo and property contained therein, shall become the property of the contractor, and the contract shall be awarded to the bidder making the proposition most advantageous to the United States: *Provided*, That such bidder shall give satisfactory security to execute the work: *Provided further*, That any money received from the sale of any such wreck, or from any contractor for the removal of wrecks, under this paragraph shall be covered into the Treasury of the United States.

(b) The owner, lessee, or operator of such vessel, boat, watercraft, raft, or other obstruction as described in this section shall be liable to the United States for the cost of removal or destruction and disposal as described which exceeds the costs recovered under subsection (a) of this section. Any amount recovered from the owner, lessee, or operator of such vessel pursuant to this subsection to recover costs in excess of the proceeds from the sale or disposition of such vessel shall be deposited in the general fund of the Treasury of the United States.

(Mar. 3, 1899, ch. 425, §19, 30 Stat. 1154; July 26, 1947, ch. 343, title II, §205(a), 61 Stat. 501; Pub. L. 99–662, title IX, §939(b), Nov. 17, 1986, 100 Stat. 4199.)

CODIFICATION

Section is from act Mar. 3, 1899, popularly known as the "Rivers and Harbors Appropriation Act of 1899".

PRIOR PROVISIONS

Section superseded act June 14, 1880, ch. 211, §4, 21 Stat. 197, and act Aug. 2, 1882, ch. 375, 22 Stat. 208, which required the Secretary of War to give notice to the persons interested in wrecks obstructing navigation of the purpose of the Secretary to remove the same unless such parties should do so, and authorized the Secretary to remove the same on the failure of the parties interested to do so, and to sell the same to the highest bidder, and also authorized the Secretary to dispose of any sunken vessel or cargo before removal.

Section also superseded act Sept. 19, 1890, ch. 907, §8, 26 Stat. 454, which authorized the Secretary of War to remove wrecks remaining for more than two months.

AMENDMENTS

1986—Pub. L. 99–662 designated existing provision as subsec. (a) and added subsec. (b).

CHANGE OF NAME

Department of War designated Department of the Army and title of Secretary of War changed to Secretary of the Army by section 205(a) of act July 26, 1947, ch. 343, title II, 61 Stat. 501. Section 205(a) of act July 26, 1947, was repealed by section 53 of act Aug. 10, 1956, ch. 1041, 70A Stat. 641. Section 1 of act Aug. 10, 1956, enacted "Title 10, Armed Forces" which in sections 3010 to 3013 continued Department of the Army under administrative supervision of Secretary of the Army.

TRANSFER OF FUNCTIONS

Functions, powers and duties of Secretary of the Army and other offices and officers of Department of the Army under section 401 of this title to extent that they relate generally to location and clearances of bridges and causeways in navigable waters of United States transferred to and vested in Secretary of Transportation by Pub. L. 89–670, §6(g)(6)(A), Oct. 15, 1966, 80 Stat. 941, which created Department of Transportation. Pub. L. 97–449 amended section 401 of this title to reflect transfer made by section 6(g)(6)(A) of Pub. L. 89–670, and repealed section 6(g)(6)(A).

For transfer of certain functions insofar as they pertain to Air Force, and to extent that they were not previously transferred to Secretary of the Air Force and Department of the Air Force from Secretary of the Army and Department of the Army, see Secretary of Defense Transfer Order No. 40 [App. A(57)], July 22, 1949.

§415. Summary removal of water craft obstructing navigation; liability of owner, lessee, or operator

(a) Removal authority

Under emergency, in the case of any vessel, boat, water craft, or raft, or other similar obstruction, sinking of grounding, or being unnecessarily delayed in any Government canal or lock, or in any navigable waters mentioned in section 414 of this title, in such manner as to stop, seriously interfere with, or specially endanger navigation, in the opinion of the Secretary of the Army, or any agent of the United States to whom the Secretary may delegate proper authority, the Secretary of the Army or any such agent shall have the right to take immediate possession of such boat, vessel, or other water craft, or raft, so far as to remove or to destroy it and to clear immediately the canal, lock, or navigable waters aforesaid of the obstruction thereby caused, using his best judgment to prevent any unnecessary injury; and no one shall interfere with or prevent such removal or destruction: *Provided*, That the officer or agent charged with the removal or destruction of an obstruction under this section may in his discretion give notice in writing to the owners of any such obstruction requiring them to remove it: *And provided further*, That the actual expense, including administrative expenses, of removing any such obstruction as aforesaid shall be a charge against such craft and cargo; and if the owners thereof fail or refuse to reimburse the United States for such expense within thirty days after notification, then the officer or agent aforesaid may sell the craft or cargo, or any part thereof that may not have been destroyed in removal, and the proceeds of such sale shall be covered into the Treasury of the United States.

(b) Removal requirement

Not later than 24 hours after the Secretary of the Department in which the Coast Guard is operating issues an order to stop or delay navigation in any navigable waters of the United States because of conditions related to the sinking or grounding of a vessel, the owner or operator of the vessel, with the approval of the Secretary of the Army, shall begin removal of the vessel using the most expeditious removal method available or, if appropriate, secure the vessel pending removal to allow navigation to resume. If the owner or operator fails to begin removal or to secure the vessel pending removal or fails to complete removal on an expedited basis, the Secretary of the Army shall remove or destroy the vessel using the summary removal procedures under subsection (a) of this section.

(c) Liability of owner, lessee, or operator

The owner, lessee, or operator of such vessel, boat, watercraft, raft, or other obstruction as described in this section shall be liable to the United States for the actual cost, including administrative costs, of removal or destruction and disposal as described which exceeds the costs recovered under subsection (a) of this section. Any amount recovered from the owner, lessee, or operator of such vessel pursuant to this subsection to recover costs in excess of the proceeds from the sale or disposition of such vessel shall be deposited in the general fund of the Treasury of the United States.

(Mar. 3, 1899, ch. 425, §20, 30 Stat. 1154; July 26, 1947, ch. 343, title II, §205(a), 61 Stat. 501; Pub. L. 99–662, title IX, §939(b), Nov. 17, 1986, 100 Stat. 4199; Pub. L. 104–303, title II, §218(b), Oct. 12, 1996, 110 Stat. 3696.)

CODIFICATION

Section is from part of section 20 of act Mar. 3, 1899, popularly known as the "Rivers and Harbors Appropriation Act of 1899". Another part of that section, appropriating money necessary to execute its provisions, is classified to section 416 of this title.

Section 20 of act Mar. 3, 1899, also contained a repealing clause with a proviso saving pending actions and rights of actions. It was amended by act Feb. 20, 1900, ch. 23, §3, 31 Stat. 32, and again amended by act June 13, 1902, ch. 1079, §12, 32 Stat. 375, by adding another proviso which is classified to section 418 of this title.

AMENDMENTS

1996—Subsec. (a). Pub. L. 104–303, §218(b)(1), substituted "actual expense, including administrative expenses, of removing" for "expense of removing".

Subsec. (b). Pub. L. 104–303, §218(b)(4), added subsec. (b). Former subsec. (b) redesignated (c).

Subsec. (c). Pub. L. 104–303, §218(b)(2), (3), redesignated subsec. (b) as (c) and substituted "actual cost, including administrative costs, of removal" for "cost of removal".

1986—Pub. L. 99–662 designated existing provision as subsec. (a) and added subsec. (b).

CHANGE OF NAME

Department of War designated Department of the Army and title of Secretary of War changed to Secretary of the Army by section 205(a) of act July 26, 1947, ch. 343, title II, 61 Stat. 501. Section 205(a) of act July 26, 1947, was repealed by section 53 of act Aug. 10, 1956, ch. 1041, 70A Stat. 641. Section 1 of act Aug. 10, 1956, enacted "Title 10, Armed Forces" which in sections 3010 to 3013 continued Department of the Army under administrative supervision of Secretary of the Army.

TRANSFER OF FUNCTIONS

For transfer of authorities, functions, personnel, and assets of the Coast Guard, including the authorities and functions of the Secretary of Transportation relating thereto, to the Department of Homeland Security, and for treatment of related references, see sections 468(b), 551(d), 552(d), and 557 of Title 6, Domestic Security, and the Department of Homeland Security Reorganization Plan of November 25, 2002, as modified, set out as a note under section 542 of Title 6.

Functions, powers, and duties of Secretary of the Army and other offices and officers of Department of the Army under section 401 of this title to extent that they relate generally to location and clearances of bridges and causeways in navigable waters of United States transferred to and vested in Secretary of Transportation by Pub. L. 89–670, §6(g)(6)(A), Oct. 15, 1966, 80 Stat. 941, which created Department of Transportation. Pub. L. 97–449 amended section 401 of this title to reflect transfer made by section 6(g)(6)(A) of Pub. L. 89–670, and repealed section 6(g)(6)(A).

For transfer of certain functions insofar as they pertain to Air Force, and to extent that they were not previously transferred to Secretary of the Air Force and Department of the Air Force from Secretary of the Army and Department of the Army, see Secretary of Defense Transfer Order No. 40 [App. A(57)], July 22, 1949.

§416. Appropriations for removal of sunken water craft

Such sum of money as may be necessary to execute sections 414 and 415 of this title is hereby appropriated out of any money in the Treasury not otherwise appropriated, to be paid out on the requisition of the Secretary of the Army.

(Mar. 3, 1899, ch. 425, §20(a), formerly §20, 30 Stat. 1155; July 26, 1947, ch. 343, title II, §205(a), 61 Stat. 501; renumbered §20(a), Pub. L. 99–662, title IX, §939(b), Nov. 17, 1986, 100 Stat. 4199.)

CODIFICATION

Section is from part of section 20(a) of act Mar. 3, 1899, popularly known as the "Rivers and Harbors Appropriation Act of 1899". See Codification and Amendment notes set out under section 415 of this title.

CHANGE OF NAME

Department of War designated Department of the Army and title of Secretary of War changed to Secretary of the Army by section 205(a) of act July 26, 1947, ch. 343, title II, 61 Stat. 501. Section 205(a) of act July 26, 1947, was repealed by section 53 of act Aug. 10, 1956, ch. 1041, 70A Stat. 641. Section 1 of act Aug. 10, 1956, enacted "Title 10, Armed Forces" which in sections 3010 to 3013 continued Department of the Army under administrative supervision of Secretary of the Army.

APPROPRIATIONS

Section 2 of act June 26, 1934, ch. 756, 48 Stat. 1225, which was classified to section 725a of former Title 31, Money and Finance, repealed the permanent appropriation under the title "Removing sunken vessels or craft obstructing or endangering navigation (8x888)" effective July 1, 1935, and provided that such portions of any acts as make permanent appropriations to be expended under such account are amended so as to authorize, in lieu thereof, annual appropriations from the general fund of the Treasury in identical terms and in such amounts as now provided by the laws providing such permanent appropriations.

§417. Expenses of investigations by Department of the Army

Expenses incurred by the Engineer Department of the Department of the Army in all investigations, inspections, hearings, reports, service of notice, or other action incidental to examination of plans or sites of bridges or other structures built or proposed to be built in or over navigable waters, or to examinations into alleged violations of laws for the protection and preservation of navigable waters, or to the establishment or marking of harbor lines, shall be payable from any funds which may be available for the improvement, maintenance, operation, or care of the waterways or harbors affected, or if such funds are not available in sums judged by the Chief of Engineers to be adequate, then from any funds available for examinations, surveys, and contingencies of rivers and harbors.

(Mar. 3, 1905, ch. 1482, §6, 33 Stat. 1148; July 26, 1947, ch. 343, title II, §205(a), 61 Stat. 501.)

CHANGE OF NAME

Department of War designated Department of the Army and title of Secretary of War changed to Secretary of the Army by section 205(a) of act July 26, 1947, ch. 343, title II, 61 Stat. 501. Section 205(a) of act July 26, 1947, was repealed by section 53 of act Aug. 10, 1956, ch. 1041, 70A Stat. 641. Section 1 of act Aug. 10, 1956, enacted "Title 10, Armed Forces" which in sections 3010 to 3013 continued Department of the Army under administrative supervision of Secretary of the Army.

TRANSFER OF FUNCTIONS

Functions, powers, and duties of Secretary of the Army and other offices and officers of Department of the Army under section 401 of this title to extent that they relate generally to location and clearances of bridges and causeways in navigable waters of United States transferred to and vested in Secretary of Transportation by Pub. L. 89–670, §6(g)(6)(A), Oct. 15, 1966, 80 Stat. 941, which created Department of Transportation. Pub. L. 97–449 amended section 401 of this title to reflect transfer made by section 6(g)(6)(A) of Pub. L. 89–670, and repealed section 6(g)(6)(A).

§418. Provisions for protection of New York Harbor unaffected

Nothing contained in sections 401, 403, 404, 406, 407, 408, 409, 411 to 416, and 502 of this title shall be construed as repealing, modifying, or in any manner affecting the provisions of subchapter III of this chapter.

(Mar. 3, 1899, ch. 425, §20(a), formerly §20, 30 Stat. 1154; Feb. 20, 1900, ch. 23, §3, 31 Stat. 32; June 13, 1902, ch. 1079, §12, 32 Stat. 375; renumbered §20(a), Pub. L. 99–662, title IX, §939(b), Nov. 17, 1986, 100 Stat. 4199.)

REFERENCES IN TEXT

Subchapter III (§441 et seq.) of this chapter, referred to in text, was in the original a reference to the Act of June 29, 1888, as amended by section 3 of the river and harbor Act of August 18, 1894.

CODIFICATION

Section is from part of section 20(a) of act Mar. 3, 1899, popularly known as the "Rivers and Harbors Appropriation Act of 1899". See Codification and Amendment notes set out under section 415 of this title.

§ 419. Regulation by Secretary governing transportation and dumping of dredgings, refuse, etc., into navigable waters; oyster lands; appropriations

The Secretary of the Army is authorized and empowered to prescribe regulations to govern the transportation and dumping into any navigable water, or waters adjacent thereto, of dredgings, earth, garbage, and other refuse materials of every kind or description, whenever in his judgment such regulations are required in the interest of navigation. Such regulations shall be posted in conspicuous and appropriate places for the information of the public; and every person or corporation which shall violate the said regulations, or any of them, shall be deemed guilty of a misdemeanor and shall be subject to the penalties prescribed in sections 411 and 412 of this title, for violation of the provisions of section 407 of this title: *Provided*, That any regulations made in pursuance hereof may be enforced as provided in section 413 of this title, the provisions whereof are made applicable to the said regulations: *Provided further*, That this section shall not apply to any waters within the jurisdictional boundaries of any State which are now or may hereafter be used for the cultivation of oysters under the laws of such State, except navigable channels which have been or may hereafter be improved by the United States, or to be designated as navigable channels by competent authority, and in making such improvements of channels, the material dredged shall not be deposited upon any ground in use in accordance with the laws of such State for the cultivation of oysters, except in compliance with said laws: *And provided further*, That any expense necessary in executing this section may be paid from funds available for the improvement of the harbor or waterway, for which regulations may be prescribed, and in case no such funds are available the said expense may be paid from appropriations made by Congress for examinations, surveys, and contingencies of rivers and harbors.

(Mar. 3, 1905, ch. 1482, § 4, 33 Stat. 1147; July 26, 1947, ch. 343, title II, § 205(a), 61 Stat. 501.)

CHANGE OF NAME

Department of War designated Department of the Army and title of Secretary of War changed to Secretary of the Army by section 205(a) of act July 26, 1947, ch. 343, title II, 61 Stat. 501. Section 205(a) of act July 26, 1947, was repealed by section 53 of act Aug. 10, 1956, ch. 1041, 70A Stat. 641. Section 1 of act Aug. 10, 1956, enacted "Title 10, Armed Forces" which in sections 3010 to 3013 continued Department of the Army under administrative supervision of Secretary of the Army.

TRANSFER OF FUNCTIONS

Functions, powers, and duties of Secretary of the Army and other offices and officers of Department of the Army under section 401 of this title to extent that they relate generally to location and clearances of bridges and causeways in navigable waters of United States transferred to and vested in Secretary of Transportation by Pub. L. 89–670, § 6(g)(6)(A), Oct. 15, 1966, 80 Stat. 941, which created Department of Transportation. Pub. L. 97–449 amended section 401 of this title to reflect transfer made by section 6(g)(6)(A) of Pub. L. 89–670, and repealed section 6(g)(6)(A).

§ 419a. Management practices to extend capacity and useful life of dredged material disposal areas

The Secretary of the Army, acting through the Chief of Engineers, shall utilize and encourage the utilization of such management practices as he determines appropriate to extend the capacity and useful life of dredged material disposal areas such that the need for new dredged material disposal areas is kept to a minimum. Management practices authorized by this section shall include, but not be limited to, the construction of dikes, consolidation and dewatering of dredged material, and construction of drainage and outflow facilities.

(Pub. L. 94–587, § 148, Oct. 22, 1976, 90 Stat. 2931.)

§ 420. Piers and cribs on Mississippi and St. Croix Rivers

The owners of sawmills on the Mississippi River and the Saint Croix River in the States of Wisconsin and Minnesota are authorized and empowered under the direction of the Secretary of the Army, to construct piers or cribs in front of their mill property on the banks of the river, for the protection of their mills and rafts against damage by floods and ice: *Provided, however*, That the piers or cribs so constructed shall not interfere with or obstruct the navigation of the river. And in case any pier or crib constructed under authority of this section shall at any time, and for any cause, be found to obstruct the navigation of the river, the Government expressly reserves the right to remove or direct the removal of it, at the cost and expense of the owners thereof.

(R.S. § 5254; May 1, 1882, ch. 112, 22 Stat. 52; July 26, 1947, ch. 343, title II, § 205(a), 61 Stat. 501.)

CODIFICATION

R.S. § 5254 derived from act Mar. 3, 1873, ch. 278, 17 Stat. 606.

AMENDMENTS

1882—Act May 1, 1882, inserted reference to Saint Croix River in the States of Wisconsin and Minnesota.

CHANGE OF NAME

Department of War designated Department of the Army and title of Secretary of War changed to Secretary of the Army by section 205(a) of act July 26, 1947, ch. 343, title II, 61 Stat. 501. Section 205(a) of act July 26, 1947, was repealed by section 53 of act Aug. 10, 1956, ch. 1041, 70A Stat. 641. Section 1 of act Aug. 10, 1956, enacted "Title 10, Armed Forces" which in sections 3010 to 3013 continued Department of the Army under administrative supervision of Secretary of the Army.

TRANSFER OF FUNCTIONS

Functions, powers, and duties of Secretary of the Army and other offices and officers of Department of the Army under section 401 of this title to extent that they relate generally to location and clearances of bridges and causeways in navigable waters of United States transferred to and vested in Secretary of Transportation by Pub. L. 89–670, § 6(g)(6)(A), Oct. 15, 1966, 80

Stat. 941, which created Department of Transportation. Pub. L. 97–449 amended section 401 of this title to reflect transfer made by section 6(g)(6)(A) of Pub. L. 89–670, and repealed section 6(g)(6)(A).

§ 421. Deposit of refuse, etc., in Lake Michigan near Chicago

It shall not be lawful to throw, discharge, dump, or deposit, or cause, suffer, or procure, to be thrown, discharged, dumped, or deposited, any refuse matter of any kind or description whatever other than that flowing from streets and sewers and passing therefrom in a liquid state into Lake Michigan, at any point opposite or in front of the county of Cook, in the State of Illinois, or the county of Lake in the State of Indiana, within eight miles from the shore of said lake, unless said material shall be placed inside of a breakwater so arranged as not to permit the escape of such refuse material into the body of the lake and cause contamination thereof; and no officer of the Government shall dump or cause or authorize to be dumped any material contrary to the provisions of this section: *Provided, however*, That the provisions of this section shall not apply to work in connection with the construction, repair, and protection of breakwaters and other structures built in aid of navigation, or for the purpose of obtaining water supply. Any person violating any provision of this section shall be guilty of a misdemeanor, and on conviction thereof shall be fined for each offense not exceeding $1,000.

(June 23, 1910, ch. 359, 36 Stat. 593.)

CODIFICATION

Section is from act June 23, 1910, popularly known as the "Rivers and Harbors Act of 1910".

§ 422. Modification and extension of harbor lines at Chicago

The Secretary of the Army is authorized, in his discretion, to modify and extend harbor lines in front of the city of Chicago in such manner as to permit park extension work which may be desired by the municipal authorities, including the changing and widening of the southern entrance to the Chicago Harbor.

(Aug. 26, 1912, ch. 408, § 5, 37 Stat. 626; July 26, 1947, ch. 343, title II, § 205(a), 61 Stat. 501.)

CODIFICATION

Section is from act Aug. 26, 1912, popularly known as the "Deficiency Appropriation Act for 1912".

CHANGE OF NAME

Department of War designated Department of the Army and title of Secretary of War changed to Secretary of the Army by section 205(a) of act July 26, 1947, ch. 343, title II, 61 Stat. 501. Section 205(a) of act July 26, 1947, was repealed by section 53 of act Aug. 10, 1956, ch. 1041, 70A Stat. 641. Section 1 of act Aug. 10, 1956, enacted "Title 10, Armed Forces" which in sections 3010 to 3013 continued Department of the Army under administrative supervision of Secretary of the Army.

TRANSFER OF FUNCTIONS

Functions, powers, and duties of Secretary of the Army and other offices and officers of Department of the Army under section 401 of this title to extent that they relate generally to location and clearances of bridges and causeways in navigable waters of United States transferred to and vested in Secretary of Transportation by Pub. L. 89–670, § 6(g)(6)(A), Oct. 15, 1966, 80 Stat. 941, which created Department of Transportation. Pub. L. 97–449 amended section 401 of this title to reflect transfer made by section 6(g)(6)(A) of Pub. L. 89–670, and repealed section 6(g)(6)(A).

§ 423. Establishment of pierhead and bulkhead lines in Wilmington Harbor, California

The Secretary of the Army is authorized to fix and establish pierhead and bulkhead lines, either or both, in the inner harbor of San Pedro, otherwise known as Wilmington Harbor, California, beyond which no piers, wharves, bulkheads, or other works shall be extended or deposits made except under such regulations as shall be prescribed from time to time by the Secretary of the Army.

(Mar. 26, 1908, No. 14, 35 Stat. 569; July 26, 1947, ch. 343, title II, § 205(a), 61 Stat. 501.)

CHANGE OF NAME

Department of War designated Department of the Army and title of Secretary of War changed to Secretary of the Army by section 205(a) of act July 26, 1947, ch. 343, title II, 61 Stat. 501. Section 205(a) of act July 26, 1947, was repealed by section 53 of act Aug. 10, 1956, ch. 1041, 70A Stat. 641. Section 1 of act Aug. 10, 1956, enacted "Title 10, Armed Forces" which in sections 3010 to 3013 continued Department of the Army under administrative supervision of Secretary of the Army.

TRANSFER OF FUNCTIONS

Functions, powers, and duties of Secretary of the Army and other offices and officers of Department of the Army under section 401 of this title to extent that they relate generally to location and clearances of bridges and causeways in navigable waters of United States transferred to and vested in Secretary of Transportation by Pub. L. 89–670, § 6(g)(6)(A), Oct. 15, 1966, 80 Stat. 941, which created Department of Transportation. Pub. L. 97–449 amended section 401 of this title to reflect transfer made by section 6(g)(6)(A) of Pub. L. 89–670, and repealed section 6(g)(6)(A).

§ 424. Establishment of pierhead or bulkhead lines in Newport Harbor, California

The Secretary of the Army is authorized and directed to fix and establish pierhead and bulkhead lines, either or both, at Newport Harbor, California, in accordance with plan dated United States Engineer Office, Los Angeles, California, March 25, 1913, and entitled "Newport Bay, California", showing harbor lines, beyond which no piers, wharfs, bulkheads, or other works shall be extended or deposit made, except under such regulations as shall be prescribed from time to time by the Secretary of the Army.

(July 27, 1916, ch. 260, § 3, 39 Stat. 411; July 26, 1947, ch. 343, title II, § 205(a), 61 Stat. 501.)

CODIFICATION

Section is from act July 27, 1916, popularly known as the "Rivers and Harbors Appropriation Act of 1916".

CHANGE OF NAME

Department of War designated Department of the Army and title of Secretary of War changed to Secretary of the Army by section 205(a) of act July 26, 1947, ch. 343, title II, 61 Stat. 501. Section 205(a) of act July 26, 1947, was repealed by section 53 of act Aug. 10, 1956, ch. 1041, 70A Stat. 641. Section 1 of act Aug. 10, 1956, enacted "Title 10, Armed Forces" which in sections 3010 to 3013 continued Department of the Army under administrative supervision of Secretary of the Army.

TRANSFER OF FUNCTIONS

Functions, powers, and duties of Secretary of the Army and other offices and officers of Department of the Army under section 401 of this title to extent that they relate generally to location and clearances of bridges and causeways in navigable waters of United States transferred to and vested in Secretary of Transportation by Pub. L. 89–670, §6(g)(6)(A), Oct. 15, 1966, 80 Stat. 941, which created Department of Transportation. Pub. L. 97–449 amended section 401 of this title to reflect transfer made by section 6(g)(6)(A) of Pub. L. 89–670, and repealed section 6(g)(6)(A).

§424a. Modification of harbor lines in Newport Harbor, California

The Secretary of the Army is authorized to modify from time to time, the harbor lines at Newport Harbor, California, established in pursuance of section 424 of this title: *Provided*, That in his opinion such modification will not injuriously affect the interests of navigation.

(Mar. 3, 1925, ch. 467, §10, 43 Stat. 1197; July 26, 1947, ch. 343, title II, §205(a), 61 Stat. 501.)

CHANGE OF NAME

Department of War designated Department of the Army and title of Secretary of War changed to Secretary of the Army by section 205(a) of act July 26, 1947, ch. 343, title II, 61 Stat. 501. Section 205(a) of act July 26, 1947, was repealed by section 53 of act Aug. 10, 1956, ch. 1041, 70A Stat. 641. Section 1 of act Aug. 10, 1956, enacted "Title 10, Armed Forces" which in sections 3010 to 3013 continued Department of the Army under administrative supervision of Secretary of the Army.

TRANSFER OF FUNCTIONS

Functions, powers, and duties of Secretary of the Army and other offices and officers of Department of the Army under section 401 of this title to extent that they relate generally to location and clearances of bridges and causeways in navigable waters of United States transferred to and vested in Secretary of Transportation by Pub. L. 89–670, §6(g)(6)(A), Oct. 15, 1966, 80 Stat. 941, which created Department of Transportation. Pub. L. 97–449 amended section 401 of this title to reflect transfer made by section 6(g)(6)(A) of Pub. L. 89–670, and repealed section 6(g)(6)(A).

§425. Omitted

CODIFICATION

Section, act June 7, 1924, ch. 316, §9, 43 Stat. 606, directed Secretary of War to investigate depositing of polluting substances into navigable streams and report the results to Congress not later than two years from June 7, 1924.

§426. Investigations concerning erosion of shores of coastal and lake waters

The Chief of Engineers of the United States Army, under the direction of the Secretary of the Army, is authorized and directed to cause investigations and studies to be made in cooperation with the appropriate agencies of the various States on the Atlantic, Pacific, and gulf coasts and on the Great Lakes, and of the States of Alaska and Hawaii, the Commonwealth of Puerto Rico, and the possessions of the United States, with a view to devising effective means of preventing erosion of the shores of coastal and lake waters by waves and currents; and any expenses incident and necessary thereto may be paid from funds appropriated for General Investigations, Civil Functions, Department of the Army: *Provided*, That the Department of the Army may release to the appropriate cooperating agencies information obtained by these investigations and studies prior to the formal transmission of reports to Congress: *Provided further*, That no money shall be expended under authority of this section in any State which does not provide for cooperation with the agents of the United States and contribute to the project such funds or services as the Secretary of the Army may deem appropriate and require; that there shall be organized under the Chief of Engineers, United States Army, a Board of seven members, of whom four shall be officers of the Corps of Engineers and three shall be civilian engineers selected by the Chief of Engineers with regard to their special fitness in the field of beach erosion and shore protection. The Board will furnish such technical assistance as may be directed by the Chief of Engineers in the conduct of such studies as may be undertaken and will review the reports of the investigations made. In the consideration of such studies as may be referred to the Board by the Chief of Engineers, the Board shall, when it considers it necessary and with the sanction of the Chief of Engineers, make, as a board or through its members, personal examination of localities under investigation: *Provided further*, That the civilian members of the Board may be paid at rates not to exceed $100 a day for each day of attendance at Board meetings, not to exceed thirty days per annum, in addition to the traveling and other necessary expenses connected with their duties on the Board in accordance with the provisions of section 5703 of title 5.

(July 3, 1930, ch. 847, §2, 46 Stat. 945; Pub. L. 86–645, title I, §103, July 14, 1960, 74 Stat. 484.)

REFERENCES IN TEXT

The Board, referred to in text, means the Beach Erosion Board, which was abolished by Pub. L. 88–172, §1, Nov. 7, 1963, 77 Stat. 304. See note set out below.

CODIFICATION

"Section 5703 of title 5" substituted in text for "section 5 of the Administrative Expenses Act of 1946, as amended (5 U.S.C. 73b–2)", on authority of Pub. L. 89–554, §7(b), Sept. 6, 1966, 80 Stat. 631, the first section of which enacted Title 5, Government Organization and Employees.

AMENDMENTS

1960—Pub. L. 86–645, among other changes, substituted provisions requiring the three civilian members of the Board to be civilian engineers selected by the Chief of Engineers with regard to their special fitness in the field of beach erosion and shore protection for provisions which required the civilian members to be selected with regard to their special fitness from among the State agencies cooperating with the Department of the Army, and provisions authorizing payment of civilian members at rates not to exceed $100 a day, for not more than 30 days per annum, for provisions which required the States to pay the salaries of the civilian members.

ABOLITION OF BEACH EROSION BOARD

Pub. L. 88–172, §1, Nov. 7, 1963, 77 Stat. 304, provided in part: "That the Board established by section 2 of the

River and Harbor Act approved July 3, 1930, as amended (33 U.S.C. 426), referred to as the Beach Erosion Board, is hereby abolished.'' For the transfer of functions of the Beach Erosion Board to the Coastal Engineering Research Center and the Board of Engineers for Rivers and Harbors, see sections 426–1 and 426–3 of this title. For termination of Board of Engineers for Rivers and Harbors 180 days after Oct. 31, 1992, and reassignment of duties and responsibilities by Secretary of Army, see section 223 of Pub. L. 102–580, set out as a note under section 541 of this title.

GREAT LAKES LEVELS STUDY

Pub. L. 99–662, title VII, § 706, Nov. 17, 1986, 100 Stat. 4158, authorized Secretary of the Army, in cooperation with National Oceanic and Atmospheric Administration, Federal Emergency Management Agency, International Joint Commission, and other appropriate Federal, State, and local agencies and the private sector, to conduct a study of shoreline protection and beach erosion control policy and related projects of the Secretary, in view of the current situation and long-term expected increases in levels of the Great Lakes and directed Secretary, within three years after Nov. 17, 1986, to transmit the study, together with supporting documentation and recommendations to Congress.

STUDY OF RISING OCEANS

Pub. L. 99–662, title VII, § 731, Nov. 17, 1986, 100 Stat. 4165, authorized Secretary of the Army, in cooperation with National Oceanic and Atmospheric Administration, Federal Emergency Management Agency, and other appropriate Federal, State, and local agencies and the private sector, to conduct a study of shoreline protection and beach erosion control policy and related projects of the Secretary, in view of the prospect for long-term increases in levels of the ocean and directed Secretary, within three years after Nov. 17, 1986, to transmit the study, together with supporting documentation and recommendations to Congress.

APPLICATION OF EXISTING LAW TO SURVEYS RELATING TO SHORE PROTECTION

Pub. L. 87–874, § 103(b), Oct. 23, 1962, 76 Stat. 1179, provided that: ''All provisions of existing law relating to surveys of rivers and harbors shall apply to surveys relating to shore protection and section 2 of the River and Harbor Act approved July 3, 1930, as amended (33 U.S.C. 426), is modified to the extent inconsistent herewith.''

§ 426–1. Coastal Engineering Research Center; establishment; powers and functions

There shall be established under the Chief of Engineers, United States Army, a Coastal Engineering Research Center which, except as hereinafter provided in section 426–3 of this title, shall be vested with all the functions of the Beach Erosion Board, including the authority to make general investigations as provided in section 426a of this title, and such additional functions as the Chief of Engineers may assign.

(Pub. L. 88–172, § 1, Nov. 7, 1963, 77 Stat. 304.)

CODIFICATION

Section was enacted as part of section 1 of Pub. L. 88–172. The remainder of said section 1, abolishing the Beach Erosion Board, is classified as a note under section 426 of this title.

ABOLITION OF BEACH EROSION BOARD

Section 1 of Pub. L. 88–172 abolished Beach Erosion Board, and is set out as a note under section 426 of this title. For the transfer of certain functions of said Board to Board of Engineers for Rivers and Harbors, see section 426–3 of this title. For termination of Board of Engineers for Rivers and Harbors 180 days after Oct. 31, 1992, and reassignment of duties and responsibilities by Secretary of Army, see section 223 of Pub. L. 102–580, set out as a note under section 541 of this title.

§ 426–2. Board on Coastal Engineering Research

The functions of the Coastal Engineering Research Center established by section 426–1 of this title, shall be conducted with the guidance and advice of a Board on Coastal Engineering Research, constituted by the Chief of Engineers in the same manner as the present Beach Erosion Board.

(Pub. L. 88–172, § 2, Nov. 7, 1963, 77 Stat. 305.)

COMPENSATION OF BOARD

Pub. L. 91–611, title I, § 105, Dec. 31, 1970, 84 Stat. 1819, provided that: ''The civilian members of the Board on Coastal Engineering Research authorized by the Act of November 7, 1963 (33 U.S.C. 426–2) may be paid at rates not to exceed the daily equivalent of the rate for GS–18 for each day of attendance at Board meetings, not to exceed thirty days per year, in addition to the traveling and other necessary expenses connected with their duties on the Board in accordance with the provisions of 5 U.S.C. 5703(b), (d), and 5707.''

[References in laws to the rates of pay for GS–16, 17, or 18, or to maximum rates of pay under the General Schedule, to be considered references to rates payable under specified sections of Title 5, Government Organization and Employees, see section 529 [title I, § 101(c)(1)] of Pub. L. 101–509, set out in a note under section 5376 of Title 5.]

ABOLITION OF BEACH EROSION BOARD

Section 1 of Pub. L. 88–172 abolished Beach Erosion Board, and is set out as a note under section 426 of this title. For transfer of functions of Board to Coastal Engineering Research Center and Board of Engineers for Rivers and Harbors, see sections 426–1 and 426–3 of this title. For termination of Board of Engineers for Rivers and Harbors 180 days after Oct. 31, 1992, and reassignment of duties and responsibilities by Secretary of Army, see section 223 of Pub. L. 102–580, set out as a note under section 541 of this title.

§ 426–3. Transfer of functions of Beach Erosion Board

All functions of the Beach Erosion Board pertaining to review of reports of investigations made concerning erosion of the shores of coastal and lake waters, and the protection of such shores, are hereby transferred to the Board established by section 541 of this title, referred to as the Board of Engineers for Rivers and Harbors.

(Pub. L. 88–172, § 3, Nov. 7, 1963, 77 Stat. 305.)

TERMINATION OF BOARD OF ENGINEERS FOR RIVERS AND HARBORS AND REASSIGNMENT OF DUTIES AND RESPONSIBILITIES

For termination of Board of Engineers for Rivers and Harbors 180 days after Oct. 31, 1992, and reassignment of duties and responsibilities by Secretary of Army, see section 223 of Pub. L. 102–580, set out as a note under section 541 of this title.

ABOLITION OF BEACH EROSION BOARD

Section 1 of Pub. L. 88–172 abolished Beach Erosion Board, and is set out as a note under section 426 of this title. For transfer of certain functions of Board to Coastal Engineering Research Center, see section 426–1 of this title.

§426a. Additional investigations concerning erosion of shores of coastal and lake waters; payment of costs; "shores" defined

In addition to participating in cooperative investigations and studies with agencies of the various States as authorized in section 426 of this title, it shall be the duty of the Chief of Engineers, through the Coastal Engineering Research Center, to make general investigations with a view to preventing erosion of the shores of the United States by waves and currents and determining the most suitable methods for the protection, restoration, and development of beaches; and to publish from time to time such useful data and information concerning the erosion and protection of beaches and shore lines as the Center may deem to be of value to the people of the United States. The cost of the general investigations authorized by sections 426a to 426d of this title shall be borne wholly by the United States. As used in said sections, the word "shores" includes the shore lines of the Atlantic and Pacific Oceans, the Gulf of Mexico, the Great Lakes, Lake Champlain, and estuaries and bays directly connected therewith.

(July 31, 1945, ch. 334, §1, 59 Stat. 508; Pub. L. 88–172, §1, Nov. 7, 1963, 77 Stat. 304.)

CODIFICATION

Coastal Engineering Research Center has been substituted for Beach Erosion Board pursuant to Pub. L. 88–172, §1, providing in part for the abolition of the Beach Erosion Board, which is set out as a note under section 426 of this title. For transfer of investigatory functions of the Beach Erosion Board to the Coastal Engineering Research Center, see section 426–1 of this title.

§426b. Applicability of existing laws; projects referred to Board of Engineers for Rivers and Harbors

All provisions of existing law relating to examinations and surveys and to works of improvement of rivers and harbors shall apply, insofar as practicable, to examinations and surveys and to works of improvement relating to shore protection; except that all projects having to do with shore protection shall be referred for consideration and recommendation to the Board of Engineers for Rivers and Harbors.

(July 31, 1945, ch. 334, §2, 59 Stat. 508; Pub. L. 88–172, §1, Nov. 7, 1963, 77 Stat. 304.)

CODIFICATION

Provision for the referral of projects having to do with shore protection for consideration and recommendation to the Beach Erosion Board have been omitted as obsolete in view of the abolition of the Beach Erosion Board and the transfer of its review function to the Board of Engineers for Rivers and Harbors by Pub. L. 88–172, §1. See section 426–3 of this title.

TERMINATION OF BOARD OF ENGINEERS FOR RIVERS AND HARBORS AND REASSIGNMENT OF DUTIES AND RESPONSIBILITIES

For termination of Board of Engineers for Rivers and Harbors 180 days after Oct. 31, 1992, and reassignment of duties and responsibilities by Secretary of Army, see section 223 of Pub. L. 102–580, set out as a note under section 541 of this title.

§426c. Report by Coastal Engineering Research Center

The Coastal Engineering Research Center, in making its report on any cooperative investigation and studies under the provisions of section 426 of this title, relating to shore protection work shall, in addition to any other matters upon which it may be required to report, state its opinion as to (a) the advisability of adopting the project; (b) what public interest, if any, is involved in the proposed improvement; and (c) what share of the expense, if any, should be borne by the United States.

(July 31, 1945, ch. 334, §3, 59 Stat. 508; Pub. L. 88–172, §1, Nov. 7, 1963, 77 Stat. 304.)

CODIFICATION

Coastal Engineering Research Center has been substituted for Beach Erosion Board pursuant to Pub. L. 88–172, §1, providing in part for the abolition of the Beach Erosion Board, which is set out as a note under section 426 of this title. For transfer of investigatory functions of the Beach Erosion Board to the Coastal Engineering Research Center see section 426–1 of this title.

§426d. Payment of expenses

Any expenses incident and necessary in the undertaking of the general investigations authorized by sections 426a to 426d of this title may be paid from funds appropriated prior to or after July 31, 1945, for examinations, surveys, and contingencies for rivers and harbors.

(July 31, 1945, ch. 334, §4, 59 Stat. 508.)

§426e. Federal aid in protection of shores

(a) Declaration of policy

With the purpose of preventing damage to the shores and beaches of the United States, its Territories and possessions and promoting and encouraging the healthful recreation of the people, it is declared to be the policy of the United States, subject to sections 426e to 426h–1 of this title, to promote shore protection projects and related research that encourage the protection, restoration, and enhancement of sandy beaches, including beach restoration and periodic beach nourishment, on a comprehensive and coordinated basis by the Federal Government, States, localities, and private enterprises. In carrying out this policy, preference shall be given to areas in which there has been a Federal investment of funds and areas with respect to which the need for prevention or mitigation of damage to shores and beaches is attributable to Federal navigation projects or other Federal activities.

(b) Federal contribution; maximum amount; exceptions

The Federal contribution in the case of any project referred to in subsection (a) of this section shall not exceed one-half of the cost of the project, and the remainder shall be paid by the State, municipality, or other political subdivision in which the project is located, except that (1) the costs allocated to the restoration and protection of Federal property shall be borne fully by the Federal Government, (2) Federal participation in the cost of a project for restoration and protection of State, county, and other publicly owned shore parks and conservation areas may be, in the discretion of the Chief of Engineers, not more than 70 per centum of the total cost exclusive of land costs, when such areas: Include a zone which excludes permanent human habitation; include but are not limited to recreational beaches; satisfy adequate criteria for conservation and development of the natural resources of the environment; extend landward a sufficient distance to include, where appropriate, protective dunes, bluffs, or other natural features which serve to protect the uplands from damage; and provide essentially full park facilities for appropriate public use, all of which shall meet with the approval of the Chief of Engineers, and (3) Federal participation in the cost of a project providing hurricane protection may be, in the discretion of the Secretary[1] not more than 70 per centum of the total cost exclusive of land costs.

(c) Periodic beach nourishment; "construction" defined

When in the opinion of the Chief of Engineers the most suitable and economical remedial measures would be provided by periodic beach nourishment, the term "construction" may be construed for the purposes of sections 426e to 426h–1 of this title to include the deposit of sand fill at suitable intervals of time to furnish sand supply to project shores for a length of time specified by the Chief of Engineers.

(d) Shores other than public

Shores other than public will be eligible for Federal assistance if there is benefit such as that arising from public use or from the protection of nearby public property or if the benefits to those shores are incidental to the project, and the Federal contribution to the project shall be adjusted in accordance with the degree of such benefits.

(e) Authorization of projects

(1) In general

No Federal contributions shall be made with respect to a project under sections 426e to 426h–1 of this title unless the plan therefor shall have been specifically adopted and authorized by Congress after investigation and study by the Coastal Engineering Research Center under the provisions of section 426 of this title as amended and supplemented, or, in the case of a small project under section 426g or 426h[2] of this title, unless the plan therefor has been approved by the Chief of Engineers.

(2) Studies

(A) In general

The Secretary shall—

(i) recommend to Congress studies concerning shore protection projects that meet the criteria established under sections 426e to 426h–1 of this title (including subparagraph (B)(iii)) and other applicable law;

(ii) conduct such studies as Congress requires under applicable laws; and

(iii) report the results of the studies to the Committee on Environment and Public Works of the Senate and the Committee on Transportation and Infrastructure of the House of Representatives.

(B) Recommendations for shore protection projects

(i) In general

The Secretary shall recommend to Congress the authorization or reauthorization of shore protection projects based on the studies conducted under subparagraph (A).

(ii) Considerations

In making recommendations, the Secretary shall consider the economic and ecological benefits of the shore protection project.

(C) Coordination of projects

In conducting studies and making recommendations for a shore protection project under this paragraph, the Secretary shall—

(i) determine whether there is any other project being carried out by the Secretary or the head of another Federal agency that may be complementary to the shore protection project; and

(ii) if there is such a complementary project, describe the efforts that will be made to coordinate the projects.

(3) Shore protection projects

(A) In general

The Secretary shall construct, or cause to be constructed, any shore protection project authorized by Congress, or separable element of such a project, for which funds have been appropriated by Congress.

(B) Agreements

(i) Requirement

After authorization by Congress, and before commencement of construction, of a shore protection project or separable element, the Secretary shall enter into a written agreement with a non-Federal interest with respect to the project or separable element.

(ii) Terms

The agreement shall—

(I) specify the life of the project; and

(II) ensure that the Federal Government and the non-Federal interest will cooperate in carrying out the project or separable element.

(C) Coordination of projects

In constructing a shore protection project or separable element under this paragraph, the Secretary shall, to the extent practicable, coordinate the project or element with any complementary project identified under paragraph (2)(C).

(Aug. 13, 1946, ch. 960, §1, 60 Stat. 1056; July 28, 1956, ch. 768, 70 Stat. 702; Pub. L. 87–874, title I, §103(a)(1)–(3), Oct. 23, 1962, 76 Stat. 1178; Pub. L. 88–172, §1, Nov. 7, 1963, 77 Stat. 304; Pub. L. 91–611, title II, §208, Dec. 31, 1970, 84 Stat. 1829; Pub. L. 104–303, title II, §227(a), (b), (e)(2)(A), (B), Oct. 12, 1996, 110 Stat. 3698, 3703.)

---

[1] So in original. Probably should be followed by a comma.

[2] See References in Text note below.

REFERENCES IN TEXT

Section 426h of this title, referred to in subsec. (e)(1), was repealed by Pub. L. 110–114, title II, §2038(b), Nov. 8, 2007, 121 Stat. 1100.

CODIFICATION

Coastal Engineering Research Center, referred to in subsec. (e), has been substituted for Beach Erosion Board pursuant to Pub. L. 88–172, §1, providing in part for the abolition of the Beach Erosion Board and for transfer of functions of the Beach Erosion Board to the Coastal Engineering Research Center. See section 426–1 of this title.

AMENDMENTS

1996—Subsec. (a). Pub. L. 104–303, §227(a), inserted "and beaches" after "damage to the shores" and substituted "sections 426e to 426h–1 of this title, to promote shore protection projects and related research that encourage the protection, restoration, and enhancement of sandy beaches, including beach restoration and periodic beach nourishment, on a comprehensive and coordinated basis by the Federal Government, States, localities, and private enterprises. In carrying out this policy, preference shall be given to areas in which there has been a Federal investment of funds and areas with respect to which the need for prevention or mitigation of damage to shores and beaches is attributable to Federal navigation projects or other Federal activities." for "the following provisions of sections 426e to 426h of this title to assist in the construction, but not the maintenance, of works for the restoration and protection against erosion, by waves and currents, of the shores of the United States, its Territories and possessions."

Subsec. (b)(3). Pub. L. 104–303, §227(e)(2), substituted "Secretary" for "Secretary of the Army, acting through the Chief of Engineers," and struck out second period at end.

Subsec. (e). Pub. L. 104–303, §227(b), (e)(2)(B), inserted subsec. heading, designated existing provisions as par. (1) and inserted heading, realigned margin, inserted "or 426h" after "under section 426g", and added pars. (2) and (3).

1970—Subsec. (b). Pub. L. 91–611 provided for designation of existing provisions as cls. (1) and (2) by insertion of "(1)" after "except that" and substitution of "(2)" for "and, further, that" and added cl. (3).

1962—Subsec. (b). Pub. L. 87–874, §103(a)(1), (2), increased maximum limit on amount of Federal contributions from one-third to one-half of project cost, provided that costs for restoration and protection of Federal property shall be borne fully by the Federal Government, and that costs for restoration and protection of State, county and other publicly owned shore parks and conservation areas may be borne by Federal Government up to not more than 70 per centum, exclusive of land costs, when such areas include a zone which excludes permanent human habitation, include recreational beaches, satisfy criteria for conservation and development of natural resources, extend landward enough to include natural features to protect uplands, and provide essentially full park facilities for public use, all of which meet with approval of Chief of Engineers.

Subsec. (e). Pub. L. 87–874, §103(a)(3), required approval of plans by Chief of Engineers in case of a small project under section 426g of this title.

1956—Act July 28, 1956, extended assistance to privately owned shores, to include shores of Territories and possessions, substituted "restoration" for "improvement", defined "construction", and struck out provisions which authorized Federal aid toward the repair and protection of seawalls constructed by political subdivisions to protect important public highways.

BEACH RECREATION

Pub. L. 106–541, title II, §220, Dec. 11, 2000, 114 Stat. 2596, provided that: "Not later than 1 year after the date of enactment of this Act [Dec. 11, 2000], the Secretary shall develop and implement procedures to ensure that all of the benefits of a beach restoration project, including those benefits attributable to recreation, hurricane and storm damage reduction, and environmental protection and restoration, are displayed in reports for such projects."

SHORE MANAGEMENT PROGRAM

Pub. L. 106–53, title II, §213, Aug. 17, 1999, 113 Stat. 291, provided that:

"(a) REVIEW.—The Secretary shall review the implementation of the Corps of Engineers shore management program, with particular attention to—

"(1) inconsistencies in implementation among the divisions and districts of the Corps of Engineers; and

"(2) complaints by or potential inequities regarding property owners in the Savannah District, including an accounting of the number and disposition of complaints in the Savannah District during the 5-year period preceding the date of enactment of this Act [Aug. 17, 1999].

"(b) REPORT.—As expeditiously as practicable, but not later than 1 year after the date of enactment of this Act [Aug. 17, 1999], the Secretary shall submit to the Committee on Transportation and Infrastructure of the House of Representatives and the Committee on Environment and Public Works of the Senate a report describing the results of the review under subsection (a)."

REPORT ON SHORES OF THE UNITED STATES

Pub. L. 106–53, title II, §215(c), Aug. 17, 1999, 113 Stat. 293, provided that:

"(1) IN GENERAL.—Not later than 3 years after the date of enactment of this Act [Aug. 17, 1999], the Secretary shall report to Congress on the state of the shores of the United States.

"(2) CONTENTS.—The report shall include—

"(A) a description of—

"(i) the extent of, and economic and environmental effects caused by, erosion and accretion along the shores of the United States; and

"(ii) the causes of such erosion and accretion;

"(B) a description of resources committed by Federal, State, and local governments to restore and renourish shores;

"(C) a description of the systematic movement of sand along the shores of the United States; and

"(D) recommendations regarding—

"(i) appropriate levels of Federal and non-Federal participation in shore protection; and

"(ii) use of a systems approach to sand management.

"(3) USE OF SPECIFIC LOCATION DATA.—In developing the report, the Secretary shall use data from specific locations on the coasts of the Atlantic Ocean, Pacific Ocean, Great Lakes, and Gulf of Mexico."

REPORT TO CONGRESS ON SHORELINE PROTECTION PROGRAMS

Pub. L. 101–640, title III, §309, Nov. 28, 1990, 104 Stat. 4638, provided that: "Not later than 1 year after the date of the enactment of this Act [Nov. 28, 1990], the Secretary shall transmit to Congress a report on the advisability of not participating in the planning, implementation, or maintenance of any beach stabilization or renourishment project involving Federal funds unless the State in which the proposed project will be located has established or committed to establish a beach front management program that includes—

"(1) restrictions on new development seaward of an erosion setback line (based on preproject beach size) of at least 30 times the annual erosion rate;

"(2) restrictions on construction of new structural stabilization projects, such as seawalls and groins, and their reconstruction if damaged by 50 percent or more;

"(3) provisions for the relocation of structures in erosion-prone areas;

"(4) provisions to assure public access to beaches stabilized or renourished with Federal funds after January 1, 1991; and

"(5) such other provisions as the Secretary may prescribe by regulation to prevent hazardous or environmentally damaging shoreline development."

§ 426e–1. Shore protection projects

(a) In general

In accordance with the Act of July 3, 1930 (33 U.S.C. 426) of this title, and notwithstanding administrative actions, it is the policy of the United States to promote beach nourishment for the purposes of flood damage reduction and hurricane and storm damage reduction and related research that encourage the protection, restoration, and enhancement of sandy beaches, including beach restoration and periodic beach renourishment for a period of 50 years, on a comprehensive and coordinated basis by the Federal Government, States, localities, and private enterprises.

(b) Preference

In carrying out the policy under subsection (a), preference shall be given to—

(1) areas in which there has been a Federal investment of funds for the purposes described in subsection (a); and

(2) areas with respect to which the need for prevention or mitigation of damage to shores and beaches is attributable to Federal navigation projects or other Federal activities.

(c) Applicability

The Secretary shall apply the policy under subsection (a) to each shore protection and beach renourishment project (including shore protection and beach renourishment projects constructed before November 8, 2007).

(Pub. L. 110–114, title II, § 2018, Nov. 8, 2007, 121 Stat. 1077.)

References in Text

The Act of July 3, 1930, referred to in subsec. (a), is act July 3, 1930, ch. 847, 46 Stat. 918. For complete classification of this Act to the Code, see Tables.

"Secretary" Defined

Secretary means the Secretary of the Army, see section 2 of Pub. L. 110–114, set out as a note under section 2201 of this title.

§ 426f. Reimbursements

(a) In general

The Secretary is authorized to reimburse non-Federal interests for work done by them, after initiation of the survey studies which form the basis for the project or separable element of the project, on authorized projects or separable elements which individually do not exceed $1,000,000 in total cost: *Provided*, That the work which may have been done on the projects or separable elements is approved by the Chief of Engineers as being in accordance with the authorized projects or separable elements: *Provided further*, That such reimbursement shall be subject to appropriations applicable thereto or funds available therefor and shall not take precedence over other pending projects or separable elements of higher priority for improvements.

(b) Agreements

(1) Requirement

After authorization of reimbursement by the Secretary under this section, and before commencement of construction, of a shore protection project, the Secretary shall enter into a written agreement with the non-Federal interest with respect to the project or separable element.

(2) Terms

The agreement shall—

(A) specify the life of the project; and

(B) ensure that the Federal Government and the non-Federal interest will cooperate in carrying out the project or separable element.

(Aug. 13, 1946, ch. 960, § 2, 60 Stat. 1056; July 26, 1947, ch. 343, title II, § 205(a), 61 Stat. 501; July 28, 1956, ch. 768, 70 Stat. 703; Pub. L. 87–874, title I, § 103(a)(4), Oct. 23, 1962, 76 Stat. 1178; Pub. L. 104–303, title II, § 227(c)(1), Oct. 12, 1996, 110 Stat. 3699.)

Amendments

1996—Pub. L. 104–303 inserted section catchline, designated existing provisions as subsec. (a), inserted heading, substituted "Secretary" for "Secretary of the Army" and "non-Federal interests" for "local interests", inserted "or separable element of the project" after "project", inserted "or separable elements" after "projects" wherever appearing, and added subsec. (b).

1962—Pub. L. 87–874 substituted provisions which authorize the Secretary of the Army to reimburse local interests for work done on authorized projects which individually do not exceed $1,000,000 in cost, and provide that such reimbursement shall be subject to applicable appropriations or available funds and not take priority over pending projects of higher priority, for provisions which authorized the Chief of Engineers to cause to be paid to the political subdivision involved the amount authorized by Congress.

1956—Act July 28, 1956, substituted "or other political subdivision involved" for "or political subdivision".

Change of Name

Department of War designated Department of the Army and title of Secretary of War changed to Secretary of the Army by section 205(a) of act July 26, 1947, ch. 343, title II, 61 Stat. 501. Section 205(a) of act July 26, 1947, was repealed by section 53 of act Aug. 10, 1956, ch. 1041, 70A Stat. 641. Section 1 of act Aug. 10, 1956, enacted "Title 10, Armed Forces" which in sections 3010 to 3013 continued Department of the Army under administrative supervision of Secretary of the Army.

Transfer of Functions

Functions, powers, and duties of Secretary of the Army and other offices and officers of Department of the Army under section 401 of this title to extent that they relate generally to location and clearances of bridges and causeways in navigable waters of United States transferred to and vested in Secretary of Transportation by Pub. L. 89–670, § 6(g)(6)(A), Oct. 15, 1966, 80 Stat. 941, which created Department of Transportation. Pub. L. 97–449 amended section 401 of this title to reflect transfer made by section 6(g)(6)(A) of Pub. L. 89–670, and repealed section 6(g)(6)(A).

§ 426g. Storm and hurricane restoration and impact minimization program

(a) Construction of small shore and beach restoration and protection projects

(1) In general

The Secretary may carry out a program for the construction of small shore and beach restoration and protection projects not specifically authorized by Congress that otherwise comply with section 426e of this title if the Secretary determines that such construction is advisable.

(2) Local cooperation

The local cooperation requirement of section 426e of this title shall apply to a project under this section.

(3) Completeness

A project under this subsection—

(A) shall be complete; and

(B) shall not commit the United States to any additional improvement to ensure the successful operation of the project; except for participation in periodic beach nourishment in accordance with—

(i) section 426e of this title; and

(ii) the procedure for projects authorized after submission of a survey report.

(b) National shoreline erosion control development and demonstration program

(1) In general

The Secretary shall conduct under the program authorized by subsection (a) a national shoreline erosion control development and demonstration program (referred to in this section as the "demonstration program").

(2) Requirements

(A) In general

The demonstration program shall include provisions for—

(i) projects consisting of planning, design, construction, and monitoring of prototype engineered and native and naturalized vegetative shoreline erosion control devices and methods;

(ii) monitoring of the applicable prototypes;

(iii) detailed engineering and environmental reports on the results of each project carried out under the demonstraton[1] program; and

(iv) technology transfers, as appropriate, to private property owners, State and local entities, nonprofit educational institutions, and nongovernmental organizations.

(B) Determination of feasibility

A project under the demonstration program shall not be carried out until the Secretary determines that the project is feasible.

(C) Emphasis

A project under the demonstration program shall emphasize, to the maximum extent practicable—

(i) the development and demonstration of innovative technologies;

(ii) efficient designs to prevent erosion at a shoreline site, taking into account the lifecycle cost of the design, including cleanup, maintenance, and amortization;

(iii) new and enhanced shore protection project design and project formulation tools the purposes of which are to improve the physical performance, and lower the lifecycle costs, of the projects;

(iv) natural designs, including the use of native and naturalized vegetation or temporary structures that minimize permanent structural alterations to the shoreline;

(v) the avoidance of negative impacts to adjacent shorefront communities;

(vi) in areas with substantial residential or commercial interests located adjacent to the shoreline, designs that do not impair the aesthetic appeal of the interests;

(vii) the potential for long-term protection afforded by the technology; and

(viii) recommendations developed from evaluations of the program established under the Shoreline Erosion Control Demonstration Act of 1974 (42 U.S.C. 1962–5 note),[2] including—

(I) adequate consideration of the subgrade;

(II) proper filtration;

(III) durable components;

(IV) adequate connection between units; and

(V) consideration of additional relevant information.

(D) Sites

(i) In general

Each project under the demonstration program may be carried out at—

(I) a privately owned site with substantial public access; or

(II) a publicly owned site on open coast or in tidal waters.

(ii) Selection

The Secretary shall develop criteria for the selection of sites for projects under the demonstration program, including criteria based on—

(I) a variety of geographic and climatic conditions;

(II) the size of the population that is dependent on the beaches for recreation or the protection of private property or public infrastructure;

(III) the rate of erosion;

(IV) significant natural resources or habitats and environmentally sensitive areas; and

(V) significant threatened historic structures or landmarks.

(3) Consultation

The Secretary shall carry out the demonstration program in consultation with—

(A) the Secretary of Agriculture, particularly with respect to native and naturalized vegetative means of preventing and controlling shoreline erosion;

(B) Federal, State, and local agencies;

(C) private organizations;

(D) the Coastal Engineering Research Center established by section 426–1 of this title; and

(E) applicable university research facilities.

[1] So in original. Probably should be "demonstration".

[2] See References in Text note below.

(4) Completion of demonstration

After carrying out the initial construction and evaluation of the performance and cost of a project under the demonstration program, the Secretary may—

(A) amend, at the request of a non-Federal interest of the project, the partnership agreement for a federally authorized shore protection project in existence on the date on which initial construction of the project under the demonstration program is complete to incorporate the project constructed under the demonstration program as a feature of the shore protection project, with the future cost sharing of the project constructed under the demonstration program to be determined by the project purposes of the shore protection project; or

(B) transfer all interest in and responsibility for the completed project constructed under the demonstration program to a non-Federal interest or another Federal agency.

(5) Agreements

The Secretary may enter into a partnership agreement with the non-Federal interest or a cooperative agreement with the head of another Federal agency under the demonstration program—

(A) to share the costs of construction, operation, maintenance, and monitoring of a project under the demonstration program;

(B) to share the costs of removing the project, or element of the project if the Secretary determines that the project or element of the project is detrimental to public or private property, public infrastructure, or public safety; or

(C) to specify ownership of the completed project if the Secretary determines that the completed project will not be part of a Corps of Engineers project.

(6) Report

Not later than December 31, 2008, and every 3 years thereafter, the Secretary shall prepare and submit to the Committee on Environment and Public Works of the Senate and the Committee on Transportation and Infrastructure of the House of Representatives a report describing—

(A) the activities carried out and accomplishments made under the demonstration program since the previous report under this paragraph; and

(B) any recommendations of the Secretary relating to the program.

(c) Authorization of appropriations

(1) In general

Subject to paragraph (2), the Secretary may expend, from any appropriations made available to the Secretary for the purpose of carrying out civil works, not more than $30,000,000 during any fiscal year to pay the Federal share of the costs of construction of small shore and beach restoration and protection projects or small projects under this section.

(2) Limitation

The total amount expended for a project under this section shall—

(A) be sufficient to pay the cost of Federal participation in the project (including periodic nourishment as provided for under section 426e of this title), as determined by the Secretary; and

(B) be not more than $5,000,000.

(Aug. 13, 1946, ch. 960, §3, 60 Stat. 1056; July 26, 1947, ch. 343, title II, §205(a), 61 Stat. 501; July 28, 1956, ch. 768, 70 Stat. 703; Pub. L. 87–874, title I, §103(a)(4), Oct. 23, 1962, 76 Stat. 1178; Pub. L. 89–298, title III, §310(b), Oct. 27, 1965, 79 Stat. 1095; Pub. L. 91–611, title I, §112(b), Dec. 31, 1970, 84 Stat. 1821; Pub. L. 99–662, title IX, §915(e), Nov. 17, 1986, 100 Stat. 4191; Pub. L. 104–303, title II, §227(e)(2)(C), Oct. 12, 1996, 110 Stat. 3703; Pub. L. 106–53, title II, §226, Aug. 17, 1999, 113 Stat. 298; Pub. L. 110–114, title II, §2038(a), Nov. 8, 2007, 121 Stat. 1097.)

REFERENCES IN TEXT

The Shoreline Erosion Control Demonstration Act of 1974, referred to in subsec. (b)(2)(C)(viii), is Pub. L. 93–251, title I, §54, Mar. 7, 1974, 88 Stat. 26, formerly set out as a note under section 1962d–5 of Title 42, The Public Health and Welfare.

AMENDMENTS

2007—Pub. L. 110–114 amended section generally. Prior to amendment, section related to authorization of small shore and beach restoration and protection projects not specifically authorized by Congress.

1999—Pub. L. 106–53 substituted "$3,000,000" for "$2,000,000".

1996—Pub. L. 104–303 substituted "Secretary" for "Secretary of the Army".

1986—Pub. L. 99–662 substituted "$30,000,000" for "$25,000,000" and "$2,000,000" for "$1,000,000".

1970—Pub. L. 91–611 increased authorized annual allotment for Federal share of project construction costs from $10,000,000 to $25,000,000 and the limitation on allotment for any single project from $500,000 to $1,000,000.

1965—Pub. L. 89–298 increased authorized annual allotment for Federal share of project construction costs from $3,000,000 to $10,000,000 and the limitation on allotment for any single project from $400,000 to $500,000.

1962—Pub. L. 87–874 substituted provisions which authorize the Secretary of the Army to undertake small shore and beach projects not specifically authorized by Congress, which otherwise comply with section 426e of this title, and to allot from any civil works appropriations hereafter made, an amount not to exceed $3,000,000 for the Federal share of such projects in any one fiscal year, provide that no such single project shall be allotted more than $400,000, including periodic nourishment, that provisions of local cooperation shall apply, and that the work shall be complete and not commit the United States to any additional improvement except for periodic beach nourishment, and as may result from procedure applying to projects authorized after submission of survey reports, for provisions which permitted the Chief of Engineers to make advance payments, not exceeding the United States pro rata part of the value of the labor and materials actually put in, and to undertake construction of restoration and protective works under sections 426e to 426h of this title upon the request of, and contribution of funds by, the interested political subdivision.

1956—Act July 28, 1956, substituted "restoration and protective works under sections 426e to 426h of this title" for "improvement and protective works".

CHANGE OF NAME

Department of War designated Department of the Army and title of Secretary of War changed to Secretary of the Army by section 205(a) of act July 26, 1947, ch. 343, title II, 61 Stat. 501. Section 205(a) of act July 26, 1947, was repealed by section 53 of act Aug. 10, 1956, ch. 1041, 70A Stat. 641. Section 1 of act Aug. 10, 1956, enacted "Title 10, Armed Forces" which in sections 3010 to 3013 continued Department of the Army under administrative supervision of Secretary of the Army.

EFFECTIVE DATE OF 1986 AMENDMENT

Section 915(i) of Pub. L. 99–662 provided that: "The amendments made by this section [amending this section and sections 426i, 577, 603a, 701g, 701r, and 701s of this title] shall not apply to any project under contract for construction on the date of enactment of this Act [Nov. 17, 1986]."

EFFECTIVE DATE OF 1970 AMENDMENT

Section 112(c) of Pub. L. 91–611 provided that: "The amendments made by this section [amending this section and section 577 of this title] shall not apply to any project under contract for construction on the date of enactment of this Act [Dec. 31, 1970]."

TRANSFER OF FUNCTIONS

Functions, powers, and duties of Secretary of the Army and other offices and officers of Department of the Army under section 401 of this title to extent that they relate generally to location and clearances of bridges and causeways in navigable waters of United States transferred to and vested in Secretary of Transportation by Pub. L. 89–670, §6(g)(6)(A), Oct. 15, 1966, 80 Stat. 941, which created Department of Transportation. Pub. L. 97–449 amended section 401 of this title to reflect transfer made by section 6(g)(6)(A) of Pub. L. 89–670, and repealed section 6(g)(6)(A).

§426g–1. State and regional plans

The Secretary may—

(1) cooperate with any State in the preparation of a comprehensive State or regional plan for the conservation of coastal resources located within the boundaries of the State;

(2) encourage State participation in the implementation of the plan; and

(3) submit to Congress reports and recommendations with respect to appropriate Federal participation in carrying out the plan.

(Aug. 13, 1946, ch. 960, §4, as added Pub. L. 104–303, title II, §227(d)(2), Oct. 12, 1996, 110 Stat. 3700.)

PRIOR PROVISIONS

A prior section 4 of act Aug. 13, 1946, was renumbered section 5 of that act, and was classified to section 426h of this title prior to repeal by Pub. L. 104–303.

§426h. Repealed. Pub. L. 110–114, title II, §2038(b), Nov. 8, 2007, 121 Stat. 1100

Section, act Aug. 13, 1946, ch. 960, §5, as added Pub. L. 104–303, title II, §227(e)(1), Oct. 12, 1996, 110 Stat. 3700; amended Pub. L. 106–53, title V, §581, Aug. 17, 1999, 113 Stat. 375; Pub. L. 109–234, title II, §2305, June 15, 2006, 120 Stat. 456; Pub. L. 110–161, div. C, title I, §113, Dec. 26, 2007, 121 Stat. 1944, related to national shoreline erosion control development and demonstration program.

A prior section 426h, acts Aug. 13, 1946, ch. 960, §5, formerly §4, 60 Stat. 1057; July 28, 1956, ch. 768, 70 Stat. 703; renumbered §5, Oct. 12, 1996, Pub. L. 104–303, title II, §227(d)(1), 110 Stat. 3700, defined the word "shores" as used in sections 426e to 426h of this title, prior to repeal by Pub. L. 104–303, title II, §227(e)(1), Oct. 12, 1996, 110 Stat. 3700.

§426h–1. Definitions

In sections 426e to 426h–1 of this title, the following definitions apply:

(1) Erosion control program

The term "erosion control program" means the national shoreline erosion control development and demonstration program established under this section.

(2) Secretary

The term "Secretary" means the Secretary of the Army.

(3) Separable element

The term "separable element" has the meaning provided by section 2213(f) of this title.

(4) Shore

The term "shore" includes each shoreline of the Atlantic and Pacific Oceans, the Gulf of Mexico, the Great Lakes, and lakes, estuaries, and bays directly connected therewith.

(5) Shore protection project

The term "shore protection project" includes a project for beach nourishment, including the replacement of sand.

(Aug. 13, 1946, ch. 960, §6, as added Pub. L. 104–303, title II, §227(e)(1), Oct. 12, 1996, 110 Stat. 3702.)

§426i. Shore damage prevention or mitigation

(a) In general

The Secretary of the Army is authorized to investigate, study, plan, and implement structural and nonstructural measures for the prevention or mitigation of shore damages attributable to Federal navigation works and shore damage attributable to the Atlantic Intracoastal Waterway and the Gulf Intracoastal Waterway, if a non-Federal public body agrees to operate and maintain such measures, and, in the case of interests in real property acquired in conjunction with nonstructural measures, to operate and maintain the property for public purposes in accordance with regulations prescribed by the Secretary.

(b) Cost sharing

The costs of implementing measures under this section shall be cost-shared in the same proportion as the cost-sharing provisions applicable to the project causing the shore damage.

(c) Requirement for specific authorization

No such project shall be initiated without specific authorization by Congress if the Federal first cost exceeds $5,000,000.

(d) Coordination

The Secretary shall—

(1) coordinate the implementation of the measures under this section with other Federal and non-Federal shore protection projects in the same geographic area; and

(2) to the extent practicable, combine mitigation projects with other shore protection projects in the same area into a comprehensive regional project.

(Pub. L. 90–483, title I, §111, Aug. 13, 1968, 82 Stat. 735; Pub. L. 99–662, title IX, §§915(f), 940, Nov. 17, 1986, 100 Stat. 4191, 4199; Pub. L. 106–53, title II, §214, Aug. 17, 1999, 113 Stat. 291.)

AMENDMENTS

1999—Pub. L. 106–53 designated first sentence as subsec. (a), inserted heading, and inserted "and shore damage attributable to the Atlantic Intracoastal Waterway and the Gulf Intracoastal Waterway" after "navigation works", designated second sentence as subsec. (b) and inserted heading, and designated third sentence as subsec. (c), inserted heading, and substituted "$5,000,000" for "$2,000,000", and added subsec. (d).

1986—Pub. L. 99–662, § 940, amended section generally. Prior to amendment, section read as follows: "The Secretary of the Army, acting through the Chief of Engineers, is authorized to investigate, study, and construct projects for the prevention or mitigation of shore damages attributable to Federal navigation works. The cost of installing, operating, and maintaining such projects shall be borne entirely by the United States. No such project shall be constructed without specific authorization by Congress if the estimated first cost exceeds $2,000,000."

Pub. L. 99–662, § 915(f), substituted "$2,000,000" for "$1,000,000".

EFFECTIVE DATE OF 1986 AMENDMENT

Amendment by section 915(f) of Pub. L. 99–662 not applicable to any project under contract for construction on Nov. 17, 1986, see section 915(i) of Pub. L. 99–662, set out as a note under section 426g of this title.

§ 426i–1. Construction of shoreline protection projects by non-Federal interests

(a) Authority

Non-Federal interests are authorized to undertake shoreline protection projects on the coastline of the United States, subject to obtaining any permits required pursuant to Federal and State laws in advance of actual construction.

(b) Studies and engineering

(1) By non-Federal interests

A non-Federal interest may prepare, for review and approval by the Secretary, the necessary studies and engineering for any construction to be undertaken under subsection (a) of this section.

(2) By Secretary

Upon request of an appropriate non-Federal interest, the Secretary may undertake all necessary studies and engineering for any construction to be undertaken under subsection (a) of this section and provide technical assistance in obtaining all necessary permits for such construction if the non-Federal interest contracts with the Secretary to furnish the United States funds for the studies and engineering during the period that the studies and engineering will be conducted.

(c) Completion of studies

The Secretary is authorized to complete and transmit to the appropriate non-Federal interests any study for shoreline protection which was initiated before October 31, 1992, or, upon the request of such non-Federal interest, to terminate the study and transmit the partially completed study to the non-Federal interest for completion. Studies subject to this subsection shall be completed without regard to the requirements of subsection (b) of this section.

(d) Authority to carry out improvement

(1) In general

Any non-Federal interest which has received from the Secretary pursuant to subsection (b) or (c) of this section a favorable recommendation to carry out a shoreline protection project or separable element thereof, based on the results of completed studies and engineering for the project or element, may carry out the project or element if a final environmental impact statement has been filed for the project or element.

(2) Permits

Any plan of improvement proposed to be implemented in accordance with this subsection shall be deemed to satisfy the requirements for obtaining the appropriate permits required under the Secretary's authority and such permits shall be granted subject to the non-Federal interest's acceptance of the terms and conditions of such permits if the Secretary determines that the applicable regulatory criteria and procedures have been satisfied.

(3) Monitoring

The Secretary shall monitor any project for which permits are granted under this subsection in order to ensure that such project is constructed (and, in those cases where such activities will not be the responsibility of the Secretary, operated and maintained) in accordance with the terms and conditions of such permits.

(e) Reimbursement

(1) General rule

Subject to the enactment of appropriation Acts, the Secretary is authorized to reimburse any non-Federal interest an amount equal to the estimate of the Federal share, without interest, of the cost of any authorized shoreline protection project, or separable element thereof, constructed under this section—

(A) if, after authorization and before initiation of construction of the project or separable element, the Secretary approves the plans for construction of such project by such non-Federal interest and enters into a written agreement with the non-Federal interest with respect to the project or separable element (including the terms of cooperation); and

(B) if the Secretary finds, after a review of studies and engineering prepared pursuant to this section, that construction of the project or separable element is economically justified and environmentally acceptable.

(2) Matters to be considered in reviewing plans

In reviewing plans under this subsection, the Secretary shall consider budgetary and programmatic priorities and other factors that the Secretary deems appropriate.

(3) Monitoring

The Secretary shall regularly monitor and audit any project for shore protection constructed under this section by a non-Federal interest in order to ensure that such construction is in compliance with the plans approved by the Secretary and that the costs are reasonable.

(4) Limitation on reimbursements

No reimbursement shall be made under this section unless and until the Secretary has certified that the work for which reimbursement is requested has been performed in accordance with applicable permits or approved plans.

(Pub. L. 102–580, title II, §206, Oct. 31, 1992, 106 Stat. 4828; Pub. L. 104–303, title II, §227(c)(2), Oct. 12, 1996, 110 Stat. 3700.)

AMENDMENTS

1996—Subsec. (e)(1)(A). Pub. L. 104–303 inserted before semicolon "and enters into a written agreement with the non-Federal interest with respect to the project or separable element (including the terms of cooperation)".

"SECRETARY" DEFINED

Secretary means the Secretary of the Army, see section 3 of Pub. L. 102–580, set out as a note under section 2201 of this title.

§426i–2. National coastal data bank

(1) Establishment of data bank

Not later than 2 years after August 17, 1999, the Secretary shall establish a national coastal data bank containing data on the geophysical and climatological characteristics of the shores of the United States.

(2) Content

To the extent practicable, the national coastal data bank shall include data regarding current and predicted shore positions, information on federally authorized shore protection projects, and data on the movement of sand along the shores of the United States, including impediments to such movement caused by natural and manmade features.

(3) Access

The national coastal data bank shall be made readily accessible to the public.

(Pub. L. 106–53, title II, §215(d), Aug. 17, 1999, 113 Stat. 293.)

"SECRETARY" DEFINED

Secretary means the Secretary of the Army, see section 2 of Pub. L. 106–53, set out as a note under section 2201 of this title.

§426j. Repealed. Pub. L. 110–114, title II, §2037(b)(1), Nov. 8, 2007, 121 Stat. 1096

Section, Pub. L. 94–587, §145, Oct. 22, 1976, 90 Stat. 2931; Pub. L. 99–662, title IX, §933, Nov. 17, 1986, 100 Stat. 4197; Pub. L. 100–676, §35, Nov. 17, 1988, 102 Stat. 4031; Pub. L. 102–580, title II, §207, Oct. 31, 1992, 106 Stat. 4829; Pub. L. 106–53, title II, §217(a), Aug. 17, 1999, 113 Stat. 294, related to placement on State beaches of sand dredged in constructing and maintaining navigation inlets and channels adjacent to such beaches.

EXISTING PROJECTS

Pub. L. 110–114, title II, §2037(b)(2), Nov. 8, 2007, 121 Stat. 1096, provided that: "The Secretary [of the Army] may complete any project being carried out under section 145 of the Water Resources Development Act of 1976 [this section] on the day before the date of enactment of this Act [Nov. 8, 2007]."

§426k. Five year demonstration program to temporarily increase diversion of water from Lake Michigan at Chicago, Illinois

(a) Authorization of Secretary of the Army; purpose; amounts of increase; incremental accomplishment; effects on Illinois Waterway; responsibilities for development, implementation, and supervision

In order to alleviate water damage on the shoreline of Lake Michigan and others of the Great Lakes during periods of abnormally high water levels in the Great Lakes, and to improve the water quality of the Illinois Waterway, the Secretary of the Army, acting through the Chief of Engineers, is authorized to carry out a five-year demonstration program to temporarily increase the diversion of water from Lake Michigan at Chicago, Illinois, for the purpose of testing the practicability of increasing the average annual diversion from the present limit of three thousand two hundred cubic feet per second to ten thousand cubic feet per second. The demonstration program will increase the controllable diversion by various amounts calculated to raise the average annual diversion above three thousand two hundred cubic feet per second up to ten thousand cubic feet per second. The increase in diversion rate will be accomplished incrementally and will take into consideration the effects of such increase on the Illinois Waterway. The program will be developed by the Chief of Engineers in cooperation with the State of Illinois and the Metropolitan Sanitary District of Greater Chicago. The program will be implemented by the State of Illinois and the Metropolitan Sanitary District of Greater Chicago under the supervision of the Chief of Engineers.

(b) Establishment of monthly controllable diversion rates; average annual level of Lake Michigan and total diversion for succeeding accounting year

During the demonstration program a controllable diversion rate will be established for each month calculated to establish an annual average diversion from three thousand two hundred cubic feet per second to not more than ten thousand cubic feet per second. When the level of Lake Michigan is below its average level, the total diversion for the succeeding accounting year shall not exceed three thousand two hundred cubic feet per second on an annual basis. The average level of Lake Michigan will be based upon the average monthly level for the period from 1900 to 1975.

(c) River stages approaching bankfull conditions on Illinois Waterway or Mississippi River or further increased diversion adversely affecting St. Lawrence Seaway water levels: limitation on diversion

When river stages approach or are predicted to approach bankfull conditions at the established flood warning stations on the Illinois Waterway or the Mississippi River, or when further increased diversion of water from Lake Michigan would adversely affect water levels necessary for navigational requirements of the Saint Lawrence Seaway in its entirety throughout the Saint Lawrence River and Great Lakes-Saint Lawrence Seaway, water shall not be diverted directly from Lake Michigan at the Wilmette, O'Brien, or Chicago River control structures other than as necessary for navigational requirements.

(d) Additional study and demonstration program: determination of effects on Great Lakes levels and Illinois Waterway water quality and susceptibility to additional flooding and investigation of other adverse or beneficial impacts; report and recommendations to Congress

The Chief of Engineers shall conduct a study and a demonstration program to determine the effects of the increased diversion on the levels of the Great Lakes, on the water quality of the Illinois Waterway, and on the susceptibility of the Illinois Waterway to additional flooding. The study and demonstration program will also investigate any adverse or beneficial impacts which result from this section. The Chief of Engineers, at the end of five years after October 22, 1976, will submit to the Congress the results of this study and demonstration program including recommendations whether to continue this authority or to change the criteria stated in subsection (b) of this section.

(e) "Controllable diversion" defined

For purposes of this section, controllable diversion is defined as that diversion at Wilmette, O'Brien, and Chicago River control structures which is not attributable to leakage or which is not necessary for navigational requirements.

(Pub. L. 94–587, § 166, Oct. 22, 1976, 90 Stat. 2934.)

§ 426*l*. Protection of Lake Ontario

(a) Plan for shoreline protection and beach erosion control; report to Congress

The Secretary of the Army, acting through the Chief of Engineers, is directed to develop a plan for shoreline protection and beach erosion control along Lake Ontario, and report on such plan to the Congress as soon as practicable. Such report shall include recommendations on measures of protection and proposals for equitable cost sharing, together with recommendations for regulating the level of Lake Ontario to assure maximum protection of the natural environment and to hold shoreline damage to a minimum.

(b) Minimization of damage and erosion to Lake Ontario shoreline

Until the Congress receives and acts upon the report required under subsection (a) of this section, all Federal agencies having responsibilities affecting the level of Lake Ontario shall, consistent with existing authority, make every effort to discharge such responsibilities in a manner so as to minimize damage and erosion to the shoreline of Lake Ontario.

(c) Authorization of appropriations

There is authorized to be appropriated to carry out this section $2,000,000.

(d) Short title

This section may be cited as the "Lake Ontario Protection Act of 1976."

(Pub. L. 94–587, § 180, Oct. 22, 1976, 90 Stat. 2939.)

§ 426m. Collection and removal of drift and debris from publicly maintained commercial boat harbors and adjacent land and water areas

(a) Congressional findings

The Congress finds that drift and debris on or in publicly maintained commercial boat harbors and the land and water areas immediately adjacent thereto threaten navigational safety, public health, recreation, and the harborfront environment.

(b) Responsibility of Secretary of the Army for development of projects; project undertakings exempt from specific Congressional approval

(1) The Secretary of the Army, acting through the Chief of Engineers, shall be responsible for developing projects for the collection and removal of drift and debris from publicly maintained commercial boat harbors and from land and water areas immediately adjacent thereto.

(2) The Secretary of the Army, acting through the Chief of Engineers, is authorized to undertake projects developed under paragraph (1) of this subsection without specific congressional approval when the total Federal cost for the project is less than $400,000.

(c) Federal share of costs; responsibility of non-Federal interests in future project development to recover cost or repair sources

The Federal share of the cost of any project developed pursuant to subsection (b) of this section shall be two-thirds of the cost of the project. The remainder of such costs shall be paid by the State, municipality, or other political subdivision in which the project is to be located, except that any costs associated with the collections and removal of drift and debris from federally owned lands shall be borne by the Federal Government. Non-Federal interests in future project development under subsection (b) of this section shall be required to recover the full cost of drift or debris removal from any identified owner of piers or other potential sources of drift or debris, or to repair such sources so that they no longer create a potential source of drift or debris.

(d) Responsibility for providing lands, easements, and right-of-way necessary for projects; agreement to maintain projects and hold United States free from damages; regulation of project area following project completion; technical advice

Any State, municipality, or other political subdivision where any project developed pursuant to subsection (b) of this section is located shall provide all lands, easements, and right-of-way necessary for the project, including suitable access and disposal areas, and shall agree to maintain such projects and hold and save the United States free from any damages which may result from the non-Federal sponsor's performance of, or failure to perform, any of its required responsibilities of cooperation for the project. Non-Fededal[1] interest shall agree to regulate any project area following project completion so

[1] So in original.

that such area will not become a future source of drift and debris. The Chief of Engineers shall provide technical advice to non-Federal interests on the implementation of this subsection.

(e) Definitions

For the purposes of this section—

(1) the term "drift" includes any buoyant material that, when floating in the navigable waters of the United States, may cause damage to a commercial or recreational vessel; and

(2) the term "debris" includes any abandoned or dilapidated structure or any sunken vessel or other object that can reasonably be expected to collapse or otherwise enter the navigable waters of the United States as drift within a reasonable period.

(f) Authorization of appropriations

There is authorized to be appropriated to carry out this section such sums as may be necessary for fiscal years beginning after September 30, 1986.

(Pub. L. 94–587, § 202, Oct. 22, 1976, 90 Stat. 2945; Pub. L. 99–662, title XI, § 1129(a), Nov. 17, 1986, 100 Stat. 4246.)

AMENDMENTS

1986—Subsec. (f). Pub. L. 99–662 amended subsec. (f) generally, substituting "such sums as may be necessary for fiscal years beginning after Sept. 30, 1986" for "not to exceed $4,000,000 per fiscal year for fiscal years 1978 and 1979".

§ 426n. Technical assistance to States and local governments; cost sharing

(a) Upon request of the Governor of a State, or the appropriate official of local government, the Secretary is authorized to provide designs, plans, and specifications, and such other technical assistance as he deems advisable to such State or local government for its use in carrying out—

(1) projects for removing accumulated snags and other debris, and clearing and straightening channels in navigable streams and tributaries thereof; and

(2) projects for renovating navigable streams and tributaries thereof by means of predominantly nonstructural methods judged by the Secretary to be cost effective, for the purpose of improved drainage, water quality, and habitat diversity.

(b) The non-Federal share of the cost of any designs, plans, specifications or technical assistance provided under subsection (a) of this section shall be 50 percent.

(Pub. L. 99–662, title IX, § 942, Nov. 17, 1986, 100 Stat. 4199.)

"SECRETARY" DEFINED

Secretary means the Secretary of the Army, see section 2201 of this title.

§ 426*o*. Great Lakes material disposal

In planning and implementing any navigation project (including maintenance thereof) on the Great Lakes and adjacent waters, the Secretary shall consult and cooperate with concerned States in selecting disposal areas for dredged material which is suitable for beach nourishment.

(Pub. L. 99–662, title XI, § 1154, Nov. 17, 1986, 100 Stat. 4256.)

"SECRETARY" DEFINED

Secretary means the Secretary of the Army, see section 2201 of this title.

§ 426*o*–1. Great Lakes dredging levels adjustment

(a) Definition of Great Lake

In this section, the term "Great Lake" means Lake Superior, Lake Michigan, Lake Huron (including Lake St. Clair), Lake Erie, and Lake Ontario (including the St. Lawrence River to the 45th parallel of latitude).

(b) Dredging levels

In operating and maintaining Federal channels and harbors of, and the connecting channels between, the Great Lakes, the Secretary shall conduct such dredging as is necessary to ensure minimal operation depths consistent with the original authorized depths of the channels and harbors when water levels in the Great Lakes are, or are forecast to be, below the International Great Lakes Datum of 1985.

(Pub. L. 106–541, title III, § 343, Dec. 11, 2000, 114 Stat. 2613.)

"SECRETARY" DEFINED

Secretary means the Secretary of the Army, see section 2 of Pub. L. 106–541, set out as a note under section 2201 of this title.

§ 426*o*–2. Great Lakes navigation and protection

(a) Great Lakes navigation

Using available funds, the Secretary shall expedite the operation and maintenance, including dredging, of the navigation features of the Great Lakes and Connecting Channels for the purpose of supporting commercial navigation to authorized project depths.

(b) Great Lakes pilot project

Using available funds, the Director of the Animal and Plant Health Inspection Service, in coordination with the Secretary, the Administrator of the Environmental Protection Agency, the Commandant of the Coast Guard, and the Director of the United States Fish and Wildlife Service, shall carry out a pilot project, on an emergency basis, to control and prevent further spreading of viral hemorrhagic septicemia in the Great Lakes and Connecting Channels.

(c) Great Lakes and Connecting Channels defined

In this section, the term "Great Lakes and Connecting Channels" includes Lakes Superior, Huron, Michigan, Erie, and Ontario, all connecting waters between and among such lakes used for commercial navigation, any navigation features in such lakes or waters that are a Federal operation or maintenance responsibility, and areas of the Saint Lawrence River that are operated or maintained by the Federal Government for commercial navigation.

(Pub. L. 110–114, title V, § 5014, Nov. 8, 2007, 121 Stat. 1195.)

"SECRETARY" DEFINED

Secretary means the Secretary of the Army, see section 2 of Pub. L. 110–114, set out as a note under section 2201 of this title.

§ 426p. Corps of Engineers

(a) Technical and other assistance

The Secretary of the Army may—

(1) provide emergency assistance to prevent or reduce damage attributable to high water levels in the Great Lakes, including provision of sandbags, sheeting, and stones and other armoring devices (taking account of flooding and erosion of other property which may be caused by such activity) but not including construction of permanent structures;

(2) provide technical assistance to individuals and local governments with respect to measures to prevent or reduce such damage; and

(3) compile and disseminate information on—

(A) water levels of the Great Lakes,

(B) techniques for prevention or reduction of such damage, and

(C) emergency relief available to persons who suffer economic injury attributable to high water levels in the Great Lakes.

(b) Issuance of permits

(1) Consideration of flooding and erosion

In issuing a permit under—

(A) section 403 of this title; or

(B) section 1344 of this title;

for any activity carried out with assistance under this title, the Secretary of the Army shall take account of flooding and erosion of other property which may be caused by such activity.

(2) Bank stabilization

(A) General rule

In issuing permits under sections 403 and 1344 of this title for a project involving dredging of any portion of the Great Lakes, the Secretary of the Army shall, if feasible, encourage for bank stabilization purposes the disposal of nonhazardous compatible sand from such project on shorelines affected by erosion.

(B) Consultation

In carrying out subparagraph (A), the Secretary of the Army shall consult affected State and local governments.

(Pub. L. 100–707, title II, § 203, Nov. 23, 1988, 102 Stat. 4712.)

REFERENCES IN TEXT

This title, referred to in subsec. (b)(1), is title II of Pub. L. 100–707, Nov. 23, 1988, 102 Stat. 4711, known as the "Great Lakes Planning Assistance Act of 1988". For complete classification of this Act to the Code, see Short Title note below and Tables.

SHORT TITLE

Pub. L. 100–707, title II, § 201, Nov. 23, 1988, 102 Stat. 4711, provided that: "This title [enacting this section, amending sections 3501 to 3503 of Title 16, Conservation, and enacting provisions set out as notes under this section and sections 3501 and 3505 of Title 16] may be cited as the 'Great Lakes Planning Assistance Act of 1988'."

GREAT LAKES DAMAGE ASSISTANCE AND PREVENTION; DAMAGE ASSISTANCE PROGRAM

Pub. L. 100–707, title II, § 202, Nov. 23, 1988, 102 Stat. 4711, provided that:

"(a) IN GENERAL.—The Director is authorized to provide assistance to Great Lakes States in the establishment of State programs to reduce and prevent damage attributable to high water levels in the Great Lakes.

"(b) GRANTS.—Upon application by a Great Lakes State within 1 year after the date of enactment of this Act [Nov. 23, 1988], the Director may make a one-time grant to the State of not more than $250,000 for use by the State for—

"(1) preparation of plans for mitigation, warning, emergency operations, and emergency assistance;

"(2) coordination of available State and Federal assistance;

"(3) development and implementation of nonstructural measures to reduce or prevent damage attributable to high water levels in the Great Lakes, including establishment of setback requirements and other conditions on construction and reconstruction of public and private facilities, mapping of flooding zones, and technical assistance; and

"(4) assisting local governments in developing and implementing plans for nonstructural reduction and prevention of damages attributable to high water levels in the Great Lakes.

"(c) TECHNICAL ASSISTANCE.—The Director may provide technical assistance to Great Lakes States for carrying out any activity carried out with assistance under this section.

"(d) STATE MATCHING.—A State which receives a grant under this section shall match the grant with an amount of funds from non-Federal sources equal to 25 percent of the amount of the grant.

"(e) AUTHORIZATION.—There are authorized to be appropriated for making grants under this section not more than $2,000,000 for fiscal years beginning after September 30, 1988."

GREAT LAKES DAMAGE ASSISTANCE AND PREVENTION; DEFINITIONS

Pub. L. 100–707, title II, § 205, Nov. 23, 1988, 102 Stat. 4715, as amended by Pub. L. 109–295, title VI, § 612(c), Oct. 4, 2006, 120 Stat. 1410, provided that: "For purposes of this title [see Short Title note above]—

"(1) DIRECTOR.—The term 'Director' means the Administrator of the Federal Emergency Management Agency.

"(2) HIGH WATER LEVELS.—The term 'high water levels' means water levels above the long-term average of water levels from 1900.

"(3) LOCAL GOVERNMENT.—The term 'local government' means a county, city, village, town, district, or other political subdivision of a Great Lakes State and an Indian tribe or authorized tribal organization.

"(4) GREAT LAKES STATE.—The term 'Great Lakes State' means Minnesota, Wisconsin, Illinois, Ohio, Michigan, Indiana, Pennsylvania, and New York."

§§ 427 to 430. Repealed. July 31, 1945, ch. 334, § 5, 59 Stat. 508

Section 427, act June 26, 1936, ch. 849, § 1, 49 Stat. 1982, related to improvement and protection of beaches and defined "beach".

Section 428, act June 26, 1936, ch. 849, § 2, 49 Stat. 1982, related to investigations by Beach Erosion Board and duties of Board. See section 426–1 of this title.

Section 429, act June 26, 1936, ch. 849, § 3, 49 Stat. 1983, related to investigative reports by Beach Erosion Board. See section 426–1 of this title.

Section 430, act June 26, 1936, ch. 849, § 4, 49 Stat. 1983, related to payment of expenses incident to investigations by Board. See section 426–1 of this title.

SUBCHAPTER II—OIL POLLUTION OF COASTAL WATERS

§§431 to 437. Repealed. Pub. L. 91–224, title I, §108, Apr. 3, 1970, 84 Stat. 113

Section 431, acts June 7, 1924, ch. 316, §1, 43 Stat. 604; Nov. 3, 1966, Pub. L. 89–753, title II, §211(a), 80 Stat. 1252, related to the short title for this subchapter.

Section 432, acts June 7, 1924, ch. 316, §2, 43 Stat. 604; Nov. 3, 1966, Pub. L. 89–753, title II, §211(a), 80 Stat. 1252, defined "oil," "person", "coastal navigable waters of the United States", and "Secretary".

Section 433, acts June 7, 1924, ch. 316, §3, 43 Stat. 605; Nov. 3, 1966, Pub. L. 89–753, title II, §211(a), 80 Stat. 1253, related to prohibition against discharge of oil generally.

Section 434, acts June 7, 1924, ch. 316, §4, 43 Stat. 605; Nov. 3, 1966, Pub. L. 89–753, title II, §211(a), 80 Stat. 1253, related to penalties for violation of oil discharge prohibition and liability of vessel.

Section 435, act June 7, 1924, ch. 316, §5, 43 Stat. 605; 1946 Reorg. Plan No. 3, §§101–104, eff. July 16, 1946, 11 F.R. 7875, 60 Stat. 1097; act Nov. 3, 1966, Pub. L. 89–753, title II, §211(a), 80 Stat. 1254, related to revocation or suspension of licenses of officers of offending vessels.

Section 436, acts June 7, 1924, ch. 316, §7, 43 Stat. 605; Nov. 3, 1966, Pub. L. 89–753, title II, §211(a), 80 Stat. 1254, related to authorization of use of certain personnel in enforcement of this subchapter and arrest of offenders.

Section 437, acts June 7, 1924, ch. 316, §8, 43 Stat. 606; Nov. 3, 1966, Pub. L. 89–753, title II, §211(a), 80 Stat. 1254, related to affect of this subchapter on preexisting laws for preservation and protection of navigable waters.

See section 1251 et seq. of this title.

SUBCHAPTER III—NEW YORK HARBOR, HARBOR OF HAMPTON ROADS, AND HARBOR OF BALTIMORE

§441. Deposit of refuse prohibited; penalty

The placing, discharging, or depositing, by any process or in any manner, of refuse, dirt, ashes, cinders, mud, sand, dredgings, sludge, acid, or any other matter of any kind, other than that flowing from streets, sewers, and passing therefrom in a liquid state, in the waters of any harbor subject to this subchapter, within the limits which shall be prescribed by the supervisor of the harbor, is strictly forbidden, and every such act is made a misdemeanor, and every person engaged in or who shall aid, abet, authorize, or instigate a violation of this section, shall, upon conviction, be punishable by fine or imprisonment, or both, such fine to be not less than $250 nor more than $2,500, and the imprisonment to be not less than thirty days nor more than one year, either or both united, as the judge before whom conviction is obtained shall decide, one-half of said fine to be paid to the person or persons giving information which shall lead to conviction of this misdemeanor.

(June 29, 1888, ch. 496, §1, 25 Stat. 209; Pub. L. 85–802, §1(1), Aug. 28, 1958, 72 Stat. 970.)

PRIOR PROVISIONS

Section 1 of act June 29, 1888, superseded act Aug. 5, 1886, ch. 929, §3, 24 Stat. 329, which provided that: "It shall not be lawful to cast, throw, empty, or unlade, or cause, suffer, or procure to be cast, thrown, emptied, or unladen, either from or out of any ship, vessel, lighter, barge, boat, or other craft, or from the shore, pier, wharf, or mills of any kind whatever, any ballast, stone, slate, gravel, earth, slack, rubbish, wreck, filth, slabs, edgings, sawdust, slag or cinders or other refuse or mill-waste of any kind, into New York Harbor: *Provided*, That nothing herein contained shall extend, or be construed to extend, to the casting out, unlading, or throwing out of any ship or vessel, lighter, barge, boat, or other craft, any stones, rocks, bricks, lime, or other materials used, or to be used, in or toward the building, repairing, or keeping in repair any quay, pier, wharf, weir, bridge, building, or other work lawfully erected or to be erected on the banks or sides of said harbor, or to the casting out, unloading or depositing of any material excavated for the improvement of navigable waters, into such places and in such manner as may be deemed by the United States officer supervising the improvement of said harbor most judicious and practicable and for the best interests of such improvement."

AMENDMENTS

1958—Pub. L. 85–802 substituted "waters of any harbor subject to this subchapter," for "tidal waters of the harbor of New York, or its adjacent or tributary waters, or in those of long Island Sound,".

EFFECTIVE DATE OF 1958 AMENDMENT

Section 2 of Pub. L. 85–802 provided that: "This Act [amending this section and sections 442, 446, 447, 449, 451, and 451a of this title and enacting section 451b of this title] shall take effect on the sixtieth day after the date of its enactment [Aug. 28, 1958]."

§442. Liability of officers of towing vessel

Any and every master and engineer, or person or persons acting in such capacity, respectively, on board of any boat or vessel, who shall knowingly engage in towing any scow, boat, or vessel loaded with any such prohibited matter to any point or place of deposit, or discharge in the waters of any harbor subject to this subchapter, or to any point or place elsewhere than within the limits defined and permitted by the supervisor of the harbor, shall be deemed guilty of a violation of section 441 of this title, and shall, upon conviction, be punishable as provided for offenses in violation of section 441 of this title, and shall also have his license revoked or suspended for a term to be fixed by the judge before whom tried and convicted.

(June 29, 1888, ch. 496, §2, 25 Stat. 209; Pub. L. 85–802, §1(2), Aug. 28, 1958, 72 Stat. 970.)

AMENDMENTS

1958—Pub. L. 85–802 substituted "any harbor subject to this subchapter" for "the harbor of New York, or in its adjacent or tributary waters, or in those of Long Island Sound", and struck out "hereinafter mentioned" after "supervisor of the harbor".

EFFECTIVE DATE OF 1958 AMENDMENT

Amendment by Pub. L. 85–802 effective on sixtieth day after Aug. 28, 1958, see section 2 of Pub. L. 85–802, set out as a note under section 441 of this title.

§443. Permit for dumping; penalty for taking or towing boat or scow without permit

In all cases of receiving on board of any scows or boats such forbidden matter or substance as described in section 441 of this title, the owner or master, or person acting in such capacity on board of such scows or boats, before proceeding to take or tow the same to the place of deposit, shall apply for and obtain from the supervisor of the harbor appointed, as provided in section 451 of this title, a permit defining the precise limits within which the discharge of such scows or boats may be made; and it shall not be lawful for the owner or master, or person acting in such capacity, of any tug or towboat to tow or move any scow or boat so loaded with such forbidden matter until such permit shall have been obtained; and every person violating the foregoing provisions of this section shall be deemed guilty of a misdemeanor, and on conviction thereof shall be punished by a fine of not more than $1,000 nor less than $500, and in addition thereto the master of any tug or towboat so offending shall have his license revoked or suspended for a term to be fixed by the judge before whom tried and convicted.

(June 29, 1888, ch. 496, §3, 25 Stat. 209; Aug. 18, 1894, ch. 299, §3, 28 Stat. 360; May 28, 1908, ch. 212, §8, 35 Stat. 426.)

CODIFICATION

Section was enacted as part of section 3 of act June 29, 1888. Said section 3 of act June 29, 1888, enacted sections 443 to 448 of this title.

Section 3 of act June 29, 1888, as originally enacted, provided as follows:

"In all cases of receiving on board of any scows or boats such forbidden matter or substance as herein described, it shall be the duty of the owner or master, or person acting in such capacity, on board of such scows or boats, before proceeding to take or tow the same to the place of deposit, to apply for and obtain from the supervisor of the harbor appointed hereunder a permit defining the precise limits within which the discharge of such scows or boats may be made; and any deviation from such dumping or discharging place specified in such permit shall be a misdemeanor within the meaning of this act; and the master and engineer, or person or persons acting in such capacity, on board of any towboat towing such scows or boats, shall be equally guilty of such offense with the master or person acting in the capacity of master of the scow, and be liable to equal punishment."

Section 3 was amended by act Aug. 18, 1894, to read as follows:

"In all cases of receiving on board of any scows or boats such forbidden matter or substance as herein described, the owner or master, or person acting in such capacity on board of such scows or boats, before proceeding to take or tow the same to the place of deposit, shall apply for and obtain from the supervisor of the harbor appointed hereunder a permit defining the precise limits within which the discharge of such scows or boats may be made; and it shall not be lawful for the owner or master, or person acting in such capacity, of any tug or towboat to tow or move any scow or boat so loaded with such forbidden matter until such permit shall have been obtained; and every person violating the foregoing provisions of this section shall be deemed guilty of a misdemeanor, and on conviction thereof shall be punished by a fine of not more than one thousand nor less than five hundred dollars, and in addition thereto the master of any tug or towboat so offending shall have his license revoked, or suspended for a term to be fixed by the judge before whom tried and convicted. And any deviation from such dumping or discharging place specified in such permit shall be a misdemeanor, and the owner and master, or person acting in the capacity of master, of any scows or boats dumping or discharging such forbidden matter in any place other than that specified in such permit shall be liable to punishment therefor as provided in section one of the said Act of June twenty-ninth, eighteen hundred and eighty-eight [section 441 of this title]; and the owner and master, or person acting in the capacity of master, of any tug or towboat towing such scows or boats shall be liable to equal punishment with the owner and master, or person acting in the capacity of master, of the scows or boats; and further, every scowman or other employee on board of both scows and towboats shall be deemed to have knowledge of the place of dumping specified in such permit, and the owners and masters, or persons acting in the capacity of masters, shall be liable to punishment, as aforesaid, for any unlawful dumping, within the meaning of this Act or of the said Act of June twenty-ninth, eighteen hundred and eighty-eight, which may be caused by the negligence or ignorance of such scowman or other employee; and, further, neither defect in machinery nor avoidable accidents to scows or towboats, nor unfavorable weather, nor improper handling or moving of scows or boats of any kind whatsoever, shall operate to release the owners and masters and employees of scows and towboats from the penalties hereinbefore mentioned. Every scow or boat engaged in the transportation of dredgings, earth, sand, mud, cellar dirt, garbage, or other offensive material of any description shall have its name or number and owner's name painted in letters and numbers at least fourteen inches long on both sides of the scow or boat; these names and numbers shall be kept distinctly legible at all times, and no scow or boat not so marked shall be used to transport or dump any such material. The supervisor of the harbor of New York, designated as provided in section five of the said Act of June twenty-ninth, eighteen hundred and eighty-eight [section 451 of this title], is authorized and directed to appoint inspectors and deputy inspectors, and, for the purpose of enforcing the provisions of this Act and of the Act aforesaid, and of detecting and bringing to punishment offenders against the same, the said supervisor of the harbor, and the inspectors and deputy inspectors so appointed by him, shall have power and authority: First. To arrest and take into custody, with or without process, any person or persons who may commit any of the acts or offenses prohibited by this section and by the Act of June twenty-ninth, eighteen hundred and eighty-eight, aforesaid, or who may violate any of the provisions of the same: Provided, That no person shall be arrested without process for any offense not committed in the presence of the supervisor or his inspectors or deputy inspectors, or either of them: And provided further, That whenever any such arrest is made the person or persons so arrested shall be brought forthwith before a commissioner, judge, or court of the United States for examination of the offenses alleged against him; and such commissioner, judge, or court shall proceed in respect thereto as authorized by law in case of crimes against the United States. Second. To go on board of any scow or towboat engaged in unlawful dumping of prohibited material, or in moving the same without a permit as required in this section of this Act, and to seize and hold said boats until they are discharged by action of the commissioner, judge, or court of the United States before whom the offending persons are brought. Third. To arrest and take into custody any witness or witnesses to such unlawful dumping of prohibited material, the said witnesses to be released under proper bonds. Fourth. To go on board of any towboat having in tow scows or boats loaded with such prohibited material, and accompany the same to the place of dumping whenever such action appears to be necessary to secure compliance with the requirements of this Act and of the Act aforesaid. Fifth. To enter gas and oil works and all other manufacturing works for the purpose of discovering the disposition made of sludge, acid, or other injurious material, whenever there is good reason to believe that such sludge, acid, or other injurious material is allowed to run into the tidal waters of the harbor in violation of section one of the aforesaid Act of June twenty-ninth, eighteen hundred and eighty-eight [section 441 of this title]. Every person who, directly or indirectly, gives any sum of money or other bribe, present, or reward or makes any offer of the same to any inspector, deputy inspector, or other employee of the office of the supervisor of the harbor with intent to influence such inspector, deputy inspector, or other employee to permit or overlook any violation of the provisions of this section or of the said Act of June twenty-ninth, eighteen hundred and eighty-eight, shall, on conviction thereof, be fined not less than five hundred dollars nor more than one thousand dollars, and be imprisoned not less than six months nor more than one year. Every permit issued in accordance with the provisions of this section of this Act which may not be taken up by an inspector or deputy inspector shall be returned within forty-eight hours after issuance to the office of the supervisor of the harbor; such permit shall bear an indorsement by the master of the towboat, or the person acting in such capacity, stating whether the permit has been used, and if so the time and place of dumping. Any person violating the provisions of this section shall be liable to a fine of not more than five hundred dollars nor less than one hundred dollars.''

Section 3 was further amended by act May 28, 1908, ch. 212, §8, to read as set forth in this section and sections 444 to 448 of this title.

§444. Dumping at other place than designated dumping grounds; penalty; person liable; excuses for deviation

Any deviation from such dumping or discharging place specified in such permit shall be a misdemeanor, and the owner and master, or person acting in the capacity of master, of any scows or boats dumping or discharging such forbidden matter in any place other than that specified in such permit shall be liable to punishment therefor as provided in section 441 of this title; and the owner and master, or person acting in the capacity of master, of any tug or towboat towing such scows or boats shall be liable to equal punishment with the owner and master, or person acting in the capacity of master, of the scows or boats; and, further, every scowman or other employee on board of both scows and towboats shall be deemed to have knowledge of the place of dumping specified in such permit, and the owners and masters, or persons acting in the capacity of masters, shall be liable to punishment, as aforesaid, for any unlawful dumping, within the meaning of this Act and this subchapter, which may be caused by the negligence or ignorance of such scowman or other employee; and, further, neither defect in machinery nor avoidable accidents to scows or towboats, nor unfavorable weather, nor improper handling or moving of scows or boats of any kind whatsoever shall operate to release the owners and master and employees of scows and towboats from the penalties mentioned in section 441 of this title.

(June 29, 1888, ch. 496, §3, 25 Stat. 209; Aug. 18, 1894, ch. 299, §3, 28 Stat. 360; May 28, 1908, ch. 212, §8, 35 Stat. 426.)

REFERENCES IN TEXT

This Act, referred to in text, is act Aug. 18, 1894, ch. 299, 28 Stat. 356, as amended, which enacted sections 1, 31, and 452 of this title and amended sections 443 to 448 and 499 of this title. For complete classification of this Act to the Code, see Tables.

CODIFICATION

Section was enacted as part of section 3 of act June 29, 1888. Said section 3 of act June 29, 1888, enacted sections 443 to 448 of this title. See Codification note set out under section 443 of this title.

§445. Equipment and marking of boats or scows

Every scow or boat engaged in the transportation of dredgings, earth, sand, mud, cellar dirt, garbage, or other offensive material of any description shall have its name or number and owner's name painted in letters and numbers at least fourteen inches long on both sides of the scow or boat; these names and numbers shall be kept distinctly legible at all times, and no scow or boat not so marked shall be used to transport or dump any such material. Each such scow or boat shall be equipped at all times with a life line or rope extending at least the length of and three feet above the deck thereof, such rope to be attached to the coaming thereof, also with a life preserver and a life buoy for each person on board thereof, also with anchor to weigh not less than two hundred and seventy-five pounds, and at least one hundred feet of cable attached thereto; a list of the names of all men employed on any such scow or boat shall be kept by the owner or master thereof and the said list shall be open to the inspection of all parties. Failure to comply with any of the foregoing provisions shall render the owner of such scow or boat liable upon conviction thereof to a penalty of not more than $500: *Provided*, That the requirements in regard to life line or rope contained in this section shall not apply to any scow or boat the deck outside the coaming or rail of which shall not exceed one foot in width: *And provided further*, That on any such scow or boat its name or number and owner's name painted in letters and numbers, at least fourteen inches long on both ends of such scow or boat, shall be a compliance with the provisions of this section in regard to name, number, and owner's name.

(June 29, 1888, ch. 496, §3, 25 Stat. 209; Aug. 18, 1894, ch. 299, §3, 28 Stat. 360; May 28, 1908, ch. 212, §8, 35 Stat. 427; Feb. 16, 1909, ch. 132, 35 Stat. 623.)

CODIFICATION

Section was enacted as part of section 3 of act June 29, 1888. Said section 3 of act June 29, 1888, enacted sections 443 to 448 of this title. See Codification note set out under section 443 of this title.

Provisos are from act Feb. 16, 1909.

§446. Inspectors; appointment, powers, and duties

Each supervisor of a harbor is authorized and directed to appoint inspectors and deputy inspectors, and for the purposes of enforcing this subchapter and the Act of August 18, 1894, entitled ''An Act making appropriations for the construction, repair, and preservation of certain public works on rivers and harbors, and for other purposes'' (28 Stat. 338), and of detecting and bringing to punishment offenders against the same, the said supervisor of the harbor, and the inspectors and deputy inspectors so appointed by him, shall have power and authority.

First. To arrest and take into custody, with or without process, any person or persons who may commit any of the acts or offenses prohibited by this subchapter, or who may violate any of the provisions of the same: *Provided*, That no person shall be arrested without process for any offense not committed in the presence of the supervisor or his inspectors or deputy inspectors, or either of them: *And provided further*, That whenever any such arrest is made the person or persons so arrested shall be brought forthwith before a magistrate judge, judge, or court of the United

States for examination of the offenses alleged against him; and such magistrate judge, judge, or court shall proceed in respect thereto as authorized by law in case of crimes against the United States.

Second. To go on board of any scow or towboat engaged in unlawful dumping of prohibited material, or in moving the same without a permit, as required in sections 443 to 448 of this title, or otherwise violating sections 443 to 448 of this title, and to seize and hold said boats until they are discharged by action of the magistrate judge, judge, or court of the United States before whom the offending persons are brought.

Third. To arrest and take into custody any witness or witnesses to such unlawful dumping of prohibited material, the said witnesses to be released under proper bonds.

Fourth. To go on board of any towboat having in tow scows or boats loaded with such prohibited material, and accompany the same to the place of dumping, whenever such action appears to be necessary to secure compliance with the requirements of this subchapter and of the Act aforesaid.

Fifth. To enter gas and oil works and all other manufacturing works for the purpose of discovering the disposition made of sludge, acid, or other injurious material, whenever there is good reason to believe that such sludge, acid, or other injurious material is allowed to run into tidal waters of the harbor in violation of section 441 of this title.

(June 29, 1888, ch. 496, §3, 25 Stat. 209; Aug. 18, 1894, ch. 299, §3, 28 Stat. 360; May 28, 1908, ch. 212, §8, 35 Stat. 427; Pub. L. 85–802, §1(3), Aug. 28, 1958, 72 Stat. 970; Pub. L. 90–578, title IV, §402(b)(2), Oct. 17, 1968, 82 Stat. 1118; Pub. L. 101–650, title III, §321, Dec. 1, 1990, 104 Stat. 5117.)

REFERENCES IN TEXT

Act of August 18, 1894, referred to in provision preceding First paragraph, and Act aforesaid, referred to in Fourth paragraph, mean act Aug. 18, 1894, ch. 299, 28 Stat. 356, as amended, which enacted sections 1, 31, and 452 of this title and amended sections 443 to 448 and 499 of this title. For complete classification of this Act to the Code, see Tables.

Sections 443 to 448 of this title, referred to in the Second paragraph, were in the original "this section of this Act" meaning section 3 of act June 29, 1888, which enacted sections 443 to 448 of this title. The provision of section 3 relating to issuance of permits is classified to section 443 of this title.

CODIFICATION

Section was enacted as part of section 3 of act June 29, 1888. Said section 3 of act June 29, 1888, enacted sections 443 to 448 of this title. See Codification note set out under section 443 of this title.

AMENDMENTS

1958—Pub. L. 85–802 substituted "Each supervisor of a harbor is authorized and directed to appoint inspectors and deputy inspectors, and, for the purposes of enforcing this subchapter" for "The supervisor of the harbor of New York, designated as provided in section 451 of this title, is authorized and directed to appoint inspectors and deputy inspectors, and for the purpose of enforcing sections 1, 31, and this subchapter".

CHANGE OF NAME

"Magistrate judge" substituted in text for "magistrate" pursuant to section 321 of Pub. L. 101–650, set out as a note under section 631 of Title 28, Judiciary and Judicial Procedure. Previously, "magistrate" substituted for "commissioner" pursuant to Pub. L. 90–578. See chapter 43 (§631 et seq.) of Title 28.

EFFECTIVE DATE OF 1958 AMENDMENT

Amendment by Pub. L. 85–802 effective on sixtieth day after Aug. 28, 1958, see section 2 of Pub. L. 85–802, set out as a note under section 441 of this title.

§447. Bribery of inspector; penalty

Every person who, directly or indirectly, gives any sum of money or other bribe, present, or reward, or makes any offer of the same to any inspector, deputy inspector, or other employee of the office of any supervisor of a harbor with intent to influence such inspector, deputy inspector, or other employee to permit or overlook any violation of the provisions of this subchapter, shall, on conviction thereof, be fined not less than $500 nor more than $1,000, and be imprisoned not less than six months nor more than one year.

(June 29, 1888, ch. 496, §3, 25 Stat. 209; Aug. 18, 1894, ch. 299, §3, 28 Stat. 360; May 28, 1908, ch. 212, §8, 35 Stat. 428; Pub. L. 85–802, §1(4), Aug. 28, 1958, 72 Stat. 970.)

CODIFICATION

Section was enacted as part of section 3 of act June 29, 1888. Said section 3 of act June 29, 1888, enacted sections 443 to 448 of this title. See Codification note set out under section 443 of this title.

AMENDMENTS

1958—Pub. L. 85–802 substituted "any supervisor of a harbor" for "the supervisor of the harbor".

EFFECTIVE DATE OF 1958 AMENDMENT

Amendment by Pub. L. 85–802 effective on sixtieth day after Aug. 28, 1958, see section 2 of Pub. L. 85–802, set out as a note under section 441 of this title.

§448. Return of permit; penalty for failure to return

Every permit issued in accordance with the provisions of sections 443 to 448 of this title, which may not be taken up by an inspector or deputy inspector, shall be returned within four days after issuance to the office of the supervisor of the harbor; such permit shall bear an indorsement by the master of the towboat, or the person acting in such capacity, stating whether the permit has been used, and, if so, the time and place of dumping. Any person violating the provisions of this section shall be liable to a fine of not more than $500 nor less than $100.

(June 29, 1888, ch. 496, §3, 25 Stat. 209; Aug. 18, 1894, ch. 299, §3, 28 Stat. 360; May 28, 1908, ch. 212, §8, 35 Stat. 428.)

REFERENCES IN TEXT

Sections 443 to 448 of this title, referred to in text, were in the original "this section of this Act", meaning section 3 of act June 29, 1888, which enacted sections 443 to 448 of this title. The provision of section 3 relating to issuance of permits is classified to section 443 of this title.

CODIFICATION

Section was enacted as part of section 3 of act June 29, 1888. Said section 3 of act June 29, 1888 enacted sections 443 to 448 of this title. See Codification note set out under section 443 of this title.

§449. Disposition of dredged matter; persons liable; penalty

All mud, dirt, sand, dredgings, and material of every kind and description whatever taken, dredged, or excavated from any slip, basin, or shoal in any harbor subject to this subchapter, and placed on any boat, scow, or vessel for the purpose of being taken or towed upon the waters of that harbor to a place of deposit, shall be deposited and discharged at such place or within such limits as shall be defined and specified by the supervisor of the harbor, as in sections 443 to 448 of this title prescribed, and not otherwise. Every person, firm, or corporation being the owner of any slip, basin, or shoal, from which such mud, dirt, sand, dredgings, and material shall be taken, dredged, or excavated, and every person, firm, or corporation in any manner engaged in the work of dredging or excavating any such slip, basin, or shoal, or of removing such mud, dirt, sand, or dredgings therefrom, shall severally be responsible for the deposit and discharge of all such mud, dirt, sand, or dredgings at such place or within such limits so defined and prescribed by said supervisor of the harbor; and for every violation of the provisions of this section the person offending shall be guilty of an offense, and shall be punished by a fine equal to the sum of $5 for every cubic yard of mud, dirt, sand, dredgings, or material not deposited or discharged as required by this section.

(June 29, 1888, ch. 496, §4, 25 Stat. 210; Pub. L. 85–802, §1(5), Aug. 28, 1958, 72 Stat. 970.)

References in Text

Sections 443 to 448 of this title, referred to in text, were in the original "the third section of this Act", meaning section 3 of act June 29, 1888, which enacted sections 443 to 448 of this title. The provision of section 3 relating to specification of the limits within which to discharge is classified to section 443 of this title.

Codification

Section was enacted as part of section 4 of act June 29, 1888, which enacted sections 449 and 450 of this title.

Amendments

1958—Pub. L. 85–802 substituted "any harbor subject to this subchapter" for "the harbor of New York, or the waters adjacent or tributary thereto" and "the waters of that harbor" for "the waters of the harbor of New York".

Effective Date of 1958 Amendment

Amendment by Pub. L. 85–802 effective on sixtieth day after Aug. 28, 1958, see section 2 of Pub. L. 85–802, set out as a note under section 441 of this title.

§450. Liability of vessel

Any boat or vessel used or employed in violating any provision of this subchapter, shall be liable to the pecuniary penalties imposed thereby, and may be proceeded against, summarily by way of libel in any district court of the United States having jurisdiction thereof.

(June 29, 1888, ch. 496, §4, 25 Stat. 210.)

Codification

Section was enacted as part of section 4 of act June 29, 1888, which enacted sections 449 and 450 of this title.

§451. Supervisor of harbor; appointment and duties

An officer of the Corps of Engineers shall, for each harbor subject to this subchapter, be designated by the Secretary of the Army as supervisor of the harbor, to act under the direction of the Chief of Engineers in enforcing the provisions of this subchapter, and in detecting offenders against the same. Each such officer shall have personal charge and supervision under the Chief of Engineers, and shall direct the patrol boats and other means to detect and bring to punishment offenders against the provisions of this subchapter.

(June 29, 1888, ch. 496, §5, 25 Stat. 210; July 26, 1947, ch. 343, title II, §205(a), 61 Stat. 501; June 29, 1949, ch. 278, 63 Stat. 300; July 12, 1952, ch. 707, 66 Stat. 596; Pub. L. 85–802, §1(6), Aug. 28, 1958, 72 Stat. 970.)

Amendments

1958—Pub. L. 85–802 inserted "for each harbor subject to this subchapter," and substituted "Each such officer" for "This officer".

1952—Act July 12, 1952, transferred enforcement responsibilities of this section from a Naval officer to the Army district engineer at New York.

1949—Act June 29, 1949, struck out "shall receive the sea-pay of his grade and" after "this officer".

Change of Name

Department of War designated Department of the Army and title of Secretary of War changed to Secretary of the Army by section 205(a) of act July 26, 1947, ch. 343, title II, 61 Stat. 501. Section 205(a) of act July 26, 1947, was repealed by section 53 of act Aug. 10, 1956, ch. 1041, 70A Stat. 641. Section 1 of act Aug. 10, 1956, enacted "Title 10, Armed Forces" which in sections 3010 to 3013 continued Department of the Army under administrative supervision of Secretary of the Army.

Effective Date of 1958 Amendment

Amendment by Pub. L. 85–802 effective on sixtieth day after Aug. 28, 1958, see section 2 of Pub. L. 85–802, set out as a note under section 441 of this title.

§451a. Harbors subject to this subchapter

The following harbors shall be subject to this subchapter:

(1) The harbor of New York.

(2) The harbor of Hampton Roads.

(3) The harbor of Baltimore.

(June 29, 1888, ch. 496, §6, 25 Stat. 210; Pub. L. 85–802, §1(7), Aug. 28, 1958, 72 Stat. 970.)

Amendments

1958—Pub. L. 85–802 substituted provisions making harbors of New York, Hampton Roads, and Baltimore subject to this subchapter for appropriation provisions.

Effective Date of 1958 Amendment

Amendment by Pub. L. 85–802 effective on sixtieth day after Aug. 28, 1958, see section 2 of Pub. L. 85–802, set out as a note under section 441 of this title.

§451b. Waters included within subchapter

For the purposes of this subchapter—

(1) The term "harbor of New York" means the tidal waters of the harbor of New York, its adjacent and tributary waters, and those of Long Island Sound.

(2) The term "harbor of Hampton Roads" means the tidal waters of the harbors of Nor-

folk, Portsmouth, Newport News, Hampton Roads, and their adjacent and tributary waters, so much of the Chesapeake Bay and its tributaries as lies within the State of Virginia, and so much of the Atlantic Ocean and its tributaries as lies within the jurisdiction of the United States within or to the east of the State of Virginia.

(3) The term "harbor of Baltimore" means the tidal waters of the harbor of Baltimore and its adjacent and tributary waters, and so much of Chesapeake Bay and its tributaries as lies within the State of Maryland.

(June 29, 1888, ch. 496, §7, as added Pub. L. 85–802, §1(8), Aug. 28, 1958, 72 Stat. 970.)

EFFECTIVE DATE

Section effective on sixtieth day after Aug. 28, 1958, see section 2 of Pub. L. 85–802, set out as an Effective Date of 1958 Amendment note under section 441 of this title.

§452. Taking shellfish or otherwise interfering with navigation in New York Harbor channels; penalty; arrest and procedure

It shall be unlawful for any person or persons to engage in fishing or dredging for shellfish in any of the channels leading to and from the harbor of New York, or to interfere in any way with the safe navigation of those channels by ocean steamships and ships of deep draft.

Any person or persons violating the foregoing provisions of this section shall be deemed guilty of a misdemeanor, and on conviction thereof shall be punished by fine or imprisonment, or both, such fine to be not more than $250 nor less than $50, and the imprisonment to be not more than six months nor less than thirty days, either or both united, as the judge before whom conviction is obtained shall decide.

It shall be the duty of the United States supervisor of the harbor to enforce this section, and the deputy inspectors of the said supervisor shall have authority to arrest and take into custody, with or without process, any person or persons, who may commit any of the acts or offenses prohibited by this section: *Provided*, That no person shall be arrested without process for any offense not committed in the presence of the supervisor or his inspector or deputy inspectors, or either of them: *And provided further*, That whenever any such arrest is made the person or persons so arrested shall be brought forthwith before a magistrate judge, judge, or court of the United States for examination of the offenses alleged against him; and such magistrate judge, judge or court shall proceed in respect thereto as authorized by law in case of crimes against the United States.

(Aug. 18, 1894, ch. 299, §2, 28 Stat. 360; Pub. L. 90–578, title IV, §402(b)(2), Oct. 17, 1968, 82 Stat. 1118; Pub. L. 101–650, title III, §321, Dec. 1, 1990, 104 Stat. 5117.)

CODIFICATION

Section was not enacted as part of act June 29, 1888, ch. 496, 25 Stat. 209, which comprises this subchapter.

CHANGE OF NAME

"Magistrate judge" substituted in text for "magistrate" pursuant to section 321 of Pub. L. 101–650, set out as a note under section 631 of Title 28, Judiciary and Judicial Procedure. Previously, "magistrate" was substituted for "commissioner" pursuant to Pub. L. 90–578. See chapter 43 (§631 et seq.) of Title 28.

§453. Regulations for navigation of Ambrose Channel; exclusion of tows and sailing vessels

The Secretary of the Army is authorized to make such rules and regulations for the navigation of Ambrose Channel as he may deem necessary or expedient to insure its safe use in all kinds of weather, night and day, for all vessels under control and running under their own power, and to this end he may, in his discretion, forbid its use to tows of every description and to sailing vessels.

(Mar. 4, 1913, ch. 144, §1, 37 Stat. 803; July 26, 1947, ch. 343, title II, §205(a), 61 Stat. 501.)

CODIFICATION

Section was not enacted as part of act June 29, 1888, ch. 496, 25 Stat. 209, which comprises this subchapter.

CHANGE OF NAME

Department of War designated Department of the Army and title of Secretary of War changed to Secretary of the Army by section 205(a) of act July 26, 1947, ch. 343, title II, 61 Stat. 501. Section 205(a) of act July 26, 1947, was repealed by section 53 of act Aug. 10, 1956, ch. 1041, 70A Stat. 641. Section 1 of act Aug. 10, 1956, enacted "Title 10, Armed Forces" which in sections 3010 to 3013 continued Department of the Army under administrative supervision of Secretary of the Army.

§454. Consent of Congress to obstruction of waters by New York City

The consent of Congress is given to the city of New York, in the State of New York, to obstruct navigation of any river or other waterway which does not form a connecting link between other navigable waters of the United States, and lying wholly within the limits of said city, by closing all or any portion of the same or by building structures in or over the same when the said city shall be lawfully authorized to do so by the State of New York: *Provided, however*, That any such obstruction shall be unlawful unless the location and plans for the proposed work or works before the commencement thereof shall have been filed with and approved by the Secretary of the Army and Chief of Engineers; and when the plans for any such obstruction have been approved by the Chief of Engineers and by the Secretary of the Army it shall not be lawful to deviate from such plans either before or after the completion of such obstruction, unless the modification of such plans has previously been submitted to and received the approval of the Chief of Engineers and the Secretary of the Army: *And provided further*, That the city of New York shall be liable for any damage that may be inflicted upon private property by reason of any of the provisions of this section.

The right to alter, amend, or repeal this section is expressly reserved, and the United States shall incur no liability for the alteration, amendment, or repeal thereof to the city of New York, or to the owner or owners, or any other persons interested in any obstruction which shall have been constructed under its provisions.

(June 25, 1910, ch. 436, §§1, 2, 36 Stat. 866, 867; July 26, 1947, ch. 343, title II, §205(a), 61 Stat. 501.)

CODIFICATION

Section was not enacted as part of act June 29, 1888, ch. 496, 25 Stat. 209, which comprises this subchapter.

CHANGE OF NAME

Department of War designated Department of the Army and title of Secretary of War changed to Secretary of the Army by section 205(a) of act July 26, 1947, ch. 343, title II, 61 Stat. 501. Section 205(a) of act July 26, 1947, was repealed by section 53 of act Aug. 10, 1956, ch. 1041, 70A Stat. 641. Section 1 of act Aug. 10, 1956, enacted "Title 10, Armed Forces" which in sections 3010 to 3013 continued Department of the Army under administrative supervision of Secretary of the Army.

TRANSFER OF FUNCTIONS

Functions, powers, and duties of Secretary of the Army and other offices and officers of Department of the Army under section 401 of this title to extent that they relate generally to location and clearances of bridges and causeways in navigable waters of United States transferred to and vested in Secretary of Transportation by Pub. L. 89–670, §6(g)(6)(A), Oct. 15, 1966, 80 Stat. 941. Pub. L. 97–449 amended section 401 of this title to reflect transfer made by section 6(g)(6)(A) of Pub. L. 89–670, and repealed section 6(g)(6)(A).

SUBCHAPTER IV—POTOMAC RIVER AND TRIBUTARIES IN DISTRICT OF COLUMBIA

§§461 to 464. Repealed. Mar. 3, 1901, ch. 854, §1636, 31 Stat. 1434

Section 461, act May 19, 1896, ch. 208, §1, 29 Stat. 126, prohibited deposit of ballast, dirt, ashes or oyster shells into Potomac River except for purpose of making a wharf and then only after approval.

Section 462, act May 19, 1896, ch. 208, §2, 29 Stat. 127, prohibited deposit of dead fish, dead animals, fruits, vegetables, ice, snow, filth or trash of any kind into Potomac River.

Section 463, act May 19, 1896, ch. 208, §3, 29 Stat. 127, related to penalties.

Section 464, act May 19, 1896, ch. 208, §4, 29 Stat. 127, provided that none of these provisions be construed to interfere with any work or improvements in harbor or river area.

SUBCHAPTER V—NAVIGABLE WATERS OF MARYLAND

§465. Authority to dredge; riparian rights of United States

Subject to the provisions of section 403 of this title authority is granted to dredge, without cost to the United States, in the navigable waters of the United States included within the State of Maryland and outside the limits of projects for improvement of navigation facilities approved by Congress, regardless of rights accruing to the United States as riparian owner under the laws of the State of Maryland: *Provided*, That in the opinion of the Chief of Engineers such dredging will improve facilities for navigation.

(July 3, 1930, ch. 847, §12, 46 Stat. 949.)

SUBCHAPTER VI—WATER POLLUTION CONTROL

§§466 to 466g. Transferred

CODIFICATION

Sections 466 to 466g of this title were transferred to sections 1151 to 1160 of this title and were subsequently omitted in the general amendment of the Federal Water Pollution Control Act by Pub. L. 92–500, §2, Oct. 18, 1972, 86 Stat. 816. See section 1251 et seq. of this title.

Section 466, acts June 30, 1948, ch. 758, §1, 62 Stat. 1155; July 9, 1956, ch. 518, §1, 70 Stat. 498; July 20, 1961, Pub. L. 87–88, §1(a), 75 Stat. 204; Oct. 2, 1965, Pub. L. 89–234, §1(a), 79 Stat. 903; 1966 Reorg. Plan No. 2, eff. May 10, 1966, §§1(a), (e)(1), 5, 31 F.R. 6857, 80 Stat. 1608, which related to Congressional declaration of policy, was transferred to section 1151 of this title.

Section 466–1, act June 30, 1948, ch. 758, §2, as added Oct. 2, 1965, Pub. L. 89–234, §2(a), 79 Stat. 903; amended 1966 Reorg. Plan. No. 2, eff. May 10, 1966, §1(a), (b), 31 F.R. 6857, 80 Stat. 1608; Apr. 3, 1970, Pub. L. 91–224, title I, §110(a), 84 Stat. 113, which provided for a Federal Water Quality Administration, was transferred to section 1152 of this title.

Section 466a, acts June 30, 1948, ch. 758, §3, formerly §2, 62 Stat. 1155; July 9, 1956, ch. 518, §1, 70 Stat. 498; July 20, 1961, Pub. L. 87–88, §§1(b), 2, 75 Stat. 204; renumbered §3, Oct. 2, 1965, Pub. L. 89–234, §2(a), 79 Stat. 903; Nov. 3, 1966, Pub. L. 89–753, title I, §101, 80 Stat. 1246, which provided for comprehensive water pollution programs, was transferred to section 1153 of this title.

Section 466b, acts June 30, 1948, ch. 758, §4, formerly §3, 62 Stat. 1157; July 9, 1956, ch. 518, §1, 70 Stat. 498; July 20, 1961, Pub. L. 87–88, §1(b), 75 Stat. 204; renumbered §4, Oct. 2, 1965, Pub. L. 89–234, §2(a), 79 Stat. 903, which provided for interstate cooperation, was transferred to section 1154 of this title.

Section 466c, acts June 30, 1948, ch. 758, §5, formerly §4, 62 Stat. 1158; July 9, 1956, ch. 518, §1, 70 Stat. 499; July 20, 1961, Pub. L. 87–88, §§1(b), (c), 3, 75 Stat. 204, 205; renumbered §5, Oct. 2, 1965, Pub. L. 89–234, §2(a), 79 Stat. 903; 1966 Reorg. Plan No. 2, eff. May 10, 1966, §1(a), 31 F.R. 6857, 80 Stat. 1608; Nov. 3, 1966, Pub. L. 89–753, title II, §201(b), (c)(1), 80 Stat. 1247, 1248; Apr. 3, 1970, Pub. L. 91–224, title I, §105, 84 Stat. 111, which provided for research, experiments, and studies, was transferred to section 1155 of this title.

Section 466c–1, act June 30, 1948, ch. 758, §6, as added Oct. 2, 1965, Pub. L. 89–234, §3, 79 Stat. 905; amended Nov. 3, 1966, Pub. L. 89–753, title II, §201(a), 80 Stat. 1246; Apr. 3, 1970, Pub. L. 91–224, title I, §106, 84 Stat. 113, which provided grants for research and development, was transferred to section 1156 of this title.

Section 466d, acts June 30, 1948, ch. 758, §7, formerly §5, 62 Stat. 1158; July 9, 1956, ch. 518, §1, 70 Stat. 499; June 25, 1959, Pub. L. 86–70, §28(a), 73 Stat. 148; July 12, 1960, Pub. L. 86–624, §23(a), 74 Stat. 417; July 20, 1961, Pub. L. 87–88, §§1(b), 4(a), (b), 75 Stat. 204, 205; renumbered §7 and amended Oct. 2, 1965, Pub. L. 89–234, §§2(a), 7(a), 79 Stat. 903, 910; Nov. 3, 1966, Pub. L. 89–753, title II, §202, 80 Stat. 1248, which provided grants for water pollution control programs, was transferred to section 1157 of this title.

Section 466e, acts June 30, 1948, ch. 758, §8, formerly §6, 62 Stat. 1158; July 9, 1956, ch. 518, §1, 70 Stat. 502; July 20, 1961, Pub. L. 87–88, §§1(b), 5, 75 Stat. 204, 206; renumbered §8 and amended Oct. 2, 1965, Pub. L. 89–234, §§2(a), 4, 7(b), 79 Stat. 903, 906, 910; Nov. 3, 1966, Pub. L. 89–753, title II, §§203(a), 204, 205, 80 Stat. 1248–1250; Apr. 3, 1970, Pub. L. 91–224, title I, §111, 84 Stat. 113, which provided grants for construction of sewerage treatment works, was transferred to section 1158 of this title.

Section 466f, acts June 30, 1948, ch. 758, §9, formerly §7, 62 Stat. 1159; July 17, 1952, ch. 927, 66 Stat. 755; July 9, 1956, ch. 518, §1, 70 Stat. 503; July 20, 1961, Pub. L. 87–88, §§1(b)–(d), 6(a), (b), 75 Stat. 204, 207; renumbered §9, Oct. 2, 1965, Pub. L. 89–234, §2(a), 79 Stat. 903; 1966 Reorg. Plan No. 2, eff. May 10, 1966, §1(a), (c)(1), (2), 31 F.R. 6857, 80 Stat. 1608, which provided for a Water Pollution Control Advisory Board, was transferred to section 1159 of this title.

Section 466g, acts June 30, 1948, ch. 758, §10, formerly §8, 62 Stat. 1159; July 17, 1952, ch. 927, 66 Stat. 755; July 9, 1956, ch. 518, §1, 70 Stat. 504; July 20, 1961, Pub. L. 87–88, §§1(b), 7, 75 Stat. 204, 207; renumbered §10 and amended Oct. 2, 1965, Pub. L. 89–234, §§2(a), 5, 7(c), (d),

79 Stat. 903, 907, 910; 1966 Reorg. Plan No. 2, eff. May 10, 1966, § 1(a), (d)(1), (2), 31 F.R. 6857, 80 Stat. 1608; Nov. 3, 1966, Pub. L. 89–753, title II, §§ 206–208, 80 Stat. 1250; Apr. 3, 1970, Pub. L. 91–224, title I, § 112, 84 Stat. 114, which provided for enforcement measures against pollution of interstate or navigable waters, was transferred to section 1160 of this title.

§ 466g–1. Controversies involving construction or application of interstate compacts and pollution of waters

(a) Jurisdiction of actions by States

The United States district courts shall have original jurisdiction (concurrent with that of the Supreme Court of the United States, and concurrent with that of any other court of the United States or of any State of the United States in matters in which the Supreme Court, or any other court, has original jurisdiction) of any case or controversy—

(1) which involves the construction or application of an interstate compact which (A) in whole or in part relates to the pollution of the waters of an interstate river system or any portion thereof, and (B) expresses the consent of the States signatory to said compact to be sued in a district court in any case or controversy involving the application or construction thereof; and

(2) which involves pollution of the waters of such river system, or any portion thereof, alleged to be in violation of the provisions of said compact; and

(3) in which one or more of the States signatory to said compact is a plaintiff or plaintiffs; and

(4) which is within the judicial power of the United States as set forth in the Constitution of the United States.

(b) Amount in controversy; residence, situs or citizenship; nature, character, or legal status of parties

The district courts shall have original jurisdiction of a case or controversy such as is referred to in subsection (a) of this section, without any requirement, limitation, or regard as to the sum or value of the matter in controversy, or of the place of residence or situs or citizenship, or of the nature, character, or legal status, of any of the proper parties plaintiff or defendant in said case or controversy other than the signatory State or States plaintiff or plaintiffs referred to in paragraph (3) of subsection (a) of this section: *Provided*, That nothing in this section shall be construed as authorizing a State to sue its own citizens in said courts.

(c) Suits between States signatory to interstate compact

The original jurisdiction conferred upon the district courts by this section shall include, but not be limited to, suits between States signatory to such interstate compact: *Provided*, That nothing in this section shall be construed as authorizing a State to sue another State which is not a signatory to such compact in said courts.

(d) Venue

The venue of such case or controversy shall be as prescribed by law: *Provided*, That in addition thereto, such case or controversy may be brought in in any judicial district in which the acts of pollution complained of, or any portion thereof, occur, regardless of the place or places of residence, or situs, of any of the parties plaintiff or defendant.

(Pub. L. 87–830, § 1, Oct. 15, 1962, 76 Stat. 957.)

Separability

Section 2 of Pub. L. 87–830 provided that: "If any part or application of this Act [this section] should be declared invalid by a court of competent jurisdiction, said invalidity shall not affect the other parts, or the other applications, of said Act."

§§ 466h to 466*l*. Transferred

Codification

Sections 466h to 466*l* of this title were transferred to sections 1171 to 1175 of this title and were subsequently omitted in the general amendment of the Federal Water Pollution Control Act by Pub. L. 92–500, § 2, Oct. 18, 1972, 86 Stat. 816. See section 1251 et seq. of this title.

Section 466h, acts June 30, 1948, ch. 758, § 21, formerly § 9, 62 Stat. 1160; July 9, 1956, ch. 518, § 1, 70 Stat. 506; July 20, 1961, Pub. L. 87–88, § 8, 75 Stat. 210; renumbered § 11 and amended Oct. 2, 1965, Pub. L. 89–234, §§ 2(a), 7(e), 79 Stat. 903, 910; 1966 Reorg. Plan No. 2, eff. May 10, 1966, § 1(a), 31 F.R. 6857, 80 Stat. 1608; renumbered § 21 and amended Apr. 3, 1970, Pub. L. 91–224, title I, §§ 102, 103, 84 Stat. 91, 107, which provided for cooperation by all Federal agencies in pollution control, was transferred to section 1171 of this title.

Section 466i, acts June 30, 1948, ch. 758, § 22, formerly § 10, 62 Stat. 1160; July 9, 1956, ch. 518, § 1, 70 Stat. 506; July 20, 1961, Pub. L. 87–88, § 1(b), (d), (e), 75 Stat. 204; renumbered § 12 and amended Oct. 2, 1965, Pub. L. 89–234, §§ 2(a), 6, 79 Stat. 903, 909; 1966 Reorg. Plan No. 2, eff. May 10, 1966, § 1(a), 31 F.R. 6857, 80 Stat. 1608; renumbered § 22 and amended Apr. 3, 1970, Pub. L. 91–224, title I, §§ 102, 104, 84 Stat. 91, 110, which provided for rules and regulations, was transferred to section 1172 of this title.

Section 466j, acts June 30, 1948, ch. 758, § 23, formerly § 11, 62 Stat. 1161; July 9, 1956, ch. 518, § 1, 70 Stat. 506; June 25, 1959, Pub. L. 86–70, § 28(b), 73 Stat. 148; July 12, 1960, Pub. L. 86–624, § 23(b), 74 Stat. 418; July 20, 1961, Pub. L. 87–88, § 9, 75 Stat. 210; renumbered § 13, Oct. 2, 1965, Pub. L. 89–234, § 2(a), 79 Stat. 903; Nov. 3, 1966, Pub. L. 89–753, title II, § 209, 80 Stat. 1251; renumbered § 23, Apr. 3, 1970, Pub. L. 91–224, title I, § 102, 84 Stat. 91, which related to definitions, was transferred to section 1173 of this title.

Section 466k, act June 30, 1948, ch. 758, § 24, formerly § 12, as added July 9, 1956, ch. 518, § 1, 70 Stat. 506; renumbered § 14, Oct. 2, 1965, Pub. L. 89–234, § 2(a), 79 Stat. 903; renumbered § 24 and amended Apr. 3, 1970, Pub. L. 91–224, title I, §§ 102, 107, 84 Stat. 91, 113, which related to application of other laws, was transferred to section 1174 of this title.

Section 466*l*, act June 30, 1948, ch. 758, § 26, formerly § 16, as added Nov. 3, 1966, Pub. L. 89–753, title II, § 210, 80 Stat. 1252; renumbered § 26, Apr. 3, 1970, Pub. L. 91–224, title I, § 102, 84 Stat. 91, which provided for studies and analysis of costs estimates and reports to Congress, was transferred to section 1175 of this title.

§§ 466m, 466n. Repealed. Pub. L. 91–224, title I, § 102, Apr. 3, 1970, 84 Stat. 91

Section 466m, act June 30, 1948, ch. 758, § 17, as added Nov. 3, 1966, Pub. L. 89–753, title II, § 210, 80 Stat. 1252, authorized a study by Secretary of the Interior, and a report to Congress not later than July 1, 1967, of the extent of pollution of the navigable waters of the United States from litter and sewage deposited into such waters from watercraft.

Section 466n, act June 30, 1948, ch. 758, § 18, as added Nov. 3, 1966, Pub. L. 89–753, title II, § 210, 80 Stat. 1252, authorized a study by Secretary of the Interior, and a report to Congress not later than Jan. 30, 1968, relating to incentives, including, but not limited to, tax and other financial incentives, to assist in the construction of industrial anti-pollution facilities.

SUBCHAPTER VII—DAM INSPECTION PROGRAM

§467. Definitions

In this subchapter, the following definitions apply:

(1) Board

The term "Board" means a National Dam Safety Review Board established under section 467f(f) of this title.

(2) Dam

The term "dam"—

(A) means any artificial barrier that has the ability to impound water, wastewater, or any liquid-borne material, for the purpose of storage or control of water, that—

(i) is 25 feet or more in height from—

(I) the natural bed of the stream channel or watercourse measured at the downstream toe of the barrier; or

(II) if the barrier is not across a stream channel or watercourse, from the lowest elevation of the outside limit of the barrier;

to the maximum water storage elevation; or

(ii) has an impounding capacity for maximum storage elevation of 50 acre-feet or more; but

(B) does not include—

(i) a levee; or

(ii) a barrier described in subparagraph (A) that—

(I) is 6 feet or less in height regardless of storage capacity; or

(II) has a storage capacity at the maximum water storage elevation that is 15 acre-feet or less regardless of height;

unless the barrier, because of the location of the barrier or another physical characteristic of the barrier, is likely to pose a significant threat to human life or property if the barrier fails (as determined by the Director).

(3) Director

The term "Director" means the Administrator of FEMA.

(4) Federal agency

The term "Federal agency" means a Federal agency that designs, finances, constructs, owns, operates, maintains, or regulates the construction, operation, or maintenance of a dam.

(5) Federal Guidelines for Dam Safety

The term "Federal Guidelines for Dam Safety" means the FEMA publication, numbered 93 and dated June 1979, that defines management practices for dam safety at all Federal agencies.

(6) FEMA

The term "FEMA" means the Federal Emergency Management Agency.

(7) Hazard reduction

The term "hazard reduction" means the reduction in the potential consequences to life and property of dam failure.

(8) ICODS

The term "ICODS" means the Interagency Committee on Dam Safety established by section 467e of this title.

(9) Program

The term "Program" means the national dam safety program established under section 467f of this title.

(10) State

The term "State" means each of the several States of the United States, the District of Columbia, the Commonwealth of Puerto Rico, the Virgin Islands, Guam, American Samoa, the Commonwealth of the Northern Mariana Islands, and any other territory or possession of the United States.

(11) State dam safety agency

The term "State dam safety agency" means a State agency that has regulatory authority over the safety of non-Federal dams.

(12) State dam safety program

The term "State dam safety program" means a State dam safety program approved and assisted under section 467f(e) of this title.

(13) United States

The term "United States", when used in a geographical sense, means all of the States.

(Pub. L. 92–367, §2, as added Pub. L. 104–303, title II, §215(c)(4), Oct. 12, 1996, 110 Stat. 3685; amended Pub. L. 107–310, §3(e)(2), Dec. 2, 2002, 116 Stat. 2451; Pub. L. 109–295, title VI, §612(c), Oct. 4, 2006, 120 Stat. 1410.)

PRIOR PROVISIONS

A prior section 467, Pub. L. 92–367, §1, Aug. 8, 1972, 86 Stat. 506; Pub. L. 99–662, title XII, §1201(a), Nov. 17, 1986, 100 Stat. 4260, defined term "dam" as used in this subchapter, prior to repeal by Pub. L. 104–303, §215(c)(1).

A prior section 2 of Pub. L. 92–367 was renumbered section 3 by section 215(c)(3) of Pub. L. 104–303 and is classified to section 467a of this title.

AMENDMENTS

2002—Par. (1). Pub. L. 107–310, §3(e)(2)(A), substituted "section 467f(f)" for "section 467f(h)".

Par. (12). Pub. L. 107–310, §3(e)(2)(B), substituted "section 467f(e)" for "section 467f(f)".

CHANGE OF NAME

"Administrator of FEMA" substituted for "Director of FEMA" in par. (3) on authority of section 612(c) of Pub. L. 109–295, set out as a note under section 313 of Title 6, Domestic Security. Any reference to the Administrator of the Federal Emergency Management Agency in title VI of Pub. L. 109–295 or an amendment by title VI to be considered to refer and apply to the Director of the Federal Emergency Management Agency until Mar. 31, 2007, see section 612(f)(2) of Pub. L. 109–295, set out as a note under section 313 of Title 6.

SHORT TITLE OF 2006 AMENDMENT

Pub. L. 109–460, §1(a), Dec. 22, 2006, 120 Stat. 3401, provided that: "This section [amending sections 467d, 467f, and 467j of this title] may be cited as the 'Dam Safety Act of 2006'."

SHORT TITLE OF 2002 AMENDMENT

Pub. L. 107–310, §1(a), Dec. 2, 2002, 116 Stat. 2450, provided that: "This Act [enacting section 467g–1 of this title and amending this section and sections 467e to 467g and 467h to 467j of this title] may be cited as the 'Dam Safety and Security Act of 2002'."

SHORT TITLE OF 1986 AMENDMENT

Section 1206 of title XII of Pub. L. 99–662 provided that: "This title [enacting sections 467f to 467n and 2311 of this title and amending this section and sections 467a and 467b of this title] may be cited as the 'Dam Safety Act of 1986'."

SHORT TITLE

Section 1 of Pub. L. 92–367, as added by Pub. L. 104–303, title II, §215(c)(1), Oct. 12, 1996, 110 Stat. 3685, provided that: "This Act [enacting this subchapter] may be cited as the 'National Dam Safety Program Act'."

TRANSFER OF FUNCTIONS

For transfer of all functions, personnel, assets, components, authorities, grant programs, and liabilities of the Federal Emergency Management Agency, including the functions of the Under Secretary for Federal Emergency Management relating thereto, to the Federal Emergency Management Agency, see section 315(a)(1) of Title 6, Domestic Security.

For transfer of functions, personnel, assets, and liabilities of the Federal Emergency Management Agency, including the functions of the Director of the Federal Emergency Management Agency relating thereto, to the Secretary of Homeland Security, and for treatment of related references, see former section 313(1) and sections 551(d), 552(d), and 557 of Title 6, Domestic Security, and the Department of Homeland Security Reorganization Plan of November 25, 2002, as modified, set out as a note under section 542 of Title 6.

CONGRESSIONAL STATEMENT OF PURPOSE; NATIONAL DAM SAFETY PROGRAM

Section 215(a) of Pub. L. 104–303 provided that: "The purpose of this section [enacting this section and sections 467d to 467j of this title, amending sections 467a to 467c of this title and section 3802 of Title 25, Indians, repealing former sections 467 and 467d to 467m of this title, and enacting provisions set out as notes under this section] is to reduce the risks to life and property from dam failure in the United States through the establishment and maintenance of an effective national dam safety program to bring together the expertise and resources of the Federal and non-Federal communities in achieving national dam safety hazard reduction. It is not the intent of this section to preempt any other Federal or State authorities nor is it the intent of this section to mandate State participation in the grant assistance program to be established under this section."

EFFECT ON OTHER DAM SAFETY PROGRAMS

Section 215(b) of Pub. L. 104–303 provided that: "Nothing in this section (including the amendments made by this section) [enacting this section and sections 467d to 467j of this title, amending sections 467a to 467c of this title and section 3802 of Title 25, Indians, repealing former sections 467 and 467d to 467m of this title, and enacting provisions set out as notes under this section] shall preempt or otherwise affect any dam safety program of a Federal agency other than the Federal Emergency Management Agency, including any program that regulates, permits, or licenses any activity affecting a dam."

§467a. Inspection of dams

(a) In general

As soon as practicable, the Secretary of the Army, acting through the Chief of Engineers, shall carry out a national program of inspection of dams for the purpose of protecting human life and property. All dams in the United States shall be inspected by the Secretary except (1) dams under the jurisdiction of the Bureau of Reclamation, the Tennessee Valley Authority, or the International Boundary and Water Commission, (2) dams which have been constructed pursuant to licenses issued under the authority of the Federal Power Act [16 U.S.C. 791a et seq.], (3) dams which have been inspected within the twelve-month period immediately prior to August 8, 1972, by a State agency and which the Governor of such State requests be excluded from inspection, and (4) dams which the Secretary of the Army determines do not pose any threat to human life or property. The Secretary may inspect dams which have been licensed under the Federal Power Act upon request of the Federal Energy Regulatory Commission and dams under the jurisdiction of the International Boundary and Water Commission upon request of such Commission.

(b) State participation

On request of a State dam safety agency, with respect to any dam the failure of which would affect the State, the head of a Federal agency shall—

(1) provide information to the State dam safety agency on the construction, operation, or maintenance of the dam; or

(2) allow any official of the State dam safety agency to participate in the Federal inspection of the dam.

(Pub. L. 92–367, §3, formerly §2, Aug. 8, 1972, 86 Stat. 506; Pub. L. 95–91, title IV, §402(a)(1)(A), Aug. 4, 1977, 91 Stat. 583; renumbered §3 and amended Pub. L. 104–303, title II, §215(c)(3), (5), Oct. 12, 1996, 110 Stat. 3685, 3687.)

REFERENCES IN TEXT

The Federal Power Act, referred to in subsec. (a), is act June 10, 1920, ch. 285, 41 Stat. 1063, as amended, which is classified generally to chapter 12 (§791a et seq.) of Title 16, Conservation. For complete classification of this Act to the Code, see section 791a of Title 16 and Tables.

PRIOR PROVISIONS

A prior section 3 of Pub. L. 92–367 was renumbered section 4 and is classified to section 467b of this title.

AMENDMENTS

1996—Pub. L. 104–303 inserted section catchline, designated existing provisions as subsec. (a) and inserted heading, and added subsec. (b).

TRANSFER OF FUNCTIONS

"Federal Energy Regulatory Commission" substituted in text for "Federal Power Commission" on authority of Pub. L. 95–91, title IV, §402(a)(1)(A), Aug. 4, 1977, 91 Stat. 583, which is classified to section 7172(a)(1)(A) of Title 42, The Public Health and Welfare.

§467b. Investigation reports to Governors

As soon as practicable after inspection of a dam, the Secretary shall notify the Governor of the State in which such dam is located the results of such investigation. In any case in which any hazardous conditions are found during an inspection, upon request by the owner, the Secretary, acting through the Chief of Engineers, may perform detailed engineering studies to determine the structural integrity of the dam, subject to reimbursement of such expense by the owner of such dam. The Secretary shall immediately notify the Governor of any hazardous conditions found during an inspection. The Secretary shall provide advice to the Governor, upon request, relating to timely remedial measures necessary to mitigate or obviate any hazardous conditions found during an inspection.

(Pub. L. 92–367, §4, formerly §3, Aug. 8, 1972, 86 Stat. 507; Pub. L. 99–662, title XII, §1204, Nov. 17, 1986, 100 Stat. 4263; renumbered §4 and amended Pub. L. 104–303, title II, §215(c)(3), (6), Oct. 12, 1996, 110 Stat. 3685, 3687.)

PRIOR PROVISIONS

A prior section 4 of Pub. L. 92–367 was renumbered section 5 and is classified to section 467c of this title.

AMENDMENTS

1996—Pub. L. 104–303 inserted section catchline.

1986—Pub. L. 99–662 inserted "In any case in which any hazardous conditions are found during an inspection, upon request by the owner, the Secretary, acting through the Chief of Engineers, may perform detailed engineering studies to determine the structural integrity of the dam, subject to reimbursement of such expense by the owner of such dam."

§467c. Determination of danger to human life and property

For the purpose of determining whether a dam (including the waters impounded by such dam) constitutes a danger to human life or property, the Secretary shall take into consideration the possibility that the dam might be endangered by overtopping, seepage, settlement, erosion, sediment, cracking, earth movement, earthquakes, failure of bulkheads, flashboard, gates on conduits, or other conditions which exist or which might occur in any area in the vicinity of the dam.

(Pub. L. 92–367, §5, formerly §4, Aug. 8, 1972, 86 Stat. 507; renumbered §5 and amended Pub. L. 104–303, title II, §215(c)(3), (7), Oct. 12, 1996, 110 Stat. 3685, 3687.)

PRIOR PROVISIONS

A prior section 5 of Pub. L. 92–367 was classified to section 467d of this title prior to repeal by Pub. L. 104–303.

AMENDMENTS

1996—Pub. L. 104–303 inserted section catchline.

§467d. National dam inventory

The Secretary of the Army shall maintain and update information on the inventory of dams in the United States. Such inventory of dams shall include any available information assessing each dam based on inspections completed by either a Federal agency or a State dam safety agency.

(Pub. L. 92–367, §6, as added Pub. L. 104–303, title II, §215(c)(8), Oct. 12, 1996, 110 Stat. 3687; amended Pub. L. 109–460, §1(b), Dec. 22, 2006, 120 Stat. 3401.)

PRIOR PROVISIONS

A prior section 467d, Pub. L. 92–367, §5, Aug. 8, 1972, 86 Stat. 507, directed Secretary report to Congress on or before July 1, 1974, on activities under this subchapter, including in report an inventory of dams in the United States, a review of each inspection made, recommendations to State Governors and implementation of those recommendations, recommendations for comprehensive national program for inspection and safety regulation, and recommendations on responsibilities which should be assumed by Federal, State, and local governments and by public and private interests, prior to repeal by Pub. L. 104–303, title II, §215(c)(2), Oct. 12, 1996, 110 Stat. 3685.

A prior section 6 of Pub. L. 92–367 was classified to section 467e of this title prior to repeal by Pub. L. 104–303.

AMENDMENTS

2006—Pub. L. 109–460 amended section generally. Prior to amendment, section read as follows: "The Secretary of the Army, acting through the Chief of Engineers, may maintain and periodically publish updated information on the inventory of dams in the United States."

§467e. Interagency Committee on Dam Safety

(a) Establishment

There is established an Interagency Committee on Dam Safety—

(1) comprised of a representative of each of the Department of Agriculture, the Department of Defense, the Department of Energy, the Department of the Interior, the Department of Labor, FEMA, the Federal Energy Regulatory Commission, the Nuclear Regulatory Commission, the Tennessee Valley Authority, and the United States Section of the International Boundary Commission; and

(2) chaired by the Director.

(b) Duties

ICODS shall encourage the establishment and maintenance of effective Federal programs, policies, and guidelines intended to enhance dam safety for the protection of human life and property through coordination and information exchange among Federal agencies concerning implementation of the Federal Guidelines for Dam Safety.

(Pub. L. 92–367, §7, as added Pub. L. 104–303, title II, §215(c)(8), Oct. 12, 1996, 110 Stat. 3687; amended Pub. L. 107–310, §2, Dec. 2, 2002, 116 Stat. 2450.)

PRIOR PROVISIONS

A prior section 467e, Pub. L. 92–367, §6, Aug. 8, 1972, 86 Stat. 507, directed that existing liabilities and obligations be unaffected, prior to repeal by Pub. L. 104–303, title II, §215(c)(2), Oct. 12, 1996, 110 Stat. 3685.

A prior section 7 of Pub. L. 92–367 was classified to section 467f of this title prior to repeal by Pub. L. 104–303.

AMENDMENTS

2002—Subsec. (b). Pub. L. 107–310 substituted "Federal programs" for "Federal and State programs" and "through coordination and information exchange among Federal agencies concerning implementation of the Federal Guidelines for Dam Safety." for "through—

"(1) coordination and information exchange among Federal agencies and State dam safety agencies; and

"(2) coordination and information exchange among Federal agencies concerning implementation of the Federal Guidelines for Dam Safety."

TRANSFER OF FUNCTIONS

For transfer of all functions, personnel, assets, components, authorities, grant programs, and liabilities of the Federal Emergency Management Agency, including the functions of the Under Secretary for Federal Emergency Management relating thereto, to the Federal Emergency Management Agency, see section 315(a)(1) of Title 6, Domestic Security.

For transfer of functions, personnel, assets, and liabilities of the Federal Emergency Management Agency, including the functions of the Director of the Federal Emergency Management Agency relating thereto, to the Secretary of Homeland Security, and for treatment of related references, see former section 313(1) and sections 551(d), 552(d), and 557 of Title 6, Domestic Security, and the Department of Homeland Security Reorganization Plan of November 25, 2002, as modified, set out as a note under section 542 of Title 6.

§ 467f. National dam safety program

(a) In general

The Director, in consultation with ICODS and State dam safety agencies, and the Board shall establish and maintain, in accordance with this section, a coordinated national dam safety program. The Program shall—

(1) be administered by FEMA to achieve the objectives set forth in subsection (c) of this section;

(2) involve, to the extent appropriate, each Federal agency; and

(3) include—

(A) each of the components described in subsection (d) of this section;

(B) the strategic plan described in subsection (b) of this section; and

(C) assistance for State dam safety programs described in subsection (e) of this section.

(b) Duties

The Director shall prepare a strategic plan—

(1) to establish goals, priorities, performance measures, and target dates toward effectively administering this subchapter in order to improve the safety of dams in the United States; and

(2) to the extent feasible, to establish cooperation and coordination with, and assistance to, interested governmental entities in all States.

(c) Objectives

The objectives of the Program are to—

(1) ensure that new and existing dams are safe through the development of technologically and economically feasible programs and procedures for national dam safety hazard reduction;

(2) encourage acceptable engineering policies and procedures to be used for dam site investigation, design, construction, operation and maintenance, and emergency preparedness;

(3) encourage the establishment and implementation of effective dam safety programs in each State based on State standards;

(4) develop and encourage public awareness projects to increase public acceptance and support of State dam safety programs;

(5) develop technical assistance materials for Federal and non-Federal dam safety programs;

(6) develop mechanisms with which to provide Federal technical assistance for dam safety to the non-Federal sector; and

(7) develop technical assistance materials, seminars, and guidelines to improve security for dams in the United States.

(d) Components

(1) In general

The Program shall consist of—

(A) a Federal element and a non-Federal element; and

(B) leadership activity, technical assistance activity, and public awareness activity.

(2) Elements

(A) Federal

The Federal element shall incorporate the activities and practices carried out by Federal agencies under section 467e of this title to implement the Federal Guidelines for Dam Safety.

(B) Non-Federal

The non-Federal element shall consist of—

(i) the activities and practices carried out by States, local governments, and the private sector to safely build, regulate, operate, and maintain dams; and

(ii) Federal activities that foster State efforts to develop and implement effective programs for the safety of dams.

(3) Functional activities

(A) Leadership

The leadership activity shall be the responsibility of FEMA and shall be exercised by chairing the Board to coordinate national efforts to improve the safety of the dams in the United States.

(B) Technical assistance

The technical assistance activity shall consist of the transfer of knowledge and technical information among the Federal and non-Federal elements described in paragraph (2).

(C) Public awareness

The public awareness activity shall provide for the education of the public, including State and local officials, in the hazards of dam failure, methods of reducing the adverse consequences of dam failure, and related matters.

(e) Assistance for State dam safety programs

(1) In general

To encourage the establishment and maintenance of effective State programs intended to ensure dam safety, to protect human life and property, and to improve State dam safety programs, the Director shall provide assistance with amounts made available under section 467j of this title to assist States in establishing, maintaining, and improving dam safety programs in accordance with the criteria specified in paragraph (2).

(2) Criteria and budgeting requirement

For a State to be eligible for assistance under this subsection, a State dam safety program must be working toward meeting the following criteria and budgeting requirement:

(A) Criteria

A State dam safety program must be authorized by State legislation to include, at a minimum—

(i) the authority to review and approve plans and specifications to construct, enlarge, modify, remove, and abandon dams;

(ii) the authority to perform periodic inspections during dam construction to ensure compliance with approved plans and specifications;

(iii) a requirement that, on completion of dam construction, State approval must be given before operation of the dam;

(iv) the authority to require or perform periodic evaluations of all dams and reservoirs to determine the extent of the threat to human life and property in case of failure;

(v)(I) the authority to require or perform the inspection, at least once every 5 years, of all dams and reservoirs that would pose a significant threat to human life and property in case of failure to determine the continued safety of the dams and reservoirs; and

(II) a procedure for more detailed and frequent safety inspections;

(vi) a requirement that all inspections be performed under the supervision of a State-registered professional engineer with related experience in dam design and construction;

(vii) the authority to issue notices, when appropriate, to require owners of dams to perform necessary maintenance or remedial work, install and monitor instrumentation, improve security, revise operating procedures, or take other actions, including breaching dams when necessary;

(viii) regulations for carrying out the legislation of the State described in this subparagraph;

(ix) provision for necessary funds—

(I) to ensure timely repairs or other changes to, or removal of, a dam in order to protect human life and property; and

(II) if the owner of the dam does not take action described in subclause (I), to take appropriate action as expeditiously as practicable;

(x) a system of emergency procedures to be used if a dam fails or if the failure of a dam is imminent; and

(xi) an identification of—

(I) each dam the failure of which could be reasonably expected to endanger human life;

(II) the maximum area that could be flooded if the dam failed; and

(III) necessary public facilities that would be affected by the flooding.

(B) Budgeting requirement

For a State to be eligible for assistance under this subsection, State appropriations must be budgeted to carry out the legislation of the State under subparagraph (A).

(3) Work plans

The Director shall enter into a[1] agreement with each State receiving assistance under paragraph (2) to develop a work plan necessary for the State dam safety program to reach a level of program performance specified in the agreement.

(4) Maintenance of effort

Assistance may not be provided to a State under this subsection for a fiscal year unless the State enters into such agreement with the Director as the Director requires to ensure that the State will maintain the aggregate expenditures of the State from all other sources for programs to ensure dam safety for the protection of human life and property at or above a level equal to the average annual level of such expenditures for the 2 fiscal years preceding the fiscal year.

(5) Approval of programs

(A) Submission

For a State to be eligible for assistance under this subsection, a plan for a State dam safety program shall be submitted to the Director for approval.

(B) Approval

A State dam safety program shall be deemed to be approved 120 days after the date of receipt by the Director unless the Director determines within the 120-day period that the State dam safety program fails to meet the requirements of paragraphs (1) through (3).

(C) Notification of disapproval

If the Director determines that a State dam safety program does not meet the requirements for approval, the Director shall immediately notify the State in writing and provide the reasons for the determination and the changes that are necessary for the plan to be approved.

(6) Review of State dam safety programs

Using the expertise of the Board, the Director shall periodically review State dam safety programs. If the Board finds that a State dam safety program has proven inadequate to reasonably protect human life and property and the Director concurs, the Director shall revoke approval of the State dam safety program, and withhold assistance under this subsection, until the State dam safety program again meets the requirements for approval.

(f) Board

(1) Establishment

The Director shall establish an advisory board to be known as the "National Dam Safety Review Board" to monitor the safety of dams in the United States, to monitor State implementation of this section, and to advise the Director on national dam safety policy.

(2) Authority

The Board may use the expertise of Federal agencies and enter into contracts for necessary studies to carry out this section.

(3) Voting membership

The Board shall consist of 11 voting members selected by the Director for expertise in dam safety, of whom—

(A) 1 member shall represent the Department of Agriculture;

[1] So in original. Probably should be "an".

(B) 1 member shall represent the Department of Defense;

(C) 1 member shall represent the Department of the Interior;

(D) 1 member shall represent FEMA;

(E) 1 member shall represent the Federal Energy Regulatory Commission;

(F) 5 members shall be selected by the Director from among State dam safety officials; and

(G) 1 member shall be selected by the Director to represent the private sector.

(4) Nonvoting membership

The Director, in consultation with the Board, may invite a representative of the National Laboratories of the Department of Energy and may invite representatives from Federal or State agencies or dam safety experts, as needed, to participate in meetings of the Board.

(5) Duties

(A) In general

The Board shall encourage the establishment and maintenance of effective programs, policies, and guidelines to enhance dam safety for the protection of human life and property throughout the United States.

(B) Coordination and information exchange among agencies

In carrying out subparagraph (A), the Board shall encourage coordination and information exchange among Federal and State dam safety agencies that share common problems and responsibilities for dam safety, including planning, design, construction, operation, emergency action planning, inspections, maintenance, regulation or licensing, technical or financial assistance, research, and data management.

(6) Work groups

The Director may establish work groups under the Board to assist the Board in accomplishing its goals. The work groups shall consist of members of the Board and other individuals selected by the Director.

(7) Compensation of members

(A) Federal employees

Each member of the Board who is an officer or employee of the United States shall serve without compensation in addition to compensation received for the services of the member as an officer or employee of the United States.

(B) Other members

Each member of the Board who is not an officer or employee of the United States shall serve without compensation.

(8) Travel expenses

(A) Representatives of Federal agencies

To the extent amounts are made available in advance in appropriations Acts, each member of the Board who represents a Federal agency shall be reimbursed of appropriations for travel expenses by his or her agency, including per diem in lieu of subsistence, at rates authorized for an employee of an agency under subchapter I of chapter 57 of title 5, while away from the home or regular place of business of the member in the performance of services for the Board.

(B) Other individuals

To the extent amounts are made available in advance in appropriations Acts, each member of the Board who represents a State agency, the member of the Board who represents the private sector, and each member of a work group created under paragraph (1) shall be reimbursed for travel expenses by FEMA, including per diem in lieu of subsistence, at rates authorized for an employee of an agency under subchapter I of chapter 57 of title 5, while away from home or regular place of business of the member in performance of services for the Board.

(9) Applicability of Federal Advisory Committee Act

The Federal Advisory Committee Act (5 U.S.C. App.) shall not apply to the Board.

(Pub. L. 92–367, §8, as added Pub. L. 104–303, title II, §215(c)(8), Oct. 12, 1996, 110 Stat. 3688; amended Pub. L. 107–310, §3(a)–(e)(1), (f), (g), Dec. 2, 2002, 116 Stat. 2450, 2451; Pub. L. 109–460, §1(c), Dec. 22, 2006, 120 Stat. 3401.)

REFERENCES IN TEXT

The Federal Advisory Committee Act, referred to in subsec. (f)(9), is Pub. L. 92–463, Oct. 6, 1972, 86 Stat. 770, as amended, which is set out in the Appendix to Title 5, Government Organization and Employees.

PRIOR PROVISIONS

A prior section 467f, Pub. L. 92–367, §7, as added Pub. L. 99–662, title XII, §1201(b), Nov. 17, 1986, 100 Stat. 4260; amended Pub. L. 102–580, title II, §209(a), Oct. 31, 1992, 106 Stat. 4830, related to funding for State dam safety programs, prior to repeal by Pub. L. 104–303, title II, §215(c)(2), Oct. 12, 1996, 110 Stat. 3685.

A prior section 8 of Pub. L. 92–367 was classified to section 467g of this title prior to repeal by Pub. L. 104–303.

AMENDMENTS

2006—Subsec. (b)(1). Pub. L. 109–460, §1(c)(1), substituted "performance measures, and target dates toward effectively administering this subchapter in order to" for "and target dates to".

Subsec. (e)(2)(A). Pub. L. 109–460, §1(c)(2)(A), struck out "substantially" after "to include" in introductory provisions.

Subsec. (e)(2)(A)(iv) to (vi). Pub. L. 109–460, §1(c)(2)(B), (C), added cl. (iv) and redesignated former cls. (iv) and (v) as (v) and (vi), respectively. Former cl. (vi) redesignated (vii).

Subsec. (e)(2)(A)(vii). Pub. L. 109–460, §1(c)(2)(B), (D), redesignated cl. (vi) as (vii) and inserted "install and monitor instrumentation," after "remedial work,". Former cl. (vii) redesignated (viii).

Subsec. (e)(2)(A)(viii) to (xi). Pub. L. 109–460, §1(c)(2)(B), redesignated cls. (vii) to (x) as (viii) to (xi), respectively.

2002—Subsec. (a)(3)(B). Pub. L. 107–310, §3(a)(1), substituted "strategic plan described in subsection (b)" for "implementation plan described in subsection (e)".

Subsec. (a)(3)(C). Pub. L. 107–310, §3(a)(2), substituted "subsection (e)" for "subsection (f)".

Subsec. (b). Pub. L. 107–310, §3(b), amended heading and text of subsec. (b) generally. Prior to amendment, text read as follows: "The Director shall—

"(1) not later than 270 days after October 12, 1996, develop the implementation plan described in subsection (e) of this section;

"(2) not later than 300 days after October 12, 1996, submit to the appropriate authorizing committees of Congress the implementation plan described in subsection (e) of this section; and

"(3) by regulation, not later than 360 days after October 12, 1996—

"(A) develop and implement the Program;

"(B) establish goals, priorities, and target dates for implementation of the Program; and

"(C) to the extent feasible, provide a method for cooperation and coordination with, and assistance to, interested governmental entities in all States."

Subsec. (c)(7). Pub. L. 107–310, §3(c), added par. (7).

Subsec. (d)(3)(A). Pub. L. 107–310, §3(d), substituted "and shall be exercised by chairing the Board to coordinate national efforts to improve the safety of the dams in the United States" for "and shall be exercised by chairing ICODS to coordinate Federal efforts in cooperation with State dam safety officials".

Subsec. (e). Pub. L. 107–310, §3(e)(1), redesignated subsec. (f) as (e) and struck out heading and text of former subsec. (e). Text read as follows: "The Director shall—

"(1) develop an implementation plan for the Program that shall set, through fiscal year 2002, year-by-year targets that demonstrate improvements in dam safety; and

"(2) recommend appropriate roles for Federal agencies and for State and local units of government, individuals, and private organizations in carrying out the implementation plan."

Subsec. (e)(1). Pub. L. 107–310, §3(f)(1), substituted "the Director shall provide assistance with amounts made available under section 467j of this title to assist States in establishing, maintaining, and improving dam safety programs in accordance with the criteria specified in paragraph (2)." for "the Director shall provide assistance with amounts made available under section 467j of this title to assist States in establishing and maintaining dam safety programs—

"(A) in accordance with the criteria specified in paragraph (2); and

"(B) in accordance with more advanced requirements and standards established by the Board and the Director with the assistance of established criteria such as the Model State Dam Safety Program published by FEMA, numbered 123 and dated April 1987, and amendments to the Model State Dam Safety Program."

Subsec. (e)(2). Pub. L. 107–310, §3(f)(2)(A), in introductory provisions, struck out "primary" after "For a State to be eligible for" and ", and for a State to be eligible for advanced assistance under this subsection, a State dam safety program must meet the following criteria and budgeting requirement and be working toward meeting the advanced requirements and standards established under paragraph (1)(B)" before colon.

Subsec. (e)(2)(A). Pub. L. 107–310, §3(f)(2)(B)(i), substituted "A State" for "For a State to be eligible for assistance under this subsection, a State" in introductory provisions.

Subsec. (e)(2)(A)(vi). Pub. L. 107–310, §3(f)(2)(B)(ii), inserted "improve security," before "revise operating procedures,".

Subsec. (e)(3). Pub. L. 107–310, §3(f)(3), substituted "agreement" for "contract" in two places.

Subsec. (f). Pub. L. 107–310, §3(e)(1), redesignated subsec. (h) as (f). Former subsec. (f) redesignated (e).

Subsec. (f)(1). Pub. L. 107–310, §3(g)(1), substituted "The Director shall establish" for "The Director may establish" and "to monitor the safety of dams in the United States, to monitor State implementation of this section, and to advise the Director on national dam safety policy" for "to monitor State implementation of this section".

Subsec. (f)(3). Pub. L. 107–310, §3(g)(2)(A), (B), substituted "Voting membership" for "Membership" in heading and "11 voting members" for "11 members" in introductory provisions.

Subsec. (f)(3)(F), (G). Pub. L. 107–310, §3(g)(2)(C), added subpars. (F) and (G) and struck out former subpars. (F) and (G) which read as follows:

"(F) 5 members shall be selected by the Director from among dam safety officials of States; and

"(G) 1 member shall be selected by the Director to represent the United States Committee on Large Dams."

Subsec. (f)(4) to (6). Pub. L. 107–310, §3(g)(3)(B), added pars. (4) to (6). Former pars. (4) to (6) redesignated (7) to (9), respectively.

Subsec. (f)(7). Pub. L. 107–310, §3(g)(3)(A), redesignated par. (4) as (7).

Subsec. (f)(8). Pub. L. 107–310, §3(g)(4), added par. (8) and struck out heading and text of former par. (8). Text read as follows: "Each member of the Board shall be allowed travel expenses, including per diem in lieu of subsistence, at rates authorized for an employee of an agency under subchapter I of chapter 57 of title 5, while away from the home or regular place of business of the member in the performance of services for the Board."

Pub. L. 107–310, §3(g)(3)(A), redesignated par. (5) as (8).

Subsec. (f)(9). Pub. L. 107–310, §3(g)(3)(A), redesignated par. (6) as (9).

Subsec. (g). Pub. L. 107–310, §3(e)(1), struck out heading and text of subsec. (g). Text read as follows: "At the request of any State that has or intends to develop a State dam safety program, the Director shall provide training for State dam safety staff and inspectors."

Subsec. (h). Pub. L. 107–310, §3(e)(1), redesignated subsec. (h) as (f).

TRANSFER OF FUNCTIONS

For transfer of all functions, personnel, assets, components, authorities, grant programs, and liabilities of the Federal Emergency Management Agency, including the functions of the Under Secretary for Federal Emergency Management relating thereto, to the Federal Emergency Management Agency, see section 315(a)(1) of Title 6, Domestic Security.

For transfer of functions, personnel, assets, and liabilities of the Federal Emergency Management Agency, including the functions of the Director of the Federal Emergency Management Agency relating thereto, to the Secretary of Homeland Security, and for treatment of related references, see former section 313(1) and sections 551(d), 552(d), and 557 of Title 6, Domestic Security, and the Department of Homeland Security Reorganization Plan of November 25, 2002, as modified, set out as a note under section 542 of Title 6.

§467f–1. Lock and dam security

(a) Standards

The Secretary, in consultation with the Federal Emergency Management Agency, the Tennessee Valley Authority, and the Coast Guard, shall develop standards for the security of locks and dams, including the testing and certification of vessel exclusion barriers.

(b) Site surveys

At the request of a lock or dam owner, the Secretary shall provide technical assistance, on a reimbursable basis, to improve lock or dam security.

(c) Cooperative agreement

The Secretary may enter into a cooperative agreement with a nonprofit alliance of public and private organizations that has the mission of promoting safe waterways and seaports to carry out testing and certification activities, and to perform site surveys, under this section.

(d) Authorization of appropriations

There is authorized to be appropriated $3,000,000 to carry out this section.

(Pub. L. 110–114, title V, §5024, Nov. 8, 2007, 121 Stat. 1203.)

CODIFICATION

Section was enacted as part of the Water Resources Development Act of 2007, and not as part of the National Dam Safety Program Act which comprises this subchapter.

"SECRETARY" DEFINED

Secretary means the Secretary of the Army, see section 2 of Pub. L. 110–114, set out as a note under section 2201 of this title.

§ 467g. Research

(a) In general

The Director, in cooperation with the Board, shall carry out a program of technical and archival research to develop and support—

(1) improved techniques, historical experience, and equipment for rapid and effective dam construction, rehabilitation, and inspection;

(2) devices for the continued monitoring of the safety of dams;

(3) development and maintenance of information resources systems needed to support managing the safety of dams; and

(4) initiatives to guide the formulation of effective public policy and advance improvements in dam safety engineering, security, and management.

(b) Consultation

The Director shall provide for State participation in research under subsection (a) of this section and periodically advise all States and Congress of the results of the research.

(Pub. L. 92–367, §9, as added Pub. L. 104–303, title II, §215(c)(8), Oct. 12, 1996, 110 Stat. 3692; amended Pub. L. 107–310, §4, Dec. 2, 2002, 116 Stat. 2453.)

PRIOR PROVISIONS

A prior section 467g, Pub. L. 92–367, §8, as added Pub. L. 99–662, title XII, §1201(b), Nov. 17, 1986, 100 Stat. 4261, set out the requisite features of State dam safety programs and provided for program approval and periodic review, prior to repeal by Pub. L. 104–303, title II, §215(c)(2), Oct. 12, 1996, 110 Stat. 3685.

A prior section 9 of Pub. L. 92–367 was classified to section 467h of this title prior to repeal by Pub. L. 104–303.

AMENDMENTS

2002—Subsec. (a). Pub. L. 107–310, §4(1), in introductory provisions, substituted "in cooperation with the Board" for "in cooperation with ICODS" and inserted "and support" after "develop".

Subsec. (a)(3), (4). Pub. L. 107–310, §4(2)–(4), added pars. (3) and (4).

§ 467g–1. Dam safety training

At the request of any State that has or intends to develop a State dam safety program, the Director shall provide training for State dam safety staff and inspectors.

(Pub. L. 92–367, §10, as added Pub. L. 107–310, §5(2), Dec. 2, 2002, 116 Stat. 2453.)

PRIOR PROVISIONS

A prior section 10 of Pub. L. 92–367 was renumbered section 11, and is classified to section 467h of this title.

Another prior section 10 of Pub. L. 92–367 was classified to section 467i of this title prior to repeal by Pub. L. 104–303.

§ 467h. Reports

Not later than 90 days after the end of each odd-numbered fiscal year, the Director shall submit a report to Congress that—

(1) describes the status of the Program;

(2) describes the progress achieved by Federal agencies during the 2 preceding fiscal years in implementing the Federal Guidelines for Dam Safety;

(3) describes the progress achieved in dam safety by States participating in the Program; and

(4) includes any recommendations for legislative and other action that the Director considers necessary.

(Pub. L. 92–367, §11, formerly §10, as added Pub. L. 104–303, title II, §215(c)(8), Oct. 12, 1996, 110 Stat. 3692; renumbered §11 and amended Pub. L. 107–310, §§5(1), 6, Dec. 2, 2002, 116 Stat. 2453.)

PRIOR PROVISIONS

A prior section 467h, Pub. L. 92–367, §9, as added Pub. L. 99–662, title XII, §1201(b), Nov. 17, 1986, 100 Stat. 4262, provided for creation of National Dam Safety Review Board, prior to repeal by Pub. L. 104–303, title II, §215(c)(2), Oct. 12, 1996, 110 Stat. 3685.

A prior section 11 of Pub. L. 92–367 was renumbered section 12, and is classified to section 467i of this title.

Another prior section 11 of Pub. L. 92–367 was classified to section 467j of this title prior to repeal by Pub. L. 104–303.

AMENDMENTS

2002—Pub. L. 107–310, §6, struck out subsec. designations and headings for subsecs. (a) and (b) and text of subsec. (a) which read as follows: "Not later than 180 days after October 12, 1996, the Director shall report to Congress on the availability of dam insurance and make recommendations concerning encouraging greater availability."

§ 467i. Statutory construction

Nothing in this subchapter and no action or failure to act under this subchapter shall—

(1) create any liability in the United States or its officers or employees for the recovery of damages caused by such action or failure to act;

(2) relieve an owner or operator of a dam of the legal duties, obligations, or liabilities incident to the ownership or operation of the dam; or

(3) preempt any other Federal or State law.

(Pub. L. 92–367, §12, formerly §11, as added Pub. L. 104–303, title II, §215(c)(8), Oct. 12, 1996, 110 Stat. 3693; renumbered §12, Pub. L. 107–310, §5(1), Dec. 2, 2002, 116 Stat. 2453.)

PRIOR PROVISIONS

A prior section 467i, Pub. L. 92–367, §10, as added Pub. L. 99–662, title XII, §1201(b), Nov. 17, 1986, 100 Stat. 4262, related to consultation of Federal officers with State officials when dam operated or proposed by Federal agency is operated or proposed in a State, prior to repeal by Pub. L. 104–303, title II, §215(c)(2), Oct. 12, 1996, 110 Stat. 3685.

A prior section 12 of Pub. L. 92–367 was renumbered section 13, and is classified to section 467j of this title.

Another prior section 12 of Pub. L. 92–367 was classified to section 467k of this title prior to repeal by Pub. L. 104–303.

§ 467j. Authorization of appropriations

(a) National dam safety program

(1) Annual amounts

There are authorized to be appropriated to FEMA to carry out sections 467e, 467f, and 467h of this title (in addition to any amounts made available for similar purposes included in any other Act and amounts made available under subsections (b) through (e) of this section), $6,500,000 for fiscal year 2007, $7,100,000 for fiscal year 2008, $7,600,000 for fiscal year 2009, $8,300,000 for fiscal year 2010, and $9,200,000 for fiscal year 2011, to remain available until expended.

(2) Allocation

(A) In general

Subject to subparagraphs (B) and (C), for each fiscal year, amounts made available under this subsection to carry out section 467f of this title shall be allocated among the States as follows:

(i) One-third among States that qualify for assistance under section 467f(e) of this title.

(ii) Two-thirds among States that qualify for assistance under section 467f(e) of this title, to each such State in proportion to—

(I) the number of dams in the State that are listed as State-regulated dams on the inventory of dams maintained under section 467d of this title; as compared to

(II) the number of dams in all States that are listed as State-regulated dams on the inventory of dams maintained under section 467d of this title.

(B) Maximum amount of allocation

The amount of funds allocated to a State under this paragraph may not exceed 50 percent of the reasonable cost of implementing the State dam safety program.

(C) Determination

The Director and the Board shall determine the amount allocated to States.

(b) National dam inventory

There is authorized to be appropriated to carry out section 467d of this title $650,000 for fiscal year 2007, $700,000 for fiscal year 2008, $750,000 for fiscal year 2009, $800,000 for fiscal year 2010, and $850,000 for fiscal year 2011.

(c) Research

There is authorized to be appropriated to carry out section 467g of this title $1,600,000 for fiscal year 2007, $1,700,000 for fiscal year 2008, $1,800,000 for fiscal year 2009, $1,900,000 for fiscal year 2010, and $2,000,000 for fiscal year 2011, to remain until expended.

(d) Dam safety training

There is authorized to be appropriated to carry out section 467g–1 of this title $550,000 for fiscal year 2007, $600,000 for fiscal year 2008, $650,000 for fiscal year 2009, $700,000 for fiscal year 2010, and $750,000 for fiscal year 2011.

(e) Staff

There is authorized to be appropriated to FEMA for the employment of such additional staff personnel as are necessary to carry out sections 467f through 467g–1 of this title $700,000 for fiscal year 2007, $800,000 for fiscal year 2008, $900,000 for fiscal year 2009, $1,000,000 for fiscal year 2010, and $1,100,000 for fiscal year 2011.

(f) Limitation on use of amounts

Amounts made available under this subchapter may not be used to construct or repair any Federal or non-Federal dam.

(Pub. L. 92–367, § 13, formerly § 12, as added Pub. L. 104–303, title II, § 215(c)(8), Oct. 12, 1996, 110 Stat. 3693; renumbered § 13 and amended Pub. L. 107–310, §§ 5(1), 7, Dec. 2, 2002, 116 Stat. 2453; Pub. L. 109–460, § 1(d), Dec. 22, 2006, 120 Stat. 3401.)

PRIOR PROVISIONS

A prior section 467j, Pub. L. 92–367, § 11, as added Pub. L. 99–662, title XII, § 1201(b), Nov. 17, 1986, 100 Stat. 4262; amended Pub. L. 102–580, title II, § 209(b), Oct. 31, 1992, 106 Stat. 4830, related to training for State dam safety inspectors, prior to repeal by Pub. L. 104–303, title II, § 215(c)(2), Oct. 12, 1996, 110 Stat. 3685.

A prior section 13 of Pub. L. 92–367 was classified to section 467*l* of this title prior to repeal by Pub. L. 104–303.

AMENDMENTS

2006—Subsec. (a)(1). Pub. L. 109–460, § 1(d)(1), substituted "$6,500,000 for fiscal year 2007, $7,100,000 for fiscal year 2008, $7,600,000 for fiscal year 2009, $8,300,000 for fiscal year 2010, and $9,200,000 for fiscal year 2011" for "$6,000,000 for each of fiscal years 2003 through 2006".

Subsec. (b). Pub. L. 109–460, § 1(d)(2), substituted "$650,000 for fiscal year 2007, $700,000 for fiscal year 2008, $750,000 for fiscal year 2009, $800,000 for fiscal year 2010, and $850,000 for fiscal year 2011" for "$500,000 for each fiscal year".

Subsec. (c). Pub. L. 109–460, § 1(d)(3), substituted "$1,600,000 for fiscal year 2007, $1,700,000 for fiscal year 2008, $1,800,000 for fiscal year 2009, $1,900,000 for fiscal year 2010, and $2,000,000 for fiscal year 2011" for "$1,500,000 for each of fiscal years 2003 through 2006".

Subsec. (d). Pub. L. 109–460, § 1(d)(4), substituted "$550,000 for fiscal year 2007, $600,000 for fiscal year 2008, $650,000 for fiscal year 2009, $700,000 for fiscal year 2010, and $750,000 for fiscal year 2011" for "$500,000 for each of fiscal years 2003 through 2006".

Subsec. (e). Pub. L. 109–460, § 1(d)(5), substituted "$700,000 for fiscal year 2007, $800,000 for fiscal year 2008, $900,000 for fiscal year 2009, $1,000,000 for fiscal year 2010, and $1,100,000 for fiscal year 2011" for "$600,000 for each of fiscal years 2003 through 2006".

2002—Subsec. (a)(1). Pub. L. 107–310, § 7(a)(2), substituted "$6,000,000 for each of fiscal years 2003 through 2006, to remain available until expended" for "$1,000,000 for fiscal year 1998, $2,000,000 for fiscal year 1999, $4,000,000 for fiscal year 2000, $4,000,000 for fiscal year 2001, and $4,000,000 for fiscal year 2002".

Pub. L. 107–310, § 7(a)(1), made technical amendment to reference in original act which appears in text as reference to section 467h of this title.

Subsec. (a)(2)(A)(i), (ii). Pub. L. 107–310, § 7(b)(1), substituted "section 467f(e)" for "section 467f(f)".

Subsec. (a)(2)(C). Pub. L. 107–310, § 7(b)(2), struck out "needing primary assistance and States needing advanced assistance under section 467f(f) of this title" before period at end.

Subsecs. (c) to (e). Pub. L. 107–310, § 7(c), added subsecs. (c) to (e) and struck out former subsecs. (c) to (e) which authorized appropriations for fiscal years 1998 through 2002 for dam safety training, research, and staff.

TRANSFER OF FUNCTIONS

For transfer of all functions, personnel, assets, components, authorities, grant programs, and liabilities of the Federal Emergency Management Agency, including the functions of the Under Secretary for Federal Emergency Management relating thereto, to the Federal Emergency Management Agency, see section 315(a)(1) of Title 6, Domestic Security.

For transfer of functions, personnel, assets, and liabilities of the Federal Emergency Management Agency, including the functions of the Director of the Federal Emergency Management Agency relating thereto, to the Secretary of Homeland Security, and for treatment of related references, see former section 313(1) and sections 551(d), 552(d), and 557 of Title 6, Domestic Security, and the Department of Homeland Security Reorganization Plan of November 25, 2002, as modified, set out as a note under section 542 of Title 6.

§§ 467k to 467m. Repealed. Pub. L. 104–303, title II, § 215(c)(2), Oct. 12, 1996, 110 Stat. 3685

Section 467k, Pub. L. 92–367, § 12, as added Pub. L. 99–662, title XII, § 1201(b), Nov. 17, 1986, 100 Stat. 4262; amended Pub. L. 100–418, title V, § 5115(c), Aug. 23, 1988, 102 Stat. 1433; Pub. L. 102–580, title II, § 209(c), Oct. 31, 1992, 106 Stat. 4830, related to development of improved dam inspection techniques.

Section 467*l*, Pub. L. 92–367, § 13, as added Pub. L. 99–662, title XII, § 1201(b), Nov. 17, 1986, 100 Stat. 4262; amended Pub. L. 102–580, title II, § 209(d), Oct. 31, 1992, 106 Stat. 4830, related to dam inventory updates.

Section 467m, Pub. L. 92–367, § 14, as added Pub. L. 99–662, title XII, § 1201(b), Nov. 17, 1986, 100 Stat. 4263, provided that inspection funds were not to be used for repair or construction of any dam.

§ 467n. Recovery of dam modification costs required for safety purposes

(a) After November 17, 1986, costs incurred in the modification by the Secretary of dams and related facilities constructed or operated by the Secretary, the cause of which results from new hydrologic or seismic data or changes in state-of-the-art design or construction criteria deemed necessary for safety purposes, shall be recovered in accordance with the provisions in this subsection:

(1) Fifteen percent of the modification costs shall be assigned to project purposes in accordance with the cost allocation in effect for the project at the time the work is initiated. Non-Federal interests shall share the costs assigned to each purpose in accord with the cost sharing in effect at the time of initial project construction: *Provided*, That the Secretary of the Interior shall recover costs assigned to irrigation in accordance with repayment provisions of Public Law 98–404.

(2) Repayment under this subsection, with the exception of costs assigned to irrigation, may be made, with interest, over a period of not more than thirty years from the date of completion of the work. The interest rate used shall be determined by the Secretary of the Treasury, taking into consideration average market yields on outstanding marketable obligations of the United States with remaining periods to maturity comparable to the applicable reimbursable period during the month preceding the fiscal year in which the costs are incurred, plus a premium of one-eighth of one percentage point for transaction costs. To the extent that more than one interest rate is determined pursuant to the preceding sentence, the Secretary of the Treasury shall establish an interest rate at the weighted average of the rates so determined.

(b) Nothing in this section affects the authority of the Secretary to perform work pursuant to Public Law 84–99, as amended (33 U.S.C. 701n) or cost sharing for such work.

(Pub. L. 99–662, title XII, § 1203, Nov. 17, 1986, 100 Stat. 4263.)

References in Text

Public Law 98–404, referred to in subsec. (a)(1), is Pub. L. 98–404, Aug. 28, 1984, 98 Stat. 1481, known as The Reclamation Safety of Dams Act Amendments of 1984, which amended sections 508 and 509 of Title 43, Public Lands. For complete classification of this Act to the Code, see Short Title of 1984 Amendment note set out under section 506 of Title 43 and Tables.

Public Law 84–99, referred to in subsec. (b), is act June 28, 1955, ch. 194, 69 Stat. 186, which amended section 701n of this title.

Codification

Section was enacted as part of the Dam Safety Act of 1986, and also as part of the Water Resources Development Act of 1986, and not as part of the National Dam Safety Program Act which comprises this subchapter.

"Secretary" Defined

Secretary means the Secretary of the Army, see section 2201 of this title.

CHAPTER 10—ANCHORAGE GROUNDS AND HARBOR REGULATIONS GENERALLY

§ 471. Establishment by Secretary of Homeland Security of anchorage grounds and regulations generally

The Secretary of Homeland Security is authorized, empowered, and directed to define and establish anchorage grounds for vessels in all harbors, rivers, bays, and other navigable waters of the United States whenever it is manifest to the said Secretary that the maritime or commercial interests of the United States require such anchorage grounds for safe navigation and the establishment of such anchorage grounds shall have been recommended by the Chief of Engineers, and to adopt suitable rules and regulations in relation thereto; and such rules and regulations shall be enforced by the Coast Guard under the direction of the Secretary of Transportation: *Provided*, That at ports or places where there is no Coast Guard vessel available such rules and regulations may be enforced by the Chief of Engineers under the direction of the Secretary of Homeland Security. In the event of the violation of any such rules and regulations by the owner, master, or person in charge of any vessel, such owner, master, or person in charge of such vessel shall be liable to a penalty of $100; and the said vessel may be holden for the payment of such penalty, and may be seized and proceeded against summarily by libel for the recovery of the same in any United States district court for the district within which such vessel may be and in the name of the officer designated by the Secretary of Homeland Security.

(Mar. 4, 1915, ch. 142, §7, 38 Stat. 1053; Aug. 4, 1949, ch. 393, §§1, 20, 63 Stat. 496, 561; Pub. L. 89–670, §6(b)(1), Oct. 15, 1966, 80 Stat. 938; Pub. L. 97–449, §2(d)(1), Jan. 12, 1983, 96 Stat. 2440; Pub. L. 109–241, title IX, §902(j), July 11, 2006, 120 Stat. 568.)

CODIFICATION

Section was from the Rivers and Harbors Appropriation Act of 1915.

PRIOR PROVISIONS

Section probably supersedes acts May 16, 1888, ch. 257, §§1, 2, 25 Stat. 151, relative to anchorage grounds in port of New York, Mar. 3, 1899, ch. 424, §1, 30 Stat. 1074, extending anchorage regulations for port of New York, Feb. 6, 1893, ch. 64, §§1, 2, 27 Stat. 431, relative to anchorage grounds in port of Chicago, and June 6, 1900, ch. 819, §§1, 2, 31 Stat. 682, relative to anchorage grounds in Kennebec River.

AMENDMENTS

2006—Pub. L. 109–241 substituted "Secretary of Homeland Security" for "Secretary of Transportation" wherever appearing in the original.

1983—Pub. L. 97–449 substituted "Secretary of Transportation" for "Secretary of War" wherever appearing. See Transfer of Functions note below.

TRANSFER OF FUNCTIONS

"Coast Guard" and "Coast Guard vessel" substituted in text for "Revenue Cutter Service" and "revenue cutter", respectively, the Revenue Cutter Service and Life-Saving Service having been combined to form the Coast Guard by act Jan. 28, 1915, ch. 20, §1, 38 Stat. 800. That act was repealed by act Aug. 4, 1949, ch. 393, §20, 63 Stat. 561, section 1 of which reestablished the Coast Guard by enacting Title 14, Coast Guard.

"Secretary of Transportation" substituted for "Secretary of the Treasury" in provision covering enforcement of rules and regulations by Coast Guard pursuant to section 6(b)(1) of Pub. L. 89–670, which transferred to Secretary of Transportation functions, powers, and duties of Secretary of the Treasury and of other offices and officers of Department of the Treasury relating to Coast Guard. Section 6(b)(2) of Pub. L. 89–670, however, provided that notwithstanding such transfer of functions, the Coast Guard shall operate as part of the Navy in time of war or when President directs as provided in section 3 of Title 14, Coast Guard. See section 108 of Title 49, Transportation. For subsequent transfers relating to the Secretary of Transportation and the Coast Guard, see below.

Section 6(g)(1)(A) of Pub. L. 89–670, transferred functions, powers, and duties of Secretary of the Army [formerly War] and other officers and offices of Department of the Army [formerly War] relating generally to water vessel anchorages under this section to Secretary of Transportation. Pub. L. 97–449 amended this section to reflect the transfer made by section 6(g)(1)(A) of Pub. L. 89–670, and repealed section 6(g)(1)(A).

For transfer of authorities, functions, personnel, and assets of the Coast Guard, including the authorities and functions of the Secretary of Transportation relating thereto, to the Department of Homeland Security, and for treatment of related references, see sections 468(b), 551(d), 552(d), and 557 of Title 6, Domestic Security, and the Department of Homeland Security Reorganization Plan of November 25, 2002, as modified, set out as a note under section 542 of Title 6.

§472. Marking anchorage grounds by Commandant of the Coast Guard

The Commandant of the Coast Guard shall provide, establish, and maintain, out of the annual appropriations for the Coast Guard, buoys or other suitable marks for marking anchorage grounds for vessels in waters of the United States, when such anchorage grounds have been defined and established by proper authority in accordance with the laws of the United States.

(Sept. 15, 1922, ch. 313, 42 Stat. 844; 1939 Reorg. Plan No. II, §2(a), eff. July 1, 1939, 4 F.R. 2731, 53 Stat. 1432.)

TRANSFER OF FUNCTIONS

"Commandant of the Coast Guard" and "Coast Guard" substituted in text for "Commissioner of Lighthouses" and "Lighthouse Service", respectively, on authority of Reorg. Plan No. II of 1939, §2(a), set out in the Appendix to Title 5, Government Organization and Employees, which transferred and consolidated the Bureau of Lighthouses (of which the Lighthouse Service was a part and of which the Commissioner of Lighthouses was the head) and its functions with the Coast Guard (of which the Commandant was the Chief).

For transfer of functions of other officers, employees, and agencies of Department of the Treasury, with certain exceptions, to Secretary of the Treasury with power to delegate, see Reorg. Plan No. 26 of 1950, §§1, 2, eff. July 31, 1950, 15 F.R. 4935, 64 Stat. 1280, 1281, set out in the Appendix to Title 5, Government Organization and Employees. Functions of Coast Guard, and Commandant of Coast Guard, excepted from transfer when Coast Guard is operating as part of Navy under sections 1 and 3 of Title 14, Coast Guard.

Coast Guard transferred to Department of Transportation, and functions, powers, and duties relating to Coast Guard of Secretary of the Treasury and of other officers and offices of Department of the Treasury transferred to Secretary of Transportation by Pub. L. 89–670, §6(b)(1), Oct. 15, 1966, 80 Stat. 938. Section 6(b)(2) of Pub. L. 89–670, however, provided that notwithstanding such transfer of functions, Coast Guard shall operate as part of the Navy in time of war or when President directs as provided in section 3 of Title 14, Coast Guard. See section 108 of Title 49, Transportation.

For transfer of authorities, functions, personnel, and assets of the Coast Guard, including the authorities and functions of the Secretary of Transportation relating thereto, to the Department of Homeland Security, and for treatment of related references, see sections 468(b), 551(d), 552(d), and 557 of Title 6, Domestic Security, and the Department of Homeland Security Reorganization Plan of November 25, 2002, as modified, set out as a note under section 542 of Title 6.

§473. Repealed. Pub. L. 89–554, §8(a), Sept. 6, 1966, 80 Stat. 637

Section, act Mar. 2, 1895, ch. 172, §2, 28 Stat. 740, provided that the powers and authority conferred upon the harbor master, District of Columbia, may in his absence or disability be exercised by the pilot of the harbor police boat.

§474. Anchorage and general regulations for St. Marys River

The Commandant of the Coast Guard is authorized and directed to adopt and prescribe suitable rules and regulations governing the movements and anchorage of vessels and rafts in Saint Marys River from Point Iroquois, on Lake Superior, to Point Detour, on Lake Huron, and for the purpose of enforcing the observance of such regulations the Secretary of Transportation is authorized to detail one or more Coast Guard vessels for duty upon the request of the Commandant of the Coast Guard on said river.

All officers of the Coast Guard who are directed to enforce the regulations prescribed by the above rules are empowered and directed, in case of necessity, or when a proper notice has been disregarded, to use the force at their command to remove from channels or stop any vessel found violating the prescribed rules.

In the event of the violation of any such regulations or rules of the Commandant of the Coast Guard by the owners, master, or person in charge of such vessel, such owners, master, or person in charge shall be liable to a penalty not exceeding $200: *Provided*, That the Commandant of the Coast Guard may remit said fine on such terms as he may prescribe: *Provided also*, That nothing in this section shall be construed to amend or repeal chapter[1] 4 of this title.

(Mar. 6, 1896, ch. 49, §§ 1–3, 29 Stat. 54, 55; Apr. 26, 1906, ch. 1874, §§ 1, 2, 34 Stat. 136; Mar. 4, 1913, ch. 141, § 1, 37 Stat. 736; 1946 Reorg. Plan No. 3, §§ 101–104, eff. July 16, 1946, 11 F.R. 7875, 60 Stat. 1097; Oct. 14, 1949, ch. 393, §§ 1, 20, 63 Stat. 496, 561; Pub. L. 89–670, § 6(b)(1), Oct. 15, 1966, 80 Stat. 938.)

REFERENCES IN TEXT

Chapter 4 of this title, referred to in last par., was in the original "the Act entitled 'An Act to regulate navigation on the Great Lakes, and their connecting and tributary waters as far east as Montreal,' approved February eighth, eighteen hundred and ninety-five", which was classified generally to chapter 4 (§ 241 et seq.) of this title and was repealed by Pub. L. 96–591, § 8(b), Dec. 24, 1980, 94 Stat. 3435, eff. Mar. 1, 1983, pursuant to 47 F.R. 15135, Apr. 8, 1982. See section 7 of Pub. L. 96–591, set out as an Effective Date note under section 2001 of this title.

TRANSFER OF FUNCTIONS

"Coast Guard vessels" and "Coast Guard" substituted in text for "revenue cutters" and "Revenue-Cutter Service", respectively, the Revenue Cutter Service and Life-Saving Service having been combined to form the Coast Guard by act Jan. 28, 1915, ch. 20, § 1, 38 Stat. 800. That act was repealed by act Aug. 4, 1949, ch. 393, § 20, 63 Stat. 561, section 1 of which reestablished the Coast Guard by enacting Title 14, Coast Guard.

Secretary of Commerce and Labor designated Secretary of Commerce by act Mar. 4, 1913, which created Department of Labor.

Functions of Secretary of Commerce under this section transferred to Commandant of Coast Guard by Reorg. Plan No. 3 of 1946, §§ 101–104, set out in the Appendix to Title 5, Government Organization and Employees.

For transfer of functions of other officers, employees, and agencies of Department of the Treasury, with certain exceptions, to Secretary of the Treasury with power to delegate, see Reorg. Plan No. 26 of 1950, §§ 1, 2, eff. July 31, 1950, 15 F.R. 4935, 64 Stat. 1280, 1281, set out in the Appendix to Title 5, Government Organization and Employees. Functions of Coast Guard, and Commandant of Coast Guard, excepted from transfer when Coast Guard is operating as part of Navy under sections 1 and 3 of Title 14, Coast Guard.

Coast Guard transferred to Department of Transportation, and functions, powers, and duties relating to Coast Guard of Secretary of the Treasury and of other officers and offices of Department of the Treasury transferred to Secretary of Transportation by Pub. L. 89–670, § 6(b)(1), Oct. 15, 1966, 80 Stat. 938. Section 6(b)(2) of Pub. L. 89–670, however, provided that notwithstanding such transfer of functions, Coast Guard shall operate as part of Navy in time of war or when President directs as provided in section 3 of Title 14, Coast Guard. See section 108 of Title 49, Transportation.

For transfer of authorities, functions, personnel, and assets of the Coast Guard, including the authorities and functions of the Secretary of Transportation relating thereto, to the Department of Homeland Security, and for treatment of related references, see sections 468(b), 551(d), 552(d), and 557 of Title 6, Domestic Security, and the Department of Homeland Security Reorganization Plan of November 25, 2002, as modified, set out as a note under section 542 of Title 6.

§ 475. Regulations for Pearl Harbor, Hawaii

For the proper control, protection, and defense of the naval station, harbor, and entrance channel at Pearl Harbor, Territory of Hawaii, the Secretary of the Navy is authorized, empowered, and directed to adopt and prescribe suitable rules and regulations governing the navigation, movement, and anchorage of vessels of whatsoever character in the waters of Pearl Harbor, island of Oahu, Hawaiian Islands, and in the entrance channel to said harbor, and to take all necessary measures for the proper enforcement of such rules and regulations.

(Aug. 22, 1912, ch. 335, 37 Stat. 341.)

CODIFICATION

Section is from the Naval Appropriation Act for 1913.

ADMISSION OF HAWAII AS STATE

Admission of Hawaii into the Union was accomplished Aug. 21, 1959, on issuance of Proc. No. 3309, Aug. 21, 1959, 24 F.R. 6868, 73 Stat. c74, as required by sections 1 and 7(c) of Pub. L. 86–3, Mar. 18, 1959, 73 Stat. 4, set out as notes preceding section 491 of Title 48, Territories and Insular Possessions.

§ 476. Restrictions on tanker traffic in Puget Sound and adjacent waters

(a) The Congress finds that—

(1) the navigable waters of Puget Sound in the State of Washington, and the natural resources therein, are a fragile and important national asset;

(2) Puget Sound and the shore area immediately adjacent thereto is threatened by increased domestic and international traffic of tankers carrying crude oil in bulk which increases the possibility of vessel collisions and oil spills; and

(3) it is necessary to restrict such tanker traffic in Puget Sound in order to protect the navigable waters thereof, the natural resources therein, and the shore area immediately adjacent thereto, from environmental harm.

(b) Notwithstanding any other provision of law, on and after October 18, 1977, no officer, employee, or other official of the Federal Government shall, or shall have authority to, issue, renew, grant, or otherwise approve any permit, license, or other authority for constructing, renovating, modifying, or otherwise altering a terminal, dock, or other facility in, on, or immediately adjacent to, or affecting the navigable waters of Puget Sound, or any other navigable waters in the State of Washington east of Port Angeles, which will or may result in any increase in the volume of crude oil capable of being handled at any such facility (measured as of October 18, 1977), other than oil to be refined for consumption in the State of Washington.

(Pub. L. 95–136, § 5, Oct. 18, 1977, 91 Stat. 1168.)

[1] See References in Text note below.

CHAPTER 11—BRIDGES OVER NAVIGABLE WATERS

SUBCHAPTER I—GENERAL PROVISIONS

SUBCHAPTER I—GENERAL PROVISIONS

§491. Approval of and deviation from plans; exemptions

When, after March 23, 1906, authority is granted by Congress to any persons to construct and maintain a bridge across or over any of the navigable waters of the United States, such bridge shall not be built or commenced until the plans and specifications for its construction, together with such drawings of the proposed construction and such map of the proposed location as may be required for a full understanding of the subject, have been submitted to the Secretary of Transportation for the Secretary's approval, nor until the Secretary shall have approved such plans and specifications and the location of such bridge and accessory works; and when the plans for any bridge to be constructed under the provisions of sections 491 to 498 of this title, have been approved by the Secretary it shall not be lawful to deviate from such plans, either before or after completion of the structure, unless the modification of such plans has previously been submitted to and received the approval of the Secretary. This section shall not apply to any bridge over waters which are not subject to the ebb and flow of the tide and which are not used and are not susceptible to use in their natural condition or by reasonable improvement as a means to transport interstate or foreign commerce.

(Mar. 23, 1906, ch. 1130, §1, 34 Stat. 84; Pub. L. 97–322, title I, §107(c), Oct. 15, 1982, 96 Stat. 1582; Pub. L. 97–449, §2(d)(1), Jan. 12, 1983, 96 Stat. 2440; Pub. L. 98–557, §17(g)(1), Oct. 30, 1984, 98 Stat. 2869.)

AMENDMENTS

1984—Pub. L. 98–557 substituted "for the Secretary's approval, nor until the Secretary" for "and Chief of Engineers for their approval, nor until they" and struck out "by the Chief of Engineers and" after "have been approved", "of the Chief of Engineers and" after "received the approval", and "of Transportation" after "by the Secretary" and after "of the Secretary".

1983—Pub. L. 97–449 substituted "Secretary of Transportation" for "Secretary of War" wherever appearing. See Transfer of Functions note below.

1982—Pub. L. 97–322 inserted sentence at end relating to exemption.

SHORT TITLE

Sections 491 to 498 of this title are popularly known as the "Bridge Act of 1906" and the "General Bridge Act of 1906".

TRANSFER OF FUNCTIONS

Functions, powers, and duties of Secretary of the Army [formerly War] and other offices and officers of Department of the Army [formerly War] under this section to extent that they relate generally to location and clearances of bridges and causeways in navigable waters of United States transferred to and vested in

Secretary of Transportation by Pub. L. 89–670, § 6(g)(6)(B), Oct. 15, 1966, 80 Stat. 941. Pub. L. 97–449 amended this section to reflect transfer made by section 6(g)(6)(B) of Pub. L. 89–670, and repealed section 6(g)(6)(B).

§ 492. Bridge as post route; limitation as to charges against Government; telegraph and telephone lines

Any bridge built in accordance with the provisions of sections 491 to 498 of this title, shall be a lawful structure and shall be recognized and known as a post route, upon which no higher charge shall be made for the transmission over the same of the mails, the troops, and the munitions of war of the United States than the rate per mile paid for the transportation over any railroad, street railway, or public highway leading to said bridge; and the United States shall have the right to construct, maintain, and repair, without any charge therefor, telegraph and telephone lines across and upon said bridge and its approaches; and equal privileges in the use of said bridge and its approaches shall be granted to all telegraph and telephone companies.

(Mar. 23, 1906, ch. 1130, § 2, 34 Stat. 85.)

§ 493. Use of railroad bridges by other railroad companies

All railroad companies desiring the use of any railroad bridge built in accordance with the provisions of sections 491 to 498 of this title, shall be entitled to equal rights and privileges relative to the passage of railway trains or cars over the same and over the approaches thereto upon payment of a reasonable compensation for such use; and in case of any disagreement between the parties in regard to the terms of such use or the sums to be paid all matters at issue shall be determined by the Secretary of Transportation upon hearing the allegations and proofs submitted to him.

(Mar. 23, 1906, ch. 1130, § 3, 34 Stat. 85; Pub. L. 97–449, § 2(d)(1), Jan. 12, 1983, 96 Stat. 2440.)

Amendments

1983—Pub. L. 97–449 substituted "Secretary of Transportation" for "Secretary of War". See Transfer of Functions note below.

Transfer of Functions

Functions, powers, and duties of Secretary of the Army [formerly War] and other offices and officers of Department of the Army [formerly War] under this section to extent that they relate generally to location and clearances of bridges and causeways in navigable waters of United States transferred to and vested in Secretary of Transportation by Pub. L. 89–670, § 6(g)(6)(B), Oct. 15, 1966, 80 Stat. 941. Pub. L. 97–449 amended this section to reflect transfer made by section 6(g)(6)(B) of Pub. L. 89–670, and repealed section 6(g)(6)(B).

§ 494. Obstruction of navigation; alterations and removals; lights and signals; draws

No bridge erected or maintained under the provisions of sections 491 to 498 of this title, shall at any time unreasonably obstruct the free navigation of the waters over which it is constructed, and if any bridge erected in accordance with the provisions of said sections, shall, in the opinion of the Secretary of Homeland Security at any time unreasonably obstruct such navigation, either on account of insufficient height, width of span, or otherwise, or if there be difficulty in passing the draw opening or the drawspan of such bridge by rafts, steamboats, or other water craft, it shall be the duty of the Secretary of Homeland Security after giving the parties interested reasonable opportunity to be heard, to notify the persons owning or controlling such bridge to so alter the same as to render navigation through or under it reasonably free, easy, and unobstructed, stating in such notice the changes required to be made, and prescribing in each case a reasonable time in which to make such changes, and if at the end of the time so specified the changes so required have not been made, the persons owning or controlling such bridge shall be deemed guilty of a violation of said sections; and all such alterations shall be made and all such obstructions shall be removed at the expense of the persons owning or operating said bridge. The persons owning or operating any such bridge shall maintain, at their own expense, such lights and other signals thereon as the Commandant of the Coast Guard shall prescribe. If the bridge shall be constructed with a draw, then the draw shall be opened promptly by the persons owning or operating such bridge upon reasonable signal for the passage of boats and other water craft.

(Mar. 23, 1906, ch. 1130, § 4, 34 Stat. 85; Mar. 4, 1913, ch. 141, § 1, 37 Stat. 736; 1946 Reorg. Plan No. 3, §§ 101–104, eff. July 16, 1946, 11 F.R. 7875, 60 Stat. 1097; Pub. L. 97–449, § 2(d)(1), Jan. 12, 1983, 96 Stat. 2440; Pub. L. 100–17, title I, § 135(a), Apr. 2, 1987, 101 Stat. 173; Pub. L. 109–241, title IX, § 902(k), July 11, 2006, 120 Stat. 568.)

Prior Provisions

Act July 5, 1884, ch. 229, § 8, 23 Stat. 148, relating to authority of Secretary of War to require owners of bridges which obstruct navigation to relieve the situation or be penalized, was probably omitted from the Code as superseded by this section and section 495 of this title, which by section 498b of this title were made applicable to bridges authorized prior to March 23, 1906.

Section would seem to supersede a provision of act Aug. 7, 1882, ch. 433, § 1, 22 Stat. 309, which read as follows: "That all parties owning, occupying, or operating bridges over any navigable river shall maintain at their own expense, from sunset to sunrise, throughout the year, such lights on their bridges as may be required by the Light-House Board for the security of navigation: and in addition thereto all persons owning, occupying, or operating any bridge over any navigable river shall, in any event, maintain all lights on their bridge that may be necessary for the security of navigation."

Amendments

2006—Pub. L. 109–241, which directed substitution of "Secretary of Homeland Security" for "Secretary of Transportation", was executed by making the substitution both places "Secretary of Transportation" appeared, to reflect the probable intent of Congress.

1987—Pub. L. 100–17 struck out last sentence relating to tolls.

1983—Pub. L. 97–449 substituted "Secretary of Transportation" for "Secretary of War" wherever appearing. See Transfer of Functions note below.

Transfer of Functions

For transfer of authorities, functions, personnel, and assets of the Coast Guard, including the authorities and functions of the Secretary of Transportation relating thereto, to the Department of Homeland Security, and for treatment of related references, see sections 468(b), 551(d), 552(d), and 557 of Title 6, Domestic Security, and the Department of Homeland Security Reorganization Plan of November 25, 2002, as modified, set out as a note under section 542 of Title 6.

Functions, powers, and duties of Secretary of the Army [formerly War] and other offices and officers of Department of the Army [formerly War] relating to reasonableness of tolls and to location and clearances of bridges and causeways in navigable waters of United States under this section transferred to and vested in Secretary of Transportation by section 6(g)(4)(A), (6)(B) of Pub. L. 89–670. Pub. L. 97–449 amended this section to reflect transfer made by section 6(g)(4)(A), (6)(B) of Pub. L. 89–670, and repealed section 6(g)(4)(A), (6)(B).

Coast Guard transferred to Department of Transportation, and functions, powers, and duties relating to Coast Guard of Secretary of the Treasury and of other officers and offices of Department of the Treasury transferred to Secretary of Transportation by Pub. L. 89–670, §6(b)(1), Oct. 15, 1966, 80 Stat. 938. Section 6(b)(2) of Pub. L. 89–670, however, provided that notwithstanding such transfer of functions, Coast Guard shall operate as part of Navy in time of war or when the President directs as provided in section 3 of Title 14, Coast Guard. See section 108 of Title 49, Transportation.

For transfer of functions of other officers, employees, and agencies of Department of the Treasury, with certain exceptions, to Secretary of the Treasury with power to delegate, see Reorg. Plan No. 26 of 1950, §§1, 2, eff. July 31, 1950, 15 F.R. 4935, 64 Stat. 1280, 1281, set out in the Appendix to Title 5, Government Organization and Employees. Functions of Coast Guard, and Commandant of Coast Guard, excepted from transfer when Coast Guard is operating as part of Navy under sections 1 and 3 of Title 14, Coast Guard.

"Commandant of the Coast Guard" substituted in text for "Secretary of Commerce" on authority of Reorg. Plan No. 3 of 1946, §§101 to 104, set out in the Appendix to Title 5, Government Organization and Employees.

Secretary of Commerce and Labor redesignated Secretary of Labor by act Mar. 4, 1913, which enacted Department of Labor.

CONNECTICUT RIVER BRIDGES

Acts Aug. 7, 1939, ch. 503, 53 Stat. 1234, and Apr. 24, 1946, ch. 214, 60 Stat. 122, were amended by act Aug. 9, 1955, ch. 631, 69 Stat. 552, to provide that the last sentence of this section should not be applicable to bridges constructed pursuant to acts Aug. 7, 1939 and Apr. 24, 1946.

§495. Violations of orders respecting bridges and accessory works

(a) Criminal penalties for violation; misdemeanor; fine; new offenses; jurisdiction: suits for recovery of removal expenses, enforcement of removal, and obstruction-to-navigation causes or questions

Any persons who shall willfully fail or refuse to comply with the lawful order of the Secretary of Transportation or the Chief of Engineers, made in accordance with the provisions of sections 491 to 498 of this title, shall be deemed guilty of a misdemeanor and on conviction thereof shall be punished in any court of competent jurisdiction by a fine not exceeding $5,000, and every month such persons shall remain in default shall be deemed a new offense and subject such persons to additional penalties therefor; and in addition to the penalties above described the Secretary of Transportation and the Chief of Engineers may, upon refusal of the persons owning or controlling any such bridge and accessory works to comply with any lawful order issued by the Secretary of Transportation or Chief of Engineers in regard thereto, cause the removal of such bridge and accessory works at the expense of the persons owning or controlling such bridge, and suit for such expense may be brought in the name of the United States against such persons, and recovery had for such expense in any court of competent jurisdiction; and the removal of any structures erected or maintained in violation of the provisions of said sections, or the order or direction of the Secretary of Transportation or Chief of Engineers made in pursuance thereof may be enforced by injunction, mandamus, or other summary process, upon application to the district court in the district in which such structure may, in whole or in part, exist, and proper proceedings to this end may be instituted under the direction of the Attorney General of the United States at the request of the Secretary of Transportation; and in case of any litigation arising from any obstruction or alleged obstruction to navigation created by the construction of any bridge under said sections, the cause or question arising may be tried before the district court of the United States in any district which any portion of said obstruction or bridge touches.

(b) Civil penalties for violation; separate offenses; notice and hearing; assessment, collection, and remission; civil actions

Whoever violates any provision of sections 491 to 498 of this title, or any order issued under sections 491 to 498 of this title, shall be liable to a civil penalty of not more than $5,000 for a violation occurring in 2004; $10,000 for a violation occurring in 2005; $15,000 for a violation occurring in 2006; $20,000 for a violation occurring in 2007; and $25,000 for a violation occurring in 2008 and any year thereafter. Each day a violation continues shall be deemed a separate offense. No penalty may be assessed under this subsection until the person charged is given notice and an opportunity for a hearing on the charge. The Secretary of Transportation may assess and collect any civil penalty incurred under this subsection and, in his discretion, may remit, mitigate, or compromise any penalty until the matter is referred to the Attorney General. If a person against whom a civil penalty is assessed under this subsection fails to pay that penalty, an action may be commenced in the district court of the United States for any district in which the violation occurs for such penalty.

(Mar. 23, 1906, ch. 1130, §5, 34 Stat. 85; Mar. 3, 1911, ch. 231, §§289, 291, 36 Stat. 1167; Pub. L. 97–322, title I, §108(c), Oct. 15, 1982, 96 Stat. 1584; Pub. L. 97–449, §2(d)(1), Jan. 12, 1983, 96 Stat. 2440; Pub. L. 108–293, title VI, §601(a), Aug. 9, 2004, 118 Stat. 1050.)

CODIFICATION

The words "district court" were substituted for "circuit court," upon incorporation into the Code, the Circuit Courts being abolished by act Mar. 3, 1911, and their powers and duties transferred to the district courts by section 291 of that act.

AMENDMENTS

2004—Subsec. (b). Pub. L. 108–293 substituted "$5,000 for a violation occurring in 2004; $10,000 for a violation occurring in 2005; $15,000 for a violation occurring in 2006; $20,000 for a violation occurring in 2007; and $25,000 for a violation occurring in 2008 and any year thereafter" for "$1,000".

1983—Subsec. (a). Pub. L. 97–449 substituted "Secretary of Transportation" for "Secretary of War" wherever appearing. See Transfer of Functions note below.

1982—Subsec. (a). Pub. L. 97–322, § 108(c)(1)–(3), designated existing provisions as subsec. (a), provided for punishment of persons who shall "willfully" fail to comply with lawful orders, and struck out "shall be deemed guilty of a violation of said sections, and any persons who shall be guilty of a violation of said sections" after "sections 491 to 498 of this title,".

Subsec. (b). Pub. L. 97–322, § 108(c)(4), added subsec. (b).

TRANSFER OF FUNCTIONS

Functions, powers, and duties of Secretary of the Army [formerly War] and other offices and officers of Department the Army [formerly War] under this section to extent that they relate generally to location and clearances of bridges and causeways in navigable waters of United States transferred to and vested in Secretary of Transportation by Pub. L. 89–670, § 6(g)(6)(B), Oct. 15, 1966, 80 Stat. 941. Pub. L. 97–449 amended this section to reflect transfer made by section 6(g)(6)(B) of Pub. L. 89–670, and repealed section 6(g)(6)(B).

§ 496. Time for commencement and completion of bridge

Whenever Congress shall after March 23, 1906, by law authorize the construction of any bridge over or across any of the navigable waters of the United States, and no time for the commencement and completion of such bridge is named in said Act, the authority thereby granted shall cease and be null and void unless the actual construction of the bridge authorized in such Act be commenced within one year and completed within three years from the date of the passage of such Act.

(Mar. 23, 1906, ch. 1130, § 6, 34 Stat. 86.)

§ 497. "Persons" defined

The word "persons" as used in sections 491 to 498 of this title, shall be construed to import both the singular and the plural, as the case demands, and shall include municipalities, quasi-municipal corporations, corporations, companies, and associations.

(Mar. 23, 1906, ch. 1130, § 7, 34 Stat. 86.)

§ 498. Reservation of right to alter or repeal

The right to alter, amend, or repeal sections 491 to 498 of this title, is expressly reserved as to any and all bridges which may be built in accordance with the provisions of said sections, and the United States shall incur no liability for the alteration, amendment, or repeal thereof to the owner or owners or any other persons interested in any bridge which shall have been constructed in accordance with its provisions.

(Mar. 23, 1906, ch. 1130, § 8, 34 Stat. 86.)

§ 498a. Repealed. Pub. L. 100–17, title I, § 135(b), Apr. 2, 1987, 101 Stat. 174

Section, act June 10, 1930, ch. 441, § 17, 46 Stat. 552, provided that, in the case of bridges authorized prior to June 10, 1930, by Acts of Congress, where Congress has specifically reserved the right to regulate tolls, such bridges, with respect to regulation of all tolls, be subject to sections 491 to 498 of this title.

§ 498b. Repealed. Pub. L. 100–17, title I, § 135(c), Apr. 2, 1987, 101 Stat. 174

Section, act June 27, 1930, ch. 640, § 1, 46 Stat. 821, provided that, in case of any bridge authorized prior to Mar. 23, 1906, by Act of Congress, where Congress has specifically reserved the right to alter, amend, or repeal such Act, regulation of all tolls be subject to sections 491 to 498 of this title.

§ 499. Regulations for drawbridges

(a) Criminal penalties for violations; enforcement; rules and regulations

It shall be the duty of all persons owning, operating, and tending the drawbridges built prior to August 18, 1894, or which may thereafter be built across the navigable rivers and other waters of the United States, to open, or cause to be opened, the draws of such bridges under such rules and regulations as in the opinion of the Secretary of Transportation the public interests require to govern the opening of drawbridges for the passage of vessels and other water crafts, and such rules and regulations, when so made and published, shall have the force of law. Every such person who shall willfully fail or refuse to open, or cause to be opened, the draw of any such bridge for the passage of a boat or boats, as provided in such regulations, shall be deemed guilty of a misdemeanor, and on conviction thereof shall be punished by a fine of not more than $2,000 nor less than $1,000, or by imprisonment (in the case of a natural person) for not exceeding one year, or by both such fine and imprisonment, in the discretion of the court: *Provided*, That the proper action to enforce the provisions of this subsection may be commenced before any magistrate judge, judge, or court of the United States, and such magistrate judge, judge, or court shall proceed in respect thereto as authorized by law in case of crimes against the United States: *Provided further*, That whenever, in the opinion of the Secretary of Transportation, the public interests require it, he may make rules and regulations to govern the opening of drawbridges for the passage of vessels and other water crafts, and such rules and regulations, when so made and published, shall have the force of law, and any willful violation thereof shall be punished as hereinbefore provided: *Provided further*, That any regulations made in pursuance of this section may be enforced as provided in section 413 of this title, the provisions whereof are made applicable to the said regulations. Any rules and regulations made in pursuance of this section shall, to the extent practical and feasible, provide for regularly scheduled openings of drawbridges during seasons of the year, and during times of the day, when scheduled openings would help reduce motor vehicle traffic delays and congestion on roads and highways linked by drawbridges.

(b) Nonstructural vessel appurtenances; unreasonable delays

No vessel owner or operator shall signal a drawbridge to open for any nonstructural vessel appurtenance which is not essential to navigation or which is easily lowered and no person shall unreasonably delay the opening of a draw after the signal required by rules or regulations under this section has been given. The Secretary of Transportation shall issue rules and regulations to implement this subsection.

(c) Civil penalties for violation; notice and hearing; assessment, collection, and remission; civil actions

Whoever violates any rule or regulation issued under subsection (a) or (b) of this section, shall be liable to a civil penalty of not more than $5,000 for a violation occurring in 2004; $10,000 for a violation occurring in 2005; $15,000 for a violation occurring in 2006; $20,000 for a violation occurring in 2007; and $25,000 for a violation occurring in 2008 and any year thereafter. No penalty may be assessed under this subsection until the person charged is given notice and an opportunity for a hearing on the charge. The Secretary of Transportation may assess and collect any civil penalty incurred under this subsection and, in his discretion, may remit, mitigate, or compromise any penalty until the matter is referred to the Attorney General. If a person against whom a civil penalty is assessed under this subsection fails to pay that penalty, an action may be commenced in the district court of the United States for any district in which the violation occurs for such penalty.

(Aug. 18, 1894, ch. 299, §5, 28 Stat. 362; June 13, 1902, ch. 1079, §6, 32 Stat. 374; Pub. L. 90–578, title IV, §402(b)(2), Oct. 17, 1968, 82 Stat. 1118; Pub. L. 97–322, title I, §108(a), Oct. 15, 1982, 96 Stat. 1582; Pub. L. 97–449, §2(d)(1), Jan. 12, 1983, 96 Stat. 2440; Pub. L. 100–448, §21, Sept. 28, 1988, 102 Stat. 1846; Pub. L. 101–650, title III, §321, Dec. 1, 1990, 104 Stat. 5117; Pub. L. 108–293, title VI, §601(b), Aug. 9, 2004, 118 Stat. 1050.)

CODIFICATION

The last proviso of subsec. (a) of this section was from a part of section 6 of act June 13, 1902, which reads as follows: "Any regulations heretofore or hereafter prescribed by the Secretary of War in pursuance of the fourth and fifth sections of the river and harbor Act of August eighteenth, eighteen hundred and ninety-four [this section and section 1 of this title], and any regulations hereafter prescribed in pursuance of the aforesaid section four as amended by section eleven of this Act [section 1 of this title], may be enforced as provided in section seventeen of the river and harbor Act of March third, eighteen hundred and ninety-nine [section 413 of this title], the provisions whereof are hereby made applicable to the said regulations."

The last paragraph of section 1 of this title is also from a part of section 6 of act June 13, 1902.

Except for the last proviso of subsec. (a), this section was from act Aug. 18, 1894.

AMENDMENTS

2004—Subsec. (c). Pub. L. 108–293 substituted "$5,000 for a violation occurring in 2004; $10,000 for a violation occurring in 2005; $15,000 for a violation occurring in 2006; $20,000 for a violation occurring in 2007; and $25,000 for a violation occurring in 2008 and any year thereafter" for "$1,000".

1988—Subsec. (a). Pub. L. 100–448 inserted at end "Any rules and regulations made in pursuance of this section shall, to the extent practical and feasible, provide for regularly scheduled openings of drawbridges during seasons of the year, and during times of the day, when scheduled openings would help reduce motor vehicle traffic delays and congestion on roads and highways linked by drawbridges."

1983—Subsec. (a). Pub. L. 97–449 substituted "Secretary of Transportation" for "Secretary of War" wherever appearing. See Transfer of Functions note below.

1982—Subsec. (a). Pub. L. 97–322, §108(a)(1)–(4), designated existing provisions as subsec. (a); struck out from second sentence after "boats," the clause "or who shall unreasonably delay the opening of said draw after reasonable signal shall have been given,"; substituted in first proviso "subsection" for "section"; and in second proviso provided for punishment of "willful" violation of rules and regulations.

Subsecs. (b), (c). Pub. L. 97–322, §108(a)(5), added subsecs. (b) and (c).

CHANGE OF NAME

"Magistrate judge" substituted in text for "magistrate" pursuant to section 321 of Pub. L. 101–650, set out as a note under section 631 of Title 28, Judiciary and Judicial Procedure. Previously, "magistrate" substituted for "commissioner" pursuant to Pub. L. 90–578. See chapter 43 (§631 et seq.) of Title 28.

TRANSFER OF FUNCTIONS

Section 6(g)(2) of Pub. L. 89–670 transferred functions, powers, and duties of Secretary of the Army [formerly War] and other officers and offices of Department of the Army [formerly War] relating to drawbridge operating regulations under this section to Secretary of Transportation. Pub. L. 97–449 amended this section to reflect transfer made by section 6(g)(2) of Pub. L. 89–670, and repealed section 6(g)(2).

§500. Deflection of current; liability to riparian owners

Whenever complaint shall be made to the Secretary of the Army that by reason of the placing in any navigable waters of the United States of any bridge pier or abutment, the current of such waters has been so deflected from its natural course as to cause by producing caving of banks or otherwise serious damage or danger to property, it shall be his duty to make inquiry, and if it shall be ascertained that the complaint is well founded, he shall cause the owners or persons operating such bridge to repair such damage or prevent such danger to property by such means as he shall indicate and within such time as he may name, and in default thereof the owners or persons operating such bridge shall be liable in any court of competent jurisdiction to the persons injured in a sum double the amount of said injury: *Provided, however*, That nothing herein contained shall be construed so as to affect any rights of action which may have existed prior to August 11, 1888.

(Aug. 11, 1888, ch. 860, §2, 25 Stat. 423; July 26, 1947, ch. 343, title II, §205(a), 61 Stat 501.)

CODIFICATION

Section was from the River and Harbor Appropriation Act of 1888.

CHANGE OF NAME

Department of War designated Department of the Army and title of Secretary of War changed to Secretary of the Army by section 205(a) of act July 26, 1947, ch. 343, title II, 61 Stat. 501. Section 205(a) of act July 26, 1947, was repealed by section 53 of act Aug. 10, 1956, ch. 1041, 70A Stat. 641. Section 1 of act Aug. 10, 1956, enacted "Title 10, Armed Forces" which in sections 3010 to 3013 continued Department of the Army under administrative supervision of Secretary of the Army.

TRANSFER OF FUNCTIONS

Functions, powers, and duties of Secretary of the Army and other offices and officers of Department of the Army under sections 491 to 498 of this title to extent that they relate generally to location and clearances of bridges and causeways in navigable waters of United States transferred to and vested in Secretary of Transportation by Pub. L. 89–670, §6(g)(6)(B), Oct. 15, 1966, 80 Stat. 931. Pub. L. 97–449 amended sections 491 to 498 of this title to reflect transfer made by section 6(g)(6)(B) of Pub. L. 89–670, and repealed section 6(g)(6)(B).

§501. Omitted

Codification

Section, R.S. §5250, gave assent of Congress to construction of bridges across the Maquoketa River in Iowa.

§502. Alteration, removal, or repair of bridge or accessory obstructions to navigation

(a) Criminal penalties for violation; alteration or removal requirements; notice and hearing; specification of changes; time for compliance; notice to United States attorney; misdemeanor; fine; new offenses

Whenever the Secretary of Transportation shall have good reason to believe that any railroad or other bridge over any of the navigable waterways of the United States is an unreasonable obstruction to the free navigation of such waters on account of insufficient height, width of span, or otherwise, or where there is difficulty in passing the draw opening or the draw span of such bridge by rafts, steamboats, or other water craft, it shall be the duty of the said Secretary, first giving the parties reasonable opportunity to be heard, to give notice to the persons or corporations owning or controlling such bridge so to alter the same as to render navigation through or under it reasonably free, easy, and unobstructed; and in giving such notice he shall specify the changes that are required to be made, and shall prescribe in each case a reasonable time in which to make them. If at the end of such time the alteration has not been made, the Secretary of Transportation shall forthwith notify the United States attorney for the district in which such bridge is situated, to the end that the criminal proceedings hereinafter in this section mentioned may be taken. If the persons, corporation, or association owning or controlling any railroad or other bridge shall, after receiving notice to that effect, as hereinbefore required, from the Secretary of Transportation and within the time prescribed by him willfully fail or refuse to remove the same or to comply with the lawful order of the Secretary of the Army in the premises, such persons, corporation, or association shall be deemed guilty of a misdemeanor and on conviction thereof shall be punished by a fine not exceeding $5,000, and every month such persons, corporation, or association shall remain in default in respect to the removal or alteration of such bridge shall be deemed a new offense, and subject the persons, corporation, or association so offending to the penalties above prescribed.

(b) Proper repair requirement

No owner or operator of any bridge, drawbridge, or causeway shall endanger, unreasonably obstruct, or make hazardous the free navigation of any navigable water of the United States by reason of the failure to keep the bridge, drawbridge, or causeway and any accessory works in proper repair.

(c) Civil penalties for violation; separate offenses; notice and hearing; assessment, collection, and remission; civil actions

Whoever violates any provision of this section, or any order issued under this section, shall be liable to a civil penalty of not more than $5,000 for a violation occurring in 2004; $10,000 for a violation occurring in 2005; $15,000 for a violation occurring in 2006; $20,000 for a violation occurring in 2007; and $25,000 for a violation occurring in 2008 and any year thereafter. Each day a violation continues shall be deemed a separate offense. No penalty may be assessed under this subsection until the person charged is given notice and an opportunity for a hearing on the charge. The Secretary of Transportation may assess and collect any civil penalty incurred under this subsection and, in his discretion, may remit, mitigate, or compromise any penalty until the matter is referred to the Attorney General. If a person against whom a civil penalty is assessed under this subsection fails to pay that penalty, an action may be commenced in the district court of the United States for any district in which the violation occurs for such penalty.

(Mar. 3, 1899, ch. 425, §18, 30 Stat. 1153; Mar. 3, 1911, ch. 231, §291, 36 Stat. 1167; Jan. 31, 1928, ch. 14, §1, 45 Stat. 54; June 25, 1948, ch. 646, §§1, 39, 62 Stat. 909, 992; Pub. L. 97–322, title I, §108(b), Oct. 15, 1982, 96 Stat. 1583; Pub. L. 108–293, title VI, §601(c), Aug. 9, 2004, 118 Stat. 1050.)

Codification

Section is from act Mar. 3, 1899, popularly known as the "Rivers and Harbors Appropriation Act of 1899".

The words "or from the existing circuit courts," which followed "district courts" in the proviso were superseded by the abolition of the circuit courts and the transfer of their jurisdiction to the district courts, by act Mar. 3, 1911.

Prior Provisions

This section superseded act Aug. 11, 1888, ch. 860, §§9, 10, 25 Stat. 424, as amended by act Sept. 19, 1890, ch. 907, §§4, 5, 26 Stat. 453, which required the Secretary of War to provide against obstructions to navigation by bridges, and prescribed a punishment on the owner's default in making the required alterations.

The Secretary of War was authorized to make the required changes in bridges obstructing navigation on the owner's failure to do so, and the Attorney General was required to institute proceedings against the owner for the recovery of the cost of such changes, by act July 5, 1884, ch. 229, §8, 23 Stat. 148.

Amendments

2004—Subsec. (c). Pub. L. 108–293 substituted "$5,000 for a violation occurring in 2004; $10,000 for a violation occurring in 2005; $15,000 for a violation occurring in 2006; $20,000 for a violation occurring in 2007; and $25,000 for a violation occurring in 2008 and any year thereafter" for "$1,000".

1982—Subsec. (a). Pub. L. 97–322 designated existing provisions as subsec. (a), substituted "Secretary of Transportation" for "Secretary of War" wherever appearing, and struck out "recommended by the Chief of Engineers" after "specify the charges".

Subsecs. (b), (c). Pub. L. 97–322 added subsecs. (b) and (c).

1948—Act June 25, 1948, §39, repealed proviso at end relating to appeals. See sections 1252 and 1253 of title 28.

CHANGE OF NAME

Act June 25, 1948, eff. Sept. 1, 1948, substituted "United States attorney" for "district attorney of the United States". See section 541 of Title 28, Judiciary and Judicial Procedure, and Historical and Revision Notes thereunder.

EFFECTIVE DATE OF 1948 AMENDMENT

Amendment by act June 25, 1948 effective Sept. 1, 1948, see section 38 of act June 25, 1948, set out as an Effective Date note preceding section 1 of Title 28, Judiciary and Judicial Procedure.

LIMITATION ON APPLICATION

Section as not applicable to bridges constructed under sections 491 to 498 of this title, see section 494 of this title.

§503 to 507. Repealed. Pub. L. 100–17, title I, §135(d), Apr. 2, 1987, 101 Stat. 174

Section 503, act Aug. 21, 1935, ch. 597, §1, 49 Stat. 670, provided that, on and after Aug. 21, 1935, tolls over any bridge over any of the navigable waters of the United States, if such bridge is used for travel or transportation in interstate or foreign commerce, be just and reasonable and specified bridges to which sections 503 to 507 of this title not apply.

Section 504, acts Aug. 21, 1935, ch. 597, §2, 49 Stat. 671; Jan. 12, 1983, Pub. L. 97–449, §2(d)(1), 96 Stat. 2440, authorized Secretary of Transportation to determine reasonableness of any toll charged for passage or transit over any bridge to which sections 503 to 507 of this title applied and to prescribe an order establishing a reasonable toll, which order was to take effect thirty days after issuance.

Section 505, acts Aug. 21, 1935, ch. 597, §3, 49 Stat. 671; June 25, 1948, ch. 646, §32(a), 62 Stat. 991; May 24, 1949, ch. 139, §127, 63 Stat. 107; Jan. 12, 1983, Pub. L. 97–449, §2(d)(1), 96 Stat. 2440, provided for judicial review of orders of the Secretary of Transportation prescribing reasonable tolls.

Section 506, acts Aug. 21, 1935, ch. 597, §4, 49 Stat. 671; Oct. 15, 1970, Pub. L. 91–452, title II, §235, 84 Stat. 930; Jan. 12, 1983, Pub. L. 97–449, §2(d)(1), 96 Stat. 2440, authorized Secretary of Transportation to hold hearings in determining reasonableness of tolls, to require attendance of witnesses, and to punish witnesses for failure to attend such hearings.

Section 507, act Aug. 21, 1935, ch. 597, §5, 49 Stat. 672, related to punishment for failure to obey an order prescribing toll.

§508. Amount of tolls

Tolls for passage or transit over any bridge constructed under the authority of the Act of March 23, 1906 (34 Stat. 84; 33 U.S.C. 491–498), commonly known as the "Bridge Act of 1906", the General Bridge Act of 1946 [33 U.S.C. 525 et seq.], and the International Bridge Act of 1972 [33 U.S.C. 535 et seq.] shall be just and reasonable.

(Pub. L. 100–17, title I, §135(i), Apr. 2, 1987, 101 Stat. 174.)

REFERENCES IN TEXT

Act of March 23, 1906 (34 Stat. 84; 33 U.S.C. 491–498), commonly known as the "Bridge Act of 1906", referred to in text, is act Mar. 23, 1906, ch. 1130, 34 Stat. 84, as amended, which enacted sections 491 to 498 of this title. For complete classification of this Act of the Code, see Short Title note set out under section 491 of this title and Tables.

The General Bridge Act of 1946, referred to in text, is title V of act Aug. 2, 1946, ch. 753, 60 Stat. 847, as amended, which is classified generally to subchapter III (§525 et seq.) of this chapter. For complete classification of this Act to the Code, see Short Title note set out under section 525 of this title and Tables.

The International Bridge Act of 1972, referred to in text, is Pub. L. 92–434, Sept. 26, 1972, 86 Stat. 731, as amended, which is classified principally to subchapter IV (§535 et seq.) of this chapter. For complete classification of this Act to the Code, see Short Title note set out under section 535 of this title and Tables.

SUBCHAPTER II—ALTERATION OF BRIDGES

§511. Definitions

When used in this subchapter, unless the context indicates otherwise—

The term "alteration" includes changes of any kind, reconstruction, or removal in whole or in part.

The term "bridge" means a lawful bridge over navigable waters of the United States, including approaches, fenders, and appurtenances thereto, which is used and operated for the purpose of carrying railroad traffic, or both railroad and highway traffic, or if a State, county, municipality, or other political subdivision is the owner or joint owner thereof, which is used and operated for the purpose of carrying highway traffic.

The term "bridge owner" means any State, county, municipality, or other political subdivision, or any corporation, association, partnership, or individual owning, or jointly owning, any bridge, and, when any bridge shall be in the possession or under the control of any trustee, receiver, trustee in a case under title 11, or lessee, such terms shall include both the owner of the legal title and the person or the entity in possession or control of such bridge.

The term "Secretary" means the Secretary of Transportation.

The term "United States", when used in a geographical sense, includes the Territories and possessions of the United States.

(June 21, 1940, ch. 409, §1, 54 Stat. 497; July 16, 1952, ch. 889, §1, 66 Stat. 732; Pub. L. 95–598, title III, §323, Nov. 6, 1978, 92 Stat. 2679; Pub. L. 97–449, §2(d)(2), Jan. 12, 1983, 96 Stat. 2440.)

AMENDMENTS

1983—Pub. L. 97–449 substituted provision that the term "Secretary" means the Secretary of Transportation for provision that it meant the Secretary of War acting directly or through the Chief of Engineers.

1978—Pub. L. 95–598 substituted in definition of "bridge owner" the phrase "trustee in a case under title 11" for "trustee in bankruptcy".

1952—Act of July 16, 1952, redefined "bridge" and "bridge owner".

EFFECTIVE DATE OF 1978 AMENDMENT

Amendment by Pub. L. 95–598 effective Oct. 1, 1979, see section 402(a) of Pub. L. 95–598, set out as an Effective Dates note preceding section 101 of Title 11, Bankruptcy.

SHORT TITLE

Sections 511 to 523 of this title are popularly known as the "Hobbs Bridge Act" and also as the "Truman-Hobbs Act".

TRANSFER OF FUNCTIONS

Section 6(g)(3) of Pub. L. 89–670 transferred functions, powers, and duties of Secretary of the Army [formerly

War] and other officers and offices of Department of the Army [formerly War] relating to obstructive bridges under this subchapter to Secretary of Transportation. Pub. L. 97–449 amended this section to reflect transfer made by section 6(g)(3) of Pub. L. 89–670, and repealed section 6(g)(3).

§512. Obstruction of navigation

No bridge shall at any time unreasonably obstruct the free navigation of any navigable waters of the United States.

(June 21, 1940, ch. 409, §2, 54 Stat. 498.)

§513. Notice, hearings, and findings

Whenever any bridge shall, in the opinion of the Secretary, at any time unreasonably obstruct such navigation, it shall be the duty of the Secretary, after notice to interested parties, to hold a hearing at which the bridge owner, those interested in water navigation thereunder or therethrough, those interested in either railroad or highway traffic thereover, and any other party or parties in interest shall have full opportunity to offer evidence and be heard as to whether any alteration of such bridge is needed, and if so what alterations are needed, having due regard to the necessity of free and unobstructed water navigation and to the necessities of the rail or highway traffic. If, upon such hearing, the Secretary determines that any alterations of such bridge are necessary in order to render navigation through or under it reasonably free, easy, and unobstructed, having due regard also for the necessities of rail or highway traffic thereover, he shall so find and shall issue and cause to be served upon interested parties an order requiring such alterations of such bridge as he finds to be reasonably necessary for the purposes of navigation.

(June 21, 1940, ch. 409, §3, 54 Stat. 498.)

§514. Submission and approval of general plans and specifications

After the service of an order under this subchapter, it shall be the duty of the bridge owner to prepare and submit to the Secretary of Transportation, within a reasonable time as prescribed by the Secretary, general plans and specifications to provide for the alteration of such bridge in accordance with such order, and for such additional alteration of such bridge as the bridge owner may desire to meet the necessities of railroad or highway traffic, or both. The Secretary may approve or reject such general plans and specifications, in whole or in part, and may require the submission of new or additional plans and specifications, but when the Secretary shall have approved general plans and specifications, they shall be final and binding upon all parties unless changes therein be afterward approved by the Secretary and the bridge owner.

(June 21, 1940, ch. 409, §4, 54 Stat. 498; Pub. L. 94–587, §119, Oct. 22, 1976, 90 Stat. 2924.)

AMENDMENTS

1976—Pub. L. 94–587 substituted provision for preparation and submission of general plans and specifications within a reasonable time as prescribed by the Secretary after the service of an order for provision for such action within ninety days after service of his order.

§515. Contracts for project; guaranty of cost

After approval of such general plans and specifications by the Secretary, and after notification of such approval, the bridge owner shall, in such manner and within such times as the Secretary may prescribe, take bids for the alteration of such bridge in accordance with such general plans and specifications. All bids, including any bid for all or part of the project submitted by the bridge owner, shall be submitted to the Secretary, together with a recommendation by the bridge owner as to the most competent bid or bids, and at the same time the bridge owner shall submit to the Secretary a written guaranty that the total cost of the project, including the cost of such work as is to be performed by the bridge owner and not included in the work to be performed by contract, shall not exceed the sum stated in said guaranty. The Secretary may direct the bridge owner to reject all bids and to take new bids, or may authorize the bridge owner to proceed with the project, by contract, or partly by contract and partly by the bridge owner, or wholly by the bridge owner. Upon such authorization and fixing of the proportionate shares of the cost as provided in section 516 of this title, the bridge owner shall, within a reasonable time to be prescribed by the Secretary, proceed with the work of alteration; and the cost thereof shall be borne by the United States and by the bridge owner, as provided in sections 516 and 517 of this title: *Provided*, That where funds have been appropriated for part only of a project, the bridge owner may take bids for part only of the work. In the event the bridge owner proceeds with the alteration through the taking of successive partial bids, the bridge owner shall, if required by the Secretary, submit a revised guaranty of cost after bids are accepted for successive parts of the work.

(June 21, 1940, ch. 409, §5, 54 Stat. 498; Pub. L. 85–640, §1(a), (b), Aug. 14, 1958, 72 Stat. 595.)

AMENDMENTS

1958—Pub. L. 85–640 struck out provisions which required bridge owner to take bids within 90 days after notification of approval of general plans and specifications, and inserted provisions permitting the taking of partial bids where funds have been appropriated for part of a project, and requiring the bridge owner, if requested, to submit a revised guaranty of cost.

§516. Apportionment of cost

At the time the Secretary shall authorize the bridge owner to proceed with the project, as provided in section 515 of this title, and after an opportunity to the bridge owner to be heard thereon, the Secretary shall determine and issue an order specifying the proportionate shares of the total cost of the project to be borne by the United States and by the bridge owner. Such apportionment shall be made on the following basis: The bridge owner shall bear such part of the cost as is attributable to the direct and special benefits which will accrue to the bridge owner as a result of the alteration, including the expectable savings in repair or maintenance costs; and that part of the cost attributable to the requirements of traffic by railroad or highway, or both, including any expenditure for increased carrying capacity of the bridge, and including such proportion of the actual capital cost of the old bridge or of such part of the old bridge as may be altered or changed or rebuilt, as the used service life of the whole or a part, as the case may be, bears to the total estimated service life of the whole or such part: *Provided*, That in the event the alteration or relocation of any bridge may be desirable for the reason that the bridge unreasonably obstructs navigation, but also for some other reason, the Secretary may require equitable contribution from any interested person, firm, association, corporation, municipality, county, or State desiring such alteration or relocation for such other reason, as a condition precedent to the making of an order for such alteration or relocation. The United States shall bear the balance of the cost, including that part attributable to the necessities of navigation: *And provided further*, That where the bridge owner proceeds with the alteration on a successive partial bid basis the Secretary is authorized to issue an order of apportionment of cost for the entire alteration based on the accepted bid for the first part of the alteration and an estimate of cost for the remainder of the work. The Secretary is authorized to revise the order of apportionment of cost, to the extent he deems reasonable and proper, to meet any changed conditions.

(June 21, 1940, ch. 409, §6, 54 Stat. 499; July 16, 1952, ch. 889, §2, 66 Stat. 733; Pub. L. 85–640, §1(c), Aug. 14, 1958, 72 Stat. 595.)

AMENDMENTS

1958—Pub. L. 85–640 permitted issuance of an order of apportionment of cost for entire alteration based on the accepted bid for first part of alteration and an estimate of cost for remainder of work where bridge owner proceeds with alteration on a successive partial bid basis.

1952—Act July 16, 1952, made railroads share equally with proprietors of highways in bearing cost of alterations necessary to remove obstacles to navigation.

§517. Payment of share of United States

Following service of the order requiring alteration of the bridge, the Secretary of Transportation may make partial payments as the work progresses to the extent that funds have been appropriated. The total payments out of Federal funds shall not exceed the proportionate share of the United States of the total cost of the project paid or incurred by the bridge owner, and, if such total cost exceeds the cost guaranteed by the bridge owner, shall not exceed the proportionate share of the United States of such guaranteed cost, except that if the cost of the work exceeds the guaranteed cost by reason of emergencies, conditions beyond the control of the owner, or unforeseen or undetermined conditions, the Secretary of Transportation may, after full review of all the circumstances, provide for additional payments by the United States to help defray such excess cost to the extent he deems to be reasonable and proper, and shall certify such additional payments to the Secretary of the Treasury for payment. All payments to any bridge owner herein provided for shall be made by the Secretary of the Treasury through the Fiscal Service upon certifications of the Secretary of Transportation.

(June 21, 1940, ch. 409, §7, 54 Stat. 499; 1940 Reorg. Plan No. III, §1(a)(1), eff. June 30, 1940, 5 F.R. 2107, 54 Stat. 1231; Pub. L. 85–640, §1(d), Aug. 14, 1958, 72 Stat. 596; Pub. L. 91–605, title I, §118, Dec. 31, 1970, 84 Stat. 1725; Pub. L. 97–449, §2(d)(1), Jan. 12, 1983, 96 Stat. 2440.)

AMENDMENTS

1983—Pub. L. 97–449 substituted "Secretary of Transportation" for "Secretary of War" wherever appearing, which substitution had previously been made by Pub. L. 91–605. See, also, Transfer of Functions note below.

1970—Pub. L. 91–605 substituted provision permitting Secretary of Transportation to make payments for design work performed prior to the actual commencement of bridge alteration but after the order to alter has been issued for provision requiring Secretary of War to approve alteration plans, the cost guaranty, the fixing of proportionate shares as between the United States and bridge owner, and the commencement of the alteration, before the Chief of Engineers may make payments for bridge alteration, inserted reference to Secretary of Transportation in second sentence, and substituted "Secretary of Transportation" for "Secretary of War" in third sentence.

1958—Pub. L. 85–640 struck out provisions which required Secretary of War to furnish to Secretary of the Treasury a certified copy of his approval of the plans and specifications and guaranty, and of his order fixing the proportionate shares, and which required the Secretary of the Treasury to set aside the share of the United States for the project.

TRANSFER OF FUNCTIONS

Section 6(g)(3) of Pub. L. 89–670 transferred functions, powers, and duties of Secretary of the Army [formerly War] and other officers and offices of Department of the Army [formerly War] relating to obstructive bridges under this subchapter to Secretary of Transportation. Pub. L. 97–449 amended this section to reflect transfer made by section 6(g)(3) of Pub. L. 89–670, and repealed section 6(g)(3).

"Fiscal Service" substituted in text for "Division of Disbursement" on authority of section 1(a)(1) of Reorg. Plan No. III of 1940, eff. June 30, 1940, 5 F.R. 2107, 54 Stat. 1231, set out in the Appendix to Title 5, Government Organization and Employees, which consolidated such division into Fiscal Service of Department of the Treasury. See section 306 of Title 31, Money and Finance.

§518. Authorization of appropriations

There are authorized to be appropriated such sums as may be necessary to carry out the provisions of this subchapter.

(June 21, 1940, ch. 409, §8, 54 Stat. 500.)

ALTERATION OF BRIDGES

Pub. L. 108–90, title II, Oct. 1, 2003, 117 Stat. 1144, provided in part: "That in fiscal year 2004 and thereafter, funds for bridge alteration projects conducted pursuant to the Act of June 21, 1940 (33 U.S.C. 511 et seq.) shall be available for such projects only to the extent that the steel, iron, and manufactured products used in such projects are produced in the United States, unless contrary to law or international agreement, or unless the Commandant of the Coast Guard determines such action to be inconsistent with the public interest or the cost unreasonable."

Similar provisions were contained in the following prior appropriation act:

Pub. L. 108–7, div. I, title I, Feb. 20, 2003, 117 Stat. 389.

§ 519. Noncompliance with orders; penalties; removal of bridge

Any bridge owner who shall willfully fail or refuse to comply with any lawful order of the Secretary, made in accordance with the provisions of this subchapter, shall be deemed guilty of a misdemeanor and on conviction thereof shall be punished in any court of competent jurisdiction by a fine not exceeding $5,000, and every month such bridge owner shall remain in default shall be deemed a new offense and subject such bridge owner to additional penalties therefor. In addition to the penalties above prescribed the Secretary may, upon the failure or refusal of any bridge owner to comply with any lawful order issued by the Secretary in regard thereto, cause the removal of any such bridge and accessory works at the expense of the bridge owner; and suit for such expense may be brought in the name of the United States against such bridge owner and recovery had for such expense in any court of competent jurisdiction. The removal of any bridge erected or maintained in violation of the provisions of this subchapter or the order or direction of the Secretary made in pursuance thereof, and compliance with any order of the Secretary made with respect to any bridge in accordance with the provisions of this subchapter, may be enforced by injunction, mandamus, or other summary process upon application to the district court of any district in which such bridge may, in whole or in part, exist, and proper proceedings to this end may be instituted under the direction of the Attorney General of the United States at the request of the Secretary.

(June 21, 1940, ch. 409, § 9, 54 Stat. 500.)

§ 520. Review of findings and orders

Any order made or issued under section 516 of this title may be reviewed by the court of appeals for any judicial circuit in which the bridge in question is wholly or partly located, if a petition for such review is filed within three months after the date such order is issued. The judgment of any such court shall be final except that it shall be subject to review by the Supreme Court of the United States upon certification or certiorari, in the manner provided in section 1254 of title 28. The review by such Court shall be limited to questions of law, and the findings of fact by the Secretary, if supported by substantial evidence, shall be conclusive. Upon such review, such Court shall have power to affirm or, if the order is not in accordance with law, to modify or to reverse the order, with or without remanding the case for a rehearing as justice may require. Proceedings under this section shall not operate as a stay of any order of the Secretary issued under provisions of this subchapter other than section 516 of this title, or relieve any bridge owner of any liability or penalty under such provisions.

(June 21, 1940, ch. 409, § 10, 54 Stat. 501; June 25, 1948, ch. 646, § 32(a), 62 Stat. 991; May 24, 1949, ch. 139, § 127, 63 Stat. 107.)

CODIFICATION

"Section 1254 of title 28" substituted in text for "sections 239 and 240 of the Judicial Code, as amended" on authority of act June 25, 1948, ch. 646, 62 Stat. 869, section 1 of which enacted Title 28, Judiciary and Judicial Procedure. Prior to the enactment of Title 28, sections 239 and 240 of the Judicial Code were classified to sections 346 and 347 of Title 28.

CHANGE OF NAME

Act June 25, 1948, as amended by act May 24, 1949, substituted "court of appeals" for "circuit court of appeals".

§ 521. Regulations and orders

The Secretary is authorized to prescribe such rules and regulations, and to make and issue such orders, as may be necessary or appropriate for carrying out the provisions of this subchapter.

(June 21, 1940, ch. 409, § 11, 54 Stat. 501.)

§ 522. Existing provisions of law

(a) Obstructing navigation; criminal penalties

The first sentence of section 494 of this title, and section 502 of this title, shall be inapplicable with respect to any bridge to which the provisions of this subchapter are applicable, except to the extent provided in this section.

(b) Construction, reconstruction, or alteration of bridges not completed on July 1, 1939; apportionment of costs

Any bridge, the construction, reconstruction, or alteration of which was required by an order of the Secretary issued prior to July 1, 1939, and was not completed on such date, and in the case of which no penalties have accrued at the time of the enactment of this subchapter, shall be constructed, reconstructed, or altered as required by such order, and not in accordance with the provisions of this subchapter. In the case of any such bridge, however, the Secretary shall apportion the cost of the project between the bridge owner and the United States, and payment of the share of the United States shall be made, in the same manner as if the provisions of this subchapter applied to such construction, reconstruction, or alteration, subject to the following limitations:

(1) In case such construction, reconstruction, or alteration has not begun on or before April 1, 1940, such apportionment of cost shall be made only if (A) the construction, reconstruction, or alteration is carried out in accordance with plans and specifications, and pursuant to bids, approved by the Secretary, and (B) the bridge owner has submitted to the Secretary a written guaranty of cost as provided for in section 515 of this title.

(2) The Secretary's determination as to such apportionment, and as to such plans and specifications and bids, shall be final.

(3) Such apportionment shall not be made if such construction, reconstruction, or alteration is not completed within the time fixed in such order of the Secretary or within such additional time as the Secretary, for good cause shown, may allow.

(c) Construction, reconstruction, or alteration of bridges not begun on July 1, 1939

Any bridge (except a bridge to which subsection (b) of this section applies) the construction, reconstruction, or alteration of which was required by an order of the Secretary issued prior to July 1, 1939, and was not begun before such date, shall be subject to the provisions of this subchapter as though such order had not been issued, and compliance with the provisions of this subchapter and with such orders as may be issued thereunder shall be considered to constitute compliance with such order issued prior to July 1, 1939, and with the provisions of law under which it was issued.

(June 21, 1940, ch. 409, §12, 54 Stat. 501.)

§523. Relocation of bridges

If the owner of any bridge and the Secretary shall agree that in order to remove an obstruction to navigation, or for any other purpose, a relocation of such bridge or the construction of a new bridge upon a new location would be preferable to an alteration of the existing bridge, such relocation or new construction may be carried out at such new site and upon such terms as may be acceptable to the bridge owner and the Secretary, and the cost of such relocation or new construction, including also any expense of changes in and additions to rights-of-way, stations, tracks, spurs, sidings, switches, signals, and other railroad facilities and property, and relocation of shippers required for railroad connection with the bridge at the new site, shall be apportioned as between the bridge owner and the United States in the manner which is provided for in section 516 of this title in the case of an alteration and the share of the United States paid from the appropriation authorized in section 518 of this title: *Provided*, That nothing in this section shall be construed as requiring the United States to pay any part of the expense of building any bridge across a navigable stream which the Secretary of Transportation shall not find to be, in fact, a relocation of an existing bridge.

(June 21, 1940, ch. 409, §13, 54 Stat. 502; July 16, 1952, ch. 889, §4, 66 Stat. 733; Pub. L. 97–449, §2(d)(1), Jan. 12, 1983, 96 Stat. 2440.)

Amendments

1983—Pub. L. 97–449 substituted "Secretary of Transportation" for "Secretary of War". See Transfer of Functions note below.

1952—Act July 16, 1952, struck out "used for railroad traffic" after "owner of any bridge".

Transfer of Functions

Section 6(g)(3) of Pub. L. 89–670 transferred functions, powers, and duties of Secretary of the Army [formerly War] and other officers and offices of Department of the Army [formerly War] relating to obstructive bridges under this subchapter to Secretary of Transportation. Pub. L. 97–449 amended this section to reflect transfer made by section 6(g)(3) of Pub. L. 89–670, and repealed section 6(g)(3).

§524. Applicability of administrative procedure provisions

In the administration of this Act, hearings and other procedures shall be exempted from the provisions of subchapter II of chapter 5, and chapter 7, of title 5, except as to the requirements of section 552 of title 5.

(July 16, 1952, ch. 889, §3, 66 Stat. 733.)

References in Text

This Act, referred to in text, is act July 16, 1952, ch. 889, 66 Stat. 732, which enacted this section and amended sections 511, 516, and 523 of this title. For complete classification of this Act to the Code, see Tables.

Codification

Section was not enacted as part of act June 21, 1940, ch. 409, 54 Stat. 497, which comprises this subchapter.

"Subchapter II of chapter 5, and chapter 7, of title 5" and "section 552 of title 5" substituted in text for "the Administrative Procedure Act (60 Stat. 237)" and "section 3 thereof", respectively, on authority of Pub. L. 89–554, §7(b), Sept. 6, 1966, 80 Stat. 631, the first section of which enacted Title 5, Government Organization and Employees.

SUBCHAPTER III—GENERAL BRIDGE AUTHORITY

§525. Construction and operation of bridges

(a) Consent of Congress

The consent of Congress is granted for the construction, maintenance, and operation of bridges and approaches thereto over the navigable waters of the United States, in accordance with the provisions of this subchapter.

(b) Approval of plans

The location and plans for such bridges shall be approved by the Secretary of Transportation before construction is commenced, and, in approving the location and plans of any bridge, the Secretary may impose any specific conditions relating to the maintenance and operation of the structure which the Secretary may deem necessary in the interest of public navigation, and the conditions so imposed shall have the force of law. This subsection shall not apply to any bridge over waters which are not subject to the ebb and flow of the tide and which are not used and are not susceptible to use in their natural condition or by reasonable improvement as a means to transport interstate or foreign commerce.

(c) Private highway toll bridges

Notwithstanding the provisions of subsections (a) and (b) of this section, it shall be unlawful to construct or commence the construction of any privately owned highway toll bridge until the location and plans thereof shall also have been submitted to and approved by the highway department or departments of the State or States in which the bridge and its approaches are situated; and where such bridge shall be between two or more States and the highway departments thereof shall be unable to agree upon the location and plans therefor, or if they, or either of them, shall fail or refuse to act upon the location and plans submitted, such location and plans then shall be submitted to the Secretary of Transportation and, if approved by the Secretary of Transportation, approval by the highway departments shall not be required.

(Aug. 2, 1946, ch. 753, title V, §502, 60 Stat. 847; June 30, 1949, ch. 288, title I, §103(a), 63 Stat. 380; 1949 Reorg. Plan No. 7, §1, eff. Aug. 19, 1949, 14 F.R. 5288, 63 Stat. 1070; Pub. L. 97–322, title I, §107(a), Oct. 15, 1982, 96 Stat. 1582; Pub. L. 97–449, §2(d)(1), (3), Jan. 12, 1983, 96 Stat. 2440; Pub. L. 98–557, §17(g)(2), Oct. 30, 1984, 98 Stat. 2869.)

AMENDMENTS

1984—Subsec. (b). Pub. L. 98–557 struck out "the Chief of Engineers and" before "the Secretary of Transportation" and substituted "the Secretary" for "they" wherever appearing.

1983—Subsec. (b). Pub. L. 97–449, §2(d)(1), substituted "Secretary of Transportation" for "Secretary of War". See Transfer of Functions note below.

Subsec. (c). Pub. L. 97–449, §2(d)(3), substituted "Secretary of Transportation" for "Public Roads Administration" wherever appearing. See Transfer of Functions note below.

1982—Subsec. (b). Pub. L. 97–322 inserted exemption provision at end.

SHORT TITLE

Section 501 of title V of act Aug. 2, 1946, provided that: "This title [enacting this subchapter] may be cited as the 'General Bridge Act of 1946'."

TRANSFER OF FUNCTIONS

Functions, powers, and duties of Secretary of the Army [formerly War] and other offices and officers of Department of the Army [formerly War] under this section to extent that they relate generally to location and clearances of bridges and causeways in navigable waters of United States transferred to and vested in Secretary of Transportation by section 6(g)(6)(C) of Pub. L. 89–670. Pub. L. 97–449 amended this section to reflect transfer made by section 6(g)(6)(C) of Pub. L. 89–670, and repealed section 6(g)(6)(C).

Functions of Public Roads Administration transferred to Bureau of Public Roads within General Services Administration by section 103(a) of act June 30, 1949. See Historical and Revision Notes under section 303(b) of Title 40, Public Buildings, Property, and Works. Section 303(b) of Title 40 was amended generally by Pub. L. 109–313, §2(a)(1), Oct. 6, 2006, 120 Stat. 1734, and, as so amended, no longer relates to the Federal Works Agency and Commissioner of Public Buildings. See 2006 Amendment note under section 303 of Title 40.

Bureau of Public Roads within General Services Administration transferred to Department of Commerce by section 1 of Reorg. Plan No. 7 of 1949.

For transfer of functions of other officers, employees, and agencies of Department of Commerce, with certain exceptions, to Secretary of Commerce, with power to delegate, see Reorg. Plan No. 5 of 1950, §§1, 2, eff. May 24, 1950, 15 F.R. 3174, 64 Stat. 1263, set out in the Appendix to Title 5, Government Organization and Employees.

Functions, powers, and duties of Secretary of Commerce and other offices and officers of Department of Commerce under subsec. (c) of this section relating generally to highways transferred to and vested in Secretary of Transportation by section 6(g)(6)(C) of Pub. L. 89–670. Pub. L. 97–449 amended this section to reflect transfer made by section 6(g)(6)(C) of Pub. L. 89–670, and repealed section 6(g)(6)(C).

RESERVATION OF RIGHT TO ALTER, AMEND, OR REPEAL

Section 511 of title V of act Aug. 2, 1946, provided that: "The right to alter, amend, or repeal this title [this subchapter] is hereby expressly reserved as to any and all bridges which may be built under authority hereof."

§526. Repealed. Pub. L. 100–17, title I, §135(e), Apr. 2, 1987, 101 Stat. 174

Section, acts Aug. 2, 1946, ch. 753, title V, §503, 60 Stat. 847; Jan. 12, 1983, Pub. L. 97–449, §2(d)(1), 96 Stat. 2440, provided that tolls charged for transit over any interstate bridge be just and reasonable and authorized Secretary of Transportation to prescribe reasonable rates of toll for such transit, which rates were to be legal rates demanded and received. See section 508 of this title.

§526a. Repealed. Pub. L. 100–17, title I, §135(f), Apr. 2, 1987, 101 Stat. 174

Section, act Pub. L. 93–87, title I, §133(b), Aug. 13, 1973, 87 Stat. 267, authorized Secretary of Transportation to promulgate regulations establishing guidelines governing any increase in tolls for use of any bridge constructed pursuant to either the General Bridge Act of 1906 or the General Bridge Act of 1946.

STUDY OF TOLL BRIDGE AUTHORITY; INVESTIGATION AND STUDY OF FEDERAL STATUTES AND REGULATIONS; REPORT TO CONGRESS

Section 133(a) of Pub. L. 93–87 directed Secretary of Transportation to study the existing Federal laws and regulations governing toll bridges over navigable waters of United States and submit a report containing recommendations regarding action to be taken to assure reasonable nationwide tolls no later than July 1, 1974, except in the case of the toll bridge at Chester, Illinois, where the Secretary was directed to submit a similar report no later than Dec. 31, 1973, prior to repeal by Pub. L. 100–17, title I, §135(f), Apr. 2, 1987, 101 Stat. 174.

§527. Acquisition of interstate bridges by public agencies; amount of damages

After the completion of any interstate toll bridge constructed by an individual, firm, or corporation, as determined by the Secretary of Transportation, either of the States in which the bridge is located, or any public agency or political subdivision of either of such States, within or adjoining which any part of such bridge is located, or any two or more of them jointly, may at any time acquire and take over all right, title, and interest in such bridge and its approaches, and any interest in real property for public purposes by condemnation or expropriation. If at any time after the expiration of five years after the completion of such bridge the same is acquired by condemnation or expropriation, the amount of damages or compensation to be allowed shall not include good will, going value, or prospective revenues or profits, but shall be limited to the sum of (1) the actual cost of constructing such bridge and its approaches, less a reasonable deduction for actual depreciation in value; (2) the actual costs of acquiring such interests in real property; (3) actual financing and promotion costs, not to exceed 10 per centum of the sum of the cost of constructing the bridge and its approaches and acquiring such interests in real property; and (4) actual expenditures for necessary improvements.

(Aug. 2, 1946, ch. 753, title V, §504, 60 Stat. 848; Pub. L. 97–449, §2(d)(1), Jan. 12, 1983, 96 Stat. 2440.)

AMENDMENTS

1983—Pub. L. 97–449 substituted "Secretary of Transportation" for "Secretary of War". See Transfer of Functions note below.

TRANSFER OF FUNCTIONS

Section 6(g)(6)(C) of Pub. L. 89–670 transferred functions, powers, and duties of Secretary of the Army [formerly War] and other offices and officers of Department of the Army [formerly War] under this subchapter to extent that they relate generally to location and clearances of bridges and causeways in navigable waters of United States to Secretary of Transportation. Pub. L. 97–449 amended this section to reflect transfer made by section 6(g)(6)(C) of Pub. L. 89–670, and repealed section 6(g)(6)(C).

§528. Statement of construction costs of privately owned interstate bridges; investigation of costs; conclusiveness of findings; review

Within ninety days after the completion of a privately owned interstate toll bridge, the owner shall file with the Secretary of Transportation and with the highway departments of the States in which the bridge is located, a sworn itemized statement showing the actual original cost of constructing the bridge and its approaches, the actual cost of acquiring any interest in real property necessary therefor, and the actual financing and promotion costs. The Secretary of Transportation may, and upon request of a highway department shall, at any time within three years after the completion of such bridge, investigate such costs and determine the accuracy and the reasonableness of the costs alleged in the statement of costs so filed, and shall make a finding of the actual and reasonable costs of constructing, financing, and promoting such bridge. For the purpose of such investigation the said individual, firm, or corporation, its successors and assigns, shall make available all of its records in connection with the construction, financing, and promotion thereof. The findings of the Secretary of Transportation as to the reasonable costs of the construction, financing, and promotion of the bridge shall be conclusive for the purposes mentioned in section 527 of this title subject only to review in a court of equity for fraud or gross mistake.

(Aug. 2, 1946, ch. 753, title V, §505, 60 Stat. 848; Pub. L. 97–449, §2(d)(1), Jan. 12, 1983, 96 Stat. 2440.)

AMENDMENTS

1983—Pub. L. 97–449 substituted "Secretary of Transportation" for "Secretary of War" wherever appearing. See Transfer of Functions note below.

TRANSFER OF FUNCTIONS

Section 6(g)(6)(C) of Pub. L. 89–670 transferred functions, powers, and duties of Secretary of the Army [formerly War] and other offices and officers of Department of the Army [formerly War] under this subchapter to extent that they relate generally to location and clearances of bridges and causeways in navigable waters of United States to Secretary of Transportation. Pub. L. 97–449 amended this section to reflect transfer made by section 6(g)(6)(C) of Pub. L. 89–670, and repealed section 6(g)(6)(C).

§529. Repealed. Pub. L. 100–17, title I, §135(e), Apr. 2, 1987, 101 Stat. 174

Section, acts Aug. 2, 1946, ch. 753, title V, §506, 60 Stat. 848; May 25, 1948, ch. 336, 62 Stat. 267, related to adjusting rates of tolls charged on an interstate bridge constructed or taken over by State or political subdivision thereof to provide fund to pay reasonable costs of maintaining and operating such bridge and a sinking fund to amortize amount paid for such bridge, with such bridge to be operated and maintained free of tolls after a sinking fund sufficient for such amortization had been provided.

§530. Bridges included and excluded

The provisions of this subchapter shall apply only to bridges over navigable waters of the United States, the construction of which is approved after August 2, 1946, under the provisions of this subchapter; and the provisions of the first proviso of section 401 of this title, and the provisions of sections 491 to 498 of this title, shall not apply to such bridges.

(Aug. 2, 1946, ch. 753, title V, §507, 60 Stat. 849.)

§531. International bridges

This subchapter shall not be construed to authorize the construction of any bridge which will connect the United States, or any Territory or possession of the United States, with any foreign country.

(Aug. 2, 1946, ch. 753, title V, §508, 60 Stat. 849.)

§532. Eminent domain

There are conferred upon any individual, his heirs, legal representatives, or assigns, any firm or corporation, its successors or assigns, or any State, political subdivision, or municipality authorized in accordance with the provisions of this subchapter to build a bridge between two or more States, all such rights and powers to enter upon lands and acquire, condemn, occupy, possess, and use real estate and other property in the respective States needed for the location, construction, operation, and maintenance of such bridge and its approaches, as are possessed by railroad corporations for railroad purposes or by bridge corporations for bridge purposes in the State in which such real estate or other property is situated, upon making just compensation therefor to be ascertained and paid according to the laws of such State, and the proceedings therefor shall be the same as in the condemnation or expropriation of property for public purposes in such State.

(Aug. 2, 1946, ch. 753, title V, §509, 60 Stat. 849.)

§533. Penalties for violations

(a) Criminal penalties for violation

Any person who willfully fails or refuses to comply with any lawful order of the Secretary of Transportation or the Chief of Engineers issued under the provisions of this subchapter, or who willfully fails to comply with any specific condition imposed by the Chief of Engineers and the Secretary of Transportation relating to the maintenance and operation of bridges, or who willfully refuses to produce books, papers, or documents in obedience to a subpena or other lawful requirement under this subchapter, or who otherwise willfully violates any provisions of this subchapter, shall, upon conviction thereof, be punished by a fine of not to exceed $5,000 or by imprisonment for not more than one year, or by both such fine and imprisonment.

(b) Civil penalties for violation; separate offenses; notice and hearing; assessment, collection, and remission; civil actions

Whoever violates any provision of this subchapter, or any order issued under this subchapter, shall be liable to a civil penalty of not more than $5,000 for a violation occurring in 2004; $10,000 for a violation occurring in 2005; $15,000 for a violation occurring in 2006; $20,000 for a violation occurring in 2007; and $25,000 for a violation occurring in 2008 and any year thereafter. Each day a violation continues shall be deemed a separate offense. No penalty may be assessed under this subsection until the person charged is given notice and an opportunity for a hearing on the charge. The Secretary of Transportation may assess and collect any civil penalty incurred under this subsection and, in his discretion, may remit, mitigate, or compromise any penalty until the matter is referred to the Attorney General. If a person against whom a civil penalty is assessed under this subsection fails to pay that penalty, an action may be commenced in the district court of the United States for any district in which the violation occurs for such penalty.

(Aug. 2, 1946, ch. 753, title V, §510, 60 Stat. 849; Pub. L. 97–322, title I, §108(d), Oct. 15, 1982, 96 Stat. 1584; Pub. L. 97–449, §2(d)(1), Jan. 12, 1983, 96 Stat. 2440; Pub. L. 108–293, title VI, §601(d), Aug. 9, 2004, 118 Stat. 1050.)

Amendments

2004—Subsec. (b). Pub. L. 108–293 substituted "$5,000 for a violation occurring in 2004; $10,000 for a violation occurring in 2005; $15,000 for a violation occurring in 2006; $20,000 for a violation occurring in 2007; and $25,000 for a violation occurring in 2008 and any year thereafter" for "$1,000".

1983—Subsec. (a). Pub. L. 97–449 substituted "Secretary of Transportation" for "Secretary of War" wherever appearing. See Transfer of Functions note below.

1982—Pub. L. 97–322 designated existing provisions as subsec. (a), made willfulness an element of the described offenses, and added subsec. (b).

Transfer of Functions

Section 6(g)(6)(C) of Pub. L. 89–670 transferred functions, powers, and duties of Secretary of the Army [formerly War] and other offices and officers of Department of the Army [formerly War] under this subchapter to extent that they relate generally to location and clearances of bridges and causeways in navigable waters of United States to Secretary of Transportation. Pub. L. 97–449 amended this section to reflect transfer made by section 6(g)(6)(C) of Pub. L. 89–670, and repealed section 6(g)(6)(C).

§ 534. Conveyance of right, title, and interest of United States in bridges transferred to States or political subdivisions; terms and conditions

The Secretary of the Army is authorized to transfer or convey to State authorities or political subdivisions thereof all right, title, and interest of the United States, in and to any and all bridges heretofore or hereafter constructed or acquired in connection with the improvement of canals, rivers and harbors, or works of flood control, together with the necessary lands, easements, or rights-of-way, upon such terms and conditions and with or without consideration, as may be determined to be in the best interest of the United States by the Chief of Engineers: *Provided*, That such transferred bridges shall be toll-free.

(May 17, 1950, ch. 188, title I, §109, 64 Stat. 168.)

Codification

Section was not enacted as part of the General Bridge Act of 1946 which comprises this subchapter.

SUBCHAPTER IV—INTERNATIONAL BRIDGES

§ 535. Congressional consent to construction, maintenance, and operation of international bridges; conditions of consent

The consent of Congress is hereby granted to the construction, maintenance, and operation of any bridge and approaches thereto, which will connect the United States with any foreign country (hereinafter in this subchapter referred to as an "international bridge") and to the collection of tolls for its use, so far as the United States has jurisdiction. Such consent shall be subject to (1) the approval of the proper authorities in the foreign country concerned; (2) the provisions of sections 491 to 498 of this title, except section 496 of this title, whether or not such bridge is to be built across or over any of the navigable waters of the United States; and (3) of the provisions of this subchapter.

(Pub. L. 92–434, §2, Sept. 26, 1972, 86 Stat. 731.)

Short Title

Section 1 of Pub. L. 92–434 provided: "That this Act [enacting this subchapter and amending section 129 of Title 23, Highways] may be cited as the 'International Bridge Act of 1972'."

§ 535a. Congressional consent to State agreements with Canada and Mexico; Secretary of State's approval of agreements

The consent of Congress is hereby granted for a State or a subdivision or instrumentality thereof to enter into agreements—

(1) with the Government of Canada, a Canadian Province, or a subdivision or instrumentality of either, in the case of a bridge connecting the United States and Canada, or

(2) with the Government of Mexico, a Mexican State, or a subdivision or instrumentality of either, in the case of a bridge connecting the United States and Mexico,

for the construction, operation, and maintenance of such bridge in accordance with the applicable provisions of this subchapter. The effectiveness of such agreement shall be conditioned on its approval by the Secretary of State.

(Pub. L. 92–434, §3, Sept. 26, 1972, 86 Stat. 731.)

§ 535b. Presidential approval; recommendations of Federal officials

No bridge may be constructed, maintained, and operated as provided in section 535 of this title unless the President has given his approval thereto. In the course of determining whether to grant such approval, the President shall secure the advice and recommendations of (1) the United States section of the International Boundary and Water Commission, United States and Mexico, in the case of a bridge connecting the United States and Mexico, and (2) the heads of such departments and agencies of the Federal Government as he deems appropriate to determine the necessity for such bridge.

(Pub. L. 92–434, §4, Sept. 26, 1972, 86 Stat. 731.)

§535c. Secretary of Transportation's approval; commencement and completion requirements; extension of time limits

The approval of the Secretary of Transportation, as required by section 491 of this title, shall be given only subsequent to the President's approval, as provided for in section 535b of this title, and shall be null and void unless the construction of the bridge is commenced within two years and completed within five years from the date of the Secretary's approval: *Provided, however*, That the Secretary, for good cause shown, may extend for a reasonable time either or both of the time limits herein provided.

(Pub. L. 92–434, §5, Sept. 26, 1972, 86 Stat. 732.)

§535d. Repealed. Pub. L. 100–17, title I, §135(g), Apr. 2, 1987, 101 Stat. 174

Section, Pub. L. 92–434, §6, Sept. 26, 1972, 86 Stat. 732, directed that tolls charged for use of an international bridge constructed or acquired under this subchapter by private individual, company, or other private entity be collected for a reasonable period for amortization of construction or acquisition costs, plus interest and reasonable return, that at end of such period the United States portion of bridge become the property of the State having jurisdiction over such United States portion, and that accurate records on expenditures and tolls collected be kept and annually reported to Secretary of Transportation, with authority for Secretary to conduct audits.

§535e. Ownership

(a) Sale, assignment, or transfer; Secretary of Transportation's approval

Nothing in this subchapter shall be deemed to prevent the individual, corporation, or other entity to which, pursuant to this subchapter, authorization has been given to construct, operate, and maintain an international bridge and the approaches thereto, from selling, assigning, or transferring the rights, powers, and privileges conferred by this subchapter: *Provided*, That such sale, assignment, or transfer shall be subject to approval by the Secretary of Transportation.

(b) State status of original applicant upon acquisition of right, title, and interest after termination of private entity licenses, contracts, or orders

Upon the acquisition by a State or States, or by a subdivision or instrumentality thereof, of the right, title, and interest of a private individual, corporation, or other private entity, in and to an international bridge, any license, contract, or order issued or entered into by the Secretary of Transportation, to or with such private individual, corporation, or other private entity, shall be deemed terminated forthwith. Thereafter, the State, subdivision, or instrumentality so acquiring shall operate and maintain such bridge in the same manner as if it had been the original applicant, and the provisions of section 535d[1] of this title shall not apply.

(Pub. L. 92–434, §8, Sept. 26, 1972, 86 Stat. 732.)

[1] See References in Text note below.

REFERENCES IN TEXT

Section 535d of this title, referred to in subsec. (b), was repealed by Pub. L. 100–17, title I, §135(g), Apr. 2, 1987, 101 Stat. 174.

§535f. Applicability of provisions

This subchapter shall apply to all international bridges constructed under the authority of this subchapter. Section 535a of this title and section 129(a)(3) of title 23, shall apply to all international bridges the construction of which has been heretofore approved by Congress, notwithstanding any conflicting provision in any Act authorizing the construction of such a bridge or in any agreement entered into by the Federal Government and a State.

(Pub. L. 92–434, §9, Sept. 26, 1972, 86 Stat. 733.)

§535g. Federal navigable waters and commerce jurisdiction unaffected

Nothing in this subchapter shall be construed to affect, impair, or diminish any right, power, or jurisdiction of the United States over or in regard to any navigable water or any interstate or foreign commerce.

(Pub. L. 92–434, §10, Sept. 26, 1972, 86 Stat. 733.)

§535h. Report of Secretary of Transportation's approval during fiscal year

The Secretary of Transportation shall make a report of all approvals granted by him during the fiscal year pursuant to section 535c of this title in each annual report of the activities of the Department required by section 308(a) of title 49.

(Pub. L. 92–434, §11, Sept. 26, 1972, 86 Stat. 733.)

CODIFICATION

"Section 308(a) of title 49" substituted in text for "section 11 of the Department of Transportation Act (49 U.S.C. 1658)" on authority of Pub. L. 97–449, §6(b), Jan. 12, 1983, 96 Stat. 2443, the first section of which enacted subtitle I (§101 et seq.) of Title 49, Transportation.

§535i. Reservation of right to alter or repeal

The right to alter, amend, or repeal this subchapter is expressly reserved.

(Pub. L. 92–434, §12, Sept. 26, 1972, 86 Stat. 733.)

CHAPTER 12—RIVER AND HARBOR IMPROVEMENTS GENERALLY

SUBCHAPTER I—GENERAL PROVISIONS

SUBCHAPTER II—PAY AND ALLOWANCES; TRAVELING EXPENSES AND SUBSISTENCE

SUBCHAPTER III—ACQUISITION OF LAND AND MATERIALS

SUBCHAPTER IV—PARTICULAR WORK OR IMPROVEMENTS

SUBCHAPTER I—GENERAL PROVISIONS

§540. Investigations and improvements; control by Department of the Army; wildlife conservation

Federal investigations and improvements of rivers, harbors, and other waterways shall be under the jurisdiction of and shall be prosecuted by the Department of the Army under the direction of the Secretary of the Army and the supervision of the Chief of Engineers, except as otherwise specifically provided by Act of Congress, which said investigations and improvements shall include a due regard for wildlife conservation.

(June 20, 1938, ch. 535, §1, 52 Stat. 802; July 26, 1947, ch. 343, title II, §205(a), 61 Stat. 501.)

PRIOR PROVISIONS

Acts Aug. 30, 1935, ch. 831, 49 Stat. 1028; Aug. 26, 1937, ch. 832, 50 Stat. 844, contained similar provisions.

CHANGE OF NAME

Department of War designated Department of the Army and title of Secretary of War changed to Secretary of the Army by section 205(a) of act July 26, 1947, ch. 343, title II, 61 Stat. 501. Section 205(a) of act July 26, 1947, was repealed by section 53 of act Aug. 10, 1956, ch. 1041, 70A Stat. 641. Section 1 of act Aug. 10, 1956, enacted "Title 10, Armed Forces" which in sections 3010 to 3013 continued Department of the Army under administrative supervision of Secretary of the Army.

WATERWAY IMPROVEMENTS STUDY AND REPORT; AVAILABILITY OF DATA TO NATIONAL TRANSPORTATION POLICY COMMISSION

Pub. L. 94–587, §158, Oct. 22, 1976, 90 Stat. 2933, directed the Secretary of the Army, acting through the Chief of Engineers, to make a comprehensive study and report on the system of waterway improvements under his jurisdiction, including a review of emergency and defense requirements and an appraisal of additional improvements necessary to optimize the system and its intermodal characteristics, and to submit a report to Congress within three years after funds were first appropriated and made available for the study, together with his recommendations. The Secretary of the Army, acting through the Chief of Engineers, was to make available to the National Transportation Policy Study Commission established by section 154 of Public Law 94–280 [set out as a note under section 101 of Title 23, Highways], the information and other data developed as a result of the study.

REIMBURSEMENT OF STATES FOR WATER RESOURCES PROJECTS; STUDY

Pub. L. 89–298, title III, §314, Oct. 27, 1965, 79 Stat. 1096, authorized the Secretary of the Army, through the Chief of Engineers, to study the need for and feasibility of Federal reimbursement of certain public entities for their expenses incurred in connection with authorized projects for improvements of rivers, harbors, and certain other waterways, for various purposes, and to submit a report to Congress no later than Jan. 31, 1967, together with his recommendations in connection therewith.

§540a. Availability of appropriations for attendance by military personnel at meetings and for printing survey reports

Appropriations in this title[1] or appropriations made in this title[1] in subsequent Energy and Water Development Appropriations Acts shall on and after October 2, 1992, be available for expenses of attendance by military personnel at meetings in the manner authorized by section 4110 of title 5, uniforms, and allowances therefor, as authorized by law (5 U.S.C. 5901–5902), and for printing, either during a recess or session of Congress, of survey reports authorized by law, and such survey reports as may be printed during a recess of Congress shall be printed, with illustrations, as documents of the next succeeding session of Congress.

(Pub. L. 102–377, title I, Oct. 2, 1992, 106 Stat. 1325.)

REFERENCES IN TEXT

This title, referred to in text, is title I of Pub. L. 102–377, Oct. 2, 1992, 106 Stat. 1315. For complete classification of title I to the Code, see Tables.

§541. Board of Engineers for Rivers and Harbors; establishment; duties and powers generally

There shall be organized in the office of the Chief of Engineers, United States Army, by detail from time to time from the Corps of Engineers, a board of seven engineer officers, a majority of whom shall be of rank not less than lieutenant colonel, whose duties shall be fixed by the Chief of Engineers, and to whom shall be referred for consideration and recommendation, in addition to any other duties assigned, so far as in the opinion of the Chief of Engineers may be necessary, all reports upon examinations and surveys provided for by Congress, and all projects or changes in projects for works of river and harbor improvement prior to June 13, 1902, or thereafter provided for. And the board shall submit to the Chief of Engineers recommenda-

[1] See References in Text note below.

tions as to the desirability of commencing or continuing any and all improvements upon which reports are required. And in the consideration of such works and projects the board shall have in view the amount and character of commerce existing or reasonably prospective which will be benefited by the improvement, and the relation of the ultimate cost of such work, both as to cost of construction and maintenance, to the public commercial interests involved, and the public necessity for the work and propriety of its construction, continuance, or maintenance at the expense of the United States. And such consideration shall be given as time permits to such works as have, prior to June 13, 1902, been provided for by Congress, the same as in the case of new works proposed. The board shall, when it considers the same necessary, and with the sanction and under orders from the Chief of Engineers, make, as a board or through its members, personal examinations of localities. And all facts, information, and arguments which are presented to the board for its consideration in connection with any matter referred to it by the Chief of Engineers shall be reduced to and submitted in writing, and made a part of the records of the office of the Chief of Engineers. It shall further be the duty of said board, upon a request transmitted to the Chief of Engineers by the Committee on Public Works and Transportation of the House of Representatives, or the Committee on Environment and Public Works of the Senate, in the same manner to examine and report through the Chief of Engineers upon any projects adopted, prior to June 13, 1902, by the Government or upon which appropriations have been made, and report upon the desirability of continuing the same or upon any modifications thereof which may be deemed desirable. As used in this section the term "commerce" shall include the use of waterways by seasonal passenger craft, yachts, house boats, fishing boats, motor boats, and other similar water craft, whether or not operated for hire.

The board shall have authority, with the approval of the Chief of Engineers, to rent quarters, if necessary, for the proper transaction of its business, and to employ such civil employees as may, in the opinion of the Chief of Engineers, be required for properly transacting the business assigned to it, and the necessary expenses of the board shall be paid from allotments made by the Chief of Engineers from any appropriations made by Congress for the work or works to which the duties of the board pertain.

(June 13, 1902, ch. 1079, § 3, 32 Stat. 372; Mar. 4, 1913, ch. 144, § 4, 37 Stat. 827; Feb. 10, 1932, ch. 26, 47 Stat. 42; Pub. L. 103–437, § 12(a), Nov. 2, 1994, 108 Stat. 4590.)

CODIFICATION

The original text of section 3 of act June 13, 1902, provided for "a board of five engineer officers, whose duties shall be fixed by the Chief of Engineers." The last proviso of act Mar. 4, 1913, provided "that said board shall consist of seven members, a majority of whom shall be of rank not less than lieutenant colonel."

Other parts of section 4 of act Mar. 4, 1913, are set out in section 542 of this title.

AMENDMENTS

1994—Pub. L. 103–437 substituted "Committee on Public Works and Transportation of the House of Representatives, or the Committee on Environment and Public Works of the Senate" for "Committee on Rivers and Harbors of the House of Representatives, or the Committee on Commerce of the Senate".

1932—Act Feb. 10, 1932, inserted sentence defining "commerce".

CHANGE OF NAME

Committee on Public Works and Transportation of House of Representatives treated as referring to Committee on Transportation and Infrastructure of House of Representatives by section 1(a) of Pub. L. 104–14, set out as a note preceding section 21 of Title 2, The Congress.

TERMINATION OF BOARD OF ENGINEERS FOR RIVERS AND HARBORS AND REASSIGNMENT OF DUTIES AND RESPONSIBILITIES

Pub. L. 102–580, title II, § 223, Oct. 31, 1992, 106 Stat. 4837, provided that: "The Board of Engineers for Rivers and Harbors, established by section 3 of the River and Harbor Act of June 13, 1902 (33 U.S.C. 541), shall cease to exist on the 180th day following the date of the enactment of this Act [Oct. 31, 1992]. The Secretary may reassign to other elements within the Department of the Army such duties and responsibilities of the Board as the Secretary determines to be necessary."

WATERWAYS COMMISSION

Act Aug. 8, 1917, ch. 49, § 18, 40 Stat. 269, created a commission to be known as the Waterways Commission, to bring into coordination and cooperation the engineering, scientific, and constructive services, bureaus, boards, etc., relating to study development, or control of waterways, etc., prior to repeal by act June 10, 1920, ch. 285, § 29, 41 Stat. 1077.

§ 542. Review by Board of Engineers of reports on examinations and surveys and special reports

All reports on examinations and surveys authorized by law shall be reviewed by the Board of Engineers for Rivers and Harbors as provided for in section 541 of this title, and all special reports ordered by Congress shall, in the discretion of the Chief of Engineers, be reviewed in like manner by said board; and the said board shall also, on request by resolution of the Committee on Environment and Public Works of the Senate or the Committee on Public Works and Transportation of the House of Representatives, submitted to the Chief of Engineers, examine and review the report of any examination or survey made pursuant to any Act or resolution of Congress, and report thereon through the Chief of Engineers, United States Army, who shall submit his conclusions thereon as in other cases: *Provided*, That in no case shall the board, in its report thus called for by committee resolution, extend the scope of the project contemplated in the original report upon which its examination and review has been requested, or in the provision of law authorizing the original examination or survey.

(Mar. 4, 1913, ch. 144, § 4, 37 Stat. 826; Pub. L. 103–437, § 12(b), Nov. 2, 1994, 108 Stat. 4590.)

CODIFICATION

Section is from part of section 4 of act Mar. 4, 1913, popularly known as the "Rivers and Harbors Act of 1913". The last proviso of said section 4 is set out in section 541 of this title.

AMENDMENTS

1994—Pub. L. 103–437 substituted "Committee on Environment and Public Works of the Senate or the Committee on Public Works and Transportation of the House of Representatives" for "Committee on Commerce of the Senate or the Committee on Rivers and Harbors of the House of Representatives".

CHANGE OF NAME

Committee on Public Works and Transportation of House of Representatives treated as referring to Committee on Transportation and Infrastructure of House of Representatives by section 1(a) of Pub. L. 104–14, set out as a note preceding section 21 of Title 2, The Congress.

TRANSFER OF FUNCTIONS

For transfer of certain functions insofar as they pertain to Air Force, and to extent that they were not previously transferred to Secretary of the Air Force and Department of the Air Force from Secretary of the Army and Department of the Army, see Secretary of Defense Transfer Order No. 40, July 22, 1949.

TERMINATION OF BOARD OF ENGINEERS FOR RIVERS AND HARBORS AND REASSIGNMENT OF DUTIES AND RESPONSIBILITIES

For termination of Board of Engineers for Rivers and Harbors 180 days after Oct. 31, 1992, and reassignment of duties and responsibilities by Secretary of Army, see section 223 of Pub. L. 102–580, set out as a note under section 541 of this title.

§543. Employment of civil engineers on western and northwestern rivers

The Chief of Engineers may, with the approval of the Secretary of the Army, employ such civil engineers, not exceeding five in number, for the purpose of executing the surveys and improvements of western and northwestern rivers, ordered by Congress, as may be necessary to the proper and diligent prosecution of the same; and the persons so employed may be allowed a reasonable compensation for their services, not to exceed the sum of $3,000 a year.

(R.S. §5253; July 26, 1947, ch. 343, title II, §205(a), 61 Stat. 501.)

CODIFICATION

R.S. §5253 derived from Res. Mar. 29, 1867, No. 27, 15 Stat. 28.

CHANGE OF NAME

Department of War designated Department of the Army and title of Secretary of War changed to Secretary of the Army by section 205(a) of act July 26, 1947, ch. 343, title II, 61 Stat. 501. Section 205(a) of act July 26, 1947, was repealed by section 53 of act Aug. 10, 1956, ch. 1041, 70A Stat. 641. Section 1 of act Aug. 10, 1956, enacted "Title 10, Armed Forces" which in sections 3010 to 3013 continued Department of the Army under administrative supervision of Secretary of the Army.

TRANSFER OF FUNCTIONS

For transfer of certain functions insofar as they pertain to Air Force, and to extent that they were not previously transferred to Secretary of the Air Force and Department of the Air Force from Secretary of the Army and Department of the Army, see Secretary of Defense Transfer Order No. 40, July 22, 1949.

§544. Repealed. Aug. 19, 1968, Pub. L. 88–448, §402(a)(9), 78 Stat. 493

Section, act June 3, 1896, ch. 314, §7, 29 Stat. 235, related to employment of retired officers of the Army or Navy on river and harbour improvements.

§544a. Repealed. Pub. L. 89–554, §8(a), Sept. 6, 1966, 80 Stat. 650

Section, act June 20, 1938, ch. 535, §5, 52 Stat. 805, related to employment of retired civil service employees. See section 3323 of Title 5, Government Organization and Employees.

§544b. Employment of physicians to examine employees; fee or employment basis; validation of prior agreements

The Chief of Engineers may authorize the employment of physicians under agreement, to make such physical examinations of employees or prospective employees as he may consider essential, on a fee or regular employment basis, and all agreements entered into prior to March 2, 1945, for such purposes are validated, and the Comptroller General is authorized and directed to allow credit in the accounts of disbursing officers for reasonable payments made prior to March 2, 1945, for such services.

(Mar. 2, 1945, ch. 19, §5, 59 Stat. 24.)

TRANSFER OF FUNCTIONS

For transfer of certain functions insofar as they pertain to Air Force, and to extent that they were not previously transferred to Secretary of the Air Force and Department of the Air Force from Secretary of the Army and Department of the Army, see Secretary of Defense Transfer Order No. 40, July 22, 1949.

§544c. Minority group participation in construction of the Tennessee-Tombigbee Waterway project; annual report to Congress

The Secretary of the Army, acting through the Chief of Engineers, is directed to make a maximum effort to assure the full participation of members of minority groups, living in the States participating in the Tennessee-Tombigbee Waterway Development Authority, in the construction of the Tennessee-Tombigbee Waterway project, including actions to encourage the use, wherever possible, of minority owned firms.

(Pub. L. 94–587, §185, Oct. 22, 1976, 90 Stat. 2941; Pub. L. 104–106, div. A, title X, §1064(e), Feb. 10, 1996, 110 Stat. 445.)

AMENDMENTS

1996—Pub. L. 104–106 struck out at end "The Chief of Engineers is directed to report on July 1 of each year to the Congress on the implementation of this section, together with recommendation for any legislation that may be needed to assure the fuller and more equitable participation of members of minority groups in this project or others under the direction of the Secretary."

§545. Preliminary examinations and reports; surveys; contents of report to Congress generally

In all cases where preliminary examinations and surveys are authorized a preliminary examination of the river, harbor, or other proposed improvement mentioned shall first be made and a report as to the advisability of its improvement shall be submitted unless a survey or estimate is expressly directed. If upon such preliminary examination the proposed improvement is not deemed advisable, no further action shall be taken thereon without the further direction of

Congress; but in case the report shall be favorable to such proposed improvement, or that a survey and estimate should be made to determine the advisability of improvement, the Secretary of the Army is authorized, in his discretion, to cause surveys to be made, and the cost and advisability to be reported to Congress. And such reports containing plans and estimates shall also contain a statement as to the rate at which the work should be prosecuted: *Provided*, That every report submitted to Congress, in addition to full information regarding the present and prospective commercial importance of the project covered by the report and the benefit to commerce likely to result from any proposed plan of improvement, shall also contain such data as it may be practicable to secure in regard to the following subjects:

(a) The existence and establishment of both private and public terminal and transfer facilities contiguous to the navigable water proposed to be improved, and, if water terminals have been constructed, the general location, description, and use made of the same, with an opinion as to their adequacy and efficiency, whether private or public. If no public terminals have been constructed, or if they are inadequate in number, there shall be included in the report an opinion in general terms as to the necessity, number, and appropriate location of the same, and also the necessary relations of such proposed terminals to the development of commerce.

(b) The development and utilization of water power for industrial and commercial purposes.

(c) Such other subjects as may be properly connected with such project: *Provided*, That in the investigation and study of these questions consideration shall be given only to their bearing upon the improvement of navigation, to the possibility and desirability of their being coordinated in a logical and proper manner with improvements for navigation to lessen the cost of such improvements and to compensate the Government for expenditures made in the interest of navigation, and to their relation to the development and regulation of commerce: *Provided further*, That the investigation and study of these questions may, upon review by the Board of Engineers for Rivers and Harbors when called for as provided by law, be extended to any work of improvement under way and to any locality the examination and survey of which has heretofore been, or may hereafter be, authorized by Congress.

(Mar. 4, 1913, ch. 144, § 3, 37 Stat. 825; July 26, 1947, ch. 343, title II, § 205(a), 61 Stat. 501.)

CODIFICATION

This section and the second paragraph of section 556 of this title are from section 3 of act Mar. 4, 1913, popularly known as the "Rivers and Harbors Appropriation Act of 1913". That section superseded similar provisions of act June 25, 1910, ch. 382, § 3, 36 Stat. 668, for reports, investigations on review by the board of Engineers and for the printing of reports.

PRIOR PROVISIONS

Provision for report of examinations of river and harbor improvements appeared in R.S. § 231, repealed by act Mar. 3, 1933, ch. 202, § 1, 47 Stat. 1428, and read as follows: "The Secretary of War shall cause to be prepared and submitted to Congress, in connection with the reports of examinations and surveys of rivers and harbors hereafter made by order of Congress, full statements of all existing facts tending to show to what extent the general commerce of the country will be promoted by the several works of improvements contemplated by such examinations and surveys, to the end that public moneys shall not be applied excepting where such improvements shall tend to subserve the general commercial and navigation interests of the United States."

CHANGE OF NAME

Department of War designated Department of the Army and title of Secretary of War changed to Secretary of the Army by section 205(a) of act July 26, 1947, ch. 343, title II, 61 Stat. 501. Section 205(a) of act July 26, 1947, was repealed by section 53 of act Aug. 10, 1956, ch. 1041, 70A Stat. 641. Section 1 of act Aug. 10, 1956, enacted "Title 10, Armed Forces" which in sections 3010 to 3013 continued Department of the Army under administrative supervision of Secretary of the Army.

TERMINATION OF BOARD OF ENGINEERS FOR RIVERS AND HARBORS AND REASSIGNMENT OF DUTIES AND RESPONSIBILITIES

For termination of Board of Engineers for Rivers and Harbors 180 days after Oct. 31, 1992, and reassignment of duties and responsibilities by Secretary of Army, see section 223 of Pub. L. 102–580, set out as a note under section 541 of this title.

TEMPORARY PROHIBITORY PROVISIONS

Provisions prohibiting supplemental reports or estimates, prohibiting the making of examination or survey for new works not designated, and providing that projects were not to be deemed entered upon until appropriations were made, appeared in various rivers and harbors appropriation acts. They are omitted from the Code as superseded or temporary.

REPORT ON IMPROVEMENTS FOR COASTAL DEFENSE PURPOSES

The Secretary of War and the Secretary of the Navy were authorized and directed to report to Congress at the earliest practicable date, such specific plans for improvement of harbors, canals and connecting channels as would best provide adequate facilities for operations of the fleet for defense of the harbors on the Atlantic, Gulf, and Pacific coasts; also the feasible extensions requisite to make existing approved projects for improvement of such harbors, canals, and channels available for such purposes, and the cost of each such several improvements, calculated upon the basis of completion under contract within five years, by act Aug. 29, 1916, ch. 417, 39 Stat. 556, omitted from the Code as special and temporary.

PRELIMINARY EXAMINATIONS AND SURVEYS OF GREAT LAKES

The Secretary of War was directed to cause preliminary examinations and surveys to be made of the harbors and connecting waters of the Great Lakes with a view to determining what additional improvements would be necessary to permit those waterways to accommodate vessels to pass through the Welland Canal when enlarged by the Dominion of Canada, including report as to the character and draft of vessels which might be expected to use the canal when so enlarged, by a provision of the Rivers and Harbors Appropriation Act of 1916, act July 27, 1916, ch. 260, § 2, 39 Stat. 411, omitted from the Code as special and temporary.

§ 545a. Discontinuance

For preliminary examinations and surveys authorized in previous river and harbor and flood-control Acts, the Secretary of the Army is directed to cause investigations and reports for navigation and allied purposes to be prepared under the supervision of the Chief of Engineers in the form of survey reports, and that preliminary examination reports shall no longer be required to be prepared.

(Pub. L. 85–500, title I, §105, July 3, 1958, 72 Stat. 300.)

REFERENCES IN TEXT

Previous river and harbor and flood-control Acts, referred to in text, means those acts prior to the River and Harbor Act of 1958 and the Flood Control Act of 1958, titles I and II, respectively, of Pub. L. 85–500.

§546. Investigation of stream flow and watersheds; surveys in connection with dams

The surveys of navigable streams shall include such stream-flow measurements and other investigations of the watersheds as may be necessary for preparation of plans of improvement and a proper consideration of all uses of the stream affecting navigation, and whenever necessary similar investigations may be made in connection with all navigable streams under improvement. Whenever permission for the construction of dams in navigable streams is granted, or is under consideration by Congress, such surveys and investigations of the sections of the streams affected may be made as are necessary to secure conformity with rational plans for the improvement of the streams for navigation.

(June 25, 1910, ch. 382, §3, 36 Stat. 669.)

CODIFICATION

Section is from section 3 of act June 25, 1910, popularly known as the "Rivers and Harbors Appropriation Act of 1910". Other provisions of such section were omitted, as superseded by section 545 of this title.

PRIOR PROVISIONS

General provisions regulating the construction of dams were made by the Dam Act of June 21, 1906, ch. 3508, 34 Stat. 386, as amended by act June 23, 1910, ch. 360, 36 Stat. 593, apparently omitted from the Code as superseded.

§546a. Information as to configuration of shore line

Every report submitted to Congress in pursuance of any provision of law for preliminary examination and survey looking to the improvement of the entrance at the mouth of any river or at any inlet, in addition to other information which the Congress has directed shall be given, shall contain information concerning the configuration of the shore line and the probable effect thereon that may be expected to result from the improvement having particular reference to erosion and/or accretion for a distance of not less than ten miles on either side of the said entrance.

(Aug. 30, 1935, ch. 831, §5, 49 Stat. 1048.)

§547. Reports as to local benefits of improvement and recommendations as to local cooperation

Every report submitted to Congress in pursuance of any provision of law for a survey, in addition to other information which the Congress has directed shall be given, shall contain a statement of special or local benefit which will accrue to localities affected by such improvement and a statement of general or national benefits, with recommendations as to what local cooperation should be required, if any, on account of such special or local benefit.

(June 5, 1920, ch. 252, §2, 41 Stat. 1010.)

CODIFICATION

Section is from act June 5, 1920, popularly known as the "Rivers and Harbors Appropriation Act of 1921".

§547a. Inclusion of regional economic development benefits in economic analysis for purposes of computing economic justification of project

In the case of any authorized navigation project which has been partially constructed, or is to be constructed, which is located in one or more States, and which serves regional needs, the Secretary of the Army, acting through the Chief of Engineers, may include in any economic analysis which is under preparation on October 22, 1976, such regional economic development benefits as he determines to be appropriate for purposes of computing the economic justification of the project.

(Pub. L. 94–587, §140, Oct. 22, 1976, 90 Stat. 2930.)

§548. Omitted

CODIFICATION

Section, act Mar. 3, 1925, ch. 467, §7, 43 Stat. 1191, required a report on projects adopted prior to March 3, 1925.

§549. Repealed. Pub. L. 96–470, title I, §104(c), Oct. 19, 1980, 94 Stat. 2238

Section, act Mar. 3, 1899, ch. 425, §7, 30 Stat. 1150, provided that Chief of Engineers, in submitting his annual reports to Congress on river and harbor improvements, report on deterioration in improvements, estimate cost of repairing or rebuilding such works, and recommend discontinuance of appropriations for any works deemed unworthy of further improvement.

§549a. Review of navigation, flood control, and water supply projects

The Secretary of the Army, acting through the Chief of Engineers, is authorized to review the operation of projects the construction of which has been completed and which were constructed by the Corps of Engineers in the interest of navigation, flood control, water supply, and related purposes, when found advisable due[1] the significantly changed physical or economic conditions, and to report thereon to Congress with recommendations on the advisability of modifying the structures or their operation, and for improving the quality of the environment in the overall public interest.

(Pub. L. 91–611, title II, §216, Dec. 31, 1970, 84 Stat. 1830.)

CODIFICATION

Section is from Pub. L. 91–611, popularly known as the "Flood Control Act of 1970".

[1] So in original. Probably should be "due to".

§ 550. Report on water terminal and transfer facilities

The Chief of Engineers, United States Army, shall indicate in his annual reports the character of the terminal and transfer facilities existing on every harbor or waterway under maintenance or improvement by the United States, and state whether they are considered adequate for existing commerce. He shall also submit one or more special reports on this subject, as soon as possible after January 18, 1918, including, among other things, the following:

(a) A brief description of such water terminals, including location and the suitability of such terminals to the existing traffic conditions, and whether such terminals are publicly or privately owned, and the terms and conditions under which they may be subjected to public use.

(b) Whether such water terminals are connected by a belt or spur line of railroad with all the railroads serving the same territory or municipality, and whether such connecting railroad is owned by the public and the conditions upon which the same may be used, and also whether there is an interchange of traffic between the water carriers and the railroad or railroads as to such traffic which is carried partly by rail and partly by water to its destination, and also whether improved and adequate highways have been constructed connecting such water terminal with the other lines of highways.

(c) If no water terminals have been constructed by the municipality or other existing public agency there shall be included in his report an expression of opinion in general terms as to the necessity, number, and appropriate location of such a terminal or terminals.

(d) An investigation of the general subject of water terminals, with descriptions and general plans of terminals of appropriate types and construction for the harbors and waterways of the United States suitable for various commercial purposes and adapted to the varying conditions of tides, floods, and other physical characteristics.

(July 18, 1918, ch. 155, § 7, 40 Stat. 911.)

CODIFICATION

Section is from act July 18, 1918, popularly known as the "Rivers and Harbors Appropriation Act of 1918".

§ 551. Policy of Government as to terminal facilities for new projects

It is declared to be the policy of the Congress that water terminals are essential at all cities and towns located upon harbors or navigable waterways and that at least one public terminal should exist, constructed, owned, and regulated by the municipality or other public agency of the State and open to the use of all on equal terms. The Secretary of the Army, through the Chief of Engineers, shall give full publicity, as far as may be practicable, to this provision.

(Mar. 2, 1919, ch. 95, § 1, 40 Stat. 1286; July 26, 1947, ch. 343, title II, § 205(a), 61 Stat. 501.)

CODIFICATION

Section is from act Mar. 2, 1919, popularly known as the "Rivers and Harbors Appropriation Act of 1919".

The original text of said section 1 read as follows: "It is hereby declared to be the policy of the Congress that water terminals are essential at all cities and towns located upon harbors or navigable waterways and that at least one public terminal should exist, constructed, owned, and regulated by the municipality, or other public agency of the State and open to the use of all on equal terms, and with the view of carrying out this policy to the fullest possible extent the Secretary of War is hereby vested with the discretion to withhold, unless the public interests would seriously suffer by delay, monies appropriated in this Act for new projects adopted herein, or for the further improvement of existing projects if, in his opinion, no water terminals exist adequate for the traffic and open to all on equal terms, or unless satisfactory assurances are received that local or other interests will provide such adequate terminal or terminals. The Secretary of War, through the Chief of Engineers, shall give full publicity, as far as may be practicable, to this provision."

CHANGE OF NAME

Department of War designated Department of the Army and title of Secretary of War changed to Secretary of the Army by section 205(a) of act July 26, 1947, ch. 343, title II, 61 Stat. 501. Section 205(a) of act July 26, 1947, was repealed by section 53 of act Aug. 10, 1956, ch. 1041, 70A Stat. 641. Section 1 of act Aug. 10, 1956, enacted "Title 10, Armed Forces" which in sections 3010 to 3013 continued Department of the Army under administrative supervision of Secretary of the Army.

§ 552. Repealed. May 29, 1928, ch. 901, § 1(28), 45 Stat. 988

Section, act Aug. 5, 1886, ch. 929, § 8, 24 Stat. 335, required reports to Congress concerning civilian engineers employed in improving rivers and harbors.

§ 553. Freight statistics

In the collection of statistics relating to traffic, the Corps of Engineers is directed to adopt a uniform system of classification for freight, and upon rivers or inland waterways to collate ton-mileage statistics as far as practicable.

(July 25, 1912, ch. 253, § 1, 37 Stat. 223.)

CODIFICATION

Section is from part of section 1 of act July 25, 1912, popularly known as the "Rivers and Harbors Appropriation Act of 1912".

§ 554. Duty of shipowners and officers to furnish information to person in local charge of improvement; penalty

Owners, agents, masters, and clerks of vessels arriving at or departing from localities where works of river and harbor improvement are carried on shall furnish, on application of the persons in local charge of the works, a comprehensive statement of vessels, passengers, freight, and tonnage.

Every person or persons offending against the provisions of this section shall, for each and every offense, be liable to a fine of $100, or imprisonment not exceeding two months, to be enforced in any district court in the United States within whose territorial jurisdiction such offense may have been committed.

(Feb. 21, 1891, ch. 252, §§ 1, 2, 26 Stat. 766.)

§ 555. Duty of shipowners and officers to furnish information required by Secretary of the Army

Owners, agents, masters, and clerks of vessels and other craft plying upon the navigable waters of the United States, and all individuals and corporations engaged in transporting their own goods upon the navigable waters of the United States, shall furnish such statements relative to vessels, passengers, freight, and tonnage as may be required by the Secretary of the Army: *Provided*, That this provision shall not apply to those rafting logs except upon a direct request upon the owner to furnish specific information.

Every person or persons offending against the provisions of this section shall, for each and every offense, be liable to a fine of not more than $5,000, or imprisonment not exceeding two months, to be enforced in any district court in the United States within whose territorial jurisdiction such offense may have been committed. In addition, the Secretary may assess a civil penalty of up to $2,500, per violation, against any person or entity that fails to provide timely, accurate statements required to be submitted pursuant to this section by the Secretary.

(Sept. 22, 1922, ch. 427, §11, 42 Stat. 1043; July 26, 1947, ch. 343, title II, §205(a), 61 Stat. 501; Pub. L. 99–662, title IX, §919(f), Nov. 17, 1986, 100 Stat. 4193.)

CODIFICATION

Section is from act Sept. 22, 1922, popularly known as the "Rivers and Harbors Appropriation Act of 1922".

AMENDMENTS

1986—Pub. L. 99–662 substituted "not more than $5,000" for "$100" and inserted "In addition, the Secretary may assess a civil penalty of up to $2,500, per violation, against any person or entity that fails to provide timely, accurate statements required to be submitted pursuant to this section by the Secretary."

CHANGE OF NAME

Department of War designated Department of the Army and title of Secretary of War changed to Secretary of the Army by section 205(a) of act July 26, 1947, ch. 343, title II, 61 Stat. 501. Section 205(a) of act July 26, 1947, was repealed by section 53 of act Aug. 10, 1956, ch. 1041, 70A Stat. 641. Section 1 of act Aug. 10, 1956, enacted "Title 10, Armed Forces" which in sections 3010 to 3013 continued Department of the Army under administrative supervision of Secretary of the Army.

§ 555a. Petroleum product information

(a) Disclosure to States

The Secretary shall disclose petroleum product information to any State taxing agency making a request under subsection (b) of this section. Such information shall be disclosed for the purpose of, and only to the extent necessary in, the administration of State tax laws.

(b) Requests for disclosure

Disclosure of information under this section shall be permitted only upon written request by the head of the State taxing agency and only to the representatives of such agency designated in such written request as the individuals who are to inspect or to receive the information on behalf of such agency. Any such representative shall be an employee or legal representative of such agency.

(c) Modes of disclosure

(1) Requests for the disclosure of information under this section, and such disclosure, shall be made in such manner and at such time and place as shall be prescribed by the Secretary.

(2) Information disclosed to any person under this section may be provided in the form of written documents or reproductions of such documents, or by any other mode or means which the Secretary determines necessary or appropriate. A reasonable fee may be prescribed for furnishing such information.

(3) Any reproduction of any document or other matter made in accordance with this subsection shall have the same legal status as the original, and any such reproduction shall, if properly authenticated, be admissible in evidence in any judicial or administrative proceeding as if it were the original, whether or not the original is in existence.

(d) Confidentiality of disclosed information

The Secretary shall not disclose information to a State taxing agency of a State under this section unless such State has in effect provisions of law which—

(1) exempt such information from disclosure under a State law requiring agencies of the State to make information available to the public, or

(2) otherwise protect the confidentiality of the information.

Nothing in the preceding sentence shall be construed to prohibit the disclosure by an officer or employee of a State of information to another officer or employer of such State (or political subdivision of such State) to the extent necessary in the administration of State tax laws.

(e) Definitions

For purposes of this section, the term—

(1) "petroleum product information" means information relating to petroleum products transported by vessel which is received by the Secretary (A) under section 555 of this title, or (B) under any other legal authority; and

(2) "State taxing agency" means any State agency, body, or commission, or its legal representative, which is charged under the laws of such State with responsibility for the administration of State tax laws.

(f) Omitted

(Pub. L. 99–662, title IX, §919, Nov. 17, 1986, 100 Stat. 4192.)

CODIFICATION

Subsec. (f) of this section amended section 555 of this title.

"SECRETARY" DEFINED

Secretary means the Secretary of the Army, see section 2201 of this title.

§ 556. Printing reports generally

The Secretary of the Army shall cause the manuscript of the annual report of the Chief of Engineers and subordinate engineers, relating to the improvement of rivers and harbors, and the report of the Mississippi River Commission to be placed in the hands of the Public Printer on or before the 15th day of October in each year, and the Public Printer shall cause said reports to be printed with an accurate and comprehensive index thereof, on or before the first Monday in December in each year, for the use of Congress.

All reports on examinations and surveys which may be prepared during the recess of Congress shall, in the discretion of the Secretary of the Army, be printed by the Public Printer as documents of the following session of Congress.

(Aug. 11, 1888, ch. 860, § 8, 25 Stat. 424; June 13, 1902, ch. 1079, § 1, 32 Stat. 367; Mar. 4, 1913, ch. 144, § 3, 37 Stat. 826; July 26, 1947, ch. 343, title II, § 205(a), 61 Stat. 501.)

CODIFICATION

The first paragraph of this section is from act Aug. 11, 1888, popularly known as the "Rivers and Harbors Appropriation Act".

The Mississippi River Commission was created by act June 28, 1879, set out as sections 641, 642, 644, 646, and 647 of this title.

The words "and Missouri" which appeared in the original text after "Mississippi" were superseded by the abolition of the Missouri River Commission by act June 13, 1902, ch. 1079, § 1, 32 Stat. 367.

The second paragraph of this section is from the last paragraph of section 3 of act Mar. 4, 1913, which superseded a similar provision of act July 25, 1912, ch. 253, 37 Stat. 231. Other parts of said section 3 are set out in section 545 of this title.

CHANGE OF NAME

Department of War designated Department of the Army and title of Secretary of War changed to Secretary of the Army by section 205(a) of act July 26, 1947, ch. 343, title II, 61 Stat. 501. Section 205(a) of act July 26, 1947, was repealed by section 53 of act Aug. 10, 1956, ch. 1041, 70A Stat. 641. Section 1 of act Aug. 10, 1956, enacted "Title 10, Armed Forces" which in sections 3010 to 3013 continued Department of the Army under administrative supervision of Secretary of the Army.

COMPILATION AND PRINTING OF LAWS

Act June 5, 1920, ch. 252, § 6, 41 Stat. 1014, as amended by act Mar. 3, 1925, ch. 467, § 4, 43 Stat. 1190, provided for compilation and printing of laws relating to improvement of rivers and harbors, passed between Mar. 4, 1913, until and including laws of second session of Sixty-eighth Congress.

§ 557. Payment of costs of printing

The printing of matter relating to river and harbor works, including all reports, compilations, regulations, and so forth, whose preparation is allowable under Department of the Army regulations, shall be done and paid for out of regular annual appropriations for printing and binding for the Department of the Army.

(July 25, 1912, ch. 253, § 13, 37 Stat. 234; July 1, 1916, ch. 209, § 1, 39 Stat. 330; July 26, 1947, ch. 343, title II, § 205(a), 61 Stat. 501.)

CODIFICATION

Section is from section 1 of act July 1, 1916, repealing section 13 of act July 25, 1912.

Section 1 of that act was a provision, following an appropriation for printing for the War Department, of the Sundry Civil Appropriation Act for 1917.

The repealed section 13 of act July 25, 1912, read as follows: "The printing of matter relating to river and harbor works, including all reports, compilations, regulations, and so forth, whose preparation is allowable under War Department regulations, may, upon recommendation of the Chief of Engineers and approval by the Secretary of War, be paid for from river and harbor appropriations."

CHANGE OF NAME

Department of War designated Department of the Army and title of Secretary of War changed to Secretary of the Army by section 205(a) of act July 26, 1947, ch. 343, title II, 61 Stat. 501. Section 205(a) of act July 26, 1947, was repealed by section 53 of act Aug. 10, 1956, ch. 1041, 70A Stat. 641. Section 1 of act Aug. 10, 1956, enacted "Title 10, Armed Forces" which in sections 3010 to 3013 continued Department of the Army under administrative supervision of Secretary of the Army.

§ 557a. Publication of pamphlets, maps, brochures, and other material

The Chief of Engineers is authorized to publish information pamphlets, maps, brochures, and other material on river and harbor, flood control, and other civil works activities, including related public park and recreation facilities, under his jurisdiction, as he may deem to be of value to the general public.

(Pub. L. 85–480, § 1, July 2, 1958, 72 Stat. 279.)

§ 557b. Sale of publications, charts, or other material; deposit of proceeds

The Chief of Engineers is authorized to provide for the sale of any of the material prepared under authority of section 557a of this title; and of publications, charts, or material prepared under his direction pursuant to other legislative authorization or appropriation, and to charge therefor a sum not less than the cost of reproduction. The money received from sales authorized by this section shall be deposited into the Treasury to the credit of miscellaneous receipts, except that in any case in which the cost of reproduction has been paid from the revolving fund established pursuant to the Civil Functions Appropriation Act, 1954, the proceeds shall be deposited to the credit of such fund.

(Pub. L. 85–480, § 2, July 2, 1958, 72 Stat. 279.)

REFERENCES IN TEXT

The Civil Functions Appropriation Act, 1954, referred to in text, is act July 27, 1953, ch. 245, 67 Stat. 197. Provisions of the Act establishing the revolving fund are classified to sections 576 and 701b–10 of this title.

§ 558. Proceeds from sale or transfer of property acquired

When any property which has been heretofore or may be hereafter purchased or acquired for the improvement of rivers and harbors is no longer needed, or is no longer serviceable and is transferred or sold, the proceeds thereof may be credited to the appropriation for the work for which it was acquired.

(June 13, 1902, ch. 1079, § 5, 32 Stat. 373; Feb. 20, 1931, ch. 235, 46 Stat. 1191; Oct. 31, 1951, ch. 654, § 4(4), 65 Stat. 709.)

CODIFICATION

Section originally began with the words "when any land or other" preceding "property". The words, "land or other", were deleted on the basis of act February 20, 1931, which provided, "that hereafter no real estate of the War Department shall be sold or disposed of without authority of Congress, and all existing Acts or parts thereof in conflict with this proviso, other than special Acts for the sale of stated tracts of land, are hereby repealed."

Section is from the first part of section 5 of act June 13, 1902, which was a provision of the Rivers and Harbors Appropriation Act for 1902. The last part of such section 5 is set out as section 631 of this title.

AMENDMENTS

1951—Act Oct. 31, 1951, struck out provisions authorizing the Secretary of the Army to sell the unserviceable property referred to, and authorizing him to direct the transfer of any property employed in river and harbor works; struck out the provision that the property so transferred should be valued and credited to the project upon which it was theretofore used and charged to the project to which it was transferred; and inserted "and is transferred or sold, the proceeds thereof may be credited to the appropriation for the work for which it was acquired".

§558a. Repealed. Oct. 31, 1951, ch. 654, §1(56), 65 Stat. 703

Section, act Aug. 30, 1935, ch. 831, §7, 49 Stat. 1048, related to sale of property no longer needed for improvement of canals, rivers and harbors.

§558b. Exchange of land or property

In any case in which it may be necessary or advisable in the execution of an authorized work of river and harbor improvement to exchange land or other property of the Government for private lands or property required for such project, the Secretary of the Army may, upon the recommendation of the Chief of Engineers, authorize such exchange upon terms and conditions deemed appropriate by him, and any conveyance of Government land or interests therein necessary to effect such exchange may be executed by the Secretary of the Army: *Provided further*, That the authority granted to the Secretary of the Army shall not extend to or include lands held or acquired by the Tennessee Valley Authority pursuant to the terms of the Tennessee Valley Authority Act [16 U.S.C. 831 et seq.]. This section shall apply to any exchanges heretofore deemed advisable in connection with the construction of the Bonneville Dam in the Columbia River.

(June 20, 1938, ch. 535, §2, 52 Stat. 804; July 26, 1947, ch. 343, title II, §205(a), 61 Stat. 501.)

REFERENCES IN TEXT

The Tennessee Valley Authority Act, referred to in text, is act May 18, 1933, ch. 32, 48 Stat. 58, as amended, known as the Tennessee Valley Authority Act of 1933, which is classified generally to chapter 12A (§831 et seq.) of Title 16, Conservation. For complete classification of this Act to the Code, see section 831 of Title 16 and Tables.

CHANGE OF NAME

Department of War designated Department of the Army and title of Secretary of War changed to Secretary of the Army by section 205(a) of act July 26, 1947, ch. 343, title II, 61 Stat. 501. Section 205(a) of act July 26, 1947, was repealed by section 53 of act Aug. 10, 1956, ch. 1041, 70A Stat. 641. Section 1 of act Aug. 10, 1956, enacted "Title 10, Armed Forces" which in sections 3010 to 3013 continued Department of the Army under administrative supervision of Secretary of the Army.

§558b–1. Application to authorized works of flood control

Section 558b of this title is made applicable to authorized works of flood control.

(Aug. 11, 1939, ch. 699, §3, 53 Stat. 1414.)

§558c. Rights-of-way over United States land

The Secretary of the Army is authorized and empowered, under such terms and conditions as are deemed advisable by him, to grant easements for rights-of-way for public roads and streets on and across lands acquired by the United States for river and harbor and flood control improvements including, whenever necessary, the privilege of occupying so much of said lands as may be necessary for the piers, abutments, and other portions of a bridge structure: *Provided*, That such rights-of-way shall be granted only upon a finding by the Secretary of the Army that the same will be in the public interest and will not substantially injure the interest of the United States in the property affected thereby: *Provided further*, That all or any part of such rights-of-way may be annulled and forfeited by the Secretary of the Army for failure to comply with the terms or conditions of any grant hereunder or for nonuse or for abandonment of rights granted under the authority hereof: *Provided further*, That the authority granted to the Secretary of the Army shall not extend to or include lands held or acquired by the Tennessee Valley Authority pursuant to the terms of the Tennessee Valley Authority Act [16 U.S.C. 831 et seq.].

(June 20, 1938, ch. 535, §10, 52 Stat. 808; July 26, 1947, ch. 343, title II, §205(a), 61 Stat. 501.)

REFERENCES IN TEXT

The Tennessee Valley Authority Act, referred to in text, is act May 18, 1933, ch. 32, 48 Stat. 58, as amended, known as the Tennessee Valley Authority Act of 1933, which is classified generally to chapter 12A (§831 et seq.) of Title 16, Conservation. For complete classification of this Act to the Code, see section 831 of Title 16 and Tables.

CHANGE OF NAME

Department of War designated Department of the Army and title of Secretary of War changed to Secretary of the Army by section 205(a) of act July 26, 1947, ch. 343, title II, 61 Stat. 501. Section 205(a) of act July 26, 1947, was repealed by section 53 of act Aug. 10, 1956, ch. 1041, 70A Stat. 641. Section 1 of act Aug. 10, 1956, enacted "Title 10, Armed Forces" which in sections 3010 to 3013 continued Department of the Army under administrative supervision of Secretary of the Army.

§559. Disposition of rentals for Government plants

Amounts paid after August 8, 1917, by private parties or other agencies for rental of plant owned by the Government in connection with the prosecution of river and harbor works shall be deposited in each case to the credit of the appropriation to which the plant belongs.

(Aug. 8, 1917, ch. 49, §13, 40 Stat. 268.)

CODIFICATION

Section is from act Aug. 8, 1917, popularly known as the "Rivers and Harbors Appropriation Act of 1917".

§560. Contributions from private parties; return of excess

The Secretary of the Army is authorized to receive from private parties such funds as may be contributed by them to be expended in connection with funds appropriated by the United States for any authorized work of public improvement of rivers and harbors whenever such work and expenditure may be considered by the

Chief of Engineers as advantageous to the interests of navigation: *Provided*, That when contributions heretofore or hereafter made by local interests for river and harbor improvements, in accordance with specific requirements or under general authority of Congress, are in excess of the actual cost of the work contemplated and properly chargeable to such contributions, such excess contributions may, with the approval of the Secretary of the Army, be returned to the proper representatives of the contributing interests, unless the provision of law under which the contribution is made requires that the entire contribution be retained by the United States.

(Mar. 4, 1915, ch. 142, § 4, 38 Stat. 1053; July 26, 1947, ch. 343, title II, § 205(a), 61 Stat. 501.)

CODIFICATION

Section is from act Mar. 4, 1915, popularly known as the "Rivers and Harbors Appropriation Act of 1915".

PRIOR PROVISIONS

Section superseded act Mar. 4, 1913, ch. 144, § 8, 37 Stat. 827, which read as follows: "The Secretary of War is hereby authorized to receive from private parties such funds as may be contributed by them to be expended in connection with funds appropriated by the United States for any authorized work of public improvement of rivers and harbors, whenever such work and expenditure may be considered by the Chief of Engineers as advantageous to the interests of navigation."

CHANGE OF NAME

Department of War designated Department of the Army and title of Secretary of War changed to Secretary of the Army by section 205(a) of act July 26, 1947, ch. 343, title II, 61 Stat. 501. Section 205(a) of act July 26, 1947, was repealed by section 53 of act Aug. 10, 1956, ch. 1041, 70A Stat. 641. Section 1 of act Aug. 10, 1956, enacted "Title 10, Armed Forces" which in sections 3010 to 3013 continued Department of the Army under administrative supervision of Secretary of the Army.

§ 561. Advances by private parties; repayment

Whenever local interests shall offer to advance funds for the prosecution of a work of river and harbor improvement duly adopted and authorized by law the Secretary of the Army may, in his discretion, receive such funds and expend the same in the immediate prosecution of such work. The Secretary of the Army is authorized and directed to repay without interest, from appropriations which may be provided by Congress for river and harbor improvements, the moneys so contributed and expended: *Provided*, That no repayment of funds which may be contributed for the purpose of meeting any conditions of local cooperation imposed by Congress, nor under the authority of section 560 of this title shall be made.

(Mar. 3, 1925, ch. 467, § 11, 43 Stat. 1197; July 26, 1947, ch. 343, title II, § 205(a), 61 Stat. 501.)

CHANGE OF NAME

Department of War designated Department of the Army and title of Secretary of War changed to Secretary of the Army by section 205(a) of act July 26, 1947, ch. 343, title II, 61 Stat. 501. Section 205(a) of act July 26, 1947, was repealed by section 53 of act Aug. 10, 1956, ch. 1041, 70A Stat. 641. Section 1 of act Aug. 10, 1956, enacted "Title 10, Armed Forces" which in sections 3010 to 3013 continued Department of the Army under administrative supervision of Secretary of the Army.

§ 561a. Contributions from local interests; reduction to meet lowered cost

When the authorization of a project of river and harbor improvement requires that local interests shall contribute a specific sum of money toward its cost, the Secretary of the Army, upon the recommendation of the Chief of Engineers, may reduce the sum to be contributed to an amount which shall be in the same ratio to the amount of the required contribution as the actual cost of the work to which said contribution is applicable bears to its original estimated cost as set forth in the project document.

(Mar. 3, 1933, ch. 216, 47 Stat. 1545; July 26, 1947, ch. 343, title II, § 205(a), 61 Stat. 501.)

CODIFICATION

A prior provision that the reduction authorized by this section was not to apply to contributions made prior to Mar. 3, 1933, was omitted as obsolete.

CHANGE OF NAME

Department of War designated Department of the Army and title of Secretary of War changed to Secretary of the Army by section 205(a) of act July 26, 1947, ch. 343, title II, 61 Stat. 501. Section 205(a) of act July 26, 1947, was repealed by section 53 of act Aug. 10, 1956, ch. 1041, 70A Stat. 641. Section 1 of act Aug. 10, 1956, enacted "Title 10, Armed Forces" which in sections 3010 to 3013 continued Department of the Army under administrative supervision of Secretary of the Army.

§ 562. Channel depths and dimensions defined

In the preparation of projects under this and subsequent river and harbor acts and after the project becomes operational, unless otherwise expressed, the channel depths referred to shall be understood to signify the depth at mean lower low water, as defined by the Department of Commerce for nautical charts and tidal predictions, in tidal waters tributary to the Atlantic and Gulf coasts and at mean lower low water, as defined by the Department of Commerce for nautical charts and tidal predictions, in tidal waters tributary to the Pacific coast and the mean depth for a continuous period of fifteen days of the lowest water, as defined by the Department of Commerce for nautical charts and tidal predictions, in the navigation season of any year in rivers and nontidal channels, and and[1] after the project becomes operational the channel dimensions specified shall be understood to admit of such increase at the entrances, bends, sidings, and turning places as may be necessary to allow of the free movement of boats.

(Mar. 4, 1915, ch. 142, § 5, 38 Stat. 1053; Pub. L. 102–580, title II, § 224, Oct. 31, 1992, 106 Stat. 4837.)

CODIFICATION

Section is from act Mar. 4, 1915, popularly known as the "Rivers and Harbors Appropriation Act of 1915".

PRIOR PROVISIONS

Section superseded act Mar. 4, 1913, ch. 144, § 9, 37 Stat. 827, which read as follows: "In the preparation of projects under this and subsequent river and harbor acts, unless otherwise expressed, the channel depths referred to shall be understood to signify the depth at

[1] So in original.

mean lower low water in tidal waters, and the mean depth during the month of lowest water in the navigation season in rivers and nontidal channels, and the channel dimensions specified shall be understood to admit of such increase at the entrances, bends, sidings, and turning places as may be necessary to allow of the free movement of boats."

AMENDMENTS

1992—Pub. L. 102–580 inserted "and after the project becomes operational" after "harbor acts", "lower" after "depth at mean", ", as defined by the Department of Commerce for nautical charts and tidal predictions," after "water" wherever appearing, and "and after the project becomes operational" before "the channel dimensions".

§562a. Project depths for national defense purposes; waterways for general commerce

The Chief of Engineers, under the direction of the Secretary of the Army, is hereby authorized to maintain authorized river and harbor projects in excess of authorized project depths where such excess depths have been provided by the United States for defense purposes and whenever the Chief of Engineers determines that such waterways also serve essential needs of general commerce.

(Pub. L. 90–483, title I, §117, Aug. 13, 1968, 82 Stat. 737.)

§563. Omitted

CODIFICATION

Section, act Sept. 22, 1922, ch. 427, §6, 42 Stat. 1042, made unexpended funds, appropriated prior to Sept. 22, 1922, for river and harbor improvements, available for preservation and maintenance of existing river and harbor works and prosecution of desirable new projects.

§564. Repealed. July 3, 1943, ch. 189, §5, 57 Stat. 374

Section, acts June 25, 1910, ch. 382, §4, 36 Stat. 676; June 5, 1920, ch. 252, §9, 41 Stat. 1015, related to settlement of claims for injury to or loss of private property.

§565. River and harbor improvement by private or municipal enterprise

Any person or persons, corporations, municipal or private, who desire to improve any navigable river, or any part thereof, at their or its own expense and risk may do so upon the approval of the plans and specifications of said proposed improvement by the Secretary of the Army and Chief of Engineers of the Army. The plan of said improvement must conform with the general plan of the Government improvements, must not impede navigation, and no toll shall be imposed on account thereof, and said improvement shall at all times be under the control and supervision of the Secretary of the Army and Chief of Engineers.

(June 13, 1902, ch. 1079, §1, 32 Stat. 371; July 26, 1947, ch. 343, title II, §205(a), 61 Stat. 501.)

CODIFICATION

Section is from act June 13, 1902, popularly known as the "Rivers and Harbors Appropriation Act for 1902". The provisions of this section followed an appropriation for emergencies.

CHANGE OF NAME

Department of War designated Department of the Army and title of Secretary of War changed to Secretary of the Army by section 205(a) of act July 26, 1947, ch. 343, title II, 61 Stat. 501. Section 205(a) of act July 26, 1947, was repealed by section 53 of act Aug. 10, 1956, ch. 1041, 70A Stat. 641. Section 1 of act Aug. 10, 1956, enacted "Title 10, Armed Forces" which in sections 3010 to 3013 continued Department of the Army under administrative supervision of Secretary of the Army.

CONSTRUCTION OF CANAL

The consent of Congress was given to the construction of a ship canal along the Government right of way connecting the waters of Puget Sound with Lake Washington, said canal, when completed, to be turned over to the United States, by act June 11, 1906, ch. 3072, 34 Stat. 231.

§566. Improvement by or under authority of State of New Jersey

Authority is given to the State of New Jersey, or, through it, to any commission, individual, corporation, or municipality, singly or collectively, designated by the legislature of said State, or by a commission appointed or authorized by said legislature, to improve the channels on the New Jersey seacoast, or any portion of said coast, or the waters adjacent thereto, lying between thirty-eight degrees fifty-six minutes and forty degrees twenty minutes north latitude, by dredging, or by the construction of piers, jetties, or breakwaters, or other river and harbor work of any description or nature adapted to attain the ends now pursued by the United States Government for the advantage of said coast or the relief of commerce: *Provided*, That such operations shall not encroach upon those portions of said coast, or the channels adjacent thereto, for which the United States Government may undertake similar work according to its own plans: *And provided*, That the plans for said work shall be placed on file with the Chief of Engineers of the Department of the Army for thirty days, during which time he is authorized to disapprove said plans and forbid such work if, in his judgment, the improvements when completed will interfere with navigation or with any works of the United States Government commenced or proposed to be made: *Provided further*, That no tolls or other charges upon commerce shall be imposed by those making such improvements: *And provided further*, That this section shall not be construed as affecting in any way the jurisdiction and control of the Federal Government over any waters that may be improved in pursuance of the provisions thereof, nor as exempting such waters from the operation of the laws heretofore or hereafter enacted by Congress for the preservation and protection of navigable waters. The right to alter, amend, or repeal this section is expressly reserved.

(June 30, 1906, ch. 3923, §§1, 2, 34 Stat. 800; July 26, 1947, ch. 343, title II, §205(a), 61 Stat. 501.)

CHANGE OF NAME

Department of War designated Department of the Army and title of Secretary of War changed to Secretary of the Army by section 205(a) of act July 26, 1947, ch. 343, title II, 61 Stat. 501. Section 205(a) of act July 26, 1947, was repealed by section 53 of act Aug. 10, 1956, ch. 1041, 70A Stat. 641. Section 1 of act Aug. 10, 1956, enacted "Title 10, Armed Forces" which in sections 3010 to 3013 continued Department of the Army under administrative supervision of Secretary of the Army.

§ 567. Navigation and flood control improvements by Minnesota, North Dakota, and South Dakota

Congress consents that the States of Minnesota, North Dakota, and South Dakota, or any two of them, may enter into any agreement or agreements with each other to aid in improving navigation and to prevent and control floods on boundary waters of said States and the waters tributary thereto. And said States, or any two of them, may agree with each other upon any project or projects for the purpose of making such improvements, and upon the amount of money to be contributed by each to carry out such projects. The Secretary of the Army is authorized and directed to make a survey of any project proposed, as aforesaid, by said States, or any two of them, to determine the feasibility and practicability thereof and the expenses of carrying the same into effect and what share of such expenses should be borne by the respective States, local interests, or by the National Government. If the Secretary of the Army approves any such projects, he may authorize the States to make such improvements at their own expense, but under his supervision.

(Aug. 8, 1917, ch. 49, § 5, 40 Stat. 266; July 26, 1947, ch. 343, title II, § 205(a), 61 Stat. 501.)

CODIFICATION

Section is from a part of section 5 of act Aug. 8, 1917, which act was popularly known as the "Rivers and Harbors Appropriation Act for 1917". The omitted part of such section read as follows: "That the sum of $25,000, or so much thereof as may be necessary, is hereby appropriated, out of any funds in the Treasury of the United States not otherwise appropriated, for the purpose of enabling the Secretary of War to make the surveys and estimates herein contemplated."

CHANGE OF NAME

Department of War designated Department of the Army and title of Secretary of War changed to Secretary of the Army by section 205(a) of act July 26, 1947, ch. 343, title II, 61 Stat. 501. Section 205(a) of act July 26, 1947, was repealed by section 53 of act Aug. 10, 1956, ch. 1041, 70A Stat. 641. Section 1 of act Aug. 10, 1956, enacted "Title 10, Armed Forces" which in sections 3010 to 3013 continued Department of the Army under administrative supervision of Secretary of the Army.

§ 567a. Flood and pollution control compacts between certain States

The consent of the Congress of the United States is given to the States of Maine, New York, New Hampshire, Vermont, Massachusetts, Rhode Island, Connecticut, Pennsylvania, West Virginia, Kentucky, Indiana, Illinois, Tennessee, and Ohio, or any two or more of them, to negotiate and enter into agreements or compacts for conserving and regulating the flow, lessening flood damage, removing sources of pollution of the waters thereof, or making other public improvements on any rivers or streams whose drainage basins lie within any two or more of the said States.

No such compact or agreement shall be binding or obligatory upon any State a party thereto unless and until it has been approved by the legislatures of each of the States whose assent is contemplated by the terms of the compact or agreement and by the Congress.

(June 8, 1936, ch. 542, §§ 1, 2, 49 Stat. 1490.)

APPROVAL OF COMPACT BY CONGRESS

Act July 11, 1940, ch. 581, 54 Stat. 752, provided in part that: "The consent and approval of Congress is hereby given to an interstate compact relating to the control and reduction of the pollution of the streams of the Ohio River drainage basin negotiated and entered into or to be entered into under authority of Public Resolution Numbered 104, Seventy-fourth Congress, approved June 8, 1936, [this section] and now ratified by the States of New York, Illinois, Kentucky, and Indiana, and by the State of Ohio (whose ratification is to go into effect at the time at which the States of New York, Pennsylvania, and West Virginia enter into said compact as parties and signatory States), also by the State of West Virginia (whose ratification is to go into effect at the time at which the States of New York, Ohio, Virginia, and Pennsylvania enter into said compact as parties and signatory States) * * *."

"SEC. 2. Without further submission of said compact, the consent of Congress is hereby given to the State of Virginia or any other State with waters in the Ohio River drainage basin, entering into said compact as a signatory State and party in addition to the States therein named or any of them.

"SEC. 3. The commissioners to represent the United States, as provided in article IV of said compact, shall be appointed by the President.

"SEC. 4. Nothing contained in this Act or in the compact herein approved shall be construed as impairing or affecting the sovereignty of the United States or any of its rights or jurisdiction in and over the area or waters which are the subject of such compact.

"SEC. 5. The right to alter, amend, or repeal the provisions of section 1 is hereby expressly reserved."

§ 567b. Pollution of Potomac drainage basin; control by State compacts

The consent of Congress is given to the States of Maryland and West Virginia and the Commonwealths of Virginia and Pennsylvania and the District of Columbia to enter into the compact to create a Potomac Valley Conservancy District and to establish an Interstate Commission on the Potomac River Basin: *Provided*, That nothing contained in such compact shall be construed as impairing or in any manner affecting any right or jurisdiction of the United States in and over the region which forms the subject of this compact.

(July 11, 1940, ch. 579, 54 Stat. 748.)

§ 567b–1. Amended compact

The consent of Congress is hereby given to the States of Maryland and West Virginia and the Commonwealths of Virginia and Pennsylvania and the District of Columbia to adopt the aforementioned amendments and enter into the amended compact hereinbefore recited and every part and article thereof: *Provided*, That nothing contained in such amended compact shall be construed as impairing or in any manner affecting any right or jurisdiction of the United States in and over the region which forms the subject of this compact: *And provided further*, That the consent herein given does not extend to section (F)(2) of article II of the amended compact.

(Pub. L. 91–407, § 1, Sept. 25, 1970, 84 Stat. 860.)

REFERENCES IN TEXT

The amended compact, referred to in text, is set out in 84 Stat. 856 to 860.

§ 568. Limitation on power of committee of Congress to consider projects

No project shall be considered by any committee of Congress with a view to its adoption, except with a view to a survey, if five years have elapsed since a report upon a survey of such project has been submitted to Congress pursuant to law.

(Sept. 22, 1922, ch. 427, § 9, 42 Stat. 1043.)

CODIFICATION

Section is from act Sept. 22, 1922, popularly known as the "Rivers and Harbors Appropriation Act of 1918".

§ 569. Personal equipment for employees; use of funds for purpose

Funds heretofore or hereafter appropriated for rivers and harbors to be expended under the supervision of the Secretary of the Army shall be available for expenditure in the purchase of such personal equipment for employees as in the opinion of the Chief of Engineers are essential for the efficient prosecution of the works.

(Jan. 21, 1927, ch. 47, § 5(b), 44 Stat. 1021; July 26, 1947, ch. 343, title II, § 205(a), 61 Stat. 501.)

CHANGE OF NAME

Department of War designated Department of the Army and title of Secretary of War changed to Secretary of the Army by section 205(a) of act July 26, 1947, ch. 343, title II, 61 Stat. 501. Section 205(a) of act July 26, 1947, was repealed by section 53 of act Aug. 10, 1956, ch. 1041, 70A Stat. 641. Section 1 of act Aug. 10, 1956, enacted "Title 10, Armed Forces" which in sections 3010 to 3013 continued Department of the Army under administrative supervision of Secretary of the Army.

TRANSFER OF FUNCTIONS

For transfer of certain functions insofar as they pertain to Air Force, and to extent that they were not previously transferred to Secretary of the Air Force and Department of the Air Force from Secretary of the Army and Department of the Army, see Secretary of Defense Transfer Order No. 40, July 22, 1949.

§ 569a. Temporary employment of experts or consultants; compensation

The Chief of Engineers is authorized to procure the temporary or intermittent services of experts or consultants or organizations thereof in connection with civil functions of the Corps of Engineers without regard to chapter 51 and subchapter III of chapter 53 of title 5: *Provided*, That individuals so engaged may be paid at rates not to exceed the daily equivalent of the rate for GS–18 for each day of their services.

(July 3, 1930, ch. 847, § 6, 46 Stat. 948; May 17, 1950, ch. 188, title I, § 105, 64 Stat. 168; Pub. L. 91–611, title I, § 104, Dec. 31, 1970, 84 Stat. 1819.)

CODIFICATION

"Chapter 51 and subchapter III of chapter 53 of title 5" substituted in text for "the Classification Act as amended" on authority of Pub. L. 89–554, § 7(b), Sept. 6, 1966, 80 Stat. 631, the first section of which enacted Title 5, Government Organization and Employees.

AMENDMENTS

1970—Pub. L. 91–611 substituted provision that compensation "may be paid at rates not to exceed the daily equivalent of the rate for GS–18 for each day of their services" for "shall not be paid in excess of $100 per day for their services".

1950—Act May 17, 1950, amended section generally, providing for employment of experts and consultants and omitting provisions relating to stenographic assistance.

REFERENCES IN OTHER LAWS TO GS–16, 17, OR 18 PAY RATES

References in laws to the rates of pay for GS–16, 17, or 18, or to maximum rates of pay under the General Schedule, to be considered references to rates payable under specified sections of Title 5, Government Organization and Employees, see section 529 [title I, § 101(c)(1)] of Pub. L. 101–509, set out in a note under section 5376 of Title 5.

§ 569b. Contracts; architect and engineering services; surveying and mapping services

Contracts for architect and engineering services, and surveying and mapping services, shall be awarded by the Chief of Engineers in accordance with title IX of the Federal Property and Administrative Services Act of 1949.[1]

(Pub. L. 98–63, title I, § 101, July 30, 1983, 97 Stat. 311.)

REFERENCES IN TEXT

The Federal Property and Administrative Services Act of 1949, referred to in text, is act June 30, 1949, ch. 288, 63 Stat. 377. Title IX of the Act, which was classified generally to subchapter VI (§ 541 et seq.) of chapter 10 of former Title 40, Public Buildings, Property, and Works, was repealed and reenacted by Pub. L. 107–217, §§ 1, 6(b), Aug. 21, 2002, 116 Stat. 1062, 1304, as chapter 11 (§ 1101 et seq.) of Title 40, Public Buildings, Property, and Works. For disposition of sections of former Title 40 to revised Title 40, see Table preceding section 101 of Title 40. For complete classification of this Act to the Code, see Tables.

§ 569c. Services of volunteers

The United States Army Chief of Engineers may accept the services of volunteers and provide for their incidental expenses to carry out any activity of the Army Corps of Engineers except policy-making or law or regulatory enforcement. Such volunteers shall not be employees of the United States Government except for the purposes of (1) chapter 171 of title 28, relating to tort claims, and (2) chapter 81 of title 5, relating to compensation for work injuries.

(Pub. L. 98–63, title I, § 101, July 30, 1983, 97 Stat. 312.)

§ 569d. Safety award and promotional materials

(a) Promotion of safety program

(1) Procurement of promotional materials

The Secretary is authorized to procure materials that, in the judgment of the Secretary, are necessary to promote the Corps of Engineers safety program.

(2) Distribution of materials to employees

The items purchased pursuant to this subsection shall be distributed to employees of the Corps of Engineers to advance the goals of the safety program.

(b) Employee recognition

The Secretary is authorized to incur necessary expenses for the honorary recognition of the

[1] See References in Text note below.

outstanding safety performance of employees of the Corps of Engineers. Such recognition may be in the form of certificates, plaques, cash, or other forms of awards.

(c) Authorization of appropriations

There is authorized to be appropriated $350,000 for each fiscal year beginning after September 30, 1992, for carrying out the purposes of this section.

(Pub. L. 102–580, title II, § 210, Oct. 31, 1992, 106 Stat. 4830.)

"SECRETARY" DEFINED

Secretary means the Secretary of the Army, see section 3 of Pub. L. 102–580, set out as a note under section 2201 of this title.

§ 569e. Use of private sector resources in surveying and mapping

To the maximum extent practicable, the Secretary shall make use of private sector resources in carrying out surveying and mapping activities in the Civil Works Program of the Corps of Engineers.

(Pub. L. 102–580, title II, § 212, Oct. 31, 1992, 106 Stat. 4831.)

"SECRETARY" DEFINED

Secretary means the Secretary of the Army, see section 3 of Pub. L. 102–580, set out as a note under section 2201 of this title.

§ 569f. Debarment of persons convicted of fraudulent use of "Made in America" labels

If the Secretary determines that a person has been convicted of intentionally affixing a label bearing a "Made in America" inscription to any product sold in or shipped to the United States which is not made in the United States and which is used in a civil works project of the Secretary, the Secretary shall debar the person from contracting with the Federal Government for a period of not less than 3 years and not more than 5 years. For purposes of this section, the term "debar" has the meaning that term has under section 2393(c) of title 10.

(Pub. L. 102–580, title II, § 226, Oct. 31, 1992, 106 Stat. 4838.)

"SECRETARY" DEFINED

Secretary means the Secretary of the Army, see section 3 of Pub. L. 102–580, set out as a note under section 2201 of this title.

§ 570. Default in contract; disposition of amounts collected

Any amounts collected from defaulting contractors or their sureties under contracts entered into in connection with river and harbor or flood-control work prosecuted by the Engineer Department, whether collected in cash or by deduction from amounts otherwise due such contractors, hereafter shall be credited in each case to the appropriation under which the contract was made.

(Aug. 30, 1935, ch. 831, § 8, 49 Stat. 1048.)

§ 571. Crediting reimbursements for lost, stolen, or damaged property

Any amounts collected from any person, persons, or corporations as a reimbursement for lost, stolen, or damaged property, purchased in connection with river and harbor or flood-control work prosecuted under the direction of the Secretary of the Army and the supervision of the Chief of Engineers, whether collected in cash or by deduction from amounts otherwise due such person, persons, or corporations, hereafter shall be credited in each case to the appropriation that bore the cost of purchase, repair, or replacement of the lost, stolen, or damaged property.

(June 20, 1938, ch. 535, § 4, 52 Stat. 805; July 26, 1947, ch. 343, title II, § 205(a), 61 Stat. 501.)

CODIFICATION

Section is also set out as section 701k of this title.

CHANGE OF NAME

Department of War designated Department of the Army and title of Secretary of War changed to Secretary of the Army by section 205(a) of act July 26, 1947, ch. 343, title II, 61 Stat. 501. Section 205(a) of act July 26, 1947, was repealed by section 53 of act Aug. 10, 1956, ch. 1041, 70A Stat. 641. Section 1 of act Aug. 10, 1956, enacted "Title 10, Armed Forces" which in sections 3010 to 3013 continued Department of the Army under administrative supervision of Secretary of the Army.

§ 572. Collection and removal of drift in Baltimore Harbor

On and after July 30, 1948, direct allotments from appropriations for the maintenance and improvement of existing river and harbor works, or from other available appropriations, may be made by the Secretary of the Army for the collection and removal of drift in Baltimore Harbor and its tributary waters, and this work shall be carried out as a separate and distinct project.

(June 30, 1948, ch. 771, title I, § 102, 62 Stat. 1173.)

§ 573. Repealed. Pub. L. 89–554, § 8(a), Sept. 6, 1966, 80 Stat. 656

Section, act May 17, 1950, ch. 188, title I, § 111, 64 Stat. 170, provided that section 607 of the Federal Employees Pay Act of 1945, as amended [former 5 U.S.C. 947], should not be construed to prevent employment of additional personnel.

§ 574. Omitted

CODIFICATION

Section, act Sept. 6, 1950, ch. 896, ch. IX, § 101, 64 Stat. 726, which related to availability of appropriation for payments to school districts, was from the Civil Functions Appropriation Act, 1951, and was not repeated in subsequent appropriation acts.

§ 574a. Training funds

(a) In general

The Secretary may include individuals not employed by the Department of the Army in training classes and courses offered by the Corps of Engineers in any case in which the Secretary determines that it is in the best interest of the Federal Government to include those individuals as participants.

(b) Expenses

(1) In general

An individual not employed by the Department of the Army attending a training class or course described in subsection (a) shall pay the full cost of the training provided to the individual.

(2) Payments

Payments made by an individual for training received under paragraph (1), up to the actual cost of the training—

(A) may be retained by the Secretary;

(B) shall be credited to an appropriations account used for paying training costs; and

(C) shall be available for use by the Secretary, without further appropriation, for training purposes.

(3) Excess amounts

Any payments received under paragraph (2) that are in excess of the actual cost of training provided shall be credited as miscellaneous receipts to the Treasury of the United States.

(Pub. L. 110–114, title II, §2016, Nov. 8, 2007, 121 Stat. 1076.)

"SECRETARY" DEFINED

Secretary means the Secretary of the Army, see section 2 of Pub. L. 110–114, set out as a note under section 2201 of this title.

§575. Availability of appropriations for expenses incident to operation of power boats or vessels; expenses defined; certification of expenditures

On and after July 31, 1947, no appropriation under the Corps of Engineers shall be available for any expenses incident to operating any power-driven boat or vessel on other than Government business, and that Government business shall be construed to include transportation, lodging, and subsistence on inspection trips of Federal and State officials, having a public interest in authorized or proposed improvements for river and harbor and flood control, and any expenses incurred therefor shall be chargeable to river and harbor and flood control appropriations heretofore or hereafter made under rules and regulations to be prescribed by the Chief of Engineers: *Provided*, That such expenditures shall be certified by the Division Engineer as necessary and proper expenditures.

(July 31, 1947, ch. 411, §1, 61 Stat. 688.)

CODIFICATION

Section is also set out as section 701b–9 of this title.

Section was formerly classified to sections 190a and 199 of Title 10 prior to the general revision and enactment of Title 10, Armed Forces, by act Aug. 10, 1956, ch. 1041, §1, 70A Stat. 1.

§576. Revolving fund; establishment; availability; reimbursement; transfer of funds; limitation

There is established a revolving fund, to be available without fiscal year limitation, for expenses necessary for the maintenance and operation of the plant and equipment of the Corps of Engineers used in civil works functions, including acquisition of plant and equipment, maintenance, repair, and purchase, operation, and maintenance of not to exceed four aircraft at any one time, temporary financing of services finally chargeable to appropriations for civil works functions, and the furnishing of facilities and services for military functions of the Department of the Army and other Government agencies and private persons, as authorized by law. In addition, the Secretary of the Army is authorized to provide capital for the fund by capitalizing the present inventories, plant and equipment of the civil works functions of the Corps of Engineers. The fund shall be credited with reimbursements or advances for the cost of equipment, facilities, and services furnished, at rates which shall include charges for overhead and related expenses, depreciation of plant and equipment, and accrued leave: *Provided*, That on July 1, 1953, (1) the fund shall assume the assets, liabilities, and obligations of the Plant accounts, as carried on the records of the Corps of Engineers as of June 30, 1953, under the appropriations for "Maintenance and improvement of existing river and harbor works", "Flood control, general", and "Flood control, Mississippi River and tributaries", and (2) there shall be transferred from said appropriations to the fund amounts equivalent to the unexpended cash balances of the Plant accounts on June 30, 1953: *Provided further*, That the total capital of said fund shall not exceed $140,000,000.

(July 27, 1953, ch. 245, §101, 67 Stat. 199.)

CODIFICATION

Section is also set out as section 701b–10 of this title.

Section was formerly classified to section 190b of Title 10 prior to the general revision and enactment of Title 10, Armed Forces, by act Aug. 10, 1956, ch. 1041, §1, 70A Stat. 1.

HEADQUARTERS AIRCRAFT; TRANSFER AND REASSIGNMENT OF PROPERTY ACCOUNTABILITY TO ARMY MILITARY ACTIVITY

Pub. L. 101–101, title I, §105, Sept. 29, 1989, 103 Stat. 649, provided that: "Notwithstanding section 110 of the Energy and Water Development Appropriation Act, 1988, Public Law 100–202 [set out below], the Secretary of the Army is authorized to transfer and reassign property accountability for the headquarters aircraft of the Corps of Engineers, Serial Number 045, from the assets of the civil works revolving fund, to the military activity of the Army that the Secretary determines is appropriate, except that the aircraft shall be made available on a priority basis as necessary for activities in support of the Army's civil works mission."

RETENTION OF THREE OPERATIONAL AIRCRAFT; NOTICE OF INTENDED USE OUTSIDE UNITED STATES

Pub. L. 100–202, §101(d) [title I, §110], Dec. 22, 1987, 101 Stat. 1329–104, 1329–112, provided that: "The Chief of Engineers is directed to retain three operational aircraft authorized pursuant to section 101 of the Act of July 27, 1953, 67 Stat. 199 [33 U.S.C. 576], together with their attendant crews, and may only dispose of any of these aircraft if authorized to do so by a future congressional enactment for that purpose. The Chief of Engineers shall provide at least thirty days advance written notification to the Appropriations Committees of the Senate and House of Representatives of any intended use of any of these aircraft for a trip destined outside the United States or its territories or possessions."

§576a. Purchase of passenger motor vehicles by Corps of Engineers

On and after March 4, 1933, the provisions of section 1343 of title 31 shall be construed as applying to the Corps of Engineers as to the purchase of motor-propelled passenger-carrying vehicles.

(Mar. 4, 1933, ch. 281, title II, §1, 47 Stat. 1599.)

CODIFICATION

"Section 1343 of title 31" substituted in text for "section 5 of the Act of July 16, 1914 (U.S.C., title 5, sec. 78)" on authority of Pub. L. 97–258, §4(b), Sept. 13, 1982, 96 Stat. 1067, the first section of which enacted Title 31, Money and Finance.

Section was formerly classified to section 638b of Title 31 prior to the general revision and enactment of Title 31, Money and Finance, by Pub. L. 97–258, Sept. 13, 1982, 96 Stat. 877.

Section was also formerly classified to section 78a of Title 5 prior to the general revision and enactment of Title 5, Government Organization and Employees, by Pub. L. 89–554, Sept. 6, 1966, 80 Stat. 378.

§576b. Lease authority

Notwithstanding any other provision of law, the Secretary may lease space available in buildings for which funding for construction or purchase was provided from the revolving fund established by the 1st section of the Civil Functions Appropriations Act, 1954 (33 U.S.C. 576; 67 Stat. 199), under such terms and conditions as are acceptable to the Secretary. The proceeds from such leases shall be credited to the revolving fund for the purposes set forth in such Act.

(Pub. L. 104–303, title II, §213, Oct. 12, 1996, 110 Stat. 3684.)

REFERENCES IN TEXT

The Civil Functions Appropriations Act, 1954, referred to in text, is act July 27, 1953, ch. 245, 67 Stat. 197. For complete classification of this Act to the Code, see Tables.

§577. Small river and harbor improvement projects

(a) Allotment from appropriations for construction

The Secretary of the Army is authorized to allot from any appropriations hereafter made for rivers and harbors not to exceed $35,000,000 for any one fiscal year for the construction of small river and harbor improvement projects not specifically authorized by Congress which will result in substantial benefits to navigation and which can be operated consistently with appropriate and economic use of the waters of the Nation for other purposes, when in the opinion of the Chief of Engineers such work is advisable, if benefits are in excess of the cost.

(b) Limitation on allotment

Not more than $7,000,000 shall be allotted for the construction of a project under this section at any single locality and the amount allotted shall be sufficient to complete the Federal participation in the project under this section.

(c) Lands, easements, and rights-of-way; indemnification; assurances of local cooperation

Local interests shall provide without cost to the United States all necessary lands, easements and rights-of-way for all projects to be constructed under the authority of this section. In addition, local interests may be required to hold and save the United States free from damages that may result from the construction and maintenance of the project and may be required to provide such additional local cooperation as the Chief of Engineers deems appropriate. A State, county, municipality or other responsible local entity shall give assurance satisfactory to the Chief of Engineers that such conditions of cooperation as are required will be accomplished.

(d) Sharing of costs by non-Federal interests

Non-Federal interests may be required to share in the cost of the project to the extent that the Chief of Engineers deems that such cost should not be borne by the Federal Government in view of the recreational or otherwise special or local nature of the project benefits.

(e) Completeness of project

Each project for which money is allotted under this section shall be complete in itself and not commit the United States to any additional improvement to insure its successful operation, other than routine maintenance, and except as may result from the normal procedure applying to projects authorized after submission of survey reports, and projects constructed under the authority of this section shall be considered as authorized projects.

(f) Low water access navigation channels from existing channel of Mississippi River

This section shall apply to, but not be limited to, the provision of low water access navigation channels from the existing channel of the Mississippi River to harbor areas heretofore or now established and located along the Mississippi River.

(Pub. L. 86–645, title I, §107, July 14, 1960, 74 Stat. 486; Pub. L. 89–298, title III, §310(a) Oct. 27, 1965, 79 Stat. 1095; Pub. L. 91–611, title I, §112(a), Dec. 31, 1970, 84 Stat. 1821; Pub. L. 94–587, §133(a), Oct. 22, 1976, 90 Stat. 2928; Pub. L. 99–662, title IX, §915(d), Nov. 17, 1986, 100 Stat. 4191; Pub. L. 110–114, title II, §2022, Nov. 8, 2007, 121 Stat. 1078.)

AMENDMENTS

2007—Subsec. (b). Pub. L. 110–114 substituted "$7,000,000" for "$4,000,000".

1986—Subsec. (a). Pub. L. 99–662 substituted "$35,000,000" for "$25,000,000".

Subsec. (b). Pub. L. 99–662 substituted "$4,000,000" for "$2,000,000".

1976—Subsec. (b). Pub. L. 94–587 substituted "$2,000,000" for "$1,000,000".

1970—Subsec. (a). Pub. L. 91–611 substituted "$25,000,000" for "$10,000,000".

Subsec. (b). Pub. L. 91–611 substituted "$1,000,000" for "$500,000".

1965—Subsec. (a). Pub. L. 89–298, §310(a)(1), substituted "$10,000,000" for "$2,000,000".

Subsec. (b). Pub. L. 89–298, §310(a)(2), substituted "$500,000" for "$200,000".

EFFECTIVE DATE OF 1986 AMENDMENT

Amendment by Pub. L. 99–662 not applicable to any project under contract for construction on Nov. 17, 1986, see section 915(i) of Pub. L. 99–662, set out as a note under section 426g of this title.

EFFECTIVE DATE OF 1976 AMENDMENT

Section 133(c) of Pub. L. 94–587 provided that: "The amendments made by this section [amending this section and section 701s of this title] shall not apply to any project under contract for construction on the date of enactment of the Water Resources Development Act of 1976 [Oct. 22, 1976]."

EFFECTIVE DATE OF 1970 AMENDMENT

Amendment by Pub. L. 91–611 not applicable to any project under contract for construction on Dec. 31, 1970, see section 112(c) of Pub. L. 91–611, set out as a note under section 426g of this title.

§577a. Small-boat navigation projects; charter fishing craft

The Chief of Engineers, for the purpose of determining Federal and non-Federal cost sharing, relating to proposed construction of small-boat navigation projects, shall consider charter fishing craft as commercial vessels.

(Pub. L. 91–611, title I, §119, Dec. 31, 1970, 84 Stat. 1822.)

§577b. Cost of operation and maintenance of general navigation features of small boat harbor projects; applicable projects

The cost of operation and maintenance of the general navigation features of small boat harbor projects shall be borne by the United States. This section shall apply to any such project authorized (A) under section 201 of the Flood Control Act of 1965 [42 U.S.C. 1962d–5], (B) under section 107 of the River and Harbor Act of 1960 [33 U.S.C. 577], (C) between January 1, 1970, and December 31, 1970, under authority of this Act, and to projects heretofore authorized in accordance with the policy set forth in the preceding sentence and to such projects authorized in this Act or which are hereafter authorized.

(Pub. L. 91–611, title I, §103, Dec. 31, 1970, 84 Stat. 1819; Pub. L. 93–251, §6, Mar. 7, 1974, 88 Stat. 15.)

REFERENCES IN TEXT

This Act, referred to in text, means Pub. L. 91–611, Dec. 31, 1970, 84 Stat. 1818, as amended. For complete classification of this Act to the Code, see Tables.

Hereafter, referred to in text, probably means after Dec. 31, 1970.

AMENDMENTS

1974—Pub. L. 93–251 amended section generally. Prior to amendment, section read as follows: "The costs of operation and maintenance of the general navigation features of small boat harbor projects authorized between January 1, 1970, and December 31, 1970, under the authority of this Act, section 201 of the Flood Control Act of 1965 [42 U.S.C. 1962d–5], or section 107 of the River and Harbor Act of 1960 [33 U.S.C. 577], shall be borne by the United States."

§578. Disposal of surplus property for development of public port or industrial facilities

(a) Conveyance by Secretary of the Army

Whenever the Secretary of the Army, upon the recommendation of the Chief of Engineers, determines that notwithstanding the provisions of the Federal Property and Administrative Services Act of 1949, as amended,[1] with respect to disposal of surplus real property, (1) the development of public port or industrial facilities on land which is part of a water resource development project under his jurisdiction will be in the public interest; (2) that such development will not interfere with the operation and maintenance of the project; and (3) that disposition of the property for these purposes under this section will serve the objectives of the project within which the land is located, he may convey the land by quitclaim deed to a State, political subdivision thereof, port district, port authority, or other body created by the State or through a compact between two or more States for the purpose of developing or encouraging the development of such facilities. In any case, where two or more political subdivisions thereof, or bodies created by, a State or group of States, seek to obtain the same land, the Secretary of the Army shall give preference to that political subdivision or body whose intended use of land will, in his opinion, best promote the purposes for which the project involved was authorized.

(b) Purchase price; conditions, reservations or restrictions

Any conveyance authorized by this section shall be made at the fair market value of the land, as determined by the Secretary of the Army, upon condition that the property shall be used for one of the purposes stated in the subsection (a) of this section only, and subject to such other conditions, reservations or restrictions as the Secretary may determine to be necessary for the development, maintenance, or operation of the project or otherwise in the public interest.

(c) Notice of proposed conveyance

Prior to the conveyance of any land under the provisions of this section, the Secretary of the Army shall, in the manner he deems reasonable, give public notice of the proposed conveyance and afford an opportunity to interested eligible bodies in the general vicinity of the land to apply for its purchase.

(d) Delegation of authority

The Secretary of the Army may delegate any authority conferred upon him by this section to any officer or employee of the Department of the Army. Any such officer or employee shall exercise the authority so delegated under rules and regulations approved by the Secretary.

(e) Deposit of proceeds

The proceeds from any conveyance made under the provisions of this section shall be covered into the Treasury as miscellaneous receipts.

(Pub. L. 86–645, title I, §108, July 14, 1960, 74 Stat. 486.)

REFERENCES IN TEXT

The Federal Property and Administrative Services Act of 1949, as amended, referred to in subsec. (a), is act June 30, 1949, ch. 288, 63 Stat. 377, as amended. Except for title III of the Act, which is classified generally to subchapter IV (§251 et seq.) of chapter 4 of Title 41, Public Contracts, the Act was repealed and reenacted by Pub. L. 107–217, §§1, 6(b), Aug. 21, 2002, 116 Stat. 1062, 1304, as chapters 1 to 11 of Title 40, Public Buildings, Property, and Works.

§579. Repealed. Pub. L. 101–640, title I, §119(b), Nov. 28, 1990, 104 Stat. 4630

Section, Pub. L. 93–251, title I, §12, Mar. 7, 1974, 88 Stat. 16; H. Res. 988, Oct. 8, 1974; Pub. L. 94–587, §157(a), Oct. 22, 1976, 90 Stat. 2933; S. Res. 4, Feb. 4, 1977, pro-

[1] See References in Text note below.

vided for deauthorization of projects of improvement of rivers and harbors and other waterways for navigation, beach erosion, flood control, and other purposes which the Secretary of the Army determined should no longer be authorized.

§ 579a. Project deauthorizations

(a) Funds to be obligated for construction to avoid deauthorization

Any project authorized for construction by this Act shall not be authorized after the last day of the 5-year period beginning on November 17, 1986, unless during such period funds have been obligated for construction, including planning and designing, of such project.

(b) Transmission to Congress of list of unconstructed projects or separable elements authorized but not receiving obligations during 10 fiscal years preceding transmission; two-year updates of list

(1) Not later than one year after November 17, 1986, the Secretary shall transmit to Congress a list of unconstructed projects, or unconstructed separable elements of projects, which have been authorized, but have received no obligations during the 10 full fiscal years preceding the transmittal of such list. A project or separable element included in such list is not authorized after December 31, 1989, if funds have not been obligated for construction of such project or element after November 17, 1986, and before December 31, 1989.

(2) Notwithstanding section 3003 of Public Law 104–66 (31 U.S.C. 1113 note; 109 Stat. 734), every year after the transmittal of the list under paragraph (1), the Secretary shall transmit to Congress a list of projects or separable elements of projects which have been authorized, but have received no obligations during the 5 full fiscal years preceding the transmittal of such list. Upon submission of such list to Congress, the Secretary shall notify each Senator in whose State, and each Member of the House of Representatives in whose district, a project (including any part thereof) on such list would be located. A project or separable element included in such list is not authorized after the date which is the last date of the fiscal year following the fiscal year in which the list is so transmitted if funds have not been obligated for the planning, design, or construction of such project or element during such period.

(c) Deauthorized list; publication in Federal Register

The Secretary shall publish in the Federal Register a list of any projects or separable elements that are deauthorized under this section.

(Pub. L. 99–662, title X, § 1001, Nov. 17, 1986, 100 Stat. 4201; Pub. L. 101–640, title I, § 119(a), Nov. 28, 1990, 104 Stat. 4630; Pub. L. 104–303, title II, § 228(a), Oct. 12, 1996, 110 Stat. 3703; Pub. L. 106–109, § 8(d), Nov. 24, 1999, 113 Stat. 1496; Pub. L. 110–114, title II, § 2046, Nov. 8, 2007, 121 Stat. 1105.)

REFERENCES IN TEXT

This Act, referred to in subsec. (a), is Pub. L. 99–662, Nov. 17, 1986, 100 Stat. 4082, known as the Water Resources Development Act of 1986. For complete classification of this Act to the Code, see Short Title note set out under section 2201 of this title and Tables.

AMENDMENTS

2007—Subsec. (b)(2). Pub. L. 110–114, § 2046(3), which directed the substitution of "such period" for "such 30 month period" in last sentence, was executed by making the substitution for "such 30-month period" to reflect the probable intent of Congress.

Pub. L. 110–114, § 2046(2), in last sentence, substituted "the last date of the fiscal year following the fiscal year in which" for "30 months after the date".

Pub. L. 110–114, § 2046(1), in first sentence, substituted "year" for "two years" and "5" for "7".

1999—Subsec. (b)(2). Pub. L. 106–109, in first sentence, substituted "Notwithstanding section 3003 of Public Law 104–66 (31 U.S.C. 1113 note; 109 Stat. 734), every" for "Every".

1996—Subsec. (b)(2). Pub. L. 104–303 substituted "7 full" for "10 full", "Upon submission" for "Before submission", and "for the planning, design, or construction" for "for construction".

1990—Subsec. (b)(2). Pub. L. 101–640 inserted after first sentence "Before submission of such list to Congress, the Secretary shall notify each Senator in whose State, and each Member of the House of Representatives in whose district, a project (including any part thereof) on such list would be located."

PROJECT DEAUTHORIZATIONS; EXTENSION OF LIMITATION ON PERIOD OF AUTHORIZATION

Pub. L. 100–676, § 52(a), Nov. 17, 1988, 102 Stat. 4044, which provided that subsecs. (a) and (c) of this section applied to projects authorized for construction by Pub. L. 100–676 (see Short Title of 1988 Amendment note set out under section 2201 of this title), except that the 5-year period during which funds had to be obligated to prevent deauthorization began on Nov. 17, 1988, and were also to apply to projects authorized for construction subsequent to Pub. L. 100–676, except that 5-year period during which funds had to be obligated to prevent deauthorization began on the date of the authorization of such projects, was repealed by Pub. L. 104–303, title II, § 228(b)(1), Oct. 12, 1996, 110 Stat. 3703.

"SECRETARY" DEFINED

Secretary means the Secretary of the Army, see section 2201 of this title.

SUBCHAPTER II—PAY AND ALLOWANCES; TRAVELING EXPENSES AND SUBSISTENCE

§ 581. Hiring special means of transportation

In their execution and inspection of river and harbor improvement work, at points beyond easy reach of ordinary regular transportation lines, Engineer officers are authorized to hire and use such transportation as they may consider desirable and advantageous to the progress of work.

(July 25, 1912, ch. 253, § 9, 37 Stat. 233.)

CODIFICATION

Section is from act July 25, 1912, popularly known as the "Rivers and Harbors Appropriation Act of 1912".

§ 582. Repealed. Pub. L. 89–554, § 8(a), Sept. 6, 1966, 80 Stat. 644

Section, act July 18, 1918, ch. 155, § 9, 40 Stat. 912, related to subsistence allowance to persons engaged in field work.

§ 583. Payment of allowances, etc., incident to change of station of Engineer officers from appropriation for improvements

When in the opinion of the Secretary of the Army the changes of a station of an officer of the Corps of Engineers is primarily in the interest of river and harbor improvement, the mileage and other allowances to which he may be entitled incident to such change of station may be paid from appropriations for such improvements.

(Mar. 3, 1925, ch. 467, § 5, 43 Stat. 1191; July 26, 1947, ch. 343, title II, § 205(a), 61 Stat. 501.)

CHANGE OF NAME

Department of War designated Department of the Army and title of Secretary of War changed to Secretary of the Army by section 205(a) of act July 26, 1947, ch. 343, title II, 61 Stat. 501. Section 205(a) of act July 26, 1947, was repealed by section 53 of act Aug. 10, 1956, ch. 1041, 70A Stat. 641. Section 1 of act Aug. 10, 1956, enacted "Title 10, Armed Forces" which in sections 3010 to 3013 continued Department of the Army under administrative supervision of Secretary of the Army.

§ 583a. Payment of pay and allowances of officers of Corps of Engineers from appropriation for improvements

Regular officers of the Corps of Engineers of the Army, and reserve officers of the Army who are assigned to the Corps of Engineers, who are employed primarily on duty connected with non-military public works prosecuted under the direction of the Chief of Engineers, including river and harbor improvements, flood control, and other such works, shall, while so employed, be paid their pay and allowances from the appropriation for the works upon which they are employed.

(Aug. 10, 1956, ch. 1041, § 36, 70A Stat. 634.)

CODIFICATION

Section is derived from the third proviso of Act June 26, 1936, ch. 839, 49 Stat. 1974, which was classified to section 181a of Title 10 prior to the general revision and enactment of Title 10, Armed Forces, by act Aug. 10, 1956, ch. 1041, § 1, 70A Stat. 1.

§§ 584, 584a. Repealed. Pub. L. 89–554, § 8(a), Sept. 6, 1966, 80 Stat. 647, 648

Section 584, act Jan. 21, 1927, ch. 47, § 5(d), 44 Stat. 1021, related to expenses incident to transportation of household effects of civilian employees.

Section 584a, act July 3, 1930, ch. 847, § 6, 46 Stat. 948, related to travel expenses of civilian employees on river and harbor works.

SUBCHAPTER III—ACQUISITION OF LAND AND MATERIALS

§ 591. Condemnation, purchase, and donation of land and materials

The Secretary of the Army may cause proceedings to be instituted, in the name of the United States, in any court having jurisdiction of such proceedings, for the acquirement by condemnation of any land, right-of-way, or material needed to enable him to maintain, operate, or prosecute works for the improvement of rivers and harbors for which provision has been made by law; such proceedings to be prosecuted in accordance with the laws relating to suits for the condemnation of property of the States wherein the proceedings may be instituted: *Provided, however*, That when the owner of such land, right-of-way, or material shall fix a price for the same, which in the opinion of the Secretary of the Army, shall be reasonable, he may purchase the same at such price without further delay: And provided further, That the Secretary of the Army is authorized to accept donations of lands or materials required for the maintenance or prosecution of such works.

(Apr. 24, 1888, ch. 194, 25 Stat. 94; July 26, 1947, ch. 343, title II, § 205(a), 61 Stat. 501.)

CHANGE OF NAME

Department of War designated Department of the Army and title of Secretary of War changed to Secretary of the Army by section 205(a) of act July 26, 1947, ch. 343, title II, 61 Stat. 501. Section 205(a) of act July 26, 1947, was repealed by section 53 of act Aug. 10, 1956, ch. 1041, 70A Stat. 641. Section 1 of act Aug. 10, 1956, enacted "Title 10, Armed Forces" which in sections 3010 to 3013 continued Department of the Army under administrative supervision of Secretary of the Army.

§ 592. Condemnation of land in aid of person, company, corporation, municipal or private

Whenever any person, company, or corporation, municipal or private, shall undertake to secure any land or easement therein needed in connection with a work of river and harbor improvement duly authorized by Congress, for the purpose of conveying the same to the United States free of cost, or for the purpose of constructing, maintaining, and operating locks, dry docks, or other works to be conveyed to the United States free of cost, and of constructing, maintaining and operating dams for use in connection therewith, and shall be unable for any reason to obtain the same by purchase and acquire a valid title thereto, the Secretary of the Army may, in his discretion, cause proceedings to be instituted in the name of the United States for the acquirement by condemnation of said land or easement, and it shall be the duty of the Attorney General of the United States to institute and conduct such proceedings upon the request of the Secretary of the Army: *Provided*, That all expenses of said proceedings and any award that may be made thereunder shall be paid by the said person, company, or corporation, to secure which payment the Secretary of the Army may require the said person, company, or corporation to execute a proper bond in such amount as he may deem necessary before said proceedings are commenced.

(May 16, 1906, ch. 2465, 34 Stat. 196; June 29, 1906, ch. 3628, 34 Stat. 632; July 26, 1947, ch. 343, title II, § 205(a), 61 Stat. 501.)

CODIFICATION

Act May 16, 1906, as originally enacted, provided that: "Whenever any person, company, or corporation, municipal or private, shall undertake to secure, for the purpose of conveying the same to the United States free of cost, any land or easement therein, needed in connection with a work of river and harbor improvement duly authorized by Congress, and shall be unable for any reason to obtain a valid title thereto, the Secretary of War may, in his discretion, cause proceedings to be instituted in the name of the United States for the acquirement by condemnation of said land or easement, and it shall be the duty of the Attorney General of the United States to institute and conduct such proceedings upon the request of the Secretary of War: Provided, That all the expenses of said proceedings and any award that may be made thereunder shall be paid by the said person, company, or corporation, to secure which payment the Secretary of War may require the said person, company, or corporation to execute a proper bond in such amount as he may deem necessary before said proceedings are commenced."

CHANGE OF NAME

Department of War designated Department of the Army and title of Secretary of War changed to Secretary of the Army by section 205(a) of act July 26, 1947, ch. 343, title II, 61 Stat. 501. Section 205(a) of act July 26, 1947, was repealed by section 53 of act Aug. 10, 1956, ch. 1041, 70A Stat. 641. Section 1 of act Aug. 10, 1956, enacted "Title 10, Armed Forces" which in sections 3010 to 3013 continued Department of the Army under administrative supervision of Secretary of the Army.

§ 593. Condemnation of land in aid of State or State agency

Whenever any State, or any reclamation, flood control or drainage district, or other public agency created by any State, shall undertake to secure any land or easement therein, needed in connection with a work of river and harbor improvement duly authorized by Congress, for the purpose of conveying the same to the United States free of cost, and shall be unable for any reason to obtain the same by purchase and acquire a valid title thereto, the Secretary of the Army may, in his discretion, cause proceedings to be instituted in the name of the United States for the acquirement by condemnation of said land or easement, and it shall be the duty of the Attorney General of the United States to institute and conduct such proceedings upon the request of the Secretary of the Army: *Provided*, That all expenses of said proceedings and any award that may be made thereunder shall be paid by such State, or reclamation, flood control or drainage district, or other public agency as aforesaid, to secure which payment the Secretary of the Army may require such State, or reclamation, flood control or drainage district, or other public agency as aforesaid, to execute a proper bond in such amount as he may deem necessary before said proceedings are commenced.

(Aug. 8, 1917, ch. 49, § 9, 40 Stat. 267; July 26, 1947, ch. 343, title II, § 205(a), 61 Stat. 501.)

CODIFICATION

Section is from act Aug. 8, 1917, popularly known as the "Rivers and Harbors Appropriation Act of 1917".

CHANGE OF NAME

Department of War designated Department of the Army and title of Secretary of War changed to Secretary of the Army by section 205(a) of act July 26, 1947, ch. 343, title II, 61 Stat. 501. Section 205(a) of act July 26, 1947, was repealed by section 53 of act Aug. 10, 1956, ch. 1041, 70A Stat. 641. Section 1 of act Aug. 10, 1956, enacted "Title 10, Armed Forces" which in sections 3010 to 3013 continued Department of the Army under administrative supervision of Secretary of the Army.

§ 594. When immediate possession of land may be taken

Whenever the Secretary of the Army, in pursuance of authority conferred on him by law, causes proceedings to be instituted in the name of the United States for the acquirement by condemnation of any lands, easements, or rights of way needed for a work of river and harbor improvements duly authorized by Congress, the United States, upon the filing of the petition in any such proceedings, shall have the right to take immediate possession of said lands, easements, or rights-of-way, to the extent of the interest to be acquired, and proceed with such public works thereon as have been authorized by Congress: *Provided*, That certain and adequate provision shall have been made for the payment of just compensation to the party or parties entitled thereto, either by previous appropriation by the United States or by the deposit of moneys or other form of security in such amount and form as shall be approved by the court in which such proceedings shall be instituted. The respondent or respondents may move at any time in the court to increase or change the amounts or securities, and the court shall make such order as shall be just in the premises and as shall adequately protect the respondents. In every case the proceedings in condemnation shall be diligently prosecuted on the part of the United States in order that such compensation may be promptly ascertained and paid.

(July 18, 1918, ch. 155, § 5, 40 Stat. 911; July 26, 1947, ch. 343, title II, § 205(a), 61 Stat. 501.)

CODIFICATION

Section is from act July 18, 1918, popularly known as the "Rivers and Harbors Appropriation Act of 1918".

CHANGE OF NAME

Department of War designated Department of the Army and title of Secretary of War changed to Secretary of the Army by section 205(a) of act July 26, 1947, ch. 343, title II, 61 Stat. 501. Section 205(a) of act July 26, 1947, was repealed by section 53 of act Aug. 10, 1956, ch. 1041, 70A Stat. 641. Section 1 of act Aug. 10, 1956, enacted "Title 10, Armed Forces" which in sections 3010 to 3013 continued Department of the Army under administrative supervision of Secretary of the Army.

§ 595. Consideration of benefits in assessing compensation

In all cases where private property shall be taken by the United States for the public use in connection with any improvement of rivers, harbors, canals, or waterways of the United States, and in all condemnation proceedings by the United States to acquire lands or easements for such improvements, where a part only of any such parcel, lot, or tract of land shall be taken, the jury or other tribunal awarding the just compensation or assessing the damages to the owner, whether for the value of the part taken or for any injury to the part not taken, shall take into consideration by way of reducing the amount of compensation or damages any special and direct benefits to the remainder arising from the improvement, and shall render their award or verdict accordingly.

(July 18, 1918, ch. 155, § 6, 40 Stat. 911.)

CODIFICATION

Section is from act July 18, 1918, popularly known as the "Rivers and Harbors Appropriation Act of 1918".

§ 595a. Compensation for taking or condemnation of property for public improvements; fair market value; partial taking; effective date

In all cases where real property shall be taken by the United States for the public use in connection with any improvement of rivers, harbors, canals, or waterways of the United States, and in all condemnation proceedings by the United States to acquire lands or easements for such improvements, the compensation to be paid for real property taken by the United States above the normal high water mark of navigable waters of the United States shall be the fair market value of such real property based upon all uses to which such real property may reasonably be put, including its highest and best use, any of which uses may be dependent upon access to or utilization of such navigable waters. In cases of partial takings of real property, no depreciation in the value of any remaining real property shall be recognized and no compensation shall be paid for any damages to such remaining real property which result from loss of or reduction of access from such remaining real property to such navigable waters because of the taking of real property or the purposes for which such real property is taken. The compensation defined herein shall apply to all acquisitions of real property after December 31, 1970, and to the determination of just compensation in any condemnation suit pending on December 31, 1970.

(Pub. L. 91–611, title I, § 111, Dec. 31, 1970, 84 Stat. 1821.)

§ 596. Repealed. Pub. L. 91–646, title III, § 306, Jan. 2, 1971, 84 Stat. 1907

Section, Pub. L. 86–645, title III, § 301, July 14, 1960, 74 Stat. 502, declared the policy of Congress with respect to payment of just and reasonable consideration to owners and tenants whose property is acquired for public works projects and payment of a purchase price in negotiation for such property which will consider such congressional policy. See provisions of Uniform Relocation Assistance and Real Property Acquisition Policies Act of 1970, classified to chapter 61 (§ 4601 et seq.) of Title 42, The Public Health and Welfare.

EFFECTIVE DATE OF REPEAL

Repeal not applicable to any State so long as sections 4630 and 4655 of title 42 are not applicable in such State; but such sections completely applicable to all States after July 1, 1972, but until such date applicable to a State to extent the State is able under its laws to comply with such sections, see section 221 of Pub. L. 91–646, set out as an Effective Date note under section 4601 of Title 42, The Public Health and Welfare.

SAVINGS PROVISION

Any rights or liabilities existing under provisions repealed by section 306 of Pub. L. 91–646 as not affected by such repeal, see section 306 of Pub. L. 91–646, set out in part as a Savings Provision note under section 4651 of Title 42, The Public Health and Welfare.

§ 597. Acquisition of lands for water resource development projects; information as to probable timing for acquisition; public meetings; regulations

Within six months after the date that Congress authorizes construction of a water resource development project under the jurisdiction of the Secretary of the Army, the Corps of Engineers shall make reasonable effort to advise owners and occupants in and adjacent to the project area as to the probable timing for the acquisition of lands for the project and for incidental rights-of-way, relocations, and any other requirements affecting owners and occupants. Within a reasonable time after initial appropriations are made for land acquisition or construction, including relocations, the Corps of Engineers shall conduct public meetings at locations convenient to owners and tenants to be displaced by the project in order to advise them of the proposed plans for acquisition and to afford them an opportunity to comment. To carry out the provisions of this section, the Chief of Engineers shall issue regulations to provide, among other things, dissemination of the following information to those affected: (1) factors considered in making the appraisals; (2) desire to purchase property without going to court; (3) legal right to submit to condemnation proceedings; (4) payments for moving expenses or other losses not covered by appraised market value; (5) occupancy during construction; (6) removal of improvements; (7) payments required from occupants of Government acquired land; (8) withdrawals by owners of deposits made in court by Government, and (9) use of land by owner when easement is acquired. The provisions of this section shall not subject the United States to any liability nor affect the validity of any acquisitions by purchase or condemnation and shall be exempt from the operations of subchapter II of chapter 5, and chapter 7, of title 5.

(Pub. L. 86–645, title III, § 302, July 14, 1960, 74 Stat. 502.)

CODIFICATION

"Subchapter II of chapter 5, and chapter 7, of title 5" substituted in text for "the Administrative Procedure Act of June 11, 1946, as amended" on authority of Pub. L. 89–554, § 7(b), Sept. 6, 1966, 80 Stat. 631, the first section of which enacted Title 5, Government Organization and Employees.

SHORT TITLE

Section 303 of Pub. L. 86–645 provided that: "Title III of this Act [enacting this section and section 596 of this title] may be cited as the 'Land Acquisition Policy Act of 1960'."

§ 598. Resettlement of displaced families, individuals, and business concerns

(a) Acquisition of land; condemnation expenses; bond

Whenever any State, or any agency or instrumentality of a State or local government, or any nonprofit incorporated body organized or chartered under the law of the State in which it is located, or any nonprofit association or combination of such bodies, agencies or instrumentalities, shall undertake to secure any lands or interests therein as a site for the resettlement of families, individuals, and business concerns displaced by a river and harbor improvement, flood control or other water resource project duly authorized by Congress, and when it has been determined by the Secretary of the Army that the State is unable to acquire necessary lands or interests in lands or is unable to acquire such lands or interests in lands with sufficient promptness, the Secretary, upon the request of the Governor of the State in which such site is located, and after consultation with appropriate Federal, State, interstate, regional, and local departments and agencies, is authorized, in the name of the United States and prior to the approval of title by the Attorney General, to acquire, enter upon, and take possession of such lands or interests in lands by purchase, donation, condemnation or otherwise in accordance with the laws of the United States (including sections 3114–3116 and 3118 of title 40). All expenses of said acquisition and any award that may be made under a condemnation proceeding, including costs of examination and abstract of title, certificate of title, appraisal, advertising, and any fees incident to acquisition, shall be paid by such State or body, agency, or instrumentality. The State, agency, instrumentality, or nonprofit body may repay such amounts from any funds made available to it for such purposes by any Federal department, agency, or instrumentality (other than the Department of the Army) having authority to make funds available for such a purpose. Pending such payment, the Secretary may expend from any funds hereafter appropriated for the project occasioning such acquisition such sums as may be necessary to carry out this section. To secure payment, the Secretary may require any such State or agency, body, or instrumentality to execute a proper bond in such amount as he may deem necessary before acquisition is commenced. Any sums paid to the Secretary by any such State or agency, body or instrumentality shall be deposited in the Treasury to the credit of the appropriation for such project.

(b) Acquisition provisions

No acquisition shall be undertaken under the authority of this section unless the Secretary has determined, after consultation with appropriate Federal, State, and local governmental agencies that (1) the development of a site is necessary in order to alleviate hardships to displaced persons; (2) the location of the site is suitable for development in relation to present or potential sources of employment; and (3) a plan for development of the site has been approved by appropriate local governmental authorities in the area or community in which such site is located.

(c) Conveyance to State, public or private nonprofit body

The Secretary is further authorized and directed by proper deed, executed in the name of the United States, to convey any lands or interests in land acquired in any State under the provisions of this section, to the State, or such public or private nonprofit body, agency, or institution in the State as the Governor may prescribe, upon such terms and conditions as may be agreed upon by the Secretary, the Governor, and the agency to which the conveyance is to be made.

(Pub. L. 90–483, title II, § 209, Aug. 13, 1968, 82 Stat. 745.)

CODIFICATION

"Sections 3114–3116 and 3118 of title 40" substituted in subsec. (a) for "the Act of February 26, 1931 (46 Stat. 1421)" on authority of Pub. L. 107–217, § 5(c), Aug. 21, 2002, 116 Stat. 1303, the first section of which enacted Title 40, Public Buildings, Property, and Works.

SUBCHAPTER IV—PARTICULAR WORK OR IMPROVEMENTS

§ 601. Mississippi River; regulation of reservoirs at headwaters

It shall be the duty of the Secretary of the Army to prescribe such rules and regulations in respect to the use and administration of the reservoirs at the headwaters of the Mississippi River as in his judgment the public interest and necessity may require; which rules and regulations shall be posted in some conspicuous place or places for the information of the public. And any person knowingly and willfully violating such rules and regulations shall be liable to a fine not exceeding $500, or imprisonment, not exceeding six months, the same to be enforced by prosecution in any district court of the United States within whose territorial jurisdiction such offense may have been committed. And the Secretary of the Army shall cause such gaugings to be made at or near Saint Paul during the annual operation of said reservoirs as shall determine accurately the discharge at that point, the cost of same to be paid out of the annual appropriation for gauging the waters of the Mississippi River and its tributaries.

(Aug. 11, 1888, ch. 860, § 1, 25 Stat. 419; July 26, 1947, ch. 343, title II, § 205(a), 61 Stat. 501.)

CODIFICATION

Section is from act Aug. 11, 1888, the River and Harbor Appropriation Act of 1888.

In the original text the words "said reservoirs" appeared instead of "reservoirs at the headwaters of the Mississippi river." The provision from which this section is derived, however, followed an appropriation "for continuing operations upon the reservoirs at the headwaters of the Mississippi river."

CHANGE OF NAME

Department of War designated Department of the Army and title of Secretary of War changed to Secretary of the Army by section 205(a) of act July 26, 1947, ch. 343, title II, 61 Stat. 501. Section 205(a) of act July 26, 1947, was repealed by section 53 of act Aug. 10, 1956, ch. 1041, 70A Stat. 641. Section 1 of act Aug. 10, 1956, enacted "Title 10, Armed Forces" which in sections 3010 to 3013 continued Department of the Army under administrative supervision of Secretary of the Army.

§ 602. Maintenance of channel of South Pass of Mississippi River

Upon the termination of the contract entered into with the late James B. Eads for the maintenance of the channel through the South Pass of the Mississippi River, the Secretary of the Army is directed to take charge of said channel, including the jetties, and all auxiliary works connected therewith, and thereafter to maintain with the utmost efficiency said South Pass Channel; and for that purpose he is authorized to draw his warrants from time to time on the Treasurer of the United States, until otherwise provided for by law, for such sums of money as may be necessary, not to exceed in the aggregate for any one year $100,000. For that purpose any available Government dredge may be used.

For the purpose of securing the uninterrupted examinations and surveys of the South Pass of the Mississippi River, the Secretary of the Army, upon the application of the Chief of Engineers, is authorized to draw his warrant or requisition from time to time upon the Secretary of the Treasury for such sums as may be necessary to do such work, not to exceed in the aggregate for each year the sum of $10,000.

(Aug. 11, 1888, ch. 860, §§1, 4, 25 Stat. 422, 424; June 6, 1900, ch. 790, §3, 31 Stat. 584; June 13, 1902, ch. 1079, §1, 32 Stat. 340; July 26, 1947, ch. 343, title II, §205(a), 61 Stat. 501; Aug. 30, 1954, ch. 1076, §1(15), 68 Stat. 967.)

CODIFICATION

Except for the last sentence, the first paragraph of this section was from a part of section 3 of act June 6, 1900. The omitted portion of the original text authorized the Secretary of War, in his discretion, to terminate the contract with James B. Eads and provided that the Secretary of War should take charge of the channel "in case of the termination of said contract, by virtue of the provisions hereof or by expiration of said contract."

The last sentence of the first paragraph of this section was from a provision of section 1 of act June 13, 1902. Further provisions of the original text, for the purchase of lands and buildings on either side of the South Pass, were temporary merely and are omitted. The original text provided for the use of "the dredge boat Beta, or any other available government dredge."

The second paragraph of this section was from section 4 of act Aug. 11, 1888. In the original text, following the words "Mississippi river," the following words appeared: "As provided for in the Act of Mar. third, eighteen hundred and seventy-five."

The words "the sum of $10,000," are substituted for "the amount appropriated in this act for such purpose." $10,000 was the amount appropriated for such purpose by section 1 of act June 13, 1902.

Act Mar. 3, 1875, ch. 134, mentioned in the original text, provided in section 4 et seq., 18 Stat. 463 to 466, for a contract with James B. Eads and others to construct jetties, etc., to maintain the channel at the South Pass.

The provisions of that act and of act Aug. 11, 1888, with regard to examinations and surveys at the South Pass, remained in force notwithstanding the termination of said contract, by a provision of act June 13, 1902.

AMENDMENTS

1954—Act Aug. 30, 1954, repealed proviso requiring that an itemized statement of expenses incurred for maintenance of the channel through, and securing uninterrupted examinations and surveys of, the South Pass of the Mississippi River, as provided in this section, should accompany the annual report of the Chief of Engineers.

CHANGE OF NAME

Department of War designated Department of the Army and title of Secretary of War changed to Secretary of the Army by section 205(a) of act July 26, 1947, ch. 343, title II, 61 Stat. 501. Section 205(a) of act July 26, 1947, was repealed by section 53 of act Aug. 10, 1956, ch. 1041, 70A Stat. 641. Section 1 of act Aug. 10, 1956, enacted "Title 10, Armed Forces" which in sections 3010 to 3013 continued Department of the Army under administrative supervision of Secretary of the Army.

APPROPRIATIONS

Section 2 of act June 26, 1934, ch. 756, 48 Stat. 1225, which was classified to section 725a of former Title 31, Money and Finance, repealed the permanent appropriation under the titles "Maintenance of channel, South Pass, Mississippi River (fiscal year) (8–961.55)" and "Examinations and surveys at South Pass, Mississippi River (fiscal year) (8–961.53)" effective July 1, 1935, and provided that such portions of any Acts as make permanent appropriations to be expended under such accounts are amended so as to authorize, in lieu thereof, annual appropriations from the general fund of the Treasury in identical terms and in such amounts as now provided by the laws providing such permanent appropriations.

§ 603. Repealed. Mar. 2, 1945, ch. 19, § 3, 59 Stat. 23

Section, acts July 25, 1912, ch. 253, §1, 37 Stat. 222; July 3, 1930, ch. 847, §3, 46 Stat. 946; Oct. 17, 1940, ch. 895, §3, 54 Stat. 1200, related to removal of temporary obstructions and to minor improvements in navigable waters. See section 603a of this title.

§ 603a. Removal of snags and debris, and straightening, clearing, and protecting channels in navigable waters

The Secretary of the Army is authorized to allot not to exceed $1,000,000 from any appropriations made prior to or after March 2, 1945, for any one fiscal year for improvement of rivers and harbors, for removing accumulated snags and other debris, and for protecting, clearing, and straightening channels in navigable harbors and navigable streams and tributaries thereof, when in the opinion of the Chief of Engineers such work is advisable in the interest of navigation or flood control.

(Mar. 2, 1945, ch. 19, §3, 59 Stat. 23; July 26, 1947, ch. 343, title II, §205(a), 61 Stat. 501; Pub. L. 99–662, title IX, §915(g), Nov. 17, 1986, 100 Stat. 4191.)

AMENDMENTS

1986—Pub. L. 99–662 substituted "$1,000,000" for "$300,000".

CHANGE OF NAME

Department of War designated Department of the Army and title of Secretary of War changed to Secretary of the Army by section 205(a) of act July 26, 1947, ch. 343, title II, 61 Stat. 501. Section 205(a) of act July 26, 1947, was repealed by section 53 of act Aug. 10, 1956, ch. 1041, 70A Stat. 641. Section 1 of act Aug. 10, 1956, enacted "Title 10, Armed Forces" which in sections 3010 to 3013 continued Department of the Army under administrative supervision of Secretary of the Army.

EFFECTIVE DATE OF 1986 AMENDMENT

Amendment by Pub. L. 99–662 not applicable to any project under contract for construction on Nov. 17, 1986, see section 915(i) of Pub. L. 99–662, set out as a note under section 426g of this title.

§ 604. Removal of snags, etc., from Mississippi River

For the purpose of removing snags, wrecks, and other obstructions in the Mississippi River, the Atchafalaya and Old Rivers from the junction with the Mississippi and Red Rivers down the Atchafalaya River as far down as Melville, Louisiana, the Secretary of the Army, upon the application of the Chief of Engineers, is authorized to draw his warrant or requisition from time to time upon the Secretary of the Treasury for such sums as may be necessary to do such work, not to exceed in the aggregate for each year the sum of $100,000.

(Aug. 11, 1888, ch. 860, §§1, 7, 25 Stat. 421, 424; Mar. 3, 1909, ch. 264, §3, 35 Stat. 817; July 26, 1947, ch. 343, title II, §205(a), 61 Stat. 501; Aug. 30, 1954, ch. 1076, §1(15), 68 Stat. 967.)

CODIFICATION

Section is from the Rivers and Harbors Appropriation Act of 1888, act Aug. 11, 1888, as affected by act Mar. 3, 1909.

Act Mar. 3, 1909, made the provisions of act Aug. 11, 1888, for the removal of snags applicable to "the Atchafalaya and Old Rivers from the junction with the Mississippi and Red Rivers down the Atchafalaya River as far as Melville, Louisiana."

Section 7 of act Aug. 11, 1888, provided for "securing the uninterrupted work of operating snag boats on the upper Mississippi River" as well as for the removal of snags. The provision for operating snag boats is set out as section 605 of this title.

The words "the sum of $100,000" are substituted for "the amounts appropriated in this act for such purposes." An appropriation of $100,000 for removal of snags is contained in section 1 of the act.

AMENDMENTS

1954—Act Aug. 30, 1954, repealed proviso requiring that an itemized statement of expenses incurred in the removal of snags, etc., as provided in this section, should accompany the annual report of the Chief of Engineers.

CHANGE OF NAME

Department of War designated Department of the Army and title of Secretary of War changed to Secretary of the Army by section 205(a) of act July 26, 1947, ch. 343, title II, 61 Stat. 501. Section 205(a) of act July 26, 1947, was repealed by section 53 of act Aug. 10, 1956, ch. 1041, 70A Stat. 641. Section 1 of act Aug. 10, 1956, enacted "Title 10, Armed Forces" which in sections 3010 to 3013 continued Department of the Army under administrative supervision of Secretary of the Army.

APPROPRIATIONS

Section 2 of act June 26, 1934, ch. 756, 48 Stat. 1225, which was classified to section 725a of former Title 31, Money and Finance, repealed the permanent appropriation under the title "Removing obstructions in Mississippi, Atchafalaya, and Old Rivers (fiscal year) (8–961.58)" effective July 1, 1935, and provided that such portions of any Acts as make permanent appropriations to be expended under such account are amended so as to authorize, in lieu thereof, annual appropriations from the general fund of the Treasury in identical terms and in such amounts as now provided by the laws providing such permanent appropriations.

§ 605. Operation of snag boats on Upper Mississippi River

For the purpose of securing the uninterrupted work of operating snag boats on the Upper Mississippi River, the Illinois River, from its mouth to Copperas Creek, and the Minnesota River and other tributaries of the Upper Mississippi River improved by the United States, the Secretary of the Army, upon the application of the Chief of Engineers, is authorized to draw his warrant or requisition from time to time upon the Secretary of the Treasury for such sums as may be necessary to do such work, not to exceed in the aggregate for each year the sum of $25,000.

(Aug. 11, 1888, ch. 860, §§ 1, 7, 25 Stat. 420, 421, 424; Mar. 2, 1907, ch. 2509, § 1, 34 Stat. 1102; Mar. 3, 1909, ch. 264, § 3, 35 Stat. 817; July 26, 1947, ch. 343, title II, § 205(a), 61 Stat. 501; Aug. 30, 1954, ch. 1076, § 1(15), 68 Stat. 967.)

CODIFICATION

Section is from act, Aug. 11, 1888, as affected by acts Mar. 2, 1907, and Mar. 3, 1909.

Section 7 of act Aug. 11, 1888, also provided for the removal of snags from the Mississippi River. (See section 604 of this title.)

The words "the sum of $25,000," are substituted for "the amounts appropriated in this act for such purposes." An appropriation of $25,000 for operating snag boats was made in section 1 of the act.

Act Mar. 2, 1907, made the provisions of the earlier Act concerning snag boats applicable to the Illinois river from its mouth to Copperas Creek.

Act Mar. 3, 1909, made such provisions applicable to "the Minnesota river and other tributaries of the upper Mississippi River now or heretofore improved by the United States."

AMENDMENTS

1954—Act Aug. 30, 1954, repealed proviso requiring that an itemized statement of expenses incurred in operation of snag boats on the Upper Mississippi River, etc., as provided in this section, should accompany the annual report of the Chief of Engineers.

CHANGE OF NAME

Department of War designated Department of the Army and title of Secretary of War changed to Secretary of the Army by section 205(a) of act July 26, 1947, ch. 343, title II, 61 Stat. 501. Section 205(a) of act July 26, 1947, was repealed by section 53 of act Aug. 10, 1956, ch. 1041, 70A Stat. 641. Section 1 of act Aug. 10, 1956, enacted "Title 10, Armed Forces" which in sections 3010 to 3013 continued Department of the Army under administrative supervision of Secretary of the Army.

APPROPRIATIONS

Section 2 of act June 26, 1934, ch. 756, 48 Stat. 1225, which was classified to section 725a of former Title 31, Money and Finance, repealed the permanent appropriation under the title "Operating snag and dredge boats on upper Mississippi, Illinois, and Minnesota Rivers (fiscal year) (8–962.60)" effective July 1, 1935, and provided that such portions of any Acts as make permanent appropriations to be expended under such account are amended so as to authorize, in lieu thereof, annual appropriations from the general fund of the Treasury in identical terms and in such amounts as now provided by the laws providing such permanent appropriations.

§ 606. Removal of snags, and so forth, from Ohio River

For the purpose of securing the uninterrupted work of operating snag boats on the Ohio River and removing snags, wrecks, and other obstructions in said river, the Secretary of the Army, upon the application of the Chief of Engineers, is authorized to draw his warrant or requisition from time to time upon the Secretary of the Treasury for such sums as may be necessary to do such work, not to exceed in the aggregate for each year the sum of $50,000.

(Sept. 19, 1890, ch. 907, § 13, 26 Stat. 455; June 3, 1896, ch. 314, § 3, 29 Stat. 234; July 26, 1947, ch. 343, title II, § 205(a), 61 Stat. 501; Aug. 30, 1954, ch. 1076, § 1(15), 68 Stat. 967.)

CODIFICATION

Section is from the Rivers and Harbors Appropriation Act of 1890, act Sept. 19, 1890, as amended by act June 3, 1896.

The section, as originally enacted, limited the amount to be drawn for the work, by the words "not to exceed in the aggregate for each year the sum of twenty-five thousand dollars." It was amended by act June 3, 1896 by inserting the words "fifty thousand dollars" for the words "twenty-five thousand dollars" therein.

AMENDMENTS

1954—Act Aug. 30, 1954, repealed proviso requiring that an itemized statement of expenses incurred in removing snags, etc., from the Ohio River, as provided in this section, should accompany the annual report of the Chief of Engineers.

CHANGE OF NAME

Department of War designated Department of the Army and title of Secretary of War changed to Secretary of the Army by section 205(a) of act July 26, 1947, ch. 343, title II, 61 Stat. 501. Section 205(a) of act July 26, 1947, was repealed by section 53 of act Aug. 10, 1956, ch. 1041, 70A Stat. 641. Section 1 of act Aug. 10, 1956, enacted "Title 10, Armed Forces" which in sections 3010 to 3013 continued Department of the Army under administrative supervision of Secretary of the Army.

APPROPRIATIONS

Section 2 of act June 26, 1934, ch. 756, 48 Stat. 1225, which was classified to section 725a of former Title 31, Money and Finance, repealed the permanent appropriation under the title "Operating snag boats on the Ohio River (fiscal year) (8–962.51)" effective July 1, 1935, and provided that such portions of any Acts as make permanent appropriations to be expended under such account are amended so as to authorize, in lieu thereof, annual appropriations from the general fund of the Treasury in identical terms and in such amounts as now provided by the laws providing such permanent appropriations.

§ 607. Removal of drift from New York Harbor

So much as may be necessary of any appropriations made for specific portions of New York Harbor and its immediate tributaries may be allotted by the Secretary of the Army for the maintenance of these waterways by the collection and removal of drift.

(Aug. 8, 1917, ch. 49, §1, 40 Stat. 252; July 26, 1947, ch. 343, title II, §205(a), 61 Stat. 501.)

CODIFICATION

Section is from act Aug. 8, 1917, the Rivers and Harbors Appropriation Act of 1917.

CHANGE OF NAME

Department of War designated Department of the Army and title of Secretary of War changed to Secretary of the Army by section 205(a) of act July 26, 1947, ch. 343, title II, 61 Stat. 501. Section 205(a) of act July 26, 1947, was repealed by section 53 of act Aug. 10, 1956, ch. 1041, 70A Stat. 641. Section 1 of act Aug. 10, 1956, enacted "Title 10, Armed Forces" which in sections 3010 to 3013 continued Department of the Army under administrative supervision of Secretary of the Army.

§ 607a. Appropriations; separate project

On and after July 3, 1930, direct allotments from appropriations for maintenance and improvement of existing river and harbor works or other available appropriation may be made by the Secretary of the Army for the collection and removal of drift in New York Harbor and its tributary waters, and this work on and after July 3, 1930, shall be carried as a separate and distinct project.

(July 3, 1930, ch. 847, §6, 46 Stat. 947; July 26, 1947, ch. 343, title II, §205(a), 61 Stat. 501.)

CHANGE OF NAME

Department of War designated Department of the Army and title of Secretary of War changed to Secretary of the Army by section 205(a) of act July 26, 1947, ch. 343, title II, 61 Stat. 501. Section 205(a) of act July 26, 1947, was repealed by section 53 of act Aug. 10, 1956, ch. 1041, 70A Stat. 641. Section 1 of act Aug. 10, 1956, enacted "Title 10, Armed Forces" which in sections 3010 to 3013 continued Department of the Army under administrative supervision of Secretary of the Army.

§ 608. Construction of fishways

Whenever river and harbor improvements shall be found to operate (whether by lock and dam or otherwise), as obstructions to the passage of fish, the Secretary of the Army may, in his discretion, direct and cause to be constructed practical and sufficient fishways, to be paid for out of the general appropriations for the streams on which such fishways may be constructed.

(Aug. 11, 1888, ch. 860, §11, 25 Stat. 425; July 26, 1947, ch. 343, title II, §205(a), 61 Stat. 501.)

CODIFICATION

Section is from act Aug. 11, 1888, the Rivers and Harbors Appropriation Act of 1888.

CHANGE OF NAME

Department of War designated Department of the Army and title of Secretary of War changed to Secretary of the Army by section 205(a) of act July 26, 1947, ch. 343, title II, 61 Stat. 501. Section 205(a) of act July 26, 1947, was repealed by section 53 of act Aug. 10, 1956, ch. 1041, 70A Stat. 641. Section 1 of act Aug. 10, 1956, enacted "Title 10, Armed Forces" which in sections 3010 to 3013 continued Department of the Army under administrative supervision of Secretary of the Army.

§ 609. Sluices and other work in dams for development of water power

In order to make possible the economical future development of water power, the Secretary of the Army, upon recommendation of the Chief of Engineers, is authorized, in his discretion, to provide in the permanent parts of any dam authorized at any time by Congress for the improvement of navigation such foundations, sluices, and other works, as may be considered desirable for the future development of its water power.

(July 25, 1912, ch. 253, §12, 37 Stat. 233; July 26, 1947, ch. 343, title II, §205(a), 61 Stat. 501.)

CODIFICATION

Section is from act July 25, 1912, the Rivers and Harbors Appropriation Act of 1912.

CHANGE OF NAME

Department of War designated Department of the Army and title of Secretary of War changed to Secretary of the Army by section 205(a) of act July 26, 1947, ch. 343, title II, 61 Stat. 501. Section 205(a) of act July 26, 1947, was repealed by section 53 of act Aug. 10, 1956, ch. 1041, 70A Stat. 641. Section 1 of act Aug. 10, 1956, enacted "Title 10, Armed Forces" which in sections 3010 to 3013 continued Department of the Army under administrative supervision of Secretary of the Army.

§ 610. Control of aquatic plant growths

(a) In general

There is hereby authorized a comprehensive program to provide for control and progressive eradication of noxious aquatic plant growths from the navigable waters, tributary streams, connecting channels, and other allied waters of the United States, in the combined interest of navigation, flood control, drainage, agriculture, fish and wildlife conservation, public health, and related purposes, including continued research for development of the most effective and economic control measures, to be administered by the Chief of Engineers, under the direction of the Secretary of the Army, in cooperation with other Federal and State agencies. Local interests shall agree to hold and save the United States free from claims that may occur from control operations and to participate to the extent of 30 per centum of the cost of such operations. Costs for research and planning undertaken pursuant to the authorities of this section shall be borne fully by the Federal Government.

(b) Appropriations

There are authorized to be appropriated such amounts, not in excess of $15,000,000 annually, as may be necessary to carry out the provisions of this section. Any such funds employed for control operations shall be allocated by the Chief of Engineers on a priority basis, based upon the urgency and need of each area, and the availability of local funds.

(c) Support

In carrying out the program under this section, the Secretary is encouraged to use contracts, cooperative agreements, and grants with colleges and universities and other non-Federal entities.

(Pub. L. 85–500, title I, § 104, July 3, 1958, 72 Stat. 300; Pub. L. 89–298, title III, § 302, Oct. 27, 1965, 79 Stat. 1092; Pub. L. 98–63, title I, § 101, July 30, 1983, 97 Stat. 313; Pub. L. 99–662, title IX, § 941, Nov. 17, 1986, 100 Stat. 4199; Pub. L. 104–303, title II, § 225, Oct. 12, 1996, 110 Stat. 3697; Pub. L. 106–53, title II, § 205, Aug. 17, 1999, 113 Stat. 285.)

AMENDMENTS

1999—Subsec. (a). Pub. L. 106–53, § 205(1), substituted "noxious aquatic plant growths from" for "water-hyacinth, alligatorweed, Eurasian water milfoil, melaleuca, and other obnoxious aquatic plant growths, from" in first sentence.

Subsec. (b). Pub. L. 106–53, § 205(2), substituted "$15,000,000" for "$12,000,000" in first sentence.

Subsec. (c). Pub. L. 106–53, § 205(3), added subsec. (c).

1996—Subsec. (a). Pub. L. 104–303 inserted "melaleuca," after "milfoil,".

1986—Subsec. (b). Pub. L. 99–662 substituted "$12,000,000" for "$10,000,000".

1983—Subsec. (b). Pub. L. 98–63 substituted "$10,000,000" for "$5,000,000".

1965—Subsec. (a). Pub. L. 89–298 designated part of existing provisions as subsec. (a), substituting "comprehensive program" and "other allied waters of the United States" for "comprehensive project" and "other allied waters in the States of North Carolina, South Carolina, Georgia, Florida, Alabama, Mississippi, Louisiana, and Texas", respectively, providing for control and eradication of Eurasian water milfoil, and striking out "in accordance with the report of the Chief of Engineers, published as House Document Numbered 37, Eighty-fifth Congress" after "Federal and State agencies".

Subsec. (b). Pub. L. 89–298 designated part of existing provisions as subsec. (b), substituting the appropriations authorization of $5,000,000 annually as first sentence for former provisions which authorized "an estimated additional cost for the expanded program over that now underway of $1,350,000 annually for five years, of which 70 per centum, presently estimated at $945,000, shall be borne by the United States and 30 per centum, presently estimated at $405,000, by local interests" and incorporating former second proviso in second sentence.

SUBCHAPTER V—PROSECUTION OF WORK GENERALLY

§ 621. By what methods river and harbor work may be authorized to be prosecuted

Any public work on canals, rivers, and harbors adopted by Congress may be prosecuted by direct appropriations, by continuing contracts, or by both direct appropriations and continuing contracts.

(Sept. 22, 1922, ch. 427, § 10, 42 Stat. 1043.)

CODIFICATION

Section is from the Rivers and Harbors Appropriation Act of 1922.

§ 622. Contracts, etc., with private industry for implementation of projects for improvements and dredging; reduction of federally owned fleet

(a) Contracts for dredging and related work

The Secretary of the Army, acting through the Chief of Engineers (hereinafter referred to as the "Secretary"), in carrying out projects for improvement of rivers and harbors (other than surveys, estimates, and gagings) shall, by contract or otherwise, carry out such work in the manner most economical and advantageous to the United States. The Secretary shall have dredging and related work done by contract if he determines private industry has the capability to do such work and it can be done at reasonable prices and in a timely manner. During the four-year period which begins on April 26, 1978, the Secretary may limit the application of the second sentence of this subsection for work for which the federally owned fleet is available to achieve an orderly transition to full implementation of this subsection.

(b) Reduction of federally owned fleet

As private industry reasonably demonstrates its capability under subsection (a) of this section to perform the work done by the federally owned fleet, at reasonable prices and in a timely manner, the federally owned fleet shall be reduced in an orderly manner, as determined by the Secretary, by retirement of plant. To carry out emergency and national defense work the Secretary shall retain only the minimum federally owned fleet capable of performing such work and he may exempt from the provisions of this section such amount of work as he determines to be reasonably necessary to keep such fleet fully operational, as determined by the Secretary, after the minimum fleet requirements have been determined. Notwithstanding the preceding sentence, in carrying out the reduction of the federally owned fleet, the Secretary may retain so much of the federally owned fleet as he determines necessary, for so long as he determines necessary, to insure the capability of the Federal Government and private industry together to carry out projects for improvements of rivers and harbors. For the purpose of making the determination required by the preceding sentence the Secretary shall not exempt any work from the requirements of this section. The minimum federally owned fleet shall be maintained to technologically modern and efficient standards, including replacement as necessary. The Secretary is authorized and directed to undertake a study to determine the minimum federally owned fleet required to perform emergency and national defense work. The study, which shall be submitted to Congress within two years after April 26, 1978, shall also include preservation of employee rights of persons presently employed on the existing federally owned fleet.

(c) Program to increase use of private hopper dredges

(1) Initiation

The Secretary shall initiate a program to increase the use of private-industry hopper dredges for the construction and maintenance of Federal navigation channels.

(2) Ready reserve status for hopper dredge Wheeler

In order to carry out this subsection, the Secretary shall place the Federal hopper dredge Wheeler in a ready reserve status not later than the earlier of 90 days after the date of completion of the rehabilitation of the hopper dredge McFarland pursuant to section 563 of the Water Resources Development Act of 1996 or October 1, 1997.

(3) Testing and use of ready reserve hopper dredge

The Secretary may periodically perform routine tests of the equipment of the vessel placed in a ready reserve status under paragraph (2) to ensure the vessel's ability to perform emergency work. The Secretary shall not assign any scheduled hopper dredging work to such vessel but shall perform any repairs needed to maintain the vessel in a fully operational condition. The Secretary may place the vessel in active status in order to perform any dredging work only if the Secretary determines that private industry has failed to submit a responsive and responsible bid for work advertised by the Secretary or to carry out the project as required pursuant to a contract with the Secretary.

(4) Repair and rehabilitation

The Secretary may undertake any repair and rehabilitation of any Federal hopper dredge, including the vessel placed in ready reserve status under paragraph (2) to allow the vessel to be placed in active status as provided in paragraph (3).

(5) Procedures

The Secretary shall develop and implement procedures to ensure that, to the maximum extent practicable, private industry hopper dredge capacity is available to meet both routine and time-sensitive dredging needs. Such procedures shall include—

(A) scheduling of contract solicitations to effectively distribute dredging work throughout the dredging season; and

(B) use of expedited contracting procedures to allow dredges performing routine work to be made available to meet time-sensitive, urgent, or emergency dredging needs.

(6) Report

Not later than 2 years after October 12, 1996, the Secretary shall report to Congress on whether the vessel placed in ready reserve status under paragraph (2) is needed to be returned to active status or continued in a ready reserve status or whether another Federal hopper dredge should be placed in a ready reserve status.

(7) Limitations

(A) Reductions in status

The Secretary may not further reduce the readiness status of any Federal hopper dredge below a ready reserve status except any vessel placed in such status for not less than 5 years that the Secretary determines has not been used sufficiently to justify retaining the vessel in such status.

(B) Increase in assignments of dredging work

For each fiscal year beginning after October 12, 1996, the Secretary shall not assign any greater quantity of dredging work to any Federal hopper dredge in active status than was assigned to that vessel in the average of the 3 prior fiscal years. This subparagraph shall not apply to the Federal hopper dredges Essayons and Yaquina of the Corps of Engineers.

(C) Remaining dredges

In carrying out the program under this section, the Secretary shall not reduce the availability and utilization of Federal hopper dredge vessels stationed on the Pacific and Atlantic coasts below that which occurred in fiscal year 1996 to meet the navigation dredging needs of the ports on those coasts.

(8) Contracts; payment of capital costs

The Secretary may enter into a contract for the maintenance and crewing of any Federal hopper dredge retained in a ready reserve status. The capital costs (including depreciation costs) of any dredge retained in such status shall be paid for out of funds made available from the Harbor Maintenance Trust Fund and shall not be charged against the Corps of Engineers' Revolving Fund Account or any individual project cost unless the dredge is specifically used in connection with that project.

(Aug. 11, 1888, ch. 860, §3, 25 Stat. 423; July 25, 1912, ch. 253, §1, 37 Stat. 222; Mar. 2, 1919, ch. 95, §3, 40 Stat. 1287; Pub. L. 95–269, §1, Apr. 26, 1978, 92 Stat. 218; Pub. L. 104–303, title II, §237, Oct. 12, 1996, 110 Stat. 3705; Pub. L. 110–114, title II, §2047(b), Nov. 8, 2007, 121 Stat. 1106.)

REFERENCES IN TEXT

Section 563 of the Water Resources Development Act of 1996, referred to in subsec. (c)(2), is section 563 of Pub. L. 104–303, Oct. 12, 1996, 110 Stat. 3784, which is not classified to the Code.

CODIFICATION

Prior to the general amendment by Pub. L. 95–269, this section was a composite of several Acts as follows:

The first sentence was from a part of section 3 of Act of Aug. 11, 1888, the Rivers and Harbors Appropriation Act of 1888. The remainder of section 3 was classified to section 623 of this title.

The second sentence, which provided that all improvement works authorized by contract may, in the discretion of the Secretary of War [now Army], be carried on by contract or otherwise, as may be most economical or advantageous to the United States, was from section 1 of the Act of July 25, 1912, the Rivers and Harbors Appropriation Act of 1912. Previous similar provisions were contained in Acts Mar. 2, 1907, ch. 2509, § 1, 34 Stat. 1110; Feb. 27, 1911, ch. 166, § 1, 36 Stat. 952.

The third sentence, which provided that in all cases where the project for a work of river or harbor improvement provides for the construction or use of Government dredging plant, the Secretary of War [now Army] may, in his discretion, have the work done by contract if reasonable prices can be obtained, was from section 3 of the Act of Mar. 2, 1919, the Rivers and Harbors Appropriation Act of 1919, which superseded a somewhat similar provision in section 3 of the Act of Aug. 8, 1917, ch. 49, 40 Stat. 261. Section 1 of the 1917 Act, 40 Stat. 255, provided in part that "the work proposed under the project adopted by the river and harbor Act approved July twenty-fifth, nineteen hundred and twelve, may be done by contract if reasonable prices can be obtained".

AMENDMENTS

2007—Subsec. (c)(7)(B). Pub. L. 110–114 inserted "This subparagraph shall not apply to the Federal hopper dredges Essayons and Yaquina of the Corps of Engineers." at end.

1996—Subsec. (c). Pub. L. 104–303 added subsec. (c).

1978—Pub. L. 95–269 designated existing provision as subsec. (a), substituted provisions relating to authority of Secretary of the Army, acting through the Chief of Engineers, to implement improvement projects by contract or otherwise and dredging and related work by contract with private industry, for provisions relating to authority of the Secretary of the Army to apply moneys appropriated for improvements by contract or otherwise and for construction or use of a Government dredging plant by contract, and added subsec. (b).

§ 623. Repealed. Oct. 31, 1951, ch. 654, § 1(57), 65 Stat. 703

Section, act Aug. 11, 1888, ch. 860, § 3, 25 Stat. 423, related to letting of contracts to lowest responsible bidder.

§ 624. Limitation on improvement work by private contract

(a) Determinations respecting comparison of private contract price with estimation of cost of performance of work by Government plant or by well-equipped contractor

No works of river and harbor improvement shall be done by private contract—

(1) if the Secretary of the Army, acting through the Chief of Engineers, determines that Government plant is reasonably available to perform the subject work and the contract price for doing the work is more than 25 per centum in excess of the estimated comparable cost of doing the work by Government plant; or

(2) in any other circumstance where the Secretary of the Army, acting through the Chief of Engineers, determines that the contract price is more than 25 per centum in excess of what he determines to be a fair and reasonable estimated cost of a well-equipped contractor doing the work.

(b) Considerations involved in determinations of estimation of cost of performance of work by Government plant

In estimating the comparable cost of doing the work under subsection (a)(1) of this section by Government plant the Secretary of the Army, acting through the Chief of Engineers shall, in addition to the cost of labor and materials, take into account proper charges for depreciation of plant, all supervising and overhead expenses, interest on the capital invested in the Government plant (but the rate of interest shall not exceed the maximum prevailing rate being paid by the United States on current issues of bonds or other evidences of indebtedness) and such other Government expenses and charges as the Chief of Engineers determines to be appropriate.

(c) Considerations involved in determinations of estimation of cost of performance of work by well-equipped contractor

In determining a fair and reasonable estimated cost of doing work by private contract under subsection (a)(2) of this section, the Secretary of the Army, acting through the Chief of Engineers, shall, in addition to the cost of labor and materials, take into account proper charges for depreciation of plant, all expenses for supervision, overhead, workmen's compensation, general liability insurance, taxes (State and local), interest on capital invested in plant, and such other expenses and charges the Secretary of the Army, acting through the Chief of Engineers, determines to be appropriate.

(Mar. 2, 1919, ch. 95, § 8, 40 Stat. 1290; Pub. L. 95–269, § 2, Apr. 26, 1978, 92 Stat. 219.)

CODIFICATION

Section is from the Rivers and Harbors Appropriation Act of 1919.

AMENDMENTS

1978—Pub. L. 95–269 designated existing provision as subsec. (a), substituted provisions relating to determinations by the Secretary of the Army, acting through the Chief of Engineers, respecting contract prices for performance of works of river and harbor improvement by a Government plant or by a well-equipped contractor as a limitation on performance of the work by private contract, for provisions relating to limitation on use of funds for works of river and harbor improvement pursuant to private contract based on estimation of cost for performance of work by Government plant and factors constituting cost estimation, and added subsecs. (b) and (c).

COMPENSATION FOR INCREASED COSTS

Provision for payment to contractors to compensate for loss occasioned by increased cost of materials during the war with Germany was made by section 10 of act Mar. 2, 1919, and act June 5, 1920, ch. 252, § 5, 41 Stat. 1014.

REPEAL OF LIMITATION ON COSTS

A provision for limitation on the costs of projects made by section 1 of act Mar. 2, 1919, was repealed by act June 5, 1920, ch. 252, § 3, 41 Stat. 1013.

§ 625. Repealed. Oct. 31, 1951, ch. 654, § 1(58), 65 Stat. 703

Section, acts Sept. 19, 1890, ch. 907, § 2, 26 Stat. 452; July 25, 1912, ch. 253, § 8, 37 Stat. 233, related to combining several projects in one contract.

§ 626. Prosecution of work when appropriation insufficient

Whenever the appropriations made, or authorized to be made, for the completion of any river and harbor work shall prove insufficient therefor, the Secretary of the Army may, in his discretion, on the recommendation of the Chief of Engineers, apply the funds so appropriated or authorized to the prosecution of such work.

(July 25, 1912, ch. 253, §8, 37 Stat. 233; July 26, 1947, ch. 343, title II, §205(a), 61 Stat. 501.)

CODIFICATION

Section is from part of section 8 of the Rivers and Harbors Appropriation Act of 1912. The omitted part of such section 8 was set out in section 625 of this title.

CHANGE OF NAME

Department of War designated Department of the Army and title of Secretary of War changed to Secretary of the Army by section 205(a) of act July 26, 1947, ch. 343, title II, 61 Stat. 501. Section 205(a) of act July 26, 1947, was repealed by section 53 of act Aug. 10, 1956, ch. 1041, 70A Stat. 641. Section 1 of act Aug. 10, 1956, enacted "Title 10, Armed Forces" which in sections 3010 to 3013 continued Department of the Army under administrative supervision of Secretary of the Army.

SIMILAR PROVISIONS

A similar provision was contained in act Mar. 2, 1907, ch. 2509, §1, 34 Stat. 1073.

§627. Application of appropriation when separate works are included therein

Where separate works or items are consolidated in River and Harbor Acts and an aggregate amount is appropriated therefor, any balances remaining to the credit of the separate works or items may be transferred to the credit of the corresponding aggregate amounts appropriated for the consolidated items, and the amounts appropriated or transferred shall, unless otherwise expressed, be expended in securing maintenance and improvement according to the respective projects adopted by Congress, after giving due regard to the respective needs of traffic. The allotments to the respective works consolidated shall be made by the Secretary of the Army upon recommendations by the Chief of Engineers. In case such works or items are consolidated and separate amounts are given with each project, the amounts so named shall be expended upon such separate projects unless, in the discretion of the Secretary of the Army, another allotment or division should be made of the same. Any balances remaining to the credit of the consolidated items shall be carried to the credit of the respective aggregate amounts appropriated for the consolidated items.

(Mar. 4, 1915, ch. 142, §3, 38 Stat. 1052; July 26, 1947, ch. 343, title II, §205(a), 61 Stat. 501.)

CODIFICATION

Section is from the Rivers and Harbors Appropriation Act of 1915.

PRIOR PROVISIONS

Section 3 of act Mar. 4, 1915, superseded act Mar. 4, 1913, ch. 144, §7, 37 Stat. 827, which read as follows:

"Where separate works or items are consolidated in this or subsequent river and harbor Acts and an aggregate amount is appropriated therefor the amounts appropriated shall, unless otherwise expressed, be expended in securing maintenance and improvement according to the respective projects adopted by Congress, after giving due regard to the respective needs of traffic. The allotments to the respective works consolidated shall be made by the Secretary of War upon recommendations by the Chief of Engineers. In case such works or items are consolidated and separate amounts are given with each project, the amounts so named shall be expended upon such separate projects unless, in the discretion of the Secretary of War, another allotment or division should be made of the same. Any balances remaining to the credit of the consolidated items shall be carried to the credit of the respective aggregate amounts appropriated for the consolidated items."

CHANGE OF NAME

Department of War designated Department of the Army and title of Secretary of War changed to Secretary of the Army by section 205(a) of act July 26, 1947, ch. 343, title II, 61 Stat. 501. Section 205(a) of act July 26, 1947, was repealed by section 53 of act Aug. 10, 1956, ch. 1041, 70A Stat. 641. Section 1 of act Aug. 10, 1956, enacted "Title 10, Armed Forces" which in sections 3010 to 3013 continued Department of the Army under administrative supervision of Secretary of the Army.

SIMILAR PROVISIONS

The Rivers and Harbors Appropriation Act, Mar. 2, 1919, ch. 95, §2, 40 Stat. 1287, contained the following provision: "Where separate works or items are consolidated herein and an aggregate amount is appropriated therefor, the amount so appropriated shall, unless otherwise expressed, be expended in securing the maintenance and improvement according to the respective projects adopted by Congress after giving due regard to the respective needs of traffic. The allotments to the respective works so consolidated shall be made by the Chief of Engineers as authorized by the Secretary of War. In case such works or items are consolidated and separate amounts are given to individual projects the amounts so named shall be expended upon such separate projects. Any balances remaining to the credit of the consolidated items shall be carried to the credit of the respective aggregate amounts appropriated for the consolidated items."

Similar provisions were contained in act July 18, 1918, ch. 155, §2, 40 Stat. 910.

§628. Expenditure for dredging within harbor lines

No money appropriated for the improvement of rivers and harbors shall be expended for dredging inside of harbor lines duly established.

(July 13, 1892, ch. 158, §5, 27 Stat. 111.)

CODIFICATION

Section is from the Rivers and Harbors Appropriation Act of 1892.

§629. Contract for hire of dredging plant

Whenever it shall become, in the opinion of the Secretary of the Army, necessary or desirable to hire a dredging plant or plants for the performance of any of the public work carried on under his direction the said Secretary may, in his discretion, agree for the same, either in the manner customary on March 2, 1907, or on the basis of an equitable reimbursement for deterioration of plant when in use by the Government, and a reasonable percentage of the total cost of the work.

(Mar. 2, 1907, ch. 2509, §5, 34 Stat. 1119; July 26, 1947, ch. 343, title II, §205(a), 61 Stat. 501.)

CODIFICATION

Section is from the Rivers and Harbors Appropriation Act of 1907.

The part of the original text omitted here repealed act Apr. 28, 1904, ch. 1761, §4, 33 Stat. 452.

CHANGE OF NAME

Department of War designated Department of the Army and title of Secretary of War changed to Secretary of the Army by section 205(a) of act July 26, 1947, ch. 343, title II, 61 Stat. 501. Section 205(a) of act July 26, 1947, was repealed by section 53 of act Aug. 10, 1956, ch. 1041, 70A Stat. 641. Section 1 of act Aug. 10, 1956, enacted "Title 10, Armed Forces" which in sections 3010 to 3013 continued Department of the Army under administrative supervision of Secretary of the Army.

§ 630. Limitation on expenditure for purchase of dredges

No money authorized to be expended for the acquirement of any dredge or dredges shall be so expended for the purchase of any dredge or dredges from private contractors, which at the time of the proposed purchase can be manufactured at any navy yard or other government-owned factory for a sum less than it can be purchased for from such private contractor.

(Sept. 22, 1922, ch. 427, §5, 42 Stat. 1042.)

CODIFICATION

Section is from part of section 5 of the Rivers and Harbors Appropriation Act for 1922.

The omitted portion of that section authorized the construction of six seagoing hopper dredges and limited the cost of each to $750,000.

§ 631. Transfer of property between projects

The Secretary of the Army may direct a temporary transfer of any property employed in the improvement of rivers and harbors whenever, in his judgment, such transfer would secure efficient or economical results, and such adjustment in the way of charges and credits shall be made between the projects affected as may be equitable.

(June 13, 1902, ch. 1079, §5, 32 Stat. 373; July 26, 1947, ch. 343, title II, §205(a), 61 Stat. 501.)

CODIFICATION

Section is from part of section 5 of the Rivers and Harbors Appropriation Act of 1902.

The omitted part of that section is set out as section 558 of this title.

CHANGE OF NAME

Department of War designated Department of the Army and title of Secretary of War changed to Secretary of the Army by section 205(a) of act July 26, 1947, ch. 343, title II, 61 Stat. 501. Section 205(a) of act July 26, 1947, was repealed by section 53 of act Aug. 10, 1956, ch. 1041, 70A Stat. 641. Section 1 of act Aug. 10, 1956, enacted "Title 10, Armed Forces" which in sections 3010 to 3013 continued Department of the Army under administrative supervision of Secretary of the Army.

§ 632. Omitted

CODIFICATION

Section, act June 25, 1910, ch. 382, §5, 36 Stat. 676, provided that the requirements of R.S. §3744, section 16 of Title 41, Public Contracts, should not apply to the lease of certain property or hire of vessels for use in connection with river and harbor improvements where the period of the lease or hire did not exceed three months. R.S. §3744, which required contracts by the Secretaries of War, Navy, and Interior to be in writing and filed in the returns office of the Interior Department, was repealed by act Oct. 21, 1941, ch. 452, 55 Stat. 743.

§ 633. Protection, alteration, reconstruction, relocation, or replacement of structures and facilities; contract standards; reasonable costs

Whenever, during the construction or reconstruction of any navigation, flood control, or related water development project under the direction of the Secretary of the Army, the Chief of Engineers determines that any structure or facility owned by an agency of government and utilized in the performance of a governmental function should be protected, altered, reconstructed, relocated, or replaced to meet the requirements of navigation or flood control, or both; or to preserve the safety or integrity of such facility when its safety or usefulness is determined by the Chief of Engineers to be adversely affected or threatened by the project, the Chief of Engineers may, if he deems such action to be in the public interest, enter into a contract providing for (1) the payment from appropriations made for the construction or maintenance of such project, of the reasonable cost of replacing, relocating, or reconstructing such facility to such standard as he deems reasonable but not to exceed the minimum standard of the State or political subdivision for the same type of facility involved, except that if the existing facility exceeds the minimum standard of the State or political subdivision, the Chief of Engineers may provide a facility of comparable standard, or (2) the payment of a lump sum representing the estimated reasonable cost thereof. This section shall not be construed as modifying any existing or future requirement of local cooperation, or as indicating a policy that local interests shall not hereafter be required to assume costs of modifying such facilities. The provisions of this section may be applied to projects hereafter authorized and to those heretofore authorized but not completed as of July 3, 1958, and notwithstanding the navigation servitude vested in the United States, they may be applied to such structures or facilities occupying the beds of navigable waters of the United States.

(Pub. L. 85–500, title I, §111, July 3, 1958, 72 Stat. 303; Pub. L. 89–298, title III, §309, Oct. 27, 1965, 79 Stat. 1094.)

AMENDMENTS

1965—Pub. L. 89–298 provided for payment of the reasonable cost of replacing, relocating, or reconstructing the facility to a reasonable standard, not exceeding minimum standard of State or political subdivision for same type of facility involved, except that if the existing facility exceeds the minimum standard of the State or political subdivision, the Chief of Engineers may provide a facility of comparable standard, in provision designated as clause (1), eliminated former provision for payment of reasonable actual cost of the remedial work, and designated existing provisions as clause (2).

CHAPTER 13—MISSISSIPPI RIVER COMMISSION

§641. Creation of Mississippi River Commission

A commission is created to be called "The Mississippi River Commission", to consist of seven members.

(June 28, 1879, ch. 43, §1, 21 Stat. 37.)

CODIFICATION

This was the first section of an act entitled "An act to provide for the appointment of a 'Mississippi River Commission' for the improvement of said river from the Head of the Passes near its mouth to its head-waters".

APPROPRIATION FOR SALARIES AND EXPENSES

Section 7 of act June 28, 1879, omitted as temporary and executed, provided for the expenditure of an appropriation of $175,000 for salaries of the commission and necessary expenses of surveys, examinations, etc.

MISSOURI RIVER COMMISSION

The Missouri River Commission was created by act July 5, 1884, ch. 229, §1, 23 Stat. 144, and repealed by act July 13, 1902, ch. 1079, §1, 32 Stat. 367.

§642. Appointment of commissioners; vacancies; chairman; tenure of office

The President of the United States shall, by and with the advice and consent of the Senate, appoint seven commissioners, three of whom shall be selected from the Engineer Corps of the Army, one from the National Ocean Survey, and three from civil life, two of whom shall be civil engineers. And any vacancy which may occur in the commission shall in like manner be filled by the President of the United States; and he shall designate one of the commissioners appointed from the Engineer Corps of the Army to be president of the commission. The commissioners appointed under sections 641 to 644, 646, and 647 of this title, except those appointed from civil life, shall remain in office subject to removal by the President of the United States. Each commissioner appointed from civil life after November 7, 1966, shall be appointed for a term of nine years.

(June 28, 1879, ch. 43, §2, 21 Stat. 37; Pub. L. 89–789, title II, §208, Nov. 7, 1966, 80 Stat. 1423.)

AMENDMENTS

1966—Pub. L. 89–789 inserted ", except those appointed from civil life," and provided a nine year term for each commissioner appointed from civil life after Nov. 7, 1966.

CHANGE OF NAME

Coast and Geodetic Survey consolidated with National Weather Bureau in 1965 to form Environmental Science Services Administration by Reorg. Plan No. 2 of 1965, eff. July 13, 1965, 30 F.R. 8819, 79 Stat. 1318. Environmental Science Services Administration abolished in 1970 and its personnel, property, records, etc., transferred to National Oceanic and Atmospheric Administration by Reorg. Plan No. 4 of 1970, eff. Oct. 3, 1970, 35 F.R. 15627, 84 Stat. 2090. By order of Acting Associate Administrator of National Oceanic Atmospheric Administration, 35 F.R. 19249, Dec. 19, 1970, Coast and Geodetic Survey redesignated National Ocean Survey. See notes set out under section 311 of Title 15, Commerce and Trade.

TRANSFER OF FUNCTIONS

Functions of all officers of Department of Commerce and functions of all officers and employees of such Department transferred, with a few exceptions, to Secretary of Commerce, with power vested in him to authorize their performance or performance of any of his functions by any of such officers, agencies and employees, by Reorg. Plan No. 5 of 1950, §§1, 2, eff. May 24, 1950, 15 F.R. 3174, 64 Stat. 1263, set out in the Appendix to Title 5, Government Organization and Employees.

§642a. Rank, pay, and allowances of Corps of Engineers officers serving as President of Mississippi River Commission

Any officer of the Corps of Engineers who has served or shall serve four years as President of the Mississippi River Commission and who has been or shall subsequently be retired, shall, from the date of such retirement, receive the rank, pay, and allowances of a retired major general.

(June 15, 1936, ch. 548 (pt.), as added Aug. 18, 1941, ch. 377, §3, 55 Stat. 644.)

CODIFICATION

Section was formerly classified to section 1026b of title 10 prior to the general revision and enactment of Title 10, Armed Forces, by act Aug. 10, 1956, ch. 1041, §1, 70A Stat. 1.

§643. Omitted

CODIFICATION

Section, acts June 28, 1879, ch. 43, §2, 21 Stat. 37; June 25, 1910, ch. 382, §1, 36 Stat. 658; Mar. 1, 1917, ch. 144, §4, 39 Stat. 951, related to compensation of commissioners. See section 702h of this title.

§644. Secretary of commission

The Secretary of the Army may detail from the Engineer Corps of the Army of the United States an officer to act as secretary of said commission.

(June 28, 1879, ch. 43, §6, 21 Stat. 38; July 26, 1947, ch. 343, title II, §205(a), 61 Stat. 501.)

CHANGE OF NAME

Department of War designated Department of the Army and title of Secretary of War changed to Secretary of the Army by section 205(a) of act July 26, 1947, ch. 343, title II, 61 Stat. 501. Section 205(a) of act July 26, 1947, was repealed by section 53 of act Aug. 10, 1956, ch. 1041, 70A Stat. 641. Section 1 of act Aug. 10, 1956, enacted "Title 10, Armed Forces" which in sections 3010 to 3013 continued Department of the Army under administrative supervision of Secretary of the Army.

§645. Repealed. Pub. L. 89–554, §8(a), Sept. 6, 1966, 80 Stat. 642

Section, act July 25, 1912, ch. 253, §1, 37 Stat. 218, related to traveling expenses of civilian members of commission and of Assistant Engineer of Board of Engineers for Rivers and Harbors.

§ 646. Headquarters and meetings of commission

The headquarters and general offices of said commission shall be located at some city or town on the Mississippi River, to be designated by the Secretary of the Army, and the meetings of the commission except such as are held on Government boats during the time of the semiannual inspection trips of the commission shall be held at said headquarters and general offices, the times of said meetings to be fixed by the president of the commission, who shall cause due notice of such meetings to be given members of the commission and the public.

(June 28, 1879, ch. 43, §8, as added Feb. 18, 1901, ch. 377, 31 Stat. 793; July 26, 1947, ch. 343, title II, §205(a), 61 Stat. 501.)

CHANGE OF NAME

Department of War designated Department of the Army and title of Secretary of War changed to Secretary of the Army by section 205(a) of act July 26, 1947, ch. 343, title II, 61 Stat. 501. Section 205(a) of act July 26, 1947, was repealed by section 53 of act Aug. 10, 1956, ch. 1041, 70A Stat. 641. Section 1 of act Aug. 10, 1956, enacted "Title 10, Armed Forces" which in sections 3010 to 3013 continued Department of the Army under administrative supervision of Secretary of the Army.

§ 647. Mississippi River survey

Detail of assistants; vessels; instruments—It shall be the duty of the Mississippi River Commission to direct and complete such surveys of the Mississippi River, between the Head of the Passes near its mouth to its headwaters as may have been in progress June 28, 1879, and to make such additional surveys, examinations, and investigations, topographical, hydrographical, and hydrometrical, of said river and its tributaries, as may be deemed necessary by said commission to carry out the objects of sections 641 to 644, 646, and 647 of this title. And to enable said commission to complete such surveys, examinations, and investigations, the Secretary of the Army shall, when requested by said commission, detail from the Engineer Corps of the Army such officers and men as may be necessary, and shall place in the charge and for the use of said commission such vessel or vessels and such machinery and instruments as may be under his control and may be deemed necessary. And the Secretary of Commerce shall, when requested by said commission in like manner detail from the National Ocean Survey such officers and men as may be necessary, and shall place in the charge and for the use of said commission such vessel or vessels and such machinery and instruments as may be under his control and may be deemed necessary. And the said commission may, with the approval of the Secretary of the Army, employ such additional force and assistants, and provide, by purchase or otherwise, such vessels or boats and such instruments and means as may be deemed necessary.

Plans; report—It shall be the duty of said commission to take into consideration and mature such plan or plans and estimates as will correct, permanently locate, and deepen the channel and protect the banks of the Mississippi River; improve and give safety and ease to the navigation thereof; prevent destructive floods; promote and facilitate commerce, trade, and the postal service; and when so prepared and matured, to submit to the Secretary of the Army a full and detailed report of their proceedings and actions, and of such plans, with estimates of the cost thereof, for the purposes aforesaid, to be by him transmitted to Congress: *Provided*, That the commission shall report in full upon the practicability, feasibility, and probable cost of the various plans known as the jetty system, the levee system, and the outlet system, as well as upon such others as they deem necessary.

Plans for immediate works—The said commission may, prior to the completion of all the surveys and examinations contemplated by sections 641 to 644, 646, and 647 of this title, prepare and submit to the Secretary of the Army, plans, specifications, and estimates of costs for such immediate works as, in the judgment of said commission, may constitute a part of the general system of works herein contemplated, to be by him transmitted to Congress.

(June 28, 1879, ch. 43, §§3–5, 21 Stat. 37, 38; Feb. 14, 1903, ch. 552, §4, 32 Stat. 826; July 26, 1947, ch. 343, title II, §205(a), 61 Stat. 501.)

CHANGE OF NAME

Coast and Geodetic Survey consolidated with National Weather Bureau in 1965 to form Environmental Science Services Administration by Reorg. Plan No. 2 of 1965, eff. July 13, 1965, 30 F.R. 8819, 79 Stat. 1318. Environmental Science Services Administration abolished in 1970 and its personnel, property, records, etc., transferred to National Oceanic and Atmospheric Administration by Reorg. Plan No. 4 of 1970, eff. Oct. 3, 1970, 35 F.R. 15627, 84 Stat. 2090. By order of Acting Associate Administrator of National Oceanic Atmospheric Administration, 35 F.R. 19249, Dec. 19, 1970, Coast and Geodetic Survey redesignated National Ocean Survey. See notes set out under section 311 of Title 15, Commerce and Trade.

Department of War designated Department of the Army and title of Secretary of War changed to Secretary of the Army by section 205(a) of act July 26, 1947, ch. 343, title II, 61 Stat. 501. Section 205(a) of act July 26, 1947, was repealed by section 53 of act Aug. 10, 1956, ch. 1041, 70A Stat. 641. Section 1 of act Aug. 10, 1956, enacted "Title 10, Armed Forces" which in sections 3010 to 3013 continued Department of the Army under administrative supervision of Secretary of the Army.

TRANSFER OF FUNCTIONS

"Secretary of Commerce" substituted for "Secretary of the Treasury" in the first par. pursuant to sections 4 and 10 of act Feb. 14, 1903, which are classified to sections 1511, 1513, 1515, and 1516 of Title 15, Commerce and Trade, and which transferred Coast and Geodetic Survey, and powers and duties pertaining thereto, from Department of the Treasury to Department of Commerce.

Functions of all officers of Department of Commerce and functions of all officers and employees of such Department transferred, with a few exceptions, to Secretary of Commerce, with power vested in him to authorize their performance or performance of any of his functions by any of such officers, agencies, and employees, by Reorg. Plan No. 5 of 1950, §§1, 2, eff. May 24, 1950, 15 F.R. 3174, 64 Stat. 1263, set out in Appendix to Title 5, Government Organization and Employees.

TRIBUTARIES

Act Mar. 3, 1881, ch. 136, 21 Stat. 474, provided in part as follows: "It shall be the duty of said commission to take into consideration, and of the Secretary of War [now Secretary of the Army] to extend operations, under their supervision, to tributaries of the Mississippi River to the extent, and not further, that may be necessary in the judgment of said commission to the perfection of the general and permanent improvement of said Mississippi River."

§648. Arkansas River; levee and bank protection

The jurisdiction of the Mississippi River Commission is extended so as to include that part of the Arkansas River between its mouth and the intersection thereof with the division line between Lincoln and Jefferson Counties, and any funds which are appropriated by Congress for improving the Mississippi River between Head of Passes and the mouth of the Ohio River, and which may be allotted to levees and bank revetment, may be expended within the limits of said extended jurisdiction under the direction of the Secretary of the Army, in accordance with the plans, specifications, and recommendations of the Mississippi River Commission, as approved by the Chief of Engineers, and upon like terms and conditions for levees and bank revetment upon any part of the Mississippi River now under the jurisdiction of said commission, and in such manner as will best promote and accomplish the purposes for which commission was created, in so far as the territory hereby added to its said jurisdiction may be involved.

(July 27, 1916, ch. 260, §1, 39 Stat. 402; July 26, 1947, ch. 343, title II, §205(a), 61 Stat. 501.)

CODIFICATION

Section is from part of section 1 of the Rivers and Harbors Appropriation Act of 1916.

CHANGE OF NAME

Department of War designated Department of the Army and title of Secretary of War changed to Secretary of the Army by section 205(a) of act July 26, 1947, ch. 343, title II, 61 Stat. 501. Section 205(a) of act July 26, 1947, was repealed by section 53 of act Aug. 10, 1956, ch. 1041, 70A Stat. 641. Section 1 of act Aug. 10, 1956, enacted "Title 10, Armed Forces" which in sections 3010 to 3013 continued Department of the Army under administrative supervision of Secretary of the Army.

§649. Vicksburg Harbor and Ohio River below Cache River

The harbor at Vicksburg, Mississippi, and the Ohio River from its mouth to the mouth of the Cache River, are transferred to and placed under the control and jurisdiction of the Mississippi River Commission: *Provided*, That no part of the improvement of the Ohio River, with a view to the construction of locks and dams, shall be considered as transferred to or placed under the control and jurisdiction of the Mississippi River Commission.

(July 27, 1916, ch. 260, §1, 39 Stat. 402.)

CODIFICATION

Section is from part of section 1 of the Rivers and Harbors Appropriation Act of 1916.

§650. Mississippi River below Rock Island; levee and bank protection

Any funds which are appropriated by Congress for improving the Mississippi River between Head of Passes and the mouth of the Ohio River, and which may be allotted to levees, may be expended, under the direction of the Secretary of the Army, in accordance with the plans, specifications, and recommendations of the Mississippi River Commission, as approved by the Chief of Engineers, for levees upon any part of said river between Head of Passes and Rock Island, Illinois, in such manner as, in their opinion, shall best improve navigation and promote the interest of commerce at all stages of the river.

(July 27, 1916, ch. 260, §1, 39 Stat. 402; July 26, 1947, ch. 343, title II, §205(a), 61 Stat. 501.)

CODIFICATION

Section is from part of section 1 of the Rivers and Harbors Appropriation Act of 1916.

PRIOR PROVISIONS

This provision superseded act June 4, 1906, ch. 2572, 34 Stat. 208, which contained similar provisions.

CHANGE OF NAME

Department of War designated Department of the Army and title of Secretary of War changed to Secretary of the Army by section 205(a) of act July 26, 1947, ch. 343, title II, 61 Stat. 501. Section 205(a) of act July 26, 1947, was repealed by section 53 of act Aug. 10, 1956, ch. 1041, 70A Stat. 641. Section 1 of act Aug. 10, 1956, enacted "Title 10, Armed Forces" which in sections 3010 to 3013 continued Department of the Army under administrative supervision of Secretary of the Army.

§651. Tributaries of Mississippi River below Cairo; levee and bank protection

The jurisdiction of the Mississippi River Commission is extended, for the purposes of levee protection and bank protection, to the tributaries and outlets of the Mississippi River between Cairo, Illinois, and the Head of the Passes, in so far as these tributaries and outlets are affected by the flood waters of the Mississippi River.

(Sept. 22, 1922, ch. 427, §13, 42 Stat. 1047.)

CODIFICATION

Section is from the Rivers and Harbors Appropriation Act for the year 1922.

§652. Upper Mississippi River Management

(a) Short title; Congressional declaration of intent

(1) This section may be cited as the "Upper Mississippi River Management Act of 1986".

(2) To ensure the coordinated development and enhancement of the Upper Mississippi River system, it is hereby declared to be the intent of Congress to recognize that system as a nationally significant ecosystem and a nationally significant commercial navigation system. Congress further recognizes that the system provides a diversity of opportunities and experiences. The system shall be administered and regulated in recognition of its several purposes.

(b) Definitions

For purposes of this section—

(1) the terms "Upper Mississippi River system" and "system" mean those river reaches having commercial navigation channels on the Mississippi River main stem north of Cairo, Il-

linois; the Minnesota River, Minnesota; Black River, Wisconsin; Saint Croix River, Minnesota and Wisconsin; Illinois River and Waterway, Illinois; and Kaskaskia River, Illinois;

(2) the term "Master Plan" means the comprehensive master plan for the management of the Upper Mississippi River system, dated January 1, 1982, prepared by the Upper Mississippi River Basin Commission and submitted to Congress pursuant to Public Law 95–502;

(3) the term "GREAT I, GREAT II, and GRRM studies" means the studies entitled "GREAT Environmental Action Team—GREAT I—A Study of the Upper Mississippi River", dated September 1980, "GREAT River Environmental Action Team—GREAT II—A Study of the Upper Mississippi River", dated December 1980, and "GREAT River Resource Management Study", dated September 1982; and

(4) the term "Upper Mississippi River Basin Association" means an association of the States of Illinois, Iowa, Minnesota, Missouri, and Wisconsin, formed for the purposes of cooperative effort and united assistance in the comprehensive planning for the use, protection, growth, and development of the Upper Mississippi River System.

(c) Congressional approval of Master Plan

(1) Congress hereby approves the Master Plan as a guide for future water policy on the Upper Mississippi River system. Such approval shall not constitute authorization of any recommendation contained in the Master Plan.

(2) Omitted.

(d) Cooperative effort and mutual assistance among States

(1) The consent of the Congress is hereby given to the States of Illinois, Iowa, Minnesota, Missouri, and Wisconsin, or any two or more of such States, to enter into negotiations for agreements, not in conflict with any law of the United States, for cooperative effort and mutual assistance in the comprehensive planning for the use, protection, growth, and development of the Upper Mississippi River system, and to establish such agencies, joint or otherwise, or designate an existing multi-State entity, as they may deem desirable for making effective such agreements. To the extent required by Article I, section 10 of the Constitution, such agreements shall become final only after ratification by an Act of Congress.

(2) The Secretary is authorized to enter into cooperative agreements with thè Upper Mississippi River Basin Association or any other agency established under paragraph (1) of this subsection to promote and facilitate active State government participation in the river system management, development, and protection.

(3) For the purpose of ensuring the coordinated planning and implementation of programs authorized in subsections (e) and (h)(2) of this section, the Secretary shall enter into an interagency agreement with the Secretary of the Interior to provide for the direct participation of, and transfer of funds to, the Fish and Wildlife Service and any other agency or bureau of the Department of the Interior for the planning, design, implementation, and evaluation of such programs.

(4) The Upper Mississippi River Basin Association or any other agency established under paragraph (1) of this subsection is hereby designated by Congress as the caretaker of the master plan. Any changes to the master plan recommended by the Secretary shall be submitted to such association or agency for review. Such association or agency may make such comments with respect to such recommendations and offer other recommended changes to the master plan as such association or agency deems appropriate and shall transmit such comments and other recommended changes to the Secretary. The Secretary shall transmit such recommendations along with the comments and other recommended changes of such association or agency to the Congress for approval within 90 days of the receipt of such comments or recommended changes.

(e) Program authority

(1) AUTHORITY.—

(A) IN GENERAL.—The Secretary, in consultation with the Secretary of the Interior and the States of Illinois, Iowa, Minnesota, Missouri, and Wisconsin, may undertake, as identified in the master plan—

(i) a program for the planning, construction, and evaluation of measures for fish and wildlife habitat rehabilitation and enhancement; and

(ii) implementation of a long-term resource monitoring, computerized data inventory and analysis, and applied research program, including research on water quality issues affecting the Mississippi River (including elevated nutrient levels) and the development of remediation strategies.

(B) ADVISORY COMMITTEE.—In carrying out subparagraph (A)(i), the Secretary shall establish an independent technical advisory committee to review projects, monitoring plans, and habitat and natural resource needs assessments.

(2) REPORTS.—Not later than December 31, 2004, and not later than December 31 of every sixth year thereafter, the Secretary, in consultation with the Secretary of the Interior and the States of Illinois, Iowa, Minnesota, Missouri, and Wisconsin, shall submit to Congress a report that—

(A) contains an evaluation of the programs described in paragraph (1);

(B) describes the accomplishments of each of the programs;

(C) provides updates of a systemic habitat needs assessment; and

(D) identifies any needed adjustments in the authorization of the programs.

(3) For purposes of carrying out paragraph (1)(A)(i) of this subsection, there is authorized to be appropriated to the Secretary $22,750,000 for fiscal year 1999 and each fiscal year thereafter.

(4) For purposes of carrying out paragraph (1)(A)(ii) of this subsection, there is authorized to be appropriated to the Secretary $10,420,000 for fiscal year 1999 and each fiscal year thereafter.

(5) AUTHORIZATION OF APPROPRIATIONS.—There is authorized to be appropriated to carry out paragraph (1)(B) $350,000 for each of fiscal years 1999 through 2009.

(6) TRANSFER OF AMOUNTS.—For fiscal year 1999 and each fiscal year thereafter, the Secretary, in consultation with the Secretary of the Interior and the States of Illinois, Iowa, Minnesota, Missouri, and Wisconsin, may transfer not to exceed 20 percent of the amounts appropriated to carry out clause (i) or (ii) of paragraph (1)(A) to the amounts appropriated to carry out the other of those clauses.

(7)(A) Notwithstanding the provisions of subsection (a)(2) of this section, the costs of each project carried out pursuant to paragraph (1)(A)(i) of this subsection shall be allocated between the Secretary and the appropriate non-Federal sponsor in accordance with the provisions of section 2283(e) of this title; except that the costs of operation and maintenance of projects located on Federal lands or lands owned or operated by a State or local government shall be borne by the Federal, State, or local agency that is responsible for management activities for fish and wildlife on such lands and, in the case of any project requiring non-Federal cost sharing, the non-Federal share of the cost of the project shall be 35 percent.

(B) Notwithstanding the provisions of subsection (a)(2) of this section, the cost of implementing the activities authorized by paragraph (1)(A)(ii) of this subsection shall be allocated in accordance with the provisions of section 2283 of this title, as if such activity was required to mitigate losses to fish and wildlife.

(8) None of the funds appropriated pursuant to any authorization contained in this subsection shall be considered to be chargeable to navigation.

(f) Recreational projects authority

(1) The Secretary, in consultation with any agency established under subsection (d)(1) of this section, is authorized to implement a program of recreational projects for the system substantially in accordance with the recommendations of the GREAT I, GREAT II, and GRRM studies and the master plan reports. In addition, the Secretary, in consultation with any such agency, shall, at Federal expense, conduct an assessment of the economic benefits generated by recreational activities in the system. The cost of each such project shall be allocated between the Secretary and the appropriate non-Federal sponsor in accordance with title I of this Act [33 U.S.C. 2211 et seq.].

(2) For purposes of carrying out the program of recreational projects authorized in paragraph (1) of this subsection, there is authorized to be appropriated to the Secretary not to exceed $500,000 per fiscal year for each of the first 15 fiscal years beginning after November 17, 1986.

(g) Increases in lock capacity

The Secretary shall, in his budget request, identify those measures developed by the Secretary, in consultation with the Secretary of Transportation and any agency established under subsection (d)(1) of this section, to be undertaken to increase the capacity of specific locks throughout the system by employing nonstructural measures and making minor structural improvements.

(h) Monitoring of traffic movements

(1) The Secretary, in consultation with any agency established under subsection (d)(1) of this section, shall monitor traffic movements on the system for the purpose of verifying lock capacity, updating traffic projections, and refining the economic evaluation so as to verify the need for future capacity expansion of the system.

(2) DETERMINATION.—

(A) IN GENERAL.—The Secretary, in consultation with the Secretary of the Interior and the States of Illinois, Iowa, Minnesota, Missouri, and Wisconsin, shall determine the need for river rehabilitation and environmental enhancement and protection based on the condition of the environment, project developments, and projected environmental impacts from implementing any proposals resulting from recommendations made under subsection (g) of this section and paragraph (1) of this subsection.

(B) REQUIREMENTS.—The Secretary shall—

(i) complete the ongoing habitat needs assessment conducted under this paragraph not later than September 30, 2000; and

(ii) include in each report under subsection (e)(2) of this section the most recent habitat needs assessment conducted under this paragraph.

(3) There is authorized to be appropriated to the Secretary such sums as may be necessary to carry out this subsection.

(i) Disposal of dredged material

(1) The Secretary shall, as he determines feasible, dispose of dredged material from the system pursuant to the recommendations of the GREAT I, GREAT II, and GRRM studies.

(2) The Secretary shall establish and request appropriate Federal funding for a program to facilitate productive uses of dredged material. The Secretary shall work with the States which have, within their boundaries, any part of the system to identify potential users of dredged material.

(j) Construction of second lock at locks and dam 26, Mississippi River, Alton, Illinois and Missouri

The Secretary is authorized to provide for the engineering, design, and construction of a second lock at locks and dam 26, Mississippi River, Alton, Illinois and Missouri, at a total cost of $220,000,000, with a first Federal cost of $220,000,000. Such second lock shall be one hundred and ten feet by six hundred feet and shall be constructed at or in the vicinity of the location of the replacement lock authorized by section 102 of Public Law 95–502. Section 2212 of this title shall apply to the project authorized by this subsection.

(Pub. L. 99–662, title XI, § 1103, Nov. 17, 1986, 100 Stat. 4225; Pub. L. 101–640, title IV, § 405, Nov. 28, 1990, 104 Stat. 4646; Pub. L. 102–580, title I, § 107, Oct. 31, 1992, 106 Stat. 4815; Pub. L. 106–53, title V, § 509, Aug. 17, 1999, 113 Stat. 339; Pub. L. 106–109, § 2, Nov. 24, 1999, 113 Stat. 1494; Pub. L. 110–114, title III, § 3177, Nov. 8, 2007, 121 Stat. 1155.)

REFERENCES IN TEXT

Public Law 95–502, referred to in subsecs. (b)(2) and (j), is Pub. L. 95–502, Oct. 21, 1978, 92 Stat. 1693, as amended. Section 102 of Pub. L. 95–502 is not classified to the Code. For complete classification of this Act to the Code, see Tables.

This Act, referred to in subsec. (f)(1), is Pub. L. 99–662, Nov. 17, 1986, 100 Stat. 4082, as amended, known as the Water Resources Development Act of 1986. Title I of this Act is classified generally to subchapter I (§ 2211 et seq.) of chapter 36 of this title. For complete classification of this Act to the Code, see Short Title note set out under section 2201 of this title and Tables.

CODIFICATION

Subsec. (c)(2) of this section amended section 101 of Pub. L. 95–502, which is set out as a note under section 1962b–3 of Title 42, The Public Health and Welfare.

AMENDMENTS

2007—Subsec. (e)(1)(A)(ii). Pub. L. 110–114 inserted ", including research on water quality issues affecting the Mississippi River (including elevated nutrient levels) and the development of remediation strategies" before period at end.

1999—Subsec. (e). Pub. L. 106–53, § 509(a), inserted subsec. heading, added par. (1), and struck out former par. (1) which read as follows: "The Secretary, in consultation with the Secretary of the Interior and the States of Illinois, Iowa, Minnesota, Missouri, and Wisconsin, is authorized to undertake, as identified in the master plan—

"(A) a program for the planning, construction, and evaluation of measures for fish and wildlife habitat rehabilitation and enhancement;

"(B) implementation of a long-term resource monitoring program; and

"(C) implementation of a computerized inventory and analysis system."

Subsec. (e)(2). Pub. L. 106–53, § 509(b), added par. (2) and struck out former par. (2) which read as follows: "Each program referred to in paragraph (1) shall be carried out for 15 years. Before the last day of such 15-year period, the Secretary, in consultation with the Secretary of the Interior and the States of Illinois, Iowa, Minnesota, Missouri, and Wisconsin, shall conduct an evaluation of such programs and submit a report on the results of such evaluation to Congress. Such evaluation shall determine each such program's effectiveness, strengths, and weaknesses and contain recommendations for the modification and continuance or termination of such program."

Subsec. (e)(3). Pub. L. 106–53, § 509(c)(1), substituted "(1)(A)(i)" for "(1)(A)" and "Secretary $22,750,000 for fiscal year 1999 and each fiscal year thereafter" for "Secretary not to exceed $8,200,000 for the first fiscal year beginning after November 17, 1986, not to exceed $12,400,000 for the second fiscal year beginning after November 17, 1986, and not to exceed $13,000,000 per fiscal year for each of the succeeding 13 fiscal years".

Subsec. (e)(4). Pub. L. 106–53, § 509(c)(2), substituted "(1)(A)(ii)" for "(1)(B)" and "Secretary $10,420,000 for fiscal year 1999 and each fiscal year thereafter" for "Secretary not to exceed $7,680,000 for the first fiscal year beginning after November 17, 1986, and not to exceed $5,080,000 per fiscal year for each of the succeeding 14 fiscal years".

Subsec. (e)(5). Pub. L. 106–109 substituted "paragraph (1)(B)" for "paragraph (1)(A)(i)".

Pub. L. 106–53, § 509(c)(3), added par. (5) and struck out former par. (5) which read as follows: "For purposes of carrying out paragraph (1)(C) of this subsection, there is authorized to be appropriated to the Secretary not to exceed $40,000 for the first fiscal year beginning after November 17, 1986, not to exceed $280,000 for the second fiscal year beginning after November 17, 1986, not to exceed $1,220,000 for the third fiscal year beginning after November 17, 1986, and not to exceed $875,000 per fiscal year for each of the succeeding 12 fiscal years".

Subsec. (e)(6). Pub. L. 106–53, § 509(d), added par. (6) and struck out former par. (6) which contained provisions limiting transfers to 20% of appropriated amounts and setting out specific maximum monetary amounts.

Subsec. (e)(7)(A). Pub. L. 106–53, § 509(e), (g)(1)(A), substituted "(1)(A)(i)" for "(1)(A)" and inserted before period at end "and, in the case of any project requiring non-Federal cost sharing, the non-Federal share of the cost of the project shall be 35 percent".

Subsec. (e)(7)(B). Pub. L. 106–53, § 509(g)(1)(B), substituted "paragraph (1)(A)(ii)" for "paragraphs (1)(B) and (1)(C)".

Subsec. (f)(2). Pub. L. 106–53, § 509(g)(2), struck out "(A)" after "(2)" and struck out subpar. (B) which read as follows: "For purposes of carrying out the assessment of the economic benefits of recreational activities as authorized in paragraph (1) of this subsection, there is authorized to be appropriated to the Secretary not to exceed $300,000 per fiscal year for the first and second fiscal years beginning after the computerized inventory and analysis system implemented pursuant to subsection (e)(1)(C) of this section is fully functional and $150,000 for the third such fiscal year".

Subsec. (h)(2). Pub. L. 106–53, § 509(f), inserted par. heading, designated existing provisions as subpar. (A) and inserted heading, and added subpar. (B).

1992—Subsec. (e)(2). Pub. L. 102–580, § 107(a)(1), which directed the substitution of "15" for "ten" each place it appears, could not be executed because "ten" did not appear subsequent to amendment by Pub. L. 101–640, § 405(1). See 1990 Amendment note below.

Subsec. (e)(6). Pub. L. 102–580, § 107(a)(3), added par. (6). Former par. (6) redesignated (7).

Subsec. (e)(7). Pub. L. 102–580, § 107(a)(2), redesignated par. (6) as (7). Former par. (7) redesignated (8).

Subsec. (e)(7)(A). Pub. L. 102–580, § 107(b), added subpar. (A) and struck out former subpar. (A) which read as follows: "Notwithstanding the provisions of subsection (a)(2) of this section, the costs of each project carried out pursuant to paragraph (1)(A) of this subsection shall be allocated between the Secretary and the appropriate non-Federal sponsor in accordance with the provisions of section 2283 of this title."

Subsec. (e)(8). Pub. L. 102–580, § 107(a)(2), redesignated par. (7) as (8).

1990—Subsec. (e)(2). Pub. L. 101–640, § 405(1), substituted "15" for "ten" in two places.

Subsec. (e)(3). Pub. L. 101–640, § 405(2), substituted "13" for "eight".

Subsec. (e)(4). Pub. L. 101–640, § 405(3), substituted "14" for "nine".

Subsec. (e)(5). Pub. L. 101–640, § 405(4), substituted "12" for "seven".

Subsec. (f)(2)(A). Pub. L. 101–640, § 405(5), substituted "15" for "ten".

UPPER MISSISSIPPI RIVER AND ILLINOIS WATER-WAY SYSTEM

Pub. L. 110–114, title VIII, Nov. 8, 2007, 121 Stat. 1283, provided that:

"SEC. 8001. DEFINITIONS.

"In this title, the following definitions apply:

"(1) PLAN.—The term 'Plan' means the project for navigation and ecosystem improvements for the Upper Mississippi River and Illinois Waterway System: Report of the Chief of Engineers, dated December 15, 2004.

"(2) UPPER MISSISSIPPI RIVER AND ILLINOIS WATERWAY SYSTEM.—The term 'Upper Mississippi River and Illinois Waterway System' means the projects for navigation and ecosystem restoration authorized by Congress for—

"(A) the segment of the Mississippi River from the confluence with the Ohio River, River Mile 0.0, to Upper St. Anthony Falls Lock in Minneapolis-St. Paul, Minnesota, River Mile 854.0; and

"(B) the Illinois Waterway from its confluence with the Mississippi River at Grafton, Illinois, River Mile 0.0, to T.J. O'Brien Lock in Chicago, Illinois, River Mile 327.0.

"SEC. 8002. NAVIGATION IMPROVEMENTS AND RESTORATION.

"Except as modified by this title, the Secretary [of the Army] shall undertake navigation improvements and restoration of the ecosystem for the Upper Mississippi River and Illinois Waterway System substantially in accordance with the Plan and subject to the conditions described therein.

"SEC. 8003. AUTHORIZATION OF CONSTRUCTION OF NAVIGATION IMPROVEMENTS.

"(a) SMALL SCALE AND NONSTRUCTURAL MEASURES.—

"(1) IN GENERAL.—The Secretary [of the Army] shall—

"(A) construct mooring facilities at Locks 12, 14, 18, 20, 22, 24, and LaGrange Lock or other alternative locations that are economically and environmentally feasible;

"(B) provide switchboats at Locks 20 through 25; and

"(C) conduct development and testing of an appointment scheduling system.

"(2) AUTHORIZATION OF APPROPRIATIONS.—The total cost of projects authorized under this subsection shall be $256,000,000. Such costs are to be paid half from amounts appropriated from the general fund of the Treasury and half from amounts appropriated from the Inland Waterways Trust Fund. Such sums shall remain available until expended.

"(b) NEW LOCKS.—

"(1) IN GENERAL.—The Secretary [of the Army] shall construct new 1,200-foot locks at Locks 20, 21, 22, 24, and 25 on the Upper Mississippi River and at LaGrange Lock and Peoria Lock on the Illinois Waterway.

"(2) AUTHORIZATION OF APPROPRIATIONS.—The total cost of projects authorized under this subsection shall be $1,948,000,000. Such costs are to be paid half from amounts appropriated from the general fund of the Treasury and half from amounts appropriated from the Inland Waterways Trust Fund. Such sums shall remain available until expended.

"(c) CONCURRENCE.—The mitigation required for the projects authorized under subsections (a) and (b), including any acquisition of lands or interests in lands, shall be undertaken or acquired concurrently with lands and interests in lands for the projects authorized under subsections (a) and (b), and physical construction required for the purposes of mitigation shall be undertaken concurrently with the physical construction of such projects.

"SEC. 8004. ECOSYSTEM RESTORATION AUTHORIZATION.

"(a) OPERATION.—To ensure the environmental sustainability of the existing Upper Mississippi River and Illinois Waterway System, the Secretary [of the Army] shall modify, consistent with requirements to avoid adverse effects on navigation, the operation of the Upper Mississippi River and Illinois Waterway System to address the cumulative environmental impacts of operation of the system and improve the ecological integrity of the Upper Mississippi River and Illinois River.

"(b) ECOSYSTEM RESTORATION PROJECTS.—

"(1) IN GENERAL.—The Secretary [of the Army] shall carry out, consistent with requirements to avoid adverse effects on navigation, ecosystem restoration projects to attain and maintain the sustainability of the ecosystem of the Upper Mississippi River and Illinois River in accordance with the general framework outlined in the Plan.

"(2) PROJECTS INCLUDED.—Ecosystem restoration projects may include—

"(A) island building;

"(B) construction of fish passages;

"(C) floodplain restoration;

"(D) water level management (including water drawdown);

"(E) backwater restoration;

"(F) side channel restoration;

"(G) wing dam and dike restoration and modification;

"(H) island and shoreline protection;

"(I) topographical diversity;

"(J) dam point control;

"(K) use of dredged material for environmental purposes;

"(L) tributary confluence restoration;

"(M) spillway, dam, and levee modification to benefit the environment; and

"(N) land and easement acquisition.

"(3) COST SHARING.—

"(A) IN GENERAL.—Except as provided in subparagraphs (B) and (C), the Federal share of the cost of carrying out an ecosystem restoration project under this subsection shall be 65 percent.

"(B) EXCEPTION FOR CERTAIN RESTORATION PROJECTS.—In the case of a project under this section for ecosystem restoration, the Federal share of the cost of carrying out the project shall be 100 percent if the project—

"(i) is located below the ordinary high water mark or in a connected backwater;

"(ii) modifies the operation of structures for navigation; or

"(iii) is located on federally owned land.

"(C) SAVINGS CLAUSE.—Nothing in this subsection affects the applicability of section 906(e) of the Water Resources Development Act of 1986 (33 U.S.C. 2283(e)).

"(D) NONGOVERNMENTAL ORGANIZATIONS.—In accordance with section 221 of the Flood Control Act of 1970 (42 U.S.C. 1962d–5b), for any project carried out under this title, a non-Federal sponsor may include a nonprofit entity, with the consent of the affected local government.

"(4) LAND ACQUISITION.—The Secretary [of the Army] may acquire land or an interest in land for an ecosystem restoration project from a willing seller through conveyance of—

"(A) fee title to the land; or

"(B) a flood plain conservation easement.

"(c) MONITORING.—The Secretary [of the Army] shall carry out a long term resource monitoring, computerized data inventory and analysis, and applied research program for the Upper Mississippi River and Illinois River to determine trends in ecosystem health, to understand systemic changes, and to help identify restoration needs. The program shall consider and adopt the monitoring program established under section 1103(e)(1)(A)(ii) of the Water Resources Development Act of 1986 (33 U.S.C. 652(e)(1)(A)(ii)).

"(d) ECOSYSTEM RESTORATION PRECONSTRUCTION ENGINEERING AND DESIGN.—

"(1) RESTORATION DESIGN.—Before initiating the construction of any individual ecosystem restoration project, the Secretary [of the Army] shall—

"(A) establish ecosystem restoration goals and identify specific performance measures designed to demonstrate ecosystem restoration;

"(B) establish the without-project condition or baseline for each performance indicator; and

"(C) for each separable element of the ecosystem restoration, identify specific target goals for each performance indicator.

"(2) OUTCOMES.—Performance measures identified under paragraph (1)(A) shall include specific measurable environmental outcomes, such as changes in water quality, hydrology, or the well-being of indicator species the population and distribution of which are representative of the abundance and diversity of ecosystem-dependent aquatic and terrestrial species.

"(3) RESTORATION DESIGN.—Restoration design carried out as part of ecosystem restoration shall include a monitoring plan for the performance measures identified under paragraph (1)(A), including—

"(A) a timeline to achieve the identified target goals; and

"(B) a timeline for the demonstration of project completion.

"(e) CONSULTATION AND FUNDING AGREEMENTS.—

"(1) IN GENERAL.—In carrying out the environmental sustainability, ecosystem restoration, and monitoring activities authorized in this section, the Secretary [of the Army] shall consult with the Secretary of the Interior and the States of Illinois, Iowa, Minnesota, Missouri, and Wisconsin.

"(2) FUNDING AGREEMENTS.—The Secretary is authorized to enter into agreements with the Secretary of the Interior, the Upper Mississippi River Basin Association, and natural resource and conservation agencies of the States of Illinois, Iowa, Minnesota, Missouri, and Wisconsin to provide for the direct participation of and transfer of funds to such entities for the planning, implementation, and evaluation of projects and programs established by this section.

"(f) SPECIFIC PROJECTS AUTHORIZATION.—

"(1) IN GENERAL.—There is authorized to be appropriated to carry out this subsection $1,717,000,000, of which not more than $245,000,000 shall be available for projects described in subsection (b)(2)(B) and not more than $48,000,000 shall be available for projects described in subsection (b)(2)(J). Such sums shall remain available until expended.

"(2) LIMITATION ON AVAILABLE FUNDS.—Of the amounts made available under paragraph (1), not more than $35,000,000 in any fiscal year may be used for land acquisition under subsection (b)(4).

"(3) INDIVIDUAL PROJECT LIMIT.—Other than for projects described in subparagraphs (B) and (J) of subsection (b)(2), the total cost of any single project carried out under this subsection shall not exceed $25,000,000.

"(4) MONITORING.—In addition to amounts authorized under paragraph (1), there are authorized $10,420,000 per fiscal year to carry out the monitoring program under subsection (c) if such sums are not appropriated pursuant to section 1103(e)(4) the Water Resources Development Act of 1986 (33 U.S.C. 652(e)(4)).

"(g) IMPLEMENTATION REPORTS.—

"(1) IN GENERAL.—Not later than June 30, 2009, and every 4 years thereafter, the Secretary [of the Army] shall submit to the Committee on Environment and Public Works of the Senate and the Committee on Transportation and Infrastructure of the House of Representatives an implementation report that—

"(A) includes baselines, milestones, goals, and priorities for ecosystem restoration projects; and

"(B) measures the progress in meeting the goals.

"(2) ADVISORY PANEL.—

"(A) IN GENERAL.—The Secretary shall appoint and convene an advisory panel to provide independent guidance in the development of each implementation report under paragraph (1).

"(B) PANEL MEMBERS.—Panel members shall include—

"(i) one representative of each of the State resource agencies (or a designee of the Governor of the State) from each of the States of Illinois, Iowa, Minnesota, Missouri, and Wisconsin;

"(ii) one representative of the Department of Agriculture;

"(iii) one representative of the Department of Transportation;

"(iv) one representative of the United States Geological Survey;

"(v) one representative of the United States Fish and Wildlife Service;

"(vi) one representative of the Environmental Protection Agency;

"(vii) one representative of affected landowners;

"(viii) two representatives of conservation and environmental advocacy groups; and

"(ix) two representatives of agriculture and industry advocacy groups.

"(C) CHAIRPERSON.—The Secretary shall serve as chairperson of the advisory panel.

"(D) APPLICATION OF FEDERAL ADVISORY COMMITTEE ACT.—The Advisory Panel and any working group established by the Advisory Panel shall not be considered an advisory committee under the Federal Advisory Committee Act (5 U.S.C. App.).

"(h) RANKING SYSTEM.—

"(1) IN GENERAL.—The Secretary [of the Army], in consultation with the Advisory Panel, shall develop a system to rank proposed projects.

"(2) PRIORITY.—The ranking system shall give greater weight to projects that restore natural river processes, including those projects listed in subsection (b)(2).

"SEC. 8005. COMPARABLE PROGRESS.

"(a) IN GENERAL.—As the Secretary [of the Army] conducts pre-engineering, design, and construction for projects authorized under this title, the Secretary shall—

"(1) select appropriate milestones;

"(2) determine, at the time of such selection, whether the projects are being carried out at comparable rates; and

"(3) make an annual report to Congress, beginning in fiscal year 2009, regarding whether the projects are being carried out at a comparable rate.

"(b) NO COMPARABLE RATE.—If the Secretary [of the Army] or Congress determines under subsection (a)(2) that projects authorized under this title are not moving toward completion at a comparable rate, annual funding requests for the projects shall be adjusted to ensure that the projects move toward completion at a comparable rate in the future."

UPPER MISSISSIPPI RIVER BASIN SEDIMENT AND NUTRIENT STUDY

Pub. L. 106–541, title IV, § 403, Dec. 11, 2000, 114 Stat. 2634, provided that:

"(a) IN GENERAL.—In conjunction with the Secretary of Agriculture and the Secretary of the Interior, the Secretary [of the Army] shall conduct a study to—

"(1) identify and evaluate significant sources of sediment and nutrients in the upper Mississippi River basin;

"(2) quantify the processes affecting mobilization, transport, and fate of those sediments and nutrients on land and in water; and

"(3) quantify the transport of those sediments and nutrients to the upper Mississippi River and the tributaries of the upper Mississippi River.

"(b) STUDY COMPONENTS.—

"(1) COMPUTER MODELING.—In carrying out the study under this section, the Secretary shall develop computer models of the upper Mississippi River basin, at the subwatershed and basin scales, to—

"(A) identify and quantify sources of sediment and nutrients; and

"(B) examine the effectiveness of alternative management measures.

"(2) RESEARCH.—In carrying out the study under this section, the Secretary shall conduct research to improve the understanding of—

"(A) fate processes and processes affecting sediment and nutrient transport, with emphasis on nitrogen and phosphorus cycling and dynamics;

"(B) the influences on sediment and nutrient losses of soil type, slope, climate, vegetation cover, and modifications to the stream drainage network; and

"(C) river hydrodynamics, in relation to sediment and nutrient transformations, retention, and transport.

"(c) USE OF INFORMATION.—On request of a Federal agency, the Secretary may provide information for use in applying sediment and nutrient reduction programs associated with land-use improvements and land management practices.

"(d) REPORTS.—

"(1) PRELIMINARY REPORT.—Not later than 2 years after the date of enactment of this Act [Dec. 11, 2000], the Secretary shall transmit to Congress a preliminary report that outlines work being conducted on the study components described in subsection (b).

"(2) FINAL REPORT.—Not later than 5 years after the date of enactment of this Act, the Secretary shall transmit to Congress a report describing the results of the study under this section, including any findings and recommendations of the study.

"(e) FUNDING.—

"(1) AUTHORIZATION OF APPROPRIATIONS.—There is authorized to be appropriated to carry out this section $4,000,000 for each of fiscal years 2001 through 2005.

"(2) FEDERAL SHARE.—The Federal share of the cost of carrying out this section shall be 50 percent."

UPPER MISSISSIPPI RIVER COMPREHENSIVE PLAN

Pub. L. 106–53, title IV, §459, Aug. 17, 1999, 113 Stat. 332, as amended by Pub. L. 106–541, title IV, §404, Dec. 11, 2000, 114 Stat. 2635, provided that:

"(a) DEVELOPMENT.—The Secretary [of the Army] shall develop a plan to address water resource and related land resource problems and opportunities in the upper Mississippi and Illinois River basins, from Cairo, Illinois, to the headwaters of the Mississippi River, in the interest of systemic flood damage reduction by means of—

"(1) structural and nonstructural flood control and floodplain management strategies;

"(2) continued maintenance of the navigation project;

"(3) management of bank caving and erosion;

"(4) watershed nutrient and sediment management;

"(5) habitat management;

"(6) recreation needs; and

"(7) other related purposes.

"(b) CONTENTS.—The plan under subsection (a) shall—

"(1) contain recommendations on management plans and actions to be carried out by the responsible Federal and non-Federal entities;

"(2) specifically address recommendations to authorize construction of a systemic flood control project for the upper Mississippi River; and

"(3) include recommendations for Federal action where appropriate and recommendations for follow-on studies for problem areas for which data or current technology does not allow immediate solutions.

"(c) CONSULTATION AND USE OF EXISTING DATA.—In carrying out this section, the Secretary shall—

"(1) consult with appropriate Federal and State agencies; and

"(2) make maximum use of data in existence on the date of enactment of this Act [Aug. 17, 1999] and ongoing programs and efforts of Federal agencies and States in developing the plan under subsection (a).

"(d) COST SHARING.—

"(1) DEVELOPMENT.—Development of the plan under subsection (a) shall be at Federal expense.

"(2) FEASIBILITY STUDIES.—Feasibility studies resulting from development of the plan shall be subject to cost sharing under section 105 of the Water Resources Development Act of 1986 (33 U.S.C. 2215).

"(e) REPORT.—Not later than 3 years after the first date on which funds are appropriated to carry out this section, the Secretary shall submit to the Committee on Transportation and Infrastructure of the House of Representatives and the Committee on Environment and Public Works of the Senate a report that includes the plan under subsection (a)."

"SECRETARY" DEFINED

Secretary means the Secretary of the Army, see section 2201 of this title.

§ 653. Extension of jurisdiction of Mississippi River Commission

The jurisdiction of the Mississippi River Commission (established by the Act of June 29, 1879[1] (33 U.S.C. 641)) is extended to include—

(1) Terrebonne Parish, Louisiana; and

(2) the area bounded by the East Atchafalaya Basin Protection Levee, the Mississippi River Levee, and Bayou Lafourche and extending from Morganza, Louisiana, to the Gulf of Mexico, insofar as such area is affected by the flood waters of the Mississippi River.

(Pub. L. 102–580, title III, §301, Oct. 31, 1992, 106 Stat. 4838.)

REFERENCES IN TEXT

Act of June 29, 1879 (33 U.S.C. 641), referred to in text, probably means the act of June 28, 1879, ch. 43, 21 Stat. 37, which enacted sections 641 to 644, 646, and 647 of this title.

§ 653a. Extension of jurisdiction of Mississippi River Commission

The jurisdiction of the Mississippi River Commission, established by section 641 of this title, is extended to include—

(1) all of the area between the eastern side of the Bayou Lafourche Ridge from Donaldsonville, Louisiana, to the Gulf of Mexico and the west guide levee of the Mississippi River from Donaldsonville, Louisiana, to the Gulf of Mexico;

(2) Alexander County, Illinois; and

(3) the area in the State of Illinois from the confluence of the Mississippi and Ohio Rivers northward to the vicinity of Mississippi River mile 39.5, including the Len Small Drainage and Levee District, insofar as such area is affected by the flood waters of the Mississippi River.

(Pub. L. 104–303, title V, §517, Oct. 12, 1996, 110 Stat. 3764.)

CHAPTER 14—CALIFORNIA DEBRIS COMMISSION

[1] See References in Text note below.

§661. Creation of commission; appointment of members; vacancies; powers generally

A commission is created, to be known as the California Debris Commission, consisting of three members. The President of the United States shall, by and with the advice and consent of the Senate, appoint the commission from officers of the Corps of Engineers, United States Army. Vacancies occurring therein shall be filled in like manner. It shall have the authority, and exercise the powers set forth in sections 662 to 685 of this title, under the supervision of the Chief of Engineers and direction of the Secretary of the Army.

(Mar. 1, 1893, ch. 183, §1, 27 Stat. 507; July 26, 1947, ch. 343, title II, §205(a), 61 Stat. 501.)

CHANGE OF NAME

Department of War designated Department of the Army and title of Secretary of War changed to Secretary of the Army by section 205(a) of act July 26, 1947, ch. 343, title II, 61 Stat. 501. Section 205(a) of act July 26, 1947, was repealed by section 53 of act Aug. 10, 1956, ch. 1041, 70A Stat. 641. Section 1 of act Aug. 10, 1956, enacted "Title 10, Armed Forces" which in sections 3010 to 3013 continued Department of the Army under administrative supervision of Secretary of the Army.

ABOLITION OF CALIFORNIA DEBRIS COMMISSION

Pub. L. 99–662, title XI, §1106, Nov. 17, 1986, 100 Stat. 4229, provided that:

"(a) The California Debris Commission established by the first section of the Act of March 1, 1893 (33 U.S.C. 661) is hereby abolished.

"(b) All authorities, powers, functions, and duties of the California Debris Commission are hereby transferred to the Secretary [meaning Secretary of the Army, see 33 U.S.C. 2201].

"(c) The assets, liabilities, contracts, property, records, and the unexpended balance of appropriations, authorizations, allocations, and other funds employed, held, used arising from, available to, or to be made available in connection with the authorities, powers, functions, and duties transferred by this section, subject to section 202 of the Budget and Accounting Procedure Act of 1950 [see 31 U.S.C. 1531], are hereby transferred to the Secretary for appropriate allocation. Unexpended funds transferred pursuant to this subsection shall be used only for the purposes for which the funds were originally authorized and appropriated.

"(d) All acquired lands, and other interests therein presently under the jurisdiction of the California Debris Commission are hereby authorized to be retained, and shall be administered under the direction of the Secretary, who is hereby authorized to take such actions as are necessary to consolidate and perfect title; to exchange for other lands or interests therein which may be required for recreation or for existing or proposed projects of the United States; to transfer to other Federal agencies or dispose of as surplus property; and to release to the coextensive fee owners any easements no longer required by the United States, under such conditions or for such consideration as the Secretary shall determine to be fair and reasonable. Except as specifically provided herein all transactions will be in accordance with existing laws and procedures."

§662. Organization; compensation of members; rules and regulations of procedure; traveling expenses

Said commission shall organize by the selection of such officers as may be required in the performance of its duties the same to be selected from the members thereof. The members of said commission shall receive no greater compensation than is now allowed by law to each, respectively, as an officer of said Corps of Engineers. It shall also adopt rules and regulations, not inconsistent with law, to govern its deliberations and prescribe the method of procedure under the provisions of this chapter. While traveling on duty the officers of the commission shall receive the mileage allowed by law.

(Mar. 1, 1893, ch. 183, §2, 27 Stat. 507; June 6, 1900, ch. 791, §1, 31 Stat. 631.)

CODIFICATION

The last sentence of this section is from a provision accompanying an appropriation for the expenses of the Commission in the Sundry Civil Appropriation Act for 1901, which originally read as follows: "So much of the Act of March third, eighteen hundred and ninety-nine, as provides that the members of the California Debris Commission shall receive only actual expenses in lieu of mileage while traveling on duty is hereby repealed, and hereafter the officers of the commission shall receive the mileage allowed by law."

Act Mar. 3, 1899, ch. 424, §1, 30 Stat. 1109, mentioned in said provision, provided that the officers of the Commission traveling on duty might be paid their actual traveling expenses, in lieu of mileage allowed by law, and should thereafter receive no mileage.

TRANSFER OF FUNCTIONS

California Debris Commission abolished and functions transferred to Secretary of the Army by Pub. L. 99–662, title XI, §1106, Nov. 17, 1986, 100 Stat. 4229, set out as a note under section 661 of this title.

§663. Territorial jurisdiction over hydraulic mining; hydraulic mining injurious to navigation prohibited

The jurisdiction of said commission, in so far as the same affects mining carried on by the hydraulic process, shall extend to all such mining in the territory drained by the Sacramento and San Joaquin River systems in the State of California. Hydraulic mining, as defined in section 668 of this title, directly or indirectly injuring the navigability of said river systems, carried on in said territory other than as permitted under the provisions of this chapter is prohibited and declared unlawful.

(Mar. 1, 1893, ch. 183, §3, 27 Stat. 507.)

TRANSFER OF FUNCTIONS

California Debris Commission abolished and functions transferred to Secretary of the Army by Pub. L. 99–662, title XI, §1106, Nov. 17, 1986, 100 Stat. 4229, set out as a note under section 661 of this title.

§ 664. General duties as to plans for protection of navigation

It shall be the duty of said commission to mature and adopt such plan or plans, from examinations and surveys made prior to March 1, 1893, and from such additional examinations and surveys as it may deem necessary, as will improve the navigability of all the rivers comprising said systems, deepen their channels, and protect their banks. Such plan or plans shall be matured with a view of making the same effective as against the encroachment of and damage from debris resulting from mining operations, natural erosion, or other causes, with a view of restoring, as near as practicable and the necessities of commerce and navigation demand, the navigability of said rivers to the condition existing in 1860, and permitting mining by the hydraulic process, as the term is understood in said State, to be carried on, provided the same can be accomplished, without injury to the navigability of said rivers or the lands adjacent thereto.

(Mar. 1, 1893, ch. 183, § 4, 27 Stat. 507.)

TRANSFER OF FUNCTIONS

California Debris Commission abolished and functions transferred to Secretary of the Army by Pub. L. 99–662, title XI, § 1106, Nov. 17, 1986, 100 Stat. 4229, set out as a note under section 661 of this title.

§ 665. Survey for debris reservoirs; study of methods of mines and mining

It shall further examine, survey, and determine the utility and practicability, for the purposes hereinafter indicated, of storage sites in the tributaries of said rivers and in the respective branches of said tributaries, or in the plains, basins, sloughs, and tule and swamp lands adjacent to or along the course of said rivers, for the storage of debris or water or as settling reservoirs, with the object of using the same by either or all of these methods to aid in the improvement and protection of said navigable rivers by preventing deposits therein of debris resulting from mining operations, natural erosion, or other causes, or for affording relief thereto in flood time and providing sufficient water to maintain scouring force therein in the summer season; and in connection therewith to investigate such hydraulic and other mines as are or may have been worked by methods intended to restrain the debris and material moved in operating such mines by impounding dams, settling reservoirs, or otherwise, and in general to make such study of and researches in the hydraulic mining industry as science, experience, and engineering skill may suggest as practicable and useful in devising a method or methods whereby such mining may be carried on as aforesaid.

(Mar. 1, 1893, ch. 183, § 5, 27 Stat. 507.)

TRANSFER OF FUNCTIONS

California Debris Commission abolished and functions transferred to Secretary of the Army by Pub. L. 99–662, title XI, § 1106, Nov. 17, 1986, 100 Stat. 4229, set out as a note under section 661 of this title.

§ 666. Noting conditions of navigable channels

The said commission shall from time to time note the conditions of the navigable channels of said river systems, by cross-section surveys or otherwise, in order to ascertain the effect therein of such hydraulic mining operations as may be permitted by its orders and such as is caused by erosion, natural or otherwise.

(Mar. 1, 1893, ch. 183, § 6, 27 Stat. 508.)

TRANSFER OF FUNCTIONS

California Debris Commission abolished and functions transferred to Secretary of the Army by Pub. L. 99–662, title XI, § 1106, Nov. 17, 1986, 100 Stat. 4229, set out as a note under section 661 of this title.

§ 667. Annual reports

Said commission shall submit to the Chief of Engineers, for the information of the Secretary of the Army, on or before the 15th day of November of each year, a report of its labors and transactions, with plans for the construction, completion, and preservation of the public works outlined in this chapter, together with estimates of the cost thereof, stating what amounts can be profitably expended thereon each year. The Secretary of the Army shall thereupon submit same to Congress on or before the meeting thereof.

(Mar. 1, 1893, ch. 183, § 7, 27 Stat. 508; July 26, 1947, ch. 343, title II, § 205(a), 61 Stat. 501.)

CHANGE OF NAME

Department of War designated Department of the Army and title of Secretary of War changed to Secretary of the Army by section 205(a) of act July 26, 1947, ch. 343, title II, 61 Stat. 501. Section 205(a) of act July 26, 1947, was repealed by section 53 of act Aug. 10, 1956, ch. 1041, 70A Stat. 641. Section 1 of act Aug. 10, 1956, enacted "Title 10, Armed Forces" which in sections 3010 to 3013 continued Department of the Army under administrative supervision of Secretary of the Army.

TRANSFER OF FUNCTIONS

California Debris Commission abolished and functions transferred to Secretary of the Army by Pub. L. 99–662, title XI, § 1106, Nov. 17, 1986, 100 Stat. 4229, set out as a note under section 661 of this title.

§ 668. "Hydraulic mining" and "mining by hydraulic process" defined

For the purposes of this chapter "hydraulic mining" and "mining by the hydraulic process" are declared to have the meaning and application given to said terms in the State of California.

(Mar. 1, 1893, ch. 183, § 8, 27 Stat 508.)

§ 669. Petition by hydraulic miners

The individual proprietor or proprietors, or in case of a corporation, its manager or agent appointed for that purpose, owning mining ground in the territory in the State of California mentioned in section 663 of this title, which it is desired to work by the hydraulic process, must file with said commission a verified petition, setting forth such facts as will comply with law and the rules prescribed by said commission.

(Mar. 1, 1893, ch. 183, § 9, 27 Stat. 508.)

TRANSFER OF FUNCTIONS

California Debris Commission abolished and functions transferred to Secretary of the Army by Pub. L. 99–662, title XI, § 1106, Nov. 17, 1986, 100 Stat. 4229, set out as a note under section 661 of this title.

§ 670. Surrender to United States of right to regulate debris of mine

Said petition shall be accompanied by an instrument duly executed and acknowledged, as required by the law of the said State, whereby the owner or owners of such mine or mines surrender to the United States the right and privilege to regulate by law, as provided in this chapter, or any law that may be enacted after March 1, 1893, or by such rules and regulations as may be prescribed by virtue thereof, the manner and method in which the debris resulting from the working of said mine or mines shall be restrained, and what amount shall be produced therefrom; it being understood that the surrender aforesaid shall not be construed as in any way affecting the right of such owner or owners to operate said mine or mines by any other process or method in use in said State on March 1, 1893: *Provided*, That they shall not interfere with the navigability of the aforesaid rivers.

(Mar. 1, 1893, ch. 183, § 10, 27 Stat. 508.)

§ 671. Petition for common dumping ground, etc.

The owners of several mining claims situated so as to require a common dumping ground or dam or other restraining works for the debris issuing therefrom in one or more sites may file a joint petition setting forth such facts in addition to the requirements of section 669 of this title; and where the owner of a hydraulic mine or owners of several such mines have and use common dumping sites for impounding debris or as settling reservoirs, which sites are located below the mine of an applicant not entitled to use same, such fact shall also be stated in said petition. Thereupon the same proceedings shall be had as provided for herein.

(Mar. 1, 1893, ch. 183, § 11, 27 Stat. 508.)

REFERENCES IN TEXT

Herein, referred to in text, means act Mar. 1, 1893, which comprises this chapter.

§ 672. Notice of petition for dumping grounds, etc.; hearing

A notice specifying briefly the contents of said petition and fixing a time previous to which all proofs are to be submitted shall be published by said commission in some newspaper or newspapers of general circulation in the communities interested in the matter set forth therein. If published in a daily paper such publication shall continue for at least ten days; if in a weekly paper in at least three issues of the same. Pending publication thereof said commission, or a committee thereof, shall examine the mine and premises described in such petition. On or before the time so fixed all parties interested, either as petitioners or contestants, whether miners or agriculturists, may file affidavits, plans, and maps in support of their respective claims. Further hearings, upon notice to all parties of record, may be granted by the commission when necessary.

(Mar. 1, 1893, ch. 183, § 12, 27 Stat. 508.)

TRANSFER OF FUNCTIONS

California Debris Commission abolished and functions transferred to Secretary of the Army by Pub. L. 99–662, title XI, § 1106, Nov. 17, 1986, 100 Stat. 4229, set out as a note under section 661 of this title.

§ 673. Order by commission directing method of mining, etc.; expenses of complying with order; exemption from mining taxes

In case a majority of the members of said commission, within thirty days after the time so fixed, concur in the decision in favor of the petitioner or petitioners, the said commission shall thereupon make an order directing the methods and specifying in detail the manner in which operations shall proceed in such mine or mines; what restraining or impounding works, if any, if facilities therefor can be found, shall be built and maintained; how and of what material; where to be located; and in general set forth such further requirements and safeguards as will protect the public interests and prevent injury to the said navigable rivers and the lands adjacent thereto, with such further conditions and limitations as will observe all the provisions of this chapter in relation to the working thereof and the payment of taxes on the gross proceeds of the same: *Provided*, That all expense incurred in complying with said order shall be borne by the owner or owners of such mine or mines: *And provided further*, That where it shall appear to said commission that hydraulic mining may be carried on without injury to the navigation of said navigable rivers and the lands adjacent thereto, an order may be made authorizing such mining to be carried on without requiring the construction of any restraining or impounding works or any settling reservoirs: *And provided also*, That where such an order is made a license to mine, no taxes provided for in this chapter on the gross proceeds of such mining operations shall be collected.

(Mar. 1, 1893, ch. 183, § 13, 27 Stat. 508; Feb. 27, 1907, ch. 2077, 34 Stat. 1001.)

AMENDMENTS

1907—Act Feb. 27, 1907, inserted "if any" after "restraining or impounding works" and inserted last two provisos.

TRANSFER OF FUNCTIONS

California Debris Commission abolished and functions transferred to Secretary of the Army by Pub. L. 99–662, title XI, § 1106, Nov. 17, 1986, 100 Stat. 4229, set out as a note under section 661 of this title.

§ 674. Plans for and supervision of work required by order; permit to commence mining

Such petitioner or petitioners must within a reasonable time present plans and specifications of all works required to be built in pursuance of said order for examination, correction, and approval by said commission; and thereupon work may immediately commence thereon under the supervision of said commission or representative thereof attached thereto from said Corps of Engineers, who shall inspect same from time to time. Upon completion thereof, if found in every respect to meet the requirements of the said order and said approved plans and specifications, permission shall thereupon be granted to the owner or owners of such mine or mines to commence mining operations, subject to the conditions of said order and the provisions of this chapter.

(Mar. 1, 1893, ch. 183, §14, 27 Stat. 509.)

TRANSFER OF FUNCTIONS

California Debris Commission abolished and functions transferred to Secretary of the Army by Pub. L. 99–662, title XI, §1106, Nov. 17, 1986, 100 Stat. 4229, set out as a note under section 661 of this title.

§675. Conditions precedent for commencement of mining operations

No permission granted to a mine owner or owners under this chapter shall take effect, so far as regards the working of a mine, until all impounding dams or other restraining works, if any are prescribed by the order granting such permission, have been completed and until the impounding dams or other restraining works or settling reservoirs provided by said commission have reached such a stage as, in the opinion of said commission, it is safe to use the same: *Provided, however*, That if said commission shall be of the opinion that the restraining and other works already constructed at the mine or mines shall be sufficient to protect the navigable rivers of said systems and the work of said commission, then the owner or owners of such mine or mines may be permitted to commence operations.

(Mar. 1, 1893, ch. 183, §15, 27 Stat. 509.)

TRANSFER OF FUNCTIONS

California Debris Commission abolished and functions transferred to Secretary of the Army by Pub. L. 99–662, title XI, §1106, Nov. 17, 1986, 100 Stat. 4229, set out as a note under section 661 of this title.

§676. Allotment of expenses for common dumping grounds; location of impounding works

In case the joint petition referred to in section 671 of this title is granted, the commission shall fix the respective amounts to be paid by each owner of such mines toward providing and building necessary impounding dams or other restraining works. In the event of a petition being filed after the entry of such order, or in case the impounding dam or dams or other restraining works have already been constructed and accepted by said commission, the commission shall fix such amount as may be reasonable for the privilege of dumping therein, which amount shall be divided between the original owners of such impounding dams or other restraining works in proportion to the amount respectively paid by each party owning same. The expense of maintaining and protecting such joint dam or works shall be divided among mine owners using the same in such proportion as the commission shall determine. In all cases where it is practicable, restraining and impounding works are to be provided, constructed, and maintained by mine owners near or below the mine or mines before reaching the main tributaries of said navigable waters.

(Mar. 1, 1893, ch. 183, §16, 27 Stat. 509.)

TRANSFER OF FUNCTIONS

California Debris Commission abolished and functions transferred to Secretary of the Army by Pub. L. 99–662, title XI, §1106, Nov. 17, 1986, 100 Stat. 4229, set out as a note under section 661 of this title.

§677. Limitation as to quantity of debris washed away

At no time shall any more debris be permitted to be washed away from any hydraulic mine or mines situated on the tributaries of said rivers and the respective branches of each, worked under the provisions of this chapter, than can be impounded within the restraining works erected.

(Mar. 1, 1893, ch. 183, §17, 27 Stat. 509.)

§678. Modification and revocation of permit to mine

The said commission may, at any time when the condition of the navigable rivers or when the capacities of all impounding and settling facilities erected by mine owners or such as may be provided by Government authority require same, modify the order granting the privilege to mine by the hydraulic mining process so as to reduce the amount thereof to meet the capacities of the facilities then in use; or, if actually required in order to protect the navigable rivers from damage or in case of failure to pay the tax prescribed by section 683 of this title within thirty days after same becomes due, may revoke same until the further notice of the commission.

(Mar. 1, 1893, ch. 183, §18, 27 Stat. 509; June 19, 1934, ch. 661, §1, 48 Stat. 1118.)

AMENDMENTS

1934—Act June 19, 1934, inserted "or in case of failure to pay the tax prescribed by section 683 of this title within thirty days after same becomes due".

TRANSFER OF FUNCTIONS

California Debris Commission abolished and functions transferred to Secretary of the Army by Pub. L. 99–662, title XI, §1106, Nov. 17, 1986, 100 Stat. 4229, set out as a note under section 661 of this title.

§679. Violation of permit to mine; penalty

An intentional violation on the part of a mine owner or owners, company, or corporation, or the agents or employees of either, of the conditions of the order granted pursuant to section 673 of this title, or such modifications thereof as may have been made by said commission, shall work a forfeiture of the privileges thereby conferred, and upon notice being served by the order of said commission upon such owner or owners, company, or corporation, or agent in charge, work shall immediately cease. Said commission shall take necessary steps to enforce its orders in case of the failure, neglect, or refusal of such owner or owners, company, or corporation, or agents thereof, to comply therewith, or in the event of any person or persons, company, or corporation working by said process in said territory contrary to law.

(Mar. 1, 1893, ch. 183, §19, 27 Stat. 510.)

TRANSFER OF FUNCTIONS

California Debris Commission abolished and functions transferred to Secretary of the Army by Pub. L. 99–662, title XI, §1106, Nov. 17, 1986, 100 Stat. 4229, set out as a note under section 661 of this title.

§680. Examination of mines; reports

Said commission, or a committee therefrom, or officer of said corps assigned to duty under its orders, shall, whenever deemed necessary, visit said territory and all mines operating under the provisions of this chapter. A report of such examination shall be placed on file.

(Mar. 1, 1893, ch. 183, § 20, 27 Stat. 510.)

TRANSFER OF FUNCTIONS

California Debris Commission abolished and functions transferred to Secretary of the Army by Pub. L. 99–662, title XI, § 1106, Nov. 17, 1986, 100 Stat. 4229, set out as a note under section 661 of this title.

§ 681. Repealed. Pub. L. 94–579, title VII, § 704(a), Oct. 21, 1976, 90 Stat. 2792

Section, act Mar. 1, 1893, ch. 183, § 21, 27 Stat. 510; 1946 Reorg. Plan No. 3, § 403, eff. July 16, 1946, 11 F.R. 7876, 60 Stat. 1100, authorized the commission to use any of the public lands, etc., of the United States, and the withdrawal of lands, etc., required from sale or entry.

EFFECTIVE DATE OF REPEAL

Section 704(a) of Pub. L. 94–579 provided that the repeal is effective on and after Oct. 21, 1976.

SAVINGS PROVISION

Repeal by Pub. L. 94–579 not to be construed as terminating any valid lease, permit, patent, etc., existing on Oct. 21, 1976, see section 701(a) of Pub. L. 94–579, set out as a note under section 1701 of Title 43, Public Lands.

§ 682. Malicious injury to works; injury to navigable waters by hydraulic mining; penalty

Any person or persons who willfully or maliciously injure, damage, or destroy, or attempt to injure, damage, or destroy, any dam or other work erected under the provisions of this chapter for restraining, impounding, or settling purposes, or for use in connection therewith, shall be guilty of a misdemeanor, and upon conviction thereof shall be fined not to exceed the sum of $5,000 or be imprisoned not to exceed five years, or by both such fine and imprisonment, in the discretion of the court. And any person or persons, company or corporation, their agents or employees, who shall mine by the hydraulic process directly or indirectly injuring the navigable waters of the United States, in violation of the provisions of this chapter shall be guilty of a misdemeanor, and upon conviction thereof shall be punished by a fine not exceeding $5,000, or by imprisonment not exceeding one year, or by both such fine and imprisonment, in the discretion of the court.

(Mar. 1, 1893, ch. 183, § 22, 27 Stat. 510.)

§ 683. Tax on operation of hydraulic mines; "debris fund"; advances by mine owners; storage for water and use of outlet facilities

Upon the construction by the said commission of dams or other works for the detention of debris from hydraulic mines and the issuing of the order provided for by this chapter to any individual, company, or corporation to work any mine or mines by hydraulic process, the individual, company, or corporation operating thereunder working any mine or mines by hydraulic process, the debris from which flows into or is in whole or in part restrained by such dams or other works erected by said commission, shall pay for each cubic yard mined from the natural bank a tax equal to the total capital cost of the dam, reservoir, and rights-of-way divided by the total capacity of the reservoir for the restraint of debris, as determined in each case by the California Debris Commission, which tax shall be paid annually on a date fixed by said commission and in accordance with regulations to be adopted by the Secretary of the Treasury, and the Treasurer of the United States is authorized to receive the same. All sums of money paid into the Treasury under this section shall be set apart and credited to a fund to be known as the "debris fund", and shall be expended by said commission under the supervision of the Chief of Engineers and direction of the Secretary of the Army, for repayment of any funds advanced by the Federal Government or other agency for the construction of restraining works and settling reservoirs, and for maintenance: *Provided*, That said commission is authorized to receive and pay into the Treasury from the owner or owners of mines worked by the hydraulic process, to whom permission may have been granted so to work under the provisions thereof, such money advances as may be offered to aid in the construction of such impounding dams, or other restraining works, or settling reservoirs, or sites thereof, as may be deemed necessary by said commission to protect the navigable channels of said river systems, on condition that all moneys so advanced shall be refunded as the said tax is paid into the said debris fund: *And provided further*, That in no event shall the Government of the United States be held liable to refund same except as directed by this section. The Secretary of the Army is authorized to enter into contracts to supply storage for water and use of outlet facilities from debris storage reservoirs, for domestic and irrigation purposes and power development upon such conditions of delivery, use, and payment as he may approve: *Provided*, That the moneys received from such contracts shall be deposited to the credit of the reservoir project from which the water is supplied, and the total capital cost of said reservoir, which is to be repaid by tax on mining operations as provided in this section, shall be reduced in the amount so received.

(Mar. 1, 1893, ch. 183, § 23, 27 Stat. 510; June 19, 1934, ch. 661, § 2, 48 Stat. 1118; June 25, 1938, ch. 653, 52 Stat. 1040; July 26, 1947, ch. 343, title II, § 205(a), 61 Stat. 501.)

AMENDMENTS

1938—Act June 25, 1938, inserted provisions relating to storage for water and use of outlet facilities.

1934—Act June 19, 1934, substituted an annual tax for each cubic yard mined from the natural bank, based on total capital cost divided by total capacity, for the 3 per centum gross proceeds tax, and required money from debris fund to be expended in repayment of Government advances for construction and maintenance, instead of authorizing the expenditure of such money in addition to appropriations for construction and maintenance.

CHANGE OF NAME

Department of War designated Department of the Army and title of Secretary of War changed to Secretary of the Army by section 205(a) of act July 26, 1947, ch. 343, title II, 61 Stat. 501. Section 205(a) of act July 26, 1947, was repealed by section 53 of act Aug. 10, 1956, ch. 1041, 70A Stat. 641. Section 1 of act Aug. 10, 1956, enacted "Title 10, Armed Forces" which in sections 3010 to 3013 continued Department of the Army under administrative supervision of Secretary of the Army.

TRANSFER OF FUNCTIONS

California Debris Commission abolished and functions transferred to Secretary of the Army by Pub. L. 99–662, title XI, §1106, Nov. 17, 1986, 100 Stat. 4229, set out as a note under section 661 of this title.

For transfer of certain functions insofar as they pertain to Air Force, and to extent that they were not previously transferred to Secretary of the Air Force and Department of the Air Force from Secretary of the Army and Department of the Army, see Secretary of Defense Transfer Order No. 40, July 22, 1949.

§684. Cooperation by commission with State authorities

For the purpose of securing harmony of action and economy in expenditures in the work to be done by the United States and the State of California, respectively, the former in its plans for the improvement and protection of the navigable streams and to prevent the depositing of mining debris or other materials within the same, and the latter in its plans authorized by law for the reclamation, drainage, and protection of its lands, or relating to the working of hydraulic mines, the said commission is empowered to consult thereon with a commission of engineers of said State, if authorized by said State for said purpose, the result of such conference to be reported to the Chief of Engineers of the United States Army, and if by him approved shall be followed by said commission.

(Mar. 1, 1893, ch. 183, §24, 27 Stat. 511.)

TRANSFER OF FUNCTIONS

California Debris Commission abolished and functions transferred to Secretary of the Army by Pub. L. 99–662, title XI, §1106, Nov. 17, 1986, 100 Stat. 4229, set out as a note under section 661 of this title.

§685. Construction by commission of restraining works, etc.; use of debris fund

Said commission, in order that such material as is now or may hereafter be lodged in the tributaries of the Sacramento and San Joaquin River systems resulting from mining operations, natural erosion, or other causes, shall be prevented from injuring the said navigable rivers or such of the tributaries of either as may be navigable and the land adjacent thereto, is directed and empowered, when appropriations are made therefor by law, or sufficient money is deposited for that purpose in said debris fund, to build at such points above the head of navigation in said rivers and on the main tributaries thereof, or branches of such tributaries, or any place adjacent to the same, which in the judgment of said commission, will effect said object (the same to be of such material as will insure safety and permanency), such restraining or impounding dams and settling reservoirs, with such canals, locks, or other works adapted and required to complete same. The recommendations contained in Executive Document Numbered 267, Fifty-first Congress, second session, and Executive Document Numbered 98, Forty-seventh Congress, first session, as far as they refer to impounding dams, or other restraining works, are adopted, and the same are directed to be made the basis of operations.

(Mar. 1, 1893, ch. 183, §25, 27 Stat. 511.)

REFERENCES IN TEXT

Executive Document Numbered 267, referred to in text, contained a report of Lieut. Col. G. H. Mendell, Corps of Engineers, U.S.A., dated Jan. 26, 1882, prepared pursuant to a provision in act June 14, 1880, ch. 211, 21 Stat. 196. Executive Document Numbered 98, also referred to in text, contained a report by a board of engineers created by act Oct. 1, 1888, ch. 1057, 25 Stat. 498.

TRANSFER OF FUNCTIONS

California Debris Commission abolished and functions transferred to Secretary of the Army by Pub. L. 99–662, title XI, §1106, Nov. 17, 1986, 100 Stat. 4229, set out as a note under section 661 of this title.

§686. Construction of restraining works in conjunction with State

The Secretary of the Army, in expending appropriations in the preparation for and construction of works for the restraining or impounding of mining debris in the State of California, is authorized to enter into an agreement that the contractor shall look solely to the State of California for one-half of such expense, to be paid out of said State's appropriation, and the United States shall in nowise be liable for said one-half.

The Secretary of the Army, in carrying out the provisions of any Act of Congress, providing for the restraining or impounding of mining debris in California, may, in his discretion, when in his judgment the aggregate of appropriations already made by said State and Congress and available therefor are sufficient to complete the same, undertake the works necessary thereto by hired labor and by purchase of supplies and materials therefor, and may accept payments on account thereof as the work progresses under and according to the provisions of the acts of the legislature of said State for such purposes.

(July 1, 1898, ch. 546, §1, 30 Stat. 631; Mar. 3, 1899, ch. 425, §1, 30 Stat. 1148; July 26, 1947, ch. 343, title II, §205(a), 61 Stat. 501.)

CODIFICATION

Section was enacted as part of act Mar. 3, 1899, popularly known as the "Rivers and Harbors Appropriation Act of 1899", and not as part of act Mar. 1, 1893, ch. 183, 27 Stat. 507, which comprises this chapter.

As originally enacted the first paragraph read as follows: "The provisions of an Act of Congress, entitled 'An Act making appropriations for sundry civil expenses of the Government for the fiscal year ending June thirtieth, eighteen hundred and ninety-nine, and for other purposes,' approved July first, eighteen hundred and ninety-eight, authorizing the Secretary of War, in expending certain specified appropriations in the preparation for and construction of certain works for the restraining or impounding of mining debris in the State of California, to enter into a contract or contracts wherein the contractor or contractors shall look solely to that State for one-half of such expense, and that the United States shall in no wise be liable for said one-half, are hereby extended to any appropriations, when made, that may hereafter be made for said purposes."

Act July 1, 1898 authorized Secretary of War, in contracting for construction of certain proposed works, to enter into an agreement that contractor should look solely to California for half of expenses.

CHANGE OF NAME

Department of War designated Department of the Army and title of Secretary of War changed to Secretary of the Army by section 205(a) of act July 26, 1947, ch. 343, title II, 61 Stat. 501. Section 205(a) of act July 26, 1947, was repealed by section 53 of act Aug. 10, 1956, ch. 1041 70A Stat. 641. Section 1 of act Aug. 10, 1956, enacted "Title 10, Armed Forces" which in sections 3010 to 3013 continued Department of the Army under administrative supervision of Secretary of the Army.

§ 687. Use of State dredge and appliances in river and harbor improvements

The Secretary of the Army is authorized to accept from the State of California the use of any dredger, or appliances owned or controlled by said State, conformably to any offer thereof by the said State; and the Secretary of the Army is authorized to use any such dredger or appliances in any river or harbor improvement that may be prosecuted therein by the United States, either on the part of the United States alone or conjointly with said State: *Provided*, That nothing shall be paid to the State of California for the use of said dredger, and that nothing herein contained shall create any liability against the United States.

(Mar. 3, 1899, ch. 425, § 1, 30 Stat. 1148; July 26, 1947, ch. 343, title II, § 205(a), 61 Stat. 501.)

Codification

Section was enacted as part of act Mar. 3, 1899, popularly known as the "Rivers and Harbors Appropriation Act of 1899", and not as part of act Mar. 1, 1983, ch. 183, 27 Stat. 507, which comprises this chapter.

Change of Name

Department of War designated Department of the Army and title of Secretary of War changed to Secretary of the Army by section 205(a) of act July 26, 1947, ch. 343, title II, 61 Stat. 501. Section 205(a) of act July 26, 1947, was repealed by section 53 of act Aug. 10, 1956, ch. 1041, 70A Stat. 641. Section 1 of act Aug. 10, 1956, enacted "Title 10, Armed Forces" which in sections 3010 to 3013 continued Department of the Army under administrative supervision of Secretary of the Army.

CHAPTER 15—FLOOD CONTROL

§701. Flood control generally

Laws applicable to works of improvement relating to flood control—All the provisions of existing law relating to examinations and surveys and to works of improvement of rivers and harbors shall apply, so far as applicable to examinations and surveys and to works of improvement relating to flood control. And all expenditures of funds appropriated for works and projects relating to flood control shall be made in accordance with and subject to the law governing the disbursement and expenditure of funds appropriated for the improvement of rivers and harbors.

Examinations and surveys; details from Government departments; reports—All examinations and surveys of projects relating to flood control shall include a comprehensive study of the watershed or watersheds, and the report thereon in addition to any other matter upon which a report is required shall give such data as it may be practicable to secure in regard to (a) the extent and character of the area to be affected by the proposed improvement; (b) the probable effect upon any navigable water or waterway; (c) the possible economical development and utilization of water power; and (d) such other uses as may be properly related to or coordinated with the project. And the heads of the several departments of the Government may, in their discretion, and shall upon the request of the Secretary of the Army, detail representatives from their respective departments to assist the Engineers of the Army in the study and examination of such watersheds, to the end that duplication of work may be avoided and the various services of the Government economically coordinated therein: *Provided*, That all reports on preliminary examinations hereafter authorized, together with the report of the Board of Engineers for Rivers and Harbors thereon and the separate report of the representative of any other department, shall be submitted to the Secretary of the Army by the Chief of Engineers, with his recommendations, and shall be transmitted by the Secretary of the Army to the House of Representatives, and are ordered to be printed when so made.

Reports by Board of Engineers for Rivers and Harbors—In the consideration of all works and projects relating to flood control which may be submitted to the Board of Engineers for Rivers and Harbors for consideration and recommendation, said board shall, in addition to any other matters upon which it may be required to report, state its opinion as to (a) what Federal interest, if any, is involved in the proposed improvement; (b) what share of the expense, if any, should be borne by the United States; and (c) the advisability of adopting the project.

(Mar. 1, 1917, ch. 144, §3, 39 Stat. 950; July 26, 1947, ch. 343, title II, §205(a), 61 Stat. 501; Pub. L. 103–437, §12(c), Nov. 2, 1994, 108 Stat. 4590.)

Codification

Sections 1 and 2 of act Mar. 1, 1917, are classified to sections 702 and 703 of this title. Section 4 amended section 643 of this title. See section 702h of this title.

Amendments

1994—Pub. L. 103–437 struck out par. at end which read as follows: "All examinations and reports which may now be made by the Board of Engineers for Rivers and Harbors upon request of the Committee on Rivers and Harbors relating to works or projects of navigation shall in like manner be made upon request of the Committee on Flood Control on all works and projects relating to flood control."

Change of Name

Department of War designated Department of the Army and title of Secretary of War changed to Secretary of the Army by section 205(a) of act July 26, 1947, ch. 343, title II, 61 Stat. 501. Section 205(a) of act July 26, 1947, was repealed by section 53 of act Aug. 10, 1956, ch. 1041, 70A Stat. 641. Section 1 of act Aug. 10, 1956, enacted "Title 10, Armed Forces" which in sections 3010 to 3013 continued Department of the Army under administrative supervision of Secretary of the Army.

TERMINATION OF BOARD OF ENGINEERS FOR RIVERS AND HARBORS AND REASSIGNMENT OF DUTIES AND RESPONSIBILITIES

For termination of Board of Engineers for Rivers and Harbors 180 days after Oct. 31, 1992, and reassignment of duties and responsibilities by Secretary of Army, see section 223 of Pub. L. 102–580, set out as a note under section 541 of this title.

FLOODPLAIN MANAGEMENT

For provisions relating to the reduction of the risk of flood loss, the minimization of the impact of floods on human safety, health, and welfare, and the management of floodplains, see Ex. Ord. No. 11988, May 24, 1977, 42 F.R. 26951, set out as a note under section 4321 of Title 42, The Public Health and Welfare.

EXECUTIVE ORDER NO. 11296

Ex. Ord. No. 11296, Aug. 10, 1966, 31 F.R. 10663, as amended by Pub. L. 90–608, ch. IV, § 402, Oct. 21, 1968, 82 Stat. 1194, which related to the evaluation of flood hazard in locating federally owned or financed buildings, roads, and other facilities, and in disposing of federal lands and properties, was revoked by Ex. Ord. No. 11988, May 24, 1977, 42 F.R. 26951, set out as a note under section 4321 of Title 42, The Public Health and Welfare.

§ 701–1. Declaration of policy of 1944 act

In connection with the exercise of jurisdiction over the rivers of the Nation through the construction of works of improvement, for navigation or flood control, as herein authorized, it is declared to be the policy of the Congress to recognize the interests and rights of the States in determining the development of the watersheds within their borders and likewise their interests and rights in water utilization and control, as herein authorized to preserve and protect to the fullest possible extent established and potential uses, for all purposes, of the waters of the Nation's rivers; to facilitate the consideration of projects on a basis of comprehensive and coordinated development; and to limit the authorization and construction of navigation works to those in which a substantial benefit to navigation will be realized therefrom and which can be operated consistently with appropriate and economic use of the waters of such rivers by other users.

In conformity with this policy:

(a) Plans, proposals, or reports of the Chief of Engineers, Department of the Army, for any works of improvement for navigation or flood control not heretofore or herein authorized, shall be submitted to the Congress only upon compliance with the provisions of this paragraph (a). Investigations which form the basis of any such plans, proposals, or reports shall be conducted in such a manner as to give to the affected State or States, during the course of the investigations, information developed by the investigations and also opportunity for consultation regarding plans and proposals, and, to the extent deemed practicable by the Chief of Engineers, opportunity to cooperate in the investigations. If such investigations in whole or part are concerned with the use or control of waters arising west of the ninety-seventh meridian, the Chief of Engineers shall give to the Secretary of the Interior, during the course of the investigations, information developed by the investigations and also opportunity for consultation regarding plans and proposals, and to the extent deemed practicable by the Chief of Engineers, opportunity to cooperate in the investigations. The relations of the Chief of Engineers with any State under this paragraph (a) shall be with the Governor of the State or such official or agency of the State as the Governor may designate. The term "affected State or States" shall include those in which the works or any part thereof are proposed to be located; those which in whole or part are both within the drainage basin involved and situated in a State lying wholly or in part west of the ninety-eighth meridian; and such of those which are east of the ninety-eighth meridian as, in the judgment of the Chief of Engineers, will be substantially affected. Such plans, proposals, or reports and related investigations shall be made to the end, among other things, of facilitating the coordination of plans for the construction and operation of the proposed works with other plans involving the waters which would be used or controlled by such proposed works. Each report submitting any such plans or proposals to the Congress shall set out therein, among other things, the relationship between the plans for construction and operation of the proposed works and the plans, if any, submitted by the affected States and by the Secretary of the Interior. The Chief of Engineers shall transmit a copy of his proposed report to each affected State, and, in case the plans or proposals covered by the report are concerned with the use or control of waters which rise in whole or in part west of the ninety-seventh meridian, to the Secretary of the Interior. Within 30 days from the date of receipt of said proposed report, the written views and recommendations of each affected State and of the Secretary of the Interior may be submitted to the Chief of Engineers. The Secretary of the Army shall transmit to the Congress, with such comments and recommendations as he deems appropriate, the proposed report together with the submitted views and recommendations of affected States and of the Secretary of the Interior. The Secretary of the Army may prepare and make said transmittal any time following said 30-day period. The letter of transmittal and its attachments shall be printed as a House or Senate document.

(b) The use for navigation, in connection with the operation and maintenance of such works herein authorized for construction, of waters arising in States lying wholly or partly west of the ninety-eighth meridian shall be only such use as does not conflict with any beneficial consumptive use, present or future, in States lying wholly or partly west of the ninety-eighth meridian, of such waters for domestic, municipal, stock water, irrigation, mining, or industrial purposes.

(c) The Secretary of the Interior, in making investigations of and reports on works for irrigation and purposes incidental thereto shall, in relation to an affected State or States (as defined in paragraph (a) of this section), and to the Secretary of the Army, be subject to the same provisions regarding investigations, plans, proposals, and reports as prescribed in paragraph (a) of this section for the Chief of Engineers and the Secretary of the Army. In the event a submission of views and recommendations, made by an affected State or by the Secretary of the Army pursuant to said provisions, sets forth objections to the plans or proposals covered by the report of the Secretary of the Interior, the proposed works shall not be deemed authorized except upon approval by an Act of Congress; and section 485h(a) of title 43 and section 590z–1(a) of title 16 are amended accordingly.

(Dec. 22, 1944, ch. 665, §1, 58 Stat. 887; July 26, 1947, ch. 343, title II, §205(a), 61 Stat. 501; Pub. L. 104–303, title II, §223, Oct. 12, 1996, 110 Stat. 3697.)

AMENDMENTS

1996—Par. (a). Pub. L. 104–303 substituted "Within 30 days" for "Within ninety days" and "30-day period" for "ninety-day period".

CHANGE OF NAME

Department of War designated Department of the Army and title of Secretary of War changed to Secretary of the Army by section 205(a) of act July 26, 1947, ch. 343, title II, 61 Stat. 501. Section 205(a) of act July 26, 1947, was repealed by section 53 of act Aug. 10, 1956, ch. 1041, 70A Stat. 641. Section 1 of act Aug. 10, 1956, enacted "Title 10, Armed Forces" which in sections 3010 to 3013 continued Department of the Army under administrative supervision of Secretary of the Army.

APPLICABILITY OF SECTION TO PROJECTS AUTHORIZED BY FLOOD CONTROL ACTS

Pub. L. 90–483, title II, §202, Aug. 13, 1968, 82 Stat. 739, provided that: "The provisions of section 1 of the Act of December 22, 1944 (Public Law Numbered 534, Seventy-eighth Congress, second session) [this section], shall govern with respect to projects authorized in this Act [Pub. L. 90–483], and the procedures therein set forth with respect to plans, proposals, or reports for works of improvement for navigation or flood control and for irrigation and purposes incidental thereto shall apply as if herein set forth in full."

Similar provisions were contained in the following prior acts:

Nov. 7, 1966, Pub. L. 89–789, title II, §202, 80 Stat. 1418.
Oct. 27, 1965, Pub. L. 89–298, title II, §203, 79 Stat. 1074.
Sept. 3, 1954, ch. 1264, title II, §202, 68 Stat. 1256.
May 17, 1950, ch. 188, title II, §202, 64 Stat. 170.

GLENDO UNIT, WYOMING, MISSOURI RIVER BASIN PROJECT

Joint Res. July 16, 1954, ch. 532, §2, 68 Stat. 486, provided, with respect to the Glendo unit (dam and reservoir), Missouri River Basin Project, at the Glendo site on the North Platte River in Wyoming, for waiver of the provisions of subsec. (c) of this section. Section 1 of the Joint Resolution provided for the construction and operation of such unit by the Secretary of the Interior.

SECTION AS UNAFFECTED BY SUBMERGED LANDS ACT

Provisions of this section as not amended, modified or repealed by the Submerged Lands Act, see section 1303 of Title 43, Public Lands.

§701a. Declaration of policy of 1936 act

It is recognized that destructive floods upon the rivers of the United States, upsetting orderly processes and causing loss of life and property, including the erosion of lands, and impairing and obstructing navigation, highways, railroads, and other channels of commerce between the States, constitute a menace to national welfare; that it is the sense of Congress that flood control on navigable waters or their tributaries is a proper activity of the Federal Government in cooperation with States, their political subdivisions, and localities thereof; that investigations and improvements of rivers and other waterways, including watersheds thereof, for flood-control purposes are in the interest of the general welfare; that the Federal Government should improve or participate in the improvement of navigable waters or their tributaries, including watersheds thereof, for flood-control purposes if the benefits to whomsoever they may accrue are in excess of the estimated costs, and if the lives and social security of people are otherwise adversely affected.

(June 22, 1936, ch. 688, §1, 49 Stat. 1570.)

§701a–1. "Flood control" defined; jurisdiction of Federal investigations

The words "flood control" as used in section 701a of this title, shall be construed to include channel and major drainage improvements and flood prevention improvements for protection from groundwater-induced damages, and Federal investigations and improvements of rivers and other waterways for flood control and allied purposes shall be under the jurisdiction of and shall be prosecuted by the Department of the Army under the direction of the Secretary of the Army and supervision of the Chief of Engineers, and Federal investigations of watersheds and measures for run-off and water-flow retardation and soil-erosion prevention on watersheds shall be under the jurisdiction of and shall be prosecuted by the Department of Agriculture under the direction of the Secretary of Agriculture, except as otherwise provided by Act of Congress.

(Dec. 22, 1944, ch. 665, §2, 58 Stat. 889; July 26, 1947, ch. 343, title II, §205(a), 61 Stat. 501; Pub. L. 99–662, title IV, §403, Nov. 17, 1986, 100 Stat. 4133.)

AMENDMENTS

1986—Pub. L. 99–662 inserted "and flood prevention improvements for protection from groundwater-induced damages" after "drainage improvements".

CHANGE OF NAME

Department of War designated Department of the Army and title of Secretary of War changed to Secretary of the Army by section 205(a) of act July 26, 1947, ch. 343, title II, 61 Stat. 501. Section 205(a) of act July 26, 1947, was repealed by section 53 of act Aug. 10, 1956, ch. 1041, 70A Stat. 641. Section 1 of act Aug. 10, 1956, enacted "Title 10, Armed Forces" which in sections 3010 to 3013 continued Department of the Army under administrative supervision of Secretary of the Army.

SAVINGS PROVISION

Authority of Secretary of Agriculture under this section as unaffected by repeal of Secretary's authority under section 701b of this title, see section 7 of act Aug. 4, 1954, set out as a note under section 701b of this title.

SECTION AS UNAFFECTED BY SUBMERGED LANDS ACT

Provisions of this section as not amended, modified or repealed by the Submerged Lands Act, see section 1303 of Title 43, Public Lands.

§701b. Supervision of Secretary of the Army; reclamation projects unaffected

Federal investigations and improvements of rivers and other waterways for flood control and allied purposes shall be under the jurisdiction of and shall be prosecuted by the Department of the Army under the direction of the Secretary of the Army and supervision of the Chief of Engineers, except as otherwise provided by Act of Congress; and in his reports upon examinations and surveys, the Secretary of the Army shall be guided as to flood-control measures by the principles set forth in section 701a of this title in the determination of the Federal interests involved: *Provided*, That the foregoing grant of authority shall not interfere with investigations and river improvements incident to reclamation projects that may now be in progress or may be hereafter undertaken by the Bureau of Reclamation of the Interior Department pursuant to any general or specific authorization of law.

(June 22, 1936, ch. 688, §2, 49 Stat. 1570; June 28, 1938, ch. 795, §1, 52 Stat. 1215; Aug. 18, 1941, ch. 377, §1, 55 Stat. 638; July 26, 1947, ch. 343, title II, §205(a), 61 Stat. 501; Aug. 4, 1954, ch. 656, §7, 68 Stat. 668.)

AMENDMENTS

1954—Act Aug. 4, 1954, repealed provisions conferring authority on the Department of Agriculture under the direction of the Secretary of Agriculture to make preliminary examinations and surveys and to prosecute works of improvement for runoff and waterflow retardation and soil erosion prevention on the watersheds of rivers and other waterways.

1941—Act Aug. 18, 1941, reenacted without change portion of section preceding semicolon.

1938—Act June 28, 1938, reenacted without change portion of section preceding semicolon.

CHANGE OF NAME

Department of War designated Department of the Army and title of Secretary of War changed to Secretary of the Army by section 205(a) of act July 26, 1947, ch. 343, title II, 61 Stat. 501. Section 205(a) of act July 26, 1947, was repealed by section 53 of act Aug. 10, 1956, ch. 1041, 70A Stat. 641. Section 1 of act Aug. 10, 1956, enacted "Title 10, Armed Forces" which in sections 3010 to 3013 continued Department of the Army under administrative supervision of Secretary of the Army.

SAVINGS PROVISION

Section 7 of act Aug. 4, 1954, which amended this section by repealing provisions relating to the Department of Agriculture, provides in part that: "(a) the authority of that Department of Agriculture, under the direction of the Secretary, to prosecute the works of improvement for runoff and waterflow retardation and soil erosion prevention authorized to be carried out by the Department by the act of December 22, 1944 (58 Stat. 887), as amended [section 701a–1 of this title], and (b) the authority of the Secretary of Agriculture to undertake emergency measures for runoff retardation and soil erosion prevention authorized to be carried out by section 7 of the act of June 28, 1938 (52 Stat. 1215), as amended by section 216 of the act of May 17, 1950 (64 Stat. 163) [section 701b–1 of this title], shall not be affected by the provisions of this section."

RISK-BASED ANALYSIS METHODOLOGY

Pub. L. 104–303, title II, §202(h), Oct. 12, 1996, 110 Stat. 3676, provided that:

"(1) IN GENERAL.—The Secretary shall enter into an agreement with the National Academy of Sciences to conduct a study of the Corps of Engineers' use of risk-based analysis for the evaluation of hydrology, hydraulics, and economics in flood damage reduction studies. The study shall include—

"(A) an evaluation of the impact of risk-based analysis on project formulation, project economic justification, and minimum engineering and safety standards; and

"(B) a review of studies conducted using risk-based analysis to determine—

"(i) the scientific validity of applying risk-based analysis in these studies; and

"(ii) the impact of using risk-based analysis as it relates to current policy and procedures of the Corps of Engineers.

"(2) REPORT.—Not later than 18 months after the date of the enactment of this Act [Oct. 12, 1996], the Secretary shall submit to Congress a report on the results of the study under paragraph (1), as well as such recommendations as the Secretary considers appropriate.

"(3) LIMITATION ON USE OF METHODOLOGY.—During the period beginning on the date of the enactment of this Act [Oct. 12, 1996] and ending 18 months after that date, if requested by a non-Federal interest, the Secretary shall refrain from using any risk-based technique required under the studies described in paragraph (1) for the evaluation and design of a project.

"(4) AUTHORIZATION OF APPROPRIATIONS.—There is authorized to be appropriated $250,000 to carry out this subsection."

§ 701b–1. Transfer of jurisdiction in certain cases to Department of Agriculture

In order to effectuate the policy declared in sections 701a and 701b of this title, and to correlate the program for the improvement of rivers and other waterways by the Department of the Army with the program for the improvement of watersheds by the Department of Agriculture, works of improvement for measures of run-off and water-flow retardation and soil-erosion prevention on the watersheds of waterways, for which works of improvement for the benefit of navigation and the control of destructive floodwaters and other provisions have been adopted and authorized to be prosecuted under the direction of the Secretary of the Army and supervision of the Chief of Engineers, are authorized to be prosecuted by the Department of Agriculture under the direction of the Secretary of Agriculture and in accordance with plans approved by him. The Secretary of Agriculture is authorized in his discretion to undertake such emergency measures for run-off retardation and soil-erosion prevention as may be needed to safeguard lives and property from floods and the products of erosion on any watershed whenever fire or any other natural element or force has caused a sudden impairment of that watershed: *Provided*, That not to exceed $300,000 out of any funds heretofore or hereafter appropriated for the prosecution by the Secretary of Agriculture of works of improvement or measures for run-off and water-flow retardation and soil-erosion prevention on watersheds may be expended during any one fiscal year for such emergency measures. For prosecuting said work and measures there is authorized to be appropriated the sum of $10,000,000 to be expended at the rate of $2,000,000 per annum during the five-year period ending June 30, 1944: *Provided*, That such works and measures which are herein authorized to be prosecuted by the Department of Agriculture may be carried out on the watersheds of the Rio Grande and Pecos Rivers subject to the proviso in section 701b of this title.

(June 28, 1938, ch. 795, §7, 52 Stat. 1225; Dec. 22, 1944, ch. 665, §15, 58 Stat. 907; July 26, 1947, ch. 343, title II, §205(a), 61 Stat. 501; May 17, 1950, ch. 188, title II, §216, 64 Stat. 184.)

AMENDMENTS

1950—Act May 17, 1950, substituted "$300,000" for "$100,000".

1944—Act Dec. 22, 1944, inserted provisions authorizing Secretary of Agriculture to undertake emergency work and limiting amount of annual expenditures for such work.

CHANGE OF NAME

Department of War designated Department of the Army and title of Secretary of War changed to Secretary of the Army by section 205(a) of act July 26, 1947, ch. 343, title II, 61 Stat. 501. Section 205(a) of act July 26, 1947, was repealed by section 53 of act Aug. 10, 1956, ch. 1041, 70A Stat. 641. Section 1 of act Aug. 10, 1956, enacted "Title 10, Armed Forces" which in sections 3010 to 3013 continued Department of the Army under administrative supervision of Secretary of the Army.

SAVINGS PROVISION

Authority of Secretary of Agriculture under this section as unaffected by repeal of Secretary's authority under section 701b of this title, see section 7 of act Aug. 4, 1954, set out as a note under section 701b of this title

SECTION AS UNAFFECTED BY SUBMERGED LANDS ACT

Provisions of this section as not amended, modified or repealed by the Submerged Lands Act, see section 1303 of Title 43, Public Lands.

§ 701b–2. Cooperation by Secretaries of the Army and Agriculture; expenditures

In carrying out the purposes of the Act of June 22, 1936 (49 Stat. 1570), as amended and supplemented, the Secretary of the Army and the Secretary of Agriculture are authorized to cooperate with institutions, organizations, and individuals, and to utilize the services of Federal, State, and other public agencies, and to pay by check to the cooperating public agency, either in advance or upon the furnishing or performance of said services, all or part of the estimated or actual cost thereof; and to make expenditures for personal services and rent in the District of Columbia and elsewhere, for purchase of reference and law books and periodicals, for printing and binding, for the purchase, exchange, operation, and maintenance of motor-propelled passenger-carrying vehicles and motorboats for official use, and for other necessary expenses. The provisions of this section shall be applicable to any funds heretofore appropriated for the prosecution by the Secretary of Agriculture of works of improvement for measures of run-off and water-flow retardation and soil-erosion prevention upon watersheds.

(June 28, 1938, ch. 795, § 5, 52 Stat. 1223; Aug. 18, 1941, ch. 377, § 8, 55 Stat. 650; July 26, 1947, ch. 343, title II, § 205(a), 61 Stat. 501.)

REFERENCES IN TEXT

Act of June 22, 1936 (49 Stat. 1570), as amended and supplemented, referred to in text, is act June 22, 1936, ch. 688, 49 Stat. 1570, as amended, popularly known as the Flood Control Act of June 22, 1936, which to the extent classified to the Code enacted sections 701a, 701b, 701c, 701d to 701f, and 701h of this title. For complete classification of this Act to the Code, see Tables.

AMENDMENTS

1941—Act Aug. 18, 1941, changed the reference near the beginning of section and inserted sentence at end.

CHANGE OF NAME

Department of War designated Department of the Army and title of Secretary of War changed to Secretary of the Army by section 205(a) of act July 26, 1947, ch. 343, title II, 61 Stat. 501. Section 205(a) of act July 26, 1947, was repealed by section 53 of act Aug. 10, 1956, ch. 1041, 70A Stat. 641. Section 1 of act Aug. 10, 1956, enacted "Title 10, Armed Forces" which in sections 3010 to 3013 continued Department of the Army under administrative supervision of Secretary of the Army.

TRANSFER OF FUNCTIONS

Functions of all officers, agencies and employees of Department of Agriculture transferred, with certain exceptions, to Secretary of Agriculture by Reorg. Plan No. 2 of 1953, § 1, eff. June 4, 1953, 18 F.R. 3219, 67 Stat. 633, set out in the Appendix to Title 5, Government Organization and Employees.

§ 701b–3. Examinations and surveys; availability of appropriations

Funds heretofore or hereafter appropriated for construction and maintenance of flood-control works by the Department of the Army shall be available for expenditure by the Department of the Army in making examinations and surveys for flood control heretofore or hereafter authorized, or in preparing reports in review thereof as authorized by law, in addition to funds heretofore authorized to be expended for such purposes by the Department of the Army.

(Aug. 11, 1939, ch. 699, § 2, 53 Stat. 1414; July 26, 1947, ch. 343, title II, § 205(a), 61 Stat. 501.)

CHANGE OF NAME

Department of War designated Department of the Army and title of Secretary of War changed to Secretary of the Army by section 205(a) of act July 26, 1947, ch. 343, title II, 61 Stat. 501. Section 205(a) of act July 26, 1947, was repealed by section 53 of act Aug. 10, 1956, ch. 1041, 70A Stat. 641. Section 1 of act Aug. 10, 1956, enacted "Title 10, Armed Forces" which in sections 3010 to 3013 continued Department of the Army under administrative supervision of Secretary of the Army.

§ 701b–4. Administration of surveys; number authorized; reports

The surveys authorized to be performed under the direction of the Secretary of the Army as well as all duties performed by the Chief of Engineers under the direction of the Secretary of the Army shall be functions of the Engineer Corps, United States Army, and its head, to be administered under the direction of the Secretary of the Army and the supervision of the Chief of Engineers except as otherwise specifically provided by Congress: *Provided*, That the power and authority conferred by the Flood Control Act of June 28, 1938, and previously conferred, upon the Federal Power Commission shall remain in full force and effect: *Provided*, That no preliminary examination, survey, project, or estimate for new works other than those designated in this Act or some prior Act or joint resolution shall be made: *Provided further*, That after the regular or formal reports made as required by law on any examination, survey, project, or work under way or proposed, are submitted, no supplemental or additional report or estimate shall be made unless authorized by law.

(Aug. 11, 1939, ch. 699, § 6, 53 Stat. 1415; July 26, 1947, ch. 343, title II, § 205(a), 61 Stat. 501.)

REFERENCES IN TEXT

The Flood Control Act of June 28, 1938, referred to in text, is act June 28, 1938, ch. 795, 52 Stat. 1215, as amended, which to the extent classified to the Code is classified to sections 701b, 701b-1, 701b-2, 701c-1, 701f-1, 701i, 701j, 702a-1½, 702a-11, and 706 of this title. For complete classification of this Act to the Code, see Tables.

This Act, referred to in text, is act Aug. 11, 1939, ch. 699, 53 Stat. 1414, as amended, which to the extent classified to the Code enacted sections 558b-1, 701b-3, 701b-4, and 707 of this title and amended sections 701c-1 and 701g of this title. For complete classification of this Act to the Code, see Tables.

CHANGE OF NAME

Department of War designated Department of the Army and title of Secretary of War changed to Secretary of the Army by section 205(a) of act July 26, 1947, ch. 343, title II, 61 Stat. 501. Section 205(a) of act July 26, 1947, was repealed by section 53 of act Aug. 10, 1956, ch. 1041, 70A Stat. 641. Section 1 of act Aug. 10, 1956, enacted "Title 10, Armed Forces" which in sections 3010 to 3013 continued Department of the Army under administrative supervision of Secretary of the Army.

TRANSFER OF FUNCTIONS

Federal Power Commission terminated and its functions, personnel, property, funds, etc., transferred to Secretary of Energy (except for certain functions transferred to Federal Energy Regulatory Commission) by sections 7151(b), 7171(a), 7172(a), 7291, and 7293 of Title 42, The Public Health and Welfare.

For transfer of functions of Federal Power Commission, with certain reservations, to chairman of such Commission, see Reorg. Plan No. 9 of 1950, §§ 1, 2, eff. May 24, 1950, 15 F.R. 3175, 64 Stat. 1265, set out in the Appendix to Title 5, Government Organization and Employees.

§ 701b-5. Omitted

CODIFICATION

Section, act Mar. 31, 1945, ch. 45, § 1, 59 Stat. 41, relating to appropriations subject to priority restrictions, was from the War Department Civil Appropriation Act, 1946, and was not repeated in subsequent appropriation acts.

§ 701b-6. Examinations and surveys by Secretary of Agriculture

That, in order to further the declaration of policy and principles declared in sections 701a and 701b of this title, and to supplement the preliminary examinations and surveys which the Secretary of the Army has heretofore been, or is hereafter, authorized and directed to make of waterways with a view to the control of their floods, the Secretary of Agriculture be, and he is, authorized and directed to cause preliminary examinations and surveys to be made for run-off and water-flow retardation and soil-erosion prevention on the watersheds of said waterways, the costs thereof to be paid from appropriations heretofore or hereafter made for such purposes.

(Aug. 28, 1937, ch. 877, § 3, 50 Stat. 877; Jan. 19, 1948, ch. 2, § 1, 62 Stat. 4; July 26, 1947, ch. 343, title II, § 205(a), 61 Stat. 501.)

AMENDMENTS

1948—Act Jan. 19, 1948, inserted "or is hereafter" after "heretofore been" to make section applicable to future preliminary surveys and examinations.

CHANGE OF NAME

Department of War designated Department of the Army and title of Secretary of War changed to Secretary of the Army by section 205(a) of act July 26, 1947, ch. 343, title II, 61 Stat. 501. Section 205(a) of act July 26, 1947, was repealed by section 53 of act Aug. 10, 1956, ch. 1041, 70A Stat. 641. Section 1 of act Aug. 10, 1956, enacted "Title 10, Armed Forces" which in sections 3010 to 3013 continued Department of the Army under administrative supervision of Secretary of the Army.

§ 701b-7. Supplemental reports to Senate Environment and Public Works Committee and House Public Works Committee

After the Secretary of Agriculture has submitted to Congress a regular or formal report made on any examination or survey, pursuant to the Flood Control Act approved June 22, 1936, as amended and supplemented, a supplemental, additional, or review report or estimate may be made if authorized by law or by resolution of the Committee on Public Works and Transportation of the House of Representatives or the Committee on Environment and Public Works of the Senate.

(Jan. 19, 1948, ch. 2, § 2, 62 Stat. 4; Pub. L. 103-437, § 12(d), Nov. 2, 1994, 108 Stat. 4590.)

REFERENCES IN TEXT

The Flood Control Act approved June 22, 1936, as amended and supplemented, referred to in text, is act June 22, 1936, ch. 688, 49 Stat. 1570, as amended, which to the extent classified to the Code enacted sections 701a, 701b, 701c, 701d to 701f, and 701h of this title. For complete classification of this Act to the Code, see Tables.

AMENDMENTS

1994—Pub. L. 103-437 substituted "Committee on Public Works and Transportation of the House of Representatives or the Committee on Environment and Public Works of the Senate" for "Committee on Public Works of the House of Representatives or the Committee on Public Works of the Senate".

CHANGE OF NAME

Committee on Public Works and Transportation of House of Representatives treated as referring to Committee on Transportation and Infrastructure of House of Representatives by section 1(a) of Pub. L. 104-14, set out as a note preceding section 21 of Title 2, The Congress.

§ 701b-8. Submission of report by Chief of Engineers

It is declared to be the policy of the Congress that the following provisions shall be observed:

No project or any modification not authorized, of a project for flood control or rivers and harbors, shall be authorized by the Congress unless a report for such project or modification has been previously submitted by the Chief of Engineers, United States Army, in conformity with existing law.

(Sept. 3, 1954, ch. 1264, title II, § 202, 68 Stat. 1256.)

CODIFICATION

Section comprises last two paragraphs of section 202 of act Sept. 3, 1954. First paragraph of section 202 is set out as a note under section 701-1 of this title.

PRIOR PROVISIONS

Provisions similar to those in this section were contained in the following prior acts:

May 17, 1950, ch. 188, title II, § 202, 64 Stat. 170.

June 30, 1948, ch. 771, title II, § 202, 62 Stat. 1175.

July 24, 1946, ch. 596, §2, 60 Stat. 641.

§701b–8a. Discontinuance of preliminary examination reports

For preliminary examinations and surveys authorized in previous river and harbor and flood control Acts, the Secretary of the Army is directed to cause investigations and reports for flood control and allied purposes, to be prepared under the supervision of the Chief of Engineers in the form of survey reports, and that preliminary examination reports shall no longer be required to be prepared.

(Pub. L. 85–500, title II, §208, July 3, 1958, 72 Stat. 319.)

REFERENCES IN TEXT

Previous river and harbor and flood-control Acts, referred to in text, means those acts prior to the River and Harbor Act of 1958 and the Flood Control Act of 1958, titles I and II of Pub. L. 85–500.

§701b–9. Availability of appropriations for expenses incident to operation of power boats or vessels; expenses defined; certification of expenditures

On and after July 31, 1947, no appropriation under the Corps of Engineers shall be available for any expenses incident to operating any power-driven boat or vessel on other than Government business, and that Government business shall be construed to include transportation, lodging, and subsistence on inspection trips of Federal and State officials, having a public interest in authorized or proposed improvements for river and harbor and flood control, and any expenses incurred therefor shall be chargeable to river and harbor and flood control appropriations heretofore or hereafter made under rules and regulations to be prescribed by the Chief of Engineers: *Provided*, That such expenditures shall be certified by the Division Engineer as necessary and proper expenditures.

(July 31, 1947, ch. 411, §1, 61 Stat. 688.)

CODIFICATION

Section is also set out as section 575 of this title.

Section was formerly classified to sections 190a and 199 of Title 10 prior to the general revision and enactment of Title 10, Armed Forces, by act Aug. 10, 1956, ch. 1041, 70A Stat. 1.

§701b–10. Revolving fund; establishment; availability; reimbursement; transfer of funds; limitation

There is established a revolving fund, to be available without fiscal year limitation, for expenses necessary for the maintenance and operation of the plant and equipment of the Corps of Engineers used in civil works functions, including acquisition of plant and equipment, maintenance, repair, and purchase, operation, and maintenance of not to exceed four aircraft at any one time, temporary financing of services finally chargeable to appropriations for civil works functions, and the furnishing of facilities and services for military functions of the Department of the Army and other Government agencies and private persons, as authorized by law, $100; and in addition, the Secretary of the Army is authorized to provide capital for the fund by capitalizing the present inventories, plant and equipment of the civil works functions of the Corps of Engineers. The fund shall be credited with reimbursements or advances for the cost of equipment, facilities, and services furnished, at rates which shall include charges for overhead and related expenses, depreciation of plant and equipment, and accrued leave: *Provided*, That on July 1, 1953, (1) the fund shall assume the assets, liabilities, and obligations of the Plant accounts, as carried on the records of the Corps of Engineers as of June 30, 1953, under the appropriations for "Maintenance and improvement of existing river and harbor works", "Flood control, general", and "Flood control, Mississippi River and tributaries", and (2) there shall be transferred from said appropriations to the fund amounts equivalent to the unexpended cash balances of the Plant accounts on June 30, 1953: *Provided further*, That the total capital of said fund shall not exceed $140,000,000.

(July 27, 1953, ch. 245, §101, 67 Stat. 199.)

CODIFICATION

Section is also set out as section 576 of this title.

Section was formerly classified to section 190b of Title 10 prior to the general revision and enactment of Title 10, Armed Forces, by act Aug. 10, 1956, ch. 1041, 70A Stat. 1.

RETENTION OF THREE OPERATIONAL AIRCRAFT; NOTICE OF INTENDED USE OUTSIDE UNITED STATES

For provision relating to retention, use, and disposal of three operational aircraft by Chief of Engineers, see section 101(d) [title I, §110] of Pub. L. 100–202, set out as a note under section 576 of this title.

§701b–11. Flood protection projects

(a) General considerations; nonstructural alternatives

In the survey, planning, or design by any Federal agency of any project involving flood protection, consideration shall be given to nonstructural alternatives to prevent or reduce flood damages including, but not limited to, floodproofing of structures; flood plain regulation; acquisition of flood plain lands for recreational, fish and wildlife, and other public purposes; and relocation with a view toward formulating the most economically, socially, and environmentally acceptable means of reducing or preventing flood damages.

(b) Non-Federal participation through nonstructural alternatives; limitation

Where a nonstructural alternative is recommended, non-Federal participation shall be comparable to the value of lands, easements, and rights-of-way which would have been required of non-Federal interests under section 701c of this title, for structural protection measures, but in no event shall exceed 20 per centum of the project costs.

(Pub. L. 93–251, title I, §73, Mar. 7, 1974, 88 Stat. 32.)

NONSTRUCTURAL FLOOD CONTROL POLICY

Pub. L. 104–303, title II, §202(d), Oct. 12, 1996, 110 Stat. 3675, provided that:

"(1) REVIEW.—The Secretary shall conduct a review of policies, procedures, and techniques relating to the evaluation and development of flood control measures with a view toward identifying impediments that may exist to justifying nonstructural flood control measures as alternatives to structural measures.

"(2) REPORT.—Not later than 1 year after the date of the enactment of this Act [Oct. 12, 1996], the Secretary shall transmit to Congress a report on the findings of the review conducted under this subsection, together with any recommendations for modifying existing law to remove any impediments identified under such review."

§ 701b–12. Floodplain management requirements

(a) Compliance with floodplain management and insurance programs

Before construction of any project for local flood protection, or any project for hurricane or storm damage reduction, that involves Federal assistance from the Secretary, the non-Federal interest shall agree to participate in and comply with applicable Federal floodplain management and flood insurance programs.

(b) Floodplain management plans

Within 1 year after the date of signing a project cooperation agreement for construction of a project to which subsection (a) of this section applies, the non-Federal interest shall prepare a floodplain management plan designed to reduce the impacts of future flood events in the project area. Such plan shall be implemented by the non-Federal interest not later than 1 year after completion of construction of the project.

(c) Guidelines

(1) In general

The Secretary shall develop guidelines for preparation of floodplain management plans by non-Federal interests under subsection (b) of this section.

(2) Required elements

The guidelines developed under paragraph (1) shall—

(A) address potential measures, practices, and policies to be undertaken by non-Federal interests to to[1] reduce loss of life, injuries, damages to property and facilities, public expenditures, and other adverse impacts associated with flooding and to preserve and enhance natural floodplain values; and

(B) address those measures to be undertaken by non-Federal interests to preserve the level of flood protection provided by a project to which subsection (a) of this section applies.

(3) Limitation on statutory construction

Nothing in this subsection shall be construed to confer any regulatory authority upon the Secretary or the Administrator of the Federal Emergency Management Agency.

(d) Technical support

The Secretary may provide technical support to a non-Federal interest for a project to which subsection (a) of this section applies for the development and implementation of plans prepared under subsection (b) of this section.

(Pub. L. 99–662, title IV, § 402, Nov. 17, 1986, 100 Stat. 4133; Pub. L. 100–676, § 14, Nov. 17, 1988, 102 Stat. 4026; Pub. L. 104–303, title II, § 202(c)(1), Oct. 12, 1996, 110 Stat. 3674; Pub. L. 106–541, title II, § 209(a), (c), Dec. 11, 2000, 114 Stat. 2591; Pub. L. 109–295, title VI, § 612(c), Oct. 4, 2006, 120 Stat. 1410.)

[1] So in original.

AMENDMENTS

2000—Subsec. (b). Pub. L. 106–541, § 209(c), substituted "Floodplain" for "Flood plain" in heading and "floodplain" for "flood plain" in first sentence.

Subsec. (c). Pub. L. 106–541, § 209(a), in first sentence substituted "The" for "Within 6 months after October 12, 1996, the", designated second sentence as par. (2), inserted heading, substituted "The guidelines developed under paragraph (1) shall—" for "Such guidelines shall", designated remainder of sentence as subpar. (A), inserted "to be undertaken by non-Federal interests to" after "policies", added subpar. (B), and redesignated former par. (2) as (3).

1996—Pub. L. 104–303 substituted "Floodplain management requirements" for "Compliance with flood plain management and insurance programs" in section catchline and amended text generally. Prior to amendment, text read as follows: "Before construction of any project for local flood protection or any project for hurricane or storm damage reduction, the non-Federal interests shall agree to participate in and comply with applicable Federal flood plain management and flood insurance programs."

1988—Pub. L. 100–676 inserted "or any project for hurricane or storm damage reduction" after "local flood protection".

CHANGE OF NAME

"Administrator of the Federal Emergency Management Agency" substituted for "Director of the Federal Emergency Management Agency" in subsec. (c)(3) on authority of section 612(c) of Pub. L. 109–295, set out as a note under section 313 of Title 6, Domestic Security. Any reference to the Administrator of the Federal Emergency Management Agency in title VI of Pub. L. 109–295 or an amendment by title VI to be considered to refer and apply to the Director of the Federal Emergency Management Agency until Mar. 31, 2007, see section 612(f)(2) of Pub. L. 109–295, set out as a note under section 313 of Title 6.

EFFECTIVE DATE OF 2000 AMENDMENT

Pub. L. 106–541, title II, § 209(b), Dec. 11, 2000, 114 Stat. 2591, provided that: "The amendments made by subsection (a) [amending this section] shall apply to any project or separable element of a project with respect to which the Secretary [of the Army] and the non-Federal interest have not entered a project cooperation agreement on or before the date of enactment of this Act [Dec. 11, 2000]."

EFFECTIVE DATE OF 1996 AMENDMENT

Section 202(c)(2) of Pub. L. 104–303 provided that: "The amendment made by paragraph (1) [amending this section] shall apply to any project or separable element thereof with respect to which the Secretary and the non-Federal interest have not entered into a project cooperation agreement on or before the date of the enactment of this Act [Oct. 12, 1996]."

REFERENCE TO PROJECT COOPERATION AGREEMENT DEEMED REFERENCE TO PROJECT PARTNERSHIP AGREEMENT

Reference to "project cooperation agreement" deemed to be reference to "project partnership agreement", see section 2003(f)(2) of Pub. L. 110–114, set out as a note under section 1962d–5b of Title 42, The Public Health and Welfare.

§ 701b–13. Construction of flood control projects by non-Federal interests

(a) Authority

Non-Federal interests are authorized to undertake flood control projects in the United States, subject to obtaining any permits required pursuant to Federal and State laws in advance of actual construction.

(b) Studies and design activities

(1) By non-Federal interests

A non-Federal interest may prepare, for review and approval by the Secretary, the necessary studies and design documents for any construction to be undertaken pursuant to subsection (a) of this section.

(2) By Secretary

Upon request of an appropriate non-Federal interest, the Secretary may undertake all necessary studies and design activities for any construction to be undertaken pursuant to subsection (a) of this section and provide technical assistance in obtaining all necessary permits for such construction if the non-Federal interest contracts with the Secretary to provide to the United States funds for the studies and design activities during the period in which the studies and design activities will be conducted.

(c) Completion of studies and design activities

In the case of any study or design documents for a flood control project that were initiated before October 12, 1996, the Secretary may complete and transmit to the appropriate non-Federal interests the study or design documents or, upon the request of such non-Federal interests, terminate the study or design activities and transmit the partially completed study or design documents to such non-Federal interests for completion. Studies and design documents subject to this subsection shall be completed without regard to the requirements of subsection (b) of this section.

(d) Authority to carry out improvement

(1) In general

(A) Studies and design activities under subsection (b)

(i) In general

A non-Federal interest may carry out construction for which studies and design documents are prepared under subsection (b) of this section only if the Secretary approves the project for construction.

(ii) Criteria for approval

The Secretary shall approve a project for construction if the Secretary determines that the project is technically sound, economically justified, and environmentally acceptable and meets the requirements for obtaining the appropriate permits required under the authority of the Secretary.

(iii) No unreasonable withholding of approval

The Secretary shall not unreasonably withhold approval of a project for construction.

(iv) No effect on regulatory authority

Nothing in this subparagraph affects any regulatory authority of the Secretary.

(B) Studies and design activities under subsection (c)

Any non-Federal interest that has received from the Secretary under subsection (c) of this section a favorable recommendation to carry out a flood control project, or separable element of a flood control project, based on the results of completed studies and design documents for the project or element may carry out the project or element if a final environmental impact statement under the National Environmental Policy Act of 1969 (42 U.S.C. 4321 et seq.) has been filed for the project or element.

(2) Permits

Any plan of improvement proposed to be implemented in accordance with this subsection (other than paragraph (1)(A)) shall be deemed to satisfy the requirements for obtaining the appropriate permits required under the Secretary's authority. Such permits shall be granted subject to the non-Federal interest's acceptance of the terms and conditions of such permits if the Secretary determines that the applicable regulatory criteria and procedures have been satisfied.

(3) Monitoring

The Secretary shall monitor any project for which a permit is granted under this subsection in order to ensure that such project is constructed, operated, and maintained in accordance with the terms and conditions of such permit.

(e) Reimbursement

(1) General rule

Subject to appropriations Acts, the Secretary may reimburse any non-Federal interest an amount equal to the estimate of the Federal share, without interest, of the cost of any authorized flood control project, or separable element of a flood control project, constructed pursuant to this section and provide credit for the non-Federal share of the project—

(A) if, after authorization and before initiation of construction of the project or separable element, the Secretary approves the plans for construction of such project by the non-Federal interest;

(B) if the Secretary finds, after a review of studies and design documents prepared pursuant to this section, that construction of the project or separable element is economically justified and environmentally acceptable; and

(C) if the construction work is substantially in accordance with plans prepared under subsection (b) of this section.

(2) Special rules

(A) Reimbursement or credit

For work (including work associated with studies, planning, design, and construction) carried out by a non-Federal interest with respect to a project described in subsection

(f) of this section, the Secretary shall, subject to the availability of appropriations, reimburse, without interest, the non-Federal interest an amount equal to the estimated Federal share of the cost of such work, or provide credit (depending on the request of the non-Federal interest) for the non-Federal share of such work, if such work is later recommended by the Chief of Engineers and approved by the Secretary.

(B) Credit

If the non-Federal interest for a project described in subsection (f) of this section carries out work before completion of a reconnaissance study by the Secretary and if such work is determined by the Secretary to be compatible with the project later recommended by the Secretary, the Secretary shall credit the non-Federal interest for its share of the cost of the project for such work.

(3) Matters to be considered in reviewing plans

In reviewing plans under this subsection, the Secretary shall consider budgetary and programmatic priorities and other factors that the Secretary considers appropriate.

(4) Monitoring

The Secretary shall regularly monitor and audit any project for flood control approved for construction under this section by a non-Federal interest to ensure that such construction is in compliance with the plans approved by the Secretary and that the costs are reasonable.

(5) Limitation on reimbursements

The Secretary may not make any reimbursement under this section until the Secretary determines that the work for which reimbursement is requested has been performed in accordance with applicable permits and approved plans.

(6) Schedule and manner of reimbursement

(A) Budgeting

The Secretary shall budget and request appropriations for reimbursements under this section on a schedule that is consistent with a Federal construction schedule.

(B) Commencement of reimbursements

Reimbursements under this section may commence on approval of a project by the Secretary.

(C) Credit

At the request of a non-Federal interest, the Secretary may reimburse the non-Federal interest by providing credit toward future non-Federal costs of the project.

(D) Scheduling

Nothing in this paragraph affects the discretion of the President to schedule new construction starts.

(f) Specific projects

For the purpose of demonstrating the potential advantages and effectiveness of non-Federal implementation of flood control projects, the Secretary shall enter into agreements pursuant to this section with non-Federal interests for development of the following flood control projects by such interests:

(1) Berryessa Creek, California

The Berryessa Creek element of the project for flood control, Coyote and Berryessa Creeks, California, authorized by section 101(a)(5) of the Water Resources Development Act of 1990 (104 Stat. 4606); except that, subject to the approval of the Secretary as provided by this section, the non-Federal interest may design and construct an alternative to such element.

(2) Los Angeles County Drainage Area, California

The project for flood control, Los Angeles County Drainage Area, California, authorized by section 101(b) of the Water Resources Development Act of 1990 (104 Stat. 4611).

(3) Stockton Metropolitan Area, California

The project for flood control, Stockton Metropolitan Area, California.

(4) Upper Guadalupe River, California

The project for flood control, Upper Guadalupe River, California.

(5) Flamingo and Tropicana Washes, Nevada

The project for flood control, Las Vegas Wash and Tributaries (Flamingo and Tropicana Washes), Nevada, authorized by section 101(13) of the Water Resources Development Act of 1992 (106 Stat. 4803).

(6) Brays Bayou, Texas

Flood control components comprising the Brays Bayou element of the project for flood control, Buffalo Bayou and tributaries, Texas, authorized by section 101(a)(21) of the Water Resources Development Act of 1990 (104 Stat. 4610); except that, subject to the approval of the Secretary as provided by this section, the non-Federal interest may design and construct an alternative to the diversion component of such element.

(7) Hunting Bayou, Texas

The Hunting Bayou element of the project for flood control, Buffalo Bayou and tributaries, Texas, authorized by such section; except that, subject to the approval of the Secretary as provided by this section, the non-Federal interest may design and construct an alternative to such element.

(8) White Oak Bayou, Texas

The project for flood control, White Oak Bayou watershed, Texas.

(12)[1] Perris, California

The project for flood control, Perris, California.

(13) Thornton Reservoir, Cook County, Illinois

An element of the project for flood control, Chicagoland Underflow Plan, Illinois.

(14) Larose to Golden Meadow, Louisiana

The project for flood control, Larose to Golden Meadow, Louisiana.

[1] So in original. There are no pars. designated "(9)", "(10)", or "(11)".

(15) Buffalo Bayou, Texas

A project for flood control, Buffalo Bayou, Texas, to provide an alternative to the project authorized by the first section of the River and Harbor Act of June 20, 1938 (52 Stat. 804) and modified by section 3a of the Flood Control Act of August 11, 1939 (53 Stat. 1414).

(16) Halls Bayou, Texas

A project for flood control, Halls Bayou, Texas, to provide an alternative to the project for flood control, Buffalo Bayou and tributaries, Texas, authorized by section 101(a)(21) of the Water Resources Development Act of 1990 (104 Stat. 4610).

(17) Menomonee River Watershed, Wisconsin

The project for the Menomonee River Watershed, Wisconsin, including—

(A) the Underwood Creek diversion facility project (Milwaukee County Grounds); and

(B) the Greater Milwaukee Rivers watershed project.

(g) Treatment of flood damage prevention measures

For the purposes of this section, flood damage prevention measures at or in the vicinity of Morgan City and Berwick, Louisiana, shall be treated as an authorized separable element of the Atchafalaya Basin feature of the project for flood control, Mississippi River and Tributaries.

(Pub. L. 104–303, title II, § 211, Oct. 12, 1996, 110 Stat. 3681; Pub. L. 106–53, title II, § 223, Aug. 17, 1999, 113 Stat. 296; Pub. L. 106–60, title VI, § 606, Sept. 29, 1999, 113 Stat. 501; Pub. L. 110–114, title V, § 5157, Nov. 8, 2007, 121 Stat. 1257.)

REFERENCES IN TEXT

The National Environmental Policy Act of 1969, referred to in subsec. (d)(1), is Pub. L. 91–190, Jan. 1, 1970, 83 Stat. 852, as amended, which is classified generally to chapter 55 (§ 4321 et seq.) of Title 42, The Public Health and Welfare. For complete classification of this Act to the Code, see Short Title note set out under section 4321 of Title 42 and Tables.

Section 101 of the Water Resources Development Act of 1990, referred to in subsec. (f)(1), (2), (6), (16), is section 101 of Pub. L. 101–640, title I, Nov. 28, 1990, 104 Stat. 4605, which is not classified to the Code.

Section 101(13) of the Water Resources Development Act of 1992, referred to in subsec. (f)(5), is section 101(13) of Pub. L. 102–580, title I, Oct. 31, 1992, 106 Stat. 4803, which is not classified to the Code.

The first section of the River and Harbor Act of June 20, 1938, referred to in subsec. (f)(15), is section 1 of act June 20, 1938, ch. 535, 52 Stat. 802, which is classified in part to section 540 of this title.

Section 3a of the Flood Control Act of August 11, 1939, referred to in subsec. (f)(15), is section 3a of act Aug. 11, 1939, ch. 699, 53 Stat. 1414, which is not classified to the Code.

AMENDMENTS

2007—Subsec. (f)(12) to (17). Pub. L. 110–114 added pars. (12) to (17).

1999—Subsec. (d)(1). Pub. L. 106–53, § 223(a)(1), added subpar. (A), designated existing provisions as subpar. (B), inserted subpar. heading, and substituted "under subsection (c)" for "pursuant to subsection (b) or (c)".

Subsec. (d)(2). Pub. L. 106–53, § 223(a)(2), inserted "(other than paragraph (1)(A))" after "this subsection" in first sentence.

Subsec. (e)(1). Pub. L. 106–53, § 223(b)(1), inserted "and provide credit for the non-Federal share of the project" after "constructed pursuant to this section" in introductory provisions, and added subpar. (C).

Subsec. (e)(2)(A). Pub. L. 106–60, which directed the amendment of subpar. (A) by striking out "in advance in appropriations Acts", could not be executed because that phrase did not appear in text subsequent to the amendment by Pub. L. 106–53, § 223(b)(2). See below.

Pub. L. 106–53, § 223(b)(2), in subpar. heading, inserted "or credit" after "Reimbursement" and, in text, substituted "subject to the availability of appropriations" for "subject to amounts being made available in advance in appropriations Acts" and inserted ", or provide credit (depending on the request of the non-Federal interest) for the non-Federal share of such work," after "the cost of such work".

Subsec. (e)(6). Pub. L. 106–53, § 223(b)(3), added par. (6).

§ 701b–14. Structural integrity evaluations

(a) In general

Upon request of a non-Federal interest, the Secretary shall evaluate the structural integrity and effectiveness of a project for flood damage reduction and, if the Secretary determines that the project does not meet such minimum standards as the Secretary may establish and absent action by the Secretary the project will fail, the Secretary may take such action as may be necessary to restore the integrity and effectiveness of the project.

(b) Priority

The Secretary shall carry out an evaluation and take such actions as may be necessary under subsection (a) for the project for flood damage reduction, Arkansas River Levees, Arkansas.

(Pub. L. 110–114, title V, § 5004, Nov. 8, 2007, 121 Stat. 1191.)

"SECRETARY" DEFINED

Secretary means the Secretary of the Army, see section 2 of Pub. L. 110–114, set out as a note under section 2201 of this title.

§ 701c. Rights-of-way, easements, etc.; acquisition by local authorities; maintenance and operation; protection of United States from liability for damages; requisites to run-off and water-flow retardation and soil erosion prevention assistance

After June 22, 1936, no money appropriated under authority of section 701f of this title shall be expended on the construction of any project until States, political subdivisions thereof, or other responsible local agencies have given assurances satisfactory to the Secretary of the Army that they will (a) provide without cost to the United States all lands, easements, and rights-of-way necessary for the construction of the project, except as otherwise provided herein; (b) hold and save the United States free from damages due to the construction works; (c) maintain and operate all the works after completion in accordance with regulations prescribed by the Secretary of the Army: *Provided*, That the construction of any dam authorized herein, may be undertaken without delay when the dam site has been acquired and the assurances prescribed herein have been furnished, without awaiting the acquisition of the easements and rights-of-way required for the reservoir area: *And provided further*, That whenever expenditures for lands, easements, and rights-of-way by States, political subdivisions thereof, or responsible local agencies for any individual project or useful part thereof shall have exceeded the present estimated construction cost therefor, the local agency concerned may be reimbursed one-half of its excess expenditures over said estimated construction cost: *And provided further*, That when benefits of any project or useful part thereof accrue to lands and property outside of the State in which said project or part thereof is located, the Secretary of the Army with the consent of the State wherein the same are located may acquire the necessary lands, easements, and rights-of-way for said project or part thereof after he has received from the States, political subdivisions thereof, or responsible local agencies benefited the present estimated cost of said lands, easements, and rights-of-way, less one-half the amount by which the estimated cost of these lands, easements, and rights-of-way exceeds the estimated construction cost corresponding thereto: *And provided further*, That the Secretary of the Army shall determine the proportion of the present estimated cost of said lands, easements, and rights-of-way that each State, political subdivision thereof, or responsible local agency should contribute in consideration for the benefits to be received by such agencies: *And provided further*, That whenever not less than 75 per centum of the benefits as estimated by the Secretary of the Army of any project or useful part thereof accrue to lands and property outside of the State in which said project or part thereof is located, provision (c) of this section shall not apply thereto; nothing herein shall impair or abridge the powers now existing in the Department of the Army with respect to navigable streams: *And provided further*, That nothing herein shall be construed to interfere with the completion of any reservoir or flood control work authorized by the Congress and now under way.

(d) As a condition to the extending of any benefits, in prosecuting measures for run-off and water-flow retardation and soil erosion prevention authorized by Act of Congress pursuant to the policy declared in section 701a of this title, to any lands not owned or controlled by the United States or any of its agencies, the Secretary of Agriculture may, insofar as he may deem necessary for the purposes of such Act, require—

(1) The enactment and reasonable safeguards for the enforcement of State and local laws imposing suitable permanent restrictions on the use of such lands and otherwise providing for run-off and waterflow retardation and soil-erosion prevention;

(2) Agreements or covenants as to the permanent use of such lands; and

(3) Contributions in money, services, materials, or otherwise to any operations conferring such benefits.

(June 22, 1936, ch. 688, §3, 49 Stat. 1571; Aug. 28, 1937, ch. 877, §4, 50 Stat. 877; July 26, 1947, ch. 343, title II, §205(a), 61 Stat. 501.)

REFERENCES IN TEXT

Herein, referred to in text, means act June 22, 1936, ch. 688, 49 Stat. 1570, as amended, popularly known as the Flood Control Act of June 22, 1936, which to the extent classified to the Code enacted sections 701a, 701b, 701c, 701d to 701f, and 701h of this title. For complete classification of this Act to the Code, see Tables. Portions of section 5 of act June 22, 1936, enumerating certain dams to be constructed, were not classified to the Code.

AMENDMENTS

1937—Act Aug. 28, 1937, added subsec. (d).

CHANGE OF NAME

Department of War designated Department of the Army and title of Secretary of War changed to Secretary of the Army by section 205(a) of act July 26, 1947, ch. 343, title II, 61 Stat. 501. Section 205(a) of act July 26, 1947, was repealed by section 53 of act Aug. 10, 1956, ch. 1041, 70A Stat. 641. Section 1 of act Aug. 10, 1956, enacted "Title 10, Armed Forces" which in sections 3010 to 3013 continued Department of the Army under administrative supervision of Secretary of the Army.

APPLICABILITY OF SECTION TO FLOOD CONTROL WORKS AUTHORIZED BY FLOOD CONTROL ACTS

Pub. L. 90–483, title II, §201, Aug. 13, 1968, 82 Stat. 739, provided that: "Section 3 of the Act approved June 22, 1936 (Public Law Numbered 738, Seventy-fourth Congress) [this section], as amended by section 2 of the Act approved June 28, 1938 (Public Law Numbered 761, Seventy-fifth Congress) [section 701c–1 of this title], shall apply to all works authorized in this title except that for any channel improvement or channel rectification project, provisions (a), (b), and (c) of section 3 of said Act of June 22, 1936 [this section], shall apply thereto, except as otherwise provided by law. The authorization for any flood control project herein authorized by this Act [Pub. L. 90–483] requiring local cooperation shall expire five years from the date on which local interests are notified in writing by the Secretary of the Army or his designee of the requirements of local cooperation, unless said interests shall within said time furnish assurances satisfactory to the Secretary of the Army that the required cooperation will be furnished."

Similar provisions were contained in the following prior acts:

Nov. 7, 1966, Pub. L. 89–789, title II, §201, 80 Stat. 1418.
Oct. 27, 1965, Pub. L. 89–298, title II, §202, 79 Stat. 1074.
Sept. 3, 1954, ch. 1264, title II, §201, 68 Stat. 1256.
May 17, 1950, ch. 188, title II, §201, 64 Stat. 170.
June 30, 1948, ch. 771, title II, §201, 62 Stat. 1175.
July 24, 1946, ch. 596, §2, 60 Stat. 641.
Dec. 22, 1944, ch. 665, §3, 58 Stat. 889.

APPLICATION OF SECTION

Act June 28, 1938, ch. 795, §2, 52 Stat. 1215, provided that this section, as theretofore amended and therein further modified, should apply to all flood control projects, except as otherwise specifically provided by law. For modification of this section by that act, see section 701c–1 of this title.

MUSKINGUM RIVER VALLEY

Provisions of act June 28, 1938, ch. 795, §2, 52 Stat. 1215, referred to above, were extended to the Muskingum River Valley dams and reservoirs by section 4 of act Aug. 11, 1939, ch. 699, 53 Stat. 1414.

§701c–1. Acquirement of titles for certain projects and to lands, easements, rights-of-way; reimbursement of local agencies

In case of any dam and reservoir project, or channel improvement or channel rectification project for flood control, herein authorized or heretofore authorized by the Act of June 22, 1936, as amended, and sections 642a, 702a, 702a–1, 702a–2 to 702d, 702e to 702h, 702i to 702m, and 704 of this title, title to all lands, easements, and rights-of-way for such project shall be acquired by the United States or by States, political subdivisions thereof or other responsible local agencies and conveyed to the United States, and provisions of clauses (a), (b), and (c) of section 701c of this title shall not apply thereto. Notwithstanding any restrictions, limitations, or requirement of prior consent provided by any other Act, the Secretary of the Army is authorized and directed to acquire in the name of the United States title to all lands, easements, and rights-of-way necessary for any dam and reservoir project or channel improvement or channel rectification project for flood control, with funds heretofore or hereafter appropriated or made available for such projects, and States, political subdivisions thereof, or other responsible local agencies, shall be granted and reimbursed, from such funds, sums equivalent to actual expenditures deemed reasonable by the Secretary of the Army and the Chief of Engineers and made by them in acquiring lands, easements, and rights-of-way for any dam and reservoir project, or any channel improvement or channel rectification project for flood control heretofore or herein authorized: *Provided*, That no reimbursement shall be made for any indirect or speculative damages: *Provided further*, That lands, easements, and rights-of-way shall include lands on which dams, reservoirs, channel improvements, and channel rectifications are located; lands or flowage rights in reservoirs and highway, railway, and utility relocation: *Provided further*, That in all cases of the acquisition hereunder by the United States from the Los Angeles County Flood Control District or the Muskingum Watershed Conservancy District of lands, easements, or rights-of-way, wherein the written opinion of the Attorney General in favor of the validity of the title to such lands, easements, or rights-of-way is or may be required or authorized by law, the Attorney General may, in his discretion, base such opinion upon a certificate of title of the district from which said lands, easements, or rights-of-way are to be acquired accompanied by an agreement, duly executed by the district in conformity with the constitutions and laws of the State where the district in question is situated to indemnify the United States against all claims, liabilities, loss, expenses, and attorneys' fees of whatsoever kind or nature, resulting from or arising out of any defect or defects whatsoever in the title to any such lands, easements, or rights-of-way so conveyed to the United States, including all just compensation, costs, and expenses which may be incurred in any condemnation proceeding deemed necessary and instituted by the United States in order to perfect title to any such lands, easements, or rights-of-way.

(June 28, 1938, ch. 795, §2, 52 Stat. 1215; Aug. 11, 1939, ch. 699, §5, 53 Stat. 1415; July 26, 1947, ch. 343, title II, §205(a), 61 Stat. 501.)

REFERENCES IN TEXT

Herein, referred to in text, means act June 28, 1938, ch. 795, 75 Stat. 1215, as amended, popularly known as the Flood Control Act of June 28, 1938, which to the extent classified to the Code enacted sections 701b, 701b–1, 701b–2, 701c–1, 701f–1, 701i, 701j, 702a–1½, 702a–11, and 706 of this title. For complete classification of this Act to the Code, see Tables.

Act of June 22, 1936, referred to in text, is act June 22, 1936, ch. 688, 49 Stat. 1570, as amended, popularly known as the Flood Control Act of June 22, 1936, which to the extent classified to the Code enacted sections 701a, 701b, 701c, 701d to 701f, and 701h of this title. For complete classification of this Act to the Code, see Tables.

CODIFICATION

Section comprises last paragraph of section 2 of act June 28, 1938. First paragraph of such section 2 is referred to in an Application of Section note under section 701c of this title.

AMENDMENTS

1939—Act Aug. 11, 1939, inserted last proviso.

CHANGE OF NAME

Department of War designated Department of the Army and title of Secretary of War changed to Secretary of the Army by section 205(a) of act July 26, 1947, ch. 343, title II, 61 Stat. 501. Section 205(a) of act July 26, 1947, was repealed by section 53 of act Aug. 10, 1956, ch. 1041, 70A Stat. 641. Section 1 of act Aug. 10, 1956, enacted "Title 10, Armed Forces" which in sections 3010 to 3013 continued Department of the Army under administrative supervision of Secretary of the Army.

§ 701c–2. Acquisition and sale of land

The provisions of sections 593 to 595 of this title relating to river and harbor improvements are made applicable to works of flood control heretofore or hereafter authorized.

(Aug. 18, 1941, ch. 377, §6, 55 Stat. 650; Oct. 31, 1951, ch. 654, §3(6), 65 Stat. 708.)

AMENDMENTS

1951—Act Oct. 31, 1951, struck out "558a and" in the reference to other sections.

§ 701c–3. Lease receipts; payment of portion to States

75 per centum of all moneys received and deposited in the Treasury of the United States during any fiscal year on account of the leasing of lands acquired by the United States for flood control, navigation, and allied purposes, including the development of hydroelectric power, shall be paid at the end of such year by the Secretary of the Treasury to the State in which such property is situated, to be expended as the State legislature may prescribe for the benefit of public schools and public roads of the county, or counties, in which such property is situated, or for defraying any of the expenses of county government in such county or counties, including public obligations of levee and drainage districts for flood control and drainage improvements: *Provided*, That when such property is situated in more than one State or county, the distributive share to each from the proceeds of such property shall be proportional to its area therein. For the purposes of this section, the term "money" includes, but is not limited to, such bonuses, royalties and rentals (and any interest or other charge paid to the United States by reason of the late payment of any royalty, rent, bonus or other amount due to the United States) paid to the United States from a mineral lease issued under the authority of the Mineral Leasing Act for Acquired Lands [30 U.S.C. 351 et seq.] or paid to the United States from a mineral

lease in existence at the time of the acquisition of the land by the United States.

(Aug. 18, 1941, ch. 377, § 7, 55 Stat. 650; July 24, 1946, ch. 596, § 5, 60 Stat. 642; June 16, 1953, ch. 114, 67 Stat. 61; Sept. 3, 1954, ch. 1264, title II, § 206, 68 Stat. 1266; Pub. L. 102–486, title XXV, § 2506(c), Oct. 24, 1992, 106 Stat. 3107.)

REFERENCES IN TEXT

The Mineral Leasing Act for Acquired Lands, referred to in text, is act Aug. 7, 1947, ch. 513, 61 Stat. 913, as amended, which is classified generally to chapter 7 (§ 351 et seq.) of Title 30, Mineral Lands and Mining. For complete classification of this Act to the Code, see Short Title note set out under section 351 of Title 30 and Tables.

AMENDMENTS

1992—Pub. L. 102–486 inserted sentence at end defining term "money" for purposes of this section.

1954—Act Sept. 3, 1954, extended the 75 percent rental provision so as also to include moneys received and deposited with respect to the leasing of lands acquired for navigation and allied purposes.

1953—Act June 16, 1953, inserted "or for defraying any of the expenses of county government in such county or counties, including public obligations of levee and drainage districts for flood control and drainage improvements" after "situated".

1946—Act July 24, 1946, increased the percentage return to the States from 25 percent to 75 percent.

§ 701d. Compacts between States; consent of Congress

The consent of Congress is given to any two or more States to enter into compacts or agreements in connection with any project or operation authorized by this Act for flood control or the prevention of damage to life or property by reason of floods upon any stream or streams and their tributaries which lie in two or more such States, for the purpose of providing, in such manner and such proportion as may be agreed upon by such States and approved by the Secretary of the Army, funds for construction and maintenance, for the payment of damages, and for the purchase of rights-of-way, lands, and easements in connection with such project or operation. No such compact or agreement shall become effective without the further consent or ratification of Congress, except a compact or agreement which provides that all money to be expended pursuant thereto and all work to be performed thereunder shall be expended and performed by the Department of the Army, with the exception of such reasonable sums as may be reserved by the States entering into the compact or agreement for the purpose of collecting taxes and maintaining the necessary State organizations for carrying out the compact or agreement.

(June 22, 1936, ch. 688, § 4, 49 Stat. 1571; July 26, 1947, ch. 343, title II, § 205(a), 61 Stat. 501.)

REFERENCES IN TEXT

This Act, referred to in text, is act June 22, 1936, ch. 688, 49 Stat. 1570, as amended, popularly known as the Flood Control Act of June 22, 1936, which to the extent classified to the Code enacted sections 701a, 701b, 701c, 701d to 701f, and 701h of this title. For complete classification of this Act to the Code, see Tables. Portions of section 5 and sections 6 and 7 of act June 22, 1936, enumerating certain projects and operations with regard to flood control, were not classified to the Code.

CHANGE OF NAME

Department of War designated Department of the Army and title of Secretary of War changed to Secretary of the Army by section 205(a) of act July 26, 1947, ch. 343, title II, 61 Stat. 501. Section 205(a) of act July 26, 1947, was repealed by section 53 of act Aug. 10, 1956, ch. 1041, 70A Stat. 641. Section 1 of act Aug. 10, 1956, enacted "Title 10, Armed Forces" which in sections 3010 to 3013 continued Department of the Army under administrative supervision of Secretary of the Army.

§ 701e. Effect of act June 22, 1936, on provisions for Mississippi River and other projects

Nothing in this Act shall be construed as repealing or amending any provision of sections 702a, 702b to 702d, 702e to 702g, 702h, 702i, 702j, 702k, 702*l*, 702m, and 704 of this title. The authority conferred by this Act and any funds appropriated pursuant thereto for expenditure are supplemental to all other authority and appropriations relating to the departments or agencies concerned, and nothing in this Act shall be construed to limit or retard any department or agency in carrying out similar and related activities heretofore or hereafter authorized, or to limit the exercise of powers conferred on any department or agency by other provisions of law is[1] carrying out similar and related activities.

(June 22, 1936, ch. 688, § 8, 49 Stat. 1596.)

REFERENCES IN TEXT

This Act, referred to in text, is act June 22, 1936, ch. 688, 49 Stat. 1570, as amended, popularly known as the Flood Control Act of June 22, 1936, which to the extent classified to the Code enacted sections 701a, 701b, 701c, 701d to 701f, and 701h of this title. For complete classification of this Act to the Code, see Tables.

§ 701f. Authorization of appropriations

The sum of $310,000,000 is authorized to be appropriated for carrying out the improvements herein and the sum of $10,000,000 is authorized to be appropriated and expended in equal amounts by the Departments of the Army and Agriculture for carrying out any examinations and surveys provided for in this Act and other Acts of Congress.

(June 22, 1936, ch. 688, § 9, 49 Stat. 1596; July 26, 1947, ch. 343, title II, § 205(a), 61 Stat. 501.)

REFERENCES IN TEXT

"Herein", and "this Act", referred to in text, means act June 22, 1936, ch. 688, 49 Stat. 1570, as amended, popularly known as the Flood Control Act of June 22, 1936, which to the extent classified to the Code enacted sections 701a, 701b, 701c, 701d to 701f, and 701h of this title. For complete classification of this Act to the Code, see Tables. Portions of section 5 of act June 22, 1936, enumerating certain improvements with regard to flood control, and sections 6 and 7 of that act, relating to examinations and surveys, were not classified to the Code.

CODIFICATION

The first proviso, relating to a limitation upon the amount of expenditure during the fiscal year 1937, was deleted as executed and obsolete. The second proviso, relating to payment from funds available to the Works Progress Administration, was also omitted as executed and obsolete. The Works Progress Administration was renamed the Work Projects Administration by Reorg.

[1] So in original. Probably should be "in".

Plan No. 1 of 1939, §306, eff. July 1, 1939, 4 F.R. 2727, 53 Stat. 1423, set out in the Appendix to Title 5, Government Organization and Employees. Liquidation was ordered by President's letter of December 4, 1942, and appropriations for it authorized by act July 12, 1943, ch. 229, title I, 57 Stat. 540.

CHANGE OF NAME

Department of War designated Department of the Army and title of Secretary of War changed to Secretary of the Army by section 205(a) of act July 26, 1947, ch. 343, title II, 61 Stat. 501. Section 205(a) of act July 26, 1947, was repealed by section 53 of act Aug. 10, 1956, ch. 1041, 70A Stat. 641. Section 1 of act Aug. 10, 1956, enacted "Title 10, Armed Forces" which in sections 3010 to 3013 continued Department of the Army under administrative supervision of Secretary of the Army.

ADOPTION OF IMPROVEMENTS

Works of improvement adopted and authorized to be prosecuted are listed in section 5 of act June 22, 1936, ch. 688, 49 Stat. 1596, referred to in this section, as amended or supplemented by acts Aug. 28, 1937, ch. 877, §1, 50 Stat. 876; June 28, 1938, ch. 795, §4, 52 Stat. 1216; Aug. 11, 1939, ch. 699, §4, 53 Stat. 1414; Aug. 18, 1941, ch. 377, §3, 55 Stat. 639; Dec. 22, 1944, ch. 665, §10, 58 Stat. 891; July 24, 1946, ch. 596, §10, 60 Stat. 643.

AUTHORIZATION OF EXAMINATIONS AND SURVEYS

Localities at which preliminary examinations and surveys are authorized to be made are listed in acts June 22, 1936, ch. 688, §6, 49 Stat. 1592; Aug. 28, 1937, ch. 877, §5, 50 Stat. 877; and June 28, 1938, ch. 795, §6, 52 Stat. 1223; Aug. 11, 1939, ch. 699, §6, 53 Stat. 1415; Aug. 18, 1941, ch. 377, §4, 55 Stat. 648; Dec. 22, 1944, ch. 665, §11, 58 Stat. 903; July 24, 1946, ch. 596, §11, 60 Stat. 651.

CONTINUANCE OF EXAMINATIONS AND SURVEYS

Localities at which the continuance of examinations and surveys already undertaken is authorized are listed in act June 22, 1936, ch. 688, §7, 49 Stat. 1596.

§ 701f–1. Additional authorization

The sum of $375,000,000 is hereby authorized to be appropriated for carrying out the improvements herein over the five-year period ending June 30, 1944, and the sum of $10,000,000 additional is authorized to be appropriated and expended in equal amounts by the Departments of the Army and Agriculture for carrying out any examinations and surveys provided for in this Act and any other Acts of Congress, to be prosecuted by said Departments. The sum of $1,500,000 additional is authorized to be appropriated and expended by the Secretary of Energy for carrying out any examinations and surveys provided for in this Act or any other Acts of Congress, to be prosecuted by the said Secretary of Energy.

(June 28, 1938, ch. 795, §9, 52 Stat. 1226; July 26, 1947, ch. 343, title II, §205(a), 61 Stat. 501; Pub. L. 95–91, title III, §301(b), Aug. 4, 1977, 91 Stat. 578.)

REFERENCES IN TEXT

"Herein" and "this Act", referred to in text, mean act June 28, 1938, ch. 795, 52 Stat. 1215, as amended, popularly known as the Flood Control Act of June 28, 1938, which to the extent classified to the Code enacted sections 701b, 701b–1, 701b–2, 701c–1, 701f–1, 701i, 701j, 702a–1½, 702a–11, and 706 of this title. For complete classification of this Act to the Code, see Tables.

CHANGE OF NAME

Department of War designated Department of the Army and title of Secretary of War changed to Secretary of the Army by section 205(a) of act July 26, 1947, ch. 343, title II, 61 Stat. 501. Section 205(a) of act July 26, 1947, was repealed by section 53 of act Aug. 10, 1956, ch. 1041, 70A Stat. 641. Section 1 of act Aug. 10, 1956, enacted "Title 10, Armed Forces" which in sections 3010 to 3013 continued Department of the Army under administrative supervision of Secretary of the Army.

TRANSFER OF FUNCTIONS

"Secretary of Energy" substituted in text for "Federal Power Commission" on authority of Pub. L. 95–91, title III, §301(b), Aug. 4, 1977, 91 Stat. 577, which is classified to section 7151(b) of Title 42, The Public Health and Welfare.

For transfer of functions of Federal Power Commission, with certain reservations, to chairman of such Commission, see Reorg. Plan No. 9 of 1950, §§1, 2, eff. May 24, 1950, 15 F.R. 3175, 64 Stat. 1265, set out in the Appendix to Title 5, Government Organization and Employees.

ADDITIONAL AUTHORIZATION

Sections 15 and 17 of act July 24, 1946, ch. 596, 60 Stat. 653, provided:

"SEC. 15. That the sum of $772,000,000 is hereby authorized to be appropriated for carrying out improvements by the War Department [now Department of the Army], the sum of $10,000,000 additional is authorized to be appropriated and expended in equal amounts by the Departments of War [now Army] and Agriculture for carrying out any examination or survey provided for in this Act and any other Acts of Congress to be prosecuted by said Departments.

"SEC. 17. That the $5,000,000 authorized to be appropriated in section 10 of the Flood Control Act approved August 18, 1941 [set out as a note under this section], is reauthorized to be appropriated, and the sum of $20,000,000 additional is authorized to be appropriated, for expenditure by the Department of Agriculture for the prosecution of the works of improvement authorized to be carried out by that Department by the Flood Control Act of December 22, 1944 [act Dec. 22, 1944, ch. 665, 58 Stat. 887]."

Act Aug. 18, 1941, ch. 377, §10, 55 Stat. 651, provided as follows: "That the sum of $275,000,000 is hereby authorized to be appropriated for carrying out the improvements herein, the sum of $10,000,000 additional is authorized to be appropriated and expended in equal amounts by the Departments of War [now Army] and Agriculture for carrying out any examinations and surveys provided for in this Act and any other Acts of Congress to be prosecuted by said departments. There is also hereby authorized to be appropriated for expenditure by the Department of Agriculture in carrying on works of improvement of the character specified in section 7 of the Flood Control Act of June 28, 1938 [section 701b–1 of this title], and which the Department is not otherwise authorized to undertake, such additional sums, not to exceed $5,000,000, as may be necessary for that purpose. All appropriations necessary for operation and maintenance of flood-control works authorized by law to be operated and maintained by the United States are hereby authorized."

§ 701f–2. Funds for specific and authorized projects merged with and accounted for under regular annual appropriation

Funds on and after May 17, 1950, appropriated for a specific and heretofore authorized project for a river, harbor, or flood-control works shall be merged with and be accounted for under the regular annual appropriation title applicable to such item.

(May 17, 1950, ch. 188, title II, §207, 64 Stat. 182.)

§ 701f–3. Expenditure in watersheds of funds appropriated for flood prevention purposes

On and after May 23, 1955, the funds appropriated for flood prevention purposes may be expended in watersheds heretofore authorized by section 13 of the Flood Control Act of December 22, 1944, as amended, for necessary measures for the prevention of erosion, floodwater, and sediment damages, including gully control, floodwater detention, and floodway structures, in areas other than those over which the Department of the Army has jurisdiction and responsibility, and where the Army does have jurisdiction and responsibility, may enter into agreements with the Army to carry out jointly the measures heretofore set out and in areas where the Secretary is authorized to purchase land rights for structural measures, the Secretary in lieu of such acquisition, may reimburse local organizations for such proportionate share of the cost of land rights furnished by local organizations as the Secretary deems equitable in consideration of the national interest.

(May 23, 1955, ch. 43, title I, § 101, 69 Stat. 54; Pub. L. 91–566, title I, § 101, Dec. 22, 1970, 84 Stat. 1484.)

REFERENCES IN TEXT

Section 13 of the Flood Control Act of December 22, 1944, referred to in text, is section 13 of act Dec. 22, 1944, ch. 665, 58 Stat. 905, which was not classified to the Code. Such section 13 authorized the following works of improvement for run-off and waterflow retardation, and soil erosion prevention: Los Angeles River Basin; Santa Ynez River Watershed; Trinity River Basin (Texas); Little Tallahatchie River Watershed; Yazoo River Watershed; Coosa River Watershed (above Rome, Georgia); Little Sioux River Watershed; Potomac River Watershed; Buffalo Creek Watershed (New York); Colorado River Watershed (Texas), and Washita River Watershed.

AMENDMENTS

1970—Pub. L. 91–566 empowered the Secretary, where the Army does have jurisdiction and responsibility, to enter into agreements with the Army to carry out jointly the measures heretofore set out and in areas where the Secretary is authorized to purchase land rights for structural measures, permitted the Secretary in lieu of such acquisition, to reimburse local organizations for such proportionate share of the cost of land rights furnished as the Secretary deems equitable in consideration of the national interest.

§ 701g. Removal of obstructions; clearing channels

The Secretary of the Army is authorized to allot not to exceed $7,500,000 from any appropriations heretofore or hereafter made for any one fiscal year for flood control, for removing accumulated snags and other debris, and clearing and straightening the channel in navigable streams and tributaries thereof, when in the opinion of the Chief of Engineers such work is advisable in the interest of flood control: *Provided*, That not more than $500,000 shall be expended for this purpose for any single tributary from the appropriations for any one fiscal year.

(Aug. 28, 1937, ch. 877, § 2, 50 Stat. 877; Aug. 11, 1939, ch. 699, § 1, 53 Stat. 1414; Aug. 18, 1941, ch. 377, § 9, 55 Stat. 650; July 24, 1946, ch. 596, § 13, 60 Stat. 652; July 26, 1947, ch. 343, title II, § 205(a), 61 Stat. 501; Sept. 3, 1954, ch. 1264, title II, § 208, 68 Stat. 1266; Pub. L. 93–251, title I, § 26, Mar. 7, 1974, 88 Stat. 20; Pub. L. 99–662, title IX, § 915(b), Nov. 17, 1986, 100 Stat. 4191.)

AMENDMENTS

1986—Pub. L. 99–662 substituted "$7,500,000" for "$5,000,000" and "$500,000" for "$250,000".

1974—Pub. L. 93–251 substituted "$5,000,000" for "$2,000,000" and "$250,000" for "$100,000".

1954—Act Sept. 3, 1954, substituted "$2,000,000" for "$1,000,000" and "$100,000" for "$50,000".

1946—Act July 24, 1946, substituted "$1,000,000" for "$500,000" and "$50,000" for "$25,000".

1941—Act Aug. 18, 1941, substituted "$500,000" for "$300,000".

1939—Act Aug. 11, 1939, authorized Secretary to allot instead of to approve amount for flood control and limited amount allotted instead of expended for any single tributary.

CHANGE OF NAME

Department of War designated Department of the Army and title of Secretary of War changed to Secretary of the Army by section 205(a) of act July 26, 1947, ch. 343, title II, 61 Stat. 501. Section 205(a) of act July 26, 1947, was repealed by section 53 of act Aug. 10, 1956, ch. 1041, 70A Stat. 641. Section 1 of act Aug. 10, 1956, enacted "Title 10, Armed Forces" which in sections 3010 to 3013 continued Department of the Army under administrative supervision of Secretary of the Army.

EFFECTIVE DATE OF 1986 AMENDMENT

Amendment by Pub. L. 99–662 not applicable to any project under contract for construction on Nov. 17, 1986, see section 915(i) of Pub. L. 99–662, set out as a note under section 426g of this title.

§ 701h. Contributions by States and political subdivisions

The Secretary of the Army is authorized to receive from States and political subdivisions thereof, such funds as may be contributed by them to be expended in connection with funds appropriated by the United States for any authorized flood control or environmental restoration work whenever such work and expenditure may be considered by the Secretary of the Army, on recommendation of the Chief of Engineers, as advantageous in the public interest, and the plans for any reservoir project may, in the discretion of the Secretary of the Army, on recommendation of the Chief of Engineers, be modified to provide additional storage capacity for domestic water supply or other conservation storage, on condition that the cost of such increased storage capacity is contributed by local agencies and that the local agencies agree to utilize such additional storage capacity in a manner consistent with Federal uses and purposes: *Provided*, That when contributions made by States and political subdivisions thereof, are in excess of the actual cost of the work contemplated and properly chargeable to such contributions, such excess contributions may, with the approval of the Secretary of the Army, be returned to the proper representatives of the contributing interests.

(June 22, 1936, ch. 688, § 5, as added July 19, 1937, ch. 511, § 1, 50 Stat. 518; July 26, 1947, ch. 343, title II, § 205(a), 61 Stat. 501; Pub. L. 106–53, title II, § 203, Aug. 17, 1999, 113 Stat. 285.)

CODIFICATION

Provisions of section 5 of act June 22, 1936, authorizing enumerated works of improvement were not classified to the Code.

AMENDMENTS

1999—Pub. L. 106–53 inserted "or environmental restoration" after "flood control".

CHANGE OF NAME

Department of War designated Department of the Army and title of Secretary of War changed to Secretary of the Army by section 205(a) of act July 26, 1947, ch. 343, title II, 61 Stat. 501. Section 205(a) of act July 26, 1947, was repealed by section 53 of act Aug. 10, 1956, ch. 1041, 70A Stat. 641. Section 1 of act Aug. 10, 1956, enacted "Title 10, Armed Forces" which in sections 3010 to 3013 continued Department of the Army under administrative supervision of Secretary of the Army.

§ 701h–1. Contributions by States and political subdivisions for immediate use on authorized flood-control work; repayment

Whenever any State or political subdivision thereof shall offer to advance funds for a flood-control project duly adopted and authorized by law the Secretary of the Army may in his discretion, receive such funds and expend the same in the immediate prosecution of such work. The Secretary of the Army is authorized and directed to repay without interest, from appropriations which may be provided by Congress for flood-control work, the moneys so contributed and expended: *Provided, however*, That no repayment of funds which may be contributed for the purpose of meeting any conditions of local cooperation imposed by Congress, or under the authority of section 701h of this title, shall be made.

(Oct. 15, 1940, ch. 884, 54 Stat. 1176; July 26, 1947, ch. 343, title II, § 205(a), 61 Stat. 501.)

CHANGE OF NAME

Department of War designated Department of the Army and title of Secretary of War changed to Secretary of the Army by section 205(a) of act July 26, 1947, ch. 343, title II, 61 Stat. 501. Section 205(a) of act July 26, 1947, was repealed by section 53 of act Aug. 10, 1956, ch. 1041, 70A Stat. 641. Section 1 of act Aug. 10, 1956, enacted "Title 10, Armed Forces" which in sections 3010 to 3013 continued Department of the Army under administrative supervision of Secretary of the Army.

§ 701i. Elimination from protection of areas subject to evacuation

In any case where the construction cost of levees or flood walls included in any authorized project can be substantially reduced by the evacuation of a portion or all of the area proposed to be protected and by the elimination of that portion or all of the area from the protection to be afforded by the project, the Chief of Engineers may modify the plan of said project so as to eliminate said portion or all of the area: *Provided*, That a sum not substantially exceeding the amount thus saved in construction cost may be expended by the Chief of Engineers, or in his discretion may be transferred to any other appropriate Federal agency for expenditure, toward the evacuation of the locality eliminated from protection and the rehabilitation of the persons so evacuated: *And provided further*, That the Chief of Engineers may, if he so desires, enter into agreement with States, local agencies, or the individuals concerned for the accomplishment by them, of such evacuation and rehabilitation and for their reimbursement from said sum for expenditures actually incurred by them for this purpose.

(June 28, 1938, ch. 795, § 3, 52 Stat. 1216.)

§ 701j. Installation in dams of facilities for future development of hydroelectric power

Penstocks or other similar facilities adapted to possible future use in the development of hydroelectric power shall be installed in any dam herein authorized when approved by the Secretary of the Army upon the recommendation of the Chief of Engineers and of the Secretary of Energy.

(June 28, 1938, ch. 795, § 4, 52 Stat. 1216; July 26, 1947, ch. 343, title II, § 205(a), 61 Stat. 501; Pub. L. 95–91, title III, § 301(b), Aug. 4, 1977, 91 Stat. 578.)

REFERENCES IN TEXT

Herein, referred to in text, means act June 28, 1938, ch. 795, 52 Stat. 1215, as amended, popularly known as the Flood Control Act of June 28, 1938, which to the extent classified to the Code enacted sections 701b, 701b–1, 701b–2, 701c–1, 701f–1, 701i, 701j, 702a–1½, 702a–11, and 706 of this title. For complete classification of this Act to the Code, see Tables.

CHANGE OF NAME

Department of War designated Department of the Army and title of Secretary of War changed to Secretary of the Army by section 205(a) of act July 26, 1947, ch. 343, title II, 61 Stat. 501. Section 205(a) of act July 26, 1947, was repealed by section 53 of act Aug. 10, 1956, ch. 1041, 70A Stat. 641. Section 1 of act Aug. 10, 1956, enacted "Title 10, Armed Forces" which in sections 3010 to 3013 continued Department of the Army under administrative supervision of Secretary of the Army.

TRANSFER OF FUNCTIONS

"Secretary of Energy" substituted in text for "Federal Power Commission" on authority of Pub. L. 95–91, title III, § 301(b), which is classified to section 7151(b) of Title 42, The Public Health and Welfare.

For transfer of functions of Federal Power Commission, with certain reservations, to chairman of such Commission, see Reorg. Plan No. 9 of 1950, §§ 1, 2, eff. May 24, 1950, 15 F.R. 3175, 64 Stat. 1265, set out in the Appendix to Title 5, Government Organization and Employees.

SIMILAR PROVISIONS

Similar provisions with reference to dams authorized in such acts were contained in acts Aug. 18, 1941, ch. 377, § 3, 55 Stat. 639; Dec. 22, 1944, ch. 665, § 10, 58 Stat. 891; July 24, 1946, ch. 596, § 10, 60 Stat. 643.

§ 701k. Crediting reimbursements for lost, stolen, or damaged property

Any amounts collected from any person, persons, or corporations as a reimbursement for lost, stolen, or damaged property, purchased in connection with river and harbor or flood control work prosecuted under the direction of the Secretary of the Army and the supervision of the Chief of Engineers, whether collected in cash or by deduction from amounts otherwise due such person, persons, or corporations, on and after June 20, 1938, shall be credited in each case to the appropriation that bore the cost of purchase, repair, or replacement of the lost, stolen, or damaged property.

(June 20, 1938, ch. 535, § 4, 52 Stat. 805; July 26, 1947, ch. 343, title II, § 205(a), 61 Stat. 501.)

CODIFICATION

Section is also set out as section 571 of this title.

CHANGE OF NAME

Department of War designated Department of the Army and title of Secretary of War changed to Secretary of the Army by section 205(a) of act July 26, 1947, ch. 343, title II, 61 Stat. 501. Section 205(a) of act July 26, 1947, was repealed by section 53 of act Aug. 10, 1956, ch. 1041, 70A Stat. 641. Section 1 of act Aug. 10, 1956, enacted "Title 10, Armed Forces" which in sections 3010 to 3013 continued Department of the Army under administrative supervision of Secretary of the Army.

§§ 701*l*, 701*l*–1. Repealed. Pub. L. 89–554, § 8(a), Sept. 6, 1966, 80 Stat. 650, 656

Section 701*l*, act June 20, 1938, ch. 535, § 5, 52 Stat. 805, related to employment of retired civil service employees. See section 3323 of Title 5, Government Organization and Employees.

Section 701*l*–1, act May 17, 1950, ch. 188, title II, § 214, 64 Stat. 184, provided that section 947 of former Title 5, Executive Departments and Government Officers and Employees, should not be construed to prevent employment of additional personnel.

§ 701m. Insufficient Congressional authorization; preparations for and modification of project

In any case where the total authorization for a project heretofore or hereafter authorized by Congress is not sufficient to complete plans that may have been made the Chief of Engineers is authorized in his discretion to plan and make expenditures on preparations for the project, such as the purchase of lands, easements, and rights-of-way; readjustments of roads, railroads, and other utilities; removal of towns, cemeteries, and dwellings from reservoir sites; and the construction of foundations. The Chief of Engineers is also authorized in his discretion to modify the plan for any dam or other work heretofore or hereafter authorized so that such dam or work will be smaller than originally planned with a view to completing a useful improvement within an authorization: *Provided*, That the smaller structure shall be located on the chosen site so that it will be feasible at some future time to enlarge the work in order to permit the full utilization of the site for all purposes of conservation such as flood control, navigation, reclamation, the development of hydroelectric power, and the abatement of pollution.

(Aug. 18, 1941, ch. 377, § 2, 55 Stat. 638.)

§ 701n. Emergency response to natural disasters

(a) Emergency fund

(1) There is authorized an emergency fund to be expended in preparation for emergency response to any natural disaster, in flood fighting and rescue operations, or in the repair or restoration of any flood control work threatened or destroyed by flood, including the strengthening, raising, extending, or other modification thereof as may be necessary in the discretion of the Chief of Engineers for the adequate functioning of the work for flood control, or in implementation of nonstructural alternatives to the repair or restoration of such flood control work if requested by the non-Federal sponsor; in the emergency protection of federally authorized hurricane or shore protection being threatened when in the discretion of the Chief of Engineers such protection is warranted to protect against imminent and substantial loss to life and property; in the repair and restoration of any federally authorized hurricane or shore protective structure damaged or destroyed by wind, wave, or water action of other than an ordinary nature when in the discretion of the Chief of Engineers such repair and restoration is warranted for the adequate functioning of the structure for hurricane or shore protection. The emergency fund may also be expended for emergency dredging for restoration of authorized project depths for Federal navigable channels and waterways made necessary by flood, drought, earthquake, or other natural disasters. In any case in which the Chief of Engineers is otherwise performing work under this section in an area for which the Governor of the affected State has requested a determination that an emergency exists or a declaration that a major disaster exists under the Disaster Relief and Emergency Assistance Act [42 U.S.C. 5121 et seq.], the Chief of Engineers is further authorized to perform on public and private lands and waters for a period of ten days following the Governor's request any emergency work made necessary by such emergency or disaster which is essential for the preservation of life and property, including, but not limited to, channel clearance, emergency shore protection, clearance and removal of debris and wreckage endangering public health and safety, and temporary restoration of essential public facilities and services. The Chief of Engineers, in the exercise of his discretion, is further authorized to provide emergency supplies of clean water, on such terms as he determines to be advisable, to any locality which he finds is confronted with a source of contaminated water causing or likely to cause a substantial threat to the public health and welfare of the inhabitants of the locality. The appropriation of such moneys for the initial establishment of this fund and for its replenishment on an annual basis, is authorized: *Provided*, That pending the appropriation of sums to such emergency fund, the Secretary of the Army may allot, from existing flood-control appropriations, such sums as may be necessary for the immediate prosecution of the work herein authorized, such appropriations to be reimbursed from the appropriation herein authorized when made. The Chief of Engineers is authorized, in the prosecution of work in connection with rescue operations, or in conducting other flood emergency work, to acquire on a rental basis such motor vehicles, including passenger cars and buses, as in his discretion are deemed necessary.

(2) In preparing a cost and benefit feasibility assessment for any emergency project described in paragraph (1), the Chief of Engineers shall consider the benefits to be gained by such project for the protection of—

(A) residential establishments;

(B) commercial establishments, including the protection of inventory; and

(C) agricultural establishments, including the protection of crops.

(b) Emergency supplies of drinking water; drought; well construction and water transportation

(1) The Secretary, upon a written request for assistance under this paragraph made by any farmer, rancher, or political subdivision within a distressed area, and after a determination by the Secretary that (A) as a result of the drought such farmer, rancher, or political subdivision has an inadequate supply of water, (B) an adequate supply of water can be made available to such farmer, rancher, or political subdivision through the construction of a well, and (C) as a result of the drought such well could not be constructed by a private business, the Secretary, subject to paragraph (3) of this subsection, may enter into an agreement with such farmer, rancher, or political subdivision for the construction of such well.

(2) The Secretary, upon a written request for assistance under this paragraph made by any farmer, rancher, or political subdivision within a distressed area, and after a determination by the Secretary that as a result of the drought such farmer, rancher, or political subdivision has an inadequate supply of water and water cannot be obtained by such farmer, rancher, or political subdivision, the Secretary may transport water to such farmer, rancher, or political subdivision by methods which include, but are not limited to, small-diameter emergency water lines and tank trucks, until such time as the Secretary determines that an adequate supply of water is available to such farmer, rancher, or political subdivision.

(3)(A) Any agreement entered into by the Secretary pursuant to paragraph (1) of this subsection shall require the farmer, rancher, or political subdivision for whom the well is constructed to pay to the United States the reasonable cost of such construction, with interest, over such number of years, not to exceed thirty, as the Secretary deems appropriate. The rate of interest shall be that rate which the Secretary determines would apply if the amount to be repaid was a loan made pursuant to section 636(b)(2) of title 15.

(B) The Secretary shall not construct any well pursuant to this subsection unless the farmer, rancher, or political subdivision for whom the well is being constructed has obtained, prior to construction, all necessary State and local permits.

(4) The Federal share for the transportation of water pursuant to paragraph (2) of this subsection shall be 100 per centum.

(5) For purposes of this subsection—

(A) the term "construction" includes construction, reconstruction, or repair;

(B) the term "distressed area" means an area which the Secretary determines due to drought conditions has an inadequate water supply which is causing, or is likely to cause, a substantial threat to the health and welfare of the inhabitants of the area including threat of damage or loss of property;

(C) the term "political subdivision" means a city, town, borough, county, parish, district, association, or other public body created by or pursuant to State law and having jurisdiction over the water supply of such public body;

(D) the term "reasonable cost" means the lesser of (i) the cost to the Secretary of constructing a well pursuant to this subsection exclusive of the cost of transporting equipment used in the construction of wells, or (ii) the cost to a private business of constructing such well;

(E) the term "Secretary" means the Secretary of the Army, acting through the Chief of Engineers; and

(F) the term "State" means a State, the District of Columbia, the Commonwealth of Puerto Rico, the Virgin Islands, Guam, American Samoa, and the Trust Territory of the Pacific Islands.

(c) Levee owners manual

(1) In general

Not later than 1 year after October 12, 1996, in accordance with chapter 5 of title 5, the Secretary of the Army shall prepare a manual describing the maintenance and upkeep responsibilities that the Corps of Engineers requires of a non-Federal interest in order for the non-Federal interest to receive Federal assistance under this section. The Secretary shall provide a copy of the manual at no cost to each non-Federal interest that is eligible to receive Federal assistance under this section.

(2) Authorization of appropriations

There is authorized to be appropriated $1,000,000 to carry out this subsection.

(3) Definitions

In this subsection, the following definitions apply:

(A) Maintenance and upkeep

The term "maintenance and upkeep" means all maintenance and general upkeep of a levee performed on a regular and consistent basis that is not repair and rehabilitation.

(B) Repair and rehabilitation

The term "repair and rehabilitation"—

(i) means the repair or rebuilding of a levee or other flood control structure, after the structure has been damaged by a flood, to the level of protection provided by the structure before the flood; but

(ii) does not include—

(I) any improvement to the structure; or

(II) repair or rebuilding described in clause (i) if, in the normal course of usage, the structure becomes structurally unsound and is no longer fit to provide the level of protection for which the structure was designed.

(Aug. 18, 1941, ch. 377, §5, 55 Stat. 650; July 24, 1946, ch. 596, §12, 60 Stat. 652; July 26, 1947, ch. 343, title II, §205(a), 61 Stat. 501; June 30, 1948, ch. 771, title II, §206, 62 Stat. 1182; May 17, 1950, ch. 188, title II, §210, 64 Stat. 183; June 28, 1955, ch. 194, 69 Stat. 186; Pub. L. 87–874, title II, §206, Oct. 23, 1962, 76 Stat. 1194; Pub. L. 93–251, title I, §82, Mar. 7, 1974, 88 Stat. 34; Pub. L. 95–51, §2, June 20, 1977, 91 Stat. 233; Pub. L. 99–662, title IX, §917, Nov. 17, 1986, 100 Stat. 4192; Pub. L. 100–45, §9, May 27, 1987, 101 Stat. 323; Pub. L. 100–707, title

I, § 109(m), Nov. 23, 1988, 102 Stat. 4709; Pub. L. 101–640, title III, § 302, Nov. 28, 1990, 104 Stat. 4633; Pub. L. 104–303, title II, § 202(e), (f), Oct. 12, 1996, 110 Stat. 3675.)

REFERENCES IN TEXT

The Disaster Relief and Emergency Assistance Act, referred to in subsec. (a)(1), is Pub. L. 93–288, May 22, 1974, 88 Stat. 143, as amended, known as the Robert T. Stafford Disaster Relief and Emergency Assistance Act, which is classified principally to chapter 68 (§ 5121 et seq.) of Title 42, The Public Health and Welfare. For complete classification of this Act to the Code, see Short Title note set out under section 5121 of Title 42 and Tables.

AMENDMENTS

1996—Subsec. (a)(1). Pub. L. 104–303, § 202(e), in first sentence, inserted ", or in implementation of nonstructural alternatives to the repair or restoration of such flood control work if requested by the non-Federal sponsor".

Subsec. (c). Pub. L. 104–303, § 202(f), added subsec. (c).

1990—Subsec. (a)(1). Pub. L. 101–640 substituted "preparation for emergency response to any natural disaster" for "flood emergency preparation" and inserted provision permitting the emergency fund to be used for emergency dredging for restoration of authorized depths for Federal navigable channels and waterways made necessary by flood, drought, earthquake, or other natural disasters.

1988—Subsec. (a)(1). Pub. L. 100–707 substituted "and Emergency Assistance Act" for "Act of 1974".

1987—Subsec. (a). Pub. L. 100–45 designated existing provisions as par. (1) and added par. (2).

1986—Subsec. (a). Pub. L. 99–662 inserted provision relating to authority of the Chief of Engineers, when the Governor of an affected State requests a determination that an emergency or major disaster exists, to perform on public and private lands and waters, for a period of ten days following the Governor's request, any emergency work made necessary by such emergency or disaster which is essential for the preservation of life and property, and substituted "clean water" for "clean drinking water" and "contaminated water" for "contaminated drinking water".

1977—Pub. L. 95–51 designated existing provisions as subsec. (a) and added subsec. (b).

1974—Pub. L. 93–251 struck out limitation of emergency fund to $15,000,000, provided for emergency supplies of clean drinking water to localities confronted with source of contaminated drinking water, and substituted in proviso "of sums to such emergency fund" for "of said sum".

1962—Pub. L. 87–874 authorized expenditures from the emergency fund for the protection of federally authorized hurricane or shore protection being threatened when such is warranted to protect against imminent and substantial loss to life and property, and for the repair and restoration of any such federally authorized hurricane or shore protective structure damaged or destroyed by wind or water action of an extraordinary nature when such is warranted for the adequate functioning of the structure for hurricane or shore protection.

1955—Act June 28, 1955, authorized expenditure for flood emergency preparation and eliminated the requirement of maintenance of flood control works threatened by flood.

1950—Act May 17, 1950, expanded scope of work considered under emergency repairs to flood-control structures, and substituted "$15,000,000" for "$2,000,000".

1948—Act June 30, 1948, inserted provisions relating to the strengthening, extending, or modification of flood-control works.

1946—Act July 24, 1946, substituted "$2,000,000" for "$1,000,000".

CHANGE OF NAME

Department of War designated Department of the Army and title of Secretary of War changed to Secretary of the Army by section 205(a) of act July 26, 1947, ch. 343, title II, 61 Stat. 501. Section 205(a) of act July 26, 1947, was repealed by section 53 of act Aug. 10, 1956, ch. 1041, 70A Stat. 641. Section 1 of act Aug. 10, 1956, enacted "Title 10, Armed Forces" which in sections 3010 to 3013 continued Department of the Army under administrative supervision of Secretary of the Army.

TERMINATION OF TRUST TERRITORY OF THE PACIFIC ISLANDS

For termination of Trust Territory of the Pacific Islands, see note set out preceding section 1681 of Title 48, Territories and Insular Possessions.

VEGETATION MANAGEMENT GUIDELINES

Section 202(g) of Pub. L. 104–303 provided that:

"(1) REVIEW.—The Secretary shall undertake a comprehensive review of the current policy guidelines on vegetation management for levees. The review shall examine current policies in view of the varied interests in providing flood control, preserving, protecting, and enhancing natural resources, protecting the rights of Native Americans pursuant to treaty and statute, and such other factors as the Secretary considers appropriate.

"(2) COOPERATION AND CONSULTATION.—The review under this section [subsection] shall be undertaken in cooperation with interested Federal agencies and in consultation with interested representatives of State and local governments and the public.

"(3) REVISION OF GUIDELINES.—Based upon the results of the review, the Secretary shall revise, not later than 270 days after the date of the enactment of this Act [Oct. 12, 1996], the policy guidelines so as to provide a coherent and coordinated policy for vegetation management for levees. Such revised guidelines shall address regional variations in levee management and resource needs and shall be incorporated in the manual proposed under section 5(c) of such Act of August 18, 1941 (33 U.S.C. 701n[(c)])."

§ 701*o*. Omitted

CODIFICATION

Section, act June 30, 1948, ch. 771, title II, § 202, 62 Stat. 1175, related to conditions precedent on unauthorized projects and modifications. Similar provisions were contained in act July 24, 1946, ch. 596, § 2, 60 Stat. 641. See section 701b–8 of this title.

§ 701p. Railroad bridge alterations at Federal expense

On and after July 24, 1946, for authorized flood protection projects which include alterations of railroad bridges the Chief of Engineers is authorized to include at Federal expense the necessary alterations of railroad bridges and approaches in connection therewith.

(July 24, 1946, ch. 596, § 3, 60 Stat. 642.)

§ 701q. Repair and protection of highways, railroads, and utilities damaged by operation of dams or reservoir

Whenever the Chief of Engineers shall find that any highway, railway, or utility has been or is being damaged or destroyed by reason of the operation of any dam or reservoir project under the control of the Department of the Army, he may utilize any funds available for the construction, maintenance, or operation of the project involved for the repair, relocation, restoration, or protection of such highway, railway, or utility: *Provided*, That this section shall not apply to highways, railways, and utilities previously provided for by the Department of the Army, unless the Chief of Engineers determines that the actual damage has or will exceed that for which provision had previously been made.

(July 24, 1946, ch. 596, §9, 60 Stat. 643; July 26, 1947, ch. 343, title II, §205(a), 61 Stat. 501.)

CHANGE OF NAME

Department of War designated Department of the Army and title of Secretary of War changed to Secretary of the Army by section 205(a) of act July 26, 1947, ch. 343, title II, 61 Stat. 501. Section 205(a) of act July 26, 1947, was repealed by section 53 of act Aug. 10, 1956, ch. 1041, 70A Stat. 641. Section 1 of act Aug. 10, 1956, enacted "Title 10, Armed Forces" which in sections 3010 to 3013 continued Department of the Army under administrative supervision of Secretary of the Army.

§701r. Protection of highways, bridge approaches, public works, and nonprofit public services

The Secretary of the Army is authorized to allot from any appropriations heretofore or hereafter made for flood control, not to exceed $15,000,000 per year, for the construction, repair, restoration, and modification of emergency streambank and shoreline protection works to prevent damage to highways, bridge approaches, and public works, churches, hospitals, schools, and other nonprofit public services, when in the opinion of the Chief of Engineers such work is advisable: *Provided*, That not more than $1,500,000 shall be allotted for this purpose at any single locality from the appropriations for any one fiscal year.

(July 24, 1946, ch. 596, §14, 60 Stat. 653; July 26, 1947, ch. 343, title II, §205(a), 61 Stat. 501; Pub. L. 93–251, title I, §27, Mar. 7, 1974, 88 Stat. 20; Pub. L. 99–662, title IX, §915(c), Nov. 17, 1986, 100 Stat. 4191; Pub. L. 104–303, title II, §219, Oct. 12, 1996, 110 Stat. 3696; Pub. L. 110–114, title II, §2023, Nov. 8, 2007, 121 Stat. 1078.)

AMENDMENTS

2007—Pub. L. 110–114 substituted "$1,500,000" for "$1,000,000".

1996—Pub. L. 104–303 substituted "$15,000,000" for "$12,500,000" and "$1,000,000" for "$500,000".

1986—Pub. L. 99–662 substituted "$12,500,000" for "$10,000,000" and "$500,000" for "$250,000".

1974—Pub. L. 93–251 substituted "$10,000,000" for "$1,000,000", "$250,000" for "$50,000", and "construction, repair, restoration, and modification of emergency streambank and shoreline protection works to prevent flood damages to highways, bridge approaches, and public works, churches, hospitals, schools, and other nonprofit public services," for "construction of emergency bank-protection works to prevent flood damages to highways, bridge approaches, and public works,".

CHANGE OF NAME

Department of War designated Department of the Army and title of Secretary of War changed to Secretary of the Army by section 205(a) of act July 26, 1947, ch. 343, title II, 61 Stat. 501. Section 205(a) of act July 26, 1947, was repealed by section 53 of act Aug. 10, 1956, ch. 1041, 70A Stat. 641. Section 1 of act Aug. 10, 1956, enacted "Title 10, Armed Forces" which in sections 3010 to 3013 continued Department of the Army under administrative supervision of Secretary of the Army.

EFFECTIVE DATE OF 1986 AMENDMENT

Amendment by Pub. L. 99–662 not applicable to any project under contract for construction on Nov. 17, 1986, see section 915(i) of Pub. L. 99–662, set out as a note under section 426g of this title.

§701r–1. Utilization of public roads

(a) Definitions

When used in this section—

(1) The term "Agency" means the Corps of Engineers, United States Army or the Bureau of Reclamation, United States Department of the Interior, whichever has jurisdiction over the project concerned.

(2) The term "head of the Agency concerned" means the Chief of Engineers or the Commissioner, Bureau of Reclamation, or their respective designees.

(3) The term "water resources projects to be constructed in the future" includes all projects not yet actually under construction, and, to the extent of work remaining to be completed, includes projects presently under construction where road relocations or identifiable components thereof are not complete as of the date of this section.

(4) The term "time of the taking" is the date of the relocation agreement, the date of the filing of a condemnation proceeding, or a date agreed upon between the parties as the date of taking.

(b) Improvement, reconstruction, and maintenance

Whenever, in connection with the construction of any authorized flood control, navigation, irrigation, or multiple purpose project for the development of water resources, the head of the Agency concerned determines it to be in the public interest to utilize existing public roads as a means of providing access to such projects during construction, such Agency may improve, reconstruct, and maintain such roads and may contract with the local authority having jurisdiction over the roads to accomplish the necessary work. The accomplishment of such work of improvement may be carried out with or without obtaining any interest in the land on which the road is located in accordance with mutual agreement between the parties: *Provided*, (1) That the head of the Agency concerned determines that such work would result in a saving in Federal cost as opposed to the cost of providing a new access road at Federal expense, (2) that, at the completion of construction, the head of the Agency concerned will, if necessary, restore the road to at least as good condition as prior to the beginning of utilization for access during construction, and (3) that, at the completion of construction, the responsibility of the Agency for improvement, reconstruction, and maintenance shall cease.

(c) Replacement roads; construction to higher standards

For water resources projects to be constructed in the future, when the taking by the Federal Government of an existing public road necessitates replacement, the substitute provided will, as nearly as practicable, serve in the same manner and reasonably as well as the existing road. The head of the agency concerned is authorized to construct such substitute roads to the design standards which the State or owning political division would use in constructing a new road under similar conditions of geography and under similar traffic loads (present and projected). In any case where a State or political subdivision thereof requests that such a substitute road be constructed to a higher standard than that provided for in the preceding provisions of this subsection, and pays, prior to commencement of such construction, the additional costs involved due to such higher standard, such agency head is authorized to construct such road to such higher standard. Federal costs under the provisions of this subsection shall be part of the nonreimbursable project costs.

(Pub. L. 86–645, title II, § 207, July 14, 1960, 74 Stat. 500; Pub. L. 87–874, title II, § 208, Oct. 23, 1962, 76 Stat. 1196; Pub. L. 93–251, title I, § 13, Mar. 7, 1974, 88 Stat. 17.)

AMENDMENTS

1974—Subsec. (c). Pub. L. 93–251 lower cased "agency" in two places, and substituted "to the design standards which the State or owning political division would use in constructing a new road under similar conditions of geography and under similar traffic loads (present and projected)." for "to design standards comparable to those of the State, or, where applicable State standards do not exist, those of the owning political division in which the road is located, for roads of the same classification as the road being replaced. The traffic existing at the time of the taking shall be used in the determination of the classification."

1962—Subsec. (a). Pub. L. 87–874 added subsec. (a). Former subsec. (a) redesignated (b).

Subsec. (b). Pub. L. 87–874 redesignated former subsec. (a) as (b), and among other changes, inserted "irrigation," before "or multiple-purpose project" and substituted references to head of the Agency concerned, for references to Chief of Engineers. Former subsec. (b) redesignated (c).

Subsec. (c). Pub. L. 87–874 redesignated former subsec. (b) as (c), substituted construction authority to head of the agency concerned for authority to Chief of Engineers, provided that where State standards do not exist, those of the owning political division in which the road is located shall be used, that where a State or political subdivision requests a substitute road to be constructed to a higher standard than provided in this subsection, and pays the additional costs, the Agency head is authorized to so construct the road, and that the Federal costs under this subsection shall be part of the nonreimbursable costs.

§ 701s. Small flood control projects; appropriations; amount limitation for single locality; conditions

The Secretary of the Army is authorized to allot from any appropriations heretofore or hereafter made for flood control, not to exceed $55,000,000 for any one fiscal year, for the implementation of small structural and nonstructural projects for flood control and related purposes not specifically authorized by Congress, which come within the provisions of section 701a of this title, when in the opinion of the Chief of Engineers such work is advisable. The amount allotted for a project shall be sufficient to complete Federal participation in the project. Not more than $7,000,000 shall be allotted under this section for a project at any single locality. The provisions of local cooperation specified in section 701c of this title shall apply. The work shall be complete in itself and not commit the United States to any additional improvement to insure its successful operation, except as may result from the normal procedure applying to projects authorized after submission of preliminary examination and survey reports.

(June 30, 1948, ch. 771, title II, § 205, 62 Stat. 1182; May 17, 1950, ch. 188, title II, § 212, 64 Stat. 183; July 11, 1956, ch. 558, 70 Stat. 522; Pub. L. 87–874, title II, § 205, Oct. 23, 1962, 76 Stat. 1194; Pub. L. 93–251, title I, § 61, Mar. 7, 1974, 88 Stat. 29; Pub. L. 94–587, § 133(b), Oct. 22, 1976, 90 Stat. 2928; Pub. L. 97–140, § 2(a), Dec. 29, 1981, 95 Stat. 1717; Pub. L. 99–662, title IX, § 915(a), Nov. 17, 1986, 100 Stat. 4191; Pub. L. 106–53, title II, § 201, Aug. 17, 1999, 113 Stat. 285; Pub. L. 106–541, title II, § 218, Dec. 11, 2000, 114 Stat. 2596; Pub. L. 110–114, title II, § 2021, Nov. 8, 2007, 121 Stat. 1078.)

AMENDMENTS

2007—Pub. L. 110–114 substituted "$55,000,000" for "$50,000,000" in first sentence.

2000—Pub. L. 106–541 substituted "$50,000,000" for "$40,000,000" in first sentence.

1999—Pub. L. 106–53, in first sentence, substituted "implementation of small structural and nonstructural projects" for "construction of small projects" and, in third sentence, substituted "$7,000,000" for "$5,000,000".

1986—Pub. L. 99–662 substituted "$40,000,000" for "$30,000,000" and "$5,000,000" for "$4,000,000".

1981—Pub. L. 97–140 substituted "Not more than $4,000,000 shall be allotted under this section for a project at any single locality" for "Not more than $2,000,000 shall be allotted under this section for a project in any single locality, except that not more than $3,000,000 shall be allotted under this section for a project at a single locality if such project protects an area which has been declared to be a major disaster area pursuant to the Disaster Relief Act of 1966 or the Disaster Relief Act of 1970 in the five-year period immediately preceding the date the Chief of Engineers deems such work advisable".

1976—Pub. L. 94–587 increased limitation on allotment for a project at a single locality from $1,000,000 to $2,000,000 and for such a project protecting a major disaster area from $2,000,000 to $3,000,000.

1974—Pub. L. 93–251, in revising provisions, increased fiscal year allotment to $30,000,000 from $25,000,000 and required allotment of $2,000,000 for a project at a single locality if such locality protects an area declared to be a major-disaster area pursuant to Disaster Relief Act of 1966 or Disaster Relief Act of 1970 in five-year period immediately preceding the date the Chief of Engineers deems such work advisable.

1962—Pub. L. 87–874 substituted "$25,000,000" for "$10,000,000", "projects for flood control and related purposes" for "flood control projects", and provisions limiting the allotment for a single project to $1,000,000 and providing that such allotment shall be sufficient to complete Federal participation, for provisions limiting the allotment for any single project to $400,000 from the appropriations for any fiscal year.

1956—Act July 11, 1956, substituted "$10,000,000" for "$3,000,000", struck out "and not within areas intended to be protected by projects so authorized" before "which come within the provisions of section 701a of this title", and substituted "$400,000" for "$150,000".

1950—Act May 17, 1950, substituted "$3,000,000" for "$2,000,000" and "$150,000" for "$100,000".

EFFECTIVE DATE OF 1986 AMENDMENT

Amendment by Pub. L. 99–662 not applicable to any project under contract for construction on Nov. 17, 1986, see section 915(i) of Pub. L. 99–662, set out as a note under section 426g of this title.

EFFECTIVE DATE OF 1981 AMENDMENT

Section 2(b) of Pub. L. 97–140 provided that: "The amendment made by this section [amending this section] shall not apply to any project under contract for construction on the date of enactment of this Act [Dec. 29, 1981].''

EFFECTIVE DATE OF 1976 AMENDMENT

Amendment by Pub. L. 94–587 not applicable to any project under contract for construction on Oct. 22, 1976, see section 133(c) of Pub. L. 94–587, set out as a note under section 577 of this title.

§ 701t. Emergency fund for flood damage; amount; commitments to be fulfilled by local interests

The sum of $25,000,000 is authorized to be appropriated as an emergency fund to be expended under the direction of the Secretary of the Army and the supervision of the Chief of Engineers for the repair, restoration, and strengthening of levees and other flood control works which have been threatened or destroyed by recent floods, or which may be threatened or destroyed by later floods, including the raising, extending, or other modification of such works as may be necessary in the discretion of the Chief of Engineers for the adequate functioning of the works for flood control: *Provided*, That local interests shall provide without cost to the United States all lands, easements, and rights of way necessary for the work and shall maintain and operate all the works after completion in a manner satisfactory to the Chief of Engineers: *Provided further*, That pending the appropriation of said sum, the Secretary of the Army may allot from existing flood-control appropriations such sums as may be necessary for the immediate prosecution of the work authorized by this section, such appropriations to be reimbursed from said emergency fund when appropriated: *And provided further*, That funds allotted under this authority shall not be diverted from the unobligated funds from the appropriation ''Flood control, general'', made available in War Department Civil Functions Appropriation Acts for specific purposes.

(June 30, 1948, ch. 771, title II, § 208, 62 Stat. 1182.)

§ 701u. International engineering or scientific conferences; attendance

The Secretary of the Army is authorized to allot from any appropriations heretofore or hereafter made for flood control or rivers and harbors, funds for payment of expenses of representatives of the Corps of Engineers engaged on flood control and river and harbor work to international engineering or scientific conferences to be held outside the United States: *Provided*, That not more than ten representatives of the Corps of Engineers shall attend any one conference.

(May 17, 1950, ch. 188, title II, § 211, 64 Stat. 183; Pub. L. 104–303, title II, § 222, Oct. 12, 1996, 110 Stat. 3697.)

AMENDMENTS

1996—Pub. L. 104–303 substituted ''outside the United States'' for ''outside the continental limits of the United States'' and struck out before period at end '': *And provided further*, That not more than $25,000 shall be allotted during any one fiscal year for this purpose''.

§ 702. Mississippi River

Authorization of flood-control work—For controlling the floods of the Mississippi River and continuing its improvement from the Head of the Passes to the mouth of the Ohio River the Secretary of the Army is empowered, authorized, and directed to carry on continuously, by hired labor or otherwise, the plans of the Mississippi River Commission, prior to March 3, 1923, or thereafter adopted, to be paid for as appropriations may from time to time be made by law.

Allotments for improvement of watercourses connected with Mississippi River—The watercourses connected with the Mississippi River to such extent as may be necessary to exclude the flood waters from the upper limits of any delta basin, together with the Ohio River from its mouth to the mouth of the Cache River, may, in the discretion of said commission, receive allotments for improvements under way March 1, 1917, or thereafter to be undertaken.

Maintenance of levees constructed for flood control—Upon the completion of any levee constructed for flood control under authority of this section, said levee shall be turned over to the levee district protected thereby for maintenance thereafter; but for all other purposes the United States shall retain such control over the same as it may have the right to exercise upon such completion.

(Mar. 1, 1917, ch. 144, § 1, 39 Stat. 948; Mar. 4, 1923, ch. 277, 42 Stat. 1505; July 26, 1947, ch. 343, title II, § 205(a), 61 Stat. 501.)

CODIFICATION

Last clause of first paragraph was originally limited to appropriations made for a period of six years beginning July 1, 1924.

The portion of the first paragraph providing ''and a sum not to exceed $10,000,000 annually is hereby authorized to be appropriated for that purpose, for a period of six years beginning July 1, 1924'' together with the fourth paragraph, relating to expenditures for improvements between Head of Passes and Rock Island, were from act Mar. 4, 1923, which superseded provisions on the same subjects contained in act Mar. 1, 1917, from which the rest of the section was derived, and were omitted as executed.

Sections 2 and 3 of act Mar. 1, 1917, are classified to sections 703 and 701, respectively, of this title, and section 4 of act Mar. 1, 1917, amended section 643 of this title.

CHANGE OF NAME

Department of War designated Department of the Army and title of Secretary of War changed to Secretary of the Army by section 205(a) of act July 26, 1947, ch. 343, title II, 61 Stat. 501. Section 205(a) of act July 26, 1947, was repealed by section 53 of act Aug. 10, 1956, ch. 1041, 70A Stat. 641. Section 1 of act Aug. 10, 1956, enacted ''Title 10, Armed Forces'' which in sections 3010 to 3013 continued Department of the Army under administrative supervision of Secretary of the Army.

§ 702a. Adoption of 1927 project; execution; creation of board; scope of authority; appropriation

The project for the flood control of the Mississippi River in its alluvial valley and for its improvement from the Head of Passes to Cape Girardeau, Missouri, in accordance with the engineering plan set forth and recommended in the report submitted by the Chief of Engineers to the Secretary of the Army dated December 1, 1927, and printed in House Document Numbered 90, Seventieth Congress, first session, is adopted and authorized to be prosecuted under the direction of the Secretary of the Army and the supervision of the Chief of Engineers: *Provided*, That a board to consist of the Chief of Engineers, the president of the Mississippi River Commission, and a civil engineer chosen from civil life to be appointed by the President, by and with the advice and consent of the Senate, whose compensation shall be fixed by the President and be paid out of the appropriations made to carry on this project, is created; and such board is authorized and directed to consider the engineering differences between the adopted project and the plans recommended by the Mississippi River Commission in its special report dated November 28, 1927, and after such study and such further surveys as may be necessary, to recommend to the President such action as it may deem necessary to be taken in respect to such engineering differences and the decision of the President upon all recommendations or questions submitted to him by such board shall be followed in carrying out the project herein adopted. The board shall not have any power or authority in respect to such project except as hereinbefore provided. Such project and the changes therein, if any, shall be executed in accordance with the provisions of section 702h of this title. Such surveys shall be made between Baton Rouge, Louisiana, and Cape Girardeau, Missouri, as the board may deem necessary to enable it to ascertain and determine the best method of securing flood relief in addition to levees, before any flood-control works other than levees and revetments are undertaken on that portion of the river: *Provided*, That all diversion works and outlets constructed under the provisions of sections 702a, 702b to 702d, 702e to 702g, 702h, 702i, 702j, 702k, 702*l*, 702m and 704 of this title shall be built in a manner and of a character which will fully and amply protect the adjacent lands: *Provided further*, That pending completion of any floodway, spillway, or diversion channel, the areas within the same shall be given the same degree of protection as is afforded by levees on the west side of the river contiguous to the levee at the head of said floodway, but nothing herein shall prevent, postpone, delay, or in anywise interfere with the execution of that part of the project on the east side of the river, including raising, strengthening, and enlarging the levees on the east side of the river. The sum of $325,000,000 is authorized to be appropriated for this purpose.

All unexpended balances of appropriations prior to May 15, 1928, made for prosecuting work of flood control on the Mississippi River in accordance with the provisions of section 702 of this title, are made available for expenditure under the provisions of sections 702a, 702b to 702d, 702e to 702g, 702h, 702i, 702j, 702k, 702*l*, and 702m of this title.

(May 15, 1928, ch. 569, § 1, 45 Stat. 534; July 26, 1947, ch. 343, title II, § 205(a), 61 Stat. 501.)

REFERENCES IN TEXT

Herein, referred to in text, means act May 15, 1928, ch. 569, 45 Stat. 534, as amended, which enacted sections 702a, 702b to 702d, 702e to 702g, 702h, 702i, 702j, 702k, 702*l*, 702m, and 704 of this title. For complete classification of this Act to the Code, see Tables.

CHANGE OF NAME

Department of War designated Department of the Army and title of Secretary of War changed to Secretary of the Army by section 205(a) of act July 26, 1947, ch. 343, title II, 61 Stat. 501. Section 205(a) of act July 26, 1947, was repealed by section 53 of act Aug. 10, 1956, ch. 1041, 70A Stat. 641. Section 1 of act Aug. 10, 1956, enacted "Title 10, Armed Forces" which in sections 3010 to 3013 continued Department of the Army under administrative supervision of Secretary of the Army.

ABANDONMENT AND REPEAL OF PROJECTS

For abandonment of Boeuf Floodway and Eudora Floodway as well as Northward Extension and back protection levee extending from head of Eudora Floodway north to Arkansas River and repeal of provisions relating to prosecution of work, see section 702a–12 of this title.

§ 702a–1. Modification of project of 1927; adoption

The project for the control of floods of the Mississippi River and its tributaries, adopted by section 702a of this title, is modified in accordance with the recommendations of section 43 of the report submitted by the Chief of Engineers to the Chairman of the Committee on Flood Control, dated February 12, 1935, and printed in House Committee on Flood Control Document Numbered 1, Seventy-fourth Congress, first session, as, in sections 642a, 702a–2 to 702a–12, 702g–1, 702j–1, 702j–2, 702k–1, and 702k–2 of this title, further modified and amended; and as so modified is adopted and authorized and directed to be prosecuted under the direction of the Secretary of the Army and the supervision of the Chief of Engineers.

(June 15, 1936, ch. 548, § 1, 49 Stat. 1508; July 26, 1947, ch. 343, title II, § 205(a), 61 Stat. 501.)

PRIOR PROVISIONS

A prior section 702a–1½, act June 28, 1938, ch. 795, § 4, 52 Stat. 1220, which related to further modification of 1927 project, was transferred to section 702a–1a of this title.

A prior section 702a–1¾, act Aug. 18, 1941, ch. 377, § 3, 55 Stat. 642, which related to further modificiation and adoption of Lower Mississippi River flood control project, was transferred to section 702a–1b of this title.

CHANGE OF NAME

Department of War designated Department of the Army and title of Secretary of War changed to Secretary of the Army by section 205(a) of act July 26, 1947, ch. 343, title II, 61 Stat. 501. Section 205(a) of act July 26, 1947, was repealed by section 53 of act Aug. 10, 1956, ch. 1041, 70A Stat. 641. Section 1 of act Aug. 10, 1956, enacted "Title 10, Armed Forces" which in sections 3010 to 3013 continued Department of the Army under administrative supervision of Secretary of the Army.

§ 702a–1a. Further modification of 1927 project; adoption; appropriation

In accordance with the recommendations of the Chief of Engineers, as set forth in his report of April 6, 1937, and published as Flood Control Committee Document Numbered 1, Seventy-fifth Congress, first session, paragraph 38(b), except subparagraph (1), the project for flood control of the Lower Mississippi River adopted by sections

642a, 702a, 702a–1, 702a–2 to 702d, 702e to 702h, 702i to 702m, and 704 of this title, is modified and, as modified, is adopted, and there is authorized to be appropriated in addition to the sums previously authorized $40,000,000 to be applied for the purposes set forth in said document covering the said recommendations, with the exceptions mentioned, subject to the provisions made in section 702a–11 of this title.

(June 28, 1938, ch. 795, §4, 52 Stat. 1220.)

CODIFICATION

Section was formerly classified to section 702a–1½ of this title.

§702a–1b. Further modification; adoption

The project for flood control of the Lower Mississippi River adopted by sections 642a, 702a to 702a–1½, 702a–2 to 702d, and 702e to 702h, 702i to 702m, and 704 of this title is modified and, as modified, is authorized and adopted.

(Aug. 18, 1941, ch. 377, §3, 55 Stat. 642.)

CODIFICATION

Section was formerly classified to section 702a–1¾ of this title.

§702a–2. Abandonment of Boeuf Floodway

The Boeuf Floodway, authorized by the provisions adopted in section 702a of this title, shall be abandoned as soon as the Eudora Floodway, provided for in Flood Control Committee Document Numbered 1, Seventy-fourth Congress, first session, is in operative condition and the back protection levee recommended in said document, extending north from the head of the Eudora Floodway, shall have been constructed.

(June 15, 1936, ch. 548, §2, 49 Stat. 1509.)

ABANDONMENT AND REPEAL OF PROJECTS

For abandonment of Boeuf Floodway and Eudora Floodway as well as Northward Extension and back protection levee extending from head of Eudora Floodway north to Arkansas River and repeal of provisions relating to prosecution of work, see section 702a–12 of this title.

§702a–3. Levees; raising and enlarging

The levees along the Mississippi River from the head of the Morganza Floodway to the head of the Atchafalaya River and down the east bank of the Atchafalaya River to intersection with the west protection levee of said Morganza Floodway shall be raised and enlarged to 1928 grade and section.

(June 15, 1936, ch. 548, §3, 49 Stat. 1509.)

§702a–4. Fuse-plug levees

After the Eudora Floodway shall have been constructed and is ready for operation, the fuse-plug levees now at the head of the Boeuf and Tensas Basins shall be constructed to the 1914 grade and the 1928 section. The fuse-plug levees at the head of the Atchafalaya Basin on the west side shall be constructed to the 1914 grade and the 1928 section. The fuse-plug levees at the head of the Atchafalaya Basin on the east side of the Atchafalaya River shall be constructed to the 1914 grade and 1928 section, and, after the Morganza Floodway has been completed, shall be raised to the 1928 grade as provided in section 702a–3 of this title. Thereafter those stretches of said levees which are left as fuse-plug levees shall be reconstructed and maintained as herein provided, subject to the provisions of section 702a–3 of this title. Any funds appropriated under authority of sections 702g–1 and 702k–1 of this title may be expended for this purpose.

(June 15, 1936, ch. 548, §10, 49 Stat. 1511.)

REFERENCES IN TEXT

Herein, referred to in text, means act June 15, 1936, ch. 548, 49 Stat. 1508, as amended, which enacted sections 642a, 702a–1, 702a–2 to 702a–12, 702g–1, 702j–1, 702j–2, 702k–1, and 702k–2 of this title. For complete classification of this Act to the Code, see Tables.

§702a–5. Back levee north of Eudora Floodway

The back-protection levee north of the Eudora Floodway shall be constructed to the same grade and section as the levees opposite on the east side of the Mississippi River: *Provided*, That this levee extending from the head of the Eudora Floodway north to the Arkansas River shall be so located as to afford adequate space for the passage of flood waters without endangering the levees opposite on the east side of the river and shall be constructed contemporaneously with the construction of the Eudora Floodway; except that, until the Eudora Floodway is in operative condition, there shall be left in this back levee north of the head of the Eudora Floodway openings which shall be sufficient, in the discretion of the Chief of Engineers, to permit the passage of all flood waters to be reasonably contemplated in the event of any break in the riverside fuse-plug levee prior to the time the Eudora Floodway shall be in operative condition.

(June 15, 1936, ch. 548, §11, 49 Stat. 1511.)

ABANDONMENT AND REPEAL OF PROJECTS

For abandonment of Boeuf Floodway and Eudora Floodway as well as Northward Extension and back protection levee extending from head of Eudora Floodway north to Arkansas River and repeal of provisions relating to prosecution of work, see section 702a–12 of this title.

§702a–6. Drainage necessitated by floodway levees

The United States shall provide the drainage made necessary by the construction of floodway levees included in the modified project.

(June 15, 1936, ch. 548, §6, 49 Stat. 1510.)

§702a–7. Railroad and highway crossings over floodways

The United States shall construct, at its own cost, one railroad and one highway crossing over the Eudora Floodway and not to exceed three railway and two highway crossings over the Morganza Floodway, and not to exceed one railway crossing (together with suitable physical connections therewith) and one highway crossing over the floodway west of the Atchafalaya River provided for in the modified project: *Provided*, That equitable agreements can be made with the railroad and highway authorities concerned and that the appropriate railroad or highway agencies agree to accept and maintain and operate these crossings without cost to the United States: *Provided further*, That the railroads crossing the Morganza and West Atchafalaya Floodways agree in consideration for the crossings constructed to waive all claims against the Government for any damages that may occur by reason of overflows in the Morganza and West Atchafalaya Floodways: *And provided further*, That other railway and highway damages shall be adjusted as provided for in section 702a–10 of this title.

(June 15, 1936, ch. 548, § 7, 49 Stat. 1510.)

§ 702a–8. Additional roads; construction by United States

In addition to the construction by the United States of roads in connection with floodways as heretofore provided, the Federal Government may, in the discretion of the Chief of Engineers, and within the limits of available funds, construct additional roads to afford access to those portions of the levee lines not otherwise accessible.

(June 15, 1936, ch. 548, § 8, 49 Stat. 1510.)

§ 702a–9. Lands, easements, and rights-of-way; acquisition by local authorities; reimbursement; protection of United States from liability for damages

No money appropriated under sections 702g–1 and 702k–1 of this title shall be expended on the construction of any reservoir project herein authorized until States, political subdivisions thereof, or other responsible local agencies have given assurances satisfactory to the Secretary of the Army that they will (a) provide without cost to the United States all lands, easements, and rights-of-way necessary for the construction of the project, except as otherwise provided herein; (b) hold and save the United States free from damages due to the construction works; (c) maintain and operate all the works after completion in accordance with regulations prescribed by the Secretary of the Army: *And provided*, That the construction of any dam authorized herein may be undertaken without delay when the dam site has been acquired and the assurances prescribed herein have been furnished, without awaiting the acquisition of the easements and rights-of-way required for the reservoir area: *And provided further*, That whenever expenditures for lands, easements, and rights-of-way by States, political subdivisions thereof, or responsible local agencies for any individual project or useful part thereof shall have exceeded the present estimated construction cost therefor, the local agency concerned may be reimbursed one-half of its excess expenditures over said estimated construction cost: *And provided further*, That when benefits of any project or useful part thereof accrue to lands and property outside of the State in which said project or part thereof is located, the Secretary of the Army may acquire the necessary lands, easements, and rights-of-way for said project or part thereof after he has received from the States, political subdivisions thereof, or responsible local agencies benefited the present estimated cost of said lands, easements, and rights-of-way, less one-half the amount by which the estimated cost of these lands, easements, and rights-of-way exceeds the estimated construction cost corresponding thereto: *And provided further*, That the Secretary of the Army shall determine the proportion of the present estimated cost of said lands, easements, and rights-of-way that each State, political subdivision thereof, or responsible local agency should contribute in consideration for the benefits to be received by such agencies: *And provided further*, That whenever not less than 75 per centum of the benefits as estimated by the Secretary of the Army of any project or useful part thereof accrue to lands and property outside of the State in which said project or part thereof is located, provision (c) of this section shall not apply thereto; nothing herein shall impair or abridge the powers now existing in the Department of the Army with respect to navigable streams: *And provided further*, That nothing herein shall be construed to interfere with the completion of any reservoir or flood control work authorized by the Congress and under way on June 15, 1936.

(June 15, 1936, ch. 548, § 8a, 49 Stat. 1510; July 26, 1947, ch. 343, title II, § 205(a), 61 Stat. 501.)

REFERENCES IN TEXT

Herein, referred to in text, means act June 15, 1936, ch. 548, 49 Stat. 1508, as amended, which enacted sections 642a, 702a–1, 702a–2 to 702a–12, 702g–1, 702j–1, 702j–2, 702k–1, and 702k–2 of this title. For complete classification of this Act to the Code, see Tables.

CHANGE OF NAME

Department of War designated Department of the Army and title of Secretary of War changed to Secretary of the Army by section 205(a) of act July 26, 1947, ch. 343, title II, 61 Stat. 501. Section 205(a) of act July 26, 1947, was repealed by section 53 of act Aug. 10, 1956, ch. 1041, 70A Stat. 641. Section 1 of act Aug. 10, 1956, enacted "Title 10, Armed Forces" which in sections 3010 to 3013 continued Department of the Army under administrative supervision of Secretary of the Army.

§ 702a–10. Flowage rights and rights-of-way; reimbursement of local authorities; highway crossings; use of properties for national forests or wildlife refuges

In order to facilitate the United States in the acquisition of flowage rights and rights-of-way for levee foundations, the Secretary of the Army is authorized to enter into agreements with the States or with local levee districts, boards, commissions, or other agencies for the acquisition and transfer to the United States of such flowage rights and levee rights-of-way, and for the reimbursement of such States or local levee districts, boards, commissions, or other agencies, for the cost thereof at prices previously agreed upon between the Secretary of the Army and the governing authority of such agencies, within the maximum limitations hereinafter prescribed: *Provided*, That no money appropriated under the authority of sections 702g–1 and 702k–1 of this title shall be expended upon the construction of the Eudora Floodway, the Morganza Floodway, the back protection levee extending north from the Eudora Floodway, or the levees extending from the head of the Morganza Floodway to the head of and down the east bank of the

Atchafalaya River to the intersection of said Morganza Floodway until 75 per centum of the value of the flowage rights and rights-of-way for levee foundations, as estimated by the Chief of Engineers, shall have been acquired or options or assurances satisfactory to the Chief of Engineers shall have been obtained for the Eudora Floodway, the Morganza Floodway, and the area lying between said back protection levee and the present front line levees: *Provided further*, That easements required in said areas in connection with roads and other public utilities owned by States or political subdivisions thereof shall be provided without cost to the United States upon the condition, that the United States shall provide suitable crossings, including surfacing of like character, over floodway guide-line levees in said areas for all improved roads now constituting a part of the State highway system, and shall repair all damage done to said highways within the said floodways by the actual use of such floodways for diversion: *Provided further*, That when such portion of said rights as to all of said areas shall have been acquired or obtained and when said easements required in connection with roads and other public utilities owned by States or political subdivisions thereof have been provided as hereinabove set forth, construction of said flood-control works in said areas shall be undertaken according to the engineering recommendations of the Report of the Chief of Engineers dated February 12, 1935 (House Committee on Flood Control Document Numbered 1, Seventy-fourth Congress, first session), and the Secretary of the Army shall cause proceedings to be instituted for the condemnation of the remainder of said rights and easements, as are needed and cannot be secured by agreement, in accordance with section 702d of this title: *Provided further*, That in no event and under no circumstances shall any of the additional money appropriated under the authority of sections 702g–1 and 702k–1 be expended for the acquisition of said 75 per centum of the flowage rights and rights-of-way hereinabove contemplated in excess of $20,000,000: *Provided further*, That the Chief of Engineers is authorized, out of the funds herein authorized to be appropriated, to purchase flowage easements over lands and properties in the floodway west of the Atchafalaya River and lying above the approximate latitude of Krotz Springs: *Provided further*, That none of such easements in said West Atchafalaya Floodway shall be purchased until options covering at least 75 per centum of the total value of such easements as estimated by the Chief of Engineers shall have been obtained at prices deemed reasonable by the Chief of Engineers and not exceeding in the aggregate $2,250,000 for said 75 per centum of said easements with respect to the floodway west of the Atchafalaya River: *Provided further*, That easements required in said West Atchafalaya Floodway in connection with roads and other public utilities owned by States or other political subdivisions shall be provided without cost to the United States upon condition that the United States shall provide suitable crossings, including surfacing of like character, over floodway guide-line levees for all improved roads in said West Atchafalaya Floodway now constituting a part of the State highway system and shall repair all damage done to said highways within said West Atchafalaya Floodway by the actual use of such floodway for diversion: *Provided further*, That no flowage easements shall be paid for by the United States over properties subject to frequent overflow in the Atchafalaya Basin below the approximate latitude of Krotz Springs: *Provided further*, That payment for rights-of-way, easements, and flowage rights acquired under this section, or reimbursement to the States or local interests furnishing them, shall be made as soon as the Chief of Engineers is satisfied that such rights-of-way, easements, or flowage rights have been acquired in conformity with local custom or legal procedure in such matters; and, thereafter, no liability of any kind shall attach to or rest upon the United States for any further damage by reason of diversions or flood waters: *And provided further*, That if the Secretary of Agriculture shall determine to acquire any of the properties within the floodways herein referred to, for national forests, wildlife refuges, or other purposes of his Department, the Secretary of the Army may, upon recommendation by the Chief of Engineers, in lieu of acquiring flowage rights, advance to or reimburse the said Secretary of Agriculture sums equal to those that would otherwise be used for the purchase of easements desired by the Department of the Army and the Secretary of Agriculture is authorized to use these sums for the purpose of acquiring properties in the floodways in question.

(June 15, 1936, ch. 548, §12, 49 Stat. 1512; July 26, 1947, ch. 343, title II, §205(a), 61 Stat. 501.)

REFERENCES IN TEXT

Herein, referred to in text, means act June 15, 1936, ch. 548, 49 Stat. 1508, as amended, which enacted sections 642a, 702a–1, 702–2 to 702a–12, 702g–1, 702j–1, 702j–2, 702k–1, and 702k–2 of this title. For complete classification of this Act to the Code, see Tables.

CHANGE OF NAME

Department of War designated Department of the Army and title of Secretary of War changed to Secretary of the Army by section 205(a) of act July 26, 1947, ch. 343, title II, 61 Stat. 501. Section 205(a) of act July 26, 1947, was repealed by section 53 of act Aug. 10, 1956, ch. 1041, 70A Stat. 641. Section 1 of act Aug. 10, 1956, enacted "Title 10, Armed Forces" which in sections 3010 to 3013 continued Department of the Army under administrative supervision of Secretary of the Army.

§702a–11. Morganza Floodway; Eudora Floodway

The United States may, within the discretion of the Chief of Engineers, irrespective of other provisions of law, proceed to acquire all easements needed and of the character considered advisable in the Morganza floodway and to construct said Morganza floodway. Said Morganza floodway may, within the discretion of the Chief of Engineers, be modified as to its design and inflow.

The said Morganza floodway may be initiated and constructed without delay; and the United States may, within the discretion of the Chief of Engineers, irrespective of other provisions of law, proceed to the acquisition of flowage rights and flowage easements in the Eudora floodway, and to its construction as authorized by existing law: *Provided*, That the intakes of such Eudora floodway shall include an automatic masonry weir with its sill at such an elevation that it will not be overtopped by stages other than those capable of producing a stage of fifty-one feet or over on the Vicksburg gage: *Provided further*, That a fuseplug levee loop may be constructed behind said sill to prevent flow into the floodway until the predicted flood exceeds the safe capacity of the main river leveed channel, with a free-board of at least three feet, but said fuseplug levee may be artificially breached when in the opinion of the Chief of Engineers such breaching is advisable to insure the safety of the main river controlling levee line: *Provided further*, That the authority to acquire lands, flowage rights, and easements for floodways shall be confined to the floodways proper and to the northward extension of Eudora: *Provided further*, That within the discretion of the Chief of Engineers, the guide line levees of the Eudora floodway may be extended south toward Old River: *Provided further*, That the Chief of Engineers is authorized to construct the said Eudora floodway at such location as he may determine, in the vicinity of Eudora. The United States may, within the discretion of the Chief of Engineers irrespective of other provisions of law, proceed to acquire flowage rights and flowage easements in the northward extension of the Eudora floodway, as authorized by existing law, provided that pending the completion of such northward extension all the Riverside fuseplug levee extending south from the vicinity of Yancopin to the vicinity of Vau Cluse, Arkansas, and so as to connect with the existing levee of 1928 grade and section, shall be reconstructed to the 1914 grade and 1928 section: *Provided further*, That if the back protection levee is constructed prior to the construction of Eudora floodway, it shall be connected with the main Mississippi River levee and subsequently connected with the Eudora floodway when constructed: *Provided further*, That the Chief of Engineers is authorized, in his discretion, to negotiate options, make agreements and offers with respect to lands, flowage rights, easements, and rights-of-way involved, as provided by law, at prices deemed reasonable by him.

The United States, irrespective of other provisions of law, may, within the discretion of the Chief of Engineers, acquire flowage easements over all lands not subject to frequent overflow in the Atchafalaya Basin below the latitude of Krotz Springs.

Said Morganza floodway shall not be operated until the Wax Lake outlet has been put into operative condition.

The fuseplug levees at the head of the Atchafalaya Basin on the east side of the Atchafalaya River shall be reconstructed to the 1928 grade and section.

The United States may, in the discretion of the Chief of Engineers, acquire all flowage rights, flowage easements, rights-of-way for levee foundations, and titles in fee simple as herein provided, either by voluntary acquisition or in accordance with the condemnation proceedings by the Secretary of the Army as provided for in section 702d of this title.

In the event the United States acquires or owns title to any lands in fee simple under the provisions of sections 702a, 702b to 702d, 702e to 702g, 702h, 702i, 702j, 702k, 702*l*, 702m, and 704 of this title, as amended and supplemented, the United States may retain the ownership thereof, or any part thereof instead of turning over such lands to the ownership of States or local interests as provided in section 702d of this title, and may lease such lands: *Provided*, That 25 per centum of all moneys received and deposited in the Treasury of the United States during any fiscal year on account of such leases shall be paid, at the end of such year, by the Secretary of the Treasury to the State in which such property is situated, to be expended as the State legislature may prescribe for the benefit of the public schools and public roads of the county or counties in which such property is situated: *Provided further*, That when such property is situated in more than one State or county the distributive share to each from the proceeds of such property shall be proportional to its area therein: *Provided further*, That no part of the appropriations herein or heretofore authorized for said Morganza and Eudora floodways and extension shall be used for any other purpose.

(June 15, 1936, ch. 548 (pt.), as added June 28, 1938, ch. 795, § 4, 52 Stat. 1220; amended July 26, 1947, ch. 343, title II, § 205(a), 61 Stat. 501.)

References in Text

Herein, referred to in text, means act June 15, 1936, ch. 548, 49 Stat. 1508, as amended, which enacted sections 642a, 702a–1, 702a–2 to 702a–12, 702g–1, 702j–1, 702j–2, 702k–1, and 702k–2 of this title. For complete classification of this Act to the Code, see Tables.

Change of Name

Department of War designated Department of the Army and title of Secretary of War changed to Secretary of the Army by section 205(a) of act July 26, 1947, ch. 343, title II, 61 Stat. 501. Section 205(a) of act July 26, 1947, was repealed by section 53 of act Aug. 10, 1956, ch. 1041, 70A Stat. 641. Section 1 of act Aug. 10, 1956, enacted "Title 10, Armed Forces" which in sections 3010 to 3013 continued Department of the Army under administrative supervision of Secretary of the Army.

Effect of Amendment

Act June 28, 1938, provided that, except as amended therein, the act of May 15, 1928, ch. 569, 45 Stat. 534, as amended by the act of June 15, 1936, as amended, should remain in full force and effect. Act May 15, 1928, is classified to sections 702a, 702b to 702d, 702e to 702g, 702h, 702i, 702j, 702k, 702*l*, 702m, and 704 of this title.

Abandonment and Repeal of Projects

For abandonment of Boeuf Floodway and Eudora Floodway as well as Northward Extension and back protection levee extending from head of Eudora Floodway north to Arkansas River and repeal of provisions relating to prosecution of work, see section 702a–12 of this title.

§ 702a–12. Modified Lower Mississippi River project as of August 18, 1941

(a) Alluvial valley, Mississippi River; Yazoo Basin levees; abandonment of Boeuf and Eudora Floodways and Northward Extension

The existing engineering plan for flood control in the alluvial valley of the Mississippi River is modified so as to provide for the construction of plan 4 as set forth in the report of the Mississippi River Commission, dated March 7, 1941, to the Chief of Engineers, except that the levees in the Yazoo Basin on the east bank of the Mississippi River south of the Coahoma-Bolivar County line in said plan shall have a three foot freeboard over the project flood, and all levees shall be constructed with adequate section and foundation to conform to increased levee heights. The Boeuf Floodway in the project adopted by sections 702a, 702b to 702d, 702e to 702g, 702h, 702i, 702j, 702k, 702*l*, 702m, and 704 of this title, and the Eudora Floodway as well as the Northward Extension and the back protection levee extending from the head of the said Eudora Floodway north to the Arkansas River in the project adopted by sections 642a, 702a–1, 702a–2 to 702a–12, 702g–1, 702j–1, 702j–2, 702k–1, and 702k–2 of this title, are abandoned, and the provisions of said sections relating to the prosecution of work on said floodways and extension are repealed; except that the Ouachita River Levees, Louisiana, authorized by section 702a of this title, shall remain as a component of the Mississippi River and Tributaries Project and afforded operation and maintenance responsibilities as provided under section 702c of this title.

(b) Yazoo River project

The project for flood control of the Yazoo River shall be as authorized by sections 642a, 702a–1, 702a–2 to 702a–12, 702g–1, 702j–1, 702j–2, 702k–1, and 702k–2 of this title, except that the Chief of Engineers may, in his discretion, from time to time, substitute therefor combinations of reservoirs, levees, and channel improvements; and except that the extension of the authorized project and improvements contemplated in plan C of the report of March 7, 1941, of the Mississippi River Commission are authorized, including the extension of the levee on the east bank of the Mississippi River generally along the west bank of the Yazoo River to a connection in the vicinity of Yazoo City with the Yazoo River levee, authorized by the existing project for protection against headwater floods of the Yazoo River system, and the adjustment in the discretion of the Chief of Engineers of the grades of the existing levees in the backwater area on the east bank of Yazoo River below Yazoo City, all at an estimated additional cost of $11,982,000: *Provided*, That the Chief of Engineers shall fix the grade of the extension levees along the Yazoo River, with higher levees in his discretion, so that their construction will give the maximum practical protection without jeopardizing the safety and integrity of the main Mississippi River levees: *And provided further*, That prior to the beginning of construction local authorities shall furnish satisfactory assurances that they will (1) maintain the levees in accordance with the provisions of section 702c of this title, and will (2) not raise the levees in the backwater above the limiting elevations established therefor by the Chief of Engineers.

(c) Tensas-Cocodrie backwater area

In the development of the authorized project, the construction of a levee and improvements contemplated in the report of March 7, 1941, of the Mississippi River Commission from the main-line levee on the west bank of the Mississippi River in the vicinity of Shaw, Louisiana, westward and northward to the vicinity of Newlight, Louisiana, for the protection of that part of the Red River backwater known as the Tensas-Cocodrie area at an estimated cost of $6,976,000 is authorized: *Provided*, That the Chief of Engineers shall fix the grade of said levee, with a higher levee in his discretion, so that its construction will give the maximum practical protection without jeopardizing the safety and integrity of the main Mississippi River levees: *And provided further*, That prior to the beginning of construction local authorities shall furnish satisfactory assurances that they will (1) maintain the levee in accordance with the provisions of section 702c of this title, and will (2) not raise the said levee above the limiting elevations established therefor by the Chief of Engineers: *Provided further*, That subject to the foregoing conditions of local cooperation the Chief of Engineers may in his discretion substitute other levees and appurtenant works for, or make such modifications of, the levees and improvements herein authorized for the protection of the Tensas-Cocodrie area as may be found after further investigation to afford protection to a larger area in the Red River Backwater at a total cost not to exceed $29,000,000 and without jeopardizing the safety and integrity of the main Mississippi River levees and without preventing or jeopardizing the diversions contemplated in the adopted project through the Atchafalaya River and Atchafalaya Basin.

(d) Reimbursement of local authorities for certain expenses

The Chief of Engineers, with approval of the Secretary of the Army, shall reimburse local authorities for actual expenditures found by the Chief of Engineers to be reasonable, for providing at the request of the United States, in accordance with local legal procedure or custom, rights-of-way and flowage easements required for future setbacks of main-line Mississippi River levees.

(e) Saint Francis River

The existing engineering plan for flood control of the Saint Francis River is modified so as to permit the substitution for the suspended portions of the original project below Oak Donnick, Arkansas, of the construction of a ditch in Cross County, Arkansas, beginning in the vicinity of the outlet end of the existing Oak Donnick to Saint Francis Bay floodway and terminating in Saint Francis Bay about two miles north of Riverfront, including the construction of a highway bridge at State Highway Numbered 42 made necessary by the ditch construction: *Provided*, That local interests give assurances satisfactory to the Secretary of the Army that they will (1) provide without cost to the United States all lands, easements, and rights-of-way necessary for the construction; (2) hold and save the United States free from damages due to the construction works; and (3) maintain the works after completion in accordance with regulations prescribed by the Secretary of the Army.

(f) Bayou Rapides, Boeuf, and Cocodrie, Louisiana, improvements

In the development of the authorized project, the construction of improvements for Bayou Rapides, Boeuf, and Cocodrie, Louisiana, contemplated in the report dated March 24, 1941, of the Special Board of Officers at an estimated cost of $2,600,000 is authorized.

(g) Increased authorizations for alluvial valley, Mississippi River

The total authorizations heretofore made for the flood control project of the alluvial valley of the Mississippi River shall not be increased by reason of any provision in this Act, except for the additional amounts necessary for the Yazoo and Red River backwater improvements, and any appropriations heretofore or hereafter made or authorized for said project as herein or heretofore modified may be expended upon any feature of the said project, notwithstanding any restrictions, limitations, or requirements of existing law: *Provided*, That funds hereafter expended for maintenance shall not be considered as reducing present remaining balances of authorizations.

(June 15, 1936, ch. 548 (pt.), as added Aug. 18, 1941, ch. 377, § 3, 55 Stat. 642; amended July 26, 1947, ch. 343, title II, § 205(a), 61 Stat. 501; May 17, 1950, ch. 188, title II, § 204(a), 64 Stat. 172; Pub. L. 110–114, title III, § 3013(b), Nov. 8, 2007, 121 Stat. 1109.)

REFERENCES IN TEXT

Herein, referred to in subsecs. (c) and (g), and this Act, referred to in subsec. (g), probably mean act June 15, 1936, ch. 548, 49 Stat. 1508, as amended, which enacted sections 642a, 702a–1, 702a–2 to 702a–12, 702g–1, 702j–1, 702j–2, 702k–1, and 702k–2 of this title. For complete classification of this Act to the Code, see Tables.

CHANGE OF NAME

Department of War designated Department of the Army and title of Secretary of War changed to Secretary of the Army by section 205(a) of act July 26, 1947, ch. 343, title II, 61 Stat. 501. Section 205(a) of act July 26, 1947, was repealed by section 53 of act Aug. 10, 1956, ch. 1041, 70A Stat. 641. Section 1 of act Aug. 10, 1956, enacted "Title 10, Armed Forces" which in sections 3010 to 3013 continued Department of the Army under administrative supervision of Secretary of the Army.

AMENDMENTS

2007—Subsec. (a). Pub. L. 110–114, in last sentence, inserted "; except that the Ouachita River Levees, Louisiana, authorized by section 702a of this title, shall remain as a component of the Mississippi River and Tributaries Project and afforded operation and maintenance responsibilities as provided under section 702c of this title" before period at end.

1950—Subsec. (c). Act May 17, 1950, substituted "$29,000,000" for "$14,000,000".

APPLICATION OF 1950 INCREASE IN AUTHORIZATION CONTAINED IN SUBSEC. (c) TO OLD AND ATCHAFALAYA RIVERS PROJECT

Section 203 of act Sept. 3, 1954, ch. 1264, title II, 68 Stat. 1258, in addition to authorizing an amount of $32,000,000 for control of the Old and Atchafalaya Rivers and a lock for navigation, provided in part that the $15,000,000 increase in authorization by act May 17, 1950 in amending subsec. (c) of this section (see 1950 Amendment note above), should be applied to such project.

§ 702b. Local contribution toward cost of flood control work

It is declared to be the sense of Congress that the principle of local contribution toward the cost of flood control work, which has been incorporated in all previous national legislation on the subject, is sound, as recognizing the special interest of the local population in its own protection, and as a means of preventing inordinate requests for unjustified items of work having no material national interest. As a full compliance with this principle in view of the great expenditure estimated at approximately $292,000,000, prior to May 15, 1928, made by the local interests in the alluvial valley of the Mississippi River for protection against the floods of that river; in view of the extent of national concern in the control of these floods in the interests of national prosperity, the flow of interstate commerce, and the movement of the United States mails; and, in view of the gigantic scale of the project, involving flood waters of a volume and flowing from a drainage area largely outside the States most affected, and far exceeding those of any other river in the United States, no local contribution to the project herein adopted is required.

(May 15, 1928, ch. 569, § 2, 45 Stat. 535.)

REFERENCES IN TEXT

Herein, referred to in text, means act May 15, 1928, ch. 569, 45 Stat. 534, as amended, which enacted sections 702a, 702b to 702d, 702e to 702g, 702h, 702i, 702j, 702k, 702*l*, 702m, and 704 of this title. For complete classification of this Act to the Code, see Tables.

§ 702c. Expenditures for construction work; conditions precedent; liability for damage from flood waters; condemnation proceedings; floodage rights

Except when authorized by the Secretary of the Army upon the recommendation of the Chief of Engineers, no money appropriated under authority of sections 702a and 702g of this title shall be expended on the construction of any item of the project until the States or levee districts have given assurances satisfactory to the Secretary of the Army that they will (a) maintain all flood-control works after their completion, except controlling and regulating spillway structures, including special relief levees; maintenance includes normally such matters as cutting grass, removal of weeds, local drainage, and minor repairs of main river levees; (b) agree to accept land turned over to them under the provisions of section 702d of this title; (c) provide without cost to the United States, all rights-of-way for levee foundations and levees on the main stem of the Mississippi River between Cape Girardeau, Missouri, and the Head of Passes.

No liability of any kind shall attach to or rest upon the United States for any damage from or by floods or flood waters at any place: *Provided, however*, That if in carrying out the purposes of sections 702a, 702b to 702d, 702e to 702g, 702h, 702i, 702j, 702k, 702*l*, 702m, and 704 of this title it shall be found that upon any stretch of the banks of the Mississippi River it is impracticable to construct levees, either because such construction is not economically justified or because such construction would unreasonably restrict the flood channel, and lands in such stretch of the river are subjected to overflow and damage which are not now overflowed or damaged by reason of the construction of levees on the opposite banks of the river it shall be the duty of the

Secretary of the Army and the Chief of Engineers to institute proceedings on behalf of the United States Government to acquire either the absolute ownership of the lands so subjected to overflow and damage or floodage rights over such lands.

(May 15, 1928, ch. 569, §3, 45 Stat. 535; July 26, 1947, ch. 343, title II, §205(a), 61 Stat. 501.)

CHANGE OF NAME

Department of War designated Department of the Army and title of Secretary of War changed to Secretary of the Army by section 205(a) of act July 26, 1947, ch. 343, title II, 61 Stat. 501. Section 205(a) of act July 26, 1947, was repealed by section 53 of act Aug. 10, 1956, ch. 1041, 70A Stat. 641. Section 1 of act Aug. 10, 1956, enacted "Title 10, Armed Forces" which in sections 3010 to 3013 continued Department of the Army under administrative supervision of Secretary of the Army.

§702d. Flowage rights; condemnation proceedings; benefits to property

The United States shall provide flowage rights for additional destructive flood waters that will pass by reason of diversions from the main channel of the Mississippi River: *Provided*, That in all cases where the execution of the flood control plan herein adopted results in benefits to property such benefits shall be taken into consideration by way of reducing the amount of compensation to be paid.

The Secretary of the Army may cause proceedings to be instituted for the acquirement by condemnation of any lands, easements, or rights of way which, in the opinion of the Secretary of the Army and the Chief of Engineers, are needed in carrying out this project, the said proceedings to be instituted in the United States district court for the district in which the land, easement, or right of way is located. In all such proceedings the practice, pleadings, forms, and modes of proceedings shall conform as near as may be to the practice, pleadings, forms, and proceedings existing at the time in like causes in the courts of record of the State within which such district court is held, any rule of the court to the contrary notwithstanding. When the owner of any land, easement, or right of way shall fix a price for the same which, in the opinion of the Secretary of the Army is reasonable, he may purchase the same at such price; and the Secretary of the Army is also authorized to accept donations of lands, easements, and rights of way required for this project. The provisions of sections 594 and 595 of this title are made applicable to the acquisition of lands, easements, or rights of way needed for works of flood control: *Provided*, That any land acquired under the provisions of this section shall be turned over without cost to the ownership of States or local interests.

(May 15, 1928, ch. 569, §4, 45 Stat. 536; Nov. 30, 1945, ch. 496, 59 Stat. 587; July 26, 1947, ch. 343, title II, §205(a), 61 Stat. 501.)

AMENDMENTS

1945—Act Nov. 30, 1945, substituted second sentence of second par. for a sentence which read "In all such proceedings the court, for the purpose of ascertaining the value of the property and assessing the compensation to be paid, shall appoint three commissioners, whose award, when confirmed by the court, shall be final."

CHANGE OF NAME

Department of War designated Department of the Army and title of Secretary of War changed to Secretary of the Army by section 205(a) of act July 26, 1947, ch. 343, title II, 61 Stat. 501. Section 205(a) of act July 26, 1947, was repealed by section 53 of act Aug. 10, 1956, ch. 1041, 70A Stat. 641. Section 1 of act Aug. 10, 1956, enacted "Title 10, Armed Forces" which in sections 3010 to 3013 continued Department of the Army under administrative supervision of Secretary of the Army.

§702d–1. Bonnet Carre Spillway and Floodway; rights-of-way, etc., over lands

The proviso in section 702d of this title "That any land acquired under the provisions of this section shall be turned over without cost to the ownership of States or local interests," shall not apply to the lands heretofore acquired or that may be hereafter acquired in connection with the construction, maintenance, or operation of the Bonnet Carre Spillway and Floodway. The Secretary of the Army is authorized to grant to any citizen, association, railroad, or other corporation, State or public agency thereof, rights-of-way, easements, and permits, over, across, in, and upon said lands for railway, highway, telephone, telegraph, and pipe-line crossings, and other purposes. The grants issued in pursuance of this authority shall be under such terms and conditions as the Secretary of the Army may deem advisable for the protection of the public interests, and may be perpetual or temporary in his discretion.

(Feb. 15, 1933, ch. 76, 47 Stat. 810; July 26, 1947, ch. 343, title II, §205(a), 61 Stat. 501.)

CHANGE OF NAME

Department of War designated Department of the Army and title of Secretary of War changed to Secretary of the Army by section 205(a) of act July 26, 1947, ch. 343, title II, 61 Stat. 501. Section 205(a) of act July 26, 1947, was repealed by section 53 of act Aug. 10, 1956, ch. 1041, 70A Stat. 641. Section 1 of act Aug. 10, 1956, enacted "Title 10, Armed Forces" which in sections 3010 to 3013 continued Department of the Army under administrative supervision of Secretary of the Army.

§702e. Maps for project; preparation

Subject to the approval of the heads of the several executive departments concerned, the Secretary of the Army, on the recommendation of the Chief of Engineers, may engage the services and assistance of the National Ocean Survey, the United States Geological Survey, or other mapping agencies of the Government, in the preparation of maps required in furtherance of this project, and funds to pay for such services may be allotted from appropriations made under authority of sections 702a and 702g of this title.

(May 15, 1928, ch. 569, §5, 45 Stat. 536; July 26, 1947, ch. 343, title II, §205(a), 61 Stat. 501; Pub. L. 102–154, title I, Nov. 13, 1991, 105 Stat. 1000.)

CHANGE OF NAME

"United States Geological Survey" substituted in text for "Geological Survey" pursuant to provision of title I of Pub. L. 102–154, set out as a note under section 31 of Title 43, Public Lands.

Coast and Geodetic Survey consolidated with National Weather Bureau in 1965 to form Environmental Science Services Administration by Reorg. Plan No. 2

of 1965, eff. July 13, 1965, 30 F.R. 8819, 79 Stat. 1318. Environmental Science Services Administration abolished in 1970, and its personnel, property, records, etc., transferred to National Oceanic and Atmospheric Administration by Reorg. Plan No. 4 of 1970, eff. Oct. 3, 1970, 35 F.R. 15627, 84 Stat. 2090. By order of Acting Associate Administrator of National Oceanic and Atmospheric Administration, 35 F.R. 19249, Dec. 19, 1970, Coast and Geodetic Survey redesignated National Ocean Survey. See notes set out under section 311 of Title 15, Commerce and Trade.

Department of War designated Department of the Army and title of Secretary of War changed to Secretary of the Army by section 205(a) of act July 26, 1947, ch. 343, title II, 61 Stat. 501. Section 205(a) of act July 26, 1947, was repealed by section 53 of act Aug. 10, 1956, ch. 1041, 70A Stat. 641. Section 1 of act Aug. 10, 1956, enacted "Title 10, Armed Forces" which in sections 3010 to 3013 continued Department of the Army under administrative supervision of Secretary of the Army.

TRANSFER OF FUNCTIONS

For transfer of functions of other officers, employees, and agencies of Department of the Interior, with certain exceptions, to Secretary of the Interior, with power to delegate, see Reorg. Plan No. 3 of 1950, §§1, 2, eff. May 24, 1950, 15 F.R. 3174, 64 Stat. 1262, set out in the Appendix to Title 5, Government Organization and Employees. The Geological Survey, referred to in text, is an agency of Department of the Interior.

§ 702f. Expenditures for earlier projects

Funds appropriated under authority of section 702a of this title may be expended for the prosecution of such works for the control of the floods of the Mississippi River as have, prior to May 15, 1928, been authorized and are not included in the present project, including levee work on the Mississippi River between Rock Island, Illinois, and Cape Girardeau, Missouri, and on the outlets and tributaries of the Mississippi River between Rock Island and Head of Passes insofar as such outlets or tributaries are affected by the backwaters of the Mississippi: *Provided*, That for such work on the Mississippi River between Rock Island, Illinois, and Cape Girardeau, Missouri, and on such tributaries, the States or levee districts shall provide rights-of-way without cost to the United States, contribute 33⅓ per centum of the costs of the works, and maintain them after completion: *And provided further*, That not more than $10,000,000 of the sums authorized in section 702a of this title, shall be expended under the provisions of this section. In an emergency, funds appropriated under authority of section 702a of this title may be expended for the maintenance of any levee when it is demonstrated to the satisfaction of the Secretary of the Army that the levee cannot be adequately maintained by the State or levee district.

(May 15, 1928, ch. 569, §6, 45 Stat. 536; July 26, 1947, ch. 343, title II, §205(a), 61 Stat. 501.)

CHANGE OF NAME

Department of War designated Department of the Army and title of Secretary of War changed to Secretary of the Army by section 205(a) of act July 26, 1947, ch. 343, title II, 61 Stat. 501. Section 205(a) of act July 26, 1947, was repealed by section 53 of act Aug. 10, 1956, ch. 1041, 70A Stat. 641. Section 1 of act Aug. 10, 1956, enacted "Title 10, Armed Forces" which in sections 3010 to 3013 continued Department of the Army under administrative supervision of Secretary of the Army.

§ 702g. Appropriation for emergency fund

The sum of $5,000,000 is authorized to be appropriated as an emergency fund to be allotted by the Secretary of the Army on the recommendation of the Chief of Engineers, in rescue work or in the repair or maintenance of any flood-control work on any tributaries of the Mississippi River threatened or destroyed by flood including the flood of 1927: *Provided*, That the unexpended and unallotted balance of said sum, or so much thereof as may be necessary, may be allotted by the Secretary of the Army on the recommendation of the Chief of Engineers in the reimbursement of levee districts or others for expenditures heretofore incurred or made for the construction, repair, or maintenance of any flood-control work on any tributaries or outlets of the Mississippi River that may be threatened, impaired, or destroyed by the flood of 1927 or subsequent flood or that have been impaired, damaged, or destroyed by flood; and also in the construction, repair, or maintenance, and in the reimbursement of levee districts or others for the construction, repair, or maintenance of any flood-control work on any of the tributaries or outlets of the Mississippi River that have been impaired, damaged, or destroyed by caving banks or that may be threatened or impaired by caving banks of such tributaries, whether or not such caving has taken place during a flood stage: *Provided further*, That if the Chief of Engineers finds that it has been or will be necessary or advisable to change the location of any such flood-control work in order to provide the protection contemplated by this section, such change may be approved and/or authorized.

(May 15, 1928, ch. 569, §7, 45 Stat. 537; June 19, 1930, ch. 542, 46 Stat. 787; July 26, 1947, ch. 343, title II, §205(a), 61 Stat. 501.)

AMENDMENTS

1930—Act June 19, 1930, inserted provisos.

CHANGE OF NAME

Department of War designated Department of the Army and title of Secretary of War changed to Secretary of the Army by section 205(a) of act July 26, 1947, ch. 343, title II, 61 Stat. 501. Section 205(a) of act July 26, 1947, was repealed by section 53 of act Aug. 10, 1956, ch. 1041, 70A Stat. 641. Section 1 of act Aug. 10, 1956, enacted "Title 10, Armed Forces" which in sections 3010 to 3013 continued Department of the Army under administrative supervision of Secretary of the Army.

§ 702g–1. Additional appropriation for emergency fund

The sum of $15,000,000 is authorized to be appropriated as an emergency fund to be allocated by the Secretary of the Army on the recommendation of the Chief of Engineers in rescue work or in the repair or maintenance of any flood-control work on any tributary of the Mississippi River threatened or destroyed by flood heretofore or hereafter occurring: *Provided*, That the unexpended and unallotted balance of said sum, or so much thereof as may be necessary, may be allotted by the Secretary of the Army, on the recommendation of the Chief of Engineers, in the reimbursement of levee districts or others for expenditures incurred or made prior to June 15, 1936 for the construction, repair, or maintenance of any flood-control work on any tributaries or outlets of the Mississippi River that may be threatened, impaired, or destroyed by the flood of 1927 or subsequent flood; and also in the construction, repair, or maintenance, and in the reimbursement of levee districts or others for the construction, repair, or maintenance of any flood-control work on any of the tributaries or outlets of the Mississippi River that may have been impaired, damaged, or destroyed by caving banks or that may be threatened or impaired by caving banks, of such tributaries, whether or not such caving has taken place during a flood stage: *Provided further*, That if the Chief of Engineers finds that it has been or will be necessary or advisable to change the location of any such flood-control work in order to provide the protection contemplated by this section, such change may be approved and authorized.

(June 15, 1936, ch. 548, §9, 49 Stat. 1511; July 26, 1947, ch. 343, title II, §205(a), 61 Stat. 501.)

CHANGE OF NAME

Department of War designated Department of the Army and title of Secretary of War changed to Secretary of the Army by section 205(a) of act July 26, 1947, ch. 343, title II, 61 Stat. 501. Section 205(a) of act July 26, 1947, was repealed by section 53 of act Aug. 10, 1956, ch. 1041, 70A Stat. 641. Section 1 of act Aug. 10, 1956, enacted "Title 10, Armed Forces" which in sections 3010 to 3013 continued Department of the Army under administrative supervision of Secretary of the Army.

§702h. Prosecution of project by Mississippi River Commission; president of commission; salaries

The project herein authorized shall be prosecuted by the Mississippi River Commission under the direction of the Secretary of the Army and supervision of the Chief of Engineers and subject to the provisions of sections 702a, 702b to 702d, 702e to 702g, 702h, 702i, 702j, 702k, 702*l*, 702m, and 704 of this title. It shall perform such functions and through such agencies as they shall designate after consultation and discussion with the president of the commission. For all other purposes the existing laws governing the constitution and activities of the commission shall remain unchanged. The commission shall make inspection trips of such frequency and duration as will enable it to acquire first-hand information as to conditions and problems germane to the matter of flood control within the area of its jurisdiction; and on such trips of inspection ample opportunity for hearings and suggestions shall be afforded persons affected by or interested in such problems. The president of the commission shall be the executive officer thereof and shall have the qualifications prescribed by law on May 15, 1928, for the Assistant Chief of Engineers, shall have the title brigadier general, Corps of Engineers, and shall have the rank, pay, and allowances of a brigadier general while actually assigned to such duty: *Provided*, That the incumbent of the office on May 15, 1928, may be appointed a brigadier general of the Army, retired, and shall be eligible for the position of president of the commission if recalled to active service by the President under the provisions of existing law.

The official salary of any officer of the United States Army or other branch of the Government appointed or employed under sections 702a, 702b to 702d, 702e to 702g, 702h, 702i, 702j, 702k, 702*l*, 702m, and 704 of this title shall be deducted from the amount of salary or compensation provided by, or which shall be fixed under, the terms of such sections.

(May 15, 1928, ch. 569, §8, 45 Stat. 537; July 26, 1947, ch. 343, title II, §205(a), 61 Stat. 501; Pub. L. 106–53, title V, §558, Aug. 17, 1999, 113 Stat. 354.)

REFERENCES IN TEXT

Herein, referred to in text, means act May 15, 1928, ch. 569, 45 Stat. 534, as amended, which enacted sections 702a, 702b to 702d, 702e to 702g, 702h, 702i, 702j, 702k, 702*l*, 702m, and 704 of this title. For complete classification of this Act to the Code, see Tables. The "project herein authorized" was specifically authorized by section 702a of this title.

CODIFICATION

Provisions of the second paragraph, as amended by Pub. L. 106–53, that read: "The salary of the president of the Mississippi River Commission shall hereafter be $10,000 per annum, and the salary of the other members of the commission shall hereafter be $21,500 per annum." were omitted as obsolete and superseded by the Classification Act of 1949, 63 Stat. 954, 972. The Classification Act of 1949 was repealed by Pub. L. 89–554, Sept. 6, 1966, §8(a), 80 Stat. 632, and reenacted as chapter 51 and subchapter III of chapter 53 of Title 5, Government Organization and Employees. Section 5102 of Title 5 contains the applicability provisions of the 1949 Act, and section 5103 of Title 5 authorizes the Office of Personnel Management to determine the applicability to specific positions and employees.

AMENDMENTS

1999—Pub. L. 106–53 amended provisions which were omitted from the second paragraph by substituting "$21,500" for "$7,500". See Codification note above.

CHANGE OF NAME

Department of War designated Department of the Army and title of Secretary of War changed to Secretary of the Army by section 205(a) of act July 26, 1947, ch. 343, title II, 61 Stat. 501. Section 205(a) of act July 26, 1947, was repealed by section 53 of act Aug. 10, 1956, ch. 1041, 70A Stat. 641. Section 1 of act Aug. 10, 1956, enacted "Title 10, Armed Forces" which in sections 3010 to 3013 continued Department of the Army under administrative supervision of Secretary of the Army.

§702h–1. Transferred

CODIFICATION

Section has been transferred to section 642a of this title.

§702i. Certain sections applicable to property and rights acquired or constructed

The provisions of sections 407, 408, 411, 412, and 413 of this title are made applicable to all lands, waters, easements, and other property and rights acquired or constructed under the provisions of sections 702a, 702b to 702d, 702e to 702g, 702h, 702i, 702j, 702k, 702*l*, 702m, and 704 of this title.

(May 15, 1928, ch. 569, §9, 45 Stat. 537.)

§702j. Projects relating to tributary streams; report to Congress; appropriation

It is the sense of Congress that the surveys of the Mississippi River and its tributaries, authorized pursuant to the Act of January 21, 1927 [ch. 47, 44 Stat. 1010], and House Document Numbered 308, Sixty-ninth Congress, first session, be prosecuted as speedily as practicable, and the Secretary of the Army, through the Corps of Engineers, United States Army, is directed to prepare and submit to Congress at the earliest practicable date projects for flood control on all tributary streams of the Mississippi River system subject to destructive floods which projects shall include: The Red River and tributaries, the Yazoo River and tributaries, the White River and tributaries, the Saint Francis River and tributaries, the Arkansas River and tributaries, the Ohio River and tributaries, the Missouri River and tributaries, and the Illinois River and tributaries; and the reports thereon, in addition to the surveys provided by said House Document 308, Sixty-ninth Congress, first session, shall include the effect on the subject of further flood control of the lower Mississippi River to be attained through the control of the flood waters in the drainage basins of the tributaries by the establishment of a reservoir system; the benefits that will accrue to navigation and agriculture from the prevention of erosion and siltage entering the stream; a determination of the capacity of the soils of the district to receive and hold waters from such reservoirs; the prospective income from the disposal of reservoired waters; the extent to which reservoired waters may be made available for public and private uses; and inquiry as to the return flow of waters placed in the soils from reservoirs, and as to their stabilizing effect on stream flow as a means of preventing erosion, siltage, and improving navigation: *Provided*, That before transmitting such reports to Congress the same shall be presented to the Mississippi River Commission, and its conclusions and recommendations thereon shall be transmitted to Congress by the Secretary of the Army with his report.

The sum of $5,000,000 is authorized to be used out of the appropriation authorized in section 702a of this title, in addition to amounts authorized in the River and Harbor Act of January 21, 1927 [ch. 47, 44 Stat. 1010], to be expended under the direction of the Secretary of the Army and the supervision of the Chief of Engineers for the preparation of the flood-control projects authorized to be submitted to Congress under this section: *Provided further*, That the flood surveys herein provided for shall be made simultaneously with the flood-control work on the Mississippi River provided for in sections 702a, 702b to 702d, 702e to 702g, 702h, 702i, 702j, 702k, 702*l*, 702m, and 704 of this title: *And provided further*, That the President shall proceed to ascertain through the Secretary of Agriculture and such other agencies as he may deem proper, the extent to and manner in which the floods in the Mississippi Valley may be controlled by proper forestry practice.

(May 15, 1928, ch. 569, § 10, 45 Stat. 538; July 26, 1947, ch. 343, title II, § 205(a), 61 Stat. 501.)

REFERENCES IN TEXT

Act of January 21, 1927 [ch. 47, 44 Stat. 1010], referred to in text, popularly known as the River and Harbor Act of January 21, 1927, was not classified to the Code, except for subsections (b) and (d) of section 5 of the act, which enacted sections 569 and 584 of this title.

Herein, referred to in text, means act May 15, 1928, ch. 569, 45 Stat. 534, as amended, which enacted sections 702a, 702b to 702d, 702e to 702g, 702h, 702i, 702j, 702k, 702*l*, 702m, and 704 of this title. For complete classification of this Act to the Code, see Tables.

CHANGE OF NAME

Department of War designated Department of the Army and title of Secretary of War changed to Secretary of the Army by section 205(a) of act July 26, 1947, ch. 343, title II, 61 Stat. 501. Section 205(a) of act July 26, 1947, was repealed by section 53 of act Aug. 10, 1956, ch. 1041, 70A Stat. 641. Section 1 of act Aug. 10, 1956, enacted "Title 10, Armed Forces" which in sections 3010 to 3013 continued Department of the Army under administrative supervision of Secretary of the Army.

TRANSFER OF FUNCTIONS

For transfer of functions of other officers, employees, and agencies of Department of Agriculture, with certain exceptions, to Secretary of Agriculture, with power to delegate, see Reorg. Plan No. 2 of 1953, § 1, eff. June 4, 1953, 18 F.R. 3219, 67 Stat. 633, set out in the Appendix to Title 5, Government Organization and Employees.

§ 702j–1. Saint Francis and Yazoo Rivers; lands and easements; alteration of highways; cooperation of States

(1) Neither of the projects for the flood control of the Saint Francis River or the Yazoo River, authorized by sections 642a, 702a–1, 702a–2 to 702a–12, 702g–1, 702j–1, 702j–2, 702k–1, and 702k–2 of this title, shall be undertaken until the States, or other qualified agencies, shall have furnished satisfactory assurances that they will undertake, without cost to the United States, all alterations of highways made necessary because of the construction of the authorized reservoirs, and meet all damages because of such highway alterations, and have agreed also to furnish without cost to the United States all lands and easements necessary to the construction of levees and drainage ditches constructed under this project: *Provided*, That the reservoirs for control of headwater flow of the Yazoo River system may be located by the Chief of Engineers, in his discretion: *And provided further*, That the Chief of Engineers may, in his discretion, substitute levees, floodways, or auxiliary channels, or any or all of them, for any or all of the seven detention reservoirs recommended in his report of February 12, 1935, for the control of floods of the Yazoo River: *And provided further*, That the Chief of Engineers, with the approval of the Secretary of the Army, may modify the project for the flood control of the Saint Francis River as recommended in said report, to include therein the construction of a detention reservoir for the reduction of floods, and the acquisition at the cost of the United States of all lands and flowage necessary to the construction of said reservoir except flowage of highways: *Provided further*, That the estimated cost to the United States of the project is not increased by reason of such detention reservoir.

(2) The Chief of Engineers may, in his discretion, modify the project for the control of floods on the Yazoo River, as authorized by paragraph (1) of this section, to substitute therefor a combined reservoir floodway and levee plan: *Provided*, That the total cost thereof does not exceed the present authorization as estimated in

House Committee on Flood Control Document Numbered 1, Seventy-fourth Congress, first session: *Provided further*, That the modified project shall be subject to the following conditions of local cooperation:

No work shall be undertaken until the States or other qualified agencies have furnished satisfactory assurances that they will—

(a) undertake, without cost to the United States, all alterations of highways made necessary because of the construction of reservoirs and meet all damages because of such highway alterations; and

(b) furnish, without cost to the United States, all lands and easements necessary to the construction of levees and drainage ditches.

(June 15, 1936, ch. 548, § 4, 49 Stat. 1509; Aug. 28, 1937, ch. 877, § 6, 50 Stat. 880; July 26, 1947, ch. 343, title II, § 205(a), 61 Stat. 501.)

CODIFICATION

Par. (1) is comprised of act June 15, 1936, and par. (2) is from act Aug. 28, 1937.

CHANGE OF NAME

Department of War designated Department of the Army and title of Secretary of War changed to Secretary of the Army by section 205(a) of act July 26, 1947, ch. 343, title II, 61 Stat. 501. Section 205(a) of act July 26, 1947, was repealed by section 53 of act Aug. 10, 1956, ch. 1041, 70A Stat. 641. Section 1 of act Aug. 10, 1956, enacted "Title 10, Armed Forces" which in sections 3010 to 3013 continued Department of the Army under administrative supervision of Secretary of the Army.

§ 702j–2. White River Levee District; rights-of-way; drainage facilities; flowage rights; acquisition by local authorities; protection of United States from liability for damages

The Chief of Engineers, under the supervision of the Secretary of the Army, shall at the expense of the United States Government construct a system of levees substantially in accordance with general plan shown on map designated as sheet numbered 1 entitled "Tributary Levee Location Survey—White River Levee District—Proposed Levee Location" accompanying report dated April 2, 1925, and filed in office of First and Second Mississippi River Commission Districts, Memphis, Tennessee. The Chief of Engineers shall have the right to alter, change, or modify said plan as to the grades and levee sections: *Provided, however*, That no work shall be commenced on the above-mentioned project until the State, levee boards, or other responsible local interests have given assurances satisfactory to the Secretary of the Army that they will (a) provide without cost to the United States all rights-of-way necessary for the construction of said project; (b) provide drainage facilities made necessary by construction of levees; (c) acquire and provide without cost to the United States all flowage and storage rights and easements over, upon, and across the lands and properties within the protected area in the event it becomes necessary in the judgment and discretion of the Secretary of the Army or the Chief of Engineers to use said area, or any part thereof, for an emergency reservoir; (d) hold and save the United States free from liability for damages on account of the use of said area for reservoir purposes during said emergency.

(June 15, 1936, ch. 548, § 5, 49 Stat. 1509; July 26, 1947, ch. 343, title II, § 205(a), 61 Stat. 501.)

CHANGE OF NAME

Department of War designated Department of the Army and title of Secretary of War changed to Secretary of the Army by section 205(a) of act July 26, 1947, ch. 343, title II, 61 Stat. 501. Section 205(a) of act July 26, 1947, was repealed by section 53 of act Aug. 10, 1956, ch. 1041, 70A Stat. 641. Section 1 of act Aug. 10, 1956, enacted "Title 10, Armed Forces" which in sections 3010 to 3013 continued Department of the Army under administrative supervision of Secretary of the Army.

§ 702k. Surveys below Cape Girardeau, Missouri; resurvey of levee in Tennessee

The Secretary of the Army shall cause the Mississippi River Commission to make an examination and survey of the Mississippi River below Cape Girardeau, Missouri, (a) at places where levees have prior to May 15, 1928, been constructed on one side of the river and the lands on the opposite side have been thereby subjected to greater overflow, and were, without unreasonably restricting the flood channel, levees can be constructed to reduce the extent of this overflow, and where the construction of such levees is economically justified, and report thereon to the Congress as soon as practicable with such recommendations as the commission may deem advisable; (b) with a view to determining the estimated effects, if any, upon lands lying between the river and adjacent hills by reason of overflow of such lands caused by the construction of levees at other points along the Mississippi River, and determining the equities of the owners of such lands and the value of the same, and the commission shall report thereon to the Congress as soon as practicable with such recommendation as it may deem advisable: *Provided*, That inasmuch as the Mississippi River Commission made a report on the 26th day of October 1912, recommending a levee to be built from Tiptonville, Tennessee, to the Obion River in Tennessee, the said Mississippi River Commission is authorized to make a resurvey of said proposed levee and a relocation of the same if necessary, and if such levee is found feasible, and is approved by the board created in section 702a of this title, and by the President the same shall be built out of appropriations made after May 15, 1928.

(May 15, 1928, ch. 569, § 11, 45 Stat. 538; July 26, 1947, ch. 343, title II, § 205(a), 61 Stat. 501.)

CHANGE OF NAME

Department of War designated Department of the Army and title of Secretary of War changed to Secretary of the Army by section 205(a) of act July 26, 1947, ch. 343, title II, 61 Stat. 501. Section 205(a) of act July 26, 1947, was repealed by section 53 of act Aug. 10, 1956, ch. 1041, 70A Stat. 641. Section 1 of act Aug. 10, 1956, enacted "Title 10, Armed Forces" which in sections 3010 to 3013 continued Department of the Army under administrative supervision of Secretary of the Army.

§ 702k–1. Authorization of appropriation

$272,000,000 is authorized to be appropriated for the carrying out of the modified adopted project, and all unexpended balances of appropriations heretofore made for the prosecution of said flood-control project are made available for the purposes of sections 642a, 702a-1, 702a-2 to 702a-12, 702g-1, 702j-1, 702j-2, 702k-1, and 702k-2 of this title.

(June 15, 1936, ch. 548, § 13, 49 Stat. 1513.)

§ 702k-2. Separability

If any provision of sections 642a, 702a-1, 702a-2 to 702a-12, 702g-1, 702j-1, 702j-2, and 702k-1 of this title, or the application thereof, to any person or circumstances, is held invalid, the remainder of the said sections, and the application of such provisions to other persons or circumstances, shall not be affected thereby.

(June 15, 1936, ch. 548, § 14, 49 Stat. 1513.)

§ 702*l*. Repeal of inconsistent laws

All laws or parts of laws inconsistent with sections 702a, 702b to 702d, 702e to 702g, 702h, 702i, 702j, and 702k of this title, are repealed.

(May 15, 1928, ch. 569, § 12, 45 Stat. 539.)

§ 702m. Interest of Members of Congress in contracts for acquisition of land

In every contract or agreement to be made or entered into for the acquisition of land either by private sale or condemnation as in sections 702a, 702b to 702d, 702e to 702g, 702h, 702i, 702j, 702k, 702*l*, 702m, and 704 of this title provided the provisions contained in section 22 of Title 41 shall be applicable.

(May 15, 1928, ch. 569, § 14, 45 Stat. 539.)

§ 702n. Levee rights-of-way; payment or reimbursement for

The Secretary of the Army is authorized, out of any money available for carrying out the provisions of sections 702a, 702b to 702d, 702e to 702g, 702h, 702i, 702j, 702k, 702*l*, 702m, and 704 of this title, to purchase from, or to reimburse States or local levee districts for the cost of, any levee rights-of-way or easements for the building of levees in the Mississippi Valley for which the United States was or is under obligation to pay under the provisions of said sections regardless of whether said States or local levee districts have furnished such rights-of-way in the past and regardless of the conditions under which such levee rights-of-way were furnished, or may be furnished in the future: *Provided*, That after careful investigation the prices are found to be reasonable: *And provided further*, That payments or reimbursements for levee rights-of-way or easements conveying the privilege of building levees may be made as soon as they have been acquired in conformity with local custom or legal procedure in such matters and to the satisfaction of the Chief of Engineers.

(Apr. 23, 1934, ch. 159, 48 Stat. 607; July 26, 1947, ch. 343, title II, § 205(a), 61 Stat. 501.)

CHANGE OF NAME

Department of War designated Department of the Army and title of Secretary of War changed to Secretary of the Army by section 205(a) of act July 26, 1947, ch. 343, title II, 61 Stat. 501. Section 205(a) of act July 26, 1947, was repealed by section 53 of act Aug. 10, 1956, ch. 1041, 70A Stat. 641. Section 1 of act Aug. 10, 1956, enacted "Title 10, Armed Forces" which in sections 3010 to 3013 continued Department of the Army under administrative supervision of Secretary of the Army.

§ 703. Sacramento River, California

Flood-control works authorized—For controlling the floods, removing the débris, and continuing the improvement of the Sacramento River, California, in accordance with the plans of the California Débris Commission, the Secretary of the Army is authorized and directed to carry on continuously, by hired labor or otherwise, the plan of said commission contained in its report submitted August 10, 1910, and printed in House Document Numbered 81, Sixty-second Congress, first session, as modified by the report of said commission submitted February 8, 1913, approved by the Chief of Engineers of the United States Army and the Board of Engineers for Rivers and Harbors, and printed in Rivers and Harbors Committee Document Numbered 5, Sixty-third Congress, first session, insofar as said plan provides for the rectification and enlargement of river channels and the construction of weirs, to be paid for as appropriations may from time to time be made by law, not to exceed in the aggregate $5,600,000: *Provided*, That not more than $1,000,000 shall be expended therefor during any one fiscal year.

Limitation on expenditure of appropriations generally—(a) All money appropriated under authority of this section shall be expended under the direction of the Secretary of the Army, in accordance with the plans, specifications, and recommendations of the California Débris Commission, as approved by the Chief of Engineers, for the control of floods, removal of débris, and the general improvement of the Sacramento River: *Provided*, That no money shall be expended under authority of this section until assurances have been given satisfactory to the Secretary of the Army (a) that the State of California will contribute annually for such work a sum equal to such sum as may be expended annually therefor by the United States under authority of this section; (b) that such equal contributions by the State of California will continue annually until the full equal share of the cost of such work shall have been contributed by said State; and (c) that the river levees contemplated in the report of the California Débris Commission, dated August 10, 1910, will be constructed to such grade and section and within such time as may be required by said commission: *Provided further*, That said State shall not be required to expend for such work, for any one year, a sum larger than that expended thereon by the United States during the same year: *And provided further*, That the total contributions so required of the State of California shall not exceed in the aggregate $5,600,000.

Expenditure of contributions by State of California; acquisition of sites, easements, etc.—(b) All money contributed by the State of California, as herein provided, shall be expended under the direction of the California Débris Commission and in such manner as it may require or approve, and no money appropriated under authority of this section shall be expended in the purchase of or payment for any right-of-way, easement, or land acquired for the purposes of this improvement, but all such rights-of-way, easements, and lands shall be provided free of cost to the United States: *Provided*, That no money paid or expense incurred therefor shall be computed as a part of the contribution of the State of California toward the work of improvement herein provided for within the meaning of paragraph (a) of this section.

Maintenance of works for flood control by State of California—(c) Upon the completion of all works for flood control herein authorized the said works shall be turned over to the State of California for maintenance thereafter; but for all other purposes the United States shall retain such control over the same as it may have the right to exercise upon such completion.

(Mar. 1, 1917, ch. 144, §2, 39 Stat. 949; July 26, 1947, ch. 343, title II, §205(a), 61 Stat. 501.)

CHANGE OF NAME

Department of War designated Department of the Army and title of Secretary of War changed to Secretary of the Army by section 205(a) of act July 26, 1947, ch. 343, title II, 61 Stat. 501. Section 205(a) of act July 26, 1947, was repealed by section 53 of act Aug. 10, 1956, ch. 1041, 70A Stat. 641. Section 1 of act Aug. 10, 1956, enacted "Title 10, Armed Forces" which in sections 3010 to 3013 continued Department of the Army under administrative supervision of Secretary of the Army.

TERMINATION OF BOARD OF ENGINEERS FOR RIVERS AND HARBORS AND REASSIGNMENT OF DUTIES AND RESPONSIBILITIES

For termination of Board of Engineers for Rivers and Harbors 180 days after Oct. 31, 1992, and reassignment of duties and responsibilities by Secretary of Army, see section 223 of Pub. L. 102–580, set out as a note under section 541 of this title.

§ 704. Modification of project

The project for the control of floods in the Sacramento River, California, adopted by section 703 of this title, is modified in accordance with the report of the California Débris Commission submitted in Senate Document Numbered 23, Sixty-ninth Congress, first session: *Provided*, That the total amounts contributed by the Federal Government, including the amounts heretofore contributed by it, shall in no event exceed in the aggregate $17,600,000.

(May 15, 1928, ch. 569, §13, 45 Stat. 539.)

§ 705. Salmon River, Alaska; flood control work authorized

The project of prevention and control of floods in the Salmon River, Alaska, recommended in the report of the Chief of Engineers, United States Army, in House Document Numbered 228, Seventy-second Congress, is adopted and authorized and shall be prosecuted under the direction of the Secretary of the Army and the supervision of the Chief of Engineers in accordance with the plan recommended in such report and subject to the conditions set forth therein.

(June 18, 1934, ch. 581, 48 Stat. 991; July 26, 1947, ch. 343, title II, §205(a), 61 Stat. 501.)

CHANGE OF NAME

Department of War designated Department of the Army and title of Secretary of War changed to Secretary of the Army by section 205(a) of act July 26, 1947, ch. 343, title II, 61 Stat. 501. Section 205(a) of act July 26, 1947, was repealed by section 53 of act Aug. 10, 1956, ch. 1041, 70A Stat. 641. Section 1 of act Aug. 10, 1956, enacted "Title 10, Armed Forces" which in sections 3010 to 3013 continued Department of the Army under administrative supervision of Secretary of the Army.

§ 706. Secretary of Commerce; current precipitation information; appropriation

There is authorized an expenditure as required, from any appropriations heretofore or hereafter made for flood control, rivers and harbors, and related purposes by the United States, for the establishment, operation, and maintenance by the Secretary of Commerce of a network of recording and nonrecording precipitation stations, known as the Hydroclimatic Network, whenever in the opinion of the Chief of Engineers and the Secretary of Commerce such service is advisable in connection with either preliminary examinations and surveys or works of improvement authorized by the law for flood control, rivers and harbors, and related purposes, and the Secretary of the Army upon the recommendation of the Chief of Engineers is authorized to allot the Secretary of Commerce funds for said expenditure.

(June 28, 1938, ch. 795, §8, 52 Stat. 1226; July 26, 1947, ch. 343, title II, §205(a), 61 Stat. 501; Sept. 3, 1954, ch. 1264, title II, §207, 68 Stat. 1266.)

AMENDMENTS

1954—Act Sept. 3, 1954, struck out $375,000 limitation on transfers to Weather Bureau for providing basic hydrologic and climatic information; inserted references to "rivers and harbors, and related purposes" after "flood control," in two places; and substituted "network of recording and nonrecording precipitation stations, known as the Hydroclimatic Network" for "current information service on precipitation, flood forecasts, and flood warnings".

CHANGE OF NAME

Department of War designated Department of the Army and title of Secretary of War changed to Secretary of the Army by section 205(a) of act July 26, 1947, ch. 343, title II, 61 Stat. 501. Section 205(a) of act July 26, 1947, was repealed by section 53 of act Aug. 10, 1956, ch. 1041, 70A Stat. 641. Section 1 of act Aug. 10, 1956, enacted "Title 10, Armed Forces" which in sections 3010 to 3013 continued Department of the Army under administrative supervision of Secretary of the Army.

TRANSFER OF FUNCTIONS

Weather Bureau of Department of Commerce consolidated with Coast and Geodetic Survey to form a new agency in Department of Commerce to be known as Environmental Science Services Administration and office of Chief of Weather Bureau abolished by Reorg. Plan No. 2 of 1965, eff. July 13, 1965, 30 F.R. 8819, 79 Stat. 1318, set out in the Appendix to Title 5, Government Organization and Employees. All functions of Bureau and Chief of Bureau transferred to Secretary of Commerce by Reorg. Plan. Subsequently, Environmental Science Services Administration abolished by Reorg. Plan No. 4 of 1970, eff. Oct. 3, 1970, 35 F.R. 15627, 84 Stat. 2090, set out in the Appendix to Title 5, which created National Oceanic and Atmospheric Administration in Department of Commerce. By Department Organization Order 25–5A, republished 39 F.R. 27486, Secretary of Commerce delegated to NOAA his functions relating to Weather Bureau. By order of Acting Associate Administrator of NOAA, organization name of Weather Bureau changed to National Weather Service. For further details, see Codification note set out under section 311 of Title 15, Commerce and Trade.

§ 707. Sumner Dam and Lake Sumner; declaration of purpose; report to Congress; appropriation

The Sumner Dam and Lake Sumner on the Pecos River, New Mexico, is authorized and declared to be for the purposes of controlling floods, regulating the flow of the Pecos River, providing for storage and for delivery of stored waters, for the reclamation of lands, and other beneficial uses, and said dam and reservoir shall be used, first, for irrigation; second, for flood control and river regulation; and third, for other purposes. The Chief of Engineers and the Secretary of the Army are directed to report to the Congress the amount of the total cost of said Sumner Dam and Lake Sumner which is properly allocable to flood control. The appropriation and transfer of such amount from the general fund of the Treasury to the reclamation fund, for credit by reduction of the maximum obligation of the Carlsbad Irrigation District to repay the total cost thereof, is authorized.

(Aug. 11, 1939, ch. 699, § 7, 53 Stat. 1417; July 26, 1947, ch. 343, title II, § 205(a), 61 Stat. 501; Pub. L. 93–447, Oct. 17, 1974, 88 Stat. 1363.)

AMENDMENTS

1974—Pub. L. 93–447 substituted "Sumner Dam and Lake Sumner" for "Alamogordo Dam and Reservoir" wherever appearing.

CHANGE OF NAME

Department of War designated Department of the Army and title of Secretary of War changed to Secretary of the Army by section 205(a) of act July 26, 1947, ch. 343, title II, 61 Stat. 501. Section 205(a) of act July 26, 1947, was repealed by section 53 of act Aug. 10, 1956, ch. 1041, 70A Stat. 641. Section 1 of act Aug. 10, 1956, enacted "Title 10, Armed Forces" which in sections 3010 to 3013 continued Department of the Army under administrative supervision of Secretary of the Army.

ALAMOGORDO DAM AND RESERVOIR REDESIGNATED AS SUMNER DAM AND LAKE SUMNER

Pub. L. 93–447 provided: "That the Alamogordo Dam and Reservoir, New Mexico, referred to in the Act of August 11, 1939 (53 Stat. 1414) [which enacted this section], are redesignated as Sumner Dam and Lake Sumner, respectively. Any law, regulation, map, document, record, or other paper of the United States in which such dam or reservoir is referred to shall be held to refer to such dam as Sumner Dam or such reservoir as Lake Sumner."

§ 708. Sale of surplus waters for domestic and industrial uses; disposition of moneys

The Secretary of the Army is authorized to make contracts with States, municipalities, private concerns, or individuals, at such prices and on such terms as he may deem reasonable, for domestic and industrial uses for surplus water that may be available at any reservoir under the control of the Department of the Army: *Provided*, That no contracts for such water shall adversely affect then existing lawful uses of such water. All moneys received from such contracts shall be deposited in the Treasury of the United States as miscellaneous receipts.

(Dec. 22, 1944, ch. 665, § 6, 58 Stat. 890; July 26, 1947, ch. 343, title II, § 205(a), 61 Stat. 501; May 23, 1952, ch. 328, § 1(a), 66 Stat. 93.)

AMENDMENTS

1952—Act May 23, 1952, revived and reenacted section.

CHANGE OF NAME

Department of War designated Department of the Army and title of Secretary of War changed to Secretary of the Army by section 205(a) of act July 26, 1947, ch. 343, title II, 61 Stat. 501. Section 205(a) of act July 26, 1947, was repealed by section 53 of act Aug. 10, 1956, ch. 1041, 70A Stat. 641. Section 1 of act Aug. 10, 1956, enacted "Title 10, Armed Forces" which in sections 3010 to 3013 continued Department of the Army under administrative supervision of Secretary of the Army.

REPEALS

Act May 23, 1952, § 1(b), repealed paragraph (59) of section 1 of act Oct. 31, 1951, ch. 654, 65 Stat. 703, which had previously repealed this section.

TRANSFER OF FUNCTIONS

For transfer of certain personal property and functions relating thereto, insofar as they pertain to Air Force, from Secretary of the Army and Department of the Army to Secretary of the Air Force and Department of the Air Force, see Secretary of Defense Transfer Order No. 39, eff. May 18, 1949, and 40 [App. B (98)], July 22, 1949.

SECTION AS UNAFFECTED BY SUBMERGED LANDS ACT

Provisions of this section as not amended, modified or repealed by the Submerged Lands Act, see section 1303 of Title 43, Public Lands.

§ 709. Regulations for use of storage waters; application to Tennessee Valley Authority

On and after December 22, 1944, it shall be the duty of the Secretary of the Army to prescribe regulations for the use of storage allocated for flood control or navigation at all reservoirs constructed wholly or in part with Federal funds provided on the basis of such purposes, and the operation of any such project shall be in accordance with such regulations: *Provided*, That this section shall not apply to the Tennessee Valley Authority, except that in case of danger from floods on the Lower Ohio and Mississippi Rivers the Tennessee Valley Authority is directed to regulate the release of water from the Tennessee River into the Ohio River in accordance with such instructions as may be issued by the Department of the Army.

(Dec. 22, 1944, ch. 665, § 7, 58 Stat. 890; July 26, 1947, ch. 343, title II, § 205(a), 61 Stat. 501.)

CHANGE OF NAME

Department of War designated Department of the Army and title of Secretary of War changed to Secretary of the Army by section 205(a) of act July 26, 1947, ch. 343, title II, 61 Stat. 501. Section 205(a) of act July 26, 1947, was repealed by section 53 of act Aug. 10, 1956, ch. 1041, 70A Stat. 641. Section 1 of act Aug. 10, 1956, enacted "Title 10, Armed Forces" which in sections 3010 to 3013 continued Department of the Army under administrative supervision of Secretary of the Army.

SECTION AS UNAFFECTED BY SUBMERGED LANDS ACT

Provisions of this section as not amended, modified or repealed by the Submerged Lands Act, see section 1303 of Title 43, Public Lands.

§ 709a. Information on floods and flood damage

(a) Compilation and dissemination

In recognition of the increasing use and development of the flood plains of the rivers of the United States and of the need for information on flood hazards to serve as a guide to such development, and as a basis for avoiding future flood hazards by regulation of use by States and political subdivisions thereof, and to assure that Federal departments and agencies may take proper cognizance of flood hazards, the Secretary of the Army, through the Chief of Engineers, is hereby authorized to compile and disseminate information on floods and flood damages, including identification of areas subject to inundation by floods of various magnitudes and frequencies, and general criteria for guidance of Federal and non-Federal interests and agencies in the use of flood plain areas; and to provide advice to other Federal agencies and local interests for their use in planning to ameliorate the flood hazard. Surveys and guides will be made for States and political subdivisions thereof only upon the request of a State or a political subdivision thereof, and upon approval by the Chief of Engineers, and such information and advice provided them only upon such request and approval.

(b) Flood prevention coordination

The Secretary shall coordinate with the Administrator of the Federal Emergency Management Agency and the heads of other Federal agencies to ensure that flood control projects and plans are complementary and integrated to the extent practicable and appropriate.

(c) Fees

The Secretary of the Army is authorized to establish and collect fees from Federal agencies and private persons for the purpose of recovering the cost of providing services pursuant to this section. Funds collected pursuant to this section shall be deposited into the account of the Treasury of the United States entitled "Contributions and Advances, Rivers and Harbor, Corps of Engineers (8862)" and shall be available until expended to carry out this section. No fees shall be collected from State, regional, or local governments or other non-Federal public agencies for services provided pursuant to this section, but the Secretary of the Army may accept funds voluntarily contributed by such entities for the purpose of expanding the scope of the services requested by the entities.

(d) Fiscal year limitation on expenditures

The Secretary of the Army is authorized to expend not to exceed $15,000,000 per fiscal year for the compilation and dissemination of information under this section.

(Pub. L. 86–645, title II, §206, July 14, 1960, 74 Stat. 500; Pub. L. 89–298, title II, §220, Oct. 27, 1965, 79 Stat. 1089; Pub. L. 89–789, title II, §206, Nov. 7, 1966, 80 Stat. 1422; Pub. L. 91–611, title II, §225, Dec. 31, 1970, 84 Stat. 1832; Pub. L. 93–251, title I, §64, Mar. 7, 1974, 88 Stat. 30; Pub. L. 101–640, title III, §321, Nov. 28, 1990, 104 Stat. 4643; Pub. L. 106–53, title II, §§202, 216, Aug. 17, 1999, 113 Stat. 285, 293; Pub. L. 109–295, title VI, §612(c), Oct. 4, 2006, 120 Stat. 1410.)

AMENDMENTS

1999—Subsec. (b). Pub. L. 106–53, §216, added subsec. (b). Former subsec. (b) redesignated (c).

Pub. L. 106–53, §202, inserted before period at end of third sentence ", but the Secretary of the Army may accept funds voluntarily contributed by such entities for the purpose of expanding the scope of the services requested by the entities".

Subsecs. (c), (d). Pub. L. 106–53, §216(1), redesignated subsecs. (b) and (c) as (c) and (d), respectively.

1990—Pub. L. 101–640 added subsec. (b) and redesignated former subsec. (b) as (c).

1974—Subsec. (b). Pub. L. 93–251 substituted "$15,000,000" for "$11,000,000".

1970—Subsec. (b). Pub. L. 91–611 substituted "$11,000,000" for "$7,000,000".

1966—Subsec. (a). Pub. L. 89–789, in amending subsec. (a) generally, substituted "political subdivisions thereof" for "municipalities" and "advice" for "engineering advice", inserted provision "to assure that Federal departments and agencies may take proper cognizance of flood hazards", provided for guidance of Federal and non-Federal interests and agencies and advice to other Federal agencies, and for surveys and guides upon request of a State or political subdivision in lieu of surveys and studies for specific localities upon request of a State or responsible local governmental agency.

Subsec. (b). Pub. L. 89–789 substituted "expend not to exceed $7,000,000 per fiscal year for the compilation and dissemination of information under this section" for "allot, from any appropriations hereafter made for flood control, sums not to exceed $2,500,000 in any one fiscal year for the compilation and dissemination of such information".

1965—Subsec. (b). Pub. L. 89–298 substituted "$2,500,000" for "$1,000,000".

CHANGE OF NAME

"Administrator of the Federal Emergency Management Agency" substituted for "Director of the Federal Emergency Management Agency" in subsec. (b) on authority of section 612(c) of Pub. L. 109–295, set out as a note under section 313 of Title 6, Domestic Security. Any reference to the Administrator of the Federal Emergency Management Agency in title VI of Pub. L. 109–295 or an amendment by title VI to be considered to refer and apply to the Director of the Federal Emergency Management Agency until Mar. 31, 2007, see section 612(f)(2) of Pub. L. 109–295, set out as a note under section 313 of Title 6.

§ 709b. Flood hazard information

The Secretary, the Administrator of the Federal Emergency Management Agency, and the Administrator of the Soil Conservation Service shall take necessary actions, including the posting and distribution of information and the preparation and distribution of educational materials and programs, to ensure that information relating to flood hazard areas is generally available to the public.

(Pub. L. 99–662, title IX, §944, Nov. 17, 1986, 100 Stat. 4200; Pub. L. 109–295, title VI, §612(c), Oct. 4, 2006, 120 Stat. 1410.)

CHANGE OF NAME

"Administrator of the Federal Emergency Management Agency" substituted for "Director of the Federal Emergency Management Agency" in text on authority of section 612(c) of Pub. L. 109–295, set out as a note under section 313 of Title 6, Domestic Security. Any reference to the Administrator of the Federal Emergency Management Agency in title VI of Pub. L. 109–295 or an amendment by title VI to be considered to refer and apply to the Director of the Federal Emergency Management Agency until Mar. 31, 2007, see section 612(f)(2) of Pub. L. 109–295, set out as a note under section 313 of Title 6.

"SECRETARY" DEFINED

Secretary means the Secretary of the Army, see section 2201 of this title.

CHAPTER 16—LIGHTHOUSES

§§ 711 to 715. Omitted

CODIFICATION

Sections related to the establishment of the Bureau of Lighthouses in the Department of Commerce. The Bureau of Lighthouses and its functions were transferred to and consolidated with the Coast Guard in the Department of the Treasury to be administered as a part thereof by Reorg. Plan No. II of 1939, §2(a), eff. July 1, 1939, 4 F.R. 2731, 53 Stat. 1432, set out in the Appendix to Title 5, Government Organization and Employees. Further provision to perfect the consolidation of the Lighthouse Service with the Coast Guard by authorizing the commissioning, appointment, and enlistment in the Coast Guard, of certain officers and employees of the Lighthouse Service, was made by act Aug. 5, 1939, ch. 477, 53 Stat. 1216.

Section 711, acts June 17, 1910, ch. 301, §4, 36 Stat. 537; Mar. 4, 1913, ch. 141, §1, 37 Stat. 736; June 5, 1920, ch. 264, §2, 41 Stat. 1059; July 3, 1930, ch. 850, 46 Stat. 1003; Aug. 16, 1937, ch. 665, §4, 50 Stat. 667, related to establishment of Bureau of Lighthouses, personnel, salaries, and annual reports.

Act June 5, 1920, ch. 264, §2, 41 Stat. 1059, formerly classified to section 711 of this title, was repealed by Pub. L. 89–554, §8(a), Sept. 6, 1966, 80 Stat. 644.

Section 712, acts July 27, 1912, ch. 255, §2, 37 Stat. 239; Mar. 4, 1913, ch. 141, §1, 37 Stat. 736, authorized designation of acting commissioner.

Section 713, acts June 17, 1910, ch. 301, §10, 36 Stat. 538; Mar. 4, 1913, ch. 141, §1, 37 Stat. 736, related to regulations for Lighthouse Service.

Section 714, acts June 17, 1910, ch. 301, §6, 36 Stat. 538; acts Mar. 4, 1913, ch. 141, §1, 37 Stat. 736, transferred duties of Lighthouse Board to Commissioner of Lighthouses.

Section 715, act June 17, 1910, ch. 301, §5, 36 Stat. 537, related to transfer of employees.

§ 716. Repealed. Aug. 4, 1949, ch. 393, § 20, 63 Stat. 561

Section, acts June 17, 1910, ch. 301, §9, 36 Stat. 538; July 27, 1939, ch. 388, §1, 53 Stat. 1130, related to employment of temporary draftsmen. See section 653 of Title 14, Coast Guard.

EFFECTIVE DATE OF REPEAL

Repeal effective first day of third month after approval by President [Aug. 4, 1949], see section 19 of act Aug. 4, 1949, set out as an Effective Date note preceding chapter 1 of Title 14, Coast Guard.

§ 717. Detail of Army engineers as construction aids

The President may detail officers of the Engineer Corps of the United States Army for consultation or to superintend the construction or repair of any aid to navigation authorized by Congress.

(June 17, 1910, ch. 301, §11, 36 Stat. 539.)

CODIFICATION

This section was enacted as part of section 11 of act June 17, 1910, which also enacted section 743 of this title.

§ 717a. Repealed. Pub. L. 89–554, § 8(a), Sept. 6, 1966, 80 Stat. 647

Section, act Feb. 25, 1929, ch. 313, §5, 45 Stat. 1262, provided for the detail of superintendents and engineers to duty at Washington.

§ 718. Repealed. Aug. 4, 1949, ch. 393, § 20, 63 Stat. 561

Section, act Feb. 26, 1907, ch. 1638, §6, 34 Stat. 997, related to traveling expenses of Army and Navy officers. See section 404 et seq. of Title 37, Pay and Allowances of the Uniformed Services.

EFFECTIVE DATE OF REPEAL

Repeal effective first day of third month after approval by President [Aug. 4, 1949], see section 19 of act Aug. 4, 1949, set out as an Effective Date note preceding chapter 1 of Title 14, Coast Guard.

§ 719. Omitted

CODIFICATION

Section, R.S. §4679, provided that no additional salary should be allowed to any civil, military, or naval officer on account of his being employed in the Light-

House Board, or being in any manner attached to the light-house service. The functions of the Light-House Board and all employees of or in the Light-House Board or the Light-House Establishment, except army and navy officers, were transferred to the Bureau of Lighthouses by act June 17, 1910, ch. 301, §§ 5, 6, 36 Stat. 537. The Bureau of Lighthouses was transferred to and consolidated in the Coast Guard by Reorg. Plan No. II of 1939, § 2(a), eff. July 1, 1939, 4 F.R. 2731, 53 Stat. 1432, set out in the Appendix to Title 5, Government Organization and Employees. Act Aug. 5, 1939, ch. 477, 53 Stat. 1216, provided for the commissioning or enlistment in the Coast Guard of former employees of the Bureau of Lighthouses.

§§ 720, 720a. Repealed. Aug. 4, 1949, ch. 393, § 20, 63 Stat. 561

Section 720, acts June 17, 1910, ch. 301, § 7, 36 Stat. 538; Mar. 4, 1913, ch. 141, § 1, 37 Stat. 736, related to general control by Commandant of Coast Guard. See section 81 of Title 14, Coast Guard.

Section 720a, act Aug. 16, 1937, ch. 665, § 3, 50 Stat. 667, related to establishment and maintenance of aids to navigation in certain waters. See section 81 of Title 14, Coast Guard.

Effective Date of Repeal

Repeal effective first day of third month after approval by President [Aug. 4, 1949], see section 19 of act Aug. 4, 1949, set out as an Effective Date note preceding chapter 1 of Title 14, Coast Guard.

§ 721. Omitted

Codification

Section, acts June 17, 1910, ch. 301, § 4, 36 Stat. 537; Mar. 4, 1913, ch. 141, § 1, 37 Stat. 736; Aug. 16, 1937, ch. 665, § 4, 50 Stat. 667, gave Commissioner the power to settle damage claims up to $500. These duties and functions of Commissioner of Lighthouses were taken over by Commandant of Coast Guard under Reorg. Plan II of 1939, § 2(a), eff. July 1, 1939, 4 F.R. 2731, 53 Stat. 1432, set out in the Appendix to Title 5, Government Organization and Employees.

§§ 721a to 724. Repealed. Aug. 4, 1949, ch. 393, § 20, 63 Stat. 561

Section 721a, acts Aug. 16, 1937, ch. 665, § 2, 50 Stat. 667; July 11, 1941, ch. 290, § 2, 55 Stat. 585, related to deposit of damage payments and disbursement. See section 642 of Title 14, Coast Guard.

Section 722, acts July 7, 1884, ch. 332, 23 Stat. 198; June 17, 1910, ch. 301, § 6, 36 Stat. 538, related to necessity for contract for expenditure of appropriations.

Section 723, act Mar. 4, 1909, ch. 299, § 1, 35 Stat. 973, related to proposals for repair of vessels and specifications.

Section 724, acts June 17, 1910, ch. 301, § 8, 36 Stat. 538; Mar. 4, 1913, ch. 141, § 1, 37 Stat. 736, related to contracts for materials and necessity for public letting.

Effective Date of Repeal

Repeal effective first day of third month after approval by President [Aug. 4, 1949], see section 19 of act Aug. 4, 1949, set out as an Effective Date note preceding chapter 1 of Title 14, Coast Guard.

§ 725. Prohibition against officers and employees being interested in contracts for materials, etc.

No Commandant of the Coast Guard, superintendent of lighthouses, lightkeeper, or other person in any manner connected with the lighthouse service, shall be interested, either directly or indirectly, in any contract for labor, materials, or supplies for the light-house service, or in any patent, plan, or mode of construction or illumination, or in any article of supply for the light-house service.

(R.S. § 4680; June 17, 1910, ch. 301, §§ 6, 13, 36 Stat. 538, 539; June 20, 1918, ch. 103, § 7, 40 Stat. 608; 1939 Reorg. Plan No. II, § 2(a), eff. July 1, 1939, 4 F.R. 2731, 53 Stat. 1432; Aug. 4, 1949, ch. 393, §§ 1, 20, 63 Stat. 496, 561.)

Codification

R.S. § 4680 derived from act Aug. 31, 1852, ch. 112, § 17, 10 Stat. 120.

Transfer of Functions

"Commandant of the Coast Guard" substituted in text for "member of the Light-House Board" on authority of sections 6 and 13 of act June 17, 1910, which abolished board and transferred its powers and duties to Commissioner of Lighthouses who was head of Bureau of Lighthouses. Said sections 6 and 13 were repealed by section 20 of act Aug. 4, 1949, section 1 of which reestablished the Coast Guard by enacting Title 14, Coast Guard. Section 2(a) of Reorg. Plan No. II of 1939, set out in the Appendix to Title 5, Government Organization and Employees, consolidated Bureau of Lighthouses with Coast Guard, Chief of which is Commandant of Coast Guard.

The words "superintendent of lighthouses" substituted for "inspector" on authority of act June 20, 1918, which transferred such officers to the positions of superintendent of lighthouses within the Bureau of Lighthouses.

The light-house service was a service under control of Commissioner of Lighthouses within Bureau of Lighthouses.

For transfer of functions of other officers, employees, and agencies of Department of the Treasury, with certain exceptions, to Secretary of the Treasury with power to delegate, see Reorg. Plan No. 26 of 1950, §§ 1, 2 eff. July 31, 1950, 15 F.R. 4935, 64 Stat. 1280, 1281, set out in the Appendix to Title 5, Government Organization and Employees. Functions of Coast Guard, and Commandant of Coast Guard, excepted from transfer when Coast Guard is operating as part of Navy under sections 1 and 3 of Title 14, Coast Guard.

Coast Guard transferred to Department of Transportation, and all functions, powers, and duties relating to Coast Guard of Secretary of the Treasury and of other officers and offices of Department of the Treasury transferred to Secretary of Transportation by Pub. L. 89–670, § 6(b)(1), Oct. 15, 1966, 80 Stat. 938. Section 6(b)(2) of Pub. L. 89–670, however, provided that notwithstanding such transfer of functions, Coast Guard shall operate as part of Navy in time of war or when President directs as provided in section 3 of Title 14. See section 108 of Title 49, Transportation.

For transfer of authorities, functions, personnel, and assets of the Coast Guard, including the authorities and functions of the Secretary of Transportation relating thereto, to the Department of Homeland Security, and for treatment of related references, see sections 468(b), 551(d), 552(d), and 557 of Title 6, Domestic Security, and the Department of Homeland Security Reorganization Plan of November 25, 2002, as modified, set out as a note under section 542 of Title 6.

§ 726. Repealed. Aug. 4, 1949, ch. 393, § 20, 63 Stat. 561

Section, act Mar. 4, 1913, ch. 168, 37 Stat. 1018, related to procurement of supplies and equipment for special works of Lighthouse Service. See section 649 of Title 14, Coast Guard.

Effective Date of Repeal

Repeal effective first day of third month after approval by the President [Aug. 4, 1949], see section 19 of act Aug. 19, 1949, set out as an Effective Date note preceding chapter 1 of Title 14, Coast Guard.

§ 727. Lighthouse and other sites; necessity for cession by State of jurisdiction

No lighthouse, beacon, public piers, or landmark, shall be built or erected on any site until cession of jurisdiction over the same has been made to the United States.

(R.S. § 4661.)

CODIFICATION

R.S. § 4661 derived from act Mar. 3, 1821, ch. 52, § 3, 3 Stat. 644.

§ 728. Sufficiency of cession by State; service of State process in lands ceded

A cession by a State of jurisdiction over a place selected as the site of a lighthouse, or other structure or work, shall be deemed sufficient within section 727 of this title, notwithstanding it contains a reservation that process issued under authority of such State may continue to be served within such place. And notwithstanding any such cession of jurisdiction contains no such reservation, all process may be served and executed within the place ceded, in the same manner as if no cession had been made.

(R.S. § 4662.)

CODIFICATION

R.S. § 4662 derived from act Mar. 2, 1795, ch. 40, §§ 1, 2, 1 Stat. 426.

§§ 729, 730. Repealed. Aug. 4, 1949, ch. 393, § 20, 63 Stat. 561

Section 729, acts June 17, 1910, ch. 301, § 9, 36 Stat. 538; Mar. 4, 1913, ch. 141, § 1, 37 Stat. 736, related to purchase by Commandant of sites for lighthouses. See sections 92(f) and 653 of Title 14, Coast Guard.

Section 730, acts Mar. 4, 1913, ch. 168, 37 Stat. 1018; Mar. 4, 1913, ch. 141, § 1, 37 Stat. 736; Oct. 22, 1913, ch. 32, 38 Stat. 225, related to purchase of additional land for lighthouses and depots. See section 92(f) of Title 14.

EFFECTIVE DATE OF REPEAL

Repeal effective first day of third month after approval by President [Aug. 4, 1949], see section 19 of act Aug. 19, 1949, set out as an Effective Date note preceding chapter 1 of Title 14, Coast Guard.

§ 730a. Sites for pierhead beacons

The Secretary of Transportation is authorized whenever he shall deem it advisable, to acquire, by donation or purchase in behalf of the United States, the right to use and occupy sites for pierhead beacons the establishment of which has been, or shall hereafter be, authorized by Congress.

(Mar. 3, 1875, ch. 130, § 1, 18 Stat. 372; Mar. 4, 1913, ch. 141, § 1, 37 Stat. 736; 1939 Reorg. Plan No. II, § 2(a), eff. July 1, 1939, 4 F.R. 2731, 53 Stat. 1432; Pub. L. 89–670, § 6(b)(1), Oct. 15, 1966, 80 Stat. 938.)

CODIFICATION

Section is based on last paragraph under heading "FOR LIFE-SAVING AND LIFE-BOAT STATIONS" of act Mar. 3, 1875, ch. 130, 18 Stat. 372, insofar as such paragraph provided for the right to use and occupy sites for pier-head beacons. Provisions of such paragraph relating to the right to use and occupy sites for Coast Guard Stations and houses of refuge were classified to section 96 of former Title 14, Coast Guard, and were repealed by act Aug. 4, 1949, ch. 393, § 20, 63 Stat. 561, and restated as section 92(f) of Title 14, Coast Guard.

TRANSFER OF FUNCTIONS

For transfer of authorities, functions, personnel, and assets of the Coast Guard, including the authorities and functions of the Secretary of Transportation relating thereto, to the Department of Homeland Security, and for treatment of related references, see sections 468(b), 551(d), 552(d), and 557 of Title 6, Domestic Security, and the Department of Homeland Security Reorganization Plan of November 25, 2002, as modified, set out as a note under section 542 of Title 6.

Coast Guard transferred to Department of Transportation, and all functions, powers, and duties relating to Coast Guard of Secretary of the Treasury and of other officers and offices of Department of the Treasury transferred to Secretary of Transportation by Pub. L. 89–670, § 6(b)(1), Oct. 15, 1966, 80 Stat. 938. Section 6(b)(2) of Pub. L. 89–670, however, provided that notwithstanding such transfer of functions, Coast Guard shall operate as part of Navy in time of war or when President directs as provided in section 3 of Title 14, Coast Guard. See section 108 of Title 49, Transportation.

Bureau of Lighthouses and its functions transferred and consolidated with Coast Guard by Reorg. Plan No. II of 1939, § 2(a), set out in the Appendix to Title 5, Government Organization and Employees.

§§ 731, 732. Repealed. Aug. 4, 1949, ch. 393, § 20, 63 Stat. 561

Section 731, acts Mar. 4, 1909, ch. 299, § 1, 35 Stat. 972; June 17, 1910, ch. 301, § 6, 36 Stat. 538, related to lease of sites for temporary lights. See section 92 of Title 14, Coast Guard.

Section 732, acts Aug. 28, 1916, ch. 414, § 2, 39 Stat. 538; July 11, 1941, ch. 290, § 1, 55 Stat. 584, related to exchange of right-of-way pertaining to Coast Guard. See section 92 of Title 14.

EFFECTIVE DATE OF REPEAL

Repeal effective first day of third month after approval by President [Aug. 4, 1949], see section 19 of act Aug. 4, 1949, set out as an Effective Date note preceding chapter 1 of Title 14, Coast Guard.

§ 733. Transferred

CODIFICATION

Section, R.S. § 355; June 28, 1930, ch. 710, 46 Stat. 828; Feb. 1, 1940, ch. 18, 54 Stat. 19; Oct. 9, 1940, ch. 793, 54 Stat. 1083; Sept. 1, 1970, Pub. L. 91–393, § 1, 84 Stat. 835, which related to approval of title prior to Federal land purchases, payment of title expenses, application to Tennessee Valley Authority, and Federal jurisdiction over acquisitions, was transferred to section 255 of former Title 40, Public Buildings, Property, and Works, and was repealed and reenacted as sections 3111 and 3112 of Title 40, Public Buildings, Property, and Works, by Pub. L. 107–217, §§ 1, 6(b), Aug. 21, 2002, 116 Stat. 1062, 1304; Pub. L. 108–178, § 2(a)(8), Dec. 15, 2003, 117 Stat. 2638.

§ 734. Repealed. Aug. 4, 1949, ch. 393, § 20, 63 Stat. 561

Section, R.S. § 4678, related to coloring and numbering buoys. See section 87 of Title 14, Coast Guard.

EFFECTIVE DATE OF REPEAL

Repeal effective first day of third month after approval by President [Aug. 4, 1949], see section 19 of act Aug. 4, 1949, set out as an Effective Date note preceding chapter 1 of Title 14, Coast Guard.

§ 735. Marking pierheads in certain lakes

The Commandant of the Coast Guard shall properly mark all pierheads belonging to the

United States situated on the northern and northwestern lakes, whenever he is duly notified by the department charged with the construction or repair of pierheads that the construction or repair of any such pierheads has been completed.

(R.S. §4677; June 17, 1910, ch. 301, §§6, 13, 36 Stat. 538, 539; 1939 Reorg. Plan No. II, §2(a), eff. July 1, 1939, 4 F.R. 2731, 53 Stat. 1432; Aug. 4, 1949, ch. 393, §§1, 20, 63 Stat. 496, 561.)

CODIFICATION

R.S. §4677 derived from act July 15, 1870, ch. 292, §3, 16 Stat. 309.

TRANSFER OF FUNCTIONS

"Commandant of the Coast Guard" substituted in text for "Light-House Board" on authority of sections 6 and 13 of act June 17, 1910, which abolished the board and transferred its powers and duties to the Commissioner of Lighthouses, who was the head of the Bureau of Lighthouses. Said sections 6 and 13 were repealed by section 20 of act Aug. 4, 1949, section 1 of which reestablished the Coast Guard by enacting Title 14, Coast Guard. Section 2(a) of Reorg. Plan No. II of 1939, set out in the Appendix to Title 5, Government Organization and Employees, consolidated the Bureau of Lighthouses with the Coast Guard, the Chief of which is the Commandant of the Coast Guard.

For transfer of functions of other officers, employees, and agencies of Department of the Treasury, with certain exceptions, to Secretary of the Treasury with power to delegate, see Reorg. Plan No. 26 of 1950, §§1, 2, eff. July 31, 1950, 15 F.R. 4935, 64 Stat. 1280, 1281, set out in the Appendix to Title 5. Functions of Coast Guard, and Commandant of Coast Guard, were excepted from transfer when Coast Guard is operating as part of Navy under sections 1 and 3 of Title 14, Coast Guard.

Coast Guard transferred to Department of Transportation, and all functions, powers, and duties relating to Coast Guard of Secretary of the Treasury and of other officers and offices of Department of the Treasury transferred to Secretary of Transportation by Pub. L. 89–670, §6(b)(1), Oct. 15, 1966, 80 Stat. 938. Section 6(b)(2) of Pub. L. 89–670, however, provided that notwithstanding such transfer of functions, Coast Guard shall operate as part of Navy in time of war or when President directs as provided in section 3 of Title 14. See section 108 of Title 49, Transportation.

For transfer of authorities, functions, personnel, and assets of the Coast Guard, including the authorities and functions of the Secretary of Transportation relating thereto, to the Department of Homeland Security, and for treatment of related references, see sections 468(b), 551(d), 552(d), and 557 of Title 6, Domestic Security, and the Department of Homeland Security Reorganization Plan of November 25, 2002, as modified, set out as a note under section 542 of Title 6.

§736. Repealed. Aug. 4, 1949, ch. 393, §20, 63 Stat. 561

Section, R.S. §4676; acts June 10, 1910, ch. 301, §6, 36 Stat. 538; Aug. 16, 1937, ch. 665, §1, 50 Stat. 666, related to placement of markers over sunken craft and other obstructions. See section 86 of Title 14, Coast Guard.

EFFECTIVE DATE OF REPEAL

Repeal effective first day of third month after approval by President [Aug. 4, 1949], see section 19 of act Aug. 4, 1949, set out as an Effective Date note preceding chapter 1 of Title 14, Coast Guard.

§§737, 738. Omitted

CODIFICATION

Section 737, act May 14, 1908, ch. 168, §4, 35 Stat. 162, as affected by act June 17, 1910, ch. 301, §6, 36 Stat. 538, related to maintenance of anchorage buoys in New York and Philadelphia harbors. See section 472 of this title.

Section 738, act June 5, 1920, ch. 235, §1, 41 Stat. 880, provided that the Lighthouse Service should cooperate with the Coast Guard in marking certain anchorage grounds. The Lighthouse Service was consolidated in the Coast Guard by Reorg. Plan No. II of 1939, §2(a), eff. July 1, 1939, 4 F.R. 2731, 53 Stat. 1432, set out in the Appendix to Title 5, Government Organization and Employees.

§§739 to 740b. Repealed. Aug. 4, 1949, ch. 393, §20, 63 Stat. 561

Section 739, R.S. §4668, related to substitution of lighthouses for lightships.

Section 740, acts Mar. 3, 1915, ch. 81, §5, 38 Stat. 927; Aug. 28, 1916, ch. 414, §3, 39 Stat. 538; June 20, 1918, ch. 103, §5, 40 Stat. 608; June 5, 1920, ch. 235, §1, 41 Stat. 927, related to post-lantern lights on particular waters.

Section 740a, act May 22, 1926, ch. 371, §6, 44 Stat. 626, related to post-lantern lights on Allegheny and Rock Rivers.

Section 740b, acts June 23, 1874, ch. 455, §1, 18 Stat. 220; June 17, 1910, ch. 301, §6, 36 Stat. 538, related to lights and buoys on Mississippi, Ohio, and Missouri Rivers.

Sections covered by section 81 of Title 14, Coast Guard.

EFFECTIVE DATE OF REPEAL

Repeal effective first day of third month after approval by President [Aug. 4, 1949], see section 19 of act Aug. 4, 1949, set out as an Effective Date note preceding chapter 1 of Title 14, Coast Guard.

§§741, 742. Repealed. June 6, 1940, ch. 257, §§5, 6, 54 Stat. 247

Section 741, acts May 14, 1908, ch. 168, §7, 35 Stat. 162; June 17, 1910, ch. 301, §6, 36 Stat. 538; Mar. 4, 1913, ch. 141, §1, 37 Stat. 736, related to reports of aids to navigation which might be discontinued.

Section 742, R.S. §4674; acts Feb. 14, 1903, ch. 552, §10, 32 Stat. 829; June 17, 1910, ch. 301, §6, 36 Stat. 538; Mar. 4, 1913, ch. 141, §1, 37 Stat. 736, related to discontinuance and reestablishment of lights.

Provisions of section 742 were substantially incorporated into sections 92 and 93 of Title 14, Coast Guard.

§743. Lighthouse districts

The ocean, gulf, and lake coasts and the rivers of the United States, Puerto Rico, and the naval station in Cuba shall be arranged into not exceeding nineteen lighthouse districts.

(June 17, 1910, ch. 301, §11, 36 Stat. 538; May 17, 1932, ch. 190, 47 Stat. 158.)

CODIFICATION

This section was enacted as part of section 11 of act June 17, 1910, which also enacted section 717 of this title.

The original text provided "that the commissioner of lighthouses, subject to the approval of the Secretary of Commerce and Labor, as soon as practicable" should rearrange the ocean, gulf and lake coasts and the rivers of the United States, Puerto Rico and the naval station in Cuba into not exceeding nineteen lighthouse districts.

PRIOR PROVISIONS

Prior provisions for the arrangement of the various lighthouse districts were made by R.S. §4670; act July 26, 1886, ch. 779, 24 Stat. 148, which were repealed by section 13 of act June 17, 1910.

CHANGE OF NAME

"Puerto Rico" substituted in text for "Porto Rico" pursuant to act May 17, 1932, which is classified to section 731a of Title 48, Territories and Insular Possessions.

§ 744. Omitted

CODIFICATION

Section, act June 20, 1918, ch. 103, §7, 40 Stat. 608, related to superintendents of lighthouses and their salaries. The Bureau of Lighthouses and its functions were transferred and consolidated with the Coast Guard by Reorg. Plan No. II of 1939, §2(a), eff. July 1, 1939, 4 F.R. 2731, 53 Stat. 1432, set out in the Appendix to Title 5, Government Organization and Employees.

§ 745. Repealed. Aug. 4, 1949, ch. 393, § 20, 63 Stat. 561

Section, R.S. §4673; act June 20, 1918, ch. 103, §8, 40 Stat. 609, related to salaries of keepers of lighthouses.

EFFECTIVE DATE OF REPEAL

Repeal effective first day of third month after approval by President [Aug. 4, 1949], see section 19 of act Aug. 4, 1949, set out as an Effective Date note preceding chapter 1 of Title 14, Coast Guard.

§ 745a. Traveling expenses of new appointees to isolated posts outside United States

In all appropriations hereafter made for "General expenses, Coast Guard," there is authorized to be made available not exceeding $1,500 in any fiscal year, under rules prescribed by the Secretary of Transportation, for paying the actual and necessary traveling expenses of new appointees from ports of embarkation in the United States to first post of duty at isolated light stations, in districts outside the continental limits of the United States.

(May 13, 1938, ch. 215, § 1, 52 Stat. 353; 1939 Reorg. Plan No. II, § 2(a), eff. July 1, 1939, 4 F.R. 2731, 53 Stat. 1432; Pub. L. 89–670, § 6(b)(1), Oct. 15, 1966, 80 Stat. 938.)

TRANSFER OF FUNCTIONS

"Coast Guard" substituted in text for "Lighthouse Service" on authority of Reorg. Plan No. II of 1939, §2(a), set out in the Appendix to Title 5, Government Organization and Employees, which transferred and consolidated Bureau of Lighthouses, of which Lighthouse Service was a part, with Coast Guard.

For transfer of functions of other officers, employees, and agencies of Department of the Treasury, with certain exceptions, to Secretary of the Treasury with power to delegate, see Reorg. Plan No. 26 of 1950, §§1, 2, eff. July 31, 1950, 15 F.R. 4935, 64 Stat. 1280, 1281, set out in the Appendix to Title 5. Functions of Coast Guard, and Commandant of Coast Guard, were excepted from transfer when Coast Guard is operating as part of Navy under sections 1 and 3 of Title 14, Coast Guard.

Coast Guard transferred to Department of Transportation, and all functions, powers, and duties relating to Coast Guard of Secretary of the Treasury and of other officers and offices of Department of the Treasury transferred to Secretary of Transportation by Pub. L. 89–670, §6(b)(1), Oct. 15, 1966, 80 Stat. 938. Section 6(b)(2) of Pub. L. 89–670, however, provided that notwithstanding such transfer of functions, Coast Guard shall operate as part of Navy in time of war or when President directs as provided in section 3 of Title 14. See section 108 of Title 49, Transportation.

For transfer of authorities, functions, personnel, and assets of the Coast Guard, including the authorities and functions of the Secretary of Transportation relating thereto, to the Department of Homeland Security, and for treatment of related references, see sections 468(b), 551(d), 552(d), and 557 of Title 6, Domestic Security, and the Department of Homeland Security Reorganization Plan of November 25, 2002, as modified, set out as a note under section 542 of Title 6.

§§ 746 to 746b. Repealed. Aug. 4, 1949, ch. 393, § 20, 63 Stat. 565

Section 746, act June 29, 1949, ch. 277, §1, 63 Stat. 299, related to compensation and pay of civilians keepers of lighthouses and civilian employees on Coast Guard vessels.

Section 746a, act June 29, 1949, ch. 277, §2, 63 Stat. 299, related to extra pay and hours of duty.

Section 746b, act June 29, 1949, ch. 277, §3, 63 Stat. 300, related to additional compensation as affecting retirement compensation.

EFFECTIVE DATE OF REPEAL

Repeal effective first day of third month after approval by President [Aug. 4, 1949], see section 19 of act Aug. 4, 1949, set out as an Effective Date note preceding chapter 1 of Title 14, Coast Guard.

§§ 747, 747a. Repealed. July 1, 1944, ch. 373, title XIII, § 1313, 58 Stat. 714

Section 747, act Aug. 28, 1916, ch. 414, §5, 39 Stat. 538, related to medical relief to lighthouse keepers. See section 763c of this title. Act Aug. 28, 1916, was also repealed, by act Aug. 4, 1949, ch. 393, §20, 63 Stat. 561.

Section 747a, act May 22, 1926, ch. 371, §3, 44 Stat. 626, related to medical relief to lighthouse keepers. See section 763c of this title. Act May 22, 1926, was also repealed by act Aug. 4, 1949, ch. 393, §20, 63 Stat. 561.

RENUMBERING OF REPEALING ACT

Section 611 of act July 1, 1944, which repealed this section, was renumbered §711 by act Aug. 13, 1946, ch. 958, §5, 60 Stat. 1049, §713 by act Feb. 28, 1948, ch. 83, §9(b), 62 Stat. 47, §813 by act July 30, 1956, ch. 779, §3(b), 70 Stat. 720, §913 by Pub. L. 88–581, §4(b), Sept. 4, 1964, 78 Stat. 919, §1013 by Pub. L. 85–239, §3(b), Oct. 5, 1965, 79 Stat. 931, §1113 by Pub. L. 91–572, §6(b), Dec. 24, 1970, 84 Stat. 1506, §1213 by Pub. L. 92–294, §3(b), May 16, 1972, 86 Stat. 137; §1313 by Pub. L. 93–154, §2(b)(2), Nov. 16, 1973, 87 Stat. 604, and was repealed by Pub. L. 93–222, §7(b), Dec. 29, 1973, 87 Stat. 936.

§ 747b. Lighthouse keepers; traveling expenses incurred in obtaining medical attention

On and after February 25, 1929, the appropriation, "General expenses, Coast Guard," shall be available, under rules prescribed by the Secretary of Transportation, for paying the actual and necessary traveling expenses of lighthouse keepers at isolated stations incurred in obtaining medical attention.

(Feb. 25, 1929, ch. 313, § 1, 45 Stat. 1261; 1939 Reorg. Plan No. II, § 2(a), eff. July 1, 1939, 4 F.R. 2731, 53 Stat. 1432; Pub. L. 89–670, § 6(b)(1), Oct. 15, 1966, 80 Stat. 938.)

TRANSFER OF FUNCTIONS

"Coast Guard" substituted in text for "Lighthouse Service" on authority of Reorg. Plan No. II of 1939, §2(a), set out in the Appendix to Title 5, Government Organization and Employees, which transferred and consolidated Bureau of Lighthouses, of which Lighthouse Service was a part, with Coast Guard.

For transfer of functions of other officers, employees, and agencies of Department of the Treasury, with certain exceptions, to Secretary of the Treasury with power to delegate, see Reorg. Plan No. 26 of 1950, §§1, 2, eff. July 31, 1950, 15 F.R. 4935, 64 Stat. 1280, 1281, set out in the Appendix to Title 5. Functions of Coast Guard, and Commandant of Coast Guard, were excepted from transfer when Coast Guard is operating as part of Navy under sections 1 and 3 of Title 14, Coast Guard.

Coast Guard transferred to Department of Transportation, and all functions, powers, and duties relating to Coast Guard of Secretary of the Treasury and of other officers and offices of Department of the Treasury transferred to Secretary of Transportation by Pub. L. 89–670, § 6(b)(1), Oct. 15, 1966, 80 Stat. 938. Section 6(b)(2) of Pub. L. 89–670, however, provided that notwithstanding such transfer of functions, Coast Guard shall operate as part of Navy in time of war or when President directs as provided in section 3 of Title 14. See section 108 of Title 49, Transportation.

For transfer of authorities, functions, personnel, and assets of the Coast Guard, including the authorities and functions of the Secretary of Transportation relating thereto, to the Department of Homeland Security, and for treatment of related references, see sections 468(b), 551(d), 552(d), and 557 of Title 6, Domestic Security, and the Department of Homeland Security Reorganization Plan of November 25, 2002, as modified, set out as a note under section 542 of Title 6.

§ 748. Teachers for children of lighthouse keepers

The appropriation, "General expenses, Coast Guard," shall be available, under regulations prescribed by the Secretary of Transportation, for the payment of traveling and subsistence expenses of teachers while actually employed by States or private persons to instruct the children of keepers of lighthouses.

(June 20, 1918, ch. 103, § 2, 40 Stat. 608; 1939 Reorg. Plan No. II, § 2(a), eff. July 1, 1939, 4 F.R. 2731, 53 Stat. 1432; Pub. L. 89–670, § 6(b)(1), Oct. 15, 1966, 80 Stat. 938.)

Transfer of Functions

"Coast Guard" substituted in text for "Lighthouse Service" on authority of Reorg. Plan No. II of 1939, § 2(a), set out in the Appendix to Title 5, Government Organization and Employees, which transferred and consolidated Bureau of Lighthouses, of which Lighthouse Service was a part, with Coast Guard.

All functions of all officers of Department of the Treasury, and all functions of all agencies and employees of such Department, transferred, with certain exceptions, to Secretary of the Treasury, with power vested in him to authorize their performance or the performance of any of his functions, by any of such officers, agencies, and employees, by Reorg. Plan No. 26 of 1950, §§ 1, 2, eff. July 31, 1950, 15 F.R. 4935, 64 Stat. 1280, set out in the Appendix to Title 5.

Coast Guard transferred to Department of Transportation, and all functions, powers, and duties relating to Coast Guard of Secretary of the Treasury and of other officers and offices of Department of the Treasury transferred to Secretary of Transportation by Pub. L. 89–670, § 6(b)(1), Oct. 15, 1966, 80 Stat. 938. Section 6(b)(2) of Pub. L. 89–670, however, provided that notwithstanding such transfer of functions, Coast Guard shall operate as part of Navy in time of war or when President directs as provided in section 3 of Title 14, Coast Guard. See section 108 of Title 49, Transportation.

For transfer of authorities, functions, personnel, and assets of the Coast Guard, including the authorities and functions of the Secretary of Transportation relating thereto, to the Department of Homeland Security, and for treatment of related references, see sections 468(b), 551(d), 552(d), and 557 of Title 6, Domestic Security, and the Department of Homeland Security Reorganization Plan of November 25, 2002, as modified, set out as a note under section 542 of Title 6.

§ 748a. Transportation expenses for school children

In all appropriations hereafter made for "General expenses, Coast Guard" there is authorized to be made available not exceeding $2,500 in any fiscal year, for the transportation, under regulations prescribed by the Secretary of Transportation, of the children of lighthouse keepers at isolated light stations where necessary to enable such children to attend school.

(May 13, 1938, ch. 215, § 2, 52 Stat. 353; 1939 Reorg. Plan No. II, § 2(a), eff. July 1, 1939, 4 F.R. 2731, 53 Stat. 1432; Pub. L. 89–670, § 6(b)(1), Oct. 15, 1966, 80 Stat. 938.)

Transfer of Functions

"Coast Guard" substituted in text for "Lighthouse Service" on authority of Reorg. Plan No. II of 1939, § 2(a), set out in the Appendix to Title 5, Government Organization and Employees, which transferred and consolidated Bureau of Lighthouses, of which Lighthouse Service was a part, with Coast Guard.

For transfer of functions of other officers, employees, and agencies of Department of the Treasury, with certain exceptions, to Secretary of the Treasury with power to delegate, see Reorg. Plan No. 26 of 1950, §§ 1, 2, eff. July 31, 1950, 15 F.R. 4935, 64 Stat. 1280, 1281, set out in the Appendix to Title 5. Functions of Coast Guard, and Commandant of Coast Guard, were excepted from transfer when Coast Guard is operating as part of Navy under sections 1 and 3 of Title 14, Coast Guard.

Coast Guard transferred to Department of Transportation, and all functions, powers, and duties relating to Coast Guard of Secretary of the Treasury and of other officers and offices of Department of the Treasury transferred to Secretary of Transportation by Pub. L. 89–670, § 6(b)(1), Oct. 15, 1966, 80 Stat. 938. Section 6(b)(2) of Pub. L. 89–670, however, provided that notwithstanding such transfer of functions, Coast Guard shall operate as part of Navy in time of war or when President directs as provided in section 3 of Title 14. See section 108 of Title 49, Transportation.

For transfer of authorities, functions, personnel, and assets of the Coast Guard, including the authorities and functions of the Secretary of Transportation relating thereto, to the Department of Homeland Security, and for treatment of related references, see sections 468(b), 551(d), 552(d), and 557 of Title 6, Domestic Security, and the Department of Homeland Security Reorganization Plan of November 25, 2002, as modified, set out as a note under section 542 of Title 6.

§ 749. Repealed. Aug. 4, 1949, ch. 393, § 20, 63 Stat. 561

Section, acts July 27, 1912, ch. 255, § 2, 37 Stat. 239; Mar. 4, 1913, ch. 141, § 1, 37 Stat. 736, related to reimbursement of lighthouse keepers for clothing, etc., furnished shipwrecked persons. See section 486 of Title 14, Coast Guard.

Effective Date of Repeal

Repeal effective first day of third month after approval by President [Aug. 4, 1949], see section 19 of act Aug. 4, 1949, set out as an Effective Date preceding chapter 1 of Title 14, Coast Guard.

§ 750. Repealed. Pub. L. 89–554, § 8(a), Sept. 6, 1966, 80 Stat. 642

Section, act Aug. 1, 1914, ch. 223, § 1, 38 Stat. 658, related to leaves of absence to employees of Lighthouse Service.

§§ 751 to 752a. Repealed. Aug. 4, 1949, ch. 393, § 20, 63 Stat. 561

Section 751, act Mar. 3, 1915, ch. 81, § 4, 38 Stat. 927, related to leave of absence to employees of Lighthouse Service. See section 6301 et seq. of Title 5, Government Organization and Employees.

Section 752, acts Mar. 4, 1913, ch. 168, 37 Stat. 1019; Mar. 4, 1913, ch. 141, § 1, 37 Stat. 736, related to sale of condemned supplies, etc., and land not used; disposition of funds. See section 93 of Title 14, Coast Guard.

Section 752a, act May 22, 1926, ch. 371, § 5, 44 Stat. 626, related to sale of equipment; disposition of receipts. See section 641 of Title 14.

EFFECTIVE DATE OF REPEAL

Repeal effective first day of third month after approval by President [Aug. 4, 1949], see section 19 of act Aug. 4, 1949, set out as an Effective Date note preceding chapter 1 of Title 14, Coast Guard.

§ 752b. Omitted

CODIFICATION

Section, act June 15, 1938, ch. 398, 52 Stat. 692, related to disposal of materials to the Boys Scouts of America. See section 641 of Title 14, Coast Guard.

§§ 753, 754. Repealed. Aug. 4, 1949, ch. 393, § 20, 63 Stat. 561

Section 753, act June 20, 1918, ch. 103, § 4, 40 Stat. 608, related to sale of publications of Lighthouse Service. See sections 1705, 1708 of Title 44, Public Printing and Documents.

Section 754, acts July 27, 1912, ch. 255, § 2, 37 Stat. 239; Mar. 4, 1913, ch. 141, § 1, 37 Stat. 736, related to sale of clothing to employees. See section 485 of Title 14, Coast Guard.

EFFECTIVE DATE OF REPEAL

Repeal effective first day of third month after approval by President [Aug. 4, 1949], see section 19 of act Aug. 4, 1949, set out as an Effective Date note preceding chapter 1 of Title 14, Coast Guard.

§ 754a. Purchase of commissary and quartermaster supplies

Officers and crews of vessels of the Lighthouse Service and light keepers and depot keepers of the Lighthouse Service shall be permitted to purchase commissary and quartermaster supplies from the Army, Navy, or Marine Corps at the price charged officers and enlisted men of the Army, Navy, or Marine Corps.

(May 22, 1926, ch. 371, § 4, 44 Stat. 626.)

TRANSFER OF FUNCTIONS

Bureau of Lighthouses, of which Lighthouse Service was a part, transferred and consolidated with Coast Guard by Reorg. Plan No. II of 1939, § 2(a), eff. July 1, 1939, 4 F.R. 2731, 53 Stat. 1432, set out in the Appendix to Title 5, Government Organization and Employees.

For transfer of functions of other officers, employees, and agencies of Department of the Treasury, with certain exceptions, to Secretary of the Treasury with power to delegate, see Reorg. Plan No. 26 of 1950, §§ 1, 2, eff. July 31, 1950, 15 F.R. 4935, 64 Stat. 1280, 1281, set out in the Appendix to Title 5. Functions of Coast Guard, and Commandant of Coast Guard, were excepted from transfer when Coast Guard is operating as part of Navy under sections 1 and 3 of Title 14, Coast Guard.

Coast Guard transferred to Department of Transportation, and all functions, powers, and duties relating to Coast Guard of Secretary of the Treasury and of other officers and offices of Department of the Treasury transferred to Secretary of Transportation by Pub. L. 89–670, § 6(b)(1), Oct. 15, 1966, 80 Stat. 938. Section 6(b)(2) of Pub. L. 89–670, however, provided that notwithstanding such transfer of functions, Coast Guard shall operate as part of Navy in time of war or when President directs as provided in section 3 of Title 14. See section 108 of Title 49, Transportation.

For transfer of authorities, functions, personnel, and assets of the Coast Guard, including the authorities and functions of the Secretary of Transportation relating thereto, to the Department of Homeland Security, and for treatment of related references, see sections 468(b), 551(d), 552(d), and 557 of Title 6, Domestic Security, and the Department of Homeland Security Reorganization Plan of November 25, 2002, as modified, set out as a note under section 542 of Title 6.

§§ 755 to 762. Repealed. Aug. 4, 1949, ch. 393, § 20, 63 Stat. 561

Section 755, act June 16, 1880, ch. 235, 21 Stat. 263, related to police powers of masters of Lighthouse Service. See section 89 of Title 14, Coast Guard.

Section 756, act Mar. 3, 1915, ch. 81, § 6, 38 Stat. 928, related to use of appropriations with Forest Service. See section 141 of Title 14.

Section 757, act Aug. 29, 1916, ch. 417, 39 Stat. 602, related to cooperation with Army and Navy Departments in time of or in preparation for war. See sections 3, 88, 92, 93, 141, 144, 145, and 632 of Title 14.

Section 758, act Aug. 29, 1916, ch. 417, 39 Stat. 602, related to transfer of vessels, equipment, etc., to Navy or Army Departments in case of vocational emergency. See sections 3, 88, 92, 93, 141, 144, 145, and 632 of Title 14.

Section 759, acts June 20, 1906, ch. 3447, § 3, 34 Stat. 324; June 17, 1910, ch. 301, § 6, 36 Stat. 538, related to unauthorized establishment of lights and penalty. See section 83 of Title 14.

Section 760, act May 14, 1908, ch. 168, § 5, 35 Stat. 162, related to failure to maintain lights on bridges and penalty. See section 85 of Title 14.

Section 761, acts May 14, 1908, ch. 168, § 6, 35 Stat. 162; June 17, 1910, ch. 301, § 6, 36 Stat. 538, related to wrongful interference with Government aids to navigation and penalty. See section 84 of Title 14.

Section 762, act Mar. 3, 1915, ch. 81, § 8, 38 Stat. 928, related to wrongful interference with private aids to navigation and penalty. See section 84 of Title 14.

EFFECTIVE DATE OF REPEAL

Repeal effective first day of third month after approval by President [Aug. 4, 1949], see section 19 of act Aug. 4, 1949, set out as an Effective Date note preceding chapter 1 of Title 14, Coast Guard.

§ 763. Retirement for age of officers and employees generally; retirement pay; waiver of retirement pay

All officers and employees engaged in the field service or on vessels of the Lighthouse Service, except persons continuously employed in district offices or shop, who (1) shall have reached the age of fifty-five years, after having been thirty years in the active service of the Government, (2) shall have reached the age of sixty-two years, after having been twenty-five years in the active service of the Government, or (3) are involuntarily separated from further performance of duty, except by removal for cause on charges of misconduct or delinquency, after completing twenty-five years in the active service of the Government, or after completing twenty years of such service and after reaching the age of fifty years, may at their option be retired from further performance of duty; and all such officers and employees who shall have reached the age of seventy years shall be compulsorily retired from further performance of duty: *Provided*, That the annual compensation of persons so retired shall be a sum equal to one-fortieth of the average annual pay received for the last three years of service for each year of active service in the Lighthouse Service, or in a department or branch of the Government having a retirement system, not to exceed in any case thirty-fortieths of such average annual pay received: *Provided further*, That the retirement pay computed under the preceding proviso for any such officer or employee retiring under clause (3) shall be reduced by one-sixth of 1 per centum for each full month the officer or employee is under fifty-five years of age at the date of retirement: *Provided further*, That such retirement pay shall not include any amount on account of subsistence or other allowance: *Provided further*, That the retirement provisions and pay shall not apply to persons in the field service of the Lighthouse Service whose duties do not require substantially all their time. Any person entitled to retirement pay under this section may decline to accept all or any part of such retirement pay by a waiver signed and filed with the Secretary of the Treasury. Such waiver may be revoked in writing at any time, but no payment of the retirement pay waived shall be made covering the period during which such waiver was in effect.

(June 20, 1918, ch. 103, § 6, 40 Stat. 608; Nov. 4, 1918, ch. 201, § 1, 40 Stat. 1036; June 21, 1955, ch. 170, § 1, 69 Stat. 166; Pub. L. 85–142, Aug. 14, 1957, 71 Stat. 365; Pub. L. 90–164, § 1, Nov. 29, 1967, 81 Stat. 519; Pub. L. 92–455, § 6(a), Oct. 2, 1972, 86 Stat. 761.)

CODIFICATION

Except for the last proviso this section was from act June 20, 1918. The last proviso was from act Nov. 4, 1918, the First Deficiency Appropriation Act, 1919.

AMENDMENTS

1972—Pub. L. 92–455 inserted cl. (3), substituted "three" for "five" years of service in first proviso, and inserted proviso for reduction of retirement pay computed under cl. (3) by one-sixth of 1 per centum for each full month the officer or employee is under fifty-five years of age at the date of retirement.

1967—Pub. L. 90–164 lowered voluntary retirement age from sixty to fifty-five years for those officers and employees having thirty years of active service.

1957—Pub. L. 85–142 inserted provisions allowing waiver of retirement pay.

1955—Act June 21, 1955, permitted retirement of officers and employees who have attained 60 years of age and have served for 30 years, or who have reached 62 years of age and have served for 25 years.

EFFECTIVE DATE OF 1972 AMENDMENT

Section 6(b) of Pub. L. 92–455 provided that: "The amendments made by subsection (a) of this section [amending this section] shall apply with respect to officers and employees to which such section 6 [amending this section] applies who are involuntarily separated or retired on or after the date of the enactment of this Act [Oct. 2, 1972]."

EFFECTIVE DATE OF 1967 AMENDMENT

Section 2 of Pub. L. 90–164 provided that: "The amendment made by this Act [amending this section] shall take effect on the first day of the second month which begins after the date of enactment of this Act [Nov. 29, 1967]."

EFFECTIVE DATE OF 1955 AMENDMENT

Section 2 of act June 21, 1955, provided that: "This Act [amending this section] shall take effect on the first day of the second month beginning after the date of enactment of this Act [June 21, 1955]."

TRANSFER OF FUNCTIONS

Bureau of Lighthouses, of which Lighthouse Service was a part, transferred and consolidated with Coast Guard by Reorg. Plan No. II of 1939, § 2(a), eff July 1, 1939, 4 F.R. 2731, 53 Stat. 1432, set out in the Appendix to Title 5, Government Organization and Employees.

For transfer of functions of other officers, employees, and agencies of Department of the Treasury, with certain exceptions, to Secretary of the Treasury with power to delegate, see Reorg. Plan No. 26 of 1950, §§ 1, 2, eff. July 31, 1950, 15 F.R. 4935, 64 Stat. 1280, 1281, set out in the Appendix to Title 5. Functions of Coast Guard, and Commandant of Coast Guard, were excepted from transfer when Coast Guard is operating as part of Navy under sections 1 and 3 of Title 14, Coast Guard.

Coast Guard transferred to Department of Transportation, and all functions, powers, and duties relating to Coast Guard of Secretary of the Treasury and of other officers and offices of Department of the Treasury transferred to Secretary of Transportation by Pub. L. 89–670, § 6(b)(1), Oct. 15, 1966, 80 Stat. 938. Section 6(b)(2) of Pub. L. 89–670, however, provided that notwithstanding such transfer of functions, Coast Guard shall operate as part of Navy in time of war or when President directs as provided in section 3 of Title 14. See section 108 of Title 49, Transportation.

For transfer of authorities, functions, personnel, and assets of the Coast Guard, including the authorities and functions of the Secretary of Transportation relating thereto, to the Department of Homeland Security, and for treatment of related references, see sections 468(b), 551(d), 552(d), and 557 of Title 6, Domestic Security, and the Department of Homeland Security Reorganization Plan of November 25, 2002, as modified, set out as a note under section 542 of Title 6.

INCREASE OF PAY OF PERSONS RETIRED ON OR BEFORE OCTOBER 1, 1972

Pub. L. 94–178, Dec. 23, 1975, 89 Stat. 1033, provided: "That the annual rate of retired pay received by a person under section 6 of the Act of June 20, 1918, as amended and supplemented (33 U.S.C. 736–765), who was retired on or before October 1, 1972, shall, effective on the first day of the calendar month following enactment of this Act [Dec. 23, 1975], be increased by $270."

INCREASE OF PAY OF PERSONS RETIRED PRIOR TO 1967

Pub. L. 90–165, Nov. 29, 1967, 81 Stat. 519, provided: "That effective on the first day of the first month which begins after the date of enactment of this Act [Nov. 29, 1967], the annual rate of retired pay of a person retired under section 6 of the Act of June 20, 1918 (33 U.S.C. 763), shall be increased by 11.3 per centum if such person retired prior to January 1, 1966, or by 4.1 per centum if such person retired after December 31, 1965, but before January 1, 1967."

INCREASE OF PAY OF PERSONS RETIRED PRIOR TO 1963

Pub. L. 89–201, Sept. 25, 1965, 79 Stat. 834, provided: "That the annual rate of retired pay of each person retired prior to January 1, 1963, under section 6 of the Act of June 20, 1918, as amended and supplemented [this section], shall be increased by 6.5 per centum, effective on the first day of the first calendar month following the date of enactment of this Act [Sept. 25, 1965]."

INCREASE OF PAY OF PERSONS RETIRED PRIOR TO 1958

Pub. L. 86–361, Sept. 22, 1959, 73 Stat. 643, provided: "That the annual rate of retired pay of each person retired prior to January 1, 1958, under section 6 of the Act of June 20, 1918, as amended and supplemented [this section], shall be increased, effective on the first day of the first calendar month following the date of enactment of this Act [Sept. 22, 1959], by 10 per centum, or $150 per annum, whichever is the greater."

INCREASE OF PAY OF PERSONS RETIRED PRIOR TO 1953

Act Aug. 27, 1954, ch. 1010, 68 Stat. 878, as amended May 11, 1955, ch. 36, 69 Stat. 47, provided: "That the annual rate of retired pay received by any person who was retired on or before June 30, 1953, under section 6 of the Act of June 20, 1918, as amended and supplemented (section 763 of this title), shall be increased, effective on the first day of the calendar month following enactment of this Act, by 15 per centum of $264, whichever is the lesser: *Provided*, That no retired pay shall be increased to an amount in excess of $2,160 by reason of this Act."

COST-OF-LIVING ADJUSTMENT TO RETIREE'S ANNUITY

Adjustment of annuities of retired officers and employees based on cost-of-living increases, see section 2 of Pub. L. 90–163, Nov. 29, 1967, 81 Stat. 518, set out as a note under section 771 of this title.

§ 763–1. Increase of retired pay

The annual rate of retired pay received by any person who was retired on or before June 29, 1949, under section 763 of this title, as amended and supplemented, shall be increased by $360 effective on the first day of the calendar month following October 29, 1949.

(Oct. 29, 1949, ch. 788, 63 Stat. 1026.)

§ 763–2. Additional increase of retired pay

The annual rate of retired pay of each person retired under section 763 of this title, as amended and supplemented, shall be increased, effective on the first day of the first calendar month following July 9, 1956, in accordance with the following schedule:

If retired pay commences between—	Retired pay not in excess of $1,500 shall be increased by—	Retired pay in excess of $1,500 shall be increased by—
June 20, 1918, and June 30, 1955.	12 per centum ..	8 per centum.
July 1, 1955, and December 31, 1955.	10 per centum ..	7 per centum.
January 1, 1956, and June 30, 1956.	8 per centum	6 per centum.
July 1, 1956, and December 31, 1956.	6 per centum	4 per centum.
January 1, 1957, and June 30, 1957.	4 per centum	2 per centum.
July 1, 1957, and December 31, 1957.	2 per centum	1 per centum.

Such annual increase in retired pay shall not exceed the sum necessary to increase such retired pay to $4,104. The monthly installment of each retired payment so increased shall be fixed at the nearest dollar.

(July 9, 1956, ch. 524, 70 Stat. 510.)

§ 763a. Repealed. Aug. 4, 1949, ch. 393, § 20, 63 Stat. 561

Section, act May 22, 1926, ch. 371, § 7, 44 Stat. 626, related to retirement of certain officers and employees of the Lighthouse Service.

EFFECTIVE DATE OF REPEAL

Repeal effective first day of third month after approval by President [Aug. 4, 1949], see section 19 of act Aug. 4, 1949, set out as an Effective Date note preceding chapter 1 of Title 14, Coast Guard.

§ 763a–1. Retirement, exceptions for age and period of service

Any officer or employee of the Lighthouse Service who, on June 30, 1939, meets the requirements (except those relating to age and period of service) of section 763 of this title, as amended or supplemented, and who shall (1) reach the age of sixty-four years prior to July 1, 1940, or (2) be the occupant of an office or position abolished prior to July 1, 1940, may in the discretion of the head of his executive department be retired with annual compensation as provided in said section: *Provided, however*, That no such officer or employee shall be retired hereunder unless he shall have been in the service of the Government not less than thirty years at the time of retirement. Any officer or employee to whom this section applies who is not retired hereunder prior to reaching the age of sixty-five years shall, upon reaching such age, become eligible for retirement in accordance with the provisions of said section 763 of this title, and may not be retired under the provisions of this section. Nothing contained in this section shall be construed to affect the application of said section to any officer or employee of the Lighthouse Service to whom this section does not apply.

(Aug. 10, 1939, ch. 642, 53 Stat. 1343.)

TRANSFER OF FUNCTIONS

Bureau of Lighthouses, of which Lighthouse Service was a part, transferred and consolidated with Coast Guard by Reorg. Plan No. II of 1939, § 2(a), eff. July 1, 1939, 4 F.R. 2731, 53 Stat. 1432, set out in the Appendix to Title 5, Government Organization and Employees.

For transfer of functions of other officers, employees, and agencies of Department of the Treasury, with certain exceptions, to Secretary of the Treasury with power to delegate, see Reorg. Plan No. 26 of 1950, §§ 1, 2, eff. July 31, 1950, 15 F.R. 4935, 64 Stat. 1280, 1281, set out in the Appendix to Title 5. Functions of Coast Guard, and Commandant of Coast Guard, were excepted from transfer when Coast Guard is operating as part of Navy under sections 1 and 3 of Title 14, Coast Guard.

Coast Guard transferred to Department of Transportation, and all functions, powers, and duties relating to Coast Guard of Secretary of the Treasury and of other officers and offices of Department of the Treasury transferred to Secretary of Transportation by Pub. L. 89–670, § 6(b)(1), Oct. 15, 1966, 80 Stat. 938. Section 6(b)(2) of Pub. L. 89–670, however, provided that notwithstanding such transfer of functions, Coast Guard shall operate as part of Navy in time of war or when President directs as provided in section 3 of Title 14. See section 108 of Title 49, Transportation.

For transfer of authorities, functions, personnel, and assets of the Coast Guard, including the authorities and functions of the Secretary of Transportation relating thereto, to the Department of Homeland Security, and for treatment of related references, see sections 468(b), 551(d), 552(d), and 557 of Title 6, Domestic Security, and the Department of Homeland Security Reorganization Plan of November 25, 2002, as modified, set out as a note under section 542 of Title 6.

§ 763a–2. Application to persons of Coast Guard

The provisions of sections 763 and 763a–1 of this title shall not apply to persons of the Coast Guard other than officers and employees of the former Lighthouse Service who, on June 30, 1939, met the requirements for retirement (except those relating to age and period of service) of said sections.

(June 6, 1940, ch. 257, § 7, 54 Stat. 247.)

CODIFICATION

Sections 763 and 763a–1 of this title, referred to in text, was, in the original: "The provisions of section 6 of the Act approved June 20, 1918 (40 Stat. 608), as amended and supplemented (U.S.C., 1934 edition, Supp. V., title 33, secs. 763 and 763a–1)".

TRANSFER OF FUNCTIONS

Bureau of Lighthouses, of which Lighthouse Service was a part, transferred and consolidated with Coast Guard by Reorg. Plan No. II of 1939, §2(a), eff. July 1, 1939, 4 F.R. 2731, 53 Stat. 1432, set out in the Appendix to Title 5, Government Organization and Employees.

For transfer of functions of other officers, employees, and agencies of Department of the Treasury, with certain exceptions, to Secretary of the Treasury with power to delegate, see Reorg. Plan No. 26 of 1950, §§1, 2, eff. July 31, 1950, 15 F.R. 4935, 64 Stat. 1280, 1281, set out in the Appendix to Title 5. Functions of Coast Guard, and Commandant of Coast Guard, were excepted from transfer when Coast Guard is operating as part of Navy under sections 1 and 3 of Title 14, Coast Guard.

Coast Guard transferred to Department of Transportation, and all functions, powers, and duties relating to Coast Guard of Secretary of the Treasury and of other officers and offices of Department of the Treasury transferred to Secretary of Transportation by Pub. L. 89–670, §6(b)(1), Oct. 15, 1966, 80 Stat. 938. Section 6(b)(2) of Pub. L. 89–670, however, provided that notwithstanding such transfer of functions, Coast Guard shall operate as part of Navy in time of war or when President directs as provided in section 3 of Title 14. See section 108 of Title 49, Transportation.

For transfer of authorities, functions, personnel, and assets of the Coast Guard, including the authorities and functions of the Secretary of Transportation relating thereto, to the Department of Homeland Security, and for treatment of related references, see sections 468(b), 551(d), 552(d), and 557 of Title 6, Domestic Security, and the Department of Homeland Security Reorganization Plan of November 25, 2002, as modified, set out as a note under section 542 of Title 6.

§763b. Repealed. July 1, 1944, ch. 373, title XIII, §1313, 58 Stat. 714

Section, act June 24, 1930, ch. 597, 46 Stat. 807, as affected by 1939 Reorg. Plans Nos. I, §§201, 205, and II, §2(a), eff. July 1, 1939, 4 F.R. 2728, 2731, 53 Stat. 1424, 1432, provided for hospital facilities for retired officers and employees of former Lighthouse Service.

RENUMBERING OF REPEALING ACT

Section 611 of act July 1, 1944, which repealed this section, was renumbered §711 by act Aug. 13, 1946, ch. 958, §5, 60 Stat. 1049, §713 by act Feb. 28, 1948, ch. 83, §9(b), 62 Stat. 47, §813 by act July 30, 1956, ch. 779, §3(b), 70 Stat. 720, §913 by Pub. L. 88–581, §4(b), Sept. 4, 1964, 78 Stat. 919, §1013 by Pub. L. 85–239, §3(b), Oct. 5, 1965, 79 Stat. 931, §1113 by Pub. L. 91–572, §6(b), Dec. 24, 1970, 84 Stat. 1506, §1213 by Pub. L. 92–294, §3(b), May 16, 1972, 86 Stat. 137; §1313 by Pub. L. 93–154, §2(b)(2), Nov. 16, 1973, 87 Stat. 604, and was repealed by Pub. L. 93–222, §7(b), Dec. 29, 1973, 87 Stat. 936.

§763c. Repealed. Pub. L. 93–222, §7(b), Dec. 29, 1973, 87 Stat. 936

Section, act July 1, 1944, ch. 373, title XIII, §1310(b), formerly title VI, §610(b), 58 Stat. 714; renumbered title VII, §710(b), by act Aug. 13, 1946, ch. 958, §5, 60 Stat. 1049; renumbered title VIII, §810(b), by act July 30, 1956, ch. 779, §3(b), 70 Stat. 721; renumbered title IX, §910(b), by Pub. L. 88–581, §4(b), Sept. 4, 1964, 78 Stat. 919; renumbered title X, §1010(b), by Pub. L. 89–239, §3(b), Oct. 6, 1965, 79 Stat. 931; renumbered title XI, §1110(b) by Pub. L. 91–572, §6(b), Dec. 24, 1970, 84 Stat. 1506; renumbered title XII, §1210(b) by Pub. L. 92–294, §3(b), May 16, 1972, 86 Stat. 137; renumbered title XIII, §1310(b), by Pub. L. 93–154, §2(b)(2), Nov. 16, 1973, 87 Stat. 604, made provision for hospital facilities for officers and employees.

§764. Omitted

CODIFICATION

Section, act Mar. 4, 1921, ch. 161, §1, 41 Stat. 1417, related to privilege granted employees of continuing service after retirement and which was limited to a ten year period after Mar. 4, 1921.

§765. Retirement for disability

Any officer or employee to whom section 763 of this title applies, who has been in the active service of the Government fifteen years or more and who is found, after examination by a medical officer of the United States, to be disabled for useful and efficient service by reason of disease or injury not due to vicious habits, intemperance, or willful misconduct on his part, shall be retired under rules to be prescribed by the Secretary of Transportation on an annuity computed in the manner provided in said section.

(Mar. 4, 1925, ch. 523, §1, 43 Stat. 1261; 1939 Reorg. Plan No. II, §2(a), eff. July 1, 1939, 4 F.R. 2731, 53 Stat. 1432; Pub. L. 89–670, §6(b)(1), Oct. 15, 1966, 80 Stat. 938.)

TRANSFER OF FUNCTIONS

The officers or employees to be retired refer to the officers and employees of the Lighthouse Service. The Lighthouse Service was under the Secretary of Commerce prior to the transfer and consolidation of the Bureau of Lighthouses, of which the Lighthouse Service was a part, with the Coast Guard which was under the Secretary of the Treasury by Reorg. Plan No. II, §2(a), set out in the Appendix to Title 5, Government Organization and Employees. Subsequently, the functions of the Secretary of the Treasury relating to the Coast Guard were transferred to the Secretary of Transportation by section 6(b)(1) of Pub. L. 89–670. See section 108 of Title 49, Transportation.

For transfer of authorities, functions, personnel, and assets of the Coast Guard, including the authorities and functions of the Secretary of Transportation relating thereto, to the Department of Homeland Security, and for treatment of related references, see sections 468(b), 551(d), 552(d), and 557 of Title 6, Domestic Security, and the Department of Homeland Security Reorganization Plan of November 25, 2002, as modified, set out as a note under section 542 of Title 6.

§766. Restoration to active duty after retirement for disability

Any officer or employee retired under section 765 of this title may, upon recovery, be restored to active duty, and shall from time to time, before reaching the age at which he may be retired under section 763 of this title be reexamined by a medical officer of the United States upon the request of the Secretary of Transportation.

(Mar. 4, 1925, ch. 523, §2, 43 Stat. 1262; 1939 Reorg. Plan No. II, §2(a), eff. July 1, 1939, 4 F.R. 2731, 53 Stat. 1432; Pub. L. 89–670, §6(b)(1), Oct. 15, 1966, 80 Stat. 938.)

TRANSFER OF FUNCTIONS

The officers or employees to be retired refer to the officers and employees of the Lighthouse Service. The Lighthouse Service was under the Secretary of Commerce prior to the transfer and consolidation of the Bureau of Lighthouses, of which the Lighthouse Service was a part, with the Coast Guard which was under the Secretary of the Treasury by Reorg. Plan No. II, §2(a), set out in the Appendix to Title 5, Government Organization and Employees. Subsequently, the functions of the Secretary of the Treasury relating to the Coast Guard were transferred to the Secretary of Transportation by section 6(b)(1) of Pub. L. 89–670. See section 108 of Title 49, Transportation.

For transfer of authorities, functions, personnel, and assets of the Coast Guard, including the authorities and functions of the Secretary of Transportation relating thereto, to the Department of Homeland Security, and for treatment of related references, see sections 468(b), 551(d), 552(d), and 557 of Title 6, Domestic Security, and the Department of Homeland Security Reorganization Plan of November 25, 2002, as modified, set out as a note under section 542 of Title 6.

§§ 767 to 769. Repealed. Aug. 4, 1949, ch. 393, § 20, 63 Stat. 561

Section 767, acts Mar. 3, 1915, ch. 81, § 7, 38 Stat. 928; June 20, 1918, ch. 103, § 7, 40 Stat. 608, related to administration of oaths to employees of Lighthouse Service.

Section 768, acts Aug. 24, 1912, ch. 355, § 8, 37 Stat. 487; Mar. 3, 1915, ch. 81, § 7, 38 Stat. 928; June 20, 1918, ch. 103, § 7, 40 Stat. 608; June 6, 1939, ch. 185, 53 Stat. 810, related to oaths to expense accounts.

Section 769, act Feb. 25, 1929, ch. 313, § 3, 45 Stat. 1262, related to aids to navigation in Panama. See section 81 of Title 14, Coast Guard.

Effective Date of Repeal

Repeal effective first day of third month after approval by President [Aug. 4, 1949], see section 19 of act Aug. 4, 1949, set out as an Effective Date note preceding chapter 1 of Title 14, Coast Guard.

§ 770. Regulations for expenditure of moneys accruing from commutation of rations and provisions

Money accruing from commutation of rations and provisions for working parties in the field, officers and crews of light vessels and tenders, and officials and other authorized persons on board of such tenders or vessels, after payment on proper vouchers to the officer in charge of the mess of such vessel or party, as provided by law, may be expended and accounted for pursuant to regulations prescribed by the Secretary of Transportation, notwithstanding the provisions of sections 1321 and 1322(a) of title 31.

(May 13, 1938, ch. 215, § 3, 52 Stat. 353; 1939 Reorg. Plan No. II, § 2(a), eff. July 1, 1939, 4 F.R. 2731, 53 Stat. 1432; Pub. L. 89–670, § 6(b)(1), Oct. 15, 1966, 80 Stat. 938.)

Codification

"Sections 1321 and 1322(a) of title 31" substituted in text for "the Act of June 26, 1934 (48 Stat. 1233) [31 U.S.C. 725s]" on authority of Pub. L. 97–258, § 4(b), Sept. 13, 1982, 96 Stat. 1067, the first section of which enacted Title 31, Money and Finance.

Transfer of Functions

The money accruing from commutation of rations and provisions refer to such moneys of persons in the Lighthouse Service. The Lighthouse Service was under the Secretary of Commerce prior to the transfer and consolidation of the Bureau of Lighthouses, of which the Lighthouse Service was a part, with the Coast Guard which was under the Secretary of the Treasury by Reorg. Plan No. II, § 2(a), set out in the Appendix to Title 5, Government Organization and Employees. Subsequently, the functions of the Secretary of the Treasury relating to the Coast Guard were transferred to the Secretary of Transportation by section 6(b)(1) of Pub. L. 89–670. See section 108 of Title 49, Transportation.

For transfer of authorities, functions, personnel, and assets of the Coast Guard, including the authorities and functions of the Secretary of Transportation relating thereto, to the Department of Homeland Security, and for treatment of related references, see sections 468(b), 551(d), 552(d), and 557 of Title 6, Domestic Security, and the Department of Homeland Security Reorganization Plan of November 25, 2002, as modified, set out as a note under section 542 of Title 6.

§ 771. Benefits for surviving spouses of Lighthouse Service employees; death of employee during retirement; amount of payment

Where—

(1) any former employee of the Lighthouse Service has died or shall hereafter die at a time when that employee was receiving or was entitled to receive retirement pay under section 763 of this title, as amended and supplemented, and

(2) the surviving spouse of the former employee was married to the former employee prior to the retirement of the former employee from the Lighthouse Service and has not remarried—

the surviving spouse, so long as the surviving spouse does not remarry, shall be paid $100 per month by the Secretary of Transportation.

(Aug. 19, 1950, ch. 761, § 1, 64 Stat. 465; Pub. L. 85–351, § 1, Mar. 28, 1958, 72 Stat. 49; Pub. L. 89–670, § 6(b)(1), Oct. 15, 1966, 80 Stat. 938; Pub. L. 90–163, § 1, Nov. 29, 1967, 81 Stat. 518; Pub. L. 90–167, § 1(a), Nov. 29, 1967, 81 Stat. 520; Pub. L. 98–557, § 15(b)(1), Oct. 30, 1984, 98 Stat. 2866.)

Amendments

1984—Pub. L. 98–557 substituted references to surviving spouse for references to widow.

1967—Pub. L. 90–167 struck out provision which exempted from coverage of this section widows of employees whose positions were classified in one of the grades of the professional and scientific service of the Classification Act of 1923, or a comparable grade of the Classification Act of 1949, or who performed duties of a position comparable to a position so classified after the enactment of law requiring the classification of such positions.

Pub. L. 90–163 substituted "$100 per month" for "$75 per month".

1958—Pub. L. 85–351 substituted "$75 per month" for "$50 per month".

Effective Date of 1967 Amendments

Section 2 of Pub. L. 90–167 provided that: "No payment shall be made by reason of the amendments made by this section [amending this section and section 772 of this title] for any period prior to the first day of the first month following the month in which this Act is enacted [Nov. 29, 1967]."

Section 1 of Pub. L. 90–163 provided that the amendment made by that section is effective on the first day of the month following Nov. 29, 1967.

Effective Date of 1958 Amendment

Section 2 of Pub. L. 85–351 provided that: "The amendments made by this Act [amending this section and section 772 of this title] shall take effect on the first day of the first month which begins after the date of the enactment of this Act [Mar. 28, 1958]."

Effective Date

Section 6 of act Aug. 19, 1950, provided that: "No payment shall be made under this Act [enacting this section and sections 772 to 775 of this title] for any period prior to the first day of the first month following the month in which this Act is enacted."

Transfer of Functions

Bureau of Lighthouses, of which Lighthouse Service was a part, transferred and consolidated with Coast Guard under Secretary of the Treasury by Reorg. Plan No. II of 1939, § 2(a), eff. July 1, 1939, 4 F.R. 2731, 33 Stat. 1432, set out in the Appendix to Title 5, Government Organization and Employees. Functions of Secretary of the Treasury relating to Coast Guard transferred to Secretary of Transportation by section 6(b)(1) of Pub. L. 89–670. See section 108 of Title 49, Transportation.

For transfer of authorities, functions, personnel, and assets of the Coast Guard, including the authorities and functions of the Secretary of Transportation relating thereto, to the Department of Homeland Security, and for treatment of related references, see sections 468(b), 551(d), 552(d), and 557 of Title 6, Domestic Security, and the Department of Homeland Security Reorganization Plan of November 25, 2002, as modified, set out as a note under section 542 of Title 6.

INCREASE IN WIDOWS BENEFITS AND EFFECTIVE DATE OF INCREASE

Pub. L. 94–170, Dec. 23, 1975, 89 Stat. 1022, provided: "That the benefits payable under section 1 or section 2 of the Act of August 19, 1950 (64 Stat. 465, 466), as amended (33 U.S.C. 771, 772) shall, effective on the first day of the calendar month following enactment of this Act [Dec. 23, 1975], be increased by $26 per month.

"SEC. 2. The increases under this Act shall apply to benefits which commence before, on, or after the date of enactment of this Act [Dec. 23, 1975], but no increase in benefits shall be paid for any period prior to the date of enactment of this Act [Dec. 23, 1975], or the date on which the eligibility for benefits commences, whichever is later."

COST-OF-LIVING ADJUSTMENT TO WIDOW'S ANNUITY

Section 2 of Pub. L. 90–163 provided that: "Each annuity payable under the Act entitled 'An Act to provide benefits for widows of certain persons who were retired or are eligible for retirement under section 6 of the Act entitled "An Act to authorize aids to navigation and for other works in the Lighthouse Service, and for other purposes", approved June 20, 1918, as amended', approved August 19, 1950 (33 U.S.C. 771–775), and each annuity payable under section 6 of the Act entitled 'An Act to authorize aids to navigation and for other works in the Lighthouse Service, and for other purposes', approved June 20, 1918 (33 U.S.C. 763), shall be increased by the same percentage, adjusted to the nearest dollar, and on the same effective date, as each increase hereafter allowed under the cost-of-living annuity adjustment provisions of section 8340(b) of title 5, United States Code."

§ 772. Death of employee due to non-service-connected causes after 15 years' service; amount of payment

Where—

(1) any employee of the Lighthouse Service has died or shall hereafter die from non-service-connected causes after fifteen or more years of employment in such service, and

(2) the surviving spouse of the employee has not since remarried,

the surviving spouse, so long as the surviving spouse does not marry, shall be paid $100 per month by the Secretary of Transportation.

(Aug. 19, 1950, ch. 761, §2, 64 Stat. 466; Pub. L. 85–351, §1, Mar. 28, 1958, 72 Stat. 49; Pub. L. 89–670, §6(b)(1), Oct. 15, 1966, 80 Stat. 938; Pub. L. 90–163, §1, Nov. 29, 1967, 81 Stat. 518; Pub. L. 90–167, §1(b), Nov. 29, 1967, 81 Stat. 520; Pub. L. 98–557, §15(b)(2), Oct. 30, 1984, 98 Stat. 2866.)

AMENDMENTS

1984—Pub. L. 98–557 substituted references to surviving spouse for references to widow.

1967—Pub. L. 90–167 struck out provisions which exempted from coverage of this section widows of employees whose positions were classified in one of grades of professional and scientific service of Classification Act of 1923, or a comparable grade of Classification Act of 1949, or who performed duties of a position comparable to a position so classified after enactment of law requiring classification of such positions.

Pub. L. 90–163 substituted "$100 per month" for "$75 per month".

1958—Pub. L. 85–351 substituted "$75 per month" for "$50 per month".

EFFECTIVE DATE OF 1967 AMENDMENTS

Amendment by Pub. L. 90–167 effective for any period subsequent to the first day of the first month following Nov. 29, 1967, see section 2 of Pub. L. 90–167, set out as a note under section 771 of this title.

Section 1 of Pub. L. 90–163 provided that the amendment made by that section is effective on the first day of the month following Nov. 29, 1967.

EFFECTIVE DATE OF 1958 AMENDMENT

Amendment effective Apr. 1, 1958, see section 2 of Pub. L. 85–351, set out as a note under section 771 of this title.

TRANSFER OF FUNCTIONS

Bureau of Lighthouses, of which Lighthouse Service was a part, transferred and consolidated with Coast Guard under Secretary of the Treasury by Reorg. Plan No. II of 1939, §2(a), eff. July 1, 1939, 4 F.R. 2731, 33 Stat. 1432, set out in the Appendix to Title 5, Government Organization and Employees. Functions of Secretary of the Treasury relating to Coast Guard transferred to Secretary of Transportation by section 6(b)(1) of Pub. L. 89–670. See section 108 of Title 49, Transportation.

For transfer of authorities, functions, personnel, and assets of the Coast Guard, including the authorities and functions of the Secretary of Transportation relating thereto, to the Department of Homeland Security, and for treatment of related references, see sections 468(b), 551(d), 552(d), and 557 of Title 6, Domestic Security, and the Department of Homeland Security Reorganization Plan of November 25, 2002, as modified, set out as a note under section 542 of Title 6.

INCREASE IN WIDOWS BENEFITS AND EFFECTIVE DATE OF INCREASE

For 1975 increase in widows benefits under this section and section 771 of this title, and effective date of such increase, see Pub. L. 94–170, Dec. 23, 1975, 89 Stat. 1022, set out as a note under section 771 of this title.

§ 773. Application for benefits

Application for the benefits of sections 771 to 775 of this title shall be made in such manner and form as the Director of the Office of Personnel Management shall prescribe.

(Aug. 19, 1950, ch. 761, §3, 64 Stat. 466; 1978 Reorg. Plan No. 2, §102, eff. Jan. 1, 1979, 43 F.R. 36037, 92 Stat. 3783.)

TRANSFER OF FUNCTIONS

"Director of the Office of Personnel Management" substituted in text for "Civil Service Commission" pursuant to Reorg. Plan No. 2 of 1978, §102, 43 F.R. 36037, 92 Stat. 3783, set out under section 1101 of Title 5, Government Organization and Employees, which transferred all functions vested by statute in Civil Service Commission to Director of Office of Personnel Management (except as otherwise specified), effective Jan. 1, 1979, as provided by section 1–102 of Ex. Ord. No. 12107, Dec. 28, 1978, 44 F.R. 1055, set out under section 1101 of Title 5.

§ 774. Rules and regulations

The Director of the Office of Personnel Management shall perform, or cause to be performed, such acts, and shall make such rules and regulations, as may be necessary or proper to carry out the provisions of sections 771 to 775 of this title.

(Aug. 19, 1950, ch. 761, § 4, 64 Stat. 466; 1978 Reorg. Plan No. 2, § 102, eff. Jan. 1, 1979, 43 F.R. 36037, 92 Stat. 3783.)

TRANSFER OF FUNCTIONS

"Director of the Office of Personnel Management" substituted in text for "Civil Service Commission" pursuant to Reorg. Plan No. 2 of 1978, § 102, 43 F.R. 36037, 92 Stat. 3783, set out under section 1101 of Title 5, Government Organization and Employees, which transferred all functions vested by statute in Civil Service Commission to Director of Office of Personnel Management (except as otherwise specified), effective Jan. 1, 1979, as provided by section 1–102 of Ex. Ord. No. 12107, Dec. 28, 1978, 44 F.R. 1055, set out under section 1101 of Title 5.

§ 775. Payments nonassignable and exempt from process

No payment under sections 771 to 775 of this title shall be assignable, either in law or in equity, or be subject to execution, levy, lien, attachment, garnishment, or other legal process.

(Aug. 19, 1950, ch. 761, § 5, 64 Stat. 466.)

§ 776. Payment out of Civil Service Retirement and Disability Fund

Annuities authorized by sections 771 to 775 of this title may, on and after December 26, 2007, be paid out of the Civil Service Retirement and Disability Fund.

(Pub. L. 110–161, div. D, title V, Dec. 26, 2007, 121 Stat. 2009.)

CODIFICATION

Section is from the appropriation act cited as the credit to this section.

PRIOR PROVISIONS

Provisions similar to those in this section were contained in the following prior appropriation acts:

Pub. L. 109–115, div. A, title VI, Nov. 30, 2005, 119 Stat. 2489.

Pub. L. 108–447, div. H, title IV, Dec. 8, 2004, 118 Stat. 3263.

Pub. L. 108–199, div. F, title IV, Jan. 23, 2004, 118 Stat. 339.

Pub. L. 108–7, div. J, title IV, Feb. 20, 2003, 117 Stat. 459.

Pub. L. 107–67, title IV, Nov. 12, 2001, 115 Stat. 542.

Pub. L. 106–554, § 1(a)(3) [title IV], Dec. 21, 2000, 114 Stat. 2763, 2763A–150.

Pub. L. 106–58, title IV, Sept. 29, 1999, 113 Stat. 463.

Pub. L. 105–277, div. A, § 101(h) [title IV], Oct. 21, 1998, 105 Stat. 2681–480, 2681–509.

Pub. L. 105–61, title IV, Oct. 10, 1997, 111 Stat. 1303.

Pub. L. 104–208, div. A, title I, § 101(f) [title IV], Sept. 30, 1996, 110 Stat. 3009–314, 3009–344.

Pub. L. 104–52, title IV, Nov. 19, 1995, 109 Stat. 489.

Pub. L. 103–329, title IV, Sept. 30, 1994, 108 Stat. 2407.

Pub. L. 103–123, title IV, Oct. 28, 1993, 107 Stat. 1249.

Pub. L. 102–393, title IV, Oct. 6, 1992, 106 Stat. 1756.

Pub. L. 102–141, title IV, Oct. 28, 1991, 105 Stat. 860.

Pub. L. 101–509, title IV, Nov. 5, 1990, 104 Stat. 1421.

Pub. L. 101–136, title IV, Nov. 3, 1989, 103 Stat. 810.

Pub. L. 100–440, title IV, Sept. 22, 1988, 102 Stat. 1745.

Pub. L. 100–202, § 101(m) [title IV], Dec. 22, 1987, 101 Stat. 1329–390, 1329–413.

Pub. L. 99–500, § 101(m) [title IV], Oct. 18, 1986, 100 Stat. 1783–308, 1783–322, and Pub. L. 99–591, § 101(m) [title IV], Oct. 30, 1986, 100 Stat. 3341–308, 3341–322.

Pub. L. 99–190, title I, § 101(h) [H.R. 3036, title IV], Dec. 19, 1985, 99 Stat. 1291.

Pub. L. 98–473, title I, § 101(j) [H.R. 5798, title IV], Oct. 12, 1984, 98 Stat. 1963.

Pub. L. 98–151, § 101(f) [H.R. 4139, title IV], Nov. 14, 1983, 97 Stat. 973.

Pub. L. 97–377, title I, § 101(a) [incorporating H.R. 4121, title IV, for FY 1982], Dec. 21, 1982, 96 Stat. 1830.

Pub. L. 97–92, § 101(a) [H.R. 4121, title IV], Dec. 15, 1981, 95 Stat. 1183.

Pub. L. 96–536, § 101(a) [incorporating Pub. L. 96–74, title IV], Dec. 16, 1980, 94 Stat. 3166.

Pub. L. 96–74, title IV, Sept. 29, 1979, 93 Stat. 571.

Pub. L. 95–429, title IV, Oct. 10, 1978, 92 Stat. 1007.

Pub. L. 95–81, title IV, July 31, 1977, 91 Stat. 347.

Pub. L. 94–363, title IV, July 14, 1976, 90 Stat. 969.

Pub. L. 94–91, title IV, Aug. 9, 1975, 89 Stat. 449.

Pub. L. 93–381, title IV, Aug. 21, 1974, 88 Stat. 620.

Pub. L. 93–143, title IV, Oct. 30, 1973, 87 Stat. 517.

CHAPTER 17—NATIONAL OCEANIC AND ATMOSPHERIC ADMINISTRATION

SUBCHAPTER I—GENERAL PROVISIONS

Sec.

SUBCHAPTER II—SURVEYS

SUBCHAPTER I—GENERAL PROVISIONS

SAFETY AND HEALTH REGULATIONS FOR SCIENTIFIC AND OCCUPATIONAL DIVING

Pub. L. 110–161, div. B, title I, §110, Dec. 26, 2007, 121 Stat. 1893, provided that: "The Secretary of Commerce is permitted to prescribe and enforce standards or regulations affecting safety and health in the context of scientific and occupational diving within the National Oceanic and Atmospheric Administration."

§851. Omitted

CODIFICATION

Section, Pub. L. 105–277, div. A, §101(b) [title II], Oct. 21, 1998, 105 Stat. 2681–50, 2681–83, which authorized in the National Oceanic and Atmospheric Administration 250 commissioned officers on the active list as of September 30, 1999, was from title II of the Departments of Commerce, Justice, and State, the Judiciary, and Related Agencies Appropriations Act, 1999, and was not repeated in subsequent appropriation acts.

Similar provisions were contained in the following prior appropriation acts:

Pub. L. 105–119, title II, Nov. 26, 1997, 111 Stat. 2477.

Pub. L. 104–208, div. A, title I, §101(a) [title II], Sept. 30, 1996, 110 Stat. 3009, 3009–37.

Pub. L. 104–134, title I, §101[(a)] [title II], Apr. 26, 1996, 110 Stat. 1321, 1321–27; renumbered title I, Pub. L. 104–140, §1(a), May 2, 1996, 110 Stat. 1327.

Pub. L. 103–317, title II, Aug. 26, 1994, 108 Stat. 1741.

Pub. L. 103–121, title II, Oct. 27, 1993, 107 Stat. 1170.

Pub. L. 102–395, title II, Oct. 6, 1992, 106 Stat. 1849.

Pub. L. 102–140, title II, Oct. 28, 1991, 105 Stat. 799.

Pub. L. 101–515, title I, Nov. 5, 1990, 104 Stat. 2104.

Pub. L. 101–162, title I, Nov. 21, 1989, 103 Stat. 992.

Pub. L. 100–459, title I, Oct. 1, 1988, 102 Stat. 2190.

Pub. L. 100–202, §101(a) [title I], Dec. 22, 1987, 101 Stat. 1329, 1329–4.

Pub. L. 99–500, §101(b) [title I], Oct. 18, 1986, 100 Stat. 1783–39, 1783–42, and Pub. L. 99–591, §101(b) [title I], Oct. 30, 1986, 100 Stat. 3341–39, 3341–42.

Pub. L. 99–180, title I, Dec. 13, 1985, 99 Stat. 1138.

Pub. L. 98–411, title I, Aug. 30, 1984, 98 Stat. 1548.

Pub. L. 98–166, title I, §101, Nov. 28, 1983, 97 Stat. 1074.

Pub. L. 97–377, title I, §101(d), Dec. 21, 1982, 96 Stat. 1867, 1869.

Pub. L. 97–92, §101(h) [incorporating H.R. 7584, title III, for FY 1981], Dec. 15, 1981, 95 Stat. 1190.

Pub. L. 96–536, §101*o*, [H.R. 7584, title III], Dec. 16, 1980, 94 Stat. 3169.

Pub. L. 96–68, title III, Sept. 24, 1979, 93 Stat. 424.

Pub. L. 95–431, title III, Oct. 10, 1978, 92 Stat. 1033.

Pub. L. 95–86, title III, Aug. 2, 1977, 91 Stat. 431.

Pub. L. 94–362, title III, July 14, 1976, 90 Stat. 949.

Pub. L. 94–121, title III, Oct. 21, 1975, 89 Stat. 625.

Pub. L. 93–433, title III, Oct. 5, 1974, 88 Stat. 1197.

Pub. L. 93–162, title III, Nov. 27, 1973, 87 Stat. 647.

Pub. L. 92–544, title III, Oct. 25, 1972, 86 Stat. 1121.

Pub. L. 92–77, title III, Aug. 10, 1971, 85 Stat. 257.

Pub. L. 91–472, title III, Oct. 21, 1970, 84 Stat. 1051.

Pub. L. 91–153, title III, Dec. 24, 1969, 83 Stat. 414.

Pub. L. 90–470, title III, Aug. 9, 1968, 82 Stat. 679.

Pub. L. 90–133, title III, Nov. 8, 1967, 81 Stat. 422.

Pub. L. 89–797, title III, Nov. 8, 1966, 80 Stat. 1491.

Pub. L. 89–164, title III, Sept. 2, 1965, 79 Stat. 631.

Pub. L. 88–527, title III, Aug. 31, 1964, 78 Stat. 722.

Pub. L. 88–245, title III, Dec. 30, 1963, 77 Stat. 787.

Pub. L. 87–843, title III, Oct. 18, 1962, 76 Stat. 1091.

Pub. L. 87–125, title II, Aug. 3, 1961, 75 Stat. 271.

Pub. L. 86–451, title I, May 13, 1960, 74 Stat. 94.

Pub. L. 86–88, title I, July 13, 1959, 73 Stat. 202.

Pub. L. 85–469, title I, June 25, 1958, 72 Stat. 229.

Pub. L. 85–52, title I, June 13, 1957, 71 Stat. 72.

June 20, 1956, ch. 415, title I, 70 Stat. 316.

June 30, 1955, ch. 253, title I, 69 Stat. 228.

July 2, 1954, ch. 456, title III, 68 Stat. 424.

Aug. 5, 1953, ch. 328, title III, 67 Stat. 378.

July 10, 1952, ch. 651, title III, 66 Stat. 564.

Oct. 22, 1951, ch. 533, title III, 65 Stat. 590.

Sept. 6, 1950, ch. 896, Ch. III, title III, 64 Stat. 624.

July 20, 1949, ch. 354, title III, 63 Stat. 466.

June 3, 1948, ch. 400, title III, 62 Stat. 325.

July 9, 1947, ch. 211, title III, 61 Stat. 298.

July 5, 1946, ch. 541, title III, 60 Stat. 470.

May 21, 1945, ch. 129, title III, 59 Stat. 191.

June 28, 1944, ch. 294, title III, 58 Stat. 420.

July 1, 1943, ch. 182, title III, 57 Stat. 296.

July 2, 1942, ch. 472, title III, 56 Stat. 495.

June 28, 1941, ch. 258, title II, 55 Stat. 283.

May 14, 1940, ch. 189, title II, 54 Stat. 198.

June 29, 1939, ch. 248, title III, 53 Stat. 916.

Apr. 27, 1938, ch. 180, title III, 52 Stat. 281.

June 16, 1937, ch. 359, title III, 50 Stat. 294.

May 15, 1936, ch. 405, 49 Stat. 1341.

Mar. 22, 1935, ch. 39, 49 Stat. 96.

Feb. 27, 1925, ch. 364, title III, 43 Stat. 1046.

TRANSFER OF FUNCTIONS

Coast and Geodetic Survey consolidated with Weather Bureau to form a new agency in Department of Commerce to be known as Environmental Science Services Administration, and offices of Director and Deputy Director of Coast and Geodetic Survey abolished, by Reorg. Plan No. 2 of 1965, eff. July 13, 1965, 30 F.R. 8819, 79 Stat. 1318, set out below. The Reorg. Plan also transferred to Secretary of Commerce all functions of Coast and Geodetic Survey and of its Director.

Reorg. Plan No. 4 of 1970, eff. Oct. 3, 1970, 35 F.R. 15627, 84 Stat. 2090, set out in the Appendix to Title 5, Government Organization and Employees, abolished Environmental Science Services Administration, including offices of Administrator and Deputy Administrator, and established National Oceanic and Atmospheric Administration within Department of Commerce. By Department Organization Order 25–5A, republished 39 F.R. 27486, July 29, 1974, Secretary of Commerce delegated to National Oceanic and Atmospheric Administration a number of functions vested in him, including his functions under this chapter of the Code. By order of Acting Associate Administrator, 35 F.R. 19249, Dec. 19, 1970, the following organizational names appearing in chapter IX of subtitle B of Title 15, Code of Federal Regulations, relating to the Administration, were changed: Environmental Science Services Administration to National Oceanic and Atmospheric Administration (ESSA to NOAA); Coast and Geodetic Survey to National Ocean Survey, and Weather Bureau to National Weather Service.

The functions of all officers of Department of Commerce and all functions of all officers and employees of such Department, were, with a few exceptions, transferred to Secretary of Commerce, with power vested in him to authorize their performance or the performance of any of his functions by any of such officers, agencies, and employees, by Reorg. Plan No. 5 of 1950, §§1, 2, eff. May 24, 1950, 15 F.R. 3174, 64 Stat. 1263, set out in the Appendix to Title 5, Government Organization and Employees. The Coast and Geodetic Survey was an agency within the Department of Commerce.

SHORT TITLE OF 2008 AMENDMENT

Pub. L. 110–386, §1, Oct. 10, 2008, 122 Stat. 4106, provided that: "This Act [amending sections 892, 892a, 892c, 892d, and 3005 of this title] may be cited as the 'Hydrographic Services Improvement Act Amendments of 2008'."

SHORT TITLE OF 2002 AMENDMENT

Pub. L. 107–372, title I, §101(a), Dec. 19, 2002, 116 Stat. 3079, provided that: "This title [amending sections 892 to 892d of this title] may be cited as the 'Hydrographic Services Improvement Act Amendments of 2002'."

SHORT TITLE OF 1998 AMENDMENT

Pub. L. 105–384, title III, §301, Nov. 13, 1998, 112 Stat. 3454, provided that: "This title [enacting subchapter IV of this chapter and amending sections 853a and 853u of this title] may be cited as the 'Hydrographic Services Improvement Act of 1998'."

SHORT TITLE OF 1992 AMENDMENT

Pub. L. 102–567, title VI, §601, Oct. 29, 1992, 106 Stat. 4299, provided that: "This title [enacting subchapter III of this chapter] may be cited as the 'NOAA Fleet Modernization Act'."

SHORT TITLE

Pub. L. 95–63, §1, July 5, 1977, 91 Stat. 265, provided: "That this Act [enacting sections 857–13 to 857–18 of this title, repealing sections 857–6 to 857–12 of this title, and enacting provisions set out as a note under section 857–13 of this title] may be cited as the 'National Advisory Committee on Oceans and Atmosphere Act of 1977'."

REORGANIZATION PLAN NO. 2 OF 1965

Eff. July 13, 1965, 30 F.R. 8819, 79 Stat. 1318, as amended Pub. L. 90–83, §10(c), Sept. 11, 1967, 81 Stat. 224

Prepared by the President and transmitted to the Senate and the House of Representatives in Congress assembled, May 13, 1965, pursuant to the provisions of the Reorganization Act of 1949, 63 Stat. 203, as amended [see 5 U.S.C. 901 et seq.].

ENVIRONMENTAL SCIENCE SERVICES ADMINISTRATION, DEPARTMENT OF COMMERCE

SECTION 1. TRANSFER OF FUNCTIONS

All functions vested by law in the Weather Bureau, the Chief of the Weather Bureau, the Coast and Geodetic Survey, the Director of the Coast and Geodetic Survey, and any officer, employee, or organizational entity of that Bureau or Survey, and not heretofore transferred to the Secretary of Commerce, hereinafter referred to as the Secretary, are hereby transferred to the Secretary.

SEC. 2. ABOLITIONS

(a) The offices of Director of the Coast and Geodetic Survey, Deputy Director of the Coast and Geodetic Survey, and Chief of the Weather Bureau are hereby abolished. The Secretary shall make such provisions as he shall deem to be necessary respecting the winding up of any outstanding affairs of the officers whose offices are abolished by the provisions of this section.

(b) The abolitions effected by the provision of subsection (a) of this section shall exclude the abolition of rights to which the present incumbents of the abolished offices would be entitled under law upon the termination of their appointments.

SEC. 3. ENVIRONMENTAL SCIENCE SERVICES ADMINISTRATION

(a) The Coast and Geodetic Survey and the Weather Bureau are hereby consolidated to form a new agency in the Department of Commerce which shall be known as the Environmental Science Services Administration, hereinafter referred to as the Administration.

(b) The Secretary shall from time to time establish such constituent organizational entities of the Administration, with such names, as he shall determine.

SEC. 4. OFFICERS OF THE ADMINISTRATION

(a) There shall be at the head of the Administration the Administrator of the Environmental Science Services Administration, hereinafter referred to as the Administrator. The Administrator shall be appointed by the President by and with the advice and consent of the Senate. He shall perform such functions as the Secretary may from time to time direct.

(b)(1) There shall be in the Administration a Deputy Administrator of the Environmental Science Services Administration, hereinafter referred to as the Deputy Administrator, who shall be appointed by the President by and with the advice and consent of the Senate, shall perform such functions as the Secretary may from time to time direct, and, unless he is compensated in pursuance of the provisions of paragraph (2), below, shall receive compensation in accordance with the Classification Act of 1949, as amended [chapter 51 and subchapter III of chapter 53 of Title 5, Government Organization and Employees].

(2) The office of Deputy Administrator may be filled at the discretion of the President by appointment (by and with the advice and consent of the Senate) from the active list of commissioned officers of the Administration in which case the appointment shall create a vacancy on the active list and while holding the office of Deputy Administrator the officer shall have rank, pay and allowances not exceeding those of a Vice Admiral.

(c) The Deputy Administrator of such other official of the Department of Commerce as the Secretary shall from time to time designate shall act as Administrator during the absence or disability of the Administrator or in the event of a vacancy in the office of Administrator.

(d) At any one time, one principal constituent organizational entity of the Administration may, if the Secretary so elects, be headed by a commissioned officer of the Administration, who shall be designated by the Secretary. Such designation of an officer shall create a vacancy on the active list and while serving under this paragraph the officer shall have rank, pay and allowances not exceeding those of a Rear Admiral (upper half).

(e) Any commissioned officer of the Administration who has served as Deputy Administrator or has served in a rank above that of Captain as the head of a principal constituent organizational entity of the Administration, and is retired while so serving or is retired after the completion of such service while serving in a lower rank or grade, shall be retired with the rank, pay and allowances authorized by law for the highest grade and rank held by him; but any such officer, upon termination of his appointment in a rank above that of Captain, shall, unless appointed or assigned to some other position for which a higher rank or grade is provided, revert to the grade and number he would have occupied had he not served in a rank above that of Captain and such officer shall be an extra number in that grade. [As amended Pub. L. 90–83, §10(c), Sept. 11, 1967, 81 Stat. 224.]

SEC. 5. AUTHORITY OF THE SECRETARY

Nothing in this organization plan shall divert the Secretary of any function vested in him by law or by Reorganization Plan No. 5 of 1950 (64 Stat. 1263) [set out in the Appendix to Title 5, Government Organization and Employees] or in any manner derogate from any authority of the Secretary thereunder.

SEC. 6. PERSONNEL, PROPERTY, RECORDS AND FUNDS

(a) The personnel (including commissioned officers) employed in the Coast and Geodetic Survey, the personnel employed in the Weather Bureau, and the property and records held or used by the Weather Bureau or the Coast and Geodetic Survey shall be deemed to be transferred to the Administration.

(b) Unexpended balances of appropriations, allocations, and other funds available or to be made available in connection with functions now administered by the Weather Bureau or by the Coast and Geodetic Survey shall be available to the Administration hereunder in connection with those functions.

(c) Such further measures and dispositions as the Director of the Bureau of the Budget shall deem to be necessary in order to effectuate the foregoing provisions of this section shall be carried out in such manner as he shall direct and by such agencies as he shall designate.

SEC. 7. INTERIM OFFICERS

(a) The President may authorize any person who immediately prior to the effective date of this reorganization plan held a position in the executive branch of the Government to act as Administrator until the office of Administrator is for the first time filled pursuant to the provisions of this reorganization plan or by recess appointment, as the case may be.

(b) The President may similarly authorize any such person to act as Deputy Administrator.

(c) The President may authorize any person who serves in an acting capacity under the foregoing provisions of this section to receive the compensation attached to the office in respect to which he so serves. Such compensation, if authorized, shall be in lieu of, but not in addition to, other compensation from the United States to which such person may be entitled.

[The Environmental Science Services Administration in the Department of Commerce, including the offices of Administrator and Deputy Administrator thereof, were abolished by Reorg. Plan No. 4 of 1970, eff. Oct. 3, 1970, 35 F.R. 15627, 84 Stat. 2090, which created the National Oceanic and Atmospheric Administration in the Department of Commerce and transferred the personnel, property, records, and unexpended balances of funds of the Environmental Science Services Administration to such newly created National Oceanic and Atmospheric Administration.]

MESSAGE OF THE PRESIDENT

To the Congress of the United States:

I transmit herewith Reorganization Plan No. 2 of 1965, prepared in accordance with the provisions of the Reorganization Act of 1949, as amended [see now section 901 et seq. of Title 5, Government Organization and Employees], and providing for the reorganization of two major agencies of the Department of Commerce: The Weather Bureau and the Coast and Geodetic Survey.

The reorganization plan consolidates the Coast and Geodetic Survey and the Weather Bureau to form a new agency in the Department of Commerce to be known as the Environmental Science Services Administration. It is the intention of the Secretary of Commerce to transfer the Central Radio Propagation Laboratory of the National Bureau of Standards to the Administration when the reorganization plan takes effect. The new Administration will then provide a single national focus for our efforts to describe, understand, and predict the state of the oceans, the state of the lower and upper atmosphere, and the size and shape of the earth.

Establishment of the Administration will mark a significant step forward in the continual search by the Federal Government for better ways to meet the needs of the Nation for environmental science services. The organizational improvements made possible by the reorganization plan will enhance our ability to develop an adequate warning system for the severe hazards of nature—for hurricanes, tornadoes, floods, earthquakes, and seismic sea waves, which have proved so disastrous to the Nation in recent years. These improvements will permit us to provide better environmental information to vital segments of the Nation's economy—to agriculture, transportation, communications, and industry, which continually require information about the physical environment. They will mean better services to other Federal departments and agencies—to those that are concerned with the national defense, the exploration of outer space, the management of our mineral and water resources, the protection of the public health against environmental pollution, and the preservation of our wilderness and recreation areas.

The new Administration will bring together a number of allied scientific disciplines that are concerned with the physical environment. The integration will better enable us to look at man's physical environment as a scientific whole and to seek to understand the interactions among air, sea, and earth and between the upper and lower atmosphere. It will facilitate the development of programs dealing with the physical environment and will permit better management of these programs. It will enhance our capability to identify and solve important long-range scientific and technological problems associated with the physical environment. The new Administration will, in consequence, promote a fresh sense of scientific dedication, discovery, and challenge, which are essential if we are to attract scientists and engineers of creativity and talent to Federal employment in this field.

The reorganization plan provides for an Administrator at the head of the Administration, and for a Deputy Administrator, each of whom will be appointed by the President by and with the advice and consent of the Senate. As authorized by the civil service and other laws and regulations, subordinate officers of the Administration will be appointed by the Secretary of Commerce or be assigned by him from among a corps of commissioned officers. The Administration will perform such functions as the Secretary of Commerce may delegate or otherwise assign to it and will be under his direction and control.

Commissioned officers of the Coast and Geodetic Survey will become commissioned officers of the Administration and may serve at the discretion of the Secretary of Commerce throughout the Administration. The reorganization plan authorizes the President at his discretion to fill the Office of Deputy Administrator by appointment, by and with the advice and consent of the Senate, from the active list of commissioned officers of the Administration.

The reorganization plan transmitted herewith abolishes—and thus excludes from the consolidation mentioned above—the offices of (1) Chief of the Weather Bureau, provided for in the act of October 1, 1890 (15 U.S.C. 312); (2) Director of the Coast and Geodetic Survey, provided for in the acts of June 4, 1920, and February 16, 1929, as amended (33 U.S.C. 852, 852a); and (3) Deputy Director of the Coast and Geodetic Survey, provided for in the act of January 19, 1942, as amended (33 U.S.C. 852b).

After investigation, I have found and hereby declare that each reorganization included in Reorganization Plan No. 2 of 1965 is necessary to accomplish one or more of the purposes set forth in section 2(a) of the Reorganization Act of 1949, as amended [see now section 901 of Title 5, Government Organization and Employees]. I have also found and hereby declare that by reason of the reorganizations made by the reorganization plan, it is necessary to include in the plan provisions for the appointment and compensation of the officers of the Administration set forth in section 4 of the reorganization plan. The rate of compensation fixed for each of these officers is that which I have found to prevail in respect of comparable officers in the executive branch of the Government.

In addition to permitting more effective management within the Department of Commerce, the new organization will ultimately produce economies. These economies will be of two types. The first, and probably the most significant, is the savings and avoidance of costs which will result from the sharing of complex and expensive facilities such as satellites, computers, communication systems, aircraft, and ships. These economies will increase in significance as developments in science and technology bring into being still more advanced equipment. Second, integration of the existing headquarters and field organizations will permit more efficient utilization of existing administrative staffs and thereby produce future economies. It is, however, impracticable to specify or itemize at this time the reductions of expenditures which it is probable will be brought about by the taking effect of the reorganizations included in the reorganization plan.

I recommend that the Congress allow the accompanying reorganization plan to become effective.

LYNDON B. JOHNSON.

THE WHITE HOUSE, May 13, 1965.

§ 851a. Repealed. June 3, 1948, ch. 390, § 22(a), formerly § 21(a), 62 Stat. 300; renumbered § 22(a), Sept. 14, 1961, Pub. L. 87–233, § 1(f), 75 Stat. 506

Section, act Jan. 19, 1942, ch. 6, § 1, 56 Stat. 6, related to distribution of the total number of commissioned officers in rank.

§§ 852 to 852b. Omitted

CODIFICATION

Sections, which made provision for a Director of the Coast and Geodetic Survey and for a Deputy Director and covered their appointment, rank, pay, and allowances, have been omitted in view of 1965 Reorg. Plan No. 2, eff. July 13, 1965, 30 F.R. 8819, 79 Stat. 1318, set out as a note under section 851 of this title, which abolished such offices and transferred their functions to the Secretary of Commerce. For further details, see Transfer of Functions note set out under section 851 of this title.

Section 852, acts June 4, 1920, ch. 228, § 1, 41 Stat. 825; June 5, 1920, ch. 235, § 1, 41 Stat. 929; Feb. 16, 1929, ch. 221, § 5, 45 Stat. 1187; Mar. 18, 1936, ch. 147, 49 Stat. 1164, provided for the appointment and reappointment of the Director of the Coast and Geodetic Survey.

Section 852a, acts Feb. 16, 1929, ch. 221, § 5, 45 Stat. 1187; Mar. 18, 1936, ch. 147, 49 Stat. 1164; June 3, 1948, ch. 390, § 21(a), formerly § 20(a), 62 Stat. 300; renumbered § 21(a), Sept. 14, 1961, Pub. L. 87–233, § 1(f), 75 Stat. 506, provided for the rank, pay, and allowances of the Director.

Section 852b, acts Jan. 19, 1942, ch. 6, § 8, 56 Stat. 8; June 3, 1948, ch. 390, § 21(b), formerly § 20(b), 62 Stat. 300; renumbered § 21(b), Sept. 14, 1961, Pub. L. 87–233, § 1(f), 75 Stat. 506; June 21, 1955, ch. 172, § 3(b), 69 Stat. 169; June 30, 1960, Pub. L. 86–554, § 1, 74 Stat. 258, provided for the appointment, active and retired rank, pay, and allowances, of the Deputy Director of the Coast and Geodetic Survey.

§ 853. Power to settle claims

The Secretary of Commerce is authorized to consider, ascertain, adjust, and determine all claims for damages, where the amount of the claim does not exceed $2,500, occasioned, subsequent to June 5, 1920, by acts for which the National Oceanic and Atmospheric Administration is responsible.

(June 5, 1920, ch. 256, 41 Stat. 1054; Pub. L. 93–608, § 1(4), Jan. 2, 1975, 88 Stat. 1967; Pub. L. 98–176, Nov. 29, 1983, 97 Stat. 1124.)

AMENDMENTS

1983—Pub. L. 98–176 amended section generally, substituting "The Secretary of Commerce is" for "The Superintendent of the Coast and Geodetic Survey, subject to the approval of the Secretary of Commerce, is hereby", "$2,500" for "$500", and "the National Oceanic and Atmospheric Administration is responsible" for "the Coast and Geodetic Survey shall be found to be responsible".

1975—Pub. L. 93–608 struck out reporting requirement to Congress of amounts ascertained and determined due for payment as legal claims out of Congressional appropriations.

REPEALS

Act Aug. 2, 1946, ch. 753, title IV, § 424(a), 60 Stat. 846, repealed this section insofar as it concerned claims cognizable under sections 921 and 922 of former Title 28, Judicial Code and Judiciary (see sections 2672 and 2673 of Title 28, Judiciary and Judicial Procedure) which are caused by the negligent or wrongful act or omission of any Government employee acting within the scope of his employment, but by section 424(b) of that act, section 946 of former Title 28 (see note set out under section 2680 of Title 28), this section is specifically saved with reference to any claim which is not caused by the negligent or wrongful act or omission of any Government employee acting within the scope of his employment.

§§ 853a to 853*l*. Repealed. Pub. L. 107–372, title II, § 271(1), Dec. 19, 2002, 116 Stat. 3094

Section 853a, acts June 3, 1948, ch. 390, § 2, 62 Stat. 297; Pub. L. 87–233, § 1(a), Sept. 14, 1961, 75 Stat. 506; 1965 Reorg. Plan No. 2, eff. July 13, 1965, 30 F.R. 8819, 79 Stat. 1318; 1970 Reorg. Plan No. 4, eff. Oct. 3, 1970, 35 F.R. 15627, 84 Stat. 2090; Pub. L. 105–384, title III, § 307(a), Nov. 13, 1998, 112 Stat. 3457, related to authorized numbers of commissioned officers on the active list of the National Oceanic and Atmospheric Administration. See sections 3004 and 3005 of this title.

Section 853b, act June 3, 1948, ch. 390, § 3, 62 Stat. 298, related to promotion by selection to grades above lieutenant. See section 3024 of this title.

Section 853c, act June 3, 1948, ch. 390, § 4, 62 Stat. 298, related to promotion to the grade of lieutenant and lieutenant commander upon completion of seven and fourteen years of service, respectively.

Section 853d, act June 3, 1948, ch. 390, § 5, 62 Stat. 298, related to promotion to the grade of commander and captain after completion of twenty-one and thirty years of service, respectively.

Section 853e, acts June 3, 1948, ch. 390, § 6, 62 Stat. 298; June 21, 1955, ch. 172, § 4(a), 69 Stat. 169; Pub. L. 87–233, § 1(b), Sept. 14, 1961, 75 Stat. 506, related to promotion and separation from service of ensigns. See section 3023 of this title.

Section 853f, act June 3, 1948, ch. 390, § 7, 62 Stat. 298, related to length of service for purposes of promotion. See section 3025 of this title.

Section 853g, acts June 3, 1948, ch. 390, § 8, 62 Stat. 298; Pub. L. 98–498, title III, § 320(a)(1), Oct. 19, 1984, 98 Stat. 2307, related to retirement or separation of officers. See section 3041 of this title.

Section 853h, acts June 3, 1948, ch. 390, § 9, 62 Stat. 299; Pub. L. 87–649, § 9(b)(1), Sept. 7, 1962, 76 Stat. 495; Pub. L. 98–498, title III, § 320(a)(1), Oct. 19, 1984, 98 Stat. 2307; Pub. L. 102–54, § 13(m)(1), June 13, 1991, 105 Stat. 277;

Pub. L. 105–85, div. A, title VI, §652(a), (b), Nov. 18, 1997, 111 Stat. 1803, 1804, related to separation pay of officers. See section 3042 of this title.

Section 853i, acts June 3, 1948, ch. 390, §10, 62 Stat. 299; June 21, 1955, ch. 172, §4(b), 69 Stat. 170, directed that appointments and promotions be made by President and authorized suspension of provisions in time of emergency. See sections 3026 and 3033 of this title.

Section 853j, act June 3, 1948, ch. 390, §11, 62 Stat. 299, required passing of examinations for promotion.

Section 853j–1, acts June 3, 1948, ch. 390, §12, as added Pub. L. 87–233, §1(d), Sept. 14, 1961, 75 Stat. 506; amended Pub. L. 98–498, title III, §320(b), Oct. 19, 1984, 98 Stat. 2308, related to temporary appointments and promotions made by President. See section 3029 of this title.

Section 853k, acts June 3, 1948, ch. 390, §13, formerly §12, 62 Stat. 299; renumbered §13, Pub. L. 87–233, §1(c), Sept. 14, 1961, 75 Stat. 506, related to retirement of officers for age. See section 3043 of this title.

Section 853*l*, acts June 3, 1948, ch. 390, §14, formerly §13, 62 Stat. 299; renumbered §14 and amended Pub. L. 87–233, §1(e), Sept. 14, 1961, 75 Stat. 506, related to retirement for length of service upon application. See section 3044 of this title.

A prior section 14 of act June 3, 1948, was classified to section 853m of this title prior to repeal by act Oct. 12, 1949.

SHORT TITLE

Section 1 of act June 3, 1948, ch. 390, 62 Stat. 297, provided that act June 3, 1948, enacting sections 853a to 853*o* and 853p to 853v of this title, amending sections 852a, 852b, 854a, and 864d of this title, and repealing sections 851a, 854b, 854c, 864b, and 864c of this title, could be cited as the "Coast and Geodetic Survey Commissioned Officers' Act of 1948", prior to repeal by Pub. L. 107–372, title II, §271(1), Dec. 19, 2002, 116 Stat. 3094.

§§853m, 853n. Repealed. Oct. 12, 1949, ch. 681, title V, §531(b)(41), 63 Stat. 840

Section 853m, act June 3, 1948, ch. 390, §14, 62 Stat. 299, related to retirement for disability. See section 1201 et seq. of Title 10, Armed Forces.

Section 853n, act June 3, 1948, ch. 390, §15, 62 Stat. 299, related to computation of service for retirement purposes. See sections 1401 et seq., 6321 et seq., and 6371 et seq. of Title 10.

EFFECTIVE DATE OF REPEAL

Repeal effective Oct. 1, 1949, see section 533(a) of act Oct. 12, 1949, set out as an Effective Date of 1949 Amendment note under section 854a of this title.

§853*o*. Repealed. Pub. L. 107–372, title II, §271(1), Dec. 19, 2002, 116 Stat. 3094

Section, acts June 3, 1948, ch. 390, §16, 62 Stat. 299; Oct. 12, 1949, ch. 681, title V, §531(b)(41), 63 Stat. 840; Pub. L. 85–422, §11(c), May 20, 1958, 72 Stat. 132; Pub. L. 87–649, §9(b)(2), Sept. 7, 1962, 76 Stat. 495; Pub. L. 96–342, title VIII, §813(g), Sept. 8, 1980, 94 Stat. 1110; Pub. L. 98–94, title IX, §§922(c), 923(e), Sept. 24, 1983, 97 Stat. 642, 643; Pub. L. 99–348, title II, §206, July 1, 1986, 100 Stat. 701, related to computation of retirement pay. See section 3045 of this title.

§853*o*–1. Credit of service as deck officer or junior engineer and certain other active service for retirement and retirement pay

Active service in the National Oceanic and Atmospheric Administration as a deck officer or junior engineer and active service counted on June 30, 1922, for longevity pay, shall be credited to commissioned officers as active commissioned service for purposes of retirement and retirement pay.

(Pub. L. 87–649, §9(c), Sept. 7, 1962, 76 Stat. 496; 1965 Reorg. Plan No. 2, eff. July 13, 1965, 30 F.R. 8819, 79 Stat. 1318; 1970 Reorg. Plan No. 4, eff. Oct. 3, 1970, 35 F.R. 15627, 84 Stat. 2090.)

CODIFICATION

Section was formerly classified to section 302 of Title 37 prior to the general revision and enactment of Title 37, Pay and Allowances of the Uniformed Services, by Pub. L. 87–649, §1, Sept. 7, 1962, 76 Stat. 451.

EFFECTIVE DATE

Section effective Nov. 1, 1962, see section 15 of Pub. L. 87–649, set out as a note preceding section 101 of Title 37, Pay and Allowances of the Uniformed Services.

TRANSFER OF FUNCTIONS

Coast and Geodetic Survey consolidated with Weather Bureau to form a new agency in Department of Commerce to be known as Environmental Science Services Administration, and commissioned officers of Survey transferred to ESSA, by Reorg. Plan No. 2 of 1965, eff. July 13, 1965, 30 F.R. 8819, 79 Stat. 1318, set out as a note under section 851 of this title. The Reorg. Plan also transferred to Secretary of Commerce all functions of Coast and Geodetic Survey and Director of Survey. Subsequently, Environmental Science Services Administration abolished, National Oceanic and Atmospheric Administration established, and Commissioned Officer Corps of ESSA redesignated Commissioned Officer Corps of NOAA by Reorg. Plan No. 4 of 1970, eff. Oct. 3, 1970, 35 F.R. 15627, 84 Stat. 2090, set out in the Appendix to Title 5, Government Organization and Employees. For further details, see note set out under section 851 of this title.

§§853p to 853r. Repealed. Pub. L. 107–372, title II, §271(1), Dec. 19, 2002, 116 Stat. 3094

Section 853p, act June 3, 1948, ch. 390, §17, 62 Stat. 300, provided that retired pay be based on highest rank held. See section 3046 of this title.

Section 853q, act June 3, 1948, ch. 390, §18, 62 Stat. 300, provided that Coast and Geodetic Survey Commissioned Officers' Act of 1948 would not affect retired rank and pay held pursuant to other laws. See section 3047 of this title.

Section 853r, act June 3, 1948, ch. 390, §19, 62 Stat. 300, related to personnel board. See section 3022 of this title.

§853s. Repealed. Pub. L. 88–431, §1(c)(2), Aug. 14, 1964, 78 Stat. 440

Section, act June 3, 1948, ch. 390, §20, as added Sept. 14, 1961, Pub. L. 87–233, §1(g), 75 Stat. 506, related to transportation of motor vehicles for commissioned officers of Survey ordered to make a permanent change of station.

§§853t to 854. Repealed. Pub. L. 107–372, title II, §271(1), (4), Dec. 19, 2002, 116 Stat. 3094

Section 853t, act June 3, 1948, ch. 390, §23, as added Pub. L. 87–233, §1(h), Sept. 14, 1961, 75 Stat. 506, related to original appointments. See section 3021 of this title.

Section 853u, act June 3, 1948, ch. 390, §24, as added Pub. L. 98–498, title III, §320(c)(1), Oct. 19, 1984, 98 Stat. 2308; amended Pub. L. 99–145, title V, §514(a)(3), Nov. 8, 1985, 99 Stat. 628; Pub. L. 105–384, title III, §307(b), Nov. 13, 1998, 112 Stat. 3458, related to designation of positions of importance and responsibility. See section 3028 of this title.

Section 853v, act June 3, 1948, ch. 390, §25, as added Pub. L. 106–65, div. A, title VI, §652(c), Oct. 5, 1999, 113 Stat. 665, related to presentation of flag upon retirement. See section 3076 of this title.

Section 854, acts May 22, 1917, ch. 20, §16, 40 Stat. 88; June 21, 1955, ch. 172, §2(a), 69 Stat. 169, required mental and physical examination prior to appointment or promotion. See section 3027 of this title.

§854a. Service credit as deck officer or junior engineer for promotion purposes

For purposes of promotion which is now or may hereafter be authorized for officers appointed after June 30, 1922, there shall be counted in addition to active commissioned service, service as deck officer and junior engineer.

(Jan. 19, 1942, ch. 6, §2, 56 Stat. 6; June 3, 1948, ch. 390, §22(a), formerly §21(a), 62 Stat. 300, renumbered §22(a), Pub. L. 87–233, §1(f), Sept. 14, 1961, 75 Stat. 506; Oct. 12, 1949, ch. 681, title V, §531(b)(32), 63 Stat. 839; June 21, 1955, ch. 172, §3(a), 69 Stat. 169.)

CODIFICATION

Provisions similar to this section are contained in section 3032 of this title.

AMENDMENTS

1955—Act June 21, 1955, credited all service as deck officer and junior engineer.

1949—Act Oct. 12, 1949, repealed that part of second proviso of subsec. (b) relating to service credit as deck officer or junior engineer for pay, longevity pay, or retirement purposes.

1948—Act June 3, 1948, repealed subsecs. (a), (c), (d) and all of subsec. (b) except for second proviso which now comprises this section.

EFFECTIVE DATE OF 1949 AMENDMENT

Section 533(a) of act Oct. 12, 1949, provided that: "Except as provided in subsections (b) and (c) of this section, this Act [see Tables for classification] shall become effective on October 1, 1949, and no pay, allowances, or benefits provided herein shall accrue to any person for any period prior thereto."

§854a–1. Temporary appointment or advancement of commissioned officers in time of war or national emergency

Personnel of the National Oceanic and Atmospheric Administration shall be subject in like manner and to the same extent as personnel of the Navy to all laws authorizing temporary appointment or advancement of commissioned officers in time of war or national emergency subject to the following limitations:

(1) Commissioned officers in the service of a military department, under the provisions of sections 854, 855, 856, 857, and 858[1] of this title may, upon the recommendation of the Secretary of the military department concerned, be temporarily promoted to higher ranks or grades.

(2) Commissioned officers in the service of the National Oceanic and Atmospheric Administration may be temporarily promoted to fill vacancies in ranks and grades caused by the transfer of commissioned officers to the service and jurisdiction of a military department under the provisions of sections 854, 855, 856, 857, and 858[1] of this title.

(3) Temporary appointments may be made in all grades to which original appointments in the National Oceanic and Atmospheric Administration are authorized: *Provided*, That the number of officers holding temporary appointments shall not exceed the number of officers transferred to a military department under the provisions of sections 854, 855, 856, 857, and 858[1] of this title.

(Dec. 3, 1942, ch. 670, §1, 56 Stat. 1038; Pub. L. 89–657, §3, Oct. 14, 1966, 80 Stat. 907; 1965 Reorg. Plan No. 2, eff. July 13, 1965, 30 F.R. 8819, 79 Stat. 1318; 1970 Reorg. Plan No. 4, eff. Oct. 3, 1970, 35 F.R. 15627, 84 Stat. 2090.)

REFERENCES IN TEXT

Sections 854, 855, 856, 857, and 858 of this title, referred to in text, were repealed by Pub. L. 107–372, title II, §271(4), Dec. 19, 2002, 116 Stat. 3094.

CODIFICATION

Provisions similar to this section are contained in section 3030 of this title.

AMENDMENTS

1966—Pub. L. 89–657 struck out reference to act of July 24, 1941 (Public, Numbered 188, Seventy-seventh Congress) which, for purposes of codification, has been changed to sections 350 to 350j of former title 34 and substituted Environmental Science Services Administration for Coast and Geodetic Survey, temporary advancement of commissioned officers for temporary promotions, military departments for Department of the Army or Navy Department, Secretary of the military department concerned for Secretary of the Army or Secretary of the Navy, and reference to temporary appointments in all grades to which original appointments in the Environmental Science Services Administration are authorized for reference to temporary appointment of regularly appointed deck officers and junior engineers to the rank and grade of ensign.

TRANSFER OF FUNCTIONS

Coast and Geodetic Survey consolidated with Weather Bureau to form a new agency in Department of Commerce to be known as Environmental Science Services Administration, and commissioned officers of Survey transferred to ESSA, by Reorg. Plan No. 2 of 1965, eff. July 13, 1965, 30 F.R. 8819, 79 Stat. 1318, set out as a note under section 851 of this title. The Reorg. Plan also transferred to Secretary of Commerce all functions of Coast and Geodetic Survey and Director of Survey. Subsequently, Environmental Science Services Administration abolished, National Oceanic and Atmospheric Administration established, and Commissioned Officer Corps of ESSA redesignated Commissioned Officer Corps of NOAA by Reorg. Plan No. 4 of 1970, eff. Oct. 3, 1970, 35 F.R. 15627, 84 Stat. 2090, set out in the Appendix to Title 5, Government Organization and Employees. For further details, see note set out under section 851 of this title.

DELEGATION OF FUNCTIONS

Functions of President under pars. (1), (2), and (3) delegated to Secretary of Commerce, see section 1(b), (i) and (j) of Ex. Ord. No. 11023, May 28, 1962, 27 F.R. 5131, set out as a note under section 301 of Title 3, The President.

§854a–2. Pay and allowances; date of acceptance of promotion

Any commissioned officer of the National Oceanic and Atmospheric Administration promoted to a higher grade at any time after December 7, 1941, shall be deemed for all purposes to have accepted his promotion to higher grade upon the date such promotion is made by the President unless he shall expressly decline such promotion, and shall receive the pay and allowances of the higher grade from such date unless

[1] See References in Text note below.

he is entitled under some other provision of law to receive the pay and allowances of the higher grade from an earlier date. No such officer who shall have subscribed to the oath of office required by section 3331 of title 5, shall be required to renew such oath or to take a new oath upon his promotion to a higher grade, if his service after the taking of such an oath shall have been continuous.

(Dec. 3, 1942, ch. 670, §3, 56 Stat. 1039; 1965 Reorg. Plan No. 2, eff. July 13, 1965, 30 F.R. 8819, 79 Stat. 1318; 1970 Reorg. Plan No. 4, eff. Oct. 3, 1970, 35 F.R. 15627, 84 Stat. 2090.)

CODIFICATION

"Section 3331 of title 5" substituted in text for "section 1757, Revised Statutes" on authority of Pub. L. 89–554, §7(b), Sept. 6, 1966, 80 Stat. 631, the first section of which enacted Title 5, Government Organization and Employees. Section 1757 of the Revised Statutes had been classified to section 16 of former Title 5, Executive Departments and Government Officers and Employees.

Provisions similar to this section are contained in section 3031 of this title.

TRANSFER OF FUNCTIONS

Coast and Geodetic Survey consolidated with Weather Bureau to form a new agency in Department of Commerce to be known as Environmental Science Services Administration, and commissioned officers of Survey transferred to ESSA, by Reorg. Plan No. 2 of 1965, eff. July 13, 1965, 30 F.R. 8819, 79 Stat. 1318, set out as a note under section 851 of this title. The Reorg. Plan also transferred to Secretary of Commerce all functions of Coast and Geodetic Survey and Director of Survey. Subsequently, Environmental Science Services Administration abolished, National Oceanic and Atmospheric Administration established, and Commissioned Officer Corps of ESSA redesignated Commissioned Officer Corps of NOAA by Reorg. Plan No. 4 of 1970, eff. Oct. 3, 1970, 35 F.R. 15627, 84 Stat. 2090, set out in the Appendix to Title 5, Government Organization and Employees. For further details, see note set out under section 851 of this title.

§§854b, 854c. Repealed. June 3, 1948, ch. 390, §22(a), formerly §21(a), 62 Stat. 300; renumbered §22(a), Sept. 14, 1961, Pub. L. 87–233, §1(f), 75 Stat. 506

Section 854b, act Jan. 19, 1942, ch. 6, §3, 56 Stat. 7, related to composition, powers and duties of a Personnel Board.

Section 854c, act Jan. 19, 1942, ch. 6, §4, 56 Stat. 7, related to submission of reports of the Personnel Boards to the President.

§855. Repealed. Pub. L. 107–372, title II, §271(4), Dec. 19, 2002, 116 Stat. 3094

Section, acts May 22, 1917, ch. 20, §16, 40 Stat. 87; 1965 Reorg. Plan No. 2, eff. July 13, 1965, 30 F.R. 8819, 79 Stat. 1318; Pub. L. 89–657, §1(1), Oct. 14, 1966, 80 Stat. 907; 1970 Reorg. Plan No. 4, eff. Oct. 3, 1970, 35 F.R. 15627, 84 Stat. 2090, related to cooperation with and transfer to military departments. See section 3061 of this title.

§855a. Repealed. Pub. L. 85–857, §14(79), Sept. 2, 1958, 72 Stat. 1272

Section, acts Dec. 3, 1942, ch. 670, §2, 56 Stat. 1038; Aug. 16, 1954, ch. 738, 68 Stat. 730, related to rights and benefits of commissioned officers of Coast and Geodetic Survey assigned to projects of Army and Navy outside continental United States or in hazardous military areas.

EFFECTIVE DATE OF REPEAL

Repeal by Pub. L. 85–857 effective Jan. 1, 1959, see section 2 of Pub. L. 85–857, set out as an Effective Date note preceding Part I of Title 38, Veterans' Benefits.

§§856 to 857–5. Repealed. Pub. L. 107–372, title II, §271(3), (4), Dec. 19, 2002, 116 Stat. 3094

Section 856, acts May 22, 1917, ch. 20, §16, 40 Stat. 88; June 21, 1955, ch. 172, §2(b), 69 Stat. 169; 1965 Reorg. Plan No. 2, eff. July 13, 1965, 30 F.R. 8819, 79 Stat. 1318; 1970 Reorg. Plan No. 4, eff. Oct. 3, 1970, 35 F.R. 15627, 84 Stat. 2090, related to relative rank of National Oceanic and Atmospheric Administration officers when serving with Army, Navy, or Air Force. See section 3062 of this title.

Section 857, acts May 22, 1917, ch. 20, §16, 40 Stat. 88; Aug. 1, 1956, ch. 837, title V, §501(d)(1), 70 Stat. 883; 1965 Reorg. Plan No. 2, eff. July 13, 1965, 30 F.R. 8819, 79 Stat. 1318; 1970 Reorg. Plan No. 4, eff. Oct. 3, 1970, 35 F.R. 15627, 84 Stat. 2090; Pub. L. 102–54, §13(m)(2), June 13, 1991, 105 Stat. 277, related to service of commissioned officers of the National Oceanic and Atmospheric Administration for purposes of servicemen's and veterans' benefits. See section 3072 of this title.

Section 857–1, Pub. L. 91–621, §1, Dec. 31, 1970, 84 Stat. 1863, related to applicable definitions. See section 3002 of this title.

Section 857–2, Pub. L. 91–621, §2, Dec. 31, 1970, 84 Stat. 1863, related to retirement grade and pay. See section 3046 of this title.

Section 857–3, Pub. L. 91–621, §3, Dec. 31, 1970, 84 Stat. 1863; Pub. L. 98–498, title III, §310(a), Oct. 19, 1984, 98 Stat. 2306; Pub. L. 102–54, §13(m)(3), June 13, 1991, 105 Stat. 277, related to service for purposes of certain statutory rights, privileges, immunities, and benefits and provision of medical and dental care. See sections 3072 and 3073 of this title.

Section 857–4, Pub. L. 91–621, §4, Dec. 31, 1970, 84 Stat. 1863, related to commissary privileges. See section 3074 of this title.

Section 857–5, Pub. L. 91–621, §5, Dec. 31, 1970, 84 Stat. 1864, related to applicability of statutes that had applied to commissioned officers of the Coast and Geodetic Survey and the Environmental Science Services Administration.

REPEALS

Pub. L. 91–621, §8, Dec. 31, 1970, 84 Stat. 1867, provided that all provisions of law inconsistent with Pub. L. 91–621 were repealed, prior to repeal by Pub. L. 107–372, title II, §271(3), Dec. 19, 2002, 116 Stat. 3094.

§§857–6 to 857–12. Repealed. Pub. L. 95–63, §7(a), July 5, 1977, 91 Stat. 267

Section 857–6, Pub. L. 92–125, §1, Aug. 16, 1971, 85 Stat. 344, established National Advisory Committee on Oceans and Atmosphere. See section 857–13 of this title.

Section 857–7, Pub. L. 92–125, §2, Aug. 16, 1971, 85 Stat. 344, provided for membership, terms of office, duties, and Chairman and Vice Chairman of Committee. See section 857–14 of this title.

Section 857–8, Pub. L. 92–125, §3, Aug. 16, 1971, 85 Stat. 344, provided for designation of a senior policy official of Federal departments and agencies to assist Committee. See section 857–17(a) of this title.

Section 857–9, Pub. L. 92–125, §4, Aug. 16, 1971, 85 Stat. 344; Pub. L. 94–69, §2, Aug. 5, 1975, 89 Stat. 384, provided for an annual report by Committee. See section 857–15 of this title.

Section 857–10, Pub. L. 92–125, §5, Aug. 16, 1971, 85 Stat. 344, provided for compensation and travel expenses of Committee members. See section 857–16 of this title.

Section 857–11, Pub. L. 92–125, §6, Aug. 16, 1971, 85 Stat. 345, provided for assistance to Committee by Federal departments and agencies. See section 857–17 of this title.

Section 857–12, Pub. L. 92–125, §7, Aug. 16, 1971, 85 Stat. 345; Pub. L. 92–567, Oct. 25, 1972, 86 Stat. 1181; Pub.

L. 94–69, § 1, Aug. 5, 1975, 89 Stat. 384, authorized appropriations for operation of the Committee. See section 857–18 of this title.

§ 857–13. National Advisory Committee on Oceans and Atmosphere

There is hereby established a committee of 18 members to be known as the National Advisory Committee on Oceans and Atmosphere (hereinafter in sections 857–13 to 857–18 of this title referred to as the "Committee").

(Pub. L. 95–63, § 2, July 5, 1977, 91 Stat. 265.)

PRIOR PROVISIONS

Provisions similar to that contained in this section, which established a National Advisory Committee on Oceans and Atmosphere with a membership of twenty-five, were contained in section 857–6 of this title prior to repeal by section 7(a) of Pub. L. 95–63.

SHORT TITLE

For short title of Pub. L. 95–63, see section 1 of Pub. L. 95–63, set out as a note under section 851 of this title.

TRANSFER OF PERSONNEL, POSITIONS, RECORDS, AND FUNDS

Section 7(b) of Pub. L. 95–63 provided that: "All personnel, positions, records, and unexpended balances of appropriations, allocations, and other funds employed, used, held, available, or to be made available in connection with the functions specified by the Act of August 16, 1971 [former sections 857–6 to 857–12 of this title] (establishing an advisory committee on oceans and atmosphere), are hereby transferred to the National Advisory Committee on Oceans and Atmosphere established by this Act [sections 857–13 to 857–18 of this title]. The personnel transferred under this subsection shall be so transferred without reduction in classification or compensation except, that after such transfer, such personnel shall be subject to reductions in classification or compensation in the same manner, to the same extent, and according to the same procedure as other employees of the United States classified and compensated according to the General Schedule in title 5, United States Code."

TERMINATION OF ADVISORY COMMITTEES

Advisory committees established after Jan. 5, 1973, to terminate not later than the expiration of the 2-year period beginning on the date of their establishment, unless, in the case of a committee established by the President or an officer of the Federal Government, such committee is renewed by appropriate action prior to the expiration of such 2-year period, or in the case of a committee established by the Congress, its duration is otherwise provided for by law. See section 14 of Pub. L. 92–463, Oct. 6, 1972, 86 Stat. 776, set out in the Appendix to Title 5, Government Organization and Employees.

§ 857–14. Membership

(a) Appointment and qualifications

The members of the Committee, who may not be full-time officers or employees of the United States, shall be appointed by the President. Members shall be appointed only from among individuals who are eminently qualified by way of knowledge and expertise in the following areas of direct concern to the Committee—

(1) one or more of the disciplines and fields included in marine science and technology, marine industry, marine-related State and local governmental functions, coastal zone management, or other fields directly appropriate for consideration of matters of ocean policy; or

(2) one or more of the disciplines and fields included in atmospheric science, atmospheric-related State and local governmental functions, or other fields directly appropriate for consideration of matters of atmospheric policy.

(b) Terms

(1) The term of office of a member of the Committee shall be 3 years; except that of the original appointees, 6 shall be appointed for a term to expire on July 1, 1979, 6 shall be appointed for a term to expire on July 1, 1980, and 6 shall be appointed for a term to expire on July 1, 1981.

(2) Any individual appointed to fill a vacancy occurring before the expiration of the term for which his or her predecessor was appointed shall be appointed only for the remainder of such term. No individual may be reappointed to the Committee for more than one additional 3-year term. A member may serve after the date of the expiration of the term of office for which appointed until his or her successor has taken office. The terms of office for members first appointed after July 5, 1977, shall begin on July 1, 1977.

(c) Chairman

The President shall designate one of the members of the Committee as the Chairman and one of the members as the Vice Chairman. The Vice Chairman shall act as Chairman in the absence or incapacity of, or in the event of a vacancy in the office of, the Chairman.

(d) Duties

The Committee shall—

(1) undertake a continuing review, on a selective basis, of national ocean policy, coastal zone management, and the status of the marine and atmospheric science and service programs of the United States; and

(2) advise the Secretary of Commerce with respect to the carrying out of the programs administered by the National Oceanic and Atmospheric Administration.

(Pub. L. 95–63, § 3, July 5, 1977, 91 Stat. 265; Pub. L. 95–304, § 1(1), June 29, 1978, 92 Stat. 347; Pub. L. 97–87, § 1(1), Dec. 1, 1981, 95 Stat. 1134.)

PRIOR PROVISIONS

Provisions similar to those contained in this section, which related to membership, terms, and duties of the National Advisory Committee on Oceans and Atmosphere as originally established on Aug. 16, 1971, were contained in section 857–7 of this title prior to repeal by section 7(a) of Pub. L. 95–63.

AMENDMENTS

1981—Subsec. (b)(2). Pub. L. 97–87 struck out ", or until ninety days after such date, whichever is earlier" after "until his or her successor has taken office".

1978—Subsec. (b)(1). Pub. L. 95–304 substituted provisions authorizing terms of members to expire on July 1, 1979, July 1, 1980, and July 1, 1981, respectively, for provisions authorizing terms of members to be for 1 year, 2 years, and 3 years, respectively.

TERMINATION OF ADVISORY COMMITTEES

Advisory committees established after Jan. 5, 1973, to terminate not later than the expiration of the 2-year period beginning on the date of their establishment, unless, in the case of a committee established by the President or an officer of the Federal Government, such committee is renewed by appropriate action prior to the expiration of such 2-year period, or in the case of a committee established by the Congress, its duration is otherwise provided for by law. See section 14 of Pub. L. 92–463, Oct. 6, 1972, 86 Stat. 776, set out in the Appendix to Title 5, Government Organization and Employees.

§857–15. Reports

(a) In general

The Committee shall submit an annual report to the President and to the Congress setting forth an assessment, on a selective basis, of the status of the Nation's marine and atmospheric activities, and shall submit such other reports as may from time to time be requested by the President or the Congress.

(b) Review by Secretary

Each annual report shall also be submitted to the Secretary of Commerce, who shall, within 60 days after receipt thereof, transmit his or her comments and recommendations to the President and to the Congress.

(c) Annual report submittal

The annual report required under subsection (a) of this section shall be submitted on or before June 30 of each year, beginning with June 30, 1978.

(Pub. L. 95–63, §4, July 5, 1977, 91 Stat. 266.)

PRIOR PROVISIONS

A provision similar to that contained in this section, which required an annual report, beginning June 30, 1972, from the National Advisory Committee on Oceans and Atmosphere as originally established on Aug. 16, 1971, was contained in section 857–9 of this title prior to repeal by section 7(a) of Pub. L. 95–63.

TERMINATION OF REPORTING REQUIREMENTS

For termination, effective May 15, 2000, of provisions in subsec. (a) of this section relating to submitting an annual report to Congress and provisions in subsec. (b) of this section relating to annually transmitting comments and recommendations to Congress, see section 3003 of Pub. L. 104–66, as amended, set out as a note under section 1113 of Title 31, Money and Finance, and pages 50 and 177 of House Document No. 103–7.

TERMINATION OF ADVISORY COMMITTEES

Advisory committees established after Jan. 5, 1973, to terminate not later than the expiration of the 2-year period beginning on the date of their establishment, unless, in the case of a committee established by the President or an officer of the Federal Government, such committee is renewed by appropriate action prior to the expiration of such 2-year period, or in the case of a committee established by the Congress, its duration is otherwise provided for by law. See section 14 of Pub. L. 92–463, Oct. 6, 1972, 86 Stat. 776, set out in the Appendix to Title 5, Government Organization and Employees.

§857–16. Compensation and travel expenses

Members of the Committee shall each be entitled to receive compensation not to exceed the daily rate for a GS–18 for each day (including traveltime) during which they are engaged in the actual performance of the duties of the Committee. In addition, while away from their homes or regular places of business in the performance of the duties of the Committee, each member of the Committee shall be allowed travel expenses, including per diem in lieu of subsistence, in the same manner as persons employed intermittently in the Government service are allowed expenses under section 5703(b)[1] of title 5.

(Pub. L. 95–63, §5, July 5, 1977, 91 Stat. 266; Pub. L. 97–87, §1(2), Dec. 1, 1981, 95 Stat. 1134.)

REFERENCES IN TEXT

Section 5703 of title 5, referred to in text, was amended generally by Pub. L. 94–22, §4, May 19, 1975, 89 Stat. 85, and, as so amended, does not contain a subsec. (b).

PRIOR PROVISIONS

A provision similar to that contained in this section, which authorized compensation and travel expenses for members of the National Advisory Committee on Oceans and Atmosphere as originally established on Aug. 16, 1971, was contained in section 857–10 of this title prior to repeal by section 7(a) of Pub. L. 95–63.

AMENDMENTS

1981—Pub. L. 97–87 substituted "not to exceed the daily rate for a GS–18" for "of $100 per day".

TERMINATION OF ADVISORY COMMITTEES

Advisory committees established after Jan. 5, 1973, to terminate not later than the expiration of the 2-year period beginning on the date of their establishment, unless, in the case of a committee established by the President or an officer of the Federal Government, such committee is renewed by appropriate action prior to the expiration of such 2-year period, or in the case of a committee established by the Congress, its duration is otherwise provided for by law. See section 14 of Pub. L. 92–463, Oct. 6, 1972, 86 Stat. 776, set out in the Appendix to Title 5, Government Organization and Employees.

REFERENCES IN OTHER LAWS TO GS–16, 17, OR 18 PAY RATES

References in laws to the rates of pay for GS–16, 17, or 18, or to maximum rates of pay under the General Schedule, to be considered references to rates payable under specified sections of Title 5, Government Organization and Employees, see section 529 [title I, §101(c)(1)] of Pub. L. 101–509, set out in a note under section 5376 of Title 5.

§857–17. Interagency cooperation and assistance

(a) Liaison

The head of each department or agency of the Federal Government concerned with marine and atmospheric matters shall designate a senior policy official to participate as observer in the work of the Committee and offer necessary assistance.

(b) Agency assistance

The Committee is authorized to request from the head of any department, agency, or independent instrumentality of the Federal Government any information and assistance it deems necessary to carry out the functions assigned under sections 857–13 to 857–18 of this title. The head of each such department, agency, or instrumentality is authorized to cooperate with the Committee, and, to the extent permitted by law, to furnish such information and assistance to

[1] See References in Text note below.

the Committee upon request made by the Chairman, without reimbursement for such services and assistance.

(c) Administrative assistance

The Secretary of Commerce shall make available to the Committee such staff, information, personnel, and administrative services and assistance as may reasonably be required to carry out the provisions of sections 857–13 to 857–18 of this title.

(Pub. L. 95–63, § 6, July 5, 1977, 91 Stat. 266.)

PRIOR PROVISIONS

Provisions similar to those contained in this section, which required the designation of senior policy officials as observers, directed the Secretary of Commerce to provide administrative assistance, and authorized requests for assistance from Federal agencies by the Federal Advisory Committee on Oceans and Atmosphere as originally established on Aug. 16, 1971, were contained in sections 857–8 and 857–11 of this title prior to repeal by section 7(a) of Pub. L. 95–63.

TERMINATION OF ADVISORY COMMITTEES

Advisory committees established after Jan. 5, 1973, to terminate not later than the expiration of the 2-year period beginning on the date of their establishment, unless, in the case of a committee established by the President or an officer of the Federal Government, such committee is renewed by appropriate action prior to the expiration of such 2-year period, or in the case of a committee established by the Congress, its duration is otherwise provided for by law. See section 14 of Pub. L. 92–463, Oct. 6, 1972, 86 Stat. 776, set out in the Appendix to Title 5, Government Organization and Employees.

§ 857–18. Authorization of appropriations

There are authorized to be appropriated for purposes of carrying out sections 857–13 to 857–18 of this title not to exceed $520,000 for the fiscal year ending September 30, 1978, $572,000 for the fiscal year ending September 30, 1979, $565,000 for the fiscal year ending September 30, 1980, $600,000 for the fiscal year ending September 30, 1981, and $555,000 for the fiscal year ending September 30, 1982. Such sums as may be appropriated under this section shall remain available until expended.

(Pub. L. 95–63, § 8, July 5, 1977, 91 Stat. 267; Pub. L. 95–304, § 1(2), June 29, 1978, 92 Stat. 347; Pub. L. 96–26, June 21, 1979, 93 Stat. 74; Pub. L. 97–87, § 1(3), Dec. 1, 1981, 95 Stat. 1134.)

PRIOR PROVISIONS

Provisions similar to those contained in this section, which authorized appropriations, beginning with an authorization of $200,000 for the fiscal year ending June 30, 1972, for the operation of the National Advisory Committee on Oceans and Atmosphere as originally established on Aug. 16, 1971, were contained in section 857–12 of this title prior to repeal by section 7(a) of Pub. L. 95–63.

AMENDMENTS

1981—Pub. L. 97–87 inserted provisions authorizing appropriations of not to exceed $555,000 for fiscal year ending Sept. 30, 1982, and provided that such sums as might be appropriated under authority of this section remain available until expended.

1979—Pub. L. 96–26 substituted provisions authorizing appropriations of $565,000 for fiscal year ending Sept. 30, 1980, and $600,000 for fiscal year ending Sept. 30, 1981, for provisions directing that sums appropriated under this section remain available until expended.

1978—Pub. L. 95–304 inserted provisions authorizing appropriations for fiscal year ending Sept. 30, 1979.

§ 857–19. Biennial report

Beginning in September, 2001, the President shall transmit to the Congress biennially a report that includes a detailed listing of all existing Federal programs related to ocean and coastal activities, including a description of each program, the current funding for the program, linkages to other Federal programs, and a projection of the funding level for the program for each of the next 5 fiscal years beginning after the report is submitted.

(Pub. L. 106–256, § 5, Aug. 7, 2000, 114 Stat. 648.)

NATIONAL OCEAN POLICY

Pub. L. 106–256, Aug. 7, 2000, 114 Stat. 644, as amended by Pub. L. 107–206, title I, § 206, Aug. 2, 2002, 116 Stat. 833; Pub. L. 107–372, title III, § 306, Dec. 19, 2002, 116 Stat. 3096, provided that:

"SECTION 1. SHORT TITLE.

"This Act may be cited as the 'Oceans Act of 2000'.

"SEC. 2. PURPOSE AND OBJECTIVES.

"The purpose of this Act is to establish a commission to make recommendations for coordinated and comprehensive national ocean policy that will promote—

"(1) the protection of life and property against natural and manmade hazards;

"(2) responsible stewardship, including use, of fishery resources and other ocean and coastal resources;

"(3) the protection of the marine environment and prevention of marine pollution;

"(4) the enhancement of marine-related commerce and transportation, the resolution of conflicts among users of the marine environment, and the engagement of the private sector in innovative approaches for sustainable use of living marine resources and responsible use of non-living marine resources;

"(5) the expansion of human knowledge of the marine environment including the role of the oceans in climate and global environmental change and the advancement of education and training in fields related to ocean and coastal activities;

"(6) the continued investment in and development and improvement of the capabilities, performance, use, and efficiency of technologies for use in ocean and coastal activities, including investments and technologies designed to promote national energy and food security;

"(7) close cooperation among all government agencies and departments and the private sector to ensure—

"(A) coherent and consistent regulation and management of ocean and coastal activities;

"(B) availability and appropriate allocation of Federal funding, personnel, facilities, and equipment for such activities;

"(C) cost-effective and efficient operation of Federal departments, agencies, and programs involved in ocean and coastal activities; and

"(D) enhancement of partnerships with State and local governments with respect to ocean and coastal activities, including the management of ocean and coastal resources and identification of appropriate opportunities for policy-making and decision-making at the State and local level; and

"(8) the preservation of the role of the United States as a leader in ocean and coastal activities, and, when it is in the national interest, the cooperation by the United States with other nations and international organizations in ocean and coastal activities.

"SEC. 3. COMMISSION ON OCEAN POLICY.

"(a) ESTABLISHMENT.—There is hereby established the Commission on Ocean Policy. The Federal Advisory

Committee Act (5 U.S.C. App.), except for sections 3, 7, and 12, does not apply to the Commission.

"(b) MEMBERSHIP.—

"(1) APPOINTMENT.—The Commission shall be composed of 16 members appointed by the President from among individuals described in paragraph (2) who are knowledgeable in ocean and coastal activities, including individuals representing State and local governments, ocean-related industries, academic and technical institutions, and public interest organizations involved with scientific, regulatory, economic, and environmental ocean and coastal activities. The membership of the Commission shall be balanced by area of expertise and balanced geographically to the extent consistent with maintaining the highest level of expertise on the Commission.

"(2) NOMINATIONS.—The President shall appoint the members of the Commission, within 90 days after the effective date of this Act, including individuals nominated as follows:

"(A) 4 members shall be appointed from a list of 8 individuals who shall be nominated by the Majority Leader of the Senate in consultation with the Chairman of the Senate Committee on Commerce, Science, and Transportation.

"(B) 4 members shall be appointed from a list of 8 individuals who shall be nominated by the Speaker of the House of Representatives in consultation with the Chairmen of the House Committees on Resources [now Natural Resources], Transportation and Infrastructure, and Science [now Science and Technology].

"(C) 2 members shall be appointed from a list of 4 individuals who shall be nominated by the Minority Leader of the Senate in consultation with the Ranking Member of the Senate Committee on Commerce, Science, and Transportation.

"(D) 2 members shall be appointed from a list of 4 individuals who shall be nominated by the Minority Leader of the House in consultation with the Ranking Members of the House Committees on Resources [now Natural Resources], Transportation and Infrastructure, and Science [now Science and Technology].

"(3) CHAIRMAN.—The Commission shall select a Chairman from among its members. The Chairman of the Commission shall be responsible for—

"(A) the assignment of duties and responsibilities among staff personnel and their continuing supervision; and

"(B) the use and expenditure of funds available to the Commission.

"(4) VACANCIES.—Any vacancy on the Commission shall be filled in the same manner as the original incumbent was appointed.

"(c) RESOURCES.—In carrying out its functions under this section, the Commission—

"(1) is authorized to secure directly from any Federal agency or department any information it deems necessary to carry out its functions under this Act, and each such agency or department is authorized to cooperate with the Commission and, to the extent permitted by law, to furnish such information (other than information described in section 552(b)(1)(A) of title 5, United States Code) to the Commission, upon the request of the Commission;

"(2) may enter into contracts, subject to the availability of appropriations for contracting, and employ such staff experts and consultants as may be necessary to carry out the duties of the Commission, as provided by section 3109 of title 5, United States Code; and

"(3) in consultation with the Ocean Studies Board of the National Research Council of the National Academy of Sciences, shall establish a multidisciplinary science advisory panel of experts in the sciences of living and non-living marine resources to assist the Commission in preparing its report, including ensuring that the scientific information considered by the Commission is based on the best scientific information available.

"(d) STAFFING.—The Chairman of the Commission may, without regard to the civil service laws and regulations, appoint and terminate an Executive Director and such other additional personnel as may be necessary for the Commission to perform its duties. The Executive Director shall be compensated at a rate not to exceed the rate payable for Level V of the Executive Schedule under section 5136 of title 5, United States Code. The employment and termination of an Executive Director shall be subject to confirmation by a majority of the members of the Commission.

"(e) MEETINGS.—

"(1) ADMINISTRATION.—All meetings of the Commission shall be open to the public, except that a meeting or any portion of it may be closed to the public if it concerns matters or information described in section 552b(c) of title 5, United States Code. Interested persons shall be permitted to appear at open meetings and present oral or written statements on the subject matter of the meeting. The Commission may administer oaths or affirmations to any person appearing before it.

"(2) NOTICE; MINUTES; PUBLIC AVAILABILITY OF DOCUMENTS.—

"(A) All open meetings of the Commission shall be preceded by timely public notice in the Federal Register of the time, place, and subject of the meeting.

"(B) Minutes of each meeting shall be kept and shall contain a record of the people present, a description of the discussion that occurred, and copies of all statements filed. Subject to section 552 of title 5, United States Code, the minutes and records of all meetings and other documents that were made available to or prepared for the Commission shall be available for public inspection and copying at a single location in the offices of the Commission.

"(3) INITIAL MEETING.—The Commission shall hold its first meeting within 30 days after all 16 members have been appointed.

"(4) REQUIRED PUBLIC MEETINGS.—The Commission shall hold at least one public meeting in Alaska and each of the following regions of the United States:

"(A) The Northeast (including the Great Lakes).

"(B) The Southeast (including the Caribbean).

"(C) The Southwest (including Hawaii and the Pacific Territories).

"(D) The Northwest.

"(E) The Gulf of Mexico.

"(f) REPORT.—

"(1) IN GENERAL.—By June 20, 2003, the Commission shall submit to Congress and the President a final report of its findings and recommendations regarding United States ocean policy.

"(2) REQUIRED MATTER.—The final report of the Commission shall include the following assessment, reviews, and recommendations:

"(A) An assessment of existing and planned facilities associated with ocean and coastal activities including human resources, vessels, computers, satellites, and other appropriate platforms and technologies.

"(B) A review of existing and planned ocean and coastal activities of Federal entities, recommendations for changes in such activities necessary to improve efficiency and effectiveness and to reduce duplication of Federal efforts.

"(C) A review of the cumulative effect of Federal laws and regulations on United States ocean and coastal activities and resources and an examination of those laws and regulations for inconsistencies and contradictions that might adversely affect those ocean and coastal activities and resources, and recommendations for resolving such inconsistencies to the extent practicable. Such review shall also consider conflicts with State ocean and coastal management regimes.

"(D) A review of the known and anticipated supply of, and demand for, ocean and coastal resources of the United States.

"(E) A review of and recommendations concerning the relationship between Federal, State, and local governments and the private sector in planning and carrying out ocean and coastal activities.

"(F) A review of opportunities for the development of or investment in new products, technologies, or markets related to ocean and coastal activities.

"(G) A review of previous and ongoing State and Federal efforts to enhance the effectiveness and integration of ocean and coastal activities.

"(H) Recommendations for any modifications to United States laws, regulations, and the administrative structure of Executive agencies, necessary to improve the understanding, management, conservation, and use of, and access to, ocean and coastal resources.

"(I) A review of the effectiveness and adequacy of existing Federal interagency ocean policy coordination mechanisms, and recommendations for changing or improving the effectiveness of such mechanisms necessary to respond to or implement the recommendations of the Commission.

"(3) CONSIDERATION OF FACTORS.—In making its assessment and reviews and developing its recommendations, the Commission shall give equal consideration to environmental, technical feasibility, economic, and scientific factors.

"(4) LIMITATIONS.—The recommendations of the Commission shall not be specific to the lands and waters within a single State.

"(g) PUBLIC AND COASTAL STATE REVIEW.—

"(1) NOTICE.—Before submitting the final report to the Congress, the Commission shall—

"(A) publish in the Federal Register a notice that a draft report is available for public review; and

"(B) provide a copy of the draft report to the Governor of each coastal State, the Committees on Resources [now Natural Resources], Transportation and Infrastructure, and Science [now Science and Technology] of the House of Representatives, and the Committee on Commerce, Science, and Transportation of the Senate.

"(2) INCLUSION OF GOVERNORS' COMMENTS.—The Commission shall include in the final report comments received from the Governor of a coastal State regarding recommendations in the draft report.

"(h) ADMINISTRATIVE PROCEDURE FOR REPORT AND REVIEW.—Chapter 5 and chapter 7 of title 5, United States Code, do not apply to the preparation, review, or submission of the report required by subsection (e) or the review of that report under subsection (f).

"(i) TERMINATION.—The Commission shall cease to exist 90 days after the date on which it submits its final report.

"(j) AUTHORIZATION OF APPROPRIATIONS.—There are authorized to be appropriated to carry out this section a total of $8,500,000 for the 3 fiscal-year period beginning with fiscal year 2001, such sums to remain available until expended.

"SEC. 4. NATIONAL OCEAN POLICY.

"(a) NATIONAL OCEAN POLICY.—Within 90 days after receiving and considering the report and recommendations of the Commission under section 3, the President shall submit to Congress a statement of proposals to implement or respond to the Commission's recommendations for a coordinated, comprehensive, and long-range national policy for the responsible use and stewardship of ocean and coastal resources for the benefit of the United States. Nothing in this Act authorizes the President to take any administrative or regulatory action regarding ocean or coastal policy, or to implement a reorganization plan, not otherwise authorized by law in effect at the time of such action.

"(b) COOPERATION AND CONSULTATION.—In the process of developing proposals for submission under subsection (a), the President shall consult with State and local governments and non-Federal organizations and individuals involved in ocean and coastal activities.

"SEC. 5. BIENNIAL REPORT.

"[Enacted this section.]

"SEC. 6. DEFINITIONS.

"In this Act:

"(1) MARINE ENVIRONMENT.—The term 'marine environment' includes—

"(A) the oceans, including coastal and offshore waters;

"(B) the continental shelf; and

"(C) the Great Lakes.

"(2) OCEAN AND COASTAL RESOURCE.—The term 'ocean and coastal resource' means any living or nonliving natural, historic, or cultural resource found in the marine environment.

"(3) COMMISSION.—The term 'Commission' means the Commission on Ocean Policy established by section 3.

"SEC. 7. EFFECTIVE DATE.

"This Act shall become effective on January 20, 2001."

[Pub. L. 107–206, title I, §206, Aug. 2, 2002, 116 Stat. 833, which directed the amendment of section (3)(f)(1) of Pub. L. 106–256, set out above, by striking "within 18 months of the establishment of the Commission" and inserting "by June 20, 2003", was executed by striking "Within 18 months after the establishment of the Commission" and inserting "By June 20, 2003", to reflect the probable intent of Congress.]

The following appropriations acts contained provisions similar to those in section 3(f)(1) of Pub. L. 106–256, set out above:

Pub. L. 107–77, title V, Nov. 28, 2001, 115 Stat. 792, as amended by Pub. L. 107–117, div. B, §207, Jan. 10, 2002, 115 Stat. 2298.

Pub. L. 106–553, §1(a)(2) [title V], Dec. 21, 2000, 114 Stat. 2762, 2762A–98.

EX. ORD. NO. 13366. COMMITTEE ON OCEAN POLICY

Ex. Ord. No. 13366, Dec. 17, 2004, 69 F.R. 76591, provided:

By the authority vested in me as President by the Constitution and the laws of the United States of America, it is hereby ordered as follows:

SECTION 1. *Policy*. It shall be the policy of the United States to:

(a) coordinate the activities of executive departments and agencies regarding ocean-related matters in an integrated and effective manner to advance the environmental, economic, and security interests of present and future generations of Americans; and

(b) facilitate, as appropriate, coordination and consultation regarding ocean-related matters among Federal, State, tribal, local governments, the private sector, foreign governments, and international organizations.

SEC. 2. *Definition*. For purposes of this order the term "ocean-related matters" means matters involving the oceans, the Great Lakes, the coasts of the United States (including its territories and possessions), and related seabed, subsoil, and natural resources.

SEC. 3. *Establishment of Committee on Ocean Policy*.

(a) There is hereby established, as a part of the Council on Environmental Quality and for administrative purposes only, the Committee on Ocean Policy (Committee).

(b) The Committee shall consist exclusively of the following:

(i) the Chairman of the Council on Environmental Quality, who shall be the Chairman of the Committee;

(ii) the Secretaries of State, Defense, the Interior, Agriculture, Health and Human Services, Commerce, Labor, Transportation, Energy, and Homeland Security, the Attorney General, the Administrator of the Environmental Protection Agency, the Director of the Office of Management and Budget, the Administrator of the National Aeronautics and Space Administration, the Director of National Intelligence, the Director of the Office of Science and Technology Policy, the Director of the National Science Foundation, and the Chairman of the Joint Chiefs of Staff;

(iii) the Assistants to the President for National Security Affairs, Homeland Security, Domestic Policy, and Economic Policy;

(iv) an employee of the United States designated by the Vice President; and

(v) such other officers or employees of the United States as the Chairman of the Committee may from time to time designate.

(c) The Chairman of the Committee, after coordination with the Assistants to the President for National Security Affairs and Homeland Security, shall regularly convene and preside at meetings of the Committee, determine its agenda, direct its work, and, as appropriate to deal with particular subject matters, establish and direct subcommittees of the Committee that shall consist exclusively of members of the Committee. The Committee shall coordinate its advice in a timely fashion.

(d) A member of the Committee may designate, to perform the Committee or subcommittee functions of the member, any person who is within such member's department, agency, or office and who is (i) an officer of the United States appointed by the President, (ii) a member of the Senior Executive Service or the Senior Intelligence Service, (iii) an officer or employee within the Executive Office of the President, or (iv) an employee of the Vice President.

(e) Consistent with applicable law and subject to the availability of appropriations, the Council on Environmental Quality shall provide the funding, including through the Office of Environmental Quality as permitted by law and as appropriate, and administrative support for the Committee necessary to implement this order.

SEC. 4. *Functions of the Committee.* To implement the policy set forth in section 1 of this order, the Committee shall:

(a) provide advice on establishment or implementation of policies concerning ocean-related matters to:

(i) the President; and

(ii) the heads of executive departments and agencies from time to time as appropriate;

(b) obtain information and advice concerning ocean-related matters from:

(i) State, local, and tribal elected and appointed officials in a manner that seeks their individual advice and does not involve collective judgment or consensus advice or deliberation; and

(ii) representatives of private entities or other individuals in a manner that seeks their individual advice and does not involve collective judgment or consensus advice or deliberation;

(c) at the request of the head of any department or agency who is a member of the Committee, unless the Chairman of the Committee declines the request, promptly review and provide advice on a policy or policy implementation action on ocean-related matters proposed by that department or agency;

(d) provide and obtain information and advice to facilitate:

(i) development and implementation of common principles and goals for the conduct of governmental activities on ocean-related matters;

(ii) voluntary regional approaches with respect to ocean-related matters;

(iii) use of science in establishment of policy on ocean-related matters; and

(iv) collection, development, dissemination, and exchange of information on ocean-related matters; and

(e) ensure coordinated government development and implementation of the ocean component of the Global Earth Observation System of Systems.

SEC. 5. *Cooperation.* To the extent permitted by law and applicable presidential guidance, executive departments and agencies shall provide the Committee such information, support, and assistance as the Committee, through the Chairman, may request.

SEC. 6. *Coordination.* The Chairman of the Council on Environmental Quality, the Assistant to the President for National Security Affairs, the Assistant to the President for Homeland Security, and, with respect to the interagency task force established by Executive Order 13340 of May 18, 2004 [33 U.S.C. 1268 note], the Administrator of the Environmental Protection Agency, shall ensure appropriate coordination of the activities of the Committee under this order and other policy coordination structures relating to ocean or maritime issues pursuant to Presidential guidance.

SEC. 7. *General Provisions.* (a) Nothing in this order shall be construed to impair or otherwise affect:

(i) authority granted by law to a executive department or agency or the head thereof; or

(ii) functions assigned by the President to the National Security Council or Homeland Security Council (including subordinate bodies) relating to matters affecting foreign affairs, national security, homeland security, or intelligence.

(b) Nothing in this order shall be construed to impair or otherwise affect the functions of the Director of the Office of Management and Budget relating to budget, administrative, or legislative proposals.

(c) This order is intended only to improve the internal management of the Federal Government and is not intended to, and does not, create any right or benefit, substantive or procedural, enforceable at law or in equity by a party against the United States, its departments, agencies, or entities, its officers or employees, or any other person.

GEORGE W. BUSH.

§ 857–20. Coordination

Not later than February 15 of each year, the Under Secretary of Commerce for Oceans and Atmosphere and the Director of the National Science Foundation shall jointly submit to the Committees on Resources and Science of the House of Representatives and the Committee on Commerce, Science, and Transportation of the Senate a report on how the oceans and coastal research activities of the National Oceanic and Atmospheric Administration, including the Coastal Ocean Program and the National Sea Grant College Program, and of the National Science Foundation will be coordinated during the fiscal year following the fiscal year in which the report is submitted. The report shall describe in detail any overlapping ocean and coastal research interests between the agencies and specify how such research interests will be pursued by the programs in a complementary manner.

(Pub. L. 107–299, § 9, Nov. 26, 2002, 116 Stat. 2348.)

CHANGE OF NAME

Committee on Resources of House of Representatives changed to Committee on Natural Resources of House of Representatives and Committee on Science of House of Representatives changed to Committee on Science and Technology of House of Representatives by House Resolution No. 6, One Hundred Tenth Congress, Jan. 5, 2007.

§§ 857a, 858. Repealed. Pub. L. 107–372, title II, § 271(2), (4), Dec. 19, 2002, 116 Stat. 3094

Section 857a, acts Aug. 10, 1956, ch. 1041, § 3, 70A Stat. 619; Pub. L. 85–861, § 3, Sept. 2, 1958, 72 Stat. 1546; Pub. L. 86–160, § 2, Aug. 14, 1959, 73 Stat. 358; Pub. L. 87–233, § 4, Sept. 14, 1961, 75 Stat. 507; Pub. L. 87–649, § 9(a), Sept. 7, 1962, 76 Stat. 495; Pub. L. 88–132, § 5(k), Oct. 2, 1963, 77 Stat. 214; Pub. L. 88–431, § 1(c)(1), Aug. 14, 1964, 78 Stat. 439; Pub. L. 89–538, § 3(a), Aug. 14, 1966, 80 Stat. 348; Pub. L. 92–425, § 5, Sept. 21, 1972, 86 Stat. 713; Pub. L. 96–215, § 1, Mar. 25, 1980, 94 Stat. 123; Pub. L. 96–357, § 4, Sept. 24, 1980, 94 Stat. 1182; Pub. L. 96–513, title V, § 507(f)(1), Dec.

12, 1980, 94 Stat. 2920; Pub. L. 98–94, title X, § 1007(d), Sept. 24, 1983, 97 Stat. 662; Pub. L. 104–106, div. A, title V, § 566(a), (b), Feb. 10, 1996, 110 Stat. 327; Pub. L. 105–85, div. A, title VI, § 653(b), title X, § 1073(f), Nov. 18, 1997, 111 Stat. 1804, 1906; Pub. L. 107–107, div. A, title VI, § 653(b), Dec. 28, 2001, 115 Stat. 1153, related to applicability of certain provisions of Title 10, Armed Forces. See section 3071 of this title.

Section 858, acts May 22, 1917, ch. 20, § 16, 40 Stat. 88; July 26, 1947, ch. 343, title II, § 205(a), 61 Stat. 501; 1965 Reorg. Plan No. 2, eff. July 13, 1965, 30 F.R. 8819, 79 Stat. 1318; Pub. L. 89–657, § 1(2), Oct. 14, 1966, 80 Stat. 907; 1970 Reorg. Plan No. 4, eff. Oct. 3, 1970, 35 F.R. 15627, 84 Stat. 2090, related to rules and regulations when cooperating with military departments. See section 3063 of this title.

§ 859. Repealed. June 16, 1942, ch. 413, § 19, 56 Stat. 369, eff. June 1, 1942

Section, act June 10, 1922, ch. 212, 42 Stat. 625–633, related to pay and allowances of commissioned officers.

§ 860. Repealed. Pub. L. 87–649, § 14b, Sept. 7, 1962, 76 Stat. 499

Section, act May 18, 1920, ch. 190, § 11 (words before the first semicolon), 41 Stat. 603, made pay and allowances of naval officers applicable to Coast and Geodetic Survey generally.

§ 861. Omitted

CODIFICATION

Section, acts Feb. 27, 1925, ch. 364, title III, 43 Stat. 1046; Apr. 29, 1926, ch. 195, title III, 44 Stat. 362, related to expenses of officers of the Coast and Geodetic Survey when traveling on Government owned vessels. See sections 404 to 411 of Title 37, Pay and Allowances of the Uniformed Services.

§ 861a. Repealed. Aug. 10, 1956, ch. 1041, § 53, 70A Stat. 641

Section, act May 18, 1920, ch. 190, § 12, 41 Stat. 604, related to transportation for families of officers and enlisted men on permanent change of station.

§§ 861b, 861c. Omitted

CODIFICATION

Section 861b, act Feb. 21, 1929, ch. 288, 45 Stat. 1254, defined the terms "child" and "children" as formerly used in section 861a of this title, and has been omitted in view of the repeal of section 861a.

Section 861c, act June 24, 1935, ch. 291, § 3, 49 Stat. 421, defined the phrase "permanent change in station" as formerly used in section 861a of this title, and has been omitted in view of the repeal of section 861a.

§ 862. Repealed. Pub. L. 87–649, § 14b, Sept. 7, 1962, 76 Stat. 498

Section, acts Mar. 4, 1907, ch. 2918, § 1, 34 Stat. 1322; Mar. 4, 1913, ch. 141, § 1, 37 Stat. 736; June 21, 1955, ch. 172, § 1, 69 Stat. 169; Sept. 26, 1961, Pub. L. 87–304, § 9(b), 75 Stat. 665, authorized commissioned officers of the Coast and Geodetic Survey to make assignments or allotments of their pay. See section 706 of Title 37, Pay and Allowances of the Uniformed Services.

§ 862a. Repealed. Aug. 10, 1956, ch. 1041, § 53, 70A Stat. 641

Section, acts Mar. 2, 1923, ch. 178, title I, 42 Stat. 1385; Aug. 4, 1949, ch. 393, § 11, 63 Stat. 559, prohibited the issuance of heat or light in kind to any person in the Coast and Geodetic Survey while such person is receiving an allowance for rental of quarters.

§ 863. Repealed. June 21, 1955, ch. 172, § 5(4), 69 Stat. 170

Section, acts Mar. 4, 1909, ch. 299, § 1, 35 Stat. 974; Mar. 4, 1913, ch. 141, § 1, 37 Stat. 736, related to leaves of absence of officers of the Coast and Geodetic Survey on duty in the Philippine Islands.

§ 864. Repealed. Pub. L. 107–372, title II, § 271(6), Dec. 19, 2002, 116 Stat. 3094

Section, act May 18, 1920, ch. 190, § 11, 41 Stat. 603; 1965 Reorg. Plan No. 2, eff. July 13, 1965, 30 F.R. 8819, 79 Stat. 1318; 1970 Reorg. Plan No. 4, eff. Oct. 3, 1970, 35 F.R. 15627, 84 Stat. 2090, provided that laws concerning retirement of commissioned Naval officers would apply to commissioned National Oceanic and Atmospheric Administration officers.

§ 864a. Repealed. Aug. 10, 1956, ch. 1041, § 53, 70A Stat. 641

Section, act May 18, 1920, ch. 190, §§ 11 (proviso), 14, 41 Stat. 604, related to service credits in computing longevity pay of officers of the Coast and Geodetic Survey.

§§ 864b, 864c. Repealed. June 3, 1948, ch. 390, § 22(a), formerly § 21(a), 62 Stat. 300; renumbered § 22(a), Sept. 14, 1961, Pub. L. 87–233, § 1(f), 75 Stat. 506

Section 864b, act Jan. 19, 1942, ch. 6, § 5, 56 Stat. 7, related to retirement of officers. See, sections 1401 et seq., 6321 et seq., and 6371 et seq. of Title 10, Armed Forces.

Section 864c, act Jan. 19, 1942, ch. 6, § 7, 56 Stat. 8, related to pay of officers retired upon recommendation of Personnel Board.

§ 864d. Repealed. Oct. 12, 1949, ch. 681, title V, § 531(b)(31), 63 Stat. 839, eff. Oct. 1, 1949

Section, acts Jan. 19, 1942, ch. 6, § 7, 56 Stat. 8; June 3, 1948, ch. 390, § 22(b), formerly § 21(b), 62 Stat. 300; renumbered § 22(b), Sept. 14, 1961, Pub. L. 87–233, § 1(f), 75 Stat. 506, related to rank or pay of officers retired for duty incurred disability. See sections 1201 et seq., 1371 et seq., and 1401 et seq. of Title 10, Armed Forces.

§ 864e. Repealed. Pub. L. 86–465, § 1, May 13, 1960, 74 Stat. 130

Section, acts June 6, 1942, ch. 383, 56 Stat. 328; Aug. 4, 1949, ch. 393, § 15, 63 Stat. 560; Oct. 12, 1949, ch. 681, title V, § 522(b), 63 Stat. 836, provided that certain commissioned officers of the Coast and Geodetic Survey who have been specially commended for performance of duty in actual combat prior to Dec. 31, 1946, shall, upon retirement, be placed upon the retired list one grade higher than the grade in which they were serving at the time of retirement.

EFFECTIVE DATE OF REPEAL

Section 2 of Pub. L. 86–465 provided that: "This Act [repealing this section] becomes effective on November 1, 1959."

§ 865. Omitted

CODIFICATION

Section, acts May 28, 1924, ch. 203, 43 Stat. 194; Feb. 11, 1925, ch. 209, 43 Stat. 872; May 21, 1926, ch. 355, 44 Stat. 604, related to computation of length of service of officers and expired with the appropriation acts of which it was a part.

§ 866. Repealed. Aug. 6, 1947, ch. 504, § 10(1), 61 Stat. 788

Section, act Jan. 31, 1925, ch. 121, 43 Stat. 802, related to seismological investigations. See section 883a of this title.

§§867, 868. Repealed. Oct. 31, 1951, ch. 654, §1(39), (60), 65 Stat. 702, 703

Section 867, act June 5, 1920, ch. 235, §1, 41 Stat. 930, related to transfer of instruments to institutions.

Section 868, act July 1, 1918, ch. 113, §1, 40 Stat. 688, related to purchase of supplies or procurement of services in the field. See section 5 of Title 41, Public Contracts.

§868a. Omitted

Codification

Section, act Jan. 19, 1942, ch. 6, §10, 56 Stat. 8; 1965 Reorg. Plan No. 2, eff. July 13, 1965, 30 F.R. 8819, 79 Stat. 1318; Oct. 14, 1966, Pub. L. 89–657, §2, 80 Stat. 907; 1970 Reorg. Plan No. 4, eff. Oct. 3, 1970, 35 F.R. 15627, 84 Stat. 2090, related to the purchase of commissary and quartermaster supplies by personnel from the National Oceanic and Atmospheric Administration, and has been superseded by former section 857–4 of this title and section 3074 of this title.

§869. Repealed. July 1, 1944, ch. 373, title XIII, §1313 58 Stat. 714

Section, act Apr. 26, 1939, ch. 92, §2, 53 Stat. 620, as affected by 1939 Reorg. Plan No. I, §§201, 205, eff. July 1, 1939, 4 F.R. 2728, 53 Stat. 1424, provided for medical, dental, etc., treatment of Coast and Geodetic Survey's personnel and their families. See section 253 of Title 42, The Public Health and Welfare.

Renumbering of Repealing Act

Section 611 of act July 1, 1944, which repealed this section, was renumbered §711 by act Aug. 13, 1946, ch. 958, §5, 60 Stat. 1049, §713 by act Feb. 28, 1948, ch. 83, §9(b), 62 Stat. 47, §813 by act July 30, 1956, ch. 779, §3(b), 70 Stat. 720, §913 by Pub. L. 88–581, §4(b), Sept. 4, 1964, 78 Stat. 919, §1013 by Pub. L. 89–239, §3(b), Oct. 5, 1965, 79 Stat. 931, §1113 by Pub. L. 91–572, §6(b), Dec. 24, 1970, 84 Stat. 1506, §1213 by Pub. L. 92–294, §3(b), May 16, 1972, 86 Stat. 137; §1313 by Pub. L. 93–154, §2(b)(2), Nov. 16, 1973, 87 Stat. 604, and was repealed by Pub. L. 93–222, §7(b), Dec. 29, 1973, 87 Stat. 936.

§870. Repealed. Aug. 1, 1956, ch. 837, title V, §502(7), 70 Stat. 886

Section, acts Jan. 19, 1942, ch. 6, §9, 56 Stat. 8; Mar. 29, 1944, ch. 141, §4, 58 Stat. 130; July 15, 1954, ch. 507, §15, 68 Stat. 481, provided for payment of death gratuity to survivors of commissioned officers of Coast and Geodetic Survey.

Effective Date of Repeal

Repeal effective Jan. 1, 1957, see section 603(a) of act Aug. 1, 1956.

§871. Repealed. Dec. 28, 1945, ch. 597, §4, 59 Stat. 662

Section, act Oct. 27, 1943, ch. 287, §6, 57 Stat. 583, provided for reimbursement for property lost or destroyed in service while serving with the Navy.

§872. Omitted

Codification

Section, Pub. L. 86–451, title I, §301, May 13, 1960, 74 Stat. 94, which prescribed the rate of extra compensation for recorders, instrument observers and other Federal employees while making oceanographic observations or tending seismographs, was from an appropriation act. See section 873 of this title, which authorizes Secretary of Commerce to establish rates of compensation for such personnel.

§873. Extra compensation for instrument observers, recorders and other Federal employees for oceanographic, seismographic and magnetic observations

The Secretary of Commerce is authorized to pay extra compensation to members of crews of vessels when assigned duties as instrument observer or recorder, and to employees of other Federal agencies while observing tides or currents, or tending seismographs or magnetographs, at such rates as may be specified from time to time by him and without regard to section 5533 of title 5.

(July 22, 1947, ch. 286, §2, 61 Stat. 400; Pub. L. 86–397, §1, Mar. 28, 1960, 74 Stat. 11; Pub. L. 88–448, title IV, §401(*l*), Aug. 19, 1964, 78 Stat. 491.)

Codification

"Section 5533 of title 5" substituted in text for "section 301 of the Dual Compensation Act [5 U.S.C. 3105]" on authority of Pub. L. 89–554, §7(b), Sept. 6, 1966, 80 Stat. 631, the first section of which enacted Title 5, Government Organization and Employees.

Amendments

1964—Pub. L. 88–448 inserted "and without regard to section 301 of the Dual Compensation Act".

1960—Pub. L. 86–397 substituted "Secretary of Commerce" for "Coast and Geodetic Survey" and "instrument observer or recorder" for "bombers or fathometer readers," inserted reference to employees tending magnetographs, and authorized Secretary to establish rates of compensation.

Effective Date of 1964 Amendment

Amendment by Pub. L. 88–448 effective on first day of first month which begins later than the ninetieth day following Aug. 19, 1964, see section 403 of Pub. L. 88–448.

§874. Repealed. Pub. L. 107–372, title II, §271(5), Dec. 19, 2002, 116 Stat. 3094

Section, act July 22, 1947, ch. 286, §1, 61 Stat. 400; 1965 Reorg. Plan No. 2, eff. July 13, 1965, 30 F.R. 8819, 79 Stat. 1318; 1970 Reorg. Plan No. 4, eff. Oct. 3, 1970, 35 F.R. 15627, 84 Stat. 2090, related to transportation of deceased officers' effects and reimbursement for supplies furnished distressed and shipwrecked persons. See section 3075 of this title.

§875. Powers of officers as notaries

In places where the National Oceanic and Atmospheric Administration is serving which are not within the jurisdiction of any one of the States of the continental United States, excluding Alaska, commanding officers of National Oceanic and Atmospheric Administration vessels, and such other officers of the National Oceanic and Atmospheric Administration as the Secretary of Commerce may designate, may exercise the general powers of the notary public in the administration of oaths for the execution, acknowledgment, and attestation of instruments and papers, and the performance of all other notarial acts. The powers conferred shall be limited to acts performed in behalf of the personnel of the National Oceanic and Atmospheric Administration or in connection with the proper execution of the functions of that agency.

(Aug. 3, 1956, ch. 932, §1, 70 Stat. 988; Pub. L. 86–624, §24, July 12, 1960, 74 Stat. 418; 1965 Reorg. Plan No. 2, eff. July 13, 1965, 30 F.R. 8819, 79 Stat.

1318; 1970 Reorg. Plan No. 4, eff. Oct. 3, 1970, 35 F.R. 15627, 84 Stat. 2090.)

AMENDMENTS

1960—Pub. L. 86–624 substituted "the States of the continental United States, excluding Alaska" for "the several States".

TRANSFER OF FUNCTIONS

Coast and Geodetic Survey consolidated with Weather Bureau to form a new agency in Department of Commerce to be known as Environmental Science Services Administration, and commissioned officers of Survey transferred to ESSA, by Reorg. Plan No. 2 of 1965, eff. July 13, 1965, 30 F.R. 8819, 79 Stat. 1318, set out as a note under section 851 of this title. The Reorg. Plan also transferred to Secretary of Commerce all functions of Coast and Geodetic Survey and Director of Survey. Subsequently, Environmental Science Services Administration abolished, National Oceanic and Atmospheric Administration established, and Commissioned Officer Corps of ESSA redesignated Commissioned Officer Corps of NOAA by Reorg. Plan No. 4 of 1970, eff. Oct. 3, 1970, 35 F.R. 15627, 84 Stat. 2090, set out in the Appendix to Title 5, Government Organization and Employees. For further details, see note set out under section 851 of this title.

§876. Fees for notarial acts; prima facie evidence of authority

No fee of any kind shall be paid to any officer for the performance of any notarial act authorized by section 875 of this title. The signature without seal together with indication of grade of any officer performing any notarial act shall be prima facie evidence of his authority.

(Aug. 3, 1956, ch. 932, §2, 70 Stat. 988.)

§877. Appropriations; advances from

Advances of money from available appropriations may be made to the National Ocean Survey and by authority of the Director thereof to chiefs of parties and accounts arising under such advances shall be rendered through and by the disbursing officer of the National Ocean Survey to the Government Accountability Office as under advances made to chiefs of parties prior to July 1, 1918.

(July 1, 1918, ch. 113, §1, 40 Stat. 688; June 5, 1920, ch. 235, §1, 41 Stat. 929; June 10, 1921, ch. 18, title III, §304, 42 Stat. 24; Pub. L. 92–310, title II, §231(z), June 6, 1972, 86 Stat. 212; Pub. L. 108–271, §8(b), July 7, 2004, 118 Stat. 814.)

CODIFICATION

Section was a provision of the Sundry Civil Appropriation Act of July 1, 1918.

Section was formerly classified to section 550 of Title 31 prior to the general revision and enactment of Title 31, Money and Finance, by Pub. L. 97–258, Sept. 13, 1982, 96 Stat. 877.

AMENDMENTS

1972—Pub. L. 92–310 struck out provisions which required chiefs of parties to give bonds.

TRANSFER OF FUNCTIONS

Coast and Geodetic Survey consolidated with National Weather Bureau to form Environmental Science Services Administration by Reorg. Plan No. 2 of 1965, eff. July 13, 1965, 30 F.R. 8819, 79 Stat. 1318. Environmental Science Services Administration abolished and its personnel, property, records, etc., transferred to National Oceanic and Atmospheric Administration by Reorg. Plan No. 4 of 1970, eff. Oct. 3, 1970, 35 F.R. 15627, 84 Stat. 2090. By order of Acting Associate Administrator of National Oceanic and Atmospheric Administration, 35 F.R. 19249, Dec. 19, 1970, Coast and Geodetic Survey redesignated National Ocean Survey. For further details, see note set out under section 851 of this title.

"Government Accountability Office" substituted in text for "General Accounting Office" pursuant to section 8(b) of Pub. L. 108–271, set out as a note under section 702 of Title 31, Money and Finance, which redesignated the General Accounting Office and any references thereto as the Government Accountability Office. Previously, "General Accounting Office" substituted in text for "Treasury Department" pursuant to act June 10, 1921, which transferred all powers and duties of Comptroller, six auditors, and certain other employees of Treasury to General Accounting Office. See section 701 et seq. of Title 31.

§878. Appropriations; purchases from

The Secretary of Commerce is authorized to purchase, from the appropriation for the National Ocean Survey, provisions, clothing, and small stores for the enlisted men, and food supplies for field parties working in remote localities, such provisions, clothing, small stores, and food supplies to be sold to the employees of said survey and the appropriation reimbursed.

(Mar. 3, 1901, ch. 853, §1, 31 Stat. 1144; Feb. 14, 1903, ch. 552, §4, 32 Stat. 826.)

CODIFICATION

Section was a provision of the Sundry Civil Appropriation Act of Mar. 3, 1901.

Upon incorporation into the Code, the words "Secretary of Commerce" were substituted for "Secretary of the Treasury" to conform to act Feb. 14, 1903.

Section was formerly classified to section 661 of Title 31 prior to the general revision and enactment of Title 31, Money and Finance, by Pub. L. 97–258, Sept. 13, 1982, 96 Stat. 877.

TRANSFER OF FUNCTIONS

Coast and Geodetic Survey consolidated with National Weather Bureau to form Environmental Science Services Administration by Reorg. Plan No. 2 of 1965, eff. July 13, 1965, 30 F.R. 8819, 79 Stat. 1318. Environmental Science Services Administration abolished and its personnel, property, records, etc., transferred to National Oceanic and Atmospheric Administration by Reorg. Plan No. 4 of 1970, eff. Oct. 3, 1970, 35 F.R. 15627, 84 Stat. 2090. By order of Acting Associate Administrator of National Oceanic and Atmospheric Administration, 35 F.R. 19249, Dec. 19, 1970, Coast and Geodetic Survey redesignated National Ocean Survey. For further details, see note set out under section 851 of this title.

§878a. Contract for development of a major program; costs; Major Program Annual Report for satellite development program

(a) Definitions

For purposes of this section—

(1) the term "Under Secretary" means Under Secretary of Commerce for Oceans and Atmosphere;

(2) the term "appropriate congressional committees" means—

(A) the Committee on Appropriations and the Committee on Commerce, Science, and Transportation of the Senate; and

(B) the Committee on Appropriations and the Committee on Science and Technology of the House of Representatives;

(3) the term "satellite" means the satellites proposed to be acquired for the National Oceanic and Atmospheric Administration, other than the National Polar-orbiting Operational Environmental Satellite System (NPOESS);

(4) the term "development" means the phase of a program following the formulation phase and beginning with the approval to proceed to implementation, as defined in NOAA Administrative Order 216–108, Department of Commerce Administrative Order 208–3, and NASA's Procedural Requirements 7120.5c, dated March 22, 2005;

(5) the term "development cost" means the total of all costs, including construction of facilities and civil servant costs, from the period beginning with the approval to proceed to implementation through the achievement of operational readiness, without regard to funding source or management control, for the life of the program;

(6) the term "life-cycle cost" means the total of the direct, indirect, recurring, and nonrecurring costs, including the construction of facilities and civil servant costs, and other related expenses incurred or estimated to be incurred in the design, development, verification, production, operation, maintenance, support, and retirement of a program over its planned lifespan, without regard to funding source or management control;

(7) the term "major program" means an activity approved to proceed to implementation that has an estimated life-cycle cost of more than $250,000,000;

(8) the term "baseline" means the program as set following contract award and critical design review of the space and ground systems.

(b) Contract requirements for major programs

(1) NOAA shall not enter into a contract for development of a major program, unless the Under Secretary determines that—

(A) the technical, cost, and schedule risks of the program are clearly identified and the program has developed a plan to manage those risks;

(B) the technologies required for the program have been demonstrated in a relevant laboratory or test environment;

(C) the program complies with all relevant policies, regulations, and directives of NOAA and the Department of Commerce;

(D) the program has demonstrated a high likelihood of accomplishing its intended goals; and

(E) the acquisition of satellites for use in the program represents a good value to accomplishing NOAA's mission.

(2) The Under Secretary shall transmit a report describing the basis for the determination required under paragraph (1) to the appropriate congressional committees at least 30 days before entering into a contract for development under a major program.

(3) The Under Secretary may not delegate the determination requirement under this subsection, except in cases in which the Under Secretary has a conflict of interest.

(c) Reports

(1) Annually, at the same time as the President's annual budget submission to the Congress, the Under Secretary shall transmit to the appropriate congressional committees a report that includes the information required by this section for the satellite development program for which NOAA proposes to expend funds in the subsequent fiscal year. The report under this paragraph shall be known as the Major Program Annual Report.

(2) The first Major Program Annual Report for NOAA's satellite development program shall include a Baseline Report that shall, at a minimum, include—

(A) the purposes of the program and key technical characteristics necessary to fulfill those purposes;

(B) an estimate of the life-cycle cost for the program, with a detailed breakout of the development cost, program reserves, and an estimate of the annual costs until development is completed;

(C) the schedule for development, including key program milestones;

(D) the plan for mitigating technical, cost, and schedule risks identified in accordance with subsection (b)(1)(A); and

(E) the name of the person responsible for making notifications under subsection (d), who shall be an individual whose primary responsibility is overseeing the program.

(3) For the major program for which a Baseline Report has been submitted, subsequent Major Program Annual Reports shall describe any changes to the information that had been provided in the Baseline Report, and the reasons for those changes.

(d) Notification to Under Secretary of excess development costs

(1) The individual identified under subsection (c)(2)(E) shall immediately notify the Under Secretary any time that individual has reasonable cause to believe that, for the major program for which he or she is responsible, the development cost of the program has exceeded the estimate provided in the Baseline Report of the program by 20 percent or more.

(2) Not later than 30 days after the notification required under paragraph (1), the individual identified under subsection (c)(2)(E) shall transmit to the Under Secretary a written notification explaining the reasons for the change in the cost of the program for which notification was provided under paragraph (1).

(3) Not later than 15 days after the Under Secretary receives a written notification under paragraph (2), the Under Secretary shall transmit the notification to the appropriate congressional committees.

(e) Determination by Under Secretary of excess development costs

Not later than 30 days after receiving a written notification under subsection (d)(2), the Under Secretary shall determine whether the development cost of the program has exceeded the estimate provided in the Baseline Report of the program by 20 percent or more. If the determination is affirmative, the Under Secretary shall—

(1) transmit to the appropriate congressional committees, not later than 15 days after mak-

ing the determination, a report that includes—

(A) a description of the increase in cost and a detailed explanation for the increase;

(B) a description of actions taken or proposed to be taken in response to the cost increase; and

(C) a description of any impacts the cost increase, or the actions described under subparagraph (B), will have on any other program within NOAA.[1]

(2) if the Under Secretary intends to continue with the program, promptly initiate an analysis of the program, which shall include, at a minimum—

(A) the projected cost and schedule for completing the program if current requirements of the program are not modified;

(B) the projected cost and the schedule for completing the program after instituting the actions described under paragraph (1)(B); and

(C) a description of, and the projected cost and schedule for, a broad range of alternatives to the program. NOAA shall complete an analysis initiated under paragraph (2) not later than 6 months after the Under Secretary makes a determination under this subsection. The Under Secretary shall transmit the analysis to the appropriate congressional committees not later than 30 days after its completion.

(f) Estimation of Geostationary Operational Environmental Satellite Program costs

For the purposes of determining whether cost of the Geostationary Operational Environmental Satellite Program exceeds 20 percent more than the baseline under this section, the estimate of the total life-cycle cost for GOES–R shall be the estimate provided with the NOAA Fiscal Year 2008 Presidential Budget justification (page 513).

(Pub. L. 110–161, div. B, title I, § 112, Dec. 26, 2007, 121 Stat. 1894.)

SUBCHAPTER II—SURVEYS

§§ 881 to 883. Repealed. Aug. 6, 1947, ch. 504, § 10(2)–(5), 61 Stat. 788

Section 881, R.S. § 4681, related to authority of the President to order surveys of coasts of the United States. See section 883a of this title.

Section 882, R.S. § 4682, related to additional authority to order surveys beyond twenty-league limit. See section 883a of this title.

Section 883, R.S. §§ 4683, 4684, related to mode of conducting surveys generally. See sections 883a and 883b of this title.

§ 883a. Surveys and other activities

To provide charts and related information for the safe navigation of marine and air commerce, and to provide basic data for engineering and scientific purposes and for other commercial and industrial needs, the Secretary of Commerce, is authorized to conduct the following activities:

(1) Hydrographic and topographic surveys;

(2) Tide and current observations;

(3) Geodetic-control surveys;

(4) Field surveys for aeronautical charts;

(5) Geomagnetic, seismological, gravity, and related geophysical measurements and investigations, and observations for the determination of variation in latitude and longitude.

(Aug. 6, 1947, ch. 504, § 1, 61 Stat. 787; Pub. L. 86–409, Apr. 5, 1960, 74 Stat. 16; 1965 Reorg. Plan No. 2, eff. July 13, 1965, 30 F.R. 8819, 79 Stat. 1318.)

AMENDMENTS

1960—Pub. L. 86–409 struck out provisions which restricted the Coast and Geodetic Survey in the conduct of its specified activities to the United States, its Territories and possessions, and which restricted hydrographic and topographic surveys to surveys of coastal water and land areas (including offlying islands, banks, shoals, and other offshore areas), and to surveys of lakes, rivers, reservoirs, and other inland waters not otherwise provided for by statute.

TRANSFER OF FUNCTIONS

Functions of Secretary and other officers of Department of Commerce under sections 883a to 883h of this title that relate to the Office of Aeronautical Charting and Cartography to provide aeronautical charts, products, and services for safe and efficient navigation of air commerce transferred to Administrator of Federal Aviation Administration effective Oct. 1, 2000, see section 44721(c)(1) of Title 49, Transportation.

Office of Director of Coast and Geodetic Survey abolished and Coast and Geodetic Survey consolidated with Weather Bureau to form a new agency in Department of Commerce to be known as Environmental Science Services Administration, by Reorg. Plan No. 2 of 1965, eff. July 13, 1965, 30 F.R. 8819, 79 Stat. 1318, set out as a note under section 851 of this title. The Reorg. Plan also transferred to Secretary of Commerce all functions of Coast and Geodetic Survey and Director. For further details, see note set out under section 851 of this title.

GREAT LAKES MAPPING

Pub. L. 100–220, title III, subtitle B, Dec. 29, 1987, 101 Stat. 1475, as amended by Pub. L. 100–629, § 3, Nov. 7, 1988, 102 Stat. 3286, provided that:

"SEC. 3201. SHORT TITLE.

"This subtitle may be cited as the 'Great Lakes Shoreline Mapping Act of 1987'.

"SEC. 3202. GREAT LAKES SHORELINE MAPPING PLAN.

"(a) PREPARATION OF PLAN.—Not later than nine months after the date of the enactment of this subtitle [Dec. 29, 1987], the Director, in consultation with the Director of the United States Geological Survey, shall submit to the Congress a plan for preparing maps of the shoreline of the Great Lakes under section 3203.

"(b) CONTENT OF PLAN.—A plan prepared under paragraph (1) shall include—

"(1) a work proposal and a division of responsibilities between the National Oceanic and Atmospheric Administration and the United States Geological Survey;

"(2) a time schedule for completion of maps;

"(3) recommendation of funding needed for preparing the maps; and

"(4) an area mapping schedule, with first priority given to shoreline areas subject to a high risk of erosion or flooding.

"SEC. 3203. PREPARATION OF GREAT LAKES SHORELINE MAPS.

"(a) IN GENERAL.—The [sic] following completion of a shoreline mapping plan under section 3202 and subject to authorization and appropriation of funds, the Direc-

[1] So in original. Probably should be "NOAA; and".

tor, in consultation with the Director of the United States Geological Survey, shall prepare maps of the shoreline areas of the Great Lakes.

"(b) CONTENT OF MAPS.—Maps prepared under this section—

"(1) shall include—

"(A) bathymetry of the nearshore area, to the extent that this area will affect coastal erosion and flooding;

"(B) topography of the adjacent shoreline, to the extent that this area will directly affect or be affected by coastal erosion and flooding;

"(C) the geological conditions of the nearshore area and shoreline to the extent that these areas will directly affect or be affected by coastal erosion and flooding;

"(D) information on the recent geological past of the nearshore area and shoreline areas described in paragraph (3); and

"(E) appropriate information for use in predicting and preventing damage caused by erosion and flooding in the Great Lakes;

"(2) shall be of appropriate scale and detail and take into account the greater informational needs of areas subject to a high risk of erosion or flooding; and

"(3) to the maximum extent practicable, shall be consistent with similar shoreline maps prepared by, or for the use of, the Government of Canada.

"(c) CONSULTATION.—In preparing maps under this section, the Director shall consult with, and take into consideration, the informational needs of—

"(1) the Army Corps of Engineers;

"(2) the Federal Emergency Management Agency;

"(3) other appropriate Federal agencies;

"(4) the States of Illinois, Indiana, Michigan, Minnesota, New York, Ohio, Pennsylvania, and Wisconsin;

"(5) appropriate local government units; and

"(6) the general public.

"(d) AVAILABILITY OF MAPS.—The Director shall make maps prepared under this section available to—

"(1) Federal agencies;

"(2) State governments;

"(3) local government units;

"(4) the Government of Canada; and

"(5) the general public.

"(e) RECOVERY OF COSTS.—The costs of reproducing and distributing maps prepared under this section may be recovered under section 9701 of title 31, United States Code, or another law.

"SEC. 3204. CONTRACT AUTHORITY.

"The Director may, subject to appropriations, enter into contracts and agreements on a reimbursable or cost-sharing basis with other Federal agencies, State governments, local governments, and private entities, to carry out this subtitle.

"SEC. 3205. DEFINITIONS.

"For purposes of this subtitle—

"(1) The term 'Director' means the Director of Charting and Geodetic Services of the National Ocean Service, within the National Oceanic and Atmospheric Administration.

"(2) The term 'Great Lakes' means Lake Erie, Lake Huron, Lake Michigan, Lake Ontario, Lake St. Clair, Lake Superior, the Saint Mary's River, the Saint Clair River, the Detroit River, the Niagara River, the Saint Lawrence River to the Canadian border, to the extent such lakes and rivers are subject to the jurisdiction of the United States.

"(3) The term 'high risk of erosion' means subject to erosion at a rate greater than 1 foot per year.

"SEC. 3206. AUTHORIZATION OF APPROPRIATIONS.

"There are authorized to be appropriated to carry out section 3202 not more than $100,000 for fiscal year 1989. Amounts appropriated pursuant to this section shall remain available until expended."

[For transfer of all functions, personnel, assets, components, authorities, grant programs, and liabilities of the Federal Emergency Management Agency, including the functions of the Under Secretary for Federal Emergency Management relating thereto, to the Federal Emergency Management Agency, see section 315(a)(1) of Title 6, Domestic Security.]

[For transfer of functions, personnel, assets, and liabilities of the Federal Emergency Management Agency, including the functions of the Director of the Federal Emergency Management Agency relating thereto, to the Secretary of Homeland Security, and for treatment of related references, see former section 313(1) and sections 551(d), 552(d), and 557 of Title 6, Domestic Security, and the Department of Homeland Security Reorganization Plan of November 25, 2002, as modified, set out as a note under section 542 of Title 6.]

§883b. Dissemination of data; further activities

In order that full public benefit may be derived from the operations of the National Ocean Survey by the dissemination of data resulting from the activities herein authorized and of related data from other sources, the Secretary of Commerce is authorized to conduct the following activities:

(1) Analysis and prediction of tide and current data;

(2) Processing and publication of data, information, compilations, and reports;

(3) Compilation and printing of nautical charts;

(4) Distribution of nautical charts and related navigational publications.

(Aug. 6, 1947, ch. 504, §2, 61 Stat. 787; 1965 Reorg. Plan No. 2, eff. July 13, 1965, 30 F.R. 8819, 79 Stat. 1318; 1970 Reorg. Plan No. 4, eff. Oct. 3, 1970, 35 F.R. 15627, 84 Stat. 2090; Pub. L. 106–181, title VI, §605(a), Apr. 5, 2000, 114 Stat. 154.)

AMENDMENTS

2000—Par. (3). Pub. L. 106–181, §605(a)(1), (2), redesignated par. (4) as (3), substituted "charts;" for "charts of the United States, its Territories, and possessions;" and struck out former par. (3) which read as follows: "Compilation and printing of aeronautical charts of the United States, its Territories, and possessions; and, in addition, the compilation and printing of such aeronautical charts covering international airways as are required primarily by United States Civil aviation;".

Par. (4). Pub. L. 106–181, §605(a)(1), (3), redesignated par. (6) as (4) and substituted "publications" for "publications for the United States, its Territories, and possessions". Former par. (4) redesignated (3).

Par. (5). Pub. L. 106–181, §605(a)(1), struck out par. (5) which read as follows: "Distribution of aeronautical charts and related navigational publications required by United States civil aviation;".

Par. (6). Pub. L. 106–181, §605(a)(1), redesignated par. (6) as (4).

EFFECTIVE DATE OF 2000 AMENDMENT

Amendment by Pub. L. 106–181 applicable only to fiscal years beginning after Sept. 30, 1999, see section 3 of Pub. L. 106–181, set out as a note under section 106 of Title 49, Transportation.

TRANSFER OF FUNCTIONS

Office of Director of Coast and Geodetic Survey abolished and Coast and Geodetic Survey consolidated with Weather Bureau to form a new agency in Department of Commerce to be known as Environmental Science Services Administration, by Reorg. Plan No. 2 of 1965, eff. July 13, 1965, 30 F.R. 8819, 79 Stat. 1318, set out as a note under section 851 of this title. The Reorg. Plan also transferred to Secretary of Commerce all functions of Coast and Geodetic Survey and Director. Subsequently, Environmental Science Services Administration abolished and National Oceanic and Atmospheric Administration established by Reorg. Plan No. 4 of 1970, eff. Oct. 3, 1970, 35 F.R. 15627, 84 Stat. 2090, set out in the Appendix to Title 5, Government Organization and Employees. By Department Organization Order 25-5A, Secretary delegated to NOAA his functions under this chapter of the Code. By order of Acting Associate Administrator of NOAA, organizational name of Coast and Geodetic Survey changed to National Ocean Survey. For further details, see note set out under section 851 of this title.

§ 883c. Geomagnetic data; collection, correlation, and dissemination

To provide for the orderly collection of geomagnetic data from domestic and foreign sources, and to assure that such data shall be readily available to Government and private agencies and individuals, the National Ocean Survey is designated as the central depository of the United States Government for geomagnetic data, and the Secretary of Commerce is authorized to collect, correlate, and disseminate such data.

(Aug. 6, 1947, ch. 504, §3, 61 Stat. 787; 1965 Reorg. Plan No. 2, eff. July 13, 1965, 30 F.R. 8819, 79 Stat. 1318; 1970 Reorg. Plan No. 4, eff. Oct. 3, 1970, 35 F.R. 15627, 84 Stat. 2090.)

Transfer of Functions

Office of Director of Coast and Geodetic Survey abolished and Coast and Geodetic Survey consolidated with Weather Bureau to form a new agency in Department of Commerce to be known as Environmental Science Services Administration, by Reorg. Plan No. 2 of 1965, eff. July 13, 1965, 30 F.R. 8819, 79 Stat. 1318, set out as a note under section 851 of this title. The Reorg. Plan also transferred to Secretary of Commerce all functions of Coast and Geodetic Survey and Director. Subsequently, Environmental Science Services Administration abolished and National Oceanic and Atmospheric Administration established by Reorg. Plan No. 4 of 1970, eff. Oct. 3, 1970, 35 F.R. 15627, 84 Stat. 2090, set out in the Appendix to Title 5, Government Organization and Employees. By Department Organization Order 25-5A, Secretary delegated to NOAA his functions under this chapter of the Code. By order of Acting Associate Administrator of NOAA, organizational name of Coast and Geodetic Survey changed to National Ocean Survey. For further details, see note set out under section 851 of this title.

§ 883d. Improvement of methods, instruments, and equipments; investigations and research

To improve the efficiency of the National Ocean Survey and to increase engineering and scientific knowledge, the Secretary of Commerce is authorized to conduct developmental work for the improvement of surveying and cartographic methods, instruments, and equipments; and to conduct investigations and research in geophysical sciences (including geodesy, oceanography, seismology, and geomagnetism).

(Aug. 6, 1947, ch. 504, §4, 61 Stat. 788; 1965 Reorg. Plan No. 2, eff. July 13, 1965, 30 F.R. 8819, 79 Stat. 1318; 1970 Reorg. Plan No. 4, eff. Oct. 3, 1970, 35 F.R. 15627, 84 Stat. 2090.)

Transfer of Functions

Office of Director of Coast and Geodetic Survey abolished and Coast and Geodetic Survey consolidated with Weather Bureau to form a new agency in Department of Commerce to be known as Environmental Science Services Administration, by Reorg. Plan No. 2 of 1965, eff. July 13, 1965, 30 F.R. 8819, 79 Stat. 1318, set out as a note under section 851 of this title. The Reorg. Plan also transferred to Secretary of Commerce all functions of Coast and Geodetic Survey and Director. Subsequently, Environmental Science Services Administration abolished and National Oceanic and Atmospheric Administration established by Reorg. Plan No. 4 of 1970, eff. Oct. 3, 1970, 35 F.R. 15627, 84 Stat. 2090, set out in the Appendix to Title 5, Government Organization and Employees. By Department Organization Order 25-5A, Secretary delegated to NOAA his functions under this chapter of the Code. By order of Acting Associate Administrator of NOAA, organizational name of Coast and Geodetic Survey changed to National Ocean Survey. For further details, see note set out under section 851 of this title.

§ 883e. Agreements for surveys and investigations; contribution of costs incurred by National Oceanic and Atmospheric Administration

(1) The Secretary of Commerce is authorized to enter into cooperative agreements, or any other agreements, with, and to receive and expend funds made available by, any State or subdivision thereof, any Federal agency, or any public or private organization, or individual, for surveys or investigations authorized herein, or for performing related surveying and mapping activities, including special-purpose maps, and for the preparation and publication of the results thereof.

(2) The Secretary of Commerce is authorized to establish the terms of any agreement entered into under this section, including the amount of funds to be received, and may contribute that portion of the costs incurred by the National Oceanic and Atmospheric Administration, including shiptime and personnel expenses, which the Secretary determines represents the amount of benefits derived by the Administration from the agreement.

(Aug. 6, 1947, ch. 504, §5, 61 Stat. 788; 1965 Reorg. Plan No. 2, eff. July 13, 1965, 30 F.R. 8819, 79 Stat. 1318; Pub. L. 99-272, title VI, §6085, Apr. 7, 1986, 100 Stat. 138; Pub. L. 106-181, title VI, §605(b), Apr. 5, 2000, 114 Stat. 154.)

Amendments

2000—Par. (1). Pub. L. 106-181, §605(b)(1), substituted "cooperative agreements, or any other agreements," for "cooperative agreements".

Par. (2). Pub. L. 106-181, §605(b)(2), which directed the striking of "cooperative", was executed by striking "cooperative" before "agreement" in two places, to reflect the probable intent of Congress.

1986—Pub. L. 99-272 designated existing provisions as par. (1), inserted "any Federal agency," after "or subdivision thereof," and added par. (2).

Effective Date of 2000 Amendment

Amendment by Pub. L. 106-181 applicable only to fiscal years beginning after Sept. 30, 1999, see section 3 of Pub. L. 106-181, set out as a note under section 106 of Title 49, Transportation.

Transfer of Functions

Office of Director of Coast and Geodetic Survey abolished and Coast and Geodetic Survey consolidated with Weather Bureau to form a new agency in Department of Commerce to be known as Environmental Science

Services Administration, by Reorg. Plan No. 2 of 1965, eff. July 13, 1965, 30 F.R. 8819, 79 Stat. 1318, set out as a note under section 851 of this title. The Reorg. Plan also transferred to Secretary of Commerce all functions of Coast and Geodetic Survey and Director. For further details, see note set out under section 851 of this title.

§883f. Contracts with qualified organizations

The Secretary of Commerce is authorized to contract with qualified organizations for the performance of any part of the authorized functions of the National Ocean Survey when he deems such procedure to be in the public interests.

(Aug. 6, 1947, ch. 504, §6, 61 Stat. 788; 1965 Reorg. Plan No. 2, eff. July 13, 1965, 30 F.R. 8819, 79 Stat. 1318; 1970 Reorg. Plan No. 4, eff. Oct. 3, 1970, 35 F.R. 15627, 84 Stat. 2090.)

TRANSFER OF FUNCTIONS

Office of Director of Coast and Geodetic Survey abolished and Coast and Geodetic Survey consolidated with Weather Bureau to form a new agency in Department of Commerce to be known as Environmental Science Services Administration, by Reorg. Plan No. 2, of 1965, eff. July 13, 1965, 30 F.R. 8819, 79 Stat. 1318, set out as a note under section 851 of this title. The Reorg. Plan also transferred to Secretary of Commerce all functions of Coast and Geodetic Survey and Director. Subsequently, Environmental Science Services Administration abolished and National Oceanic and Atmospheric Administration established by Reorg. Plan No. 4 of 1970, eff. Oct. 3, 1970, 35 F.R. 15627, 84 Stat. 2090, set out in the Appendix to Title 5, Government Organization and Employees. By Department Organization Order 25–5A, Secretary delegated to NOAA his functions under this chapter of the Code. By order of Acting Associate Administrator of NOAA, organizational name of Coast and Geodetic Survey changed to National Ocean Survey. For further details, see note set out under section 851 of this title.

§883g. Repealed. Pub. L. 88–611, §4(a)(2), Oct. 2, 1964, 78 Stat. 991

Section, act Aug. 6, 1947, ch. 504, §7, 61 Stat. 788, provided for acceptance of gifts or bequests and exemption from Federal taxes. See sections 1522 and 1523 of Title 15, Commerce and Trade.

§883h. Employment of public vessels

The President is authorized to cause to be employed such of the public vessels as he deems it expedient to employ, and to give such instructions for regulating their conduct as he deems proper in order to carry out the provisions of this subchapter.

(Aug. 6, 1947, ch. 504, §8, 61 Stat. 788.)

DELEGATION OF FUNCTIONS

Functions of President under this section delegated to Secretary of Commerce, see section 1(*l*) of Ex. Ord. No. 11023, May 28, 1962, 27 F.R. 5131, as amended, set out as a note under section 301 of Title 3, The President.

§883i. Authorization of appropriations

There are authorized to be appropriated such funds as may be necessary to acquire, construct, maintain, and operate ships, stations, equipment, and facilities and for such other expenditures, including personal services at the seat of government and elsewhere and including the erection of temporary observatory buildings and lease of sites therefor, as may be necessary for the conduct of the activities herein authorized.

(Aug. 6, 1947, ch. 504, §9, 61 Stat. 788.)

REFERENCES IN TEXT

Herein, referred to in text, means act Aug. 6, 1947, ch. 504, 61 Stat. 787, as amended, which is classified generally to this subchapter (§883a et seq.). For complete classification of this Act to the Code, see Tables.

§883j. Ocean satellite data

The Administrator of the National Oceanic and Atmospheric Administration (hereinafter referred to in this subtitle[1] as the "Administration") shall take such actions, including the sponsorship of applied research, as may be necessary to assure the future availability and usefulness of ocean satellite data to the maritime community.

(Pub. L. 99–272, title VI, §6082, Apr. 7, 1986, 100 Stat. 135.)

REFERENCES IN TEXT

This subtitle, referred to in text, is subtitle H (§§6081–6085) of title VI of Pub. L. 99–272, Apr. 7, 1986, 100 Stat. 135, which enacted this section and section 1530 of Title 15, Commerce and Trade, amended section 883e of this title and sections 330e, 2903 and 2904 of Title 15, and repealed section 2905 of Title 15. For complete classification of this subtitle to the Code, see Tables.

TRANSFER OF FUNCTIONS

Functions of Secretary and other officers of Department of Commerce under this section that relate to the Office of Aeronautical Charting and Cartography to provide aeronautical charts, products, and services for safe and efficient navigation of air commerce transferred to Administrator of Federal Aviation Administration effective Oct. 1, 2000, see section 44721(c)(2) of Title 49, Transportation.

REPORT ON SATELLITE OCEANOGRAPHY

Pub. L. 102–567, title I, §116, Oct. 29, 1992, 106 Stat. 4279, provided that:

"(a) IN GENERAL.—The Federal Coordinating Council for Science, Engineering, and Technology through the Committee on Earth and Environmental Sciences, in consultation with Federal, academic, and commercial users of remotely sensed data, shall consider and develop findings and recommendations regarding—

"(1) the most urgent current needs of oceanographic researchers within the Federal Government, the academic community, and the private sector, for remote sensing capabilities and remotely sensed data, including findings regarding the present inadequacies in these capabilities and data; and

"(2) the major goals of satellite oceanography for the next 10 years.

"(b) REPORT.—Not later than one year after the date of enactment of this Act [Oct. 29, 1992], the Federal Coordinating Council for Science, Engineering, and Technology shall submit to the Congress a report which describes the findings and recommendations of the Committee on Earth and Environmental Sciences, including recommendations for, or a description of actions to be taken toward—

"(1) correcting the inadequacies in remote sensing capabilities;

"(2) improving the availability of remotely sensed data; and

"(3) achieving the major goals of satellite oceanography developed pursuant to subsection (a)(2)."

[1] See References in Text note below.

§ 883k. Acquisition of land for facilities

For fiscal year 1990 and hereafter funds appropriated under this heading shall be available for acquisition of land for facilities.

(Pub. L. 101–162, title I, Nov. 21, 1989, 103 Stat. 992.)

REFERENCES IN TEXT

Funds appropriated under this heading, referred to in text, refers to funds appropriated under the headings "NATIONAL OCEANIC AND ATMOSPHERIC ADMINISTRATION" and "OPERATIONS, RESEARCH, AND FACILITIES" of title I, "Department of Commerce", of the Departments of Commerce, Justice, and State, the Judiciary, and Related Agencies Appropriations Act, 1990, Pub. L. 101–162.

§ 883*l*. Contracts for surveying and mapping services

On and after February 20, 2003, the Secretary of Commerce may award contracts for hydrographic, geodetic, and photogrammetric surveying and mapping services in accordance with title IX of the Federal Property and Administrative Services Act of 1949.[1]

(Pub. L. 108–7, div. B, title II, § 206, Feb. 20, 2003, 117 Stat. 77.)

REFERENCES IN TEXT

The Federal Property and Administrative Services Act of 1949, referred to in text, is act June 30, 1949, ch. 288, 63 Stat. 377. Title IX of the Act, which was classified generally to subchapter VI (§ 541 et seq.) of chapter 10 of former Title 40, Public Buildings, Property, and Works, was repealed and reenacted by Pub. L. 107–217, §§ 1, 6(b), Aug. 21, 2002, 116 Stat. 1062, 1304, as chapter 11 (§ 1101 et seq.) of Title 40, Public Buildings, Property, and Works. For disposition of sections of former Title 40 to revised Title 40, see Table preceding section 101 of Title 40. For complete classification of this Act to the Code, see Tables.

PRIOR PROVISIONS

Similar provisions were contained in the following prior appropriation acts:

Pub. L. 107–77, title II, § 206, Nov. 28, 2001, 115 Stat. 778.

Pub. L. 106–553, § 1(a)(2) [title II, § 207], Dec. 21, 2000, 114 Stat. 2762, 2762A–79.

Pub. L. 106–113, div. B, § 1000(a)(1) [title II, § 208], Nov. 29, 1999, 113 Stat. 1535, 1501A–32.

Pub. L. 105–277, div. A, § 101(b) [title II, § 208], Oct. 21, 1998, 112 Stat. 2681–50, 2681–87.

Pub. L. 105–119, title II, § 208, Nov. 26, 1997, 111 Stat. 2480.

Pub. L. 104–208, div. A, title I, § 101(a) [title II, § 209], Sept. 30, 1996, 110 Stat. 3009, 3009–41.

Pub. L. 104–134, title I, § 101(a) [title II, § 212], Apr. 26, 1996, 110 Stat. 1321, 1321–32.

§ 884. Power to use books, maps, etc., and to employ persons

The President is authorized, in executing the provisions of title 56 of the Revised Statutes relating to the coast survey, to use all maps, charts, books, instruments, and apparatus belonging to the United States, and to direct where the same shall be deposited, and to employ all persons in the land or naval service of the United States, and such astronomers and other persons as he shall deem proper.

(R.S. § 4685.)

[1] See References in Text note below.

REFERENCES IN TEXT

Title 56 of the Revised Statutes, referred to in text, was in the original "this Title", meaning title 56 of the Revised Statutes, consisting of R.S. §§ 4681 to 4691 of the Revised Statutes, which are classified to sections 881 to 883 and 884 to 888 of this title. For complete classification of R.S. §§ 4681 to 4691 to the Code, see Tables.

CODIFICATION

Section was not enacted as part of act Aug. 6, 1947, ch. 504, 61 Stat. 787, which comprises this subchapter.

R.S. § 4685 derived from act July 10, 1832, ch. 191, § 2, 4 Stat. 571.

§ 885. Repealed. Aug. 6, 1947, ch. 504, § 10(6), 61 Stat. 788

Section, R.S. § 4686, related to use of public vessels on coast surveys. See section 883h of this title.

§§ 886, 887. Repealed. June 21, 1955, ch. 172, § 5(1), (2), 69 Stat. 170

Section 886, R.S. § 4687, related to employment of officers of Army and Navy in the work of surveying the coast of the United States.

Section 887, R.S. § 4688; acts Aug. 30, 1890, ch. 837, § 1, 26 Stat. 382; June 5, 1920, ch. 235, § 1, 41 Stat. 929, provided for allowance for subsistence to officers of Army and Navy while employed on coast survey service.

ADDITIONAL REPEAL

Sections were also repealed by act Aug. 10, 1956, ch. 1041, § 53, 70A Stat. 641. Section 49(a) of act Aug. 10, 1956, provided in part that laws effective after Mar. 31, 1955, inconsistent with that act, should be considered as superseding it to the extent of the inconsistency.

§ 888. Omitted

CODIFICATION

Section, R.S. §§ 264, 4690; acts Feb. 14, 1903, ch. 552, §§ 4, 10, 32 Stat. 826, 829; Mar. 4, 1913, ch. 141, § 1, 37 Stat. 736; June 5, 1920, ch. 235, § 1, 41 Stat. 929, relating to an annual statement on coast surveys by the Coast and Geodetic Survey [now the National Ocean Survey], was partially repealed by acts May 29, 1928, ch. 901, § 1(104), 45 Stat. 994; Aug. 7, 1946, ch. 770, § 1(5), 60 Stat. 866; and Aug. 30, 1954, ch. 1076, § 1(13), 68 Stat. 967.

§§ 889, 890. Repealed. June 21, 1955, ch. 172, § 5(5), 69 Stat. 170

Section 889, acts Mar. 4, 1909, ch. 313, § 1, 35 Stat. 1064; Mar. 4, 1913, ch. 141, § 1, 37 Stat. 736, authorized cooperation with North Carolina State Fish Commission in survey of waters of State.

Section 890, acts Mar. 4, 1909, ch. 313, § 2, 35 Stat. 1065; Mar. 4, 1913, ch. 141, § 1, 37 Stat. 736, provided for marking triangulation points of North Carolina survey.

SUBCHAPTER III—NOAA FLEET MODERNIZATION

§ 891. Definitions

In this subchapter, the term—

(1) "NOAA" means the National Oceanic and Atmospheric Administration within the Department of Commerce.

(2) "NOAA fleet" means the fleet of research vessels owned or operated by NOAA.

(3) "Plan" means the NOAA Fleet Replacement and Modernization Plan described in section 891b of this title.

(4) "Secretary" means the Secretary of Commerce.

(5) "UNOLS" means University-National Oceanographic Laboratory System.

(Pub. L. 102–567, title VI, §602, Oct. 29, 1992, 106 Stat. 4299.)

SHORT TITLE

For short title of this subchapter as the "NOAA Fleet Modernization Act", see section 601 of Pub. L. 102–567, set out as a Short Title of 1992 Amendment note under section 851 of this title.

§891a. Fleet replacement and modernization program

The Secretary is authorized to implement, subject to the requirements of this subchapter, a 15-year program to replace and modernize the NOAA fleet.

(Pub. L. 102–567, title VI, §603, Oct. 29, 1992, 106 Stat. 4300.)

REFERENCES IN TEXT

This subchapter, referred to in text, was in the original "this Act", and was translated as reading "this title", meaning title VI of Pub. L. 102–567, which enacted this subchapter, to reflect the probable intent of Congress.

§891b. Fleet replacement and modernization Plan

(a) In general

To carry out the program authorized in section 891a of this title, the Secretary shall develop and submit to Congress a replacement and modernization Plan for the NOAA fleet covering the years authorized under section 891h of this title.

(b) Timing

The Plan required in subsection (a) of this section shall be submitted to Congress within 30 days of October 29, 1992, and updated on an annual basis.

(c) Plan elements

The Plan required in subsection (a) of this section shall include the following—

(1) the number of vessels proposed to be modernized or replaced, the schedule for their modernization or replacement, and anticipated funding requirements;

(2) the number of vessels proposed to be constructed, leased, or chartered;

(3) the number of vessels, or days at sea, that can be obtained by using the vessels of the UNOLS;

(4) the number of vessels that will be made available to NOAA by the Secretary of the Navy, or any other federal[1] official, and the terms and conditions for their availability;

(5) the proposed acquisition of modern scientific instrumentation for the NOAA fleet, including acoustic systems, data transmission positioning and communication systems, physical, chemical, and meteorological oceanographic systems, and data acquisition and processing systems; and

(6) the appropriate role of the NOAA Corps in operating and maintaining the NOAA fleet.

(d) Contracting limitation

The Secretary may not enter into any contract for the construction, lease, or service life extension of a vessel of the NOAA fleet before the date of the submission to Congress of the Plan required in subsection (a) of this section.

[1] So in original. Probably should be capitalized.

(Pub. L. 102–567, title VI, §604, Oct. 29, 1992, 106 Stat. 4300.)

FISHERY SURVEY VESSEL ACQUISITION

Pub. L. 106–450, title III, Nov. 7, 2000, 114 Stat. 1945, provided that:

"SEC. 301. SHORT TITLE.

"This title may be cited as the 'Fisheries Survey Vessel Authorization Act of 2000'.

"SEC. 302. ACQUISITION OF FISHERY SURVEY VESSELS.

"(a) IN GENERAL.—The Secretary, subject to the availability of appropriations, may in accordance with this section acquire, by purchase, lease, lease-purchase, or charter, and equip up to six fishery survey vessels in accordance with this section.

"(b) VESSEL REQUIREMENTS.—Any vessel acquired and equipped under this section must—

"(1) be capable of—

"(A) staying at sea continuously for at least 30 days;

"(B) conducting fishery population surveys using hydroacoustic, longlining, deep water, and pelagic trawls, and other necessary survey techniques; and

"(C) conducting other work necessary to provide fishery managers with the accurate and timely data needed to prepare and implement fishery management plans; and

"(2) have a hull that meets the International Council for Exploration of the Sea standard regarding acoustic quietness.

"(c) AUTHORIZATION.—To carry out this section there are authorized to be appropriated to the Secretary $60,000,000 for each of fiscal years 2002 and 2003."

DEACTIVATION OF NOAA RESEARCH VESSELS

Section 401(b)(4) of Pub. L. 102–567 provided that:

"(A) Unless necessary for safety reasons, the Secretary of Commerce shall not deactivate the ALBATROSS IV (if active), until an equivalent replacement vessel is operational.

"(B) The Secretary of Commerce shall notify the Committee on Commerce, Science, and Transportation of the Senate and the Committee on Merchant Marine and Fisheries [now Committee on Science and Technology] of the House of Representatives 60 days prior to the proposed deactivation of any other research vessel of the National Oceanic and Atmospheric Administration, if an equivalent replacement vessel will not become operational at the time of deactivation."

§891c. Design of NOAA vessels

(a) Design requirement

Except for the vessel designs identified under subsection (b) of this section, the Secretary, working through the Office of the NOAA Corps Operations and the Systems Procurement Office, shall—

(1) prepare requirements for each class of vessel to be constructed or converted under the Plan; and

(2) contract competitively from nongovernmental entities with expertise in shipbuilding for vessel design and construction based on the requirements for each class of vessel to be acquired.

(b) Exception

The Secretary shall—

(1) report to Congress identifying any existing vessel design or design proposal that meets

the requirements of the Plan within 30 days after October 29, 1992, and shall promptly advise the Congress of any modification of these designs; and

(2) submit to Congress as part of the annual update of the Plan required in section 891b of this title, any subsequent existing vessel design or design proposals that meet the requirements of the Plan.

(Pub. L. 102–567, title VI, §605, Oct. 29, 1992, 106 Stat. 4300.)

§891d. Contract authority

(a) Multiyear contracts

(1) In general

Subject to paragraphs (2) and (3), and notwithstanding section 1341 of title 31 and section 11 of title 41, the Secretary may acquire vessels for the NOAA fleet by purchase, lease, lease-purchase, or otherwise, under one or more multiyear contracts.

(2) Required findings

The Secretary may not enter into a contract pursuant to this subsection unless the Secretary finds with respect to that contract that—

(A) there is a reasonable expectation that throughout the contemplated contract period the Secretary will request from Congress funding for the contract at the level required to avoid contract termination; and

(B) the use of the contract will promote the best interests of the United States by encouraging competition and promoting economic efficiency in the operation of the NOAA fleet.

(3) Required contract provisions

The Secretary may not enter into a contract pursuant to this subsection unless the contract includes—

(A) a provision under which the obligation of the United States to make payments under the contract for any fiscal year is subject to the availability of appropriations provided in advance for those payments;

(B) a provision that specifies the term of effectiveness of the contract; and

(C) appropriate provisions under which, in case of any termination of the contract before the end of the term specified pursuant to subparagraph (B), the United States shall only be liable for the lesser of—

(i) an amount specified in the contract for such a termination; or

(ii) amounts that—

(I) were appropriated before the date of the termination for the performance of the contract or for procurement of the type of acquisition covered by the contract; and

(II) are unobligated on the date of the termination.

(b) Service contracts

Notwithstanding any other provision of law, the Secretary may enter into multiyear contracts for oceanographic research, fisheries research, and mapping and charting services to assist the Secretary in fulfilling NOAA missions. The Secretary may only enter into these contracts if—

(1) the Secretary finds that it is in the public interest to do so;

(2) the contract is for not more than 7 years; and

(3)(A) the cost of the contract is less than the cost (including the cost of operation, maintenance, and personnel) to the NOAA of obtaining those services on NOAA vessels; or

(B) NOAA vessels are not available or cannot provide those services.

(c) Bonding authority

Notwithstanding any other law, the Secretary may not require a contractor for the construction, alteration, repair or maintenance of a NOAA vessel to provide a bid bond, payment bond, performance bond, completion bond, or other surety instrument in an amount greater than 20 percent of the value of the base contract quantity (excluding options) unless the Secretary determines that requiring an instrument in that amount will not prevent a responsible bidder or offeror from competing for the award of the contract.

(Pub. L. 102–567, title VI, §606, Oct. 29, 1992, 106 Stat. 4301.)

§891e. Restriction with respect to certain shipyard subsidies

(a) In general

The Secretary of Commerce may not award a contract for the construction, repair (except emergency repairs), or alteration of any vessel of the National Oceanic and Atmospheric Administration in a shipyard, if that vessel benefits or would benefit from significant subsidies for the construction, repair, or alteration of vessels in that shipyard.

(b) "Significant subsidy" defined

In this section, the term "significant subsidy" includes, but is not limited to, any of the following:

(1) Officially supported export credits.

(2) Direct official operating support to the commercial shipbuilding and repair industry, or to a related entity that favors the operation of shipbuilding and repair, including but not limited to—

(A) grants;

(B) loans and loan guarantees other than those available on the commercial market;

(C) forgiveness of debt;

(D) equity infusions on terms inconsistent with commercially reasonable investment practices; and

(E) preferential provision of goods and services.

(3) Direct official support for investment in the commercial shipbuilding and repair industry, or to a related entity that favors the operation of shipbuilding and repair, including but not limited to the kinds of support listed in paragraph (2)(A) through (E), and any restructuring support, except public support for social purposes directly and effectively linked to shipyard closures.

(4) Assistance in the form of grants, preferential loans, preferential tax treatment, or

otherwise, that benefits or is directly related to shipbuilding and repair for purposes of research and development that is not equally open to domestic and foreign enterprises.

(5) Tax policies and practices that favor the shipbuilding and repair industry, directly or indirectly, such as tax credits, deductions, exemptions, and preferences, including accelerated depreciation, if such benefits are not generally available to persons or firms not engaged in shipbuilding or repair.

(6) Any official regulation or practice that authorizes or encourages persons or firms engaged in shipbuilding or repair to enter into anticompetitive arrangements.

(7) Any indirect support directly related, in law or in fact, to shipbuilding and repair at national yards, including any public assistance favoring shipowners with an indirect effect on shipbuilding or repair activities, and any assistance provided to suppliers of significant inputs to shipbuilding, which results in benefits to domestic shipbuilders.

(8) Any export subsidy identified in the Illustrative List of Export Subsidies in the Annex to the Agreement on Subsidies and Countervailing Measures referred to in section 3511(d)(12) of title 19, or any other export subsidy prohibited by that agreement.

(Pub. L. 102–567, title VI, §607, Oct. 29, 1992, 106 Stat. 4302; Pub. L. 106–36, title I, §1002(f), June 25, 1999, 113 Stat. 133.)

AMENDMENTS

1999—Subsec. (b)(8). Pub. L. 106–36 substituted "Agreement on Subsidies and Countervailing Measures referred to in section 3511(d)(12) of title 19, or any other export subsidy prohibited by that agreement" for "Agreement on Interpretation and Application of Articles VI, XVI, and XXIII of the General Agreement on Tariffs and Trade or any other export subsidy that may be prohibited as a result of the Uruguay Round of trade negotiations."

FISHERIES RESEARCH VESSEL PROCUREMENT

Pub. L. 106–450, title IV, §401, Nov. 7, 2000, 114 Stat. 1945, provided that: "Notwithstanding section 644 of title 15, United States Code, and section 19.502–2 of title 48, Code of Federal Regulations, the Secretary of Commerce shall seek to procure Fisheries Research Vessels through full and open competition from responsible United States shipbuilding companies irrespective of size."

§891e–1. Shipyards located outside of the United States

On and after December 26, 2007, none of the funds made available in this Act or any other Act may be used for the construction, repair (other than emergency repair), overhaul, conversion, or modernization of vessels for the National Oceanic and Atmospheric Administration in shipyards located outside of the United States.

(Pub. L. 110–161, div. B, title V, §506, Dec. 26, 2007, 121 Stat. 1925.)

REFERENCES IN TEXT

This Act, referred to in text, is div. B of Pub. L. 110–161, Dec. 26, 2007, 121 Stat. 1884, known as the Commerce, Justice, Science, and Related Agencies Appropriations Act, 2008. For complete classification of this Act to the Code, see Tables.

CODIFICATION

Section was enacted as part of the Commerce, Justice, Science, and Related Agencies Appropriations Act, 2008, and also as part of the Consolidated Appropriations Act, 2008, and not as part of the NOAA Fleet Modernization Act which comprises this subchapter.

§891f. Use of vessels

(a) Vessel agreements

In implementing the NOAA fleet replacement and modernization program, the Secretary shall use excess capacity of UNOLS vessels where appropriate and may enter into memoranda of agreement with the operators of these vessels to carry out this requirement.

(b) Report to Congress

Within one year after October 29, 1992, the Comptroller General of the United States shall provide a report to Congress, in consultation with the Secretary, comparing the cost-efficiency, accounting, and operating practices of the vessels of NOAA, UNOLS, other Federal agencies, and the United States private sector in meeting the missions of NOAA.

(Pub. L. 102–567, title VI, §608, Oct. 29, 1992, 106 Stat. 4303.)

§891g. Interoperability

The Secretary shall consult with the Oceanographer of the Navy regarding appropriate measures that should be taken, on a reimbursable basis, to ensure that NOAA vessels are interoperable with vessels of the Department of the Navy, including with respect to operation, maintenance, and repair of those vessels.

(Pub. L. 102–567, title VI, §609, Oct. 29, 1992, 106 Stat. 4303.)

INTEROPERABILITY OF VESSELS

Section 401(b)(5) of Pub. L. 102–567 provided that: "The Secretary of Commerce shall consult with the Oceanographer of the Navy regarding appropriate cost effective and practical measures to allow vessels of the National Oceanic and Atmospheric Administration to be interoperable with vessels of the Department of the Navy, including with respect to operation, maintenance, and repair of those vessels."

§891h. Authorization of appropriations

(a) In general

There are authorized to be appropriated to the Secretary for carrying out this subchapter—

(1) $50,000,000 for fiscal year 1993;

(2) $100,000,000 for fiscal year 1994; and

(3) such sums as are necessary for each of the fiscal years 1995, 1996, and 1997.

(b) Limitation on fleet modernization activities

All National Oceanic and Atmospheric Administration fleet modernization shipbuilding, and conversion shall be conducted in accordance with this subchapter.

(Pub. L. 102–567, title VI, §610, Oct. 29, 1992, 106 Stat. 4303.)

SUBCHAPTER IV—NOAA HYDROGRAPHIC SERVICES

§892. Definitions

In this subchapter:

(1) Administrator

The term "Administrator" means the Administrator of the National Oceanic and Atmospheric Administration.

(2) Administration

The term "Administration" means the National Oceanic and Atmospheric Administration.

(3) Hydrographic data

The term "hydrographic data" means information that—

(A) is acquired through—

(i) hydrographic, bathymetric, photogrammetric, lidar, radar, remote sensing, or shoreline and other ocean- and coastal-related surveying;

(ii) geodetic, geospatial, or geomagnetic measurements;

(iii) tide, water level, and current observations; or

(iv) other methods; and

(B) is used in providing hydrographic services.

(4) Hydrographic services

The term "hydrographic services" means—

(A) the management, maintenance, interpretation, certification, and dissemination of bathymetric, hydrographic, shoreline, geodetic, geospatial, geomagnetic, and tide, water level, and current information, including the production of nautical charts, nautical information databases, and other products derived from hydrographic data;

(B) the development of nautical information systems; and

(C) related activities.

(5) Coast and Geodetic Survey Act

The term "Coast and Geodetic Survey Act" means the Act entitled "An Act to define the functions and duties of the Coast and Geodetic Survey, and for other purposes", approved August 6, 1947 (33 U.S.C. 883a et seq.).

(Pub. L. 105–384, title III, § 302, Nov. 13, 1998, 112 Stat. 3454; Pub. L. 107–372, title I, § 102, Dec. 19, 2002, 116 Stat. 3079; Pub. L. 110–386, § 2, Oct. 10, 2008, 122 Stat. 4106.)

References in Text

This subchapter, referred to in text, was in the original "this title", meaning title III of Pub. L. 105–384, Nov. 13, 1998, 112 Stat. 3454, which is classified principally to this subchapter. For complete classification of this title to the Code, see Short Title of 1998 Amendment note set out under section 851 of this title and Tables.

Act of August 6, 1947, referred to in par. (5), is act Aug. 6, 1947, ch. 504, 61 Stat. 787, as amended, which is classified generally to subchapter II of this chapter. For complete classification of this Act to the Code, see Tables.

Amendments

2008—Pars. (3) to (5). Pub. L. 110–386, which directed the amendment of section "303 of the Hydrographic Services Improvement Act of 1998 (33 U.S.C. 892)" by adding pars. (3) to (5) and striking out former pars. (3) to (5), was executed to this section, which is section 302 of the Hydrographic Services Improvement Act of 1998, to reflect the probable intent of Congress. Prior to amendment, pars. (3) to (5) defined the terms "hydrographic data", "hydrographic services", and "Act of 1947", respectively.

2002—Par. (3). Pub. L. 107–372, § 102(1), inserted ", geospatial, or geomagnetic" after "geodetic".

Par. (4). Pub. L. 107–372, § 102(2), inserted "geospatial, geomagnetic," after "geodetic,".

Short Title

For short title of this subchapter as the "Hydrographic Services Improvement Act of 1998", see section 301 of Pub. L. 105–384, set out as a Short Title of 1998 Amendment note under section 851 of this title.

§ 892a. Functions of the Administrator

(a) Responsibilities

To fulfill the data gathering and dissemination duties of the Administration under the Coast and Geodetic Survey Act, promote safe, efficient and environmentally sound marine transportation, and otherwise fulfill the purposes of this subchapter, the Administrator shall—

(1) acquire and disseminate hydrographic data and provide hydrographic services;

(2) promulgate standards for hydrographic data used by the Administration in providing hydrographic services;

(3) promulgate standards for hydrographic services provided by the Administration;

(4) ensure comprehensive geographic coverage of hydrographic services, in cooperation with other appropriate Federal agencies;

(5) maintain a national database of hydrographic data, in cooperation with other appropriate Federal agencies;

(6) provide hydrographic services in uniform, easily accessible formats;

(7) participate in the development of, and implement for the United States in cooperation with other appropriate Federal agencies, international standards for hydrographic data and hydrographic services; and

(8) to the greatest extent practicable and cost-effective, fulfill the requirements of paragraphs (1) and (6) through contracts or other agreements with private sector entities.

(b) Authorities

To fulfill the data gathering and dissemination duties of the Administration under the Coast and Geodetic Survey Act, promote safe, efficient, and environmentally sound marine transportation, and otherwise fulfill the purposes of this subchapter, subject to the availability of appropriations, the Administrator—

(1) may procure, lease, evaluate, test, develop, and operate vessels, equipment, and technologies necessary to ensure safe navigation and maintain operational expertise in hydrographic data acquisition and hydrographic services;

(2) shall, subject to the availability of appropriations, design, install, maintain, and operate real-time hydrographic monitoring systems to enhance navigation safety and efficiency; and[1]

(3) where appropriate and to the extent that it does not detract from the promotion of safe and efficient navigation, may acquire hydro-

[1] So in original. The word "and" probably should not appear.

graphic data and provide hydrographic services to support the conservation and management of coastal and ocean resources;

(4) where appropriate, may acquire hydrographic data and provide hydrographic services to save and protect life and property and support the resumption of commerce in response to emergencies, natural and man-made disasters, and homeland security and maritime domain awareness needs, including obtaining mission assignments (as defined in section 741 of title 6);

(5) may create, support, and maintain such joint centers with other Federal agencies and other entities as the Administrator deems appropriate or necessary to carry out the purposes of this subchapter; and

(6) notwithstanding the existence of such joint centers, shall award contracts for the acquisition of hydrographic data in accordance with subchapter VI of chapter 10 of title 40.[2]

(c) Conservation and management of coastal and ocean resources

Where appropriate and to the extent that it does not detract from the promotion of safe and efficient navigation, the Secretary may use hydrographic data and services to support the conservation and management of coastal and ocean resources.

(Pub. L. 105–384, title III, §303, Nov. 13, 1998, 112 Stat. 3454; Pub. L. 107–372, title I, §103, Dec. 19, 2002, 116 Stat. 3079; Pub. L. 110–386, §3, Oct. 10, 2008, 122 Stat. 4107.)

REFERENCES IN TEXT

This subchapter, referred to in subsecs. (a) and (b), was in the original "this Act", and was translated, to reflect the probable intent of Congress, as reading "this title", meaning title III of Pub. L. 105–384, Nov. 13, 1998, 112 Stat. 3454, known as the Hydrographic Services Improvement Act of 1998, which is classified principally to this subchapter. For complete classification of title III to the Code, see Short Title of 1998 Amendment note set out under section 851 of this title and Tables.

Subchapter VI of chapter 10 of title 40, referred to in subsec. (b)(6), probably means title IX of the Federal Property and Administrative Services Act of 1949, act June 30, 1949, ch. 288, as added Pub. L. 92–582, Oct. 27, 1972, 86 Stat. 1278. Title IX of the Act, which was classified generally to subchapter VI (§541 et seq.) of chapter 10 of former Title 40, Public Buildings, Property, and Works, was repealed and reenacted by Pub. L. 107–217, §§1, 6(b), Aug. 21, 2002, 116 Stat. 1062, 1304, as chapter 11 (§1101 et seq.) of Title 40, Public Buildings, Property, and Works. For disposition of sections of former Title 40 to revised Title 40, see Table preceding section 101 of Title 40. For complete classification of act June 30, 1949, to the Code, see Tables.

AMENDMENTS

2008—Subsec. (a). Pub. L. 110–386, §3(1), substituted "the Coast and Geodetic Survey Act, promote safe, efficient and environmentally sound marine transportation, and otherwise fulfill the purposes of this subchapter," for "the Act of 1947," in introductory provisions.

Subsec. (a)(1). Pub. L. 110–386, §3(2), substituted "data and provide hydrographic services;" for "data;".

Subsec. (b). Pub. L. 110–386, §3(3), added subsec. (b) and struck out former subsec. (b) which related to actions of Administrator to fulfill data gathering and dissemination duties of the Administration under the Act of 1947.

2002—Subsec. (b)(4). Pub. L. 107–372, §103(a), amended par. (4) generally. Prior to amendment, par. (4) read as follows: "may design and install where appropriate Physical Oceanographic Real-Time Systems to enhance navigation safety and efficiency."

Subsec. (c). Pub. L. 107–372, §103(b), added subsec. (c).

HYDROGRAPHIC SURVEY

Pub. L. 106–541, title V, §554, Dec. 11, 2000, 114 Stat. 2679, provided that: "The Secretary [of the Army] shall enter into an agreement with the Administrator of the National Oceanic and Atmospheric Administration—

"(1) to require the Secretary, not later than 60 days after the Corps of Engineers completes a project involving dredging of a channel, to provide data to the Administration in a standard digital format on the results of a hydrographic survey of the channel conducted by the Corps of Engineers; and

"(2) to require the Administrator to provide the final charts with respect to the project to the Secretary in digital format, at no charge, for the purpose of enhancing the mission of the Corps of Engineers of maintaining Federal navigation projects."

§892b. Quality assurance program

(a) Definition

For purposes of this section, the term "hydrographic product" means any publicly or commercially available product produced by a non-Federal entity that includes or displays hydrographic data.

(b) Program

(1) In general

The Administrator—

(A) by not later than 2 years after December 19, 2002, shall, subject to the availability of appropriations, develop and implement a quality assurance program that is equally available to all applicants, under which the Administrator may certify hydrographic products that satisfy the standards promulgated by the Administrator under section 892a(a)(3) of this title;

(B) may authorize the use of the emblem or any trademark of the Administration on a hydrographic product certified under subparagraph (A); and

(C) may charge a fee for such certification and use.

(2) Limitation on fee amount

Any fee under paragraph (1)(C) shall not exceed the costs of conducting the quality assurance testing, evaluation, or studies necessary to determine whether the hydrographic product satisfies the standards adopted under section 892a(a)(3) of this title, including the cost of administering such a program.

(c) Limitation on liability

The Government of the United States shall not be liable for any negligence by a person that produces hydrographic products certified under this section.

(d) Hydrographic Services Account

(1) Establishment

There is established in the Treasury a separate account, which shall be known as the "Hydrographic Services Account".

(2) Content

The account shall consist of—

[2] See References in Text note below.

(A) amounts received by the United States as fees charged under subsection (b)(1)(C) of this section; and

(B) such other amounts as may be provided by law.

(3) Use

Amounts in the account shall be available to the Administrator, without further appropriation, for hydrographic services.

(e) Limitation on new fees and increases in existing fees for hydrographic services

After November 13, 1998, the Administrator may not—

(1) establish any fee or other charge for the provision of any hydrographic service except as authorized by this section; or

(2) increase the amount of any fee or other charge for the provision of any hydrographic service except as authorized by this section and section 1307 of title 44.

(Pub. L. 105–384, title III, § 304, Nov. 13, 1998, 112 Stat. 3455; Pub. L. 107–372, title I, § 104(a), Dec. 19, 2002, 116 Stat. 3080.)

AMENDMENTS

2002—Subsec. (b)(1). Pub. L. 107–372 reenacted heading without change and amended text generally. Prior to amendment, text read as follows: "The Administrator may—

"(A) develop and implement a quality assurance program that is equally available to all applicants, under which the Administrator may certify hydrographic products that satisfy the standards promulgated by the Administrator under section 892a(a)(3) of this title;

"(B) authorize the use of the emblem or any trademark of the Administration on a hydrographic product certified under subparagraph (A); and

"(C) charge a fee for such certification and use."

§ 892c. Hydrographic Services Review Panel

(a) Establishment

No later than 1 year after December 19, 2002, the Secretary shall establish the Hydrographic Services Review Panel.

(b) Duties

(1) In general

The panel shall advise the Administrator on matters related to the responsibilities and authorities set forth in section 892a of this title and such other appropriate matters as the Administrator refers to the panel for review and advice.

(2) Administrative resources

The Administrator shall make available to the panel such information, personnel, and administrative services and assistance as it may reasonably require to carry out its duties.

(c) Membership

(1) In general

(A) The panel shall consist of 15 voting members who shall be appointed by the Administrator. The Co-directors of the Center for Coastal and Ocean Mapping/Joint Hydrographic Center and no more than 2 employees of the National Oceanic and Atmospheric Administration appointed by the Administrator shall serve as nonvoting members of the panel. The voting members of the panel shall be individuals who, by reason of knowledge, experience, or training, are especially qualified in 1 or more of the disciplines and fields relating to hydrographic data and hydrographic services, marine transportation, port administration, vessel pilotage, coastal and fishery management, and other disciplines as determined appropriate by the Administrator.

(B) An individual may not be appointed as a voting member of the panel if the individual is a full-time officer or employee of the United States.

(C) Any voting member of the panel who is an applicant for, or beneficiary (as determined by the Secretary) of, any assistance under this subchapter shall disclose to the panel that relationship, and may not vote on any matter pertaining to that assistance.

(2) Terms

(A) The term of office of a voting member of the panel shall be 4 years, except that of the original appointees, five shall be appointed for a term of 2 years, five shall be appointed for a term of 3 years, and five shall be appointed for a term of 4 years, as specified by the Administrator at the time of appointment.

(B) Any individual appointed to a partial or full term may be reappointed for one additional full term. A voting member may serve after the date of the expiration of the term of office for which appointed until his or her successor has taken office.

(3) Nominations

At least once each year, the Secretary shall publish a notice in the Federal Register soliciting nominations for membership on the panel.

(4) Chairman and Vice Chairman

(A) The panel shall select one voting member to serve as the Chairman and another voting member to serve as the Vice Chairman.

(B) The Vice Chairman shall act as Chairman in the absence or incapacity of the Chairman.

(d) Compensation

Voting members of the panel shall—

(1) receive compensation at a rate established by the Secretary, not to exceed the maximum daily rate payable under section 5376 of title 5 when actually engaged in the performance of duties for such panel; and

(2) be reimbursed for actual and reasonable expenses incurred in the performance of such duties.

(e) Meetings

The panel shall meet on a biannual basis and, at any other time, at the call of the Chairman or upon the request of a majority of the voting members or of the Secretary.

(f) Powers

The panel may exercise such powers as are reasonably necessary in order to carry out its duties under subsection (b) of this section.

(Pub. L. 105–384, title III, § 305, Nov. 13, 1998, 112 Stat. 3456; Pub. L. 105–383, title IV, § 432(c), Nov.

13, 1998, 112 Stat. 3445; Pub. L. 107–372, title I, §105, Dec. 19, 2002, 116 Stat. 3080; Pub. L. 110–386, §4, Oct. 10, 2008, 122 Stat. 4107.)

REFERENCES IN TEXT

This subchapter, referred to in subsec. (c)(1)(C), was in the original "this Act", and was translated, to reflect the probable intent of Congress, as reading "this title", meaning title III of Pub. L. 105–384, Nov. 13, 1998, 112 Stat. 3454, known as the Hydrographic Services Improvement Act of 1998, which is classified principally to this subchapter. For complete classification of title III to the Code, see Short Title of 1998 Amendment note set out under section 851 of this title and Tables.

AMENDMENTS

2008—Subsec. (c)(1)(A). Pub. L. 110–386 amended subpar. (A) generally. Prior to amendment, subpar. (A) read as follows: "The panel shall consist of 15 voting members who shall be appointed by the Administrator. The Director of the Joint Hydrographic Institute and no more than 2 employees of the National Oceanic and Atmospheric Administration appointed by the Administrator shall serve as nonvoting members of the panel. The voting members of the panel shall be individuals who, by reason of knowledge, experience, or training, are especially qualified in one or more of the disciplines and fields relating to hydrographic surveying, tide, current geodetic and geospatial measurement, marine transportation, port administration, vessel pilotage, and coastal and fishery management."

2002—Pub. L. 107–372 amended section generally, substituting provisions establishing Hydrographic Services Review Panel for provisions requiring report, not later than 6 months after November 13, 1998, on a plan to ensure maintenance of Federal competence and expertise in hydrographic surveying.

1998—Pub. L. 105–383, which directed the amendment of this section by striking out subsecs. (a) and (d), was executed by striking out subsec. (a), because no subsec. (d) has been enacted. Prior to amendment, subsec. (a) read as follows:

"(a) PORTS.—Not later than 6 months after November 13, 1998, the Administrator and the Commandant of the Coast Guard shall report to the Congress on—

"(1) the status of implementation of real-time tide and current data systems in United States ports;

"(2) existing safety and efficiency needs in United States ports that could be met by increased use of those systems; and

"(3) a plan for expanding those systems to meet those needs, including an estimate of the cost of implementing those systems in priority locations."

EFFECTIVE DATE OF 1998 AMENDMENT

Pub. L. 105–383, title IV, §432(a), Nov. 13, 1998, 112 Stat. 3444, provided that: "Subsections (b) and (c) [amending this section and section 892d of this title] shall take effect immediately after the later of—

"(1) the enactment of the Hydrographic Services Improvement Act of 1998 [Pub. L. 105–384, title III, Nov. 13, 1998]; or

"(2) the enactment of this Act [Nov. 13, 1998]."

§892d. Authorization of appropriations

There are authorized to be appropriated to the Administrator the following:

(1) To carry out nautical mapping and charting functions under sections 892b and 892c of this title, except for conducting hydrographic surveys—

(A) $55,000,000 for fiscal year 2009;
(B) $56,000,000 for fiscal year 2010;
(C) $57,000,000 for fiscal year 2011; and
(D) $58,000,000 for fiscal year 2012.

(2) To contract for hydrographic surveys under section 892b(b)(1) of this title, including the leasing or time chartering of vessels—

(A) $32,130,000 for fiscal year 2009;
(B) $32,760,000 for fiscal year 2010;
(C) $33,390,000 for fiscal year 2011; and
(D) $34,020,000 for fiscal year 2012.

(3) To operate hydrographic survey vessels owned by the United States and operated by the Administration—

(A) $25,900,000 for fiscal year 2009;
(B) $26,400,000 for fiscal year 2010;
(C) $26,900,000 for fiscal year 2011; and
(D) $27,400,000 for fiscal year 2012.

(4) To carry out geodetic functions under this subchapter—

(A) $32,640,000 for fiscal year 2009;
(B) $33,280,000 for fiscal year 2010;
(C) $33,920,000 for fiscal year 2011; and
(D) $34,560,000 for fiscal year 2012.

(5) To carry out tide and current measurement functions under this subchapter—

(A) $27,000,000 for fiscal year 2009;
(B) $27,500,000 for fiscal year 2010;
(C) $28,000,000 for fiscal year 2011; and
(D) $28,500,000 for fiscal year 2012.

(6) To acquire a replacement hydrographic survey vessel capable of staying at sea continuously for at least 30 days $75,000,000.

(Pub. L. 105–384, title III, §306, Nov. 13, 1998, 112 Stat. 3457; Pub. L. 105–383, title IV, §432(b), Nov. 13, 1998, 112 Stat. 3445; Pub. L. 107–372, title I, §106, Dec. 19, 2002, 116 Stat. 3081; Pub. L. 110–386, §5, Oct. 10, 2008, 122 Stat. 4108.)

REFERENCES IN TEXT

This subchapter, referred to in pars. (4) and (5), was in the original "this title", meaning title III of Pub. L. 105–384, Nov. 13, 1998, 112 Stat. 3454, which is classified principally to this subchapter. For complete classification of this title to the Code, see Short Title of 1998 Amendment note set out under section 851 of this title and Tables.

AMENDMENTS

2008—Pub. L. 110–386 amended section generally. Prior to amendment, section authorized appropriations for fiscal years 2003 through 2007.

2002—Pub. L. 107–372 reenacted section catchline without change and amended text generally. Prior to amendment, text read as follows: "There is authorized to be appropriated to the Administrator the following:

"(1) To carry out nautical mapping and charting functions under the Act of 1947 and sections 892a and 892b of this title, except for conducting hydrographic surveys, $33,000,000 for fiscal year 1999, $34,000,000 for fiscal year 2000, and $35,000,000 for fiscal year 2001.

"(2) To conduct hydrographic surveys under section 892a(a)(1) of this title, including the leasing of ships, $33,000,000 for fiscal year 1999, $35,000,000 for fiscal year 2000, and $37,000,000 for fiscal year 2001. Of these amounts, no more than $16,000,000 is authorized for any one fiscal year to operate hydrographic survey vessels owned and operated by the Administration.

"(3) To carry out geodetic functions under the Act of 1947, $25,000,000 for fiscal year 1999, $30,000,000 for fiscal year 2000, and $30,000,000 for fiscal year 2001.

"(4) To carry out tide and current measurement functions under the Act of 1947, $22,500,000 for each of fiscal years 1999 through 2001. Of these amounts $4,500,000 is authorized for each fiscal year to implement and operate a national quality control system for real-time tide and current and maintain the national tide network, and $7,000,000 is authorized for each fiscal year to design and install real-time tide and current data measurement systems under section 892a(b)(4) of this title."

1998—Pub. L. 105–383 amended section generally, substituting present provisions for substantially identical provisions.

EFFECTIVE DATE OF 1998 AMENDMENT

Amendment by Pub. L. 105–383 effective immediately after enactment of Pub. L. 105–384, Nov. 13, 1998, see section 432(a) of Pub. L. 105–383, set out as a note under section 892c of this title.

SUBCHAPTER V—RESEARCH, DEVELOPMENT, EDUCATION, AND INNOVATION

§893. Ocean and atmospheric research and development program

The Administrator of the National Oceanic and Atmospheric Administration, in consultation with the Director of the National Science Foundation and the Administrator of the National Aeronautics and Space Administration, shall establish a coordinated program of ocean, coastal, Great Lakes, and atmospheric research and development, in collaboration with academic institutions and other nongovernmental entities, that shall focus on the development of advanced technologies and analytical methods that will promote United States leadership in ocean and atmospheric science and competitiveness in the applied uses of such knowledge.

(Pub. L. 110–69, title IV, §4001, Aug. 9, 2007, 121 Stat. 599.)

§893a. NOAA ocean and atmospheric science education programs

(a) In general

The Administrator of the National Oceanic and Atmospheric Administration shall conduct, develop, support, promote, and coordinate formal and informal educational activities at all levels to enhance public awareness and understanding of ocean, coastal, Great Lakes, and atmospheric science and stewardship by the general public and other coastal stakeholders, including underrepresented groups in ocean and atmospheric science and policy careers. In conducting those activities, the Administrator shall build upon the educational programs and activities of the agency.

(b) NOAA science education plan

The Administrator, appropriate National Oceanic and Atmospheric Administration programs, ocean atmospheric science and education experts, and interested members of the public shall develop a science education plan setting forth education goals and strategies for the Administration, as well as programmatic actions to carry out such goals and priorities over the next 20 years, and evaluate and update such plan every 5 years.

(c) Construction

Nothing in this section may be construed to affect the application of section 1232a of title 20 or sections 794 and 794d of title 29.

(Pub. L. 110–69, title IV, §4002, Aug. 9, 2007, 121 Stat. 600.)

§893b. NOAA's contribution to innovation

(a) Participation in interagency activities

The National Oceanic and Atmospheric Administration shall be a full participant in any interagency effort to promote innovation and economic competitiveness through near-term and long-term basic scientific research and development and the promotion of science, technology, engineering, and mathematics education, consistent with the agency mission, including authorized activities.

(b) Historic foundation

In order to carry out the participation described in subsection (a), the Administrator of the National Oceanic and Atmospheric Administration shall build on the historic role of the National Oceanic and Atmospheric Administration in stimulating excellence in the advancement of ocean and atmospheric science and engineering disciplines and in providing opportunities and incentives for the pursuit of academic studies in science, technology, engineering, and mathematics.

(Pub. L. 110–69, title IV, §4003, Aug. 9, 2007, 121 Stat. 600.)

CHAPTER 18—LONGSHORE AND HARBOR WORKERS' COMPENSATION

§ 901. Short title

This chapter may be cited as "Longshore and Harbor Workers' Compensation Act."

(Mar. 4, 1927, ch. 509, §1, 44 Stat. 1424; Pub. L. 98–426, §27(d)(1), Sept. 28, 1984, 98 Stat. 1654.)

Amendments

1984—Pub. L. 98–426 substituted "Longshore" for "Longshoremen's".

Effective Date of 1984 Amendment

Section 28(a)–(g) of Pub. L. 98–426 provided that:

"(a) Except as otherwise provided in this section, the amendments made by this Act [enacting section 942 of this title, amending this section, sections 902 to 910, 912 to 914, 917 to 919, 921 to 923, 928 to 935, 938 to 940, 944, and 948a of this title, and section 932 of Title 30, Mineral Lands and Mining, repealing sections 945 to 947 of this title, and enacting provisions set out as notes under this section and section 907 of this title] shall be effective on the date of enactment of this Act [Sept. 28, 1984] and shall apply both with respect to claims filed after such date and to claims pending on such date.

"(b) The amendments made by sections 7(a), 7(e), 8(f), 11(b), 11(c), and 13 [amending sections 907, 908, 912, and 914 of this title] shall be effective 90 days after the date of enactment of this Act [Sept. 28, 1984] and shall apply both with respect to claims filed after such 90th day and to claims pending on such 90th day.

"(c) The amendments made by sections 2(a), 3(a), 5, and 8(b) [amending sections 902, 903, 905, and 908 of this title] shall apply with respect to any injury after the date of enactment of this Act [Sept. 28, 1984].

"(d) The amendments made by sections 6(a), 8(d), and 9 [amending sections 906, 908, and 909 of this title] shall apply with respect to any death after the date of enactment of this Act [Sept. 28, 1984].

"(e)(1) The amendments made by sections 2(c), 8(c)(1), 8(e)(4), 8(e)(5), 8(g), 10(b), 15 through 20, and 22 through 27 [enacting section 942 of this title, amending this section and sections 902, 908 to 910, 914, 918, 919, 921 to 923, 928 to 932, 934, 935, 938 to 940, 944, and 948a of this title, repealing sections 945 to 947, and enacting provisions set out as a note under this section] shall be effective on the date of enactment of this Act [Sept. 24, 1984].

"(2) The amendments made by sections 7(b), 7(c), 7(d), and 8(h) [amending sections 907 and 908 of this title] shall be effective 90 days after the date of enactment of this Act [Sept. 28, 1984].

"(f) The amendments made by section 6(b) [amending section 906 of this title] shall apply with respect to any injury, disability, or death after the date of enactment of this Act [Sept. 28, 1984].

"(g) For the purpose of this section—

"(1) in the case of an occupational disease which does not immediately result in a disability or death, an injury shall be deemed to arise on the date on which the employee or claimant becomes aware, or in the exercise of reasonable diligence or by reason of medical advice should have been aware, of the disease; and

"(2) the term 'disability' has the meaning given such term by section 2(10) of the Act [section 902(10) of this title] as amended by this Act."

Effective Date

Section 52, formerly §51, of act Mar. 4, 1927, renumbered Oct. 27, 1972, Pub. L. 92–576, §19, 86 Stat. 1263, provided that: "Sections 39 to 48, 50 to 52 [50 to 52, formerly 49 to 51, renumbered Pub. L. 92–576, §19], inclusive [sections 939 to 948, 949, and 950 of this title], shall become effective upon the passage of this Act [Mar. 4, 1927], and the remainder of this Act shall become effective on July 1, 1927."

Short Title of 1984 Amendment

Section 1(a) of Pub. L. 98–426 provided that: "this Act [enacting section 942 of this title, amending this section, sections 902 to 910, 912 to 914, 917 to 919, 921 to 923, 928 to 935, 938 to 940, 944, and 948a of this title, and section 932 of Title 30, Mineral Lands and Mining, repealing sections 945 to 947 of this title, and enacting provisions set out as notes under this section and section 907 of this title] may be cited as the 'Longshore and Harbor Workers' Compensation Act Amendments of 1984'."

Short Title of 1972 Amendment

Pub. L. 92–576, §1, Oct. 27, 1972, 86 Stat. 1251, provided: "That this Act [enacting section 948a, amending sections 902, 903, 905 to 910, 912 to 914, 917, 919, 921, 921a, 923, 927, 928, 933, 935, 939, 940, and 944 of this title, and enacting and amending provisions set out as notes under this section and section 902 of this title] may be cited as the 'Longshoremen's and Harbor Workers' Compensation Act Amendments of 1972'."

References to Longshoremen's and Harbor Workers' Compensation Act

Section 27(d)(2) of Pub. L. 98–426 provided that: "Reference in any other statute, regulation, order, or other document to the Longshoremen's and Harbor Workers' Compensation Act shall be deemed to refer to the Longshore and Harbor Workers' Compensation Act."

§ 902. Definitions

When used in this chapter—

(1) The term "person" means individual, partnership, corporation, or association.

(2) The term "injury" means accidental injury or death arising out of and in the course of employment, and such occupational disease or infection as arises naturally out of such employment or as naturally or unavoidably results from such accidental injury, and includes an injury caused by the willful act of a third person directed against an employee because of his employment.

(3) The term "employee" means any person engaged in maritime employment, including any longshoreman or other person engaged in longshoring operations, and any harbor-worker including a ship repairman, shipbuilder, and ship-breaker, but such term does not include—

(A) individuals employed exclusively to perform office clerical, secretarial, security, or data processing work;

(B) individuals employed by a club, camp, recreational operation, restaurant, museum, or retail outlet;

(C) individuals employed by a marina and who are not engaged in construction, replacement, or expansion of such marina (except for routine maintenance);

(D) individuals who (i) are employed by suppliers, transporters, or vendors, (ii) are temporarily doing business on the premises of an employer described in paragraph (4), and (iii) are not engaged in work normally performed by employees of that employer under this chapter;

(E) aquaculture workers;

(F) individuals employed to build, repair, or dismantle any recreational vessel under sixty-five feet in length;

(G) a master or member of a crew of any vessel; or

(H) any person engaged by a master to load or unload or repair any small vessel under eighteen tons net;

if individuals described in clauses (A) through (F) are subject to coverage under a State workers' compensation law.

(4) The term "employer" means an employer any of whose employees are employed in maritime employment, in whole or in part, upon the navigable waters of the United States (including any adjoining pier, wharf, dry dock, terminal, building way, marine railway, or other adjoining area customarily used by an employer in loading, unloading, repairing, or building a vessel).

(5) The term "carrier" means any person or fund authorized under section 932 of this title to insure under this chapter and includes self-insurers.

(6) The term "Secretary" means the Secretary of Labor.

(7) The term "deputy commissioner" means the deputy commissioner having jurisdiction in respect of an injury or death.

(8) The term "State" includes a Territory and the District of Columbia.

(9) The term "United States" when used in a geographical sense means the several States and Territories and the District of Columbia, including the territorial waters thereof.

(10) "Disability" means incapacity because of injury to earn the wages which the employee was receiving at the time of injury in the same or any other employment; but such term shall mean permanent impairment, determined (to the extent covered thereby) under the guides to the evaluation of permanent impairment promulgated and modified from time to time by the American Medical Association, in the case of an individual whose claim is described in section 910(d)(2) of this title.

(11) "Death" as a basis for a right to compensation means only death resulting from an injury.

(12) "Compensation" means the money allowance payable to an employee or to his dependents as provided for in this chapter, and includes funeral benefits provided therein.

(13) The term "wages" means the money rate at which the service rendered by an employee is compensated by an employer under the contract of hiring in force at the time of the injury, including the reasonable value of any advantage which is received from the employer and included for purposes of any withholding of tax under subtitle C of title 26 (relating to employment taxes). The term wages does not include fringe benefits, including (but not limited to) employer payments for or contributions to a retirement, pension, health and welfare, life insurance, training, social security or other employee or dependent benefit plan for the employee's or dependent's benefit, or any other employee's dependent entitlement.

(14) "Child" shall include a posthumous child, a child legally adopted prior to the injury of the employee, a child in relation to whom the deceased employee stood in loco parentis for at least one year prior to the time of injury, and a stepchild or acknowledged illegitimate child dependent upon the deceased, but does not include married children unless wholly dependent on him. "Grandchild" means a child as above defined of a child as above defined. "Brother" and "sister" includes stepbrothers and stepsisters, half brothers and half sisters, and brothers and sisters by adoption, but does not include married brothers nor married sisters unless wholly dependent on the employee. "Child", "grandchild", "brother", and "sister" include only a person who is under eighteen years of age, or who, though eighteen years of age or over, is (1) wholly dependent upon the employee and incapable of self-support by reason of mental or physical disability, or (2) a student as defined in paragraph (19) of this section.

(15) The term "parent" includes step-parents and parents by adoption, parents-in-law, and any person who for more than three years prior to the death of the deceased employee stood in the place of a parent to him, if dependent on the injured employee.

(16) The terms "widow or widower" includes only the decedent's wife or husband living with or dependent for support upon him or her at the time of his or her death; or living apart for justifiable cause or by reason of his or her desertion at such time.

(17) The terms "adoption" or "adopted" mean legal adoption prior to the time of the injury.

(18) The term "student" means a person regularly pursuing a full-time course of study or training at an institution which is—

(A) a school or college or university operated or directly supported by the United States, or by any State or local government or political subdivision thereof,

(B) a school or college or university which has been accredited by a State or by a State recognized or nationally recognized accrediting agency or body,

(C) a school or college or university not so accredited but whose credits are accepted, on transfer, by not less than three institutions which are so accredited, for credit on the same basis as if transferred from an institution so accredited, or

(D) an additional type of educational or training institution as defined by the Secretary,

but not after he reaches the age of twenty-three or has completed four years of education beyond the high school level, except that, where his twenty-third birthday occurs during a semester or other enrollment period, he shall continue to be considered a student until the end of such semester or other enrollment period. A child shall not be deemed to have ceased to be a student during any interim between school years if the interim does not exceed five months and if he shows to the satisfaction of the Secretary that he has a bona fide intention of continuing to pursue a full-time course of education or training during the semester or other enrollment period immediately following the interim or during periods of reasonable duration during which, in the judgment of the Secretary, he is prevented by factors beyond his control from pursuing his education. A child shall not be deemed to be a student under this chapter during a period of service in the Armed Forces of the United States.

(19) The term "national average weekly wage" means the national average weekly earnings of production or nonsupervisory workers on private nonagricultural payrolls.

(20) The term "Board" shall mean the Benefits Review Board.

(21) Unless the context requires otherwise, the term "vessel" means any vessel upon which or in connection with which any person entitled to benefits under this chapter suffers injury or death arising out of or in the course of his employment, and said vessel's owner, owner pro hac vice, agent, operator, charter or bare boat charterer, master, officer, or crew member.

(22) The singular includes the plural and the masculine includes the feminine and neuter.

(Mar. 4, 1927, ch. 509, §2, 44 Stat. 1424; June 25, 1938, ch. 685, §1, 52 Stat. 1164; Pub. L. 92–576, §§2(a), (b), 3, 5(b), 15(c), 18(b), 20(c)(1), Oct. 27, 1972, 86 Stat. 1251, 1253, 1262, 1263, 1265; Pub. L. 98–426, §§2, 5(a)(2), 27(a)(1), Sept. 28, 1984, 98 Stat. 1639, 1641, 1654.)

References in Text

The phrase "a student as defined in paragraph (19) of this section", referred to in par. (14), probably means a student as defined in paragraph (18) of this section.

Amendments

1984—Par. (3). Pub. L. 98–426, §2(a), amended par. (3) generally. Prior to amendment, par. (3) read as follows: "The term 'employee' means any person engaged in maritime employment, including any longshoreman or other person engaged in longshoring operations, and any harborworker including a ship repairman, shipbuilder, and shipbreaker, but such term does not include a master or member of a crew of any vessel, or any person engaged by the master to load or unload or repair any small vessel under eighteen tons net."

Par. (6). Pub. L. 98–426, §27(a)(1), substituted "The term 'Secretary' means the Secretary of Labor" for "The term 'commission' means the United States Employees' Compensation Commission".

Par. (10). Pub. L. 98–426, §2(b), inserted "; but such term shall mean permanent impairment, determined (to the extent covered thereby) under the guides to the evaluation of permanent impairment promulgated and modified from time to time by the American Medical Association, in the case of an individual whose claim is described in section 910(d)(2) of this title".

Par. (13). Pub. L. 98–426, §2(c), amended par. (13) generally. Prior to amendment, par. (13) read as follows: "'Wages' means the money rate at which the service rendered is recompensed under the contract of hiring in force at the time of the injury, including the reasonable value of board, rent, housing, lodging, or similar advantage received from the employer, and gratuities received in the course of employment from others than the employer".

Par. (21). Pub. L. 98–426, §5(a)(2), substituted "Unless the context requires otherwise, the" for "The".

1972—Par. (3). Pub. L. 92–576, §2(a), defined "employee" to mean any person engaged in maritime employment, including any longshoreman or other person engaged in longshoring operations, and any harborworker including a ship repairman, shipbuilder, and shipbreaker and substituted "or" for "nor" before "any person engaged by the master".

Par. (4). Pub. L. 92–576, §2(b), defined "employer" to include an employer any of whose employees are employed in maritime employment upon the navigable waters of the United States, including any adjoining pier, wharf, dry dock, terminal, building way, marine railway, or other adjoining area customarily used by an employer in loading, unloading, repairing, or building a vessel.

Par. (14). Pub. L. 92–576, §3(b), defined "child, grandchild, brother, and sister" to include a student as defined in par. (19) of this section.

Par. (16). Pub. L. 92–576, §20(c)(1), consolidated provisions of former par. (16) definition of "widow" and former par. (17) definition of "widower" in one definition of "widow or widower"; and in redefining "widower", substituted provision for decedent's husband living with or dependent upon wife for support at time of her death, for prior provision for decedent's husband living with and dependent upon wife for support at time of her death, and included decedent's husband living apart from wife for justifiable cause or by reason of her desertion at time of her death.

Par. (17). Pub. L. 92–576, §20(c)(1), redesignated former par. (18) definition of "adoption" or "adopted" as par. (17). Former par. (17) definition of "widower" incorporated in par. (16).

Par. (18). Pub. L. 92–576, §§3(a), 20(c)(1), added par. (19) definition of "student" and redesignated such par. (19) as par. (18). Former par. (18) definition of "adoption" or "adopted" redesignated par. (17).

Par. (19). Pub. L. 92–576, §§5(b), 20(c)(1), added par. (20) definition of "national average weekly wage" and redesignated such par. (20) as par. (19). Former par. (19) definition of "student" redesignated par. (18).

Par. (20). Pub. L. 92–576, §§15(c), 20(c)(1), added par. (21) definition of "Board" and redesignated such par. (21) as par. (20). Former par. (20) definition of "national average weekly wage" redesignated par. (19).

Par. (21). Pub. L. 92–576, §§18(b), 20(c)(1), added par. (22) definition of "vessel" and redesignated such par. (22) as par. (21). Former par. (21) definition of "Board" redesignated par. (20).

Par. (22). Pub. L. 92–576, §§3(a), 5(b), 15(c), 18(b), 20(c)(1), redesignated former par. (19) definition of "singular" as pars. (20), (21), (22), (23), and (22) again. Former par. (22) definition of "vessel" redesignated par. (21).

1938—Par. (14). Act June 25, 1938, included within definition of child, "a child in relation to whom the deceased employee stood in loco parentis for at least one year prior to the time of injury" and within definition of child, grandchild, brother, and sister "persons who though eighteen years of age or over, are wholly dependent upon the deceased employee and incapable of self-support by reason of mental or physical disability".

Effective Date of 1984 Amendment

Amendment by sections 2(a) and 5(a)(2) of Pub. L. 98–426 applicable with respect to any injury after Sept. 28, 1984, amendment by section 2(b) of Pub. L. 98–426 effective Sept. 28, 1984, and applicable both with respect to claims filed after such date and to claims pending as of such date, and amendment by sections 2(c) and 27(a)(1) of Pub. L. 98–426 effective Sept. 28, 1984, see section 28(a), (c), (e)(1) of Pub. L. 98–426, set out as a note under section 901 of this title.

Effective Date of 1972 Amendment

Section 20(c)(3) of Pub. L. 92–576 provided that: "The amendments made by this subsection [amending this section and section 909 of this title] shall apply only with respect to deaths or injuries occurring after the enactment of this Act, [Oct. 27, 1972]."

Section 22 of Pub. L. 92–576 provided that: "The amendments made by this Act [see Short Title note set out under section 901 of this title] shall become effective thirty days after the date of enactment of this Act [Oct. 27, 1972].''

TRANSFER OF FUNCTIONS

Prior to the amendment of this chapter by Pub. L. 98–426 the word ''Secretary'' meaning the Secretary of Labor had been substituted for the word ''commission'' meaning the United States Employees' Compensation Commission throughout this chapter even when not expressly so directed by statute in view of the transfer of the functions of the commission first to the Federal Security Administrator by Reorg. Plan No. 2 of 1946, §3, eff. July 16, 1946, 11 F.R. 7873, 60 Stat. 1095, and later to the Secretary of Labor by Reorg. Plan No. 19 of 1950, §1, eff. May 24, 1950, 15 F.R. 3178, 64 Stat. 1271. Where such substitution had thus been made the statutory substitution of terms by Pub. L. 98–426 required no change in text.

§903. Coverage

(a) Disability or death; injuries occurring upon navigable waters of United States

Except as otherwise provided in this section, compensation shall be payable under this chapter in respect of disability or death of an employee, but only if the disability or death results from an injury occurring upon the navigable waters of the United States (including any adjoining pier, wharf, dry dock, terminal, building way, marine railway, or other adjoining area customarily used by an employer in loading, unloading, repairing, dismantling, or building a vessel).

(b) Governmental officers and employees

No compensation shall be payable in respect of the disability or death of an officer or employee of the United States, or any agency thereof, or of any State or foreign government, or any subdivision thereof.

(c) Intoxication; willful intention to kill

No compensation shall be payable if the injury was occasioned solely by the intoxication of the employee or by the willful intention of the employee to injure or kill himself or another.

(d) Small vessels

(1) No compensation shall be payable to an employee employed at a facility of an employer if, as certified by the Secretary, the facility is engaged in the business of building, repairing, or dismantling exclusively small vessels (as defined in paragraph (3) of this subsection), unless the injury occurs while upon the navigable waters of the United States or while upon any adjoining pier, wharf, dock, facility over land for launching vessels, or facility over land for hauling, lifting, or drydocking vessels.

(2) Notwithstanding paragraph (1), compensation shall be payable to an employee—

(A) who is employed at a facility which is used in the business of building, repairing, or dismantling small vessels if such facility receives Federal maritime subsidies; or

(B) if the employee is not subject to coverage under a State workers' compensation law.

(3) For purposes of this subsection, a small vessel means—

(A) a commercial barge which is under 900 lightship displacement tons; or

(B) a commercial tugboat, towboat, crew boat, supply boat, fishing vessel, or other work vessel which is under 1,600 tons gross as measured under section 14502 of title 46, or an alternate tonnage measured under section 14302 of that title as prescribed by the Secretary under section 14104 of that title.

(e) Credit for benefits paid under other laws

Notwithstanding any other provision of law, any amounts paid to an employee for the same injury, disability, or death for which benefits are claimed under this chapter pursuant to any other workers' compensation law or section 30104 of title 46 shall be credited against any liability imposed by this chapter.

(Mar. 4, 1927, ch. 509, §3, 44 Stat. 1426; Pub. L. 92–576, §§2(c), 21, Oct. 27, 1972, 86 Stat. 1251, 1265; Pub. L. 98–426, §3, Sept. 28, 1984, 98 Stat. 1640; Pub. L. 104–324, title VII, §703, Oct. 19, 1996, 110 Stat. 3933.)

CODIFICATION

In subsec. (e), ''section 30104 of title 46'' substituted for ''section 20 of the Act of March 4, 1915 (38 Stat. 1185, chapter 153; 46 U.S.C. 688) (relating to recovery for injury to or death of seamen)'' on authority of Pub. L. 109–304, §18(c), Oct. 6, 2006, 120 Stat. 1709, which Act enacted section 30104 of Title 46, Shipping.

AMENDMENTS

1996—Subsec. (d)(3)(B). Pub. L. 104–324 inserted before period at end ''as measured under section 14502 of title 46, or an alternate tonnage measured under section 14302 of that title as prescribed by the Secretary under section 14104 of that title''.

1984—Subsec. (a). Pub. L. 98–426, §3(a), inserted introductory language relating to exceptions provided for elsewhere in this section, redesignated existing par. (1) as subsec. (b), and struck out existing par. (2) which had excepted from coverage masters and crew members or persons engaged by such masters or crew members to load, unload, or repair vessels under 18 tons net.

Subsec. (b). Pub. L. 98–426, §3(a), redesignated as subsec. (b) provisions formerly set out in subsec. (a)(2). Former subsec. (b) redesignated (c).

Subsecs. (c) to (e). Pub. L. 98–426, §3(a), (b), redesignated former subsec. (b) as (c) and added subsecs. (d) and (e).

1972—Subsec. (a). Pub. L. 92–576, §2(c), substituted provisions respecting coverage of injuries occurring upon navigable waters of the United States, including any adjoining pier, wharf, dry dock, terminal, building way, marine railway, or other adjoining area customarily used by an employer in loading, unloading, repairing, or building a vessel, for prior provisions respecting coverage of such injuries upon navigable waters and if recovery for the disability or death through workmen's compensation proceedings may not validly be provided by State law.

Subsec. (a)(1). Pub. L. 92–576, §21, substituted ''or'' for ''nor'' before ''any person engaged by the master''.

EFFECTIVE DATE OF 1984 AMENDMENT

Amendment by section 3(a) of Pub. L. 98–426 applicable with respect to any injury after Sept. 28, 1984, and amendment by section 3(b) of Pub. L. 98–426 effective Sept. 28, 1984, and applicable both with respect to claims filed after Sept. 28, 1984, and to claims pending on that date, see section 28(a), (c) of Pub. L. 98–426, set out as a note under section 901 of this title.

EFFECTIVE DATE OF 1972 AMENDMENT

Amendment by Pub. L. 92–576 effective 30 days after Oct. 27, 1972, see section 22 of Pub. L. 92–576, set out as a note under section 902 of this title.

DISTRICT OF COLUMBIA

The Longshoremen's and Harbor Workers' Compensation Act [this chapter] was made applicable in respect to the injury or death of an employee of an employer carrying on any employment in the District of Columbia, by act May 17, 1928, ch. 612, 45 Stat. 600, as amended.

§ 904. Liability for compensation

(a) Every employer shall be liable for and shall secure the payment to his employees of the compensation payable under sections 907, 908, and 909 of this title. In the case of an employer who is a subcontractor, only if such subcontractor fails to secure the payment of compensation shall the contractor be liable for and be required to secure the payment of compensation. A subcontractor shall not be deemed to have failed to secure the payment of compensation if the contractor has provided insurance for such compensation for the benefit of the subcontractor.

(b) Compensation shall be payable irrespective of fault as a cause for the injury.

(Mar. 4, 1927, ch. 509, §4, 44 Stat. 1426; Pub. L. 98–426, §4(a), Sept. 28, 1984, 98 Stat. 1641.)

AMENDMENTS

1984—Subsec. (a). Pub. L. 98–426 amended subsec. (a) generally. Prior to amendment, subsec. (a) read as follows: "Every employer shall be liable for and shall secure the payment to his employees of the compensation payable under sections 907, 908, and 909 of this title. In the case of an employer who is a subcontractor, the contractor shall be liable for and shall secure the payment of such compensation to employees of the subcontractor unless the subcontractor has secured such payment."

EFFECTIVE DATE OF 1984 AMENDMENT

Amendment by Pub. L. 98–426 effective Sept. 28, 1984, and applicable both with respect to claims filed after Sept. 28, 1984, and to claims pending on that date, see section 28(a) of Pub. L. 98–426, set out as a note under section 901 of this title.

§ 905. Exclusiveness of liability

(a) Employer liability; failure of employer to secure payment of compensation

The liability of an employer prescribed in section 904 of this title shall be exclusive and in place of all other liability of such employer to the employee, his legal representative, husband or wife, parents, dependents, next of kin, and anyone otherwise entitled to recover damages from such employer at law or in admiralty on account of such injury or death, except that if an employer fails to secure payment of compensation as required by this chapter, an injured employee, or his legal representative in case death results from the injury, may elect to claim compensation under the chapter, or to maintain an action at law or in admiralty for damages on account of such injury or death. In such action the defendant may not plead as a defense that the injury was caused by the negligence of a fellow servant, or that the employee assumed the risk of his employment, or that the injury was due to the contributory negligence of the employee. For purposes of this subsection, a contractor shall be deemed the employer of a subcontractor's employees only if the subcontractor fails to secure the payment of compensation as required by section 904 of this title.

(b) Negligence of vessel

In the event of injury to a person covered under this chapter caused by the negligence of a vessel, then such person, or anyone otherwise entitled to recover damages by reason thereof, may bring an action against such vessel as a third party in accordance with the provisions of section 933 of this title, and the employer shall not be liable to the vessel for such damages directly or indirectly and any agreements or warranties to the contrary shall be void. If such person was employed by the vessel to provide stevedoring services, no such action shall be permitted if the injury was caused by the negligence of persons engaged in providing stevedoring services to the vessel. If such person was employed to provide shipbuilding, repairing, or breaking services and such person's employer was the owner, owner pro hac vice, agent, operator, or charterer of the vessel, no such action shall be permitted, in whole or in part or directly or indirectly, against the injured person's employer (in any capacity, including as the vessel's owner, owner pro hac vice, agent, operator, or charterer) or against the employees of the employer. The liability of the vessel under this subsection shall not be based upon the warranty of seaworthiness or a breach thereof at the time the injury occurred. The remedy provided in this subsection shall be exclusive of all other remedies against the vessel except remedies available under this chapter.

(c) Outer Continental Shelf

In the event that the negligence of a vessel causes injury to a person entitled to receive benefits under this Act by virtue of section 1333 of title 43, then such person, or anyone otherwise entitled to recover damages by reason thereof, may bring an action against such vessel in accordance with the provisions of subsection (b) of this section. Nothing contained in subsection (b) of this section shall preclude the enforcement according to its terms of any reciprocal indemnity provision whereby the employer of a person entitled to receive benefits under this chapter by virtue of section 1333 of title 43 and the vessel agree to defend and indemnify the other for cost of defense and loss or liability for damages arising out of or resulting from death or bodily injury to their employees.

(Mar. 4, 1927, ch. 509, §5, 44 Stat. 1426; Pub. L. 92–576, §18(a), Oct. 27, 1972, 86 Stat. 1263; Pub. L. 98–426, §§4(b), 5(a)(1), (b), Sept. 28, 1984, 98 Stat. 1641.)

AMENDMENTS

1984—Subsec. (a). Pub. L. 98–426, §4(b), inserted at end "For purposes of this subsection, a contractor shall be deemed the employer of a subcontractor's employees only if the subcontractor fails to secure the payment of compensation as required by section 904 of this title."

Subsec. (b). Pub. L. 98–426, §5(a)(1), substituted "If such person was employed to provide shipbuilding, repairing, or breaking services and such person's employer was the owner, owner pro hac vice, agent, operator, or charterer of the vessel, no such action shall be permitted, in whole or in part or directly or indirectly, against the injured person's employer (in any capacity, including as the vessel's owner, owner pro hac vice, agent, operator, or charterer) or against the employees of the employer" for "If such person was employed by the vessel to provide ship building or repair services, no such action shall be permitted if the injury was caused by the negligence of persons engaged in providing ship building or repair services to the vessel".

Subsec. (c). Pub. L. 98–426, § 5(b), added subsec. (c).

1972—Pub. L. 92–576 designated existing provisions as subsec. (a), substituted "the chapter" for "this chapter", and added subsec. (b).

EFFECTIVE DATE OF 1984 AMENDMENT

Amendment by section 4(b) of Pub. L. 98–426 effective Sept. 28, 1984, and applicable both with respect to claims filed after Sept. 28, 1984, and to claims pending on that date, and amendment by section 5(a)(1), (b) of Pub. L. 98–426 applicable with respect to any injury after Sept. 28, 1984, see section 28(a), (c) of Pub. L. 98–426, set out as a note under section 901 of this title.

EFFECTIVE DATE OF 1972 AMENDMENT

Amendment by Pub. L. 92–576 effective 30 days after Oct. 27, 1972, see section 22 of Pub. L. 92–576, set out as a note under section 902 of this title.

§ 906. Compensation

(a) Time for commencement

No compensation shall be allowed for the first three days of the disability, except the benefits provided for in section 907 of this title: *Provided, however*, That in case the injury results in disability of more than fourteen days the compensation shall be allowed from the date of the disability.

(b) Maximum rate of compensation

(1) Compensation for disability or death (other than compensation for death required by this chapter to be paid in a lump sum) shall not exceed an amount equal to 200 per centum of the applicable national average weekly wage, as determined by the Secretary under paragraph (3).

(2) Compensation for total disability shall not be less than 50 per centum of the applicable national average weekly wage determined by the Secretary under paragraph (3), except that if the employee's average weekly wages as computed under section 910 of this title are less than 50 per centum of such national average weekly wage, he shall receive his average weekly wages as compensation for total disability.

(3) As soon as practicable after June 30 of each year, and in any event prior to October 1 of such year, the Secretary shall determine the national average weekly wage for the three consecutive calendar quarters ending June 30. Such determination shall be the applicable national average weekly wage for the period beginning with October 1 of that year and ending with September 30 of the next year. The initial determination under this paragraph shall be made as soon as practicable after October 27, 1972.

(c) Applicability of determinations

Determinations under subsection (b)(3) of this section with respect to a period shall apply to employees or survivors currently receiving compensation for permanent total disability or death benefits during such period, as well as those newly awarded compensation during such period.

(Mar. 4, 1927, ch. 509, § 6, 44 Stat. 1426; June 24, 1948, ch. 623, § 1, 62 Stat. 602; July 26, 1956, ch. 735, § 1, 70 Stat. 654; Pub. L. 87–87, § 1, July 14, 1961, 75 Stat. 203; Pub. L. 92–576, §§ 4, 5(a), Oct. 27, 1972, 86 Stat. 1252; Pub. L. 98–426, § 6, Sept. 28, 1984, 98 Stat. 1641.)

AMENDMENTS

1984—Subsec. (b)(1). Pub. L. 98–426, § 6(a), substituted provisions setting a maximum compensation for disability on death of 200 per centum of the applicable national average weekly wage as determined by the Secretary for former provisions which had set out a schedule of progressive percentages of 125 per centum or $167, whichever is greater, during the period ending September 30, 1973, 150 per centum during the period beginning October 1, 1973, and ending September 30, 1974, 175 per centum during the period beginning October 1, 1974, and ending September 30, 1975, and 200 per centum beginning October 1, 1975.

Subsecs. (c), (d). Pub. L. 98–426, § 6(b), redesignated subsec. (d) as (c) and substituted "under subsection (b)(3) of this section" for "under this subsection". Former subsec. (c), which had directed that the maximum rate of compensation for a nonappropriated fund instrumentality employee be equal to 66⅔ per centum of the maximum rate of basic pay established for a Federal employee in grade GS–12 by section 5332 of title 5 and the minimum rate of compensation for such an employee be equal to 66⅔ per centum of the minimum rate of basic pay established for a Federal employee in grade GS–2 by such section, was struck out.

1972—Subsec. (a). Pub. L. 92–576, § 4, substituted "fourteen days" for "twenty-eight days".

Subsecs. (b) to (d). Pub. L. 92–576, § 5(a) added subsecs. (b) to (d) and struck out former subsec. (b) compensation for disability provisions which prescribed a $70 per week limit, a $18 per week minimum for total disability, and provided that if the employee's average weekly wages, as computed under section 910 of this title, were less than $18 per week he should receive as compensation for total disability his average weekly wages.

1961—Subsec. (b). Pub. L. 87–87 increased limitation on compensation for disability from "$54" to "$70" per week.

1956—Subsec. (a). Act July 26, 1956, substituted "three days" for "seven days" and "twenty-eight days" for "forty-nine days".

Subsec. (b). Act July 26, 1956, substituted "$54" for "$35", and "$18" for "$12" in two places.

1948—Subsec. (b). Act June 24, 1948, increased maximum weekly compensation from $25 to $35 and the minimum from $9 to $12 in two places.

EFFECTIVE DATE OF 1984 AMENDMENT

Amendment by section 6(a) of Pub. L. 98–426 applicable with respect to any death after Sept. 28, 1984, and amendment by section 6(b) of Pub. L. 98–426 applicable with respect to any injury, disability, or death after Sept. 28, 1984, see section 28(d), (f) of Pub. L. 98–426, set out as a note under section 901 of this title.

EFFECTIVE DATE OF 1972 AMENDMENT

Amendment by Pub. L. 92–576 effective 30 days after Oct. 27, 1972, see section 22 of Pub. L. 92–576, set out as a note under section 902 of this title.

EFFECTIVE DATE OF 1961 AMENDMENT

Section 4 of Pub. L. 87–87 provided that: "The amendments made by the foregoing provisions of this Act [amending this section and sections 909 and 914 of this title] shall become effective as to injuries or death sustained on or after the date of enactment [July 14, 1961]."

EFFECTIVE DATE OF 1956 AMENDMENT

Section 9 of act July 26, 1956, provided that: "The amendments made by the first section and sections 2, 4, and 5 of this Act [amending this section and sections 908, 909, and 914 of this title] shall be applicable only with respect to injuries and death occurring on or after the date of enactment of this Act [July 26, 1956] notwithstanding the provisions of the Act of December 2, 1942, as amended (42 U.S.C. sec. 1701 et seq.)."

EFFECTIVE DATE OF 1948 AMENDMENT

Section 6 of act June 24, 1948, provided that: "The provisions of this Act [amending this section and sections 908, 909, 910, and 914 of this title] shall be applicable only to injuries or deaths occurring on or after the effective date hereof [June 24, 1948]."

§907. Medical services and supplies

(a) General requirement

The employer shall furnish such medical, surgical, and other attendance or treatment, nurse and hospital service, medicine, crutches, and apparatus, for such period as the nature of the injury or the process of recovery may require.

(b) Physician selection; administrative supervision; change of physicians and hospitals

The employee shall have the right to choose an attending physician authorized by the Secretary to provide medical care under this chapter as hereinafter provided. If, due to the nature of the injury, the employee is unable to select his physician and the nature of the injury requires immediate medical treatment and care, the employer shall select a physician for him. The Secretary shall actively supervise the medical care rendered to injured employees, shall require periodic reports as to the medical care being rendered to injured employees, shall have authority to determine the necessity, character, and sufficiency of any medical aid furnished or to be furnished, and may, on his own initiative or at the request of the employer, order a change of physicians or hospitals when in his judgment such change is desirable or necessary in the interest of the employee or where the charges exceed those prevailing within the community for the same or similar services or exceed the provider's customary charges. Change of physicians at the request of employees shall be permitted in accordance with regulations of the Secretary.

(c) Physicians and health care providers not authorized to render medical care or provide medical services

(1)(A) The Secretary shall annually prepare a list of physicians and health care providers in each compensation district who are not authorized to render medical care or provide medical services under this chapter. The names of physicians and health care providers contained on the list required under this subparagraph shall be made available to employees and employers in each compensation district through posting and in such other forms as the Secretary may prescribe.

(B) Physicians and health care providers shall be included on the list of those not authorized to provide medical care and medical services pursuant to subparagraph (A) when the Secretary determines under this section, in accordance with the procedures provided in subsection (j) of this section, that such physician or health care provider—

(i) has knowingly and willfully made, or caused to be made, any false statement or misrepresentation of a material fact for use in a claim for compensation or claim for reimbursement of medical expenses under this chapter;

(ii) has knowingly and willfully submitted, or caused to be submitted, a bill or request for payment under this chapter containing a charge which the Secretary finds to be substantially in excess of the charge for the service, appliance, or supply prevailing within the community or in excess of the provider's customary charges, unless the Secretary finds there is good cause for the bill or request containing the charge;

(iii) has knowingly and willfully furnished a service, appliance, or supply which is determined by the Secretary to be substantially in excess of the need of the recipient thereof or to be of a quality which substantially fails to meet professionally recognized standards;

(iv) has been convicted under any criminal statute (without regard to pending appeal thereof) for fraudulent activities in connection with any Federal or State program for which payments are made to physicians or providers of similar services, appliances, or supplies; or

(v) has otherwise been excluded from participation in such program.

(C) Medical services provided by physicians or health care providers who are named on the list published by the Secretary pursuant to subparagraph (A) of this section shall not be reimbursable under this chapter; except that the Secretary shall direct the reimbursement of medical claims for services rendered by such physicians or health care providers in cases where the services were rendered in an emergency.

(D) A determination under subparagraph (B) shall remain in effect for a period of not less than three years and until the Secretary finds and gives notice to the public that there is reasonable assurance that the basis for the determination will not reoccur.

(E) A provider of a service, appliance, or supply shall provide to the Secretary such information and certification as the Secretary may require to assure that this subsection is enforced.

(2) Whenever the employer or carrier acquires knowledge of the employee's injury, through written notice or otherwise as prescribed by the chapter, the employer or carrier shall forthwith authorize medical treatment and care from a physician selected by an employee pursuant to subsection (b) of this section. An employee may not select a physician who is on the list required by paragraph (1) of this subsection. An employee may not change physicians after his initial choice unless the employer, carrier, or deputy commissioner has given prior consent for such change. Such consent shall be given in cases where an employee's initial choice was not of a specialist whose services are necessary for and appropriate to the proper care and treatment of the compensable injury or disease. In all other cases, consent may be given upon a showing of good cause for change.

(d) Request of treatment or services prerequisite to recovery of expenses; formal report of injury and treatment; suspension of compensation for refusal of treatment or examination; justification

(1) An employee shall not be entitled to recover any amount expended by him for medical or other treatment or services unless—

(A) the employer shall have refused or neglected a request to furnish such services and the employee has complied with subsections (b) and (c) of this section and the applicable regulations; or

(B) the nature of the injury required such treatment and services and the employer or his superintendent or foreman having knowledge of such injury shall have neglected to provide or authorize same.

(2) No claim for medical or surgical treatment shall be valid and enforceable against such employer unless, within ten days following the first treatment, the physician giving such treatment furnishes to the employer and the deputy commissioner a report of such injury or treatment, on a form prescribed by the Secretary. The Secretary may excuse the failure to furnish such report within the ten-day period whenever he finds it to be in the interest of justice to do so.

(3) The Secretary may, upon application by a party in interest, make an award for the reasonable value of such medical or surgical treatment so obtained by the employee.

(4) If at any time the employee unreasonably refuses to submit to medical or surgical treatment, or to an examination by a physician selected by the employer, the Secretary or administrative law judge may, by order, suspend the payment of further compensation during such time as such refusal continues, and no compensation shall be paid at any time during the period of such suspension, unless the circumstances justified the refusal.

(e) Physical examination; medical questions; report of physical impairment; review or reexamination; costs

In the event that medical questions are raised in any case, the Secretary shall have the power to cause the employee to be examined by a physician employed or selected by the Secretary and to obtain from such physician a report containing his estimate of the employee's physical impairment and such other information as may be appropriate. Any party who is dissatisfied with such report may request a review or reexamination of the employee by one or more different physicians employed or selected by the Secretary. The Secretary shall order such review or reexamination unless he finds that it is clearly unwarranted. Such review or reexamination shall be completed within two weeks from the date ordered unless the Secretary finds that because of extraordinary circumstances a longer period is required. The Secretary shall have the power in his discretion to charge the cost of examination or review under this subsection to the employer, if he is a self-insurer, or to the insurance company which is carrying the risk, in appropriate cases, or to the special fund in section 944 of this title.

(f) Place of examination; exclusion of physicians other than examining physician of Secretary; good cause for conclusions of other physicians respecting impairment; examination by employer's physician; suspension of proceedings and compensation for refusal of examination

An employee shall submit to a physical examination under subsection (e) of this section at such place as the Secretary may require. The place, or places, shall be designated by the Secretary and shall be reasonably convenient for the employee. No physician selected by the employer, carrier, or employee shall be present at or participate in any manner in such examination, nor shall conclusions of such physicians as to the nature or extent of impairment or the cause of impairment be available to the examining physician unless otherwise ordered, for good cause, by the Secretary. Such employer or carrier shall, upon request, be entitled to have the employee examined immediately thereafter and upon the same premises by a qualified physician or physicians in the presence of such physician as the employee may select, if any. Proceedings shall be suspended and no compensation shall be payable for any period during which the employee may refuse to submit to examination.

(g) Fees and charges for examinations, treatment, or service; limitation; regulations

All fees and other charges for medical examinations, treatment, or service shall be limited to such charges as prevail in the community for such treatment, and shall be subject to regulation by the Secretary. The Secretary shall issue regulations limiting the nature and extent of medical expenses chargeable against the employer without authorization by the employer or the Secretary.

(h) Third party liability

The liability of an employer for medical treatment as herein provided shall not be affected by the fact that his employee was injured through the fault or negligence of a third party not in the same employ, or that suit has been brought against such third party. The employer shall, however, have a cause of action against such third party to recover any amounts paid by him for such medical treatment in like manner as provided in section 933(b) of this title.

(i) Physicians' ineligibility for subsection (e) physical examinations and reviews because of workmen's compensation claim employment or fee acceptance or participation

Unless the parties to the claim agree, the Secretary shall not employ or select any physician for the purpose of making examinations or reviews under subsection (e) of this section who, during such employment, or during the period of two years prior to such employment, has been employed by, or accepted or participated in any fee relating to a workmen's compensation claim from any insurance carrier or any self-insurer.

(j) Procedure; judicial review

(1) The Secretary shall have the authority to make rules and regulations and to establish procedures, not inconsistent with the provisions of this chapter, which are necessary or appropriate

to carry out the provisions of subsection (c) of this section, including the nature and extent of the proof and evidence necessary for actions under this section and the methods of taking and furnishing such proof and evidence.

(2) Any decision to take action with respect to a physician or health care provider under this section shall be based on specific findings of fact by the Secretary. The Secretary shall provide notice of these findings and an opportunity for a hearing pursuant to section 556 of title 5 for a provider who would be affected by a decision under this section. A request for a hearing must be filed with the Secretary within thirty days after notice of the findings is received by the provider making such request. If a hearing is held, the Secretary shall, on the basis of evidence adduced at the hearing, affirm, modify, or reverse the findings of fact and proposed action under this section.

(3) For the purpose of any hearing, investigation, or other proceeding authorized or directed under this section, the provisions of section[1] 49 and 50 of title 15 (relating to the attendance of witnesses and the production of books, papers, and documents) shall apply to the jurisdiction, powers, and duties of the Secretary or any officer designated by him.

(4) Any physician or health care provider, after any final decision of the Secretary made after a hearing to which he was a party, irrespective of the amount in controversy, may obtain a review of such decision by a civil action commenced within sixty days after the mailing to him of notice of such decision, but the pendency of such review shall not operate as a stay upon the effect of such decision. Such action shall be brought in the court of appeals of the United States for the judicial circuit in which the plaintiff resides or has his principal place of business, or the Court of Appeals for the District of Columbia. As part of his answer, the Secretary shall file a certified copy of the transcript of the record of the hearing, including all evidence submitted in connection therewith. The findings of fact of the Secretary, if based on substantial evidence in the record as a whole, shall be conclusive.

(k) Refusal of treatment on religious grounds

(1) Nothing in this chapter prevents an employee whose injury or disability has been established under this chapter from relying in good faith on treatment by prayer or spiritual means alone, in accordance with the tenets and practice of a recognized church or religious denomination, by an accredited practitioner of such recognized church or religious denomination, and on nursing services rendered in accordance with such tenets and practice, without suffering loss or diminution of the compensation or benefits under this chapter. Nothing in this subsection shall be construed to except an employee from all physical examinations required by this chapter.

(2) If an employee refuses to submit to medical or surgical services solely because, in adherence to the tenets and practice of a recognized church or religious denomination, the employee relies upon prayer or spiritual means alone for healing, such employee shall not be considered to have unreasonably refused medical or surgical treatment under subsection (d) of this section.

(Mar. 4, 1927, ch. 509, §7, 44 Stat. 1427; May 26, 1934, ch. 354, §1, 48 Stat. 806; June 25, 1938, ch. 685, §§2, 3, 52 Stat. 1165; Pub. L. 86–757, Sept. 13, 1960, 74 Stat. 900; Pub. L. 92–576, §6, Oct. 27, 1972, 86 Stat. 1254; Pub. L. 98–426, §7, Sept. 28, 1984, 98 Stat. 1642.)

AMENDMENTS

1984—Subsec. (b). Pub. L. 98–426, §7(a), inserted "or where the charges exceed those prevailing within the community for the same or similar services or exceed the provider's customary charges".

Subsec. (c). Pub. L. 98–426, §7(b), substituted provisions respecting physicians and health care providers not authorized to render medical care or services under this chapter for former provision respecting physicians designated by the Secretary as authorized to render such care and whose names shall be available to employees through posting or in such other form as the Secretary may prescribe.

Subsec. (d). Pub. L. 98–426, §7(c), substituted provisions for the recovery by the employee of amounts spent on medical services which the employer failed to provide; for the procedure to be followed for recovery; and for suspension of any payments made if the employee unreasonably refuses to submit to treatment or examination for former provisions which required a request for treatment or services and the filing of a physician's report for recovery, and permitted the Secretary to excuse a failure to file a report when justified and to suspend payment if the employee unreasonably refuses treatment or examination.

Subsec. (j). Pub. L. 98–426, §7(d), added subsec. (j).

Subsec. (k). Pub. L. 98–426, §7(e), added subsec. (k).

1972—Subsec. (a). Pub. L. 92–576 reenacted provisions without change.

Subsec. (b). Pub. L. 92–576, substituted provisions for employee's choosing of an attending physician authorized by the Secretary, for prior provisions for such a choosing from a panel of physicians named by the employer and employer's selection of a physician for an employee when nature of injury requires immediate medical treatment and care for prior provisions for employer's selection of a physician from the panel; required Secretary's supervision of medical care rendered and periodic reports of medical care furnished; provided for initiative of the Secretary or the request of the employer for making change of hospitals or physicians and that the change be in the interest of the employee; provided for change of physicians pursuant to regulations of the Secretary; and deleted prior provision authorizing a second choice of a physician from the panel and for selection of physicians for specialized services.

Subsec. (c). Pub. L. 92–576 substituted provisions respecting Secretary's designation of physicians in community authorized to render medical care and posting of their names for prior provisions respecting deputy commissioner's determination of size of panel of physicians (named by employer) following statutory criteria and approval of their qualifications, and requirement of posting of names and addresses of physicians so as to afford reasonable notice.

Subsec. (d). Pub. L. 92–576 substituted the Secretary for the deputy commissioner as the person to exercise the various authorities, struck out introductory provisions respecting employer's failure to maintain a panel of physicians for examination purposes or to permit the employee to choose an attending physician from the panel and employee's procurement of treatment and services and selection of a physician at expense of employer, decreased from twenty to ten days the period within which to make the formal report of injury and treatment, and authorized suspension of compensation for refusal to submit to an examination by a physician of the employer.

[1] So in original. Probably should be "sections".

Subsec. (e). Pub. L. 92–576 substituted provisions respecting physical examination to determine medical questions by a physician employed or selected by the Secretary, such physician's report of the physical impairment, review or reexamination of the employee, and the charging of costs to an employer, who is a self-insurer, or the insurance company carrying the risk or the special fund for prior provisions respecting examination of employee by a physician selected by the deputy commissioner (who shall submit a report of the disability) whenever the deputy commissioner was of the opinion that the employer's physician was partial in his estimate of the degree of permanent disability or the extent of temporary disability and charging cost of examination to the employer, if he was a self-insurer, or to the insurance company which was carrying the risk when the physician's estimate was not impartial.

Subsec. (f). Pub. L. 92–576 added subsec. (f). Former subsec. (f) redesignated (g).

Subsec. (g). Pub. L. 92–576 redesignated former subsec. (f) as (g) and substituted "medical examinations, treatment, or service" for "such treatment or service", "charges as prevail in the community for such treatment" for "charges as prevail in the same community for similar treatment of injured persons of like standard of living", "regulation by the Secretary" for "regulation by the deputy commissioner", and prescribed issuance of regulations respecting medical expenses chargeable against employer. Former subsec. (g) redesignated (h).

Subsec. (h). Pub. L. 92–576 redesignated former subsec. (g) as (h) and inserted "that" before "suit".

Subsec. (i). Pub. L. 92–576 added subsec. (i).

1960—Subsec. (a). Pub. L. 86–757 designated first sentence as subsec. (a). Remainder of former subsec. (a) redesignated (d).

Subsecs. (b), (c). Pub. L. 86–757 added subsecs. (b) and (c). Former subsecs. (b) and (c) redesignated (e) and (f).

Subsec. (d). Pub. L. 86–757 redesignated all but first sentence of former subsec. (a) as (d), substituting "If the employer fails to provide the medical or other treatment, services, and supplies required to be furnished by subsec. (a) of this section, after request by the injured employee, or fails to maintain a panel of physicians as required by subsec. (c) of this section, or fails to permit the employee to choose an attending physician from such panel, such injured employee may procure such medical or other treatment, services, and supplies and select a physician to render treatment and services at the expense of the employer" for "If the employer fails to provide the same, after request by the injured employee, such injured employee may do so at the expense of the employer." Former subsec. (d) redesignated (g).

Subsecs. (e) to (g). Pub. L. 86–757 redesignated former subsecs. (b) to (d) as (e) to (g), striking out "unless and until notice of election to sue has been given as required by section 933(a) of this title" and "without the giving of such notice" before and after "or suit has been brought against such third party" in subsec. (g).

1938—Subsec. (a). Act June 25, 1938, §2, authorized deputy commissioner to excuse failure to furnish prescribed medical report.

Subsec. (d). Act June 25, 1938, §3, added subsec. (d).

1934—Subsec. (a). Act May 26, 1934, authorized deputy commissioner to suspend payment of compensation for refusal, without justification, to submit to medical or surgical treatment.

EFFECTIVE DATE OF 1984 AMENDMENT

Amendment by section 7(a), (e) of Pub. L. 98–426 effective 90 days after Sept. 28, 1984, and applicable both with respect to claims filed after such 90th day and to claims pending on such 90th day, and amendment by section 7(b)–(d) of Pub. L. 98–426 effective 90 days after Sept. 28, 1984, see section 28(b), (e)(2) of Pub. L. 98–426, set out as a note under section 901 of this title.

EFFECTIVE DATE OF 1972 AMENDMENT

Amendment by Pub. L. 92–576 effective 30 days after Oct. 27, 1972, see section 22 of Pub. L. 92–576, set out as a note under section 902 of this title.

CLAIMS FILED UNDER BLACK LUNG BENEFITS ACT

Section 28(h)(1) of Pub. L. 98–426 provided that: "The amendments made by section 7 of this Act [amending this section] shall not apply to claims filed under the Black Lung Benefits Act (30 U.S.C. 901 et seq.)."

§ 908. Compensation for disability

Compensation for disability shall be paid to the employee as follows:

(a) Permanent total disability: In case of total disability adjudged to be permanent 66⅔ per centum of the average weekly wages shall be paid to the employee during the continuance of such total disability. Loss of both hands, or both arms, or both feet, or both legs, or both eyes, or of any two thereof shall, in the absence of conclusive proof to the contrary, constitute permanent total disability. In all other cases permanent total disability shall be determined in accordance with the facts.

(b) Temporary total disability: In case of disability total in character but temporary in quality 66⅔ per centum of the average weekly wages shall be paid to the employee during the continuance thereof.

(c) Permanent partial disability: In case of disability partial in character but permanent in quality the compensation shall be 66⅔ per centum of the average weekly wages, which shall be in addition to compensation for temporary total disability or temporary partial disability paid in accordance with subsection (b) or subsection (e) of this section, respectively, and shall be paid to the employee, as follows:

(1) Arm lost, three hundred and twelve weeks' compensation.

(2) Leg lost, two hundred and eighty-eight weeks' compensation.

(3) Hand lost, two hundred and forty-four weeks' compensation.

(4) Foot lost, two hundred and five weeks' compensation.

(5) Eye lost, one hundred and sixty weeks' compensation.

(6) Thumb lost, seventy-five weeks' compensation.

(7) First finger lost, forty-six weeks' compensation.

(8) Great toe lost, thirty-eight weeks' compensation.

(9) Second finger lost, thirty weeks' compensation.

(10) Third finger lost, twenty-five weeks' compensation.

(11) Toe other than great toe lost, sixteen weeks' compensation.

(12) Fourth finger lost, fifteen weeks' compensation.

(13) Loss of hearing:

(A) Compensation for loss of hearing in one ear, fifty-two weeks.

(B) Compensation for loss of hearing in both ears, two-hundred weeks.

(C) An audiogram shall be presumptive evidence of the amount of hearing loss sustained as of the date thereof, only if (i) such audiogram was administered by a licensed or certified audiologist or a physician who is certified in otolaryngology, (ii) such audiogram, with the report thereon, was provided to the employee at the time it was administered, and (iii) no contrary audiogram made at that time is produced.

(D) The time for filing a notice of injury, under section 912 of this title, or a claim for compensation, under section 913 of this title, shall not begin to run in connection with any claim for loss of hearing under this section, until the employee has received an audiogram, with the accompanying report thereon, which indicates that the employee has suffered a loss of hearing.

(E) Determinations of loss of hearing shall be made in accordance with the guides for the evaluation of permanent impairment as promulgated and modified from time to time by the American Medical Association.

(14) Phalanges: Compensation for loss of more than one phalange of a digit shall be the same as for loss of the entire digit. Compensation for loss of the first phalange shall be one-half of the compensation for loss of the entire digit.

(15) Amputated arm or leg: Compensation for an arm or a leg, if amputated at or above the elbow or the knee, shall be the same as for a loss of the arm or leg; but, if amputated between the elbow and the wrist or the knee and the ankle, shall be the same as for loss of a hand or foot.

(16) Binocular vision or per centum of vision: Compensation for loss of binocular vision or for 80 per centum or more of the vision of an eye shall be the same as for loss of the eye.

(17) Two or more digits: Compensation for loss of two or more digits, or one or more phalanges of two or more digits, of a hand or foot may be proportioned to the loss of use of the hand or foot occasioned thereby, but shall not exceed the compensation for loss of a hand or foot.

(18) Total loss of use: Compensation for permanent total loss of use of a member shall be the same as for loss of the member.

(19) Partial loss or partial loss of use: Compensation for permanent partial loss or loss of use of a member may be for proportionate loss or loss of use of the member.

(20) Disfigurement: Proper and equitable compensation not to exceed $7,500 shall be awarded for serious disfigurement of the face, head, or neck or of other normally exposed areas likely to handicap the employee in securing or maintaining employment.

(21) Other cases: In all other cases in the class of disability, the compensation shall be 66⅔ per centum of the difference between the average weekly wages of the employee and the employee's wage-earning capacity thereafter in the same employment or otherwise, payable during the continuance of partial disability.

(22) In any case in which there shall be a loss of, or loss of use of, more than one member or parts of more than one member set forth in paragraphs (1) to (19) of this subsection, not amounting to permanent total disability, the award of compensation shall be for the loss of, or loss of use of, each such member or part thereof, which awards shall run consecutively, except that where the injury affects only two or more digits of the same hand or foot, paragraph (17) of this subsection shall apply.

(23) Notwithstanding paragraphs (1) through (22), with respect to a claim for permanent partial disability for which the average weekly wages are determined under section 910(d)(2) of this title, the compensation shall be 66⅔ per centum of such average weekly wages multiplied by the percentage of permanent impairment, as determined under the guides referred to in section 902(10) of this title, payable during the continuance of such impairment.

(d)(1) If an employee who is receiving compensation for permanent partial disability pursuant to subsection (c)(1)–(20) of this section dies from causes other than the injury, the total amount of the award unpaid at the time of death shall be payable to or for the benefit of his survivors, as follows:

(A) if the employee is survived only by a widow or widower, such unpaid amount of the award shall be payable to such widow or widower,

(B) if the employee is survived only by a child or children, such unpaid amount of the award shall be paid to such child or children in equal shares,

(C) if the employee is survived by a widow or widower and a child or children, such unpaid amount of the award shall be payable to such survivors in equal shares,

(D) if there be no widow or widower and no surviving child or children, such unpaid amount of the award shall be paid to the survivors specified in section 909(d) of this title (other than a wife, husband, or child); and the amount to be paid each such survivor shall be determined by multiplying such unpaid amount of the award by the appropriate percentage specified in section 909(d) of this title, but if the aggregate amount to which all such survivors are entitled, as so determined, is less than such unpaid amount of the award, the excess amount shall be divided among such survivors pro rata according to the amount otherwise payable to each under this subparagraph.

(2) Notwithstanding any other limitation in section 909 of this title, the total amount of any award for permanent partial disability pursuant to subsection (c)(1)–(20) of this section unpaid at time of death shall be payable in full in the appropriate distribution.

(3) An award for disability may be made after the death of the injured employee. Except where compensation is payable under subsection (c)(21) of this section if there be no survivors as prescribed in this section, then the compensation payable under this subsection shall be paid to the special fund established under section 944(a) of this title.

(e) Temporary partial disability: In case of temporary partial disability resulting in decrease of earning capacity the compensation shall be two-thirds of the difference between the injured employee's average weekly wages before the injury and his wage-earning capacity after the injury in the same or another employment, to be paid during the continuance of such disability, but shall not be paid for a period exceeding five years.

(f) Injury increasing disability:

(1) In any case in which an employee having an existing permanent partial disability suf-

fers injury, the employer shall provide compensation for such disability as is found to be attributable to that injury based upon the average weekly wages of the employee at the time of the injury. If following an injury falling within the provisions of subsection (c)(1)–(20) of this section, the employee is totally and permanently disabled, and the disability is found not to be due solely to that injury, the employer shall provide compensation for the applicable prescribed period of weeks provided for in that section for the subsequent injury, or for one hundred and four weeks, whichever is the greater, except that, in the case of an injury falling within the provisions of subsection (c)(13) of this section, the employer shall provide compensation for the lesser of such periods. In all other cases of total permanent disability or of death, found not to be due solely to that injury, of an employee having an existing permanent partial disability, the employer shall provide in addition to compensation under subsections (b) and (e) of this section, compensation payments or death benefits for one hundred and four weeks only. If following an injury falling within the provisions of subsection (c)(1)–(20) of this section, the employee has a permanent partial disability and the disability is found not to be due solely to that injury, and such disability is materially and substantially greater than that which would have resulted from the subsequent injury alone, the employer shall provide compensation for the applicable period of weeks provided for in that section for the subsequent injury, or for one hundred and four weeks, whichever is the greater, except that, in the case of an injury falling within the provisions of subsection (c)(13) of this section, the employer shall provide compensation for the lesser of such periods.

In all other cases in which the employee has a permanent partial disability, found not to be due solely to that injury, and such disability is materially and substantially greater than that which would have resulted from the subsequent injury alone, the employer shall provide in addition to compensation under subsections (b) and (e) of this section, compensation for one hundred and four weeks only.

(2)(A) After cessation of the payments for the period of weeks provided for herein, the employee or his survivor entitled to benefits shall be paid the remainder of the compensation that would be due out of the special fund established in section 944 of this title, except that the special fund shall not assume responsibility with respect to such benefits (and such payments shall not be subject to cessation) in the case of any employer who fails to comply with section 932(a) of this title.

(B) After cessation of payments for the period of weeks provided for in this subsection, the employer or carrier responsible for payment of compensation shall remain a party to the claim, retain access to all records relating to the claim, and in all other respects retain all rights granted under this chapter prior to cessation of such payments.

(3) Any request, filed after September 28, 1984, for apportionment of liability to the special fund established under section 944 of this title for the payment of compensation benefits, and a statement of the grounds therefore, shall be presented to the deputy commissioner prior to the consideration of the claim by the deputy commissioner. Failure to present such request prior to such consideration shall be an absolute defense to the special fund's liability for the payment of any benefits in connection with such claim, unless the employer could not have reasonably anticipated the liability of the special fund prior to the issuance of a compensation order.

(g) Maintenance for employees undergoing vocational rehabilitation: An employee who as a result of injury is or may be expected to be totally or partially incapacitated for a remunerative occupation and who, under the direction of the Secretary as provided by section 939(c) of this title, is being rendered fit to engage in a remunerative occupation, shall receive additional compensation necessary for his maintenance, but such additional compensation shall not exceed $25 a week. The expense shall be paid out of the special fund established in section 944 of this title.

(h) The wage-earning capacity of an injured employee in cases of partial disability under subsection (c)(21) of this section or under subsection (e) of this section shall be determined by his actual earnings if such actual earnings fairly and reasonably represent his wage-earning capacity: *Provided, however*, That if the employee has no actual earnings or his actual earnings do not fairly and reasonably represent his wage-earning capacity, the deputy commissioner may, in the interest of justice, fix such wage-earning capacity as shall be reasonable, having due regard to the nature of his injury, the degree of physical impairment, his usual employment, and any other factors or circumstances in the case which may affect his capacity to earn wages in his disabled condition, including the effect of disability as it may naturally extend into the future.

(i)(1) Whenever the parties to any claim for compensation under this chapter, including survivors benefits, agree to a settlement, the deputy commissioner or administrative law judge shall approve the settlement within thirty days unless it is found to be inadequate or procured by duress. Such settlement may include future medical benefits if the parties so agree. No liability of any employer, carrier, or both for medical, disability, or death benefits shall be discharged unless the application for settlement is approved by the deputy commissioner or administrative law judge. If the parties to the settlement are represented by counsel, then agreements shall be deemed approved unless specifically disapproved within thirty days after submission for approval.

(2) If the deputy commissioner disapproves an application for settlement under paragraph (1), the deputy commissioner shall issue a written statement within thirty days containing the reasons for disapproval. Any party to the settlement may request a hearing before an administrative law judge in the manner prescribed by this chapter. Following such hearing, the ad-

ministrative law judge shall enter an order approving or rejecting the settlement.

(3) A settlement approved under this section shall discharge the liability of the employer or carrier, or both. Settlements may be agreed upon at any stage of the proceeding including after entry of a final compensation order.

(4) The special fund shall not be liable for reimbursement of any sums paid or payable to an employee or any beneficiary under such settlement, or otherwise voluntarily paid prior to such settlement by the employer or carrier, or both.

(j)(1) The employer may inform a disabled employee of his obligation to report to the employer not less than semiannually any earnings from employment or self-employment, on such forms as the Secretary shall specify in regulations.

(2) An employee who—

(A) fails to report the employee's earnings under paragraph (1) when requested, or

(B) knowingly and willfully omits or understates any part of such earnings,

and who is determined by the deputy commissioner to have violated clause (A) or (B) of this paragraph, forfeits his right to compensation with respect to any period during which the employee was required to file such report.

(3) Compensation forfeited under this subsection, if already paid, shall be recovered by a deduction from the compensation payable to the employee in any amount and on such schedule as determined by the deputy commissioner.

(Mar. 4, 1927, ch. 509, §8, 44 Stat. 1427; May 26, 1934, ch. 354, §§2, 3, 48 Stat. 806; June 25, 1938, ch. 685, §§4, 5, 52 Stat. 1165; June 24, 1948, ch. 623, §2, 62 Stat. 602; July 26, 1956, ch. 735, §§2, 3, 70 Stat. 655; Pub. L. 92–576, §§5(c), 7, 9, 20(a), Oct. 27, 1972, 86 Stat. 1253, 1255, 1257, 1264; Pub. L. 98–426, §§8, 27(a)(2), Sept. 28, 1984, 98 Stat. 1644, 1654.)

AMENDMENTS

1984—Subsec. (c)(13). Pub. L. 98–426, §8(a), redesignated compensation for loss of hearing in one ear as subpar. (A) and for loss in both ears as subpar. (B) and added subpars. (C), (D), and (E) respecting establishing proof of hearing loss.

Subsec. (c)(20). Pub. L. 98–426, §8(b), substituted "$7,500" for "$3,500".

Subsec. (c)(21). Pub. L. 98–426, §8(c)(1), substituted "the average weekly wages of the employee and the employee's" for "his average weekly wages and his"; and struck out ", but subject to reconsideration of the degree of such impairment by the deputy commissioner on his own motion or upon application of any party in interest".

Subsec. (c)(23). Pub. L. 98–426, §8(c)(2), added par. (23).

Subsec. (d)(3), (4). Pub. L. 98–426, §8(d), redesignated par. (4) as par. (3). Former par. (3), which provided that if an employee who was receiving compensation for permanent partial disability pursuant to subsection (c)(21) of this section died from causes other than the injury, his survivors would receive death benefits as provided in section 909(b)–(g) of this title, except that the percentage figures therein would be applied to the weekly compensation payable to the employee at the time of his death multiplied by 1.5, rather than to his average weekly wages, was struck out.

Subsec. (f)(1). Pub. L. 98–426, §8(e)(1), inserted at end of second and fourth sentences ", except that, in the case of an injury falling within the provisions of section 908(c)(3) of this title, the employer shall provide compensation for the lesser of such periods".

Subsec. (f)(2)(A). Pub. L. 98–426, §8(e)(2), designated existing provisions of par. (2) as subpar. (A).

Pub. L. 98–426, §8(e)(3), inserted ", except that the special fund shall not assume responsibility with respect to such benefits (and such payments shall not be subject to cessation) in the case of any employer who fails to comply with section 932(a) of this title".

Subsec. (f)(2)(B). Pub. L. 98–426, §8(e)(4), added subpar. (B).

Subsec. (f)(3). Pub. L. 98–426, §8(e)(5), added par. (3).

Subsec. (g). Pub. L. 98–426, §27(a)(2), substituted "Secretary" for "commission". See Transfer of Functions note set out under section 902 of this title.

Subsec. (i)(1) to (3). Pub. L. 98–426, §8(f), substituted pars. (1) to (3) respecting procedures for approval of a settlement by the deputy commissioner or administrative law judge for former pars. (A) and (B) respecting settlements approved by the deputy commissioner or Secretary.

Subsec. (i)(4). Pub. L. 98–426, §8(g), added par. (4).

Subsec. (j). Pub. L. 98–426, §8(h), added subsec. (j).

1972—Subsec. (c)(20). Pub. L. 92–576, §7, included compensation for serious disfigurement of the neck and other normally exposed areas likely to handicap the employee in securing or maintaining employment.

Subsec. (d). Pub. L. 92–576, §5(c), in revising provisions substituted par. (1), subpars. (A) to (D) and pars. (2) to (4) for former provisions having an introductory par. and pars. (1) to (5), making the following changes:

Par. (1) incorporated former introductory par. providing for payments to survivors rather than for payments "for the benefit of the persons after"; subpar. (A) incorporated former par. (1) providing for a widower rather than dependent husband;

Subpar. (B) incorporated former par. (4), striking out reference to children under eighteen years, and providing for payment in equal shares;

Subpar. (C) incorporated former par. (2) for payment in equal shares rather than one half to surviving wife or dependent husband and one half to surviving child or children, substituting reference to "widow or widower" for "surviving wife or dependent husband", and striking out reference to "surviving" before "child or children";

Subpar. (D) added;

Pars. (2) and (3) added and former par. (3) struck out, such par. making it discretionary with the deputy commissioner to appoint a guardian for receipt of minor child's compensation; and

Par. (4) incorporated former par. (5), inserting provision for payment of compensation to the special fund except where payable under subsec. (c)(21) of this section.

Subsec. (f)(1). Pub. L. 92–576, §9(a) added par. (1) and struck out former par. (1) which provided that if an employee received an injury which of itself would only cause permanent partial disability but which, combined with a previous disability did in fact cause permanent total disability, the employer should provide compensation only for the disability caused by the subsequent injury, and proviso of such former par. (1) providing that in addition to compensation for the permanent partial disability, and after the cessation of the payments for the prescribed period of weeks, the employee should be paid the remainder of the compensation that would be due for permanent total disability and provision that additional compensation should be paid out of the special fund established in section 944 of this title. See par. (2) of this subsection.

Subsec. (f)(2). Pub. L. 92–576, §9, incorporated proviso of first sentence and second sentence of former par. (1) in provisions designated as par. (2) and struck out former par. (2) which stated that in all other cases in which, following a previous disability, an employee received an injury which was not covered by former par. (1), the employer should provide compensation only for the disability caused by the subsequent injury, and in determining compensation for the subsequent injury or for death resulting therefrom, the average weekly wages should be such sum as would reasonably represent the earning capacity of the employee at the time of the subsequent injury. See par. (1) of this subsection.

Subsec. (i). Pub. L. 92–576, § 20(a), designated existing provisions as subpar. (A), substituted "Whenever" for "In cases under subsection (c)(21) and subsection (e) of this section, whenever", "he may approve" for "he may, with the approval of the Secretary, approve", and "deputy commissioner" for "Secretary", and struck out after "*Provided*," where first appearing "That the sum so agreed upon shall be payable in installments as provided in section 914(b) of this title, which installments shall be subject to commutation under section 914(j) of this title; *And provided further*," and added subpar. (B).

1956—Subsec. (c). Act July 26, 1956, § 2, increased periods in schedule of compensation as follows:

Par. (1) Arm lost, increased from two hundred and eighty to three hundred and twelve weeks' compensation.

Par. (2) Leg lost, increased from two hundred and forty-eight to two hundred and eighty-eight weeks' compensation.

Par. (3) Hand lost, increased from two hundred and twelve to two hundred and forty-four weeks' compensation.

Par. (4) Foot lost, increased from one hundred and seventy-three weeks to two hundred and five weeks' compensation.

Par. (5) Eye lost, increased from one hundred and forty to one hundred and sixty weeks' compensation.

Par. (6) Thumb lost, increased from fifty-one to seventy-five weeks' compensation.

Par. (7) First finger lost, increased from twenty-eight to forty-six weeks' compensation.

Par. (8) Great toe lost, increased from twenty-six to thirty-eight weeks' compensation.

Par. (9) Second finger lost, increased from eighteen to thirty weeks' compensation.

Par. (10) Third finger lost, increased from seventeen to twenty-five weeks' compensation.

Par. (11) Toe other than great toe lost, increased from eight to sixteen weeks' compensation.

Par. (12) Fourth finger lost, increased from seven to fifteen weeks' compensation.

Subsec. (g). Act July 26, 1956, § 3, substituted "$25" for "$10".

1948—Subsec. (c). Act June 24, 1948, inserted in opening par. "or temporary partial disability", "or subsection (e)", and "respectively".

1938—Subsec. (c). Act June 25, 1938, § 4, in par. (22), inserted exception clause.

Subsecs. (h), (i). Act June 25, 1938, § 5 added subsecs. (h) and (i).

1934—Subsec. (c). Act May 26, 1934, § 2, inserted in opening par. "which shall be in addition to compensation for temporary total disability paid in accordance with subsection (b) of this section" and decreased periods in schedule of compensation of pars. (1) to (12).

Subsec. (c). Act May 26, 1934, § 3, substituted new par. (22), providing that "In any case in which there shall be a loss of, or loss of use of, more than one member or parts of more than one member set forth in paragraphs (1) to (19) of this subdivision, not amounting to permanent total disability, the award of compensation shall be for the loss of, or loss of use of, each such member or part thereof, which awards shall run consecutively.", for former provisions, providing that "In case of temporary total disability and permanent partial disability, both resulting from the same injury, if the temporary total disability continues for a longer period than the number of weeks set forth in the following schedule, the period of temporary total disability in excess of such number of weeks shall be added to the compensation period provided in this subdivision: Arm, thirty-two weeks; leg, forty weeks; hand, thirty-two weeks; foot, thirty-two weeks; eye, twenty weeks; thumb, twenty-four weeks; first finger, eighteen weeks; great toe, twelve weeks; second finger, twelve weeks; third finger, eight weeks; fourth finger, eight weeks; toe other than great toe, eight weeks.

"In any case resulting in loss or partial loss of arm, leg, hand, foot, eye, thumb, finger, or toe, where the temporary total disability does not extend beyond the periods above mentioned for such injury, compensation shall be limited to the schedule contained in this subdivision."

EFFECTIVE DATE OF 1984 AMENDMENT

Amendment by section 8(a), (c)(2), (e)(1), (2) of Pub. L. 98–426 effective Sept. 28, 1984, and applicable both with respect to claims filed after such date and to claims pending on such date, amendment by section 8(b) of Pub. L. 98–426 applicable with respect to any injury after Sept. 28, 1984, amendment by sections 8(c)(1), (e)(4), (5), (g), and 27(a)(2) of Pub. L. 98–426 effective Sept. 28, 1984, amendment by section 8(d) of Pub. L. 98–426 applicable with respect to any death after Sept. 28, 1984, amendment by section 8(f) of Pub. L. 98–426 effective 90 days after Sept. 28, 1984, and applicable both with respect to claims filed after such 90th day and to claims pending on such 90th day, and amendment by section 8(h) of Pub. L. 98–426 effective 90 days after Sept. 28, 1984, see section 28(a)–(e) of Pub. L. 98–426, set out as a note under section 901 of this title.

EFFECTIVE DATE OF 1972 AMENDMENT

Amendment by Pub. L. 92–576 effective 30 days after Oct. 27, 1972, see section 22 of Pub. L. 92–576, set out as a note under section 902 of this title.

EFFECTIVE DATE OF 1956 AMENDMENT

Amendment by act July 26, 1956, applicable only with respect to injuries and death occurring on or after July 26, 1956, see section 9 of act July 26, 1956, set out as a note under section 906 of this title.

EFFECTIVE DATE OF 1948 AMENDMENT

Amendment by act June 24, 1948, applicable to death or injuries occurring after June 24, 1948, see section 6 of act June 24, 1948, set out as a note under section 906 of this title.

§ 909. Compensation for death

If the injury causes death, the compensation therefore shall be known as a death benefit and shall be payable in the amount and to or for the benefit of the persons following:

(a) Reasonable funeral expenses not exceeding $3,000.

(b) If there be a widow or widower and no child of the deceased, to such widow or widower 50 per centum of the average wages of the deceased, during widowhood, or dependent widowerhood, with two years' compensation in one sum upon remarriage; and if there be a surviving child or children of the deceased, the additional amount of 16⅔ per centum of such wages for each such child; in case of the death or remarriage of such widow or widower, if there be one surviving child of the deceased employee, such child shall have his compensation increased to 50 per centum of such wages, and if there be more than one surviving child of the deceased employee, to such children, in equal parts, 50 per centum of such wages increased by 16⅔ per centum of such wages for each child in excess of one: *Provided*, That the total amount payable shall in no case exceed 66⅔ per centum of such wages. The deputy commissioner having jurisdiction over the claim may, in his discretion, require the appointment of a guardian for the purpose of receiving the compensation of a minor child. In the absence of such a requirement the appointment of a guardian for such purposes shall not be necessary.

(c) If there be one surviving child of the deceased, but no widow or widower, then for the support of such child 50 per centum of the wages of the deceased; and if there be more than one surviving child of the deceased, but no widow or dependent husband, then for the support of such children, in equal parts 50 per centum of such wages increased by 16⅔ per centum of such wages for each child in excess of one: *Provided*, That the total amount payable shall in no case exceed 66⅔ per centum of such wages.

(d) If there be no surviving wife or husband or child, or if the amount payable to a surviving wife or husband and to children shall be less in the aggregate than 66⅔ per centum of the average wages of the deceased; then for the support of grandchildren or brothers and sisters, if dependent upon the deceased at the time of the injury, and any other persons who satisfy the definition of the term "dependent" in section 152 of title 26, but are not otherwise eligible under this section, 20 per centum of such wages for the support of each such person during such dependency and for the support of each parent, or grandparent, of the deceased if dependent upon him at the time of the injury, 25 per centum of such wages during such dependency. But in no case shall the aggregate amount payable under this subsection exceed the difference between 66⅔ per centum of such wages and the amount payable as hereinbefore provided to widow or widower and for the support of surviving child or children.

(e) In computing death benefits, the average weekly wages of the deceased shall not be less than the national average weekly wage as prescribed in section 906(b) of this title, but—

(1) the total weekly benefits shall not exceed the lesser of the average weekly wages of the deceased or the benefit which the deceased employee would have been eligible to receive under section 906(b)(1) of this title; and

(2) in the case of a claim based on death due to an occupational disease for which the time of injury (as determined under section 910(i) of this title) occurs after the employee has retired, the total weekly benefits shall not exceed one fifty-second part of the employee's average annual earnings during the 52-week period preceding retirement.

(f) All questions of dependency shall be determined as of the time of the injury.

(g) Aliens: Compensation under this chapter to aliens not residents (or about to become nonresidents) of the United States or Canada shall be the same in amount as provided for residents, except that dependents in any foreign country shall be limited to surviving wife and child or children, or if there be no surviving wife or child or children, to surviving father or mother whom the employee has supported, either wholly or in part, for the period of one year prior to the date of the injury, and except that the Secretary may, at his option or upon the application of the insurance carrier shall, commute all future installments of compensation to be paid to such aliens by paying or causing to be paid to them one-half of the commuted amount of such future installments of compensation as determined by the Secretary.

(Mar. 4, 1927, ch. 509, §9, 44 Stat. 1429; June 25, 1938, ch. 685, §6, 52 Stat. 1166; June 24, 1948, ch. 623, §3, 62 Stat. 602; July 26, 1956, ch. 735, §4, 70 Stat. 655; Pub. L. 87–87, §2, July 14, 1961, 75 Stat. 203; Pub. L. 92–576, §§5(d), 10, 20(c)(2), Oct. 27, 1972, 86 Stat. 1253, 1257, 1265; Pub. L. 98–426, §§9, 27(a)(2), Sept. 28, 1984, 98 Stat. 1647, 1654.)

AMENDMENTS

1984—Pub. L. 98–426, §9(a), amended generally provision preceding subsec. (a), striking out "or if the employee who sustains permanent total disability due to the injury thereafter dies from causes other than the injury," after "injury causes death".

Subsec. (a). Pub. L. 98–426, §9(b), substituted "$3,000" for "$1,000".

Subsec. (e). Pub. L. 98–426, §9(c), amended subsec. (e) generally. Prior to amendment, subsec. (e) read as follows: "In computing death benefits the average weekly wages of the deceased shall be considered to have been not less than the applicable national average weekly wage as prescribed in section 906(b) of this title but the total weekly benefits shall not exceed the average weekly wages of the deceased".

Subsec. (g). Pub. L. 98–426, §27(a)(2), substituted "Secretary" for "commission". See Transfer of Functions note set out under section 902 of this title.

1972—Pub. L. 92–576, §5(d), added to introductory provision that the compensation shall be known as a death benefit if the employee who sustains permanent total disability due to the injury thereafter dies from causes other than the injury.

Subsec. (a). Pub. L. 92–576, §10(a), substituted "$1,000" for "$400".

Subsec. (b). Pub. L. 92–576, §§10(b), 20(c)(2), substituted "50" for "35" per centum in three places and "16⅔" for "15" per centum in two places and "widow or widower" for "surviving wife or dependent husband" in three places.

Subsec. (c). Pub. L. 92–576, §§10(b), 20(c)(2), substituted "50" for "35" per centum in two places and "16⅔" for "15" per centum and "widow or widower" for "surviving wife or dependent husband".

Subsec. (d). Pub. L. 92–576, §§10(c), 20(c)(2), in first sentence, substituted "husband or child," and "husband" for "dependent husband or child" and "dependent husband" and "20" for "15" per centum, and inserted "and any other persons who satisfy the definition of the term 'dependent' in section 152 of title 26, but are not otherwise eligible under this section" after "time of the injury," and "during such dependency" after "support of each such person", and in second sentence, substituted "widow or widower" for "surviving wife or dependent husband", respectively.

Subsec. (e). Pub. L. 92–576, §10(d), substituted "less than the applicable national average weekly wage as prescribed in section 906(b) of this title but the total weekly benefits shall not exceed the average weekly wages of the deceased" for "more than $105 nor less than $27 but the total weekly compensation shall not exceed the weekly wages of the deceased".

1961—Subsec. (e). Pub. L. 87–87 increased the maximum limitation with respect to average weekly wages from "$81" to "$105" in the computation of death benefits.

1956—Subsec. (e). Act July 26, 1956, substituted "$81" for "$52.50" and "$27" for "$18".

1948—Subsec. (a). Act June 24, 1948, increased funeral expenses from $200 to $400.

Subsec. (b). Act June 24, 1948, increased benefits to children of deceased workmen from 10 percent to 15 percent.

Subsec. (c). Act June 24, 1948, increased death benefits of orphaned children from 15 percent to 35 percent.

Subsec. (e). Act June 24, 1948, correlated basis for computing death benefits with basis for computing disability benefits under section 906(b) of this title.

1938—Subsecs. (b) to (d). Act June 25, 1938, struck out references to children as being under eighteen years of age.

EFFECTIVE DATE OF 1984 AMENDMENT

Amendment by section 9 of Pub. L. 98–426 applicable with respect to any death after Sept. 28, 1984, and amendment by section 27(a)(2) of Pub. L. 98–426 effective Sept. 28, 1984, see section 28(d), (e)(1) of Pub. L. 98–426, set out as a note under section 901 of this title.

EFFECTIVE DATE OF 1972 AMENDMENT

Amendment by section 20(c)(2) of Pub. L. 92–576 applicable only with respect to deaths or injuries occurring after Oct. 27, 1972, see section 20(c)(3) of Pub. L. 92–576, set out as a note under section 902 of this title.

Amendment by Pub. L. 92–576 effective 30 days after Oct. 27, 1972, see section 22 of Pub. L. 92–576, set out as a note under section 902 of this title.

EFFECTIVE DATE OF 1961 AMENDMENT

Amendment by Pub. L. 87–87 effective as to death sustained on or after July 14, 1961, see section 4 of Pub. L. 87–87, set out as a note under section 906 of this title.

EFFECTIVE DATE OF 1956 AMENDMENT

Amendment by act July 26, 1956, applicable only with respect to injuries and death occurring on or after July 26, 1956, see section 9 of act July 26, 1956, set out as a note under section 906 of this title.

EFFECTIVE DATE OF 1948 AMENDMENT

Amendment by act June 24, 1948, applicable to death or injuries occurring after June 24, 1948, see section 6 of act June 24, 1948, set out as a note under section 906 of this title.

§910. Determination of pay

Except as otherwise provided in this chapter, the average weekly wage of the injured employee at the time of the injury shall be taken as the basis upon which to compute compensation and shall be determined as follows:

(a) If the injured employee shall have worked in the employment in which he was working at the time of the injury, whether for the same or another employer, during substantially the whole of the year immediately preceding his injury, his average annual earnings shall consist of three hundred times the average daily wage or salary for a six-day worker and two hundred and sixty times the average daily wage or salary for a five-day worker, which he shall have earned in such employment during the days when so employed.

(b) If the injured employee shall not have worked in such employment during substantially the whole of such year, his average annual earnings, if a six-day worker, shall consist of three hundred times the average daily wage or salary, and, if a five-day worker, two hundred and sixty times the average daily wage or salary, which an employee of the same class working substantially the whole of such immediately preceding year in the same or in similar employment in the same or a neighboring place shall have earned in such employment during the days when so employed.

(c) If either of the foregoing methods of arriving at the average annual earnings of the injured employee cannot reasonably and fairly be applied, such average annual earnings shall be such sum as, having regard to the previous earnings of the injured employee in the employment in which he was working at the time of the injury, and of other employees of the same or most similar class working in the same or most similar employment in the same or neighboring locality, or other employment of such employee, including the reasonable value of the services of the employee if engaged in self-employment, shall reasonably represent the annual earning capacity of the injured employee.

(d)(1) The average weekly wages of an employee shall be one fifty-second part of his average annual earnings.

(2) Notwithstanding paragraph (1), with respect to any claim based on a death or disability due to an occupational disease for which the time of injury (as determined under subsection (i) of this section) occurs—

(A) within the first year after the employee has retired, the average weekly wages shall be one fifty-second part of his average annual earnings during the 52-week period preceding retirement; or

(B) more than one year after the employee has retired, the average weekly wage shall be deemed to be the national average weekly wage (as determined by the Secretary pursuant to section 906(b) of this title) applicable at the time of the injury.

(e) If it be established that the injured employee was a minor when injured, and that under normal conditions his wages should be expected to increase during the period of disability the fact may be considered in arriving at his average weekly wages.

(f) Effective October 1 of each year, the compensation or death benefits payable for permanent total disability or death arising out of injuries subject to this chapter shall be increased by the lesser of—

(1) a percentage equal to the percentage (if any) by which the applicable national weekly wage for the period beginning on such October 1, as determined under section 906(b) of this title, exceeds the applicable national average weekly wage, as so determined, for the period beginning with the preceding October 1; or

(2) 5 per centum.

(g) The weekly compensation after adjustment under subsection (f) of this section shall be fixed at the nearest dollar. No adjustment of less than $1 shall be made, but in no event shall compensation or death benefits be reduced.

(h)(1) Not later than ninety days after October 27, 1972, the compensation to which an employee or his survivor is entitled due to total permanent disability or death which commenced or occurred prior to October 27, 1972, shall be adjusted. The amount of such adjustment shall be determined in accordance with regulations of the Secretary by designating as the employee's average weekly wage the applicable national average weekly wage determined under section 906(b) of this title and (A) computing the compensation to which such employee or survivor would be entitled if the disabling injury or death had occurred on the day following October 27, 1972, and (B) subtracting therefrom the compensation to which such employee or survivor was entitled on October 27, 1972; except that no such employee or survivor shall receive total compensation amounting to less than that to which he was entitled on October 27, 1972. Notwithstanding the foregoing sentence, where such an employee or his survivor was awarded compensation as the result of death or permanent total disability at less than the maximum rate that was provided in this chapter at the time of the injury which resulted in the death or disability, then his average weekly wage shall be determined by increasing his average weekly wage at the time of such injury by the percentage which the applicable national average weekly wage has increased between the year in which the injury occurred and the first day of the first month following October 27, 1972. Where such injury occurred prior to 1947, the Secretary shall determine, on the basis of such economic data as he deems relevant, the amount by which the employee's average weekly wage shall be increased for the pre-1947 period.

(2) Fifty per centum of any additional compensation or death benefit paid as a result of the adjustment required by paragraphs (1) and (3) of this subsection shall be paid out of the special fund established under section 944 of this title, and 50 per centum shall be paid from appropriations.

(3) For the purposes of subsections (f) and (g) of this section an injury which resulted in permanent total disability or death which occurred prior to October 27, 1972, shall be considered to have occurred on the day following such date.

(i) For purposes of this section with respect to a claim for compensation for death or disability due to an occupational disease which does not immediately result in death or disability, the time of injury shall be deemed to be the date on which the employee or claimant becomes aware, or in the exercise of reasonable diligence or by reason of medical advice should have been aware, of the relationship between the employment, the disease, and the death or disability.

(Mar. 4, 1927, ch. 509, §10, 44 Stat. 1431; June 24, 1948, ch. 623, §4, 62 Stat. 603; Pub. L. 92–576, §11, Oct. 27, 1972, 86 Stat. 1258; Pub. L. 98–426, §10, Sept. 28, 1984, 98 Stat. 1647.)

AMENDMENTS

1984—Subsec. (d). Pub. L. 98–426, §10(a)(1), designated existing provisions as par. (1) and added par. (2).

Subsec. (f). Pub. L. 98–426, §10(b), substituted "subject to this chapter" for "sustained after October 27, 1972," and inserted "the lesser of—" after "by" in introductory language, designated balance of existing provisions as par. (1), substituted "; or" for a period at end of par. (1), and added par. (2).

Subsec. (i). Pub. L. 98–426, §10(a)(2), added subsec. (i).

1972—Subsecs. (f) to (h). Pub. L. 92–576 added subsecs. (f) to (h).

1948—Subsec. (a). Act June 24, 1948, included a factor (a 260 multiplier) so as to make this subsec. useful in 5-day week employments.

Subsec. (b). Act June 24, 1948, included the new factor (a 260 multiplier) to make this subsec. consistent with subsec. (a).

Subsec. (c). Act June 24, 1948, permitted the inclusion of all earnings of the injured workman in determining the employee's annual earning capacity.

EFFECTIVE DATE OF 1984 AMENDMENT

Amendment by section 10(a) of Pub. L. 98–426 effective Sept. 28, 1984, and applicable both with respect to claims filed after such date and to claims pending on such date, and amendment by section 10(b) of Pub. L. 98–426 effective Sept. 28, 1984, see section 28(a), (e)(1) of Pub. L. 98–426, set out as a note under section 901 of this title.

EFFECTIVE DATE OF 1972 AMENDMENT

Amendment by Pub. L. 92–576 effective 30 days after Oct. 27, 1972, see section 22 of Pub. L. 92–576, set out as a note under section 902 of this title.

EFFECTIVE DATE OF 1948 AMENDMENT

Amendment by act June 24, 1948, applicable to death or injuries occurring after June 24, 1948, see section 6 of act June 24, 1948, set out as a note under section 906 of this title.

§911. Guardian for minor or incompetent

The deputy commissioner may require the appointment by a court of competent jurisdiction, for any person who is mentally incompetent or a minor, of a guardian or other representative to receive compensation payable to such person under this chapter and to exercise the powers granted to or to perform the duties required of such person under this chapter.

(Mar. 4, 1927, ch. 509, §11, 44 Stat. 1431.)

§912. Notice of injury or death

(a) Time limitation

Notice of an injury or death in respect of which compensation is payable under this chapter shall be given within thirty days after the date of such injury or death, or thirty days after the employee or beneficiary is aware, or in the exercise of reasonable diligence or by reason of medical advice should have been aware, of a relationship between the injury or death and the employment, except that in the case of an occupational disease which does not immediately result in a disability or death, such notice shall be given within one year after the employee or claimant becomes aware, or in the exercise of reasonable diligence or by reason of medical advice should have been aware, of the relationship between the employment, the disease, and the death or disability. Notice shall be given (1) to the deputy commissioner in the compensation district in which the injury or death occurred, and (2) to the employer.

(b) Form and content

Such notice shall be in writing, shall contain the name and address of the employee and a statement of the time, place, nature, and cause of the injury or death, and shall be signed by the employee or by some person on his behalf, or in case of death, by any person claiming to be entitled to compensation for such death or by a person on his behalf.

(c) Delivery requirements

Notice shall be given to the deputy commissioner by delivering it to him or sending it by mail addressed to his office, and to the employer by delivering it to him or by sending it by mail addressed to him at his last known place of business. If the employer is a partnership, such notice may be given to any partner, or if a corporation, such notice may be given to any agent or officer thereof upon whom legal process may be served or who is in charge of the business in the place where the injury occurred. Each employer shall designate those agents or other responsible officials to receive such notice, except that the employer shall designate as its representatives individuals among first line supervisors, local plant management, and personnel office officials. Such designations shall be made in accordance with regulations prescribed by the Secretary and the employer shall notify his employees and the Secretary of such designation in a manner prescribed by the Secretary in regulations.

(d) Failure to give notice

Failure to give such notice shall not bar any claim under this chapter (1) if the employer (or his agent or agents or other responsible official or officials designated by the employer pursuant to subsection (c) of this section) or the carrier had knowledge of the injury or death, (2) the deputy commissioner determines that the employer or carrier has not been prejudiced by failure to give such notice, or (3) if the deputy commissioner excuses such failure on the ground that (i) notice, while not given to a responsible official designated by the employer pursuant to subsection (c) of this section, was given to an official of the employer or the employer's insurance carrier, and that the employer or carrier was not prejudiced due to the failure to provide notice to a responsible official designated by the employer pursuant to subsection (c) of this section, or (ii) for some satisfactory reason such notice could not be given; nor unless objection to such failure is raised before the deputy commissioner at the first hearing of a claim for compensation in respect of such injury or death.

(Mar. 4, 1927, ch. 509, §12, 44 Stat. 1431; Pub. L. 92–576, §12(a), Oct. 27, 1972, 86 Stat. 1259; Pub. L. 98–426, §11, Sept. 28, 1984, 98 Stat. 1648.)

AMENDMENTS

1984—Subsec. (a). Pub. L. 98–426, §11(a), inserted a comma after "aware" and "only by reason of medical advice" after "diligence" and inserted "except that in the case of an occupational disease which does not immediately result in a disability or death, such notice shall be given within one year after the employee or claimant becomes aware, or in the exercise of reasonable diligence or by reason of medical advice should have been aware, of the relationship between the employment, the disease, and the death or disability" in first sentence.

Subsec. (c). Pub. L. 98–426, §11(b), inserted at end "Each employer shall designate those agents or other responsible officials to receive such notice, except that the employer shall designate as its representatives individuals among first line supervisors, local plant management, and personnel office officials. Such designations shall be made in accordance with regulations prescribed by the Secretary and the employer shall notify his employees and the Secretary of such designation in a manner prescribed by the Secretary in regulations."

Subsec. (d)(1). Pub. L. 98–426, §11(c), substituted "(or his agent or agents or other responsible official or officials designated by the employer pursuant to subsection (c) of this section)" for "(or his agent in charge of the business in the place where the injury occurred)", substituted "injury or death, (2)" for "injury or death and", and substituted "or (3)" for "or (2)".

Pub. L. 98–426, §11(c)(4), inserted "(i) notice, while not given to a responsible official designated by the employer pursuant to subsection (c) of this section, was given to an official of the employer or the employer's insurance carrier, and that the employer or carrier was not prejudiced due to the failure to provide notice to a responsible official designated by the employer pursuant to subsection (c) of this title, or (ii)".

1972—Subsec. (a). Pub. L. 92–576 provided for notice of an injury or death within thirty days after the employee or beneficiary is aware or in the exercise of reasonable diligence should have been aware of a relationship between the injury or death and the employment.

EFFECTIVE DATE OF 1984 AMENDMENT

Amendment by section 11(a) of Pub. L. 98–426 effective Sept. 28, 1984, and applicable both with respect to claims filed after such date and to claims pending on such date, and amendment by section 11(b), (c) of Pub. L. 98–426 effective 90 days after Sept. 28, 1984, and applicable both with respect to claims filed after such 90th day and to claims pending on such 90th day, see section 28(a), (b) of Pub. L. 98–426, set out as a note under section 901 of this title.

EFFECTIVE DATE OF 1972 AMENDMENT

Amendment by Pub. L. 92–576 effective 30 days after Oct. 27, 1972, see section 22 of Pub. L. 92–576, set out as a note under section 902 of this title.

§913. Filing of claims

(a) Time to file

Except as otherwise provided in this section, the right to compensation for disability or death under this chapter shall be barred unless a claim therefore is filed within one year after the injury or death. If payment of compensation has been made without an award on account of such injury or death, a claim may be filed within one year after the date of the last payment. Such claim shall be filed with the deputy commissioner in the compensation district in which such injury or death occurred. The time for filing a claim shall not begin to run until the employee or beneficiary is aware, or by the exercise of reasonable diligence should have been aware, of the relationship between the injury or death and the employment.

(b) Failure to file

(1) Notwithstanding the provisions of subsection (a) of this section failure to file a claim within the period prescribed in such subsection shall not be a bar to such right unless objection to such failure is made at the first hearing of such claim in which all parties in interest are given reasonable notice and opportunity to be heard.

(2) Notwithstanding the provisions of subsection (a) of this section, a claim for compensation for death or disability due to an occupational disease which does not immediately result in such death or disability shall be timely if filed within two years after the employee or claimant becomes aware, or in the exercise of reasonable diligence or by reason of medical advice should have been aware, of the relationship between the employment, the disease, and the death or disability, or within one year of the date of the last payment of compensation, whichever is later.

(c) Effect on incompetents and minors

If a person who is entitled to compensation under this chapter is mentally incompetent or a minor, the provisions of subsection (a) of this section shall not be applicable so long as such person has no guardian or other authorized representative, but shall be applicable in the case of a person who is mentally incompetent or a minor from the date of appointment of such guardian or other representative, or in the case of a minor, if no guardian is appointed before he becomes of age, from the date he becomes of age.

(d) Tolling provision

Where recovery is denied to any person, in a suit brought at law or in admiralty to recover damages in respect of injury or death, on the ground that such person was an employee and that the defendant was an employer within the meaning of this chapter and that such employer had secured compensation to such employee under this chapter, the limitation of time prescribed in subsection (a) of this section shall begin to run only from the date of termination of such suit.

(Mar. 4, 1927, ch. 509, §13, 44 Stat. 1432; Pub. L. 92–576, §12(b), Oct. 27, 1972, 86 Stat. 1259; Pub. L. 98–426, §12, Sept. 28, 1984, 98 Stat. 1649.)

AMENDMENTS

1984—Subsec. (b). Pub. L. 98–426 designated existing provisions as par. (1) and added par. (2).

1972—Subsec. (a). Pub. L. 92–576 inserted "Except as otherwise provided in this section" and provided that the time for filing a claim shall not begin to run until the employee or beneficiary is aware, or by the exercise of reasonable diligence should have been aware, of the relationship between the injury or death and the employment.

EFFECTIVE DATE OF 1984 AMENDMENT

Amendment by Pub. L. 98–426 effective Sept. 28, 1984, and applicable both with respect to claims filed after such date and to claims pending on such date, see section 28(a) of Pub. L. 98–426, set out as a note under section 901 of this title.

EFFECTIVE DATE OF 1972 AMENDMENT

Amendment by Pub. L. 92–576 effective 30 days after Oct. 27, 1972, see section 22 of Pub. L. 92–576, set out as a note under section 902 of this title.

§914. Payment of compensation

(a) Manner of payment

Compensation under this chapter shall be paid periodically, promptly, and directly to the person entitled thereto, without an award, except where liability to pay compensation is controverted by the employer.

(b) Period of installment payments

The first installment of compensation shall become due on the fourteenth day after the employer has been notified pursuant to section 912 of this title, or the employer has knowledge of the injury or death, on which date all compensation then due shall be paid. Thereafter compensation shall be paid in installments, semimonthly, except where the deputy commissioner determines that payment in installments should be made monthly or at some other period.

(c) Notification of commencement or suspension of payment

Upon making the first payment, and upon suspension of payment for any cause, the employer shall immediately notify the deputy commissioner, in accordance with a form prescribed by the Secretary, that payment of compensation has begun or has been suspended, as the case may be.

(d) Right to compensation controverted

If the employer controverts the right to compensation he shall file with the deputy commissioner on or before the fourteenth day after he has knowledge of the alleged injury or death, a notice, in accordance with a form prescribed by the Secretary stating that the right to compensation is controverted, the name of the claimant, the name of the employer, the date of the alleged injury or death, and the grounds upon which the right to compensation is controverted.

(e) Additional compensation for overdue installment payments payable without award

If any installment of compensation payable without an award is not paid within fourteen days after it becomes due, as provided in subsection (b) of this section, there shall be added to such unpaid installment an amount equal to 10 per centum thereof, which shall be paid at the same time as, but in addition to, such installment, unless notice is filed under subsection (d) of this section, or unless such nonpayment is excused by the deputy commissioner after a showing by the employer that owing to conditions over which he had no control such installment could not be paid within the period prescribed for the payment.

(f) Additional compensation for overdue installment payments payable under terms of award

If any compensation, payable under the terms of an award, is not paid within ten days after it becomes due, there shall be added to such unpaid compensation an amount equal to 20 per centum thereof, which shall be paid at the same time as, but in addition to, such compensation, unless review of the compensation order making such award is had as provided in section 921 of this title and an order staying payment has been issued by the Board or court.

(g) Notice of payment; penalty

Within sixteen days after final payment of compensation has been made, the employer shall send to the deputy commissioner a notice, in accordance with a form prescribed by the Secretary, stating that such final payment has been made, the total amount of compensation paid, the name of the employee and of any other person to whom compensation has been paid, the date of the injury or death, and the date to which compensation has been paid. If the employer fails to so notify the deputy commissioner within such time the Secretary shall assess against such employer a civil penalty in the amount of $100.

(h) Investigations, examinations, and hearings for controverted, stopped, or suspended payments

The deputy commissioner (1) may upon his own initiative at any time in a case in which payments are being made without an award, and (2) shall in any case where right to compensation is controverted, or where payments of compensation have been stopped or suspended, upon receipt of notice from any person entitled to compensation, or from the employer, that the right to compensation is controverted, or that payments of compensation have been stopped or suspended, make such investigations, cause such medical examinations to be made, or hold such hearings, and take such further action as he considers will properly protect the rights of all parties.

(i) Deposit by employer

Whenever the deputy commissioner deems it advisable he may require any employer to make a deposit with the Treasurer of the United States to secure the prompt and convenient payment of such compensation, and payments therefrom upon any awards shall be made upon order of the deputy commissioner.

(j) Reimbursement for advance payments

If the employer has made advance payments of compensation, he shall be entitled to be reimbursed out of any unpaid installment or installments of compensation due.

(k) Receipt for payment

An injured employee, or in case of death his dependents or personal representative, shall give receipts for payment of compensation to the employer paying the same and such employer shall produce the same for inspection by the deputy commissioner, whenever required.

(Mar. 4, 1927, ch. 509, §14, 44 Stat. 1432; May 26, 1934, ch. 354, §4, 48 Stat. 807; June 25, 1938, ch. 685, §7, 52 Stat. 1167; June 24, 1948, ch. 623, §5, 62 Stat. 603; July 26, 1956, ch. 735, §5, 70 Stat. 655; Pub. L. 87–87, §3, July 14, 1961, 75 Stat. 203; Pub. L. 92–576, §§5(e), 15(d), Oct. 27, 1972, 86 Stat. 1254, 1262; Pub. L. 98–426, §§13, 27(a)(2), Sept. 28, 1984, 98 Stat. 1649, 1654.)

AMENDMENTS

1984—Subsec. (b). Pub. L. 98–426, §13(a), substituted "employer has been notified pursuant to section 912 of this title, or the employer," for "employer".

Subsecs. (c), (d), (g). Pub. L. 98–426, §27(a)(2), substituted "Secretary" for "commission". See Transfer of Functions note set out under section 902 of this title.

Subsecs. (j) to (*l*). Pub. L. 98–426, §13(b), redesignated subsecs. (k) and (*l*) as (j) and (k), respectively, and struck out former subsec. (j) which provided that whenever the deputy commissioner determines that it was in the interest of justice, the liability of the employer for compensation, or any part thereof as determined by the deputy commissioner with the approval of the Secretary, could be discharged by the payment of a lump sum equal to the present value of future compensation payments commuted, computed at 4 per centum true discount compounded annually, that the probability of the death of the injured employee or other person entitled to compensation before the expiration of the period during which he was entitled to compensation would be determined in accordance with the American Experience Table of Mortality, and the probability of the remarriage of the surviving wife would be determined in accordance with the remarriage tables of the Dutch Royal Insurance Institution, and that the probability of the happening of any other contingency affecting the amount or duration of the compensation would be disregarded, was struck out.

1972—Subsec. (f). Pub. L. 92–576, §15(d), substituted "order staying payment has been issued by the Board or court" for "interlocutory injunction staying payments is allowed by the court as provided therein".

Subsec. (m). Pub. L. 92–576, §5(e), repealed subsec. (m) limiting aggregate money allowance for an injury under this chapter to $24,000, making the limitation inapplicable to cases of permanent total disability or death, and providing that in applying the limitation there shall not be taken into account any amount payable under section 908(g) of this title for maintenance during rehabilitation or any amount of additional compensation required to be paid under this section for delay or default in the payment of compensation or any amount accruing as interest upon defaulted compensation collectible under section 918 of this title.

1961—Subsec. (m). Pub. L. 87–87 increased limitation on total money allowance as compensation for injury from "$17,280" to "$24,000".

1956—Subsec. (m). Act July 26, 1956, provided for maximum money allowance of $17,280 in lieu of total compensation of $11,000, struck out additional former limit of $10,000 for disabilities compensable under section 908(c)(21) of this title, and inserted provision excepting from $17,280 limitation, amounts payable under section 908(g) of this title for maintenance during rehabilitation, and amounts payable under this section for delay or default in payment of compensation or interest collectible under section 918 of this title.

1948—Subsec. (m). Act June 24, 1948, increased overall statutory maximum limitation upon compensation for disability from $7,500 to $11,000, and fixed a sublimitation of $10,000 upon that particular compensation for permanent partial disability which is payable when the case is classified as one in which compensation shall be payable under section 908(c)(21) of this title, but neither limitation shall apply for permanent total disability or death.

1938—Subsec. (f). Act June 25, 1938, inserted "and an interlocutory injunction staying payments is allowed by the court as provided therein".

1934—Subsec. (j). Act May 26, 1934, substituted "in the interest of justice" for "for the best interests of a person entitled to compensation", inserted "or any part thereof as determined by the deputy commissioner with the approval of the Commission", and inserted provision for determining probability of remarriage.

EFFECTIVE DATE OF 1984 AMENDMENT

Amendment by section 13 of Pub. L. 98–426 effective 90 days after Sept. 28, 1984, and applicable both with respect to claims filed after such 90th day and to claims pending on such 90th day, and amendment by section 27(a)(2) of Pub. L. 98–426 effective Sept. 28, 1984, see section 28(b), (e)(1) of Pub. L. 98–426, set out as a note under section 901 of this title.

EFFECTIVE DATE OF 1972 AMENDMENT

Amendment by Pub. L. 92–576 effective 30 days after Oct. 27, 1972, see section 22 of Pub. L. 92–576, set out as a note under section 902 of this title.

EFFECTIVE DATE OF 1961 AMENDMENT

Amendment by Pub. L. 87–87 effective as to injuries sustained on or after July 14, 1961, see section 4 of Pub. L. 87–87, set out as a note under section 906 of this title.

EFFECTIVE DATE OF 1956 AMENDMENT

Amendment by act July 26, 1956, applicable only with respect to injuries and death occurring on or after July 26, 1956, see section 9 of act July 26, 1956, set out as a note under section 906 of this title.

EFFECTIVE DATE OF 1948 AMENDMENT

Amendment by act June 24, 1948, applicable to death or injuries occurring after June 24, 1948, see section 6 of act June 24, 1948, set out as a note under section 906 of this title.

§915. Invalid agreements

(a) No agreement by an employee to pay any portion of premium paid by his employer to a carrier or to contribute to a benefit fund or department maintained by such employer for the purpose of providing compensation or medical services and supplies as required by this chapter shall be valid, and any employer who makes a deduction for such purpose from the pay of any employee entitled to the benefits of this chapter shall be guilty of a misdemeanor, and upon conviction thereof shall be punished by a fine of not more than $1,000.

(b) No agreement by an employee to waive his right to compensation under this chapter shall be valid.

(Mar. 4, 1927, ch. 509, §15, 44 Stat. 1434.)

§916. Assignment and exemption from claims of creditors

No assignment, release, or commutation of compensation or benefits due or payable under this chapter, except as provided by this chapter, shall be valid, and such compensation and benefits shall be exempt from all claims of creditors and from levy, execution, and attachment or other remedy for recovery or collection of a debt, which exemption may not be waived.

(Mar. 4, 1927, ch. 509, §16, 44 Stat. 1434.)

§917. Lien against compensation

Where a trust fund which complies with section 186(c) of title 29 established pursuant to a collective-bargaining agreement in effect between an employer and an employee covered under this chapter has paid disability benefits to an employee which the employee is legally obligated to repay by reason of his entitlement to compensation under this chapter or under a settlement, the Secretary shall authorize a lien on such compensation in favor of the trust fund for the amount of such payments.

(Mar. 4, 1927, ch. 509, §17, 44 Stat. 1434; June 25, 1938, ch. 685, §8, 52 Stat. 1167; Pub. L. 92–576, §20(b), Oct. 27, 1972, 86 Stat. 1264; Pub. L. 95–598, title III, §324, Nov. 6, 1978, 92 Stat. 2679; Pub. L. 98–426, §14, Sept. 28, 1984, 98 Stat. 1649.)

AMENDMENTS

1984—Pub. L. 98–426 struck out "(b)" before "Where a trust fund which complies", substituted "covered under this chapter" for "entitled to compensation under this chapter", and substituted "this chapter or under a settlement, the Secretary shall authorize" for "this chapter, the Secretary may authorize".

1978—Subsec. (a). Pub. L. 95–598 repealed provision for lien of person entitled to compensation without limit of amount against assets of carrier or employer and for preference and priority in distribution of assets of such carrier or employer, or both upon insolvency, bankruptcy, or reorganization in bankruptcy proceedings of the carrier or employer, or both.

1972—Pub. L. 92–576 designated existing provisions as subsec. (a) and added subsec. (b).

1938—Act June 25, 1938, amended section generally. Prior to amendment, section read as follows: "Compensation shall have the same preference of lien against the assets of the carrier or employer without limit of amount as is now or may hereafter be allowed by law to the claimant for unpaid wages or otherwise".

EFFECTIVE DATE OF 1984 AMENDMENT

Amendment by Pub. L. 98–426 effective Sept. 28, 1984, and applicable both with respect to claims filed after such date and to claims pending on such date, see section 28(a) of Pub. L. 98–426, set out as a note under section 901 of this title.

EFFECTIVE DATE OF 1978 AMENDMENT

Amendment by Pub. L. 95–598 effective Oct. 1, 1979, see section 402(a) of Pub. L. 95–598, set out as an Effective Date note preceding section 101 of Title 11, Bankruptcy.

EFFECTIVE DATE OF 1972 AMENDMENT

Amendment by Pub. L. 92–576 effective 30 days after Oct. 27, 1972, see section 22 of Pub. L. 92–576, set out as a note under section 902 of this title.

§918. Collection of defaulted payments; special fund

(a) In case of default by the employer in the payment of compensation due under any award of compensation for a period of thirty days after the compensation is due and payable, the person to whom such compensation is payable may, within one year after such default, make application to the deputy commissioner making the compensation order or[1] a supplementary order declaring the amount of the default. After investigation, notice, and hearing, as provided in section 919 of this title, the deputy commissioner shall make a supplementary order, declaring the amount of the default, which shall be filed in the same manner as the compensation order. In case the payment in default is an installment of the award, the deputy commissioner may, in his discretion, declare the whole of the award as the amount in default. The applicant may file a certified copy of such supplementary order with the clerk of the Federal district court for the judicial district in which the employer has his principal place of business or maintains an office, or for the judicial district in which the injury occurred. In case such principal place of business or office or place where the injury occurred is in the District of Columbia, a copy of such supplementary order may be filed with the clerk of the United States District Court for the District of Columbia. Such supplementary order of the deputy commissioner shall be final, and the court shall, upon the filing of the copy, enter judgment for the amount declared in default by the supplementary order if such supplementary order is in accordance with law. Review of the judgment so entered may be had as in civil suits for damages at common law. Final proceedings to execute the judgment may be had by writ of execution in the form used by the court in suits at common law in actions of assumpsit. No fee shall be required for filing the supplementary order nor for entry of judgment thereon, and the applicant shall not be liable for costs in a proceeding for review of the judgment unless the court shall otherwise direct. The court shall modify such judgment to conform to any later compensation order upon presentation of a certified copy thereof to the court.

(b) In cases where judgment cannot be satisfied by reason of the employer's insolvency or other circumstances precluding payment, the Secretary of Labor may, in his discretion and to the extent he shall determine advisable after consideration of current commitments payable from the special fund established in section 944 of this title, make payment from such fund upon any award made under this chapter, and in addition, provide any necessary medical, surgical, and other treatment required by section 907 of this title in any case of disability where there has been a default in furnishing medical treatment by reason of the insolvency of the employer. Such an employer shall be liable for pay-

[1] So in original. Probably should be "for".

ment into such fund of the amounts paid therefrom by the Secretary of Labor under this subsection; and for the purpose of enforcing this liability, the Secretary of Labor for the benefit of the fund shall be subrogated to all the rights of the person receiving such payment or benefits as against the employer and may by a proceeding in the name of the Secretary of Labor under this section or under subsection (c) of section 921 of this title, or both, seek to recover the amount of the default or so much thereof as in the judgment of the Secretary is possible, or the Secretary may settle and compromise any such claim.

(Mar. 4, 1927, ch. 509, §18, 44 Stat. 1434; June 25, 1936, ch. 804, 49 Stat. 1921; June 25, 1948, ch. 646, §32(b), 62 Stat. 991; May 24, 1949, ch. 139, §127, 63 Stat. 107; July 26, 1956, ch. 735, §6, 70 Stat. 655; Pub. L. 98–426, §27(b), Sept. 28, 1984, 98 Stat. 1654.)

CODIFICATION

As originally enacted, subsec. (a) contained a reference to the Supreme Court of the District of Columbia. Act June 25, 1936, substituted "the district court of the United States for the District of Columbia" for "the Supreme Court of the District of Columbia", and act June 25, 1948, as amended by act May 24, 1949, substituted "United States District Court for the District of Columbia" for "district court of the United States for the District of Columbia".

AMENDMENTS

1984—Subsec. (b). Pub. L. 98–426 struck out ", including the right of lien and priority provided for by section 917 of this title," after "shall be subrogated to all the rights of the person receiving such payment or benefits".

1956—Act July 26, 1956, designated existing provisions as subsec. (a) and added subsec. (b).

EFFECTIVE DATE OF 1984 AMENDMENT

Amendment by Pub. L. 98–426 effective Sept. 28, 1984, see section 28(e)(1) of Pub. L. 98–426, set out as a note under section 901 of this title.

§919. Procedure in respect of claims

(a) Filing of claim

Subject to the provisions of section 913 of this title a claim for compensation may be filed with the deputy commissioner in accordance with regulations prescribed by the Secretary at any time after the first seven days of disability following any injury, or at any time after death, and the deputy commissioner shall have full power and authority to hear and determine all questions in respect of such claim.

(b) Notice of claim

Within ten days after such claim is filed the deputy commissioner, in accordance with regulations prescribed by the Secretary, shall notify the employer and any other person (other than the claimant), whom the deputy commissioner considers an interested party, that a claim has been filed. Such notice may be served personally upon the employer or other person, or sent to such employer or person by registered mail.

(c) Investigations; order for hearing; notice; rejection or award

The deputy commissioner shall make or cause to be made such investigations as he considers necessary in respect of the claim, and upon application of any interested party shall order a hearing thereon. If a hearing on such claim is ordered the deputy commissioner shall give the claimant and other interested parties at least ten days' notice of such hearing, served personally upon the claimant and other interested parties or sent to such claimant and other interested parties by registered mail or by certified mail, and shall within twenty days after such hearing is had, by order, reject the claim or make an award in respect of the claim. If no hearing is ordered within twenty days after notice is given as provided in subsection (b) of this section, the deputy commissioner shall, by order, reject the claim or make an award in respect of the claim.

(d) Provisions governing conduct of hearing; administrative law judges

Notwithstanding any other provisions of this chapter, any hearing held under this chapter shall be conducted in accordance with the provisions of section 554 of title 5. Any such hearing shall be conducted by a[1] administrative law judge qualified under section 3105 of that title. All powers, duties, and responsibilities vested by this chapter, on October 27, 1972, in the deputy commissioners with respect to such hearings shall be vested in such administrative law judges.

(e) Filing and mailing of order rejecting claim or making award

The order rejecting the claim or making the award (referred to in this chapter as a compensation order) shall be filed in the office of the deputy commissioner, and a copy thereof shall be sent by registered mail or by certified mail to the claimant and to the employer at the last known address of each.

(f) Awards after death of employee

An award of compensation for disability may be made after the death of an injured employee.

(g) Transfer of case

At any time after a claim has been filed with him, the deputy commissioner may, with the approval of the Secretary, transfer such case to any other deputy commissioner for the purpose of making investigation, taking testimony, making physical examinations or taking such other necessary action therein as may be directed.

(h) Physical examination of injured employee

An injured employee claiming or entitled to compensation shall submit to such physical examination by a medical officer of the United States or by a duly qualified physician designated or approved by the Secretary as the deputy commissioner may require. The place or places shall be reasonably convenient for the employee. Such physician or physicians as the employee, employer, or carrier may select and pay for may participate in an examination if the employee, employer, or carrier so requests. Proceedings shall be suspended and no compensation be payable for any period during which the employee may refuse to submit to examination.

[1] So in original. Probably should be "an".

(Mar. 4, 1927, ch. 509, §19, 44 Stat. 1435; June 25, 1938, ch. 685, §9, 52 Stat. 1167; Pub. L. 86–507, §1(30), (31), June 11, 1960, 74 Stat. 202; Pub. L. 92–576, §14, Oct. 27, 1972, 86 Stat. 1261; Pub. L. 95–251, §2(a)(10), Mar. 27, 1978, 92 Stat. 183; Pub. L. 98–426, §27(a)(2), Sept. 28, 1984, 98 Stat. 1654.)

AMENDMENTS

1984—Subsecs. (a), (b), (g), (h). Pub. L. 98–426, §27(a)(2), substituted "Secretary" for "commission". See Transfer of Functions note under section 902 of this title.

1978—Subsec. (d). Pub. L. 95–251 substituted references to administrative law judges for references to hearing examiners.

1972—Subsec. (d). Pub. L. 92–576 substituted provisions for conduct of hearings under section 554 of title 5 by a hearing examiner qualified under section 3105 of title 5 and vesting in hearing examiners the powers, duties, and responsibilities vested in deputy commissioners on Oct. 27, 1972, for former provisions authorizing claimant and employer to present evidence with respect to claims and for representation of a claimant under a written authorization.

1960—Subsecs. (c), (e). Pub. L. 86–507 inserted "or by certified mail" after "registered mail".

1938—Subsec. (g). Act June 25, 1938, authorized transfer of cases, with administrative approval, at any time after filing of claim for the additional purposes of making investigations and taking other necessary action instead of after issuance of compensation order without anyone's approval.

EFFECTIVE DATE OF 1984 AMENDMENT

Amendment by Pub. L. 98–426 effective Sept. 28, 1984, see section 28(e)(1) of Pub. L. 98–426, set out as a note under section 901 of this title.

EFFECTIVE DATE OF 1972 AMENDMENT

Amendment by Pub. L. 92–576 effective 30 days after Oct. 27, 1972, see section 22 of Pub. L. 92–576, set out as a note under section 902 of this title.

§920. Presumptions

In any proceeding for the enforcement of a claim for compensation under this chapter it shall be presumed, in the absence of substantial evidence to the contrary—

(a) That the claim comes within the provisions of this chapter.

(b) That sufficient notice of such claim has been given.

(c) That the injury was not occasioned solely by the intoxication of the injured employee.

(d) That the injury was not occasioned by the willful intention of the injured employee to injure or kill himself or another.

(Mar. 4, 1927, ch. 509, §20, 44 Stat. 1436.)

§921. Review of compensation orders

(a) Effectiveness and finality of orders

A compensation order shall become effective when filed in the office of the deputy commissioner as provided in section 919 of this title, and, unless proceedings for the suspension or setting aside of such order are instituted as provided in subsection (b) of this section, shall become final at the expiration of the thirtieth day thereafter.

(b) Benefits Review Board; establishment; members; chairman; quorum; voting; questions reviewable; record; conclusiveness of findings; stay of payments; remand

(1) There is hereby established a Benefits Review Board which shall be composed of five members appointed by the Secretary from among individuals who are especially qualified to serve on such Board. The Secretary shall designate one of the members of the Board to serve as chairman. The Chairman shall have the authority, as delegated by the Secretary, to exercise all administrative functions necessary to operate the Board.

(2) For the purpose of carrying out its functions under this chapter, three members of the Board shall constitute a quorum and official action can be taken only on the affirmative vote of at least three members.

(3) The Board shall be authorized to hear and determine appeals raising a substantial question of law or fact taken by any party in interest from decisions with respect to claims of employees under this chapter and the extensions thereof. The Board's orders shall be based upon the hearing record. The findings of fact in the decision under review by the Board shall be conclusive if supported by substantial evidence in the record considered as a whole. The payment of the amounts required by an award shall not be stayed pending final decision in any such proceeding unless ordered by the Board. No stay shall be issued unless irreparable injury would otherwise ensue to the employer or carrier.

(4) The Board may, on its own motion or at the request of the Secretary, remand a case to the administrative law judge for further appropriate action. The consent of the parties in interest shall not be a prerequisite to a remand by the Board.

(5) Notwithstanding paragraphs (1) through (4), upon application of the Chairman of the Board, the Secretary may designate up to four Department of Labor administrative law judges to serve on the Board temporarily, for not more than one year. The Board is authorized to delegate to panels of three members any or all of the powers which the Board may exercise. Each such panel shall have no more than one temporary member. Two members shall constitute a quorum of a panel. Official adjudicative action may be taken only on the affirmative vote of at least two members of a panel. Any party aggrieved by a decision of a panel of the Board may, within thirty days after the date of entry of the decision, petition the entire permanent Board for review of the panel's decision. Upon affirmative vote of the majority of the permanent members of the Board, the petition shall be granted. The Board shall amend its Rules of Practice to conform with this paragraph. Temporary members, while serving as members of the Board, shall be compensated at the same rate of compensation as regular members.

(c) Court of appeals; jurisdiction; persons entitled to review; petition; record; determination and enforcement; service of process; stay of payments

Any person adversely affected or aggrieved by a final order of the Board may obtain a review of that order in the United States court of appeals for the circuit in which the injury occurred, by filing in such court within sixty days following the issuance of such Board order a written petition praying that the order be modified or set aside. A copy of such petition shall be forthwith transmitted by the clerk of the court, to the Board, and to the other parties, and thereupon the Board shall file in the court the record in the proceedings as provided in section 2112 of title 28. Upon such filing, the court shall have jurisdiction of the proceeding and shall have the power to give a decree affirming, modifying, or setting aside, in whole or in part, the order of the Board and enforcing same to the extent that such order is affirmed or modified. The orders, writs, and processes of the court in such proceedings may run, be served, and be returnable anywhere in the United States. The payment of the amounts required by an award shall not be stayed pending final decision in any such proceeding unless ordered by the court. No stay shall be issued unless irreparable injury would otherwise ensue to the employer or carrier. The order of the court allowing any stay shall contain a specific finding, based upon evidence submitted to the court and identified by reference thereto, that irreparable damage would result to the employer, and specifying the nature of the damage.

(d) District court; jurisdiction; enforcement of orders; application of beneficiaries of awards or deputy commissioner; process for compliance with orders

If any employer or his officers or agents fails to comply with a compensation order making an award, that has become final, any beneficiary of such award or the deputy commissioner making the order, may apply for the enforcement of the order to the Federal district court for the judicial district in which the injury occurred (or to the United States District Court for the District of Columbia if the injury occurred in the District). If the court determines that the order was made and served in accordance with law, and that such employer or his officers or agents have failed to comply therewith, the court shall enforce obedience to the order by writ of injunction or by other proper process, mandatory or otherwise, to enjoin upon such person and his officers and agents compliance with the order.

(e) Institution of proceedings for suspension, setting aside, or enforcement of compensation orders

Proceedings for suspending, setting aside, or enforcing a compensation order, whether rejecting a claim or making an award, shall not be instituted otherwise than as provided in this section and section 918 of this title.

(Mar. 4, 1927, ch. 509, §21, 44 Stat. 1436; June 25, 1936, ch. 804, 49 Stat. 1921; June 25, 1948, ch. 646, §32(b), 62 Stat. 991; May 24, 1949, ch. 139, §127, 63 Stat. 107; Pub. L. 92–576, §15(a), (b), Oct. 27, 1972, 86 Stat. 1261, 1262; Pub. L. 95–251, §2(a)(10), Mar. 27, 1978, 92 Stat. 183; Pub. L. 98–426, §15, Sept. 28, 1984, 98 Stat. 1649.)

CODIFICATION

As originally enacted, subsec. (d) contained a reference to the Supreme Court of the District of Columbia. Act June 25, 1936, substituted "the district court of the United States for the District of Columbia" for "the Supreme Court of the District of Columbia", and act June 25, 1948, as amended by act May 24, 1949, substituted "United States District Court for the District of Columbia" for "district court of the United States for the District of Columbia".

AMENDMENTS

1984—Subsec. (b)(1). Pub. L. 98–426, §15(1), (2), substituted "five" for "three", and inserted "The Chairman shall have the authority, as delegated by the Secretary, to exercise all administrative functions necessary to operate the Board."

Subsec. (b)(2). Pub. L. 98–426, §15(3), substituted "three" for "two" wherever appearing.

Subsec. (b)(5). Pub. L. 98–426, §15(4), added par. (5).

1978—Subsec. (b)(4). Pub. L. 95–251 substituted "administrative law judge" for "hearing examiner".

1972—Subsec. (b). Pub. L. 92–576, §15(a), added subsec. (b). Former provisions of subsec. (b) for injunction proceedings to suspend or set aside a compensation order by a party in interest against a deputy commissioner in Federal district court for judicial district where injury occurred superseded by subsec. (c) of this section and former provisions of such subsec. (b) respecting service of process and stay of payments, except for the procedural requirement of an interlocutory injunction to the court and hearing on at least three days' notice to the parties in interest and the deputy commissioner, incorporated in subsec. (c) of this section.

Subsecs. (c) to (e). Pub. L. 92–576, §15(a), (b), added subsec. (c) and redesignated former subsecs. (c) and (d) as (d) and (e), respectively.

EFFECTIVE DATE OF 1984 AMENDMENT

Amendment by Pub. L. 98–426 effective Sept. 28, 1984, see section 28(e)(1) of Pub. L. 98–426, set out as a note under section 901 of this title.

EFFECTIVE DATE OF 1972 AMENDMENT

Amendment by Pub. L. 92–576 effective 30 days after Oct. 27, 1972, see section 22 of Pub. L. 92–576, set out as a note under section 902 of this title.

REVIEW OF DECISIONS MADE BY OR PENDING BEFORE BENEFITS REVIEW BOARD

Pub. L. 108–447, div. F, title I, Dec. 8, 2004, 118 Stat. 3121, which provided in part that no funds made available by div. F were to be used by the Solicitor of Labor or the Secretary of Labor to review certain decisions made by or pending before the Benefits Review Board under the Longshore and Harbor Workers' Compensation Act, and deemed such decisions pending review by the Board for more than 1 year to be affirmed by and the final order of the Board for purposes of obtaining review in the United States courts of appeals, was from the Departments of Labor, Health and Human Services, and Education, and Related Agencies Appropriations Act, 2005, and was not repeated in subsequent appropriations acts. Similar provisions were contained in the following prior appropriation acts:

Pub. L. 108–199, div. E, title I, Jan. 23, 2004, 118 Stat. 234.

Pub. L. 108–7, div. G, title I, Feb. 20, 2003, 117 Stat. 306.

Pub. L. 107–116, title I, Jan. 10, 2002, 115 Stat. 2184.

Pub. L. 106–554, §1(a)(1) [title I], Dec. 21, 2000, 114 Stat. 2763, 2763A–10.

Pub. L. 106–113, div. B, §1000(a)(4) [title I], Nov. 29, 1999, 113 Stat. 1535, 1501A–224.

Pub. L. 105–277, div. A, §101(f) [title I], Oct. 21, 1998, 105 Stat. 2681–337, 2681–345.

Pub. L. 105–78, title I, Nov. 13, 1997, 111 Stat. 1475.

Pub. L. 104–208, div. A, title I, §101(e) [title I], Sept. 30, 1996, 110 Stat. 3009–233, 3009–241.

Pub. L. 104–134, title I, §101(d) [title I], Apr. 26, 1996, 110 Stat. 1321–211, 1321–218; renumbered title I, Pub. L. 104–140, §1(a), May 2, 1996, 110 Stat. 1327.

§921a. Appearance of attorneys for Secretary, deputy commissioner, or Board

Attorneys appointed by the Secretary shall represent the Secretary, the deputy commissioner, or the Board in any court proceedings under section 921 of this title or other provisions of this chapter except for proceedings in the Supreme Court of the United States.

(May 4, 1928, ch. 502, 45 Stat. 490; June 25, 1948, ch. 646, §1, 62 Stat. 909; Pub. L. 92–576, §16, Oct. 27, 1972, 86 Stat. 1262.)

CODIFICATION

Section was not enacted as part of the Longshore and Harbor Workers' Compensation Act which comprises this chapter.

AMENDMENTS

1972—Pub. L. 92–576 substituted provisions for representation of the Secretary, the deputy commissioner, or the Board by attorneys appointed by the Secretary except for proceedings in the Supreme Court, for former provisions requiring the United States attorney in the judicial district in which the case is pending to appear as attorney or counsel on behalf of the Secretary of Labor or his deputy commissioner when either is a party to the case or interested, and to represent such Secretary or deputy in any court in which such case may be carried on appeal.

CHANGE OF NAME

Act June 25, 1948, eff. Sept. 1, 1948, substituted "United States attorney" for "district attorney of the United States". See section 541 of Title 28, Judiciary and Judicial Procedure, and Historical and Revision note thereunder.

EFFECTIVE DATE OF 1972 AMENDMENT

Amendment by Pub. L. 92–576 effective 30 days after Oct. 27, 1972, see section 22 of Pub. L. 92–576, set out as a note under section 902 of this title.

§922. Modification of awards

Upon his own initiative, or upon the application of any party in interest (including an employer or carrier which has been granted relief under section 908(f) of this title), on the ground of a change in conditions or because of a mistake in a determination of fact by the deputy commissioner, the deputy commissioner may, at any time prior to one year after the date of the last payment of compensation, whether or not a compensation order has been issued, or at any time prior to one year after the rejection of a claim, review a compensation case (including a case under which payments are made pursuant to section 944(i) of this title) in accordance with the procedure prescribed in respect of claims in section 919 of this title, and in accordance with such section issue a new compensation order which may terminate, continue, reinstate, increase, or decrease such compensation, or award compensation. Such new order shall not affect any compensation previously paid, except that an award increasing the compensation rate may be made effective from the date of the injury, and if any part of the compensation due or to become due is unpaid, an award decreasing the compensation rate may be made effective from the date of the injury, and any payment made prior thereto in excess of such decreased rate shall be deducted from any unpaid compensation, in such manner and by such method as may be determined by the deputy commissioner with the approval of the Secretary. This section does not authorize the modification of settlements.

(Mar. 4, 1927, ch. 509, §22, 44 Stat. 1437; May 26, 1934, ch. 354, §5, 48 Stat. 807; June 25, 1938, ch. 685, §10, 52 Stat. 1167; Pub. L. 98–426, §§16, 27(a)(2), Sept. 28, 1984, 98 Stat. 1650, 1654.)

AMENDMENTS

1984—Pub. L. 98–426, §16, inserted "(including an employer or carrier which has been granted relief under section 908(f) of this title)" after "party in interest" and "(including a case under which payments are made pursuant to section 941(i) of this title)" after "review a compensation case" and inserted at end "This section does not authorize the modification of settlements."

Pub. L. 98–426, §27(a)(2), substituted "Secretary" for "commission". See Transfer of Functions note set out under section 902 of this title.

1938—Act June 25, 1938, permitted review of compensation case at any time prior to one year after rejection of claim and authorized award of compensation.

1934—Act May 26, 1934, permitted review based on a mistake in a determination of fact; substituted provision for review of compensation case at any time prior to one year after date of last payment of compensation, whether or not compensation order was issued, for original provision for review at any time during term of award and after compensation order in respect of such award had become final; authorized reinstatement of compensation; and inserted exception clause.

EFFECTIVE DATE OF 1984 AMENDMENT

Amendment by Pub. L. 98–426 effective Sept. 28, 1984, see section 28(e)(1) of Pub. L. 98–426, set out as a note under section 901 of this title.

§923. Procedure before deputy commissioner or Board

(a) In making an investigation or inquiry or conducting a hearing the deputy commissioner or Board shall not be bound by common law or statutory rules of evidence or by technical or formal rules of procedure, except as provided by this chapter; but may make such investigation or inquiry or conduct such hearing in such manner as to best ascertain the rights of the parties. Declarations of a deceased employee concerning the injury in respect of which the investigation or inquiry is being made or the hearing conducted shall be received in evidence and shall, if corroborated by other evidence, be sufficient to establish the injury.

(b) Hearings before a deputy commissioner or Board shall be open to the public and shall be stenographically reported, and the deputy commissioners or Board, subject to the approval of the Secretary, are authorized to contract for the reporting of such hearings. The Secretary shall by regulation provide for the preparation of a record of the hearings and other proceedings before the deputy commissioners or Board.

(Mar. 4, 1927, ch. 509, §23, 44 Stat. 1437; Pub. L. 92–576, §15(e), Oct. 27, 1972, 86 Stat. 1262; Pub. L. 98–426, §27(a)(2), Sept. 28, 1984, 98 Stat. 1654.)

AMENDMENTS

1984—Subsec. (b). Pub. L. 98–426 substituted "Secretary" for "commission". See Transfer of Functions note set out under section 902 of this title.

1972—Pub. L. 92–576 inserted references to the Board in subsecs. (a) and (b).

EFFECTIVE DATE OF 1984 AMENDMENT

Amendment by Pub. L. 98–426 effective Sept. 28, 1984, see section 28(e)(1) of Pub. L. 98–426, set out as a note under section 901 of this title.

EFFECTIVE DATE OF 1972 AMENDMENT

Amendment by Pub. L. 92–576 effective 30 days after Oct. 27, 1972, see section 22 of Pub. L. 92–576, set out as a note under section 902 of this title.

§ 924. Witnesses

No person shall be required to attend as a witness in any proceeding before a deputy commissioner at a place outside of the State of his residence and more than one hundred miles from his place of residence, unless his lawful mileage and fee for one day's attendance shall be first paid or tendered to him; but the testimony of any witness may be taken by deposition or interrogatories according to the rules of practice of the Federal district court for the judicial district in which the case is pending (or of the United States District Court for the District of Columbia if the case is pending in the District).

(Mar. 4, 1927, ch. 509, § 24, 44 Stat. 1437; June 25, 1936, ch. 804, 49 Stat. 1921; June 25, 1948, ch. 646, § 32(b), 62 Stat. 991; May 24, 1949, ch. 139, § 127, 63 Stat. 107.)

CODIFICATION

As originally enacted, this section contained a reference to the Supreme Court of the District of Columbia. Act June 25, 1936, substituted "the district court of the United States for the District of Columbia" for "the Supreme Court of the District of Columbia", and act June 25, 1948, as amended by act May 24, 1949, substituted "United States District Court for the District of Columbia" for "district court of the United States for the District of Columbia".

§ 925. Witness fees

Witnesses summoned in a proceeding before a deputy commissioner or whose depositions are taken shall receive the same fees and mileage as witnesses in courts of the United States.

(Mar. 4, 1927, ch. 509, § 25, 44 Stat. 1437.)

§ 926. Costs in proceedings brought without reasonable grounds

If the court having jurisdiction of proceedings in respect of any claim or compensation order determines that the proceedings in respect of such claim or order have been instituted or continued without reasonable ground, the costs of such proceedings shall be assessed against the party who has so instituted or continued such proceedings.

(Mar. 4, 1927, ch. 509, § 26, 44 Stat. 1438.)

§ 927. Powers of deputy commissioners or Board

(a) The deputy commissioner or Board shall have power to preserve and enforce order during any such proceedings; to issue subpoenas for, to administer oaths to, and to compel the attendance and testimony of witnesses, or the production of books, papers, documents, and other evidence, or the taking of depositions before any designated individual competent to administer oaths; to examine witnesses; and to do all things conformable to law which may be necessary to enable him effiectively[1] to discharge the duties of his office.

(b) If any person in proceedings before a deputy commissioner or Board disobeys or resists any lawful order or process, or misbehaves during a hearing or so near the place thereof as to obstruct the same, or neglects to produce, after having been ordered to do so, any pertinent book, paper, or document, or refuses to appear after having been subpoenaed, or upon appearing refuses to take the oath as a witness, or after having taken the oath refuses to be examined according to law, the deputy commissioner or Board shall certify the facts to the district court having jurisdiction in the place in which he is sitting (or to the United States District Court for the District of Columbia if he is sitting in such District) which shall thereupon in a summary manner hear the evidence as to the acts complained of, and if the evidence so warrants, punish such person in the same manner and to the same extent as for a contempt committed before the court, or commit such person upon the same conditions as if the doing of the forbidden act had occurred with reference to the process of or in the presence of the court.

(Mar. 4, 1927, ch. 509, § 27, 44 Stat. 1438; June 25, 1936, ch. 804, 49 Stat. 1921; June 25, 1948, ch. 646, § 32(b), 62 Stat. 991; May 24, 1949, ch. 139, § 127, 63 Stat. 107; Pub. L. 92–576, § 15(e), Oct. 27, 1972, 86 Stat. 1262.)

CODIFICATION

As originally enacted, subsec. (b) contained a reference to the Supreme Court of the District of Columbia. Act June 25, 1936, substituted "the district court of the United States for the District of Columbia" for "the Supreme Court of the District of Columbia", and act June 25, 1948, as amended by act May 24, 1949, substituted "United States District Court for the District of Columbia" for "district court of the United States for the District of Columbia".

AMENDMENTS

1972—Subsecs. (a), (b). Pub. L. 92–576 inserted references to the Board.

EFFECTIVE DATE OF 1972 AMENDMENT

Amendment by Pub. L. 92–576 effective 30 days after Oct. 27, 1972, see section 22 of Pub. L. 92–576, set out as a note under section 902 of this title.

§ 928. Fees for services

(a) Attorney's fee; successful prosecution of claim

If the employer or carrier declines to pay any compensation on or before the thirtieth day after receiving written notice of a claim for compensation having been filed from the deputy commissioner, on the ground that there is no liability for compensation within the provisions of this chapter and the person seeking benefits shall thereafter have utilized the services of an attorney at law in the successful prosecution of his claim, there shall be awarded, in addition to the award of compensation, in a compensation order, a reasonable attorney's fee against the employer or carrier in an amount approved by the deputy commissioner, Board, or court, as the case may be, which shall be paid directly by the employer or carrier to the attorney for the claimant in a lump sum after the compensation order becomes final.

(b) Attorney's fee; successful prosecution for additional compensation; independent medical evaluation of disability controversy; restriction of other assessments

If the employer or carrier pays or tenders payment of compensation without an award pursu-

[1] So in original. Probably should be "effectively".

ant to section 914(a) and (b) of this title, and thereafter a controversy develops over the amount of additional compensation, if any, to which the employee may be entitled, the deputy commissioner or Board shall set the matter for an informal conference and following such conference the deputy commissioner or Board shall recommend in writing a disposition of the controversy. If the employer or carrier refuse to accept such written recommendation, within fourteen days after its receipt by them, they shall pay or tender to the employee in writing the additional compensation, if any, to which they believe the employee is entitled. If the employee refuses to accept such payment or tender of compensation, and thereafter utilizes the services of an attorney at law, and if the compensation thereafter awarded is greater than the amount paid or tendered by the employer or carrier, a reasonable attorney's fee based solely upon the difference between the amount awarded and the amount tendered or paid shall be awarded in addition to the amount of compensation. The foregoing sentence shall not apply if the controversy relates to degree or length of disability, and if the employer or carrier offers to submit the case for evaluation by physicians employed or selected by the Secretary, as authorized in section 907(e) of this title and offers to tender an amount of compensation based upon the degree or length of disability found by the independent medical report at such time as an evaluation of disability can be made. If the claimant is successful in review proceedings before the Board or court in any such case an award may be made in favor of the claimant and against the employer or carrier for a reasonable attorney's fee for claimant's counsel in accord with the above provisions. In all other cases any claim for legal services shall not be assessed against the employer or carrier.

(c) Approval; payment; lien

In all cases fees for attorneys representing the claimant shall be approved in the manner herein provided. If any proceedings are had before the Board or any court for review of any action, award, order, or decision, the Board or court may approve an attorney's fee for the work done before it by the attorney for the claimant. An approved attorney's fee, in cases in which the obligation to pay the fee is upon the claimant, may be made a lien upon the compensation due under an award; and the deputy commissioner, Board, or court shall fix in the award approving the fee, such lien and manner of payment.

(d) Costs; witnesses' fees and mileage; prohibition against diminution of compensation to claimant

In cases where an attorney's fee is awarded against an employer or carrier there may be further assessed against such employer or carrier as costs, fees and mileage for necessary witnesses attending the hearing at the instance of claimant. Both the necessity for the witness and the reasonableness of the fees of expert witnesses must be approved by the hearing officer, the Board, or the court, as the case may be. The amounts awarded against an employer or carrier as attorney's fees, costs, fees and mileage for witnesses shall not in any respect affect or diminish the compensation payable under this chapter.

(e) Unapproved fees; solicitation; penalty

A person who receives a fee, gratuity, or other consideration on account of services rendered as a representative of a claimant, unless the consideration is approved by the deputy commissioner, administrative law judge, Board, or court, or who makes it a business to solicit employment for a lawyer, or for himself, with respect to a claim or award for compensation under this chapter, shall, upon conviction thereof, for each offense be punished by a fine of not more than $1,000 or be imprisoned for not more than one year, or both.

(Mar. 4, 1927, ch. 509, § 28, 44 Stat. 1438; Pub. L. 92–576, § 13, Oct. 27, 1972, 86 Stat. 1259; Pub. L. 98–426, § 17, Sept. 28, 1984, 98 Stat. 1650.)

AMENDMENTS

1984—Subsec. (e). Pub. L. 98–426 substituted "a fee, gratuity, or other consideration" for "any fees, other consideration, or any gratuity"; "with respect to" for "in respect of"; and "both" for "by both such fine and imprisonment"; and inserted "under this chapter," after "compensation".

1972—Subsec. (a). Pub. L. 92–576 substituted provisions respecting payment of attorney's fee for successful prosecution of claim for former provisions respecting approval by deputy commissioner or court of claims for legal services or for any other services rendered in respect of a claim or award for compensation and for lien upon the compensation in the manner and to the extent fixed by the deputy commissioner or the court. See subsec. (c).

Subsecs. (b) to (e). Pub. L. 92–576 added subsecs. (b) to (d), redesignated former subsec. (b) as (e), and in subsec. (e), as so redesignated, struck out item (1) and (2) designations before "who", substituted "services rendered as a representative of a claimant" for "services so rendered", and included approval by the Board.

EFFECTIVE DATE OF 1984 AMENDMENT

Amendment by Pub. L. 98–426 effective Sept. 28, 1984, see section 28(e)(1) of Pub. L. 98–426, set out as a note under section 901 of this title.

EFFECTIVE DATE OF 1972 AMENDMENT

Amendment by Pub. L. 92–576 effective 30 days after Oct. 27, 1972, see section 22 of Pub. L. 92–576, set out as a note under section 902 of this title.

§ 929. Record of injury or death

Every employer shall keep a record in respect of any injury to an employee. Such record shall contain such information of disease, other disability, or death in respect of such injury as the Secretary may by regulation require, and shall be available to inspection by the Secretary or by any State authority at such times and under such conditions as the Secretary may by regulation prescribe.

(Mar. 4, 1927, ch. 509, § 29, 44 Stat. 1438; Pub. L. 98–426, § 27(a)(2), Sept. 28, 1984, 98 Stat. 1654.)

AMENDMENTS

1984—Pub. L. 98–426, § 27(a)(2), substituted "Secretary" for "commission". See Transfer of Functions note set out under section 902 of this title.

EFFECTIVE DATE OF 1984 AMENDMENT

Amendment by Pub. L. 98–426 effective Sept. 28, 1984, see section 28(e)(1) of Pub. L. 98–426, set out as a note under section 901 of this title.

§ 930. Reports to Secretary

(a) Time for sending; contents; copy to deputy commissioner

Within ten days from the date of any injury, which causes loss of one or more shifts of work, or death or from the date that the employer has knowledge of a disease or infection in respect of such injury, the employer shall send to the Secretary a report setting forth (1) the name, address, and business of the employer; (2) the name, address, and occupation of the employee; (3) the cause and nature of the injury or death; (4) the year, month, day, and hour when and the particular locality where the injury or death occurred; and (5) such other information as the Secretary may require. A copy of such report shall be sent at the same time to the deputy commissioner in the compensation district in which the injury occurred. Notwithstanding the requirements of this subsection, each employer shall keep a record of each and every injury regardless of whether such injury results in the loss of one or more shifts of work.

(b) Additional reports

Additional reports in respect of such injury and of the condition of such employee shall be sent by the employer to the Secretary and to such deputy commissioner at such times and in such manner as the Secretary may prescribe.

(c) Use as evidence

Any report provided for in subsection (a) or (b) of this section shall not be evidence of any fact stated in such report in any proceeding in respect of such injury or death on account of which the report is made.

(d) Compliance by mailing

The mailing of any such report and copy in a stamped envelope, within the time prescribed in subsections (a) or (b) of this section, to the Secretary and deputy commissioner, respectively, shall be a compliance with this section.

(e) Penalty for failure or refusal to send report

Any employer, insurance carrier, or self-insured employer who knowingly and willfully fails or refuses to send any report required by this section or knowingly or willfully makes a false statement or misrepresentation in any such report shall be subject to a civil penalty not to exceed $10,000 for each such failure, refusal, false statement, or misrepresentation.

(f) Tolling provision

Where the employer or the carrier has been given notice, or the employer (or his agent in charge of the business in the place where the injury occurred) or the carrier has knowledge, of any injury or death of an employee and fails, neglects, or refuses to file report thereof as required by the provisions of subsection (a) of this section, the limitations in subsection (a) of section 913 of this title shall not begin to run against the claim of the injured employee or his dependents entitled to compensation, or in favor of either the employer or the carrier, until such report shall have been furnished as required by the provisions of subsection (a) of this section.

(Mar. 4, 1927, ch. 509, § 30, 44 Stat. 1439; June 25, 1938, ch. 685, § 11, 52 Stat. 1167; Pub. L. 98–426, §§ 18, 27(a)(2), Sept. 28, 1984, 98 Stat. 1650, 1654.)

AMENDMENTS

1984—Subsec. (a). Pub. L. 98–426, § 18(a)(1), inserted ", which causes loss of one or more shifts of work," after "Within ten days from the date of any injury".

Pub. L. 98–426, § 27(a)(2), substituted "Secretary" for "commission". See Transfer of Functions note set out under section 902 of this title.

Pub. L. 98–426, § 18(a)(2), inserted at end "Notwithstanding the requirements of this subsection, each employer shall keep a record of each and every injury regardless of whether such injury results in the loss of one or more shifts of work."

Subsecs. (b), (d). Pub. L. 98–426, § 27(a)(2), substituted "Secretary" for "commission". See Transfer of Functions note set out under section 902 of this title.

Subsec. (e). Pub. L. 98–426, § 18(b), amended subsec. (e) generally. Prior to amendment, subsec. (e) read as follows: "Any employer who fails or refuses to send any report required of him by this section shall be subject to a civil penalty not to exceed $500 for each such failure or refusal."

1938—Subsec. (f). Act June 25, 1938, added subsec. (f).

EFFECTIVE DATE OF 1984 AMENDMENT

Amendment by Pub. L. 98–426 effective Sept. 28, 1984, see section 28(e)(1) of Pub. L. 98–426, set out as a note under section 901 of this title.

§ 931. Penalty for misrepresentation

(a) Felony; fine; imprisonment

(1) Any claimant or representative of a claimant who knowingly and willfully makes a false statement or representation for the purpose of obtaining a benefit or payment under this chapter shall be guilty of a felony, and on conviction thereof shall be punished by a fine not to exceed $10,000, by imprisonment not to exceed five years, or by both.

(2) The United States attorney for the district in which the injury is alleged to have occurred shall make every reasonable effort to promptly investigate each complaint made under this subsection.

(b) List of persons disqualified from representing claimants

(1) No representation fee of a claimant's representative shall be approved by the deputy commissioner, an administrative law judge, the Board, or a court pursuant to section 928 of this title, if the claimant's representative is on the list of individuals who are disqualified from representing claimants under this chapter maintained by the Secretary pursuant to paragraph (2) of this subsection.

(2)(A) The Secretary shall annually prepare a list of those individuals in each compensation district who have represented claimants for a fee in cases under this chapter and who are not authorized to represent claimants. The names of individuals contained on the list required under this subparagraph shall be made available to employees and employers in each compensation district through posting and in such other forms as the Secretary may prescribe.

(B) Individuals shall be included on the list of those not authorized to represent claimants under this chapter if the Secretary determines under this section, in accordance with the procedure provided in subsection (j) of section 907 of this title, that such individual—

(i) has been convicted (without regard to pending appeal) of any crime in connection with the representation of a claimant under this chapter or any workers' compensation statute;

(ii) has engaged in fraud in connection with the presentation of a claim under this or any workers' compensation statute, including, but not limited to, knowingly making false representations, concealing or attempting to conceal material facts with respect to a claim, or soliciting or otherwise procuring false testimony;

(iii) has been prohibited from representing claimants before any other workers' compensation agency for reasons of professional misconduct which are similar in nature to those which would be grounds for disqualification under this paragraph; or

(iv) has accepted fees for representing claimants under this chapter which were not approved, or which were in excess of the amount approved pursuant to section 928 of this title.

(C) Notwithstanding subparagraph (B), no individual who is on the list required to be maintained by the Secretary pursuant to this section shall be prohibited from presenting his or her own claim or from representing without fee, a claimant who is a spouse, mother, father, sister, brother, or child of such individual.

(D) A determination under subparagraph (A) shall remain in effect for a period of not less than three years and until the Secretary finds and gives notice to the public that there is reasonable assurance that the basis for the determination will not reoccur.

(3) No employee shall be liable to pay a representation fee to any representative whose fee has been disallowed by reason of the operation of this paragraph.

(4) The Secretary shall issue such rules and regulations as are necessary to carry out this section.

(c) False statements or representation to reduce, deny, or terminate benefits

A person including, but not limited to, an employer, his duly authorized agent, or an employee of an insurance carrier who knowingly and willfully makes a false statement or representation for the purpose of reducing, denying, or terminating benefits to an injured employee, or his dependents pursuant to section 909 of this title if the injury results in death, shall be punished by a fine not to exceed $10,000, by imprisonment not to exceed five years, or by both.

(Mar. 4, 1927, ch. 509, §31, 44 Stat. 1439; Pub. L. 98–426, §19, Sept. 28, 1984, 98 Stat. 1650.)

AMENDMENTS

1984—Pub. L. 98–426 designated existing provisions as subsec. (a)(1), substituted "Any claimant or representative of a claimant who knowingly and willfully makes a false statement or representation for the purpose of obtaining a benefit or payment under this chapter shall be guilty of a felony, and on conviction thereof shall be punished by a fine not to exceed $10,000, by imprisonment not to exceed five years, or by both" for "Any person who willfully makes any false or misleading statement or representation for the purpose of obtaining any benefit or payment under this chapter shall be guilty of a misdemeanor and on conviction thereof shall be punished by a fine of not to exceed $1,000 or by imprisonment of not to exceed one year, or by both such fine and imprisonment", and added subsecs. (a)(2), (b), and (c).

EFFECTIVE DATE OF 1984 AMENDMENT

Amendment by Pub. L. 98–426 effective Sept. 28, 1984, see section 28(e)(1) of Pub. L. 98–426, set out as a note under section 901 of this title.

§932. Security for compensation

(a) Every employer shall secure the payment of compensation under this chapter—

(1) By insuring and keeping insured the payment of such compensation with any stock company or mutual company or association, or with any other person or fund, while such person or fund is authorized (A) under the laws of the United States or of any State, to insure workmen's compensation, and (B) by the Secretary, to insure payment of compensation under this chapter; or

(2) By furnishing satisfactory proof to the Secretary of his financial ability to pay such compensation and receiving an authorization from the Secretary to pay such compensation directly. The Secretary may, as a condition to such authorization, require such employer to deposit in a depository designated by the Secretary either an indemnity bond or securities (at the option of the employer) of a kind and in an amount determined by the Secretary, based on the employer's financial condition, the employer's previous record of payments, and other relevant factors, and subject to such conditions as the Secretary may prescribe, which shall include authorization to the Secretary in case of default to sell any such securities sufficient to pay compensation awards or to bring suit upon such bonds, to procure prompt payment of compensation under this chapter. Any employer securing compensation in accordance with the provisions of this paragraph shall be known as a self-insurer.

(b) In granting authorization to any carrier to insure payment of compensation under this chapter the Secretary may take into consideration the recommendation of any State authority having supervision over carriers or over workmen's compensation, and may authorize any carrier to insure the payment of compensation under this chapter in a limited territory. Any marine protection and indemnity mutual insurance corporation or association, authorized to write insurance against liability for loss or damage from personal injury and death, and for other losses and damages, incidental to or in respect of the ownership, operation, or chartering of vessels on a mutual assessment plan, shall be deemed a qualified carrier to insure compensation under this chapter. The Secretary may suspend or revoke any such authorization for good cause shown after a hearing at which the carrier shall be entitled to be heard in person or by counsel and to present evidence. No suspension or revocation shall affect the liability of any carrier already incurred.

(Mar. 4, 1927, ch. 509, §32, 44 Stat. 1439; Pub. L. 98–426, §§20, 27(a)(2), Sept. 28, 1984, 98 Stat. 1652, 1654.)

AMENDMENTS

1984—Subsec. (a)(1). Pub. L. 98–426, § 27(a)(2), substituted "Secretary" for "commission". See Transfer of Functions note set out under section 902 of this title.

Subsec. (a)(2). Pub. L. 98–426, § 20, inserted "based on the employer's financial condition, the employer's previous record of payments, and other relevant factors," after "in an amount determined by the commission,".

Pub. L. 98–426, § 27(a)(2), substituted "Secretary" for "commission". See Transfer of Functions note set out under section 902 of this title.

Subsec. (b). Pub. L. 98–426, § 27(a)(2), substituted "Secretary" for "commission". See Transfer of Functions note set out under section 902 of this title.

EFFECTIVE DATE OF 1984 AMENDMENT

Amendment by Pub. L. 98–426 effective Sept. 28, 1984, see section 28(e)(1) of Pub. L. 98–426, set out as a note under section 901 of this title.

§ 933. Compensation for injuries where third persons are liable

(a) Election of remedies

If on account of a disability or death for which compensation is payable under this chapter the person entitled to such compensation determines that some person other than the employer or a person or persons in his employ is liable in damages, he need not elect whether to receive such compensation or to recover damages against such third person.

(b) Acceptance of compensation operating as assignment

Acceptance of compensation under an award in a compensation order filed by the deputy commissioner, an administrative law judge, or the Board shall operate as an assignment to the employer of all rights of the person entitled to compensation to recover damages against such third person unless such person shall commence an action against such third person within six months after such acceptance. If the employer fails to commence an action against such third person within ninety days after the cause of action is assigned under this section, the right to bring such action shall revert to the person entitled to compensation. For the purpose of this subsection, the term "award" with respect to a compensation order means a formal order issued by the deputy commissioner, an administrative law judge, or Board.

(c) Payment into section 944 fund operating as assignment

The payment of such compensation into the fund established in section 944 of this title shall operate as an assignment to the employer of all right of the legal representative of the deceased (hereinafter referred to as "representative") to recover damages against such third person.

(d) Institution of proceedings or compromise by assignee

Such employer on account of such assignment may either institute proceedings for the recovery of such damages or may compromise with such third person either without or after instituting such proceeding.

(e) Recoveries by assignee

Any amount recovered by such employer on account of such assignment, whether or not as the result of a compromise, shall be distributed as follows:

(1) The employer shall retain an amount equal to—

(A) the expenses incurred by him in respect to such proceedings or compromise (including a reasonable attorney's fee as determined by the deputy commissioner or Board);

(B) the cost of all benefits actually furnished by him to the employee under section 907 of this title;

(C) all amounts paid as compensation;

(D) the present value of all amounts thereafter payable as compensation, such present value to be computed in accordance with a schedule prepared by the Secretary, and the present value of the cost of all benefits thereafter to be furnished under section 907 of this title, to be estimated by the deputy commissioner, and the amounts so computed and estimated to be retained by the employer as a trust fund to pay such compensation and the cost of such benefits as they become due, and to pay any sum finally remaining in excess thereof to the person entitled to compensation or to the representative; and

(2) The employer shall pay any excess to the person entitled to compensation or to the representative.

(f) Institution of proceedings by person entitled to compensation

If the person entitled to compensation institutes proceedings within the period prescribed in subsection (b) of this section the employer shall be required to pay as compensation under this chapter a sum equal to the excess of the amount which the Secretary determines is payable on account of such injury or death over the net amount recovered against such third person. Such net amount shall be equal to the actual amount recovered less the expenses reasonably incurred by such person in respect to such proceedings (including reasonable attorneys' fees).

(g) Compromise obtained by person entitled to compensation

(1) If the person entitled to compensation (or the person's representative) enters into a settlement with a third person referred to in subsection (a) of this section for an amount less than the compensation to which the person (or the person's representative) would be entitled under this chapter, the employer shall be liable for compensation as determined under subsection (f) of this section only if written approval of the settlement is obtained from the employer and the employer's carrier, before the settlement is executed, and by the person entitled to compensation (or the person's representative). The approval shall be made on a form provided by the Secretary and shall be filed in the office of the deputy commissioner within thirty days after the settlement is entered into.

(2) If no written approval of the settlement is obtained and filed as required by paragraph (1), or if the employee fails to notify the employer of any settlement obtained from or judgment rendered against a third person, all rights to

compensation and medical benefits under this chapter shall be terminated, regardless of whether the employer or the employer's insurer has made payments or acknowledged entitlement to benefits under this chapter.

(3) Any payments by the special fund established under section 944 of this title shall be a lien upon the proceeds of any settlement obtained from or judgment rendered against a third person referred to under subsection (a) of this section. Notwithstanding any other provision of law, such lien shall be enforceable against such proceeds, regardless of whether the Secretary on behalf of the special fund has agreed to or has received actual notice of the settlement or judgment.

(4) Any payments by a trust fund described in section 917 of this title shall be a lien upon the proceeds of any settlement obtained from or judgment recorded against a third person referred to under subsection (a) of this section. Such lien shall have priority over a lien under paragraph (3) of this subsection.

(h) Subrogation

Where the employer is insured and the insurance carrier has assumed the payment of the compensation, the insurance carrier shall be subrogated to all the rights of the employer under this section.

(i) Right to compensation as exclusive remedy

The right to compensation or benefits under this chapter shall be the exclusive remedy to an employee when he is injured, or to his eligible survivors or legal representatives if he is killed, by the negligence or wrong of any other person or persons in the same employ: *Provided*, That this provision shall not affect the liability of a person other than an officer or employee of the employer.

(Mar. 4, 1927, ch. 509, §33, 44 Stat. 1440; June 25, 1938, ch. 685, §§12, 13, 52 Stat. 1168; Pub. L. 86–171, Aug. 18, 1959, 73 Stat. 391; Pub. L. 92–576, §15(f)–(h), Oct. 27, 1972, 86 Stat. 1262; Pub. L. 98–426, §21, Sept. 28, 1984, 98 Stat. 1652.)

AMENDMENTS

1984—Subsec. (b). Pub. L. 98–426, §21(a), substituted "Acceptance of compensation under an award in a compensation order filed by the deputy commissioner, an administrative law judge, or the Board shall operate as an assignment to the employer of all rights of the person entitled to compensation to recover damages against such third person unless such person shall commence an action against such third person within six months after such acceptance" for "Acceptance of such compensation under an award in a compensation order filed by the deputy commissioner or Board shall operate as an assignment to the employer of all right of the person entitled to compensation to recover damages against such third person unless such person shall commence an action against such third person within six months after such award" and inserted at end "If the employer fails to commence an action against such third person within ninety days after the cause of action is assigned under this section, the right to bring such action shall revert to the person entitled to compensation. For the purpose of this subsection, the term 'award' with respect to a compensation order means a formal order issued by the deputy commissioner, an administrative law judge, or Board."

Subsec. (e)(2). Pub. L. 98–426, §21(b), struck out ", less one-fifth of such excess which shall belong to the employer" after "or to the representative".

Subsec. (f). Pub. L. 98–426, §21(c)(1), inserted "net" before "amount recovered".

Pub. L. 98–426, §21(c)(2), inserted at end "Such net amount shall be equal to the actual amount recovered less the expenses reasonably incurred by such person in respect to such proceedings (including reasonable attorneys' fees)."

Subsec. (g). Pub. L. 98–426, §21(d), designated existing provisions as par. (1), substituted "If the person entitled to compensation (or the person's representative) enters into a settlement with a third person referred to in subsection (a) of this section for an amount less than the compensation to which the person (or the person's representative) would be entitled under this chapter, the employer shall be liable for compensation as determined under subsection (f) of this section only if written approval of the settlement is obtained from the employer and the employer's carrier, before the settlement is executed, and by the person entitled to compensation (or the person's representative)" for "If compromise with such third person is made by the person entitled to compensation or such representative of an amount less than the compensation to which such person or representative would be entitled to under this chapter the employer shall be liable for compensation as determined in subsection (f) of this section only if the written approval of such compromise is obtained from the employer and its insurance carrier by the person entitled to compensation or such representative at the time of or prior to such compromise on a form provided by the Secretary and filed in the office of the deputy commissioner having jurisdiction of such injury or death within thirty days after such compromise is made", inserted at end "The approval shall be made on a form provided by the Secretary and shall be filed in the office of the deputy commissioner within thirty days after the settlement is entered into.", and added pars. (2) to (4).

1972—Subsecs. (b), (e)(1)(A). Pub. L. 92–576, §15(f), (g), inserted "or Board" after "deputy commissioner".

Subsec. (g). Pub. L. 92–576, §15(h), substituted "if the written approval of such compromise is obtained from the employer and its insurance carrier by the person entitled to compensation or such representative at the time of or prior to such compromise on a form provided by the Secretary and filed in the office of the deputy commissioner having jurisdiction of such injury or death within thirty days after such compromise is made" for "if such compromise is made with his written approval".

1959—Subsec. (a). Pub. L. 86–171 inserted "or a person or persons in his employ" after "employer" and substituted "he need not elect whether" for "he may elect, by giving notice to the deputy commissioner in such manner as the Secretary may provide,".

Subsec. (b). Pub. L. 86–171 inserted "unless such person shall commence an action against such third person within six months after such award".

Subsec. (c). Pub. L. 86–171 struck out ", whether or not the representative has notified the deputy commissioner of his election" after "third person".

Subsec. (d). Pub. L. 86–171 reenacted subsec. (d) without change.

Subsec. (e). Pub. L. 86–171 substituted "Secretary" for "Commission" in par. (1)(D) and inserted in par. (2) "less one-fifth of such excess which shall belong to the employer".

Subsec. (f). Pub. L. 86–171 struck out "or the representative elects to recover damages against such third person and notifies the Secretary of his election and" before "institutes" and substituted "subsection (b) of this section" for "section 913 of this title" and "Secretary" for "Commission".

Subsec. (g). Pub. L. 86–171 corrected reference to "subsection (e)" to read "subsection (f)".

Subsecs. (h), (i). Pub. L. 86–171 redesignated subsec. (i) as (h) and struck out former subsec. (h) that permitted the deputy commissioner to make an election for a minor or to authorize the parent or guardian to make the election.

1938—Subsec. (b). Act June 25, 1938, §12, inserted "under an award in a compensation order filed by the deputy commissioner" and struck out ", whether or not the person entitled to compensation has notified the deputy commissioner of his election" at end of sentence.

Subsec. (e). Act June 25, 1938, §12, redesignated par. (1)(C) as par. (1)(C) and (D) and included in said par. (1)(D) the present value of the cost of benefits furnished.

Subsec. (i). Act June 25, 1938, §13, added subsec. (i).

EFFECTIVE DATE OF 1984 AMENDMENT

Amendment by Pub. L. 98–426 effective Sept. 28, 1984, and applicable both with respect to claims filed after such date and to claims pending on such date, see section 28(a) of Pub. L. 98–426, set out as a note under section 901 of this title.

EFFECTIVE DATE OF 1972 AMENDMENT

Amendment by Pub. L. 92–576 effective 30 days after Oct. 27, 1972, see section 22 of Pub. L. 92–576, set out as a note under section 902 of this title.

§934. Compensation notice

Every employer who has secured compensation under the provisions of this chapter shall keep posted in a conspicuous place or places in and about his place or places of business typewritten or printed notices, in accordance with a form prescribed by the Secretary, stating that such employer has secured the payment of compensation in accordance with the provisions of this chapter. Such notices shall contain the name and address of the carrier, if any, with whom the employer has secured payment of compensation and the date of the expiration of the policy.

(Mar. 4, 1927, ch. 509, §34, 44 Stat. 1441; Pub. L. 98–426, §27(a)(2), Sept. 28, 1984, 98 Stat. 1654.)

AMENDMENTS

1984—Pub. L. 98–426 substituted "Secretary" for "commission". See Transfer of Functions note set out under section 902 of this title.

EFFECTIVE DATE OF 1984 AMENDMENT

Amendment by Pub. L. 98–426 effective Sept. 28, 1984, see section 28(e)(1) of Pub. L. 98–426, set out as a note under section 901 of this title.

§935. Substitution of carrier for employer

In any case where the employer is not a self-insurer, in order that the liability for compensation imposed by this chapter may be most effectively discharged by the employer, and in order that the administration of this chapter in respect of such liability may be facilitated, the Secretary shall by regulation provide for the discharge, by the carrier for such employer, of such obligations and duties of the employer in respect to such liability, imposed by this chapter upon the employer, as it considers proper in order to effectuate the provisions of this chapter. For such purposes (1) notice to or knowledge of an employer of the occurrence of the injury shall be notice to or knowledge of the carrier, (2) jurisdiction of the employer by a deputy commissioner, the Board, or the Secretary, or any court under this chapter shall be jurisdiction of the carrier, and (3) any requirement by a deputy commissioner, the Board, or the Secretary, or any court under any compensation order, finding, or decision shall be binding upon the carrier in the same manner and to the same extent as upon the employer.

(Mar. 4, 1927, ch. 509, §35, 44 Stat. 1441; Pub. L. 92–576, §15(i), Oct. 27, 1972, 86 Stat. 1262; Pub. L. 98–426, §27(a)(2), Sept. 28, 1984, 98 Stat. 1654.)

AMENDMENTS

1984—Pub. L. 98–426 substituted "Secretary" for "commission". See Transfer of Functions note set out under section 902 of this title.

1972—Pub. L. 92–576 inserted reference to the Board in cls. (2) and (3).

EFFECTIVE DATE OF 1984 AMENDMENT

Amendment by Pub. L. 98–426 effective Sept. 28, 1984, see section 28(e)(1) of Pub. L. 98–426, set out as a note under section 901 of this title.

EFFECTIVE DATE OF 1972 AMENDMENT

Amendment by Pub. L. 92–576 effective 30 days after Oct. 27, 1972, see section 22 of Pub. L. 92–576, set out as a note under section 902 of this title.

§936. Insurance policies

(a) Every policy or contract of insurance issued under authority of this chapter shall contain (1) a provision to carry out the provisions of section 935 of this title, and (2) a provision that insolvency or bankruptcy of the employer and/or discharge therein shall not relieve the carrier from payment of compensation for disability or death sustained by an employee during the life of such policy or contract.

(b) No contract or policy of insurance issued by a carrier under this chapter shall be canceled prior to the date specified in such contract or policy for its expiration until at least thirty days have elapsed after a notice of cancellation has been sent to the deputy commissioner and to the employer in accordance with the provisions of subsection (c) of section 912 of this title.

(Mar. 4, 1927, ch. 509, §36, 44 Stat. 1441.)

§937. Certificate of compliance with chapter

No stevedoring firm shall be employed in any compensation district by a vessel or by hull owners until it presents to such vessel or hull owners a certificate issued by a deputy commissioner assigned to such district that it has complied with the provisions of this chapter requiring the securing of compensation to its employees. Any person violating the provisions of this section shall be punished by a fine of not more than $1,000, or by imprisonment for not more than one year, or by both such fine and imprisonment.

(Mar. 4, 1927, ch. 509, §37, 44 Stat. 1442.)

§938. Penalties

(a) Failure to secure payment of compensation

Any employer required to secure the payment of compensation under this chapter who fails to secure such compensation shall be guilty of a misdemeanor and, upon conviction thereof, shall be punished by a fine of not more than $10,000, or by imprisonment for not more than one year, or by both such fine and imprisonment; and in any case where such employer is a corporation, the president, secretary, and treasurer thereof shall be also severally liable to such fine or imprisonment as herein provided for the failure of such corporation to secure the payment of compensation; and such president, secretary, and treasurer shall be severally personally liable, jointly with such corporation, for any compensation or other benefit which may accrue under the said chapter in respect to any injury which may occur to any employee of such corporation while it shall so fail to secure the payment of compensation as required by section 932 of this title.

(b) Avoiding payment of compensation

Any employer who knowingly transfers, sells, encumbers, assigns, or in any manner disposes of, conceals, secretes, or destroys any property belonging to such employer, after one of his employees has been injured within the purview of this chapter, and with intent to avoid the payment of compensation under this chapter to such employee or his dependents, shall be guilty of a misdemeanor and, upon conviction thereof, shall be punished by a fine of not more than $10,000, or by imprisonment for not more than one year, or by both such fine and imprisonment; and in any case where such employer is a corporation, the president, secretary, and treasurer thereof shall be also severally liable to such penalty of imprisonment as well as jointly liable with such corporation for such fine.

(c) Effect on other liability of employer

This section shall not affect any other liability of the employer under this chapter.

(Mar. 4, 1927, ch. 509, §38, 44 Stat. 1442; June 25, 1938, ch. 685, §14, 52 Stat. 1168; Pub. L. 98–426, §22, Sept. 28, 1984, 98 Stat. 1653.)

AMENDMENTS

1984—Subsecs. (a), (b). Pub. L. 98–426 substituted "$10,000" for "$1,000" wherever appearing.

1938—Act June 25, 1938, amended section generally, designating first sentence as subsec. (a) and inserting provisions respecting liability of corporate officers, adding subsec. (b), and designating second sentence as subsec. (c).

EFFECTIVE DATE OF 1984 AMENDMENT

Amendment by Pub. L. 98–426 effective Sept. 28, 1984, see section 28(e)(1) of Pub. L. 98–426, set out as a note under section 901 of this title.

§939. Administration by Secretary

(a) Prescribing rules and regulations; appointing and fixing compensation of employees; making expenditures

Except as otherwise specifically provided, the Secretary shall administer the provisions of this chapter, and for such purpose the Secretary is authorized (1) to make such rules and regulations; (2) to appoint and fix the compensation of such temporary technical assistants and medical advisers, and, subject to the provisions of the civil service laws, to appoint, and, in accordance with chapter 51 and subchapter III of chapter 53 of title 5, to fix the compensation of such deputy commissioners (except deputy commissioners appointed under subsection (a) of section 940 of this title) and other officers and employees; and (3) to make such expenditures (including expenditures for personal services and rent at the seat of government and elsewhere, for law books, books of reference, periodicals, and for printing and binding) as may be necessary in the administration of this chapter. All expenditures of the Secretary in the administration of this chapter shall be allowed and paid as provided in section 945[1] of this title upon the presentation of itemized vouchers therefor approved by the Secretary.

(b) Establishing compensation districts

The Secretary shall establish compensation districts, to include the high seas and the areas within the United States to which this chapter applies, and shall assign to each such district one or more deputy commissioners, as the Secretary deems advisable. Judicial proceedings under sections 918 and 921 of this title in respect of any injury or death occurring on the high seas shall be instituted in the district court within whose territorial jurisdiction is located the office of the deputy commissioner having jurisdiction in respect of such injury or death (or in the United States District Court for the District of Columbia if such office is located in such District).

(c) Furnishing information and assistance; directing vocational rehabilitation

(1) The Secretary shall, upon request, provide persons covered by this chapter with information and assistance relating to the chapter's coverage and compensation and the procedures for obtaining such compensation and including assistance in processing a claim. The Secretary may, upon request, provide persons covered by this chapter with legal assistance in processing a claim. The Secretary shall also provide employees receiving compensation information on medical, manpower, and vocational rehabilitation services and assist such employees in obtaining the best such services available.

(2) The Secretary shall direct the vocational rehabilitation of permanently disabled employees and shall arrange with the appropriate public or private agencies in States or Territories, possessions, or the District of Columbia for such rehabilitation. The Secretary may in his discretion furnish such prosthetic appliances or other apparatus made necessary by an injury upon which an award has been made under this chapter to render a disabled employee fit to engage in a remunerative occupation. Where necessary rehabilitation services are not available otherwise, the Secretary of Labor may, in his discretion, use the fund provided for in section 944 of this title in such amounts as may be necessary to procure such services, including necessary prosthetic appliance or other apparatus. This fund shall also be available in such amounts as may be authorized in annual appropriations for the Department of Labor for the costs of administering this subsection.

(Mar. 4, 1927, ch. 509, §39, 44 Stat. 1442; June 25, 1936, ch. 804, 49 Stat. 1921; June 25, 1948, ch. 646, §32(b), 62 Stat. 991; May 24, 1949, ch. 139, §127, 63 Stat. 107; Oct. 28, 1949, ch. 782, title XI, §1106(a), 63 Stat. 972; July 26, 1956, ch. 735, §7, 70 Stat. 656; Pub. L. 92–576, §17, Oct. 27, 1972, 86 Stat. 1262; Pub. L. 98–426, §27(a)(2), (c), Sept. 28, 1984, 98 Stat. 1654.)

[1] See References in Text note below.

REFERENCES IN TEXT

The civil service laws, referred to in subsec. (a), are set forth in Title 5, Government Organization and Employees. See, particularly, section 3301 et seq. of Title 5.

Section 945 of this title, referred to in subsec. (a), was repealed by Pub. L. 98–426, § 25, Sept. 28, 1984, 98 Stat. 1654. See section 944 of this title.

CODIFICATION

In subsec. (a) "chapter 51 and subchapter III of chapter 53 of title 5" substituted for "the Classification Act of 1949, as amended" on authority of Pub. L. 89–554, § 7(b), Sept. 6, 1966, 80 Stat. 631, the first section of which enacted Title 5, Government Organization and Employees.

As originally enacted, subsec. (b) contained a reference to the Supreme Court of the District of Columbia. Act June 25, 1936, substituted "the district court of the United States for the District of Columbia" for "the Supreme Court of the District of Columbia", and act June 25, 1948, as amended by act May 24, 1949, substituted "United States District Court for the District of Columbia" for "district court of the United States for the District of Columbia".

Former second sentence of subsec. (c), providing that the Federal Board for Vocational Education should cooperate with the Employees' Compensation Commission in such educational work has been omitted. The functions of the Board were transferred to the Department of the Interior by Ex. Ord. No. 6166, § 15, June 10, 1933, and then to the Federal Security Agency by Reorg. Plan No. 1 of 1939, §§ 201, 204, eff. July 1, 1939, 4 F.R. 2728, 53 Stat. 1424. The Commission was abolished and its functions transferred to the Federal Security Administrator and the Federal Board for Vocational Education was abolished by Reorg. Plan No. 2 of 1946, former sections 3 and 8, respectively, set out in the Appendix to Title 5, Government Organization and Employees.

AMENDMENTS

1984—Subsec. (a). Pub. L. 98–426, § 27(c), substituted "Secretary" for "United States Employees' Compensation Commission". See Transfer of Functions note set out under section 902 of this title.

Subsecs. (b), (c)(2). Pub. L. 98–426, § 27(a)(2), substituted "Secretary" for "commission". See Transfer of Functions note set out under section 902 of this title.

1972—Subsec. (c). Pub. L. 92–576 added par. (1) and redesignated existing provisions as par. (2).

1956—Subsec. (c). Act July 26, 1956, substituted "rehabilitation" for "education" at end of first sentence, and substituted last two sentences, relating to use of special fund where necessary rehabilitation services are not available, and availability of fund in amounts authorized annually for the Department of Labor for former sentence which provided that "If any surplus is left in any fiscal year in the fund provided for in section 944 of this title, such surplus may be used in subsequent fiscal years for the purposes of administration and investigation."

1949—Subsec. (a). Act Oct. 28, 1949, substituted "Classification Act of 1949" for "Classification Act of 1923".

EFFECTIVE DATE OF 1984 AMENDMENT

Amendment by Pub. L. 98–426 effective Sept. 28, 1984, see section 28(e)(1) of Pub. L. 98–426, set out as a note under section 901 of this title.

EFFECTIVE DATE OF 1972 AMENDMENT

Amendment by Pub. L. 92–576 effective 30 days after Oct. 27, 1972, see section 22 of Pub. L. 92–576, set out as a note under section 902 of this title.

REPEALS

Act Oct. 28, 1949, ch. 782, cited as a credit to this section, was repealed (subject to a savings clause) by Pub. L. 89–554, Sept. 6, 1966, § 8, 80 Stat. 632, 655.

§ 940. Deputy commissioners

(a) Appointment; use of personnel and facilities of boards, commissions, or other agencies; expenses and salaries

The Secretary may appoint as deputy commissioners any member of any board, commission, or other agency of a State to act as deputy commissioner for any compensation district or part thereof in such State, and may make arrangements with such board, commission, or other agency for the use of the personnel and facilities thereof in the administration of this chapter. The Secretary may make such arrangements as may be deemed advisable by him for the payment of expenses of such board, commission, or other agency, incurred in the administration of this chapter pursuant to this section, and for the payment of salaries to such board, commission, or other agency, or the members thereof, and may pay any amounts agreed upon to the proper officers of the State, upon vouchers approved by the Secretary.

(b) Appointment in Territories and District of Columbia; compensation

In any Territory of the United States or in the District of Columbia a person holding an office under the United States may be appointed deputy commissioner and for services rendered as deputy commissioner may be paid compensation, in addition to that he is receiving from the United States, in an amount fixed by the Secretary in accordance with chapter 51 and subchapter III of chapter 53 of title 5.

(c) Transfers to other districts; temporary details

Deputy commissioners (except deputy commissioners appointed under subsection (a) of this section) may be transferred from one compensation district to another and may be temporarily detailed from one compensation district for service in another in the discretion of the Secretary.

(d) Maintaining offices

Each deputy commissioner shall maintain and keep open during reasonable business hours an office, at a place designated by the Secretary, for the transaction of business under this chapter, at which office he shall keep his official records and papers. Such office shall be furnished and equipped by the Secretary, who shall also furnish the deputy commissioner with all necessary clerical and other assistants, records, books, blanks, and supplies. Wherever practicable such office shall be located in a building owned or leased by the United States; otherwise the Secretary shall rent suitable quarters.

(e) Records and papers

If any deputy commissioner is removed from office, or for any reason ceases to act as such deputy commissioner, all of his official records and papers and office equipment shall be transferred to his successor in office or, if there be no successor, then to the Secretary or to a deputy commissioner designated by the Secretary.

(f) Conflict of interest

Neither a deputy commissioner or Board member nor any business associate of a deputy commissioner or Board member shall appear as attorney in any proceeding under this chapter, and no deputy commissioner or Board member shall act in any such case in which he is interested, or when he is employed by any party in interest or related to any party in interest by consanguinity or affinity within the third degree, as determined by the common law.

(Mar. 4, 1927, ch. 509, §40, 44 Stat. 1443; Oct. 28, 1949, ch. 782, title XI, §1106(a), 63 Stat. 972; Pub. L. 92–576, §15(j), Oct. 27, 1972, 86 Stat. 1262; Pub. L. 98–426, §27(a)(2), Sept. 28, 1984, 98 Stat. 1654.)

CODIFICATION

In subsec. (b) "chapter 51 and subchapter III of chapter 53 of title 5" substituted for "the Classification Act of 1949, as amended" on authority of Pub. L. 89–554, §7(b), Sept. 6, 1966, 80 Stat. 631, the first section of which enacted Title 5, Government Organization and Employees.

AMENDMENTS

1984—Subsecs. (a) to (e). Pub. L. 98–426 substituted "Secretary" for "commission". See Transfer of Functions note set out under section 902 of this title.

1972—Subsec. (f). Pub. L. 92–576 inserted references to Board member.

1949—Subsec. (b). Act Oct. 28, 1949, substituted "Classification Act of 1949" for "Classification Act of 1923".

EFFECTIVE DATE OF 1984 AMENDMENT

Amendment by Pub. L. 98–426 effective Sept. 28, 1984, see section 28(e)(1) of Pub. L. 98–426, set out as a note under section 901 of this title.

EFFECTIVE DATE OF 1972 AMENDMENT

Amendment by Pub. L. 92–576 effective 30 days after Oct. 27, 1972, see section 22 of Pub. L. 92–576, set out as a note under section 902 of this title.

REPEALS

Act Oct. 28, 1949, ch. 782, cited as a credit to this section, was repealed (subject to a savings clause) by Pub. L. 89–554, Sept. 6, 1966, §8, 80 Stat. 632, 655.

TRANSFER OF FUNCTIONS

For transfer of functions to the Secretary of Labor, see note set out under section 902 of this title.

§941. Safety rules and regulations

(a) Safe place of employment; installation of safety devices and safeguards

Every employer shall furnish and maintain employment and places of employment which shall be reasonably safe for his employees in all employments covered by this chapter and shall install, furnish, maintain, and use such devices and safeguards with particular reference to equipment used by and working conditions established by such employers as the Secretary may determine by regulation or order to be reasonably necessary to protect the life, health, and safety of such employees, and to render safe such employment and places of employment, and to prevent injury to his employees. However, the Secretary may not make determinations by regulation or order under this section as to matters within the scope of title 52 of the Revised Statutes and Acts supplementary or amendatory thereto, the Act of June 15, 1917 (ch. 30, 40 Stat. 220), as amended, or section 1333(e) of title 43.

(b) Studies and investigations by Secretary

The Secretary, in enforcing and administering the provisions of this section, is authorized in addition to such other powers and duties as are conferred upon him—

(1) to make studies and investigations with respect to safety provisions and the causes and prevention of injuries in employments covered by this chapter, and in making such studies and investigations to cooperate with any agency of the United States or with any State agency engaged in similar work;

(2) to utilize the services of any agency of the United States or any State agency engaged in similar work (with the consent of such agency) in connection with the administration of this section;

(3) to promote uniformity in safety standards in employments covered by this chapter through cooperative action with any agency of the United States or with any State agency engaged in similar work;

(4) to provide for the establishment and supervision of programs for the education and training of employers and employees in the recognition, avoidance, and prevention of unsafe working conditions in employments covered by this chapter, and to consult with and advise employers as to the best means of preventing injuries;

(5) to hold such hearings, issue such orders, and make such decisions, based upon findings of fact, as are deemed to be necessary to enforce the provisions of this section, and for such purposes the Secretary and the district courts shall have the authority and jurisdiction provided by section 39 of title 41, and the Secretary shall be represented in any court proceedings as provided in section 921a of this title.

(c) Inspection of places and practices of employment

The Secretary or his authorized representative may inspect such places of employment, question such employees, and investigate such conditions, practices, or matters in connection with employment subject to this chapter, as he may deem appropriate to determine whether any person has violated any provision of this section, or any rule or regulation issued thereunder, or which may aid in the enforcement of the provisions of this section. No employer or other person shall refuse to admit the Secretary or his authorized representatives to any such place or shall refuse to permit any such inspection.

(d) Requests for advice; variations from safety rules and regulations

Any employer may request the advice of the Secretary or his authorized representative, in complying with the requirements of any rule or regulation adopted to carry out the provisions of this section. In case of practical difficulties or unnecessary hardships, the Secretary in his discretion may grant variations from any such rule or regulation, or particular provisions thereof, and permit the use of other or different devices if he finds that the purpose of the rule or regulation will be observed by the variation and the safety of employees will be equally secured thereby. Any person affected by such rule or regulation, or his agent, may request the Secretary to grant such variation, stating in writing the grounds on which his request is based. Any authorization by the Secretary of a variation shall be in writing, shall describe the conditions under which the variation shall be permitted, and shall be published as provided in section 552 of title 5. A properly indexed record of all variations shall be kept in the office of the Secretary and open to public inspection.

(e) Jurisdiction to restrain violations

The United States district courts shall have jurisdiction for cause shown, in any action brought by the Secretary, represented as provided in section 921a of this title, to restrain violations of this section or of any rule, regulation, or order of the Secretary adopted to carry out the provisions of this section.

(f) Violations and penalties

Any employer who, willfully, violates or fails or refuses to comply with the provisions of subsection (a) of this section, or with any lawful rule, regulation, or order adopted to carry out the provisions of this section, and any employer or other person who willfully interferes with, hinders, or delays the Secretary or his authorized representative in carrying out his duties under subsection (c) of this section by refusing to admit the Secretary or his authorized representative to any place, or to permit the inspection or examination of any employment or place of employment, or who willfully hinders or delays the Secretary or his authorized representative in the performance of his duties in the enforcement of this section, shall be guilty of an offense, and, upon conviction thereof, shall be punished for each offense by a fine of not less than $100 nor more than $3,000; and in any case where such employer is a corporation, the officer who willfully permits any such violation to occur shall be guilty of an offense, and, upon conviction thereof, shall be punished also for each offense by a fine of not less than $100 nor more than $3,000. The liability hereunder shall not affect any other liability of the employer under this chapter.

(g) Inapplicability to certain employments

(1) The provisions of this section shall not apply in the case of any employment relating to the operations for the exploration, production, or transportation by pipeline of mineral resources upon the navigable waters of the United States, nor under the authority of the Act of August 7, 1953 (ch. 345, 67 Stat. 462) [43 U.S.C. 1331 et seq.], nor in the case of any employment in connection with lands (except filled in, made or reclaimed lands) beneath the navigable waters as defined in the Act of May 22, 1953 (ch. 65, 67 Stat. 29) [43 U.S.C. 1301 et seq.], nor in the case of any employment for which compensation in case of disability or death is provided for employees under the authority of the Act of May 17, 1928 (ch. 612, 45 Stat. 600), as amended, nor under the authority of the Act of August 16, 1941 (ch. 357, 55 Stat. 622), as amended [42 U.S.C. 1651 et seq.].

(2) The provisions of this section, with the exception of paragraph (1) of subsection (b) of this section, shall not be applied under the authority of subchapter I of chapter 81 of title 5.

(Mar. 4, 1927, ch. 509, §41, 44 Stat. 1444; Pub. L. 85–742, §1, Aug. 23, 1958, 72 Stat. 835; Pub. L. 97–375, title I, §110(b), Dec. 21, 1982, 96 Stat. 1820.)

REFERENCES IN TEXT

Title 52 of the Revised Statutes, referred to in subsec. (a), consisted of R.S. §§4399 to 4500, which were classified to sections 170, 214, 215, 222, 224, 224a, 226, 228, 229, 230 to 234, 239, 240, 361, 362, 364, 371 to 373, 375 to 382, 384, 385, 391, 391a, 392 to 394, 399 to 404, 405 to 416, 435 to 440, 451 to 453, 460, 461 to 463, 464, 466, 467 to 482, and 489 to 498 of former Title 46, Shipping. For complete classification of R.S. §§4399 to 4500 to the Code, see Tables. A majority of such sections of the Revised Statutes were repealed and various provisions thereof were reenacted in Title 46, Shipping, by Pub. L. 98–89, Aug. 26, 1983, 97 Stat. 500. For disposition of sections of former Title 46 into revised Title 46, see Disposition Table preceding section 101 of Title 46.

Act of June 15, 1917, referred to in subsec. (a), is act June 15, 1917, ch. 30, 40 Stat. 217, as amended. For complete classification of this Act to the Code, see Tables.

Act of August 7, 1953, referred to in subsec. (g)(1), is known as the Outer Continental Shelf Lands Act, and is classified to subchapter III (§1331 et seq.) of chapter 29 of Title 43, Public Lands. For complete classification of this Act to the Code, see Short Title note set out under section 1331 of Title 43 and Tables.

Act of May 22, 1953, referred to in subsec. (g)(1), is known as the Submerged Lands Act, and is classified generally to subchapters I and II (§§1301 et seq., 1311 et seq.) of chapter 29 of Title 43. For complete classification of this Act to the Code, see Short Title note set out under section 1301 of Title 43 and Tables.

Act of May 17, 1928, referred to in subsec. (g)(1), extended the applicability of this chapter in respect to the injury or death of an employee of an employer carrying on any employment in the District of Columbia.

Act of August 16, 1941, referred to in subsec. (g)(1), is known as the Defense Base Act and is classified generally to chapter 11 (§1651 et seq.) of Title 42, The Public Health and Welfare. For complete classification of this Act to the Code, see Short Title note set out under section 1651 of Title 42 and Tables.

CODIFICATION

In subsec. (d) "section 552 of title 5" substituted for "section 3 of the Administrative Procedure Act (ch. 324, 60 Stat. 237), as amended", and in subsec. (g)(2) "subchapter I of chapter 81 of title 5" substituted for "the Act of September 7, 1916 (ch. 458, 39 Stat. 742), as amended", on authority of Pub. L. 89–554, §7(b), Sept. 6, 1966, 80 Stat. 631, the first section of which enacted Title 5, Government Organization and Employees. Said section 3 of the Administrative Procedure Act had been classified to section 1002 of former Title 5, Executive Departments and Government Officers and Employees. Said act of Sept. 7, 1916, was known as the "Federal Employees' Compensation Act" and had been classified to section 751 et seq. of former Title 5.

As originally enacted, subsec. (e) contained the phrase ", together with the District Court for the Territory of Alaska," following "the United States district courts". The phrase has been deleted as superfluous in view of Pub. L. 85–508, July 7, 1958, 72 Stat. 339 (set out as a note preceding section 21 of Title 48, Territories and Insular Possessions) which admitted Alaska into the union and enacted section 81A of Title 28, Judiciary and Judicial Procedure, constituting Alaska as one judicial district and in view of section 132 of Title 28 which provides that: "There shall be in each judicial district a district court which shall be a court of record known as the United States District Court for the district."

AMENDMENTS

1982—Subsec. (b)(1). Pub. L. 97–375 struck out "and from time to time make to Congress such recommendations as he may deem proper as to the best means of preventing such injuries" after "by this chapter".

1958—Pub. L. 85–742 amended section generally and, among other changes, empowered the Secretary of Labor to prescribe, by regulation or order, safety rules for the furnishing and maintenance of safe places of employment and for the installation, furnishing and maintenance of safety devices and safeguards, authorized the Secretary to provide for the establishment and supervision of safety programs, permitted the inspection of places of employment and investigation of employment conditions and practices, granted jurisdiction to the district courts to restrain violations of this section or of any rules, regulations or orders of the Secretary, and to prescribe penalties for violations.

"SECRETARY" DEFINED

Section 2 of Pub. L. 85–742 provided that: "The term 'Secretary' as used in this Act and in amendments made by this Act [to this section] means the Secretary of Labor."

§942. Annual report

The Secretary shall make to Congress at the end of each fiscal year,[1] a report of the administration of this chapter for the preceding fiscal year, including a detailed statement of receipts of and expenditures from the fund established in section 944 of this title, together with such recommendations as the Secretary deems advisable. Such report shall include the annual report required under section 936(b) of title 30 and shall be identified as the Annual Report of the Office of Workers' Compensation Programs.

(Mar. 4, 1927, ch. 509, §42, as added Pub. L. 98–426, §23, Sept. 28, 1984, 98 Stat. 1653; amended Pub. L. 104–66, title I, §1102(b)(1), Dec. 21, 1995, 109 Stat. 722.)

PRIOR PROVISIONS

A prior section 942, act Mar. 4, 1927, ch. 509, §42, 44 Stat. 1444, related to travel and subsistence expenses. See section 5701 et seq. of Title 5, Government Organization and Employees.

AMENDMENTS

1995—Pub. L. 104–66 substituted "end of each fiscal year" for "beginning of each regular session, commencing at the beginning of the second regular session after September 28, 1984" and inserted at end "Such report shall include the annual report required under section 936(b) of title 30 and shall be identified as the Annual Report of the Office of Workers' Compensation Programs."

EFFECTIVE DATE

Section effective Sept. 28, 1984, see section 28(e)(1) of Pub. L. 98–426, set out as an Effective Date of 1984 Amendment note under section 901 of this title.

§943. Repealed. Pub. L. 89–348, §1(15), Nov. 8, 1965, 79 Stat. 1311

Section, act Mar. 4, 1927, ch. 509, §43, 44 Stat. 1444, required Secretary to make a report to Congress at beginning of each regular session of the administration of this chapter for preceding fiscal year, including a detailed statement of receipts of and expenditures from funds established in sections 944 and 945 of this title.

§944. Special fund

(a) Establishment; administration; custody, trust

There is established in the Treasury of the United States a special fund. Such fund shall be administered by the Secretary. The Treasurer of the United States shall be the custodian of such fund, and all moneys and securities in such fund shall be held in trust by such Treasurer and shall not be money or property of the United States.

(b) Disbursements; bond of custodian

The Treasurer is authorized to disburse moneys from such fund only upon order of the Secretary. He shall be required to give bond in an amount to be fixed and with securities to be approved by the Secretary of the Treasury and the Comptroller General of the United States conditioned upon the faithful performance of his duty as custodian of such fund.

(c) Payments into fund

Payments into such fund shall be made as follows:

(1) Whenever the Secretary determines that there is no person entitled under this chapter to compensation for the death of an employee which would otherwise be compensable under this chapter, the appropriate employer shall pay $5,000 as compensation for the death of such an employee.

(2) At the beginning of each calendar year the Secretary shall estimate the probable expenses of the fund during that calendar year and the amount of payments required (and the schedule therefor) to maintain adequate reserves in the fund. Each carrier and self-insurer shall make payments into the fund on a prorated assessment by the Secretary determined by—

(A) computing the ratio (expressed as a percent) of (i) the carrier's or self-insured's workers' compensation payments under this chapter during the preceding calendar year, to (ii) the total of such payments by all carriers and self-insureds under this chapter during such year;

(B) computing the ratio (expressed as a percent) of (i) the payments under section 908(f) of this title during the preceding calendar year which are attributable to the carrier or self-insured, to (ii) the total of such payments during such year attributable to all carriers and self-insureds;

(C) dividing the sum of the percentages computed under subparagraphs (A) and (B) for the carrier or self-insured by two; and

(D) multiplying the percent computed under subparagraph (C) by such probable expenses of the fund (as determined under the first sentence of this paragraph).

(3) All amounts collected as fines and penalties under the provisions of this chapter shall be paid into such fund.

(d) Investigations; records, availability; recordkeeping; provisions of sections 49 and 50 of title 15 applicable to Secretary

(1) For the purpose of making rules, regulations, and determinations under this section under and for providing enforcement thereof, the Secretary may investigate and gather appropriate data from each carrier and self-insurer. For that purpose, the Secretary may enter and inspect such places and records (and make such transcriptions thereof), question such employees, and investigate such facts, conditions, practices, or matters as he may deem necessary or appropriate.

[1] So in original. The comma probably should not appear.

(2) Each carrier and self-insurer shall make, keep, and preserve such records, and make such reports and provide such additional information, as prescribed by regulation or order of the Secretary, as the Secretary deems necessary or appropriate to carry out his responsibilities under this section.

(3) For the purpose of any hearing or investigation related to determinations or the enforcement of the provisions of this section, the provisions of sections 49 and 50 of title 15 (relating to the attendance of witnesses and the production of books, papers, and documents) are hereby made applicable to the jurisdiction, powers, and duties of the Secretary of Labor.

(e) Depositories; investments

The Treasurer of the United States shall deposit any moneys paid into such fund into such depository banks as the Secretary may designate and may invest any portion of the funds which, in the opinion of the Secretary, is not needed for current requirements, in bonds or notes of the United States or of any Federal land bank.

(f) Limitation of liability

Neither the United States nor the Secretary shall be liable in respect of payments authorized under section 908 of this title in an amount greater than the money or property deposited in or belonging to such fund.

(g) Audit by Comptroller General; finality of payment determinations; credits of disbursing officers

The Comptroller General of the United States shall audit the account for such fund, but the action of the Secretary in making payments from such fund shall be final and not subject to review, and the Comptroller General is authorized and directed to allow credit in the accounts of any disbursing officer of the Secretary for payments made from such fund authorized by the Secretary.

(h) Civil actions for civil penalties and unpaid assessments

All civil penalties and unpaid assessments provided for in this chapter shall be collected by civil suit brought by the Secretary.

(i) Proceeds available for certain payments

The proceeds of this fund shall be available for payments:

(1) Pursuant to sections[1] 910 of this title with respect to certain initial and subsequent annual adjustments in compensation for total permanent disability or death.

(2) Under section 908(f) and (g), under section 918(b), and under section 939(c) of this title.

(3) To repay the sums deposited in the fund pursuant to subsection (d) of this section.

(4) To defray the expense of making examinations as provided in section 907(e) of this title.

(j) Audit to Congress

The fund shall be audited annually and the results of such audit shall be included in the annual report required by section 942 of this title.

[1] So in original. Probably should be "section".

(Mar. 4, 1927, ch. 509, §44, 44 Stat. 1444; July 26, 1956, ch. 735, §8, 70 Stat. 656; Pub. L. 92–576, §8, Oct. 27, 1972, 86 Stat. 1256; Pub. L. 98–426, §§24, 27(a)(2), Sept. 28, 1984, 98 Stat. 1653, 1654.)

AMENDMENTS

1984—Subsecs. (a), (b). Pub. L. 98–426, §27(a)(2), substituted "Secretary" for "commission". See Transfer of Functions note set out under section 902 of this title.

Subsec. (c)(2). Pub. L. 98–426, §24(a), substituted provisions requiring that, at the beginning of each calendar year the Secretary estimate the probable expenses of the fund during that calendar year and the amount of payments required (and the schedule therefor) to maintain adequate reserves in the fund and that each carrier and self-insurer make payments into the fund on a prorated assessment by the Secretary determined by (A) computing the ratio (expressed as a percent) of (i) the carrier's or self-insured's workers' compensation payments under this chapter during the preceding calendar year, to (ii) the total of such payments by all carriers and self-insureds under this chapter during such year; (B) computing the ratio (expressed as a percent) of (i) the payments under section 908(f) of this title during the preceding calendar year which are attributable to the carrier or self-insured, to (ii) the total of such payments during such year attributable to all carriers and self-insureds; (C) dividing the sum of the percentages computed under (A) and (B) for the carrier or self-insured by two; and (D) multiplying the percent computed under (C) by such probable expenses of the fund (as determined under the first sentence of this paragraph) for provisions which had formerly required that at the beginning of each calendar year the Secretary estimate the probable expenses of the fund during that calendar year and each carrier or self-insurer make payments into the fund on a prorated assessment by the Secretary in the proportion that the total compensation and medical payments made on risks covered by this chapter by each carrier and self-insurer bore to the total of such payments made by all carriers and self-insurers under the chapter in the prior calendar year in accordance with a formula and schedule to be determined from time to time by the Secretary to maintain adequate reserves in the fund.

Subsec. (e). Pub. L. 98–426, §24(b), redesignated subsec. (f) as (e). Former subsec. (e), which authorized the appropriation to the Secretary of the sum of $2,000,000 which the Secretary was required to deposit into the fund and directed that, upon deposit in the fund such moneys would be treated as the property of such fund, that the sum, without additional payments for interest, would be repaid from the money or property belonging to the fund on a schedule of repayment set by the Secretary, that full repayment had to be made no later than five years from the date of deposit into the fund, and that each such repayment, as made, would be covered into the Treasury of the United States as miscellaneous receipts, was struck out.

Pub. L. 98–426, §27(a)(2), substituted "Secretary" for "commission". See Transfer of Functions note set out under section 902 of this title.

Subsec. (f). Pub. L. 98–426, §24(b), redesignated subsec. (g) as (f). Former subsec. (f) redesignated (e).

Pub. L. 98–426, §27(a)(2), substituted "Secretary" for "commission". See Transfer of Functions note set out under section 902 of this title.

Subsec. (g). Pub. L. 98–426, §24(b), redesignated subsec. (h) as (g). Former subsec. (g) redesignated (f).

Pub. L. 98–426, §27(a)(2), substituted "Secretary" for "commission". See Transfer of Functions note set out under section 902 of this title.

Subsec. (h). Pub. L. 98–426, §24(b), redesignated subsec. (i) as (h). Former subsec. (h) redesignated (g).

Pub. L. 98–426, §24(c), inserted "and unpaid assessments" after "civil penalties".

Pub. L. 98–426, §27(a)(2), substituted "Secretary" for "commission". See Transfer of Functions note set out under section 902 of this title.

Subsec. (i). Pub. L. 98–426, §24(b), redesignated subsec. (j) as (i). Former subsec. (i) redesignated (h).

Subsec. (i)(1). Pub. L. 98–426, §24(d)(1), struck out "and 911" after "sections 910", inserted "certain" before "initial", and struck out "which occurred prior to the effective date of this subsection" after "disability or death".

Subsec. (i)(4). Pub. L. 98–426, §24(d)(2), inserted "(e)" after "section 907".

Subsec. (j). Pub. L. 98–426, §24(b), redesignated (k) as (j). Former subsec. (j) redesignated (i).

Pub. L. 98–426, §24(e), substituted "The fund shall be audited annually and the results of such audit shall be included in the annual report required by section 942 of this title" for "At the close of each fiscal year the Secretary shall submit to the Congress a complete audit of the fund".

Subsec. (k). Pub. L. 98–426, §24(b), redesignated subsec. (k) as (j).

1972—Subsec. (a). Pub. L. 92–576, §8(a), substituted "special fund" for "special fund for the purpose of making payments in accordance with the provisions of subsections (f) and (g) of section 908, of subsection (b) of section 918, and of subsection (c) of section 939 of this title".

Subsec. (c)(1). Pub. L. 92–576, §8(b), increased compensation payment for death to $5,000 from $1,000; inserted provision for compensation which would otherwise be compensable under this chapter; deleted second sentence, less two provisos, now incorporated in subsec. (j)(2) of this section; deleted first such proviso for priority of payments authorized by subsec. (f) over other payments authorized from the fund; and deleted second such proviso, now incorporated in subsec. (k) of this section.

Subsec. (c)(2), (3). Pub. L. 92–576, §8(b), added par. (2) and redesignated former par. (2) as (3).

Subsec. (d). Pub. L. 92–576, §8(b), added subsec. (d). Former subsec. (d) redesignated (f).

Subsec. (e). Pub. L. 92–576, §8(b), added subsec. (e). Former subsec. (e) redesignated (g).

Subsecs. (f) to (i). Pub. L. 92–576, §8(b), redesignated former subsecs. (d) to (g) as (f) to (i), respectively.

Subsec. (j). Pub. L. 92–576, §8(d), added pars. (1), (3), and (4), and incorporated former part of first sentence of subsec. (a) and former second sentence, less provisos, of subsec. (c)(1), in provisions designated as par. (2).

Subsec. (k). Pub. L. 92–576, §8(d), incorporated former provisions of subsec. (c)(1), last proviso, in provisions designated as subsec. (k).

1956—Subsec. (a). Act July 26, 1956, §8(a), substituted ", of subsection (b) of section 918 of this title, and of subsection (c) of section 939 of this title" for "of this title."

Subsec. (c)(1). Act July 26, 1956, §8(b), substituted provisions relating to availability of fund for payments under sections 908(f) and (g), 918(b), and 939(c) of this title, proviso that subsec. (f) payments have priority, and further proviso requiring annual audit, for former provision that fifty per centum of each payment shall be available for the payments under section 908(f) and (g) of this title.

EFFECTIVE DATE OF 1984 AMENDMENT

Amendment by Pub. L. 98–426 effective Sept. 28, 1984, see section 28(e)(1) of Pub. L. 98–426, set out as a note under section 901 of this title.

EFFECTIVE DATE OF 1972 AMENDMENT

Amendment by Pub. L. 92–576 effective 30 days after Oct. 27, 1972, see section 22 of Pub. L. 92–576, set out as a note under section 902 of this title.

TRANSFER OF FUNCTIONS

For transfer of functions of other officers, employees, and agencies of Department of the Treasury, with certain exceptions, to Secretary of the Treasury with power to delegate, see Reorg. Plan No. 26 of 1950, §§1, 2, eff. July 31, 1950, 15 F.R. 4935, 64 Stat. 1280, 1281, set out in the Appendix to Title 5, Government Organization and Employees. Functions of Coast Guard, and Commandant of Coast Guard, were excepted from transfer when Coast Guard is operating as part of Navy under sections 1 and 3 of Title 14, Coast Guard.

§§945 to 947. Repealed. Pub. L. 98–426, §25, Sept. 28, 1984, 98 Stat. 1654

Section 945, act Mar. 4, 1927, ch. 509, §45, 44 Stat. 1445, provided for creation of a fund to provide for payment of all expenses connected with administration of this chapter. See section 944 of this title.

Section 946, act Mar. 4, 1927, ch. 509, §46, 44 Stat. 1445, appropriated $250,000 to be available for expenses of administration of this chapter for fiscal years ending June 30, 1927, and June 30, 1928.

Section 947, act Mar. 4, 1927, ch. 509, §47, 44 Stat. 1445, provided for availability of appropriations for salaries and contingent expenses in administration of this chapter.

EFFECTIVE DATE OF REPEAL

Repeal effective Sept. 28, 1984, see section 28(e)(1) of Pub. L. 98–426, set out as an Effective Date of 1984 Amendment note under section 901 of this title.

§948. Laws inapplicable

Nothing in sections 4283, 4284, 4285, 4286, or 4289 of the Revised Statutes, as amended, nor in section 18 of the Act entitled "An act to remove certain burdens on the American merchant marine and encourage the American foreign carrying trade, and for other purposes," approved June 26, 1884, as amended, shall be held to limit the amount for which recovery may be had (1) in any suit at law or in admiralty where an employer has failed to secure compensation as required by this chapter, or (2) in any proceeding for compensation, any addition to compensation, or any civil penalty.

(Mar. 4, 1927, ch. 509, §48, 44 Stat. 1446.)

REFERENCES IN TEXT

Sections 4283, 4284, 4285, 4286, and 4289 of the Revised Statutes, referred to in text, were classified to sections 183, 184, 185, 186, and 188, respectively, of the former Appendix to Title 46, Shipping, and were repealed and restated in chapter 305 of Title 46, Shipping, by Pub. L. 109–304, §§6(c), 19, Oct. 6, 2006, 120 Stat. 1509, 1710. For disposition of sections of the former Appendix to Title 46, see Disposition Table preceding section 101 of Title 46.

Section 18 of the Act entitled "An act to remove certain burdens on the American merchant marine and encourage the American foreign carrying trade, and for other purposes," approved June 26, 1884, as amended, referred to in text, is section 18 of act June 26, 1884, ch. 121, 23 Stat. 57, which was classified to section 189 of the former Appendix to Title 46, Shipping, and was repealed and restated in section 30505 of Title 46, Shipping, by Pub. L. 109–304, §§6(c), 19, Oct. 6, 2006, 120 Stat. 1509, 1710.

§948a. Discrimination against employees who bring proceedings; penalties; deposit of payments in special fund; civil actions; entitlement to restoration of employment and compensation, qualifications requirement; liability of employer for penalties and payments; insurance policy exemption from liability

It shall be unlawful for any employer or his duly authorized agent to discharge or in any other manner discriminate against an employee as to his employment because such employee has claimed or attempted to claim compensation from such employer, or because he has testified or is about to testify in a proceeding under this chapter. The discharge or refusal to employ a person who has been adjudicated to have filed a fraudulent claim for compensation is not a violation of this section. Any employer who violates this section shall be liable to a penalty of not less than $1,000 or more than $5,000, as may be determined by the deputy commissioner. All such penalties shall be paid to the deputy commissioner for deposit in the special fund as described in section 944 of this title, and if not paid may be recovered in a civil action brought in the appropriate United States district court. Any employee so discriminated against shall be restored to his employment and shall be compensated by his employer for any loss of wages arising out of such discrimination: *Provided*, That if such employee shall cease to be qualified to perform the duties of his employment, he shall not be entitled to such restoration and compensation. The employer alone and not his carrier shall be liable for such penalties and payments. Any provision in an insurance policy undertaking to relieve the employer from the liability for such penalties and payments shall be void.

(Mar. 4, 1927, ch. 509, §49, as added Pub. L. 92–576, §19, Oct. 27, 1972, 86 Stat. 1263; amended Pub. L. 98–426, §26, Sept. 28, 1984, 98 Stat. 1654.)

AMENDMENTS

1984—Pub. L. 98–426 inserted after first sentence "The discharge or refusal to employ a person who has been adjudicated to have filed a fraudulent claim for compensation is not a violation of this section.", substituted "$1,000" for "$100", and substituted "$5,000" for "$1,000".

EFFECTIVE DATE OF 1984 AMENDMENT

Amendment by Pub. L. 98–426 effective Sept. 28, 1984, see section 28(e)(1) of Pub. L. 98–426, set out as a note under section 901 of this title.

EFFECTIVE DATE

Section effective 30 days after Oct. 27, 1972, see section 22 of Pub. L. 92–576, set out as an Effective Date of 1972 Amendment note under section 902 of this title.

§949. Effect of unconstitutionality

If any part of this chapter is adjudged unconstitutional by the courts, and such adjudication has the effect of invalidating any payment of compensation under this chapter, the period intervening between the time the injury was sustained and the time of such adjudication shall not be computed as a part of the time prescribed by law for the commencement of any action against the employer in respect of such injury; but the amount of any compensation paid under this chapter on account of such injury shall be deducted from the amount of damages awarded in such action in respect of such injury.

(Mar. 4, 1927, ch. 509, §50 formerly §49, 44 Stat. 1446; renumbered §50, Pub. L. 92–576, §19, Oct. 27, 1972, 86 Stat. 1263.)

§950. Separability

If any provision of this chapter is declared unconstitutional or the applicability thereof to any person or circumstances is held invalid, the validity of the remainder of the chapter and the applicability of such provision to other persons and circumstances shall not be affected thereby.

(Mar. 4, 1927, ch. 509, §51 formerly §50, 44 Stat. 1446; renumbered §51, Pub. L. 92–576, §19, Oct. 27, 1972, 86 Stat. 1263.)

CHAPTER 19—SAINT LAWRENCE SEAWAY

§981. Creation of Saint Lawrence Seaway Development Corporation

There is hereby created, subject to the direction and supervision of the Secretary of Transportation, a body corporate to be known as the Saint Lawrence Seaway Development Corporation (hereinafter referred to as the "Corporation").

(May 13, 1954, ch. 201, §1, 68 Stat. 93; Pub. L. 89–670, §8(g)(1), Oct. 15, 1966, 80 Stat. 943.)

AMENDMENTS

1966—Pub. L. 89–670 substituted "Secretary of Transportation" for "President, or the head of such agency as he may designate".

EFFECTIVE DATE OF 1966 AMENDMENT

Amendment by Pub. L. 89–670 effective Apr. 1, 1967, as prescribed by the President and published in the Federal Register, see section 16(a), formerly §15(a), of Pub. L. 89–670 and Ex. Ord. No. 11340, Mar. 30, 1967, 32 F.R. 5453.

SEPARABILITY

Section 11 of act May 13, 1954, provided: "If any provision of this Act [enacting this chapter and amending section 846 of Title 31, Money and Finance] or the application of such provision to any person or circumstances shall be held invalid, the remainder of the Act and the application of such provision to persons or circumstances other than those to which it is held invalid shall not be affected thereby."

ADMINISTRATOR TO REPORT DIRECTLY TO SECRETARY OF TRANSPORTATION

Pub. L. 89–670, §8(g)(2), which provided that the Administrator of the St. Lawrence Seaway Development Corporation report directly to the Secretary notwithstanding any other provision of the Department of Transportation Act (Pub. L. 89–670), was repealed by Pub. L. 97–449, §7(b), Jan. 12, 1983, 96 Stat. 2444, except for rights and duties that matured, penalties that were incurred, and proceedings that were begun before Jan. 12, 1983.

EXECUTIVE ORDER NO. 10534

Ex. Ord. No. 10534, June 9, 1954, 19 F.R. 3413, as amended by Ex. Ord. No. 10771, June 23, 1958, 23 F.R. 4525, which related to the direction and supervision of the St. Lawrence Seaway Development Corporation, was revoked by section 16 of Ex. Ord. No. 11382, Nov. 28, 1967, 32 F.R. 16247.

§982. Management of Corporation; appointment of Administrator; terms; vacancy; Advisory Board; establishment; membership; meetings; duties; compensation and expenses

(a) The management of the corporation shall be vested in an Administrator who shall be appointed by the President, by and with the advice and consent of the Senate, for a term of seven years. Any Administrator appointed to fill a vacancy in that position prior to the expiration of the term for which his predecessor was appointed shall be appointed for the remainder of such term.

(b) There is established the Advisory Board of the Saint Lawrence Seaway Development Corporation which shall be composed of five members appointed by the President, by and with the advice and consent of the Senate, not more than three of whom shall belong to the same political party. The Advisory Board shall meet at the call of the Administrator, who shall require it to meet not less often than once each ninety days; shall review the general policies of the Corporation, including its policies in connection with design and construction of facilities and the establishment of rules of measurement for vessels and cargo and rates of charges or tolls; and shall advise the Administrator with respect thereto. Members of the Advisory Board shall receive for their services as members compensation of not to exceed $50 per diem when actually engaged in the performance of their duties, together with their necessary traveling expenses while going to and coming from meetings.

(May 13, 1954, ch. 201, §2, 68 Stat. 93; Pub. L. 93–615, §1, Jan. 2, 1975, 88 Stat. 1977.)

AMENDMENTS

1975—Subsec. (a). Pub. L. 93–615, §1(a), amended subsec. (a) generally, inserting provisions relating to a term of seven years and the length of the term of any Administrator appointed to fill a vacancy in the position of the Administrator prior to the expiration of the term for which his predecessor was appointed.

Subsecs. (b), (c). Pub. L. 93–615, §1(b), redesignated subsec. (c) as (b). Former subsec. (b), relating to the appointment and duties of a Deputy Administrator, was repealed.

EFFECTIVE DATE OF 1975 AMENDMENT

Section 2 of Pub. L. 93–615 provided that: "The amendments made to section 2 of the Act of May 13, 1954, by the first section of this Act [amending this section] shall (1) take effect upon the first appointment of an Administrator of the Saint Lawrence Seaway Development Corporation which is made after the date of enactment of this Act [Jan. 2, 1975], and (2) be applicable to such first appointment and to each subsequent appointment to such position."

TERMINATION OF ADVISORY BOARDS

Advisory boards in existence on Jan. 5, 1973, to terminate not later than the expiration of the 2-year period following Jan. 5, 1973, unless, in the case of a board established by the President or an officer of the Federal Government, such board is renewed by appropriate action prior to the expiration of such 2-year period, or in the case of a board established by the Congress, its duration is otherwise provided by law. See sections 3(2) and 14 of Pub. L. 92–463, Oct. 6, 1972, 86 Stat. 770, 776, set out in the Appendix to Title 5, Government Organization and Employees.

§983. Functions of Corporation

(a) Construction of deep-water navigation works in Saint Lawrence River; conditions precedent

The Corporation is authorized and directed to construct, in United States territory, deep-water navigation works substantially in accordance with the "Controlled single stage project, 238–242" (with a controlling depth of twenty-seven feet in channels and canals and locks at least eight hundred feet long, eighty feet wide, and thirty feet over the sills), designated as "works solely for navigation" in the joint report dated January 3, 1941, of the Canadian Temporary Great Lakes-Saint Lawrence Basin Committee and the United States Saint Lawrence Advisory Committee, in the International Rapids section of the Saint Lawrence River together with necessary dredging in the Thousand Islands section; and to operate and maintain such works in coordination with the Saint Lawrence Seaway Authority of Canada, created by chapter 24 of the acts of the fifth session of the Twenty-first Parliament of Canada 15–16, George VI (assented to December 21, 1951): *Provided*, That the Corporation shall not proceed with the aforesaid construction unless and until—

(1) the Saint Lawrence Seaway Authority of Canada, provides assurances satisfactory to the Corporation that it will complete the Canadian portions of the navigation works authorized by section 10, chapter 24 of the acts of the fifth session of the Twenty-first Parliament of Canada 15–16, George VI, 1951, as nearly as possible concurrently with the completion of the works authorized by this section;

(2) the Corporation has received assurances satisfactory to it that the State of New York, or an entity duly designated by it, or other licensee of the Federal Energy Regulatory Commission, in conjunction with an appropriate agency in Canada, as nearly as possible concurrently with the navigation works herein authorized, will construct and complete the dams and power works approved by the International Joint Commission in its order of October 29, 1952 (docket 68) or any amendment or modification thereof.

(b) Coordination of activities regarding power projects

The Corporation shall make necessary arrangements to assure the coordination of its activities with those of the Saint Lawrence Seaway Authority of Canada and the entity designated by the State of New York, or other licensee of the Federal Energy Regulatory Commission, authorized to construct and operate the dams and power works authorized by the International Joint Commission in its order of October 29, 1952 (docket 68) or any amendment or modification thereof.

(May 13, 1954, ch. 201, §3, 68 Stat. 93; Pub. L. 95–91, title IV, §402(a)(1)(A), Aug. 4, 1977, 91 Stat. 583.)

TRANSFER OF FUNCTIONS

"Federal Energy Regulatory Commission" substituted for "Federal Power Commission" in subsecs. (a)(2) and (b), on authority of Pub. L. 95–91, title IV, §402(a)(1)(A), Aug. 4, 1977, 91 Stat. 583, which is classified to section 7172(a)(1)(A) of Title 42, The Public Health and Welfare.

§ 984. General powers of Corporation

(a) For the purpose of carrying out its functions under this chapter the Corporation—

(1) shall have succession in its corporate name;

(2) may adopt and use a corporate seal, which shall be judicially noticed;

(3) may sue and be sued in its corporate name;

(4) may adopt, amend, and repeal bylaws, rules, and regulations governing the manner in which its business may be conducted and the powers vested in it may be exercised;

(5) may make and carry out such contracts or agreements as are necessary or advisable in the conduct of its business;

(6) shall be held to be an inhabitant and resident of the northern judicial district of New York within the meaning of the laws of the United States relating to venue of civil suits;

(7) may appoint and fix the compensation, in accordance with the provisions of chapter 51 and subchapter III of chapter 53 of title 5, of such officers, attorneys, and employees as may be necessary for the conduct of its business, define their authority and duties, and delegate to them such of the powers vested in the Corporation as the Administrator may determine;

(8) may acquire, by purchase, lease, condemnation, or donation such real and personal property and any interest therein, and may sell, lease, or otherwise dispose of such real and personal property, as the Administrator deems necessary for the conduct of its business;

(9) shall determine the character of and the necessity for its obligations and expenditures, and the manner in which they shall be incurred, allowed and paid, subject to provisions of law specifically applicable to Government corporations;

(10) may retain toll revenues for purposes of eventual reinvestment in the Seaway.[1]

(11) may provide services and facilities necessary in the maintenance and operation of the seaway, including but not limited to providing, at reasonable prices, services to vessels using the seaway and to visitors to the seaway, but not to include overnight housing accommodations for visitors;

(12) may participate with the Saint Lawrence Seaway Authority of Canada, or its designee, in the ownership and operation of a toll bridge company: *Provided*, That the United States' portion of the revenue from the tolls charged to the users of any toll bridge operated under this section shall be applied solely to the cost of the bridge and approaches, including maintenance and operation, amortization of principal and interest, as established by the Secretary of the Treasury; and

(13)[2] shall be credited with amounts received from any of the activities authorized by clauses (10) and (11)[3] of this subsection.

(13)[2] shall accept such amounts as may be transferred to the Corporation under section 9505(c)(1) of title 26, except that such amounts shall be available only for the purpose of operating and maintaining those works which the Corporation is obligated to operate and maintain under subsection (a) of section 983 of this title.

(b) Amounts credited under subsection (a)(12)[3] of this section are available to pay any obligation or expense of the Corporation under this chapter, except as specifically provided in subsection (a)(11)[3] of this section.

(May 13, 1954, ch. 201, §4, 68 Stat. 94; Pub. L. 85–108, §1(1)–(3), July 17, 1957, 71 Stat. 307; Pub. L. 92–310, title II, §232, June 6, 1972, 86 Stat. 214; Pub. L. 97–369, title III, §311, Dec. 18, 1982, 96 Stat. 1783; Pub. L. 99–662, title XIV, §805(a)(1)–(3), Nov. 17, 1986, 100 Stat. 4272.)

CODIFICATION

In subsec. (a)(7), "chapter 51 and subchapter III of chapter 53 of title 5" substituted for "the Classification Act of 1949" on authority of Pub. L. 89–554, §7(b), Sept. 6, 1966, 80 Stat. 631, the first section of which enacted Title 5, Government Organization and Employees.

AMENDMENTS

1986—Subsec. (a)(13). Pub. L. 99–662 added par. (13) relating to acceptance of amounts transferred to the Corporation under section 9505(c) of title 26.

1982—Subsec. (a)(10) to (13). Pub. L. 97–369 added par. (10) and redesignated former pars. (10) to (12) as (11) to (13), respectively.

1972—Subsec. (a)(7). Pub. L. 92–310 struck out provisions which empowered the Corporation to require bonds from such officers, attorneys, and employees as the Administrator might designate.

1957—Subsecs. (a)(10) to (12), (b). Pub. L. 85–108 added pars. (10) to (12) and subsec. (b).

EFFECTIVE DATE OF 1986 AMENDMENT

Section 805(b) of Pub. L. 99–662 provided that: "The amendments made by this section [enacting section 988a of this title and amending this section] shall take effect on April 1, 1987."

§ 984a. Repealed. June 28, 1955, ch. 189, § 12(c)(11), 69 Stat. 181

Section, act Aug. 26, 1954, ch. 935, ch. VIII, §801, 68 Stat. 818, authorized Administrator to place not more than four positions in grades 16, 17, or 18 of General Schedule established by Classification Act of 1949.

§ 985. Bonds; issuance; maturity; redemption; interest; purchase of obligations by Secretary of the Treasury

(a) To finance its activities, the Corporation may issue revenue bonds payable from corporate revenue to the Secretary of the Treasury. The

[1] So in original. The period probably should be a semicolon.

[2] So in original. There are two pars. designated (13).

[3] Clauses (10), (11), and (12) redesignated (11), (12), and (13) by Pub. L. 97–369.

total face value of all bonds so issued shall not be greater than $140,000,000. Not more than fifty per centum of the bonds may be issued during any one year. Such obligations shall have maturities agreed upon by the Corporation and the Secretary of the Treasury, not in excess of fifty years. Such obligations may be redeemable at the option of the Corporation before maturity in such manner as may be stipulated in such obligations, but the obligations thus redeemed shall not be refinanced by the Corporation. The Secretary of the Treasury is authorized and directed to purchase any obligations of the Corporation to be issued hereunder and for such purpose the Secretary of the Treasury is authorized to use as a public debt transaction the proceeds from the sale of any securities issued under chapter 31 of title 31, and the purposes for which securities may be issued under chapter 31 of title 31 are extended to include any purchases of the Corporation's obligations hereunder.

(b) Effective as of October 21, 1970, the obligations of the Corporation incurred under subsection (a) of this section shall bear no interest, and the obligation of the Corporation to pay the unpaid interest which has accrued on such obligations is terminated.

(May 13, 1954, ch. 201, §5, 68 Stat. 94; Pub. L. 85–108, §1(4), July 17, 1957, 71 Stat. 307; Pub. L. 91–469, §43(a), Oct. 21, 1970, 84 Stat. 1038.)

CODIFICATION

In subsec. (a), "chapter 31 of title 31" substituted for "the Second Liberty Bond Act, as amended" on authority of Pub. L. 97–258, §4(b), Sept. 13, 1982, 96 Stat. 1067, the first section of which enacted Title 31, Money and Finance.

AMENDMENTS

1970—Subsec. (a). Pub. L. 91–469, §43(a)(1), designated existing provisions as subsec. (a) and struck out fourth, fifth, and eighth sentences which provided for deferral, with approval of Secretary of the Treasury, of interest payments on bonds but required interest payments so deferred to bear interest after June 30, 1960; prohibited charging of deferred interest against debt limitation of $140,000,000; and prescribed for each obligation a rate of interest determined by the Secretary, taking into consideration the current average rate on current marketable obligations of the United States of comparable maturities as of the last day of the month preceding the issuance of the obligation of the Corporation.

Subsec. (b). Pub. L. 91–469, §43(a)(2), added subsec. (b).

1957—Pub. L. 85–108 increased Corporation's borrowing authority from $105,000,000 to $140,000,000; omitted first year bond issue limitation, and raised limits of bond issues for any year from 40 to 50 per centum of total borrowing power; and authorized deferment of interest payments on borrowings, excluding such deferred interest charges from the debt limitation of $140,000,000.

§985a. Cancellation of bonds issued under section 985

Notwithstanding any other provision of law, any bond issued under section 985 of this title, is hereby canceled together with the obligation to pay such bond.

(Pub. L. 97–369, title III, §311, Dec. 18, 1982, 96 Stat. 1782.)

CODIFICATION

Section was enacted as part of the Department of Transportation and Related Agencies Appropriations Act, 1983, and not as part of act May 13, 1954, ch. 201, 68 Stat. 903, which comprises this chapter.

Section consists of a part of section 311 of Pub. L. 97–369. The remainder of section 311 of Pub. L. 97–369 amended sections 984 and 988 of this title.

§986. Payments to States and local governments in lieu of taxes; tax exemption of Corporation

The Corporation is authorized to make payments to State and local governments in lieu of property taxes upon property which was subject to State and local taxation before acquisition by the Corporation. Such payments may be in the amounts, at the times, and upon the terms the Corporation deems appropriate, but the Corporation shall be guided by the policy of making payments not in excess of the taxes which would have been payable for such property in the condition in which it was acquired, except in cases where special burdens are placed upon the State or local government by the activities of the Corporation or its agents. The Corporation, its property, franchises, and income are expressly exempted from taxation in any manner or form by any State, county, municipality, or any subdivision thereof, but such exemption shall not extend to contractors for the Corporation.

(May 13, 1954, ch. 201, §7, 68 Stat. 95.)

§987. Services and facilities of other agencies

(a) Utilization of personnel, services, facilities, and information

The Corporation may, with the consent of the agency concerned, accept and utilize, on a reimbursable basis, the officers, employees, services, facilities, and information of any agency of the Federal Government, except that any such agency having custody of any data relating to any of the matters within the jurisdiction of the Corporation shall, upon request of the Administrator, make such data available to the Corporation without reimbursement.

(b) Contributions to retirement and disability, and employees' compensation, funds; payment of costs

The Corporation shall contribute to the civil-service retirement and disability fund, on the basis of annual billings as determined by the Director of the Office of Personnel Management, for the Government's share of the cost of the civil-service retirement system applicable to the Corporation's employees and their beneficiaries. The Corporation shall also contribute to the employee's compensation fund, on the basis of annual billings as determined by the Secretary of Labor, for the benefit payments made from such fund on account of the Corporation's employees. The annual billings shall also include a statement of the fair portion of the cost of the administration of the respective funds, which shall be paid by the Corporation into the Treasury as miscellaneous receipts.

(May 13, 1954, ch. 201, §8, 68 Stat. 95; 1978 Reorg. Plan No. 2, §102, eff. Jan. 1, 1979, 43 F.R. 36037, 92 Stat. 3783.)

TRANSFER OF FUNCTIONS

"Director of the Office of Personnel Management" substituted for "Civil Service Commission" and "Commission" in subsec. (b) pursuant to Reorg. Plan No. 2 of 1978, § 102, 43 F.R. 36037, 92 Stat. 3783, set out under section 1101 of Title 5, Government Organization and Employees, which transferred all functions vested by statute in United States Civil Service Commission to Director of Office of Personnel Management (except as otherwise specified), effective Jan. 1, 1979, as provided by section 1–102 of Ex. Ord. No. 12107, Dec. 28, 1978, 44 F.R. 1055, set out under section 1101 of Title 5.

§ 988. Rates of charges or tolls

(a) Negotiation with Canadian authorities; revenue sharing formula; consideration of American financing costs, including interest and debt principal; rules of measurement; hearings and rehearings; approval by President; court review

The Corporation is further authorized and directed to negotiate with the Saint Lawrence Seaway Authority of Canada, or such other agency as may be designated by the Government of Canada, an agreement as to the rules for the measurement of vessels and cargoes and the rates of charges or tolls to be levied for the use of the Saint Lawrence Seaway, and for an equitable division of the revenues of the seaway between the Corporation and the Saint Lawrence Seaway Authority of Canada. Any formula for a division of revenues which takes into consideration annual debt charges shall include the total cost, including both interest and debt principal, incurred by the United States in financing activities authorized by this chapter, whether or not reimbursable by the Corporation. Such rules for the measurement of vessels and cargoes and rates of charges or tolls shall, to the extent practicable, be established or changed only after giving due notice and holding a public hearing. In the event that such negotiations shall not result in agreement, the Corporation is authorized and directed to establish unilaterally such rules of measurement and rates of charges or tolls for the use of the works under its administration: *Provided, however*, That the Corporation shall give three months' notice, by publication in the Federal Register, of any proposals to establish or change unilaterally the basic rules of measurement and of any proposals to establish or change unilaterally the rates of charges or tolls, during which period a public hearing shall be conducted. Any such establishment of or changes in basic rules of measurement or rates of charges or tolls shall be subject to and shall take effect thirty days following the date of approval thereof by the President, and shall be final and conclusive, subject to review as hereinafter provided. Any person aggrieved by an order of the Corporation establishing or changing such rules or rates may, within such thirty-day period, apply to the Corporation for a rehearing of the matter upon the basis of which the order was entered. The Corporation shall have power to grant or deny the application for rehearing and upon such rehearing or without further hearing to abrogate or modify its order. The action of the Corporation in denying an application for rehearing or in abrogating or modifying its order shall be final and conclusive thirty days after its approval by the President unless within such thirty-day period a petition for review is filed by a person aggrieved by such action in the United States Court of Appeals for the circuit in which the works to which the order applies are located or in the United States Court of Appeals for the District of Columbia. The court in which such petition is filed shall have the same jurisdiction and powers as in the case of petitions to review orders of the Federal Energy Regulatory Commission filed under section 825*l* of title 16. The judgment of the court shall be final subject to review by the Supreme Court upon certiorari or certification as provided in sections 1254(1) and 1254(2) of title 28. The filing of an application for rehearing shall not, unless specifically ordered by the Corporation, operate as a stay of the Corporation's order. The filing of a petition for review shall not, unless specifically ordered by the court, operate as a stay of the Corporation's order.

(b) Principles governing establishment of rates

In the course of its negotiations, or in the establishment, unilaterally, of the rates of charges or tolls as provided in subsection (a) of this section, the Corporation shall be guided by the following principles:

(1) That the rates shall be fair and equitable and shall give due consideration to encouragement of increased utilization of the navigation facilities, and to the special character of bulk agricultural, mineral, and other raw materials.

(2) That rates shall vary according to the character of cargo with the view that each classification of cargo shall so far as practicable derive relative benefits from the use of these facilities.

(3) That the rates on vessels in ballast without passengers or cargo may be less than the rates for vessels with passengers or cargo.

(4) That the rates prescribed shall be calculated to cover, as nearly as practicable, all costs of operating and maintaining the works under the administration of the Corporation, including depreciation and payments in lieu of taxes.

(May 13, 1954, ch. 201, § 12, 68 Stat. 96; Pub. L. 91–469, § 43(b), Oct. 21, 1970, 84 Stat. 1038; Pub. L. 95–91, title IV, § 402(a)(1)(B), Aug. 4, 1977, 91 Stat. 583; Pub. L. 97–369, title III, § 311, Dec. 18, 1982, 96 Stat. 1782; Pub. L. 100–352, § 6(h), June 27, 1988, 102 Stat. 664.)

Amendments

1988—Subsec. (a). Pub. L. 100–352 substituted "1254(2)" for "1254(3)".

1982—Subsec. (b)(5). Pub. L. 97–369 struck out par. (5) which directed that the rates provide for revenues sufficient to amortize the principal of the debts and obligations of the Corporation over a period of not to exceed 50 years.

1970—Subsec. (a). Pub. L. 91–469, § 43(b)(1), inserted requirement that any formula for a division of revenues which takes into consideration annual debt charges shall include the total cost, including both interest and debt principal, incurred by the United States in financing activities authorized by this chapter, whether or not reimbursable by the Corporation.

Subsec. (b)(4). Pub. L. 91–469, § 43(b)(2), struck out ", payment of interest on the obligations of the Corporation," after "depreciation".

Effective Date of 1988 Amendment

Amendment by Pub. L. 100–352 effective ninety days after June 27, 1988, except that such amendment not to apply to cases pending in Supreme Court on such effective date or affect right to review or manner of reviewing judgment or decree of court which was entered before such effective date, see section 7 of Pub. L. 100–352, set out as a note under section 1254 of Title 28, Judiciary and Judicial Procedure.

TRANSFER OF FUNCTIONS

"Federal Energy Regulatory Commission" substituted for "Federal Power Commission" in subsec. (a) on authority of Pub. L. 95–91, title IV, §402(a)(1)(B), Aug. 4, 1977, 91 Stat. 583, which is classified to section 7172(a)(1)(B) of Title 42, The Public Health and Welfare.

GREAT LAKES AND SAINT LAWRENCE SEAWAY

Pub. L. 101–101, title I, Sept. 29, 1989, 103 Stat. 642, provided: "That within available funds, the Secretary of the Army, acting through the Chief of Engineers, is directed to initiate and complete a reconnaissance study for the Saint Lawrence Seaway and Great Lakes-Financing Navigational Improvements Study, as authorized in section 47(d) of Public Law 100–676 [set out below], in accordance with the cost sharing provisions of Public Law 99–662 [Nov. 17, 1986, 100 Stat. 4082]."

Pub. L. 100–676, §47(d), Nov. 17, 1988, 102 Stat. 4042, provided that:

"(1) STUDY OF FINANCING NAVIGATIONAL IMPROVEMENTS.—The Secretary, in cooperation with other Federal agencies and private persons, is authorized and directed to contract with an independent party to conduct a study of cost recovery options and alternative methods of financing navigational improvements on the Great Lakes connecting channels and Saint Lawrence Seaway, including modernization of the Eisenhower and Snell Locks of the Saint Lawrence Seaway.

"(2) REPORT.—Not later than 18 months after the date of the enactment of this Act [Nov. 17, 1988], the Secretary shall transmit to Congress a report on the results of the study carried out under this subsection together with recommendations.

"(3) COST SHARING.—The non-Federal share of the cost of the study under this subsection shall be 50 percent; except that not more than 1/2 of such non-Federal share may be made by the provision of services, materials, supplies, or other in-kind services necessary to carry out the study."

REPORT ON REDUCTION OR ELIMINATION OF TOLLS ON GREAT LAKES AND SAINT LAWRENCE SEAWAY

Pub. L. 99–662, title XIV, §1406, Nov. 17, 1986, 100 Stat. 4272, provided that: "Not later than 2 years after the date of enactment of this Act [Nov. 17, 1986], the Secretary of State, in consultation with the Secretary of Transportation, shall initiate discussions with the Government of Canada with the objective of reducing or eliminating all tolls on the international Great Lakes and the Saint Lawrence Seaway, and the Secretary of Transportation shall report to the Congress on the progress of such discussions and on the economic effects upon waterborne commerce in the United States of any proposed reduction or elimination in tolls."

§988a. Waiver of collection of charges or tolls

(a) Notwithstanding section 988 of this title or any other provision of law, the Corporation shall not collect any charge or toll established pursuant to section 988 of this title with respect to a commercial vessel (as defined in section 4462(a)(4) of title 26).

(b) The Corporation will maintain a record of the annual amount of each charge or toll that would have been collected with respect to each such commercial vessel if it were not for paragraph (a) of this section.

(May 13, 1954, ch. 201, §13, as added Pub. L. 99–662, title XIV, §805(a)(4), Nov. 17, 1986, 100 Stat. 4272; amended Pub. L. 103–331, title III, §339, Sept. 30, 1994, 108 Stat. 2496.)

AMENDMENTS

1994—Pub. L. 103–331 substituted "Waiver of collection" for "Rebate of" in section catchline and amended text generally. Prior to amendment, text read as follows:

"(a) The Corporation shall transfer to the Harbor Maintenance Trust Fund, at such times and under such terms and conditions as the Secretary of the Treasury may prescribe, all revenues derived from the collection of charges or tolls established under section 988 of this title.

"(b)(1) The Corporation shall certify to the Secretary of the Treasury, in such form and at such times as the Secretary of the Treasury shall prescribe—

"(A) the identity of any person who pays a charge or toll to the Corporation pursuant to section 988 of this title with respect to a commercial vessel (as defined in section 4462(a)(4) of title 26),

"(B) the amount of the toll or charge paid by such person with respect to such vessel.

"(2) Within 30 days of the receipt of a certification described in paragraph (1), the Secretary of the Treasury shall rebate, out of the Harbor Maintenance Trust Fund, to the person described in paragraph (1) the amount of the charge or toll paid pursuant to section 988 of this title."

EFFECTIVE DATE

Section effective April 1, 1987, see section 805(b) of Pub. L. 99–662, set out as an Effective Date of 1986 Amendment note under section 984 of this title.

§989. Special reports

(a) Repealed. Pub. L. 104–66, title I, §1121(j), Dec. 21, 1995, 109 Stat. 724.

(b) The Corporation, after July 17, 1957, shall submit special reports to the Congress whenever there is proposed a new feature, design, or phase of the seaway project, not heretofore included in estimates, or whenever there is proposed an abandonment of any feature, design, or phase, heretofore included in estimates, involving an estimated value exceeding one million dollars, and such special reports shall include justification for the modifications.

(May 13, 1954, ch. 201, §10, 68 Stat. 96; Pub. L. 85–108, §1(5), July 17, 1957, 71 Stat. 308; Pub. L. 104–66, title I, §1121(j), Dec. 21, 1995, 109 Stat. 724.)

AMENDMENTS

1995—Subsec. (a). Pub. L. 104–66 struck out subsec. (a) which read as follows: "The Corporation shall submit to the President for transmission to the Congress at the beginning of each regular session an annual report of its operations under this chapter."

1957—Pub. L. 85–108 designated existing provisions as subsec. (a) and added subsec. (b).

§990. Offenses and penalties

(a) Application of penal statutes

All general penal statutes relating to the larceny, embezzlement, or conversion, of public moneys or property of the United States shall apply to the moneys and property of the Corporation.

(b) Frauds and false entries, reports, or statements

Any person who, with intent to defraud the Corporation, or to deceive any director, officer, or employee of the Corporation or any officer or employee of the United States, (1) makes any false entry in any book of the Corporation, or (2) makes any false report or statement for the Corporation, shall, upon conviction thereof, be fined not more than $10,000 or imprisoned not more than five years, or both.

(c) Receipt of compensation, or conspiracy, with intent to defraud, etc.

Any person who shall receive any compensation, rebate, or reward, or shall enter into any conspiracy, collusion, or agreement, express or implied, with intent to defraud the Corporation or wrongfully and unlawfully to defeat its purposes, shall, on conviction thereof, be fined not more than $5,000 or imprisoned not more than five years, or both.

(May 13, 1954, ch. 201, § 9, 68 Stat. 96.)

CHAPTER 20—POLLUTION OF THE SEA BY OIL

§§ 1001 to 1011. Repealed. Pub. L. 96–478, § 12, Oct. 21, 1980, 94 Stat. 2303

Section 1001, Pub. L. 87–167, § 2, Aug. 30, 1961, 75 Stat. 402; Pub. L. 89–551, § 1(2), Sept. 1, 1966, 80 Stat. 372; Pub. L. 89–670, § 6(g)(5), Oct. 15, 1966, 80 Stat. 941; Pub. L. 93–119, § 2(1), Oct. 4, 1973, 87 Stat. 424; Pub. L. 97–449, § 2(e)(1), Jan. 12, 1983, 96 Stat. 2440, defined terms used in this chapter.

Section 1002, Pub. L. 87–167, § 3, Aug. 30, 1961, 75 Stat. 402; Pub. L. 89–551, § 1(3), Sept. 1, 1966, 80 Stat. 373; Pub. L. 93–119, § 2(2), Oct. 4, 1973, 87 Stat. 425, prohibited discharge of oil or oily mixtures, but included certain permissible discharges.

Section 1003, Pub. L. 87–167, § 4, Aug. 30, 1961, 75 Stat. 402; Pub. L. 89–551, § 1(4), Sept. 1, 1966, 80 Stat. 373; Pub. L. 93–119, § 2(3), Oct. 4, 1973, 87 Stat. 425, excepted from the prohibition of section 1002 of this title discharges relating to securing safety of ship, prevention of damage to ship or cargo, saving life, and resulting from a damaged ship or unavoidable leakage.

Section 1004, Pub. L. 87–167, § 5, Aug. 30, 1961, 75 Stat. 403; Pub. L. 89–551, § 1(5), Sept. 1, 1966, 80 Stat. 374; Pub. L. 93–119, § 2(4), Oct. 4, 1973, 87 Stat. 425, excepted from the prohibition of section 1002 of this title discharges relating to tanker ballast from cargo tank.

Section 1004a, Pub. L. 87–167, § 6, as added Pub. L. 93–119, § 2(5), Oct. 4, 1973, 87 Stat. 425, provided construction standards for United States tankers, the subsections relating to following subject matter: subsec. (a) tank arrangement and tank size limitation pursuant to provisions of annex C to convention and building contracts placed on or after effective date; subsec. (b) building contracts placed or keel laid before effective date; subsec. (c) domestic tankers without certificate of compliance or exemption prohibited from engaging in domestic or foreign trade; subsec. (d) foreign tankers with foreign registry but without certificate of compliance, consultation with foreign government, and denial of access; subsec. (e) foreign tankers without foreign registry and denial of access.

Section 1005, Pub. L. 87–167, § 7, formerly § 6, Aug. 30, 1961, 75 Stat. 403; renumbered and amended Pub. L. 93–119, § 2(6), Oct. 4, 1973, 87 Stat. 426, related to penalties for violations, the subsections providing for following subject matter: subsec. (a) criminal penalties for willful violations and separate violations; subsec. (b) civil penalties for willful or negligent and other violations and separate violations; subsec. (c) liability of vessel and venue; and subsec. (d) administrative proceedings, assessment of civil penalties, remission, mitigation, or compromise of any penalty, notice and hearing, judicial proceedings, civil actions by Attorney General for collection of penalties, and trial de novo.

Section 1006, Pub. L. 87–167, § 8, formerly § 7, Aug. 30, 1961, 75 Stat. 403; renumbered Pub. L. 93–119, § 2(7), Oct. 4, 1973, 87 Stat. 427, provided for suspension or revocation of license of officers of offending vessels.

Section 1007, Pub. L. 87–167, § 9, formerly § 8, Aug. 30, 1961, 75 Stat. 403; Pub. L. 90–578, title IV, § 402(b)(2), Oct. 17, 1968, 82 Stat. 1118; renumbered and amended Pub. L. 93–119, § 2(8), Oct. 4, 1973, 87 Stat. 427, related to personnel for enforcement of provisions, arrest of offenders and procedure, and ship fittings and equipment.

Section 1008, Pub. L. 87–167, § 10, formerly § 9, Aug. 30, 1961, 75 Stat. 404; Pub. L. 89–551, § 1(6), Sept. 1, 1966, 80 Stat. 374; renumbered and amended Pub. L. 93–119, § 2(9), Oct. 4, 1973, 87 Stat. 427, provided for oil record books, the subsections relating to following subject matter: subsec. (a) printing and regulations of the Secretary; subsec. (b) supplying the books without charge and their inspection and surrender; subsec. (c) operations requiring recordation; subsec. (d) entries and signatures; and subsec. (e) rules and regulations.

Section 1009, Pub. L. 87–167, § 11, formerly § 10, Aug. 30, 1961, 75 Stat. 404; Pub. L. 89–551, § 1(7), Sept. 1, 1966, 80 Stat. 375; renumbered and amended Pub. L. 93–119, § 2(10), Oct. 4, 1973, 87 Stat. 428, authorized the Secretary to promulgate regulations for the administration of specific sections of this chapter.

Section 1010, Pub. L. 87–167, § 12, formerly § 11, Aug. 30, 1961, 75 Stat. 404; renumbered and amended Pub. L. 93–119, § 2(11), Oct. 4, 1973, 87 Stat. 428, related to boarding of ships, production of records, and evidence of violations by foreign ships.

Section 1011, Pub. L. 87–167, § 12, Aug. 30, 1961, 75 Stat. 404; Pub. L. 89–551, § 1(8), Sept. 1, 1966, 80 Stat. 375, specified prohibited zones and provided for reduction or extension of such zones.

Effective Date of Repeal

Repeal effective Oct. 2, 1983, see section 14(a) of Pub. L. 96–478, set out as an Effective Date note under section 1901 of this title.

Short Title

Pub. L. 87–167, § 1, Aug. 30, 1961, 75 Stat. 402, as amended by Pub. L. 89–551, § 1(1), Sept. 1, 1966, 80 Stat. 372, which provided that Pub. L. 87–167 could be cited as the "Oil Pollution Act, 1961, as amended", was repealed by Pub. L. 96–478, § 12, Oct. 21, 1980, 94 Stat. 2303.

Pub. L. 93–119, § 1, Oct. 4, 1973, 87 Stat. 424, which provided that Pub. L. 93–119 could be cited as the "Oil Pollution Act Amendments of 1973" was repealed by Pub. L. 96–478, § 12, Oct. 21, 1980, 94 Stat. 2303.

Savings Provision

Section 12(a) of Pub. L. 96–478 provided in part that any criminal or civil penalty proceeding under this chapter for a violation occurring prior to Oct. 2, 1983, may be initiated or continued to conclusion as though this chapter had not been repealed.

Any rights or liabilities existing on Oct. 2, 1983, not to be affected and any regulations or procedures promulgated or effected pursuant to this chapter to remain in effect until modified or superseded, see section 14(c) of Pub. L. 96–478, set out as a note under section 1901 of this title.

Separability

Pub. L. 87–167, § 14, formerly § 15, Aug. 30, 1961, 75 Stat. 407, renumbered by Pub. L. 93–119, § 2(13), Oct. 4, 1973, 87 Stat. 428, which provided for the separability of the provisions of Pub. L. 87–167, was repealed by Pub. L. 96–478, § 12, Oct. 21, 1980, 94 Stat. 2303.

§ 1012. Repealed. Pub. L. 89–551, § 1(9), Sept. 1, 1966, 80 Stat. 375

Section, Pub. L. 87–167, § 13, Aug. 30, 1961, 75 Stat. 405, set out the form and required entries for the oil record book.

§§1013 to 1016. Repealed. Pub. L. 96–478, §12, Oct. 21, 1980, 94 Stat. 2303

Section 1013, Pub. L. 87–167, §13, formerly §14, Aug. 30, 1961, 75 Stat. 407; renumbered Pub. L. 93–119, §2(13), Oct. 4, 1973, 87 Stat. 428, authorized appropriations to carry out this chapter.

Section 1014, Pub. L. 87–167, §15, formerly §16, Aug. 30, 1961, 75 Stat. 407; renumbered and amended Pub. L. 93–119, §2(14), Oct. 4, 1973, 87 Stat. 428, related to effect of this chapter on section 1321 of this title and section 89 of Title 14, Coast Guard.

Section 1015, Pub. L. 87–167, §17, Aug. 30, 1961, 75 Stat. 407; Pub. L. 89–551, §1(10), Sept. 1, 1966, 80 Stat. 375, specified the effective date of this chapter and provided savings provision for rights, liabilities, procedures, or regulations existing on the effective date of this chapter. Pub. L. 93–119, §2(15), Oct. 4, 1973, 87 Stat. 428, which provided for the repeal of this section was repealed by section 12 of Pub. L. 96–478.

Section 1016, Pub. L. 93–119, §3, Oct. 4, 1973, 87 Stat. 428, provided effective date of 1973 amendments to this chapter by Pub. L. 93–119, the subsections covering the following subject matter: subsec. (a) general effective date; subsec. (b) savings provision; and subsec. (c) effective date of section 1004(d) and (e) of this title.

Effective Date of Repeal

Repeal effective Oct. 2, 1983, see section 14(a) of Pub. L. 96–478, set out as an Effective Date note under section 1901 of this title.

CHAPTER 21—INTERNATIONAL REGULATIONS FOR PREVENTING COLLISIONS AT SEA

Prior Provisions

For prior provisions, see note set out under section 1602 of this title.

§§1051 to 1053, 1061 to 1094. Repealed. Pub. L. 95–75, §10, July 27, 1977, 91 Stat. 311

Section 1051, Pub. L. 88–131, §1, Sept. 24, 1963, 77 Stat. 194, authorized the President to proclaim the International Regulations for Preventing Collisions at Sea. See section 1602 of this title.

Section 1052, Pub. L. 88–131, §2, Sept. 24, 1963, 77 Stat. 194, provided for certification for alternative compliance covering Navy and Coast Guard vessels of special construction or purpose. See section 1605 of this title.

Section 1053, Pub. L. 88–131, §4, Sept. 24, 1963, 77 Stat. 195, constituted an introductory statement for the regulations. See section 1602 of this title.

Section 1061, Pub. L. 88–131, §4, Sept. 24, 1963, 77 Stat. 195, generally described the scope of sections 1061 to 1094.

Section 1062, Pub. L. 88–131, §4, Sept. 24, 1963, 77 Stat. 196, set out the requirements for vessels while under way.

Section 1063, Pub. L. 88–131, §4, Sept. 24, 1963, 77 Stat. 197, set the requirements for towing or pushing other vessels or seaplanes.

Section 1064, Pub. L. 88–131, §4, Sept. 24, 1963, 77 Stat. 197, related to vessels and seaplanes not under command, and vessels engaged in certain operations.

Section 1065, Pub. L. 88–131, §4, Sept. 24, 1963, 77 Stat. 198, related to sailing vessels under way, vessels or seaplanes being towed, and vessels being pushed ahead.

Section 1066, Pub. L. 88–131, §4, Sept. 24, 1963, 77 Stat. 199, related to vessels in bad weather.

Section 1067, Pub. L. 88–131, §4, Sept. 24, 1963, 77 Stat. 199, related to substitute lights for power-driven vessels towing or pushing other vessels, vessels under oars or sails, vessels being towed or pushed ahead, and rowing boats.

Section 1068, Pub. L. 88–131, §4, Sept. 24, 1963, 77 Stat. 200, related to pilot-vessels on and off duty.

Section 1069, Pub. L. 88–131, §4, Sept. 24, 1963, 77 Stat. 201, related to fishing vessels and trawling vessels.

Section 1070, Pub. L. 88–131, §4, Sept. 24, 1963, 77 Stat. 202, related to stern and tail lights.

Section 1071, Pub. L. 88–131, §4, Sept. 24, 1963, 77 Stat. 202, related to vessels and sea lanes at anchor and aground.

Section 1072, Pub. L. 88–131, §4, Sept. 24, 1963, 77 Stat. 203, provided for the use of additional lights and signals when necessary.

Section 1073, Pub. L. 88–131, §4, Sept. 24, 1963, 77 Stat. 203, related to ships of war, convoy vessels, fishing vessels, seaplanes in water, and naval and military vessels and seaplanes of special construction.

Section 1074, Pub. L. 88–131, §4, Sept. 24, 1963, 77 Stat. 203, related to vessels proceeding under sail when also propelled by machinery.

Section 1075, Pub. L. 88–131, §4, Sept. 24, 1963, 77 Stat. 203, set out general considerations concerning radar.

Section 1076, Pub. L. 88–131, §4, Sept. 24, 1963, 77 Stat. 203, related to sound signals.

Section 1077, Pub. L. 88–131, §4, Sept. 24, 1963, 77 Stat. 203, related to speed in weather restricting visibility.

Section 1078, Pub. L. 88–131, §4, Sept. 24, 1963, 77 Stat. 205, set out the general considerations related to steering and sailing.

Section 1079, Pub. L. 88–131, §4, Sept. 24, 1963, 77 Stat. 205, related to sailing vessels approaching one another.

Section 1080, Pub. L. 88–131, §4, Sept. 24, 1963, 77 Stat. 205, related to power-driven vessels meeting end on.

Section 1081, Pub. L. 88–131, §4, Sept. 24, 1963, 77 Stat. 206, related to power-driven vessels crossing.

Section 1082, Pub. L. 88–131, §4, Sept. 24, 1963, 77 Stat. 206, related to vessels or seaplanes meeting.

Section 1083, Pub. L. 88–131, §4, Sept. 24, 1963, 77 Stat. 206, related to vessels having the right of way and the duty in aiding to avert a collision.

Section 1084, Pub. L. 88–131, §4, Sept. 24, 1963, 77 Stat. 206, related to the duty to take positive action to keep out of the way.

Section 1085, Pub. L. 88–131, §4, Sept. 24, 1963, 77 Stat. 206, related to duty to slacken speed, stop, or reverse.

Section 1086, Pub. L. 88–131, §4, Sept. 24, 1963, 77 Stat. 206, related to duty of overtaking vessels to keep out of the way.

Section 1087, Pub. L. 88–131, §4, Sept. 24, 1963, 77 Stat. 207, related to duties of power-driven vessels in narrow channels.

Section 1088, Pub. L. 88–131, §4, Sept. 24, 1963, 77 Stat. 207, related to right-of-way of fishing vessels.

Section 1089, Pub. L. 88–131, Sept. 24, 1963, 77 Stat. 207, related to departure from rules in special circumstances to avoid immediate danger.

Section 1090, Pub. L. 88–131, §4, Sept. 24, 1963, 77 Stat. 207, related to sound signals indicating course.

Section 1091, Pub. L. 88–131, §4, Sept. 24, 1963, 77 Stat. 208, related to additional precautions.

Section 1092, Pub. L. 88–131, §4, Sept. 24, 1963, 77 Stat. 208, related to rules for harbours and inland navigation.

Section 1093, Pub. L. 88–131, §4, Sept. 24, 1963, 77 Stat. 208, related to distress signals.

Section 1094, Pub. L. 88–131, §4, Sept. 24, 1963, 77 Stat. 209, set out general considerations and recommendations on the use of radar information as an aid to avoiding collisions at sea.

Effective Date of Repeal

Repeal effective July 15, 1977, see section 10 of Pub. L. 95–75, set out in part as a note under section 1601 of this title.

Executive Order No. 11239

Ex. Ord. No. 11239, July 31, 1965, 30 F.R. 9671, as amended by Ex. Ord. No. 13286, §65, Feb. 28, 2003, 68 F.R. 10629, which enforced the Convention for the Safety of Life at Sea, 1960, was superseded, to the extent that the International Convention for the Safety of Life at Sea, 1974, signed at London on Nov. 1, 1974, replaced and abrogated the International Convention for the Safety of Life at Sea, 1960, signed at London on June 17, 1960, by Ex. Ord. No. 12234, Sept. 3, 1980, 45 F.R. 58801, set out as a note under section 1602 of this title.

PROCLAMATION NO. 3632

Proc. No. 3632, Dec. 29, 1964, 29 F.R. 19167, was the enabling proclamation for adopting Regulations for Preventing Collisions at Sea, 1960, under Pub. L. 88–131, Sept. 24, 1963, 77 Stat. 194.

CHAPTER 22—SEA GRANT COLLEGES AND MARINE SCIENCE DEVELOPMENT

SUBCHAPTER I—MARINE RESOURCES AND ENGINEERING DEVELOPMENT

SUBCHAPTER I—MARINE RESOURCES AND ENGINEERING DEVELOPMENT

§1101. Congressional declaration of policy and objectives

(a) It is hereby declared to be the policy of the United States to develop, encourage, and maintain a coordinated, comprehensive, and long-range national program in marine science for the benefit of mankind to assist in protection of health and property, enhancement of commerce, transportation, and national security, rehabilitation of our commercial fisheries, and increased utilization of these and other resources.

(b) The marine science activities of the United States should be conducted so as to contribute to the following objectives:

(1) The accelerated development of the resources of the marine environment.

(2) The expansion of human knowledge of the marine environment.

(3) The encouragement of private investment enterprise in exploration, technological development, marine commerce, and economic utilization of the resources of the marine environment.

(4) The preservation of the role of the United States as a leader in marine science and resource development.

(5) The advancement of education and training in marine science.

(6) The development and improvement of the capabilities, performance, use, and efficiency of vehicles, equipment, and instruments for use in exploration, research, surveys, the recovery of resources, and the transmission of energy in the marine environment.

(7) The effective utilization of the scientific and engineering resources of the Nation, with close cooperation among all interested agencies, public and private, in order to avoid unnecessary duplication of effort, facilities, and equipment, or waste.

(8) The cooperation by the United States with other nations and groups of nations and international organizations in marine science activities when such cooperation is in the national interest.

(Pub. L. 89–454, title I, §2, June 17, 1966, 80 Stat. 203.)

SHORT TITLE

Section 1 of title I of Pub. L. 89–454, as renumbered and amended by Pub. L. 89–688, §2(a), Oct. 15, 1966, 80 Stat. 1001, provided that: "This title [enacting this subchapter] may be cited as the 'Marine Resources and Engineering Development Act of 1966'."

§1102. Omitted

CODIFICATION

Section, Pub. L. 89–454, title I, §3, June 17, 1966, 80 Stat. 204; Pub. L. 89–670, §8(j), Oct. 15, 1966, 80 Stat. 943; Pub. L. 90–242, §2, Jan. 2, 1968, 81 Stat. 780; Pub. L. 91–15, §1, May 23, 1969, 83 Stat. 10; Pub. L. 91–414, Sept. 25, 1970, 84 Stat. 865, established the National Council on Marine Resources and Engineering Development. The provisions of this chapter with respect to the Council expired on June 30, 1971, and the Council terminated on Apr. 30, 1971, for lack of funds.

§1103. Executive responsibilities; utilization of staff, interagency, and non-Government advisory arrangements; consultation with agencies; solicitation of views of non-Federal agencies

(a) In conformity with the provisions of section 1101 of this title, it shall be the duty of the President with the advice and assistance of the Council to—

(1) survey all significant marine science activities, including the policies, plans, programs, and accomplishments of all departments and agencies of the United States engaged in such activities;

(2) develop a comprehensive program of marine science activities, including, but not limited to, exploration, description and prediction of the marine environment, exploitation and conservation of the resources of the marine environment, marine engineering, studies of air-sea interaction, transmission of energy, and communications, to be conducted by departments and agencies of the United States, independently or in cooperation with such non-Federal organizations as States, institutions and industry;

(3) designate and fix responsibility for the conduct of the foregoing marine science activities by departments and agencies of the United States;

(4) insure cooperation and resolve differences arising among departments and agencies of the United States with respect to marine science activities under this subchapter, including differences as to whether a particular project is a marine science activity;

(5) undertake a comprehensive study, by contract or otherwise, of the legal problems arising out of the management, use, development, recovery, and control of the resources of the marine environment;

(6) establish long-range studies of the potential benefits to the United States economy, security, health, and welfare to be gained from marine resources, engineering, and science, and the costs involved in obtaining such benefits; and

(7) review annually all marine science activities conducted by departments and agencies of the United States in light of the policies, plans, programs, and priorities developed pursuant to this chapter.

(b) In the planning and conduct of a coordinated Federal program the President and the Council shall utilize such staff, interagency, and non-Government advisory arrangements as they may find necessary and appropriate and shall consult with departments and agencies concerned with marine science activities and solicit the views of non-Federal organizations and individuals with capabilities in marine sciences.

(Pub. L. 89–454, title I, § 4, June 17, 1966, 80 Stat. 205; Pub. L. 89–688, § 2(b), Oct. 15, 1966, 80 Stat. 1001.)

AMENDMENTS

1966—Subsec. (a). Pub. L. 89–688, in par. (4), substituted "this title" for "this Act", which, for purposes of codification has been changed to "this subchapter".

TERMINATION OF COUNCIL

National Council on Marine Resources and Engineering, established under section 1102 of this title, terminated Apr. 30, 1971, for lack of funds. See Codification note set out under section 1102 of this title.

§§ 1104, 1105. Omitted

CODIFICATION

Section 1104, Pub. L. 89–454, title I, § 5, June 17, 1966, 80 Stat. 205; Pub. L. 89–688, § 2(b), Oct. 15, 1966, 80 Stat. 1001; Pub. L. 90–242, § 1, Jan. 2, 1968, 81 Stat. 780, established the Commission on Marine Science, Engineering, and Resources. For expiration of the Commission, see Codification note set out under section 1102 of this title.

Section 1105, Pub. L. 89–454, title I, § 6, June 17, 1966, 80 Stat. 207, provided for the National Council on Marine Resources and Engineering Development to coordinate a program of international cooperation with respect to work done pursuant to this chapter. For expiration of the Council, see Codification note set out under section 1102 of this title.

§ 1106. Reports to Congress

(a) The President shall transmit to the Congress biennially in January a report, which shall include (1) a comprehensive description of the activities and the accomplishments of all agencies and departments of the United States in the field of marine science during the preceding fiscal year, and (2) an evaluation of such activities and accomplishments in terms of the objectives set forth pursuant to this chapter.

(b) Reports made under this section shall contain such recommendations for legislation as the President may consider necessary or desirable for the attainment of the objectives of this chapter, and shall contain an estimate of funding requirements of each agency and department of the United States for marine science activities during the succeeding fiscal year.

(Pub. L. 89–454, title I, § 7, June 17, 1966, 80 Stat. 207; Pub. L. 99–386, title II, § 203(a), Aug. 22, 1986, 100 Stat. 823.)

AMENDMENTS

1986—Subsec. (a). Pub. L. 99–386 substituted "biennially in January" for "in January of each year".

§ 1107. Definitions

For the purposes of this subchapter, the term "marine science" shall be deemed to apply to oceanographic and scientific endeavors and disciplines, and engineering and technology in and with relation to the marine environment; and the term "marine environment" shall be deemed to include (a) the oceans, (b) the Continental Shelf of the United States, (c) the Great Lakes, (d) seabed and subsoil of the submarine areas adjacent to the coasts of the United States to the depth of two hundred meters, or beyond that limit, to where the depths of the superjacent waters admit of the exploitation of the natural resources of such areas, (e) the seabed and subsoil of similar submarine areas adjacent to the coasts of islands which comprise United States territory, and (f) the resources thereof.

(Pub. L. 89–454, title I, § 8, June 17, 1966, 80 Stat. 208; Pub. L. 89–688, § 2(b), Oct. 15, 1966, 80 Stat. 1001.)

AMENDMENTS

1966—Pub. L. 89–688 substituted "this title" for "this Act", which, for purposes of codification, has been changed to "this subchapter".

§ 1108. Authorization of appropriations

There are hereby authorized to be appropriated such sums as may be necessary to carry out this subchapter, but sums appropriated for any one fiscal year shall not exceed $1,200,000.

(Pub. L. 89–454, title I, § 9, June 17, 1966, 80 Stat. 208; Pub. L. 89–688, § 2(b), Oct. 15, 1966, 80 Stat. 1001; Pub. L. 91–15, § 2, May 23, 1969, 83 Stat. 10.)

AMENDMENTS

1969—Pub. L. 91–15 substituted "$1,200,000" for "$1,500,000".

1966—Pub. L. 89–688 substituted "this title" for "this Act", which, for purposes of codification, has been changed to "this subchapter".

SUBCHAPTER II—NATIONAL SEA GRANT COLLEGE PROGRAM

§ 1121. Congressional declaration of policy

(a) Findings

The Congress finds and declares the following:

(1) The national interest requires a strategy to—

(A) provide for the understanding and wise use of ocean, coastal, and Great Lakes resources and the environment;

(B) foster economic competitiveness;

(C) promote public stewardship and wise economic development of the coastal ocean and its margins, the Great Lakes, and the exclusive economic zone;

(D) encourage the development of preparation, forecast, analysis, mitigation, response, and recovery systems for coastal hazards;

(E) understand global environmental processes and their impacts on ocean, coastal, and Great Lakes resources; and

(F) promote domestic and international cooperative solutions to ocean, coastal, and Great Lakes issues.

(2) Investment in a strong program of integrated research, education, extension, training, technology transfer, and public service is essential for this strategy.

(3) The expanding use and development of ocean, coastal, and Great Lakes resources resulting from growing coastal area populations and the increasing pressures on the coastal and Great Lakes environment challenge the ability of the United States to manage such resources wisely.

(4) The vitality of the Nation and the quality of life of its citizens depend increasingly on the understanding, assessment, development, management, utilization, and conservation of ocean, coastal, and Great Lakes resources. These resources supply food, energy, and minerals and contribute to human health, the quality of the environment, national security, and the enhancement of commerce.

(5) The understanding, assessment, development, management, utilization, and conservation of such resources require a broad commitment and an intense involvement on the part of the Federal Government in continuing partnership with State and local governments, private industry, universities, organizations, and individuals concerned with or affected by ocean, coastal, and Great Lakes resources.

(6) The National Oceanic and Atmospheric Administration, through the national sea grant college program, offers the most suitable locus and means for such commitment and engagement through the promotion of activities that will result in greater such understanding, assessment, development, management, management,[1] utilization, and conservation of ocean, coastal, and Great Lakes resources. The most cost-effective way to promote such activities is through continued and increased Federal support of the establishment, development, management, and operation of programs and projects by sea grant colleges, sea grant institutes, and other institutions, including strong collaborations between Administration scientists and research and outreach personnel at academic institutions.

(b) Objective

The objective of this subchapter is to increase the understanding, assessment, development, management, utilization, and conservation of the Nation's ocean, coastal, and Great Lakes resources by providing assistance to promote a strong educational base, responsive research and training activities, broad and prompt dissemination of knowledge and techniques, and multidisciplinary approaches to environmental problems.

[1] So in original.

(c) Purpose

It is the purpose of the Congress to achieve the objective of this subchapter by extending and strengthening the national sea grant program, initially established in 1966, to promote integrated research, education, training, and extension services and activities in fields related to ocean, coastal, and Great Lakes resources.

(Pub. L. 89–454, title II, §202, as added Pub. L. 89–688, §1, Oct. 15, 1966, 80 Stat. 998; amended Pub. L. 94–461, §2, Oct. 8, 1976, 90 Stat. 1961; Pub. L. 95–428, §2(b), Oct. 7, 1978, 92 Stat. 999; Pub. L. 100–220, title III, §§3103, 3104(b)(1)(A), (B), Dec. 29, 1987, 101 Stat. 1469, 1470; Pub. L. 105–160, §3, Mar. 6, 1998, 112 Stat. 21; Pub. L. 107–299, §2, Nov. 26, 2002, 116 Stat. 2345; Pub. L. 110–394, §3, Oct. 13, 2008, 122 Stat. 4205.)

AMENDMENTS

2008—Subsec. (a). Pub. L. 110–394, §3(c), inserted "management," after "development," wherever appearing.

Subsec. (a)(1)(D), (E). Pub. L. 110–394, §3(a)(1), added subpars. (D) and (E) and struck out former subpars. (D) and (E) which read as follows:

"(D) encourage the development of forecast and analysis systems for coastal hazards;

"(E) understand global environmental processes; and".

Subsec. (a)(2). Pub. L. 110–394, §3(a)(2), substituted "program of integrated research, education, extension," for "program of research, education,".

Subsec. (a)(6). Pub. L. 110–394, §3(a)(3), added par. (6) and struck out former par. (6) which read as follows: "The National Oceanic and Atmospheric Administration, through the national sea grant college program, offers the most suitable locus and means for such commitment and involvement through the promotion of activities that will result in greater such understanding, assessment, development, utilization, and conservation. The most cost-effective way to promote such activities is through continued and increased Federal support of the establishment, development, and operation of programs and projects by sea grant colleges, sea grant institutes, and other institutions, including strong collaborations between Administration scientists and scientists at academic institutions."

Subsec. (b). Pub. L. 110–394, §3(c), inserted "management," after "development,".

Subsec. (c). Pub. L. 110–394, §3(b), substituted "to promote integrated research, education, training, and extension services and activities" for "to promote research, education, training, and advisory service activities".

2002—Subsec. (a)(6). Pub. L. 107–299 inserted ", including strong collaborations between Administration scientists and scientists at academic institutions" before period at end.

1998—Subsec. (a)(1)(D) to (F). Pub. L. 105–160, §3(a), added subpar. (D) and redesignated former subpars. (D) and (E) as (E) and (F), respectively.

Subsec. (a)(6). Pub. L. 105–160, §3(b), substituted "The most cost-effective way to promote such activities is through continued and increased Federal support of the establishment, development, and operation of programs and projects by sea grant colleges, sea grant institutes, and other institutions." for "Continued and increased Federal support of the establishment, development, and operation of programs and projects by sea grant colleges, sea grant regional consortia, institutions of higher education, institutes, laboratories, and other appropriate public and private entities is the most cost-effective way to promote such activities."

1987—Subsec. (a). Pub. L. 100–220, §§3103(1), 3104(b)(1)(A), added pars. (1) to (3), redesignated former pars. (1) to (3) as (4) to (6), respectively, and substituted "ocean, coastal, and Great Lakes resources" for "ocean and coastal resources" in pars. (4) and (5).

Subsec. (b). Pub. L. 100–220, §3103(2), substituted "ocean, coastal, and Great Lakes resources by providing assistance to promote a strong educational base, responsive research and training activities, broad and prompt dissemination of knowledge and techniques, and multidisciplinary approaches to environmental problems." for "ocean and coastal resources by providing assistance to promote a strong educational base, responsive research and training activities, and broad and prompt dissemination of knowledge and techniques."

Subsec. (c). Pub. L. 100–220, §3104(b)(1)(B), substituted "ocean, coastal, and Great Lakes resources" for "ocean and coastal resources".

1978—Subsec. (a)(3). Pub. L. 95–428 substituted "national sea grant college program" for "national sea grant program".

1976—Pub. L. 94–461 completely rewrote the Congressional statement of findings, objectives, and purposes of the National Sea Grant Program Act to reflect the extension and strengthening of the national sea grant program to promote research, education, training, and advisory service activities in fields related to ocean and coastal resources through federal support to sea grant colleges, sea grant regional consortia, and other institutions through the National Oceanic and Atmospheric Administration, and to make education, training, research, and advisory services responsive to state, local, regional, or national needs and problems.

SHORT TITLE OF 2008 AMENDMENT

Pub. L. 110–394, §1, Oct. 13, 2008, 122 Stat. 4205, provided that: "This Act [amending this section and sections 1122 to 1124, 1126 to 1128, and 1131 of this title and enacting provisions set out as a note under section 1128 of this title] may be cited as the 'National Sea Grant College Program Amendments Act of 2008'."

SHORT TITLE OF 2002 AMENDMENT

Pub. L. 107–299, §1, Nov. 26, 2002, 116 Stat. 2345, provided that: "This Act [enacting section 857–20 of this title, amending this section and sections 1123, 1124, 1126 to 1128, and 1131 of this title, and enacting provisions set out as a note under section 1123 of this title] may be cited as the 'National Sea Grant College Program Act Amendments of 2002'."

SHORT TITLE OF 1998 AMENDMENT

Pub. L. 105–160, §1, Mar. 6, 1998, 112 Stat. 21, provided that: "This Act [enacting section 1541 of Title 15, Commerce and Trade, amending this section and sections 1122, 1123, 1126 to 1128, and 1131 of this title, repealing section 1124a of this title, and enacting provisions set out as notes under sections 1123 and 1131 of this title] may be cited as the 'National Sea Grant College Program Reauthorization Act of 1998'."

SHORT TITLE OF 1991 AMENDMENT

Pub. L. 102–186, §1, Dec. 4, 1991, 105 Stat. 1282, provided that: "This Act [amending sections 1122 to 1124, 1127, 1128, and 1131 of this title and section 4741 of Title 16, Conservation, and repealing sections 1125 and 1130 of this title] may be cited as the 'National Sea Grant College Program Authorization Act of 1991'."

SHORT TITLE OF 1987 AMENDMENT

Section 3001 of title III of Pub. L. 100–220 provided that: "This title [amending this section and sections 1122 to 1131 of this title and enacting provisions set out as notes under this section and sections 883a and 1125 of this title] may be cited as the 'Marine Science, Technology, and Policy Development Act of 1987'."

Section 3101 of subtitle A (§§3101–3111) of title III of Pub. L. 100–220 provided that: "This subtitle [amending this section and sections 1122 to 1131 of this title and enacting provisions set out as a note under section 1125 of this title] may be cited as the 'National Sea Grant College Program Authorization Act of 1987'."

SHORT TITLE OF 1976 AMENDMENT

Section 1 of Pub. L. 94–461 provided: "That this Act [enacting sections 1124a, 1125, 1126, 1127, 1128, 1129, 1130, and 1131 of this title and amending this section, sections 1122, 1123, and 1124 of this title, sections 5314 and 5315 of Title 5, Government Organization and Employees, and provisions set out as notes under this section, section 1511 of Title 15, Commerce and Trade, and in the Appendix to Title 5, Government Organization and Employees] may be cited as the 'Sea Grant Program Improvement Act of 1976'."

SHORT TITLE

Section 201 of title II of Pub. L. 89–454, as added by section 1 of Pub. L. 89–688, and amended by Pub. L. 94–461, §2, Oct. 8, 1976, 90 Stat. 1961; Pub. L. 95–428, §2(a), Oct. 7, 1978, 92 Stat. 999, provided that: "This title [enacting this subchapter] may be cited as the 'National Sea Grant College Program Act'."

§1122. Definitions

As used in this subchapter—

(1) The term "Administration" means the National Oceanic and Atmospheric Administration.

(2) The term "Director" means the Director of the national sea grant college program, appointed pursuant to section 1123(b)[1] of this title.

(3) the[2] term "director of a sea grant college" means a person designated by his or her institution to direct a sea grant college or sea grant institute.

(4) The term "field related to ocean, coastal, and Great Lakes resources" means any discipline or field, including marine affairs, resource management, technology, education, or science, which is concerned with or likely to improve the understanding, assessment, development, management, utilization, or conservation of ocean, coastal, or Great Lakes resources.

(5) The term "institution" means any public or private institution of higher education, institute, laboratory, or State or local agency.

(6) The term "includes" and variants thereof should be read as if the phrase "but is not limited to" were also set forth.

(7) The term "ocean, coastal, and Great Lakes resources" means the resources that are located in, derived from, or traceable to, the seabed, subsoil, and waters of—

(A) the coastal zone, as defined in section 1453(1) of title 16;

(B) the Great Lakes;

(C) Lake Champlain (to the extent that such resources have hydrological, biological, physical, or geological characteristics and problems similar or related to those of the Great Lakes);

(D) the territorial sea;

(E) the exclusive economic zone;

(F) the Outer Continental Shelf; and

(G) the high seas.

(8) The term "resource" means—

(A) living resources (including natural and cultured plant life, fish, shellfish, marine mammals, and wildlife);

(B) nonliving resources (including energy sources, minerals, and chemical substances);

[1] See References in Text note below.

[2] So in original. Probably should be capitalized.

(C) the habitat of a living resource, the coastal space, the ecosystems, the nutrient-rich areas, and the other components of the marine environment that contribute to or provide (or which are capable of contributing to or providing) recreational, scenic, esthetic, biological, habitational, commercial, economic, or conservation values; and

(D) man-made, tangible, intangible, actual, or potential resources.

(9) The term "Board" means the National Sea Grant Advisory Board established under section 1128 of this title.

(10) The term "person" means any individual; any public or private corporation, partnership, or other association or entity (including any sea grant college, sea grant institute or other institution); or any State, political subdivision of a State, or agency or officer thereof.

(11) The term "project" means any individually described activity in a field related to ocean, coastal, and Great Lakes resources involving research, education, training, or extension services administered by a person with expertise in such a field.

(12) The term "sea grant college" means any institution, or any association or alliance of two or more such institutions, designated as such by the Secretary under section 1126 of this title.

(13) The term "sea grant institute" means any institution, or any association or alliance of two or more such institutions, designated as such by the Secretary under section 1126 of this title.

(14) The term "sea grant program" means a program of research and outreach which is administered by one or more sea grant colleges or sea grant institutes.

(15) The term "Secretary" means the Secretary of Commerce, acting through the Under Secretary of Commerce for Oceans and Atmosphere.

(16) The term "State" means any State of the United States, the District of Columbia, the Commonwealth of Puerto Rico, the Virgin Islands, Guam, American Samoa, the Commonwealth of the Mariana Islands, or any other territory or possession of the United States.

(Pub. L. 89–454, title II, §203, as added Pub. L. 89–688, §1, Oct. 15, 1966, 80 Stat. 999; amended Pub. L. 90–477, §1(1), Aug. 11, 1968, 82 Stat. 704; Pub. L. 91–349, July 23, 1970, 84 Stat. 448; Pub. L. 93–73, §1(1), (5), July 10, 1973, 87 Stat. 170; Pub. L. 94–461, §2, Oct. 8, 1976, 90 Stat. 1962; Pub. L. 95–428, §2(b), Oct. 7, 1978, 92 Stat. 999; Pub. L. 96–289, §1(1), June 28, 1980, 94 Stat. 605; Pub. L. 100–220, title II, §3104(a), (b)(1)(C), Dec. 29, 1987, 101 Stat. 1470; Pub. L. 102–186, §5(b)(1), Dec. 4, 1991, 105 Stat. 1284; Pub. L. 102–251, title III, §307(a), Mar. 9, 1992, 106 Stat. 66; Pub. L. 105–160, §4(a), Mar. 6, 1998, 112 Stat. 21; Pub. L. 105–174, title III, §10003, May 1, 1998, 112 Stat. 99; Pub. L. 110–394, §§4, 9(a)(4)(B), Oct. 13, 2008, 122 Stat. 4206, 4208.)

REFERENCES IN TEXT

Section 1123 of this title, referred to in par. (2), was amended generally by Pub. L. 105–160, §5, Mar. 6, 1998, 112 Stat. 22, and, as so amended, provisions relating to appointment of the Director of the National Sea Grant College Program, which formerly appeared in subsec. (b), are contained in subsec. (d).

AMENDMENTS

2008—Par. (4). Pub. L. 110–394, §4(a)(1), inserted "management," after "development,".

Par. (6)(F), (G). Pub. L. 110–394, §4(b), repealed section 307(a) of Pub. L. 102–251. See 1992 Amendment note below.

Par. (9). Pub. L. 110–394, §9(a)(4)(B), amended par. (9) generally. Prior to amendment, par. (9) read as follows: "The term 'panel' means the sea grant review panel established under section 1128 of this title."

Par. (11). Pub. L. 110–394, §4(a)(2), substituted "extension services" for "advisory services".

Pars. (12), (13). Pub. L. 110–394, §4(a)(3), made technical amendment to reference in original act which appears in text as reference to "section 1126 of this title", requiring no change in text.

1998—Par. (3). Pub. L. 105–160, §4(a)(1), substituted "his or her" for "their university or" and "college or sea grant institute" for "college, programs, or regional consortium".

Par. (4). Pub. L. 105–160, §4(a)(2), added par. (4) and struck out former par. (4) which read as follows: "The term 'field related to ocean, coastal, and Great Lakes resources' means any discipline or field (including marine science (and the physical, natural, and biological sciences, and engineering, included therein), marine technology, education, marine affairs and resource management, economics, sociology, communications, planning, law, international affairs, and public administration) which is concerned with or likely to improve the understanding, assessment, development, utilization, or conservation of ocean, coastal, and Great Lakes resources."

Par. (5). Pub. L. 105–174, §10003(1), redesignated par. (6) as (5) and struck out former par. (5) which read as follows: "The term 'Great Lakes' includes Lake Champlain."

Pub. L. 105–160, §4(a)(3), added par. (5). Former par. (5) redesignated (7).

Par. (6). Pub. L. 105–174, §10003(1), redesignated par. (7) as (6). Former par. (6) redesignated (5).

Pub. L. 105–160, §4(a)(3), added par. (6). Former par. (6) redesignated (8).

Par. (7). Pub. L. 105–174, §10003, redesignated par. (8) as (7), added subpar. (C), and redesignated former subpars. (C) to (F) as (D) to (G), respectively. Former par. (7) redesignated (6).

Pub. L. 105–160, §4(a)(3), redesignated par. (5) as (7). Former par. (7) redesignated (9).

Pars. (8) to (10). Pub. L. 105–174, §10003(1), redesignated pars. (9) to (11) as (8) to (10), respectively. Former par. (8) redesignated (7).

Pub. L. 105–160, §4(a)(3), redesignated pars. (6) to (8) as (8) to (10), respectively. Former pars. (9) and (10) redesignated (11) and (12), respectively.

Par. (11). Pub. L. 105–174, §10003(1), redesignated par. (12) as (11). Former par. (11) redesignated (10).

Pub. L. 105–160, §4(a)(3), (4), redesignated par. (9) as (11) and substituted "institute or other institution" for "regional consortium, institution of higher education, institute, or laboratory". Former par. (11) redesignated (13).

Pars. (12) to (17). Pub. L. 105–174, §10003(1), redesignated pars. (13) to (17) as (12) to (16), respectively. Former par. (12) redesignated (11).

Pub. L. 105–160, §4(a)(5), added pars. (12) to (17) and struck out former pars. (12) to (17) which defined "sea grant college", "sea grant program", "sea grant regional consortium", "Secretary", "State", and "Under Secretary", respectively.

Pub. L. 105–160, §4(a)(3), redesignated pars. (10) to (15) as (12) to (17), respectively.

1992—Par. (6)(F), (G). Pub. L. 102–251, §307(a), which directed addition of subpar. (F) and redesignation of former subpar. (F) as (G), was repealed by section 4(b) of Pub. L. 110–394. See Effective Date of 1992 Amendment note below.

1991—Par. (4). Pub. L. 102–186 inserted "marine affairs and resource management," after "education,".

1987—Pars. (2), (3). Pub. L. 100–220, §3104(a)(1), (2), added par. (3), redesignated former par. (3) as (2), and struck out former par. (2) which read as follows: "The term 'Administrator' means the Administrator of the National Oceanic and Atmospheric Administration."

Par. (4). Pub. L. 100–220, §3104(b)(1)(C), substituted "ocean, coastal, and Great Lakes resources" for "ocean and coastal resources" in two places.

Par. (6). Pub. L. 100–220, §3104(a)(3), added par. (6) and struck out former par. (6) which read as follows: "The term 'marine environment' means the coastal zone, as defined in section 1453(1) of title 16; the seabed, subsoil, and waters of the Great Lakes and the territorial sea of the United States; the waters of any zone over which the United States asserts exclusive fishery management authority; the waters of the high seas; and the seabed and subsoil of and beyond the outer Continental Shelf."

Par. (7). Pub. L. 100–220, §3104(a)(3), added par. (7) and struck out former par. (7) which read as follows: "The term 'ocean and coastal resource' means any resource (whether living, nonliving, manmade, tangible, intangible, actual, or potential) which is located in, derived from, or traceable to, the marine environment. Such term includes the habitat of any such living resource, the coastal space, the ecosystems, the nutrient-rich areas, and the other components of the marine environment which contribute to or provide (or which are capable of contributing to or providing) recreational, scenic, esthetic, biological, habitational, commercial, economic, or conservation values. Living resources include natural and cultured plant life, fish, shellfish, marine mammals, and wildlife. Nonliving resources include energy sources, minerals, and chemical substances."

Par. (11). Pub. L. 100–220, §3104(b)(1)(C), substituted "ocean, coastal, and Great Lakes resources" for "ocean and coastal resources".

Par. (15). Pub. L. 100–220, §3104(a)(4), added par. (15).

1980—Par. (6). Pub. L. 96–289 extended term "marine environment" to include waters of Great Lakes.

1978—Pub. L. 95–428 substituted "national sea grant college program" for "national sea grant program".

1976—Pub. L. 94–461 substituted provisions defining terms used in this subchapter for provisions designating Secretary of Commerce as administering authority for national sea grant program and authorizing appropriations through fiscal 1976.

1973—Subsec. (a). Pub. L. 93–73, §1(5), substituted "Secretary of Commerce" and "Secretary" for "National Science Foundation" and "Foundation", respectively.

Subsec. (b)(1). Pub. L. 93–73, §1(1), (5), authorized appropriations of $30,000,000; $40,000,000; and $50,000,000 for fiscal years ending June 30, 1974, 1975, and 1976, and substituted "Secretary" for "Foundation".

1970—Subsec. (b)(1). Pub. L. 91–349 authorized appropriations for fiscal year ending June 30, 1971, not to exceed the sum of $20,000,000, for fiscal year ending June 30, 1972, not to exceed the sum of $25,000,000, and for fiscal year ending June 30, 1973, not to exceed the sum of $30,000,000.

1968—Subsec. (b)(1). Pub. L. 90–477 authorized appropriations for fiscal year ending June 30, 1969, not to exceed the sum of $6,000,000, and for fiscal year ending June 30, 1970, not to exceed the sum of $15,000,000.

EFFECTIVE DATE OF 1992 AMENDMENT

Amendment by Pub. L. 102–251 effective on date on which Agreement between the United States and the Union of Soviet Socialist Republics on the Maritime Boundary, signed June 1, 1990, enters into force for United States, with authority to prescribe implementing regulations effective Mar. 9, 1992, but with no such regulation to be effective until date on which Agreement enters into force for United States, see section 308 of Pub. L. 102–251, set out as a note under section 773 of Title 16, Conservation.

TERRITORIAL SEA OF UNITED STATES

For extension of territorial sea of United States, see Proc. No. 5928, set out as a note under section 1331 of Title 43, Public Lands.

§1123. National sea grant college program

(a) Program maintenance

The Secretary shall maintain within the Administration a program to be known as the national sea grant college program. The national sea grant college program shall be administered by a national sea grant office within the Administration.

(b) Program elements

The national sea grant college program shall consist of the financial assistance and other activities authorized in this subchapter, and shall provide support for the following elements—

(1) sea grant programs that comprise a national sea grant college program network, including international projects conducted within such programs and regional and national projects conducted among such programs;

(2) administration of the national sea grant college program and this subchapter by the national sea grant office and the Administration;

(3) the fellowship program under section 1127 of this title; and

(4) any regional or national strategic investments in fields relating to ocean, coastal, and Great Lakes resources developed in consultation with the Board and with the approval of the sea grant colleges and the sea grant institutes.

(c) Responsibilities of Secretary

(1) The Secretary, in consultation with the Board, sea grant colleges, and sea grant institutes, shall develop at least every 4 years a strategic plan that establishes priorities for the national sea grant college program, provides an appropriately balanced response to local, regional, and national needs, and is reflective of integration with the relevant portions of the strategic plans of the Department of Commerce and of the Administration.

(2) The Secretary, in consultation with the Board, sea grant colleges, and sea grant institutes, shall establish guidelines related to the activities and responsibilities of sea grant colleges and sea grant institutes. Such guidelines shall include requirements for the conduct of merit review by the sea grant colleges and sea grant institutes of proposals for grants and contracts to be awarded under section 1124 of this title, providing, at a minimum, for standardized documentation of such proposals and peer review of all research projects.

(3) The Secretary shall by regulation prescribe the qualifications required for designation of sea grant colleges and sea grant institutes under section 1126 of this title.

(4) To carry out the provisions of this subchapter, the Secretary may—

(A) appoint, assign the duties, transfer, and fix the compensation of such personnel as may be necessary, in accordance with civil service laws;

(B) make appointments with respect to temporary and intermittent services to the extent authorized by section 3109 of title 5;

(C) publish or arrange for the publication of, and otherwise disseminate, in cooperation with other offices and programs in the Administration and without regard to section 501 of title 44, any information of research, educational, training or other value in fields related to ocean, coastal, or Great Lakes resources;

(D) enter into contracts, cooperative agreements, and other transactions without regard to section 5 of title 41;

(E) notwithstanding section 1342 of title 31, accept donations and voluntary and uncompensated services;

(F) accept funds from other Federal departments and agencies, including agencies within the Administration, to pay for and add to grants made and contracts entered into by the Secretary; and

(G) promulgate such rules and regulations as may be necessary and appropriate.

(d) Director of National Sea Grant College Program

(1) The Secretary shall appoint, as the Director of the National Sea Grant College Program, a qualified individual who has appropriate administrative experience and knowledge or expertise in fields related to ocean, coastal, and Great Lakes resources. The Director shall be appointed and compensated, without regard to the provisions of title 5 governing appointments in the competitive service, at a rate payable under section 5376 of title 5.

(2) Subject to the supervision of the Secretary, the Director shall administer the national sea grant college program and oversee the operation of the national sea grant office. In addition to any other duty prescribed by law or assigned by the Secretary, the Director shall—

(A) facilitate and coordinate the development of a strategic plan under subsection (c)(1) of this section;

(B) advise the Secretary with respect to the expertise and capabilities which are available within or through the national sea grant college program and encourage the use of such expertise and capabilities, on a cooperative or other basis, by other offices and activities within the Administration, and other Federal departments and agencies;

(C) advise the Secretary on the designation of sea grant colleges and sea grant institutes, and, if appropriate, on the termination or suspension of any such designation; and

(D) encourage the establishment and growth of sea grant programs, and cooperation and coordination with other Federal activities in fields related to ocean, coastal, and Great Lakes resources.

(3) With respect to sea grant colleges and sea grant institutes, the Director shall—

(A) evaluate and assess the performance of the programs of sea grant colleges and sea grant institutes, using the priorities, guidelines, and qualifications established by the Secretary under subsection (c) of this section, and determine which of the programs are the best managed and carry out the highest quality research, education, extension, and training activities;

(B) subject to the availability of appropriations, allocate funding among sea grant colleges and sea grant institutes so as to—

(i) promote healthy competition among sea grant colleges and institutes;

(ii) encourage collaborations among sea grant colleges and sea grant institutes to address regional and national priorities established under subsection (c)(1);

(iii) ensure successful implementation of sea grant programs;

(iv) to the maximum extent consistent with other provisions of this subchapter, provide a stable base of funding for sea grant colleges and institutes;

(v) encourage and promote coordination and cooperation between the research, education, and outreach programs of the Administration and those of academic institutions; and

(vi) encourage cooperation with Minority Serving Institutions to enhance collaborative research opportunities and increase the number of such students graduating in NOAA science areas; and

(C) ensure compliance with the guidelines for merit review under subsection (c)(2) of this section.

(Pub. L. 89–454, title II, §204, as added Pub. L. 89–688, §1, Oct. 15, 1966, 80 Stat. 999; amended Pub. L. 90–477, §1(2), Aug. 11, 1968, 82 Stat. 704; Pub. L. 93–73, §1(2)–(7), July 10, 1973, 87 Stat. 170; Pub. L. 94–461, §2, Oct. 8, 1976, 90 Stat. 1963; Pub. L. 95–428, §§2(b), 3(1), Oct. 7, 1978, 92 Stat. 999; Pub. L. 96–289, §1(2), June 28, 1980, 94 Stat. 605; Pub. L. 100–220, title III, §§3104(b)(1)(D), (2), (c), 3105(b), Dec. 29, 1987, 101 Stat. 1470, 1471; Pub. L. 102–186, §§2, 4(b)(1)(A), Dec. 4, 1991, 105 Stat. 1282, 1283; Pub. L. 105–160, §5, Mar. 6, 1998, 112 Stat. 22; Pub. L. 107–299, §3(a), (b)(1), (c), Nov. 26, 2002, 116 Stat. 2345, 2346; Pub. L. 110–394, §§5, 9(a)(4)(C)(i), Oct. 13, 2008, 122 Stat. 4206, 4208.)

REFERENCES IN TEXT

The civil service laws, referred to in subsec. (c)(4)(A), are set forth in Title 5, Government Organization and Employees. See, particularly, section 3301 et seq. of Title 5.

The provisions of title 5 governing appointments in the competitive service, referred to in subsec. (d)(1), are classified generally to section 3301 et seq. of Title 5, Government Organization and Employees.

This subchapter, referred to in subsec. (d)(3)(B)(iv), was in the original "this Act" and was translated as reading "this title" meaning title II of Pub. L. 89–454, which enacted this subchapter, to reflect the probable intent of Congress.

AMENDMENTS

2008—Subsec. (b)(1). Pub. L. 110–394, §5(a)(1), amended par. (1) generally. Prior to amendment, par. (1) read as follows: "sea grant programs which comprise a national sea grant college program network, including international projects conducted within such programs;".

Subsec. (b)(2). Pub. L. 110–394, §5(a)(2), amended par. (2) generally. Prior to amendment, par. (2) read as follows: "administration of the national sea grant college program and this subchapter by the national sea grant office, the Administration, and the panel;".

Subsec. (b)(4). Pub. L. 110–394, §5(a)(3), amended par. (4) generally. Prior to amendment, par. (4) read as follows: "any national strategic investments in fields relating to ocean, coastal, and Great Lakes resources developed with the approval of the panel, the sea grant colleges, and the sea grant institutes."

Subsec. (c)(1). Pub. L. 110–394, §9(a)(4)(C)(i), substituted "Board" for "panel".

Subsec. (c)(2). Pub. L. 110–394, §§5(b), 9(a)(4)(C)(i), substituted "The" for "Within 6 months of March 6, 1998, the" and "Board" for "panel".

Subsec. (d)(2)(A). Pub. L. 110–394, §5(c)(1), which directed the striking out of "long range", was executed by striking out "long-range" before "strategic plan" to reflect the probable intent of Congress.

Subsec. (d)(3)(A). Pub. L. 110–394, §5(c)(2), substituted "evaluate and assess" for "evaluate" and "activities;" for "activities; and", struck out cl. (i) designation before "evaluate", and struck out cl. (ii) which read as follows: "rate the programs according to their relative performance (as determined under clause (i)) into no less than 5 categories, with each of the 2 best-performing categories containing no more than 25 percent of the programs;".

Subsec. (d)(3)(B)(ii). Pub. L. 110–394, §5(c)(3)(A), added cl. (ii). Former cl. (ii) redesignated (iii).

Subsec. (d)(3)(B)(iii). Pub. L. 110–394, §5(c)(3)(A), (B), redesignated cl. (ii) as (iii) and substituted "ensure" for "encourage". Former cl. (iii) redesignated (iv).

Subsec. (d)(3)(B)(iv), (v). Pub. L. 110–394, §5(c)(3)(A), redesignated cls. (iii) and (iv) as (iv) and (v), respectively.

Subsec. (d)(3)(B)(vi). Pub. L. 110–394, §5(c)(3)(C), (D), added cl. (vi).

2002—Subsec. (c)(1). Pub. L. 107–299, §3(a), amended par. (1) generally. Prior to amendment, par. (1) read as follows: "The Secretary, in consultation with the panel, sea grant colleges, and sea grant institutes, shall develop a long-range strategic plan which establishes priorities for the national sea grant college program and which provides an appropriately balanced response to local, regional, and national needs."

Subsec. (d)(3)(A). Pub. L. 107–299, §3(b)(1), amended subpar. (A) generally. Prior to amendment, subpar. (A) read as follows: "evaluate the programs of sea grant colleges and sea grant institutes, using the priorities, guidelines, and qualifications established by the Secretary;".

Subsec. (d)(3)(B)(iv). Pub. L. 107–299, §3(c), added cl. (iv).

1998—Pub. L. 105–160 amended section catchline and text generally. Prior to amendment text consisted of subsecs. (a) to (d) relating to maintenance within the Administration of the National Sea Grant College Program, appointment and compensation of a Director of the program, duties of the Director, and powers of the Secretary to carry out the provisions of this subchapter.

1991—Subsec. (a). Pub. L. 102–186, §2(a), amended subsec. (a) generally. Prior to amendment, subsec. (a) read as follows: "The Secretary shall maintain, within the Administration, a program to be known as the national sea grant college program. The national sea grant college program shall consist of the financial assistance and other activities provided for in this subchapter. The Secretary shall establish long-range planning guidelines and priorities for, and adequately evaluate, this program."

Subsec. (c)(3). Pub. L. 102–186, §4(b)(1)(A), substituted "section 1124" for "sections 1124 and 1125".

Subsec. (c)(8). Pub. L. 102–186, §2(b), added par. (8).

Subsec. (d)(6). Pub. L. 102–186, §2(c), inserted "and add" after "to pay for".

1987—Subsec. (b)(1)(A). Pub. L. 100–220, §3104(b)(1)(D), substituted "ocean, coastal, and Great Lakes resources" for "ocean and coastal resources".

Subsec. (c). Pub. L. 100–220, §3104(c), substituted "Under Secretary" for "Administrator" wherever appearing in introductory provisions and par. (2).

Subsec. (c)(5). Pub. L. 100–220, §3104(b)(2), substituted "ocean, coastal, and Great Lakes resources" for "ocean and coastal resource".

Subsec. (d)(3). Pub. L. 100–220, §3104(b)(1)(D), substituted "ocean, coastal, and Great Lakes resources" for "ocean and coastal resources" in two places.

Subsec. (d)(6). Pub. L. 100–220, §3105(b), struck out "under section 1124(a) of this title" after "Secretary".

1980—Subsec. (c)(5) to (7). Pub. L. 96–289 added par. (5) and redesignated former pars. (5) and (6) as (6) and (7), respectively.

1978—Subsecs. (a) to (c). Pub. L. 95–428, §2(b), substituted "national sea grant college program" for "national sea grant program" wherever appearing.

Subsec. (d)(6), (7). Pub. L. 95–428, §3(1)(B), (C), added par. (6) and redesignated former par. (6) as (7).

1976—Pub. L. 94–461 substituted provisions covering the establishment and administration of the national sea grant program for provisions covering the marine resource development programs.

1973—Subsec. (a). Pub. L. 93–73, §1(2), (5), deleted item (1) designation for provision respecting consultation with experts and Federal agencies, deleted item (2) provision for seeking advice and counsel from the National Council on Marine Resources and Engineering Development, and substituted "Secretary" for "Foundation".

Subsec. (b). Pub. L. 93–73, §1(5), substituted "Secretary" for "Foundation" and "his authority" for "its authority".

Subsec. (d)(1). Pub. L. 93–73, §1(3), (5), authorized Federal contributions exceeding percentage limitation to programs limited to one percent of appropriations for the fiscal year when reducing or eliminating matching payments by a participant when Secretary determines it would be inequitable relevant to the benefits derived by the participant from the program to require the participant to make a one-third payment of the cost, and substituted "Secretary" for "Foundation" in last sentence.

Subsec. (d)(2). Pub. L. 93–73, §1(4), (5), made prohibitions of paragraph inapplicable to non-self-propelled habitats, buoys, platforms, or other similar devices or structures, used principally for research purposes and substituted "Secretary" for "foundation".

Subsecs. (d)(3), (e). Pub. L. 93–73, §1(5), substituted "Secretary" for "Foundation".

Subsec. (f). Pub. L. 93–73, §1(5), substituted "Secretary" for "Foundation" and "his functions" for "its functions".

Subsec. (g). Pub. L. 93–73, §1(6), substituted provisions for exercise of powers and authority under this subchapter by the Secretary rather than the Foundation under the powers and authority of the National Science Foundation Act of 1950, as amended.

Subsec. (h). Pub. L. 93–73, §1(5), substituted "Secretary" for "Foundation" and "his functions" for "its functions".

Subsec. (i)(3). Pub. L. 93–73, §1(7), inserted "and which is so designated by the Secretary" after "marine resources".

Subsec. (i)(4)(A) to (C). Pub. L. 93–73, §1(5), substituted "Secretary" for "Foundation".

1968—Subsec. (d)(1). Pub. L. 90–477 struck out "in any fiscal year" after "The total amount of payments" and "by any participants".

REVIEW OF EVALUATION AND RATING PROCESS

Pub. L. 107–299, §3(b)(2), Nov. 26, 2002, 116 Stat. 2346, provided that:

"(A) After 3 years after the date of the enactment of this Act [Nov. 26, 2002], the Secretary of Commerce, acting through the Under Secretary of Commerce for Oceans and Atmosphere, shall contract with the National Academy of Sciences—

"(i) to review the effectiveness of the evaluation and rating system under the amendment made by paragraph (1) [amending this section] in determining the relative performance of programs of sea grant colleges and sea grant institutes;

"(ii) to evaluate whether the sea grant programs have improved as a result of the evaluation process; and

"(iii) to make appropriate recommendations to improve the overall effectiveness of the evaluation process.

"(B) The National Academy of Sciences shall submit a report to the Congress on the findings and recommendations of the panel under subparagraph (A) by not later than 4 years after the date of the enactment of this Act [Nov. 26, 2002]."

NOTICE OF REORGANIZATION

Pub. L. 105–160, §9(d), Mar. 6, 1998, 112 Stat. 27, provided that: "The Secretary of Commerce shall provide notice to the Committees on Science [now Science and Technology], Resources [now Natural Resources], and Appropriations of the House of Representatives and the Committees on Commerce, Science, and Transportation and Appropriations of the Senate, not later than 45 days before any major reorganization of any program, project, or activity of the National Sea Grant College Program."

§1124. Program or project grants and contracts

(a) Authorization; purposes; limitation on amount

The Secretary may make grants and enter into contracts under this subsection to assist any sea grant program or project if the Secretary finds that such program or project will—

(1) implement the objective set forth in section 1121(b) of this title; and

(2) be responsive to the needs or problems of individual States or regions.

The total amount paid pursuant to any such grant or contract may equal 66⅔ percent, or any lesser percent, of the total cost of the sea grant program or project involved; except that this limitation shall not apply in the case of grants or contracts paid for with funds accepted by the Secretary under section 1123(c)(4)(F) of this title or that are appropriated under section 1127(b) of this title.

(b) Special grants; maximum amount; prerequisites

The Secretary may make special grants under this subsection to implement the objective set forth in section 1121(b) of this title. The amount of any such grant may equal 100 percent, or any lesser percent, of the total cost of the project involved. No grant may be made under this subsection unless the Secretary finds that—

(1) no reasonable means is available through which the applicant can meet the matching requirement for a grant under subsection (a) of this section;

(2) the probable benefit of such project outweighs the public interest in such matching requirement; and

(3) the same or equivalent benefit cannot be obtained through the award of a contract or grant under subsection (a) of this section.

The total amount that may be provided for grants under this subsection during any fiscal year shall not exceed an amount equal to 5 percent of the total funds appropriated for such year under section 1131 of this title.

(c) Eligibility and procedure

Any person may apply to the Secretary for a grant or contract under this section. Application shall be made in such form and manner, and with such content and other submissions, as the Secretary shall by regulation prescribe. The Secretary shall act upon each such application within 6 months after the date on which all required information is received.

(d) Terms and conditions

(1) Any grant made, or contract entered into, under this section shall be subject to the limitations and provisions set forth in paragraphs (2), (3), and (4) and to such other terms, conditions, and requirements as the Secretary deems necessary or appropriate. Terms, conditions, and requirements imposed by the Secretary under this paragraph shall minimize any requirement of prior Federal approval.

(2) No payment under any grant or contract under this section may be applied to—

(A) the purchase or rental of any land; or

(B) the purchase, rental, construction, preservation, or repair of any building, dock, or vessel;

except that payment under any such grant or contract may be applied to the short-term rental of buildings or facilities for meetings which are in direct support of any sea grant program or project and may, if approved by the Secretary, be applied to the purchase, rental, construction, preservation, or repair of non-self-propelled habitats, buoys, platforms, and other similar devices or structures, or to the rental of any research vessel which is used in direct support of activities under any sea grant program or project.

(3) The total amount which may be obligated for payment pursuant to grants made to, and contracts entered into with, persons under this section within any one State in any fiscal year shall not exceed an amount equal to 15 percent of the total funds appropriated for such year pursuant to section 1131 of this title.

(4) Any person who receives or utilizes any proceeds of any grant or contract under this section shall keep such records as the Secretary shall by regulation prescribe as being necessary and appropriate to facilitate effective audit and evaluation, including records which fully disclose the amount and disposition by such recipient of such proceeds, the total cost of the program or project in connection with which such proceeds were used, and the amount, if any, of such cost which was provided through other sources. Such records shall be maintained for 3 years after the completion of such a program or project. The Secretary and the Comptroller General of the United States, or any of their duly authorized representatives, shall have access, for the purpose of audit and evaluation, to any books, documents, papers, and records of receipts which, in the opinion of the Secretary or of the Comptroller General, may be related or pertinent to such grants and contracts.

(Pub. L. 89–454, title II, §205, as added Pub. L. 89–688, §1, Oct. 15, 1966, 80 Stat. 1001; amended Pub. L. 93–73, §1(8), July 10, 1973, 87 Stat. 170; Pub. L. 94–461, §2, Oct. 8, 1976, 90 Stat. 1964; Pub. L. 95–428, §3(2), Oct. 7, 1978, 92 Stat. 999; Pub. L. 96–289, §1(3), June 28, 1980, 94 Stat. 605; Pub. L. 100–220, title III, §3105(a), Dec. 29, 1987, 101 Stat. 1471; Pub. L. 102–186, §4(b)(1)(B), Dec. 4, 1991, 105 Stat. 1283; Pub. L. 107–299, §4, Nov. 26, 2002, 116 Stat. 2346; Pub. L. 110–394, §6, Oct. 13, 2008, 122 Stat. 4207.)

AMENDMENTS

2008—Subsec. (a). Pub. L. 110–394, §6(1), substituted "1123(c)(4)(F) of this title or that are appropriated under section 1127(b) of this title." for "1123(c)(4)(F) of this title."

Subsec. (b). Pub. L. 110–394, §6(2), inserted concluding provisions and struck out former concluding provisions which read as follows: "The total amount which may be provided for grants under this subsection during any fiscal year shall not exceed an amount equal to 1 percent of the total funds appropriated for such year pursuant to section 1131 of this title."

2002—Subsec. (a). Pub. L. 107–299 substituted "section 1123(c)(4)(F)" for "section 1123(d)(6)" in concluding provisions.

1991—Subsec. (b)(3). Pub. L. 102–186 struck out reference to section 1125 of this title after reference to subsection (a) of this section.

1987—Subsec. (d)(1). Pub. L. 100–220 inserted at end "Terms, conditions, and requirements imposed by the Secretary under this paragraph shall minimize any requirement of prior Federal approval."

1980—Subsec. (d)(2). Pub. L. 96–289 authorized application of any payment under a grant or contract to the short-term rental of buildings or facilities for meetings which are in direct support of any sea grant program or project.

1978—Subsec. (a). Pub. L. 95–428 made the percentage limitation inapplicable to grants or contracts paid for with funds accepted by the Secretary under section 1123(d)(6) of this title.

1976—Pub. L. 94–461 substituted provisions covering program or project grants and contracts for provisions authorizing the study of ways to share with other countries the results of marine research useful in the exploration, development, conservation, and management of marine resources.

1973—Pub. L. 93–73 substituted provisions for study of international marine technology transfer for prior provisions respecting advisory functions of National Council on Marine Resources and Development.

§1124a. Repealed. Pub. L. 105–160, §6, Mar. 6, 1998, 112 Stat. 24

Section, Pub. L. 94–461, §3, Oct. 8, 1976, 90 Stat. 1969; Pub. L. 95–58, §2, June 29, 1977, 91 Stat. 254; Pub. L. 95–428, §4(2), (3), Oct. 7, 1978, 92 Stat. 1000; Pub. L. 96–289, §§2, 3, June 28, 1980, 94 Stat. 605; Pub. L. 98–623, title V, §501(b), Nov. 8, 1984, 98 Stat. 3410; Pub. L. 100–220, title III, §3111, Dec. 29, 1987, 101 Stat. 1474; Pub. L. 102–251, title III, §307(b), Mar. 9, 1992, 106 Stat. 66, related to sea grant international program.

§1125. Repealed. Pub. L. 102–186, §4(a), Dec. 4, 1991, 105 Stat. 1283

Section, Pub. L. 89–454, title II, §206, as added Pub. L. 94–461, §2, Oct. 8, 1976, 90 Stat. 1965; amended Pub. L. 95–58, §1, June 29, 1977, 91 Stat. 254; Pub. L. 95–428, §3(3), Oct. 7, 1978, 92 Stat. 999; Pub. L. 96–289, §1(4), June 28, 1980, 94 Stat. 605; Pub. L. 100–220, title III, §3106(a), Dec. 29, 1987, 101 Stat. 1471, required development of a sea grant strategic research plan and authorized grants and contracts to carry out the program.

§1126. Sea grant colleges and sea grant institutes

(a) Designation

(1) A sea grant college or sea grant institute shall meet the following qualifications—

(A) have an existing broad base of competence in fields related to ocean, coastal, and Great Lakes resources;

(B) make a long-term commitment to the objective in section 1121(b) of this title, as determined by the Secretary;

(C) cooperate with other sea grant colleges and institutes and other persons to solve problems or meet needs relating to ocean, coastal, and Great Lakes resources;

(D) have received financial assistance under section 1124 of this title;

(E) be recognized for excellence in fields related to ocean, coastal, and Great Lakes resources (including marine resources management and science), as determined by the Secretary; and

(F) meet such other qualifications as the Secretary, in consultation with the Board, considers necessary or appropriate.

(2) The Secretary may designate an institution, or an association or alliance of two or more such institutions, as a sea grant college if the institution, association, or alliance—

(A) meets the qualifications in paragraph (1); and

(B) maintains a program of research, extension services, training, and education in fields related to ocean, coastal, and Great Lakes resources.

(3) The Secretary may designate an institution, or an association or alliance of two or more such institutions, as a sea grant institute if the institution, association, or alliance—

(A) meets the qualifications in paragraph (1); and

(B) maintains a program which includes, at a minimum, research and extension services.

(b) Existing designees

Any institution, or association or alliance of two or more such institutions, designated as a sea grant college or awarded institutional program status by the Director prior to March 6, 1998, shall not have to reapply for designation as a sea grant college or sea grant institute, respectively, after March 6, 1998, if the Director determines that the institution, or association or alliance of institutions, meets the qualifications in subsection (a) of this section.

(c) Suspension or termination of designation

The Secretary may, for cause and after an opportunity for hearing, suspend or terminate any designation under subsection (a) of this section.

(d) Duties

Subject to any regulations prescribed or guidelines established by the Secretary, it shall be the responsibility of each sea grant college and sea grant institute—

(1) to develop and implement, in consultation with the Secretary and the Board, a program that is consistent with the guidelines and priorities established under section 1123(c) of this title; and

(2) to conduct a merit review of all proposals for grants and contracts to be awarded under section 1124 of this title.

(e) Annual report on progress

(1) Report requirement

The Secretary shall report annually to the Committee on Resources and the Committee on Science of the House of Representatives, and to the Committee on Commerce, Science, and Transportation of the Senate, on efforts and progress made by colleges, universities, institutions, associations, and alliances to become designated under this section as sea grant colleges or sea grant institutes, including efforts and progress made by sea grant institutes in being designated as sea grant colleges.

(2) Territories and freely associated States

The report shall include description of—

(A) efforts made by colleges, universities, associations, institutions, and alliances in United States territories and freely associated States to develop the expertise necessary to be designated as a sea grant institute or sea grant college;

(B) the administrative, technical, and financial assistance provided by the Secretary to those entities seeking to be designated; and

(C) the additional actions or activities necessary for those entities to meet the qualifications for such designation under subsection (a)(1) of this section.

(Pub. L. 89–454, title II, § 207, as added Pub. L. 94–461, § 2, Oct. 8, 1976, 90 Stat. 1966; amended Pub. L. 100–220, title III, § 3104(b)(1)(E), Dec. 29, 1987, 101 Stat. 1470; Pub. L. 105–160, § 7, Mar. 6, 1998, 112 Stat. 24; Pub. L. 107–299, § 8, Nov. 26, 2002, 116 Stat. 2348; Pub. L. 110–394, §§ 7, 9(a)(4)(C)(ii), Oct. 13, 2008, 122 Stat. 4207, 4208.)

AMENDMENTS

2008—Subsec. (a)(1)(F). Pub. L. 110–394, § 9(a)(4)(C)(ii), substituted "Board" for "panel".

Subsec. (a)(2)(B), (3)(B). Pub. L. 110–394, § 7, substituted "extension services" for "advisory services".

Subsec. (d)(1). Pub. L. 110–394, § 9(a)(4)(C)(ii), substituted "Board" for "panel".

2002—Subsec. (e). Pub. L. 107–299 added subsec. (e).

1998—Pub. L. 105–160 amended section catchline and text generally. Prior to amendment text consisted of subsecs. (a) to (c) relating to authorization of the Secretary to designate sea grant college and sea grant regional consortia with certain prerequisites, requirement of regulations to prescribe qualifications and guidelines, and authorization of the Secretary to suspend or terminate any designation.

1987—Subsec. (a)(2)(A), (3)(A), (B). Pub. L. 100–220 substituted "ocean, coastal, and Great Lakes resources" for "ocean and coastal resources".

CHANGE OF NAME

Committee on Resources of House of Representatives changed to Committee on Natural Resources of House of Representatives and Committee on Science of House of Representatives changed to Committee on Science and Technology of House of Representatives by House Resolution No. 6, One Hundred Tenth Congress, Jan. 5, 2007.

§ 1127. Fellowships

(a) In general

To carry out the educational and training objectives of this subchapter, the Secretary shall support a program of fellowships for qualified individuals at the graduate and post-graduate level. The fellowships shall be related to ocean, coastal, and Great Lakes resources and awarded pursuant to guidelines established by the Secretary. The Secretary shall strive to ensure equal access for minority and economically disadvantaged students to the program carried out under this subsection. Every 2 years, the Secretary shall submit a report to the Congress describing the efforts by the Secretary to ensure equal access for minority and economically disadvantaged students to the program carried out under this subsection, and the results of such efforts.

(b) Dean John A. Knauss Marine Policy Fellowship

The Secretary may award marine policy fellowships to support the placement of individuals at the graduate level of education in fields related to ocean, coastal and Great Lakes resources in positions with the executive and legislative branches of the United States Government. A fellowship awarded under this subsection shall be for a period of not more than 1 year.

(c) Restriction on use of funds

Amounts available for fellowships under this section, including amounts accepted under section 1123(c)(4)(F) of this title or appropriated under section 1131 of this title to implement this section, shall be used only for award of such fellowships and administrative costs of implementing this section.

(Pub. L. 89–454, title II, § 208, as added Pub. L. 94–461, § 2, Oct. 8, 1976, 90 Stat. 1966; amended Pub. L. 100–66, § 3, July 10, 1987, 101 Stat. 384; Pub. L. 100–220, title III, § 3107, Dec. 29, 1987, 101 Stat. 1472; Pub. L. 102–186, § 4(b)(1)(C), (D), Dec. 4, 1991, 105 Stat. 1283; Pub. L. 105–160, § 4(b)(2), Mar. 6, 1998, 112 Stat. 22; Pub. L. 107–299, § 5, Nov. 26, 2002, 116 Stat. 2346; Pub. L. 110–394, § 8, Oct. 13, 2008, 122 Stat. 4207.)

REFERENCES IN TEXT

This subchapter, referred to in subsec. (a), was in the original "this Act" and was translated as reading "this title" meaning title II of Pub. L. 89–454, which enacted this subchapter, to reflect the probable intent of Congress.

AMENDMENTS

2008—Subsec. (a). Pub. L. 110–394, § 8(1), substituted "Every 2 years," for "Not later than 1 year after November 26, 2002, and every 2 years thereafter,".

Subsec. (c). Pub. L. 110–394, § 8(2), added subsec. (c).

2002—Subsec. (a). Pub. L. 107–299, § 5(a), inserted at end "The Secretary shall strive to ensure equal access for minority and economically disadvantaged students to the program carried out under this subsection. Not later than 1 year after November 26, 2002, and every 2 years thereafter, the Secretary shall submit a report to the Congress describing the efforts by the Secretary to ensure equal access for minority and economically disadvantaged students to the program carried out under this subsection, and the results of such efforts."

Subsec. (c). Pub. L. 107–299, § 5(b), struck out heading and text of subsec. (c). Text read as follows: "The Secretary shall establish and administer a program of postdoctoral fellowships to accelerate research in critical subject areas. The fellowship awards—

"(1) shall be for 2 years;

"(2) may be renewed once for not more than 2 years;

"(3) shall be awarded on a nationally competitive basis;

"(4) may be used at any institution of post-secondary education involved in the national sea grant college program;

"(5) shall be for up to 100 percent of the total cost of the fellowship; and

"(6) may be made to recipients of terminal professional degrees, as well as doctoral degree recipients."

1998—Pub. L. 105–160 substituted "Secretary" for "Under Secretary" in subsec. (a) in two places and in subsecs. (b) and (c).

1991—Subsec. (c)(5) to (7). Pub. L. 102–186 inserted "and" after semicolon at end of par. (5), redesignated par. (7) as (6), and struck out former par. (6) which read as follows: "may be made for any of the priority areas of research identified in the sea grant strategic research plan in effect under section 1125 of this title; and".

1987—Subsec. (a). Pub. L. 100–220 amended subsec. (a) generally. Prior to amendment, subsec. (a) read as follows: "The Secretary shall support a sea grant fellowship program to provide educational and training assistance to qualified individuals at the undergraduate and graduate levels of education in fields related to ocean and coastal resources. Such fellowships shall be awarded pursuant to guidelines established by the Secretary. Except as provided in subsection (b) of this section, sea grant fellowships may only be awarded by sea grant colleges, sea grant regional consortia, institutions of higher education, and professional associations and institutes."

Pub. L. 100–66, § 3(1), substituted "Except as provided in subsection (b) of this section, sea" for "Sea".

Subsec. (b). Pub. L. 100–220 amended subsec. (b) generally. Prior to amendment, subsec. (b) read as follows:

"(1) As part of the sea grant fellowship program, the Secretary may award sea grant fellowships to support the placement of qualified individuals in positions with the executive and legislative branches of the United States Government. No fellowship may be awarded under this paragraph for a period exceeding one year.

"(2) For purposes of this subsection, the term 'qualified individual' means an individual at the graduate level of education in fields related to ocean and coastal resources."

Pub. L. 100–66, § 3(2), (3), added subsec. (b) and redesignated former subsec. (b) as (c).

Subsec. (c). Pub. L. 100–220 amended subsec. (c) generally. Prior to amendment, subsec. (c) read as follows: "The total amount which may be provided for grants under the sea grant fellowship program during any fiscal year shall not exceed an amount equal to 5 percent of the total funds appropriated for such year pursuant to section 1131 of this title."

Pub. L. 100–66, § 3(2), redesignated former subsec. (b) as (c).

EFFECTIVE DATE OF 1987 AMENDMENT

Section 4 of Pub. L. 100–66 provided that: "The amendment made by section 3 [amending this section] shall take effect January 1, 1978."

§ 1128. National Sea Grant Advisory Board

(a) Establishment

There shall be an independent committee to be known as the National Sea Grant Advisory Board.

(b) Duties

(1) In general

The Board shall advise the Secretary and the Director concerning—

(A) strategies for utilizing the sea grant college program to address the Nation's highest priorities regarding the understanding, assessment, development, management, utilization, and conservation of ocean, coastal, and Great Lakes resources;

(B) the designation of sea grant colleges and sea grant institutes; and

(C) such other matters as the Secretary refers to the Board for review and advice.

(2) Biennial report

The Board shall report to the Congress every two years on the state of the national sea grant college program. The Board shall indicate in each such report the progress made toward meeting the priorities identified in the strategic plan in effect under section 1123(c) of this title. The Secretary shall make available to the Board such information, personnel, and administrative services and assistance as it may reasonably require to carry out its duties under this subchapter.

(c) Membership, terms, and powers

(1) The Board shall consist of 15 voting members who shall be appointed by the Secretary. The Director and a director of a sea grant program who is elected by the various directors of sea grant programs shall serve as nonvoting members of the Board. Not less than 8 of the voting members of the Board shall be individuals who, by reason of knowledge, experience, or training, are especially qualified in one or more of the disciplines and fields included in marine science. The other voting members shall be individuals who, by reason of knowledge, experience, or training, are especially qualified in, or representative of, education, marine affairs and resource management, coastal management, extension services, State government, industry, economics, planning, or any other activity which is appropriate to, and important for, any effort to enhance the understanding, assessment, development, management, utilization, or conservation of ocean, coastal, and Great Lakes resources. No individual is eligible to be a voting member of the Board if the individual is (A) the director of a sea grant college or sea grant institute; (B) an applicant for, or beneficiary (as determined by the Secretary) of, any grant or contract under section 1124 of this title; or (C) a full-time officer or employee of the United States.

(2) The term of office of a voting member of the Board shall be 3 years for a member appointed before November 26, 2002, and 4 years for a member appointed or reappointed after November 26, 2002. The Director may extend the term of office of a voting member of the Board appointed before November 26, 2002, by up to 1 year. At least once each year, the Secretary shall publish a notice in the Federal Register soliciting nominations for membership on the Board.

(3) Any individual appointed to a partial or full term may be reappointed for one additional full term. The Director may extend the term of office of a voting member of the Board once by up to 1 year.

(4) The Board shall select one voting member to serve as the Chairman and another voting member to serve as the Vice Chairman. The Vice Chairman shall act as Chairman in the absence or incapacity of the Chairman.

(5) Voting members of the Board shall—

(A) receive compensation at a rate established by the Secretary, not to exceed the maximum daily rate payable under section 5376 of title 5, when actually engaged in the performance of duties for such Board; and

(B) be reimbursed for actual and reasonable expenses incurred in the performance of such duties.

(6) The Board shall meet on a biannual basis and, at any other time, at the call of the Chairman or upon the request of a majority of the voting members or of the Director.

(7) The Board may exercise such powers as are reasonably necessary in order to carry out its duties under subsection (b) of this section.

(8) The Board may establish such subcommittees as are reasonably necessary to carry out its duties under subsection (b). Such subcommittees may include individuals who are not Board members.

(Pub. L. 89–454, title II, §209, as added Pub. L. 94–461, §2, Oct. 8, 1976, 90 Stat. 1967; amended Pub. L. 96–289, §1(5), June 28, 1980, 94 Stat. 605; Pub. L. 100–220, title III, §§3104(b)(1)(F), 3108, Dec. 29, 1987, 101 Stat. 1471, 1473; Pub. L. 102–186, §§4(b)(1)(E), (F), 5(b)(2), Dec. 4, 1991, 105 Stat. 1283, 1284; Pub. L. 105–160, §§4(b)(1), 8, Mar. 6, 1998, 112 Stat. 22, 25; Pub. L. 107–299, §6, Nov. 26, 2002, 116 Stat. 2346; Pub. L. 110–394, §9(a)(4)(A), (C)(iii)–(e), Oct. 13, 2008, 122 Stat. 4208.)

AMENDMENTS

2008—Pub. L. 110–394, §9(a)(4)(A), substituted "National Sea Grant Advisory Board" for "Sea grant review panel" in section catchline.

Subsec. (a). Pub. L. 110–394, §9(a)(4)(A), added subsec. (a) and struck out former subsec. (a). Prior to amendment, text read as follows: "There shall be established an independent committee to be known as the sea grant review panel."

Subsec. (b). Pub. L. 110–394, §9(b), amended subsec. (b) generally. Prior to amendment, subsec. (b) related to duties of sea grant review panel.

Subsec. (c). Pub. L. 110–394, §9(a)(4)(C)(iii), substituted "Board" for "panel" wherever appearing.

Subsec. (c)(1). Pub. L. 110–394, §9(c), inserted "coastal management," after "resource management," and "management," after "development,".

Subsec. (c)(3). Pub. L. 110–394, §9(d), substituted "The Director may extend the term of office of a voting member of the Board once by up to 1 year." for "A voting member may serve after the date of the expiration of the term of office for which appointed until his or her successor has taken office."

Subsec. (c)(8). Pub. L. 110–394, §9(e), added par. (8).

2002—Subsec. (c)(2). Pub. L. 107–299 inserted first and second sentences and struck out former first sentence which read as follows: "The term of office of a voting member of the panel shall be 3 years, except that of the original appointees, five shall be appointed for a term of 1 year, five shall be appointed for a term of 2 years, and five shall be appointed for a term of 3 years."

1998—Subsec. (a). Pub. L. 105–160, §8(a), struck out at end "The panel shall, on the 60th day after October 8, 1976, supersede the sea grant advisory panel in existence before October 8, 1976."

Subsec. (b). Pub. L. 105–160, §§4(b)(1), 8(b)(1), inserted heading and in introductory provisions substituted "The panel" for "The Panel" and struck out ", the Under Secretary," after "the Secretary".

Subsec. (b)(1). Pub. L. 105–160, §8(b)(2), struck out "and section 1124a of this title" before semicolon at end.

Subsec. (b)(3). Pub. L. 105–160, §8(b)(3), substituted "institutes" for "regional consortia".

Subsec. (c)(1)(A). Pub. L. 105–160, §8(c)(1), substituted "college or sea grant institute" for "college, sea grant regional consortium, or sea grant program".

Subsec. (c)(5)(A). Pub. L. 105–160, §8(c)(2), added subpar. (A) and struck out former subpar. (A) which read as follows: "receive compensation at the daily rate for GS–18 of the General Schedule under section 5332 of title 5 when actually engaged in the performance of duties for such panel; and".

1991—Subsec. (b)(1). Pub. L. 102–186, §4(b)(1)(E), substituted "section 1124" for "sections 1124 and 1125".

Subsec. (c)(1). Pub. L. 102–186, §§4(b)(1)(F), 5(b)(2), inserted "marine affairs and resource management," after "education," in fourth sentence and struck out "or 1125" after "1124" in last sentence.

1987—Subsec. (b). Pub. L. 100–220, §3108(1), in introductory provisions, substituted "The Panel shall advise the Secretary, the Under Secretary, and the Director concerning—" for "The panel shall take such steps as may be necessary to review, and shall advise the Secretary, the Administrator, and the Director with respect to—", and in par. (1), inserted "and section 1124a of this title".

Subsec. (c)(1). Pub. L. 100–220, §§3104(b)(1)(F), 3108(2)(A), (B), amended second sentence generally, substituted "8" for "five" in third sentence, and substituted "ocean, coastal, and Great Lakes resources" for "ocean and coastal resources" in fourth sentence. Prior to amendment, second sentence read as follows: "The Director shall serve as a nonvoting member of the panel."

Subsec. (c)(2). Pub. L. 100–220, §3108(2)(C), inserted at end "At least once each year, the Secretary shall publish a notice in the Federal Register soliciting nominations for membership on the panel."

Subsec. (c)(3). Pub. L. 100–220, §3108(2)(D), struck out ", or until 90 days after such date, whichever is earlier" after "office" at end of second sentence.

1980—Subsec. (c)(3). Pub. L. 96–289 substituted authorization for reappointment for one additional full term of an appointee to a partial or full term for prior authorization for filling vacancies for remainder of appointee's term and prohibition against status as a voting member after service of one full term as such voting member.

CHANGE OF NAME

Pub. L. 110–394, §9(a)(1)–(3), Oct. 13, 2008, 122 Stat. 4207, provided that:

"(1) REDESIGNATION.—The sea grant review panel established by section 209 of the National Sea Grant College Program Act (33 U.S.C. 1128), as in effect before the date of the enactment of this Act [Oct. 13, 2008], is redesignated as the National Sea Grant Advisory Board.

"(2) MEMBERSHIP NOT AFFECTED.—An individual serving as a member of the sea grant review panel immediately before date of the enactment of this Act may continue to serve as a member of the National Sea Grant Advisory Board until the expiration of such member's term under section 209(c) of such Act (33 U.S.C. 1128(c)).

"(3) REFERENCES.—Any reference in a law, map, regulation, document, paper, or other record of the United States to such sea grant review panel is deemed to be a reference to the National Sea Grant Advisory Board."

§1129. Interagency cooperation

Each department, agency, or other instrumentality of the Federal Government which is engaged in or concerned with, or which has authority over, matters relating to ocean, coastal, and Great Lakes resources—

(1) may, upon a written request from the Secretary, make available, on a reimbursable basis or otherwise any personnel (with their consent and without prejudice to their position and rating), service, or facility which the Secretary deems necessary to carry out any provision of this subchapter;

(2) shall, upon a written request from the Secretary, furnish any available data or other information which the Secretary deems necessary to carry out any provision of this subchapter; and

(3) shall cooperate with the Administration and duly authorized officials thereof.

(Pub. L. 89–454, title II, §210, as added Pub. L. 94–461, §2, Oct. 8, 1976, 90 Stat. 1968; amended Pub. L. 100–220, title III, §3104(b)(1)(G), Dec. 29, 1987, 101 Stat. 1471.)

AMENDMENTS

1987—Pub. L. 100–220 substituted "ocean, coastal, and Great Lakes resources" for "ocean and coastal resources" in introductory provisions.

§ 1130. Repealed. Pub. L. 102–186, § 5(a), Dec. 4, 1991, 105 Stat. 1283

Section, Pub. L. 89–454, title II, § 211, as added Pub. L. 94–461, § 2, Oct. 8, 1976, 90 Stat. 1968; amended Pub. L. 95–428, §§ 2(b), 3(4), Oct. 7, 1978, 92 Stat. 999; Pub. L. 100–220, title III, § 3109, Dec. 29, 1987, 101 Stat. 1473, authorized grants for graduate programs in marine affairs and resource management during fiscal years 1988 through 1990.

§ 1131. Authorization of appropriations

(a) Authorization

(1) In general

There are authorized to be appropriated to the Secretary to carry out this subchapter—

(A) $72,000,000 for fiscal year 2009;

(B) $75,600,000 for fiscal year 2010;

(C) $79,380,000 for fiscal year 2011;

(D) $83,350,000 for fiscal year 2012;

(E) $87,520,000 for fiscal year 2013; and

(F) $91,900,000 for fiscal year 2014.

(2) Priority activities

In addition to the amounts authorized under paragraph (1), there are authorized to be appropriated for each of fiscal years 2009 through 2014—

(A) $5,000,000 for competitive grants for university research on the biology, prevention, and control of aquatic nonnative species;

(B) $5,000,000 for competitive grants for university research on oyster diseases, oyster restoration, and oyster-related human health risks;

(C) $5,000,000 for competitive grants for university research on the biology, prevention, and forecasting of harmful algal blooms; and

(D) $3,000,000 for competitive grants for fishery extension activities conducted by sea grant colleges or sea grant institutes to enhance, and not supplant, existing core program funding.

(b) Limitations

(1) Administration

There may not be used for administration of programs under this subchapter in a fiscal year more than 5 percent of the lesser of—

(A) the amount authorized to be appropriated under this subchapter for the fiscal year; or

(B) the amount appropriated under this subchapter for the fiscal year.

(2) Use for other offices or programs

Sums appropriated under the authority of subsection (a)(2) of this section shall not be available for administration of this subchapter by the National Sea Grant Office, for any other Administration or department program, or for any other administrative expenses.

(c) Distribution of funds

In any fiscal year in which the appropriations made under subsection (a)(1) of this section exceed the amounts appropriated for fiscal year 2003 for the purposes described in such subsection, the Secretary shall distribute any excess amounts (except amounts used for the administration of the sea grant program) to any combination of the following:

(1) sea grant programs, according to their performance assessments;

(2) regional or national strategic investments authorized under section 1123(b)(4) of this title;

(3) a college, university, institution, association, or alliance for activities that are necessary for it to be designated as a sea grant college or sea grant institute; and

(4) a sea grant college or sea grant institute designated after November 26, 2002, but not yet evaluated under section 1123(d)(3)(A) of this title.

(d) Availability of sums

Sums appropriated pursuant to this section shall remain available until expended.

(e) Reversion of unobligated amounts

The amount of any grant, or portion of a grant, made to a person under any section of this subchapter that is not obligated by that person during the first fiscal year for which it was authorized to be obligated or during the next fiscal year thereafter shall revert to the Secretary. The Secretary shall add that reverted amount to the funds available for grants under the section for which the reverted amount was originally made available.

(Pub. L. 89–454, title II, § 212, as added Pub. L. 94–461, § 2, Oct. 8, 1976, 90 Stat. 1968; amended Pub. L. 95–58, § 1, June 29, 1977, 91 Stat. 254; Pub. L. 95–428, § 3(5), Oct. 7, 1978, 92 Stat. 1000; Pub. L. 96–289, § 1(6), June 28, 1980, 94 Stat. 605; Pub. L. 98–623, title V, § 501(a), Nov. 8, 1984, 98 Stat. 3410; Pub. L. 100–220, title III, § 3110, Dec. 29, 1987, 101 Stat. 1474; Pub. L. 102–186, § 3, Dec. 4, 1991, 105 Stat. 1282; Pub. L. 105–160, § 9(a), (b), Mar. 6, 1998, 112 Stat. 26; Pub. L. 107–299, § 7, Nov. 26, 2002, 116 Stat. 2347; Pub. L. 110–394, § 10, Oct. 13, 2008, 122 Stat. 4209.)

REFERENCES IN TEXT

This subchapter, referred to in subsec. (e), was in the original "this Act" and was translated as reading "this title" meaning title II of Pub. L. 89–454, which enacted this subchapter, to reflect the probable intent of Congress.

AMENDMENTS

2008—Subsec. (a)(1). Pub. L. 110–394, § 10(1), added par. (1) and struck out former par. (1) which authorized appropriations for fiscal years 2003 through 2008.

Subsec. (a)(2). Pub. L. 110–394, § 10(2)(A), substituted "fiscal years 2009 through 2014—" for "fiscal years 2003 through 2008—" in introductory provisions.

Subsec. (a)(2)(A). Pub. L. 110–394, § 10(2)(B), substituted "biology, prevention, and control of aquatic" for "biology and control of zebra mussels and other important aquatic".

Subsec. (a)(2)(C). Pub. L. 110–394, § 10(2)(C), substituted "blooms; and" for "blooms, including Pfiesteria piscicida; and".

Subsec. (c)(1). Pub. L. 110–394, § 10(3), substituted "performance assessments" for "rating under section 1123(d)(3)(A) of this title".

Subsec. (c)(2). Pub. L. 110–394, § 10(4), added par. (2) and struck out former par. (2) which read as follows:

"national strategic investments authorized under section 1123(b)(4) of this title;".

2002—Subsecs. (a) to (c). Pub. L. 107–299 amended subsecs. (a) to (c) generally, substituting provisions relating to authorization, limitations, and distribution of funds for provisions relating to authorization, program elements, and priority oyster disease research.

1998—Subsec. (a). Pub. L. 105–160, § 9(a), inserted heading and amended text of subsec. (a) generally. Prior to amendment, text read as follows: "There is authorized to be appropriated to carry out the provisions of sections 1124 and 1127 of this title, and section 1124a of this title, an amount—

"(1) for fiscal year 1991, not to exceed $44,398,000;

"(2) for fiscal year 1992, not to exceed $46,014,000;

"(3) for fiscal year 1993, not to exceed $47,695,000;

"(4) for fiscal year 1994, not to exceed $49,443,000; and

"(5) for fiscal year 1995, not to exceed $51,261,000."

Subsec. (b). Pub. L. 105–160, § 9(b), inserted subsec. heading and amended par. (1) generally. Prior to amendment, par. (1) read as follows: "There is authorized to be appropriated for administration of this subchapter, including section 1128 of this title, by the National Sea Grant Office and the Administration, an amount—

"(A) for fiscal year 1991, not to exceed $2,500,000;

"(B) for fiscal year 1992, not to exceed $2,600,000;

"(C) for fiscal year 1993, not to exceed $2,700,000;

"(D) for fiscal year 1994, not to exceed $2,800,000; and

"(E) for fiscal year 1995, not to exceed $2,900,000."

1991—Subsecs. (a) to (c). Pub. L. 102–186 amended subsecs. (a) to (c) generally. Prior to amendment, subsecs. (a) to (c) read as follows:

"(a) There is authorized to be appropriated to carry out the provisions of this subchapter other than sections 1125 and 1130 of this title, an amount—

"(1) for fiscal year 1988, not to exceed $41,500,000;

"(2) for fiscal year 1989, not to exceed $50,500,000; and

"(3) for fiscal year 1990, not to exceed $51,000,000.

"(b) There is authorized to be appropriated to carry out section 1125 of this title and section 1127(c) of this title, an amount—

"(1) for fiscal year 1988, not to exceed $500,000;

"(2) for fiscal year 1989, not to exceed $5,000,000; and

"(3) for fiscal year 1990, not to exceed $10,000,000.

"(c) There is authorized to be appropriated to carry out section 1130 of this title, an amount—

"(1) for fiscal year 1988, not to exceed $2,000,000;

"(2) for fiscal year 1989, not to exceed $2,500,000; and

"(3) for fiscal year 1990, not to exceed $3,000,000."

1987—Pub. L. 100–220 amended section generally, substituting provisions of subsecs. (a) to (e) relating to appropriations authorizations for fiscal years 1988, 1989, and 1990, for provisions formerly contained in a single unlettered paragraph relating to appropriations authorizations for fiscal years 1978 to 1983 and 1985 to 1987.

1984—Par. (4). Pub. L. 98–623 added par. (4).

1980—Par. (3). Pub. L. 96–289 added par. (3).

1978—Pub. L. 95–428 substituted appropriations authorization of $50,000,000 for fiscal years 1977, and 1978, for prior $50,000,000 authorization for fiscal years ending Sept. 30, 1977, and 1978, and authorized appropriation of $55,000,000 for fiscal years 1979 and 1980.

1977—Pub. L. 95–58 substituted "each of the fiscal years ending September 30, 1977, and September 30, 1978" for "the fiscal year ending September 30, 1977".

NOTICE OF REPROGRAMMING

Pub. L. 105–160, § 9(c), Mar. 6, 1998, 112 Stat. 26, provided that: "If any funds authorized by this section are subject to a reprogramming action that requires notice to be provided to the Appropriations Committees of the House of Representatives and the Senate, notice of such action shall concurrently be provided to the Committees on Science [now Science and Technology] and Resources [now Natural Resources] of the House of Representatives and the Committee on Commerce, Science, and Transportation of the Senate."

CHAPTER 23—POLLUTION CONTROL OF NAVIGABLE WATERS

§§ 1151 to 1165. Omitted

CODIFICATION

Sections 1151 to 1165 of this title were omitted as superseded by Pub. L. 92–500, § 2, Oct. 18, 1972, 86 Stat. 816. See section 1251 et seq. of this title.

Section 1151, acts June 30, 1948, ch. 758, § 1, 62 Stat. 1155; July 9, 1956, ch. 518, § 1, 70 Stat. 498; July 20, 1961, Pub. L. 87–88, § 1(a), 75 Stat. 204; Oct. 2, 1965, Pub. L. 89–234, § 1(a), 79 Stat. 903; 1966 Reorg. Plan No. 2, §§ 1(a), (e)(1), 5, eff. May 10, 1966, 31 F.R. 6857, 80 Stat. 1608; 1970 Reorg. Plan No. 3, § 2(a)(1), eff. Dec. 2, 1970, 35 F.R. 15623, 84 Stat. 2087, related to Congressional declaration of policy in controlling water pollution.

Section 1152, act June 30, 1948, ch. 758, § 2, as added Oct. 2, 1965, Pub. L. 89–234, § 2(a), 79 Stat. 903; amended 1966 Reorg. Plan No. 2, § 1(a), (b), eff. May 10, 1966, 31 F.R. 6857, 80 Stat. 1608; Apr. 3, 1970, Pub. L. 91–224, title I, § 110(a), 84 Stat. 113, created within the Department of the Interior a Federal Water Quality Administration. Reorg. Plan No. 3 of 1970, §§ 1, 2(a)(1), 6(a)(1), eff. Dec. 2, 1970, 35 F.R. 15623, 84 Stat. 2086, 2087, 2089, created Environmental Protection Agency, abolished Federal Water Quality Administration in Department of the Interior, and transferred to Administrator of Environmental Protection Agency all functions vested by law in Secretary of the Interior and Department of the Interior which had been administered through Federal Water Quality Administration.

Section 1153, acts June 30, 1948, ch. 758, § 3, formerly § 2, 62 Stat. 1155; July 9, 1956, ch. 518, § 1, 70 Stat. 498; July 20, 1961, Pub. L. 87–88, §§ 1(b), 2, 75 Stat. 204; renumbered Oct. 2, 1965, Pub. L. 89–234, § 2(a), 79 Stat. 903; amended Nov. 3, 1966, Pub. L. 89–753, title I, § 101, 80 Stat. 1246; 1970 Reorg. Plan No. 3, § 2(a)(1), eff. Dec. 2, 1970, 35 F.R. 15623, 84 Stat. 2086, related to preparation and development of comprehensive water pollution programs.

Section 1154, acts June 30, 1948, ch. 758, § 4, formerly § 3, 62 Stat. 1157; July 9, 1956, ch. 518, § 1, 70 Stat. 498; July 20, 1961, Pub. L. 87–88, § 1(b), 75 Stat. 204; renumbered Oct. 2, 1965, Pub. L. 89–234, § 2(a), 79 Stat. 903; 1970 Reorg. Plan No. 3, § 2(a)(1), eff. Dec. 2, 1970, 35 F.R. 15623, 84 Stat. 2086, related to interstate cooperation for prevention and control of water pollution.

Section 1155, acts June 30, 1948, ch. 758, § 5, formerly § 4, 62 Stat. 1158; July 9, 1956, ch. 518, § 1, 70 Stat. 499; July 20, 1961, Pub. L. 87–88, §§ 1(b), (c), 3, 75 Stat. 204, 205; renumbered Oct. 2, 1965, Pub. L. 89–234, § 2(a), 79 Stat. 903; amended 1966 Reorg. Plan No. 2, § 1(a), eff. May 10, 1966, 31 F.R. 6857, 80 Stat. 1608; Nov. 3, 1966, Pub. L. 89–753, title II, § 201(b), (c)(1), 80 Stat. 1247; Apr. 3, 1970, Pub. L. 91–224, title I, § 105, 84 Stat. 111; 1970 Reorg. Plan No. 3, § 2(a)(1), eff. Dec. 2, 1970, 35 F.R. 15623, 84 Stat. 2086; Oct. 13, 1971, Pub. L. 92–137, § 1, 85 Stat. 379; Mar. 1, 1972, Pub. L. 92–240, § 1, 86 Stat. 47, related to research, investigations, experiments, demonstrations, and studies in prevention and control of water pollution.

Section 1156, act June 30, 1948, ch. 758, § 6, as added Oct. 2, 1965, Pub. L. 89–234, § 3, 79 Stat. 905; amended Nov. 3, 1966, Pub. L. 89–753, title II, § 201(a), 80 Stat. 1246; Apr. 3, 1970, Pub. L. 91–224, title I, § 106, 84 Stat. 113; 1970 Reorg. Plan No. 3, § 2(a)(1), eff. Dec. 2, 1970, 35 F.R. 15623, 84 Stat. 2087, related to grants for research and development of methods to prevent and control water pollution.

Section 1157, acts June 30, 1948, ch. 758, § 7, formerly § 5, 62 Stat. 1158; July 9, 1956, ch. 518, § 1, 70 Stat. 499; June 25, 1959, Pub. L. 86–70, § 28(a), 73 Stat. 148; July 12, 1960, Pub. L. 86–624, § 23(a), 74 Stat. 417; July 20, 1961, Pub. L. 87–88, §§ 1(b), 4(a), (b), 75 Stat. 204, 205; renumbered and amended Oct. 2, 1965, Pub. L. 89–234, §§ 2(a), 7(a), 79 Stat. 903, 910; Nov. 3, 1966, Pub. L. 89–753, title II, § 202, 80 Stat. 1248; 1970 Reorg. Plan No. 3, § 2(a)(1), eff. Dec. 2, 1970, 35 F.R. 15623, 84 Stat. 2086; July 9, 1971,

Pub. L. 92–50, §2, 85 Stat. 124; Oct. 13, 1971, Pub. L. 92–137, §3, 85 Stat. 379; Mar. 1, 1972, Pub. L. 92–240, §2, 86 Stat. 47, related to grants for water pollution control programs.

Section 1158, acts June 30, 1948, ch. 758, §8, formerly §6, 62 Stat. 1158; July 9, 1956, ch. 518, §1, 70 Stat. 502; July 20, 1961, Pub. L. 87–88, §§1(b), 5, 75 Stat. 204, 206; renumbered and amended Oct. 2, 1965, Pub. L. 89–234, §§2(a), 4, 7(b), 79 Stat. 903, 906, 910; Nov. 3, 1966, Pub. L. 89–753, title II, §§203(a), 204, 205, 80 Stat. 1248–1250; Apr. 3, 1970, Pub. L. 91–224, title I, §111, 84 Stat. 113; 1970 Reorg. Plan No. 2, §§102, 103, eff. July 1, 1970, 35 F.R. 7959, 84 Stat. 2085; 1970 Reorg. Plan No. 3, §2(a)(1), eff. Dec. 2, 1970, 15 F.R. 15623, 84 Stat. 2087; July 9, 1971, Pub. L. 92–50, §3, 85 Stat. 124; Oct. 13, 1971, Pub. L. 92–137, §4, 85 Stat. 379; Mar. 1, 1972, Pub. L. 92–240, §3, 86 Stat. 48, related to grants for construction of sewerage treatment works.

Section 1159, acts June 30, 1948, ch. 758, §9, formerly §7, 62 Stat. 1159; July 17, 1952, ch. 927, 66 Stat. 755; July 9, 1956, ch. 518, §1, 70 Stat. 503; July 20, 1961, Pub. L. 87–88, §§1(b)–(d), 6(a), (b), 75 Stat. 204, 207; renumbered Oct. 2, 1965, Pub. L. 89–234, §2(a), 79 Stat. 903; amended 1966 Reorg. Plan No. 2, §1(a), (c)(1), (2), eff. May 10, 1966, 31 F.R. 6857, 80 Stat. 1608; 1970 Reorg. Plan No. 3, §2(a)(1), (b)(1)(i), eff. Dec. 3, 1970, 35 F.R. 15623, 84 Stat. 2087, related to establishment, composition, and duties of the Water Pollution Control Advisory Board.

Section 1160, acts June 30, 1948, ch. 758, §10, formerly §8, 62 Stat. 1159; July 17, 1952, ch. 927, 66 Stat. 755; July 9, 1956, ch. 518, §1, 70 Stat. 504; July 20, 1961, Pub. L. 87–88, §§1(b), 7, 75 Stat. 204, 207; renumbered and amended Oct. 2, 1965, Pub. L. 89–234, §§2(a), 5, 7(c), (d), 79 Stat. 903, 907, 910; 1966 Reorg. Plan No. 2, §1(a), (d)(1), (2), eff. May 10, 1966, 31 F.R. 6857, 80 Stat. 1608; Nov. 3, 1966, Pub. L. 89–753, title II, §§206–208, 80 Stat. 1250; Apr. 3, 1970, Pub. L. 91–224, title I, §112, 84 Stat. 114; 1970 Reorg. Plan No. 3, §2(a)(1), eff. Dec. 2, 1970, 35 F.R. 15623, 84 Stat. 2087, related to enforcement measures against pollution of interstate or navigable waters.

Section 1161, act June 30, 1948, ch. 758, §11, as added Apr. 3, 1970, Pub. L. 91–224, title I, §102, 84 Stat. 91; amended 1970 Reorg. Plan No. 3, §2(a)(1), eff. Dec. 2, 1970, 35 F.R. 15623, 84 Stat. 2087, Dec. 31, 1970, Pub. L. 91–611, title I, §120 84 Stat. 1823, related to control of pollution by oil.

Section 1162, act June 30, 1948, ch. 758, §12, as added Apr. 3, 1970, Pub. L. 91–224, title I, §102, 84 Stat. 98, related to control of pollution by hazardous substances.

Section 1163, act June 30, 1948, ch. 758, §13, as added Apr. 3, 1970, Pub. L. 91–224, title I, §102, 84 Stat. 100; amended 1970 Reorg. Plan No. 3, §2(a)(1), eff. Dec. 2, 1970, 35 F.R. 15623, 84 Stat. 2087, related to control of sewage from vessels.

Section 1164, act June 30, 1948, ch. 758, §14, as added Apr. 3, 1970, Pub. L. 91–224, title I, §102, 84 Stat. 103; amended 1970 Reorg. Plan No. 3, §2(a)(1), eff. Dec. 2, 1970, 35 F.R. 15623, 84 Stat. 2087, related to acid and other mine water pollution elimination or control projects.

Section 1165, act June 30, 1948, ch. 758, §15, as added Apr. 3, 1970, Pub. L. 91–224, title I, §102, 84 Stat. 104; amended 1970 Reorg. Plan No. 3, §2(a)(1), eff. Dec. 2, 1970, 35 F.R. 15623, 84 Stat. 2087, related to Great Lakes pollution elimination or control projects.

§1165a. Transferred

CODIFICATION

Section transferred to section 1293a of this title.

§§1166 to 1175. Omitted

CODIFICATION

Sections 1166 to 1175 of this title were omitted as superseded by Pub. L. 92–500, §2, Oct. 18, 1972, 88 Stat. 816. See section 1251 et seq. of this title.

Section 1166, act June 30, 1948, ch. 758, §16, as added Apr. 3, 1970, Pub. L. 91–224, title I, §102, 84 Stat. 104; amended 1970 Reorg. Plan No. 3, §2(a)(1), eff. Dec. 2, 1970, 35 F.R. 15623, 84 Stat. 2087, related to training grants to and contracts with institutions of higher education for water quality control programs or projects.

Section 1167, act June 30, 1948, ch. 758, §17, as added Apr. 3, 1970, Pub. L. 91–224, title I, §102, 84 Stat. 105; amended 1970 Reorg. Plan No. 3, §2(a)(1), eff. Dec. 3, 1970, 35 F.R. 15623, 84 Stat. 2087, related to applications for training grants or contracts.

A prior section 17 of act June 30, 1948, formerly classified to section 466m of this title, was repealed by Pub. L. 91–224, title 1, §102, Apr. 3, 1970, 84 Stat. 91, in the general reorganization of act June 30, 1948 by Pub. L. 91–224.

Section 1168, act June 30, 1948, ch. 758, §18, as added Apr. 3, 1970, Pub. L. 91–224, title I, §102, 84 Stat. 105; amended 1970 Reorg. Plan No. 3, §2(a)(1), eff. Dec. 2, 1970, 35 F.R. 15623, 84 Stat. 2087, related to awarding of scholarships for undergraduate study of operation and maintenance of treatment works.

A prior section 18 of act June 30, 1948, formerly classified to section 466n of this title, was repealed by Pub. L. 91–224, title I, §102, Apr. 3, 1970, 84 Stat. 91, in the general reorganization of act June 30, 1948 by Pub. L. 91–224.

Section 1169, act June 30, 1948, ch. 758, §19, as added Apr. 3, 1970, Pub. L. 91–224, title I, §102, 84 Stat. 106; amended 1970 Reorg. Plan No. 3, §2(a)(1), eff. Dec. 2, 1970, 35 F.R. 15623, 84 Stat. 2087, related to an annual report by the Administrator of the Environmental Protection Agency, appropriations for certain fiscal years, and defined certain terms as used in this chapter.

Section 1170, act June 30, 1948, ch. 758, §20, as added Apr. 3, 1970, Pub. L. 91–224, title I, §102, 84 Stat. 107; amended 1970 Reorg. Plan No. 3, §2(a)(1), eff. Dec. 2, 1970, 35 F.R. 15623, 84 Stat. 2087, related to Alaska village safe water and pollution elimination or control projects.

Section 1171, act June 30, 1948, ch. 758, §21, formerly §9, 62 Stat. 1160; July 9, 1956, ch. 518, §1, 70 Stat. 506; July 20, 1961. Pub. L. 87–88, §8, 75 Stat. 210; renumbered §11 and amended Oct. 2, 1965, Pub. L. 89–234, §§2(a), 7(e), 79 Stat. 903, 910; 1966 Reorg. Plan No. 2, §1(a), eff. May 10, 1966, 31 F.R. 6857, 80 Stat. 1608; renumbered §21 and amended Apr. 3, 1970, Pub. L. 91–224, title I, §§102, 103, 84 Stat. 91, 107; 1970 Reorg. Plan No. 3, §2(a)(1), eff. Dec. 2, 1970, 35 F.R. 15623, 84 Stat. 2087, related to cooperation by all Federal agencies in pollution control.

Section 1172, act June 30, 1948, ch. 758, §22, formerly §10, 62 Stat. 1160; July 9, 1956, ch. 518, §1 70 Stat. 506; July 20, 1961, Pub. L. 87–88, §1(b), (d), (e), 75 Stat. 204; renumbered §12 and amended Oct. 2, 1965, Pub. L. 89–234, §§2(a), 6, 79 Stat. 903, 909; 1966 Reorg. Plan No. 2, §1(a), eff. May 10, 1966, 31 F.R. 6857, 80 Stat. 1608; renumbered §22 and amended Apr. 3, 1970, Pub. L. 91–224, title I, §§102, 104, 84 Stat. 91, 110; 1970 Reorg. Plan No. 3, §2(a)(1), eff. Dec. 2, 1970, 35 F.R. 15623, 84 Stat. 2087, related to administration of water pollution control program under this chapter.

Section 1173, act June 30, 1948, ch. 758, §23, formerly §11, 62 Stat. 1161; July 9, 1956, ch. 518, §1, 70 Stat. 506; June 25, 1959, Pub. L. 86–70, §28(b), 73 Stat. 148; July 12, 1960, Pub. L. 86–624, §23(b), 74 Stat. 418; July 20, 1961, Pub. L. 87–88, §9, 75 Stat. 210; renumbered §13, Oct. 2, 1965, Pub. L. 89–234, §2(a), 79 Stat. 903; amended Nov. 3, 1966, Pub. L. 89–753, title II, §209, 80 Stat. 1251; renumbered §23, Apr. 3, 1970, Pub. L. 91–224, title I, §102, 84 Stat. 91, related to definitions of terms used in this chapter.

Section 1174, act June 30, 1948, ch. 758, §24, formerly §12, as added July 9, 1956, ch. 518, §1, 70 Stat. 506; renumbered §14, Oct. 2, 1965, Pub. L. 89–234, §2(a), 79 Stat. 903; renumbered §24 and amended Apr. 3, 1970, Pub. L. 91–224, §§102, 107, 84 Stat. 91, 113, related to application of this chapter to other laws.

Section 1175, act June 30, 1948, ch. 758, §26, formerly §16, as added Nov. 3, 1966, Pub. L. 89–753, title II, §210, 80 Stat. 1252; renumbered Apr. 3, 1970, Pub. L. 91–224, title I, §102, 84 Stat. 91; amended 1970 Reorg. Plan No. 3, §2(a)(1), eff. Dec. 2, 1970, 35 F.R. 15623, 84 Stat. 2087, related to cost estimates, studies, and analysis by the Administrator of Environmental Protection Agency.

CHAPTER 24—VESSEL BRIDGE-TO-BRIDGE COMMUNICATION

§1201. Statement of purpose

It is the purpose of this chapter to provide a positive means whereby the operators of approaching vessels can communicate their intentions to one another through voice radio, located convenient to the operator's navigation station. To effectively accomplish this, there is need for a specific frequency or frequencies dedicated to the exchange of navigational information, on navigable waters of the United States.

(Pub. L. 92–63, §2, Aug. 4, 1971, 85 Stat. 164.)

SHORT TITLE

Section 1 of Pub. L. 92–63 provided: "That this Act [enacting this chapter] may be cited as the 'Vessel Bridge-to-Bridge Radiotelephone Act'."

EFFECTIVE DATE

Section 10 of Pub. L. 92–63 provided that: "This Act [enacting this chapter] shall become effective May 1, 1971, or six months after the promulgation of regulations which would implement its provisions, whichever is later." See 47 CFR 83.701 et seq.

§1202. Definitions

For the purpose of this chapter—

(1) "Secretary" means the Secretary of the Department in which the Coast Guard is operating;

(2) "power-driven vessel" means any vessel propelled by machinery; and

(3) "towing vessel" means any commercial vessel engaged in towing another vessel astern, alongside, or by pushing ahead.

(Pub. L. 92–63, §3, Aug. 4, 1971, 85 Stat. 164.)

TRANSFER OF FUNCTIONS

For transfer of authorities, functions, personnel, and assets of the Coast Guard, including the authorities and functions of the Secretary of Transportation relating thereto, to the Department of Homeland Security, and for treatment of related references, see sections 468(b), 551(d), 552(d), and 557 of Title 6, Domestic Security, and the Department of Homeland Security Reorganization Plan of November 25, 2002, as modified, set out as a note under section 542 of Title 6.

§1203. Radiotelephone requirement

(a) Vessel coverage; exchange of navigational information

Except as provided in section 1206 of this title—

(1) every power-driven vessel of twenty meters or over in length while navigating;

(2) every vessel of one hundred gross tons as measured under section 14502 of title 46, or an alternate tonnage measured under section 14302 of that title as prescribed by the Secretary under section 14104 of that title, and upward carrying one or more passengers for hire while navigating;

(3) every towing vessel of twenty-six feet or over in length while navigating; and

(4) every dredge and floating plant engaged in or near a channel or fairway in operations likely to restrict or affect navigation of other vessels—

shall have a radiotelephone capable of operation from its navigational bridge or, in the case of a dredge, from its main control station and capable of transmitting and receiving on the frequency or frequencies within the 156–162 Mega-Hertz band using the classes of emissions designated by the Federal Communications Commission, after consultation with other cognizant agencies, for the exchange of navigational information.

(b) Vessels upon navigable waters of United States inside high seas lines

The radiotelephone required by subsection (a) of this section shall be carried on board the described vessels, dredges, and floating plants upon the navigable waters of the United States, which includes all waters of the territorial sea of the United States as described in Presidential Proclamation 5928 of December 27, 1988.

(Pub. L. 92–63, §4, Aug. 4, 1971, 85 Stat. 164; Pub. L. 102–241, §16, Dec. 19, 1991, 105 Stat. 2213; Pub. L. 104–324, title VII, §704, Oct. 19, 1996, 110 Stat. 3933; Pub. L. 107–295, title III, §321, Nov. 25, 2002, 116 Stat. 2103.)

REFERENCES IN TEXT

Presidential Proclamation 5928 of December 27, 1988, referred to in subsec. (b), is set out as a note under section 1331 of Title 43, Public Lands.

AMENDMENTS

2002—Subsec. (b). Pub. L. 107–295 substituted "United States, which includes all waters of the territorial sea of the United States as described in Presidential Proclamation 5928 of December 27, 1988" for "United States inside the lines established pursuant to section 151 of this title".

1996—Subsec. (a)(2). Pub. L. 104–324 inserted "as measured under section 14502 of title 46, or an alternate tonnage measured under section 14302 of that title as prescribed by the Secretary under section 14104 of that title," after "one hundred gross tons".

1991—Subsec. (a)(1). Pub. L. 102–241 amended par. (1) generally, substituting "twenty meters or over in length" for "three hundred gross tons and upward".

VESSEL COMMUNICATION EQUIPMENT REGULATIONS

Pub. L. 101–380, title IV, §4118, Aug. 18, 1990, 104 Stat. 523, provided that: "The Secretary shall, not later than one year after the date of the enactment of this Act [Aug. 18, 1990], issue regulations necessary to ensure that vessels subject to the Vessel Bridge-to-Bridge Radiotelephone Act of 1971 (33 U.S.C. 1203) are also equipped as necessary to—

"(1) receive radio marine navigation safety warnings; and

"(2) engage in radio communications on designated frequencies with the Coast Guard, and such other vessels and stations as may be specified by the Secretary.''

§1204. Radiotelephone for exclusive use of master, person in charge, or pilot; frequency listening watch; portable radiotelephone equipment

The radiotelephone required by this chapter is for the exclusive use of the master or person in charge of the vessel, or the person designated by the master or person in charge to pilot or direct the movement of the vessel, who shall maintain a listening watch on the designated frequency. Nothing contained herein shall be interpreted as precluding the use of portable radiotelephone equipment to satisfy the requirements of this chapter.

(Pub. L. 92–63, §5, Aug. 4, 1971, 85 Stat. 165.)

§1205. Radiotelephone capability; maintenance; restoration; consequences of loss: navigation of vessel

Whenever radiotelephone capability is required by this chapter, a vessel's radiotelephone equipment shall be maintained in effective operating condition. If the radiotelephone equipment carried aboard a vessel ceases to operate, the master shall exercise due diligence to restore it or cause it to be restored to effective operating condition at the earliest practicable time. The failure of a vessel's radiotelephone equipment shall not, in itself, constitute a violation of this chapter, nor shall it obligate the master of any vessel to moor or anchor his vessel; however, the loss of radiotelephone capability shall be given consideration in the navigation of the vessel.

(Pub. L. 92–63, §6, Aug. 4, 1971, 85 Stat. 165.)

§1206. Exemptions; terms and conditions

The Secretary may, if he considers that marine navigational safety will not be adversely affected or where a local communication system fully complies with the intent of this concept but does not conform in detail, issue exemptions from any provisions of this chapter, on such terms and conditions as he considers appropriate.

(Pub. L. 92–63, §7, Aug. 4, 1971, 85 Stat. 165.)

§1207. Regulations

(a) Operating and technical conditions and characteristics; frequencies, emission, and power of radiotelephone equipment

The Federal Communications Commission shall, after consultation with other cognizant agencies, prescribe regulations necessary to specify operating and technical conditions and characteristics including frequencies, emission, and power of radiotelephone equipment required under this chapter.

(b) Enforcement

The Secretary shall, subject to the concurrence of the Federal Communications Commission, prescribe regulations for the enforcement of this chapter.

(Pub. L. 92–63, §8, Aug. 4, 1971, 85 Stat. 165.)

§1208. Penalties

(a) Master, person in charge, or pilot subject to penalty

Whoever, being the master or person in charge of a vessel subject to this chapter, fails to enforce or comply with this chapter or the regulation, hereunder; or

Whoever, being designated by the master or person in charge of a vessel subject to this chapter to pilot or direct the movement of the vessel, fails to enforce or comply with this chapter or the regulations hereunder—

Is liable to a civil penalty of not more than $500 to be assessed by the Secretary.

(b) Vessels subject to penalty; jurisdiction

Every vessel navigating in violation of this chapter or the regulations hereunder is liable to a civil penalty of not more than $500 to be assessed by the Secretary for which the vessel may be proceeded against in any district court of the United States having jurisdiction.

(c) Remission or mitigation

Any penalty assessed under this section may be remitted or mitigated by the Secretary upon such terms as he may deem proper.

(Pub. L. 92–63, §9, Aug. 4, 1971, 85 Stat. 165.)

CHAPTER 25—PORTS AND WATERWAYS SAFETY PROGRAM

§1221. Statement of policy

The Congress finds and declares—

(a) that navigation and vessel safety, protection of the marine environment, and safety and security of United States ports and waterways are matters of major national importance;

(b) that increased vessel traffic in the Nation's ports and waterways creates substantial hazard to life, property, and the marine environment;

(c) that increased supervision of vessel and port operations is necessary in order to—

(1) reduce the possibility of vessel or cargo loss, or damage to life, property, or the marine environment;

(2) prevent damage to structures in, on, or immediately adjacent to the navigable waters of the United States or the resources within such waters;

(3) insure that vessels operating in the navigable waters of the United States shall comply with all applicable standards and requirements for vessel construction, equipment, manning, and operational procedures; and

(4) insure that the handling of dangerous articles and substances on the structures in, on, or immediately adjacent to the navigable waters of the United States is conducted in accordance with established standards and requirements; and

(d) that advance planning is critical in determining proper and adequate protective measures for the Nation's ports and waterways and the marine environment, with continuing consultation with other Federal agencies, State representatives, affected users, and the general public, in the development and implementation of such measures.

(Pub. L. 92–340, § 2, formerly title I, § 101, July 10, 1972, 86 Stat. 424; renumbered and amended Pub. L. 95–474, § 2, Oct. 17, 1978, 92 Stat. 1471; Pub. L. 107–295, title IV, § 443(1), Nov. 25, 2002, 116 Stat. 2132.)

AMENDMENTS

2002—Subsec. (a). Pub. L. 107–295 substituted "safety, protection of the marine environment, and safety and security of United States ports and waterways" for "safety and protection of the marine environment".

1978—Pub. L. 95–474 substituted provision relating to Congressional declaration of findings for provision relating to the authority of the Secretary of the department in which the Coast Guard is operating to prevent damage to vessels, bridges, and other structures and to protect navigable waters from environmental harm.

SHORT TITLE OF 1986 AMENDMENT

Pub. L. 99–399, title IX, § 901, Aug. 27, 1986, 100 Stat. 889, provided that: "This title [enacting section 1226 of this title and sections 1801 to 1809 of the former Appendix to Title 46, Shipping] may be cited as the 'International Maritime and Port Security Act'."

SHORT TITLE OF 1978 AMENDMENT

Section 1 of Pub. L. 95–474 provided: "That this Act [enacting sections 1225, 1228 to 1231, and 1232 of this title, amending this section, sections 1222 to 1224, 1226, and 1227 of this title, and sections 214 and 391a of Title 46, Shipping, and enacting provisions set out as notes under this section and section 1224 of this title and section 391a of former Title 46] may be cited as the 'Port and Tanker Safety Act of 1978'."

SHORT TITLE

Section 1 of Pub. L. 92–340, as amended by Pub. L. 95–474, § 2, Oct. 17, 1978, 92 Stat. 1471, provided that: "This Act [this chapter] may be cited as the 'Ports and Waterways Safety Act'."

SAVINGS PROVISION

Section 6(a) of Pub. L. 95–474 provided that: "Regulations previously issued under statutory provisions which are amended by section 2 of this Act [amending this section and sections 1222 to 1227, of this title] shall continue in effect as though issued under the authority of the Ports and Waterways Safety Act of 1972, as amended by this Act [this chapter], until expressly abrogated, modified, or amended by the Secretary. Any proceeding under title I of Public Law 92–340 [which enacted this section and sections 1222 to 1227 of this title] for a violation which occurred before the effective date of this Act [Oct. 17, 1978] may be initiated or continued to conclusion as though such public law had not been amended by this Act [amendment by section 2 of Pub. L. 95–474]."

SEPARABILITY

Section 6(c) of Pub. L. 95–474 provided that: "If a provision of this Act [see Short Title of 1978 Amendment note above] or the application of such provision to any person or circumstances shall be held invalid, the remainder of the Act and the application of such provision to persons or circumstances other than those to which it is held invalid shall not be affected thereby."

ESTABLISHMENT OF VESSEL TRAFFIC CONTROL SYSTEM FOR PRINCE WILLIAM SOUND AND VALDEZ, ALASKA

Pub. L. 93–153, title IV, § 402, Nov. 16, 1973, 87 Stat. 589, provided that: "The Secretary of the Department in which the Coast Guard is operating is hereby directed to establish a vessel traffic control system for Prince William Sound and Valdez, Alaska, pursuant to authority contained in title I of the Ports and Waterways Safety Act of 1972 (86 Stat. 424, Public Law 92–340) [this chapter, prior to the amendment by Pub. L. 95–474, Oct. 17, 1978, 92 Stat. 1471]."

§ 1222. Definitions

As used in this chapter, unless the context otherwise requires—

(1) "Marine environment" means the navigable waters of the United States and the land and resources therein and thereunder; the waters and fishery resources of any area over which the United States asserts exclusive fishery management authority; the seabed and subsoil of the Outer Continental Shelf of the United States, the resources thereof and the waters superjacent thereto; and the recreational, economic, and scenic values of such waters and resources.

(2) "Secretary" means the Secretary of the department in which the Coast Guard is operating, except that "Secretary" means the Secretary of Transportation with respect to the application of this chapter to the Saint Lawrence Seaway.

(3) "State" includes each of the several States of the United States, the District of Columbia, the Commonwealth of Puerto Rico, the Canal Zone, Guam, American Samoa, the United States Virgin Islands, the Trust Territories of the Pacific Islands, the Commonwealth of the Northern Marianas, and any other commonwealth, territory, or possession of the United States.

(4) "United States", when used in geographical context, means all the States thereof.

(5) "Navigable waters of the United States" includes all waters of the territorial sea of the United States as described in Presidential Proclamation No. 5928 of December 27, 1988.

(Pub. L. 92–340, § 3, formerly title I, § 102, July 10, 1972, 86 Stat. 425; renumbered and amended Pub. L. 95–474, § 2, Oct. 17, 1978, 92 Stat. 1471; Pub. L. 105–383, title III, § 301(a), Nov. 13, 1998, 112 Stat. 3417; Pub. L. 108–293, title III, § 304, Aug. 9, 2004, 118 Stat. 1042.)

REFERENCES IN TEXT

For definition of Canal Zone, referred to in par. (3), see section 3602(b) of Title 22, Foreign Relations and Intercourse.

Presidential Proclamation No. 5928, referred to in par. (5), is set out under section 1331 of Title 43, Public Lands.

AMENDMENTS

2004—Par. (2). Pub. L. 108–293 inserted ", except that 'Secretary' means the Secretary of Transportation with respect to the application of this chapter to the Saint Lawrence Seaway" after "in which the Coast Guard is operating".

1998—Par. (5). Pub. L. 105–383, which directed the amendment of section 102 of the Ports and Waterways Safety Act by adding par. (5), was executed to this section, which is section 3 of that act, to reflect the probable intent of Congress and the renumbering of section 102 as section 3 by Pub. L. 95–474.

1978—Pub. L. 95–474 substituted provision relating to definitions for provision defining "United States", permitting higher State or local safety standards, and providing for consultation with appropriate agencies, the inapplicability of this chapter to the Panama Canal, delegation of powers with respect to the Saint Lawrence Seaway, and factors to be considered in issuance of regulations.

TRANSFER OF FUNCTIONS

For transfer of authorities, functions, personnel, and assets of the Coast Guard, including the authorities and functions of the Secretary of Transportation relating thereto, to the Department of Homeland Security, and for treatment of related references, see sections 468(b), 551(d), 552(d), and 557 of Title 6, Domestic Security, and the Department of Homeland Security Reorganization Plan of November 25, 2002, as modified, set out as a note under section 542 of Title 6.

TERMINATION OF TRUST TERRITORY OF THE PACIFIC ISLANDS

For termination of Trust Territory of the Pacific Islands, see note set out preceding section 1681 of Title 48, Territories and Insular Possessions.

§1223. Vessel operating requirements

(a) In general

Subject to the requirements of section 1224 of this title, the Secretary—

(1) in any port or place under the jurisdiction of the United States, in the navigable waters of the United States, or in any area covered by an international agreement negotiated pursuant to section 1230 of this title, may construct, operate, maintain, improve, or expand vessel traffic services, consisting of measures for controlling or supervising vessel traffic or for protecting navigation and the marine environment and may include, but need not be limited to one or more of the following: reporting and operating requirements, surveillance and communications systems, routing systems, and fairways;

(2) shall require appropriate vessels which operate in an area of a vessel traffic service to utilize or comply with that service;

(3) may require vessels to install and use specified navigation equipment, communications equipment, electronic relative motion analyzer equipment, or any electronic or other device necessary to comply with a vessel traffic service or which is necessary in the interests of vessel safety: *Provided*, That the Secretary shall not require fishing vessels under 300 gross tons as measured under section 14502 of title 46, or an alternate tonnage measured under section 14302 of that title as prescribed by the Secretary under section 14104 of that title or recreational vessels 65 feet or less to possess or use the equipment or devices required by this subsection solely under the authority of this chapter;

(4) may control vessel traffic in areas subject to the jurisdiction of the United States which the Secretary determines to be hazardous, or under conditions of reduced visibility, adverse weather, vessel congestion, or other hazardous circumstances by—

(A) specifying times of entry, movement, or departure;

(B) establishing vessel traffic routing schemes;

(C) establishing vessel size, speed, draft limitations and vessel operating conditions; and

(D) restricting operation, in any hazardous area or under hazardous conditions, to vessels which have particular operating characteristics or capabilities which he considers necessary for safe operation under the circumstances;

(5) may require the receipt of prearrival messages from any vessel, destined for a port or place subject to the jurisdiction of the United States, in sufficient time to permit advance vessel traffic planning prior to port entry, which shall include any information which is not already a matter of record and which the Secretary determines necessary for the control of the vessel and the safety of the port or the marine environment; and

(6) may prohibit the use on vessels of electronic or other devices that interfere with communication and navigation equipment, except that such authority shall not apply to electronic or other devices certified to transmit in the maritime services by the Federal Communications Commission and used within the frequency bands 157.1875–157.4375 MHz and 161.7875–162.0375 MHz.

(b) Special powers

The Secretary may order any vessel, in a port or place subject to the jurisdiction of the United States or in the navigable waters of the United States, to operate or anchor in a manner he directs if—

(1) he has reasonable cause to believe such vessel does not comply with any regulation issued under this chapter or any other applicable law or treaty;

(2) he determines that such vessel does not satisfy the conditions for port entry set forth in section 1228 of this title; or

(3) by reason of weather, visibility, sea conditions, port congestion, other hazardous circumstances, or the condition of such vessel, he is satisfied that such directive is justified in the interest of safety.

(c) Port access routes

(1) In order to provide safe access routes for the movement of vessel traffic proceeding to or from ports or places subject to the jurisdiction of the United States, and subject to the requirements of paragraph (3) hereof, the Secretary shall designate necessary fairways and traffic separation schemes for vessels operating in the

territorial sea of the United States and in high seas approaches, outside the territorial sea, to such ports or places. Such a designation shall recognize, within the designated area, the paramount right of navigation over all other uses.

(2) No designation may be made by the Secretary pursuant to this subsection, if such a designation, as implemented, would deprive any person of the effective exercise of a right granted by a lease or permit executed or issued under other applicable provisions of law: *Provided*, That such right has become vested prior to the time of publication of the notice required by clause (A) of paragraph (3) hereof: *Provided further*, That the determination as to whether the designation would so deprive any such person shall be made by the Secretary, after consultation with the responsible official under whose authority the lease was executed or the permit issued.

(3) Prior to making a designation pursuant to paragraph (1) hereof, and in accordance with the requirements of section 1224 of this title, the Secretary shall—

(A) within six months after date of enactment of this Act (and may, from time to time thereafter), undertake a study of the potential traffic density and the need for safe access routes for vessels in any area for which fairways or traffic separation schemes are proposed or which may otherwise be considered and shall publish notice of such undertaking in the Federal Register;

(B) in consultation with the Secretary of State, the Secretary of the Interior, the Secretary of Commerce, the Secretary of the Army, and the Governors of affected States, as their responsibilities may require, take into account all other uses of the area under consideration (including, as appropriate, the exploration for, or exploitation of, oil, gas, or other mineral resources, the construction or operation of deepwater ports or other structures on or above the seabed or subsoil of the submerged lands or the Outer Continental Shelf of the United States, the establishment or operation of marine or estuarine sanctuaries, and activities involving recreational or commercial fishing); and

(C) to the extent practicable, reconcile the need for safe access routes with the needs of all other reasonable uses of the area involved.

(4) In carrying out his responsibilities under paragraph (3), the Secretary shall proceed expeditiously to complete any study undertaken. Thereafter, he shall promptly issue a notice of proposed rule-making for the designation contemplated or shall have published in the Federal Register a notice that no designation is contemplated as a result of the study and the reason for such determination.

(5) In connection with a designation made pursuant to this subsection, the Secretary—

(A) shall issue reasonable rules and regulations governing the use of such designated areas, including the applicability of rules 9 and 10 of the International Regulations for Preventing Collisions at Sea, 1972, relating to narrow channels and traffic separation schemes, respectively, in waters where such regulations apply;

(B) to the extent that he finds reasonable and necessary to effectuate the purposes of the designation, make the use of designated fairways and traffic separation schemes mandatory for specific types and sizes of vessels, foreign and domestic, operating in the territorial sea of the United States and for specific types and sizes of vessels of the United States operating on the high seas beyond the territorial sea of the United States;

(C) may, from time to time, as necessary, adjust the location or limits of designated fairways or traffic separation schemes, in order to accommodate the needs of other uses which cannot be reasonably accommodated otherwise: *Provided*, That such an adjustment will not, in the judgement of the Secretary, unacceptably adversely affect the purpose for which the existing designation was made and the need for which continues; and

(D) shall, through appropriate channels, (i) notify cognizant international organizations of any designation, or adjustment thereof, and (ii) take action to seek the cooperation of foreign States in making it mandatory for vessels under their control to use any fairway or traffic separation scheme designated pursuant to this subsection in any area of the high seas, to the same extent as required by the Secretary for vessels of the United States.

(d) Exception

Except pursuant to international treaty, convention, or agreement, to which the United States is a party, this chapter shall not apply to any foreign vessel that is not destined for, or departing from, a port or place subject to the jurisdiction of the United States and that is in—

(1) innocent passage through the territorial sea of the United States, or

(2) transit through the navigable waters of the United States which form a part of an international strait.

(e) Cooperative agreements

(1) The Secretary may enter into cooperative agreements with public or private agencies, authorities, associations, institutions, corporations, organizations, or other persons to carry out the functions under subsection (a)(1) of this section.

(2) A nongovernmental entity may not under this subsection carry out an inherently governmental function.

(3) As used in this paragraph, the term "inherently governmental function" means any activity that is so intimately related to the public interest as to mandate performance by an officer or employee of the Federal Government, including an activity that requires either the exercise of discretion in applying the authority of the Government or the use of judgment in making a decision for the Government.

(Pub. L. 92–340, § 4, formerly title I, § 103, July 10, 1972, 86 Stat. 426; renumbered and amended Pub. L. 95–474, § 2, Oct. 17, 1978, 92 Stat. 1472; Pub. L. 101–380, title IV, § 4107(a), Aug. 18, 1990, 104 Stat. 514; Pub. L. 104–324, title VII, § 705, Oct. 19, 1996, 110 Stat. 3934; Pub. L. 108–293, title III, § 302, Aug. 9, 2004, 118 Stat. 1041; Pub. L. 109–241, title IX, § 901(d), July 11, 2006, 120 Stat. 564.)

REFERENCES IN TEXT

The date of enactment of this Act, referred to in subsec. (c)(3)(A), probably means the date of enactment of Pub. L. 95–474, which was approved Oct. 17, 1978.

The International Regulations for Preventing Collisions at Sea, 1972, referred to in subsec. (c)(5)(A), are maintained and published by the United States Coast Guard, U.S. Department of Homeland Security, in the publication *Navigation Rules*, which is available for sale by the Superintendent of Documents, U.S. Government Printing Office, Washington, D.C. 20402. See International Regulations for Preventing Collisions at Sea, 1972 note under section 1602 of this title.

AMENDMENTS

2006—Subsecs. (a)(6), (e). Pub. L. 109–241 amended directory language of Pub. L. 108–293, §302. See 2004 Amendment note below.

2004—Subsec. (a)(6). Pub. L. 108–293, §302(1), as amended by Pub. L. 109–241, added par. (6).

Subsec. (e). Pub. L. 108–293, §302(2), as amended by Pub. L. 109–241, which directed the addition of subsec. (e) at the end of subsec. (a) of this section, was executed by adding subsec. (e) at the end of this section.

1996—Subsec. (a)(3). Pub. L. 104–324 inserted "as measured under section 14502 of title 46, or an alternate tonnage measured under section 14302 of that title as prescribed by the Secretary under section 14104 of that title" after "300 gross tons".

1990—Subsec. (a). Pub. L. 101–380, §4107(a)(1), substituted "Secretary—" for "Secretary may—".

Subsec. (a)(1). Pub. L. 101–380, §4107(a)(2), substituted "may construct, operate, maintain, improve, or expand" for "establish, operate, and maintain".

Subsec. (a)(2). Pub. L. 101–380, §4107(a)(3), substituted "shall require appropriate" for "require".

Subsec. (a)(3). Pub. L. 101–380, §4107(a)(4), inserted "may" before "require", which was executed by making the insertion before "require" the first place it appeared to reflect the probable intent of Congress.

Subsec. (a)(4). Pub. L. 101–380, §4107(a)(5), inserted "may" before "control".

Subsec. (a)(5). Pub. L. 101–380, §4107(a)(6), inserted "may" before "require".

1978—Pub. L. 95–474 substituted provision relating to vessel operating requirements for provision relating to the investigatory powers of the Secretary, production of witnesses and documents, and fees and allowances for witnesses.

EFFECTIVE DATE OF 2006 AMENDMENT

Pub. L. 109–241, title IX, §901(d), July 11, 2006, 120 Stat. 564, provided in part that the amendment made by section 901(d) is effective Aug. 9, 2004.

EFFECTIVE DATE OF 1990 AMENDMENT

Amendment by Pub. L. 101–380 applicable to incidents occurring after Aug. 18, 1990, see section 1020 of Pub. L. 101–380, set out as an Effective Date note under section 2701 of this title.

NOTICE OF ARRIVAL FOR FOREIGN VESSELS ON THE OUTER CONTINENTAL SHELF

Pub. L. 109–347, title I, §109, Oct. 13, 2006, 120 Stat. 1893, provided that:

"(a) NOTICE OF ARRIVAL.—Not later than 180 days after the date of the enactment of this Act [Oct. 13, 2006], the Secretary of the department in which the Coast Guard is operating shall update and finalize the rulemaking on notice of arrival for foreign vessels on the Outer Continental Shelf.

"(b) CONTENT OF REGULATIONS.—The regulations promulgated pursuant to subsection (a) shall be consistent with information required under the Notice of Arrival under section 160.206 of title 33, Code of Federal Regulations, as in effect on the date of the enactment of this Act [Oct. 13, 2006]."

DIRECTION OF VESSEL MOVEMENT STUDY; SUBMITTAL OF REPORT TO CONGRESS

Section 4107(b) of Pub. L. 101–380 provided that:

"(1) STUDY.—The Secretary shall conduct a study—

"(A) of whether the Secretary should be given additional authority to direct the movement of vessels on navigable waters and should exercise such authority; and

"(B) to determine and prioritize the United States ports and channels that are in need of new, expanded, or improved vessel traffic service systems, by evaluating—

"(i) the nature, volume, and frequency of vessel traffic;

"(ii) the risks of collisions, spills, and damages associated with that traffic;

"(iii) the impact of installation, expansion, or improvement of a vessel traffic service system; and

"(iv) all other relevant costs and data.

"(2) REPORT.—Not later than 1 year after the date of the enactment of this Act [Aug. 18, 1990], the Secretary shall submit to the Congress a report on the results of the study conducted under paragraph (1) and recommendations for implementing the results of that study."

TERRITORIAL SEA OF UNITED STATES

For extension of territorial sea of United States, see Proc. No. 5928, set out as a note under section 1331 of Title 43, Public Lands.

§1223a. Electronic charts

(a) System requirements

(1) Requirements

Subject to paragraph (2), the following vessels, while operating on the navigable waters of the United States, shall be equipped with and operate electronic charts under regulations prescribed by the Secretary of the department in which the Coast Guard is operating:

(A) A self-propelled commercial vessel of at least 65 feet overall length.

(B) A vessel carrying more than a number of passengers for hire determined by the Secretary.

(C) A towing vessel of more than 26 feet in overall length and 600 horsepower.

(D) Any other vessel for which the Secretary decides that electronic charts are necessary for the safe navigation of the vessel.

(2) Exemptions and waivers

The Secretary may—

(A) exempt a vessel from paragraph (1), if the Secretary finds that electronic charts are not necessary for the safe navigation of the vessel on the waters on which the vessel operates; and

(B) waive the application of paragraph (1) with respect to operation of vessels on navigable waters of the United States specified by the Secretary, if the Secretary finds that electronic charts are not needed for safe navigation on those waters.

(b) Regulations

The Secretary of the department in which the Coast Guard is operating shall prescribe regulations implementing subsection (a) of this section before January 1, 2007, including requirements for the operation and maintenance of the electronic charts required under subsection (a) of this section.

(Pub. L. 92–340, §4A, as added Pub. L. 108–293, title IV, §410, Aug. 9, 2004, 118 Stat. 1045.)

§ 1224. Considerations by Secretary

In carrying out his duties and responsibilities under section 1223 of this title, the Secretary shall—

(a) take into account all relevant factors concerning navigation and vessel safety, protection of the marine environment, and the safety and security of United States ports and waterways, including but not limited to—

(1) the scope and degree of the risk or hazard involved;

(2) vessel traffic characteristics and trends, including traffic volume, the sizes and types of vessels involved, potential interference with the flow of commercial traffic, the presence of any unusual cargoes, and other similar factors;

(3) port and waterway configurations and variations in local conditions of geography, climate, and other similar factors;

(4) the need for granting exemptions for the installation and use of equipment or devices for use with vessel traffic services for certain classes of small vessels, such as self-propelled fishing vessels and recreational vessels;

(5) the proximity of fishing grounds, oil and gas drilling and production operations, or any other potential or actual conflicting activity;

(6) environmental factors;

(7) economic impact and effects;

(8) existing vessel traffic services; and

(9) local practices and customs, including voluntary arrangements and agreements within the maritime community; and

(b) at the earliest possible time, consult with and receive and consider the views of representatives of the maritime community, ports and harbor authorities or associations, environmental groups, and other parties who may be affected by the proposed actions.

(Pub. L. 92–340, § 5, formerly title I, § 104, July 10, 1972, 86 Stat. 427; renumbered and amended Pub. L. 95–474, § 2, Oct. 17, 1978, 92 Stat. 1474; Pub. L. 107–295, title IV, § 443(2), Nov. 25, 2002, 116 Stat. 2132.)

AMENDMENTS

2002—Subsec. (a). Pub. L. 107–295 substituted "safety, protection of the marine environment, and the safety and security of United States ports and waterways," for "safety and protection of the marine environment," in introductory provisions.

1978—Pub. L. 95–474 substituted provision relating to factors to be considered by the Secretary and to consultation by the Secretary with affected groups for provision relating to the issuance of rules and regulations by the Secretary.

STUDY OF DESIRABILITY AND FEASIBILITY OF SHORE-STATION SYSTEMS FOR MONITORING VESSELS

Section 3 of Pub. L. 95–474 authorized the Secretary, in consultation with the Secretary of Commerce and other appropriate departments or agencies of the Federal Government to study the desirability and feasibility of shore-station systems for monitoring vessels within the Fishery Conservation Zone as defined in former section 1802(8) of Title 16, Conservation, required the Secretary to report his findings to Congress, within two years after Oct. 17, 1978, and authorized appropriations for such study for fiscal years 1979 and 1980.

§ 1225. Waterfront safety

(a) In general

The Secretary may take such action as is necessary to—

(1) prevent damage to, or the destruction of, any bridge or other structure on or in the navigable waters of the United States, or any land structure or shore area immediately adjacent to such waters; and

(2) protect the navigable waters and the resources therein from harm resulting from vessel or structure damage, destruction, or loss. Such action may include, but need not be limited to—

(A) establishing procedures, measures, and standards for the handling, loading, unloading, storage, stowage, and movement on the structure (including the emergency removal, control, and disposition) of explosives or other dangerous articles and substances, including oil or hazardous material as those terms are defined in section 2101 of title 46;

(B) prescribing minimum safety equipment requirements for the structure to assure adequate protection from fire, explosion, natural disaster, and other serious accidents or casualties;

(C) establishing water or waterfront safety zones, or other measures for limited, controlled, or conditional access and activity when necessary for the protection of any vessel, structure, waters, or shore area; and

(D) establishing procedures for examination to assure compliance with the requirements prescribed under this section.

(b) State law

Nothing contained in this section, with respect to structures, prohibits a State or political subdivision thereof from prescribing higher safety equipment requirements or safety standards than those which may be prescribed by regulations hereunder.

(Pub. L. 92–340, § 6, formerly title I, § 105, July 10, 1972, 86 Stat. 427; renumbered and amended Pub. L. 95–474, § 2, Oct. 17, 1978, 92 Stat. 1475.)

CODIFICATION

In subsec. (a)(2)(A), "section 2101 of title 46" substituted for "section 4417a of the Revised Statutes [46 U.S.C. 391a]" on authority of Pub. L. 98–89, § 2(b), Aug. 26, 1983, 97 Stat. 598, section 1 of which enacted Title 46, Shipping.

AMENDMENTS

1978—Pub. L. 95–474 substituted provisions relating to waterfront safety for provision requiring the Secretary to report to Congress within one year his recommendations for legislation to achieve coordination between functions authorized under Pub. L. 92–340 and the functions of any other agencies and to eliminate duplication of these functions.

§ 1226. Port, harbor, and coastal facility security

(a) General authority

The Secretary may take actions described in subsection (b) of this section to prevent or respond to an act of terrorism against—

(1) an individual, vessel, or public or commercial structure, that is—

(A) subject to the jurisdiction of the United States; and

(B) located within or adjacent to the marine environment; or

(2) a vessel of the United States or an individual on board that vessel.

(b) Specific authority

Under subsection (a) of this section, the Secretary may—

(1) carry out or require measures, including inspections, port and harbor patrols, the establishment of security and safety zones, and the development of contingency plans and procedures, to prevent or respond to acts of terrorism;

(2) recruit members of the Regular Coast Guard and the Coast Guard Reserve and train members of the Regular Coast Guard and the Coast Guard Reserve in the techniques of preventing and responding to acts of terrorism; and

(3) dispatch properly trained and qualified armed Coast Guard personnel on vessels and public or commercial structures on or adjacent to waters subject to United States jurisdiction to deter or respond to acts of terrorism or transportation security incidents, as defined in section 70101 of title 46.

(c) Nondisclosure of port security plans

Notwithstanding any other provision of law, information related to security plans, procedures, or programs for passenger vessels or passenger terminals authorized under this chapter is not required to be disclosed to the public.

(Pub. L. 92–340, §7, as added Pub. L. 99–399, title IX, §906, Aug. 27, 1986, 100 Stat. 890; amended Pub. L. 104–324, title III, §302, Oct. 19, 1996, 110 Stat. 3917; Pub. L. 107–295, title I, §107(a), Nov. 25, 2002, 116 Stat. 2088.)

PRIOR PROVISIONS

A prior section 1226, Pub. L. 92–340, §7, formerly title I, §106, July 10, 1972, 86 Stat. 427; renumbered §7 and amended Pub. L. 95–474, §2, Oct. 17, 1978, 92 Stat. 1475, related to requirement respecting federally licensed pilots on any foreign or domestic self-propelled vessel engaged in the foreign trade when operating in the navigable waters of the United States in areas, etc., where a pilot is not otherwise required by State law, prior to repeal by Pub. L. 98–557, §29(g), Oct. 30, 1984, 98 Stat. 2875.

AMENDMENTS

2002—Subsec. (b)(3). Pub. L. 107–295 added par. (3).

1996—Subsec. (c). Pub. L. 104–324 added subsec. (c).

TRANSFER OF FUNCTIONS

For transfer of authorities, functions, personnel, and assets of the Coast Guard, including the authorities and functions of the Secretary of Transportation relating thereto, to the Department of Homeland Security, and for treatment of related references, see sections 468(b), 551(d), 552(d), and 557 of Title 6, Domestic Security, and the Department of Homeland Security Reorganization Plan of November 25, 2002, as modified, set out as a note under section 542 of Title 6.

REPORT ON USE OF NON-COAST GUARD PERSONNEL

Pub. L. 107–295, title I, §107(b), Nov. 25, 2002, 116 Stat. 2088, provided that: "The Secretary of the department in which the Coast Guard is operating shall evaluate and report to the Congress on—

"(1) the potential use of Federal, State, or local government personnel, and documented United States Merchant Marine personnel, to supplement Coast Guard personnel under section 7(b)(3) of the Ports and Waterways Safety Act (33 U.S.C. 1226(b)(3));

"(2) the possibility of using personnel other than Coast Guard personnel to carry out Coast Guard personnel functions under that section and whether additional legal authority would be necessary to use such personnel for such functions; and

"(3) the possibility of utilizing the United States Merchant Marine Academy, State maritime academies, or Coast Guard approved maritime industry schools in the United States, to provide training under that section."

§1227. Investigatory powers

(a) Secretary

The Secretary may investigate any incident, accident, or act involving the loss or destruction of, or damage to any structure subject to this chapter, or which affects or may affect the safety or environmental quality of the ports, harbors, or navigable waters of the United States.

(b) Powers

In an investigation under this section, the Secretary may issue subpenas to require the attendance of witnesses and the production of documents or other evidence relating to such incident, accident, or act. If any person refuses to obey a subpena, the Secretary may request the Attorney General to invoke the aid of the appropriate district court of the United States to compel compliance with the subpena. Any district court of the United States may, in the case of refusal to obey a subpena, issue an order requiring compliance with the subpena, and failure to obey the order may be punished by the court as contempt. Witnesses may be paid fees for travel and attendance at rates not exceeding those allowed in a district court of the United States.

(Pub. L. 92–340, §8, formerly title I, §107, July 10, 1972, 86 Stat. 427; renumbered and amended Pub. L. 95–474, §2, Oct. 17, 1978, 92 Stat. 1476.)

AMENDMENTS

1978—Pub. L. 95–474 substituted provision relating to the investigatory powers of the Secretary for provision relating to criminal penalties.

§1228. Conditions for entry to ports in the United States

(a) In general

No vessel, subject to the provisions of chapter 37 of title 46, shall operate in the navigable waters of the United States or transfer cargo or residue in any port or place under the jurisdiction of the United States, if such vessel—

(1) has a history of accidents, pollution incidents, or serious repair problems which, as determined by the Secretary, creates reason to believe that such vessel may be unsafe or may create a threat to the marine environment; or

(2) fails to comply with any applicable regulation issued under this chapter, chapter 37 of title 46, or under any other applicable law or treaty; or

(3) discharges oil or hazardous material in violation of any law of the United States or in a manner or quantities inconsistent with the provisions of any treaty to which the United States is a party; or

(4) does not comply with any applicable vessel traffic service requirements; or

(5) is manned by one or more officers who are licensed by a certificating state which the Secretary has determined, pursuant to section 9101 of title 46, does not have standards for licensing and certification of seafarers which are comparable to or more stringent than United States standards or international standards which are accepted by the United States; or

(6) is not manned in compliance with manning levels as determined by the Secretary to be necessary to insure the safe navigation of the vessel; or

(7) while underway, does not have at least one licensed deck officer on the navigation bridge who is capable of clearly understanding English.

(b) Exceptions

The Secretary may allow provisional entry of a vessel not in compliance with subsection (a) of this section, if the owner or operator of such vessel proves, to the satisfaction of the Secretary, that such vessel is not unsafe or a threat to the marine environment, and if such entry is necessary for the safety of the vessel or persons aboard. In addition, paragraphs (1), (2), (3), and (4) of subsection (a) of this section shall not apply if the owner or operator of such vessel proves, to the satisfaction of the Secretary, that such vessel is no longer unsafe or a threat to the marine environment, and is no longer in violation of any applicable law, treaty, regulation or condition, as appropriate. Clauses (5) and (6) of subsection (a) of this section shall become applicable eighteen months after October 17, 1978.

(Pub. L. 92–340, §9, as added Pub. L. 95–474, §2, Oct. 17, 1978, 92 Stat. 1476; amended Pub. L. 101–380, title IV, §4106(c), Aug. 18, 1990, 104 Stat. 514.)

AMENDMENTS

1990—Subsec. (a). Pub. L. 101–380, §4106(c)(1), substituted "chapter 37 of title 46" for "section 4417a of the Revised Statutes, as amended" in provisions preceding par. (1) and in par. (2) and substituted "section 9101 of title 46" for "section 4417a(11) of the Revised Statutes, as amended" in par. (5).

EFFECTIVE DATE OF 1990 AMENDMENT

Amendment by Pub. L. 101–380 applicable to incidents occurring after Aug. 18, 1990, see section 1020 of Pub. L. 101–380, set out as an Effective Date note under section 2701 of this title.

§ 1229. Applicability

This chapter shall not apply to the Panama Canal. The authority granted to the Secretary under sections 1223, 1224, and 1225 of this title shall not be delegated with respect to the Saint Lawrence Seaway to any agency other than the Saint Lawrence Seaway Development Corporation. Any other authority granted the Secretary under this chapter shall be delegated to the Saint Lawrence Seaway Development Corporation to the extent he determines such delegation is necessary for the proper operation of the Saint Lawrence Seaway.

(Pub. L. 92–340, §10, as added Pub. L. 95–474, §2, Oct. 17, 1978, 92 Stat. 1477; amended Pub. L. 98–557, §29(h), Oct. 30, 1984, 98 Stat. 2875.)

AMENDMENTS

1984—Pub. L. 98–557 struck out reference to section 1226 of this title.

§ 1230. International agreements

(a) Transmittal of regulations

The Secretary shall transmit, via the Secretary of State, to appropriate international bodies or forums, any regulations issued under this chapter, for consideration as international standards.

(b) Agreements

The President is authorized and encouraged to—

(1) enter into negotiations and conclude and execute agreements with neighboring nations, to establish compatible vessel standards and vessel traffic services, and to establish, operate, and maintain international vessel traffic services, in areas and under circumstances of mutual concern; and

(2) enter into negotiations, through appropriate international bodies, and conclude and execute agreements to establish vessel traffic services in appropriate areas of the high seas.

(c) Operations

The Secretary, pursuant to any agreement negotiated under subsection (b) of this section which is binding upon the United States in accordance with constitutional requirements, may—

(1) require vessels in the vessel traffic service area to utilize or to comply with the vessel traffic service, including the carrying or installation of equipment and devices as necessary for the use of the service; and

(2) waive, by order or regulation, the application of any United States law or regulation concerning the design, construction, operation, equipment, personnel qualifications, and manning standards for vessels operating in waters over which the United States exercises jurisdiction if such vessel is not en route to or from a United States port or place, and if vessels en route to or from a United States port or place are accorded equivalent waivers of laws and regulations of the neighboring nation, when operating in waters over which that nation exercises jurisdiction.

(d) Ship reporting systems

The Secretary, in cooperation with the International Maritime Organization, is authorized to implement and enforce two mandatory ship reporting systems, consistent with international law, with respect to vessels subject to such reporting systems entering the following areas of the Atlantic Ocean: Cape Cod Bay, Massachusetts Bay, and Great South Channel (in the area generally bounded by a line starting from a point on Cape Ann, Massachusetts at 42 deg. 39' N., 70 deg. 37' W; then northeast to 42 deg. 45' N., 70 deg. 13' W; then southeast to 42 deg. 10' N., 68 deg. 31 W, then south to 41 deg. 00' N., 68 deg. 31' W; then west to 41 deg. 00' N., 69 deg. 17' W; then northeast to 42 deg. 05' N., 70 deg. 02' W, then west to 42 deg. 04' N., 70 deg. 10' W; and then along the Massachusetts shoreline of Cape Cod Bay and Massachusetts Bay back to the point on

Cape Ann at 42 deg. 39' N., 70 deg. 37' W) and in the coastal waters of the Southeastern United States within about 25 nm along a 90 nm stretch of the Atlantic seaboard (in an area generally extending from the shoreline east to longitude 80 deg. 51.6' W with the southern and northern boundary at latitudes 30 deg. 00' N., 31 deg. 27' N., respectively).

(Pub. L. 92–340, §11, as added Pub. L. 95–474, §2, Oct. 17, 1978, 92 Stat. 1477; amended Pub. L. 105–383, title III, §313, Nov. 13, 1998, 112 Stat. 3424.)

AMENDMENTS

1998—Subsec. (d). Pub. L. 105–383 added subsec. (d).

§1231. Regulations

(a) In general

In accordance with the provisions of section 553 of title 5, the Secretary shall issue, and may from time to time amend or repeal, regulations necessary to implement this chapter.

(b) Procedures

The Secretary, in the exercise of this regulatory authority, shall establish procedures for consulting with, and receiving and considering the views of all interested parties, including—

(1) interested Federal departments and agencies,

(2) officials of State and local governments,

(3) representatives of the maritime community,

(4) representatives of port and harbor authorities or associations,

(5) representatives of environmental groups,

(6) any other interested parties who are knowledgeable or experienced in dealing with problems involving vessel safety, port and waterways safety, and protection of the marine environment, and

(7) advisory committees consisting of all interested segments of the public when the establishment of such committees is considered necessary because the issues involved are highly complex or controversial.

(Pub. L. 92–340, §12, as added Pub. L. 95–474, §2, Oct. 17, 1978, 92 Stat. 1477.)

§1231a. Towing Safety Advisory Committee

(a) Establishment; membership

There is established a Towing Safety Advisory Committee (hereinafter referred to as the "Committee"). The Committee shall consist of sixteen members with particular expertise, knowledge, and experience regarding shallow-draft inland and coastal waterway navigation and towing safety as follows:

(1) seven members from the barge and towing industry, reflecting a regional geographic balance;

(2) one member from the offshore mineral and oil supply vessel industry; and

(3) two members from each of the following—

(A) port districts, authorities, or terminal operators;

(B) maritime labor;

(C) shippers (of whom at least one shall be engaged in the shipment of oil or hazardous materials by barge); and

(D) the general public.

(b) Appointments; Chairman, Vice Chairman, and observers; publication in Federal Register

The Secretary of the department in which the Coast Guard is operating (hereinafter referred to as the "Secretary") shall appoint the members of the Committee. The Secretary shall designate one of the members of the Committee as the Chairman and one of the members as the Vice Chairman. The Vice Chairman shall act as Chairman in the absence or incapacity of, or in the event of a vacancy in the office of, the Chairman. The Secretary may request the Secretary of the Army and the Secretary of Commerce to each designate a representative to participate as an observer on the Committee. The Secretary shall, not less often than once a year, publish notice in the Federal Register for solicitation of nominations for membership on the Committee.

(c) Functions; meetings; public proceedings and records; disclosures to Congress

The Committee shall advise, consult with, and make recommendations to the Secretary on matters relating to shallow-draft inland and coastal waterway navigation and towing safety. Any advice or recommendation made by the Committee to the Secretary shall reflect the independent judgment of the Committee on the matter concerned. The Secretary shall consult with the Committee before taking any significant action affecting shallow-draft inland and coastal waterway navigation and towing safety. The Committee shall meet at the call of the Secretary, but in any event not less than once during each calendar year. All proceedings of the Committee shall be open to the public, and a record of the proceedings shall be made available for public inspection. The Committee is authorized to make available to Congress any information, advice, and recommendations which the Committee is authorized to give to the Secretary.

(d) Compensation and travel expenses; administrative services; personnel; authorization of appropriations

Members of the Committee who are not officers or employees of the United States shall serve without pay and members of the Committee who are officers or employees of the United States shall receive no additional pay on account of their service on the Committee. While away from their homes or regular places of business, members of the Committee may be allowed travel expenses, including per diem in lieu of subsistence, as authorized by section 5703 of title 5. The Secretary shall furnish to the Committee an executive secretary and such secretarial, clerical, and other services as are considered necessary for the conduct of its business. There are authorized to be appropriated such sums as may be necessary to implement the provisions of this subsection.

(e) Termination

Unless extended by subsequent Act of Congress, the Committee shall terminate on September 30, 2010.

(Pub. L. 96–380, Oct. 6, 1980, 94 Stat. 1521; Pub. L. 97–322, title I, § 118(d), Oct. 15, 1982, 96 Stat. 1587; Pub. L. 98–557, § 16(a), Oct. 30, 1984, 98 Stat. 2866; Pub. L. 101–225, title I, § 105(b), Dec. 12, 1989, 103 Stat. 1910; Pub. L. 104–324, title III, § 304(c), Oct. 19, 1996, 110 Stat. 3917; Pub. L. 107–295, title III, § 336, Nov. 25, 2002, 116 Stat. 2105; Pub. L. 108–293, title IV, § 418(g), Aug. 9, 2004, 118 Stat. 1049.)

CODIFICATION

Section was not enacted as part of the Ports and Waterways Safety Act which comprises this chapter.

AMENDMENTS

2004—Subsec. (e). Pub. L. 108–293 substituted "September 30, 2010" for "September 30, 2005".

2002—Subsec. (e). Pub. L. 107–295 substituted "September 30, 2005" for "September 30, 2000".

1996—Subsec. (e). Pub. L. 104–324 substituted "September 30, 2000" for "September 30, 1995".

1989—Subsec. (e). Pub. L. 101–225 substituted "September 30, 1995" for "September 30, 1990".

1984—Subsec. (e). Pub. L. 98–557 substituted "on September 30, 1990" for "five years from the date of enactment of this Act".

1982—Subsec. (b). Pub. L. 97–322, § 118(d)(1), required the Secretary, not less often than once a year, to publish notice in the Federal Register for solicitation of nominations for membership on the Committee.

Subsec. (c). Pub. L. 97–322, § 118(d)(2), authorized the Committee to make available to Congress any information, advice, and recommendations which the Committee is authorized to give to the Secretary.

Subsec. (d). Pub. L. 97–322, § 118(d)(3), inserted introductory provisions respecting compensation and travel expenses of members of the Committee.

TRANSFER OF FUNCTIONS

For transfer of authorities, functions, personnel, and assets of the Coast Guard, including the authorities and functions of the Secretary of Transportation relating thereto, to the Department of Homeland Security, and for treatment of related references, see sections 468(b), 551(d), 552(d), and 557 of Title 6, Domestic Security, and the Department of Homeland Security Reorganization Plan of November 25, 2002, as modified, set out as a note under section 542 of Title 6.

§ 1232. Enforcement provisions

(a) Civil penalty

(1) Any person who is found by the Secretary, after notice and an opportunity for a hearing, to have violated this chapter or a regulation issued hereunder shall be liable to the United States for a civil penalty, not to exceed $25,000 for each violation. Each day of a continuing violation shall constitute a separate violation. The amount of such civil penalty shall be assessed by the Secretary, or his designee, by written notice. In determining the amount of such penalty, the Secretary shall take into account the nature, circumstances, extent and gravity of the prohibited acts committed and, with respect to the violator, the degree of culpability, any history of prior offenses, ability to pay, and such other matters as justice may require.

(2) The Secretary may compromise, modify, or remit, with or without conditions, any civil penalty which is subject to imposition or which has been imposed under this section.

(3) If any person fails to pay an assessment of a civil penalty after it has become final, the Secretary may refer the matter to the Attorney General of the United States, for collection in any appropriate district court of the United States.

(b) Criminal penalty

(1) Any person who willfully and knowingly violates this chapter or any regulation issued hereunder commits a class D felony.

(2) Any person who, in the willfull[1] and knowing violation of this chapter or of any regulation issued hereunder, uses a dangerous weapon, or engages in conduct that causes bodily injury or fear of imminent bodily injury to any officer authorized to enforce the provisions of this chapter or the regulations issued hereunder, commits a class C felony.

(c) In rem liability

Any vessel subject to the provisions of this chapter, which is used in violation of this chapter, or any regulations issued hereunder, shall be liable in rem for any civil penalty assessed pursuant to subsection (a) of this section and may be proceeded against in the United States district court for any district in which such vessel may be found.

(d) Injunction

The United States district courts shall have jurisdiction to restrain violations of this chapter or of regulations issued hereunder, for cause shown.

(e) Denial of entry

Except as provided in section 1228 of this title, the Secretary may, subject to recognized principles of international law, deny entry into the navigable waters of the United States to any port or place under the jurisdiction of the United States or to any vessel not in compliance with the provisions of this chapter or the regulations issued hereunder.

(f) Withholding of clearance

(1) If any owner, operator, or individual in charge of a vessel is liable for a penalty or fine under this section, or if reasonable cause exists to believe that the owner, operator, or individual in charge may be subject to a penalty or fine under this section, the Secretary of the Treasury, upon the request of the Secretary, shall with respect to such vessel refuse or revoke any clearance required by section 60105 of title 46.

(2) Clearance refused or revoked under this subsection may be granted upon filing of a bond or other surety satisfactory to the Secretary.

(Pub. L. 92–340, § 13, as added Pub. L. 95–474, § 2, Oct. 17, 1978, 92 Stat. 1478; amended Pub. L. 101–380, title IV, § 4302(j), Aug. 18, 1990, 104 Stat. 539; Pub. L. 104–324, title III, § 312(b), Oct. 19, 1996, 110 Stat. 3920.)

CODIFICATION

In subsec. (f)(1), "section 60105 of title 46" substituted for "section 4197 of the Revised Statutes of the United States (46 App. U.S.C. 91)" on authority of Pub. L. 109–304, § 18(c), Oct. 6, 2006, 120 Stat. 1709, which Act enacted section 60105 of Title 46, Shipping.

AMENDMENTS

1996—Subsec. (f). Pub. L. 104–324 amended heading and text of subsec. (f) generally. Prior to amendment, text

[1] So in original. Probably should be "willful".

read as follows: "The Secretary of the Treasury shall withhold or revoke, at the request of the Secretary, the clearance, required by section 91 of title 46, Appendix, of any vessel, the owner or operator of which is subject to any of the penalties in this section. Clearance may be granted in such cases upon the filing of a bond or other surety satisfactory to the Secretary."

1990—Subsec. (b)(1). Pub. L. 101–380, §4302(j)(1), substituted "commits a class D felony" for "shall be fined not more than $50,000 for each violation or imprisoned for not more than five years, or both".

Subsec. (b)(2). Pub. L. 101–380, §4302(j)(2), which directed the substitution of "commits a class C felony." for "shall, in lieu of the penalties prescribed in paragraph (1), be fined not more than $100,000, or imprisoned for not more than 10 years, or both.", was executed by making the substitution for "shall, in lieu of the penalties prescribed in paragraph (1), be fined not more than $100,000, or imprisoned for not more than ten years, or both."

EFFECTIVE DATE OF 1990 AMENDMENT

Amendment by Pub. L. 101–380 applicable to incidents occurring after Aug. 18, 1990, see section 1020 of Pub. L. 101–380, set out as an Effective Date note under section 2701 of this title.

§1232a. Navigational hazards

(a) Reporting procedure

The Secretary shall establish a program to encourage fishermen and other vessel operators to report potential or existing navigational hazards involving pipelines to the Secretary through Coast Guard field offices.

(b) Secretary's response

(1) Upon notification by the operator of a pipeline of a hazard to navigation with respect to that pipeline, the Secretary shall immediately notify Coast Guard headquarters, the Office of Pipeline Safety, other affected Federal and State agencies, and vessel owners and operators in the pipeline's vicinity.

(2) Upon notification by any other person of a hazard or potential hazard to navigation with respect to a pipeline, the Secretary shall promptly determine whether a hazard exists, and if so shall immediately notify Coast Guard headquarters, the Office of Pipeline Safety, other affected Federal and State agencies, vessel owners and operators in the pipeline's vicinity, and the owner and operator of the pipeline.

(c) Establishment of standards

The Secretary shall, within six months after November 16, 1990, establish standards, for the purposes of this section, for what constitutes a hazard to navigation.

(d) "Pipelines" defined

For purposes of this section, the term "pipelines" has the meaning given the term "pipeline facilities" in section 60101(a)(18) of title 49.

(Pub. L. 92–340, §14, as added Pub. L. 101–599, §2, Nov. 16, 1990, 104 Stat. 3040.)

CODIFICATION

In subsec. (d), "section 60101(a)(18) of title 49" substituted for "the Natural Gas Pipeline Safety Act of 1968 [49 App. U.S.C. 1671 et seq.] and the Hazardous Liquid Pipeline Safety Act of 1979 [49 App. U.S.C. 2001 et seq.]" on authority of Pub. L. 103–272, §6(b), July 5, 1994, 108 Stat. 1378, the first section of which enacted subtitles II, III, and V to X of Title 49, Transportation.

TRANSFER OF FUNCTIONS

For transfer of authorities, functions, personnel, and assets of the Coast Guard, including the authorities and functions of the Secretary of Transportation relating thereto, to the Department of Homeland Security, and for treatment of related references, see sections 468(b), 551(d), 552(d), and 557 of Title 6, Domestic Security, and the Department of Homeland Security Reorganization Plan of November 25, 2002, as modified, set out as a note under section 542 of Title 6.

§1232b. Requirement to notify Coast Guard of release of objects into the navigable waters of the United States

(a) Requirement

As soon as a person has knowledge of any release from a vessel or facility into the navigable waters of the United States of any object that creates an obstruction prohibited under section 403 of this title, such person shall notify the Secretary and the Secretary of the Army of such release.

(b) Restriction on use of notification

Any notification provided by an individual in accordance with subsection (a) may not be used against such individual in any criminal case, except a prosecution for perjury or for giving a false statement.

(Pub. L. 92–340, §15, as added Pub. L. 109–241, title VI, §602, July 11, 2006, 120 Stat. 553.)

§1233. Regulations as to regattas or marine parades

The Commandant of the Coast Guard is authorized and empowered in his discretion to issue from time to time regulations, not contrary to law, to promote the safety of life on navigable waters during regattas or marine parades.

(Apr. 28, 1908, ch. 151, §1, 35 Stat. 69; Mar. 4, 1913, ch. 141, §1, 37 Stat. 736; 1946 Reorg. Plan No. 3, §§101–104, eff. July 16, 1946, 11 F.R. 7875, 60 Stat. 1097.)

CODIFICATION

Section was not enacted as part of the Ports and Waterways Safety Act which comprises this chapter.

Section was formerly classified to section 454 of former Title 46, Shipping.

TRANSFER OF FUNCTIONS

For transfer of authorities, functions, personnel, and assets of the Coast Guard, including the authorities and functions of the Secretary of Transportation relating thereto, to the Department of Homeland Security, and for treatment of related references, see sections 468(b), 551(d), 552(d), and 557 of Title 6, Domestic Security, and the Department of Homeland Security Reorganization Plan of November 25, 2002, as modified, set out as a note under section 542 of Title 6.

Coast Guard transferred to Department of Transportation, and all functions, powers, and duties relating to Coast Guard of Secretary of the Treasury and of other officers and offices of Department of the Treasury transferred to Secretary of Transportation by Pub. L. 89–670, §6(b)(1), Oct. 15, 1966, 80 Stat. 938. Section 6(b)(2) of Pub. L. 89–670, however, provided that notwithstanding such transfer of functions, Coast Guard shall operate as part of Navy in time of war or when President directs as provided in section 3 of Title 14, Coast Guard. See section 108 of Title 49, Transportation.

For transfer of functions of other officers, employees, and agencies of Department of the Treasury, with certain exceptions, to Secretary of the Treasury with power to delegate, see Reorg. Plan No. 26 of 1950, §§ 1, 2, eff. July 31, 1950, 15 F.R. 4935, 64 Stat. 1280, 1281, set out in the Appendix to Title 5, Government Organization and Employees. Functions of Coast Guard, and Commandant of Coast Guard, were excepted from transfer when Coast Guard is operating as part of Navy under sections 1 and 3 of Title 14.

"Commandant of the Coast Guard" substituted for "Secretary of Commerce" on authority of Reorg. Plan No. 3 of 1946, §§ 101–104, set out in the Appendix to Title 5.

Upon incorporation into the Code, the words "Secretary of Commerce" were substituted for "Secretary of Commerce and Labor" to conform to act Mar. 4, 1913, which provided that the Secretary of Commerce and Labor should be called the Secretary of Commerce.

§ 1234. Enforcement of regulations; use of public or private vessels

To enforce such regulations the Commandant of the Coast Guard may detail any public vessel in the service of the Coast Guard and make use of any private vessel tendered gratuitously for the purpose, or upon the request of the Commandant of the Coast Guard the head of any other department may enforce the regulations issued under sections 1233 and 1235 of this title by means of any public vessel of such department and of any private vessel tendered gratuitously for the purpose.

(Apr. 28, 1908, ch. 151, § 2, 35 Stat. 69; Mar. 4, 1913, ch. 141, § 1, 37 Stat. 736; 1946 Reorg. Plan No. 3, §§ 101–104, eff. July 16, 1946, 11 F.R. 7875, 60 Stat. 1097.)

Codification

Section was not enacted as part of the Ports and Waterways Safety Act which comprises this chapter.

Section was formerly classified to section 455 of former Title 46, Shipping.

Transfer of Functions

For transfer of authorities, functions, personnel, and assets of the Coast Guard, including the authorities and functions of the Secretary of Transportation relating thereto, to the Department of Homeland Security, and for treatment of related references, see sections 468(b), 551(d), 552(d), and 557 of Title 6, Domestic Security, and the Department of Homeland Security Reorganization Plan of November 25, 2002, as modified, set out as a note under section 542 of Title 6.

Coast Guard transferred to Department of Transportation, and all functions, powers, and duties relating to Coast Guard of Secretary of the Treasury and of other officers and offices of Department of the Treasury transferred to Secretary of Transportation by Pub. L. 89–670, § 6(b)(1), Oct. 15, 1966, 80 Stat. 938. Section 6(b)(2) of Pub. L. 89–670, however, provided that notwithstanding such transfer of functions, Coast Guard shall operate as part of Navy in time of war or when President directs as provided in section 3 of Title 14, Coast Guard. See section 108 of Title 49, Transportation.

For transfer of functions of other officers, employees, and agencies of Department of the Treasury, with certain exceptions, to Secretary of the Treasury with power to delegate, see Reorg. Plan No. 26 of 1950, §§ 1, 2, eff. July 31, 1950, 15 F.R. 4935, 64 Stat. 1280, 1281, set out in the Appendix to Title 5, Government Organization and Employees. Functions of Coast Guard, and Commandant of Coast Guard, were excepted from transfer when Coast Guard is operating as part of Navy under sections 1 and 3 of Title 14.

"Commandant of the Coast Guard" substituted for "Secretary of Commerce" and a reference to Department of Commerce changed to Coast Guard on authority of Reorg. Plan No. 3 of 1946, §§ 101–104, set out in the Appendix to Title 5.

Upon incorporation into the Code, the words "Secretary of Commerce" were substituted for "Secretary of Commerce and Labor" to conform to act Mar. 4, 1913, which provided that the Secretary of Commerce and Labor should be called the Secretary of Commerce.

§ 1235. Transfer of authority to regulate to head of other department

The authority and power bestowed upon the Commandant of the Coast Guard by sections 1233 and 1234 of this title may be transferred for any special occasion to the head of another department by the President whenever in his judgment such transfer is desirable.

(Apr. 28, 1908, ch. 151, § 3, 35 Stat. 69; Mar. 4, 1913, ch. 141, § 1, 37 Stat. 736; 1946 Reorg. Plan No. 3, §§ 101–104, eff. July 16, 1946, 11 F.R. 7875, 60 Stat. 1097.)

Codification

Section was not enacted as part of the Ports and Waterways Safety Act which comprises this chapter.

Section was formerly classified to section 456 of former Title 46, Shipping.

Transfer of Functions

For transfer of authorities, functions, personnel, and assets of the Coast Guard, including the authorities and functions of the Secretary of Transportation relating thereto, to the Department of Homeland Security, and for treatment of related references, see sections 468(b), 551(d), 552(d), and 557 of Title 6, Domestic Security, and the Department of Homeland Security Reorganization Plan of November 25, 2002, as modified, set out as a note under section 542 of Title 6.

Coast Guard transferred to Department of Transportation, and all functions, powers, and duties relating to Coast Guard of Secretary of the Treasury and of other officers and offices of Department of the Treasury transferred to Secretary of Transportation by Pub. L. 89–670, § 6(b)(1), Oct. 15, 1966, 80 Stat. 938. Section 6(b)(2) of Pub. L. 89–670, however, provided that notwithstanding such transfer of functions, Coast Guard shall operate as part of Navy in time of war or when President directs as provided in section 3 of Title 14, Coast Guard. See section 108 of Title 49, Transportation.

For transfer of functions of other officers, employees, and agencies of Department of the Treasury, with certain exceptions, to Secretary of the Treasury with power to delegate, see Reorg. Plan No. 26 of 1950, §§ 1, 2, eff. July 31, 1950, 15 F.R. 4935, 64 Stat. 1280, 1281, set out in the Appendix to Title 5, Government Organization and Employees. Functions of Coast Guard, and Commandant of Coast Guard, were excepted from transfer when Coast Guard is operating as part of Navy under sections 1 and 3 of Title 14.

"Commandant of the Coast Guard" substituted for "Secretary of Commerce" on authority of Reorg. Plan No. 3 of 1946, §§ 101–104, set out in the Appendix to Title 5.

Upon incorporation into the Code, the words "Secretary of Commerce" were substituted for "Secretary of Commerce and Labor" to conform to act Mar. 4, 1913, which provided that the Secretary of Commerce and Labor should be called the Secretary of Commerce.

§ 1236. Penalties for violations of regulations

For any violation of regulations issued pursuant to sections 1233 to 1235 of this title the following penalties shall be incurred:

(a) A licensed officer shall be liable to suspension or revocation of license in the manner now prescribed by law for incompetency or misconduct.

(b) Any person in charge of the navigation of a vessel other than a licensed officer shall be liable to a penalty of $5,000.

(c) The owner of a vessel (including any corporate officer of a corporation owning the vessel) actually on board shall be liable to a penalty of $5,000, unless the violation of regulations shall have occurred without his knowledge.

(d) Any other person shall be liable to a penalty of $2,500.

The Commandant of the Coast Guard is authorized and empowered to mitigate or remit any penalty herein provided for in the manner prescribed by law for the mitigation or remission of penalties for violation of the navigation laws.

(Apr. 28, 1908, ch. 151, §4, 35 Stat. 69; Mar. 4, 1913, ch. 141, §1, 37 Stat. 736; 1946 Reorg. Plan No. 3, §§101–104, eff. July 16, 1946, 11 F.R. 7875, 60 Stat. 1097; Pub. L. 101–380, title IV, §4302(k), Aug. 18, 1990, 104 Stat. 539.)

REFERENCES IN TEXT

The navigation laws, referred to in text, are classified generally to this title.

CODIFICATION

Section was not enacted as part of the Ports and Waterways Safety Act which comprises this chapter.

Section was formerly classified to section 457 of former Title 46, Shipping.

AMENDMENTS

1990—Subsecs. (b) to (d). Pub. L. 101–380 substituted "$5,000" for "$500" in subsecs. (b) and (c) and "$2,500" for "$250" in subsec. (d).

EFFECTIVE DATE OF 1990 AMENDMENT

Amendment by Pub. L. 101–380 applicable to incidents occurring after Aug. 18, 1990, see section 1020 of Pub. L. 101–380, set out as an Effective Date note under section 2701 of this title.

TRANSFER OF FUNCTIONS

For transfer of authorities, functions, personnel, and assets of the Coast Guard, including the authorities and functions of the Secretary of Transportation relating thereto, to the Department of Homeland Security, and for treatment of related references, see sections 468(b), 551(d), 552(d), and 557 of Title 6, Domestic Security, and the Department of Homeland Security Reorganization Plan of November 25, 2002, as modified, set out as a note under section 542 of Title 6.

Coast Guard transferred to Department of Transportation, and all functions, powers, and duties relating to Coast Guard of Secretary of the Treasury and of other officers and offices of Department of the Treasury transferred to Secretary of Transportation by Pub. L. 89–670, §6(b)(1), Oct. 15, 1966, 80 Stat. 938. Section 6(b)(2) of Pub. L. 89–670, however, provided that notwithstanding such transfer of functions, Coast Guard shall operate as part of Navy in time of war or when President directs as provided in section 3 of Title 14, Coast Guard. See section 108 of Title 49, Transportation.

For transfer of functions of other officers, employees, and agencies of Department of the Treasury, with certain exceptions, to Secretary of the Treasury with power to delegate, see Reorg. Plan No. 26 of 1950, §§1, 2, eff. July 31, 1950, 15 F.R. 4935, 64 Stat. 1280, 1281, set out in the Appendix to Title 5, Government Organization and Employees. Functions of Coast Guard, and Commandant of Coast Guard, were excepted from transfer when Coast Guard is operating as part of Navy under sections 1 and 3 of Title 14.

"Commandant of the Coast Guard" substituted for "Secretary of Commerce" on authority of Reorg. Plan No. 3 of 1946, §§101–104, set out in the Appendix to Title 5.

Upon incorporation into the Code, the words "Secretary of Commerce" were substituted for "Secretary of Commerce and Labor" to conform to act Mar. 4, 1913, which provided that the Secretary of Commerce and Labor should be called the Secretary of Commerce.

CHAPTER 26—WATER POLLUTION PREVENTION AND CONTROL

SUBCHAPTER I—RESEARCH AND RELATED PROGRAMS

SUBCHAPTER II—GRANTS FOR CONSTRUCTION OF TREATMENT WORKS

CODIFICATION

The Federal Water Pollution Control Act, comprising this chapter, was originally enacted by act June 30, 1948, ch. 758, 62 Stat. 1155, and amended by acts July 17, 1952, ch. 927, 66 Stat. 755; July 9, 1956, ch. 518, §§1, 2, 70 Stat. 498–507; June 25, 1959, Pub. L. 86–70, 73 Stat. 141; July 12, 1960, Pub. L. 86–624, 74 Stat. 411; July 20, 1961, Pub. L. 87–88, 75 Stat. 204; Oct. 2, 1965, Pub. L. 89–234, 79 Stat. 903; Nov. 3, 1966, Pub. L. 89–753, 80 Stat. 1246; Apr. 3, 1970, Pub. L. 91–224, 84 Stat. 91; Dec. 31, 1970, Pub. L. 91–611, 84 Stat. 1818; July 9, 1971, Pub. L. 92–50, 85 Stat. 124; Oct. 13, 1971, Pub. L. 92–137, 85 Stat. 379; Mar. 1, 1972, Pub. L. 92–240, 86 Stat. 47, and was formerly classified first to section 466 et seq. of this title and later to section 1151 et seq. of this title. The act is shown herein, however, as having been added by Pub. L. 92–500 without reference to such intervening amendments because of the extensive amendment, reorganization, and expansion of the act's provisions by Pub. L. 92–500.

SUBCHAPTER I—RESEARCH AND RELATED PROGRAMS

§ 1251. Congressional declaration of goals and policy

(a) Restoration and maintenance of chemical, physical and biological integrity of Nation's waters; national goals for achievement of objective

The objective of this chapter is to restore and maintain the chemical, physical, and biological integrity of the Nation's waters. In order to achieve this objective it is hereby declared that, consistent with the provisions of this chapter—

(1) it is the national goal that the discharge of pollutants into the navigable waters be eliminated by 1985;

(2) it is the national goal that wherever attainable, an interim goal of water quality which provides for the protection and propagation of fish, shellfish, and wildlife and provides for recreation in and on the water be achieved by July 1, 1983;

(3) it is the national policy that the discharge of toxic pollutants in toxic amounts be prohibited;

(4) it is the national policy that Federal financial assistance be provided to construct publicly owned waste treatment works;

(5) it is the national policy that areawide waste treatment management planning processes be developed and implemented to assure adequate control of sources of pollutants in each State;

(6) it is the national policy that a major research and demonstration effort be made to develop technology necessary to eliminate the discharge of pollutants into the navigable waters, waters of the contiguous zone, and the oceans; and

(7) it is the national policy that programs for the control of nonpoint sources of pollution be developed and implemented in an expeditious manner so as to enable the goals of this chapter to be met through the control of both point and nonpoint sources of pollution.

(b) Congressional recognition, preservation, and protection of primary responsibilities and rights of States

It is the policy of the Congress to recognize, preserve, and protect the primary responsibilities and rights of States to prevent, reduce, and eliminate pollution, to plan the development and use (including restoration, preservation, and enhancement) of land and water resources, and to consult with the Administrator in the exercise of his authority under this chapter. It is the policy of Congress that the States manage the construction grant program under this chapter and implement the permit programs under sections 1342 and 1344 of this title. It is further the policy of the Congress to support and aid research relating to the prevention, reduction, and elimination of pollution and to provide Federal technical services and financial aid to State and interstate agencies and municipalities in connection with the prevention, reduction, and elimination of pollution.

(c) Congressional policy toward Presidential activities with foreign countries

It is further the policy of Congress that the President, acting through the Secretary of State and such national and international organizations as he determines appropriate, shall take such action as may be necessary to insure that to the fullest extent possible all foreign countries shall take meaningful action for the prevention, reduction, and elimination of pollution in their waters and in international waters and for the achievement of goals regarding the elimination of discharge of pollutants and the improvement of water quality to at least the same extent as the United States does under its laws.

(d) Administrator of Environmental Protection Agency to administer chapter

Except as otherwise expressly provided in this chapter, the Administrator of the Environmental Protection Agency (hereinafter in this chapter called "Administrator") shall administer this chapter.

(e) Public participation in development, revision, and enforcement of any regulation, etc.

Public participation in the development, revision, and enforcement of any regulation, standard, effluent limitation, plan, or program established by the Administrator or any State under this chapter shall be provided for, encouraged, and assisted by the Administrator and the States. The Administrator, in cooperation with the States, shall develop and publish regulations specifying minimum guidelines for public participation in such processes.

(f) Procedures utilized for implementing chapter

It is the national policy that to the maximum extent possible the procedures utilized for implementing this chapter shall encourage the drastic minimization of paperwork and interagency decision procedures, and the best use of available manpower and funds, so as to prevent needless duplication and unnecessary delays at all levels of government.

(g) Authority of States over water

It is the policy of Congress that the authority of each State to allocate quantities of water within its jurisdiction shall not be superseded, abrogated or otherwise impaired by this chapter. It is the further policy of Congress that nothing in this chapter shall be construed to supersede or abrogate rights to quantities of water which have been established by any State. Federal agencies shall co-operate with State and local agencies to develop comprehensive solutions to prevent, reduce and eliminate pollution in concert with programs for managing water resources.

(June 30, 1948, ch. 758, title I, §101, as added Pub. L. 92–500, §2, Oct. 18, 1972, 86 Stat. 816; amended Pub. L. 95–217, §§5(a), 26(b), Dec. 27, 1977, 91 Stat. 1567, 1575; Pub. L. 100–4, title III, §316(b), Feb. 4, 1987, 101 Stat. 60.)

AMENDMENTS

1987—Subsec. (a)(7). Pub. L. 100–4 added par. (7).

1977—Subsec. (b). Pub. L. 95–217, §26(b), inserted provisions expressing Congressional policy that the States manage the construction grant program under this chapter and implement the permit program under sections 1342 and 1344 of this title.

Subsec. (g). Pub. L. 95–217, §5(a), added subsec. (g).

SHORT TITLE OF 2008 AMENDMENT

Pub. L. 110–365, §1, Oct. 8, 2008, 122 Stat. 4021, provided that: "This Act [amending sections 1268 and 1271a of this title] may be cited as the 'Great Lakes Legacy Reauthorization Act of 2008'."

Pub. L. 110–288, §1, July 29, 2008, 122 Stat. 2650, provided that: "This Act [amending sections 1322, 1342, and 1362 of this title] may be cited as the 'Clean Boating Act of 2008'."

SHORT TITLE OF 2002 AMENDMENT

Pub. L. 107–303, §1(a), Nov. 27, 2002, 116 Stat. 2355, provided that: "This Act [enacting section 1271a of this title, amending sections 1254, 1266, 1268, 1270, 1285, 1290, 1324, 1329, 1330, and 1375 of this title, enacting provisions set out as notes under this section, section 1254 of this title, and section 1113 of Title 31, Money and Finance, and repealing provisions set out as a note under section 50 of Title 20, Education] may be cited as the 'Great Lakes and Lake Champlain Act of 2002'."

Pub. L. 107–303, title I, §101, Nov. 27, 2002, 116 Stat. 2355, provided that: "This title [enacting section 1271a of this title and amending section 1268 of this title] may be cited as the 'Great Lakes Legacy Act of 2002'."

Pub. L. 107–303, title II, §201, Nov. 27, 2002, 116 Stat. 2358, provided that: "This title [amending section 1270 of this title] may be cited as the 'Daniel Patrick Moynihan Lake Champlain Basin Program Act of 2002'."

SHORT TITLE OF 2000 AMENDMENTS

Pub. L. 106–457, title II, §201, Nov. 7, 2000, 114 Stat. 1967, provided that: "This title [amending section 1267 of this title and enacting provisions set out as a note under section 1267 of this title] may be cited as the 'Chesapeake Bay Restoration Act of 2000'."

Pub. L. 106–457, title IV, §401, Nov. 7, 2000, 114 Stat. 1973, provided that: "This title [amending section 1269 of this title] may be cited as the 'Long Island Sound Restoration Act'."

Pub. L. 106–457, title V, §501, Nov. 7, 2000, 114 Stat. 1973, provided that: "This title [enacting section 1273 of this title] may be cited as the 'Lake Pontchartrain Basin Restoration Act of 2000'."

Pub. L. 106–457, title VI, §601, Nov. 7, 2000, 114 Stat. 1975, provided that: "This title [enacting section 1300 of this title] may be cited as the 'Alternative Water Sources Act of 2000'."

Pub. L. 106–284, §1, Oct. 10, 2000, 114 Stat. 870, provided that: "This Act [enacting sections 1346 and 1375a of this title and amending sections 1254, 1313, 1314, 1362, and 1377 of this title] may be cited as the 'Beaches Environmental Assessment and Coastal Health Act of 2000'."

SHORT TITLE OF 1994 AMENDMENT

Pub. L. 103–431, §1, Oct. 31, 1994, 108 Stat. 4396, provided that: "This Act [amending section 1311 of this title] may be cited as the 'Ocean Pollution Reduction Act'."

SHORT TITLE OF 1990 AMENDMENT

Pub. L. 101–596, §1, Nov. 16, 1990, 104 Stat. 3000, provided that: "This Act [enacting sections 1269 and 1270 of this title, amending sections 1268, 1324, and 1416 of this title, and enacting provisions set out as notes under this section and section 1270 of this title] may be cited as the 'Great Lakes Critical Programs Act of 1990'."

Pub. L. 101–596, title II, § 201, Nov. 16, 1990, 104 Stat. 3004, provided that: "This part [probably means title, enacting section 1269 of this title and amending section 1416 of this title] may be cited as the 'Long Island Sound Improvement Act of 1990'."

Pub. L. 101–596, title III, § 301, Nov. 16, 1990, 104 Stat. 3006, provided that: "This title [enacting section 1270 of this title, amending section 1324 of this title, and enacting provisions set out as a note under section 1270 of this title] may be cited as the 'Lake Champlain Special Designation Act of 1990'."

SHORT TITLE OF 1988 AMENDMENT

Pub. L. 100–653, title X, § 1001, Nov. 14, 1988, 102 Stat. 3835, provided that: "This title [amending section 1330 of this title and enacting provisions set out as notes under section 1330 of this title] may be cited as the 'Massachusetts Bay Protection Act of 1988'."

SHORT TITLE OF 1987 AMENDMENT

Section 1(a) of Pub. L. 100–4 provided that: "This Act [enacting sections 1254a, 1267, 1268, 1281b, 1329, 1330, 1377, 1381 to 1387, and 1414a of this title, amending this section and sections 1254, 1256, 1262, 1281, 1282 to 1285, 1287, 1288, 1291, 1311 to 1313, 1314, 1317 to 1322, 1324, 1342, 1344, 1345, 1361, 1362, 1365, 1369, 1375, and 1376 of this title, and enacting provisions set out as notes under this section, sections 1284, 1311, 1317, 1319, 1330, 1342, 1345, 1362, 1375, and 1414a of this title, and section 1962d–20 of Title 42, The Public Health and Welfare] may be cited as the 'Water Quality Act of 1987'."

SHORT TITLE OF 1981 AMENDMENT

Pub. L. 97–117, § 1, Dec. 29, 1981, 95 Stat. 1623, provided that: "This Act [enacting sections 1298, 1299, and 1313a of this title, amending sections 1281 to 1285, 1287, 1291, 1292, 1296, 1311, and 1314 of this title, and enacting provisions set out as notes under sections 1311 and 1375 of this title] may be cited as the 'Municipal Wastewater Treatment Construction Grant Amendments of 1981'."

SHORT TITLE OF 1977 AMENDMENT

Section 1 of Pub. L. 95–217 provided: "That this Act [enacting sections 1281a, 1294 to 1296, and 1297 of this title, amending this section and sections 1252, 1254 to 1256, 1259, 1262, 1263, 1281, 1282 to 1288, 1291, 1292, 1311, 1314, 1315, 1317 to 1319, 1321 to 1324, 1328, 1341, 1342, 1344, 1345, 1362, 1364, 1375, and 1376 of this title, enacting provisions set out as notes under this section and sections 1284, 1286, 1314, 1321, 1342, 1344, and 1376 of this title, and amending provisions set out as a note under this section] may be cited as the 'Clean Water Act of 1977'."

SHORT TITLE

Section 1 of Pub. L. 92–500 provided that: "That this Act [enacting this chapter, amending section 24 of Title 12, Banks and Banking, sections 633 and 636 of Title 15, Commerce and Trade, and section 711 of former Title 31, Money and Finance, and enacting provisions set out as notes under this section and sections 1281 and 1361 of this title] may be cited as the 'Federal Water Pollution Control Act Amendments of 1972'."

Section 519, formerly section 518, of Act June 30, 1948, ch. 758, title V, as added Oct. 18, 1972, Pub. L. 92–500, § 2, 86 Stat. 896, and amended Dec. 27, 1977, Pub. L. 95–217, § 2, 91 Stat. 1566, and renumbered § 519, Feb. 4, 1987, Pub. L. 100–4, title V, § 506, 101 Stat. 76, provided that: "This Act [this chapter] may be cited as the 'Federal Water Pollution Control Act' (commonly referred to as the Clean Water Act)."

SAVINGS PROVISION

Section 4 of Pub. L. 92–500 provided that:

"(a) No suit, action, or other proceeding lawfully commenced by or against the Administrator or any other officer or employee of the United States in his official capacity or in relation to the discharge of his official duties under the Federal Water Pollution Control Act as in effect immediately prior to the date of enactment of this Act [Oct. 18, 1972] shall abate by reason of the taking effect of the amendment made by section 2 of this Act [which enacted this chapter]. The court may, on its own motion or that of any party made at any time within twelve months after such taking effect, allow the same to be maintained by or against the Administrator or such officer or employee.

"(b) All rules, regulations, orders, determinations, contracts, certifications, authorizations, delegations, or other actions duly issued, made, or taken by or pursuant to the Federal Water Pollution Control Act as in effect immediately prior to the date of enactment of this Act [Oct. 18, 1972], and pertaining to any functions, powers, requirements, and duties under the Federal Water Pollution Control Act as in effect immediately prior to the date of enactment of this Act [Oct. 18, 1972] shall continue in full force and effect after the date of enactment of this Act [Oct. 18, 1972] until modified or rescinded in accordance with the Federal Water Pollution Control Act as amended by this Act [this chapter].

"(c) The Federal Water Pollution Control Act as in effect immediately prior to the date of enactment of this Act [Oct. 18, 1972] shall remain applicable to all grants made from funds authorized for the fiscal year ending June 30, 1972, and prior fiscal years, including any increases in the monetary amount of any such grant which may be paid from authorizations for fiscal years beginning after June 30, 1972, except as specifically otherwise provided in section 202 of the Federal Water Pollution Control Act as amended by this Act [section 1282 of this title] and in subsection (c) of section 3 of this Act."

SEPARABILITY

Section 512 of act June 30, 1948, ch. 758, title V, as added Oct. 18, 1972, Pub. L. 92–500, § 2, 86 Stat. 894, provided that: "If any provision of this Act [this chapter], or the application of any provision of this Act [this chapter] to any person or circumstance, is held invalid, the application of such provision to other persons or circumstances, and the remainder of this Act [this chapter], shall not be affected thereby."

NATIONAL SHELLFISH INDICATOR PROGRAM

Pub. L. 102–567, title III, § 308, Oct. 29, 1992, 106 Stat. 4286; as amended by Pub. L. 105–362, title II, § 201(b), Nov. 10, 1998, 112 Stat. 3282, provided that:

"(a) ESTABLISHMENT OF A RESEARCH PROGRAM.—The Secretary of Commerce, in cooperation with the Secretary of Health and Human Services and the Administrator of the Environmental Protection Agency, shall establish and administer a 5-year national shellfish research program (hereafter in this section referred to as the 'Program') for the purpose of improving existing classification systems for shellfish growing waters using the latest technological advancements in microbiology and epidemiological methods. Within 12 months after the date of enactment of this Act [Oct. 29, 1992], the Secretary of Commerce, in cooperation with the advisory committee established under subsection (b) and the Consortium, shall develop a comprehensive 5-year plan for the Program which shall at a minimum provide for—

"(1) an environmental assessment of commercial shellfish growing areas in the United States, including an evaluation of the relationships between indicators of fecal contamination and human enteric pathogens;

"(2) the evaluation of such relationships with respect to potential health hazards associated with human consumption of shellfish;

"(3) a comparison of the current microbiological methods used for evaluating indicator bacteria and human enteric pathogens in shellfish and shellfish growing waters with new technological methods designed for this purpose;

"(4) the evaluation of current and projected systems for human sewage treatment in eliminating viruses and other human enteric pathogens which accumulate in shellfish;

"(5) the design of epidemiological studies to relate microbiological data, sanitary survey data, and human shellfish consumption data to actual hazards to health associated with such consumption; and

"(6) recommendations for revising Federal shellfish standards and improving the capabilities of Federal and State agencies to effectively manage shellfish and ensure the safety of shellfish intended for human consumption.

"(b) ADVISORY COMMITTEE.—(1) For the purpose of providing oversight of the Program on a continuing basis, an advisory committee (hereafter in this section referred to as the 'Committee') shall be established under a memorandum of understanding between the Interstate Shellfish Sanitation Conference and the National Marine Fisheries Service.

"(2) The Committee shall—

"(A) identify priorities for achieving the purpose of the Program;

"(B) review and recommend approval or disapproval of Program work plans and plans of operation;

"(C) review and comment on all subcontracts and grants to be awarded under the Program;

"(D) receive and review progress reports from the Consortium and program subcontractors and grantees; and

"(E) provide such other advice on the Program as is appropriate.

"(3) The Committee shall consist of at least ten members and shall include—

"(A) three members representing agencies having authority under State law to regulate the shellfish industry, of whom one shall represent each of the Atlantic, Pacific, and Gulf of Mexico shellfish growing regions;

"(B) three members representing persons engaged in the shellfish industry in the Atlantic, Pacific, and Gulf of Mexico shellfish growing regions (who shall be appointed from among at least six recommendations by the industry members of the Interstate Shellfish Sanitation Conference Executive Board), of whom one shall represent the shellfish industry in each region;

"(C) three members, of whom one shall represent each of the following Federal agencies: the National Oceanic and Atmospheric Administration, the Environmental Protection Agency, and the Food and Drug Administration; and

"(D) one member representing the Shellfish Institute of North America.

"(4) The Chairman of the Committee shall be selected from among the Committee members described in paragraph (3)(A).

"(5) The Committee shall establish and maintain a subcommittee of scientific experts to provide advice, assistance, and information relevant to research funded under the Program, except that no individual who is awarded, or whose application is being considered for, a grant or subcontract under the Program may serve on such subcommittee. The membership of the subcommittee shall, to the extent practicable, be regionally balanced with experts who have scientific knowledge concerning each of the Atlantic, Pacific, and Gulf of Mexico shellfish growing regions. Scientists from the National Academy of Sciences and appropriate Federal agencies (including the National Oceanic and Atmospheric Administration, Food and Drug Administration, Centers for Disease Control, National Institutes of Health, Environmental Protection Agency, and National Science Foundation) shall be considered for membership on the subcommittee.

"(6) Members of the Committee and its scientific subcommittee established under this subsection shall not be paid for serving on the Committee or subcommittee, but shall receive travel expenses as authorized by section 5703 of title 5, United States Code.

"(c) CONTRACT WITH CONSORTIUM.—Within 30 days after the date of enactment of this Act [Oct. 29, 1992], the Secretary of Commerce shall seek to enter into a cooperative agreement or contract with the Consortium under which the Consortium will—

"(1) be the academic administrative organization and fiscal agent for the Program;

"(2) award and administer such grants and subcontracts as are approved by the Committee under subsection (b);

"(3) develop and implement a scientific peer review process for evaluating grant and subcontractor applications prior to review by the Committee;

"(4) in cooperation with the Secretary of Commerce and the Committee, procure the services of a scientific project director;

"(5) develop and submit budgets, progress reports, work plans, and plans of operation for the Program to the Secretary of Commerce and the Committee; and

"(6) make available to the Committee such staff, information, and assistance as the Committee may reasonably require to carry out its activities.

"(d) AUTHORIZATION OF APPROPRIATIONS.—(1) Of the sums authorized under section 4(a) of the National Oceanic and Atmospheric Administration Marine Fisheries Program Authorization Act (Public Law 98–210; 97 Stat. 1409), there are authorized to be appropriated to the Secretary of Commerce $5,200,000 for each of the fiscal years 1993 through 1997 for carrying out the Program. Of the amounts appropriated pursuant to this authorization, not more than 5 percent of such appropriation may be used for administrative purposes by the National Oceanic and Atmospheric Administration. The remaining 95 percent of such appropriation shall be used to meet the administrative and scientific objectives of the Program.

"(2) The Interstate Shellfish Sanitation Conference shall not administer appropriations authorized under this section, but may be reimbursed from such appropriations for its expenses in arranging for travel, meetings, workshops, or conferences necessary to carry out the Program.

"(e) DEFINITIONS.—As used in this section, the term—

"(1) 'Consortium' means the Louisiana Universities Marine Consortium; and

"(2) 'shellfish' means any species of oyster, clam, or mussel that is harvested for human consumption."

LIMITATION ON PAYMENTS

Section 2 of Pub. L. 100–4 provided that: "No payments may be made under this Act [see Short Title of 1987 Amendment note above] except to the extent provided in advance in appropriation Acts."

SEAFOOD PROCESSING STUDY; SUBMITTAL OF RESULTS TO CONGRESS NOT LATER THAN JANUARY 1, 1979

Pub. L. 95–217, §74, Dec. 27, 1977, 91 Stat. 1609, provided that the Administrator of the Environmental Protection Agency conduct a study to examine the geographical, hydrological, and biological characteristics of marine waters to determine the effects of seafood processes which dispose of untreated natural wastes into such waters and to include in this study an examination of technologies which may be used in such processes to facilitate the use of the nutrients in these wastes or to reduce the discharge of such wastes into the marine environment and to submit the result of this study to Congress not later than Jan. 1, 1979.

STANDARDS

For provisions relating to the responsibility of the head of each Executive agency for compliance with applicable pollution control standards, see Ex. Ord. No. 12088, Oct. 13, 1978, 43 F.R. 47707, set out as a note under section 4321 of Title 42, The Public Health and Welfare.

OVERSIGHT STUDY

Section 5 of Pub. L. 92–500 authorized the Comptroller General of the United States to conduct a study and review of the research, pilot, and demonstration programs related to prevention and control of water pollution conducted, supported, or assisted by any Federal agency pursuant to any Federal law or regulation and assess conflicts between these programs and their coordination and efficacy, and to report to Congress thereon by Oct. 1, 1973.

INTERNATIONAL TRADE STUDY

Section 6 of Pub. L. 92–500 provided that:

"(a) The Secretary of Commerce, in cooperation with other interested Federal agencies and with representatives of industry and the public, shall undertake immediately an investigation and study to determine—

"(1) the extent to which pollution abatement and control programs will be imposed on, or voluntarily undertaken by, United States manufacturers in the near future and the probable short- and long-range effects of the costs of such programs (computed to the greatest extent practicable on an industry-by-industry basis) on (A) the production costs of such domestic manufacturers, and (B) the market prices of the goods produced by them;

"(2) the probable extent to which pollution abatement and control programs will be implemented in foreign industrial nations in the near future and the extent to which the production costs (computed to the greatest extent practicable on an industry-by-industry basis) of foreign manufacturers will be affected by the costs of such programs;

"(3) the probable competitive advantage which any article manufactured in a foreign nation will likely have in relation to a comparable article made in the United States if that foreign nation—

"(A) does not require its manufacturers to implement pollution abatement and control programs,

"(B) requires a lesser degree of pollution abatement and control in its programs, or

"(C) in any way reimburses or otherwise subsidizes its manufacturers for the costs of such program;

"(4) alternative means by which any competitive advantage accruing to the products of any foreign nation as a result of any factor described in paragraph (3) may be (A) accurately and quickly determined, and (B) equalized, for example, by the imposition of a surcharge or duty, on a foreign product in an amount necessary to compensate for such advantage; and

"(5) the impact, if any, which the imposition of a compensating tariff of other equalizing measure may have in encouraging foreign nations to implement pollution and abatement control programs.

"(b) The Secretary shall make an initial report to the President and Congress within six months after the date of enactment of this section [Oct. 18, 1972] of the results of the study and investigation carried out pursuant to this section and shall make additional reports thereafter at such times as he deems appropriate taking into account the development of relevant data, but not less than once every twelve months."

INTERNATIONAL AGREEMENTS

Section 7 of Pub. L. 92–500 provided that: "The President shall undertake to enter into international agreement to apply uniform standards of performance for the control of the discharge and emission of pollutants from new sources, uniform controls over the discharge and emission of toxic pollutants, and uniform controls over the discharge of pollutants into the ocean. For this purpose the President shall negotiate multilateral treaties, conventions, resolutions, or other agreements, and formulate, present, or support proposals at the United Nations and other appropriate international forums."

NATIONAL POLICIES AND GOAL STUDY

Section 10 of Pub. L. 92–500 directed President to make a full and complete investigation and study of all national policies and goals established by law to determine what the relationship should be between these policies and goals, taking into account the resources of the Nation, and to report results of his investigation and study together with his recommendations to Congress not later than two years after Oct. 18, 1972.

EFFICIENCY STUDY

Section 11 of Pub. L. 92–500 directed President, by utilization of the General Accounting Office, to conduct a full and complete investigation and study of ways and means of most effectively using all of the various resources, facilities, and personnel of the Federal Government in order to most efficiently carry out the provisions of this chapter and to report results of his investigation and study together with his recommendations to Congress not later than two hundred and seventy days after Oct. 18, 1972.

SEX DISCRIMINATION

Section 13 of Pub. L. 92–500 provided that: "No person in the United States shall on the ground of sex be excluded from participation in, be denied the benefits of, or be subjected to discrimination under any program or activity receiving Federal assistance under this Act [see Short Title note above] the Federal Water Pollution Control Act [this chapter], or the Environmental Financing Act [set out as a note under section 1281 of this title]. This section shall be enforced through agency provisions and rules similar to those already established, with respect to racial and other discrimination, under title VI of the Civil Rights Act of 1964 [section 2000d et seq. of Title 42, The Public Health and Welfare]. However, this remedy is not exclusive and will not prejudice or cut off any other legal remedies available to a discriminatee."

CONTIGUOUS ZONE OF UNITED STATES

For extension of contiguous zone of United States, see Proc. No. 7219, set out as a note under section 1331 of Title 43, Public Lands.

PREVENTION, CONTROL, AND ABATEMENT OF ENVIRONMENTAL POLLUTION AT FEDERAL FACILITIES

Ex. Ord. No. 12088, Oct. 13, 1978, 43 F.R. 47707, set out as a note under section 4321 of Title 42, The Public Health and Welfare, provides for the prevention, control, and abatement of environmental pollution at federal facilities.

EXECUTIVE ORDER NO. 11548

Ex. Ord. No. 11548, July 20, 1970, 35 F.R. 11677, which related to the delegation of Presidential functions, was superseded by Ex. Ord. No. 11735, Aug. 3, 1973, 38 F.R. 21243, formerly set out as a note under section 1321 of this title.

EX. ORD. NO. 11742. DELEGATION OF FUNCTIONS TO SECRETARY OF STATE RESPECTING THE NEGOTIATION OF INTERNATIONAL AGREEMENTS RELATING TO THE ENHANCEMENT OF THE ENVIRONMENT

Ex. Ord. No. 11742, Oct. 23, 1973, 38 F.R. 29457, provided:

Under and by virtue of the authority vested in me by section 301 of title 3 of the United States Code and as President of the United States, I hereby authorize and empower the Secretary of State, in coordination with the Council on Environmental Quality, the Environmental Protection Agency, and other appropriate Federal agencies, to perform, without the approval, ratification, or other action of the President, the functions vested in the President by Section 7 of the Federal Water Pollution Control Act Amendments of 1972 (Public Law 92–500; 86 Stat. 898) with respect to international agreements relating to the enhancement of the environment.

RICHARD NIXON.

DEFINITION OF "ADMINISTRATOR"

Section 1(d) of Pub. L. 100–4 provided that: "For purposes of this Act [see Short Title of 1987 Amendment note above], the term 'Administrator' means the Administrator of the Environmental Protection Agency."

§1252. Comprehensive programs for water pollution control

(a) Preparation and development

The Administrator shall, after careful investigation, and in cooperation with other Federal agencies, State water pollution control agencies, interstate agencies, and the municipalities and industries involved, prepare or develop comprehensive programs for preventing, reducing, or eliminating the pollution of the navigable waters and ground waters and improving the sanitary condition of surface and underground waters. In the development of such comprehensive programs due regard shall be given to the improvements which are necessary to conserve such waters for the protection and propagation of fish and aquatic life and wildlife, recreational purposes, and the withdrawal of such waters for public water supply, agricultural, industrial, and other purposes. For the purpose of this section, the Administrator is authorized to make joint investigations with any such agencies of the condition of any waters in any State or States, and of the discharges of any sewage, industrial wastes, or substance which may adversely affect such waters.

(b) Planning for reservoirs; storage for regulation of streamflow

(1) In the survey or planning of any reservoir by the Corps of Engineers, Bureau of Reclamation, or other Federal agency, consideration shall be given to inclusion of storage for regulation of streamflow, except that any such storage and water releases shall not be provided as a substitute for adequate treatment or other methods of controlling waste at the source.

(2) The need for and the value of storage for regulation of streamflow (other than for water quality) including but not limited to navigation, salt water intrusion, recreation, esthetics, and fish and wildlife, shall be determined by the Corps of Engineers, Bureau of Reclamation, or other Federal agencies.

(3) The need for, the value of, and the impact of, storage for water quality control shall be determined by the Administrator, and his views on these matters shall be set forth in any report or presentation to Congress proposing authorization or construction of any reservoir including such storage.

(4) The value of such storage shall be taken into account in determining the economic value of the entire project of which it is a part, and costs shall be allocated to the purpose of regulation of streamflow in a manner which will insure that all project purposes, share equitably in the benefit of multiple-purpose construction.

(5) Costs of regulation of streamflow features incorporated in any Federal reservoir or other impoundment under the provisions of this chapter shall be determined and the beneficiaries identified and if the benefits are widespread or national in scope, the costs of such features shall be nonreimbursable.

(6) No license granted by the Federal Energy Regulatory Commission for a hydroelectric power project shall include storage for regulation of streamflow for the purpose of water quality control unless the Administrator shall recommend its inclusion and such reservoir storage capacity shall not exceed such proportion of the total storage required for the water quality control plan as the drainage area of such reservoir bears to the drainage area of the river basin or basins involved in such water quality control plan.

(c) Basins; grants to State agencies

(1) The Administrator shall, at the request of the Governor of a State, or a majority of the Governors when more than one State is involved, make a grant to pay not to exceed 50 per centum of the administrative expenses of a planning agency for a period not to exceed three years, which period shall begin after October 18, 1972, if such agency provides for adequate representation of appropriate State, interstate, local, or (when appropriate) international interests in the basin or portion thereof involved and is capable of developing an effective, comprehensive water quality control plan for a basin or portion thereof.

(2) Each planning agency receiving a grant under this subsection shall develop a comprehensive pollution control plan for the basin or portion thereof which—

(A) is consistent with any applicable water quality standards effluent and other limitations, and thermal discharge regulations established pursuant to current law within the basin;

(B) recommends such treatment works as will provide the most effective and economical means of collection, storage, treatment, and elimination of pollutants and recommends means to encourage both municipal and industrial use of such works;

(C) recommends maintenance and improvement of water quality within the basin or portion thereof and recommends methods of adequately financing those facilities as may be necessary to implement the plan; and

(D) as appropriate, is developed in cooperation with, and is consistent with any comprehensive plan prepared by the Water Resources Council, any areawide waste management plans developed pursuant to section 1288 of this title, and any State plan developed pursuant to section 1313(e) of this title.

(3) For the purposes of this subsection the term "basin" includes, but is not limited to, rivers and their tributaries, streams, coastal waters, sounds, estuaries, bays, lakes, and portions thereof as well as the lands drained thereby.

(June 30, 1948, ch. 758, title I, §102, as added Pub. L. 92–500, §2, Oct. 18, 1972, 86 Stat. 817; amended Pub. L. 95–91, title IV, §402(a)(1)(A), Aug. 4, 1977, 91 Stat. 583; Pub. L. 95–217, §5(b), Dec. 27, 1977, 91 Stat. 1567; Pub. L. 104–66, title II, §2021(a), Dec. 21, 1995, 109 Stat. 726.)

AMENDMENTS

1995—Subsec. (d). Pub. L. 104–66 struck out subsec. (d) which read as follows: "The Administrator, after consultation with the States, and River Basin Commissions established under the Water Resources Planning Act, shall submit a report to Congress on or before July 1, 1978, which analyzes the relationship between programs under this chapter, and the programs by which State and Federal agencies allocate quantities of water. Such report shall include recommendations concerning the policy in section 1251(g) of this title to improve coordination of efforts to reduce and eliminate pollution in concert with programs for managing water resources."

1977—Subsec. (d). Pub. L. 95–217 added subsec. (d).

TRANSFER OF FUNCTIONS

"Federal Energy Regulatory Commission" substituted for "Federal Power Commission" in subsec. (b)(6) on authority of Pub. L. 95–91, title IV, § 402(a)(1)(A), Aug. 4, 1977, 91 Stat. 583, which is classified to section 7172(a)(1)(A) of Title 42, The Public Health and Welfare.

EXECUTIVE ORDER NO. 10014

Ex. Ord. No. 10014, Nov. 3, 1948, 13 F.R. 6601, which related to the cooperation of Federal and State agencies to prevent pollution of surface and underground waters, was superseded by Ex. Ord. No. 11258, Nov. 17, 1965, 30 F.R. 14483.

§ 1252a. Reservoir projects, water storage; modification; storage for other than for water quality, opinion of Federal agency, committee resolutions of approval; provisions inapplicable to projects with certain prescribed water quality benefits in relation to total project benefits

In the case of any reservoir project authorized for construction by the Corps of Engineers, Bureau of Reclamation, or other Federal agency when the Administrator of the Environmental Protection Agency determines pursuant to section 1252(b) of this title that any storage in such project for regulation of streamflow for water quality is not needed, or is needed in a different amount, such project may be modified accordingly by the head of the appropriate agency, and any storage no longer required for water quality may be utilized for other authorized purposes of the project when, in the opinion of the head of such agency, such use is justified. Any such modification of a project where the benefits attributable to water quality are 15 per centum or more but not greater than 25 per centum of the total project benefits shall take effect only upon the adoption of resolutions approving such modification by the appropriate committees of the Senate and House of Representatives. The provisions of the section shall not apply to any project where the benefits attributable to water quality exceed 25 per centum of the total project benefits.

(Pub. L. 93–251, title I, § 65, Mar. 7, 1974, 88 Stat. 30.)

CODIFICATION

Section was not enacted as part of the Federal Water Pollution Control Act which comprises this chapter.

§ 1253. Interstate cooperation and uniform laws

(a) The Administrator shall encourage cooperative activities by the States for the prevention, reduction, and elimination of pollution, encourage the enactment of improved and, so far as practicable, uniform State laws relating to the prevention, reduction, and elimination of pollution; and encourage compacts between States for the prevention and control of pollution.

(b) The consent of the Congress is hereby given to two or more States to negotiate and enter into agreements or compacts, not in conflict with any law or treaty of the United States, for (1) cooperative effort and mutual assistance for the prevention and control of pollution and the enforcement of their respective laws relating thereto, and (2) the establishment of such agencies, joint or otherwise, as they may deem desirable for making effective such agreements and compacts. No such agreement or compact shall be binding or obligatory upon any State a party thereto unless and until it has been approved by the Congress.

(June 30, 1948, ch. 758, title I, § 103, as added Pub. L. 92–500, § 2, Oct. 18, 1972, 86 Stat. 818.)

§ 1254. Research, investigations, training, and information

(a) Establishment of national programs; cooperation; investigations; water quality surveillance system; reports

The Administrator shall establish national programs for the prevention, reduction, and elimination of pollution and as part of such programs shall—

(1) in cooperation with other Federal, State, and local agencies, conduct and promote the coordination and acceleration of, research, investigations, experiments, training, demonstrations, surveys, and studies relating to the causes, effects, extent, prevention, reduction, and elimination of pollution;

(2) encourage, cooperate with, and render technical services to pollution control agencies and other appropriate public or private agencies, institutions, and organizations, and individuals, including the general public, in the conduct of activities referred to in paragraph (1) of this subsection;

(3) conduct, in cooperation with State water pollution control agencies and other interested agencies, organizations and persons, public investigations concerning the pollution of any navigable waters, and report on the results of such investigations;

(4) establish advisory committees composed of recognized experts in various aspects of pollution and representatives of the public to assist in the examination and evaluation of research progress and proposals and to avoid duplication of research;

(5) in cooperation with the States, and their political subdivisions, and other Federal agencies establish, equip, and maintain a water quality surveillance system for the purpose of monitoring the quality of the navigable waters and ground waters and the contiguous zone and the oceans and the Administrator shall, to the extent practicable, conduct such surveillance by utilizing the resources of the National Aeronautics and Space Administration, the National Oceanic and Atmospheric Administration, the United States Geological Survey, and the Coast Guard, and shall report on such quality in the report required under subsection (a) of section 1375 of this title; and

(6) initiate and promote the coordination and acceleration of research designed to develop the most effective practicable tools and

techniques for measuring the social and economic costs and benefits of activities which are subject to regulation under this chapter; and shall transmit a report on the results of such research to the Congress not later than January 1, 1974.

(b) Authorized activities of Administrator

In carrying out the provisions of subsection (a) of this section the Administrator is authorized to—

(1) collect and make available, through publications and other appropriate means, the results of and other information, including appropriate recommendations by him in connection therewith, pertaining to such research and other activities referred to in paragraph (1) of subsection (a) of this section;

(2) cooperate with other Federal departments and agencies, State water pollution control agencies, interstate agencies, other public and private agencies, institutions, organizations, industries involved, and individuals, in the preparation and conduct of such research and other activities referred to in paragraph (1) of subsection (a) of this section;

(3) make grants to State water pollution control agencies, interstate agencies, other public or nonprofit private agencies, institutions, organizations, and individuals, for purposes stated in paragraph (1) of subsection (a) of this section;

(4) contract with public or private agencies, institutions, organizations, and individuals, without regard to section 3324(a) and (b) of title 31 and section 5 of title 41, referred to in paragraph (1) of subsection (a) of this section;

(5) establish and maintain research fellowships at public or nonprofit private educational institutions or research organizations;

(6) collect and disseminate, in cooperation with other Federal departments and agencies, and with other public or private agencies, institutions, and organizations having related responsibilities, basic data on chemical, physical, and biological effects of varying water quality and other information pertaining to pollution and the prevention, reduction, and elimination thereof; and

(7) develop effective and practical processes, methods, and prototype devices for the prevention, reduction, and elimination of pollution.

(c) Research and studies on harmful effects of pollutants; cooperation with Secretary of Health and Human Services

In carrying out the provisions of subsection (a) of this section the Administrator shall conduct research on, and survey the results of other scientific studies on, the harmful effects on the health or welfare of persons caused by pollutants. In order to avoid duplication of effort, the Administrator shall, to the extent practicable, conduct such research in cooperation with and through the facilities of the Secretary of Health and Human Services.

(d) Sewage treatment; identification and measurement of effects of pollutants; augmented streamflow

In carrying out the provisions of this section the Administrator shall develop and demonstrate under varied conditions (including conducting such basic and applied research, studies, and experiments as may be necessary):

(1) Practicable means of treating municipal sewage, and other waterborne wastes to implement the requirements of section 1281 of this title;

(2) Improved methods and procedures to identify and measure the effects of pollutants, including those pollutants created by new technological developments; and

(3) Methods and procedures for evaluating the effects on water quality of augmented streamflows to control pollution not susceptible to other means of prevention, reduction, or elimination.

(e) Field laboratory and research facilities

The Administrator shall establish, equip, and maintain field laboratory and research facilities, including, but not limited to, one to be located in the northeastern area of the United States, one in the Middle Atlantic area, one in the southeastern area, one in the midwestern area, one in the southwestern area, one in the Pacific Northwest, and one in the State of Alaska, for the conduct of research, investigations, experiments, field demonstrations and studies, and training relating to the prevention, reduction and elimination of pollution. Insofar as practicable, each such facility shall be located near institutions of higher learning in which graduate training in such research might be carried out. In conjunction with the development of criteria under section 1343 of this title, the Administrator shall construct the facilities authorized for the National Marine Water Quality Laboratory established under this subsection.

(f) Great Lakes water quality research

The Administrator shall conduct research and technical development work, and make studies, with respect to the quality of the waters of the Great Lakes, including an analysis of the present and projected future water quality of the Great Lakes under varying conditions of waste treatment and disposal, an evaluation of the water quality needs of those to be served by such waters, an evaluation of municipal, industrial, and vessel waste treatment and disposal practices with respect to such waters, and a study of alternate means of solving pollution problems (including additional waste treatment measures) with respect to such waters.

(g) Treatment works pilot training programs; employment needs forecasting; training projects and grants; research fellowships; technical training; report to the President and transmittal to Congress

(1) For the purpose of providing an adequate supply of trained personnel to operate and maintain existing and future treatment works and related activities, and for the purpose of enhancing substantially the proficiency of those engaged in such activities, the Administrator shall finance pilot programs, in cooperation with State and interstate agencies, municipalities, educational institutions, and other organizations and individuals, of manpower development and training and retraining of persons in, on entering into, the field of operation and mainte-

nance of treatment works and related activities. Such program and any funds expended for such a program shall supplement, not supplant, other manpower and training programs and funds available for the purposes of this paragraph. The Administrator is authorized, under such terms and conditions as he deems appropriate, to enter into agreements with one or more States, acting jointly or severally, or with other public or private agencies or institutions for the development and implementation of such a program.

(2) The Administrator is authorized to enter into agreements with public and private agencies and institutions, and individuals to develop and maintain an effective system for forecasting the supply of, and demand for, various professional and other occupational categories needed for the prevention, reduction, and elimination of pollution in each region, State, or area of the United States and, from time to time, to publish the results of such forecasts.

(3) In furtherance of the purposes of this chapter, the Administrator is authorized to—

(A) make grants to public or private agencies and institutions and to individuals for training projects, and provide for the conduct of training by contract with public or private agencies and institutions and with individuals without regard to section 3324(a) and (b) of title 31 and section 5 of title 41;

(B) establish and maintain research fellowships in the Environmental Protection Agency with such stipends and allowances, including traveling and subsistence expenses, as he may deem necessary to procure the assistance of the most promising research fellows; and

(C) provide, in addition to the program established under paragraph (1) of this subsection, training in technical matters relating to the causes, prevention, reduction, and elimination of pollution for personnel of public agencies and other persons with suitable qualifications.

(4) The Administrator shall submit, through the President, a report to the Congress not later than December 31, 1973, summarizing the actions taken under this subsection and the effectiveness of such actions, and setting forth the number of persons trained, the occupational categories for which training was provided, the effectiveness of other Federal, State, and local training programs in this field, together with estimates of future needs, recommendations on improving training programs, and such other information and recommendations, including legislative recommendations, as he deems appropriate.

(h) Lake pollution

The Administrator is authorized to enter into contracts with, or make grants to, public or private agencies and organizations and individuals for (A) the purpose of developing and demonstrating new or improved methods for the prevention, removal, reduction, and elimination of pollution in lakes, including the undesirable effects of nutrients and vegetation, and (B) the construction of publicly owned research facilities for such purpose.

(i) Oil pollution control studies

The Administrator, in cooperation with the Secretary of the Department in which the Coast Guard is operating, shall—

(1) engage in such research, studies, experiments, and demonstrations as he deems appropriate, relative to the removal of oil from any waters and to the prevention, control, and elimination of oil and hazardous substances pollution;

(2) publish from time to time the results of such activities; and

(3) from time to time, develop and publish in the Federal Register specifications and other technical information on the various chemical compounds used in the control of oil and hazardous substances spills.

In carrying out this subsection, the Administrator may enter into contracts with, or make grants to, public or private agencies and organizations and individuals.

(j) Solid waste disposal equipment for vessels

The Secretary of the department in which the Coast Guard is operating shall engage in such research, studies, experiments, and demonstrations as he deems appropriate relative to equipment which is to be installed on board a vessel and is designed to receive, retain, treat, or discharge human body wastes and the wastes from toilets and other receptacles intended to receive or retain body wastes with particular emphasis on equipment to be installed on small recreational vessels. The Secretary of the department in which the Coast Guard is operating shall report to Congress the results of such research, studies, experiments, and demonstrations prior to the effective date of any regulations established under section 1322 of this title. In carrying out this subsection the Secretary of the department in which the Coast Guard is operating may enter into contracts with, or make grants to, public or private organizations and individuals.

(k) Land acquisition

In carrying out the provisions of this section relating to the conduct by the Administrator of demonstration projects and the development of field laboratories and research facilities, the Administrator may acquire land and interests therein by purchase, with appropriated or donated funds, by donation, or by exchange for acquired or public lands under his jurisdiction which he classifies as suitable for disposition. The values of the properties so exchanged either shall be approximately equal, or if they are not approximately equal, the values shall be equalized by the payment of cash to the grantor or to the Administrator as the circumstances require.

(*l*) Collection and dissemination of scientific knowledge on effects and control of pesticides in water

(1) The Administrator shall, after consultation with appropriate local, State, and Federal agencies, public and private organizations, and interested individuals, as soon as practicable but not later than January 1, 1973, develop and issue to the States for the purpose of carrying out this chapter the latest scientific knowledge available

in indicating the kind and extent of effects on health and welfare which may be expected from the presence of pesticides in the water in varying quantities. He shall revise and add to such information whenever necessary to reflect developing scientific knowledge.

(2) The President shall, in consultation with appropriate local, State, and Federal agencies, public and private organizations, and interested individuals, conduct studies and investigations of methods to control the release of pesticides into the environment which study shall include examination of the persistency of pesticides in the water environment and alternatives thereto. The President shall submit reports, from time to time, on such investigations to Congress together with his recommendations for any necessary legislation.

(m) Waste oil disposal study

(1) The Administrator shall, in an effort to prevent degradation of the environment from the disposal of waste oil, conduct a study of (A) the generation of used engine, machine, cooling, and similar waste oil, including quantities generated, the nature and quality of such oil, present collecting methods and disposal practices, and alternate uses of such oil; (B) the long-term, chronic biological effects of the disposal of such waste oil; and (C) the potential market for such oils, including the economic and legal factors relating to the sale of products made from such oils, the level of subsidy, if any, needed to encourage the purchase by public and private nonprofit agencies of products from such oil, and the practicability of Federal procurement, on a priority basis, of products made from such oil. In conducting such study, the Administrator shall consult with affected industries and other persons.

(2) The Administrator shall report the preliminary results of such study to Congress within six months after October 18, 1972, and shall submit a final report to Congress within 18 months after such date.

(n) Comprehensive studies of effects of pollution on estuaries and estuarine zones

(1) The Administrator shall, in cooperation with the Secretary of the Army, the Secretary of Agriculture, the Water Resources Council, and with other appropriate Federal, State, interstate, or local public bodies and private organizations, institutions, and individuals, conduct and promote, and encourage contributions to, continuing comprehensive studies of the effects of pollution, including sedimentation, in the estuaries and estuarine zones of the United States on fish and wildlife, on sport and commercial fishing, on recreation, on water supply and water power, and on other beneficial purposes. Such studies shall also consider the effect of demographic trends, the exploitation of mineral resources and fossil fuels, land and industrial development, navigation, flood and erosion control, and other uses of estuaries and estuarine zones upon the pollution of the waters therein.

(2) In conducting such studies, the Administrator shall assemble, coordinate, and organize all existing pertinent information on the Nation's estuaries and estuarine zones; carry out a program of investigations and surveys to supplement existing information in representative estuaries and estuarine zones; and identify the problems and areas where further research and study are required.

(3) The Administrator shall submit to Congress, from time to time, reports of the studies authorized by this subsection but at least one such report during any six-year period. Copies of each such report shall be made available to all interested parties, public and private.

(4) For the purpose of this subsection, the term "estuarine zones" means an environmental system consisting of an estuary and those transitional areas which are consistently influenced or affected by water from an estuary such as, but not limited to, salt marshes, coastal and intertidal areas, bays, harbors, lagoons, inshore waters, and channels, and the term "estuary" means all or part of the mouth of a river or stream or other body of water having unimpaired natural connection with open sea and within which the sea water is measurably diluted with fresh water derived from land drainage.

(*o*) Methods of reducing total flow of sewage and unnecessary water consumption; reports

(1) The Administrator shall conduct research and investigations on devices, systems, incentives, pricing policy, and other methods of reducing the total flow of sewage, including, but not limited to, unnecessary water consumption in order to reduce the requirements for, and the costs of, sewage and waste treatment services. Such research and investigations shall be directed to develop devices, systems, policies, and methods capable of achieving the maximum reduction of unnecessary water consumption.

(2) The Administrator shall report the preliminary results of such studies and investigations to the Congress within one year after October 18, 1972, and annually thereafter in the report required under subsection (a) of section 1375 of this title. Such report shall include recommendations for any legislation that may be required to provide for the adoption and use of devices, systems, policies, or other methods of reducing water consumption and reducing the total flow of sewage. Such report shall include an estimate of the benefits to be derived from adoption and use of such devices, systems, policies, or other methods and also shall reflect estimates of any increase in private, public, or other cost that would be occasioned thereby.

(p) Agricultural pollution

In carrying out the provisions of subsection (a) of this section the Administrator shall, in cooperation with the Secretary of Agriculture, other Federal agencies, and the States, carry out a comprehensive study and research program to determine new and improved methods and the better application of existing methods of preventing, reducing, and eliminating pollution from agriculture, including the legal, economic, and other implications of the use of such methods.

(q) Sewage in rural areas; national clearinghouse for alternative treatment information; clearinghouse on small flows

(1) The Administrator shall conduct a comprehensive program of research and investigation and pilot project implementation into new and improved methods of preventing, reducing, storing, collecting, treating, or otherwise eliminating pollution from sewage in rural and other areas where collection of sewage in conventional, communitywide sewage collection systems is impractical, uneconomical, or otherwise infeasible, or where soil conditions or other factors preclude the use of septic tank and drainage field systems.

(2) The Administrator shall conduct a comprehensive program of research and investigation and pilot project implementation into new and improved methods for the collection and treatment of sewage and other liquid wastes combined with the treatment and disposal of solid wastes.

(3) The Administrator shall establish, either within the Environmental Protection Agency, or through contract with an appropriate public or private non-profit organization, a national clearinghouse which shall (A) receive reports and information resulting from research, demonstrations, and other projects funded under this chapter related to paragraph (1) of this subsection and to subsection (e)(2) of section 1255 of this title; (B) coordinate and disseminate such reports and information for use by Federal and State agencies, municipalities, institutions, and persons in developing new and improved methods pursuant to this subsection; and (C) provide for the collection and dissemination of reports and information relevant to this subsection from other Federal and State agencies, institutions, universities, and persons.

(4) SMALL FLOWS CLEARINGHOUSE.—Notwithstanding section 1285(d) of this title, from amounts that are set aside for a fiscal year under section 1285(i) of this title and are not obligated by the end of the 24-month period of availability for such amounts under section 1285(d) of this title, the Administrator shall make available $1,000,000 or such unobligated amount, whichever is less, to support a national clearinghouse within the Environmental Protection Agency to collect and disseminate information on small flows of sewage and innovative or alternative wastewater treatment processes and techniques, consistent with paragraph (3). This paragraph shall apply with respect to amounts set aside under section 1285(i) of this title for which the 24-month period of availability referred to in the preceding sentence ends on or after September 30, 1986.

(r) Research grants to colleges and universities

The Administrator is authorized to make grants to colleges and universities to conduct basic research into the structure and function of freshwater aquatic ecosystems, and to improve understanding of the ecological characteristics necessary to the maintenance of the chemical, physical, and biological integrity of freshwater aquatic ecosystems.

(s) River Study Centers

The Administrator is authorized to make grants to one or more institutions of higher education (regionally located and to be designated as "River Study Centers") for the purpose of conducting and reporting on interdisciplinary studies on the nature of river systems, including hydrology, biology, ecology, economics, the relationship between river uses and land uses, and the effects of development within river basins on river systems and on the value of water resources and water related activities. No such grant in any fiscal year shall exceed $1,000,000.

(t) Thermal discharges

The Administrator shall, in cooperation with State and Federal agencies and public and private organizations, conduct continuing comprehensive studies of the effects and methods of control of thermal discharges. In evaluating alternative methods of control the studies shall consider (1) such data as are available on the latest available technology, economic feasibility including cost-effectiveness analysis, and (2) the total impact on the environment, considering not only water quality but also air quality, land use, and effective utilization and conservation of freshwater and other natural resources. Such studies shall consider methods of minimizing adverse effects and maximizing beneficial effects of thermal discharges. The results of these studies shall be reported by the Administrator as soon as practicable, but not later than 270 days after October 18, 1972, and shall be made available to the public and the States, and considered as they become available by the Administrator in carrying out section 1326 of this title and by the States in proposing thermal water quality standards.

(u) Authorization of appropriations

There is authorized to be appropriated (1) not to exceed $100,000,000 per fiscal year for the fiscal year ending June 30, 1973, the fiscal year ending June 30, 1974, and the fiscal year ending June 30, 1975, not to exceed $14,039,000 for the fiscal year ending September 30, 1980, not to exceed $20,697,000 for the fiscal year ending September 30, 1981, not to exceed $22,770,000 for the fiscal year ending September 30, 1982, such sums as may be necessary for fiscal years 1983 through 1985, and not to exceed $22,770,000 per fiscal year for each of the fiscal years 1986 through 1990, for carrying out the provisions of this section, other than subsections (g)(1) and (2), (p), (r), and (t) of this section, except that such authorizations are not for any research, development, or demonstration activity pursuant to such provisions; (2) not to exceed $7,500,000 for fiscal years 1973, 1974, and 1975, $2,000,000 for fiscal year 1977, $3,000,000 for fiscal year 1978, $3,000,000 for fiscal year 1979, $3,000,000 for fiscal year 1980, $3,000,000 for fiscal year 1981, $3,000,000 for fiscal year 1982, such sums as may be necessary for fiscal years 1983 through 1985, and $3,000,000 per fiscal year for each of the fiscal years 1986 through 1990, for carrying out the provisions of subsection (g)(1) of this section; (3) not to exceed $2,500,000 for fiscal years 1973, 1974, and 1975, $1,000,000 for fiscal year 1977, $1,500,000 for fiscal year 1978, $1,500,000 for fiscal year 1979, $1,500,000 for fiscal year 1980, $1,500,000 for fiscal year 1981, $1,500,000 for fiscal year 1982, such sums as may be necessary for fiscal years 1983 through 1985, and $1,500,000 per fiscal year for each of the fiscal years 1986 through

1990, for carrying out the provisions of subsection (g)(2) of this section; (4) not to exceed $10,000,000 for each of the fiscal years ending June 30, 1973, June 30, 1974, and June 30, 1975, for carrying out the provisions of subsection (p) of this section; (5) not to exceed $15,000,000 per fiscal year for the fiscal years ending June 30, 1973, June 30, 1974, and June 30, 1975, for carrying out the provisions of subsection (r) of this section; and (6) not to exceed $10,000,000 per fiscal year for the fiscal years ending June 30, 1973, June 30, 1974, and June 30, 1975, for carrying out the provisions of subsection (t) of this section.

(v) Studies concerning pathogen indicators in coastal recreation waters

Not later than 18 months after October 10, 2000, after consultation and in cooperation with appropriate Federal, State, tribal, and local officials (including local health officials), the Administrator shall initiate, and, not later than 3 years after October 10, 2000, shall complete, in cooperation with the heads of other Federal agencies, studies to provide additional information for use in developing—

(1) an assessment of potential human health risks resulting from exposure to pathogens in coastal recreation waters, including nongastrointestinal effects;

(2) appropriate and effective indicators for improving detection in a timely manner in coastal recreation waters of the presence of pathogens that are harmful to human health;

(3) appropriate, accurate, expeditious, and cost-effective methods (including predictive models) for detecting in a timely manner in coastal recreation waters the presence of pathogens that are harmful to human health; and

(4) guidance for State application of the criteria for pathogens and pathogen indicators to be published under section 1314(a)(9) of this title to account for the diversity of geographic and aquatic conditions.

(June 30, 1948, ch. 758, title I, §104, as added Pub. L. 92–500, §2, Oct. 18, 1972, 86 Stat. 819; amended Pub. L. 93–207, §1(1), Dec. 28, 1973, 87 Stat. 906; Pub. L. 93–592, §1, Jan. 2, 1975, 88 Stat. 1924; Pub. L. 95–217, §§4(a), (b), 6, 7, Dec. 27, 1977, 91 Stat. 1566, 1567; Pub. L. 95–576, §1(a), Nov. 2, 1978, 92 Stat. 2467; Pub. L. 96–88, title V, §509(b), Oct. 17, 1979, 93 Stat. 695; Pub. L. 96–483, §1(a), Oct. 21, 1980, 94 Stat. 2360; Pub. L. 100–4, title I, §§101(a), 102, Feb. 4, 1987, 101 Stat. 8, 9; Pub. L. 102–154, title I, Nov. 13, 1991, 105 Stat. 1000; Pub. L. 105–362, title V, §501(a)(1), (d)(2)(A), Nov. 10, 1998, 112 Stat. 3283; Pub. L. 106–284, §3(a), Oct. 10, 2000, 114 Stat. 871; Pub. L. 107–303, title III, §302(b)(1), Nov. 27, 2002, 116 Stat. 2361.)

CODIFICATION

In subsecs. (b)(4) and (g)(3)(A), "section 3324(a) and (b) of title 31" substituted for reference to section 3648 of the Revised Statutes [31 U.S.C. 529] on authority of Pub. L. 97–258, §4(b), Sept. 13, 1982, 96 Stat. 1067, the first section of which enacted Title 31, Money and Finance.

AMENDMENTS

2002—Subsecs. (a)(5), (n)(3), (4), (*o*)(2). Pub. L. 107–303 repealed Pub. L. 105–362, §501(a), (d). See 1998 Amendment notes below.

2000—Subsec. (v). Pub. L. 106–284 added subsec. (v).

1998—Subsec. (a)(5). Pub. L. 105–362, §501(d)(2)(A)(i), which directed the substitution of "not later than 90 days after the date of convening of each session of Congress" for "in the report required under subsection (a) of section 1375 of this title", was repealed by Pub. L. 107–303. See Effective Date of 2002 Amendment note below.

Subsec. (n)(3), (4). Pub. L. 105–362, §501(a)(1), which directed the redesignation of par. (4) as (3) and striking out of former par. (3), was repealed by Pub. L. 107–303. See Effective Date of 2002 Amendment note below.

Subsec. (*o*)(2). Pub. L. 105–362, §501(d)(2)(A)(ii), which directed the substitution of "not later than 90 days after the date of convening of each session of Congress" for "in the report required under subsection (a) of section 1375 of this title", was repealed by Pub. L. 107–303. See Effective Date of 2002 Amendment note below.

1987—Subsec. (q)(4). Pub. L. 100–4, §102, added par. (4).

Subsec. (u). Pub. L. 100–4, §101(a), in cl. (1) struck out "and" after "1975,", "1980,", and "1981," and inserted "such sums as may be necessary for fiscal years 1983 through 1985, and not to exceed $22,770,000 per fiscal year for each of the fiscal years 1986 through 1990,", in cl. (2) struck out "and" after "1981," and inserted "such sums as may be necessary for fiscal years 1983 through 1985, and $3,000,000 per fiscal year for each of the fiscal years 1986 through 1990,", and in cl. (3) struck out "and" after "1981," and inserted "such sums as may be necessary for fiscal years 1983 through 1985, and $1,500,000 per fiscal year for each of the fiscal years 1986 through 1990,".

1980—Subsec. (u). Pub. L. 96–483 in par. (1) inserted authorization of not to exceed $20,697,000 and $22,770,000 for fiscal years ending Sept. 30, 1981, and 1982, respectively; in par. (2) inserted authorization of the sum of $3,000,000 for each of fiscal years 1981 and 1982; and in par. (3) inserted authorization of the sum of $1,500,000 for each of fiscal years 1981 and 1982.

1978—Subsec. (u)(1). Pub. L. 95–576 authorized appropriation of not to exceed $14,039,000 for fiscal year ending Sept. 30, 1980 and prohibited use of authorizations for any research, development, or demonstration activity pursuant to provisions of this section.

1977—Subsec. (n)(3). Pub. L. 95–217, §6, substituted "any six-year period" for "any three year period".

Subsec. (q)(3). Pub. L. 95–217, §7, added par. (3).

Subsec. (u)(2). Pub. L. 95–217, §4(a), substituted "1975, $2,000,000 for fiscal year 1977, $3,000,000 for fiscal year 1978, $3,000,000 for fiscal year 1979, and $3,000,000 for fiscal year 1980," for "1975".

Subsec. (u)(3). Pub. L. 95–217, §4(b), substituted "1975, $1,000,000 for fiscal year 1977, $1,500,000 for fiscal year 1978, $1,500,000 for fiscal year 1979, and $1,500,000 for fiscal year 1980," for "1975".

1975—Subsec. (u)(1). Pub. L. 93–592, §1(a), substituted "the fiscal year ending June 30, 1974, and the fiscal year ending June 30, 1975," for "and the fiscal year ending June 30, 1974,".

Subsec. (u)(2). Pub. L. 93–592, §1(b), substituted "fiscal years 1973, 1974, and 1975" for "fiscal years 1973 and 1974".

Subsec. (u)(3). Pub. L. 93–592, §1(c), substituted "fiscal years 1973, 1974, and 1975" for "fiscal year 1973".

Subsec. (u)(4), (5), (6). Pub. L. 93–592, §1(d)–(f), substituted "June 30, 1974, and June 30, 1975," for "and June 30, 1974,".

1973—Subsec. (u)(2). Pub. L. 93–207 substituted "fiscal years 1973 and 1974" for "fiscal year 1973".

CHANGE OF NAME

"United States Geological Survey" substituted for "Geological Survey" in subsec. (a)(5) pursuant to provision of title I of Pub. L. 102–154, set out as a note under section 31 of Title 43, Public Lands.

"Secretary of Health and Human Services" substituted for "Secretary of Health, Education, and Welfare" in subsec. (c) pursuant to section 509(b) of Pub. L. 96–88 which is classified to section 3508(b) of Title 20, Education.

EFFECTIVE DATE OF 2002 AMENDMENT

Pub. L. 107–303, title III, §302(b), Nov. 27, 2002, 116 Stat. 2361, provided that:

"(1) IN GENERAL.—Effective November 10, 1998, section 501 of the Federal Reports Elimination Act of 1998 (Public Law 105–362; 112 Stat. 3283) is amended by striking subsections (a) [amending this section and section 1330 of this title], (b) [amending section 1324 of this title], (c) [amending section 1329 of this title], and (d) [amending this section and sections 1266, 1285, 1290, and 1375 of this title].

"(2) APPLICABILITY.—The Federal Water Pollution Control Act (33 U.S.C. 1254(n)(3)) [33 U.S.C. 1251 et seq.] shall be applied and administered on and after the date of enactment of this Act [Nov. 27, 2002] as if the amendments made by subsections (a), (b), (c), and (d) of section 501 of the Federal Reports Elimination Act of 1998 (Public Law 105–362; 112 Stat. 3283) had not been enacted."

TRANSFER OF FUNCTIONS

For transfer of authorities, functions, personnel, and assets of the Coast Guard, including the authorities and functions of the Secretary of Transportation relating thereto, to the Department of Homeland Security, and for treatment of related references, see sections 468(b), 551(d), 552(d), and 557 of Title 6, Domestic Security, and the Department of Homeland Security Reorganization Plan of November 25, 2002, as modified, set out as a note under section 542 of Title 6.

Enforcement functions of Secretary or other official in Department of Agriculture, insofar as they involve lands and programs under jurisdiction of that Department, related to compliance with this chapter with respect to pre-construction, construction, and initial operation of transportation system for Canadian and Alaskan natural gas were transferred to the Federal Inspector, Office of Federal Inspector for the Alaska Natural Gas Transportation System, until the first anniversary of date of initial operation of the Alaska Natural Gas Transportation System, see Reorg. Plan No. 1 of 1979, §§102(f), 203(a), 44 F.R. 33663, 33666, 93 Stat. 1373, 1376, effective July 1, 1979, set out in the Appendix to Title 5, Government Organization and Employees. Office of Federal Inspector for the Alaska Natural Gas Transportation System abolished and functions and authority vested in Inspector transferred to Secretary of Energy by section 3012(b) of Pub. L. 102–486, set out as an Abolition of Office of Federal Inspector note under section 719e of Title 15, Commerce and Trade. Functions and authority vested in Secretary of Energy subsequently transferred to Federal Coordinator for Alaska Natural Gas Transportation Projects by section 720d(f) of Title 15.

COLUMBIA RIVER BASIN SYSTEM; PROTECTION FROM OIL SPILLS AND DISCHARGES; CRITERIA FOR EVALUATION AND REPORT TO CONGRESS BY COMMANDANT OF COAST GUARD IN CONSULTATION WITH FEDERAL, ETC., AGENCIES

Pub. L. 95–308, §8, June 30, 1978, 92 Stat. 359, set forth Congressional findings and declarations and evaluation criteria with respect to protection from oil spills and discharges and betterment of the Columbia River Basin system, with such evaluation by the Commandant of the Coast Guard to begin within 180 days after June 30, 1978, and immediate submission of the evaluation to appropriate Congressional committees.

CONTIGUOUS ZONE OF UNITED STATES

For extension of contiguous zone of United States, see Proc. No. 7219, set out as a note under section 1331 of Title 43, Public Lands.

§ 1254a. Research on effects of pollutants

In carrying out the provisions of section 1254(a) of this title, the Administrator shall conduct research on the harmful effects on the health and welfare of persons caused by pollutants in water, in conjunction with the United States Fish and Wildlife Service, the National Oceanic and Atmospheric Administration, and other Federal, State, and interstate agencies carrying on such research. Such research shall include, and shall place special emphasis on, the effect that bioaccumulation of these pollutants in aquatic species has upon reducing the value of aquatic commercial and sport industries. Such research shall further study methods to reduce and remove these pollutants from the relevant affected aquatic species so as to restore and enhance these valuable resources.

(Pub. L. 100–4, title I, §105, Feb. 4, 1987, 101 Stat. 15.)

CODIFICATION

Section was enacted as part of the Water Quality Act of 1987, and not as part of the Federal Water Pollution Control Act which comprises this chapter.

DEFINITION

Administrator means the Administrator of the Environmental Protection Agency, see section 1(d) of Pub. L. 100–4, set out as a note under section 1251 of this title.

§ 1255. Grants for research and development

(a) Demonstration projects covering storm waters, advanced waste treatment and water purification methods, and joint treatment systems for municipal and industrial wastes

The Administrator is authorized to conduct in the Environmental Protection Agency, and to make grants to any State, municipality, or intermunicipal or interstate agency for the purpose of assisting in the development of—

(1) any project which will demonstrate a new or improved method of preventing, reducing, and eliminating the discharge into any waters of pollutants from sewers which carry storm water or both storm water and pollutants; or

(2) any project which will demonstrate advanced waste treatment and water purification methods (including the temporary use of new or improved chemical additives which provide substantial immediate improvements to existing treatment processes), or new or improved methods of joint treatment systems for municipal and industrial wastes;

and to include in such grants such amounts as are necessary for the purpose of reports, plans, and specifications in connection therewith.

(b) Demonstration projects for advanced treatment and environmental enhancement techniques to control pollution in river basins

The Administrator is authorized to make grants to any State or States or interstate agency to demonstrate, in river basins or portions thereof, advanced treatment and environmental enhancement techniques to control pollution from all sources, within such basins or portions thereof, including nonpoint sources, together with in stream[1] water quality improvement techniques.

[1] So in original.

(c) Research and demonstration projects for prevention of water pollution by industry

In order to carry out the purposes of section 1311 of this title, the Administrator is authorized to (1) conduct in the Environmental Protection Agency, (2) make grants to persons, and (3) enter into contracts with persons, for research and demonstration projects for prevention of pollution of any waters by industry including, but not limited to, the prevention, reduction, and elimination of the discharge of pollutants. No grant shall be made for any project under this subsection unless the Administrator determines that such project will develop or demonstrate a new or improved method of treating industrial wastes or otherwise prevent pollution by industry, which method shall have industry-wide application.

(d) Accelerated and priority development of waste management and waste treatment methods and identification and measurement methods

In carrying out the provisions of this section, the Administrator shall conduct, on a priority basis, an accelerated effort to develop, refine, and achieve practical application of:

(1) waste management methods applicable to point and nonpoint sources of pollutants to eliminate the discharge of pollutants, including, but not limited to, elimination of runoff of pollutants and the effects of pollutants from inplace or accumulated sources;

(2) advanced waste treatment methods applicable to point and nonpoint sources, including inplace or accumulated sources of pollutants, and methods for reclaiming and recycling water and confining pollutants so they will not migrate to cause water or other environmental pollution; and

(3) improved methods and procedures to identify and measure the effects of pollutants on the chemical, physical, and biological integrity of water, including those pollutants created by new technological developments.

(e) Research and demonstration projects covering agricultural pollution and pollution from sewage in rural areas; dissemination of information

(1) The Administrator is authorized to (A) make, in consultation with the Secretary of Agriculture, grants to persons for research and demonstration projects with respect to new and improved methods of preventing, reducing, and eliminating pollution from agriculture, and (B) disseminate, in cooperation with the Secretary of Agriculture, such information obtained under this subsection, section 1254(p) of this title, and section 1314 of this title as will encourage and enable the adoption of such methods in the agricultural industry.

(2) The Administrator is authorized, (A) in consultation with other interested Federal agencies, to make grants for demonstration projects with respect to new and improved methods of preventing, reducing, storing, collecting, treating, or otherwise eliminating pollution from sewage in rural and other areas where collection of sewage in conventional, community-wide sewage collection systems is impractical, uneconomical, or otherwise infeasible, or where soil conditions or other factors preclude the use of septic tank and drainage field systems, and (B) in cooperation with other interested Federal and State agencies, to disseminate such information obtained under this subsection as will encourage and enable the adoption of new and improved methods developed pursuant to this subsection.

(f) Limitations

Federal grants under subsection (a) of this section shall be subject to the following limitations:

(1) No grant shall be made for any project unless such project shall have been approved by the appropriate State water pollution control agency or agencies and by the Administrator;

(2) No grant shall be made for any project in an amount exceeding 75 per centum of cost thereof as determined by the Administrator; and

(3) No grant shall be made for any project unless the Administrator determines that such project will serve as a useful demonstration for the purpose set forth in clause (1) or (2) of subsection (a) of this section.

(g) Maximum grants

Federal grants under subsections (c) and (d) of this section shall not exceed 75 per centum of the cost of the project.

(h) Authorization of appropriations

For the purpose of this section there is authorized to be appropriated $75,000,000 per fiscal year for the fiscal year ending June 30, 1973, the fiscal year ending June 30, 1974, and the fiscal year ending June 30, 1975, and from such appropriations at least 10 per centum of the funds actually appropriated in each fiscal year shall be available only for the purposes of subsection (e) of this section.

(i) Assistance for research and demonstration projects

The Administrator is authorized to make grants to a municipality to assist in the costs of operating and maintaining a project which received a grant under this section, section 1254 of this title, or section 1263 of this title prior to December 27, 1977, so as to reduce the operation and maintenance costs borne by the recipients of services from such project to costs comparable to those for projects assisted under subchapter II of this chapter.

(j) Assistance for recycle, reuse, and land treatment projects

The Administrator is authorized to make a grant to any grantee who received an increased grant pursuant to section 1282(a)(2) of this title. Such grant may pay up to 100 per centum of the costs of technical evaluation of the operation of the treatment works, costs of training of persons (other than employees of the grantee), and costs of disseminating technical information on the operation of the treatment works.

(June 30, 1948, ch. 758, title I, §105, as added Pub. L. 92–500, §2, Oct. 18, 1972, 86 Stat. 825; amended Pub. L. 93–592, §2, Jan. 2, 1975, 88 Stat. 1925; Pub. L. 95–217, §§8, 9, Dec. 27, 1977, 91 Stat. 1568.)

AMENDMENTS

1977—Subsecs. (i), (j). Pub. L. 95–217 added subsecs. (i) and (j).

1975—Subsec. (h). Pub. L. 93–592 substituted "the fiscal year ending June 30, 1974, and the fiscal year ending June 30, 1975," for "and the fiscal year ending June 30, 1974,".

TRANSFER OF FUNCTIONS

Enforcement functions of Secretary or other official in Department of Agriculture, insofar as they involve lands and programs under jurisdiction of that Department, related to compliance with this chapter with respect to pre-construction, construction, and initial operation of transportation system for Canadian and Alaskan natural gas were transferred to the Federal Inspector, Office of Federal Inspector for the Alaska Natural Gas Transportation System, until the first anniversary of date of initial operation of the Alaska Natural Gas Transportation System, see Reorg. Plan No. 1 of 1979, §§102(f), 203(a), 44 F.R. 33663, 33666, 93 Stat. 1373, 1376, effective July 1, 1979, set out in the Appendix to Title 5, Government Organization and Employees. Office of Federal Inspector for the Alaska Natural Gas Transportation System abolished and functions and authority vested in Inspector transferred to Secretary of Energy by section 3012(b) of Pub. L. 102–486, set out as an Abolition of Office of Federal Inspector note under section 719e of Title 15, Commerce and Trade. Functions and authority vested in Secretary of Energy subsequently transferred to Federal Coordinator for Alaska Natural Gas Transportation Projects by section 720d(f) of Title 15.

§1256. Grants for pollution control programs

(a) Authorization of appropriations for State and interstate programs

There are hereby authorized to be appropriated the following sums, to remain available until expended, to carry out the purpose of this section—

(1) $60,000,000 for the fiscal year ending June 30, 1973; and

(2) $75,000,000 for the fiscal year ending June 30, 1974, and the fiscal year ending June 30, 1975, $100,000,000 per fiscal year for the fiscal years 1977, 1978, 1979, and 1980, $75,000,000 per fiscal year for the fiscal years 1981 and 1982, such sums as may be necessary for fiscal years 1983 through 1985, and $75,000,000 per fiscal year for each of the fiscal years 1986 through 1990;

for grants to States and to interstate agencies to assist them in administering programs for the prevention, reduction, and elimination of pollution, including enforcement directly or through appropriate State law enforcement officers or agencies.

(b) Allotments

From the sums appropriated in any fiscal year, the Administrator shall make allotments to the several States and interstate agencies in accordance with regulations promulgated by him on the basis of the extent of the pollution problem in the respective States.

(c) Maximum annual payments

The Administrator is authorized to pay to each State and interstate agency each fiscal year either—

(1) the allotment of such State or agency for such fiscal year under subsection (b) of this section, or

(2) the reasonable costs as determined by the Administrator of developing and carrying out a pollution program by such State or agency during such fiscal year,

which ever amount is the lesser.

(d) Limitations

No grant shall be made under this section to any State or interstate agency for any fiscal year when the expenditure of non-Federal funds by such State or interstate agency during such fiscal year for the recurrent expenses of carrying out its pollution control program are less than the expenditure by such State or interstate agency of non-Federal funds for such recurrent program expenses during the fiscal year ending June 30, 1971.

(e) Grants prohibited to States not establishing water quality monitoring procedures or adequate emergency and contingency plans

Beginning in fiscal year 1974 the Administrator shall not make any grant under this section to any State which has not provided or is not carrying out as a part of its program—

(1) the establishment and operation of appropriate devices, methods, systems, and procedures necessary to monitor, and to compile and analyze data on (including classification according to eutrophic condition), the quality of navigable waters and to the extent practicable, ground waters including biological monitoring; and provision for annually updating such data and including it in the report required under section 1315 of this title;

(2) authority comparable to that in section 1364 of this title and adequate contingency plans to implement such authority.

(f) Conditions

Grants shall be made under this section on condition that—

(1) Such State (or interstate agency) files with the Administrator within one hundred and twenty days after October 18, 1972:

(A) a summary report of the current status of the State pollution control program, including the criteria used by the State in determining priority of treatment works; and

(B) such additional information, data, and reports as the Administrator may require.

(2) No federally assumed enforcement as defined in section 1319(a)(2) of this title is in effect with respect to such State or interstate agency.

(3) Such State (or interstate agency) submits within one hundred and twenty days after October 18, 1972, and before October 1 of each year thereafter for the Administrator's approval of its program for the prevention, reduction, and elimination of pollution in accordance with purposes and provisions of this chapter in such form and content as the Administrator may prescribe.

(g) Reallotment of unpaid allotments

Any sums allotted under subsection (b) of this section in any fiscal year which are not paid shall be reallotted by the Administrator in accordance with regulations promulgated by him.

(June 30, 1948, ch. 758, title I, §106, as added Pub. L. 92–500, §2, Oct. 18, 1972, 86 Stat. 827; amended Pub. L. 93–592, §3, Jan. 2, 1975, 88 Stat. 1925; Pub.

L. 94–273, §3(20), Apr. 21, 1976, 90 Stat. 377; Pub. L. 95–217, §4(c), Dec. 27, 1977, 91 Stat. 1566; Pub. L. 96–483, §1(b), Oct. 21, 1980, 94 Stat. 2360; Pub. L. 100–4, title I, §101(b), Feb. 4, 1987, 101 Stat. 9.)

AMENDMENTS

1987—Subsec. (a)(2). Pub. L. 100–4 inserted ", such sums as may be necessary for fiscal years 1983 through 1985, and $75,000,000 per fiscal year for each of the fiscal years 1986 through 1990" after "1982".

1980—Subsec. (a)(2). Pub. L. 96–483 inserted authorization of the sum of $75,000,000 per fiscal year for fiscal years 1981 and 1982.

1977—Subsec. (a)(2). Pub. L. 95–217 substituted "and the fiscal year ending June 30, 1975, $100,000,000 per fiscal year for the fiscal years 1977, 1978, 1979, and 1980" for "and the fiscal year ending June 30, 1975".

1976—Subsec. (f)(3). Pub. L. 94–273 substituted "October" for "July".

1975—Subsec. (a)(2). Pub. L. 93–592 substituted "June 30, 1974, and the fiscal year ending June 30, 1975;" for "June 30, 1974;".

§1257. Mine water pollution control demonstrations

(a) Comprehensive approaches to elimination or control of mine water pollution

The Administrator in cooperation with the Appalachian Regional Commission and other Federal agencies is authorized to conduct, to make grants for, or to contract for, projects to demonstrate comprehensive approaches to the elimination or control of acid or other mine water pollution resulting from active or abandoned mining operations and other environmental pollution affecting water quality within all or part of a watershed or river basin, including siltation from surface mining. Such projects shall demonstrate the engineering and economic feasibility and practicality of various abatement techniques which will contribute substantially to effective and practical methods of acid or other mine water pollution elimination or control, and other pollution affecting water quality, including techniques that demonstrate the engineering and economic feasibility and practicality of using sewage sludge materials and other municipal wastes to diminish or prevent pollution affecting water quality from acid, sedimentation, or other pollutants and in such projects to restore affected lands to usefulness for forestry, agriculture, recreation, or other beneficial purposes.

(b) Consistency of projects with objectives of subtitle IV of title 40

Prior to undertaking any demonstration project under this section in the Appalachian region (as defined in section 14102(a)(1) and (b) of title 40), the Appalachian Regional Commission shall determine that such demonstration project is consistent with the objectives of subtitle IV of title 40.

(c) Watershed selection

The Administrator, in selecting watersheds for the purposes of this section, shall be satisfied that the project area will not be affected adversely by the influx of acid or other mine water pollution from nearby sources.

(d) Conditions upon Federal participation

Federal participation in such projects shall be subject to the conditions—

(1) that the State shall acquire any land or interests therein necessary for such project; and

(2) that the State shall provide legal and practical protection to the project area to insure against any activities which will cause future acid or other mine water pollution.

(e) Authorization of appropriations

There is authorized to be appropriated $30,000,000 to carry out the provisions of this section, which sum shall be available until expended.

(June 30, 1948, ch. 758, title I, §107, as added Pub. L. 92–500, §2, Oct. 18, 1972, 86 Stat. 828.)

CODIFICATION

In subsec. (b), "section 14102(a)(1) and (b) of title 40" substituted for "section 403 of the Appalachian Regional Development Act of 1965, as amended" and "subtitle IV of title 40" substituted for "the Appalachian Regional Development Act of 1965, as amended" on authority of Pub. L. 107–217, §5(c), Aug. 21, 2002, 116 Stat. 1303, the first section of which enacted Title 40, Public Buildings, Property, and Works.

§1257a. State demonstration programs for cleanup of abandoned mines for use as waste disposal sites; authorization of appropriations

The Administrator of the Environmental Protection Agency is authorized to make grants to States to undertake a demonstration program for the cleanup of State-owned abandoned mines which can be used as hazardous waste disposal sites. The State shall pay 10 per centum of project costs. At a minimum, the Administrator shall undertake projects under such program in the States of Ohio, Illinois, and West Virginia. There are authorized to be appropriated $10,000,000 per fiscal year for each of the fiscal years ending September 30, 1982, September 30, 1983, and September 30, 1984, to carry out this section. Such projects shall be undertaken in accordance with all applicable laws and regulations.

(Pub. L. 96–483, §12, Oct. 21, 1980, 94 Stat. 2363.)

CODIFICATION

Section was not enacted as part of the Federal Water Pollution Control Act which comprises this chapter.

§1258. Pollution control in the Great Lakes

(a) Demonstration projects

The Administrator, in cooperation with other Federal departments, agencies, and instrumentalities is authorized to enter into agreements with any State, political subdivision, interstate agency, or other public agency, or combination thereof, to carry out one or more projects to demonstrate new methods and techniques and to develop preliminary plans for the elimination or control of pollution, within all or any part of the watersheds of the Great Lakes. Such projects shall demonstrate the engineering and economic feasibility and practicality of removal of pollutants and prevention of any polluting matter from entering into the Great Lakes in the future and other reduction and remedial techniques which will contribute substantially to effective and practical methods of pollution prevention, reduction, or elimination.

(b) Conditions of Federal participation

Federal participation in such projects shall be subject to the condition that the State, political subdivision, interstate agency, or other public agency, or combination thereof, shall pay not less than 25 per centum of the actual project costs, which payment may be in any form, including, but not limited to, land or interests therein that is needed for the project, and personal property or services the value of which shall be determined by the Administrator.

(c) Authorization of appropriations

There is authorized to be appropriated $20,000,000 to carry out the provisions of subsections (a) and (b) of this section, which sum shall be available until expended.

(d) Lake Erie demonstration program

(1) In recognition of the serious conditions which exist in Lake Erie, the Secretary of the Army, acting through the Chief of Engineers, is directed to design and develop a demonstration waste water management program for the rehabilitation and environmental repair of Lake Erie. Prior to the initiation of detailed engineering and design, the program, along with the specific recommendations of the Chief of Engineers, and recommendations for its financing, shall be submitted to the Congress for statutory approval. This authority is in addition to, and not in lieu of, other waste water studies aimed at eliminating pollution emanating from select sources around Lake Erie.

(2) This program is to be developed in cooperation with the Environmental Protection Agency, other interested departments, agencies, and instrumentalities of the Federal Government, and the States and their political subdivisions. This program shall set forth alternative systems for managing waste water on a regional basis and shall provide local and State governments with a range of choice as to the type of system to be used for the treatment of waste water. These alternative systems shall include both advanced waste treatment technology and land disposal systems including aerated treatment-spray irrigation technology and will also include provisions for the disposal of solid wastes, including sludge. Such program should include measures to control point sources of pollution, area sources of pollution, including acid-mine drainage, urban runoff and rural runoff, and in place sources of pollution, including bottom loads, sludge banks, and polluted harbor dredgings.

(e) Authorization of appropriations for Lake Erie demonstration program

There is authorized to be appropriated $5,000,000 to carry out the provisions of subsection (d) of this section, which sum shall be available until expended.

(June 30, 1948, ch. 758, title I, § 108, as added Pub. L. 92–500, § 2, Oct. 18, 1972, 86 Stat. 828.)

§ 1259. Training grants and contracts

(a) The Administrator is authorized to make grants to or contracts with institutions of higher education, or combinations of such institutions, to assist them in planning, developing, strengthening, improving, or carrying out programs or projects for the preparation of undergraduate students to enter an occupation which involves the design, operation, and maintenance of treatment works, and other facilities whose purpose is water quality control. Such grants or contracts may include payment of all or part of the cost of programs or projects such as—

(A) planning for the development or expansion of programs or projects for training persons in the operation and maintenance of treatment works;

(B) training and retraining of faculty members;

(C) conduct of short-term or regular session institutes for study by persons engaged in, or preparing to engage in, the preparation of students preparing to enter an occupation involving the operation and maintenance of treatment works;

(D) carrying out innovative and experimental programs of cooperative education involving alternate periods of full-time or part-time academic study at the institution and periods of full-time or part-time employment involving the operation and maintenance of treatment works; and

(E) research into, and development of, methods of training students or faculty, including the preparation of teaching materials and the planning of curriculum.

(b)(1) The Administrator may pay 100 per centum of any additional cost of construction of treatment works required for a facility to train and upgrade waste treatment works operation and maintenance personnel and for the costs of other State treatment works operator training programs, including mobile training units, classroom rental, specialized instructors, and instructional material.

(2) The Administrator shall make no more than one grant for such additional construction in any State (to serve a group of States, where, in his judgment, efficient training programs require multi-State programs), and shall make such grant after consultation with and approval by the State or States on the basis of (A) the suitability of such facility for training operation and maintenance personnel for treatment works throughout such State or States; and (B) a commitment by the State agency or agencies to carry out at such facility a program of training approved by the Administrator. In any case where a grant is made to serve two or more States, the Administrator is authorized to make an additional grant for a supplemental facility in each such State.

(3) The Administrator may make such grant out of the sums allocated to a State under section 1285 of this title, except that in no event shall the Federal cost of any such training facilities exceed $500,000.

(4) The Administrator may exempt a grant under this section from any requirement under section 1284(a)(3) of this title. Any grantee who received a grant under this section prior to enactment of the Clean Water Act of 1977 shall be eligible to have its grant increased by funds made available under such Act.

(June 30, 1948, ch. 758, title I, §109, as added Pub. L. 92–500, §2, Oct. 18, 1972, 86 Stat. 829; amended Pub. L. 95–217, §10, Dec. 27, 1977, 91 Stat. 1568.)

REFERENCES IN TEXT

Prior to the date of enactment of the Clean Water Act of 1977, referred to in subsec. (b)(4), means prior to the enactment of Pub. L. 95–217, Dec. 27, 1977, 91 Stat. 1566, which was approved Dec. 27, 1977.

Such Act, referred to in subsec. (b)(4), means Pub. L. 95–217, Dec. 27, 1977, 91 Stat. 1566, as amended, known as the Clean Water Act of 1977. For complete classification of this Act to the Code, see Short Title of 1977 Amendment note set out under section 1251 of this title and Tables.

AMENDMENTS

1977—Subsec. (b)(1). Pub. L. 95–217, §10(c), (d), substituted "cost of construction of treatment works required for a facility to train and upgrade waste treatment works operation and maintenance personnel and for the costs of other State treatment works operator training programs, including mobile training units, classroom rental, specialized instructors, and instructional material" for "cost of construction of a treatment works required for a facility to train and upgrade waste treatment works operation and maintenance personnel".

Subsec. (b)(2). Pub. L. 95–217, §10(e), authorized Administrator to make an additional grant for a supplemental facility in each of the States in any case where a grant is made to serve two or more States.

Subsec. (b)(3). Pub. L. 95–217, §10(a), substituted "$500,000" for "$250,000".

Subsec. (b)(4). Pub. L. 95–217, §10(b), added par. (4).

§1260. Applications; allocation

(1) A grant or contract authorized by section 1259 of this title may be made only upon application to the Administrator at such time or times and containing such information as he may prescribe, except that no such application shall be approved unless it—

(A) sets forth programs, activities, research, or development for which a grant is authorized under section 1259 of this title and describes the relation to any program set forth by the applicant in an application, if any, submitted pursuant to section 1261 of this title;

(B) provides such fiscal control and fund accounting procedures as may be necessary to assure proper disbursement of and accounting for Federal funds paid to the applicant under this section; and

(C) provides for making such reports, in such form and containing such information, as the Administrator may require to carry out his functions under this section, and for keeping such records and for affording such access thereto as the Administrator may find necessary to assure the correctness and verification of such reports.

(2) The Administrator shall allocate grants or contracts under section 1259 of this title in such manner as will most nearly provide an equitable distribution of the grants or contracts throughout the United States among institutions of higher education which show promise of being able to use funds effectively for the purpose of this section.

(3)(A) Payments under this section may be used in accordance with regulations of the Administrator, and subject to the terms and conditions set forth in an application approved under paragraph (1), to pay part of the compensation of students employed in connection with the operation and maintenance of treatment works, other than as an employee in connection with the operation and maintenance of treatment works or as an employee in any branch of the Government of the United States, as part of a program for which a grant has been approved pursuant to this section.

(B) Departments and agencies of the United States are encouraged, to the extent consistent with efficient administration, to enter into arrangements with institutions of higher education for the full-time, part-time, or temporary employment, whether in the competitive or excepted service, of students enrolled in programs set forth in applications approved under paragraph (1).

(June 30, 1948, ch. 758, title I, §110, as added Pub. L. 92–500, §2, Oct. 18, 1972, 86 Stat. 830.)

§1261. Scholarships

(1) The Administrator is authorized to award scholarships in accordance with the provisions of this section for undergraduate study by persons who plan to enter an occupation involving the operation and maintenance of treatment works. Such scholarships shall be awarded for such periods as the Administrator may determine but not to exceed four academic years.

(2) The Administrator shall allocate scholarships under this section among institutions of higher education with programs approved under the provisions of this section for the use of individuals accepted into such programs in such manner and according to such plan as will insofar as practicable—

(A) provide an equitable distribution of such scholarships throughout the United States; and

(B) attract recent graduates of secondary schools to enter an occupation involving the operation and maintenance of treatment works.

(3) The Administrator shall approve a program of any institution of higher education for the purposes of this section only upon application by the institution and only upon his finding—

(A) that such program has a principal objective the education and training of persons in the operation and maintenance of treatment works;

(B) that such program is in effect and of high quality, or can be readily put into effect and may reasonably be expected to be of high quality;

(C) that the application describes the relation of such program to any program, activity, research, or development set forth by the applicant in an application, if any, submitted pursuant to section 1260 of this title; and

(D) that the application contains satisfactory assurances that (i) the institution will recommend to the Administrator for the award of scholarships under this section, for study in such program, only persons who have demonstrated to the satisfaction of the institution a serious intent, upon completing the program, to enter an occupation involving the operation and maintenance of treatment works, and (ii) the institution will make reasonable continuing efforts to encourage recipients of scholarships under this section, enrolled in such program, to enter occupations involving the operation and maintenance of treatment works upon completing the program.

(4)(A) The Administrator shall pay to persons awarded scholarships under this section such stipends (including such allowances for subsistence and other expenses for such persons and their dependents) as he may determine to be consistent with prevailing practices under comparable federally supported programs.

(B) The Administrator shall (in addition to the stipends paid to persons under paragraph (1)) pay to the institution of higher education at which such person is pursuing his course of study such amount as he may determine to be consistent with prevailing practices under comparable federally supported programs.

(5) A person awarded a scholarship under the provisions of this section shall continue to receive the payments provided in this section only during such periods as the Administrator finds that he is maintaining satisfactory proficiency and devoting full time to study or research in the field in which such scholarship was awarded in an institution of higher education, and is not engaging in gainful employment other than employment approved by the Administrator by or pursuant to regulation.

(6) The Administrator shall by regulation provide that any person awarded a scholarship under this section shall agree in writing to enter and remain in an occupation involving the design, operation, or maintenance of treatment works for such period after completion of his course of studies as the Administrator determines appropriate.

(June 30, 1948, ch. 758, title I, § 111, as added Pub. L. 92–500, § 2, Oct. 18, 1972, 86 Stat. 831.)

§ 1262. Definitions and authorizations

(a) As used in sections 1259 through 1262 of this title—

(1) The term "institution of higher education" means an educational institution described in the first sentence of section 1001 of title 20 (other than an institution of any agency of the United States) which is accredited by a nationally recognized accrediting agency or association approved by the Administrator for this purpose. For purposes of this subsection, the Administrator shall publish a list of nationally recognized accrediting agencies or associations which he determines to be reliable authority as to the quality of training offered.

(2) The term "academic year" means an academic year or its equivalent, as determined by the Administrator.

(b) The Administrator shall annually report his activities under sections 1259 through 1262 of this title, including recommendations for needed revisions in the provisions thereof.

(c) There are authorized to be appropriated $25,000,000 per fiscal year for the fiscal years ending June 30, 1973, June 30, 1974, and June 30, 1975, $6,000,000 for the fiscal year ending September 30, 1977, $7,000,000 for the fiscal year ending September 30, 1978, $7,000,000 for the fiscal year ending September 30, 1979, $7,000,000 for the fiscal year ending September 30, 1980, $7,000,000 for the fiscal year ending September 30, 1981, $7,000,000 for the fiscal year ending September 30, 1982, such sums as may be necessary for fiscal years 1983 through 1985, and $7,000,000 per fiscal year for each of the fiscal years 1986 through 1990, to carry out sections 1259 through 1262 of this title.

(June 30, 1948, ch. 758, title I, § 112, as added Pub. L. 92–500, § 2, Oct. 18, 1972, 86 Stat. 832; amended Pub. L. 93–592, § 4, Jan. 2, 1975, 88 Stat. 1925; Pub. L. 95–217, § 4(d), Dec. 27, 1977, 91 Stat. 1566; Pub. L. 96–483, § 1(c), Oct. 21, 1980, 94 Stat. 2360; Pub. L. 100–4, title I, § 101(c), Feb. 4, 1987, 101 Stat. 9; Pub. L. 105–244, title I, § 102(a)(11), Oct. 7, 1998, 112 Stat. 1620.)

AMENDMENTS

1998—Subsec. (a)(1). Pub. L. 105–244 substituted "section 1001" for "section 1141".

1987—Subsec. (c). Pub. L. 100–4 struck out "and" after "1981," and inserted "such sums as may be necessary for fiscal years 1983 through 1985, and $7,000,000 per fiscal year for each of the fiscal years 1986 through 1990," after "1982,".

1980—Subsec. (c). Pub. L. 96–483 inserted authorization of the sum of $7,000,000 for each of fiscal years ending Sept. 30, 1981 and 1982.

1977—Subsec. (c). Pub. L. 95–217 substituted "June 30, 1975, $6,000,000 for the fiscal year ending September 30, 1977, $7,000,000 for the fiscal year ending September 30, 1978, $7,000,000 for the fiscal year ending September 30, 1979, and $7,000,000 for the fiscal year ending September 30, 1980," for "June 30, 1975,".

1975—Subsec. (c). Pub. L. 93–592 substituted "June 30, 1974, and June 30, 1975," for "and June 30, 1974,".

EFFECTIVE DATE OF 1998 AMENDMENT

Amendment by Pub. L. 105–244 effective Oct. 1, 1998, except as otherwise provided in Pub. L. 105–244, see section 3 of Pub. L. 105–244, set out as a note under section 1001 of Title 20, Education.

§ 1263. Alaska village demonstration projects

(a) Central community facilities for safe water; elimination or control of pollution

The Administrator is authorized to enter into agreements with the State of Alaska to carry out one or more projects to demonstrate methods to provide for central community facilities for safe water and eliminate or control of pollution in those native villages of Alaska without such facilities. Such project shall include provisions for community safe water supply systems, toilets, bathing and laundry facilities, sewage disposal facilities, and other similar facilities, and educational and informational facilities and programs relating to health and hygiene. Such demonstration projects shall be for the further purpose of developing preliminary plans for providing such safe water and such elimination or control of pollution for all native villages in such State.

(b) Utilization of personnel and facilities of Department of Health and Human Services

In carrying out this section the Administrator shall cooperate with the Secretary of Health and Human Services for the purpose of utilizing such of the personnel and facilities of that Department as may be appropriate.

(c) Omitted

(d) Authorization of appropriations

There is authorized to be appropriated not to exceed $2,000,000 to carry out this section. In addition, there is authorized to be appropriated to carry out this section not to exceed $200,000 for the fiscal year ending September 30, 1978, and $220,000 for the fiscal year ending September 30, 1979.

(e) Study to develop comprehensive program for achieving sanitation services; report to Congress

The Administrator is authorized to coordinate with the Secretary of the Department of Health and Human Services, the Secretary of the Department of Housing and Urban Development, the Secretary of the Department of the Interior, the Secretary of the Department of Agriculture, and the heads of any other departments or agencies he may deem appropriate to conduct a joint study with representatives of the State of Alaska and the appropriate Native organizations (as defined in Public Law 92–203) to develop a comprehensive program for achieving adequate sanitation services in Alaska villages. This study shall be coordinated with the programs and projects authorized by sections 1254(q) and 1255(e)(2) of this title. The Administrator shall submit a report of the results of the study, together with appropriate supporting data and such recommendations as he deems desirable, to the Committee on Environment and Public Works of the Senate and to the Committee on Public Works and Transportation of the House of Representatives not later than December 31, 1979. The Administrator shall also submit recommended administrative actions, procedures, and any proposed legislation necessary to implement the recommendations of the study no later than June 30, 1980.

(f) Technical, financial, and management assistance

The Administrator is authorized to provide technical, financial and management assistance for operation and maintenance of the demonstration projects constructed under this section, until such time as the recommendations of subsection (e) of this section are implemented.

(g) "Village" and "sanitation services" defined

For the purpose of this section, the term "village" shall mean an incorporated or unincorporated community with a population of ten to six hundred people living within a two-mile radius. The term "sanitation services" shall mean water supply, sewage disposal, solid waste disposal and other services necessary to maintain generally accepted standards of personal hygiene and public health.

(June 30, 1948, ch. 758, title I, §113, as added Pub. L. 92–500, §2, Oct. 18, 1972, 86 Stat. 832; amended Pub. L. 95–217, §11, Dec. 27, 1977, 91 Stat. 1568; Pub. L. 96–88, title V, §509(b), Oct. 17, 1979, 93 Stat. 695.)

REFERENCES IN TEXT

Public Law 92–203, referred to in subsec. (e), is Pub. L. 92–203, Dec. 18, 1971, 85 Stat. 688, as amended, known as the Alaska Native Claims Settlement Act, which is classified generally to chapter 33 (§1601 et seq.) of Title 43, Public Lands. For complete classification of this Act to the Code, see Short Title note set out under section 1601 of Title 43 and Tables.

CODIFICATION

Subsec. (c) authorized the Administrator to report to Congress the results of the demonstration project accompanied by his recommendations for the establishment of a statewide project not later than July 1, 1973.

AMENDMENTS

1977—Subsec. (d). Pub. L. 95–217, §11(b), authorized additional appropriations of not to exceed $200,000 for the fiscal year ending Sept. 30, 1978, and $220,000, for the fiscal year ending Sept. 30, 1979, to carry out this section.

Subsecs. (e) to (g). Pub. L. 95–217, §11(a), added subsecs. (e), (f), and (g).

CHANGE OF NAME

"Secretary of Health and Human Services" substituted for "Secretary of Health, Education, and Welfare" in subsec. (b), and "Secretary of the Department of Health and Human Services" substituted for "Secretary of the Department of Health, Education, and Welfare" in subsec. (e), pursuant to section 509(b) of Pub. L. 96–88 which is classified to section 3508(b) of Title 20, Education.

Committee on Public Works and Transportation of House of Representatives treated as referring to Committee on Transportation and Infrastructure of House of Representatives by section 1(a) of Pub. L. 104–14, set out as a note preceding section 21 of Title 2, The Congress.

CORPS CAPABILITY STUDY, ALASKA

Pub. L. 104–303, title IV, §401, Oct. 12, 1996, 110 Stat. 3740, provided that: "Not later than 18 months after the date of the enactment of this Act [Oct. 12, 1996], the Secretary shall report to Congress on the advisability and capability of the Corps of Engineers to implement rural sanitation projects for rural and Native villages in Alaska."

§1263a. Grants to Alaska to improve sanitation in rural and Native villages

(a) In general

The Administrator of the Environmental Protection Agency may make grants to the State of Alaska for the benefit of rural and Native villages in Alaska to pay the Federal share of the cost of—

(1) the development and construction of public water systems and wastewater systems to improve the health and sanitation conditions in the villages; and

(2) training, technical assistance, and educational programs relating to the operation and management of sanitation services in rural and Native villages.

(b) Federal share

The Federal share of the cost of the activities described in subsection (a) of this section shall be 50 percent.

(c) Administrative expenses

The State of Alaska may use an amount not to exceed 4 percent of any grant made available under this subsection[1] for administrative expenses necessary to carry out the activities described in subsection (a) of this section.

(d) Consultation with State of Alaska

The Administrator shall consult with the State of Alaska on a method of prioritizing the

[1] So in original. Probably should be "section".

allocation of grants under subsection (a) of this section according to the needs of, and relative health and sanitation conditions in, each eligible village.

(e) Authorization of appropriations

There are authorized to be appropriated to carry out this section $40,000,000 for each of fiscal years 2001 through 2005.

(Pub. L. 104–182, title III, § 303, Aug. 6, 1996, 110 Stat. 1683; Pub. L. 106–457, title IX, § 903, Nov. 7, 2000, 114 Stat. 1982.)

CODIFICATION

Section was enacted as part of the Safe Drinking Water Act Amendments of 1996, and not as part of the Federal Water Pollution Control Act which comprises this chapter.

AMENDMENTS

2000—Subsec. (e). Pub. L. 106–457 substituted "to carry out this section $40,000,000 for each of fiscal years 2001 through 2005" for "$15,000,000 for each of the fiscal years 1997 through 2000 to carry out this section".

§ 1264. Omitted

CODIFICATION

Section, act June 30, 1948, ch. 758, title I, § 114, as added Oct. 18, 1972, Pub. L. 92–500, § 2, 86 Stat. 833, authorized the Administrator, in consultation with the Tahoe Regional Planning Agency, the Secretary of Agriculture, other Federal agencies, representatives of State and local governments, and members of the public, to conduct a thorough and complete study on the need of extending Federal oversight and control in order to preserve the fragile ecology of Lake Tahoe and to report the results of this study to Congress not later than one year after Oct. 18, 1972.

§ 1265. In-place toxic pollutants

The Administrator is directed to identify the location of in-place pollutants with emphasis on toxic pollutants in harbors and navigable waterways and is authorized, acting through the Secretary of the Army, to make contracts for the removal and appropriate disposal of such materials from critical port and harbor areas. There is authorized to be appropriated $15,000,000 to carry out the provisions of this section, which sum shall be available until expended.

(June 30, 1948, ch. 758, title I, § 115, as added Pub. L. 92–500, § 2, Oct. 18, 1972, 86 Stat. 833.)

§ 1266. Hudson River reclamation demonstration project

(a) The Administrator is authorized to enter into contracts and other agreements with the State of New York to carry out a project to demonstrate methods for the selective removal of polychlorinated biphenyls contaminating bottom sediments of the Hudson River, treating such sediments as required, burying such sediments in secure landfills, and installing monitoring systems for such landfills. Such demonstration project shall be for the purpose of determining the feasibility of indefinite storage in secure landfills of toxic substances and of ascertaining the improvement of the rate of recovery of a toxic contaminated national waterway. No pollutants removed pursuant to this paragraph shall be placed in any landfill unless the Administrator first determines that disposal of the pollutants in such landfill would provide a higher standard of protection of the public health, safety, and welfare than disposal of such pollutants by any other method including, but not limited to, incineration or a chemical destruction process.

(b) The Administrator is authorized to make grants to the State of New York to carry out this section from funds allotted to such State under section 1285(a) of this title, except that the amount of any such grant shall be equal to 75 per centum of the cost of the project and such grant shall be made on condition that non-Federal sources provide the remainder of the cost of such project. The authority of this section shall be available until September 30, 1983. Funds allotted to the State of New York under section 1285(a) of this title shall be available under this subsection only to the extent that funds are not available, as determined by the Administrator, to the State of New York for the work authorized by this section under section 1265 or 1321 of this title or a comprehensive hazardous substance response and clean up fund. Any funds used under the authority of this subsection shall be deducted from any estimate of the needs of the State of New York prepared under section 1375(b) of this title. The Administrator may not obligate or expend more than $20,000,000 to carry out this section.

(June 30, 1948, ch. 758, title I, § 116, as added Pub. L. 96–483, § 10, Oct. 21, 1980, 94 Stat. 2363; amended Pub. L. 105–362, title V, § 501(d)(2)(B), Nov. 10, 1998, 112 Stat. 3284; Pub. L. 107–303, title III, § 302(b)(1), Nov. 27, 2002, 116 Stat. 2361.)

AMENDMENTS

2002—Subsec. (b). Pub. L. 107–303 repealed Pub. L. 105–362, § 501(d)(2)(B). See 1998 Amendment note below.

1998—Subsec. (b). Pub. L. 105–362, § 501(d)(2)(B), which directed the substitution of "section 1375 of this title" for "section 1375(b) of this title" in penultimate sentence, was repealed by Pub. L. 107–303. See Effective Date of 2002 Amendment note below.

EFFECTIVE DATE OF 2002 AMENDMENT

Amendment by Pub. L. 107–303 effective Nov. 10, 1998, and Federal Water Pollution Act (33 U.S.C. 1251 et seq.) to be applied and administered on and after Nov. 27, 2002, as if amendments made by section 501(a)–(d) of Pub. L. 105–362 had not been enacted, see section 302(b) of Pub. L. 107–303, set out as a note under section 1254 of this title.

§ 1267. Chesapeake Bay

(a) Definitions

In this section, the following definitions apply:

(1) Administrative cost

The term "administrative cost" means the cost of salaries and fringe benefits incurred in administering a grant under this section.

(2) Chesapeake Bay Agreement

The term "Chesapeake Bay Agreement" means the formal, voluntary agreements executed to achieve the goal of restoring and protecting the Chesapeake Bay ecosystem and the living resources of the Chesapeake Bay ecosystem and signed by the Chesapeake Executive Council.

(3) Chesapeake Bay ecosystem

The term "Chesapeake Bay ecosystem" means the ecosystem of the Chesapeake Bay and its watershed.

(4) Chesapeake Bay Program

The term "Chesapeake Bay Program" means the program directed by the Chesapeake Executive Council in accordance with the Chesapeake Bay Agreement.

(5) Chesapeake Executive Council

The term "Chesapeake Executive Council" means the signatories to the Chesapeake Bay Agreement.

(6) Signatory jurisdiction

The term "signatory jurisdiction" means a jurisdiction of a signatory to the Chesapeake Bay Agreement.

(b) Continuation of Chesapeake Bay Program

(1) In general

In cooperation with the Chesapeake Executive Council (and as a member of the Council), the Administrator shall continue the Chesapeake Bay Program.

(2) Program Office

(A) In general

The Administrator shall maintain in the Environmental Protection Agency a Chesapeake Bay Program Office.

(B) Function

The Chesapeake Bay Program Office shall provide support to the Chesapeake Executive Council by—

(i) implementing and coordinating science, research, modeling, support services, monitoring, data collection, and other activities that support the Chesapeake Bay Program;

(ii) developing and making available, through publications, technical assistance, and other appropriate means, information pertaining to the environmental quality and living resources of the Chesapeake Bay ecosystem;

(iii) in cooperation with appropriate Federal, State, and local authorities, assisting the signatories to the Chesapeake Bay Agreement in developing and implementing specific action plans to carry out the responsibilities of the signatories to the Chesapeake Bay Agreement;

(iv) coordinating the actions of the Environmental Protection Agency with the actions of the appropriate officials of other Federal agencies and State and local authorities in developing strategies to—

(I) improve the water quality and living resources in the Chesapeake Bay ecosystem; and

(II) obtain the support of the appropriate officials of the agencies and authorities in achieving the objectives of the Chesapeake Bay Agreement; and

(v) implementing outreach programs for public information, education, and participation to foster stewardship of the resources of the Chesapeake Bay.

(c) Interagency agreements

The Administrator may enter into an interagency agreement with a Federal agency to carry out this section.

(d) Technical assistance and assistance grants

(1) In general

In cooperation with the Chesapeake Executive Council, the Administrator may provide technical assistance, and assistance grants, to nonprofit organizations, State and local governments, colleges, universities, and interstate agencies to carry out this section, subject to such terms and conditions as the Administrator considers appropriate.

(2) Federal share

(A) In general

Except as provided in subparagraph (B), the Federal share of an assistance grant provided under paragraph (1) shall be determined by the Administrator in accordance with guidance issued by the Administrator.

(B) Small watershed grants program

The Federal share of an assistance grant provided under paragraph (1) to carry out an implementing activity under subsection (g)(2) of this section shall not exceed 75 percent of eligible project costs, as determined by the Administrator.

(3) Non-Federal share

An assistance grant under paragraph (1) shall be provided on the condition that non-Federal sources provide the remainder of eligible project costs, as determined by the Administrator.

(4) Administrative costs

Administrative costs shall not exceed 10 percent of the annual grant award.

(e) Implementation and monitoring grants

(1) In general

If a signatory jurisdiction has approved and committed to implement all or substantially all aspects of the Chesapeake Bay Agreement, on the request of the chief executive of the jurisdiction, the Administrator—

(A) shall make a grant to the jurisdiction for the purpose of implementing the management mechanisms established under the Chesapeake Bay Agreement, subject to such terms and conditions as the Administrator considers appropriate; and

(B) may make a grant to a signatory jurisdiction for the purpose of monitoring the Chesapeake Bay ecosystem.

(2) Proposals

(A) In general

A signatory jurisdiction described in paragraph (1) may apply for a grant under this subsection for a fiscal year by submitting to the Administrator a comprehensive proposal to implement management mechanisms established under the Chesapeake Bay Agreement.

(B) Contents

A proposal under subparagraph (A) shall include—

(i) a description of proposed management mechanisms that the jurisdiction commits to take within a specified time period, such as reducing or preventing pollution in the Chesapeake Bay and its watershed or meeting applicable water quality standards or established goals and objectives under the Chesapeake Bay Agreement; and

(ii) the estimated cost of the actions proposed to be taken during the fiscal year.

(3) Approval

If the Administrator finds that the proposal is consistent with the Chesapeake Bay Agreement and the national goals established under section 1251(a) of this title, the Administrator may approve the proposal for an award.

(4) Federal share

The Federal share of a grant under this subsection shall not exceed 50 percent of the cost of implementing the management mechanisms during the fiscal year.

(5) Non-Federal share

A grant under this subsection shall be made on the condition that non-Federal sources provide the remainder of the costs of implementing the management mechanisms during the fiscal year.

(6) Administrative costs

Administrative costs shall not exceed 10 percent of the annual grant award.

(7) Reporting

On or before October 1 of each fiscal year, the Administrator shall make available to the public a document that lists and describes, in the greatest practicable degree of detail—

(A) all projects and activities funded for the fiscal year;

(B) the goals and objectives of projects funded for the previous fiscal year; and

(C) the net benefits of projects funded for previous fiscal years.

(f) Federal facilities and budget coordination

(1) Subwatershed planning and restoration

A Federal agency that owns or operates a facility (as defined by the Administrator) within the Chesapeake Bay watershed shall participate in regional and subwatershed planning and restoration programs.

(2) Compliance with agreement

The head of each Federal agency that owns or occupies real property in the Chesapeake Bay watershed shall ensure that the property, and actions taken by the agency with respect to the property, comply with the Chesapeake Bay Agreement, the Federal Agencies Chesapeake Ecosystem Unified Plan, and any subsequent agreements and plans.

(3) Budget coordination

(A) In general

As part of the annual budget submission of each Federal agency with projects or grants related to restoration, planning, monitoring, or scientific investigation of the Chesapeake Bay ecosystem, the head of the agency shall submit to the President a report that describes plans for the expenditure of the funds under this section.

(B) Disclosure to the Council

The head of each agency referred to in subparagraph (A) shall disclose the report under that subparagraph with the Chesapeake Executive Council as appropriate.

(g) Chesapeake Bay Program

(1) Management strategies

The Administrator, in coordination with other members of the Chesapeake Executive Council, shall ensure that management plans are developed and implementation is begun by signatories to the Chesapeake Bay Agreement to achieve and maintain—

(A) the nutrient goals of the Chesapeake Bay Agreement for the quantity of nitrogen and phosphorus entering the Chesapeake Bay and its watershed;

(B) the water quality requirements necessary to restore living resources in the Chesapeake Bay ecosystem;

(C) the Chesapeake Bay Basinwide Toxins Reduction and Prevention Strategy goal of reducing or eliminating the input of chemical contaminants from all controllable sources to levels that result in no toxic or bioaccumulative impact on the living resources of the Chesapeake Bay ecosystem or on human health;

(D) habitat restoration, protection, creation, and enhancement goals established by Chesapeake Bay Agreement signatories for wetlands, riparian forests, and other types of habitat associated with the Chesapeake Bay ecosystem; and

(E) the restoration, protection, creation, and enhancement goals established by the Chesapeake Bay Agreement signatories for living resources associated with the Chesapeake Bay ecosystem.

(2) Small watershed grants program

The Administrator, in cooperation with the Chesapeake Executive Council, shall—

(A) establish a small watershed grants program as part of the Chesapeake Bay Program; and

(B) offer technical assistance and assistance grants under subsection (d) of this section to local governments and nonprofit organizations and individuals in the Chesapeake Bay region to implement—

(i) cooperative tributary basin strategies that address the water quality and living resource needs in the Chesapeake Bay ecosystem; and

(ii) locally based protection and restoration programs or projects within a watershed that complement the tributary basin strategies, including the creation, restoration, protection, or enhancement of habitat associated with the Chesapeake Bay ecosystem.

(h) Study of Chesapeake Bay Program

(1) In general

Not later than April 22, 2003, and every 5 years thereafter, the Administrator, in coordination with the Chesapeake Executive Council, shall complete a study and submit to Congress a comprehensive report on the results of the study.

(2) Requirements

The study and report shall—

(A) assess the state of the Chesapeake Bay ecosystem;

(B) compare the current state of the Chesapeake Bay ecosystem with its state in 1975, 1985, and 1995;

(C) assess the effectiveness of management strategies being implemented on November 7, 2000, and the extent to which the priority needs are being met;

(D) make recommendations for the improved management of the Chesapeake Bay Program either by strengthening strategies being implemented on November 7, 2000, or by adopting new strategies; and

(E) be presented in such a format as to be readily transferable to and usable by other watershed restoration programs.

(i) Special study of living resource response

(1) In general

Not later than 180 days after November 7, 2000, the Administrator shall commence a 5-year special study with full participation of the scientific community of the Chesapeake Bay to establish and expand understanding of the response of the living resources of the Chesapeake Bay ecosystem to improvements in water quality that have resulted from investments made through the Chesapeake Bay Program.

(2) Requirements

The study shall—

(A) determine the current status and trends of living resources, including grasses, benthos, phytoplankton, zooplankton, fish, and shellfish;

(B) establish to the extent practicable the rates of recovery of the living resources in response to improved water quality condition;

(C) evaluate and assess interactions of species, with particular attention to the impact of changes within and among trophic levels; and

(D) recommend management actions to optimize the return of a healthy and balanced ecosystem in response to improvements in the quality and character of the waters of the Chesapeake Bay.

(j) Authorization of appropriations

There is authorized to be appropriated to carry out this section $40,000,000 for each of fiscal years 2001 through 2005. Such sums shall remain available until expended.

(June 30, 1948, ch. 758, title I, §117, as added Pub. L. 100–4, title I, §103, Feb. 4, 1987, 101 Stat. 10; amended Pub. L. 106–457, title II, §203, Nov. 7, 2000, 114 Stat. 1967.)

CODIFICATION

November 7, 2000, referred to in subsecs. (h)(2)(C), (D), and (i)(1), was in the original "the date of enactment of this section", which was translated as meaning the date of enactment of Pub. L. 106–457, which amended this section generally, to reflect the probable intent of Congress.

AMENDMENTS

2000—Pub. L. 106–457 amended section generally, substituting subsecs. (a) to (j) for former subsecs. (a) to (d), which related to continuation of the Chesapeake Bay Program and establishment and maintenance in the Environmental Protection Agency of an office, division, or branch of Chesapeake Bay Programs, interstate development plan grants, progress reports from grant recipient States, and authorization of appropriations.

FINDINGS AND PURPOSES

Pub. L. 106–457, title II, §202, Nov. 7, 2000, 114 Stat. 1967, provided that:

"(a) FINDINGS.—Congress finds that—

"(1) the Chesapeake Bay is a national treasure and a resource of worldwide significance;

"(2) over many years, the productivity and water quality of the Chesapeake Bay and its watershed were diminished by pollution, excessive sedimentation, shoreline erosion, the impacts of population growth and development in the Chesapeake Bay watershed, and other factors;

"(3) the Federal Government (acting through the Administrator of the Environmental Protection Agency), the Governor of the State of Maryland, the Governor of the Commonwealth of Virginia, the Governor of the Commonwealth of Pennsylvania, the Chairperson of the Chesapeake Bay Commission, and the mayor of the District of Columbia, as Chesapeake Bay Agreement signatories, have committed to a comprehensive cooperative program to achieve improved water quality and improvements in the productivity of living resources of the Bay;

"(4) the cooperative program described in paragraph (3) serves as a national and international model for the management of estuaries; and

"(5) there is a need to expand Federal support for monitoring, management, and restoration activities in the Chesapeake Bay and the tributaries of the Bay in order to meet and further the original and subsequent goals and commitments of the Chesapeake Bay Program.

"(b) PURPOSES.—The purposes of this title [amending this section and enacting provisions set out as a note under section 1251 of this title] are—

"(1) to expand and strengthen cooperative efforts to restore and protect the Chesapeake Bay; and

"(2) to achieve the goals established in the Chesapeake Bay Agreement."

NUTRIENT LOADING RESULTING FROM DREDGED MATERIAL DISPOSAL

Pub. L. 106–53, title IV, §457, Aug. 17, 1999, 113 Stat. 332, provided that:

"(a) STUDY.—The Secretary shall conduct a study of nutrient loading that occurs as a result of discharges of dredged material into open-water sites in the Chesapeake Bay.

"(b) REPORT.—Not later than 18 months after the date of enactment of this Act [Aug. 17, 1999], the Secretary shall submit to Congress a report on the results of the study."

§1268. Great Lakes

(a) Findings, purpose, and definitions

(1) Findings

The Congress finds that—

(A) the Great Lakes are a valuable national resource, continuously serving the people of the United States and other nations as an important source of food, fresh water, recreation, beauty, and enjoyment;

(B) the United States should seek to attain the goals embodied in the Great Lakes

Water Quality Agreement of 1978, as amended by the Water Quality Agreement of 1987 and any other agreements and amendments, with particular emphasis on goals related to toxic pollutants; and

(C) the Environmental Protection Agency should take the lead in the effort to meet those goals, working with other Federal agencies and State and local authorities.

(2) Purpose

It is the purpose of this section to achieve the goals embodied in the Great Lakes Water Quality Agreement of 1978, as amended by the Water Quality Agreement of 1987 and any other agreements and amendments, through improved organization and definition of mission on the part of the Agency, funding of State grants for pollution control in the Great Lakes area, and improved accountability for implementation of such agreement.

(3) Definitions

For purposes of this section, the term—

(A) "Agency" means the Environmental Protection Agency;

(B) "Great Lakes" means Lake Ontario, Lake Erie, Lake Huron (including Lake St. Clair), Lake Michigan, and Lake Superior, and the connecting channels (Saint Mary's River, Saint Clair River, Detroit River, Niagara River, and Saint Lawrence River to the Canadian Border);

(C) "Great Lakes System" means all the streams, rivers, lakes, and other bodies of water within the drainage basin of the Great Lakes;

(D) "Program Office" means the Great Lakes National Program Office established by this section;

(E) "Research Office" means the Great Lakes Research Office established by subsection (d) of this section;

(F) "area of concern" means a geographic area located within the Great Lakes, in which beneficial uses are impaired and which has been officially designated as such under Annex 2 of the Great Lakes Water Quality Agreement;

(G) "Great Lakes States" means the States of Illinois, Indiana, Michigan, Minnesota, New York, Ohio, Pennsylvania, and Wisconsin;

(H) "Great Lakes Water Quality Agreement" means the bilateral agreement, between the United States and Canada which was signed in 1978 and amended by the Protocol of 1987;

(I) "Lakewide Management Plan" means a written document which embodies a systematic and comprehensive ecosystem approach to restoring and protecting the beneficial uses of the open waters of each of the Great Lakes, in accordance with article VI and Annex 2 of the Great Lakes Water Quality Agreement;

(J) "Remedial Action Plan" means a written document which embodies a systematic and comprehensive ecosystem approach to restoring and protecting the beneficial uses of areas of concern, in accordance with article VI and Annex 2 of the Great Lakes Water Quality Agreement;

(K) "site characterization" means a process for monitoring and evaluating the nature and extent of sediment contamination in accordance with the Environmental Protection Agency's guidance for the assessment of contaminated sediment in an area of concern located wholly or partially within the United States; and

(L) "potentially responsible party" means an individual or entity that may be liable under any Federal or State authority that is being used or may be used to facilitate the cleanup and protection of the Great Lakes.

(b) Great Lakes National Program Office

The Great Lakes National Program Office (previously established by the Administrator) is hereby established within the Agency. The Program Office shall be headed by a Director who, by reason of management experience and technical expertise relating to the Great Lakes, is highly qualified to direct the development of programs and plans on a variety of Great Lakes issues. The Great Lakes National Program Office shall be located in a Great Lakes State.

(c) Great Lakes management

(1) Functions

The Program Office shall—

(A) in cooperation with appropriate Federal, State, tribal, and international agencies, and in accordance with section 1251(e) of this title, develop and implement specific action plans to carry out the responsibilities of the United States under the Great Lakes Water Quality Agreement of 1978, as amended by the Water Quality Agreement of 1987 and any other agreements and amendments,;[1]

(B) establish a Great Lakes system-wide surveillance network to monitor the water quality of the Great Lakes, with specific emphasis on the monitoring of toxic pollutants;

(C) serve as the liaison with, and provide information to, the Canadian members of the International Joint Commission and the Canadian counterpart to the Agency;

(D) coordinate actions of the Agency (including actions by headquarters and regional offices thereof) aimed at improving Great Lakes water quality; and

(E) coordinate actions of the Agency with the actions of other Federal agencies and State and local authorities, so as to ensure the input of those agencies and authorities in developing water quality strategies and obtain the support of those agencies and authorities in achieving the objectives of such agreement.

(2) Great Lakes water quality guidance

(A) By June 30, 1991, the Administrator, after consultation with the Program Office, shall publish in the Federal Register for public notice and comment proposed water quality guidance for the Great Lakes System. Such guidance shall conform with the objectives and provisions of the Great Lakes Water Quality Agreement, shall be no less restrictive than the provisions of this chapter and na-

[1] So in original.

tional water quality criteria and guidance, shall specify numerical limits on pollutants in ambient Great Lakes waters to protect human health, aquatic life, and wildlife, and shall provide guidance to the Great Lakes States on minimum water quality standards, antidegradation policies, and implementation procedures for the Great Lakes System.

(B) By June 30, 1992, the Administrator, in consultation with the Program Office, shall publish in the Federal Register, pursuant to this section and the Administrator's authority under this chapter, final water quality guidance for the Great Lakes System.

(C) Within two years after such Great Lakes guidance is published, the Great Lakes States shall adopt water quality standards, antidegradation policies, and implementation procedures for waters within the Great Lakes System which are consistent with such guidance. If a Great Lakes State fails to adopt such standards, policies, and procedures, the Administrator shall promulgate them not later than the end of such two-year period. When reviewing any Great Lakes State's water quality plan, the agency shall consider the extent to which the State has complied with the Great Lakes guidance issued pursuant to this section.

(3) Remedial Action Plans

(A) For each area of concern for which the United States has agreed to draft a Remedial Action Plan, the Program Office shall ensure that the Great Lakes State in which such area of concern is located—

(i) submits a Remedial Action Plan to the Program Office by June 30, 1991;

(ii) submits such Remedial Action Plan to the International Joint Commission by January 1, 1992; and

(iii) includes such Remedial Action Plans within the State's water quality plan by January 1, 1993.

(B) For each area of concern for which Canada has agreed to draft a Remedial Action Plan, the Program Office shall, pursuant to subparagraph (c)(1)(C) of this section, work with Canada to assure the submission of such Remedial Action Plans to the International Joint Commission by June 30, 1991, and to finalize such Remedial Action Plans by January 1, 1993.

(C) For any area of concern designated as such subsequent to November 16, 1990, the Program Office shall (i) if the United States has agreed to draft the Remedial Action Plan, ensure that the Great Lakes State in which such area of concern is located submits such Plan to the Program Office within two years of the area's designation, submits it to the International Joint Commission no later than six months after submitting it to the Program Office, and includes such Plan in the State's water quality plan no later than one year after submitting it to the Commission; and (ii) if Canada has agreed to draft the Remedial Action Plan, work with Canada, pursuant to subparagraph (c)(1)(C) of this section, to ensure the submission of such Plan to the International Joint Commission within two years of the area's designation and the finalization of such Plan no later than eighteen months after submitting it to such Commission.

(D) The Program Office shall compile formal comments on individual Remedial Action Plans made by the International Joint Commission pursuant to section 4(d) of Annex 2 of the Great Lakes Water Quality Agreement and, upon request by a member of the public, shall make such comments available for inspection and copying. The Program Office shall also make available, upon request, formal comments made by the Environmental Protection Agency on individual Remedial Action Plans.

(E) REPORT.—Not later than 1 year after November 27, 2002, the Administrator shall submit to Congress a report on such actions, time periods, and resources as are necessary to fulfill the duties of the Agency relating to oversight of Remedial Action Plans under—

(i) this paragraph; and

(ii) the Great Lakes Water Quality Agreement.

(4) Lakewide Management Plans

The Administrator, in consultation with the Program Office shall—

(A) by January 1, 1992, publish in the Federal Register a proposed Lakewide Management Plan for Lake Michigan and solicit public comments;

(B) by January 1, 1993, submit a proposed Lakewide Management Plan for Lake Michigan to the International Joint Commission for review; and

(C) by January 1, 1994, publish in the Federal Register a final Lakewide Management Plan for Lake Michigan and begin implementation.

Nothing in this subparagraph shall preclude the simultaneous development of Lakewide Management Plans for the other Great Lakes.

(5) Spills of oil and hazardous materials

The Program Office, in consultation with the Coast Guard, shall identify areas within the Great Lakes which are likely to experience numerous or voluminous spills of oil or other hazardous materials from land based facilities, vessels, or other sources and, in consultation with the Great Lakes States, shall identify weaknesses in Federal and State programs and systems to prevent and respond to such spills. This information shall be included on at least a biennial basis in the report required by this section.

(6) 5-year plan and program

The Program Office shall develop, in consultation with the States, a five-year plan and program for reducing the amount of nutrients introduced into the Great Lakes. Such program shall incorporate any management program for reducing nutrient runoff from nonpoint sources established under section 1329 of this title and shall include a program for monitoring nutrient runoff into, and ambient levels in, the Great Lakes.

(7) 5-year study and demonstration projects

(A) The Program Office shall carry out a five-year study and demonstration projects relating to the control and removal of toxic pollutants in the Great Lakes, with emphasis on the removal of toxic pollutants from bottom sediments. In selecting locations for conducting demonstration projects under this paragraph, priority consideration shall be given to projects at the following locations: Saginaw Bay, Michigan; Sheboygan Harbor, Wisconsin; Grand Calumet River, Indiana; Ashtabula River, Ohio; and Buffalo River, New York.

(B) The Program Office shall—

(i) by December 31, 1990, complete chemical, physical, and biological assessments of the contaminated sediments at the locations selected for the study and demonstration projects;

(ii) by December 31, 1990, announce the technologies that will be demonstrated at each location and the numerical standard of protection intended to be achieved at each location;

(iii) by December 31, 1992, complete full or pilot scale demonstration projects on site at each location of promising technologies to remedy contaminated sediments; and

(iv) by December 31, 1993, issue a final report to Congress on its findings.

(C) The Administrator, after providing for public review and comment, shall publish information concerning the public health and environmental consequences of contaminants in Great Lakes sediment. Information published pursuant to this subparagraph shall include specific numerical limits to protect health, aquatic life, and wildlife from the bioaccumulation of toxins. The Administrator shall, at a minimum, publish information pursuant to this subparagraph within 2 years of November 16, 1990.

(8) Administrator's responsibility

The Administrator shall ensure that the Program Office enters into agreements with the various organizational elements of the Agency involved in Great Lakes activities and the appropriate State agencies specifically delineating—

(A) the duties and responsibilities of each such element in the Agency with respect to the Great Lakes;

(B) the time periods for carrying out such duties and responsibilities; and

(C) the resources to be committed to such duties and responsibilities.

(9) Budget item

The Administrator shall, in the Agency's annual budget submission to Congress, include a funding request for the Program Office as a separate budget line item.

(10) Comprehensive report

Within 90 days after the end of each fiscal year, the Administrator shall submit to Congress a comprehensive report which—

(A) describes the achievements in the preceding fiscal year in implementing the Great Lakes Water Quality Agreement of 1978, as amended by the Water Quality Agreement of 1987 and any other agreements and amendments, and shows by categories (including judicial enforcement, research, State cooperative efforts, and general administration) the amounts expended on Great Lakes water quality initiatives in such preceding fiscal year;

(B) describes the progress made in such preceding fiscal year in implementing the system of surveillance of the water quality in the Great Lakes System, including the monitoring of groundwater and sediment, with particular reference to toxic pollutants;

(C) describes the long-term prospects for improving the condition of the Great Lakes; and

(D) provides a comprehensive assessment of the planned efforts to be pursued in the succeeding fiscal year for implementing the Great Lakes Water Quality Agreement of 1978, as amended by the Water Quality Agreement of 1987 and any other agreements and amendments,,[1] which assessment shall—

(i) show by categories (including judicial enforcement, research, State cooperative efforts, and general administration) the amount anticipated to be expended on Great Lakes water quality initiatives in the fiscal year to which the assessment relates; and

(ii) include a report of current programs administered by other Federal agencies which make available resources to the Great Lakes water quality management efforts.

(11) Confined disposal facilities

(A) The Administrator, in consultation with the Assistant Secretary of the Army for Civil Works, shall develop and implement, within one year of November 16, 1990, management plans for every Great Lakes confined disposal facility.

(B) The plan shall provide for monitoring of such facilities, including—

(i) water quality at the site and in the area of the site;

(ii) sediment quality at the site and in the area of the site;

(iii) the diversity, productivity, and stability of aquatic organisms at the site and in the area of the site; and

(iv) such other conditions as the Administrator deems appropriate.

(C) The plan shall identify the anticipated use and management of the site over the following twenty-year period including the expected termination of dumping at the site, the anticipated need for site management, including pollution control, following the termination of the use of the site.

(D) The plan shall identify a schedule for review and revision of the plan which shall not be less frequent than five years after adoption of the plan and every five years thereafter.

(12) Remediation of sediment contamination in areas of concern

(A) In general

In accordance with this paragraph, the Administrator, acting through the Program Office, may carry out projects that meet the requirements of subparagraph (B).

(B) Eligible projects

A project meets the requirements of this subparagraph if the project is to be carried out in an area of concern located wholly or partially in the United States and the project—

(i) monitors or evaluates contaminated sediment;

(ii) subject to subparagraph (D), implements a plan to remediate contaminated sediment, including activities to restore aquatic habitat that are carried out in conjunction with a project for the remediation of contaminated sediment; or

(iii) prevents further or renewed contamination of sediment.

(C) Priority

In selecting projects to carry out under this paragraph, the Administrator shall give priority to a project that—

(i) constitutes remedial action for contaminated sediment;

(ii)(I) has been identified in a Remedial Action Plan submitted under paragraph (3); and

(II) is ready to be implemented;

(iii) will use an innovative approach, technology, or technique that may provide greater environmental benefits, or equivalent environmental benefits at a reduced cost; or

(iv) includes remediation to be commenced not later than 1 year after the date of receipt of funds for the project.

(D) Limitations

The Administrator may not carry out a project under this paragraph for remediation of contaminated sediments located in an area of concern—

(i) if an evaluation of remedial alternatives for the area of concern has not been conducted, including a review of the short-term and long-term effects of the alternatives on human health and the environment;

(ii) if the Administrator determines that the area of concern is likely to suffer significant further or renewed contamination from existing sources of pollutants causing sediment contamination following completion of the project;

(iii) unless each non-Federal sponsor for the project has entered into a written project agreement with the Administrator under which the party agrees to carry out its responsibilities and requirements for the project; or

(iv) unless the Administrator provides assurance that the Agency has conducted a reasonable inquiry to identify potentially responsible parties connected with the site.

(E) Non-Federal share

(i) In general

The non-Federal share of the cost of a project carried out under this paragraph shall be at least 35 percent.

(ii) In-kind contributions

(I) In general

The non-Federal share of the cost of a project carried out under this paragraph may include the value of an in-kind contribution provided by a non-Federal sponsor.

(II) Credit

A project agreement described in subparagraph (D)(iii) may provide, with respect to a project, that the Administrator shall credit toward the non-Federal share of the cost of the project the value of an in-kind contribution made by the non-Federal sponsor, if the Administrator determines that the material or service provided as the in-kind contribution is integral to the project.

(III) Work performed before project agreement

In any case in which a non-Federal sponsor is to receive credit under subclause (II) for the cost of work carried out by the non-Federal sponsor and such work has not been carried out by the non-Federal sponsor as of October 8, 2008, the Administrator and the non-Federal sponsor shall enter into an agreement under which the non-Federal sponsor shall carry out such work, and only work carried out following the execution of the agreement shall be eligible for credit.

(IV) Limitation

Credit authorized under this clause for a project carried out under this paragraph—

(aa) shall not exceed the non-Federal share of the cost of the project; and

(bb) shall not exceed the actual and reasonable costs of the materials and services provided by the non-Federal sponsor, as determined by the Administrator.

(V) Inclusion of certain contributions

In this subparagraph, the term "in-kind contribution" may include the costs of planning (including data collection), design, construction, and materials that are provided by the non-Federal sponsor for implementation of a project under this paragraph.

(iii) Treatment of credit between projects

Any credit provided under this subparagraph towards the non-Federal share of the cost of a project carried out under this paragraph may be applied towards the non-Federal share of the cost of any other project carried out under this paragraph by the same non-Federal sponsor for a site within the same area of concern.

(iv) Non-Federal share

The non-Federal share of the cost of a project carried out under this paragraph—

(I) may include monies paid pursuant to, or the value of any in-kind contribution performed under, an administrative order on consent or judicial consent decree; but

(II) may not include any funds paid pursuant to, or the value of any in-kind contribution performed under, a unilateral administrative order or court order.

(v) Operation and maintenance

The non-Federal share of the cost of the operation and maintenance of a project carried out under this paragraph shall be 100 percent.

(F) Site characterization

(i) In general

The Administrator, in consultation with any affected State or unit of local government, shall carry out at Federal expense the site characterization of a project under this paragraph for the remediation of contaminated sediment.

(ii) Limitation

For purposes of clause (i), the Administrator may carry out one site assessment per discrete site within a project at Federal expense.

(G) Coordination

In carrying out projects under this paragraph, the Administrator shall coordinate with the Secretary of the Army, and with the Governors of States in which the projects are located, to ensure that Federal and State assistance for remediation in areas of concern is used as efficiently as practicable.

(H) Authorization of appropriations

(i) In general

In addition to other amounts authorized under this section, there is authorized to be appropriated to carry out this paragraph $50,000,000 for each of fiscal years 2004 through 2010.

(ii) Availability

Funds made available under clause (i) shall remain available until expended.

(iii) Allocation of funds

Not more than 20 percent of the funds appropriated pursuant to clause (i) for a fiscal year may be used to carry out subparagraph (F).

(13) Public information program

(A) In general

The Administrator, acting through the Program Office and in coordination with States, Indian tribes, local governments, and other entities, may carry out a public information program to provide information relating to the remediation of contaminated sediment to the public in areas of concern that are located wholly or partially in the United States.

(B) Authorization of appropriations

There is authorized to be appropriated to carry out this paragraph $1,000,000 for each of fiscal years 2004 through 2010.

(d) Great Lakes research

(1) Establishment of Research Office

There is established within the National Oceanic and Atmospheric Administration the Great Lakes Research Office.

(2) Identification of issues

The Research Office shall identify issues relating to the Great Lakes resources on which research is needed. The Research Office shall submit a report to Congress on such issues before the end of each fiscal year which shall identify any changes in the Great Lakes system[2] with respect to such issues.

(3) Inventory

The Research Office shall identify and inventory Federal, State, university, and tribal environmental research programs (and, to the extent feasible, those of private organizations and other nations) relating to the Great Lakes system,[2] and shall update that inventory every four years.

(4) Research exchange

The Research Office shall establish a Great Lakes research exchange for the purpose of facilitating the rapid identification, acquisition, retrieval, dissemination, and use of information concerning research projects which are ongoing or completed and which affect the Great Lakes System.

(5) Research program

The Research Office shall develop, in cooperation with the Coordination Office, a comprehensive environmental research program and data base for the Great Lakes system.[2] The data base shall include, but not be limited to, data relating to water quality, fisheries, and biota.

(6) Monitoring

The Research Office shall conduct, through the Great Lakes Environmental Research Laboratory, the National Sea Grant College program, other Federal laboratories, and the private sector, appropriate research and monitoring activities which address priority issues and current needs relating to the Great Lakes.

(7) Location

The Research Office shall be located in a Great Lakes State.

(e) Research and management coordination

(1) Joint plan

Before October 1 of each year, the Program Office and the Research Office shall prepare a joint research plan for the fiscal year which begins in the following calendar year.

(2) Contents of plan

Each plan prepared under paragraph (1) shall—

(A) identify all proposed research dedicated to activities conducted under the Great Lakes Water Quality Agreement of 1978, as amended by the Water Quality Agreement of 1987 and any other agreements and amendments,;[3]

---

[2] So in original. Probably should be capitalized.

[3] So in original.

(B) include the Agency's assessment of priorities for research needed to fulfill the terms of such Agreement; and

(C) identify all proposed research that may be used to develop a comprehensive environmental data base for the Great Lakes System and establish priorities for development of such data base.

(3) Health research report

(A) Not later than September 30, 1994, the Program Office, in consultation with the Research Office, the Agency for Toxic Substances and Disease Registry, and Great Lakes States shall submit to the Congress a report assessing the adverse effects of water pollutants in the Great Lakes System on the health of persons in Great Lakes States and the health of fish, shellfish, and wildlife in the Great Lakes System. In conducting research in support of this report, the Administrator may, where appropriate, provide for research to be conducted under cooperative agreements with Great Lakes States.

(B) There is authorized to be appropriated to the Administrator to carry out this section not to exceed $3,000,000 for each of fiscal years 1992, 1993, and 1994.

(f) Interagency cooperation

The head of each department, agency, or other instrumentality of the Federal Government which is engaged in, is concerned with, or has authority over programs relating to research, monitoring, and planning to maintain, enhance, preserve, or rehabilitate the environmental quality and natural resources of the Great Lakes, including the Chief of Engineers of the Army, the Chief of the Soil Conservation Service, the Commandant of the Coast Guard, the Director of the Fish and Wildlife Service, and the Administrator of the National Oceanic and Atmospheric Administration, shall submit an annual report to the Administrator with respect to the activities of that agency or office affecting compliance with the Great Lakes Water Quality Agreement of 1978, as amended by the Water Quality Agreement of 1987 and any other agreements and amendments,.[3]

(g) Relationship to existing Federal and State laws and international treaties

Nothing in this section shall be construed—

(1) to affect the jurisdiction, powers, or prerogatives of any department, agency, or officer of the Federal Government or of any State government, or of any tribe, nor any powers, jurisdiction, or prerogatives of any international body created by treaty with authority relating to the Great Lakes; or

(2) to affect any other Federal or State authority that is being used or may be used to facilitate the cleanup and protection of the Great Lakes.

(h) Authorizations of Great Lakes appropriations

There are authorized to be appropriated to the Administrator to carry out this section not to exceed—

(1) $11,000,000 per fiscal year for the fiscal years 1987, 1988, 1989, and 1990, and $25,000,000 for fiscal year 1991;

(2) such sums as are necessary for each of fiscal years 1992 through 2003; and

(3) $25,000,000 for each of fiscal years 2004 through 2008.

(June 30, 1948, ch. 758, title I, §118, as added Pub. L. 100–4, title I, §104, Feb. 4, 1987, 101 Stat. 11; amended Pub. L. 100–688, title I, §1008, Nov. 18, 1988, 102 Stat. 4151; Pub. L. 101–596, title I, §§101–106, Nov. 16, 1990, 104 Stat. 3000–3004; Pub. L. 107–303, title I, §§102–105, Nov. 27, 2002, 116 Stat. 2355–2358; Pub. L. 110–365, §§2, 3, Oct. 8, 2008, 122 Stat. 4021.)

CODIFICATION

November 16, 1990, referred to in subsec. (c)(3)(C), (7)(C), was in the original "the enactment of this Act", and "the date of the enactment of this title" which were translated as meaning the date of enactment of Pub. L. 101–596, title I of which enacted subsec. (c)(3), (7)(C), to reflect the probable intent of Congress.

AMENDMENTS

2008—Subsec. (a)(3)(K), (L). Pub. L. 110–365, §2, added subpars. (K) and (L).

Subsec. (c)(12)(B)(ii). Pub. L. 110–365, §3(a), substituted "sediment, including activities to restore aquatic habitat that are carried out in conjunction with a project for the remediation of contaminated sediment" for "sediment".

Subsec. (c)(12)(D). Pub. L. 110–365, §3(b)(1), substituted "Limitations" for "Limitation" in heading.

Subsec. (c)(12)(D)(iii), (iv). Pub. L. 110–365, §3(b)(2)–(4), added cls. (iii) and (iv).

Subsec. (c)(12)(E)(ii). Pub. L. 110–365, §3(c), amended cl. (ii) generally. Prior to amendment, text read as follows: "The non-Federal share of the cost of a project carried out under this paragraph may include the value of in-kind services contributed by a non-Federal sponsor."

Subsec. (c)(12)(E)(iii). Pub. L. 110–365, §3(d)(2), added cl. (iii). Former cl. (iii) redesignated (iv).

Subsec. (c)(12)(E)(iv). Pub. L. 110–365, §3(d)(1), (3), redesignated cl. (iii) as (iv) and substituted "contribution" for "service" in two places. Former cl. (iv) redesignated (v).

Subsec. (c)(12)(E)(v). Pub. L. 110–365, §3(d)(1), redesignated cl. (iv) as (v).

Subsec. (c)(12)(F). Pub. L. 110–365, §3(e), amended subpar. (F) generally. Prior to amendment, text read as follows: "The Administrator may not carry out a project under this paragraph unless the non-Federal sponsor enters into such agreements with the Administrator as the Administrator may require to ensure that the non-Federal sponsor will maintain its aggregate expenditures from all other sources for remediation programs in the area of concern in which the project is located at or above the average level of such expenditures in the 2 fiscal years preceding the date on which the project is initiated."

Subsec. (c)(12)(H)(i). Pub. L. 110–365, §3(f)(1), added cl. (i) and struck out former cl. (i). Prior to amendment, text read as follows: "In addition to other amounts authorized under this section, there is authorized to be appropriated to carry out this paragraph $50,000,000 for each of fiscal years 2004 through 2008."

Subsec. (c)(12)(H)(iii). Pub. L. 110–365, §3(f)(2), added cl. (iii).

Subsec. (c)(13)(B). Pub. L. 110–365, §3(g), substituted "2010" for "2008".

2002—Subsec. (c)(3)(E). Pub. L. 107–303, §102, added subpar. (E).

Subsec. (c)(12), (13). Pub. L. 107–303, §103, added pars. (12) and (13).

Subsec. (g). Pub. L. 107–303, §104, substituted "construed—" for "construed to affect", inserted "(1) to affect" before "the jurisdiction", substituted "Lakes; or" for "Lakes.", and added par. (2).

Subsec. (h). Pub. L. 107–303, § 105, substituted "not to exceed—" for "not to exceed $11,000,000", inserted "(1) $11,000,000" before "per fiscal year for", substituted "1991;" for "1991.", added pars. (2) and (3), and struck out former last sentence which read as follows: "Of the amounts appropriated each fiscal year—

"(1) 40 percent shall be used by the Great Lakes National Program Office on demonstration projects on the feasibility of controlling and removing toxic pollutants;

"(2) 7 percent shall be used by the Great Lakes National Program Office for the program of nutrient monitoring; and

"(3) 30 percent or $3,300,000, whichever is the lesser, shall be transferred to the National Oceanic and Atmospheric Administration for use by the Great Lakes Research Office."

1990—Subsec. (a)(3)(F) to (J). Pub. L. 101–596, § 103, added subpars. (F) to (J).

Subsec. (c)(2) to (11). Pub. L. 101–596, §§ 101, 102, 104, added pars. (2) to (5) after par. (1) and renumbered existing paragraphs accordingly, which was executed by renumbering pars. (2) to (6) as (6) to (10), respectively, redesignated existing provisions of par. (7) as subpar. (A) and added subpars. (B) and (C), and added par. (11).

Subsec. (e)(3). Pub. L. 101–596, § 106, added par. (3).

Subsec. (h). Pub. L. 101–596, § 105, substituted "and 1990, and $25,000,000 for fiscal year 1991" for "1990, and 1991" in introductory provisions and inserted "or $3,300,000, whichever is the lesser," after "30 percent" in par. (3).

1988—Subsecs. (a)(1)(B), (2), (c)(1)(A), (6)(A), (D), (e)(2)(A), (f). Pub. L. 100–688 inserted ", as amended by the Water Quality Agreement of 1987 and any other agreements and amendments," after "the Great Lakes Water Quality Agreement of 1978".

TRANSFER OF FUNCTIONS

For transfer of authorities, functions, personnel, and assets of the Coast Guard, including the authorities and functions of the Secretary of Transportation relating thereto, to the Department of Homeland Security, and for treatment of related references, see sections 468(b), 551(d), 552(d), and 557 of Title 6, Domestic Security, and the Department of Homeland Security Reorganization Plan of November 25, 2002, as modified, set out as a note under section 542 of Title 6.

FUNDS CONTRIBUTED BY A NON-FEDERAL SPONSOR

Pub. L. 108–447, div. I, title III, Dec. 8, 2004, 118 Stat. 3332, provided in part that: "The Administrator [of the Environmental Protection Agency] may hereafter receive and use funds contributed by a non-Federal sponsor as its share of the cost of a project to carry out a project under paragraph (c)(12) of section 118 of the Federal Water Pollution Control Act [33 U.S.C. 1268(c)(12)], as amended."

GREAT LAKES REMEDIAL ACTION PLANS AND SEDIMENT REMEDIATION

Pub. L. 101–640, title IV, § 401, Nov. 28, 1990, 104 Stat. 4644, as amended by Pub. L. 104–303, title V, § 515, Oct. 12, 1996, 110 Stat. 3763; Pub. L. 106–53, title V, § 505, Aug. 17, 1999, 113 Stat. 338; Pub. L. 106–541, title III, § 344, Dec. 11, 2000, 114 Stat. 2613; Pub. L. 110–114, title V, § 5012, Nov. 8, 2007, 121 Stat. 1195, provided that:

"(a) GREAT LAKES REMEDIAL ACTION PLANS.—

"(1) IN GENERAL.—The Secretary may provide technical, planning, and engineering assistance to State and local governments and nongovernmental entities designated by a State or local government in the development and implementation of remedial action plans for Areas of Concern in the Great Lakes identified under the Great Lakes Water Quality Agreement of 1978.

"(2) NON-FEDERAL SHARE.—

"(A) IN GENERAL.—Non-Federal interests shall contribute, in cash or by providing in-kind contributions, 35 percent of costs of activities for which assistance is provided under paragraph (1).

"(B) CONTRIBUTIONS BY ENTITIES.—Nonprofit public or private entities may contribute all or a portion of the non-Federal share.

"(b) SEDIMENT REMEDIATION PROJECTS.—

"(1) IN GENERAL.—The Secretary, in consultation with the Administrator of the Environmental Protection Agency (acting through the Great Lakes National Program Office), may conduct pilot- and full-scale projects of promising technologies to remediate contaminated sediments in freshwater coastal regions in the Great Lakes basin. The Secretary shall conduct not fewer than 3 full-scale projects under this subsection.

"(2) SITE SELECTION FOR PROJECTS.—In selecting the sites for the technology projects, the Secretary shall give priority consideration to Saginaw Bay, Michigan, Sheboygan Harbor, Wisconsin, Grand Calumet River, Indiana, Ashtabula River, Ohio, Buffalo River, New York, and Duluth-Superior Harbor, Minnesota and Wisconsin.

"(3) NON-FEDERAL SHARE.—Non-Federal interests shall contribute 35 percent of costs of projects under this subsection. Such costs may be paid in cash or by providing in-kind contributions.

"(c) AUTHORIZATION OF APPROPRIATIONS.—There is authorized to be appropriated to the Secretary to carry out this section $10,000,000 for each of fiscal years 2001 through 2012."

EX. ORD. NO. 13340. ESTABLISHMENT OF GREAT LAKES INTERAGENCY TASK FORCE AND PROMOTION OF A REGIONAL COLLABORATION OF NATIONAL SIGNIFICANCE FOR THE GREAT LAKES

Ex. Ord. No. 13340, May 18, 2004, 69 F.R. 29043, provided:

By the authority vested in me as President by the Constitution and the laws of the United States of America, and to help establish a regional collaboration of national significance for the Great Lakes, it is hereby ordered as follows:

SECTION 1. *Policy*. The Great Lakes are a national treasure constituting the largest freshwater system in the world. The United States and Canada have made great progress addressing past and current environmental impacts to the Great Lakes ecology. The Federal Government is committed to making progress on the many significant challenges that remain. Along with numerous State, tribal, and local programs, over 140 Federal programs help fund and implement environmental restoration and management activities throughout the Great Lakes system. A number of intergovernmental bodies are providing leadership in the region to address environmental and resource management issues in the Great Lakes system. These activities would benefit substantially from more systematic collaboration and better integration of effort. It is the policy of the Federal Government to support local and regional efforts to address environmental challenges and to encourage local citizen and community stewardship. To this end, the Federal Government will partner with the Great Lakes States, tribal and local governments, communities, and other interests to establish a regional collaboration to address nationally significant environmental and natural resource issues involving the Great Lakes. It is the further policy of the Federal Government that its executive departments and agencies will ensure that their programs are funding effective, coordinated, and environmentally sound activities in the Great Lakes system.

SEC. 2. *Definitions*. For purposes of this order:

(a) "Great Lakes" means Lake Ontario, Lake Erie, Lake Huron (including Lake Saint Clair), Lake Michigan, and Lake Superior, and the connecting channels (Saint Marys River, Saint Clair River, Detroit River, Niagara River, and Saint Lawrence River to the Canadian Border).

(b) "Great Lakes system" means all the streams, rivers, lakes, and other bodies of water within the drainage basin of the Great Lakes.

SEC. 3. *Great Lakes Interagency Task Force*.

(a) Task Force Purpose. To further the policy described in section 1 of this order, there is established, within the Environmental Protection Agency for administrative purposes, the "Great Lakes Interagency Task Force" (Task Force) to:

(i) Help convene and establish a process for collaboration among the members of the Task Force and the members of the Working Group that is established in paragraph b(ii) of this section, with the Great Lakes States, local communities, tribes, regional bodies, and other interests in the Great Lakes region regarding policies, strategies, plans, programs, projects, activities, and priorities for the Great Lakes system.

(ii) Collaborate with Canada and its provinces and with bi-national bodies involved in the Great Lakes region regarding policies, strategies, projects, and priorities for the Great Lakes system.

(iii) Coordinate the development of consistent Federal policies, strategies, projects, and priorities for addressing the restoration and protection of the Great Lakes system and assisting in the appropriate management of the Great Lakes system.

(iv) Develop outcome-based goals for the Great Lakes system relying upon, among other things, existing data and science-based indicators of water quality and related environmental factors. These goals shall focus on outcomes such as cleaner water, sustainable fisheries, and biodiversity of the Great Lakes system and ensure that Federal policies, strategies, projects, and priorities support measurable results.

(v) Exchange information regarding policies, strategies, projects, and activities of the agencies represented on the Task Force related to the Great Lakes system.

(vi) Work to coordinate government action associated with the Great Lakes system.

(vii) Ensure coordinated Federal scientific and other research associated with the Great Lakes system.

(viii) Ensure coordinated government development and implementation of the Great Lakes portion of the Global Earth Observation System of Systems.

(ix) Provide assistance and support to agencies represented on the Task Force in their activities related to the Great Lakes system.

(x) Submit a report to the President by May 31, 2005, and thereafter as appropriate, that summarizes the activities of the Task Force and provides any recommendations that would, in the judgment of the Task Force, advance the policy set forth in section 1 of this order.

(b) Membership and Operation.

(i) The Task Force shall consist exclusively of the following officers of the United States: the Administrator of the Environmental Protection Agency (who shall chair the Task Force), the Secretary of State, the Secretary of the Interior, the Secretary of Agriculture, the Secretary of Commerce, the Secretary of Housing and Urban Development, the Secretary of Transportation, the Secretary of Homeland Security, the Secretary of the Army, and the Chairman of the Council on Environmental Quality. A member of the Task Force may designate, to perform the Task Force functions of the member, any person who is part of the member's department, agency, or office and who is either an officer of the United States appointed by the President or a full-time employee serving in a position with pay equal to or greater than the minimum rate payable for GS–15 of the General Schedule. The Task Force shall report to the President through the Chairman of the Council on Environmental Quality.

(ii) The Task Force shall establish a "Great Lakes Regional Working Group" (Working Group) composed of the appropriate regional administrator or director with programmatic responsibility for the Great Lakes system for each agency represented on the Task Force including: the Great Lakes National Program Office of the Environmental Protection Agency; the United States Fish and Wildlife Service, National Park Service, and United States Geological Survey within the Department of the Interior; the Natural Resources Conservation Service and the Forest Service of the Department of Agriculture; the National Oceanic and Atmospheric Administration of the Department of Commerce; the Department of Housing and Urban Development; the Department of Transportation; the Coast Guard within the Department of Homeland Security; and the Army Corps of Engineers within the Department of the Army. The Working Group will coordinate and make recommendations on how to implement the policies, strategies, projects, and priorities of the Task Force.

(c) Management Principles for Regional Collaboration of National Significance. To further the policy described in section 1, the Task Force shall recognize and apply key principles and foster conditions to ensure successful collaboration. To that end, the Environmental Protection Agency will coordinate the development of a set of principles of successful collaboration.

SEC. 4. *Great Lakes National Program Office.* The Great Lakes National Program Office of the Environmental Protection Agency shall assist the Task Force and the Working Group in the performance of their functions. The Great Lakes National Program Manager shall serve as chair of the Working Group.

SEC. 5. *Preservation of Authority.* Nothing in this order shall be construed to impair or otherwise affect the functions of the Director of the Office of Management and Budget relating to budget, administrative, regulatory, and legislative proposals. Nothing in this order shall be construed to affect the statutory authority or obligations of any Federal agency or any bi-national agreement with Canada.

SEC. 6. *Judicial Review.* This order is intended only to improve the internal management of the Federal Government and is not intended to, and does not, create any right, benefit, or trust responsibility, substantive or procedural, enforceable at law or in equity by a party against the United States, its departments, agencies, instrumentalities or entities, its officers or employees, or any other person.

GEORGE W. BUSH.

§ 1269. Long Island Sound

(a) Office of Management Conference of the Long Island Sound Study

The Administrator shall continue the Management Conference of the Long Island Sound Study (hereinafter referred to as the "Conference") as established pursuant to section 1330 of this title, and shall establish an office (hereinafter referred to as the "Office") to be located on or near Long Island Sound.

(b) Administration and staffing of Office

The Office shall be headed by a Director, who shall be detailed by the Administrator, following consultation with the Administrators of EPA regions I and II, from among the employees of the Agency who are in civil service. The Administrator shall delegate to the Director such authority and detail such additional staff as may be necessary to carry out the duties of the Director under this section.

(c) Duties of Office

The Office shall assist the Management Conference of the Long Island Sound Study in carrying out its goals. Specifically, the Office shall—

(1) assist and support the implementation of the Comprehensive Conservation and Management Plan for Long Island Sound developed pursuant to section 1330 of this title, including

efforts to establish, within the process for granting watershed general permits, a system for promoting innovative methodologies and technologies that are cost-effective and consistent with the goals of the Plan;

(2) conduct or commission studies deemed necessary for strengthened implementation of the Comprehensive Conservation and Management Plan including, but not limited to—

(A) population growth and the adequacy of wastewater treatment facilities,

(B) the use of biological methods for nutrient removal in sewage treatment plants,

(C) contaminated sediments, and dredging activities,

(D) nonpoint source pollution abatement and land use activities in the Long Island Sound watershed,

(E) wetland protection and restoration,

(F) atmospheric deposition of acidic and other pollutants into Long Island Sound,

(G) water quality requirements to sustain fish, shellfish, and wildlife populations, and the use of indicator species to assess environmental quality,

(H) State water quality programs, for their adequacy pursuant to implementation of the Comprehensive Conservation and Management Plan, and

(I) options for long-term financing of wastewater treatment projects and water pollution control programs.

(3) coordinate the grant, research and planning programs authorized under this section;

(4) coordinate activities and implementation responsibilities with other Federal agencies which have jurisdiction over Long Island Sound and with national and regional marine monitoring and research programs established pursuant to the Marine Protection, Research, and Sanctuaries Act [16 U.S.C. 1431 et seq., 1447 et seq.; 33 U.S.C. 1401 et seq., 2801 et seq.];

(5) provide administrative and technical support to the conference;

(6) collect and make available to the public publications, and other forms of information the conference determines to be appropriate, relating to the environmental quality of Long Island Sound;

(7) not more than two years after the date of the issuance of the final Comprehensive Conservation and Management Plan for Long Island Sound under section 1330 of this title, and biennially thereafter, issue a report to the Congress which—

(A) summarizes the progress made by the States in implementing the Comprehensive Conservation and Management Plan;

(B) summarizes any modifications to the Comprehensive Conservation and Management Plan in the twelve-month period immediately preceding such report; and

(C) incorporates specific recommendations concerning the implementation of the Comprehensive Conservation and Management Plan; and

(8) convene conferences and meetings for legislators from State governments and political subdivisions thereof for the purpose of making recommendations for coordinating legislative efforts to facilitate the environmental restoration of Long Island Sound and the implementation of the Comprehensive Conservation and Management Plan.

(d) Grants

(1) The Administrator is authorized to make grants for projects and studies which will help implement the Long Island Sound Comprehensive Conservation and Management Plan. Special emphasis shall be given to implementation, research and planning, enforcement, and citizen involvement and education.

(2) State, interstate, and regional water pollution control agencies, and other public or nonprofit private agencies, institutions, and organizations held to be eligible for grants pursuant to this subsection.

(3) Citizen involvement and citizen education grants under this subsection shall not exceed 95 per centum of the costs of such work. All other grants under this subsection shall not exceed 50 per centum of the research, studies, or work. All grants shall be made on the condition that the non-Federal share of such costs are provided from non-Federal sources.

(e) Assistance to distressed communities

(1) Eligible communities

For the purposes of this subsection, a distressed community is any community that meets affordability criteria established by the State in which the community is located, if such criteria are developed after public review and comment.

(2) Priority

In making assistance available under this section for the upgrading of wastewater treatment facilities, the Administrator may give priority to a distressed community.

(f) Authorizations

(1) There is authorized to be appropriated to the Administrator for the implementation of this section, other than subsection (d) of this section, such sums as may be necessary for each of the fiscal years 2001 through 2010.

(2) There is authorized to be appropriated to the Administrator for the implementation of subsection (d) of this section not to exceed $40,000,000 for each of fiscal years 2001 through 2010.

(June 30, 1948, ch. 758, title I, §119, as added Pub. L. 101–596, title II, §202, Nov. 16, 1990, 104 Stat. 3004; amended Pub. L. 104–303, title V, §583, Oct. 12, 1996, 110 Stat. 3791; Pub. L. 106–457, title IV, §§402—404, Nov. 7, 2000, 114 Stat. 1973; Pub. L. 109–137, §1, Dec. 22, 2005, 119 Stat. 2646.)

REFERENCES IN TEXT

The Marine Protection, Research, and Sanctuaries Act, referred to in subsec. (c)(4), probably means the Marine Protection, Research, and Sanctuaries Act of 1972, Pub. L. 92–532, Oct. 23, 1972, 86 Stat. 1052, as amended, which is classified generally to chapters 32 (§1431 et seq.) and 32A (§1447 et seq.) of Title 16, Conservation, and chapters 27 (§1401 et seq.) and 41 (§2801 et seq.) of this title. For complete classification of this Act to the Code, see Short Title note set out under section 1401 of this title and Tables.

AMENDMENTS

2005—Subsec. (f). Pub. L. 109–137 substituted "2010" for "2005" in pars. (1) and (2).

2000—Subsec. (c)(1). Pub. L. 106–457, §402, inserted before semicolon at end ", including efforts to establish, within the process for granting watershed general permits, a system for promoting innovative methodologies and technologies that are cost-effective and consistent with the goals of the Plan".

Subsec. (e). Pub. L. 106–457, §403(2), added subsec. (e). Former subsec. (e) redesignated (f).

Subsec. (f). Pub. L. 106–457, §§403(1), 404, redesignated subsec. (e) as (f) and substituted "2001 through 2005" for "1991 through 2001" in par. (1) and "not to exceed $40,000,000 for each of fiscal years 2001 through 2005" for "not to exceed $3,000,000 for each of the fiscal years 1991 through 2001" in par. (2).

1996—Subsec. (e). Pub. L. 104–303 substituted "2001" for "1996" in pars. (1) and (2).

LONG ISLAND SOUND STEWARDSHIP

Pub. L. 109–359, Oct. 16, 2006, 120 Stat. 2049, provided that:

"SECTION 1. SHORT TITLE.

"This Act may be cited as the 'Long Island Sound Stewardship Act of 2006'.

"SEC. 2. FINDINGS AND PURPOSE.

"(a) FINDINGS.—Congress finds that—

"(1) Long Island Sound is a national treasure of great cultural, environmental, and ecological importance;

"(2) 8,000,000 people live within the Long Island Sound watershed and 28,000,000 people (approximately 10 percent of the population of the United States) live within 50 miles of Long Island Sound;

"(3) activities that depend on the environmental health of Long Island Sound contribute more than $5,000,000,000 each year to the regional economy;

"(4) the portion of the shoreline of Long Island Sound that is accessible to the general public (estimated at less than 20 percent of the total shoreline) is not adequate to serve the needs of the people living in the area;

"(5) existing shoreline facilities are in many cases overburdened and underfunded;

"(6) large parcels of open space already in public ownership are strained by the effort to balance the demand for recreation with the needs of sensitive natural resources;

"(7) approximately 1/3 of the tidal marshes of Long Island Sound have been filled, and much of the remaining marshes have been ditched, diked, or impounded, reducing the ecological value of the marshes; and

"(8) much of the remaining exemplary natural landscape is vulnerable to further development.

"(b) PURPOSE.—The purpose of this Act is to establish the Long Island Sound Stewardship Initiative to identify, protect, and enhance upland sites within the Long Island Sound ecosystem with significant ecological, educational, open space, public access, or recreational value through a bi-State network of sites best exemplifying these values.

"SEC. 3. DEFINITIONS.

"In this Act, the following definitions apply:

"(1) ADMINISTRATOR.—The term 'Administrator' means the Administrator of the Environmental Protection Agency.

"(2) ADVISORY COMMITTEE.—The term 'Advisory Committee' means the Long Island Sound Stewardship Advisory Committee established by section 8.

"(3) REGION.—The term 'Region' means the Long Island Sound Stewardship Initiative Region established by section 4(a).

"(4) STATE.—The term 'State' means each of the States of Connecticut and New York.

"(5) STEWARDSHIP.—The term 'stewardship' means land acquisition, land conservation agreements, site planning, plan implementation, land and habitat management, public access improvements, site monitoring, and other activities designed to enhance and preserve natural resource-based recreation and ecological function of upland areas.

"(6) STEWARDSHIP SITE.—The term 'stewardship site' means any area of State, local, or tribal government, or privately owned land within the Region that is designated by the Administrator under section 5(a).

"(7) SYSTEMATIC SITE SELECTION.—The term 'systematic site selection' means a process of selecting stewardship sites that—

"(A) has explicit goals, methods, and criteria;

"(B) produces feasible, repeatable, and defensible results;

"(C) provides for consideration of natural, physical, and biological patterns;

"(D) addresses replication, connectivity, species viability, location, and public recreation values;

"(E) uses geographic information systems technology and algorithms to integrate selection criteria; and

"(F) will result in achieving the goals of stewardship site selection at the lowest cost.

"(8) QUALIFIED APPLICANTS.—The term 'qualified applicant' means a non-Federal person that owns title to property located within the borders of the Region.

"(9) THREAT.—The term 'threat' means a threat that is likely to destroy or seriously degrade a conservation target or a recreation area.

"SEC. 4. LONG ISLAND SOUND STEWARDSHIP INITIATIVE REGION.

"(a) ESTABLISHMENT.—There is established in the States of Connecticut and New York the Long Island Sound Stewardship Initiative Region.

"(b) BOUNDARIES.—The Region consists of the immediate coastal upland areas along—

"(1) Long Island Sound between mean high water and the inland boundary, as described on the map entitled 'Long Island Sound Stewardship Region' and dated April 21, 2004; and

"(2) the Peconic Estuary as described on the map entitled 'Peconic Estuary Program Study Area Boundaries' and included in the Comprehensive Conservation and Management Plan for the Peconic Estuary Program and dated November 15, 2001.

"SEC. 5. DESIGNATION OF STEWARDSHIP SITES.

"(a) IN GENERAL.—The Administrator may designate a stewardship site in accordance with this Act any area that contributes to accomplishing the purpose of this Act.

"(b) PUBLICATION OF LIST OF RECOMMENDED SITES.—The Administrator shall—

"(1) publish in the Federal Register and make available in general circulation in the States of Connecticut and New York the list of sites recommended by the Advisory Committee; and

"(2) provide a 90-day period for—

"(A) the submission of public comment on the list; and

"(B) an opportunity for owners of such sites to decline designation of such sites as stewardship sites.

"(c) OPINION REGARDING OWNER'S RESPONSIBILITIES.—The Administrator may not designate an area as a stewardship site under this Act unless the Administrator provides to the owner of the area, and the owner acknowledges to the Administrator receipt of, a comprehensive opinion in plain English setting forth expressly the responsibility of the owner that arises from such designation.

"(d) DESIGNATION OF STEWARDSHIP SITES.—Not later than 150 days after receiving from the Advisory Committee its list of recommended sites, the Administrator—

"(1) shall review the recommendations of the Advisory Committee; and

"(2) may designate as a stewardship site any site included in the list.

"SEC. 6. RECOMMENDATIONS BY ADVISORY COMMITTEE.

"(a) IN GENERAL.—The Advisory Committee shall—

"(1) in accordance with this section, evaluate applications—

"(A) for designation of areas as stewardship sites;

"(B) to develop management plans to address threats to stewardship sites; and

"(C) to act on opportunities to protect and enhance stewardship sites;

"(2) develop recommended guidelines, criteria, schedules, and due dates for the submission of applications and the evaluation by the Advisory Committee of information to recommend areas for designation as stewardship sites that fulfill terms of a multi-year management plan;

"(3) recommend to the Administrator a list of sites for designation as stewardship sites that further the purpose of this Act;

"(4) develop management plans to address threats to stewardship sites;

"(5) raise awareness of the values of and threats to stewardship sites;

"(6) recommend that the Administrator award grants to qualified applicants; and

"(7) recommend to the Administrator ways to leverage additional resources for improved stewardship of the Region.

"(b) IDENTIFICATION OF SITES.—

"(1) IN GENERAL.—Any qualified applicant may submit an application to the Advisory Committee to have a site recommended to the Administrator for designation as a stewardship site.

"(2) IDENTIFICATION.—The Advisory Committee shall review each application submitted under this subsection to determine whether the site exhibits values that promote the purpose of this Act.

"(3) NATURAL RESOURCE-BASED RECREATION AREAS.—In reviewing an application for recommendation of a recreation area for designation as a stewardship site, the Advisory Committee may use a selection technique that includes consideration of—

"(A) public access;

"(B) community support;

"(C) high population density;

"(D) environmental justice (as defined in section 385.3 of title 33, Code of Federal Regulations (or successor regulations));

"(E) open spaces; and

"(F) cultural, historic, and scenic characteristics.

"(4) NATURAL AREAS WITH ECOLOGICAL VALUE.—In reviewing an application for recommendation of a natural area with ecological value for designation as a stewardship site, the Advisory Committee may use a selection technique that includes consideration of—

"(A) measurable conservation targets for the Region; and

"(B) prioritizing new sites using systematic site selection, which shall include consideration of—

"(i) ecological uniqueness;

"(ii) species viability;

"(iii) habitat heterogeneity;

"(iv) size;

"(v) quality;

"(vi) open spaces;

"(vii) land cover;

"(viii) scientific, research, or educational value; and

"(ix) threats.

"(5) DEVIATION FROM PROCESS.—The Advisory Committee may accept an application to recommend a site other than as provided in this subsection, if the Advisory Committee—

"(A) determines that the site makes significant ecological or recreational contributions to the Region; and

"(B) provides to the Administrator the reasons for deviating from the process otherwise described in this subsection.

"(c) SUBMISSION OF LIST OF RECOMMENDED SITES.—

"(1) IN GENERAL.—After completion of the site identification process set forth in subsection (b), the Advisory Committee shall submit to the Administrator its list of sites recommended for designation as stewardship sites.

"(2) LIMITATION.—The Advisory Committee shall not include a site in the list submitted under this subsection unless, prior to submission of the list, the owner of the site is—

"(A) notified of the inclusion of the site in the list; and

"(B) allowed to decline inclusion of the site in the list.

"(3) PUBLIC COMMENT.—In identifying sites for inclusion in the list, the Advisory Committee shall provide an opportunity for submission of, and consider, public comments.

"SEC. 7. GRANTS AND ASSISTANCE.

"(a) IN GENERAL.—The Administrator may provide grants, subject to the availability of appropriations, and other assistance for projects to fulfill the purpose of this Act.

"(b) FEDERAL SHARE.—The Federal share of the cost of an activity carried out using any assistance or grant under this Act shall not exceed 60 percent of the total cost of the activity.

"SEC. 8. LONG ISLAND SOUND STEWARDSHIP ADVISORY COMMITTEE.

"(a) ESTABLISHMENT.—There is established a committee to be known as the 'Long Island Sound Stewardship Advisory Committee'.

"(b) MEMBERSHIP.—

"(1) IN GENERAL.—The Administrator may appoint the members of the Advisory Committee in accordance with this subsection and the guidance in section 320(c) of the Federal Water Pollution Control Act (33 U.S.C. 1330(c)), except that the Governor of each State may appoint 2 members of the Advisory Committee.

"(2) ADDITIONAL MEMBERS.—In addition to the other members appointed under this subsection, the Advisory Committee may include—

"(A) a representative of the Regional Plan Association;

"(B) a representative of marine trade organizations; and

"(C) a representative of private landowner interests.

"(3) CONSIDERATION OF INTERESTS.—In appointing members of the Advisory Committee, the Administrator shall consider—

"(A) Federal, State, and local government interests and tribal interests;

"(B) the interests of nongovernmental organizations;

"(C) academic interests;

"(D) private interests including land, agriculture, and business interests; and

"(E) recreational and commercial fishing interests.

"(4) CHAIRPERSON.—In addition to the other members appointed under this subsection, the Administrator may appoint as a member of the Advisory Committee an individual to serve as the Chairperson, who may be the Director of the Long Island Sound Office of the Environmental Protection Agency.

"(5) COMPLETION OF APPOINTMENTS.—The Administrator shall complete the appointment of all members of the Advisory Committee by not later than 180 days after the date of enactment of this Act [Oct. 16, 2006].

"(A) [sic] VACANCIES.—A vacancy on the Advisory Committee—

"(i) shall be filled not later than 90 days after the vacancy occurs;

"(ii) shall not affect the powers of the Advisory Committee; and

"(iii) shall be filled in the same manner as the original appointment was made.

"(c) TERM.—

"(1) IN GENERAL.—A member of the Advisory Committee shall be appointed for a term of 4 years.

"(2) MULTIPLE TERMS.—An individual may be appointed as a member of the Advisory Committee for more than 1 term.

"(d) POWERS.—The Advisory Committee may hold such hearings, meet and act at such times and places, take such testimony, and receive such evidence as the Advisory Committee considers advisable to carry out this Act.

"(e) MEETINGS.—

"(1) IN GENERAL.—The Advisory Committee shall meet at the call of the Chairperson, but no fewer than 4 times each year.

"(2) INITIAL MEETING.—Not later than 30 days after the date on which all members of the Advisory Committee have been appointed, the Chairperson shall call the initial meeting of the Advisory Committee.

"(3) QUORUM.—A majority of the members of the Advisory Committee shall constitute a quorum, but a lesser number of members may hold hearings.

"(f) ADAPTIVE MANAGEMENT.—

"(1) IN GENERAL.—The Advisory Committee shall use an adaptive management framework to identify the best policy initiatives and actions through—

"(A) definition of strategic goals;

"(B) definition of policy options for methods to achieve strategic goals;

"(C) establishment of measures of success;

"(D) identification of uncertainties;

"(E) development of informative models of policy implementation;

"(F) separation of the landscape into geographic units;

"(G) monitoring key responses at different spatial and temporal scales; and

"(H) evaluation of outcomes and incorporation into management strategies.

"(2) APPLICATION OF ADAPTIVE MANAGEMENT FRAMEWORK.—The Advisory Committee shall apply the adaptive management framework to the process for making recommendations under subsections (b) through (f) of section 6 to the Administrator regarding sites that should be designated as stewardship sites.

"(3) ADAPTIVE MANAGEMENT.—The adaptive management framework required by this subsection shall consist of a scientific process—

"(A) for—

"(i) developing predictive models;

"(ii) making management policy decisions based upon the model outputs;

"(iii) revising the management policies as data become available with which to evaluate the policies; and

"(iv) acknowledging uncertainty, complexity, and variance in the spatial and temporal aspects of natural systems; and

"(B) that requires that management be viewed as experimental.

"(g) TERMINATION OF ADVISORY COMMITTEE.—The Advisory Committee shall terminate on December 31, 2011.

"SEC. 9. REPORTS.

"(a) ADMINISTRATOR.—The Administrator shall publish and make available to the public on the Internet and in paper form—

"(1) not later than 1 year after the date of enactment of this Act [Oct. 16, 2006], a report that—

"(A) assesses the role of this Act in protecting the Long Island Sound;

"(B) establishes in coordination with the Advisory Committee guidelines, criteria, schedules, and due dates for evaluating information to designate stewardship sites;

"(C) includes information about any grants that are available for the purchase of land or property rights to protect stewardship sites; and

"(D) accounts for funds received and expended during the previous fiscal year;

"(2) an update of such report, at least every other year; and

"(3) information on funding and any new stewardship sites more frequently than every other year.

"(b) ADVISORY COMMITTEE.—

"(1) REPORT.—For each of fiscal years 2007 through 2011, the Advisory Committee shall submit to the Administrator and the decisionmaking body of the Long Island Sound Study Management Conference established under section 320 of the Federal Water Pollution Control Act (33 U.S.C. 1330), an annual report that contains—

"(A) a detailed statement of the findings and conclusions of the Advisory Committee since the last report under this subsection;

"(B) a description of all sites recommended by the Advisory Committee to the Administrator for designation as stewardship sites;

"(C) the recommendations of the Advisory Committee for such legislation and administrative actions as the Advisory Committee considers appropriate; and

"(D) in accordance with paragraph (2), the recommendations of the Advisory Committee for the awarding of grants.

"(2) RECOMMENDATION FOR GRANTS.—

"(A) IN GENERAL.—The Advisory Committee shall recommend that the Administrator award grants to qualified applicants to help to secure and improve the open space, public access, or ecological values of stewardship sites, through—

"(i) purchase of the property of a stewardship site;

"(ii) purchase of relevant property rights to a stewardship site; or

"(iii) entering into any other binding legal arrangement that ensures that the values of a stewardship site are sustained, including entering into an arrangement with a land manager or property owner to develop or implement a management plan that is necessary for the conservation of natural resources.

"(B) EQUITABLE DISTRIBUTION OF FUNDS.—The Advisory Committee shall exert due diligence to ensure that its recommendations result in an equitable distribution of funds between the States.

"SEC. 10. PRIVATE PROPERTY PROTECTION; NO REGULATORY AUTHORITY.

"(a) ACCESS TO PRIVATE PROPERTY.—Nothing in this Act—

"(1) requires any private property owner to allow public access (including Federal, State, or local government access) to the private property; or

"(2) modifies the application of any provision of Federal, State, or local law with regard to public access to or use of private property, except as entered into by voluntary agreement of the owner or custodian of the property.

"(b) LIABILITY.—Establishment of the Region does not create any liability, or have any effect on any liability under any other law, of any private property owner with respect to any person injured on the private property.

"(c) RECOGNITION OF AUTHORITY TO CONTROL LAND USE.—Nothing in this Act modifies the authority of Federal, State, or local governments to regulate land use.

"(d) PARTICIPATION OF PRIVATE PROPERTY OWNERS NOT REQUIRED.—Nothing in this Act requires the owner of any private property located within the boundaries of the Region to participate in any land conservation, financial or technical assistance, or other programs established under this Act.

"(e) PURCHASE OF LAND OR INTEREST IN LAND FROM WILLING SELLERS ONLY.—Funds appropriated to carry out this Act may be used to purchase land or interests in land only from willing sellers.

"(f) MANNER OF ACQUISITION.—All acquisitions of land under this Act shall be made in a voluntary manner and shall not be the result of forced takings.

"(g) EFFECT OF ESTABLISHMENT.—

"(1) IN GENERAL.—The boundaries of the Region represent the area within which Federal funds appropriated for the purpose of this Act may be expended.

"(2) REGULATORY AUTHORITY.—The establishment of the Region and the boundaries of the Region do not provide any regulatory authority not in existence immediately before the enactment of this Act [Oct. 16, 2006] on land use in the Region by any management entity, except for such property rights as may be purchased from or donated by the owner of the property (including public lands donated by a State or local government).

"SEC. 11. AUTHORIZATION OF APPROPRIATIONS.

"(a) IN GENERAL.—There is authorized to be appropriated to the Administrator $25,000,000 for each of fiscal years 2007 through 2011 to carry out this Act, including for—

"(1) acquisition of land and interests in land;

"(2) development and implementation of site management plans;

"(3) site enhancements to reduce threats or promote stewardship; and

"(4) administrative expenses of the Advisory Committee and the Administrator.

"(b) USE OF FUNDS.—Amounts made available to the Administrator under this section each fiscal year shall be used by the Administrator after reviewing the recommendations included in the annual reports of the Advisory Committee under section 9.

"(c) AUTHORIZATION OF GIFTS, DEVISES, AND BEQUESTS FOR SYSTEM.—In furtherance of the purpose of this Act, the Administrator may accept and use any gift, devise, or bequest of real or personal property, proceeds therefrom, or interests therein, to carry out this Act. Such acceptance may be subject to the terms of any restrictive or affirmative covenant, or condition of servitude, if such terms are considered by the Administrator to be in accordance with law and compatible with the purpose for which acceptance is sought.

"(d) LIMITATION ON ADMINISTRATIVE COSTS.—Of the amount available each fiscal year to carry out this Act, not more than 8 percent may be used for administrative costs."

§ 1270. Lake Champlain Basin Program

(a) Establishment

(1) In general

There is established a Lake Champlain Management Conference to develop a comprehensive pollution prevention, control, and restoration plan for Lake Champlain. The Administrator shall convene the management conference within ninety days of November 16, 1990.

(2) Implementation

The Administrator—

(A) may provide support to the State of Vermont, the State of New York, and the New England Interstate Water Pollution Control Commission for the implementation of the Lake Champlain Basin Program; and

(B) shall coordinate actions of the Environmental Protection Agency under subparagraph (A) with the actions of other appropriate Federal agencies.

(b) Membership

The Members of the Management Conference shall be comprised of—

(1) the Governors of the States of Vermont and New York;

(2) each interested Federal agency, not to exceed a total of five members;

(3) the Vermont and New York Chairpersons of the Vermont, New York, Quebec Citizens Advisory Committee for the Environmental Management of Lake Champlain;

(4) four representatives of the State legislature of Vermont;

(5) four representatives of the State legislature of New York;

(6) six persons representing local governments having jurisdiction over any land or water within the Lake Champlain basin, as determined appropriate by the Governors; and

(7) eight persons representing affected industries, nongovernmental organizations, public and private educational institutions, and the general public, as determined appropriate by the trigovernmental Citizens Advisory Committee for the Environmental Management of Lake Champlain, but not to be current members of the Citizens Advisory Committee.

(c) Technical Advisory Committee

(1) The Management Conference shall, not later than one hundred and twenty days after November 16, 1990, appoint a Technical Advisory Committee.

(2) Such Technical Advisory Committee shall consist of officials of: appropriate departments and agencies of the Federal Government; the State governments of New York and Vermont; and governments of political subdivisions of such States; and public and private research institutions.

(d) Research program

The Management Conference shall establish a multi-disciplinary environmental research program for Lake Champlain. Such research program shall be planned and conducted jointly with the Lake Champlain Research Consortium.

(e) Pollution prevention, control, and restoration plan

(1) Not later than three years after November 16, 1990, the Management Conference shall publish a pollution prevention, control, and restoration plan for Lake Champlain.

(2) The Plan developed pursuant to this section shall—

(A) identify corrective actions and compliance schedules addressing point and nonpoint sources of pollution necessary to restore and maintain the chemical, physical, and biological integrity of water quality, a balanced, indigenous population of shellfish, fish and wildlife, recreational, and economic activities in and on the lake;

(B) incorporate environmental management concepts and programs established in State and Federal plans and programs in effect at the time of the development of such plan;

(C) clarify the duties of Federal and State agencies in pollution prevention and control activities, and to the extent allowable by law, suggest a timetable for adoption by the appropriate Federal and State agencies to accomplish such duties within a reasonable period of time;

(D) describe the methods and schedules for funding of programs, activities, and projects identified in the Plan, including the use of Federal funds and other sources of funds;

(E) include a strategy for pollution prevention and control that includes the promotion of pollution prevention and management practices to reduce the amount of pollution generated in the Lake Champlain basin; and

(F) be reviewed and revised, as necessary, at least once every 5 years, in consultation with the Administrator and other appropriate Federal agencies.

(3) The Administrator, in cooperation with the Management Conference, shall provide for public review and comment on the draft Plan. At a minimum, the Management Conference shall conduct one public meeting to hear comments on the draft plan in the State of New York and one such meeting in the State of Vermont.

(4) Not less than one hundred and twenty days after the publication of the Plan required pursuant to this section, the Administrator shall approve such plan if the plan meets the requirements of this section and the Governors of the States of New York and Vermont concur.

(5) Upon approval of the plan, such plan shall be deemed to be an approved management program for the purposes of section 1329(h) of this title and such plan shall be deemed to be an approved comprehensive conservation and management plan pursuant to section 1330 of this title.

(f) Grant assistance

(1) The Administrator may, in consultation with participants in the Lake Champlain Basin Program, make grants to State, interstate, and regional water pollution control agencies, and public or nonprofit agencies, institutions, and organizations.

(2) Grants under this subsection shall be made for assisting research, surveys, studies, and modeling and technical and supporting work necessary for the development and implementation of the Plan.

(3) The amount of grants to any person under this subsection for a fiscal year shall not exceed 75 per centum of the costs of such research, survey, study and work and shall be made available on the condition that non-Federal share of such costs are provided from non-Federal sources.

(4) The Administrator may establish such requirements for the administration of grants as he determines to be appropriate.

(g) Definitions

In this section:

(1) Lake Champlain Basin Program

The term "Lake Champlain Basin Program" means the coordinated efforts among the Federal Government, State governments, and local governments to implement the Plan.

(2) Lake Champlain drainage basin

The term "Lake Champlain drainage basin" means all or part of Clinton, Franklin, Hamilton, Warren, Essex, and Washington counties in the State of New York and all or part of Franklin, Grand Isle, Chittenden, Addison, Rutland, Bennington, Lamoille, Orange, Washington, Orleans, and Caledonia counties in Vermont, that contain all of the streams, rivers, lakes, and other bodies of water, including wetlands, that drain into Lake Champlain.

(3) Plan

The term "Plan" means the plan developed under subsection (e) of this section.

(h) No effect on certain authority

Nothing in this section—

(1) affects the jurisdiction or powers of—

(A) any department or agency of the Federal Government or any State government; or

(B) any international organization or entity related to Lake Champlain created by treaty or memorandum to which the United States is a signatory;

(2) provides new regulatory authority for the Environmental Protection Agency; or

(3) affects section 304 of the Great Lakes Critical Programs Act of 1990 (Public Law 101–596; 33 U.S.C. 1270 note).

(i) Authorization

There are authorized to be appropriated to the Environmental Protection Agency to carry out this section—

(1) $2,000,000 for each of fiscal years 1991, 1992, 1993, 1994, and 1995;

(2) such sums as are necessary for each of fiscal years 1996 through 2003; and

(3) $11,000,000 for each of fiscal years 2004 through 2008.

(June 30, 1948, ch. 758, title I, §120, as added Pub. L. 101–596, title III, §303, Nov. 16, 1990, 104 Stat. 3006; amended Pub. L. 107–303, title II, §202, Nov. 27, 2002, 116 Stat. 2358.)

AMENDMENTS

2002—Pub. L. 107–303, §202(1), substituted "Lake Champlain Basin Program" for "Lake Champlain Management Conference" in section catchline.

Subsec. (a). Pub. L. 107–303, §202(1), (2), designated existing provisions as par. (1), inserted heading, and added par. (2).

Subsec. (d). Pub. L. 107–303, §202(3), struck out par. (1) designation before "The Management".

Subsec. (e)(1). Pub. L. 107–303, §202(4)(A), struck out "(hereafter in this section referred to as the 'Plan')" after "restoration plan".

Subsec. (e)(2)(F). Pub. L. 107–303, §202(4)(B), added subpar. (F).

Subsec. (f)(1). Pub. L. 107–303, §202(5)(A), substituted "participants in the Lake Champlain Basin Program," for "the Management Conference,".

Subsec. (f)(2). Pub. L. 107–303, §202(5)(B), substituted "development and implementation of the Plan" for "development of the Plan and for retaining expert consultants in support of litigation undertaken by the State of New York and the State of Vermont to compel cleanup or obtain cleanup damage costs from persons responsible for pollution of Lake Champlain".

Subsec. (g). Pub. L. 107–303, §202(6)(A), substituted "Definitions" for "'Lake Champlain drainage basin' defined" in subsec. heading, inserted introductory provisions, added par. (1), inserted par. (2) designation and heading after par. (1) and inserted "The term" before "'Lake Champlain drainage".

Subsec. (g)(2). Pub. L. 107–303, §202(6)(B), inserted "Hamilton," after "Franklin," and "Bennington," after "Rutland,".

Subsec. (g)(3). Pub. L. 107–303, §202(6)(C), added par. (3).

Subsec. (h). Pub. L. 107–303, §202(7), added subsec. (h) and struck out heading and text of former subsec. (h). Text read as follows: "Nothing in this section shall be construed so as to affect the jurisdiction or powers of—

"(1) any department or agency of the Federal Government or any State government; or

"(2) any international organization or entity related to Lake Champlain created by treaty or memorandum to which the United States is a signatory."

Subsec. (i). Pub. L. 107–303, §202(8), substituted "section—" for "section $2,000,000", inserted "(1) $2,000,000" before "for each of fiscal years 1991,", substituted "1995;" for "1995.", and added pars. (2) and (3).

FEDERAL PROGRAM COORDINATION

Section 304 of Pub. L. 101–596, as amended by Pub. L. 104–127, title III, §336(a)(2)(F), Apr. 4, 1996, 110 Stat. 1005, provided that:

"(a) DESIGNATION OF LAKE CHAMPLAIN AS A PRIORITY AREA UNDER THE ENVIRONMENTAL QUALITY INCENTIVES PROGRAM.—

"(1) IN GENERAL.—Notwithstanding any other provision of law, the Lake Champlain basin, as defined under section 120(h) of the Federal Water Pollution Control Act [33 U.S.C. 1270(h)], shall be designated by the Secretary of Agriculture as a priority area under the environmental quality incentives program established under chapter 4 of subtitle D of title XII of the Food Security Act of 1985 [16 U.S.C. 3839aa et seq.].

"(2) TECHNICAL ASSISTANCE REIMBURSEMENT.—To carry out the purposes of this subsection, the technical assistance reimbursement from the Agricultural Stabilization and Conservation Service authorized under the Soil Conservation and Domestic Allotment Act [16 U.S.C. 590a et seq.], shall be increased from 5 per centum to 10 per centum.

"(3) COMPREHENSIVE AGRICULTURAL MONITORING.—The Secretary, in consultation with the Management Conference and appropriate State and Federal agencies, shall develop a comprehensive agricultural monitoring and evaluation network for all major drainages within the Lake Champlain basin.

"(4) ALLOCATION OF FUNDS.—In allocating funds under this subsection, the Secretary of Agriculture shall consult with the Management Conference established under section 120 of the Federal Water Pollution Control Act and to the extent allowable by law, allocate funds to those agricultural enterprises located at sites that the Management Conference determines to be priority sites, on the basis of a concern for ensuring implementation of nonpoint source pollution controls throughout the Lake Champlain basin.

"(b) COOPERATION OF THE UNITED STATES GEOLOGICAL SURVEY OF THE DEPARTMENT OF THE INTERIOR.—For the purpose of enhancing and expanding basic data collection and monitoring in operation in the Lake Champlain basin, as defined under section 120 of the Federal Water Pollution Control Act [33 U.S.C. 1270], the Secretary of the Interior, acting through the heads of water resources divisions of the New York and New England districts of the United States Geological Survey, shall—

"(1) in cooperation with appropriate universities and private research institutions, and the appropriate officials of the appropriate departments and agencies of the States of New York and Vermont, develop an integrated geographic information system of the Lake Champlain basin;

"(2) convert all partial recording sites in the Lake Champlain basin to continuous monitoring stations with full gauging capabilities and status; and

"(3) establish such additional continuous monitoring station sites in the Lake Champlain basin as are necessary to carry out basic data collection and monitoring, as defined by the Secretary of the Interior, including groundwater mapping, and water quality and sediment data collection.

"(c) COOPERATION OF THE UNITED STATES FISH AND WILDLIFE SERVICE OF THE DEPARTMENT OF THE INTERIOR.—

"(1) RESOURCE CONSERVATION PROGRAM.—The Secretary of the Interior, acting through the United States Fish and Wildlife Service, in cooperation with the Lake Champlain Fish and Wildlife Management Cooperative and the Management Conference established pursuant to this subsection shall—

"(A) establish and implement a fisheries resources restoration, development and conservation program, including dedicating a level of hatchery production within the Lake Champlain basin at or above the level that existed immediately preceding the date of enactment of this Act [Nov. 16, 1990]; and

"(B) conduct a wildlife species and habitat assessment survey in the Lake Champlain basin, including—

"(i) a survey of Federal threatened and endangered species, listed or proposed for listing under the Endangered Species Act of 1973 (16 U.S.C. 1531 et seq.), New York State and State of Vermont threatened and endangered species and other species of special concern, migratory nongame species of management concern, and national resources plan species;

"(ii) a survey of wildlife habitats such as islands, wetlands, and riparian areas; and

"(iii) a survey of migratory bird populations breeding, migrating and wintering within the Lake Champlain basin.

"(2) To accomplish the purposes of paragraph (1), the Director of the United States Fish and Wildlife Service is authorized to carry out activities related to—

"(A) controlling sea lampreys and other nonindigenous aquatic animal nuisances;

"(B) improving the health of fishery resources;

"(C) conducting investigations about and assessing the status of fishery resources, and disseminating that information to all interested parties; and

"(D) conducting and periodically updating a survey of the fishery resources and their habitats and food chains in the Lake Champlain basin.

"(d) AUTHORIZATIONS.—(1) There is authorized to be appropriated to the Department of Agriculture $2,000,000 for each of fiscal years 1991, 1992, 1993, 1994, and 1995 to carry out subsection (a) of this section.

"(2) There is authorized to be appropriated to the Department of [the] Interior $1,000,000 for each of fiscal years 1991, 1992, 1993, 1994, and 1995 to carry out subsections (b) and (c) of this section."

§1271. Sediment survey and monitoring

(a) Survey

(1) In general

The Administrator, in consultation with the Administrator of the National Oceanic and Atmospheric Administration and the Secretary, shall conduct a comprehensive national survey of data regarding aquatic sediment quality in the United States. The Administrator shall compile all existing information on the quantity, chemical and physical composition, and geographic location of pollutants in aquatic sediment, including the probable source of such pollutants and identification of those sediments which are contaminated pursuant to section 501(b)(4).[1]

(2) Report

Not later than 24 months after October 31, 1992, the Administrator shall report to the Congress the findings, conclusions, and recommendations of such survey, including recommendations for actions necessary to prevent contamination of aquatic sediments and to control sources of contamination.

(b) Monitoring

(1) In general

The Administrator, in consultation with the Administrator of the National Oceanic and At-

[1] See References in Text note below.

mospheric Administration and the Secretary, shall conduct a comprehensive and continuing program to assess aquatic sediment quality. The program conducted pursuant to this subsection shall, at a minimum—

(A) identify the location of pollutants in aquatic sediment;

(B) identify the extent of pollutants in sediment and those sediments which are contaminated pursuant to section 501(b)(4);[1]

(C) establish methods and protocols for monitoring the physical, chemical, and biological effects of pollutants in aquatic sediment and of contaminated sediment;

(D) develop a system for the management, storage, and dissemination of data concerning aquatic sediment quality;

(E) provide an assessment of aquatic sediment quality trends over time;

(F) identify locations where pollutants in sediment may pose a threat to the quality of drinking water supplies, fisheries resources, and marine habitats; and

(G) establish a clearing house for information on technology, methods, and practices available for the remediation, decontamination, and control of sediment contamination.

(2) Report

The Administrator shall submit to Congress a report on the findings of the monitoring under paragraph (1) on the date that is 2 years after the date specified in subsection (a)(2) of this section and biennially thereafter.

(Pub. L. 102–580, title V, §503, Oct. 31, 1992, 106 Stat. 4865.)

REFERENCES IN TEXT

Section 501(b)(4), referred to in subsecs. (a)(1) and (b)(1)(B), means section 501(b)(4) of Pub. L. 102–580, which is set out below.

CODIFICATION

Section was enacted as part of the Water Resources Development Act of 1992 and also as part of the National Contaminated Sediment Assessment and Management Act, and not as part of the Federal Water Pollution Control Act which comprises this chapter.

AVAILABILITY OF CONTAMINATED SEDIMENTS INFORMATION

Section 327 of Pub. L. 102–580 directed Secretary to conduct national study on information that was currently available on contaminated sediments of surface waters of United States and compile information obtained for the purpose of identifying location and nature of contaminated sediments and, not later than 1 year after Oct. 31, 1992, to transmit to Congress a report on the results of the study.

NATIONAL CONTAMINATED SEDIMENT ASSESSMENT AND MANAGEMENT; SHORT TITLE; DEFINITIONS; TASK FORCE

Sections 501 and 502 of title V of Pub. L. 102–580 provided that:

"SEC. 501. SHORT TITLE AND DEFINITIONS.

"(a) SHORT TITLE.—This title [enacting this section, amending sections 1412 to 1416, 1420, and 1421 of this title, and enacting provisions set out below] may be cited as the 'National Contaminated Sediment Assessment and Management Act'.

"(b) DEFINITIONS.—For the purposes of sections 502 and 503 of this title [enacting this section and provisions set out below]—

"(1) the term 'aquatic sediment' means sediment underlying the navigable waters of the United States;

"(2) the term 'navigable waters' has the same meaning as in section 502(7) of the Federal Water Pollution Control Act (33 U.S.C. 1362(7));

"(3) the term 'pollutant' has the same meaning as in section 502(6) of the Federal Water Pollution Control Act (33 U.S.C. 1362(6)); except that such term does not include dredge spoil, rock, sand, or cellar dirt;

"(4) the term 'contaminated sediment' means aquatic sediment which—

"(A) contains chemical substances in excess of appropriate geochemical, toxicological or sediment quality criteria or measures; or

"(B) is otherwise considered by the Administrator to pose a threat to human health or the environment; and

"(5) the term 'Administrator' means the Administrator of the Environmental Protection Agency.

"SEC. 502. NATIONAL CONTAMINATED SEDIMENT TASK FORCE.

"(a) ESTABLISHMENT.—There is established a National Contaminated Sediment Task Force (hereinafter referred to in this section as the 'Task Force'). The Task Force shall—

"(1) advise the Administrator and the Secretary in the implementation of this title;

"(2) review and comment on reports concerning aquatic sediment quality and the extent and seriousness of aquatic sediment contamination throughout the Nation;

"(3) review and comment on programs for the research and development of aquatic sediment restoration methods, practices, and technologies;

"(4) review and comment on the selection of pollutants for development of aquatic sediment criteria and the schedule for the development of such criteria;

"(5) advise appropriate officials in the development of guidelines for restoration of contaminated sediment;

"(6) make recommendations to appropriate officials concerning practices and measures—

"(A) to prevent the contamination of aquatic sediments; and

"(B) to control sources of sediment contamination; and

"(7) review and assess the means and methods for locating and constructing permanent, cost-effective long-term disposal sites for the disposal of dredged material that is not suitable for ocean dumping (as determined under the Marine Protection, Research, and Sanctuaries Act of 1972 (33 U.S.C. 1401 et seq.) [also 16 U.S.C. 1431 et seq., 1447 et seq.; 33 U.S.C. 2801 et seq.]).

"(b) MEMBERSHIP.—

"(1) IN GENERAL.—The membership of the Task Force shall include 1 representative of each of the following:

"(A) The Administrator.

"(B) The Secretary.

"(C) The National Oceanic and Atmospheric Administration.

"(D) The United States Fish and Wildlife Service.

"(E) The Geological Survey [now United States Geological Survey].

"(F) The Department of Agriculture.

"(2) ADDITIONAL MEMBERS.—Additional members of the Task Force shall be jointly selected by the Administrator and the Secretary, and shall include—

"(A) not more than 3 representatives of States;

"(B) not more than 3 representatives of ports, agriculture, and manufacturing; and

"(C) not more than 3 representatives of public interest organizations with a demonstrated interest in aquatic sediment contamination.

"(3) COCHAIRMEN.—The Administrator and the Secretary shall serve as cochairmen of the Task Force.

"(4) CLERICAL AND TECHNICAL ASSISTANCE.—Such clerical and technical assistance as may be necessary to discharge the duties of the Task Force shall be provided by the personnel of the Environmental Protection Agency and the Army Corps of Engineers.

"(5) COMPENSATION FOR ADDITIONAL MEMBERS.—The additional members of the Task Force selected under paragraph (2) shall, while attending meetings or conferences of the Task Force, be compensated at a rate to be fixed by the cochairmen, but not to exceed the daily equivalent of the base rate of pay in effect for grade GS–15 of the General Schedule under section 5332 of title 5, United States Code, for each day (including travel time) during which they are engaged in the actual performance of duties vested in the Task Force. While away from their homes or regular places of business in the performance of services for the Task Force, such members shall be allowed travel expenses, including per diem in lieu of subsistence, in the same manner as persons employed intermittently in the Government service are allowed expenses under section 5703(b) of title 5, United States Code.

"(c) REPORT.—Within 2 years after the date of the enactment of this Act [Oct. 31, 1992], the Task Force shall submit to Congress a report stating the findings and recommendations of the Task Force."

AUTHORIZATION OF APPROPRIATIONS

Section 509(b) of Pub. L. 102–580 provided that: "There is authorized to be appropriated to the Administrator to carry out sections 502 and 503 [enacting this section and provisions set out above] such sums as may be necessary."

"SECRETARY" DEFINED

Secretary means the Secretary of the Army, see section 3 of Pub. L. 102–580, set out as a note under section 2201 of this title.

§ 1271a. Research and development program

(a) In general

In coordination with other Federal, State, and local officials, the Administrator of the Environmental Protection Agency may conduct research on the development and use of innovative approaches, technologies, and techniques for the remediation of sediment contamination in areas of concern that are located wholly or partially in the United States.

(b) Authorization of appropriations

(1) In general

In addition to any amounts authorized under other provisions of law, there is authorized to be appropriated to carry out this section $3,000,000 for each of fiscal years 2004 through 2010.

(2) Availability

Funds appropriated under paragraph (1) shall remain available until expended.

(Pub. L. 107–303, title I, § 106, Nov. 27, 2002, 116 Stat. 2358; Pub. L. 110–365, § 4, Oct. 8, 2008, 122 Stat. 4023.)

CODIFICATION

Section was enacted as part of the Great Lakes Legacy Act of 2002, and also as part of the Great Lakes and Lake Champlain Act of 2002, and not as part of the Federal Water Pollution Control Act which comprises this chapter.

AMENDMENTS

2008—Subsec. (b)(1). Pub. L. 110–365 added par. (1) and struck out former par. (1). Prior to amendment, text read as follows: "In addition to amounts authorized under other laws, there is authorized to be appropriated to carry out this section $3,000,000 for each of fiscal years 2004 through 2008."

§ 1272. Environmental dredging

(a) Operation and maintenance of navigation projects

Whenever necessary to meet the requirements of the Federal Water Pollution Control Act [33 U.S.C. 1251 et seq.], the Secretary, in consultation with the Administrator of the Environmental Protection Agency, may remove and remediate, as part of operation and maintenance of a navigation project, contaminated sediments outside the boundaries of and adjacent to the navigation channel.

(b) Nonproject specific

(1) In general

The Secretary may remove and remediate contaminated sediments from the navigable waters of the United States for the purpose of environmental enhancement and water quality improvement if such removal and remediation is requested by a non-Federal sponsor and the sponsor agrees to pay 35 percent of the cost of such removal and remediation.

(2) Maximum amount

The Secretary may not expend more than $50,000,000 in a fiscal year to carry out this subsection.

(c) Joint plan requirement

The Secretary may only remove and remediate contaminated sediments under subsection (b) of this section in accordance with a joint plan developed by the Secretary and interested Federal, State, and local government officials. Such plan must include an opportunity for public comment, a description of the work to be undertaken, the method to be used for dredged material disposal, the roles and responsibilities of the Secretary and non-Federal sponsors, and identification of sources of funding.

(d) Disposal costs

Costs of disposal of contaminated sediments removed under this section shall be a[1] shared as a cost of construction.

(e) Limitation on statutory construction

Nothing in this section shall be construed to affect the rights and responsibilities of any person under the Comprehensive Environmental Response, Compensation, and Liability Act of 1980 [42 U.S.C. 9601 et seq.].

(f) Priority work

In carrying out this section, the Secretary shall give priority to work in the following areas:

(1) Brooklyn Waterfront, New York.

(2) Buffalo Harbor and River, New York.

(3) Ashtabula River, Ohio.

(4) Mahoning River, Ohio.

(5) Lower Fox River, Wisconsin.

(6) Passaic River and Newark Bay, New Jersey.

(7) Snake Creek, Bixby, Oklahoma.

(8) Willamette River, Oregon.

[1] So in original. The word "a" probably should not appear.

(g) Nonprofit entities

Notwithstanding section 1962d–5b of title 42, for any project carried out under this section, a non-Federal sponsor may include a nonprofit entity, with the consent of the affected local government.

(Pub. L. 101–640, title III, § 312, Nov. 28, 1990, 104 Stat. 4639; Pub. L. 104–303, title II, § 205, Oct. 12, 1996, 110 Stat. 3679; Pub. L. 106–53, title II, § 224, Aug. 17, 1999, 113 Stat. 297; Pub. L. 106–541, title II, § 210(a), Dec. 11, 2000, 114 Stat. 2592.)

REFERENCES IN TEXT

The Federal Water Pollution Control Act, referred to in subsec. (a), is act June 30, 1948, ch. 758, as amended generally by Pub. L. 92–500, § 2, Oct. 18, 1972, 86 Stat. 816, which is classified generally to this chapter (§ 1251 et seq.). For complete classification of this Act to the Code, see Short Title note set out under section 1251 of this title and Tables.

The Comprehensive Environmental Response, Compensation, and Liability Act of 1980, referred to in subsec. (e), is Pub. L. 96–510, Dec. 11, 1980, 94 Stat. 2767, as amended, which is classified principally to chapter 103 (§ 9601 et seq.) of Title 42, The Public Health and Welfare. For complete classification of this Act to the Code, see Short Title note set out under section 9601 of Title 42 and Tables.

CODIFICATION

Section was formerly set out as a note under section 1252 of this title.

Section was enacted as part of the Water Resources Development Act of 1990, and not as part of the Federal Water Pollution Control Act which comprises this chapter.

AMENDMENTS

2000—Subsec. (g). Pub. L. 106–541 added subsec. (g).

1999—Subsec. (b)(1). Pub. L. 106–53, § 224(1)(A), substituted "35 percent" for "50 percent".

Subsec. (b)(2). Pub. L. 106–53, § 224(1)(B), substituted "$50,000,000" for "$20,000,000".

Subsec. (d). Pub. L. 106–53, § 224(2), substituted "shared as a cost of construction" for "non-Federal responsibility".

Subsec. (f)(6) to (8). Pub. L. 106–53, § 224(3), added pars. (6) to (8).

1996—Subsec. (a). Pub. L. 104–303, § 205(1), inserted "and remediate" after "remove".

Subsec. (b)(1). Pub. L. 104–303, § 205(1), (2)(A), inserted "and remediate" after "remove" and inserted "and remediation" after "removal" in two places.

Subsec. (b)(2). Pub. L. 104–303, § 205(2)(B), substituted "$20,000,000" for "$10,000,000".

Subsec. (c). Pub. L. 104–303, § 205(1), inserted "and remediate" after "remove".

Subsec. (f). Pub. L. 104–303, § 205(3), added subsec. (f) and struck out heading and text of former subsec. (f). Text read as follows: "This section shall not be effective after the last day of the 5-year period beginning on November 28, 1990; except that the Secretary may complete any project commenced under this section on or before such last day."

§ 1273. Lake Pontchartrain Basin

(a) Establishment of restoration program

The Administrator shall establish within the Environmental Protection Agency the Lake Pontchartrain Basin Restoration Program.

(b) Purpose

The purpose of the program shall be to restore the ecological health of the Basin by developing and funding restoration projects and related scientific and public education projects.

(c) Duties

In carrying out the program, the Administrator shall—

(1) provide administrative and technical assistance to a management conference convened for the Basin under section 1330 of this title;

(2) assist and support the activities of the management conference, including the implementation of recommendations of the management conference;

(3) support environmental monitoring of the Basin and research to provide necessary technical and scientific information;

(4) develop a comprehensive research plan to address the technical needs of the program;

(5) coordinate the grant, research, and planning programs authorized under this section; and

(6) collect and make available to the public publications, and other forms of information the management conference determines to be appropriate, relating to the environmental quality of the Basin.

(d) Grants

The Administrator may make grants—

(1) for restoration projects and studies recommended by a management conference convened for the Basin under section 1330 of this title; and

(2) for public education projects recommended by the management conference.

(e) Definitions

In this section, the following definitions apply:

(1) Basin

The term "Basin" means the Lake Pontchartrain Basin, a 5,000 square mile watershed encompassing 16 parishes in the State of Louisiana and 4 counties in the State of Mississippi.

(2) Program

The term "program" means the Lake Pontchartrain Basin Restoration Program established under subsection (a) of this section.

(f) Authorization of appropriations

(1) In general

There is authorized to be appropriated to carry out this section $20,000,000 for each of fiscal years 2001 through 2011. Such sums shall remain available until expended.

(2) Public education projects

Not more than 15 percent of the amount appropriated pursuant to paragraph (1) in a fiscal year may be expended on grants for public education projects under subsection (d)(2) of this section.

(June 30, 1948, ch. 758, title I, § 121, as added Pub. L. 106–457, title V, § 502, Nov. 7, 2000, 114 Stat. 1973; amended Pub. L. 109–392, § 1, Dec. 12, 2006, 120 Stat. 2703.)

PRIOR PROVISIONS

Another section 121 of act June 30, 1948, was renumbered section 122 and is classified to section 1274 of this title.

AMENDMENTS

2006—Subsec. (f)(1). Pub. L. 109–392 substituted "2011" for "2005".

MANAGEMENT CONFERENCE

Pub. L. 110–114, title V, §5084, Nov. 8, 2007, 121 Stat. 1228, provided that: "For purposes of carrying out section 121 of the Federal Water Pollution Control Act (33 U.S.C. 1273), the Lake Pontchartrain, Louisiana, basin stakeholders conference convened by the Environmental Protection Agency, National Oceanic and Atmospheric Administration, and United States Geological Survey on February 25, 2002, shall be treated as being a management conference convened under section 320 of such Act (33 U.S.C. 1330)."

§1274. Wet weather watershed pilot projects

(a) In general

The Administrator, in coordination with the States, may provide technical assistance and grants for treatment works to carry out pilot projects relating to the following areas of wet weather discharge control:

(1) Watershed management of wet weather discharges

The management of municipal combined sewer overflows, sanitary sewer overflows, and stormwater discharges, on an integrated watershed or subwatershed basis for the purpose of demonstrating the effectiveness of a unified wet weather approach.

(2) Stormwater best management practices

The control of pollutants from municipal separate storm sewer systems for the purpose of demonstrating and determining controls that are cost-effective and that use innovative technologies in reducing such pollutants from stormwater discharges.

(b) Administration

The Administrator, in coordination with the States, shall provide municipalities participating in a pilot project under this section the ability to engage in innovative practices, including the ability to unify separate wet weather control efforts under a single permit.

(c) Funding

(1) In general

There is authorized to be appropriated to carry out this section $10,000,000 for fiscal year 2002, $15,000,000 for fiscal year 2003, and $20,000,000 for fiscal year 2004. Such funds shall remain available until expended.

(2) Stormwater

The Administrator shall make available not less than 20 percent of amounts appropriated for a fiscal year pursuant to this subsection to carry out the purposes of subsection (a)(2) of this section.

(3) Administrative expenses

The Administrator may retain not to exceed 4 percent of any amounts appropriated for a fiscal year pursuant to this subsection for the reasonable and necessary costs of administering this section.

(d) Report to Congress

Not later than 5 years after December 21, 2000, the Administrator shall transmit to Congress a report on the results of the pilot projects conducted under this section and their possible application nationwide.

(June 30, 1948, ch. 758, title I, §122, formerly §121, as added Pub. L. 106–554, §1(a)(4) [div. B, title I, §112(b)], Dec. 21, 2000, 114 Stat. 2763, 2763A–225; renumbered §122, Pub. L. 109–392, §2, Dec. 12, 2006, 120 Stat. 2703.)

SUBCHAPTER II—GRANTS FOR CONSTRUCTION OF TREATMENT WORKS

§1281. Congressional declaration of purpose

(a) Development and implementation of waste treatment management plans and practices

It is the purpose of this subchapter to require and to assist the development and implementation of waste treatment management plans and practices which will achieve the goals of this chapter.

(b) Application of technology: confined disposal of pollutants; consideration of advanced techniques

Waste treatment management plans and practices shall provide for the application of the best practicable waste treatment technology before any discharge into receiving waters, including reclaiming and recycling of water, and confined disposal of pollutants so they will not migrate to cause water or other environmental pollution and shall provide for consideration of advanced waste treatment techniques.

(c) Waste treatment management area and scope

To the extent practicable, waste treatment management shall be on an areawide basis and provide control or treatment of all point and nonpoint sources of pollution, including in place or accumulated pollution sources.

(d) Waste treatment management construction of revenue producing facilities

The Administrator shall encourage waste treatment management which results in the construction of revenue producing facilities providing for—

(1) the recycling of potential sewage pollutants through the production of agriculture, silviculture, or aquaculture products, or any combination thereof;

(2) the confined and contained disposal of pollutants not recycled;

(3) the reclamation of wastewater; and

(4) the ultimate disposal of sludge in a manner that will not result in environmental hazards.

(e) Waste treatment management integration of facilities

The Administrator shall encourage waste treatment management which results in integrating facilities for sewage treatment and recycling with facilities to treat, dispose of, or utilize other industrial and municipal wastes, including but not limited to solid waste and waste heat and thermal discharges. Such integrated facilities shall be designed and operated to produce revenues in excess of capital and operation and maintenance costs and such revenues shall be used by the designated regional management agency to aid in financing other environmental improvement programs.

(f) Waste treatment management "open space" and recreational considerations

The Administrator shall encourage waste treatment management which combines "open space" and recreational considerations with such management.

(g) Grants to construct publicly owned treatment works

(1) The Administrator is authorized to make grants to any State, municipality, or intermunicipal or interstate agency for the construction of publicly owned treatment works. On and after October 1, 1984, grants under this subchapter shall be made only for projects for secondary treatment or more stringent treatment, or any cost effective alternative thereto, new interceptors and appurtenances, and infiltration-in-flow correction. Notwithstanding the preceding sentences, the Administrator may make grants on and after October 1, 1984, for (A) any project within the definition set forth in section 1292(2) of this title, other than for a project referred to in the preceding sentence, and (B) any purpose for which a grant may be made under sections[1] 1329(h) and (i) of this title (including any innovative and alternative approaches for the control of nonpoint sources of pollution), except that not more than 20 per centum (as determined by the Governor of the State) of the amount allotted to a State under section 1285 of this title for any fiscal year shall be obligated in such State under authority of this sentence.

(2) The Administrator shall not make grants from funds authorized for any fiscal year beginning after June 30, 1974, to any State, municipality, or intermunicipal or interstate agency for the erection, building, acquisition, alteration, remodeling, improvement, or extension of treatment works unless the grant applicant has satisfactorily demonstrated to the Administrator that—

(A) alternative waste management techniques have been studied and evaluated and the works proposed for grant assistance will provide for the application of the best practicable waste treatment technology over the life of the works consistent with the purposes of this subchapter; and

(B) as appropriate, the works proposed for grant assistance will take into account and allow to the extent practicable the application of technology at a later date which will provide for the reclaiming or recycling of water or otherwise eliminate the discharge of pollutants.

(3) The Administrator shall not approve any grant after July 1, 1973, for treatment works under this section unless the applicant shows to the satisfaction of the Administrator that each sewer collection system discharging into such treatment works is not subject to excessive infiltration.

(4) The Administrator is authorized to make grants to applicants for treatment works grants under this section for such sewer system evaluation studies as may be necessary to carry out the requirements of paragraph (3) of this subsection. Such grants shall be made in accordance with rules and regulations promulgated by the Administrator. Initial rules and regulations shall be promulgated under this paragraph not later than 120 days after October 18, 1972.

(5) The Administrator shall not make grants from funds authorized for any fiscal year beginning after September 30, 1978, to any State, municipality, or intermunicipal or interstate agency for the erection, building, acquisition, alteration, remodeling, improvement, or extension of treatment works unless the grant applicant has satisfactorily demonstrated to the Administrator that innovative and alternative wastewater treatment processes and techniques which provide for the reclaiming and reuse of water, otherwise eliminate the discharge of pollutants, and utilize recycling techniques, land treatment, new or improved methods of waste treatment management for municipal and industrial waste (discharged into municipal systems) and the confined disposal of pollutants, so that pollutants will not migrate to cause water or other environmental pollution, have been fully studied and evaluated by the applicant taking into account subsection (d) of this section and taking into account and allowing to the extent practicable the more efficient use of energy and resources.

(6) The Administrator shall not make grants from funds authorized for any fiscal year beginning after September 30, 1978, to any State, municipality, or intermunicipal or interstate agency for the erection, building, acquisition, alteration, remodeling, improvement, or extension of treatment works unless the grant applicant has satisfactorily demonstrated to the Administrator that the applicant has analyzed the potential recreation and open space opportunities in the planning of the proposed treatment works.

(h) Grants to construct privately owned treatment works

A grant may be made under this section to construct a privately owned treatment works serving one or more principal residences or small commercial establishments constructed prior to, and inhabited on, December 27, 1977, where the Administrator finds that—

(1) a public body otherwise eligible for a grant under subsection (g) of this section has applied on behalf of a number of such units and certified that public ownership of such works is not feasible;

(2) such public body has entered into an agreement with the Administrator which guarantees that such treatment works will be properly operated and maintained and will comply with all other requirements of section 1284 of this title and includes a system of charges to assure that each recipient of waste treatment services under such a grant will pay its proportionate share of the cost of operation and maintenance (including replacement); and

(3) the total cost and environmental impact of providing waste treatment services to such

[1] So in original. Probably should be "section".

residences or commercial establishments will be less than the cost of providing a system of collection and central treatment of such wastes.

(i) Waste treatment management methods, processes, and techniques to reduce energy requirements

The Administrator shall encourage waste treatment management methods, processes, and techniques which will reduce total energy requirements.

(j) Grants for treatment works utilizing processes and techniques of guidelines under section 1314(d)(3) of this title

The Administrator is authorized to make a grant for any treatment works utilizing processes and techniques meeting the guidelines promulgated under section 1314(d)(3) of this title, if the Administrator determines it is in the public interest and if in the cost effectiveness study made of the construction grant application for the purpose of evaluating alternative treatment works, the life cycle cost of the treatment works for which the grant is to be made does not exceed the life cycle cost of the most cost effective alternative by more than 15 per centum.

(k) Limitation on use of grants for publicly owned treatment works

No grant made after November 15, 1981, for a publicly owned treatment works, other than for facility planning and the preparation of construction plans and specifications, shall be used to treat, store, or convey the flow of any industrial user into such treatment works in excess of a flow per day equivalent to fifty thousand gallons per day of sanitary waste. This subsection shall not apply to any project proposed by a grantee which is carrying out an approved project to prepare construction plans and specifications for a facility to treat wastewater, which received its grant approval before May 15, 1980. This subsection shall not be in effect after November 15, 1981.

(*l*) Grants for facility plans, or plans, specifications, and estimates for proposed project for construction of treatment works; limitations, allotments, advances, etc.

(1) After December 29, 1981, Federal grants shall not be made for the purpose of providing assistance solely for facility plans, or plans, specifications, and estimates for any proposed project for the construction of treatment works. In the event that the proposed project receives a grant under this section for construction, the Administrator shall make an allowance in such grant for non-Federal funds expended during the facility planning and advanced engineering and design phase at the prevailing Federal share under section 1282(a) of this title, based on the percentage of total project costs which the Administrator determines is the general experience for such projects.

(2)(A) Each State shall use a portion of the funds allotted to such State each fiscal year, but not to exceed 10 per centum of such funds, to advance to potential grant applicants under this subchapter the costs of facility planning or the preparation of plans, specifications, and estimates.

(B) Such an advance shall be limited to the allowance for such costs which the Administrator establishes under paragraph (1) of this subsection, and shall be provided only to a potential grant applicant which is a small community and which in the judgment of the State would otherwise be unable to prepare a request for a grant for construction costs under this section.

(C) In the event a grant for construction costs is made under this section for a project for which an advance has been made under this paragraph, the Administrator shall reduce the amount of such grant by the allowance established under paragraph (1) of this subsection. In the event no such grant is made, the State is authorized to seek repayment of such advance on such terms and conditions as it may determine.

(m) Grants for State of California projects

(1) Notwithstanding any other provisions of this subchapter, the Administrator is authorized to make a grant from any funds otherwise allotted to the State of California under section 1285 of this title to the project (and in the amount) specified in Order WQG 81–1 of the California State Water Resources Control Board.

(2) Notwithstanding any other provision of this chapter, the Administrator shall make a grant from any funds otherwise allotted to the State of California to the city of Eureka, California, in connection with project numbered C–06–2772, for the purchase of one hundred and thirty-nine acres of property as environmental mitigation for siting of the proposed treatment plant.

(3) Notwithstanding any other provision of this chapter, the Administrator shall make a grant from any funds otherwise allotted to the State of California to the city of San Diego, California, in connection with that city's aquaculture sewage process (total resources recovery system) as an innovative and alternative waste treatment process.

(n) Water quality problems; funds, scope, etc.

(1) On and after October 1, 1984, upon the request of the Governor of an affected State, the Administrator is authorized to use funds available to such State under section 1285 of this title to address water quality problems due to the impacts of discharges from combined storm water and sanitary sewer overflows, which are not otherwise eligible under this subsection, where correction of such discharges is a major priority for such State.

(2) Beginning fiscal year 1983, the Administrator shall have available $200,000,000 per fiscal year in addition to those funds authorized in section 1287 of this title to be utilized to address water quality problems of marine bays and estuaries subject to lower levels of water quality due to the impacts of discharges from combined storm water and sanitary sewer overflows from adjacent urban complexes, not otherwise eligible under this subsection. Such sums may be used as deemed appropriate by the Administrator as provided in paragraphs (1) and (2) of this subsection, upon the request of and demonstration of water quality benefits by the Governor of an affected State.

(*o*) Capital financing plan

The Administrator shall encourage and assist applicants for grant assistance under this subchapter to develop and file with the Administrator a capital financing plan which, at a minimum—

(1) projects the future requirements for waste treatment services within the applicant's jurisdiction for a period of no less than ten years;

(2) projects the nature, extent, timing, and costs of future expansion and reconstruction of treatment works which will be necessary to satisfy the applicant's projected future requirements for waste treatment services; and

(3) sets forth with specificity the manner in which the applicant intends to finance such future expansion and reconstruction.

(p) Time limit on resolving certain disputes

In any case in which a dispute arises with respect to the awarding of a contract for construction of treatment works by a grantee of funds under this subchapter and a party to such dispute files an appeal with the Administrator under this subchapter for resolution of such dispute, the Administrator shall make a final decision on such appeal within 90 days of the filing of such appeal.

(June 30, 1948, ch. 758, title II, §201, as added Pub. L. 92–500, §2, Oct. 18, 1972, 86 Stat. 833; amended Pub. L. 95–217, §§12–16, Dec. 27, 1977, 91 Stat. 1569, 1570; Pub. L. 96–483, §§2(d), 3, Oct. 21, 1980, 94 Stat. 2361; Pub. L. 97–117, §§2(a), 3(a), 4–6, 10(c), Dec. 29, 1981, 95 Stat. 1623–1626; Pub. L. 100–4, title II, §201, title III, §316(c), Feb. 4, 1987, 101 Stat. 15, 60.)

AMENDMENTS

1987—Subsec. (g)(1). Pub. L. 100–4, §316(c), substituted "sentences, the Administrator" for "sentence, the Administrator" and inserted "(A)" after "October 1, 1984, for" and "and (B) any purpose for which a grant may be made under sections 1329(h) and (i) of this title (including any innovative and alternative approaches for the control of nonpoint sources of pollution)," before "except that".

Subsec. (p). Pub. L. 100–4, §201, added subsec. (p).

1981—Subsec. (g)(1). Pub. L. 97–117, §2(a), inserted provisions restricting, on or after Oct. 1, 1984, the categories of projects eligible for grants under this subchapter and providing an exception to the restriction for projects, other than specified projects, within the definition set forth in section 1292(2) of this title, but limiting such exception to not more than 20 per centum, as determined by the Governor of the State, of the amount allotted to a State under section 1285 of this title for any fiscal year.

Subsec. (k). Pub. L. 97–117, §10(c), inserted provision that subsection not be in effect after Nov. 15, 1981.

Subsec. (*l*). Pub. L. 97–117, §3(a), added subsec. (*l*).

Subsec. (m). Pub. L. 97–117, §4, added subsec. (m).

Subsec. (n). Pub. L. 97–117, §5, added subsec. (n).

Subsec. (*o*). Pub. L. 97–117, §6, added subsec. (*o*).

1980—Subsec. (h). Pub. L. 96–483, §2(d), struck out text following par. (3), relating to payment to the United States by commercial users of that portion of the cost of construction applicable to treatment of commercial wastes to the extent attributable to the Federal share of the cost of construction.

Subsec. (k). Pub. L. 96–483, §3, added subsec. (k).

1977—Subsec. (g)(5). Pub. L. 95–217, §12, added par. (5).

Subsec. (g)(6). Pub. L. 95–217, §13, added par. (6).

Subsec. (h). Pub. L. 95–217, §14, added subsec. (h).

Subsec. (i). Pub. L. 95–217, §15, added subsec. (i).

Subsec. (j). Pub. L. 95–217, §16, added subsec. (j).

EFFECTIVE DATE OF 1980 AMENDMENT

Section 2(g) of Pub. L. 96–483 provided that: "The amendments made by this section [amending sections 1281, 1284, and 1293 of this title, enacting provisions set out as notes under section 1284 of this title, and amending provisions set out as a note under section 1284 of this title] shall take effect on December 27, 1977."

ENVIRONMENTAL PROTECTION AGENCY STATE AND TRIBAL ASSISTANCE GRANTS

Pub. L. 105–174, title III, May 1, 1998, 112 Stat. 92, provided that: "Notwithstanding any other provision of law, eligible recipients of the funds appropriated to the Environmental Protection Agency in the State and Tribal Assistance Grants account since fiscal year 1997 and hereafter for multi-media or single media grants, other than Performance Partnership Grants authorized pursuant to Public Law 104–134 and Public Law 105–65 [see Grants to Indian Tribes for Pollution Prevention, Control, and Abatement notes set out below], for pollution prevention, control, and abatement and related activities have been and shall be those entities eligible for grants under the Agency's organic statutes."

PRIVATIZATION OF INFRASTRUCTURE ASSETS

Pub. L. 104–303, title V, §586, Oct. 12, 1996, 110 Stat. 3791, provided that:

"(a) IN GENERAL.—Notwithstanding the provisions of title II of the Federal Water Pollution Control Act (33 U.S.C. 1281 et seq.), Executive Order 12803 [5 U.S.C. 601 note], or any other law or authority, an entity that received Federal grant assistance for an infrastructure asset under the Federal Water Pollution Control Act [33 U.S.C. 1251 et seq.] shall not be required to repay any portion of the grant upon the lease or concession of the asset only if—

"(1) ownership of the asset remains with the entity that received the grant; and

"(2) the Administrator of the Environmental Protection Agency determines that the lease or concession furthers the purposes of such Act and approves the lease or concession.

"(b) LIMITATION.—The Administrator shall not approve a total of more than 5 leases and concessions under this section."

GRANTS TO STATES TO ADMINISTER COMPLETION AND CLOSEOUT OF CONSTRUCTION GRANTS PROGRAM

Pub. L. 104–204, title III, Sept. 26, 1996, 110 Stat. 2912, provided in part: "That notwithstanding any other provision of law, beginning in fiscal year 1997 the Administrator may make grants to States, from funds available for obligation in the State under title II of the Federal Water Pollution Control Act [33 U.S.C. 1281 et seq.], as amended, for administering the completion and closeout of the State's construction grants program, based on a budget annually negotiated with the State".

WASTEWATER ASSISTANCE TO COLONIAS

Pub. L. 104–182, title III, §307, Aug. 6, 1996, 110 Stat. 1688, provided that:

"(a) DEFINITIONS.—As used in this section:

"(1) BORDER STATE.—The term 'border State' means Arizona, California, New Mexico, and Texas.

"(2) ELIGIBLE COMMUNITY.—The term 'eligible community' means a low-income community with economic hardship that—

"(A) is commonly referred to as a colonia;

"(B) is located along the United States-Mexico border (generally in an unincorporated area); and

"(C) lacks basic sanitation facilities such as household plumbing or a proper sewage disposal system.

"(3) TREATMENT WORKS.—The term 'treatment works' has the meaning provided in section 212(2) of the Federal Water Pollution Control Act (33 U.S.C. 1292(2)).

"(b) GRANTS FOR WASTEWATER ASSISTANCE.—The Administrator of the Environmental Protection Agency and the heads of other appropriate Federal agencies are authorized to award grants to a border State to provide assistance to eligible communities for the planning, design, and construction or improvement of sewers, treatment works, and appropriate connections for wastewater treatment.

"(c) USE OF FUNDS.—Each grant awarded pursuant to subsection (b) shall be used to provide assistance to one or more eligible communities with respect to which the residents are subject to a significant health risk (as determined by the Administrator or the head of the Federal agency making the grant) attributable to the lack of access to an adequate and affordable treatment works for wastewater.

"(d) COST SHARING.—The amount of a grant awarded pursuant to this section shall not exceed 50 percent of the costs of carrying out the project that is the subject of the grant.

"(e) AUTHORIZATION OF APPROPRIATIONS.—There are authorized to be appropriated to carry out this section $25,000,000 for each of the fiscal years 1997 through 1999."

GRANTS TO INDIAN TRIBES FOR POLLUTION PREVENTION, CONTROL AND ABATEMENT

Pub. L. 105–65, title III, Oct. 27, 1997, 111 Stat. 1373, provided in part that: "$745,000,000 for grants to States, federally recognized tribes, and air pollution control agencies for multi-media or single media pollution prevention, control and abatement and related activities pursuant to the provisions set forth under this heading in Public Law 104–134 [see below], provided that eligible recipients of these funds and the funds made available for this purpose since fiscal year 1996 and hereafter include States, federally recognized tribes, interstate agencies, tribal consortia, and air pollution control agencies, as provided in authorizing statutes, subject to such terms and conditions as the Administrator shall establish, and for making grants under section 103 of the Clean Air Act [42 U.S.C. 7403] for particulate matter monitoring and data collection activities".

Pub. L. 105–65, title III, Oct. 27, 1997, 111 Stat. 1374, provided in part: "That, hereafter from funds appropriated under this heading ["ENVIRONMENTAL PROTECTION AGENCY" and "STATE AND TRIBAL ASSISTANCE GRANTS"], the Administrator is authorized to make grants to federally recognized Indian governments for the development of multi-media environmental programs: *Provided further*, That, hereafter, the funds available under this heading for grants to States, federally recognized tribes, and air pollution control agencies for multi-media or single media pollution prevention, control and abatement and related activities may also be used for the direct implementation by the Federal Government of a program required by law in the absence of an acceptable State or tribal program".

Similar provisions were contained in the following prior appropriation acts:

Pub. L. 104–204, title III, Sept. 26, 1996, 110 Stat. 2912.

Pub. L. 104–134, title I, §101(e) [title III], Apr. 26, 1996, 110 Stat. 1321–257, 1321–299, renumbered title I, Pub. L. 104–140, §1(a), May 2, 1996, 110 Stat. 1327.

Pub. L. 103–327, title III, Sept. 28, 1994, 108 Stat. 2320.

Pub. L. 103–124, title III, Oct. 28, 1993, 107 Stat. 1293.

Pub. L. 102–389, title III, Oct. 6, 1992, 106 Stat. 1597.

Pub. L. 102–139, title III, Oct. 28, 1991, 105 Stat. 762.

Pub. L. 101–507, title III, Nov. 5, 1990, 104 Stat. 1372.

Pub. L. 104–134, title I, §101(e) [title III], Apr. 26, 1996, 110 Stat. 1321–257, 1321–299; renumbered title I, Pub. L. 104–140, §1(a), May 2, 1996, 110 Stat. 1327, provided in part: "That beginning in fiscal year 1996 and each fiscal year thereafter, and notwithstanding any other provision of law, the Administrator is authorized to make grants annually from funds appropriated under this heading ["ENVIRONMENTAL PROTECTION AGENCY" and "STATE AND TRIBAL ASSISTANCE GRANTS"], subject to such terms and conditions as the Administrator shall establish, to any State or federally recognized Indian tribe for multimedia or single media pollution prevention, control and abatement and related environmental activities at the request of the Governor or other appropriate State official or the tribe".

STATE MANAGEMENT OF CONSTRUCTION GRANT ACTIVITIES

Pub. L. 104–134, title I, §101(e) [title III], Apr. 26, 1996, 110 Stat. 1321–257, 1321–299; renumbered title I, Pub. L. 104–140, §1(a), May 2, 1996, 110 Stat. 1327, provided in part: "That of the funds appropriated in the Construction Grants and Water Infrastructure/State Revolving Funds accounts since the appropriation for the fiscal year ending September 30, 1992, and hereafter, for making grants for wastewater treatment works construction projects, portions may be provided by the recipients to States for managing construction grant activities, on condition that the States agree to reimburse the recipients from State funding sources".

GRANTS TO TRUST TERRITORY OF THE PACIFIC ISLANDS, AMERICAN SAMOA, GUAM, NORTHERN MARIANA ISLANDS, AND VIRGIN ISLANDS; WAIVER OF COLLECTOR SEWERS LIMITATION

Pub. L. 99–396, §12(b), Aug. 27, 1986, 100 Stat. 841, provided that: "In awarding grants to the Trust Territory of the Pacific Islands, American Samoa, Guam, the Northern Mariana Islands and the Virgin Islands under section 201(g)(1) of the Clean Water Act (33 U.S.C. 1251 et seq.) [subsec. (g)(1) of this section], the Administrator of the Environmental Protection Agency may waive limitations regarding grant eligibility for sewerage facilities and related appurtenances, insofar as such limitations relate to collector sewers, based upon a determination that applying such limitations could hinder the alleviation of threats to public health and water quality. In making such a determination, the Administrator shall take into consideration the public health and water quality benefits to be derived and the availability of alternate funding sources. The Administrator shall not award grants under this section for the operation and maintenance of sewerage facilities, for construction of facilities which are not an essential component of the sewerage facilities, or any other activities or facilities which are not concerned with the management of wastewater to alleviate threats to public health and water quality." [For termination of Trust Territory of the Pacific Islands, see note set out preceding section 1681 of Title 48, Territories and Insular Possessions.]

ENVIRONMENTAL FINANCING AUTHORITY

Section 12 of Pub. L. 92–500, as amended by Pub. L. 97–258, §4(b), Sept. 13, 1982, 96 Stat. 1067, provided that:

"(a) [Short Title] This section may be cited as the Environmental Financing Act of 1972.

"(b) [Establishment] There is hereby created a body corporate to be known as the Environmental Financing Authority, which shall have succession until dissolved by Act of Congress. The Authority shall be subject to the general supervision and direction of the Secretary of the Treasury. The Authority shall be an instrumentality of the United States Government and shall maintain such offices as may be necessary or appropriate in the conduct of its business.

"(c) [Congressional Declaration of Purpose] The purpose of this section is to assure that inability to borrow necessary funds on reasonable terms does not prevent any State or local public body from carrying out any project for construction of waste treatment works determined eligible for assistance pursuant to subsection (e) of this section.

"(d) [Board of Directors] (1) The Authority shall have a Board of Directors consisting of five persons, one of whom shall be the Secretary of the Treasury or his designee as Chairman of the Board, and four of whom shall be appointed by the President from among the officers or employees of the Authority or of any department or agency of the United States Government.

"(2) The Board of Directors shall meet at the call of its Chairman. The Board shall determine the general policies which shall govern the operations of the Authority. The Chairman of the Board shall select and effect the appointment of qualified persons to fill the offices as may be provided for in the bylaws, with such executive functions, powers, and duties as may be prescribed by the bylaws or by the Board of Directors, and such persons shall be the executive officers of the Authority and shall discharge all such executive functions, powers, and duties. The members of the Board, as such, shall not receive compensation for their services.

"(e) [Purchase of State and Local Obligations] (1) Until July 1, 1975, the Authority is authorized to make commitments to purchase, and to purchase on terms and conditions determined by the Authority, any obligation or participation therein which is issued by a State or local public body to finance the non-Federal share of the cost of any project for the construction of waste treatment works which the Administrator of the Environmental Protection Agency has determined to be eligible for Federal financial assistance under the Federal Water Pollution Control Act [this chapter].

"(2) No commitment shall be entered into, and no purchase shall be made, unless the Administrator of the Environmental Protection Agency (A) has certified that the public body is unable to obtain on reasonable terms sufficient credit to finance its actual needs; (B) has approved the project as eligible under the Federal Water Pollution Control Act [this chapter], and (C) has agreed to guarantee timely payment of principal and interest on the obligation. The Administrator is authorized to guarantee such timely payments and to issue regulations as he deems necessary and proper to protect such guarantees. Appropriations are hereby authorized to be made to the Administrator in such sums as are necessary to make payments under such guarantees, and such payments are authorized to be made from such appropriations.

"(3) No purchase shall be made of obligations issued to finance projects, the permanent financing of which occurred prior to the enactment of this section [Oct. 18, 1972].

"(4) Any purchase by the Authority shall be upon such terms and conditions as to yield a return at a rate determined by the Secretary of the Treasury taking into consideration (A) the current average yield on outstanding marketable obligations of the United States of comparable maturity or in its stead whenever the Authority has sufficient of its own long-term obligations outstanding, the current average yield on outstanding obligations of the Authority of comparable maturity; and (B) the market yields on municipal bonds.

"(5) The Authority is authorized to charge fees for its commitments and other services adequate to cover all expenses and to provide for the accumulation of reasonable contingency reserves and such fees shall be included in the aggregate project costs.

"(f) [Initial Capital] To provide initial capital to the Authority the Secretary of the Treasury is authorized to advance the funds necessary for this purpose. Each such advance shall be upon such terms and conditions as to yield a return at a rate not less than a rate determined by the Secretary of the Treasury taking into consideration the current average yield on outstanding marketable obligations of the United States of comparable maturities. Interest payments on such advances may be deferred, at the discretion of the Secretary, but any such deferred payments shall themselves bear interest at the rate specified in this section. There is authorized to be appropriated not to exceed $100,000,000, which shall be available for the purposes of this subsection.

"(g) [Issuance of Obligations] (1) The Authority is authorized, with the approval of the Secretary of the Treasury, to issue and have outstanding obligations having such maturities and bearing such rate or rates of interest as may be determined by the Authority. Such obligations may be redeemable at the option of the Authority before maturity in such manner as may be stipulated therein.

"(2) As authorized in appropriation Acts, and such authorizations may be without fiscal year limitations, the Secretary of the Treasury may in his discretion purchase or agree to purchase any obligations issued pursuant to paragraph (1) of this subsection, and for such purpose the Secretary of the Treasury is authorized to use as a public debt transaction the proceeds of the sale of any securities hereafter issued under chapter 31 of title 31, as now or hereafter in force, and the purposes for which securities may be issued under chapter 31 of title 31, as now or hereafter in force, are extended to include such purchases. Each purchase of obligations by the Secretary of the Treasury under this subsection shall be upon such terms and conditions as to yield a return at a rate not less than a rate determined by the Secretary of the Treasury, taking into consideration the current average yield on outstanding marketable obligations of the United States of comparable maturities. The Secretary of the Treasury may sell, upon such terms and conditions and at such price or prices as he shall determine, any of the obligations acquired by him under this paragraph. All purchases and sales by the Secretary of the Treasury of such obligations under this paragraph shall be treated as public debt transactions of the United States. (As amended Pub. L. 97–258, §4(b), Sept. 13, 1982, 96 Stat. 1067.)

"(h) [Interest Differential] The Secretary of the Treasury is authorized and directed to make annual payments to the Authority in such amounts as are necessary to equal the amount by which the dollar amount of interest expense accrued by the Authority on account of its obligations exceeds the dollar amount of interest income accrued by the Authority on account of obligations purchased by it pursuant to subsection (e) of this section.

"(i) [Powers] The Authority shall have power—

"(1) to sue and be sued, complain and defend, in its corporate name;

"(2) to adopt, alter, and use a corporate seal, which shall be judicially noticed;

"(3) to adopt, amend, and repeal bylaws, rules, and regulations as may be necessary for the conduct of its business;

"(4) to conduct its business, carry on its operations, and have offices and exercise the powers granted by this section in any State without regard to any qualification or similar statute in any State;

"(5) to lease, purchase, or otherwise acquire, own, hold, improve, use, or otherwise deal in and with any property, real, personal, or mixed, or any interest therein, wherever situated;

"(6) to accept gifts or donations of services, or of property, real, personal, or mixed, tangible or intangible, in aid of any of the purposes of the Authority;

"(7) to sell, convey, mortgage, pledge, lease, exchange, and otherwise dispose of its property and assets;

"(8) to appoint such officers, attorneys, employees, and agents as may be required, to define their duties, to fix and to pay such compensation for their services as may be determined, subject to the civil service and classification laws, to require bonds for them and pay the premium thereof; and

"(9) to enter into contracts, to execute instruments, to incur liabilities, and to do all things as are necessary or incidental to the proper management of its affairs and the proper conduct of its business.

"(j) [Tax Exemption, Exemptions] The Authority, its property, its franchise, capital, reserves, surplus, security holdings, and other funds, and its income shall be exempt from all taxation now or hereafter imposed by the United States or by any State or local taxing authority; except that (A) any real property and any tangible personal property of the Authority shall be subject to Federal, State, and local taxation to the same extent according to its value as other such property is taxed, and (B) any and all obligations issued by the Authority shall be subject both as to principal and interest to Federal, State, and local taxation to the same extent as the obligations of private corporations are taxed.

"(k) [Nature of Obligations] All obligations issued by the Authority shall be lawful investments, and may be accepted as security for all fiduciary, trust, and public funds, the investment or deposit of which shall be under authority or control of the United States or of any officer or officers thereof. All obligations issued by the Authority pursuant to this section shall be deemed to be exempt securities within the meaning of laws administered by the Securities and Exchange Commission, to the same extent as securities which are issued by the United States.

"(*l*) [Preparation of Obligations by Secretary of the Treasury] In order to furnish obligations for delivery by the Authority, the Secretary of the Treasury is authorized to prepare such obligations in such form as the Authority may approve, such obligations when prepared to be held in the Treasury subject to delivery upon order by the Authority. The engraved plates, dies, bed pieces, and so forth, executed in connection therewith, shall remain in the custody of the Secretary of the Treasury. The Authority shall reimburse the Secretary of the Treasury for any expenditures made in the preparation, custody, and delivery of such obligations.

"(m) [Annual Report to Congress] The Authority shall, as soon as practicable after the end of each fiscal year, transmit to the President and the Congress an annual report of its operations and activities.

"(n) [Subsec. (n) amended section 24 of Title 12, Banks and Banking, and is not set out herein.]

"(*o*) [Financial Controls] The budget and audit provisions of chapter 91 of title 31 shall be applicable to the Environmental Financing Authority in the same manner as they are applied to the wholly owned Government corporations. (As amended Pub. L. 97–258, §4(b), Sept. 13, 1982, 96 Stat. 1067.)

"(p) [Subsec. (p) amended section 711 of former Title 31, Money and Finance, and is not set out herein.]"

§ 1281a. Total treatment system funding

Notwithstanding any other provision of law, in any case where the Administrator of the Environmental Protection Agency finds that the total of all grants made under section 1281 of this title for the same treatment works exceeds the actual construction costs for such treatment works (as defined in this chapter) such excess amount shall be a grant of the Federal share (as defined in this chapter) of the cost of construction of a sewage collection system if—

(1) such sewage collection system was constructed as part of the same total treatment system as the treatment works for which such grants under section 1281 of this title were approved, and

(2) an application for assistance for the construction of such sewage collection system was filed in accordance with section 3102 of title 42 before all such grants under section 1281 of this title were made and such grant under section 3102 of title 42 could not be approved due to lack of funding under such section 3102 of title 42.

The total of all grants for sewage collection systems made under this section shall not exceed $2,800,000.

(Pub. L. 95–217, §78, Dec. 27, 1977, 91 Stat. 1611.)

References in Text

Section 3102 of title 42, referred to in par. (2), was omitted from the Code pursuant to section 5316 of Title 42, The Public Health and Welfare, which terminated the authority to make grants or loans under that section after Jan. 1, 1975.

Codification

Section was enacted as part of the Clean Water Act of 1977, Pub. L. 95–217, and not as part of the Federal Water Pollution Control Act which comprises this chapter.

§ 1281b. Availability of Farmers Home Administration funds for non-Federal share

Notwithstanding any other provision of law, Federal assistance made available by the Farmers Home Administration to any political subdivision of a State may be used to provide the non-Federal share of the cost of any construction project carried out under section 1281 of this title.

(Pub. L. 100–4, title II, §202(f), Feb. 4, 1987, 101 Stat. 16.)

Codification

Section was enacted as part of the Water Quality Act of 1987, and not as part of the Federal Water Pollution Control Act which comprises this chapter.

§ 1282. Federal share

(a) Amount of grants for treatment works

(1) The amount of any grant for treatment works made under this chapter from funds authorized for any fiscal year beginning after June 30, 1971, and ending before October 1, 1984, shall be 75 per centum of the cost of construction thereof (as approved by the Administrator), and for any fiscal year beginning on or after October 1, 1984, shall be 55 per centum of the cost of construction thereof (as approved by the Administrator), unless modified to a lower percentage rate uniform throughout a State by the Governor of that State with the concurrence of the Administrator. Within ninety days after October 21, 1980, the Administrator shall issue guidelines for concurrence in any such modification, which shall provide for the consideration of the unobligated balance of sums allocated to the State under section 1285 of this title, the need for assistance under this subchapter in such State, and the availability of State grant assistance to replace the Federal share reduced by such modification. The payment of any such reduced Federal share shall not constitute an obligation on the part of the United States or a claim on the part of any State or grantee to reimbursement for the portion of the Federal share reduced in any such State. Any grant (other than for reimbursement) made prior to October 18, 1972, from any funds authorized for any fiscal year beginning after June 30, 1971, shall, upon the request of the applicant, be increased to the applicable percentage under this section. Notwithstanding the first sentence of this paragraph, in any case where a primary, secondary, or advanced waste treatment facility or its related interceptors or a project for infiltration-in-flow correction has received a grant for erection, building, acquisition, alteration, remodeling, improvement, extension, or correction before October 1, 1984, all segments and phases of such facility, interceptors, and project for infiltration-in-flow correction shall be eligible for grants at 75 per centum of the cost of construction thereof for any grant made pursuant to a State obligation which obligation occurred before October 1, 1990. Notwithstanding the first sentence of this paragraph, in the case of a project for which an application for a grant under this subchapter has been made to

the Administrator before October 1, 1984, and which project is under judicial injunction on such date prohibiting its construction, such project shall be eligible for grants at 75 percent of the cost of construction thereof. Notwithstanding the first sentence of this paragraph, in the case of the Wyoming Valley Sanitary Authority project mandated by judicial order under a proceeding begun prior to October 1, 1984, and a project for wastewater treatment for Altoona, Pennsylvania, such projects shall be eligible for grants at 75 percent of the cost of construction thereof.

(2) The amount of any grant made after September 30, 1978, and before October 1, 1981, for any eligible treatment works or significant portion thereof utilizing innovative or alternative wastewater treatment processes and techniques referred to in section 1281(g)(5) of this title shall be 85 per centum of the cost of construction thereof, unless modified by the Governor of the State with the concurrence of the Administrator to a percentage rate no less than 15 per centum greater than the modified uniform percentage rate in which the Administrator has concurred pursuant to paragraph (1) of this subsection. The amount of any grant made after September 30, 1981, for any eligible treatment works or unit processes and techniques thereof utilizing innovative or alternative wastewater treatment processes and techniques referred to in section 1281(g)(5) of this title shall be a percentage of the cost of construction thereof equal to 20 per centum greater than the percentage in effect under paragraph (1) of this subsection for such works or unit processes and techniques, but in no event greater than 85 per centum of the cost of construction thereof. No grant shall be made under this paragraph for construction of a treatment works in any State unless the proportion of the State contribution to the non-Federal share of construction costs for all treatment works in such State receiving a grant under this paragraph is the same as or greater than the proportion of the State contribution (if any) to the non-Federal share of construction costs for all treatment works receiving grants in such State under paragraph (1) of this subsection.

(3) In addition to any grant made pursuant to paragraph (2) of this subsection, the Administrator is authorized to make a grant to fund all of the costs of the modification or replacement of any facilities constructed with a grant made pursuant to paragraph (2) if the Administrator finds that such facilities have not met design performance specifications unless such failure is attributable to negligence on the part of any person and if such failure has significantly increased capital or operating and maintenance expenditures. In addition, the Administrator is authorized to make a grant to fund all of the costs of the modification or replacement of biodisc equipment (rotating biological contactors) in any publicly owned treatment works if the Administrator finds that such equipment has failed to meet design performance specifications, unless such failure is attributable to negligence on the part of any person, and if such failure has significantly increased capital or operating and maintenance expenditures.

(4) For the purposes of this section, the term "eligible treatment works" means those treatment works in each State which meet the requirements of section 1281(g)(5) of this title and which can be fully funded from funds available for such purpose in such State.

(b) Amount of grants for construction of treatment works not commenced prior to July 1, 1971

The amount of the grant for any project approved by the Administrator after January 1, 1971, and before July 1, 1971, for the construction of treatment works, the actual erection, building or acquisition of which was not commenced prior to July 1, 1971, shall, upon the request of the applicant, be increased to the applicable percentage under subsection (a) of this section for grants for treatment works from funds for fiscal years beginning after June 30, 1971, with respect to the cost of such actual erection, building, or acquisition. Such increased amount shall be paid from any funds allocated to the State in which the treatment works is located without regard to the fiscal year for which such funds were authorized. Such increased amount shall be paid for such project only if—

(1) a sewage collection system that is a part of the same total waste treatment system as the treatment works for which such grant was approved is under construction or is to be constructed for use in conjunction with such treatment works, and if the cost of such sewage collection system exceeds the cost of such treatment works, and

(2) the State water pollution control agency or other appropriate State authority certifies that the quantity of available ground water will be insufficient, inadequate, or unsuitable for public use, including the ecological preservation and recreational use of surface water bodies, unless effluents from publicly-owned treatment works after adequate treatment are returned to the ground water consistent with acceptable technological standards.

(c) Availability of sums allotted to Puerto Rico

Notwithstanding any other provision of law, sums allotted to the Commonwealth of Puerto Rico under section 1285 of this title for fiscal year 1981 shall remain available for obligation for the fiscal year for which authorized and for the period of the next succeeding twenty-four months. Such sums and any unobligated funds available to Puerto Rico from allotments for fiscal years ending prior to October 1, 1981, shall be available for obligation by the Administrator of the Environmental Protection Agency only to fund the following systems: Aguadilla, Arecibo, Mayaguez, Carolina, and Camuy Hatillo. These funds may be used by the commonwealth of Puerto Rico to fund the non-Federal share of the costs of such projects. To the extent that these funds are used to pay the non-Federal share, the Commonwealth of Puerto Rico shall repay to the Environmental Protection Agency such amounts on terms and conditions developed and approved by the Administrator in consultation with the Governor of the Commonwealth of Puerto Rico. Agreement on such terms and conditions, including the payment of interest to be determined by the Secretary of the Treasury, shall be reached prior to the use of these funds for the Commonwealth's non-Federal share. No

Federal funds awarded under this provision shall be used to replace local governments funds previously expended on these projects.

(June 30, 1948, ch. 758, title II, § 202, as added Pub. L. 92–500, § 2, Oct. 18, 1972, 86 Stat. 834; amended Pub. L. 95–217, § 17, Dec. 27, 1977, 91 Stat. 1571; Pub. L. 96–483, § 9, Oct. 21, 1980, 94 Stat. 2362; Pub. L. 97–117, §§ 7, 8(a), (b), Dec. 29, 1981, 95 Stat. 1625; Pub. L. 97–357, title V, § 501, Oct. 19, 1982, 96 Stat. 1712; Pub. L. 100–4, title II, § 202(a)–(d), Feb. 4, 1987, 101 Stat. 15, 16.)

AMENDMENTS

1987—Subsec. (a)(1). Pub. L. 100–4, § 202(a), inserted "for any grant made pursuant to a State obligation which obligation occurred before October 1, 1990" before period at end of last sentence.

Pub. L. 100–4, § 202(b), inserted at end "Notwithstanding the first sentence of this paragraph, in the case of a project for which an application for a grant under this subchapter has been made to the Administrator before October 1, 1984, and which project is under judicial injunction on such date prohibiting its construction, such project shall be eligible for grants at 75 percent of the cost of construction thereof."

Pub. L. 100–4, § 202(c), inserted at end "Notwithstanding the first sentence of this paragraph, in the case of the Wyoming Valley Sanitary Authority project mandated by judicial order under a proceeding begun prior to October 1, 1984, and a project for wastewater treatment for Altoona, Pennsylvania, such projects shall be eligible for grants at 75 percent of the cost of construction thereof."

Subsec. (a)(3). Pub. L. 100–4, § 202(d), inserted at end "In addition, the Administrator is authorized to make a grant to fund all of the costs of the modification or replacement of biodisc equipment (rotating biological contactors) in any publicly owned treatment works if the Administrator finds that such equipment has failed to meet design performance specifications, unless such failure is attributable to negligence on the part of any person, and if such failure has significantly increased capital or operating and maintenance expenditures."

1982—Subsec. (c). Pub. L. 97–357 added subsec. (c).

1981—Subsec. (a)(1). Pub. L. 97–117, § 7, inserted "and ending before October 30, 1984," after "June 30, 1971," and "and for any fiscal year beginning on or after October 1, 1984, shall be 55 per centum of the cost of construction thereof (as approved by the Administrator)," after "(as approved by the Administrator)," and provision that notwithstanding first sentence of this paragraph, in any case where primary, secondary, or advanced waste treatment facility or its related interceptors or a project for infiltration-in-flow correction has received a grant for building, acquisition, etc., before Oct. 1, 1984, all segments and phases be eligible for grants at 75 per centum of the cost of construction.

Subsec. (a)(2). Pub. L. 97–117, § 8(a), inserted provision that the amount of any grant made after Sept. 30, 1981, for any eligible treatment works or unit processes or techniques, utilizing innovative or alternative wastewater treatment processes or techniques referred to in section 1281(g)(5) of this title be a percentage of the cost of construction equal to 20 per centum greater than the percentage in effect under par. (1) of this subsection, but in no event greater than 85 per centum of the cost of construction.

Subsec. (a)(4). Pub. L. 97–117, § 8(b), struck out "in the fiscal years ending September 30, 1979, September 30, 1980, and September 30, 1981" after "purpose in such State" and provision that excluded from term "eligible treatment works" collector sewers, interceptors, storm or sanitary sewers or the separation thereof, or major sewer rehabilitation.

1980—Subsec. (a)(1). Pub. L. 96–483, § 9(a), inserted provisions relating to modification to a lower percentage rate by the Governor of the State and issuance of guidelines by the Administrator for the concurrence in any such modification.

Subsec. (a)(2). Pub. L. 96–483, § 9(b), inserted provision relating to the modification by the Governor of the State to a percentage rate no less than 15 per centum greater than the modified uniform rate in which the Administrator has concurred.

1977—Subsec. (a). Pub. L. 95–217 designated existing provisions as par. (1) and added pars. (2) to (4).

PROMULGATION OF FEDERAL SHARES

Act July 9, 1956, ch. 518, § 4, 70 Stat. 507, authorized the Surgeon General to promulgate Federal shares under the Federal Water Pollution Control Grant Program as soon as possible after July 9, 1956, in the manner specified in the Water Pollution Control Act, act June 30, 1948, ch. 758, 62 Stat. 1155, and provided that such shares were to be conclusive for the purposes of section 5 of act June 30, 1948.

§ 1283. Plans, specifications, estimates, and payments

(a) Submission; contractual nature of approval by Administrator; agreement on eligible costs; single grant

(1) Each applicant for a grant shall submit to the Administrator for his approval, plans, specifications, and estimates for each proposed project for the construction of treatment works for which a grant is applied for under section 1281(g)(1) of this title from funds allotted to the State under section 1285 of this title and which otherwise meets the requirements of this chapter. The Administrator shall act upon such plans, specifications, and estimates as soon as practicable after the same have been submitted, and his approval of any such plans, specifications, and estimates shall be deemed a contractual obligation of the United States for the payment of its proportional contribution to such project.

(2) AGREEMENT ON ELIGIBLE COSTS.—

(A) LIMITATION ON MODIFICATIONS.—Before taking final action on any plans, specifications, and estimates submitted under this subsection after the 60th day following February 4, 1987, the Administrator shall enter into a written agreement with the applicant which establishes and specifies which items of the proposed project are eligible for Federal payments under this section. The Administrator may not later modify such eligibility determinations unless they are found to have been made in violation of applicable Federal statutes and regulations.

(B) LIMITATION ON EFFECT.—Eligibility determinations under this paragraph shall not preclude the Administrator from auditing a project pursuant to section 1361 of this title, or other authority, or from withholding or recovering Federal funds for costs which are found to be unreasonable, unsupported by adequate documentation, or otherwise unallowable under applicable Federal cost principles, or which are incurred on a project which fails to meet the design specifications or effluent limitations contained in the grant agreement and permit pursuant to section 1342 of this title for such project.

(3) In the case of a treatment works that has an estimated total cost of $8,000,000 or less (as determined by the Administrator), and the population of the applicant municipality is twenty-five thousand or less (according to the most re-

cent United States census), upon completion of an approved facility plan, a single grant may be awarded for the combined Federal share of the cost of preparing construction plans and specifications, and the building and erection of the treatment works.

(b) Periodic payments

The Administrator shall, from time to time as the work progresses, make payments to the recipient of a grant for costs of construction incurred on a project. These payments shall at no time exceed the Federal share of the cost of construction incurred to the date of the voucher covering such payment plus the Federal share of the value of the materials which have been stockpiled in the vicinity of such construction in conformity to plans and specifications for the project.

(c) Final payments

After completion of a project and approval of the final voucher by the Administrator, he shall pay out of the appropriate sums the unpaid balance of the Federal share payable on account of such project.

(d) Projects eligible

Nothing in this chapter shall be construed to require, or to authorize the Administrator to require, that grants under this chapter for construction of treatment works be made only for projects which are operable units usable for sewage collection, transportation, storage, waste treatment, or for similar purposes without additional construction.

(e) Technical and legal assistance in administration and enforcement of contracts; intervention in civil actions

At the request of a grantee under this subchapter, the Administrator is authorized to provide technical and legal assistance in the administration and enforcement of any contract in connection with treatment works assisted under this subchapter, and to intervene in any civil action involving the enforcement of such a contract.

(f) Design/build projects

(1) Agreement

Consistent with State law, an applicant who proposes to construct waste water treatment works may enter into an agreement with the Administrator under this subsection providing for the preparation of construction plans and specifications and the erection of such treatment works, in lieu of proceeding under the other provisions of this section.

(2) Limitation on projects

Agreements under this subsection shall be limited to projects under an approved facility plan which projects are—

(A) treatment works that have an estimated total cost of $8,000,000 or less; and

(B) any of the following types of waste water treatment systems: aerated lagoons, trickling filters, stabilization ponds, land application systems, sand filters, and subsurface disposal systems.

(3) Required terms

An agreement entered into under this subsection shall—

(A) set forth an amount agreed to as the maximum Federal contribution to the project, based upon a competitively bid document of basic design data and applicable standard construction specifications and a determination of the federally eligible costs of the project at the applicable Federal share under section 1282 of this title;

(B) set forth dates for the start and completion of construction of the treatment works by the applicant and a schedule of payments of the Federal contribution to the project;

(C) contain assurances by the applicant that (i) engineering and management assistance will be provided to manage the project; (ii) the proposed treatment works will be an operable unit and will meet all the requirements of this subchapter; and (iii) not later than 1 year after the date specified as the date of completion of construction of the treatment works, the treatment works will be operating so as to meet the requirements of any applicable permit for such treatment works under section 1342 of this title;

(D) require the applicant to obtain a bond from the contractor in an amount determined necessary by the Administrator to protect the Federal interest in the project; and

(E) contain such other terms and conditions as are necessary to assure compliance with this subchapter (except as provided in paragraph (4) of this subsection).

(4) Limitation on application

Subsections (a), (b), and (c) of this section shall not apply to grants made pursuant to this subsection.

(5) Reservation to assure compliance

The Administrator shall reserve a portion of the grant to assure contract compliance until final project approval as defined by the Administrator. If the amount agreed to under paragraph (3)(A) exceeds the cost of designing and constructing the treatment works, the Administrator shall reallot the amount of the excess to the State in which such treatment works are located for the fiscal year in which such audit is completed.

(6) Limitation on obligations

The Administrator shall not obligate more than 20 percent of the amount allotted to a State for a fiscal year under section 1285 of this title for grants pursuant to this subsection.

(7) Allowance

The Administrator shall determine an allowance for facilities planning for projects constructed under this subsection in accordance with section 1281(*l*) of this title.

(8) Limitation on Federal contributions

In no event shall the Federal contribution for the cost of preparing construction plans and specifications and the building and erection of treatment works pursuant to this subsection exceed the amount agreed upon under paragraph (3).

(9) Recovery action

In any case in which the recipient of a grant made pursuant to this subsection does not comply with the terms of the agreement entered into under paragraph (3), the Administrator is authorized to take such action as may be necessary to recover the amount of the Federal contribution to the project.

(10) Prevention of double benefits

A recipient of a grant made pursuant to this subsection shall not be eligible for any other grants under this subchapter for the same project.

(June 30, 1948, ch. 758, title II, § 203, as added Pub. L. 92–500, § 2, Oct. 18, 1972, 86 Stat. 835; amended Pub. L. 93–243, § 2, Jan. 2, 1974, 87 Stat. 1069; Pub. L. 95–217, §§ 18, 19, Dec. 27, 1977, 91 Stat. 1571, 1572; Pub. L. 96–483, § 6, Oct. 21, 1980, 94 Stat. 2362; Pub. L. 97–117, § 9, Dec. 29, 1981, 95 Stat. 1626; Pub. L. 100–4, title II, §§ 203, 204, Feb. 4, 1987, 101 Stat. 16, 17.)

AMENDMENTS

1987—Subsec. (a). Pub. L. 100–4, § 203, designated provision relating to submission of plans, specifications, and estimates, and provision relating to contractual nature of approval by Administrator as par. (1), designated provision relating to requirements for awarding single grant for combined Federal share of cost of preparing plans and specifications, and building and erection of treatment works as par. (3), and added par. (2).

Subsec. (f). Pub. L. 100–4, § 204, added subsec. (f).

1981—Subsec. (a). Pub. L. 97–117 substituted "$8,000,000" for "$4,000,000" and struck out provision that, if any State is found by the Administrator to have unusually high costs of construction, the Administrator may authorize a single grant where the estimated total cost of the treatment works does not exceed $5,000,000.

1980—Subsec. (a). Pub. L. 96–483 substituted "$4,000,000" and "$5,000,000" for "$2,000,000" and "$3,000,000", respectively.

1977—Subsec. (a). Pub. L. 95–217, § 18, provided that, in the case of a treatment works that has an estimated total cost of $2,000,000 or less (as determined by the Administrator), and the population of the applicant municipality is twenty-five thousand or less (according to the most recent United States census), upon completion of an approved facility plan, a single grant may be awarded for the combined Federal share of the cost of preparing construction plans and specifications, and the building and erection of the treatment works, and that, if any State is found by the Administrator to have unusually high costs of construction, the Administrator may authorize a single grant where the estimated total cost of the treatment works does not exceed $3,000,000.

Subsec. (e). Pub. L. 95–217, § 19, added subsec. (e).

1974—Subsec. (d). Pub. L. 93–243 added subsec. (d).

§ 1284. Limitations and conditions

(a) Determinations by Administrator

Before approving grants for any project for any treatment works under section 1281(g)(1) of this title the Administrator shall determine—

(1) that any required areawide waste treatment management plan under section 1288 of this title (A) is being implemented for such area and the proposed treatment works are included in such plan, or (B) is being developed for such area and reasonable progress is being made toward its implementation and the proposed treatment works will be included in such plan;

(2) that (A) the State in which the project is to be located (i) is implementing any required plan under section 1313(e) of this title and the proposed treatment works are in conformity with such plan, or (ii) is developing such a plan and the proposed treatment works will be in conformity with such plan, and (B) such State is in compliance with section 1315(b) of this title;

(3) that such works have been certified by the appropriate State water pollution control agency as entitled to priority over such other works in the State in accordance with any applicable State plan under section 1313(e) of this title, except that any priority list developed pursuant to section 1313(e)(3)(H) of this title may be modified by such State in accordance with regulations promulgated by the Administrator to give higher priority for grants for the Federal share of the cost of preparing construction drawings and specifications for any treatment works utilizing processes and techniques meeting the guidelines promulgated under section 1314(d)(3) of this title and for grants for the combined Federal share of the cost of preparing construction drawings and specifications and the building and erection of any treatment works meeting the requirements of the next to the last sentence of section 1283(a) of this title which utilizes processes and techniques meeting the guidelines promulgated under section 1314(d)(3) of this title.[1]

(4) that the applicant proposing to construct such works agrees to pay the non-Federal costs of such works and has made adequate provisions satisfactory to the Administrator for assuring proper and efficient operation, including the employment of trained management and operations personnel, and the maintenance of such works in accordance with a plan of operation approved by the State water pollution control agency or, as appropriate, the interstate agency, after construction thereof;

(5) that the size and capacity of such works relate directly to the needs to be served by such works, including sufficient reserve capacity. The amount of reserve capacity provided shall be approved by the Administrator on the basis of a comparison of the cost of constructing such reserves as a part of the works to be funded and the anticipated cost of providing expanded capacity at a date when such capacity will be required, after taking into account, in accordance with regulations promulgated by the Administrator, efforts to reduce total flow of sewage and unnecessary water consumption. The amount of reserve capacity eligible for a grant under this subchapter shall be determined by the Administrator taking into account the projected population and associated commercial and industrial establishments within the jurisdiction of the applicant to be served by such treatment works as identified in an approved facilities plan, an areawide plan under section 1288 of this title, or an

[1] So in original. The period probably should be a semicolon.

applicable municipal master plan of development. For the purpose of this paragraph, section 1288 of this title, and any such plan, projected population shall be determined on the basis of the latest information available from the United States Department of Commerce or from the States as the Administrator, by regulation, determines appropriate. Beginning October 1, 1984, no grant shall be made under this subchapter to construct that portion of any treatment works providing reserve capacity in excess of existing needs (including existing needs of residential, commercial, industrial, and other users) on the date of approval of a grant for the erection, building, acquisition, alteration, remodeling, improvement, or extension of a project for secondary treatment or more stringent treatment or new interceptors and appurtenances, except that in no event shall reserve capacity of a facility and its related interceptors to which this subsection applies be in excess of existing needs on October 1, 1990. In any case in which an applicant proposes to provide reserve capacity greater than that eligible for Federal financial assistance under this subchapter, the incremental costs of the additional reserve capacity shall be paid by the applicant;

(6) that no specification for bids in connection with such works shall be written in such a manner as to contain proprietary, exclusionary, or discriminatory requirements other than those based upon performance, unless such requirements are necessary to test or demonstrate a specific thing or to provide for necessary interchangeability of parts and equipment. When in the judgment of the grantee, it is impractical or uneconomical to make a clear and accurate description of the technical requirements, a "brand name or equal" description may be used as a means to define the performance or other salient requirements of a procurement, and in doing so the grantee need not establish the existence of any source other than the brand or source so named.

(b) Additional determinations; issuance of guidelines; approval by Administrator; system of charges

(1) Notwithstanding any other provision of this subchapter, the Administrator shall not approve any grant for any treatment works under section 1281(g)(1) of this title after March 1, 1973, unless he shall first have determined that the applicant (A) has adopted or will adopt a system of charges to assure that each recipient of waste treatment services within the applicant's jurisdiction, as determined by the Administrator, will pay its proportionate share (except as otherwise provided in this paragraph) of the costs of operation and maintenance (including replacement) of any waste treatment services provided by the applicant; and (B) has legal, institutional, managerial, and financial capability to insure adequate construction, operation, and maintenance of treatment works throughout the applicant's jurisdiction, as determined by the Administrator. In any case where an applicant which, as of December 27, 1977, uses a system of dedicated ad valorem taxes and the Administrator determines that the applicant has a system of charges which results in the distribution of operation and maintenance costs for treatment works within the applicant's jurisdiction, to each user class, in proportion to the contribution to the total cost of operation and maintenance of such works by each user class (taking into account total waste water loading of such works, the constituent elements of the wastes, and other appropriate factors), and such applicant is otherwise in compliance with clause (A) of this paragraph with respect to each industrial user, then such dedicated ad valorem tax system shall be deemed to be the user charge system meeting the requirements of clause (A) of this paragraph for the residential user class and such small non-residential user classes as defined by the Administrator. In defining small non-residential users, the Administrator shall consider the volume of wastes discharged into the treatment works by such users and the constituent elements of such wastes as well as such other factors as he deems appropriate. A system of user charges which imposes a lower charge for low-income residential users (as defined by the Administrator) shall be deemed to be a user charge system meeting the requirements of clause (A) of this paragraph if the Administrator determines that such system was adopted after public notice and hearing.

(2) The Administrator shall, within one hundred and eighty days after October 18, 1972, and after consultation with appropriate State, interstate, municipal, and intermunicipal agencies, issue guidelines applicable to payment of waste treatment costs by industrial and nonindustrial recipients of waste treatment services which shall establish (A) classes of users of such services, including categories of industrial users; (B) criteria against which to determine the adequacy of charges imposed on classes and categories of users reflecting all factors that influence the cost of waste treatment, including strength, volume, and delivery flow rate characteristics of waste; and (C) model systems and rates of user charges typical of various treatment works serving municipal-industrial communities.

(3) Approval by the Administrator of a grant to an interstate agency established by interstate compact for any treatment works shall satisfy any other requirement that such works be authorized by Act of Congress.

(4) A system of charges which meets the requirement of clause (A) of paragraph (1) of this subsection may be based on something other than metering the sewage or water supply flow of residential recipients of waste treatment services, including ad valorem taxes. If the system of charges is based on something other than metering the Administrator shall require (A) the applicant to establish a system by which the necessary funds will be available for the proper operation and maintenance of the treatment works; and (B) the applicant to establish a procedure under which the residential user will be notified as to that portion of his total payment which will be allocated to the cost of the waste treatment services.

(c) Applicability of reserve capacity restrictions to primary, secondary, or advanced waste treatment facilities or related interceptors

The next to the last sentence of paragraph (5) of subsection (a) of this section shall not apply in any case where a primary, secondary, or advanced waste treatment facility or its related interceptors has received a grant for erection, building, acquisition, alteration, remodeling, improvement, or extension before October 1, 1984, and all segments and phases of such facility and interceptors shall be funded based on a 20-year reserve capacity in the case of such facility and a 20-year reserve capacity in the case of such interceptors, except that, if a grant for such interceptors has been approved prior to December 29, 1981, such interceptors shall be funded based on the approved reserve capacity not to exceed 40 years.

(d) Engineering requirements; certification by owner and operator; contractual assurances, etc.

(1) A grant for the construction of treatment works under this subchapter shall provide that the engineer or engineering firm supervising construction or providing architect engineering services during construction shall continue its relationship to the grant applicant for a period of one year after the completion of construction and initial operation of such treatment works. During such period such engineer or engineering firm shall supervise operation of the treatment works, train operating personnel, and prepare curricula and training material for operating personnel. Costs associated with the implementation of this paragraph shall be eligible for Federal assistance in accordance with this subchapter.

(2) On the date one year after the completion of construction and initial operation of such treatment works, the owner and operator of such treatment works shall certify to the Administrator whether or not such treatment works meet the design specifications and effluent limitations contained in the grant agreement and permit pursuant to section 1342 of this title for such works. If the owner and operator of such treatment works cannot certify that such treatment works meet such design specifications and effluent limitations, any failure to meet such design specifications and effluent limitations shall be corrected in a timely manner, to allow such affirmative certification, at other than Federal expense.

(3) Nothing in this section shall be construed to prohibit a grantee under this subchapter from requiring more assurances, guarantees, or indemnity or other contractual requirements from any party to a contract pertaining to a project assisted under this subchapter, than those provided under this subsection.

(June 30, 1948, ch. 758, title II, § 204, as added Pub. L. 92–500, § 2, Oct. 18, 1972, 86 Stat. 835; amended Pub. L. 95–217, §§ 20–24, Dec. 27, 1977, 91 Stat. 1572, 1573; Pub. L. 96–483, § 2(a), (b), Oct. 21, 1980, 94 Stat. 2360, 2361; Pub. L. 97–117, §§ 10(a), (b), 11, 12, Dec. 29, 1981, 95 Stat. 1626, 1627; Pub. L. 100–4, title II, § 205(a)–(c), Feb. 4, 1987, 101 Stat. 18.)

AMENDMENTS

1987—Subsec. (a)(1). Pub. L. 100–4, § 205(a), amended par. (1) generally. Prior to amendment, par. (1) read as follows: "that such works are included in any applicable areawide waste treatment management plan developed under section 1288 of this title;".

Subsec. (a)(2). Pub. L. 100–4, § 205(b), amended par. (2) generally. Prior to amendment, par. (2) read as follows: "that such works are in conformity with any applicable State plan under section 1313(e) of this title;".

Subsec. (b)(1). Pub. L. 100–4, § 205(c), inserted at end "A system of user charges which imposes a lower charge for low-income residential users (as defined by the Administrator) shall be deemed to be a user charge system meeting the requirements of clause (A) of this paragraph if the Administrator determines that such system was adopted after public notice and hearing."

1981—Subsec. (a)(5). Pub. L. 97–117, § 10(a), inserted provision that beginning Oct. 1, 1984, no grant be made under this subchapter to construct that portion of any treatment works providing reserve capacity in excess of existing needs on the date of approval of a grant for the erection, building, etc., of a project for secondary treatment or more stringent treatment or new interceptors and appurtenances, except that in no event shall reserve capacity of a facility and its related interceptors to which this subsection applies be in excess of existing needs on Oct. 1, 1990, and that in any case in which an applicant proposes to provide reserve capacity greater than that eligible for Federal financial assistance under this subchapter, the incremental costs of the additional reserve capacity be paid by the applicant.

Subsec. (a)(6). Pub. L. 97–117, § 11, struck out ", or at least two brand names or trade names of comparable quality or utility are listed and are followed by the words 'or equal' " after "parts and equipment" and inserted provision that when in the judgment of the grantee, it is impractical or uneconomical to make a clear and accurate description of the technical requirements, a "brand name or equal" description be used as a means to define performance or other salient requirements of a procurement, and in doing so the grantee need not establish the existence of any source other than the brand or source so named.

Subsec. (c). Pub. L. 97–117, § 10(b), added subsec. (c).

Subsec. (d). Pub. L. 97–117, § 12, added subsec. (d).

1980—Subsec. (b)(1). Pub. L. 96–483, § 2(a), redesignated cl. (C) as (B). Former cl. (B) relating to payment, as a condition of approval of a grant, to an applicant by industrial users of that portion of cost of construction allocable to the treatment of such industrial waste to the extent attributable to the Federal share of the cost of construction, was struck out.

Subsec. (b)(3) to (6). Pub. L. 96–483, § 2(b), redesignated pars. (4) and (5) as (3) and (4), respectively. Former par. (3) relating to a formula determining the amount the grantee shall retain of the revenues derived from the payment of costs by industrial users of waste treatment services, to the extent costs are attributable to the Federal share of eligible project costs, and former par. (6) relating to the exemption from the requirements of par. (1)(B) of industrial users with a flow of twenty-five thousand gallons or less per day, were struck out.

1977—Subsec. (a)(3). Pub. L. 95–217, § 20, provided that any priority list developed pursuant to section 1313(e)(3)(H) of this title may be modified by such State in accordance with regulations promulgated by the Administrator to give higher priority for grants for the Federal share of the cost of preparing construction drawings and specifications for any treatment works utilizing processes and techniques meeting the guidelines promulgated under section 1314(d)(3) of this title and for grants for the combined Federal share of the cost of preparing construction drawings and specifications and the building and erection of any treatment works meeting the requirements of the next to the last sentence of section 1283(a) of this title which utilizes processes and techniques meeting the guidelines promulgated under section 1314(d)(3) of this title.

Subsec. (a)(5). Pub. L. 95–217, §21, provided that efforts to reduce total flow of sewage and unnecessary water consumption be taken into account, in accordance with regulations promulgated by the Administrator, that the amount of reserve capacity eligible for a grant under this subchapter be determined by the Administrator taking into account the projected population and associated commercial and industrial establishments within the jurisdiction of the applicant to be served by such treatment works as identified in an approved facilities plan, an areawide plan under section 1288 of this title, or an applicable municipal master plan of development, and that, for the purpose of this paragraph, section 1288 of this title, and any such plan, projected population be determined on the basis of the latest information available from the United States Department of Commerce or from the States as the Administrator, by regulation, determines appropriate.

Subsec. (b)(1). Pub. L. 95–217, §§22(a)(1), (2), 24(c), inserted "(except as otherwise provided in this paragraph)" after "proportionate share" in cl. (A) and "(which such portion, in the discretion of the applicant, may be recovered from industrial users of the total waste treatment system as distinguished from the treatment works for which the grant is made)" in cl. (B) and, at end of existing provisions, inserted sentences under which a dedicated ad valorem tax system is to be deemed the user charge system meeting the requirements of cl. (A) for the residential user class and such small non-residential user classes as defined by the Administrator in cases where an applicant, as of Dec. 27, 1977, uses a system of dedicated ad valorem taxes and the Administrator determines that the applicant has a system of charges which results in the distribution of operation and maintenance costs for treatment works within the applicant's jurisdiction, to each user class, in proportion to the contribution to the total cost of operation and maintenance of such works by each user class (taking into account total waste water loading of such works, the constituent elements of the wastes, and other appropriate factors), and such applicant is otherwise in compliance with cl. (A) of this paragraph with respect to each industrial user.

Subsec. (b)(3). Pub. L. 95–217, §§23, 24(a), substituted "necessary for the administrative costs associated with the requirement of paragraph (1)(B) of this subsection and future expansion" for "necessary for future expansion" in cl. (B) and, at end of existing provisions, inserted sentence under which, subject to the approval of the Administrator, the following: "Not a grantee that received a grant prior to Dec. 27, 1977, may reduce the amounts required to be paid to such grantee by any industrial user of waste treatment services under such paragraph, if such grantee requires such industrial user to adopt other means of reducing the demand for waste treatment services through reduction in the total flow of sewage or unnecessary water consumption, in proportion to such reduction as determined in accordance with regulations promulgated by the Administrator".

Subsec. (b)(5), (6). Pub. L. 95–217, §§22(b), 24(b), added pars. (5) and (6).

EFFECTIVE DATE OF 1987 AMENDMENT

Section 205(d) of Pub. L. 100–4 provided that: "This section [amending this section] shall take effect on the date of the enactment of this Act [Feb. 4, 1987], except that the amendments made by subsections (a) and (b) [amending this section] shall take effect on the last day of the two-year period beginning on such date of enactment."

EFFECTIVE DATE OF 1980 AMENDMENT

Amendment by Pub. L. 96–483 effective Dec. 27, 1977, see section 2(g) of Pub. L. 96–483, set out as a note under section 1281 of this title.

ELIMINATION OF INAPPLICABLE CONDITIONS OR REQUIREMENTS FROM CERTAIN GRANTS

Section 2(c) of Pub. L. 96–483 provided that: "The Administrator of the Environmental Protection Agency shall take such action as may be necessary to remove from any grant made under section 201(g)(1) of the Federal Water Pollution Control Act [section 1281(g)(1) of this title] after March 1, 1973, and prior to the date of enactment of this Act [Oct. 21, 1980], any condition or requirement no longer applicable as a result of the repeals made by subsections (a) and (b) of this section [amending subsec. (b) of this section] or release any grant recipient of the obligations established by such conditions or other requirement."

Section 2(c) of Pub. L. 96–483, set out above, effective Dec. 27, 1977, see section 2(g) of Pub. L. 96–483, set out as an Effective Date of 1980 Amendment note under section 1281 of this title.

COST RECOVERY; SUSPENSION OF GRANT REQUIREMENTS THAT INDUSTRIAL USERS MAKE PAYMENTS

Section 75 of Pub. L. 95–217, as amended by Pub. L. 96–148, §1, Dec. 16, 1979, 93 Stat. 1088; Pub. L. 96–483, §2(f), Oct. 21, 1980, 94 Stat. 2361, directed Administrator of Environmental Protection Agency to study and report to Congress not later than last day of twelfth month which begins after Dec. 27, 1977, cost recovery procedures from industrial users of treatment works to the extent construction costs are attributable to the Federal share of the cost of construction.

§1285. Allotment of grant funds

(a) Funds for fiscal years during period June 30, 1972, and September 30, 1977; determination of amount

Sums authorized to be appropriated pursuant to section 1287 of this title for each fiscal year beginning after June 30, 1972, and before September 30, 1977, shall be allotted by the Administrator not later than the January 1st immediately preceding the beginning of the fiscal year for which authorized, except that the allotment for fiscal year 1973 shall be made not later than 30 days after October 18, 1972. Such sums shall be allotted among the States by the Administrator in accordance with regulations promulgated by him, in the ratio that the estimated cost of constructing all needed publicly owned treatment works in each State bears to the estimated cost of construction of all needed publicly owned treatment works in all of the States. For the fiscal years ending June 30, 1973, and June 30, 1974, such ratio shall be determined on the basis of table III of House Public Works Committee Print No. 92–50. For the fiscal year ending June 30, 1975, such ratio shall be determined one-half on the basis of table I of House Public Works Committee Print Numbered 93–28 and one-half on the basis of table II of such print, except that no State shall receive an allotment less than that which it received for the fiscal year ending June 30, 1972, as set forth in table III of such print. Allotments for fiscal years which begin after the fiscal year ending June 30, 1975, shall be made only in accordance with a revised cost estimate made and submitted to Congress in accordance with section 1375(b) of this title and only after such revised cost estimate shall have been approved by law specifically enacted after October 18, 1972.

(b) Availability and use of funds allotted for fiscal years during period June 30, 1972, and September 30, 1977; reallotment

(1) Any sums allotted to a State under subsection (a) of this section shall be available for obligation under section 1283 of this title on and after the date of such allotment. Such sums shall continue available for obligation in such State for a period of one year after the close of the fiscal year for which such sums are authorized. Any amounts so allotted which are not obligated by the end of such one-year period shall be immediately reallotted by the Administrator, in accordance with regulations promulgated by him, generally on the basis of the ratio used in making the last allotment of sums under this section. Such reallotted sums shall be added to the last allotments made to the States. Any sum made available to a State by reallotment under this subsection shall be in addition to any funds otherwise allotted to such State for grants under this subchapter during any fiscal year.

(2) Any sums which have been obligated under section 1283 of this title and which are released by the payment of the final voucher for the project shall be immediately credited to the State to which such sums were last allotted. Such released sums shall be added to the amounts last allotted to such State and shall be immediately available for obligation in the same manner and to the same extent as such last allotment.

(c) Funds for fiscal years during period October 1, 1977, and September 30, 1981; funds for fiscal years 1982 to 1990; determination of amount

(1) Sums authorized to be appropriated pursuant to section 1287 of this title for the fiscal years during the period beginning October 1, 1977, and ending September 30, 1981, shall be allotted for each such year by the Administrator not later than the tenth day which begins after December 27, 1977. Notwithstanding any other provision of law, sums authorized for the fiscal years ending September 30, 1978, September 30, 1979, September 30, 1980, and September 30, 1981, shall be allotted in accordance with table 3 of Committee Print Numbered 95-30 of the Committee on Public Works and Transportation of the House of Representatives.

(2) Sums authorized to be appropriated pursuant to section 1287 of this title for the fiscal years 1982, 1983, 1984, and 1985 shall be allotted for each such year by the Administrator not later than the tenth day which begins after December 29, 1981. Notwithstanding any other provision of law, sums authorized for the fiscal year ending September 30, 1982, shall be allotted in accordance with table 3 of Committee Print Numbered 95-30 of the Committee on Public Works and Transportation of the House of Representatives. Sums authorized for the fiscal years ending September 30, 1983, September 30, 1984, September 30, 1985, and September 30, 1986, shall be allotted in accordance with the following table:

States:	Fiscal years 1983 through 1985[1]
Alabama	.011398
Alaska	.006101
Arizona	.006885
Arkansas	.006668
California	.072901
Colorado	.008154
Connecticut	.012487
Delaware	.004965
District of Columbia	.004965
Florida	.034407
Georgia	.017234
Hawaii	.007895
Idaho	.004965
Illinois	.046101
Indiana	.024566
Iowa	.013796
Kansas	.009201
Kentucky	.012973
Louisiana	.011205
Maine	.007788
Maryland	.024653
Massachusetts	.034608
Michigan	.043829
Minnesota	.018735
Mississippi	.009184
Missouri	.028257
Montana	.004965
Nebraska	.005214
Nevada	.004965
New Hampshire	.010186
New Jersey	.041654
New Mexico	.004965
New York	.113097
North Carolina	.018396
North Dakota	.004965
Ohio	.057383
Oklahoma	.008235
Oregon	.011515
Pennsylvania	.040377
Rhode Island	.006750
South Carolina	.010442
South Dakota	.004965
Tennessee	.014807
Texas	.038726
Utah	.005371
Vermont	.004965
Virginia	.020861
Washington	.017726
West Virginia	.015890
Wisconsin	.027557
Wyoming	.004965
Samoa	.000915
Guam	.000662
Northern Marianas	.000425
Puerto Rico	.013295
Pacific Trust Territories	.001305
Virgin Islands	.000531
United States totals	.999996

(3) FISCAL YEARS 1987–1990.—Sums authorized to be appropriated pursuant to section 1287 of this title for the fiscal years 1987, 1988, 1989, and 1990 shall be allotted for each such year by the Administrator not later than the 10th day which begins after February 4, 1987. Sums authorized for such fiscal years shall be allotted in accordance with the following table:

States:	
Alabama	.011309
Alaska	.006053
Arizona	.006831
Arkansas	.006616
California	.072333

[1] So in original. Probably should be "1986".

States:	
Colorado	.008090
Connecticut	.012390
Delaware	.004965
District of Columbia	.004965
Florida	.034139
Georgia	.017100
Hawaii	.007833
Idaho	.004965
Illinois	.045741
Indiana	.024374
Iowa	.013688
Kansas	.009129
Kentucky	.012872
Louisiana	.011118
Maine	.007829
Maryland	.024461
Massachusetts	.034338
Michigan	.043487
Minnesota	.018589
Mississippi	.009112
Missouri	.028037
Montana	.004965
Nebraska	.005173
Nevada	.004965
New Hampshire	.010107
New Jersey	.041329
New Mexico	.004965
New York	.111632
North Carolina	.018253
North Dakota	.004965
Ohio	.056936
Oklahoma	.008171
Oregon	.011425
Pennsylvania	.040062
Rhode Island	.006791
South Carolina	.010361
South Dakota	.004965
Tennessee	.014692
Texas	.046226
Utah	.005329
Vermont	.004965
Virginia	.020698
Washington	.017588
West Virginia	.015766
Wisconsin	.027342
Wyoming	.004965
American Samoa	.000908
Guam	.000657
Northern Marianas	.000422
Puerto Rico	.013191
Pacific Trust Territories	.001295
Virgin Islands	.000527

(d) Availability and use of funds; reallotment

Sums allotted to the States for a fiscal year shall remain available for obligation for the fiscal year for which authorized and for the period of the next succeeding twelve months. The amount of any allotment not obligated by the end of such twenty-four-month period shall be immediately reallotted by the Administrator on the basis of the same ratio as applicable to sums allotted for the then current fiscal year, except that none of the funds reallotted by the Administrator for fiscal year 1978 and for fiscal years thereafter shall be allotted to any State which failed to obligate any of the funds being reallotted. Any sum made available to a State by reallotment under this subsection shall be in addition to any funds otherwise allotted to such State for grants under this subchapter during any fiscal year.

(e) Minimum allotment; additional appropriations; ratio of amount available

For the fiscal years 1978, 1979, 1980, 1981, 1982, 1983, 1984, 1985, 1986, 1987, 1988, 1989, and 1990, no State shall receive less than one-half of 1 per centum of the total allotment under subsection (c) of this section, except that in the case of Guam, Virgin Islands, American Samoa, and the Trust Territories not more than thirty-three one-hundredths of 1 per centum in the aggregate shall be allotted to all four of these jurisdictions. For the purpose of carrying out this subsection there are authorized to be appropriated, subject to such amounts as are provided in appropriation Acts, not to exceed $75,000,000 for each of fiscal years 1978, 1979, 1980, 1981, 1982, 1983, 1984, 1985, 1986, 1987, 1988, 1989, and 1990. If for any fiscal year the amount appropriated under authority of this subsection is less than the amount necessary to carry out this subsection, the amount each State receives under this subsection for such year shall bear the same ratio to the amount such State would have received under this subsection in such year if the amount necessary to carry it out had been appropriated as the amount appropriated for such year bears to the amount necessary to carry out this subsection for such year.

(f) Omitted

(g) Reservation of funds; State management assistance

(1) The Administrator is authorized to reserve each fiscal year not to exceed 2 per centum of the amount authorized under section 1287 of this title for purposes of the allotment made to each State under this section on or after October 1, 1977, except in the case of any fiscal year beginning on or after October 1, 1981, and ending before October 1, 1994, in which case the percentage authorized to be reserved shall not exceed 4 per centum.[2] or $400,000 whichever amount is the greater. Sums so reserved shall be available for making grants to such State under paragraph (2) of this subsection for the same period as sums are available from such allotment under subsection (d) of this section, and any such grant shall be available for obligation only during such period. Any grant made from sums reserved under this subsection which has not been obligated by the end of the period for which available shall be added to the amount last allotted to such State under this section and shall be immediately available for obligation in the same manner and to the same extent as such last allotment. Sums authorized to be reserved by this paragraph shall be in addition to and not in lieu of any other funds which may be authorized to carry out this subsection.

(2) The Administrator is authorized to grant to any State from amounts reserved to such State under this subsection, the reasonable costs of administering any aspects of sections 1281, 1283, 1284, and 1292 of this title the responsibility for administration of which the Administrator has delegated to such State. The Administrator may increase such grant to take into account the reasonable costs of administering an approved program under section 1342 or 1344 of this title, administering a state-wide waste treatment management planning program under section 1288(b)(4) of this title, and manag-

[2] So in original. The period probably should be a comma.

ing waste treatment construction grants for small communities.

(h) Alternate systems for small communities

The Administrator shall set aside from funds authorized for each fiscal year beginning on or after October 1, 1978, a total (as determined by the Governor of the State) of not less than 4 percent nor more than 7½ percent of the sums allotted to any State with a rural population of 25 per centum or more of the total population of such State, as determined by the Bureau of the Census. The Administrator may set aside no more than 7½ percent of the sums allotted to any other State for which the Governor requests such action. Such sums shall be available only for alternatives to conventional sewage treatment works for municipalities having a population of three thousand five hundred or less, or for the highly dispersed sections of larger municipalities, as defined by the Administrator.

(i) Set-aside for innovative and alternative projects

Not less than ½ of 1 percent of funds allotted to a State for each of the fiscal years ending September 30, 1979, through September 30, 1990, under subsection (c) of this section shall be expended only for increasing the Federal share of grants for construction of treatment works utilizing innovative processes and techniques pursuant to section 1282(a)(2) of this title. Including the expenditures authorized by the preceding sentence, a total of 2 percent of the funds allotted to a State for each of the fiscal years ending September 30, 1979, and September 30, 1980, and 3 percent of the funds allotted to a State for the fiscal year ending September 30, 1981, under subsection (c) of this section shall be expended only for increasing grants for construction of treatment works pursuant to section 1282(a)(2) of this title. Including the expenditures authorized by the first sentence of this subsection, a total (as determined by the Governor of the State) of not less than 4 percent nor more than 7½ percent of the funds allotted to such State under subsection (c) of this section for each of the fiscal years ending September 30, 1982, through September 30, 1990, shall be expended only for increasing the Federal share of grants for construction of treatment works pursuant to section 1282(a)(2) of this title.

(j) Water quality management plan; reservation of funds for nonpoint source management

(1) The Administrator shall reserve each fiscal year not to exceed 1 per centum of the sums allotted and available for obligation to each State under this section for each fiscal year beginning on or after October 1, 1981, or $100,000, whichever amount is the greater.

(2) Such sums shall be used by the Administrator to make grants to the States to carry out water quality management planning, including, but not limited to—

(A) identifying most cost effective and locally acceptable facility and non-point measures to meet and maintain water quality standards;

(B) developing an implementation plan to obtain State and local financial and regulatory commitments to implement measures developed under subparagraph (A);

(C) determining the nature, extent, and causes of water quality problems in various areas of the State and interstate region, and reporting on these annually; and

(D) determining those publicly owned treatment works which should be constructed with assistance under this subchapter, in which areas and in what sequence, taking into account the relative degree of effluent reduction attained, the relative contributions to water quality of other point or nonpoint sources, and the consideration of alternatives to such construction, and implementing section 1313(e) of this title.

(3) In carrying out planning with grants made under paragraph (2) of this subsection, a State shall develop jointly with local, regional, and interstate entities, a plan for carrying out the program and give funding priority to such entities and designated or undesignated public comprehensive planning organizations to carry out the purposes of this subsection. In giving such priority, the State shall allocate at least 40 percent of the amount granted to such State for a fiscal year under paragraph (2) of this subsection to regional public comprehensive planning organizations in such State and appropriate interstate organizations for the development and implementation of the plan described in this paragraph. In any fiscal year for which the Governor, in consultation with such organizations and with the approval of the Administrator, determines that allocation of at least 40 percent of such amount to such organizations will not result in significant participation by such organizations in water quality management planning and not significantly assist in development and implementation of the plan described in this paragraph and achieving the goals of this chapter, the allocation to such organization may be less than 40 percent of such amount.

(4) All activities undertaken under this subsection shall be in coordination with other related provisions of this chapter.

(5) NONPOINT SOURCE RESERVATION.—In addition to the sums reserved under paragraph (1), the Administrator shall reserve each fiscal year for each State 1 percent of the sums allotted and available for obligation to such State under this section for each fiscal year beginning on or after October 1, 1986, or $100,000, whichever is greater, for the purpose of carrying out section 1329 of this title. Sums so reserved in a State in any fiscal year for which such State does not request the use of such sums, to the extent such sums exceed $100,000, may be used by such State for other purposes under this subchapter.

(k) New York City Convention Center

The Administrator shall allot to the State of New York from sums authorized to be appropriated for the fiscal year ending September 30, 1982, an amount necessary to pay the entire cost of conveying sewage from the Convention Center of the city of New York to the Newtown sewage treatment plant, Brooklyn-Queens area, New York. The amount allotted under this subsection shall be in addition to and not in lieu of any other amounts authorized to be allotted to such State under this chapter.

(*l*) Marine estuary reservation

(1) Reservation of funds

(A) General rule

Prior to making allotments among the States under subsection (c) of this section, the Administrator shall reserve funds from sums appropriated pursuant to section 1287 of this title for each fiscal year beginning after September 30, 1986.

(B) Fiscal years 1987 and 1988

For each of fiscal years 1987 and 1988 the reservation shall be 1 percent of the sums appropriated pursuant to section 1287 of this title for such fiscal year.

(C) Fiscal years 1989 and 1990

For each of fiscal years 1989 and 1990 the reservation shall be 1½ percent of the funds appropriated pursuant to section 1287 of this title for such fiscal year.

(2) Use of funds

Of the sums reserved under this subsection, two-thirds shall be available to address water quality problems of marine bays and estuaries subject to lower levels of water quality due to the impacts of discharges from combined storm water and sanitary sewer overflows from adjacent urban complexes, and one-third shall be available for the implementation of section 1330 of this title, relating to the national estuary program.

(3) Period of availability

Sums reserved under this subsection shall be subject to the period of availability for obligation established by subsection (d) of this section.

(4) Treatment of certain body of water

For purposes of this section and section 1281(n) of this title, Newark Bay, New Jersey, and the portion of the Passaic River up to Little Falls, in the vicinity of Beatties Dam, shall be treated as a marine bay and estuary.

(m) Discretionary deposits into State water pollution control revolving funds

(1) From construction grant allotments

In addition to any amounts deposited in a water pollution control revolving fund established by a State under subchapter VI of this chapter, upon request of the Governor of such State, the Administrator shall make available to the State for deposit, as capitalization grants, in such fund in any fiscal year beginning after September 30, 1986, such portion of the amounts allotted to such State under this section for such fiscal year as the Governor considers appropriate; except that (A) in fiscal year 1987, such deposit may not exceed 50 percent of the amounts allotted to such State under this section for such fiscal year, and (B) in fiscal year 1988, such deposit may not exceed 75 percent of the amounts allotted to such State under this section for this fiscal year.

(2) Notice requirement

The Governor of a State may make a request under paragraph (1) for a deposit into the water pollution control revolving fund of such State—

(A) in fiscal year 1987 only if no later than 90 days after February 4, 1987, and

(B) in each fiscal year thereafter only if 90 days before the first day of such fiscal year,

the State provides notice of its intent to make such deposit.

(3) Exception

Sums reserved under section 1285(j) of this title shall not be available for obligation under this subsection.

(June 30, 1948, ch. 758, title II, §205, as added Pub. L. 92–500, §2, Oct. 18, 1972, 86 Stat. 837; amended Pub. L. 93–243, §1, Jan. 2, 1974, 87 Stat. 1069; Pub. L. 95–217, §§25, 26(a), 27, 28, Dec. 27, 1977, 91 Stat. 1574, 1575; Pub. L. 96–483, §11, Oct. 21, 1980, 94 Stat. 2363; Pub. L. 97–117, §§8(c), 13–16, Dec. 29, 1981, 95 Stat. 1625, 1627–1629; Pub. L. 100–4, title II, §§206(a)–(c), 207–210, 212(b), title III, §316(d), Feb. 4, 1987, 101 Stat. 19–21, 27, 60; Pub. L. 105–362, title V, §501(d)(2)(C), Nov. 10, 1998, 112 Stat. 3284; Pub. L. 107–303, title III, §302(b)(1), Nov. 27, 2002, 116 Stat. 2361.)

CODIFICATION

Subsec. (f) provided that sums made available for obligation between Jan. 1, 1975, and Mar. 1, 1975, be available for obligation until Sept. 30, 1978.

AMENDMENTS

2002—Subsec. (a). Pub. L. 107–303 repealed Pub. L. 105–362, §501(d)(2)(C). See 1998 Amendment note below.

1998—Subsec. (a). Pub. L. 105–362, §501(d)(2)(C), which directed the substitution of "section 1375 of this title" for "section 1375(b) of this title" in last sentence, was repealed by Pub. L. 107–303. See Effective Date of 2002 Amendment note below.

1987—Subsec. (c)(2). Pub. L. 100–4, §206(a)(1), substituted "September 30, 1985, and September 30, 1986" for "and September 30, 1985".

Subsec. (c)(3). Pub. L. 100–4, §206(a)(2), added par. (3).

Subsec. (e). Pub. L. 100–4, §206(b), substituted "1985, 1986, 1987, 1988, 1989, and 1990" for "and 1985" in two places.

Subsec. (g)(1). Pub. L. 100–4, §206(c), substituted "October 1, 1994" for "October 1, 1985".

Subsec. (h). Pub. L. 100–4, §207, substituted "a total (as determined by the Governor of the State) of not less than 4 percent nor more than 7½ percent" for "four per centum" and "7½ per cent" for "four per centum".

Subsec. (i). Pub. L. 100–4, §208, amended subsec. (i) generally. Prior to amendment, subsec. (i) read as follows: "Not less than one-half of one per centum of funds allotted to a State for each of the fiscal years ending September 30, 1979, September 30, 1980, September 30, 1981, September 30, 1982, September 30, 1983, September 30, 1984, and September 30, 1985, under subsection (a) of this section shall be expended only for increasing the Federal share of grants for construction of treatment works utilizing innovative processes and techniques pursuant to section 1282(a)(2) of this title. Including the expenditures authorized by the preceding sentence, a total of two per centum of the funds allotted to a State for each of the fiscal years ending September 30, 1979, and September 30, 1980, and 3 per centum of the funds allotted to a State for the fiscal year ending September 30, 1981, under subsection (a) of this section shall be expended only for increasing grants for construction of treatment works from 75 per centum to 85 per centum pursuant to section 1282(a)(2) of this title. Including the expenditures authorized by the first sentence of this subsection, a total (as determined by the Governor of the State) of not less than 4 per centum nor more than 7½ per centum of the funds allotted to such State for any fiscal year beginning after September 30, 1981, under subsection (c) of this section shall be expended only for increasing the Federal share of grants for construction of treatment works pursuant to section 1282(a)(2) of this title."

Subsec. (j)(3). Pub. L. 100–4, §209, inserted provision directing State to allocate at least 40 percent of amount granted under par. (2) to regional public comprehensive planning organizations and appropriate interstate organizations for development and implementation of plan, with exception for less than 40 percent allocation in certain circumstances.

Subsec. (j)(5). Pub. L. 100–4, §316(d), added par. (5).

Subsec. (*l*). Pub. L. 100–4, §210, added subsec. (*l*).

Subsec. (m). Pub. L. 100–4, §212(b), added subsec. (m).

1981—Subsec. (c). Pub. L. 97–117, §13(a), designated existing provision as par. (1) and added par. (2).

Subsec. (e). Pub. L. 97–117, §13(b), substituted "1981, 1982, 1983, 1984, and 1985" for "and 1981" in two places.

Subsec. (g)(1). Pub. L. 97–117, §14, inserted "except in the case of any fiscal year beginning on or after October 1, 1981, and ending before October 1, 1985, in which case the percentage authorized to be reserved shall not exceed 4 per centum," after "October 1, 1977," and provision that sums authorized to be reserved be in addition to and not in lieu of any other funds which may be authorized to carry out this subsection.

Subsec. (i). Pub. L. 97–117, §8(c), substituted "September 30, 1981, September 30, 1982, September 30, 1983, September 30, 1984, and September 30, 1985" for "and September 30, 1981", struck out "from 75 per centum to 85 per centum" after "innovative processes and techniques", and inserted provision that including the expenditures authorized by the first sentence of this subsection, a total, as determined by the State Governor, of not less than 4 per centum nor more than 7½ per centum of the funds allotted to such State for any fiscal year beginning after Sept. 30, 1981, under subsec. (c) of this section be expended only for increasing the Federal share of grants for construction of treatment works pursuant to section 1282(a)(2) of this title.

Subsecs. (j), (k). Pub. L. 97–117, §§15, 16, added subsecs. (j) and (k).

1980—Subsec. (g)(1). Pub. L. 96–483 inserted "of the amount authorized under section 1287 of this title for purposes" after "2 per centum".

1977—Subsec. (a). Pub. L. 95–217, §25(a), substituted "each fiscal year beginning after June 30, 1972, and before September 30, 1977" for "each fiscal year beginning after June 30, 1972".

Subsecs. (c) to (f). Pub. L. 95–217, §25(b), added subsecs. (c) to (f).

Subsecs. (g) to (i). Pub. L. 95–217, §§26(a), 27, 28, added subsecs. (g) to (i).

1974—Subsec. (a). Pub. L. 93–243 inserted provisions that for the fiscal year ending June 30, 1975, the ratio shall be determined one-half on the basis of table I of House Public Works Committee Print Numbered 93–28 and one-half on the basis of table II of such print, except that no State shall receive an allotment less than that which it received for the fiscal year ending June 30, 1972, as set forth in table III of such print and substituted "June 30, 1975" for "June 30, 1974" in sentence beginning "Allotments for fiscal years".

CHANGE OF NAME

Committee on Public Works and Transportation of House of Representatives treated as referring to Committee on Transportation and Infrastructure of House of Representatives by section 1(a) of Pub. L. 104–14, set out as a note preceding section 21 of Title 2, The Congress.

EFFECTIVE DATE OF 2002 AMENDMENT

Amendment by Pub. L. 107–303 effective Nov. 10, 1998, and Federal Water Pollution Act (33 U.S.C. 1251 et seq.) to be applied and administered on and after Nov. 27, 2002, as if amendments made by section 501(a)–(d) of Pub. L. 105–362 had not been enacted, see section 302(b) of Pub. L. 107–303, set out as a note under section 1254 of this title.

TERMINATION OF TRUST TERRITORY OF THE PACIFIC ISLANDS

For termination of Trust Territory of the Pacific Islands, see note set out preceding section 1681 of Title 48, Territories and Insular Possessions.

AVAILABILITY OF ALLOTTED SUMS IN SUBSEQUENT YEARS; REALLOTMENT OF UNOBLIGATED SUMS

Section 7 of Pub. L. 96–483 provided that: "Notwithstanding section 205(d) of the Federal Water Pollution Control Act (33 U.S.C. 1285), sums allotted to the States for the fiscal year 1979 shall remain available for obligation for the fiscal year for which authorized and for the period of the next succeeding twenty-four months. The amount of any allotment not obligated by the end of such thirty-six month period shall be immediately reallotted by the Administrator on the basis of the same ratio as applicable to sums allotted for the then current fiscal year, except that none of the funds reallotted by the Administrator for fiscal year 1979 shall be allotted to any State which failed to obligate any of the funds being reallotted. Any sum made available to a State by reallotment under this section shall be in addition to any funds otherwise allotted to such State for grants under title II of the Federal Water Pollution Control Act [this subchapter] during any fiscal year. This section shall take effect on September 30, 1980."

§1286. Reimbursement and advanced construction

(a) Publicly owned treatment works construction initiated after June 30, 1966, but before July 1, 1973; reimbursement formula

Any publicly owned treatment works in a State on which construction was initiated after June 30, 1966, but before July 1, 1973, which was approved by the appropriate State water pollution control agency and which the Administrator finds meets the requirements of section 1158 of this title in effect at the time of the initiation of construction shall be reimbursed a total amount equal to the difference between the amount of Federal financial assistance, if any, received under such section 1158 of this title for such project and 50 per centum of the cost of such project, or 55 per centum of the project cost where the Administrator also determines that such treatment works was constructed in conformity with a comprehensive metropolitan treatment plan as described in section 1158(f) of this title as in effect immediately prior to October 18, 1972. Nothing in this subsection shall result in any such works receiving Federal grants from all sources in excess of 80 per centum of the cost of such project.

(b) Publicly owned treatment works construction initiated between June 30, 1956, and June 30, 1966; reimbursement formula

Any publicly owned treatment works constructed with or eligible for Federal financial assistance under this Act in a State between June 30, 1956, and June 30, 1966, which was approved by the State water pollution control agency and which the Administrator finds meets the requirements of section 1158 of this title prior to October 18, 1972 but which was constructed without assistance under such section 1158 of this title or which received such assistance in an amount less than 30 per centum of the cost of such project shall qualify for payments and reimbursement of State or local funds used for such project from sums allocated to such State under this section in an amount which shall not exceed the difference between the amount of such assistance, if any, received for such project and 30 per centum of the cost of such project.

(c) Application for reimbursement

No publicly owned treatment works shall receive any payment or reimbursement under subsection (a) or (b) of this section unless an application for such assistance is filed with the Administrator within the one year period which begins on October 18, 1972. Any application filed within such one year period may be revised from time to time, as may be necessary.

(d) Allocation of funds

The Administrator shall allocate to each qualified project under subsection (a) of this section each fiscal year for which funds are appropriated under subsection (e) of this section an amount which bears the same ratio to the unpaid balance of the reimbursement due such project as the total of such funds for such year bears to the total unpaid balance of reimbursement due all such approved projects on the date of enactment of such appropriation. The Administrator shall allocate to each qualified project under subsection (b) of this section each fiscal year for which funds are appropriated under subsection (e) of this section an amount which bears the same ratio to the unpaid balance of the reimbursement due such project as the total of such funds for such year bears to the total unpaid balance of reimbursement due all such approved projects on the date of enactment of such appropriation.

(e) Authorization of appropriations

There is authorized to be appropriated to carry out subsection (a) of this section not to exceed $2,600,000,000 and, to carry out subsection (b) of this section, not to exceed $750,000,000. The authorizations contained in this subsection shall be the sole source of funds for reimbursements authorized by this section.

(f) Additional funds

(1) In any case where a substantial portion of the funds allotted to a State for the current fiscal year under this subchapter have been obligated under section 1281(g) of this title, or will be so obligated in a timely manner (as determined by the Administrator), and there is construction of any treatment works project without the aid of Federal funds and in accordance with all procedures and all requirements applicable to treatment works projects, except those procedures and requirements which limit construction of projects to those constructed with the aid of previously allotted Federal funds, the Administrator, upon his approval of an application made under this subsection therefor, is authorized to pay the Federal share of the cost of construction of such project when additional funds are allotted to the State under this subchapter if prior to the construction of the project the Administrator approves plans, specifications, and estimates therefor in the same manner as other treatment works projects. The Administrator may not approve an application under this subsection unless an authorization is in effect for the first fiscal year in the period for which the application requests payment and such requested payment for that fiscal year does not exceed the State's expected allotment from such authorization. The Administrator shall not be required to make such requested payment for any fiscal year—

(A) to the extent that such payment would exceed such State's allotment of the amount appropriated for such fiscal year; and

(B) unless such payment is for a project which, on the basis of an approved funding priority list of such State, is eligible to receive such payment based on the allotment and appropriation for such fiscal year.

To the extent that sufficient funds are not appropriated to pay the full Federal share with respect to a project for which obligations under the provisions of this subsection have been made, the Administrator shall reduce the Federal share to such amount less than 75 per centum as such appropriations do provide.

(2) In determining the allotment for any fiscal year under this subchapter, any treatment works project constructed in accordance with this section and without the aid of Federal funds shall not be considered completed until an application under the provisions of this subsection with respect to such project has been approved by the Administrator, or the availability of funds from which this project is eligible for reimbursement has expired, whichever first occurs.

(June 30, 1948, ch. 758, title II, §206, as added Pub. L. 92–500, §2, Oct. 18, 1972, 86 Stat. 838; amended Pub. L. 93–207, §1(2), Dec. 28, 1973, 87 Stat. 906; Pub. L. 95–217, §29(a), Dec. 27, 1977, 91 Stat. 1576; Pub. L. 96–483, §5, Oct. 21, 1980, 94 Stat. 2361.)

REFERENCES IN TEXT

Section 1158 of this title, referred to in subsecs. (a) and (b), refers to section 8 of act June 30, 1948, ch. 758, 62 Stat. 1158, prior to the supersedure and reenactment of act June 30, 1948, by act Oct. 18, 1972, Pub. L. 92–500, 86 Stat. 816. Provisions of section 1158 of this title are covered by this subchapter.

This Act, referred to in subsec. (b), means act June 30, 1948, ch. 758, 62 Stat. 1155, prior to the supersedure and reenactment of act June 30, 1948 by act Oct. 18, 1972, Pub. L. 92–500, 86 Stat. 816. Act June 30, 1948, ch. 758, as added by act Oct. 18, 1972, Pub. L. 92–500, 86 Stat. 816, enacted this chapter.

AMENDMENTS

1980—Subsec. (f)(1). Pub. L. 96–483 substituted "In any case where a substantial portion of the funds allotted to a State for the current fiscal year under this subchapter have been obligated under section 1281(g) of this title, or will be so obligated in a timely manner (as determined by the Administrator)" for "In any case where all funds allotted to a State under this subchapter have been obligated under section 1283 of this title", substituted "first fiscal year" for "future fiscal year", inserted "in the period" before "for which the application", substituted "and such requested payment for that fiscal year does not exceed the State's expected allotment from such authorization. The Administrator shall not be required to make such requested payment for any fiscal year—" for "which authorization will insure such payment without exceeding the State's expected allotment from such authorization.", and added subpars. (A), (B), and provisions following subpar. (B).

1977—Subsec. (a). Pub. L. 95–217 substituted "July 1, 1973" for "July 1, 1972".

1973—Subsec. (e). Pub. L. 93–207 substituted "$2,600,000,000" for "$2,000,000,000".

APPLICATION FOR ASSISTANCE FOR PUBLICLY OWNED TREATMENT WORKS WHERE GRANTS WERE MADE BEFORE JULY 2, 1972, AND ON WHICH CONSTRUCTION WAS INITIATED BEFORE JULY 1, 1973

Section 29(b) of Pub. L. 95–217 provided that applications for assistance for publicly owned treatment works for which a grant was made under this chapter before July 1, 1972, and on which construction was initiated before July 1, 1973, be filed not later than the ninetieth day after Dec. 27, 1977.

APPLICATION FOR ASSISTANCE

Section 2 of Pub. L. 93–207 provided that notwithstanding the requirements of subsec. (c) of this section, applications for assistance under this section could have been filed with the Administrator until Jan. 31, 1974.

ALLOCATION OF CONSTRUCTION GRANTS APPROPRIATED FOR THE YEAR ENDING JUNE 30, 1973; INTERIM PAYMENTS; LIMITATIONS

Section 3 of Pub. L. 93–207 provided that: "Funds available for reimbursement under Public Law 92–399 [making appropriations for Agriculture-Environmental and Consumer Protection Programs for the fiscal year ending June 30, 1973] shall be allocated in accordance with subsection (d) of section 206 of the Federal Water Pollution Control Act (86 Stat. 838) [subsec. (d) of this section], pro rata among all projects eligible under subsection (a) of such section 206 [subsec. (a) of this section] for which applications have been submitted and approved by the Administrator pursuant to such Act [this chapter]. Notwithstanding the provisions of subsection (d) of such section 206, (1) the Administrator is authorized to make interim payments to each such project for which an application has been approved on the basis of estimates of maximum pro rata entitlement of all applicants under section 206(a) and (2) for the purpose of determining allocation of sums available under Public Law 92–399, the unpaid balance of reimbursement due such projects shall be computed as of January 31, 1974. Upon completion by the Administrator of his audit and approval of all projects for which an application has been filed under subsection (a) of such section 206, the Administrator shall, within the limits of appropriated funds, allocate to each such qualified project the amount remaining, if any, of its total entitlement. Amounts allocated to projects which are later determined to be in excess of entitlement shall be available for reallocation, until expended, to other qualified projects under subsection (a) of such section 206. In no event, however, shall any payments exceed the Federal share of the cost of construction incurred to the date of the voucher covering such payment plus the Federal share of the value of the materials which have been stockpiled in the vicinity of such construction in conformity to plans and specifications for the project."

§ 1287. Authorization of appropriations

There is authorized to be appropriated to carry out this subchapter, other than sections 1286(e), 1288 and 1289 of this title, for the fiscal year ending June 30, 1973, not to exceed $5,000,000,000, for the fiscal year ending June 30, 1974, not to exceed $6,000,000,000, and for the fiscal year ending June 30, 1975, not to exceed $7,000,000,000, and subject to such amounts as are provided in appropriation Acts, for the fiscal year ending September 30, 1977, $1,000,000,000 for the fiscal year ending September 30, 1978, $4,500,000,000 and for the fiscal years ending September 30, 1979, September 30, 1980, not to exceed $5,000,000,000; for the fiscal year ending September 30, 1981, not to exceed $2,548,837,000; and for the fiscal years ending September 30, 1982, September 30, 1983, September 30, 1984, and September 30, 1985, not to exceed $2,400,000,000 per fiscal year; and for each of the fiscal years ending September 30, 1986, September 30, 1987, and September 30, 1988, not to exceed $2,400,000,000; and for each of the fiscal years ending September 30, 1989, and September 30, 1990, not to exceed $1,200,000,000.

(June 30, 1948, ch. 758, title II, § 207, as added Pub. L. 92–500, § 2, Oct. 18, 1972, 86 Stat. 839; amended Pub. L. 93–207, § 1(3), Dec. 28, 1973, 87 Stat. 906; Pub. L. 95–217, § 30, Dec. 27, 1977, 91 Stat. 1576; Pub. L. 97–35, title XVIII, § 1801(a), Aug. 13, 1981, 95 Stat. 764; Pub. L. 97–117, § 17, Dec. 29, 1981, 95 Stat. 1630; Pub. L. 100–4, title II, § 211, Feb. 4, 1987, 101 Stat. 21.)

AMENDMENTS

1987—Pub. L. 100–4 inserted "; and for each of the fiscal years ending September 30, 1986, September 30, 1987, and September 30, 1988, not to exceed $2,400,000,000; and for each of the fiscal years ending September 30, 1989, and September 30, 1990, not to exceed $1,200,000,000" before period at end.

1981—Pub. L. 97–117 substituted "and for the fiscal years ending September 30, 1982, September 30, 1983, September 30, 1984, and September 30, 1985, not to exceed $2,400,000,000 per fiscal year" for "and for the fiscal year ending September 30, 1982, not to exceed $0, unless there is enacted legislation establishing an allotment formula for fiscal year 1982 construction grant funds and otherwise reforming the municipal sewage treatment construction grant program under this subchapter, in which case the authorization for fiscal year 1982 shall be an amount not to exceed $2,400,000,000".

Pub. L. 97–35 substituted provisions authorizing not to exceed $2,548,837,000 for fiscal year ending Sept. 30, 1981, and not to exceed $0 for the fiscal year ending Sept. 30, 1982, unless an allotment formula is enacted, in which case the authorization is not to exceed $2,400,000,000, for provisions authorizing not to exceed $5,000,000,000 for fiscal years ending Sept. 30, 1981 and 1982.

1977—Pub. L. 95–217 inserted "and subject to such amounts as are provided in appropriation Acts, for the fiscal year ending September 30, 1977, $1,000,000,000 for the fiscal year ending September 30, 1978, $4,500,000,000 and for the fiscal years ending September 30, 1979, September 30, 1980, September 30, 1981, and September 30, 1982, not to exceed $5,000,000,000 per fiscal year".

1973—Pub. L. 93–207 inserted reference to section 1286(e) of this title.

ADDITIONAL AUTHORIZATION OF APPROPRIATIONS

Pub. L. 94–369, title III, § 301, July 22, 1976, 90 Stat. 1011, provided for authorization to carry out this subchapter, other than sections 1286, 1288, and 1289, for the fiscal year ending Sept. 30, 1977, not to exceed $700,000,000, which sum (subject to amounts provided in appropriation Acts) was to be allotted to each State listed in column 1 of table IV contained in House Public Works and Transportation Committee Print numbered 94–25 in accordance with the percentages provided for such State (if any) in column 5 of such table, and such sum to be in addition to, and not in lieu of, any funds otherwise authorized and to be available until expended.

§1288. Areawide waste treatment management

(a) Identification and designation of areas having substantial water quality control problems

For the purpose of encouraging and facilitating the development and implementation of areawide waste treatment management plans—

(1) The Administrator, within ninety days after October 18, 1972, and after consultation with appropriate Federal, State, and local authorities, shall by regulation publish guidelines for the identification of those areas which, as a result of urban-industrial concentrations or other factors, have substantial water quality control problems.

(2) The Governor of each State, within sixty days after publication of the guidelines issued pursuant to paragraph (1) of this subsection, shall identify each area within the State which, as a result of urban-industrial concentrations or other factors, has substantial water quality control problems. Not later than one hundred and twenty days following such identification and after consultation with appropriate elected and other officials of local governments having jurisdiction in such areas, the Governor shall designate (A) the boundaries of each such area, and (B) a single representative organization, including elected officials from local governments or their designees, capable of developing effective areawide waste treatment management plans for such area. The Governor may in the same manner at any later time identify any additional area (or modify an existing area) for which he determines areawide waste treatment management to be appropriate, designate the boundaries of such area, and designate an organization capable of developing effective areawide waste treatment management plans for such area.

(3) With respect to any area which, pursuant to the guidelines published under paragraph (1) of this subsection, is located in two or more States, the Governors of the respective States shall consult and cooperate in carrying out the provisions of paragraph (2), with a view toward designating the boundaries of the interstate area having common water quality control problems and for which areawide waste treatment management plans would be most effective, and toward designating, within one hundred and eighty days after publication of guidelines issued pursuant to paragraph (1) of this subsection, of a single representative organization capable of developing effective areawide waste treatment management plans for such area.

(4) If a Governor does not act, either by designating or determining not to make a designation under paragraph (2) of this subsection, within the time required by such paragraph, or if, in the case of an interstate area, the Governors of the States involved do not designate a planning organization within the time required by paragraph (3) of this subsection, the chief elected officials of local governments within an area may by agreement designate (A) the boundaries for such an area, and (B) a single representative organization including elected officials from such local governments, or their designees, capable of developing an areawide waste treatment management plan for such area.

(5) Existing regional agencies may be designated under paragraphs (2), (3), and (4) of this subsection.

(6) The State shall act as a planning agency for all portions of such State which are not designated under paragraphs (2), (3), or (4) of this subsection.

(7) Designations under this subsection shall be subject to the approval of the Administrator.

(b) Planning process

(1)(A) Not later than one year after the date of designation of any organization under subsection (a) of this section such organization shall have in operation a continuing areawide waste treatment management planning process consistent with section 1281 of this title. Plans prepared in accordance with this process shall contain alternatives for waste treatment management, and be applicable to all wastes generated within the area involved. The initial plan prepared in accordance with such process shall be certified by the Governor and submitted to the Administrator not later than two years after the planning process is in operation.

(B) For any agency designated after 1975 under subsection (a) of this section and for all portions of a State for which the State is required to act as the planning agency in accordance with subsection (a)(6) of this section, the initial plan prepared in accordance with such process shall be certified by the Governor and submitted to the Administrator not later than three years after the receipt of the initial grant award authorized under subsection (f) of this section.

(2) Any plan prepared under such process shall include, but not be limited to—

(A) the identification of treatment works necessary to meet the anticipated municipal and industrial waste treatment needs of the area over a twenty-year period, annually updated (including an analysis of alternative waste treatment systems), including any requirements for the acquisition of land for treatment purposes; the necessary waste water collection and urban storm water runoff systems; and a program to provide the necessary financial arrangements for the development of such treatment works, and an identification of open space and recreation opportunities that can be expected to result from improved water quality, including consideration of potential use of lands associated with treatment works and increased access to water-based recreation;

(B) the establishment of construction priorities for such treatment works and time schedules for the initiation and completion of all treatment works;

(C) the establishment of a regulatory program to—

(i) implement the waste treatment management requirements of section 1281(c) of this title,

(ii) regulate the location, modification, and construction of any facilities within such area which may result in any discharge in such area, and

(iii) assure that any industrial or commercial wastes discharged into any treatment works in such area meet applicable pretreatment requirements;

(D) the identification of those agencies necessary to construct, operate, and maintain all facilities required by the plan and otherwise to carry out the plan;

(E) the identification of the measures necessary to carry out the plan (including financing), the period of time necessary to carry out the plan, the costs of carrying out the plan within such time, and the economic, social, and environmental impact of carrying out the plan within such time;

(F) a process to (i) identify, if appropriate, agriculturally and silviculturally related nonpoint sources of pollution, including return flows from irrigated agriculture, and their cumulative effects, runoff from manure disposal areas, and from land used for livestock and crop production, and (ii) set forth procedures and methods (including land use requirements) to control to the extent feasible such sources;

(G) a process to (i) identify, if appropriate, mine-related sources of pollution including new, current, and abandoned surface and underground mine runoff, and (ii) set forth procedures and methods (including land use requirements) to control to the extent feasible such sources;

(H) a process to (i) identify construction activity related sources of pollution, and (ii) set forth procedures and methods (including land use requirements) to control to the extent feasible such sources;

(I) a process to (i) identify, if appropriate, salt water intrusion into rivers, lakes, and estuaries resulting from reduction of fresh water flow from any cause, including irrigation, obstruction, ground water extraction, and diversion, and (ii) set forth procedures and methods to control such intrusion to the extent feasible where such procedures and methods are otherwise a part of the waste treatment management plan;

(J) a process to control the disposition of all residual waste generated in such area which could affect water quality; and

(K) a process to control the disposal of pollutants on land or in subsurface excavations within such area to protect ground and surface water quality.

(3) Areawide waste treatment management plans shall be certified annually by the Governor or his designee (or Governors or their designees, where more than one State is involved) as being consistent with applicable basin plans and such areawide waste treatment management plans shall be submitted to the Administrator for his approval.

(4)(A) Whenever the Governor of any State determines (and notifies the Administrator) that consistency with a statewide regulatory program under section 1313 of this title so requires, the requirements of clauses (F) through (K) of paragraph (2) of this subsection shall be developed and submitted by the Governor to the Administrator for approval for application to a class or category of activity throughout such State.

(B) Any program submitted under subparagraph (A) of this paragraph which, in whole or in part, is to control the discharge or other placement of dredged or fill material into the navigable waters shall include the following:

(i) A consultation process which includes the State agency with primary jurisdiction over fish and wildlife resources.

(ii) A process to identify and manage the discharge or other placement of dredged or fill material which adversely affects navigable waters, which shall complement and be coordinated with a State program under section 1344 of this title conducted pursuant to this chapter.

(iii) A process to assure that any activity conducted pursuant to a best management practice will comply with the guidelines established under section 1344(b)(1) of this title, and sections 1317 and 1343 of this title.

(iv) A process to assure that any activity conducted pursuant to a best management practice can be terminated or modified for cause including, but not limited to, the following:

(I) violation of any condition of the best management practice;

(II) change in any activity that requires either a temporary or permanent reduction or elimination of the discharge pursuant to the best management practice.

(v) A process to assure continued coordination with Federal and Federal-State water-related planning and reviewing processes, including the National Wetlands Inventory.

(C) If the Governor of a State obtains approval from the Administrator of a statewide regulatory program which meets the requirements of subparagraph (B) of this paragraph and if such State is administering a permit program under section 1344 of this title, no person shall be required to obtain an individual permit pursuant to such section, or to comply with a general permit issued pursuant to such section, with respect to any appropriate activity within such State for which a best management practice has been approved by the Administrator under the program approved by the Administrator pursuant to this paragraph.

(D)(i) Whenever the Administrator determines after public hearing that a State is not administering a program approved under this section in accordance with the requirements of this section, the Administrator shall so notify the State, and if appropriate corrective action is not taken within a reasonable time, not to exceed ninety days, the Administrator shall withdraw approval of such program. The Administrator shall not withdraw approval of any such program unless he shall first have notified the State, and made public, in writing, the reasons for such withdrawal.

(ii) In the case of a State with a program submitted and approved under this paragraph, the Administrator shall withdraw approval of such program under this subparagraph only for a substantial failure of the State to administer its program in accordance with the requirements of this paragraph.

(c) Regional operating agencies

(1) The Governor of each State, in consultation with the planning agency designated under subsection (a) of this section, at the time a plan is submitted to the Administrator, shall designate one or more waste treatment management agencies (which may be an existing or newly created local, regional, or State agency or political subdivision) for each area designated under subsection (a) of this section and submit such designations to the Administrator.

(2) The Administrator shall accept any such designation, unless, within 120 days of such designation, he finds that the designated management agency (or agencies) does not have adequate authority—

(A) to carry out appropriate portions of an areawide waste treatment management plan developed under subsection (b) of this section;

(B) to manage effectively waste treatment works and related facilities serving such area in conformance with any plan required by subsection (b) of this section;

(C) directly or by contract, to design and construct new works, and to operate and maintain new and existing works as required by any plan developed pursuant to subsection (b) of this section;

(D) to accept and utilize grants, or other funds from any source, for waste treatment management purposes;

(E) to raise revenues, including the assessment of waste treatment charges;

(F) to incur short- and long-term indebtedness;

(G) to assure in implementation of an areawide waste treatment management plan that each participating community pays its proportionate share of treatment costs;

(H) to refuse to receive any wastes from any municipality or subdivision thereof, which does not comply with any provisions of an approved plan under this section applicable to such area; and

(I) to accept for treatment industrial wastes.

(d) Conformity of works with area plan

After a waste treatment management agency having the authority required by subsection (c) of this section has been designated under such subsection for an area and a plan for such area has been approved under subsection (b) of this section, the Administrator shall not make any grant for construction of a publicly owned treatment works under section 1281(g)(1) of this title within such area except to such designated agency and for works in conformity with such plan.

(e) Permits not to conflict with approved plans

No permit under section 1342 of this title shall be issued for any point source which is in conflict with a plan approved pursuant to subsection (b) of this section.

(f) Grants

(1) The Administrator shall make grants to any agency designated under subsection (a) of this section for payment of the reasonable costs of developing and operating a continuing areawide waste treatment management planning process under subsection (b) of this section.

(2) For the two-year period beginning on the date the first grant is made under paragraph (1) of this subsection to an agency, if such first grant is made before October 1, 1977, the amount of each such grant to such agency shall be 100 per centum of the costs of developing and operating a continuing areawide waste treatment management planning process under subsection (b) of this section, and thereafter the amount granted to such agency shall not exceed 75 per centum of such costs in each succeeding one-year period. In the case of any other grant made to an agency under such paragraph (1) of this subsection, the amount of such grant shall not exceed 75 per centum of the costs of developing and operating a continuing areawide waste treatment management planning process in any year.

(3) Each applicant for a grant under this subsection shall submit to the Administrator for his approval each proposal for which a grant is applied for under this subsection. The Administrator shall act upon such proposal as soon as practicable after it has been submitted, and his approval of that proposal shall be deemed a contractual obligation of the United States for the payment of its contribution to such proposal, subject to such amounts as are provided in appropriation Acts. There is authorized to be appropriated to carry out this subsection not to exceed $50,000,000 for the fiscal year ending June 30, 1973, not to exceed $100,000,000 for the fiscal year ending June 30, 1974, not to exceed $150,000,000 per fiscal year for the fiscal years ending June 30, 1975, September 30, 1977, September 30, 1978, September 30, 1979, and September 30, 1980, not to exceed $100,000,000 per fiscal year for the fiscal years ending September 30, 1981, and September 30, 1982, and such sums as may be necessary for fiscal years 1983 through 1990.

(g) Technical assistance by Administrator

The Administrator is authorized, upon request of the Governor or the designated planning agency, and without reimbursement, to consult with, and provide technical assistance to, any agency designated under subsection (a) of this section in the development of areawide waste treatment management plans under subsection (b) of this section.

(h) Technical assistance by Secretary of the Army

(1) The Secretary of the Army, acting through the Chief of Engineers, in cooperation with the Administrator is authorized and directed, upon request of the Governor or the designated planning organization, to consult with, and provide technical assistance to, any agency designed[1] under subsection (a) of this section in developing and operating a continuing areawide waste treatment management planning process under subsection (b) of this section.

(2) There is authorized to be appropriated to the Secretary of the Army, to carry out this subsection, not to exceed $50,000,000 per fiscal

[1] So in original. Probably should be "designated".

year for the fiscal years ending June 30, 1973, and June 30, 1974.

(i) State best management practices program

(1) The Secretary of the Interior, acting through the Director of the United States Fish and Wildlife Service, shall, upon request of the Governor of a State, and without reimbursement, provide technical assistance to such State in developing a statewide program for submission to the Administrator under subsection (b)(4)(B) of this section and in implementing such program after its approval.

(2) There is authorized to be appropriated to the Secretary of the Interior $6,000,000 to complete the National Wetlands Inventory of the United States, by December 31, 1981, and to provide information from such Inventory to States as it becomes available to assist such States in the development and operation of programs under this chapter.

(j) Agricultural cost sharing

(1) The Secretary of Agriculture, with the concurrence of the Administrator, and acting through the Soil Conservation Service and such other agencies of the Department of Agriculture as the Secretary may designate, is authorized and directed to establish and administer a program to enter into contracts, subject to such amounts as are provided in advance by appropriation acts, of not less than five years nor more than ten years with owners and operators having control of rural land for the purpose of installing and maintaining measures incorporating best management practices to control nonpoint source pollution for improved water quality in those States or areas for which the Administrator has approved a plan under subsection (b) of this section where the practices to which the contracts apply are certified by the management agency designated under subsection (c)(1) of this section to be consistent with such plans and will result in improved water quality. Such contracts may be entered into during the period ending not later than September 31, 1988. Under such contracts the land owner or operator shall agree—

(i) to effectuate a plan approved by a soil conservation district, where one exists, under this section for his farm, ranch, or other land substantially in accordance with the schedule outlined therein unless any requirement thereof is waived or modified by the Secretary;

(ii) to forfeit all rights to further payments or grants under the contract and refund to the United States all payments and grants received thereunder, with interest, upon his violation of the contract at any stage during the time he has control of the land if the Secretary, after considering the recommendations of the soil conservation district, where one exists, and the Administrator, determines that such violation is of such a nature as to warrant termination of the contract, or to make refunds or accept such payment adjustments as the Secretary may deem appropriate if he determines that the violation by the owner or operator does not warrant termination of the contract;

(iii) upon transfer of his right and interest in the farm, ranch, or other land during the contract period to forfeit all rights to further payments or grants under the contract and refund to the United States all payments or grants received thereunder, with interest, unless the transferee of any such land agrees with the Secretary to assume all obligations of the contract;

(iv) not to adopt any practice specified by the Secretary on the advice of the Administrator in the contract as a practice which would tend to defeat the purposes of the contract;

(v) to such additional provisions as the Secretary determines are desirable and includes in the contract to effectuate the purposes of the program or to facilitate the practical administration of the program.

(2) In return for such agreement by the landowner or operator the Secretary shall agree to provide technical assistance and share the cost of carrying out those conservation practices and measures set forth in the contract for which he determines that cost sharing is appropriate and in the public interest and which are approved for cost sharing by the agency designated to implement the plan developed under subsection (b) of this section. The portion of such cost (including labor) to be shared shall be that part which the Secretary determines is necessary and appropriate to effectuate the installation of the water quality management practices and measures under the contract, but not to exceed 50 per centum of the total cost of the measures set forth in the contract; except the Secretary may increase the matching cost share where he determines that (1) the main benefits to be derived from the measures are related to improving offsite water quality, and (2) the matching share requirement would place a burden on the landowner which would probably prevent him from participating in the program.

(3) The Secretary may terminate any contract with a landowner or operator by mutual agreement with the owner or operator if the Secretary determines that such termination would be in the public interest, and may agree to such modification of contracts previously entered into as he may determine to be desirable to carry out the purposes of the program or facilitate the practical administration thereof or to accomplish equitable treatment with respect to other conservation, land use, or water quality programs.

(4) In providing assistance under this subsection the Secretary will give priority to those areas and sources that have the most significant effect upon water quality. Additional investigations or plans may be made, where necessary, to supplement approved water quality management plans, in order to determine priorities.

(5) The Secretary shall, where practicable, enter into agreements with soil conservation districts, State soil and water conservation agencies, or State water quality agencies to administer all or part of the program established in this subsection under regulations developed by the Secretary. Such agreements shall provide for the submission of such reports as the Secretary deems necessary, and for payment by the United States of such portion of the costs incurred in the administration of the program as the Secretary may deem appropriate.

(6) The contracts under this subsection shall be entered into only in areas where the management agency designated under subsection (c)(1) of this section assures an adequate level of participation by owners and operators having control of rural land in such areas. Within such areas the local soil conservation district, where one exists, together with the Secretary of Agriculture, will determine the priority of assistance among individual land owners and operators to assure that the most critical water quality problems are addressed.

(7) The Secretary, in consultation with the Administrator and subject to section 1314(k) of this title, shall, not later than September 30, 1978, promulgate regulations for carrying out this subsection and for support and cooperation with other Federal and non-Federal agencies for implementation of this subsection.

(8) This program shall not be used to authorize or finance projects that would otherwise be eligible for assistance under the terms of Public Law 83–566 [16 U.S.C. 1001 et seq.].

(9) There are hereby authorized to be appropriated to the Secretary of Agriculture $200,000,000 for fiscal year 1979, $400,000,000 for fiscal year 1980, $100,000,000 for fiscal year 1981, $100,000,000 for fiscal year 1982, and such sums as may be necessary for fiscal years 1983 through 1990, to carry out this subsection. The program authorized under this subsection shall be in addition to, and not in substitution of, other programs in such area authorized by this or any other public law.

(June 30, 1948, ch. 758, title II, § 208, as added Pub. L. 92–500, § 2, Oct. 18, 1972, 86 Stat. 839; amended Pub. L. 95–217, §§ 4(e), 31, 32, 33(a), 34, 35, Dec. 27, 1977, 91 Stat. 1566, 1576–1579; Pub. L. 96–483, § 1(d), (e), Oct. 21, 1980, 94 Stat. 2360; Pub. L. 100–4, title I, § 101(d), (e), Feb. 4, 1987, 101 Stat. 9.)

REFERENCES IN TEXT

Public Law 83–566, referred to in subsec. (j)(8), is act Aug. 4, 1954, ch. 656, 68 Stat. 666, as amended, known as the Watershed Protection and Flood Prevention Act, which is classified generally to chapter 18 (§ 1001 et seq.) of Title 16, Conservation. For complete classification of this Act to the Code, see Short Title note set out under section 1001 of Title 16 and Tables.

AMENDMENTS

1987—Subsec. (f)(3). Pub. L. 100–4, § 101(d), struck out "and" after "1974," and "1980," and inserted ", and such sums as may be necessary for fiscal years 1983 through 1990" after "1982".

Subsec. (j)(9). Pub. L. 100–4, § 101(e), struck out "and" after "1981," and inserted "and such sums as may be necessary for fiscal years 1983 through 1990," after "1982,".

1980—Subsec. (f)(3). Pub. L. 96–483, § 1(d), inserted authorization of not to exceed $100,000,000 per fiscal year for fiscal years ending Sept. 30, 1981 and 1982.

Subsec. (j)(9). Pub. L. 96–483, § 1(e), inserted reference to authorization of $100,000,000 for each of fiscal years 1981 and 1982.

1977—Subsec. (b)(1). Pub. L. 95–217, § 31(a), designated existing provisions as subpar. (A) and added subpar. (B).

Subsec. (b)(2)(A). Pub. L. 95–217, § 32, inserted ", and an identification of open space and recreation opportunities that can be expected to result from improved water quality, including consideration of potential use of lands associated with treatment works and increased access to water-based recreation" after "development of such treatment works".

Subsec. (b)(2)(F). Pub. L. 95–217, § 33(a), substituted "sources of pollution, including return flows from irrigated agriculture, and their cumulative effects," for "sources of pollution, including".

Subsec. (b)(4). Pub. L. 95–217, § 34(a), designated existing provisions as subpar. (A), substituted "to the Administrator for approval for application to a class or category of activity throughout such State" for "to the Administrator for application to all regions within such State", and added subpars. (B) to (D).

Subsec. (f)(2). Pub. L. 95–217, § 31(b), substituted "For the two-year period beginning on the date the first grant is made under paragraph (1) of this subsection to an agency, if such first grant is made before October 1, 1977, the amount of each such grant to such agency shall be 100 per centum of the costs of developing and operating a continuing areawide waste treatment management planning process under subsection (b) of this section, and thereafter the amount granted to such agency shall not exceed 75 per centum of such costs in each succeeding one-year period" for "The amount granted to any agency under paragraph (1) of this subsection shall be 100 per centum of the costs of developing and operating a continuing areawide waste treatment management planning process under subsection (b) of this section for each of the fiscal years ending on June 30, 1973, June 30, 1974, and June 30, 1975, and shall not exceed 75 per centum of such costs in each succeeding fiscal year" and inserted "In the case of any other grant made to an agency under such paragraph (1) of this subsection, the amount of such grant shall not exceed 75 per centum of the costs of developing and operating a continuing areawide waste treatment management planning process in any year."

Subsec. (f)(3). Pub. L. 95–217, §§ 4(e), 31(c), substituted "and not to exceed $150,000,000 per fiscal year for the fiscal years ending June 30, 1975, September 30, 1977, September 30, 1978, September 30, 1979, and September 30, 1980" for "and not to exceed $150,000,000 for the fiscal year ending June 30, 1975" and inserted "subject to such amounts as are provided in appropriation Acts" after "contractual obligation of the United States for the payment of its contribution to such proposal".

Subsec. (i). Pub. L. 95–217, § 34(b), added subsec. (i).

Subsec. (j). Pub. L. 95–217, § 35, added subsec. (j).

TRANSFER OF FUNCTIONS

Enforcement functions of Secretary or other official in Department of Agriculture, insofar as they involve lands and programs under jurisdiction of that Department, relating to compliance with this chapter with respect to pre-construction, construction, and initial operation of transportation system for Canadian and Alaskan natural gas were transferred to the Federal Inspector, Office of Federal Inspector for the Alaska Natural Gas Transportation System, until the first anniversary of the date of initial operation of the Alaska Natural Gas Transportation System, see Reorg. Plan No. 1 of 1979, §§ 102(f), 203(a), 44 F.R. 33663, 33666, 93 Stat. 1373, 1376, effective July 1, 1979, set out in the Appendix to Title 5, Government Organization and Employees. Office of Federal Inspector for the Alaska Natural Gas Transportation System abolished and functions and authority vested in Inspector transferred to Secretary of Energy by section 3012(b) of Pub. L. 102–486, set out as an Abolition of Office of Federal Inspector note under section 719e of Title 15, Commerce and Trade. Functions and authority vested in Secretary of Energy subsequently transferred to Federal Coordinator for Alaska Natural Gas Transportation Projects by section 720d(f) of Title 15.

§ 1289. Basin planning

(a) Preparation of Level B plans

The President, acting through the Water Resources Council, shall, as soon as practicable, prepare a Level B plan under the Water Resources Planning Act [42 U.S.C. 1962 et seq.] for all basins in the United States. All such plans shall be completed not later than January 1, 1980, except that priority in the preparation of such plans shall be given to those basins and portions thereof which are within those areas designated under paragraphs (2), (3), and (4) of subsection (a) of section 1288 of this title.

(b) Reporting requirements

The President, acting through the Water Resources Council, shall report annually to Congress on progress being made in carrying out this section. The first such report shall be submitted not later than January 31, 1973.

(c) Authorization of appropriations

There is authorized to be appropriated to carry out this section not to exceed $200,000,000.

(June 30, 1948, ch. 758, title II, § 209, as added Pub. L. 92–500, § 2, Oct. 18, 1972, 86 Stat. 843.)

REFERENCES IN TEXT

The Water Resources Planning Act, referred to in subsec. (a), is Pub. L. 89–80, July 22, 1965, 79 Stat. 244, as amended, which is classified generally to chapter 19B (§ 1962 et seq.) of Title 42, The Public Health and Welfare. For complete classification of this Act to the Code, see Short Title note set out under section 1962 of Title 42 and Tables.

§ 1290. Annual survey

The Administrator shall annually make a survey to determine the efficiency of the operation and maintenance of treatment works constructed with grants made under this chapter, as compared to the efficiency planned at the time the grant was made. The results of such annual survey shall be included in the report required under section 1375(a) of this title.

(June 30, 1948, ch. 758, title II, § 210, as added Pub. L. 92–500, § 2, Oct. 18, 1972, 86 Stat. 843; amended Pub. L. 105–362, title V, § 501(d)(2)(D), Nov. 10, 1998, 112 Stat. 3284; Pub. L. 107–303, title III, § 302(b)(1), Nov. 27, 2002, 116 Stat. 2361.)

AMENDMENTS

2002—Pub. L. 107–303 repealed Pub. L. 105–362, § 501(d)(2)(D). See 1998 Amendment note below.

1998—Pub. L. 105–362, § 501(d)(2)(D), which directed the substitution of "shall be reported to Congress not later than 90 days after the date of convening of each session of Congress" for "shall be included in the report required under section 1375(a) of this title", was repealed by Pub. L. 107–303. See Effective Date of 2002 Amendment note below.

EFFECTIVE DATE OF 2002 AMENDMENT

Amendment by Pub. L. 107–303 effective Nov. 10, 1998, and Federal Water Pollution Act (33 U.S.C. 1251 et seq.) to be applied and administered on and after Nov. 27, 2002, as if amendments made by section 501(a)–(d) of Pub. L. 105–362 had not been enacted, see section 302(b) of Pub. L. 107–303, set out as a note under section 1254 of this title.

§ 1291. Sewage collection systems

(a) Existing and new systems

No grant shall be made for a sewage collection system under this subchapter unless such grant (1) is for replacement or major rehabilitation of an existing collection system and is necessary to the total integrity and performance of the waste treatment works servicing such community, or (2) is for a new collection system in an existing community with sufficient existing or planned capacity adequately to treat such collected sewage and is consistent with section 1281 of this title.

(b) Use of population density as test

If the Administrator uses population density as a test for determining the eligibility of a collector sewer for assistance it shall be only for the purpose of evaluating alternatives and determining the needs for such system in relation to ground or surface water quality impact.

(c) Pollutant discharges from separate storm sewer systems

No grant shall be made under this subchapter from funds authorized for any fiscal year during the period beginning October 1, 1977, and ending September 30, 1990, for treatment works for control of pollutant discharges from separate storm sewer systems.

(June 30, 1948, ch. 758, title II, § 211, as added Pub. L. 92–500, § 2, Oct. 18, 1972, 86 Stat. 843; amended Pub. L. 95–217, § 36, Dec. 27, 1977, 91 Stat. 1581; Pub. L. 97–117, § 2(b), Dec. 29, 1981, 95 Stat. 1623; Pub. L. 100–4, title II, § 206(d), Feb. 4, 1987, 101 Stat. 20.)

AMENDMENTS

1987—Subsec. (c). Pub. L. 100–4 substituted "1990" for "1985".

1981—Subsec. (c). Pub. L. 97–117 substituted "September 30, 1985" for "September 30, 1982".

1977—Pub. L. 95–217 designated existing provisions as subsec. (a) and added subsecs. (b) and (c).

§ 1292. Definitions

As used in this subchapter—

(1) The term "construction" means any one or more of the following: preliminary planning to determine the feasibility of treatment works, engineering, architectural, legal, fiscal, or economic investigations or studies, surveys, designs, plans, working drawings, specifications, procedures, field testing of innovative or alternative waste water treatment processes and techniques meeting guidelines promulgated under section 1314(d)(3) of this title, or other necessary actions, erection, building, acquisition, alteration, remodeling, improvement, or extension of treatment works, or the inspection or supervision of any of the foregoing items.

(2)(A) The term "treatment works" means any devices and systems used in the storage, treatment, recycling, and reclamation of municipal sewage or industrial wastes of a liquid nature to implement section 1281 of this title, or necessary to recycle or reuse water at the most economical cost over the estimated life of the works, including intercepting sewers, outfall sewers, sewage collection systems, pumping, power, and other equipment, and their appurtenances; extensions, improvements, remodeling, additions, and alterations thereof; elements essential to provide a reliable recycled supply such as standby treatment units and clear well facilities; and any works, including site acquisition of the land that will be an integral part of the treatment process (including land used for the storage of treated wastewater in land treatment systems prior to land application) or is used for ultimate disposal of residues resulting from such treatment.

(B) In addition to the definition contained in subparagraph (A) of this paragraph, "treatment works" means any other method or system for preventing, abating, reducing, storing, treating, separating, or disposing of municipal waste, including storm water runoff, or industrial waste, including waste in combined storm water and sanitary sewer systems. Any application for construction grants which includes wholly or in part such methods or systems shall, in accordance with guidelines published by the Administrator pursuant to subparagraph (C) of this paragraph, contain adequate data and analysis demonstrating such proposal to be, over the life of such works, the most cost efficient alternative to comply with sections 1311 or 1312 of this title, or the requirements of section 1281 of this title.

(C) For the purposes of subparagraph (B) of this paragraph, the Administrator shall, within one hundred and eighty days after October 18, 1972, publish and thereafter revise no less often than annually, guidelines for the evaluation of methods, including cost-effective analysis, described in subparagraph (B) of this paragraph.

(3) The term "replacement" as used in this subchapter means those expenditures for obtaining and installing equipment, accessories, or appurtenances during the useful life of the treatment works necessary to maintain the capacity and performance for which such works are designed and constructed.

(June 30, 1948, ch. 758, title II, §212, as added Pub. L. 92–500, §2, Oct. 18, 1972, 86 Stat. 844; amended Pub. L. 95–217, §37, Dec. 27, 1977, 91 Stat. 1581; Pub. L. 97–117, §8(d), Dec. 29, 1981, 95 Stat. 1626.)

AMENDMENTS

1981—Par. (1). Pub. L. 97–117 inserted "field testing of innovative or alternative waste water treatment processes and techniques meeting guidelines promulgated under section 1314(d)(3) of this title," after "procedures,".

1977—Par. (2)(A). Pub. L. 95–217 inserted "(including land used for the storage of treated wastewater in land treatment systems prior to land application)" after "integral part of the treatment process".

§ 1293. Loan guarantees

(a) State or local obligations issued exclusively to Federal Financing Bank for publicly owned treatment works; determination of eligibility of project by Administrator

Subject to the conditions of this section and to such terms and conditions as the Administrator determines to be necessary to carry out the purposes of this subchapter, the Administrator is authorized to guarantee, and to make commitments to guarantee, the principal and interest (including interest accruing between the date of default and the date of the payment in full of the guarantee) of any loan, obligation, or participation therein of any State, municipality, or intermunicipal or interstate agency issued directly and exclusively to the Federal Financing Bank to finance that part of the cost of any grant-eligible project for the construction of publicly owned treatment works not paid for with Federal financial assistance under this subchapter (other than this section), which project the Administrator has determined to be eligible for such financial assistance under this subchapter, including, but not limited to, projects eligible for reimbursement under section 1286 of this title.

(b) Conditions for issuance

No guarantee, or commitment to make a guarantee, may be made pursuant to this section—

(1) unless the Administrator certifies that the issuing body is unable to obtain on reasonable terms sufficient credit to finance its actual needs without such guarantee; and

(2) unless the Administrator determines that there is a reasonable assurance of repayment of the loan, obligation, or participation therein.

A determination of whether financing is available at reasonable rates shall be made by the Secretary of the Treasury with relationship to the current average yield on outstanding marketable obligations of municipalities of comparable maturity.

(c) Fees for application investigation and issuance of commitment guarantee

The Administrator is authorized to charge reasonable fees for the investigation of an application for a guarantee and for the issuance of a commitment to make a guarantee.

(d) Commitment for repayment

The Administrator, in determining whether there is a reasonable assurance of repayment, may require a commitment which would apply to such repayment. Such commitment may include, but not be limited to, any funds received by such grantee from the amounts appropriated under section 1286 of this title.

(June 30, 1948, ch. 758, title II, §213, as added Pub. L. 94–558, Oct. 19, 1976, 90 Stat. 2639; amended Pub. L. 96–483, §2(e), Oct. 21, 1980, 94 Stat. 2361.)

AMENDMENTS

1980—Subsec. (d). Pub. L. 96–483 struck out "(1) all or any portion of the funds retained by such grantee under section 1284(b)(3) of this title, and (2)" after "limited to".

EFFECTIVE DATE OF 1980 AMENDMENT

Amendment by Pub. L. 96–483 effective Dec. 27, 1977, see section 2(g) of Pub. L. 96–483, set out as a note under section 1281 of this title.

§ 1293a. Contained spoil disposal facilities

(a) Construction, operation, and maintenance; period; conditions; requirements

The Secretary of the Army, acting through the Chief of Engineers, is authorized to construct, operate, and maintain, subject to the provisions of subsection (c) of this section, contained spoil disposal facilities of sufficient capacity for a period not to exceed ten years, to meet the requirements of this section. Before establishing each such facility, the Secretary of the Army shall obtain the concurrence of appropriate local governments and shall consider the views and recommendations of the Administrator of the Environmental Protection Agency and shall comply with requirements of section 1171 of this title, and of the National Environmental Policy Act of 1969 [42 U.S.C. 4321 et seq.]. Section 401 of this title shall not apply to any facility authorized by this section.

(b) Time for establishment; consideration of area needs; requirements

The Secretary of the Army, acting through the Chief of Engineers, shall establish the contained spoil disposal facilities authorized in subsection (a) of this section at the earliest practicable date, taking into consideration the views and recommendations of the Administrator of the Environmental Protection Agency as to those areas which, in the Administrator's judgment, are most urgently in need of such facilities and pursuant to the requirements of the National Environmental Policy Act of 1969 [42 U.S.C. 4321 et seq.] and the Federal Water Pollution Control Act [33 U.S.C. 1251 et seq.].

(c) Written agreement requirement; terms of agreement

Prior to construction of any such facility, the appropriate State or States, interstate agency, municipality, or other appropriate political subdivision of the State shall agree in writing to (1) furnish all lands, easements, and rights-of-way necessary for the construction, operation, and maintenance of the facility; (2) contribute to the United States 25 per centum of the construction costs, such amount to be payable either in cash prior to construction, in installments during construction, or in installments, with interest at a rate to be determined by the Secretary of the Treasury, as of the beginning of the fiscal year in which construction is initiated, on the basis of the computed average interest rate payable by the Treasury upon its outstanding marketable public obligations, which are neither due or callable for redemption for fifteen years from date of issue; (3) hold and save the United States free from damages due to construction, operation, and maintenance of the facility; and (4) except as provided in subsection (f) of this section, maintain the facility after completion of its use for disposal purposes in a manner satisfactory to the Secretary of the Army.

(d) Waiver of construction costs contribution from non-Federal interests; findings of participation in waste treatment facilities for general geographical area and compliance with water quality standards; waiver of payments in event of written agreement before occurrence of findings

The requirement for appropriate non-Federal interest or interests to furnish an agreement to contribute 25 per centum of the construction costs as set forth in subsection (c) of this section shall be waived by the Secretary of the Army upon a finding by the Administrator of the Environmental Protection Agency that for the area to which such construction applies, the State or States involved, interstate agency, municipality, and other appropriate political subdivision of the State and industrial concerns are participating in and in compliance with an approved plan for the general geographical area of the dredging activity for construction, modification, expansion, or rehabilitation of waste treatment facilities and the Administrator has found that applicable water quality standards are not being violated. In the event such findings occur after the appropriate non-Federal interest or interests have entered into the agreement required by subsection (c) of this section, any payments due after the date of such findings as part of the required local contribution of 25 per centum of the construction costs shall be waived by the Secretary of the Army.

(e) Federal payment of costs for disposal of dredged spoil from project

Notwithstanding any other provision of law, all costs of disposal of dredged spoil from the project for the Great Lakes connecting channels, Michigan, shall be borne by the United States.

(f) Title to lands, easements, and rights-of-way; retention by non-Federal interests; conveyance of facilities; agreement of transferee

The participating non-Federal interest or interests shall retain title to all lands, easements, and rights-of-way furnished by it pursuant to subsection (c) of this section. A spoil disposal facility owned by a non-Federal interest or interests may be conveyed to another party only after completion of the facility's use for disposal purposes and after the transferee agrees in writing to use or maintain the facility in a manner which the Secretary of the Army determines to be satisfactory.

(g) Federal licenses or permits; charges; remission of charge

Any spoil disposal facilities constructed under the provisions of this section shall be made available to Federal licensees or permittees upon payment of an appropriate charge for such use. Twenty-five per centum of such charge shall be remitted to the participating non-Federal interest or interests except for those excused from contributing to the construction costs under subsections (d) and (e) of this section.

(h) Provisions applicable to Great Lakes and their connecting channels

This section, other than subsection (i), shall be applicable only to the Great Lakes and their connecting channels.

(i) Research, study, and experimentation program relating to dredged spoil extended to navigable waters, etc.; cooperative program; scope of program; utilization of facilities and personnel of Federal agency

The Chief of Engineers, under the direction of the Secretary of the Army, is hereby authorized to extend to all navigable waters, connecting channels, tributary streams, other waters of the United States and waters contiguous to the United States, a comprehensive program of research, study, and experimentation relating to dredged spoil. This program shall be carried out in cooperation with other Federal and State agencies, and shall include, but not be limited to, investigations on the characteristics of dredged spoil, and alternative methods of its disposal. To the extent that such study shall include the effects of such dredge spoil on water quality, the facilities and personnel of the Environmental Protection Agency shall be utilized.

(j) Period for depositing dredged materials

The Secretary of the Army, acting through the Chief of Engineers, is authorized to continue to deposit dredged materials into a contained spoil disposal facility constructed under this section until the Secretary determines that such facility is no longer needed for such purpose or that such facility is completely full.

(k) Study and monitoring program

(1) Study

The Secretary of the Army, acting through the Chief of Engineers, shall conduct a study of the materials disposed of in contained spoil disposal facilities constructed under this section for the purpose of determining whether or not toxic pollutants are present in such facilities and for the purpose of determining the concentration levels of each of such pollutants in such facilities.

(2) Report

Not later than 1 year after November 17, 1988, the Secretary shall transmit to Congress a report on the results of the study conducted under paragraph (1).

(3) Inspection and monitoring program

The Secretary shall conduct a program to inspect and monitor contained spoil disposal facilities constructed under this section for the purpose of determining whether or not toxic pollutants are leaking from such facilities.

(4) Toxic pollutant defined

For purposes of this subsection, the term "toxic pollutant" means those toxic pollutants referred to in section 1311(b)(2)(C) and 1311(b)(2)(D) of this title and such other pollutants as the Secretary, in consultation with the Administrator of the Environmental Protection Agency, determines are appropriate based on their effects on human health and the environment.

(Pub. L. 91–611, title I, §123, Dec. 31, 1970, 84 Stat. 1823; Pub. L. 93–251, title I, §23, Mar. 7, 1974, 88 Stat. 20; Pub. L. 100–676, §24, Nov. 17, 1988, 102 Stat. 4027.)

REFERENCES IN TEXT

Section 1171 of this title, referred to in subsec. (a), was omitted as superseded.

The National Environmental Policy Act of 1969, referred to in subsecs. (a) and (b), is Pub. L. 91–190, Jan. 1, 1970, 83 Stat. 852, as amended, which is classified generally to chapter 55 (§4321 et seq.) of Title 42, The Public Health and Welfare. For complete classification of this Act to the Code, see Short Title note set out under section 4321 of Title 42 and Tables.

The Federal Water Pollution Control Act, referred to in subsec. (b), is act June 30, 1948, ch. 758, as amended generally by Pub. L. 92–500, §2, Oct. 18, 1972, 86 Stat. 816, which is classified generally to this chapter (§1251 et seq.). For complete classification of this Act to the Code, see Short Title note set out under section 1251 of this title and Tables.

CODIFICATION

Section was formerly classified to section 1165a of this title.

Section was not enacted as a part of the Federal Water Pollution Control Act which comprises this chapter.

AMENDMENTS

1988—Subsec. (j). Pub. L. 100–676, §24(a), added subsec. (j).

Subsec. (k). Pub. L. 100–676, §24(b), added subsec. (k).

1974—Subsec. (d). Pub. L. 93–251 inserted provision for waiver of payments in event of a written agreement before occurrence of findings.

GREAT LAKES CONFINED DISPOSAL FACILITIES

Pub. L. 104–303, title V, §513, Oct. 12, 1996, 110 Stat. 3762, provided that:

"(a) ASSESSMENT.—Pursuant to the responsibilities of the Secretary under section 123 of the River and Harbor Act of 1970 (33 U.S.C. 1293a), the Secretary shall conduct an assessment of the general conditions of confined disposal facilities in the Great Lakes.

"(b) REPORT.—Not later than 3 years after the date of the enactment of this Act [Oct. 12, 1996], the Secretary shall transmit to Congress a report on the results of the assessment conducted under subsection (a), including the following:

"(1) A description of the cumulative effects of confined disposal facilities in the Great Lakes.

"(2) Recommendations for specific remediation actions for each confined disposal facility in the Great Lakes.

"(3) An evaluation of, and recommendations for, confined disposal facility management practices and technologies to conserve capacity at such facilities and to minimize adverse environmental effects at such facilities throughout the Great Lakes system."

§1294. Public information and education on recycling and reuse of wastewater, use of land treatment, and reduction of wastewater volume

The Administrator shall develop and operate within one year of December 27, 1977, a continuing program of public information and education on recycling and reuse of wastewater (including sludge), the use of land treatment, and methods for the reduction of wastewater volume.

(June 30, 1948, ch. 758, title II, §214, as added Pub. L. 95–217, §38, Dec. 27, 1977, 91 Stat. 1581.)

§1295. Requirements for American materials

Notwithstanding any other provision of law, no grant for which application is made after February 1, 1978, shall be made under this subchapter for any treatment works unless only such unmanufactured articles, materials, and supplies as have been mined or produced in the United States, and only such manufactured articles, materials, and supplies as have been manufactured in the United States, substantially all from articles, materials, or supplies mined, produced, or manufactured, as the case may be, in the United States will be used in such treatment works. This section shall not apply in any case where the Administrator determines, based upon those factors the Administrator deems relevant, including the available resources of the agency, it to be inconsistent with the public interest (including multilateral government procurement agreements) or the cost to be unreasonable, or if articles, materials, or supplies of the class or kind to be used or the articles, materials, or supplies from which they are manufactured are not mined, produced, or manufactured, as the case may be, in the United States in sufficient and reasonably available commercial quantities and of a satisfactory quality.

(June 30, 1948, ch. 758, title II, §215, as added Pub. L. 95–217, §39, Dec. 27, 1977, 91 Stat. 1581.)

§1296. Determination of priority of projects

Notwithstanding any other provision of this chapter, the determination of the priority to be given each category of projects for construction of publicly owned treatment works within each State shall be made solely by that State, except that if the Administrator, after a public hearing, determines that a specific project will not result in compliance with the enforceable requirements of this chapter, such project shall be removed from the State's priority list and such State shall submit a revised priority list. These categories shall include, but not be limited to (A) secondary treatment, (B) more stringent treatment, (C) infiltration-in-flow correction, (D) major sewer system rehabilitation, (E) new collector sewers and appurtenances, (F) new interceptors and appurtenances, and (G) correction of combined sewer overflows. Not less than 25 per centum of funds allocated to a State in any fiscal year under this subchapter for construction of publicly owned treatment works in such State shall be obligated for those types of projects referred to in clauses (D), (E), (F), and (G) of this section, if such projects are on such State's priority list for that year and are otherwise eligible for funding in that fiscal year. It is the policy of Congress that projects for wastewater treatment and management undertaken with Federal financial assistance under this chapter by any State, municipality, or intermunicipal or interstate agency shall be projects which, in the estimation of the State, are designed to achieve optimum water quality management, consistent with the public health and water quality goals and requirements of this chapter.

(June 30, 1948, ch. 758, title II, §216, as added Pub. L. 95–217, §40, Dec. 27, 1977, 91 Stat. 1582; amended Pub. L. 97–117, §18, Dec. 29, 1981, 95 Stat. 1630.)

AMENDMENTS

1981—Pub. L. 97–117 inserted provision that it is the policy of Congress that projects for wastewater treatment and management undertaken with Federal financial assistance under this chapter by any State, municipality, or intermunicipal or interstate agency be projects which, in the estimation of the State, are designed to achieve optimum water quality management, consistent with the public health and water quality goals and requirements of this chapter.

§1297. Guidelines for cost-effectiveness analysis

Any guidelines for cost-effectiveness analysis published by the Administrator under this subchapter shall provide for the identification and selection of cost effective alternatives to comply with the objectives and goals of this chapter and sections 1281(b), 1281(d), 1281(g)(2)(A), and 1311(b)(2)(B) of this title.

(June 30, 1948, ch. 758, title II, §217, as added Pub. L. 95–217, §41, Dec. 27, 1977, 91 Stat. 1582.)

§1298. Cost effectiveness

(a) Congressional statement of policy

It is the policy of Congress that a project for waste treatment and management undertaken with Federal financial assistance under this chapter by any State, municipality, or intermunicipal or interstate agency shall be considered as an overall waste treatment system for waste treatment and management, and shall be that system which constitutes the most economical and cost-effective combination of devices and systems used in the storage, treatment, recycling, and reclamation of municipal sewage or industrial wastes of a liquid nature to implement section 1281 of this title, or necessary to recycle or reuse water at the most economical cost over the estimated life of the works, including intercepting sewers, outfall sewers, sewage collection systems, pumping power, and other equipment, and their appurtenances; extension, improvements, remodeling, additions, and alterations thereof; elements essential to provide a reliable recycled supply such as standby treatment units and clear well facilities; and any works, including site acquisition of the land that will be an integral part of the treatment process (including land use for the storage of treated wastewater in land treatment systems prior to land application) or which is used for ultimate disposal of residues resulting from such treatment; water efficiency measures and devices; and any other method or system for preventing, abating, reducing, storing, treating, separating, or disposing of municipal waste, including storm water runoff, or industrial waste, including waste in combined storm water and sanitary sewer systems; to meet the requirements of this chapter.

(b) Determination by Administrator as prerequisite to approval of grant

In accordance with the policy set forth in subsection (a) of this section, before the Administrator approves any grant to any State, municipality, or intermunicipal or interstate agency for the erection, building, acquisition, alteration, remodeling, improvement, or extension of any treatment works the Administrator shall determine that the facilities plan of which such treatment works are a part constitutes the most economical and cost-effective combination of treatment works over the life of the project to meet the requirements of this chapter, including, but not limited to, consideration of construction costs, operation, maintenance, and replacement costs.

(c) Value engineering review

In furtherance of the policy set forth in subsection (a) of this section, the Administrator shall require value engineering review in connection with any treatment works, prior to approval of any grant for the erection, building, acquisition, alteration, remodeling, improvement, or extension of such treatment works, in any case in which the cost of such erection, building, acquisition, alteration, remodeling, improvement, or extension is projected to be in excess of $10,000,000. For purposes of this subsection, the term "value engineering review" means a specialized cost control technique which uses a systematic and creative approach to identify and to focus on unnecessarily high cost in a project in order to arrive at a cost saving without sacrificing the reliability or efficiency of the project.

(d) Projects affected

This section applies to projects for waste treatment and management for which no treatment works including a facilities plan for such project have received Federal financial assistance for the preparation of construction plans and specifications under this chapter before December 29, 1981.

(June 30, 1948, ch. 758, title II, §218, as added Pub. L. 97–117, §19, Dec. 29, 1981, 95 Stat. 1630.)

§1299. State certification of projects

Whenever the Governor of a State which has been delegated sufficient authority to administer the construction grant program under this subchapter in that State certifies to the Administrator that a grant application meets applicable requirements of Federal and State law for assistance under this subchapter, the Administrator shall approve or disapprove such application within 45 days of the date of receipt of such application. If the Administrator does not approve or disapprove such application within 45 days of receipt, the application shall be deemed approved. If the Administrator disapproves such application the Administrator shall state in writing the reasons for such disapproval. Any grant approved or deemed approved under this section shall be subject to amounts provided in appropriation Acts.

(June 30, 1948, ch. 758, title II, §219, as added Pub. L. 97–117, §20, Dec. 29, 1981, 95 Stat. 1631.)

§1300. Pilot program for alternative water source projects

(a) Policy

Nothing in this section shall be construed to affect the application of section 1251(g) of this title and all of the provisions of this section shall be carried out in accordance with the provisions of section 1251(g) of this title.

(b) In general

The Administrator may establish a pilot program to make grants to State, interstate, and intrastate water resource development agencies (including water management districts and water supply authorities), local government agencies, private utilities, and nonprofit entities for alternative water source projects to meet critical water supply needs.

(c) Eligible entity

The Administrator may make grants under this section to an entity only if the entity has authority under State law to develop or provide water for municipal, industrial, and agricultural uses in an area of the State that is experiencing critical water supply needs.

(d) Selection of projects

(1) Limitation

A project that has received funds under the reclamation and reuse program conducted under the Reclamation Projects Authorization and Adjustment Act of 1992 (43 U.S.C. 390h et seq.) shall not be eligible for grant assistance under this section.

(2) Additional consideration

In making grants under this section, the Administrator shall consider whether the project is located within the boundaries of a State or area referred to in section 391 of title 43, and within the geographic scope of the reclamation and reuse program conducted under the Reclamation Projects Authorization and Adjustment Act of 1992 (43 U.S.C. 390h et seq.).

(3) Geographical distribution

Alternative water source projects selected by the Administrator under this section shall reflect a variety of geographical and environmental conditions.

(e) Committee resolution procedure

(1) In general

No appropriation shall be made for any alternative water source project under this section, the total Federal cost of which exceeds $3,000,000, if such project has not been approved by a resolution adopted by the Committee on Transportation and Infrastructure of the House of Representatives or the Committee on Environment and Public Works of the Senate.

(2) Requirements for securing consideration

For purposes of securing consideration of approval under paragraph (1), the Administrator shall provide to a committee referred to in paragraph (1) such information as the committee requests and the non-Federal sponsor shall provide to the committee information on the costs and relative needs for the alternative water source project.

(f) Uses of grants

Amounts from grants received under this section may be used for engineering, design, construction, and final testing of alternative water source projects designed to meet critical water supply needs. Such amounts may not be used for planning, feasibility studies or for operation, maintenance, replacement, repair, or rehabilitation.

(g) Cost sharing

The Federal share of the eligible costs of an alternative water source project carried out using assistance made available under this section shall not exceed 50 percent.

(h) Reports

On or before September 30, 2004, the Administrator shall transmit to Congress a report on the results of the pilot program established under this section, including progress made toward meeting the critical water supply needs of the participants in the pilot program.

(i) Definitions

In this section, the following definitions apply:

(1) Alternative water source project

The term "alternative water source project" means a project designed to provide municipal, industrial, and agricultural water supplies in an environmentally sustainable manner by conserving, managing, reclaiming, or reusing water or wastewater or by treating wastewater. Such term does not include water treatment or distribution facilities.

(2) Critical water supply needs

The term "critical water supply needs" means existing or reasonably anticipated future water supply needs that cannot be met by existing water supplies, as identified in a comprehensive statewide or regional water supply plan or assessment projected over a planning period of at least 20 years.

(j) Authorization of appropriations

There is authorized to be appropriated to carry out this section a total of $75,000,000 for fiscal years 2002 through 2004. Such sums shall remain available until expended.

(June 30, 1948, ch. 758, title II, §220, as added Pub. L. 106–457, title VI, §602, Nov. 7, 2000, 114 Stat. 1975.)

References in Text

The Reclamation Projects Authorization and Adjustment Act of 1992, referred to in subsec. (d)(1), (2), is Pub. L. 102–575, Oct. 30, 1992, 106 Stat. 4600, as amended. Provisions relating to the reclamation and reuse program are classified generally to section 390h et seq. of Title 43, Public Lands. For complete classification of this Act to the Code, see Short Title of 1992 Amendment note set out under section 371 of Title 43 and Tables.

§1301. Sewer overflow control grants

(a) In general

In any fiscal year in which the Administrator has available for obligation at least $1,350,000,000 for the purposes of section 1381 of this title—

(1) the Administrator may make grants to States for the purpose of providing grants to a municipality or municipal entity for planning, design, and construction of treatment works to intercept, transport, control, or treat municipal combined sewer overflows and sanitary sewer overflows; and

(2) subject to subsection (g) of this section, the Administrator may make a direct grant to a municipality or municipal entity for the purposes described in paragraph (1).

(b) Prioritization

In selecting from among municipalities applying for grants under subsection (a) of this section, a State or the Administrator shall give priority to an applicant that—

(1) is a municipality that is a financially distressed community under subsection (c) of this section;

(2) has implemented or is complying with an implementation schedule for the nine minimum controls specified in the CSO control policy referred to in section 1342(q)(1) of this title and has begun implementing a long-term municipal combined sewer overflow control plan or a separate sanitary sewer overflow control plan;

(3) is requesting a grant for a project that is on a State's intended use plan pursuant to section 1386(c) of this title; or

(4) is an Alaska Native Village.

(c) Financially distressed community

(1) Definition

In subsection (b) of this section, the term "financially distressed community" means a community that meets affordability criteria established by the State in which the community is located, if such criteria are developed after public review and comment.

(2) Consideration of impact on water and sewer rates

In determining if a community is a distressed community for the purposes of subsection (b) of this section, the State shall consider, among other factors, the extent to which the rate of growth of a community's tax base has been historically slow such that implementing a plan described in subsection (b)(2) of this section would result in a significant increase in any water or sewer rate charged by the community's publicly owned wastewater treatment facility.

(3) Information to assist States

The Administrator may publish information to assist States in establishing affordability criteria under paragraph (1).

(d) Cost-sharing

The Federal share of the cost of activities carried out using amounts from a grant made under subsection (a) of this section shall be not less than 55 percent of the cost. The non-Federal share of the cost may include, in any amount, public and private funds and in-kind services, and may include, notwithstanding section 1383(h) of this title, financial assistance, including loans, from a State water pollution control revolving fund.

(e) Administrative reporting requirements

If a project receives grant assistance under subsection (a) of this section and loan assistance from a State water pollution control revolving fund and the loan assistance is for 15 percent or more of the cost of the project, the project may be administered in accordance with State water pollution control revolving fund administrative reporting requirements for the purposes of streamlining such requirements.

(f) Authorization of appropriations

There is authorized to be appropriated to carry out this section $750,000,000 for each of fiscal years 2002 and 2003. Such sums shall remain available until expended.

(g) Allocation of funds

(1) Fiscal year 2002

Subject to subsection (h) of this section, the Administrator shall use the amounts appropriated to carry out this section for fiscal year 2002 for making grants to municipalities and municipal entities under subsection (a)(2) of this section, in accordance with the criteria set forth in subsection (b) of this section.

(2) Fiscal year 2003

Subject to subsection (h) of this section, the Administrator shall use the amounts appropriated to carry out this section for fiscal year 2003 as follows:

(A) Not to exceed $250,000,000 for making grants to municipalities and municipal entities under subsection (a)(2) of this section, in accordance with the criteria set forth in subsection (b) of this section.

(B) All remaining amounts for making grants to States under subsection (a)(1) of this section, in accordance with a formula to be established by the Administrator, after providing notice and an opportunity for public comment, that allocates to each State a proportional share of such amounts based on the total needs of the State for municipal combined sewer overflow controls and sanitary sewer overflow controls identified in the most recent survey conducted pursuant to section 1375(b)(1) of this title.

(h) Administrative expenses

Of the amounts appropriated to carry out this section for each fiscal year—

(1) the Administrator may retain an amount not to exceed 1 percent for the reasonable and necessary costs of administering this section; and

(2) the Administrator, or a State, may retain an amount not to exceed 4 percent of any grant made to a municipality or municipal entity under subsection (a) of this section, for the reasonable and necessary costs of administering the grant.

(i) Reports

Not later than December 31, 2003, and periodically thereafter, the Administrator shall transmit to Congress a report containing recommended funding levels for grants under this section. The recommended funding levels shall be sufficient to ensure the continued expeditious implementation of municipal combined sewer overflow and sanitary sewer overflow controls nationwide.

(June 30, 1948, ch. 758, title II, §221, as added Pub. L. 106–554, §1(a)(4) [div. B, title I, §112(c)], Dec. 21, 2000, 114 Stat. 2763, 2763A–225.)

INFORMATION ON CSOS AND SSOS

Pub. L. 106–554, §1(a)(4) [div. B, title I, §112(d)], Dec. 21, 2000, 114 Stat. 2763, 2763A–227, provided that:

"(1) REPORT TO CONGRESS.—Not later than 3 years after the date of enactment of this Act [Dec. 21, 2000], the Administrator of the Environmental Protection Agency shall transmit to Congress a report summarizing—

"(A) the extent of the human health and environmental impacts caused by municipal combined sewer overflows and sanitary sewer overflows, including the location of discharges causing such impacts, the volume of pollutants discharged, and the constituents discharged;

"(B) the resources spent by municipalities to address these impacts; and

"(C) an evaluation of the technologies used by municipalities to address these impacts.

"(2) TECHNOLOGY CLEARINGHOUSE.—After transmitting a report under paragraph (1), the Administrator shall maintain a clearinghouse of cost-effective and efficient technologies for addressing human health and environmental impacts due to municipal combined sewer overflows and sanitary sewer overflows."

SUBCHAPTER III—STANDARDS AND ENFORCEMENT

§1311. Effluent limitations

(a) Illegality of pollutant discharges except in compliance with law

Except as in compliance with this section and sections 1312, 1316, 1317, 1328, 1342, and 1344 of this title, the discharge of any pollutant by any person shall be unlawful.

(b) Timetable for achievement of objectives

In order to carry out the objective of this chapter there shall be achieved—

(1)(A) not later than July 1, 1977, effluent limitations for point sources, other than publicly owned treatment works, (i) which shall require the application of the best practicable control technology currently available as defined by the Administrator pursuant to section 1314(b) of this title, or (ii) in the case of a discharge into a publicly owned treatment works which meets the requirements of subparagraph (B) of this paragraph, which shall require compliance with any applicable pretreatment requirements and any requirements under section 1317 of this title; and

(B) for publicly owned treatment works in existence on July 1, 1977, or approved pursuant to section 1283 of this title prior to June 30, 1974 (for which construction must be completed within four years of approval), effluent limitations based upon secondary treatment as defined by the Administrator pursuant to section 1314(d)(1) of this title; or,

(C) not later than July 1, 1977, any more stringent limitation, including those necessary to meet water quality standards, treatment standards, or schedules of compliance, established pursuant to any State law or regulations (under authority preserved by section 1370 of this title) or any other Federal law or regulation, or required to implement any applicable water quality standard established pursuant to this chapter.

(2)(A) for pollutants identified in subparagraphs (C), (D), and (F) of this paragraph, effluent limitations for categories and classes of point sources, other than publicly owned treatment works, which (i) shall require application of the best available technology economically achievable for such category or class, which will result in reasonable further progress toward the national goal of eliminating the discharge of all pollutants, as determined in accordance with regulations issued by the Administrator pursuant to section 1314(b)(2) of this title, which such effluent limitations shall require the elimination of discharges of all pollutants if the Administrator finds, on the basis of information available to him (including information developed pursuant to section 1325 of this title), that such elimination is technologically and economically achievable for a category or class of point sources as determined in accordance with regulations issued by the Administrator pursuant to section 1314(b)(2) of this title, or (ii) in the case of the introduction of a pollutant into a publicly owned treatment works which meets the requirements of subparagraph

(B) of this paragraph, shall require compliance with any applicable pretreatment requirements and any other requirement under section 1317 of this title;

(B) Repealed. Pub. L. 97–117, §21(b), Dec. 29, 1981, 95 Stat. 1632.

(C) with respect to all toxic pollutants referred to in table 1 of Committee Print Numbered 95–30 of the Committee on Public Works and Transportation of the House of Representatives compliance with effluent limitations in accordance with subparagraph (A) of this paragraph as expeditiously as practicable but in no case later than three years after the date such limitations are promulgated under section 1314(b) of this title, and in no case later than March 31, 1989;

(D) for all toxic pollutants listed under paragraph (1) of subsection (a) of section 1317 of this title which are not referred to in subparagraph (C) of this paragraph compliance with effluent limitations in accordance with subparagraph (A) of this paragraph as expeditiously as practicable, but in no case later than three years after the date such limitations are promulgated under section 1314(b) of this title, and in no case later than March 31, 1989;

(E) as expeditiously as practicable but in no case later than three years after the date such limitations are promulgated under section 1314(b) of this title, and in no case later than March 31, 1989, compliance with effluent limitations for categories and classes of point sources, other than publicly owned treatment works, which in the case of pollutants identified pursuant to section 1314(a)(4) of this title shall require application of the best conventional pollutant control technology as determined in accordance with regulations issued by the Administrator pursuant to section 1314(b)(4) of this title; and

(F) for all pollutants (other than those subject to subparagraphs (C), (D), or (E) of this paragraph) compliance with effluent limitations in accordance with subparagraph (A) of this paragraph as expeditiously as practicable but in no case later than 3 years after the date such limitations are established, and in no case later than March 31, 1989.

(3)(A) for effluent limitations under paragraph (1)(A)(i) of this subsection promulgated after January 1, 1982, and requiring a level of control substantially greater or based on fundamentally different control technology than under permits for an industrial category issued before such date, compliance as expeditiously as practicable but in no case later than three years after the date such limitations are promulgated under section 1314(b) of this title, and in no case later than March 31, 1989; and

(B) for any effluent limitation in accordance with paragraph (1)(A)(i), (2)(A)(i), or (2)(E) of this subsection established only on the basis of section 1342(a)(1) of this title in a permit issued after February 4, 1987, compliance as expeditiously as practicable but in no case later than three years after the date such limitations are established, and in no case later than March 31, 1989.

(c) Modification of timetable

The Administrator may modify the requirements of subsection (b)(2)(A) of this section with respect to any point source for which a permit application is filed after July 1, 1977, upon a showing by the owner or operator of such point source satisfactory to the Administrator that such modified requirements (1) will represent the maximum use of technology within the economic capability of the owner or operator; and (2) will result in reasonable further progress toward the elimination of the discharge of pollutants.

(d) Review and revision of effluent limitations

Any effluent limitation required by paragraph (2) of subsection (b) of this section shall be reviewed at least every five years and, if appropriate, revised pursuant to the procedure established under such paragraph.

(e) All point discharge source application of effluent limitations

Effluent limitations established pursuant to this section or section 1312 of this title shall be applied to all point sources of discharge of pollutants in accordance with the provisions of this chapter.

(f) Illegality of discharge of radiological, chemical, or biological warfare agents, high-level radioactive waste, or medical waste

Notwithstanding any other provisions of this chapter it shall be unlawful to discharge any radiological, chemical, or biological warfare agent, any high-level radioactive waste, or any medical waste, into the navigable waters.

(g) Modifications for certain nonconventional pollutants

(1) General authority

The Administrator, with the concurrence of the State, may modify the requirements of subsection (b)(2)(A) of this section with respect to the discharge from any point source of ammonia, chlorine, color, iron, and total phenols (4AAP) (when determined by the Administrator to be a pollutant covered by subsection (b)(2)(F) of this section) and any other pollutant which the Administrator lists under paragraph (4) of this subsection.

(2) Requirements for granting modifications

A modification under this subsection shall be granted only upon a showing by the owner or operator of a point source satisfactory to the Administrator that—

(A) such modified requirements will result at a minimum in compliance with the requirements of subsection (b)(1)(A) or (C) of this section, whichever is applicable;

(B) such modified requirements will not result in any additional requirements on any other point or nonpoint source; and

(C) such modification will not interfere with the attainment or maintenance of that water quality which shall assure protection of public water supplies, and the protection and propagation of a balanced population of shellfish, fish, and wildlife, and allow recreational activities, in and on the water and such modification will not result in the discharge of pollutants in quantities which may reasonably be anticipated to pose an unacceptable risk to human health or the environment because of bioaccumulation, persistency in the environment, acute toxicity, chronic toxicity (including carcinogenicity, mutagenicity or teratogenicity), or synergistic propensities.

(3) Limitation on authority to apply for subsection (c) modification

If an owner or operator of a point source applies for a modification under this subsection with respect to the discharge of any pollutant, such owner or operator shall be eligible to apply for modification under subsection (c) of this section with respect to such pollutant only during the same time period as he is eligible to apply for a modification under this subsection.

(4) Procedures for listing additional pollutants

(A) General authority

Upon petition of any person, the Administrator may add any pollutant to the list of pollutants for which modification under this section is authorized (except for pollutants identified pursuant to section 1314(a)(4) of this title, toxic pollutants subject to section 1317(a) of this title, and the thermal component of discharges) in accordance with the provisions of this paragraph.

(B) Requirements for listing

(i) Sufficient information

The person petitioning for listing of an additional pollutant under this subsection shall submit to the Administrator sufficient information to make the determinations required by this subparagraph.

(ii) Toxic criteria determination

The Administrator shall determine whether or not the pollutant meets the criteria for listing as a toxic pollutant under section 1317(a) of this title.

(iii) Listing as toxic pollutant

If the Administrator determines that the pollutant meets the criteria for listing as a toxic pollutant under section 1317(a) of this title, the Administrator shall list the pollutant as a toxic pollutant under section 1317(a) of this title.

(iv) Nonconventional criteria determination

If the Administrator determines that the pollutant does not meet the criteria for listing as a toxic pollutant under such section and determines that adequate test methods and sufficient data are available to make the determinations required by paragraph (2) of this subsection with respect to the pollutant, the Administrator shall add the pollutant to the list of pollutants specified in paragraph (1) of this subsection for which modifications are authorized under this subsection.

(C) Requirements for filing of petitions

A petition for listing of a pollutant under this paragraph—

(i) must be filed not later than 270 days after the date of promulgation of an applicable effluent guideline under section 1314 of this title;

(ii) may be filed before promulgation of such guideline; and

(iii) may be filed with an application for a modification under paragraph (1) with respect to the discharge of such pollutant.

(D) Deadline for approval of petition

A decision to add a pollutant to the list of pollutants for which modifications under this subsection are authorized must be made within 270 days after the date of promulgation of an applicable effluent guideline under section 1314 of this title.

(E) Burden of proof

The burden of proof for making the determinations under subparagraph (B) shall be on the petitioner.

(5) Removal of pollutants

The Administrator may remove any pollutant from the list of pollutants for which modifications are authorized under this subsection if the Administrator determines that adequate test methods and sufficient data are no longer available for determining whether or not modifications may be granted with respect to such pollutant under paragraph (2) of this subsection.

(h) Modification of secondary treatment requirements

The Administrator, with the concurrence of the State, may issue a permit under section 1342 of this title which modifies the requirements of subsection (b)(1)(B) of this section with respect to the discharge of any pollutant from a publicly owned treatment works into marine waters, if the applicant demonstrates to the satisfaction of the Administrator that—

(1) there is an applicable water quality standard specific to the pollutant for which the modification is requested, which has been identified under section 1314(a)(6) of this title;

(2) the discharge of pollutants in accordance with such modified requirements will not interfere, alone or in combination with pollutants from other sources, with the attainment or maintenance of that water quality which assures protection of public water supplies and the protection and propagation of a balanced, indigenous population of shellfish, fish, and wildlife, and allows recreational activities, in and on the water;

(3) the applicant has established a system for monitoring the impact of such discharge on a representative sample of aquatic biota, to the extent practicable, and the scope of such monitoring is limited to include only those scientific investigations which are necessary to study the effects of the proposed discharge;

(4) such modified requirements will not result in any additional requirements on any other point or nonpoint source;

(5) all applicable pretreatment requirements for sources introducing waste into such treatment works will be enforced;

(6) in the case of any treatment works serving a population of 50,000 or more, with respect

to any toxic pollutant introduced into such works by an industrial discharger for which pollutant there is no applicable pretreatment requirement in effect, sources introducing waste into such works are in compliance with all applicable pretreatment requirements, the applicant will enforce such requirements, and the applicant has in effect a pretreatment program which, in combination with the treatment of discharges from such works, removes the same amount of such pollutant as would be removed if such works were to apply secondary treatment to discharges and if such works had no pretreatment program with respect to such pollutant;

(7) to the extent practicable, the applicant has established a schedule of activities designed to eliminate the entrance of toxic pollutants from nonindustrial sources into such treatment works;

(8) there will be no new or substantially increased discharges from the point source of the pollutant to which the modification applies above that volume of discharge specified in the permit;

(9) the applicant at the time such modification becomes effective will be discharging effluent which has received at least primary or equivalent treatment and which meets the criteria established under section 1314(a)(1) of this title after initial mixing in the waters surrounding or adjacent to the point at which such effluent is discharged.

For the purposes of this subsection the phrase "the discharge of any pollutant into marine waters" refers to a discharge into deep waters of the territorial sea or the waters of the contiguous zone, or into saline estuarine waters where there is strong tidal movement and other hydrological and geological characteristics which the Administrator determines necessary to allow compliance with paragraph (2) of this subsection, and section 1251(a)(2) of this title. For the purposes of paragraph (9), "primary or equivalent treatment" means treatment by screening, sedimentation, and skimming adequate to remove at least 30 percent of the biological oxygen demanding material and of the suspended solids in the treatment works influent, and disinfection, where appropriate. A municipality which applies secondary treatment shall be eligible to receive a permit pursuant to this subsection which modifies the requirements of subsection (b)(1)(B) of this section with respect to the discharge of any pollutant from any treatment works owned by such municipality into marine waters. No permit issued under this subsection shall authorize the discharge of sewage sludge into marine waters. In order for a permit to be issued under this subsection for the discharge of a pollutant into marine waters, such marine waters must exhibit characteristics assuring that water providing dilution does not contain significant amounts of previously discharged effluent from such treatment works. No permit issued under this subsection shall authorize the discharge of any pollutant into saline estuarine waters which at the time of application do not support a balanced indigenous population of shellfish, fish and wildlife, or allow recreation in and on the waters or which exhibit ambient water quality below applicable water quality standards adopted for the protection of public water supplies, shellfish, fish and wildlife or recreational activities or such other standards necessary to assure support and protection of such uses. The prohibition contained in the preceding sentence shall apply without regard to the presence or absence of a causal relationship between such characteristics and the applicant's current or proposed discharge. Notwithstanding any other provisions of this subsection, no permit may be issued under this subsection for discharge of a pollutant into the New York Bight Apex consisting of the ocean waters of the Atlantic Ocean westward of 73 degrees 30 minutes west longitude and northward of 40 degrees 10 minutes north latitude.

(i) Municipal time extensions

(1) Where construction is required in order for a planned or existing publicly owned treatment works to achieve limitations under subsection (b)(1)(B) or (b)(1)(C) of this section, but (A) construction cannot be completed within the time required in such subsection, or (B) the United States has failed to make financial assistance under this chapter available in time to achieve such limitations by the time specified in such subsection, the owner or operator of such treatment works may request the Administrator (or if appropriate the State) to issue a permit pursuant to section 1342 of this title or to modify a permit issued pursuant to that section to extend such time for compliance. Any such request shall be filed with the Administrator (or if appropriate the State) within 180 days after February 4, 1987. The Administrator (or if appropriate the State) may grant such request and issue or modify such a permit, which shall contain a schedule of compliance for the publicly owned treatment works based on the earliest date by which such financial assistance will be available from the United States and construction can be completed, but in no event later than July 1, 1988, and shall contain such other terms and conditions, including those necessary to carry out subsections (b) through (g) of section 1281 of this title, section 1317 of this title, and such interim effluent limitations applicable to that treatment works as the Administrator determines are necessary to carry out the provisions of this chapter.

(2)(A) Where a point source (other than a publicly owned treatment works) will not achieve the requirements of subsections (b)(1)(A) and (b)(1)(C) of this section and—

(i) if a permit issued prior to July 1, 1977, to such point source is based upon a discharge into a publicly owned treatment works; or

(ii) if such point source (other than a publicly owned treatment works) had before July 1, 1977, a contract (enforceable against such point source) to discharge into a publicly owned treatment works; or

(iii) if either an application made before July 1, 1977, for a construction grant under this chapter for a publicly owned treatment works, or engineering or architectural plans or working drawings made before July 1, 1977, for a publicly owned treatment works, show that such point source was to discharge into such publicly owned treatment works, and such publicly owned treatment works is presently unable to accept such discharge without construction, and in the case of a discharge to an existing publicly owned treatment works, such treatment works has an extension pursuant to paragraph (1) of this subsection, the owner or operator of such point source may request the Administrator (or if appropriate the State) to issue or modify such a permit pursuant to such section 1342 of this title to extend such time for compliance. Any such request shall be filed with the Administrator (or if appropriate the State) within 180 days after December 27, 1977, or the filing of a request by the appropriate publicly owned treatment works under paragraph (1) of this subsection, whichever is later. If the Administrator (or if appropriate the State) finds that the owner or operator of such point source has acted in good faith, he may grant such request and issue or modify such a permit, which shall contain a schedule of compliance for the point source to achieve the requirements of subsections (b)(1)(A) and (C) of this section and shall contain such other terms and conditions, including pretreatment and interim effluent limitations and water conservation requirements applicable to that point source, as the Administrator determines are necessary to carry out the provisions of this chapter.

(B) No time modification granted by the Administrator (or if appropriate the State) pursuant to paragraph (2)(A) of this subsection shall extend beyond the earliest date practicable for compliance or beyond the date of any extension granted to the appropriate publicly owned treatment works pursuant to paragraph (1) of this subsection, but in no event shall it extend beyond July 1, 1988; and no such time modification shall be granted unless (i) the publicly owned treatment works will be in operation and available to the point source before July 1, 1988, and will meet the requirements of subsections (b)(1)(B) and (C) of this section after receiving the discharge from that point source; and (ii) the point source and the publicly owned treatment works have entered into an enforceable contract requiring the point source to discharge into the publicly owned treatment works, the owner or operator of such point source to pay the costs required under section 1284 of this title, and the publicly owned treatment works to accept the discharge from the point source; and (iii) the permit for such point source requires that point source to meet all requirements under section 1317(a) and (b) of this title during the period of such time modification.

(j) Modification procedures

(1) Any application filed under this section for a modification of the provisions of—

(A) subsection (b)(1)(B) of this section under subsection (h) of this section shall be filed not later that[1] the 365th day which begins after December 29, 1981, except that a publicly owned treatment works which prior to December 31, 1982, had a contractual arrangement to use a portion of the capacity of an ocean outfall operated by another publicly owned treatment works which has applied for or received modification under subsection (h) of this section, may apply for a modification of subsection (h) of this section in its own right not later than 30 days after February 4, 1987, and except as provided in paragraph (5);

(B) subsection (b)(2)(A) of this section as it applies to pollutants identified in subsection (b)(2)(F) of this section shall be filed not later than 270 days after the date of promulgation of an applicable effluent guideline under section 1314 of this title or not later than 270 days after December 27, 1977, whichever is later.

(2) Subject to paragraph (3) of this section, any application for a modification filed under subsection (g) of this section shall not operate to stay any requirement under this chapter, unless in the judgment of the Administrator such a stay or the modification sought will not result in the discharge of pollutants in quantities which may reasonably be anticipated to pose an unacceptable risk to human health or the environment because of bioaccumulation, persistency in the environment, acute toxicity, chronic toxicity (including carcinogenicity, mutagenicity, or teratogenicity), or synergistic propensities, and that there is a substantial likelihood that the applicant will succeed on the merits of such application. In the case of an application filed under subsection (g) of this section, the Administrator may condition any stay granted under this paragraph on requiring the filing of a bond or other appropriate security to assure timely compliance with the requirements from which a modification is sought.

(3) COMPLIANCE REQUIREMENTS UNDER SUBSECTION (g).—

(A) EFFECT OF FILING.—An application for a modification under subsection (g) of this section and a petition for listing of a pollutant as a pollutant for which modifications are authorized under such subsection shall not stay the requirement that the person seeking such modification or listing comply with effluent limitations under this chapter for all pollutants not the subject of such application or petition.

(B) EFFECT OF DISAPPROVAL.—Disapproval of an application for a modification under subsection (g) of this section shall not stay the requirement that the person seeking such modification comply with all applicable effluent limitations under this chapter.

(4) DEADLINE FOR SUBSECTION (g) DECISION.—An application for a modification with respect to a pollutant filed under subsection (g) of this section must be approved or disapproved not later than 365 days after the date of such filing; except that in any case in which a petition for listing such pollutant as a pollutant for which modifications are authorized under such subsection is approved, such application must be approved or disapproved not later than 365 days after the date of approval of such petition.

(5) EXTENSION OF APPLICATION DEADLINE.—

(A) IN GENERAL.—In the 180-day period beginning on October 31, 1994, the city of San Diego, California, may apply for a modification pursuant to subsection (h) of this section of the requirements of subsection (b)(1)(B) of this section with respect to biological oxygen de-

[1] So in original. Probably should be "than".

mand and total suspended solids in the effluent discharged into marine waters.

(B) APPLICATION.—An application under this paragraph shall include a commitment by the applicant to implement a waste water reclamation program that, at a minimum, will—

(i) achieve a system capacity of 45,000,000 gallons of reclaimed waste water per day by January 1, 2010; and

(ii) result in a reduction in the quantity of suspended solids discharged by the applicant into the marine environment during the period of the modification.

(C) ADDITIONAL CONDITIONS.—The Administrator may not grant a modification pursuant to an application submitted under this paragraph unless the Administrator determines that such modification will result in removal of not less than 58 percent of the biological oxygen demand (on an annual average) and not less than 80 percent of total suspended solids (on a monthly average) in the discharge to which the application applies.

(D) PRELIMINARY DECISION DEADLINE.—The Administrator shall announce a preliminary decision on an application submitted under this paragraph not later than 1 year after the date the application is submitted.

(k) Innovative technology

In the case of any facility subject to a permit under section 1342 of this title which proposes to comply with the requirements of subsection (b)(2)(A) or (b)(2)(E) of this section by replacing existing production capacity with an innovative production process which will result in an effluent reduction significantly greater than that required by the limitation otherwise applicable to such facility and moves toward the national goal of eliminating the discharge of all pollutants, or with the installation of an innovative control technique that has a substantial likelihood for enabling the facility to comply with the applicable effluent limitation by achieving a significantly greater effluent reduction than that required by the applicable effluent limitation and moves toward the national goal of eliminating the discharge of all pollutants, or by achieving the required reduction with an innovative system that has the potential for significantly lower costs than the systems which have been determined by the Administrator to be economically achievable, the Administrator (or the State with an approved program under section 1342 of this title, in consultation with the Administrator) may establish a date for compliance under subsection (b)(2)(A) or (b)(2)(E) of this section no later than two years after the date for compliance with such effluent limitation which would otherwise be applicable under such subsection, if it is also determined that such innovative system has the potential for industrywide application.

(*l*) Toxic pollutants

Other than as provided in subsection (n) of this section, the Administrator may not modify any requirement of this section as it applies to any specific pollutant which is on the toxic pollutant list under section 1317(a)(1) of this title.

(m) Modification of effluent limitation requirements for point sources

(1) The Administrator, with the concurrence of the State, may issue a permit under section 1342 of this title which modifies the requirements of subsections (b)(1)(A) and (b)(2)(E) of this section, and of section 1343 of this title, with respect to effluent limitations to the extent such limitations relate to biochemical oxygen demand and pH from discharges by an industrial discharger in such State into deep waters of the territorial seas, if the applicant demonstrates and the Administrator finds that—

(A) the facility for which modification is sought is covered at the time of the enactment of this subsection by National Pollutant Discharge Elimination System permit number CA0005894 or CA0005282;

(B) the energy and environmental costs of meeting such requirements of subsections (b)(1)(A) and (b)(2)(E) of this section and section 1343 of this title exceed by an unreasonable amount the benefits to be obtained, including the objectives of this chapter;

(C) the applicant has established a system for monitoring the impact of such discharges on a representative sample of aquatic biota;

(D) such modified requirements will not result in any additional requirements on any other point or nonpoint source;

(E) there will be no new or substantially increased discharges from the point source of the pollutant to which the modification applies above that volume of discharge specified in the permit;

(F) the discharge is into waters where there is strong tidal movement and other hydrological and geological characteristics which are necessary to allow compliance with this subsection and section 1251(a)(2) of this title;

(G) the applicant accepts as a condition to the permit a contractural[2] obligation to use funds in the amount required (but not less than $250,000 per year for ten years) for research and development of water pollution control technology, including but not limited to closed cycle technology;

(H) the facts and circumstances present a unique situation which, if relief is granted, will not establish a precedent or the relaxation of the requirements of this chapter applicable to similarly situated discharges; and

(I) no owner or operator of a facility comparable to that of the applicant situated in the United States has demonstrated that it would be put at a competitive disadvantage to the applicant (or the parent company or any subsidiary thereof) as a result of the issuance of a permit under this subsection.

(2) The effluent limitations established under a permit issued under paragraph (1) shall be sufficient to implement the applicable State water quality standards, to assure the protection of public water supplies and protection and propagation of a balanced, indigenous population of shellfish, fish, fauna, wildlife, and other aquatic organisms, and to allow recreational activities in and on the water. In setting such limitations,

[2] So in original. Probably should be "contractual".

the Administrator shall take into account any seasonal variations and the need for an adequate margin of safety, considering the lack of essential knowledge concerning the relationship between effluent limitations and water quality and the lack of essential knowledge of the effects of discharges on beneficial uses of the receiving waters.

(3) A permit under this subsection may be issued for a period not to exceed five years, and such a permit may be renewed for one additional period not to exceed five years upon a demonstration by the applicant and a finding by the Administrator at the time of application for any such renewal that the provisions of this subsection are met.

(4) The Administrator may terminate a permit issued under this subsection if the Administrator determines that there has been a decline in ambient water quality of the receiving waters during the period of the permit even if a direct cause and effect relationship cannot be shown: *Provided*, That if the effluent from a source with a permit issued under this subsection is contributing to a decline in ambient water quality of the receiving waters, the Administrator shall terminate such permit.

(n) Fundamentally different factors

(1) General rule

The Administrator, with the concurrence of the State, may establish an alternative requirement under subsection (b)(2) of this section or section 1317(b) of this title for a facility that modifies the requirements of national effluent limitation guidelines or categorical pretreatment standards that would otherwise be applicable to such facility, if the owner or operator of such facility demonstrates to the satisfaction of the Administrator that—

(A) the facility is fundamentally different with respect to the factors (other than cost) specified in section 1314(b) or 1314(g) of this title and considered by the Administrator in establishing such national effluent limitation guidelines or categorical pretreatment standards;

(B) the application—

(i) is based solely on information and supporting data submitted to the Administrator during the rulemaking for establishment of the applicable national effluent limitation guidelines or categorical pretreatment standard specifically raising the factors that are fundamentally different for such facility; or

(ii) is based on information and supporting data referred to in clause (i) and information and supporting data the applicant did not have a reasonable opportunity to submit during such rulemaking;

(C) the alternative requirement is no less stringent than justified by the fundamental difference; and

(D) the alternative requirement will not result in a non-water quality environmental impact which is markedly more adverse than the impact considered by the Administrator in establishing such national effluent limitation guideline or categorical pretreatment standard.

(2) Time limit for applications

An application for an alternative requirement which modifies the requirements of an effluent limitation or pretreatment standard under this subsection must be submitted to the Administrator within 180 days after the date on which such limitation or standard is established or revised, as the case may be.

(3) Time limit for decision

The Administrator shall approve or deny by final agency action an application submitted under this subsection within 180 days after the date such application is filed with the Administrator.

(4) Submission of information

The Administrator may allow an applicant under this subsection to submit information and supporting data until the earlier of the date the application is approved or denied or the last day that the Administrator has to approve or deny such application.

(5) Treatment of pending applications

For the purposes of this subsection, an application for an alternative requirement based on fundamentally different factors which is pending on February 4, 1987, shall be treated as having been submitted to the Administrator on the 180th day following February 4, 1987. The applicant may amend the application to take into account the provisions of this subsection.

(6) Effect of submission of application

An application for an alternative requirement under this subsection shall not stay the applicant's obligation to comply with the effluent limitation guideline or categorical pretreatment standard which is the subject of the application.

(7) Effect of denial

If an application for an alternative requirement which modifies the requirements of an effluent limitation or pretreatment standard under this subsection is denied by the Administrator, the applicant must comply with such limitation or standard as established or revised, as the case may be.

(8) Reports

By January 1, 1997, and January 1 of every odd-numbered year thereafter, the Administrator shall submit to the Committee on Environment and Public Works of the Senate and the Committee on Transportation and Infrastructure of the House of Representatives a report on the status of applications for alternative requirements which modify the requirements of effluent limitations under section 1311 or 1314 of this title or any national categorical pretreatment standard under section 1317(b) of this title filed before, on, or after February 4, 1987.

(*o*) Application fees

The Administrator shall prescribe and collect from each applicant fees reflecting the reasonable administrative costs incurred in reviewing and processing applications for modifications submitted to the Administrator pursuant to subsections (c), (g), (i), (k), (m), and (n) of this section, section 1314(d)(4) of this title, and section 1326(a) of this title. All amounts collected by the Administrator under this subsection shall be deposited into a special fund of the Treasury entitled "Water Permits and Related Services" which shall thereafter be available for appropriation to carry out activities of the Environmental Protection Agency for which such fees were collected.

(p) Modified permit for coal remining operations

(1) In general

Subject to paragraphs (2) through (4) of this subsection, the Administrator, or the State in any case which the State has an approved permit program under section 1342(b) of this title, may issue a permit under section 1342 of this title which modifies the requirements of subsection (b)(2)(A) of this section with respect to the pH level of any pre-existing discharge, and with respect to pre-existing discharges of iron and manganese from the remined area of any coal remining operation or with respect to the pH level or level of iron or manganese in any pre-existing discharge affected by the remining operation. Such modified requirements shall apply the best available technology economically achievable on a case-by-case basis, using best professional judgment, to set specific numerical effluent limitations in each permit.

(2) Limitations

The Administrator or the State may only issue a permit pursuant to paragraph (1) if the applicant demonstrates to the satisfaction of the Administrator or the State, as the case may be, that the coal remining operation will result in the potential for improved water quality from the remining operation but in no event shall such a permit allow the pH level of any discharge, and in no event shall such a permit allow the discharges of iron and manganese, to exceed the levels being discharged from the remined area before the coal remining operation begins. No discharge from, or affected by, the remining operation shall exceed State water quality standards established under section 1313 of this title.

(3) Definitions

For purposes of this subsection—

(A) Coal remining operation

The term "coal remining operation" means a coal mining operation which begins after February 4, 1987 at a site on which coal mining was conducted before August 3, 1977.

(B) Remined area

The term "remined area" means only that area of any coal remining operation on which coal mining was conducted before August 3, 1977.

(C) Pre-existing discharge

The term "pre-existing discharge" means any discharge at the time of permit application under this subsection.

(4) Applicability of strip mining laws

Nothing in this subsection shall affect the application of the Surface Mining Control and Reclamation Act of 1977 [30 U.S.C. 1201 et seq.] to any coal remining operation, including the application of such Act to suspended solids.

(June 30, 1948, ch. 758, title III, §301, as added Pub. L. 92–500, §2, Oct. 18, 1972, 86 Stat. 844; amended Pub. L. 95–217, §§42–47, 53(c), Dec. 27, 1977, 91 Stat. 1582–1586, 1590; Pub. L. 97–117, §§21, 22(a)–(d), Dec. 29, 1981, 95 Stat. 1631, 1632; Pub. L. 97–440, Jan. 8, 1983, 96 Stat. 2289; Pub. L. 100–4, title III, §§301(a)–(e), 302(a)–(d), 303(a), (b)(1), (c)–(f), 304(a), 305, 306(a), (b), 307, Feb. 4, 1987, 101 Stat. 29–37; Pub. L. 100–688, title III, §3202(b), Nov. 18, 1988, 102 Stat. 4154; Pub. L. 103–431, §2, Oct. 31, 1994, 108 Stat. 4396; Pub. L. 104–66, title II, §2021(b), Dec. 21, 1995, 109 Stat. 727.)

REFERENCES IN TEXT

The Surface Mining Control and Reclamation Act of 1977, referred to in subsec. (p)(4), is Pub. L. 95–87, Aug. 3, 1977, 91 Stat. 445, as amended, which is classified generally to chapter 25 (§1201 et seq.) of Title 30, Mineral Lands and Mining. For complete classification of this Act to the Code, see Short Title note set out under section 1201 of Title 30 and Tables.

AMENDMENTS

1995—Subsec. (n)(8). Pub. L. 104–66 substituted "By January 1, 1997, and January 1 of every odd-numbered year thereafter, the Administrator shall submit to the Committee on Environment and Public Works of the Senate and the Committee on Transportation and Infrastructure" for "Every 6 months after February 4, 1987, the Administrator shall submit to the Committee on Environment and Public Works of the Senate and the Committee on Public Works and Transportation".

1994—Subsec. (j)(1)(A). Pub. L. 103–431, §2(1), inserted before semicolon at end ", and except as provided in paragraph (5)".

Subsec. (j)(5). Pub. L. 103–431, §2(2), added par. (5).

1988—Subsec. (f). Pub. L. 100–688 substituted ", any high-level radioactive waste, or any medical waste," for "or high-level radioactive waste".

1987—Subsec. (b)(2)(C). Pub. L. 100–4, §301(a), struck out "not later than July 1, 1984," before "with respect" and inserted "as expeditiously as practicable but in no case later than three years after the date such limitations are promulgated under section 1314(b) of this title, and in no case later than March 31, 1989" after "of this paragraph".

Subsec. (b)(2)(D). Pub. L. 100–4, §301(b), substituted "as expeditiously as practicable, but in no case later than three years after the date such limitations are promulgated under section 1314(b) of this title, and in no case later than March 31, 1989" for "not later than three years after the date such limitations are established".

Subsec. (b)(2)(E). Pub. L. 100–4, §301(c), substituted "as expeditiously as practicable but in no case later than three years after the date such limitations are promulgated under section 1314(b) of this title, and in no case later than March 31, 1989, compliance with" for "not later than July 1, 1984,".

Subsec. (b)(2)(F). Pub. L. 100–4, §301(d), substituted "as expeditiously as practicable but in no case" for "not" and "and in no case later than March 31, 1989" for "or not later than July 1, 1984, whichever is later, but in no case later than July 1, 1987".

Subsec. (b)(3). Pub. L. 100–4, §301(e), added par. (3).

Subsec. (g)(1). Pub. L. 100–4, §302(a), substituted par. (1) for introductory provisions of former par. (1) which read as follows: "The Administrator, with the concurrence of the State, shall modify the requirements of subsection (b)(2)(A) of this section with respect to the discharge of any pollutant (other than pollutants identified pursuant to section 1314(a)(4) of this title, toxic pollutants subject to section 1317(a) of this title, and the thermal component of discharges) from any point source upon a showing by the owner or operator of such point source satisfactory to the Administrator that—''. Subpars (A) to (C) of former par. (1) were redesignated as subpars. (A) to (C) of par. (2).

Subsec. (g)(2). Pub. L. 100–4, §302(a), (d)(2), inserted introductory provisions of par. (2), and by so doing, redesignated subpars. (A) to (C) of former par. (1) as subpars. (A) to (C) of par. (2), realigned such subpars. with subpar. (A) of par. (4), and redesignated former par. (2) as (3).

Subsec. (g)(3). Pub. L. 100–4, §302(a), (d)(1), redesignated former par. (2) as (3), inserted heading, and aligned par. (3) with par. (4).

Subsec. (g)(4), (5). Pub. L. 100–4, §302(b), added pars. (4) and (5).

Subsec. (h). Pub. L. 100–4, §303(d)(2), (e), in closing provisions, inserted provision defining ''primary or equivalent treatment'' for purposes of par. (9) and provisions placing limitations on issuance of permits for discharge of pollutant into marine waters and saline estuarine waters and prohibiting issuance of permit for discharge of pollutant into New York Bight Apex.

Subsec. (h)(2). Pub. L. 100–4, §303(a), substituted ''the discharge of pollutants in accordance with such modified requirements will not interfere, alone or in combination with pollutants from other sources,'' for ''such modified requirements will not interfere''.

Subsec. (h)(3). Pub. L. 100–4, §303(b)(1), inserted '', and the scope of such monitoring is limited to include only those scientific investigations which are necessary to study the effects of the proposed discharge'' before semicolon at end.

Subsec. (h)(6) to (9). Pub. L. 100–4, §303(c), (d)(1), added par. (6), redesignated former pars. (6) and (7) as (7) and (8), respectively, substituted semicolon for period at end of par. (8), and added par. (9).

Subsec. (i)(1). Pub. L. 100–4, §304(a), substituted ''February 4, 1987'' for ''December 27, 1977''.

Subsec. (j)(1)(A). Pub. L. 100–4, §303(f), inserted before semicolon at end '', except that a publicly owned treatment works which prior to December 31, 1982, had a contractual arrangement to use a portion of the capacity of an ocean outfall operated by another publicly owned treatment works which has applied for or received modification under subsection (h) of this section, may apply for a modification of subsection (h) of this section in its own right not later than 30 days after February 4, 1987''.

Subsec. (j)(2). Pub. L. 100–4, §302(c)(1), substituted ''Subject to paragraph (3) of this section, any'' for ''Any''.

Subsec. (j)(3), (4). Pub. L. 100–4, §302(c)(2), added pars. (3) and (4).

Subsec. (k). Pub. L. 100–4, §305, substituted ''two years after the date for compliance with such effluent limitation which would otherwise be applicable under such subsection'' for ''July 1, 1987'' and inserted ''or (b)(2)(E)'' after ''(b)(2)(A)'' in two places.

Subsec. (*l*). Pub. L. 100–4, §306(b), substituted ''Other than as provided in subsection (n) of this section, the'' for ''The''.

Subsecs. (n), (*o*). Pub. L. 100–4, §306(a), added subsecs. (n) and (*o*).

Subsec. (p). Pub. L. 100–4, §307, added subsec. (p).

1983—Subsec. (m). Pub. L. 97–440 added subsec. (m).

1981—Subsec. (b)(2)(B). Pub. L. 97–117, §21(b), struck out subpar. (B) which required that, not later than July 1, 1983, compliance by all publicly owned treatment works with the requirements in section 1281(g)(2)(A) of this title be achieved.

Subsec. (h). Pub. L. 97–117, §22(a) to (c), struck out in provision preceding par. (1) ''in an existing discharge'' after ''discharge of any pollutant'', struck out par. (8), which required the applicant to demonstrate to the satisfaction of the Administrator that any funds available to the owner of such treatment works under subchapter II of this chapter be used to achieve the degree of effluent reduction required by section 1281(b) and (g)(2)(A) of this title or to carry out the requirements of this subsection, and inserted in provision following par. (7) a further provision that a municipality which applies secondary treatment be eligible to receive a permit which modifies the requirements of subsec. (b)(1)(B) of this section with respect to the discharge of any pollutant from any treatment works owned by such municipality into marine waters and that no permit issued under this subsection authorize the discharge of sewage sludge into marine waters.

Subsec. (i)(1), (2)(B). Pub. L. 97–117, §21(a), substituted ''July 1, 1988,'' for ''July 1, 1983,'' wherever appearing. Par. (2)(B) contained a reference to ''July 1, 1983;'' which was changed to ''July 1, 1988;'' as the probable intent of Congress in that reference to July 1, 1983, was to the outside date for compliance for a point source other than a publicly owned treatment works and subpar. (B) allows a time extension for such a point source up to the date granted in an extension for a publicly owned treatment works, which date was extended to July 1, 1988, by Pub. L. 97–117.

Subsec. (j)(1)(A). Pub. L. 97–117, §22(d), substituted ''that the 365th day which begins after December 29, 1981'' for ''than 270 days after December 27, 1977''.

1977—Subsec. (b)(2)(A). Pub. L. 95–217, §42(b), substituted ''for pollutants identified in subparagraphs (C), (D), and (F) of this paragraph'' for ''not later than July 1, 1983''.

Subsec. (b)(2)(C) to (F). Pub. L. 95–217, §42(a), added subpars. (C) to (F).

Subsec. (g). Pub. L. 95–217, §43, added subsec. (g).

Subsec. (h). Pub. L. 95–217, §44, added subsec. (h).

Subsec. (i). Pub. L. 95–217, §45, added subsec. (i).

Subsec. (j). Pub. L. 95–217, §46, added subsec. (j).

Subsec. (k). Pub. L. 95–217, §47, added subsec. (k).

Subsec. (*l*). Pub. L. 95–217, §53(c), added subsec. (*l*).

CHANGE OF NAME

Committee on Public Works and Transportation of House of Representatives treated as referring to Committee on Transportation and Infrastructure of House of Representatives by section 1(a) of Pub. L. 104–14, set out as a note preceding section 21 of Title 2, The Congress.

EFFECTIVE DATE OF 1987 AMENDMENT

Section 302(e) of Pub. L. 100–4 provided that:

''(1) GENERAL RULE.—Except as provided in paragraph (2), the amendments made by this section [amending this section] shall apply to all requests for modifications under section 301(g) of the Federal Water Pollution Control Act [33 U.S.C. 1311(g)] pending on the date of the enactment of this Act [Feb. 4, 1987] and shall not have the effect of extending the deadline established in section 301(j)(1)(B) of such Act.

''(2) EXCEPTION.—The amendments made by this section shall not affect any application for a modification with respect to the discharge of ammonia, chlorine, color, iron, or total phenols (4AAP) under section 301(g) of the Federal Water Pollution Control Act pending on the date of the enactment of this Act; except that the Administrator must approve or disapprove such application not later than 365 days after the date of such enactment.''

Section 303(b)(2) of Pub. L. 100–4 provided that: ''The amendment made by subsection (b) [amending this section] shall only apply to modifications and renewals of modifications which are tentatively or finally approved after the date of the enactment of this Act [Feb. 4, 1987].''

Section 303(g) of Pub. L. 100–4 provided that: ''The amendments made by subsections (a), (c), (d), and (e) of this section [amending this section] shall not apply to an application for a permit under section 301(h) of the Federal Water Pollution Control Act [33 U.S.C. 1311(h)] which has been tentatively or finally approved by the Administrator before the date of the enactment of this Act [Feb. 4, 1987]; except that such amendments shall apply to all renewals of such permits after such date of enactment.''

Section 304(b) of Pub. L. 100–4 provided that: ''The amendment made by subsection (a) [amending this section] shall not apply to those treatment works which are subject to a compliance schedule established before the date of the enactment of this Act [Feb. 4, 1987] by a court order or a final administrative order."

EFFECTIVE DATE OF 1981 AMENDMENT

Section 22(e) of Pub. L. 97–117 provided that: "The amendments made by this section [amending this section] shall take effect on the date of enactment of this Act [Dec. 29, 1981], except that no applicant, other than the city of Avalon, California, who applies after the date of enactment of this Act for a permit pursuant to subsection (h) of section 301 of the Federal Water Pollution Control Act [33 U.S.C. 1311(h)] which modifies the requirements of subsection (b)(1)(B) of section 301 of such Act [33 U.S.C. 1311(b)(1)(B)] shall receive such permit during the one-year period which begins on the date of enactment of this Act."

REGULATIONS

Section 301(f) of Pub. L. 100–4 provided that: "The Administrator shall promulgate final regulations establishing effluent limitations in accordance with sections 301(b)(2)(A) and 307(b)(1) of the Federal Water Pollution Control Act [33 U.S.C. 1311(b)(2)(A), 1317(b)(1)] for all toxic pollutants referred to in table 1 of Committee Print Numbered 95–30 of the Committee on Public Works and Transportation of the House of Representatives which are discharged from the categories of point sources in accordance with the following table:

"Category	Date by which the final regulation shall be promulgated
Organic chemicals and plastics and synthetic fibers	December 31, 1986.
Pesticides	December 31, 1986."

PHOSPHATE FERTILIZER EFFLUENT LIMITATION

Amendment by section 306(a), (b) of Pub. L. 100–4 not to be construed (A) to require the Administrator to permit the discharge of gypsum or gypsum waste into the navigable waters, (B) to affect the procedures and standards applicable to the Administrator in issuing permits under section 1342(a)(1)(B) of this title, and (C) to affect the authority of any State to deny or condition certification under section 1314 of this title with respect to the issuance of permits under section 1342(a)(1)(B) of this title, see section 306(c) of Pub. L. 100–4, set out as a note under section 1342 of this title.

DISCHARGES FROM POINT SOURCES IN UNITED STATES VIRGIN ISLANDS ATTRIBUTABLE TO MANUFACTURE OF RUM; EXEMPTION FROM FEDERAL WATER POLLUTION CONTROL REQUIREMENTS; CONDITIONS

Pub. L. 98–67, title II, § 214(g), Aug. 5, 1983, 97 Stat. 393, as amended by Pub. L. 99–514, § 2, Oct. 22, 1986, 100 Stat. 2095, provided that: "Any discharge from a point source in the United States Virgin Islands in existence on the date of the enactment of this subsection [Aug. 5, 1983] which discharge is attributable to the manufacture of rum (as defined in paragraphs (3) of section 7652(c) of the Internal Revenue Code of 1986 [formerly I.R.C. 1954]) [26 U.S.C. 7652(c)(3)] shall not be subject to the requirements of section 301 (other than toxic pollutant discharges), section 306 or section 403 of the Federal Water Pollution Control Act [33 U.S.C. 1311, 1316, 1343] if—

"(1) such discharge occurs at least one thousand five hundred feet into the territorial sea from the line of ordinary low water from that portion of the coast which is in direct contact with the sea, and

"(2) the Governor of the United States Virgin Islands determines that such discharge will not interfere with the attainment or maintenance of that water quality which shall assure protection of public water supplies, and the protection and propagation of a balanced population of shellfish, fish, and wildlife, and allow recreational activities, in and on the water and will not result in the discharge of pollutants in quantities which may reasonably be anticipated to pose an unacceptable risk to human health or the environment because of bioaccumulation, persistency in the environment, acute toxicity, chronic toxicity (including carcinogenicity, mutagenicity, or teratogenicity), or synergistic propensities."

CERTAIN MUNICIPAL COMPLIANCE DEADLINES UNAFFECTED; EXCEPTION

Section 21(a) of Pub. L. 97–117 provided in part that: "The amendment made by this subsection [amending this section] shall not be interpreted or applied to extend the date for compliance with section 301(b)(1)(B) or (C) of the Federal Water Pollution Control Act [33 U.S.C. 1311(b)(1)(B), (C)] beyond schedules for compliance in effect as of the date of enactment of this Act [Dec. 29, 1981], except in cases where reductions in the amount of financial assistance under this Act [Pub. L. 97–117, see Short Title of 1981 Amendment note set out under section 1251 of this title] or changed conditions affecting the rate of construction beyond the control of the owner or operator will make it impossible to complete construction by July 1, 1983."

TERRITORIAL SEA AND CONTIGUOUS ZONE OF UNITED STATES

For extension of territorial sea and contiguous zone of United States, see Proc. No. 5928 and Proc. No. 7219, respectively, set out as notes under section 1331 of Title 43, Public Lands.

§ 1312. Water quality related effluent limitations

(a) Establishment

Whenever, in the judgment of the Administrator or as identified under section 1314(*l*) of this title, discharges of pollutants from a point source or group of point sources, with the application of effluent limitations required under section 1311(b)(2) of this title, would interfere with the attainment or maintenance of that water quality in a specific portion of the navigable waters which shall assure protection of public health, public water supplies, agricultural and industrial uses, and the protection and propagation of a balanced population of shellfish, fish and wildlife, and allow recreational activities in and on the water, effluent limitations (including alternative effluent control strategies) for such point source or sources shall be established which can reasonably be expected to contribute to the attainment or maintenance of such water quality.

(b) Modifications of effluent limitations

(1) Notice and hearing

Prior to establishment of any effluent limitation pursuant to subsection (a) of this section, the Administrator shall publish such proposed limitation and within 90 days of such publication hold a public hearing.

(2) Permits

(A) No reasonable relationship

The Administrator, with the concurrence of the State, may issue a permit which modifies the effluent limitations required by subsection (a) of this section for pollutants other than toxic pollutants if the applicant demonstrates at such hearing that (whether or not technology or other alternative control strategies are available) there is no reasonable relationship between the economic and social costs and the benefits to be obtained (including attainment of the objective of this chapter) from achieving such limitation.

(B) Reasonable progress

The Administrator, with the concurrence of the State, may issue a permit which modifies the effluent limitations required by subsection (a) of this section for toxic pollutants for a single period not to exceed 5 years if the applicant demonstrates to the satisfaction of the Administrator that such modified requirements (i) will represent the maximum degree of control within the economic capability of the owner and operator of the source, and (ii) will result in reasonable further progress beyond the requirements of section 1311(b)(2) of this title toward the requirements of subsection (a) of this section.

(c) Delay in application of other limitations

The establishment of effluent limitations under this section shall not operate to delay the application of any effluent limitation established under section 1311 of this title.

(June 30, 1948, ch. 758, title III, §302, as added Pub. L. 92–500, §2, Oct. 18, 1972, 86 Stat. 846; amended Pub. L. 100–4, title III, §308(e), Feb. 4, 1987, 101 Stat. 39.)

AMENDMENTS

1987—Subsec. (a). Pub. L. 100–4, §308(e)(2), inserted "or as identified under section 1314(*l*) of this title" after "Administrator" and "public health," after "protection of".

Subsec. (b). Pub. L. 100–4, §308(e)(1), amended subsec. (b) generally. Prior to amendment, subsec. (b) read as follows:

"(1) Prior to establishment of any effluent limitation pursuant to subsection (a) of this section, the Administrator shall issue notice of intent to establish such limitation and within ninety days of such notice hold a public hearing to determine the relationship of the economic and social costs of achieving any such limitation or limitations, including any economic or social dislocation in the affected community or communities, to the social and economic benefits to be obtained (including the attainment of the objective of this chapter) and to determine whether or not such effluent limitations can be implemented with available technology or other alternative control strategies.

"(2) If a person affected by such limitation demonstrates at such hearing that (whether or not such technology or other alternative control strategies are available) there is no reasonable relationship between the economic and social costs and the benefits to be obtained (including attainment of the objective of this chapter), such limitation shall not become effective and the Administrator shall adjust such limitation as it applies to such person."

§1313. Water quality standards and implementation plans

(a) Existing water quality standards

(1) In order to carry out the purpose of this chapter, any water quality standard applicable to interstate waters which was adopted by any State and submitted to, and approved by, or is awaiting approval by, the Administrator pursuant to this Act as in effect immediately prior to October 18, 1972, shall remain in effect unless the Administrator determined that such standard is not consistent with the applicable requirements of this Act as in effect immediately prior to October 18, 1972. If the Administrator makes such a determination he shall, within three months after October 18, 1972, notify the State and specify the changes needed to meet such requirements. If such changes are not adopted by the State within ninety days after the date of such notification, the Administrator shall promulgate such changes in accordance with subsection (b) of this section.

(2) Any State which, before October 18, 1972, has adopted, pursuant to its own law, water quality standards applicable to intrastate waters shall submit such standards to the Administrator within thirty days after October 18, 1972. Each such standard shall remain in effect, in the same manner and to the same extent as any other water quality standard established under this chapter unless the Administrator determines that such standard is inconsistent with the applicable requirements of this Act as in effect immediately prior to October 18, 1972. If the Administrator makes such a determination he shall not later than the one hundred and twentieth day after the date of submission of such standards, notify the State and specify the changes needed to meet such requirements. If such changes are not adopted by the State within ninety days after such notification, the Administrator shall promulgate such changes in accordance with subsection (b) of this section.

(3)(A) Any State which prior to October 18, 1972, has not adopted pursuant to its own laws water quality standards applicable to intrastate waters shall, not later than one hundred and eighty days after October 18, 1972, adopt and submit such standards to the Administrator.

(B) If the Administrator determines that any such standards are consistent with the applicable requirements of this Act as in effect immediately prior to October 18, 1972, he shall approve such standards.

(C) If the Administrator determines that any such standards are not consistent with the applicable requirements of this Act as in effect immediately prior to October 18, 1972, he shall, not later than the ninetieth day after the date of submission of such standards, notify the State and specify the changes to meet such requirements. If such changes are not adopted by the State within ninety days after the date of notification, the Administrator shall promulgate such standards pursuant to subsection (b) of this section.

(b) Proposed regulations

(1) The Administrator shall promptly prepare and publish proposed regulations setting forth water quality standards for a State in accordance with the applicable requirements of this Act as in effect immediately prior to October 18, 1972, if—

(A) the State fails to submit water quality standards within the times prescribed in subsection (a) of this section.

(B) a water quality standard submitted by such State under subsection (a) of this section is determined by the Administrator not to be consistent with the applicable requirements of subsection (a) of this section.

(2) The Administrator shall promulgate any water quality standard published in a proposed

regulation not later than one hundred and ninety days after the date he publishes any such proposed standard, unless prior to such promulgation, such State has adopted a water quality standard which the Administrator determines to be in accordance with subsection (a) of this section.

(c) Review; revised standards; publication

(1) The Governor of a State or the State water pollution control agency of such State shall from time to time (but at least once each three year period beginning with October 18, 1972) hold public hearings for the purpose of reviewing applicable water quality standards and, as appropriate, modifying and adopting standards. Results of such review shall be made available to the Administrator.

(2)(A) Whenever the State revises or adopts a new standard, such revised or new standard shall be submitted to the Administrator. Such revised or new water quality standard shall consist of the designated uses of the navigable waters involved and the water quality criteria for such waters based upon such uses. Such standards shall be such as to protect the public health or welfare, enhance the quality of water and serve the purposes of this chapter. Such standards shall be established taking into consideration their use and value for public water supplies, propagation of fish and wildlife, recreational purposes, and agricultural, industrial, and other purposes, and also taking into consideration their use and value for navigation.

(B) Whenever a State reviews water quality standards pursuant to paragraph (1) of this subsection, or revises or adopts new standards pursuant to this paragraph, such State shall adopt criteria for all toxic pollutants listed pursuant to section 1317(a)(1) of this title for which criteria have been published under section 1314(a) of this title, the discharge or presence of which in the affected waters could reasonably be expected to interfere with those designated uses adopted by the State, as necessary to support such designated uses. Such criteria shall be specific numerical criteria for such toxic pollutants. Where such numerical criteria are not available, whenever a State reviews water quality standards pursuant to paragraph (1), or revises or adopts new standards pursuant to this paragraph, such State shall adopt criteria based on biological monitoring or assessment methods consistent with information published pursuant to section 1314(a)(8) of this title. Nothing in this section shall be construed to limit or delay the use of effluent limitations or other permit conditions based on or involving biological monitoring or assessment methods or previously adopted numerical criteria.

(3) If the Administrator, within sixty days after the date of submission of the revised or new standard, determines that such standard meets the requirements of this chapter, such standard shall thereafter be the water quality standard for the applicable waters of that State. If the Administrator determines that any such revised or new standard is not consistent with the applicable requirements of this chapter, he shall not later than the ninetieth day after the date of submission of such standard notify the State and specify the changes to meet such requirements. If such changes are not adopted by the State within ninety days after the date of notification, the Administrator shall promulgate such standard pursuant to paragraph (4) of this subsection.

(4) The Administrator shall promptly prepare and publish proposed regulations setting forth a revised or new water quality standard for the navigable waters involved—

(A) if a revised or new water quality standard submitted by such State under paragraph (3) of this subsection for such waters is determined by the Administrator not to be consistent with the applicable requirements of this chapter, or

(B) in any case where the Administrator determines that a revised or new standard is necessary to meet the requirements of this chapter.

The Administrator shall promulgate any revised or new standard under this paragraph not later than ninety days after he publishes such proposed standards, unless prior to such promulgation, such State has adopted a revised or new water quality standard which the Administrator determines to be in accordance with this chapter.

(d) Identification of areas with insufficient controls; maximum daily load; certain effluent limitations revision

(1)(A) Each State shall identify those waters within its boundaries for which the effluent limitations required by section 1311(b)(1)(A) and section 1311(b)(1)(B) of this title are not stringent enough to implement any water quality standard applicable to such waters. The State shall establish a priority ranking for such waters, taking into account the severity of the pollution and the uses to be made of such waters.

(B) Each State shall identify those waters or parts thereof within its boundaries for which controls on thermal discharges under section 1311 of this title are not stringent enough to assure protection and propagation of a balanced indigenous population of shellfish, fish, and wildlife.

(C) Each State shall establish for the waters identified in paragraph (1)(A) of this subsection, and in accordance with the priority ranking, the total maximum daily load, for those pollutants which the Administrator identifies under section 1314(a)(2) of this title as suitable for such calculation. Such load shall be established at a level necessary to implement the applicable water quality standards with seasonal variations and a margin of safety which takes into account any lack of knowledge concerning the relationship between effluent limitations and water quality.

(D) Each State shall estimate for the waters identified in paragraph (1)(B) of this subsection the total maximum daily thermal load required to assure protection and propagation of a balanced, indigenous population of shellfish, fish, and wildlife. Such estimates shall take into account the normal water temperatures, flow rates, seasonal variations, existing sources of heat input, and the dissipative capacity of the identified waters or parts thereof. Such estimates shall include a calculation of the maximum heat input that can be made into each such part and shall include a margin of safety which takes into account any lack of knowledge concerning the development of thermal water quality criteria for such protection and propagation in the identified waters or parts thereof.

(2) Each State shall submit to the Administrator from time to time, with the first such submission not later than one hundred and eighty days after the date of publication of the first identification of pollutants under section 1314(a)(2)(D) of this title, for his approval the waters identified and the loads established under paragraphs (1)(A), (1)(B), (1)(C), and (1)(D) of this subsection. The Administrator shall either approve or disapprove such identification and load not later than thirty days after the date of submission. If the Administrator approves such identification and load, such State shall incorporate them into its current plan under subsection (e) of this section. If the Administrator disapproves such identification and load, he shall not later than thirty days after the date of such disapproval identify such waters in such State and establish such loads for such waters as he determines necessary to implement the water quality standards applicable to such waters and upon such identification and establishment the State shall incorporate them into its current plan under subsection (e) of this section.

(3) For the specific purpose of developing information, each State shall identify all waters within its boundaries which it has not identified under paragraph (1)(A) and (1)(B) of this subsection and estimate for such waters the total maximum daily load with seasonal variations and margins of safety, for those pollutants which the Administrator identifies under section 1314(a)(2) of this title as suitable for such calculation and for thermal discharges, at a level that would assure protection and propagation of a balanced indigenous population of fish, shellfish, and wildlife.

(4) LIMITATIONS ON REVISION OF CERTAIN EFFLUENT LIMITATIONS.—

(A) STANDARD NOT ATTAINED.—For waters identified under paragraph (1)(A) where the applicable water quality standard has not yet been attained, any effluent limitation based on a total maximum daily load or other waste load allocation established under this section may be revised only if (i) the cumulative effect of all such revised effluent limitations based on such total maximum daily load or waste load allocation will assure the attainment of such water quality standard, or (ii) the designated use which is not being attained is removed in accordance with regulations established under this section.

(B) STANDARD ATTAINED.—For waters identified under paragraph (1)(A) where the quality of such waters equals or exceeds levels necessary to protect the designated use for such waters or otherwise required by applicable water quality standards, any effluent limitation based on a total maximum daily load or other waste load allocation established under this section, or any water quality standard established under this section, or any other permitting standard may be revised only if such revision is subject to and consistent with the antidegradation policy established under this section.

(e) Continuing planning process

(1) Each State shall have a continuing planning process approved under paragraph (2) of this subsection which is consistent with this chapter.

(2) Each State shall submit not later than 120 days after October 18, 1972, to the Administrator for his approval a proposed continuing planning process which is consistent with this chapter. Not later than thirty days after the date of submission of such a process the Administrator shall either approve or disapprove such process. The Administrator shall from time to time review each State's approved planning process for the purpose of insuring that such planning process is at all times consistent with this chapter. The Administrator shall not approve any State permit program under subchapter IV of this chapter for any State which does not have an approved continuing planning process under this section.

(3) The Administrator shall approve any continuing planning process submitted to him under this section which will result in plans for all navigable waters within such State, which include, but are not limited to, the following:

(A) effluent limitations and schedules of compliance at least as stringent as those required by section 1311(b)(1), section 1311(b)(2), section 1316, and section 1317 of this title, and at least as stringent as any requirements contained in any applicable water quality standard in effect under authority of this section;

(B) the incorporation of all elements of any applicable area-wide waste management plans under section 1288 of this title, and applicable basin plans under section 1289 of this title;

(C) total maximum daily load for pollutants in accordance with subsection (d) of this section;

(D) procedures for revision;

(E) adequate authority for intergovernmental cooperation;

(F) adequate implementation, including schedules of compliance, for revised or new water quality standards, under subsection (c) of this section;

(G) controls over the disposition of all residual waste from any water treatment processing;

(H) an inventory and ranking, in order of priority, of needs for construction of waste treatment works required to meet the applicable requirements of sections 1311 and 1312 of this title.

(f) Earlier compliance

Nothing in this section shall be construed to affect any effluent limitation, or schedule of compliance required by any State to be implemented prior to the dates set forth in sections 1311(b)(1) and 1311(b)(2) of this title nor to preclude any State from requiring compliance with any effluent limitation or schedule of compliance at dates earlier than such dates.

(g) Heat standards

Water quality standards relating to heat shall be consistent with the requirements of section 1326 of this title.

(h) Thermal water quality standards

For the purposes of this chapter the term "water quality standards" includes thermal water quality standards.

(i) Coastal recreation water quality criteria

(1) Adoption by States

(A) Initial criteria and standards

Not later than 42 months after October 10, 2000, each State having coastal recreation waters shall adopt and submit to the Administrator water quality criteria and standards for the coastal recreation waters of the State for those pathogens and pathogen indicators for which the Administrator has published criteria under section 1314(a) of this title.

(B) New or revised criteria and standards

Not later than 36 months after the date of publication by the Administrator of new or revised water quality criteria under section 1314(a)(9) of this title, each State having coastal recreation waters shall adopt and submit to the Administrator new or revised water quality standards for the coastal recreation waters of the State for all pathogens and pathogen indicators to which the new or revised water quality criteria are applicable.

(2) Failure of States to adopt

(A) In general

If a State fails to adopt water quality criteria and standards in accordance with paragraph (1)(A) that are as protective of human health as the criteria for pathogens and pathogen indicators for coastal recreation waters published by the Administrator, the Administrator shall promptly propose regulations for the State setting forth revised or new water quality standards for pathogens and pathogen indicators described in paragraph (1)(A) for coastal recreation waters of the State.

(B) Exception

If the Administrator proposes regulations for a State described in subparagraph (A) under subsection (c)(4)(B) of this section, the Administrator shall publish any revised or new standard under this subsection not later than 42 months after October 10, 2000.

(3) Applicability

Except as expressly provided by this subsection, the requirements and procedures of subsection (c) of this section apply to this subsection, including the requirement in subsection (c)(2)(A) of this section that the criteria protect public health and welfare.

(June 30, 1948, ch. 758, title III, §303, as added Pub. L. 92–500, §2, Oct. 18, 1972, 86 Stat. 846; amended Pub. L. 100–4, title III, §308(d), title IV, §404(b), Feb. 4, 1987, 101 Stat. 39, 68; Pub. L. 106–284, §2, Oct. 10, 2000, 114 Stat. 870.)

REFERENCES IN TEXT

This Act, referred to in subsecs. (a)(1), (2), (3)(B), (C) and (b)(1), means act June 30, 1948, ch. 758, 62 Stat. 1155, prior to the supersedure and reenactment of act June 30, 1948 by act Oct. 18, 1972, Pub. L. 92–500, 86 Stat. 816. Act June 30, 1948, ch. 758, as added by act Oct. 18, 1972, Pub. L. 92–500, 86 Stat. 816, enacted this chapter.

AMENDMENTS

2000—Subsec. (i). Pub. L. 106–284 added subsec. (i).

1987—Subsec. (c)(2). Pub. L. 100–4, §308(d), designated existing provision as subpar. (A) and added subpar. (B).

Subsec. (d)(4). Pub. L. 100–4, §404(b), added par. (4).

§1313a. Revised water quality standards

The review, revision, and adoption or promulgation of revised or new water quality standards pursuant to section 303(c) of the Federal Water Pollution Control Act [33 U.S.C. 1313(c)] shall be completed by the date three years after December 29, 1981. No grant shall be made under title II of the Federal Water Pollution Control Act [33 U.S.C. 1281 et seq.] after such date until water quality standards are reviewed and revised pursuant to section 303(c), except where the State has in good faith submitted such revised water quality standards and the Administrator has not acted to approve or disapprove such submission within one hundred and twenty days of receipt.

(Pub. L. 97–117, §24, Dec. 29, 1981, 95 Stat. 1632.)

REFERENCES IN TEXT

The Federal Water Pollution Control Act, referred to in text, is act June 30, 1948, ch. 758, as amended generally by Pub. L. 92–500, §2, Oct. 18, 1972, 86 Stat. 816. Title II of the Act is classified generally to subchapter II (§1281 et seq.) of this chapter. For complete classification of this Act to the Code, see Short Title note set out under section 1251 of this title and Tables.

CODIFICATION

Section was enacted as part of the Municipal Wastewater Treatment Construction Grant Amendments of 1981, and not as part of the Federal Water Pollution Control Act which comprises this chapter.

§1314. Information and guidelines

(a) Criteria development and publication

(1) The Administrator, after consultation with appropriate Federal and State agencies and other interested persons, shall develop and publish, within one year after October 18, 1972 (and from time to time thereafter revise) criteria for water quality accurately reflecting the latest scientific knowledge (A) on the kind and extent of all identifiable effects on health and welfare including, but not limited to, plankton, fish, shellfish, wildlife, plant life, shorelines, beaches, esthetics, and recreation which may be expected from the presence of pollutants in any body of water, including ground water; (B) on the concentration and dispersal of pollutants, or their byproducts, through biological, physical, and chemical processes; and (C) on the effects of pollutants on biological community diversity, productivity, and stability, including information on the factors affecting rates of eutrophication and rates of organic and inorganic sedimentation for varying types of receiving waters.

(2) The Administrator, after consultation with appropriate Federal and State agencies and other interested persons, shall develop and pub-

lish, within one year after October 18, 1972 (and from time to time thereafter revise) information (A) on the factors necessary to restore and maintain the chemical, physical, and biological integrity of all navigable waters, ground waters, waters of the contiguous zone, and the oceans; (B) on the factors necessary for the protection and propagation of shellfish, fish, and wildlife for classes and categories of receiving waters and to allow recreational activities in and on the water; and (C) on the measurement and classification of water quality; and (D) for the purpose of section 1313 of this title, on and the identification of pollutants suitable for maximum daily load measurement correlated with the achievement of water quality objectives.

(3) Such criteria and information and revisions thereof shall be issued to the States and shall be published in the Federal Register and otherwise made available to the public.

(4) The Administrator shall, within 90 days after December 27, 1977, and from time to time thereafter, publish and revise as appropriate information identifying conventional pollutants, including but not limited to, pollutants classified as biological oxygen demanding, suspended solids, fecal coliform, and pH. The thermal component of any discharge shall not be identified as a conventional pollutant under this paragraph.

(5)(A) The Administrator, to the extent practicable before consideration of any request under section 1311(g) of this title and within six months after December 27, 1977, shall develop and publish information on the factors necessary for the protection of public water supplies, and the protection and propagation of a balanced population of shellfish, fish and wildlife, and to allow recreational activities, in and on the water.

(B) The Administrator, to the extent practicable before consideration of any application under section 1311(h) of this title and within six months after December 27, 1977, shall develop and publish information on the factors necessary for the protection of public water supplies, and the protection and propagation of a balanced indigenous population of shellfish, fish and wildlife, and to allow recreational activities, in and on the water.

(6) The Administrator shall, within three months after December 27, 1977, and annually thereafter, for purposes of section 1311(h) of this title publish and revise as appropriate information identifying each water quality standard in effect under this chapter or State law, the specific pollutants associated with such water quality standard, and the particular waters to which such water quality standard applies.

(7) GUIDANCE TO STATES.—The Administrator, after consultation with appropriate State agencies and on the basis of criteria and information published under paragraphs (1) and (2) of this subsection, shall develop and publish, within 9 months after February 4, 1987, guidance to the States on performing the identification required by subsection (*l*)(1) of this section.

(8) INFORMATION ON WATER QUALITY CRITERIA.—The Administrator, after consultation with appropriate State agencies and within 2 years after February 4, 1987, shall develop and publish information on methods for establishing and measuring water quality criteria for toxic pollutants on other bases than pollutant-by-pollutant criteria, including biological monitoring and assessment methods.

(9) REVISED CRITERIA FOR COASTAL RECREATION WATERS.—

(A) IN GENERAL.—Not later than 5 years after October 10, 2000, after consultation and in cooperation with appropriate Federal, State, tribal, and local officials (including local health officials), the Administrator shall publish new or revised water quality criteria for pathogens and pathogen indicators (including a revised list of testing methods, as appropriate), based on the results of the studies conducted under section 1254(v) of this title, for the purpose of protecting human health in coastal recreation waters.

(B) REVIEWS.—Not later than the date that is 5 years after the date of publication of water quality criteria under this paragraph, and at least once every 5 years thereafter, the Administrator shall review and, as necessary, revise the water quality criteria.

(b) Effluent limitation guidelines

For the purpose of adopting or revising effluent limitations under this chapter the Administrator shall, after consultation with appropriate Federal and State agencies and other interested persons, publish within one year of October 18, 1972, regulations, providing guidelines for effluent limitations, and, at least annually thereafter, revise, if appropriate, such regulations. Such regulations shall—

(1)(A) identify, in terms of amounts of constituents and chemical, physical, and biological characteristics of pollutants, the degree of effluent reduction attainable through the application of the best practicable control technology currently available for classes and categories of point sources (other than publicly owned treatment works); and

(B) specify factors to be taken into account in determining the control measures and practices to be applicable to point sources (other than publicly owned treatment works) within such categories or classes. Factors relating to the assessment of best practicable control technology currently available to comply with subsection (b)(1) of section 1311 of this title shall include consideration of the total cost of application of technology in relation to the effluent reduction benefits to be achieved from such application, and shall also take into account the age of equipment and facilities involved, the process employed, the engineering aspects of the application of various types of control techniques, process changes, nonwater quality environmental impact (including energy requirements), and such other factors as the Administrator deems appropriate;

(2)(A) identify, in terms of amounts of constituents and chemical, physical, and biological characteristics of pollutants, the degree of effluent reduction attainable through the application of the best control measures and practices achievable including treatment techniques, process and procedure innovations, operating methods, and other alternatives for classes and categories of point sources (other than publicly owned treatment works); and

(B) specify factors to be taken into account in determining the best measures and practices available to comply with subsection (b)(2) of section 1311 of this title to be applicable to any point source (other than publicly owned treatment works) within such categories or classes. Factors relating to the assessment of best available technology shall take into account the age of equipment and facilities involved, the process employed, the engineering aspects of the application of various types of control techniques, process changes, the cost of achieving such effluent reduction, non-water quality environmental impact (including energy requirements), and such other factors as the Administrator deems appropriate;

(3) identify control measures and practices available to eliminate the discharge of pollutants from categories and classes of point sources, taking into account the cost of achieving such elimination of the discharge of pollutants; and

(4)(A) identify, in terms of amounts of constituents and chemical, physical, and biological characteristics of pollutants, the degree of effluent reduction attainable through the application of the best conventional pollutant control technology (including measures and practices) for classes and categories of point sources (other than publicly owned treatment works); and

(B) specify factors to be taken into account in determining the best conventional pollutant control technology measures and practices to comply with section 1311(b)(2)(E) of this title to be applicable to any point source (other than publicly owned treatment works) within such categories or classes. Factors relating to the assessment of best conventional pollutant control technology (including measures and practices) shall include consideration of the reasonableness of the relationship between the costs of attaining a reduction in effluents and the effluent reduction benefits derived, and the comparison of the cost and level of reduction of such pollutants from the discharge from publicly owned treatment works to the cost and level of reduction of such pollutants from a class or category of industrial sources, and shall take into account the age of equipment and facilities involved, the process employed, the engineering aspects of the application of various types of control techniques, process changes, non-water quality environmental impact (including energy requirements), and such other factors as the Administrator deems appropriate.

(c) Pollution discharge elimination procedures

The Administrator, after consultation, with appropriate Federal and State agencies and other interested persons, shall issue to the States and appropriate water pollution control agencies within 270 days after October 18, 1972 (and from time to time thereafter) information on the processes, procedures, or operating methods which result in the elimination or reduction of the discharge of pollutants to implement standards of performance under section 1316 of this title. Such information shall include technical and other data, including costs, as are available on alternative methods of elimination or reduction of the discharge of pollutants. Such information, and revisions thereof, shall be published in the Federal Register and otherwise shall be made available to the public.

(d) Secondary treatment information; alternative waste treatment management techniques; innovative and alternative wastewater treatment processes; facilities deemed equivalent of secondary treatment

(1) The Administrator, after consultation with appropriate Federal and State agencies and other interested persons, shall publish within sixty days after October 18, 1972 (and from time to time thereafter) information, in terms of amounts of constituents and chemical, physical, and biological characteristics of pollutants, on the degree of effluent reduction attainable through the application of secondary treatment.

(2) The Administrator, after consultation with appropriate Federal and State agencies and other interested persons, shall publish within nine months after October 18, 1972 (and from time to time thereafter) information on alternative waste treatment management techniques and systems available to implement section 1281 of this title.

(3) The Administrator, after consultation with appropriate Federal and State agencies and other interested persons, shall promulgate within one hundred and eighty days after December 27, 1977, guidelines for identifying and evaluating innovative and alternative wastewater treatment processes and techniques referred to in section 1281(g)(5) of this title.

(4) For the purposes of this subsection, such biological treatment facilities as oxidation ponds, lagoons, and ditches and trickling filters shall be deemed the equivalent of secondary treatment. The Administrator shall provide guidance under paragraph (1) of this subsection on design criteria for such facilities, taking into account pollutant removal efficiencies and, consistent with the objectives of this chapter, assuring that water quality will not be adversely affected by deeming such facilities as the equivalent of secondary treatment.

(e) Best management practices for industry

The Administrator, after consultation with appropriate Federal and State agencies and other interested persons, may publish regulations, supplemental to any effluent limitations specified under subsections (b) and (c) of this section for a class or category of point sources, for any specific pollutant which the Administrator is charged with a duty to regulate as a toxic or hazardous pollutant under section 1317(a)(1) or 1321 of this title, to control plant site runoff, spillage or leaks, sludge or waste disposal, and drainage from raw material storage which the Administrator determines are associated with or ancillary to the industrial manufacturing or treatment process within such class or category of point sources and may contribute significant amounts of such pollutants to navigable waters. Any applicable controls established under this subsection shall be included as a requirement for the purposes of section 1311, 1312, 1316, 1317, or 1343 of this title, as the case may be, in any permit issued to a point source pursuant to section 1342 of this title.

(f) Identification and evaluation of nonpoint sources of pollution; processes, procedures, and methods to control pollution

The Administrator, after consultation with appropriate Federal and State agencies and other interested persons, shall issue to appropriate Federal agencies, the States, water pollution control agencies, and agencies designated under section 1288 of this title, within one year after October 18, 1972 (and from time to time thereafter) information including (1) guidelines for identifying and evaluating the nature and extent of nonpoint sources of pollutants, and (2) processes, procedures, and methods to control pollution resulting from—

(A) agricultural and silvicultural activities, including runoff from fields and crop and forest lands;

(B) mining activities, including runoff and siltation from new, currently operating, and abandoned surface and underground mines;

(C) all construction activity, including runoff from the facilities resulting from such construction;

(D) the disposal of pollutants in wells or in subsurface excavations;

(E) salt water intrusion resulting from reductions of fresh water flow from any cause, including extraction of ground water, irrigation, obstruction, and diversion; and

(F) changes in the movement, flow, or circulation of any navigable waters or ground waters, including changes caused by the construction of dams, levees, channels, causeways, or flow diversion facilities.

Such information and revisions thereof shall be published in the Federal Register and otherwise made available to the public.

(g) Guidelines for pretreatment of pollutants

(1) For the purpose of assisting States in carrying out programs under section 1342 of this title, the Administrator shall publish, within one hundred and twenty days after October 18, 1972, and review at least annually thereafter and, if appropriate, revise guidelines for pretreatment of pollutants which he determines are not susceptible to treatment by publicly owned treatment works. Guidelines under this subsection shall be established to control and prevent the discharge into the navigable waters, the contiguous zone, or the ocean (either directly or through publicly owned treatment works) of any pollutant which interferes with, passes through, or otherwise is incompatible with such works.

(2) When publishing guidelines under this subsection, the Administrator shall designate the category or categories of treatment works to which the guidelines shall apply.

(h) Test procedures guidelines

The Administrator shall, within one hundred and eighty days from October 18, 1972, promulgate guidelines establishing test procedures for the analysis of pollutants that shall include the factors which must be provided in any certification pursuant to section 1341 of this title or permit application pursuant to section 1342 of this title.

(i) Guidelines for monitoring, reporting, enforcement, funding, personnel, and manpower

The Administrator shall (1) within sixty days after October 18, 1972, promulgate guidelines for the purpose of establishing uniform application forms and other minimum requirements for the acquisition of information from owners and operators of point-sources of discharge subject to any State program under section 1342 of this title, and (2) within sixty days from October 18, 1972, promulgate guidelines establishing the minimum procedural and other elements of any State program under section 1342 of this title, which shall include:

(A) monitoring requirements;

(B) reporting requirements (including procedures to make information available to the public);

(C) enforcement provisions; and

(D) funding, personnel qualifications, and manpower requirements (including a requirement that no board or body which approves permit applications or portions thereof shall include, as a member, any person who receives, or has during the previous two years received, a significant portion of his income directly or indirectly from permit holders or applicants for a permit).

(j) Lake restoration guidance manual

The Administrator shall, within 1 year after February 4, 1987, and biennially thereafter, publish and disseminate a lake restoration guidance manual describing methods, procedures, and processes to guide State and local efforts to improve, restore, and enhance water quality in the Nation's publicly owned lakes.

(k) Agreements with Secretaries of Agriculture, Army, and the Interior to provide maximum utilization of programs to achieve and maintain water quality; transfer of funds; authorization of appropriations

(1) The Administrator shall enter into agreements with the Secretary of Agriculture, the Secretary of the Army, and the Secretary of the Interior, and the heads of such other departments, agencies, and instrumentalities of the United States as the Administrator determines, to provide for the maximum utilization of other Federal laws and programs for the purpose of achieving and maintaining water quality through appropriate implementation of plans approved under section 1288 of this title and nonpoint source pollution management programs approved under section 1329 of this title.

(2) The Administrator is authorized to transfer to the Secretary of Agriculture, the Secretary of the Army, and the Secretary of the Interior and the heads of such other departments, agencies, and instrumentalities of the United States as the Administrator determines, any funds appropriated under paragraph (3) of this subsection to supplement funds otherwise appropriated to programs authorized pursuant to any agreement under paragraph (1).

(3) There is authorized to be appropriated to carry out the provisions of this subsection,

$100,000,000 per fiscal year for the fiscal years 1979 through 1983 and such sums as may be necessary for fiscal years 1984 through 1990.

(*l*) Individual control strategies for toxic pollutants

(1) State list of navigable waters and development of strategies

Not later than 2 years after February 4, 1987, each State shall submit to the Administrator for review, approval, and implementation under this subsection—

(A) a list of those waters within the State which after the application of effluent limitations required under section 1311(b)(2) of this title cannot reasonably be anticipated to attain or maintain (i) water quality standards for such waters reviewed, revised, or adopted in accordance with section 1313(c)(2)(B) of this title, due to toxic pollutants, or (ii) that water quality which shall assure protection of public health, public water supplies, agricultural and industrial uses, and the protection and propagation of a balanced population of shellfish, fish and wildlife, and allow recreational activities in and on the water;

(B) a list of all navigable waters in such State for which the State does not expect the applicable standard under section 1313 of this title will be achieved after the requirements of sections 1311(b), 1316, and 1317(b) of this title are met, due entirely or substantially to discharges from point sources of any toxic pollutants listed pursuant to section 1317(a) of this title;

(C) for each segment of the navigable waters included on such lists, a determination of the specific point sources discharging any such toxic pollutant which is believed to be preventing or impairing such water quality and the amount of each such toxic pollutant discharged by each such source; and

(D) for each such segment, an individual control strategy which the State determines will produce a reduction in the discharge of toxic pollutants from point sources identified by the State under this paragraph through the establishment of effluent limitations under section 1342 of this title and water quality standards under section 1313(c)(2)(B) of this title, which reduction is sufficient, in combination with existing controls on point and nonpoint sources of pollution, to achieve the applicable water quality standard as soon as possible, but not later than 3 years after the date of the establishment of such strategy.

(2) Approval or disapproval

Not later than 120 days after the last day of the 2-year period referred to in paragraph (1), the Administrator shall approve or disapprove the control strategies submitted under paragraph (1) by any State.

(3) Administrator's action

If a State fails to submit control strategies in accordance with paragraph (1) or the Administrator does not approve the control strategies submitted by such State in accordance with paragraph (1), then, not later than 1 year after the last day of the period referred to in paragraph (2), the Administrator, in cooperation with such State and after notice and opportunity for public comment, shall implement the requirements of paragraph (1) in such State. In the implementation of such requirements, the Administrator shall, at a minimum, consider for listing under this subsection any navigable waters for which any person submits a petition to the Administrator for listing not later than 120 days after such last day.

(m) Schedule for review of guidelines

(1) Publication

Within 12 months after February 4, 1987, and biennially thereafter, the Administrator shall publish in the Federal Register a plan which shall—

(A) establish a schedule for the annual review and revision of promulgated effluent guidelines, in accordance with subsection (b) of this section;

(B) identify categories of sources discharging toxic or nonconventional pollutants for which guidelines under subsection (b)(2) of this section and section 1316 of this title have not previously been published; and

(C) establish a schedule for promulgation of effluent guidelines for categories identified in subparagraph (B), under which promulgation of such guidelines shall be no later than 4 years after February 4, 1987, for categories identified in the first published plan or 3 years after the publication of the plan for categories identified in later published plans.

(2) Public review

The Administrator shall provide for public review and comment on the plan prior to final publication.

(June 30, 1948, ch. 758, title III, § 304, as added Pub. L. 92–500, § 2, Oct. 18, 1972, 86 Stat. 850; amended Pub. L. 95–217, §§ 48–51, 62(b), Dec. 27, 1977, 91 Stat. 1587, 1588, 1598; Pub. L. 97–117, § 23, Dec. 29, 1981, 95 Stat. 1632; Pub. L. 100–4, title I, § 101(f), title III, §§ 308(a), (c), (f), 315(c), 316(e), Feb. 4, 1987, 101 Stat. 9, 38–40, 52, 61; Pub. L. 106–284, § 3(b), Oct. 10, 2000, 114 Stat. 871.)

CODIFICATION

Section 50 of Pub. L. 95–217 provided in part that, upon the enactment of subsec. (e) of this section by Pub. L. 95–217 and the concurrent redesignation of former subsecs. (e) to (j) of this section as (f) to (k), respectively, all references to former subsecs. (e) to (j) be changed to (f) to (k), respectively.

AMENDMENTS

2000—Subsec. (a)(9). Pub. L. 106–284 added par. (9).

1987—Subsec. (a)(7), (8). Pub. L. 100–4, § 308(c), added pars. (7) and (8).

Subsec. (j). Pub. L. 100–4, § 315(c), amended subsec. (j) generally. Prior to amendment, subsec. (j) read as follows: "The Administrator shall issue information biennially on methods, procedures, and processes as may be appropriate to restore and enhance the quality of the Nation's publicly owned freshwater lakes."

Subsec. (k)(1). Pub. L. 100–4, § 316(e), inserted "and nonpoint source pollution management programs approved under section 1329 of this title" before period at end.

Subsec. (k)(3). Pub. L. 100–4, §101(f), inserted "and such sums as may be necessary for fiscal years 1984 through 1990" after "1983".

Subsec. (*l*). Pub. L. 100–4, §308(a), added subsec. (*l*).

Subsec. (m). Pub. L. 100–4, §308(f), added subsec. (m).

1981—Subsec. (d)(4). Pub. L. 97–117 added par. (4).

1977—Subsec. (a)(4) to (6). Pub. L. 95–217, §48(a), added pars. (4) to (6).

Subsec. (b)(4). Pub. L. 95–217, §48(b), added par. (4).

Subsec. (d)(3). Pub. L. 95–217, §49, added par. (3).

Subsecs. (e) to (i). Pub. L. 95–217, §50, added subsec. (e) and redesignated former subsecs. (e) to (h) as (f) to (i), respectively. Former subsec. (i) redesignated (j).

Subsec. (j). Pub. L. 95–217, §§50, 62(b), redesignated former subsec. (i) as (j) and substituted "shall issue information biennially on methods" for "shall, within 270 days after October 18, 1972 (and from time to time thereafter), issue such information on methods". Former subsec. (j) redesignated (k).

Subsec. (k). Pub. L. 95–217, §§50, 51, redesignated former subsec. (j) as (k), substituted "The Administrator shall enter into agreements with the Secretary of Agriculture, the Secretary of the Army, and the Secretary of the Interior, and the heads of such other departments, agencies, and instrumentalities of the United States as the Administrator determines, to provide the maximum utilization of other Federal laws and programs" for "The Administrator shall, within six months from October 18, 1972, enter into agreements with the Secretary of Agriculture, the Secretary of the Army, and the Secretary of the Interior to provide for the maximum utilization of the appropriate programs authorized under other Federal law to be carried out by such Secretaries" in par. (1), made conforming amendments in par. (2), and in par. (3) authorized appropriations for fiscal years 1979 through 1983.

TRANSFER OF FUNCTIONS

Enforcement functions of Secretary or other official in Department of Agriculture, insofar as they involve lands and programs under jurisdiction of that Department, relating to compliance with this chapter with respect to pre-construction, construction, and initial operation of transportation system for Canadian and Alaskan natural gas were transferred to the Federal Inspector, Office of Federal Inspector for the Alaska Natural Gas Transportation System, until the first anniversary of the date of initial operation of the Alaska Natural Gas Transportation System, see Reorg. Plan No. 1 of 1979, §§102(f), 203(a), 44 F.R. 33663, 33666, 93 Stat. 1373, 1376, effective July 1, 1979, set out in the Appendix to Title 5, Government Organization and Employees. Office of Federal Inspector for the Alaska Natural Gas Transportation System abolished and functions and authority vested in Inspector transferred to Secretary of Energy by section 3012(b) of Pub. L. 102–486, set out as an Abolition of Office of Federal Inspector note under section 719e of Title 15, Commerce and Trade. Functions and authority vested in Secretary of Energy subsequently transferred to Federal Coordinator for Alaska Natural Gas Transportation Projects by section 720d(f) of Title 15.

REVIEW OF EFFLUENT GUIDELINES PROMULGATED PRIOR TO DECEMBER 27, 1977

Section 73 of Pub. L. 95–217 directed Administrator, within 90 days after Dec. 27, 1977, to review every effluent guideline promulgated prior to that date which was final or interim final (other than those applicable to industrial categories listed in table 2 of Committee Print Numbered 95–30 of Committee on Public Works and Transportation of House of Representatives) and which applied to those pollutants identified pursuant to 33 U.S.C. 1314(a)(4) and, on or before July 1, 1980, to review every guideline applicable to industrial categories listed in such table 2, authorized Administrator, upon completion of each such review to make such adjustments in any such guidelines as may be necessary to carry out 33 U.S.C. 1314(b)(4), directed Administrator to publish the results of each such review, and provided for judicial review of Administrator's actions.

CONTIGUOUS ZONE OF UNITED STATES

For extension of contiguous zone of United States, see Proc. No. 7219, set out as a note under section 1331 of Title 43, Public Lands.

§1315. State reports on water quality

(a) Omitted

(b)(1) Each State shall prepare and submit to the Administrator by April 1, 1975, and shall bring up to date by April 1, 1976, and biennially thereafter, a report which shall include—

(A) a description of the water quality of all navigable waters in such State during the preceding year, with appropriate supplemental descriptions as shall be required to take into account seasonal, tidal, and other variations, correlated with the quality of water required by the objective of this chapter (as identified by the Administrator pursuant to criteria published under section 1314(a) of this title) and the water quality described in subparagraph (B) of this paragraph;

(B) an analysis of the extent to which all navigable waters of such State provide for the protection and propagation of a balanced population of shellfish, fish, and wildlife, and allow recreational activities in and on the water;

(C) an analysis of the extent to which the elimination of the discharge of pollutants and a level of water quality which provides for the protection and propagation of a balanced population of shellfish, fish, and wildlife and allows recreational activities in and on the water, have been or will be achieved by the requirements of this chapter, together with recommendations as to additional action necessary to achieve such objectives and for what waters such additional action is necessary;

(D) an estimate of (i) the environmental impact, (ii) the economic and social costs necessary to achieve the objective of this chapter in such State, (iii) the economic and social benefits of such achievement, and (iv) an estimate of the date of such achievement; and

(E) a description of the nature and extent of nonpoint sources of pollutants, and recommendations as to the programs which must be undertaken to control each category of such sources, including an estimate of the costs of implementing such programs.

(2) The Administrator shall transmit such State reports, together with an analysis thereof, to Congress on or before October 1, 1975, and October 1, 1976, and biennially thereafter.

(June 30, 1948, ch. 758, title III, §305, as added Pub. L. 92–500, §2, Oct. 18, 1972, 86 Stat. 853; amended Pub. L. 95–217, §52, Dec. 27, 1977, 91 Stat. 1589.)

CODIFICATION

Subsec. (a) authorized the Administrator, in cooperation with the States and Federal agencies, to prepare a report describing the specific quality, during 1973, of all navigable waters and waters of the contiguous zone, including an inventory of all point sources of discharge of pollutants into these waters, and identifying those navigable waters capable of supporting fish and wildlife populations and allowing recreational activities, those which could reasonably be expected to attain this level by 1977 or 1983, and those which could attain this level sooner, and submit this report to Congress on or before Jan. 1, 1974.

AMENDMENTS

1977—Subsec. (b)(1). Pub. L. 95–217, § 52(1), substituted "April 1, 1975, and shall bring up to date by April 1, 1976, and biennially thereafter" for "January 1, 1975, and shall bring up to date each year thereafter" in provisions preceding subpar. (A).

Subsec. (b)(2). Pub. L. 95–217, § 52(2), substituted "on or before October 1, 1975, and October 1, 1976, and biennially thereafter" for "on or before October 1, 1975, and annually thereafter".

§ 1316. National standards of performance

(a) Definitions

For purposes of this section:

(1) The term "standard of performance" means a standard for the control of the discharge of pollutants which reflects the greatest degree of effluent reduction which the Administrator determines to be achievable through application of the best available demonstrated control technology, processes, operating methods, or other alternatives, including, where practicable, a standard permitting no discharge of pollutants.

(2) The term "new source" means any source, the construction of which is commenced after the publication of proposed regulations prescribing a standard of performance under this section which will be applicable to such source, if such standard is thereafter promulgated in accordance with this section.

(3) The term "source" means any building, structure, facility, or installation from which there is or may be the discharge of pollutants.

(4) The term "owner or operator" means any person who owns, leases, operates, controls, or supervises a source.

(5) The term "construction" means any placement, assembly, or installation of facilities or equipment (including contractual obligations to purchase such facilities or equipment) at the premises where such equipment will be used, including preparation work at such premises.

(b) Categories of sources; Federal standards of performance for new sources

(1)(A) The Administrator shall, within ninety days after October 18, 1972, publish (and from time to time thereafter shall revise) a list of categories of sources, which shall, at the minimum, include:

pulp and paper mills;
paperboard, builders paper and board mills;
meat product and rendering processing;
dairy product processing;
grain mills;
canned and preserved fruits and vegetables processing;
canned and preserved seafood processing;
sugar processing;
textile mills;
cement manufacturing;
feedlots;
electroplating;
organic chemicals manufacturing;
inorganic chemicals manufacturing;
plastic and synthetic materials manufacturing;
soap and detergent manufacturing;
fertilizer manufacturing;
petroleum refining;
iron and steel manufacturing;
nonferrous metals manufacturing;
phosphate manufacturing;
steam electric powerplants;
ferroalloy manufacturing;
leather tanning and finishing;
glass and asbestos manufacturing;
rubber processing; and
timber products processing.

(B) As soon as practicable, but in no case more than one year, after a category of sources is included in a list under subparagraph (A) of this paragraph, the Administrator shall propose and publish regulations establishing Federal standards of performance for new sources within such category. The Administrator shall afford interested persons an opportunity for written comment on such proposed regulations. After considering such comments, he shall promulgate, within one hundred and twenty days after publication of such proposed regulations, such standards with such adjustments as he deems appropriate. The Administrator shall, from time to time, as technology and alternatives change, revise such standards following the procedure required by this subsection for promulgation of such standards. Standards of performance, or revisions thereof, shall become effective upon promulgation. In establishing or revising Federal standards of performance for new sources under this section, the Administrator shall take into consideration the cost of achieving such effluent reduction, and any non-water quality, environmental impact and energy requirements.

(2) The Administrator may distinguish among classes, types, and sizes within categories of new sources for the purpose of establishing such standards and shall consider the type of process employed (including whether batch or continuous).

(3) The provisions of this section shall apply to any new source owned or operated by the United States.

(c) State enforcement of standards of performance

Each State may develop and submit to the Administrator a procedure under State law for applying and enforcing standards of performance for new sources located in such State. If the Administrator finds that the procedure and the law of any State require the application and enforcement of standards of performance to at least the same extent as required by this section, such State is authorized to apply and enforce such standards of performance (except with respect to new sources owned or operated by the United States).

(d) Protection from more stringent standards

Notwithstanding any other provision of this chapter, any point source the construction of which is commenced after October 18, 1972, and which is so constructed as to meet all applicable standards of performance shall not be subject to any more stringent standard of performance during a ten-year period beginning on the date of completion of such construction or during the period of depreciation or amortization of such facility for the purposes of section 167 or 169 (or both) of title 26 whichever period ends first.

(e) Illegality of operation of new sources in violation of applicable standards of performance

After the effective date of standards of performance promulgated under this section, it shall be unlawful for any owner or operator of any new source to operate such source in violation of any standard of performance applicable to such source.

(June 30, 1948, ch. 758, title III, §306, as added Pub. L. 92–500, §2, Oct. 18, 1972, 86 Stat. 854.)

DISCHARGES FROM POINT SOURCES IN UNITED STATES VIRGIN ISLANDS ATTRIBUTABLE TO MANUFACTURE OF RUM; EXEMPTION; CONDITIONS

Discharges from point sources in the United States Virgin Islands in existence on Aug. 5, 1983, attributable to the manufacture of rum not to be subject to the requirements of this section under certain conditions, see section 214(g) of Pub. L. 98–67, set out as a note under section 1311 of this title.

§ 1317. Toxic and pretreatment effluent standards

(a) Toxic pollutant list; revision; hearing; promulgation of standards; effective date; consultation

(1) On and after December 27, 1977, the list of toxic pollutants or combination of pollutants subject to this chapter shall consist of those toxic pollutants listed in table 1 of Committee Print Numbered 95–30 of the Committee on Public Works and Transportation of the House of Representatives, and the Administrator shall publish, not later than the thirtieth day after December 27, 1977, that list. From time to time thereafter, the Administrator may revise such list and the Administrator is authorized to add to or remove from such list any pollutant. The Administrator in publishing any revised list, including the addition or removal of any pollutant from such list, shall take into account toxicity of the pollutant, its persistence, degradability, the usual or potential presence of the affected organisms in any waters, the importance of the affected organisms, and the nature and extent of the effect of the toxic pollutant on such organisms. A determination of the Administrator under this paragraph shall be final except that if, on judicial review, such determination was based on arbitrary and capricious action of the Administrator, the Administrator shall make a redetermination.

(2) Each toxic pollutant listed in accordance with paragraph (1) of this subsection shall be subject to effluent limitations resulting from the application of the best available technology economically achievable for the applicable category or class of point sources established in accordance with sections 1311(b)(2)(A) and 1314(b)(2) of this title. The Administrator, in his discretion, may publish in the Federal Register a proposed effluent standard (which may include a prohibition) establishing requirements for a toxic pollutant which, if an effluent limitation is applicable to a class or category of point sources, shall be applicable to such category or class only if such standard imposes more stringent requirements. Such published effluent standard (or prohibition) shall take into account the toxicity of the pollutant, its persistence, degradability, the usual or potential presence of the affected organisms in any waters, the importance of the affected organisms and the nature and extent of the effect of the toxic pollutant on such organisms, and the extent to which effective control is being or may be achieved under other regulatory authority. The Administrator shall allow a period of not less than sixty days following publication of any such proposed effluent standard (or prohibition) for written comment by interested persons on such proposed standard. In addition, if within thirty days of publication of any such proposed effluent standard (or prohibition) any interested person so requests, the Administrator shall hold a public hearing in connection therewith. Such a public hearing shall provide an opportunity for oral and written presentations, such cross-examination as the Administrator determines is appropriate on disputed issues of material fact, and the transcription of a verbatim record which shall be available to the public. After consideration of such comments and any information and material presented at any public hearing held on such proposed standard or prohibition, the Administrator shall promulgate such standard (or prohibition) with such modification as the Administrator finds are justified. Such promulgation by the Administrator shall be made within two hundred and seventy days after publication of proposed standard (or prohibition). Such standard (or prohibition) shall be final except that if, on judicial review, such standard was not based on substantial evidence, the Administrator shall promulgate a revised standard. Effluent limitations shall be established in accordance with sections 1311(b)(2)(A) and 1314(b)(2) of this title for every toxic pollutant referred to in table 1 of Committee Print Numbered 95–30 of the Committee on Public Works and Transportation of the House of Representatives as soon as practicable after December 27, 1977, but no later than July 1, 1980. Such effluent limitations or effluent standards (or prohibitions) shall be established for every other toxic pollutant listed under paragraph (1) of this subsection as soon as practicable after it is so listed.

(3) Each such effluent standard (or prohibition) shall be reviewed and, if appropriate, revised at least every three years.

(4) Any effluent standard promulgated under this section shall be at that level which the Administrator determines provides an ample margin of safety.

(5) When proposing or promulgating any effluent standard (or prohibition) under this section, the Administrator shall designate the category or categories of sources to which the effluent standard (or prohibition) shall apply. Any disposal of dredged material may be included in such a category of sources after consultation with the Secretary of the Army.

(6) Any effluent standard (or prohibition) established pursuant to this section shall take effect on such date or dates as specified in the order promulgating such standard, but in no case, more than one year from the date of such

promulgation. If the Administrator determines that compliance within one year from the date of promulgation is technologically infeasible for a category of sources, the Administrator may establish the effective date of the effluent standard (or prohibition) for such category at the earliest date upon which compliance can be feasibly attained by sources within such category, but in no event more than three years after the date of such promulgation.

(7) Prior to publishing any regulations pursuant to this section the Administrator shall, to the maximum extent practicable within the time provided, consult with appropriate advisory committees, States, independent experts, and Federal departments and agencies.

(b) Pretreatment standards; hearing; promulgation; compliance period; revision; application to State and local laws

(1) The Administrator shall, within one hundred and eighty days after October 18, 1972, and from time to time thereafter, publish proposed regulations establishing pretreatment standards for introduction of pollutants into treatment works (as defined in section 1292 of this title) which are publicly owned for those pollutants which are determined not to be susceptible to treatment by such treatment works or which would interfere with the operation of such treatment works. Not later than ninety days after such publication, and after opportunity for public hearing, the Administrator shall promulgate such pretreatment standards. Pretreatment standards under this subsection shall specify a time for compliance not to exceed three years from the date of promulgation and shall be established to prevent the discharge of any pollutant through treatment works (as defined in section 1292 of this title) which are publicly owned, which pollutant interferes with, passes through, or otherwise is incompatible with such works. If, in the case of any toxic pollutant under subsection (a) of this section introduced by a source into a publicly owned treatment works, the treatment by such works removes all or any part of such toxic pollutant and the discharge from such works does not violate that effluent limitation or standard which would be applicable to such toxic pollutant if it were discharged by such source other than through a publicly owned treatment works, and does not prevent sludge use or disposal by such works in accordance with section 1345 of this title, then the pretreatment requirements for the sources actually discharging such toxic pollutant into such publicly owned treatment works may be revised by the owner or operator of such works to reflect the removal of such toxic pollutant by such works.

(2) The Administrator shall, from time to time, as control technology, processes, operating methods, or other alternatives change, revise such standards following the procedure established by this subsection for promulgation of such standards.

(3) When proposing or promulgating any pretreatment standard under this section, the Administrator shall designate the category or categories of sources to which such standard shall apply.

(4) Nothing in this subsection shall affect any pretreatment requirement established by any State or local law not in conflict with any pretreatment standard established under this subsection.

(c) New sources of pollutants into publicly owned treatment works

In order to insure that any source introducing pollutants into a publicly owned treatment works, which source would be a new source subject to section 1316 of this title if it were to discharge pollutants, will not cause a violation of the effluent limitations established for any such treatment works, the Administrator shall promulgate pretreatment standards for the category of such sources simultaneously with the promulgation of standards of performance under section 1316 of this title for the equivalent category of new sources. Such pretreatment standards shall prevent the discharge of any pollutant into such treatment works, which pollutant may interfere with, pass through, or otherwise be incompatible with such works.

(d) Operation in violation of standards unlawful

After the effective date of any effluent standard or prohibition or pretreatment standard promulgated under this section, it shall be unlawful for any owner or operator of any source to operate any source in violation of any such effluent standard or prohibition or pretreatment standard.

(e) Compliance date extension for innovative pretreatment systems

In the case of any existing facility that proposes to comply with the pretreatment standards of subsection (b) of this section by applying an innovative system that meets the requirements of section 1311(k) of this title, the owner or operator of the publicly owned treatment works receiving the treated effluent from such facility may extend the date for compliance with the applicable pretreatment standard established under this section for a period not to exceed 2 years—

(1) if the Administrator determines that the innovative system has the potential for industrywide application, and

(2) if the Administrator (or the State in consultation with the Administrator, in any case in which the State has a pretreatment program approved by the Administrator)—

(A) determines that the proposed extension will not cause the publicly owned treatment works to be in violation of its permit under section 1342 of this title or of section 1345 of this title or to contribute to such a violation, and

(B) concurs with the proposed extension.

(June 30, 1948, ch. 758, title III, §307, as added Pub. L. 92–500, §2, Oct. 18, 1972, 86 Stat. 856; amended Pub. L. 95–217, §§53(a), (b), 54(a), Dec. 27, 1977, 91 Stat. 1589–1591; Pub. L. 100–4, title III, §309(a), Feb. 4, 1987, 101 Stat. 41.)

AMENDMENTS

1987—Subsec. (e). Pub. L. 100–4 added subsec. (e).

1977—Subsec. (a)(1). Pub. L. 95–217, §53(a), substituted "On and after December 27, 1977, the list of toxic pollutants or combination of pollutants subject to this chapter shall consist of those toxic pollutants listed in table 1 of Committee Print Numbered 95–30 of the Committee on Public Works and Transportation of the House of Representatives, and the Administrator shall publish, not later than the thirtieth day after December 27, 1977, that list" for "The Administrator shall, within ninety days after October 18, 1972, publish (and from time to time thereafter revise) a list which includes any toxic pollutant or combination of such pollutants for which an effluent standard (which may include a prohibition of the discharge of such pollutants or combination of such pollutants) will be established under this section" and inserted provision for the revision of the list and for the finality of the Administrator's determination except when that determination is arbitrary and capricious.

Subsec. (a)(2). Pub. L. 95–217, §53(a), expanded provisions covering effluent limitations and the establishment of effluent standards (or prohibitions), introduced provisions relating to the application of the best available technology economically achievable for the applicable category or class of point sources established in accordance with sections 1311(b)(2)(A) and 1314(b)(2) of this title, inserted provision that published effluent standards take into account the extent to which effective control is being or may be achieved under other regulatory authority, inserted provision for a sixty day minimum period following publication of proposed effluent standards for written comment, substituted two hundred and seventy days for six months as the period following publication of proposed standards during which period standards (or prohibitions) must be promulgated, and inserted provision for the finality of effluent limitations (or prohibitions) except if, on judicial review, the standard was not based on substantial evidence.

Subsec. (a)(3). Pub. L. 95–217, §53(a), struck out provision for the immediate promulgation of revised effluent standards (or prohibitions) for pollutants or combinations of pollutants if, after public hearings, the Administrator found that a modification of such proposed standards (or prohibitions) was justified. See subsec. (a)(2) of this section.

Subsec. (a)(6). Pub. L. 95–217, §53(b), inserted provision that if the Administrator determines that compliance with effluent standards (or prohibitions) within one year from the date of promulgation is technologically infeasible for a category of sources, the Administrator may establish the effective date of the effluent standard (or prohibition) for that category at the earliest date upon which compliance can be feasibly attained by sources within such category, but in no event more than three years after the date of such promulgation.

Subsec. (b)(1). Pub. L. 95–217, §54(a), inserted provision that if, in the case of any toxic pollutant under subsection (a) of this section introduced by a source into a publicly owned treatment works, the treatment by the works removes all or any part of the toxic pollutant and the discharge from the works does not violate that effluent limitation or standard which would be applicable to the toxic pollutant if it were discharged by the source other than through a publicly owned treatment works, and does not prevent sludge use or disposal by the works in accordance with section 1345 of this title, then the pretreatment requirements for the sources actually discharging the toxic pollutant into the publicly owned treatment works may be revised by the owner or operator of the works to reflect the removal of the toxic pollutant by the works.

CHANGE OF NAME

Committee on Public Works and Transportation of House of Representatives treated as referring to Committee on Transportation and Infrastructure of House of Representatives by section 1(a) of Pub. L. 104–14, set out as a note preceding section 21 of Title 2, The Congress.

INCREASE IN EPA EMPLOYEES

Section 309(b) of Pub. L. 100–4 provided that: "The Administrator shall take such actions as may be necessary to increase the number of employees of the Environmental Protection Agency in order to effectively implement pretreatment requirements under section 307 of the Federal Water Pollution Control Act [33 U.S.C. 1317]."

§1318. Records and reports; inspections

(a) Maintenance; monitoring equipment; entry; access to information

Whenever required to carry out the objective of this chapter, including but not limited to (1) developing or assisting in the development of any effluent limitation, or other limitation, prohibition, or effluent standard, pretreatment standard, or standard of performance under this chapter; (2) determining whether any person is in violation of any such effluent limitation, or other limitation, prohibition or effluent standard, pretreatment standard, or standard of performance; (3) any requirement established under this section; or (4) carrying out sections 1315, 1321, 1342, 1344 (relating to State permit programs), 1345, and 1364 of this title—

(A) the Administrator shall require the owner or operator of any point source to (i) establish and maintain such records, (ii) make such reports, (iii) install, use, and maintain such monitoring equipment or methods (including where appropriate, biological monitoring methods), (iv) sample such effluents (in accordance with such methods, at such locations, at such intervals, and in such manner as the Administrator shall prescribe), and (v) provide such other information as he may reasonably require; and

(B) the Administrator or his authorized representative (including an authorized contractor acting as a representative of the Administrator), upon presentation of his credentials—

(i) shall have a right of entry to, upon, or through any premises in which an effluent source is located or in which any records required to be maintained under clause (A) of this subsection are located, and

(ii) may at reasonable times have access to and copy any records, inspect any monitoring equipment or method required under clause (A), and sample any effluents which the owner or operator of such source is required to sample under such clause.

(b) Availability to public; trade secrets exception; penalty for disclosure of confidential information

Any records, reports, or information obtained under this section (1) shall, in the case of effluent data, be related to any applicable effluent limitations, toxic, pretreatment, or new source performance standards, and (2) shall be available to the public, except that upon a showing satisfactory to the Administrator by any person that records, reports, or information, or particular part thereof (other than effluent data), to which the Administrator has access under this section, if made public would divulge methods or processes entitled to protection as trade secrets of such person, the Administrator shall consider such record, report, or information, or particular portion thereof confidential in accordance with the purposes of section 1905 of title 18. Any authorized representative of the Administrator (including an authorized contractor acting as a representative of the Administrator) who knowingly or willfully publishes, divulges, discloses, or makes known in any manner or to any extent not authorized by law any information which is required to be considered confidential under this subsection shall be fined not more than $1,000 or imprisoned not more than 1 year, or both. Nothing in this subsection shall prohibit the Administrator or an authorized representative of the Administrator (including any authorized contractor acting as a representative of the Administrator) from disclosing records, reports, or information to other officers, employees, or authorized representatives of the United States concerned with carrying out this chapter or when relevant in any proceeding under this chapter.

(c) Application of State law

Each State may develop and submit to the Administrator procedures under State law for inspection, monitoring, and entry with respect to point sources located in such State. If the Administrator finds that the procedures and the law of any State relating to inspection, monitoring, and entry are applicable to at least the same extent as those required by this section, such State is authorized to apply and enforce its procedures for inspection, monitoring, and entry with respect to point sources located in such State (except with respect to point sources owned or operated by the United States).

(d) Access by Congress

Notwithstanding any limitation contained in this section or any other provision of law, all information reported to or otherwise obtained by the Administrator (or any representative of the Administrator) under this chapter shall be made available, upon written request of any duly authorized committee of Congress, to such committee.

(June 30, 1948, ch. 758, title III, § 308, as added Pub. L. 92–500, § 2, Oct. 18, 1972, 86 Stat. 858; amended Pub. L. 95–217, § 67(c)(1), Dec. 27, 1977, 91 Stat. 1606; Pub. L. 100–4, title III, § 310, title IV, § 406(d)(1), Feb. 4, 1987, 101 Stat. 41, 73.)

AMENDMENTS

1987—Subsec. (a). Pub. L. 100–4, § 406(d)(1), substituted "1345, and 1364" for "and 1364" in cl. (4).

Subsec. (a)(B). Pub. L. 100–4, § 310(a)(2), inserted "(including an authorized contractor acting as a representative of the Administrator)" after "representative".

Subsec. (b). Pub. L. 100–4, § 310(a)(1), substituted a period and "Any authorized representative of the Administrator (including an authorized contractor acting as a representative of the Administrator) who knowingly or willfully publishes, divulges, discloses, or makes known in any manner or to any extent not authorized by law any information which is required to be considered confidential under this subsection shall be fined not more than $1,000 or imprisoned not more than 1 year, or both. Nothing in this subsection shall prohibit the Administrator or an authorized representative of the Administrator (including any authorized contractor acting as a representative of the Administrator) from disclosing records, reports, or information to other officers, employees, or authorized representatives of the United States concerned with carrying out this chapter or when relevant in any proceeding under this chapter." for ", except that such record, report, or information may be disclosed to other officers, employees, or authorized representatives of the United States concerned with carrying out this chapter or when relevant in any proceeding under this chapter."

Subsec. (d). Pub. L. 100–4, § 310(b), added subsec. (d).

1977—Subsec. (a)(4). Pub. L. 95–217 inserted "1344 (relating to State permit programs)," after "sections 1315, 1321, 1342," in provisions preceding subpar. (A).

§ 1319. Enforcement

(a) State enforcement; compliance orders

(1) Whenever, on the basis of any information available to him, the Administrator finds that any person is in violation of any condition or limitation which implements section 1311, 1312, 1316, 1317, 1318, 1328, or 1345 of this title in a permit issued by a State under an approved permit program under section 1342 or 1344 of this title he shall proceed under his authority in paragraph (3) of this subsection or he shall notify the person in alleged violation and such State of such finding. If beyond the thirtieth day after the Administrator's notification the State has not commenced appropriate enforcement action, the Administrator shall issue an order requiring such person to comply with such condition or limitation or shall bring a civil action in accordance with subsection (b) of this section.

(2) Whenever, on the basis of information available to him, the Administrator finds that violations of permit conditions or limitations as set forth in paragraph (1) of this subsection are so widespread that such violations appear to result from a failure of the State to enforce such permit conditions or limitations effectively, he shall so notify the State. If the Administrator finds such failure extends beyond the thirtieth day after such notice, he shall give public notice of such finding. During the period beginning with such public notice and ending when such State satisfies the Administrator that it will enforce such conditions and limitations (hereafter referred to in this section as the period of "federally assumed enforcement"), except where an extension has been granted under paragraph (5)(B) of this subsection, the Administrator shall enforce any permit condition or limitation with respect to any person—

(A) by issuing an order to comply with such condition or limitation, or

(B) by bringing a civil action under subsection (b) of this section.

(3) Whenever on the basis of any information available to him the Administrator finds that any person is in violation of section 1311, 1312, 1316, 1317, 1318, 1328, or 1345 of this title, or is in violation of any permit condition or limitation implementing any of such sections in a permit issued under section 1342 of this title by him or by a State or in a permit issued under section 1344 of this title by a State, he shall issue an order requiring such person to comply with such section or requirement, or he shall bring a civil action in accordance with subsection (b) of this section.

(4) A copy of any order issued under this subsection shall be sent immediately by the Administrator to the State in which the violation oc-

curs and other affected States. In any case in which an order under this subsection (or notice to a violator under paragraph (1) of this subsection) is issued to a corporation, a copy of such order (or notice) shall be served on any appropriate corporate officers. An order issued under this subsection relating to a violation of section 1318 of this title shall not take effect until the person to whom it is issued has had an opportunity to confer with the Administrator concerning the alleged violation.

(5)(A) Any order issued under this subsection shall be by personal service, shall state with reasonable specificity the nature of the violation, and shall specify a time for compliance not to exceed thirty days in the case of a violation of an interim compliance schedule or operation and maintenance requirement and not to exceed a time the Administrator determines to be reasonable in the case of a violation of a final deadline, taking into account the seriousness of the violation and any good faith efforts to comply with applicable requirements.

(B) The Administrator may, if he determines (i) that any person who is a violator of, or any person who is otherwise not in compliance with, the time requirements under this chapter or in any permit issued under this chapter, has acted in good faith, and has made a commitment (in the form of contracts or other securities) of necessary resources to achieve compliance by the earliest possible date after July 1, 1977, but not later than April 1, 1979; (ii) that any extension under this provision will not result in the imposition of any additional controls on any other point or nonpoint source; (iii) that an application for a permit under section 1342 of this title was filed for such person prior to December 31, 1974; and (iv) that the facilities necessary for compliance with such requirements are under construction, grant an extension of the date referred to in section 1311(b)(1)(A) of this title to a date which will achieve compliance at the earliest time possible but not later than April 1, 1979.

(6) Whenever, on the basis of information available to him, the Administrator finds (A) that any person is in violation of section 1311(b)(1)(A) or (C) of this title, (B) that such person cannot meet the requirements for a time extension under section 1311(i)(2) of this title, and (C) that the most expeditious and appropriate means of compliance with this chapter by such person is to discharge into a publicly owned treatment works, then, upon request of such person, the Administrator may issue an order requiring such person to comply with this chapter at the earliest date practicable, but not later than July 1, 1983, by discharging into a publicly owned treatment works if such works concur with such order. Such order shall include a schedule of compliance.

(b) Civil actions

The Administrator is authorized to commence a civil action for appropriate relief, including a permanent or temporary injunction, for any violation for which he is authorized to issue a compliance order under subsection (a) of this section. Any action under this subsection may be brought in the district court of the United States for the district in which the defendant is located or resides or is doing business, and such court shall have jurisdiction to restrain such violation and to require compliance. Notice of the commencement of such action shall be given immediately to the appropriate State.

(c) Criminal penalties

(1) Negligent violations

Any person who—

(A) negligently violates section 1311, 1312, 1316, 1317, 1318, 1321(b)(3), 1328, or 1345 of this title, or any permit condition or limitation implementing any of such sections in a permit issued under section 1342 of this title by the Administrator or by a State, or any requirement imposed in a pretreatment program approved under section 1342(a)(3) or 1342(b)(8) of this title or in a permit issued under section 1344 of this title by the Secretary of the Army or by a State; or

(B) negligently introduces into a sewer system or into a publicly owned treatment works any pollutant or hazardous substance which such person knew or reasonably should have known could cause personal injury or property damage or, other than in compliance with all applicable Federal, State, or local requirements or permits, which causes such treatment works to violate any effluent limitation or condition in any permit issued to the treatment works under section 1342 of this title by the Administrator or a State;

shall be punished by a fine of not less than $2,500 nor more than $25,000 per day of violation, or by imprisonment for not more than 1 year, or by both. If a conviction of a person is for a violation committed after a first conviction of such person under this paragraph, punishment shall be by a fine of not more than $50,000 per day of violation, or by imprisonment of not more than 2 years, or by both.

(2) Knowing violations

Any person who—

(A) knowingly violates section 1311, 1312, 1316, 1317, 1318, 1321(b)(3), 1328, or 1345 of this title, or any permit condition or limitation implementing any of such sections in a permit issued under section 1342 of this title by the Administrator or by a State, or any requirement imposed in a pretreatment program approved under section 1342(a)(3) or 1342(b)(8) of this title or in a permit issued under section 1344 of this title by the Secretary of the Army or by a State; or

(B) knowingly introduces into a sewer system or into a publicly owned treatment works any pollutant or hazardous substance which such person knew or reasonably should have known could cause personal injury or property damage or, other than in compliance with all applicable Federal, State, or local requirements or permits, which causes such treatment works to violate any effluent limitation or condition in a permit issued to the treatment works under section 1342 of this title by the Administrator or a State;

shall be punished by a fine of not less than $5,000 nor more than $50,000 per day of violation, or by imprisonment for not more than 3 years, or by both. If a conviction of a person is for a violation committed after a first conviction of such person under this paragraph, punishment shall be by a fine of not more than $100,000 per day of violation, or by imprisonment of not more than 6 years, or by both.

(3) Knowing endangerment

(A) General rule

Any person who knowingly violates section 1311, 1312, 1313, 1316, 1317, 1318, 1321(b)(3), 1328, or 1345 of this title, or any permit condition or limitation implementing any of such sections in a permit issued under section 1342 of this title by the Administrator or by a State, or in a permit issued under section 1344 of this title by the Secretary of the Army or by a State, and who knows at that time that he thereby places another person in imminent danger of death or serious bodily injury, shall, upon conviction, be subject to a fine of not more than $250,000 or imprisonment of not more than 15 years, or both. A person which is an organization shall, upon conviction of violating this subparagraph, be subject to a fine of not more than $1,000,000. If a conviction of a person is for a violation committed after a first conviction of such person under this paragraph, the maximum punishment shall be doubled with respect to both fine and imprisonment.

(B) Additional provisions

For the purpose of subparagraph (A) of this paragraph—

(i) in determining whether a defendant who is an individual knew that his conduct placed another person in imminent danger of death or serious bodily injury—

(I) the person is responsible only for actual awareness or actual belief that he possessed; and

(II) knowledge possessed by a person other than the defendant but not by the defendant himself may not be attributed to the defendant;

except that in proving the defendant's possession of actual knowledge, circumstantial evidence may be used, including evidence that the defendant took affirmative steps to shield himself from relevant information;

(ii) it is an affirmative defense to prosecution that the conduct charged was consented to by the person endangered and that the danger and conduct charged were reasonably foreseeable hazards of—

(I) an occupation, a business, or a profession; or

(II) medical treatment or medical or scientific experimentation conducted by professionally approved methods and such other person had been made aware of the risks involved prior to giving consent;

and such defense may be established under this subparagraph by a preponderance of the evidence;

(iii) the term "organization" means a legal entity, other than a government, established or organized for any purpose, and such term includes a corporation, company, association, firm, partnership, joint stock company, foundation, institution, trust, society, union, or any other association of persons; and

(iv) the term "serious bodily injury" means bodily injury which involves a substantial risk of death, unconsciousness, extreme physical pain, protracted and obvious disfigurement, or protracted loss or impairment of the function of a bodily member, organ, or mental faculty.

(4) False statements

Any person who knowingly makes any false material statement, representation, or certification in any application, record, report, plan, or other document filed or required to be maintained under this chapter or who knowingly falsifies, tampers with, or renders inaccurate any monitoring device or method required to be maintained under this chapter, shall upon conviction, be punished by a fine of not more than $10,000, or by imprisonment for not more than 2 years, or by both. If a conviction of a person is for a violation committed after a first conviction of such person under this paragraph, punishment shall be by a fine of not more than $20,000 per day of violation, or by imprisonment of not more than 4 years, or by both.

(5) Treatment of single operational upset

For purposes of this subsection, a single operational upset which leads to simultaneous violations of more than one pollutant parameter shall be treated as a single violation.

(6) Responsible corporate officer as "person"

For the purpose of this subsection, the term "person" means, in addition to the definition contained in section 1362(5) of this title, any responsible corporate officer.

(7) Hazardous substance defined

For the purpose of this subsection, the term "hazardous substance" means (A) any substance designated pursuant to section 1321(b)(2)(A) of this title, (B) any element, compound, mixture, solution, or substance designated pursuant to section 9602 of title 42, (C) any hazardous waste having the characteristics identified under or listed pursuant to section 3001 of the Solid Waste Disposal Act [42 U.S.C. 6921] (but not including any waste the regulation of which under the Solid Waste Disposal Act [42 U.S.C. 6901 et seq.] has been suspended by Act of Congress), (D) any toxic pollutant listed under section 1317(a) of this title, and (E) any imminently hazardous chemical substance or mixture with respect to which the Administrator has taken action pursuant to section 2606 of title 15.

(d) Civil penalties; factors considered in determining amount

Any person who violates section 1311, 1312, 1316, 1317, 1318, 1328, or 1345 of this title, or any permit condition or limitation implementing any of such sections in a permit issued under section 1342 of this title by the Administrator, or by a State, or in a permit issued under section 1344 of this title by a State,,[1] or any requirement imposed in a pretreatment program approved under section 1342(a)(3) or 1342(b)(8) of this title, and any person who violates any order issued by the Administrator under subsection (a) of this section, shall be subject to a civil penalty not to exceed $25,000 per day for each violation. In determining the amount of a civil penalty the court shall consider the seriousness of the violation or violations, the economic benefit (if any) resulting from the violation, any history of such violations, any good-faith efforts to comply with the applicable requirements, the economic impact of the penalty on the violator, and such other matters as justice may require. For purposes of this subsection, a single operational upset which leads to simultaneous violations of more than one pollutant parameter shall be treated as a single violation.

(e) State liability for judgments and expenses

Whenever a municipality is a party to a civil action brought by the United States under this section, the State in which such municipality is located shall be joined as a party. Such State shall be liable for payment of any judgment, or any expenses incurred as a result of complying with any judgment, entered against the municipality in such action to the extent that the laws of that State prevent the municipality from raising revenues needed to comply with such judgment.

(f) Wrongful introduction of pollutant into treatment works

Whenever, on the basis of any information available to him, the Administrator finds that an owner or operator of any source is introducing a pollutant into a treatment works in violation of subsection (d) of section 1317 of this title, the Administrator may notify the owner or operator of such treatment works and the State of such violation. If the owner or operator of the treatment works does not commence appropriate enforcement action within 30 days of the date of such notification, the Administrator may commence a civil action for appropriate relief, including but not limited to, a permanent or temporary injunction, against the owner or operator of such treatment works. In any such civil action the Administrator shall join the owner or operator of such source as a party to the action. Such action shall be brought in the district court of the United States in the district in which the treatment works is located. Such court shall have jurisdiction to restrain such violation and to require the owner or operator of the treatment works and the owner or operator of the source to take such action as may be necessary to come into compliance with this chapter. Notice of commencement of any such action shall be given to the State. Nothing in this subsection shall be construed to limit or prohibit any other authority the Administrator may have under this chapter.

(g) Administrative penalties

(1) Violations

Whenever on the basis of any information available—

(A) the Administrator finds that any person has violated section 1311, 1312, 1316, 1317, 1318, 1328, or 1345 of this title, or has violated any permit condition or limitation implementing any of such sections in a permit issued under section 1342 of this title by the Administrator or by a State, or in a permit issued under section 1344 of this title by a State, or

(B) the Secretary of the Army (hereinafter in this subsection referred to as the "Secretary") finds that any person has violated any permit condition or limitation in a permit issued under section 1344 of this title by the Secretary,

the Administrator or Secretary, as the case may be, may, after consultation with the State in which the violation occurs, assess a class I civil penalty or a class II civil penalty under this subsection.

(2) Classes of penalties

(A) Class I

The amount of a class I civil penalty under paragraph (1) may not exceed $10,000 per violation, except that the maximum amount of any class I civil penalty under this subparagraph shall not exceed $25,000. Before issuing an order assessing a civil penalty under this subparagraph, the Administrator or the Secretary, as the case may be, shall give to the person to be assessed such penalty written notice of the Administrator's or Secretary's proposal to issue such order and the opportunity to request, within 30 days of the date the notice is received by such person, a hearing on the proposed order. Such hearing shall not be subject to section 554 or 556 of title 5, but shall provide a reasonable opportunity to be heard and to present evidence.

(B) Class II

The amount of a class II civil penalty under paragraph (1) may not exceed $10,000 per day for each day during which the violation continues; except that the maximum amount of any class II civil penalty under this subparagraph shall not exceed $125,000. Except as otherwise provided in this subsection, a class II civil penalty shall be assessed and collected in the same manner, and subject to the same provisions, as in the case of civil penalties assessed and collected after notice and opportunity for a hearing on the record in accordance with section 554 of title 5. The Administrator and the Secretary may issue rules for discovery procedures for hearings under this subparagraph.

(3) Determining amount

In determining the amount of any penalty assessed under this subsection, the Administrator or the Secretary, as the case may be, shall take into account the nature, circumstances, extent and gravity of the violation, or violations, and, with respect to the violator, ability to pay, any prior history of such violations, the degree of culpability, economic benefit or savings (if any) resulting from the violation, and such other matters as justice may require. For purposes of this subsection, a sin-

[1] So in original.

gle operational upset which leads to simultaneous violations of more than one pollutant parameter shall be treated as a single violation.

(4) Rights of interested persons

(A) Public notice

Before issuing an order assessing a civil penalty under this subsection the Administrator or Secretary, as the case may be, shall provide public notice of and reasonable opportunity to comment on the proposed issuance of such order.

(B) Presentation of evidence

Any person who comments on a proposed assessment of a penalty under this subsection shall be given notice of any hearing held under this subsection and of the order assessing such penalty. In any hearing held under this subsection, such person shall have a reasonable opportunity to be heard and to present evidence.

(C) Rights of interested persons to a hearing

If no hearing is held under paragraph (2) before issuance of an order assessing a penalty under this subsection, any person who commented on the proposed assessment may petition, within 30 days after the issuance of such order, the Administrator or Secretary, as the case may be, to set aside such order and to provide a hearing on the penalty. If the evidence presented by the petitioner in support of the petition is material and was not considered in the issuance of the order, the Administrator or Secretary shall immediately set aside such order and provide a hearing in accordance with paragraph (2)(A) in the case of a class I civil penalty and paragraph (2)(B) in the case of a class II civil penalty. If the Administrator or Secretary denies a hearing under this subparagraph, the Administrator or Secretary shall provide to the petitioner, and publish in the Federal Register, notice of and the reasons for such denial.

(5) Finality of order

An order issued under this subsection shall become final 30 days after its issuance unless a petition for judicial review is filed under paragraph (8) or a hearing is requested under paragraph (4)(C). If such a hearing is denied, such order shall become final 30 days after such denial.

(6) Effect of order

(A) Limitation on actions under other sections

Action taken by the Administrator or the Secretary, as the case may be, under this subsection shall not affect or limit the Administrator's or Secretary's authority to enforce any provision of this chapter; except that any violation—

(i) with respect to which the Administrator or the Secretary has commenced and is diligently prosecuting an action under this subsection,

(ii) with respect to which a State has commenced and is diligently prosecuting an action under a State law comparable to this subsection, or

(iii) for which the Administrator, the Secretary, or the State has issued a final order not subject to further judicial review and the violator has paid a penalty assessed under this subsection, or such comparable State law, as the case may be,

shall not be the subject of a civil penalty action under subsection (d) of this section or section 1321(b) of this title or section 1365 of this title.

(B) Applicability of limitation with respect to citizen suits

The limitations contained in subparagraph (A) on civil penalty actions under section 1365 of this title shall not apply with respect to any violation for which—

(i) a civil action under section 1365(a)(1) of this title has been filed prior to commencement of an action under this subsection, or

(ii) notice of an alleged violation of section 1365(a)(1) of this title has been given in accordance with section 1365(b)(1)(A) of this title prior to commencement of an action under this subsection and an action under section 1365(a)(1) of this title with respect to such alleged violation is filed before the 120th day after the date on which such notice is given.

(7) Effect of action on compliance

No action by the Administrator or the Secretary under this subsection shall affect any person's obligation to comply with any section of this chapter or with the terms and conditions of any permit issued pursuant to section 1342 or 1344 of this title.

(8) Judicial review

Any person against whom a civil penalty is assessed under this subsection or who commented on the proposed assessment of such penalty in accordance with paragraph (4) may obtain review of such assessment—

(A) in the case of assessment of a class I civil penalty, in the United States District Court for the District of Columbia or in the district in which the violation is alleged to have occurred, or

(B) in the case of assessment of a class II civil penalty, in United States Court of Appeals for the District of Columbia Circuit or for any other circuit in which such person resides or transacts business,

by filing a notice of appeal in such court within the 30-day period beginning on the date the civil penalty order is issued and by simultaneously sending a copy of such notice by certified mail to the Administrator or the Secretary, as the case may be, and the Attorney General. The Administrator or the Secretary shall promptly file in such court a certified copy of the record on which the order was issued. Such court shall not set aside or remand such order unless there is not substantial evidence in the record, taken as a whole, to support the finding of a violation or unless the Administrator's or Secretary's assessment of the penalty constitutes an abuse of discretion and shall not impose additional civil penalties for the same violation unless the Administrator's or Secretary's assessment of the penalty constitutes an abuse of discretion.

(9) Collection

If any person fails to pay an assessment of a civil penalty—

(A) after the order making the assessment has become final, or

(B) after a court in an action brought under paragraph (8) has entered a final judgment in favor of the Administrator or the Secretary, as the case may be,

the Administrator or the Secretary shall request the Attorney General to bring a civil action in an appropriate district court to recover the amount assessed (plus interest at currently prevailing rates from the date of the final order or the date of the final judgment, as the case may be). In such an action, the validity, amount, and appropriateness of such penalty shall not be subject to review. Any person who fails to pay on a timely basis the amount of an assessment of a civil penalty as described in the first sentence of this paragraph shall be required to pay, in addition to such amount and interest, attorneys fees and costs for collection proceedings and a quarterly nonpayment penalty for each quarter during which such failure to pay persists. Such nonpayment penalty shall be in an amount equal to 20 percent of the aggregate amount of such person's penalties and nonpayment penalties which are unpaid as of the beginning of such quarter.

(10) Subpoenas

The Administrator or Secretary, as the case may be, may issue subpoenas for the attendance and testimony of witnesses and the production of relevant papers, books, or documents in connection with hearings under this subsection. In case of contumacy or refusal to obey a subpoena issued pursuant to this paragraph and served upon any person, the district court of the United States for any district in which such person is found, resides, or transacts business, upon application by the United States and after notice to such person, shall have jurisdiction to issue an order requiring such person to appear and give testimony before the administrative law judge or to appear and produce documents before the administrative law judge, or both, and any failure to obey such order of the court may be punished by such court as a contempt thereof.

(11) Protection of existing procedures

Nothing in this subsection shall change the procedures existing on the day before February 4, 1987, under other subsections of this section for issuance and enforcement of orders by the Administrator.

(June 30, 1948, ch. 758, title III, §309, as added Pub. L. 92–500, §2, Oct. 18, 1972, 86 Stat. 859; amended Pub. L. 95–217, §§54(b), 55, 56, 67(c)(2), Dec. 27, 1977, 91 Stat. 1591, 1592, 1606; Pub. L. 100–4, title III, §§312, 313(a)(1), (b)(1), (c), 314(a), Feb. 4, 1987, 101 Stat. 42, 45, 46; Pub. L. 101–380, title IV, §4301(c), Aug. 18, 1990, 104 Stat. 537.)

REFERENCES IN TEXT

The Solid Waste Disposal Act, referred to in subsec. (c)(7), is title II of Pub. L. 89–272, Oct. 20, 1965, 79 Stat. 997, as amended generally by Pub. L. 94–580, §2, Oct. 21, 1976, 90 Stat. 2795, which is classified generally to chapter 82 (§6901 et seq.) of Title 42, The Public Health and Welfare. For complete classification of this Act to the Code, see Short Title note set out under section 6901 of Title 42 and Tables.

AMENDMENTS

1990—Subsec. (c)(1)(A), (2)(A), (3)(A). Pub. L. 101–380 inserted "1321(b)(3)," after "1318,".

1987—Subsec. (c). Pub. L. 100–4, §312, amended subsec. (c) generally, revising provisions of par. (1), adding pars. (2), (3), (5), and (7), redesignating former pars. (2) and (4) as (3) and (6), respectively, and revising provisions of redesignated par. (4).

Subsec. (d). Pub. L. 100–4, §313(a)(1), inserted ", or any requirement imposed in a pretreatment program approved under section 1342(a)(3) or 1342(b)(8) of this title," after second reference to "State,".

Pub. L. 100–4, §313(b)(1), substituted "$25,000 per day for each violation" for "$10,000 per day of such violation".

Pub. L. 100–4, §313(c), inserted at end "In determining the amount of a civil penalty the court shall consider the seriousness of the violation or violations, the economic benefit (if any) resulting from the violation, any history of such violations, any good-faith efforts to comply with the applicable requirements, the economic impact of the penalty on the violator, and such other matters as justice may require. For purposes of this subsection, a single operational upset which leads to simultaneous violations of more than one pollutant parameter shall be treated as a single violation."

Subsec. (g). Pub. L. 100–4, §314(a), added subsec. (g).

1977—Subsec. (a)(1). Pub. L. 95–217, §§55(a), 67(c)(2)(A), substituted "1318, 1328, or 1345 of this title" for "or 1318 of this title" and "1342 or 1344 of this title" for "1342 of this title".

Subsec. (a)(2). Pub. L. 95–217, §56(a), substituted "except where an extension has been granted under paragraph (5)(B) of this subsection, the Administrator shall enforce any permit condition or limitation" for "the Administrator shall enforce any permit condition or limitation".

Subsec. (a)(3). Pub. L. 95–217, §§55(b), 67(c)(2)(B), substituted "1318, 1328, or 1345 of this title" for "or 1318 of this title" and inserted "or in a permit issued under section 1344 of this title by a State" after "in a permit issued under section 1342 of this title by him or by a State".

Subsec. (a)(4). Pub. L. 95–217, §56(b), struck out provision that any order issued under this subsection had to be by personal service and had to state with reasonable specificity the nature of the violation and a time for compliance, not to exceed thirty days, which the Administrator determined to be reasonable, taking into account the seriousness of the violation and any good faith efforts to comply with applicable requirements. See section subsec. (a)(5) of this section.

Subsec. (a)(5), (6). Pub. L. 95–217, §56(c), added pars. (5) and (6).

Subsec. (c)(1). Pub. L. 95–217, §67(c)(2)(C), substituted "by a State or in a permit issued under section 1344 of this title by a State, shall be punished" for "by a State, shall be punished".

Subsec. (d). Pub. L. 95–217, §§55(c), 67(c)(2)(D), substituted "1318, 1328, or 1345 of this title" for "or 1318 of this title" and inserted "or in a permit issued under section 1344 of this title by a State," after "permit issued under section 1342 of this title by the Administrator, or by a State,".

Subsec. (f). Pub. L. 95–217, §54(b), added subsec. (f).

EFFECTIVE DATE OF 1990 AMENDMENT

Amendment by Pub. L. 101–380 applicable to incidents occurring after Aug. 18, 1990, see section 1020 of Pub. L.

101–380, set out as an Effective Date note under section 2701 of this title.

SAVINGS PROVISION

Section 313(a)(2) of Pub. L. 100–4 provided that: "No State shall be required before July 1, 1988, to modify a permit program approved or submitted under section 402 of the Federal Water Pollution Control Act [33 U.S.C. 1342] as a result of the amendment made by paragraph (1) [amending this section]."

DEPOSIT OF CERTAIN PENALTIES INTO OIL SPILL LIABILITY TRUST FUND

Penalties paid pursuant to subsection (c) of this section and sections 1321 and 1501 et seq. of this title to be deposited in the Oil Spill Liability Trust Fund created under section 9509 of Title 26, Internal Revenue Code, see section 4304 of Pub. L. 101–380, set out as a note under section 9509 of Title 26.

INCREASED PENALTIES NOT REQUIRED UNDER STATE PROGRAMS

Section 313(b)(2) of Pub. L. 100–4 provided that: "The Federal Water Pollution Control Act [33 U.S.C. 1251 et seq.] shall not be construed as requiring a State to have a civil penalty for violations described in section 309(d) of such Act [33 U.S.C. 1319(d)] which has the same monetary amount as the civil penalty established by such section, as amended by paragraph (1) [amending this section]. Nothing in this paragraph shall affect the Administrator's authority to establish or adjust by regulation a minimum acceptable State civil penalty.

ACTIONS BY SURGEON GENERAL RELATING TO INTERSTATE POLLUTION

Act July 9, 1956, ch. 518, §5, 70 Stat. 507, provided that actions by the Surgeon General with respect to water pollutants under section 2(d) of act June 30, 1948, ch. 758, 62 Stat. 1155, as in effect prior to July 9, 1956, which had been completed prior to such date, would still be subject to the terms of section 2(d) of act June 30, 1948, in effect prior to the July 9, 1956 amendment, but that actions with respect to such pollutants would nevertheless subsequently be possible in accordance with the terms of act June 30, 1948, as amended by act July 9, 1956.

§1320. International pollution abatement

(a) Hearing; participation by foreign nations

Whenever the Administrator, upon receipts of reports, surveys, or studies from any duly constituted international agency, has reason to believe that pollution is occurring which endangers the health or welfare of persons in a foreign country, and the Secretary of State requests him to abate such pollution, he shall give formal notification thereof to the State water pollution control agency of the State or States in which such discharge or discharges originate and to the appropriate interstate agency, if any. He shall also promptly call such a hearing, if he believes that such pollution is occurring in sufficient quantity to warrant such action, and if such foreign country has given the United States essentially the same rights with respect to the prevention and control of pollution occurring in that country as is given that country by this subsection. The Administrator, through the Secretary of State, shall invite the foreign country which may be adversely affected by the pollution to attend and participate in the hearing, and the representative of such country shall, for the purpose of the hearing and any further proceeding resulting from such hearing, have all the rights of a State water pollution control agency. Nothing in this subsection shall be construed to modify, amend, repeal, or otherwise affect the provisions of the 1909 Boundary Waters Treaty between Canada and the United States or the Water Utilization Treaty of 1944 between Mexico and the United States (59 Stat. 1219), relative to the control and abatement of pollution in waters covered by those treaties.

(b) Functions and responsibilities of Administrator not affected

The calling of a hearing under this section shall not be construed by the courts, the Administrator, or any person as limiting, modifying, or otherwise affecting the functions and responsibilities of the Administrator under this section to establish and enforce water quality requirements under this chapter.

(c) Hearing board; composition; findings of fact; recommendations; implementation of board's decision

The Administrator shall publish in the Federal Register a notice of a public hearing before a hearing board of five or more persons appointed by the Administrator. A majority of the members of the board and the chairman who shall be designated by the Administrator shall not be officers or employees of Federal, State, or local governments. On the basis of the evidence presented at such hearing, the board shall within sixty days after completion of the hearing make findings of fact as to whether or not such pollution is occurring and shall thereupon by decision, incorporating its findings therein, make such recommendations to abate the pollution as may be appropriate and shall transmit such decision and the record of the hearings to the Administrator. All such decisions shall be public. Upon receipt of such decision, the Administrator shall promptly implement the board's decision in accordance with the provisions of this chapter.

(d) Report by alleged polluter

In connection with any hearing called under this subsection, the board is authorized to require any person whose alleged activities result in discharges causing or contributing to pollution to file with it in such forms as it may prescribe, a report based on existing data, furnishing such information as may reasonably be required as to the character, kind, and quantity of such discharges and the use of facilities or other means to prevent or reduce such discharges by the person filing such a report. Such report shall be made under oath or otherwise, as the board may prescribe, and shall be filed with the board within such reasonable period as it may prescribe, unless additional time is granted by it. Upon a showing satisfactory to the board by the person filing such report that such report or portion thereof (other than effluent data), to which the Administrator has access under this section, if made public would divulge trade secrets or secret processes of such person, the board shall consider such report or portion thereof confidential for the purposes of section 1905 of title 18. If any person required to file any report under this paragraph shall fail to do so within the time fixed by the board for filing the same, and such failure shall continue for thirty days after notice of such default, such person shall forfeit to the United States the sum of $1,000 for each and every day of the continuance of such failure, which forfeiture shall be payable into the Treasury of the United States, and shall be recoverable in a civil suit in the name of the United States in the district court of the United States where such person has his principal office or in any district in which he does business. The Administrator may upon application therefor remit or mitigate any forfeiture provided for under this subsection.

(e) Compensation of board members

Board members, other than officers or employees of Federal, State, or local governments, shall be for each day (including travel-time) during which they are performing board business, entitled to receive compensation at a rate fixed by the Administrator but not in excess of the maximum rate of pay for grade GS–18, as provided in the General Schedule under section 5332 of title 5, and shall, notwithstanding the limitations of sections 5703 and 5704 of title 5, be fully reimbursed for travel, subsistence and related expenses.

(f) Enforcement proceedings

When any such recommendation adopted by the Administrator involves the institution of enforcement proceedings against any person to obtain the abatement of pollution subject to such recommendation, the Administrator shall institute such proceedings if he believes that the evidence warrants such proceedings. The district court of the United States shall consider and determine de novo all relevant issues, but shall receive in evidence the record of the proceedings before the conference or hearing board. The court shall have jurisdiction to enter such judgment and orders enforcing such judgment as it deems appropriate or to remand such proceedings to the Administrator for such further action as it may direct.

(June 30, 1948, ch. 758, title III, §310, as added Pub. L. 92–500, §2, Oct. 18, 1972, 86 Stat. 860.)

REFERENCES IN OTHER LAWS TO GS–16, 17, OR 18 PAY RATES

References in laws to the rates of pay for GS–16, 17, or 18, or to maximum rates of pay under the General Schedule, to be considered references to rates payable under specified sections of Title 5, Government Organization and Employees, see section 529 [title I, §101(c)(1)] of Pub. L. 101–509, set out in a note under section 5376 of Title 5.

§1321. Oil and hazardous substance liability

(a) Definitions

For the purpose of this section, the term—

(1) "oil" means oil of any kind or in any form, including, but not limited to, petroleum, fuel oil, sludge, oil refuse, and oil mixed with wastes other than dredged spoil;

(2) "discharge" includes, but is not limited to, any spilling, leaking, pumping, pouring, emitting, emptying or dumping, but excludes (A) discharges in compliance with a permit under section 1342 of this title, (B) discharges resulting from circumstances identified and reviewed and made a part of the public record with respect to a permit issued or modified under section 1342 of this title, and subject to a condition in such permit,,[1] (C) continuous or anticipated intermittent discharges from a point source, identified in a permit or permit application under section 1342 of this title, which are caused by events occurring within the scope of relevant operating or treatment systems, and (D) discharges incidental to mechanical removal authorized by the President under subsection (c) of this section;

(3) "vessel" means every description of watercraft or other artificial contrivance used, or capable of being used, as a means of transportation on water other than a public vessel;

(4) "public vessel" means a vessel owned or bareboat-chartered and operated by the United States, or by a State or political subdivision thereof, or by a foreign nation, except when such vessel is engaged in commerce;

(5) "United States" means the States, the District of Columbia, the Commonwealth of Puerto Rico, the Commonwealth of the Northern Mariana Islands, Guam, American Samoa, the Virgin Islands, and the Trust Territory of the Pacific Islands;

(6) "owner or operator" means (A) in the case of a vessel, any person owning, operating, or chartering by demise, such vessel, and (B) in the case of an onshore facility, and an offshore facility, any person owning or operating such onshore facility or offshore facility, and (C) in the case of any abandoned offshore facility, the person who owned or operated such facility immediately prior to such abandonment;

(7) "person" includes an individual, firm, corporation, association, and a partnership;

(8) "remove" or "removal" refers to containment and removal of the oil or hazardous substances from the water and shorelines or the taking of such other actions as may be necessary to prevent, minimize, or mitigate damage to the public health or welfare, including, but not limited to, fish, shellfish, wildlife, and public and private property, shorelines, and beaches;

(9) "contiguous zone" means the entire zone established or to be established by the United States under article 24 of the Convention on the Territorial Sea and the Contiguous Zone;

(10) "onshore facility" means any facility (including, but not limited to, motor vehicles and rolling stock) of any kind located in, on, or under, any land within the United States other than submerged land;

(11) "offshore facility" means any facility of any kind located in, on, or under, any of the navigable waters of the United States, and any facility of any kind which is subject to the jurisdiction of the United States and is located in, on, or under any other waters, other than a vessel or a public vessel;

(12) "act of God" means an act occasioned by an unanticipated grave natural disaster;

(13) "barrel" means 42 United States gallons at 60 degrees Fahrenheit;

[1] So in original.

(14) "hazardous substance" means any substance designated pursuant to subsection (b)(2) of this section;

(15) "inland oil barge" means a non-self-propelled vessel carrying oil in bulk as cargo and certificated to operate only in the inland waters of the United States, while operating in such waters;

(16) "inland waters of the United States" means those waters of the United States lying inside the baseline from which the territorial sea is measured and those waters outside such baseline which are a part of the Gulf Intracoastal Waterway;

(17) "otherwise subject to the jurisdiction of the United States" means subject to the jurisdiction of the United States by virtue of United States citizenship, United States vessel documentation or numbering, or as provided for by international agreement to which the United States is a party;

(18) "Area Committee" means an Area Committee established under subsection (j) of this section;

(19) "Area Contingency Plan" means an Area Contingency Plan prepared under subsection (j) of this section;

(20) "Coast Guard District Response Group" means a Coast Guard District Response Group established under subsection (j) of this section;

(21) "Federal On-Scene Coordinator" means a Federal On-Scene Coordinator designated in the National Contingency Plan;

(22) "National Contingency Plan" means the National Contingency Plan prepared and published under subsection (d) of this section;

(23) "National Response Unit" means the National Response Unit established under subsection (j) of this section;

(24) "worst case discharge" means—

(A) in the case of a vessel, a discharge in adverse weather conditions of its entire cargo; and

(B) in the case of an offshore facility or onshore facility, the largest foreseeable discharge in adverse weather conditions;

(25) "removal costs" means—

(A) the costs of removal of oil or a hazardous substance that are incurred after it is discharged; and

(B) in any case in which there is a substantial threat of a discharge of oil or a hazardous substance, the costs to prevent, minimize, or mitigate that threat; and

(26) "nontank vessel" means a self-propelled vessel that—

(A) is at least 400 gross tons as measured under section 14302 of title 46 or, for vessels not measured under that section, as measured under section 14502 of that title;

(B) is not a tank vessel;

(C) carries oil of any kind as fuel for main propulsion; and

(D) operates on the navigable waters of the United States, as defined in section 2101(17a) of that title.

(b) Congressional declaration of policy against discharges of oil or hazardous substances; designation of hazardous substances; study of higher standard of care incentives and report to Congress; liability; penalties; civil actions: penalty limitations, separate offenses, jurisdiction, mitigation of damages and costs, recovery of removal costs, alternative remedies, and withholding clearance of vessels

(1) The Congress hereby declares that it is the policy of the United States that there should be no discharges of oil or hazardous substances into or upon the navigable waters of the United States, adjoining shorelines, or into or upon the waters of the contiguous zone, or in connection with activities under the Outer Continental Shelf Lands Act [43 U.S.C. 1331 et seq.] or the Deepwater Port Act of 1974 [33 U.S.C. 1501 et seq.], or which may affect natural resources belonging to, appertaining to, or under the exclusive management authority of the United States (including resources under the Magnuson-Stevens Fishery Conservation and Management Act [16 U.S.C. 1801 et seq.]).

(2)(A) The Administrator shall develop, promulgate, and revise as may be appropriate, regulations designating as hazardous substances, other than oil as defined in this section, such elements and compounds which, when discharged in any quantity into or upon the navigable waters of the United States or adjoining shorelines or the waters of the contiguous zone or in connection with activities under the Outer Continental Shelf Lands Act [43 U.S.C. 1331 et seq.] or the Deepwater Port Act of 1974 [33 U.S.C. 1501 et seq.], or which may affect natural resources belonging to, appertaining to, or under the exclusive management authority of the United States (including resources under the Magnuson-Stevens Fishery Conservation and Management Act [16 U.S.C. 1801 et seq.]), present an imminent and substantial danger to the public health or welfare, including, but not limited to, fish, shellfish, wildlife, shorelines, and beaches.

(B) The Administrator shall within 18 months after the date of enactment of this paragraph, conduct a study and report to the Congress on methods, mechanisms, and procedures to create incentives to achieve a higher standard of care in all aspects of the management and movement of hazardous substances on the part of owners, operators, or persons in charge of onshore facilities, offshore facilities, or vessels. The Administrator shall include in such study (1) limits of liability, (2) liability for third party damages, (3) penalties and fees, (4) spill prevention plans, (5) current practices in the insurance and banking industries, and (6) whether the penalty enacted in subclause (bb) of clause (iii) of subparagraph (B) of subsection (b)(2) of section 311 of Public Law 92–500 should be enacted.

(3) The discharge of oil or hazardous substances (i) into or upon the navigable waters of the United States, adjoining shorelines, or into or upon the waters of the contiguous zone, or (ii) in connection with activities under the Outer Continental Shelf Lands Act [43 U.S.C. 1331 et seq.] or the Deepwater Port Act of 1974 [33 U.S.C. 1501 et seq.], or which may affect natural resources belonging to, appertaining to, or under

the exclusive management authority of the United States (including resources under the Magnuson-Stevens Fishery Conservation and Management Act [16 U.S.C. 1801 et seq.]), in such quantities as may be harmful as determined by the President under paragraph (4) of this subsection, is prohibited, except (A) in the case of such discharges into the waters of the contiguous zone or which may affect natural resources belonging to, appertaining to, or under the exclusive management authority of the United States (including resources under the Magnuson-Stevens Fishery Conservation and Management Act), where permitted under the Protocol of 1978 Relating to the International Convention for the Prevention of Pollution from Ships, 1973, and (B) where permitted in quantities and at times and locations or under such circumstances or conditions as the President may, by regulation, determine not to be harmful. Any regulations issued under this subsection shall be consistent with maritime safety and with marine and navigation laws and regulations and applicable water quality standards.

(4) The President shall by regulation determine for the purposes of this section those quantities of oil and any hazardous substances the discharge of which may be harmful to the public health or welfare or the environment of the United States, including but not limited to fish, shellfish, wildlife, and public and private property, shorelines, and beaches.

(5) Any person in charge of a vessel or of an onshore facility or an offshore facility shall, as soon as he has knowledge of any discharge of oil or a hazardous substance from such vessel or facility in violation of paragraph (3) of this subsection, immediately notify the appropriate agency of the United States Government of such discharge. The Federal agency shall immediately notify the appropriate State agency of any State which is, or may reasonably be expected to be, affected by the discharge of oil or a hazardous substance. Any such person (A) in charge of a vessel from which oil or a hazardous substance is discharged in violation of paragraph (3)(i) of this subsection, or (B) in charge of a vessel from which oil or a hazardous substance is discharged in violation of paragraph (3)(ii) of this subsection and who is otherwise subject to the jurisdiction of the United States at the time of the discharge, or (C) in charge of an onshore facility or an offshore facility, who fails to notify immediately such agency of such discharge shall, upon conviction, be fined in accordance with title 18, or imprisoned for not more than 5 years, or both. Notification received pursuant to this paragraph shall not be used against any such natural person in any criminal case, except a prosecution for perjury or for giving a false statement.

(6) ADMINISTRATIVE PENALTIES.—

(A) VIOLATIONS.—Any owner, operator, or person in charge of any vessel, onshore facility, or offshore facility—

(i) from which oil or a hazardous substance is discharged in violation of paragraph (3), or

(ii) who fails or refuses to comply with any regulation issued under subsection (j) of this section to which that owner, operator, or person in charge is subject,

may be assessed a class I or class II civil penalty by the Secretary of the department in which the Coast Guard is operating or the Administrator.

(B) CLASSES OF PENALTIES.—

(i) CLASS I.—The amount of a class I civil penalty under subparagraph (A) may not exceed $10,000 per violation, except that the maximum amount of any class I civil penalty under this subparagraph shall not exceed $25,000. Before assessing a civil penalty under this clause, the Administrator or Secretary, as the case may be, shall give to the person to be assessed such penalty written notice of the Administrator's or Secretary's proposal to assess the penalty and the opportunity to request, within 30 days of the date the notice is received by such person, a hearing on the proposed penalty. Such hearing shall not be subject to section 554 or 556 of title 5, but shall provide a reasonable opportunity to be heard and to present evidence.

(ii) CLASS II.—The amount of a class II civil penalty under subparagraph (A) may not exceed $10,000 per day for each day during which the violation continues; except that the maximum amount of any class II civil penalty under this subparagraph shall not exceed $125,000. Except as otherwise provided in this subsection, a class II civil penalty shall be assessed and collected in the same manner, and subject to the same provisions, as in the case of civil penalties assessed and collected after notice and opportunity for a hearing on the record in accordance with section 554 of title 5. The Administrator and Secretary may issue rules for discovery procedures for hearings under this paragraph.

(C) RIGHTS OF INTERESTED PERSONS.—

(i) PUBLIC NOTICE.—Before issuing an order assessing a class II civil penalty under this paragraph the Administrator or Secretary, as the case may be, shall provide public notice of and reasonable opportunity to comment on the proposed issuance of such order.

(ii) PRESENTATION OF EVIDENCE.—Any person who comments on a proposed assessment of a class II civil penalty under this paragraph shall be given notice of any hearing held under this paragraph and of the order assessing such penalty. In any hearing held under this paragraph, such person shall have a reasonable opportunity to be heard and to present evidence.

(iii) RIGHTS OF INTERESTED PERSONS TO A HEARING.—If no hearing is held under subparagraph (B) before issuance of an order assessing a class II civil penalty under this paragraph, any person who commented on the proposed assessment may petition, within 30 days after the issuance of such order, the Administrator or Secretary, as the case may be, to set aside such order and to provide a hearing on the penalty. If the evidence presented by the petitioner in support of the petition is material and was not considered in the issuance of the order, the Administrator or Secretary shall immediately set aside such order and provide a hearing in accordance with subparagraph (B)(ii). If the

Administrator or Secretary denies a hearing under this clause, the Administrator or Secretary shall provide to the petitioner, and publish in the Federal Register, notice of and the reasons for such denial.

(D) FINALITY OF ORDER.—An order assessing a class II civil penalty under this paragraph shall become final 30 days after its issuance unless a petition for judicial review is filed under subparagraph (G) or a hearing is requested under subparagraph (C)(iii). If such a hearing is denied, such order shall become final 30 days after such denial.

(E) EFFECT OF ORDER.—Action taken by the Administrator or Secretary, as the case may be, under this paragraph shall not affect or limit the Administrator's or Secretary's authority to enforce any provision of this chapter; except that any violation—

(i) with respect to which the Administrator or Secretary has commenced and is diligently prosecuting an action to assess a class II civil penalty under this paragraph, or

(ii) for which the Administrator or Secretary has issued a final order assessing a class II civil penalty not subject to further judicial review and the violator has paid a penalty assessed under this paragraph,

shall not be the subject of a civil penalty action under section 1319(d), 1319(g), or 1365 of this title or under paragraph (7).

(F) EFFECT OF ACTION ON COMPLIANCE.—No action by the Administrator or Secretary under this paragraph shall affect any person's obligation to comply with any section of this chapter.

(G) JUDICIAL REVIEW.—Any person against whom a civil penalty is assessed under this paragraph or who commented on the proposed assessment of such penalty in accordance with subparagraph (C) may obtain review of such assessment—

(i) in the case of assessment of a class I civil penalty, in the United States District Court for the District of Columbia or in the district in which the violation is alleged to have occurred, or

(ii) in the case of assessment of a class II civil penalty, in United States Court of Appeals for the District of Columbia Circuit or for any other circuit in which such person resides or transacts business,

by filing a notice of appeal in such court within the 30-day period beginning on the date the civil penalty order is issued and by simultaneously sending a copy of such notice by certified mail to the Administrator or Secretary, as the case may be, and the Attorney General. The Administrator or Secretary shall promptly file in such court a certified copy of the record on which the order was issued. Such court shall not set aside or remand such order unless there is not substantial evidence in the record, taken as a whole, to support the finding of a violation or unless the Administrator's or Secretary's assessment of the penalty constitutes an abuse of discretion and shall not impose additional civil penalties for the same violation unless the Administrator's or Secretary's assessment of the penalty constitutes an abuse of discretion.

(H) COLLECTION.—If any person fails to pay an assessment of a civil penalty—

(i) after the assessment has become final, or

(ii) after a court in an action brought under subparagraph (G) has entered a final judgment in favor of the Administrator or Secretary, as the case may be,

the Administrator or Secretary shall request the Attorney General to bring a civil action in an appropriate district court to recover the amount assessed (plus interest at currently prevailing rates from the date of the final order or the date of the final judgment, as the case may be). In such an action, the validity, amount, and appropriateness of such penalty shall not be subject to review. Any person who fails to pay on a timely basis the amount of an assessment of a civil penalty as described in the first sentence of this subparagraph shall be required to pay, in addition to such amount and interest, attorneys fees and costs for collection proceedings and a quarterly nonpayment penalty for each quarter during which such failure to pay persists. Such nonpayment penalty shall be in an amount equal to 20 percent of the aggregate amount of such person's penalties and nonpayment penalties which are unpaid as of the beginning of such quarter.

(I) SUBPOENAS.—The Administrator or Secretary, as the case may be, may issue subpoenas for the attendance and testimony of witnesses and the production of relevant papers, books, or documents in connection with hearings under this paragraph. In case of contumacy or refusal to obey a subpoena issued pursuant to this subparagraph and served upon any person, the district court of the United States for any district in which such person is found, resides, or transacts business, upon application by the United States and after notice to such person, shall have jurisdiction to issue an order requiring such person to appear and give testimony before the administrative law judge or to appear and produce documents before the administrative law judge, or both, and any failure to obey such order of the court may be punished by such court as a contempt thereof.

(7) CIVIL PENALTY ACTION.—

(A) DISCHARGE, GENERALLY.—Any person who is the owner, operator, or person in charge of any vessel, onshore facility, or offshore facility from which oil or a hazardous substance is discharged in violation of paragraph (3), shall be subject to a civil penalty in an amount up to $25,000 per day of violation or an amount up to $1,000 per barrel of oil or unit of reportable quantity of hazardous substances discharged.

(B) FAILURE TO REMOVE OR COMPLY.—Any person described in subparagraph (A) who, without sufficient cause—

(i) fails to properly carry out removal of the discharge under an order of the President pursuant to subsection (c) of this section; or

(ii) fails to comply with an order pursuant to subsection (e)(1)(B) of this section;

shall be subject to a civil penalty in an amount up to $25,000 per day of violation or an amount up to 3 times the costs incurred by the Oil Spill Liability Trust Fund as a result of such failure.

(C) FAILURE TO COMPLY WITH REGULATION.—Any person who fails or refuses to comply with any regulation issued under subsection (j) of this section shall be subject to a civil penalty in an amount up to $25,000 per day of violation.

(D) GROSS NEGLIGENCE.—In any case in which a violation of paragraph (3) was the result of gross negligence or willful misconduct of a person described in subparagraph (A), the person shall be subject to a civil penalty of not less than $100,000, and not more than $3,000 per barrel of oil or unit of reportable quantity of hazardous substance discharged.

(E) JURISDICTION.—An action to impose a civil penalty under this paragraph may be brought in the district court of the United States for the district in which the defendant is located, resides, or is doing business, and such court shall have jurisdiction to assess such penalty.

(F) LIMITATION.—A person is not liable for a civil penalty under this paragraph for a discharge if the person has been assessed a civil penalty under paragraph (6) for the discharge.

(8) DETERMINATION OF AMOUNT.—In determining the amount of a civil penalty under paragraphs (6) and (7), the Administrator, Secretary, or the court, as the case may be, shall consider the seriousness of the violation or violations, the economic benefit to the violator, if any, resulting from the violation, the degree of culpability involved, any other penalty for the same incident, any history of prior violations, the nature, extent, and degree of success of any efforts of the violator to minimize or mitigate the effects of the discharge, the economic impact of the penalty on the violator, and any other matters as justice may require.

(9) MITIGATION OF DAMAGE.—In addition to establishing a penalty for the discharge of oil or a hazardous substance, the Administrator or the Secretary of the department in which the Coast Guard is operating may act to mitigate the damage to the public health or welfare caused by such discharge. The cost of such mitigation shall be deemed a cost incurred under subsection (c) of this section for the removal of such substance by the United States Government.

(10) RECOVERY OF REMOVAL COSTS.—Any costs of removal incurred in connection with a discharge excluded by subsection (a)(2)(C) of this section shall be recoverable from the owner or operator of the source of the discharge in an action brought under section 1319(b) of this title.

(11) LIMITATION.—Civil penalties shall not be assessed under both this section and section 1319 of this title for the same discharge.

(12) WITHHOLDING CLEARANCE.—If any owner, operator, or person in charge of a vessel is liable for a civil penalty under this subsection, or if reasonable cause exists to believe that the owner, operator, or person in charge may be subject to a civil penalty under this subsection, the Secretary of the Treasury, upon the request of the Secretary of the department in which the Coast Guard is operating or the Administrator, shall with respect to such vessel refuse or revoke—

(A) the clearance required by section 60105 of title 46;

(B) a permit to proceed under section 4367 of the Revised Statutes of the United States (46 U.S.C. App. 313);[2] and

(C) a permit to depart required under section 1443[2] of title 19;

as applicable. Clearance or a permit refused or revoked under this paragraph may be granted upon the filing of a bond or other surety satisfactory to the Secretary of the department in which the Coast Guard is operating or the Administrator.

(c) Federal removal authority

(1) General removal requirement

(A) The President shall, in accordance with the National Contingency Plan and any appropriate Area Contingency Plan, ensure effective and immediate removal of a discharge, and mitigation or prevention of a substantial threat of a discharge, of oil or a hazardous substance—

(i) into or on the navigable waters;

(ii) on the adjoining shorelines to the navigable waters;

(iii) into or on the waters of the exclusive economic zone; or

(iv) that may affect natural resources belonging to, appertaining to, or under the exclusive management authority of the United States.

(B) In carrying out this paragraph, the President may—

(i) remove or arrange for the removal of a discharge, and mitigate or prevent a substantial threat of a discharge, at any time;

(ii) direct or monitor all Federal, State, and private actions to remove a discharge; and

(iii) remove and, if necessary, destroy a vessel discharging, or threatening to discharge, by whatever means are available.

(2) Discharge posing substantial threat to public health or welfare

(A) If a discharge, or a substantial threat of a discharge, of oil or a hazardous substance from a vessel, offshore facility, or onshore facility is of such a size or character as to be a substantial threat to the public health or welfare of the United States (including but not limited to fish, shellfish, wildlife, other natural resources, and the public and private beaches and shorelines of the United States), the President shall direct all Federal, State, and private actions to remove the discharge or to mitigate or prevent the threat of the discharge.

(B) In carrying out this paragraph, the President may, without regard to any other provision of law governing contracting procedures or employment of personnel by the Federal Government—

(i) remove or arrange for the removal of the discharge, or mitigate or prevent the substantial threat of the discharge; and

[2] See References in Text note below.

(ii) remove and, if necessary, destroy a vessel discharging, or threatening to discharge, by whatever means are available.

(3) Actions in accordance with National Contingency Plan

(A) Each Federal agency, State, owner or operator, or other person participating in efforts under this subsection shall act in accordance with the National Contingency Plan or as directed by the President.

(B) An owner or operator participating in efforts under this subsection shall act in accordance with the National Contingency Plan and the applicable response plan required under subsection (j) of this section, or as directed by the President, except that the owner or operator may deviate from the applicable response plan if the President or the Federal On-Scene Coordinator determines that deviation from the response plan would provide for a more expeditious or effective response to the spill or mitigation of its environmental effects.

(4) Exemption from liability

(A) A person is not liable for removal costs or damages which result from actions taken or omitted to be taken in the course of rendering care, assistance, or advice consistent with the National Contingency Plan or as otherwise directed by the President relating to a discharge or a substantial threat of a discharge of oil or a hazardous substance.

(B) Subparagraph (A) does not apply—

(i) to a responsible party;

(ii) to a response under the Comprehensive Environmental Response, Compensation, and Liability Act of 1980 (42 U.S.C. 9601 et seq.);

(iii) with respect to personal injury or wrongful death; or

(iv) if the person is grossly negligent or engages in willful misconduct.

(C) A responsible party is liable for any removal costs and damages that another person is relieved of under subparagraph (A).

(5) Obligation and liability of owner or operator not affected

Nothing in this subsection affects—

(A) the obligation of an owner or operator to respond immediately to a discharge, or the threat of a discharge, of oil; or

(B) the liability of a responsible party under the Oil Pollution Act of 1990 [33 U.S.C. 2701 et seq.].

(6) "Responsible party" defined

For purposes of this subsection, the term "responsible party" has the meaning given that term under section 1001 of the Oil Pollution Act of 1990 [33 U.S.C. 2701].

(d) National Contingency Plan

(1) Preparation by President

The President shall prepare and publish a National Contingency Plan for removal of oil and hazardous substances pursuant to this section.

(2) Contents

The National Contingency Plan shall provide for efficient, coordinated, and effective action to minimize damage from oil and hazardous substance discharges, including containment, dispersal, and removal of oil and hazardous substances, and shall include, but not be limited to, the following:

(A) Assignment of duties and responsibilities among Federal departments and agencies in coordination with State and local agencies and port authorities including, but not limited to, water pollution control and conservation and trusteeship of natural resources (including conservation of fish and wildlife).

(B) Identification, procurement, maintenance, and storage of equipment and supplies.

(C) Establishment or designation of Coast Guard strike teams, consisting of—

(i) personnel who shall be trained, prepared, and available to provide necessary services to carry out the National Contingency Plan;

(ii) adequate oil and hazardous substance pollution control equipment and material; and

(iii) a detailed oil and hazardous substance pollution and prevention plan, including measures to protect fisheries and wildlife.

(D) A system of surveillance and notice designed to safeguard against as well as ensure earliest possible notice of discharges of oil and hazardous substances and imminent threats of such discharges to the appropriate State and Federal agencies.

(E) Establishment of a national center to provide coordination and direction for operations in carrying out the Plan.

(F) Procedures and techniques to be employed in identifying, containing, dispersing, and removing oil and hazardous substances.

(G) A schedule, prepared in cooperation with the States, identifying—

(i) dispersants, other chemicals, and other spill mitigating devices and substances, if any, that may be used in carrying out the Plan,

(ii) the waters in which such dispersants, other chemicals, and other spill mitigating devices and substances may be used, and

(iii) the quantities of such dispersant, other chemicals, or other spill mitigating device or substance which can be used safely in such waters,

which schedule shall provide in the case of any dispersant, chemical, spill mitigating device or substance, or waters not specifically identified in such schedule that the President, or his delegate, may, on a case-by-case basis, identify the dispersants, other chemicals, and other spill mitigating devices and substances which may be used, the waters in which they may be used, and the quantities which can be used safely in such waters.

(H) A system whereby the State or States affected by a discharge of oil or hazardous substance may act where necessary to remove such discharge and such State or States may be reimbursed in accordance with the Oil Pollution Act of 1990 [33 U.S.C. 2701 et seq.], in the case of any discharge of oil from a vessel or facility, for the reasonable costs incurred for that removal, from the Oil Spill Liability Trust Fund.

(I) Establishment of criteria and procedures to ensure immediate and effective Federal identification of, and response to, a discharge, or the threat of a discharge, that results in a substantial threat to the public health or welfare of the United States, as required under subsection (c)(2) of this section.

(J) Establishment of procedures and standards for removing a worst case discharge of oil, and for mitigating or preventing a substantial threat of such a discharge.

(K) Designation of the Federal official who shall be the Federal On-Scene Coordinator for each area for which an Area Contingency Plan is required to be prepared under subsection (j) of this section.

(L) Establishment of procedures for the coordination of activities of—

(i) Coast Guard strike teams established under subparagraph (C);

(ii) Federal On-Scene Coordinators designated under subparagraph (K);

(iii) District Response Groups established under subsection (j) of this section; and

(iv) Area Committees established under subsection (j) of this section.

(M) A fish and wildlife response plan, developed in consultation with the United States Fish and Wildlife Service, the National Oceanic and Atmospheric Administration, and other interested parties (including State fish and wildlife conservation officials), for the immediate and effective protection, rescue, and rehabilitation of, and the minimization of risk of damage to, fish and wildlife resources and their habitat that are harmed or that may be jeopardized by a discharge.

(3) Revisions and amendments

The President may, from time to time, as the President deems advisable, revise or otherwise amend the National Contingency Plan.

(4) Actions in accordance with National Contingency Plan

After publication of the National Contingency Plan, the removal of oil and hazardous substances and actions to minimize damage from oil and hazardous substance discharges shall, to the greatest extent possible, be in accordance with the National Contingency Plan.

(e) Civil enforcement

(1) Orders protecting public health

In addition to any action taken by a State or local government, when the President determines that there may be an imminent and substantial threat to the public health or welfare of the United States, including fish, shellfish, and wildlife, public and private property, shorelines, beaches, habitat, and other living and nonliving natural resources under the jurisdiction or control of the United States, because of an actual or threatened discharge of oil or a hazardous substance from a vessel or facility in violation of subsection (b) of this section, the President may—

(A) require the Attorney General to secure any relief from any person, including the owner or operator of the vessel or facility, as may be necessary to abate such endangerment; or

(B) after notice to the affected State, take any other action under this section, including issuing administrative orders, that may be necessary to protect the public health and welfare.

(2) Jurisdiction of district courts

The district courts of the United States shall have jurisdiction to grant any relief under this subsection that the public interest and the equities of the case may require.

(f) Liability for actual costs of removal

(1) Except where an owner or operator can prove that a discharge was caused solely by (A) an act of God, (B) an act of war, (C) negligence on the part of the United States Government, or (D) an act or omission of a third party without regard to whether any such act or omission was or was not negligent, or any combination of the foregoing clauses, such owner or operator of any vessel from which oil or a hazardous substance is discharged in violation of subsection (b)(3) of this section shall, notwithstanding any other provision of law, be liable to the United States Government for the actual costs incurred under subsection (c) of this section for the removal of such oil or substance by the United States Government in an amount not to exceed, in the case of an inland oil barge $125 per gross ton of such barge, or $125,000, whichever is greater, and in the case of any other vessel, $150 per gross ton of such vessel (or, for a vessel carrying oil or hazardous substances as cargo, $250,000), whichever is greater, except that where the United States can show that such discharge was the result of willful negligence or willful misconduct within the privity and knowledge of the owner, such owner or operator shall be liable to the United States Government for the full amount of such costs. Such costs shall constitute a maritime lien on such vessel which may be recovered in an action in rem in the district court of the United States for any district within which any vessel may be found. The United States may also bring an action against the owner or operator of such vessel in any court of competent jurisdiction to recover such costs.

(2) Except where an owner or operator of an onshore facility can prove that a discharge was caused solely by (A) an act of God, (B) an act of war, (C) negligence on the part of the United States Government, or (D) an act or omission of a third party without regard to whether any such act or omission was or was not negligent, or any combination of the foregoing clauses, such owner or operator of any such facility from which oil or a hazardous substance is discharged in violation of subsection (b)(3) of this section shall be liable to the United States Government for the actual costs incurred under subsection (c) of this section for the removal of such oil or substance by the United States Government in an amount not to exceed $50,000,000, except that

where the United States can show that such discharge was the result of willful negligence or willful misconduct within the privity and knowledge of the owner, such owner or operator shall be liable to the United States Government for the full amount of such costs. The United States may bring an action against the owner or operator of such facility in any court of competent jurisdiction to recover such costs. The Administrator is authorized, by regulation, after consultation with the Secretary of Commerce and the Small Business Administration, to establish reasonable and equitable classifications of those onshore facilities having a total fixed storage capacity of 1,000 barrels or less which he determines because of size, type, and location do not present a substantial risk of the discharge of oil or a hazardous substance in violation of subsection (b)(3) of this section, and apply with respect to such classifications differing limits of liability which may be less than the amount contained in this paragraph.

(3) Except where an owner or operator of an offshore facility can prove that a discharge was caused solely by (A) an act of God, (B) an act of war, (C) negligence on the part of the United States Government, or (D) an act or omission of a third party without regard to whether any such act or omission was or was not negligent, or any combination of the foregoing clauses, such owner or operator of any such facility from which oil or a hazardous substance is discharged in violation of subsection (b)(3) of this section shall, notwithstanding any other provision of law, be liable to the United States Government for the actual costs incurred under subsection (c) of this section for the removal of such oil or substance by the United States Government in an amount not to exceed $50,000,000, except that where the United States can show that such discharge was the result of willful negligence or willful misconduct within the privity and knowledge of the owner, such owner or operator shall be liable to the United States Government for the full amount of such costs. The United States may bring an action against the owner or operator of such a facility in any court of competent jurisdiction to recover such costs.

(4) The costs of removal of oil or a hazardous substance for which the owner or operator of a vessel or onshore or offshore facility is liable under subsection (f) of this section shall include any costs or expenses incurred by the Federal Government or any State government in the restoration or replacement of natural resources damaged or destroyed as a result of a discharge of oil or a hazardous substance in violation of subsection (b) of this section.

(5) The President, or the authorized representative of any State, shall act on behalf of the public as trustee of the natural resources to recover for the costs of replacing or restoring such resources. Sums recovered shall be used to restore, rehabilitate, or acquire the equivalent of such natural resources by the appropriate agencies of the Federal Government, or the State government.

(g) Third party liability

Where the owner or operator of a vessel (other than an inland oil barge) carrying oil or hazardous substances as cargo or an onshore or offshore facility which handles or stores oil or hazardous substances in bulk, from which oil or a hazardous substance is discharged in violation of subsection (b) of this section, alleges that such discharge was caused solely by an act or omission of a third party, such owner or operator shall pay to the United States Government the actual costs incurred under subsection (c) of this section for removal of such oil or substance and shall be entitled by subrogation to all rights of the United States Government to recover such costs from such third party under this subsection. In any case where an owner or operator of a vessel, of an onshore facility, or of an offshore facility, from which oil or a hazardous substance is discharged in violation of subsection (b)(3) of this section, proves that such discharge of oil or hazardous substance was caused solely by an act or omission of a third party, or was caused solely by such an act or omission in combination with an act of God, an act of war, or negligence on the part of the United States Government, such third party shall, notwithstanding any other provision of law, be liable to the United States Government for the actual costs incurred under subsection (c) of this section for removal of such oil or substance by the United States Government, except where such third party can prove that such discharge was caused solely by (A) an act of God, (B) an act of war, (C) negligence on the part of the United States Government, or (D) an act or omission of another party without regard to whether such act or omission was or was not negligent, or any combination of the foregoing clauses. If such third party was the owner or operator of a vessel which caused the discharge of oil or a hazardous substance in violation of subsection (b)(3) of this section, the liability of such third party under this subsection shall not exceed, in the case of an inland oil barge $125 per gross ton of such barge, or $125,000, whichever is greater, and in the case of any other vessel, $150 per gross ton of such vessel (or, for a vessel carrying oil or hazardous substances as cargo, $250,000), whichever is greater. In any other case the liability of such third party shall not exceed the limitation which would have been applicable to the owner or operator of the vessel or the onshore or offshore facility from which the discharge actually occurred if such owner or operator were liable. If the United States can show that the discharge of oil or a hazardous substance in violation of subsection (b)(3) of this section was the result of willful negligence or willful misconduct within the privity and knowledge of such third party, such third party shall be liable to the United States Government for the full amount of such removal costs. The United States may bring an action against the third party in any court of competent jurisdiction to recover such removal costs.

(h) Rights against third parties who caused or contributed to discharge

The liabilities established by this section shall in no way affect any rights which (1) the owner or operator of a vessel or of an onshore facility or an offshore facility may have against any third party whose acts may in any way have caused or contributed to such discharge, or (2) the United States Government may have against any third party whose actions may in any way have caused or contributed to the discharge of oil or hazardous substance.

(i) Recovery of removal costs

In any case where an owner or operator of a vessel or an onshore facility or an offshore facility from which oil or a hazardous substance is discharged in violation of subsection (b)(3) of this section acts to remove such oil or substance in accordance with regulations promulgated pursuant to this section, such owner or operator shall be entitled to recover the reasonable costs incurred in such removal upon establishing, in a suit which may be brought against the United States Government in the United States Court of Federal Claims, that such discharge was caused solely by (A) an act of God, (B) an act of war, (C) negligence on the part of the United States Government, or (D) an act or omission of a third party without regard to whether such act or omission was or was not negligent, or of any combination of the foregoing causes.

(j) National Response System

(1) In general

Consistent with the National Contingency Plan required by subsection (c)(2) of this section, as soon as practicable after October 18, 1972, and from time to time thereafter, the President shall issue regulations consistent with maritime safety and with marine and navigation laws (A) establishing methods and procedures for removal of discharged oil and hazardous substances, (B) establishing criteria for the development and implementation of local and regional oil and hazardous substance removal contingency plans, (C) establishing procedures, methods, and equipment and other requirements for equipment to prevent discharges of oil and hazardous substances from vessels and from onshore facilities and offshore facilities, and to contain such discharges, and (D) governing the inspection of vessels carrying cargoes of oil and hazardous substances and the inspection of such cargoes in order to reduce the likelihood of discharges of oil from vessels in violation of this section.

(2) National Response Unit

The Secretary of the department in which the Coast Guard is operating shall establish a National Response Unit at Elizabeth City, North Carolina. The Secretary, acting through the National Response Unit—

(A) shall compile and maintain a comprehensive computer list of spill removal resources, personnel, and equipment that is available worldwide and within the areas designated by the President pursuant to paragraph (4), and of information regarding previous spills, including data from universities, research institutions, State governments, and other nations, as appropriate, which shall be disseminated as appropriate to response groups and area committees, and which shall be available to Federal and State agencies and the public;

(B) shall provide technical assistance, equipment, and other resources requested by a Federal On-Scene Coordinator;

(C) shall coordinate use of private and public personnel and equipment to remove a worst case discharge, and to mitigate or prevent a substantial threat of such a discharge, from a vessel, offshore facility, or onshore facility operating in or near an area designated by the President pursuant to paragraph (4);

(D) may provide technical assistance in the preparation of Area Contingency Plans required under paragraph (4);

(E) shall administer Coast Guard strike teams established under the National Contingency Plan;

(F) shall maintain on file all Area Contingency Plans approved by the President under this subsection; and

(G) shall review each of those plans that affects its responsibilities under this subsection.

(3) Coast Guard District Response Groups

(A) The Secretary of the department in which the Coast Guard is operating shall establish in each Coast Guard district a Coast Guard District Response Group.

(B) Each Coast Guard District Response Group shall consist of—

(i) the Coast Guard personnel and equipment, including firefighting equipment, of each port within the district;

(ii) additional prepositioned equipment; and

(iii) a district response advisory staff.

(C) Coast Guard district response groups—

(i) shall provide technical assistance, equipment, and other resources when required by a Federal On-Scene Coordinator;

(ii) shall maintain all Coast Guard response equipment within its district;

(iii) may provide technical assistance in the preparation of Area Contingency Plans required under paragraph (4); and

(iv) shall review each of those plans that affect its area of geographic responsibility.

(4) Area Committees and Area Contingency Plans

(A) There is established for each area designated by the President an Area Committee comprised of members appointed by the President from qualified personnel of Federal, State, and local agencies.

(B) Each Area Committee, under the direction of the Federal On-Scene Coordinator for its area, shall—

(i) prepare for its area the Area Contingency Plan required under subparagraph (C);

(ii) work with State and local officials to enhance the contingency planning of those officials and to assure preplanning of joint response efforts, including appropriate procedures for mechanical recovery, dispersal, shoreline cleanup, protection of sensitive environmental areas, and protection, rescue, and rehabilitation of fisheries and wildlife; and

(iii) work with State and local officials to expedite decisions for the use of dispersants and other mitigating substances and devices.

(C) Each Area Committee shall prepare and submit to the President for approval an Area

Contingency Plan for its area. The Area Contingency Plan shall—

(i) when implemented in conjunction with the National Contingency Plan, be adequate to remove a worst case discharge, and to mitigate or prevent a substantial threat of such a discharge, from a vessel, offshore facility, or onshore facility operating in or near the area;

(ii) describe the area covered by the plan, including the areas of special economic or environmental importance that might be damaged by a discharge;

(iii) describe in detail the responsibilities of an owner or operator and of Federal, State, and local agencies in removing a discharge, and in mitigating or preventing a substantial threat of a discharge;

(iv) list the equipment (including firefighting equipment), dispersants or other mitigating substances and devices, and personnel available to an owner or operator and Federal, State, and local agencies, to ensure an effective and immediate removal of a discharge, and to ensure mitigation or prevention of a substantial threat of a discharge;

(v) compile a list of local scientists, both inside and outside Federal Government service, with expertise in the environmental effects of spills of the types of oil typically transported in the area, who may be contacted to provide information or, where appropriate, participate in meetings of the scientific support team convened in response to a spill, and describe the procedures to be followed for obtaining an expedited decision regarding the use of dispersants;

(vi) describe in detail how the plan is integrated into other Area Contingency Plans and vessel, offshore facility, and onshore facility response plans approved under this subsection, and into operating procedures of the National Response Unit;

(vii) include any other information the President requires; and

(viii) be updated periodically by the Area Committee.

(D) The President shall—

(i) review and approve Area Contingency Plans under this paragraph; and

(ii) periodically review Area Contingency Plans so approved.

(5) Tank vessel, nontank vessel, and facility response plans

(A)(i) The President shall issue regulations which require an owner or operator of a tank vessel or facility described in subparagraph (C) to prepare and submit to the President a plan for responding, to the maximum extent practicable, to a worst case discharge, and to a substantial threat of such a discharge, of oil or a hazardous substance.

(ii) The President shall also issue regulations which require an owner or operator of a nontank vessel to prepare and submit to the President a plan for responding, to the maximum extent practicable, to a worst case discharge, and to a substantial threat of such a discharge, of oil.

(B) The Secretary of the Department in which the Coast Guard is operating may issue regulations which require an owner or operator of a tank vessel, a nontank vessel, or a facility described in subparagraph (C) that transfers noxious liquid substances in bulk to or from a vessel to prepare and submit to the Secretary a plan for responding, to the maximum extent practicable, to a worst case discharge, and to a substantial threat of such a discharge, of a noxious liquid substance that is not designated as a hazardous substance or regulated as oil in any other law or regulation. For purposes of this paragraph, the term "noxious liquid substance" has the same meaning when that term is used in the MARPOL Protocol described in section 1901(a)(3)[2] of this title.

(C) The tank vessels, nontank vessels, and facilities referred to in subparagraphs (A) and (B) are the following:

(i) A tank vessel, as defined under section 2101 of title 46.

(ii) A nontank vessel.

(iii) An offshore facility.

(iv) An onshore facility that, because of its location, could reasonably be expected to cause substantial harm to the environment by discharging into or on the navigable waters, adjoining shorelines, or the exclusive economic zone.

(D) A response plan required under this paragraph shall—

(i) be consistent with the requirements of the National Contingency Plan and Area Contingency Plans;

(ii) identify the qualified individual having full authority to implement removal actions, and require immediate communications between that individual and the appropriate Federal official and the persons providing personnel and equipment pursuant to clause (iii);

(iii) identify, and ensure by contract or other means approved by the President the availability of, private personnel and equipment necessary to remove to the maximum extent practicable a worst case discharge (including a discharge resulting from fire or explosion), and to mitigate or prevent a substantial threat of such a discharge;

(iv) describe the training, equipment testing, periodic unannounced drills, and response actions of persons on the vessel or at the facility, to be carried out under the plan to ensure the safety of the vessel or facility and to mitigate or prevent the discharge, or the substantial threat of a discharge;

(v) be updated periodically; and

(vi) be resubmitted for approval of each significant change.

(E) With respect to any response plan submitted under this paragraph for an onshore facility that, because of its location, could reasonably be expected to cause significant and substantial harm to the environment by discharging into or on the navigable waters or adjoining shorelines or the exclusive economic zone, and with respect to each response plan submitted under this paragraph for a tank vessel, nontank vessel, or offshore facility, the President shall—

(i) promptly review such response plan;

(ii) require amendments to any plan that does not meet the requirements of this paragraph;

(iii) approve any plan that meets the requirements of this paragraph;

(iv) review each plan periodically thereafter; and

(v) in the case of a plan for a nontank vessel, consider any applicable State-mandated response plan in effect on August 9, 2004, and ensure consistency to the extent practicable.

(F) A tank vessel, nontank vessel, offshore facility, or onshore facility required to prepare a response plan under this subsection may not handle, store, or transport oil unless—

(i) in the case of a tank vessel, nontank vessel, offshore facility, or onshore facility for which a response plan is reviewed by the President under subparagraph (E), the plan has been approved by the President; and

(ii) the vessel or facility is operating in compliance with the plan.

(G) Notwithstanding subparagraph (E), the President may authorize a tank vessel, nontank vessel, offshore facility, or onshore facility to operate without a response plan approved under this paragraph, until not later than 2 years after the date of the submission to the President of a plan for the tank vessel, nontank vessel, or facility, if the owner or operator certifies that the owner or operator has ensured by contract or other means approved by the President the availability of private personnel and equipment necessary to respond, to the maximum extent practicable, to a worst case discharge or a substantial threat of such a discharge.

(H) The owner or operator of a tank vessel, nontank vessel, offshore facility, or onshore facility may not claim as a defense to liability under title I of the Oil Pollution Act of 1990 [33 U.S.C. 2701 et seq.] that the owner or operator was acting in accordance with an approved response plan.

(I) The Secretary shall maintain, in the Vessel Identification System established under chapter 125 of title 46, the dates of approval and review of a response plan under this paragraph for each tank vessel and nontank vessel that is a vessel of the United States.

(6) Equipment requirements and inspection

The President may require—

(A) periodic inspection of containment booms, skimmers, vessels, and other major equipment used to remove discharges; and

(B) vessels operating on navigable waters and carrying oil or a hazardous substance in bulk as cargo, and nontank vessels carrying oil of any kind as fuel for main propulsion, to carry appropriate removal equipment that employs the best technology economically feasible and that is compatible with the safe operation of the vessel.

(7) Area drills

The President shall periodically conduct drills of removal capability, without prior notice, in areas for which Area Contingency Plans are required under this subsection and under relevant tank vessel, nontank vessel, and facility response plans. The drills may include participation by Federal, State, and local agencies, the owners and operators of vessels and facilities in the area, and private industry. The President may publish annual reports on these drills, including assessments of the effectiveness of the plans and a list of amendments made to improve plans.

(8) United States Government not liable

The United States Government is not liable for any damages arising from its actions or omissions relating to any response plan required by this section.

(k) Repealed. Pub. L. 101–380, title II, §2002(b)(2), Aug. 18, 1990, 104 Stat. 507

(*l*) Administration

The President is authorized to delegate the administration of this section to the heads of those Federal departments, agencies, and instrumentalities which he determines to be appropriate. Each such department, agency, and instrumentality, in order to avoid duplication of effort, shall, whenever appropriate, utilize the personnel, services, and facilities of other Federal departments, agencies, and instrumentalities.

(m) Administrative provisions

(1) For vessels

Anyone authorized by the President to enforce the provisions of this section with respect to any vessel may, except as to public vessels—

(A) board and inspect any vessel upon the navigable waters of the United States or the waters of the contiguous zone,

(B) with or without a warrant, arrest any person who in the presence or view of the authorized person violates the provisions of this section or any regulation issued thereunder, and

(C) execute any warrant or other process issued by an officer or court of competent jurisdiction.

(2) For facilities

(A) Recordkeeping

Whenever required to carry out the purposes of this section, the Administrator or the Secretary of the Department in which the Coast Guard is operating shall require the owner or operator of a facility to which this section applies to establish and maintain such records, make such reports, install, use, and maintain such monitoring equipment and methods, and provide such other information as the Administrator or Secretary, as the case may be, may require to carry out the objectives of this section.

(B) Entry and inspection

Whenever required to carry out the purposes of this section, the Administrator or the Secretary of the Department in which the Coast Guard is operating or an authorized representative of the Administrator or Secretary, upon presentation of appropriate credentials, may—

(i) enter and inspect any facility to which this section applies, including any facility at which any records are required to be maintained under subparagraph (A); and

(ii) at reasonable times, have access to and copy any records, take samples, and inspect any monitoring equipment or methods required under subparagraph (A).

(C) Arrests and execution of warrants

Anyone authorized by the Administrator or the Secretary of the department in which the Coast Guard is operating to enforce the provisions of this section with respect to any facility may—

(i) with or without a warrant, arrest any person who violates the provisions of this section or any regulation issued thereunder in the presence or view of the person so authorized; and

(ii) execute any warrant or process issued by an officer or court of competent jurisdiction.

(D) Public access

Any records, reports, or information obtained under this paragraph shall be subject to the same public access and disclosure requirements which are applicable to records, reports, and information obtained pursuant to section 1318 of this title.

(n) Jurisdiction

The several district courts of the United States are invested with jurisdiction for any actions, other than actions pursuant to subsection (i)(1) of this section, arising under this section. In the case of Guam and the Trust Territory of the Pacific Islands, such actions may be brought in the district court of Guam, and in the case of the Virgin Islands such actions may be brought in the district court of the Virgin Islands. In the case of American Samoa and the Trust Territory of the Pacific Islands, such actions may be brought in the District Court of the United States for the District of Hawaii and such court shall have jurisdiction of such actions. In the case of the Canal Zone, such actions may be brought in the United States District Court for the District of the Canal Zone.

(*o*) Obligation for damages unaffected; local authority not preempted; existing Federal authority not modified or affected

(1) Nothing in this section shall affect or modify in any way the obligations of any owner or operator of any vessel, or of any owner or operator of any onshore facility or offshore facility to any person or agency under any provision of law for damages to any publicly owned or privately owned property resulting from a discharge of any oil or hazardous substance or from the removal of any such oil or hazardous substance.

(2) Nothing in this section shall be construed as preempting any State or political subdivision thereof from imposing any requirement or liability with respect to the discharge of oil or hazardous substance into any waters within such State, or with respect to any removal activities related to such discharge.

(3) Nothing in this section shall be construed as affecting or modifying any other existing authority of any Federal department, agency, or instrumentality, relative to onshore or offshore facilities under this chapter or any other provision of law, or to affect any State or local law not in conflict with this section.

(p) Repealed. Pub. L. 101–380, title II, §2002(b)(4), Aug. 18, 1990, 104 Stat. 507

(q) Establishment of maximum limit of liability with respect to onshore or offshore facilities

The President is authorized to establish, with respect to any class or category of onshore or offshore facilities, a maximum limit of liability under subsections (f)(2) and (3) of this section of less than $50,000,000, but not less than $8,000,000.

(r) Liability limitations not to limit liability under other legislation

Nothing in this section shall be construed to impose, or authorize the imposition of, any limitation on liability under the Outer Continental Shelf Lands Act [43 U.S.C. 1331 et seq.] or the Deepwater Port Act of 1974 [33 U.S.C. 1501 et seq.].

(s) Oil Spill Liability Trust Fund

The Oil Spill Liability Trust Fund established under section 9509 of title 26 shall be available to carry out subsections (b), (c), (d), (j), and (*l*) of this section as those subsections apply to discharges, and substantial threats of discharges, of oil. Any amounts received by the United States under this section shall be deposited in the Oil Spill Liability Trust Fund.

(June 30, 1948, ch. 758, title III, §311, as added Pub. L. 92–500, §2, Oct. 18, 1972, 86 Stat. 862; amended Pub. L. 93–207, §1(4), Dec. 28, 1973, 87 Stat. 906; Pub. L. 95–217, §§57, 58(a)–(g), (i), (k)–(m), Dec. 27, 1977, 91 Stat. 1593–1596; Pub. L. 95–576, §1(b), Nov. 2, 1978, 92 Stat. 2467; Pub. L. 96–478, §13(b), Oct. 21, 1980, 94 Stat. 2303; Pub. L. 96–483, §8, Oct. 21, 1980, 94 Stat. 2362; Pub. L. 96–561, title II, §238(b), Dec. 22, 1980, 94 Stat. 3300; Pub. L. 97–164, title I, §161(5), Apr. 2, 1982, 96 Stat. 49; Pub. L. 100–4, title V, §502(b), Feb. 4, 1987, 101 Stat. 75; Pub. L. 101–380, title II, §2002(b), title IV, §§4201(a), (b), (b)[(c)], 4202(a), (c), 4204, 4301(a), (b), 4305, 4306, Aug. 18, 1990, 104 Stat. 507, 523–527, 532, 533, 540, 541; Pub. L. 102–388, title III, §349, Oct. 6, 1992, 106 Stat. 1554; Pub. L. 102–572, title IX, §902(b)(1), Oct. 29, 1992, 106 Stat. 4516; Pub. L. 104–208, div. A, title I, §101(a) [title II, §211(b)], Sept. 30, 1996, 110 Stat. 3009, 3009–41; Pub. L. 104–324, title XI, §§1143, 1144, Oct. 19, 1996, 110 Stat. 3992; Pub. L. 105–383, title IV, §411, Nov. 13, 1998, 112 Stat. 3432; Pub. L. 108–293, title VII, §701(a), (b), (d), Aug. 9, 2004, 118 Stat. 1067, 1068; Pub. L. 109–241, title VI, §608, title IX, §901(i), July 11, 2006, 120 Stat. 558, 564.)

References in Text

The Outer Continental Shelf Lands Act, referred to in subsecs. (b)(1), (2)(A), (3) and (r), is act Aug. 7, 1953, ch. 345, 67 Stat. 462, as amended, which is classified generally to subchapter III (§1331 et seq.) of chapter 29 of Title 43, Public Lands. For complete classification of this Act to the Code, see Short Title note set out under section 1331 of Title 43 and Tables.

The Deepwater Port Act of 1974, referred to in subsecs. (b)(1), (2)(A), (3) and (r), is Pub. L. 93–627, Jan. 3, 1975, 88 Stat. 2126, as amended, which is classified generally to chapter 29 (§1501 et seq.) of this title. For complete classification of this Act to the Code, see Short Title note set out under section 1501 of this title and Tables.

The Magnuson-Stevens Fishery Conservation and Management Act, referred to in subsec. (b)(1), (2)(A), (3), is Pub. L. 94–265, Apr. 13, 1976, 90 Stat. 331, as amended, which is classified principally to chapter 38 (§ 1801 et seq.) of Title 16, Conservation. For complete classification of this Act to the Code, see Short Title note set out under section 1801 of Title 16 and Tables.

The date of enactment of this paragraph, referred to in subsec. (b)(2)(B), probably means the date of enactment of Pub. L. 95–576, which amended subsec. (b)(2)(B) and which was approved Nov. 2, 1978.

The penalty enacted in subclause (bb) of clause (iii) of subparagraph (B) of subsection (b)(2) of section 311 of Public Law 92–500, referred to in subsec. (b)(2)(B), probably means the penalty provision of subsec. (b)(2)(B)(iii)(bb) of this section as added by Pub. L. 92–500, § 2, Oct. 18, 1972, 86 Stat. 864, prior to the amendment to subsec. (b)(2)(B) by section 1(b)(3) of Pub. L. 95–576. Prior to amendment, subsec. (b)(2)(B)(iii)(bb) read as follows: "a penalty determined by the number of units discharged multiplied by the amount established for such unit under clause (iv) of this subparagraph, but such penalty shall not be more than $5,000,000 in the case of a discharge from a vessel and $500,000 in the case of a discharge from an onshore or offshore facility."

Section 4367 of the Revised Statutes of the United States (46 U.S.C. App. 313), referred to in subsec. (b)(12)(B), was repealed by Pub. L. 103–182, title VI, § 690(a)(21), Dec. 8, 1993, 107 Stat. 2223.

Section 1443 of title 19, referred to in subsec. (b)(12)(C), was repealed by Pub. L. 103–182, title VI, § 690(b)(6), Dec. 8, 1993, 107 Stat. 2223.

The Comprehensive Environmental Response, Compensation, and Liability Act of 1980, referred to in subsec. (c)(4)(B)(ii), is Pub. L. 96–510, Dec. 11, 1980, 94 Stat. 2767, as amended, which is classified principally to chapter 103 (§ 9601 et seq.) of Title 42, The Public Health and Welfare. For complete classification of this Act to the Code, see Short Title note set out under section 9601 of Title 42 and Tables.

The Oil Pollution Act of 1990, referred to in subsecs. (c)(5)(B), (d)(2)(H), and (j)(5)(H), is Pub. L. 101–380, Aug. 18, 1990, 104 Stat. 484, which is classified principally to chapter 40 (§ 2701 et seq.) of this title. Title I of the Act is classified generally to subchapter I (§ 2701 et seq.) of chapter 40 of this title. For complete classification of this Act to the Code, see Short Title note set out under section 2701 of this title and Tables.

Par. (3) of section 1901(a) of this title, referred to in subsec. (j)(5)(B), was redesignated par. (4) by Pub. L. 110–280, § 3(1), July 21, 2008, 122 Stat. 2611.

Codification

In subsec. (b)(12)(A), "section 60105 of title 46" substituted for "section 4197 of the Revised Statutes of the United States (46 U.S.C. App. 91)" on authority of Pub. L. 109–304, § 18(c), Oct. 6, 2006, 120 Stat. 1709, which Act enacted section 60105 of Title 46, Shipping.

Amendments

2006—Subsec. (a)(26). Pub. L. 109–241, § 608, amended par. (26) generally. Prior to amendment, par. (26) read as follows: "'nontank vessel' means a self-propelled vessel of 400 gross tons as measured under section 14302 of title 46 or greater, other than a tank vessel, that carries oil of any kind as fuel for main propulsion and that—

"(A) is a vessel of the United States; or

"(B) operates on the navigable waters of the United States."

Subsec. (j)(5)(A)(ii), (B), (F), and (G). Pub. L. 109–241, § 901(i)(1), substituted "nontank" for "non-tank" wherever appearing.

Subsec. (j)(5)(H). Pub. L. 109–241, § 901(i)(2), amended directory language of Pub. L. 108–293, § 701(b)(9). See 2004 Amendment note below.

2004—Subsec. (a)(26). Pub. L. 108–293, § 701(a), added par. (26).

Subsec. (j)(5). Pub. L. 108–293, § 701(b)(1), inserted ", nontank vessel," after "vessel" in heading.

Subsec. (j)(5)(A). Pub. L. 108–293, § 701(b)(2), (d)(3), designated existing text as cl. (i), substituted "subparagraph (C)" for "subparagraph (B)", and added cl. (ii).

Subsec. (j)(5)(B). Pub. L. 108–293, § 701(d)(2), added subpar. (B). Former subpar. (B) redesignated (C).

Pub. L. 108–293, § 701(b)(3), (4), inserted ", nontank vessels," after "vessels" in introductory provisions, added cl. (ii), and redesignated former cls. (ii) and (iii) as (iii) and (iv), respectively.

Subsec. (j)(5)(C). Pub. L. 108–293, § 701(d)(1), (4), redesignated subpar. (B) as (C) and substituted "subparagraphs (A) and (B)" for "subparagraph (A)" in introductory provisions. Former subpar. (C) redesignated (D).

Subsec. (j)(5)(D). Pub. L. 108–293, § 701(d)(1), redesignated subpar. (C) as (D). Former subpar (D) redesignated (E).

Pub. L. 108–293, § 701(b)(5), inserted ", nontank vessel," after "vessel" in introductory provisions and added cl. (v).

Subsec. (j)(5)(E). Pub. L. 108–293, § 701(d)(1), redesignated subpar. (D) as (E). Former subpar. (E) redesignated (F).

Pub. L. 108–293, § 701(b)(6), inserted "non-tank vessel," after "vessel," in two places.

Subsec. (j)(5)(F). Pub. L. 108–293, § 701(d)(1), (5), redesignated subpar. (E) as (F) and substituted "subparagraph (E)," for "subparagraph (D)," in cl. (i). Former subpar. (F) redesignated (G).

Pub. L. 108–293, § 701(b)(7), inserted "non-tank vessel," after "vessel," and substituted "vessel, non-tank vessel, or" for "vessel or".

Subsec. (j)(5)(G). Pub. L. 108–293, § 701(d)(1), redesignated subpar. (F) as (G). Former subpar. (G) redesignated (H).

Pub. L. 108–293, § 701(b)(8), inserted "nontank vessel," after "vessel,".

Subsec. (j)(5)(H). Pub. L. 108–293, § 701(d)(1), redesignated subpar. (G) as (H). Former subpar. (H) redesignated (I).

Pub. L. 108–293, § 701(b)(9), as amended by Pub. L. 109–241, § 901(i)(2), inserted "and nontank vessel" after "each tank vessel".

Subsec. (j)(5)(I). Pub. L. 108–293, § 701(d)(1), redesignated subpar. (H) as (I).

Subsec. (j)(6). Pub. L. 108–293, § 701(b)(10), substituted "The President may require—" for "Not later than 2 years after August 18, 1990, the President shall require—" in introductory provisions.

Subsec. (j)(6)(B). Pub. L. 108–293, § 701(b)(11), inserted ", and nontank vessels carrying oil of any kind as fuel for main propulsion," after "cargo".

Subsec. (j)(7). Pub. L. 108–293, § 701(b)(12), inserted ", nontank vessel," after "vessel".

1998—Subsec. (a)(2). Pub. L. 105–383, § 411(b), substituted ", (C)" for "and (C)" and inserted ", and (D) discharges incidental to mechanical removal authorized by the President under subsection (c) of this section" before semicolon at end.

Subsec. (a)(8). Pub. L. 105–383, § 411(a)(1), substituted "to prevent, minimize, or mitigate damage" for "to minimize or mitigate damage".

Subsec. (a)(25). Pub. L. 105–383, § 411(a)(2), added par. (25).

Subsec. (c)(4)(A). Pub. L. 105–383, § 411(a)(3), inserted "relating to a discharge or a substantial threat of a discharge of oil or a hazardous substance" before period at end.

1996—Subsec. (b)(1), (2)(A), (3). Pub. L. 104–208 substituted "Magnuson-Stevens Fishery" for "Magnuson Fishery" wherever appearing.

Subsec. (c)(3)(B). Pub. L. 104–324, § 1144, inserted ", except that the owner or operator may deviate from the applicable response plan if the President or the Federal On-Scene Coordinator determines that deviation from the response plan would provide for a more expeditious or effective response to the spill or mitigation of its environmental effects" before period at end.

Subsec. (j)(2)(A). Pub. L. 104–324, §1143(1), inserted "and of information regarding previous spills, including data from universities, research institutions, State governments, and other nations, as appropriate, which shall be disseminated as appropriate to response groups and area committees, and" after "paragraph (4),".

Subsec. (j)(4)(C)(v). Pub. L. 104–324, §1143(2), inserted "compile a list of local scientists, both inside and outside Federal Government service, with expertise in the environmental effects of spills of the types of oil typically transported in the area, who may be contacted to provide information or, where appropriate, participate in meetings of the scientific support team convened in response to a spill, and" before "describe".

1992—Subsec. (b)(12). Pub. L. 102–388 added par. (12).

Subsec. (i). Pub. L. 102–572 substituted "United States Court of Federal Claims" for "United States Claims Court".

1990—Subsec. (a)(8). Pub. L. 101–380, §4201(b)(1)[(c)(1)], inserted "containment and" after "refers to".

Subsec. (a)(16). Pub. L. 101–380, §4201(b)(2)[(c)(2)], substituted semicolon for period at end.

Subsec. (a)(17). Pub. L. 101–380, §4201(b)(3)[(c)(3)], substituted "otherwise" for "Otherwise" and semicolon for period at end.

Subsec. (a)(18) to (24). Pub. L. 101–380, §4201(b)(4)[(c)(4)], added pars. (18) to (24).

Subsec. (b)(4). Pub. L. 101–380, §4204, inserted "or the environment" after "the public health or welfare".

Subsec. (b)(5). Pub. L. 101–380, §4301(a), inserted after first sentence "The Federal agency shall immediately notify the appropriate State agency of any State which is, or may reasonably be expected to be, affected by the discharge of oil or a hazardous substance.", substituted "fined in accordance with title 18, United States Code, or imprisoned for not more than 5 years, or both" for "fined not more than $10,000, or imprisoned for not more than one year, or both", struck out "or information obtained by the exploitation of such notification" before "shall not be used", and inserted "natural" before "person in any".

Subsec. (b)(6) to (11). Pub. L. 101–380, §4301(b), added pars. (6) to (11) and struck out former par. (6) which related to assessment of civil penalties, limited to $5,000 for each offense, against any owner, operator, or person in charge of any onshore or offshore facility from which oil or a hazardous substance was discharged in violation of par. (3).

Subsec. (c). Pub. L. 101–380, §4201(a), amended subsec. (c) generally, substituting present provisions for provisions authorizing President to arrange for removal of discharge of oil or a hazardous substance into or upon the navigable waters of the U.S., unless he determined such removal would be properly conducted by owner or operator of the vessel causing discharge, and directed President to prepare and publish a National Contingency Plan within 60 days after October 18, 1972.

Subsec. (d). Pub. L. 101–380, §4201(b), amended subsec. (d) generally. Prior to amendment, subsec. (d) read as follows: "Whenever a marine disaster in or upon the navigable waters of the United States has created a substantial threat of a pollution hazard to the public health or welfare of the United States, including, but not limited to, fish, shellfish, and wildlife and the public and private shorelines and beaches of the United States, because of a discharge, or an imminent discharge, of large quantities of oil, or of a hazardous substance from a vessel the United States may (A) coordinate and direct all public and private efforts directed at the removal or elimination of such threat; and (B) summarily remove, and, if necessary, destroy such vessel by whatever means are available without regard to any provisions of law governing the employment of personnel or the expenditure of appropriated funds. Any expense incurred under this subsection or under the Intervention on the High Seas Act (or the convention defined in section 2(3) thereof) shall be a cost incurred by the United States Government for the purposes of subsection (f) of this section in the removal of oil or hazardous substance."

Subsec. (e). Pub. L. 101–380, §4306, amended subsec. (e) generally. Prior to amendment, subsec. (e) read as follows: "In addition to any other action taken by a State or local government, when the President determines there is an imminent and substantial threat to the public health or welfare of the United States, including, but not limited to, fish, shellfish, and wildlife and public and private property, shorelines, and beaches within the United States, because of an actual or threatened discharge of oil or hazardous substance into or upon the navigable waters of the United States from an onshore or offshore facility, the President may require the United States attorney of the district in which the threat occurs to secure such relief as may be necessary to abate such threat, and the district courts of the United States shall have jurisdiction to grant such relief as the public interest and the equities of the case may require."

Subsec. (i). Pub. L. 101–380, §2002(b)(1), struck out par. (1) designation before "In any case" and struck out pars. (2) and (3) which read as follows:

"(2) The provisions of this subsection shall not apply in any case where liability is established pursuant to the Outer Continental Shelf Lands Act, or the Deepwater Port Act of 1974.

"(3) Any amount paid in accordance with a judgment of the United States Claims Court pursuant to this section shall be paid from the funds established pursuant to subsection (k) of this section."

Subsec. (j). Pub. L. 101–380, §4202(a), amended heading, inserted heading for par. (1) and realigned its margin, added pars. (2) to (8), and struck out former par. (2) which read as follows: "Any owner or operator of a vessel or an onshore facility or an offshore facility and any other person subject to any regulation issued under paragraph (1) of this subsection who fails or refuses to comply with the provisions of any such regulations, shall be liable to a civil penalty of not more than $5,000 for each such violation. This paragraph shall not apply to any owner or operator of any vessel from which oil or a hazardous substance is discharged in violation of paragraph (3)(ii) of subsection (b) of this section unless such owner, operator, or person in charge is otherwise subject to the jurisdiction of the United States. Each violation shall be a separate offense. The President may assess and compromise such penalty. No penalty shall be assessed until the owner, operator, or other person charged shall have been given notice and an opportunity for a hearing on such charge. In determining the amount of the penalty, or the amount agreed upon in compromise, the gravity of the violation, and the demonstrated good faith of the owner, operator, or other person charged in attempting to achieve rapid compliance, after notification of a violation, shall be considered by the President."

Subsec. (k). Pub. L. 101–380, §2002(b)(2), struck out subsec. (k) which authorized appropriations and supplemental appropriations to create and maintain a revolving fund to carry out subsecs. (c), (d), (i), and (*l*) of this section.

Subsec. (*l*). Pub. L. 101–380, §2002(b)(3), struck out after first sentence "Any moneys in the fund established by subsection (k) of this section shall be available to such Federal departments, agencies, and instrumentalities to carry out the provisions of subsections (c) and (i) of this section."

Subsec. (m). Pub. L. 101–380, §4305, amended subsec. (m) generally. Prior to amendment, subsec. (m) read as follows: "Anyone authorized by the President to enforce the provisions of this section may, except as to public vessels, (A) board and inspect any vessel upon the navigable waters of the United States or the waters of the contiguous zone, (B) with or without a warrant arrest any person who violates the provisions of this section or any regulation issued thereunder in his presence or view, and (C) execute any warrant or other process issued by an officer or court of competent jurisdiction."

Subsec. (*o*)(2). Pub. L. 101–380, §4202(c), inserted ", or with respect to any removal activities related to such discharge" after "within such State".

Subsec. (p). Pub. L. 101–380, §2002(b)(4), struck out subsec. (p) which provided for establishment and maintenance of evidence of financial responsibility by vessels over 300 gross tons carrying oil or hazardous substances.

Subsec. (s). Pub. L. 101–380, §2002(b)(5), added subsec. (s).

1987—Subsec. (a)(5). Pub. L. 100–4 substituted "the Commonwealth of the Northern Mariana Islands" for "the Canal Zone".

1982—Subsec. (i)(1), (3). Pub. L. 97–164 substituted "Claims Court" for "Court of Claims".

1980—Subsec. (b)(1), (2)(A), (3). Pub. L. 96–561 substituted "Magnuson Fishery Conservation and Management Act" for "Fishery Conservation and Management Act of 1976".

Subsec. (b)(3)(A). Pub. L. 96–478 struck out "of oil" after "in the case of such discharges" and substituted "Protocol of 1978 Relating to the International Convention for the Prevention of Pollution from Ships, 1973" for "International Convention for the Prevention of Pollution of the Sea by Oil, 1954, as amended".

Subsec. (c)(1). Pub. L. 96–561 substituted "Magnuson Fishery Conservation and Management Act" for "Fishery Conservation and Management Act of 1976".

Subsec. (k). Pub. L. 96–483 designated existing provisions as par. (1) and added par. (2).

1978—Subsec. (a)(2). Pub. L. 95–576, §1(b)(1), excluded discharges described in cls. (A) to (C) from term "discharge".

Subsec. (a)(17). Pub. L. 95–576, §1(b)(2), added par. (17).

Subsec. (b)(2)(B). Pub. L. 95–576, §1(b)(3), substituted requirement that a study be made respecting methods, mechanisms, and procedures for creating incentives to achieve higher standard of care in management and movement of hazardous substances, including consideration of enumerated items, and a report made to Congress within 18 months after Nov. 2, 1978, for provisions concerning actual removability of any designated hazardous substance, liability during two year period commencing Oct. 18, 1972 based on toxicity, degradability, and dispersal characteristics of the substance limited to $50,000 and without limitation in cases of willful negligence or willful misconduct, liability after such two year period ranging from $500 to $5,000 based on toxicity, etc., or liability for penalty determined by number of units discharged multiplied by amount established for the unit limited to $5,000,000 in the case of a discharge from a vessel and to $500,000 in the case of a discharge from onshore or offshore facility, establishment by regulation of a unit of measurement based upon the usual trade practice for each designated hazardous substance and establishment for such unit a fixed monetary amount ranging from $100 to $1,000 based on toxicity, etc.

Subsec. (b)(3). Pub. L. 95–576, §1(b)(4), substituted "such quantities as may be harmful" for "harmful quantities".

Subsec. (b)(4). Pub. L. 95–576, §1(b)(5), struck out ", to be issued as soon as possible after October 18, 1972," after "regulation" and substituted "substances" for "substance" and "discharge of which may be harmful" for "discharge of which, at such times, locations, circumstances, and conditions, will be harmful".

Subsec. (b)(5). Pub. L. 95–576, §1(b)(6), inserted "at the time of the discharge" after "otherwise subject to the jurisdiction of the United States".

Subsec. (b)(6)(A) to (E). Pub. L. 95–576, §1(b)(7), designated existing provisions as subpar. (A), inserted "at the time of the discharge" after "jurisdiction of the United States", and added subpars. (B) to (E).

1977—Subsec. (a)(11). Pub. L. 95–217, §58(k), inserted ", and any facility of any kind which is subject to the jurisdiction of the United States and is located in, on, or under any other waters," after "United States".

Subsec. (a)(15), (16). Pub. L. 95–217, §58(d)(1), added pars. (15) and (16).

Subsec. (b)(1). Pub. L. 95–217, §58(a)(1), inserted reference to activities under the Outer Continental Shelf Lands Act or the Deepwater Port Act of 1974, or which may affect natural resources belonging to, appertaining to, or under the exclusive management authority of the United States (including resources under the Fishery Conservation and Management Act of 1976).

Subsec. (b)(2)(A). Pub. L. 95–217, §58(a)(2), inserted reference to activities under the Outer Continental Shelf Lands Act or the Deepwater Port Act of 1974, or which may affect natural resources belonging to, appertaining to, or under the exclusive management authority of the United States (including resources under the Fishery Conservation and Management Act of 1976).

Subsec. (b)(2)(B)(v). Pub. L. 95–217, §57, added cl. (v).

Subsec. (b)(3). Pub. L. 95–217, §58(a)(3), (4), designated part of existing provisions preceding cl. (A) as cl. (i) and added cl. (ii), and, in cl. (A), inserted "or which may affect natural resources belonging to, appertaining to, or under the exclusive management authority of the United States (including resources under the Fishery Conservation and Management Act of 1976)" after "waters of the contiguous zone" and struck out "article IV of" before "the International Convention for the Prevention of Pollution of the Sea by Oil, 1954".

Subsec. (b)(4). Pub. L. 95–217, §58(a)(5), struck out provisions under which, in the case of the discharge of oil into or upon the waters of the contiguous zone, only those discharges which threatened the fishery resources of the contiguous zone or threatened to pollute or contribute to the pollution of the territory or the territorial sea of the United States could be determined to be harmful.

Subsec. (b)(5). Pub. L. 95–217, §58(a)(6), added cls. (A), (B), and (C) between "Any such person" and "who fails to notify".

Subsec. (b)(6). Pub. L. 95–217, §58(a)(7), (8), substituted "Any owner, operator, or person in charge of any onshore facility, or offshore facility" for "Any owner or operator of any vessel, onshore facility, or offshore facility" in provision relating to violations of par. (3) of this subsection, and inserted provisions directing the assessment of a civil penalty of not more than $5,000 for each offense by the Secretary of the department in which the Coast Guard is operating to be assessed against any owner, operator, or person in charge of any vessel from which oil or a hazardous substance is discharged in violation of paragraph (3)(i) of this subsection, and any owner, operator, or person in charge of a vessel from which oil or a hazardous substance is discharged in violation of paragraph (3)(ii) who is otherwise subject to the jurisdiction of the United States.

Subsec. (c)(1). Pub. L. 95–217, §58(b), (c)(1), inserted "or there is a substantial threat of such discharge," after "Whenever any oil or a hazardous substance is discharged," and "or in connection with activities under the Outer Continental Shelf Lands Act or the Deepwater Port Act of 1974, or which may affect natural resources belonging to, appertaining to, or under the exclusive management authority of the United States (including resources under the Fishery Conservation and Management Act of 1976)" after "waters of the contiguous zone,".

Subsec. (c)(2)(D). Pub. L. 95–217, §58(e), substituted "and imminent threats of such discharges to the appropriate State and Federal agencies;" for "to the appropriate Federal agency;".

Subsec. (d). Pub. L. 95–217, §58(c)(2), inserted "or under the Intervention on the High Seas Act (or the convention defined in section 2(3) thereof)" after "Any expense incurred under this subsection".

Subsec. (f)(1). Pub. L. 95–217, §58(d)(2), substituted ", in the case of an inland oil barge $125 per gross ton of such barge, or $125,000, whichever is greater, and in the case of any other vessel, $150 per gross ton of such vessel (or, for a vessel carrying oil or hazardous substances as cargo, $250,000), whichever is greater," for "$100 per gross ton of such vessel or $14,000,000, whichever is lesser,".

Subsec. (f)(2), (3). Pub. L. 95–217, §58(d)(5), (6), substituted "$50,000,000" for "$8,000,000".

Subsec. (f)(4), (5). Pub. L. 95–217, §58(g), added pars. (4) and (5).

Subsec. (g). Pub. L. 95–217, § 58(d)(3), (f), substituted ", in the case of an inland oil barge $125 per gross ton of such barge, or $125,000, whichever is greater, and in the case of any other vessel, $150 per gross ton of such vessel (or, for a vessel carrying oil or hazardous substances as cargo, $250,000), whichever is greater" for "$100 per gross ton of such vessel or $14,000,000, whichever is the lesser" in the existing provisions and inserted provision under which, where the owner or operator of a vessel (other than an inland oil barge) carrying oil or hazardous substances as cargo or an onshore or offshore facility which handles or stores oil or hazardous substances in bulk, from which oil or a hazardous substance is discharged in violation of subsec. (b) of this section, alleges that the discharge was caused solely by an act or omission of a third party, the owner or operator must pay to the United States Government the actual costs incurred under subsec. (c) of this section for removal of the oil or substance and shall be entitled by subrogation to all rights of the United States Government to recover the costs from the third party under this subsection.

Subsec. (i)(2). Pub. L. 95–217, § 58(m), inserted reference to the Deepwater Port Act of 1974.

Subsec. (j)(2). Pub. L. 95–217, § 58(c)(3), inserted provision that subsec. (j)(2) shall not apply to any owner or operator of any vessel from which oil or a hazardous substance is discharged in violation of subsec. (b)(3)(ii) of this section unless the owner, operator, or person in charge is otherwise subject to the jurisdiction of the United States.

Subsec. (k). Pub. L. 95–217, § 58(*l*), substituted "such sums as may be necessary to maintain such fund at a level of $35,000,000" for "not to exceed $35,000,000".

Subsec. (p)(1). Pub. L. 95–217, § 58(d)(4), substituted ", in the case of an inland oil barge $125 per gross ton of such barge, or $125,000, whichever is greater, and in the case of any other vessel, $150 per gross ton of such vessel (or, for a vessel carrying oil or hazardous substances as cargo, $250,000), whichever is greater," for "$100 per gross ton, or $14,000,000 whichever is the lesser,".

Subsecs. (q), (r). Pub. L. 95–217, § 58(i), added subsecs. (q) and (r).

1973—Subsec. (f). Pub. L. 93–207, § 1(4)(A), (B), substituted "(b)(3)" for "(b)(2)" wherever appearing in pars. (1) to (3), and substituted "Administrator" for "Secretary" in last sentence of par. (2).

Subsecs. (g), (i). Pub. L. 93–207, § 1(4)(C), substituted "(b)(3)" for "(b)(2)" wherever appearing.

Effective Date of 2006 Amendment

Pub. L. 109–241, title IX, § 901(i)(2), July 11, 2006, 120 Stat. 564, provided in part that the amendment made by section 901(i)(2) is effective Aug. 9, 2004.

Effective Date of 1996 Amendment

Section 101(a) [title II, § 211(b)] of div. A of Pub. L. 104–208 provided that the amendment made by that section is effective 15 days after Oct. 11, 1996.

Effective Date of 1992 Amendment

Amendment by Pub. L. 102–572 effective Oct. 29, 1992, see section 911 of Pub. L. 102–572, set out as a note under section 171 of Title 28, Judiciary and Judicial Procedure.

Effective Date of 1990 Amendment

Amendment by Pub. L. 101–380 applicable to incidents occurring after Aug. 18, 1990, see section 1020 of Pub. L. 101–380, set out as an Effective Date note under section 2701 of this title.

Effective Date of 1982 Amendment

Amendment by Pub. L. 97–164 effective Oct. 1, 1982, see section 402 of Pub. L. 97–164, set out as a note under section 171 of Title 28, Judiciary and Judicial Procedure.

Effective Date of 1980 Amendments

Section 238(b) of Pub. L. 96–561 provided that the amendment made by that section is effective 15 days after Dec. 22, 1980.

Amendment by Pub. L. 96–478 effective Oct. 2, 1983, see section 14(a) of Pub. L. 96–478, set out as an Effective Date note under section 1901 of this title.

Effective Date of 1977 Amendment

Section 58(h) of Pub. L. 95–217 provided that: "The amendments made by paragraphs (5) and (6) of subsection (d) of this section [amending this section] shall take effect 180 days after the date of enactment of the Clean Water Act of 1977 [Dec. 27, 1977]."

Transfer of Functions

For transfer of authorities, functions, personnel, and assets of the Coast Guard, including the authorities and functions of the Secretary of Transportation relating thereto, to the Department of Homeland Security, and for treatment of related references, see sections 468(b), 551(d), 552(d), and 557 of Title 6, Domestic Security, and the Department of Homeland Security Reorganization Plan of November 25, 2002, as modified, set out as a note under section 542 of Title 6.

Enforcement functions of Administrator or other official of the Environmental Protection Agency under this section relating to spill prevention, containment and countermeasure plans with respect to pre-construction, construction, and initial operation of transportation system for Canadian and Alaskan natural gas were transferred to the Federal Inspector, Office of Federal Inspector for the Alaska Natural Gas Transportation System, until the first anniversary of the date of initial operation of the Alaska Natural Gas Transportation System, see Reorg. Plan No. 1 of 1979, §§ 102(a), 203(a), 44 F.R. 33663, 33666, 93 Stat. 1373, 1376, effective July 1, 1979, set out in the Appendix to Title 5, Government Organization and Employees. Office of Federal Inspector for the Alaska Natural Gas Transportation System abolished and functions and authority vested in Inspector transferred to Secretary of Energy by section 3012(b) of Pub. L. 102–486, set out as an Abolition of Office of Federal Inspector note under section 719e of Title 15, Commerce and Trade. Functions and authority vested in Secretary of Energy subsequently transferred to Federal Coordinator for Alaska Natural Gas Transportation Projects by section 720d(f) of Title 15.

Delegation of Functions

For delegation of certain functions of President under this section, see Ex. Ord. No. 12580, Jan. 23, 1987, 52 F.R. 2923, as amended, set out as a note under section 9615 of Title 42, The Public Health and Welfare.

Termination of Trust Territory of the Pacific Islands

For termination of Trust Territory of the Pacific Islands, see note set out preceding section 1681 of Title 48, Territories and Insular Possessions.

Termination of United States District Court for the District of the Canal Zone

For termination of the United States District Court for the District of the Canal Zone at end of the "transition period", being the 30-month period beginning Oct. 1, 1979, and ending midnight Mar. 31, 1982, see Paragraph 5 of Article XI of the Panama Canal Treaty of 1977 and sections 2101 and 2201 to 2203 of Pub. L. 96–70, title II, Sept. 27, 1979, 93 Stat. 493, formerly classified to sections 3831 and 3841 to 3843, respectively, of Title 22, Foreign Relations and Intercourse.

Implementation Date for Vessel Response Plans for Nontank Vessels

Pub. L. 108–293, title VII, § 701(c), Aug. 9, 2004, 118 Stat. 1068, provided that: "No later than one year after the date of enactment of this Act [Aug. 9, 2004], the owner or operator of a nontank vessel (as defined [sic] section 311(j)(9) [311(a)(26)] of the Federal Water Pollution Control Act (33 U.S.C. 1321(j)(9) [1321(a)(26)], as amended by this section) shall prepare and submit a vessel response plan for such vessel.''

REPORT ON OIL SPILL RESPONDER IMMUNITY

Pub. L. 107–295, title IV, §440, Nov. 25, 2002, 116 Stat. 2130, provided that:

''(a) REPORT TO CONGRESS.—Not later than January 1, 2004, the Secretary of the department in which the Coast Guard is operating, jointly with the Secretary of Commerce and the Secretary of the Interior, and after consultation with the Administrator of the Environmental Protection Agency and the Attorney General, shall submit a report to the Committee on Commerce, Science, and Transportation of the Senate and the Committee on Transportation and Infrastructure of the House of Representatives on the immunity from criminal and civil penalties provided under existing law of a private responder (other than a responsible party) in the case of the incidental take of federally listed fish or wildlife that results from, but is not the purpose of, carrying out an otherwise lawful activity conducted by that responder during an oil spill removal activity where the responder was acting in a manner consistent with the National Contingency Plan or as otherwise directed by the Federal On-Scene Coordinator for the spill, and on the circumstances under which such penalties have been or could be imposed on a private responder. The report shall take into consideration the procedures under the Inter-Agency Memorandum for addressing incidental takes.

''(b) DEFINITIONS.—In this section—

''(1) the term 'Federal On-Scene Coordinator' has the meaning given that term in section 311 of the Federal Water Pollution Control Act (33 U.S.C. 1321);

''(2) the term 'incidental take' has the meaning given that term in the Inter-Agency Memorandum;

''(3) the term 'Inter-Agency Memorandum' means the Inter-Agency Memorandum of Agreement Regarding Oil Spill Planning and Response Activities under the Federal Water Pollution Control Act's National Oil and Hazardous Substances Pollution Contingency Plan and the Endangered Species Act [of 1973, 16 U.S.C. 1531 et seq.], effective on July 22, 2001;

''(4) the terms 'National Contingency Plan', 'removal', and 'responsible party' have the meanings given those terms under section 1001 of the Oil Pollution Act of 1990 (33 U.S.C. 2701); and

''(5) the term 'private responder' means a nongovernmental entity or individual that is carrying out an oil spill removal activity at the direction of a Federal agency or a responsible party.''

OIL SPILL LIABILITY UNDER OIL POLLUTION ACT OF 1990

Section 2002(a) of Pub. L. 101–380 provided that: ''Subsections (f), (g), (h), and (i) of section 311 of the Federal Water Pollution Control Act (33 U.S.C. 1321) shall not apply with respect to any incident for which liability is established under section 1002 of this Act [33 U.S.C. 2702].''

TRANSFER OF MONEYS TO OIL SPILL LIABILITY TRUST FUND

Section 2002(b)(2) of Pub. L. 101–380 provided that: ''Subsection (k) [of this section] is repealed. Any amounts remaining in the revolving fund established under that subsection shall be deposited in the [Oil Spill Liability Trust] Fund. The Fund shall assume all liability incurred by the revolving fund established under that subsection.''

REVISION OF NATIONAL CONTINGENCY PLAN

Section 4201(c)[(d)] of Pub. L. 101–380 provided that: ''Not later than one year after the date of the enactment of this Act [Aug. 18, 1990], the President shall revise and republish the National Contingency Plan prepared under section 311(c)(2) of the Federal Water Pollution Control Act [33 U.S.C. 1321(c)(2)] (as in effect immediately before the date of the enactment of this Act) to implement the amendments made by this section and section 4202 [amending this section].''

[For delegation of functions of President under section 4201(c) of Pub. L. 101–380, set out above, see Ex. Ord. No. 12580, Jan. 23, 1987, 52 F.R. 2923, as amended, set out as a note under section 9615 of Title 42, The Public Health and Welfare.]

IMPLEMENTATION OF NATIONAL PLANNING AND RESPONSE SYSTEM

Section 4202(b) of Pub. L. 101–380 provided that:

''(1) AREA COMMITTEES AND CONTINGENCY PLANS.—(A) Not later than 6 months after the date of the enactment of this Act [Aug. 18, 1990], the President shall designate the areas for which Area Committees are established under section 311(j)(4) of the Federal Water Pollution Control Act [33 U.S.C. 1321(j)(4)], as amended by this Act. In designating such areas, the President shall ensure that all navigable waters, adjoining shorelines, and waters of the exclusive economic zone are subject to an Area Contingency Plan under that section.

''(B) Not later than 18 months after the date of the enactment of this Act, each Area Committee established under that section shall submit to the President the Area Contingency Plan required under that section.

''(C) Not later than 24 months after the date of the enactment of this Act, the President shall—

''(i) promptly review each plan;

''(ii) require amendments to any plan that does not meet the requirements of section 311(j)(4) of the Federal Water Pollution Control Act; and

''(iii) approve each plan that meets the requirements of that section.

''(2) NATIONAL RESPONSE UNIT.—Not later than one year after the date of the enactment of this Act, the Secretary of the department in which the Coast Guard is operating shall establish a National Response Unit in accordance with section 311(j)(2) of the Federal Water Pollution Control Act, as amended by this Act.

''(3) COAST GUARD DISTRICT RESPONSE GROUPS.—Not later than 1 year after the date of the enactment of this Act, the Secretary of the department in which the Coast Guard is operating shall establish Coast Guard District Response Groups in accordance with section 311(j)(3) of the Federal Water Pollution Control Act, as amended by this Act.

''(4) TANK VESSEL AND FACILITY RESPONSE PLANS; TRANSITION PROVISION; EFFECTIVE DATE OF PROHIBITION.—(A) Not later than 24 months after the date of the enactment of this Act, the President shall issue regulations for tank vessel and facility response plans under section 311(j)(5) of the Federal Water Pollution Control Act, as amended by this Act.

''(B) During the period beginning 30 months after the date of the enactment of this paragraph [Aug. 18, 1990] and ending 36 months after that date of enactment, a tank vessel or facility for which a response plan is required to be prepared under section 311(j)(5) of the Federal Water Pollution Control Act, as amended by this Act, may not handle, store, or transport oil unless the owner or operator thereof has submitted such a plan to the President.

''(C) Subparagraph (E) of section 311(j)(5) of the Federal Water Pollution Control Act, as amended by this Act, shall take effect 36 months after the date of the enactment of this Act.''

DEPOSIT OF CERTAIN PENALTIES INTO OIL SPILL LIABILITY TRUST FUND

Penalties paid pursuant to this section and sections 1319(c) and 1501 et seq. of this title to be deposited in the Oil Spill Liability Trust Fund created under section 9509 of Title 26, Internal Revenue Code, see section

4304 of Pub. L. 101–380, set out as a note under section 9509 of Title 26.

ALLOWABLE DELAY IN ESTABLISHING FINANCIAL RESPONSIBILITY FOR INCREASE IN AMOUNTS UNDER 1977 AMENDMENT

Section 58(j) of Pub. L. 95–217 provided that: "No vessel subject to the increased amounts which result from the amendments made by subsections (d)(2), (d)(3), and (d)(4) of this section [amending this section] shall be required to establish any evidence of financial responsibility under section 311(p) of the Federal Water Pollution Control Act [subsec. (p) of this section] for such increased amounts before October 1, 1978."

TERRITORIAL SEA AND CONTIGUOUS ZONE OF UNITED STATES

For extension of territorial sea and contiguous zone of United States, see Proc. No. 5928 and Proc. No. 7219, respectively, set out as notes under section 1331 of Title 43, Public Lands.

EXECUTIVE ORDER NO. 11735

Ex. Ord. No. 11735, Aug. 3, 1973, 38 F.R. 21243, as amended by Ex. Ord. No. 12418, May 5, 1983, 48 F.R. 20891, which assigned functions of the President regarding water pollution, was revoked by Ex. Ord. No. 12777, §8(i), Oct. 18, 1991, 56 F.R. 54769, set out below.

EXECUTIVE ORDER NO. 12418

Ex. Ord. No. 12418, May 5, 1983, 48 F.R. 20891, which transferred certain functions relating to the financial responsibility of vessels for water pollution and established authority of Federal agencies to respond to discharges or substantial threats of discharges of oil and hazardous substances, was revoked by Ex. Ord. No. 12777, §8(i), Oct. 18, 1991, 56 F.R. 54769, set out below.

EX. ORD. NO. 12777. IMPLEMENTATION OF THIS SECTION AND OIL POLLUTION ACT OF 1990

Ex. Ord. No. 12777, Oct. 18, 1991, 56 F.R. 54757, as amended by Ex. Ord. No. 13286, §34, Feb. 28, 2003, 68 F.R. 10625, provided:

By the authority vested in me as President by the Constitution and the laws of the United States of America, including Section 311 of the Federal Water Pollution Control Act, ("FWPCA") (33 U.S.C. 1321), as amended by the Oil Pollution Act of 1990 (Public Law 101–380) ("OPA"), and by Section 301 of Title 3 of the United States Code, it is hereby ordered as follows:

SECTION 1. *National Contingency Plan, Area Committees, and Area Contingency Plans.* (a) Section 1 of Executive Order No. 12580 of January 23, 1987 [42 U.S.C. 9615 note], is amended to read as follows:

"SECTION 1. *National Contingency Plan.* (a)(1) The National Contingency Plan ("the NCP"), shall provide for a National Response Team ("the NRT") composed of representatives of appropriate Federal departments and agencies for national planning and coordination of preparedness and response actions, and Regional Response Teams as the regional counterparts to the NRT for planning and coordination of regional preparedness and response actions.

"(2) The following agencies (in addition to other appropriate agencies) shall provide representatives to the National and Regional Response Teams to carry out their responsibilities under the NCP: Department of State, Department of Defense, Department of Justice, Department of the Interior, Department of Agriculture, Department of Commerce, Department of Labor, Department of Health and Human Services, Department of Transportation, Department of Energy, Environmental Protection Agency, Federal Emergency Management Agency, United States Coast Guard, and the Nuclear Regulatory Commission.

"(3) Except for periods of activation because of response action, the representative of the Environmental Protection Agency ("EPA") shall be the chairman, and the representative of the United States Coast Guard shall be the vice chairman, of the NRT and these agencies' representatives shall be co-chairs of the Regional Response Teams ("the RRTs"). When the NRT or an RRT is activated for a response action, the EPA representative shall be the chairman when the release or threatened release or discharge or threatened discharge occurs in the inland zone, and the United States Coast Guard representative shall be the chairman when the release or threatened release or discharge or threatened discharge occurs in the coastal zone, unless otherwise agreed upon by the EPA and the United States Coast Guard representatives (inland and coastal zones are defined in the NCP).

"(4) The RRTs may include representatives from State governments, local governments (as agreed upon by the States), and Indian tribal governments. Subject to the functions and authorities delegated to Executive departments and agencies in other sections of this order, the NRT shall provide policy and program direction to the RRTs.

"(b)(1) The responsibility for the revision of the NCP and all the other functions vested in the President by Sections 105(a), (b), (c), and (g), 125, and 301(f) of the Act, by Section 311(d)(1) of the Federal Water Pollution Control Act, and by Section 4201(c) of the Oil Pollution Act of 1990 is delegated to the Administrator of the Environmental Protection Agency ("the Administrator").

"(2) The function vested in the President by Section 118(p) of the Superfund Amendments and Reauthorization Act of 1986 (Pub. L. 99–499) ("SARA") is delegated to the Administrator.

"(c) In accord with Section 107(f)(2)(A) of the Act, Section 311(f)(5) of the Federal Water Pollution Control Act, as amended (33 U.S.C. 1321(f)(5)), and Section 1006(b)(1) and (2) of the Oil Pollution Act of 1990, the following shall be among those designated in the NCP as Federal trustees for natural resources:

["](1) Secretary of Defense;
["](2) Secretary of the Interior;
["](3) Secretary of Agriculture;
["](4) Secretary of Commerce;
["](5) Secretary of Energy.

["]In the event of a spill, the above named Federal trustees for natural resources shall designate one trustee to act as Lead Administrative Trustee, the duties of which shall be defined in the regulations promulgated pursuant to Section 1006(e)(1) of OPA. If there are natural resource trustees other than those designated above which are acting in the event of a spill, those other trustees may join with the Federal trustees to name a Lead Administrative Trustee which shall exercise the duties defined in the regulations promulgated pursuant to Section 1006(e)(1) of OPA.

"(d) Revisions to the NCP shall be made in consultation with members of the NRT prior to publication for notice and comment.

"(e) All revisions to the NCP, whether in proposed or final form, shall be subject to review and approval by the Director of the Office of Management and Budget ("OMB")."

(b) The functions vested in the President by Section 311(j)(4) of FWPCA, and Section 4202(b)(1) of OPA [set out as a note above], respecting the designation of Areas, the appointment of Area Committee members, the requiring of information to be included in Area Contingency Plans, and the review and approval of Area Contingency Plans are delegated to the Administrator of the Environmental Protection Agency ("Administrator") for the inland zone and the Secretary of the Department in which the Coast Guard is operating for the coastal zone (inland and coastal zones are defined in the NCP).

SEC. 2. *National Response System.* (a) The functions vested in the President by Section 311(j)(1)(A) of FWPCA, respecting the establishment of methods and procedures for the removal of discharged oil and hazardous substances, and by Section 311(j)(1)(B) of FWPCA respecting the establishment of criteria for the development and implementation of local and regional oil and hazardous substance removal contingency plans, are delegated to the Administrator for the inland zone and the Secretary of the Department in which the Coast Guard is operating for the coastal zone.

(b)(1) The functions vested in the President by Section 311(j)(1)(C) of FWPCA, respecting the establishment of procedures, methods, and equipment and other requirements for equipment to prevent and to contain discharges of oil and hazardous substances from non-transportation-related onshore facilities, are delegated to the Administrator.

(2) The functions vested in the President by Section 311(j)(1)(C) of FWPCA, respecting the establishment of procedures, methods, and equipment and other requirements for equipment to prevent and to contain discharges of oil and hazardous substances from vessels and transportation-related onshore facilities and deepwater ports subject to the Deepwater Ports [Port] Act of 1974 ("DPA") [33 U.S.C. 1501 et seq.], are delegated to the Secretary of Transportation and the Secretary of the Department in which the Coast Guard is operating.

(3) The functions vested in the President by Section 311(j)(1)(C) of FWPCA, respecting the establishment of procedures, methods, and equipment and other requirements for equipment to prevent and to contain discharges of oil and hazardous substances from offshore facilities, including associated pipelines, other than deepwater ports subject to the DPA, are delegated to the Secretary of the Interior.

(c) The functions vested in the President by Section 311(j)(1)(D) of FWPCA, respecting the inspection of vessels carrying cargoes of oil and hazardous substances and the inspection of such cargoes, are delegated to the Secretary of the Department in which the Coast Guard is operating.

(d)(1) The functions vested in the President by Section 311(j)(5) of FWPCA and Section 4202(b)(4) of OPA [set out as a note above], respecting the issuance of regulations requiring the owners or operators of non-transportation-related onshore facilities to prepare and submit response plans, the approval of means to ensure the availability of private personnel and equipment, the review and approval of such response plans, and the authorization of non-transportation-related onshore facilities to operate without approved response plans, are delegated to the Administrator.

(2) The functions vested in the President by Section 311(j)(5) of FWPCA and Section 4202(b)(4) of OPA, respecting the issuance of regulations requiring the owners or operators of tank vessels, transportation-related onshore facilities and deepwater ports subject to the DPA, to prepare and submit response plans, the approval of means to ensure the availability of private personnel and equipment, the review and approval of such response plans, and the authorization of tank vessels, transportation-related onshore facilities and deepwater ports subject to the DPA to operate without approved response plans, are delegated to the Secretary of Transportation and the Secretary of the Department in which the Coast Guard is operating.

(3) The functions vested in the President by Section 311(j)(5) of FWPCA and Section 4202(b)(4) of OPA, respecting the issuance of regulations requiring the owners or operators of offshore facilities, including associated pipelines, other than deepwater ports subject to the DPA, to prepare and submit response plans, the approval of means to ensure the availability of private personnel and equipment, the review and approval of such response plans, and the authorization of offshore facilities, including associated pipelines, other than deepwater ports subject to the DPA, to operate without approved response plans, are delegated to the Secretary of the Interior.

(e)(1) The functions vested in the President by Section 311(j)(6)(A) of FWPCA, respecting the requirements for periodic inspections of containment booms and equipment used to remove discharges at non-transportation-related onshore facilities, are delegated to the Administrator.

(2) The functions vested in the President by Section 311(j)(6)(A) of FWPCA, respecting the requirements for periodic inspections of containment booms and equipment used to remove discharges on vessels, and at transportation-related onshore facilities and deepwater ports subject to the DPA, are delegated to the Secretary of the Department in which the Coast Guard is operating.

(3) The functions vested in the President by Section 311(j)(6)(A) of FWPCA, respecting the requirements for periodic inspections of containment booms and equipment used to remove discharges at offshore facilities, including associated pipelines, other than deepwater ports subject to the DPA, are delegated to the Secretary of the Interior.

(f) The functions vested in the President by Section 311(j)(6)(B) of FWPCA, respecting requirements for vessels to carry appropriate removal equipment, are delegated to the Secretary of the Department in which the Coast Guard is operating.

(g)(1) The functions vested in the President by Section 311(j)(7) of FWPCA, respecting periodic drills of removal capability under relevant response plans for onshore and offshore facilities located in the inland zone, and the publishing of annual reports on those drills, are delegated to the Administrator.

(2) The functions vested in the President by Section 311(j)(7) of FWPCA, respecting periodic drills of removal capability under relevant response plans for tank vessels, and for onshore and offshore facilities located in the coastal zone, and the publishing of annual reports on those drills, are delegated to the Secretary of the Department in which the Coast Guard is operating.

(h) No provision of Section 2 of this order, including, but not limited to, any delegation or assignment of any function hereunder, shall in any way affect, or be construed or interpreted to affect the authority of any Department or agency, or the head of any Department or agency under any provision of law other than Section 311(j) of FWPCA or Section 4202(b)(4) of OPA.

(i) The functions vested in the President by Section 311(j) of FWPCA or Section 4202(b)(4) of OPA which have been delegated or assigned by Section 2 of this order may be redelegated to the head of any Executive department or agency with his or her consent.

SEC. 3. *Removal.* The functions vested in the President by Section 311(c) of FWPCA and Section 1011 of OPA [33 U.S.C. 2711], respecting an effective and immediate removal or arrangement for removal of a discharge and mitigation or prevention of a substantial threat of a discharge of oil or a hazardous substance, the direction and monitoring of all Federal, State and private actions, the removal and destruction of a vessel, the issuance of directions, consulting with affected trustees, and removal completion determinations, are delegated to the Administrator for the inland zone and to the Secretary of the Department in which the Coast Guard is operating for the coastal zone.

SEC. 4. *Liability Limit Adjustment.* (a) The functions vested in the President by Section 1004(d) of OPA [33 U.S.C. 2704(d)], respecting the establishment of limits of liability, with respect to classes or categories of non-transportation-related onshore facilities, the reporting to Congress on the desirability of adjusting limits of liability with respect to non-transportation-related onshore facilities, and the adjustment of limits of liability to reflect significant increases in the Consumer Price Index with respect to non-transportation-related onshore facilities, are delegated to the Administrator, acting in consultation with the Secretary of Transportation, the Secretary of Energy, and the Attorney General.

(b) The functions vested in the President by Section 1004(d) of OPA, respecting the establishment of limits of liability, with respect to classes or categories of transportation-related onshore facilities, the reporting to Congress on the desirability of adjusting limits of liability, with respect to vessels or transportation-related onshore facilities and deepwater ports subject to the DPA, and the adjustment of limits of liability to reflect significant increases in the Consumer Price Index with respect to vessels or transportation-related onshore facilities and deepwater ports subject to the DPA, are delegated to the Secretary of Transportation.

(c) The functions vested in the President by Section 1004(d) of OPA, respecting the reporting to Congress on the desirability of adjusting limits of liability with respect to offshore facilities, including associated pipelines, other than deepwater ports subject to the DPA, and the adjustment of limits of liability to reflect significant increases in the Consumer Price Index with respect to offshore facilities, including associated pipelines, other than deepwater ports subject to the DPA, are delegated to the Secretary of the Interior.

SEC. 5. *Financial Responsibility*. (a)(1) The functions vested in the President by Section 1016(e) of OPA [33 U.S.C. 2716(e)], respecting (in the case of offshore facilities other than deepwater ports) the issuance of regulations concerning financial responsibility, the determination of acceptable methods of financial responsibility, and the specification of necessary or unacceptable terms, conditions, or defenses, are delegated to the Secretary of the Interior.

(2) The functions vested in the President by Section 1016(e) of OPA, respecting (in the case of deepwater ports) the issuance of regulations concerning financial responsibility, the determination of acceptable methods of financial responsibility, and the specification of necessary or unacceptable terms, conditions, or defenses, are delegated to the Secretary of the Department in which the Coast Guard is operating.

(b)(1) The functions vested in the President by Section 4303 of OPA [33 U.S.C. 2716a], respecting (in cases involving vessels) the assessment of civil penalties, the compromising, modification or remission, with or without condition, and the referral for collection of such imposed penalties, and requests to the Attorney General to secure necessary judicial relief, are delegated to the Secretary of the Department in which the Coast Guard is operating.

(2) The functions vested in the President by Section 4303 of OPA, respecting (in cases involving offshore facilities other than deepwater ports) the assessment of civil penalties, the compromising, modification or remission, with or without condition, and the referral for collection of such imposed penalties, and requests to the Attorney General to secure necessary judicial relief, are delegated to the Secretary of the Interior.

(3) The functions vested in the President by Section 4303 of OPA, respecting (in cases involving deepwater ports) the assessment of civil penalties, the compromising, modification or remission, with or without condition, and the referral for collection of such imposed penalties, and requests to the Attorney General to secure necessary judicial relief, are delegated to the Secretary of the Department in which the Coast Guard is operating.

SEC. 6. *Enforcement*. (a) The functions vested in the President by Section 311(m)(1) of FWPCA, respecting the enforcement of Section 311 with respect to vessels, are delegated to the Secretary of the Department in which the Coast Guard is operating.

(b) The functions vested in the President by Section 311(e) of FWPCA, respecting determinations of imminent and substantial threat, requesting the Attorney General to secure judicial relief, and other action including issuing administrative orders, are delegated to the Administrator for the inland zone and to the Secretary of the Department in which the Coast Guard is operating for the coastal zone.

SEC. 7. *Management of the Oil Spill Liability Trust Fund and Claims*. (a)(1)(A) The functions vested in the President by Section 1012(a)(1), (3), and (4) of OPA [33 U.S.C. 2712(a)(1), (3), (4)] respecting payment of removal costs and claims and determining consistency with the National Contingency Plan (NCP) are delegated to the Secretary of the Department in which the Coast Guard is operating.

(B) The functions vested in the President by Section 6002(b) of the OPA [33 U.S.C. 2752(b)] respecting making amounts, not to exceed $50,000,000 and subject to normal budget controls, in any fiscal year, available from the Fund (i) to carry out Section 311(c) of FWPCA, and (ii) to initiate the assessment of natural resources damages required under Section 1006 of OPA [33 U.S.C. 2706] are delegated to the Secretary of the Department in which the Coast Guard is operating. Such Secretary shall make amounts available from the Fund to initiate the assessment of natural resources damages exclusively to the Federal trustees designated in the NCP. Such Federal trustees shall allocate such amounts among all trustees required to assess natural resources damages under Section 1006 of OPA.

(2) The functions vested in the President by Section 1012(a)(2) of OPA [33 U.S.C. 2712(a)(2)], respecting the payment of costs and determining consistency with the NCP, are delegated to the Federal trustees designated in the NCP.

(3) The functions vested in the President by Section 1012(a)(5) of OPA, respecting the payment of costs and expenses of departments and agencies having responsibility for the implementation, administration, and enforcement of the Oil Pollution Act of 1990 and subsections (b), (c), (d), (j) and (*l*) of Section 311 of FWPCA, are delegated to each head of such department and agency.

(b) The functions vested in the President by Section 1012(c) of OPA, respecting designation of Federal officials who may obligate money, are delegated to each head of the departments and agencies to whom functions have been delegated under section 7(a) of this order for the purpose of carrying out such functions.

(c)(1) The functions vested in the President by Section 1012(d) and (e) of OPA, respecting the obligation of the Trust Fund on the request of a Governor or pursuant to an agreement with a State, entrance into agreements with States, agreement upon terms and conditions, and the promulgation of regulations concerning such obligation and entrance into such agreement, are delegated to the Secretary of the Department in which the Coast Guard is operating, in consultation with the Administrator.

(2) The functions vested in the President by Section 1013(e) of OPA [33 U.S.C. 2713(e)], respecting the promulgation and amendment of regulations for the presentation, filing, processing, settlement, and adjudication of claims under OPA against the Trust Fund, are delegated to the Secretary of the Department in which the Coast Guard is operating, in consultation with the Attorney General.

(3) The functions vested in the President by Section 1012(a) of OPA, respecting the payment of costs, damages, and claims, delegated herein to the Secretary of the Department in which the Coast Guard is operating, include, *inter alia*, the authority to process, settle, and administratively adjudicate such costs, damages, and claims, regardless of amount.

(d)(1) The Coast Guard is designated the "appropriate agency" for the purpose of receiving the notice of discharge of oil or hazardous substances required by Section 311(b)(5) of FWPCA, and the Secretary of the Department in which the Coast Guard is operating is authorized to issue regulations implementing this designation.

(2) The functions vested in the President by Section 1014 of OPA [33 U.S.C. 2714], respecting designation of sources of discharges or threats, notification to responsible parties, promulgation of regulations respecting advertisements, the advertisement of designation, and notification of claims procedures, are delegated to the Secretary of the Department in which the Coast Guard is operating.

SEC. 8. *Miscellaneous*. (a) The functions vested in the President by Section 311(b)(3) and (4) of FWPCA, as amended by the Oil Pollution Act of 1990, respecting the determination of quantities of oil and any hazardous substances the discharge of which may be harmful to the public health or welfare or the environment and the determinations of quantities, time, locations, circumstances, or conditions, which are not harmful, are delegated to the Administrator.

(b) The functions vested in the President by Section 311(d)(2)(G) of FWPCA, respecting schedules of dispersant, chemical, and other spill mitigating devices or substances, are delegated to the Administrator.

(c) The functions vested in the President by Section 1006(b)(3) and (4) of OPA [33 U.S.C. 2706(b)(3), (4)] respecting the receipt of designations of State and Indian tribe trustees for natural resources are delegated to the Administrator.

(d) The function vested in the President by Section 3004 of OPA [104 Stat. 508], with respect to encouraging the development of an international inventory of equipment and personnel, is delegated to the Secretary of the Department in which the Coast Guard is operating, in consultation with the Secretary of State.

(e) The functions vested in the President by Section 4113 of OPA [104 Stat. 516], respecting a study on the use of liners or other secondary means of containment for onshore facilities, and the implementation of the recommendations of the study, are delegated to the Administrator.

(f) The function vested in the President by Section 5002(c)(2)(D) of OPA [33 U.S.C. 2732(c)(2)(D)], respecting the designating of an employee of the Federal Government who shall represent the Federal Government on the Oil Terminal Facilities and Oil Tanker Operations Associations, is delegated to the Secretary of the Department in which the Coast Guard is operating.

(g) The functions vested in the President by Section 5002(*o*) of OPA, respecting the annual certification of alternative voluntary advisory groups, are delegated to the Secretary of the Department in which the Coast Guard is operating.

(h) The function vested in the President by Section 7001(a)(3) of OPA [33 U.S.C. 2761(a)(3)], respecting the appointment of Federal agencies to membership on the Interagency Coordinating Committee on Oil Pollution Research, is delegated to the Secretary of the Department in which the Coast Guard is operating.

(i) Executive Order No. 11735 of August 3, 1973, Executive Order No. 12123 of February 26, 1979, Executive Order No. 12418 of May 5, 1983 and the memorandum of August 24, 1990, delegating certain authorities of the President under the Oil Pollution Act of 1990 are revoked.

SEC. 9. *Consultation*. Authorities and functions delegated or assigned by this order shall be exercised subject to consultation with the Secretaries of departments and the heads of agencies with statutory responsibilities which may be significantly affected, including, but not limited to, the Department of Justice.

SEC. 10. *Litigation*. (a) Notwithstanding any other provision of this order, any representation pursuant to or under this order in any judicial proceedings shall be by or through the Attorney General. The conduct and control of all litigation arising under the Oil Pollution Act of 1990 [see Short Title note set out under section 2701 of this title] shall be the responsibility of the Attorney General.

(b) Notwithstanding any other provision of this order, the authority under the Oil Pollution Act of 1990 to require the Attorney General to commence litigation is retained by the President.

(c) Notwithstanding any other provision of this order, the Secretaries of the Departments of Transportation, Commerce, Interior, Agriculture, the Secretary of the Department in which the Coast Guard is operating, and/or the Administrator of the Environmental Protection Agency may request that the Attorney General commence litigation under the Oil Pollution Act of 1990.

(d) The Attorney General, in his discretion, is authorized to require that, with respect to a particular oil spill, an agency refrain from taking administrative enforcement action without first consulting with the Attorney General.

§ 1322. Marine sanitation devices

(a) Definitions

For the purpose of this section, the term—

(1) "new vessel" includes every description of watercraft or other artificial contrivance used, or capable of being used, as a means of transportation on the navigable waters, the construction of which is initiated after promulgation of standards and regulations under this section;

(2) "existing vessel" includes every description of watercraft or other artificial contrivance used, or capable of being used, as a means of transportation on the navigable waters, the construction of which is initiated before promulgation of standards and regulations under this section;

(3) "public vessel" means a vessel owned or bareboat chartered and operated by the United States, by a State or political subdivision thereof, or by a foreign nation, except when such vessel is engaged in commerce;

(4) "United States" includes the States, the District of Columbia, the Commonwealth of Puerto Rico, the Virgin Islands, Guam, American Samoa, the Canal Zone, and the Trust Territory of the Pacific Islands;

(5) "marine sanitation device" includes any equipment for installation on board a vessel which is designed to receive, retain, treat, or discharge sewage, and any process to treat such sewage;

(6) "sewage" means human body wastes and the wastes from toilets and other receptacles intended to receive or retain body wastes except that, with respect to commercial vessels on the Great Lakes, such term shall include graywater;

(7) "manufacturer" means any person engaged in the manufacturing, assembling, or importation of marine sanitation devices or of vessels subject to standards and regulations promulgated under this section;

(8) "person" means an individual, partnership, firm, corporation, association, or agency of the United States, but does not include an individual on board a public vessel;

(9) "discharge" includes, but is not limited to, any spilling, leaking, pumping, pouring, emitting, emptying or dumping;

(10) "commercial vessels" means those vessels used in the business of transporting property for compensation or hire, or in transporting property in the business of the owner, lessee, or operator of the vessel;

(11) "graywater" means galley, bath, and shower water;

(12) "discharge incidental to the normal operation of a vessel"—

(A) means a discharge, including—

(i) graywater, bilge water, cooling water, weather deck runoff, ballast water, oil water separator effluent, and any other pollutant discharge from the operation of a marine propulsion system, shipboard maneuvering system, crew habitability system, or installed major equipment, such as an aircraft carrier elevator or a catapult, or from a protective, preservative, or absorptive application to the hull of the vessel; and

(ii) a discharge in connection with the testing, maintenance, and repair of a system described in clause (i) whenever the vessel is waterborne; and

(B) does not include—

(i) a discharge of rubbish, trash, garbage, or other such material discharged overboard;

(ii) an air emission resulting from the operation of a vessel propulsion system, motor driven equipment, or incinerator; or

(iii) a discharge that is not covered by part 122.3 of title 40, Code of Federal Regulations (as in effect on February 10, 1996);

(13) "marine pollution control device" means any equipment or management practice, for installation or use on board a vessel of the Armed Forces, that is—

(A) designed to receive, retain, treat, control, or discharge a discharge incidental to the normal operation of a vessel; and

(B) determined by the Administrator and the Secretary of Defense to be the most effective equipment or management practice to reduce the environmental impacts of the discharge consistent with the considerations set forth in subsection (n)(2)(B) of this section; and

(14) "vessel of the Armed Forces" means—

(A) any vessel owned or operated by the Department of Defense, other than a time or voyage chartered vessel; and

(B) any vessel owned or operated by the Department of Transportation that is designated by the Secretary of the department in which the Coast Guard is operating as a vessel equivalent to a vessel described in subparagraph (A).

(b) Federal standards of performance

(1) As soon as possible, after October 18, 1972, and subject to the provisions of section 1254(j) of this title, the Administrator, after consultation with the Secretary of the department in which the Coast Guard is operating, after giving appropriate consideration to the economic costs involved, and within the limits of available technology, shall promulgate Federal standards of performance for marine sanitation devices (hereafter in this section referred to as "standards") which shall be designed to prevent the discharge of untreated or inadequately treated sewage into or upon the navigable waters from new vessels and existing vessels, except vessels not equipped with installed toilet facilities. Such standards and standards established under subsection (c)(1)(B) of this section shall be consistent with maritime safety and the marine and navigation laws and regulations and shall be coordinated with the regulations issued under this subsection by the Secretary of the department in which the Coast Guard is operating. The Secretary of the department in which the Coast Guard is operating shall promulgate regulations, which are consistent with standards promulgated under this subsection and subsection (c) of this section and with maritime safety and the marine and navigation laws and regulations governing the design, construction, installation, and operation of any marine sanitation device on board such vessels.

(2) Any existing vessel equipped with a marine sanitation device on the date of promulgation of initial standards and regulations under this section, which device is in compliance with such initial standards and regulations, shall be deemed in compliance with this section until such time as the device is replaced or is found not to be in compliance with such initial standards and regulations.

(c) Initial standards; effective dates; revision; waiver

(1)(A) Initial standards and regulations under this section shall become effective for new vessels two years after promulgation; and for existing vessels five years after promulgation. Revisions of standards and regulations shall be effective upon promulgation, unless another effective date is specified, except that no revision shall take effect before the effective date of the standard or regulation being revised.

(B) The Administrator shall, with respect to commercial vessels on the Great Lakes, establish standards which require at a minimum the equivalent of secondary treatment as defined under section 1314(d) of this title. Such standards and regulations shall take effect for existing vessels after such time as the Administrator determines to be reasonable for the upgrading of marine sanitation devices to attain such standard.

(2) The Secretary of the department in which the Coast Guard is operating with regard to his regulatory authority established by this section, after consultation with the Administrator, may distinguish among classes, type, and sizes of vessels as well as between new and existing vessels, and may waive applicability of standards and regulations as necessary or appropriate for such classes, types, and sizes of vessels (including existing vessels equipped with marine sanitation devices on the date of promulgation of the initial standards required by this section), and, upon application, for individual vessels.

(d) Vessels owned and operated by the United States

The provisions of this section and the standards and regulations promulgated hereunder apply to vessels owned and operated by the United States unless the Secretary of Defense finds that compliance would not be in the interest of national security. With respect to vessels owned and operated by the Department of Defense, regulations under the last sentence of subsection (b)(1) of this section and certifications under subsection (g)(2) of this section shall be promulgated and issued by the Secretary of Defense.

(e) Pre-promulgation consultation

Before the standards and regulations under this section are promulgated, the Administrator and the Secretary of the department in which the Coast Guard is operating shall consult with the Secretary of State; the Secretary of Health and Human Services; the Secretary of Defense; the Secretary of the Treasury; the Secretary of Commerce; other interested Federal agencies; and the States and industries interested; and otherwise comply with the requirements of section 553 of title 5.

(f) Regulation by States or political subdivisions thereof; complete prohibition upon discharge of sewage

(1)(A) Except as provided in subparagraph (B), after the effective date of the initial standards and regulations promulgated under this section, no State or political subdivision thereof shall adopt or enforce any statute or regulation of such State or political subdivision with respect to the design, manufacture, or installation or use of any marine sanitation device on any vessel subject to the provisions of this section.

(B) A State may adopt and enforce a statute or regulation with respect to the design, manufacture, or installation or use of any marine sanitation device on a houseboat, if such statute or regulation is more stringent than the standards and regulations promulgated under this section. For purposes of this paragraph, the term "houseboat" means a vessel which, for a period of time determined by the State in which the vessel is located, is used primarily as a residence and is not used primarily as a means of transportation.

(2) If, after promulgation of the initial standards and regulations and prior to their effective date, a vessel is equipped with a marine sanitation device in compliance with such standards and regulations and the installation and operation of such device is in accordance with such standards and regulations, such standards and regulations shall, for the purposes of paragraph (1) of this subsection, become effective with respect to such vessel on the date of such compliance.

(3) After the effective date of the initial standards and regulations promulgated under this section, if any State determines that the protection and enhancement of the quality of some or all of the waters within such State require greater environmental protection, such State may completely prohibit the discharge from all vessels of any sewage, whether treated or not, into such waters, except that no such prohibition shall apply until the Administrator determines that adequate facilities for the safe and sanitary removal and treatment of sewage from all vessels are reasonably available for such water to which such prohibition would apply. Upon application of the State, the Administrator shall make such determination within 90 days of the date of such application.

(4)(A) If the Administrator determines upon application by a State that the protection and enhancement of the quality of specified waters within such State requires such a prohibition, he shall by regulation completely prohibit the discharge from a vessel of any sewage (whether treated or not) into such waters.

(B) Upon application by a State, the Administrator shall, by regulation, establish a drinking water intake zone in any waters within such State and prohibit the discharge of sewage from vessels within that zone.

(g) Sales limited to certified devices; certification of test device; recordkeeping; reports

(1) No manufacturer of a marine sanitation device shall sell, offer for sale, or introduce or deliver for introduction in interstate commerce, or import into the United States for sale or resale any marine sanitation device manufactured after the effective date of the standards and regulations promulgated under this section unless such device is in all material respects substantially the same as a test device certified under this subsection.

(2) Upon application of the manufacturer, the Secretary of the department in which the Coast Guard is operating shall so certify a marine sanitation device if he determines, in accordance with the provisions of this paragraph, that it meets the appropriate standards and regulations promulgated under this section. The Secretary of the department in which the Coast Guard is operating shall test or require such testing of the device in accordance with procedures set forth by the Administrator as to standards of performance and for such other purposes as may be appropriate. If the Secretary of the department in which the Coast Guard is operating determines that the device is satisfactory from the standpoint of safety and any other requirements of maritime law or regulation, and after consideration of the design, installation, operation, material, or other appropriate factors, he shall certify the device. Any device manufactured by such manufacturer which is in all material respects substantially the same as the certified test device shall be deemed to be in conformity with the appropriate standards and regulations established under this section.

(3) Every manufacturer shall establish and maintain such records, make such reports, and provide such information as the Administrator or the Secretary of the department in which the Coast Guard is operating may reasonably require to enable him to determine whether such manufacturer has acted or is acting in compliance with this section and regulations issued thereunder and shall, upon request of an officer or employee duly designated by the Administrator or the Secretary of the department in which the Coast Guard is operating, permit such officer or employee at reasonable times to have access to and copy such records. All information reported to or otherwise obtained by the Administrator or the Secretary of the Department in which the Coast Guard is operating or their representatives pursuant to this subsection which contains or relates to a trade secret or other matter referred to in section 1905 of title 18 shall be considered confidential for the purpose of that section, except that such information may be disclosed to other officers or employees concerned with carrying out this section. This paragraph shall not apply in the case of the construction of a vessel by an individual for his own use.

(h) Sale and resale of properly equipped vessels; operability of certified marine sanitation devices

After the effective date of standards and regulations promulgated under this section, it shall be unlawful—

(1) for the manufacturer of any vessel subject to such standards and regulations to manufacture for sale, to sell or offer for sale, or to distribute for sale or resale any such vessel unless it is equipped with a marine sanitation device which is in all material respects sub-

stantially the same as the appropriate test device certified pursuant to this section;

(2) for any person, prior to the sale or delivery of a vessel subject to such standards and regulations to the ultimate purchaser, wrongfully to remove or render inoperative any certified marine sanitation device or element of design of such device installed in such vessel;

(3) for any person to fail or refuse to permit access to or copying of records or to fail to make reports or provide information required under this section; and

(4) for a vessel subject to such standards and regulations to operate on the navigable waters of the United States, if such vessel is not equipped with an operable marine sanitation device certified pursuant to this section.

(i) Jurisdiction to restrain violations; contempts

The district courts of the United States shall have jurisdictions to restrain violations of subsection (g)(1) of this section and subsections (h)(1) through (3) of this section. Actions to restrain such violations shall be brought by, and in, the name of the United States. In case of contumacy or refusal to obey a subpena served upon any person under this subsection, the district court of the United States for any district in which such person is found or resides or transacts business, upon application by the United States and after notice to such person, shall have jurisdiction to issue an order requiring such person to appear and give testimony or to appear and produce documents, and any failure to obey such order of the court may be punished by such court as a contempt thereof.

(j) Penalties

Any person who violates subsection (g)(1) of this section, clause (1) or (2) of subsection (h) of this section, or subsection (n)(8) of this section shall be liable to a civil penalty of not more than $5,000 for each violation. Any person who violates clause (4) of subsection (h) of this section or any regulation issued pursuant to this section shall be liable to a civil penalty of not more than $2,000 for each violation. Each violation shall be a separate offense. The Secretary of the department in which the Coast Guard is operating may assess and compromise any such penalty. No penalty shall be assessed until the person charged shall have been given notice and an opportunity for a hearing on such charge. In determining the amount of the penalty, or the amount agreed upon in compromise, the gravity of the violation, and the demonstrated good faith of the person charged in attempting to achieve rapid compliance, after notification of a violation, shall be considered by said Secretary.

(k) Enforcement authority

The provisions of this section shall be enforced by the Secretary of the department in which the Coast Guard is operating and he may utilize by agreement, with or without reimbursement, law enforcement officers or other personnel and facilities of the Administrator, other Federal agencies, or the States to carry out the provisions of this section. The provisions of this section may also be enforced by a State.

(*l*) Boarding and inspection of vessels; execution of warrants and other process

Anyone authorized by the Secretary of the department in which the Coast Guard is operating to enforce the provisions of this section may, except as to public vessels, (1) board and inspect any vessel upon the navigable waters of the United States and (2) execute any warrant or other process issued by an officer or court of competent jurisdiction.

(m) Enforcement in United States possessions

In the case of Guam and the Trust Territory of the Pacific Islands, actions arising under this section may be brought in the district court of Guam, and in the case of the Virgin Islands such actions may be brought in the district court of the Virgin Islands. In the case of American Samoa and the Trust Territory of the Pacific Islands, such actions may be brought in the District Court of the United States for the District of Hawaii and such court shall have jurisdiction of such actions. In the case of the Canal Zone, such actions may be brought in the District Court for the District of the Canal Zone.

(n) Uniform national discharge standards for vessels of Armed Forces

(1) Applicability

This subsection shall apply to vessels of the Armed Forces and discharges, other than sewage, incidental to the normal operation of a vessel of the Armed Forces, unless the Secretary of Defense finds that compliance with this subsection would not be in the national security interests of the United States.

(2) Determination of discharges required to be controlled by marine pollution control devices

(A) In general

The Administrator and the Secretary of Defense, after consultation with the Secretary of the department in which the Coast Guard is operating, the Secretary of Commerce, and interested States, shall jointly determine the discharges incidental to the normal operation of a vessel of the Armed Forces for which it is reasonable and practicable to require use of a marine pollution control device to mitigate adverse impacts on the marine environment. Notwithstanding subsection (a)(1) of section 553 of title 5, the Administrator and the Secretary of Defense shall promulgate the determinations in accordance with such section. The Secretary of Defense shall require the use of a marine pollution control device on board a vessel of the Armed Forces in any case in which it is determined that the use of such a device is reasonable and practicable.

(B) Considerations

In making a determination under subparagraph (A), the Administrator and the Secretary of Defense shall take into consideration—

(i) the nature of the discharge;

(ii) the environmental effects of the discharge;

(iii) the practicability of using the marine pollution control device;

(iv) the effect that installation or use of the marine pollution control device would have on the operation or operational capability of the vessel;

(v) applicable United States law;

(vi) applicable international standards; and

(vii) the economic costs of the installation and use of the marine pollution control device.

(3) Performance standards for marine pollution control devices

(A) In general

For each discharge for which a marine pollution control device is determined to be required under paragraph (2), the Administrator and the Secretary of Defense, in consultation with the Secretary of the department in which the Coast Guard is operating, the Secretary of State, the Secretary of Commerce, other interested Federal agencies, and interested States, shall jointly promulgate Federal standards of performance for each marine pollution control device required with respect to the discharge. Notwithstanding subsection (a)(1) of section 553 of title 5, the Administrator and the Secretary of Defense shall promulgate the standards in accordance with such section.

(B) Considerations

In promulgating standards under this paragraph, the Administrator and the Secretary of Defense shall take into consideration the matters set forth in paragraph (2)(B).

(C) Classes, types, and sizes of vessels

The standards promulgated under this paragraph may—

(i) distinguish among classes, types, and sizes of vessels;

(ii) distinguish between new and existing vessels; and

(iii) provide for a waiver of the applicability of the standards as necessary or appropriate to a particular class, type, age, or size of vessel.

(4) Regulations for use of marine pollution control devices

The Secretary of Defense, after consultation with the Administrator and the Secretary of the department in which the Coast Guard is operating, shall promulgate such regulations governing the design, construction, installation, and use of marine pollution control devices on board vessels of the Armed Forces as are necessary to achieve the standards promulgated under paragraph (3).

(5) Deadlines; effective date

(A) Determinations

The Administrator and the Secretary of Defense shall—

(i) make the initial determinations under paragraph (2) not later than 2 years after February 10, 1996; and

(ii) every 5 years—

(I) review the determinations; and

(II) if necessary, revise the determinations based on significant new information.

(B) Standards

The Administrator and the Secretary of Defense shall—

(i) promulgate standards of performance for a marine pollution control device under paragraph (3) not later than 2 years after the date of a determination under paragraph (2) that the marine pollution control device is required; and

(ii) every 5 years—

(I) review the standards; and

(II) if necessary, revise the standards, consistent with paragraph (3)(B) and based on significant new information.

(C) Regulations

The Secretary of Defense shall promulgate regulations with respect to a marine pollution control device under paragraph (4) as soon as practicable after the Administrator and the Secretary of Defense promulgate standards with respect to the device under paragraph (3), but not later than 1 year after the Administrator and the Secretary of Defense promulgate the standards. The regulations promulgated by the Secretary of Defense under paragraph (4) shall become effective upon promulgation unless another effective date is specified in the regulations.

(D) Petition for review

The Governor of any State may submit a petition requesting that the Secretary of Defense and the Administrator review a determination under paragraph (2) or a standard under paragraph (3), if there is significant new information, not considered previously, that could reasonably result in a change to the particular determination or standard after consideration of the matters set forth in paragraph (2)(B). The petition shall be accompanied by the scientific and technical information on which the petition is based. The Administrator and the Secretary of Defense shall grant or deny the petition not later than 2 years after the date of receipt of the petition.

(6) Effect on other laws

(A) Prohibition on regulation by States or political subdivisions of States

Beginning on the effective date of—

(i) a determination under paragraph (2) that it is not reasonable and practicable to require use of a marine pollution control device regarding a particular discharge incidental to the normal operation of a vessel of the Armed Forces; or

(ii) regulations promulgated by the Secretary of Defense under paragraph (4);

except as provided in paragraph (7), neither a State nor a political subdivision of a State may adopt or enforce any statute or regulation of the State or political subdivision with respect to the discharge or the design, construction, installation, or use of any marine pollution control device required to control discharges from a vessel of the Armed Forces.

(B) Federal laws

This subsection shall not affect the application of section 1321 of this title to discharges incidental to the normal operation of a vessel.

(7) Establishment of State no-discharge zones

(A) State prohibition

(i) In general

After the effective date of—

(I) a determination under paragraph (2) that it is not reasonable and practicable to require use of a marine pollution control device regarding a particular discharge incidental to the normal operation of a vessel of the Armed Forces; or

(II) regulations promulgated by the Secretary of Defense under paragraph (4);

if a State determines that the protection and enhancement of the quality of some or all of the waters within the State require greater environmental protection, the State may prohibit 1 or more discharges incidental to the normal operation of a vessel, whether treated or not treated, into the waters. No prohibition shall apply until the Administrator makes the determinations described in subclauses (II) and (III) of subparagraph (B)(i).

(ii) Documentation

To the extent that a prohibition under this paragraph would apply to vessels of the Armed Forces and not to other types of vessels, the State shall document the technical or environmental basis for the distinction.

(B) Prohibition by the Administrator

(i) In general

Upon application of a State, the Administrator shall by regulation prohibit the discharge from a vessel of 1 or more discharges incidental to the normal operation of a vessel, whether treated or not treated, into the waters covered by the application if the Administrator determines that—

(I) the protection and enhancement of the quality of the specified waters within the State require a prohibition of the discharge into the waters;

(II) adequate facilities for the safe and sanitary removal of the discharge incidental to the normal operation of a vessel are reasonably available for the waters to which the prohibition would apply; and

(III) the prohibition will not have the effect of discriminating against a vessel of the Armed Forces by reason of the ownership or operation by the Federal Government, or the military function, of the vessel.

(ii) Approval or disapproval

The Administrator shall approve or disapprove an application submitted under clause (i) not later than 90 days after the date on which the application is submitted to the Administrator. Notwithstanding clause (i)(II), the Administrator shall not disapprove an application for the sole reason that there are not adequate facilities to remove any discharge incidental to the normal operation of a vessel from vessels of the Armed Forces.

(C) Applicability to foreign flagged vessels

A prohibition under this paragraph—

(i) shall not impose any design, construction, manning, or equipment standard on a foreign flagged vessel engaged in innocent passage unless the prohibition implements a generally accepted international rule or standard; and

(ii) that relates to the prevention, reduction, and control of pollution shall not apply to a foreign flagged vessel engaged in transit passage unless the prohibition implements an applicable international regulation regarding the discharge of oil, oily waste, or any other noxious substance into the waters.

(8) Prohibition relating to vessels of the Armed Forces

After the effective date of the regulations promulgated by the Secretary of Defense under paragraph (4), it shall be unlawful for any vessel of the Armed Forces subject to the regulations to—

(A) operate in the navigable waters of the United States or the waters of the contiguous zone, if the vessel is not equipped with any required marine pollution control device meeting standards established under this subsection; or

(B) discharge overboard any discharge incidental to the normal operation of a vessel in waters with respect to which a prohibition on the discharge has been established under paragraph (7).

(9) Enforcement

This subsection shall be enforceable, as provided in subsections (j) and (k) of this section, against any agency of the United States responsible for vessels of the Armed Forces notwithstanding any immunity asserted by the agency.

(*o*) Management practices for recreational vessels

(1) Applicability

This subsection applies to any discharge, other than a discharge of sewage, from a recreational vessel that is—

(A) incidental to the normal operation of the vessel; and

(B) exempt from permitting requirements under section 1342(r) of this title.

(2) Determination of discharges subject to management practices

(A) Determination

(i) In general

The Administrator, in consultation with the Secretary of the department in which the Coast Guard is operating, the Secretary of Commerce, and interested States, shall determine the discharges incidental to the normal operation of a recreational vessel for which it is reasonable and practicable to develop management practices to mitigate adverse impacts on the waters of the United States.

(ii) Promulgation

The Administrator shall promulgate the determinations under clause (i) in accordance with section 553 of title 5.

(iii) Management practices

The Administrator shall develop management practices for recreational vessels in any case in which the Administrator determines that the use of those practices is reasonable and practicable.

(B) Considerations

In making a determination under subparagraph (A), the Administrator shall consider—

(i) the nature of the discharge;

(ii) the environmental effects of the discharge;

(iii) the practicability of using a management practice;

(iv) the effect that the use of a management practice would have on the operation, operational capability, or safety of the vessel;

(v) applicable Federal and State law;

(vi) applicable international standards; and

(vii) the economic costs of the use of the management practice.

(C) Timing

The Administrator shall—

(i) make the initial determinations under subparagraph (A) not later than 1 year after July 29, 2008; and

(ii) every 5 years thereafter—

(I) review the determinations; and

(II) if necessary, revise the determinations based on any new information available to the Administrator.

(3) Performance standards for management practices

(A) In general

For each discharge for which a management practice is developed under paragraph (2), the Administrator, in consultation with the Secretary of the department in which the Coast Guard is operating, the Secretary of Commerce, other interested Federal agencies, and interested States, shall promulgate, in accordance with section 553 of title 5, Federal standards of performance for each management practice required with respect to the discharge.

(B) Considerations

In promulgating standards under this paragraph, the Administrator shall take into account the considerations described in paragraph (2)(B).

(C) Classes, types, and sizes of vessels

The standards promulgated under this paragraph may—

(i) distinguish among classes, types, and sizes of vessels;

(ii) distinguish between new and existing vessels; and

(iii) provide for a waiver of the applicability of the standards as necessary or appropriate to a particular class, type, age, or size of vessel.

(D) Timing

The Administrator shall—

(i) promulgate standards of performance for a management practice under subparagraph (A) not later than 1 year after the date of a determination under paragraph (2) that the management practice is reasonable and practicable; and

(ii) every 5 years thereafter—

(I) review the standards; and

(II) if necessary, revise the standards, in accordance with subparagraph (B) and based on any new information available to the Administrator.

(4) Regulations for the use of management practices

(A) In general

The Secretary of the department in which the Coast Guard is operating shall promulgate such regulations governing the design, construction, installation, and use of management practices for recreational vessels as are necessary to meet the standards of performance promulgated under paragraph (3).

(B) Regulations

(i) In general

The Secretary shall promulgate the regulations under this paragraph as soon as practicable after the Administrator promulgates standards with respect to the practice under paragraph (3), but not later than 1 year after the date on which the Administrator promulgates the standards.

(ii) Effective date

The regulations promulgated by the Secretary under this paragraph shall be effective upon promulgation unless another effective date is specified in the regulations.

(iii) Consideration of time

In determining the effective date of a regulation promulgated under this paragraph, the Secretary shall consider the period of time necessary to communicate the existence of the regulation to persons affected by the regulation.

(5) Effect of other laws

This subsection shall not affect the application of section 1321 of this title to discharges incidental to the normal operation of a recreational vessel.

(6) Prohibition relating to recreational vessels

After the effective date of the regulations promulgated by the Secretary of the department in which the Coast Guard is operating under paragraph (4), the owner or operator of a recreational vessel shall neither operate in nor discharge any discharge incidental to the normal operation of the vessel into, the waters of the United States or the waters of the contiguous zone, if the owner or operator of the vessel is not using any applicable management practice meeting standards established under this subsection.

(June 30, 1948, ch. 758, title III, §312, as added Pub. L. 92–500, §2, Oct. 18, 1972, 86 Stat. 871;

amended Pub. L. 95–217, § 59, Dec. 27, 1977, 91 Stat. 1596; Pub. L. 96–88, title V, § 509(b), Oct. 17, 1979, 93 Stat. 695; Pub. L. 100–4, title III, § 311, Feb. 4, 1987, 101 Stat. 42; Pub. L. 104–106, div. A, title III, § 325(b)–(c)(2), Feb. 10, 1996, 110 Stat. 254–259; Pub. L. 110–288, § 4, July 29, 2008, 122 Stat. 2650.)

REFERENCES IN TEXT

For definition of Canal Zone, referred to in subsecs. (a)(4) and (m), see section 3602(b) of Title 22, Foreign Relations and Intercourse.

AMENDMENTS

2008—Subsec. (*o*). Pub. L. 110–288 added subsec. (*o*).

1996—Subsec. (a)(8). Pub. L. 104–106, § 325(c)(1)(A), substituted "corporation, association, or agency of the United States," for "corporation, or association,".

Subsec. (a)(12) to (14). Pub. L. 104–106, § 325(c)(1)(B), (C), added pars. (12) to (14).

Subsec. (j). Pub. L. 104–106, § 325(c)(2), substituted "subsection (g)(1) of this section, clause (1) or (2) of subsection (h) of this section, or subsection (n)(8) of this section shall be liable" for "subsection (g)(1) of this section or clause (1) or (2) of subsection (h) of this section shall be liable".

Subsec. (n). Pub. L. 104–106, § 325(b), added subsec. (n).

1987—Subsec. (f)(1). Pub. L. 100–4, § 311(a), designated existing provision as subpar. (A), substituted "Except as provided in subparagraph (B), after" for "After", and added subpar. (B).

Subsec. (k). Pub. L. 100–4, § 311(b), inserted at end "The provisions of this section may also be enforced by a State."

1977—Subsec. (a)(6). Pub. L. 95–217, § 59(a), inserted "except that, with respect to commercial vessels on the Great Lakes, such term shall include graywater" after "receive or retain body wastes".

Subsec. (a)(10), (11). Pub. L. 95–217, § 59(b), added pars. (10) and (11).

Subsec. (b)(1). Pub. L. 95–217, § 59(c), inserted references to standards established under subsec. (c)(1)(B) of this section and to standards promulgated under subsec. (c) of this section.

Subsec. (c)(1). Pub. L. 95–217, § 59(d), designated existing provisions as subpar. (A) and added subpar. (B).

Subsec. (f)(4). Pub. L. 95–217, § 59(e), designated existing provisions as subpar. (A) and added subpar. (B).

CHANGE OF NAME

"Secretary of Health and Human Services" substituted for "Secretary of Health, Education, and Welfare" in subsec. (e) pursuant to section 509(b) of Pub. L. 96–88 which is classified to section 3508(b) of Title 20, Education.

TRANSFER OF FUNCTIONS

For transfer of authorities, functions, personnel, and assets of the Coast Guard, including the authorities and functions of the Secretary of Transportation relating thereto, to the Department of Homeland Security, and for treatment of related references, see sections 468(b), 551(d), 552(d), and 557 of Title 6, Domestic Security, and the Department of Homeland Security Reorganization Plan of November 25, 2002, as modified, set out as a note under section 542 of Title 6.

TERMINATION OF TRUST TERRITORY OF THE PACIFIC ISLANDS

For termination of Trust Territory of the Pacific Islands, see note set out preceding section 1681 of Title 48, Territories and Insular Possessions.

TERMINATION OF UNITED STATES DISTRICT COURT FOR THE DISTRICT OF THE CANAL ZONE

For termination of the United States District Court for the District of the Canal Zone at end of the "transition period", being the 30-month period beginning Oct. 1, 1979, and ending midnight Mar. 31, 1982, see Paragraph 5 of Article XI of the Panama Canal Treaty of 1977 and sections 2101 and 2201 to 2203 of Pub. L. 96–70, title II, Sept. 27, 1979, 93 Stat. 493, formerly classified to sections 3831 and 3841 to 3843, respectively, of Title 22, Foreign Relations and Intercourse.

PURPOSE OF 1996 AMENDMENT

Section 325(a) of Pub. L. 104–106 provided that: "The purposes of this section [amending this section and section 1362 of this title and enacting provisions set out as a note below] are to—

"(1) enhance the operational flexibility of vessels of the Armed Forces domestically and internationally;

"(2) stimulate the development of innovative vessel pollution control technology; and

"(3) advance the development by the United States Navy of environmentally sound ships."

COOPERATION IN NATIONAL DISCHARGE STANDARDS DEVELOPMENT

Section 325(d) of Pub. L. 104–106 provided that: "The Administrator of the Environmental Protection Agency and the Secretary of Defense may, by mutual agreement, with or without reimbursement, provide for the use of information, reports, personnel, or other resources of the Environmental Protection Agency or the Department of Defense to carry out section 312(n) of the Federal Water Pollution Control Act [33 U.S.C. 1322(n)] (as added by subsection (b)), including the use of the resources—

"(1) to determine—

"(A) the nature and environmental effect of discharges incidental to the normal operation of a vessel of the Armed Forces;

"(B) the practicability of using marine pollution control devices on vessels of the Armed Forces; and

"(C) the effect that installation or use of marine pollution control devices on vessels of the Armed Forces would have on the operation or operational capability of the vessels; and

"(2) to establish performance standards for marine pollution control devices on vessels of the Armed Forces."

CLEAN VESSELS

Pub. L. 102–587, title V, subtitle F, Nov. 4, 1992, 106 Stat. 5086, as amended by Pub. L. 109–59, title X, § 10131, Aug. 10, 2005, 119 Stat. 1931, provided that:

"SEC. 5601. SHORT TITLE.

"This subtitle may be cited as the 'Clean Vessel Act of 1992'.

"SEC. 5602. FINDINGS; PURPOSE.

"(a) FINDINGS.—The Congress finds the following:

"(1) The discharge of untreated sewage by vessels is prohibited under Federal law in all areas within the navigable waters of the United States.

"(2) The discharge of treated sewage by vessels is prohibited under either Federal or State law in many of the United States bodies of water where recreational boaters operate.

"(3) There is currently an inadequate number of pumpout stations for type III marine sanitation devices where recreational vessels normally operate.

"(4) Sewage discharged by recreational vessels because of an inadequate number of pumpout stations is a substantial contributor to localized degradation of water quality in the United States.

"(b) PURPOSE.—The purpose of this subtitle is to provide funds to States for the construction, renovation, operation, and maintenance of pumpout stations and waste reception facilities.

"SEC. 5603. DETERMINATION AND PLAN REGARDING STATE MARINE SANITATION DEVICE PUMPOUT STATION NEEDS.

"(a) SURVEY.—Within 3 months after the notification under section 5605(b), each coastal State shall conduct a survey to determine—

"(1) the number and location of all operational pumpout stations and waste reception facilities at public and private marinas, mooring areas, docks, and other boating access facilities within the coastal zone of the State; and

"(2) the number of recreational vessels in the coastal waters of the State with type III marine sanitation devices or portable toilets, and the areas of those coastal waters where those vessels congregate.

"(b) PLAN.—Within 6 months after the notification under section 5605(b), and based on the survey conducted under subsection (a), each coastal State shall—

"(1) develop and submit to the Secretary of the Interior a plan for any construction or renovation of pumpout stations and waste reception facilities that are necessary to ensure that, based on the guidance issued under section 5605(a), there are pumpout stations and waste reception facilities in the State that are adequate and reasonably available to meet the needs of recreational vessels using the coastal waters of the State; and

"(2) submit to the Secretary of the Interior with that plan a list of all stations and facilities in the coastal zone of the State which are operational on the date of submittal.

"(c) PLAN APPROVAL.—

"(1) IN GENERAL.—Not later than 60 days after a plan is submitted by a State under subsection (b), the Secretary of the Interior shall approve or disapprove the plan, based on—

"(A) the adequacy of the survey conducted by the State under subsection (a); and

"(B) the ability of the plan, based on the guidance issued under section 5605(a), to meet the construction and renovation needs of the recreational vessels identified in the survey.

"(2) NOTIFICATION OF STATE; MODIFICATION.—The Secretary of the Interior shall promptly notify the affected Governor of the approval or disapproval of a plan. If a plan is disapproved, the Secretary of the Interior shall recommend necessary modifications and return the plan to the affected Governor.

"(3) RESUBMITTAL.—Not later than 60 days after receiving a plan returned by the Secretary of the Interior, the Governor shall make the appropriate changes and resubmit the plan.

"(d) INDICATION OF STATIONS AND FACILITIES ON NOAA CHARTS.—

"(1) IN GENERAL.—The Under Secretary of Commerce for Oceans and Atmosphere shall indicate, on charts published by the National Oceanic and Atmospheric Administration for the use of operators of recreational vessels, the locations of pumpout stations and waste reception facilities.

"(2) NOTIFICATION OF NOAA.—

"(A) LISTS OF STATIONS AND FACILITIES.—The Secretary of the Interior shall transmit to the Under Secretary of Commerce for Oceans and Atmosphere each list of operational stations and facilities submitted by a State under subsection (b)(2), by not later than 30 days after the date of receipt of that list.

"(B) COMPLETION OF PROJECT.—The Director of the United States Fish and Wildlife Service shall notify the Under Secretary of the location of each station or facility at which a construction or renovation project is completed by a State with amounts made available under the Act of August 9, 1950 (16 U.S.C. 777a et seq. [16 U.S.C. 777 et seq.]), as amended by this subtitle, by not later than 30 days after the date of notification by a State of the completion of the project.

"SEC. 5604. FUNDING.

"(a) TRANSFER.—[Amended section 777c of Title 16, Conservation.]

"(b) ACCESS INCREASE.—[Amended section 777g of Title 16, Conservation.]

"(c) GRANT PROGRAM.—

"(1) MATCHING GRANTS.—The Secretary of the Interior may obligate an amount not to exceed the amount made available under section 4(b)(2) of the Act of August 9, 1950 (16 U.S.C. 777c(b)(2), as amended by this Act), to make grants to—

"(A) coastal States to pay not more than 75 percent of the cost to a coastal State of—

"(i) conducting a survey under section 5603(a);

"(ii) developing and submitting a plan and accompanying list under section 5603(b);

"(iii) constructing and renovating pumpout stations and waste reception facilities; and

"(iv) conducting a program to educate recreational boaters about the problem of human body waste discharges from vessels and inform them of the location of pumpout stations and waste reception facilities.

"(B) inland States, which can demonstrate to the Secretary of the Interior that there are an inadequate number of pumpout stations and waste reception facilities to meet the needs of recreational vessels in the waters of that State, to pay 75 percent of the cost to that State of—

"(i) constructing and renovating pumpout stations and waste reception facilities in the inland State; and

"(ii) conducting a program to educate recreational boaters about the problem of human body waste discharges from vessels and inform them of the location of pumpout stations and waste reception facilities.

"(2) PRIORITY.—In awarding grants under this subsection, the Secretary of the Interior shall give priority consideration to grant applications that—

"(A) provide for public/private partnership efforts to develop and operate pumpout stations and waste reception facilities; and

"(B) propose innovative ways to increase the availability and use of pumpout stations and waste reception facilities.

"(d) DISCLAIMER.—Nothing in this subtitle shall be interpreted to preclude a State from carrying out the provisions of this subtitle with funds other than those described in this section.

"SEC. 5605. GUIDANCE AND NOTIFICATION.

"(a) ISSUANCE OF GUIDANCE.—Not later than 3 months after the date of the enactment of this subtitle [Nov. 4, 1992], the Secretary of the Interior shall, after consulting with the Administrator of the Environmental Protection Agency, the Under Secretary of Commerce for Oceans and Atmosphere, and the Commandant of the Coast Guard, issue for public comment pumpout station and waste reception facility guidance. The Secretary of the Interior shall finalize the guidance not later than 6 months after the date of enactment of this subtitle. The guidance shall include—

"(1) guidance regarding the types of pumpout stations and waste reception facilities that may be appropriate for construction, renovation, operation, or maintenance with amounts available under the Act of August 9, 1950 (16 U.S.C. 777a et seq. [16 U.S.C. 777 et seq.]), as amended by this subtitle, and appropriate location of the stations and facilities within a marina or boatyard;

"(2) guidance defining what constitutes adequate and reasonably available pumpout stations and waste reception facilities in boating areas;

"(3) guidance on appropriate methods for disposal of vessel sewage from pumpout stations and waste reception facilities;

"(4) guidance on appropriate connector fittings to facilitate the sanitary and expeditious discharge of sewage from vessels;

"(5) guidance on the waters most likely to be affected by the discharge of sewage from vessels; and

"(6) other information that is considered necessary to promote the establishment of pumpout facilities to reduce sewage discharges from vessels and to protect United States waters.

"(b) NOTIFICATION.—Not later than one month after the guidance issued under subsection (a) is finalized, the Secretary of the Interior shall provide notification in writing to the fish and wildlife, water pollution control, and coastal zone management authorities of each State, of—

"(1) the availability of amounts under the Act of August 9, 1950 (16 U.S.C. 777a et seq. [16 U.S.C. 777 et seq.]) to implement the Clean Vessel Act of 1992; and

"(2) the guidance developed under subsection (a).

"SEC. 5606. EFFECT ON STATE FUNDING ELIGIBILITY.

"This subtitle shall not be construed or applied to jeopardize any funds available to a coastal State under the Act of August 9, 1950 (16 U.S.C. 777a et seq. [16 U.S.C. 777 et seq.]), if the coastal State is, in good faith, pursuing a survey and plan designed to meet the purposes of this subtitle.

"SEC. 5607. APPLICABILITY.

"The requirements of section 5603 shall not apply to a coastal State if within six months after the date of enactment of this subtitle [Nov. 4, 1992] the Secretary of the Interior certifies that—

"(1) the State has developed and is implementing a plan that will ensure that there will be pumpout stations and waste reception facilities adequate to meet the needs of recreational vessels in the coastal waters of the State; or

"(2) existing pumpout stations and waste reception facilities in the coastal waters of the State are adequate to meet those needs.

"SEC. 5608. DEFINITIONS.

"For the purposes of this subtitle the term:

"(1) 'coastal State'—

"(A) means a State of the United States in, or bordering on the Atlantic, Pacific, or Arctic Ocean; the Gulf of Mexico; Long Island Sound; or one or more of the Great Lakes;

"(B) includes Puerto Rico, the Virgin Islands, Guam, the Commonwealth of the Northern Mariana Islands, and American Samoa; and

"(C) does not include a State for which the ratio of the number of recreational vessels in the State numbered under chapter 123 of title 46, United States Code, to number of miles of shoreline (as that term is defined in section 926.2(d) of title 15, Code of Federal Regulations, as in effect on January 1, 1991), is less than one.

"(2) 'coastal waters' means—

"(A) in the Great Lakes area, the waters within the territorial jurisdiction of the United States consisting of the Great Lakes, their connecting waters, harbors, roadsteads, and estuary-type areas such as bays, shallows, and marshes; and

"(B) in other areas, those waters, adjacent to the shorelines, which contain a measurable percentage of sea water, including sounds, bay, lagoons, bayous, ponds, and estuaries.

"(3) 'coastal zone' has the same meaning that term has in section 304(1) of the Coastal Zone Management Act of 1972 (16 U.S.C. 1453(1));

"(4) 'inland State' means a State which is not a coastal state;

"(5) 'type III marine sanitation device' means any equipment for installation on board a vessel which is specifically designed to receive, retain, and discharge human body wastes;

"(6) 'pumpout station' means a facility that pumps or receives human body wastes out of type III marine sanitation devices installed on board vessels;

"(7) 'recreational vessel' means a vessel—

"(A) manufactured for operation, or operated, primarily for pleasure; or

"(B) leased, rented, or chartered to another for the latter's pleasure; and

"(8) 'waste reception facility' means a facility specifically designed to receive wastes from portable toilets carried on vessels, and does not include lavatories."

CONTIGUOUS ZONE OF UNITED STATES

For extension of contiguous zone of United States, see Proc. No. 7219, set out as a note under section 1331 of Title 43, Public Lands.

§ 1323. Federal facilities pollution control

(a) Each department, agency, or instrumentality of the executive, legislative, and judicial branches of the Federal Government (1) having jurisdiction over any property or facility, or (2) engaged in any activity resulting, or which may result, in the discharge or runoff of pollutants, and each officer, agent, or employee thereof in the performance of his official duties, shall be subject to, and comply with, all Federal, State, interstate, and local requirements, administrative authority, and process and sanctions respecting the control and abatement of water pollution in the same manner, and to the same extent as any nongovernmental entity including the payment of reasonable service charges. The preceding sentence shall apply (A) to any requirement whether substantive or procedural (including any recordkeeping or reporting requirement, any requirement respecting permits and any other requirement, whatsoever), (B) to the exercise of any Federal, State, or local administrative authority, and (C) to any process and sanction, whether enforced in Federal, State, or local courts or in any other manner. This subsection shall apply notwithstanding any immunity of such agencies, officers, agents, or employees under any law or rule of law. Nothing in this section shall be construed to prevent any department, agency, or instrumentality of the Federal Government, or any officer, agent, or employee thereof in the performance of his official duties, from removing to the appropriate Federal district court any proceeding to which the department, agency, or instrumentality or officer, agent, or employee thereof is subject pursuant to this section, and any such proceeding may be removed in accordance with section 1441 et seq. of title 28. No officer, agent, or employee of the United States shall be personally liable for any civil penalty arising from the performance of his official duties, for which he is not otherwise liable, and the United States shall be liable only for those civil penalties arising under Federal law or imposed by a State or local court to enforce an order or the process of such court. The President may exempt any effluent source of any department, agency, or instrumentality in the executive branch from compliance with any such a requirement if he determines it to be in the paramount interest of the United States to do so; except that no exemption may be granted from the requirements of section 1316 or 1317 of this title. No such exemptions shall be granted due to lack of appropriation unless the President shall have specifically requested such appropriation as a part of the budgetary process and the Congress shall have failed to make available such requested appropriation. Any exemption shall be for a period not in excess of one year, but additional exemptions may be granted for periods of not to exceed one year upon the President's making a new determination. The President shall report each January to the Congress all exemptions from the requirements of this section granted during the preceding calendar year, together with his reason for granting such exemption. In addition to any such exemption of a particular effluent source, the President may, if he determines it to be in the paramount interest of the United States to do so, issue regulations exempting from compliance with the requirements of this section any weaponry, equipment, aircraft, vessels, vehicles, or other classes or categories of property, and access to such property, which are owned or operated by the Armed Forces of the United States (including the Coast Guard) or by the National Guard of any State and which are uniquely military in nature. The President shall reconsider the need for such regulations at three-year intervals.

(b)(1) The Administrator shall coordinate with the head of each department, agency, or instrumentality of the Federal Government having jurisdiction over any property or facility utilizing federally owned wastewater facilities to develop a program of cooperation for utilizing wastewater control systems utilizing those innovative treatment processes and techniques for which guidelines have been promulgated under section 1314(d)(3) of this title. Such program shall include an inventory of property and facilities which could utilize such processes and techniques.

(2) Construction shall not be initiated for facilities for treatment of wastewater at any Federal property or facility after September 30, 1979, if alternative methods for wastewater treatment at such property or facility utilizing innovative treatment processes and techniques, including but not limited to methods utilizing recycle and reuse techniques and land treatment are not utilized, unless the life cycle cost of the alternative treatment works exceeds the life cycle cost of the most cost effective alternative by more than 15 per centum. The Administrator may waive the application of this paragraph in any case where the Administrator determines it to be in the public interest, or that compliance with this paragraph would interfere with the orderly compliance with conditions of a permit issued pursuant to section 1342 of this title.

(June 30, 1948, ch. 758, title III, §313, as added Pub. L. 92–500, §2, Oct. 18, 1972, 86 Stat. 875; amended Pub. L. 95–217, §§60, 61(a), Dec. 27, 1977, 91 Stat. 1597, 1598.)

AMENDMENTS

1977—Subsec. (a). Pub. L. 95–217, §§60, 61(a), designated existing provisions as subsec. (a) and inserted provisions making officers, agents, or employees of Federal departments, agencies, or instrumentalities subject to Federal, State, interstate, and local requirements, administrative authority, process, and sanctions respecting the control and abatement of water pollution in the same manner and to the same extent as non-governmental entities, including the payment of reasonable service charges, inserted provisions covering Federal employee liability, and inserted provisions relating to military source exemptions and the issuance of regulations covering those exemptions.

Subsec. (b). Pub. L. 95–217, §60, added subsec. (b).

TRANSFER OF FUNCTIONS

For transfer of authorities, functions, personnel, and assets of the Coast Guard, including the authorities and functions of the Secretary of Transportation relating thereto, to the Department of Homeland Security, and for treatment of related references, see sections 468(b), 551(d), 552(d), and 557 of Title 6, Domestic Security, and the Department of Homeland Security Reorganization Plan of November 25, 2002, as modified, set out as a note under section 542 of Title 6.

MARINE GUIDANCE SYSTEMS

Pub. L. 105–383, title IV, §425(b), Nov. 13, 1998, 112 Stat. 3441, provided that: "The Secretary of Transportation shall, within 12 months after the date of the enactment of this Act [Nov. 13, 1998], evaluate and report to the Congress on the suitability of marine sector laser lighting, cold cathode lighting, and ultraviolet enhanced vision technologies for use in guiding marine vessels and traffic."

FEDERAL COMPLIANCE WITH POLLUTION CONTROL STANDARDS

For provisions relating to the responsibility of the head of each Executive agency for compliance with applicable pollution control standards, see Ex. Ord. No. 12088, Oct. 13, 1978, 43 F.R. 47707, set out as a note under section 4321 of Title 42, The Public Health and Welfare.

EXECUTIVE ORDER NO. 11258

Ex. Ord. No. 11258, Nov. 17, 1965, 30 F.R. 14483, which related to prevention, control, and abatement of water pollution by federal activities, was superseded by Ex. Ord. No. 11288, July 2, 1966, 31 F.R. 9261.

EXECUTIVE ORDER NO. 11288

Ex. Ord. No. 11288, July 2, 1966, 31 F.R. 9261, which provided for prevention, control, and abatement of water pollution from federal activities, was superseded by Ex. Ord. No. 11507, Feb. 4, 1970, 35 F.R. 2573.

§1324. Clean lakes

(a) Establishment and scope of program

(1) State program requirements

Each State on a biennial basis shall prepare and submit to the Administrator for his approval—

(A) an identification and classification according to eutrophic condition of all publicly owned lakes in such State;

(B) a description of procedures, processes, and methods (including land use requirements), to control sources of pollution of such lakes;

(C) a description of methods and procedures, in conjunction with appropriate Federal agencies, to restore the quality of such lakes;

(D) methods and procedures to mitigate the harmful effects of high acidity, including innovative methods of neutralizing and restoring buffering capacity of lakes and methods of removing from lakes toxic metals and other toxic substances mobilized by high acidity;

(E) a list and description of those publicly owned lakes in such State for which uses are known to be impaired, including those lakes which are known not to meet applicable water quality standards or which require implementation of control programs to maintain compliance with applicable standards and those lakes in which water quality has deteriorated as a result of high acidity that may reasonably be due to acid deposition; and

(F) an assessment of the status and trends of water quality in lakes in such State, including but not limited to, the nature and extent of pollution loading from point and nonpoint sources and the extent to which the use of lakes is impaired as a result of such pollution, particularly with respect to toxic pollution.

(2) Submission as part of 1315(b)(1) report

The information required under paragraph (1) shall be included in the report required under section 1315(b)(1) of this title, beginning with the report required under such section by April 1, 1988.

(3) Report of Administrator

Not later than 180 days after receipt from the States of the biennial information required under paragraph (1), the Administrator shall submit to the Committee on Public Works and Transportation of the House of Representatives and the Committee on Environment and Public Works of the Senate a report on the status of water quality in lakes in the United States, including the effectiveness of the methods and procedures described in paragraph (1)(D).

(4) Eligibility requirement

Beginning after April 1, 1988, a State must have submitted the information required under paragraph (1) in order to receive grant assistance under this section.

(b) Financial assistance to States

The Administrator shall provide financial assistance to States in order to carry out methods and procedures approved by him under subsection (a) of this section. The Administrator shall provide financial assistance to States to prepare the identification and classification surveys required in subsection (a)(1) of this section.

(c) Maximum amount of grant; authorization of appropriations

(1) The amount granted to any State for any fiscal year under subsection (b) of this section shall not exceed 70 per centum of the funds expended by such State in such year for carrying out approved methods and procedures under subsection (a) of this section.

(2) There is authorized to be appropriated $50,000,000 for each of fiscal years 2001 through 2005 for grants to States under subsection (b) of this section which such sums shall remain available until expended. The Administrator shall provide for an equitable distribution of such sums to the States with approved methods and procedures under subsection (a) of this section.

(d) Demonstration program

(1) General requirements

The Administrator is authorized and directed to establish and conduct at locations throughout the Nation a lake water quality demonstration program. The program shall, at a minimum—

(A) develop cost effective technologies for the control of pollutants to preserve or enhance lake water quality while optimizing multiple lakes uses;

(B) control nonpoint sources of pollution which are contributing to the degradation of water quality in lakes;

(C) evaluate the feasibility of implementing regional consolidated pollution control strategies;

(D) demonstrate environmentally preferred techniques for the removal and disposal of contaminated lake sediments;

(E) develop improved methods for the removal of silt, stumps, aquatic growth, and other obstructions which impair the quality of lakes;

(F) construct and evaluate silt traps and other devices or equipment to prevent or abate the deposit of sediment in lakes; and

(G) demonstrate the costs and benefits of utilizing dredged material from lakes in the reclamation of despoiled land.

(2) Geographical requirements

Demonstration projects authorized by this subsection shall be undertaken to reflect a variety of geographical and environmental conditions. As a priority, the Administrator shall undertake demonstration projects at Lake Champlain, New York and Vermont; Lake Houston, Texas; Beaver Lake, Arkansas; Greenwood Lake and Belcher Creek, New Jersey; Deal Lake, New Jersey; Alcyon Lake, New Jersey; Gorton's Pond, Rhode Island; Lake Washington, Rhode Island; Lake Bomoseen, Vermont; Sauk Lake, Minnesota; Otsego Lake, New York; Oneida Lake, New York; Raystown Lake, Pennsylvania; Swan Lake, Itasca County, Minnesota; Walker Lake, Nevada; Lake Tahoe, California and Nevada; Ten Mile Lakes, Oregon; Woahink Lake, Oregon; Highland Lake, Connecticut; Lily Lake, New Jersey; Strawbridge Lake, New Jersey; Baboosic Lake, New Hampshire; French Pond, New Hampshire; Dillon Reservoir, Ohio; Tohopekaliga Lake, Florida; Lake Apopka, Florida; Lake George, New York; Lake Wallenpaupack, Pennsylvania; Lake Allatoona, Georgia; and Lake Worth, Texas.

(3) Reports

Notwithstanding section 3003 of the Federal Reports Elimination and Sunset Act of 1995 (31 U.S.C. 1113 note; 109 Stat. 734–736), by January 1, 1997, and January 1 of every odd-numbered year thereafter, the Administrator shall report to the Committee on Transportation and Infrastructure of the House of Representatives and the Committee on Environment and Public Works of the Senate on work undertaken pursuant to this subsection. Upon completion of the program authorized by this subsection, the Administrator shall submit to such committees a final report on the results of such program, along with recommendations for further measures to improve the water quality of the Nation's lakes.

(4) Authorization of appropriations

(A) In general

There is authorized to be appropriated to carry out this subsection not to exceed $40,000,000 for fiscal years beginning after September 30, 1986, to remain available until expended.

(B) Special authorizations

(i) Amount

There is authorized to be appropriated to carry out subsection (b) of this section with respect to subsection (a)(1)(D) of this section not to exceed $25,000,000 for fiscal years beginning after September 30, 1986, to remain available until expended.

(ii) Distribution of funds

The Administrator shall provide for an equitable distribution of sums appropriated pursuant to this subparagraph among States carrying out approved methods and procedures. Such distribution shall be based on the relative needs of each such State for the mitigation of the harmful effects on lakes and other surface waters of high acidity that may reasonably be due to acid deposition or acid mine drainage.

(iii) Grants as additional assistance

The amount of any grant to a State under this subparagraph shall be in addition to, and not in lieu of, any other Federal financial assistance.

(June 30, 1948, ch. 758, title III, §314, as added Pub. L. 92–500, §2, Oct. 18, 1972, 86 Stat. 875; amended Pub. L. 95–217, §§4(f), 62(a), Dec. 27, 1977, 91 Stat. 1567, 1598; Pub. L. 96–483, §1(f), Oct. 21, 1980, 94 Stat. 2360; Pub. L. 100–4, title I, §101(g), title III, §315(a), (b), (d), Feb. 4, 1987, 101 Stat. 9, 49, 50, 52; Pub. L. 101–596, title III, §302, Nov. 16, 1990, 104 Stat. 3006; Pub. L. 104–66, title II, §2021(c), Dec. 21, 1995, 109 Stat. 727; Pub. L. 105–362, title V, §501(b), Nov. 10, 1998, 112 Stat. 3283; Pub. L. 106–457, title VII, §§701, 702, Nov. 7, 2000, 114 Stat. 1976; Pub. L. 107–303, title III, §302(b)(1), Nov. 27, 2002, 116 Stat. 2361.)

REFERENCES IN TEXT

Section 3003 of the Federal Reports Elimination and Sunset Act of 1995, referred to in subsec. (d)(3), is section 3003 of Pub. L. 104–66, which is set out as a note under section 1113 of Title 31, Money and Finance.

AMENDMENTS

2002—Subsec. (a)(3), (4). Pub. L. 107–303 repealed Pub. L. 105–362, §501(b). See 1998 Amendment note below.

2000—Subsec. (c)(2). Pub. L. 106–457, §701, substituted "$50,000,000 for each of fiscal years 2001 through 2005" for "$50,000,000 for the fiscal year ending June 30, 1973; $100,000,000 for the fiscal year 1974; $150,000,000 for the fiscal year 1975, $50,000,000 for fiscal year 1977, $60,000,000 for fiscal year 1978, $60,000,000 for fiscal year 1979, $60,000,000 for fiscal year 1980, $30,000,000 for fiscal year 1981, $30,000,000 for fiscal year 1982, such sums as may be necessary for fiscal years 1983 through 1985, and $30,000,000 per fiscal year for each of the fiscal years 1986 through 1990".

Subsec. (d)(2). Pub. L. 106–457, §702(1), inserted "Otsego Lake, New York; Oneida Lake, New York; Raystown Lake, Pennsylvania; Swan Lake, Itasca County, Minnesota; Walker Lake, Nevada; Lake Tahoe, California and Nevada; Ten Mile Lakes, Oregon; Woahink Lake, Oregon; Highland Lake, Connecticut; Lily Lake, New Jersey; Strawbridge Lake, New Jersey; Baboosic Lake, New Hampshire; French Pond, New Hampshire; Dillon Reservoir, Ohio; Tohopekaliga Lake, Florida; Lake Apopka, Florida; Lake George, New York; Lake Wallenpaupack, Pennsylvania; Lake Allatoona, Georgia;" after "Sauk Lake, Minnesota;".

Subsec. (d)(3). Pub. L. 106–457, §702(2), substituted "Notwithstanding section 3003 of the Federal Reports Elimination and Sunset Act of 1995 (31 U.S.C. 1113 note; 109 Stat. 734–736), by" for "By".

Subsec. (d)(4)(B)(i). Pub. L. 106–457, §702(3), substituted "$25,000,000" for "$15,000,000".

1998—Subsec. (a)(3), (4). Pub. L. 105–362, §501(b), which directed the redesignation of par. (4) as (3) and striking out of heading and text of par. (3), was repealed by Pub. L. 107–303. See Effective Date of 2002 Amendment note below.

1995—Subsec. (d)(3). Pub. L. 104–66 substituted "By January 1, 1997, and January 1 of every odd-numbered year thereafter, the Administrator shall report to the Committee on Transportation and Infrastructure" for "The Administrator shall report annually to the Committee on Public Works and Transportation".

1990—Subsec. (d)(2). Pub. L. 101–596 inserted "Lake Champlain, New York and Vermont;" before "Lake Houston, Texas".

1987—Subsec. (a). Pub. L. 100–4, §315(a), amended subsec. (a) generally. Prior to amendment, subsec. (a) read as follows: "Each State shall prepare or establish, and submit to the Administrator for his approval—

"(1) an identification and classification according to eutrophic condition of all publicly owned fresh water lakes in such State;

"(2) procedures, processes, and methods (including land use requirements), to control sources of pollution of such lakes; and

"(3) methods and procedures, in conjunction with appropriate Federal agencies, to restore the quality of such lakes."

Subsec. (b). Pub. L. 100–4, §315(d)(1), substituted "subsection (a) of this section" for "this section" in first sentence.

Subsec. (c)(1). Pub. L. 100–4, §315(d)(2), substituted "subsection (b) of this section" for first reference to "this section" and "subsection (a) of this section" for second reference to "this section".

Subsec. (c)(2). Pub. L. 100–4, §§101(g), 315(d)(3), struck out "and" after "1981," and inserted ", such sums as may be necessary for fiscal years 1983 through 1985, and $30,000,000 per fiscal year for each of the fiscal years 1986 through 1990" after "1982", and substituted "subsection (b) of this section" for first reference to "this section" and "subsection (a) of this section" for second reference to "this section".

Subsec. (d). Pub. L. 100–4, §315(b), added subsec. (d).

1980—Subsec. (c)(2). Pub. L. 96–483 inserted authorization of $30,000,000 for each of fiscal years 1981 and 1982.

1977—Subsec. (b). Pub. L. 95–217, §62(a), inserted provision directing the Administrator to provide financial assistance to States to prepare the identification and classification surveys required in subsec. (a)(1) of this section.

Subsec. (c)(2). Pub. L. 95–217, §4(f), substituted "$150,000,000 for the fiscal year 1975, $50,000,000 for fiscal year 1977, $60,000,000 for fiscal year 1978, $60,000,000 for fiscal year 1979, and $60,000,000 for fiscal year 1980" for "and $150,000,000 for the fiscal year 1975".

EFFECTIVE DATE OF 2002 AMENDMENT

Amendment by Pub. L. 107–303 effective Nov. 10, 1998, and Federal Water Pollution Act (33 U.S.C. 1251 et seq.) to be applied and administered on and after Nov. 27, 2002, as if amendments made by section 501(a)–(d) of Pub. L. 105–362 had not been enacted, see section 302(b) of Pub. L. 107–303, set out as a note under section 1254 of this title.

§1325. National Study Commission

(a) Establishment

There is established a National Study Commission, which shall make a full and complete investigation and study of all of the technological aspects of achieving, and all aspects of the total economic, social, and environmental effects of achieving or not achieving, the effluent limitations and goals set forth for 1983 in section 1311(b)(2) of this title.

(b) Membership; chairman

Such Commission shall be composed of fifteen members, including five members of the Senate, who are members of the Environment and Public Works committee, appointed by the President of the Senate, five members of the House, who are members of the Public Works and Transportation committee, appointed by the Speaker of the House, and five members of the public appointed by the President. The Chairman of such Commission shall be elected from among its members.

(c) Contract authority

In the conduct of such study, the Commission is authorized to contract with the National Academy of Sciences and the National Academy of Engineering (acting through the National Research Council), the National Institute of Ecology, Brookings Institution, and other nongovernmental entities, for the investigation of matters within their competence.

(d) Cooperation of departments, agencies, and instrumentalities of executive branch

The heads of the departments, agencies and instrumentalities of the executive branch of the Federal Government shall cooperate with the Commission in carrying out the requirements of this section, and shall furnish to the Commission such information as the Commission deems necessary to carry out this section.

(e) Report to Congress

A report shall be submitted to the Congress of the results of such investigation and study, together with recommendations, not later than three years after October 18, 1972.

(f) Compensation and allowances

The members of the Commission who are not officers or employees of the United States, while attending conferences or meetings of the Commission or while otherwise serving at the request of the Chairman shall be entitled to receive compensation at a rate not in excess of the maximum rate of pay for Grade GS–18, as provided in the General Schedule under section 5332 of title 5, including traveltime and while away from their homes or regular places of business they may be allowed travel expenses, including per diem in lieu of subsistence as authorized by law for persons in the Government service employed intermittently.

(g) Appointment of personnel

In addition to authority to appoint personnel subject to the provisions of title 5 governing appointments in the competitive service, and to pay such personnel in accordance with the provisions of chapter 51 and subchapter III of chapter 53 of such title relating to classification and General Schedule pay rates, the Commission shall have authority to enter into contracts with private or public organizations who shall furnish the Commission with such administrative and technical personnel as may be necessary to carry out the purpose of this section. Personnel furnished by such organizations under this subsection are not, and shall not be considered to be, Federal employees for any purposes, but in the performance of their duties shall be guided by the standards which apply to employees of the legislative branches under rules 41 and 43[1] of the Senate and House of Representatives, respectively.

(h) Authorization of appropriation

There is authorized to be appropriated, for use in carrying out this section, not to exceed $17,250,000.

(June 30, 1948, ch. 758, title III, §315, as added Pub. L. 92–500, §2, Oct. 18, 1972, 86 Stat. 875; amended Pub. L. 93–207, §1(5), Dec. 28, 1973, 87 Stat. 906; Pub. L. 93–592, §5, Jan. 2, 1975, 88 Stat. 1925; Pub. L. 94–238, Mar. 23, 1976, 90 Stat. 250; H. Res. 988, Oct. 8, 1974; S. Res. 4, Feb. 4, 1977.)

REFERENCES IN TEXT

Travel expenses, including per diem in lieu of subsistence as authorized by law, referred to subsec. (f), probably refers to the allowances authorized by section 5703 of Title 5, Government Organization and Employees.

The General Schedule, referred to in subsec. (g), is set out under section 5332 of Title 5.

The Rules of the House of Representatives for the One Hundred Sixth Congress were adopted and amended generally by House Resolution No. 5, One Hundred Sixth Congress, Jan. 6, 1999. Provisions formerly appearing in rule 43, referred to in subsec. (g), were contained in rule XXIV, which was subsequently renumbered Rule XXIII by House Resolution No. 5, One Hundred Seventh Congress, Jan. 3, 2001.

AMENDMENTS

1976—Subsec. (h). Pub. L. 94–238 substituted "$17,250,000" for "$17,000,000".

1975—Subsec. (h). Pub. L. 93–592 substituted "$17,000,000" for "$15,000,000".

1973—Subsecs. (g), (h). Pub. L. 93–207 added subsec. (g) and redesignated former subsec. (g) as (h).

CHANGE OF NAME

Committee on Public Works of Senate abolished and replaced by Committee on Environment and Public Works of Senate, effective Feb. 11, 1977. See Rule XXV of Standing Rules of Senate, as amended by Senate Resolution No. 4 (popularly cited as the "Committee System Reorganization Amendments of 1977"), approved Feb. 4, 1977.

Committee on Public Works of House of Representatives changed to Committee on Public Works and Transportation of House of Representatives, effective Jan. 3, 1975, by House Resolution No. 988, 93d Congress. Committee on Public Works and Transportation of House of Representatives treated as referring to Committee on Transportation and Infrastructure of House of Representatives by section 1(a) of Pub. L. 104–14, set out as a note preceding section 21 of Title 2, The Congress.

REFERENCES IN OTHER LAWS TO GS–16, 17, OR 18 PAY RATES

References in laws to the rates of pay for GS–16, 17, or 18, or to maximum rates of pay under the General Schedule, to be considered references to rates payable under specified sections of Title 5, Government Organization and Employees, see section 529 [title I, §101(c)(1)] of Pub. L. 101–509, set out in a note under section 5376 of Title 5.

§ 1326. Thermal discharges

(a) Effluent limitations that will assure protection and propagation of balanced, indigenous population of shellfish, fish, and wildlife

With respect to any point source otherwise subject to the provisions of section 1311 of this

[1] See References in Text note below.

title or section 1316 of this title, whenever the owner or operator of any such source, after opportunity for public hearing, can demonstrate to the satisfaction of the Administrator (or, if appropriate, the State) that any effluent limitation proposed for the control of the thermal component of any discharge from such source will require effluent limitations more stringent than necessary to assure the projection and propagation of a balanced, indigenous population of shellfish, fish, and wildlife in and on the body of water into which the discharge is to be made, the Administrator (or, if appropriate, the State) may impose an effluent limitation under such sections for such plant, with respect to the thermal component of such discharge (taking into account the interaction of such thermal component with other pollutants), that will assure the protection and propagation of a balanced, indigenous population of shellfish, fish, and wildlife in and on that body of water.

(b) Cooling water intake structures

Any standard established pursuant to section 1311 of this title or section 1316 of this title and applicable to a point source shall require that the location, design, construction, and capacity of cooling water intake structures reflect the best technology available for minimizing adverse environmental impact.

(c) Period of protection from more stringent effluent limitations following discharge point source modification commenced after October 18, 1972

Notwithstanding any other provision of this chapter, any point source of a discharge having a thermal component, the modification of which point source is commenced after October 18, 1972, and which, as modified, meets effluent limitations established under section 1311 of this title or, if more stringent, effluent limitations established under section 1313 of this title and which effluent limitations will assure protection and propagation of a balanced, indigenous population of shellfish, fish, and wildlife in or on the water into which the discharge is made, shall not be subject to any more stringent effluent limitation with respect to the thermal component of its discharge during a ten year period beginning on the date of completion of such modification or during the period of depreciation or amortization of such facility for the purpose of section 167 or 169 (or both) of title 26, whichever period ends first.

(June 30, 1948, ch. 758, title III, §316, as added Pub. L. 92–500, §2, Oct. 18, 1972, 86 Stat. 876; amended Pub. L. 99–514, §2, Oct. 22, 1986, 100 Stat. 2095.)

AMENDMENTS

1986—Subsec. (c). Pub. L. 99–514 substituted "Internal Revenue Code of 1986" for "Internal Revenue Code of 1954", which for purposes of codification was translated as "title 26" thus requiring no change in text.

§ 1327. Omitted

CODIFICATION

Section, act June 30, 1948, ch. 758, title III, §317, as added Oct. 18, 1972, Pub. L. 92–500, §2, 86 Stat. 877, authorized Administrator to investigate and study feasibility of alternate methods of financing cost of preventing, controlling, and abating pollution as directed by Water Quality Improvement Act of 1970 and to report to Congress, not later than two years after Oct. 18, 1972, the results of investigation and study accompanied by recommendations for financing these programs for fiscal years beginning after 1976.

§ 1328. Aquaculture

(a) Authority to permit discharge of specific pollutants

The Administrator is authorized, after public hearings, to permit the discharge of a specific pollutant or pollutants under controlled conditions associated with an approved aquaculture project under Federal or State supervision pursuant to section 1342 of this title.

(b) Procedures and guidelines

The Administrator shall by regulation establish any procedures and guidelines which the Administrator deems necessary to carry out this section. Such regulations shall require the application to such discharge of each criterion, factor, procedure, and requirement applicable to a permit issued under section 1342 of this title, as the Administrator determines necessary to carry out the objective of this chapter.

(c) State administration

Each State desiring to administer its own permit program within its jurisdiction for discharge of a specific pollutant or pollutants under controlled conditions associated with an approved aquaculture project may do so if upon submission of such program the Administrator determines such program is adequate to carry out the objective of this chapter.

(June 30, 1948, ch. 758, title III, §318, as added Pub. L. 92–500, §2, Oct. 18, 1972, 86 Stat. 877; amended Pub. L. 95–217, §63, Dec. 27, 1977, 91 Stat. 1599.)

AMENDMENTS

1977—Subsec. (a). Pub. L. 95–217 inserted "pursuant to section 1342 of this title" after "Federal or State supervision".

Subsec. (b). Pub. L. 95–217 struck out ", not later than January 1, 1974," after "The Administrator shall by regulation" in existing provisions and inserted provisions that the regulations require the application to the discharge of each criterion, factor, procedure, and requirement applicable to a permit issued under section 1342 of this title, as the Administrator determines necessary to carry out the objectives of this chapter.

Subsec. (c). Pub. L. 95–217 added subsec. (c).

§ 1329. Nonpoint source management programs

(a) State assessment reports

(1) Contents

The Governor of each State shall, after notice and opportunity for public comment, prepare and submit to the Administrator for approval, a report which—

(A) identifies those navigable waters within the State which, without additional action to control nonpoint sources of pollution, cannot reasonably be expected to attain or maintain applicable water quality standards or the goals and requirements of this chapter;

(B) identifies those categories and subcategories of nonpoint sources or, where appropriate, particular nonpoint sources which add significant pollution to each portion of the navigable waters identified under subparagraph (A) in amounts which contribute to such portion not meeting such water quality standards or such goals and requirements;

(C) describes the process, including intergovernmental coordination and public participation, for identifying best management practices and measures to control each category and subcategory of nonpoint sources and, where appropriate, particular nonpoint sources identified under subparagraph (B) and to reduce, to the maximum extent practicable, the level of pollution resulting from such category, subcategory, or source; and

(D) identifies and describes State and local programs for controlling pollution added from nonpoint sources to, and improving the quality of, each such portion of the navigable waters, including but not limited to those programs which are receiving Federal assistance under subsections (h) and (i) of this section.

(2) Information used in preparation

In developing the report required by this section, the State (A) may rely upon information developed pursuant to sections 1288, 1313(e), 1314(f), 1315(b), and 1324 of this title, and other information as appropriate, and (B) may utilize appropriate elements of the waste treatment management plans developed pursuant to sections 1288(b) and 1313 of this title, to the extent such elements are consistent with and fulfill the requirements of this section.

(b) State management programs

(1) In general

The Governor of each State, for that State or in combination with adjacent States, shall, after notice and opportunity for public comment, prepare and submit to the Administrator for approval a management program which such State proposes to implement in the first four fiscal years beginning after the date of submission of such management program for controlling pollution added from nonpoint sources to the navigable waters within the State and improving the quality of such waters.

(2) Specific contents

Each management program proposed for implementation under this subsection shall include each of the following:

(A) An identification of the best management practices and measures which will be undertaken to reduce pollutant loadings resulting from each category, subcategory, or particular nonpoint source designated under paragraph (1)(B), taking into account the impact of the practice on ground water quality.

(B) An identification of programs (including, as appropriate, nonregulatory or regulatory programs for enforcement, technical assistance, financial assistance, education, training, technology transfer, and demonstration projects) to achieve implementation of the best management practices by the categories, subcategories, and particular nonpoint sources designated under subparagraph (A).

(C) A schedule containing annual milestones for (i) utilization of the program implementation methods identified in subparagraph (B), and (ii) implementation of the best management practices identified in subparagraph (A) by the categories, subcategories, or particular nonpoint sources designated under paragraph (1)(B). Such schedule shall provide for utilization of the best management practices at the earliest practicable date.

(D) A certification of the attorney general of the State or States (or the chief attorney of any State water pollution control agency which has independent legal counsel) that the laws of the State or States, as the case may be, provide adequate authority to implement such management program or, if there is not such adequate authority, a list of such additional authorities as will be necessary to implement such management program. A schedule and commitment by the State or States to seek such additional authorities as expeditiously as practicable.

(E) Sources of Federal and other assistance and funding (other than assistance provided under subsections (h) and (i) of this section) which will be available in each of such fiscal years for supporting implementation of such practices and measures and the purposes for which such assistance will be used in each of such fiscal years.

(F) An identification of Federal financial assistance programs and Federal development projects for which the State will review individual assistance applications or development projects for their effect on water quality pursuant to the procedures set forth in Executive Order 12372 as in effect on September 17, 1983, to determine whether such assistance applications or development projects would be consistent with the program prepared under this subsection; for the purposes of this subparagraph, identification shall not be limited to the assistance programs or development projects subject to Executive Order 12372 but may include any programs listed in the most recent Catalog of Federal Domestic Assistance which may have an effect on the purposes and objectives of the State's nonpoint source pollution management program.

(3) Utilization of local and private experts

In developing and implementing a management program under this subsection, a State shall, to the maximum extent practicable, involve local public and private agencies and organizations which have expertise in control of nonpoint sources of pollution.

(4) Development on watershed basis

A State shall, to the maximum extent practicable, develop and implement a management program under this subsection on a watershed-by-watershed basis within such State.

(c) Administrative provisions

(1) Cooperation requirement

Any report required by subsection (a) of this section and any management program and report required by subsection (b) of this section shall be developed in cooperation with local, substate regional, and interstate entities which are actively planning for the implementation of nonpoint source pollution controls and have either been certified by the Administrator in accordance with section 1288 of this title, have worked jointly with the State on water quality management planning under section 1285(j) of this title, or have been designated by the State legislative body or Governor as water quality management planning agencies for their geographic areas.

(2) Time period for submission of reports and management programs

Each report and management program shall be submitted to the Administrator during the 18-month period beginning on February 4, 1987.

(d) Approval or disapproval of reports and management programs

(1) Deadline

Subject to paragraph (2), not later than 180 days after the date of submission to the Administrator of any report or management program under this section (other than subsections (h), (i), and (k) of this section), the Administrator shall either approve or disapprove such report or management program, as the case may be. The Administrator may approve a portion of a management program under this subsection. If the Administrator does not disapprove a report, management program, or portion of a management program in such 180-day period, such report, management program, or portion shall be deemed approved for purposes of this section.

(2) Procedure for disapproval

If, after notice and opportunity for public comment and consultation with appropriate Federal and State agencies and other interested persons, the Administrator determines that—

(A) the proposed management program or any portion thereof does not meet the requirements of subsection (b)(2) of this section or is not likely to satisfy, in whole or in part, the goals and requirements of this chapter;

(B) adequate authority does not exist, or adequate resources are not available, to implement such program or portion;

(C) the schedule for implementing such program or portion is not sufficiently expeditious; or

(D) the practices and measures proposed in such program or portion are not adequate to reduce the level of pollution in navigable waters in the State resulting from nonpoint sources and to improve the quality of navigable waters in the State;

the Administrator shall within 6 months of the receipt of the proposed program notify the State of any revisions or modifications necessary to obtain approval. The State shall thereupon have an additional 3 months to submit its revised management program and the Administrator shall approve or disapprove such revised program within three months of receipt.

(3) Failure of State to submit report

If a Governor of a State does not submit the report required by subsection (a) of this section within the period specified by subsection (c)(2) of this section, the Administrator shall, within 30 months after February 4, 1987, prepare a report for such State which makes the identifications required by paragraphs (1)(A) and (1)(B) of subsection (a) of this section. Upon completion of the requirement of the preceding sentence and after notice and opportunity for comment, the Administrator shall report to Congress on his actions pursuant to this section.

(e) Local management programs; technical assistance

If a State fails to submit a management program under subsection (b) of this section or the Administrator does not approve such a management program, a local public agency or organization which has expertise in, and authority to, control water pollution resulting from nonpoint sources in any area of such State which the Administrator determines is of sufficient geographic size may, with approval of such State, request the Administrator to provide, and the Administrator shall provide, technical assistance to such agency or organization in developing for such area a management program which is described in subsection (b) of this section and can be approved pursuant to subsection (d) of this section. After development of such management program, such agency or organization shall submit such management program to the Administrator for approval. If the Administrator approves such management program, such agency or organization shall be eligible to receive financial assistance under subsection (h) of this section for implementation of such management program as if such agency or organization were a State for which a report submitted under subsection (a) of this section and a management program submitted under subsection (b) of this section were approved under this section. Such financial assistance shall be subject to the same terms and conditions as assistance provided to a State under subsection (h) of this section.

(f) Technical assistance for States

Upon request of a State, the Administrator may provide technical assistance to such State in developing a management program approved under subsection (b) of this section for those portions of the navigable waters requested by such State.

(g) Interstate management conference

(1) Convening of conference; notification; purpose

If any portion of the navigable waters in any State which is implementing a management program approved under this section is not meeting applicable water quality standards or the goals and requirements of this chapter as a result, in whole or in part, of pollution from nonpoint sources in another State, such State may petition the Administrator to convene, and the Administrator shall convene, a management conference of all States which contribute significant pollution resulting from nonpoint sources to such portion. If, on the basis of information available, the Administrator determines that a State is not meeting applicable water quality standards or the goals and requirements of this chapter as a result, in whole or in part, of significant pollution from nonpoint sources in another State, the Administrator shall notify such States. The Administrator may convene a management conference under this paragraph not later than 180 days after giving such notification, whether or not the State which is not meeting such standards requests such conference. The purpose of such conference shall be to develop an agreement among such States to reduce the level of pollution in such portion resulting from nonpoint sources and to improve the water quality of such portion. Nothing in such agreement shall supersede or abrogate rights to quantities of water which have been established by interstate water compacts, Supreme Court decrees, or State water laws. This subsection shall not apply to any pollution which is subject to the Colorado River Basin Salinity Control Act [43 U.S.C. 1571 et seq.]. The requirement that the Administrator convene a management conference shall not be subject to the provisions of section 1365 of this title.

(2) State management program requirement

To the extent that the States reach agreement through such conference, the management programs of the States which are parties to such agreements and which contribute significant pollution to the navigable waters or portions thereof not meeting applicable water quality standards or goals and requirements of this chapter will be revised to reflect such agreement. Such management programs shall be consistent with Federal and State law.

(h) Grant program

(1) Grants for implementation of management programs

Upon application of a State for which a report submitted under subsection (a) of this section and a management program submitted under subsection (b) of this section is approved under this section, the Administrator shall make grants, subject to such terms and conditions as the Administrator considers appropriate, under this subsection to such State for the purpose of assisting the State in implementing such management program. Funds reserved pursuant to section 1285(j)(5) of this title may be used to develop and implement such management program.

(2) Applications

An application for a grant under this subsection in any fiscal year shall be in such form and shall contain such other information as the Administrator may require, including an identification and description of the best management practices and measures which the State proposes to assist, encourage, or require in such year with the Federal assistance to be provided under the grant.

(3) Federal share

The Federal share of the cost of each management program implemented with Federal assistance under this subsection in any fiscal year shall not exceed 60 percent of the cost incurred by the State in implementing such management program and shall be made on condition that the non-Federal share is provided from non-Federal sources.

(4) Limitation on grant amounts

Notwithstanding any other provision of this subsection, not more than 15 percent of the amount appropriated to carry out this subsection may be used to make grants to any one State, including any grants to any local public agency or organization with authority to control pollution from nonpoint sources in any area of such State.

(5) Priority for effective mechanisms

For each fiscal year beginning after September 30, 1987, the Administrator may give priority in making grants under this subsection, and shall give consideration in determining the Federal share of any such grant, to States which have implemented or are proposing to implement management programs which will—

(A) control particularly difficult or serious nonpoint source pollution problems, including, but not limited to, problems resulting from mining activities;

(B) implement innovative methods or practices for controlling nonpoint sources of pollution, including regulatory programs where the Administrator deems appropriate;

(C) control interstate nonpoint source pollution problems; or

(D) carry out ground water quality protection activities which the Administrator determines are part of a comprehensive nonpoint source pollution control program, including research, planning, ground water assessments, demonstration programs, enforcement, technical assistance, education, and training to protect ground water quality from nonpoint sources of pollution.

(6) Availability for obligation

The funds granted to each State pursuant to this subsection in a fiscal year shall remain available for obligation by such State for the fiscal year for which appropriated. The amount of any such funds not obligated by the end of such fiscal year shall be available to the Administrator for granting to other States under this subsection in the next fiscal year.

(7) Limitation on use of funds

States may use funds from grants made pursuant to this section for financial assistance to persons only to the extent that such assistance is related to the costs of demonstration projects.

(8) Satisfactory progress

No grant may be made under this subsection in any fiscal year to a State which in the preceding fiscal year received a grant under this subsection unless the Administrator determines that such State made satisfactory progress in such preceding fiscal year in meeting the schedule specified by such State under subsection (b)(2) of this section.

(9) Maintenance of effort

No grant may be made to a State under this subsection in any fiscal year unless such State enters into such agreements with the Administrator as the Administrator may require to ensure that such State will maintain its aggregate expenditures from all other sources for programs for controlling pollution added to the navigable waters in such State from nonpoint sources and improving the quality of such waters at or above the average level of such expenditures in its two fiscal years preceding February 4, 1987.

(10) Request for information

The Administrator may request such information, data, and reports as he considers necessary to make the determination of continuing eligibility for grants under this section.

(11) Reporting and other requirements

Each State shall report to the Administrator on an annual basis concerning (A) its progress in meeting the schedule of milestones submitted pursuant to subsection (b)(2)(C) of this section, and (B) to the extent that appropriate information is available, reductions in nonpoint source pollutant loading and improvements in water quality for those navigable waters or watersheds within the State which were identified pursuant to subsection (a)(1)(A) of this section resulting from implementation of the management program.

(12) Limitation on administrative costs

For purposes of this subsection, administrative costs in the form of salaries, overhead, or indirect costs for services provided and charged against activities and programs carried out with a grant under this subsection shall not exceed in any fiscal year 10 percent of the amount of the grant in such year, except that costs of implementing enforcement and regulatory activities, education, training, technical assistance, demonstration projects, and technology transfer programs shall not be subject to this limitation.

(i) Grants for protecting groundwater quality

(1) Eligible applicants and activities

Upon application of a State for which a report submitted under subsection (a) of this section and a plan submitted under subsection (b) of this section is approved under this section, the Administrator shall make grants under this subsection to such State for the purpose of assisting such State in carrying out groundwater quality protection activities which the Administrator determines will advance the State toward implementation of a comprehensive nonpoint source pollution control program. Such activities shall include, but not be limited to, research, planning, groundwater assessments, demonstration programs, enforcement, technical assistance, education and training to protect the quality of groundwater and to prevent contamination of groundwater from nonpoint sources of pollution.

(2) Applications

An application for a grant under this subsection shall be in such form and shall contain such information as the Administrator may require.

(3) Federal share; maximum amount

The Federal share of the cost of assisting a State in carrying out groundwater protection activities in any fiscal year under this subsection shall be 50 percent of the costs incurred by the State in carrying out such activities, except that the maximum amount of Federal assistance which any State may receive under this subsection in any fiscal year shall not exceed $150,000.

(4) Report

The Administrator shall include in each report transmitted under subsection (m) of this section a report on the activities and programs implemented under this subsection during the preceding fiscal year.

(j) Authorization of appropriations

There is authorized to be appropriated to carry out subsections (h) and (i) of this section not to exceed $70,000,000 for fiscal year 1988, $100,000,000 per fiscal year for each of fiscal years 1989 and 1990, and $130,000,000 for fiscal year 1991; except that for each of such fiscal years not to exceed $7,500,000 may be made available to carry out subsection (i) of this section. Sums appropriated pursuant to this subsection shall remain available until expended.

(k) Consistency of other programs and projects with management programs

The Administrator shall transmit to the Office of Management and Budget and the appropriate Federal departments and agencies a list of those assistance programs and development projects identified by each State under subsection (b)(2)(F) of this section for which individual assistance applications and projects will be reviewed pursuant to the procedures set forth in Executive Order 12372 as in effect on September 17, 1983. Beginning not later than sixty days after receiving notification by the Administrator, each Federal department and agency shall modify existing regulations to allow States to review individual development projects and assistance applications under the identified Federal assistance programs and shall accommodate, according to the requirements and definitions of Executive Order 12372, as in effect on September 17, 1983, the concerns of the State regarding the consistency of such applications or projects with the State nonpoint source pollution management program.

***(l)* Collection of information**

The Administrator shall collect and make available, through publications and other appropriate means, information pertaining to management practices and implementation methods, including, but not limited to, (1) information concerning the costs and relative efficiencies of best management practices for reducing nonpoint source pollution; and (2) available data concerning the relationship between water quality and implementation of various management practices to control nonpoint sources of pollution.

(m) Reports of Administrator

(1) Annual reports

Not later than January 1, 1988, and each January 1 thereafter, the Administrator shall transmit to the Committee on Public Works and Transportation of the House of Representatives and the Committee on Environment and Public Works of the Senate, a report for the preceding fiscal year on the activities and programs implemented under this section and the progress made in reducing pollution in the navigable waters resulting from nonpoint sources and improving the quality of such waters.

(2) Final report

Not later than January 1, 1990, the Administrator shall transmit to Congress a final report on the activities carried out under this section. Such report, at a minimum, shall—

(A) describe the management programs being implemented by the States by types and amount of affected navigable waters, categories and subcategories of nonpoint sources, and types of best management practices being implemented;

(B) describe the experiences of the States in adhering to schedules and implementing best management practices;

(C) describe the amount and purpose of grants awarded pursuant to subsections (h) and (i) of this section;

(D) identify, to the extent that information is available, the progress made in reducing pollutant loads and improving water quality in the navigable waters;

(E) indicate what further actions need to be taken to attain and maintain in those navigable waters (i) applicable water quality standards, and (ii) the goals and requirements of this chapter;

(F) include recommendations of the Administrator concerning future programs (including enforcement programs) for controlling pollution from nonpoint sources; and

(G) identify the activities and programs of departments, agencies, and instrumentalities of the United States which are inconsistent with the management programs submitted by the States and recommend modifications so that such activities and programs are consistent with and assist the States in implementation of such management programs.

(n) Set aside for administrative personnel

Not less than 5 percent of the funds appropriated pursuant to subsection (j) of this section for any fiscal year shall be available to the Administrator to maintain personnel levels at the Environmental Protection Agency at levels which are adequate to carry out this section in such year.

(June 30, 1948, ch. 758, title III, § 319, as added Pub. L. 100–4, title III, § 316(a), Feb. 4, 1987, 101 Stat. 52; amended Pub. L. 105–362, title V, § 501(c), Nov. 10, 1998, 112 Stat. 3283; Pub. L. 107–303, title III, § 302(b)(1), Nov. 27, 2002, 116 Stat. 2361.)

REFERENCES IN TEXT

Executive Order 12372, referred to in subsecs. (b)(2)(F) and (k), is Ex. Ord. No. 12372, July 14, 1982, 47 F.R. 30959, as amended, which is set out under section 6506 of Title 31, Money and Finance.

The Colorado River Basin Salinity Control Act, referred to in subsec. (g)(1), is Pub. L. 93–320, June 24, 1974, 88 Stat. 266, as amended, which is classified principally to chapter 32A (§ 1571 et seq.) of Title 43, Public Lands. For complete classification of this Act to the Code, see Short Title note set out under section 1571 of Title 43 and Tables.

AMENDMENTS

2002—Subsecs. (i)(4), (m), (n). Pub. L. 107–303 repealed Pub. L. 105–362, § 501(c). See 1998 Amendment note below.

1998—Subsec. (i)(4). Pub. L. 105–362, § 501(c)(1), which directed the striking out of heading and text of par. (4), was repealed by Pub. L. 107–303. See Effective Date of 2002 Amendment note below.

Subsecs. (m), (n). Pub. L. 105–362, § 501(c)(2), (3), which directed the redesignation of subsec. (n) as (m) and striking out of heading and text of former subsec. (m), was repealed by Pub. L. 107–303. See Effective Date of 2002 Amendment note below.

CHANGE OF NAME

Committee on Public Works and Transportation of House of Representatives treated as referring to Committee on Transportation and Infrastructure of House of Representatives by section 1(a) of Pub. L. 104–14, set out as a note preceding section 21 of Title 2, The Congress.

EFFECTIVE DATE OF 2002 AMENDMENT

Amendment by Pub. L. 107–303 effective Nov. 10, 1998, and Federal Water Pollution Act (33 U.S.C. 1251 et seq.) to be applied and administered on and after Nov. 27, 2002, as if amendments made by section 501(a)–(d) of Pub. L. 105–362 had not been enacted, see section 302(b) of Pub. L. 107–303, set out as a note under section 1254 of this title.

§ 1330. National estuary program

(a) Management conference

(1) Nomination of estuaries

The Governor of any State may nominate to the Administrator an estuary lying in whole or in part within the State as an estuary of national significance and request a management conference to develop a comprehensive management plan for the estuary. The nomination shall document the need for the conference, the likelihood of success, and information relating to the factors in paragraph (2).

(2) Convening of conference

(A) In general

In any case where the Administrator determines, on his own initiative or upon nomination of a State under paragraph (1), that the attainment or maintenance of that water quality in an estuary which assures protection of public water supplies and the protection and propagation of a balanced, indigenous population of shellfish, fish, and wildlife, and allows recreational activities, in and on the water, requires the control of point and nonpoint sources of pollution to supplement existing controls of pollution in more than one State, the Administrator shall select such estuary and convene a management conference.

(B) Priority consideration

The Administrator shall give priority consideration under this section to Long Island Sound, New York and Connecticut; Narragansett Bay, Rhode Island; Buzzards Bay, Massachusetts; Massachusetts Bay, Massachusetts (including Cape Cod Bay and Boston Harbor); Puget Sound, Washington; New York-New Jersey Harbor, New York and New Jersey; Delaware Bay, Delaware and New Jersey; Delaware Inland Bays, Delaware; Albemarle Sound, North Carolina; Sarasota Bay, Florida; San Francisco Bay, California; Santa Monica Bay, California; Galveston Bay, Texas; Barataria-Terrebonne Bay estuary complex, Louisiana; Indian River Lagoon, Florida; Lake Pontchartrain Basin, Louisiana and Mississippi; and Peconic Bay, New York.

(3) Boundary dispute exception

In any case in which a boundary between two States passes through an estuary and such boundary is disputed and is the subject of an action in any court, the Administrator shall not convene a management conference with respect to such estuary before a final adjudication has been made of such dispute.

(b) Purposes of conference

The purposes of any management conference convened with respect to an estuary under this subsection shall be to—

(1) assess trends in water quality, natural resources, and uses of the estuary;

(2) collect, characterize, and assess data on toxics, nutrients, and natural resources within the estuarine zone to identify the causes of environmental problems;

(3) develop the relationship between the inplace loads and point and nonpoint loadings of pollutants to the estuarine zone and the potential uses of the zone, water quality, and natural resources;

(4) develop a comprehensive conservation and management plan that recommends priority corrective actions and compliance schedules addressing point and nonpoint sources of pollution to restore and maintain the chemical, physical, and biological integrity of the estuary, including restoration and maintenance of water quality, a balanced indigenous population of shellfish, fish and wildlife, and recreational activities in the estuary, and assure that the designated uses of the estuary are protected;

(5) develop plans for the coordinated implementation of the plan by the States as well as Federal and local agencies participating in the conference;

(6) monitor the effectiveness of actions taken pursuant to the plan; and

(7) review all Federal financial assistance programs and Federal development projects in accordance with the requirements of Executive Order 12372, as in effect on September 17, 1983, to determine whether such assistance program or project would be consistent with and further the purposes and objectives of the plan prepared under this section.

For purposes of paragraph (7), such programs and projects shall not be limited to the assistance programs and development projects subject to Executive Order 12372, but may include any programs listed in the most recent Catalog of Federal Domestic Assistance which may have an effect on the purposes and objectives of the plan developed under this section.

(c) Members of conference

The members of a management conference convened under this section shall include, at a minimum, the Administrator and representatives of—

(1) each State and foreign nation located in whole or in part in the estuarine zone of the estuary for which the conference is convened;

(2) international, interstate, or regional agencies or entities having jurisdiction over all or a significant part of the estuary;

(3) each interested Federal agency, as determined appropriate by the Administrator;

(4) local governments having jurisdiction over any land or water within the estuarine zone, as determined appropriate by the Administrator; and

(5) affected industries, public and private educational institutions, and the general public, as determined appropriate by the Administrator.

(d) Utilization of existing data

In developing a conservation and management plan under this section, the management conference shall survey and utilize existing reports, data, and studies relating to the estuary that have been developed by or made available to Federal, interstate, State, and local agencies.

(e) Period of conference

A management conference convened under this section shall be convened for a period not to exceed 5 years. Such conference may be extended by the Administrator, and if terminated after the initial period, may be reconvened by the Administrator at any time thereafter, as may be necessary to meet the requirements of this section.

(f) Approval and implementation of plans

(1) Approval

Not later than 120 days after the completion of a conservation and management plan and after providing for public review and comment, the Administrator shall approve such plan if the plan meets the requirements of this section and the affected Governor or Governors concur.

(2) Implementation

Upon approval of a conservation and management plan under this section, such plan shall be implemented. Funds authorized to be appropriated under subchapters II and VI of this chapter and section 1329 of this title may be used in accordance with the applicable requirements of this chapter to assist States with the implementation of such plan.

(g) Grants

(1) Recipients

The Administrator is authorized to make grants to State, interstate, and regional water pollution control agencies and entities, State coastal zone management agencies, interstate agencies, other public or nonprofit private agencies, institutions, organizations, and individuals.

(2) Purposes

Grants under this subsection shall be made to pay for activities necessary for the development and implementation of a comprehensive conservation and management plan under this section.

(3) Federal share

The Federal share of a grant to any person (including a State, interstate, or regional agency or entity) under this subsection for a fiscal year—

(A) shall not exceed—

(i) 75 percent of the annual aggregate costs of the development of a comprehensive conservation and management plan; and

(ii) 50 percent of the annual aggregate costs of the implementation of the plan; and

(B) shall be made on condition that the non-Federal share of the costs are provided from non-Federal sources.

(h) Grant reporting

Any person (including a State, interstate, or regional agency or entity) that receives a grant under subsection (g) of this section shall report to the Administrator not later than 18 months after receipt of such grant and biennially thereafter on the progress being made under this section.

(i) Authorization of appropriations

There are authorized to be appropriated to the Administrator not to exceed $35,000,000 for each of fiscal years 2001 through 2010 for—

(1) expenses related to the administration of management conferences under this section, not to exceed 10 percent of the amount appropriated under this subsection;

(2) making grants under subsection (g) of this section; and

(3) monitoring the implementation of a conservation and management plan by the management conference or by the Administrator, in any case in which the conference has been terminated.

The Administrator shall provide up to $5,000,000 per fiscal year of the sums authorized to be appropriated under this subsection to the Administrator of the National Oceanic and Atmospheric Administration to carry out subsection (j) of this section.

(j) Research

(1) Programs

In order to determine the need to convene a management conference under this section or at the request of such a management conference, the Administrator shall coordinate and implement, through the National Marine Pollution Program Office and the National Marine Fisheries Service of the National Oceanic and Atmospheric Administration, as appropriate, for one or more estuarine zones—

(A) a long-term program of trend assessment monitoring measuring variations in pollutant concentrations, marine ecology, and other physical or biological environmental parameters which may affect estuarine zones, to provide the Administrator the capacity to determine the potential and actual effects of alternative management strategies and measures;

(B) a program of ecosystem assessment assisting in the development of (i) baseline studies which determine the state of estuarine zones and the effects of natural and anthropogenic changes, and (ii) predictive models capable of translating information on specific discharges or general pollutant loadings within estuarine zones into a set of probable effects on such zones;

(C) a comprehensive water quality sampling program for the continuous monitoring of nutrients, chlorine, acid precipitation dissolved oxygen, and potentially toxic pollutants (including organic chemicals and metals) in estuarine zones, after consultation with interested State, local, interstate, or international agencies and review and analysis of all environmental sampling data presently collected from estuarine zones; and

(D) a program of research to identify the movements of nutrients, sediments and pollutants through estuarine zones and the impact of nutrients, sediments, and pollutants on water quality, the ecosystem, and designated or potential uses of the estuarine zones.

(2) Reports

The Administrator, in cooperation with the Administrator of the National Oceanic and Atmospheric Administration, shall submit to the Congress no less often than biennially a comprehensive report on the activities authorized under this subsection including—

(A) a listing of priority monitoring and research needs;

(B) an assessment of the state and health of the Nation's estuarine zones, to the extent evaluated under this subsection;

(C) a discussion of pollution problems and trends in pollutant concentrations with a direct or indirect effect on water quality, the ecosystem, and designated or potential uses of each estuarine zone, to the extent evaluated under this subsection; and

(D) an evaluation of pollution abatement activities and management measures so far implemented to determine the degree of improvement toward the objectives expressed in subsection (b)(4) of this section.

(k) Definitions

For purposes of this section, the terms "estuary" and "estuarine zone" have the meanings such terms have in section 1254(n)(4) of this title, except that the term "estuarine zone" shall also include associated aquatic ecosystems and those portions of tributaries draining into the estuary up to the historic height of migration of anadromous fish or the historic head of tidal influence, whichever is higher.

(June 30, 1948, ch. 758, title III, § 320, as added Pub. L. 100–4, title III, § 317(b), Feb. 4, 1987, 101 Stat. 61; amended Pub. L. 100–202, § 101(f) [title II, 201], Dec. 22, 1987, 101 Stat. 1329–187, 1329–197; Pub. L. 100–653, title X, § 1004, Nov. 14, 1988, 102 Stat. 3836; Pub. L. 100–688, title II, § 2001, Nov. 18, 1988, 102 Stat. 4151; Pub. L. 105–362, title V, § 501(a)(2), Nov. 10, 1998, 112 Stat. 3283; Pub. L. 106–457, title III, §§ 301—303, Nov. 7, 2000, 114 Stat. 1972; Pub. L. 107–303, title III, § 302(b)(1), Nov. 27, 2002, 116 Stat. 2361; Pub. L. 108–399, § 1, Oct. 30, 2004, 118 Stat. 2253.)

REFERENCES IN TEXT

Executive Order 12372, referred to in subsec. (b), is Ex. Ord. No. 12372, July 14, 1982, 47 F.R. 30959, as amended, which is set out under section 6506 of Title 31, Money and Finance.

AMENDMENTS

2004—Subsec. (i). Pub. L. 108–399 substituted "2010" for "2005" in introductory provisions.

2002—Subsec. (k). Pub. L. 107–303 repealed Pub. L. 105–362, § 501(a)(2). See 1998 Amendment note below.

2000—Subsec. (a)(2)(B). Pub. L. 106–457, § 301, inserted "Lake Pontchartrain Basin, Louisiana and Mississippi;" before "and Peconic Bay, New York."

Subsec. (g)(2), (3). Pub. L. 106–457, § 302, added pars. (2) and (3) and struck out former pars. (2) and (3) which read as follows:

"(2) PURPOSES.—Grants under this subsection shall be made to pay for assisting research, surveys, studies, and modeling and other technical work necessary for the development of a conservation and management plan under this section.

"(3) FEDERAL SHARE.—The amount of grants to any person (including a State, interstate, or regional agency or entity) under this subsection for a fiscal year shall not exceed 75 percent of the costs of such research, survey, studies, and work and shall be made on condition that the non-Federal share of such costs are provided from non-Federal sources."

Subsec. (i). Pub. L. 106–457, § 303, substituted "$35,000,000 for each of fiscal years 2001 through 2005" for "$12,000,000 per fiscal year for each of fiscal years 1987, 1988, 1989, 1990, and 1991".

1998—Subsec. (k). Pub. L. 105–362, § 501(a)(2), which directed the substitution of "section 1254(n)(3)" for "section 1254(n)(4)", was repealed by Pub. L. 107–303. See Effective Date of 2002 Amendment note below.

1988—Subsec. (a)(2)(B). Pub. L. 100–653, § 1004, and Pub. L. 100–688, § 2001(1), made identical amendments, inserting "Massachusetts Bay, Massachusetts (including Cape Cod Bay and Boston Harbor);" after "Buzzards Bay, Massachusetts;".

Pub. L. 100–688, § 2001(2), substituted "California; Galveston" for "California; and Galveston".

Pub. L. 100–688, § 2001(3), which directed insertion of "; Barataria-Terrebonne Bay estuary complex, Louisiana; Indian River Lagoon, Florida; and Peconic Bay, New York" after "Galveston Bay, Texas;" was executed by making insertion after "Galveston Bay, Texas" as probable intent of Congress.

1987—Subsec. (a)(2)(B). Pub. L. 100–202 inserted "Santa Monica Bay, California;".

EFFECTIVE DATE OF 2002 AMENDMENT

Amendment by Pub. L. 107–303 effective Nov. 10, 1998, and Federal Water Pollution Act (33 U.S.C. 1251 et seq.) to be applied and administered on and after Nov. 27, 2002, as if amendments made by section 501(a)–(d) of Pub. L. 105–362 had not been enacted, see section 302(b) of Pub. L. 107–303, set out as a note under section 1254 of this title.

MASSACHUSETTS BAY PROTECTION; DEFINITION; FINDINGS AND PURPOSE; FUNDING SOURCES

Sections 1002, 1003, 1005 of title X of Pub. L. 100–653 provided that:

"SEC. 1002. DEFINITION.

"For purposes of this title [amending section 1330 of this title and enacting provisions set out as notes under sections 1251 and 1330 of this title], the term 'Massachusetts Bay' includes Massachusetts Bay, Cape Cod Bay, and Boston Harbor, consisting of an area extending from Cape Ann, Massachusetts south to the northern reach of Cape Cod, Massachusetts.

"SEC. 1003. FINDINGS AND PURPOSE.

"(a) FINDINGS.—The Congress finds and declares that—

"(1) Massachusetts Bay comprises a single major estuarine and oceanographic system extending from Cape Ann, Massachusetts south to the northern reaches of Cape Cod, encompassing Boston Harbor, Massachusetts Bay, and Cape Cod Bay;

"(2) several major riverine systems, including the Charles, Neponset, and Mystic Rivers, drain the watersheds of eastern Massachusetts into the Bay;

"(3) the shorelines of Massachusetts Bay, first occupied in the middle 1600's, are home to over 4 million people and support a thriving industrial and recreational economy;

"(4) Massachusetts Bay supports important commercial fisheries, including lobsters, finfish, and shellfisheries, and is home to or frequented by several endangered species and marine mammals;

"(5) Massachusetts Bay also constitutes an important recreational resource, providing fishing, swimming, and boating opportunities to the region;

"(6) rapidly expanding coastal populations and pollution pose increasing threats to the long-term health and integrity of Massachusetts Bay;

"(7) while the cleanup of Boston Harbor will contribute significantly to improving the overall environmental quality of Massachusetts Bay, expanded efforts encompassing the entire ecosystem will be necessary to ensure its long-term health;

"(8) the concerted efforts of all levels of Government, the private sector, and the public at large will be necessary to protect and enhance the environmental integrity of Massachusetts Bay; and

"(9) the designation of Massachusetts Bay as an Estuary of National Significance and the development of a comprehensive plan for protecting and restoring the Bay may contribute significantly to its long-term health and environmental integrity.

"(b) PURPOSE.—The purpose of this title is to protect and enhance the environmental quality of Massachusetts Bay by providing for its designation as an Estuary of National Significance and by providing for the preparation of a comprehensive restoration plan for the Bay.

"SEC. 1005. FUNDING SOURCES.

"Within one year of enactment [Nov. 14, 1988], the Administrator of the United States Environmental Protection Agency and the Governor of Massachusetts shall undertake to identify and make available sources of funding to support activities pertaining to Massachusetts Bay undertaken pursuant to or authorized by section 320 of the Clean Water Act [33 U.S.C. 1330], and shall make every effort to coordinate existing research, monitoring or control efforts with such activities."

PURPOSES AND POLICIES OF NATIONAL ESTUARY PROGRAM

Section 317(a) of Pub. L. 100–4 provided that:

"(1) FINDINGS.—Congress finds and declares that—

"(A) the Nation's estuaries are of great importance for fish and wildlife resources and recreation and economic opportunity;

"(B) maintaining the health and ecological integrity of these estuaries is in the national interest;

"(C) increasing coastal population, development, and other direct and indirect uses of these estuaries threaten their health and ecological integrity;

"(D) long-term planning and management will contribute to the continued productivity of these areas, and will maximize their utility to the Nation; and

"(E) better coordination among Federal and State programs affecting estuaries will increase the effectiveness and efficiency of the national effort to protect, preserve, and restore these areas.

"(2) PURPOSES.—The purposes of this section [enacting this section] are to—

"(A) identify nationally significant estuaries that are threatened by pollution, development, or overuse;

"(B) promote comprehensive planning for, and conservation and management of, nationally significant estuaries;

"(C) encourage the preparation of management plans for estuaries of national significance; and

"(D) enhance the coordination of estuarine research."

SUBCHAPTER IV—PERMITS AND LICENSES

§ 1341. Certification

(a) Compliance with applicable requirements; application; procedures; license suspension

(1) Any applicant for a Federal license or permit to conduct any activity including, but not limited to, the construction or operation of facilities, which may result in any discharge into the navigable waters, shall provide the licensing or permitting agency a certification from the State in which the discharge originates or will originate, or, if appropriate, from the interstate water pollution control agency having jurisdiction over the navigable waters at the point where the discharge originates or will originate, that any such discharge will comply with the applicable provisions of sections 1311, 1312, 1313, 1316, and 1317 of this title. In the case of any such activity for which there is not an applicable effluent limitation or other limitation under sections 1311(b) and 1312 of this title, and there is not an applicable standard under sections 1316 and 1317 of this title, the State shall so certify, except that any such certification shall not be deemed to satisfy section 1371(c) of this title. Such State or interstate agency shall establish procedures for public notice in the case of all applications for certification by it and, to the extent it deems appropriate, procedures for public hearings in connection with specific applications. In any case where a State or interstate agency has no authority to give such a certification, such certification shall be from the Administrator. If the State, interstate agency, or Administrator, as the case may be, fails or refuses to act on a request for certification, within a reasonable period of time (which shall not exceed one year) after receipt of such request, the certification requirements of this subsection shall be waived with respect to such Federal application. No license or permit shall be granted until the certification required by this section has been obtained or has been waived as provided in the preceding sentence. No license or permit shall be granted if certification has been denied by the State, interstate agency, or the Administrator, as the case may be.

(2) Upon receipt of such application and certification the licensing or permitting agency shall immediately notify the Administrator of such application and certification. Whenever such a discharge may affect, as determined by the Administrator, the quality of the waters of any other State, the Administrator within thirty days of the date of notice of application for such Federal license or permit shall so notify such other State, the licensing or permitting agency, and the applicant. If, within sixty days after receipt of such notification, such other State determines that such discharge will affect the quality of its waters so as to violate any water quality requirements in such State, and within such sixty-day period notifies the Administrator and the licensing or permitting agency in writing of its objection to the issuance of such license or permit and requests a public hearing on such objection, the licensing or permitting agency shall hold such a hearing. The Administrator shall at such hearing submit his evaluation and recommendations with respect to any such objection to the licensing or permitting agency. Such agency, based upon the recommendations of such State, the Administrator, and upon any additional evidence, if any, presented to the agency at the hearing, shall condition such license or permit in such manner as may be necessary to insure compliance with applicable water quality requirements. If the imposition of conditions cannot insure such compliance such agency shall not issue such license or permit.

(3) The certification obtained pursuant to paragraph (1) of this subsection with respect to the construction of any facility shall fulfill the requirements of this subsection with respect to certification in connection with any other Federal license or permit required for the operation of such facility unless, after notice to the certifying State, agency, or Administrator, as the case may be, which shall be given by the Federal agency to whom application is made for such operating license or permit, the State, or if appropriate, the interstate agency or the Administrator, notifies such agency within sixty days after receipt of such notice that there is no longer reasonable assurance that there will be compliance with the applicable provisions of sections 1311, 1312, 1313, 1316, and 1317 of this title because of changes since the construction license or permit certification was issued in (A) the construction or operation of the facility, (B) the characteristics of the waters into which such discharge is made, (C) the water quality criteria applicable to such waters or (D) applicable effluent limitations or other requirements. This paragraph shall be inapplicable in any case where the applicant for such operating license or permit has failed to provide the certifying State, or, if appropriate, the interstate agency or the Administrator, with notice of any proposed changes in the construction or operation of the facility with respect to which a construction license or permit has been granted, which changes may result in violation of section 1311, 1312, 1313, 1316, or 1317 of this title.

(4) Prior to the initial operation of any federally licensed or permitted facility or activity which may result in any discharge into the navigable waters and with respect to which a certification has been obtained pursuant to paragraph (1) of this subsection, which facility or activity

is not subject to a Federal operating license or permit, the licensee or permittee shall provide an opportunity for such certifying State, or, if appropriate, the interstate agency or the Administrator to review the manner in which the facility or activity shall be operated or conducted for the purposes of assuring that applicable effluent limitations or other limitations or other applicable water quality requirements will not be violated. Upon notification by the certifying State, or if appropriate, the interstate agency or the Administrator that the operation of any such federally licensed or permitted facility or activity will violate applicable effluent limitations or other limitations or other water quality requirements such Federal agency may, after public hearing, suspend such license or permit. If such license or permit is suspended, it shall remain suspended until notification is received from the certifying State, agency, or Administrator, as the case may be, that there is reasonable assurance that such facility or activity will not violate the applicable provisions of section 1311, 1312, 1313, 1316, or 1317 of this title.

(5) Any Federal license or permit with respect to which a certification has been obtained under paragraph (1) of this subsection may be suspended or revoked by the Federal agency issuing such license or permit upon the entering of a judgment under this chapter that such facility or activity has been operated in violation of the applicable provisions of section 1311, 1312, 1313, 1316, or 1317 of this title.

(6) Except with respect to a permit issued under section 1342 of this title, in any case where actual construction of a facility has been lawfully commenced prior to April 3, 1970, no certification shall be required under this subsection for a license or permit issued after April 3, 1970, to operate such facility, except that any such license or permit issued without certification shall terminate April 3, 1973, unless prior to such termination date the person having such license or permit submits to the Federal agency which issued such license or permit a certification and otherwise meets the requirements of this section.

(b) Compliance with other provisions of law setting applicable water quality requirements

Nothing in this section shall be construed to limit the authority of any department or agency pursuant to any other provision of law to require compliance with any applicable water quality requirements. The Administrator shall, upon the request of any Federal department or agency, or State or interstate agency, or applicant, provide, for the purpose of this section, any relevant information on applicable effluent limitations, or other limitations, standards, regulations, or requirements, or water quality criteria, and shall, when requested by any such department or agency or State or interstate agency, or applicant, comment on any methods to comply with such limitations, standards, regulations, requirements, or criteria.

(c) Authority of Secretary of the Army to permit use of spoil disposal areas by Federal licensees or permittees

In order to implement the provisions of this section, the Secretary of the Army, acting through the Chief of Engineers, is authorized, if he deems it to be in the public interest, to permit the use of spoil disposal areas under his jurisdiction by Federal licensees or permittees, and to make an appropriate charge for such use. Moneys received from such licensees or permittees shall be deposited in the Treasury as miscellaneous receipts.

(d) Limitations and monitoring requirements of certification

Any certification provided under this section shall set forth any effluent limitations and other limitations, and monitoring requirements necessary to assure that any applicant for a Federal license or permit will comply with any applicable effluent limitations and other limitations, under section 1311 or 1312 of this title, standard of performance under section 1316 of this title, or prohibition, effluent standard, or pretreatment standard under section 1317 of this title, and with any other appropriate requirement of State law set forth in such certification, and shall become a condition on any Federal license or permit subject to the provisions of this section.

(June 30, 1948, ch. 758, title IV, §401, as added Pub. L. 92–500, §2, Oct. 18, 1972, 86 Stat. 877; amended Pub. L. 95–217, §§61(b), 64, Dec. 27, 1977, 91 Stat. 1598, 1599.)

AMENDMENTS

1977—Subsec. (a). Pub. L. 95–217 inserted reference to section 1313 of this title in pars. (1), (3), (4), and (5), struck out par. (6) which provided that no Federal agency be deemed an applicant for purposes of this subsection, and redesignated par. (7) as (6).

§1342. National pollutant discharge elimination system

(a) Permits for discharge of pollutants

(1) Except as provided in sections 1328 and 1344 of this title, the Administrator may, after opportunity for public hearing issue a permit for the discharge of any pollutant, or combination of pollutants, notwithstanding section 1311(a) of this title, upon condition that such discharge will meet either (A) all applicable requirements under sections 1311, 1312, 1316, 1317, 1318, and 1343 of this title, or (B) prior to the taking of necessary implementing actions relating to all such requirements, such conditions as the Administrator determines are necessary to carry out the provisions of this chapter.

(2) The Administrator shall prescribe conditions for such permits to assure compliance with the requirements of paragraph (1) of this subsection, including conditions on data and information collection, reporting, and such other requirements as he deems appropriate.

(3) The permit program of the Administrator under paragraph (1) of this subsection, and permits issued thereunder, shall be subject to the same terms, conditions, and requirements as apply to a State permit program and permits issued thereunder under subsection (b) of this section.

(4) All permits for discharges into the navigable waters issued pursuant to section 407 of this title shall be deemed to be permits issued under this subchapter, and permits issued under

this subchapter shall be deemed to be permits issued under section 407 of this title, and shall continue in force and effect for their term unless revoked, modified, or suspended in accordance with the provisions of this chapter.

(5) No permit for a discharge into the navigable waters shall be issued under section 407 of this title after October 18, 1972. Each application for a permit under section 407 of this title, pending on October 18, 1972, shall be deemed to be an application for a permit under this section. The Administrator shall authorize a State, which he determines has the capability of administering a permit program which will carry out the objectives of this chapter to issue permits for discharges into the navigable waters within the jurisdiction of such State. The Administrator may exercise the authority granted him by the preceding sentence only during the period which begins on October 18, 1972, and ends either on the ninetieth day after the date of the first promulgation of guidelines required by section 1314(i)(2) of this title, or the date of approval by the Administrator of a permit program for such State under subsection (b) of this section, whichever date first occurs, and no such authorization to a State shall extend beyond the last day of such period. Each such permit shall be subject to such conditions as the Administrator determines are necessary to carry out the provisions of this chapter. No such permit shall issue if the Administrator objects to such issuance.

(b) State permit programs

At any time after the promulgation of the guidelines required by subsection (i)(2) of section 1314 of this title, the Governor of each State desiring to administer its own permit program for discharges into navigable waters within its jurisdiction may submit to the Administrator a full and complete description of the program it proposes to establish and administer under State law or under an interstate compact. In addition, such State shall submit a statement from the attorney general (or the attorney for those State water pollution control agencies which have independent legal counsel), or from the chief legal officer in the case of an interstate agency, that the laws of such State, or the interstate compact, as the case may be, provide adequate authority to carry out the described program. The Administrator shall approve each submitted program unless he determines that adequate authority does not exist:

(1) To issue permits which—

(A) apply, and insure compliance with, any applicable requirements of sections 1311, 1312, 1316, 1317, and 1343 of this title;

(B) are for fixed terms not exceeding five years; and

(C) can be terminated or modified for cause including, but not limited to, the following:

(i) violation of any condition of the permit;

(ii) obtaining a permit by misrepresentation, or failure to disclose fully all relevant facts;

(iii) change in any condition that requires either a temporary or permanent reduction or elimination of the permitted discharge;

(D) control the disposal of pollutants into wells;

(2)(A) To issue permits which apply, and insure compliance with, all applicable requirements of section 1318 of this title; or

(B) To inspect, monitor, enter, and require reports to at least the same extent as required in section 1318 of this title;

(3) To insure that the public, and any other State the waters of which may be affected, receive notice of each application for a permit and to provide an opportunity for public hearing before a ruling on each such application;

(4) To insure that the Administrator receives notice of each application (including a copy thereof) for a permit;

(5) To insure that any State (other than the permitting State), whose waters may be affected by the issuance of a permit may submit written recommendations to the permitting State (and the Administrator) with respect to any permit application and, if any part of such written recommendations are not accepted by the permitting State, that the permitting State will notify such affected State (and the Administrator) in writing of its failure to so accept such recommendations together with its reasons for so doing;

(6) To insure that no permit will be issued if, in the judgment of the Secretary of the Army acting through the Chief of Engineers, after consultation with the Secretary of the department in which the Coast Guard is operating, anchorage and navigation of any of the navigable waters would be substantially impaired thereby;

(7) To abate violations of the permit or the permit program, including civil and criminal penalties and other ways and means of enforcement;

(8) To insure that any permit for a discharge from a publicly owned treatment works includes conditions to require the identification in terms of character and volume of pollutants of any significant source introducing pollutants subject to pretreatment standards under section 1317(b) of this title into such works and a program to assure compliance with such pretreatment standards by each such source, in addition to adequate notice to the permitting agency of (A) new introductions into such works of pollutants from any source which would be a new source as defined in section 1316 of this title if such source were discharging pollutants, (B) new introductions of pollutants into such works from a source which would be subject to section 1311 of this title if it were discharging such pollutants, or (C) a substantial change in volume or character of pollutants being introduced into such works by a source introducing pollutants into such works at the time of issuance of the permit. Such notice shall include information on the quality and quantity of effluent to be introduced into such treatment works and any anticipated impact of such change in the quantity or quality of effluent to be discharged from such publicly owned treatment works; and

(9) To insure that any industrial user of any publicly owned treatment works will comply with sections 1284(b), 1317, and 1318 of this title.

(c) Suspension of Federal program upon submission of State program; withdrawal of approval of State program; return of State program to Administrator

(1) Not later than ninety days after the date on which a State has submitted a program (or revision thereof) pursuant to subsection (b) of this section, the Administrator shall suspend the issuance of permits under subsection (a) of this section as to those discharges subject to such program unless he determines that the State permit program does not meet the requirements of subsection (b) of this section or does not conform to the guidelines issued under section 1314(i)(2) of this title. If the Administrator so determines, he shall notify the State of any revisions or modifications necessary to conform to such requirements or guidelines.

(2) Any State permit program under this section shall at all times be in accordance with this section and guidelines promulgated pursuant to section 1314(i)(2) of this title.

(3) Whenever the Administrator determines after public hearing that a State is not administering a program approved under this section in accordance with requirements of this section, he shall so notify the State and, if appropriate corrective action is not taken within a reasonable time, not to exceed ninety days, the Administrator shall withdraw approval of such program. The Administrator shall not withdraw approval of any such program unless he shall first have notified the State, and made public, in writing, the reasons for such withdrawal.

(4) LIMITATIONS ON PARTIAL PERMIT PROGRAM RETURNS AND WITHDRAWALS.—A State may return to the Administrator administration, and the Administrator may withdraw under paragraph (3) of this subsection approval, of—

(A) a State partial permit program approved under subsection (n)(3) of this section only if the entire permit program being administered by the State department or agency at the time is returned or withdrawn; and

(B) a State partial permit program approved under subsection (n)(4) of this section only if an entire phased component of the permit program being administered by the State at the time is returned or withdrawn.

(d) Notification of Administrator

(1) Each State shall transmit to the Administrator a copy of each permit application received by such State and provide notice to the Administrator of every action related to the consideration of such permit application, including each permit proposed to be issued by such State.

(2) No permit shall issue (A) if the Administrator within ninety days of the date of his notification under subsection (b)(5) of this section objects in writing to the issuance of such permit, or (B) if the Administrator within ninety days of the date of transmittal of the proposed permit by the State objects in writing to the issuance of such permit as being outside the guidelines and requirements of this chapter. Whenever the Administrator objects to the issuance of a permit under this paragraph such written objection shall contain a statement of the reasons for such objection and the effluent limitations and conditions which such permit would include if it were issued by the Administrator.

(3) The Administrator may, as to any permit application, waive paragraph (2) of this subsection.

(4) In any case where, after December 27, 1977, the Administrator, pursuant to paragraph (2) of this subsection, objects to the issuance of a permit, on request of the State, a public hearing shall be held by the Administrator on such objection. If the State does not resubmit such permit revised to meet such objection within 30 days after completion of the hearing, or, if no hearing is requested within 90 days after the date of such objection, the Administrator may issue the permit pursuant to subsection (a) of this section for such source in accordance with the guidelines and requirements of this chapter.

(e) Waiver of notification requirement

In accordance with guidelines promulgated pursuant to subsection (i)(2) of section 1314 of this title, the Administrator is authorized to waive the requirements of subsection (d) of this section at the time he approves a program pursuant to subsection (b) of this section for any category (including any class, type, or size within such category) of point sources within the State submitting such program.

(f) Point source categories

The Administrator shall promulgate regulations establishing categories of point sources which he determines shall not be subject to the requirements of subsection (d) of this section in any State with a program approved pursuant to subsection (b) of this section. The Administrator may distinguish among classes, types, and sizes within any category of point sources.

(g) Other regulations for safe transportation, handling, carriage, storage, and stowage of pollutants

Any permit issued under this section for the discharge of pollutants into the navigable waters from a vessel or other floating craft shall be subject to any applicable regulations promulgated by the Secretary of the department in which the Coast Guard is operating, establishing specifications for safe transportation, handling, carriage, storage, and stowage of pollutants.

(h) Violation of permit conditions; restriction or prohibition upon introduction of pollutant by source not previously utilizing treatment works

In the event any condition of a permit for discharges from a treatment works (as defined in section 1292 of this title) which is publicly owned is violated, a State with a program approved under subsection (b) of this section or the Administrator, where no State program is approved or where the Administrator determines pursuant to section 1319(a) of this title that a State with an approved program has not commenced appropriate enforcement action with respect to such permit, may proceed in a court of competent jurisdiction to restrict or prohibit the introduction of any pollutant into such treatment works by a source not utilizing such treatment works prior to the finding that such condition was violated.

(i) Federal enforcement not limited

Nothing in this section shall be construed to limit the authority of the Administrator to take action pursuant to section 1319 of this title.

(j) Public information

A copy of each permit application and each permit issued under this section shall be available to the public. Such permit application or permit, or portion thereof, shall further be available on request for the purpose of reproduction.

(k) Compliance with permits

Compliance with a permit issued pursuant to this section shall be deemed compliance, for purposes of sections 1319 and 1365 of this title, with sections 1311, 1312, 1316, 1317, and 1343 of this title, except any standard imposed under section 1317 of this title for a toxic pollutant injurious to human health. Until December 31, 1974, in any case where a permit for discharge has been applied for pursuant to this section, but final administrative disposition of such application has not been made, such discharge shall not be a violation of (1) section 1311, 1316, or 1342 of this title, or (2) section 407 of this title, unless the Administrator or other plaintiff proves that final administrative disposition of such application has not been made because of the failure of the applicant to furnish information reasonably required or requested in order to process the application. For the 180-day period beginning on October 18, 1972, in the case of any point source discharging any pollutant or combination of pollutants immediately prior to such date which source is not subject to section 407 of this title, the discharge by such source shall not be a violation of this chapter if such a source applies for a permit for discharge pursuant to this section within such 180-day period.

(*l*) Limitation on permit requirement

(1) Agricultural return flows

The Administrator shall not require a permit under this section for discharges composed entirely of return flows from irrigated agriculture, nor shall the Administrator directly or indirectly, require any State to require such a permit.

(2) Stormwater runoff from oil, gas, and mining operations

The Administrator shall not require a permit under this section, nor shall the Administrator directly or indirectly require any State to require a permit, for discharges of stormwater runoff from mining operations or oil and gas exploration, production, processing, or treatment operations or transmission facilities, composed entirely of flows which are from conveyances or systems of conveyances (including but not limited to pipes, conduits, ditches, and channels) used for collecting and conveying precipitation runoff and which are not contaminated by contact with, or do not come into contact with, any overburden, raw material, intermediate products, finished product, byproduct, or waste products located on the site of such operations.

(m) Additional pretreatment of conventional pollutants not required

To the extent a treatment works (as defined in section 1292 of this title) which is publicly owned is not meeting the requirements of a permit issued under this section for such treatment works as a result of inadequate design or operation of such treatment works, the Administrator, in issuing a permit under this section, shall not require pretreatment by a person introducing conventional pollutants identified pursuant to section 1314(a)(4) of this title into such treatment works other than pretreatment required to assure compliance with pretreatment standards under subsection (b)(8) of this section and section 1317(b)(1) of this title. Nothing in this subsection shall affect the Administrator's authority under sections 1317 and 1319 of this title, affect State and local authority under sections 1317(b)(4) and 1370 of this title, relieve such treatment works of its obligations to meet requirements established under this chapter, or otherwise preclude such works from pursuing whatever feasible options are available to meet its responsibility to comply with its permit under this section.

(n) Partial permit program

(1) State submission

The Governor of a State may submit under subsection (b) of this section a permit program for a portion of the discharges into the navigable waters in such State.

(2) Minimum coverage

A partial permit program under this subsection shall cover, at a minimum, administration of a major category of the discharges into the navigable waters of the State or a major component of the permit program required by subsection (b) of this section.

(3) Approval of major category partial permit programs

The Administrator may approve a partial permit program covering administration of a major category of discharges under this subsection if—

(A) such program represents a complete permit program and covers all of the discharges under the jurisdiction of a department or agency of the State; and

(B) the Administrator determines that the partial program represents a significant and identifiable part of the State program required by subsection (b) of this section.

(4) Approval of major component partial permit programs

The Administrator may approve under this subsection a partial and phased permit program covering administration of a major component (including discharge categories) of a State permit program required by subsection (b) of this section if—

(A) the Administrator determines that the partial program represents a significant and identifiable part of the State program required by subsection (b) of this section; and

(B) the State submits, and the Administrator approves, a plan for the State to assume administration by phases of the remainder of the State program required by subsection (b) of this section by a specified date not more than 5 years after submission of the partial program under this subsection and agrees to make all reasonable efforts to assume such administration by such date.

(*o*) Anti-backsliding

(1) General prohibition

In the case of effluent limitations established on the basis of subsection (a)(1)(B) of this section, a permit may not be renewed, reissued, or modified on the basis of effluent guidelines promulgated under section 1314(b) of this title subsequent to the original issuance of such permit, to contain effluent limitations which are less stringent than the comparable effluent limitations in the previous permit. In the case of effluent limitations established on the basis of section 1311(b)(1)(C) or section 1313(d) or (e) of this title, a permit may not be renewed, reissued, or modified to contain effluent limitations which are less stringent than the comparable effluent limitations in the previous permit except in compliance with section 1313(d)(4) of this title.

(2) Exceptions

A permit with respect to which paragraph (1) applies may be renewed, reissued, or modified to contain a less stringent effluent limitation applicable to a pollutant if—

(A) material and substantial alterations or additions to the permitted facility occurred after permit issuance which justify the application of a less stringent effluent limitation;

(B)(i) information is available which was not available at the time of permit issuance (other than revised regulations, guidance, or test methods) and which would have justified the application of a less stringent effluent limitation at the time of permit issuance; or

(ii) the Administrator determines that technical mistakes or mistaken interpretations of law were made in issuing the permit under subsection (a)(1)(B) of this section;

(C) a less stringent effluent limitation is necessary because of events over which the permittee has no control and for which there is no reasonably available remedy;

(D) the permittee has received a permit modification under section 1311(c), 1311(g), 1311(h), 1311(i), 1311(k), 1311(n), or 1326(a) of this title; or

(E) the permittee has installed the treatment facilities required to meet the effluent limitations in the previous permit and has properly operated and maintained the facilities but has nevertheless been unable to achieve the previous effluent limitations, in which case the limitations in the reviewed, reissued, or modified permit may reflect the level of pollutant control actually achieved (but shall not be less stringent than required by effluent guidelines in effect at the time of permit renewal, reissuance, or modification).

Subparagraph (B) shall not apply to any revised waste load allocations or any alternative grounds for translating water quality standards into effluent limitations, except where the cumulative effect of such revised allocations results in a decrease in the amount of pollutants discharged into the concerned waters, and such revised allocations are not the result of a discharger eliminating or substantially reducing its discharge of pollutants due to complying with the requirements of this chapter or for reasons otherwise unrelated to water quality.

(3) Limitations

In no event may a permit with respect to which paragraph (1) applies be renewed, reissued, or modified to contain an effluent limitation which is less stringent than required by effluent guidelines in effect at the time the permit is renewed, reissued, or modified. In no event may such a permit to discharge into waters be renewed, reissued, or modified to contain a less stringent effluent limitation if the implementation of such limitation would result in a violation of a water quality standard under section 1313 of this title applicable to such waters.

(p) Municipal and industrial stormwater discharges

(1) General rule

Prior to October 1, 1994, the Administrator or the State (in the case of a permit program approved under this section) shall not require a permit under this section for discharges composed entirely of stormwater.

(2) Exceptions

Paragraph (1) shall not apply with respect to the following stormwater discharges:

(A) A discharge with respect to which a permit has been issued under this section before February 4, 1987.

(B) A discharge associated with industrial activity.

(C) A discharge from a municipal separate storm sewer system serving a population of 250,000 or more.

(D) A discharge from a municipal separate storm sewer system serving a population of 100,000 or more but less than 250,000.

(E) A discharge for which the Administrator or the State, as the case may be, determines that the stormwater discharge contributes to a violation of a water quality standard or is a significant contributor of pollutants to waters of the United States.

(3) Permit requirements

(A) Industrial discharges

Permits for discharges associated with industrial activity shall meet all applicable provisions of this section and section 1311 of this title.

(B) Municipal discharge

Permits for discharges from municipal storm sewers—

(i) may be issued on a system- or jurisdiction-wide basis;

(ii) shall include a requirement to effectively prohibit non-stormwater discharges into the storm sewers; and

(iii) shall require controls to reduce the discharge of pollutants to the maximum extent practicable, including management practices, control techniques and system, design and engineering methods, and such other provisions as the Administrator or the State determines appropriate for the control of such pollutants.

(4) Permit application requirements

(A) Industrial and large municipal discharges

Not later than 2 years after February 4, 1987, the Administrator shall establish regulations setting forth the permit application requirements for stormwater discharges described in paragraphs (2)(B) and (2)(C). Applications for permits for such discharges shall be filed no later than 3 years after February 4, 1987. Not later than 4 years after February 4, 1987, the Administrator or the State, as the case may be, shall issue or deny each such permit. Any such permit shall provide for compliance as expeditiously as practicable, but in no event later than 3 years after the date of issuance of such permit.

(B) Other municipal discharges

Not later than 4 years after February 4, 1987, the Administrator shall establish regulations setting forth the permit application requirements for stormwater discharges described in paragraph (2)(D). Applications for permits for such discharges shall be filed no later than 5 years after February 4, 1987. Not later than 6 years after February 4, 1987, the Administrator or the State, as the case may be, shall issue or deny each such permit. Any such permit shall provide for compliance as expeditiously as practicable, but in no event later than 3 years after the date of issuance of such permit.

(5) Studies

The Administrator, in consultation with the States, shall conduct a study for the purposes of—

(A) identifying those stormwater discharges or classes of stormwater discharges for which permits are not required pursuant to paragraphs (1) and (2) of this subsection;

(B) determining, to the maximum extent practicable, the nature and extent of pollutants in such discharges; and

(C) establishing procedures and methods to control stormwater discharges to the extent necessary to mitigate impacts on water quality.

Not later than October 1, 1988, the Administrator shall submit to Congress a report on the results of the study described in subparagraphs (A) and (B). Not later than October 1, 1989, the Administrator shall submit to Congress a report on the results of the study described in subparagraph (C).

(6) Regulations

Not later than October 1, 1993, the Administrator, in consultation with State and local officials, shall issue regulations (based on the results of the studies conducted under paragraph (5)) which designate stormwater discharges, other than those discharges described in paragraph (2), to be regulated to protect water quality and shall establish a comprehensive program to regulate such designated sources. The program shall, at a minimum, (A) establish priorities, (B) establish requirements for State stormwater management programs, and (C) establish expeditious deadlines. The program may include performance standards, guidelines, guidance, and management practices and treatment requirements, as appropriate.

(q) Combined sewer overflows

(1) Requirement for permits, orders, and decrees

Each permit, order, or decree issued pursuant to this chapter after December 21, 2000, for a discharge from a municipal combined storm and sanitary sewer shall conform to the Combined Sewer Overflow Control Policy signed by the Administrator on April 11, 1994 (in this subsection referred to as the "CSO control policy").

(2) Water quality and designated use review guidance

Not later than July 31, 2001, and after providing notice and opportunity for public comment, the Administrator shall issue guidance to facilitate the conduct of water quality and designated use reviews for municipal combined sewer overflow receiving waters.

(3) Report

Not later than September 1, 2001, the Administrator shall transmit to Congress a report on the progress made by the Environmental Protection Agency, States, and municipalities in implementing and enforcing the CSO control policy.

(r) Discharges incidental to the normal operation of recreational vessels

No permit shall be required under this chapter by the Administrator (or a State, in the case of a permit program approved under subsection (b)) for the discharge of any graywater, bilge water, cooling water, weather deck runoff, oil water separator effluent, or effluent from properly functioning marine engines, or any other discharge that is incidental to the normal operation of a vessel, if the discharge is from a recreational vessel.

(June 30, 1948, ch. 758, title IV, §402, as added Pub. L. 92–500, §2, Oct. 18, 1972, 86 Stat. 880; amended Pub. L. 95–217, §§33(c), 50, 54(c)(1), 65, 66, Dec. 27, 1977, 91 Stat. 1577, 1588, 1591, 1599, 1600; Pub. L. 100–4, title IV, §§401–404(a), 404(c), formerly 404(d), 405, Feb. 4, 1987, 101 Stat. 65–67, 69, renumbered §404(c), Pub. L. 104–66, title II, §2021(e)(2), Dec. 21, 1995, 109 Stat. 727; Pub. L. 102–580, title III, §364, Oct. 31, 1992, 106 Stat. 4862; Pub. L. 106–554, §1(a)(4) [div. B, title I, §112(a)], Dec. 21, 2000, 114 Stat. 2763, 2763A–224; Pub. L. 110–288, §2, July 29, 2008, 122 Stat. 2650.)

AMENDMENTS

2008—Subsec. (r). Pub. L. 110–288 added subsec. (r).

2000—Subsec. (q). Pub. L. 106–554 added subsec. (q).

1992—Subsec. (p)(1), (6). Pub. L. 102–580 substituted "October 1, 1994" for "October 1, 1992" in par. (1) and "October 1, 1993" for "October 1, 1992" in par. (6).

1987—Subsec. (a)(1). Pub. L. 100–4, §404(c), inserted cl. (A) and (B) designations.

Subsec. (c)(1). Pub. L. 100–4, §403(b)(2), substituted "as to those discharges" for "as to those navigable waters".

Subsec. (c)(4). Pub. L. 100–4, §403(b)(1), added par. (4).

Subsec. (*l*). Pub. L. 100–4, §401, inserted "Limitation on permit requirement" as subsec. heading designated existing provisions as par. (1) and inserted par. heading, added par. (2), and aligned pars. (1) and (2).

Subsecs. (m) to (p). Pub. L. 100–4, §§402, 403(a), 404(a), 405, added subsecs. (m) to (p).

1977—Subsec. (a)(5). Pub. L. 95–217, §50, substituted "section 1314(i)(2)" for "section 1314(h)(2)".

Subsec. (b). Pub. L. 95–217, §50, substituted in provisions preceding par. (1) "subsection (i)(2) of section 1314" for "subsection (h)(2) of section 1314".

Subsec. (b)(8). Pub. L. 95–217, §54(c)(1), inserted reference to identification in terms of character and volume of pollutants of any significant source introducing pollutants subject to pretreatment standards under section 1317(b) of this title into treatment works and programs to assure compliance with pretreatment standards by each source.

Subsec. (c)(1), (2). Pub. L. 95–217, §50, substituted "section 1314(i)(2)" for "section 1314(h)(2)".

Subsec. (d)(2). Pub. L. 95–217, §65(b), inserted provision requiring that, whenever the Administrator objects to the issuance of a permit under subsec. (d)(2) of this section, the written objection contain a statement of the reasons for the objection and the effluent limitations and conditions which the permit would include if it were issued by the Administrator.

Subsec. (d)(4). Pub. L. 95–217, §65(a), added par. (4).

Subsec. (e). Pub. L. 95–217, §50, substituted "subsection (i)(2) of section 1314" for "subsection (h)(2) of section 1314".

Subsec. (h). Pub. L. 95–217, §66, substituted "where no State program is approved or where the Administrator determines pursuant to section 1319(a) of this title that a State with an approved program has not commenced appropriate enforcement action with respect to such permit," for "where no State program is approved,".

Subsec. (*l*). Pub. L. 95–217, §33(c), added subsec. (*l*).

TRANSFER OF FUNCTIONS

For transfer of authorities, functions, personnel, and assets of the Coast Guard, including the authorities and functions of the Secretary of Transportation relating thereto, to the Department of Homeland Security, and for treatment of related references, see sections 468(b), 551(d), 552(d), and 557 of Title 6, Domestic Security, and the Department of Homeland Security Reorganization Plan of November 25, 2002, as modified, set out as a note under section 542 of Title 6.

Enforcement functions of Administrator or other official of the Environmental Protection Agency under this section relating to compliance with national pollutant discharge elimination system permits with respect to pre-construction, construction, and initial operation of transportation system for Canadian and Alaskan natural gas were transferred to the Federal Inspector, Office of Federal Inspector for the Alaska Natural Gas Transportation System, until the first anniversary of the date of initial operation of the Alaska Natural Gas Transportation System, see Reorg. Plan No. 1 of 1979, §§102(a), 203(a), 44 F.R. 33663, 33666, 93 Stat. 1373, 1376, effective July 1, 1979, set out in the Appendix to Title 5, Government Organization and Employees. Office of Federal Inspector for the Alaska Natural Gas Transportation System abolished and functions and authority vested in Inspector transferred to Secretary of Energy by section 3012(b) of Pub. L. 102–486, set out as an Abolition of Office of Federal Inspector note under section 719e of Title 15, Commerce and Trade. Functions and authority vested in Secretary of Energy subsequently transferred to Federal Coordinator for Alaska Natural Gas Transportation Projects by section 720d(f) of Title 15.

PERMIT REQUIREMENTS FOR DISCHARGES FROM CERTAIN VESSELS

Pub. L. 110–299, §§1, 2, July 31, 2008, 122 Stat. 2995, provided that:

"SECTION 1. DEFINITIONS.

"In this Act:

"(1) ADMINISTRATOR.—The term 'Administrator' means the Administrator of the Environmental Protection Agency.

"(2) COVERED VESSEL.—The term 'covered vessel' means a vessel that is—

"(A) less than 79 feet in length; or

"(B) a fishing vessel (as defined in section 2101 of title 46, United States Code), regardless of the length of the vessel.

"(3) OTHER TERMS.—The terms 'contiguous zone', 'discharge', 'ocean', and 'State' have the meanings given the terms in section 502 of the Federal Water Pollution Control Act (33 U.S.C. 1362).

"SEC. 2. DISCHARGES INCIDENTAL TO NORMAL OPERATION OF VESSELS.

"(a) NO PERMIT REQUIREMENT.—Except as provided in subsection (b), during the 2-year period beginning on the date of enactment of this Act [July 31, 2008], the Administrator, or a State in the case of a permit program approved under section 402 of the Federal Water Pollution Control Act (33 U.S.C. 1342), shall not require a permit under that section for a covered vessel for—

"(1) any discharge of effluent from properly functioning marine engines;

"(2) any discharge of laundry, shower, and galley sink wastes; or

"(3) any other discharge incidental to the normal operation of a covered vessel.

"(b) EXCEPTIONS.—Subsection (a) shall not apply with respect to—

"(1) rubbish, trash, garbage, or other such materials discharged overboard;

"(2) other discharges when the vessel is operating in a capacity other than as a means of transportation, such as when—

"(A) used as an energy or mining facility;

"(B) used as a storage facility or a seafood processing facility;

"(C) secured to a storage facility or a seafood processing facility; or

"(D) secured to the bed of the ocean, the contiguous zone, or waters of the United States for the purpose of mineral or oil exploration or development;

"(3) any discharge of ballast water; or

"(4) any discharge in a case in which the Administrator or State, as appropriate, determines that the discharge—

"(A) contributes to a violation of a water quality standard; or

"(B) poses an unacceptable risk to human health or the environment."

STORMWATER PERMIT REQUIREMENTS

Pub. L. 102–240, title I, §1068, Dec. 18, 1991, 105 Stat. 2007, provided that:

"(a) GENERAL RULE.—Notwithstanding the requirements of sections 402(p)(2)(B), (C), and (D) of the Federal Water Pollution Control Act [33 U.S.C. 1342(p)(2)(B), (C), (D)], permit application deadlines for stormwater discharges associated with industrial activities from facilities that are owned or operated by a municipality shall be established by the Administrator of the Environmental Protection Agency (hereinafter in this section referred to as the 'Administrator') pursuant to the requirements of this section.

"(b) PERMIT APPLICATIONS.—

"(1) INDIVIDUAL APPLICATIONS.—The Administrator shall require individual permit applications for discharges described in subsection (a) on or before October 1, 1992; except that any municipality that has participated in a timely part I group application for an industrial activity discharging stormwater that is denied such participation in a group application or for which a group application is denied shall not be required to submit an individual application until the 180th day following the date on which the denial is made.

"(2) GROUP APPLICATIONS.—With respect to group applications for permits for discharges described in subsection (a), the Administrator shall require—

"(A) part I applications on or before September 30, 1991, except that any municipality with a population of less than 250,000 shall not be required to submit a part I application before May 18, 1992; and

"(B) part II applications on or before October 1, 1992, except that any municipality with a population of less than 250,000 shall not be required to submit a part II application before May 17, 1993.

"(c) MUNICIPALITIES WITH LESS THAN 100,000 POPULATION.—The Administrator shall not require any municipality with a population of less than 100,000 to apply for or obtain a permit for any stormwater discharge associated with an industrial activity other than an airport, powerplant, or uncontrolled sanitary landfill owned or operated by such municipality before October 1, 1992, unless such permit is required by section 402(p)(2)(A) or (E) of the Federal Water Pollution Control Act [33 U.S.C. 1342(p)(2)(A), (E)].

"(d) UNCONTROLLED SANITARY LANDFILL DEFINED.—For the purposes of this section, the term 'uncontrolled sanitary landfill' means a landfill or open dump, whether in operation or closed, that does not meet the requirements for run-on and run-off controls established pursuant to subtitle D of the Solid Waste Disposal Act [42 U.S.C. 6941 et seq.].

"(e) LIMITATION ON STATUTORY CONSTRUCTION.—Nothing in this section shall be construed to affect any application or permit requirement, including any deadline, to apply for or obtain a permit for stormwater discharges subject to section 402(p)(2)(A) or (E) of the Federal Water Pollution Control Act [33 U.S.C. 1342(p)(2)(A), (E)].

"(f) REGULATIONS.—The Administrator shall issue final regulations with respect to general permits for stormwater discharges associated with industrial activity on or before February 1, 1992."

PHOSPHATE FERTILIZER EFFLUENT LIMITATION

Section 306(c) of Pub. L. 100–4 provided that:

"(1) ISSUANCE OF PERMIT.—As soon as possible after the date of the enactment of this Act [Feb. 4, 1987], but not later than 180 days after such date of enactment, the Administrator shall issue permits under section 402(a)(1)(B) of the Federal Water Pollution Control Act [33 U.S.C. 1342(a)(1)(B)] with respect to facilities—

"(A) which were under construction on or before April 8, 1974, and

"(B) for which the Administrator is proposing to revise the applicability of the effluent limitation established under section 301(b) of such Act [33 U.S.C. 1311(b)] for phosphate subcategory of the fertilizer manufacturing point source category to exclude such facilities.

"(2) LIMITATIONS ON STATUTORY CONSTRUCTION.—Nothing in this section [amending section 1311 of this title and enacting this note] shall be construed—

"(A) to require the Administrator to permit the discharge of gypsum or gypsum waste into the navigable waters,

"(B) to affect the procedures and standards applicable to the Administrator in issuing permits under section 402(a)(1)(B) of the Federal Water Pollution Control Act [33 U.S.C. 1342(a)(1)(B)], and

"(C) to affect the authority of any State to deny or condition certification under section 401 of such Act [33 U.S.C. 1341] with respect to the issuance of permits under section 402(a)(1)(B) of such Act."

LOG TRANSFER FACILITIES

Section 407 of Pub. L. 100–4 provided that:

"(a) AGREEMENT.—The Administrator and Secretary of the Army shall enter into an agreement regarding coordination of permitting for log transfer facilities to designate a lead agency and to process permits required under sections 402 and 404 of the Federal Water Pollution Control Act [33 U.S.C. 1342, 1344], where both such sections apply, for discharges associated with the construction and operation of log transfer facilities. The Administrator and Secretary are authorized to act in accordance with the terms of such agreement to assure that, to the maximum extent practicable, duplication, needless paperwork and delay in the issuance of permits, and inequitable enforcement between and among facilities in different States, shall be eliminated.

"(b) APPLICATIONS AND PERMITS BEFORE OCTOBER 22, 1985.—Where both of sections 402 and 404 of the Federal Water Pollution Control Act [33 U.S.C. 1342, 1344] apply, log transfer facilities which have received a permit under section 404 of such Act before October 22, 1985, shall not be required to submit a new application for a permit under section 402 of such Act. If the Administrator determines that the terms of a permit issued on or before October 22, 1985, under section 404 of such Act satisfies the applicable requirements of sections 301, 302, 306, 307, 308, and 403 of such Act [33 U.S.C. 1311, 1312, 1316, 1317, 1318, and 1343], a separate application for a permit under section 402 of such Act shall not thereafter be required. In any case where the Administrator demonstrates, after an opportunity for a hearing, that the terms of a permit issued on or before October 22, 1985, under section 404 of such Act do not satisfy the applicable requirements of sections 301, 302, 306, 307, 308, and 403 of such Act, modifications to the existing permit under section 404 of such Act to incorporate such applicable requirements shall be issued by the Administrator as an alternative to issuance of a separate new permit under section 402 of such Act.

"(c) LOG TRANSFER FACILITY DEFINED.—For the purposes of this section, the term 'log transfer facility' means a facility which is constructed in whole or in part in waters of the United States and which is utilized for the purpose of transferring commercially harvested logs to or from a vessel or log raft, including the formation of a log raft."

ALLOWABLE DELAY IN MODIFYING EXISTING APPROVED STATE PERMIT PROGRAMS TO CONFORM TO 1977 AMENDMENT

Section 54(c)(2) of Pub. L. 95–217 provided that any State permit program approved under this section before Dec. 27, 1977, which required modification to conform to the amendment made by section 54(c)(1) of Pub. L. 95–217, which amended subsec. (b)(8) of this section, not be required to be modified before the end of the one year period which began on Dec. 27, 1977, unless in order to make the required modification a State must amend or enact a law in which case such modification not be required for such State before the end of the two year period which began on Dec. 27, 1977.

§ 1343. Ocean discharge criteria

(a) Issuance of permits

No permit under section 1342 of this title for a discharge into the territorial sea, the waters of the contiguous zone, or the oceans shall be issued, after promulgation of guidelines established under subsection (c) of this section, except in compliance with such guidelines. Prior to the promulgation of such guidelines, a permit may be issued under such section 1342 of this title if the Administrator determines it to be in the public interest.

(b) Waiver

The requirements of subsection (d) of section 1342 of this title may not be waived in the case of permits for discharges into the territorial sea.

(c) Guidelines for determining degradation of waters

(1) The Administrator shall, within one hundred and eighty days after October 18, 1972 (and from time to time thereafter), promulgate

guidelines for determining the degradation of the waters of the territorial seas, the contiguous zone, and the oceans, which shall include:

(A) the effect of disposal of pollutants on human health or welfare, including but not limited to plankton, fish, shellfish, wildlife, shorelines, and beaches;

(B) the effect of disposal of pollutants on marine life including the transfer, concentration, and dispersal of pollutants or their byproducts through biological, physical, and chemical processes; changes in marine ecosystem diversity, productivity, and stability; and species and community population changes;

(C) the effect of disposal, of pollutants on esthetic, recreation, and economic values;

(D) the persistence and permanence of the effects of disposal of pollutants;

(E) the effect of the disposal of varying rates, of particular volumes and concentrations of pollutants;

(F) other possible locations and methods of disposal or recycling of pollutants including land-based alternatives; and

(G) the effect on alternate uses of the oceans, such as mineral exploitation and scientific study.

(2) In any event where insufficient information exists on any proposed discharge to make a reasonable judgment on any of the guidelines established pursuant to this subsection no permit shall be issued under section 1342 of this title.

(June 30, 1948, ch. 758, title IV, §403, as added Pub. L. 92–500, §2, Oct. 18, 1972, 86 Stat. 883.)

DISCHARGES FROM POINT SOURCES IN UNITED STATES VIRGIN ISLANDS ATTRIBUTABLE TO MANUFACTURE OF RUM; EXEMPTION; CONDITIONS

Discharges from point sources in the United States Virgin Islands in existence on Aug. 5, 1983, attributable to the manufacture of rum not to be subject to the requirements of this section under certain conditions, see section 214(g) of Pub. L. 98–67, set out as a note under section 1311 of this title.

TERRITORIAL SEA AND CONTIGUOUS ZONE OF UNITED STATES

For extension of territorial sea and contiguous zone of United States, see Proc. No. 5928 and Proc. No. 7219, respectively, set out as notes under section 1331 of Title 43, Public Lands.

§1344. Permits for dredged or fill material

(a) Discharge into navigable waters at specified disposal sites

The Secretary may issue permits, after notice and opportunity for public hearings for the discharge of dredged or fill material into the navigable waters at specified disposal sites. Not later than the fifteenth day after the date an applicant submits all the information required to complete an application for a permit under this subsection, the Secretary shall publish the notice required by this subsection.

(b) Specification for disposal sites

Subject to subsection (c) of this section, each such disposal site shall be specified for each such permit by the Secretary (1) through the application of guidelines developed by the Administrator, in conjunction with the Secretary, which guidelines shall be based upon criteria comparable to the criteria applicable to the territorial seas, the contiguous zone, and the ocean under section 1343(c) of this title, and (2) in any case where such guidelines under clause (1) alone would prohibit the specification of a site, through the application additionally of the economic impact of the site on navigation and anchorage.

(c) Denial or restriction of use of defined areas as disposal sites

The Administrator is authorized to prohibit the specification (including the withdrawal of specification) of any defined area as a disposal site, and he is authorized to deny or restrict the use of any defined area for specification (including the withdrawal of specification) as a disposal site, whenever he determines, after notice and opportunity for public hearings, that the discharge of such materials into such area will have an unacceptable adverse effect on municipal water supplies, shellfish beds and fishery areas (including spawning and breeding areas), wildlife, or recreational areas. Before making such determination, the Administrator shall consult with the Secretary. The Administrator shall set forth in writing and make public his findings and his reasons for making any determination under this subsection.

(d) "Secretary" defined

The term "Secretary" as used in this section means the Secretary of the Army, acting through the Chief of Engineers.

(e) General permits on State, regional, or nationwide basis

(1) In carrying out his functions relating to the discharge of dredged or fill material under this section, the Secretary may, after notice and opportunity for public hearing, issue general permits on a State, regional, or nationwide basis for any category of activities involving discharges of dredged or fill material if the Secretary determines that the activities in such category are similar in nature, will cause only minimal adverse environmental effects when performed separately, and will have only minimal cumulative adverse effect on the environment. Any general permit issued under this subsection shall (A) be based on the guidelines described in subsection (b)(1) of this section, and (B) set forth the requirements and standards which shall apply to any activity authorized by such general permit.

(2) No general permit issued under this subsection shall be for a period of more than five years after the date of its issuance and such general permit may be revoked or modified by the Secretary if, after opportunity for public hearing, the Secretary determines that the activities authorized by such general permit have an adverse impact on the environment or such activities are more appropriately authorized by individual permits.

(f) Non-prohibited discharge of dredged or fill material

(1) Except as provided in paragraph (2) of this subsection, the discharge of dredged or fill material—

(A) from normal farming, silviculture, and ranching activities such as plowing, seeding, cultivating, minor drainage, harvesting for the production of food, fiber, and forest products, or upland soil and water conservation practices;

(B) for the purpose of maintenance, including emergency reconstruction of recently damaged parts, of currently serviceable structures such as dikes, dams, levees, groins, riprap, breakwaters, causeways, and bridge abutments or approaches, and transportation structures;

(C) for the purpose of construction or maintenance of farm or stock ponds or irrigation ditches, or the maintenance of drainage ditches;

(D) for the purpose of construction of temporary sedimentation basins on a construction site which does not include placement of fill material into the navigable waters;

(E) for the purpose of construction or maintenance of farm roads or forest roads, or temporary roads for moving mining equipment, where such roads are constructed and maintained, in accordance with best management practices, to assure that flow and circulation patterns and chemical and biological characteristics of the navigable waters are not impaired, that the reach of the navigable waters is not reduced, and that any adverse effect on the aquatic environment will be otherwise minimized;

(F) resulting from any activity with respect to which a State has an approved program under section 1288(b)(4) of this title which meets the requirements of subparagraphs (B) and (C) of such section,

is not prohibited by or otherwise subject to regulation under this section or section 1311(a) or 1342 of this title (except for effluent standards or prohibitions under section 1317 of this title).

(2) Any discharge of dredged or fill material into the navigable waters incidental to any activity having as its purpose bringing an area of the navigable waters into a use to which it was not previously subject, where the flow or circulation of navigable waters may be impaired or the reach of such waters be reduced, shall be required to have a permit under this section.

(g) State administration

(1) The Governor of any State desiring to administer its own individual and general permit program for the discharge of dredged or fill material into the navigable waters (other than those waters which are presently used, or are susceptible to use in their natural condition or by reasonable improvement as a means to transport interstate or foreign commerce shoreward to their ordinary high water mark, including all waters which are subject to the ebb and flow of the tide shoreward to their mean high water mark, or mean higher high water mark on the west coast, including wetlands adjacent thereto) within its jurisdiction may submit to the Administrator a full and complete description of the program it proposes to establish and administer under State law or under an interstate compact. In addition, such State shall submit a statement from the attorney general (or the attorney for those State agencies which have independent legal counsel), or from the chief legal officer in the case of an interstate agency, that the laws of such State, or the interstate compact, as the case may be, provide adequate authority to carry out the described program.

(2) Not later than the tenth day after the date of the receipt of the program and statement submitted by any State under paragraph (1) of this subsection, the Administrator shall provide copies of such program and statement to the Secretary and the Secretary of the Interior, acting through the Director of the United States Fish and Wildlife Service.

(3) Not later than the ninetieth day after the date of the receipt by the Administrator of the program and statement submitted by any State, under paragraph (1) of this subsection, the Secretary and the Secretary of the Interior, acting through the Director of the United States Fish and Wildlife Service, shall submit any comments with respect to such program and statement to the Administrator in writing.

(h) Determination of State's authority to issue permits under State program; approval; notification; transfers to State program

(1) Not later than the one-hundred-twentieth day after the date of the receipt by the Administrator of a program and statement submitted by any State under paragraph (1) of this subsection, the Administrator shall determine, taking into account any comments submitted by the Secretary and the Secretary of the Interior, acting through the Director of the United States Fish and Wildlife Service, pursuant to subsection (g) of this section, whether such State has the following authority with respect to the issuance of permits pursuant to such program:

(A) To issue permits which—

(i) apply, and assure compliance with, any applicable requirements of this section, including, but not limited to, the guidelines established under subsection (b)(1) of this section, and sections 1317 and 1343 of this title;

(ii) are for fixed terms not exceeding five years; and

(iii) can be terminated or modified for cause including, but not limited to, the following:

(I) violation of any condition of the permit;

(II) obtaining a permit by misrepresentation, or failure to disclose fully all relevant facts;

(III) change in any condition that requires either a temporary or permanent reduction or elimination of the permitted discharge.

(B) To issue permits which apply, and assure compliance with, all applicable requirements of section 1318 of this title, or to inspect, monitor, enter, and require reports to at least the same extent as required in section 1318 of this title.

(C) To assure that the public, and any other State the waters of which may be affected, receive notice of each application for a permit and to provide an opportunity for public hearing before a ruling on each such application.

(D) To assure that the Administrator receives notice of each application (including a copy thereof) for a permit.

(E) To assure that any State (other than the permitting State), whose waters may be affected by the issuance of a permit may submit written recommendations to the permitting State (and the Administrator) with respect to any permit application and, if any part of such written recommendations are not accepted by the permitting State, that the permitting State will notify such affected State (and the Administrator) in writing of its failure to so accept such recommendations together with its reasons for so doing.

(F) To assure that no permit will be issued if, in the judgment of the Secretary, after consultation with the Secretary of the department in which the Coast Guard is operating, anchorage and navigation of any of the navigable waters would be substantially impaired thereby.

(G) To abate violations of the permit or the permit program, including civil and criminal penalties and other ways and means of enforcement.

(H) To assure continued coordination with Federal and Federal-State water-related planning and review processes.

(2) If, with respect to a State program submitted under subsection (g)(1) of this section, the Administrator determines that such State—

(A) has the authority set forth in paragraph (1) of this subsection, the Administrator shall approve the program and so notify (i) such State and (ii) the Secretary, who upon subsequent notification from such State that it is administering such program, shall suspend the issuance of permits under subsections (a) and (e) of this section for activities with respect to which a permit may be issued pursuant to such State program; or

(B) does not have the authority set forth in paragraph (1) of this subsection, the Administrator shall so notify such State, which notification shall also describe the revisions or modifications necessary so that such State may resubmit such program for a determination by the Administrator under this subsection.

(3) If the Administrator fails to make a determination with respect to any program submitted by a State under subsection (g)(1) of this section within one-hundred-twenty days after the date of the receipt of such program, such program shall be deemed approved pursuant to paragraph (2)(A) of this subsection and the Administrator shall so notify such State and the Secretary who, upon subsequent notification from such State that it is administering such program, shall suspend the issuance of permits under subsection (a) and (e) of this section for activities with respect to which a permit may be issued by such State.

(4) After the Secretary receives notification from the Administrator under paragraph (2) or (3) of this subsection that a State permit program has been approved, the Secretary shall transfer any applications for permits pending before the Secretary for activities with respect to which a permit may be issued pursuant to such State program to such State for appropriate action.

(5) Upon notification from a State with a permit program approved under this subsection that such State intends to administer and enforce the terms and conditions of a general permit issued by the Secretary under subsection (e) of this section with respect to activities in such State to which such general permit applies, the Secretary shall suspend the administration and enforcement of such general permit with respect to such activities.

(i) Withdrawal of approval

Whenever the Administrator determines after public hearing that a State is not administering a program approved under subsection (h)(2)(A) of this section, in accordance with this section, including, but not limited to, the guidelines established under subsection (b)(1) of this section, the Administrator shall so notify the State, and, if appropriate corrective action is not taken within a reasonable time, not to exceed ninety days after the date of the receipt of such notification, the Administrator shall (1) withdraw approval of such program until the Administrator determines such corrective action has been taken, and (2) notify the Secretary that the Secretary shall resume the program for the issuance of permits under subsections (a) and (e) of this section for activities with respect to which the State was issuing permits and that such authority of the Secretary shall continue in effect until such time as the Administrator makes the determination described in clause (1) of this subsection and such State again has an approved program.

(j) Copies of applications for State permits and proposed general permits to be transmitted to Administrator

Each State which is administering a permit program pursuant to this section shall transmit to the Administrator (1) a copy of each permit application received by such State and provide notice to the Administrator of every action related to the consideration of such permit application, including each permit proposed to be issued by such State, and (2) a copy of each proposed general permit which such State intends to issue. Not later than the tenth day after the date of the receipt of such permit application or such proposed general permit, the Administrator shall provide copies of such permit application or such proposed general permit to the Secretary and the Secretary of the Interior, acting through the Director of the United States Fish and Wildlife Service. If the Administrator intends to provide written comments to such State with respect to such permit application or such proposed general permit, he shall so notify such State not later than the thirtieth day after the date of the receipt of such application or such proposed general permit and provide such written comments to such State, after consideration of any comments made in writing with respect to such application or such proposed general permit by the Secretary and the Secretary of the Interior, acting through the Director of the United States Fish and Wildlife Service, not later than the ninetieth day after the date of such receipt. If such State is so notified by the Administrator, it shall not issue the proposed permit until after the receipt of such comments from the Administrator, or after such ninetieth day, whichever first occurs. Such State shall not issue such proposed permit after such ninetieth day if it has received such written comments in which the Administrator objects (A) to the issuance of such proposed permit and such proposed permit is one that has been submitted to the Administrator pursuant to subsection (h)(1)(E) of this section, or (B) to the issuance of such proposed permit as being outside the requirements of this section, including, but not limited to, the guidelines developed under subsection (b)(1) of this section unless it modifies such proposed permit in accordance with such comments. Whenever the Administrator objects to the issuance of a permit under the preceding sentence such written objection shall contain a statement of the reasons for such objection and the conditions which such permit would include if it were issued by the Administrator. In any case where the Administrator objects to the issuance of a permit, on request of the State, a public hearing shall be held by the Administrator on such objection. If the State does not resubmit such permit revised to meet such objection within 30 days after completion of the hearing or, if no hearing is requested within 90 days after the date of such objection, the Secretary may issue the permit pursuant to subsection (a) or (e) of this section, as the case may be, for such source in accordance with the guidelines and requirements of this chapter.

(k) Waiver

In accordance with guidelines promulgated pursuant to subsection (i)(2) of section 1314 of this title, the Administrator is authorized to waive the requirements of subsection (j) of this section at the time of the approval of a program pursuant to subsection (h)(2)(A) of this section for any category (including any class, type, or size within such category) of discharge within the State submitting such program.

(*l*) Categories of discharges not subject to requirements

The Administrator shall promulgate regulations establishing categories of discharges which he determines shall not be subject to the requirements of subsection (j) of this section in any State with a program approved pursuant to subsection (h)(2)(A) of this section. The Administrator may distinguish among classes, types, and sizes within any category of discharges.

(m) Comments on permit applications or proposed general permits by Secretary of the Interior acting through Director of United States Fish and Wildlife Service

Not later than the ninetieth day after the date on which the Secretary notifies the Secretary of the Interior, acting through the Director of the United States Fish and Wildlife Service that (1) an application for a permit under subsection (a) of this section has been received by the Secretary, or (2) the Secretary proposes to issue a general permit under subsection (e) of this section, the Secretary of the Interior, acting through the Director of the United States Fish and Wildlife Service, shall submit any comments with respect to such application or such proposed general permit in writing to the Secretary.

(n) Enforcement authority not limited

Nothing in this section shall be construed to limit the authority of the Administrator to take action pursuant to section 1319 of this title.

(*o*) Public availability of permits and permit applications

A copy of each permit application and each permit issued under this section shall be available to the public. Such permit application or portion thereof, shall further be available on request for the purpose of reproduction.

(p) Compliance

Compliance with a permit issued pursuant to this section, including any activity carried out pursuant to a general permit issued under this section, shall be deemed compliance, for purposes of sections 1319 and 1365 of this title, with sections 1311, 1317, and 1343 of this title.

(q) Minimization of duplication, needless paperwork, and delays in issuance; agreements

Not later than the one-hundred-eightieth day after December 27, 1977, the Secretary shall enter into agreements with the Administrator, the Secretaries of the Departments of Agriculture, Commerce, Interior, and Transportation, and the heads of other appropriate Federal agencies to minimize, to the maximum extent practicable, duplication, needless paperwork, and delays in the issuance of permits under this section. Such agreements shall be developed to assure that, to the maximum extent practicable, a decision with respect to an application for a permit under subsection (a) of this section will be made not later than the ninetieth day after the date the notice for such application is published under subsection (a) of this section.

(r) Federal projects specifically authorized by Congress

The discharge of dredged or fill material as part of the construction of a Federal project specifically authorized by Congress, whether prior to or on or after December 27, 1977, is not prohibited by or otherwise subject to regulation under this section, or a State program approved under this section, or section 1311(a) or 1342 of this title (except for effluent standards or prohibitions under section 1317 of this title), if information on the effects of such discharge, including consideration of the guidelines developed under subsection (b)(1) of this section, is included in an environmental impact statement for such project pursuant to the National Environmental Policy Act of 1969 [42 U.S.C. 4321 et seq.] and such environmental impact statement has been submitted to Congress before the actual discharge of dredged or fill material in connection with the construction of such project and prior to either authorization of such project or an appropriation of funds for such construction.

(s) Violation of permits

(1) Whenever on the basis of any information available to him the Secretary finds that any

person is in violation of any condition or limitation set forth in a permit issued by the Secretary under this section, the Secretary shall issue an order requiring such person to comply with such condition or limitation, or the Secretary shall bring a civil action in accordance with paragraph (3) of this subsection.

(2) A copy of any order issued under this subsection shall be sent immediately by the Secretary to the State in which the violation occurs and other affected States. Any order issued under this subsection shall be by personal service and shall state with reasonable specificity the nature of the violation, specify a time for compliance, not to exceed thirty days, which the Secretary determines is reasonable, taking into account the seriousness of the violation and any good faith efforts to comply with applicable requirements. In any case in which an order under this subsection is issued to a corporation, a copy of such order shall be served on any appropriate corporate officers.

(3) The Secretary is authorized to commence a civil action for appropriate relief, including a permanent or temporary injunction for any violation for which he is authorized to issue a compliance order under paragraph (1) of this subsection. Any action under this paragraph may be brought in the district court of the United States for the district in which the defendant is located or resides or is doing business, and such court shall have jurisdiction to restrain such violation and to require compliance. Notice of the commencement of such acton[1] shall be given immediately to the appropriate State.

(4) Any person who violates any condition or limitation in a permit issued by the Secretary under this section, and any person who violates any order issued by the Secretary under paragraph (1) of this subsection, shall be subject to a civil penalty not to exceed $25,000 per day for each violation. In determining the amount of a civil penalty the court shall consider the seriousness of the violation or violations, the economic benefit (if any) resulting from the violation, any history of such violations, any good-faith efforts to comply with the applicable requirements, the economic impact of the penalty on the violator, and such other matters as justice may require.

(t) Navigable waters within State jurisdiction

Nothing in this section shall preclude or deny the right of any State or interstate agency to control the discharge of dredged or fill material in any portion of the navigable waters within the jurisdiction of such State, including any activity of any Federal agency, and each such agency shall comply with such State or interstate requirements both substantive and procedural to control the discharge of dredged or fill material to the same extent that any person is subject to such requirements. This section shall not be construed as affecting or impairing the authority of the Secretary to maintain navigation.

(June 30, 1948, ch. 758, title IV, §404, as added Pub. L. 92–500, §2, Oct. 18, 1972, 86 Stat. 884; amended Pub. L. 95–217, §67(a), (b), Dec. 27, 1977, 91 Stat. 1600; Pub. L. 100–4, title III, §313(d), Feb. 4, 1987, 101 Stat. 45.)

[1] So in original. Probably should be "action".

REFERENCES IN TEXT

The National Environmental Policy Act of 1969, referred to in subsec. (r), is Pub. L. 91–190, Jan. 1, 1970, 83 Stat. 852, as amended, which is classified generally to chapter 55 (§4321 et seq.) of Title 42, The Public Health and Welfare. For complete classification of this Act to the Code, see Short Title note set out under section 4321 of Title 42 and Tables.

AMENDMENTS

1987—Subsec. (s). Pub. L. 100–4 redesignated par. (5) as (4), substituted "$25,000 per day for each violation" for "$10,000 per day of such violation", inserted provision specifying factors to consider in determining the penalty amount, and struck out former par. (4) which read as follows:

"(A) Any person who willfully or negligently violates any condition or limitation in a permit issued by the Secretary under this section shall be punished by a fine of not less than $2,500 nor more than $25,000 per day of violation, or by imprisonment for not more than one year, or by both. If the conviction is for a violation committed after a first conviction of such person under this paragraph, punishment shall be by a fine of not more than $50,000 per day of violation, or by imprisonment for not more than two years, or by both.

"(B) For the purposes of this paragraph, the term 'person' shall mean, in addition to the definition contained in section 1362(5) of this title, any responsible corporate officer."

1977—Subsec. (a). Pub. L. 95–217, §67(a)(1), substituted "The Secretary" for "The Secretary of the Army, acting through the Chief of Engineers," and inserted provision that, not later than the fifteenth day after the date an applicant submits all the information required to complete an application for a permit under this subsection, the Secretary publish the notice required by this subsection.

Subsecs. (b), (c). Pub. L. 95–217, §67(a)(2), substituted "the Secretary" for "the Secretary of the Army".

Subsecs. (d) to (t). Pub. L. 95–217, §67(b), added subsecs. (d) to (t).

TRANSFER OF FUNCTIONS

For transfer of authorities, functions, personnel, and assets of the Coast Guard, including the authorities and functions of the Secretary of Transportation relating thereto, to the Department of Homeland Security, and for treatment of related references, see sections 468(b), 551(d), 552(d), and 557 of Title 6, Domestic Security, and the Department of Homeland Security Reorganization Plan of November 25, 2002, as modified, set out as a note under section 542 of Title 6.

Enforcement functions of Administrator or other official of the Environmental Protection Agency and of Secretary or other official in Department of the Interior relating to review of the Corps of Engineers' dredged and fill material permits and such functions of Secretary of the Army, Chief of Engineers, or other official in Corps of Engineers of the United States Army relating to compliance with dredged and fill material permits issued under this section with respect to preconstruction, construction, and initial operation of transportation system for Canadian and Alaskan natural gas were transferred to the Federal Inspector, Office of Federal Inspector for the Alaska Natural Gas Transportation System, until the first anniversary of the date of initial operation of the Alaska Natural Gas Transportation System, see Reorg. Plan No. 1 of 1979, §§102(a), (b), (e), 203(a), 44 F.R. 33663, 33666, 93 Stat. 1373, 1376, effective July 1, 1979, set out in the Appendix to Title 5, Government Organization and Employees. Office of Federal Inspector for the Alaska Natural Gas Transportation System abolished and functions and authority vested in Inspector transferred to Secretary of Energy by section 3012(b) of Pub. L. 102–486, set out as an Abolition of Office of Federal Inspector note under section 719e of Title 15, Commerce and Trade. Functions and authority vested in Secretary of Energy subsequently transferred to Federal Coordinator for Alaska Natural Gas Transportation Projects by section 720d(f) of Title 15.

MITIGATION AND MITIGATION BANKING REGULATIONS

Pub. L. 108–136, div. A, title III, § 314(b), Nov. 24, 2003, 117 Stat. 1431, provided that:

"(1) To ensure opportunities for Federal agency participation in mitigation banking, the Secretary of the Army, acting through the Chief of Engineers, shall issue regulations establishing performance standards and criteria for the use, consistent with section 404 of the Federal Water Pollution Control Act (33 U.S.C. 1344), of on-site, off-site, and in-lieu fee mitigation and mitigation banking as compensation for lost wetlands functions in permits issued by the Secretary of the Army under such section. To the maximum extent practicable, the regulatory standards and criteria shall maximize available credits and opportunities for mitigation, provide flexibility for regional variations in wetland conditions, functions and values, and apply equivalent standards and criteria to each type of compensatory mitigation.

"(2) Final regulations shall be issued not later than two years after the date of the enactment of this Act [Nov. 24, 2003]."

REGULATORY PROGRAM

Pub. L. 106–377, § 1(a)(2) [title I], Oct. 27, 2000, 114 Stat. 1441, 1441A–63, provided in part that: "For expenses necessary for administration of laws pertaining to regulation of navigable waters and wetlands, $125,000,000, to remain available until expended: *Provided*, That the Secretary of the Army, acting through the Chief of Engineers, is directed to use funds appropriated herein to: (1) by March 1, 2001, supplement the report, Cost Analysis For the 1999 Proposal to Issue and Modify Nationwide Permits, to reflect the Nationwide Permits actually issued on March 9, 2000, including changes in the acreage limits, preconstruction notification requirements and general conditions between the rule proposed on July 21, 1999, and the rule promulgated and published in the Federal Register; (2) after consideration of the cost analysis for the 1999 proposal to issue and modify nationwide permits and the supplement prepared pursuant to this Act [H.R. 5483, as enacted by section 1(a)(2) of Pub. L. 106–377, see Tables for classification] and by September 30, 2001, prepare, submit to Congress and publish in the Federal Register a Permit Processing Management Plan by which the Corps of Engineers will handle the additional work associated with all projected increases in the number of individual permit applications and preconstruction notifications related to the new and replacement permits and general conditions. The Permit Processing Management Plan shall include specific objective goals and criteria by which the Corps of Engineers' progress towards reducing any permit backlog can be measured; (3) beginning on December 31, 2001, and on a biannual basis thereafter, report to Congress and publish in the Federal Register, an analysis of the performance of its program as measured against the criteria set out in the Permit Processing Management Plan; (4) implement a 1-year pilot program to publish quarterly on the U.S. Army Corps of Engineer's Regulatory Program website all Regulatory Analysis and Management Systems (RAMS) data for the South Pacific Division and North Atlantic Division beginning within 30 days of the enactment of this Act [Oct. 27, 2000]; and (5) publish in Division Office websites all findings, rulings, and decisions rendered under the administrative appeals process for the Corps of Engineers Regulatory Program as established in Public Law 106–60 [113 Stat. 486]: *Provided further*, That, through the period ending on September 30, 2003, the Corps of Engineers shall allow any appellant to keep a verbatim record of the proceedings of the appeals conference under the aforementioned administrative appeals process: *Provided further*, That within 30 days of the enactment of this Act, the Secretary of the Army, acting through the Chief of Engineers, shall require all U.S. Army Corps of Engineers Divisions and Districts to record the date on which a section 404 individual permit application or nationwide permit notification is filed with the Corps of Engineers: *Provided further*, That the Corps of Engineers, when reporting permit processing times, shall track both the date a permit application is first received and the date the application is considered complete, as well as the reason that the application is not considered complete upon first submission."

AUTHORITY TO DELEGATE TO STATE OF WASHINGTON FUNCTIONS OF THE SECRETARY RELATING TO LAKE CHELAN, WASHINGTON

Section 76 of Pub. L. 95–217 provided that: "The Secretary of the Army, acting through the Chief of Engineers, is authorized to delegate to the State of Washington upon its request all or any part of those functions vested in such Secretary by section 404 of the Federal Water Pollution Control Act [this section] and by sections 9, 10, and 13 of the Act of March 3, 1899 [sections 401, 403, and 407 of this title], relating to Lake Chelan, Washington, if the Secretary determines (1) that such State has the authority, responsibility, and capability to carry out such functions, and (2) that such delegation is in the public interest. Such delegation shall be subject to such terms and conditions as the Secretary deems necessary, including, but not limited to, suspension and revocation for cause of such delegation."

CONTIGUOUS ZONE OF UNITED STATES

For extension of contiguous zone of United States, see Proc. No. 7219, set out as a note under section 1331 of Title 43, Public Lands.

§ 1345. Disposal or use of sewage sludge

(a) Permit

Notwithstanding any other provision of this chapter or of any other law, in any case where the disposal of sewage sludge resulting from the operation of a treatment works as defined in section 1292 of this title (including the removal of in-place sewage sludge from one location and its deposit at another location) would result in any pollutant from such sewage sludge entering the navigable waters, such disposal is prohibited except in accordance with a permit issued by the Administrator under section 1342 of this title.

(b) Issuance of permit; regulations

The Administrator shall issue regulations governing the issuance of permits for the disposal of sewage sludge subject to subsection (a) of this section and section 1342 of this title. Such regulations shall require the application to such disposal of each criterion, factor, procedure, and requirement applicable to a permit issued under section 1342 of this title.

(c) State permit program

Each State desiring to administer its own permit program for disposal of sewage sludge subject to subsection (a) of this section within its jurisdiction may do so in accordance with section 1342 of this title.

(d) Regulations

(1) Regulations

The Administrator, after consultation with appropriate Federal and State agencies and other interested persons, shall develop and publish, within one year after December 27, 1977, and from time to time thereafter, regulations providing guidelines for the disposal of sludge and the utilization of sludge for various purposes. Such regulations shall—

(A) identify uses for sludge, including disposal;

(B) specify factors to be taken into account in determining the measures and practices applicable to each such use or disposal (including publication of information on costs);

(C) identify concentrations of pollutants which interfere with each such use or disposal.

The Administrator is authorized to revise any regulation issued under this subsection.

(2) Identification and regulation of toxic pollutants

(A) On basis of available information

(i) Proposed regulations

Not later than November 30, 1986, the Administrator shall identify those toxic pollutants which, on the basis of available information on their toxicity, persistence, concentration, mobility, or potential for exposure, may be present in sewage sludge in concentrations which may adversely affect public health or the environment, and propose regulations specifying acceptable management practices for sewage sludge containing each such toxic pollutant and establishing numerical limitations for each such pollutant for each use identified under paragraph (1)(A).

(ii) Final regulations

Not later than August 31, 1987, and after opportunity for public hearing, the Administrator shall promulgate the regulations required by subparagraph (A)(i).

(B) Others

(i) Proposed regulations

Not later than July 31, 1987, the Administrator shall identify those toxic pollutants not identified under subparagraph (A)(i) which may be present in sewage sludge in concentrations which may adversely affect public health or the environment, and propose regulations specifying acceptable management practices for sewage sludge containing each such toxic pollutant and establishing numerical limitations for each pollutant for each such use identified under paragraph (1)(A).

(ii) Final regulations

Not later than June 15, 1988, the Administrator shall promulgate the regulations required by subparagraph (B)(i).

(C) Review

From time to time, but not less often than every 2 years, the Administrator shall review the regulations promulgated under this paragraph for the purpose of identifying additional toxic pollutants and promulgating regulations for such pollutants consistent with the requirements of this paragraph.

(D) Minimum standards; compliance date

The management practices and numerical criteria established under subparagraphs (A), (B), and (C) shall be adequate to protect public health and the environment from any reasonably anticipated adverse effects of each pollutant. Such regulations shall require compliance as expeditiously as practicable but in no case later than 12 months after their publication, unless such regulations require the construction of new pollution control facilities, in which case the regulations shall require compliance as expeditiously as practicable but in no case later than two years from the date of their publication.

(3) Alternative standards

For purposes of this subsection, if, in the judgment of the Administrator, it is not feasible to prescribe or enforce a numerical limitation for a pollutant identified under paragraph (2), the Administrator may instead promulgate a design, equipment, management practice, or operational standard, or combination thereof, which in the Administrator's judgment is adequate to protect public health and the environment from any reasonably anticipated adverse effects of such pollutant. In the event the Administrator promulgates a design or equipment standard under this subsection, the Administrator shall include as part of such standard such requirements as will assure the proper operation and maintenance of any such element of design or equipment.

(4) Conditions on permits

Prior to the promulgation of the regulations required by paragraph (2), the Administrator shall impose conditions in permits issued to publicly owned treatment works under section 1342 of this title or take such other measures as the Administrator deems appropriate to protect public health and the environment from any adverse effects which may occur from toxic pollutants in sewage sludge.

(5) Limitation on statutory construction

Nothing in this section is intended to waive more stringent requirements established by this chapter or any other law.

(e) Manner of sludge disposal

The determination of the manner of disposal or use of sludge is a local determination, except that it shall be unlawful for any person to dispose of sludge from a publicly owned treatment works or any other treatment works treating domestic sewage for any use for which regulations have been established pursuant to subsection (d) of this section, except in accordance with such regulations.

(f) Implementation of regulations

(1) Through section 1342 permits

Any permit issued under section 1342 of this title to a publicly owned treatment works or any other treatment works treating domestic sewage shall include requirements for the use and disposal of sludge that implement the regulations established pursuant to subsection (d) of this section, unless such requirements have been included in a permit issued under the appropriate provisions of subtitle C of the Solid Waste Disposal Act [42 U.S.C. 6921 et seq.], part C of the Safe Drinking Water Act [42 U.S.C. 300h et seq.], the Marine Protection, Research, and Sanctuaries Act of 1972 [16 U.S.C. 1431 et seq., 1447 et seq.; 33 U.S.C. 1401 et seq., 2801 et seq.], or the Clean Air Act [42 U.S.C. 7401 et seq.], or under State permit programs approved by the Administrator, where the Administrator determines that such programs assure compliance with any applicable requirements of this section. Not later than December 15, 1986, the Administrator shall promulgate procedures for approval of State programs pursuant to this paragraph.

(2) Through other permits

In the case of a treatment works described in paragraph (1) that is not subject to section 1342 of this title and to which none of the other above listed permit programs nor approved State permit authority apply, the Administrator may issue a permit to such treatment works solely to impose requirements for the use and disposal of sludge that implement the regulations established pursuant to subsection (d) of this section. The Administrator shall include in the permit appropriate requirements to assure compliance with the regulations established pursuant to subsection (d) of this section. The Administrator shall establish procedures for issuing permits pursuant to this paragraph.

(g) Studies and projects

(1) Grant program; information gathering

The Administrator is authorized to conduct or initiate scientific studies, demonstration projects, and public information and education projects which are designed to promote the safe and beneficial management or use of sewage sludge for such purposes as aiding the restoration of abandoned mine sites, conditioning soil for parks and recreation areas, agricultural and horticultural uses, and other beneficial purposes. For the purposes of carrying out this subsection, the Administrator may make grants to State water pollution control agencies, other public or nonprofit agencies, institutions, organizations, and individuals. In cooperation with other Federal departments and agencies, other public and private agencies, institutions, and organizations, the Administrator is authorized to collect and disseminate information pertaining to the safe and beneficial use of sewage sludge.

(2) Authorization of appropriations

For the purposes of carrying out the scientific studies, demonstration projects, and public information and education projects authorized in this section, there is authorized to be appropriated for fiscal years beginning after September 30, 1986, not to exceed $5,000,000.

(June 30, 1948, ch. 758, title IV, §405, as added Pub. L. 92–500, §2, Oct. 18, 1972, 86 Stat. 884; amended Pub. L. 95–217, §§54(d), 68, Dec. 27, 1977, 91 Stat. 1591, 1606; Pub. L. 100–4, title IV, §406(a)–(c), (f), Feb. 4, 1987, 101 Stat. 71, 72, 74.)

REFERENCES IN TEXT

The Solid Waste Disposal Act, referred to in subsec. (f)(1), is title II of Pub. L. 89–272, Oct. 20, 1965, 79 Stat. 997, as amended generally by Pub. L. 94–580, §2, Oct. 21, 1976, 90 Stat. 2795. Subtitle C of the Solid Waste Disposal Act is classified generally to subchapter III (§6921 et seq.) of chapter 82 of Title 42, The Public Health and Welfare. For complete classification of this Act to the Code, see Short Title note set out under section 6901 of Title 42 and Tables.

The Safe Drinking Water Act, referred to in subsec. (f)(1), is title XIV of act July 1, 1944, as added Dec. 16, 1974, Pub. L. 93–523, §2(a), 88 Stat. 1660, as amended. Part C of the Act is classified generally to part C (§300h et seq.) of subchapter XII of chapter 6A of Title 42. For complete classification of this Act to the Code, see Short Title note set out under section 201 of Title 42 and Tables.

The Marine Protection, Research, and Sanctuaries Act of 1972, referred to in subsec. (f)(1), is Pub. L. 92–532, Oct. 23, 1972, 86 Stat. 1052, as amended, which is classified generally to chapters 32 (§1431 et seq.) and 32A (§1447 et seq.) of Title 16, Conservation, and chapters 27 (§1401 et seq.) and 41 (§2801 et seq.) of this title. For complete classification of this Act to the Code, see Short Title note set out under section 1401 of this title and Tables.

The Clean Air Act, referred to in subsec. (f)(1), is act July 14, 1955, ch. 360, 69 Stat. 322, as amended, which is classified generally to chapter 85 (§7401 et seq.) of Title 42, The Public Health and Welfare. For complete classification of this Act to the Code, see Short Title note set out under section 7401 of Title 42 and Tables.

AMENDMENTS

1987—Subsec. (d). Pub. L. 100–4, §406(a), designated existing provision as par. (1), inserted heading, redesignated former pars. (1) to (3) as subpars. (A) to (C), and added pars. (2) to (5).

Pub. L. 100–4, §406(f), inserted heading "Regulations" and aligned par. (1) with par. (3) and subpars. (A) to (C) of par. (1) with subpar. (C) of par. (2).

Subsec. (e). Pub. L. 100–4, §406(b), amended subsec. (e) generally. Prior to amendment, subsec. (e) read as follows: "The determination of the manner of disposal or use of sludge is a local determination except that it shall be unlawful for the owner or operator of any publicly owned treatment works to dispose of sludge from such works for any use for which guidelines have been established pursuant to subsection (d) of this section, except in accordance with such guidelines."

Subsecs. (f), (g). Pub. L. 100–4, §406(c), added subsecs. (f) and (g).

1977—Subsec. (a). Pub. L. 95–217, §68(a), substituted "under section 1342 of this title" for "under this section".

Subsec. (b). Pub. L. 95–217, §§54(d)(1), 68(b), (c), substituted "sewage sludge subject to subsection (a) of this section and section 1342 of this title" for "sewage sludge subject to this section" and struck out ", as the Administrator determines necessary to carry out the objective of this chapter" after "permit issued under section 1342 of this title".

Subsec. (c). Pub. L. 95–217, §§54(d)(2), 68(d), substituted "disposal of sewage sludge subject to subsection (a) of this section within its jurisdiction may do so in accordance with section 1342 of this title" for "disposal of sewage sludge within its jurisdiction may do so if upon submission of such program the Administrator determines such program is adequate to carry out the objective of this chapter".

Subsecs. (d), (e). Pub. L. 95–217, §54(d)(3), added subsecs. (d) and (e).

REMOVAL CREDITS

Section 406(e) of Pub. L. 100–4 provided that: "The part of the decision of Natural Resources Defense Council, Inc. v. U.S. Environmental Protection Agency, No. 84–3530 (3d. Cir. 1986), which addresses section 405(d) of the Federal Water Pollution Control Act [33 U.S.C. 1345(d)] is stayed until August 31, 1987, with respect to—

"(1) those publicly owned treatment works the owner or operator of which received authority to revise pretreatment requirements under section 307(b)(1) of such Act [33 U.S.C. 1317(b)(1)] before the date of the enactment of this section [Feb. 4, 1987], and

"(2) those publicly owned treatment works the owner or operator of which has submitted an application for authority to revise pretreatment requirements under such section 307(b)(1) which application is pending on such date of enactment and is approved before August 31, 1987.

The Administrator shall not authorize any other removal credits under such Act [33 U.S.C. 1251 et seq.] until the Administrator issues the regulations required by paragraph (2)(A)(ii) of section 405(d) of such Act, as amended by subsection (a) of this section."

§1346. Coastal recreation water quality monitoring and notification

(a) Monitoring and notification

(1) In general

Not later than 18 months after October 10, 2000, after consultation and in cooperation with appropriate Federal, State, tribal, and local officials (including local health officials), and after providing public notice and an opportunity for comment, the Administrator shall publish performance criteria for—

(A) monitoring and assessment (including specifying available methods for monitoring) of coastal recreation waters adjacent to beaches or similar points of access that are used by the public for attainment of applicable water quality standards for pathogens and pathogen indicators; and

(B) the prompt notification of the public, local governments, and the Administrator of any exceeding of or likelihood of exceeding applicable water quality standards for coastal recreation waters described in subparagraph (A).

(2) Level of protection

The performance criteria referred to in paragraph (1) shall provide that the activities described in subparagraphs (A) and (B) of that paragraph shall be carried out as necessary for the protection of public health and safety.

(b) Program development and implementation grants

(1) In general

The Administrator may make grants to States and local governments to develop and implement programs for monitoring and notification for coastal recreation waters adjacent to beaches or similar points of access that are used by the public.

(2) Limitations

(A) In general

The Administrator may award a grant to a State or a local government to implement a monitoring and notification program if—

(i) the program is consistent with the performance criteria published by the Administrator under subsection (a) of this section;

(ii) the State or local government prioritizes the use of grant funds for particular coastal recreation waters based on the use of the water and the risk to human health presented by pathogens or pathogen indicators;

(iii) the State or local government makes available to the Administrator the factors used to prioritize the use of funds under clause (ii);

(iv) the State or local government provides a list of discrete areas of coastal recreation waters that are subject to the program for monitoring and notification for which the grant is provided that specifies any coastal recreation waters for which fiscal constraints will prevent consistency with the performance criteria under subsection (a) of this section; and

(v) the public is provided an opportunity to review the program through a process that provides for public notice and an opportunity for comment.

(B) Grants to local governments

The Administrator may make a grant to a local government under this subsection for implementation of a monitoring and notification program only if, after the 1-year period beginning on the date of publication of performance criteria under subsection (a)(1) of this section, the Administrator determines that the State is not implementing a program that meets the requirements of this subsection, regardless of whether the State has received a grant under this subsection.

(3) Other requirements

(A) Report

A State recipient of a grant under this subsection shall submit to the Administrator, in such format and at such intervals as the Administrator determines to be appropriate, a report that describes—

(i) data collected as part of the program for monitoring and notification as described in subsection (c) of this section; and

(ii) actions taken to notify the public when water quality standards are exceeded.

(B) Delegation

A State recipient of a grant under this subsection shall identify each local government to which the State has delegated or intends to delegate responsibility for implementing a monitoring and notification program consistent with the performance criteria published under subsection (a) of this section (including any coastal recreation waters for which the authority to implement a monitoring and notification program would be subject to the delegation).

(4) Federal share

(A) In general

The Administrator, through grants awarded under this section, may pay up to 100 percent of the costs of developing and implementing a program for monitoring and notification under this subsection.

(B) Non-Federal share

The non-Federal share of the costs of developing and implementing a monitoring and notification program may be—

(i) in an amount not to exceed 50 percent, as determined by the Administrator in consultation with State, tribal, and local government representatives; and

(ii) provided in cash or in kind.

(c) Content of State and local government programs

As a condition of receipt of a grant under subsection (b) of this section, a State or local government program for monitoring and notification under this section shall identify—

(1) lists of coastal recreation waters in the State, including coastal recreation waters adjacent to beaches or similar points of access that are used by the public;

(2) in the case of a State program for monitoring and notification, the process by which the State may delegate to local governments responsibility for implementing the monitoring and notification program;

(3) the frequency and location of monitoring and assessment of coastal recreation waters based on—

(A) the periods of recreational use of the waters;

(B) the nature and extent of use during certain periods;

(C) the proximity of the waters to known point sources and nonpoint sources of pollution; and

(D) any effect of storm events on the waters;

(4)(A) the methods to be used for detecting levels of pathogens and pathogen indicators that are harmful to human health; and

(B) the assessment procedures for identifying short-term increases in pathogens and pathogen indicators that are harmful to human health in coastal recreation waters (including increases in relation to storm events);

(5) measures for prompt communication of the occurrence, nature, location, pollutants involved, and extent of any exceeding of, or likelihood of exceeding, applicable water quality standards for pathogens and pathogen indicators to—

(A) the Administrator, in such form as the Administrator determines to be appropriate; and

(B) a designated official of a local government having jurisdiction over land adjoining the coastal recreation waters for which the failure to meet applicable standards is identified;

(6) measures for the posting of signs at beaches or similar points of access, or functionally equivalent communication measures that are sufficient to give notice to the public that the coastal recreation waters are not meeting or are not expected to meet applicable water quality standards for pathogens and pathogen indicators; and

(7) measures that inform the public of the potential risks associated with water contact activities in the coastal recreation waters that do not meet applicable water quality standards.

(d) Federal agency programs

Not later than 3 years after October 10, 2000, each Federal agency that has jurisdiction over coastal recreation waters adjacent to beaches or similar points of access that are used by the public shall develop and implement, through a process that provides for public notice and an opportunity for comment, a monitoring and notification program for the coastal recreation waters that—

(1) protects the public health and safety;

(2) is consistent with the performance criteria published under subsection (a) of this section;

(3) includes a completed report on the information specified in subsection (b)(3)(A) of this section, to be submitted to the Administrator; and

(4) addresses the matters specified in subsection (c) of this section.

(e) Database

The Administrator shall establish, maintain, and make available to the public by electronic and other means a national coastal recreation water pollution occurrence database that provides—

(1) the data reported to the Administrator under subsections (b)(3)(A)(i) and (d)(3) of this section; and

(2) other information concerning pathogens and pathogen indicators in coastal recreation waters that—

(A) is made available to the Administrator by a State or local government, from a coastal water quality monitoring program of the State or local government; and

(B) the Administrator determines should be included.

(f) Technical assistance for monitoring floatable material

The Administrator shall provide technical assistance to States and local governments for the development of assessment and monitoring procedures for floatable material to protect public health and safety in coastal recreation waters.

(g) List of waters

(1) In general

Beginning not later than 18 months after the date of publication of performance criteria under subsection (a) of this section, based on information made available to the Administrator, the Administrator shall identify, and maintain a list of, discrete coastal recreation waters adjacent to beaches or similar points of access that are used by the public that—

(A) specifies any waters described in this paragraph that are subject to a monitoring and notification program consistent with the performance criteria established under subsection (a) of this section; and

(B) specifies any waters described in this paragraph for which there is no monitoring and notification program (including waters for which fiscal constraints will prevent the State or the Administrator from performing monitoring and notification consistent with the performance criteria established under subsection (a) of this section).

(2) Availability

The Administrator shall make the list described in paragraph (1) available to the public through—

(A) publication in the Federal Register; and

(B) electronic media.

(3) Updates

The Administrator shall update the list described in paragraph (1) periodically as new information becomes available.

(h) EPA implementation

In the case of a State that has no program for monitoring and notification that is consistent with the performance criteria published under subsection (a) of this section after the last day of the 3-year period beginning on the date on which the Administrator lists waters in the State under subsection (g)(1)(B) of this section, the Administrator shall conduct a monitoring and notification program for the listed waters based on a priority ranking established by the Administrator using funds appropriated for grants under subsection (i) of this section—

(1) to conduct monitoring and notification; and

(2) for related salaries, expenses, and travel.

(i) Authorization of appropriations

There is authorized to be appropriated for making grants under subsection (b) of this section, including implementation of monitoring and notification programs by the Administrator under subsection (h) of this section, $30,000,000 for each of fiscal years 2001 through 2005.

(June 30, 1948, ch. 758, title IV, §406, as added Pub. L. 106–284, §4, Oct. 10, 2000, 114 Stat. 872.)

SUBCHAPTER V—GENERAL PROVISIONS

§1361. Administration

(a) Authority of Administrator to prescribe regulations

The Administrator is authorized to prescribe such regulations as are necessary to carry out his functions under this chapter.

(b) Utilization of other agency officers and employees

The Administrator, with the consent of the head of any other agency of the United States, may utilize such officers and employees of such agency as may be found necessary to assist in carrying out the purposes of this chapter.

(c) Recordkeeping

Each recipient of financial assistance under this chapter shall keep such records as the Administrator shall prescribe, including records which fully disclose the amount and disposition by such recipient of the proceeds of such assistance, the total cost of the project or undertaking in connection with which such assistance is given or used, and the amount of that portion of the cost of the project or undertaking supplied by other sources, and such other records as will facilitate effective audit.

(d) Audit

The Administrator and the Comptroller General of the United States, or any of their duly authorized representatives, shall have access, for the purpose of audit and examination, to any books, documents, papers, and records of the recipients that are pertinent to the grants received under this chapter. For the purpose of carrying out audits and examinations with respect to recipients of Federal assistance under this chapter, the Administrator is authorized to enter into noncompetitive procurement contracts with independent State audit organizations, consistent with chapter 75 of title 31. Such contracts may only be entered into to the extent and in such amounts as may be provided in advance in appropriation Acts.

(e) Awards for outstanding technological achievement or innovative processes, methods, or devices in waste treatment and pollution abatement programs

(1) It is the purpose of this subsection to authorize a program which will provide official recognition by the United States Government to those industrial organizations and political subdivisions of States which during the preceding year demonstrated an outstanding technological achievement or an innovative process, method, or device in their waste treatment and pollution abatement programs. The Administrator shall, in consultation with the appropriate State water pollution control agencies, establish regulations under which such recognition may be applied for and granted, except that no applicant shall be eligible for an award under this subsection if such applicant is not in total compliance with all applicable water quality requirements under this chapter, or otherwise does not have a satisfactory record with respect to environmental quality.

(2) The Administrator shall award a certificate or plaque of suitable design to each industrial organization or political subdivision which qualifies for such recognition under regulations established under this subsection.

(3) The President of the United States, the Governor of the appropriate State, the Speaker of the House of Representatives, and the President pro tempore of the Senate shall be notified of the award by the Administrator and the awarding of such recognition shall be published in the Federal Register.

(f) Detail of Environmental Protection Agency personnel to State water pollution control agencies

Upon the request of a State water pollution control agency, personnel of the Environmental Protection Agency may be detailed to such agency for the purpose of carrying out the provisions of this chapter.

(June 30, 1948, ch. 758, title V, §501, as added Pub. L. 92–500, §2, Oct. 18, 1972, 86 Stat. 885; amended Pub. L. 100–4, title V, §501, Feb. 4, 1987, 101 Stat. 75.)

AMENDMENTS

1987—Subsec. (d). Pub. L. 100–4 inserted provision at end authorizing Administrator to enter into noncompetitive procurement contracts with independent

State audit organizations, consistent with chapter 75 of title 31, but only to extent and in such amounts as provided in advance in appropriations Acts.

ENVIRONMENTAL COURT FEASIBILITY STUDY

Section 9 of Pub. L. 92–500 authorized the President, acting through the Attorney General, to study the feasibility of establishing a separate court or court system with jurisdiction over environmental matters and required him to report the results of his study, together with his recommendations, to Congress not later than one year after Oct. 18, 1972.

TRANSFER OF PUBLIC HEALTH SERVICE OFFICERS

Pub. L. 89–234, § 2(b)–(k), Oct. 2, 1965, 79 Stat. 904, 905, authorized the transfer of certain commissioned officers of the Public Health Service to classified positions in the Federal Water Pollution Control Administration, now the Environmental Protection Agency, where such transfer was requested within six months after the establishment of the Administration and made certain administrative provisions relating to pension and retirement rights of the transferees, sick leave benefits, group life insurance, and certain other miscellaneous provisions.

§ 1362. Definitions

Except as otherwise specifically provided, when used in this chapter:

(1) The term "State water pollution control agency" means the State agency designated by the Governor having responsibility for enforcing State laws relating to the abatement of pollution.

(2) The term "interstate agency" means an agency of two or more States established by or pursuant to an agreement or compact approved by the Congress, or any other agency of two or more States, having substantial powers or duties pertaining to the control of pollution as determined and approved by the Administrator.

(3) The term "State" means a State, the District of Columbia, the Commonwealth of Puerto Rico, the Virgin Islands, Guam, American Samoa, the Commonwealth of the Northern Mariana Islands, and the Trust Territory of the Pacific Islands.

(4) The term "municipality" means a city, town, borough, county, parish, district, association, or other public body created by or pursuant to State law and having jurisdiction over disposal of sewage, industrial wastes, or other wastes, or an Indian tribe or an authorized Indian tribal organization, or a designated and approved management agency under section 1288 of this title.

(5) The term "person" means an individual, corporation, partnership, association, State, municipality, commission, or political subdivision of a State, or any interstate body.

(6) The term "pollutant" means dredged spoil, solid waste, incinerator residue, sewage, garbage, sewage sludge, munitions, chemical wastes, biological materials, radioactive materials, heat, wrecked or discarded equipment, rock, sand, cellar dirt and industrial, municipal, and agricultural waste discharged into water. This term does not mean (A) "sewage from vessels or a discharge incidental to the normal operation of a vessel of the Armed Forces" within the meaning of section 1322 of this title; or (B) water, gas, or other material which is injected into a well to facilitate production of oil or gas, or water derived in association with oil or gas production and disposed of in a well, if the well used either to facilitate production or for disposal purposes is approved by authority of the State in which the well is located, and if such State determines that such injection or disposal will not result in the degradation of ground or surface water resources.

(7) The term "navigable waters" means the waters of the United States, including the territorial seas.

(8) The term "territorial seas" means the belt of the seas measured from the line of ordinary low water along that portion of the coast which is in direct contact with the open sea and the line marking the seaward limit of inland waters, and extending seaward a distance of three miles.

(9) The term "contiguous zone" means the entire zone established or to be established by the United States under article 24 of the Convention of the Territorial Sea and the Contiguous Zone.

(10) The term "ocean" means any portion of the high seas beyond the contiguous zone.

(11) The term "effluent limitation" means any restriction established by a State or the Administrator on quantities, rates, and concentrations of chemical, physical, biological, and other constituents which are discharged from point sources into navigable waters, the waters of the contiguous zone, or the ocean, including schedules of compliance.

(12) The term "discharge of a pollutant" and the term "discharge of pollutants" each means (A) any addition of any pollutant to navigable waters from any point source, (B) any addition of any pollutant to the waters of the contiguous zone or the ocean from any point source other than a vessel or other floating craft.

(13) The term "toxic pollutant" means those pollutants, or combinations of pollutants, including disease-causing agents, which after discharge and upon exposure, ingestion, inhalation or assimilation into any organism, either directly from the environment or indirectly by ingestion through food chains, will, on the basis of information available to the Administrator, cause death, disease, behavioral abnormalities, cancer, genetic mutations, physiological malfunctions (including malfunctions in reproduction) or physical deformations, in such organisms or their offspring.

(14) The term "point source" means any discernible, confined and discrete conveyance, including but not limited to any pipe, ditch, channel, tunnel, conduit, well, discrete fissure, container, rolling stock, concentrated animal feeding operation, or vessel or other floating craft, from which pollutants are or may be discharged. This term does not include agricultural stormwater discharges and return flows from irrigated agriculture.

(15) The term "biological monitoring" shall mean the determination of the effects on aquatic life, including accumulation of pollutants in tissue, in receiving waters due to the discharge of pollutants (A) by techniques and procedures, including sampling of organisms representative of appropriate levels of the food chain appropriate to the volume and the physical, chemical, and biological characteristics of the effluent, and (B) at appropriate frequencies and locations.

(16) The term "discharge" when used without qualification includes a discharge of a pollutant, and a discharge of pollutants.

(17) The term "schedule of compliance" means a schedule of remedial measures including an enforceable sequence of actions or operations leading to compliance with an effluent limitation, other limitation, prohibition, or standard.

(18) The term "industrial user" means those industries identified in the Standard Industrial Classification Manual, Bureau of the Budget, 1967, as amended and supplemented, under the category of "Division D—Manufacturing" and such other classes of significant waste producers as, by regulation, the Administrator deems appropriate.

(19) The term "pollution" means the man-made or man-induced alteration of the chemical, physical, biological, and radiological integrity of water.

(20) The term "medical waste" means isolation wastes; infectious agents; human blood and blood products; pathological wastes; sharps; body parts; contaminated bedding; surgical wastes and potentially contaminated laboratory wastes; dialysis wastes; and such additional medical items as the Administrator shall prescribe by regulation.

(21) COASTAL RECREATION WATERS.—

(A) IN GENERAL.—The term "coastal recreation waters" means—

(i) the Great Lakes; and

(ii) marine coastal waters (including coastal estuaries) that are designated under section 1313(c) of this title by a State for use for swimming, bathing, surfing, or similar water contact activities.

(B) EXCLUSIONS.—The term "coastal recreation waters" does not include—

(i) inland waters; or

(ii) waters upstream of the mouth of a river or stream having an unimpaired natural connection with the open sea.

(22) FLOATABLE MATERIAL.—

(A) IN GENERAL.—The term "floatable material" means any foreign matter that may float or remain suspended in the water column.

(B) INCLUSIONS.—The term "floatable material" includes—

(i) plastic;

(ii) aluminum cans;

(iii) wood products;

(iv) bottles; and

(v) paper products.

(23) PATHOGEN INDICATOR.—The term "pathogen indicator" means a substance that indicates the potential for human infectious disease.

(24) OIL AND GAS EXPLORATION AND PRODUCTION.—The term "oil and gas exploration, production, processing, or treatment operations or transmission facilities" means all field activities or operations associated with exploration, production, processing, or treatment operations, or transmission facilities, including activities necessary to prepare a site for drilling and for the movement and placement of drilling equipment, whether or not such field activities or operations may be considered to be construction activities.

(25) RECREATIONAL VESSEL.—

(A) IN GENERAL.—The term "recreational vessel" means any vessel that is—

(i) manufactured or used primarily for pleasure; or

(ii) leased, rented, or chartered to a person for the pleasure of that person.

(B) EXCLUSION.—The term "recreational vessel" does not include a vessel that is subject to Coast Guard inspection and that—

(i) is engaged in commercial use; or

(ii) carries paying passengers.

(June 30, 1948, ch. 758, title V, § 502, as added Pub. L. 92–500, § 2, Oct. 18, 1972, 86 Stat. 886; amended Pub. L. 95–217, § 33(b), Dec. 27, 1977, 91 Stat. 1577; Pub. L. 100–4, title V, §§ 502(a), 503, Feb. 4, 1987, 101 Stat. 75; Pub. L. 100–688, title III, § 3202(a), Nov. 18, 1988, 102 Stat. 4154; Pub. L. 104–106, div. A, title III, § 325(c)(3), Feb. 10, 1996, 110 Stat. 259; Pub. L. 106–284, § 5, Oct. 10, 2000, 114 Stat. 875; Pub. L. 109–58, title III, § 323, Aug. 8, 2005, 119 Stat. 694; Pub. L. 110–288, § 3, July 29, 2008, 122 Stat. 2650.)

AMENDMENTS

2008—Par. (25). Pub. L. 110–288 added par. (25).

2005—Par. (24). Pub. L. 109–58 added par. (24).

2000—Pars. (21) to (23). Pub. L. 106–284 added pars. (21) to (23).

1996—Par. (6)(A). Pub. L. 104–106 substituted "'sewage from vessels or a discharge incidental to the normal operation of a vessel of the Armed Forces'" for "'sewage from vessels'".

1988—Par. (20). Pub. L. 100–688 added par. (20).

1987—Par. (3). Pub. L. 100–4, § 502(a), inserted "the Commonwealth of the Northern Mariana Islands," after "Samoa,".

Par. (14). Pub. L. 100–4, § 503, inserted "agricultural stormwater discharges and" after "does not include".

1977—Par. (14). Pub. L. 95–217 inserted provision that "point source" does not include return flows from irrigated agriculture.

TERMINATION OF TRUST TERRITORY OF THE PACIFIC ISLANDS

For termination of Trust Territory of the Pacific Islands, see note set out preceding section 1681 of Title 48, Territories and Insular Possessions.

TERRITORIAL SEA AND CONTIGUOUS ZONE OF UNITED STATES

For extension of territorial sea and contiguous zone of United States, see Proc. No. 5928 and Proc. No. 7219, respectively, set out as notes under section 1331 of Title 43, Public Lands.

DEFINITION OF "POINT SOURCE"

Section 507 of Pub. L. 100–4 provided that: "For purposes of the Federal Water Pollution Control Act [33 U.S.C. 1251 et seq.], the term 'point source' includes a landfill leachate collection system."

§ 1363. Water Pollution Control Advisory Board

(a) Establishment; composition; terms of office

(1) There is hereby established in the Environmental Protection Agency a Water Pollution Control Advisory Board, composed of the Administrator or his designee, who shall be Chairman, and nine members appointed by the President, none of whom shall be Federal officers or employees. The appointed members, having due regard for the purposes of this chapter, shall be selected from among representatives of various State, interstate, and local governmental agen-

cies, of public or private interests contributing to, affected by, or concerned with pollution, and of other public and private agencies, organizations, or groups demonstrating an active interest in the field of pollution prevention and control, as well as other individuals who are expert in this field.

(2)(A) Each member appointed by the President shall hold office for a term of three years, except that (i) any member appointed to fill a vacancy occurring prior to the expiration of the term for which his predecessor was appointed shall be appointed for the remainder of such term, and (ii) the terms of office of the members first taking office after June 30, 1956, shall expire as follows: three at the end of one year after such date, three at the end of two years after such date, and three at the end of three years after such date, as designated by the President at the time of appointment, and (iii) the term of any member under the preceding provisions shall be extended until the date on which his successor's appointment is effective. None of the members appointed by the President shall be eligible for reappointment within one year after the end of his preceding term.

(B) The members of the Board who are not officers or employees of the United States, while attending conferences or meetings of the Board or while serving at the request of the Administrator, shall be entitled to receive compensation at a rate to be fixed by the Administrator, but not exceeding $100 per diem, including traveltime, and while away from their homes or regular places of business they may be allowed travel expenses, including per diem in lieu of subsistence, as authorized by law for persons in the Government service employed intermittently.

(b) Functions

The Board shall advise, consult with, and make recommendations to the Administrator on matters of policy relating to the activities and functions of the Administrator under this chapter.

(c) Clerical and technical assistance

Such clerical and technical assistance as may be necessary to discharge the duties of the Board shall be provided from the personnel of the Environmental Protection Agency.

(June 30, 1948, ch. 758, title V, §503, as added Pub. L. 92–500, §2, Oct. 18, 1972, 86 Stat. 887.)

REFERENCES IN TEXT

Travel expenses, including per diem in lieu of subsistence as authorized by law, referred to in subsec. (a)(2)(B), probably means the allowances authorized by section 5703 of Title 5, Government Organization and Employees.

CONTINUATION OF TERM OF OFFICE

Pub. L. 87–88, §6(c), July 20, 1961, 75 Stat. 207, provided that members of the Water Pollution Control Advisory Board holding office immediately preceding July 20, 1961 were to remain in office as members of the Board as established by section 6(a) of Pub. L. 87–88 until the expiration of the terms of office for which they were originally appointed.

TERMS OF OFFICE OF MEMBERS OF WATER POLLUTION CONTROL ADVISORY BOARD

Act July 9, 1956, ch. 518, §3, 70 Stat. 507, provided that the terms of office of members of the Water Pollution Control Advisory Board, holding office on July 9, 1956, were to terminate at the close of business on that date.

TERMINATION OF ADVISORY BOARDS

Advisory boards in existence on Jan. 5, 1973, to terminate not later than the expiration of the 2-year period following Jan. 5, 1973, unless, in the case of a board established by the President or an officer of the Federal Government, such board is renewed by appropriate action prior to the expiration of such 2-year period, or in the case of a board established by the Congress, its duration is otherwise provided for by law. See sections 3(2) and 14 of Pub. L. 92–463, Oct. 6, 1972, 86 Stat. 770, 776, set out in the Appendix to Title 5, Government Organization and Employees.

§1364. Emergency powers

(a) Emergency powers

Notwithstanding any other provision of this chapter, the Administrator upon receipt of evidence that a pollution source or combination of sources is presenting an imminent and substantial endangerment to the health of persons or to the welfare of persons where such endangerment is to the livelihood of such persons, such as inability to market shellfish, may bring suit on behalf of the United States in the appropriate district court to immediately restrain any person causing or contributing to the alleged pollution to stop the discharge of pollutants causing or contributing to such pollution or to take such other action as may be necessary.

(b) Repealed. Pub. L. 96–510, title III, §304(a), Dec. 11, 1980, 94 Stat. 2809

(June 30, 1948, ch. 758, title V, §504, as added Pub. L. 92–500, §2, Oct. 18, 1972, 86 Stat. 888; amended Pub. L. 95–217, §69, Dec. 27, 1977, 91 Stat. 1607; Pub. L. 96–510, title III, §304(a), Dec. 11, 1980, 94 Stat. 2809.)

AMENDMENTS

1980—Subsec. (b). Pub. L. 96–510 struck out subsec. (b) which related to emergency assistance, establishment of an emergency fund, and preparation of a contingency plan for such emergencies.

1977—Pub. L. 95–217 designated existing provisions as subsec. (a) and added subsec. (b).

EFFECTIVE DATE OF 1980 AMENDMENT

Amendment by Pub. L. 96–510 effective Dec. 11, 1980, see section 9652 of Title 42, The Public Health and Welfare.

§1365. Citizen suits

(a) Authorization; jurisdiction

Except as provided in subsection (b) of this section and section 1319(g)(6) of this title, any citizen may commence a civil action on his own behalf—

(1) against any person (including (i) the United States, and (ii) any other governmental instrumentality or agency to the extent permitted by the eleventh amendment to the Constitution) who is alleged to be in violation of (A) an effluent standard or limitation under this chapter or (B) an order issued by the Administrator or a State with respect to such a standard or limitation, or

(2) against the Administrator where there is alleged a failure of the Administrator to perform any act or duty under this chapter which is not discretionary with the Administrator.

The district courts shall have jurisdiction, without regard to the amount in controversy or the citizenship of the parties, to enforce such an effluent standard or limitation, or such an order, or to order the Administrator to perform such act or duty, as the case may be, and to apply any appropriate civil penalties under section 1319(d) of this title.

(b) Notice

No action may be commenced—

(1) under subsection (a)(1) of this section—

(A) prior to sixty days after the plaintiff has given notice of the alleged violation (i) to the Administrator, (ii) to the State in which the alleged violation occurs, and (iii) to any alleged violator of the standard, limitation, or order, or

(B) if the Administrator or State has commenced and is diligently prosecuting a civil or criminal action in a court of the United States, or a State to require compliance with the standard, limitation, or order, but in any such action in a court of the United States any citizen may intervene as a matter of right.

(2) under subsection (a)(2) of this section prior to sixty days after the plaintiff has given notice of such action to the Administrator,

except that such action may be brought immediately after such notification in the case of an action under this section respecting a violation of sections 1316 and 1317(a) of this title. Notice under this subsection shall be given in such manner as the Administrator shall prescribe by regulation.

(c) Venue; intervention by Administrator; United States interests protected

(1) Any action respecting a violation by a discharge source of an effluent standard or limitation or an order respecting such standard or limitation may be brought under this section only in the judicial district in which such source is located.

(2) In such action under this section, the Administrator, if not a party, may intervene as a matter of right.

(3) PROTECTION OF INTERESTS OF UNITED STATES.—Whenever any action is brought under this section in a court of the United States, the plaintiff shall serve a copy of the complaint on the Attorney General and the Administrator. No consent judgment shall be entered in an action in which the United States is not a party prior to 45 days following the receipt of a copy of the proposed consent judgment by the Attorney General and the Administrator.

(d) Litigation costs

The court, in issuing any final order in any action brought pursuant to this section, may award costs of litigation (including reasonable attorney and expert witness fees) to any prevailing or substantially prevailing party, whenever the court determines such award is appropriate. The court may, if a temporary restraining order or preliminary injunction is sought, require the filing of a bond or equivalent security in accordance with the Federal Rules of Civil Procedure.

(e) Statutory or common law rights not restricted

Nothing in this section shall restrict any right which any person (or class of persons) may have under any statute or common law to seek enforcement of any effluent standard or limitation or to seek any other relief (including relief against the Administrator or a State agency).

(f) Effluent standard or limitation

For purposes of this section, the term "effluent standard or limitation under this chapter" means (1) effective July 1, 1973, an unlawful act under subsection (a) of section 1311 of this title; (2) an effluent limitation or other limitation under section 1311 or 1312 of this title; (3) standard of performance under section 1316 of this title; (4) prohibition, effluent standard or pretreatment standards under section 1317 of this title; (5) certification under section 1341 of this title; (6) a permit or condition thereof issued under section 1342 of this title, which is in effect under this chapter (including a requirement applicable by reason of section 1323 of this title); or (7) a regulation under section 1345(d) of this title,.[1]

(g) "Citizen" defined

For the purposes of this section the term "citizen" means a person or persons having an interest which is or may be adversely affected.

(h) Civil action by State Governors

A Governor of a State may commence a civil action under subsection (a) of this section, without regard to the limitations of subsection (b) of this section, against the Administrator where there is alleged a failure of the Administrator to enforce an effluent standard or limitation under this chapter the violation of which is occurring in another State and is causing an adverse effect on the public health or welfare in his State, or is causing a violation of any water quality requirement in his State.

(June 30, 1948, ch. 758, title V, §505, as added Pub. L. 92–500, §2, Oct. 18, 1972, 86 Stat. 888; amended Pub. L. 100–4, title III, §314(c), title IV, §406(d)(2), title V, §§504, 505(c), Feb. 4, 1987, 101 Stat. 49, 73, 75, 76.)

REFERENCES IN TEXT

The Federal Rules of Civil Procedure, referred to in subsec. (d), are set out in the Appendix to Title 28, Judiciary and Judicial Procedure.

AMENDMENTS

1987—Subsec. (a). Pub. L. 100–4, §314(c), inserted "and section 1319(g)(6) of this title" after "subsection (b) of this section" in introductory text.

Subsec. (c)(3). Pub. L. 100–4, §504, added par. (3).

Subsec. (d). Pub. L. 100–4, §505(c), inserted "prevailing or substantially prevailing" before "party".

Subsec. (f). Pub. L. 100–4, §406(d)(2), added cl. (7).

§1366. Appearance

The Administrator shall request the Attorney General to appear and represent the United States in any civil or criminal action instituted under this chapter to which the Administrator is a party. Unless the Attorney General notifies

[1] So in original.

the Administrator within a reasonable time, that he will appear in a civil action, attorneys who are officers or employees of the Environmental Protection Agency shall appear and represent the United States in such action.

(June 30, 1948, ch. 758, title V, § 506, as added Pub. L. 92–500, § 2, Oct. 18, 1972, 86 Stat. 889.)

§ 1367. Employee protection

(a) Discrimination against persons filing, instituting, or testifying in proceedings under this chapter prohibited

No person shall fire, or in any other way discriminate against, or cause to be fired or discriminated against, any employee or any authorized representative of employees by reason of the fact that such employee or representative has filed, instituted, or caused to be filed or instituted any proceeding under this chapter, or has testified or is about to testify in any proceeding resulting from the administration or enforcement of the provisions of this chapter.

(b) Application for review; investigation; hearing; review

Any employee or a representative of employees who believes that he has been fired or otherwise discriminated against by any person in violation of subsection (a) of this section may, within thirty days after such alleged violation occurs, apply to the Secretary of Labor for a review of such firing or alleged discrimination. A copy of the application shall be sent to such person who shall be the respondent. Upon receipt of such application, the Secretary of Labor shall cause such investigation to be made as he deems appropriate. Such investigation shall provide an opportunity for a public hearing at the request of any party to such review to enable the parties to present information relating to such alleged violation. The parties shall be given written notice of the time and place of the hearing at least five days prior to the hearing. Any such hearing shall be of record and shall be subject to section 554 of title 5. Upon receiving the report of such investigation, the Secretary of Labor shall make findings of fact. If he finds that such violation did occur, he shall issue a decision, incorporating an order therein and his findings, requiring the party committing such violation to take such affirmative action to abate the violation as the Secretary of Labor deems appropriate, including, but not limited to, the rehiring or reinstatement of the employee or representative of employees to his former position with compensation. If he finds that there was no such violation, he shall issue an order denying the application. Such order issued by the Secretary of Labor under this subparagraph shall be subject to judicial review in the same manner as orders and decisions of the Administrator are subject to judicial review under this chapter.

(c) Costs and expenses

Whenever an order is issued under this section to abate such violation, at the request of the applicant, a sum equal to the aggregate amount of all costs and expenses (including the attorney's fees), as determined by the Secretary of Labor, to have been reasonably incurred by the applicant for, or in connection with, the institution and prosecution of such proceedings, shall be assessed against the person committing such violation.

(d) Deliberate violations by employee acting without direction from his employer or his agent

This section shall have no application to any employee who, acting without direction from his employer (or his agent) deliberately violates any prohibition of effluent limitation or other limitation under section 1311 or 1312 of this title, standards of performance under section 1316 of this title, effluent standard, prohibition or pretreatment standard under section 1317 of this title, or any other prohibition or limitation established under this chapter.

(e) Investigations of employment reductions

The Administrator shall conduct continuing evaluations of potential loss or shifts of employment which may result from the issuance of any effluent limitation or order under this chapter, including, where appropriate, investigating threatened plant closures or reductions in employment allegedly resulting from such limitation or order. Any employee who is discharged or laid-off, threatened with discharge or lay-off, or otherwise discriminated against by any person because of the alleged results of any effluent limitation or order issued under this chapter, or any representative of such employee, may request the Administrator to conduct a full investigation of the matter. The Administrator shall thereupon investigate the matter and, at the request of any party, shall hold public hearings on not less than five days notice, and shall at such hearings require the parties, including the employer involved, to present information relating to the actual or potential effect of such limitation or order on employment and on any alleged discharge, lay-off, or other discrimination and the detailed reasons or justification therefor. Any such hearing shall be of record and shall be subject to section 554 of title 5. Upon receiving the report of such investigation, the Administrator shall make findings of fact as to the effect of such effluent limitation or order on employment and on the alleged discharge, lay-off, or discrimination and shall make such recommendations as he deems appropriate. Such report, findings, and recommendations shall be available to the public. Nothing in this subsection shall be construed to require or authorize the Administrator to modify or withdraw any effluent limitation or order issued under this chapter.

(June 30, 1948, ch. 758, title V, § 507, as added Pub. L. 92–500, § 2, Oct. 18, 1972, 86 Stat. 890.)

§ 1368. Federal procurement

(a) Contracts with violators prohibited

No Federal agency may enter into any contract with any person, who has been convicted of any offense under section 1319(c) of this title, for the procurement of goods, materials, and services if such contract is to be performed at any facility at which the violation which gave rise to such conviction occurred, and if such facility is owned, leased, or supervised by such person. The prohibition in the preceding sentence shall continue until the Administrator certifies that the condition giving rise to such conviction has been corrected.

(b) Notification of agencies

The Administrator shall establish procedures to provide all Federal agencies with the notification necessary for the purposes of subsection (a) of this section.

(c) Omitted

(d) Exemptions

The President may exempt any contract, loan, or grant from all or part of the provisions of this section where he determines such exemption is necessary in the paramount interest of the United States and he shall notify the Congress of such exemption.

(e) Annual report to Congress

The President shall annually report to the Congress on measures taken in compliance with the purpose and intent of this section, including, but not limited to, the progress and problems associated with such compliance.

(f) Contractor certification or contract clause in acquisition of commercial items

(1) No certification by a contractor, and no contract clause, may be required in the case of a contract for the acquisition of commercial items in order to implement a prohibition or requirement of this section or a prohibition or requirement issued in the implementation of this section.

(2) In paragraph (1), the term "commercial item" has the meaning given such term in section 403(12) of title 41.

(June 30, 1948, ch. 758, title V, §508, as added Pub. L. 92–500, §2, Oct. 18, 1972, 86 Stat. 891; amended Pub. L. 103–355, title VIII, §8301(a), Oct. 13, 1994, 108 Stat. 3396.)

CODIFICATION

Subsec. (c) of this section authorized the President to cause to be issued, not more than 180 days after October 18, 1972, an order (1) requiring each Federal agency authorized to enter into contracts or to extend Federal assistance by way of grant, loan, or contract, to effectuate the purpose and policy of this chapter, and (2) setting forth procedures, sanctions and penalties as the President determines necessary to carry out such requirement.

AMENDMENTS

1994—Subsec. (f). Pub. L. 103–355 added subsec. (f).

EFFECTIVE DATE OF 1994 AMENDMENT

For effective date and applicability of amendment by Pub. L. 103–355, see section 10001 of Pub. L. 103–355, set out as a note under section 251 of Title 41, Public Contracts.

ADMINISTRATION OF CHAPTER WITH RESPECT TO FEDERAL CONTRACTS, GRANTS, OR LOANS

For provisions concerning the administration of this chapter with respect to Federal contracts, grants, or loans, see Ex. Ord. No. 11738, Sept. 10, 1973, 38 F.R. 25161, set out as a note under section 7606 of Title 42, The Public Health and Welfare.

§1369. Administrative procedure and judicial review

(a) Subpenas

(1) For purposes of obtaining information under section 1315 of this title, or carrying out section 1367(e) of this title, the Administrator may issue subpenas for the attendance and testimony of witnesses and the production of relevant papers, books, and documents, and he may administer oaths. Except for effluent data, upon a showing satisfactory to the Administrator that such papers, books, documents, or information or particular part thereof, if made public, would divulge trade secrets or secret processes, the Administrator shall consider such record, report, or information or particular portion thereof confidential in accordance with the purposes of section 1905 of title 18, except that such paper, book, document, or information may be disclosed to other officers, employees, or authorized representatives of the United States concerned with carrying out this chapter, or when relevant in any proceeding under this chapter. Witnesses summoned shall be paid the same fees and mileage that are paid witnesses in the courts of the United States. In case of contumacy or refusal to obey a subpena served upon any person under this subsection, the district court of the United States for any district in which such person is found or resides or transacts business, upon application by the United States and after notice to such person, shall have jurisdiction to issue an order requiring such person to appear and give testimony before the Administrator, to appear and produce papers, books, and documents before the Administrator, or both, and any failure to obey such order of the court may be punished by such court as a contempt thereof.

(2) The district courts of the United States are authorized, upon application by the Administrator, to issue subpenas for attendance and testimony of witnesses and the production of relevant papers, books, and documents, for purposes of obtaining information under sections 1314(b) and (c) of this title. Any papers, books, documents, or other information or part thereof, obtained by reason of such a subpena shall be subject to the same requirements as are provided in paragraph (1) of this subsection.

(b) Review of Administrator's actions; selection of court; fees

(1) Review of the Administrator's action (A) in promulgating any standard of performance under section 1316 of this title, (B) in making any determination pursuant to section 1316(b)(1)(C) of this title, (C) in promulgating any effluent standard, prohibition, or pretreatment standard under section 1317 of this title, (D) in making any determination as to a State permit program submitted under section 1342(b) of this title, (E) in approving or promulgating any effluent limitation or other limitation under section 1311, 1312, 1316, or 1345 of this title, (F) in issuing or denying any permit under section 1342 of this title, and (G) in promulgating any individual control strategy under section 1314(*l*) of this title, may be had by any interested person in the Circuit Court of Appeals of the United States for the Federal judicial district in which such person resides or transacts business which is directly affected by such action upon application by such person. Any such application shall be made within 120 days from the date of such determination, approval, pro-

mulgation, issuance or denial, or after such date only if such application is based solely on grounds which arose after such 120th day.

(2) Action of the Administrator with respect to which review could have been obtained under paragraph (1) of this subsection shall not be subject to judicial review in any civil or criminal proceeding for enforcement.

(3) AWARD OF FEES.—In any judicial proceeding under this subsection, the court may award costs of litigation (including reasonable attorney and expert witness fees) to any prevailing or substantially prevailing party whenever it determines that such award is appropriate.

(c) Additional evidence

In any judicial proceeding brought under subsection (b) of this section in which review is sought of a determination under this chapter required to be made on the record after notice and opportunity for hearing, if any party applies to the court for leave to adduce additional evidence, and shows to the satisfaction of the court that such additional evidence is material and that there were reasonable grounds for the failure to adduce such evidence in the proceeding before the Administrator, the court may order such additional evidence (and evidence in rebuttal thereof) to be taken before the Administrator, in such manner and upon such terms and conditions as the court may deem proper. The Administrator may modify his findings as to the facts, or make new findings, by reason of the additional evidence so taken and he shall file such modified or new findings, and his recommendation, if any, for the modification or setting aside of his original determination, with the return of such additional evidence.

(June 30, 1948, ch. 758, title V, § 509, as added Pub. L. 92–500, § 2, Oct. 18, 1972, 86 Stat. 891; amended Pub. L. 93–207, § 1(6), Dec. 28, 1973, 87 Stat. 906; Pub. L. 100–4, title III, § 308(b), title IV, § 406(d)(3), title V, § 505(a), (b), Feb. 4, 1987, 101 Stat. 39, 73, 75; Pub. L. 100–236, § 2, Jan. 8, 1988, 101 Stat. 1732.)

AMENDMENTS

1988—Subsec. (b)(3), (4). Pub. L. 100–236 redesignated par. (4) as (3) and struck out former par. (3) relating to venue, which provided for selection procedure in subpar. (A), administrative provisions in subpar. (B), and transfers in subpar. (C).

1987—Subsec. (b)(1). Pub. L. 100–4, §§ 308(b), 406(d)(3), 505(a), substituted "transacts business which is directly affected by such action" for "transacts such business", "120" for "ninety", and "120th" for "ninetieth", substituted "1316, or 1345 of this title" for "or 1316 of this title" in cl. (E), and added cl. (G).

Subsec. (b)(3), (4). Pub. L. 100–4, § 505(b), added pars. (3) and (4).

1973—Subsec. (b)(1)(C). Pub. L. 93–207 substituted "pretreatment" for "treatment".

EFFECTIVE DATE OF 1988 AMENDMENT

Amendment by Pub. L. 100–236 effective 180 days after Jan. 8, 1988, see section 3 of Pub. L. 100–236, set out as a note under section 2112 of Title 28, Judiciary and Judicial Procedure.

§ 1370. State authority

Except as expressly provided in this chapter, nothing in this chapter shall (1) preclude or deny the right of any State or political subdivision thereof or interstate agency to adopt or enforce (A) any standard or limitation respecting discharges of pollutants, or (B) any requirement respecting control or abatement of pollution; except that if an effluent limitation, or other limitation, effluent standard, prohibition, pretreatment standard, or standard of performance is in effect under this chapter, such State or political subdivision or interstate agency may not adopt or enforce any effluent limitation, or other limitation, effluent standard, prohibition, pretreatment standard, or standard of performance which is less stringent than the effluent limitation, or other limitation, effluent standard, prohibition, pretreatment standard, or standard of performance under this chapter; or (2) be construed as impairing or in any manner affecting any right or jurisdiction of the States with respect to the waters (including boundary waters) of such States.

(June 30, 1948, ch. 758, title V, § 510, as added Pub. L. 92–500, § 2, Oct. 18, 1972, 86 Stat. 893.)

§ 1371. Authority under other laws and regulations

(a) Impairment of authority or functions of officials and agencies; treaty provisions

This chapter shall not be construed as (1) limiting the authority or functions of any officer or agency of the United States under any other law or regulation not inconsistent with this chapter; (2) affecting or impairing the authority of the Secretary of the Army (A) to maintain navigation or (B) under the Act of March 3, 1899, (30 Stat. 1112); except that any permit issued under section 1344 of this title shall be conclusive as to the effect on water quality of any discharge resulting from any activity subject to section 403 of this title, or (3) affecting or impairing the provisions of any treaty of the United States.

(b) Discharges of pollutants into navigable waters

Discharges of pollutants into the navigable waters subject to the Rivers and Harbors Act of 1910 (36 Stat. 593; 33 U.S.C. 421) and the Supervisory Harbors Act of 1888 (25 Stat. 209; 33 U.S.C. 441–451b) shall be regulated pursuant to this chapter, and not subject to such Act of 1910 and the Act of 1888 except as to effect on navigation and anchorage.

(c) Action of the Administrator deemed major Federal action; construction of the National Environmental Policy Act of 1969

(1) Except for the provision of Federal financial assistance for the purpose of assisting the construction of publicly owned treatment works as authorized by section 1281 of this title, and the issuance of a permit under section 1342 of this title for the discharge of any pollutant by a new source as defined in section 1316 of this title, no action of the Administrator taken pursuant to this chapter shall be deemed a major Federal action significantly affecting the quality of the human environment within the meaning of the National Environmental Policy Act of 1969 (83 Stat. 852) [42 U.S.C. 4321 et seq.]; and

(2) Nothing in the National Environmental Policy Act of 1969 (83 Stat. 852) shall be deemed to—

(A) authorize any Federal agency authorized to license or permit the conduct of any activity which may result in the discharge of a pollutant into the navigable waters to review any effluent limitation or other requirement established pursuant to this chapter or the adequacy of any certification under section 1341 of this title; or

(B) authorize any such agency to impose, as a condition precedent to the issuance of any license or permit, any effluent limitation other than any such limitation established pursuant to this chapter.

(d) Consideration of international water pollution control agreements

Notwithstanding this chapter or any other provision of law, the Administrator (1) shall not require any State to consider in the development of the ranking in order of priority of needs for the construction of treatment works (as defined in subchapter II of this chapter), any water pollution control agreement which may have been entered into between the United States and any other nation, and (2) shall not consider any such agreement in the approval of any such priority ranking.

(June 30, 1948, ch. 758, title V, §511, as added Pub. L. 92–500, §2, Oct. 18, 1972, 86 Stat. 893; amended Pub. L. 93–243, §3, Jan. 2, 1974, 87 Stat. 1069.)

REFERENCES IN TEXT

Act of March 3, 1899, referred to in subsec. (a), is act Mar. 3, 1899, ch. 425, 30 Stat. 1121, as amended, which enacted sections 401, 403, 404, 406, 407, 408, 409, 411 to 416, 418, 502, 549, and 687 of this title and amended section 686 of this title. For complete classification of this Act to the Code, see Tables.

The Rivers and Harbors Act of 1910, referred to in subsec. (b), probably means act June 23, 1910, ch. 359, 36 Stat. 593.

The Supervisory Harbors Act of 1888, referred to in subsec. (b), probably means act June 29, 1888, ch. 496, 25 Stat. 209, as amended, which is classified generally to subchapter III (§441 et seq.) of chapter 9 of this title. For complete classification of this Act to the Code, see Tables.

The National Environmental Policy Act of 1969, referred to in subsec. (c), is Pub. L. 91–190, Jan. 1, 1970, 83 Stat. 852, as amended, which is classified generally to chapter 55 (§4321 et seq.) of Title 42, The Public Health and Welfare. For complete classification of this Act to the Code, see Short Title note set out under section 4321 of Title 42 and Tables.

AMENDMENTS

1974—Subsec. (d). Pub. L. 93–243 added subsec. (d).

§1372. Labor standards

The Administrator shall take such action as may be necessary to insure that all laborers and mechanics employed by contractors or subcontractors on treatment works for which grants are made under this chapter shall be paid wages at rates not less than those prevailing for the same type of work on similar construction in the immediate locality, as determined by the Secretary of Labor, in accordance with sections 3141–3144, 3146, and 3147 of title 40. The Secretary of Labor shall have, with respect to the labor standards specified in this subsection,[1] the authority and functions set forth in Reorganization Plan Numbered 14 of 1950 (15 F.R. 3176) and section 3145 of title 40.

(June 30, 1948, ch. 758, title V, §513, as added Pub. L. 92–500, §2, Oct. 18, 1972, 86 Stat. 894.)

REFERENCES IN TEXT

Reorganization Plan Numbered 14 of 1950, referred to in text, is Reorg. Plan No. 14 of 1950, eff. May 24, 1950, 15 F.R. 3176, 64 Stat. 1267, which is set out in the Appendix to Title 5, Government Organization and Employees.

CODIFICATION

In text, "sections 3141–3144, 3146, and 3147 of title 40" substituted for "the Act of March 3, 1931, as amended, known as the Davis-Bacon Act (46 Stat. 1494; 40 U.S.C., sec. 276a through 276a–5)" and "section 3145 of title 40" substituted for "section 2 of the Act of June 13, 1934, as amended (48 Stat. 948; 40 U.S.C. 276c)" on authority of Pub. L. 107–217, §5(c), Aug. 21, 2002, 116 Stat. 1303, the first section of which enacted Title 40, Public Buildings, Property, and Works.

§1373. Public health agency coordination

The permitting agency under section 1342 of this title shall assist the applicant for a permit under such section in coordinating the requirements of this chapter with those of the appropriate public health agencies.

(June 30, 1948, ch. 758, title V, §514, as added Pub. L. 92–500, §2, Oct. 18, 1972, 86 Stat. 894.)

§1374. Effluent Standards and Water Quality Information Advisory Committee

(a) Establishment; membership; term

(1) There is established an Effluent Standards and Water Quality Information Advisory Committee, which shall be composed of a Chairman and eight members who shall be appointed by the Administrator within sixty days after October 18, 1972.

(2) All members of the Committee shall be selected from the scientific community, qualified by education, training, and experience to provide, assess, and evaluate scientific and technical information on effluent standards and limitations.

(3) Members of the Committee shall serve for a term of four years, and may be reappointed.

(b) Action on proposed regulations

(1) No later than one hundred and eighty days prior to the date on which the Administrator is required to publish any proposed regulations required by section 1314(b) of this title, any proposed standard of performance for new sources required by section 1316 of this title, or any proposed toxic effluent standard required by section 1317 of this title, he shall transmit to the Committee a notice of intent to propose such regulations. The Chairman of the Committee within ten days after receipt of such notice may publish a notice of a public hearing by the Committee, to be held within thirty days.

(2) No later than one hundred and twenty days after receipt of such notice, the Committee shall transmit to the Administrator such scientific and technical information as is in its possession, including that presented at any public hearing, related to the subject matter contained in such notice.

[1] So in original. Probably should be "section,".

(3) Information so transmitted to the Administrator shall constitute a part of the administrative record and comments on any proposed regulations or standards as information to be considered with other comments and information in making any final determinations.

(4) In preparing information for transmittal, the Committee shall avail itself of the technical and scientific services of any Federal agency, including the United States Geological Survey and any national environmental laboratories which may be established.

(c) Secretary; legal counsel; compensation

(1) The Committee shall appoint and prescribe the duties of a Secretary, and such legal counsel as it deems necessary. The Committee shall appoint such other employees as it deems necessary to exercise and fulfill its powers and responsibilities. The compensation of all employees appointed by the Committee shall be fixed in accordance with chapter 51 and subchapter III of chapter 53 of title 5.

(2) Members of the Committee shall be entitled to receive compensation at a rate to be fixed by the President but not in excess of the maximum rate of pay for grade GS–18, as provided in the General Schedule under section 5332 of title 5.

(d) Quorum; special panel

Five members of the Committee shall constitute a quorum, and official actions of the Committee shall be taken only on the affirmative vote of at least five members. A special panel composed of one or more members upon order of the Committee shall conduct any hearing authorized by this section and submit the transcript of such hearing to the entire Committee for its action thereon.

(e) Rules

The Committee is authorized to make such rules as are necessary for the orderly transaction of its business.

(June 30, 1948, ch. 758, title V, § 515, as added Pub. L. 92–500, § 2, Oct. 18, 1972, 86 Stat. 894.)

TERMINATION OF ADVISORY COMMITTEES

Advisory committees in existence on Jan. 5, 1973, to terminate not later than the expiration of the 2-year period following Jan. 5, 1973, unless, in the case of a committee established by the President or an officer of the Federal Government, such committee is renewed by appropriate action prior to the expiration of such 2-year period, or in the case of a committee established by the Congress, its duration is otherwise provided by law. See section 14 of Pub. L. 92–463, Oct. 6, 1972, 86 Stat. 776, set out in the Appendix to Title 5, Government Organization and Employees.

REFERENCES IN OTHER LAWS TO GS–16, 17, OR 18 PAY RATES

References in laws to the rates of pay for GS–16, 17, or 18, or to maximum rates of pay under the General Schedule, to be considered references to rates payable under specified sections of Title 5, Government Organization and Employees, see section 529 [title I, § 101(c)(1)] of Pub. L. 101–509, set out in a note under section 5376 of Title 5.

§ 1375. Reports to Congress; detailed estimates and comprehensive study on costs; State estimates

(a) Implementation of chapter objectives; status and progress of programs

Within ninety days following the convening of each session of Congress, the Administrator shall submit to the Congress a report, in addition to any other report required by this chapter, on measures taken toward implementing the objective of this chapter, including, but not limited to, (1) the progress and problems associated with developing comprehensive plans under section 1252 of this title, areawide plans under section 1288 of this title, basin plans under section 1289 of this title, and plans under section 1313(e) of this title; (2) a summary of actions taken and results achieved in the field of water pollution control research, experiments, studies, and related matters by the Administrator and other Federal agencies and by other persons and agencies under Federal grants or contracts; (3) the progress and problems associated with the development of effluent limitations and recommended control techniques; (4) the status of State programs,including a detailed summary of the progress obtained as compared to that planned under State program plans for development and enforcement of water quality requirements; (5) the identification and status of enforcement actions pending or completed under this chapter during the preceding year; (6) the status of State, interstate, and local pollution control programs established pursuant to, and assisted by, this chapter; (7) a summary of the results of the survey required to be taken under section 1290 of this title; (8) his activities including recommendations under sections 1259 through 1261 of this title; and (9) all reports and recommendations made by the Water Pollution Control Advisory Board.

(b) Detailed estimates and comprehensive study on costs; State estimates, survey form

(1) The Administrator, in cooperation with the States, including water pollution control agencies and other water pollution control planning agencies, shall make (A) a detailed estimate of the cost of carrying out the provisions of this chapter; (B) a detailed estimate, biennially revised, of the cost of construction of all needed publicly owned treatment works in all of the States and of the cost of construction of all needed publicly owned treatment works in each of the States; (C) a comprehensive study of the economic impact on affected units of government of the cost of installation of treatment facilities; and (D) a comprehensive analysis of the national requirements for and the cost of treating municipal, industrial, and other effluent to attain the water quality objectives as established by this chapter or applicable State law. The Administrator shall submit such detailed estimate and such comprehensive study of such cost to the Congress no later than February 10 of each odd-numbered year. Whenever the Administrator, pursuant to this subsection, requests and receives an estimate of cost from a State, he shall furnish copies of such estimate together with such detailed estimate to Congress.

(2) Notwithstanding the second sentence of paragraph (1) of this subsection, the Administrator shall make a preliminary detailed estimate called for by subparagraph (B) of such paragraph and shall submit such preliminary detailed estimate to the Congress no later than September 3, 1974. The Administrator shall require each State to prepare an estimate of cost for such State, and shall utilize the survey form EPA–1, O.M.B. No. 158–R0017, prepared for the 1973 detailed estimate, except that such estimate shall include all costs of compliance with section 1281(g)(2)(A) of this title and water quality standards established pursuant to section 1313 of this title, and all costs of treatment works as defined in section 1292(2) of this title, including all eligible costs of constructing sewage collection systems and correcting excessive infiltration or inflow and all eligible costs of correcting combined storm and sanitary sewer problems and treating storm water flows. The survey form shall be distributed by the Administrator to each State no later than January 31, 1974.

(c) Status of combined sewer overflows in municipal treatment works operations

The Administrator shall submit to the Congress by October 1, 1978, a report on the status of combined sewer overflows in municipal treatment works operations. The report shall include (1) the status of any projects funded under this chapter to address combined sewer overflows (2) a listing by State of combined sewer overflow needs identified in the 1977 State priority listings, (3) an estimate for each applicable municipality of the number of years necessary, assuming an annual authorization and appropriation for the construction grants program of $5,000,000,000, to correct combined sewer overflow problems, (4) an analysis using representative municipalities faced with major combined sewer overflow needs, of the annual discharges of pollutants from overflows in comparison to treated effluent discharges, (5) an analysis of the technological alternatives available to municipalities to correct major combined sewer overflow problems, and (6) any recommendations of the Administrator for legislation to address the problem of combined sewer overflows, including whether a separate authorization and grant program should be established by the Congress to address combined sewer overflows.

(d) Legislative recommendations on program requiring coordination between water supply and wastewater control plans as condition for construction grants; public hearing

The Administrator, in cooperation with the States, including water pollution control agencies, and other water pollution control planning agencies, and water supply and water resources agencies of the States and the United States shall submit to Congress, within two years of December 27, 1977, a report with recommendations for legislation on a program to require coordination between water supply and wastewater control plans as a condition to grants for construction of treatment works under this chapter. No such report shall be submitted except after opportunity for public hearings on such proposed report.

(e) State revolving fund report

(1) In general

Not later than February 10, 1990, the Administrator shall submit to Congress a report on the financial status and operations of water pollution control revolving funds established by the States under subchapter VI of this chapter. The Administrator shall prepare such report in cooperation with the States, including water pollution control agencies and other water pollution control planning and financing agencies.

(2) Contents

The report under this subsection shall also include the following:

(A) an inventory of the facilities that are in significant noncompliance with the enforceable requirements of this chapter;

(B) an estimate of the cost of construction necessary to bring such facilities into compliance with such requirements;

(C) an assessment of the availability of sources of funds for financing such needed construction, including an estimate of the amount of funds available for providing assistance for such construction through September 30, 1999, from the water pollution control revolving funds established by the States under subchapter VI of this chapter;

(D) an assessment of the operations, loan portfolio, and loan conditions of such revolving funds;

(E) an assessment of the effect on user charges of the assistance provided by such revolving funds compared to the assistance provided with funds appropriated pursuant to section 1287 of this title; and

(F) an assessment of the efficiency of the operation and maintenance of treatment works constructed with assistance provided by such revolving funds compared to the efficiency of the operation and maintenance of treatment works constructed with assistance provided under section 1281 of this title.

(June 30, 1948, ch. 758, title V, §516, as added Pub. L. 92–500, §2, Oct. 18, 1972, 86 Stat. 895; amended Pub. L. 93–243, §4, Jan. 2, 1974, 87 Stat. 1069; Pub. L. 95–217, §§70–72, Dec. 27, 1977, 91 Stat. 1608, 1609; Pub. L. 100–4, title II, §212(c), Feb. 4, 1987, 101 Stat. 27; Pub. L. 104–66, title II, §2021(d), Dec. 21, 1995, 109 Stat. 727; Pub. L. 105–362, title V, §501(d)(1), Nov. 10, 1998, 112 Stat. 3283; Pub. L. 107–303, title III, §302(b)(1), Nov. 27, 2002, 116 Stat. 2361.)

AMENDMENTS

2002—Subsecs. (a) to (e). Pub. L. 107–303 repealed Pub. L. 105–362, §501(d)(1). See 1998 Amendment notes below.

1998—Subsec. (a). Pub. L. 105–362, §501(d)(1)(A), which directed the striking out of subsec. (a), was repealed by Pub. L. 107–303. See Effective Date of 2002 Amendment note below.

Subsec. (b). Pub. L. 105–362, §501(d), which directed the striking out of par. (1) designation, redesignation of subpars. (A) to (D) as pars. (1) to (4), respectively, and striking out of par. (2), was repealed by Pub. L. 107–303. See Effective Date of 2002 Amendment note below.

Subsecs. (c) to (e). Pub. L. 105–362, §501(d)(1)(A), which directed the striking out of subsecs. (c) to (e), was repealed by Pub. L. 107–303. See Effective Date of 2002 Amendment note below.

1995—Subsecs. (d), (e), (g). Pub. L. 104–66 redesignated subsecs. (e) and (g) as (d) and (e), respectively, and struck out former subsec. (d) which related to status reports on the use of municipal secondary effluent and sludge for agricultural and other purposes that utilize the nutrient value of treated wastewater effluent.

1987—Subsec. (g). Pub. L. 100–4 added subsec. (g).

1977—Subsecs. (c) to (e). Pub. L. 95–217 added subsecs. (c) to (e).

1974—Subsec. (b). Pub. L. 93–243 designated existing paragraph as par. (1) and cls. (1) to (4) as (A) to (D), and added par. (2).

EFFECTIVE DATE OF 2002 AMENDMENT

Amendment by Pub. L. 107–303 effective Nov. 10, 1998, and Federal Water Pollution Act (33 U.S.C. 1251 et seq.) to be applied and administered on and after Nov. 27, 2002, as if amendments made by section 501(a)–(d) of Pub. L. 105–362 had not been enacted, see section 302(b) of Pub. L. 107–303, set out as a note under section 1254 of this title.

STUDIES AND REPORTS

Pub. L. 100–4, title III, § 308(g), Feb. 4, 1987, 101 Stat. 40, directed Administrator to conduct a water quality improvement study and report results of such study to specified Congressional committees not later than 2 years after Feb. 4, 1987.

Pub. L. 100–4, title III, § 314(b), Feb. 4, 1987, 101 Stat. 49, directed Secretary of the Army and Administrator to each prepare a report on enforcement mechanisms and to submit the reports to Congress not later than Dec. 1, 1988.

Pub. L. 100–4, title IV, § 404(c), Feb. 4, 1987, 101 Stat. 69, directed Administrator to study extent to which States have adopted water quality standards in accordance with section 1313a of this title and extent to which modifications of permits issued under section 1342(a)(1)(B) of this title for the purpose of reflecting revisions of water quality standards be encouraged and to submit a report on such study to Congress not later than 2 years after Feb. 4, 1987, prior to repeal by Pub. L. 104–66, title II, § 2021(e)(1), Dec. 21, 1995, 109 Stat. 727.

Pub. L. 100–4, title V, § 516, Feb. 4, 1987, 101 Stat. 86, directed Administrator to conduct a study of de minimis discharges and report results of such study to specified Congressional committees not later than 1 year after Feb. 4, 1987.

Pub. L. 100–4, title V, § 517, Feb. 4, 1987, 101 Stat. 86, directed Administrator to conduct a study of effectiveness of innovative and alternative wastewater processes and techniques and report results of such study to specified Congressional committees not later than 1 year after Feb. 4, 1987.

Pub. L. 100–4, title V, § 518, Feb. 4, 1987, 101 Stat. 86, directed Administrator to conduct a study of testing procedures established under section 1314(h) of this title for analysis of pollutants and report results of such study to specified Congressional committees not later than 1 year after Feb. 4, 1987.

Pub. L. 100–4, title V, § 519, Feb. 4, 1987, 101 Stat. 87, directed Administrator to conduct a study of pretreatment of toxic pollutants and report results of such study to specified Congressional committees not later than 4 years after Feb. 4, 1987.

Pub. L. 100–4, title V, § 520, Feb. 4, 1987, 101 Stat. 87, directed Administrator, in conjunction with State and local agencies, to conduct studies of water pollution problems in aquifers and report result of such studies to Congress not later than 2 years after Feb. 4, 1987.

Pub. L. 100–4, title V, § 522, Feb. 4, 1987, 101 Stat. 88, directed Administrator to conduct a study on sulfide corrosion in collection and treatment systems and report results of such study to specified Congressional committees not later than 1 year after Feb. 4, 1987.

Pub. L. 100–4, title V, § 523, Feb. 4, 1987, 101 Stat. 89, directed Administrator to conduct a study of rainfall induced infiltration into sewer systems and report results of such study to Congress not later than 1 year after Feb. 4, 1987.

Pub. L. 100–4, title V, § 524, Feb. 4, 1987, 101 Stat. 89, directed Administrator to conduct a study of dam water quality and report results of such study to Congress not later than Dec. 31, 1987.

Pub. L. 100–4, title V, § 525, Feb. 4, 1987, 101 Stat. 89, directed Administrator to conduct a study of pollution in Lake Pend Oreille, Idaho, and the Clark Fork River and its tributaries, Idaho, Montana, and Washington, and to report to Congress findings and recommendations.

DETAILED ESTIMATES, COMPREHENSIVE STUDY, AND COMPREHENSIVE ANALYSIS; REPORT TO CONGRESS NOT LATER THAN DECEMBER 31, 1982

Pub. L. 97–117, § 25, Dec. 29, 1981, 95 Stat. 1633, provided that the Administrator of the Environmental Protection Agency submit to the Congress, not later than December 31, 1982, a report containing the detailed estimates, comprehensive study, and comprehensive analysis required by section 1375(b) of this title, including an estimate of the total cost and the amount of Federal funds necessary for the construction of needed publicly owned treatment facilities, such report to reflect the changes made in the Federal water pollution control program by Pub. L. 97–117 [see Short Title of 1981 Amendment note set out under section 1251 of this title]. The Administrator was to give emphasis to the effects of the amendment made by section 2(a) of Pub. L. 97–117 [amending section 1281(g)(1) of this title] in addressing water quality needs adequately and appropriately.

STUDY AND REPORT TO CONGRESS BY SECRETARY OF THE INTERIOR OF FINANCING WATER POLLUTION PREVENTION, CONTROL, AND ABATEMENT PROGRAMS

Pub. L. 91–224, title I, § 109, Apr. 3, 1970, 34 Stat. 113, directed the Secretary of the Interior to conduct a full and complete investigation and study of the feasibility of all methods of financing the cost of preventing, controlling, and abating water pollution, other than methods authorized by existing law, with results of such investigation and study to be reported to Congress no later than Dec. 31, 1970, together with the recommendations of the Secretary for financing the programs for preventing, controlling, and abating water pollution for the fiscal years beginning after fiscal year 1971, including any necessary legislation.

TERMINATION OF ADVISORY BOARDS

Advisory boards in existence on Jan. 5, 1973, to terminate not later than the expiration of the 2-year period following Jan. 5, 1973, unless, in the case of a board established by the President or an officer of the Federal Government, such board is renewed by appropriate action prior to the expiration of such 2-year period, or in the case of a board established by the Congress, its duration is otherwise provided by law. see sections 3(2) and 14 of Pub. L. 92–463, Oct. 6, 1972, 86 Stat. 770, 776, set out in the Appendix to Title 5, Government Organization and Employees.

§ 1375a. Report on coastal recreation waters

(a) In general

Not later than 4 years after October 10, 2000, and every 4 years thereafter, the Administrator of the Environmental Protection Agency shall submit to Congress a report that includes—

(1) recommendations concerning the need for additional water quality criteria for pathogens and pathogen indicators and other actions that should be taken to improve the quality of coastal recreation waters;

(2) an evaluation of Federal, State, and local efforts to implement this Act, including the amendments made by this Act; and

(3) recommendations on improvements to methodologies and techniques for monitoring of coastal recreation waters.

(b) Coordination

The Administrator of the Environmental Protection Agency may coordinate the report under this section with other reporting requirements under the Federal Water Pollution Control Act (33 U.S.C. 1251 et seq.).

(Pub. L. 106–284, §7, Oct. 10, 2000, 114 Stat. 876.)

REFERENCES IN TEXT

This Act, referred to in subsec. (a)(2), is Pub. L. 106–284, Oct. 10, 2000, 114 Stat. 870, known as the Beaches Environmental Assessment and Coastal Health Act of 2000. For complete classification of this Act to the Code, see Short Title of 2000 Amendment note set out under section 1251 of this title and Tables.

The Federal Water Pollution Control Act, referred to in subsec. (b), is act June 30, 1948, ch. 758, as amended generally by Pub. L. 92–500, §2, Oct. 18, 1972, 86 Stat. 816, which is classified generally to this chapter. For complete classification of this Act to the Code, see Short Title note set out under section 1251 of this title and Tables.

CODIFICATION

Section was enacted as part of the Beaches Environmental Assessment and Coastal Health Act of 2000, and not as part of the Federal Water Pollution Control Act which comprises this chapter.

§ 1376. Authorization of appropriations

There are authorized to be appropriated to carry out this chapter, other than sections 1254, 1255, 1256(a), 1257, 1258, 1262, 1263, 1264, 1265, 1286, 1287, 1288(f) and (h), 1289, 1314, 1321(c), (d), (i), (*l*), and (k),[1] 1324, 1325, and 1327 of this title, $250,000,000 for the fiscal year ending June 30, 1973, $300,000,000 for the fiscal year ending June 30, 1974, $350,000,000 for the fiscal year ending June 30, 1975, $100,000,000 for the fiscal year ending September 30, 1977, $150,000,000 for the fiscal year ending September 30, 1978, $150,000,000 for the fiscal year ending September 30, 1979, $150,000,000 for the fiscal year ending September 30, 1980, $150,000,000 for the fiscal year ending September 30, 1981, $161,000,000 for the fiscal year ending September 30, 1982, such sums as may be necessary for fiscal years 1983 through 1985, and $135,000,000 per fiscal year for each of the fiscal years 1986 through 1990.

(June 30, 1948, ch. 758, title V, §517, as added Pub. L. 92–500, §2, Oct. 18, 1972, 86 Stat. 896; amended Pub. L. 95–217, §4(g), Dec. 27, 1977, 91 Stat. 1567; Pub. L. 96–483, §1(g), Oct. 21, 1980, 94 Stat. 2360; Pub. L. 100–4, title I, §101(h), Feb. 4, 1987, 101 Stat. 9.)

REFERENCES IN TEXT

Section 1321(k) of this title, referred to in text, was repealed by Pub. L. 101–380, title II, §2002(b)(2), Aug. 18, 1990, 104 Stat. 507.

AMENDMENTS

1987—Pub. L. 100–4 struck out "and" after "1981," and inserted ", such sums as may be necessary for fiscal years 1983 through 1985, and $135,000,000 per fiscal year for each of the fiscal years 1986 through 1990" after "1982".

1980—Pub. L. 96–483 inserted authorization of $150,000,000 for fiscal year ending Sept. 30, 1981 and $161,000,000 for fiscal year ending Sept. 30, 1982.

1977—Pub. L. 95–217 substituted "$350,000,000 for the fiscal year ending June 30, 1975, $100,000,000 for the fiscal year ending September 30, 1977, $150,000,000 for the fiscal year ending September 30, 1978, $150,000,000 for the fiscal year ending September 30, 1979, and $150,000,000 for the fiscal year ending September 30, 1980" for "and $350,000,000 for the fiscal year ending June 30, 1975".

AUTHORIZATION APPROVAL FOR FUNDS APPROPRIATED BEFORE DECEMBER 27, 1977, FOR EXPENDITURES THROUGH FISCAL YEAR ENDING SEPTEMBER 30, 1977

Section 3 of Pub. L. 95–217 provided that funds appropriated before Dec. 27, 1977 for expenditure during the fiscal year ending June 30, 1976, the transition quarter ending September 30, 1976, and the fiscal year ending September 30, 1977, under authority of this chapter were authorized for those purposes for which appropriated.

§ 1377. Indian tribes

(a) Policy

Nothing in this section shall be construed to affect the application of section 1251(g) of this title, and all of the provisions of this section shall be carried out in accordance with the provisions of such section 1251(g) of this title. Indian tribes shall be treated as States for purposes of such section 1251(g) of this title.

(b) Assessment of sewage treatment needs; report

The Administrator, in cooperation with the Director of the Indian Health Service, shall assess the need for sewage treatment works to serve Indian tribes, the degree to which such needs will be met through funds allotted to States under section 1285 of this title and priority lists under section 1296 of this title, and any obstacles which prevent such needs from being met. Not later than one year after February 4, 1987, the Administrator shall submit a report to Congress on the assessment under this subsection, along with recommendations specifying (1) how the Administrator intends to provide assistance to Indian tribes to develop waste treatment management plans and to construct treatment works under this chapter, and (2) methods by which the participation in and administration of programs under this chapter by Indian tribes can be maximized.

(c) Reservation of funds

The Administrator shall reserve each fiscal year beginning after September 30, 1986, before allotments to the States under section 1285(e) of this title, one-half of one percent of the sums appropriated under section 1287 of this title. Sums reserved under this subsection shall be available only for grants for the development of waste treatment management plans and for the construction of sewage treatment works to serve Indian tribes, as defined in subsection (h) of this section and former Indian reservations in Oklahoma (as determined by the Secretary of the Interior) and Alaska Native Villages as defined in Public Law 92–203 [43 U.S.C. 1601 et seq.].

(d) Cooperative agreements

In order to ensure the consistent implementation of the requirements of this chapter, an Indian tribe and the State or States in which the lands of such tribe are located may enter into a

[1] See References in Text note below.

cooperative agreement, subject to the review and approval of the Administrator, to jointly plan and administer the requirements of this chapter.

(e) Treatment as States

The Administrator is authorized to treat an Indian tribe as a State for purposes of subchapter II of this chapter and sections 1254, 1256, 1313, 1315, 1318, 1319, 1324, 1329, 1341, 1342, 1344, and 1346 of this title to the degree necessary to carry out the objectives of this section, but only if—

(1) the Indian tribe has a governing body carrying out substantial governmental duties and powers;

(2) the functions to be exercised by the Indian tribe pertain to the management and protection of water resources which are held by an Indian tribe, held by the United States in trust for Indians, held by a member of an Indian tribe if such property interest is subject to a trust restriction on alienation, or otherwise within the borders of an Indian reservation; and

(3) the Indian tribe is reasonably expected to be capable, in the Administrator's judgment, of carrying out the functions to be exercised in a manner consistent with the terms and purposes of this chapter and of all applicable regulations.

Such treatment as a State may include the direct provision of funds reserved under subsection (c) of this section to the governing bodies of Indian tribes, and the determination of priorities by Indian tribes, where not determined by the Administrator in cooperation with the Director of the Indian Health Service. The Administrator, in cooperation with the Director of the Indian Health Service, is authorized to make grants under subchapter II of this chapter in an amount not to exceed 100 percent of the cost of a project. Not later than 18 months after February 4, 1987, the Administrator shall, in consultation with Indian tribes, promulgate final regulations which specify how Indian tribes shall be treated as States for purposes of this chapter. The Administrator shall, in promulgating such regulations, consult affected States sharing common water bodies and provide a mechanism for the resolution of any unreasonable consequences that may arise as a result of differing water quality standards that may be set by States and Indian tribes located on common bodies of water. Such mechanism shall provide for explicit consideration of relevant factors including, but not limited to, the effects of differing water quality permit requirements on upstream and downstream dischargers, economic impacts, and present and historical uses and quality of the waters subject to such standards. Such mechanism should provide for the avoidance of such unreasonable consequences in a manner consistent with the objective of this chapter.

(f) Grants for nonpoint source programs

The Administrator shall make grants to an Indian tribe under section 1329 of this title as though such tribe was a State. Not more than one-third of one percent of the amount appropriated for any fiscal year under section 1329 of this title may be used to make grants under this subsection. In addition to the requirements of section 1329 of this title, an Indian tribe shall be required to meet the requirements of paragraphs (1), (2), and (3) of subsection (d)[1] of this section in order to receive such a grant.

(g) Alaska Native organizations

No provision of this chapter shall be construed to—

(1) grant, enlarge, or diminish, or in any way affect the scope of the governmental authority, if any, of any Alaska Native organization, including any federally-recognized tribe, traditional Alaska Native council, or Native council organized pursuant to the Act of June 18, 1934 (48 Stat. 987), over lands or persons in Alaska;

(2) create or validate any assertion by such organization or any form of governmental authority over lands or persons in Alaska; or

(3) in any way affect any assertion that Indian country, as defined in section 1151 of title 18, exists or does not exist in Alaska.

(h) Definitions

For purposes of this section, the term—

(1) "Federal Indian reservation" means all land within the limits of any Indian reservation under the jurisdiction of the United States Government, notwithstanding the issuance of any patent, and including rights-of-way running through the reservation; and

(2) "Indian tribe" means any Indian tribe, band, group, or community recognized by the Secretary of the Interior and exercising governmental authority over a Federal Indian reservation.

(June 30, 1948, ch. 758, title V, §518, as added Pub. L. 100–4, title V, §506, Feb. 4, 1987, 101 Stat. 76; amended Pub. L. 100–581, title II, §207, Nov. 1, 1988, 102 Stat. 2940; Pub. L. 106–284, §6, Oct. 10, 2000, 114 Stat. 876.)

REFERENCES IN TEXT

Public Law 92–203, referred to in subsec. (c), is Pub. L. 92–203, Dec. 18, 1971, 85 Stat. 688, as amended, known as the Alaska Native Claims Settlement Act, which is classified generally to chapter 33 (§1601 et seq.) of Title 43, Public Lands. The term "Alaska Native Villages" is defined in section 3 of Pub. L. 92–203 which is classified to section 1602 of Title 43. For complete classification of this Act to the Code, see Short Title note set out under section 1601 of Title 43 and Tables.

Act of June 18, 1934 (48 Stat. 987), referred to in subsec. (g)(1), is act June 18, 1934, ch. 576, 48 Stat. 984, as amended, popularly known as the Indian Reorganization Act, which enacted sections 461, 462, 463, 464, 465, 466 to 470, 471, 472, 473, 474, 475, 476 to 478, and 479 of Title 25, Indians. For complete classification of this Act to the Code, see Short Title note set out under section 461 of Title 25 and Tables.

PRIOR PROVISIONS

A prior section 518 of act June 30, 1948, was renumbered section 519 and is set out as a note under section 1251 of this title.

AMENDMENTS

2000—Subsec. (e). Pub. L. 106–284 substituted "1344, and 1346 of this title" for "and 1344 of this title" in introductory provisions.

[1] So in original. Probably should be subsection "(e)".

1988—Subsec. (c). Pub. L. 100–581 inserted ", as defined in subsection (h) of this section and former Indian reservations in Oklahoma (as determined by the Secretary of the Interior) and Alaska Native Villages as defined in Public Law 92–203" before period at end.

GRANTS FOR CONSTRUCTION OF WATER FACILITIES AND FOR WATER QUALITY PROTECTION

Pub. L. 109–54, title II, Aug. 2, 2005, 119 Stat. 530, provided in part: "That, notwithstanding this or any other appropriations Act, heretofore and hereafter, after consultation with the House and Senate Committees on Appropriations and for the purpose of making technical corrections, the Administrator is authorized to award grants under this heading [State and Tribal Assistance Grants] to entities and for purposes other than those listed in the joint explanatory statements of the managers accompanying the Agency's appropriations Acts for the construction of drinking water, wastewater and stormwater infrastructure and for water quality protection."

GRANTS TO INDIAN TRIBES

Provisions stating that for fiscal year 2006 and notwithstanding section 1377(f) of this title, the Administrator was authorized to use the amounts appropriated for any fiscal year under section 1329 of this title to make grants to Indian tribes pursuant to sections 1329(h) and 1377(e) of this title, were contained in the Department of the Interior, Environment, and Related Agencies Appropriations Act, 2006, Pub. L. 109–54, title II, Aug. 2, 2005, 119 Stat. 530, and were repeated in provisions of subsequent appropriations acts which are not set out in the Code. Similar provisions were contained in the following prior appropriations acts:

Pub. L. 108–447, div. I, title III, Dec. 8, 2004, 118 Stat. 3330.

Pub. L. 108–199, div. G, title III, Jan. 23, 2004, 118 Stat. 406.

Pub. L. 108–7, div. K, title III, Feb. 20, 2003, 117 Stat. 512.

Pub. L. 107–73, title III, Nov. 26, 2001, 115 Stat. 685.

Pub. L. 106–377, §1(a)(1) [title III], Oct. 27, 2000, 114 Stat. 1441, 1441A–43.

Pub. L. 106–74, title III, Oct. 20, 1999, 113 Stat. 1083.

SUBCHAPTER VI—STATE WATER POLLUTION CONTROL REVOLVING FUNDS

§ 1381. Grants to States for establishment of revolving funds

(a) General authority

Subject to the provisions of this subchapter, the Administrator shall make capitalization grants to each State for the purpose of establishing a water pollution control revolving fund for providing assistance (1) for construction of treatment works (as defined in section 1292 of this title) which are publicly owned, (2) for implementing a management program under section 1329 of this title, and (3) for developing and implementing a conservation and management plan under section 1330 of this title.

(b) Schedule of grant payments

The Administrator and each State shall jointly establish a schedule of payments under which the Administrator will pay to the State the amount of each grant to be made to the State under this subchapter. Such schedule shall be based on the State's intended use plan under section 1386(c) of this title, except that—

(1) such payments shall be made in quarterly installments, and

(2) such payments shall be made as expeditiously as possible, but in no event later than the earlier of—

(A) 8 quarters after the date such funds were obligated by the State, or

(B) 12 quarters after the date such funds were allotted to the State.

(June 30, 1948, ch. 758, title VI, §601, as added Pub. L. 100–4, title II, §212(a), Feb. 4, 1987, 101 Stat. 22.)

§ 1382. Capitalization grant agreements

(a) General rule

To receive a capitalization grant with funds made available under this subchapter and section 1285(m) of this title, a State shall enter into an agreement with the Administrator which shall include but not be limited to the specifications set forth in subsection (b) of this section.

(b) Specific requirements

The Administrator shall enter into an agreement under this section with a State only after the State has established to the satisfaction of the Administrator that—

(1) the State will accept grant payments with funds to be made available under this subchapter and section 1285(m) of this title in accordance with a payment schedule established jointly by the Administrator under section 1381(b) of this title and will deposit all such payments in the water pollution control revolving fund established by the State in accordance with this subchapter;

(2) the State will deposit in the fund from State moneys an amount equal to at least 20 percent of the total amount of all capitalization grants which will be made to the State with funds to be made available under this subchapter and section 1285(m) of this title on or before the date on which each quarterly grant payment will be made to the State under this subchapter;

(3) the State will enter into binding commitments to provide assistance in accordance with the requirements of this subchapter in an amount equal to 120 percent of the amount of each such grant payment within 1 year after the receipt of such grant payment;

(4) all funds in the fund will be expended in an expeditious and timely manner;

(5) all funds in the fund as a result of capitalization grants under this subchapter and section 1285(m) of this title will first be used to assure maintenance of progress, as determined by the Governor of the State, toward compliance with enforceable deadlines, goals, and requirements of this chapter, including the municipal compliance deadline;

(6) treatment works eligible under section 1383(c)(1) of this title which will be constructed in whole or in part before fiscal year 1995 with funds directly made available by capitalization grants under this subchapter and section 1285(m) of this title will meet the requirements of, or otherwise be treated (as determined by the Governor of the State) under sections 1281(b), 1281(g)(1), 1281(g)(2), 1281(g)(3), 1281(g)(5), 1281(g)(6), 1281(n)(1), 1281(*o*), 1284(a)(1), 1284(a)(2), 1284(b)(1), 1284(d)(2), 1291, 1298, 1371(c)(1), and 1372 of this title in the same manner as treatment works constructed with assistance under subchapter II of this chapter;

(7) in addition to complying with the requirements of this subchapter, the State will commit or expend each quarterly grant payment which it will receive under this subchapter in accordance with laws and procedures applicable to the commitment or expenditure of revenues of the State;

(8) in carrying out the requirements of section 1386 of this title, the State will use accounting, audit, and fiscal procedures conforming to generally accepted government accounting standards;

(9) the State will require as a condition of making a loan or providing other assistance, as described in section 1383(d) of this title, from the fund that the recipient of such assistance will maintain project accounts in accordance with generally accepted government accounting standards; and

(10) the State will make annual reports to the Administrator on the actual use of funds in accordance with section 1386(d) of this title.

(June 30, 1948, ch. 758, title VI, §602, as added Pub. L. 100–4, title II, §212(a), Feb. 4, 1987, 101 Stat. 22.)

§ 1383. Water pollution control revolving loan funds

(a) Requirements for obligation of grant funds

Before a State may receive a capitalization grant with funds made available under this subchapter and section 1285(m) of this title, the State shall first establish a water pollution control revolving fund which complies with the requirements of this section.

(b) Administration

Each State water pollution control revolving fund shall be administered by an instrumentality of the State with such powers and limitations as may be required to operate such fund in accordance with the requirements and objectives of this chapter.

(c) Projects eligible for assistance

The amounts of funds available to each State water pollution control revolving fund shall be used only for providing financial assistance (1) to any municipality, intermunicipal, interstate, or State agency for construction of publicly owned treatment works (as defined in section 1292 of this title), (2) for the implementation of a management program established under section 1329 of this title, and (3) for development and implementation of a conservation and management plan under section 1330 of this title. The fund shall be established, maintained, and credited with repayments, and the fund balance shall be available in perpetuity for providing such financial assistance.

(d) Types of assistance

Except as otherwise limited by State law, a water pollution control revolving fund of a State under this section may be used only—

(1) to make loans, on the condition that—

(A) such loans are made at or below market interest rates, including interest free loans, at terms not to exceed 20 years;

(B) annual principal and interest payments will commence not later than 1 year after completion of any project and all loans will be fully amortized not later than 20 years after project completion;

(C) the recipient of a loan will establish a dedicated source of revenue for repayment of loans; and

(D) the fund will be credited with all payments of principal and interest on all loans;

(2) to buy or refinance the debt obligation of municipalities and intermunicipal and interstate agencies within the State at or below market rates, where such debt obligations were incurred after March 7, 1985;

(3) to guarantee, or purchase insurance for, local obligations where such action would improve credit market access or reduce interest rates;

(4) as a source of revenue or security for the payment of principal and interest on revenue or general obligation bonds issued by the State if the proceeds of the sale of such bonds will be deposited in the fund;

(5) to provide loan guarantees for similar revolving funds established by municipalities or intermunicipal agencies;

(6) to earn interest on fund accounts; and

(7) for the reasonable costs of administering the fund and conducting activities under this subchapter, except that such amounts shall not exceed 4 percent of all grant awards to such fund under this subchapter.

(e) Limitation to prevent double benefits

If a State makes, from its water pollution revolving fund, a loan which will finance the cost of facility planning and the preparation of plans, specifications, and estimates for construction of publicly owned treatment works, the State shall ensure that if the recipient of such loan receives a grant under section 1281(g) of this title for construction of such treatment works and an allowance under section 1281(*l*)(1) of this title for non-Federal funds expended for such planning and preparation, such recipient will promptly repay such loan to the extent of such allowance.

(f) Consistency with planning requirements

A State may provide financial assistance from its water pollution control revolving fund only with respect to a project which is consistent with plans, if any, developed under sections 1285(j), 1288, 1313(e), 1329, and 1330 of this title.

(g) Priority list requirement

The State may provide financial assistance from its water pollution control revolving fund only with respect to a project for construction of a treatment works described in subsection (c)(1) of this section if such project is on the State's priority list under section 1296 of this title. Such assistance may be provided regardless of the rank of such project on such list.

(h) Eligibility of non-Federal share of construction grant projects

A State water pollution control revolving fund may provide assistance (other than under subsection (d)(1) of this section) to a municipality or intermunicipal or interstate agency with respect to the non-Federal share of the costs of a treatment works project for which such municipality or agency is receiving assistance from the

Administrator under any other authority only if such assistance is necessary to allow such project to proceed.

(June 30, 1948, ch. 758, title VI, § 603, as added Pub. L. 100–4, title II, § 212(a), Feb. 4, 1987, 101 Stat. 23.)

§ 1384. Allotment of funds

(a) Formula

Sums authorized to be appropriated to carry out this section for each of fiscal years 1989 and 1990 shall be allotted by the Administrator in accordance with section 1285(c) of this title.

(b) Reservation of funds for planning

Each State shall reserve each fiscal year 1 percent of the sums allotted to such State under this section for such fiscal year, or $100,000, whichever amount is greater, to carry out planning under sections 1285(j) and 1313(e) of this title.

(c) Allotment period

(1) Period of availability for grant award

Sums allotted to a State under this section for a fiscal year shall be available for obligation by the State during the fiscal year for which sums are authorized and during the following fiscal year.

(2) Reallotment of unobligated funds

The amount of any allotment not obligated by the State by the last day of the 2-year period of availability established by paragraph (1) shall be immediately reallotted by the Administrator on the basis of the same ratio as is applicable to sums allotted under subchapter II of this chapter for the second fiscal year of such 2-year period. None of the funds reallotted by the Administrator shall be reallotted to any State which has not obligated all sums allotted to such State in the first fiscal year of such 2-year period.

(June 30, 1948, ch. 758, title VI, § 604, as added Pub. L. 100–4, title II, § 212(a), Feb. 4, 1987, 101 Stat. 25.)

USE OF CAPITALIZATION GRANT FUNDS FOR CONSTRUCTION GRANTS

Pub. L. 101–144, title III, Nov. 9, 1989, 103 Stat. 858, as amended by Pub. L. 101–302, title II, May 25, 1990, 104 Stat. 238, provided: "That, notwithstanding any other provision of law, sums heretofore, herein or hereafter appropriated under this heading ["ENVIRONMENTAL PROTECTION AGENCY" and "CONSTRUCTION GRANTS"] allotted for title VI [33 U.S.C. 1381 et seq.] capitalization grants to American Samoa, Commonwealth of the Northern Mariana Islands, Guam, the Republic of Palau (or its successor entity), Virgin Islands and the District of Columbia, may be used for title II [33 U.S.C. 1281 et seq.] construction grants at the request of the chief executive of each of the above named entities, and sums appropriated in fiscal year 1989 shall remain available for obligation until September 30, 1992."

§ 1385. Corrective action

(a) Notification of noncompliance

If the Administrator determines that a State has not complied with its agreement with the Administrator under section 1382 of this title or any other requirement of this subchapter, the Administrator shall notify the State of such noncompliance and the necessary corrective action.

(b) Withholding of payments

If a State does not take corrective action within 60 days after the date a State receives notification of such action under subsection (a) of this section, the Administrator shall withhold additional payments to the State until the Administrator is satisfied that the State has taken the necessary corrective action.

(c) Reallotment of withheld payments

If the Administrator is not satisfied that adequate corrective actions have been taken by the State within 12 months after the State is notified of such actions under subsection (a) of this section, the payments withheld from the State by the Administrator under subsection (b) of this section shall be made available for reallotment in accordance with the most recent formula for allotment of funds under this subchapter.

(June 30, 1948, ch. 758, title VI, § 605, as added Pub. L. 100–4, title II, § 212(a), Feb. 4, 1987, 101 Stat. 25.)

§ 1386. Audits, reports, and fiscal controls; intended use plan

(a) Fiscal control and auditing procedures

Each State electing to establish a water pollution control revolving fund under this subchapter shall establish fiscal controls and accounting procedures sufficient to assure proper accounting during appropriate accounting periods for—

(1) payments received by the fund;

(2) disbursements made by the fund; and

(3) fund balances at the beginning and end of the accounting period.

(b) Annual Federal audits

The Administrator shall, at least on an annual basis, conduct or require each State to have independently conducted reviews and audits as may be deemed necessary or appropriate by the Administrator to carry out the objectives of this section. Audits of the use of funds deposited in the water pollution revolving fund established by such State shall be conducted in accordance with the auditing procedures of the Government Accountability Office, including chapter 75 of title 31.

(c) Intended use plan

After providing for public comment and review, each State shall annually prepare a plan identifying the intended uses of the amounts available to its water pollution control revolving fund. Such intended use plan shall include, but not be limited to—

(1) a list of those projects for construction of publicly owned treatment works on the State's priority list developed pursuant to section 1296 of this title and a list of activities eligible for assistance under sections 1329 and 1330 of this title;

(2) a description of the short- and long-term goals and objectives of its water pollution control revolving fund;

(3) information on the activities to be supported, including a description of project categories, discharge requirements under subchapters III and IV of this chapter, terms of financial assistance, and communities served;

(4) assurances and specific proposals for meeting the requirements of paragraphs (3), (4), (5), and (6) of section 1382(b) of this title; and

(5) the criteria and method established for the distribution of funds.

(d) Annual report

Beginning the first fiscal year after the receipt of payments under this subchapter, the State shall provide an annual report to the Administrator describing how the State has met the goals and objectives for the previous fiscal year as identified in the plan prepared for the previous fiscal year pursuant to subsection (c) of this section, including identification of loan recipients, loan amounts, and loan terms and similar details on other forms of financial assistance provided from the water pollution control revolving fund.

(e) Annual Federal oversight review

The Administrator shall conduct an annual oversight review of each State plan prepared under subsection (c) of this section, each State report prepared under subsection (d) of this section, and other such materials as are considered necessary and appropriate in carrying out the purposes of this subchapter. After reasonable notice by the Administrator to the State or the recipient of a loan from a water pollution control revolving fund, the State or loan recipient shall make available to the Administrator such records as the Administrator reasonably requires to review and determine compliance with this subchapter.

(f) Applicability of subchapter II provisions

Except to the extent provided in this subchapter, the provisions of subchapter II of this chapter shall not apply to grants under this subchapter.

(June 30, 1948, ch. 758, title VI, §606, as added Pub. L. 100–4, title II, §212(a), Feb. 4, 1987, 101 Stat. 25; amended Pub. L. 108–271, §8(b), July 7, 2004, 118 Stat. 814.)

AMENDMENTS

2004—Subsec. (b). Pub. L. 108–271 substituted "Government Accountability Office" for "General Accounting Office".

§ 1387. Authorization of appropriations

There is authorized to be appropriated to carry out the purposes of this subchapter the following sums:

(1) $1,200,000,000 per fiscal year for each of fiscal years 1989 and 1990;

(2) $2,400,000,000 for fiscal year 1991;

(3) $1,800,000,000 for fiscal year 1992;

(4) $1,200,000,000 for fiscal year 1993; and

(5) $600,000,000 for fiscal year 1994.

(June 30, 1948, ch. 758, title VI, §607, as added Pub. L. 100–4, title II, §212(a), Feb. 4, 1987, 101 Stat. 26.)

CHAPTER 27—OCEAN DUMPING

§ 1401. Congressional finding, policy, and declaration of purpose

(a) Dangers of unregulated dumping

Unregulated dumping of material into ocean waters endangers human health, welfare, and amenities, and the marine environment, ecological systems, and economic potentialities.

(b) Policy of regulation and prevention or limitation

The Congress declares that it is the policy of the United States to regulate the dumping of all types of materials into ocean waters and to prevent or strictly limit the dumping into ocean waters of any material which would adversely affect human health, welfare, or amenities, or the marine environment, ecological systems, or economic potentialities.

(c) Regulation of dumping and transportation for dumping purposes

It is the purpose of this Act to regulate (1) the transportation by any person of material from the United States and, in the case of United States vessels, aircraft, or agencies, the transportation of material from a location outside the United States, when in either case the transportation is for the purpose of dumping the material into ocean waters, and (2) the dumping of material transported by any person from a location outside the United States, if the dumping occurs in the territorial sea or the contiguous zone of the United States.

(Pub. L. 92–532, §2, Oct. 23, 1972, 86 Stat. 1052; Pub. L. 93–254, §1(1), Mar. 22, 1974, 88 Stat. 50.)

REFERENCES IN TEXT

This Act, referred to in subsec. (c), means Pub. L. 92–532, which is classified generally to this chapter,

chapter 41 (§2801 et seq.) of this title, and chapters 32 (§1431 et seq.) and 32A (§1447 et seq.) of Title 16, Conservation.

AMENDMENTS

1974—Subsec. (b). Pub. L. 93–254 struck out statement of the purpose of this Act as being the regulation of transportation of material from the United States for dumping into ocean waters, and the dumping of material, transported from outside the United States, if the dumping occurs in ocean waters over which the United States has jurisdiction or over which it may exercise control, under accepted principles of international law, in order to protect its territory or territorial sea, now covered by subsec. (c) of this section.

Subsec. (c). Pub. L. 93–254 added subsec. (c).

EFFECTIVE DATE OF 1974 AMENDMENT

Section 2 of Pub. L. 93–254 provided in part that amendment of subsecs. (b) and (c) of this section and sections 1402, 1411, and 1412(a), other than last sentence of subsec. (a), of this title, by Pub. L. 93–254 shall become effective Mar. 22, 1974.

SHORT TITLE OF 1988 AMENDMENT

Pub. L. 100–688, title I, §1001, Nov. 18, 1988, 102 Stat. 4139, provided that: "This title [enacting sections 1414b and 1414c of this title, amending sections 1268, 1412a, and 1414a of this title, and amending provisions set out as a note under section 2267 of this title] may be cited as the 'Ocean Dumping Ban Act of 1988'."

SHORT TITLE

Section 1 of Pub. L. 92–532 provided: "That this Act [enacting this chapter, chapter 41 (§2801 et seq.) of this title, and chapters 32 (§1431 et seq.) and 32A (§1447 et seq.) of Title 16, Conservation] may be cited as the 'Marine Protection, Research, and Sanctuaries Act of 1972'."

TERRITORIAL SEA AND CONTIGUOUS ZONE OF UNITED STATES

For extension of territorial sea and contiguous zone of United States, see Proc. No. 5928 and Proc. No. 7219, respectively, set out as notes under section 1331 of Title 43, Public Lands.

ENVIRONMENTAL EFFECTS ABROAD OF MAJOR FEDERAL ACTIONS

For provisions relating to environmental effects abroad of major federal actions, see Ex. Ord. No. 12114, Jan. 4, 1979, 44 F.R. 1957, set out as a note under section 4321 of Title 42, The Public Health and Welfare.

FEDERAL COMPLIANCE WITH POLLUTION CONTROL STANDARDS

For provisions relating to the responsibility of the head of each Executive agency for compliance with applicable pollution control standards, see Ex. Ord. No. 12088, Oct. 13, 1978, 43 F.R. 47707, set out as a note under section 4321 of Title 42, The Public Health and Welfare.

§1402. Definitions

For the purposes of this Act the term—

(a) "Administrator" means the Administrator of the Environmental Protection Agency.

(b) "Ocean waters" means those waters of the open seas lying seaward of the base line from which the territorial sea is measured, as provided for in the Convention on the Territorial Sea and the Contiguous Zone (15 UST 1606; TIAS 5639).

(c) "Material" means matter of any kind or description, including, but not limited to, dredged material, solid waste, incinerator residue, garbage, sewage, sewage sludge, munitions, radiological, chemical, and biological warfare agents, radioactive materials, chemicals, biological and laboratory waste, wreck or discarded equipment, rock, sand, excavation debris, and industrial, municipal, agricultural, and other waste; but such term does not mean sewage from vessels within the meaning of section 1322 of this title. Oil within the meaning of section 1321 of this title shall be included only to the extent that such oil is taken on board a vessel or aircraft for the purpose of dumping.

(d) "United States" includes the several States, the District of Columbia, the Commonwealth of Puerto Rico, the Canal Zone, the territories and possessions of the United States, and the Trust Territory of the Pacific Islands.

(e) "Person" means any private person or entity, or any officer, employee, agent, department, agency, or instrumentality of the Federal Government, of any State or local unit of government, or of any foreign government.

(f) "Dumping" means a disposition of material: *Provided*, That it does not mean a disposition of any effluent from any outfall structure to the extent that such disposition is regulated under the provisions of the Federal Water Pollution Control Act, as amended [33 U.S.C. 1251 et seq.], under the provisions of section 407 of this title, or under the provisions of the Atomic Energy Act of 1954, as amended [42 U.S.C. 2011 et seq.], nor does it mean a routine discharge of effluent incidental to the propulsion of, or operation of motor-driven equipment on, vessels: *Provided, further*, That it does not mean the construction of any fixed structure or artificial island nor the intentional placement of any device in ocean waters or on or in the submerged land beneath such waters, for a purpose other than disposal, when such construction or such placement is otherwise regulated by Federal or State law or occurs pursuant to an authorized Federal or State program: *And provided further*, That it does not include the deposit of oyster shells, or other materials when such deposit is made for the purpose of developing, maintaining, or harvesting fisheries resources and is otherwise regulated by Federal or State law or occurs pursuant to an authorized Federal or State program.

(g) "District court of the United States" includes the District Court of Guam, the District Court of the Virgin Islands, the District Court of Puerto Rico, the District Court of the Canal Zone, and in the case of American Samoa and the Trust Territory of the Pacific Islands, the District Court of the United States for the District of Hawaii, which court shall have jurisdiction over actions arising therein.

(h) "Secretary" means the Secretary of the Army.

(i) "Dredged material" means any material excavated or dredged from the navigable waters of the United States.

(j) "High-level radioactive waste" means the aqueous waste resulting from the operation of the first cycle solvent extraction system, or equivalent and the concentrated waste from subsequent extraction cycles, or equivalent, in a facility for reprocessing irradiated reactor fuels, or irradiated fuel from nuclear power reactors.

(k) "Medical waste" means isolation wastes; infectious agents; human blood and blood products; pathological wastes; sharps; body parts; contaminated bedding; surgical wastes and potentially contaminated laboratory wastes; dialysis wastes; and such additional medical items as the Administrator shall prescribe by regulation.

(*l*) "Transport" or "transportation" refers to the carriage and related handling of any material by a vessel, or by any other vehicle, including aircraft.

(m) "Convention" means the Convention on the Prevention of Marine Pollution by Dumping of Wastes and Other Matter.

(Pub. L. 92–532, § 3, Oct. 23, 1972, 86 Stat. 1052; Pub. L. 93–254, § 1(2), Mar. 22, 1974, 88 Stat. 50; Pub. L. 100–688, title III, § 3201(a), Nov. 18, 1988, 102 Stat. 4153.)

REFERENCES IN TEXT

This Act, referred to in text, means Pub. L. 92–532, which is classified generally to this chapter, chapter 41 (§ 2801 et seq.) of this title, and chapters 32 (§ 1431 et seq.) and 32A (§ 1447 et seq.) of Title 16, Conservation.

For definition of Canal Zone, referred to in subsec. (d), see section 3602(b) of Title 22, Foreign Relations and Intercourse.

The Federal Water Pollution Control Act, as amended, referred to in subsec. (f), is act June 30, 1948, ch. 758, as amended generally by Pub. L. 92–500, § 2, Oct. 18, 1972, 86 Stat. 816, which is classified generally to chapter 26 (§ 1251 et seq.) of this title. For complete classification of this Act to the Code, see Short Title note set out under section 1251 of this title and Tables.

The Atomic Energy Act of 1954, as amended, referred to in subsec. (f), is act Aug. 1, 1946, ch. 724, as added by act Aug. 30, 1954, ch. 1073, § 1, 68 Stat. 921, and amended, which is classified generally to chapter 23 (§ 2011 et seq.) of Title 42, The Public Health and Welfare. For complete classification of this Act to the Code, see Short Title note set out under section 2011 of Title 42 and Tables.

AMENDMENTS

1988—Subsecs. (k) to (m). Pub. L. 100–688 added subsec. (k) and redesignated former subsecs. (k) and (*l*) as (*l*) and (m), respectively.

1974—Subsec. (c). Pub. L. 93–254, § 1(2)(A), substituted "sewage from vessels within the meaning of section 1322 of this title. Oil within the meaning of section 1321 of this title shall be included only to the extent that such oil is taken on board a vessel or aircraft for the purpose of dumping." for "oil within the meaning of section 11 of the Federal Water Pollution Control Act and does not mean sewage from vessels within the meaning of section 13 of such Act."

Subsec. (*l*). Pub. L. 93–254, § 1(2)(C), added subsec. (*l*).

EFFECTIVE DATE OF 1974 AMENDMENT

Amendment by Pub. L. 93–254 effective Mar. 22, 1974, see section 2 of Pub. L. 93–254, set out in part as a note under section 1401 of this title.

TERMINATION OF TRUST TERRITORY OF THE PACIFIC ISLANDS

For termination of Trust Territory of the Pacific Islands, see note set out preceding section 1681 of Title 48, Territories and Insular Possessions.

TERMINATION OF UNITED STATES DISTRICT COURT FOR THE DISTRICT OF THE CANAL ZONE

For termination of the United States District Court for the District of the Canal Zone at end of the "transition period", being the 30-month period beginning Oct. 1, 1979, and ending midnight Mar. 31, 1982, see Paragraph 5 of Article XI of the Panama Canal Treaty of 1977 and sections 2101 and 2201 to 2203 of Pub. L. 96–70, title II, Sept. 27, 1979, 93 Stat. 493, formerly classified to sections 3831 and 3841 to 3843, respectively, of Title 22, Foreign Relations and Intercourse.

TERRITORIAL SEA AND CONTIGUOUS ZONE OF UNITED STATES

For extension of territorial sea and contiguous zone of United States, see Proc. No. 5928 and Proc. No. 7219, respectively, set out as notes under section 1331 of Title 43, Public Lands.

SUBCHAPTER I—REGULATION

§ 1411. Prohibited acts

(a) Except as may be authorized by a permit issued pursuant to section 1412 or section 1413 of this title, and subject to regulations issued pursuant to section 1418 of this title,

(1) no person shall transport from the United States, and

(2) in the case of a vessel or aircraft registered in the United States or flying the United States flag or in the case of a United States department, agency, or instrumentality, no person shall transport from any location

any material for the purpose of dumping it into ocean waters.

(b) Except as may be authorized by a permit issued pursuant to section 1412 of this title, and subject to regulations issued pursuant to section 1418 of this title, no person shall dump any material transported from a location outside the United States (1) into the territorial sea of the United States, or (2) into a zone contiguous to the territorial sea of the United States, extending to a line twelve nautical miles seaward from the base line from which the breadth of the territorial sea is measured, to the extent that it may affect the territorial sea or the territory of the United States.

(Pub. L. 92–532, title I, § 101, Oct. 23, 1972, 86 Stat. 1053; Pub. L. 93–254, § 1(3), Mar. 22, 1974, 88 Stat. 51.)

AMENDMENTS

1974—Subsec. (a). Pub. L. 93–254 incorporated existing provisions in introductory text, substituting reference to permits issued under section 1412 or section 1413 of this title for prior reference to such issuance under this subchapter; incorporated existing provisions in item designated (1); added item (2); and substituted prohibition against transportation of any material for ocean dumping for former prohibition against such dumping of any radiological, chemical, or biological warfare agent or any high-level radioactive waste, or any other material.

Subsec. (b). Pub. L. 93–254 substituted reference to permits issued under section 1412 of this title for former reference to such issuance under this subchapter, made any ocean dumping subject to regulations issued under section 1418 of this title, and substituted prohibition against dumping of any material for former prohibition against dumping of any radiological, chemical, or biological warfare agent or any high-level radioactive waste, or any other material.

Subsec. (c). Pub. L. 93–254 struck out subsec. (c) which prohibited any officer, employee, agent, department, agency, or instrumentality of the United States from transporting from any location outside the United States any radiological, chemical, or biological warfare agent or any high-level radioactive waste, or, except as may be authorized in a permit, any other material for purpose of dumping in ocean waters. See subsec. (b) of this section.

EFFECTIVE DATE OF 1974 AMENDMENT

Amendment by Pub. L. 93–254 effective Mar. 22, 1974, see section 2 of Pub. L. 93–254, set out in part as a note under section 1401 of this title.

EFFECTIVE DATE

Section 110(a) of title I of Pub. L. 92–532 provided that: "This title [this subchapter] shall take effect six months after the date of the enactment of this Act [Oct. 23, 1972]."

SAVINGS PROVISION

Section 110(b) of title I of Pub. L. 92–532 provided that: "No legal action begun, or right of action accrued, prior to the effective date of this title [this subchapter] shall be affected by any provision of this title [this subchapter]."

TERRITORIAL SEA AND CONTIGUOUS ZONE OF UNITED STATES

For extension of territorial sea and contiguous zone of United States, see Proc. No. 5928 and Proc. No. 7219, respectively, set out as notes under section 1331 of Title 43, Public Lands.

§ 1412. Dumping permit program

(a) Environmental Protection Agency permits

Except in relation to dredged material, as provided for in section 1413 of this title, and in relation to radiological, chemical, and biological warfare agents, high-level radioactive waste, and medical waste, for which no permit may be issued, the Administrator may issue permits, after notice and opportunity for public hearings, for the transportation from the United States or, in the case of an agency or instrumentality of the United States, or in the case of a vessel or aircraft registered in the United States or flying the United States flag, for the transportation from a location outside the United States, of material for the purpose of dumping it into ocean waters, or for the dumping of material into the waters described in section 1411(b) of this title, where the Administrator determines that such dumping will not unreasonably degrade or endanger human health, welfare, or amenities, or the marine environment, ecological systems, or economic potentialities. The Administrator shall establish and apply criteria for reviewing and evaluating such permit applications, and, in establishing or revising such criteria, shall consider, but not be limited in his consideration to, the following:

(A) The need for the proposed dumping.

(B) The effect of such dumping on human health and welfare, including economic, esthetic, and recreational values.

(C) The effect of such dumping on fisheries resources, plankton, fish, shellfish, wildlife, shore lines and beaches.

(D) The effect of such dumping on marine ecosystems, particularly with respect to—

(i) the transfer, concentration, and dispersion of such material and its byproducts through biological, physical, and chemical processes,

(ii) potential changes in marine ecosystem diversity, productivity, and stability, and

(iii) species and community population dynamics.

(E) The persistence and permanence of the effects of the dumping.

(F) The effect of dumping particular volumes and concentrations of such materials.

(G) Appropriate locations and methods of disposal or recycling, including land-based alternatives and the probable impact of requiring use of such alternate locations or methods upon considerations affecting the public interest.

(H) The effect on alternate uses of oceans, such as scientific study, fishing, and other living resource exploitation, and non-living resource exploitation.

(I) In designating recommended sites, the Administrator shall utilize wherever feasible locations beyond the edge of the Continental Shelf.

In establishing or revising such criteria, the Administrator shall consult with Federal, State, and local officials, and interested members of the general public, as may appear appropriate to the Administrator. With respect to such criteria as may affect the civil works program of the Department of the Army, the Administrator shall also consult with the Secretary. In reviewing applications for permits, the Administrator shall make such provision for consultation with interested Federal and State agencies as he deems useful or necessary. No permit shall be issued for a dumping of material which will violate applicable water quality standards. To the extent that he may do so without relaxing the requirements of this subchapter, the Administrator, in establishing or revising such criteria, shall apply the standards and criteria binding upon the United States under the Convention, including its Annexes.

(b) Permit categories

The Administrator may establish and issue various categories of permits, including the general permits described in section 1414(c) of this title.

(c) Designation of sites

(1) In general

The Administrator shall, in a manner consistent with the criteria established pursuant to subsection (a) of this section, designate sites or time periods for dumping. The Administrator shall designate sites or time periods for dumping that will mitigate adverse impact on the environment to the greatest extent practicable.

(2) Prohibitions regarding site or time period

In any case where the Administrator determines that, with respect to certain materials, it is necessary to prohibit dumping at a site or during a time period, the Administrator shall prohibit the dumping of such materials in such site or during such time period. This prohibition shall apply to any dumping at the site or during such time period. This prohibition shall apply to any dumping at the site or during the time period, including any dumping under section 1413(e) of this title.

(3) Dredged material disposal sites

In the case of dredged material disposal sites, the Administrator, in conjunction with the Secretary, shall develop a site management plan for each site designated pursuant to this section. In developing such plans, the Administrator and the Secretary shall provide opportunity for public comment. Such plans shall include, but not be limited to—

(A) a baseline assessment of conditions at the site;

(B) a program for monitoring the site;

(C) special management conditions or practices to be implemented at each site that are necessary for protection of the environment;

(D) consideration of the quantity of the material to be disposed of at the site, and the presence, nature, and bioavailability of the contaminants in the material;

(E) consideration of the anticipated use of the site over the long term, including the anticipated closure date for the site, if applicable, and any need for management of the site after the closure of the site; and

(F) a schedule for review and revision of the plan (which shall not be reviewed and revised less frequently than 10 years after adoption of the plan, and every 10 years thereafter).

(4) General site management plan requirement; prohibitions

After January 1, 1995, no site shall receive a final designation unless a management plan has been developed pursuant to this section. Beginning on January 1, 1997, no permit for dumping pursuant to this Act or authorization for dumping under section 1413(e) of this title shall be issued for a site (other than the site located off the coast of Newport Beach, California, which is known as "LA–3") unless such site has received a final designation pursuant to this subsection or an alternative site has been selected pursuant to section 1413(b) of this title. Beginning January 1, 2011, no permit for dumping pursuant to this Act or authorization for dumping under section 1413(e) of this title shall be issued for the site located off the coast of Newport Beach, California, which is known as "LA–3", unless such site has received a final designation pursuant to this subsection or an alternative site has been selected pursuant to section 1413(b) of this title.

(5) Management plans for previously designated sites

The Administrator shall develop a site management plan for any site designated prior to January 1, 1995, as expeditiously as practicable, but not later than January 1, 1997, giving priority consideration to management plans for designated sites that are considered to have the greatest impact on the environment.

(d) Fish wastes

No permit is required under this subchapter for the transportation for dumping or the dumping of fish wastes, except when deposited in harbors or other protected or enclosed coastal waters, or where the Administrator finds that such deposits could endanger health, the environment, or ecological systems in a specific location. Where the Administrator makes such a finding, such material may be deposited only as authorized by a permit issued by the Administrator under this section.

(e) Foreign State permits; acceptance

In the case of transportation of material, by an agency or instrumentality of the United States or by a vessel or aircraft registered in the United States or flying the United States flag, from a location in a foreign State Party to the Convention, a permit issued pursuant to the authority of that foreign State Party, in accordance with Convention requirements, and which otherwise could have been issued pursuant to subsection (a) of this section, shall be accepted, for the purposes of this subchapter, as if it were issued by the Administrator under the authority of this section: *Provided*, That in the case of an agency or instrumentality of the United States, no application shall be made for a permit to be issued pursuant to the authority of a foreign State Party to the Convention unless the Administrator concurs in the filing of such application.

(Pub. L. 92–532, title I, §102, Oct. 23, 1972, 86 Stat. 1054; Pub. L. 93–254, §1(4), Mar. 22, 1974, 88 Stat. 51; Pub. L. 96–572, §3, Dec. 22, 1980, 94 Stat. 3345; Pub. L. 100–688, title III, §3201(b), Nov. 18, 1988, 102 Stat. 4153; Pub. L. 102–580, title V, §506(a), Oct. 31, 1992, 106 Stat. 4868; Pub. L. 104–303, title V, §582, Oct. 12, 1996, 110 Stat. 3791; Pub. L. 106–53, title V, §562, Aug. 17, 1999, 113 Stat. 355; Pub. L. 110–114, title V, §5046, Nov. 8, 2007, 121 Stat. 1209.)

REFERENCES IN TEXT

This Act, referred to in subsec. (c)(4), means Pub. L. 92–532, which is classified generally to this chapter, chapter 41 (§2801 et seq.) of this title, and chapters 32 (§1431 et seq.) and 32A (§1447 et seq.) of Title 16, Conservation.

AMENDMENTS

2007—Subsec. (c)(4). Pub. L. 110–114 substituted "January 1, 2011" for "January 1, 2003" in third sentence.

1999—Subsec. (c)(4). Pub. L. 106–53 substituted "January 1, 2003" for "January 1, 2000" in third sentence.

1996—Subsec. (e)(4). Pub. L. 104–303 inserted "(other than the site located off the coast of Newport Beach, California, which is known as 'LA–3')" after "for a site" and inserted at end "Beginning January 1, 2000, no permit for dumping pursuant to this Act or authorization for dumping under section 1413(e) of this title shall be issued for the site located off the coast of Newport Beach, California, which is known as 'LA–3', unless such site has received a final designation pursuant to this subsection or an alternative site has been selected pursuant to section 1413(b) of this title."

1992—Subsec. (c). Pub. L. 102–580 amended subsec. (c) generally. Prior to amendment, subsec. (c) read as follows: "The Administrator may, considering the criteria established pursuant to subsection (a) of this section, designate recommended sites or times for dumping and, when he finds it necessary to protect critical areas, shall, after consultation with the Secretary, also designate sites or times within which certain materials may not be dumped."

1988—Subsec. (a). Pub. L. 100–688 substituted "agents, high-level" for "agents and high-level" and inserted "and medical waste," after "radioactive waste,".

1980—Subsec. (e). Pub. L. 96–572 inserted applicability to United States agency or instrumentality, and proviso respecting such agency or instrumentality.

1974—Subsec. (a). Pub. L. 93–254, §1(4)(A), substituted "for which no permit may be issued," for "as provided for in section 1411 of this title,", inserted "or in the case of a vessel or aircraft registered in the United States or flying the United States flag," after "instrumentality of the United States,", and required the Administrator to apply the standards and criteria binding upon the United States under the Convention, including its Annexes.

Subsec. (e). Pub. L. 93–254, §1(4)(B), added subsec. (e).

EFFECTIVE DATE OF 1974 AMENDMENT

Section 2 of Pub. L. 93–254 provided in part that: "The amendments made by subparagraph 1(4)(A)(iii) and paragraph 1(4)(B) of this Act [enacting provision of subsec. (a) respecting application of standards by Administrator and subsec. (e) of this section] shall become effective on the date that the Convention on the Prevention of Marine Pollution by Dumping of Wastes and Other Matters enters into force for the United States." [The Convention entered into force for the United States Aug. 30, 1975.]

Amendment of subsec. (a) of this section, other than last sentence, by Pub. L. 93–254 effective Mar. 22, 1974, see section 2 of Pub. L. 93–254, set out in part as a note under section 1401 of this title.

§1412a. Emergency dumping of industrial waste

(a) Issuance of emergency permits

Notwithstanding section 104B of the Marine Protection, Research, and Sanctuaries Act of 1972 [33 U.S.C. 1414b], after December 31, 1981, the Administrator may issue emergency permits under title I of such Act [33 U.S.C. 1411 et seq.] for the dumping of industrial waste into ocean waters, or into waters described in such section 101(b) [33 U.S.C. 1411(b)], if the Administrator determines that there has been demonstrated to exist an emergency, requiring the dumping of such waste, which poses an unacceptable risk relating to human health and admits of no other feasible solution. As used herein, "emergency" refers to situations requiring action with a marked degree of urgency.

(b) "Industrial waste" defined

For purposes of this section, the term "industrial waste" means any solid, semisolid, or liquid waste generated by a manufacturing or processing plant.

(Pub. L. 95–153, §4, Nov. 4, 1977, 91 Stat. 1255; Pub. L. 96–572, §2, Dec. 22, 1980, 94 Stat. 3344; Pub. L. 100–688, title I, §1003(a), Nov. 18, 1988, 102 Stat. 4149.)

REFERENCES IN TEXT

The Marine Protection, Research, and Sanctuaries Act of 1972, referred to in subsec. (a), is Pub. L. 92–532, Oct. 23, 1972, 86 Stat. 1052, as amended. Title I of the Act is classified generally to this subchapter. For complete classification of this Act to the Code, see Short Title note set out under section 1401 of this title and Tables.

Such section 101(b), referred to in subsec. (b), means section 101(b) of the Marine Protection, Research, and Sanctuaries Act of 1972.

CODIFICATION

Section was not enacted as part of the Marine Protection, Research, and Sanctuaries Act of 1972 which comprises this chapter.

AMENDMENTS

1988—Subsec. (a). Pub. L. 100–688, §1003(a)(1), (3)–(5), redesignated subsec. (c) as (a), substituted "Notwithstanding section 104B of the Marine Protection, Research, and Sanctuaries Act of 1972 after" for "After", and "title I of such Act" for "such title I". Former subsec. (a), which related to cessation of dumping, with exceptions, was struck out.

Subsec. (b). Pub. L. 100–688, §1003(a)(2), (7), added subsec. (b). Former subsec. (b), which related to issuance of permits for dumping of industrial waste, was struck out.

Subsec. (c). Pub. L. 100–688, §1003(a)(3), redesignated subsec. (c) as (a).

Subsec. (d). Pub. L. 100–688, §1003(a)(6), struck out subsec. (d) which related to definitions.

1980—Subsec. (a). Pub. L. 96–572, §2(1), inserted applicability to industrial waste, exceptions respecting subsecs. (b) and (c) of this section, and conforming changes in phraseology.

Subsec. (b). Pub. L. 96–572, §2(2), added subsec. (b). Former subsec. (b), defining "sewage sludge", was struck out.

Subsecs. (c), (d). Pub. L. 96–572, §2(2), added subsecs. (c) and (d).

§1413. Dumping permit program for dredged material

(a) Issuance by Secretary of the Army

Subject to the provisions of subsections (b), (c), and (d) of this section, the Secretary may issue permits, after notice and opportunity for public hearings, for the transportation of dredged material for the purpose of dumping it into ocean waters, where the Secretary determines that the dumping will not unreasonably degrade or endanger human health, welfare, or amenities, or the marine environment, ecological systems, or economic potentialities.

(b) Independent determination of need for dumping, other methods of disposal, and appropriate locations; alternative sites

In making the determination required by subsection (a) of this section, the Secretary shall apply those criteria, established pursuant to section 1412(a) of this title, relating to the effects of the dumping. Based upon an evaluation of the potential effect of a permit denial on navigation, economic and industrial development, and foreign and domestic commerce of the United States, the Secretary shall make an independent determination as to the need for the dumping. The Secretary shall also make an independent determination as to other possible methods of disposal and as to appropriate locations for the dumping. In considering appropriate locations, he shall, to the maximum extent feasible, utilize the recommended sites designated by the Administrator pursuant to section 1412(c) of this title. In any case in which the use of a designated site is not feasible, the Secretary may, with the concurrence of the Administrator, select an alternative site. The criteria and factors established in section 1412(a) of this title relating to site selection shall be used in selecting the alternative site in a manner consistent with the application of such factors and criteria pursuant to section 1412(c) of this title. Disposal at or in the vicinity of an alternative site shall be limited to a period of not greater than 5 years unless the site is subsequently designated pursuant to section 1412(c) of this title; except that an alternative site may continue to be used for an additional period of time that shall not exceed 5 years if—

(1) no feasible disposal site has been designated by the Administrator;

(2) the continued use of the alternative site is necessary to maintain navigation and facilitate interstate or international commerce; and

(3) the Administrator determines that the continued use of the site does not pose an unacceptable risk to human health, aquatic resources, or the environment.

(c) Concurrence by Administrator

(1) Notification

Prior to issuing a permit to any person under this section, the Secretary shall first notify the Administrator of the Secretary's intention to do so and provide necessary and appropriate information concerning the permit to the Administrator. Within 30 days of receiving such information, the Administrator shall review the information and request any additional information the Administrator deems necessary to evaluate the proposed permit.

(2) Concurrence by Administrator

Within 45 days after receiving from the Secretary all information the Administrator considers to be necessary to evaluate the proposed permit, the Administrator shall, in writing, concur with (either entirely or with conditions) or decline to concur with the determination of the Secretary as to compliance with the criteria, conditions, and restrictions established pursuant to sections 1412(a) and 1412(c) of this title relating to the environmental impact of the permit. The Administrator may request one 45-day extension in writing and the Secretary shall grant such request on receipt of the request.

(3) Effect of concurrence

In any case where the Administrator makes a determination to concur (with or without conditions) or to decline to concur within the time period specified in paragraph (2) the determination shall prevail. If the Administrator declines to concur in the determination of the Secretary no permit shall be issued. If the Administrator concurs with conditions the permit shall include such conditions. The Administrator shall state in writing the reasons for declining to concur or for the conditions of the concurrence.

(4) Failure to act

If no written documentation is made by the Administrator within the time period provided for in paragraph (2), the Secretary may issue the permit.

(5) Compliance with criteria and restrictions

Unless the Administrator grants a waiver pursuant to subsection (d) of this section, any permit issued by the Secretary shall require compliance with such criteria and restrictions.

(d) Waiver of requirements

If, in any case, the Secretary finds that, in the disposition of dredged material, there is no economically feasible method or site available other than a dumping site the utilization of which would result in non-compliance with the criteria established pursuant to section 1412(a) of this title relating to the effects of dumping or with the restrictions established pursuant to section 1412(c) of this title relating to critical areas, he shall so certify and request a waiver from the Administrator of the specific requirements involved. Within thirty days of the receipt of the waiver request, unless the Administrator finds that the dumping of the material will result in an unacceptably adverse impact on municipal water supplies, shell-fish beds, wildlife, fisheries (including spawning and breeding areas), or recreational areas, he shall grant the waiver.

(e) Federal projects involving dredged material

In connection with Federal projects involving dredged material, the Secretary may, in lieu of the permit procedure, issue regulations which will require the application to such projects of the same criteria, other factors to be evaluated, the same procedures, and the same requirements which apply to the issuance of permits under subsections (a), (b), (c), and (d) of this section and section 1414(a) and (d) of this title.

(Pub. L. 92–532, title I, § 103, Oct. 23, 1972, 86 Stat. 1055; Pub. L. 102–580, title V, §§ 504, 506(b), Oct. 31, 1992, 106 Stat. 4866, 4869.)

AMENDMENTS

1992—Subsec. (b). Pub. L. 102–580, § 506(b), inserted "maximum" before "extent feasible" and inserted three sentences at end.

Subsec. (c). Pub. L. 102–580, § 504(a), amended subsec. (c) generally. Prior to amendment, subsec. (c) read as follows: "Prior to issuing any permit under this section, the Secretary shall first notify the Administrator of his intention to do so. In any case in which the Administrator disagrees with the determination of the Secretary as to compliance with the criteria established pursuant to section 1412(a) of this title relating to the effects of the dumping or with the restrictions established pursuant to section 1412(c) of this title relating to critical areas, the determination of the Administrator shall prevail. Unless the Administrator grants a waiver pursuant to subsection (d) of this section, the Secretary shall not issue a permit which does not comply with such criteria and with such restrictions."

Subsec. (e). Pub. L. 102–580, § 504(b), inserted before period at end "and section 1414(a) and (d) of this title".

§ 1414. Permit conditions

(a) Designated and included conditions

Permits issued under this subchapter shall designate and include (1) the type of material authorized to be transported for dumping or to be dumped; (2) the amount of material authorized to be transported for dumping or to be dumped; (3) the location where such transport for dumping will be terminated or where such dumping will occur; (4) such requirements, limitations, or conditions as are necessary to assure consistency with any site management plan approved pursuant to section 1412(c) of this title; (5) any special provisions deemed necessary by the Administrator or the Secretary, as the case may be, after consultation with the Secretary of the Department in which the Coast Guard is operating, for the monitoring and surveillance of the transportation or dumping; and (6) such other matters as the Administrator or the Secretary, as the case may be, deems appropriate. Permits issued under this subchapter shall be issued for a period of not to exceed 7 years.

(b) Permit processing fees; reporting requirements

The Administrator or the Secretary, as the case may be, may prescribe such processing fees for permits and such reporting requirements for actions taken pursuant to permits issued by him under this subchapter as he deems appropriate.

(c) General permits

Consistent with the requirements of sections 1412 and 1413 of this title, but in lieu of a requirement for specific permits in such case, the Administrator or the Secretary, as the case may be, may issue general permits for the transportation for dumping, or dumping, or both, of specified materials or classes of materials for which he may issue permits, which he determines will have a minimal adverse environmental impact.

(d) Review

Any permit issued under this subchapter shall be reviewed periodically and, if appropriate, revised. The Administrator or the Secretary, as the case may be, may limit or deny the issuance of permits, or he may alter or revoke partially or entirely the terms of permits issued by him under this subchapter, for the transportation for dumping, or for the dumping, or both, of specified materials or classes of materials, where he finds, based upon monitoring data from the dump site and surrounding area, that such materials cannot be dumped consistently with the criteria and other factors required to be applied in evaluating the permit application. No action shall be taken under this subsection unless the affected person or permittee shall have been given notice and opportunity for a hearing on such action as proposed.

(e) Information for review and evaluation of applications

The Administrator or the Secretary, as the case may be, shall require an applicant for a permit under this subchapter to provide such information as he may consider necessary to review and evaluate such application.

(f) Public information

Information received by the Administrator or the Secretary, as the case may be, as a part of any application or in connection with any permit granted under this subchapter shall be available to the public as a matter of public record, at every stage of the proceeding. The final determination of the Administrator or the Secretary, as the case may be, shall be likewise available.

(g) Display of issued permits

A copy of any permit issued under this subchapter shall be placed in a conspicuous place in the vessel which will be used for the transportation or dumping authorized by such permit, and an additional copy shall be furnished by the issuing official to the Secretary of the department in which the Coast Guard is operating, or its designee.

(h) Low-level radioactive waste; research purposes

Notwithstanding any provision of this subchapter to the contrary, during the two-year period beginning on January 6, 1983, no permit may be issued under this subchapter that authorizes the dumping of any low-level radioactive waste unless the Administrator of the Environmental Protection Agency determines—

(1) that the proposed dumping is necessary to conduct research—

(A) on new technology related to ocean dumping, or

(B) to determine the degree to which the dumping of such substance will degrade the marine environment;

(2) that the scale of the proposed dumping is limited to the smallest amount of such material and the shortest duration of time that is necessary to fulfill the purposes of the research, such that the dumping will have minimal adverse impact upon human health, welfare, and amenities, and the marine environment, ecological systems, economic potentialities, and other legitimate uses;

(3) after consultation with the Secretary of Commerce, that the potential benefits of such research will outweigh any such adverse impact; and

(4) that the proposed dumping will be preceded by appropriate baseline monitoring studies of the proposed dump site and its surrounding environment.

Each permit issued pursuant to this subsection shall be subject to such conditions and restrictions as the Administrator determines to be necessary to minimize possible adverse impacts of such dumping.

(i) Radioactive Material Disposal Impact Assessment; Congressional approval

(1) Two years after January 6, 1983, the Administrator may not issue a permit under this subchapter for the disposal of radioactive waste material until the applicant, in addition to complying with all other requirements of this subchapter, prepares, with respect to the site at which the disposal is proposed, a Radioactive Material Disposal Impact Assessment which shall include—

(A) a listing of all radioactive materials in each container to be disposed, the number of containers to be dumped, the structural diagrams of each container, the number of curies of each material in each container, and the exposure levels in rems at the inside and outside of each container;

(B) an analysis of the environmental impact of the proposed action, at the site at which the applicant desires to dispose of the material, upon human health and welfare and marine life;

(C) any adverse environmental effects at the site which cannot be avoided should the proposal be implemented;

(D) an analysis of the resulting environmental and economic conditions if the containers fail to contain the radioactive waste material when initially deposited at the specific site;

(E) a plan for the removal or containment of the disposed nuclear material if the container leaks or decomposes;

(F) a determination by each affected State whether the proposed action is consistent with its approved Coastal Zone Management Program;

(G) an analysis of the economic impact upon other users of marine resources;

(H) alternatives to the proposed action;

(I) comments and results of consultation with State officials and public hearings held in the coastal States that are nearest to the affected areas;

(J) a comprehensive monitoring plan to be carried out by the applicant to determine the full effect of the disposal on the marine environment, living resources, or human health, which plan shall include, but not be limited to, the monitoring of exterior container radiation samples, the taking of water and sediment samples, and fish and benthic animal samples, adjacent to the containers, and the acquisition of such other information as the Administrator may require; and

(K) such other information which the Administrator may require in order to determine the full effects of such disposal.

(2) The Administrator shall include, in any permit to which paragraph (1) applies, such terms and conditions as may be necessary to ensure that the monitoring plan required under paragraph (1)(J) is fully implemented, including the analysis by the Administrator of the samples required to be taken under the plan.

(3) The Administrator shall submit a copy of the assessment prepared under paragraph (1) with respect to any permit to the Committee on Merchant Marine and Fisheries of the House of Representatives and the Committee on Environment and Public Works of the Senate.

(4)(A) Upon a determination by the Administrator that a permit to which this subsection applies should be issued, the Administrator shall transmit such a recommendation to the House of Representatives and the Senate.

(B) No permit may be issued by the Administrator under this Act for the disposal of radioactive materials in the ocean unless the Congress, by approval of a resolution described in paragraph (D) within 90 days of continuous session of the Congress beginning on the date after the date of receipt by the Senate and the House of Representatives of such recommendation, authorizes the Administrator to grant a permit to dispose of radioactive material under this Act.

(C) For purposes of this subsection—

(1) continuity of session of the Congress is broken only by an adjournment sine die;

(2) the days on which either House is not in session because of an adjournment of more than three days to a day certain are excluded in the computation of the 90 day calendar period.

(D) For the purposes of this subsection, the term "resolution" means a joint resolution, the resolving clause of which is as follows: "That the House of Representatives and the Senate approve and authorize the Administrator of the Environmental Protection Agency to grant a permit to ________ under the Marine Protection, Research, and Sanctuaries Act of 1972 to dispose of radioactive materials in the ocean as recommended by the Administrator to the Congress on ________, 19__."; the first blank space therein to be filled with the appropriate applicant to dispose of nuclear material and the second blank therein to be filled with the date on which the Administrator submits the recommendation to the House of Representatives and the Senate.

(Pub. L. 92–532, title I, §104, Oct. 23, 1972, 86 Stat. 1056; Pub. L. 97–424, title IV, §424(a), Jan. 6, 1983, 96 Stat. 2165; Pub. L. 100–17, title I, §133(c)(1), Apr. 2, 1987, 101 Stat. 172; Pub. L. 102–580, title V, §507, Oct. 31, 1992, 106 Stat. 4869.)

REFERENCES IN TEXT

This Act and the Marine Protection, Research, and Sanctuaries Act of 1972, referred to in subsec. (i)(4)(B), (D), is Pub. L. 92–532, Oct. 23, 1972, 86 Stat. 1052, as amended, which is classified generally to this chapter, chapter 41 (§2801 et seq.) of this title, and chapters 32 (§1431 et seq.) and 32A (§1447 et seq.) of Title 16, Conservation. For complete classification of this Act to the Code, see Short Title note set out under section 1401 of this title and Tables.

AMENDMENTS

1992—Subsec. (a). Pub. L. 102–580, §507(b), inserted at end "Permits issued under this subchapter shall be issued for a period of not to exceed 7 years."

Pub. L. 102–580, §507(a), amended cl. (4) generally. Prior to amendment, cl. (4) read as follows: "the length of time for which the permits are valid and their expiration date;".

Subsec. (d). Pub. L. 102–580, §507(c), inserted ", based upon monitoring data from the dump site and surrounding area," after "where he finds".

1987—Subsec. (i)(4)(D). Pub. L. 100–17 inserted "to ________" after "grant a permit".

1983—Subsecs. (h), (i). Pub. L. 97–424 added subsecs. (h) and (i).

TRANSFER OF FUNCTIONS

For transfer of authorities, functions, personnel, and assets of the Coast Guard, including the authorities and functions of the Secretary of Transportation relating thereto, to the Department of Homeland Security, and for treatment of related references, see sections 468(b), 551(d), 552(d), and 557 of Title 6, Domestic Security, and the Department of Homeland Security Reorganization Plan of November 25, 2002, as modified, set out as a note under section 542 of Title 6.

ABOLITION OF HOUSE COMMITTEE ON MERCHANT MARINE AND FISHERIES

Committee on Merchant Marine and Fisheries of House of Representatives abolished and its jurisdiction transferred by House Resolution No. 6, One Hundred Fourth Congress, Jan. 4, 1995. For treatment of references to Committee on Merchant Marine and Fisheries, see section 1(b)(3) of Pub. L. 104–14, set out as a note preceding section 21 of Title 2, The Congress.

§1414a. Special provisions regarding certain dumping sites

(a) New York Bight Apex

(1) For purposes of this subsection—

(A) The term "Apex" means the New York Bight Apex consisting of the ocean waters of the Atlantic Ocean westward of 73 degrees 30 minutes west longitude and northward of 40 degrees 10 minutes north latitude.

(B) The term "Apex site" means that site within the Apex at which the dumping of municipal sludge occurred before October 1, 1983.

(C) The term "eligible authority" means any sewerage authority or other unit of State or local government that on November 2, 1983, was authorized under court order to dump municipal sludge at the Apex site.

(2) No person may apply for a permit under this subchapter in relation to the dumping of, or

the transportation for purposes of dumping, municipal sludge within the Apex unless that person is an eligible authority.

(3) The Administrator may not issue, or renew, any permit under this subchapter that authorizes the dumping of, or the transportation for purposes of dumping, municipal sludge within the Apex after the earlier of—

(A) December 15, 1987; or

(B) the day determined by the Administrator to be the first day on which municipal sludge generated by eligible authorities can reasonably be dumped at a site designated under section 1412 of this title other than a site within the Apex.

(b) Restriction on use of 106-mile site

The Administrator may not issue or renew any permit under this subchapter which authorizes any person, other than a person that is an eligible authority within the meaning of subsection (a)(1)(C) of this section, to dump, or to transport for the purposes of dumping, municipal sludge within the site designated under section 1412(c) of this title by the Administrator and known as the "106-Mile Ocean Waste Dump Site" (as described in 49 F.R. 19005).

(Pub. L. 92–532, title I, §104A, as added Pub. L. 99–662, title XI, §1172(b), Nov. 17, 1986, 100 Stat. 4259; Pub. L. 100–4, title V, §508(b), Feb. 4, 1987, 101 Stat. 79; Pub. L. 100–688, title I, §1002, Nov. 18, 1988, 102 Stat. 4139.)

AMENDMENTS

1988—Pub. L. 100–688 repealed the second of two identical sections 104A of Pub. L. 92–532, both classified to this section and enacted by Pub. L. 99–662 and Pub. L. 100–4, thereby involving no change in text.

NEW YORK BIGHT APEX NOT SUITABLE FOR DUMPING

Section 1172(a) of Pub. L. 99–662 provided that: "The Congress finds that the New York Bight Apex is no longer a suitable location for the ocean dumping of municipal sludge."

An identical provision was enacted by Pub. L. 100–4, title V, §508(a), Feb. 4, 1987, 101 Stat. 79.

§1414b. Ocean dumping of sewage sludge and industrial waste

(a) Termination of dumping

(1) Prohibitions on dumping

Notwithstanding any other provision of law—

(A) on and after the 270th day after November 18, 1988, no person (including a person described in section 1414a(a)(1)(C) of this title) shall dump into ocean waters, or transport for the purpose of dumping into ocean waters, sewage sludge or industrial waste, unless such person—

(i) has entered into a compliance agreement or enforcement agreement which meets the requirements of subsection (c)(2) or (3) of this section, as applicable; and

(ii) has obtained a permit issued under section 1412 of this title which authorizes such transportation and dumping; and

(B) after December 31, 1991, it shall be unlawful for any person to dump into ocean waters, or to transport for the purposes of dumping into ocean waters, sewage sludge or industrial waste.

(2) Prohibition on new entrants

The Administrator shall not issue any permit under this Act which authorizes a person to dump into ocean waters, or to transport for the purposes of dumping into ocean waters, sewage sludge or industrial waste, unless that person was authorized by a permit issued under section 1412 of this title or by a court order to dump into ocean waters, or to transport for the purpose of dumping into ocean waters, sewage sludge or industrial waste on September 1, 1988.

(b) Special dumping fees

(1) In general

Subject to paragraph (4), any person who dumps into ocean waters, or transports for the purpose of dumping into ocean waters, sewage sludge or industrial waste shall be liable for a fee equal to—

(A) $100 for each dry ton (or equivalent) of sewage sludge or industrial waste transported or dumped by the person on or after the 270th day after November 18, 1988, and before January 1, 1990;

(B) $150 for each dry ton (or equivalent) of sewage sludge or industrial waste transported or dumped by the person on or after January 1, 1990, and before January 1, 1991; and

(C) $200 for each dry ton (or equivalent) of sewage sludge or industrial waste transported or dumped by the person on or after January 1, 1991, and before January 1, 1992.

(2) Payment of fees

Of the amount of fees under paragraph (1) for which a person is liable, such person—

(A) shall pay into a trust account established by the person in accordance with subsection (e) of this section a sum equal to 85 percent of such amount;

(B) shall pay to the Administrator a sum equal to $15 per dry ton (or equivalent) of sewage sludge and industrial waste transported or dumped by such person, for use for agency activities as provided in subsection (f)(1) of this section;

(C) subject to paragraph (5), shall pay into the Clean Oceans Fund established by the State in which the person is located a sum equal to 50 percent of the balance of such amount after application of subparagraphs (A) and (B); and

(D) subject to paragraph (5), shall pay to the State in which the person is located a sum equal to the balance of such amount after application of subparagraphs (A), (B), and (C), for deposit into the water pollution control revolving fund established by the State under title VI of the Federal Water Pollution Control Act [33 U.S.C. 1381 et seq.], as provided in subsection (f)(2) of this section.

(3) Schedule for payment

Fees under this subsection shall be paid on a quarterly basis.

(4) Waiver of fees

(A) The Administrator shall waive all fees under this subsection, other than the portion of fees required to be paid to the Administrator under paragraph (2)(B) for agency activities, for any person who has entered into a compliance agreement which meets the requirements of subsection (c)(2) of this section.

(B) The Administrator shall reimpose fees under this subsection for a person for whom such fees are waived under subparagraph (A) if the Administrator determines that—

(i) the person has failed to comply with the terms of a compliance agreement which the person entered into under subsection (c)(2) of this section; and

(ii) such failure is likely to result in the person not being able to terminate by December 31, 1991, dumping of sewage sludge or industrial waste into ocean waters.

(C) The Administrator may waive fees reimposed for a person under subparagraph (B) if the Administrator determines that the person has returned to compliance with a compliance agreement which the person entered into under subsection (c)(2) of this section.

(5) Payments prior to establishment of account

(A) In any case in which a State has not established a Clean Oceans Fund or a water pollution control revolving fund under title VI of the Federal Water Pollution Control Act [33 U.S.C. 1381 et seq.], fees required to be paid by a person in that State under paragraph (2)(C) or (D), as applicable, shall be paid to the Administrator.

(B) Amounts paid to the Administrator pursuant to this paragraph shall be held by the Administrator in escrow until the establishment of the fund into which such amounts are required to be paid under paragraph (2), or until the last day of the 1-year period beginning on the date of such payment, whichever is earlier, and thereafter—

(i) if such fund has been established, shall be paid by the Administrator into the fund; or

(ii) if such fund has not been established, shall revert to the general fund of the Treasury.

(c) Compliance agreements and enforcement agreements

(1) In general

As a condition of issuing a permit under section 1412 of this title which authorizes a person to transport or dump sewage sludge or industrial waste, the Administrator shall require that, before the issuance of such permit, the person and the State in which the person is located enter into with the Administrator—

(A) a compliance agreement which meets the requirements of paragraph (2); or

(B) an enforcement agreement which meets the requirements of paragraph (3).

(2) Compliance agreements

An agreement shall be a compliance agreement for purposes of this section only if—

(A) it includes a plan negotiated by the person, the State in which the person is located, and the Administrator that will, in the opinion of the Administrator, if adhered to by the person in good faith, result in the phasing out and termination of ocean dumping, and transportation for the purpose of ocean dumping, of sewage sludge and industrial waste by such person by not later than December 31, 1991, through the design, construction, and full implementation of an alternative system for the management of sewage sludge and industrial waste transported or dumped by the person;

(B) it includes a schedule which—

(i) in the opinion of the Administrator, specifies reasonable dates by which the person shall complete the various activities that are necessary for the timely implementation of the alternative system referred to in subparagraph (A); and

(ii) meets the requirements of paragraph (4);

(C) it requires the person to notify in a timely manner the Administrator and the Governor of the State of any problems the person has in complying with the schedule referred to in subparagraph (B);

(D) it requires the Administrator and the Governor of the State to evaluate on an ongoing basis the compliance of the person with the schedule referred to in subparagraph (B);

(E) it requires the person to pay in accordance with this section all fees and penalties the person is liable for under this section; and

(F) it authorizes the person to use interim measures before completion of the alternative system referred to in subparagraph (A).

(3) Enforcement agreements

An agreement shall be an enforcement agreement for purposes of this section only if—

(A) it includes a plan negotiated by the person, the State in which the person is located, and the Administrator that will, in the opinion of the Administrator, if adhered to by the person in good faith, result in the phasing out and termination of ocean dumping, and transportation for the purpose of ocean dumping, of sewage sludge and industrial waste by such person through the design, construction, and full implementation of an alternative system for the management of sewage sludge and industrial waste transported or dumped by the person;

(B) it includes a schedule which—

(i) in the opinion of the Administrator, specifies reasonable dates by which the person shall complete the various activities that are necessary for the timely implementation of the alternative system referred to in subparagraph (A); and

(ii) meets the requirements of paragraph (4);

(C) it requires the person to notify in a timely manner the Administrator and the Governor of the State of any problems the person has in complying with the schedule referred to in subparagraph (B);

(D) it requires the Administrator and the Governor of the State to evaluate on an ongoing basis the compliance of the person with the schedule referred to in subparagraph (B);

(E) it requires the person to pay in accordance with this section all fees and penalties the person is liable for under this section; and

(F) it authorizes the person to use interim measures before completion of the alternative system referred to in subparagraph (A).

(4) Schedules

A schedule included in a compliance agreement pursuant to paragraph (2)(B) or an enforcement agreement pursuant to paragraph (3)(B) shall establish deadlines for—

(A) preparation of engineering designs and related specifications for the alternative system referred to in paragraph (2)(A) or paragraph (3)(A), as applicable;

(B) compliance with appropriate Federal, State, and local statutes, regulations, and ordinances;

(C) site and equipment acquisitions for such alternative system;

(D) construction and testing of such alternative system;

(E) operation of such alternative system at full capacity; and

(F) any other activities, including interim measures, that the Administrator considers necessary or appropriate.

(5) Clean oceans funds

(A) Each State that is a party to a compliance agreement or an enforcement agreement under this subsection shall establish an interest bearing account, to be known as a Clean Oceans Fund, into which a person shall pay fees and penalties in accordance with subsections (b)(2)(C) and (d)(2)(C)(i) of this section, respectively.

(B) A State which establishes a Clean Oceans Fund pursuant to this paragraph shall allocate and pay from the fund each year, to each person in the State which has entered into a compliance agreement or enforcement agreement under this subsection, a portion of amounts in the fund on the last day of that year which is equal to the sum of—

(i) amounts paid by the person into the fund in that year as fees pursuant to subsection (b)(2)(C) of this section and as penalties pursuant to subsection (d)(2)(C)(i) of this section;

(ii) amounts paid by the Administrator into the fund in that year as fees held in escrow for the person pursuant to subsection (b)(5)(B) of this section; and

(iii) interest on such amounts.

(C) Amounts allocated and paid to a person pursuant to subparagraph (B)—

(i) shall be used for the purposes described in subsection (e)(2)(B) of this section; and

(ii) may be used for matching Federal grants.

(D) A Clean Oceans Fund established by a State pursuant to this paragraph shall be subject to such accounting, reporting, and other requirements as may be established by the Administrator to assure accountability of payments into and out of the fund.

(6) Public participation

The Administrator shall provide an opportunity for public comment regarding the establishment and implementation of compliance agreements and enforcement agreements entered into pursuant to this section.

(d) Penalties

(1) In general

In lieu of any other civil penalty under this Act, any person who has entered into a compliance agreement or enforcement agreement under subsection (c) of this section and who dumps or transports sewage sludge or industrial waste in violation of subsection (a)(1)(B) of this section shall be liable for a civil penalty, to be assessed by the Administrator, as follows:

(A) For each dry ton (or equivalent) of sewage sludge or industrial waste dumped or transported by the person in violation of this subsection in calendar year 1992, $600.

(B) For each dry ton (or equivalent) of sewage sludge or industrial waste dumped or transported by the person in violation of this subsection in any year after calendar year 1992, a sum equal to—

(i) the amount of penalty per dry ton (or equivalent) for a violation occurring in the preceding calendar year, plus

(ii) a percentage of such amount equal to 10 percent of such amount, plus an additional 1 percent of such amount for each full calendar year since December 31, 1991.

(2) Payment of penalty

Of the amount of penalties under paragraph (1) for which a person is liable, such person—

(A) shall pay into a trust account established by the person in accordance with subsection (e) of this section a sum which is a percentage of such amount equal to—

(i) 90 percent of such amount, reduced by

(ii) 5 percent of such amount for each full calendar year since December 31, 1991;

(B) shall pay to the Administrator a sum equal to $15 per dry ton (or equivalent) of sewage sludge and industrial waste transported or dumped by such person in that year, for use for agency activities as provided in subsection (f)(1) of this section;

(C) for violations in any year before calendar year 1995—

(i) subject to paragraph (4), shall pay into the Clean Oceans Fund established by the State in which the person is located a sum equal to 50 percent of the balance of such amount; and

(ii) subject to paragraph (4), shall pay to the State in which the person is located a sum equal to the portion of such amount which is not paid as provided in subparagraphs (A), (B), and (C), for deposit into the water pollution control revolving fund established by the State under title VI of the Federal Water Pollution Control Act [33 U.S.C. 1381 et seq.], as provided in subsection (f)(2) of this section; and

(D) for violations in any year after calendar year 1994, shall pay to the State in which the person is located a sum equal to the balance of such amount, for use by the State for providing assistance under subsection (f)(3) of this section.

(3) Schedule for payment

Penalties under this subsection shall be paid on a quarterly basis.

(4) Payments prior to establishment of account

In any case in which a State has not established a Clean Oceans Fund or a water pollution control revolving fund under title VI of the Federal Water Pollution Control Act, penalties required to be paid by a person in that State under paragraph (2)(C)(i) or (ii), as applicable, shall be paid to the Administrator for holding and payment or reversion, as applicable, in the same manner as fees are held and paid or revert under subsection (b)(5) of this section.

(e) Trust account

(1) In general

A person who enters into a compliance agreement or an enforcement agreement under subsection (c) of this section shall establish a trust account for the payment and use of fees and penalties under this section.

(2) Trust account requirements

An account shall be a trust account for purposes of this subsection only if it meets, to the satisfaction of the Administrator, the following requirements:

(A) Amounts in the account may be used only with the concurrence of the person who establishes the account and the Administrator; except that the person may use amounts in the account for a purpose authorized by subparagraph (B) after 60 days after notification of the Administrator if the Administrator does not disapprove such use before the end of such 60-day period.

(B) Amounts in the account may be used only for projects which will identify, develop, and implement—

(i) an alternative system, and any interim measures, for the management of sewage sludge and industrial waste, including but not limited to any such system or measures utilizing resource recovery, recycling, thermal reduction, or composting techniques; or

(ii) improvements in pretreatment, treatment, and storage techniques for sewage sludge and industrial waste to facilitate the implementation of such alternative system or interim measures.

(C) Upon a finding by the Administrator that a person did not pay fees or penalties into an account as required by this section, or did not use amounts in the account in accordance with this subsection, the balance of the amounts in the account shall be paid to the State in which the person is located, for deposit into the water pollution control revolving fund established by the State under title VI of the Federal Water Pollution Control Act [33 U.S.C. 1381 et seq.], as provided in subsection (f)(2) of this section.

(3) Use of unexpended amounts

Upon a determination by the Administrator that a person has terminated ocean dumping of sewage sludge or industrial waste, the balance of amounts in an account established by the person under this subsection shall be paid to the person for use—

(A) for debts incurred by the person in complying with this Act or the Federal Water Pollution Control Act [33 U.S.C. 1251 et seq.];

(B) in meeting the requirements of the Federal Water Pollution Control Act (33 U.S.C. 1251 et seq.) which apply to the person, including operations and maintenance; and

(C) for matching Federal grants.

(4) Use for matching Federal grants

Amounts in a trust account under this subsection may be used for matching Federal grants.

(f) Use of fees and penalties

(1) Agency activities

Of the total amount of fees and penalties paid to the Administrator in a fiscal year pursuant to subsections (b)(2)(B) and (d)(2)(B) of this section, respectively—

(A) not to exceed one-third of such total amount shall be used by the Administrator for—

(i) costs incurred or expected to be incurred in undertaking activities directly associated with the issuance under this Act of permits for the transportation or dumping of sewage sludge and industrial waste, including the costs of any environmental assessment of the direct effects of dumping under the permits;

(ii) preparation of reports under subsection (i) of this section; and

(iii) such other research, studies, and projects the Administrator considers necessary for, and consistent with, the development and implementation of alternative systems for the management of sewage sludge and industrial waste;

(B) not to exceed one-third of such total amount shall be transferred to the Secretary of the department in which the Coast Guard is operating for use for—

(i) Coast Guard surveillance of transportation and dumping of sewage sludge and industrial waste subject to this Act; and

(ii) such enforcement activities conducted by the Coast Guard with respect to such transportation and dumping as may be necessary to ensure to the maximum extent practicable complete compliance with the requirements of this Act; and

(C) not to exceed one-third of such total amount shall be transferred to the Under Secretary of Commerce for Oceans and Atmosphere for use for—

(i) monitoring, research, and related activities consistent with the program developed pursuant to subsection (j)(1) of this section; and

(ii) preparing annual reports to the Congress pursuant to subsection (j)(4)[1] of this section which describe the results of such monitoring, research, and activities.

(2) Deposits into State water pollution control revolving fund

(A) Amounts paid to a State pursuant to subsection (b)(2)(D), (d)(2)(C)(ii), or (e)(2)(C) of this section shall be deposited into the water pollution control revolving fund established by the State pursuant to title VI of the Federal Water Pollution Control Act [33 U.S.C. 1381 et seq.].

(B) Amounts deposited into a State water pollution control revolving fund pursuant to this paragraph—

(i) shall not be used by the State to provide assistance to the person who paid such amounts for development or implementation of any alternative system;

(ii) shall not be considered to be State matching amounts under title VI of the Federal Water Pollution Control Act; and

(iii) shall not be subject to State matching requirements under such title.

(3) Penalty payments to States after 1994

(A) Amounts paid to a State as penalties pursuant to subsection (d)(2)(D) of this section may be used by the State—

(i) for providing assistance to any person in the State—

(I) for implementing a management program under section 319 of the Federal Water Pollution Control Act [33 U.S.C. 1329];

(II) for developing and implementing a conservation and management plan under section 320 of such Act [33 U.S.C. 1330]; or

(III) for implementing technologies and management practices necessary for controlling pollutant inputs adversely affecting the New York Bight, as such inputs are identified in the New York Bight Restoration Plan prepared under section 2301 of the Marine Plastic Pollution Research and Control Act of 1987; and

(ii) for providing assistance to any person in the State who was not required to pay such penalties for construction of treatment works (as defined in section 212 of the Federal Water Pollution Control Act [33 U.S.C. 1292]) which are publicly owned.

(B) Amounts paid to a State as penalties pursuant to subsection (d)(2)(D) of this section which are not used in accordance with subparagraph (A) shall be deposited into the water pollution control revolving fund established by the State under title VI of the Federal Water Pollution Control Act. Amounts deposited into such a fund pursuant to this subparagraph—

(i) shall not be used by the State to provide assistance to the person who paid such amounts;

(ii) shall not be considered to be State matching amounts under title VI of the Federal Water Pollution Control Act; and

(iii) shall not be subject to State matching requirements under such title.

(4) Deposits into Treasury as offsetting collections

Amounts of fees and penalties paid to the Administrator pursuant to subsection (b)(2)(B) or (d)(2)(B) of this section which are used by an agency in accordance with paragraph (1) shall be deposited into the Treasury as offsetting collections of the agency.

(g) Enforcement

(1) In general

Whenever, on the basis of any information available, the Administrator finds that a person is dumping or transporting sewage sludge or industrial waste in violation of subsection (a)(1) of this section, the Administrator shall issue an order requiring such person to terminate such dumping or transporting (as applicable) until such person—

(A) enters into a compliance agreement or an enforcement agreement under subsection (c) of this section; and

(B) obtains a permit under section 1412 of this title which authorizes such dumping or transporting.

(2) Requirements of order

Any order issued by the Administrator under this subsection—

(A) shall be delivered by personal service to the person named in the order;

(B) shall state with reasonable specificity the nature of the violation for which the order is issued; and

(C) shall require that the person named in the order, as a condition of dumping into ocean waters, or transporting for the purpose of dumping into ocean waters, sewage sludge or industrial waste—

(i) shall enter into a compliance agreement or an enforcement agreement under subsection (c) of this section; and

(ii) shall obtain a permit under section 1412 of this title which authorizes such dumping or transporting.

(3) Actions

The Administrator may request the Attorney General to commence a civil action for appropriate relief, including a temporary or permanent injunction and the imposition of civil penalties authorized by subsection (d)(1) of this section, for any violation of subsection (a)(1) of this section or of an order issued by the Administrator under this section. Such an action may be brought in the district court of the United States for the district in which the defendant is located, resides, or is doing business, and such court shall have jurisdiction to restrain such violation and require compliance with subsection (a)(1) of this section and any such order.

(h) State progress reports

(1) In general

The Governor of each State that is a party to a compliance agreement or an enforcement agreement under subsection (c) of this section shall submit to the Administrator on Septem-

[1] See References in Text note below.

ber 30 of 1989 and of every year thereafter until the Administrator determines that ocean dumping of sewage sludge and industrial waste by persons located in that State has terminated, a report which describes—

(A) the efforts of each person located in the State to comply with a compliance agreement or enforcement agreement entered into by the person pursuant to subsection (c) of this section, including the extent to which such person has complied with deadlines established by the schedule included in such agreement;

(B) activity of the State regarding permits for the construction and operation of each alternative system; and

(C) an accounting of amounts paid into and withdrawn from a Clean Oceans Fund established by the State.

(2) Failure to submit report

If a State fails to submit a report in accordance with this subsection, the Administrator shall withhold funds reserved for such State under section 205(g) of the Federal Water Pollution Control Act (33 U.S.C. 1285(g)). Funds withheld pursuant to this paragraph may, at the discretion of the Administrator, be restored to a State upon compliance with this subsection.

(i) EPA progress reports

(1) In general

Not later than December 31 of 1989 and of each year thereafter until the Administrator determines that ocean dumping of sewage sludge and industrial waste has terminated, the Administrator shall prepare and submit to the Congress a report on—

(A) progress being made by persons issued permits under section 1412 of this title for transportation or dumping of sewage sludge or industrial waste in developing alternative systems for managing sewage sludge and industrial waste;

(B) the efforts of each such person to comply with a compliance agreement or enforcement agreement entered into by the person pursuant to subsection (c) of this section, including the extent to which such person has complied with deadlines established by the schedule included in such agreement;

(C) progress being made by the Administrator and others in identifying and implementing alternative systems for the management of sewage sludge and industrial waste; and

(D) progress being made toward the termination of ocean dumping of sewage sludge and industrial waste.

(2) Referral to Congressional committees

Each report submitted to the Congress under this subsection shall be referred to each standing committee of the House of Representatives and of the Senate having jurisdiction over any part of the subject matter of the report.

(j) Environmental monitoring

(1) In general

The Administrator, in cooperation with the Under Secretary of Commerce for Oceans and Atmosphere, shall design a program for monitoring environmental conditions—

(A) at the Apex site (as that term is defined in section 1414a of this title);

(B) at the site designated by the Administrator under section 1412(c) of this title and known as the "106-Mile Ocean Waste Dump Site" (as described in 49 F.R. 19005);

(C) at the site at which industrial waste is dumped; and

(D) within the potential area of influence of the sewage sludge and industrial waste dumped at those sites.

(2) Program requirements

The program designed under paragraph (1) shall include, but is not limited to—

(A) sampling of an appropriate number of fish and shellfish species and other organisms to assess the effects of environmental conditions on living marine organisms in these areas; and

(B) use of satellite and other advanced technologies in conducting the program.

(3) Monitoring activities

The Administrator and the Under Secretary of Commerce for Oceans and Atmosphere shall each conduct monitoring activities consistent with the program designed under paragraph (1).

(4) Omitted

(k) Definitions

For purposes of this section—

(1) the term "alternative system" means any method for the management of sewage sludge or industrial waste which does not require a permit under this Act;

(2) the term "Clean Oceans Fund" means such a fund established by a State in accordance with subsection (c)(5) of this section;

(3) the term "excluded material" means—

(A) any dredged material discharged by the United States Army Corps of Engineers or discharged pursuant to a permit issued by the Secretary in accordance with section 1413 of this title; and

(B) any waste from a tuna cannery operation located in American Samoa or Puerto Rico discharged pursuant to a permit issued by the Administrator under section 1412 of this title;

(4) the term "industrial waste" means any solid, semisolid, or liquid waste generated by a manufacturing or processing plant, other than an excluded material;

(5) the term "interim measure" means any short-term method for the management of sewage sludge or industrial waste, which—

(A) is used before implementation of an alternative system; and

(B) does not require a permit under this Act; and

(6) the term "sewage sludge" means any solid, semisolid, or liquid waste generated by a wastewater treatment plant, other than an excluded material.

(Pub. L. 92–532, title I, §104B, as added Pub. L. 100–688, title I, §1002, Nov. 18, 1988, 102 Stat. 4139.)

REFERENCES IN TEXT

This Act, referred to in subsecs. (a)(2), (d)(1), (e)(3)(A), (f)(1)(A)(i), (B), and (k)(1), (5)(B), means Pub. L. 92–532, which is classified generally to this chapter, chapter 41 (§2801 et seq.) of this title, and chapters 32 (§1431 et seq.) and 32A (§1447 et seq.) of Title 16, Conservation.

The Federal Water Pollution Control Act, referred to in subsecs. (b)(2)(D), (5)(A), (d)(2)(C)(ii), (4), (e)(2)(C), (3)(A), (B), (f)(2)(A), (B)(ii), (iii), and (3)(B), is act June 30, 1948, ch. 758, as amended generally by Pub. L. 92–500, §2, Oct. 18, 1972, 86 Stat. 816, which is classified generally to chapter 26 (§1251 et seq.) of this title. Title VI of that Act is classified to subchapter VI (§1381 et seq.) of chapter 26 of this title. For complete classification of this Act to the Code, see Short Title note set out under section 1251 of this title and Tables.

Subsection (j)(4) of this section, referred to in subsec. (f)(1)(C)(ii), was omitted from the Code. See Codification note below.

Section 2301 of the Marine Plastic Pollution Research and Control Act of 1987, referred to in subsec. (f)(3)(A)(i)(III), is section 2301 of Pub. L. 100–220 which is set out as a note under section 2267 of this title.

CODIFICATION

Subsec. (j)(4)(A) of this section directed the Administrator, in cooperation with the Under Secretary of Commerce for Oceans and Atmosphere, to submit to Congress a report describing the program designed pursuant to subsec. (j)(1) of this section not later than one year after Nov. 18, 1988.

Subsec. (j)(4)(B) of this section, which required the Administrator and the Under Secretary of Commerce for Oceans and Atmosphere to report annually to Congress on monitoring activities conducted under the program designed pursuant to subsec. (j)(1) of this section, terminated, effective May 15, 2000, pursuant to section 3003 of Pub. L. 104–66, as amended, set out as a note under section 1113 of Title 31, Money and Finance. See, also, page 148 of House Document No. 103–7.

TRANSFER OF FUNCTIONS

For transfer of authorities, functions, personnel, and assets of the Coast Guard, including the authorities and functions of the Secretary of Transportation relating thereto, to the Department of Homeland Security, and for treatment of related references, see sections 468(b), 551(d), 552(d), and 557 of Title 6, Domestic Security, and the Department of Homeland Security Reorganization Plan of November 25, 2002, as modified, set out as a note under section 542 of Title 6.

§1414c. Prohibition on disposal of sewage sludge at landfills on Staten Island

(a) In general

No person shall dispose of sewage sludge at any landfill located on Staten Island, New York.

(b) Exclusion from penalties

(1) In general

Subject to paragraph (2), a person who violates this section shall not be subject to any penalty under this Act.

(2) Injunction

Paragraph (1) shall not prohibit the bringing of an action for, or the granting of, an injunction under section 1415 of this title with respect to a violation of this section.

(c) "Sewage sludge" defined

For purposes of this section, the term "sewage sludge" has the meaning such term has in section 1414b of this title.

(Pub. L. 92–532, title I, §104C, as added Pub. L. 100–688, title I, §1005, Nov. 18, 1988, 102 Stat. 4150.)

REFERENCES IN TEXT

This Act, referred to in subsec. (b)(1), means Pub. L. 92–532, which is classified generally to this chapter, chapter 41 (§2801 et seq.) of this title, and chapters 32 (§1431 et seq.) and 32A (§1447 et seq.) of Title 16, Conservation.

§1415. Penalties

(a) Assessment of civil penalty by Administrator; remission or mitigation; court action for appropriate relief

Any person who violates any provision of this subchapter, or of the regulations promulgated under this subchapter, or a permit issued under this subchapter shall be liable to a civil penalty of not more than $50,000 for each violation to be assessed by the Administrator. In addition, any person who violates this subchapter or any regulation issued under this subchapter by engaging in activity involving the dumping of medical waste shall be liable for a civil penalty of not more than $125,000 for each violation, to be assessed by the Administrator after written notice and an opportunity for a hearing. No penalty shall be assessed until the person charged shall have been given notice and an opportunity for a hearing of such violation. In determining the amount of the penalty, the gravity of the violation, prior violations, and the demonstrated good faith of the person charged in attempting to achieve rapid compliance after notification of a violation shall be considered by said Administrator. For good cause shown, the Administrator may remit or mitigate such penalty. Upon failure of the offending party to pay the penalty, the Administrator may request the Attorney General to commence an action in the appropriate district court of the United States for such relief as may be appropriate.

(b) Criminal penalties

In addition to any action that may be brought under subsection (a) of this section—

(1) any person who knowingly violates any provision of this subchapter, any regulation promulgated under this subchapter, or a permit issued under this subchapter, shall be fined under title 18 or imprisoned for not more than 5 years, or both; and

(2) any person who is convicted of such a violation pursuant to paragraph (1) shall forfeit to the United States—

(A) any property constituting or derived from any proceeds that the person obtained, directly or indirectly, as a result of such violation; and

(B) any of the property of the person which was used, or intended to be used in any manner or part, to commit or to facilitate the commission of the violation.

(c) Separate offenses

For the purpose of imposing civil penalties and criminal fines under this section, each day of a continuing violation shall constitute a separate offense as shall the dumping from each of several vessels, or other sources.

(d) Injunctive relief

The Attorney General or his delegate may bring actions for equitable relief to enjoin an imminent or continuing violation of this subchapter, of regulations promulgated under this subchapter, or of permits issued under this subchapter, and the district courts of the United States shall have jurisdiction to grant such relief as the equities of the case may require.

(e) Liability of vessels in rem

A vessel, except a public vessel within the meaning of section 13 of the Federal Water Pollution Control Act, as amended, used in a violation, shall be liable in rem for any civil penalty assessed or criminal fine imposed and may be proceeded against in any district court of the United States having jurisdiction thereof; but no vessel shall be liable unless it shall appear that one or more of the owners, or bareboat charterers, was at the time of the violation a consenting party or privy to such violation.

(f) Revocation and suspension of permits

If the provisions of any permit issued under section 1412 or 1413 of this title are violated, the Administrator or the Secretary, as the case may be, may revoke the permit or may suspend the permit for a specified period of time. No permit shall be revoked or suspended unless the permittee shall have been given notice and opportunity for a hearing on such violation and proposed suspension or revocation.

(g) Civil suits by private persons

(1) Except as provided in paragraph (2) of this subsection any person may commence a civil suit on his own behalf to enjoin any person, including the United States and any other governmental instrumentality or agency (to the extent permitted by the eleventh amendment to the Constitution), who is alleged to be in violation of any prohibition, limitation, criterion, or permit established or issued by or under this subchapter. The district courts shall have jurisdiction, without regard to the amount in controversy or the citizenship of the parties, to enforce such prohibition, limitation, criterion, or permit, as the case may be.

(2) No action may be commenced—

(A) prior to sixty days after notice of the violation has been given to the Administrator or to the Secretary, and to any alleged violator of the prohibition, limitation, criterion, or permit; or

(B) if the Attorney General has commenced and is diligently prosecuting a civil action in a court of the United States to require compliance with the prohibition, limitation, criterion, or permit; or

(C) if the Administrator has commenced action to impose a penalty pursuant to subsection (a) of this section, or if the Administrator, or the Secretary, has initiated permit revocation or suspension proceedings under subsection (f) of this section; or

(D) if the United States has commenced and is diligently prosecuting a criminal action in a court of the United States or a State to redress a violation of this subchapter.

(3)(A) Any suit under this subsection may be brought in the judicial district in which the violation occurs.

(B) In any such suit under this subsection in which the United States is not a party, the Attorney General, at the request of the Administrator or Secretary, may intervene on behalf of the United States as a matter of right.

(4) The court, in issuing any final order in any suit brought pursuant to paragraph (1) of this subsection may award costs of litigation (including reasonable attorney and expert witness fees) to any party, whenever the court determines such award is appropriate.

(5) The injunctive relief provided by this subsection shall not restrict any right which any person (or class of persons) may have under any statute or common law to seek enforcement of any standard or limitation or to seek any other relief (including relief against the Administrator, the Secretary, or a State agency).

(h) Emergencies

No person shall be subject to a civil penalty or to a criminal fine or imprisonment for dumping materials from a vessel if such materials are dumped in an emergency to safeguard life at sea. Any such emergency dumping shall be reported to the Administrator under such conditions as he may prescribe.

(i) Seizure and forfeiture

(1) In general

Any vessel used to commit an act for which a penalty is imposed under subsection (b) of this section shall be subject to seizure and forfeiture to the United States under procedures established for seizure and forfeiture of conveyances under sections 853 and 881 of title 21.

(2) Limitation on application

This subsection does not apply to an act committed substantially in accordance with a compliance agreement or enforcement agreement entered into by the Administrator under section 1414b(c) of this title.

(Pub. L. 92–532, title I, §105, Oct. 23, 1972, 86 Stat. 1057; Pub. L. 100–688, title III, §3201(c), (d), Nov. 18, 1988, 102 Stat. 4153; Pub. L. 102–580, title V, §508, Oct. 31, 1992, 106 Stat. 4869.)

References in Text

Section 13 of the Federal Water Pollution Control Act, referred to in subsec. (e), is section 13 of act June 30, 1948, ch. 758, as added by act Apr. 3, 1970, Pub. L. 91–224, title I, §102, 84 Stat. 100, which was classified to section 1163 of this title and was superseded by Pub. L. 92–500, Oct. 18, 1972, 86 Stat. 816. See section 1322 of this title.

Amendments

1992—Subsec. (b). Pub. L. 102–580, §508(a), amended subsec. (b) generally. Prior to amendment, subsec. (b) read as follows:

"(1) In addition to any action which may be brought under subsection (a) of this section, a person who knowingly violates this subchapter, regulations promulgated under this subchapter, or a permit issued under this subchapter shall be fined not more than $50,000, or imprisoned for not more than one year, or both.

"(2) In addition to any action which may be brought under subsection (a) of this section, any person—

"(A) who knowingly violates any provision of this subchapter by engaging in activity involving the dumping into ocean waters of medical waste shall upon conviction be fined not more than $250,000, or imprisoned for not more than 5 years, or both; and

"(B) convicted of a violation involving such activity shall forfeit to the United States any property constituting or derived from any proceeds the person obtained, directly or indirectly, as a result of such violation, and any of the property of the person which was used, or intended to be used in any manner or part, to commit or to facilitate the commission of the violation."

Subsec. (i). Pub. L. 102–508, §508(b), added subsec. (i).

1988—Subsec. (a). Pub. L. 100–688, §3201(c), inserted provisions relating to civil penalty of not more than $125,000 for engaging in activity involving dumping of medical waste.

Subsec. (b). Pub. L. 100–688, §3201(d), designated existing provisions as par. (1) and added par. (2).

§1416. Relationship to other laws

(a) Voiding of preexisting licenses

After the effective date of this subchapter, all licenses, permits, and authorizations other than those issued pursuant to this subchapter shall be void and of no legal effect, to the extent that they purport to authorize any activity regulated by this subchapter, and whether issued before or after the effective date of this subchapter.

(b) Actions under authority of Rivers and Harbors Act

The provisions of subsection (a) of this section shall not apply to actions taken before the effective date of this subchapter under the authority of the Rivers and Harbors Act of 1899 (30 Stat. 1151), as amended (33 U.S.C. 401 et seq.).

(c) Impairment of navigation

Prior to issuing any permit under this subchapter, if it appears to the Administrator that the disposition of material, other than dredged material, may adversely affect navigation in the territorial sea of the United States, or in the approaches to any harbor of the United States, or may create an artificial island on the Outer Continental Shelf, the Administrator shall consult with the Secretary and no permit shall be issued if the Secretary determines that navigation will be unreasonably impaired.

(d) State programs

(1) State rights preserved

Except as expressly provided in this subsection, nothing in this subchapter shall preclude or deny the right of any State to adopt or enforce any requirements respecting dumping of materials into ocean waters within the jurisdiction of the State.

(2) Federal projects

In the case of a Federal project, a State may not adopt or enforce a requirement that is more stringent than a requirement under this subchapter if the Administrator finds that such requirement—

(A) is not supported by relevant scientific evidence showing the requirement to be protective of human health, aquatic resources, or the environment;

(B) is arbitrary or capricious; or

(C) is not applicable or is not being applied to all projects without regard to Federal, State, or private participation and the Secretary of the Army concurs in such finding.

(3) Exemption from State requirements

The President may exempt a Federal project from any State requirement respecting dumping of materials into ocean waters if it is in the paramount interest of the United States to do so.

(4) Consideration of site of origin prohibited

Any requirement respecting dumping of materials into ocean waters applied by a State shall be applied without regard to the site of origin of the material to be dumped.

(e) Existing conservation programs not affected

Nothing in this subchapter shall be deemed to affect in any manner or to any extent any provision of the Fish and Wildlife Coordination Act as amended (16 U.S.C. 661–666c).

(f) Dumping of dredged material in Long Island Sound from any Federal, etc., project

In addition to other provisions of law and not withstanding the specific exclusion relating to dredged material in the first sentence in section 1412(a) of this title, the dumping of dredged material in Long Island Sound from any Federal project (or pursuant to Federal authorization) or from a dredging project by a non-Federal applicant exceeding 25,000 cubic yards shall comply with the requirements of this subchapter.

(g) Savings clause

Nothing in this Act shall restrict, affect or modify the rights of any person (1) to seek damages or enforcement of any standard or limitation under State law, including State common law, or (2) to seek damages under other Federal law, including maritime tort law, resulting from noncompliance with any requirement of this Act or any permit under this Act.

(Pub. L. 92–532, title I, §106, Oct. 23, 1972, 86 Stat. 1058; Pub. L. 96–572, §4, Dec. 22, 1980, 94 Stat. 3345; Pub. L. 99–499, title I, §127(d), Oct. 17, 1986, 100 Stat. 1693; Pub. L. 101–596, title II, §203, Nov. 16, 1990, 104 Stat. 3006; Pub. L. 102–580, title V, §505, Oct. 31, 1992, 106 Stat. 4867.)

References in Text

The effective date of this subchapter, referred to in subsecs. (a) and (b), means the effective date of title I of Pub. L. 92–532, which is six months after Oct. 23, 1972. See section 110(a) of Pub. L. 92–532, set out as an Effective Date note under section 1411 of this title.

The Rivers and Harbors Act of 1899, referred to in subsec. (b), is act Mar. 3, 1899, ch. 425, 30 Stat. 1151, as amended, which enacted sections 401, 403, 404, 406 to 409, 411 to 416, 418, 502, 549, 686, and 687 of this title. For complete classification of this Act to the Code, see Tables.

The Fish and Wildlife Coordination Act referred to in subsec. (e), is act Mar. 10, 1934, ch. 55, 48 Stat. 401, as amended, which is classified generally to sections 661 to 666c of Title 16, Conservation. For complete classification of this Act to the Code, see Short Title note set out under section 661 of Title 16 and Tables.

This Act, referred to in subsec. (g), means Pub. L. 92–532, which is classified generally to this chapter, chapter 41 (§2801 et seq.) of this title, and chapters 32 (§1431 et seq.) and 32A (§1447 et seq.) of Title 16.

Amendments

1992—Subsec. (d). Pub. L. 102–580 amended subsec. (d) generally. Prior to amendment, subsec. (d) read as follows: "After the effective date of this subchapter, no State shall adopt or enforce any rule or regulation relating to any activity regulated by this subchapter. Any State may, however, propose to the Administrator criteria relating to the dumping of materials into ocean waters within its jurisdiction, or into other ocean waters to the extent that such dumping may affect waters within the jurisdiction of such State, and if the Administrator determines, after notice and opportunity for hearing, that the proposed criteria are not inconsistent with the purposes of this subchapter, may adopt those criteria and may issue regulations to implement such criteria. Such determination shall be made by the Administrator within one hundred and twenty days of receipt of the proposed criteria. For the purposes of this subsection, the term 'State' means any State, interstate or regional authority, Federal territory or Commonwealth or the District of Columbia."

1990—Subsec. (f). Pub. L. 101–596, which directed the substitution of "the requirements of this subchapter" for all after "shall comply with" in "subsection 116(g) of the Marine Protection Research and Sanctuaries Act (33 U.S.C. 1416(g))", was executed by making the substitution for "the criteria established pursuant to the second sentence of section 1412(a) of this title relating to the effects of dumping. Subsection (d) of this section shall not apply to this subsection." which followed "shall comply with" in section 106(f) of the Marine Protection Research and Sanctuaries Act of 1972, which is classified to subsec. (f) of this section, to reflect the probable intent of Congress.

1986—Subsec. (g). Pub. L. 99–499 added subsec. (g).

1980—Subsec. (f). Pub. L. 96–572 added subsec. (f).

TERRITORIAL SEA OF UNITED STATES

For extension of territorial sea of United States, see Proc. No. 5928, set out as a note under section 1331 of Title 43, Public Lands.

§1417. Enforcement

(a) Utilization of other departments, agencies, and instrumentalities

The Administrator or the Secretary, as the case may be, may, whenever appropriate, utilize by agreement, the personnel, services and facilities of other Federal departments, agencies, and instrumentalities, or State agencies or instrumentalities, whether on a reimbursable or a nonreimbursable basis, in carrying out his responsibilities under this subchapter.

(b) Delegation of review and evaluation authority

The Administrator or the Secretary may delegate responsibility and authority for reviewing and evaluating permit applications, including the decision as to whether a permit will be issued, to an officer of his agency, or he may delegate, by agreement, such responsibility and authority to the heads of other Federal departments or agencies, whether on a reimbursable or nonreimbursable basis.

(c) Surveillance and other enforcement activity

The Secretary of the department in which the Coast Guard is operating shall conduct surveillance and other appropriate enforcement activity to prevent unlawful transportation of material for dumping, or unlawful dumping. Such enforcement activity shall include, but not be limited to, enforcement of regulations issued by him pursuant to section 1418 of this title, relating to safe transportation, handling, carriage, storage, and stowage. The Secretary of the Department in which the Coast Guard is operating shall supply to the Administrator and to the Attorney General, as appropriate, such information of enforcement activities and such evidentiary material assembled as they may require in carrying out their duties relative to penalty assessments, criminal prosecutions, or other actions involving litigation pursuant to the provisions of this subchapter.

(Pub. L. 92–532, title I, §107, Oct. 23, 1972, 86 Stat. 1059.)

TRANSFER OF FUNCTIONS

For transfer of authorities, functions, personnel, and assets of the Coast Guard, including the authorities and functions of the Secretary of Transportation relating thereto, to the Department of Homeland Security, and for treatment of related references, see sections 468(b), 551(d), 552(d), and 557 of Title 6, Domestic Security, and the Department of Homeland Security Reorganization Plan of November 25, 2002, as modified, set out as a note under section 542 of Title 6.

§1418. Regulations

In carrying out the responsibilities and authority conferred by this subchapter, the Administrator, the Secretary, and the Secretary of the department in which the Coast Guard is operating are authorized to issue such regulations as they may deem appropriate.

(Pub. L. 92–532, title I, §108, Oct. 23, 1972, 86 Stat. 1059.)

TRANSFER OF FUNCTIONS

For transfer of authorities, functions, personnel, and assets of the Coast Guard, including the authorities and functions of the Secretary of Transportation relating thereto, to the Department of Homeland Security, and for treatment of related references, see sections 468(b), 551(d), 552(d), and 557 of Title 6, Domestic Security, and the Department of Homeland Security Reorganization Plan of November 25, 2002, as modified, set out as a note under section 542 of Title 6.

§1419. International cooperation

The Secretary of State, in consultation with the Administrator, shall seek effective international action and cooperation to insure protection of the marine environment, and may, for this purpose, formulate, present, or support specific proposals in the United Nations and other component international organizations for the development of appropriate international rules and regulations in support of the policy of this Act.

(Pub. L. 92–532, title I, §109, Oct. 23, 1972, 86 Stat. 1060.)

REFERENCES IN TEXT

This Act, referred to in text, means Pub. L. 92–532, which is classified generally to this chapter, chapter 41 (§2801 et seq.) of this title, and chapters 32 (§1431 et seq.) and 32A (§1447 et seq.) of Title 16, Conservation.

§1420. Authorization of appropriations

There are authorized to be appropriated, for purposes of carrying out this subchapter, not to exceed $12,000,000 for fiscal year 1993 and not to exceed $14,000,000 for each of the fiscal years 1994, 1995, 1996, and 1997, to remain available until expended.

(Pub. L. 92–532, title I, §111, Oct. 23, 1972, 86 Stat. 1060; Pub. L. 93–472, Oct. 26, 1974, 88 Stat. 1430; Pub. L. 94–62, §1, July 25, 1975, 89 Stat. 303; Pub. L. 94–326, §1, June 30, 1976, 90 Stat. 725; Pub. L. 95–153, §1, Nov. 4, 1977, 91 Stat. 1255; Pub. L.

96–572, §1, Dec. 22, 1980, 94 Stat. 3344; Pub. L. 97–16, June 23, 1981, 95 Stat. 100; Pub. L. 100–536, Oct. 28, 1988, 102 Stat. 2710; Pub. L. 102–580, title V, §509(a), Oct. 31, 1992, 106 Stat. 4870.)

AMENDMENTS

1992—Pub. L. 102–580 substituted "for fiscal year 1993 and not to exceed $14,000,000 for each of the fiscal years 1994, 1995, 1996, and 1997, to remain available until expended" for "for each of fiscal years 1989, 1990, and 1991".

1988—Pub. L. 100–536 amended section generally, substituting provisions authorizing appropriations not to exceed $12,000,000 for each of fiscal years 1989, 1990, and 1991, for provisions authorizing appropriations for fiscal years 1973 to 1982.

1981—Pub. L. 97–16 increased to $4,213,000 from $2,000,000 the authorization of appropriation for fiscal year 1982.

1980—Pub. L. 96–572 inserted provisions authorizing appropriations for fiscal years 1980, 1981, and 1982.

1977—Pub. L. 95–153 inserted provision authorizing appropriations not to exceed $4,800,000 for fiscal year 1978.

1976—Pub. L. 94–326 inserted provision authorizing appropriations not to exceed $4,800,000 for fiscal year 1977.

1975—Pub. L. 94–62 substituted "not to exceed $5,500,000 for each of the fiscal years 1974 and 1975" for "and not to exceed $5,500,000 for fiscal years 1974 and 1975", and inserted provisions authorizing appropriation of an amount not to exceed $5,300,000 for fiscal year 1976, and not to exceed $1,325,000 for the transition period (July 1 through Sept. 30, 1976).

1974—Pub. L. 93–472 substituted "fiscal years 1974 and 1975," for "fiscal year 1974,".

§1421. Omitted

CODIFICATION

Section, Pub. L. 92–532, title I, §112, Oct. 23, 1972, 86 Stat. 1060; Pub. L. 94–326, §2, June 30, 1976, 90 Stat. 725; Pub. L. 96–470, title II, §209(f), Oct. 19, 1980, 94 Stat. 2245; Pub. L. 102–580, title V, §510, Oct. 31, 1992, 106 Stat. 4870, which required the Administrator of the Environmental Protection Agency to report annually to Congress on the administration of this subchapter, terminated, effective May 15, 2000, pursuant to section 3003 of Pub. L. 104–66, as amended, set out as a note under section 1113 of Title 31, Money and Finance. See, also, page 163 of House Document No. 103–7.

SUBCHAPTER II—RESEARCH

§1441. Monitoring and research program

The Secretary of Commerce, in coordination with the Secretary of the Department in which the Coast Guard is operating and with the Administrator shall, within six months of October 23, 1972, initiate a comprehensive and continuing program of monitoring and research regarding the effects of the dumping of material into ocean waters or other coastal waters where the tide ebbs and flows or into the Great Lakes or their connecting waters.

(Pub. L. 92–532, title II, §201, Oct. 23, 1972, 86 Stat. 1060; Pub. L. 99–272, title VI, §6061, Apr. 7, 1986, 100 Stat. 131.)

AMENDMENTS

1986—Pub. L. 99–272 struck out provision which had required the Secretary of Commerce to report from time to time, not less frequently than annually, his findings under this section (including an evaluation of the short-term ecological effects and the social and economic factors involved) to the Congress.

TRANSFER OF FUNCTIONS

For transfer of authorities, functions, personnel, and assets of the Coast Guard, including the authorities and functions of the Secretary of Transportation relating thereto, to the Department of Homeland Security, and for treatment of related references, see sections 468(b), 551(d), 552(d), and 557 of Title 6, Domestic Security, and the Department of Homeland Security Reorganization Plan of November 25, 2002, as modified, set out as a note under section 542 of Title 6.

§1442. Research program respecting possible long-range effects of pollution, overfishing, and man-induced changes of ocean ecosystems

(a) Secretary of Commerce

(1) The Secretary of Commerce, in close consultation with other appropriate Federal departments, agencies, and instrumentalities shall, within six months of October 23, 1972, initiate a comprehensive and continuing program of research with respect to the possible long-range effects of pollution, overfishing, and man-induced changes of ocean ecosystems. These responsibilities shall include the scientific assessment of damages to the natural resources from spills of petroleum or petroleum products. In carrying out such research, the Secretary of Commerce shall take into account such factors as existing and proposed international policies affecting oceanic problems, economic considerations involved in both the protection and the use of the oceans, possible alternatives to existing programs, and ways in which the health of the oceans may best be preserved for the benefit of succeeding generations of mankind.

(2) The Secretary of Commerce shall ensure that the program under this section complements, when appropriate, the activities undertaken by other Federal agencies pursuant to subchapter I of this chapter and section 1443 of this title. That program shall include but not be limited to—

(A) the development and assessment of scientific techniques to define and quantify the degradation of the marine environment;

(B) the assessment of the capacity of the marine environment to receive materials without degradation;

(C) continuing monitoring programs to assess the health of the marine environment, including but not limited to the monitoring of bottom oxygen concentrations, contaminant levels in biota, sediments, and the water column, diseases in fish and shellfish, and changes in types and abundance of indicator species;

(D) the development of methodologies, techniques, and equipment for disposal of waste materials to minimize degradation of the marine environment.

(3) The Secretary of Commerce shall ensure that the comprehensive and continuing research program conducted under this subsection is consistent with the comprehensive plan for ocean pollution research and development and monitoring prepared under section 1703[1] of this title.

(b) Action with other nations

In carrying out his responsibilities under this section, the Secretary of Commerce, under the foreign policy guidance of the President and

[1] See References in Text note below.

pursuant to international agreements and treaties made by the President with the advice and consent of the Senate, may act alone or in conjunction with any other nation or group of nations, and shall make known the results of his activities by such channels of communication as may appear appropriate.

(c) Cooperation of other departments, agencies, and independent instrumentalities

Each department, agency, and independent instrumentality of the Federal Government is authorized and directed to cooperate with the Secretary of Commerce in carrying out the purposes of this section and, to the extent permitted by law, to furnish such information as may be requested.

(d) Utilization of personnel, services, and facilities; inter-agency agreements

The Secretary of Commerce, in carrying out his responsibilities under this section, shall, to the extent feasible utilize the personnel, services, and facilities of other Federal departments, agencies, and instrumentalities (including those of the Coast Guard for monitoring purposes), and is authorized to enter into appropriate inter-agency agreements to accomplish this action.

(Pub. L. 92–532, title II, §202, Oct. 23, 1972, 86 Stat. 1060; Pub. L. 94–62, §2, July 25, 1975, 89 Stat. 303; Pub. L. 96–381, §3, Oct. 6, 1980, 94 Stat. 1524; Pub. L. 96–470, title II, §201(f), Oct. 19, 1980, 94 Stat. 2242; Pub. L. 99–272, title VI, §6062, Apr. 7, 1986, 100 Stat. 131; Pub. L. 100–627, title I, §101, Nov. 7, 1988, 102 Stat. 3213.)

REFERENCES IN TEXT

Section 1703 of this title, referred to in subsec. (a)(3), was repealed by Pub. L. 102–567, title II, §204, Oct. 29, 1992, 106 Stat. 4282.

AMENDMENTS

1988—Subsec. (a)(3). Pub. L. 100–627 added par. (3).

1986—Subsec. (a). Pub. L. 99–272, §6062(1)–(3), designated existing provisions as par. (1), substituted "in close consultation" for "in consultation", and added par. (2).

Subsec. (c). Pub. L. 99–272, §6062(4), redesignated subsec. (d) as (c), and struck out former subsec. (c) which required the Secretary of Commerce to make an annual report to Congress, in March of each year, on the results of activities undertaken by him pursuant to this section during the previous fiscal year, and to include in that report the report to Congress required by section 665 of title 16 on activities of the Department of Commerce under that section.

Subsecs. (d), (e). Pub. L. 99–272, §6062(4), redesignated subsec. (e) as (d). Former subsec. (d) redesignated (c).

1980—Subsec. (a). Pub. L. 96–381 inserted provision including within the responsibilities of the Secretary the scientific assessment of damages to natural resources from spills of petroleum or petroleum products.

Subsec. (c). Pub. L. 96–470 inserted provision requiring the Secretary to include in his annual report the report on activities of the Department of Commerce under section 665 of title 16.

1975—Subsec. (c). Pub. L. 94–62 substituted "March" for "January".

TRANSFER OF FUNCTIONS

For transfer of authorities, functions, personnel, and assets of the Coast Guard, including the authorities and functions of the Secretary of Transportation relating thereto, to the Department of Homeland Security, and for treatment of related references, see sections 468(b), 551(d), 552(d), and 557 of Title 6, Domestic Security, and the Department of Homeland Security Reorganization Plan of November 25, 2002, as modified, set out as a note under section 542 of Title 6.

§1443. Research program respecting ocean dumping and other methods of waste disposal

(a) Cooperation with public authorities, agencies, and institutions, private agencies and institutions, and individuals

The Administrator of the Environmental Protection Agency shall—

(1) conduct research, investigations, experiments, training, demonstrations, surveys, and studies for the purpose of—

(A) determining means of minimizing or ending, as soon as possible after October 6, 1980, the dumping into ocean waters, or waters described in section 1411(b) of this title, of material which may unreasonably degrade or endanger human health, welfare, or amenities, or the marine environment, ecological systems, or economic potentialities, and

(B) developing disposal methods as alternatives to the dumping described in subparagraph (A); and

(2) encourage, cooperate with, promote the coordination of, and render financial and other assistance to appropriate public authorities, agencies, and institutions (whether Federal, State, interstate, or local) and appropriate private agencies, institutions, and individuals in the conduct of research and other activities described in paragraph (1).

(b) Termination date for ocean dumping of sewage sludge not affected

Nothing in this section shall be construed to affect in any way the December 31, 1981, termination date, established in section 1412a of this title, for the ocean dumping of sewage sludge.

(c) Regional management plans for waste disposal

The Administrator, in cooperation with the Secretary, the Secretary of Commerce, and other officials of appropriate Federal, State, and local agencies, shall assess the feasibility in coastal areas of regional management plans for the disposal of waste materials. Such plans should integrate where appropriate Federal, State, regional, and local waste disposal activities into a comprehensive regional disposal strategy. These plans should address, among other things—

(1) the sources, quantities, and types of materials that require and will require disposal;

(2) the environmental, economic, social, and human health factors (and the methods used to assess these factors) associated with disposal alternatives;

(3) the improvements in production processes, methods of disposal, and recycling to reduce the adverse effects associated with such disposal alternatives;

(4) the applicable laws and regulations governing waste disposal; and

(5) improvements in permitting processes to reduce administrative burdens.

(d) Report on sewage disposal in New York metropolitan area

The Administrator, in cooperation with the Secretary of Commerce, shall submit to the Congress and the President, not later than one year after April 7, 1986, a report on sewage sludge disposal in the New York City metropolitan region. The report shall—

(1) consider the factors listed in subsection (c) of this section as they relate to landfilling, incineration, ocean dumping, or any other feasible disposal or reuse/recycling option;

(2) include an assessment of the cost of these alternatives; and

(3) recommend such regulatory or legislative changes as may be necessary to reduce the adverse impacts associated with sewage sludge disposal.

(Pub. L. 92–532, title II, §203, Oct. 23, 1972, 86 Stat. 1061; Pub. L. 96–381, §1, Oct. 6, 1980, 94 Stat. 1523; Pub. L. 99–272, title VI, §6063, Apr. 7, 1986, 100 Stat. 131.)

CODIFICATION

In subsec. (a)(1)(A), October 6, 1980, was substituted for "the date of the enactment of this section", which has been translated to reflect the probable intent of Congress as meaning the date of enactment of Pub. L. 96–381 which amended this section generally and which was approved Oct. 6, 1980.

AMENDMENTS

1986—Subsecs. (c), (d). Pub. L. 99–272 added subsecs. (c) and (d).

1980—Pub. L. 96–381 substituted provision authorizing the Administrator of the Environmental Protection Agency to conduct research, etc., and to encourage and cooperate with public authorities, etc., for the purpose of determining means of minimizing or ending, as soon as possible after Oct. 6, 1980, dumping in ocean waters, or waters described in section 1411(b) of this title, of materials which may unreasonably degrade or endanger human health or the marine environment and to develop disposal methods as alternatives to dumping for provision authorizing the Secretary of Commerce to conduct research, etc., and to encourage and cooperate with public authorities, etc., for the purpose of minimizing or ending all dumping of materials within five years after the effective date of Pub. L. 92–532, which was approved Oct. 23, 1972, and inserted provision directing that nothing in this section be construed to affect in any way the Dec. 31, 1981, termination date, established by section 1412a of this title for ocean dumping of sewage sludge.

§1444. Annual reports

(a) Report by Secretary of Commerce

In March of each year, the Secretary of Commerce shall report to the Congress on his activities under this subchapter during the previous fiscal year. The report shall include—

(1) the Secretary's findings made under section 1441 of this title, including an evaluation of the short-term ecological effects and the social and economic factors involved with the dumping;

(2) the results of activities undertaken pursuant to section 1442 of this title;

(3) with the concurrence of the Administrator and after consulting with officials of other appropriate Federal agencies, an identification of the short- and long-term research requirements associated with activities under subchapter I of this chapter, and a description of how Federal research under this subchapter and subchapter I of this chapter will meet those requirements; and

(4) activities of the Department of Commerce under section 665 of title 16.

(b) Report by Administrator

In March of each year, the Administrator shall report to the Congress on his activities during the previous fiscal year under section 1443 of this title.

(c) Report by Under Secretary

On October 31 of each year, the Under Secretary shall report to the Congress the specific programs that the National Oceanic and Atmospheric Administration and the Environmental Protection Agency carried out pursuant to this subchapter in the previous fiscal year, specifically listing the amount of funds allocated to those specific programs in the previous fiscal year.

(Pub. L. 92–532, title II, §204, formerly §205, as added Pub. L. 96–572, §5, Dec. 22, 1980, 94 Stat. 3345; renumbered §204 and amended Pub. L. 99–272, title VI, §6065, Apr. 7, 1986, 100 Stat. 132; Pub. L. 100–627, title I, §102, Nov. 7, 1988, 102 Stat. 3213.)

PRIOR PROVISIONS

A prior section 204 of Pub. L. 92–532, which was classified to this section, was renumbered section 205 and is classified to section 1445 of this title.

AMENDMENTS

1988—Subsec. (c). Pub. L. 100–627 added subsec. (c).

1986—Pub. L. 99–272 amended section generally. Prior to amendment, section read as follows: "The Administrator of the Environmental Protection Agency is authorized to conduct a study to assist the city of New York in evaluating the technological options available for the removal of heavy metals and other toxic organic materials from the sewage sludge of the city of New York. The study shall also examine options available to reduce the amount of such pollutants entering the sewage system. The study is to be completed by July 1, 1981."

§1445. Authorization of appropriations

There are authorized to be appropriated for the first fiscal year after October 23, 1972, and for the next two fiscal years thereafter such sums as may be necessary to carry out this subchapter, but the sums appropriated for any such fiscal year may not exceed $6,000,000. There are authorized to be appropriated not to exceed $1,500,000 for the transition period (July 1 through September 30, 1976), not to exceed $5,600,000 for fiscal year 1977, and not to exceed $6,500,000 for fiscal year 1978, not to exceed $11,396,000 for fiscal year 1981, not to exceed $12,000,000 for fiscal year 1982, not to exceed $10,635,000 for fiscal year 1986, not to exceed $11,114,000 for fiscal year 1987, not to exceed $13,500,000 for fiscal year 1989, and not to exceed $14,500,000 for fiscal year 1990.

(Pub. L. 92–532, title II, §205, formerly §204, Oct. 23, 1972, 86 Stat. 1061; Pub. L. 94–62, §3, July 25, 1975, 89 Stat. 303; Pub. L. 94–326, §3, June 30, 1976, 90 Stat. 725; Pub. L. 95–153, §2, Nov. 4, 1977, 91 Stat. 1255; Pub. L. 96–381, §2, Oct. 6, 1980, 94 Stat.

1523; renumbered §205 and amended Pub. L. 99–272, title VI, §6064, Apr. 7, 1986, 100 Stat. 132; Pub. L. 100–627, title I, §103, Nov. 7, 1988, 102 Stat. 3213.)

PRIOR PROVISIONS

A prior section 205 of Pub. L. 92–532, which was classified to this section, was renumbered section 204 and is classified to section 1444 of this title.

AMENDMENTS

1988—Pub. L. 100–627 inserted provision authorizing appropriations not to exceed $13,500,000 for fiscal year 1989 and not to exceed $14,500,000 for fiscal year 1990.

1986—Pub. L. 99–272 inserted provision authorizing appropriations not to exceed $10,635,000 for fiscal year 1986 and not to exceed $11,114,000 for fiscal year 1987.

1980—Pub. L. 96–381 inserted provision authorizing appropriations not to exceed $11,396,000 for fiscal year 1981 and not to exceed $12,000,000 for fiscal year 1982.

1977—Pub. L. 95–153 inserted provision authorizing appropriations not to exceed $6,500,000 for fiscal year 1978.

1976—Pub. L. 94–326 inserted provision authorizing appropriations not to exceed $5,600,000 for fiscal year 1977.

1975—Pub. L. 94–62 inserted provision authorizing appropriations not to exceed $1,500,000 for the transition period (July 1, through Sept. 30, 1976).

CHAPTER 28—POLLUTION CASUALTIES ON THE HIGH SEAS: UNITED STATES INTERVENTION

§ 1471. Definitions

As used in this chapter—

(1) "a substance other than convention oil" means those oils, noxious substances, liquefied gases, and radioactive substances—

(A) enumerated in the protocol, or

(B) otherwise determined to be hazardous under section 1473(a) of this title;

(2) "convention" means the International Convention Relating to Intervention on the High Seas in Cases of Oil Pollution Casualties, 1969, including annexes thereto;

(3) "convention oil" means crude oil, fuel oil, diesel oil, and lubricating oil;

(4) "Secretary" means the Secretary of the department in which the Coast Guard is operating;

(5) "ship" means—

(A) a seagoing vessel of any type whatsoever, and

(B) any floating craft, except an installation or device engaged in the exploration and exploitation of the resources of the seabed and the ocean floor and the subsoil thereof;

(6) "protocol" means the Protocol Relating to Intervention on the High Seas in Cases of Marine Pollution by Substances Other Than Oil, 1973, including annexes thereto; and

(7) "United States" means the States, the District of Columbia, the Commonwealth of Puerto Rico, the Canal Zone, Guam, American Samoa, the United States Virgin Islands, the Trust Territory of the Pacific Islands, the Commonwealth of the Northern Marianas, and any other commonwealth, territory, or possession of the United States.

(Pub. L. 93–248, §2, Feb. 5, 1974, 88 Stat. 8; Pub. L. 95–302, §1(1), June 26, 1978, 92 Stat. 344.)

REFERENCES IN TEXT

For definition of Canal Zone, referred to in par. (7), see section 3602(b) of Title 22, Foreign Relations and Intercourse.

AMENDMENTS

1978—Pub. L. 95–302 in cl. (1) substituted definition of "a substance other than convention oil" for definition of "ship", in cl. (2) substituted definition of "convention" for definition of "oil", in cl. (3) substituted definition of "convention oil" for definition of "convention", in cl. (5) substituted definition of "ship" for definition of "United States", and added cls. (6) and (7).

EFFECTIVE DATE OF 1978 AMENDMENT

For effective date of amendment by Pub. L. 95–302, see section 2 of Pub. L. 95–302, set out as a note under section 1487 of this title.

SHORT TITLE

Section 1 of Pub. L. 93–248 provided: "That this Act [enacting this chapter] may be cited as the 'Intervention on the High Seas Act'."

TRANSFER OF FUNCTIONS

For transfer of authorities, functions, personnel, and assets of the Coast Guard, including the authorities and functions of the Secretary of Transportation relating thereto, to the Department of Homeland Security, and for treatment of related references, see sections 468(b), 551(d), 552(d), and 557 of Title 6, Domestic Security, and the Department of Homeland Security Reorganization Plan of November 25, 2002, as modified, set out as a note under section 542 of Title 6.

TERMINATION OF TRUST TERRITORY OF THE PACIFIC ISLANDS

For termination of Trust Territory of the Pacific Islands, see note set out preceding section 1681 of Title 48, Territories and Insular Possessions.

§1472. Grave and imminent danger from oil pollution casualties to coastline or related interests of United States; Federal nonliability for Federal preventive measures on the high seas

Whenever a ship collision, stranding, or other incident of navigation or other occurrence on board a ship or external to it resulting in material damage or imminent threat of material damage to the ship or her cargo creates, as determined by the Secretary, a grave and imminent danger to the coastline or related interests of the United States from pollution or threat of pollution of the sea by convention oil or of the sea or atmosphere by a substance other than convention oil which may reasonably be expected to result in major harmful consequences, the Secretary may, except as provided for in section 1479 of this title, without liability for any damage to the owners or operators of the ship, to her cargo or crew, to underwriters or other parties interested therein, take measures on the high seas, in accordance with the provisions of the convention, the protocol and this chapter, to prevent, mitigate, or eliminate that danger.

(Pub. L. 93–248, §3, Feb. 5, 1974, 88 Stat. 8; Pub. L. 95–302, §1(2), June 26, 1978, 92 Stat. 344.)

AMENDMENTS

1978—Pub. L. 95–302 substituted "convention oil or of the sea or atmosphere by a substance other than convention oil" for "oil", and "convention, the protocol" for "Convention".

EFFECTIVE DATE OF 1978 AMENDMENT

For effective date of amendment by Pub. L. 95–302, see section 2 of Pub. L. 95–302, set out as a note under section 1487 of this title.

§1473. Consultations and determinations respecting creation of hazards to human health, etc.; criteria for determinations respecting grave and imminent dangers of major harmful consequences to United States coastline or related interests

(a) The Secretary, after consultation with the Administrator of the Environmental Protection Agency and the Secretary of Commerce, shall determine when a substance other than those enumerated in the protocol is liable to create a hazard to human health, to harm living resources, to damage amenities, or to interfere with other legitimate uses of the sea.

(b) In determining whether there is grave and imminent danger of major harmful consequences to the coastline or related interests of the United States, the Secretary shall consider the interests of the United States directly threatened or affected including but not limited to, human health, fish, shellfish, and other living marine resources, wildlife, coastal zone and estuarine activities, and public and private shorelines and beaches.

(Pub. L. 93–248, §4, Feb. 5, 1974, 88 Stat. 9; Pub. L. 95–302, §1(3), June 26, 1978, 92 Stat. 344.)

AMENDMENTS

1978—Pub. L. 95–302 added subsec. (a), designated existing provisions as subsec. (b), and inserted "human health," before "fish".

EFFECTIVE DATE OF 1978 AMENDMENT

For effective date of amendment by Pub. L. 95–302, see section 2 of Pub. L. 95–302, set out as a note under section 1487 of this title.

§1474. Federal intervention actions

Upon a determination under section 1472 of this title of a grave and imminent danger to the coastline or related interests of the United States, the Secretary may—

(1) coordinate and direct all public and private efforts directed at the removal or elimination of the threatened pollution damage;

(2) directly or indirectly undertake the whole or any part of any salvage or other action he could require or direct under subsection (1) of this section; and

(3) remove, and, if necessary, destroy the ship and cargo which is the source of the danger.

(Pub. L. 93–248, §5, Feb. 5, 1974, 88 Stat. 9.)

§1475. Consultation procedure

Before taking any measure under section 1474 of this title, the Secretary shall—

(1) consult, through the Secretary of State, with other countries affected by the marine casualty, and particularly with the flag country of any ship involved;

(2) notify without delay the Administrator of the Environmental Protection Agency and any other persons known to the Secretary, or of whom he later becomes aware, who have interests which can reasonably be expected to be affected by any proposed measures; and

(3) consider any views submitted in response to the consultation or notification required by subsections (1) and (2) of this section.

(Pub. L. 93–248, §6, Feb. 5, 1974, 88 Stat. 9.)

§1476. Emergencies

In cases of extreme urgency requiring measures to be taken immediately, the Secretary may take those measures rendered necessary by the urgency of the situation without the prior consultation or notification as required by section 1475 of this title or without the continuation of consultations already begun.

(Pub. L. 93–248, §7, Feb. 5, 1974, 88 Stat. 9.)

§1477. Reasonable measures; considerations

(a) Measures directed or conducted under this chapter shall be proportionate to the damage, actual or threatened, to the coastline or related interests of the United States and may not go beyond what is reasonably necessary to prevent, mitigate, or eliminate that damage.

(b) In considering whether measures are proportionate to the damage the Secretary shall, among other things, consider—

(1) the extent and probability of imminent damage if those measures are not taken;

(2) the likelihood of effectiveness of those measures; and

(3) the extent of the damage which may be caused by those measures.

(Pub. L. 93–248, §8, Feb. 5, 1974, 88 Stat. 9.)

§1478. Personal, flag state, and foreign state considerations

In the direction and conduct of measures under this chapter the Secretary shall use his best endeavors to—

(1) assure the avoidance of risk to human life;

(2) render all possible aid to distressed persons, including facilitating repatriation of ships' crews; and

(3) not unnecessarily interfere with rights and interests of others, including the flag state of any ship involved, other foreign states threatened by damage, and persons otherwise concerned.

(Pub. L. 93–248, §9, Feb. 5, 1974, 88 Stat. 9.)

§1479. Federal liability for unreasonable damages

(a) Payment of compensation

The United States shall be obliged to pay compensation to the extent of the damage caused by measures which exceed those reasonably necessary to achieve the end mentioned in section 1472 of this title.

(b) Jurisdiction

Actions against the United States seeking compensation for any excessive measures may be brought in the United States Court of Federal Claims, in any district court of the United States, and in those courts enumerated in section 460 of title 28. For purposes of this chapter, American Samoa shall be included within the judicial district of the District Court of the United States for the District of Hawaii, and the Trust Territory of the Pacific Islands shall be included within the judicial districts of both the District Court of the United States for the District of Hawaii and the District Court of Guam.

(c) Burden of proof

With respect to intervention for a substance identified pursuant to section 1473(a) of this title, the United States has the burden of establishing that, under the circumstances present at the time of the intervention, the substance could reasonably pose a grave and imminent danger analogous to that posed by a substance enumerated in the protocol.

(Pub. L. 93–248, §10, Feb. 5, 1974, 88 Stat. 10; Pub. L. 95–302, §1(4), June 26, 1978, 92 Stat. 345; Pub. L. 97–164, title I, §161(6), Apr. 2, 1982, 96 Stat. 49; Pub. L. 102–572, title IX, §902(b)(1), Oct. 29, 1992, 106 Stat. 4516.)

AMENDMENTS

1992—Subsec. (b). Pub. L. 102–572 substituted "United States Court of Federal Claims" for "United States Claims Court".

1982—Subsec. (b). Pub. L. 97–164 substituted "Claims Court" for "Court of Claims".

1978—Subsec. (c). Pub. L. 95–302 added subsec. (c).

EFFECTIVE DATE OF 1992 AMENDMENT

Amendment by Pub. L. 102–572 effective Oct. 29, 1992, see section 911 of Pub. L. 102–572, set out as a note under section 171 of Title 28, Judiciary and Judicial Procedure.

EFFECTIVE DATE OF 1982 AMENDMENT

Amendment by Pub. L. 97–164 effective Oct. 1, 1982, see section 402 of Pub. L. 97–164, set out as a note under section 171 of Title 28, Judiciary and Judicial Procedure.

EFFECTIVE DATE OF 1978 AMENDMENT

For effective date of amendment by Pub. L. 95–302, see section 2 of Pub. L. 95–302, set out as a note under section 1487 of this title.

TERMINATION OF TRUST TERRITORY OF THE PACIFIC ISLANDS

For termination of Trust Territory of the Pacific Islands, see note set out preceding section 1681 of Title 48, Territories and Insular Possessions.

§1480. Notification by Secretary of State

The Secretary of State shall notify without delay foreign states concerned, the Secretary-General of the Inter-Governmental Maritime Consultative Organization, and persons affected by measures taken under this chapter.

(Pub. L. 93–248, §11, Feb. 5, 1974, 88 Stat. 10.)

§1481. Violations; penalties

(a) A person commits a class A misdemeanor if that person—

(1) willfully violates a provision of this chapter or a regulation issued thereunder; or

(2) willfully refuses or fails to comply with any lawful order or direction given pursuant to this chapter; or

(3) willfully obstructs any person who is acting in compliance with an order or direction under this chapter.

(b) In a criminal proceeding for an offense under paragraph (1) or (2) of subsection (a) of this section it shall be a defense for the accused to prove that he used all due diligence to comply with any order or direction that he had reasonable cause to believe that compliance would have resulted in serious risk to human life.

(Pub. L. 93–248, §12, Feb. 5, 1974, 88 Stat. 10; Pub. L. 101–380, title IV, §4302(*l*), Aug. 18, 1990, 104 Stat. 539.)

AMENDMENTS

1990—Subsec. (a). Pub. L. 101–380 substituted "A person commits a class A misdemeanor if that person" for "Any person who" in introductory provisions and struck out ", shall be fined not more than $10,000 or imprisoned not more than one year, or both" after "under this chapter" in par. (3).

EFFECTIVE DATE OF 1990 AMENDMENT

Amendment by Pub. L. 101–380 applicable to incidents occurring after Aug. 18, 1990, see section 1020 of Pub. L. 101–380, set out as an Effective Date note under section 2701 of this title.

§1482. Consultation for nomination and nomination of experts, negotiators, etc.; proposal of amendments to list of substances other than convention oil; Presidential acceptance of amendments

(a) Nomination of experts and proposal of amendments to list of substances

The Secretary, in consultation with the Secretary of State and the Administrator of the Environmental Protection Agency, may nominate individuals to the list of experts provided for in article III of the convention and article II of the protocol and may propose amendments to the list of substances other than convention oil in accordance with article III of the protocol.

(b) Consultations for designation or nomination of negotiators, etc., provided for by convention and protocol

The Secretary of State, in consultation with the Secretary, shall designate or nominate, as appropriate and necessary, the negotiators, conciliators, or arbitrators provided for by the convention and the protocol.

(c) Presidential acceptance of amendments to list of substances other than convention oil in accordance with protocol

The President may accept amendments to the list of substances other than convention oil in accordance with article III of the protocol.

(Pub. L. 93–248, §13, Feb. 5, 1974, 88 Stat. 10; Pub. L. 95–302, §1(5), June 26, 1978, 92 Stat. 345.)

AMENDMENTS

1978—Subsec. (a). Pub. L. 95–302, §1(5)(A), inserted provisions relating to applicability of article II of the protocol and provisions for proposal of amendments to the list of substances other than convention oil.

Subsec. (b). Pub. L. 95–302, §1(5)(B), substituted "protocol" for "annexes thereto".

Subsec. (c). Pub. L. 95–302, §1(5)(C), added subsec. (c).

EFFECTIVE DATE OF 1978 AMENDMENT

For effective date of amendment by Pub. L. 95–302, see section 2 of Pub. L. 95–302, set out as a note under section 1487 of this title.

§1483. Foreign government ships; immunity

No measures may be taken under authority of this chapter against any warship or other ship owned or operated by a country and used, for the time being, only on Government noncommercial service.

(Pub. L. 93–248, §14, Feb. 5, 1974, 88 Stat. 10.)

§1484. Interpretation and administration; other right, duty, privilege, or immunity and other remedy unaffected

This chapter shall be interpreted and administered in a manner consistent with the convention, the protocol, and other international law. Except as specifically provided, nothing in this chapter may be interpreted to prejudice any otherwise applicable right, duty, privilege, or immunity or deprive any country or person of any remedy otherwise applicable.

(Pub. L. 93–248, §15, Feb. 5, 1974, 88 Stat. 10; Pub. L. 95–302, §1(6), June 26, 1978, 92 Stat. 345.)

AMENDMENTS

1978—Pub. L. 95–302 inserted ", the protocol," after "convention".

EFFECTIVE DATE OF 1978 AMENDMENT

For effective date of amendment by Pub. L. 95–302, see section 2 of Pub. L. 95–302, set out as a note under section 1487 of this title.

§1485. Rules and regulations

The Secretary may issue reasonable rules and regulations which he considers appropriate and necessary for the effective implementation of this chapter.

(Pub. L. 93–248, §16, Feb. 5, 1974, 88 Stat. 10.)

§1486. Oil Spill Liability Trust Fund

The Oil Spill Liability Trust Fund shall be available to the Secretary for actions taken under sections 1474 and 1476 of this title.

(Pub. L. 93–248, §17, Feb. 5, 1974, 88 Stat. 10; Pub. L. 101–380, title II, §2001, Aug. 18, 1990, 104 Stat. 506.)

AMENDMENTS

1990—Pub. L. 101–380 amended section generally. Prior to amendment, section read as follows: "The revolving fund established under section 1321(k) of this title shall be available to the Secretary for Federal actions and activities under section 1474 of this title."

EFFECTIVE DATE OF 1990 AMENDMENT

Amendment by Pub. L. 101–380 applicable to incidents occurring after Aug. 18, 1990, see section 1020 of Pub. L. 101–380, set out as an Effective Date note under section 2701 of this title.

§1487. Effective date

This chapter shall be effective upon February 5, 1974, or upon the date the convention becomes effective as to the United States, whichever is later.

(Pub. L. 93–248, §18, Feb. 5, 1974, 88 Stat. 10.)

REFERENCES IN TEXT

The date the convention became effective as to the United States, referred to in text, is May 6, 1975.

EFFECTIVE DATE OF 1978 AMENDMENT

Pub. L. 95–302, §2, June 26, 1978, 92 Stat. 345, provided that: "This Act [amending sections 1471 to 1473, 1479, 1482, and 1484 of this title] shall be effective upon the date of enactment [June 26, 1978], or upon the date the protocol becomes effective as to the United States, whichever is later." [The protocol was adopted by the United States on Sept. 7, 1978, to be effective as to the United States upon its adoption by 15 countries. The protocol became effective as to the United States Mar. 30, 1983.

CHAPTER 29—DEEPWATER PORTS

§ 1501. Congressional declaration of policy

(a) It is declared to be the purposes of the Congress in this chapter to—

(1) authorize and regulate the location, ownership, construction, and operation of deepwater ports in waters beyond the territorial limits of the United States;

(2) provide for the protection of the marine and coastal environment to prevent or minimize any adverse impact which might occur as a consequence of the development of such ports;

(3) protect the interests of the United States and those of adjacent coastal States in the location, construction, and operation of deepwater ports;

(4) protect the rights and responsibilities of States and communities to regulate growth, determine land use, and otherwise protect the environment in accordance with law;

(5) promote the construction and operation of deepwater ports as a safe and effective means of importing oil or natural gas into the United States and transporting oil or natural gas from the outer continental shelf[1] while minimizing tanker traffic and the risks attendant thereto; and

(6) promote oil or natural gas production on the outer continental shelf[1] by affording an economic and safe means of transportation of outer continental shelf[1] oil or natural gas to the United States mainland.

(b) The Congress declares that nothing in this chapter shall be construed to affect the legal status of the high seas, the superjacent airspace, or the seabed and subsoil, including the Continental Shelf.

(Pub. L. 93–627, § 2, Jan. 3, 1975, 88 Stat. 2126; Pub. L. 104–324, title V, § 502(b), Oct. 19, 1996, 110 Stat. 3925; Pub. L. 107–295, title I, § 106(a)(1), Nov. 25, 2002, 116 Stat. 2086.)

AMENDMENTS

2002—Subsec. (a)(5), (6). Pub. L. 107–295 inserted "or natural gas" after "oil" wherever appearing.

1996—Subsec. (a)(5), (6). Pub. L. 104–324 added pars. (5) and (6).

SHORT TITLE OF 1996 AMENDMENT

Section 501 of title V of Pub. L. 104–324 provided that: "This title [amending this section and sections 1502 to 1504, 1507, and 1509 of this title, repealing section 1506 of this title, and enacting provisions set out as a note under this section] may be cited as the 'Deepwater Port Modernization Act'."

SHORT TITLE OF 1984 AMENDMENT

Pub. L. 98–419, § 1, Sept. 25, 1984, 98 Stat. 1607, provided: "That this Act [amending sections 1502, 1503, 1504, 1506, 1507, 1517, and 1518 of this title and enacting provisions set out as a note under section 1518 of this title] may be cited as the 'Deepwater Port Act Amendments of 1984'."

SHORT TITLE

Section 1 of Pub. L. 93–627 provided: "That this Act [enacting this chapter and amending section 1333 of Title 43, Public Lands] may be cited as the 'Deepwater Port Act of 1974'."

CONGRESSIONAL PURPOSES FOR 1996 AMENDMENTS

Section 502(a) of title V of Pub. L. 104–324 provided that: "The purposes of this title [see Short Title of 1996 Amendment note above] are to—

"(1) update and improve the Deepwater Port Act of 1974 [33 U.S.C. 1501 et seq.];

"(2) assure that the regulation of deepwater ports is not more burdensome or stringent than necessary in comparison to the regulation of other modes of importing or transporting oil;

"(3) recognize that deepwater ports are generally subject to effective competition from alternative transportation modes and eliminate, for as long as a port remains subject to effective competition, unnecessary Federal regulatory oversight or involvement in the ports' business and economic decisions; and

"(4) promote innovation, flexibility, and efficiency in the management and operation of deepwater ports by removing or reducing any duplicative, unnecessary, or overly burdensome Federal regulations or license provisions."

DEPOSIT OF CERTAIN PENALTIES INTO OIL SPILL LIABILITY TRUST FUND

Penalties paid pursuant to this chapter and sections 1319(c) and 1321 of this title to be deposited in the Oil Spill Liability Trust Fund created under section 9509 of Title 26, Internal Revenue Code, see section 4304 of Pub. L. 101–380, set out as a note under section 9509 of Title 26.

ENVIRONMENTAL EFFECTS ABROAD OF MAJOR FEDERAL ACTIONS

For provisions relating to environmental effects abroad of major Federal actions, see Ex. Ord. No. 12114, Jan. 4, 1979, 44 F.R. 1957, set out as a note under section 4321 of Title 42, The Public Health and Welfare.

§ 1502. Definitions

As used in this chapter, unless the context otherwise requires, the term—

(1) "adjacent coastal State" means any coastal State which (A) would be directly connected by pipeline to a deepwater port, as proposed in an application; (B) would be located within 15 miles of any such proposed deepwater port; or (C) is designated by the Secretary in accordance with section 1508(a)(2) of this title;

(2) "affiliate" means any entity owned or controlled by, any person who owns or controls, or any entity which is under common ownership or control with an applicant, licensee, or any person required to be disclosed pursuant to section 1504(c)(2)(A) or (B) of this title;

(3) "application" means an application submitted under this Act for a license for the ownership, construction, and operation of a deepwater port;

(4) "citizen of the United States" means any person who is a United States citizen by law, birth, or naturalization, any State, any agency of a State or a group of States, or any corporation, partnership, or association organized under the laws of any State which has as its president or other executive officer and as its chairman of the board of directors, or holder of a similar office, a person who is a United States citizen by law, birth or naturalization and which has no more of its directors who are

[1] So in original. Probably should be capitalized.

not United States citizens by law, birth or naturalization than constitute a minority of the number required for a quorum necessary to conduct the business of the board;

(5) "coastal environment" means the navigable waters (including the lands therein and thereunder) and the adjacent shorelines including[1] waters therein and thereunder). The term includes transitional and intertidal areas, bays, lagoons, salt marshes, estuaries, and beaches; the fish, wildlife and other living resources thereof; and the recreational and scenic values of such lands, waters and resources;

(6) "coastal State" means any State of the United States in or bordering on the Atlantic, Pacific, or Arctic Oceans, or the Gulf of Mexico;

(7) "construction" means the supervising, inspection, actual building, and all other activities incidental to the building, repairing, or expanding of a deepwater port or any of its components, including, but not limited to, pile driving and bulkheading, and alterations, modifications, or additions to the deepwater port;

(8) "control" means the power, directly or indirectly, to determine the policy, business practices, or decisionmaking process of another person, whether by stock or other ownership interest, by representation on a board of directors or similar body, by contract or other agreement with stockholders or others, or otherwise;

(9) "deepwater port"—

(A) means any fixed or floating manmade structure other than a vessel, or any group of such structures, that are located beyond State seaward boundaries and that are used or intended for use as a port or terminal for the transportation, storage, or further handling of oil or natural gas for transportation to any State, except as otherwise provided in section 1522 of this title, and for other uses not inconsistent with the purposes of this chapter, including transportation of oil or natural gas from the United States outer continental shelf;

(B) includes all components and equipment, including pipelines, pumping stations, service platforms, buoys, mooring lines, and similar facilities to the extent they are located seaward of the high water mark;

(C) in the case of a structure used or intended for such use with respect to natural gas, includes all components and equipment, including pipelines, pumping or compressor stations, service platforms, buoys, mooring lines, and similar facilities that are proposed or approved for construction and operation as part of a deepwater port, to the extent that they are located seaward of the high water mark and do not include interconnecting facilities; and

(D) shall be considered a "new source" for purposes of the Clean Air Act (42 U.S.C. 7401 et seq.), and the Federal Water Pollution Control Act (33 U.S.C. 1251 et seq.);

[1] So in original. Probably should be preceded by an opening parenthesis.

(10) "Governor" means the Governor of a State or the person designated by State law to exercise the powers granted to the Governor pursuant to this chapter;

(11) "licensee" means a citizen of the United States holding a valid license for the ownership, construction, and operation of a deepwater port that was issued, transferred, or renewed pursuant to this chapter;

(12) "marine environment" includes the coastal environment, waters of the contiguous zone, and waters of the high seas; the fish, wildlife, and other living resources of such waters; and the recreational and scenic values of such waters and resources;

(13) "natural gas" means either natural gas unmixed, or any mixture of natural or artificial gas, including compressed or liquefied natural gas, natural gas liquids, liquefied petroleum gas, and condensate recovered from natural gas;

(14) "oil" means petroleum, crude oil, and any substance refined from petroleum or crude oil;

(15) "person" includes an individual, a public or private corporation, a partnership or other association, or a government entity;

(16) "safety zone" means the safety zone established around a deepwater port as determined by the Secretary in accordance with section 1509(d) of this title;

(17) "Secretary" means the Secretary of Transportation;

(18) "State" includes each of the States of the United States, the District of Columbia, the Commonwealth of Puerto Rico, and the territories and possessions of the United States; and

(19) "vessel" means every description of watercraft or other artificial contrivance used as a means of transportation on or through the water.

(Pub. L. 93–627, §3, Jan. 3, 1975, 88 Stat. 2127; Pub. L. 98–419, §2(a), Sept. 25, 1984, 98 Stat. 1607; Pub. L. 104–324, title V, §503, Oct. 19, 1996, 110 Stat. 3926; Pub. L. 107–295, title I, §106(b), Nov. 25, 2002, 116 Stat. 2086; Pub. L. 109–58, title III, §321(b), Aug. 8, 2005, 119 Stat. 694.)

References in Text

The Clean Air Act, referred to in par. (9)(D), is act July 14, 1955, ch. 360, 69 Stat. 322, as amended, which is classified generally to chapter 85 (§7401 et seq.) of Title 42, The Public Health and Welfare. For complete classification of this Act to the Code, see Short Title note set out under section 7401 of Title 42 and Tables.

The Federal Water Pollution Control Act, as amended, referred to in par. (9)(D), is act June 30, 1948, ch. 758, as amended generally by Pub. L. 92–500, §2, Oct. 18, 1972, 86 Stat. 816, which is classified generally to chapter 26 (§1251 et seq.) of this title. For complete classification of this Act to the Code, see Short Title note set out under section 1251 of this title and Tables.

Amendments

2005—Par. (13). Pub. L. 109–58 inserted ", natural gas liquids, liquefied petroleum gas, and condensate recovered from natural gas" before semicolon at end.

2002—Par. (9). Pub. L. 107–295, §106(b)(2), amended par. (9) generally. Prior to amendment, par. (9) read as follows: "'deepwater port' means any fixed or floating manmade structures other than a vessel, or any group of structures, located beyond the territorial sea and off the coast of the United States and which are used or intended for use as a port or terminal for the transportation, storage, and further handling of oil for transportation to any State, except as otherwise provided in section 1522 of this title, and for other uses not inconsistent with the purposes of this chapter, including transportation of oil from the United States outer continental shelf. The term includes all associated components and equipment, including pipelines, pumping stations, service platforms, mooring buoys, and similar appurtenances to the extent they are located seaward of the high water mark. A deepwater port shall be considered a 'new source' for purposes of the Clean Air Act, as amended, and the Federal Water Pollution Control Act, as amended;".

Pars. (13) to (19). Pub. L. 107–295, § 106(b)(1), (3), added par. (13) and redesignated former pars. (13) to (18) as (14) to (19), respectively.

1996—Pars. (3) to (8). Pub. L. 104–324, § 503(a), redesignated pars. (4) to (9) as (3) to (8), respectively, and struck out former par. (3) which read as follows: "'antitrust laws' includes the Act of July 2, 1890, as amended, the Act of October 15, 1914, as amended, the Federal Trade Commission Act (15 U.S.C. 41 et seq.), and sections 73 and 74 of the Act of August 27, 1894, as amended;".

Par. (9). Pub. L. 104–324, § 503(a)(2), (b), redesignated par. (10) as (9) and substituted "structures, located beyond the territorial sea and off the coast of the United States and which are used or intended for use as a port or terminal for the transportation, storage, and further handling of oil for transportation to any State, except as otherwise provided in section 1522 of this title, and for other uses not inconsistent with the purposes of this chapter, including transportation of oil from the United States outer continental shelf." for "such structures, located beyond the territorial sea and off the coast of the United States and which are used or intended for use as a port or terminal for the loading or unloading and further handling of oil for transportation to any State, except as otherwise provided in section 1522 of this title." Former par. (9) redesignated (8).

Pars. (10) to (19). Pub. L. 104–324, § 503(a)(2), redesignated pars. (11) to (19) as (10) to (18), respectively. Former par. (10) redesignated (9).

1984—Par. (4). Pub. L. 98–419 substituted "means an application" for "means any application", struck out designation "(A)" before "for a license", and struck out cls. (B) and (C) which provided that "application" meant any application submitted under this chapter for transfer of any license referred to in this paragraph, or for any substantial change in any of the conditions and provisions of any such license.

TERRITORIAL SEA AND CONTIGUOUS ZONE OF UNITED STATES

For extension of territorial sea and contiguous zone of United States, see Proc. No. 5928 and Proc. No. 7219, respectively, set out as notes under section 1331 of Title 43, Public Lands.

§ 1503. License for ownership, construction, and operation of deepwater port

(a) Requirement

No person may engage in the ownership, construction, or operation of a deepwater port except in accordance with a license issued pursuant to this chapter. No person may transport or otherwise transfer any oil or natural gas between a deepwater port and the United States unless such port has been so licensed and the license is in force.

(b) Issuance, transfer, amendment, or reinstatement

The Secretary may—

(1) on application, issue a license for the ownership, construction, and operation of a deepwater port; and

(2) on petition of the licensee, amend, transfer, or reinstate a license issued under this chapter.

(c) Conditions for issuance

The Secretary may issue a license in accordance with the provisions of this chapter if—

(1) he determines that the applicant is financially responsible and will meet the requirements of section 2716 of this title[1]

(2) he determines that the applicant can and will comply with applicable laws, regulations, and license conditions;

(3) he determines that the construction and operation of the deepwater port will be in the national interest and consistent with national security and other national policy goals and objectives, including energy sufficiency and environmental quality;

(4) he determines that the deepwater port will not unreasonably interfere with international navigation or other reasonable uses of the high seas, as defined by treaty, convention, or customary international law;

(5) he determines, in accordance with the environmental review criteria established pursuant to section 1505 of this title, that the applicant has demonstrated that the deepwater port will be constructed and operated using best available technology, so as to prevent or minimize adverse impact on the marine environment;

(6) he has not been informed, within 45 days of the last public hearing on a proposed license for a designated application area, by the Administrator of the Environmental Protection Agency that the deepwater port will not conform with all applicable provisions of the Clean Air Act, as amended [42 U.S.C. 7401 et seq.], the Federal Water Pollution Control Act, as amended [33 U.S.C. 1251 et seq.], or the Marine Protection, Research and Sanctuaries Act, as amended [16 U.S.C. 1431 et seq., 1447 et seq.; 33 U.S.C. 1401 et seq., 2801 et seq.];

(7) he has consulted with the Secretary of the Army, the Secretary of State, and the Secretary of Defense, to determine their views on the adequacy of the application, and its effect on programs within their respective jurisdictions;

(8) the Governor of the adjacent coastal State of States, pursuant to section 1508 of this title, approves, or is presumed to approve, issuance of the license; and

(9) the adjacent coastal State to which the deepwater port is to be directly connected by pipeline has developed, or is making, at the time the application is submitted, reasonable progress, as determined in accordance with section 1508(c) of this title, toward developing, an approved coastal zone management program pursuant to the Coastal Zone Management Act of 1972 [16 U.S.C. 1451 et seq.].

[1] So in original. Probably should be followed by a semicolon.

(d) Application for license subject to examination and comparison of economic, social, and environmental effects of deepwater port facility and deep draft channel and harbor; finality of determination

If an application is made under this chapter for a license to construct a deepwater port facility off the coast of a State, and a port of the State which will be directly connected by pipeline with such deepwater port, on the date of such application—

(1) has existing plans for construction of a deep draft channel and harbor; and

(2) has either (A) an active study by the Secretary of the Army relating to the construction of a deep draft channel and harbor, or (B) a pending application for a permit under section 403 of this title for such construction; and

(3) applies to the Secretary for a determination under this section within 30 days of the date of the license application;

the Secretary shall not issue a license under this chapter until he has examined and compared the economic, social, and environmental effects of the construction and operation of the deepwater port with the economic, social and environmental effects of the construction, expansion, deepening, and operation of such State port, and has determined which project best serves the national interest or that both developments are warranted. The Secretary's determination shall be discretionary and nonreviewable.

(e) Additional conditions; removal requirements, waiver; Outer Continental Shelf Lands Act applicable to utilization of components upon waiver of removal requirements

(1) In issuing a license for the ownership, construction, and operation of a deepwater port, the Secretary shall prescribe those conditions which the Secretary deems necessary to carry out the provisions and requirements of this chapter[2] or which are otherwise required by any Federal department or agency pursuant to the terms of this chapter.[2] To the extent practicable, conditions required to carry out the provisions and requirements of this chapter[2] shall be addressed in license conditions rather than by regulation and, to the extent practicable, the license shall allow a deepwater port's operating procedures to be stated in an operations manual, approved by the Coast Guard, in accordance with section 1509(a) of this title, rather than in detailed and specific license conditions or regulations; except that basic standards and conditions shall be addressed in regulations. On petition of a licensee, the Secretary shall review any condition of a license issued under this chapter to determine if that condition is uniform, insofar as practicable, with the conditions of other licenses issued under this chapter, reasonable, and necessary to meet the objectives of this chapter. The Secretary shall amend or rescind any condition that is no longer necessary or otherwise required by any Federal department or agency under this chapter.

(2) No license shall be issued, transferred, or renewed under this chapter unless the licensee or transferee first agrees in writing that (A) there will be no substantial change from the plans, operational systems, and methods, procedures, and safeguards set forth in his license, as approved, without prior approval in writing from the Secretary; and (B) he will comply with any condition the Secretary may prescribe in accordance with the provisions of this chapter.

(3) The Secretary shall establish such bonding requirements or other assurances as he deems necessary to assure that, upon the revocation or termination of a license, the licensee will remove all components of the deepwater port. In the case of components lying in the subsoil below the seabed, the Secretary is authorized to waive the removal requirements if he finds that such removal is not otherwise necessary and that the remaining components do not constitute any threat to navigation or to the environment. At the request of the licensee, the Secretary, after consultation with the Secretary of the Interior, is authorized to waive the removal requirement as to any components which he determines may be utilized in connection with the transportation of oil, natural gas, or other minerals, pursuant to a lease granted under the provisions of the Outer Continental Shelf Lands Act [43 U.S.C. 1331 et seq.], after which waiver the utilization of such components shall be governed by the terms of the Outer Continental Shelf Lands Act.

(f) Amendments, transfers, and reinstatements

The Secretary may amend, transfer, or reinstate a license issued under this chapter[2] if the Secretary finds that the amendment, transfer, or reinstatement is consistent with the requirements of this chapter.

(g) Eligible citizens

Any citizen of the United States who otherwise qualifies under the terms of this chapter shall be eligible to be issued a license for the ownership, construction, and operation of a deepwater port.

(h) Term of license

A license issued under this chapter remains in effect unless suspended or revoked by the Secretary or until surrendered by the licensee.

(i) Liquefied natural gas facilities

To promote the security of the United States, the Secretary shall give top priority to the processing of a license under this chapter for liquefied natural gas facilities that will be supplied with liquefied natural gas by United States flag vessels.

(Pub. L. 93–627, §4, Jan. 3, 1975, 88 Stat. 2128; Pub. L. 98–419, §2(b)–(e), Sept. 25, 1984, 98 Stat. 1607; Pub. L. 101–380, title II, §2003(a)(1), Aug. 18, 1990, 104 Stat. 507; Pub. L. 104–324, title V, §504, Oct. 19, 1996, 110 Stat. 3926; Pub. L. 107–295, title I, §106(a)(2), Nov. 25, 2002, 116 Stat. 2086; Pub. L. 109–241, title III, §304(b), July 11, 2006, 120 Stat. 527.)

REFERENCES IN TEXT

The Clean Air Act, referred to in subsec. (c)(6), is act July 14, 1955, ch. 360, 69 Stat. 322, as amended, which is classified generally to chapter 85 (§7401 et seq.) of Title 42, The Public Health and Welfare. For complete classi-

[2] See References in Text note below.

fication of this Act to the Code, see Short Title note set out under section 7401 of Title 42 and Tables.

The Federal Water Pollution Control Act, as amended, referred to in subsec. (c)(6), is act June 30, 1948, ch. 758, as amended generally by Pub. L. 92–500, §2, Oct. 18, 1972, 86 Stat. 816, which is classified generally to chapter 26 (§1251 et seq.) of this title. For complete classification of this Act to the Code, see Short Title note set out under section 1251 of this title and Tables.

The Marine Protection, Research and Sanctuaries Act, referred to subsec. (c)(6), probably means Pub. L. 92–532, Oct. 23, 1972, 86 Stat. 1052, as amended, known as the Marine Protection, Research, and Sanctuaries Act of 1972, which is classified generally to chapters 27 (§1401 et seq.) and 41 (§2801 et seq.) of this title and chapters 32 (§1431 et seq.) and 32A (§1447 et seq.) of Title 16, Conservation. For complete classification of this Act to the Code, see Short Title note set out under section 1401 of this title and Tables.

The Coastal Zone Management Act of 1972, referred to in subsec. (c)(9), is title III of Pub. L. 89–454, as added by Pub. L. 92–583, Oct. 27, 1972, 86 Stat. 1280, as amended, which is classified generally to chapter 33 (§1451 et seq.) of Title 16, Conservation. For complete classification of this Act to the Code, see Short Title note set out under section 1451 of Title 16 and Tables.

This chapter, referred to first three times in subsec. (e)(1) and first time in subsec. (f), was in the original "this title" and was translated as reading "this Act", meaning Pub. L. 93–627, which is classified generally to this chapter, to reflect the probable intent of Congress, because Pub. L. 93–627 does not contain titles.

The Outer Continental Shelf Lands Act, referred to in subsec. (e)(3), is act Aug. 7, 1953, ch. 345, 67 Stat. 462, as amended, which is classified generally to subchapter III (§1331 et seq.) of chapter 29 of Title 43, Public Lands. For complete classification of this Act to the Code, see Short Title note set out under section 1331 of Title 43 and Tables.

AMENDMENTS

2006—Subsec. (i). Pub. L. 109–241 added subsec. (i).

2002—Subsec. (a). Pub. L. 107–295 inserted "or natural gas" after "oil".

1996—Subsec. (a). Pub. L. 104–324, §504(a), struck out at end "A deepwater port, licensed pursuant to the provisions of this chapter, may not be utilized—

"(1) for the loading and unloading of commodities or materials (other than oil) transported from the United States, other than materials to be used in the construction, maintenance, or operation of the high seas oil port, to be used as ship supplies, including bunkering for vessels utilizing the high seas oil port,

"(2) for the transshipment of commodities or materials, to the United States, other than oil,

"(3) except in cases where the Secretary otherwise by rule provides, for the transshipment of oil, destined for locations outside the United States."

Subsec. (c)(7) to (10). Pub. L. 104–324, §504(b), redesignated pars. (8) to (10) as (7) to (9), respectively, and struck out former par. (7) which read as follows: "he has received the opinions of the Federal Trade Commission and the Attorney General, pursuant to section 1506 of this title, as to whether issuance of the license would adversely affect competition, restrain trade, promote monopolization, or otherwise create a situation in contravention of the antitrust laws;".

Subsec. (e)(1). Pub. L. 104–324, §504(c), substituted "In issuing a license for the ownership, construction, and operation of a deepwater port, the Secretary shall prescribe those conditions which the Secretary deems necessary to carry out the provisions and requirements of this chapter or which are otherwise required by any Federal department or agency pursuant to the terms of this chapter. To the extent practicable, conditions required to carry out the provisions and requirements of this chapter shall be addressed in license conditions rather than by regulation and, to the extent practicable, the license shall allow a deepwater port's operating procedures to be stated in an operations manual, approved by the Coast Guard, in accordance with section 1509(a) of this title, rather than in detailed and specific license conditions or regulations; except that basic standards and conditions shall be addressed in regulations." for "In issuing a license for the ownership, construction, and operation of a deepwater port, the Secretary shall prescribe any conditions which he deems necessary to carry out the provisions of this chapter, or which are otherwise required by any Federal department or agency pursuant to the terms of this chapter."

Subsec. (e)(2). Pub. L. 104–324, §504(d), substituted "his license" for "his application".

Subsec. (f). Pub. L. 104–324, §504(e), inserted heading and amended text generally. Prior to amendment, text read as follows: "The Secretary may amend, transfer, or reinstate a license issued under this chapter if the amendment, transfer, or reinstatement is consistent with the findings made at the time the license was issued."

1990—Subsec. (c)(1). Pub. L. 101–380 substituted "section 2716 of this title" for "section 1517(*l*) of this title;".

1984—Subsec. (b). Pub. L. 98–419, §2(b), substituted provisions authorizing the Secretary, on application, to issue a license for the ownership, construction, and operation of a deepwater port and, on petition of the licensee, to amend, transfer, or reinstate a license issued under this chapter for provisions which had authorized the Secretary, upon application and in accordance with the provisions of this chapter, to issue, transfer, amend, or renew a license for the ownership, construction, and operation of a deepwater port.

Subsec. (e)(1). Pub. L. 98–419, §2(e), inserted provision that on petition of a licensee, the Secretary shall review any condition of a license issued under this chapter to determine if that condition is uniform, insofar as practicable, with the conditions of other licenses issued under this chapter and is reasonable, and necessary to meet the objectives of this chapter, and that the Secretary shall amend or rescind any condition that is no longer necessary or otherwise required by any Federal department or agency under this chapter.

Subsec. (f). Pub. L. 98–419, §2(c), substituted provisions authorizing the Secretary to amend, transfer, or reinstate a license issued under this chapter if the amendment, transfer, or reinstatement is consistent with the findings made at the time the license was issued for provisions which had authorized the Secretary to transfer such licenses if the Secretary determined that such transfer was in the public interest and that the transferee met the requirements of this chapter and the prerequisites to issuance under subsec. (c) of this section.

Subsec. (h). Pub. L. 98–419, §2(d), substituted provision that a license issued under this chapter remain in effect unless suspended or revoked by the Secretary or until surrendered by the licensee for provisions which had limited the terms of licenses to not more than 20 years and which had granted each licensee a preferential right of renewal for not more than 10 years, subject to subsec. (c), upon such conditions and for such term as determined by the Secretary to be reasonable and appropriate.

EFFECTIVE DATE OF 1990 AMENDMENT

Amendment by Pub. L. 101–380 applicable to incidents occurring after Aug. 18, 1990, see section 1020 of Pub. L. 101–380, set out as an Effective Date note under section 2701 of this title.

TRANSFER OF FUNCTIONS

For transfer of authorities, functions, personnel, and assets of the Coast Guard, including the authorities and functions of the Secretary of Transportation relating thereto, to the Department of Homeland Security, and for treatment of related references, see sections 468(b), 551(d), 552(d), and 557 of Title 6, Domestic Security, and the Department of Homeland Security Reorganization Plan of November 25, 2002, as modified, set out as a note under section 542 of Title 6.

LNG TANKERS

Pub. L. 109–241, title III, §304(a), July 11, 2006, 120 Stat. 527, provided that: "The Secretary of Transportation shall develop and implement a program to promote the transportation of liquefied natural gas to the United States on United States flag vessels."

§1504. Procedure

(a) Regulations; issuance, amendment, or rescission; scope

The Secretary shall, as soon as practicable after January 3, 1975, and after consultation with other Federal agencies, issue regulations to carry out the purposes and provisions of this chapter in accordance with the provisions of section 553 of title 5, without regard to subsection (a) thereof. Such regulations shall pertain to, but need not be limited to, application, issuance, transfer, renewal, suspension, and termination of licenses. Such regulations shall provide for full consultation and cooperation with all other interested Federal agencies and departments and with any potentially affected coastal State, and for consideration of the views of any interested members of the general public. The Secretary is further authorized, consistent with the purposes and provisions of this chapter, to amend or rescind any such regulation.

(b) Additional regulations; criteria for site evaluation and preconstruction testing

The Secretary, in consultation with the Secretary of the Interior and the Administrator of the National Oceanic and Atmospheric Administration, shall, as soon as practicable after January 3, 1975, prescribe regulations relating to those activities involved in site evaluation and preconstruction testing at potential deepwater port locations that may (1) adversely affect the environment; (2) interfere with authorized uses of the Outer Continental Shelf; or (3) pose a threat to human health and welfare. Such activity may thenceforth not be undertaken except in accordance with regulations prescribed pursuant to this subsection. Such regulations shall be consistent with the purposes of this chapter.

(c) Plans; submittal to Secretary of Transportation; publication in Federal Register; application contents; exemption

(1) Any person making an application under this chapter shall submit detailed plans to the Secretary. Within 21 days after the receipt of an application, the Secretary shall determine whether the application appears to contain all of the information required by paragraph (2) hereof. If the Secretary determines that such information appears to be contained in the application, the Secretary shall, no later than 5 days after making such a determination, publish notice of the application and a summary of the plans in the Federal Register. If the Secretary determines that all of the required information does not appear to be contained in the application, the Secretary shall notify the applicant and take no further action with respect to the application until such deficiencies have been remedied.

(2) Each application shall include such financial, technical, and other information as the Secretary deems necessary or appropriate. Such information shall include, but need not be limited to—

(A) the name, address, citizenship, telephone number, and the ownership interest in the applicant, of each person having any ownership interest in the applicant of greater than 3 per centum;

(B) to the extent feasible, the name, address, citizenship, and telephone number of any person with whom the applicant has made, or proposes to make, a significant contract for the construction or operation of the deepwater port and a copy of any such contract;

(C) the name, address, citizenship, and telephone number of each affiliate of the applicant and of any person required to be disclosed pursuant to subparagraphs (A) or (B) of this paragraph, together with a description of the manner in which such affiliate is associated with the applicant or any person required to be disclosed under subparagraph (A) or (B) of this paragraph;

(D) the proposed location and capacity of the deepwater port, including all components thereof;

(E) the type and design of all components of the deepwater port and any storage facilities associated with the deepwater port;

(F) with respect to construction in phases, a detailed description of each phase, including anticipated dates of completion for each of the specific components thereof;

(G) the location and capacity of existing and proposed storage facilities and pipelines which will store or transport oil transported through the deepwater port, to the extent known by the applicant or any person required to be disclosed pursuant to subparagraphs (A), (B), or (C) of this paragraph;

(H) with respect to any existing and proposed refineries which will receive oil transported through the deepwater port, the location and capacity of each such refinery and the anticipated volume of such oil to be refined by each such refinery, to the extent known by the applicant or any person required to be disclosed pursuant to subparagraphs (A), (B), or (C) of this paragraph;

(I) the financial and technical capabilities of the applicant to construct or operate the deepwater port;

(J) other qualifications of the applicant to hold a license under this chapter;

(K) the nation of registry for, and the nationality or citizenship of officers and crew serving on board, vessels transporting natural gas that are reasonably anticipated to be servicing the deepwater port;

(L) a description of procedures to be used in constructing, operating, and maintaining the deepwater port, including systems of oil spill prevention, containment, and cleanup; and

(M) such other information as may be required by the Secretary to determine the environmental impact of the proposed deepwater port.

(3) Upon written request of any person subject to this subsection, the Secretary may make a determination in writing to exempt such person from any of the informational filing provisions enumerated in this subsection or the regulations

implementing this section if the Secretary determines that such information is not necessary to facilitate the Secretary's determinations under section 1503 of this title and that such exemption will not limit public review and evaluation of the deepwater port project.

(d) Application area; publication in Federal Register; "application area" defined; submission of other applications; notice of intent and submission of completed applications; denial of pending application prior to consideration of other untimely applications

(1) At the time notice of an application is published pursuant to subsection (c) of this section, the Secretary shall publish a description in the Federal Register of an application area encompassing the deepwater port site proposed by such application and within which construction of the proposed deepwater port would eliminate, at the time such application was submitted, the need for any other deepwater port within that application area.

(2) As used in this section, "application area" means any reasonable geographical area within which a deepwater port may be constructed and operated. Such application area shall not exceed a circular zone, the center of which is the principal point of loading and unloading at the port, and the radius of which is the distance from such point to the high water mark of the nearest adjacent coastal State.

(3) The Secretary shall accompany such publication with a call for submission of any other applications for licenses for the ownership, construction, and operation of a deepwater port within the designated application area. Persons intending to file applications for such license shall submit a notice of intent to file an application with the Secretary not later than 60 days after the publication of notice pursuant to subsection (c) of this section and shall submit the completed application no later than 90 days after publication of such notice. The Secretary shall publish notice of any such application received in accordance with subsection (c) of this section. No application for a license for the ownership, construction, and operation of a deepwater port within the designated application area for which a notice of intent to file was received after such 60-day period, or which is received after such 90-day period has elapsed, shall be considered until the application pending with respect to such application area have been denied pursuant to this chapter.

(4) This subsection shall not apply to deepwater ports for natural gas.

(e) Recommendations to Secretary of Transportation; application for all Federal authorizations; copies of application to Federal agencies and departments with jurisdiction; recommendation of approval or disapproval and of manner of amendment to comply with laws or regulations

(1) Not later than 30 days after January 3, 1975, the Secretary of the Interior, the Administrator of the Environmental Protection Agency, the Chief of Engineers of the United States Army Corps of Engineers, the Administrator of the National Oceanic and Atmospheric Administration, and the heads of any other Federal department or agencies having expertise concerning, or jurisdiction over, any aspect of the construction or operation of deepwater ports shall transmit to the Secretary written comments as to their expertise or statutory responsibilities pursuant to this chapter or any other Federal law.

(2) An application filed with the Secretary shall constitute an application for all Federal authorizations required for ownership, construction, and operation of a deepwater port. At the time notice of any application is published pursuant to subsection (c) of this section, the Secretary shall forward a copy of such application to those Federal agencies and departments with jurisdiction over any aspect of such ownership, construction, or operation for comment, review, or recommendation as to conditions and for such other action as may be required by law. Each agency or department involved shall review the application and, based upon legal considerations within its area of responsibility, recommend to the Secretary, the approval or disapproval of the application not later than 45 days after the last public hearing on a proposed license for a designated application area. In any case in which the agency or department recommends disapproval, it shall set forth in detail the manner in which the application does not comply with any law or regulation within its area of responsibility and shall notify the Secretary how the application may be amended so as to bring it into compliance with the law or regulation involved.

(f) NEPA compliance

For all applications, the Secretary, in cooperation with other involved Federal agencies and departments, shall comply with the National Environmental Policy Act of 1969 (42 U.S.C. 4332) [42 U.S.C. 4321 et seq.]. Such compliance shall fulfill the requirement of all Federal agencies in carrying out their responsibilities under the National Environmental Policy Act of 1969 pursuant to this chapter.

(g) Public notice and hearings; evidentiary hearing in District of Columbia; decision of Secretary based on evidentiary record; consolidation of hearings

A license may be issued only after public notice and public hearings in accordance with this subsection. At least one such public hearing shall be held in each adjacent coastal State. Any interested person may present relevant material at any hearing. After hearings in each adjacent coastal State are concluded if the Secretary determines that there exists one or more specific and material factual issues which may be resolved by a formal evidentiary hearing, at least one adjudicatory hearing shall be held in accordance with the provisions of section 554 of title 5 in the District of Columbia. The record developed in any such adjudicatory hearing shall be basis for the Secretary's decision to approve or deny a license. Hearings held pursuant to this subsection shall be consolidated insofar as practicable with hearings held by other agencies. All public hearings on all applications for any designated application area shall be consolidated and shall be concluded not later than 240 days after notice of the initial application has been published pursuant to subsection (c) of this section.

(h) Nonrefundable application fee; processing costs; State fees; "land-based facilities directly related to a deepwater port facility" defined; fair market rental value, advance payment

(1) Each person applying for a license pursuant to this chapter shall remit to the Secretary at the time the application is filed a nonrefundable application fee established by regulation by the Secretary. In addition, an applicant shall also reimburse the United States and the appropriate adjacent coastal State for any additional costs incurred in processing an application.

(2) Notwithstanding any other provision of this chapter, and unless prohibited by law, an adjacent coastal State may fix reasonable fees for the use of a deepwater port facility, and such State and any other State in which land-based facilities directly related to a deepwater port facility are located may set reasonable fees for the use of such land-based facilities. Fees may be fixed under authority of this paragraph as compensation for any economic cost attributable to the construction and operation of such deepwater port and such land-based facilities, which cannot be recovered under other authority of such State or political subdivision thereof, including, but not limited to, ad valorem taxes, and for environmental and administrative costs attributable to the construction and operation of such deepwater port and such land-based facilities. Fees under this paragraph shall not exceed such economic, environmental, and administrative costs of such State. Such fees shall be subject to the approval of the Secretary. As used in this paragraph, the term "land-based facilities directly related to a deepwater port facility" means the onshore tank farm and pipelines connecting such tank farm to the deepwater port facility.

(3) A licensee shall pay annually in advance the fair market rental value (as determined by the Secretary of the Interior) of the subsoil and seabed of the Outer Continental Shelf of the United States to be utilized by the deepwater port, including the fair market rental value of the right-of-way necessary for the pipeline segment of the port located on such subsoil and seabed.

(i) Application approval; period for determination; priorities; criteria for determination of application best serving national interest

(1) The Secretary shall approve or deny any application for a designated application area submitted pursuant to this chapter not later than 90 days after the last public hearing on a proposed license for that area.

(2) In the event more than one application is submitted for an application area, the Secretary, unless one of the proposed deepwater ports clearly best serves the national interest, shall issue a license according to the following order of priorities:

(A) to an adjacent coastal State (or combination of States), any political subdivision thereof, or agency or instrumentality, including a wholly owned corporation of any such government;

(B) to a person who is neither (i) engaged in producing, refining, or marketing oil, nor (ii) an affiliate of any person who is engaged in producing, refining, or marketing oil or an affiliate of any such affiliate;

(C) to any other person.

(3) In determining whether any one proposed deepwater port clearly best serves the national interest, the Secretary shall consider the following factors:

(A) the degree to which the proposed deepwater ports affect the environment, as determined under criteria established pursuant to section 1505 of this title;

(B) any significant differences between anticipated completion dates for the proposed deepwater ports; and

(C) any differences in costs of construction and operation of the proposed deepwater ports, to the extent that such differential may significantly affect the ultimate cost of oil to the consumer.

(4) The Secretary shall approve or deny any application for a deepwater port for natural gas submitted pursuant to this chapter not later than 90 days after the last public hearing on a proposed license. Paragraphs (1), (2), and (3) of this subsection shall not apply to an application for a deepwater port for natural gas.

(Pub. L. 93–627, §5, Jan. 3, 1975, 88 Stat. 2131; Pub. L. 98–419, §2(f), Sept. 25, 1984, 98 Stat. 1607; Pub. L. 104–324, title V, §505, Oct. 19, 1996, 110 Stat. 3927; Pub. L. 107–295, title I, §106(c), (f), (g), Nov. 25, 2002, 116 Stat. 2086–2088; Pub. L. 109–241, title III, §304(c)(1), July 11, 2006, 120 Stat. 527.)

REFERENCES IN TEXT

The National Environmental Policy Act of 1969, referred to in subsec. (f), is Pub. L. 91–190, Jan. 1, 1970, 83 Stat. 852, as amended, which is classified generally to chapter 55 (§4321 et seq.) of Title 42, The Public Health and Welfare. For complete classification of this Act to the Code, see Short Title note set out under section 4321 of Title 42 and Tables.

AMENDMENTS

2006—Subsec. (c)(2)(K) to (M). Pub. L. 109–241 added subpar. (K) and redesignated former subpars. (K) and (L) as (L) and (M), respectively.

2002—Subsec. (d)(4). Pub. L. 107–295, §106(c)(1), added par. (4).

Subsec. (f). Pub. L. 107–295, §106(f), substituted "NEPA compliance" for "Environmental impact statement for single application area; criteria" in heading and amended text generally. Prior to amendment, text read as follows: "For all timely applications covering a single application area, the Secretary, in cooperation with other involved Federal agencies and departments, shall, pursuant to section 4332(2)(C) of title 42, prepare a single, detailed environmental impact statement, which shall fulfill the requirement of all Federal agencies in carrying out their responsibilities pursuant to this chapter to prepare an environmental impact statement. In preparing such statement the Secretary shall consider the criteria established under section 1505 of this title."

Subsec. (h)(2). Pub. L. 107–295, §106(g), inserted "and unless prohibited by law," after "Notwithstanding any other provision of this chapter,".

Subsec. (i)(4). Pub. L. 107–295, §106(c)(2), added par. (4).

1996—Subsec. (c)(3). Pub. L. 104–324 added par. (3).

1984—Subsec. (g). Pub. L. 98–419 substituted "issued" for "issued, transferred, or renewed".

REGULATIONS

Pub. L. 107–295, title I, §106(e), Nov. 25, 2002, 116 Stat. 2087, provided that:

"(1) AGENCY AND DEPARTMENT EXPERTISE AND RESPONSIBILITIES.—Not later than 30 days after the date of the enactment of this Act [Nov. 25, 2002], the heads of Federal departments or agencies having expertise concerning, or jurisdiction over, any aspect of the construction or operation of deepwater ports for natural gas shall transmit to the Secretary of Transportation written comments as to such expertise or statutory responsibilities pursuant to the Deepwater Port Act of 1974 (33 U.S.C. 1501 et seq.) or any other Federal law.

"(2) INTERIM FINAL RULE.—The Secretary may issue an interim final rule as a temporary regulation implementing this section [amending this section and sections 1501 to 1503, 1507, and 1520 of this title] (including the amendments made by this section) as soon as practicable after the date of enactment of this section, without regard to the provisions of chapter 5 of title 5, United States Code.

"(3) FINAL RULES.—As soon as practicable after the date of the enactment of this Act, the Secretary of Transportation shall issue additional final rules that, in the discretion of the Secretary, are determined to be necessary under the Deepwater Port Act of 1974 (33 U.S.C. 1501 et seq.) for the application and issuance of licenses for a deepwater port for natural gas."

INFORMATION TO BE PROVIDED

Pub. L. 109–241, title III, §304(c)(2), July 11, 2006, 120 Stat. 527, provided that: "When the Coast Guard is operating as a contributing agency in the Federal Energy Regulatory Commission's shoreside licensing process for a liquefied natural gas or liquefied petroleum gas terminal located on shore or within State seaward boundaries, the Coast Guard shall provide to the Commission the information described in section 5(c)(2)(K) of the Deepwater Port Act of 1974 (33 U.S.C. 1504(c)(2)(K)) with respect to vessels reasonably anticipated to be servicing that port."

§1505. Environmental review criteria

(a) Establishment; evaluation of proposed deepwater ports

The Secretary, in accordance with the recommendations of the Administrator of the Environmental Protection Agency and the Administrator of the National Oceanic and Atmospheric Administration and after consultation with any other Federal departments and agencies having jurisdiction over any aspect of the construction or operation of a deepwater port, shall establish, as soon as practicable after January 3, 1975, environmental review criteria consistent with the National Environmental Policy Act [42 U.S.C. 4321 et seq.]. Such criteria shall be used to evaluate a deepwater port as proposed in an application, including—

(1) the effect on the marine environment;

(2) the effect on oceanographic currents and wave patterns;

(3) the effect on alternate uses of the oceans and navigable waters, such as scientific study, fishing, and exploitation of other living and nonliving resources;

(4) the potential dangers to a deepwater port from waves, winds, weather, and geological conditions, and the steps which can be taken to protect against or minimize such dangers;

(5) effects of land-based developments related to deepwater port development;

(6) the effect on human health and welfare; and

(7) such other considerations as the Secretary deems necessary or appropriate.

(b) Review and revision

The Secretary shall periodically review and, whenever necessary, revise in the same manner as originally developed, criteria established pursuant to subsection (a) of this section.

(c) Concurrent development of criteria and regulations

Criteria established pursuant to this section shall be developed concurrently with the regulations in subsection (a) of section 1504 of this title and in accordance with the provisions of that subsection.

(Pub. L. 93–627, §6, Jan. 3, 1975, 88 Stat. 2135.)

REFERENCES IN TEXT

The National Environmental Policy Act, referred to in subsec. (a), is Pub. L. 91–190, §2, Jan. 1970, 83 Stat. 852, as amended, which is classified generally to chapter 55 (§4321 et seq.) of Title 42, The Public Health and Welfare. For complete classification of this Act to the Code, see Short Title note set out under section 4321 of Title 42 and Tables.

§1506. Repealed. Pub. L. 104–324, title V, §506, Oct. 19, 1996, 110 Stat. 3927

Section, Pub. L. 93–627, §7, Jan. 3, 1975, 88 Stat. 2135; Pub. L. 98–419, §2(g), (h), Sept. 25, 1984, 98 Stat. 1607, provided for antitrust review by Attorney General and Federal Trade Commission prior to issuance of license for ownership, construction, and operation of deepwater port.

§1507. Common carrier status

(a) Status of deepwater ports and storage facilities

A deepwater port and a storage facility serviced directly by that deepwater port shall operate as a common carrier under applicable provisions of part I of the Interstate Commerce Act and subtitle IV of title 49, and shall accept, transport, or convey without discrimination all oil delivered to the deepwater port with respect to which its license is issued, except as provided by subsection (b) of this section.

(b) Discrimination prohibition; exceptions

A licensee is not discriminating under this section and is not subject to common carrier regulations under subsection (a) of this section when that licensee—

(1) is subject to effective competition for the transportation of oil from alternative transportation systems; and

(2) sets its rates, fees, charges, and conditions of service on the basis of competition, giving consideration to other relevant business factors such as the market value of services provided, licensee's cost of operation, and the licensee's investment in the deepwater port and a storage facility, and components thereof, serviced directly by that deepwater port.

(c) Enforcement, suspension, or termination proceedings

When the Secretary has reason to believe that a licensee is not in compliance with this section, the Secretary shall commence an appropriate proceeding before the Federal Energy Regulatory Commission or request the Attorney General to take appropriate steps to enforce compliance with this section and, when appropriate, to secure the imposition of appropriate sanctions. In addition, the Secretary may suspend or revoke the license of a licensee not complying with its obligations under this section.

(d) Managed access

Subsections (a) and (b) of this section shall not apply to deepwater ports for natural gas. A licensee of a deepwater port for natural gas, or an affiliate thereof, may exclusively utilize the entire capacity of the deepwater port and storage facilities for the acceptance, transport, storage, regasification, or conveyance of natural gas produced, processed, marketed, or otherwise obtained by agreement by such licensee or its affiliates. The licensee may make unused capacity of the deepwater port and storage facilities available to other persons, pursuant to reasonable terms and conditions imposed by the licensee, if such use does not otherwise interfere in any way with the acceptance, transport, storage, regasification, or conveyance of natural gas produced, processed, marketed, or otherwise obtained by agreement by such licensee or its affiliates.

(e) Jurisdiction

Notwithstanding any provision of the Natural Gas Act (15 U.S.C. 717 et seq.), any regulation or rule issued thereunder, or section 1518 of this title as it pertains to such Act, this chapter shall apply with respect to the licensing, siting, construction, or operation of a deepwater natural gas port or the acceptance, transport, storage, regasification, or conveyance of natural gas at or through a deepwater port, to the exclusion of the Natural Gas Act or any regulation or rule issued thereunder.

(Pub. L. 93–627, §8, Jan. 3, 1975, 88 Stat. 2136; Pub. L. 98–419, §3(a), Sept. 25, 1984, 98 Stat. 1608; Pub. L. 104–324, title V, §507, Oct. 19, 1996, 110 Stat. 3927; Pub. L. 107–295, title I, §106(d), Nov. 25, 2002, 116 Stat. 2087.)

REFERENCES IN TEXT

The Interstate Commerce Act, referred to in subsec. (a), is act Feb. 4, 1887, ch. 104, 24 Stat. 379, as amended. Part I of the Act, which was classified to chapter 1 (§1 et seq.) of former Title 49, Transportation, was repealed by Pub. L. 95-473, §4(b), Oct. 17, 1978, 92 Stat. 1467, the first section of which enacted subtitle IV (§10101 et seq.) of Title 49. For distribution of former sections of Title 49 into the revised Title 49, see Table at the beginning of Title 49.

The Natural Gas Act, referred to in subsec. (e), is act June 21, 1938, ch. 556, 52 Stat. 821, as amended, which is classified generally to chapter 15B (§717 et seq.) of Title 15, Commerce and Trade. For complete classification of this Act to the Code, see section 717w of Title 15 and Tables.

AMENDMENTS

2002—Subsecs. (d), (e). Pub. L. 107–295 added subsecs. (d) and (e).

1996—Subsec. (a). Pub. L. 104–324, §507(a), inserted "and shall accept, transport, or convey without discrimination all oil delivered to the deepwater port with respect to which its license is issued," after "subtitle IV of title 49,".

Subsec. (b). Pub. L. 104–324, §507(b), substituted "A licensee is not discriminating under this section and" for "A licensee under this chapter shall accept, transport, or convey without discrimination all oil delivered to the deepwater port with respect to which its license is issued. However, a licensee".

1984—Subsec. (a). Pub. L. 98–419 substituted provision that a deepwater port and a storage facility serviced directly by that deepwater port shall operate as a common carrier under applicable provisions of part I of the Interstate Commerce Act and subtitle IV of title 49 except as provided by subsec. (b), for provision that such port and such facilities were subject to regulations as a common carrier in accordance with the Interstate Commerce Act, as amended, for purposes of chapter 39 of title 18 and former sections 1 to 27 of title 49.

Subsec. (b). Pub. L. 98–419 inserted provisions enumerating conditions under which a licensee is not subject to common carrier regulations under subsec. (a). Provisions dealing with enforcement, suspension, or termination proceedings, were redesignated as subsec. (c).

Subsec. (c). Pub. L. 98–419 redesignated a portion of provisions of subsec. (b) as subsec. (c), and in subsec. (c) as so redesignated substituted provisions authorizing the Secretary to commence proceedings before the Federal Energy Regulatory Commission, or to suspend or revoke licenses of noncomplying licensees, in the event of noncompliance with this section, for provisions which had authorized the Secretary to commence proceedings before the Interstate Commerce Commission or to suspend or terminate licenses of noncomplying licensees as provided in section 1511 of this title, in the event of noncompliance by a licensee with its obligations as a common carrier.

§1508. Adjacent coastal States

(a) Designation; direct pipeline connections; mileage; risk of damage to coastal environment, time for designation

(1) The Secretary, in issuing notice of application pursuant to section 1504(c) of this title, shall designate as an "adjacent coastal State" any coastal State which (A) would be directly connected by pipeline to a deepwater port as proposed in an application, or (B) would be located within 15 miles of any such proposed deepwater port.

(2) The Secretary shall, upon request of a State, and after having received the recommendations of the Administrator of the National Oceanic and Atmospheric Administration, designate such State as an "adjacent coastal State" if he determines that there is a risk of damage to the coastal environment of such State equal to or greater than the risk posed to a State directly connected by pipeline to the proposed deepwater port. This paragraph shall apply only with respect to requests made by a State not later than the 14th day after the date of publication of notice of an application for a proposed deepwater port in the Federal Register in accordance with section 1504(c) of this title. The Secretary shall make the designation required by this paragraph not later than the 45th day after the date he receives such a request from a State.

(b) Applications; submittal to Governors for approval or disapproval; consistency of Federal licenses and State programs; views of other interested States

(1) Not later than 10 days after the designation of adjacent coastal States pursuant to this chapter, the Secretary shall transmit a complete copy of the application to the Governor of each adjacent coastal State. The Secretary shall not issue a license without the approval of the Governor of each adjacent coastal State. If the Governor fails to transmit his approval or disapproval to the Secretary not later than 45 days after the last public hearing on applications for

a particular application area, such approval shall be conclusively presumed. If the Governor notifies the Secretary that an application, which would otherwise be approved pursuant to this paragraph, is inconsistent with State programs relating to environmental protection, land and water use, and coastal zone management, the Secretary shall condition the license granted so as to make it consistent with such State programs.

(2) Any other interested State shall have the opportunity to make its views known to, and shall be given full consideration by, the Secretary regarding the location, construction, and operation of a deepwater port.

(c) Reasonable progress toward development of coastal zone management program; planning grants

The Secretary shall not issue a license unless the adjacent coastal State to which the deepwater port is to be directly connected by pipeline has developed, or is making, at the time the application is submitted, reasonable progress toward developing an approved coastal zone management program pursuant to the Coastal Zone Management Act of 1972 [16 U.S.C. 1451 et seq.] in the area to be directly and primarily impacted by land and water development in the coastal zone resulting from such deepwater port. For the purposes of this chapter, a State shall be considered to be making reasonable progress if it is receiving a planning grant pursuant to section 305 of the Coastal Zone Management Act [16 U.S.C. 1454].

(d) State agreements or compacts

The consent of Congress is given to two or more coastal States to negotiate and enter into agreements or compacts, not in conflict with any law or treaty of the United States, (1) to apply for a license for the ownership, construction, and operation of a deepwater port or for the transfer of such license, and (2) to establish such agencies, joint or otherwise, as are deemed necessary or appropriate for implementing and carrying out the provisions of any such agreement or compact. Such agreement or compact shall be binding and obligatory upon any State or party thereto without further approval by Congress.

(Pub. L. 93–627, § 9, Jan. 3, 1975, 88 Stat. 2136.)

REFERENCES IN TEXT

The Coastal Zone Management Act of 1972, referred to in subsec. (c), is title III of Pub. L. 89–454 as added by Pub. L. 92–583, Oct. 27, 1972, 86 Stat. 1280, as amended, which is classified generally to chapter 33 (§ 1451 et seq.) of Title 16, Conservation. For complete classification of this Act to the Code, see Short Title note set out under section 1451 of Title 16, and Tables.

§ 1509. Marine environmental protection and navigational safety

(a) Regulations and procedures

Subject to recognized principles of international law and the provision of adequate opportunities for public involvement, the Secretary shall prescribe and enforce procedures, either by regulation (for basic standards and conditions) or by the licensee's operations manual, with respect to rules governing vessel movement, loading and unloading procedures, designation and marking of anchorage areas, maintenance, law enforcement, and the equipment, training, and maintenance required (A) to prevent pollution of the marine environment, (B) to clean up any pollutants which may be discharged, and (C) to otherwise prevent or minimize any adverse impact from the construction and operation of such deepwater port.

(b) Safety of property and life; regulations

The Secretary shall issue and enforce regulations with respect to lights and other warning devices, safety equipment, and other matters relating to the promotion of safety of life and property in any deepwater port and the waters adjacent thereto.

(c) Marking of components; payment of cost

The Secretary shall mark, for the protection of navigation, any component of a deepwater port whenever the licensee fails to mark such component in accordance with applicable regulations. The licensee shall pay the cost of such marking.

(d) Safety zones; designation; construction period; permitted activities

(1) Subject to recognized principles of international law and after consultation with the Secretary of the Interior, the Secretary of Commerce, the Secretary of State, and the Secretary of Defense, the Secretary shall designate a zone of appropriate size around and including any deepwater port for the purpose of navigational safety. In such zone, no installations, structures, or uses will be permitted that are incompatible with the operation of the deepwater port. The Secretary shall by regulation define permitted activities within such zone. The Secretary shall, not later than 30 days after publication of notice pursuant to section 1504(c) of this title, designate such safety zone with respect to any proposed deepwater port.

(2) In addition to any other regulations, the Secretary is authorized, in accordance with this subsection, to establish a safety zone to be effective during the period of construction of a deepwater port and to issue rules and regulations relating thereto.

(Pub. L. 93–627, § 10, Jan. 3, 1975, 88 Stat. 2137; Pub. L. 104–324, title V, § 508, Oct. 19, 1996, 110 Stat. 3927.)

AMENDMENTS

1996—Subsec. (a). Pub. L. 104–324, § 507(a), inserted "and the provision of adequate opportunities for public involvement" after "international law" and substituted "shall prescribe and enforce procedures, either by regulation (for basic standards and conditions) or by the licensee's operations manual, with respect to" for "shall prescribe by regulation and enforce procedures with respect to any deepwater port, including, but not limited to,".

§ 1510. International agreements

The Secretary of State, in consultation with the Secretary, shall seek effective international action and cooperation in support of the policy and purposes of this chapter and may formulate, present, or support specific proposals in the

United Nations and other competent international organizations for the development of appropriate international rules and regulations relative to the construction, ownership, and operation of deepwater ports, with particular regard for measures that assure protection of such facilities as well as the promotion of navigational safety in the vicinity thereof.

(Pub. L. 93–627, § 11, Jan. 3, 1975, 88 Stat. 2138.)

§ 1511. Suspension or termination of licenses

(a) Proceedings by Attorney General; venue; conditions subsequent

Whenever a licensee fails to comply with any applicable provision of this chapter, or any applicable rule, regulation, restriction, or condition issued or imposed by the Secretary under the authority of this chapter, the Attorney General, at the request of the Secretary, may file an appropriate action in the United States district court nearest to the location of the proposed or actual deepwater port, as the case may be, or in the district in which the licensee resides or may be found, to—

(1) suspend the license; or

(2) if such failure is knowing and continues for a period of thirty days after the Secretary mails notification of such failure by registered letter to the licensee at his record post office address, revoke such license.

No proceeding under this subsection is necessary if the license, by its terms, provides for automatic suspension or termination upon the occurrence of a fixed or agreed upon condition, event, or time.

(b) Public health or safety; danger to environment; completion of proceedings

If the Secretary determines that immediate suspension of the construction or operation of a deepwater port or any component thereof is necessary to protect public health or safety or to eliminate imminent and substantial danger to the environment, he shall order the licensee to cease or alter such construction or operation pending the completion of a judicial proceeding pursuant to subsection (a) of this section.

(Pub. L. 93–627, § 12, Jan. 3, 1975, 88 Stat. 2138.)

CODIFICATION

In subsec. (a), "chapter" substituted for "title" to conform to other substitutions for "Act" and as reflecting intent of Congress manifest throughout Pub. L. 93–627 in the use of the term "Act".

§ 1512. Recordkeeping and inspection

(a) Regulations; regulations under other provisions unaffected

Each licensee shall establish and maintain such records, make such reports, and provide such information as the Secretary, after consultation with other interested Federal departments and agencies, shall by regulation prescribe to carry out the provision of this chapter. Such regulations shall not amend, contradict or duplicate regulations established pursuant to part I of the Interstate Commerce Act or any other law. Each licensee shall submit such reports and shall make such records and information available as the Secretary may request.

(b) Access to deepwater ports in enforcement proceedings and execution of official duties; inspections and tests; notification of results

All United States officials, including those officials responsible for the implementation and enforcement of United States laws applicable to a deepwater port, shall at all times be afforded reasonable access to a deepwater port licensed under this chapter for the purpose of enforcing laws under their jurisdiction or otherwise carrying out their responsibilities. Each such official may inspect, at reasonable times, records, files, papers, processes, controls, and facilities and may test any feature of a deep water port. Each inspection shall be conducted with reasonable promptness, and such licensee shall be notified of the results of such inspection.

(Pub. L. 93–627, § 13, Jan. 3, 1975, 88 Stat. 2139.)

REFERENCES IN TEXT

The Interstate Commerce Act, referred to in subsec. (a), is act Feb. 4, 1887, ch. 104, 24 Stat. 379, as amended. Part I of the Act, which was classified to chapter 1 (§ 1 et seq.) of former Title 49, Transportation, was repealed by Pub. L. 95-473, § 4(b), Oct. 17, 1978, 92 Stat. 1467, the first section of which enacted subtitle IV (§ 10101 et seq.) of Title 49. For distribution of former sections of Title 49 into the revised Title 49, see Table at the beginning of Title 49.

§ 1513. Public access to information

(a) Inspection of copies; reproduction costs; protected information

Copies of any communication, document, report, or information transmitted between any official of the Federal Government and any person concerning a deepwater port (other than contracts referred to in section 1504(c)(2)(B) of this title) shall be made available to the public for inspection, and shall be available for the purpose of reproduction at a reasonable cost, to the public upon identifiable request, unless such information may not be publicly released under the terms of subsection (b) of this section. Except as provided in subsection (b) of this section, nothing contained in this section shall be construed to require the release of any information of the kind described in subsection (b) of section 552 of title 5 or which is otherwise protected by law from disclosure to the public.

(b) Information disclosure prohibition; confidentiality of certain disclosures

The Secretary shall not disclose information obtained by him under this chapter that concerns or relates to a trade secret, referred to in section 1905 of title 18, or to a contract referred to in section 1504(c)(2)(B) of this title, except that such information may be disclosed, in a manner which is designed to maintain confidentiality—

(1) to other Federal and adjacent coastal State government departments and agencies for official use, upon request;

(2) to any committee of Congress having jurisdiction over the subject matter to which the information relates, upon request;

(3) to any person in any judicial proceeding, under a court order formulated to preserve such confidentiality without impairing the proceedings; and

(4) to the public in order to protect health and safety, after notice and opportunity for comment in writing or for discussion in closed session within fifteen days by the party to which the information pertains (if the delay resulting from such notice and opportunity for comment would not be detrimental to the public health and safety).

(Pub. L. 93–627, §14, Jan. 3, 1975, 88 Stat. 2139.)

§1514. Remedies

(a) Criminal penalties

Any person who willfully violates any provision of this chapter or any rule, order, or regulation issued pursuant thereto commits a class A misdemeanor for each day of violation.

(b) Orders of compliance; Attorney General's civil action; jurisdiction and venue

(1) Whenever on the basis of any information available to him the Secretary finds that any person is in violation of any provision of this chapter or any rule, regulation, order, license, or condition thereof, or other requirements under this chapter, he shall issue an order requiring such person to comply with such provision or requirement, or he shall bring a civil action in accordance with paragraph (3) of this subsection.

(2) Any order issued under this subsection shall state with reasonable specificity the nature of the violation and a time for compliance, not to exceed thirty days, which the Secretary determines is reasonable, taking into account the seriousness of the violation and any good faith efforts to comply with applicable requirements.

(3) Upon a request by the Secretary, the Attorney General shall commence a civil action for appropriate relief, including a permanent or temporary injunction or a civil penalty not to exceed $25,000 per day of such violation, for any violation for which the Secretary is authorized to issue a compliance order under paragraph (1) of this subsection. Any action under this subsection may be brought in the district court of the United States for the district in which the defendant is located or resides, or is doing business, and such court shall have jurisdiction to restrain such violation, require compliance, or impose such penalty.

(c) Attorney General's action for equitable relief; scope of relief

Upon a request by the Secretary, the Attorney General shall bring an action in an appropriate district court of the United States for equitable relief to redress a violation by any person of any provision of this chapter, any regulation under this chapter, or any license condition. The district courts of the United States shall have jurisdiction to grant such relief as is necessary or appropriate, including mandatory or prohibitive injunctive relief, interim equitable relief, compensatory damages, and punitive damages.

(d) Vessels; liability in rem; exempt vessels; consent or privy of owners or bareboat charterers

Any vessel, except a public vessel engaged in noncommercial activities, used in a violation of this chapter or of any rule or regulation issued pursuant to this chapter, shall be liable in rem for any civil penalty assessed or criminal fine imposed and may be proceeded against in any district court of the United States having jurisdiction thereof; but no vessel shall be liable unless it shall appear that one or more of the owners, or bareboat charterers, was at the time of the violation, a consenting party or privy to such violation.

(Pub. L. 93–627, §15, Jan. 3, 1975, 88 Stat. 2140; Pub. L. 101–380, title IV, §4302(m), Aug. 18, 1990, 104 Stat. 539.)

AMENDMENTS

1990—Subsec. (a). Pub. L. 101–380 substituted "commits a class A misdemeanor for each day of violation" for "shall on conviction be fined not more than $25,000 for each day of violation or imprisoned for not more than 1 year, or both".

EFFECTIVE DATE OF 1990 AMENDMENT

Amendment by Pub. L. 101–380 applicable to incidents occurring after Aug. 18, 1990, see section 1020 of Pub. L. 101–380, set out as an Effective Date note under section 2701 of this title.

DEPOSIT OF CERTAIN PENALTIES INTO OIL SPILL LIABILITY TRUST FUND

Penalties paid pursuant to this chapter and sections 1319(c) and 1321 of this title to be deposited in the Oil Spill Liability Trust Fund created under section 9509 of Title 26, Internal Revenue Code, see section 4304 of Pub. L. 101–380, set out as a note under section 9509 of Title 26.

§1515. Citizen civil action

(a) Equitable relief; case or controversy; district court jurisdiction

Except as provided in subsection (b) of this section, any person may commence a civil action for equitable relief on his own behalf, whenever such action constitutes a case or controversy—

(1) against any person (including (A) the United States, and (B) any other governmental instrumentality or agency to the extent permitted by the eleventh amendment to the Constitution) who is alleged to be in violation of any provision of this chapter or any condition of a license issued pursuant to this chapter; or

(2) against the Secretary where there is alleged a failure of the Secretary to perform any act or duty under this chapter which is not discretionary with the Secretary. Any action brought against the Secretary under this paragraph shall be brought in the district court for the District of Columbia or the district of the appropriate adjacent coastal State.

In suits brought under this chapter, the district court shall have jurisdiction, without regard to the amount in controversy or the citizenship of the parties, to enforce any provision of this chapter or any condition of a license issued pursuant to this chapter, or to order the Secretary to perform such act or duty, as the case may be.

(b) Notice; intervention of right by person

No civil action may be commenced—

(1) under subsection (a)(1) of this section—

(A) prior to 60 days after the plaintiff has given notice of the violation (i) to the Secretary and (ii) to any alleged violator; or

(B) if the Secretary or the Attorney General has commenced and is diligently prosecuting a civil or criminal action with respect to such matters in a court of the United States, but in any such action any person may intervene as a matter of right; or

(2) under subsection (a)(2) of this section prior to 60 days after the plaintiff has given notice of such action to the Secretary.

Notice under this subsection shall be given in such a manner as the Secretary shall prescribe by regulation.

(c) Intervention of right by Secretary or Attorney General

In any action under this section, the Secretary or the Attorney General, if not a party, may intervene as a matter of right.

(d) Costs of litigation; attorney and witness fees

The Court, in issuing any final order in any action brought pursuant to subsection (a) of this section, may award costs of litigation (including reasonable attorney and expert witness fees) to any party whenever the court determines that such an award is appropriate.

(e) Statutory or common law rights unaffected

Nothing in this section shall restrict any right which any person (or class of persons) may have under any statute or common law to seek enforcement or to seek any other relief.

(Pub. L. 93–627, §16, Jan. 3, 1975, 88 Stat. 2140.)

§1516. Judicial review; persons aggrieved; jurisdiction of courts of appeal

Any person suffering legal wrong, or who is adversely affected or aggrieved by the Secretary's decision to issue, transfer, modify, renew, suspend, or revoke a license may, not later than 60 days after any such decision is made, seek judicial review of such decision in the United States Court of Appeals for the circuit within which the nearest adjacent coastal State is located. A person shall be deemed to be aggrieved by the Secretary's decision within the meaning of this chapter if he—

(A) has participated in the administrative proceedings before the Secretary (or if he did not so participate, he can show that his failure to do so was caused by the Secretary's failure to provide the required notice); and

(B) is adversely affected by the Secretary's action.

(Pub. L. 93–627, §17, Jan. 3, 1975, 88 Stat. 2141.)

§1517. Repealed. Pub. L. 101–380, title II, §2003(a)(2), Aug. 18, 1990, 104 Stat. 507

Section, Pub. L. 93–627, §18, Jan. 3, 1975, 88 Stat. 2141; Pub. L. 98–419, §4(a), Sept. 25, 1984, 98 Stat. 1608, set penalties for discharge of oil into marine environment and provided for creation and maintenance of a Deepwater Port Liability Fund.

DEEPWATER PORT LIABILITY FUND

Amounts remaining in Deepwater Port Liability Fund established under former subsec. (f) of this section to be deposited in Oil Spill Liability Trust Fund established under section 9509 of Title 26, Internal Revenue Code, with that Fund to assume all liability incurred by the Deepwater Port Liability Fund, see section 2003(b) of Pub. L. 101–380, set out as a note under section 9509 of Title 26.

EFFECTIVE DATE OF REPEAL

Repeal applicable to incidents occurring after Aug. 18, 1990, see section 1020 of Pub. L. 101–380, set out as an Effective Date note under section 2701 of this title.

§1517a. Omitted

CODIFICATION

Section, Pub. L. 101–164, title I, Nov. 21, 1989, 103 Stat. 1073, which authorized Secretary of Transportation to issue, and Secretary of the Treasury to purchase, notes or other obligations to meet obligations of Deepwater Port Liability Fund, applied to fiscal year ending Sept. 30, 1990, and was not repeated in subsequent appropriation acts.

Similar provisions were contained in the following prior appropriation acts:

Pub. L. 100–457, title I, Sept. 30, 1988, 102 Stat. 2128.

Pub. L. 100–202, §101(*l*) [title I], Dec. 22, 1987, 101 Stat. 1329–358, 1329–361.

Pub. L. 99–500, §101(*l*) [H.R. 5205, title I], Oct. 18, 1986, 100 Stat. 1783–308, and Pub. L. 99–591, §101(*l*) [H.R. 5205, title I], Oct. 30, 1986, 100 Stat. 3341–308.

Pub. L. 99–190, §101(e) [title I], Dec. 19, 1985, 99 Stat. 1267, 1270.

Pub. L. 98–473, title I, §101(i) [title I], Oct. 12, 1984, 98 Stat. 1944, 1947.

Pub. L. 98–78, title I, Aug. 15, 1983, 97 Stat. 455.

Pub. L. 97–369, title I, Dec. 18, 1982, 95 Stat. 1767.

Pub. L. 97–102, title I, Dec. 23, 1981, 95 Stat. 1444.

Pub. L. 97–12, title I, June 5, 1981, 95 Stat. 67.

§1518. Relationship to other laws

(a) Federal Constitution, laws, and treaties applicable; other Federal requirements applicable; status of deepwater port; Federal or State authorities and responsibilities within territorial seas unaffected; notification by Secretary of State of intent to exercise jurisdiction; objections by foreign governments

(1) The Constitution, laws, and treaties of the United States shall apply to a deepwater port licensed under this chapter and to activities connected, associated, or potentially interfering with the use or operation of any such port, in the same manner as if such port were an area of exclusive Federal jurisdiction located within a State. Nothing in this chapter shall be construed to relieve, exempt, or immunize any person from any other requirement imposed by Federal law, regulation, or treaty. Deepwater ports licensed under this chapter do not possess the status of islands and have no territorial seas of their own.

(2) Except as otherwise provided by this chapter, nothing in this chapter shall in any way alter the responsibilities and authorities of a State or the United States within the territorial seas of the United States.

(3) The Secretary of State shall notify the government of each foreign state having vessels registered under its authority or flying its flag which may call at or otherwise utilize a deepwater port but which do not currently have an agreement in effect as provided in subsection (c)(2)(A)(i) of this section that the United States intends to exercise jurisdiction over vessels calling at or otherwise utilizing a deepwater port and the persons on board such vessels. The Sec-

retary of State shall notify the government of each such state that, absent its objection, its vessels will be subject to the jurisdiction of the United States whenever they—

(A) are calling at or otherwise utilizing a deepwater port; and

(B) are within the safety zone of such a deepwater port and are engaged in activities connected, associated, or potentially interfering with the use and operation of the deepwater port.

The Secretary of State shall promptly inform licensees of deepwater ports of all objections received from governments of foreign states in response to notifications made under this paragraph.

(b) Law of nearest adjacent coastal State as applicable Federal law; Federal administration and enforcement of such law; nearest adjacent coastal State defined

The law of the nearest adjacent coastal State, now in effect or hereafter adopted, amended, or repealed, is declared to be the law of the United States, and shall apply to any deepwater port licensed pursuant to this chapter, to the extent applicable and not inconsistent with any provision or regulation under this chapter or other Federal laws and regulations now in effect or hereafter adopted, amended, or repealed. All such applicable laws shall be administered and enforced by the appropriate officers and courts of the United States. For purposes of this subsection, the nearest adjacent coastal State shall be that State whose seaward boundaries, if extended beyond 3 miles, would encompass the site of the deepwater port.

(c) Vessels of United States and foreign states subject to Federal jurisdiction; objections to jurisdiction; designation of agent for service of process; duty of licensee

(1) The jurisdiction of the United States shall apply to vessels of the United States and persons on board such vessels. The jurisdiction of the United States shall also apply to vessels, and persons on board such vessels, registered in or flying the flags of foreign states, whenever such vessels are—

(A) calling at or otherwise utilizing a deepwater port; and

(B) are within the safety zone of such a deepwater port, and are engaged in activities connected, associated, or potentially interfering with the use and operation of the deepwater port.

The jurisdiction of the United States under this paragraph shall not, however, apply to vessels registered in or flying the flag of any foreign state that has objected to the application of such jurisdiction.

(2) Except in a situation involving force majeure, a licensee shall not permit a vessel registered in or flying the flag of a foreign state to call at or otherwise utilize a deepwater port licensed under this chapter unless—

(A)(i) the foreign state involved, by specific agreement with the United States, has agreed to recognize the jurisdiction of the United States over the vessels registered in or flying the flag of that state and persons on board such vessels in accordance with the provisions of paragraph (1) of this subsection, while the vessel is located within the safety zone, or

(ii) the foreign state has not objected to the application of the jurisdiction of the United States to any vessel, or persons on board such vessel, while the vessel is located within the safety zone; and

(B) the vessel owner or operator has designated an agent in the United States for receipt of service of process in the event of any claim or legal proceeding resulting from activities of the vessel or its personnel while located within such a safety zone.

(3) For purposes of paragraph (2)(A)(ii) of this subsection, a licensee shall not be obliged to prohibit a call at or use of a deepwater port by a vessel registered in or flying the flag of an objecting state unless the licensee has been informed by the Secretary of State as required by subsection (a)(3) of this section.

(d) Customs laws inapplicable to deepwater port; duties and taxes on foreign articles imported into customs territory of United States

The customs laws administered by the Secretary of the Treasury shall not apply to any deepwater port licensed under this chapter, but all foreign articles to be used in the construction of any such deepwater port, including any component thereof, shall first be made subject to all applicable duties and taxes which would be imposed upon or by reason of their importation if they were imported for consumption in the United States. Duties and taxes shall be paid thereon in accordance with laws applicable to merchandise imported into the customs territory of the United States.

(e) Federal district courts; original jurisdiction; venue

The United States district courts shall have original jurisdiction of cases and controversies arising out of or in connection with the construction and operation of deepwater ports, and proceedings with respect to any such case or controversy may be instituted in the judicial district in which any defendant resides or may be found, or in the judicial district of the adjacent coastal State nearest the place where the cause of action arose.

(Pub. L. 93–627, §19(a)–(e), Jan. 3, 1975, 88 Stat. 2145, 2146; Pub. L. 98–419, §5(a), (b), Sept. 25, 1984, 98 Stat. 1609.)

REFERENCES IN TEXT

The customs laws, referred to in subsec. (d), are classified generally to Title 19, Customs Duties.

CODIFICATION

Section 19(f) of Pub. L. 93–627 amended section 1333(a)(2) of Title 43, Public Lands.

AMENDMENTS

1984—Subsec. (a)(3). Pub. L. 98–419, §5(a), added par. (3).

Subsec. (c)(1). Pub. L. 98–419, §5(b), added par. (1). Former cl. (1) redesignated cl. (A)(i) of par. (2).

Subsec. (c)(2). Pub. L. 98–419, §5(b), redesignated existing provisions of subsec. (c) as par. (2)(A)(i) and (B) thereof, substituted reference to provisions of par. (1) for former reference to provisions of this chapter in par. (2)(A)(i) as so redesignated, and added par. (2)(A)(ii).

Subsec. (c)(3). Pub. L. 98–419, §5(b), added par. (3).

EFFECTIVE DATE OF 1984 AMENDMENT

Section 5(c) of Pub. L. 98–419 provided that: "The amendment made by subsection (b) of this section [amending this section] shall be effective on the ninetieth day following the date of enactment of this Act [Sept. 25, 1984]. The Secretary of State shall make the first series of notifications referred to in section 19(a)(3) of the Deepwater Port Act of 1974 [subsec. (a)(3) of this section], as added by subsection (a) of this section, prior to the thirtieth day following the date of enactment of this Act [Sept. 25, 1984]."

§1519. Repealed. Pub. L. 104–66, title I, §1121(a), Dec. 21, 1995, 109 Stat. 724

Section, Pub. L. 93–627, §20, Jan. 3, 1975, 88 Stat. 2146, related to annual report and recommendations by Secretary of Transportation to Congress.

§1520. Pipeline safety and operation

(a) Standards and regulations for Outer Continental Shelf

The Secretary, in cooperation with the Secretary of the Interior, shall establish and enforce such standards and regulations as may be necessary to assure the safe construction and operation of oil or natural gas pipelines on the Outer Continental Shelf.

(b), (c) Omitted

(Pub. L. 93–627, §21, Jan. 3, 1975, 88 Stat. 2146; Pub. L. 107–295, title I, §106(a)(3), Nov. 25, 2002, 116 Stat. 2086.)

CODIFICATION

Subsec. (b) directed the Secretary to report to the Congress within 60 days after Jan. 3, 1975, on appropriations and staffing needed to monitor pipelines on Federal lands and the Outer Continental Shelf.

Subsec. (c) directed the Secretary to review all laws and regulations relating to the construction, operation, and maintenance of pipelines on Federal lands and the Outer Continental Shelf and to report to Congress within 6 months after Jan. 3, 1975, on administrative changes needed and recommendations for new legislation.

AMENDMENTS

2002—Subsec. (a). Pub. L. 107–295 inserted "or natural gas" after "oil".

§1521. Negotiations with Canada and Mexico; report to Congress

The President of the United States is authorized and requested to enter into negotiations with the Governments of Canada and Mexico to determine:

(1) the need for intergovernmental understandings, agreements, or treaties to protect the interests of the people of Canada, Mexico, and the United States and of any party or parties involved with the construction or operation of deepwater ports; and

(2) the desirability of undertaking joint studies and investigations designed to insure protection of the environment and to eliminate any legal and regulatory uncertainty, to assure that the interests of the people of Canada, Mexico, and the United States are adequately met.

The President shall report to the Congress the actions taken, the progress achieved, the areas of disagreement, and the matters about which more information is needed, together with his recommendations for further action.

(Pub. L. 93–627, §22, Jan. 3, 1975, 88 Stat. 2147.)

§1522. Limitations on export provisions of section 185(u) of title 30 unaffected

Nothing in this chapter shall be construed to amend, restrict, or otherwise limit the application of section 185(u) of title 30.

(Pub. L. 93–627, §23, Jan. 3, 1975, 88 Stat. 2147.)

§1523. General procedures; issuance and enforcement of orders; scope of authority; evidentiary matters

The Secretary or his delegate shall have the authority to issue and enforce orders during proceedings brought under this chapter. Such authority shall include the authority to issue subpenas, administer oaths, compel the attendance and testimony of witnesses and the production of books, papers, documents, and other evidence, to take depositions before any designated individual competent to administer oaths, and to examine witnesses.

(Pub. L. 93–627, §24, Jan. 3, 1975, 88 Stat. 2147.)

§1524. Authorization of appropriations

There is authorized to be appropriated for administration of this chapter, not to exceed $2,500,000 per fiscal year for the fiscal years ending June 30, 1975, June 30, 1976, September 30, 1977, September 30, 1978, September 30, 1979, and September 30, 1980.

(Pub. L. 93–627, §25, Jan. 3, 1975, 88 Stat. 2147; Pub. L. 95–36, June 1, 1977, 91 Stat. 177.)

AMENDMENTS

1977—Pub. L. 95–36 authorized appropriations of not to exceed $2,500,000 per fiscal year for fiscal years ending Sept. 30, 1977, Sept. 30, 1978, Sept. 30, 1979, and Sept. 30, 1980.

CHAPTER 30—INTERNATIONAL REGULATIONS FOR PREVENTING COLLISIONS AT SEA

§1601. Definitions

For the purposes of this chapter—

(1) "vessel" means every description of watercraft, including nondisplacement craft and seaplanes, used or capable of being used as a means of transportation on water; and

(2) "high seas" means all parts of the sea that are not included in the territorial sea or in the internal waters of any nation.

(Pub. L. 95–75, § 2, July 27, 1977, 91 Stat. 308.)

REFERENCES IN TEXT

This chapter, referred to in opening par., was in the original "this Act", meaning Pub. L. 95–75, July 27, 1977, 91 Stat. 308, known as the "International Navigational Rules Act of 1977", which enacted this chapter, repealed sections 1051 to 1094 of this title, enacted provisions set out as notes under this section, and repealed provision set out as a note under section 1051 of this title.

EFFECTIVE DATE OF INTERNATIONAL REGULATIONS; REPEAL OF FORMER REGULATIONS

Section 10 of Pub. L. 95–75 provided in part that Pub. L. 88–131, enacting sections 1051 to 1094 of this title and a provision set out as a note under section 1051 of this title which sections included the former International Regulations for Preventing Collisions at Sea, was repealed effective on the date on which the International Regulations [promulgated pursuant to this chapter] entered into force for the United States [July 15, 1977]. See Proclamation dated Jan. 19, 1977, set out as a note under section 1602 of this title.

REFERENCES TO FORMER REGULATIONS

Section 10 of Pub. L. 95–75 provided in part that: "The reference in any other law to Public Law 88–131 [enacting sections 1051 to 1094 of this title and enacting a provision set out as a note under section 1051 of this title], or to the regulations set forth in section 4 of that Act [sections 1061 to 1094 of this title], shall be considered a reference, respectively, to this Act [this chapter], or to the International Regulations proclaimed hereunder [set out as a note under section 1602 of this title]."

SHORT TITLE

Section 1 of Pub. L. 95–75 provided: "That this Act [enacting this chapter, repealing sections 1051 to 1094 of this title, enacting provisions set out as notes under this section, and repealing provisions set out as a note under section 1051 of this title] may be cited as the 'International Navigational Rules Act of 1977'."

§ 1602. International Regulations

(a) Proclamation by President; effective date

The President is authorized to proclaim the International Regulations for Preventing Collisions at Sea, 1972 (hereinafter referred to as the "International Regulations"). The effective date of the International Regulations for the United States shall be specified in the proclamation and shall be the date as near as possible to, but no earlier than, the date on which the Convention on the International Regulations for Preventing Collisions at Sea, 1972 (hereinafter referred to as the "Convention"), signed at London, England, under date of October 20, 1972, enters into force for the United States. The International Regulations proclaimed shall consist of the rules and other annexes attached to the Convention.

(b) Publication of proclamation in Federal Register

The proclamation shall include the International Regulations and shall be published in the Federal Register. On the date specified in the proclamation, the International Regulations shall enter into force for the United States and shall have effect as if enacted by statute.

(c) Amendment of International Regulations

Subject to the provisions of subsection (d) of this section, the President is also authorized to proclaim any amendment to the International Regulations hereafter adopted in accordance with the provisions of article VI of the Convention, and to which the United States does not object. The effective date of the amendment shall be specified in the proclamation and shall be in accordance with the provisions of the said article VI. The proclamation shall include the adopted amendment and shall be published in the Federal Register. On the date specified in the proclamation, the amendment shall enter into force for the United States as a constituent part of the International Regulations, as amended, and shall have effect as if enacted by statute.

(d) Notification to Congress of proposed amendments; Congressional resolution of disapproval

(1) Upon receiving a proposed amendment to the International Regulations, communicated to the United States pursuant to clause 3 of article VI of the Convention, the President shall promptly notify the Congress of the proposed amendment. If, within sixty days after receipt of such notification by the Congress, or ten days prior to the date under clause 4 of article VI for registering an objection, whichever comes first, the Congress adopts a resolution of disapproval, such resolution shall be transmitted to the President and shall constitute an objection by the United States to the proposed amendment. If, upon receiving notification of the resolution of disapproval, the President has not already notified the Inter-Governmental Maritime Consultative Organization of an objection to the United States to the proposed amendment, he shall promptly do so.

(2) For the purposes of this subsection, "resolution of disapproval" means a concurrent resolution initiated by either House of the Congress, the matter after the resolving clause of which is to read as follows: "That the (the concurring) does not favor the proposed amendment to the International Regulations for Preventing Collisions at Sea, 1972, relating to , and forwarded to the Congress by the President on .", the first blank space therein to be filled with the name of the resolving House, the second blank space therein to be filled with the name of the concurring House, the third blank space therein to be filled with the subject matter of the proposed amendment, and the fourth blank space therein to be filled with the day, month, and year.

(3) Any proposed amendment transmitted to the Congress by the President and any resolution of disapproval pertaining thereto shall be referred, in the House of Representatives, to the Committee on Transportation and Infrastructure, and shall be referred, in the Senate, to the Committee on Commerce, Science, and Transportation.

(Pub. L. 95–75, § 3, July 27, 1977, 91 Stat. 308; Pub. L. 107–295, title IV, § 408(b)(1), Nov. 25, 2002, 116 Stat. 2117.)

PRIOR PROVISIONS

The original rules for the prevention of collisions on the water were contained in R.S. § 4233, which consisted of 26 rules. R.S. § 4412, which authorized the board of supervising inspectors to establish such regulations to be observed by all steam vessels in passing each other, as they should from time to time deem necessary for safety, and provided that copies of such regulations should be furnished to all of such vessels, to be kept posted up in conspicuous places in such vessels, and R.S. §4413, which prescribed a penalty for neglecting or willfully refusing to observe the regulations established pursuant to said section 4412.

The rules prescribed by R.S. §4233 were superseded as to navigation on the high seas and in all coast waters of the United States, except such as were otherwise provided for, by the adoption of the "Revised International Regulations" by act March 3, 1885, ch. 354, 23 Stat. 438, which rules were superseded by the passage and adoption of act Aug. 19, 1890, ch. 802, 26 Stat. 322, section 1 of which enacted a set of regulations for preventing collisions at sea to be followed by all public and private vessels of the United States upon the high seas and in all waters connected therewith, navigable by seagoing vessels.

Act Aug. 19, 1890, ch. 802, §1, consisted of 31 articles. Section 2 of act Aug. 19, 1890, ch. 802, repealed all laws and parts of laws inconsistent with the regulations for preventing collisions at sea for the navigation of all public and private vessels of the United States upon the high seas, and in all waters connected therewith navigable by seagoing vessels, prescribed by section 1 of that act.

The rules prescribed by R.S. §4233, were further superseded as to navigation on the Great Lakes and their connecting and tributary waters as far east as Montreal by act Feb. 8, 1895, ch. 64, 28 Stat. 645, section 1 of which enacted rules for preventing collisions to be followed in the navigation of all public and private vessels of the United States upon the Great Lakes and their connecting and tributary waters as far east as Montreal. Section 1 contained 28 articles. Section 2 of the act Feb. 8, 1895, ch. 64, prescribed a fine for violations of the act. Section 3 of the act Feb. 8, 1895, ch. 64, gave the Secretary of the Treasury authority to establish all necessary regulations not inconsistent with the act, necessary to carry the act into effect, and gave the Board of Supervising Inspectors of the United States authority to establish such regulations to be observed by all steam vessels in passing each other, not inconsistent with the act, as they should from time to time deem necessary, and provided that the regulations so adopted, when approved by the Secretary of the Treasury, should have the force of law. Section 4 of the act Feb. 8, 1895, ch. 64, repealed all laws or parts of laws, so far as applicable to the navigation of the Great Lakes and their connecting and tributary waters as far east as Montreal, inconsistent with the rules promulgated by the act.

The rules prescribed by R.S. §4233, and by R.S. §§4412, 4414, and the regulations pursuant thereto, were required to be followed on the harbors, rivers, and inland waters of the United States, and the provisions of said sections were made special rules, duly made by local authority, relative to the navigation of harbors, rivers, and inland waters, as provided for by article 30 of the act Aug. 19, 1890, ch. 802, §1, by act Feb. 19, 1895, ch. 102, §1, 28 Stat. 672. Section 2 of the act Feb. 19, 1895, ch. 102, authorized the Secretary of the Treasury to designate and define by the suitable bearing or range with light houses, light vessels, buoys, or coast objects, the lines dividing the high seas from rivers, harbors, and inland waters. Section 3 of the act Feb. 19, 1895, ch. 102, required collectors or other chief officers of the customs to require sail vessels to be furnished with proper signal lights, and prescribed a penalty to be assessed against vessels navigated without complying with the statutes of the United States, or the regulations lawfully made thereunder. Section 4 of the act Feb. 19, 1895, ch. 102, provided that the words "inland waters" should not be held to include the Great Lakes and their connecting and tributary waters as far east as Montreal, and provided that the act should not modify or affect the provisions of act Feb. 8, 1895, ch. 64, which was the act prescribing rules for preventing collisions to be followed in the navigation of all public and private vessels upon the Great Lakes and their connecting and tributary waters as far east as Montreal.

The rules prescribed by R.S. §4233, were further superseded as to the navigation of all harbors, rivers, and inland waters of the United States, except the Great Lakes and their connecting and tributary waters as far east as Montreal and the Red River of the North and rivers emptying into the Gulf of Mexico and their tributaries, by act June 7, 1897, ch. 4, 30 Stat. 96, section 1 of which enacted a set of regulations for preventing collisions, to be followed by all vessels navigating all harbors, rivers, and inland waters of the United States, except the Great Lakes and their connecting and tributary waters as far east as Montreal and the Red River of the North and rivers emptying into the Gulf of Mexico and their tributaries. Said section 1 consisted of 31 articles. Section 2 of the act June 7, 1897, ch. 4, authorized the supervising inspectors of steam-vessels and the Supervising Inspector-General to establish rules to be observed by steam vessels in passing each other and as to the lights to be carried by ferry-boats and by barges and canal-boats, when in tow of steam-vessels, not inconsistent with the provisions of the act, such rules, when approved by the Secretary of the Treasury, to be special rules duly made by local authority, as provided for by article 30 of the act Aug. 19, 1890, ch. 802, §1 which article provided that nothing in the rules contained in that act should interfere with the operation of special rules, duly made by local authority, relative to the navigation of any harbor, river, or inland waters. Section 3 of the act June 7, 1897, ch. 4, prescribed a penalty for violations of the provisions of the act or the regulations established pursuant to section 2. Section 4 of the act June 7, 1897, ch. 4, also prescribed a penalty to be assessed against vessels navigated without compliance with the provisions of the act. Section 5 of the act June 7, 1897, ch. 4, repealed R.S. §§4233, 4412 (with the regulations made in pursuance thereof, except the rules and regulations for the government of pilots of steamers navigating the Red River of the North and rivers emptying into the Gulf of Mexico and their tributaries, and except the rules for the Great Lakes and their connecting and tributary waters as far east as Montreal), §4413, act March 3, 1893, ch. 202, 27 Stat. 557, which amended R.S. §4233, act Feb. 19, 1895, ch. 102, §§1, 3, and act March 3, 1897, ch. 389, §§5, 12, 13, 29 Stat. 689, 690, and all amendments thereto insofar as the harbors, rivers, and inland waters of the United States (except the Great Lakes and their connecting and tributary waters as far east as Montreal and the Red River of the North and rivers emptying into the Gulf of Mexico, and their tributaries) were concerned.

This legislation resulted in the following situation: Navigation on the high seas was governed by act Aug. 19, 1890, ch. 802, with its amendatory and supplementary acts, which was superseded by act Oct. 11, 1951, ch. 495, formerly set forth in chapter 2 of this title; navigation on all harbors, rivers, and inland waters of the United States, except the Great Lakes and their connecting and tributary waters as far east as Montreal and the Red River of the North and rivers emptying into the Gulf of Mexico and their tributaries, was governed by act June 7, 1897, ch. 4, as amended, formerly set forth in chapter 3 of this title; navigation on the Great Lakes and their connecting and tributary waters as far east as Montreal was governed by act Feb. 8, 1895, ch. 64, formerly set forth in section 301 et seq. of this title; and navigation on the Red River of the North and rivers emptying into the Gulf of Mexico and their tributaries was governed by R.S. §4233, as amended and supplemented, formerly set forth in section 301 et seq. of this title.

See also Codification notes to sections 154, 241, and 301 of this title.

Regulations for Preventing Collisions at Sea, 1948, approved by the International Conference on Safety of Life at Sea, 1948, covering substantially the same subject matter included under these rules, were set out as sections 143 to 147d of this title.

Regulations for Preventing Collisions at Sea, 1960, approved by the International Conference on the Safety of Life at Sea, 1960, covering substantially the same subject matter included under these rules, were set out as sections 1051 to 1094 of this title.

AMENDMENTS

2002—Subsec. (d)(3). Pub. L. 107–295 substituted "Transportation and Infrastructure" for "Merchant Marine and Fisheries".

INTERNATIONAL CONVENTION FOR SAFETY OF LIFE AT SEA, 1948

The convention, known as the International Convention for Safety of Life at Sea, was signed at London on June 10, 1948, and was ratified by the United States on April 20, 1949 (see Senate Report No. 838, Sept. 26, 1951, to accompany H.R. 5013, 82nd Cong.). The "International Regulations for Preventing Collisions at Sea, 1948", approved by the 1948 London conference, were adopted by section 6 of act Oct. 11, 1951, and were classified to section 144 et seq. of this title.

INTERNATIONAL CONVENTION FOR THE SAFETY OF LIFE AT SEA, 1960

The convention, known as the International Convention for the Safety of Life at Sea, was signed at London on June 17, 1960, and was ratified by the United States on May 26, 1965 (see Senate Report No. 477, Aug. 30, 1963, to accompany H.R. 6012, 88th Cong.). The "Regulations for Preventing Collisions at Sea, 1960", approved by the 1960 London conference, were adopted by section 4 of Pub. L. 88–131, Sept. 24, 1963, 77 Stat. 194, and were classified to section 1051 et seq. of this title.

INTERNATIONAL REGULATIONS FOR PREVENTING COLLISIONS AT SEA, 1972

The Convention on the International Regulations for Preventing Collisions at Sea, 1972, was proclaimed by the President on Jan. 19, 1977. The President's proclamation provided that the Convention enter into force for the United States on July 15, 1977. The proclamation and the International Regulations were published in the Federal Register on Mar. 31, 1977, 42 F.R. 17112, with corrections to the International Regulations published on Apr. 7, 1977, 42 F.R. 18401 and on Apr. 21, 1977, 42 F.R. 20625. The International Regulations, as amended, are maintained and published by the United States Coast Guard, U.S. Department of Homeland Security, in the publication *Navigation Rules*, which is available for sale by the Superintendent of Documents, U.S. Government Printing Office, Washington, D.C. 20402.

EX. ORD. NO. 11964. IMPLEMENTATION OF CONVENTION ON THE INTERNATIONAL REGULATIONS FOR PREVENTING COLLISIONS AT SEA, 1972

Ex. Ord. No. 11964, Jan. 19, 1977, 42 F.R. 4327, provided:

By virtue of the authority vested in me by the Constitution and statutes of the United States of America, including Section 301 of Title 3 of the United States Code, and as President of the United States of America and Commander-in-Chief of the Armed Forces, in order to provide for the coming into force on July 15, 1977, of the Convention on the International Regulations for Preventing Collisions at Sea, 1972 (Senate Executive W, 93d Cong., 1st Sess.), it is hereby ordered as follows:

SECTION 1. (a) With respect to vessels of special construction or purpose, the Secretary of the Navy, for vessels of the Navy, and the Secretary of the Department in which the Coast Guard is operating, for all other vessels, shall determine and certify, in accord with Rule I of the International Regulations for Preventing Collisions at Sea, 1972, hereinafter referred to as the International Regulations, as to which such vessels cannot comply fully with the provisions of any of the International Regulations with respect to the number, positions, range or arc of visibility of lights or shapes, as well as to the disposition and characteristics of sound-signalling appliances, without interfering with the special function of the vessel.

(b) With respect to vessels for which a certification is issued, the Secretary issuing the certification shall certify as to such other provisions which are the closest possible compliance by that vessel with the International Regulations.

(c) Notice of any certification issued shall be published in the FEDERAL REGISTER.

SEC. 2. The Secretary of the Navy is authorized to promulgate special rules with respect to additional station or signal lights or whistle signals for ships of war or vessels proceeding under convoy, and the Secretary of the Department in which the Coast Guard is operating is authorized, to the extent permitted by law, including the provisions of Title 14 of the United States Code, to promulgate special rules with respect to additional station or signal lights for fishing vessels engaged in fishing as a fleet. In accord with Rule I of the International Regulations, the additional station or signal lights or whistle signals contained in the special rules shall be, as far as possible, such as they cannot be mistaken for any light or signal authorized by the International Regulations. Notice of such special rules for fishing vessels shall be published in the FEDERAL REGISTER.

SEC. 3. The Secretary of the Navy, for vessels of the Navy, and the Secretary of the Department in which the Coast Guard is operating, for all other vessels, are authorized to exempt, in accord with Rule 38 of the International Regulations, any vessel or class of vessels, the keel of which is laid, or which is at a corresponding stage of construction, before July 15, 1977, from full compliance with the International Regulations, provided that such vessel or class of vessels complies with the requirements of the International Regulations for Preventing Collisions at Sea, 1960. Notice of any exemption granted shall be published in the FEDERAL REGISTER.

SEC. 4. The Secretary of the Department in which the Coast Guard is operating is authorized, to the extent permitted by law, to promulgate such rules and regulations that are necessary to implement the provisions of the Convention and International Regulations. He shall cause to be published in the FEDERAL REGISTER any implementing regulations or interpretive rulings promulgated pursuant to this Order, and shall promptly publish in the FEDERAL REGISTER the full text of the International Regulations.

GERALD R. FORD.

EX. ORD. NO. 12234. ENFORCEMENT OF CONVENTION FOR THE SAFETY OF LIFE AT SEA, 1974

Ex. Ord. No. 12234, Sept. 3, 1980, 45 F.R. 58801, provided:

By the authority vested in me as President by the Constitution and the laws of the United States of America, and in order to implement the International Convention for the Safety of Life at Sea, 1974, it is hereby ordered as follows:

1–101. The International Convention for the Safety of Life at Sea, 1974, signed at London on November 1, 1974, and proclaimed by the President of the United States on January 28, 1980 (TIAS 9700), entered into force for the United States on May 25, 1980.

1–102. The Secretary of State, the Secretary of the Department in which the Coast Guard is operating, the Secretary of Commerce, and the Federal Communications Commission shall (a) perform those functions prescribed in the Convention that are within their respective areas of responsibility, and (b) cooperate and assist each other in carrying out those functions.

1–103. (a) The Secretary of the Department in which the Coast Guard is operating, or the head of any other Executive agency authorized by law, shall be responsible for the issuance of certificates as required by the Convention.

(b) If a certificate is to include matter that pertains to functions vested by law in another Executive agency, the issuing agency shall first ascertain from the other Executive agency the decision regarding that matter. The decision of that agency shall be final and binding on the issuing agency.

1–104. The Secretary of the Department in which the Coast Guard is operating may use the services of the American Bureau of Shipping as long as that Bureau is operated in compliance with Section 25 of the Act of June 5, 1920, as amended (46 U.S.C. 881), to perform the functions under the Convention. The Secretary may also use the services of the National Cargo Bureau to perform functions under Chapter VI (Carriage of Grain) of the Convention.

1–105. The Secretary of the Department in which the Coast Guard is operating shall promulgate regulations necessary to implement the provisions of the Convention.

1–106. To the extent that the International Convention for the Safety of Life at Sea, 1974, replaces and abrogates the International Convention for the Safety of Life at Sea, 1960 (TIAS 5780), this Order supersedes Executive Order No. 11239 of July 31, 1965, entitled "Enforcement of the Convention for the Safety of Life at Sea, 1960."

1–107. Executive Order No. 10402 of October 30, 1952, entitled "Enforcement of the Convention for the Safety of Life at Sea, 1948," is revoked.

JIMMY CARTER.

§1603. Vessels subject to International Regulations

Except as provided in section 1604 of this title and subject to the provisions of section 1605 of this title, the International Regulations, as proclaimed under section 1602 of this title, shall be applicable to, and shall be complied with by—

(1) all vessels, public and private, subject to the jurisdiction of the United States, while upon the high seas or in waters connected therewith navigable by seagoing vessels, and

(2) all other vessels when on waters subject to the jurisdiction of the United States.

(Pub. L. 95–75, §4, July 27, 1977, 91 Stat. 309.)

§1604. Vessels not subject to International Regulations

(a) The International Regulations do not apply to vessels while in the waters of the United States shoreward of the navigational demarcation lines dividing the high seas from harbors, rivers, and other inland waters of the United States.

(b) Whenever a vessel subject to the jurisdiction of the United States is in the territorial waters of a foreign state the International Regulations shall be applicable to, and shall be complied with by, that vessel to the extent that the laws and regulations of the foreign state are not in conflict therewith.

(Pub. L. 95–75, §5, July 27, 1977, 91 Stat. 309; Pub. L. 96–591, §6(1), Dec. 24, 1980, 94 Stat. 3434.)

AMENDMENTS

1980—Subsec. (a). Pub. L. 96–591 substituted provision providing that the International Regulations do not apply to vessels while in the waters of the United States shoreward of the navigational demarcation lines dividing the high seas from harbors, rivers, and other inland waters of the United States for provisions that had made specific reference to harbors, rivers, and other inland waters of the United States, as defined in section 154 of this title, to the Great Lakes of North America and their connecting and tributary waters, as defined in section 241 of this title, and to the Red River of the North and rivers emptying into the Gulf of Mexico and their tributaries, as defined in section 301 of this title.

EFFECTIVE DATE OF 1980 AMENDMENT

Amendment by Pub. L. 96–591 effective 12 months after Dec. 24, 1981, see section 7 of Pub. L. 96–591, set out as an Effective Date note under section 2001 of this title.

§1605. Navy and Coast Guard vessels of special construction or purpose

(a) Certification for alternative compliance

Any requirement of the International Regulations with respect to the number, position, range, or arc of visibility of lights, with respect to shapes, or with respect to the disposition and characteristics of sound-signaling appliances, shall not be applicable to a vessel of special construction or purpose, whenever the Secretary of the Navy, for any vessel of the Navy, or the Secretary of the department in which the Coast Guard is operating, for any other vessel of the United States, shall certify that the vessel cannot comply fully with that requirement without interfering with the special function of the vessel.

(b) Closest possible compliance by vessels covered by certification for alternative compliance

Whenever a certification is issued under the authority of subsection (a) of this section, the vessel involved shall comply with the requirement as to which the certification is made to the extent that the Secretary issuing the certification shall certify as the closest possible compliance by that vessel.

(c) Publication of certifications in Federal Register

Notice of the certifications issued pursuant to subsections (a) and (b) of this section shall be published in the Federal Register.

(d) Issuance of certification for a class of vessels

A certification authorized by this section may be issued for a class of vessels.

(Pub. L. 95–75, §6, July 27, 1977, 91 Stat. 309; Pub. L. 96–591, §6(2), Dec. 24, 1980, 94 Stat. 3434.)

AMENDMENTS

1980—Subsec. (d). Pub. L. 96–591 added subsec. (d).

TRANSFER OF FUNCTIONS

For transfer of authorities, functions, personnel, and assets of the Coast Guard, including the authorities and functions of the Secretary of Transportation relating thereto, to the Department of Homeland Security, and for treatment of related references, see sections 468(b), 551(d), 552(d), and 557 of Title 6, Domestic Security, and the Department of Homeland Security Reorganization Plan of November 25, 2002, as modified, set out as a note under section 542 of Title 6.

§1606. Special rules for ships of war, vessels proceeding under convoy, and fishing vessels engaged in fishing as a fleet

(a) The Secretary of the Navy is authorized to promulgate special rules with respect to additional station or signal lights or whistle signals for ships of war or vessels proceeding under convoy, and the Secretary of the department in which the Coast Guard is operating is authorized to promulgate special rules with respect to additional station or signal lights for fishing vessels engaged in fishing as a fleet.

(b) The additional station or signal lights or whistle signals contained in the special rules authorized under subsection (a) of this section shall be, as far as possible, such that they cannot be mistaken for any light or signal authorized by the International Regulations. Notice of such special rules shall be published in the Federal Register and, after the effective date specified in such notice, they shall have effect as if they were a part of the International Regulations.

(Pub. L. 95–75, § 7, July 27, 1977, 91 Stat. 310.)

TRANSFER OF FUNCTIONS

For transfer of authorities, functions, personnel, and assets of the Coast Guard, including the authorities and functions of the Secretary of Transportation relating thereto, to the Department of Homeland Security, and for treatment of related references, see sections 468(b), 551(d), 552(d), and 557 of Title 6, Domestic Security, and the Department of Homeland Security Reorganization Plan of November 25, 2002, as modified, set out as a note under section 542 of Title 6.

§ 1607. Implementation by rules and regulations; authority to promulgate

The Secretary of the department in which the Coast Guard is operating is authorized to promulgate such reasonable rules and regulations as are necessary to implement the provisions of this chapter and the International Regulations proclaimed hereunder.

(Pub. L. 95–75, § 8, July 27, 1977, 91 Stat. 310.)

TRANSFER OF FUNCTIONS

For transfer of authorities, functions, personnel, and assets of the Coast Guard, including the authorities and functions of the Secretary of Transportation relating thereto, to the Department of Homeland Security, and for treatment of related references, see sections 468(b), 551(d), 552(d), and 557 of Title 6, Domestic Security, and the Department of Homeland Security Reorganization Plan of November 25, 2002, as modified, set out as a note under section 542 of Title 6.

§ 1608. Civil penalties

(a) Liability of vessel operator for violations

Whoever operates a vessel, subject to the provisions of this chapter, in violation of this chapter or of any regulation promulgated pursuant to section 1607 of this title, shall be liable to a civil penalty of not more than $5,000 for each such violation.

(b) Liability of vessel for violations; seizure of vessel

Every vessel subject to the provisions of this chapter, other than a public vessel being used for noncommercial purposes, which is operated in violation of this chapter or of any regulation promulgated pursuant to section 1607 of this title, shall be liable to a civil penalty of not more than $5,000 for each such violation, for which penalty the vessel may be seized and proceeded against in the district court of the United States of any district within which such vessel may be found.

(c) Assessment of penalties; notice; opportunity for hearing; remission, mitigation, and compromise of penalty; action for collection

The Secretary of the department in which the Coast Guard is operating may assess any civil penalty authorized by this section. No such penalty may be assessed until the person charged, or the owner of the vessel charged, as appropriate, shall have been given notice of the violation involved and an opportunity for a hearing. For good cause shown, the Secretary may remit, mitigate, or compromise any penalty assessed. Upon the failure of the person charged, or the owner of the vessel charged, to pay an assessed penalty, as it may have been mitigated or compromised, the Secretary may request the Attorney General to commence an action in the appropriate district court of the United States for collection of the penalty as assessed, without regard to the amount involved, together with such other relief as may be appropriate.

(Pub. L. 95–75, § 9, July 27, 1977, 91 Stat. 310; Pub. L. 96–591, § 6(3), (4), Dec. 24, 1980, 94 Stat. 3435.)

AMENDMENTS

1980—Subsec. (a). Pub. L. 96–591, § 6(3), substituted "$5,000" for "$500".

Subsec. (b). Pub. L. 96–591, § 6(4), substituted "not more than $5,000" for "$500".

TRANSFER OF FUNCTIONS

For transfer of authorities, functions, personnel, and assets of the Coast Guard, including the authorities and functions of the Secretary of Transportation relating thereto, to the Department of Homeland Security, and for treatment of related references, see sections 468(b), 551(d), 552(d), and 557 of Title 6, Domestic Security, and the Department of Homeland Security Reorganization Plan of November 25, 2002, as modified, set out as a note under section 542 of Title 6.

CHAPTER 31—OCEAN POLLUTION RESEARCH AND DEVELOPMENT AND MONITORING PLANNING

§§ 1701 to 1709. Repealed. Pub. L. 102–567, title II, § 204, Oct. 29, 1992, 106 Stat. 4282

Section 1701, Pub. L. 95–273, § 2, May 8, 1978, 92 Stat. 228; Pub. L. 99–272, title VI, § 6071, Apr. 7, 1986, 100 Stat. 133, provided findings and purposes for chapter.

Section 1702, Pub. L. 95–273, § 3, May 8, 1978, 92 Stat. 228; Pub. L. 99–272, title VI, § 6072(1), Apr. 7, 1986, 100 Stat. 133; Pub. L. 100–636, § 1(1)–(4), Nov. 8, 1988, 102 Stat. 3324, provided definitions for chapter.

Section 1702a, Pub. L. 95–273, § 3A, as added Pub. L. 99–272, title VI, § 6072(2), Apr. 7, 1986, 100 Stat. 133; amended Pub. L. 100–636, § 1(5)–(7), Nov. 8, 1988, 102 Stat. 3324, provided for a National Ocean Pollution Program Office and a National Ocean Pollution Policy Board.

Section 1703, Pub. L. 95–273, § 4, May 8, 1978, 92 Stat. 229; Pub. L. 96–255, § 2, May 30, 1980, 94 Stat. 420; Pub. L. 97–375, title II, § 202(c), Dec. 21, 1982, 96 Stat. 1822; Pub. L. 99–272, title VI, § 6073, Apr. 7, 1986, 100 Stat. 134; Pub. L. 100–636, § 1(5), Nov. 8, 1988, 102 Stat. 3324, provided for a comprehensive Federal Plan relating to ocean pollution.

Section 1704, Pub. L. 95–273, § 5, May 8, 1978, 92 Stat. 230; Pub. L. 100–636, § 1(5), Nov. 8, 1988, 102 Stat. 3324, provided for a comprehensive ocean pollution program in NOAA.

Section 1705, Pub. L. 95–273, § 6, May 8, 1978, 92 Stat. 231; Pub. L. 100–636, § 1(5), Nov. 8, 1988, 102 Stat. 3324, provided for Federal financial assistance for programs under this chapter.

Section 1706, Pub. L. 95–273, §7, May 8, 1978, 92 Stat. 232; Pub. L. 100–636, §1(5), Nov. 8, 1988, 102 Stat. 3324, provided for interagency cooperation in carrying out this chapter.

Section 1707, Pub. L. 95–273, §8, May 8, 1978, 92 Stat. 232; Pub. L. 99–272, title VI, §6074, Apr. 7, 1986, 100 Stat. 135; Pub. L. 100–636, §1(5), Nov. 8, 1988, 102 Stat. 3324, provided for dissemination of information on ocean and Great Lakes pollution research activities.

Section 1708, Pub. L. 95–273, §9, May 8, 1978, 92 Stat. 232, related to effect of this chapter on other laws.

Section 1709, Pub. L. 95–273, §10, May 8, 1978, 92 Stat. 232; Pub. L. 96–17, June 4, 1979, 93 Stat. 34; Pub. L. 96–255, §1, May 30, 1980, 94 Stat. 420; Pub. L. 99–272, title VI, §6075, Apr. 7, 1986, 100 Stat. 135; Pub. L. 100–636, §1(8), Nov. 8, 1988, 102 Stat. 3324, authorized appropriations to carry out this chapter.

SHORT TITLE

Section 1 of Pub. L. 95–273, as amended by Pub. L. 96–255, §3, May 30, 1980, 94 Stat. 420, which provided that this chapter could be cited as the "National Ocean Pollution Planning Act of 1978", was repealed by Pub. L. 102–567, title II, §204, Oct. 29, 1992, 106 Stat. 4282.

CHAPTER 32—INLAND WATERWAYS TRUST FUND

§§1801, 1802. Repealed. Pub. L. 99–662, title XIV, §1405(b), Nov. 17, 1986, 100 Stat. 4271

Section 1801, Pub. L. 95–502, title II, §203, Oct. 21, 1978, 92 Stat. 1697, established Inland Waterways Trust Fund. See section 9506 of Title 26, Internal Revenue Code.

Section 1802, Pub. L. 95–502, title II, §204, Oct. 21, 1978, 92 Stat. 1698, made Inland Waterways Trust Fund available for expenditures for navigation construction and rehabilitation projects on inland waterways. See section 9506 of Title 26.

EFFECTIVE DATE OF REPEAL

Repeal effective Jan. 1, 1987, see section 1405(d)(1) of Pub. L. 99–662, set out as an Effective Date note under section 9506 of Title 26, Internal Revenue Code.

§1803. Study with respect to inland waterway user taxes and charges

(a) Study directed

The Secretary of Transportation, and the Secretary of Commerce, in consultation with the Secretary of the Treasury, the Secretary of Agriculture, the Secretary of Energy, the Attorney General of the United States, the Secretary of the Army, the Chairman of the Water Resources Council, and the Director of the Office of Management and Budget, shall—

(1) make a full and complete study with respect to inland waterway user taxes and charges, and

(2) make findings and policy recommendations with respect thereto.

Such study shall include (but shall not be limited to) a consideration of the matters listed in subsections (b), (c), (d), (e), and (f) of this section.

(b) Considerations relating to the taxing mechanism

(1) The extent to which the Federal Government should seek to recover some or all of Federal expenditures for the benefit of inland waterway transportation from the users of the facilities for which such expenditures are made.

(2) The various forms of inland waterway user taxes and charges which could be established.

(3) The various methods of collecting inland waterway user taxes and charges, and the administrative costs of such taxes and charges.

(4) The classes and categories of users and other persons on whom inland waterway user taxes and charges should be imposed.

(5) The waterways of the United States (including the Great Lakes, deep draft channels, and coastal ports) which should be included in any system of user taxes and charges, together with the economic effects of such taxes and charges.

(6) The use of revenues derived from inland waterway user taxes and charges, including consideration of changes in, or alternatives to, the Trust Fund mechanism.

(c) Considerations relating to economic effects

The economic effects of waterway user taxes and charges on—

(1) Carriers and users

On—

(A) carriers and shippers using the inland waterways, and

(B) users (including ultimate consumers) of commodities which are transported on the inland waterways.

(2) Regions, etc.

On—

(A) existing investment in industrial plants, agricultural interests, and commercial enterprises, and on related employment, in regions of the country served by inland water transportation directly or in combination with other modes, and

(B) future economic growth prospects in such regions, including anticipated shifts of industry and employment to other areas together with an evaluation of effects on regional economies and their development, including consistency with Federal policies as set forth in other legislation.

(3) Small business and industrial concentration and competition

On—

(A) small business enterprise, and

(B) industrial concentration and competition, both within the transportation industry and in any line of commerce (within the meaning of the antitrust laws).

(4) Competitors

On the freight rates charged by other modes of transportation and the extent of short-term and long-term diversion of traffic from the inland waterways to such other modes. In considering such diversion of traffic, there shall also be considered the effects of such diversion on—

(A) the development of alternative sources of supply and on alternative modes of transportation and alternative routing to market,

(B) the comparative safety of the handling and transportation of hazardous materials, and

(C) the comparative energy efficiency of the modes and routes of the transportation involved.

(5) Prices

On prices of commodities shipped by inland waterways and by competing modes, including the costs of energy materials and the effects on electric power rates.

(6) Balance of payments

On the balance of payments of the United States based on our international trade.

(d) Considerations relating to economic feasibility of waterway improvement projects; level of benefits from waterway expenditures

(1) The effects of inland waterway user taxes and charges on the economic feasibility of inland waterway improvement projects.

(2) The comparative levels of benefits received from Federal expenditures on inland waterways for—

(A) commercial uses, and

(B) other uses, including (but not limited to) recreation, reclamation, water supply, low-flow augmentation, fish and wildlife enhancement, hydroelectric power, flood control, and irrigation uses.

(e) Considerations relating to Federal assistance

(1) The extent of past, present, and expected future Federal assistance to the several modes of freight transportation. Such consideration shall include an evaluation and comparison of the public benefits resulting from such assistance to each of the several transportation modes in terms of adequacy, efficiency, and economy of service, safety, technological progress, and energy conservation. The Federal assistance considered under this paragraph shall include all forms of such assistance, such as tax advantages, direct grants, rate adjustments for improvement purposes, assumption of pension fund liabilities, loans, guarantees, capital participation, revenues from land grants, and provision of right-of-way operation, maintenance, and improvement.

(2) The competitive effects of past, present, and expected future Federal expenditures on inland waterways on competitive modes of transportation.

(3) The need for Federal assistance to agricultural, industrial, and other interests affected by inland waterway user taxes and charges.

(f) Considerations relating to policy and future development

The effects of inland waterway user taxes and charges on—

(1) The achievement of the objectives of the National Transportation Policy as set forth in sections 10101 and 13101 of title 49.

(2) The expansion and improvement of the inland waterways determined to be necessary by the Secretary of the Army under section 158 of the Water Resources Development Act of 1976 (Public Law 94–587) or estimated to be necessary under paragraph (3).

(3) The requirements of the Nation through the year 2000 for transportation service, the portion thereof which should be provided by inland waterway carriers, and an estimate of the expansion and improvement of inland waterway capacity necessary to meet such requirements.

(g) "Inland waterway user taxes and charges" defined

For purposes of this section, the term "inland waterway user taxes and charges" means taxes imposed on the use of the inland and intracoastal waterways of the United States and all alternatives to such taxes.

(h) Report

Not later than September 30, 1981, the Secretary of Transportation shall transmit to Congress a final report of the study required by this section, together with his findings and recommendations (including necessary legislation) and the findings and recommendations of the Secretary of Commerce, the Secretary of the Treasury, the Secretary of Agriculture, the Secretary of Energy, the Attorney General of the United States, the Secretary of the Army, the Chairman of the Water Resources Council, and the Director of the Office of Management and Budget.

(i) Authorization of appropriations

There are hereby authorized to be appropriated from time to time to the Secretary of Transportation such sums, not to exceed $8,000,000 in the aggregate, as may be necessary to carry out the study required by this section.

(Pub. L. 95–502, title II, § 205, Oct. 21, 1978, 92 Stat. 1698; Pub. L. 104–88, title III, § 338, Dec. 29, 1995, 109 Stat. 954.)

CODIFICATION

Section 158 of the Water Resources Development Act of 1976 (Public Law 94–587), referred to in subsec. (f)(2), is section 158 of Pub. L. 94–587, Oct. 22, 1976, 90 Stat. 2933, which is set out as a note under section 540 of this title.

AMENDMENTS

1995—Subsec. (f)(1). Pub. L. 104–88 substituted "as set forth in sections 10101 and 13101 of title 49" for "as set forth in the preamble to the Transportation Act of 1940".

EFFECTIVE DATE OF 1995 AMENDMENT

Amendment by Pub. L. 104–88 effective Jan. 1, 1996, see section 2 of Pub. L. 104–88, set out as an Effective Date note under section 701 of Title 49, Transportation.

SHORT TITLE

For short title of title II of Pub. L. 95–502 as the "Inland Waterways Revenue Act of 1978", see section 201 of Pub. L. 95–502, set out as a Short Title of 1978 Amendment note under section 1 of Title 26, Internal Revenue Code.

§ 1804. Inland and intracoastal waterways of the United States

For purposes of section 4042 of title 26 (relating to tax on fuel used in commercial transportation on inland waterways) and for purposes of section 1802[1] of this title, the following inland

[1] See References in Text note below.

and intracoastal waterways of the United States are described in this section:

(1) Alabama-Coosa Rivers: From junction with the Tombigbee River at river mile (hereinafter referred to as RM) 0 to junction with Coosa River at RM 314.

(2) Allegheny River: From confluence with the Monongahela River to form the Ohio River at RM 0 to the head of the existing project at East Brady, Pennsylvania, RM 72.

(3) Apalachicola-Chattahoochee and Flint Rivers: Apalachicola River from mouth at Apalachicola Bay (intersection with the Gulf Intracoastal Waterway) RM 0 to junction with Chattachoochee[2] and Flint Rivers at RM 107.8. Chattachoochee[2] River from junction with Apalachicola and Flint Rivers at RM 0 to Columbus, Georgia, at RM 155 and Flint River, from junction with Apalachicola and Chattahoochee Rivers at RM 0 to Bainbridge, Georgia, at RM 28.

(4) Arkansas River (McClellan-Kerr Arkansas River Navigation System): From junction with Mississippi River at RM 0 to port of Catoosa, Oklahoma, at RM 448.2.

(5) Atchafalaya River: From RM 0 at its intersection with the Gulf Intracoastal Waterway at Morgan City, Louisiana, upstream to junction with Red River at RM 116.8.

(6) Atlantic Intracoastal Waterway: Two inland water routes approximately paralleling the Atlantic coast between Norfolk, Virginia, and Miami, Florida, for 1,192 miles via both the Albermarle[3] and Chesapeake Canal and Great Dismal Swamp Canal routes.

(7) Black Warrior-Tombigbee-Mobile Rivers: Black Warrior River System from RM 2.9, Mobile River (at Chickasaw Creek) to confluence with Tombigbee River at RM 45. Tombigbee River (to Demopolis at RM 215.4) to port of Birmingham, RM's 374–411 and upstream to head of navigation on Mulberry Fork (RM 429.6), Locust Fork (RM 407.8), and Sipsey Fork (RM 430.4).

(8) Columbia River (Columbia-Snake Rivers Inland Waterways): From The Dalles at RM 191.5 to Pasco, Washington (McNary Pool), at RM 330, Snake River from RM 0 at the mouth to RM 231.5 at Johnson Bar Landing, Idaho.

(9) Cumberland River: Junction with Ohio River at RM 0 to head of navigation, upstream to Carthage, Tennessee, at RM 313.5.

(10) Green and Barren Rivers: Green River from junction with the Ohio River at RM 0 to head of navigation at RM 149.1.

(11) Gulf Intracoastal Waterway: From St. Mark's River, Florida, to Brownsville, Texas, 1,134.5 miles.

(12) Illinois Waterway (Calumet-Sag Channel): From the junction of the Illinois River with the Mississippi River RM 0 to Chicago Harbor at Lake Michigan, approximately RM 350.

(13) Kanawha River: From junction with Ohio River at RM 0 to RM 90.6 at Deepwater, West Virginia.

(14) Kaskaskia River: From junction with the Mississippi River at RM 0 to RM 36.2 at Fayetteville, Illinois.

(15) Kentucky River: From junction with Ohio River at RM 0 to confluence of Middle and North Forks at RM 258.6.

(16) Lower Mississippi River: From Baton Rouge, Louisiana, RM 233.9 to Cairo, Illinois, RM 953.8.

(17) Upper Mississippi River: From Cairo, Illinois, RM 953.8 to Minneapolis, Minnesota, RM 1,811.4.

(18) Missouri River: From junction with Mississippi River at RM 0 to Sioux City, Iowa, at RM 734.8.

(19) Monongahela River: From junction with Allegheny River to form the Ohio River at RM 0 to junction of the Tygart and West Fork Rivers, Fairmont, West Virginia, at RM 128.7.

(20) Ohio River: From junction with the Mississippi River at RM 0 to junction of the Allegheny and Monongahela Rivers at Pittsburgh, Pennsylvania, at RM 981.

(21) Ouachita-Black Rivers: From the mouth of the Black River at its junction with the Red River at RM 0 to RM 351 at Camden, Arkansas.

(22) Pearl River: From junction of West Pearl River with the Rigolets at RM 0 to Bogalusa, Louisiana, RM 58.

(23) Red River: From RM 0 to the mouth of Cypress Bayou at RM 236.

(24) Tennessee River: From junction with Ohio River at RM 0 to confluence with Holstein and French Rivers at RM 652.

(25) White River: From RM 9.8 to RM 255 at Newport, Arkansas.

(26) Willamette River: From RM 21 upstream of Portland, Oregon, to Harrisburg, Oregon, at RM 194.

(27) Tennessee-Tombigbee Waterway: From its confluence with the Tennessee River to the Warrior River at Demopolis, Alabama.

(Pub. L. 95–502, title II, §206, Oct. 21, 1978, 92 Stat. 1700; Pub. L. 99–514, §2, Oct. 22, 1986, 100 Stat. 2095; Pub. L. 99–662, title XIV, §1404(b), Nov. 17, 1986, 100 Stat. 4270.)

REFERENCES IN TEXT

Section 1802 of this title, referred to in text, was repealed by Pub. L. 99–662, title XIV, §1405(b), Nov. 17, 1986, 100 Stat. 4271.

AMENDMENTS

1986—Pub. L. 99–514, in introductory provisions, substituted "Internal Revenue Code of 1986" for "Internal Revenue Code of 1954", which for purposes of codification was translated as "title 26" thus requiring no change in text.

Par. (27). Pub. L. 99–662 added par. (27).

EFFECTIVE DATE OF 1986 AMENDMENT

Amendment by Pub. L. 99–662 effective Jan. 1, 1987, see section 1404(c) of Pub. L. 99–662 set out as a note under section 4042 of Title 26, Internal Revenue Code.

CHAPTER 33—PREVENTION OF POLLUTION FROM SHIPS

[2] So in original. Probably should be "Chattahoochee".

[3] So in original. Probably should be "Albemarle".

§ 1901. Definitions

(a) Unless the context indicates otherwise, as used in this chapter—

(1) "Administrator" means the Administrator of the Environmental Protection Agency;

(2) "Antarctica" means the area south of 60 degrees south latitude;

(3) "Antarctic Protocol" means the Protocol on Environmental Protection to the Antarctic Treaty, signed October 4, 1991, in Madrid, and all annexes thereto, and includes any future amendments thereto which have entered into force;

(4) "MARPOL Protocol" means the Protocol of 1978 relating to the International Convention for the Prevention of Pollution from Ships, 1973, and includes the Convention;

(5) "Convention" means the International Convention for the Prevention of Pollution from Ships, 1973, including Protocols I and II and Annexes I, II, V, and VI thereto, including any modification or amendments to the Convention, Protocols, or Annexes which have entered into force for the United States;

(6) "discharge", "emission", "garbage", "harmful substance", and "incident" shall have the meanings provided in the Convention;

(7) "navigable waters" includes the territorial sea of the United States (as defined in Presidential Proclamation 5928 of December 27, 1988) and the internal waters of the United States;

(8) "owner" means any person holding title to, or in the absence of title, any other indicia of ownership of, a ship or terminal, but does not include a person who, without participating in the management or operation of a ship or terminal, holds indicia of ownership primarily to protect a security interest in the ship or terminal;

(9) "operator" means—

(a) in the case of a ship, a charterer by demise or any other person, except the owner, who is responsible for the operation, manning, victualing, and supplying of the vessel, or

(b) in the case of a terminal, any person, except the owner, responsible for the operation of the terminal by agreement with the owner;

(10) "person" means an individual, firm, public or private corporation, partnership, association, State, municipality, commission, political subdivision of a State, or any interstate body;

(11) "Secretary" means the Secretary of the department in which the Coast Guard is operating;

(12) "ship" means a vessel of any type whatsoever, including hydrofoils, air-cushion vehicles, submersibles, floating craft whether self-propelled or not, and fixed or floating platforms;

(13) "submersible" means a submarine, or any other vessel designed to operate under water; and

(14) "terminal" means an onshore facility or an offshore structure located in the navigable waters of the United States or subject to the jurisdiction of the United States and used, or intended to be used, as a port or facility for the transfer or other handling of a harmful substance.

(b) For purposes of this chapter, the requirements of Annex V shall apply to the navigable waters of the United States, as well as to all other waters and vessels over which the United States has jurisdiction.

(c) For the purposes of this chapter, the requirements of Annex IV to the Antarctic Protocol shall apply in Antarctica to all vessels over which the United States has jurisdiction.

(Pub. L. 96–478, §2, Oct. 21, 1980, 94 Stat. 2297; Pub. L. 100–220, title II, §2101, Dec. 29, 1987, 101 Stat. 1460; Pub. L. 103–160, div. A, title X, §1003(f), Nov. 30, 1993, 107 Stat. 1748; Pub. L. 104–227, title II, §201(a), Oct. 2, 1996, 110 Stat. 3042; Pub. L. 110–280, §3, July 21, 2008, 122 Stat. 2611.)

References in Text

This chapter, referred to in text, was in the original "this Act", meaning Pub. L. 96–478, Oct. 21, 1980, 94 Stat. 2297, known as the "Act to Prevent Pollution from Ships". For complete classification of this Act to the Code, see Short Title note below and Tables.

Presidential Proclamation 5928, referred to in subsec. (a)(7), is set out under section 1331 of Title 43, Public Lands.

Amendments

2008—Subsec. (a). Pub. L. 110–280 added par. (1), redesignated pars. (1) to (5) as (2) to (6), respectively, in par. (5) substituted "V, and VI" for "and V", in par. (6) substituted "'discharge', 'emission', 'garbage', 'harmful substance', and 'incident'" for "'discharge' and 'garbage' and 'harmful substance' and 'incident'", added par. (7), and redesignated pars. (6) to (12) as (8) to (14), respectively.

1996—Subsec. (a). Pub. L. 104–227, §201(a)(1), (2), added pars. (1) and (2) and redesignated former pars. (1) to (10) as (3) to (12), respectively.

Subsec. (c). Pub. L. 104–227, §201(a)(3), added subsec. (c).

1993—Subsec. (a)(9), (10). Pub. L. 103–160 added par. (9) and redesignated former par. (9) as (10).

1987—Subsec. (a). Pub. L. 100–220, §2101(1), designated existing provisions as subsec. (a).

Subsec. (a)(1). Pub. L. 100–220, §2101(2), amended par. (1) generally. Prior to amendment, par. (1) read as follows: "'MARPOL Protocol' means the Protocol of 1978 Relating to the International Convention for the Prevention of Pollution from Ships, 1973, done at London on February 17, 1978. This Protocol incorporates and modifies the International Convention for the Prevention of Pollution from Ships, 1973, done at London on November 2, 1973;".

Subsec. (a)(2). Pub. L. 100–220, §2101(3), substituted "Annexes I, II, and V thereto, including any modification or amendments to the Convention, Protocols, or Annexes which have entered into force for the United States" for "Annexes I and II attached thereto".

Subsec. (a)(3). Pub. L. 100–220, §2101(4), inserted "and 'garbage'".

Subsec. (b). Pub. L. 100–220, §2101(5), added subsec. (b).

EFFECTIVE DATE OF 1987 AMENDMENT

Section 2002 of title II of Pub. L. 100–220 provided that:

"(a) IN GENERAL.—Except as provided in subsections (b) and (c), this title [enacting sections 1912 to 1915 of this title, amending this section and sections 1902, 1903, 1905, and 1907 to 1909 of this title, and enacting provisions set out as notes under this section, section 2267 of this title, and section 6981 of Title 42, The Public Health and Welfare] shall be effective on the date on which Annex V to the International Convention for the Prevention of Pollution from Ships, 1973, enters into force for the United States. [Annex V entered into force for the United States Dec. 31, 1988.]

"(b) EXCEPTIONS.—Sections 2001, 2002, 2003, 2108, 2202, 2203, 2204, and subtitle C of this title [enacting sections 1912, 1914, and 1915 of this title, and provisions set out as notes under this section, section 2267 of this title, and section 6981 of Title 42] shall be effective on the date of the enactment of this title [Dec. 29, 1987].

"(c) ISSUANCE OF REGULATIONS.—

"(1) IN GENERAL.—The authority to prescribe regulations pursuant to this title shall be effective on the date of enactment of this title [Dec. 29, 1987].

"(2) EFFECTIVE DATE OF REGULATIONS.—Any regulation prescribed pursuant to this title shall not be effective before the effective date of the provision of this title under which the regulation is prescribed."

EFFECTIVE DATE

Section 14(a), (b) of Pub. L. 96–478 provided:

"(a) Except as provided in subsection (b) of this section, this Act [see Short Title note below] is effective upon the date of enactment [Oct. 21, 1980], or on the date the MARPOL Protocol becomes effective as to the United States, whichever is later. [The MARPOL Protocol became effective as to the United States Oct. 2, 1983.]

"(b) The Secretary and the heads of Federal departments shall have the authority to issue regulations, standards, and certifications under sections 3(c), 3(d), 4(b), 5(a), 6(a), 6(c), and 6(f) [sections 1902(c), (d), 1903(b), 1904(a), and 1905(a), (c), (f) of this title] effective on the date of enactment of this Act [Oct. 21, 1980]. Section 13(a)(2) [amending section 391a(3)(E) of former Title 46, Shipping] is effective upon the date of enactment of this Act [Oct. 21, 1980]."

SHORT TITLE OF 2008 AMENDMENT

Pub. L. 110–280, §1, July 21, 2008, 122 Stat. 2611, provided that: "This Act [amending this section and sections 1902, 1903 to 1905, and 1907 to 1911 of this title] may be cited as the 'Maritime Pollution Prevention Act of 2008'."

SHORT TITLE OF 1987 AMENDMENT

Section 2001 of title II of Pub. L. 100–220 provided that: "This title [see Effective Date of 1987 Amendment note above] may be cited as the 'Marine Plastic Pollution Research and Control Act of 1987'."

SHORT TITLE

Section 1 of Pub. L. 96–478 provided: "That this Act [enacting this chapter, amending section 1321 of this title and section 742c(c) of Title 16, Conservation, and section 391a of former Title 46, Shipping, repealing sections 1001 to 1011 and 1013 to 1016 of this title, and enacting provisions set out as notes under section 1001 of this title, and section 742c of Title 16] may be cited as the 'Act to Prevent Pollution from Ships'."

SAVINGS PROVISION: REGULATIONS IN EFFECT UNTIL SUPERSEDED

Section 14(c) of Pub. L. 96–478 provided that: "Any rights or liabilities existing on the effective date of this Act [see Effective Date note above] shall not be affected by this enactment [see Short Title note above]. Any regulations or procedures promulgated or effected pursuant to the Oil Pollution Act, 1961, as amended [section 1001 et seq. of this title], remain in effect until modified or superseded by regulations promulgated under the authority of the MARPOL Protocol or this Act."

TRANSFER OF FUNCTIONS

For transfer of authorities, functions, personnel, and assets of the Coast Guard, including the authorities and functions of the Secretary of Transportation relating thereto, to the Department of Homeland Security, and for treatment of related references, see sections 468(b), 551(d), 552(d), and 557 of Title 6, Domestic Security, and the Department of Homeland Security Reorganization Plan of November 25, 2002, as modified, set out as a note under section 542 of Title 6.

INTERIM AUTHORITY FOR DRY BULK CARGO RESIDUE DISPOSAL

Pub. L. 108–293, title VI, §623, Aug. 9, 2004, 118 Stat. 1063, provided that:

"(a) EXTENSION OF INTERIM AUTHORITY.—The Secretary of the Department in which the Coast Guard is operating shall continue to implement and enforce United States Coast Guard 1997 Enforcement Policy for Cargo Residues on the Great Lakes (hereinafter in this section referred to as the 'Policy') or revisions thereto, in accordance with that policy, for the purpose of regulating incidental discharges from vessels of residues of dry bulk cargo into the waters of the Great Lakes under the jurisdiction of the United States, until the earlier of—

"(1) the date regulations are promulgated under subsection (b) for the regulation of incidental discharges from vessels of dry bulk cargo residue into the waters of the Great Lakes under the jurisdiction of the United States; or

"(2) September 30, 2008.

"(b) PERMANENT AUTHORITY.—Notwithstanding any other law, the Commandant of the Coast Guard may promulgate regulations governing the discharge of dry bulk cargo residue on the Great Lakes.

"(c) ENVIRONMENTAL ASSESSMENT.—No later than 90 days after the date of the enactment of this Act [Aug. 9, 2004], the Secretary of the department in which the Coast Guard is operating shall commence the environmental assessment necessary to promulgate the regulations under subsection (b)."

STUDY AND REGULATION OF GREAT LAKES CARGO RESIDUES

Pub. L. 106–554, §1(a)(4) [div. A, §1117(b), (c)], Dec. 21, 2000, 114 Stat. 2763, 2763A–209, provided that:

"(b) The Secretary shall conduct a study of the effectiveness of the United States 1997 Enforcement Policy for Cargo Residues on the Great Lakes ('Policy') by September 30, 2002.

"(c) The Secretary is authorized to promulgate regulations to implement and enforce a program to regulate incidental discharges from vessels of residues of non-hazardous and non-toxic dry bulk cargo into the waters of the Great Lakes, which takes into account the finding in the study required under subsection (b). This program shall be consistent with the Policy."

CERTAIN ALASKAN CRUISE SHIP OPERATIONS

Pub. L. 106–554, §1(a)(4) [div. B, title XIV], Dec. 21, 2000, 114 Stat. 2763, 2763A–315, provided that:

"SEC. 1401. PURPOSE.

"The purpose of this title is to:

"(1) Ensure that cruise vessels operating in the waters of the Alexander Archipelago and the navigable waters of the United States within the State of Alaska and within the Kachemak Bay National Estuarine Research Reserve comply with all applicable environmental laws, including, but not limited to, the Federal Water Pollution Control Act, as amended (33 U.S.C. 1251 et seq.), the Act to Prevent Pollution from Ships, as amended (33 U.S.C. 1901 et seq.), and the protections contained within this title.

"(2) Ensure that cruise vessels do not discharge untreated sewage within the waters of the Alexander Archipelago, the navigable waters of the United States in the State of Alaska, or within the Kachemak Bay National Estuarine Research Reserve.

"(3) Prevent the unregulated discharge of treated sewage and graywater while in ports in the State of Alaska or traveling near the shore in the Alexander Archipelago and the navigable waters of the United States in the State of Alaska or within the Kachemak Bay National Estuarine Research Reserve.

"(4) Ensure that discharges of sewage and graywater from cruise vessels operating in the Alexander Archipelago and the navigable waters of the United States in the State of Alaska or within the Kachemak Bay National Estuarine Research Reserve can be monitored for compliance with the requirements contained in this title.

"SEC. 1402. APPLICABILITY.

"This title applies to all cruise vessels authorized to carry 500 or more passengers for hire.

"SEC. 1403. PROHIBITION ON DISCHARGE OF UNTREATED SEWAGE.

"No person shall discharge any untreated sewage from a cruise vessel into the waters of the Alexander Archipelago or the navigable waters of the United States within the State of Alaska or within the Kachemak Bay National Estuarine Research Reserve.

"SEC. 1404. LIMITATIONS ON DISCHARGE OF TREATED SEWAGE OR GRAYWATER.

"(a) No person shall discharge any treated sewage or graywater from a cruise vessel into the waters of the Alexander Archipelago or the navigable waters of the United States within the State of Alaska or within the Kachemak Bay National Estuarine Research Reserve unless—

"(1) the cruise vessel is underway and proceeding at a speed of not less than six knots;

"(2) the cruise vessel is not less than one nautical mile from the nearest shore, except in areas designated by the Secretary, in consultation with the State of Alaska;

"(3) the discharge complies with all applicable cruise vessel effluent standards established pursuant to this title and any other applicable law; and

"(4) the cruise vessel is not in an area where the discharge of treated sewage or graywater is prohibited.

"(b) The Administrator, in consultation with the Secretary, may promulgate regulations allowing the discharge of treated sewage or graywater, otherwise prohibited under paragraphs (a)(1) and (a)(2) of this section, where the discharge meets effluent standards determined by the Administrator as appropriate for discharges into the marine environment. In promulgating such regulations, the Administrator shall take into account the best available scientific information on the environmental effects of the regulated discharges. The effluent discharge standards promulgated under this section shall, at a minimum, be consistent with all relevant State of Alaska water quality standards in force at the time of the enactment of this title [Dec. 21, 2000].

"(c) Until such time as the Administrator promulgates regulations under paragraph (b) of this section, treated sewage and graywater may be discharged from vessels subject to this title in circumstances otherwise prohibited under paragraphs (a)(1) and (a)(2) of this section, provided that—

"(1) the discharge satisfies the minimum level of effluent quality specified in 40 CFR 133.102, as in effect on the date of enactment of this section [Dec. 21, 2000];

"(2) the geometric mean of the samples from the discharge during any 30-day period does not exceed 20 fecal coliform/100 ml and not more than 10 percent of the samples exceed 40 fecal coliform/100 ml;

"(3) concentrations of total residual chlorine may not exceed 10.0 µg/l; and

"(4) prior to any such discharge occurring, the owner, operator or master, or other person in charge of a cruise vessel, can demonstrate test results from at least five samples taken from the vessel representative of the effluent to be discharged, on different days over a 30-day period, conducted in accordance with the guidelines promulgated by the Administrator in 40 CFR Part 136, which confirm that the water quality of the effluents proposed for discharge is in compliance with paragraphs (1), (2), and (3) of this subsection. To the extent not otherwise being done by the owner, operator, master or other person in charge of a cruise vessel pursuant to section 1406, the owner, operator, master or other person in charge of a cruise vessel shall demonstrate continued compliance through periodic sampling. Such sampling and test results shall be considered environmental compliance records that must be made available for inspection pursuant to section 1406(d) of this title.

"SEC. 1405. SAFETY EXCEPTION.

"Sections 1403 and 1404 of this title shall not apply to discharges made for the purpose of securing the safety of the cruise vessel or saving life at sea, provided that all reasonable precautions have been taken for the purpose of preventing or minimizing the discharge.

"SEC. 1406. INSPECTION AND SAMPLING REGIME.

"(a) The Secretary shall incorporate into the commercial vessel examination program an inspection regime sufficient to verify that cruise vessels visiting ports in the State of Alaska or operating in the waters of the Alexander Archipelago or the navigable waters of the United States within the State of Alaska or within the Kachemak Bay National Estuarine Research Reserve are in full compliance with this title, the Federal Water Pollution Control Act [33 U.S.C. 1251 et seq.], as amended, and any regulations issued thereunder, other applicable Federal laws and regulations, and all applicable international treaty requirements.

"(b) The inspection regime shall, at a minimum, include—

"(1) examination of environmental compliance records and procedures; and

"(2) inspection of the functionality and proper operation of installed equipment for abatement and control of any discharge.

"(c) The inspection regime may—

"(1) include unannounced inspections of any aspect of cruise vessel operations, equipment or discharges pertinent to the verification under subsection (a) of this section; and

"(2) require the owner, operator or master, or other person in charge of a cruise vessel subject to this title to maintain and produce a logbook detailing the times, types, volumes or flow rates and locations of any discharges of sewage or graywater under this title.

"(d) The inspection regime shall incorporate a plan for sampling and testing cruise vessel discharges to ensure that any discharges of sewage or graywater are in compliance with this title, the Federal Water Pollution Control Act [33 U.S.C. 1251 et seq.], as amended, and any other applicable laws and regulations, and may require the owner, operator or master, or other person in charge of a cruise vessel subject to this title to conduct such samples or tests, and to produce any records of such sampling or testing at the request of the Secretary or Administrator.

"SEC. 1407. CRUISE VESSEL EFFLUENT STANDARDS.

"Pursuant to this title and the authority of the Federal Water Pollution Control Act [33 U.S.C. 1251 et seq.], as amended, the Administrator may promulgate effluent standards for treated sewage and graywater from cruise vessels operating in the waters of the Alexander Archipelago or the navigable waters of the United States within the State of Alaska or within the Kachemak Bay National Estuarine Research Reserve. Regulations implementing such standards shall take into account the best available scientific information on the environmental effects of the regulated discharges and the availability of new technologies for wastewater treatment. Until such time as the Administrator promulgates such effluent standards, treated sewage effluent discharges shall not have a fecal coliform bacterial count of greater than 200 per 100 milliliters nor suspended solids greater than 150 milligrams per liter.

"SEC. 1408. REPORTS.

"(a) Any owner, operator or master, or other person in charge of a cruise vessel who has knowledge of a discharge from the cruise vessel in violation of section 1403 or 1404 or pursuant to section 1405 of this title, or any regulations promulgated thereunder, shall immediately report that discharge to the Secretary, who shall provide a copy to the Administrator upon request.

"(b) The Secretary may prescribe the form of reports required under this section.

"SEC. 1409. ENFORCEMENT.

"(a) ADMINISTRATIVE PENALTIES.—

"(1) VIOLATIONS.—Any person who violates section 1403, 1404, 1408, or 1413 of this title, or any regulations promulgated pursuant to this title may be assessed a class I or class II civil penalty by the Secretary or Administrator.

"(2) CLASSES OF PENALTIES.—

"(A) CLASS I.—The amount of a class I civil penalty under this section may not exceed $10,000 per violation, except that the maximum amount of any class I civil penalty under this section shall not exceed $25,000. Before assessing a civil penalty under this clause, the Secretary or Administrator, as the case may be, shall give to the person to be assessed such penalty written notice of the Secretary's or Administrator's proposal to assess the penalty and the opportunity to request, within 30 days of the date the notice is received by such person, a hearing on the proposed penalty. Such hearing shall not be subject to section 554 or 556 of title 5, but shall provide a reasonable opportunity to be heard and to present evidence.

"(B) CLASS II.—The amount of a class II civil penalty under this section may not exceed $10,000 per day for each day during which the violation continues, except that the maximum amount of any class II civil penalty under this section shall not exceed $125,000. Except as otherwise provided in this subsection, a class II civil penalty shall be assessed and collected in the same manner, and subject to the same provisions as in the case of civil penalties assessed and collected after notice and an opportunity for a hearing on the record in accordance with section 554 of title 5, United States Code. The Secretary and Administrator may issue rules for discovery procedures for hearings under this paragraph.

"(3) RIGHTS OF INTERESTED PERSONS.—

"(A) PUBLIC NOTICE.—Before issuing an order assessing a class II civil penalty under this section, the Secretary or Administrator, as the case may be, shall provide public notice of and reasonable opportunity to comment on the proposed issuance of each order.

"(B) PRESENTATION OF EVIDENCE.—Any person who comments on a proposed assessment of a class II civil penalty under this section shall be given notice of any hearing held under this paragraph and of the order assessing such penalty. In any hearing held under this paragraph, such person shall have a reasonable opportunity to be heard and present evidence.

"(C) RIGHTS OF INTERESTED PERSONS TO A HEARING.—If no hearing is held under subsection (2) before issuance of an order assessing a class II civil penalty under this section, any person who commented on the proposed assessment may petition, within 30 days after the issuance of such order, the Administrator or Secretary, as the case may be, to set aside such order and to provide a hearing on the penalty. If the evidence presented by the petitioner in support of the petition is material and was not considered in the issuance of the order, the Administrator or Secretary shall immediately set aside such order and provide a hearing in accordance with subsection (2)(B). If the Administrator or Secretary denies a hearing under this clause, the Administrator or Secretary shall provide to the petitioner, and publish in the Federal Register, notice of and the reasons for such denial.

"(4) FINALITY OF ORDER.—An order assessing a class II civil penalty under this paragraph shall become final 30 days after its issuance unless a petition for judicial review is filed under subparagraph (6) or a hearing is requested under subsection (3)(C). If such a hearing is denied, such order shall become final 30 days after such denial.

"(5) EFFECT OF ACTION ON COMPLIANCE.—No action by the Administrator or Secretary under this paragraph shall affect any person's obligation to comply with any section of this title.

"(6) JUDICIAL REVIEW.—Any person against whom a civil penalty is assessed under this paragraph or who commented on the proposed assessment of such penalty in accordance with subsection (3) may obtain review of such assessment—

"(A) in the case of assessment of a class I civil penalty, in the United States District Court for the District of Columbia or in the District of Alaska; or

"(B) in the case of assessment of a class II civil penalty, in the United States Court of Appeals for the District of Columbia Circuit or for any other circuit in which such person resides or transacts business, by filing a notice of appeal in such court within the 30-day period beginning on the date the civil penalty order is issued and by simultaneously sending a copy of such notice by certified mail to the Administrator or Secretary, as the case may be, and the Attorney General. The Administrator or Secretary shall promptly file in such court a certified copy of the record on which the order was issued. Such court shall not set aside or remand such order unless there is not substantial evidence in the record, taken as a whole, to support the finding of a violation or unless the Administrator's or Secretary's assessment of the penalty constitutes an abuse of discretion and shall not impose additional civil penalties for the same violation unless the Administrator's or Secretary's assessment of the penalty constitutes an abuse of discretion.

"(7) COLLECTION.—If any person fails to pay an assessment of a civil penalty—

"(A) after the assessment has become final, or

"(B) after a court in an action brought under subsection (6) has entered a final judgment in favor of the Administrator or Secretary, as the case may be, the Administrator or Secretary shall request the Attorney General to bring a civil action in an appropriate district court to recover the amount assessed (plus interest at currently prevailing rates from the date of the final order or the date of the final judgment, as the case may be). In such an action, the validity, amount, and appropriateness of such penalty shall not be subject to review. Any person who fails to pay on a timely basis the amount of an assessment of a civil penalty as described in the first sentence of this subparagraph shall be required to pay, in addition to such amount and interest, attorneys fees and costs for collection proceedings and a quarterly nonpayment penalty for each quarter during which such failure to pay persists. Such nonpayment penalty shall be in an amount equal to 20 percent of the aggregate amount of such person's penalties and nonpayment penalties which are unpaid as of the beginning of such quarter.

"(8) SUBPOENAS.—The Administrator or Secretary, as the case may be, may issue subpoenas for the attendance and testimony of witnesses and the production of relevant papers, books, or documents in connection with hearings under this section. In case of contumacy or refusal to obey a subpoena issued pursuant to this subsection and served upon any person, the district court of the United States for any district in which such person is found, resides, or transacts business, upon application by the United States and after notice to such person, shall have jurisdiction to issue an order requiring such person to appear and give testimony before the Administrator or Secretary or to appear and produce documents before the Administrator or Secretary, or both, and any failure to obey such order of the court may be punished by such court as a contempt thereof.

"(b) CIVIL PENALTIES.—

"(1) IN GENERAL.—Any person who violates section 1403, 1404, 1408, or 1413 of this title, or any regulations promulgated pursuant to this title shall be subject to a civil penalty not to exceed $25,000 per day for each violation. Each day a violation continues constitutes a separate violation.

"(2) JURISDICTION.—An action to impose a civil penalty under this section may be brought in the district court of the United States for the district in which the defendant is located, resides, or transacts business, and such court shall have jurisdiction to assess such penalty.

"(3) LIMITATION.—A person is not liable for a civil judicial penalty under this paragraph for a violation if the person has been assessed a civil administrative penalty under paragraph (a) for the violation.

"(c) DETERMINATION OF AMOUNT.—In determining the amount of a civil penalty under paragraphs (a) or (b) of this section, the court, the Secretary or the Administrator, as the case may be, shall consider the seriousness of the violation or violations, the economic benefit (if any) resulting from the violation, any history of such violations, any good-faith efforts to comply with the applicable requirements, the economic impact of the penalty on the violator, and other such matters as justice may require.

"(d) CRIMINAL PENALTIES.—

"(1) NEGLIGENT VIOLATIONS.—Any person who negligently violates section 1403, 1404, 1408, or 1413 of this title, or any regulations promulgated pursuant to this title commits a Class A misdemeanor.

"(2) KNOWING VIOLATIONS.—Any person who knowingly violates section 1403, 1404, 1408, or 1413 of this title, or any regulations promulgated pursuant to this title commits a Class D felony.

"(3) FALSE STATEMENTS.—Any person who knowingly makes any false statement, representation, or certification in any record, report or other document filed or required to be maintained under this title or the regulations issued thereunder, or who falsifies, tampers with, or knowingly renders inaccurate any testing or monitoring device or method required to be maintained under this title, or the regulations issued thereunder, commits a Class D felony.

"(e) AWARDS.—

"(1) The Secretary, the Administrator, or the court, when assessing any fines or civil penalties, as the case may be, may pay from any fines or civil penalties collected under this section an amount not to exceed one-half of the penalty or fine collected, to any individual who furnishes information which leads to the payment of the penalty or fine. If several individuals provide such information, the amount shall be divided equitably among such individuals. No officer or employee of the United States, the State of Alaska or any federally recognized Tribe who furnishes information or renders service in the performance of his or her official duties shall be eligible for payment under this subsection.

"(2) The Secretary, Administrator or the court, when assessing any fines or civil penalties, as the case may be, may pay, from any fines or civil penalties collected under this section, to the State of Alaska or to any federally recognized Tribe providing information or investigative assistance which leads to payment of the penalty or fine, an amount which reflects the level of information or investigative assistance provided. Should the State of Alaska or a federally recognized Tribe and an individual under paragraph (1) of this section be eligible for an award, the Secretary, the Administrator, or the court, as the case may be, shall divide the amount equitably.

"(f) LIABILITY IN REM.—A cruise vessel operated in violation of this title or the regulations issued thereunder is liable in rem for any fine imposed under subsection (d) of this section or for any civil penalty imposed under subsections (a) or (b) of this section, and may be proceeded against in the United States district court of any district in which the cruise vessel may be found.

"(g) COMPLIANCE ORDERS.—

"(1) IN GENERAL.—Whenever on the basis of any information available to him the Administrator finds that any person is in violation of section 1403, 1404, 1408, or 1413 of this title, or any regulations promulgated pursuant to this title, the Administrator shall issue an order requiring such person to comply with such section or requirement, or shall bring a civil action in accordance with subsection (b).

"(2) COPIES OF ORDERS, SERVICE.—A copy of any order issued under this subsection shall be sent immediately by the Administrator to the State of Alaska. In any case in which an order under this subsection is issued to a corporation, a copy of such order shall be served on any appropriate corporate officer. Any order issued under this subsection shall be by personal service, shall state with reasonable specificity the nature of the violation, and shall specify a time for compliance not to exceed 30 days in the case of a violation of an interim compliance schedule or operation and maintenance requirement and not to exceed a time the Administrator determines to be reasonable in the case of a violation of a final deadline, taking into account the seriousness of the violation and any good faith efforts to comply with applicable requirements.

"(h) CIVIL ACTIONS.—The Administrator is authorized to commence a civil action for appropriate relief, including a permanent or temporary injunction, for any violation for which he is authorized to issue a compliance order under this subsection. Any action under subsection (h) may be brought in the district court of the United States for the district in which the defendant is located or resides or is doing business, and such court shall have jurisdiction to restrain such violation and to require compliance. Notice of the commencement of such action shall be given immediately to the State of Alaska.

"SEC. 1410. DESIGNATION OF CRUISE VESSEL NO-DISCHARGE ZONES.

"If the State of Alaska determines that the protection and enhancement of the quality of some or all of the waters of the Alexander Archipelago or the navigable waters of the United States within the State of Alaska or within the Kachemak Bay National Estuarine Research Reserve require greater environmental protection, the State of Alaska may petition the Administrator to prohibit the discharge of graywater and sewage from cruise vessels operating in such waters. The establishment of such a prohibition shall be achieved in the same manner as the petitioning process and prohibition of the discharge of sewage pursuant to section 312(f) of the Federal Water Pollution Control Act [33 U.S.C. 1322(f)], as amended, and the regulations promulgated thereunder.

"SEC. 1411. SAVINGS CLAUSE.

"(a) Nothing in this title shall be construed as restricting, affecting, or amending any other law or the authority of any department, instrumentality, or agency of the United States.

"(b) Nothing in this title shall in any way affect or restrict, or be construed to affect or restrict, the authority of the State of Alaska or any political subdivision thereof—

"(1) to impose additional liability or additional requirements; or

"(2) to impose, or determine the amount of a fine or penalty (whether criminal or civil in nature) for any violation of law; relating to the discharge of sewage (whether treated or untreated) or graywater in the waters of the Alexander Archipelago and the navigable waters of the United States within the State of Alaska or within the Kachemak Bay National Estuarine Research Reserve.

"SEC. 1412. REGULATIONS.

"The Secretary and the Administrator each may prescribe any regulations necessary to carry out the provisions of this title.

"SEC. 1413. INFORMATION GATHERING AUTHORITY.

"The authority of sections 308(a) and (b) of the Federal Water Pollution Control Act [33 U.S.C. 1318(a), (b)], as amended, shall be available to the Administrator to carry out the provisions of this title. The Administrator and the Secretary shall minimize, to the extent practicable, duplication of or inconsistency with the inspection, sampling, testing, recordkeeping, and reporting requirements established by the Secretary under section 1406 of this title.

"SEC. 1414. DEFINITIONS.

"In this title:

"(1) ADMINISTRATOR.—The term 'Administrator' means the Administrator of the United States Environmental Protection Agency.

"(2) CRUISE VESSEL.—The term 'cruise vessel' means a passenger vessel as defined in section 2101(22) of title 46, United States Code. The term 'cruise vessel' does not include a vessel of the United States operated by the Federal Government or a vessel owned and operated by the government of a State.

"(3) DISCHARGE.—The term 'discharge' means any release however caused from a cruise vessel, and includes any escape, disposal, spilling, leaking, pumping, emitting, or emptying.

"(4) GRAYWATER.—The term 'graywater' means only galley, dishwasher, bath, and laundry waste water. The term does not include other wastes or waste streams.

"(5) NAVIGABLE WATERS.—The term 'navigable waters' has the same meaning as in section 502 of the Federal Water Pollution Control Act [33 U.S.C. 1362], as amended.

"(6) PERSON.—The term 'person' means an individual, corporation, partnership, limited liability company, association, State, municipality, commission, or political subdivision of a State, or any federally recognized tribe.

"(7) SECRETARY.—The term 'Secretary' means the Secretary of the department in which the United States Coast Guard is operating.

"(8) SEWAGE.—The term 'sewage' means human body wastes and the wastes from toilets and other receptacles intended to receive or retain body waste.

"(9) TREATED SEWAGE.—The term 'treated sewage' means sewage meeting all applicable effluent limitation standards and processing requirements of the Federal Water Pollution Control Act [33 U.S.C. 1251 et seq.], as amended[,] and of this title, and regulations promulgated under either.

"(10) UNTREATED SEWAGE.—The term 'untreated sewage' means sewage that is not treated sewage.

"(11) WATERS OF THE ALEXANDER ARCHIPELAGO.—The term 'waters of the Alexander Archipelago' means all waters under the sovereignty of the United States within or near Southeast Alaska, beginning at a point 58°11′41″N, 136°39′25″W [near Cape Spencer Light], thence southeasterly along a line three nautical miles seaward of the baseline from which the breadth of the territorial sea is measured in the Pacific Ocean and the Dixon Entrance, except where this line intersects geodesics connecting the following five pairs of points:

"(1) 58°05′17″N, 136°33′49″W and 58°11′41″N, 136°39′25″W [Cross Sound].

"(2) 56°09′40″N, 134°40′00″W and 55°49′15″N, 134°17′40″W [Chatham Strait].

"(3) 55°49′15″N, 134°17′40″W and 55°50′30″N, 133°54′15″W [Sumner Strait].

"(4) 54°41′30″N, 132°01′00″W and 54°51′30″N, 131°20′45″W [Clarence Strait].

"(5) 54°51′30″N, 131°20′45″W and 54°46′15″N, 130°52′00″W [Revillagigedo Channel].

"The portion of each such geodesic situated beyond three nautical miles from the baseline from which the breadth of the territorial sea is measured forms the outer limit of the waters of the Alexander Archipelago in those five locations."

PREEMPTION; ADDITIONAL STATE REQUIREMENTS

Section 2003 of title II of Pub. L. 100–220 provided that:

"(a) PREEMPTION.—Except as specifically provided in this title [see Effective Date of 1987 Amendment note above], nothing in this title shall be interpreted or construed to supersede or preempt any other provision of Federal or State law, either statutory or common.

"(b) ADDITIONAL STATE REQUIREMENTS.—Nothing in this title shall be construed or interpreted as preempting any State from imposing any additional requirements."

§ 1902. Ships subject to preventive measures

(a) Included vessels

This chapter shall apply—

(1) to a ship of United States registry or nationality, or one operated under the authority of the United States, wherever located;

(2) with respect to Annexes I and II to the Convention, to a ship, other than a ship referred to in paragraph (1), while in the navigable waters of the United States;

(3) with respect to the requirements of Annex V to the Convention, to a ship, other than a ship referred to in paragraph (1), while in the navigable waters or the exclusive economic zone of the United States;

(4) with respect to regulations prescribed under section 1905 of this title, any port or terminal in the United States; and

(5) with respect to Annex VI to the Convention, and other than with respect to a ship referred to in paragraph (1)—

(A) to a ship that is in a port, shipyard, offshore terminal, or the internal waters of the United States;

(B) to a ship that is bound for, or departing from, a port, shipyard, offshore terminal, or the internal waters of the United States, and is in—

(i) the navigable waters or the exclusive economic zone of the United States;

(ii) an emission control area designated pursuant to section 1903 of this title; or

(iii) any other area that the Administrator, in consultation with the Secretary and each State in which any part of the area is located, has designated by order as being an area from which emissions from ships are of concern with respect to protection of public health, welfare, or the environment;

(C) to a ship that is entitled to fly the flag of, or operating under the authority of, a party to Annex VI, and is in—

(i) the navigable waters or the exclusive economic zone of the United States;

(ii) an emission control area designated under section 1903 of this title; or

(iii) any other area that the Administrator, in consultation with the Secretary and each State in which any part of the area is located, has designated by order as being an area from which emissions from ships are of concern with respect to protection of public health, welfare, or the environment; and

(D) to any other ship, to the extent that, and in the same manner as, such ship may be boarded by the Secretary to implement or enforce any other law of the United States or Annex I, II, or V of the Convention, and is in—

(i) the exclusive economic zone of the United States;

(ii) the navigable waters of the United States;

(iii) an emission control area designated under section 1903 of this title; or

(iv) any other area that the Administrator, in consultation with the Secretary and each State in which any part of the area is located, has designated by order as being an area from which emissions from ships are of concern with respect to protection of public health, welfare, or the environment.

(b) Excluded vessels

(1) Except as provided in paragraphs (2) and (3), this chapter shall not apply to—

(A) a warship, naval auxiliary, or other ship owned or operated by the United States when engaged in noncommercial service; or

(B) any other ship specifically excluded by the MARPOL Protocol or the Antarctic Protocol.

(2)(A) Notwithstanding any provision of the MARPOL Protocol, and subject to subparagraph (B) of this paragraph, the requirements of Annex V to the Convention shall apply as follows:

(i) After December 31, 1993, to all ships referred to in paragraph (1)(A) of this subsection other than those owned or operated by the Department of the Navy.

(ii) Except as provided in subsection (c)[1] of this section, after December 31, 1998, to all ships referred to in paragraph (1)(A) of this subsection other than submersibles owned or operated by the Department of the Navy.

(iii) Except as provided in subsection (c)[1] of this section, after December 31, 2008, to all ships referred to in paragraph (1)(A) of this subsection.

(B) This paragraph shall not apply during time of war or a declared national emergency.

(3) With respect to Annex VI the Administrator, or the Secretary, as relevant to their authorities pursuant to this chapter, may determine that some or all of the requirements under this chapter shall apply to one or more classes of public vessels, except that such a determination by the Administrator shall have no effect unless the head of the Department or agency under which the vessels operate concurs in the determination. This paragraph does not apply during time of war or during a declared national emergency.

(c) Application to other persons

This chapter shall apply to all persons to the extent necessary to ensure compliance with Annex VI to the Convention.

(d) Discharges in special areas

(1) Except as provided in paragraphs (2) and (3), not later than December 31, 2000, all surface ships owned or operated by the Department of the Navy, and not later than December 31, 2008, all submersibles owned or operated by the Department of the Navy, shall comply with the special area requirements of Regulation 5 of Annex V to the Convention.

(2)(A) Subject to subparagraph (B), any ship described in subparagraph (C) may discharge, without regard to the special area requirements of Regulation 5 of Annex V to the Convention, the following non-plastic, non-floating garbage:

(i) A slurry of seawater, paper, cardboard, or food waste that is capable of passing through a screen with openings no larger than 12 millimeters in diameter.

(ii) Metal and glass that have been shredded and bagged so as to ensure negative buoyancy.

(iii) With regard to a submersible, nonplastic garbage that has been compacted and weighted to ensure negative buoyancy.

(B)(i) Garbage described in subparagraph (A)(i) may not be discharged within 3 nautical miles of land.

(ii) Garbage described in clauses (ii) and (iii) of subparagraph (A) may not be discharged within 12 nautical miles of land.

(C) This paragraph applies to any ship that is owned or operated by the Department of the Navy that, as determined by the Secretary of the Navy—

(i) has unique military design, construction, manning, or operating requirements; and

(ii) cannot fully comply with the special area requirements of Regulation 5 of Annex V to the Convention because compliance is not technologically feasible or would impair the operations or operational capability of the ship.

(3)(A) Not later than December 31, 2000, the Secretary of the Navy shall prescribe and publish in the Federal Register standards to ensure that each ship described in subparagraph (B) is, to the maximum extent practicable without impairing the operations or operational capabilities of the ship, operated in a manner that is consistent with the special area requirements of Regulation 5 of Annex V to the Convention.

(B) Subparagraph (A) applies to surface ships that are owned or operated by the Department of the Navy that the Secretary plans to decommission during the period beginning on January 1, 2001, and ending on December 31, 2005.

(C) At the same time that the Secretary publishes standards under subparagraph (A), the Secretary shall publish in the Federal Register a list of the ships covered by subparagraph (B).

(e) Regulations

The Secretary or the Administrator, consistent with section 1903 of this title, shall prescribe

[1] See References in Text note below.

regulations applicable to the ships of a country not a party to the MARPOL Protocol (or the applicable Annex), including regulations conforming to and giving effect to the requirements of Annex V and Annex VI as they apply under subsection (a) of this section, to ensure that their treatment is not more favorable than that accorded ships to parties to the MARPOL Protocol.

(f) Compliance by excluded vessels

(1) The Secretary of the Navy shall develop and, as appropriate, support the development of technologies and practices for solid waste management aboard ships owned or operated by the Department of the Navy, including technologies and practices for the reduction of the waste stream generated aboard such ships, that are necessary to ensure the compliance of such ships with Annex V to the Convention on or before the dates referred to in subsections (b)(2)(A) and (c)(1) of this section.

(2) Notwithstanding any effective date of the application of this section to a ship, the provisions of Annex V to the Convention with respect to the disposal of plastic shall apply to ships equipped with plastic processors required for the long-term collection and storage of plastic aboard ships of the Navy upon the installation of such processors in such ships.

(3) Except when necessary for the purpose of securing the safety of the ship, the health of the ship's personnel, or saving life at sea, it shall be a violation of this chapter for a ship referred to in subsection (b)(1)(A) of this section that is owned or operated by the Department of the Navy:

(A) With regard to a submersible, to discharge buoyant garbage or plastic.

(B) With regard to a surface ship, to discharge plastic contaminated by food during the last 3 days before the ship enters port.

(C) With regard to a surface ship, to discharge plastic, except plastic that is contaminated by food, during the last 20 days before the ship enters port.

(4) The Secretary of Defense shall publish in the Federal Register:

(A) Each year, the amount and nature of the discharges in special areas, not otherwise authorized under this chapter, during the preceding year from ships referred to in subsection (b)(1)(A) of this section owned or operated by the Department of the Navy.

(B) Beginning on October 1, 1996, and each year thereafter until October 1, 1998, a list of the names of such ships equipped with plastic processors pursuant to section 1003(e) of the National Defense Authorization Act for Fiscal Year 1994.

(g) Waiver authority

The President may waive the effective dates of the requirements set forth in subsection (c)[1] of this section and in subsection 1003(e) of the National Defense Authorization Act for Fiscal Year 1994 if the President determines it to be in the paramount interest of the United States to do so. Any such waiver shall be for a period not in excess of one year. The President shall submit to the Congress each January a report on all waivers from the requirements of this section granted during the preceding calendar year, together with the reasons for granting such waivers.

(h) Noncommercial shipping standards

The heads of Federal departments and agencies shall prescribe standards applicable to ships excluded from this chapter by subsection (b)(1) of this section and for which they are responsible. Standards prescribed under this subsection shall ensure, so far as is reasonable and practicable without impairing the operations or operational capabilities of such ships, that such ships act in a manner consistent with the MARPOL Protocol.

(i) Savings clause

Nothing in this section shall be construed to restrict in a manner inconsistent with international law navigational rights and freedoms as defined by United States law, treaty, convention, or customary international law.

(Pub. L. 96–478, §3, Oct. 21, 1980, 94 Stat. 2297; Pub. L. 100–220, title II, §2102, Dec. 29, 1987, 101 Stat. 1461; Pub. L. 103–160, div. A, title X, §1003(a)–(d), Nov. 30, 1993, 107 Stat. 1745–1747; Pub. L. 104–201, div. A, title III, §324(a), (d), Sept. 23, 1996, 110 Stat. 2480, 2481; Pub. L. 104–227, title II, §201(b), Oct. 2, 1996, 110 Stat. 3042; Pub. L. 105–261, div. A, title III, §326, Oct. 17, 1998, 112 Stat. 1965; Pub. L. 110–280, §4, July 21, 2008, 122 Stat. 2611.)

REFERENCES IN TEXT

Subsection (c) of this section, referred to in subsecs. (b)(2)(A)(ii), (iii), (f)(1), and (g), was redesignated subsection (d) by Pub. L. 110–280, §4(3), July 21, 2008, 122 Stat. 2613.

Section 1003(e) of the National Defense Authorization Act for Fiscal Year 1994, referred to in subsecs. (f)(4)(B) and (g), is section 1003(e) of Pub. L. 103–160, which is set out below.

AMENDMENTS

2008—Subsec. (a)(5). Pub. L. 110–280, §4(1), added par. (5).

Subsec. (b)(1). Pub. L. 110–280, §4(2)(A), substituted "paragraphs (2) and (3)," for "paragraph (2)," in introductory provisions.

Subsec. (b)(3). Pub. L. 110–280, §4(2)(B), added par. (3).

Subsecs. (c), (d). Pub. L. 110–280, §4(3), added subsec. (c) and redesignated former subsec. (c) as (d). Former subsec. (d) redesignated (e).

Subsec. (e). Pub. L. 110–280, §4(4)(C), substituted "Protocol (or the applicable Annex), including regulations conforming to and giving effect to the requirements of Annex V and Annex VI" for "Protocol, including regulations conforming to and giving effect to the requirements of Annex V".

Pub. L. 110–280, §4(4)(B), made technical amendment to reference in original act which appears in text as reference to "of this section" requiring no change in text.

Pub. L. 110–280, §4(4)(A), inserted "or the Administrator, consistent with section 1903 of this title," after "Secretary".

Pub. L. 110–280, §4(3), redesignated subsec. (d) as (e). Former subsec. (e) redesignated (f).

Subsecs. (f) to (h). Pub. L. 110–280, §4(3), redesignated subsecs. (e) to (g) as (f) to (h), respectively.

Subsec. (i). Pub. L. 110–280, §4(5), added subsec. (i).

1998—Subsec. (c)(2)(A)(iii). Pub. L. 105–261, §326(a)(1), added cl. (iii).

Subsec. (c)(2)(B)(ii). Pub. L. 105–261, §326(a)(2), substituted "clauses (ii) and (iii) of subparagraph (A)" for "subparagraph (A)(ii)".

Subsec. (e)(3)(A). Pub. L. 105–261, § 326(b), struck out "garbage that contains more than the minimum amount practicable of" after "buoyant garbage or".

1996—Subsec. (b)(1)(B). Pub. L. 104–227 inserted "or the Antarctic Protocol" after "MARPOL Protocol".

Subsec. (c)(1). Pub. L. 104–201, § 324(a)(1), substituted "Except as provided in paragraphs (2) and (3), not later than" for "Not later than".

Subsec. (c)(2) to (4). Pub. L. 104–201, § 324(a)(2), added pars. (2) and (3) and struck out former pars. (2) to (4) which required the Secretary of the Navy to submit to Congress a plan for compliance of Navy ships with the requirements set forth in par. (1) of this subsec. and provided for modification of the applicability of par. (1) as appropriate.

Subsec. (e)(4)(A). Pub. L. 104–201, § 324(d), amended subpar. (A) generally. Prior to amendment, subpar. (A) read as follows: "Beginning on October 1, 1994, and each year thereafter until October 1, 2000, the amount and nature of the discharges in special areas, not otherwise authorized under Annex V to the Convention, during the preceding year from ships referred to in subsection (b)(1)(A) of this section owned or operated by the Department of the Navy."

1993—Subsec. (b)(2)(A). Pub. L. 103–160, § 1003(a), substituted "as follows:" and cls. (i) to (iii) for "after 5 years after the effective date of this paragraph to a ship referred to in paragraph (1)(A)."

Subsecs. (c), (d). Pub. L. 103–160, § 1003(b), added subsec. (c) and redesignated former subsec. (c) as (d). Former subsec. (d) redesignated (g).

Subsecs. (e), (f). Pub. L. 103–160, § 1003(c), (d), added subsecs. (e) and (f).

Subsec. (g). Pub. L. 103–160, § 1003(b)(1), redesignated subsec. (d) as (g).

1987—Subsec. (a). Pub. L. 100–220, § 2102(a), amended subsec. (a) generally. Prior to amendment, subsec. (a) read as follows: "This chapter applies to—

"(1) a ship of United States registry or nationality, or one operated under the authority of the United States, wherever located;

"(2) a ship registered in or of the nationality of a country party to the MARPOL Protocol, or one operated under the authority of a country party to the MARPOL Protocol, while in the navigable waters of the United States; and

"(3) a ship registered in or of the nationality of a country not a party to the MARPOL Protocol, under subsection (c) of this section, while in the navigable waters of the United States."

Subsec. (b). Pub. L. 100–220, § 2102(b), amended subsec. (b) generally. Prior to amendment, subsec. (b) read as follows: "This chapter does not apply to—

"(1) a warship, naval auxiliary, or other ship owned or operated by the United States when engaged in noncommercial service; or

"(2) any other ship specifically excluded by the MARPOL Protocol."

Subsec. (c). Pub. L. 100–220, § 2102(c), amended subsec. (c) generally. Prior to amendment, subsec. (c) read as follows: "The Secretary shall prescribe regulations applicable to the ships of a country not a party to the MARPOL Protocol to ensure that their treatment is not more favorable than that accorded ships of parties to the MARPOL Protocol."

EFFECTIVE DATE OF 1987 AMENDMENT

Amendment by Pub. L. 100–220 effective Dec. 31, 1988, the date on which Annex V to the International Convention for the Prevention of Pollution from Ships, 1973, entered into force for the United States, see section 2002(a) of Pub. L. 100–220, set out as a note under section 1901 of this title.

EFFECTIVE DATE

Subsecs. (c) and (d) of this section effective Oct. 21, 1980, see section 14(b) of Pub. L. 96–478, set out as a note under section 1901 of this title.

INSTALLATION SCHEDULE FOR PLASTICS PROCESSOR EQUIPMENT ABOARD SHIPS; REQUEST FOR PROPOSALS FOR EQUIPMENT

Section 1003(e) of Pub. L. 103–160 provided that:

"(1) Not later than October 1, 1994, the Secretary of the Navy shall release a request for proposals for equipment (hereinafter in this subsection referred to as 'plastics processor') required for the long-term collection and storage of plastic aboard ships owned or operated by the Navy.

"(2) Not later than July 1, 1996, the Secretary shall install the first production unit of the plastics processor on board a ship owned or operated by the Navy.

"(3) Not later than March 1, 1997, the Secretary shall complete the installation of plastics processors on board not less than 25 percent of the ships owned or operated by the Navy that require plastics processors to comply with section 3 of the Act to Prevent Pollution from Ships [33 U.S.C. 1902], as amended by subsections (a), (b), and (c) of this section.

"(4) Not later than July 1, 1997, the Secretary shall complete the installation of plastics processors on board not less than 50 percent of the ships owned or operated by the Navy that require processors to comply with section 3 of such Act, as amended by subsections (a), (b), and (c) of this section.

"(5) Not later than July 1, 1998, the Secretary shall complete the installation of plastics processors on board not less than 75 percent of the ships owned or operated by the Navy that require processors to comply with section 3 of such Act, as amended by subsections (a), (b), and (c) of this section.

"(6) Not later than December 31, 1998, the Secretary shall complete the installation of plastics processors on board all ships owned or operated by the Navy that require processors to comply with section 3 of such Act, as amended by subsections (a), (b), and (c) of this section."

§ 1902a. Discharge of agricultural cargo residue

Notwithstanding any other provision of law, the discharge from a vessel of any agricultural cargo residue material in the form of hold washings shall be governed exclusively by the provisions of the Act to Prevent Pollution from Ships (33 U.S.C. 1901 et seq.) that implement Annex V to the International Convention for the Prevention of Pollution from Ships.

(Pub. L. 107–295, title II, § 204, Nov. 25, 2002, 116 Stat. 2094.)

REFERENCES IN TEXT

The Act to Prevent Pollution from Ships, referred to in text, is Pub. L. 96–478, Oct. 21, 1980, 94 Stat. 2297, as amended, which is classified principally to this chapter (§ 1901 et seq.). For complete classification of this Act to the Code, see Short Title note set out under section 1901 of this title and Tables.

CODIFICATION

Section was enacted as part of the Maritime Policy Improvement Act of 2002 and as part of the Maritime Transportation Security Act of 2002, and not as part of the Act to Prevent Pollution from Ships which comprises this chapter.

§ 1903. Administration and enforcement

(a) Duty of Secretary; Annexes of Convention applicable to seagoing vessels

Unless otherwise specified in this chapter, the Secretary shall administer and enforce the

MARPOL Protocol, Annex IV to the Antarctic Protocol, and this chapter. In the administration and enforcement of the MARPOL Protocol and this chapter, Annexes I and II of the Convention apply only to seagoing ships.

(b) Duty of the Administrator

In addition to other duties specified in this chapter, the Administrator and the Secretary, respectively, shall have the following duties and authorities:

(1) The Administrator shall, and no other person may, issue Engine International Air Pollution Prevention certificates in accordance with Annex VI and the International Maritime Organization's Technical Code on Control of Emissions of Nitrogen Oxides from Marine Diesel Engines, on behalf of the United States for a vessel of the United States as that term is defined in section 116 of title 46. The issuance of Engine International Air Pollution Prevention certificates shall be consistent with any applicable requirements of the Clean Air Act [42 U.S.C. 7401 et seq.] or regulations prescribed under that Act.

(2) The Administrator shall have authority to administer regulations 12, 13, 14, 15, 16, 17, 18, and 19 of Annex VI to the Convention.

(3) The Administrator shall, only as specified in section 1907(f) of this title, have authority to enforce Annex VI of the Convention.

(c) Regulations; refuse record books; waste management plans; notification of crew and passengers

(1) The Secretary shall prescribe any necessary or desired regulations to carry out the provisions of the MARPOL Protocol, Annex IV to the Antarctic Protocol, or this chapter.

(2) In addition to the authority the Secretary has to prescribe regulations under this chapter, the Administrator shall also prescribe any necessary or desired regulations to carry out the provisions of regulations 12, 13, 14, 15, 16, 17, 18, and 19 of Annex VI to the Convention.

(3) In prescribing any regulations under this section, the Secretary and the Administrator shall consult with each other, and with respect to regulation 19, with the Secretary of the Interior.

(4) The Secretary of the department in which the Coast Guard is operating shall—

(A) prescribe regulations which—

(i) require certain ships described in section 1902(a)(1) of this title to maintain refuse record books and shipboard management plans, and to display placards which notify the crew and passengers of the requirements of Annex V to the Convention and of Annex IV to the Antarctic Protocol; and

(ii) specify the ships described in section 1902(a)(1) of this title to which the regulations apply;

(B) seek an international agreement or international agreements which apply requirements equivalent to those described in subparagraph (A)(i) to all vessels subject to Annex V to the Convention; and

(C) within 2 years after the effective date of this paragraph, report to the Congress—

(i) regarding activities of the Secretary under subparagraph (B); and

(ii) if the Secretary has not obtained agreements pursuant to subparagraph (B) regarding the desirability of applying the requirements described in subparagraph (A)(i) to all vessels described in section 1902(a) of this title which call at United States ports.

(5) No standard issued by any person or Federal authority, with respect to emissions from tank vessels subject to regulation 15 of Annex VI to the Convention, shall be effective until 6 months after the required notification to the International Maritime Organization by the Secretary.

(d) Utilization of personnel, facilities, or equipment of other Federal departments and agencies

The Secretary may utilize by agreement, with or without reimbursement, personnel, facilities, or equipment of other Federal departments and agencies in administering the MARPOL Protocol, this chapter, or the regulations thereunder.

(Pub. L. 96–478, §4, Oct. 21, 1980, 94 Stat. 2298; Pub. L. 100–220, title II, §2107, Dec. 29, 1987, 101 Stat. 1464; Pub. L. 104–227, title II, §201(c), Oct. 2, 1996, 110 Stat. 3042; Pub. L. 110–280, §5, July 21, 2008, 122 Stat. 2613.)

REFERENCES IN TEXT

The Clean Air Act, referred to in subsec. (b)(1), is act July 14, 1955, ch. 360, 69 Stat. 322, which is classified generally to chapter 85 (§7401 et seq.) of Title 42, The Public Health and Welfare. For complete classification of this Act to the Code, see Short Title note set out under section 7401 of Title 42 and Tables.

The effective date of this paragraph, referred to in subsec. (c)(4)(C), is Dec. 31, 1988, the effective date of section 2107(b) of Pub. L. 100–220. See Effective Date of 1987 Amendment note below.

AMENDMENTS

2008—Subsec. (b). Pub. L. 110–280, §5(1), added subsec. (b). Former subsec. (b) redesignated (c).

Subsec. (c). Pub. L. 110–280 redesignated subsec. (b) as (c), added pars. (2), (3), and (5), and redesignated former par. (2) as (4). Former subsec. (c) redesignated (d).

Subsec. (d). Pub. L. 110–280, §5(1), redesignated subsec. (c) as (d).

1996—Subsec. (a). Pub. L. 104–227, §201(c)(1), inserted ", Annex IV to the Antarctic Protocol," after "the MARPOL Protocol" in first sentence.

Subsec. (b)(1). Pub. L. 104–227, §201(c)(2), inserted ", Annex IV to the Antarctic Protocol," after "the MARPOL Protocol".

Subsec. (b)(2)(A). Pub. L. 104–227, §201(c)(3), (4), struck out "within 1 year after the effective date of this paragraph," before "prescribe" in introductory provisions and inserted "and of Annex IV to the Antarctic Protocol" after "the Convention" in cl. (i).

1987—Subsec. (a). Pub. L. 100–220, §2107(a), amended subsec. (a) generally. Prior to amendment, subsec. (a) read as follows: "Unless otherwise specified herein, the Secretary shall administer and enforce the MARPOL Protocol and this chapter. In the administration and enforcement of the MARPOL Protocol and this chapter, Annexes I and II of the MARPOL Protocol shall be applicable only to seagoing ships."

Subsec. (b). Pub. L. 100–220, §2107(b), designated existing provisions as par. (1) and added par. (2).

EFFECTIVE DATE OF 1987 AMENDMENT

Amendment by Pub. L. 100–220 effective Dec. 31, 1988, the date on which Annex V to the International Convention for the Prevention of Pollution from Ships, 1973, entered into force for the United States, see section 2002(a) of Pub. L. 100–220, set out as a note under section 1901 of this title.

EFFECTIVE DATE

Subsec. (b) of this section effective Oct. 21, 1980, see section 14(b) of Pub. L. 96–478, set out as a note under section 1901 of this title.

TRANSFER OF FUNCTIONS

For transfer of authorities, functions, personnel, and assets of the Coast Guard, including the authorities and functions of the Secretary of Transportation relating thereto, to the Department of Homeland Security, and for treatment of related references, see sections 468(b), 551(d), 552(d), and 557 of Title 6, Domestic Security, and the Department of Homeland Security Reorganization Plan of November 25, 2002, as modified, set out as a note under section 542 of Title 6.

§ 1904. Certificates

(a) Issuance by authorized designees; restriction on issuance

Except as provided in section 1903(b)(1) of this title, the Secretary shall designate those persons authorized to issue on behalf of the United States the certificates required by the MARPOL Protocol. A certificate required by the MARPOL Protocol shall not be issued to a ship which is registered in or of the nationality of a country which is not a party to the MARPOL Protocol.

(b) Validity of foreign certificates

A certificate issued by a country which is a party to the MARPOL Protocol has the same validity as a certificate issued by the Secretary or the Administrator under the authority of this chapter.

(c) Location onboard vessel; inspection of vessels subject to jurisdiction of the United States

A ship required by the MARPOL Protocol to have a certificate—

(1) shall carry a valid certificate onboard in the manner prescribed by the authority issuing the certificate; and

(2) is subject to inspection while in a port or terminal under the jurisdiction of the United States.

(d) Onboard inspections; other Federal inspection authority unaffected

An inspection conducted under subsection (c)(2) of this section is limited to verifying whether or not a valid certificate is onboard, unless clear grounds exist which reasonably indicate that the condition of the ship or its equipment does not substantially agree with the particulars of its certificate. This section shall not limit the authority of any official or employee of the United States under any other treaty, law, or regulation to board and inspect a ship or its equipment.

(e) Detention orders; duration of detention; shipyard option

In addition to the penalties prescribed in section 1908 of this title, a ship required by the MARPOL Protocol to have a certificate—

(1) which does not have a valid certificate onboard; or

(2) whose condition or whose equipment's condition does not substantially agree with the particulars of the certificate onboard;

shall be detained by order of the Secretary at the port or terminal where the violation is discovered until, in the opinion of the Secretary, the ship can proceed to sea without presenting an unreasonable threat of harm to the marine environment or the public health and welfare. The detention order may authorize the ship to proceed to the nearest appropriate available shipyard rather than remaining at the place where the violation was discovered.

(f) Ship clearance or permits; refusal or revocation

If a ship is under a detention order under this section, the Secretary of the Treasury, upon the request of the Secretary, may refuse or revoke—

(1) the clearance required by section 60105 of title 46; or

(2) a permit to proceed under section 4367 of the Revised Statutes of the United States (46 U.S.C. 313)[1] or section 1443[2] of title 19.

(g) Review of detention orders; petition; determination by Secretary

A person whose ship is subject to a detention order under this section may petition the Secretary, in the manner prescribed by regulation, to review the detention order. Upon receipt of a petition under this subsection, the Secretary shall affirm, modify, or withdraw the detention order within the time prescribed by regulation.

(h) Compensation for loss or damage

A ship unreasonably detained or delayed by the Secretary acting under the authority of this chapter is entitled to compensation for any loss or damage suffered thereby.

(Pub. L. 96–478, §5, Oct. 21, 1980, 94 Stat. 2298; Pub. L. 110–280, §6, July 21, 2008, 122 Stat. 2614.)

REFERENCES IN TEXT

Section 4367 of the Revised Statutes of the United States (46 U.S.C. 313), referred to in subsec. (f)(2), was classified to section 313 of the former Appendix to Title 46, Shipping, prior to repeal by Pub. L. 103–182, title VI, §690(a)(21), Dec. 8, 1993, 107 Stat. 2223.

CODIFICATION

In subsec. (f)(1), "section 60105 of title 46" substituted for "section 4197 of the Revised Statutes of the United States, as amended (46 U.S.C. 91)" on authority of Pub. L. 109–304, §18(c), Oct. 6, 2006, 120 Stat. 1709, which Act enacted section 60105 of Title 46, Shipping.

Section 1443 of title 19, referred to in subsec. (f)(2), was in the original section 442 of the Tariff Act of 1930, as amended (19 U.S.C. 1443). Although section 442 of the Tariff Act of 1930, June 17, 1930, ch. 497, title IV, 46 Stat. 713, is classified to section 1442 of Title 19, Customs Duties, the reference was translated as meaning section 443 of the Tariff Act of 1930, which was classified to section 1443 of title 19 prior to repeal by Pub. L. 103–182, title VI, §690(b)(6), Dec. 8, 1993, 107 Stat. 2223.

AMENDMENTS

2008—Subsec. (a). Pub. L. 110–280, §6(1), substituted "Except as provided in section 1903(b)(1) of this title, the Secretary" for "The Secretary".

Subsec. (b). Pub. L. 110–280, §6(2), substituted "Secretary or the Administrator under the authority of this chapter." for "Secretary under the authority of the MARPOL Protocol."

---

[1] See References in Text note below.

[2] See Codification note below.

Subsec. (e). Pub. L. 110–280, § 6(3), substituted "environment or the public health and welfare." for "environment." in concluding provisions.

EFFECTIVE DATE

Subsec. (a) of this section effective Oct. 21, 1980, see section 14(b) of Pub. L. 96–478, set out as a note under section 1901 of this title.

§ 1905. Pollution reception facilities

(a) Adequacy; criteria

(1) The Secretary, after consultation with the Administrator of the Environmental Protection Agency, shall establish regulations setting criteria for determining the adequacy of a port's or terminal's reception facilities for mixtures containing oil or noxious liquid substances and shall establish procedures whereby a person in charge of a port or terminal may request the Secretary to certify that the port's or terminal's facilities for receiving the residues and mixtures containing oil or noxious liquid substance from seagoing ships are adequate.

(2) The Secretary, after consulting with appropriate Federal agencies, shall establish regulations setting criteria for determining the adequacy of reception facilities for garbage at a port or terminal, and stating such additional measures and requirements as are appropriate to ensure such adequacy. Persons in charge of ports and terminals shall provide reception facilities, or ensure that such facilities are available, for receiving garbage in accordance with those regulations.

(3) The Secretary and the Administrator, after consulting with appropriate Federal agencies, shall jointly prescribe regulations setting criteria for determining the adequacy of reception facilities for receiving ozone depleting substances, equipment containing such substances, and exhaust gas cleaning residues at a port or terminal, and stating any additional measures and requirements as are appropriate to ensure such adequacy. Persons in charge of ports and terminals shall provide reception facilities, or ensure that reception facilities are available, in accordance with those regulations. The Secretary and the Administrator may jointly prescribe regulations to certify, and may issue certificates to the effect, that a port's or terminal's facilities for receiving ozone depleting substances, equipment containing such substances, and exhaust gas cleaning residues from ships are adequate.

(b) Traffic considerations

In determining the adequacy of reception facilities required by the MARPOL Protocol or the Antarctic Protocol at a port or terminal, and in establishing regulations under subsection (a) of this section, the Secretary or the Administrator may consider, among other things, the number and types of ships or seagoing ships using the port or terminal, including their principal trades.

(c) Certificate; issuance; validity; inspection; review of suspension or revocation by Secretary

(1) If reception facilities of a port or terminal meet the requirements of Annex I and Annex II to the Convention and the regulations prescribed under subsection (a)(1) of this section, the Secretary shall, after consultation with the Administrator of the Environmental Protection Agency, issue a certificate to that effect to the applicant.

(2)(A) Subject to subparagraph (B), if reception facilities of a port or terminal meet the requirements of Annex V to the Convention and the regulations prescribed under subsection (a)(2) of this section, the Secretary may, after consultation with appropriate Federal agencies, issue a certificate to that effect to the person in charge of the port or terminal.

(B) The Secretary may not issue a certificate attesting to the adequacy of reception facilities under this paragraph unless, prior to the issuance of the certificate, the Secretary conducts an inspection of the reception facilities of the port or terminal that is the subject of the certificate.

(C) The Secretary may, with respect to certificates issued under this paragraph prior to October 19, 1996, prescribe by regulation differing periods of validity for such certificates.

(3) A certificate issued under this subsection—

(A) is valid for the 5-year period beginning on the date of issuance of the certificate, except that if—

(i) the charge for operation of the port or terminal is transferred to a person or entity other than the person or entity that is the operator on the date of issuance of the certificate—

(I) the certificate shall expire on the date that is 30 days after the date of the transfer; and

(II) the new operator shall be required to submit an application for a certificate before a certificate may be issued for the port or terminal; or

(ii) the certificate is suspended or revoked by the Secretary, the certificate shall cease to be valid; and

(B) shall be available for inspection upon the request of the master, other person in charge, or agent of a ship using or intending to use the port or terminal.

(4) The suspension or revocation of a certificate issued under this subsection may be appealed to the Secretary and acted on by the Secretary in the manner prescribed by regulation.

(d) Publication of list of certificated ports or terminals

(1) The Secretary shall maintain a list of ports or terminals with respect to which a certificate issued under this section—

(A) is in effect; or

(B) has been revoked or suspended.

(2) The Secretary shall make the list referred to in paragraph (1) available to the general public.

(e) Entry; denial

(1) Except in the case of force majeure, the Secretary shall deny entry to a seagoing ship required by the Convention or the Antarctic Protocol to retain onboard while at sea, residues and mixtures containing oil or noxious liquid substances, if—

(A) the port or terminal is one required by Annexes I and II of the Convention or Article 9 of Annex IV to the Antarctic Protocol or regulations hereunder to have adequate reception facilities; and

(B) the port or terminal does not hold a valid certificate issued by the Secretary under this section.

(2) The Secretary may deny the entry of a ship to a port or terminal required by the MARPOL Protocol, this chapter, or regulations prescribed under this section relating to the provision of adequate reception facilities for garbage, ozone depleting substances, equipment containing those substances, or exhaust gas cleaning residues, if the port or terminal is not in compliance with the MARPOL Protocol, this chapter, or those regulations.

(f) Surveys

(1) The Secretary and the Administrator are authorized to conduct surveys of existing reception facilities in the United States to determine measures needed to comply with the MARPOL Protocol or the Antarctic Protocol.

(2) Not later than 18 months after October 19, 1996, the Secretary shall promulgate regulations that require the operator of each port or terminal that is subject to any requirement of the MARPOL Protocol relating to reception facilities to post a placard in a location that can easily be seen by port and terminal users. The placard shall state, at a minimum, that a user of a reception facility of the port or terminal should report to the Secretary any inadequacy of the reception facility.

(Pub. L. 96–478, §6, Oct. 21, 1980, 94 Stat. 2299; Pub. L. 100–220, title II, §2103, Dec. 29, 1987, 101 Stat. 1461; Pub. L. 101–225, title II, §201(1), Dec. 12, 1989, 103 Stat. 1910; Pub. L. 104–227, title II, §201(d), Oct. 2, 1996, 110 Stat. 3042; Pub. L. 104–324, title VIII, §801, Oct. 19, 1996, 110 Stat. 3943; Pub. L. 110–280, §7, July 21, 2008, 122 Stat. 2614.)

AMENDMENTS

2008—Subsec. (a)(3). Pub. L. 110–280, §7(1), added par. (3).

Subsec. (b). Pub. L. 110–280, §7(2), inserted "or the Administrator" after "Secretary".

Subsec. (e)(2). Pub. L. 110–280, §7(3), added par. (2) and struck out former par. (2). Prior to amendment, text read as follows: "The Secretary may deny the entry of a ship to a port or terminal required by regulations issued under this section to provide adequate reception facilities for garbage if the port or terminal is not in compliance with those regulations."

Subsec. (f)(1). Pub. L. 110–280, §7(4), substituted "Secretary and the Administrator are" for "Secretary is".

Subsec. (f)(2). Pub. L. 110–280, §7(5), struck out subpar. (A) designation before "Not later".

1996—Subsec. (b). Pub. L. 104–227, §201(d)(1), inserted "or the Antarctic Protocol" after "the MARPOL Protocol".

Subsec. (c)(2). Pub. L. 104–324, §801(a)(1), (2), designated existing provisions as subpar. (A), substituted "Subject to subparagraph (B), if" for "If", and added subpars. (B) and (C).

Subsec. (c)(3)(A). Pub. L. 104–324, §801(a)(3), added subpar. (A) and struck out former subpar. (A) which read as follows: "is valid until suspended or revoked by the Secretary for cause or because of changed conditions; and".

Subsec. (d). Pub. L. 104–324, §801(a)(4), added subsec. (d) and struck out former subsec. (d) which read as follows: "The Secretary shall periodically cause to be published in the Federal Register a list of the ports or terminals holding a valid certificate issued under this section."

Subsec. (e)(1). Pub. L. 104–227, §201(d)(2), (3), inserted "or the Antarctic Protocol" after "the Convention" in introductory provisions and inserted "or Article 9 of Annex IV to the Antarctic Protocol" after "the Convention" in subpar. (A).

Subsec. (f). Pub. L. 104–324, §801(b), designated existing provisions as par. (1) and added par. (2)(A).

Pub. L. 104–227, §201(d)(4), inserted "or the Antarctic Protocol" after "the MARPOL Protocol".

1989—Subsec. (c)(1). Pub. L. 101–225 substituted "Annex I and Annex II" for "Annex V".

1987—Subsec. (a). Pub. L. 100–220, §2103(a), designated existing provisions as par. (1), substituted "a port's or terminal's reception facilities for mixtures containing oil or noxious liquid substances" for "reception facilities of a port or terminal", and added par. (2).

Subsec. (b). Pub. L. 100–220, §2103(b), inserted "and in establishing regulations under subsection (a) of this section," and "ships or".

Subsec. (c). Pub. L. 100–220, §2103(c), amended subsec. (c) generally. Prior to amendment, subsec. (c) read as follows: "If, upon inspection, reception facilities of a port or terminal are adequate to meet the requirements of the MARPOL Protocol and the regulations established hereunder, the Secretary shall, after consultation with the Administrator of the Environmental Protection Agency, issue a certificate to that effect to the applicant. A certificate issued under this subsection—

"(1) is valid until suspended or revoked by the Secretary for cause or because of changed conditions; and

"(2) shall be available for inspection upon the request of the master, other person in charge, or agent of a seagoing ship using or intending to use the port or terminal.

The suspension or revocation of a certificate issued under this subsection may be appealed to the Secretary and acted on by him in the manner prescribed by regulation."

Subsec. (e). Pub. L. 100–220, §2103(d), designated existing provisions as par. (1), redesignated former pars. (1) and (2) as subpars. (A) and (B), respectively, in subpar. (A), substituted "Annexes I and II of the Convention" for "the MARPOL Protocol", and added par. (2).

EFFECTIVE DATE OF 1987 AMENDMENT

Amendment by Pub. L. 100–220 effective Dec. 31, 1988, the date on which Annex V to the International Convention for the Prevention of Pollution from Ships, 1973, entered into force for the United States, see section 2002(a) of Pub. L. 100–220, set out as a note under section 1901 of this title.

EFFECTIVE DATE

Subsecs. (a), (c), and (f) of this section effective Oct. 21, 1980, see section 14(b) of Pub. L. 96–478, set out as a note under section 1901 of this title.

§1906. Incidents involving ships

(a) Requirement to report incident

The master, person in charge, owner, charterer, manager, or operator of a ship involved in an incident shall report the incident in the manner prescribed by Article 8 of the Convention in accordance with regulations promulgated by the Secretary for that purpose.

(b) Requirement to report discharge, probable discharge, or presence of oil

The master or person in charge of—

(1) a ship of United States registry or nationality, or operated under the authority of the United States, wherever located;

(2) another ship while in the navigable waters of the United States; or

(3) a sea port or oil handling facility subject to the jurisdiction of the United States,

shall report a discharge, probable discharge, or presence of oil in the manner prescribed by Article 4 of the International Convention on Oil Pollution Preparedness, Response and Cooperation, 1990 (adopted at London, November 30, 1990), in accordance with regulations promulgated by the Secretary for that purpose.

(Pub. L. 96–478, §7, Oct. 21, 1980, 94 Stat. 2300; Pub. L. 102–241, §39, Dec. 19, 1991, 105 Stat. 2225.)

AMENDMENTS

1991—Pub. L. 102–241 amended section generally. Prior to amendment, section read as follows:

"(a) As soon as he has knowledge of an incident, the master or other person in charge of a ship shall report it to the Secretary in the manner prescribed by Article 8 of the Convention.

"(b) Upon receipt of the report of an incident involving a ship, other than one of United States registry or nationality or one operated under the authority of the United States, the Secretary shall take the action required by Article 8 of the Convention."

§1907. Violations

(a) General prohibition; cooperation and enforcement; detection and monitoring measures; reports; evidence

It is unlawful to act in violation of the MARPOL Protocol, Annex IV to the Antarctic Protocol, this chapter, or the regulations issued thereunder. The Secretary shall cooperate with other parties to the MARPOL Protocol or to the Antarctic Protocol in the detection of violations and in enforcement of the MARPOL Protocol and Annex IV to the Antarctic Protocol. The Secretary shall use all appropriate and practical measures of detection and environmental monitoring, and shall establish adequate procedures for reporting violations and accumulating evidence.

(b) Investigations; subpenas: issuance by Secretary, enforcement; action by Secretary; information to party

Upon receipt of evidence that a violation has occurred, the Secretary shall cause the matter to be investigated. In any investigation under this section the Secretary may issue subpenas to require the attendance of any witness and the production of documents and other evidence. In case of refusal to obey a subpena issued to any person, the Secretary may request the Attorney General to invoke the aid of the appropriate district court of the United States to compel compliance. Upon completion of the investigation, the Secretary shall take the action required by the MARPOL Protocol or the Antarctic Protocol and whatever further action he considers appropriate under the circumstances. If the initial evidence was provided by a party to the MARPOL Protocol or the Antarctic Protocol, the Secretary, acting through the Secretary of State, shall inform that party of the action taken or proposed.

(c) Ship inspections; reports to Secretary; additional action

(1) This subsection applies to inspections relating to possible violations of Annex I or Annex II to the Convention, of Article 3 or Article 4 of Annex IV to the Antarctic Protocol, or of this chapter by any seagoing ship referred to in section 1902(a)(2) of this title.

(2) While at a port or terminal subject to the jurisdiction of the United States, a ship to which the MARPOL Protocol or the Antarctic Protocol applies may be inspected by the Secretary—

(A) to verify whether or not the ship has discharged a harmful substance in violation of the MARPOL Protocol, Annex IV to the Antarctic Protocol, or this chapter; or

(B) to comply with a request from a party to the MARPOL Protocol or the Antarctic Protocol for an investigation as to whether the ship may have discharged a harmful substance anywhere in violation of the MARPOL Protocol or Annex IV to the Antarctic Protocol. An investigation may be undertaken under this clause only when the requesting party has furnished sufficient evidence to allow the Secretary reasonably to believe that a discharge has occurred.

If an inspection under this subsection indicates that a violation has occurred, the investigating officer shall forward a report to the Secretary for appropriate action. The Secretary shall undertake to notify the master of the ship concerned and, acting in coordination with the Secretary of State, shall take any additional action required by Article 6 of the Convention.

(d) Garbage disposal inspections; covered ships; enforcement actions

(1) The Secretary may inspect a ship referred to in section 1902(a)(3) of this title to verify whether the ship has disposed of garbage in violation of Annex V to the Convention, Article 5 of Annex IV to the Antarctic Protocol, or this chapter.

(2) If an inspection under this subsection indicates that a violation has occurred, the Secretary may undertake enforcement action under section 1908 of this title.

(e) Harmful substance or garbage disposal inspections; covered ships; enforcement actions

(1) The Secretary may inspect at any time a ship of United States registry or nationality or operating under the authority of the United States to which the MARPOL Protocol or the Antarctic Protocol applies to verify whether the ship has discharged a harmful substance or disposed of garbage in violation of those Protocols or this chapter.

(2) If an inspection under this subsection indicates that a violation of the MARPOL Protocol, of Annex IV to the Antarctic Protocol, or of this chapter has occurred the Secretary may undertake enforcement action under section 1908 of this title.

(f) Inspections; enforcement

(1) The Secretary may inspect a ship to which this chapter applies as provided under section 1902(a)(5) of this title, to verify whether the ship is in compliance with Annex VI to the Convention and this chapter.

(2) If an inspection under this subsection or any other information indicates that a violation

has occurred, the Secretary, or the Administrator in a matter referred by the Secretary, may undertake enforcement action under this section.

(3) Notwithstanding subsection (b) and paragraph (2) of this subsection, the Administrator shall have all of the authorities of the Secretary, as specified in subsection (b) of this section, for the purposes of enforcing regulations 17 and 18 of Annex VI to the Convention to the extent that shoreside violations are the subject of the action and in any other matter referred to the Administrator by the Secretary.

(Pub. L. 96–478, § 8, Oct. 21, 1980, 94 Stat. 2300; Pub. L. 100–220, title II, § 2104, Dec. 29, 1987, 101 Stat. 1462; Pub. L. 101–225, title II, § 201(2), (3), Dec. 12, 1989, 103 Stat. 1910; Pub. L. 104–227, title II, § 201(e), Oct. 2, 1996, 110 Stat. 3043; Pub. L. 110–280, § 8, July 21, 2008, 122 Stat. 2614.)

AMENDMENTS

2008—Subsec. (f). Pub. L. 110–280 amended subsec. (f) generally. Prior to amendment, text read as follows: "Remedies and requirements of this chapter supplement and neither amend nor repeal any other provisions of law, except as expressly provided in this chapter. Nothing in this chapter shall limit, deny, amend, modify, or repeal any other remedy available to the United States or any other person, except as expressly provided in this chapter."

1996—Subsec. (a). Pub. L. 104–227, § 201(e)(1), (2), inserted "Annex IV to the Antarctic Protocol," after "violation of the MARPOL Protocol,", "or to the Antarctic Protocol" after "to the MARPOL Protocol", and "and Annex IV to the Antarctic Protocol" after "enforcement of the MARPOL Protocol".

Subsec. (b). Pub. L. 104–227, § 201(e)(3), inserted "or the Antarctic Protocol" after "MARPOL Protocol" in two places.

Subsec. (c)(1). Pub. L. 104–227, § 201(e)(4), inserted ", of Article 3 or Article 4 of Annex IV to the Antarctic Protocol," after "to the Convention".

Subsec. (c)(2). Pub. L. 104–227, § 201(e)(5), (6), inserted "or the Antarctic Protocol" after "which the MARPOL Protocol" in introductory provisions, ", Annex IV to the Antarctic Protocol," after "MARPOL Protocol" in subpar. (A), and "or the Antarctic Protocol" after "to the MARPOL Protocol" and "or Annex IV to the Antarctic Protocol" after "of the MARPOL Protocol" in subpar. (B).

Subsec. (d)(1). Pub. L. 104–227, § 201(e)(8), inserted ", Article 5 of Annex IV to the Antarctic Protocol," after "Convention".

Subsec. (e)(1). Pub. L. 104–227, § 201(e)(9), inserted "or the Antarctic Protocol" after "MARPOL Protocol" and substituted "those Protocols" for "that Protocol".

Subsec. (e)(2). Pub. L. 104–227, § 201(e)(10), inserted ", of Annex IV to the Antarctic Protocol," after "MARPOL Protocol".

1989—Subsecs. (c)(1), (e)(2). Pub. L. 101–225 inserted "or of this chapter".

1987—Subsec. (c). Pub. L. 100–220, § 2104(a), added par. (1), designated existing provisions as par. (2), redesignated former pars. (1) and (2) as subpars. (A) and (B), respectively, and in closing provisions of par. (2) substituted "The" for "If a report made under this subsection involves a ship, other than one of United States registry or nationality or one operated under the authority of the United States, the".

Subsecs. (d) to (f). Pub. L. 100–220, § 2104(b), added subsecs. (d) and (e) and redesignated former subsec. (d) as (f).

EFFECTIVE DATE OF 1987 AMENDMENT

Amendment by Pub. L. 100–220 effective Dec. 31, 1988, the date on which Annex V to the International Convention for the Prevention of Pollution from Ships, 1973, entered into force for the United States, see section 2002(a) of Pub. L. 100–220, set out as a note under section 1901 of this title.

§ 1908. Penalties for violations

(a) Criminal penalties; payment for information leading to conviction

A person who knowingly violates the MARPOL Protocol, Annex IV to the Antarctic Protocol, this chapter, or the regulations issued thereunder commits a class D felony. In the discretion of the Court, an amount equal to not more than ½ of such fine may be paid to the person giving information leading to conviction.

(b) Civil penalties; separate violations; assessment notice; considerations affecting amount; payment for information leading to assessment of penalty

A person who is found by the Secretary, or the Administrator as provided for in this chapter, after notice and an opportunity for a hearing, to have—

(1) violated the MARPOL Protocol, Annex IV to the Antarctic Protocol, this chapter, or the regulations issued thereunder shall be liable to the United States for a civil penalty, not to exceed $25,000 for each violation; or

(2) made a false, fictitious, or fraudulent statement or representation in any matter in which a statement or representation is required to be made to the Secretary, or the Administrator as provided for in this chapter, under the MARPOL Protocol, Annex IV to the Antarctic Protocol, this chapter, or the regulations thereunder, shall be liable to the United States for a civil penalty, not to exceed $5,000 for each statement or representation.

Each day of a continuing violation shall constitute a separate violation. The amount of the civil penalty shall be assessed by the Secretary, or the Administrator as provided for in this chapter or his designee, by written notice. In determining the amount of the penalty, the Secretary, or the Administrator as provided for in this chapter, shall take into account the nature, circumstances, extent, and gravity of the prohibited acts committed and, with respect to the violator, the degree of culpability, any history of prior offenses, ability to pay, and other matters as justice may require. An amount equal to not more than ½ of such penalties may be paid by the Secretary, or the Administrator as provided for in this chapter, to the person giving information leading to the assessment of such penalties.

(c) Abatement of civil penalties; collection by Attorney General

The Secretary, or the Administrator as provided for in this chapter, may compromise, modify, or remit, with or without conditions, any civil penalty which is subject to assessment or which has been assessed under this section. If any person fails to pay an assessment of a civil penalty after it has become final, the Secretary, or the Administrator as provided for in this chapter, may refer the matter to the Attorney General of the United States for collection in any appropriate district court of the United States.

(d) Liability in rem; district court jurisdiction

A ship operated in violation of the MARPOL Protocol, Annex IV to the Antarctic Protocol, this chapter, or the regulations thereunder is liable in rem for any fine imposed under subsection (a) of this section or civil penalty assessed pursuant to subsection (b) of this section, and may be proceeded against in the United States district court of any district in which the ship may be found.

(e) Ship clearance or permits; refusal or revocation; bond or other surety

If any ship subject to the MARPOL Protocol, Annex IV to the Antarctic Protocol, or this chapter, its owner, operator, or person in charge is liable for a fine or civil penalty under this section, or if reasonable cause exists to believe that the ship, its owner, operator, or person in charge may be subject to a fine or civil penalty under this section, the Secretary of the Treasury, upon the request of the Secretary, shall refuse or revoke the clearance required by section 60105 of title 46. Clearance may be granted upon the filing of a bond or other surety satisfactory to the Secretary.

(f) Referrals for appropriate action by foreign country

Notwithstanding subsection (a), (b), or (d) of this section, if the violation is by a ship registered in or of the nationality of a country party to the MARPOL Protocol or the Antarctic Protocol, or one operated under the authority of a country party to the MARPOL Protocol or the Antarctic Protocol, the Secretary, or the Administrator as provided for in this chapter acting in coordination with the Secretary of State, may refer the matter to the government of the country of the ship's registry or nationality, or under whose authority the ship is operating for appropriate action, rather than taking the actions required or authorized by this section.

(Pub. L. 96–478, §9, Oct. 21, 1980, 94 Stat. 2301; Pub. L. 100–220, title II, §2105, Dec. 29, 1987, 101 Stat. 1463; Pub. L. 101–380, title IV, §4302(n), Aug. 18, 1990, 104 Stat. 539; Pub. L. 103–182, title VI, §688, Dec. 8, 1993, 107 Stat. 2222; Pub. L. 104–227, title II, §201(f), Oct. 2, 1996, 110 Stat. 3043; Pub. L. 110–280, §10, July 21, 2008, 122 Stat. 2615.)

CODIFICATION

In subsec. (e), "section 60105 of title 46" substituted for "section 4197 of the Revised Statutes of the United States (46 U.S.C. App. 91)" on authority of Pub. L. 109–304, §18(c), Oct. 6, 2006, 120 Stat. 1709, which Act enacted section 60105 of Title 46, Shipping.

AMENDMENTS

2008—Pub. L. 110–280, §10(1), substituted "MARPOL Protocol," for "MARPOL Protocol,," wherever appearing in subsecs. (a), (b), and (d).

Subsec. (b). Pub. L. 110–280, §10(2)(C), in concluding provisions, inserted "or the Administrator as provided for in this chapter" after "Secretary," and ", or the Administrator as provided for in this chapter," after "Secretary" in two places.

Pub. L. 110–280, §10(2)(A), in introductory provisions, inserted "or the Administrator as provided for in this chapter," after "Secretary,".

Subsec. (b)(2). Pub. L. 110–280, §10(2)(B), inserted ", or the Administrator as provided for in this chapter," after "Secretary".

Subsec. (c). Pub. L. 110–280, §10(3), inserted ", or the Administrator as provided for in this chapter," after "Secretary" in two places.

Subsec. (f). Pub. L. 110–280, §10(4), inserted "or the Administrator as provided for in this chapter" after "Secretary,".

1996—Subsec. (a). Pub. L. 104–227, §201(f)(1), inserted ", Annex IV to the Antarctic Protocol," after "MARPOL Protocol,".

Subsec. (b). Pub. L. 104–227, §201(f)(2), (3), inserted ", Annex IV to the Antarctic Protocol," after "MARPOL Protocol," in pars. (1) and (2).

Subsec. (d). Pub. L. 104–227, §201(f)(4), inserted ", Annex IV to the Antarctic Protocol," after "MARPOL Protocol,".

Subsec. (e). Pub. L. 104–227, §201(f)(5), inserted ", Annex IV to the Antarctic Protocol," after "MARPOL Protocol".

Subsec. (f). Pub. L. 104–227, §201(f)(6), inserted "or the Antarctic Protocol" after "MARPOL Protocol" in two places.

1993—Subsec. (e). Pub. L. 103–182 substituted "shall refuse or revoke the clearance required by section 91 of title 46, Appendix. Clearance may be granted upon the filing of a bond or other surety satisfactory to the Secretary." for "shall refuse or revoke—

"(1) the clearance required by section 91 of title 46, Appendix; or

"(2) a permit to proceed under section 313 of title 46, Appendix, or section 1443 of title 19.

Clearance or a permit to proceed may be granted upon the filing of a bond or other surety satisfactory to the Secretary."

1990—Subsec. (a). Pub. L. 101–380 substituted "commits a class D felony" for "shall, for each violation, be fined not more than $50,000 or be imprisoned for not more than 5 years, or both".

1987—Subsec. (a). Pub. L. 100–220, §2105(a)(1), inserted at end "In the discretion of the Court, an amount equal to not more than ½ of such fine may be paid to the person giving information leading to conviction."

Subsec. (b). Pub. L. 100–220, §2105(a)(2), inserted at end "An amount equal to not more than ½ of such penalties may be paid by the Secretary to the person giving information leading to the assessment of such penalties."

Subsec. (f). Pub. L. 100–220, §2105(b), substituted "to the government of the country of the ship's registry or nationality, or under whose authority the ship is operating" for "to that country".

EFFECTIVE DATE OF 1990 AMENDMENT

Amendment by Pub. L. 101–380 applicable to incidents occurring after Aug. 18, 1990, see section 1020 of Pub. L. 101–380, set out as an Effective Date note under section 2701 of this title.

EFFECTIVE DATE OF 1987 AMENDMENT

Amendment by Pub. L. 100–220 effective Dec. 31, 1988, the date on which Annex V to the International Convention for the Prevention of Pollution from Ships, 1973, entered into force for the United States, see section 2002(a) of Pub. L. 100–220, set out as a note under section 1901 of this title.

§1909. MARPOL Protocol; proposed amendments

(a) Acceptance of certain amendments by the President

A proposed amendment to the MARPOL Protocol received by the United States from the Secretary-General of the International Maritime Organization pursuant to Article VI of the MARPOL Protocol, may be accepted on behalf of the United States by the President following the advice and consent of the Senate, except as provided for in subsection (b) of this section.

(b) Action on certain amendments by the Secretary of State

A proposed amendment to Annex I, II, V, or VI to the Convention, appendices to those Annexes, or Protocol I of the Convention received by the United States from the Secretary-General of the International Maritime Organization pursuant to Article VI of the MARPOL Protocol, may be the subject of appropriate action on behalf of the United States by the Secretary of State following consultation with the Secretary, or the Administrator as provided for in this chapter, who shall inform the Secretary of State as to what action he considers appropriate at least 30 days prior to the expiration of the period specified in Article VI of the MARPOL Protocol during which objection may be made to any amendment received.

(c) Declaration of nonacceptance by the Secretary of State

Following consultation with the Secretary, the Secretary of State may make a declaration that the United States does not accept an amendment proposed pursuant to Article VI of the MARPOL Protocol.

(Pub. L. 96–478, § 10, Oct. 21, 1980, 94 Stat. 2302; Pub. L. 100–220, title II, § 2106, Dec. 29, 1987, 101 Stat. 1463; Pub. L. 110–280, § 9, July 21, 2008, 122 Stat. 2615.)

AMENDMENTS

2008—Subsec. (b). Pub. L. 110–280 substituted "Annex I, II, V, or VI" for "Annex I, II, or V" and inserted "or the Administrator as provided for in this chapter," after "Secretary,".

1987—Subsec. (a). Pub. L. 100–220, § 2106(1), substituted "International Maritime Organization" for "Inter-Governmental Maritime Consultative Organization".

Subsec. (b). Pub. L. 100–220, § 2106(2), substituted "Annex I, II, or V to the Convention, appendices to those Annexes, or Protocol I of the Convention" for "Annex I or II, appendices to the Annexes, or Protocol I of the MARPOL Protocol," and "International Maritime Organization" for "Inter-Governmental Maritime Consultative Organization".

EFFECTIVE DATE OF 1987 AMENDMENT

Amendment by Pub. L. 100–220 effective Dec. 31, 1988, the date on which Annex V to the International Convention for the Prevention of Pollution from Ships, 1973, entered into force for the United States, see section 2002(a) of Pub. L. 100–220, set out as a note under section 1901 of this title.

§ 1910. Legal actions

(a) Persons with adversely affected interests as plaintiffs; defendants

Except as provided in subsection (b) of this section, any person having an interest which is, or can be, adversely affected, may bring an action on his own behalf—

(1) against any person alleged to be in violation of the provisions of this chapter, or regulations issued hereunder;

(2) against the Secretary where there is alleged a failure of the Secretary to perform any act or duty under this chapter which is not discretionary with the Secretary;

(3) against the Administrator where there is alleged a failure of the Administrator to perform any act or duty under this chapter which is not discretionary; or

(4) against the Secretary of the Treasury where there is alleged a failure of the Secretary of the Treasury to take action under section 1908(e) of this title.

(b) Commencement conditions

No action may be commenced under subsection (a) of this section—

(1) prior to 60 days after the plaintiff has given notice, in writing and under oath, to the alleged violator, the Secretary concerned or the Administrator, and the Attorney General; or

(2) if the Secretary or the Administrator has commenced enforcement or penalty action with respect to the alleged violation and is conducting such procedures diligently.

(c) Venue

Any suit brought under this section shall be brought—

(1) in a case concerning an onshore facility or port, in the United States district court for the judicial district where the onshore facility or port is located;

(2) in a case concerning an offshore facility or offshore structure under the jurisdiction of the United States, in the United States district court for the judicial district nearest the offshore facility or offshore structure;

(3) in a case concerning a ship, in the United States district court for any judicial district wherein the ship or its owner or operator may be found; or

(4) in any case, in the District Court for the District of Columbia.

(d) Costs; attorney fees; witness fees

The court, in issuing any final order in any action brought pursuant to this section, may award costs of litigation (including reasonable attorney and expert witness fees) to any party including the Federal Government.

(e) Federal intervention

In any action brought under this section, if the Secretary or Attorney General are not parties of record, the United States, through the Attorney General, shall have the right to intervene.

(Pub. L. 96–478, § 11, Oct. 21, 1980, 94 Stat. 2302; Pub. L. 110–280, § 12, July 21, 2008, 122 Stat. 2615.)

AMENDMENTS

2008—Subsec. (a)(3), (4). Pub. L. 110–280, § 12(1), added par. (3) and redesignated former par. (3) as (4).

Subsec. (b)(1). Pub. L. 110–280, § 12(2), substituted "concerned or the Administrator," for "concerned,".

Subsec. (b)(2). Pub. L. 110–280, § 12(3), inserted "or the Administrator" after "Secretary".

§ 1911. Effect on other laws

Authorities, requirements, and remedies of this chapter supplement and neither amend nor repeal any other authorities, requirements, or remedies conferred by any other provision of law. Nothing in this chapter shall limit, deny, amend, modify, or repeal any other authority, requirement, or remedy available to the United States or any other person, except as expressly provided in this chapter.

(Pub. L. 96–478, § 15, Oct. 21, 1980, 94 Stat. 2303; Pub. L. 110–280, § 11, July 21, 2008, 122 Stat. 2615.)

AMENDMENTS

2008—Pub. L. 110–280 amended section generally. Prior to amendment, section read as follows: "Nothing in this chapter shall be construed as limiting, diminishing, or otherwise restricting any of the authority of the Secretary under the Port and Tanker Safety Act of 1978."

§1912. International law

Any action taken under this chapter shall be taken in accordance with international law.

(Pub. L. 96–478, §17, as added Pub. L. 100–220, title II, §2108, Dec. 29, 1987, 101 Stat. 1464.)

§1913. Compliance reports

(a) In general

Within 1 year after the effective date of this section, and triennially thereafter, the Secretary of the department in which the Coast Guard is operating, in consultation with the Secretary of Agriculture and the Secretary of Commerce, shall report to the Congress regarding compliance with Annex V to the International Convention for the Prevention of Pollution from Ships, 1973, in United States waters and, not later than 1 year after October 19, 1996, and annually thereafter, shall publish in the Federal Register a list of the enforcement actions taken against any domestic or foreign ship (including any commercial or recreational ship) pursuant to the Act to Prevent Pollution from Ships (33 U.S.C. 1901 et seq.).

(b) Report on inability to comply

Within 3 years after the effective date of this section, the head of each Federal agency that operates or contracts for the operation of any ship referred to in section 3(b)(1)(A) of the Act to Prevent Pollution from Ships [33 U.S.C. 1902(b)(1)(A)] that may not be able to comply with the requirements of that section shall report to the Congress describing—

(1) the technical and operational impediments to achieving that compliance;

(2) an alternative schedule for achieving that compliance as rapidly as is technologically feasible;

(3) the ships operated or contracted for operation by the agency for which full compliance with section 3(b)(2)(A) [33 U.S.C. 1902(b)(2)(A)] is not technologically feasible; and

(4) any other information which the agency head considers relevant and appropriate.

(c) Congressional action

Upon receipt of the compliance report under subsection (b) of this section, the Congress shall modify the applicability of Annex V to ships referred to in section 3(b)(1)(A) of the Act to Prevent Pollution from Ships [33 U.S.C. 1902(b)(1)(A)], as may be appropriate with respect to the requirements of Annex V to the Convention.

(Pub. L. 100–220, title II, §2201, Dec. 29, 1987, 101 Stat. 1464; Pub. L. 104–66, title I, §1121(c), Dec. 21, 1995, 109 Stat. 724; Pub. L. 104–324, title VIII, §802(a), Oct. 19, 1996, 110 Stat. 3944.)

REFERENCES IN TEXT

For effective date of this section, referred to in subsecs. (a) and (b), see section 2002 of Pub. L. 100–220, set out as an Effective Date of 1987 Amendment note under section 1901 of this title.

The Act to Prevent Pollution from Ships, referred to in subsec. (a), is Pub. L. 96–478, Oct. 21, 1980, 94 Stat. 2297, as amended, which is classified principally to this chapter (§1901 et seq.). For complete classification of this Act to the Code, see Short Title note set out under section 1901 of this title and Tables.

CODIFICATION

Section was formerly set out as a note under section 1902 of this title.

Section was enacted as part of the Marine Plastic Pollution Research and Control Act of 1987 and as part of the United States-Japan Fishery Agreement Approval Act of 1987, and not as part of the Act to Prevent Pollution from Ships which comprises this chapter.

AMENDMENTS

1996—Subsec. (a). Pub. L. 104–324 struck out "for a period of 6 years" after "triennially thereafter" and inserted "and, not later than 1 year after October 19, 1996, and annually thereafter, shall publish in the Federal Register a list of the enforcement actions taken against any domestic or foreign ship (including any commercial or recreational ship) pursuant to the Act to Prevent Pollution from Ships (33 U.S.C. 1901 et seq.)" before period at end.

1995—Subsec. (a). Pub. L. 104–66 substituted "triennially" for "biennially".

TRANSFER OF FUNCTIONS

For transfer of authorities, functions, personnel, and assets of the Coast Guard, including the authorities and functions of the Secretary of Transportation relating thereto, to the Department of Homeland Security, and for treatment of related references, see sections 468(b), 551(d), 552(d), and 557 of Title 6, Domestic Security, and the Department of Homeland Security Reorganization Plan of November 25, 2002, as modified, set out as a note under section 542 of Title 6.

§1914. Coordination

(a) Establishment of Interagency Marine Debris Coordinating Committee

There is established an Interagency Marine Debris Coordinating Committee to coordinate a comprehensive program of marine debris research and activities among Federal agencies, in cooperation and coordination with non-governmental organizations, industry, universities, and research institutions, States, Indian tribes, and other nations, as appropriate.

(b) Membership

The Committee shall include a senior official from—

(1) the National Oceanic and Atmospheric Administration, who shall serve as the Chairperson of the Committee;

(2) the Environmental Protection Agency;

(3) the United States Coast Guard;

(4) the United States Navy; and

(5) such other Federal agencies that have an interest in ocean issues or water pollution prevention and control as the Secretary of Commerce determines appropriate.

(c) Meetings

The Committee shall meet at least twice a year to provide a public, interagency forum to ensure the coordination of national and international research, monitoring, education, and regulatory actions addressing the persistent marine debris problem.

(d) Monitoring

The Secretary of Commerce, acting through the Administrator of the National Oceanic and Atmospheric Administration, in cooperation with the Administrator of the Environmental Protection Agency, shall utilize the marine debris data derived under title V of the Marine Protection, Research, and Sanctuaries Act of 1972 (33 U.S.C. 2801 et seq.) to assist—

(1) the Committee in ensuring coordination of research, monitoring, education and regulatory actions; and

(2) the United States Coast Guard in assessing the effectiveness of this Act and the Act to Prevent Pollution from Ships [33 U.S.C. 1901 et seq.] in ensuring compliance under section 1913 of this title.

(Pub. L. 100–220, title II, §2203, Dec. 29, 1987, 101 Stat. 1466; Pub. L. 104–324, title VIII, §802(b), Oct. 19, 1996, 110 Stat. 3944; Pub. L. 109–449, §5(a), Dec. 22, 2006, 120 Stat. 3337.)

REFERENCES IN TEXT

The Marine Protection, Research, and Sanctuaries Act of 1972, referred to in subsec. (d), is Pub. L. 92–532, Oct. 23, 1972, 86 Stat. 1052, as amended. Title V of the Act, popularly known as the National Coastal Monitoring Act, is classified generally to chapter 41 (§2801 et seq.) of this title. For complete classification of title V to the Code, see Short Title note set out under section 2801 of this title and Tables.

This Act, referred to in subsec. (d)(2), probably should be "this title" meaning title II of Pub. L. 100–220, Dec. 29, 1987, 101 Stat. 1460, as amended, known as the Marine Plastic Pollution Research and Control Act of 1987. For complete classification of title II to the Code, see Short Title of 1987 Amendment note set out under section 1901 of this title and Tables.

The Act to Prevent Pollution from Ships, referred to in subsec. (d)(2), is Pub. L. 96–478, Oct. 21, 1980, 94 Stat. 2297, as amended, which is classified principally to this chapter (§1901 et seq.). For complete classification of this Act to the Code, see Short Title note set out under section 1901 of this title and Tables.

CODIFICATION

Section was enacted as part of the Marine Plastic Pollution Research and Control Act of 1987 and as part of the United States-Japan Fishery Agreement Approval Act of 1987, and not as part of the Act to Prevent Pollution from Ships which comprises this chapter.

AMENDMENTS

2006—Subsec. (a). Pub. L. 109–449, §5(a)(1), added subsec. (a) and struck out former subsec. (a). Text read as follows: "The Secretary of Commerce shall establish a Marine Debris Coordinating Committee."

Subsec. (c). Pub. L. 109–449, §5(a)(2), inserted "public, interagency" before "forum".

1996—Pub. L. 104–324 amended section generally. Prior to amendment, section read as follows: "Not later than September 30, 1988, the Secretary of Commerce shall submit to the Congress a report on the effects of plastic materials on the marine environment. The report shall—

"(1) identify and quantify the harmful effects of plastic materials on the marine environment;

"(2) assess the specific effects of plastic materials on living marine resources in the marine environment;

"(3) identify the types and classes of plastic materials that pose the greatest potential hazard to living marine resources;

"(4) analyze, in consultation with the Director of the National Bureau of Standards, plastic materials which are claimed to be capable of reduction to environmentally benign submits under the action of normal environmental forces (including biological decomposition, photodegradation, and hydrolysis); and

"(5) recommend legislation which is necessary to prohibit, tax, or regulate sources of plastic materials that enter the marine environment."

TRANSFER OF FUNCTIONS

For transfer of authorities, functions, personnel, and assets of the Coast Guard, including the authorities and functions of the Secretary of Transportation relating thereto, to the Department of Homeland Security, and for treatment of related references, see sections 468(b), 551(d), 552(d), and 557 of Title 6, Domestic Security, and the Department of Homeland Security Reorganization Plan of November 25, 2002, as modified, set out as a note under section 542 of Title 6.

§1915. Plastic pollution public education program

(a) Outreach program

(1) In general

Not later than April 1, 1988, the Administrator of the National Oceanic and Atmospheric Administration and the Administrator of the Environmental Protection Agency, in consultation with the Secretary of Transportation, shall jointly commence and thereafter conduct a public outreach program to educate the public (including recreational boaters, fishermen, and other users of the marine environment) regarding—

(A) the harmful effects of plastic pollution;

(B) the need to reduce such pollution;

(C) the need to recycle plastic materials;

(D) the need to reduce the quantity of plastic debris in the marine environment; and

(E) the requirements under this Act and the Act to Prevent Pollution from Ships (33 U.S.C. 1901 et seq.) with respect to ships and ports, and the authority of citizens to report violations of this Act and the Act to Prevent Pollution from Ships (33 U.S.C. 1901 et seq.).

(2) Authorized activities

(A) Public outreach program

A public outreach program under paragraph (1) may include—

(i) developing and implementing a voluntary boaters' pledge program;

(ii) workshops with interested groups;

(iii) public service announcements;

(iv) distribution of leaflets and posters; and

(v) any other means appropriate to educating the public.

(B) Grants and cooperative agreements

To carry out this section, the Secretary of the department in which the Coast Guard is operating, the Secretary of Commerce, and the Administrator of the Environmental Protection Agency are authorized to award grants, enter into cooperative agreements with appropriate officials of other Federal agencies and agencies of States and political subdivisions of States and with public and private entities, and provide other financial assistance to eligible recipients.

(C) Consultation

In developing outreach initiatives for groups that are subject to the requirements of this title and the Act to Prevent Pollution from Ships (33 U.S.C. 1901 et seq.), the Secretary of the department in which the Coast Guard is operating, in consultation with the Secretary of Commerce, acting through the Administrator of the National Oceanic and Atmospheric Administration, and the Administrator of the Environmental Protection Agency, shall consult with—

(i) the heads of State agencies responsible for implementing State boating laws; and

(ii) the heads of other enforcement agencies that regulate boaters or commercial fishermen.

(b) Citizen Pollution Patrols

The Secretary of Commerce, along with the Administrator of the Environmental Protection Agency and the Secretary of the Department in which the Coast Guard is operating, shall conduct a program to encourage the formation of volunteer groups, to be designated as "Citizen Pollution Patrols", to assist in monitoring, reporting, cleanup, and prevention of ocean and shoreline pollution.

(Pub. L. 100–220, title II, §2204, Dec. 29, 1987, 101 Stat. 1466; Pub. L. 104–324, title VIII, §802(c), Oct. 19, 1996, 110 Stat. 3945.)

REFERENCES IN TEXT

This Act and this title, referred to in subsec. (a)(1)(E), (2)(C), probably should all be "this title" meaning title II of Pub. L. 100–220, Dec. 29, 1987, 101 Stat. 1460, as amended, known as the Marine Plastic Pollution Research and Control Act of 1987. For complete classification of title II to the Code, see Short Title of 1987 Amendment note set out under section 1901 of this title and Tables.

The Act to Prevent Pollution from Ships, referred to in subsec. (a)(1)(E), (2)(C), is Pub. L. 96–478, Oct. 21, 1980, 94 Stat. 2297, as amended, which is classified principally to this chapter (§1901 et seq.). For complete classification of this Act to the Code, see Short Title note set out under section 1901 of this title and Tables.

CODIFICATION

Section was formerly set out as a note under section 6981 of Title 42, The Public Health and Welfare.

Section was enacted as part of the Marine Plastic Pollution Research and Control Act of 1987 and as part of the United States-Japan Fishery Agreement Approval Act of 1987, and not as part of the Act to Prevent Pollution from Ships which comprises this chapter.

AMENDMENTS

1996—Subsec. (a)(1). Pub. L. 104–324, §802(c)(1)–(4), struck out "for a period of at least 3 years," after "conduct" in introductory provisions and added subpar. (E).

Subsec. (a)(2). Pub. L. 104–324, §802(c)(5), added par. (2) and struck out heading and text of former par. (2). Text read as follows: "A public outreach program under paragraph (1) may include—

"(A) workshops with interested groups;

"(B) public service announcements;

"(C) distribution of leaflets and posters; and

"(D) any other means appropriate to educating the public."

TRANSFER OF FUNCTIONS

For transfer of authorities, functions, personnel, and assets of the Coast Guard, including the authorities and functions of the Secretary of Transportation relating thereto, to the Department of Homeland Security, and for treatment of related references, see sections 468(b), 551(d), 552(d), and 557 of Title 6, Domestic Security, and the Department of Homeland Security Reorganization Plan of November 25, 2002, as modified, set out as a note under section 542 of Title 6.

CHAPTER 33A—MARINE DEBRIS RESEARCH, PREVENTION, AND REDUCTION

§1951. Purposes

The purposes of this chapter are—

(1) to help identify, determine sources of, assess, reduce, and prevent marine debris and its adverse impacts on the marine environment and navigation safety;

(2) to reactivate the Interagency Marine Debris Coordinating Committee; and

(3) to develop a Federal marine debris information clearinghouse.

(Pub. L. 109–449, §2, Dec. 22, 2006, 120 Stat. 3333.)

REFERENCES IN TEXT

This chapter, referred to in text, was in the original "this Act", meaning Pub. L. 109–449, Dec. 22, 2006, 120 Stat. 3333, which is classified generally to this chapter. For complete classification of this Act to the Code, see Short Title note set out below and Tables.

SHORT TITLE

Pub. L. 109–449, §1, Dec. 22, 2006, 120 Stat. 3333, provided that: "This Act [enacting this chapter and amending section 1914 of this title] may be cited as the 'Marine Debris Research, Prevention, and Reduction Act'."

§1952. NOAA Marine Debris Prevention and Removal Program

(a) Establishment of Program

There is established, within the National Oceanic and Atmospheric Administration, a Marine Debris Prevention and Removal Program to reduce and prevent the occurrence and adverse impacts of marine debris on the marine environment and navigation safety.

(b) Program components

The Administrator, acting through the Program and subject to the availability of appropriations, shall carry out the following activities:

(1) Mapping, identification, impact assessment, removal, and prevention

The Administrator shall, in consultation with relevant Federal agencies, undertake marine debris mapping, identification, impact assessment, prevention, and removal efforts, with a focus on marine debris posing a threat to living marine resources and navigation safety, including—

(A) the establishment of a process, building on existing information sources maintained by Federal agencies such as the Environmental Protection Agency and the Coast Guard, for cataloguing and maintaining an inventory of marine debris and its impacts found in the navigable waters of the United States and the United States exclusive economic zone, including location, material, size, age, and origin, and impacts on habitat, living marine resources, human health, and navigation safety;

(B) measures to identify the origin, location, and projected movement of marine debris within United States navigable waters, the United States exclusive economic zone, and the high seas, including the use of oceanographic, atmospheric, satellite, and remote sensing data; and

(C) development and implementation of strategies, methods, priorities, and a plan for preventing and removing marine debris from United States navigable waters and within the United States exclusive economic zone, including development of local or regional protocols for removal of derelict fishing gear and other marine debris.

(2) Reducing and preventing loss of gear

The Administrator shall improve efforts to reduce adverse impacts of lost and discarded fishing gear on living marine resources and navigation safety, including—

(A) research and development of alternatives to gear posing threats to the marine environment, and methods for marking gear used in specific fisheries to enhance the tracking, recovery, and identification of lost and discarded gear; and

(B) development of effective nonregulatory measures and incentives to cooperatively reduce the volume of lost and discarded fishing gear and to aid in its recovery.

(3) Outreach

The Administrator shall undertake outreach and education of the public and other stakeholders, such as the fishing industry, fishing gear manufacturers, and other marine-dependent industries, and the plastic and waste management industries, on sources of marine debris, threats associated with marine debris and approaches to identify, determine sources of, assess, reduce, and prevent marine debris and its adverse impacts on the marine environment and navigational safety, including outreach and education activities through public-private initiatives. The Administrator shall coordinate outreach and education activities under this paragraph with any outreach programs conducted under section 1915 of this title.

(c) Grants, cooperative agreements, and contracts

(1) In general

The Administrator, acting through the Program, shall enter into cooperative agreements and contracts and provide financial assistance in the form of grants for projects to accomplish the purpose set forth in section 1951(1) of this title.

(2) Grant cost sharing requirement

(A) In general

Except as provided in subparagraph (B), Federal funds for any grant under this section may not exceed 50 percent of the total cost of such project. For purposes of this subparagraph, the non-Federal share of project costs may be provided by in-kind contributions and other noncash support.

(B) Waiver

The Administrator may waive all or part of the matching requirement under subparagraph (A) if the Administrator determines that no reasonable means are available through which applicants can meet the matching requirement and the probable benefit of such project outweighs the public interest in such matching requirement.

(3) Amounts paid and services rendered under consent

(A) Consent decrees and orders

If authorized by the Administrator or the Attorney General, as appropriate, the non-Federal share of the cost of a project carried out under this chapter may include money paid pursuant to, or the value of any in-kind service performed under, an administrative order on consent or judicial consent decree that will remove or prevent marine debris.

(B) Other decrees and orders

The non-Federal share of the cost of a project carried out under this chapter may not include any money paid pursuant to, or the value of any in-kind service performed under, any other administrative order or court order.

(4) Eligibility

Any State, local, or tribal government whose activities affect research or regulation of marine debris, and any institution of higher education, nonprofit organization, or commercial organization with expertise in a field related to marine debris, is eligible to submit to the Administrator a marine debris proposal under the grant program.

(5) Grant criteria and guidelines

Within 180 days after December 22, 2006, the Administrator shall promulgate necessary guidelines for implementation of the grant program, including development of criteria and priorities for grants. In developing those guidelines, the Administrator shall consult with—

(A) the Interagency Committee;

(B) regional fishery management councils established under the Magnuson-Stevens Fishery Conservation and Management Act (16 U.S.C. 1801 et seq.);

(C) State, regional, and local governmental entities with marine debris experience;

(D) marine-dependent industries; and

(E) nongovernmental organizations involved in marine debris research, prevention, or removal activities.

(6) Project review and approval

The Administrator shall—

(A) review each marine debris project proposal to determine if it meets the grant criteria and supports the goals of this chapter;

(B) after considering any written comments and recommendations based on the review, approve or disapprove the proposal; and

(C) provide notification of that approval or disapproval to the person who submitted the proposal.

(7) Project reporting

Each grantee under this section shall provide periodic reports as required by the Administrator. Each report shall include all information required by the Administrator for evaluating the progress and success in meeting its stated goals, and impact of the grant activities on the marine debris problem.

(Pub. L. 109–449, §3, Dec. 22, 2006, 120 Stat. 3333.)

REFERENCES IN TEXT

This chapter, referred to in subsec. (c)(3), (6)(A), was in the original "this Act", meaning Pub. L. 109–449, Dec. 22, 2006, 120 Stat. 3333, which is classified generally to this chapter. For complete classification of this Act to the Code, see Short Title note set out under section 1951 of this title and Tables.

The Magnuson-Stevens Fishery Conservation and Management Act, referred to in subsec. (c)(5)(B), is Pub. L. 94–265, Apr. 13, 1976, 90 Stat. 331, which is classified principally to chapter 38 (§1801 et seq.) of Title 16, Conservation. For complete classification of this Act to the Code, see Short Title note set out under section 1801 of Title 16 and Tables.

§ 1953. Coast Guard program

(a) Strategy

The Commandant of the Coast Guard, in consultation with the Interagency Committee, shall—

(1) take actions to reduce violations of and improve implementation of MARPOL Annex V and the Act to Prevent Pollution from Ships (33 U.S.C. 1901 et seq.) with respect to the discard of plastics and other garbage from vessels;

(2) take actions to cost-effectively monitor and enforce compliance with MARPOL Annex V and the Act to Prevent Pollution from Ships (33 U.S.C. 1901 et seq.), including through cooperation and coordination with other Federal and State enforcement programs;

(3) take actions to improve compliance with requirements under MARPOL Annex V and section 6 of the Act to Prevent Pollution from Ships (33 U.S.C. 1905) that all United States ports and terminals maintain and monitor the adequacy of receptacles for the disposal of plastics and other garbage, including through promoting voluntary government-industry partnerships;

(4) develop and implement a plan, in coordination with industry and recreational boaters, to improve ship-board waste management, including recordkeeping, and access to waste reception facilities for ship-board waste;

(5) take actions to improve international cooperation to reduce marine debris; and

(6) establish a voluntary reporting program for commercial vessel operators and recreational boaters to report incidents of damage to vessels and disruption of navigation caused by marine debris, and observed violations of laws and regulations relating to the disposal of plastics and other marine debris.

(b) Report

Not later than 180 days after December 22, 2006, the Commandant of the Coast Guard shall submit to the Committee on Commerce, Science, and Transportation of the Senate and the Committee on Transportation and Infrastructure of the House of Representatives a report evaluating the Coast Guard's progress in implementing subsection (a).

(c) External evaluation and recommendations on Annex V

(1) In general

The Commandant of the Coast Guard shall enter into an arrangement with the National Research Council under which the National Research Council shall submit, by not later than 18 months after December 22, 2006, and in consultation with the Commandant and the Interagency Committee, to the Committee on Commerce, Science, and Transportation of the Senate and the Committee on Transportation and Infrastructure of the House of Representatives a comprehensive report on the effectiveness of international and national measures to prevent and reduce marine debris and its impact.

(2) Contents

The report required under paragraph (1) shall include—

(A) an evaluation of international and domestic implementation of MARPOL Annex V and the Act to Prevent Pollution from Ships (33 U.S.C. 1901 et seq.) and recommendations of cost-effective actions to improve implementation and compliance with such measures to reduce impacts of marine debris;

(B) recommendation of additional Federal or international actions, including changes to international and domestic law or regulations, needed to further reduce the impacts of marine debris; and

(C) evaluation of the role of floating fish aggregation devices in the generation of marine debris and existing legal mechanisms to reduce impacts of such debris, focusing on impacts in the Western Pacific and Central Pacific regions.

(Pub. L. 109–449, §4, Dec. 22, 2006, 120 Stat. 3335.)

REFERENCES IN TEXT

The Act to Prevent Pollution from Ships, referred to in subsecs. (a)(1), (2) and (c)(2)(A), is Pub. L. 96–478, Oct. 21, 1980, 94 Stat. 2297, which is classified principally to chapter 33 (§1901 et seq.) of this title. For complete classification of this Act to the Code, see Short Title note set out under section 1901 of this title and Tables.

§ 1954. Interagency coordination

(a) Omitted

(b) Definition of marine debris

The Administrator and the Commandant of the Coast Guard, in consultation with the Interagency Committee established under subsection (a),[1] shall jointly develop and promulgate

[1] See Codification note below.

through regulations a definition of the term "marine debris" for purposes of this chapter.

(c) Reports

(1) Interagency report on marine debris impacts and strategies

(A) In general

Not later than 12 months after December 22, 2006, the Interagency Committee, through the chairperson, shall complete and submit to the Committee on Commerce, Science, and Transportation of the Senate and the Committee on Transportation and Infrastructure and the Committee on Resources of the House of Representatives a report that—

(i) identifies[2] sources of marine debris;

(ii) the ecological and economic impact of marine debris;

(iii) alternatives for reducing, mitigating, preventing, and controlling the harmful affects of marine debris;

(iv) the social and economic costs and benefits of such alternatives; and

(v) recommendations to reduce marine debris both domestically and internationally.

(B) Recommendations

The report shall provide strategies and recommendations on—

(i) establishing priority areas for action to address leading problems relating to marine debris;

(ii) developing strategies and approaches to prevent, reduce, remove, and dispose of marine debris, including through private-public partnerships;

(iii) establishing effective and coordinated education and outreach activities; and

(iv) ensuring Federal cooperation with, and assistance to, the coastal States (as that term is defined in section 1453 of title 16), Indian tribes, and local governments in the identification, determination of sources, prevention, reduction, management, mitigation, and control of marine debris and its adverse impacts.

(2) Annual progress reports

Not later than 3 years after December 22, 2006, and biennially thereafter, the Interagency Committee, through the chairperson, shall submit to the Committee on Commerce, Science, and Transportation of the Senate and the Committee on Transportation and Infrastructure and the Committee on Resources of the House of Representatives a report that evaluates United States and international progress in meeting the purpose of this chapter. The report shall include—

(A) the status of implementation of any recommendations and strategies of the Interagency Committee and analysis of their effectiveness;

(B) a summary of the marine debris inventory to be maintained by the National Oceanic and Atmospheric Administration;

(C) a review of the National Oceanic and Atmospheric Administration program authorized by section 1952 of this title, including projects funded and accomplishments relating to reduction and prevention of marine debris;

(D) a review of Coast Guard programs and accomplishments relating to marine debris removal, including enforcement and compliance with MARPOL requirements; and

(E) estimated Federal and non-Federal funding provided for marine debris and recommendations for priority funding needs.

(Pub. L. 109–449, § 5, Dec. 22, 2006, 120 Stat. 3337.)

REFERENCES IN TEXT

This chapter, referred to in subsecs. (b) and (c)(2), was in the original "this Act", meaning Pub. L. 109–449, Dec. 22, 2006, 120 Stat. 3333, which is classified generally to this chapter. For complete classification of this Act to the Code, see Short Title note set out under section 1951 of this title and Tables.

CODIFICATION

Section is comprised of section 5 of Pub. L. 109–449. Subsec. (a) of section 5 of Pub. L. 109–449 amended section 1914 of this title.

CHANGE OF NAME

Committee on Resources of House of Representatives changed to Committee on Natural Resources of House of Representatives by House Resolution No. 6, One Hundred Tenth Congress, Jan. 5, 2007.

§ 1955. Federal information clearinghouse

The Administrator, in coordination with the Interagency Committee, shall—

(1) maintain a Federal information clearinghouse on marine debris that will be available to researchers and other interested persons to improve marine debris source identification, data sharing, and monitoring efforts through collaborative research and open sharing of data; and

(2) take the necessary steps to ensure the confidentiality of such information (especially proprietary information), for any information required by the Administrator to be submitted by the fishing industry under this section.

(Pub. L. 109–449, § 6, Dec. 22, 2006, 120 Stat. 3338.)

§ 1956. Definitions

In this chapter:

(1) Administrator

The term "Administrator" means the Administrator of the National Oceanic and Atmospheric Administration.

(2) Interagency Committee

The term "Interagency Committee" means the Interagency Marine Debris Coordinating Committee established under section 1914 of this title.

(3) United States exclusive economic zone

The term "United States exclusive economic zone" means the zone established by Presidential Proclamation Numbered 5030, dated March 10, 1983, including the ocean waters of the areas referred to as "eastern special areas" in article 3(1) of the Agreement be-

[2] So in original. The word "identifies" probably should follow "a report that".

tween the United States of America and the Union of Soviet Socialist Republics on the Maritime Boundary, signed June 1, 1990.

(4) MARPOL; Annex V; Convention

The terms "MARPOL", "Annex V", and "Convention" have the meaning given those terms under section 1901(a) of this title.

(5) Navigable waters

The term "navigable waters" means waters of the United States, including the territorial sea.

(6) Territorial sea

The term "territorial sea" means the waters of the United States referred to in Presidential Proclamation No. 5928, dated December 27, 1988.

(7) Program

The term "Program" means the Marine Debris Prevention and Removal Program established under section 1952 of this title.

(8) State

The term "State" means—

(A) any State of the United States that is impacted by marine debris within its seaward or Great Lakes boundaries;

(B) the District of Columbia;

(C) American Samoa, Guam, the Northern Mariana Islands, Puerto Rico, and the Virgin Islands; and

(D) any other territory or possession of the United States, or separate sovereign in free association with the United States, that is impacted by marine debris within its seaward boundaries.

(Pub. L. 109–449, § 7, Dec. 22, 2006, 120 Stat. 3338.)

References in Text

This chapter, referred to in text, was in the original "this Act", meaning Pub. L. 109–449, Dec. 22, 2006, 120 Stat. 3333, which is classified generally to this chapter. For complete classification of this Act to the Code, see Short Title note set out under section 1951 of this title and Tables.

Presidential Proclamation Numbered 5030, referred to in par. (3), is set out as a note under section 1453 of Title 16, Conservation.

Presidential Proclamation No. 5928, referred to in par. (6), is set out as a note under section 1331 of Title 43, Public Lands.

§ 1957. Relationship to Outer Continental Shelf Lands Act

Nothing in this chapter supersedes, or limits the authority of the Secretary of the Interior under, the Outer Continental Shelf Lands Act (43 U.S.C. 1331 et seq.).

(Pub. L. 109–449, § 8, Dec. 22, 2006, 120 Stat. 3339.)

References in Text

This chapter, referred to in text, was in the original "this Act", meaning Pub. L. 109–449, Dec. 22, 2006, 120 Stat. 3333, which is classified generally to this chapter. For complete classification of this Act to the Code, see Short Title note set out under section 1951 of this title and Tables.

The Outer Continental Shelf Lands Act, referred to in text, is act Aug. 7, 1953, ch. 345, 67 Stat. 462, which is classified generally to subchapter III (§ 1331 et seq.) of chapter 29 of Title 43, Public Lands. For complete classification of this Act to the Code, see Short Title note set out under section 1331 of Title 43 and Tables.

§ 1958. Authorization of appropriations

There are authorized to be appropriated for each fiscal year 2006 through 2010—

(1) to the Administrator for carrying out sections 1952 and 1955 of this title, $10,000,000, of which no more than 10 percent may be for administrative costs; and

(2) to the Secretary of the Department in which the Coast Guard is operating, for the use of the Commandant of the Coast Guard in carrying out section 1953 of this title, $2,000,000, of which no more than 10 percent may be used for administrative costs.

(Pub. L. 109–449, § 9, Dec. 22, 2006, 120 Stat. 3339.)

CHAPTER 34—INLAND NAVIGATIONAL RULES

SUBCHAPTER I—RULES

PART A—GENERAL

SUBCHAPTER I—RULES

PART A—GENERAL

§2001. Application (Rule 1)

(a) United States inland waters and Canadian waters of the Great Lakes

These Rules apply to all vessels upon the inland waters of the United States, and to vessels of the United States on the Canadian waters of the Great Lakes to the extent that there is no conflict with Canadian law.

(b) International Regulations

(i) These Rules constitute special rules made by an appropriate authority within the meaning of Rule 1(b) of the International Regulations.

(ii) All vessels complying with the construction and equipment requirements of the International Regulations are considered to be in compliance with these Rules.

(c) Special rules

Nothing in these Rules shall interfere with the operation of any special rules made by the Secretary of the Navy with respect to additional station or signal lights and shapes or whistle signals for ships of war and vessels proceeding under convoy, or by the Secretary with respect to additional station or signal lights and shapes for fishing vessels engaged in fishing as a fleet. These additional station or signal lights and shapes or whistle signals shall, so far as possible, be such that they cannot be mistaken for any light, shape, or signal authorized elsewhere under these Rules. Notice of such special rules shall be published in the Federal Register and, after the effective date specified in such notice, they shall have effect as if they were a part of these Rules.

(d) Vessel traffic service regulations

Traffic separation schemes may be established for the purpose of these Rules. Vessel traffic service regulations may be in effect in certain areas.

(e) Alternative compliance

Whenever the Secretary determines that a vessel or class of vessels of special construction or purpose cannot comply fully with the provisions of any of these Rules with respect to the number, position, range, or arc of visibility of lights or shapes, as well as to the disposition and characteristics of sound-signaling appliances, the vessel shall comply with such other provisions in regard to the number, position, range, or arc of visibility of lights or shapes, as well as to the disposition and characteristics of sound-signaling appliances, as the Secretary shall have determined to be the closest possible compliance with these Rules. The Secretary may issue a certificate of alternative compliance for a vessel or class of vessels specifying the closest possible compliance with these Rules. The Secretary of the Navy shall make these determinations and issue certificates of alternative compliance for vessels of the Navy.

(f) Acceptance of certificates of alternative compliance from contracting parties to International Regulations

The Secretary may accept a certificate of alternative compliance issued by a contracting party to the International Regulations if he determines that the alternative compliance standards of the contracting party are substantially the same as those of the United States.

(Pub. L. 96–591, §2, Dec. 24, 1980, 94 Stat. 3415; Pub. L. 102–241, §21(1), Dec. 19, 1991, 105 Stat. 2217; Pub. L. 102–587, title V, §5206[(1)], Nov. 4, 1992, 106 Stat. 5074.)

REPEAL OF SECTION

Pub. L. 108–293, title III, §303(a), (c), Aug. 9, 2004, 118 Stat. 1042, provided that this section is repealed effective on the effective date of final regulations prescribed by the Secretary of the Department in which the Coast Guard is operating under section 2071 of this title.

REFERENCES IN TEXT

These Rules, referred to in pars. (a), (b), (c), and (e), are the Inland Navigational Rules which are classified to this subchapter.

The International Regulations, referred to in pars. (b) and (f), are the International Regulations for Preventing Collisions at Sea, 1972, which are maintained and published by the United States Coast Guard, U.S. Department of Homeland Security, in the publication *Navigation Rules*, which is available for sale by the Superintendent of Documents, U.S. Government Printing Office, Washington, D.C. 20402. See International Regulations for Preventing Collisions at Sea, 1972 note under section 1602 of this title.

CODIFICATION

Section was enacted as part of section 2 of Pub. L. 96–591 which enacted the Inland Navigational Rules which comprise this subchapter.

AMENDMENTS

1992—Par. (d). Pub. L. 102–587 amended par. (d) generally. Prior to amendment, par. (d) read as follows: "Vessel traffic service regulations may be in effect in certain areas."

1991—Par. (e). Pub. L. 102–241 struck out "without interfering with the special function of the vessel," before "the vessel shall comply".

EFFECTIVE DATE OF REPEAL

Pub. L. 108–293, title III, §303(c), Aug. 9, 2004, 118 Stat. 1042, provided that: "Subsection (a) [repealing this subchapter] is effective on the effective date of final regulations prescribed by the Secretary of the Department in which the Coast Guard is operating under section 3 of the Inland Navigation Rules Act of 1980 (33 U.S.C. 2001) [33 U.S.C. 2071], as amended by this Act."

EFFECTIVE DATE

Section 7 of Pub. L. 96–591 provided that: "Sections 2, 4, 6(1), and 8(a) [enacting this section and sections 2002 to 2038 and 2072 of this title, amending section 1604 of this title, and repealing sections 154 to 159, 171 to 183, 191, 192, 201 to 213, 221, 222, 231, 232, 301 to 303, 311 to 323, 331, 341–356, 360, and 360a of this title and sections 526b, 526c, and 526d of former Title 46, Shipping] are effective 12 months after the date of enactment of this Act [Dec. 24, 1980], except that on the Great Lakes, the effective date of sections 2 and 4 [enacting this section and sections 2002 to 2038 and 2072 of this title] will be established by the Secretary. [The effective date on the Great Lakes was established as Mar. 1, 1983. See 47 F.R. 15135, Apr. 8, 1982.] Section 5 [enacting section 2073 of this title] is effective on October 1, 1981."

SHORT TITLE

Section 1 of Pub. L. 96–591 provided: "That this Act [enacting this chapter, amending sections 151, 1604, 1605, and 1608 of this title, repealing sections 154 to 159, 171 to 183, 191, 192, 201 to 213, 221, 222, 231, 232, 241 to 244, 251 to 262, 271, 272, 281 to 295, 301 to 303, 311 to 323, 331, 341 to 356, 360, and 360a of this title and sections 526b, 526c, and 526d of former Title 46, Shipping, and enacting provisions set out as notes under this section] may be cited as the 'Inland Navigational Rules Act of 1980'."

REPEAL OF PREDECESSOR PROVISIONS; SAVINGS PROVISIONS

Section 8(a) of Pub. L. 96–591 provided in part that: "The laws specified in the following schedules are repealed. Any prior rights or liabilities existing under these laws are not affected by their repeal." [The schedules repealed sections 154 to 159, 171 to 183, 191, 192, 201 to 213, 221, 222, 231, 232, 301 to 303, 311 to 323, 331, 341 to 356, 360, and 360a of this title and sections 526b, 526c, and 526d of former Title 46, Shipping.]

Section 8(b) of Pub. L. 96–591 provided in part that: "The following laws [sections 241 to 244, 251 to 262, 271, 272, and 281 to 295 of this title] are repealed when the Secretary establishes an effective date under section 7 [set out as a note above]."

§2002. Responsibility (Rule 2)

(a) Exoneration

Nothing in these Rules shall exonerate any vessel, or the owner, master, or crew thereof, from the consequences of any neglect to comply with these Rules or of the neglect of any precaution which may be required by the ordinary practice of seamen, or by the special circumstances of the case.

(b) Departure from rules when necessary to avoid immediate danger

In construing and complying with these Rules due regard shall be had to all dangers of navigation and collision and to any special circumstances, including the limitations of the vessels involved, which may make a departure from these Rules necessary to avoid immediate danger.

(Pub. L. 96–591, §2, Dec. 24, 1980, 94 Stat. 3416.)

REPEAL OF SECTION

Pub. L. 108–293, title III, §303(a), (c), Aug. 9, 2004, 118 Stat. 1042, provided that this section is repealed effective on the effective date of final regulations prescribed by the Secretary of the Department in which the Coast Guard is operating under section 2071 of this title.

REFERENCES IN TEXT

These Rules, referred to in text, are the Inland Navigational Rules which are classified to this subchapter.

CODIFICATION

Section was enacted as part of section 2 of Pub. L. 96–591 which enacted the Inland Navigational Rules which comprise this subchapter.

§2003. Definitions (Rule 3)

For the purpose of these Rules and this chapter, except where the context otherwise requires:

(a) The word "vessel" includes every description of water craft, including nondisplacement craft and seaplanes, used or capable of being used as a means of transportation on water;

(b) The term "power-driven vessel" means any vessel propelled by machinery;

(c) The term "sailing vessel" means any vessel under sail provided that propelling machinery, if fitted, is not being used;

(d) The term "vessel engaged in fishing" means any vessel fishing with nets, lines, trawls, or other fishing apparatus which restricts maneuverability, but does not include a vessel fishing with trolling lines or other fishing apparatus which do not restrict maneuverability;

(e) The word "seaplane" includes any aircraft designed to maneuver on the water;

(f) The term "vessel not under command" means a vessel which through some exceptional circumstance is unable to maneuver as required by these Rules and is therefore unable to keep out of the way of another vessel;

(g) The term "vessel restricted in her ability to maneuver" means a vessel which from the nature of her work is restricted in her ability to maneuver as required by these Rules and is therefore unable to keep out of the way of another vessel; vessels restricted in their ability to maneuver include, but are not limited to:

(i) a vessel engaged in laying, servicing, or picking up a navigation mark, submarine cable, or pipeline;

(ii) a vessel engaged in dredging, surveying, or underwater operations;

(iii) a vessel engaged in replenishment or transferring persons, provisions, or cargo while underway;

(iv) a vessel engaged in the launching or recovery of aircraft;

(v) a vessel engaged in mineclearance operations; and

(vi) a vessel engaged in a towing operation such as severely restricts the towing vessel and her tow in their ability to deviate from their course.

(h) The word "underway" means that a vessel is not at anchor, or made fast to the shore, or aground;

(i) The words "length" and "breadth" of a vessel mean her length overall and greatest breadth;

(j) Vessels shall be deemed to be in sight of one another only when one can be observed visually from the other;

(k) The term "restricted visibility" means any condition in which visibility is restricted by fog, mist, falling snow, heavy rainstorms, sandstorms, or any other similar causes;

(*l*) "Western Rivers" means the Mississippi River, its tributaries, South Pass, and Southwest Pass, to the navigational demarcation lines dividing the high seas from harbors, rivers, and other inland waters of the United States, and the Port Allen-Morgan City Alternate Route, and that part of the Atchafalaya River above its junction with the Port Allen-Morgan City Alternate Route including the Old River and the Red River;

(m) "Great Lakes" means the Great Lakes and their connecting and tributary waters including the Calumet River as far as the Thomas J. O'Brien Lock and Controlling Works (between mile 326 and 327), the Chicago River as far as the east side of the Ashland Avenue Bridge (between mile 321 and 322), and the Saint Lawrence River as far east as the lower exit of Saint Lambert Lock;

(n) "Secretary" means the Secretary of the department in which the Coast Guard is operating;

(*o*) "Inland Waters" means the navigable waters of the United States shoreward of the navigational demarcation lines dividing the high seas from harbors, rivers, and other inland waters of the United States and the waters of the Great Lakes on the United States side of the International Boundary;

(p) "Inland Rules" or "Rules" mean the Inland Navigational Rules and the annexes thereto, which govern the conduct of vessels and specify the lights, shapes, and sound signals that apply on inland waters; and

(q) "International Regulations" means the International Regulations for Preventing Collisions at Sea, 1972, including annexes currently in force for the United States.

(Pub. L. 96–591, §2, Dec. 24, 1980, 94 Stat. 3416; Pub. L. 100–448, §14(1), Sept. 28, 1988, 102 Stat. 1844.)

REPEAL OF SECTION

Pub. L. 108–293, title III, §303(a), (c), Aug. 9, 2004, 118 Stat. 1042, provided that this section is repealed effective on the effective date of final regulations prescribed by the Secretary of the Department in which the Coast Guard is operating under section 2071 of this title.

REFERENCES IN TEXT

These Rules and Inland Rules, referred to in text, mean the Inland Navigational Rules which are classified to this subchapter.

This chapter, referred to in text, was in the original "this Act", meaning Pub. L. 96–591, Dec. 24, 1980, 94 Stat. 3415, as amended, known as the Inland Navigational Rules Act of 1980, which enacted this chapter, amended sections 151, 1604, 1605, and 1608 of this title, repealed sections 154 to 159, 171 to 183, 191, 192, 201 to 213, 221, 222, 232, 241 to 244, 251 to 262, 271, 272, 281 to 295, 301 to 303, 311 to 323, 331, 341 to 356, 360, and 360a of this title and sections 526b, 526c, and 526d of former Title 46, Shipping, and enacted provisions set out as notes under section 2001 of this title. For complete classification of this Act to the Code see Short Title note set out under section 2001 of this title and Tables.

The International Regulations for Preventing Collisions at Sea, 1972, referred to in par. (q), are maintained and published by the United States Coast Guard, U.S. Department of Homeland Security, in the publication *Navigation Rules*, which is available for sale by the Superintendent of Documents, U.S. Government Printing Office, Washington, D.C. 20402. See International Regulations for Preventing Collisions at Sea, 1972 note under section 1602 of this title.

CODIFICATION

Section was enacted as part of section 2 of Pub. L. 96–591 which enacted the Inland Navigational Rules which comprise this subchapter.

AMENDMENTS

1988—Par. (g)(v). Pub. L. 100–448 substituted "mineclearance" for "minesweeping".

TRANSFER OF FUNCTIONS

For transfer of authorities, functions, personnel, and assets of the Coast Guard, including the authorities and functions of the Secretary of Transportation relating thereto, to the Department of Homeland Security, and for treatment of related references, see sections 468(b), 551(d), 552(d), and 557 of Title 6, Domestic Security, and the Department of Homeland Security Reorganization Plan of November 25, 2002, as modified, set out as a note under section 542 of Title 6.

PART B—STEERING AND SAILING RULES

SUBPART I—CONDUCT OF VESSELS IN ANY CONDITION OF VISIBILITY

§ 2004. Application (Rule 4)

Rules in this subpart apply in any condition of visibility.

(Pub. L. 96–591, §2, Dec. 24, 1980, 94 Stat. 3417.)

REPEAL OF SECTION

Pub. L. 108–293, title III, §303(a), (c), Aug. 9, 2004, 118 Stat. 1042, provided that this section is repealed effective on the effective date of final regulations prescribed by the Secretary of the Department in which the Coast Guard is operating under section 2071 of this title.

REFERENCES IN TEXT

Rules in this subpart, referred to in text, means sections 2004 to 2010 of this title.

CODIFICATION

Section was enacted as part of section 2 of Pub. L. 96–591 which enacted the Inland Navigational Rules which comprise this subchapter.

§ 2005. Look-out (Rule 5)

Every vessel shall at all times maintain a proper look-out by sight and hearing as well as by all available means appropriate in the prevailing circumstances and conditions so as to make a full appraisal of the situation and of the risk of collision.

(Pub. L. 96–591, §2, Dec. 24, 1980, 94 Stat. 3418.)

REPEAL OF SECTION

Pub. L. 108–293, title III, §303(a), (c), Aug. 9, 2004, 118 Stat. 1042, provided that this section is repealed effective on the effective date of final regulations prescribed by the Secretary of the Department in which the Coast Guard is operating under section 2071 of this title.

CODIFICATION

Section was enacted as part of section 2 of Pub. L. 96–591 which enacted the Inland Navigational Rules which comprise this subchapter.

§ 2006. Safe speed (Rule 6)

Every vessel shall at all times proceed at a safe speed so that she can take proper and effective action to avoid collision and be stopped within a distance appropriate to the prevailing circumstances and conditions.

In determining a safe speed the following factors shall be among those taken into account:

(a) By all vessels:

(i) the state of visibility;

(ii) the traffic density including concentration of fishing vessels or any other vessels;

(iii) the maneuverability of the vessel with special reference to stopping distance and turning ability in the prevailing conditions;

(iv) at night the presence of background light such as from shores lights or from back scatter of her own lights;

(v) the state of wind, sea, and current, and the proximity of navigational hazards;

(vi) the draft in relation to the available depth of water.

(b) Additionally, by vessels with operational radar:

(i) the characteristics, efficiency and limitations of the radar equipment;

(ii) any constraints imposed by the radar range scale in use;

(iii) the effect on radar detection of the sea state, weather, and other sources of interference;

(iv) the possibility that small vessels, ice and other floating objects may not be detected by radar at an adequate range;

(v) the number, location, and movement of vessels detected by radar; and

(vi) the more exact assessment of the visibility that may be possible when radar is used to determine the range of vessels or other objects in the vicinity.

(Pub. L. 96–591, §2, Dec. 24, 1980, 94 Stat. 3418.)

REPEAL OF SECTION

Pub. L. 108–293, title III, §303(a), (c), Aug. 9, 2004, 118 Stat. 1042, provided that this section is repealed effective on the effective date of final regulations prescribed by the Secretary of the Department in which the Coast Guard is operating under section 2071 of this title.

CODIFICATION

Section was enacted as part of section 2 of Pub. L. 96–591 which enacted the Inland Navigational Rules which comprise this subchapter.

§ 2007. Risk of collision (Rule 7)

(a) Determination if risk exists

Every vessel shall use all available means appropriate to the prevailing circumstances and conditions to determine if risk of collision exists. If there is any doubt such risk shall be deemed to exist.

(b) Radar

Proper use shall be made of radar equipment if fitted and operational, including long-range scanning to obtain early warning of risk of collision and radar plotting or equivalent systematic observation of detected objects.

(c) Scanty information

Assumptions shall not be made on the basis of scanty information, especially scanty radar information.

(d) Considerations taken into account in determining if risk exists

In determining if risk of collision exists the following considerations shall be among those taken into account:

(i) such risk shall be deemed to exist if the compass bearing of an approaching vessel does not appreciably change; and

(ii) such risk may sometimes exist even when an appreciable bearing change is evident, particularly when approaching a very large vessel or a tow or when approaching a vessel at close range.

(Pub. L. 96–591, §2, Dec. 24, 1980, 94 Stat. 3418.)

REPEAL OF SECTION

Pub. L. 108–293, title III, §303(a), (c), Aug. 9, 2004, 118 Stat. 1042, provided that this section is repealed effective on the effective date of final regulations prescribed by the Secretary of the Department in which the Coast Guard is operating under section 2071 of this title.

CODIFICATION

Section was enacted as part of section 2 of Pub. L. 96–591 which enacted the Inland Navigational Rules which comprise this subchapter.

§ 2008. Action to avoid collision (Rule 8)

(a) General characteristics of action taken to avoid collision

Any action taken to avoid collision shall, if the circumstances of the case admit, be positive, made in ample time and with due regard to the observance of good seamanship.

(b) Readily apparent alterations in course or speed

Any alteration of course or speed to avoid collision shall, if the circumstances of the case admit, be large enough to be readily apparent to another vessel observing visually or by radar; a succession of small alterations of course or speed should be avoided.

(c) Alteration of course to avoid close-quarters situation

If there is sufficient sea room, alteration of course alone may be the most effective action to avoid a close-quarters situation provided that it is made in good time, is substantial and does not result in another close-quarters situation.

(d) Action to result in passing at safe distance

Action taken to avoid collision with another vessel shall be such as to result in passing at a safe distance. The effectiveness of the action shall be carefully checked until the other vessel is finally past and clear.

(e) Slackening of vessel speed; stopping or reversing means of propulsion

If necessary to avoid collision or allow more time to assess the situation, a vessel shall slacken her speed or take all way off by stopping or reversing her means of propulsion.

(f) Early action to allow room for safe passage

(i) A vessel which, by any of these Rules, is required not to impede the passage or safe passage of another vessel shall, when required by the circumstances of the case, take early action to allow sufficient sea room for the safe passage of the other vessel.

(ii) A vessel required not to impede the passage or safe passage of another vessel is not relieved of this obligation if approaching the other vessel so as to involve risk of collision and shall, when taking action, have full regard to the action which may be required by the Rules of this part.

(iii) A vessel the passage of which is not to be impeded remains fully obliged to comply with the Rules of this part when the two vessels are approaching one another so as to involve risk of collision.

(Pub. L. 96–591, §2, Dec. 24, 1980, 94 Stat. 3419; Pub. L. 102–241, §21(2), Dec. 19, 1991, 105 Stat. 2217.)

REPEAL OF SECTION

Pub. L. 108–293, title III, § 303(a), (c), Aug. 9, 2004, 118 Stat. 1042, provided that this section is repealed effective on the effective date of final regulations prescribed by the Secretary of the Department in which the Coast Guard is operating under section 2071 of this title.

CODIFICATION

Section was enacted as part of section 2 of Pub. L. 96–591 which enacted the Inland Navigational Rules which comprise this subchapter.

AMENDMENTS

1991—Par. (f). Pub. L. 102–241 added par. (f).

§ 2009. Narrow channels (Rule 9)

(a) Keeping near to outer limit of channel or fairway which lies on vessel's starboard side; exception

(i) A vessel proceeding along the course of a narrow channel or fairway shall keep as near to the outer limit of the channel or fairway which lies on her starboard side as is safe and practicable.

(ii) Notwithstanding paragraph (a)(i) and Rule 14(a), a power-driven vessel operating in narrow channels or fairways on the Great Lakes, Western Rivers, or waters specified by the Secretary, and proceeding downbound with a following current shall have the right-of-way over an upbound vessel, shall propose the manner and place of passage, and shall initiate the maneuvering signals prescribed by Rule 34(a)(i), as appropriate. The vessel proceeding upbound against the current shall hold as necessary to permit safe passing.

(b) Vessels of less than 20 meters in length; sailing vessels

A vessel of less than 20 meters in length or a sailing vessel shall not impede the passage of a vessel that can safely navigate only within a narrow channel or fairway.

(c) Vessels engaged in fishing

A vessel engaged in fishing shall not impede the passage of any other vessel navigating within a narrow channel or fairway.

(d) Crossing narrow channels or fairways

A vessel shall not cross a narrow channel or fairway if such crossing impedes the passage of a vessel which can safely navigate only within that channel or fairway. The latter vessel shall use the danger signal prescribed in Rule 34(d) if in doubt as to the intention of the crossing vessel.

(e) Overtaking vessels

(i) In a narrow channel or fairway when overtaking, the power-driven vessel intending to overtake another power-driven vessel shall indicate her intention by sounding the appropriate signal prescribed in Rule 34(c) and take steps to permit safe passing. The power-driven vessel being overtaken, if in agreement, shall sound the same signal and may, if specifically agreed to[1] take steps to permit safe passing. If in doubt she shall sound the danger signal prescribed in Rule 34(d).

(ii) This Rule does not relieve the overtaking vessel of her obligation under Rule 13.

(f) Areas of obscured visibility due to intervening obstructions

A vessel nearing a bend or an area of a narrow channel or fairway where other vessels may be obscured by an intervening obstruction shall navigate with particular alertness and caution and shall sound the appropriate signal prescribed in Rule 34(e).

(g) Avoidance of anchoring in narrow channels

Every vessel shall, if the circumstances of the case admit, avoid anchoring in a narrow channel.

(Pub. L. 96–591, §2, Dec. 24, 1980, 94 Stat. 3419; Pub. L. 104–324, title VII, §701(1), Oct. 19, 1996, 110 Stat. 3932.)

REPEAL OF SECTION

Pub. L. 108–293, title III, § 303(a), (c), Aug. 9, 2004, 118 Stat. 1042, provided that this section is repealed effective on the effective date of final regulations prescribed by the Secretary of the Department in which the Coast Guard is operating under section 2071 of this title.

REFERENCES IN TEXT

Rule 14, referred to in par. (a)(ii), is classified to section 2014 of this title.

Rule 34, referred to in pars. (a)(ii), (d), (e)(i), and (f), is classified to section 2034 of this title.

Rule 13, referred to in par. (e)(ii), is classified to section 2013 of this title.

CODIFICATION

Section was enacted as part of section 2 of Pub. L. 96–591 which enacted the Inland Navigational Rules which comprise this subchapter.

AMENDMENTS

1996—Par. (e)(i). Pub. L. 104–324 amended par. (e)(i) generally. Prior to amendment, par. (e)(i) read as follows: "In a narrow channel or fairway when overtaking, the vessel intending to overtake shall indicate her intention by sounding the appropriate signal prescribed in Rule 34(c) and take steps to permit safe passing. The overtaken vessel, if in agreement, shall sound the same signal. If in doubt she shall sound the danger signal prescribed in Rule 34(d)."

§ 2010. Traffic separation schemes (Rule 10)

(a) Obligations under other Rules unaffected

This Rule applies to traffic separation schemes and does not relieve any vessel of her obligation under any other Rule.

(b) Duties for vessel using scheme

A vessel using a traffic separation scheme shall:

[1] So in original. Probably should be followed by a comma.

(i) proceed in the appropriate traffic lane in the general direction of traffic flow for that lane;

(ii) so far as practicable keep clear of a traffic separation line or separation zone;

(iii) normally join or leave a traffic lane at the termination of the lane, but when joining or leaving from either side shall do so at as small an angle to the general direction of traffic flow as practicable.

(c) Crossing traffic lanes

A vessel shall, so far as practicable, avoid crossing traffic lanes but if obliged to do so shall cross on a heading as nearly as practicable at right angles to the general direction of traffic flow.

(d) Use of inshore traffic lane

(i) A vessel shall not use an inshore traffic zone when she can safely use the appropriate traffic lane within the adjacent traffic separation scheme. However, vessels of less than twenty meters in length, sailing vessels, and vessels engaged in fishing may use the inshore traffic zone.

(ii) Notwithstanding subparagraph (d)(i), a vessel may use an inshore traffic zone when en route to or from a port, offshore installation or structure, pilot station, or any other place situated within the inshore traffic zone, or to avoid immediate danger.

(e) Entering separation zone or crossing separation line

A vessel other than a crossing vessel or a vessel joining or leaving a lane shall not normally enter a separation zone or cross a separation line except:

(i) in cases of emergency to avoid immediate danger; or

(ii) to engage in fishing within a separation zone.

(f) Caution in areas near termination of scheme

A vessel navigating in areas near the terminations of traffic separation schemes shall do so with particular caution.

(g) Anchoring

A vessel shall so far as practicable avoid anchoring in a traffic separation scheme or in areas near its terminations.

(h) Avoidance of scheme

A vessel not using a traffic separation scheme shall avoid it by as wide a margin as is practicable.

(i) Fishing vessels

A vessel engaged in fishing shall not impede the passage of any vessel following a traffic lane.

(j) Power-driven vessels

A vessel of less than twenty meters in length or a sailing vessel shall not impede the safe passage of a power-driven vessel following a traffic lane.

(k) Exemption; maintenance of safety of navigation

A vessel restricted in her ability to maneuver when engaged in an operation for the maintenance of safety of navigation in a traffic separation scheme is exempted from complying with this Rule to the extent necessary to carry out the operation.

(1)[1] Exemption; laying, servicing, or picking up submarine cable

A vessel restricted in her ability to maneuver when engaged in an operation for the laying, servicing, or picking up of a submarine cable, within a traffic separation scheme, is exempted from complying with this Rule to the extent necessary to carry out the operation.

(Pub. L. 96–591, §2, Dec. 24, 1980, 94 Stat. 3420; Pub. L. 102–587, title V, §5206(2), Nov. 4, 1992, 106 Stat. 5074.)

REPEAL OF SECTION

Pub. L. 108–293, title III, § 303(a), (c), Aug. 9, 2004, 118 Stat. 1042, provided that this section is repealed effective on the effective date of final regulations prescribed by the Secretary of the Department in which the Coast Guard is operating under section 2071 of this title.

CODIFICATION

Section was enacted as part of section 2 of Pub. L. 96–591 which enacted the Inland Navigational Rules which comprise this subchapter.

AMENDMENTS

1992—Pub. L. 102–587 amended section generally. Prior to amendment, section read as follows: "Each vessel required by regulation to participate in a vessel traffic service shall comply with the applicable regulations."

SUBPART II—CONDUCT OF VESSELS IN SIGHT OF ONE ANOTHER

§ 2011. Application (Rule 11)

Rules in this subpart apply to vessels in sight of one another.

(Pub. L. 96–591, §2, Dec. 24, 1980, 94 Stat. 3420.)

REPEAL OF SECTION

Pub. L. 108–293, title III, § 303(a), (c), Aug. 9, 2004, 118 Stat. 1042, provided that this section is repealed effective on the effective date of final regulations prescribed by the Secretary of the Department in which the Coast Guard is operating under section 2071 of this title.

REFERENCES IN TEXT

Rules in this subpart, referred to in text, means sections 2011 to 2018 of this title.

CODIFICATION

Section was enacted as part of section 2 of Pub. L. 96–591 which enacted the Inland Navigational Rules which comprise this subchapter.

§ 2012. Sailing vessels (Rule 12)

(a) Keeping out of the way

When two sailing vessels are approaching one another, so as to involve risk of collision, one of them shall keep out of the way of the other as follows:

(i) when each has the wind on a different side, the vessel which has the wind on the port side shall keep out of the way of the other;

[1] So in original. Probably should be "(*l*)".

(ii) when both have the wind on the same side, the vessel which is to windward shall keep out of the way of the vessel which is to leeward; and

(iii) if a vessel with the wind on the port side sees a vessel to windward and cannot determine with certainty whether the other vessel has the wind on the port or on the starboard side, she shall keep out of the way of the other.

(b) Windward side

For the purpose of this Rule the windward side shall be deemed to be the side opposite to that on which the mainsail is carried or, in the case of a square-rigged vessel, the side opposite to that on which the largest fore-and-aft sail is carried.

(Pub. L. 96–591, §2, Dec. 24, 1980, 94 Stat. 3420.)

REPEAL OF SECTION

Pub. L. 108–293, title III, §303(a), (c), Aug. 9, 2004, 118 Stat. 1042, provided that this section is repealed effective on the effective date of final regulations prescribed by the Secretary of the Department in which the Coast Guard is operating under section 2071 of this title.

CODIFICATION

Section was enacted as part of section 2 of Pub. L. 96–591 which enacted the Inland Navigational Rules which comprise this subchapter.

§ 2013. Overtaking (Rule 13)

(a) Overtaking vessel to keep out of the overtaken vessel's way

Notwithstanding anything contained in Rules 4 through 18, any vessel overtaking any other shall keep out of the way of the vessel being overtaken.

(b) Overtaking vessel defined

A vessel shall be deemed to be overtaking when coming up with another vessel from a direction more than 22.5 degrees abaft her beam; that is, in such a position with reference to the vessel she is overtaking, that at night she would be able to see only the sternlight of that vessel but neither of her sidelights.

(c) Assumption that vessel is overtaking another in cases of doubt

When a vessel is in any doubt as to whether she is overtaking another, she shall assume that this is the case and act accordingly.

(d) Overtaking vessel to become crossing vessel only when finally past and clear

Any subsequent alteration of the bearing between the two vessels shall not make the overtaking vessel a crossing vessel within the meaning of these Rules or relieve her of the duty of keeping clear of the overtaken vessel until she is finally past and clear.

(Pub. L. 96–591, §2, Dec. 24, 1980, 94 Stat. 3420.)

REPEAL OF SECTION

Pub. L. 108–293, title III, §303(a), (c), Aug. 9, 2004, 118 Stat. 1042, provided that this section is repealed effective on the effective date of final regulations prescribed by the Secretary of the Department in which the Coast Guard is operating under section 2071 of this title.

REFERENCES IN TEXT

Rules 4 through 18, referred to in par. (a), are classified to sections 2004 through 2018 of this title.

These Rules, referred to in par. (d), are the Inland Navigational Rules which are classified to this subchapter.

CODIFICATION

Section was enacted as part of section 2 of Pub. L. 96–591 which enacted the Inland Navigational Rules which comprise this subchapter.

§ 2014. Head-on situation (Rule 14)

(a) Course alterations to starboard; port side passage

Unless otherwise agreed, when two power-driven vessels are meeting on reciprocal or nearly reciprocal courses so as to involve risk of collision each shall alter her course to starboard so that each shall pass on the port side of the other.

(b) Existence of head-on situation

Such a situation shall be deemed to exist when a vessel sees the other ahead or nearly ahead and by night she could see the masthead lights of the other in a line or nearly in a line or both sidelights and by day she observes the corresponding aspect of the other vessel.

(c) Assumption that head-on situation exists in cases of doubt

When a vessel is in any doubt as to whether such a situation exists she shall assume that it does exist and act accordingly.

(d) Vessel operating on Great Lakes, Western Rivers, or other specified waters, and proceeding downbound with following current

Notwithstanding paragraph (a) of this Rule, a power-driven vessel operating on the Great Lakes, Western Rivers, or waters specified by the Secretary, and proceeding downbound with a following current shall have the right-of-way over an upbound vessel, shall propose the manner of passage, and shall initiate the maneuvering signals prescribed by Rule 34(a)(i), as appropriate.

(Pub. L. 96–591, §2, Dec. 24, 1980, 94 Stat. 3421; Pub. L. 98–557, §16(c), Oct. 30, 1984, 98 Stat. 2867.)

REPEAL OF SECTION

Pub. L. 108–293, title III, §303(a), (c), Aug. 9, 2004, 118 Stat. 1042, provided that this section is repealed effective on the effective date of final regulations prescribed by the Secretary of the Department in which the Coast Guard is operating under section 2071 of this title.

REFERENCES IN TEXT

Rule 34(a)(i), referred to in par. (d), is classified to section 2034(a)(i) of this title.

CODIFICATION

Section was enacted as part of section 2 of Pub. L. 96–591 which enacted the Inland Navigational Rules which comprise this subchapter.

AMENDMENTS

1984—Par. (a). Pub. L. 98–557, §16(c)(1), substituted "Unless otherwise agreed, when" for "When".

Par. (d). Pub. L. 98–557, §16(c)(2), added par. (d).

§2015. Crossing situation (Rule 15)

(a) Vessel which must keep out of the other vessel's way

When two power-driven vessels are crossing so as to involve risk of collision, the vessel which has the other on her starboard side shall keep out of the way and shall, if the circumstances of the case admit, avoid crossing ahead of the other vessel.

(b) Vessels crossing river

Notwithstanding paragraph (a), on the Great Lakes, Western Rivers, or water specified by the Secretary, a power-driven vessel crossing a river shall keep out of the way of a power-driven vessel ascending or descending the river.

(Pub. L. 96–591, §2, Dec. 24, 1980, 94 Stat. 3421; Pub. L. 104–324, title VII, §701(2), Oct. 19, 1996, 110 Stat. 3932.)

REPEAL OF SECTION

Pub. L. 108–293, title III, §303(a), (c), Aug. 9, 2004, 118 Stat. 1042, provided that this section is repealed effective on the effective date of final regulations prescribed by the Secretary of the Department in which the Coast Guard is operating under section 2071 of this title.

CODIFICATION

Section was enacted as part of section 2 of Pub. L. 96–591 which enacted the Inland Navigational Rules which comprise this subchapter.

AMENDMENTS

1996—Par. (b). Pub. L. 104–324 inserted "power-driven" after "Secretary, a".

§2016. Action by give-way vessel (Rule 16)

Every vessel which is directed to keep out of the way of another vessel shall, so far as possible, take early and substantial action to keep well clear.

(Pub. L. 96–591, §2, Dec. 24, 1980, 94 Stat. 3421.)

REPEAL OF SECTION

Pub. L. 108–293, title III, §303(a), (c), Aug. 9, 2004, 118 Stat. 1042, provided that this section is repealed effective on the effective date of final regulations prescribed by the Secretary of the Department in which the Coast Guard is operating under section 2071 of this title.

CODIFICATION

Section was enacted as part of section 2 of Pub. L. 96–591 which enacted the Inland Navigational Rules which comprise this subchapter.

§2017. Action by stand-on vessel (Rule 17)

(a) Stand-on vessel to keep course and speed; action allowed when give-way vessel fails to take appropriate action

(i) Where one of two vessels is to keep out of the way, the other shall keep her course and speed.

(ii) The latter vessel may, however, take action to avoid collision by her maneuver alone, as soon as it becomes apparent to her that the vessel required to keep out of the way is not taking appropriate action in compliance with these Rules.

(b) Action by stand-on vessel allowed when action by give-way vessel alone cannot avoid collision

When, from any cause, the vessel required to keep her course and speed finds herself so close that collision cannot be avoided by the action of the give-way vessel alone, she shall take such action as will best aid to avoid collision.

(c) Crossing situations

A power-driven vessel which takes action in a crossing situation in accordance with subparagraph (a)(ii) of this Rule to avoid collision with another power-driven vessel shall, if the circumstances of the case admit, not alter course to port for a vessel on her own port side.

(d) Give-way vessel not relieved of obligation to keep out of the way

This Rule does not relieve the give-way vessel of her obligation to keep out of the way.

(Pub. L. 96–591, §2, Dec. 24, 1980, 94 Stat. 3421.)

REPEAL OF SECTION

Pub. L. 108–293, title III, §303(a), (c), Aug. 9, 2004, 118 Stat. 1042, provided that this section is repealed effective on the effective date of final regulations prescribed by the Secretary of the Department in which the Coast Guard is operating under section 2071 of this title.

REFERENCES IN TEXT

These Rules, referred to in par. (a)(ii), are the Inland Navigational Rules which are classified to this subchapter.

CODIFICATION

Section was enacted as part of section 2 of Pub. L. 96–591 which enacted the Inland Navigational Rules which comprise this subchapter.

§2018. Responsibilities between vessels (Rule 18)

Except where Rules 9, 10, and 13 otherwise require:

(a) Power-driven vessels underway

A power-driven vessel underway shall keep out of the way of:

(i) a vessel not under command;

(ii) a vessel restricted in her ability to maneuver;

(iii) a vessel engaged in fishing; and

(iv) a sailing vessel.

(b) Sailing vessels underway

A sailing vessel underway shall keep out of the way of:

(i) a vessel not under command;

(ii) a vessel restricted in her ability to maneuver; and

(iii) a vessel engaged in fishing.

(c) Vessels engaged in fishing when underway

A vessel engaged in fishing when underway shall, so far as possible, keep out of the way of:

(i) a vessel not under command; and

(ii) a vessel restricted in her ability to maneuver.

(d) Seaplanes on the water

A seaplane on the water shall, in general, keep well clear of all vessels and avoid impeding their navigation. In circumstances, however, where risk of collision exists, she shall comply with the Rules of this Part.

(Pub. L. 96–591, § 2, Dec. 24, 1980, 94 Stat. 3422.)

REPEAL OF SECTION

Pub. L. 108–293, title III, § 303(a), (c), Aug. 9, 2004, 118 Stat. 1042, provided that this section is repealed effective on the effective date of final regulations prescribed by the Secretary of the Department in which the Coast Guard is operating under section 2071 of this title.

REFERENCES IN TEXT

Rules 9, 10, and 13, referred to in text, are classified to sections 2009, 2010, and 2013, respectively, of this title.

Rules of this Part, referred to in par. (d), mean sections 2004 to 2019 of this title.

CODIFICATION

Section was enacted as part of section 2 of Pub. L. 96–591 which enacted the Inland Navigational Rules which comprise this subchapter.

SUBPART III—CONDUCT OF VESSELS IN RESTRICTED VISIBILITY

§ 2019. Conduct of vessels in restricted visibility (Rule 19)

(a) Vessels to which rule applies

This Rule applies to vessels not in sight of one another when navigating in or near an area of restricted visibility.

(b) Safe speed; engines ready for immediate maneuver

Every vessel shall proceed at a safe speed adapted to the prevailing circumstances and conditions of restricted visibility. A power-driven vessel shall have her engines ready for immediate maneuver.

(c) Due regard to prevailing circumstances and conditions

Every vessel shall have due regard to the prevailing circumstances and conditions of restricted visibility when complying with Rules 4 through 10.

(d) Detection of vessel by radar alone

A vessel which detects by radar alone the presence of another vessel shall determine if a close-quarters situation is developing or risk of collision exists. If so, she shall take avoiding action in ample time, provided that when such action consists of an alteration of course, so far as possible the following shall be avoided:

(i) an alteration of course to port for a vessel forward of the beam, other than for a vessel being overtaken; and

(ii) an alteration of course toward a vessel abeam or abaft the beam.

(e) Reduction of speed to minimum

Except where it has been determined that a risk of collision does not exist, every vessel which hears apparently forward of her beam the fog signal of another vessel, or which cannot avoid a close-quarters situation with another vessel forward of her beam, shall reduce her speed to the minimum at which she can be kept on course. She shall if necessary take all her way off and, in any event, navigate with extreme caution until danger of collision is over.

(Pub. L. 96–591, § 2, Dec. 24, 1980, 94 Stat. 3422.)

REPEAL OF SECTION

Pub. L. 108–293, title III, § 303(a), (c), Aug. 9, 2004, 118 Stat. 1042, provided that this section is repealed effective on the effective date of final regulations prescribed by the Secretary of the Department in which the Coast Guard is operating under section 2071 of this title.

REFERENCES IN TEXT

Rules 4 through 10, referred to in par. (c), are classified to sections 2004 through 2010 of this title.

CODIFICATION

Section was enacted as part of section 2 of Pub. L. 96–591 which enacted the Inland Navigational Rules which comprise this subchapter.

PART C—LIGHTS AND SHAPES

§ 2020. Application (Rule 20)

(a) Compliance in all weathers

Rules in this Part shall be complied with in all weathers.

(b) Rules concerning lights complied with from sunset to sunrise; other lights

The Rules concerning lights shall be complied with from sunset to sunrise, and during such times no other lights shall be exhibited, except such lights as cannot be mistaken for the lights specified in these Rules or do not impair their visibility or distinctive character, or interfere with the keeping of a proper lookout.

(c) Lights during daylight hours in restricted visibility; other circumstances

The lights prescribed by these Rules shall, if carried, also be exhibited from sunrise to sunset in restricted visibility and may be exhibited in all other circumstances when it is deemed necessary.

(d) Rules concerning shapes; compliance by day

The Rules concerning shapes shall be complied with by day.

(e) Annex

The lights and shapes specified in these Rules shall comply with the provisions of Annex I of these Rules.

(Pub. L. 96–591, § 2, Dec. 24, 1980, 94 Stat. 3423.)

REPEAL OF SECTION

Pub. L. 108–293, title III, § 303(a), (c), Aug. 9, 2004, 118 Stat. 1042, provided that this section is repealed effective on the effective date of final regulations prescribed by the Secretary of the Department in which the Coast Guard is operating under section 2071 of this title.

REFERENCES IN TEXT

Rules in this Part, referred to in par. (a), mean sections 2020 to 2031 of this title.

The Rules, referred to in pars. (b) and (d), and these Rules, referred to in pars. (c) and (e), respectively, are the Inland Navigational Rules which are classified to this subchapter.

Annex I of these Rules, referred to in par. (e), is to be established by the Secretary under section 2071 of this title.

CODIFICATION

Section was enacted as part of section 2 of Pub. L. 96–591 which enacted the Inland Navigational Rules which comprise this subchapter.

§2021. Definitions (Rule 21)

(a) "Masthead light" means a white light placed over the fore and aft centerline of the vessel showing an unbroken light over an arc of the horizon of 225 degrees and so fixed as to show the light from right ahead to 22.5 degrees abaft the beam on either side of the vessel, except that on a vessel of less than 12 meters in length the masthead light shall be placed as nearly as practicable to the fore and aft centerline of the vessel.

(b) "Sidelights" mean a green light on the starboard side and a red light on the port side each showing an unbroken light over an arc of the horizon of 112.5 degrees and so fixed as to show the light from right ahead to 22.5 degrees abaft the beam on its respective side. On a vessel of less than 20 meters in length the side lights may be combined in one lantern carried on the fore and aft centerline of the vessel, except that on a vessel of less than 12 meters in length the sidelights when combined in one lantern shall be placed as nearly as practicable to the fore and aft centerline of the vessel.

(c) "Sternlight" means a white light placed as nearly as practicable at the stern showing an unbroken light over an arc of the horizon of 135 degrees and so fixed as to show the light 67.5 degrees from right aft on each side of the vessel.

(d) "Towing light" means a yellow light having the same characteristics as the "sternlight" defined in paragraph (c) of this Rule.

(e) "All-round light" means a light showing an unbroken light over an arc of the horizon of 360 degrees.

(f) "Flashing light" means a light flashing at regular intervals at a frequency of 120 flashes or more per minute.

(g) "Special flashing light" means a yellow light flashing at regular intervals at a frequency of 50 to 70 flashes per minute, placed as far forward and as nearly as practicable on the fore and aft centerline of the tow and showing an unbroken light over an arc of the horizon of not less than 180 degrees nor more than 225 degrees and so fixed as to show the light from right ahead to abeam and no more than 22.5 degrees abaft the beam on either side of the vessel.

(Pub. L. 96–591, §2, Dec. 24, 1980, 94 Stat. 3423.)

REPEAL OF SECTION

Pub. L. 108–293, title III, §303(a), (c), Aug. 9, 2004, 118 Stat. 1042, provided that this section is repealed effective on the effective date of final regulations prescribed by the Secretary of the Department in which the Coast Guard is operating under section 2071 of this title.

CODIFICATION

Section was enacted as part of section 2 of Pub. L. 96–591 which enacted the Inland Navigational Rules which comprise this subchapter.

§2022. Visibility of lights (Rule 22)

The lights prescribed in these Rules shall have an intensity as specified in Annex I to these Rules, so as to be visible at the following minimum ranges:

(a) Vessels of 50 meters or more in length

In a vessel of 50 meters or more in length:
a masthead light, 6 miles;
a sidelight, 3 miles;
a sternlight, 3 miles;
a towing light, 3 miles;
a white, red, green or yellow all-round light, 3 miles; and
a special flashing light, 2 miles.

(b) Vessels of 12 meters or more but less than 50 meters in length

In a vessel of 12 meters or more in length but less than 50 meters in length:
a masthead light, 5 miles; except that where the length of the vessel is less than 20 meters, 3 miles;
a sidelight, 2 miles;
a sternlight, 2 miles;
a towing light, 2 miles;
a white, red, green or yellow all-round light, 2 miles; and
a special flashing light, 2 miles.

(c) Vessels of less than 12 meters in length

In a vessel of less than 12 meters in length:
a masthead light, 2 miles;
a sidelight, 1 mile;
a sternlight, 2 miles;
a towing light, 2 miles;
a white, red, green or yellow all-round light, 2 miles; and
a special flashing light, 2 miles.

(d) Inconspicuous, partly submerged vessels or objects being towed

In an inconspicuous, partly submerged vessel or object being towed:
a white all-round light, 3 miles.

(Pub. L. 96–591, §2, Dec. 24, 1980, 94 Stat. 3424.)

REPEAL OF SECTION

Pub. L. 108–293, title III, §303(a), (c), Aug. 9, 2004, 118 Stat. 1042, provided that this section is repealed effective on the effective date of final regulations prescribed by the Secretary of the Department in which the Coast Guard is operating under section 2071 of this title.

REFERENCES IN TEXT

These Rules, referred to in text, are the Inland Navigational Rules which are classified to this subchapter.

Annex I to these Rules, referred to in text, is to be established by the Secretary under section 2071 of this title.

CODIFICATION

Section was enacted as part of section 2 of Pub. L. 96–591 which enacted the Inland Navigational Rules which comprise this subchapter.

§2023. Power-driven vessels underway (Rule 23)

(a) Lights exhibited by power-driven vessels underway

A power-driven vessel underway shall exhibit:
(i) a masthead light forward;

(ii) a second masthead light abaft of and higher than the forward one; except that a vessel of less than 50 meters in length shall not be obliged to exhibit such light but may do so;

(iii) sidelights; and

(iv) a sternlight.

(b) Air-cushion vessels

An air-cushion vessel when operating in the nondisplacement mode shall, in addition to the lights prescribed in paragraph (a) of this Rule, exhibit an all-round flashing yellow light where it can best be seen.

(c) Alternative lights for power-driven vessels of less than 12 meters in length

A power-driven vessel of less than 12 meters in length may, in lieu of the lights prescribed in paragraph (a) of this Rule, exhibit an all-round white light and sidelights.

(d) Power-driven vessels when operating on Great Lakes

A power-driven vessel when operating on the Great Lakes may carry an all-round white light in lieu of the second masthead light and sternlight prescribed in paragraph (a) of this Rule. The light shall be carried in the position of the second masthead light and be visible at the same minimum range.

(Pub. L. 96–591, §2, Dec. 24, 1980, 94 Stat. 3424; Pub. L. 104–324, title VII, §701(3), Oct. 19, 1996, 110 Stat. 3932.)

REPEAL OF SECTION

Pub. L. 108–293, title III, § 303(a), (c), Aug. 9, 2004, 118 Stat. 1042, provided that this section is repealed effective on the effective date of final regulations prescribed by the Secretary of the Department in which the Coast Guard is operating under section 2071 of this title.

CODIFICATION

Section was enacted as part of section 2 of Pub. L. 96–591 which enacted the Inland Navigational Rules which comprise this subchapter.

AMENDMENTS

1996—Par. (a)(i). Pub. L. 104–324, which directed the striking out of "except that a vessel of less than 20 meters in length need not exhibit this light forward of amidships but shall exhibit it as far forward as is practicable;" after "masthead light forward", was executed by striking out that language, which appeared after "masthead light forward;" to reflect the probable intent of Congress.

§ 2024. Towing and pushing (Rule 24)

(a) Power-driven vessels when towing astern

A power-driven vessel when towing astern shall exhibit:

(i) instead of the light prescribed either in Rule 23(a)(i) or 23(a)(ii), two masthead lights in a vertical line. When the length of the tow, measuring from the stern of the towing vessel to the after end of the tow exceeds 200 meters, three such lights in a vertical line;

(ii) sidelights;

(iii) a sternlight;

(iv) a towing light in a vertical line above the sternlight; and

(v) when the length of the tow exceeds 200 meters, a diamond shape where it can best be seen.

(b) Pushing vessel and pushed vessel rigidly connected in composite unit

When a pushing vessel and a vessel being pushed ahead are rigidly connected in a composite unit they shall be regarded as a power-driven vessel and exhibit the lights prescribed in Rule 23.

(c) Power-driven vessel when pushing ahead or towing alongside

A power-driven vessel when pushing ahead or towing alongside, except as required by paragraphs (b) and (i) of this Rule, shall exhibit:

(i) instead of the light prescribed either in Rule 23(a)(i) or 23(a)(ii), two masthead lights in a vertical line;

(ii) sidelights; and

(iii) two towing lights in a vertical line.

(d) Compliance with other requirements

A power-driven vessel to which paragraphs (a) or (c) of this Rule apply shall also comply with Rule 23(a)(i) and 23(a)(ii).

(e) Vessels being towed

A vessel or object other than those referred to in paragraph (g) of this Rule being towed shall exhibit:

(i) sidelights;

(ii) a sternlight; and

(iii) when the length of the tow exceeds 200 meters, a diamond shape where it can best be seen.

(f) Vessels being towed alongside or pushed in a group

Provided that any number of vessels being towed alongside or pushed in a group shall be lighted as one vessel, except as provided in paragraph (iii)—

(i) a vessel being pushed ahead, not being part of a composite unit, shall exhibit at the forward end, sidelights and a special flashing light;

(ii) a vessel being towed alongside shall exhibit a sternlight and at the forward end, sidelights and a special flashing light; and

(iii) when vessels are towed alongside on both sides of the towing vessels a stern light[1] shall be exhibited on the stern of the outboard vessel on each side of the towing vessel, and a single set of sidelights as far forward and as far outboard as is practicable, and a single special flashing light.

(g) Inconspicuous, partly submerged vessel or object being towed

An inconspicuous, partly submerged vessel or object being towed shall exhibit:

(i) if it is less than 25 meters in breadth, one all-round white light at or near each end;

(ii) if it is 25 meters or more in breadth, four all-round white lights to mark its length and breadth;

(iii) if it exceeds 100 meters in length, additional all-round white lights between the lights prescribed in subparagraphs (i) and (ii) so that the distance between the lights shall not exceed 100 meters: *Provided*, That any vessels or objects being towed alongside each other shall be lighted as one vessel or object;

[1] So in original. Probably should be "sternlight".

(iv) a diamond shape at or near the aftermost extremity of the last vessel or object being towed; and

(v) the towing vessel may direct a searchlight in the direction of the tow to indicate its presence to an approaching vessel.

(h) Alternative lighting of vessel or object being towed

Where from any sufficient cause it is impracticable for a vessel or object being towed to exhibit the lights prescribed in paragraph (e) or (g) of this Rule, all possible measures shall be taken to light the vessel or object towed or at least to indicate the presence of the unlighted vessel or object.

(i) Western Rivers or other specified waters; exception

Notwithstanding paragraph (c), on the Western Rivers (except below the Huey P. Long Bridge on the Mississippi River) and on waters specified by the Secretary, a power-driven vessel when pushing ahead or towing alongside, except as paragraph (b) applies, shall exhibit:

(i) sidelights; and

(ii) two towing lights in a vertical line.

(j) Towing another vessel in distress or otherwise in need of assistance

Where from any sufficient cause it is impracticable for a vessel not normally engaged in towing operations to display the lights prescribed by paragraph (a), (c) or (i) of this Rule, such vessel shall not be required to exhibit those lights when engaged in towing another vessel in distress or otherwise in need of assistance. All possible measures shall be taken to indicate the nature of the relationship between the towing vessel and the vessel being assisted. The searchlight authorized by Rule 36 may be used to illuminate the tow.

(Pub. L. 96–591, §2, Dec. 24, 1980, 94 Stat. 3425; Pub. L. 98–557, §16(b)(1), Oct. 30, 1984, 98 Stat. 2866; Pub. L. 104–324, title VII, §701(4), Oct. 19, 1996, 110 Stat. 3932.)

REPEAL OF SECTION

Pub. L. 108–293, title III, §303(a), (c), Aug. 9, 2004, 118 Stat. 1042, provided that this section is repealed effective on the effective date of final regulations prescribed by the Secretary of the Department in which the Coast Guard is operating under section 2071 of this title.

REFERENCES IN TEXT

Rule 23, referred to in pars. (a)(i), (b), (c)(i), and (d), is classified to section 2023 of this title.

Rule 36, referred to in par. (j), is classified to section 2036 of this title.

CODIFICATION

Section was enacted as part of section 2 of Pub. L. 96–591 which enacted the Inland Navigational Rules which comprise this subchapter.

AMENDMENTS

1996—Par. (f). Pub. L. 104–324 amended par. (f) generally. Prior to amendment, par. (f) read as follows: "Provided that any number of vessels being towed alongside or pushed in a group shall be lighted as one vessel:

"(i) a vessel being pushed ahead, not being part of a composite unit, shall exhibit at the forward end sidelights, and a special flashing light; and

"(ii) a vessel being towed alongside shall exhibit a sternlight and at the forward end sidelights."

1984—Par. (i). Pub. L. 98–557 inserted exception for below the Long Bridge on the Mississippi River.

§2025. Sailing vessels underway and vessels under oars (Rule 25)

(a) Sailing vessels underway

A sailing vessel underway shall exhibit:

(i) sidelights; and

(ii) a sternlight.

(b) Sailing vessels of less than 20 meters in length

In a sailing vessel of less than 20 meters in length the lights prescribed in paragraph (a) of this Rule may be combined in one lantern carried at or near the top of the mast where it can best be seen.

(c) Additional lights

A sailing vessel underway may, in addition to the lights prescribed in paragraph (a) of this Rule, exhibit at or near the top of the mast, where they can best be seen, two all-round lights in a vertical line, the upper being red and the lower green, but these lights shall not be exhibited in conjunction with the combined lantern permitted by paragraph (b) of this Rule.

(d) Sailing vessels of less than 7 meters in length; vessels under oars

(i) A sailing vessel of less than 7 meters in length shall, if practicable, exhibit the lights prescribed in paragraph (a) or (b) of this Rule, but if she does not, she shall have ready at hand an electric torch or lighted lantern showing a white light which shall be exhibited in sufficient time to prevent collision.

(ii) A vessel under oars may exhibit the lights prescribed in this Rule for sailing vessels, but if she does not, she shall have ready at hand an electric torch or lighted lantern showing a white light which shall be exhibited in sufficient time to prevent collision.

(e) Vessels proceeding under sail

A vessel proceeding under sail when also being propelled by machinery shall exhibit forward where it can best be seen a conical shape, apex downward. A vessel of less than 12 meters in length is not required to exhibit this shape, but may do so.

(Pub. L. 96–591, §2, Dec. 24, 1980, 94 Stat. 3426.)

REPEAL OF SECTION

Pub. L. 108–293, title III, §303(a), (c), Aug. 9, 2004, 118 Stat. 1042, provided that this section is repealed effective on the effective date of final regulations prescribed by the Secretary of the Department in which the Coast Guard is operating under section 2071 of this title.

CODIFICATION

Section was enacted as part of section 2 of Pub. L. 96–591 which enacted the Inland Navigational Rules which comprise this subchapter.

§2026. Fishing vessels (Rule 26)

(a) Exhibition of only prescribed lights and shapes

A vessel engaged in fishing, whether underway or at anchor, shall exhibit only the lights and shapes prescribed in this Rule.

(b) Vessels engaged in trawling

A vessel when engaged in trawling, by which is meant the dragging through the water of a dredge net or other apparatus used as a fishing appliance, shall exhibit:

(i) two all-round lights in a vertical line, the upper being green and the lower white, or a shape consisting of two cones with their apexes together in a vertical line one above the other;

(ii) a masthead light abaft of and higher than the all-round green light; a vessel of less than 50 meters in length shall not be obliged to exhibit such a light but may do so; and

(iii) when making way through the water, in addition to the lights prescribed in this paragraph, sidelights and a sternlight.

(c) Vessels engaged in fishing other than trawling

A vessel engaged in fishing, other than trawling, shall exhibit:

(i) two all-round lights in a vertical line, the upper being red and the lower white, or a shape consisting of two cones with apexes together in a vertical line one above the other;

(ii) when there is outlying gear extending more than 150 meters horizontally from the vessel, an all-round white light or a cone apex upward in the direction of the gear; and

(iii) when making way through the water, in addition to the lights prescribed in this paragraph, sidelights and a sternlight.

(d) Vessels engaged in fishing in close proximity to other vessels engaged in fishing

The additional signals described in Annex II to these Rules apply to a vessel engaged in fishing in close proximity to other vessels engaged in fishing.

(e) Vessels when not engaged in fishing

A vessel when not engaged in fishing shall not exhibit the lights or shapes prescribed in this Rule, but only those prescribed for a vessel of her length.

(Pub. L. 96–591, §2, Dec. 24, 1980, 94 Stat. 3427; Pub. L. 104–324, title VII, §701(5), Oct. 19, 1996, 110 Stat. 3933.)

REPEAL OF SECTION

Pub. L. 108–293, title III, §303(a), (c), Aug. 9, 2004, 118 Stat. 1042, provided that this section is repealed effective on the effective date of final regulations prescribed by the Secretary of the Department in which the Coast Guard is operating under section 2071 of this title.

REFERENCES IN TEXT

Annex II to these Rules, referred to in par. (d), is to be established by the Secretary under section 2071 of this title.

CODIFICATION

Section was enacted as part of section 2 of Pub. L. 96–591 which enacted the Inland Navigational Rules which comprise this subchapter.

AMENDMENTS

1996—Pars. (b)(i), (c)(i). Pub. L. 104–324, §701(5)(A), struck out "a vessel of less than 20 meters in length may instead of this shape exhibit a basket;" after "above the other;".

Par. (d). Pub. L. 104–324 amended par. (d) generally. Prior to amendment, par. (d) read as follows: "A vessel engaged in fishing in close proximity to other vessels engaged in fishing may exhibit the additional signals described in Annex II to these Rules."

§2027. Vessels not under command or restricted in their ability to maneuver (Rule 27)

(a) Vessels not under command

A vessel not under command shall exhibit:

(i) two all-round red lights in a vertical line where they can best be seen;

(ii) two balls or similar shapes in a vertical line where they can best be seen; and

(iii) when making way through the water, in addition to the lights prescribed in this paragraph, sidelights and a sternlight.

(b) Vessels restricted in their ability to maneuver

A vessel restricted in her ability to maneuver, except a vessel engaged in mineclearance operations, shall exhibit:

(i) three all-round lights in a vertical line where they can best be seen. The highest and lowest of these lights shall be red and the middle light shall be white;

(ii) three shapes in a vertical line where they can best be seen. The highest and lowest of these shapes shall be balls and the middle one a diamond;

(iii) when making way through the water, masthead lights, sidelights and a sternlight, in addition to the lights prescribed in subparagraph (b)(i); and

(iv) when at anchor, in addition to the lights or shapes prescribed in subparagraphs (b)(i) and (ii), the light, lights or shapes prescribed in Rule 30.

(c) Vessels engaged in towing operations

A vessel engaged in a towing operation which severely restricts the towing vessel and her tow in their ability to deviate from their course shall, in addition to the lights or shapes prescribed in subparagraphs (b)(i) and (ii) of this Rule, exhibit the lights or shape prescribed in Rule 24.

(d) Vessels engaged in dredging or underwater operations

A vessel engaged in dredging or underwater operations, when restricted in her ability to maneuver, shall exhibit the lights and shapes prescribed in subparagraphs (b)(i), (ii), and (iii) of this Rule and shall in addition, when an obstruction exists, exhibit:

(i) two all-round red lights or two balls in a vertical line to indicate the side on which the obstruction exists;

(ii) two all-round green lights or two diamonds in a vertical line to indicate the side on which another vessel may pass; and

(iii) when at anchor, the lights or shape prescribed by this paragraph, instead of the lights or shapes prescribed in Rule 30 for anchored vessels.

(e) Vessels engaged in diving operations

Whenever the size of a vessel engaged in diving operations makes it impracticable to exhibit all lights and shapes prescribed in paragraph (d) of this Rule, the following shall instead be exhibited:

(i) Three all-round lights in a vertical line where they can best be seen. The highest and lowest of these lights shall be red and the middle light shall be white.

(ii) A rigid replica of the international Code flag "A" not less than 1 meter in height. Measures shall be taken to insure its all-round visibility.

(f) Vessels engaged in mineclearance operations

A vessel engaged in mineclearance operations shall, in addition to the lights prescribed for a power-driven vessel in Rule 23 or to the lights or shape prescribed for a vessel at anchor in Rule 30, as appropriate, exhibit three all-round green lights or three balls. One of these lights or shapes shall be exhibited near the foremast head and one at each end of the fore yard. These lights or shapes indicate that it is dangerous for another vessel to approach within 1,000 meters of the mineclearance vessel.

(g) Vessels of less than 12 meters in length

A vessel of less than 12 meters in length, except when engaged in diving operations, is not required to exhibit the lights or shapes prescribed in this Rule.

(h) Signals of vessels in distress and requiring assistance

The signals prescribed in this Rule are not signals of vessels in distress and requiring assistance. Such signals are contained in Annex IV to these Rules.

(Pub. L. 96–591, §2, Dec. 24, 1980, 94 Stat. 3427; Pub. L. 100–448, §14(2), (3), Sept. 28, 1988, 102 Stat. 1844.)

REPEAL OF SECTION

Pub. L. 108–293, title III, §303(a), (c), Aug. 9, 2004, 118 Stat. 1042, provided that this section is repealed effective on the effective date of final regulations prescribed by the Secretary of the Department in which the Coast Guard is operating under section 2071 of this title.

REFERENCES IN TEXT

Rule 30, referred to in pars. (b)(iv), (d)(iii), and (f), is classified to section 2030 of this title.

Rule 24, referred to in par. (c), is classified to section 2024 of this title.

Rule 23, referred to in par. (f), is classified to section 2023 of this title.

Annex IV to these Rules, referred to in par. (h), is to be established by the Secretary under section 2071 of this title.

CODIFICATION

Section was enacted as part of section 2 of Pub. L. 96–591 which enacted the Inland Navigational Rules which comprise this subchapter.

AMENDMENTS

1988—Par. (b). Pub. L. 100–448, §14(2), substituted "mineclearance" for "minesweeping" in introductory provisions.

Par. (f). Pub. L. 100–448, §14(3), amended par. (f) generally. Prior to amendment, par. (f) read as follows: "A vessel engaged in minesweeping operations shall, in addition to the lights prescribed for a power-driven vessel in Rule 23, exhibit three all-round green lights or three balls. One of these lights or shapes shall be exhibited near the foremast head and one at each end of the fore yard. These lights or shapes indicate that it is dangerous for another vessel to approach closer than 1,000 meters astern or 500 meters on either side of the minesweeper."

§ 2028. [Reserved] (Rule 28)

§ 2029. Pilot vessels (Rule 29)

(a) Vessels engaged on pilotage duty

A vessel engaged on pilotage duty shall exhibit:

(i) at or near the masthead, two all-round lights in a vertical line, the upper being white and the lower red;

(ii) when underway, in addition, sidelights and a sternlight; and

(iii) when at anchor, in addition to the lights prescribed in subparagraph (i), the anchor light, lights, or shape prescribed in Rule 30 for anchored vessels.

(b) Vessels when not engaged on pilotage duty

A pilot vessel when not engaged on pilotage duty shall exhibit the lights or shapes prescribed for a vessel of her length.

(Pub. L. 96–591, §2, Dec. 24, 1980, 94 Stat. 3428.)

REPEAL OF SECTION

Pub. L. 108–293, title III, §303(a), (c), Aug. 9, 2004, 118 Stat. 1042, provided that this section is repealed effective on the effective date of final regulations prescribed by the Secretary of the Department in which the Coast Guard is operating under section 2071 of this title.

REFERENCES IN TEXT

Rule 30, referred to in par. (a)(iii), is classified to section 2030 of this title.

CODIFICATION

Section was enacted as part of section 2 of Pub. L. 96–591 which enacted the Inland Navigational Rules which comprise this subchapter.

§ 2030. Anchored vessels and vessels aground (Rule 30)

(a) Vessels at anchor

A vessel at anchor shall exhibit where it can best be seen:

(i) in the fore part, an all-round white light or one ball; and

(ii) at or near the stern and at a lower level than the light prescribed in subparagraph (i), an all-round white light.

(b) Vessels of less than 50 meters in length; alternative light

A vessel of less than 50 meters in length may exhibit an all-round white light where it can best be seen instead of the lights prescribed in paragraph (a) of this Rule.

(c) Illumination of decks

A vessel at anchor may, and a vessel of 100 meters or more in length shall, also use the available working or equivalent lights to illuminate her decks.

(d) Vessels aground

A vessel aground shall exhibit the lights prescribed in paragraph (a) or (b) of this Rule and in addition, if practicable, where they can best be seen:

(i) two all-round red lights in a vertical line; and

(ii) three balls in a vertical line.

(e) Vessels of less than 7 meters in length when at anchor

A vessel of less than 7 meters in length, when at anchor, not in or near a narrow channel, fairway, anchorage, or where other vessels normally navigate, shall not be required to exhibit the lights or shape prescribed in paragraphs (a) and (b) of this Rule.

(f) Vessels of less than 12 meters in length when aground

A vessel of less than 12 meters in length when aground shall not be required to exhibit the lights or shapes prescribed in subparagraphs (d)(i) and (ii) of this Rule.

(g) Vessels of less than 20 meters in length while at anchor in special anchorage

A vessel of less than 20 meters in length, when at anchor in a special anchorage area designated by the Secretary, shall not be required to exhibit the anchor lights and shapes required by this Rule.

(Pub. L. 96–591, §2, Dec. 24, 1980, 94 Stat. 3429.)

REPEAL OF SECTION

Pub. L. 108–293, title III, § 303(a), (c), Aug. 9, 2004, 118 Stat. 1042, provided that this section is repealed effective on the effective date of final regulations prescribed by the Secretary of the Department in which the Coast Guard is operating under section 2071 of this title.

CODIFICATION

Section was enacted as part of section 2 of Pub. L. 96–591 which enacted the Inland Navigational Rules which comprise this subchapter.

§ 2031. Seaplanes (Rule 31)

Where it is impracticable for a seaplane to exhibit lights and shapes of the characteristics or in the positions prescribed in the Rules of this Part she shall exhibit lights and shapes as closely similar in characteristics and position as is possible.

(Pub. L. 96–591, §2, Dec. 24, 1980, 94 Stat. 3429.)

REPEAL OF SECTION

Pub. L. 108–293, title III, § 303(a), (c), Aug. 9, 2004, 118 Stat. 1042, provided that this section is repealed effective on the effective date of final regulations prescribed by the Secretary of the Department in which the Coast Guard is operating under section 2071 of this title.

REFERENCES IN TEXT

Rules of this Part, referred to in text, means sections 2020 to 2031 of this title.

CODIFICATION

Section was enacted as part of section 2 of Pub. L. 96–591 which enacted the Inland Navigational Rules which comprise this subchapter.

PART D—SOUND AND LIGHT SIGNALS

§ 2032. Definitions (Rule 32)

(a) The word "whistle" means any sound signaling appliance capable of producing the prescribed blasts and which complies with specifications in Annex III to these Rules.

(b) The term "short blast" means a blast of about 1 second's duration.

(c) The term "prolonged blast" means a blast of from 4 to 6 seconds' duration.

(Pub. L. 96–591, §2, Dec. 24, 1980, 94 Stat. 3429.)

REPEAL OF SECTION

Pub. L. 108–293, title III, § 303(a), (c), Aug. 9, 2004, 118 Stat. 1042, provided that this section is repealed effective on the effective date of final regulations prescribed by the Secretary of the Department in which the Coast Guard is operating under section 2071 of this title.

REFERENCES IN TEXT

Annex III to these Rules, referred to in par. (a), is to be established by the Secretary under section 2071 of this title.

CODIFICATION

Section was enacted as part of section 2 of Pub. L. 96–591 which enacted the Inland Navigational Rules which comprise this subchapter.

§ 2033. Equipment for sound signals (Rule 33)

(a) Vessels of 12 meters or more in length

A vessel of 12 meters or more in length shall be provided with a whistle and a bell and a vessel of 100 meters or more in length shall, in addition, be provided with a gong, the tone and sound of which cannot be confused with that of the bell. The whistle, bell and gong shall comply with the specifications in Annex III to these Rules. The bell or gong or both may be replaced by other equipment having the same respective sound characteristics, provided that manual sounding of the prescribed signals shall always be possible.

(b) Vessels of less than 12 meters in length

A vessel of less than 12 meters in length shall not be obliged to carry the sound signaling appliances prescribed in paragraph (a) of this Rule but if she does not, she shall be provided with some other means of making an efficient sound signal.

(Pub. L. 96–591, §2, Dec. 24, 1980, 94 Stat. 3430.)

REPEAL OF SECTION

Pub. L. 108–293, title III, § 303(a), (c), Aug. 9, 2004, 118 Stat. 1042, provided that this section is repealed effective on the effective date of final regulations prescribed by the Secretary of the Department in which the Coast Guard is operating under section 2071 of this title.

REFERENCES IN TEXT

Annex III to these Rules, referred to in par. (a), is to be established by the Secretary under section 2071 of this title.

CODIFICATION

Section was enacted as part of section 2 of Pub. L. 96–591 which enacted the Inland Navigational Rules which comprise this subchapter.

§ 2034. Maneuvering and warning signals (Rule 34)

(a) Whistle signals

When power-driven vessels are in sight of one another and meeting or crossing at a distance within half a mile of each other, each vessel underway, when maneuvering as authorized or required by these Rules:

(i) shall indicate that maneuver by the following signals on her whistle: one short blast to mean "I intend to leave you on my port side"; two short blasts to mean "I intend to leave you on my starboard side"; and three short blasts to mean "I am operating astern propulsion".

(ii) upon hearing the one or two blast signal of the other shall, if in agreement, sound the same whistle signal and take the steps necessary to effect a safe passing. If, however, from any cause, the vessel doubts the safety of the proposed maneuver, she shall sound the danger signal specified in paragraph (d) of this Rule and each vessel shall take appropriate precautionary action until a safe passing agreement is made.

(b) Light signals

A vessel may supplement the whistle signals prescribed in paragraph (a) of this Rule by light signals:

(i) These signals shall have the following significance: one flash to mean "I intend to leave you on my port side"; two flashes to mean "I intend to leave you on my starboard side"; three flashes to mean "I am operating astern propulsion";

(ii) The duration of each flash shall be about 1 second; and

(iii) The light used for this signal shall, if fitted, be one all-round white or yellow light, visible at a minimum range of 2 miles, synchronized with the whistle, and shall comply with the provisions of Annex I to these Rules.

(c) Overtaking situations

When in sight of one another:

(i) a power-driven vessel intending to overtake another power-driven vessel shall indicate her intention by the following signals on her whistle: one short blast to mean "I intend to overtake you on your starboard side"; two short blasts to mean "I intend to overtake you on your port side"; and

(ii) the power-driven vessel about to be overtaken shall, if in agreement, sound a similar sound signal. If in doubt she shall sound the danger signal prescribed in paragraph (d).

(d) Doubts or failure to understand signals

When vessels in sight of one another are approaching each other and from any cause either vessel fails to understand the intentions or actions of the other, or is in doubt whether sufficient action is being taken by the other to avoid collision, the vessel in doubt shall immediately indicate such doubt by giving at least five short and rapid blasts on the whistle. This signal may be supplemented by a light signal of at least five short and rapid flashes.

(e) Vessels in areas of obscured visibility due to intervening obstructions

A vessel nearing a bend or an area of a channel or fairway where other vessels may be obscured by an intervening obstruction shall sound one prolonged blast. This signal shall be answered with a prolonged blast by any approaching vessel that may be within hearing around the bend or behind the intervening obstruction.

(f) Use of one whistle only on a vessel

If whistles are fitted on a vessel at a distance apart of more than 100 meters, one whistle only shall be used for giving maneuvering and warning signals.

(g) Power-driven vessels leaving dock or berth

When a power-driven vessel is leaving a dock or berth, she shall sound one prolonged blast.

(h) Agreement between vessels using radiotelephone

A vessel that reaches agreement with another vessel in a head-on, crossing, or overtaking situation, as for example, by using the radiotelephone as prescribed by the Vessel Bridge-to-Bridge Radiotelephone Act (85 Stat. 164; 33 U.S.C. 1201 et seq.), is not obliged to sound the whistle signals prescribed by this rule,[1] but may do so. If agreement is not reached, then whistle signals shall be exchanged in a timely manner and shall prevail.

(Pub. L. 96–591, §2, Dec. 24, 1980, 94 Stat. 3430; Pub. L. 104–324, title VII, §701(6), Oct. 19, 1996, 110 Stat. 3933.)

REPEAL OF SECTION

Pub. L. 108–293, title III, §303(a), (c), Aug. 9, 2004, 118 Stat. 1042, provided that this section is repealed effective on the effective date of final regulations prescribed by the Secretary of the Department in which the Coast Guard is operating under section 2071 of this title.

REFERENCES IN TEXT

These Rules, referred to in par. (a), are the Inland Navigational Rules which are classified to this subchapter.

Annex I to these Rules, referred to in par. (b)(iii), is to be established by the Secretary under section 2071 of this title.

The Vessel Bridge-to-Bridge Radiotelephone Act, referred to in par. (h), is Pub. L. 92–63, Aug. 4, 1971, 85 Stat. 164, as amended, which is classified generally to chapter 24 (§1201 et seq.) of this title. For complete classification of this Act to the Code, see Short Title note set out under section 1201 of this title and Tables.

CODIFICATION

Section was enacted as part of section 2 of Pub. L. 96–591 which enacted the Inland Navigational Rules which comprise this subchapter.

AMENDMENTS

1996—Par. (h). Pub. L. 104–324 amended par. (h) generally. Prior to amendment, par. (h) read as follows: "A vessel that reaches agreement with another vessel in a meeting, crossing, or overtaking situation by using the radiotelephone as prescribed by the Bridge-to-Bridge Radiotelephone Act (85 Stat. 165; 33 U.S.C. 1207), is not obliged to sound the whistle signals prescribed by this Rule, but may do so. If agreement is not reached, then whistle signals shall be exchanged in a timely manner and shall prevail."

§2035. Sound signals in restricted visibility (Rule 35)

In or near an area of restricted visibility, whether by day or night, the signals prescribed in this Rule shall be used as follows:

[1] So in original. Probably should be capitalized.

(a) Power-driven vessels making way through the water

A power-driven vessel making way through the water shall sound at intervals of not more than 2 minutes one prolonged blast.

(b) Power-driven vessels underway but stopped and making no way through the water

A power-driven vessel underway but stopped and making no way through the water shall sound at intervals of not more than 2 minutes two prolonged blasts in succession with an interval of about 2 seconds between them.

(c) Vessels not under command; vessels restricted in ability to maneuver; sailing vessels; vessels engaged in fishing; vessels engaged in towing or pushing

A vessel not under command; a vessel restricted in her ability to maneuver, whether underway or at anchor; a sailing vessel; a vessel engaged in fishing, whether underway or at anchor; and a vessel engaged in towing or pushing another vessel shall, instead of the signals prescribed in paragraphs (a) or (b) of this Rule, sound at intervals of not more than 2 minutes, three blasts in succession; namely, one prolonged followed by two short blasts.

(d) Vessels towed

A vessel towed or if more than one vessel is towed the last vessel of the tow, if manned, shall at intervals of not more than 2 minutes sound four blasts in succession; namely, one prolonged followed by three short blasts. When practicable, this signal shall be made immediately after the signal made by the towing vessel.

(e) Pushing and pushed vessels connected in composite unit

When a pushing vessel and a vessel being pushed ahead are rigidly connected in a composite unit they shall be regarded as a power-driven vessel and shall give the signals prescribed in paragraphs (a) or (b) of this Rule.

(f) Vessels at anchor

A vessel at anchor shall at intervals of not more than 1 minute ring the bell rapidly for about 5 seconds. In a vessel of 100 meters or more in length the bell shall be sounded in the forepart of the vessel and immediately after the ringing of the bell the gong shall be sounded rapidly for about 5 seconds in the after part of the vessel. A vessel at anchor may in addition sound three blasts in succession; namely, one short, one prolonged and one short blast, to give warning of her position and of the possibility of collision to an approaching vessel.

(g) Vessels aground

A vessel aground shall give the bell signal and if required the gong signal prescribed in paragraph (f) of this Rule and shall, in addition, give three separate and distinct strokes on the bell immediately before and after the rapid ringing of the bell. A vessel aground may in addition sound an appropriate whistle signal.

(h) Vessels of less than 12 meters in length

A vessel of less than 12 meters in length shall not be obliged to give the above-mentioned signals but, if she does not, shall make some other efficient sound signal at intervals of not more than 2 minutes.

(i) Pilot vessels

A pilot vessel when engaged on pilotage duty may in addition to the signals prescribed in paragraphs (a), (b) or (f) of this Rule sound an identity signal consisting of four short blasts.

(j) Vessels anchored in special anchorage areas

The following vessels shall not be required to sound signals as prescribed in paragraph (f) of this Rule when anchored in a special anchorage area designated by the Secretary:

(i) a vessel of less than 20 meters in length; and

(ii) a barge, canal boat, scow, or other nondescript craft.

(Pub. L. 96–591, §2, Dec. 24, 1980, 94 Stat. 3431.)

REPEAL OF SECTION

Pub. L. 108–293, title III, §303(a), (c), Aug. 9, 2004, 118 Stat. 1042, provided that this section is repealed effective on the effective date of final regulations prescribed by the Secretary of the Department in which the Coast Guard is operating under section 2071 of this title.

CODIFICATION

Section was enacted as part of section 2 of Pub. L. 96–591 which enacted the Inland Navigational Rules which comprise this subchapter.

§2036. Signals to attract attention (Rule 36)

If necessary to attract the attention of another vessel, any vessel may make light or sound signals that cannot be mistaken for any signal authorized elsewhere in these Rules, or may direct the beam of her searchlight in the direction of the danger, in such a way as not to embarrass any vessel.

(Pub. L. 96–591, §2, Dec. 24, 1980, 94 Stat. 3432.)

REPEAL OF SECTION

Pub. L. 108–293, title III, §303(a), (c), Aug. 9, 2004, 118 Stat. 1042, provided that this section is repealed effective on the effective date of final regulations prescribed by the Secretary of the Department in which the Coast Guard is operating under section 2071 of this title.

REFERENCES IN TEXT

These Rules, referred to in text, are the Inland Navigational Rules which are classified to this subchapter.

CODIFICATION

Section was enacted as part of section 2 of Pub. L. 96–591 which enacted the Inland Navigational Rules which comprise this subchapter.

§2037. Distress signals (Rule 37)

When a vessel is in distress and requires assistance she shall use or exhibit the signals described in Annex IV to these Rules.

(Pub. L. 96–591, §2, Dec. 24, 1980, 94 Stat. 3432.)

REPEAL OF SECTION

Pub. L. 108–293, title III, §303(a), (c), Aug. 9, 2004, 118 Stat. 1042, provided that this section is repealed effective on the effective date of final regulations prescribed by the Secretary of the

Department in which the Coast Guard is operating under section 2071 of this title.

REFERENCES IN TEXT

Annex IV to these Rules, referred to in text, is to be established by the Secretary under section 2071 of this title.

CODIFICATION

Section was enacted as part of section 2 of Pub. L. 96–591 which enacted the Inland Navigational Rules which comprise this subchapter.

PART E—EXEMPTIONS

§2038. Exemptions (Rule 38)

Any vessel or class of vessels, the keel of which is laid or which is at a corresponding stage of construction before December 24, 1980, provided that she complies with the requirements of—

(a) Chapter 3 of this title for vessels navigating the waters subject to that chapter;

(b) Chapter 5 of this title for vessels navigating the waters subject to that chapter;

(c) Chapter 4 of this title for vessels navigating the waters subject to that chapter; or

(d) Sections 3, 4, and 5 of the Act of April 25, 1940 (54 Stat. 163), as amended (46 U.S.C. 526b, c, and d) for motorboats navigating the waters subject to that statute; shall be exempted from compliance with the technical Annexes to these Rules as follows:

(i) the installation of lights with ranges prescribed in Rule 22, until 4 years after the effective date of these Rules, except that vessels of less than 20 meters in length are permanently exempt;

(ii) the installation of lights with color specifications as prescribed in Annex I to these Rules, until 4 years after the effective date of these Rules, except that vessels of less than 20 meters in length are permanently exempt;

(iii) the repositioning of lights as a result of conversion to metric units and rounding off measurement figures, are permanently exempt; and

(iv) the horizontal repositioning of masthead lights prescribed by Annex I to these Rules:

(1) on vessels of less than 150 meters in length, permanent exemption.

(2) on vessels of 150 meters or more in length, until 9 years after the effective date of these Rules.

(v) the restructuring or repositioning of all lights to meet the prescriptions of Annex I to these Rules, until 9 years after the effective date of these Rules;

(vi) power-driven vessels of 12 meters or more but less than 20 meters in length are permanently exempt from the provisions of Rule 23(a)(i) and 23(a)(iv) provided that, in place of these lights, the vessel exhibits a white light aft visible all round the horizon; and

(vii) the requirements for sound signal appliances prescribed in Annex III to these Rules, until 9 years after the effective date of these Rules.

(Pub. L. 96–591, §2, Dec. 24, 1980, 94 Stat. 3432.)

REPEAL OF SECTION

Pub. L. 108–293, title III, §303(a), (c), Aug. 9, 2004, 118 Stat. 1042, provided that this section is repealed effective on the effective date of final regulations prescribed by the Secretary of the Department in which the Coast Guard is operating under section 2071 of this title.

REFERENCES IN TEXT

Chapter 3 of this title, referred to in par. (a), was in the original "The Act of June 7, 1897 (30 Stat. 96), as amended (33 U.S.C. 154–232)", which was repealed by section 8(a) of Pub. L. 96–591.

Chapter 5 of this title, referred to in par. (b), was in the original "Section 4233 of the Revised Statutes (33 U.S.C. 301–356)", which was repealed by section 8(a) of Pub. L. 96–591.

Chapter 4 of this title, referred to in par. (c), was in the original "The Act of February 8, 1895 (28 Stat. 645), as amended (33 U.S.C. 241–295)", which was repealed by section 8(b) of Pub. L. 96–591.

Sections 3, 4, and 5 of the Act of April 25, 1940 (54 Stat. 163), as amended (46 U.S.C. 526b, c, and d), referred to in par. (d), were repealed effective 12 months after Dec. 24, 1980, by section 8(a) of Pub. L. 96–591.

Annexes and Annexes I and III to these Rules, referred to in par. (d), are to be established by the Secretary under section 2071 of this title.

Rule 22, referred to in par. (d)(i), is classified to section 2022 of this title.

The effective date of these Rules, referred to in par. (d), is 12 months after Dec. 24, 1980, except on the Great Lakes, where the effective date was established as Mar. 1, 1983. See section 7 of Pub. L. 96–591, set out as an Effective Date note under section 2001 of this title.

Rule 23, referred to in par. (d)(vi), is classified to section 2023 of this title.

CODIFICATION

Section was enacted as part of section 2 of Pub. L. 96–591 which enacted the Inland Navigational Rules which comprise this subchapter.

SUBCHAPTER II—MISCELLANEOUS PROVISIONS

§2071. Inland navigation rules

The Secretary of the Department in which the Coast Guard is operating may issue inland navigation regulations applicable to all vessels upon the inland waters of the United States and technical annexes that are as consistent as possible with the respective annexes to the International Regulations.

(Pub. L. 96–591, §3, Dec. 24, 1980, 94 Stat. 3433; Pub. L. 108–293, title III, §303(b), Aug. 9, 2004, 118 Stat. 1042.)

REFERENCES IN TEXT

The International Regulations, referred to in text, are the International Regulations for Preventing Collisions at Sea, 1972, which are maintained and published by the United States Coast Guard, U.S. Department of Homeland Security, in the publication *Navigation Rules*, which is available for sale by the Superintendent of Documents, U.S. Government Printing Office, Washington, D.C. 20402. See International Regulations for Preventing Collisions at Sea, 1972 note under section 1602 of this title.

AMENDMENTS

2004—Pub. L. 108–293 amended section catchline and text generally. Prior to amendment, text read as follows: "The Secretary may issue regulations necessary to implement and interpret this chapter. The Secretary shall establish the following technical annexes to these Rules: Annex I, Positioning and Technical Details of Lights and Shapes; Annex II, Additional Signals for Fishing Vessels Fishing in Close Proximity; Annex III,

Technical Details of Sound Appliances; and Annex IV, Distress Signals. These annexes shall be as consistent as possible with the respective annexes to the International Regulations. The Secretary may establish other technical annexes, including local pilot rules."

§2072. Violations of Inland Navigational Rules

(a) Liability of operator for civil penalty

Whoever operates a vessel in violation of this chapter, or of any regulation issued thereunder, or in violation of a certificate of alternative compliance issued under Rule 1 is liable to a civil penalty of not more than $5,000 for each violation.

(b) Liability of vessel for civil penalty; seizure of vessel

Every vessel subject to this chapter, other than a public vessel being used for noncommercial purposes, that is operated in violation of this chapter, or of any regulation issued thereunder, or in violation of a certificate of alternative compliance issued under Rule 1 is liable to a civil penalty of not more than $5,000 for each violation, for which penalty the vessel may be seized and proceeded against in the district court of the United States of any district within which the vessel may be found.

(c) Assessment of civil penalty by Secretary; collection

The Secretary may assess any civil penalty authorized by this section. No such penalty may be assessed until the person charged, or the owner of the vessel charged, as appropriate, shall have been given notice of the violation involved and an opportunity for a hearing. For good cause shown, the Secretary may remit, mitigate, or compromise any penalty assessed. Upon the failure of the person charged, or the owner of the vessel charged, to pay an assessed penalty, as it may have been mitigated or compromised, the Secretary may request the Attorney General to commence an action in the appropriate district court of the United States for collection of the penalty as assessed, without regard to the amount involved, together with such other relief as may be appropriate.

(d) Withholding of clearance

(1) If any owner, operator, or individual in charge of a vessel is liable for a penalty under this section, or if reasonable cause exists to believe that the owner, operator, or individual in charge may be subject to a penalty under this section, the Secretary of the Treasury, upon the request of the Secretary, shall with respect to such vessel refuse or revoke any clearance required by section 60105 of title 46.

(2) Clearance or a permit refused or revoked under this subsection may be granted upon filing of a bond or other surety satisfactory to the Secretary.

(Pub. L. 96–591, §4, Dec. 24, 1980, 94 Stat. 3433; Pub. L. 104–324, title III, §312(c), Oct. 19, 1996, 110 Stat. 3920.)

References in Text

Rule 1, referred to in pars. (a) and (b), is classified to section 2001 of this title.

Codification

In subsec. (d)(1), "section 60105 of title 46" substituted for "section 4197 of the Revised Statutes of the United States (46 App. U.S.C. 91)" on authority of Pub. L. 109–304, §18(c), Oct. 6, 2006, 120 Stat. 1709, which Act enacted section 60105 of Title 46, Shipping.

Amendments

1996—Par. (d). Pub. L. 104–324 inserted heading and amended text generally. Prior to amendment, text read as follows: "The Secretary of the Treasury shall withhold or revoke, at the request of the Secretary, the clearance, required by section 91 of title 46, Appendix, of any vessel, the owner or operator of which is subject to any of the penalties in this section. Clearance may be granted in such cases upon the filing of a bond or other surety satisfactory to the Secretary."

§2073. Navigation Safety Advisory Council

(a) Establishment; membership; Council panels; publication in Federal Register

The Secretary shall establish a Navigation Safety Advisory Council (hereinafter referred to as the Council) not exceeding 21 members. To assure balanced representation, members shall be chosen, insofar as practical, from the following groups: (1) recognized experts and leaders in organizations having an active interest in the Rules of the Road and vessel and port safety, (2) representatives of owners and operators of vessels, professional mariners, recreational boaters, and the recreational boating industry, (3) individuals with an interest in maritime law, and (4) Federal and State officials with responsibility for vessel and port safety. Additional persons may be appointed to panels of the Council to assist the Council in the performance of its functions. The Secretary shall, not less often than once a year, publish notice in the Federal Register for solicitation of nominations for membership on the Council.

(b) Functions and purpose of Council

The Council shall advise, consult with, and make recommendations to the Secretary on matters relating to the prevention of collisions, rammings, and groundings, including the Inland Rules of the Road, the International Rules of the Road, navigation regulations and equipment, routing measures, marine information, diving safety, and aids to navigation systems. Any advice or recommendation made by the Council to the Secretary shall reflect the independent judgment of the Council on the matter concerned. The Council shall meet at the call of the Secretary, but in any event not less than twice during each calendar year. All proceedings of the Council shall be public, and a record of the proceedings shall be made available for public inspection.

(c) Executive secretary; staff; travel expenses and status of members

The Secretary shall furnish to the Council an executive secretary and such secretarial, clerical, and other services as are deemed necessary for the conduct of its business. Members of the Council, while away from their home or regular places of business, may be allowed travel expenses, including per diem in lieu of subsistence, as authorized by section 5703 of title 5. Payments under this section shall not render members of the Council officers or employees of the United States for any purpose.

(d) Termination of Council

Unless extended by subsequent Act of Congress, the Council shall terminate on September 30, 2010.

(Pub. L. 96–591, §5, Dec. 24, 1980, 94 Stat. 3434; Pub. L. 97–322, title I, §118(c), Oct. 15, 1982, 96 Stat. 1586; Pub. L. 98–557, §16(b)(2), Oct. 30, 1984, 98 Stat. 2866; Pub. L. 101–225, title I, §105(a)(1), Dec. 12, 1989, 103 Stat. 1909; Pub. L. 104–324, title III, §304(a), (g), Oct. 19, 1996, 110 Stat. 3917, 3918; Pub. L. 107–295, title III, §334, Nov. 25, 2002, 116 Stat. 2105; Pub. L. 108–293, title IV, §418(e), Aug. 9, 2004, 118 Stat. 1049.)

AMENDMENTS

2004—Subsec. (d). Pub. L. 108–293 substituted "September 30, 2010" for "September 30, 2005".

2002—Subsec. (d). Pub. L. 107–295 substituted "September 30, 2005" for "September 30, 2000".

1996—Pub. L. 104–324, §304(g), which directed the general amendment of the "section heading for section 5(d) of the Inland Navigational Rules Act of 1980 (33 U.S.C. 2073)", was executed by inserting section catchline, to reflect the probable intent of Congress.

Par. (d). Pub. L. 104–324, §304(a), substituted "September 30, 2000" for "September 30, 1995".

1989—Par. (a). Pub. L. 101–225, §105(a)(1)(A), substituted "Navigation Safety Advisory Council" for "Rules of the Road Advisory Council".

Par. (b). Pub. L. 101–225, §105(a)(1)(B), amended par. (b) generally. Prior to amendment, par. (b) read as follows: "The Council shall advise, consult with, and make recommendations to the Secretary on matters relating to any major proposals for changes to the Inland Rules. The Council may recommend changes to the Inland Rules and International Regulations to the Secretary. Any advice or recommendation made by the Council to the Secretary shall reflect the independent judgment of the Council on the matter concerned. The Council shall meet at the call of the Secretary, but in any event not less than once during each calendar year. All proceedings of the Council shall be public, and a record of the proceedings shall be made available for public inspection. The Council is authorized to make available to Congress any information, advice, and recommendations which the Council is authorized to give to the Secretary."

Par. (d). Pub. L. 101–225, §105(a)(1)(C), substituted "September 30, 1995" for "September 30, 1990".

1984—Par. (c). Pub. L. 98–557, §16(b)(2)(A), struck out provisions authorizing members who are not officers or employees of the United States to receive compensation at a rate not exceeding the daily equivalent of the current rate of basic pay for GS–18 of the General Schedule under section 5332 of title 5.

Par. (d). Pub. L. 98–557, §16(b)(2)(B), substituted "on September 30, 1990" for "5 years from the date of enactment of this Act".

1982—Par. (a). Pub. L. 97–322, §118(c)(1), directed Secretary, not less often than once a year, to publish notice in Federal Register for solicitation of nominations for membership on Council.

Par. (b). Pub. L. 97–322, §118(c)(2), authorized Council to make available to Congress any information, advice, and recommendations which Council is authorized to give to Secretary.

Par. (c). Pub. L. 97–322, §118(c)(3), struck out "or while otherwise engaged in the business of the Council" after "meetings of the Council", and ", including traveltime" after "section 5332 of title 5".

REFERENCES IN OTHER LAWS

Section 105(a)(2) of Pub. L. 101–225 provided that: "Each reference to the Rules of the Road Advisory Council in a law, regulation, order, document, record, or paper of the United States is deemed to be a reference to the Navigation Safety Advisory Council."

CHAPTER 35—ARTIFICIAL REEFS

§2101. Congressional statement of findings and purpose

(a) The Congress finds that—

(1) although fishery products provide an important source of protein and industrial products for United States consumption, United States fishery production annually falls far short of satisfying United States demand;

(2) overfishing and the degradation of vital fishery resource habitats have caused a reduction in the abundance and diversity of United States fishery resources;

(3) escalated energy costs have had a negative effect on the economics of United States commercial and recreational fisheries;

(4) commercial and recreational fisheries are a prominent factor in United States coastal economies and the direct and indirect returns to the United States economy from commercial and recreational fishing expenditures are threefold; and

(5) properly designed, constructed, and located artificial reefs in waters covered under this chapter can enhance the habitat and diversity of fishery resources; enhance United States recreational and commercial fishing opportunities; increase the production of fishery products in the United States; increase the energy efficiency of recreational and commercial fisheries; and contribute to the United States and coastal economies.

(b) The purpose of this chapter is to promote and facilitate responsible and effective efforts to establish artificial reefs in waters covered under this chapter.

(Pub. L. 98–623, title II, §202, Nov. 8, 1984, 98 Stat. 3394.)

REFERENCES IN TEXT

This chapter, referred to in text, was in the original "this title", meaning title II of Pub. L. 98–623, which in addition to enacting this chapter also enacted section 1220d of Title 16, Conservation, and amended sections 1220, 1220a, 1220b, and 1220c of Title 16.

SHORT TITLE

Section 201 of title II of Pub. L. 98–623 provided that: "This title [enacting this chapter and section 1220d of Title 16, Conservation, and amending sections 1220 to 1220c of Title 16] may be cited as the 'National Fishing Enhancement Act of 1984'."

§2102. Establishment of standards

Based on the best scientific information available, artificial reefs in waters covered under this chapter shall be sited and constructed, and subsequently monitored and managed in a manner which will—

(1) enhance fishery resources to the maximum extent practicable;

(2) facilitate access and utilization by United States recreational and commercial fishermen;

(3) minimize conflicts among competing uses of waters covered under this chapter and the resources in such waters;

(4) minimize environmental risks and risks to personal health and property; and

(5) be consistent with generally accepted principles of international law and shall not create any unreasonable obstruction to navigation.

(Pub. L. 98–623, title II, § 203, Nov. 8, 1984, 98 Stat. 3395.)

§ 2103. National artificial reef plan

Not later than one year after November 8, 1984, the Secretary of Commerce, in consultation with the Secretary of the Interior, the Secretary of Defense, the Administrator of the Environmental Protection Agency, the Secretary of the Department in which the Coast Guard is operating, the Regional Fishery Managment[1] Councils, interested States, Interstate Fishery Commissions, and representatives of the private sector, shall develop and publish a long-term plan which will meet the purpose of this chapter and be consistent with the standards established under section 2102 of this chapter. The plan must include—

(1) geographic, hydrographic, geologic, biological, ecological, social, economic, and other criteria for siting artificial reefs;

(2) design, material, and other criteria for constructing artificial reefs;

(3) mechanisms and methodologies for monitoring the compliance of artificial reefs with the requirements of permits issued under section 2104 of this title;

(4) mechanisms and methodologies for managing the use of artificial reefs;

(5) a synopsis of existing information on artificial reefs and needs for further research on artificial reef technology and management strategies; and

(6) an evaluation of alternatives for facilitating the transfer of artificial reef construction materials to persons holding permits issued pursuant to section 2104 of this title, including, but not limited to, credits for environmental mitigation and modified tax obligations.

(Pub. L. 98–623, title II, § 204, Nov. 8, 1984, 98 Stat. 3395.)

Transfer of Functions

For transfer of authorities, functions, personnel, and assets of the Coast Guard, including the authorities and functions of the Secretary of Transportation relating thereto, to the Department of Homeland Security, and for treatment of related references, see sections 468(b), 551(d), 552(d), and 557 of Title 6, Domestic Security, and the Department of Homeland Security Reorganization Plan of November 25, 2002, as modified, set out as a note under section 542 of Title 6.

[1] So in original. Probably should be "Management".

§ 2104. Permits for construction and management of artificial reefs

(a) Secretarial action on permits

In issuing a permit for artificial reefs under section 403 of this title, section 1344 of this title, or section 1333(e) of title 43, the Secretary of the Army (hereinafter in this section referred to as the "Secretary") shall—

(1) consult with and consider the views of appropriate Federal agencies, States, local governments, and other interested parties;

(2) ensure that the provisions for siting, constructing, monitoring, and managing the artificial reef are consistent with the criteria and standards established under this chapter;

(3) ensure that the title to the artificial reef construction material is unambiguous, and that responsibility for maintenance and the financial ability to assume liability for future damages are clearly established; and

(4) consider the plan developed under section 2103 of this title and notify the Secretary of Commerce of any need to deviate from that plan.

(b) Terms and conditions of permits

(1) Each permit issued by the Secretary subject to this section shall specify the design and location for construction of the artificial reef and the types and quantities of materials that may be used in constructing such artificial reef. In addition, each such permit shall specify such terms and conditions for the construction, operation, maintenance, monitoring, and managing the use of the artificial reef as are necessary for compliance with all applicable provisions of law and as are necessary to ensure the protection of the environment and human safety and property.

(2) Before issuing a permit under section 1342 of this title for any activity relating to the siting, design, construction, operation, maintenance, monitoring, or managing of an artificial reef, the Administrator of the Environmental Protection Agency shall consult with the Secretary to ensure that such permit is consistent with any permit issued by the Secretary subject to this section.

(c) Liability of permittee

(1) A person to whom a permit is issued in accordance with subsection (a) of this section and any insurer of that person shall not be liable for damages caused by activities required to be undertaken under any terms and conditions of the permit, if the permittee is in compliance with such terms and conditions.

(2) A person to whom a permit is issued in accordance with subsection (a) of this section and any insurer of that person shall be liable, to the extent determined under applicable law, for damages to which paragraph (1) does not apply.

(3) The Secretary may not issue a permit subject to this section to a person unless that person demonstrates to the Secretary the financial ability to assume liability for all damages that may arise with respect to an artificial reef and for which such permittee may be liable.

(4) Any person who has transferred title to artificial reef construction materials to a person to whom a permit is issued in accordance with

subsection (a) of this section shall not be liable for damages arising from the use of such materials in an artificial reef, if such materials meet applicable requirements of the plan published under section 2103 of this title and are not otherwise defective at the time title is transferred.

(d) Liability of the United States

Nothing in this chapter creates any liability on the part of the United States.

(e) Civil penalty

Any person who, after notice and an opportunity for a hearing, is found to have violated any provision of a permit issued in accordance with subsection (a) of this section shall be liable to the United States for a civil penalty, not to exceed $10,000 for each violation. The amount of the civil penalty shall be assessed by the Secretary by written notice. In determining the amount of such penalty, the Secretary shall take into account the nature, circumstances, extent, and gravity of the violation. The Secretary may compromise, modify, or remit with or without conditions, any civil penalty which is subject to imposition or which has been imposed under this section. If any person fails to pay an assessment of a civil penalty after it has become final, the Secretary may refer the matter to the Attorney General for collection.

(Pub. L. 98–623, title II, §205, Nov. 8, 1984, 98 Stat. 3396.)

§2105. Definitions

For purposes of this chapter—

(1) The term "artificial reef" means a structure which is constructed or placed in waters covered under this chapter for the purpose of enhancing fishery resources and commercial and recreational fishing opportunities.

(2) The term "State" means a State of the United States, the District of Columbia, Puerto Rico, the United States Virgin Islands, American Samoa, Guam, Johnston Island, Midway Island, and Wake Island.

(3) The term "waters covered under this chapter" means the navigable waters of the United States and the waters superjacent to the Outer Continental Shelf as defined in section 1331 of title 43, to the extent such waters exist in or are adjacent to any State.

(Pub. L. 98–623, title II, §206, Nov. 8, 1984, 98 Stat. 3397.)

§2106. Savings clauses

(a) Tennessee Valley Authority jurisdiction

Nothing in this chapter shall be construed as replacing or superseding section 831y–1 of title 16.

(b) State jurisdiction

Nothing in this chapter shall be construed as extending or diminishing the jurisdiction or authority of any State over the siting, construction, monitoring, or managing of artificial reefs within its boundaries.

(Pub. L. 98–623, title II, §208, Nov. 8, 1984, 98 Stat. 3398.)

CHAPTER 36—WATER RESOURCES DEVELOPMENT

§2201. "Secretary" defined

For purposes of this Act, the term "Secretary" means the Secretary of the Army.

(Pub. L. 99–662, §2, Nov. 17, 1986, 100 Stat. 4082.)

References in Text

This Act, referred to in text, is Pub. L. 99–662, Nov. 17, 1986, 100 Stat. 4082, as amended, known as the Water Resources Development Act of 1986. For complete classification of this Act to the Code, see Short Title note set out below and Tables.

Short Title of 2007 Amendment

Pub. L. 110–114, §1(a), Nov. 8, 2007, 121 Stat. 1041, provided that: "This Act [see Tables for classification] may be cited as the 'Water Resources Development Act of 2007'."

Short Title of 2000 Amendment

Pub. L. 106–541, §1(a), Dec. 11, 2000, 114 Stat. 2572, provided that: "This Act [see Tables for classification] may be cited as the 'Water Resources Development Act of 2000'."

Short Title of 1999 Amendment

Pub. L. 106–53, §1(a), Aug. 17, 1999, 113 Stat. 269, provided that: "This Act [see Tables for classification] may be cited as the 'Water Resources Development Act of 1999'."

Short Title of 1996 Amendment

Pub. L. 104–303, §1(a), Oct. 12, 1996, 110 Stat. 3658, provided that: "This Act [see Tables for classification] may be cited as the 'Water Resources Development Act of 1996'."

Short Title of 1992 Amendment

Pub. L. 102–580, §1(a), Oct. 31, 1992, 106 Stat. 4797, provided that: "This Act [enacting sections 59gg, 426i–1, 569d to 569f, 653, 1271, 2268, and 2325 to 2329 of this title, amending sections 426j, 467f, 467j to 467*l*, 562, 652, 1342, 1412, 1413, 1414, 1415, 1416, 1420, 1421, 2211, 2213, 2283, and 2309a of this title, section 3036 of Title 10, Armed Forces, sections 460tt, 4702, and 4711 of Title 16, Conservation, and section 1962d–16 of Title 42, The Public Health and Welfare, and enacting provisions set out as notes under this section and sections 541, 1271, 2211, 2239, 2267, and 2281 of this title, section 9505 of Title 26, Internal Revenue Code, and sections 390h–4 and 390h–5 of Title 43, Public Lands] may be cited as the 'Water Resources Development Act of 1992'."

Short Title of 1990 Amendment

Pub. L. 101–640, §1(a), Nov. 28, 1990, 104 Stat. 4604, provided that: "This Act [enacting sections 59bb and 2316 to 2324 of this title, amending sections 579a, 652, 701n, 709a, 2213, 2215, 2232, 2238, 2281, 2309a, and 2314a of this title, section 460tt of Title 16, Conservation, and section 1962d–16 of Title 42, The Public Health and Welfare, repealing sections 579 and 2239 of this title, enacting provisions set out as notes under this section, sections 426e, 1252, 1268, 2213, 2232, 2239, 2313, and 2317 of this title, and section 1405c of Title 48, Territories and Insular Possessions, and amending provisions set out as notes under sections 2294 and 2314 of this title and section 460d of Title 16] may be cited as the 'Water Resources Development Act of 1990'."

SHORT TITLE OF 1988 AMENDMENT

Pub. L. 100–676, §1(a), Nov. 17, 1988, 102 Stat. 4012, provided that: "This Act [enacting sections 59j–1, 59y, 59z, and 2312 to 2315 of this title, amending sections 426j, 701b–12, 1293a, 2211, 2239, 2280, and 2291 of this title and section 1962d–5a of Title 42, The Public Health and Welfare, enacting provisions set out as notes under this section, sections 579a, 988, 2211, 2294, 2300, and 2314 of this title, and section 1962d–5g of Title 42, and amending provisions set out as a note under section 2294 of this title] may be cited as the 'Water Resources Development Act of 1988'."

SHORT TITLE

Section 1(a) of Pub. L. 99–662 provided that: "This Act [enacting this chapter and sections 59n–1, 59v, 59w, 403b, 426n, 426*o*, 467f to 467n, 555a, 579a, 652, 701b–12, 709b, 988a, and 1414a of this title, sections 460tt of Title 16, Conservation, sections 4461, 4462, 9505, and 9506 of Title 26, Internal Revenue Code, section 483d of former Title 40, Public Buildings, Property, and Works, and sections 1962d–11b and 1962d–20 of Title 42, The Public Health and Welfare, amending sections 409, 414, 415, 426g, 426i, 426j, 426m, 467, 467b, 555, 557, 603a, 610, 701a–1, 701g, 701n, 701r, 701s, 984, and 1804 of this title, section 3036 of Title 10, Armed Forces, sections 460ee and 1002 of Title 16, section 4042 of Title 26, sections 1962d–5a, 1962d–5b, 1962d–5d, 1962d–5f, and 1962d–16 of Title 42, sections 390 and 390b of Title 43, Public Lands, and section 1121–1 of Title 46, Appendix, Shipping, repealing sections 1801 and 1802 of this title, enacting provisions set out as notes under this section, sections 426, 426g, 467, 661, 984, 988, 1414a, and 2294 of this title, sections 460d and 1004 of Title 16, sections 1, 4042, 4461, 9505, and 9506 of Title 26, sections 1962d–5b, 1962d–20, and 10301 of Title 42, and section 390b of Title 43, and amending provisions set out as a note under section 1962b–3 of Title 42] may be cited as the 'Water Resources Development Act of 1986'."

Section 215 of title II of Pub. L. 99–662 provided that: "This title [enacting subchapter II of this chapter] may be cited as the 'Harbor Development and Navigation Improvement Act of 1986'."

FUNDING TO PROCESS PERMITS

Pub. L. 106–541, title II, §214, Dec. 11, 2000, 114 Stat. 2594, as amended by Pub. L. 108–137, title I, §114, Dec. 1, 2003, 117 Stat. 1836; Pub. L. 109–99, §1, Nov. 11, 2005, 119 Stat. 2169; Pub. L. 109–209, §1, Mar. 24, 2006, 120 Stat. 318; Pub. L. 109–434, §1, Dec. 20, 2006, 120 Stat. 3197; Pub. L. 110–114, title II, §2002, Nov. 8, 2007, 121 Stat. 1067, provided that:

"(a) IN GENERAL.—The Secretary, after public notice, may accept and expend funds contributed by non-Federal public entities to expedite the evaluation of permits under the jurisdiction of the Department of the Army.

"(b) EFFECT ON PERMITTING.—In carrying out this section, the Secretary shall ensure that the use of funds accepted under subsection (a) will not impact impartial decisionmaking with respect to permits, either substantively or procedurally.

"(c) DURATION OF AUTHORITY.—The authority provided under this section shall be in effect from October 1, 2000, through December 31, 2009."

MONITORING

Pub. L. 106–541, title II, §223, Dec. 11, 2000, 114 Stat. 2597, provided that:

"(a) IN GENERAL.—The Secretary shall conduct a monitoring program of the economic and environmental results of up to 5 eligible projects selected by the Secretary.

"(b) DURATION.—The monitoring of a project selected by the Secretary under this section shall be for a period of not less than 12 years beginning on the date of its selection.

"(c) REPORTS.—The Secretary shall transmit to Congress every 3 years a report on the performance of each project selected under this section.

"(d) ELIGIBLE PROJECT DEFINED.—In this section, the term 'eligible project' means a water resources project, or separable element thereof—

"(1) for which a contract for physical construction has not been awarded before the date of enactment of this Act [Dec. 11, 2000];

"(2) that has a total cost of more than $25,000,000; and

"(3)(A) that has as a benefit-to-cost ratio of less than 1.5 to 1; or

"(B) that has significant environmental benefits or significant environmental mitigation components.

"(e) COSTS.—The cost of conducting monitoring under this section shall be a Federal expense."

WATER CONTROL MANAGEMENT

Pub. L. 106–53, title V, §511, Aug. 17, 1999, 113 Stat. 341, provided that:

"(a) IN GENERAL.—In evaluating potential improvements for water control management activities and consolidation of water control management centers, the Secretary may consider a regionalized water control management plan but may not implement such a plan until the date on which a report is submitted under subsection (b).

"(b) REPORT.—Not later than 180 days after the date of enactment of this Act [Aug. 17, 1999], the Secretary shall submit to the Committee on Transportation and Infrastructure and the Committee on Appropriations of the House of Representatives and the Committee on Environment and Public Works and the Committee on Appropriations of the Senate a report containing—

"(1) a description of the primary objectives of streamlining water control management activities;

"(2) a description of the benefits provided by streamlining water control management activities through consolidation of centers for those activities;

"(3) a determination whether the benefits to users of establishing regional water control management centers will be retained in each district office of the Corps of Engineers that does not have a regional center;

"(4) a determination whether users of regional centers will receive a higher level of benefits from streamlining water control management activities; and

"(5) a list of the members of Congress who represent a district that includes a water control management center that is to be eliminated under a proposed regionalized plan."

BUY AMERICAN; SENSE OF CONGRESS; REQUIREMENT REGARDING NOTICE

Pub. L. 106–53, title II, §222, Aug. 17, 1999, 113 Stat. 295, provided that:

"(a) IN GENERAL.—It is the sense of Congress that, to the extent practicable, all equipment and products purchased with funds made available under this Act [see Tables for classification] should be American made.

"(b) NOTICE TO RECIPIENTS OF ASSISTANCE.—In providing financial assistance under this Act, the Secretary, to the greatest extent practicable, shall provide to each recipient of the assistance a notice describing the statement made in subsection (a)."

Pub. L. 104–303, title II, §235, Oct. 12, 1996, 110 Stat. 3704, provided that:

"(a) PURCHASE OF AMERICAN-MADE EQUIPMENT AND PRODUCTS.—It is the sense of Congress that, to the greatest extent practicable, all equipment and products purchased with funds made available under this Act [see Tables for classification] should be American-made.

"(b) NOTICE TO RECIPIENTS OF ASSISTANCE.—In providing financial assistance under this Act, the Secretary, to the greatest extent practicable, shall provide to each recipient of the assistance a notice describing the statement made in subsection (a)."

BUDGET ACT REQUIREMENTS

Section 948 of Pub. L. 99–662 provided that: "Any spending authority under this Act [see Short Title note above] shall be effective only to such extent and in such amounts as are provided in appropriation Acts. For purposes of this Act, the term 'spending authority' has the meaning provided in section 401(c)(2) of the Congressional Budget Act of 1974 [2 U.S.C. 651(c)(2)], except that such term does not include spending authority for which an exception is made under section 401(d) of such Act."

"SECRETARY" DEFINED

Pub. L. 110–114, § 2, Nov. 8, 2007, 121 Stat. 1049, provided that: "In this Act [see Tables for classification], the term 'Secretary' means the Secretary of the Army."

Pub. L. 106–541, § 2, Dec. 11, 2000, 114 Stat. 2575, provided that: "In this Act [see Tables for classification], the term 'Secretary' means the Secretary of the Army."

Pub. L. 106–53, § 2, Aug. 17, 1999, 113 Stat. 273, provided that: "In this Act [see Tables for classification], the term 'Secretary' means the Secretary of the Army."

Pub. L. 104–303, § 2, Oct. 12, 1996, 110 Stat. 3662, provided that: "In this Act [see Tables for classification], the term 'Secretary' means the Secretary of the Army."

Pub. L. 102–580, § 3, Oct. 31, 1992, 106 Stat. 4801, provided that: "For purposes of this Act [see Short Title of 1992 Amendment note above], the term 'Secretary' means the Secretary of the Army."

Pub. L. 101–640, § 2, Nov. 28, 1990, 104 Stat. 4605, provided that: "For purposes of this Act [see Short Title of 1990 Amendment note above], the term 'Secretary' means the Secretary of the Army."

Pub. L. 100–676, § 2, Nov. 17, 1988, 102 Stat. 4013, provided that: "For purposes of this Act [see Short Title of 1988 Amendment note above], the term 'Secretary' means the Secretary of the Army."

SUBCHAPTER I—COST SHARING

§ 2211. Harbors

(a) Construction

(1) Payments during construction

The non-Federal interests for a navigation project for a harbor or inland harbor, or any separable element thereof, on which a contract for physical construction has not been awarded before November 17, 1986, shall pay, during the period of construction of the project, the following costs associated with general navigation features:

(A) 10 percent of the cost of construction of the portion of the project which has a depth not in excess of 20 feet; plus

(B) 25 percent of the cost of construction of the portion of the project which has a depth in excess of 20 feet but not in excess of 45 feet; plus

(C) 50 percent of the cost of construction of the portion of the project which has a depth in excess of 45 feet.

(2) Additional 10 percent payment over 30 years

The non-Federal interests for a project to which paragraph (1) applies shall pay an additional 10 percent of the cost of the general navigation features of the project in cash over a period not to exceed 30 years, at an interest rate determined pursuant to section 2216 of this title. The value of lands, easements, rights-of-way, and relocations provided under paragraph (3) and the costs of relocations borne by the non-Federal interests under paragraph (4) shall be credited toward the payment required under this paragraph.

(3) Lands, easements, and rights-of-way

Except as provided under section 2283(c) of this title, the non-Federal interests for a project to which paragraph (1) applies shall provide the lands, easements, rights-of-way, and relocations (other than utility relocations under paragraph (4)) necessary for the project, including any lands, easements, rights-of-way, and relocations (other than utility relocations accomplished under paragraph (4)) that are necessary for dredged material disposal facilities.

(4) Utility relocations

The non-Federal interests for a project to which paragraph (1) applies shall perform or assure the performance of all relocations of utilities necessary to carry out the project, except that in the case of a project for a deep-draft harbor and in the case of a project constructed by non-Federal interests under section 2232 of this title, one-half of the cost of each such relocation shall be borne by the owner of the facility being relocated and one-half of the cost of each such relocation shall be borne by the non-Federal interests.

(5) Dredged material disposal facilities for project construction

In this subsection, the term "general navigation features" includes constructed land-based and aquatic dredged material disposal facilities that are necessary for the disposal of dredged material required for project construction and for which a contract for construction has not been awarded on or before October 12, 1996.

(b) Operation and maintenance

(1) In general

The Federal share of the cost of operation and maintenance of each navigation project for a harbor or inland harbor constructed by the Secretary pursuant to this Act or any other law approved after November 17, 1986, shall be 100 percent, except that in the case of a deep-draft harbor, the non-Federal interests shall be responsible for an amount equal to 50 percent of the excess of the cost of the operation and maintenance of such project over the cost which the Secretary determines would be incurred for operation and maintenance of such project if such project had a depth of 45 feet.

(2) Dredged material disposal facilities

The Federal share of the cost of constructing land-based and aquatic dredged material disposal facilities that are necessary for the disposal of dredged material required for the operation and maintenance of a project and for which a contract for construction has not been awarded on or before October 12, 1996, shall be determined in accordance with subsection (a) of this section. The Federal share of operating and maintaining such facilities shall be determined in accordance with paragraph (1).

(c) Erosion or shoaling attributable to Federal navigation works

Costs of constructing projects or measures for the prevention or mitigation of erosion or shoaling damages attributable to Federal navigation works shall be shared in the same proportion as the cost sharing provisions applicable to the project causing such erosion or shoaling. The non-Federal interests for the project causing the erosion or shoaling shall agree to operate and maintain such measures.

(d) Non-Federal payments during construction

The amount of any non-Federal share of the cost of any navigation project for a harbor or inland harbor shall be paid to the Secretary. Amounts required to be paid during construction shall be paid on an annual basis during the period of construction, beginning not later than one year after construction is initiated.

(e) Agreement

Before initiation of construction of a project to which this section applies, the Secretary and the non-Federal interests shall enter into a cooperative agreement according to the provisions of section 1962d–5b of title 42. The non-Federal interests shall agree to—

(1) provide to the Federal Government lands, easements, and rights-of-way, including those necessary for dredged material disposal facilities, and perform the necessary relocations required for construction, operation, and maintenance of such project;

(2) hold and save the United States free from damages due to the construction or operation and maintenance of the project, except for damages due to the fault or negligence of the United States or its contractors;

(3) provide to the Federal Government the non-Federal share of all other costs of construction of such project; and

(4) in the case of a deep-draft harbor, be responsible for the non-Federal share of operation and maintenance required by subsection (b) of this section.

(f) Consideration of funding requirements and equitable apportionment

The Secretary shall ensure, to the extent practicable, that—

(1) funding requirements for operation and maintenance dredging of commercial navigation harbors are considered before Federal funds are obligated for payment of the Federal share of costs associated with the construction of dredged material disposal facilities in accordance with subsections (a) and (b) of this section;

(2) funds expended for such construction are apportioned equitably in accordance with regional needs; and

(3) use of a dredged material disposal facility designed, constructed, managed, or operated by a private entity is not precluded if, consistent with economic and environmental considerations, the facility is the least-cost alternative.

(Pub. L. 99–662, title I, §101, Nov. 17, 1986, 100 Stat. 4082; Pub. L. 100–676, §13(a), Nov. 17, 1988, 102 Stat. 4025; Pub. L. 102–580, title III, §333(b)(1), Oct. 31, 1992, 106 Stat. 4852; Pub. L. 104–303, title II, §201(a)–(d), Oct. 12, 1996, 110 Stat. 3671, 3672.)

REFERENCES IN TEXT

This Act, referred to in subsec. (b)(1), is Pub. L. 99–662, Nov. 17, 1986, 100 Stat. 4082, as amended, known as the Water Resources Development Act of 1986. For complete classification of this Act to the Code, see Short Title note set out under section 2201 of this title and Tables.

AMENDMENTS

1996—Subsec. (a)(2). Pub. L. 104–303, §201(a)(1), inserted last sentence and struck out former last sentence which read as follows: "The value of lands, easements, rights-of-way, relocations, and dredged material disposal areas provided under paragraph (3) and the costs of relocations borne by the non-Federal interests under paragraph (4) shall be credited toward the payment required under this paragraph."

Subsec. (a)(3). Pub. L. 104–303, §201(a)(2), inserted "and" after "rights-of-way,", struck out ", and dredged material disposal areas" after "relocations under paragraph (4))", and inserted before period at end ", including any lands, easements, rights-of-way, and relocations (other than utility relocations accomplished under paragraph (4)) that are necessary for dredged material disposal facilities".

Subsec. (a)(5). Pub. L. 104–303, §201(a)(3), added par. (5).

Subsec. (b). Pub. L. 104–303, §201(b), designated existing provisions as par. (1), inserted heading, realigned margins, and substituted "by the Secretary pursuant to this Act or any other law approved after November 17, 1986" for "pursuant to this Act", and added par. (2).

Subsec. (e)(1). Pub. L. 104–303, §201(c), substituted "including those necessary for dredged material disposal facilities," for "and to provide dredged material disposal areas".

Subsec. (f). Pub. L. 104–303, §201(d), added subsec. (f).

1992—Subsec. (a)(3). Pub. L. 102–580 substituted "Except as provided under section 906(c), the non-Federal" for "The non-Federal".

1988—Subsec. (a)(2). Pub. L. 100–676 added par. (2) and struck out former par. (2) which read as follows: "The non-Federal interests for a project to which paragraph (1) applies shall pay an additional 10 percent of the cost of the general navigation features of the project in cash over a period not to exceed 30 years, at an interest rate determined pursuant to section 2216 of this title. The value of lands, easements, rights-of-way, relocations, and dredged material disposal areas provided under paragraph (3) shall be credited toward the payment required under this paragraph."

EFFECTIVE DATE OF 1988 AMENDMENT

Section 13(b) of Pub. L. 100–676 provided that: "The amendment made by subsection (a) [amending this section] shall take effect on November 17, 1986."

DEEP DRAFT HARBOR COST SHARING

Pub. L. 106–53, title IV, §401, Aug. 17, 1999, 113 Stat. 322, provided that:

"(a) IN GENERAL.—The Secretary shall undertake a study of non-Federal cost-sharing requirements for the construction and operation and maintenance of deep draft harbor projects to determine whether—

"(1) cost sharing adversely affects United States port development or domestic and international trade; and

"(2) any revision of the cost-sharing requirements would benefit United States domestic and international trade.

"(b) RECOMMENDATIONS.—

"(1) IN GENERAL.—Not later than May 30, 2001, the Secretary shall submit to the Committee on Environment and Public Works of the Senate and the Committee on Transportation and Infrastructure of the House of Representatives any recommendations that the Secretary may have in light of the study under subsection (a).

"(2) CONSIDERATIONS.—In making recommendations, the Secretary shall consider—

"(A) the potential economic, environmental, and budgetary impacts of any proposed revision of the cost-sharing requirements; and

"(B) the effect that any such revision would have on regional port competition."

AMENDMENT OF COOPERATION AGREEMENT

Section 201(f) of Pub. L. 104–303 provided that: "If requested by the non-Federal interest, the Secretary shall amend a project cooperation agreement executed on or before the date of the enactment of this Act [Oct. 12, 1996] to reflect the application of the amendments made by this section [amending this section and section 2241 of this title] to any project for which a contract for construction has not been awarded on or before that date."

INCREASES IN NON-FEDERAL SHARE OF COSTS

Section 201(g) of Pub. L. 104–303 provided that: "Nothing in this section [amending this section and section 2241 of this title and enacting provisions set out above] (including the amendments made by this section) shall increase, or result in the increase of, the non-Federal share of the costs of—

"(1) expanding any confined dredged material disposal facility that is operated by the Secretary and that is authorized for cost recovery through the collection of tolls;

"(2) any confined dredged material disposal facility for which the invitation for bids for construction was issued before the date of the enactment of this Act [Oct. 12, 1996]; and

"(3) expanding any confined dredged material disposal facility constructed under section 123 of the River and Harbor Act of 1970 (33 U.S.C. 1293a) if the capacity of the confined dredged material disposal facility was exceeded in less than 6 years."

DREDGED MATERIAL DISPOSAL AREAS STUDY

Section 216 of Pub. L. 102–580 directed Secretary to conduct a study on the need for changes in Federal law and policy with respect to dredged material disposal areas for construction and maintenance of harbors and inland harbors by Secretary and, not later than 18 months after Oct. 31, 1992, to transmit to Congress a report on the results of the study, together with recommendations of the Secretary.

§ 2212. Inland waterway transportation

(a) Construction

One-half of the costs of construction—

(1) of each project authorized by title III of this Act,

(2) of the project authorized by section 652(j) of this title, and

(3) allocated to inland navigation for the project authorized by section 844 of this Act,

shall be paid only from amounts appropriated from the general fund of the Treasury. One-half of such costs shall be paid only from amounts appropriated from the Inland Waterways Trust Fund. For purposes of this subsection, the term "construction" shall include planning, designing, engineering, surveying, the acquisition of all lands, easements, and rights-of-way necessary for the project, including lands for disposal of dredged material, and relocations necessary for the project.

(b) Operation and maintenance

The Federal share of the cost of operation and maintenance of any project for navigation on the inland waterways is 100 percent.

(c) Authorizations from general fund

Any Federal responsibility—

(1) with respect to a project authorized by title III or section 652(j) of this title, or

(2) with respect to the portion of the project authorized by section 844 allocated to inland navigation,

which responsibility is not provided for in subsection (a) of this section shall be paid only from amounts appropriated from the general fund of the Treasury.

(Pub. L. 99–662, title I, § 102, Nov. 17, 1986, 100 Stat. 4084.)

REFERENCES IN TEXT

Title III of this Act, referred to in subsecs. (a)(1) and (c)(1), is title III of Pub. L. 99–662, Nov. 17, 1986, 100 Stat. 4109, consisting of sections 301 and 302. The projects authorized by title III probably mean the projects authorized by section 301 of Pub. L. 99–662, which is not classified to the Code. Section 302 of Pub. L. 99–662, which established the Inland Waterways Users Board, is classified to section 2251 of this title.

Section 844 of this Act, referred to in subsecs. (a)(3) and (c)(2), is section 844 of Pub. L. 99–662, Nov. 17, 1986, 100 Stat. 4177, which is not classified to the Code.

§ 2213. Flood control and other purposes

(a) Flood control

(1) General rule

The non-Federal interests for a project with costs assigned to flood control (other than a nonstructural project) shall—

(A) pay 5 percent of the cost of the project assigned to flood control during construction of the project;

(B) provide all lands, easements, rights-of-way, and dredged material disposal areas required only for flood control and perform all related necessary relocations; and

(C) provide that portion of the joint costs of lands, easements, rights-of-way, dredged material disposal areas, and relocations which is assigned to flood control.

(2) 35 percent minimum contribution

If the value of the contributions required under paragraph (1) of this subsection is less than 35 percent of the cost of the project assigned to flood control, the non-Federal interest shall pay during construction of the project such additional amounts as are necessary so that the total contribution of the non-Federal interests under this subsection is equal to 35 percent of the cost of the project assigned to flood control.

(3) 50 percent maximum

The non-Federal share under paragraph (1) shall not exceed 50 percent of the cost of the project assigned to flood control. The preceding sentence does not modify the requirement of paragraph (1)(A) of this subsection.

(4) Deferred payment of amount exceeding 30 percent

If the total amount of the contribution required under paragraph (1) of this subsection exceeds 30 percent of the cost of the project assigned to flood control, the non-Federal interests may pay the amount of the excess to the Secretary over a 15-year period (or such shorter period as may be agreed to by the Secretary and the non-Federal interests) beginning on the date construction of the project or separable element is completed, at an interest rate determined pursuant to section 2216 of this title. The preceding sentence does not modify the requirement of paragraph (1)(A) of this subsection.

(b) Nonstructural flood control projects

(1) In general

The non-Federal share of the cost of nonstructural flood control measures shall be 35 percent of the cost of such measures. The non-Federal interests for any such measures shall be required to provide all lands, easements, rights-of-way, dredged material disposal areas, and relocations necessary for the project, but shall not be required to contribute any amount in cash during construction of the project.

(2) Non-Federal contribution in excess of 35 percent

At any time during construction of a project, if the Secretary determines that the costs of land, easements, rights-of-way, dredged material disposal areas, and relocations for the project, in combination with other costs contributed by the non-Federal interests, will exceed 35 percent, any additional costs for the project (not to exceed 65 percent of the total costs of the project) shall be a Federal responsibility and shall be contributed during construction as part of the Federal share.

(c) Other purposes

The non-Federal share of the cost assigned to other project purposes shall be as follows:

(1) hydroelectric power: 100 percent, except that the marketing of such power and the recovery of costs of constructing, operating, maintaining, and rehabilitating such projects shall be in accordance with existing law: *Provided*, That after November 17, 1986, the Secretary shall not submit to Congress any proposal for the authorization of any water resources project that has a hydroelectric power component unless such proposal contains the comments of the appropriate Power Marketing Administrator designated pursuant to section 7152 of title 42 concerning the appropriate Power Marketing Administration's ability to market the hydroelectric power expected to be generated and not required in the operation of the project under the applicable Federal power marketing law, so that, 100 percent of operation, maintenance and replacement costs, 100 percent of the capital investment allocated to the purpose of hydroelectric power (with interest at rates established pursuant to or prescribed by applicable law), and any other costs assigned in accordance with law for return from power revenues can be returned within the period set for the return of such costs by or pursuant to such applicable Federal power marketing law;

(2) municipal and industrial water supply: 100 percent;

(3) agricultural water supply: 35 percent;

(4) recreation, including recreational navigation: 50 percent of separable costs and, in the case of any harbor or inland harbor or channel project, 50 percent of joint and separable costs allocated to recreational navigation;

(5) hurricane and storm damage reduction: 35 percent;

(6) aquatic plant control: 50 percent of control operations; and

(7) environmental protection and restoration: 35 percent; except that nothing in this paragraph shall affect or limit the applicability of section 2283 of this title.

(d) Certain other costs assigned to project purposes

(1) Construction

Costs of constructing projects or measures for beach erosion control and water quality enhancement shall be assigned to appropriate project purposes listed in subsections (a), (b), and (c) of this section and shall be shared in the same percentage as the purposes to which the costs are assigned, except that all costs assigned to benefits to privately owned shores (where use of such shores is limited to private interests) or to prevention of losses of private lands shall be borne by non-Federal interests and all costs assigned to the protection of federally owned shores shall be borne by the United States.

(2) Periodic nourishment

(A) In general

In the case of a project authorized for construction after December 31, 1999, except for a project for which a District Engineer's Report is completed by that date, the non-Federal cost of the periodic nourishment of the project, or any measure for shore protection or beach erosion control for the project, that is carried out—

(i) after January 1, 2001, shall be 40 percent;

(ii) after January 1, 2002, shall be 45 percent; and

(iii) after January 1, 2003, shall be 50 percent.

(B) Benefits to privately owned shores

All costs assigned to benefits of periodic nourishment projects or measures to privately owned shores (where use of such shores is limited to private interests) or to prevention of losses of private land shall be borne by the non-Federal interest.

(C) Benefits to federally owned shores

All costs assigned to the protection of federally owned shores for periodic nourishment measures shall be borne by the United States.

(e) Applicability

(1) In general

This section applies to any project (including any small project which is not specifically authorized by Congress and for which the Secretary has not approved funding before November 17, 1986), or separable element thereof, on which physical construction is initiated after April 30, 1986, as determined by the Secretary, except as provided in paragraph (2). For the purpose of the preceding sentence, physical construction shall be considered to be initiated on the date of the award of a construction contract.

(2) Exceptions

This section shall not apply to the Yazoo Basin, Mississippi, Demonstration Erosion Control Program, authorized by Public Law 98–8, or to the Harlan, Kentucky, or Barbourville, Kentucky, elements of the project authorized by section 202 of Public Law 96–367.

(f) "Separable element" defined

For purposes of this Act, the term "separable element" means a portion of a project—

(1) which is physically separable from other portions of the project; and

(2) which—

(A) achieves hydrologic effects, or

(B) produces physical or economic benefits,

which are separately identifiable from those produced by other portions of the project.

(g) Deferral of payment

(1) With respect to the projects listed in paragraph (2), no amount of the non-Federal share required under this section shall be required to be paid during the three-year period beginning on November 17, 1986.

(2) The projects referred to in paragraph (1) are the following:

(A) Boeuf and Tensas Rivers, Tensas Basin, Louisiana and Arkansas, authorized by the Flood Control Act of 1946;

(B) Eight Mile Creek, Arkansas, authorized by Public Law 99–88; and

(C) Rocky Bayou Area, Yazoo Backwater Area, Yazoo Basin, Mississippi, authorized by the Flood Control Act approved August 18, 1941.

(h) Assigned joint and separable costs

The share of the costs specified under this section for each project purpose shall apply to the joint and separable costs of construction of each project assigned to that purpose, except as otherwise specified in this Act.

(i) Lands, easements, rights-of-way, dredged material disposal areas, and relocations

Except as provided under section 2283(c) of this title, the non-Federal interests for a project to which this section applies shall provide all lands, easements, rights-of-way, and dredged material disposal areas required for the project and perform all necessary relocations, except to the extent limited by any provision of this section. The value of any contribution under the preceding sentence shall be included in the non-Federal share of the project specified in this section.

(j) Agreement

(1) Requirement for agreement

Any project to which this section applies (other than a project for hydroelectric power) shall be initiated only after non-Federal interests have entered into binding agreements with the Secretary to pay 100 percent of the operation, maintenance, and replacement and rehabilitation costs of the project, to pay the non-Federal share of the costs of construction required by this section, and to hold and save the United States free from damages due to the construction or operation and maintenance of the project, except for damages due to the fault or negligence of the United States or its contractors.

(2) Elements of agreement

The agreement required pursuant to paragraph (1) shall be in accordance with the requirements of section 1962d–5b of title 42 and shall provide for the rights and duties of the United States and the non-Federal interest with respect to the construction, operation, and maintenance of the project, including, but not limited to, provisions specifying that, in the event the non-Federal interest fails to provide the required non-Federal share of costs for such work, the Secretary—

(A) shall terminate or suspend work on the project unless the Secretary determines that continuation of the work is in the interest of the United States or is necessary in order to satisfy agreements with other non-Federal interests in connection with the project; and

(B) may terminate or adjust the rights and privileges of the non-Federal interest to project outputs under the terms of the agreement.

(k) Payment options

Except as otherwise provided in this section, the Secretary may permit the full non-Federal contribution to be made without interest during construction of the project or separable element, or with interest at a rate determined pursuant to section 2216 of this title over a period of not more than thirty years from the date of completion of the project or separable element. Repayment contracts shall provide for recalculation of the interest rate at five-year intervals.

(*l*) Delay of initial payment

At the request of any non-Federal interest the Secretary may permit such non-Federal interest to delay the initial payment of any non-Federal contribution under this section or section 2211 of this title for up to one year after the date when construction is begun on the project for which such contribution is to be made. Any such delay in initial payment shall be subject to interest charges for up to six months at a rate determined pursuant to section 2216 of this title.

(m) Ability to pay

(1) In general

Any cost-sharing agreement under this section for a feasibility study, or for construction of an environmental protection and restoration project, a flood control project, a project for navigation, storm damage protection, shoreline erosion, hurricane protection, or recreation, or an agricultural water supply project, shall be subject to the ability of the non-Federal interest to pay.

(2) Criteria and procedures

The ability of a non-Federal interest to pay shall be determined by the Secretary in accordance with criteria and procedures in effect under paragraph (3) on the day before December 11, 2000; except that such criteria and procedures shall be revised, and new criteria and procedures shall be developed, not later than December 31, 2007, to reflect the requirements of such paragraph (3).

(3) Revision of criteria and procedures

In revising criteria and procedures pursuant to paragraph (2), the Secretary—

(A) shall consider—

(i) per capita income data for the county or counties in which the project is to be located; and

(ii) the per capita non-Federal cost of construction of the project for the county or counties in which the project is to be located; and

(B) may consider additional criteria relating to the non-Federal interest's financial ability to carry out its cost-sharing responsibilities, to the extent that the application of such criteria does not eliminate areas from eligibility for a reduction in the non-Federal share as determined under subparagraph (A).

(4) Non-Federal share

Notwithstanding subsection (a) of this section, the Secretary may reduce the requirement that a non-Federal interest make a cash contribution for any project that is determined to be eligible for a reduction in the non-Federal share under criteria and procedures in effect under paragraphs (1), (2), and (3).

(n) Non-Federal contributions

(1) Prohibition on solicitation of excess contributions

The Secretary may not—

(A) solicit contributions from non-Federal interests for costs of constructing authorized water resources projects or measures in excess of the non-Federal share assigned to the appropriate project purposes listed in subsections (a), (b), and (c); or

(B) condition Federal participation in such projects or measures on the receipt of such contributions.

(2) Limitation on statutory construction

Nothing in this subsection shall be construed to affect the Secretary's authority under section 903(c).[1]

(Pub. L. 99–662, title I, § 103, Nov. 17, 1986, 100 Stat. 4084; Pub. L. 101–640, title III, § 305(a), Nov. 28, 1990, 104 Stat. 4635; Pub. L. 102–580, title II, § 201(a), title III, § 333(b)(2), Oct. 31, 1992, 106 Stat. 4825, 4852; Pub. L. 104–303, title II, §§ 202(a)(1)(A), (2), (b)(1), 210(a), Oct. 12, 1996, 110 Stat. 3673, 3681; Pub. L. 106–53, title II, §§ 215(a), 219(c), Aug. 17, 1999, 113 Stat. 292, 295; Pub. L. 106–109, § 5, Nov. 24, 1999, 113 Stat. 1495; Pub. L. 106–541, title II, § 204, Dec. 11, 2000, 114 Stat. 2589; Pub. L. 110–114, title II, §§ 2001, 2019(a), Nov. 8, 2007, 121 Stat. 1067, 1078.)

[1] See References in Text note below.

REFERENCES IN TEXT

Public Law 98–8, referred to in subsec. (e)(2), is Pub. L. 98–8, Mar. 24, 1983, 97 Stat. 13. For complete classification of this Act to the Code, see Tables.

Section 202 of Public Law 96–367, referred to in subsec. (e)(2), is section 202 of Pub. L. 96–367, title II, Oct. 1, 1980, 94 Stat. 1339, which is not classified to the Code.

This Act, referred to in subsecs. (f) and (h), is Pub. L. 99–662, Nov. 17, 1986, 100 Stat. 4082, as amended, known as the Water Resources Development Act of 1986. For complete classification of this Act to the Code, see Short Title note set out under section 2201 of this title and Tables.

The Flood Control Act of 1946, referred to in subsec. (g)(2)(A), is act July 24, 1946, ch. 596, 60 Stat. 641, as amended. For complete classification of this Act to the Code, see Tables.

Public Law 99–88, referred to in subsec. (g)(2)(B), is Pub. L. 99–88, Aug. 15, 1985, 99 Stat. 293, known as the Supplemental Appropriations Act, 1985. Provisions of Pub. L. 99–88 authorizing the project for Eight Mile Creek, Arkansas, are not classified to the Code. For complete classification of this Act to the Code, see Tables.

The Flood Control Act approved August 18, 1941, referred to in subsec. (g)(2)(C), is act Aug. 18, 1941, ch. 377, 55 Stat. 638. For complete classification of this Act to the Code, see Tables.

Section 903(c), referred to in subsec. (n)(2), is section 903(c) of Pub. L. 99–662, title IX, Nov. 17, 1986, 100 Stat. 4184, which is not classified to the Code.

AMENDMENTS

2007—Subsec. (m)(2). Pub. L. 110–114, § 2019(a), substituted "December 31, 2007" for "180 days after December 11, 2000".

Subsec. (n). Pub. L. 110–114, § 2001, added subsec. (n).

2000—Subsec. (m)(1), (2). Pub. L. 106–541, § 204(1), added pars. (1) and (2) and struck out former pars. (1) and (2) which required any cost-sharing agreement to be subject to the ability of a non-Federal interest to pay and required the Secretary to determine ability to pay using certain criteria and procedures.

Subsec. (m)(3)(B), (C). Pub. L. 106–541, § 204(2), redesignated subpar. (C) as (B) and struck out former subpar. (B) which read as follows: "shall not consider criteria (other than criteria described in subparagraph (A)) in effect on the day before October 12, 1996; and".

1999—Subsec. (b). Pub. L. 106–53, § 219(c)(1), which directed insertion of the par. (1) designation and heading before "The non-Federal", was executed by making the insertion before that phrase the first place it appeared to reflect the probable intent of Congress.

Subsec. (b)(2). Pub. L. 106–53, § 219(c)(2), added par. (2).

Subsec. (d). Pub. L. 106–53, § 215(a), designated existing provisions as par. (1), inserted heading, and added par. (2).

Subsec. (d)(2)(A). Pub. L. 106–109 substituted "except for a project for which a District Engineer's Report is completed by that date," for "or for which a feasibility study is completed after that date,".

1996—Subsecs. (a)(2), (b). Pub. L. 104–303, § 202(a)(1)(A), substituted "35 percent" for "25 percent" wherever appearing.

Subsec. (c)(7). Pub. L. 104–303, § 210(a), added par. (7).

Subsec. (e)(1). Pub. L. 104–303, § 202(a)(2), inserted at end "For the purpose of the preceding sentence, physical construction shall be considered to be initiated on the date of the award of a construction contract."

Subsec. (m). Pub. L. 104–303, § 202(b)(1), reenacted heading without change and amended text generally.

Prior to amendment, text read as follows: "Any cost-sharing agreement under this section for flood control or agricultural water supply shall be subject to the ability of a non-Federal interest to pay. The ability of any non-Federal interest to pay shall be determined by the Secretary in accordance with procedures established by the Secretary."

1992—Subsec. (i). Pub. L. 102–580, §333(b)(2), substituted "Except as provided under section 2283(c) of this title, the non-Federal" for "The non-Federal".

Subsec. (m). Pub. L. 102–580, §201(a), amended subsec. (m) generally. Prior to amendment, subsec. (m) read as follows:

"(1) GENERAL RULE.—Any cost-sharing agreement under this section for flood control or agricultural water supply shall be subject to the ability of a non-Federal interest to pay.

"(2) PROCEDURES.—

"(A) IN GENERAL.—The ability of any non-Federal interest to pay shall be determined by the Secretary in accordance with procedures established by the Secretary.

"(B) LIMITATIONS.—The procedures established pursuant to this subsection shall provide for a reduction in any non-Federal cash contribution required under subsection (a)(2) of this section. In addition, such procedures shall provide for determination of the eligibility of the non-Federal interest for a reduction in the required cash contribution on the basis of local, not statewide, economic and financial data.

"(C) REGULATIONS.—Not later than 1 year after November 28, 1990, the Secretary shall issue regulations establishing the procedures required by this paragraph."

1990—Subsec. (m). Pub. L. 101–640 amended subsec. (m) generally. Prior to amendment, subsec. (m) read as follows: "Any cost-sharing agreement under this section for flood control or agricultural water supply shall be subject to the ability of a non-Federal interest to pay. The ability of any non-Federal interest to pay shall be determined by the Secretary in accordance with procedures established by the Secretary."

EFFECTIVE DATE OF 1996 AMENDMENT

Section 202(a)(1)(B) of Pub. L. 104–303 provided that: "The amendments made by subparagraph (A) [amending this section] shall apply to any project authorized after the date of the enactment of this Act [Oct. 12, 1996] and to any flood control project that is not specifically authorized by Congress for which a Detailed Project Report is approved after such date of enactment or, in the case of a project for which no Detailed Project Report is prepared, construction is initiated after such date of enactment."

Section 202(b)(2) of Pub. L. 104–303 provided that:

"(A) GENERALLY.—Subject to subparagraph (C), the amendment made by paragraph (1) [amending this section] shall apply to any project, or separable element thereof, with respect to which the Secretary and the non-Federal interest enter into a project cooperation agreement after December 31, 1997.

"(B) AMENDMENT OF COOPERATION AGREEMENT.—If requested by the non-Federal interest, the Secretary shall amend a project cooperation agreement executed on or before the date of the enactment of this Act [Oct. 12, 1996] to reflect the application of the amendment made by paragraph (1) to any project for which a contract for construction has not been awarded on or before such date of enactment.

"(C) NON-FEDERAL OPTION.—If requested by the non-Federal interest, the Secretary shall apply the criteria and procedures established pursuant to section 103(m) of the Water Resources Development Act of 1986 [subsec. (m) of this section] as in effect on the day before the date of the enactment of this Act for projects that are authorized before the date of the enactment of this Act."

[Reference to "project cooperation agreement" deemed to be reference to "project partnership agreement", see section 2003(f)(2) of Pub. L. 110–114, set out as a note under section 1962d–5b of Title 42, The Public Health and Welfare.]

Section 210(b) of Pub. L. 104–303 provided that: "The amendments made by subsection (a) [amending this section] apply only to projects authorized after the date of the enactment of this Act [Oct. 12, 1996]."

CONTINUATION OF EXISTING REGULATIONS

Section 305(b) of Pub. L. 101–640 provided that: "Regulations issued to carry out section 103(m) of the Water Resources Development Act of 1986 [33 U.S.C. 2213(m)] before the date of the enactment of this Act [Nov. 28, 1990] and in effect on such date shall continue in effect until regulations are issued pursuant to paragraph (2)(C) of such section, as added by subsection (a) of this section."

REPORTS TO CONGRESS

Pub. L. 100–71, title I, July 11, 1987, 101 Stat. 401, provided that: "The Secretary of the Army shall file a report with the appropriate committees of the House of Representatives and the Senate within ninety days after a written request is made pursuant to the provisions of subsection (m) of section 103 of Public Law 99–662 [33 U.S.C. 2213(m)] indicating the action taken on the request. In addition, the Secretary of the Army shall file a report with the appropriate committees of the House of Representatives and the Senate within ninety days after enactment of this Act [July 11, 1987] listing any project or study falling under the provisions of subsection (e)(1) of section 103 of Public Law 99–662."

§2214. General credit for flood control

(a) Guidelines

Within one year after November 17, 1986, the Secretary shall issue guidelines to carry out this section, consistent with the principles and guidelines on project formulation. The guidelines shall include criteria for determining whether work carried out by non-Federal interests is compatible with a project for flood control and procedures for making such determinations. The guidelines under this section shall be promulgated after notice in the Federal Register and opportunity for comment.

(b) Analysis of costs and benefits

The guidelines established under subsection (a) of this section shall provide for the Secretary to consider, in analyzing the costs and benefits of a proposed project for flood control, the costs and benefits produced by any flood control work carried out by non-Federal interests that the Secretary determines to be compatible with the project. For purposes of the preceding sentence the Secretary may consider only work carried out after the date which is 5 years before the first obligation of funds for the reconnaissance study for such project. In no case may work which was carried out more than 5 years before November 17, 1986, be considered under this subsection, unless otherwise provided in this Act.

(c) Crediting of non-Federal share

The guidelines established under subsection (a) of this section shall provide for crediting the cost of work carried out by the non-Federal interests against the non-Federal share of the cost of an authorized project for flood control as follows:

(1) Work which is carried out after the end of the reconnaissance study and before the submission to Congress of the final report of the Chief of Engineers on the project and which is

determined by the Secretary to be compatible with the project shall be included as part of the project and shall be recommended by the Secretary in the final report for credit against the non-Federal share of the cost of the project.

(2) Work which is carried out after submission of the final report of the Chief of Engineers to Congress and which is determined by the Secretary to be compatible with the project shall be considered as part of the project and shall be credited by the Secretary against the non-Federal share of the cost of the project in accordance with the guidelines promulgated pursuant to subsection (a) of this section.

In no event may work which was carried out more than 5 years before November 17, 1986, be considered under this subsection, unless otherwise provided in this Act.

(d) Procedure for work done before November 17, 1986

The Secretary shall consider, under subsections (b) and (c) of this section, work carried out before November 17, 1986, by non-Federal interests on a project for flood control, if the non-Federal interests apply to the Secretary for consideration of such work not later than March 31, 1987. The Secretary shall make determinations under subsections (b) and (c) of this section with respect to such work not later than 6 months after guidelines are issued under subsection (a) of this section.

(e) Procedure for work done after November 17, 1986

The Secretary shall consider work carried out after November 17, 1986, by non-Federal interests on a project for flood control under subsections (b) and (c) of this section in accordance with the guidelines issued under subsection (a) of this section. The guidelines shall require prior approval by the Secretary of any flood control work carried out after November 17, 1986, in order to be considered under this section, taking into account the economic and environmental feasibility of the project.

(f) Limitation not applicable

Any flood control work included as part of the non-Federal share of the cost of a project under this section shall not be subject to the limitation contained in the last sentence of section 1962d–5a(a) of title 42.

(g) Cash contribution not affected

Nothing in this section affects the requirement of section 2213(a)(1)(A) of this title.

(Pub. L. 99–662, title I, §104, Nov. 17, 1986, 100 Stat. 4087.)

REFERENCES IN TEXT

This Act, referred to in subsecs. (b) and (c), is Pub. L. 99–662, Nov. 17, 1986, 100 Stat. 4082, as amended, known as the Water Resources Development Act of 1986. For complete classification of this Act to the Code, see Short Title note set out under section 2201 of this title and Tables.

§2215. Feasibility studies; planning, engineering, and design

(a) Feasibility studies

(1) Cost sharing

(A) In general

The Secretary shall not initiate any feasibility study for a water resources project after November 17, 1986, until appropriate non-Federal interests agree, by contract, to contribute 50 percent of the cost of the study.

(B) Payment of cost share during period of study

During the period of the study, the non-Federal share of the cost of the study payable under subparagraph (A) shall be 50 percent of the sum of—

(i) the cost estimate for the study as contained in the feasibility cost-sharing agreement; and

(ii) any excess of the cost of the study over the cost estimate if the excess results from—

(I) a change in Federal law; or

(II) a change in the scope of the study requested by the non-Federal interests.

(C) Payment of cost share on authorization of project or termination of study

(i) Project timely authorized

Except as otherwise agreed to by the Secretary and the non-Federal interests and subject to clause (ii), the non-Federal share of any excess of the cost of the study over the cost estimate (excluding any excess cost described in subparagraph (B)(ii)) shall be payable on the date on which the Secretary and the non-Federal interests enter into an agreement pursuant to section 2211(e) or 2213(j) of this title with respect to the project.

(ii) Project not timely authorized

If the project that is the subject of the study is not authorized by the date that is 5 years after the completion of the final report of the Chief of Engineers concerning the study or the date that is 2 years after the termination of the study, the non-Federal share of any excess of the cost of the study over the cost estimate (excluding any excess cost described in subparagraph (B)(ii)) shall be payable to the United States on that date.

(D) Amendment of cost estimate

The cost estimate referred to in subparagraph (B)(i) may be amended only by agreement of the Secretary and the non-Federal interests.

(E) In-kind contributions

The non-Federal share required under this paragraph may be satisfied by the provision of services, materials, supplies, or other in-kind services necessary to prepare the feasibility report.

(2) Applicability

This subsection shall not apply to any water resources study primarily designed for the purposes of navigational improvements in the nature of dams, locks, and channels on the Nation's system of inland waterways.

(3) Detailed project reports

The requirements of this subsection that apply to a feasibility study also shall apply to a study that results in a detailed project report, except that—

(A) the first $100,000 of the costs of a study that results in a detailed project report shall be a Federal expense; and

(B) paragraph (1)(C)(ii) shall not apply to such a study.

(b) Planning and engineering

The Secretary shall not initiate any planning or engineering for a water resources project until appropriate non-Federal interests agree, by contract, to contribute 50 percent of the cost of the planning and engineering during the period of the planning and engineering. Costs of planning and engineering of projects for which non-Federal interests contributed 50 percent of the cost of the feasibility study shall be treated as costs of construction.

(c) Design

Costs of design of a water resources project shall be shared in the same percentage as the purposes of such project.

(d) Definitions

In this section, the following definitions apply:

(1) Detailed project report

The term "detailed project report" means a report for a project not specifically authorized by Congress in law or otherwise that determines the feasibility of the project with a level of detail appropriate to the scope and complexity of the recommended solution and sufficient to proceed directly to the preparation of contract plans and specifications. The term includes any associated environmental impact statement and mitigation plan. For a project for which the Federal cost does not exceed $1,000,000, the term includes a planning and design analysis document.

(2) Feasibility study

The term "feasibility study" means a study that results in a feasibility report under section 2282 of this title, and any associated environmental impact statement and mitigation plan, prepared by the Corps of Engineers for a water resources project. The term includes a study that results in a project implementation report prepared under title VI of the Water Resources Development Act of 2000 (114 Stat. 2680–2694), a general reevaluation report, and a limited reevaluation report.

(Pub. L. 99–662, title I, § 105, Nov. 17, 1986, 100 Stat. 4088; Pub. L. 101–640, title III, § 301, Nov. 28, 1990, 104 Stat. 4633; Pub. L. 104–303, title II, § 203(a), Oct. 12, 1996, 110 Stat. 3677; Pub. L. 106–541, title II, § 225, Dec. 11, 2000, 114 Stat. 2598; Pub. L. 110–114, title II, § 2043(a), Nov. 8, 2007, 121 Stat. 1101.)

REFERENCES IN TEXT

The Water Resources Development Act of 2000, referred to in subsec. (d)(2), is Pub. L. 106–541, Dec. 11, 2000, 114 Stat. 2572. Title VI of the Act is not classified to the Code. For complete classification of this Act to the Code, see Short Title of 2000 Amendment note set out under section 2201 of this title and Tables.

AMENDMENTS

2007—Subsec. (a)(3). Pub. L. 110–114, § 2043(a)(1), added par. (3).

Subsec. (b). Pub. L. 110–114, § 2043(a)(2), struck out "authorized by this Act" before "for a water resources project".

Subsec. (d). Pub. L. 110–114, § 2043(a)(3), added subsec. (d).

2000—Subsec. (a)(1)(E). Pub. L. 106–541 substituted "The" for "Not more than ½ of the".

1996—Subsec. (a)(1). Pub. L. 104–303, § 203(a)(1), inserted heading and amended text of par. (1) generally. Prior to amendment text read as follows: "The Secretary shall not initiate any feasibility study for a water resources project after November 17, 1986, until appropriate non-Federal interests agree, by contract, to contribute 50 percent of the cost for such study during the period of such study. Not more than one-half of such non-Federal contribution may be made by the provision of services, materials, supplies, or other in-kind services necessary to prepare the feasibility report."

Subsec. (a)(2). Pub. L. 104–303, § 203(a)(2), inserted heading.

1990—Subsec. (b). Pub. L. 101–640 inserted at end "Costs of planning and engineering of projects for which non-Federal interests contributed 50 percent of the cost of the feasibility study shall be treated as costs of construction."

EFFECTIVE DATE OF 1996 AMENDMENT

Section 203(b) of Pub. L. 104–303 provided that: "The amendments made by subsection (a) [amending this section] shall apply notwithstanding any feasibility cost-sharing agreement entered into by the Secretary and the non-Federal interests. On request of the non-Federal interest, the Secretary shall amend any feasibility cost-sharing agreements in effect on the date of the enactment of this Act [Oct. 12, 1996] so as to conform the agreements with the amendments."

NO REQUIREMENT OF REIMBURSEMENT

Section 203(c) of Pub. L. 104–303 provided that: "Nothing in this section [amending this section and enacting provisions set out above] or any amendment made by this section requires the Secretary to reimburse the non-Federal interests for funds previously contributed for a study."

§ 2216. Rate of interest

Whenever a non-Federal interest is required or elects to repay an amount under this Act over a period of time, the amount to be repaid shall include interest at a rate determined by the Secretary of the Treasury, taking into consideration the average market yields on outstanding marketable obligations of the United States with remaining periods to maturity comparable to the reimbursement period, during the month preceding the fiscal year in which costs for the construction of the project are first incurred (or in the case of recalculation the fiscal year in which the recalculation is made), plus a premium of one-eighth of one percentage point for transaction costs; except that such rates for hydroelectric power shall be in accordance with existing law.

(Pub. L. 99–662, title I, § 106, Nov. 17, 1986, 100 Stat. 4089.)

REFERENCES IN TEXT

This Act, referred to in text, is Pub. L. 99–662, Nov. 17, 1986, 100 Stat. 4082, as amended, known as the Water Resources Development Act of 1986. For complete classification of this Act to the Code, see Short Title note set out under section 2201 of this title and Tables.

§2217. Limitation on applicability of certain provisions in reports

If any provision in any report designated by this Act recommends that a State contribute in cash 5 percent of the construction costs allocated to non-vendible project purposes and 10 percent of the construction costs allocated to vendible project purposes, such provision shall not apply to the project recommended in such report.

(Pub. L. 99–662, title I, §107, Nov. 17, 1986, 100 Stat. 4089.)

REFERENCES IN TEXT

This Act, referred to in text, is Pub. L. 99–662, Nov. 17, 1986, 100 Stat. 4082, as amended, known as the Water Resources Development Act of 1986. For complete classification of this Act to the Code, see Short Title note set out under section 2201 of this title and Tables.

§2218. General applicability of cost sharing

Unless otherwise specified, the cost sharing provisions of this subchapter shall apply to all projects in this Act. The Federal share of any cost of a project authorized by this Act for which cost a Federal share is not established in this subchapter, shall be the share of such cost otherwise provided by law.

(Pub. L. 99–662, title I, §108, Nov. 17, 1986, 100 Stat. 4089.)

REFERENCES IN TEXT

This Act, referred to in text, is Pub. L. 99–662, Nov. 17, 1986, 100 Stat. 4082, as amended, known as the Water Resources Development Act of 1986. For complete classification of this Act to the Code, see Short Title note set out under section 2201 of this title and Tables.

§2219. Definitions

For purposes of this subchapter, terms shall have the meanings given by section 2241 of this title.

(Pub. L. 99–662, title I, §109, Nov. 17, 1986, 100 Stat. 4089.)

§2220. Rivers and harbors and other waterways projects for benefit of navigation, flood control, hurricane protection, beach erosion control, and other purposes

(a) Congressional declaration of policy; purchase of indebtedness and loans to local interests to meet contribution requirements

In the prosecution of projects for rivers and harbors and other waterways for the benefit of navigation, the control of destructive flood waters, hurricane protection, beach erosion control, and for other purposes, authorized to be prosecuted under the direction of the Secretary of the Army under the supervision of the Chief of Engineers in accordance with plans adopted and authorized by the Congress, it is hereby declared to be the policy of the Congress, that whenever such projects are located wholly or partially within an area which is eligible for financial assistance under the Public Works and Economic Development Act of 1965 [42 U.S.C. 3121 et seq.], the Secretary of Commerce is authorized to purchase evidences of indebtedness and to make loans for a period not exceeding fifty years to enable responsible local interests to meet the requirements of local cooperation pertaining to contributions toward the cost of construction of such projects within such areas.

(b) Authorization of appropriations

There is hereby authorized to be appropriated to carry out this section, not to exceed $10,000,000 per fiscal year for the fiscal year ending June 30, 1966, and for each fiscal year thereafter through and including the fiscal year ending June 30, 1970.

(Pub. L. 89–298, title II, §217, Oct. 27, 1965, 79 Stat. 1088.)

REFERENCES IN TEXT

The Public Works and Economic Development Act of 1965, referred to in subsec. (a), is Pub. L. 89–136, Aug. 26, 1965, 79 Stat. 552, as amended, which is classified generally to chapter 38 (§3121 et seq.) of Title 42, The Public Health and Welfare. For complete classification of this Act to the Code, see Short Title note set out under section 3121 of Title 42 and Tables.

CODIFICATION

Section was formerly classified to section 3142a of Title 42, The Public Health and Welfare.

Section was not enacted as part of the Water Resources Development Act of 1986 which comprises this chapter.

§2221. Cost limitations on projects

Beginning in fiscal year 2006 and thereafter, agreements proposed for execution by the Assistant Secretary of the Army for Civil Works or the United States Army Corps of Engineers after November 19, 2005, pursuant to section 560 of this title; section 561 of this title; the Civil Functions Appropriations Act, 1936, Public Law 75–208[1]; section 1962d–5a of title 42; sections 2214, 2231, and 2232 of this title; section 426i–1 of this title; section 701b–13 of this title; and any other specific project authority, shall be limited to total credits and reimbursements for all applicable projects not to exceed $100,000,000 in each fiscal year.

(Pub. L. 109–103, title I, §102, Nov. 19, 2005, 119 Stat. 2253.)

REFERENCES IN TEXT

The Civil Functions Appropriations Act, 1936, Public Law 75–208, referred to in text, may mean the War Department Civil Appropriation Act, 1938, act July 19, 1937, ch. 511, 50 Stat. 515, 518, which amended act June 22, 1936, ch. 688, §5, by adding the proviso classified to section 701h of this title.

CODIFICATION

Section was enacted as part of the Energy and Water Development Appropriations Act, 2006, and not as part of the Water Resources Development Act of 1986 which comprises this chapter.

PRIOR PROVISIONS

Provisions similar to those in this section were contained in the following prior appropriation acts:

Pub. L. 108–447, div. C, title I, §101, Dec. 8, 2004, 118 Stat. 2941; Pub. L. 109–13, div. A, title VI, §6005, May 11, 2005, 119 Stat. 282.

[1] See References in Text note below.

Pub. L. 108–137, title I, § 101, Dec. 1, 2003, 117 Stat. 1833.
Pub. L. 108–7, div. D, title I, § 101, Feb. 20, 2003, 117 Stat. 138.
Pub. L. 107–66, title I, § 103, Nov. 12, 2001, 115 Stat. 493.
Pub. L. 106–377, § 1(a)(2) [title I, § 102], Oct. 27, 2000, 114 Stat. 1441, 1441A–65.
Pub. L. 106–60, title I, § 102, Sept. 29, 1999, 113 Stat. 487.

§ 2222. Use of other Federal funds

The non-Federal interest for a water resources study or project may use, and the Secretary shall accept, funds provided by a Federal agency under any other Federal program, to satisfy, in whole or in part, the non-Federal share of the cost of the study or project if the Federal agency that provides the funds determines that the funds are authorized to be used to carry out the study or project.

(Pub. L. 110–114, title II, § 2007, Nov. 8, 2007, 121 Stat. 1073.)

CODIFICATION

Section was enacted as part of the Water Resources Development Act of 2007, and not as part of the Water Resources Development Act of 1986 which comprises this chapter.

"SECRETARY" DEFINED

Secretary means the Secretary of the Army, see section 2 of Pub. L. 110–114, set out as a note under section 2201 of this title.

SUBCHAPTER II—HARBOR DEVELOPMENT

§ 2231. Studies of projects by non-Federal interests

(a) Submission to Secretary

A non-Federal interest may on its own undertake a feasibility study of a proposed harbor or inland harbor project and submit it to the Secretary. To assist non-Federal interests, the Secretary shall, as soon as practicable, promulgate guidelines for studies of harbors or inland harbors to provide sufficient information for the formulation of studies.

(b) Review by Secretary

The Secretary shall review each study submitted under subsection (a) of this section for the purpose of determining whether or not such study and the process under which such study was developed comply with Federal laws and regulations applicable to feasibility studies of navigation projects for harbors or inland harbors.

(c) Submission to Congress

Not later than 180 days after receiving any study submitted under subsection (a) of this section, the Secretary shall transmit to the Congress, in writing, the results of such review and any recommendations the Secretary may have concerning the project described in such plan and design.

(d) Credit and reimbursement

If a project for which a study has been submitted under subsection (a) of this section is authorized by any provision of Federal law enacted after the date of such submission, the Secretary shall credit toward the non-Federal share of the cost of construction of such project an amount equal to the portion of the cost of developing such study that would be the responsibility of the United States if such study were developed by the Secretary.

(Pub. L. 99–662, title II, § 203, Nov. 17, 1986, 100 Stat. 4098.)

SHORT TITLE

For short title of title II of Pub. L. 99–662, enacting this subchapter, as the Harbor Development and Navigation Improvement Act of 1986, see section 215 of Pub. L. 99–662, set out as a note under section 2201 of this title.

§ 2232. Construction of projects by non-Federal interests

(a) Authority

In addition to projects undertaken pursuant to sections 201 and 202 of this title, any non-Federal interest is authorized to undertake navigational improvements in harbors or inland harbors of the United States, subject to obtaining any permits required pursuant to Federal and State laws in advance of the actual construction of such improvements.

(b) Studies and engineering

When requested by an appropriate non-Federal interest the Secretary is authorized to undertake all necessary studies and engineering for any construction to be undertaken under the terms of subsection (a) of this section, and provide technical assistance in obtaining all necessary permits, if the non-Federal interest contracts with the Secretary to furnish the United States funds for such studies and engineering during the period that they are conducted.

(c) Completion of studies

The Secretary is authorized to complete and transmit to the appropriate non-Federal interest any study for improvements to harbors or inland harbors of the United States which were initiated prior to November 17, 1986, or, upon the request of such non-Federal interest, to terminate such study and transmit such partially completed study to the non-Federal interest. The Secretary is further authorized to complete and transmit to the appropriate non-Federal interest any study for improvement to harbors or inland harbors of the United States that is initiated pursuant to section 577 of this title or, upon request of such non-Federal interest, to terminate such study and transmit such partially completed study to the non-Federal interest. Studies under this subsection shall be completed without regard to the requirements of subsection (b) of this section.

(d) Authority to carry out improvement

Any non-Federal interest which has requested and received from the Secretary pursuant to subsection (b) or (c) of this section, the completed study and engineering for an improvement to a harbor or an inland harbor, or separable element thereof, for the purpose of constructing such improvement and for which improvement a final environmental impact statement has been filed, shall be authorized to carry out the terms of the plan for such improvement. Any plan of improvement proposed to be implemented in accordance with this subsection shall be deemed to satisfy the requirements for obtaining the appropriate permits required under the Secretary's authority and such permits shall be granted subject to the non-Federal interest's acceptance of the terms and conditions of such permits: Provided, That the Secretary determines that the applicable regulatory criteria and procedures have been satisfied. The Secretary shall monitor any project for which permits are granted under this subsection in order to ensure that such project is constructed (and, in those cases where such activities will not be the responsibility of the Secretary, operated and maintained) in accordance with the terms and conditions of such permits.

(e) Reimbursement

(1) General rule

Subject to the enactment of appropriation Acts, the Secretary is authorized to reimburse any non-Federal interest an amount equal to the estimate of Federal share, without interest, of the cost of any authorized harbor or inland harbor improvement, or separable element thereof, including any small navigation project approved pursuant to section 577 of this title, constructed under the terms of this section if—

(A) after authorization of the project (or, in the case of a small navigation project, after completion of a favorable project report by the Corps of Engineers) and before initiation of construction of the project or separable element—

(i) the Secretary approves the plans of construction of such project by such non-Federal interest, and

(ii) such non-Federal interest enters into an agreement to pay the non-Federal share, if any, of the cost of operation and maintenance of such project; and

(B) the Secretary finds before approval of the plans of construction of the project that the project, or separable element, is economically justified and environmentally acceptable.

(2) Matters to be considered in reviewing plans

In reviewing such plans, the Secretary shall consider budgetary and programmatic priorities, potential impacts on the cost of dredging projects nationwide, and other factors that the Secretary deems appropriate.

(3) Monitoring

The Secretary shall regularly monitor and audit any project for a harbor or inland harbor constructed under this subsection by a non-Federal interest in order to ensure that such construction is in compliance with the plans approved by the Secretary, and that costs are reasonable. No reimbursement shall be made unless and until the Secretary has certified that the work for which reimbursement is requested has been performed in accordance with applicable permits and the approved plans.

(f) Operation and maintenance

Whenever a non-Federal interest constructs improvements to any harbor or inland harbor, the Secretary shall be responsible for maintenance in accordance with section 2211(b) of this title if—

(1) the Secretary determines, before construction, that the improvements, or separable elements thereof, are economically justified, environmentally acceptable, and consistent with the purposes of this subchapter;

(2) the Secretary certifies that the project is constructed in accordance with applicable permits and the appropriate engineering and design standards; and

(3) the Secretary does not find that the project, or separable element thereof, is no longer economically justified or environmentally acceptable.

(g) Demonstration of non-Federal interests acting as agent of Secretary

For the purpose of demonstrating the potential advantages and efficiencies of non-Federal management of projects, the Secretary may approve as many as two proposals pursuant to which the non-Federal interests will undertake part or all of a harbor project authorized by Congress as the agent of the Secretary by utilizing its own personnel or by procuring outside services, so long as the cost of doing so will not exceed the cost of the Secretary undertaking the project.

(Pub. L. 99–662, title II, §204, Nov. 17, 1986, 100 Stat. 4099; Pub. L. 101–640, title III, §303, Nov. 28, 1990, 104 Stat. 4634.)

REFERENCES IN TEXT

Sections 201 and 202 of this title, referred to in subsec. (a), are sections 201 and 202 of title II of Pub. L. 99–662, Nov. 17, 1986, 100 Stat. 4089, 4091, which are not classified to the Code.

This subchapter, referred to in subsec. (f)(1), was in the original "this title" which, in addition to this subchapter, consisted of sections 201 and 202 of Pub. L. 99–662, which are not classified to the Code.

AMENDMENTS

1990—Subsec. (c). Pub. L. 101–640, §303(a), inserted after first sentence "The Secretary is further authorized to complete and transmit to the appropriate non-Federal interest any study for improvement to harbors or inland harbors of the United States that is initiated pursuant to section 577 of this title or, upon request of such non-Federal interest, to terminate such study and transmit such partially completed study to the non-Federal interest."

Subsec. (e). Pub. L. 101–640, §303(b)(1), redesignated subsec. (e), relating to operation and maintenance, as (f).

Subsec. (e)(1). Pub. L. 101–640, §303(b)(2), (3), in introductory provisions inserted "including any small navigation project approved pursuant to section 577 of this title," after "or separable element thereof," and in subpar. (A) inserted "(or, in the case of a small navigation project, after completion of a favorable project report by the Corps of Engineers)" after "authorization of the project".

Subsec. (f). Pub. L. 101–640, §303(b)(1), redesignated subsec. (e), relating to operation and maintenance, as (f). Former subsec. (f) redesignated (g).

Subsec. (g). Pub. L. 101–640, §303(b)(1), redesignated subsec. (f) as (g).

DEMONSTRATION OF CONSTRUCTION OF FEDERAL PROJECT BY NON-FEDERAL INTERESTS

Section 404 of Pub. L. 101–640 provided that:

"(a) IN GENERAL.—For purposes of demonstrating the safety benefits and economic efficiencies which would accrue as a consequence of non-Federal management of harbor improvement projects, the Secretary shall enter into agreements with 2 non-Federal interests pursuant to which the non-Federal interests will undertake part or all of a harbor project authorized by law, by utilizing their own personnel or by procuring outside services, if the cost of doing so will not exceed the cost of the Secretary undertaking the project. If proposals for such agreements meet the criteria of section 204 of the Water Resources Development Act of 1986 [33 U.S.C. 2232], the agreements shall be entered into not later than 1 year after the date of the enactment of this Act [Nov. 28, 1990].

"(b) LIMITATION.—At least 1 project carried out pursuant to this section shall pertain to improvements to a major ship channel which carries a substantial volume of both passenger and cargo traffic.

"(c) REPORT.—The Secretary shall transmit to Congress a report regarding the safety benefits and economic efficiencies accrued from entering into agreements with non-Federal interests under this section."

§ 2233. Coordination and scheduling of Federal, State, and local actions

(a) Notice of intent

The Secretary, on request from an appropriate non-Federal interest in the form of a written notice of intent to construct a navigation project for a harbor or inland harbor under section 2232 of this title or this section, shall initiate procedures to establish a schedule for consolidating Federal, State, and local agency environmental assessments, project reviews, and issuance of all permits for the construction of the project, including associated access channels, berthing areas, and onshore port-related facilities, before the initiation of construction. The non-Federal interest shall submit, with the notice of intent, studies and documentation, including environmental reviews, that may be required by Federal law for decisionmaking on the proposed project. A State shall not be required to participate in carrying out this section.

(b) Procedural requirements

Within 15 days after receipt of notice under subsection (a) of this section, the Secretary shall publish such notice in the Federal Register. The Secretary also shall provide written notification of the receipt of a notice under subsection (a) of this section to all State and local agencies that may be required to issue permits for the construction of the project or related activities. The Secretary shall solicit the cooperation of those agencies and request their entry into a memorandum of agreement described in subsection (c) of this section. Within 30 days after publication of the notice in the Federal Register, State and local agencies that intend to enter into the memorandum of agreement shall notify the Secretary of their intent in writing.

(c) Scheduling agreement

Within 90 days after receipt of notice under subsection (a) of this section, the Secretary of the Interior, the Secretary of Commerce, the Administrator of the Environmental Protection Agency, and any State or local agencies that have notified the Secretary under subsection (b) of this section shall enter into an agreement with the Secretary establishing a schedule of decisionmaking for approval of the project and permits associated with it and with related activities. Such schedule may not exceed two and one-half years from the date of the agreement.

(d) Contents of agreement

The agreement entered into under subsection (c) of this section, to the extent practicable, shall consolidate hearing and comment periods, procedures for data collection and report preparation, and the environmental review and permitting processes associated with the project and related activities. The agreement shall detail, to the extent possible, the non-Federal interest's responsibilities for data development and information that may be necessary to process each permit, including a schedule when the information and data will be provided to the appropriate Federal, State, or local agency.

(e) Preliminary decision

The agreement shall include a date by which the Secretary, taking into consideration the views of all affected Federal agencies, shall provide to the non-Federal interest in writing a preliminary determination whether the project and Federal permits associated with it are reasonably likely to receive approval.

(f) Revision of agreement

The Secretary may revise the agreement once to extend the schedule to allow the non-Federal interest the minimum amount of additional time necessary to revise its original application to meet the objections of a Federal, State, or local agency which is a party to the agreement.

(g) Progress reports

Six months before the final date of the schedule, the Secretary shall provide to Congress a written progress report for each navigation project for a harbor or inland harbor subject to this section. The Secretary shall transmit the report to the Committee on Public Works and Transportation of the House of Representatives and the Committee on Environment and Public Works of the Senate. The report shall summarize all work completed under the agreement and shall include a detailed work program that will assure completion of all remaining work under the agreement.

(h) Final decision

Not later than the final day of the schedule, the Secretary shall notify the non-Federal interest of the final decision on the project and whether the permit or permits have been issued.

(i) Report on timesavings methods

Not later than one year after November 17, 1986, the Secretary shall prepare and transmit to Congress a report estimating the time required for the issuance of all Federal, State, and local permits for the construction of navigation projects for harbors or inland harbors and associated activities. The Secretary shall include in that report recommendations for further reducing the amount of time required for the issuance of those permits, including any proposed changes in existing law.

(Pub. L. 99–662, title II, § 205, Nov. 17, 1986, 100 Stat. 4101.)

CHANGE OF NAME

Committee on Public Works and Transportation of House of Representatives treated as referring to Committee on Transportation and Infrastructure of House of Representatives by section 1(a) of Pub. L. 104–14, set out as a note preceding section 21 of Title 2, The Congress.

§ 2234. Nonapplicability to Saint Lawrence Seaway

Sections 2231, 2232, and 2233 of this title do not apply to any harbor or inland harbor project for that portion of the Saint Lawrence Seaway administered by the Saint Lawrence Seaway Development Corporation.

(Pub. L. 99–662, title II, § 206, Nov. 17, 1986, 100 Stat. 4102.)

§ 2235. Construction in usable increments

Any navigation project for a harbor or inland harbor authorized by this subchapter or any other provision of law enacted before, on, or after November 17, 1986, may be constructed in usable increments.

(Pub. L. 99–662, title II, § 207, Nov. 17, 1986, 100 Stat. 4102.)

§ 2236. Port or harbor dues

(a) Consent of Congress

Subject to the following conditions, a non-Federal interest may levy port or harbor dues (in the form of tonnage duties or fees) on a vessel engaged in trade entering or departing from a harbor and on cargo loaded on or unloaded from that vessel under clauses 2 and 3 of section 10, and under clause 3 of section 8, of Article 1 of the Constitution:

(1) Purposes

Port or harbor dues may be levied only in conjunction with a harbor navigation project whose construction is complete (including a usable increment of the project) and for the following purposes and in amounts not to exceed those necessary to carry out those purposes:

(A)(i) to finance the non-Federal share of construction and operation and maintenance costs of a navigation project for a harbor under the requirements of section 2211 of this title; or

(ii) to finance the cost of construction and operation and maintenance of a navigation project for a harbor under section 2232 or 2233 of this title; and

(B) provide emergency response services in the harbor, including contingency planning, necessary personnel training, and the procurement of equipment and facilities.

(2) Limitation on port or harbor dues for emergency service

Port or harbor dues may not be levied for the purposes described in paragraph (1)(B) of this subsection after the dues cease to be levied for the purposes described in paragraph (1)(A) of this subsection.

(3) General limitations

(A) Port or harbor dues may not be levied under this section in conjunction with a deepening feature of a navigation improvement project on any vessel if that vessel, based on its design draft, could have utilized the project at mean low water before construction. In the case of project features which solely—

(i) widen channels or harbors,

(ii) create or enlarge bend easings, turning basins or anchorage areas, or provide protected areas, or

(iii) remove obstructions to navigation,

only vessels at least comparable in size to those used to justify these features may be charged under this section.

(B) In developing port or harbor dues that may be charged under this section on vessels for project features constructed under this subchapter, the non-Federal interest may consider such criteria as: elapsed time of passage, safety of passage, vessel economy of scale, under keel clearance, vessel draft, vessel squat, vessel speed, sinkage, and trim.

(C) Port or harbor dues authorized by this section shall not be imposed on—

(i) vessels owned and operated by the United States Government, a foreign country, a State, or a political subdivision of a country or State, unless engaged in commercial services;

(ii) towing vessels, vessels engaged in dredging activities, or vessels engaged in intraport movements; or

(iii) vessels with design drafts of 20 feet or less when utilizing general cargo and deep-draft navigation projects.

(4) Formulation of port or harbor dues

Port or harbor dues may be levied only on a vessel entering or departing from a harbor and its cargo on a fair and equitable basis. In formulating port and harbor dues, the non-Federal interest shall consider—

(A) the direct and indirect cost of construction, operations, and maintenance, and providing the facilities and services under paragraph (1) of this subsection;

(B) the value of those facilities and services to the vessel and cargo;

(C) the public policy or interest served; and

(D) any other pertinent factors.

(5) Notice and hearing

(A) Before the initial levy of or subsequent modification to port or harbor dues under this section, a non-Federal interest shall transmit to the Secretary—

(i) the text of the proposed law, regulation, or ordinance that would establish the port or harbor dues, including provisions for their administration, collection, and enforcement;

(ii) the name, address, and telephone number of an official to whom comments on and requests for further information on the proposal are to be directed;

(iii) the date by which comments on the proposal are due and a date for a public hearing on the proposal at which any interested party may present a statement; however, the non-Federal interest may not set a hearing date earlier than 45 days after the date of publication of the notice in the Federal Register required by subparagraph (B) of this paragraph or set a deadline for receipt of comments earlier than 60 days after the date of publication; and

(iv) a written statement signed by an appropriate official that the non-Federal interest agrees to be governed by the provisions of this section.

(B) On receiving from a non-Federal interest the information required by subparagraph (A) of this paragraph, the Secretary shall transmit the material required by clauses (i) through (iii) of subparagraph (A) of this paragraph to the Federal Register for publication.

(C) Port or harbor dues may be imposed by a non-Federal interest only after meeting the conditions of this paragraph.

(6) Requirements on non-Federal interest

A non-Federal interest shall—

(A) file a schedule of any port or harbor dues levied under this subsection with the Secretary and the Federal Maritime Commission, which the Commission shall make available for public inspection;

(B) provide to the Comptroller General of the United States on request of the Comptroller General any records or other evidence that the Comptroller General considers to be necessary and appropriate to enable the Comptroller General to carry out the audit required under subsection (b)[1] of this section;

(C) designate an officer or authorized representative, including the Secretary of the Treasury acting on a cost-reimbursable basis, to receive tonnage certificates and cargo manifests from vessels which may be subject to the levy of port or harbor dues, export declarations from shippers, consignors, and terminal operators, and such other documents as the non-Federal interest may by law, regulation, or ordinance require for the imposition, computation, and collection of port or harbor dues; and

(D) consent expressly to the exclusive exercise of Federal jurisdiction under subsection (c)[1] of this section.

(b) Jurisdiction

(1) The district court of the United States for the district in which is located a non-Federal interest that levies port or harbor dues under this section has original and exclusive jurisdiction over any matter arising out of or concerning, the imposition, computation, collection, and enforcement of port or harbor dues by a non-Federal interest under this section.

(2) Any person who suffers legal wrong or is adversely affected or aggrieved by the imposition by a non-Federal interest of a proposed scheme or schedule of port or harbor dues under this section may, not later than 180 days after the date of hearing under subsection (a)(5)(A)(iii) of this section, commence an action to seek judicial review of that proposed scheme or schedule in the appropriate district court under paragraph (1).

(3) On petition of the Attorney General or any other party, that district court may—

(A) grant appropriate injunctive relief to restrain an action by that non-Federal interest violating the conditions of consent in subsection (a) of this section;

(B) order the refund of any port or harbor dues not lawfully collected; and

(C) grant other appropriate relief or remedy.

(c) Collection of duties

(1)[2] Delivery of certificate and manifest

(A) Upon arrival of vessel

Upon the arrival of a vessel in a harbor in which the vessel may be subject to the levy of port or harbor dues under this section, the master of that vessel shall, within forty-eight hours after arrival and before any cargo is unloaded from that vessel, deliver to the appropriate authorized representative appointed under subsection (a)(6)(C) of this section a tonnage certificate for the vessel and a manifest of the cargo aboard that vessel or, if the vessel is in ballast, a declaration to that effect.

(B) Before departure of vessel

The shipper, consignor, or terminal operator having custody of any cargo to be loaded on board a vessel while the vessel is in a harbor in which the vessel may be subject to the levy of port or harbor dues under this section shall, within forty-eight hours before departure of that vessel, deliver to the appropriate authorized representative appointed under subsection (a)(6)(C) of this section an export declaration specifying the cargo to be loaded on board that vessel.

(d) Enforcement

At the request of an authorized representative referred to in subsection (a)(6)(C) of this section, the Secretary of the Treasury may:

(1) withhold the clearance required by section 60105 of title 46 for a vessel if the master, owner, or operator of a vessel subject to port or harbor dues under this section fails to comply with the provisions of this section including any non-Federal law, regulation or ordinance issued hereunder; and

(2) assess a penalty or initiate a forfeiture of the cargo in the same manner and under the same procedures as are applicable for failure to pay customs duties under the Tariff Act of 1930 (19 U.S.C. 1202 et seq.) if the shipper, consignor, consignee, or terminal operator having title to or custody of cargo subject to port or harbor dues under this section fails to comply with the provisions of this section including any non-Federal law, regulation, or ordinance issued hereunder.

(e) Maritime Lien

Port or harbor dues levied under this section against a vessel constitute a maritime lien against the vessel and port or harbor dues levied against cargo constitute a lien against the cargo that may be recovered in an action in the district court of the United States for the district in which the vessel or cargo is found.

(Pub. L. 99–662, title II, §208, Nov. 17, 1986, 100 Stat. 4102; Pub. L. 104–66, title I, §1021(g), Dec. 21, 1995, 109 Stat. 713.)

[1] See References in Text note below.

[2] So in original. No par. (2) has been enacted.

REFERENCES IN TEXT

Subsection (b) of this section, referred to in subsec. (a)(6)(B), which related to audits, was struck out by Pub. L. 104–66 and subsec. (c) was redesignated as subsec. (b).

Subsection (c) of this section, referred to in subsec. (a)(6)(D), which related to jurisdiction, was redesignated as subsec. (b) by Pub. L. 104–66.

The Tariff Act of 1930, referred to in subsec. (d)(2), is act June 17, 1930, ch. 497, 46 Stat. 590, as amended, which is classified generally to chapter 4 (§1202 et seq.) of Title 19, Customs Duties. For complete classification of this Act to the Code, see section 1654 of Title 19 and Tables.

CODIFICATION

In subsec. (d)(1), "section 60105 of title 46" substituted for "section 4197 of the Revised Statutes of the United States (46 U.S.C. App. 91)" on authority of Pub. L. 109–304, §18(c), Oct. 6, 2006, 120 Stat. 1709, which Act enacted section 60105 of Title 46, Shipping.

AMENDMENTS

1995—Subsecs. (b) to (f). Pub. L. 104–66 redesignated subsecs. (c) to (f) as (b) to (e), respectively, and struck out heading and text of former subsec. (b). Text read as follows: "The Comptroller General of the United States shall—

"(1) carry out periodic audits of the operations of non-Federal interests that elect to levy port or harbor dues under this section to determine if the conditions of subsection (a) of this section are being complied with;

"(2) submit to each House of the Congress a written report containing the findings resulting from each audit; and

"(3) make any recommendations that the Comptroller General considers appropriate regarding the compliance of those non-Federal interests with the requirements of this section."

§2237. Information for national security

Any non-Federal interest shall provide the United States the information necessary for military readiness planning and harbor, inland harbor, and national security, including information necessary to obtain national security clearances for individuals employed in critical harbor and inland harbor positions.

(Pub. L. 99–662, title II, §209, Nov. 17, 1986, 100 Stat. 4106.)

§2238. Authorization of appropriations

(a) Trust fund

There are authorized to be appropriated out of the Harbor Maintenance Trust Fund, established by section 9505 of title 26, for each fiscal year such sums as may be necessary to pay—

(1) 100 percent of the eligible operations and maintenance costs of those portions of the Saint Lawrence Seaway operated and maintained by the Saint Lawrence Seaway Development Corporation for such fiscal year; and

(2) up to 100 percent of the eligible operations and maintenance costs assigned to commercial navigation of all harbors and inland harbors within the United States.

(b) General fund

There are authorized to be appropriated out of the general fund of the Treasury of the United States for each fiscal year such sums as may be necessary to pay the balance of all eligible operations and maintenance costs not provided by payments from the Harbor Maintenance Trust Fund under this section.

(Pub. L. 99–662, title II, §210, Nov. 17, 1986, 100 Stat. 4106; Pub. L. 101–640, title III, §316, Nov. 28, 1990, 104 Stat. 4641.)

AMENDMENTS

1990—Subsec. (a)(2). Pub. L. 101–640 substituted "up to 100 percent" for "not more than 40 percent".

§2239. Repealed. Pub. L. 101–640, title IV, §412(f), Nov. 28, 1990, 104 Stat. 4650

Section, Pub. L. 99–662, title II, §211, Nov. 17, 1986, 100 Stat. 4106; Pub. L. 100–676, §32, Nov. 17, 1988, 102 Stat. 4030, directed Administrator of Environmental Protection Agency to designate one or more sites for disposal of dredged material as an alternative to disposal at the Mud Dump in New Jersey.

SEDIMENTS DECONTAMINATION TECHNOLOGY

Pub. L. 102–580, title IV, §405, Oct. 31, 1992, 106 Stat. 4863, as amended by Pub. L. 104–303, title II, §226, Oct. 12, 1996, 110 Stat. 3697; Pub. L. 106–53, title II, §204, Aug. 17, 1999, 113 Stat. 285, provided that:

"(a) DECONTAMINATION PROJECT.—

"(1) SELECTION OF TECHNOLOGIES.—Based upon a review of decontamination technologies identified pursuant to section 412(c) of the Water Resources Development Act of 1990 [Pub. L. 101–640, set out below], the Administrator of the Environmental Protection Agency and the Secretary shall, within 1 year after the date of the enactment of this Act [Oct. 31, 1992], jointly select removal, pre-treatment, post-treatment, and decontamination technologies for contaminated marine sediments for a decontamination project in the New York/New Jersey Harbor.

"(2) RECOMMENDED PROGRAM.—Upon selection of technologies, the Administrator and the Secretary shall jointly recommend a program of selected technologies to assess their effectiveness in rendering sediments acceptable for unrestricted ocean disposal or beneficial reuse, or both.

"(3) PROJECT PURPOSE.—The purpose of the project to be carried out under this section is to provide for the development of 1 or more sediment decontamination technologies on a pilot scale demonstrating a capacity of at least 500,000 cubic yards per year.

"(4) PRACTICAL END-USE PRODUCTS.—Technologies selected for demonstration at the pilot scale shall be intended to result in practical end-use products.

"(5) ASSISTANCE BY THE SECRETARY.—The Secretary shall assist the project to ensure expeditious completion by providing sufficient quantities of contaminated dredged material to conduct the full-scale demonstrations to stated capacity.

"(b) DECONTAMINATION DEFINED.—For purposes of this section, 'decontamination' may include local or remote prototype or production and laboratory decontamination technologies, sediment pre-treatment and post-treatment processes, and siting, economic, or other measures necessary to develop a matrix for selection of interim prototype of long-term processes. Decontamination techniques need not be preproven in terms of likely success.

"(c) AUTHORIZATION OF APPROPRIATIONS.—There is authorized to be appropriated to carry out this section $22,000,000 to complete technology testing, technology commercialization, and the development of full scale processing facilities within the New York/New Jersey Harbor. Such sums shall remain available until expended.

"(d) REPORTS.—Not later than September 30, 1998, and periodically thereafter, the Administrator and the Secretary shall transmit to Congress a report on the results of the project to be carried out under this section, including an assessment of the progress made in achieving the purpose of the project set forth in subsection (a)(3).

"(e) SUPPORT.—In carrying out the program under this section, the Secretary is encouraged to use contracts, cooperative agreements, and grants with colleges and universities and other non-Federal entities."

ALTERNATIVES TO MUD DUMP SITE FOR DISPOSAL OF DREDGED MATERIAL

Section 412 of Pub. L. 101–640 provided that:

"(a) REPORT.—Within 90 days after the date of the enactment of this Act [Nov. 28, 1990], the Administrator of the Environmental Protection Agency shall submit to the Congress a final report on the feasibility of designating an alternative site to the Mud Dump Site at a distance not less than 20 miles from the shoreline.

"(b) PLAN.—Within 180 days after the date of the enactment of this Act [Nov. 28, 1990], the Secretary and the Administrator of the Environmental Protection Agency shall submit to Congress a plan for the long-term management of dredged material from the New York/New Jersey Harbor region. The plan shall include—

"(1) an identification of the source, quantities, and characteristics of material to be dredged;

"(2) a discussion of potential alternative sites for disposal of dredged material, including the feasibility of altering the boundaries of the Mud Dump Site;

"(3) measures to reduce the quantities of dredged material proposed for ocean disposal;

"(4) measures to reduce the amount of contaminants in materials proposed to be dredged from the Harbor through source controls and decontamination technology;

"(5) a program for monitoring the physical, chemical, and biological effects of dumping dredged material at the Mud Dump Site; and

"(6) a study of the characteristics of the bottom sediments, including type and distribution.

"(c) DEMONSTRATION PROJECT.—The Secretary, in consultation with the Administrator of the Environmental Protection Agency, shall implement a demonstration project for disposing on an annual basis up to 10 percent of the material dredged from the New York/New Jersey Harbor region in an environmentally sound manner other than by ocean disposal. Environmentally sound alternatives may include, among others, capping of borrow pits, construction of a containment island, application for landfill cover, habitat restoration, and use of decontamination technology.

"(d) MUD DUMP SITE DEFINED.—For purposes of this section, the term 'Mud Dump Site' means the area located approximately 5¾ miles east of Sandy Hook, New Jersey, with boundary coordinates of 40 degrees, 23 minutes, 48 seconds North, 73 degrees, 51 minutes, 28 seconds West; 40 degrees, 21 minutes, 48 seconds North, 73 degrees, 50 minutes, 00 seconds West; 40 degrees, 21 minutes, 48 seconds North; 73 degrees, 51 minutes, 28 seconds West; and 40 degrees, 23 minutes, 48 seconds North; 73 degrees, 50 minutes, 00 seconds West.

"(e) AUTHORIZATION OF APPROPRIATIONS.—There are authorized to be appropriated to the Secretary for fiscal year 1991, $3,000,000 to implement subsection (b) and $1,000,000 to implement subsection (c), and such sums as may be necessary for fiscal year 1992.

"(f) REPEAL.—Section 211 of the Water Resources Development Act of 1986 (33 U.S.C. 2239) is repealed."

§ 2240. Emergency response services

(a) Grants

The Secretary is authorized to make grants to any non-Federal interest operating a project for a harbor for provision of emergency response services in such harbor (including contingency planning, necessary personnel training, and the procurement of equipment and facilities either by the non-Federal interest, by a local agency or municipality, or by a combination of local agencies or municipalities on a cost-reimbursable basis, either by a cooperative agreement, mutual aid plan, or mutual assistance plan entered into between one or more non-Federal interests, public agencies, or local municipalities).

(b) Authorization of appropriations

There is authorized to be appropriated for fiscal years beginning after September 30, 1986, and ending before October 1, 1992, $5,000,000.

(Pub. L. 99–662, title II, § 212, Nov. 17, 1986, 100 Stat. 4107.)

§ 2241. Definitions

For purposes of this subchapter—

(1) Deep-draft harbor

The term "deep-draft harbor" means a harbor which is authorized to be constructed to a depth of more than 45 feet (other than a project which is authorized by section 202 of this title).

(2) Eligible operations and maintenance

(A) Except as provided in subparagraph (B), the term "eligible operations and maintenance" means all Federal operations, maintenance, repair, and rehabilitation, including (i) maintenance dredging reasonably necessary to maintain the width and nominal depth of any harbor or inland harbor; (ii) the construction of dredged material disposal facilities that are necessary for the operation and maintenance of any harbor or inland harbor; (iii) dredging and disposing of contaminated sediments that are in or that affect the maintenance of Federal navigation channels; (iv) mitigating for impacts resulting from Federal navigation operation and maintenance activities; and (v) operating and maintaining dredged material disposal facilities.

(B) As applied to the Saint Lawrence Seaway, the term "eligible operations and maintenance" means all operations, maintenance, repair, and rehabilitation, including maintenance dredging reasonably necessary to keep such Seaway or navigation improvements operated or maintained by the Saint Lawrence Seaway Development Corporation in operation and reasonable state of repair.

(C) The term "eligible operations and maintenance" does not include providing any lands, easements, or rights-of-way, or performing relocations required for project operations and maintenance.

(3) General cargo harbor

The term "general cargo harbor" means a harbor for which a project is authorized by section 202 of this title and any other harbor which is authorized to be constructed to a depth of more than 20 feet but not more than 45 feet;

(4) Harbor

The term "harbor" means any channel or harbor, or element thereof, in the United States, capable of being utilized in the transportation of commercial cargo in domestic or foreign waterborne commerce by commercial vessels. The term does not include—

(A) an inland harbor;

(B) the Saint Lawrence Seaway;

(C) local access or berthing channels;

(D) channels or harbors constructed or maintained by nonpublic interests; and

(E) any portion of the Columbia River other than the channels on the downstream side of Bonneville lock and dam.

(5) Inland harbor

The term "inland harbor" means a navigation project which is used principally for the accommodation of commercial vessels and the receipt and shipment of waterborne cargoes on inland waters. The term does not include—

(A) projects on the Great Lakes;

(B) projects that are subject to tidal influence;

(C) projects with authorized depths of greater than 20 feet;

(D) local access or berthing channels; and

(E) projects constructed or maintained by nonpublic interests.

(6) Nominal depth

The term "nominal depth" means, in relation to the stated depth for any navigation improvement project, such depth, including any greater depths which must be maintained for any harbor or inland harbor or element thereof included within such project in order to ensure the safe passage at mean low tide of any vessel requiring the stated depth.

(7) Non-Federal interest

The term "non-Federal interest" has the meaning such term has under section 1962d–5b of title 42 and includes any interstate agency and port authority established under a compact entered into between two or more States with the consent of Congress under section 10 of Article I of the Constitution.

(8) United States

The term "United States" means all areas included within the territorial boundaries of the United States, including the several States, the District of Columbia, the Commonwealth of Puerto Rico, the Virgin Islands, Guam, American Samoa, the Trust Territory of the Pacific Islands, the Northern Mariana Islands, and any other territory or possession over which the United States exercises jurisdiction.

(Pub. L. 99–662, title II, §214, Nov. 17, 1986, 100 Stat. 4108; Pub. L. 104–303, title II, §201(e), Oct. 12, 1996, 110 Stat. 3672.)

REFERENCES IN TEXT

Section 202 of this title, referred to in pars. (1) and (3), is section 202 of title II of Pub. L. 99–662, Nov. 17, 1986, 100 Stat. 4091, which is not classified to the Code.

AMENDMENTS

1996—Par. (2)(A). Pub. L. 104–303, §201(e)(1), inserted "Federal" after "means all" and "(i)" after "including", and inserted before period at end a semicolon and cls. (ii) to (v).

Par. (2)(C). Pub. L. 104–303, §201(e)(2), substituted "or rights-of-way," for "rights-of-way, or dredged material disposal areas,".

INCREASES IN NON-FEDERAL SHARE OF COSTS

Amendment by Pub. L. 104–303 not to increase, or result in increase of, non-Federal share of costs of expanding any confined dredged material disposal facility that is operated by Secretary and authorized for cost recovery through collection of tolls, any confined dredged material disposal facility for which invitation for bids for construction was issued before Oct. 12, 1996, and expanding any confined dredged material disposal facility constructed under section 1293a of this title if capacity of confined dredged material disposal facility was exceeded in less than 6 years, see section 201(g) of Pub. L. 104–303, set out as a note under section 2211 of this title.

TERMINATION OF TRUST TERRITORY OF THE PACIFIC ISLANDS

For termination of Trust Territory of the Pacific Islands, see note set out preceding section 1681 of Title 48, Territories and Insular Possessions.

§2242. Remote and subsistence harbors

(a) In general

In conducting a study of harbor and navigation improvements, the Secretary may recommend a project without the need to demonstrate that the project is justified solely by national economic development benefits if the Secretary determines that—

(1)(A) the community to be served by the project is at least 70 miles from the nearest surface accessible commercial port and has no direct rail or highway link to another community served by a surface accessible port or harbor; or

(B) the project would be located in the State of Hawaii, the Commonwealth of Puerto Rico, Guam, the Commonwealth of the Northern Mariana Islands, the United States Virgin Islands, or American Samoa;

(2) the harbor is economically critical such that over 80 percent of the goods transported through the harbor would be consumed within the community served by the harbor and navigation improvement; and

(3) the long-term viability of the community would be threatened without the harbor and navigation improvement.

(b) Justification

In considering whether to recommend a project under subsection (a), the Secretary shall consider the benefits of the project to—

(1) public health and safety of the local community, including access to facilities designed to protect public health and safety;

(2) access to natural resources for subsistence purposes;

(3) local and regional economic opportunities;

(4) welfare of the local population; and

(5) social and cultural value to the community.

(Pub. L. 110–114, title II, §2006, Nov. 8, 2007, 121 Stat. 1073.)

CODIFICATION

Section was enacted as part of the Water Resources Development Act of 2007, and not as part of the Water Resources Development Act of 1986 which comprises this chapter.

"SECRETARY" DEFINED

Secretary means the Secretary of the Army, see section 2 of Pub. L. 110–114, set out as a note under section 2201 of this title.

SUBCHAPTER III—INLAND WATERWAY TRANSPORTATION SYSTEM

§2251. Inland Waterways Users Board

(a) Establishment of Users Board

There is hereby established an Inland Waterway Users Board (hereinafter in this section referred to as the "Users Board") composed of the eleven members selected by the Secretary, one of whom shall be designated by the Secretary as Chairman. The members shall be selected so as to represent various regions of the country and a spectrum of the primary users and shippers utilizing the inland and intracoastal waterways for commercial purposes. Due consideration shall be given to assure a balance among the members based on the ton-mile shipments of the various categories of commodities shipped on inland waterways. The Secretary of the Army shall designate, and the Secretaries of Agriculture, Transportation, and Commerce may each designate, a representative to act as an observer of the Users Board.

(b) Duties

The Users Board shall meet at least semi-annually to develop and make recommendations to the Secretary regarding construction and rehabilitation priorities and spending levels on the commercial navigational features and components of the inland waterways and inland harbors of the United States for the following fiscal years. Any advice or recommendation made by the Users Board to the Secretary shall reflect the independent judgment of the Users Board. Notwithstanding section 3003 of Public Law 104–66 (31 U.S.C. 1113 note; 109 Stat. 734), the Users Board shall, by December 31, 1987, and annually thereafter file such recommendations with the Secretary and with the Congress.

(c) Administration

The Users Board shall be subject to the Federal Advisory Committee Act, other than section 14, and, with the consent of the appropriate agency head, the Users Board may use the facilities and services of any Federal agency. Non-Federal members of the Users Board while engaged in the performance of their duties away from their homes or regular places of business, may be allowed travel expenses, including per diem in lieu of subsistence, as authorized by section 5703 of title 5.

(Pub. L. 99–662, title III, §302, Nov. 17, 1986, 100 Stat. 4111; Pub. L. 106–109, §8(a), Nov. 24, 1999, 113 Stat. 1495.)

REFERENCES IN TEXT

The Federal Advisory Committee Act, referred to in subsec. (c), is Pub. L. 92–463, Oct. 6, 1972, 86 Stat. 770, as amended, which is set out in the Appendix to Title 5, Government Organization and Employees.

AMENDMENTS

1999—Subsec. (b). Pub. L. 106–109, in last sentence, substituted "Notwithstanding section 3003 of Public Law 104–66 (31 U.S.C. 1113 note; 109 Stat. 734), the" for "The".

SUBCHAPTER IV—WATER RESOURCES STUDIES

§2261. Territories development study

The Secretary is hereby authorized and directed to make studies in cooperation with the Secretary of the Interior and the governments of the Virgin Islands, Guam, American Samoa, the Trust Territory of the Pacific Islands, and the Commonwealth of the Northern Mariana Islands for the purposes of providing plans for the development, utilization, and conservation of water and related land resources of such jurisdiction, at a total cost of $2,000,000 for each of the five studies. Such studies shall include appropriate consideration of the needs for flood protection, wise use of flood plain lands, navigation facilities, hydroelectric power generation, regional water supply and waste water management facilities systems, general recreation facilities, enhancement and control of water quality, enhancement and conservation of fish and wildlife, and other measures for environmental enhancement, economic and human resources development. Such studies shall be compatible with comprehensive development plans formulated by local planning agencies and other interested Federal agencies. Any funds made available under this section for a study for any such jurisdiction which is not needed for such study shall be available to the Secretary to construct authorized water resources projects in such jurisdiction and to implement the findings of such study with appropriate cost sharing as provided in this Act.

(Pub. L. 99–662, title VII, §702, Nov. 17, 1986, 100 Stat. 4156.)

REFERENCES IN TEXT

This Act, referred to in text, is Pub. L. 99–662, Nov. 17, 1986, 100 Stat. 4082, as amended, known as the Water Resources Development Act of 1986. For complete classification of this Act to the Code, see Short Title note set out under section 2201 of this title and Tables.

TERMINATION OF TRUST TERRITORY OF THE PACIFIC ISLANDS

For termination of Trust Territory of the Pacific Islands, see note set out preceding section 1681 of Title 48, Territories and Insular Possessions.

§2262. Survey of potential for use of certain facilities as hydroelectric facilities

(a) Survey authority

The Secretary shall, upon the request of local public officials, survey the potential and methods for rehabilitating former industrial sites, millraces, and similar types of facilities already constructed for use as hydroelectric facilities. The Secretary shall, upon request, provide technical assistance to local public agencies, including electric cooperatives, in designing projects to rehabilitate sites that have been surveyed, or are qualified for such survey, under this section. The non-Federal share of the cost of carrying out this section shall be 50 percent.

(b) Authorization of appropriations

There is authorized to be appropriated to the Secretary, to implement this section, the sum of $5,000,000 for each of the fiscal years ending September 30, 1988, through September 30, 1992, such sums to remain available until expended.

(Pub. L. 99–662, title VII, §703, Nov. 17, 1986, 100 Stat. 4156.)

§ 2263. Study of Corps capability to conserve fish and wildlife

(a) Investigation and study

The Secretary shall investigate and study the feasibility of utilizing the capabilities of the United States Army Corps of Engineers to conserve fish and wildlife (including their habitats) where such fish and wildlife are indigenous to the United States, its possessions, or its territories. The scope of such study shall include the use of engineering or construction capabilities to create alternative habitats, or to improve, enlarge, develop, or otherwise beneficially modify existing habitats of such fish and wildlife. The study shall be conducted in consultation with the Director of the Fish and Wildlife Service of the Department of the Interior, the Assistant Administrator for Fisheries of the National Oceanic and Atmospheric Administration, and the Administrator of the Environmental Protection Agency, and shall be transmitted within the 30-month period beginning on November 17, 1986, by the Secretary to Congress, together with the findings, conclusions, and recommendations of the Chief of Engineers. The Secretary, in consultation with the Federal officers referred to in the preceding sentence, shall undertake a continuing review of the matters covered in the study and shall transmit to Congress, on a biennial basis, any revisions to the study that may be required as a result of the review, together with the findings, conclusions, and recommendations of the Chief of Engineers.

(b) Projects

(1) In general

The Secretary is further authorized to conduct projects of alternative or beneficially modified habitats for fish and wildlife, including but not limited to man-made reefs for fish. There is authorized to be appropriated not to exceed $50,000,000 to carry out such projects.

(2) Inclusions

Such projects shall be developed, and their effectiveness evaluated, in consultation with the Director of the Fish and Wildlife Service and the Assistant Administrator for Fisheries of the National Oceanic and Atmospheric Administration. Such projects shall include—

(A) the construction of a reef for fish habitat in Lake Erie in the vicinity of Buffalo, New York;

(B) the construction of a reef for fish habitat in the Atlantic Ocean in the vicinity of Fort Lauderdale, Florida;

(C) the construction of a reef for fish habitat in Lake Ontario in the vicinity of the town of Newfane, New York; and

(D) the restoration and rehabilitation of habitat for fish, including native oysters, in the Chesapeake Bay and its tributaries in Virginia and Maryland, including—

(i) the construction of oyster bars and reefs;

(ii) the rehabilitation of existing marginal habitat;

(iii) the use of appropriate alternative substrate material in oyster bar and reef construction;

(iv) the construction and upgrading of oyster hatcheries; and

(v) activities relating to increasing the output of native oyster broodstock for seeding and monitoring of restored sites to ensure ecological success.

(3) Restoration and rehabilitation activities

The restoration and rehabilitation activities described in paragraph (2)(D) shall be—

(A) for the purpose of establishing permanent sanctuaries and harvest management areas; and

(B) consistent with plans and strategies for guiding the restoration of the Chesapeake Bay oyster resource and fishery.

(4) Cost sharing

(A) In general

The non-Federal share of the cost of any project under this subsection shall be 25 percent.

(B) Form

The non-Federal share may be provided through in-kind services, including the provision by the non-Federal interest of shell stock material that is determined by the Chief of Engineers to be suitable for use in carrying out the project.

(C) Applicability

The non-Federal interest shall be credited with the value of in-kind services provided on or after October 1, 2000, for a project described in paragraph (1) completed on or after that date, if the Secretary determines that the work is integral to the project.

(5) Definition of ecological success

In this subsection, the term "ecological success" means—

(A) achieving a tenfold increase in native oyster biomass by the year 2010, from a 1994 baseline; and

(B) the establishment of a sustainable fishery as determined by a broad scientific and economic consensus.

In carrying out paragraph (4),[1] the Chief of Engineers may solicit participation by and the services of commercial watermen in the construction of the reefs.

(Pub. L. 99–662, title VII, §704, Nov. 17, 1986, 100 Stat. 4157; Pub. L. 104–303, title V, §505, Oct. 12, 1996, 110 Stat. 3757; Pub. L. 106–541, title III, §342, Dec. 11, 2000, 114 Stat. 2612; Pub. L. 107–66, title I, §113, Nov. 12, 2001, 115 Stat. 496; Pub. L. 109–103, title I, §126, Nov. 19, 2005, 119 Stat. 2259; Pub. L. 110–114, title V, §5021, Nov. 8, 2007, 121 Stat. 1202.)

REFERENCES IN TEXT

Paragraph (4), referred to in concluding provisions of subsec. (b), meaning subsec. (b)(4) of this section, was redesignated subsec. (b)(1)(D) by Pub. L. 107–66, title I,

[1] See References in Text note below.

§113(1), (2), Nov. 12, 2001, 115 Stat. 496. Subsequently, Pub. L. 110–114, title V, §5021(1), (2)(B), (3), Nov. 8, 2007, 121 Stat. 1202, redesignated subsec. (b)(1)(D) as (b)(2)(D), struck it out, added a new subsec. (b)(2)(D), and redesignated former subsec. (b)(2) as (b)(4).

AMENDMENTS

2007—Subsec. (b)(1). Pub. L. 110–114, §5021(2), substituted "$50,000,000" for "$30,000,000" in second sentence and designated last sentence as par. (2).

Subsec. (b)(2). Pub. L. 110–114, §5021(2)(B), designated last sentence of par. (1) as (2) and inserted heading. Former par. (2) redesignated (4).

Subsec. (b)(2)(D). Pub. L. 110–114, §5021(3), added subpar. (D) and struck out former subpar. (D) which read as follows: "the construction of reefs and related clean shell substrate for fish habitat, including manmade 3-dimensional oyster reefs, in the Chesapeake Bay and its tributaries in Maryland and Virginia if the reefs are preserved as permanent sanctuaries by the non-Federal interests, consistent with the recommendations of the scientific consensus document on Chesapeake Bay oyster restoration dated June 1999."

Subsec. (b)(3), (4). Pub. L. 110–114, §5021(1), (3), added par. (3) and redesignated par. (2) as (4).

Subsec. (b)(5). Pub. L. 110–114, §5021(4), which directed addition of par. (5) at end of subsec. (b), was executed by adding par. (5) after par. (4) to reflect the probable intent of Congress.

2005—Subsec. (b)(1). Pub. L. 109–103 substituted "$30,000,000" for "$20,000,000" in introductory provisions.

2001—Subsec. (b). Pub. L. 107–66 inserted subsec. heading, designated introductory provisions as par. (1), inserted par. (1) heading, redesignated former pars. (1) to (4) as subpars. (A) to (D), respectively, of par. (1), and substituted par. (2) for first sentence of concluding provisions which read "The non-Federal share of the cost of any project under this section shall be 25 percent."

2000—Subsec. (b). Pub. L. 106–541, §342(1), (3), substituted "$20,000,000" for "$7,000,000" in second sentence of introductory provisions and inserted at end of concluding provisions "In carrying out paragraph (4), the Chief of Engineers may solicit participation by and the services of commercial watermen in the construction of the reefs."

Subsec. (b)(4). Pub. L. 106–541, §342(2), added par. (4) and struck out former par. (4) which read as follows: "the construction of a reef for fish habitat in the Chesapeake Bay in Maryland and Virginia."

1996—Subsec. (b). Pub. L. 104–303 substituted "$7,000,000" for "$5,000,000" in introductory provisions and inserted "and Virginia" after "Maryland" in par. (4).

TERMINATION OF REPORTING REQUIREMENTS

For termination, effective May 15, 2000, of provisions of law requiring submittal to Congress of any annual, semiannual, or other regular periodic report listed in House Document No. 103–7 (in which a report required under subsec. (a) of this section is listed on page 68), see section 3003 of Pub. L. 104–66, as amended, set out as a note under section 1113 of Title 31, Money and Finance.

§ 2264. Deauthorization of studies

(a) Notwithstanding section 3003 of Public Law 104–66 (31 U.S.C. 1113 note; 109 Stat. 734), not later than one year after November 17, 1986, and annually thereafter, the Secretary shall submit to Congress a list of incomplete water resources studies which have been authorized, but for which no funds have been appropriated during the 5 full fiscal years preceding the submission of such list. For each such study the Secretary shall include the following information:

(1) the date of authorization and the manner in which the study was authorized;

(2) a description of the purposes of the study;

(3) a description of funding that has been made available for the study;

(4) a description of any work that has been performed in carrying out the study and the results and conclusions, if any, of such work; and

(5) a description of any work that remains to be done in carrying out the study and the time necessary for and estimated cost of completing such work.

(b) Each study included in a list under subsection (a) of this section is not authorized on and after the 90th day following the submission to Congress of such list if no funds have been appropriated for such study after the list is submitted and before such 90th day.

(Pub. L. 99–662, title VII, §710, Nov. 17, 1986, 100 Stat. 4160; Pub. L. 106–109, §8(b), Nov. 24, 1999, 113 Stat. 1495.)

AMENDMENTS

1999—Subsec. (a). Pub. L. 106–109, in first sentence, substituted "Notwithstanding section 3003 of Public Law 104–66 (31 U.S.C. 1113 note; 109 Stat. 734), not" for "Not".

§ 2265. Columbia River/Arkansas River Basin transfers

(a) No Federal agency shall study or participate in the study of any regional or river basin plan or any plan for any Federal water and related land resource project which has as its objective the transfer of water from the Columbia River Basin to any other region or any other major river basin of the United States, unless such study is approved by the Governors of all affected States.

(b) For a period of 5 years after November 17, 1986, no Federal agency shall study or participate in the study of any regional or river basin plan or any plan for any Federal water and related land resource project which has as its objective the transfer of water from the Arkansas River Basin to any other region or any other major river basin of the United States, unless such study is approved by the Governors of all affected States.

(Pub. L. 99–662, title VII, §715, Nov. 17, 1986, 100 Stat. 4161.)

§ 2266. Canadian tidal power study

(a) Study authority

The Secretary, after consultation with the National Oceanic and Atmospheric Administration, the National Marine Fisheries Service, the United States Fish and Wildlife Service, and other appropriate governmental agencies, and the National Research Council of the National Academy of Sciences, is authorized and directed to undertake studies to identify the impacts on the United States of potential Canadian tidal power development in the Bay of Fundy, and submit such studies to the appropriate committees of the Congress.

(b) Study phases

The Secretary shall conduct the studies authorized in subsection (a) of this section in two phases:

(1) Studies to be completed not later than October 1, 1988, to (A) identify effects of any such projects on tidal ranges and resulting impacts to beaches and estuarine areas, and (B) identify further studies which would be needed to meet the requirements of paragraph (2) of this subsection; and

(2) Studies to be completed not later than October 1, 1990, to (A) determine further environmental, social, economic, and institutional impacts of such tidal power development, and (B) determine what measures could be taken in Canada and the United States to offset or minimize any adverse impacts of such development on the United States.

(c) Authorization of appropriations

In the fiscal year ending September 30, 1987, or in any fiscal year thereafter, there is authorized to be appropriated to the Secretary the sum of $1,100,000 for the purposes of subsection (b)(1) of this section, and the sum of $8,900,000 for the purposes of subsection (b)(2) of this section, such sums to remain available until expended.

(Pub. L. 99–662, title VII, §724, Nov. 17, 1986, 100 Stat. 4163.)

§2267. New York Bight study

(a) Study authority

The Secretary shall study a hydro-environmental monitoring and information system in the New York Bight in the form of a system using computerized buoys and radio telemetry that allows for the continual monitoring (at strategically located sites throughout the New York Bight) of the following: wind, wave, current, salinity and thermal gradients and sea chemistry, in order to measure the effect of changes due to air and water pollution, including changes due to continued dumping in the Bight.

(b) Study of physical hydraulic model

In addition, the Secretary shall study a proper physical hydraulic model of the New York Bight and for such an offshore model to be tied into the existing inshore physical hydraulic model of the Port of New York and New Jersey operated by the United States Army Corps of Engineers.

(c) Agency coordination; findings and recommendations

The Secretary shall coordinate fully with the Administrator of the Environmental Protection Agency in carrying out the study described in this section and shall report any findings and recommendations to Congress. The Secretary and the Administrator shall also consider the views of other appropriate Federal, State, and local agencies, academic institutions, and members of the public who are concerned about water quality in the New York Bight.

(d) Authorization of appropriations

There is authorized to be appropriated not more than $1,000,000 per fiscal year for each of fiscal years 1987, 1988, 1989, 1990, and 1991.

(Pub. L. 99–662, title VII, §728, Nov. 17, 1986, 100 Stat. 4164.)

NEW YORK BIGHT AND HARBOR STUDY

Pub. L. 102–580, title III, §326, Oct. 31, 1992, 106 Stat. 4850, as amended by Pub. L. 104–303, title IV, §433, Oct. 12, 1996, 110 Stat. 3746, provided that:

"(a) IN GENERAL.—As a continuation of the study pursuant to section 728 of the Water Resources Development Act of 1986 [33 U.S.C. 2267], the Secretary shall study a hydro-environmental monitoring and information system in the New York Bight and New York Harbor and tributaries to the head of tide, in the form of a system using computerized buoys and radio telemetry that allows for the continual monitoring (at strategically located sites throughout the New York Bight and Harbor region) of the following: wind, wave, current, salinity, and thermal gradients and sea chemistry, in order to measure the effect of changes due to air and water pollution, including changes due to continued dumping in the Bight. This effort will include the study of a verified, nested, high-resolution Harbor/Bight Apex numerical model, and supportive monitoring and information systems.

"(b) HYDRAULIC MODEL.—In addition, the Secretary shall study a proper physical hydraulic model of the New York Bight and the tying in of such model to the existing inshore physical hydraulic model of the Port of New York and New Jersey operated by the United States Army Corps of Engineers.

"(c) PURPOSE.—This New York Bight and Harbor effort will address the engineering, environmental, and social impacts of natural and man-made changes to the New York Bight, including water quality parameters such as contaminant and sediment transport effects, and nutrient eutrophication.

"(d) COORDINATION WITH EPA; REPORTS.—The Secretary shall coordinate fully with the Administrator of the Environmental Protection Agency in carrying out the study described in the section and shall report any findings and recommendations to Congress. The Secretary and the Administrator shall also consider the views of other appropriate Federal, State, and local agencies, academic institutions, and members of the public who are concerned about water and sediment quality in the New York Bight and Harbor region.

"(e) REMEDIATION TECHNIQUES.—

"(1) IN GENERAL.—To test and verify contaminant and sediment tracking ability of the models, and to reduce the problems associated with the dredging and disposal of dioxin contaminated sediments in the region, a study shall be performed to identify appropriate remediation techniques (including isolation and treatment) for mitigating dioxin contaminated sediments at their sources. The study and report are not intended to encumber civil works projects under development or scheduled to be maintained. Work on these projects shall proceed along the present schedule.

"(2) REPORT.—Not later than 1 year after the date of the enactment of this Act [Oct. 31, 1992], the Secretary shall submit to the Committee on Environment and Public Works of the Senate, the Committee on Public Works and Transportation of the House of Representatives, and to the State of New Jersey a report on—

"(A) the dioxin study and monitoring required in this subsection; and

"(B) the effectiveness and costs of all reasonable remediation measures, including recommendations as to a plan for implementation of the most time and cost-effective measures.

"(f) FUNDING.—There is authorized to be appropriated $3,000,000 for fiscal years beginning after September 30, 1992. Such sums shall remain available until expended."

Pub. L. 100–220, title II, subtitle C, Dec. 29, 1987, 101 Stat. 1467, as amended by Pub. L. 100–688, title I, §1003(b), (c), Nov. 18, 1988, 102 Stat. 4150, directed Administrator of the Environmental Protection Agency, within 3 years after Dec. 29, 1987, in consultation with Administrator of the National Oceanic and Atmospheric Administration and other Federal, State, and interstate agencies, to prepare and submit to Congress a New York Bight Restoration Plan and a detailed schedule and two preliminary reports at specified times, and further directed Administrator to conduct a study of problems associated with plastic debris in the New York Bight and report to Congress within 6 months after Dec. 29, 1987.

§ 2267a. Watershed and river basin assessments

(a) In general

The Secretary may assess the water resources needs of river basins and watersheds of the United States, including needs relating to—

(1) ecosystem protection and restoration;

(2) flood damage reduction;

(3) navigation and ports;

(4) watershed protection;

(5) water supply; and

(6) drought preparedness.

(b) Cooperation

An assessment under subsection (a) of this section shall be carried out in cooperation and coordination with—

(1) the Secretary of the Interior;

(2) the Secretary of Agriculture;

(3) the Secretary of Commerce;

(4) the Administrator of the Environmental Protection Agency; and

(5) the heads of other appropriate agencies.

(c) Consultation

In carrying out an assessment under subsection (a) of this section, the Secretary shall consult with Federal, tribal, State, interstate, and local governmental entities.

(d) Priority river basins and watersheds

In selecting river basins and watersheds for assessment under this section, the Secretary shall give priority to—

(1) the Delaware River basin;

(2) the Kentucky River basin;

(3) the Potomac River basin;

(4) the Susquehanna River basin;

(5) the Willamette River basin;

(6) Tuscarawas River Basin, Ohio;

(7) Sauk River Basin, Snohomish and Skagit Counties, Washington;

(8) Niagara River Basin, New York;

(9) Genesee River Basin, New York; and

(10) White River Basin, Arkansas and Missouri.

(e) Acceptance of contributions

In carrying out an assessment under subsection (a) of this section, the Secretary may accept contributions, in cash or in kind, from Federal, tribal, State, interstate, and local governmental entities to the extent that the Secretary determines that the contributions will facilitate completion of the assessment.

(f) Cost-sharing requirements

(1) Non-Federal share

The non-Federal share of the costs of an assessment carried out under this section on or after December 11, 2000, shall be 25 percent.

(2) Credit

(A) In general

Subject to subparagraph (B), the Secretary may credit toward the non-Federal share of an assessment under this section the cost of services, materials, supplies, or other in-kind contributions provided by the non-Federal interests for the assessment.

(B) Maximum amount of credit

The credit under subparagraph (A) may not exceed an amount equal to 25 percent of the costs of the assessment.

(Pub. L. 99–662, title VII, § 729, Nov. 17, 1986, 100 Stat. 4164; Pub. L. 106–541, title II, § 202, Dec. 11, 2000, 114 Stat. 2587; Pub. L. 110–114, title II, § 2010, Nov. 8, 2007, 121 Stat. 1074.)

AMENDMENTS

2007—Subsec. (d)(6) to (10). Pub. L. 110–114, § 2010(1), added pars. (6) to (10).

Subsec. (f)(1). Pub. L. 110–114, § 2010(2), added par. (1) and struck out heading and text of former par. (1). Text read as follows: "The non-Federal share of the costs of an assessment carried out under this section shall be 50 percent."

Subsec. (g). Pub. L. 110–114, § 2010(3), struck out heading and text of subsec. (g). Text read as follows: "There is authorized to be appropriated to carry out this section $15,000,000."

2000—Pub. L. 106–541 amended section catchline and text generally. Prior to amendment, section read as follows:

"(a) The Secretary, in coordination with the Secretary of the Interior and in consultation with appropriate Federal, State, and local agencies, is authorized to study the water resources needs of river basins and regions of the United States. The Secretaries shall report the results of such study to Congress not later than October 1, 1988.

"(b) In carrying out the studies authorized under subsection (a) of this section, the Secretaries shall consult with State, interstate, and local governmental entities.

"(c) There is authorized to be appropriated $5,000,000 for fiscal years beginning after September 30, 1986, to carry out this section."

§ 2268. Marine technology review

(a) Dredging needs

The Secretary is authorized to conduct such studies as are necessary to provide a report to Congress on the dredging needs of the national ports and harbors of the United States. The report shall include existing and projected future project depths, types and sizes of ships in use, and world trade patterns, an assessment of the future national waterside infrastructure needs, and a comparison of drafts of United States and selected world ports.

(b) Authorization of appropriations

There is authorized to be appropriated $2,500,000 to carry out this section for fiscal years beginning after September 30, 1992. Such sums shall remain available until expended.

(Pub. L. 102–580, title IV, § 402, Oct. 31, 1992, 106 Stat. 4862.)

CODIFICATION

Section was enacted as part of the Water Resources Development Act of 1992, and not as part of the Water Resources Development Act of 1986 which comprises this chapter.

"SECRETARY" DEFINED

Secretary means the Secretary of the Army, see section 3 of Pub. L. 102–580, set out as a note under section 2201 of this title.

§2269. Tribal partnership program

(a) Definition of Indian tribe

In this section, the term "Indian tribe" has the meaning given the term in section 450b of title 25.

(b) Program

(1) In general

In cooperation with Indian tribes and the heads of other Federal agencies, the Secretary may carry out water-related planning activities and study and determine the feasibility of carrying out water resources development projects that—

(A) will substantially benefit Indian tribes; and

(B) are located primarily within Indian country (as defined in section 1151 of title 18, and including lands that are within the jurisdictional area of an Oklahoma Indian tribe, as determined by the Secretary of the Interior, and are recognized by the Secretary of the Interior as eligible for trust land status under part 151 of title 25, Code of Federal Regulations) or in proximity to Alaska Native villages.

(2) Matters to be studied

A study conducted under paragraph (1) may address—

(A) projects for flood damage reduction, environmental restoration and protection, and preservation of cultural and natural resources;

(B) watershed assessments and planning activities; and

(C) such other projects as the Secretary, in cooperation with Indian tribes and the heads of other Federal agencies, determines to be appropriate.

(c) Consultation and coordination with Secretary of the Interior

(1) In general

In recognition of the unique role of the Secretary of the Interior concerning trust responsibilities with Indian tribes and in recognition of mutual trust responsibilities, the Secretary shall consult with the Secretary of the Interior concerning studies conducted under subsection (b) of this section.

(2) Integration of activities

The Secretary shall—

(A) integrate civil works activities of the Department of the Army with activities of the Department of the Interior to avoid conflicts, duplications of effort, or unanticipated adverse effects on Indian tribes; and

(B) consider the authorities and programs of the Department of the Interior and other Federal agencies in any recommendations concerning carrying out projects studied under subsection (b) of this section.

(d) Cost sharing

(1) Ability to pay

(A) In general

Any cost-sharing agreement for a study under subsection (b) of this section shall be subject to the ability of the non-Federal interest to pay.

(B) Use of procedures

The ability of a non-Federal interest to pay shall be determined by the Secretary in accordance with procedures established by the Secretary.

(2) Credit

The Secretary may credit toward the non-Federal share of the costs of a study under subsection (b) of this section the cost of services, studies, supplies, or other in-kind contributions provided by the non-Federal interest if the Secretary determines that the services, studies, supplies, and other in-kind contributions will facilitate completion of the study.

(e) Authorization of appropriations

There is authorized to be appropriated to carry out subsection (b) of this section $5,000,000 for each of fiscal years 2002 through 2012, of which not more than $1,000,000 may be used with respect to any 1 Indian tribe.

(Pub. L. 106–541, title II, §203, Dec. 11, 2000, 114 Stat. 2588; Pub. L. 110–114, title II, §2011, Nov. 8, 2007, 121 Stat. 1074.)

CODIFICATION

Section was enacted as part of the Water Resources Development Act of 2000, and not as part of the Water Resources Development Act of 1986 which comprises this chapter.

AMENDMENTS

2007—Subsec. (b)(1). Pub. L. 110–114, §2011(a)(1), inserted "carry out water-related planning activities and" after "the Secretary may" in introductory provisions.

Subsec. (b)(1)(B). Pub. L. 110–114, §2011(a)(2), inserted ", and including lands that are within the jurisdictional area of an Oklahoma Indian tribe, as determined by the Secretary of the Interior, and are recognized by the Secretary of the Interior as eligible for trust land status under part 151 of title 25, Code of Federal Regulations" after "section 1151 of title 18".

Subsec. (b)(2). Pub. L. 110–114, §2011(a)(3), added subpar. (B) and redesignated former subpar. (B) as (C).

Subsec. (e). Pub. L. 110–114, §2011(b), substituted "2012" for "2006".

"SECRETARY" DEFINED

Secretary means the Secretary of the Army, see section 2 of Pub. L. 106–541, set out as a note under section 2201 of this title.

SUBCHAPTER V—GENERAL PROVISIONS

§2280. Maximum cost of projects

In order to insure against cost overruns, each total cost set forth with respect to a project for water resources development and conservation and related purposes authorized to be carried out by the Secretary in this Act or in a law enacted after the date of the enactment of this Act, including the Water Resources Development Act of 1988, or in an amendment made by this Act or any later law with respect to such a project shall be the maximum cost of that project, except that such maximum amount—

(1) may be increased by the Secretary for modifications which do not materially alter

the scope or functions of the project as authorized, but not by more than 20 percent of the total cost stated for the project in this Act, in any later law, or in an amendment made by this Act or any later law; and

(2) shall be automatically increased for—

(A) changes in construction costs applied to unconstructed features (including real property acquisitions, preconstruction studies, planning, engineering, and design) from the date of enactment of this Act or any later law (unless otherwise specified) as indicated by engineering and other appropriate cost indexes; and

(B) additional studies, modifications, and actions (including mitigation and other environmental actions) authorized by this Act or any later law or required by changes in Federal law.

(Pub. L. 99–662, title IX, § 902, Nov. 17, 1986, 100 Stat. 4183; Pub. L. 100–676, § 3(b), Nov. 17, 1988, 102 Stat. 4014.)

REFERENCES IN TEXT

This Act, referred to in text, is Pub. L. 99–662, Nov. 17, 1986, 100 Stat. 4082, as amended, known as the Water Resources Development Act of 1986. For complete classification of this Act to the Code, see Short Title note set out under section 2201 of this title and Tables.

The date of enactment of this Act, referred to in text, is the date of enactment of Pub. L. 99–662, which was approved Nov. 17, 1986.

The Water Resources Development Act of 1988, referred to in text, is Pub. L. 100–676, Nov. 17, 1988, 102 Stat. 4012. For complete classification of this Act to the Code, see Short Title of 1988 Amendment note set out under section 2201 of this title and Tables.

AMENDMENTS

1988—Pub. L. 100–676, § 3(b)(1), substituted "with respect to a project for water resources development and conservation and related purposes authorized to be carried out by the Secretary in this Act or in a law enacted after the date of the enactment of this Act, including the Water Resources Development Act of 1988, or in an amendment made by this Act or any later law with respect to such a project" for "in this Act, or an amendment made by this Act, for a project".

Par. (1). Pub. L. 100–676, § 3(b)(2), inserted ", in any later law," after "in this Act", and "or any later law" after "by this Act".

Par. (2). Pub. L. 100–676, § 3(b)(3), (4), inserted "or any later law" after "of this Act" in subpars. (A) and (B).

§ 2281. Matters to be addressed in planning

(a) In general

Enhancing national economic development (including benefits to particular regions of the Nation not involving the transfer of economic activity to such regions from other regions), the quality of the total environment (including preservation and enhancement of the environment), the well-being of the people of the United States, the prevention of loss of life, and the preservation of cultural and historical values shall be addressed in the formulation and evaluation of water resources projects to be carried out by the Secretary, and the associated benefits and costs, both quantifiable and unquantifiable, and information regarding potential loss of human life that may be associated with flooding and coastal storm events, shall be displayed in the benefits and costs of such projects.

(b) Assessments

For all feasibility reports for water resources projects completed after December 31, 2007, the Secretary shall assess whether—

(1) the water resources project and each separable element is cost-effective; and

(2) the water resources project complies with Federal, State, and local laws (including regulations) and public policies.

(Pub. L. 99–662, title IX, § 904, Nov. 17, 1986, 100 Stat. 4185; Pub. L. 101–640, title III, § 315, Nov. 28, 1990, 104 Stat. 4641; Pub. L. 104–303, title II, § 231, Oct. 12, 1996, 110 Stat. 3704; Pub. L. 110–114, title II, § 2033(a), Nov. 8, 2007, 121 Stat. 1084.)

AMENDMENTS

2007—Pub. L. 110–114 designated existing provisions as subsec. (a), inserted heading, and added subsec. (b).

1996—Pub. L. 104–303 inserted "and information regarding potential loss of human life that may be associated with flooding and coastal storm events," after "unquantifiable,".

1990—Pub. L. 101–640 inserted "(including preservation and enhancement of the environment)" after "environment".

RURAL PROJECT EVALUATION AND SELECTION CRITERIA

Pub. L. 102–580, title II, § 214, Oct. 31, 1992, 106 Stat. 4831, directed Comptroller General, not later than 18 months after Oct. 31, 1992, to report to Congress with specific legislative and other recommendations on improving the equitable distribution of water resources development projects in rural areas, prior to repeal by Pub. L. 104–316, title I, § 117, Oct. 19, 1996, 110 Stat. 3835.

§ 2282. Feasibility reports

(a) Preparation of reports

(1) In general

In the case of any water resources project-related study authorized to be undertaken by the Secretary that results in recommendations concerning a project or the operation of a project and that requires specific authorization by Congress in law or otherwise, the Secretary shall perform a reconnaissance study and prepare a feasibility report, subject to section 2215 of this title.

(2) Contents of feasibility reports

A feasibility report shall describe, with reasonable certainty, the economic, environmental, and social benefits and detriments of the recommended plan and alternative plans considered by the Secretary and the engineering features (including hydrologic and geologic information), the public acceptability, and the purposes, scope, and scale of the recommended plan. A feasibility report shall also include the views of other Federal agencies and non-Federal agencies with regard to the recommended plan, a description of a nonstructural alternative to the recommended plan when such plan does not have significant nonstructural features, and a description of the Federal and non-Federal participation in such plan, and shall demonstrate that States, other non-Federal interests, and Federal agencies have been consulted in the development of the recommended plan.

(3) Applicability

This subsection shall not apply to—

(A) any study with respect to which a report has been submitted to Congress before November 17, 1986;

(B) any study for a project, which project is authorized for construction by this Act and is not subject to section 903(b);[1]

(C) any study for a project which does not require specific authorization by Congress in law or otherwise; and

(D) general studies not intended to lead to recommendation of a specific water resources project.

(4) Feasibility report defined

In this subsection, the term "feasibility report" means each feasibility report, and any associated environmental impact statement and mitigation plan, prepared by the Corps of Engineers for a water resources project. The term includes a project implementation report prepared under title VI of the Water Resources Development Act of 2000 (114 Stat. 2680–2694), a general reevaluation report, and a limited reevaluation report.

(b) Reconnaissance studies

Before initiating any feasibility study under subsection (a) of this section after November 17, 1986, the Secretary shall first perform, at Federal expense, a reconnaissance study of the water resources problem in order to identify potential solutions to such problem in sufficient detail to enable the Secretary to determine whether or not planning to develop a project should proceed to the preparation of a feasibility report. Such reconnaissance study shall include a preliminary analysis of the Federal interest, costs, benefits, and environmental impacts of such project, and an estimate of the costs of preparing the feasibility report. The duration of a reconnaissance study shall normally be no more than twelve months, but in all cases is to be limited to eighteen months.

(c) Projects not specifically authorized by Congress

In the case of any water resources project-related study authorized to be undertaken by the Secretary without specific authorization by Congress in law or otherwise, the Secretary shall prepare a detailed project report.

(d) Indian tribes

For purposes of studies undertaken pursuant to this section, the Secretary is authorized to consider benefits which may accrue to Indian tribes as a result of a project resulting from such a study.

(e) Standard and uniform procedures and practices

The Secretary shall undertake such measures as are necessary to ensure that standard and uniform procedures and practices are followed by each district office (and each division office for any area in which there is no district office) of the United States Army Corps of Engineers in the preparation of feasibility reports on water resources projects.

[1] See References in Text note below.

(f) Enhanced public participation

(1) In general

The Secretary shall establish procedures to enhance public participation in the development of each feasibility study under subsection (a) of this section, including, if appropriate, establishment of a stakeholder advisory group to assist the Secretary with the development of the study.

(2) Membership

If the Secretary provides for the establishment of a stakeholder advisory group under this subsection, the membership of the advisory group shall include balanced representation of social, economic, and environmental interest groups, and such members shall serve on a voluntary, uncompensated basis.

(3) Limitation

Procedures established under this subsection shall not delay development of any feasibility study under subsection (a) of this section.

(Pub. L. 99–662, title IX, § 905, Nov. 17, 1986, 100 Stat. 4185; Pub. L. 106–541, title II, § 222(a), Dec. 11, 2000, 114 Stat. 2597; Pub. L. 110–114, title II, § 2043(b), Nov. 8, 2007, 121 Stat. 1101.)

REFERENCES IN TEXT

This Act, referred to in subsec. (a)(3)(B), is Pub. L. 99–662, Nov. 17, 1986, 100 Stat. 4082, known as the Water Resources Development Act of 1986. For complete classification of this Act to the Code, see Short Title note set out under section 2201 of this title and Tables.

Section 903(b), referred to in subsec. (a)(3)(B), is section 903(b) of Pub. L. 99–662, title IX, Nov. 17, 1986, 100 Stat. 4184, which is not classified to the Code.

The Water Resources Development Act of 2000, referred to in subsec. (a)(4), is Pub. L. 106–541, Dec. 11, 2000, 114 Stat. 2572. Title VI of the Act is not classified to the Code. For complete classification of this Act to the Code, see Short Title of 2000 Amendment note set out under section 2201 of this title and Tables.

AMENDMENTS

2007—Subsec. (a). Pub. L. 110–114, § 2043(b)(1), designated first sentence of existing provisions as par. (1) and inserted subsec. (a) and par. (1) headings, substituted "the Secretary that results in recommendations concerning a project or the operation of a project and that requires specific authorization by Congress in law or otherwise, the Secretary shall perform a reconnaissance study and" for "the Secretary, the Secretary shall" in par. (1), designated second and third sentences of existing provisions as par. (2) and inserted heading, substituted "A feasibility report" for "Such feasibility report" and "The feasibility report" in par. (2), added pars. (3) and (4), and struck out last sentence of existing provisions which read as follows: "This subsection shall not apply to (1) any study with respect to which a report has been submitted to Congress before November 17, 1986, (2) any study for a project, which project is authorized for construction by this Act and is not subject to section 903(b), (3) any study for a project which is authorized under any of the following sections: section 205 of the Flood Control Act of 1948 (33 U.S.C. 701s), section 2 of the Flood Control Act of August 28, 1946 (33 U.S.C. 701r), section 107 of the River and Harbor Act of 1960 (33 U.S.C. 577), section 3 of the Act entitled 'An Act authorizing Federal participation in the cost of protecting the shores of publicly owned property', approved August 13, 1946 (33 U.S.C. 426g), and section 111 of the River and Harbor Act of 1968 (33 U.S.C. 426i), and (4) general studies not intended to lead to recommendation of a specific water resources project."

Subsec. (b). Pub. L. 110–114, § 2043(b)(2)(A), inserted heading.

Subsecs. (c) to (f). Pub. L. 110–114, § 2043(b)(2)(B)–(E), added subsec. (c), redesignated former subsecs. (c) to (e) as (d) to (f), respectively, and inserted headings in subsecs. (d) and (e).

2000—Subsec. (e). Pub. L. 106–541 added subsec. (e).

NATIONAL ACADEMY OF SCIENCES STUDY

Pub. L. 106–541, title II, § 216, Dec. 11, 2000, 114 Stat. 2595, provided that:

"(a) DEFINITIONS.—In this section, the following definitions apply:

"(1) ACADEMY.—The term 'Academy' means the National Academy of Sciences.

"(2) METHOD.—The term 'method' means a method, model, assumption, or other pertinent planning tool used in conducting an economic or environmental analysis of a water resources project, including the formulation of a feasibility report.

"(3) FEASIBILITY REPORT.—The term 'feasibility report' means each feasibility report, and each associated environmental impact statement and mitigation plan, prepared by the Corps of Engineers for a water resources project.

"(4) WATER RESOURCES PROJECT.—The term 'water resources project' means a project for navigation, a project for flood control, a project for hurricane and storm damage reduction, a project for emergency streambank and shore protection, a project for ecosystem restoration and protection, and a water resources project of any other type carried out by the Corps of Engineers.

"(b) INDEPENDENT PEER REVIEW OF PROJECTS.—

"(1) IN GENERAL.—Not later than 90 days after the date of enactment of this Act [Dec. 11, 2000], the Secretary [of the Army] shall contract with the Academy to study, and make recommendations relating to, the independent peer review of feasibility reports.

"(2) STUDY ELEMENTS.—In carrying out a contract under paragraph (1), the Academy shall study the practicality and efficacy of the independent peer review of the feasibility reports, including—

"(A) the cost, time requirements, and other considerations relating to the implementation of independent peer review; and

"(B) objective criteria that may be used to determine the most effective application of independent peer review to feasibility reports for each type of water resources project.

"(3) ACADEMY REPORT.—Not later than 1 year after the date of a contract under paragraph (1), the Academy shall submit to the Secretary, the Committee on Transportation and Infrastructure of the House of Representatives, and the Committee on Environment and Public Works of the Senate a report that includes—

"(A) the results of the study conducted under paragraphs (1) and (2); and

"(B) in light of the results of the study, specific recommendations, if any, on a program for implementing independent peer review of feasibility reports.

"(4) AUTHORIZATION OF APPROPRIATIONS.—There is authorized to be appropriated to carry out this subsection $1,000,000, to remain available until expended.

"(c) INDEPENDENT PEER REVIEW OF METHODS FOR PROJECT ANALYSIS.—

"(1) IN GENERAL.—Not later than 90 days after the date of enactment of this Act [Dec. 11, 2000], the Secretary [of the Army] shall contract with the Academy to conduct a study that includes—

"(A) a review of state-of-the-art methods;

"(B) a review of the methods currently used by the Secretary;

"(C) a review of a sample of instances in which the Secretary has applied the methods identified under subparagraph (B) in the analysis of each type of water resources project; and

"(D) a comparative evaluation of the basis and validity of state-of-the-art methods identified under subparagraph (A) and the methods identified under subparagraphs (B) and (C).

"(2) ACADEMY REPORT.—Not later than 1 year after the date of a contract under paragraph (1), the Academy shall transmit to the Secretary, the Committee on Transportation and Infrastructure of the House of Representatives, and the Committee on Environment and Public Works of the Senate a report that includes—

"(A) the results of the study conducted under paragraph (1); and

"(B) in light of the results of the study, specific recommendations for modifying any of the methods currently used by the Secretary for conducting economic and environmental analyses of water resources projects.

"(3) AUTHORIZATION OF APPROPRIATIONS.—There is authorized to be appropriated to carry out this subsection $2,000,000. Such sums shall remain available until expended."

ENGINEERING CONSULTING SERVICES

Pub. L. 106–541, title II, § 219, Dec. 11, 2000, 114 Stat. 2596, provided that: "In conducting a feasibility study for a water resources project, the Secretary [of the Army], to the maximum extent practicable, should not employ a person for engineering and consulting services if the same person is also employed by the non-Federal interest for such services unless there is only 1 qualified and responsive bidder for such services."

§ 2282a. Planning

(a) Omitted

(b) Planning process improvements

The Chief of Engineers—

(1) shall adopt a risk analysis approach to project cost estimates for water resources projects; and

(2) not later than one year after November 8, 2007, shall—

(A) issue procedures for risk analysis for cost estimation for water resources projects; and

(B) submit to Congress a report that includes any recommended amendments to section 2280 of this title.

(c) Benchmarks

(1) In general

Not later than 12 months after November 8, 2007, the Chief of Engineers shall establish benchmarks for determining the length of time it should take to conduct a feasibility study for a water resources project and its associated review process under the National Environmental Policy Act of 1969 (42 U.S.C. 4321 et seq.). The Chief of Engineers shall use such benchmarks as a management tool to make the feasibility study process more efficient in all districts of the Corps of Engineers.

(2) Benchmark goals

The Chief of Engineers shall establish, to the extent practicable, under paragraph (1) benchmark goals for completion of feasibility studies for water resources projects generally within 2 years. In the case of feasibility studies that the Chief of Engineers determines may require additional time based on the project type, size, cost, or complexity, the benchmark goal for completion shall be generally within 4 years.

(d) Calculation of benefits and costs for flood damage reduction projects

A feasibility study for a project for flood damage reduction shall include, as part of the calculation of benefits and costs—

(1) a calculation of the residual risk of flooding following completion of the proposed project;

(2) a calculation of the residual risk of loss of human life and residual risk to human safety following completion of the proposed project;

(3) a calculation of any upstream or downstream impacts of the proposed project; and

(4) calculations to ensure that the benefits and costs associated with structural and nonstructural alternatives are evaluated in an equitable manner.

(e) Centers of specialized planning expertise

(1) Establishment

The Secretary may establish centers of expertise to provide specialized planning expertise for water resources projects to be carried out by the Secretary in order to enhance and supplement the capabilities of the districts of the Corps of Engineers.

(2) Duties

A center of expertise established under this subsection shall—

(A) provide technical and managerial assistance to district commanders of the Corps of Engineers for project planning, development, and implementation;

(B) provide agency peer reviews of new major scientific, engineering, or economic methods, models, or analyses that will be used to support decisions of the Secretary with respect to feasibility studies for water resources projects;

(C) provide support for independent peer review panels under section 2343 of this title; and

(D) carry out such other duties as are prescribed by the Secretary.

(f) Completion of Corps of Engineers reports

(1) Alternatives

(A) In general

Feasibility and other studies and assessments for a water resources project shall include recommendations for alternatives—

(i) that, as determined in coordination with the non-Federal interest for the project, promote integrated water resources management; and

(ii) for which the non-Federal interest is willing to provide the non-Federal share for the studies or assessments.

(B) Constraints

The alternatives contained in studies and assessments described in subparagraph (A) shall not be constrained by budgetary or other policy.

(C) Reports of Chief of Engineers

The reports of the Chief of Engineers shall identify any recommendation that is not the best technical solution to water resource needs and problems and the reason for the deviation.

(2) Report completion

The completion of a report of the Chief of Engineers for a water resources project—

(A) shall not be delayed while consideration is being given to potential changes in policy or priority for project consideration; and

(B) shall be submitted, on completion, to—

(i) the Committee on Environment and Public Works of the Senate; and

(ii) the Committee on Transportation and Infrastructure of the House of Representatives.

(g) Completion review

(1) In general

Except as provided in paragraph (2), not later than 120 days after the date of completion of a report of the Chief of Engineers that recommends to Congress a water resources project, the Secretary shall—

(A) review the report; and

(B) provide any recommendations of the Secretary regarding the water resources project to Congress.

(2) Prior reports

Not later than 180 days after November 8, 2007, with respect to any report of the Chief of Engineers recommending a water resources project that is complete prior to November 8, 2007, the Secretary shall complete review of, and provide recommendations to Congress for, the report in accordance with paragraph (1).

(Pub. L. 110–114, title II, §2033, Nov. 8, 2007, 121 Stat. 1084.)

REFERENCES IN TEXT

The National Environmental Policy Act of 1969, referred to in subsec. (c)(1), is Pub. L. 91–190, Jan. 1, 1970, 83 Stat. 852, which is classified generally to chapter 55 (§4321 et seq.) of Title 42, The Public Health and Welfare. For complete classification of this Act to the Code, see Short Title note set out under section 4321 of Title 42 and Tables.

CODIFICATION

Section is comprised of section 2033 of Pub. L. 110–114. Subsec. (a) of section 2033 of Pub. L. 110–114 amended section 2281 of this title.

Section was enacted as part of the Water Resources Development Act of 2007, and not as part of the Water Resources Development Act of 1986 which comprises this chapter.

"SECRETARY" DEFINED

Secretary means the Secretary of the Army, see section 2 of Pub. L. 110–114, set out as a note under section 2201 of this title.

§2283. Fish and wildlife mitigation

(a) Steps to be taken prior to or concurrently with construction

(1) In the case of any water resources project which is authorized to be constructed by the Secretary before, on, or after November 17, 1986, construction of which has not commenced as of November 17, 1986, and which necessitates the mitigation of fish and wildlife losses, including

the acquisition of lands or interests in lands to mitigate losses to fish and wildlife, as a result of such project, such mitigation, including acquisition of the lands or interests—

(A) shall be undertaken or acquired before any construction of the project (other than such acquisition) commences, or

(B) shall be undertaken or acquired concurrently with lands and interests in lands for project purposes (other than mitigation of fish and wildlife losses),

whichever the Secretary determines is appropriate, except that any physical construction required for the purposes of mitigation may be undertaken concurrently with the physical construction of such project.

(2) For the purposes of this subsection, any project authorized before November 17, 1986, on which more than 50 percent of the land needed for the project, exclusive of mitigation lands, has been acquired shall be deemed to have commenced construction under this subsection.

(b) Acquisition of lands or interests in lands for mitigation

(1) After consultation with appropriate Federal and non-Federal agencies, the Secretary is authorized to mitigate damages to fish and wildlife resulting from any water resources project under his jurisdiction, whether completed, under construction, or to be constructed. Such mitigation may include the acquisition of lands, or interests therein, except that—

(A) acquisition under this paragraph shall not be by condemnation in the case of projects completed as of November 17, 1986, or on which at least 10 percent of the physical construction on the project has been completed as of November 17, 1986; and

(B) acquisition of water, or interests therein, under this paragraph, shall not be by condemnation.

The Secretary, shall, under the terms of this paragraph, obligate no more than $30,000,000 in any fiscal year. With respect to any water resources project, the authority under this subsection shall not apply to measures that cost more than $7,500,000 or 10 percent of the cost of the project, whichever is greater.

(2) Whenever, after his review, the Secretary determines that such mitigation features under this subsection are likely to require condemnation under subparagraph (A) or (B) of paragraph (1) of this subsection, the Secretary shall transmit to Congress a report on such proposed modification, together with his recommendations.

(c) Allocation of mitigation costs

Costs incurred after November 17, 1986, including lands, easements, rights-of-way, and relocations, for implementation and operation, maintenance, and rehabilitation to mitigate damages to fish and wildlife shall be allocated among authorized project purposes in accordance with applicable cost allocation procedures, and shall be subject to cost sharing or reimbursement to the same extent as such other project costs are shared or reimbursed, except that when such costs are covered by contracts entered into prior to November 17, 1986, such costs shall not be recovered without the consent of the non-Federal interests or until such contracts are complied with or renegotiated.

(d) Mitigation plans as part of project proposals

(1) In general

After November 17, 1986, the Secretary shall not submit any proposal for the authorization of any water resources project to Congress in any report, and shall not select a project alternative in any report, unless such report contains (A) a recommendation with a specific plan to mitigate fish and wildlife losses created by such project, or (B) a determination by the Secretary that such project will have negligible adverse impact on fish and wildlife. Specific mitigation plans shall ensure that impacts to bottomland hardwood forests are mitigated in-kind, and other habitat types are mitigated to not less than in-kind conditions, to the extent possible. In carrying out this subsection, the Secretary shall consult with appropriate Federal and non-Federal agencies.

(2) Design of mitigation projects

The Secretary shall design mitigation projects to reflect contemporary understanding of the science of mitigating the adverse environmental impacts of water resources projects.

(3) Mitigation requirements

(A) In general

To mitigate losses to flood damage reduction capabilities and fish and wildlife resulting from a water resources project, the Secretary shall ensure that the mitigation plan for each water resources project complies with the mitigation standards and policies established pursuant to the regulatory programs administered by the Secretary.

(B) Inclusions

A specific mitigation plan for a water resources project under paragraph (1) shall include, at a minimum—

(i) a plan for monitoring the implementation and ecological success of each mitigation measure, including the cost and duration of any monitoring, and, to the extent practicable, a designation of the entities that will be responsible for the monitoring;

(ii) the criteria for ecological success by which the mitigation will be evaluated and determined to be successful based on replacement of lost functions and values of the habitat, including hydrologic and vegetative characteristics;

(iii) a description of the land and interests in land to be acquired for the mitigation plan and the basis for a determination that the land and interests are available for acquisition;

(iv) a description of—

(I) the types and amount of restoration activities to be conducted;

(II) the physical action to be undertaken to achieve the mitigation objectives within the watershed in which such losses occur and, in any case in which the mitigation will occur outside the watershed, a detailed explanation for undertaking the mitigation outside the watershed; and

(III) the functions and values that will result from the mitigation plan; and

(v) a contingency plan for taking corrective actions in cases in which monitoring demonstrates that mitigation measures are not achieving ecological success in accordance with criteria under clause (ii).

(C) Responsibility for monitoring

In any case in which it is not practicable to identify in a mitigation plan for a water resources project the entity responsible for monitoring at the time of a final report of the Chief of Engineers or other final decision document for the project, such entity shall be identified in the partnership agreement entered into with the non-Federal interest under section 1962d–5b of title 42.

(4) Determination of success

(A) In general

A mitigation plan under this subsection shall be considered to be successful at the time at which the criteria under paragraph (3)(B)(ii) are achieved under the plan, as determined by monitoring under paragraph (3)(B)(i).

(B) Consultation

In determining whether a mitigation plan is successful under subparagraph (A), the Secretary shall consult annually with appropriate Federal agencies and each State in which the applicable project is located on at least the following:

(i) The ecological success of the mitigation as of the date on which the report is submitted.

(ii) The likelihood that the mitigation will achieve ecological success, as defined in the mitigation plan.

(iii) The projected timeline for achieving that success.

(iv) Any recommendations for improving the likelihood of success.

(5) Monitoring

Mitigation monitoring shall continue until it has been demonstrated that the mitigation has met the ecological success criteria.

(e) First enhancement costs as Federal costs

In those cases when the Secretary, as part of any report to Congress, recommends activities to enhance fish and wildlife resources, the first costs of such enhancement shall be a Federal cost when—

(1) such enhancement provides benefits that are determined to be national, including benefits to species that are identified by the National Marine Fisheries Service as of national economic importance, species that are subject to treaties or international convention to which the United States is a party, and anadromous fish;

(2) such enhancement is designed to benefit species that have been listed as threatened or endangered by the Secretary of the Interior under the terms of the Endangered Species Act, as amended (16 U.S.C. 1531, et seq.), or

(3) such activities are located on lands managed as a national wildlife refuge.

When benefits of enhancement do not qualify under the preceding sentence, 25 percent of such first costs of enhancement shall be provided by non-Federal interests under a schedule of reimbursement determined by the Secretary. Not more than 80 percent of the non-Federal share of such first costs may be satisfied through in-kind contributions, including facilities, supplies, and services that are necessary to carry out the enhancement project. The non-Federal share of operation, maintenance, and rehabilitation of activities to enhance fish and wildlife resources shall be 25 percent.

(f) National benefits from enhancement measures for Atchafalaya Floodway System and Mississippi Delta Region projects

Fish and wildlife enhancement measures carried out as part of the project for Atchafalaya Floodway System, Louisiana, authorized by Public Law 99–88, and the project for Mississippi Delta Region, Louisiana, authorized by the Flood Control Act of 1965, shall be considered to provide benefits that are national for purposes of this section.

(g) Fish and Wildlife Coordination Act supplementation

The provisions of subsections (a), (b), and (d) of this section shall be deemed to supplement the responsibility and authority of the Secretary pursuant to the Fish and Wildlife Coordination Act [16 U.S.C. 661 et seq.], and nothing in this section is intended to affect that Act.

(Pub. L. 99–662, title IX, §906, Nov. 17, 1986, 100 Stat. 4186; Pub. L. 102–580, title III, §333(a), Oct. 31, 1992, 106 Stat. 4852; Pub. L. 106–53, title II, §221, Aug. 17, 1999, 113 Stat. 295; Pub. L. 106–541, title II, §224(a), Dec. 11, 2000, 114 Stat. 2597; Pub. L. 110–114, title II, §2036(a), Nov. 8, 2007, 121 Stat. 1092.)

REFERENCES IN TEXT

The Endangered Species Act, as amended, referred to in subsec. (e)(2), probably means the Endangered Species Act of 1973, Pub. L. 93–205, Dec. 28, 1973, 87 Stat. 884, as amended, which is classified generally to chapter 35 (§1531 et seq.) of Title 16, Conservation. For complete classification of this Act to the Code, see Short Title note set out under section 1531 of Title 16 and Tables.

Public Law 99–88, referred to in subsec. (f), is Pub. L. 99–88, Aug. 15, 1985, 99 Stat. 293, known as the Supplemental Appropriations Act, 1985. Provisions of Pub. L. 99–88 authorizing the project for the Atchafalaya Floodway System, Louisiana, are not classified to the Code. For complete classification of this Act to the Code, see Tables.

The Flood Control Act of 1965, referred to in subsec. (f), is title II of Pub. L. 89–298, Oct. 27, 1965, 79 Stat. 1073. Provisions of that Act authorizing the project for Mississippi Delta Region, Louisiana, are not classified to the Code. For complete classification of this Act to the Code, see Tables.

The Fish and Wildlife Coordination Act referred to in subsec. (g), is act Mar. 10, 1934, ch. 55, 48 Stat. 401, as amended, which is classified generally to sections 661 to 666c of Title 16, Conservation. For complete classification of this Act to the Code, see Short Title note set out under section 661 of Title 16 and Tables.

AMENDMENTS

2007—Subsec. (d)(1). Pub. L. 110–114, §2036(a)(1), (2), substituted "to Congress in any report, and shall not select a project alternative in any report," for "to the Congress" and inserted ", and other habitat types are mitigated to not less than in-kind conditions" after "mitigated in-kind".

Subsec. (d)(3) to (5). Pub. L. 110–114, § 2036(a)(3), added pars. (3) to (5).

2000—Subsec. (d). Pub. L. 106–541 inserted subsec. heading, designated existing provisions as par. (1), inserted par. heading, realigned margins, substituted "November 17, 1986" for "the date of enactment of this Act", redesignated former cls. (1) and (2) as (A) and (B), respectively, and added par. (2).

1999—Subsec. (e). Pub. L. 106–53 inserted after second sentence "Not more than 80 percent of the non-Federal share of such first costs may be satisfied through in-kind contributions, including facilities, supplies, and services that are necessary to carry out the enhancement project."

1992—Subsec. (c). Pub. L. 102–580 inserted ", including lands, easements, rights-of-way, and relocations," before "for implementation and operation".

CONCURRENT MITIGATION

Pub. L. 106–541, title II, § 224(b), Dec. 11, 2000, 114 Stat. 2598, provided that:

"(1) INVESTIGATION.—

"(A) IN GENERAL.—The Comptroller General shall conduct an investigation of the effectiveness of the concurrent mitigation requirements of section 906 of the Water Resources Development Act of 1986 (33 U.S.C. 2283). In carrying out the investigation, the Comptroller General shall determine—

"(i) whether or not there are instances in which less than 50 percent of required mitigation is completed before initiation of project construction and the number of such instances; and

"(ii) the extent to which mitigation projects restore natural hydrologic conditions, restore native vegetation, and otherwise support native fish and wildlife species.

"(B) SPECIAL RULE.—In carrying out subparagraph (A)(ii), the Comptroller General shall—

"(i) establish a panel of independent scientists, comprised of individuals with expertise and experience in applicable scientific disciplines, to assist the Comptroller General; and

"(ii) assess methods used by the Corps of Engineers to monitor and evaluate mitigation projects, and compare Corps of Engineers mitigation project design, construction, monitoring, and evaluation practices with those used in other publicly and privately financed mitigation projects.

"(2) REPORT.—Not later than 1 year after the date of enactment of this Act [Dec. 11, 2000], the Comptroller General shall transmit to Congress a report on the results of the investigation."

§ 2283a. Status report

(1) In general

Concurrent with the President's submission to Congress of the President's request for appropriations for the Civil Works Program for a fiscal year, the Secretary shall submit to the Committee on Transportation and Infrastructure of the House of Representatives and the Committee on Environment and Public Works of the Senate a report on the status of construction of projects that require mitigation under section 2283 of this title, the status of such mitigation, and the results of the consultation under subsection (d)(4)(B) of such section.

(2) Projects included

The status report shall include the status of—

(A) all projects that are under construction as of the date of the report;

(B) all projects for which the President requests funding for the next fiscal year; and

(C) all projects that have undergone or completed construction, but have not completed the mitigation required under section 2283 of this title.

(3) Availability of information

The Secretary shall make information contained in the status report available to the public, including on the Internet.

(Pub. L. 110–114, title II, § 2036(b), Nov. 8, 2007, 121 Stat. 1094.)

CODIFICATION

Section was enacted as part of the Water Resources Development Act of 2007, and not as part of the Water Resources Development Act of 1986 which comprises this chapter.

"SECRETARY" DEFINED

Secretary means the Secretary of the Army, see section 2 of Pub. L. 110–114, set out as a note under section 2201 of this title.

§ 2284. Benefits and costs attributable to environmental measures

In the evaluation by the Secretary of benefits and costs of a water resources project, the benefits attributable to measures included in a project for the purpose of environmental quality, including improvement of the environment and fish and wildlife enhancement, shall be deemed to be at least equal to the costs of such measures.

(Pub. L. 99–662, title IX, § 907, Nov. 17, 1986, 100 Stat. 4188.)

§ 2284a. Benefits to navigation

In evaluating potential improvements to navigation and the maintenance of navigation projects, the Secretary shall consider, and include for purposes of project justification, economic benefits generated by cruise ships as commercial navigation benefits.

(Pub. L. 104–303, title II, § 230, Oct. 12, 1996, 110 Stat. 3704.)

CODIFICATION

Section was enacted as part of the Water Resources Development Act of 1996, and not as part of the Water Resources Development Act of 1986 which comprises this chapter.

"SECRETARY" DEFINED

Secretary means the Secretary of the Army, see section 2 of Pub. L. 104–303, set out as a note under section 2201 of this title.

§ 2284b. Scenic and aesthetic considerations

In conducting studies of potential water resources projects, the Secretary shall consider measures to preserve and enhance scenic and aesthetic qualities in the vicinity of such projects.

(Pub. L. 104–303, title II, § 232, Oct. 12, 1996, 110 Stat. 3704.)

CODIFICATION

Section was enacted as part of the Water Resources Development Act of 1996, and not as part of the Water Resources Development Act of 1986 which comprises this chapter.

"SECRETARY" DEFINED

Secretary means the Secretary of the Army, see section 2 of Pub. L. 104–303, set out as a note under section 2201 of this title.

§ 2285. Environmental Protection and Mitigation Fund

There is established an Environmental Protection and Mitigation Fund. There is authorized to be appropriated to such fund $35,000,000 for fiscal years beginning after September 30, 1986. Amounts in the fund[1] shall be available for undertaking, in advance of construction of any water resources project authorized to be constructed by the Secretary, such measures authorized as part of such project, including the acquisition of lands and interests therein, as may be necessary to ensure that project-induced losses to fish and wildlife production and habitat will be mitigated. The Secretary shall reimburse the Fund for any amounts expended under this section for a water resources project from the first appropriations made for construction, including planning and designing, of such project.

(Pub. L. 99–662, title IX, § 908, Nov. 17, 1986, 100 Stat. 4188.)

§ 2286. Acceptance of certain funds for mitigation

The Secretary is authorized to accept funds from any entity, public or private, in accordance with the Pacific Northwest Electric Power Planning and Conservation Act [16 U.S.C. 839 et seq.] to be used to protect, mitigate, and enhance fish and wildlife in connection with projects constructed or operated by the Secretary. The Secretary may accept and use funds for such purposes without regard to any limitation established under any other provision of law or rule of law.

(Pub. L. 99–662, title XI, § 1146, Nov. 17, 1986, 100 Stat. 4253.)

REFERENCES IN TEXT

The Pacific Northwest Electric Power Planning and Conservation Act, referred to in text, is Pub. L. 96–501, Dec. 5, 1980, 94 Stat. 2697, which is classified principally to chapter 12H (§ 839 et seq.) of Title 16, Conservation. For complete classification of this Act to the Code, see Short Title note set out under section 839 of Title 16 and Tables.

§ 2287. Continued planning and investigations

(a) Pre-authorization planning and engineering

After the Chief of Engineers transmits his recommendations for a water resources development project to the Secretary for transmittal to the Congress, as authorized in section 701–1 of this title, and before authorization for construction of such project, the Chief of Engineers is authorized to undertake continued planning and engineering (other than preparation of plans and specifications) for such project if the Chief of Engineers finds that the project is without substantial controversy and justifies further engineering, economic, and environmental investigations and the Chief of Engineers transmits to the Committee on Public Works and Transportation of the House of Representatives and the Committee on Environment and Public Works of the Senate a statement of such findings. In the one-year period after authorization for construction of such project, the Chief of Engineers is authorized to undertake planning, engineering, and design for such project.

(b) Omitted

(c) Authorizations as additions to other authorizations

The authorization made by this section shall be in addition to any other authorizations for planning, engineering, and design of water resources development projects and shall not be construed as a limitation on any other such authorization.

(Pub. L. 99–662, title IX, § 910, Nov. 17, 1986, 100 Stat. 4189.)

CODIFICATION

Subsec. (b) of this section, which required the Secretary to prepare and transmit an annual report to certain committees of Congress on activities undertaken under this section, terminated, effective May 15, 2000, pursuant to section 3003 of Pub. L. 104–66, as amended, set out as a note under section 1113 of Title 31, Money and Finance. See, also, page 72 of House Document No. 103–7.

CHANGE OF NAME

Committee on Public Works and Transportation of House of Representatives treated as referring to Committee on Transportation and Infrastructure of House of Representatives by section 1(a) of Pub. L. 104–14, set out as a note preceding section 21 of Title 2, The Congress.

§ 2288. Review of cost effectiveness of design

During the design of each water resources project which has a total cost in excess of $10,000,000, which is authorized before, on, or after November 17, 1986, and undertaken by the Secretary, and on which construction has not been initiated as of November 17, 1986, the Secretary shall require a review of the cost effectiveness of such design. The review shall employ cost control techniques which will ensure that such project is designed in the most cost-effective way for the life of the project.

(Pub. L. 99–662, title IX, § 911, Nov. 17, 1986, 100 Stat. 4189.)

§ 2289. Urban and rural flood control frequency

In the preparation of feasibility reports for projects for flood damage prevention in urban and rural areas, the Secretary may consider and evaluate measures to reduce or eliminate damages from flooding without regard to frequency of flooding, drainage area, and amount of runoff. This section shall apply with respect to any project, or separable element thereof, the Federal share of the cost of which is less than $3,000,000.

(Pub. L. 99–662, title IX, § 914, Nov. 17, 1986, 100 Stat. 4190.)

§ 2290. Flood control in Trust Territory of the Pacific Islands

The Secretary is authorized to use the authority contained in section 205 of the Flood Control

[1] So in original. Probably should be capitalized.

Act of 1948 (33 U.S.C. 701s), section 2 of the Flood Control Act of August 28, 1937 (33 U.S.C. 701g), section 14 of the Flood Control Act of 1946 (33 U.S.C. 701r), section 107 of the River and Harbor Act of 1960 (33 U.S.C. 577), section 3 of the Act entitled "An Act authorizing Federal participation in the cost of protecting the shores of publicly owned property", approved August 13, 1946 (33 U.S.C. 426g), and section 111 of the River and Harbor Act of 1968 (33 U.S.C. 426i) in the Trust Territory of the Pacific Islands.

(Pub. L. 99–662, title IX, § 915(h), Nov. 17, 1986, 100 Stat. 4191.)

TERMINATION OF TRUST TERRITORY OF THE PACIFIC ISLANDS

For termination of Trust Territory of the Pacific Islands, see note set out preceding section 1681 of Title 48, Territories and Insular Possessions.

§ 2291. Federal Project Repayment District

(a) The Secretary may enter into a contract providing for the payment or recovery of an appropriate share of the costs of a project under his responsibility with a Federal Project Repayment District or other political subdivision of a State prior to the construction, operation, improvement, or financing of such project. The Federal Project Repayment District shall include lands and improvements which receive identifiable benefits from the construction or operation of such project. Such districts shall be established in accordance with State law, shall have specific boundaries which may be changed from time to time based upon further evaluations of benefits, and shall have the power to recover benefits through any cost-recovery approach that is consistent with State law and satisfies the applicable cost-recovery requirement under subsection (b) of this section.

(b) Prior to execution of an agreement pursuant to subsection (a) of this section, the Secretary shall require and approve a study from the State or political subdivision demonstrating that the revenues to be derived from a contract under this section, or an agreement with a Federal Project Repayment District, will be sufficient to equal or exceed the cost recovery requirements over the term of repayment required by Federal law.

(Pub. L. 99–662, title IX, § 916, Nov. 17, 1986, 100 Stat. 4191; Pub. L. 100–676, § 15, Nov. 17, 1988, 102 Stat. 4026.)

AMENDMENTS

1988—Subsec. (a). Pub. L. 100–676 substituted "have the power to recover benefits through any cost-recovery approach that is consistent with State law and satisfies the applicable cost-recovery requirement under subsection (b) of this section" for "include the power to collect a portion of the transfer price from any transaction involving the sale, transfer, or change in beneficial ownership of lands and improvements within the district boundaries".

§ 2292. Surveying and mapping

Any surveying or mapping services to be performed in connection with a water resources project which is or has been authorized to be undertaken by the Secretary shall be procured in accordance with title IX of the Federal Property and Administrative Services Act of 1949.[1]

(Pub. L. 99–662, title IX, § 918, Nov. 17, 1986, 100 Stat. 4192.)

REFERENCES IN TEXT

The Federal Property and Administrative Services Act of 1949, referred to in text, is act June 30, 1949, ch. 288, 63 Stat. 377. Title IX of the Act, which was classified generally to subchapter VI (§ 541 et seq.) of chapter 10 of former Title 40, Public Buildings, Property, and Works, was repealed and reenacted by Pub. L. 107–217, §§ 1, 6(b), Aug. 21, 2002, 116 Stat. 1062, 1304, as chapter 11 (§ 1101 et seq.) of Title 40, Public Buildings, Property, and Works. For disposition of sections of former Title 40 to revised Title 40, see Table preceding section 101 of Title 40. For complete classification of this Act to the Code, see Tables.

§ 2293. Reprogramming during national emergencies

(a) Termination or deferment of civil works projects; application of resources to national defense projects

In the event of a declaration of war or a declaration by the President of a national emergency in accordance with the National Emergencies Act [50 U.S.C. 1601 et seq.] that requires or may require use of the Armed Forces, the Secretary, without regard to any other provision of law, may (1) terminate or defer the construction, operation, maintenance, or repair of any Department of the Army civil works project that he deems not essential to the national defense, and (2) apply the resources of the Department of the Army's civil works program, including funds, personnel, and equipment, to construct or assist in the construction, operation, maintenance, and repair of authorized civil works, military construction, and civil defense projects that are essential to the national defense.

(b) Termination of state of war or national emergency

The Secretary shall immediately notify the appropriate committees of Congress of any actions taken pursuant to the authorities provided by this section, and cease to exercise such authorities not later than 180 calendar days after the termination of the state of war or national emergency, whichever occurs later.

(Pub. L. 99–662, title IX, § 923, Nov. 17, 1986, 100 Stat. 4194.)

REFERENCES IN TEXT

The National Emergencies Act, referred to in subsec. (a), is Pub. L. 94–412, Sept. 14, 1976, 90 Stat. 1255, as amended, which is classified principally to chapter 34 (§ 1601 et seq.) of Title 50, War and National Defense. For complete classification of this Act to the Code, see Short Title note set out under section 1601 of Title 50 and Tables.

§ 2293a. Reprogramming of funds for projects by Corps of Engineers

None of the funds made available before, on, or after June 15, 2006, in an appropriations Act may be expended to prevent or limit any reprogram-

[1] See References in Text note below.

ming of funds for a project to be carried out by the Corps of Engineers using funds appropriated in any Act making appropriations for energy and water development, based on whether the project was included by the President in the budget transmitted under section 1105(a) of title 31 or is otherwise proposed by the President or considered part of the budget by the Office of Management and Budget, if the project received funds in an Act making appropriations for energy and water development or any other appropriations Act making additional funds available for energy and water development.

(Pub. L. 109–234, title II, §2307, June 15, 2006, 120 Stat. 457.)

CODIFICATION

Section was enacted as part of the Emergency Supplemental Appropriations Act for Defense, the Global War on Terror, and Hurricane Recovery, 2006, and not as part of the Water Resources Development Act of 1986 which comprises this chapter.

§2294. Office of Environmental Policy

The Secretary shall establish in the Directorate of Civil Works of the Office of the Chief of Engineers an Office of Environmental Policy. Such Office shall be responsible for the formulation, coordination, and implementation of all matters concerning environmental quality and policy as they relate to the water resources program of the United States Army Corps of Engineers. Such Office shall, among other things, develop, and monitor compliance with, guidelines for the consideration of environmental quality in formulation and planning of water resources projects carried out by the Secretary, the preparation and coordination of environmental impact statements for such projects, and the coordination with Federal, State, and local agencies of environmental aspects of such projects and regulatory responsibilities of the Secretary.

(Pub. L. 99–662, title IX, §924, Nov. 17, 1986, 100 Stat. 4194.)

§2295. Compilation of laws; annual reports

(a) Federal laws relating to improvements of rivers and harbors, flood control, beach erosion, and other water resources development

Within one year after November 17, 1986, the laws of the United States relating to the improvement of rivers and harbors, flood control, beach erosion, and other water resources development enacted after November 8, 1966, and before January 1, 1987, shall be compiled under the direction of the Secretary and the Chief of Engineers and printed for the use of the Department of the Army, the Congress, and the general public. The Secretary shall reprint the volumes containing such laws enacted before November 8, 1966. In addition, the Secretary shall include an index in each volume so compiled or reprinted. The Secretary shall transmit copies of each such volume to Congress.

(b) Annual report

The Secretary shall prepare and submit the annual report required by section 556 of this title, in two volumes. Volume I shall consist of a summary and highlights of Corps of Engineers' activities, authorities, and accomplishments. Volume II shall consist of detailed information and field reports on Corps of Engineers' activities. The Secretary shall publish an index with each annual report.

(c) Biennial reports for each State

The Secretary shall prepare biennially for public information a report for each State containing a description of each water resources project under the jurisdiction of the Secretary in such State and the status of each such project. Each report shall include an index. The report for each State shall be prepared in a separate volume. The reports under this subsection shall be published at the same time and the first such reports shall be published not later than one year after November 17, 1986.

(Pub. L. 99–662, title IX, §925, Nov. 17, 1986, 100 Stat. 4194.)

COMPILATION OF LAWS

Pub. L. 110–114, title II, §2004, Nov. 8, 2007, 121 Stat. 1071, provided that:

"(a) COMPILATION OF LAWS ENACTED AFTER NOVEMBER 8, 1966.—The Secretary [of the Army] and the Chief of Engineers shall prepare a compilation of the laws of the United States relating to the improvement of rivers and harbors, flood damage reduction, beach and shoreline erosion, hurricane and storm damage reduction, ecosystem and environmental restoration, and other water resources development enacted after November 8, 1966, and before January 1, 2008, and have such compilation printed for the use of the Department of the Army, Congress, and the general public.

"(b) REPRINT OF LAWS ENACTED BEFORE NOVEMBER 8, 1966.—The Secretary shall have the volumes containing the laws referred to in subsection (a) enacted before November 8, 1966, reprinted.

"(c) INDEX.—The Secretary shall include an index in each volume compiled, and each volume reprinted, pursuant to this section.

"(d) CONGRESSIONAL COPIES.—Not later than April 1, 2008, the Secretary shall transmit at least 25 copies of each volume compiled, and of each volume reprinted, pursuant to this section to each of the Committee on Transportation and Infrastructure of the House of Representatives and the Committee on Environment and Public Works of the Senate.

"(e) AVAILABILITY.—The Secretary [of the Army] shall ensure that each volume compiled, and each volume reprinted, pursuant to this section are available through electronic means, including on the Internet."

§2296. Acquisition of recreation lands

(a) In the case of any water resources project which is authorized to be constructed by the Secretary before, on, or after November 17, 1986, construction of which has not commenced before November 17, 1986, and which involves the acquisition of lands or interests in lands for recreation purposes, such lands or interests shall be acquired along with the acquisition of lands and interests in lands for other project purposes.

(b) The Secretary is authorized to acquire real property by condemnation, purchase, donation, exchange, or otherwise, as a part of any water resources development project for use for public park and recreation purposes, including but not limited to, real property not contiguous to the principal part of the project.

(Pub. L. 99–662, title IX, §926, Nov. 17, 1986, 100 Stat. 4195.)

§2297. Operation and maintenance on recreation lands

The Secretary shall not require, under section 460d of title 16, and the Federal Water Project Recreation Act [16 U.S.C. 460*l*–12 et seq.], non-Federal interests to assume operation and maintenance of any recreational facility operated by the Secretary at any water resources project as a condition to the construction of new recreational facilities at such project or any other water resources project.

(Pub. L. 99–662, title IX, §927, Nov. 17, 1986, 100 Stat. 4195.)

REFERENCES IN TEXT

The Federal Water Project Recreation Act, referred to in text, is Pub. L. 89–72, July 9, 1965, 79 Stat. 213, as amended, which is classified principally to part C (§460*l*–12 et seq.) of subchapter LXIX of chapter 1 of Title 16, Conservation. For complete classification of this Act to the Code, see Short Title note set out under section 460*l*–12 of Title 16 and Tables.

§2298. Impact of proposed projects on existing recreation facilities

Any report describing a project having recreation benefits that is submitted after November 17, 1986, to the Committee on Environment and Public Works of the Senate or the Committee on Public Works and Transportation of the House of Representatives by the Secretary, or by the Secretary of Agriculture under authority of the Watershed Protection and Flood Protection Act (68 Stat. 666; 16 U.S.C. 1001 et seq.), shall describe the usage of other, similar public recreational facilities within the general area of the project, and the anticipated impact of the proposed project on the usage of such existing recreational facilities.

(Pub. L. 99–662, title IX, §928, Nov. 17, 1986, 100 Stat. 4195.)

REFERENCES IN TEXT

The Watershed Protection and Flood Prevention Act, referred to in text, is act Aug. 4, 1954, ch. 656, 68 Stat. 666, as amended, which is classified generally to chapter 18 (§1001 et seq.) of Title 16, Conservation. For complete classification of this Act to the Code, see Short Title note set out under section 1001 of Title 16 and Tables.

CHANGE OF NAME

Committee on Public Works and Transportation of House of Representatives treated as referring to Committee on Transportation and Infrastructure of House of Representatives by section 1(a) of Pub. L. 104–14, set out as a note preceding section 21 of Title 2, The Congress.

§2299. Acquisition of beach fill

Notwithstanding any other provision of law, in any case in which the use of fill material for beach erosion and beach nourishment is authorized as a purpose of an authorized water resources project, the Secretary is authorized to acquire by purchase, exchange, or otherwise from nondomestic sources and utilize such material for such purposes if such materials are not available from domestic sources for environmental or economic reasons.

(Pub. L. 99–662, title IX, §935, Nov. 17, 1986, 100 Stat. 4197.)

§2300. Study of Corps capabilities

The Secretary shall study and evaluate the measures necessary to increase the capabilities of the United States Army Corps of Engineers to undertake the planning and construction of water resources projects on an expedited basis and to adequately comply with all requirements of law applicable to the water resources program of the Corps of Engineers. As part of such study the Secretary shall consider appropriate measures to increase reliance on the private sector in the conduct of the water resources program of the Corps of Engineers. The Secretary shall implement such measures as may be necessary to improve the capabilities referred to in the first sentence of this section, including the establishment of increased levels of personnel, changes in project planning and construction procedures designed to lessen the time required for such planning and construction, and procedures for expediting the coordination of water resources projects with Federal, State, and local agencies.

(Pub. L. 99–662, title IX, §936, Nov. 17, 1986, 100 Stat. 4197.)

GAO REVIEW OF CIVIL WORKS PROGRAM

Pub. L. 100–676, §44, Nov. 17, 1988, 102 Stat. 4041, provided that the Comptroller General was to conduct a review of the Civil Works Program of the United States Army Corps of Engineers and to transmit the review to Congress with any recommendations the Comptroller General may make.

§§2301, 2302. Omitted

CODIFICATION

Section 2301, Pub. L. 99–662, title IX, §937, Nov. 17, 1986, 100 Stat. 4198, which required the Secretary of the Army to transmit to certain committees of Congress annual reports on electricity generated by water resource projects constructed by the Secretary and revenues and costs associated with the projects, terminated, effective May 15, 2000, pursuant to section 3003 of Pub. L. 104–66, as amended, set out as a note under section 1113 of Title 31, Money and Finance. See, also, page 72 of House Document No. 103–7.

Subsec. (a) of section 2302, Pub. L. 99–662, title IX, §938(a), Nov. 17, 1986, 100 Stat. 4198, which required the Secretary of the Army to transmit an annual report to certain committees of Congress describing contracts awarded, broken down by Engineer District of the Army Corps of Engineers, including the number and dollar amount of contracts set aside for small business concerns, awarded to small business or small disadvantaged business concerns, available for competition by qualified firms of all sizes, and awarded to other than small business or small disadvantaged business concerns, terminated, effective May 15, 2000, pursuant to section 3003 of Pub. L. 104–66, as amended, set out as a note under section 1113 of Title 31, Money and Finance. See, also, page 69 of House Document No. 103–7.

Subsec. (b) of section 2302, Pub. L. 99–662, title IX, §938(b), Nov. 17, 1986, 100 Stat. 4198, directed the Comptroller General to conduct a study of the contracting procedures of the Secretary of the Army for civil works projects, examining whether potential bidders or offerors, regardless of their size, are allowed to compete fairly in the interest of lowering cost on contracts for construction, and to report findings and recommendations to Congress within two years of Nov. 17, 1986.

§2303. Historical properties

The Secretary is authorized to preserve, restore, and maintain those historic properties located on water resource development project lands under the jurisdiction of the Department of the Army if such properties have been entered into the National Register of Historic Places.

(Pub. L. 99–662, title IX, §943, Nov. 17, 1986, 100 Stat. 4200.)

§2304. Separability

If any provision of this Act, or the application of any provision of this Act to any person or circumstance, is held invalid, the application of such provision to other persons or circumstances, and the remainder of this Act, shall not be affected thereby.

(Pub. L. 99–662, title IX, §949, Nov. 17, 1986, 100 Stat. 4201.)

References in Text

This Act, referred to in text, is Pub. L. 99–662, Nov. 17, 1986, 100 Stat. 4082, as amended, known as the Water Resources Development Act of 1986. For complete classification of this Act to the Code, see Short Title note set out under section 2201 of this title and Tables.

§2305. Use of FMHA funds

Notwithstanding any other provision of law, Federal assistance made available by the Farmers Home Administration may be used to pay the non-Federal share of any other Federal grant-in-aid program for any project for water resources, including water pollution control.

(Pub. L. 99–662, title IX, §950, Nov. 17, 1986, 100 Stat. 4201.)

§2306. Reports

If any report required to be transmitted under this Act to the Committee on Public Works and Transportation of the House of Representatives or the Committee on Environment and Public Works of the Senate pertains in whole or in part to fish and wildlife mitigation, benthic environmental repercussions, or ecosystem mitigation, the Federal officer required to prepare or transmit that report also shall transmit a copy of the report to the Committee on Merchant Marine and Fisheries of the House of Representatives.

(Pub. L. 99–662, title IX, §951, Nov. 17, 1986, 100 Stat. 4201.)

References in Text

This Act, referred to in text, is Pub. L. 99–662, Nov. 17, 1986, 100 Stat. 4082, as amended, known as the Water Resources Development Act of 1986. For complete classification of this Act to the Code, see Short Title note set out under section 2201 of this title and Tables.

Change of Name

Committee on Public Works and Transportation of House of Representatives treated as referring to Committee on Transportation and Infrastructure of House of Representatives by section 1(a) of Pub. L. 104–14, set out as a note preceding section 21 of Title 2, The Congress.

Abolition of House Committee on Merchant Marine and Fisheries

Committee on Merchant Marine and Fisheries of House of Representatives abolished and its jurisdiction transferred by House Resolution No. 6, One Hundred Fourth Congress, Jan. 4, 1995. Committee on Merchant Marine and Fisheries of House of Representatives treated as referring to Committee on Resources of House of Representatives in case of provisions relating to fisheries, wildlife, international fishing agreements, marine affairs (including coastal zone management) except for measures relating to oil and other pollution of navigable waters, or oceanography by section 1(b)(3) of Pub. L. 104–14, set out as a note preceding section 21 of Title 2, The Congress. Committee on Resources of House of Representatives changed to Committee on Natural Resources of House of Representatives by House Resolution No. 6, One Hundred Tenth Congress, Jan. 5, 2007.

§2307. Control of ice

(a) Program authority

The Secretary shall undertake a program of research for the control of ice, and to assist communities in breaking up ice, which otherwise is likely to cause or aggravate flood damage or severe streambank erosion.

(b) Assistance to units of local government

The Secretary is further authorized to provide technical assistance to units of local government to implement local plans to control or break up such ice. As part of such authority, the Secretary shall acquire necessary ice-control or ice-breaking equipment, which shall be loaned to units of local government together with operating assistance, where appropriate.

(c) Authorization of appropriations

There is authorized to be appropriated $5,000,000 per fiscal year for each of the fiscal years 1988, 1989, 1990, 1991, and 1992 for purposes of carrying out subsections (a) and (b) of this section, such sums to remain available until expended.

(d) Hardwick, Vermont, demonstration program

To implement further the purposes of this section, the Secretary, in consultation and cooperation with local officials, is authorized and directed to undertake a demonstration program for the control of ice at Hardwick, Vermont. The work authorized by this subsection shall be designed to minimize the danger of flooding due to ice problems in the vicinity of such community. In the design, construction, and location of ice-control structures for this project, full consideration will be given to the recreational, scenic, and environmental values of the reach of river affected by the project, in order to minimize project impacts on these values. Full opportunity shall be given to interested environmental and recreational organizations to participate in such planning. There is authorized to be appropriated $900,000 for fiscal years beginning after September 30, 1986, for the purposes of carrying out this subsection, such sum to remain available until expended.

(e) Salmon, Idaho, experimental program

(1) The Secretary is directed to complete an experimental program placing screens in the Salmon River in the vicinity of Salmon, Idaho, to trap frazil ice, and thus to eliminate flooding caused by ice dams in the river. Within one year of November 17, 1986, the Secretary shall report to the Congress on the feasibility of such experiment, including consideration of any adverse environmental or social effects that could result from such experiment. If, in the Secretary's

judgment, such experiment is not feasible or acceptable, the Secretary is authorized to consult with local public interests to develop a plan that is workable and practical, and then to submit such plan to Congress.

(2) There is authorized to be appropriated $1,000,000 for fiscal years beginning after September 30, 1986, for purposes of carrying out this subsection, such sum to remain available until expended.

(f) Wilmington, Illinois, project

(1) To implement further the purposes of this section, the Secretary shall carry out a project for the control of ice on the Kankakee River in the vicinity of Wilmington, Illinois. The Secretary shall report to Congress not later than one year after November 17, 1986, and annually thereafter on the effectiveness of the program under this section with respect to the Kankakee River in the vicinity of Wilmington, Illinois.

(2) There is authorized to be appropriated $3,000,000 for fiscal years beginning after September 30, 1986, for purposes of carrying out this subsection, such sum to remain available until expended.

(g) Cost sharing

Cost sharing applicable to flood control projects under section 2213 of this title shall apply to projects under this section.

(h) Report to Congress

Not later than March 1, 1989, the Secretary shall report to the Congress on activities under this section.

(Pub. L. 99–662, title XI, § 1101, Nov. 17, 1986, 100 Stat. 4223.)

TERMINATION OF REPORTING REQUIREMENTS

For termination, effective May 15, 2000, of provisions in subsec. (f)(1) of this section relating to the requirement that the Secretary report annually to Congress on the effectiveness of the program under this section, see section 3003 of Pub. L. 104–66, as amended, set out as a note under section 1113 of Title 31, Money and Finance, and page 71 of House Document No. 103–7.

§ 2308. Campgrounds for senior citizens

(a) Establishment and development

The Secretary may establish and develop separate campgrounds for individuals sixty-two years of age or older at any lake or reservoir under the jurisdiction of the Secretary where camping is permitted.

(b) Control of campground use and access

The Secretary may prescribe regulations to control the use of and the access to any separate campground established and developed under subsection (a) of this section.

(c) Authorization of appropriations

There are authorized to be appropriated such sums as may be necessary for fiscal years beginning after September 30, 1986, to carry out subsection (a) of this section.

(d) Campground at Sam Rayburn Dam and Reservoir, Texas

The Secretary shall establish and develop the parcel of land (located in the State of Texas at the Sam Rayburn Dam and Reservoir) described in subsection (g) of this section as a separate campground for individuals sixty-two years of age or older.

(e) Control of use and access to campground at Sam Rayburn Dam and Reservoir, Texas

The Secretary shall prescribe regulations to control the use of and the access to the separate campground established and developed pursuant to subsection (d) of this section.

(f) Authorization of appropriations

There are authorized to be appropriated for fiscal years beginning after September 30, 1986, $600,000 to carry out subsection (d) of this section.

(g) Boundaries of campground at Sam Rayburn Dam and Reservoir, Texas

The parcel of land to be established and developed as a separate campground pursuant to subsection (d) of this section is a tract of land of approximately 50 acres which is located in the county of Angelina in the State of Texas and which is part of the Thomas Hanks survey. The boundary of the parcel begins at a point at the corner furthest west of tract numbered 3420 of the Sam Rayburn Dam and Reservoir:

thence north 81 degrees 30 minutes east, approximately 2,800 feet to a point at the edge of the water;

thence south along the edge of the water approximately 2,600 feet;

thence north 80 degrees 30 minutes west, approximately 1,960 feet to a point at the reentrant corner of tract numbered 3419 of the Sam Rayburn Dam and Reservoir;

thence along the boundary line of tract numbered 3419 north 46 degrees 15 minutes west, 220 feet to a point at the center line of a road at the corner common to tract numbered 3419 and tract numbered 3420;

thence along the southwestern boundary line of tract numbered 3420 north 46 degrees 15 minutes west, 230 feet to a point at the corner furthest east of tract numbered 3424 of the Sam Rayburn Dam and Reservoir;

thence along the boundary line of tract numbered 3424 south 32 degrees 4 minutes west, 420 feet to a point;

thence along the boundary line of tract numbered 3424 north 28 degrees 34 minutes west, 170 feet to a point;

thence along the boundary line of tract numbered 3424 north 38 degrees 15 minutes east, 248 feet to a point;

thence along the boundary line of tract numbered 3424 north 32 degrees 44 minutes east, 120 feet to a point at the corner furthest north of tract numbered 3424;

thence along the southwestern boundary line of tract numbered 3420 north 46 degrees 15 minutes west, 460 feet to the beginning point.

(Pub. L. 99–662, title XI, § 1127, Nov. 17, 1986, 100 Stat. 4245.)

§ 2309. Great Lakes Commodities Marketing Board

(a) Congressional declaration of purpose

To ensure the coordinated economic revitalization and environmental enhancement of the

Great Lakes and their connecting channels and the Saint Lawrence Seaway (hereinafter in this section referred to as the "Great Lakes"), known as the "Fourth Seacoast" of the United States, it is hereby declared to be the intent of Congress to recognize the importance of the economic vitality of the Great Lakes region, the importance of exports from the region in the United States balance of trade, and the need to assure an environmentally and socially responsible navigation system for the Great Lakes. Congress finds that the Great Lakes provide a diversity of agricultural, commercial, environmental, recreational, and related opportunities based on their extensive water resources and water transportation systems.

(b) Establishment; strategy development; composition of Board; Director; report; termination

(1) There is hereby established a Board to be known as the Great Lakes Commodities Marketing Board (hereinafter in this subsection referred to as the "Board").

(2)(A) The Board shall develop a strategy to improve the capacity of the Great Lakes region to produce, market, and transport commodities in a timely manner and to maximize the efficiency and benefits of marketing products produced in the Great Lakes region and products shipped through the Great Lakes.

(B) The strategy shall address, among other things, environmental issues relating to transportation on the Great Lakes and marketing difficulties experienced due to late harvest seasons in the Great Lakes region. The strategy shall include, as appropriate alternative storage, sales, marketing, multimodal transportation systems, and other systems, to assure optimal economic benefits to the region from agricultural and other commercial activities. The strategy shall develop—

(i) methods to improve and promote both bulk and general cargo trade through Great Lakes ports;

(ii) methods to accelerate the movement of grains and other agricultural commodities through the Great Lakes;

(iii) methods to provide needed flexibility to farmers in the Great Lakes region to market grains and other agricultural commodities; and

(iv) methods and materials to promote trade from the Great Lakes region and through Great Lakes ports, particularly with European, Mediterranean, African, Caribbean, Central American, and South American nations.

(C) In developing the strategy, the Board shall conduct and consider the results of—

(i) an analysis of the feasibility and costs of using iron ore vessels, which are not being utilized, to move grain and other agricultural commodities on the Great Lakes;

(ii) an economic analysis of transshipping such commodities through Montreal, Canada, and other ports;

(iii) an analysis of the economic feasibility of storing such commodities during the non-navigation season of the Great Lakes and the feasibility of and need for construction of new storage facilities for such commodities;

(iv) an analysis of the constraints on the flexibility of farmers in the Great Lakes region to market grains and other agricultural commodities, including harvest dates for such commodities and the availability of transport and storage facilities for such commodities; and

(v) an analysis of the amount of grain and other agricultural commodities produced in the United States which are being diverted to Canada by rail but which could be shipped on the Great Lakes if vessels were available for shipping such products during the navigation season.

(D) In developing the strategy, the Board shall consider weather problems and related costs and marketing problems resulting from the late harvest of agricultural commodities (including wheat and sunflower seeds) in the Great Lakes region.

(E) In developing the strategy, the Board shall consult United States ports on the Great Lakes and their users, including farm organizations (such as wheat growers and soybean growers), port authorities, water carrier organizations, and other interested persons.

(3) The Board shall be composed of seven members as follows:

(A) the chairman of the Great Lakes Commission or his or her delegate,

(B) the Secretary or his or her delegate,

(C) the Secretary of Transportation or his or her delegate,

(D) the Secretary of Commerce or his or her delegate,

(E) the Administrator of the Saint Lawrence Seaway Development Corporation or his or her delegate,

(F) the Secretary of Agriculture or his or her delegate, and

(G) the Administrator of the Environmental Protection Agency or his or her delegate.

(4)(A) Members of the Board shall serve for the life of the Board.

(B) Members of the Board shall serve without pay and those members who are full time officers or employees of the United States shall receive no additional pay by reason of their service on the Board, except that members of the Board shall be allowed travel or transportation expenses under subchapter I of chapter 57 of title 5 while away from their homes or regular places of business and engaged in the actual performance of duties vested in the Board.

(C) Four members of the Board shall constitute a quorum but a lesser number may hold hearings.

(D) The co-chairmen of the Board shall be the Secretary or his or her delegate and the Administrator of the Saint Lawrence Seaway Development Corporation or his or her delegate.

(E) The Board shall meet at the call of the co-chairmen or a majority of its members.

(5)(A) The Board shall, without regard to section 5311(b) [1] of title 5, have a Director, who shall be appointed by the Board and shall be paid at a rate which the Board considers appropriate.

(B) Subject to such rules as may be prescribed by the Board, without regard to 5311(b) [1] of title

[1] See References in Text note below.

5, the Board may appoint and fix the pay of such additional personnel as the Board considers appropriate.

(C) Upon request of the Board, the head of any Federal agency is authorized to detail, on a reimbursable basis, any of the personnel of such agency to the Board to assist the Board in carrying out its duties under this subsection.

(6)(A) The Board may, for purposes of carrying out this subsection, hold such hearings, sit and act at such times and places, take such testimony, and receive such evidence, as the Board considers appropriate.

(B) Any member or agent of the Board may, if so authorized by the Board, take any action which the Board is authorized to take by this paragraph.

(C) The Board may secure directly from any department or agency of the United States any information necessary to enable it to carry out this subsection. Upon request of the co-chairmen of the Board, the head of such department or agency shall furnish such information to the Board.

(D) The Board may use the United States mail in the same manner and under the same conditions as other departments and agencies of the United States.

(E) The Administrator of General Services shall provide to the Board on a reimbursable basis such administrative support services as the Board may request.

(7) Not later than September 30, 1989, the Board shall transmit to the President and to each House of the Congress a report stating the strategy developed under this subsection and the results of each analysis conducted under this subsection. Such report shall contain a detailed statement of the findings and conclusions of the Board together with its recommendations for such legislative and administrative actions as it considers appropriate to carry out such strategy and to assure maximum economic benefits to the users of the Great Lakes and to the Great Lakes region.

(8) The Board shall cease to exist 180 days after submitting its report pursuant to this subsection.

(9) The non-Federal share of the cost of carrying out this subsection shall be 25 percent. There is authorized to be appropriated such sums as may be necessary to carry out the Federal share of this subsection for fiscal years beginning after September 30, 1986, and ending before October 1, 1990.

(c) International advisory group

(1) The President shall invite the Government of Canada to join in the formation of an international advisory group whose duty it shall be (A) to develop a bilateral program for improving navigation, through a coordinated strategy, on the Great Lakes, and (B) to conduct investigations on a continuing basis and make recommendations for a system-wide navigation improvement program to facilitate optimum use of the Great Lakes. The advisory group shall be composed of five members representing the United States, five members representing Canada, and two members from the International Joint Commission established by the treaty between the United States and Great Britain relating to boundary waters between the United States and Canada, signed at Washington, January 11, 1909 (36 Stat. 2448). The five members representing the United States shall include the Secretary of State, one member of the Great Lakes Commodities Marketing Board (as designated by the Board), and three individuals appointed by the President representing commercial, shipping, and environmental interests, respectively.

(2) The United States representatives to the international advisory group shall serve without pay and the United States representatives to the advisory group who are full time officers or employees of the United States shall receive no additional pay by reason of their service on the advisory group, except that the United States representatives shall be allowed travel or transportation expenses under subchapter I of chapter 57 of title 5 while away from their homes or regular place of business and engaged in the actual performance of duties vested in the advisory group.

(3) The international advisory group established by this subsection shall report to Congress and to the Canadian Parliament on its progress in carrying out the duties set forth in this subsection not later than one year after the formation of such group and biennially thereafter.

(d) Review of environmental, economic, and social impacts of navigation in United States portion of Great Lakes

The Secretary and the Administrator of the Environmental Protection Agency, in cooperation with the Secretary of the Interior, the Administrator of the National Oceanic and Atmospheric Administration, and other appropriate Federal and non-Federal entities, shall carry out a review of the environmental, economic, and social impacts of navigation in the United States portion of the Great Lakes. In carrying out such review, the Secretary and the Administrator shall use existing research, studies, and investigations relating to such impacts to the maximum extent possible. Special emphasis shall be made in such review of the impacts of navigation on the shoreline and on fish and wildlife habitat, including, but not limited to, impacts associated with resuspension of bottom sediment. The Secretary and the Administrator shall submit to Congress an interim report of such review not later than September 30, 1988, and a final report of such review along with recommendations not later than September 30, 1990.

(Pub. L. 99–662, title XI, § 1132, Nov. 17, 1986, 100 Stat. 4246.)

REFERENCES IN TEXT

Section 5311(b) of title 5, referred to in subsec. (b)(5)(A), (B), was repealed by Pub. L. 101–509, title V, § 529 [title I, § 104(c)(1)], Nov. 5, 1990, 104 Stat. 1427, 1447.

TERMINATION OF REPORTING REQUIREMENTS

For termination, effective May 15, 2000, of provisions in subsec. (c)(3) of this section relating to the requirement that the international advisory group report biennially to Congress, see section 3003 of Pub. L. 104–66, as amended, set out as a note under section 1113 of Title 31, Money and Finance, and page 193 of House Document No. 103–7.

§2309a. Project modifications for improvement of environment

(a) Determination of need

The Secretary is authorized to review water resources projects constructed by the Secretary to determine the need for modifications in the structures and operations of such projects for the purpose of improving the quality of the environment in the public interest and to determine if the operation of such projects has contributed to the degradation of the quality of the environment.

(b) Authority to make modifications

The Secretary is authorized to carry out a program for the purpose of making such modifications in the structures and operations of water resources projects constructed by the Secretary which the Secretary determines (1) are feasible and consistent with the authorized project purposes, and (2) will improve the quality of the environment in the public interest.

(c) Restoration of environmental quality

(1) In general

If the Secretary determines that construction of a water resources project by the Secretary or operation of a water resources project constructed by the Secretary has contributed to the degradation of the quality of the environment, the Secretary may undertake measures for restoration of environmental quality and measures for enhancement of environmental quality that are associated with the restoration, through modifications either at the project site or at other locations that have been affected by the construction or operation of the project, if such measures do not conflict with the authorized project purposes.

(2) Control of sea lamprey

Congress finds that—

(A) the Great Lakes navigation system has been instrumental in the spread of sea lamprey and the associated impacts on its fishery; and

(B) the use of the authority under this subsection for control of sea lamprey at any Great Lakes basin location is appropriate.

(d) Non-Federal share; limitation on maximum Federal expenditure

The non-Federal share of the cost of any modifications or measures carried out or undertaken pursuant to subsection (b) or (c) of this section shall be 25 percent. Not more than 80 percent of the non-Federal share may be in kind, including a facility, supply, or service that is necessary to carry out the modification or measure. Not more than $5,000,000 in Federal funds may be expended on any single modification or measure carried out or undertaken pursuant to this section.

(e) Coordination of actions

The Secretary shall coordinate any actions taken pursuant to this section with appropriate Federal, State, and local agencies.

(f) Omitted

(g) Nonprofit entities

Notwithstanding section 1962d–5b of title 42, a non-Federal sponsor for any project carried out under this section may include a nonprofit entity, with the consent of the affected local government.

(h) Authorization of appropriations

There is authorized to be appropriated not to exceed $40,000,000 annually to carry out this section.

(i) Definition

In this section, the term "water resources project constructed by the Secretary" includes a water resources project constructed or funded jointly by the Secretary and the head of any other Federal agency (including the Natural Resources Conservation Service).

(Pub. L. 99–662, title XI, §1135, Nov. 17, 1986, 100 Stat. 4251; Pub. L. 100–676, §41, Nov. 17, 1988, 102 Stat. 4040; Pub. L. 101–640, title III, §304, Nov. 28, 1990, 104 Stat. 4634; Pub. L. 102–580, title II, §202, Oct. 31, 1992, 106 Stat. 4826; Pub. L. 104–303, title II, §204, Oct. 12, 1996, 110 Stat. 3678; Pub. L. 106–53, title V, §506, Aug. 17, 1999, 113 Stat. 338; Pub. L. 106–541, title II, §210(c), Dec. 11, 2000, 114 Stat. 2592; Pub. L. 110–114, title II, §2024, Nov. 8, 2007, 121 Stat. 1079.)

CODIFICATION

Subsec. (f) of this section, which required the Secretary to transmit biennial reports to Congress on the results of reviews conducted under subsec. (a) of this section and on the programs conducted under subsecs. (b) and (c) of this section, terminated, effective May 15, 2000, pursuant to section 3003 of Pub. L. 104–66, as amended, set out as a note under section 1113 of Title 31, Money and Finance. See, also, page 72 of House Document No. 103–7.

Section was formerly set out as a note under section 2294 of this title.

AMENDMENTS

2007—Subsec. (h). Pub. L. 110–114 substituted "$40,000,000" for "$25,000,000".

2000—Subsecs. (g) to (i). Pub. L. 106–541 added subsec. (g) and redesignated former subsecs. (g) and (h) as (h) and (i), respectively.

1999—Subsec. (c). Pub. L. 106–53 designated existing provisions as par. (1), inserted heading, and added par. (2).

1996—Subsec. (a). Pub. L. 104–303, §204(a), struck out "the operation of" after "to review" and inserted before period at end "and to determine if the operation of such projects has contributed to the degradation of the quality of the environment".

Subsec. (b). Pub. L. 104–303, §204(b), struck out at end "The non-Federal share of the cost of any modifications carried out under this section shall be 25 percent. No modification shall be carried out under this section without specific authorization by Congress if the estimated cost exceeds $5,000,000."

Subsecs. (c), (d). Pub. L. 104–303, §204(c)(2), added subsecs. (c) and (d). Former subsecs. (c) and (d) redesignated (e) and (f), respectively.

Subsec. (e). Pub. L. 104–303, §204(c)(1), redesignated subsec. (c) as (e). Former subsec. (e) redesignated (g).

Subsec. (f). Pub. L. 104–303, §204(c)(1), (3), redesignated subsec. (d) as (f) and substituted "programs conducted under subsections (b) and (c) of this section" for "program conducted under subsection (b) of this section".

Subsec. (g). Pub. L. 104–303, §204(c)(1), redesignated subsec. (e) as (g).

Subsec. (h). Pub. L. 104–303, §204(d), added subsec. (h).

1992—Subsec. (b). Pub. L. 102–580, §202(1), inserted at end "No modification shall be carried out under this section without specific authorization by Congress if the estimated cost exceeds $5,000,000."

Subsec. (e). Pub. L. 102–580, § 202(2), substituted "$25,000,000" for "$15,000,000".

1990—Subsec. (a). Pub. L. 101–640, § 304(a), struck out "before the date of enactment of this Act" after "constructed by the Secretary".

Subsec. (b). Pub. L. 101–640, § 304(b), substituted "program" for "demonstration program in the 5-year period beginning on the date of enactment of this Act" and struck out "before the date of enactment of this Act" after "constructed by the Secretary".

Subsec. (d). Pub. L. 101–640, § 304(c), amended subsec. (d) generally. Prior to amendment, subsec. (d) read as follows: "Not later than 5 years after the date of enactment of this Act, the Secretary shall transmit to Congress a report on the results of the review conducted under subsection (a) and on the demonstration program conducted under subsection (b). Such report shall contain any recommendations of the Secretary concerning modification and extension of such program."

Subsec. (e). Pub. L. 101–640, § 304(d), substituted "$15,000,000 annually to carry out this section" for "$25,000,000 to carry out this section".

1988—Subsec. (b). Pub. L. 100–676, § 41(a), substituted "5-year period" for "two-year period".

Subsec. (d). Pub. L. 100–676, § 41(b), substituted "5 years" for "two years".

§ 2310. Cost sharing for Territories

The Secretary shall waive local cost-sharing requirements up to $200,000 for all studies and projects in American Samoa, Guam, the Northern Mariana Islands, the Virgin Islands, and the Trust Territory of the Pacific Islands.

(Pub. L. 99–662, title XI, § 1156, Nov. 17, 1986, 100 Stat. 4256.)

TERMINATION OF TRUST TERRITORY OF THE PACIFIC ISLANDS

For termination of Trust Territory of the Pacific Islands, see note set out preceding section 1681 of Title 48, Territories and Insular Possessions.

§ 2311. Report to Congress covering proposals for water impoundment facilities

Any report that is submitted to the Committee on Environment and Public Works of the Senate or the Committee on Public Works and Transportation of the House of Representatives by the Secretary, or the Secretary of Agriculture acting under Public Law 83–566, as amended [16 U.S.C. 1001 et seq.], which proposes construction of a water impoundment facility, shall include information on the consequences of failure and geologic or design factors which could contribute to the possible failure of such facility.

(Pub. L. 99–662, title XII, § 1202, Nov. 17, 1986, 100 Stat. 4263.)

REFERENCES IN TEXT

Public Law 83–566, as amended, referred to in text, is act Aug. 4, 1954, ch. 656, 68 Stat. 666, as amended, known as the Watershed Protection and Flood Prevention Act, which is classified generally to chapter 18 (§ 1001 et seq.) of Title 16, Conservation. For complete classification of this Act to the Code, see Short Title note set out under section 1001 of Title 16 and Tables.

CHANGE OF NAME

Committee on Public Works and Transportation of House of Representatives treated as referring to Committee on Transportation and Infrastructure of House of Representatives by section 1(a) of Pub. L. 104–14, set out as a note preceding section 21 of Title 2, The Congress.

§ 2312. Comments on certain changes in operations of reservoirs

Before the Secretary may make changes in the operation of any reservoir which will result in or require a reallocation of storage space in such reservoir or will significantly affect any project purpose, the Secretary shall provide an opportunity for public review and comment.

(Pub. L. 100–676, § 5, Nov. 17, 1988, 102 Stat. 4022.)

CODIFICATION

Section was enacted as part of the Water Resources Development Act of 1988, and not as part of the Water Resources Development Act of 1986 which comprises this chapter.

"SECRETARY" DEFINED

Secretary means the Secretary of the Army, see section 2 of Pub. L. 100–676, set out as a note under section 2201 of this title.

§ 2313. Collaborative research and development

(a) In general

For the purpose of improving the state of engineering and construction in the United States and consistent with the civil works mission of the Army Corps of Engineers, the Secretary is authorized to utilize Army Corps of Engineers laboratories and research centers to undertake, on a cost-shared basis, collaborative research and development with non-Federal entities, including State and local government, colleges and universities, and corporations, partnerships, sole proprietorships, and trade associations which are incorporated or established under the laws of any of the several States of the United States or the District of Columbia.

(b) Pre-agreement temporary protection of technology

(1) In general

If the Secretary determines that information developed as a result of research and development activities conducted by the Corps of Engineers is likely to be subject to a cooperative research and development agreement within 2 years of its development and that such information would be a trade secret or commercial or financial information that would be privileged or confidential if the information had been obtained from a non-Federal party participating in a cooperative research and development agreement under section 12 of the Stevenson-Wydler Technology Innovation Act of 1980 (15 U.S.C. 3710a), the Secretary may provide appropriate protection against the dissemination of such information, including exemption from subchapter II of chapter 5 of title 5, until the earlier of the date the Secretary enters into such an agreement with respect to such technology or the last day of the 2-year period beginning on the date of such determination.

(2) Treatment

Any technology covered by this section that becomes the subject of a cooperative research and development agreement shall be accorded the protection provided under section 12(c)(7)(B) of such Act (15 U.S.C. 3710a(c)(7)(B)) as if such technology had been developed under a cooperative research and development agreement.

(c) Administrative provisions

In carrying out this section, the Secretary may consider the recommendations of a non-Federal entity in identifying appropriate research or development projects and may enter into a cooperative research and development agreement, as defined in section 12 of the Stevenson-Wydler Technology Innovation Act of 1980 (15 U.S.C. 3710a); except that in such agreement, the Secretary may agree to provide not more than 50 percent of the cost of any research or development project selected by the Secretary under this section. Not less than 5 percent of the non-Federal entity's share of the cost of any such project shall be paid in cash.

(d) Applicability of other laws

The research, development, or utilization of any technology pursuant to an agreement under subsection (c) of this section, including the terms under which such technology may be licensed and the resulting royalties may be distributed, shall be subject to the provisions of the Stevenson-Wydler Technology Innovation Act of 1980 (15 U.S.C. 3701–3714).

(e) Authorization of appropriations

To carry out the purposes of this section, there is authorized to be appropriated to the Secretary of the Army civil works funds $3,000,000 for fiscal year 1989, $4,000,000 for fiscal year 1990, $5,000,000 for fiscal year 1991, and $6,000,000 for each fiscal year thereafter.

(f) Funding from other Federal sources

The Secretary may accept and expend additional funds from other Federal programs, including other Department of Defense programs, to carry out this section.

(Pub. L. 100–676, §7, Nov. 17, 1988, 102 Stat. 4022; Pub. L. 104–303, title II, §214, Oct. 12, 1996, 110 Stat. 3684.)

REFERENCES IN TEXT

The Stevenson-Wydler Technology Innovation Act of 1980, referred to in subsec. (d), is Pub. L. 96–480, Oct. 21, 1980, 94 Stat. 2311, as amended, which is classified generally to chapter 63 (§3701 et seq.) of Title 15, Commerce and Trade. For complete classification of this Act to the Code, see Short Title note set out under section 3701 of Title 15 and Tables.

CODIFICATION

Section was enacted as part of the Water Resources Development Act of 1988, and not as part of the Water Resources Development Act of 1986 which comprises this chapter.

AMENDMENTS

1996—Subsec. (a). Pub. L. 104–303, §214(a)(1), inserted "civil works" before "mission".

Subsecs. (b), (c). Pub. L. 104–303, §214(b)(1), (2), added subsec. (b) and redesignated former subsec. (b) as (c). Former subsec. (c) redesignated (d).

Subsec. (d). Pub. L. 104–303, §214(b)(1), (3), redesignated subsec. (c) as (d) and substituted "subsection (c)" for "subsection (b)". Former subsec. (d) redesignated (e).

Subsec. (e). Pub. L. 104–303, §214(b)(1), redesignated subsec. (d) as (e). Former subsec. (e) redesignated (f).

Pub. L. 104–303, §214(a)(2), added subsec. (e) and struck out heading and text of former subsec. (e). Text read as follows: "Notwithstanding the third proviso under the heading 'GENERAL INVESTIGATIONS' of title I of the Energy and Water Development Appropriations Act, 1989 (102 Stat. 857), an additional $3,000,000 of the funds appropriated under such heading shall be available to the Secretary for obligation to carry out the purposes of this section in fiscal year 1989."

Subsec. (f). Pub. L. 104–303, §214(b)(1), redesignated subsec. (e) as (f).

MAGNETIC LEVITATION TECHNOLOGY

Pub. L. 101–640, title IV, §417, Nov. 28, 1990, 104 Stat. 4652, provided that:

"(a) RESEARCH AND DEVELOPMENT.—The Secretary is authorized, in cooperation with the Secretary of Transportation, to conduct research and development activities on magnetic levitation technology or to provide for such research and development.

"(b) COLLABORATION.—The Secretary is authorized to collaborate with non-Federal entities (including State and local governments, colleges and universities, and corporations, partnerships, sole proprietorships, and trade associations which are incorporated or established under laws of a State or the District of Columbia) in carrying out research and development on magnetic levitation technology.

"(c) COOPERATIVE RESEARCH CONTRACTS.—In carrying out this section, the Secretary may enter into contracts or cooperative research and development agreements under section 12 of the Stevenson-Wydler Technology Innovation Act of 1980 (15 U.S.C. 3710a), except that the Secretary may fund up to 50 percent of the cost of each collaborative research and development project undertaken.

"(d) LICENSING OF RESEARCH AND DEVELOPMENT.—The research, development, and use of any technology developed under an agreement entered into pursuant to this section, including the terms under which such technology may be licensed and the resulting royalties may be distributed, shall be subject to the provisions of the Stevenson-Wydler Technology Innovation Act of 1980 (15 U.S.C. 3701–3714). In addition, the Secretary may require the non-Federal entity to certify that such research and development will be performed substantially in the United States and that products embodying inventions made under an agreement entered into pursuant to this section or produced through the use of such inventions will be manufactured substantially in the United States.

"(e) AUTHORIZATION OF APPROPRIATIONS.—For purposes of carrying out this section, there is authorized to be appropriated $1,000,000 for fiscal year 1990 and $4,000,000 for fiscal year 1991. Such funds shall remain available until expended. No funds are authorized to be appropriated under this section for any fiscal year beginning after September 30, 1991."

"SECRETARY" DEFINED

Secretary means the Secretary of the Army, see section 2 of Pub. L. 100–676, set out as a note under section 2201 of this title.

§2313a. Engineering and environmental innovations of national significance

(a) Surveys, plans, and studies

To encourage innovative and environmentally sound engineering solutions and innovative environmental solutions to problems of national significance, the Secretary may undertake surveys, plans, and studies and prepare reports that may lead to work under existing civil works authorities or to recommendations for authorizations.

(b) Funding

(1) Authorization of appropriations

There is authorized to be appropriated to carry out this section $1,000,000 for each of fiscal years 1997 through 2000.

(2) Funding from other sources

The Secretary may accept and expend additional funds from other Federal agencies, States, or non-Federal entities for purposes of carrying out this section.

(Pub. L. 104–303, title II, §212, Oct. 12, 1996, 110 Stat. 3684.)

CODIFICATION

Section was enacted as part of the Water Resources Development Act of 1996, and not as part of the Water Resources Development Act of 1986 which comprises this chapter.

"SECRETARY" DEFINED

Secretary means the Secretary of the Army, see section 2 of Pub. L. 104–303, set out as a note under section 2201 of this title.

§2313b. Support of Army civil works program

(a) General authority

In carrying out research and development in support of the civil works program of the Department of the Army, the Secretary may utilize contracts, cooperative research and development agreements, cooperative agreements, and grants with non-Federal entities, including State and local governments, colleges and universities, consortia, professional and technical societies, public and private scientific and technical foundations, research institutions, educational organizations, and nonprofit organizations.

(b) Commercial application

With respect to contracts for research and development, the Secretary may include requirements that have potential commercial application and may use such potential application as an evaluation factor where appropriate.

(Pub. L. 104–303, title II, §229, Oct. 12, 1996, 110 Stat. 3703.)

CODIFICATION

Section was enacted as part of the Water Resources Development Act of 1996, and not as part of the Water Resources Development Act of 1986 which comprises this chapter.

"SECRETARY" DEFINED

Secretary means the Secretary of the Army, see section 2 of Pub. L. 104–303, set out as a note under section 2201 of this title.

§2314. Innovative technology

(a) Use

The Secretary shall, whenever feasible, seek to promote long- and short-term cost savings, increased efficiency, reliability, and safety, and improved environmental results through the use of innovative technology in all phases of water resources development projects and programs under the Secretary's jurisdiction. To further this goal, Congress encourages the Secretary to—

(1) use procurement and contracting procedures that encourage innovative project design, construction, rehabilitation, repair, and operation and maintenance technologies;

(2) frequently review technical and design criteria to remove or modify unnecessary impediments to innovation;

(3) increase timely exchange of technical information with universities, private companies, government agencies, and individuals;

(4) foster design competition; and

(5) encourage greater participation by non-Federal project sponsors in the development and implementation of projects.

(b) Accelerated adoption of innovative technologies for management of contaminated sediments

(1) Test projects

The Secretary shall approve an appropriate number of projects to test, under actual field conditions, innovative technologies for environmentally sound management of contaminated sediments.

(2) Demonstration projects

The Secretary may approve an appropriate number of projects to demonstrate innovative technologies that have been pilot tested under paragraph (1).

(3) Conduct of projects

Each pilot project under paragraph (1) and demonstration project under paragraph (2) shall be conducted by a university with proven expertise in the research and development of contaminated sediment treatment technologies and innovative applications using waste materials.

(4) Location

At least 1 of the projects under this subsection shall be conducted in New England by the University of New Hampshire.

(c) Reports

Within 2 years after November 17, 1988, and thereafter at the Secretary's discretion, the Secretary shall provide Congress with a report on the results of, and recommendations to increase, the development and use of innovative technology in water resources development projects under the Secretary's jurisdiction. Such report shall also contain information regarding innovative technologies which the Secretary has considered and rejected for use in water resources development projects under the Secretary's jurisdiction.

(d) "Innovative technology" defined

For the purpose of this section, the term "innovative technology" means designs, materials, or methods which the Secretary determines are previously undemonstrated or are too new to be considered standard practice.

(Pub. L. 100–676, §8, Nov. 17, 1988, 102 Stat. 4023; Pub. L. 106–53, title V, §503(b), Aug. 17, 1999, 113 Stat. 337.)

CODIFICATION

Section was enacted as part of the Water Resources Development Act of 1988, and not as part of the Water

Resources Development Act of 1986 which comprises this chapter.

AMENDMENTS

1999—Subsecs. (b) to (d). Pub. L. 106–53 added subsec. (b) and redesignated former subsecs. (b) and (c) as (c) and (d), respectively.

DESIGN-BUILD CONTRACTING

Pub. L. 106–541, title II, §221, Dec. 11, 2000, 114 Stat. 2596, provided that:

"(a) PILOT PROGRAM.—The Secretary [of the Army] may conduct a pilot program consisting of not more than 5 authorized projects to test the design-build method of project delivery on various authorized civil works projects of the Corps of Engineers, including levees, pumping plants, revetments, dikes, dredging, weirs, dams, retaining walls, generation facilities, mattress laying, recreation facilities, and other water resources facilities.

"(b) DESIGN-BUILD DEFINED.—In this section, the term 'design-build' means an agreement between the Federal Government and a contractor that provides for both the design and construction of a project by a single contract.

"(c) REPORT.—Not later than 4 years after the date of enactment of this Act [Dec. 11, 2000], the Secretary shall transmit to Congress a report on the results of the pilot program."

REVIEW OF INNOVATIVE DREDGING TECHNOLOGIES

Pub. L. 106–53, title V, §503(a), Aug. 17, 1999, 113 Stat. 337, provided that:

"(1) IN GENERAL.—Not later than June 1, 2001, the Secretary shall complete a review of innovative dredging technologies designed to minimize or eliminate contamination of a water column upon removal of contaminated sediments.

"(2) TESTING.—

"(A) SELECTION OF TECHNOLOGY.—After completion of the review under paragraph (1), the Secretary shall select, from among the technologies reviewed, the technology that the Secretary determines will best increase the effectiveness of removing contaminated sediments and significantly reduce contamination of the water column.

"(B) AGREEMENT.—Not later than December 31, 2001, the Secretary shall enter into an agreement with a public or private entity to test the selected technology in the vicinity of Peoria Lakes, Illinois.

"(3) AUTHORIZATION OF APPROPRIATIONS.—There is authorized to be appropriated to carry out this subsection $2,000,000."

BENEFICIAL USE OF WASTE TIRE RUBBER

Pub. L. 106–53, title V, §561, Aug. 17, 1999, 113 Stat. 355, provided that:

"(a) IN GENERAL.—The Secretary shall, when appropriate, encourage the beneficial use of waste tire rubber (including crumb rubber and baled tire products) recycled from tires.

"(b) INCLUDED BENEFICIAL USES.—Beneficial uses under subsection (a) may include marine pilings, underwater framing, floating docks with built-in flotation, utility poles, and other uses associated with transportation and infrastructure projects receiving Federal funds.

"(c) USE OF WASTE TIRE RUBBER.—The Secretary shall encourage the use, when appropriate, of waste tire rubber (including crumb rubber) in projects described in subsection (b)."

"SECRETARY" DEFINED

Secretary means the Secretary of the Army, see section 2 of Pub. L. 100–676, set out as a note under section 2201 of this title.

§2314a. Technical assistance program

(a) In general

The Secretary is authorized to provide technical assistance, on a nonexclusive basis, to any United States firm which is competing for, or has been awarded, a contract for the planning, design, or construction of a project outside the United States, if the United States firm provides, in advance of fiscal obligation by the United States, funds to cover all costs of such assistance. In determining whether to provide such assistance, the Secretary shall consider the effects on the Department of the Army civil works mission, personnel, and facilities. Prior to the Secretary providing such assistance, a United States firm must—

(1) certify to the Secretary that such assistance is not otherwise reasonably and expeditiously available; and

(2) agree to hold and save the United States free from damages due to the planning, design, construction, operation, or maintenance of the project.

(b) Federal employees' inventions

As to an invention made or conceived by a Federal employee while providing assistance pursuant to this section, if the Secretary decides not to retain all rights in such invention, the Secretary may—

(1) grant or agree to grant in advance, to a United States firm, a patent license or assignment, or an option thereto, retaining a nonexclusive, nontransferable, irrevocable, paid-up license to practice the invention or have the invention practiced throughout the world by or on behalf of the United States and such other rights as the Secretary deems appropriate; or

(2) waive, subject to reservation by the United States of a nonexclusive, irrevocable, paid-up license to practice the invention or have the invention practiced throughout the world by or on behalf of the United States, in advance, in whole, or in part, any right which the United States may have to such invention.

(c) Protection of confidential information

Information of a confidential nature, such as proprietary or classified information, provided to a United States firm pursuant to this section shall be protected. Such information may be released by a United States firm only after written approval by the Secretary.

(d) Definitions

For purposes of this section—

(1) United States firm

The term "United States firm" means a corporation, partnership, limited partnership, or sole proprietorship that is incorporated or established under the laws of any of the United States with its principal place of business in the United States.

(2) United States

The term "United States", when used in a geographical sense, means the several States of the United States and the District of Columbia.

(Pub. L. 100–676, §9, Nov. 17, 1988, 102 Stat. 4024; Pub. L. 101–640, title III, §318(c), Nov. 28, 1990, 104 Stat. 4642.)

CODIFICATION

Section was formerly set out as a note under section 2314 of this title.

Section was enacted as part of the Water Resources Development Act of 1988, and not as part of the Water Resources Development Act of 1986 which comprises this chapter.

AMENDMENTS

1990—Pub. L. 101–640, §318(c)(1), struck out "demonstration" after "Technical assistance" in section catchline.

Subsec. (a). Pub. L. 101–640, §318(c)(2), struck out "to undertake a demonstration program for a 2-year period, which shall begin within 6 months after the date of enactment of this Act," after "The Secretary is authorized".

Subsecs. (d), (e). Pub. L. 101–640, §318(c)(3), (4), redesignated subsec. (e) as (d) and struck out former subsec. (d) which read as follows: "Within 6 months after the end of the demonstration program authorized by this section, the Secretary shall submit to Congress a report on the results of such demonstration program."

"SECRETARY" DEFINED

Secretary means the Secretary of the Army, see section 2 of Pub. L. 100–676, set out as a note under section 2201 of this title.

§ 2315. Periodic statements

Upon receipt of a request from a non-Federal sponsor of a water resources development project under construction by the Secretary, the Secretary shall provide such sponsor with periodic statements of project expenditures. Such statements shall include an estimate of all Federal and non-Federal funds expended by the Secretary, including overhead expenditures, the purpose for expenditures, and a schedule of anticipated expenditures during the remaining period of construction. Statements shall be provided to the sponsor at intervals of no greater than 6 months.

(Pub. L. 100–676, §10, Nov. 17, 1988, 102 Stat. 4024.)

CODIFICATION

Section was enacted as part of the Water Resources Development Act of 1988, and not as part of the Water Resources Development Act of 1986 which comprises this chapter.

"SECRETARY" DEFINED

Secretary means the Secretary of the Army, see section 2 of Pub. L. 100–676, set out as a note under section 2201 of this title.

§ 2316. Environmental protection mission

(a) General rule

The Secretary shall include environmental protection as one of the primary missions of the Corps of Engineers in planning, designing, constructing, operating, and maintaining water resources projects.

(b) Limitation

Nothing in this section affects—

(1) existing Corps of Engineers' authorities, including its authorities with respect to navigation and flood control;

(2) pending Corps of Engineers permit applications or pending lawsuits involving permits or water resources projects; or

(3) the application of public interest review procedures for Corps of Engineers permits.

(Pub. L. 101–640, title III, §306, Nov. 28, 1990, 104 Stat. 4635.)

CODIFICATION

Section was enacted as part of the Water Resources Development Act of 1990, and not as part of the Water Resources Development Act of 1986 which comprises this chapter.

"SECRETARY" DEFINED

Secretary means the Secretary of the Army, see section 2 of Pub. L. 101–640, set out as a note under section 2201 of this title.

§ 2317. Wetlands

(a) Goals and action plan

(1) Goals

There is established, as part of the Corps of Engineers water resources development program, an interim goal of no overall net loss of the Nation's remaining wetlands base, as defined by acreage and function, and a long-term goal to increase the quality and quantity of the Nation's wetlands, as defined by acreage and function.

(2) Use of authorities

The Secretary shall utilize all appropriate authorities, including those to restore and create wetlands, in meeting the interim and long-term goals.

(3) Action plan

(A) Development

The Secretary shall develop, in consultation with the Environmental Protection Agency, the Fish and Wildlife Service, and other appropriate Federal agencies, a wetlands action plan to achieve the goals established by this subsection as soon as possible.

(B) Contents

The plan shall include and identify actions to be taken by the Secretary in achieving the goals and any new authorities which may be necessary to accelerate attainment of the goals.

(C) Completion deadline

The Secretary shall complete the plan not later than 1 year after November 28, 1990.

(b) Constructed wetlands for Mud Creek, Arkansas

Notwithstanding any other provision of law, the Secretary is authorized and directed to establish and carry out a research and pilot project to evaluate and demonstrate—

(1) the use of constructed wetlands for wastewater treatment, and

(2) methods by which such projects contribute—

(A) to meeting the objective of the Federal Water Pollution Control Act [33 U.S.C. 1251 et seq.] to restore and maintain the physical, chemical, and biological integrity of the Nation's waters, and

(B) to attaining the goals established by subsection (a) of this section.

The project under this subsection shall be carried out to improve the quality of effluent discharged from publicly owned treatment works operated by the city of Fayetteville, Arkansas, into Mud Creek or its tributaries.

(c) Non-Federal responsibilities

For the project conducted under subsection (b) of this section, the non-Federal interest shall agree—

(1) to provide, without cost to the United States, all lands, easements, rights-of-way, relocations, and dredged material disposal areas necessary for construction and subsequent research and demonstration work;

(2) to hold and save the United States free from damages due to construction, operation, and maintenance of the project, except damages due to the fault or negligence of the United States or its contractors; and

(3) to operate and maintain the restored or constructed wetlands in accordance with good management practices; except that nothing in this paragraph shall be construed as precluding a Federal agency from agreeing to operate and maintain the restored or reconstructed wetlands.

The value of the non-Federal lands, easements, rights-of-way, relocations, and dredged material disposal areas provided by the non-Federal interest shall be credited toward the non-Federal share of project design and construction costs. The non-Federal share of project design and construction costs shall be 25 percent.

(d) Wetlands restoration and enhancement demonstration program

(1) Establishment and implementation

The Secretary, in consultation with the Administrator, is authorized to establish and implement a demonstration program for the purpose of determining the feasibility of wetlands restoration, enhancement, and creation as a means of contributing to the goals established by subsection (a) of this section.

(2) Goal

The goal of the program under this subsection shall be to establish a limited number of demonstration wetlands restoration, enhancement, and creation areas in districts of the Corps of Engineers for the purpose of evaluating the technical and scientific long-term feasibility of such areas as a means of contributing to the attainment of the goals established by subsection (a) of this section. Federal and State land-owning agencies and private parties may contribute to such areas.

(3) Factors to consider

In establishing the demonstration program under this subsection, the Secretary shall consider—

(A) past experience with wetlands restoration, enhancement, and creation;

(B) the appropriate means of measuring benefits of compensatory mitigation activities, including enhancement or restoration of existing wetlands or creation of wetlands;

(C) the appropriate geographic scope for which wetlands loss may be offset by restoration, enhancement, and creation efforts;

(D) the technical feasibility and scientific likelihood that wetlands can be successfully restored, enhanced, and created;

(E) means of establishing liability for, and long-term ownership of, wetlands restoration, enhancement, and creation areas; and

(F) responsibilities for short- and long-term project monitoring.

(4) Reporting

(A) To the Chief of Engineers

The district engineer for each district of the Corps of Engineers in which a wetlands restoration, enhancement, and creation area is established under this subsection shall transmit annual reports to the Chief of Engineers describing the amount and value of wetlands restored, enhanced, and created for the area and a summary of whether the area is contributing to the goal established in paragraph (2).

(B) To Congress

Not later than 3 years after November 28, 1990, the Secretary shall transmit to Congress a report evaluating the use of wetlands restoration, enhancement, and creation areas in fulfilling the goal established by paragraph (2), together with recommendations on whether or not to continue use of such areas as a means of meeting the goals established by subsection (a) of this section.

(5) Effect on other laws

Nothing in this subsection affects any requirements under section 404 of the Federal Water Pollution Control Act (33 U.S.C. 1344) or section 403 of this title.

(e) Training and certification of delineators

(1) In general

The Secretary is authorized to establish a program for the training and certification of individuals as wetlands delineators. As part of such program, the Secretary shall carry out demonstration projects in districts of the Corps of Engineers. The program shall include training and certification of delineators and procedures for expediting consideration and acceptance of delineations performed by certified delineators.

(2) Reports

The Secretary shall transmit to Congress periodic reports concerning the status of the program and any recommendations on improving the content and implementation of the Federal Manual for Identifying and Delineating Jurisdictional Wetlands.

(Pub. L. 101–640, title III, §307, Nov. 28, 1990, 104 Stat. 4635.)

REFERENCES IN TEXT

The Federal Water Pollution Control Act, referred to in subsec. (b)(2)(A), is act June 30, 1948, ch. 758, as amended generally by Pub. L. 92–500, §2, Oct. 18, 1972, 86 Stat. 816, which is classified generally to chapter 26 (§1251 et seq.) of this title. For complete classification of this Act to the Code, see Short Title note set out under section 1251 of this title and Tables.

CODIFICATION

Section was enacted as part of the Water Resources Development Act of 1990, and not as part of the Water Resources Development Act of 1986 which comprises this chapter.

TERMINATION OF REPORTING REQUIREMENTS

For termination, effective May 15, 2000, of provisions of law requiring submittal to Congress of any annual, semiannual, or other regular periodic report listed in House Document No. 103–7 (in which a report required under subsec. (e)(2) of this section is listed on page 70), see section 3003 of Pub. L. 104–66, as amended, set out as a note under section 1113 of Title 31, Money and Finance.

WETLANDS ENHANCEMENT OPPORTUNITIES

Section 409 of Pub. L. 101–640 provided that: "Not later than January 20, 1992, the Secretary shall transmit to Congress a list which specifically identifies opportunities of enhancing wetlands in connection with construction and operation of water resource projects."

"SECRETARY" DEFINED

Secretary means the Secretary of the Army, see section 2 of Pub. L. 101–640, set out as a note under section 2201 of this title.

§ 2317a. Cooperative agreements

(a) In general

For the purpose of expediting the cost-effective design and construction of wetlands restoration that is part of an authorized water resources project, the Secretary may enter into cooperative agreements under section 6305 of title 31 with nonprofit organizations with expertise in wetlands restoration to carry out such design and construction on behalf of the Secretary.

(b) Limitations

(1) Per project limit

A cooperative agreement under this section may not obligate the Secretary to pay the nonprofit organization more than $1,000,000 for any single wetlands restoration project.

(2) Annual limit

The total value of work carried out under cooperative agreements under this section may not exceed $5,000,000 in any fiscal year.

(Pub. L. 110–114, title II, § 2015, Nov. 8, 2007, 121 Stat. 1076.)

CODIFICATION

Section was enacted as part of the Water Resources Development Act of 2007, and not as part of the Water Resources Development Act of 1986 which comprises this chapter.

"SECRETARY" DEFINED

Secretary means the Secretary of the Army, see section 2 of Pub. L. 110–114, set out as a note under section 2201 of this title.

§ 2317b. Wetlands mitigation

(1) In general

In carrying out a water resources project that involves wetlands mitigation and that has impacts that occur within the service area of a mitigation bank, the Secretary, where appropriate, shall first consider the use of the mitigation bank if the bank contains sufficient available credits to offset the impact and the bank is approved in accordance with the Federal Guidance for the Establishment, Use and Operation of Mitigation Banks (60 Fed. Reg. 58605) or other applicable Federal law (including regulations).

(2) Service area

To the maximum extent practicable, the service area of the mitigation bank under paragraph (1) shall be in the same watershed as the affected habitat.

(3) Responsibility for monitoring

(A) In general

Purchase of credits from a mitigation bank for a water resources project relieves the Secretary and the non-Federal interest from responsibility for monitoring or demonstrating mitigation success.

(B) Applicability

The relief of responsibility under subparagraph (A) applies only in any case in which the Secretary determines that monitoring of mitigation success is being conducted by the Secretary or by the owner or operator of the mitigation bank.

(Pub. L. 110–114, title II, § 2036(c), Nov. 8, 2007, 121 Stat. 1094.)

CODIFICATION

Section was enacted as part of the Water Resources Development Act of 2007, and not as part of the Water Resources Development Act of 1986 which comprises this chapter.

"SECRETARY" DEFINED

Secretary means the Secretary of the Army, see section 2 of Pub. L. 110–114, set out as a note under section 2201 of this title.

§ 2318. Flood plain management

(a) Exclusion of elements from benefit-cost analysis

The Secretary shall not include in the benefit base for justifying Federal flood damage reduction projects—

(1)(A) any new or substantially improved structure (other than a structure necessary for conducting a water-dependent activity) built in the 100-year flood plain with a first floor elevation less than the 100-year flood elevation after July 1, 1991; or

(B) in the case of a county substantially located within the 100-year flood plain, any new or substantially improved structure (other than a structure necessary for conducting a water-dependent activity) built in the 10-year flood plain after July 1, 1991; and

(2) any structure which becomes located in the 100-year flood plain with a first floor elevation less than the 100-year flood elevation or in the 10-year flood plain, as the case may be, by virtue of constrictions placed in the flood plain after July 1, 1991.

(b) Flood damage reduction benefits

(1) In general

In calculating the benefits of a proposed project for nonstructural flood damage reduction, the Secretary shall calculate the benefits of the nonstructural project using methods similar to those used for calculating the benefits of structural projects, including similar treatment in calculating the benefits from losses avoided.

(2) Avoidance of double counting

In carrying out paragraph (1), the Secretary should avoid double counting of benefits.

(c) Counties substantially located within 100-year flood plain

For the purposes of subsection (a) of this section, a county is substantially located within the 100-year flood plain—

(1) if the county is comprised of lands of which 50 percent or more are located in the 100-year flood plain; and

(2) if the Secretary determines that application of the requirement contained in subsection (a)(1)(A) of this section with respect to the county would unreasonably restrain continued economic development or unreasonably limit the availability of needed flood control measures.

(d) Cost sharing

Not later than January 1, 1992, the Secretary shall transmit to Congress a report on the feasibility and advisability of increasing the non-Federal share of costs for new projects in areas where new or substantially improved structures and other constrictions are built or placed in the 100-year flood plain or the 10-year flood plain, as the case may be, after the initial date of the affected governmental unit's entry into the regular program of the national flood insurance program of the National Flood Insurance Act of 1968 [42 U.S.C. 4001 et seq.].

(e) Regulations

Not later than 6 months after the date on which a report is transmitted to Congress under subsection (c) of this section, the Secretary, in consultation with the Director of the Federal Emergency Management Agency, shall issue regulations to implement subsection (a) of this section. Such regulations shall define key terms, such as new or substantially improved structure, constriction, 10-year flood plain, and 100-year flood plain.

(f) Applicability

The provisions of this section shall not apply to any project, or separable element thereof, for which a final report of the Chief of Engineers has been forwarded to the Secretary before the last day of the 6-month period beginning on the date on which regulations are issued pursuant to subsection (a) of this section but not later than July 1, 1993.

(Pub. L. 101–640, title III, §308, Nov. 28, 1990, 104 Stat. 4638; Pub. L. 106–53, title II, §219(a), Aug. 17, 1999, 113 Stat. 294.)

REFERENCES IN TEXT

The National Flood Insurance Act of 1968, referred to in subsec. (d), is title XIII of Pub. L. 90–448, Aug. 1, 1968, 82 Stat. 572, as amended, which is classified principally to chapter 50 (§4001 et seq.) of Title 42, The Public Health and Welfare. For complete classification of this Act to the Code, see Short Title note set out under section 4001 of Title 42 and Tables.

CODIFICATION

Section was enacted as part of the Water Resources Development Act of 1990, and not as part of the Water Resources Development Act of 1986 which comprises this chapter.

AMENDMENTS

1999—Subsec. (a). Pub. L. 106–53, §219(a)(1), inserted "Exclusion of elements from" before "benefit-cost" in heading.

Subsecs. (b) to (d). Pub. L. 106–53, §219(a)(2), (3), added subsec. (b) and redesignated former subsecs. (b) and (c) as (c) and (d), respectively. Former subsec. (d) redesignated (e).

Subsec. (e). Pub. L. 106–53, §219(a)(2), (4), redesignated subsec. (d) as (e) and substituted "subsection (c)" for "subsection (b)". Former subsec. (e) redesignated (f).

Subsec. (f). Pub. L. 106–53, §219(a)(2), redesignated subsec. (e) as (f).

CHANGE OF NAME

References to the Director of the Federal Emergency Management Agency to be considered to refer and apply to the Administrator of the Federal Emergency Management Agency, see section 612(c) of Pub. L. 109–295, set out as a note under section 313 of Title 6, Domestic Security.

TRANSFER OF FUNCTIONS

For transfer of all functions, personnel, assets, components, authorities, grant programs, and liabilities of the Federal Emergency Management Agency, including the functions of the Under Secretary for Federal Emergency Management relating thereto, to the Federal Emergency Management Agency, see section 315(a)(1) of Title 6, Domestic Security.

For transfer of functions, personnel, assets, and liabilities of the Federal Emergency Management Agency, including the functions of the Director of the Federal Emergency Management Agency relating thereto, to the Secretary of Homeland Security, and for treatment of related references, see former section 313(1) and sections 551(d), 552(d), and 557 of Title 6, Domestic Security, and the Department of Homeland Security Reorganization Plan of November 25, 2002, as modified, set out as a note under section 542 of Title 6.

REEVALUATION OF FLOOD CONTROL PROJECTS

Pub. L. 106–53, title II, §219(b), Aug. 17, 1999, 113 Stat. 295, provided that: "At the request of a non-Federal interest for a flood control project, the Secretary shall conduct a reevaluation of a project authorized before the date of enactment of this Act [Aug. 17, 1999] to consider nonstructural alternatives in light of the amendments made by subsection (a) [amending this section]."

"SECRETARY" DEFINED

Secretary means the Secretary of the Army, see section 2 of Pub. L. 101–640, set out as a note under section 2201 of this title.

§2319. Reservoir management

The Secretary shall ensure that, in developing or revising reservoir operating manuals of the Corps of Engineers, the Corps shall provide significant opportunities for public participation, including opportunities for public hearings. The Secretary shall issue regulations to implement this section, including a requirement that all appropriate informational materials relating to proposed management decisions of the Corps be made available to the public sufficiently in advance of public hearings. Not later than January 1, 1992, the Secretary shall transmit to Congress a report on measures taken pursuant to this section.

(Pub. L. 101–640, title III, §310, Nov. 28, 1990, 104 Stat. 4639; Pub. L. 104–303, title II, §233, Oct. 12, 1996, 110 Stat. 3704.)

CODIFICATION

Section was enacted as part of the Water Resources Development Act of 1990, and not as part of the Water Resources Development Act of 1986 which comprises this chapter.

AMENDMENTS

1996—Subsec. (a). Pub. L. 104–303, §233(1), struck out heading and text of subsec. (a). Text read as follows: "Not later than 2 years after November 28, 1990, the Secretary shall establish for major reservoirs under the jurisdiction of the Corps of Engineers a technical advisory committee to provide to the Secretary and Corps of Engineers recommendations on reservoir monitoring and options for reservoir research. The Secretary shall determine the membership of the committee, except that the Secretary may not appoint more than 6 members and shall ensure a predominance of members with appropriate academic, technical, or scientific qualifications. Members shall serve without pay, and the Secretary shall provide any necessary facilities, staff, and other support services in accordance with the Federal Advisory Committee Act (5 U.S.C. App. 1 et seq.)."

Subsec. (b). Pub. L. 104–303, §233(2), struck out "(b) PUBLIC PARTICIPATION.—" before "The Secretary shall ensure", and substituted "section" for "subsection" in two places.

"SECRETARY" DEFINED

Secretary means the Secretary of the Army, see section 2 of Pub. L. 101–640, set out as a note under section 2201 of this title.

§2320. Protection of recreational and commercial uses

(a) General rule

In planning any water resources project, the Secretary shall consider the impact of the project on existing and future recreational and commercial uses in the area surrounding the project.

(b) Maintenance

Whenever the Secretary maintains, repairs, rehabilitates, or reconstructs a water resources project which will result in a change in the configuration of a structure which is a part of such project, the Secretary, to the maximum extent practicable, shall carry out such maintenance, repair, rehabilitation, or reconstruction in a manner which will not adversely affect any recreational use established with respect to such project before the date of such maintenance, repair, rehabilitation, or reconstruction.

(c) Mitigation

(1) In general

If maintenance, repair, rehabilitation, or reconstruction of a water resources project by the Secretary results in a change in the configuration of any structure which is a part of such project and has an adverse effect on a recreational use established with respect to such project before the date of such maintenance, repair, rehabilitation, or reconstruction, the Secretary, to the maximum extent practicable, shall take such actions as may be necessary to restore such recreational use or provide alternative opportunities for comparable recreational use.

(2) Maximum amount

The Secretary may not expend more than $2,000,000 in a fiscal year to carry out this subsection.

(3) Termination date

This subsection shall not be effective after the last day of the 5-year period beginning on November 28, 1990; except that the Secretary may complete any restoration commenced under this subsection on or before such last day.

(d) Applicability

(1) General rule

Subsections (b) and (c) of this section shall apply to maintenance, repair, rehabilitation, or reconstruction for which physical construction is initiated after May 1, 1988.

(2) Limitation

Subsections (b) and (c) of this section shall not apply to any action of the Secretary which is necessary to discontinue the operation of a water resources project.

(e) Cost sharing

Costs incurred by the Secretary to carry out the objectives of this section shall be allocated to recreation and shall be payable by the beneficiaries of the recreation.

(Pub. L. 101–640, title III, §313, Nov. 28, 1990, 104 Stat. 4640.)

CODIFICATION

Section was enacted as part of the Water Resources Development Act of 1990, and not as part of the Water Resources Development Act of 1986 which comprises this chapter.

"SECRETARY" DEFINED

Secretary means the Secretary of the Army, see section 2 of Pub. L. 101–640, set out as a note under section 2201 of this title.

§2321. Operation and maintenance of hydroelectric facilities

Activities currently performed by personnel under the direction of the Secretary in connection with the operation and maintenance of hydroelectric power generating facilities at Corps of Engineers water resources projects are to be considered as inherently governmental functions and not commercial activities. This section does not prohibit contracting out major maintenance or other functions which are currently contracted out or studying services not directly connected with project maintenance and operations.

(Pub. L. 101–640, title III, §314, Nov. 28, 1990, 104 Stat. 4641.)

CODIFICATION

Section was enacted as part of the Water Resources Development Act of 1990, and not as part of the Water Resources Development Act of 1986 which comprises this chapter.

"SECRETARY" DEFINED

Secretary means the Secretary of the Army, see section 2 of Pub. L. 101–640, set out as a note under section 2201 of this title.

§2321a. Hydroelectric power project uprating

(a) In general

In carrying out the operation, maintenance, rehabilitation, and modernization of a hydroelectric power generating facility at a water resources project under the jurisdiction of the Department of the Army, the Secretary may, to the extent funds are made available in appropriations Acts or in accordance with subsection (c) of this section, take such actions as are necessary to optimize the efficiency of energy production or increase the capacity of the facility, or both, if, after consulting with the heads of other appropriate Federal and State agencies, the Secretary determines that such actions—

(1) are economically justified and financially feasible;

(2) will not result in any significant adverse effect on the other purposes for which the project is authorized;

(3) will not result in significant adverse environmental impacts;

(4) will not involve major structural or operational changes in the project; and

(5) will not adversely affect the use, management, or protection of existing Federal, State, or tribal water rights.

(b) Consultation

Before proceeding with any proposed uprating under subsection (a) of this section, the Secretary shall provide affected State, tribal, and Federal agencies with a copy of the proposed determinations under subsection (a) of this section. If the agencies submit comments, the Secretary shall accept those comments or respond in writing to any objections those agencies raise to the proposed determinations.

(c) Use of funds provided by preference customers

In carrying out this section, the Secretary may accept and expend funds provided by preference customers under Federal law relating to the marketing of power.

(d) Application

This section does not apply to any facility of the Department of the Army that is authorized to be funded under section 839d–1 of title 16.

(e) Effect on other authority

This section shall not affect the authority of the Secretary and the Administrator of the Bonneville Power Administration under section 839d–1 of title 16.

(Pub. L. 104–303, title II, §216, Oct. 12, 1996, 110 Stat. 3694; Pub. L. 106–541, title II, §212, Dec. 11, 2000, 114 Stat. 2593.)

CODIFICATION

Section was enacted as part of the Water Resources Development Act of 1996, and not as part of the Water Resources Development Act of 1986 which comprises this chapter.

AMENDMENTS

2000—Subsec. (a). Pub. L. 106–541, §212(1), inserted introductory provisions and struck out former introductory provisions which read as follows: "In carrying out the maintenance, rehabilitation, and modernization of a hydroelectric power generating facility at a water resources project under the jurisdiction of the Department of the Army, the Secretary may take, to the extent funds are made available in appropriations Acts, such actions as are necessary to increase the efficiency of energy production or the capacity of the facility, or both, if, after consulting with the heads of other appropriate Federal and State agencies, the Secretary determines that the increase—".

Subsec. (a)(1). Pub. L. 106–541, §212(1), substituted "are" for "is" before "economically justified".

Subsec. (b). Pub. L. 106–541, §212(2), substituted "any proposed uprating" for "the proposed uprating" in first sentence.

Subsecs. (c) to (e). Pub. L. 106–541, §212(3), (4), added subsecs. (c) and (d) and redesignated former subsec. (c) as (e).

"SECRETARY" DEFINED

Secretary means the Secretary of the Army, see section 2 of Pub. L. 104–303, set out as a note under section 2201 of this title.

§ 2322. Single entities

For purposes of Federal participation in water resource development projects which are to be carried out by the Secretary, benefits which are to be provided to a facility owned by a State (including the District of Columbia and a territory or possession of the United States), county, municipality, or other public entity shall not be treated as benefits to be provided a single owner or single entity. The Secretary shall not treat such a facility as a single owner or single entity for any purpose.

(Pub. L. 101–640, title III, §317, Nov. 28, 1990, 104 Stat. 4641.)

CODIFICATION

Section was enacted as part of the Water Resources Development Act of 1990, and not as part of the Water Resources Development Act of 1986 which comprises this chapter.

"SECRETARY" DEFINED

Secretary means the Secretary of the Army, see section 2 of Pub. L. 101–640, set out as a note under section 2201 of this title.

§ 2323. Technical assistance to private entities

(a) Use of Corps research and development labs

The Secretary is authorized to use Corps of Engineers research and development laboratories to provide research and development assistance to corporations, partnerships, limited partnerships, consortia, public and private foundations, universities, and nonprofit organizations operating within the United States, territories or possessions of the United States, and the Commonwealths of Puerto Rico and the Northern Mariana Islands—

(1) if the entity furnishes in advance of fiscal obligation by the United States such funds as are necessary to cover any and all costs of such research and development assistance;

(2) if the Secretary determines that the research and development assistance to be provided is within the mission of the Corps of Engineers and is in the public interest;

(3) if the entity has certified to the Secretary that provision of such research and development assistance is not otherwise reasonably and expeditiously obtainable from the private sector; and

(4) if the entity has agreed to hold and save the United States free from any damages due to any such research and development assistance.

(b) Contract

The Secretary may provide research and development assistance under subsection (a) of this section, or any part thereof, by contract.

(c) Omitted

(Pub. L. 101–640, title III, § 318, Nov. 28, 1990, 104 Stat. 4641.)

CODIFICATION

Section is comprised of section 318 of Pub. L. 101–640. Subsec. (c) of section 318 of Pub. L. 101–640 amended section 2314a of this title.

Section was enacted as part of the Water Resources Development Act of 1990, and not as part of the Water Resources Development Act of 1986 which comprises this chapter.

"SECRETARY" DEFINED

Secretary means the Secretary of the Army, see section 2 of Pub. L. 101–640, set out as a note under section 2201 of this title.

§ 2323a. Interagency and international support authority

(a) In general

The Secretary may engage in activities (including contracting) in support of other Federal agencies, international organizations, or foreign governments to address problems of national significance to the United States.

(b) Consultation

The Secretary may engage in activities in support of international organizations only after consulting with the Department of State.

(c) Use of Corps' expertise

The Secretary may use the technical and managerial expertise of the Corps of Engineers to address domestic and international problems related to water resources, infrastructure development, and environmental protection.

(d) Funding

There is authorized to be appropriated to carry out this section $1,000,000 for fiscal year 2008 and each fiscal year thereafter. The Secretary may accept and expend additional funds from other Federal agencies, international organizations, or foreign governments to carry out this section.

(Pub. L. 104–303, title II, § 234, Oct. 12, 1996, 110 Stat. 3704; Pub. L. 106–541, title II, § 207, Dec. 11, 2000, 114 Stat. 2590; Pub. L. 110–114, title II, § 2030, Nov. 8, 2007, 121 Stat. 1081.)

CODIFICATION

Section was enacted as part of the Water Resources Development Act of 1996, and not as part of the Water Resources Development Act of 1986 which comprises this chapter.

AMENDMENTS

2007—Subsec. (a). Pub. L. 110–114, § 2030(1), added subsec. (a) and struck out heading and text of former subsec. (a). Text read as follows: "The Secretary may engage in activities in support of other Federal agencies or international organizations to address problems of national significance to the United States."

Subsec. (b). Pub. L. 110–114, § 2030(2), substituted "Department of State" for "Secretary of State".

Subsec. (d). Pub. L. 110–114, § 2030(3), substituted "$1,000,000 for fiscal year 2008" for "$250,000 for fiscal year 2001" and ", international organizations, or foreign governments" for "or international organizations".

2000—Subsec. (d). Pub. L. 106–541 substituted "There is authorized to be appropriated to carry out this section $250,000 for fiscal year 2001 and each fiscal year thereafter." for "There is authorized to be appropriated $1,000,000 to carry out this section." and inserted "out" after "carry" in second sentence.

NATIONAL RECREATION RESERVATION SERVICE

Pub. L. 106–541, title II, § 206, Dec. 11, 2000, 114 Stat. 2590, provided that: "Notwithstanding section 611 of the Treasury and General Government Appropriations Act, 1999 (112 Stat. 2681–515), the Secretary [of the Army] may—

"(1) participate in the National Recreation Reservation Service on an interagency basis; and

"(2) pay the Department of the Army's share of the activities required to implement, operate, and maintain the Service."

"SECRETARY" DEFINED

Secretary means the Secretary of the Army, see section 2 of Pub. L. 104–303, set out as a note under section 2201 of this title.

§ 2324. Reduced pricing for certain water supply storage

(a) Provision of storage space

If a low income community requests the Secretary to provide water supply storage space in a water resources development project operated by the Secretary and if the amount of space requested is available or could be made available through reallocation of water supply storage space in the project or through modifications to operation of the project, the Secretary may provide such space to the community at a price determined under subsection (c) of this section.

(b) Maximum amount of storage space

The maximum amount of water supply storage space which may be provided to a community under this section may not exceed an amount of water supply storage space sufficient to yield 2,000,000 gallons of water per day.

(c) Price

The Secretary shall provide water supply storage space under this section at a price which is the greater of—

(1) the updated construction cost of the project allocated to provide such amount of water supply storage space or $100 per acre foot of storage space, whichever is less; and

(2) the value of the benefits which are lost as a result of providing such water supply storage space.

(d) Determinations

For purposes of subsection (c) of this section, the determinations of updated construction costs and value of benefits lost shall be made by the Secretary on the basis of the most recent information available.

(e) Inflation adjustment of dollar amount

The $100 amount set forth in subsection (c) of this section shall be adjusted annually by the Secretary for changes in the Consumer Price Index of All Urban Consumers published by the Bureau of Labor Statistics.

(f) Non-Federal responsibilities

Nothing in this section shall be construed as affecting the responsibility of non-Federal interests to provide operation and maintenance costs assigned to water supply storage provided under this section.

(g) "Low income community" defined

The term "low income community" means a community with a population of less than 20,000 which is located in a county with a per capita income less than the per capita income of two-thirds of the counties in the United States.

(Pub. L. 101–640, title III, §322, Nov. 28, 1990, 104 Stat. 4643.)

CODIFICATION

Section was enacted as part of the Water Resources Development Act of 1990, and not as part of the Water Resources Development Act of 1986 which comprises this chapter.

"SECRETARY" DEFINED

Secretary means the Secretary of the Army, see section 2 of Pub. L. 101–640, set out as a note under section 2201 of this title.

§2325. Voluntary contributions for environmental and recreation projects

(a) Acceptance

In connection with carrying out a water resources project for environmental protection and restoration or a water resources project for recreation, the Secretary is authorized to accept contributions of cash, funds, materials, and services from persons, including governmental entities but excluding the project sponsor.

(b) Deposit

Any cash or funds received by the Secretary under subsection (a) of this section shall be deposited into the account in the Treasury of the United States entitled "Contributions and Advances, Rivers and Harbors, Corps of Engineers (8862)" and shall be available until expended to carry out water resources projects described in subsection (a) of this section.

(Pub. L. 102–580, title II, §203, Oct. 31, 1992, 106 Stat. 4826; Pub. L. 104–303, title II, §236(a), Oct. 12, 1996, 110 Stat. 3705.)

CODIFICATION

Section was enacted as part of the Water Resources Development Act of 1992, and not as part of the Water Resources Development Act of 1986 which comprises this chapter.

AMENDMENTS

1996—Subsec. (b). Pub. L. 104–303 substituted "(8862)" for "(8662)".

"SECRETARY" DEFINED

Secretary means the Secretary of the Army, see section 3 of Pub. L. 102–580, set out as a note under section 2201 of this title.

§2326. Regional sediment management

(a) In general

(1) Sediment use

For sediment obtained through the construction, operation, or maintenance of an authorized Federal water resources project, the Secretary shall develop, at Federal expense, regional sediment management plans and carry out projects at locations identified in plans developed under this section, or identified jointly by the non-Federal interest and the Secretary, for use in the construction, repair, modification, or rehabilitation of projects associated with Federal water resources projects for purposes listed in paragraph (3).

(2) Cooperation

The Secretary shall develop plans under this subsection in cooperation with the appropriate Federal, State, regional, and local agencies.

(3) Purposes for sediment use in projects

The purposes of using sediment for the construction, repair, modification, or rehabilitation of Federal water resources projects are—

(A) to reduce storm damage to property;

(B) to protect, restore, and create aquatic and ecologically related habitats, including wetlands; and

(C) to transport and place suitable sediment.

(b) Secretarial findings

Subject to subsection (c), projects carried out under subsection (a) may be carried out in any case in which the Secretary finds that—

(1) the environmental, economic, and social benefits of the project, both monetary and nonmonetary, justify the cost of the project; and

(2) the project will not result in environmental degradation.

(c) Determination of project costs

(1) Costs of construction

(A) In general

Costs associated with construction of a project under this section or identified in a regional sediment management plan shall be limited solely to construction costs that are in excess of the costs necessary to carry out the dredging for construction, operation, or maintenance of an authorized Federal water resources project in the most cost-effective way, consistent with economic, engineering, and environmental criteria.

(B) Cost sharing

(i) In general

Except as provided in clause (ii), the non-Federal share of the construction cost of a project under this section shall be determined as provided in subsections (a) through (d) of section 2213 of this title.

(ii) Special rule

Construction of a project under this section for one or more of the purposes of protection, restoration, or creation of aquatic and ecologically related habitat, the cost of which does not exceed $750,000 and which is located in a disadvantaged community as determined by the Secretary, may be carried out at Federal expense.

(C) Total cost

The total Federal costs associated with construction of a project under this section may not exceed $5,000,000.

(2) Operation, maintenance, replacement, and rehabilitation costs

Operation, maintenance, replacement, and rehabilitation costs associated with a project under this section are the responsibility of the non-Federal interest.

(d) Selection of dredged material disposal method for environmental purposes

(1) In general

In developing and carrying out a Federal water resources project involving the disposal of dredged material, the Secretary may select, with the consent of the non-Federal interest, a disposal method that is not the least cost option if the Secretary determines that the incremental costs of the disposal method are reasonable in relation to the environmental benefits, including the benefits to the aquatic environment to be derived from the creation of wetlands and control of shoreline erosion.

(2) Federal share

The Federal share of such incremental costs shall be determined in accordance with subsection (c).

(e) State and regional plans

The Secretary may—

(1) cooperate with any State in the preparation of a comprehensive State or regional sediment management plan within the boundaries of the State;

(2) encourage State participation in the implementation of the plan; and

(3) submit to Congress reports and recommendations with respect to appropriate Federal participation in carrying out the plan.

(f) Priority areas

In carrying out this section, the Secretary shall give priority to a regional sediment management project in the vicinity of each of the following:

(1) Little Rock Slackwater Harbor, Arkansas.

(2) Fletcher Cove, California.

(3) Egmont Key, Florida.

(4) Calcasieu Ship Channel, Louisiana.

(5) Delaware River Estuary, New Jersey and Pennsylvania.

(6) Fire Island Inlet, Suffolk County, New York.

(7) Smith Point Park Pavilion and the TWA Flight 800 Memorial, Brookhaven, New York.

(8) Morehead City, North Carolina.

(9) Toledo Harbor, Lucas County, Ohio.

(10) Galveston Bay, Texas.

(11) Benson Beach, Washington.

(g) Authorization of appropriations

There is authorized to be appropriated to carry out this section $30,000,000 per fiscal year, of which not more than $5,000,000 per fiscal year may be used for the development of regional sediment management plans authorized by subsection (e) and of which not more than $3,000,000 per fiscal year may be used for construction of projects to which subsection (c)(1)(B)(ii) applies. Such funds shall remain available until expended.

(Pub. L. 102–580, title II, § 204, Oct. 31, 1992, 106 Stat. 4826; Pub. L. 104–303, title II, § 207, Oct. 12, 1996, 110 Stat. 3680; Pub. L. 106–53, title II, § 209, Aug. 17, 1999, 113 Stat. 287; Pub. L. 110–114, title II, § 2037(a), Nov. 8, 2007, 121 Stat. 1094.)

CODIFICATION

Section was enacted as part of the Water Resources Development Act of 1992, and not as part of the Water Resources Development Act of 1986 which comprises this chapter.

AMENDMENTS

2007—Pub. L. 110–114 amended section generally. Prior to amendment, section related to beneficial uses of dredged material.

1999—Subsec. (c). Pub. L. 106–53, § 209(1), in introductory provisions, substituted "binding agreement with the Secretary" for "cooperative agreement in accordance with the requirements of section 1962d–5b of title 42".

Subsec. (g). Pub. L. 106–53, § 209(2), added subsec. (g).

1996—Subsecs. (e), (f). Pub. L. 104–303 added subsec. (e) and redesignated former subsec. (e) as (f).

"SECRETARY" DEFINED

Secretary means the Secretary of the Army, see section 3 of Pub. L. 102–580, set out as a note under section 2201 of this title.

§ 2326a. Dredged material disposal facility partnerships

(a) Additional capacity

(1) Provided by Secretary

At the request of a non-Federal interest with respect to a project, the Secretary may provide additional capacity at a dredged material disposal facility constructed by the Secretary beyond the capacity that would be required for project purposes if the non-Federal interest agrees to pay, during the period of construction, all costs associated with the construction of the additional capacity.

(2) Cost recovery authority

The non-Federal interest may recover the costs assigned to the additional capacity through fees assessed on third parties whose dredged material is deposited at the facility and who enter into agreements with the non-Federal interest for the use of the facility. The amount of such fees may be determined by the non-Federal interest.

(b) Non-Federal use of disposal facilities

(1) In general

The Secretary—

(A) may permit the use of any dredged material disposal facility under the jurisdiction of, or managed by, the Secretary by a non-Federal interest if the Secretary determines that such use will not reduce the availability of the facility for project purposes; and

(B) may impose fees to recover capital, operation, and maintenance costs associated with such use.

(2) Use of fees

Notwithstanding section 1341(c) of this title but subject to advance appropriations, any monies received through collection of fees under this subsection shall be available to the Secretary, and shall be used by the Secretary, for the operation and maintenance of the disposal facility from which the fees were collected.

(c) Dredged material facility

(1) In general

The Secretary may enter into a partnership agreement under section 1962d–5b of title 42 with one or more non-Federal interests with respect to a water resources project, or group of water resources projects within a geographic region, if appropriate, for the acquisition, design, construction, management, or operation of a dredged material processing, treatment, contaminant reduction, or disposal facility (including any facility used to demonstrate potential beneficial uses of dredged material, which may include effective sediment contaminant reduction technologies) using funds provided in whole or in part by the Federal Government.

(2) Performance

One or more of the parties to a partnership agreement under this subsection may perform the acquisition, design, construction, management, or operation of a dredged material processing, treatment, contaminant reduction, or disposal facility.

(3) Multiple projects

If appropriate, the Secretary may combine portions of separate water resources projects with appropriate combined cost-sharing among the various water resources projects in a partnership agreement for a facility under this subsection if the facility serves to manage dredged material from multiple water resources projects located in the geographic region of the facility.

(4) Specified Federal funding sources and cost sharing

(A) Specified Federal funding

A partnership agreement with respect to a facility under this subsection shall specify—

(i) the Federal funding sources and combined cost-sharing when applicable to multiple water resources projects; and

(ii) the responsibilities and risks of each of the parties relating to present and future dredged material managed by the facility.

(B) Management of sediments

(i) In general

A partnership agreement under this subsection may include the management of sediments from the maintenance dredging of Federal water resources projects that do not have partnership agreements.

(ii) Payments

A partnership agreement under this subsection may allow the non-Federal interest to receive reimbursable payments from the Federal Government for commitments made by the non-Federal interest for disposal or placement capacity at dredged material processing, treatment, contaminant reduction, or disposal facilities.

(C) Credit

A partnership agreement under this subsection may allow costs incurred by the non-Federal interest before execution of the partnership agreement to be credited in accordance with section 1962d–5b of title 42.

(5) Credit

(A) Effect on existing agreements

Nothing in this subsection supersedes or modifies an agreement in effect on November 8, 2007, between the Federal Government and any non-Federal interest for the cost-sharing, construction, and operation and maintenance of a water resources project.

(B) Credit for funds

Subject to the approval of the Secretary and in accordance with law (including regulations and policies) in effect on November 8, 2007, a non-Federal interest for a water resources project may receive credit for funds provided for the acquisition, design, construction, management, or operation of a dredged material processing, treatment, contaminant reduction, or disposal facility to the extent the facility is used to manage dredged material from the project.

(C) Non-Federal interest responsibilities

A non-Federal interest entering into a partnership agreement under this subsection for a facility shall—

(i) be responsible for providing all necessary lands, easements, relocations, and rights-of-way associated with the facility; and

(ii) receive credit toward the non-Federal share of the cost of the project with respect to which the agreement is being entered into for those items.

(d) Public-private partnerships

(1) In general

The Secretary may carry out a program to evaluate and implement opportunities for public-private partnerships in the design, construction, management, or operation and maintenance of dredged material processing, treatment, contaminant reduction, or disposal facilities in connection with construction or maintenance of Federal navigation projects. If a non-Federal interest is a sponsor of the project, the Secretary shall consult with the non-Federal interest in carrying out the program with respect to the project.

(2) Private financing

(A) Agreements

In carrying out this subsection, the Secretary may enter into an agreement with a non-Federal interest with respect to a project, a private entity, or both for the acquisition, design, construction, management, or operation and maintenance of a dredged material processing, treatment, contaminant reduction, or disposal facility (including any facility used to demonstrate potential beneficial uses of dredged material) using funds provided in whole or in part by the private entity.

(B) Reimbursement

If any funds provided by a private entity are used to carry out a project under this subsection, the Secretary may reimburse the private entity over a period of time agreed to by the parties to the agreement through the payment of subsequent user fees. Such fees may include the payment of a disposal or tipping fee for placement of suitable dredged material at the facility.

(C) Amount of fees

User fees paid pursuant to subparagraph (B) shall be sufficient to repay funds contributed by the private entity plus a reasonable return on investment approved by the Secretary in cooperation with the non-Federal interest with respect to the project and the private entity.

(D) Federal share

The Federal share of such fees shall be equal to the percentage of the total cost that would otherwise be borne by the Federal Government as required pursuant to existing cost-sharing requirements, including section 2213 of this title and section 2326 of this title.

(E) Budget Act compliance

Any spending authority (as defined in section 651(c)(2) of title 2) authorized by this section shall be effective only to such extent and in such amounts as are provided in appropriation Acts.

(Pub. L. 104–303, title II, § 217, Oct. 12, 1996, 110 Stat. 3694; Pub. L. 110–114, title II, § 2005, Nov. 8, 2007, 121 Stat. 1071.)

REFERENCES IN TEXT

The Budget Act, referred to in subsec. (d)(2)(E) heading, probably means the Congressional Budget Act of 1974, titles I through IX of Pub. L. 93–344, July 12, 1974, 88 Stat. 297, as amended. For complete classification of this Act to the Code, see Short Title note set out under section 621 of Title 2, The Congress, and Tables.

CODIFICATION

Section was enacted as part of the Water Resources Development Act of 1996, and not as part of the Water Resources Development Act of 1986 which comprises this chapter.

AMENDMENTS

2007—Subsec. (c). Pub. L. 110–114, § 2005(2), added subsec. (c). Former subsec. (c) redesignated (d).

Subsec. (d). Pub. L. 110–114, § 2005(1), redesignated subsec. (c) as (d).

Subsec. (d)(1). Pub. L. 110–114, § 2005(3), inserted "and maintenance" after "operation" and "processing, treatment, contaminant reduction, or" after "dredged material".

Subsec. (d)(2)(A). Pub. L. 110–114, § 2005(3), inserted "and maintenance" after "operation" and "processing, treatment, contaminant reduction, or" after "of a dredged material".

"SECRETARY" DEFINED

Secretary means the Secretary of the Army, see section 2 of Pub. L. 104–303, set out as a note under section 2201 of this title.

§ 2326b. Sediment management

(a) In general

The Secretary may enter into cooperation agreements with non-Federal interests with respect to navigation projects, or other appropriate non-Federal entities, for the development of long-term management strategies for controlling sediments at such projects.

(b) Contents of strategies

Each strategy developed under subsection (a) of this section shall—

(1) include assessments of sediment rates and composition, sediment reduction options, dredging practices, long-term management of any dredged material disposal facilities, remediation of such facilities, and alternative disposal and reuse options;

(2) include a timetable for implementation of the strategy; and

(3) incorporate relevant ongoing planning efforts, including remedial action planning, dredged material management planning, harbor and waterfront development planning, and watershed management planning.

(c) Consultation

In developing strategies under subsection (a) of this section, the Secretary shall consult with interested Federal agencies, States, and Indian tribes and provide an opportunity for public comment.

(d) Dredged material disposal

(1) Study

The Secretary shall conduct a study to determine the feasibility of constructing and operating an underwater confined dredged material disposal site in the Port of New York-New Jersey that could accommodate as much as 250,000 cubic yards of dredged material for the purpose of demonstrating the feasibility of an underwater confined disposal pit as an environmentally suitable method of containing certain sediments.

(2) Report

The Secretary shall transmit to Congress a report on the results of the study conducted under paragraph (1), together with any recommendations of the Secretary that may be developed in a strategy under subsection (a) of this section.

(e) Great Lakes tributary model

(1) In general

In consultation and coordination with the Great Lakes States, the Secretary shall develop a tributary sediment transport model for each major river system or set of major river systems depositing sediment into a Great Lakes federally authorized commercial harbor, channel maintenance project site, or Area of Concern identified under the Great Lakes Water Quality Agreement of 1978. Such model may be developed as a part of a strategy developed under subsection (a) of this section.

(2) Requirements for models

In developing a tributary sediment transport model under this subsection, the Secretary shall build on data and monitoring information generated in earlier studies and programs of the Great Lakes and their tributaries.

(3) Report

Not later than December 31, 2003, the Secretary shall transmit to Congress a report on the Secretary's activities under this subsection.

(f) "Great Lakes States" defined

In this section, the term "Great Lakes States" means the States of Illinois, Indiana, Michigan, Minnesota, New York, Ohio, Pennsylvania, and Wisconsin.

(g) Authorization of appropriations

(1) In general

There is authorized to be appropriated to the Secretary to carry out this section $5,000,000 for each of fiscal years 1998 through 2001.

(2) Great Lakes tributary model

In addition to amounts made available under paragraph (1), there is authorized to be appropriated to carry out subsection (e) of this section $5,000,000 for each of fiscal years 2002 through 2012.

(Pub. L. 104–303, title V, §516, Oct. 12, 1996, 110 Stat. 3763; Pub. L. 106–541, title V, §505, Dec. 11, 2000, 114 Stat. 2645; Pub. L. 110–114, title V, §5013, Nov. 8, 2007, 121 Stat. 1195.)

CODIFICATION

Section was enacted as part of the Water Resources Development Act of 1996, and not as part of the Water Resources Development Act of 1986 which comprises this chapter.

AMENDMENTS

2007—Subsec. (g)(2). Pub. L. 110–114 substituted "through 2012" for "through 2006".

2000—Subsec. (e)(3). Pub. L. 106–541, §505(1), added par. (3).

Subsec. (g). Pub. L. 106–541, §505(2), designated existing provisions as par. (1), inserted heading, realigned margins, and added par. (2).

NEW YORK-NEW JERSEY HARBOR, NEW YORK AND NEW JERSEY

Pub. L. 106–53, title V, §540, Aug. 17, 1999, 113 Stat. 350, provided that:

"(a) IN GENERAL.—The Secretary shall conduct a study to analyze the economic and environmental benefits and costs of potential sediment management and contaminant reduction measures.

"(b) COOPERATIVE AGREEMENTS.—In conducting the study, the Secretary may enter into cooperative agreements with non-Federal interests to investigate, develop, and support measures for sediment management and reduction of sources of contaminant that affect navigation in the Port of New York-New Jersey and the environmental conditions of the New York-New Jersey Harbor estuary."

"SECRETARY" DEFINED

Secretary means the Secretary of the Army, see section 2 of Pub. L. 104–303, set out as a note under section 2201 of this title.

§ 2326c. Dredged material marketing and recycling

(a) Dredged material marketing

(1) In general

Not later than 180 days after December 11, 2000, the Secretary shall establish a program to allow the direct marketing of dredged material to public agencies and private entities.

(2) Limitations

The Secretary shall not establish the program under paragraph (1) unless the Secretary determines that the program is in the interest of the United States and is economically justified, equitable, and environmentally acceptable.

(3) Regional responsibility

The program described in paragraph (1) may authorize each of the 8 division offices of the Corps of Engineers to market to public agencies and private entities any dredged material from projects under the jurisdiction of the regional office. Any revenues generated from any sale of dredged material to such entities shall be deposited in the United States Treasury.

(4) Reports

Not later than 180 days after December 11, 2000, and annually thereafter for a period of 4 years, the Secretary shall transmit to Congress a report on the program established under paragraph (1).

(5) Authorization of appropriations

There is authorized to be appropriated to carry out this subsection $2,000,000 for each fiscal year.

(b) Dredged material recycling

(1) Pilot program

The Secretary shall conduct a pilot program to provide incentives for the removal of dredged material from confined disposal facilities associated with Corps of Engineer navigation projects for the purpose of recycling the dredged material and extending the life of the confined disposal facilities.

(2) Report

Not later than 90 days after the date of completion of the pilot program, the Secretary shall transmit to Congress a report on the results of the program.

(3) Authorization of appropriations

There is authorized to be appropriated to carry out this subsection $2,000,000, except that not to exceed $1,000,000 may be expended with respect to any project.

(Pub. L. 106–541, title II, §215, Dec. 11, 2000, 114 Stat. 2594.)

CODIFICATION

Section was enacted as part of the Water Resources Development Act of 2000, and not as part of the Water Resources Development Act of 1986 which comprises this chapter.

"SECRETARY" DEFINED

Secretary means the Secretary of the Army, see section 2 of Pub. L. 106–541, set out as a note under section 2201 of this title.

§ 2327. Definition of rehabilitation for inland waterway projects

For purposes of laws relating to navigation on inland and intracoastal waterways of the United States, the term "rehabilitation" means—

(1) major project feature restoration—

(A) which consists of structural work on an inland navigation facility operated and maintained by the Corps of Engineers;

(B) which will significantly extend the physical life of the feature;

(C) which is economically justified by a benefit-cost analysis;

(D) which will take at least 2 years to complete; and

(E)(i) which is initially funded before October 1, 1994, and will require at least $5,000,000 in capital outlays; or

(ii) which is initially funded on or after such date and will require at least $8,000,000 in capital outlays; and

(2) structural modification of a major project component (not exhibiting reliability problems)—

(A) which will enhance the operational efficiency of such component or any other major component of the project by increasing benefits beyond the original project design; and

(B) which will require at least $1,000,000 in capital outlays.

Such term does not include routine or deferred maintenance. The dollar amounts referred to in paragraphs (1) and (2) shall be adjusted annually according to the economic assumption published each year as guidance in the Annual Program and Budget Request for Civil Works Activities of the Corps of Engineers.

(Pub. L. 102–580, title II, §205, Oct. 31, 1992, 106 Stat. 4827.)

CODIFICATION

Section was enacted as part of the Water Resources Development Act of 1992, and not as part of the Water Resources Development Act of 1986 which comprises this chapter.

§2328. Challenge cost-sharing program for management of recreation facilities

(a) In general

The Secretary is authorized to develop and implement a program to share the cost of managing recreation facilities and natural resources at water resource development projects under the Secretary's jurisdiction.

(b) Cooperative agreements

To implement the program under this section, the Secretary is authorized to enter into cooperative agreements with non-Federal public and private entities to provide for operation and management of recreation facilities and natural resources at civil works projects under the Secretary's jurisdiction where such facilities and resources are being maintained at complete Federal expense.

(c) Contributions

For purposes of carrying out this section the Secretary may accept contributions of funds, materials, and services from non-Federal public and private entities. Any funds received by the Secretary under this section shall be deposited into the account in the Treasury of the United States entitled "Contributions and Advances, Rivers and Harbors, Corps of Engineers (8862)" and shall be available until expended to carry out the purposes of this section.

(Pub. L. 102–580, title II, §225, Oct. 31, 1992, 106 Stat. 4838; Pub. L. 104–303, title II, §236(b), Oct. 12, 1996, 110 Stat. 3705.)

CODIFICATION

Section was enacted as part of the Water Resources Development Act of 1992, and not as part of the Water Resources Development Act of 1986 which comprises this chapter.

AMENDMENTS

1996—Subsec. (c). Pub. L. 104–303 substituted "(8862)" for "(8662)".

RECREATION PARTNERSHIP INITIATIVE

Section 519 of Pub. L. 104–303, as amended by Pub. L. 106–53, title III, §350(a), Aug. 17, 1999, 113 Stat. 310, provided that:

"(a) IN GENERAL.—The Secretary shall promote Federal, non-Federal, and private sector cooperation in creating public recreation opportunities and developing the necessary supporting infrastructure at water resources projects of the Corps of Engineers.

"(b) INFRASTRUCTURE IMPROVEMENTS.—

"(1) RECREATION INFRASTRUCTURE IMPROVEMENTS.—In determining the feasibility of the public-private cooperative under subsection (a), the Secretary shall provide such infrastructure improvements as are necessary to support a potential private recreational development at the Raystown Lake Project, Pennsylvania, generally in accordance with the Master Plan Update (1994) for the project.

"(2) AGREEMENT.—The Secretary shall enter into an agreement with an appropriate non-Federal public entity to ensure that the infrastructure improvements constructed by the Secretary on non-project lands pursuant to paragraph (1) are transferred to and operated and maintained by the non-Federal public entity.

"(3) ENGINEERING AND DESIGN SERVICES.—The Secretary may perform engineering and design services for project infrastructure expected to be associated with the development of the site at Raystown Lake, Hesston, Pennsylvania.

"(4) AUTHORIZATION OF APPROPRIATIONS.—There is authorized to be appropriated to carry out this subsection $3,000,000.

"(c) REPORT.—Not later than December 31, 1998, the Secretary shall transmit to Congress a report on the results of the cooperative efforts carried out under this section, including the improvements required by subsection (b)."

"SECRETARY" DEFINED

Secretary means the Secretary of the Army, see section 3 of Pub. L. 102–580, set out as a note under section 2201 of this title.

§2329. International outreach program

(a) In general

The Secretary is authorized to engage in activities to inform the United States maritime industry and port authorities of technological innovations abroad that could significantly improve waterborne transportation in the United States, both inland and deep draft. Such activities may include—

(1) development, monitoring, assessment, and dissemination of information about foreign water transportation and port facilities that could significantly improve water transportation in the United States;

(2) research, development, training, and other forms of technology transfer and exchange; and

(3) offering technical services which cannot be readily obtained in the private sector to be incorporated in the proposals of port authorities or other water transportation developers if the costs for assistance will be recovered under the terms of each project.

(b) Cooperation

The Secretary may carry out the provisions of this section in cooperation with Federal departments and agencies, State and local agencies, authorities, institutions, corporations (profit or nonprofit), foreign governments, or other organizations.

(c) Funding

The funds to carry out the provisions of this section shall include funds deposited in a special account with the Secretary of the Treasury for such purposes by any cooperating entity or organization according to cost-sharing agreements proscribed by the Secretary. Reimbursement for services provided under this section shall be credited to the appropriation concerned.

(Pub. L. 102–580, title IV, §401, Oct. 31, 1992, 106 Stat. 4862.)

CODIFICATION

Section was enacted as part of the Water Resources Development Act of 1992, and not as part of the Water Resources Development Act of 1986 which comprises this chapter.

"SECRETARY" DEFINED

Secretary means the Secretary of the Army, see section 3 of Pub. L. 102–580, set out as a note under section 2201 of this title.

§2330. Aquatic ecosystem restoration

(a) General authority

(1) In general

The Secretary may carry out a project to restore and protect an aquatic ecosystem or estuary if the Secretary determines that the project—

(A)(i) will improve the quality of the environment and is in the public interest; or

(ii) will improve the elements and features of an estuary (as defined in section 2902 of this title); and

(B) is cost-effective.

(2) Dam removal

A project under this section may include removal of a dam.

(b) Cost sharing

(1) In general

Non-Federal interests shall provide 35 percent of the cost of construction of any project carried out under this section, including provision of all lands, easements, rights-of-way, and necessary relocations.

(2) Form

Before October 1, 2003, the Federal share of the cost of a project under this section may be provided in the form of reimbursements of project costs.

(c) Agreements

(1) In general

Construction of a project under this section shall be initiated only after a non-Federal interest has entered into a binding agreement with the Secretary to pay the non-Federal share of the costs of construction required by this section and to pay 100 percent of any operation, maintenance, and replacement and rehabilitation costs with respect to the project in accordance with regulations prescribed by the Secretary.

(2) Nonprofit entities

Notwithstanding section 1962d–5b of title 42, for any project carried out under this section, a non-Federal interest may include a nonprofit entity, with the consent of the affected local government.

(d) Cost limitation

Not more than $5,000,000 in Federal funds may be allotted under this section for a project at any single locality.

(e) Funding

There is authorized to be appropriated to carry out this section $50,000,000 for each fiscal year.

(Pub. L. 104–303, title II, §206, Oct. 12, 1996, 110 Stat. 3679; Pub. L. 106–53, title II, §210, Aug. 17, 1999, 113 Stat. 287; Pub. L. 110–114, title II, §2020, Nov. 8, 2007, 121 Stat. 1078.)

CODIFICATION

Section was enacted as part of the Water Resources Development Act of 1996, and not as part of the Water Resources Development Act of 1986 which comprises this chapter.

AMENDMENTS

2007—Subsec. (a). Pub. L. 110–114, §2020(1), added subsec. (a) and struck out former subsec. (a), which read as follows:

"(a) GENERAL AUTHORITY.—The Secretary may carry out an aquatic ecosystem restoration and protection project if the Secretary determines that the project—

"(1) will improve the quality of the environment and is in the public interest; and

"(2) is cost-effective."

Subsec. (e). Pub. L. 110–114, §2020(2), substituted "$50,000,000" for "$25,000,000".

1999—Subsec. (b). Pub. L. 106–53, §210(1), designated existing provisions as par. (1), inserted heading, and added par. (2).

Subsec. (c). Pub. L. 106–53, §210(2), designated existing provisions as par. (1), inserted heading, and added par. (2).

"SECRETARY" DEFINED

Secretary means the Secretary of the Army, see section 2 of Pub. L. 104–303, set out as a note under section 2201 of this title.

§2330a. Monitoring ecosystem restoration

(a) In general

In conducting a feasibility study for a project (or a component of a project) for ecosystem restoration, the Secretary shall ensure that the recommended project includes, as an integral part of the project, a plan for monitoring the success of the ecosystem restoration.

(b) Monitoring plan

The monitoring plan shall—

(1) include a description of the monitoring activities to be carried out, the criteria for ecosystem restoration success, and the estimated cost and duration of the monitoring; and

(2) specify that the monitoring shall continue until such time as the Secretary determines that the criteria for ecosystem restoration success will be met.

(c) Cost share

For a period of 10 years from completion of construction of a project (or a component of a project) for ecosystem restoration, the Secretary shall consider the cost of carrying out the monitoring as a project cost. If the monitoring plan under subsection (b) requires monitoring beyond the 10-year period, the cost of monitoring shall be a non-Federal responsibility.

(Pub. L. 110–114, title II, §2039, Nov. 8, 2007, 121 Stat. 1100.)

CODIFICATION

Section was enacted as part of the Water Resources Development Act of 2007, and not as part of the Water Resources Development Act of 1986 which comprises this chapter.

"SECRETARY" DEFINED

Secretary means the Secretary of the Army, see section 2 of Pub. L. 110–114, set out as a note under section 2201 of this title.

§2331. Use of continuing contracts for construction of certain projects

(a) In general

Notwithstanding any other provision of law, the Secretary shall not implement a fully allocated funding policy with respect to a water resource project if initiation of construction has occurred but sufficient funds are not available to complete the project.

(b) Continuing contracts

The Secretary shall enter into a continuing contract for a project described in subsection (a) of this section.

(c) Initiation of construction clarified

For the purposes of this section, initiation of construction for a project occurs on the date of enactment of an Act that appropriates funds for the project from 1 of the following appropriation accounts:

(1) Construction, General.

(2) Operation and Maintenance, General.

(3) Flood Control, Mississippi River and Tributaries.

(Pub. L. 106–53, title II, §206, Aug. 17, 1999, 113 Stat. 286.)

CODIFICATION

Section was enacted as part of the Water Resources Development Act of 1999, and not as part of the Water Resources Development Act of 1986 which comprises this chapter.

"SECRETARY" DEFINED

Secretary means the Secretary of the Army, see section 2 of Pub. L. 106–53, set out as a note under section 2201 of this title.

§2332. Flood mitigation and riverine restoration program

(a) In general

The Secretary may undertake a program for the purpose of conducting projects to reduce flood hazards and restore the natural functions and values of rivers throughout the United States.

(b) Studies and projects

(1) Authority

In carrying out the program, the Secretary may conduct studies to identify appropriate flood damage reduction, conservation, and restoration measures and may design and implement projects described in subsection (a) of this section.

(2) Consultation and coordination

The studies and projects carried out under this section shall be conducted, to the maximum extent practicable, in consultation and coordination with the Federal Emergency Management Agency and other appropriate Federal agencies, and in consultation and coordination with appropriate State and local agencies and tribes.

(3) Nonstructural approaches

The studies and projects shall emphasize, to the maximum extent practicable and appropriate, nonstructural approaches to preventing or reducing flood damages.

(4) Participation

The studies and projects shall be conducted, to the maximum extent practicable, in cooperation with State and local agencies and tribes to ensure the coordination of local flood damage reduction or riverine and wetland restoration studies with projects that conserve, restore, and manage hydrologic and hydraulic regimes and restore the natural functions and values of floodplains.

(c) Cost-sharing requirements

(1) Studies

Studies conducted under this section shall be subject to cost sharing in accordance with section 2215 of this title.

(2) Environmental restoration and nonstructural flood control projects

(A) In general

The non-Federal interests shall pay 35 percent of the cost of any environmental restoration or nonstructural flood control project carried out under this section.

(B) Items provided by non-Federal interests

The non-Federal interests shall provide all land, easements, rights-of-way, dredged material disposal areas, and relocations necessary for such projects.

(C) Credit

The value of such land, easements, rights-of-way, dredged material disposal areas, and relocations shall be credited toward the payment required under this paragraph.

(3) Structural flood control projects

Any structural flood control projects carried out under this section shall be subject to cost sharing in accordance with section 2213(a) of this title.

(4) Operation and maintenance

The non-Federal interests shall be responsible for all costs associated with operating, maintaining, replacing, repairing, and rehabilitating all projects carried out under this section.

(d) Project justification

(1) In general

Notwithstanding any other provision of law or requirement for economic justification established under section 1962–2 of title 42, the Secretary may implement a project under this section if the Secretary determines that the project—

(A) will significantly reduce potential flood damages;

(B) will improve the quality of the environment; and

(C) is justified considering all costs and beneficial outputs of the project.

(2) Establishment of selection and rating criteria and policies

(A) In general

Not later than 180 days after August 17, 1999, the Secretary, in cooperation with State and local agencies and tribes, shall—

(i) develop, and submit to the Committee on Transportation and Infrastructure of the House of Representatives and the Committee on Environment and Public Works of the Senate, criteria for selecting and rating projects to be carried out under this section; and

(ii) establish policies and procedures for carrying out the studies and projects undertaken under this section.

(B) Criteria

The criteria referred to in subparagraph (A)(i) shall include, as a priority, the extent to which the appropriate State government supports the project.

(e) Priority areas

In carrying out this section, the Secretary shall examine appropriate locations, including—

(1) Pima County, Arizona, at Paseo De Las Iglesias and Rillito River;

(2) Coachella Valley, Riverside County, California;

(3) Los Angeles and San Gabriel Rivers, California;

(4) Murrieta Creek, California;

(5) Napa River Valley watershed, California, at Yountville, St. Helena, Calistoga, and American Canyon;

(6) Santa Clara basin, California, at Upper Guadalupe River and Tributaries, San Francisquito Creek, and Upper Penitencia Creek;

(7) Pond Creek, Kentucky;

(8) Red River of the North, Minnesota, North Dakota, and South Dakota;

(9) Connecticut River, New Hampshire;

(10) Pine Mount Creek, New Jersey;

(11) Southwest Valley, Albuquerque, New Mexico;

(12) Upper Delaware River, New York;

(13) Briar Creek, North Carolina;

(14) Chagrin River, Ohio;

(15) Mill Creek, Cincinnati, Ohio;

(16) Tillamook County, Oregon;

(17) Willamette River basin, Oregon;

(18) Blair County, Pennsylvania, at Altoona and Frankstown Township;

(19) Delaware River, Pennsylvania;

(20) Schuylkill River, Pennsylvania;

(21) Providence County, Rhode Island;

(22) Shenandoah River, Virginia;

(23) Lincoln Creek, Wisconsin;

(24) Perry Creek, Iowa;

(25) Lester, St. Louis, East Savanna, and Floodwood Rivers, Duluth, Minnesota;

(26) Lower Hudson River and tributaries, New York;

(27) Susquehanna River watershed, Bradford County, Pennsylvania;

(28) Clear Creek, Harris, Galveston, and Brazoria Counties, Texas;

(29) Ascension Parish, Louisiana;

(30) East Baton Rouge Parish, Louisiana;

(31) Iberville Parish, Louisiana;

(32) Livingston Parish, Louisiana; and

(33) Pointe Coupee Parish, Louisiana.

(f) Program review

(1) In general

The program established under this section shall be subject to an independent review to evaluate the efficacy of the program in achieving the dual goals of flood hazard mitigation and riverine restoration.

(2) Report

Not later than April 15, 2003, the Secretary shall submit to the Committee on Transportation and Infrastructure of the House of Representatives and the Committee on Environment and Public Works of the Senate a report on the findings of the review conducted under this subsection with any recommendations concerning continuation of the program.

(g) Maximum Federal cost per project

Not more than $30,000,000 may be expended by the United States on any single project under this section.

(h) Procedure

(1) All projects

The Secretary shall not implement any project under this section until—

(A) the Secretary submits to the Committee on Environment and Public Works of the Senate and the Committee on Transportation and Infrastructure of the House of Representatives a written notification describing the project and the determinations made under subsection (d)(1) of this section; and

(B) 21 calendar days have elapsed after the date on which the notification was received by the committees.

(2) Projects exceeding $15,000,000

(A) Limitation on appropriations

No appropriation shall be made to construct any project under this section the total Federal cost of construction of which exceeds $15,000,000 if the project has not been approved by resolutions adopted by the Committee on Transportation and Infrastructure of the House of Representatives and the Committee on Environment and Public Works of the Senate.

(B) Report

For the purpose of securing consideration of approval under this paragraph, the Secretary shall submit a report on the proposed project, including all relevant data and information on all costs.

(i) Authorization of appropriations

(1) In general

There are authorized to be appropriated to carry out this section $20,000,000.

(2) Full funding

All studies and projects carried out under this section from Army Civil Works appropriations shall be fully funded within the program funding levels provided in this subsection.

(Pub. L. 106–53, title II, §212, Aug. 17, 1999, 113 Stat. 288; Pub. L. 106–541, title II, §227, Dec. 11, 2000, 114 Stat. 2599; Pub. L. 110–114, title V, §5005, Nov. 8, 2007, 121 Stat. 1192.)

CODIFICATION

Section was enacted as part of the Water Resources Development Act of 1999, and not as part of the Water Resources Development Act of 1986 which comprises this chapter.

AMENDMENTS

2007—Subsec. (e)(23). Pub. L. 110–114, §5005(a)(1), struck out "and" at end.

Subsec. (e)(29) to (33). Pub. L. 110–114, §5005(a), added pars. (29) to (33).

Subsec. (i)(1). Pub. L. 110–114, §5005(b), substituted "section $20,000,000" for "section—

"(A) $20,000,000 for fiscal year 2001;

"(B) $30,000,000 for fiscal year 2002; and

"(C) $50,000,000 for each of fiscal years 2003 through 2005".

2000—Subsec. (e)(24) to (28). Pub. L. 106–541 added pars. (24) to (28).

TRANSFER OF FUNCTIONS

For transfer of all functions, personnel, assets, components, authorities, grant programs, and liabilities of the Federal Emergency Management Agency, including the functions of the Under Secretary for Federal Emergency Management relating thereto, to the Federal Emergency Management Agency, see section 315(a)(1) of Title 6, Domestic Security.

For transfer of functions, personnel, assets, and liabilities of the Federal Emergency Management Agency, including the functions of the Director of the Federal Emergency Management Agency relating thereto, to the Secretary of Homeland Security, and for treatment of related references, see former section 313(1) and sections 551(d), 552(d), and 557 of Title 6, Domestic Security, and the Department of Homeland Security Reorganization Plan of November 25, 2002, as modified, set out as a note under section 542 of Title 6.

"SECRETARY" DEFINED

Secretary means the Secretary of the Army, see section 2 of Pub. L. 106–53, set out as a note under section 2201 of this title.

§2333. Irrigation diversion protection and fisheries enhancement assistance

(a) In general

The Secretary may provide technical planning and design assistance to non-Federal interests and may conduct other site-specific studies to formulate and evaluate fish screens, fish passages devices, and other measures to decrease the incidence of juvenile and adult fish inadvertently entering irrigation systems.

(b) Cooperation

Measures under subsection (a) of this section—

(1) shall be developed in cooperation with Federal and State resource agencies; and

(2) shall not impair the continued withdrawal of water for irrigation purposes.

(c) Priority

In providing assistance under subsection (a) of this section, the Secretary shall give priority based on—

(1) the objectives of the Endangered Species Act of 1973 (16 U.S.C. 1531 et seq.);

(2) cost-effectiveness; and

(3) the potential for reducing fish mortality.

(d) Non-Federal share

(1) In general

The non-Federal share of the cost of measures under subsection (a) of this section shall be 50 percent.

(2) In-kind contributions

Not more than 50 percent of the non-Federal contribution may be made through the provision of services, materials, supplies, or other in-kind contributions.

(e) No construction activity

This section does not authorize any construction activity.

(f) Report

Not later than 2 years after August 17, 1999, the Secretary shall submit to Congress a report on—

(1) fish mortality caused by irrigation water intake devices;

(2) appropriate measures to reduce fish mortality;

(3) the extent to which those measures are currently being employed in arid States;

(4) the construction costs associated with those measures; and

(5) the appropriate Federal role, if any, to encourage the use of those measures.

(Pub. L. 106–53, title V, §515, Aug. 17, 1999, 113 Stat. 344.)

REFERENCES IN TEXT

The Endangered Species Act of 1973, referred to in subsec. (c)(1), is Pub. L. 93–205, Dec. 28, 1973, 87 Stat. 884, as amended, which is classified generally to chapter 35 (§1531 et seq.) of Title 16, Conservation. For complete classification of this Act to the Code, see Short Title note set out under section 1531 of Title 16 and Tables.

CODIFICATION

Section was enacted as part of the Water Resources Development Act of 1999, and not as part of the Water Resources Development Act of 1986 which comprises this chapter.

"SECRETARY" DEFINED

Secretary means the Secretary of the Army, see section 2 of Pub. L. 106–53, set out as a note under section 2201 of this title.

§2334. Innovative technologies for watershed restoration

The Secretary shall examine using, and, if appropriate, encourage the use of, innovative treatment technologies, including membrane technologies, for watershed and environmental restoration and protection projects involving water quality.

(Pub. L. 106–53, title V, §516, Aug. 17, 1999, 113 Stat. 344.)

CODIFICATION

Section was enacted as part of the Water Resources Development Act of 1999, and not as part of the Water Resources Development Act of 1986 which comprises this chapter.

"SECRETARY" DEFINED

Secretary means the Secretary of the Army, see section 2 of Pub. L. 106–53, set out as a note under section 2201 of this title.

§2335. Coastal aquatic habitat management

(a) In general

The Secretary may cooperate with the Secretaries of Agriculture and the Interior, the Administrators of the Environmental Protection Agency and the National Oceanic and Atmospheric Administration, other appropriate Federal, State, and local agencies, and affected private entities, in the development of a management strategy to address problems associated with toxic microorganisms and the resulting degradation of ecosystems in the tidal and nontidal wetlands and waters of the United States.

(b) Assistance

As part of the management strategy, the Secretary may provide planning, design, and other technical assistance to each participating State in the development and implementation of nonregulatory measures to mitigate environmental problems and restore aquatic resources.

(c) Cost sharing

The Federal share of the cost of measures undertaken under this section shall not exceed 65 percent.

(d) Operation and maintenance

The non-Federal share of operation and maintenance costs for projects constructed with assistance provided under this section shall be 100 percent.

(e) Authorization of appropriations

There is authorized to be appropriated to carry out this section $7,000,000 for the period beginning with fiscal year 2000.

(Pub. L. 106–53, title V, §559, Aug. 17, 1999, 113 Stat. 354.)

CODIFICATION

Section was enacted as part of the Water Resources Development Act of 1999, and not as part of the Water Resources Development Act of 1986 which comprises this chapter.

"SECRETARY" DEFINED

Secretary means the Secretary of the Army, see section 2 of Pub. L. 106–53, set out as a note under section 2201 of this title.

§2336. Abandoned and inactive noncoal mine restoration

(a) In general

The Secretary may provide technical, planning, and design assistance to Federal and non-Federal interests for carrying out projects to address water quality problems caused by drainage and related activities from abandoned and inactive noncoal mines.

(b) Specific measures

Assistance provided under subsection (a) of this section may be in support of projects for the purposes of—

(1) managing drainage from abandoned and inactive noncoal mines;

(2) restoring and protecting streams, rivers, wetlands, other waterbodies, and riparian areas degraded by drainage from abandoned and inactive noncoal mines; and

(3) demonstrating management practices and innovative and alternative treatment technologies to minimize or eliminate adverse environmental effects associated with drainage from abandoned and inactive noncoal mines.

(c) Non-Federal share

The non-Federal share of the cost of assistance under subsection (a) of this section shall be 50 percent, except that the Federal share with respect to projects located on land owned by the United States shall be 100 percent.

(d) Effect on authority of Secretary of the Interior

Nothing in this section affects the authority of the Secretary of the Interior under title IV of the Surface Mining Control and Reclamation Act of 1977 (30 U.S.C. 1231 et seq.).

(e) Technology database for reclamation of abandoned mines

The Secretary may provide assistance to non-Federal and nonprofit entities to develop, manage, and maintain a database of conventional and innovative, cost-effective technologies for reclamation of abandoned and inactive noncoal mine sites. Such assistance shall be provided through the Rehabilitation of Abandoned Mine Sites Program managed by the Sacramento District Office of the Corps of Engineers.

(f) Authorization of appropriations

There is authorized to be appropriated to carry out this section $20,000,000.

(Pub. L. 106–53, title V, §560, Aug. 17, 1999, 113 Stat. 354; Pub. L. 108–137, title I, §118, Dec. 1, 2003, 117 Stat. 1836; Pub. L. 110–114, title II, §2025, Nov. 8, 2007, 121 Stat. 1079.)

REFERENCES IN TEXT

The Surface Mining Control and Reclamation Act of 1977, referred to in subsec. (d), is Pub. L. 95–87, Aug. 3, 1977, 91 Stat. 445, as amended. Title IV of the Act is classified generally to subchapter IV (§1231 et seq.) of chapter 25 of Title 30, Mineral Lands and Mining. For complete classification of this Act to the Code, see Short Title note set out under section 1201 of Title 30 and Tables.

CODIFICATION

Section was enacted as part of the Water Resources Development Act of 1999, and not as part of the Water Resources Development Act of 1986 which comprises this chapter.

AMENDMENTS

2007—Subsec. (f). Pub. L. 110–114 substituted "$20,000,000" for "$7,500,000".

2003—Subsec. (f). Pub. L. 108–137 substituted "$7,500,000" for "$5,000,000".

"SECRETARY" DEFINED

Secretary means the Secretary of the Army, see section 2 of Pub. L. 106–53, set out as a note under section 2201 of this title.

§2337. Property protection program

(a) In general

The Secretary may carry out a program to reduce vandalism and destruction of property at water resources development projects under the jurisdiction of the Department of the Army.

(b) Provision of rewards

In carrying out the program, the Secretary may provide rewards (including cash rewards) to individuals who provide information or evidence leading to the arrest and prosecution of individuals causing damage to Federal property.

(c) Authorization of appropriations

There is authorized to be appropriated to carry out this section $500,000 for fiscal year 2001 and each fiscal year thereafter.

(Pub. L. 106–541, title II, § 205, Dec. 11, 2000, 114 Stat. 2590.)

CODIFICATION

Section was enacted as part of the Water Resources Development Act of 2000, and not as part of the Water Resources Development Act of 1986 which comprises this chapter.

"SECRETARY" DEFINED

Secretary means the Secretary of the Army, see section 2 of Pub. L. 106–541, set out as a note under section 2201 of this title.

§ 2338. Reburial and conveyance authority

(a) Definition of Indian tribe

In this section, the term "Indian tribe" has the meaning given the term in section 450b of title 25.

(b) Reburial

(1) Reburial areas

In consultation with affected Indian tribes, the Secretary may identify and set aside areas at civil works projects of the Department of the Army that may be used to rebury Native American remains that—

(A) have been discovered on project land; and

(B) have been rightfully claimed by a lineal descendant or Indian tribe in accordance with applicable Federal law.

(2) Reburial

In consultation with and with the consent of the lineal descendant or the affected Indian tribe, the Secretary may recover and rebury, at Federal expense, the remains at the areas identified and set aside under subsection (b)(1) of this section.

(c) Conveyance authority

(1) In general

Subject to paragraph (2), notwithstanding any other provision of law, the Secretary may convey to an Indian tribe for use as a cemetery an area at a civil works project that is identified and set aside by the Secretary under subsection (b)(1) of this section.

(2) Retention of necessary property interests

In carrying out paragraph (1), the Secretary shall retain any necessary right-of-way, easement, or other property interest that the Secretary determines to be necessary to carry out the authorized purposes of the project.

(Pub. L. 106–541, title II, § 208, Dec. 11, 2000, 114 Stat. 2590.)

CODIFICATION

Section was enacted as part of the Water Resources Development Act of 2000, and not as part of the Water Resources Development Act of 1986 which comprises this chapter.

"SECRETARY" DEFINED

Secretary means the Secretary of the Army, see section 2 of Pub. L. 106–541, set out as a note under section 2201 of this title.

§ 2339. Assistance programs

(a) Conservation and recreation management

To further training and educational opportunities at water resources development projects under the jurisdiction of the Secretary, the Secretary may enter into cooperative agreements with non-Federal public and nonprofit entities for services relating to natural resources conservation or recreation management.

(b) Rural community assistance

In carrying out studies and projects under the jurisdiction of the Secretary, the Secretary may enter into cooperative agreements with multistate regional private nonprofit rural community assistance entities for services, including water resource assessment, community participation, planning, development, and management activities.

(c) Cooperative agreements

A cooperative agreement entered into under this section shall not be considered to be, or treated as being, a cooperative agreement to which chapter 63 of title 31 applies.

(Pub. L. 106–541, title II, § 213, Dec. 11, 2000, 114 Stat. 2593.)

CODIFICATION

Section was enacted as part of the Water Resources Development Act of 2000, and not as part of the Water Resources Development Act of 1986 which comprises this chapter.

"SECRETARY" DEFINED

Secretary means the Secretary of the Army, see section 2 of Pub. L. 106–541, set out as a note under section 2201 of this title.

§ 2340. Revision of project partnership agreement; cost sharing

(a) Federal allocation

Upon authorization by law of an increase in the maximum amount of Federal funds that may be allocated for a water resources project or an increase in the total cost of a water resources project authorized to be carried out by the Secretary, the Secretary shall enter into a revised partnership agreement for the project to take into account the change in Federal participation in the project.

(b) Cost sharing

An increase in the maximum amount of Federal funds that may be allocated for a water resources project, or an increase in the total cost of a water resources project, authorized to be carried out by the Secretary shall not affect any cost-sharing requirement applicable to the project.

(c) Cost estimates

The estimated Federal and non-Federal costs of water resources projects authorized to be carried out by the Secretary before, on, or after November 8, 2007, are for informational purposes only and shall not be interpreted as affecting the cost-sharing responsibilities established by law.

(Pub. L. 110–114, title II, §2008, Nov. 8, 2007, 121 Stat. 1073.)

CODIFICATION

Section was enacted as part of the Water Resources Development Act of 2007, and not as part of the Water Resources Development Act of 1986 which comprises this chapter.

REFERENCE TO PARTNERSHIP AGREEMENT DEEMED REFERENCE TO COOPERATION AGREEMENT

Reference to partnership agreement deemed to be reference to cooperation agreement, see section 2003(f)(3) of Pub. L. 110–114, set out as a note under section 1962d–5b of Title 42, The Public Health and Welfare.

"SECRETARY" DEFINED

Secretary means the Secretary of the Army, see section 2 of Pub. L. 110–114, set out as a note under section 2201 of this title.

§2341. Expedited actions for emergency flood damage reduction

The Secretary shall expedite any authorized planning, design, and construction of any project for flood damage reduction for an area that, within the preceding 5 years, has been subject to flooding that resulted in the loss of life and caused damage of sufficient severity and magnitude to warrant a declaration of a major disaster by the President under the Robert T. Stafford Disaster Relief and Emergency Assistance Act (42 U.S.C. 5121 et seq.).

(Pub. L. 110–114, title II, §2009, Nov. 8, 2007, 121 Stat. 1074.)

REFERENCES IN TEXT

The Robert T. Stafford Disaster Relief and Emergency Assistance Act, referred to in text, is Pub. L. 93–288, May 22, 1974, 88 Stat. 143, which is classified principally to chapter 68 (§5121 et seq.) of Title 42, The Public Health and Welfare. For complete classification of this Act to the Code, see Short Title note set out under section 5121 of Title 42 and Tables.

CODIFICATION

Section was enacted as part of the Water Resources Development Act of 2007, and not as part of the Water Resources Development Act of 1986 which comprises this chapter.

"SECRETARY" DEFINED

Secretary means the Secretary of the Army, see section 2 of Pub. L. 110–114, set out as a note under section 2201 of this title.

§2342. Access to water resource data

(a) In general

The Secretary shall carry out a program to provide public access to water resources and related water quality data in the custody of the Corps of Engineers.

(b) Data

Public access under subsection (a) shall—

(1) include, at a minimum, access to data generated in water resources project development and regulation under section 1344 of this title; and

(2) appropriately employ geographic information system technology and linkages to water resource models and analytical techniques.

(c) Partnerships

To the maximum extent practicable, in carrying out activities under this section, the Secretary shall develop partnerships, including cooperative agreements, with State, tribal, and local governments and other Federal agencies.

(d) Authorization of appropriations

There is authorized to be appropriated to carry out this section $3,000,000 for each fiscal year.

(Pub. L. 110–114, title II, §2017, Nov. 8, 2007, 121 Stat. 1077.)

CODIFICATION

Section was enacted as part of the Water Resources Development Act of 2007, and not as part of the Water Resources Development Act of 1986 which comprises this chapter.

"SECRETARY" DEFINED

Secretary means the Secretary of the Army, see section 2 of Pub. L. 110–114, set out as a note under section 2201 of this title.

§2343. Independent peer review

(a) Project studies subject to independent peer review

(1) In general

Project studies shall be subject to a peer review by an independent panel of experts as determined under this section.

(2) Scope

The peer review may include a review of the economic and environmental assumptions and projections, project evaluation data, economic analyses, environmental analyses, engineering analyses, formulation of alternative plans, methods for integrating risk and uncertainty, models used in evaluation of economic or environmental impacts of proposed projects, and any biological opinions of the project study.

(3) Project studies subject to peer review

(A) Mandatory

A project study shall be subject to peer review under paragraph (1) if—

(i) the project has an estimated total cost of more than $45,000,000, including mitigation costs, and is not determined by the Chief of Engineers to be exempt from peer review under paragraph (6);

(ii) the Governor of an affected State requests a peer review by an independent panel of experts; or

(iii) the Chief of Engineers determines that the project study is controversial considering the factors set forth in paragraph (4).

(B) Discretionary

(i) Agency request

A project study shall be considered by the Chief of Engineers for peer review under this section if the head of a Federal or State agency charged with reviewing the project study determines that the project is likely to have a significant adverse impact on environmental, cultural, or other resources under the jurisdiction of the agency after implementation of proposed mitigation plans and requests a peer review by an independent panel of experts.

(ii) Deadline for decision

A decision of the Chief of Engineers under this subparagraph whether to conduct a peer review shall be made within 21 days of the date of receipt of the request by the head of the Federal or State agency under clause (i).

(iii) Reasons for not conducting peer review

If the Chief of Engineers decides not to conduct a peer review following a request under clause (i), the Chief shall make publicly available, including on the Internet, the reasons for not conducting the peer review.

(iv) Appeal to Chairman of Council on Environmental Quality

A decision by the Chief of Engineers not to conduct a peer review following a request under clause (i) shall be subject to appeal by a person referred to in clause (i) to the Chairman of the Council on Environmental Quality if such appeal is made within the 30-day period following the date of the decision being made available under clause (iii). A decision of the Chairman on an appeal under this clause shall be made within 30 days of the date of the appeal.

(4) Factors to consider

In determining whether a project study is controversial under paragraph (3)(A)(iii), the Chief of Engineers shall consider if—

(A) there is a significant public dispute as to the size, nature, or effects of the project; or

(B) there is a significant public dispute as to the economic or environmental costs or benefits of the project.

(5) Project studies excluded from peer review

The Chief of Engineers may exclude a project study from peer review under paragraph (1)—

(A) if the project study does not include an environmental impact statement and is a project study subject to peer review under paragraph (3)(A)(i) that the Chief of Engineers determines—

(i) is not controversial;

(ii) has no more than negligible adverse impacts on scarce or unique cultural, historic, or tribal resources;

(iii) has no substantial adverse impacts on fish and wildlife species and their habitat prior to the implementation of mitigation measures; and

(iv) has, before implementation of mitigation measures, no more than a negligible adverse impact on a species listed as endangered or threatened species under the Endangered Species Act of 1973 (16 U.S.C. 1531 et seq.) or the critical habitat of such species designated under such Act;

(B) if the project study—

(i) involves only the rehabilitation or replacement of existing hydropower turbines, lock structures, or flood control gates within the same footprint and for the same purpose as an existing water resources project;

(ii) is for an activity for which there is ample experience within the Corps of Engineers and industry to treat the activity as being routine; and

(iii) has minimal life safety risk; or

(C) if the project study does not include an environmental impact statement and is a project study pursued under section 701s of this title, section 701g of this title, section 701r of this title, section 577(a) of this title, section 426g of this title, section 426i of this title, section 603a of this title, section 2309a of this title, or section 2330 of this title.

(6) Determination of total cost

For purposes of determining the estimated total cost of a project under paragraph (3)(A), the total cost shall be based upon the reasonable estimates of the Chief of Engineers at the completion of the reconnaissance study for the project. If the reasonable estimate of total costs is subsequently determined to be in excess of the amount in paragraph (3)(A), the Chief of Engineers shall make a determination whether a project study is required to be reviewed under this section.

(b) Timing of peer review

(1) In general

The Chief of Engineers shall determine the timing of a peer review of a project study under subsection (a). In all cases, the peer review shall occur during the period beginning on the date of the signing of the feasibility cost-sharing agreement for the study and ending on the date established under subsection (e)(1)(A) for the peer review and shall be accomplished concurrent with the conducting of the project study.

(2) Factors to consider

In any case in which the Chief of Engineers has not initiated a peer review of a project study, the Chief of Engineers shall consider, at a minimum, whether to initiate a peer review at the time that—

(A) the without-project conditions are identified;

(B) the array of alternatives to be considered are identified; and

(C) the preferred alternative is identified.

(3) Limitation on multiple peer review

Nothing in this subsection shall be construed to require the Chief of Engineers to conduct multiple peer reviews for a project study.

(c) Establishment of panels

(1) In general

For each project study subject to peer review under subsection (a), as soon as practicable after the Chief of Engineers determines that a project study will be subject to peer review, the Chief of Engineers shall contract with the National Academy of Sciences or a similar independent scientific and technical advisory organization or an eligible organization to establish a panel of experts to conduct a peer review for the project study.

(2) Membership

A panel of experts established for a project study under this section shall be composed of independent experts who represent a balance of areas of expertise suitable for the review being conducted.

(3) Limitation on appointments

The National Academy of Sciences or any other organization the Chief of Engineers contracts with under paragraph (1) to establish a panel of experts shall apply the National Academy of Science's policy for selecting committee members to ensure that members selected for the panel of experts have no conflict with the project being reviewed.

(4) Congressional notification

Upon identification of a project study for peer review under this section, but prior to initiation of the review, the Chief of Engineers shall notify the Committee on Environment and Public Works of the Senate and the Committee on Transportation and Infrastructure of the House of Representatives of the review.

(d) Duties of panels

A panel of experts established for a peer review for a project study under this section shall—

(1) conduct the peer review for the project study;

(2) assess the adequacy and acceptability of the economic, engineering, and environmental methods, models, and analyses used by the Chief of Engineers;

(3) receive from the Chief of Engineers the public written and oral comments provided to the Chief of Engineers;

(4) provide timely written and oral comments to the Chief of Engineers throughout the development of the project study, as requested; and

(5) submit to the Chief of Engineers a final report containing the panel's economic, engineering, and environmental analysis of the project study, including the panel's assessment of the adequacy and acceptability of the economic, engineering, and environmental methods, models, and analyses used by the Chief of Engineers, to accompany the publication of the report of the Chief of Engineers for the project.

(e) Duration of project study peer reviews

(1) Deadline

A panel of experts established under this section shall—

(A) complete its peer review under this section for a project study and submit a report to the Chief of Engineers under subsection (d)(5) not more than 60 days after the last day of the public comment period for the draft project study, or, if the Chief of Engineers determines that a longer period of time is necessary, such period of time determined necessary by the Chief of Engineers; and

(B) terminate on the date of initiation of the State and agency review required by section 701–1 of this title.

(2) Failure to meet deadline

If a panel of experts does not complete its peer review of a project study under this section and submit a report to the Chief of Engineers under subsection (d)(5) on or before the deadline established by paragraph (1) for the peer review, the Chief of Engineers shall complete the project study without delay.

(f) Recommendations of panel

(1) Consideration by the Chief of Engineers

After receiving a report on a project study from a panel of experts under this section and before entering a final record of decision for the project, the Chief of Engineers shall consider any recommendations contained in the report and prepare a written response for any recommendations adopted or not adopted.

(2) Public availability and transmittal to Congress

After receiving a report on a project study from a panel of experts under this section, the Chief of Engineers shall—

(A) make a copy of the report and any written response of the Chief of Engineers on recommendations contained in the report available to the public by electronic means, including the Internet; and

(B) transmit to the Committee on Environment and Public Works of the Senate and the Committee on Transportation and Infrastructure of the House of Representatives a copy of the report, together with any such written response, on the date of a final report of the Chief of Engineers or other final decision document for the project study.

(g) Costs

(1) In general

The costs of a panel of experts established for a peer review under this section—

(A) shall be a Federal expense; and

(B) shall not exceed $500,000.

(2) Waiver

The Chief of Engineers may waive the $500,000 limitation contained in paragraph (1)(B) in cases that the Chief of Engineers determines appropriate.

(h) Applicability

This section shall apply to—

(1) project studies initiated during the 2-year period preceding November 8, 2007, and for which the array of alternatives to be considered has not been identified; and

(2) project studies initiated during the period beginning on November 8, 2007, and ending 7 years after November 8, 2007.

(i) Reports

(1) Initial report

Not later than 3 years after November 8, 2007, the Chief of Engineers shall submit to the

Committee on Environment and Public Works of the Senate and the Committee on Transportation and Infrastructure of the House of Representatives a report on the implementation of this section.

(2) Additional report

Not later than 6 years after November 8, 2007, the Chief of Engineers shall update the report under paragraph (1) taking into account any further information on implementation of this section and submit such updated report to the Committee on Environment and Public Works of the Senate and the Committee on Transportation and Infrastructure of the House of Representatives.

(j) Nonapplicability of FACA

The Federal Advisory Committee Act (5 U.S.C. App.) shall not apply to a peer review panel established under this section.

(k) Savings clause

Nothing in this section shall be construed to affect any authority of the Chief of Engineers to cause or conduct a peer review of a water resources project existing on November 8, 2007.

(*l*) Definitions

In this section, the following definitions apply:

(1) Project study

The term "project study" means—

(A) a feasibility study or reevaluation study for a water resources project, including the environmental impact statement prepared for the study; and

(B) any other study associated with a modification of a water resources project that includes an environmental impact statement, including the environmental impact statement prepared for the study.

(2) Affected State

The term "affected State", as used with respect to a water resources project, means a State all or a portion of which is within the drainage basin in which the project is or would be located and would be economically or environmentally affected as a consequence of the project.

(3) Eligible organization

The term "eligible organization" means an organization that—

(A) is described in section 501(c)(3), and exempt from Federal tax under section 501(a), of title 26;

(B) is independent;

(C) is free from conflicts of interest;

(D) does not carry out or advocate for or against Federal water resources projects; and

(E) has experience in establishing and administering peer review panels.

(4) Total cost

The term "total cost", as used with respect to a water resources project, means the cost of construction (including planning and designing) of the project. In the case of a project for hurricane and storm damage reduction or flood damage reduction that includes periodic nourishment over the life of the project, the term includes the total cost of the nourishment.

(Pub. L. 110–114, title II, § 2034, Nov. 8, 2007, 121 Stat. 1086.)

REFERENCES IN TEXT

The Endangered Species Act of 1973, referred to in subsec. (a)(5)(A)(iv), is Pub. L. 93–205, Dec. 28, 1973, 87 Stat. 884, which is classified principally to chapter 35 (§ 1531 et seq.) of Title 16, Conservation. For complete classification of this Act to the Code, see Short Title note set out under section 1531 of Title 16 and Tables.

The Federal Advisory Committee Act, referred to in subsec. (j), is Pub. L. 92–463, Oct. 6, 1972, 86 Stat. 770, which is set out in the Appendix to Title 5, Government Organization and Employees.

CODIFICATION

Section was enacted as part of the Water Resources Development Act of 2007, and not as part of the Water Resources Development Act of 1986 which comprises this chapter.

§ 2344. Safety assurance review

(a) Projects subject to safety assurance review

The Chief of Engineers shall ensure that the design and construction activities for hurricane and storm damage reduction and flood damage reduction projects are reviewed by independent experts under this section if the Chief of Engineers determines that a review by independent experts is necessary to assure public health, safety, and welfare.

(b) Factors

In determining whether a review of design and construction of a project is necessary under this section, the Chief of Engineers shall consider whether—

(1) the failure of the project would pose a significant threat to human life;

(2) the project involves the use of innovative materials or techniques;

(3) the project design lacks redundancy; or

(4) the project has a unique construction sequencing or a reduced or overlapping design construction schedule.

(c) Safety assurance review

(1) Initiation of review

At the appropriate point in the development of detailed engineering and design specifications for each water resources project subject to review under this section, the Chief of Engineers shall initiate a safety assurance review by independent experts on the design and construction activities for the project.

(2) Selection of reviewers

A safety assurance review under this section shall include participation by experts selected by the Chief of Engineers from among individuals who are distinguished experts in engineering, hydrology, or other appropriate disciplines. The Chief of Engineers shall apply the National Academy of Science's policy for selecting reviewers to ensure that reviewers have no conflict of interest with the project being reviewed.

(3) Compensation

An individual serving as an independent reviewer under this section shall be compensated at a rate of pay to be determined by the Secretary and shall be allowed travel expenses.

(d) Scope of safety assurance reviews

A safety assurance review under this section shall include a review of the design and construction activities prior to the initiation of physical construction and periodically thereafter until construction activities are completed on a regular schedule sufficient to inform the Chief of Engineers on the adequacy, appropriateness, and acceptability of the design and construction activities for the purpose of assuring public health, safety, and welfare. The Chief of Engineers shall ensure that reviews under this section do not create any unnecessary delays in design and construction activities.

(e) Safety assurance review record

The written recommendations of a reviewer or panel of reviewers under this section and the responses of the Chief of Engineers shall be available to the public, including through electronic means on the Internet.

(f) Applicability

This section shall apply to any project in design or under construction on November 8, 2007, and to any project with respect to which design or construction is initiated during the period beginning on November 8, 2007, and ending 7 years after November 8, 2007.

(Pub. L. 110–114, title II, §2035, Nov. 8, 2007, 121 Stat. 1091.)

CODIFICATION

Section was enacted as part of the Water Resources Development Act of 2007, and not as part of the Water Resources Development Act of 1986 which comprises this chapter.

"SECRETARY" DEFINED

Secretary means the Secretary of the Army, see section 2 of Pub. L. 110–114, set out as a note under section 2201 of this title.

§2345. Electronic submission of permit applications

(a) In general

Not later than 2 years after November 8, 2007, the Secretary shall implement a program to allow electronic submission of permit applications for permits under the jurisdiction of the Secretary.

(b) Limitations

This section does not preclude the submission of a physical copy.

(c) Authorization of appropriations

There is authorized to be appropriated to carry out this section $3,000,000.

(Pub. L. 110–114, title II, §2040, Nov. 8, 2007, 121 Stat. 1100.)

CODIFICATION

Section was enacted as part of the Water Resources Development Act of 2007, and not as part of the Water Resources Development Act of 1986 which comprises this chapter.

"SECRETARY" DEFINED

Secretary means the Secretary of the Army, see section 2 of Pub. L. 110–114, set out as a note under section 2201 of this title.

§2346. Project administration

(a) Project tracking

The Secretary shall assign a unique tracking number to each water resources project under the jurisdiction of the Secretary to be used by each Federal agency throughout the life of the project.

(b) Report repository

(1) In general

The Secretary shall provide to the Library of Congress a copy of each final feasibility study, final environmental impact statement, final reevaluation report, record of decision, and report to Congress prepared by the Corps of Engineers.

(2) Availability to public

Each document described in paragraph (1) shall be made available to the public, and an electronic copy of each document shall be made permanently available to the public through the Internet.

(Pub. L. 110–114, title II, §2041, Nov. 8, 2007, 121 Stat. 1100.)

CODIFICATION

Section was enacted as part of the Water Resources Development Act of 2007, and not as part of the Water Resources Development Act of 1986 which comprises this chapter.

"SECRETARY" DEFINED

Secretary means the Secretary of the Army, see section 2 of Pub. L. 110–114, set out as a note under section 2201 of this title.

§2347. Coordination and scheduling of Federal, State, and local actions

(a) Notice of intent

Upon request of the non-Federal interest in the form of a written notice of intent to construct or modify a non-Federal water supply, wastewater infrastructure, flood damage reduction, storm damage reduction, ecosystem restoration, or navigation project that requires the approval of the Secretary, the Secretary shall initiate, subject to subsection (c), procedures to establish a schedule for consolidating Federal, State, and local agency and Indian tribe environmental assessments, project reviews, and issuance of all permits for the construction or modification of the project. All States and Indian tribes having jurisdiction over the proposed project shall be invited by the Secretary, but shall not be required, to participate in carrying out this section with respect to the project.

(b) Coordination

The Secretary shall seek, to the extent practicable, to consolidate hearing and comment periods, procedures for data collection and report preparation, and the environmental review and permitting processes associated with the project and related activities. The Secretary shall notify, to the extent possible, the non-Federal interest of its responsibilities for data development and information that may be necessary to process each permit required for the project, including a schedule when the information and data should be provided to the appropriate Federal, State, or local agency or Indian tribe.

(c) Costs of coordination

The costs incurred by the Secretary to establish and carry out a schedule to consolidate Federal, State, and local agency and Indian tribe environmental assessments, project reviews, and permit issuance for a project under this section shall be paid by the non-Federal interest.

(d) Report on timesavings methods

Not later than 3 years after November 8, 2007, the Secretary shall prepare and transmit to Congress a report estimating the time required for the issuance of all Federal, State, local, and tribal permits for the construction of non-Federal projects for water supply, wastewater infrastructure, flood damage reduction, storm damage reduction, ecosystem restoration, and navigation.

(Pub. L. 110–114, title II, §2044, Nov. 8, 2007, 121 Stat. 1102.)

CODIFICATION

Section was enacted as part of the Water Resources Development Act of 2007, and not as part of the Water Resources Development Act of 1986 which comprises this chapter.

"SECRETARY" DEFINED

Secretary means the Secretary of the Army, see section 2 of Pub. L. 110–114, set out as a note under section 2201 of this title.

§ 2348. Project streamlining

(a) Policy

The benefits of water resources projects are important to the Nation's economy and environment, and recommendations to Congress regarding such projects should not be delayed due to uncoordinated or inefficient reviews or the failure to timely resolve disputes during the development of water resources projects.

(b) Scope

This section shall apply to each study initiated after November 8, 2007, to develop a feasibility report under section 2282 of this title, or a reevaluation report, for a water resources project if the Secretary determines that such study requires an environmental impact statement under the National Environmental Policy Act of 1969 (42 U.S.C. 4321 et seq.).

(c) Water resources project review process

The Secretary shall develop and implement a coordinated review process for the development of water resources projects.

(d) Coordinated reviews

The coordinated review process under this section may provide that all reviews, analyses, opinions, permits, licenses, and approvals that must be issued or made by a Federal, State, or local government agency or Indian tribe for the development of a water resources project described in subsection (b) will be conducted, to the maximum extent practicable, concurrently and completed within a time period established by the Secretary in cooperation with the agencies identified under subsection (e) with respect to the project.

(e) Identification of jurisdictional agencies

With respect to the development of each water resources project, the Secretary shall identify, as soon as practicable, all Federal, State, and local government agencies and Indian tribes that may—

(1) have jurisdiction over the project;

(2) be required by law to conduct or issue a review, analysis, or opinion for the project; or

(3) be required to make a determination on issuing a permit, license, or approval for the project.

(f) State authority

If the coordinated review process is being implemented under this section by the Secretary with respect to the development of a water resources project described in subsection (b) within the boundaries of a State, the State, consistent with State law, may choose to participate in the process and to make subject to the process all State agencies that—

(1) have jurisdiction over the project;

(2) are required to conduct or issue a review, analysis, or opinion for the project; or

(3) are required to make a determination on issuing a permit, license, or approval for the project.

(g) Memorandum of understanding

The coordinated review process developed under this section may be incorporated into a memorandum of understanding for a water resources project between the Secretary, the heads of Federal, State, and local government agencies, Indian tribes identified under subsection (e), and the non-Federal interest for the project.

(h) Effect of failure to meet deadline

(1) Notification

If the Secretary determines that a Federal, State, or local government agency, Indian tribe, or non-Federal interest that is participating in the coordinated review process under this section with respect to the development of a water resources project has not met a deadline established under subsection (d) for the project, the Secretary shall notify, within 30 days of the date of such determination, the agency, Indian tribe, or non-Federal interest about the failure to meet the deadline.

(2) Agency report

Not later than 30 days after the date of receipt of a notice under paragraph (1), the Federal, State, or local government agency, Indian tribe, or non-Federal interest involved may submit a report to the Secretary, explaining why the agency, Indian tribe, or non-Federal interest did not meet the deadline and what actions it intends to take to complete or issue the required review, analysis, or opinion or determination on issuing a permit, license, or approval.

(3) Report to Congress

Not later than 30 days after the date of receipt of a report under paragraph (2), the Secretary shall compile and submit a report to the Committee on Transportation and Infrastructure of the House of Representatives, the

Committee on Environment and Public Works of the Senate, and the Council on Environmental Quality, describing any deadlines identified in paragraph (1), and any information provided to the Secretary by the Federal, State, or local government agency, Indian tribe, or non-Federal interest involved under paragraph (2).

(i) Limitations

Nothing in this section shall preempt or interfere with—

(1) any statutory requirement for seeking public comment;

(2) any power, jurisdiction, or authority that a Federal, State, or local government agency, Indian tribe, or non-Federal interest has with respect to carrying out a water resources project; or

(3) any obligation to comply with the provisions of the National Environmental Policy Act of 1969 [42 U.S.C. 4321 et seq.] and the regulations issued by the Council on Environmental Quality to carry out such Act.

(Pub. L. 110–114, title II, §2045, Nov. 8, 2007, 121 Stat. 1103.)

REFERENCES IN TEXT

The National Environmental Policy Act of 1969, referred to in subsecs. (b) and (i)(3), is Pub. L. 91–190, Jan. 1, 1970, 83 Stat. 852, which is classified generally to chapter 55 (§4321 et seq.) of Title 42, The Public Health and Welfare. For complete classification of this Act to the Code, see Short Title note set out under section 4321 of Title 42 and Tables.

CODIFICATION

Section was enacted as part of the Water Resources Development Act of 2007, and not as part of the Water Resources Development Act of 1986 which comprises this chapter.

"SECRETARY" DEFINED

Secretary means the Secretary of the Army, see section 2 of Pub. L. 110–114, set out as a note under section 2201 of this title.

CHAPTER 37—ORGANOTIN ANTIFOULING PAINT CONTROL

Sec.

§2401. Findings; purpose

(a) Findings

The Congress finds the following:

(1) Antifouling paints containing organotin biocides are used to prevent the build-up of barnacles and other encrusting organisms on vessels.

(2) Laboratory and field studies show that organotin is very toxic to marine and freshwater organisms at very low levels.

(3) Vessels that are less than 25 meters in length and are coated with organotin antifouling paint account for a large amount of the organotin released into the aquatic environment.

(4) The Environmental Protection Agency has determined that concentrations of organotin currently in the waters of the United States may pose unreasonable risks to oysters, clams, fish, and other aquatic life.

(b) Purpose

The purpose of this chapter is to protect the aquatic environment by reducing immediately the quantities of organotin entering the waters of the United States.

(Pub. L. 100–333, §2, June 16, 1988, 102 Stat. 605.)

EFFECTIVE DATE; USE OF EXISTING STOCKS

Section 12 of Pub. L. 100–333 provided that:

"(a) IN GENERAL.—Except as provided in subsection (b), this Act [enacting this chapter] shall take effect on the date of its enactment [June 16, 1988].

"(b) TERMINATION OF INTERIM PROHIBITION.—Section 5(a) [section 2404(a) of this title] shall remain in effect until a final decision regarding the release of organotin into the aquatic environment by antifouling paints, pursuant to the process initiated by the Administrator's Position Document 1 dated January 8, 1986—

"(1) is issued by the Administrator; and

"(2) takes effect.

"(c) FINAL DECISION DEFINED.—For purposes of subsection (b), a final decision shall be considered to have taken effect upon the date of the expiration of the time for making any appeal with respect to such decision or, in the case of any such appeal, the resolution of such appeal.

"(d) USE OF EXISTING STOCKS.—Notwithstanding the prohibitions contained in sections 4 and 5 [sections 2403 and 2404 of this title], the Administrator, not later than 90 days after the date of the enactment of this Act [June 16, 1988], shall provide reasonable times—

"(1) not to exceed 180 days after the date of the enactment of this Act, for the continued sale, delivery, purchase, and receipt of any antifouling paints containing organotin and organotin additives that exist before the date of the enactment of this Act; and

"(2) not to exceed one year after the date of the enactment of this Act, for the application of any antifouling paints containing organotin and organotin additives that exist before the date of the enactment of this Act."

SHORT TITLE

Section 1 of Pub. L. 100–333 provided that: "This Act [enacting this chapter] may be cited as the 'Organotin Antifouling Paint Control Act of 1988'."

§2402. Definitions

For purposes of this chapter:

(1) The term "Administrator" means the Administrator of the Environmental Protection Agency.

(2) The term "antifouling paint" means a coating, paint, or treatment that is applied to a vessel to control fresh water or marine fouling organisms.

(3) The term "estuary" means a body of water having an unimpaired connection with open sea, where the sea water is measurably diluted with fresh water derived from land drainage, and such term includes the Chesapeake Bay and estuary-type areas of the Great Lakes.

(4) The term "organotin" means any compound of tin used as a biocide in an antifouling paint.

(5) The term "person" means any individual, and partnership, association, corporation, or organized group of persons whether incorporated or not, or any government entity, including the military.

(6) The term "qualified antifouling paint containing organotin" means an antifouling paint containing organotin that—

(A) is allowed to be used under the terms of the final decision referred to in section 12(c); or

(B) until such final decision takes effect, is certified by the Administrator under section 2405 of this title as having a release rate of not more than 4.0 micrograms per square centimeter per day.

(7) The term "release rate" means the rate at which organotin is released from an antifouling paint over the long term, as determined by the Administrator, using—

(A) the American Society for Testing Materials (ASTM) standard test method which the Environmental Protection Agency required in its July 29, 1986, data call-in notice on tributyltin compounds used in antifouling paints; or

(B) any similar test method specified by the Administrator.

(8) The term "retail" means the transfer of title to tangible personal property other than for resale, after manufacturing or processing.

(9) The term "Secretary" means the Secretary of the Navy.

(10) The term "State" means a State of the United States, the District of Columbia, the Commonwealth of Puerto Rico, the Commonwealth of the Northern Mariana Islands, or any territory or possession of the United States.

(11) The term "vessel" includes every description of watercraft or other artificial contrivance used, or capable of being used, as a means of transportation on water.

(Pub. L. 100–333, § 3, June 16, 1988, 102 Stat. 605.)

REFERENCES IN TEXT

Section 12(c), referred to in par. (6)(A), is section 12(c) of Pub. L. 100–333, which is set out as a note under section 2401 of this title.

§ 2403. Prohibition on application of organotin antifouling paints on certain vessels

(a) Prohibition

Subject to section 12(d), and except as provided in subsection (b) of this section, no person in any State may apply to a vessel that is less than 25 meters in length an antifouling paint containing organotin.

(b) Exceptions

Subsection (a) of this section shall not prohibit the application of a qualified antifouling paint containing organotin on—

(1) the aluminum hull of a vessel that is less than 25 meters in length; or

(2) the outboard motor or lower drive unit of a vessel that is less than 25 meters in length.

(Pub. L. 100–333, § 4, June 16, 1988, 102 Stat. 606.)

REFERENCES IN TEXT

Section 12(d), referred to in subsec. (a), is section 12(d) of Pub. L. 100–333, which is set out as a note under section 2401 of this title.

§ 2404. Prohibition of certain organotin antifouling paints and organotin additives used to make such paints

(a) Interim prohibition of certain organotin antifouling paints

Subject to section 12(d), no person in any State may—

(1) sell or deliver to, or purchase or receive from, another person an antifouling paint containing organotin; or

(2) apply to a vessel an antifouling paint containing organotin;

unless the antifouling paint is certified by the Administrator as being a qualified antifouling paint containing organotin.

(b) Prohibition of certain organotin additives

Subject to section 12(d), no person in any State may sell or deliver to, or purchase or receive from, another person at retail any substance containing organotin for the purpose of adding such substance to paint to create an antifouling paint.

(Pub. L. 100–333, § 5, June 16, 1988, 102 Stat. 606.)

REFERENCES IN TEXT

Section 12(d), referred to in text, is section 12(d) of Pub. L. 100–333, which is set out as a note under section 2401 of this title.

EFFECTIVE DATE

Section effective June 16, 1988, with subsec. (a) to remain in effect until a final decision, as defined in section 12(c) of Pub. L. 100–333, regarding release of organotin into the aquatic environment by antifouling paints, is issued and takes effect, see section 12(a) to (c) of Pub. L. 100–333, set out as an Effective Date; Use of Existing Stocks note under section 2401 of this title.

§ 2405. Certification

(a) Initial certification

Not later than 90 days after June 16, 1988, the Administrator shall certify each antifouling paint containing organotin that the Administrator determines has a release rate of not more than 4.0 micrograms per square centimeter per day on the basis of the information submitted to the Environmental Protection Agency before June 16, 1988, in response to its July 29, 1986, data call-in notice on tributyltin or any other data call-in notice.

(b) Subsequent certification

After the initial period of certification required by subsection (a) of this section, and not later than 90 days after the receipt of information with regard to an antifouling paint containing organotin submitted—

(1) in response to a data call-in referred to in subsection (a) of this section; or

(2) under any provision of law;

the Administrator shall certify such paint if, on the basis of such information, the Administrator determines that such paint has a release rate of not more than 4.0 micrograms per square centimeter per day.

(Pub. L. 100–333, §6, June 16, 1988, 102 Stat. 607.)

§2406. Monitoring and research of ecological effects

(a) Estuarine monitoring

The Administrator, in consultation with the Under Secretary of Commerce for Oceans and Atmosphere, shall monitor the concentrations of organotin in the water column, sediments, and aquatic organisms of representative estuaries and near-coastal waters in the United States. This monitoring program shall remain in effect until 10 years after June 16, 1988. The Administrator shall submit a report annually to the Speaker of the House of Representatives and to the President pro tempore of the Senate detailing the results of such monitoring program for the preceding year.

(b) Navy home port monitoring

The Secretary shall provide for periodic monitoring, not less than quarterly, of waters serving as the home port for any Navy vessel coated with an antifouling paint containing organotin to determine the concentration of organotin in the water column, sediments, and aquatic organisms of such waters.

(c) Navy research of ecological effects

The Secretary shall continue existing Navy programs evaluating the laboratory toxicity and environmental risks associated with the use of antifouling paints containing organotin.

(d) Assistance to States

To the extent practicable, the Administrator shall assist States in monitoring waters in such States for the presence of organotin and in analyzing samples taken during such monitoring.

(e) Five-year report

At the end of the 5-year period beginning on June 16, 1988, the Administrator shall submit a report to the Speaker of the House of Representatives and to the President pro tempore of the Senate providing an assessment of—

(1) the effectiveness of existing laws and rules concerning organotin compounds in ensuring protection of human health and the environment;

(2) compliance with water quality criteria established pursuant to section 2408 of this title and any applicable water quality standards; and

(3) recommendations for additional measures to protect human health and the environment.

(Pub. L. 100–333, §7, June 16, 1988, 102 Stat. 607; Pub. L. 104–106, div. A, title X, §1064(f), Feb. 10, 1996, 110 Stat. 445.)

AMENDMENTS

1996—Subsecs. (d) to (f). Pub. L. 104–106 redesignated subsecs. (e) and (f) as (d) and (e), respectively, and struck out heading and text of former subsec. (d). Text read as follows: "The Secretary shall submit a report annually to the Administrator and to the Governor of each State in which a home port for the Navy is monitored under subsection (b) of this section detailing the results of such monitoring in the State. Such reports shall be included in the annual report required to be submitted under subsection (a) of this section."

NAVY PROGRAM TO MONITOR ECOLOGICAL EFFECTS OF ORGANOTIN

Pub. L. 104–201, div. A, title III, §333, Sept. 23, 1996, 110 Stat. 2485, as amended by Pub. L. 106–65, div. A, title X, §1067(5), Oct. 5, 1999, 113 Stat. 774, provided that:

"(a) MONITORING REQUIREMENT.—The Secretary of the Navy shall, in consultation with the Administrator of the Environmental Protection Agency, develop and implement a program to monitor the concentrations of organotin in the water column, sediments, and aquatic organisms of representative estuaries and near-coastal waters in the United States, as described in section 7(a) of the Organotin Antifouling Paint Control Act of 1988 (33 U.S.C. 2406(a)). The program shall be designed to produce high-quality data to enable the Environmental Protection Agency to develop water quality criteria concerning organotin compounds.

"(b) FUNDING.—The Administrator of the Environmental Protection Agency shall provide, in advance, such sums as are necessary to the Secretary of the Navy for the costs of developing and implementing the program under subsection (a).

"(c) WRITTEN AGREEMENT.—The Secretary of the Navy and the Administrator of the Environmental Protection Agency shall enter into a written agreement setting forth the actions that the Secretary plans to take under subsection (a) and the funding that the Administrator agrees to provide under subsection (b). If the Secretary determines that the Administrator will not enter into such an agreement, the Secretary shall notify the Committee on Armed Services of the House of Representatives and the Committee on Armed Services of the Senate not later than 30 days after such determination.

"(d) NONIMPAIRMENT OF MISSION.—Compliance with subsection (a) shall be conducted in such a manner so as not to impair the ability of the Department of the Navy to meet its operational requirements.

"(e) REPORT.—Not later than June 1, 1997, the Secretary of the Navy shall submit to Congress a report containing the following:

"(1) A description of the monitoring program developed pursuant to subsection (a).

"(2) An analysis of the results of the monitoring program as of the date of the submission of the report.

"(3) Information about the progress of Navy programs, referred to in section 7(c) of the Organotin Antifouling Paint Control Act of 1988 (33 U.S.C. 2406(c)), for evaluating the laboratory toxicity and environmental risks associated with the use of antifouling paints containing organotin.

"(4) An assessment, developed in consultation with the Administrator of the Environmental Protection Agency, of the effectiveness of existing laws and rules concerning organotin compounds in ensuring protection of human health and the environment.

"(f) SENSE OF CONGRESS.—(1) It is the sense of Congress that the Administrator of the Environmental Protection Agency, in consultation with the Secretary of the Navy, should develop, for purposes of the national pollutant discharge elimination system, a model permit for the discharge of organotin compounds at shipbuilding and ship repair facilities.

"(2) For purposes of this subsection, the term 'organotin' has the meaning provided in section 3 of the Organotin Antifouling Paint Control Act of 1988 (33 U.S.C. 2402).

"(g) TERMINATION.—The program required by subsection (a) shall terminate five years after the date of the enactment of this Act [Sept. 23, 1996]."

§2407. Alternative antifouling research

(a) Research

The Secretary and the Administrator shall conduct research into chemical and nonchemical alternatives to antifouling paints containing organotin.

(b) Report

At the end of the 4-year period beginning on June 16, 1988, the Administrator, in consultation with the Secretary, shall submit a report to the Speaker of the House of Representatives and to the President pro tempore of the Senate detailing the results of the research conducted pursuant to subsection (a) of this section.

(Pub. L. 100–333, §8, June 16, 1988, 102 Stat. 608.)

§2408. Water quality criteria document

Not later than March 30, 1989, the Administrator shall issue a final water quality criteria document concerning organotin compounds pursuant to section 1314(a) of this title.

(Pub. L. 100–333, §9, June 16, 1988, 102 Stat. 608.)

§2409. Penalties

(a) Civil penalties

(1) Any person violating section 2403 or 2404 of this title shall be assessed a civil penalty of not more than $5,000 for each offense.

(2) After notice and an opportunity for a hearing, a person found by the Administrator to have violated section 2403 or 2404 of this title is liable to the United States Government for the civil penalty assessed under subsection (a) of this section. The amount of the civil penalty shall be assessed by the Administrator by written notice. In determining the amount of the penalty, the Administrator shall consider the nature, circumstances, extent, and gravity of the prohibited acts committed and, with respect to the violator, the degree of culpability, any history of prior offenses, ability to pay, and other matters that justice requires.

(3) The Administrator may compromise, modify, or remit, with or without consideration, a civil penalty assessed under this section until the assessment is referred to the Attorney General.

(4) If a person fails to pay an assessment of a civil penalty after it has become final, the Administrator may refer the matter to the Attorney General for collection in the appropriate United States district court.

(b) Criminal penalties

Any person knowingly violating section 2403 or 2404 of this title shall be fined not more than $25,000, or imprisoned for not more than one year, or both.

(Pub. L. 100–333, §10, June 16, 1988, 102 Stat. 608.)

§2410. Other authorities; State laws

(a) Other authorities of Administrator

Nothing in this chapter shall limit or prevent the Administrator from establishing a lower permissible release rate for organotin under authorities other than this chapter.

(b) State laws

Nothing in this chapter shall preclude or deny any State or political subdivision thereof the right to adopt or enforce any requirement regarding antifouling paint or any other substance containing organotin. Compliance with the requirements of any State or political subdivision thereof respecting antifouling paint or any other substance containing organotin shall not relieve any person of the obligation to comply with the provisions of this chapter.

(Pub. L. 100–333, §11, June 16, 1988, 102 Stat. 608.)

CHAPTER 38—DUMPING OF MEDICAL WASTE BY PUBLIC VESSELS

§2501. Findings

The Congress finds the following:

(1) The washing ashore of potentially infectious medical wastes from public vessels of the United States may pose serious and widespread risks to public health and to the welfare of coastal communities.

(2) Current Federal law provides inadequate protections against the disposal of such wastes from such vessels into ocean waters.

(3) Operators of such vessels must take immediate action to stop disposing of such wastes into ocean waters.

(Pub. L. 100–688, title III, §3102, Nov. 18, 1988, 102 Stat. 4152.)

SHORT TITLE

Section 3101 of subtitle A [§§3101–3105] of title III of Pub. L. 100–688 provided that: "This subtitle [enacting this chapter] may be cited as the 'United States Public Vessel Medical Waste Anti-Dumping Act of 1988'."

§2502. Definitions

For the purposes of this chapter:

(1) Potentially infectious medical waste

The term "potentially infectious medical waste" includes isolation wastes; infectious agents; human blood and blood products; pathological wastes; sharps; body parts; contaminated bedding; surgical wastes; and other disposable medical equipment and material that may pose a risk to the public health, welfare or the marine environment.

(2) Public vessel

The term "public vessel" means a vessel of any type whatsoever (including hydrofoils, air-cushion vehicles, submersibles, floating craft whether propelled or not, and fixed or floating platforms) that is owned, or demise chartered, and operated by the United States Government, and is not engaged in commercial service.

(Pub. L. 100–688, title III, §3103, Nov. 18, 1988, 102 Stat. 4152.)

§2503. Prohibition

After 6 months after November 18, 1988, no public vessel shall dispose of potentially infectious medical waste into ocean waters unless—

(1)(A) the health or safety of individuals on board the vessel is threatened; or

(B) during time of war or a declared national emergency;

(2) the waste is disposed of beyond 50 nautical miles from the nearest land; and

(3)(A) in the case of a public vessel which is not a submersible, the waste is sterilized, properly packaged, and sufficiently weighted to prevent the waste from coming ashore after disposal; and

(B) in the case of a public vessel which is a submersible, the waste is properly packaged and sufficiently weighted to prevent the waste from coming ashore after disposal.

(Pub. L. 100–688, title III, §3104, Nov. 18, 1988, 102 Stat. 4152.)

§2504. Guidance

Not later than 3 months after November 18, 1988, the Secretary of Defense and the head of each affected agency, in consultation with the Administrator of the Environmental Protection Agency, shall each issue guidance for public vessels under the jurisdiction of their agency regarding implementation of section 2503 of this title.

(Pub. L. 100–688, title III, §3105, Nov. 18, 1988, 102 Stat. 4153.)

CHAPTER 39—SHORE PROTECTION FROM MUNICIPAL OR COMMERCIAL WASTE

SUBCHAPTER I—SHORE PROTECTION

SUBCHAPTER II—RELATED PROVISIONS

SUBCHAPTER I—SHORE PROTECTION

§2601. Definitions

In this chapter—

(1) "Administrator" means the Administrator of the Environmental Protection Agency.

(2) "coastal waters" means—

(A) the territorial sea of the United States;

(B) the Great Lakes and their connecting waters;

(C) the marine and estuarine waters of the United States up to the head of tidal influence; and

(D) the Exclusive Economic Zone as established by Presidential Proclamation Number 5030, dated March 10, 1983.

(3) "municipal or commercial waste" means solid waste (as defined in section 6903 of title 42) except—

(A) solid waste identified and listed under section 6921 of title 42;

(B) waste generated by the vessel during normal operations;

(C) debris solely from construction activities;

(D) sewage sludge subject to regulation under title I of the Marine Protection, Research, and Sanctuaries Act of 1972 [33 U.S.C. 1411 et seq.]; and

(E) dredged or fill material subject to regulation under title I of the Marine Protection, Research, and Sanctuaries Act of 1972 [33 U.S.C. 1411 et seq.], the Federal Water Pollution Control Act (33 U.S.C. 1251 et seq.), or the Rivers and Harbors Appropriation Act of 1899 (33 U.S.C. 401 et seq.).

(4) "person" means an individual, trust, firm, joint stock company, corporation (including a government corporation), partnership, association, State, municipality, commission, political subdivision of a State, or any interstate body.

(5) "receiving facility" means a facility or operation where municipal or commercial waste is unloaded from a vessel.

(6) "United States", when used in a geographic sense, means the States of the United States, Puerto Rico, the District of Columbia, the Virgin Islands, American Samoa, Guam, the Northern Mariana Islands, and any other territory or possession of the United States.

(7) "waste source" means a facility or vessel from which municipal or commercial waste is loaded onto a vessel, including any rolling stock or motor vehicles from which that waste is directly loaded.

(Pub. L. 100–688, title IV, §4101, Nov. 18, 1988, 102 Stat. 4154.)

REFERENCES IN TEXT

Presidential Proclamation Number 5030, referred to in par. (2)(D), is set out under section 1453 of Title 16, Conservation.

The Marine Protection, Research, and Sanctuaries Act of 1972, referred to in par. (3)(D) and (E), is Pub. L. 92–532, Oct. 23, 1972, 86 Stat. 1052, as amended. Title I of that Act is classified generally to subchapter I (§1411 et seq.) of chapter 27 of this title. For complete classification of this Act to the Code, see Short Title note set out under section 1401 of this title and Tables.

The Federal Water Pollution Control Act, referred to in par. (3)(E), is act June 30, 1948, ch. 758, as amended generally by Pub. L. 92–500, §2, Oct. 18, 1972, 86 Stat. 816, which is classified generally to chapter 26 (§1251 et seq.) of this title. For complete classification of this Act to the Code, see Short Title note set out under section 1251 of this title and Tables.

The Rivers and Harbors Appropriation Act of 1899, referred to in par. (3)(E), is act Mar. 3, 1899, ch. 425, 30 Stat. 1151, as amended, which enacted sections 401, 403, 404, 406 to 409, 411 to 416, 418, 502, 549, 686, and 687 of this title. For complete classification of this Act to the Code, see Tables.

SHORT TITLE

Section 4001 of title IV of Pub. L. 100–688 provided that: "This title [enacting this chapter] may be cited as the 'Shore Protection Act of 1988'."

TERRITORIAL SEA OF UNITED STATES

For extension of territorial sea of United States, see Proc. No. 5928, set out as a note under section 1331 of Title 43, Public Lands.

§2602. Vessel permits and numbers

(a) In general

A vessel (except a public vessel as defined in section 2101 of title 46) may not transport municipal or commercial waste in coastal waters without—

(1) a permit for that vessel from the Secretary of Transportation; and

(2) displaying a number or other marking on the vessel as prescribed by the Secretary under chapter 123 or section 12502(b) of title 46.

(b) Permit applications

Application for a permit required by subsection (a) of this section shall be made by the vessel owner or operator and include—

(1) the name, address, and telephone number of the vessel owner and operator;

(2) the vessel's name and identification number;

(3) the vessel's area of operation;

(4) the vessel's transport capacity;

(5) a history of the types of cargo transported by that vessel during the previous year, including identifying the type of municipal or commercial waste transported as—

(A) municipal waste;

(B) commercial waste;

(C) medical waste; or

(D) waste of another character.

(6) any other information the Secretary may require; and

(7) an acknowledgment.

(c) Effective date of permits

A permit issued under this section—

(1) is effective 30 days after the date on which it was issued;

(2) may be issued only for a period of not more than 5 years after the effective date of the permit;

(3) may be renewed for periods of not more than 5 years only by the vessel owner or operator that applied for the original permit; and

(4) is terminated when the vessel is sold.

(d) Denial of permits

The Secretary may, or at the request of the Administrator shall, deny the issuance of a permit for any vessel if the owner or operator of the vessel has a record of a pattern of serious violations of—

(1) this subchapter;

(2) the Solid Waste Disposal Act (42 U.S.C. 6901 et seq.);

(3) the Marine Protection, Research, and Sanctuaries Act of 1972 [16 U.S.C. 1431 et seq., 1447 et seq.; 33 U.S.C. 1401 et seq., 2801 et seq.];

(4) the Rivers and Harbors Appropriation Act of 1899 (33 U.S.C. 401 et seq.); or

(5) the Federal Water Pollution Control Act (33 U.S.C. 1251 et seq.).

(e) Permit decision

The Secretary, after consultation with the Administrator, shall issue or deny a vessel permit under this section within 30 days after receiving a complete application. On denying the issuance of the permit for a vessel the Secretary shall—

(1) notify the applicant of the denial and the reasons for the denial; and

(2) provide an opportunity for a hearing on the denial.

(f) Maintaining permit

(1) In general

The permit issued for a vessel under this chapter shall be maintained in a manner prescribed by the Secretary.

(2) Endorsements

If a vessel is a documented vessel, the Secretary may endorse a permit on the vessel's certificate of documentation.

(g) Vessel information system

The Secretary may include information in a permit in the vessel information system maintained under chapter 125 of title 46.

(Pub. L. 100–688, title IV, § 4102, Nov. 18, 1988, 102 Stat. 4155.)

REFERENCES IN TEXT

The Solid Waste Disposal Act, referred to in subsec. (d)(2), is title II of Pub. L. 89–272, Oct. 20, 1965, 79 Stat. 997, as amended generally by Pub. L. 94–580, § 2, Oct. 21, 1976, 90 Stat. 2795, which is classified generally to chapter 82 (§ 6901 et seq.) of Title 42, The Public Health and Welfare. For complete classification of this Act to the Code, see Short Title note set out under section 6901 of Title 42 and Tables.

The Marine Protection, Research, and Sanctuaries Act of 1972, referred to in subsec. (d)(3), is Pub. L. 92–532, Oct. 23, 1972, 86 Stat. 1052, as amended, which is classified generally to chapters 27 (§ 1401 et seq.) and 41 (§ 2801 et seq.) of this title and chapters 32 (§ 1431 et seq.) and 32A (§ 1447 et seq.) of Title 16, Conservation. For complete classification of this Act to the Code, see Short Title note set out under section 1401 of this title and Tables.

The Rivers and Harbors Appropriation Act of 1899, referred to in subsec. (d)(4), is act Mar. 3, 1899, ch. 425, 30 Stat. 1151, as amended, which enacted sections 401, 403, 404, 406 to 409, 411 to 416, 418, 502, 549, 686, and 687 of this title. For complete classification of this Act to the Code, see Tables.

The Federal Water Pollution Control Act, referred to in subsec. (d)(5), is act June 30, 1948, ch. 758, as amended generally by Pub. L. 92–500, § 2, Oct. 18, 1972, 86 Stat. 816, which is classified generally to chapter 26 (§ 1251 et seq.) of this title. For complete classification of this Act to the Code, see Short Title note set out under section 1251 of this title and Tables.

EFFECTIVE DATE

Section 4204(b) of Pub. L. 100–688 provided that: "Section 4102(a) of this Act [33 U.S.C. 2602(a)] is effective 240 days after the date of enactment of this Act [Nov. 18, 1988]."

AVAILABILITY OF APPLICATIONS

Section 4204(a) of Pub. L. 100–688 provided that: "The Secretary shall make vessel applications for permits to be issued under section 4102 of this Act [33 U.S.C. 2602] publicly available within 60 days after the date of enactment of this Act [Nov. 18, 1988]."

§ 2603. Waste handling practices

(a) In general

(1) Loading

The owner or operator of the waste source shall take all reasonable steps to assure that all municipal or commercial waste is loaded onto a vessel in a manner that assures that waste deposited in coastal waters is minimized.

(2) Securing

The owner or operator of a vessel shall assure that all municipal or commercial waste loaded onto the vessel is secured by netting or other means to assure that waste will not be deposited into coastal waters during transport.

(3) **Offloading**

The owner or operator of the receiving facility shall take all reasonable steps to assure that any municipal or commercial waste is offloaded from a vessel in a manner that assures that waste deposited into coastal waters is minimized.

(4) **Cleaning up**

The owner or operator of any waste source or receiving facility shall provide adequate control measures to clean up any municipal or commercial waste which is deposited into coastal waters.

(b) Regulations

The Administrator, in consultation with the Secretary of Transportation, shall prescribe regulations—

(1) requiring that waste sources, receiving facilities, and vessels provide the means and facilities to assure that the waste will not be deposited into coastal waters during loading, offloading, and transport;

(2) requiring, as appropriate, the submission and adoption by each responsible party of an operation and maintenance manual identifying procedures to be used to prevent, report, and clean up any deposit of municipal or commercial waste into coastal waters, including record keeping requirements; and

(3) if the Administrator determines that tracking systems are required to assure adequate enforcement of laws preventing the deposit of municipal or commercial waste into coastal waters, requiring installation of the appropriate systems within 18 months after the Administrator makes that determination.

(Pub. L. 100–688, title IV, §4103, Nov. 18, 1988, 102 Stat. 4156.)

EFFECTIVE DATE

Section 4204(c) of Pub. L. 100–688 provided that: "Section 4103 of this Act [33 U.S.C. 2603] takes effect 60 days after the date of enactment of this Act [Nov. 18, 1988]."

§2604. Suspension, revocation, and injunctions

(a) Suspension and revocation

After notice and opportunity for a hearing, the Secretary of Transportation may, and at the request of the Administrator shall, suspend or revoke a permit issued to a vessel under this chapter for a violation of this chapter or a regulation prescribed under this chapter.

(b) Injunctions

The Secretary or the Administrator may bring a civil action to enjoin any operation in violation of this chapter or a regulation prescribed under this chapter in the district court of the United States for the district in which the violation occurred.

(Pub. L. 100–688, title IV, §4104, Nov. 18, 1988, 102 Stat. 4157.)

§2605. Enforcement

(a) General authority

The Secretary of Transportation shall enforce this chapter under section 89 of title 14. The Secretary may authorize other officers or employees of the United States Government to enforce this chapter under that section.

(b) Periodic examinations

The Secretary shall conduct periodic examinations of vessels operating under this chapter transporting municipal or commercial waste to determine that each of these vessels has a permit issued under section 2602 of this title.

(c) Refusal of clearance

The Secretary of the Treasury may refuse the clearance required by section 60105 of title 46, to any vessel subject to this chapter which does not have a permit required under section 2602 of this title.

(d) Denial of entry and detention

If a vessel does not comply with this chapter, the Secretary of Transportation may—

(1) deny entry to any place in the United States; and

(2) detain at the place in the United States from which it is about to depart.

(e) Persistent violators

The Administrator shall conduct an investigation of the owner or operator of a vessel or facility if the owner has 5 or more separate violations during a 6-month period.

(Pub. L. 100–688, title IV, §4105, Nov. 18, 1988, 102 Stat. 4157.)

CODIFICATION

In subsec. (c), "section 60105 of title 46" substituted for "section 4197 of the Revised Statutes of the United States (46 App. U.S.C. 91)" on authority of Pub. L. 109–304, §18(c), Oct. 6, 2006, 120 Stat. 1709, which Act enacted section 60105 of Title 46, Shipping.

§2606. Subpena authority

(a) General authority

In an investigation under this chapter, the attendance and testimony of witnesses, including parties in interest, and the production of any evidence may be compelled by subpena. The subpena authority granted by this section is coextensive with that of a district court of the United States, in civil matters, for the district in which the investigation is conducted.

(b) Subpena authority

An official designated by the Secretary of Transportation or Administrator to conduct an investigation under this chapter may issue subpenas as provided in this section and administer oaths to witnesses.

(c) Failure to comply

When a person fails to obey a subpena issued under this section, the district court of the United States for the district in which the investigation is conducted or in which the person failing to obey is found, shall on proper application issue an order directing that person to comply with the subpena. The court may punish as contempt any disobedience of its order.

(d) Witness fees

A witness complying with a subpena issued under this section may be paid for actual travel and attendance at the rate provided for witnesses in the district courts of the United States.

(Pub. L. 100–688, title IV, §4106, Nov. 18, 1988, 102 Stat. 4157.)

REFERENCES IN TEXT

This chapter, referred to in subsec. (b), was in the original "this part" and was translated as reading "this title" to reflect the probable intent of Congress.

§2607. Fees

The Secretary of Transportation may collect a fee under section 9701 of title 31 of not more than $1,000, from each person to whom a permit is issued under this subchapter for a permitting system and to maintain information.

(Pub. L. 100–688, title IV, §4107, Nov. 18, 1988, 102 Stat. 4158.)

§2608. Civil penalty procedures

(a) General procedures

After notice and an opportunity for a hearing, a person found by the Secretary of Transportation to have violated this chapter or a regulation prescribed under this chapter for which a civil penalty is provided, is liable to the United States Government for the civil penalty provided. The amount of the civil penalty shall be assessed by the Secretary by written notice. In determining the amount of the penalty, the Secretary shall consider the nature, circumstances, extent, and gravity of the prohibited acts committed and, with respect to the violator, the degree of culpability, any history of prior offenses, ability to pay, and other matters that justice requires.

(b) Compromising penalties

The Secretary may compromise, modify, or remit, with or without consideration, a civil penalty under this chapter until the assessment is referred to the Attorney General.

(c) Referral to Attorney General

If a person fails to pay an assessment of a civil penalty after it has become final, the Secretary may refer the matter to the Attorney General for collection in an appropriate district court of the United States.

(d) Refund of penalty

The Secretary may refund or remit a civil penalty collected under this chapter if—

(1) application has been made for refund or remission of the penalty within one year from the date of payment; and

(2) the Secretary finds that the penalty was unlawfully, improperly, or excessively imposed.

(Pub. L. 100–688, title IV, §4108, Nov. 18, 1988, 102 Stat. 4158.)

§2609. Penalties

(a) General penalty

Except as provided in subsection (b) of this section, a person violating this chapter is liable to the United States Government for a civil penalty of not more than $25,000. Each day of a continuing violation is a separate violation. A vessel involved in the violation also is liable in rem for the penalty.

(b) Operating without a permit

A person violating section 2602 of this title is liable to the United States Government for a civil penalty of not more than $10,000. Each day of a continuing violation is a separate violation. A vessel involved in the violation also is liable in rem for the penalty.

(c) Criminal penalty

Any person that knowingly violates, or that knowingly aids, abets, authorizes, or instigates a violation of this chapter, shall be fined under title 18, imprisoned for not more than 3 years, or both.

(d) Payments for information

The court, the Secretary of Transportation, or the Administrator, as the case may be, may pay up to one-half of a fine or penalty to any person giving information leading to the assessment of the fine or penalty.

(Pub. L. 100–688, title IV, §4109, Nov. 18, 1988, 102 Stat. 4158.)

SUBCHAPTER II—RELATED PROVISIONS

§2621. Study and recommendations

(a) Study

The Administrator, in consultation with the Secretary of Transportation, shall conduct a study to determine the need for, and effectiveness of additional tracking systems for vessels to assure that municipal or commercial waste is not deposited in coastal waters. In conducting this study, the Administrator shall use the data collected from its permitting and enforcement activities under this chapter. In determining the effectiveness of tracking systems, the Administrator shall rely on the information provided by the Secretary under subsection (b) of this section. The report shall include a recommendation whether additional tracking systems are needed. This study shall be submitted to Congress within 24 months after November 18, 1988.

(b) Recommendations

The Secretary shall provide recommendations to the Administrator concerning the various tracking systems that might be applicable to vessels transporting municipal or commercial waste which the Secretary currently is studying. The Secretary shall consider the relative effectiveness of various systems and the relative costs of the systems both to the United States Government and to the vessel owner.

(Pub. L. 100–688, title IV, §4201, Nov. 18, 1988, 102 Stat. 4159.)

§2622. Relation to other laws

(a) Effect on Federal and State laws

This chapter does not affect the application of any other Federal or State law, statutory or common, including the Marine Protection, Research, and Sanctuaries Act of 1972 [16 U.S.C. 1431 et seq., 1447 et seq.; 33 U.S.C. 1401 et seq., 2801 et seq.] and the Solid Waste Disposal Act (42 U.S.C. 6901 et seq.).

(b) Effect on foreign vessels

This chapter shall be carried out with respect to foreign vessels consistent with the obligations of the United States under international law.

(Pub. L. 100–688, title IV, §4202, Nov. 18, 1988, 102 Stat. 4159.)

REFERENCES IN TEXT

The Marine Protection, Research, and Sanctuaries Act of 1972, referred to in subsec. (a), is Pub. L. 92–532, Oct. 23, 1972, 86 Stat. 1052, as amended, which is classified generally to chapters 27 (§1401 et seq.) and 41 (§2801 et seq.) of this title and chapters 32 (§1431 et seq.) and 32A (§1447 et seq.) of Title 16, Conservation. For complete classification of this Act to the Code, see Short Title note set out under section 1401 of this title and Tables.

The Solid Waste Disposal Act, referred to in subsec. (a), is title II of Pub. L. 89–272, Oct. 20, 1965, 79 Stat. 997, as amended generally by Pub. L. 94–580, §2, Oct. 21, 1976, 90 Stat. 2795, which is classified generally to chapter 82 (§6901 et seq.) of Title 42, The Public Health and Welfare. For complete classification of this Act to the Code, see Short Title note set out under section 6901 of Title 42 and Tables.

§2623. Authorization of appropriations

There are authorized to be appropriated $1,500,000 for each of the fiscal years 1989 and 1990, to carry out this chapter.

(Pub. L. 100–688, title IV, §4203, Nov. 18, 1988, 102 Stat. 4160.)

CHAPTER 40—OIL POLLUTION

SUBCHAPTER I—OIL POLLUTION LIABILITY AND COMPENSATION

SUBCHAPTER I—OIL POLLUTION LIABILITY AND COMPENSATION

§2701. Definitions

For the purposes of this Act, the term—

(1) "act of God" means an unanticipated grave natural disaster or other natural phenomenon of an exceptional, inevitable, and irresistible character the effects of which could not have been prevented or avoided by the exercise of due care or foresight;

(2) "barrel" means 42 United States gallons at 60 degrees fahrenheit;

(3) "claim" means a request, made in writing for a sum certain, for compensation for damages or removal costs resulting from an incident;

(4) "claimant" means any person or government who presents a claim for compensation under this subchapter;

(5) "damages" means damages specified in section 2702(b) of this title, and includes the cost of assessing these damages;

(6) "deepwater port" is a facility licensed under the Deepwater Port Act of 1974 (33 U.S.C. 1501–1524);

(7) "discharge" means any emission (other than natural seepage), intentional or unintentional, and includes, but is not limited to, spilling, leaking, pumping, pouring, emitting, emptying, or dumping;

(8) "exclusive economic zone" means the zone established by Presidential Proclamation Numbered 5030, dated March 10, 1983, including the ocean waters of the areas referred to as "eastern special areas" in Article 3(1) of the Agreement between the United States of America and the Union of Soviet Socialist Republics on the Maritime Boundary, signed June 1, 1990;

(9) "facility" means any structure, group of structures, equipment, or device (other than a vessel) which is used for one or more of the following purposes: exploring for, drilling for, producing, storing, handling, transferring, processing, or transporting oil. This term includes any motor vehicle, rolling stock, or pipeline used for one or more of these purposes;

(10) "foreign offshore unit" means a facility which is located, in whole or in part, in the territorial sea or on the continental shelf of a foreign country and which is or was used for one or more of the following purposes: exploring for, drilling for, producing, storing, handling, transferring, processing, or transporting oil produced from the seabed beneath the foreign country's territorial sea or from the foreign country's continental shelf;

(11) "Fund" means the Oil Spill Liability Trust Fund, established by section 9509 of title 26;

(12) "gross ton" has the meaning given that term by the Secretary under part J of title 46;

(13) "guarantor" means any person, other than the responsible party, who provides evidence of financial responsibility for a responsible party under this Act;

(14) "incident" means any occurrence or series of occurrences having the same origin, involving one or more vessels, facilities, or any

combination thereof, resulting in the discharge or substantial threat of discharge of oil;

(15) "Indian tribe" means any Indian tribe, band, nation, or other organized group or community, but not including any Alaska Native regional or village corporation, which is recognized as eligible for the special programs and services provided by the United States to Indians because of their status as Indians and has governmental authority over lands belonging to or controlled by the tribe;

(16) "lessee" means a person holding a leasehold interest in an oil or gas lease on lands beneath navigable waters (as that term is defined in section 1301(a) of title 43) or on submerged lands of the Outer Continental Shelf, granted or maintained under applicable State law or the Outer Continental Shelf Lands Act (43 U.S.C. 1331 et seq.);

(17) "liable" or "liability" shall be construed to be the standard of liability which obtains under section 1321 of this title;

(18) "mobile offshore drilling unit" means a vessel (other than a self-elevating lift vessel) capable of use as an offshore facility;

(19) "National Contingency Plan" means the National Contingency Plan prepared and published under section 1321(d) of this title or revised under section 105 of the Comprehensive Environmental Response, Compensation, and Liability Act (42 U.S.C. 9605);

(20) "natural resources" includes land, fish, wildlife, biota, air, water, ground water, drinking water supplies, and other such resources belonging to, managed by, held in trust by, appertaining to, or otherwise controlled by the United States (including the resources of the exclusive economic zone), any State or local government or Indian tribe, or any foreign government;

(21) "navigable waters" means the waters of the United States, including the territorial sea;

(22) "offshore facility" means any facility of any kind located in, on, or under any of the navigable waters of the United States, and any facility of any kind which is subject to the jurisdiction of the United States and is located in, on, or under any other waters, other than a vessel or a public vessel;

(23) "oil" means oil of any kind or in any form, including petroleum, fuel oil, sludge, oil refuse, and oil mixed with wastes other than dredged spoil, but does not include any substance which is specifically listed or designated as a hazardous substance under subparagraphs (A) through (F) of section 101(14) of the Comprehensive Environmental Response, Compensation, and Liability Act (42 U.S.C. 9601) and which is subject to the provisions of that Act [42 U.S.C. 9601 et seq.];

(24) "onshore facility" means any facility (including, but not limited to, motor vehicles and rolling stock) of any kind located in, on, or under, any land within the United States other than submerged land;

(25) the term "Outer Continental Shelf facility" means an offshore facility which is located, in whole or in part, on the Outer Continental Shelf and is or was used for one or more of the following purposes: exploring for, drilling for, producing, storing, handling, transferring, processing, or transporting oil produced from the Outer Continental Shelf;

(26) "owner or operator"—

(A) means—

(i) in the case of a vessel, any person owning, operating, or chartering by demise, the vessel;

(ii) in the case of an onshore or offshore facility, any person owning or operating such facility;

(iii) in the case of any abandoned offshore facility, the person who owned or operated such facility immediately prior to such abandonment;

(iv) in the case of any facility, title or control of which was conveyed due to bankruptcy, foreclosure, tax delinquency, abandonment, or similar means to a unit of State or local government, any person who owned, operated, or otherwise controlled activities at such facility immediately beforehand;

(v) notwithstanding subparagraph (B)(i), and in the same manner and to the same extent, both procedurally and substantively, as any nongovernmental entity, including for purposes of liability under section 2702 of this title, any State or local government that has caused or contributed to a discharge or substantial threat of a discharge of oil from a vessel or facility ownership or control of which was acquired involuntarily through—

(I) seizure or otherwise in connection with law enforcement activity;

(II) bankruptcy;

(III) tax delinquency;

(IV) abandonment; or

(V) other circumstances in which the government involuntarily acquires title by virtue of its function as sovereign;

(vi) notwithstanding subparagraph (B)(ii), a person that is a lender and that holds indicia of ownership primarily to protect a security interest in a vessel or facility if, while the borrower is still in possession of the vessel or facility encumbered by the security interest, the person—

(I) exercises decision making control over the environmental compliance related to the vessel or facility, such that the person has undertaken responsibility for oil handling or disposal practices related to the vessel or facility; or

(II) exercises control at a level comparable to that of a manager of the vessel or facility, such that the person has assumed or manifested responsibility—

(aa) for the overall management of the vessel or facility encompassing day-to-day decision making with respect to environmental compliance; or

(bb) over all or substantially all of the operational functions (as distinguished from financial or administrative functions) of the vessel or facility other than the function of environmental compliance; and

(B) does not include—

(i) A unit of state or local government that acquired ownership or control of a vessel or facility involuntarily through—

(I) seizure or otherwise in connection with law enforcement activity;

(II) bankruptcy;

(III) tax delinquency;

(IV) abandonment; or

(V) other circumstances in which the government involuntarily acquires title by virtue of its function as sovereign;

(ii) a person that is a lender that does not participate in management of a vessel or facility, but holds indicia of ownership primarily to protect the security interest of the person in the vessel or facility; or

(iii) a person that is a lender that did not participate in management of a vessel or facility prior to foreclosure, notwithstanding that the person—

(I) forecloses on the vessel or facility; and

(II) after foreclosure, sells, re-leases (in the case of a lease finance transaction), or liquidates the vessel or facility, maintains business activities, winds up operations, undertakes a removal action under section 1321(c) of this title or under the direction of an on-scene coordinator appointed under the National Contingency Plan, with respect to the vessel or facility, or takes any other measure to preserve, protect, or prepare the vessel or facility prior to sale or disposition,

if the person seeks to sell, re-lease (in the case of a lease finance transaction), or otherwise divest the person of the vessel or facility at the earliest practicable, commercially reasonable time, on commercially reasonable terms, taking into account market conditions and legal and regulatory requirements;

(27) "person" means an individual, corporation, partnership, association, State, municipality, commission, or political subdivision of a State, or any interstate body;

(28) "permittee" means a person holding an authorization, license, or permit for geological exploration issued under section 11 of the Outer Continental Shelf Lands Act (43 U.S.C. 1340) or applicable State law;

(29) "public vessel" means a vessel owned or bareboat chartered and operated by the United States, or by a State or political subdivision thereof, or by a foreign nation, except when the vessel is engaged in commerce;

(30) "remove" or "removal" means containment and removal of oil or a hazardous substance from water and shorelines or the taking of other actions as may be necessary to minimize or mitigate damage to the public health or welfare, including, but not limited to, fish, shellfish, wildlife, and public and private property, shorelines, and beaches;

(31) "removal costs" means the costs of removal that are incurred after a discharge of oil has occurred or, in any case in which there is a substantial threat of a discharge of oil, the costs to prevent, minimize, or mitigate oil pollution from such an incident;

(32) "responsible party" means the following:

(A) VESSELS.—In the case of a vessel, any person owning, operating, or demise chartering the vessel.

(B) ONSHORE FACILITIES.—In the case of an onshore facility (other than a pipeline), any person owning or operating the facility, except a Federal agency, State, municipality, commission, or political subdivision of a State, or any interstate body, that as the owner transfers possession and right to use the property to another person by lease, assignment, or permit.

(C) OFFSHORE FACILITIES.—In the case of an offshore facility (other than a pipeline or a deepwater port licensed under the Deepwater Port Act of 1974 (33 U.S.C. 1501 et seq.)), the lessee or permittee of the area in which the facility is located or the holder of a right of use and easement granted under applicable State law or the Outer Continental Shelf Lands Act (43 U.S.C. 1301–1356) for the area in which the facility is located (if the holder is a different person than the lessee or permittee), except a Federal agency, State, municipality, commission, or political subdivision of a State, or any interstate body, that as owner transfers possession and right to use the property to another person by lease, assignment, or permit.

(D) DEEPWATER PORTS.—In the case of a deepwater port licensed under the Deepwater Port Act of 1974 (33 U.S.C. 1501–1524), the licensee.

(E) PIPELINES.—In the case of a pipeline, any person owning or operating the pipeline.

(F) ABANDONMENT.—In the case of an abandoned vessel, onshore facility, deepwater port, pipeline, or offshore facility, the persons who would have been responsible parties immediately prior to the abandonment of the vessel or facility.

(33) "Secretary" means the Secretary of the department in which the Coast Guard is operating;

(34) "tank vessel" means a vessel that is constructed or adapted to carry, or that carries, oil or hazardous material in bulk as cargo or cargo residue, and that—

(A) is a vessel of the United States;

(B) operates on the navigable waters; or

(C) transfers oil or hazardous material in a place subject to the jurisdiction of the United States;

(35) "territorial seas" means the belt of the seas measured from the line of ordinary low water along that portion of the coast which is in direct contact with the open sea and the line marking the seaward limit of inland waters, and extending seaward a distance of 3 miles;

(36) "United States" and "State" mean the several States of the United States, the District of Columbia, the Commonwealth of Puerto Rico, Guam, American Samoa, the United States Virgin Islands, the Commonwealth of the Northern Marianas, and any other territory or possession of the United States;

(37) "vessel" means every description of watercraft or other artificial contrivance used, or capable of being used, as a means of transportation on water, other than a public vessel;

(38) "participate in management"—

(A)(i) means actually participating in the management or operational affairs of a vessel or facility; and

(ii) does not include merely having the capacity to influence, or the unexercised right to control, vessel or facility operations; and

(B) does not include—

(i) performing an act or failing to act prior to the time at which a security interest is created in a vessel or facility;

(ii) holding a security interest or abandoning or releasing a security interest;

(iii) including in the terms of an extension of credit, or in a contract or security agreement relating to the extension, a covenant, warranty, or other term or condition that relates to environmental compliance;

(iv) monitoring or enforcing the terms and conditions of the extension of credit or security interest;

(v) monitoring or undertaking one or more inspections of the vessel or facility;

(vi) requiring a removal action or other lawful means of addressing a discharge or substantial threat of a discharge of oil in connection with the vessel or facility prior to, during, or on the expiration of the term of the extension of credit;

(vii) providing financial or other advice or counseling in an effort to mitigate, prevent, or cure default or diminution in the value of the vessel or facility;

(viii) restructuring, renegotiating, or otherwise agreeing to alter the terms and conditions of the extension of credit or security interest, exercising forbearance;

(ix) exercising other remedies that may be available under applicable law for the breach of a term or condition of the extension of credit or security agreement; or

(x) conducting a removal action under section 1321(c) of this title or under the direction of an on-scene coordinator appointed under the National Contingency Plan,

if such actions do not rise to the level of participating in management under subparagraph (A) of this paragraph and paragraph (26)(A)(vi);

(39) "extension of credit" has the meaning provided in section 101(20)(G)(i) of the Comprehensive Environmental Response, Compensation and Liability Act of 1980 (42 U.S.C. 9601(20)(G)(i));

(40) "financial or administrative function" has the meaning provided in section 101(20)(G)(ii) of the Comprehensive Environmental Response, Compensation and Liability Act of 1980 (42 U.S.C. 9601(20)(G)(ii));

(41) "foreclosure" and "foreclose" each has the meaning provided in section 101(20)(G)(iii) of the Comprehensive Environmental Response, Compensation and Liability Act of 1980 (42 U.S.C. 9601(20)(G)(iii));

(42) "lender" has the meaning provided in section 101(20)(G)(iv) of the Comprehensive Environmental Response, Compensation and Liability Act of 1980 (42 U.S.C. 9601(20)(G)(iv));

(43) "operational function" has the meaning provided in section 101(20)(G)(v) of the Comprehensive Environmental Response, Compensation and Liability Act of 1980 (42 U.S.C. 9601(20)(G)(v)); and

(44) "security interest" has the meaning provided in section 101(20)(G)(vi) of the Comprehensive Environmental Response, Compensation and Liability Act of 1980 (42 U.S.C. 9601(20)(G)(vi)).

(Pub. L. 101–380, title I, §1001, Aug. 18, 1990, 104 Stat. 486; Pub. L. 105–383, title III, §307(a), Nov. 13, 1998, 112 Stat. 3421; Pub. L. 108–293, title VII, §703(a), (b), Aug. 9, 2004, 118 Stat. 1069, 1071.)

REFERENCES IN TEXT

This Act, referred to in text, is Pub. L. 101–380, Aug. 18, 1990, 104 Stat. 484, as amended, known as the Oil Pollution Act of 1990, which is classified principally to this chapter. For complete classification of this Act to the Code, see Short Title note set out below and Tables.

The Deepwater Port Act of 1974, referred to in pars. (6) and (32)(C), (D), is Pub. L. 93–627, Jan. 3, 1975, 88 Stat. 2126, as amended, which is classified generally to chapter 29 (§1501 et seq.) of this title. For complete classification of this Act to the Code, see Short Title note set out under section 1501 of this title and Tables.

Presidential Proclamation Numbered 5030, referred to in par. (8), is Proc. No. 5030, Mar. 10, 1983, 48 F.R. 10605, which is set out as a note under section 1453 of Title 16, Conservation.

The Outer Continental Shelf Lands Act, referred to in pars. (16) and (32)(C), is act Aug. 7, 1953, ch. 345, 67 Stat. 462, as amended, which is classified generally to subchapter III (§1331 et seq.) of chapter 29 of Title 43, Public Lands. For complete classification of this Act to the Code, see Short Title note set out under section 1331 of Title 43 and Tables.

The Comprehensive Environmental Response, Compensation, and Liability Act, referred to in par. (23), probably means the Comprehensive Environmental Response, Compensation, and Liability Act of 1980, Pub. L. 96–510, Dec. 11, 1980, 94 Stat. 2767, as amended, which is classified principally to chapter 103 (§9601 et seq.) of Title 42, The Public Health and Welfare. For complete classification of this Act to the Code, see Short Title note set out under section 9601 of Title 42 and Tables.

AMENDMENTS

2004—Par. (26). Pub. L. 108–293, §703(a), amended par. (26) generally. Prior to amendment, par. (26) read as follows: "'owner or operator' means (A) in the case of a vessel, any person owning, operating, or chartering by demise, the vessel, and (B) in the case of an onshore facility, and an offshore facility, any person owning or operating such onshore facility or offshore facility, and (C) in the case of any abandoned offshore facility, the person who owned or operated such facility immediately prior to such abandonment;".

Pars. (38) to (44). Pub. L. 108–293, §703(b), added pars. (38) to (44).

1998—Par. (23). Pub. L. 105–383 amended par. (23) generally. Prior to amendment, par. (23) read as follows: "'oil' means oil of any kind or in any form, including, but not limited to, petroleum, fuel oil, sludge, oil refuse, and oil mixed with wastes other than dredged spoil, but does not include petroleum, including crude oil or any fraction thereof, which is specifically listed or designated as a hazardous substance under subparagraphs (A) through (F) of section 101(14) of the Comprehensive Environmental Response, Compensation, and Liability Act (42 U.S.C. 9601) and which is subject to the provisions of that Act;".

EFFECTIVE DATE

Section 1020 of title I of Pub. L. 101–380 provided that: "This Act [see Short Title of 1990 Amendments note below for classification] shall apply to an incident occurring after the date of the enactment of this Act [Aug. 18, 1990]."

SHORT TITLE OF 2006 AMENDMENT

Pub. L. 109–241, title VI, §601, July 11, 2006, 120 Stat. 553, provided that: "This title [enacting sections 1232b and 2762 of this title, amending sections 1321, 2704, and 2761 of this title, and enacting provisions set out as notes under section 2704 of this title] may be cited as the 'Delaware River Protection Act of 2006'."

SHORT TITLE OF 1995 AMENDMENT

Pub. L. 104–55, §1, Nov. 20, 1995, 109 Stat. 546, provided that: "This Act [enacting section 2720 of this title and amending sections 2704 and 2716 of this title] may be cited as the 'Edible Oil Regulatory Reform Act'."

SHORT TITLE OF 1990 AMENDMENTS

Pub. L. 101–537, title II, §2001, Nov. 8, 1990, 104 Stat. 2375, and Pub. L. 101–646, title IV, §4001, Nov. 29, 1990, 104 Stat. 4788, as amended by Pub. L. 104–332, §2(h)(1), Oct. 26, 1996, 110 Stat. 4091, provided that: "This title [amending section 2761 of this title] may be cited as the 'Great Lakes Oil Pollution Research and Development Act'."

SHORT TITLE

Section 1 of Pub. L. 101–380 provided that: "This Act [enacting this chapter, sections 1642 and 1656 of Title 43, Public Lands, sections 3703a and 7505 of Title 46, Shipping, and section 1274a of the Appendix to Title 46, amending sections 1223, 1228, 1232, 1236, 1319, 1321, 1481, 1486, 1503, 1514, and 1908 of this title, section 3145 of Title 16, Conservation, sections 4612 and 9509 of Title 26, Internal Revenue Code, sections 1334, 1350, and 1653 of Title 43, sections 2101, 2302, 3318, 3715, 3718, 5116, 6101, 7101, 7106, 7107, 7109, 7302, 7502, 7503, 7701 to 7703, 8101, 8104, 8502, 8503, 8702, 9101, 9102, 9302, 9308, and 12106 of Title 46, and section 1274 of the Appendix to Title 46, repealing section 1517 of this title and sections 1811 and 1812 to 1824 of Title 43, enacting provisions set out as notes under this section, sections 1203, 1223, and 1321, of this title, section 92 of Title 14, Coast Guard, section 9509 of Title 26, sections 1334, 1651, and 1653 of Title 43, sections 3703, 3703a, and 7106 of Title 46, and section 1295 of the Appendix to Title 46, amending provisions set out as a note under section 401 of Title 23, Highways, and repealing provisions set out as a note under section 1811 of Title 43] may be cited as the 'Oil Pollution Act of 1990'."

TRANSFER OF FUNCTIONS

For transfer of authorities, functions, personnel, and assets of the Coast Guard, including the authorities and functions of the Secretary of Transportation relating thereto, to the Department of Homeland Security, and for treatment of related references, see sections 468(b), 551(d), 552(d), and 557 of Title 6, Domestic Security, and the Department of Homeland Security Reorganization Plan of November 25, 2002, as modified, set out as a note under section 542 of Title 6.

§2702. Elements of liability

(a) In general

Notwithstanding any other provision or rule of law, and subject to the provisions of this Act, each responsible party for a vessel or a facility from which oil is discharged, or which poses the substantial threat of a discharge of oil, into or upon the navigable waters or adjoining shorelines or the exclusive economic zone is liable for the removal costs and damages specified in subsection (b) of this section that result from such incident.

(b) Covered removal costs and damages

(1) Removal costs

The removal costs referred to in subsection (a) of this section are—

(A) all removal costs incurred by the United States, a State, or an Indian tribe under subsection (c), (d), (e), or (*l*) of section 1321 of this title, under the Intervention on the High Seas Act (33 U.S.C. 1471 et seq.), or under State law; and

(B) any removal costs incurred by any person for acts taken by the person which are consistent with the National Contingency Plan.

(2) Damages

The damages referred to in subsection (a) of this section are the following:

(A) Natural resources

Damages for injury to, destruction of, loss of, or loss of use of, natural resources, including the reasonable costs of assessing the damage, which shall be recoverable by a United States trustee, a State trustee, an Indian tribe trustee, or a foreign trustee.

(B) Real or personal property

Damages for injury to, or economic losses resulting from destruction of, real or personal property, which shall be recoverable by a claimant who owns or leases that property.

(C) Subsistence use

Damages for loss of subsistence use of natural resources, which shall be recoverable by any claimant who so uses natural resources which have been injured, destroyed, or lost, without regard to the ownership or management of the resources.

(D) Revenues

Damages equal to the net loss of taxes, royalties, rents, fees, or net profit shares due to the injury, destruction, or loss of real property, personal property, or natural resources, which shall be recoverable by the Government of the United States, a State, or a political subdivision thereof.

(E) Profits and earning capacity

Damages equal to the loss of profits or impairment of earning capacity due to the injury, destruction, or loss of real property, personal property, or natural resources, which shall be recoverable by any claimant.

(F) Public services

Damages for net costs of providing increased or additional public services during or after removal activities, including protection from fire, safety, or health hazards, caused by a discharge of oil, which shall be recoverable by a State, or a political subdivision of a State.

(c) Excluded discharges

This subchapter does not apply to any discharge—

(1) permitted by a permit issued under Federal, State, or local law;

(2) from a public vessel; or

(3) from an onshore facility which is subject to the Trans-Alaska Pipeline Authorization Act (43 U.S.C. 1651 et seq.).

(d) Liability of third parties

(1) In general

(A) Third party treated as responsible party

Except as provided in subparagraph (B), in any case in which a responsible party establishes that a discharge or threat of a discharge and the resulting removal costs and damages were caused solely by an act or omission of one or more third parties described in section 2703(a)(3) of this title (or solely by such an act or omission in combination with an act of God or an act of war), the third party or parties shall be treated as the responsible party or parties for purposes of determining liability under this subchapter.

(B) Subrogation of responsible party

If the responsible party alleges that the discharge or threat of a discharge was caused solely by an act or omission of a third party, the responsible party—

(i) in accordance with section 2713 of this title, shall pay removal costs and damages to any claimant; and

(ii) shall be entitled by subrogation to all rights of the United States Government and the claimant to recover removal costs or damages from the third party or the Fund paid under this subsection.

(2) Limitation applied

(A) Owner or operator of vessel or facility

If the act or omission of a third party that causes an incident occurs in connection with a vessel or facility owned or operated by the third party, the liability of the third party shall be subject to the limits provided in section 2704 of this title as applied with respect to the vessel or facility.

(B) Other cases

In any other case, the liability of a third party or parties shall not exceed the limitation which would have been applicable to the responsible party of the vessel or facility from which the discharge actually occurred if the responsible party were liable.

(Pub. L. 101–380, title I, § 1002, Aug. 18, 1990, 104 Stat. 489.)

REFERENCES IN TEXT

This Act, referred to in subsec. (a), is Pub. L. 101–380, Aug. 18, 1990, 104 Stat. 484, as amended, known as the Oil Pollution Act of 1990, which is classified principally to this chapter. For complete classification of this Act to the Code, see Short Title note set out under section 2701 of this title and Tables.

The Intervention on the High Seas Act, referred to in subsec. (b)(1)(A), is Pub. L. 93–248, Feb. 5, 1974, 88 Stat. 8, as amended, which is classified generally to chapter 28 (§ 1471 et seq.) of this title. For complete classification of this Act to the Code, see Short Title note set out under section 1471 of this title and Tables.

The Trans-Alaska Pipeline Authorization Act, referred to in subsec. (c)(3), is title II of Pub. L. 93–153, Nov. 16, 1973, 87 Stat. 584, which is classified generally to chapter 34 (§ 1651 et seq.) of Title 43, Public Lands. For complete classification of this Act to the Code, see Short Title note set out under section 1651 of Title 43 and Tables.

§ 2703. Defenses to liability

(a) Complete defenses

A responsible party is not liable for removal costs or damages under section 2702 of this title if the responsible party establishes, by a preponderance of the evidence, that the discharge or substantial threat of a discharge of oil and the resulting damages or removal costs were caused solely by—

(1) an act of God;

(2) an act of war;

(3) an act or omission of a third party, other than an employee or agent of the responsible party or a third party whose act or omission occurs in connection with any contractual relationship with the responsible party (except where the sole contractual arrangement arises in connection with carriage by a common carrier by rail), if the responsible party establishes, by a preponderance of the evidence, that the responsible party—

(A) exercised due care with respect to the oil concerned, taking into consideration the characteristics of the oil and in light of all relevant facts and circumstances; and

(B) took precautions against foreseeable acts or omissions of any such third party and the foreseeable consequences of those acts or omissions; or

(4) any combination of paragraphs (1), (2), and (3).

(b) Defenses as to particular claimants

A responsible party is not liable under section 2702 of this title to a claimant, to the extent that the incident is caused by the gross negligence or willful misconduct of the claimant.

(c) Limitation on complete defense

Subsection (a) of this section does not apply with respect to a responsible party who fails or refuses—

(1) to report the incident as required by law if the responsible party knows or has reason to know of the incident;

(2) to provide all reasonable cooperation and assistance requested by a responsible official in connection with removal activities; or

(3) without sufficient cause, to comply with an order issued under subsection (c) or (e) of section 1321 of this title or the Intervention on the High Seas Act (33 U.S.C. 1471 et seq.).

(d) Definition of contractual relationship

(1) In general

For purposes of subsection (a)(3) of this section the term "contractual relationship" includes, but is not limited to, land contracts, deeds, easements, leases, or other instruments transferring title or possession, unless—

(A) the real property on which the facility concerned is located was acquired by the responsible party after the placement of the oil on, in, or at the real property on which the facility concerned is located;

(B) one or more of the circumstances described in subparagraph (A), (B), or (C) of paragraph (2) is established by the responsible party by a preponderance of the evidence; and

(C) the responsible party complies with paragraph (3).

(2) Required circumstance

The circumstances referred to in paragraph (1)(B) are the following:

(A) At the time the responsible party acquired the real property on which the facility is located the responsible party did not know and had no reason to know that oil that is the subject of the discharge or substantial threat of discharge was located on, in, or at the facility.

(B) The responsible party is a government entity that acquired the facility—

(i) by escheat;

(ii) through any other involuntary transfer or acquisition; or

(iii) through the exercise of eminent domain authority by purchase or condemnation.

(C) The responsible party acquired the facility by inheritance or bequest.

(3) Additional requirements

For purposes of paragraph (1)(C), the responsible party must establish by a preponderance of the evidence that the responsible party—

(A) has satisfied the requirements of subsection (a)(3)(A) and (B) of this section;

(B) has provided full cooperation, assistance, and facility access to the persons that are authorized to conduct removal actions, including the cooperation and access necessary for the installation, integrity, operation, and maintenance of any complete or partial removal action;

(C) is in compliance with any land use restrictions established or relied on in connection with the removal action; and

(D) has not impeded the effectiveness or integrity of any institutional control employed in connection with the removal action.

(4) Reason to know

(A) Appropriate inquiries

To establish that the responsible party had no reason to know of the matter described in paragraph (2)(A), the responsible party must demonstrate to a court that—

(i) on or before the date on which the responsible party acquired the real property on which the facility is located, the responsible party carried out all appropriate inquiries, as provided in subparagraphs (B) and (D), into the previous ownership and uses of the real property on which the facility is located in accordance with generally accepted good commercial and customary standards and practices; and

(ii) the responsible party took reasonable steps to—

(I) stop any continuing discharge;

(II) prevent any substantial threat of discharge; and

(III) prevent or limit any human, environmental, or natural resource exposure to any previously discharged oil.

(B) Regulations establishing standards and practices

Not later than 2 years after August 9, 2004, the Secretary, in consultation with the Administrator of the Environmental Protection Agency, shall by regulation establish standards and practices for the purpose of satisfying the requirement to carry out all appropriate inquiries under subparagraph (A).

(C) Criteria

In promulgating regulations that establish the standards and practices referred to in subparagraph (B), the Secretary shall include in such standards and practices provisions regarding each of the following:

(i) The results of an inquiry by an environmental professional.

(ii) Interviews with past and present owners, operators, and occupants of the facility and the real property on which the facility is located for the purpose of gathering information regarding the potential for oil at the facility and on the real property on which the facility is located.

(iii) Reviews of historical sources, such as chain of title documents, aerial photographs, building department records, and land use records, to determine previous uses and occupancies of the real property on which the facility is located since the property was first developed.

(iv) Searches for recorded environmental cleanup liens against the facility and the real property on which the facility is located that are filed under Federal, State, or local law.

(v) Reviews of Federal, State, and local government records, waste disposal records, underground storage tank records, and waste handling, generation, treatment, disposal, and spill records, concerning oil at or near the facility and on the real property on which the facility is located.

(vi) Visual inspections of the facility, the real property on which the facility is located, and adjoining properties.

(vii) Specialized knowledge or experience on the part of the responsible party.

(viii) The relationship of the purchase price to the value of the facility and the real property on which the facility is located, if oil was not at the facility or on the real property.

(ix) Commonly known or reasonably ascertainable information about the facility and the real property on which the facility is located.

(x) The degree of obviousness of the presence or likely presence of oil at the facility and on the real property on which the facility is located, and the ability to detect the oil by appropriate investigation.

(D) Interim standards and practices

(i) Real property purchased before May 31, 1997

With respect to real property purchased before May 31, 1997, in making a determination with respect to a responsible party described in subparagraph (A), a court shall take into account—

(I) any specialized knowledge or experience on the part of the responsible party;

(II) the relationship of the purchase price to the value of the facility and the real property on which the facility is located, if the oil was not at the facility or on the real property;

(III) commonly known or reasonably ascertainable information about the facility and the real property on which the facility is located;

(IV) the obviousness of the presence or likely presence of oil at the facility and on the real property on which the facility is located; and

(V) the ability of the responsible party to detect oil by appropriate inspection.

(ii) Real property purchased on or after May 31, 1997

With respect to real property purchased on or after May 31, 1997, until the Secretary promulgates the regulations described in clause (ii), the procedures of the American Society for Testing and Materials, including the document known as "Standard E1527–97", entitled "Standard Practice for Environmental Site Assessment: Phase I Environmental Site Assessment Process", shall satisfy the requirements in subparagraph (A).

(E) Site inspection and title search

In the case of real property for residential use or other similar use purchased by a nongovernmental or noncommercial entity, inspection and title search of the facility and the real property on which the facility is located that reveal no basis for further investigation shall be considered to satisfy the requirements of this paragraph.

(5) Previous owner or operator

Nothing in this paragraph or in subsection (a)(3) of this section shall diminish the liability of any previous owner or operator of such facility who would otherwise be liable under this Act. Notwithstanding this paragraph, if a responsible party obtained actual knowledge of the discharge or substantial threat of discharge of oil at such facility when the responsible party owned the facility and then subsequently transferred ownership of the facility or the real property on which the facility is located to another person without disclosing such knowledge, the responsible party shall be treated as liable under 2702(a)[1] of this title and no defense under subsection (a) of this section shall be available to such responsible party.

(6) Limitation on defense

Nothing in this paragraph shall affect the liability under this Act of a responsible party who, by any act or omission, caused or contributed to the discharge or substantial threat of discharge of oil which is the subject of the action relating to the facility.

(Pub. L. 101–380, title I, § 1003, Aug. 18, 1990, 104 Stat. 491; Pub. L. 108–293, title VII, § 703(c), Aug. 9, 2004, 118 Stat. 1072.)

REFERENCES IN TEXT

The Intervention on the High Seas Act, referred to in subsec. (c)(3), is Pub. L. 93–248, Feb. 5, 1974, 88 Stat. 8, as amended, which is classified generally to chapter 28 (§ 1471 et seq.) of this title. For complete classification of this Act to the Code, see Short Title note set out under section 1471 of this title and Tables.

This Act, referred to in subsec. (d)(5), (6), is Pub. L. 101–380, Aug. 18, 1990, 104 Stat. 484, as amended, known as the Oil Pollution Act of 1990, which is classified principally to this chapter. For complete classification of this Act to the Code, see Short Title note set out under section 2701 of this title and Tables.

AMENDMENTS

2004—Subsec. (d). Pub. L. 108–293 added subsec. (d).

§ 2704. Limits on liability

(a) General rule

Except as otherwise provided in this section, the total of the liability of a responsible party under section 2702 of this title and any removal costs incurred by, or on behalf of, the responsible party, with respect to each incident shall not exceed—

(1) for a tank vessel the greater of—

(A) with respect to a single-hull vessel, including a single-hull vessel fitted with double sides only or a double bottom only, $3,000 per gross ton;

(B) with respect to a vessel other than a vessel referred to in subparagraph (A), $1,900 per gross ton; or

(C)(i) with respect to a vessel greater than 3,000 gross tons that is—

(I) a vessel described in subparagraph (A), $22,000,000; or

(II) a vessel described in subparagraph (B), $16,000,000; or

(ii) with respect to a vessel of 3,000 gross tons or less that is—

(I) a vessel described in subparagraph (A), $6,000,000; or

(II) a vessel described in subparagraph (B), $4,000,000;

(2) for any other vessel, $950 per gross ton or $800,000,,[1] whichever is greater;

(3) for an offshore facility except a deepwater port, the total of all removal costs plus $75,000,000; and

(4) for any onshore facility and a deepwater port, $350,000,000.

(b) Division of liability for mobile offshore drilling units

(1) Treated first as tank vessel

For purposes of determining the responsible party and applying this Act and except as provided in paragraph (2), a mobile offshore drilling unit which is being used as an offshore facility is deemed to be a tank vessel with respect to the discharge, or the substantial

[1] So in original. Probably should be preceded by "section".

[1] So in original. The second comma probably should not appear.

threat of a discharge, of oil on or above the surface of the water.

(2) Treated as facility for excess liability

To the extent that removal costs and damages from any incident described in paragraph (1) exceed the amount for which a responsible party is liable (as that amount may be limited under subsection (a)(1) of this section), the mobile offshore drilling unit is deemed to be an offshore facility. For purposes of applying subsection (a)(3) of this section, the amount specified in that subsection shall be reduced by the amount for which the responsible party is liable under paragraph (1).

(c) Exceptions

(1) Acts of responsible party

Subsection (a) of this section does not apply if the incident was proximately caused by—

(A) gross negligence or willful misconduct of, or

(B) the violation of an applicable Federal safety, construction, or operating regulation by,

the responsible party, an agent or employee of the responsible party, or a person acting pursuant to a contractual relationship with the responsible party (except where the sole contractual arrangement arises in connection with carriage by a common carrier by rail).

(2) Failure or refusal of responsible party

Subsection (a) of this section does not apply if the responsible party fails or refuses—

(A) to report the incident as required by law and the responsible party knows or has reason to know of the incident;

(B) to provide all reasonable cooperation and assistance requested by a responsible official in connection with removal activities; or

(C) without sufficient cause, to comply with an order issued under subsection (c) or (e) of section 1321 of this title or the Intervention on the High Seas Act (33 U.S.C. 1471 et seq.).

(3) OCS facility or vessel

Notwithstanding the limitations established under subsection (a) of this section and the defenses of section 2703 of this title, all removal costs incurred by the United States Government or any State or local official or agency in connection with a discharge or substantial threat of a discharge of oil from any Outer Continental Shelf facility or a vessel carrying oil as cargo from such a facility shall be borne by the owner or operator of such facility or vessel.

(4) Certain tank vessels

Subsection (a)(1) of this section shall not apply to—

(A) a tank vessel on which the only oil carried as cargo is an animal fat or vegetable oil, as those terms are used in section 2720 of this title; and

(B) a tank vessel that is designated in its certificate of inspection as an oil spill response vessel (as that term is defined in section 2101 of title 46) and that is used solely for removal.

(d) Adjusting limits of liability

(1) Onshore facilities

Subject to paragraph (2), the President may establish by regulation, with respect to any class or category of onshore facility, a limit of liability under this section of less than $350,000,000, but not less than $8,000,000, taking into account size, storage capacity, oil throughput, proximity to sensitive areas, type of oil handled, history of discharges, and other factors relevant to risks posed by the class or category of facility.

(2) Deepwater ports and associated vessels

(A) Study

The Secretary shall conduct a study of the relative operational and environmental risks posed by the transportation of oil by vessel to deepwater ports (as defined in section 1502 of this title) versus the transportation of oil by vessel to other ports. The study shall include a review and analysis of offshore lightering practices used in connection with that transportation, an analysis of the volume of oil transported by vessel using those practices, and an analysis of the frequency and volume of oil discharges which occur in connection with the use of those practices.

(B) Report

Not later than 1 year after August 18, 1990, the Secretary shall submit to the Congress a report on the results of the study conducted under subparagraph (A).

(C) Rulemaking proceeding

If the Secretary determines, based on the results of the study conducted under this[2] subparagraph (A), that the use of deepwater ports in connection with the transportation of oil by vessel results in a lower operational or environmental risk than the use of other ports, the Secretary shall initiate, not later than the 180th day following the date of submission of the report to the Congress under subparagraph (B), a rulemaking proceeding to lower the limits of liability under this section for deepwater ports as the Secretary determines appropriate. The Secretary may establish a limit of liability of less than $350,000,000, but not less than $50,000,000, in accordance with paragraph (1).

(3) Periodic reports

The President shall, within 6 months after August 18, 1990, and from time to time thereafter, report to the Congress on the desirability of adjusting the limits of liability specified in subsection (a) of this section.

(4) Adjustment to reflect Consumer Price Index

The President, by regulations issued not later than 3 years after July 11, 2006, and not less than every 3 years thereafter, shall adjust the limits on liability specified in subsection (a) to reflect significant increases in the Consumer Price Index.

(Pub. L. 101–380, title I, §1004, Aug. 18, 1990, 104 Stat. 491; Pub. L. 104–55, §2(d)(1), Nov. 20, 1995,

[2] So in original. The word "this" probably should not appear.

109 Stat. 546; Pub. L. 105–383, title IV, § 406, Nov. 13, 1998, 112 Stat. 3429; Pub. L. 109–241, title VI, § 603(a)(1), (2), (b), July 11, 2006, 120 Stat. 553, 554.)

REFERENCES IN TEXT

This Act, referred to in subsec. (b)(1), is Pub. L. 101–380, Aug. 18, 1990, 104 Stat. 484, as amended, known as the Oil Pollution Act of 1990, which is classified principally to this chapter. For complete classification of this Act to the Code, see Short Title note set out under section 2701 of this title and Tables.

The Intervention on the High Seas Act, referred to in subsec. (c)(2)(C), is Pub. L. 93–248, Feb. 5, 1974, 88 Stat. 8, as amended, which is classified generally to chapter 28 (§ 1471 et seq.) of this title. For complete classification of this Act to the Code, see Short Title note set out under section 1471 of this title and Tables.

AMENDMENTS

2006—Subsec. (a)(1)(A) to (C). Pub. L. 109–241, § 603(a)(1), added subpars. (A) to (C) and struck out former subpars. (A) and (B), which read as follows:

"(A) $1,200 per gross ton; or

"(B)(i) in the case of a vessel greater than 3,000 gross tons, $10,000,000; or

"(ii) in the case of a vessel of 3,000 gross tons or less, $2,000,000;".

Subsec. (a)(2). Pub. L. 109–241, § 603(a)(2), substituted "$950 per gross ton" for "$600 per gross ton" and "$800,000," for "$500,000".

Subsec. (d)(4). Pub. L. 109–241, § 603(b), amended heading and text of par. (4) generally. Prior to amendment, text read as follows: "The President shall, by regulations issued not less often than every 3 years, adjust the limits of liability specified in subsection (a) of this section to reflect significant increases in the Consumer Price Index."

1998—Subsec. (a)(1). Pub. L. 105–383, § 406(1), substituted comma for "(except a tank vessel on which the only oil carried as cargo is an animal fat or vegetable oil, as those terms are used in section 2720 of this title)" after "tank vessel".

Subsec. (c)(4). Pub. L. 105–383, § 406(2), added par. (4).

1995—Subsec. (a)(1). Pub. L. 104–55 substituted "for a tank vessel (except a tank vessel on which the only oil carried as cargo is an animal fat or vegetable oil, as those terms are used in section 2720 of this title)" for "for a tank vessel,".

EFFECTIVE DATE OF 2006 AMENDMENT

Pub. L. 109–241, title VI, § 603(a)(3), July 11, 2006, 120 Stat. 554, provided that: "In the case of an incident occurring before the 90th day following the date of enactment of this Act [July 11, 2006], section 1004(a)(1) of the Oil Pollution Act of 1990 (33 U.S.C. 2704(a)(1)) shall apply as in effect immediately before the effective date of this subsection [July 11, 2006]."

DELEGATION OF FUNCTIONS

Specific functions of President under subsec. (d) of this section delegated to Administrator of Environmental Protection Agency, Secretary of Transportation, and Secretary of the Interior by section 4 of Ex. Ord. No. 12777, Oct. 18, 1991, 56 F.R. 54763, set out as a note under section 1321 of this title.

REPORT

Pub. L. 109–241, title VI, § 603(c), July 11, 2006, 120 Stat. 554, provided that:

"(1) INITIAL REPORT.—Not later than 45 days after the date of enactment of this Act [July 11, 2006], the Secretary of the department in which the Coast Guard is operating shall submit a report on liability limits described in paragraph (2) to the Committee on Commerce, Science, and Transportation of the Senate and the Committee on Transportation and Infrastructure of the House of Representatives.

"(2) CONTENTS.—The report shall include, at a minimum, the following:

"(A) An analysis of the extent to which oil discharges from vessels and nonvessel sources have or are likely to result in removal costs and damages (as defined in section 1001 of the Oil Pollution Act of 1990 (33 U.S.C. 2701)) for which no defense to liability exists under section 1003 of such Act [33 U.S.C. 2703] and that exceed the liability limits established in section 1004 of such Act [33 U.S.C. 2704], as amended by this section.

"(B) An analysis of the impacts that claims against the Oil Spill Liability Trust Fund for amounts exceeding such liability limits will have on the Fund.

"(C) Based on analyses under this paragraph and taking into account other factors impacting the Fund, recommendations on whether the liability limits need to be adjusted in order to prevent the principal of the Fund from declining to levels that are likely to be insufficient to cover expected claims.

"(3) ANNUAL UPDATES.—The Secretary shall provide an update of the report to the Committees referred to in paragraph (1) on an annual basis."

§ 2705. Interest; partial payment of claims

(a) General rule

The responsible party or the responsible party's guarantor is liable to a claimant for interest on the amount paid in satisfaction of a claim under this Act for the period described in subsection (b) of this section. The responsible party shall establish a procedure for the payment or settlement of claims for interim, short-term damages. Payment or settlement of a claim for interim, short-term damages representing less than the full amount of damages to which the claimant ultimately may be entitled shall not preclude recovery by the claimant for damages not reflected in the paid or settled partial claim.

(b) Period

(1) In general

Except as provided in paragraph (2), the period for which interest shall be paid is the period beginning on the 30th day following the date on which the claim is presented to the responsible party or guarantor and ending on the date on which the claim is paid.

(2) Exclusion of period due to offer by guarantor

If the guarantor offers to the claimant an amount equal to or greater than that finally paid in satisfaction of the claim, the period described in paragraph (1) does not include the period beginning on the date the offer is made and ending on the date the offer is accepted. If the offer is made within 60 days after the date on which the claim is presented under section 2713(a) of this title, the period described in paragraph (1) does not include any period before the offer is accepted.

(3) Exclusion of periods in interests of justice

If in any period a claimant is not paid due to reasons beyond the control of the responsible party or because it would not serve the interests of justice, no interest shall accrue under this section during that period.

(4) Calculation of interest

The interest paid under this section shall be calculated at the average of the highest rate for commercial and finance company paper of maturities of 180 days or less obtaining on each of the days included within the period for which interest must be paid to the claimant, as published in the Federal Reserve Bulletin.

(5) Interest not subject to liability limits

(A) In general

Interest (including prejudgment interest) under this paragraph is in addition to damages and removal costs for which claims may be asserted under section 2702 of this title and shall be paid without regard to any limitation of liability under section 2704 of this title.

(B) Payment by guarantor

The payment of interest under this subsection by a guarantor is subject to section 2716(g) of this title.

(Pub. L. 101–380, title I, §1005, Aug. 18, 1990, 104 Stat. 493; Pub. L. 104–324, title XI, §1142(a), Oct. 19, 1996, 110 Stat. 3991.)

REFERENCES IN TEXT

This Act, referred to in subsec. (a), is Pub. L. 101–380, Aug. 18, 1990, 104 Stat. 484, as amended, known as the Oil Pollution Act of 1990, which is classified principally to this chapter. For complete classification of this Act to the Code, see Short Title note set out under section 2701 of this title and Tables.

AMENDMENTS

1996—Pub. L. 104–324, §1142(a)(1), inserted "; partial payment of claims" after "Interest" in section catchline.

Subsec. (a). Pub. L. 104–324, §1142(a)(2), inserted at end "The responsible party shall establish a procedure for the payment or settlement of claims for interim, short-term damages. Payment or settlement of a claim for interim, short-term damages representing less than the full amount of damages to which the claimant ultimately may be entitled shall not preclude recovery by the claimant for damages not reflected in the paid or settled partial claim."

§2706. Natural resources

(a) Liability

In the case of natural resource damages under section 2702(b)(2)(A) of this title, liability shall be—

(1) to the United States Government for natural resources belonging to, managed by, controlled by, or appertaining to the United States;

(2) to any State for natural resources belonging to, managed by, controlled by, or appertaining to such State or political subdivision thereof;

(3) to any Indian tribe for natural resources belonging to, managed by, controlled by, or appertaining to such Indian tribe; and

(4) in any case in which section 2707 of this title applies, to the government of a foreign country for natural resources belonging to, managed by, controlled by, or appertaining to such country.

(b) Designation of trustees

(1) In general

The President, or the authorized representative of any State, Indian tribe, or foreign government, shall act on behalf of the public, Indian tribe, or foreign country as trustee of natural resources to present a claim for and to recover damages to the natural resources.

(2) Federal trustees

The President shall designate the Federal officials who shall act on behalf of the public as trustees for natural resources under this Act.

(3) State trustees

The Governor of each State shall designate State and local officials who may act on behalf of the public as trustee for natural resources under this Act and shall notify the President of the designation.

(4) Indian tribe trustees

The governing body of any Indian tribe shall designate tribal officials who may act on behalf of the tribe or its members as trustee for natural resources under this Act and shall notify the President of the designation.

(5) Foreign trustees

The head of any foreign government may designate the trustee who shall act on behalf of that government as trustee for natural resources under this Act.

(c) Functions of trustees

(1) Federal trustees

The Federal officials designated under subsection (b)(2) of this section—

(A) shall assess natural resource damages under section 2702(b)(2)(A) of this title for the natural resources under their trusteeship;

(B) may, upon request of and reimbursement from a State or Indian tribe and at the Federal officials' discretion, assess damages for the natural resources under the State's or tribe's trusteeship; and

(C) shall develop and implement a plan for the restoration, rehabilitation, replacement, or acquisition of the equivalent, of the natural resources under their trusteeship.

(2) State trustees

The State and local officials designated under subsection (b)(3) of this section—

(A) shall assess natural resource damages under section 2702(b)(2)(A) of this title for the purposes of this Act for the natural resources under their trusteeship; and

(B) shall develop and implement a plan for the restoration, rehabilitation, replacement, or acquisition of the equivalent, of the natural resources under their trusteeship.

(3) Indian tribe trustees

The tribal officials designated under subsection (b)(4) of this section—

(A) shall assess natural resource damages under section 2702(b)(2)(A) of this title for the purposes of this Act for the natural resources under their trusteeship; and

(B) shall develop and implement a plan for the restoration, rehabilitation, replacement, or acquisition of the equivalent, of the natural resources under their trusteeship.

(4) Foreign trustees

The trustees designated under subsection (b)(5) of this section—

(A) shall assess natural resource damages under section 2702(b)(2)(A) of this title for the purposes of this Act for the natural resources under their trusteeship; and

(B) shall develop and implement a plan for the restoration, rehabilitation, replacement, or acquisition of the equivalent, of the natural resources under their trusteeship.

(5) Notice and opportunity to be heard

Plans shall be developed and implemented under this section only after adequate public notice, opportunity for a hearing, and consideration of all public comment.

(d) Measure of damages

(1) In general

The measure of natural resource damages under section 2702(b)(2)(A) of this title is—

(A) the cost of restoring, rehabilitating, replacing, or acquiring the equivalent of, the damaged natural resources;

(B) the diminution in value of those natural resources pending restoration; plus

(C) the reasonable cost of assessing those damages.

(2) Determine costs with respect to plans

Costs shall be determined under paragraph (1) with respect to plans adopted under subsection (c) of this section.

(3) No double recovery

There shall be no double recovery under this Act for natural resource damages, including with respect to the costs of damage assessment or restoration, rehabilitation, replacement, or acquisition for the same incident and natural resource.

(e) Damage assessment regulations

(1) Regulations

The President, acting through the Under Secretary of Commerce for Oceans and Atmosphere and in consultation with the Administrator of the Environmental Protection Agency, the Director of the United States Fish and Wildlife Service, and the heads of other affected agencies, not later than 2 years after August 18, 1990, shall promulgate regulations for the assessment of natural resource damages under section 2702(b)(2)(A) of this title resulting from a discharge of oil for the purpose of this Act.

(2) Rebuttable presumption

Any determination or assessment of damages to natural resources for the purposes of this Act made under subsection (d) of this section by a Federal, State, or Indian trustee in accordance with the regulations promulgated under paragraph (1) shall have the force and effect of a rebuttable presumption on behalf of the trustee in any administrative or judicial proceeding under this Act.

(f) Use of recovered sums

Sums recovered under this Act by a Federal, State, Indian, or foreign trustee for natural resource damages under section 2702(b)(2)(A) of this title shall be retained by the trustee in a revolving trust account, without further appropriation, for use only to reimburse or pay costs incurred by the trustee under subsection (c) of this section with respect to the damaged natural resources. Any amounts in excess of those required for these reimbursements and costs shall be deposited in the Fund.

(g) Compliance

Review of actions by any Federal official where there is alleged to be a failure of that official to perform a duty under this section that is not discretionary with that official may be had by any person in the district court in which the person resides or in which the alleged damage to natural resources occurred. The court may award costs of litigation (including reasonable attorney and expert witness fees) to any prevailing or substantially prevailing party. Nothing in this subsection shall restrict any right which any person may have to seek relief under any other provision of law.

(Pub. L. 101–380, title I, §1006, Aug. 18, 1990, 104 Stat. 494.)

REFERENCES IN TEXT

This Act, referred to in subsecs. (b)(2)–(5), (c)(2)(A), (3)(A), (4)(A), (d)(3), (e), and (f), is Pub. L. 101–380, Aug. 18, 1990, 104 Stat. 484, as amended, known as the Oil Pollution Act of 1990, which is classified principally to this chapter. For complete classification of this Act to the Code, see Short Title note set out under section 2701 of this title and Tables.

DELEGATION OF FUNCTIONS

Functions of President under subsec. (b)(3) and (4) of this section delegated to Administrator of Environmental Protection Agency by section 8(c) of Ex. Ord. No. 12777, Oct. 18, 1991, 56 F.R. 54768, set out as a note under section 1321 of this title.

NOAA OIL AND HAZARDOUS SUBSTANCE SPILL COST REIMBURSEMENT

Pub. L. 102–567, title II, §205, Oct. 29, 1992, 106 Stat. 4282, provided that:

"(a) TREATMENT OF AMOUNTS RECEIVED AS REIMBURSEMENT OF EXPENSES.—Notwithstanding any other provision of law, amounts received by the United States as reimbursement of expenses related to oil or hazardous substance spill response activities, or natural resource damage assessment, restoration, rehabilitation, replacement, or acquisition activities, conducted (or to be conducted) by the National Oceanic and Atmospheric Administration—

"(1) shall be deposited into the Fund;

"(2) shall be available, without fiscal year limitation and without apportionment, for use in accordance with the law under which the activities are conducted; and

"(3) shall not be considered to be an augmentation of appropriations.

"(b) APPLICATION.—Subsection (a) shall apply to amounts described in subsection (a) that are received—

"(1) after the date of the enactment of this Act [Oct. 29, 1992]; or

"(2) with respect to the oil spill associated with the grounding of the EXXON VALDEZ.

"(c) DEFINITIONS.—For purposes of this section—

"(1) the term 'Fund' means the Damage Assessment and Restoration Revolving Fund of the National Oceanic and Atmospheric Administration referred to in title I of Public Law 101–515 under the heading 'National Oceanic and Atmospheric Administration' (104 Stat. 2105) [set out as a note below]; and

"(2) the term 'expenses' includes incremental and base salaries, ships, aircraft, and associated indirect costs, except the term does not include base salaries and benefits of National Oceanic and Atmospheric Administration Support Coordinators."

DAMAGE ASSESSMENT AND RESTORATION REVOLVING FUND; DEPOSITS; AVAILABILITY; TRANSFER

Pub. L. 101–515, title I, Nov. 5, 1990, 104 Stat. 2105, provided that: "For contingency planning, response and natural resource damage assessment and restoration activities, pursuant to the Comprehensive Environmental Response, Compensation[,] and Liability Act [of 1980], as amended [42 U.S.C. 9601 et seq.], the Federal Water Pollution Control Act, as amended [33 U.S.C. 1251 et seq.], the Marine Protection, Research[,] and Sanctuaries Act [of 1972], as amended [16 U.S.C. 1431et seq., 1447 et seq.; 33 U.S.C. 1401 et seq., 2801 et seq.], and the Oil Pollution Act of 1990 [33 U.S.C. 2701 et seq.], $5,000,000 to remain available until expended: *Provided*, That notwithstanding any other provision of law, in fiscal year 1991 and thereafter, sums provided by any party or governmental entity for natural resource damage assessment, response or restoration activities conducted or to be conducted by the National Oceanic and Atmospheric Administration as a result of any injury to the marine environment and/or resources for which the National Oceanic and Atmospheric Administration acts as trustee of said marine environment and/or resources, shall be deposited in the Damage Assessment and Restoration Revolving Fund and said funds so deposited shall remain available until expended: *Provided further*, That for purposes of obligation and expenditure in fiscal year 1991 and thereafter, sums available in the Damage Assessment and Restoration Revolving Fund may be transferred, upon the approval of the Secretary of Commerce or his delegate, to the Operations, Research, and Facilities appropriation of the National Oceanic and Atmospheric Administration."

§2707. Recovery by foreign claimants

(a) Required showing by foreign claimants

(1) In general

In addition to satisfying the other requirements of this Act, to recover removal costs or damages resulting from an incident a foreign claimant shall demonstrate that—

(A) the claimant has not been otherwise compensated for the removal costs or damages; and

(B) recovery is authorized by a treaty or executive agreement between the United States and the claimant's country, or the Secretary of State, in consultation with the Attorney General and other appropriate officials, has certified that the claimant's country provides a comparable remedy for United States claimants.

(2) Exceptions

Paragraph (1)(B) shall not apply with respect to recovery by a resident of Canada in the case of an incident described in subsection (b)(4) of this section.

(b) Discharges in foreign countries

A foreign claimant may make a claim for removal costs and damages resulting from a discharge, or substantial threat of a discharge, of oil in or on the territorial sea, internal waters, or adjacent shoreline of a foreign country, only if the discharge is from—

(1) an Outer Continental Shelf facility or a deepwater port;

(2) a vessel in the navigable waters;

(3) a vessel carrying oil as cargo between 2 places in the United States; or

(4) a tanker that received the oil at the terminal of the pipeline constructed under the Trans-Alaska Pipeline Authorization Act (43 U.S.C. 1651 et seq.), for transportation to a place in the United States, and the discharge or threat occurs prior to delivery of the oil to that place.

(c) "Foreign claimant" defined

In this section, the term "foreign claimant" means—

(1) a person residing in a foreign country;

(2) the government of a foreign country; and

(3) an agency or political subdivision of a foreign country.

(Pub. L. 101–380, title I, §1007, Aug. 18, 1990, 104 Stat. 496.)

References in Text

This Act, referred to in subsec. (a)(1), is Pub. L. 101–380, Aug. 18, 1990, 104 Stat. 484, as amended, known as the Oil Pollution Act of 1990, which is classified principally to this chapter. For complete classification of this Act to the Code, see Short Title note set out under section 2701 of this title and Tables.

The Trans-Alaska Pipeline Authorization Act, referred to in subsec. (b)(4), is title II of Pub. L. 93–153, Nov. 16, 1973, 87 Stat. 584, which is classified generally to chapter 34 (§1651 et seq.) of Title 43, Public Lands. For complete classification of this Act to the Code, see Short Title note set out under section 1651 of Title 43 and Tables.

§2708. Recovery by responsible party

(a) In general

The responsible party for a vessel or facility from which oil is discharged, or which poses the substantial threat of a discharge of oil, may assert a claim for removal costs and damages under section 2713 of this title only if the responsible party demonstrates that—

(1) the responsible party is entitled to a defense to liability under section 2703 of this title; or

(2) the responsible party is entitled to a limitation of liability under section 2704 of this title.

(b) Extent of recovery

A responsible party who is entitled to a limitation of liability may assert a claim under section 2713 of this title only to the extent that the sum of the removal costs and damages incurred by the responsible party plus the amounts paid by the responsible party, or by the guarantor on behalf of the responsible party, for claims asserted under section 2713 of this title exceeds the amount to which the total of the liability under section 2702 of this title and removal costs and damages incurred by, or on behalf of, the responsible party is limited under section 2704 of this title.

(Pub. L. 101–380, title I, §1008, Aug. 18, 1990, 104 Stat. 497.)

§2709. Contribution

A person may bring a civil action for contribution against any other person who is liable or potentially liable under this Act or another law. The action shall be brought in accordance with section 2717 of this title.

(Pub. L. 101–380, title I, §1009, Aug. 18, 1990, 104 Stat. 497.)

References in Text

This Act, referred to in text, is Pub. L. 101–380, Aug. 18, 1990, 104 Stat. 484, as amended, known as the Oil Pollution Act of 1990, which is classified principally to this chapter. For complete classification of this Act to the Code, see Short Title note set out under section 2701 of this title and Tables.

§2710. Indemnification agreements

(a) Agreements not prohibited

Nothing in this Act prohibits any agreement to insure, hold harmless, or indemnify a party to such agreement for any liability under this Act.

(b) Liability not transferred

No indemnification, hold harmless, or similar agreement or conveyance shall be effective to transfer liability imposed under this Act from a responsible party or from any person who may be liable for an incident under this Act to any other person.

(c) Relationship to other causes of action

Nothing in this Act, including the provisions of subsection (b) of this section, bars a cause of action that a responsible party subject to liability under this Act, or a guarantor, has or would have, by reason of subrogation or otherwise, against any person.

(Pub. L. 101–380, title I, §1010, Aug. 18, 1990, 104 Stat. 498.)

References in Text

This Act, referred to in text, is Pub. L. 101–380, Aug. 18, 1990, 104 Stat. 484, as amended, known as the Oil Pollution Act of 1990, which is classified principally to this chapter. For complete classification of this Act to the Code, see Short Title note set out under section 2701 of this title and Tables.

§2711. Consultation on removal actions

The President shall consult with the affected trustees designated under section 2706 of this title on the appropriate removal action to be taken in connection with any discharge of oil. For the purposes of the National Contingency Plan, removal with respect to any discharge shall be considered completed when so determined by the President in consultation with the Governor or Governors of the affected States. However, this determination shall not preclude additional removal actions under applicable State law.

(Pub. L. 101–380, title I, §1011, Aug. 18, 1990, 104 Stat. 498.)

Delegation of Functions

Functions of President under this section delegated to Administrator of Environmental Protection Agency for inland zone and to Secretary of Department in which Coast Guard is operating for coastal zone by section 3 of Ex. Ord. No. 12777, Oct. 18, 1991, 56 F.R. 54757, set out as a note under section 1321 of this title.

§2712. Uses of Fund

(a) Uses generally

The Fund shall be available to the President for—

(1) the payment of removal costs, including the costs of monitoring removal actions, determined by the President to be consistent with the National Contingency Plan—

(A) by Federal authorities; or

(B) by a Governor or designated State official under subsection (d) of this section;

(2) the payment of costs incurred by Federal, State, or Indian tribe trustees in carrying out their functions under section 2706 of this title for assessing natural resource damages and for developing and implementing plans for the restoration, rehabilitation, replacement, or acquisition of the equivalent of damaged resources determined by the President to be consistent with the National Contingency Plan;

(3) the payment of removal costs determined by the President to be consistent with the National Contingency Plan as a result of, and damages resulting from, a discharge, or a substantial threat of a discharge, of oil from a foreign offshore unit;

(4) the payment of claims in accordance with section 2713 of this title for uncompensated removal costs determined by the President to be consistent with the National Contingency Plan or uncompensated damages;

(5) the payment of Federal administrative, operational, and personnel costs and expenses reasonably necessary for and incidental to the implementation, administration, and enforcement of this Act (including, but not limited to, sections 1004(d)(2), 1006(e), 4107, 4110, 4111, 4112, 4117, 5006, 8103, and title VII) and subsections (b), (c), (d), (j), and (*l*) of section 1321 of this title with respect to prevention, removal, and enforcement related to oil discharges, provided that—

(A) not more than $25,000,000 in each fiscal year shall be available to the Secretary for operating expenses incurred by the Coast Guard;

(B) not more than $30,000,000 each year through the end of fiscal year 1992 shall be available to establish the National Response System under section 1321(j) of this title, including the purchase and prepositioning of oil spill removal equipment; and

(C) not more than $27,250,000 in each fiscal year shall be available to carry out subchapter IV of this chapter; and

(6) the making of loans pursuant to the program established under section 2713(f) of this title.

(b) Defense to liability for Fund

The Fund shall not be available to pay any claim for removal costs or damages to a particular claimant, to the extent that the incident, removal costs, or damages are caused by the gross negligence or willful misconduct of that claimant.

(c) Obligation of Fund by Federal officials

The President may promulgate regulations designating one or more Federal officials who may obligate money in accordance with subsection (a) of this section.

(d) Access to Fund by State officials

(1) Immediate removal

In accordance with regulations promulgated under this section, the President, upon the request of the Governor of a State or pursuant to an agreement with a State under paragraph (2), may obligate the Fund for payment in an amount not to exceed $250,000 for removal costs consistent with the National Contingency Plan required for the immediate removal of a discharge, or the mitigation or prevention of a substantial threat of a discharge, of oil.

(2) Agreements

(A) In general

The President shall enter into an agreement with the Governor of any interested State to establish procedures under which the Governor or a designated State official may receive payments from the Fund for removal costs pursuant to paragraph (1).

(B) Terms

Agreements under this paragraph—

(i) may include such terms and conditions as may be agreed upon by the President and the Governor of a State;

(ii) shall provide for political subdivisions of the State to receive payments for reasonable removal costs; and

(iii) may authorize advance payments from the Fund to facilitate removal efforts.

(e) Regulations

The President shall—

(1) not later than 6 months after August 18, 1990, publish proposed regulations detailing the manner in which the authority to obligate the Fund and to enter into agreements under this subsection shall be exercised; and

(2) not later than 3 months after the close of the comment period for such proposed regulations, promulgate final regulations for that purpose.

(f) Rights of subrogation

Payment of any claim or obligation by the Fund under this Act shall be subject to the United States Government acquiring by subrogation all rights of the claimant or State to recover from the responsible party.

(g) Audits

The Comptroller General shall audit all payments, obligations, reimbursements, and other uses of the Fund, to assure that the Fund is being properly administered and that claims are being appropriately and expeditiously considered. The Comptroller General shall submit to the Congress an interim report one year after August 18, 1990. The Comptroller General shall thereafter audit the Fund as is appropriate. Each Federal agency shall cooperate with the Comptroller General in carrying out this subsection.

(h) Period of limitations for claims

(1) Removal costs

No claim may be presented under this subchapter for recovery of removal costs for an incident unless the claim is presented within 6 years after the date of completion of all removal actions for that incident.

(2) Damages

No claim may be presented under this section for recovery of damages unless the claim is presented within 3 years after the date on which the injury and its connection with the discharge in question were reasonably discoverable with the exercise of due care, or in the case of natural resource damages under section 2702(b)(2)(A) of this title, if later, the date of completion of the natural resources damage assessment under section 2706(e) of this title.

(3) Minors and incompetents

The time limitations contained in this subsection shall not begin to run—

(A) against a minor until the earlier of the date when such minor reaches 18 years of age or the date on which a legal representative is duly appointed for the minor, or

(B) against an incompetent person until the earlier of the date on which such incompetent's incompetency ends or the date on which a legal representative is duly appointed for the incompetent.

(i) Limitation on payment for same costs

In any case in which the President has paid an amount from the Fund for any removal costs or damages specified under subsection (a) of this section, no other claim may be paid from the Fund for the same removal costs or damages.

(j) Obligation in accordance with plan

(1) In general

Except as provided in paragraph (2), amounts may be obligated from the Fund for the restoration, rehabilitation, replacement, or acquisition of natural resources only in accordance with a plan adopted under section 2706(c) of this title.

(2) Exception

Paragraph (1) shall not apply in a situation requiring action to avoid irreversible loss of natural resources or to prevent or reduce any continuing danger to natural resources or similar need for emergency action.

(k) Preference for private persons in area affected by discharge

(1) In general

In the expenditure of Federal funds for removal of oil, including for distribution of supplies, construction, and other reasonable and appropriate activities, under a contract or agreement with a private person, preference shall be given, to the extent feasible and practicable, to private persons residing or doing business primarily in the area affected by the discharge of oil.

(2) Limitation

This subsection shall not be considered to restrict the use of Department of Defense resources.

(Pub. L. 101–380, title I, §1012, Aug. 18, 1990, 104 Stat. 498; Pub. L. 108–293, title VII, §708(b), Aug. 9, 2004, 118 Stat. 1077.)

REFERENCES IN TEXT

This Act, referred to in subsecs. (a)(5) and (f), is Pub. L. 101–380, Aug. 18, 1990, 104 Stat. 484, known as the Oil Pollution Act of 1990, which is classified principally to this chapter. Sections 1004(d)(2) and 1006(e) are classified to sections 2704(d)(2) and 2706(e), respectively, of this title. Section 4107 amended section 1223 of this title and enacted provisions set out as a note under section 1223 of this title. Sections 4110 and 4111 enacted provisions set out as a note and formerly set out as a note under section 3703 of Title 46, Shipping. Section 4112 is not classified to the Code. Section 4117 enacted provisions set out as a note under section 1295 of the former Appendix to Title 46. Section 5006 is classified to section 2736 of this title. Section 8103 enacted provisions formerly set out as a note under section 1651 of Title 43, Public Lands. Title VII is classified to subchapter IV of this chapter. For complete classification of this Act to the Code, see Short Title note set out under section 2701 of this title and Tables.

AMENDMENTS

2004—Subsec. (a)(6). Pub. L. 108–293 added par. (6).

TRANSFER OF FUNCTIONS

For transfer of authorities, functions, personnel, and assets of the Coast Guard, including the authorities and functions of the Secretary of Transportation relating thereto, to the Department of Homeland Security, and for treatment of related references, see sections 468(b), 551(d), 552(d), and 557 of Title 6, Domestic Security, and the Department of Homeland Security Reorganization Plan of November 25, 2002, as modified, set out as a note under section 542 of Title 6.

DELEGATION OF FUNCTIONS

Functions of President under subsecs. (a)(1), (3), (4), (d), and (e) of this section delegated to Secretary of Department in which Coast Guard is operating by section 7(a)(1)(A), (c)(1), (3) of Ex. Ord. No. 12777, Oct. 18, 1991, 56 F.R. 54766, 54767, set out as a note under section 1321 of this title.

Functions of President under subsec. (a)(2) of this section delegated to Federal trustees designated in National Contingency Plan by section 7(a)(2) of Ex. Ord. No. 12777.

Functions of President under subsecs. (a)(5) and (c) of this section delegated to each head of departments and agencies having responsibility for implementation, administration, and enforcement of the Oil Pollution Act of 1990 (Pub. L. 101–380, see Tables for classification) and section 1321(b), (c), (d), (j), (*l*) of this title by section 7(a)(3), (b) of Ex. Ord. No. 12777.

Memorandum of the President of the United States, Aug. 24, 1990, 55 F.R. 35291, which delegated to the Secretary of the Department in which the Coast Guard is operating authority to make available from the Oil Spill Liability Trust Fund not to exceed $50,000,000 in any fiscal year to remove discharged oil or hazardous substances from navigable waters, was revoked by Ex. Ord. No. 12777, §8(i), Oct. 18, 1991, 56 F.R. 54769, set out as a note under section 1321 of this title.

§ 2713. Claims procedure

(a) Presentation

Except as provided in subsection (b) of this section, all claims for removal costs or damages shall be presented first to the responsible party or guarantor of the source designated under section 2714(a) of this title.

(b) Presentation to Fund

(1) In general

Claims for removal costs or damages may be presented first to the Fund—

(A) if the President has advertised or otherwise notified claimants in accordance with section 2714(c) of this title;

(B) by a responsible party who may assert a claim under section 2708 of this title;

(C) by the Governor of a State for removal costs incurred by that State; or

(D) by a United States claimant in a case where a foreign offshore unit has discharged oil causing damage for which the Fund is liable under section 2712(a) of this title.

(2) Limitation on presenting claim

No claim of a person against the Fund may be approved or certified during the pendency of an action by the person in court to recover costs which are the subject of the claim.

(c) Election

If a claim is presented in accordance with subsection (a) of this section and—

(1) each person to whom the claim is presented denies all liability for the claim, or

(2) the claim is not settled by any person by payment within 90 days after the date upon which (A) the claim was presented, or (B) advertising was begun pursuant to section 2714(b) of this title, whichever is later,

the claimant may elect to commence an action in court against the responsible party or guarantor or to present the claim to the Fund.

(d) Uncompensated damages

If a claim is presented in accordance with this section, including a claim for interim, short-term damages representing less than the full amount of damages to which the claimant ultimately may be entitled, and full and adequate compensation is unavailable, a claim for the uncompensated damages and removal costs may be presented to the Fund.

(e) Procedure for claims against Fund

The President shall promulgate, and may from time to time amend, regulations for the presentation, filing, processing, settlement, and adjudication of claims under this Act against the Fund.

(f) Loan program

(1) In general

The President shall establish a loan program under the Fund to provide interim assistance to fishermen and aquaculture producer claimants during the claims procedure.

(2) Eligibility for loan

A loan may be made under paragraph (1) only to a fisherman or aquaculture producer that—

(A) has incurred damages for which claims are authorized under section 2702 of this title;

(B) has made a claim pursuant to this section that is pending; and

(C) has not received an interim payment under section 2705(a) of this title for the amount of the claim, or part thereof, that is pending.

(3) Terms and conditions of loans

A loan awarded under paragraph (1)—

(A) shall have flexible terms, as determined by the President;

(B) shall be for a period ending on the later of—

(i) the date that is 5 years after the date on which the loan is made; or

(ii) the date on which the fisherman or aquaculture producer receives payment for the claim to which the loan relates under the procedure established by subsections (a) through (e) of this section; and

(C) shall be at a low interest rate, as determined by the President.

(Pub. L. 101–380, title I, §1013, Aug. 18, 1990, 104 Stat. 501; Pub. L. 104–324, title XI, §1142(b), Oct. 19, 1996, 110 Stat. 3991; Pub. L. 108–293, title VII, §708(a), Aug. 9, 2004, 118 Stat. 1077.)

REFERENCES IN TEXT

This Act, referred to in subsec. (e), is Pub. L. 101–380, Aug. 18, 1990, 104 Stat. 484, as amended, known as the Oil Pollution Act of 1990, which is classified principally to this chapter. For complete classification of this Act to the Code, see Short Title note set out under section 2701 of this title and Tables.

AMENDMENTS

2004—Subsec. (f). Pub. L. 108–293 added subsec.(f).

1996—Subsec. (d). Pub. L. 104–324 substituted "section, including a claim for interim, short-term damages representing less than the full amount of damages to which the claimant ultimately may be entitled," for "section".

DELEGATION OF FUNCTIONS

Functions of President under subsec. (e) of this section delegated to Secretary of Department in which Coast Guard is operating by section 7(c)(2) of Ex. Ord. No. 12777, Oct. 18, 1991, 56 F.R. 54767, set out as a note under section 1321 of this title.

§2714. Designation of source and advertisement

(a) Designation of source and notification

When the President receives information of an incident, the President shall, where possible and appropriate, designate the source or sources of the discharge or threat. If a designated source is a vessel or a facility, the President shall immediately notify the responsible party and the guarantor, if known, of that designation.

(b) Advertisement by responsible party or guarantor

(1) If a responsible party or guarantor fails to inform the President, within 5 days after receiving notification of a designation under subsection (a) of this section, of the party's or the guarantor's denial of the designation, such party or guarantor shall advertise the designation and the procedures by which claims may be presented, in accordance with regulations promulgated by the President. Advertisement under the preceding sentence shall begin no later than 15 days after the date of the designation made under subsection (a) of this section. If advertisement is not otherwise made in accordance with this subsection, the President shall promptly and at the expense of the responsible party or the guarantor involved, advertise the designation and the procedures by which claims may be presented to the responsible party or guarantor. Advertisement under this subsection shall continue for a period of no less than 30 days.

(2) An advertisement under paragraph (1) shall state that a claimant may present a claim for interim, short-term damages representing less than the full amount of damages to which the claimant ultimately may be entitled and that payment of such a claim shall not preclude recovery for damages not reflected in the paid or settled partial claim.

(c) Advertisement by President

If—

(1) the responsible party and the guarantor both deny a designation within 5 days after receiving notification of a designation under subsection (a) of this section,

(2) the source of the discharge or threat was a public vessel, or

(3) the President is unable to designate the source or sources of the discharge or threat under subsection (a) of this section,

the President shall advertise or otherwise notify potential claimants of the procedures by which claims may be presented to the Fund.

(Pub. L. 101–380, title I, §1014, Aug. 18, 1990, 104 Stat. 501; Pub. L. 104–324, title XI, §1142(c), Oct. 19, 1996, 110 Stat. 3991.)

AMENDMENTS

1996—Subsec. (b). Pub. L. 104–324 designated existing provisions as par. (1) and added par. (2).

DELEGATION OF FUNCTIONS

Functions of President under this section delegated to Secretary of Department in which Coast Guard is operating by section 7(d)(2) of Ex. Ord. No. 12777, Oct. 18, 1991, 56 F.R. 54768, set out as a note under section 1321 of this title.

§2715. Subrogation

(a) In general

Any person, including the Fund, who pays compensation pursuant to this Act to any claimant for removal costs or damages shall be subrogated to all rights, claims, and causes of action that the claimant has under any other law.

(b) Interim damages

(1) In general

If a responsible party, a guarantor, or the Fund has made payment to a claimant for interim, short-term damages representing less than the full amount of damages to which the claimant ultimately may be entitled, subrogation under subsection (a) of this section shall apply only with respect to the portion of the claim reflected in the paid interim claim.

(2) Final damages

Payment of such a claim shall not foreclose a claimant's right to recovery of all damages to which the claimant otherwise is entitled under this Act or under any other law.

(c) Actions on behalf of Fund

At the request of the Secretary, the Attorney General shall commence an action on behalf of the Fund to recover any compensation paid by the Fund to any claimant pursuant to this Act, and all costs incurred by the Fund by reason of the claim, including interest (including prejudgment interest), administrative and adjudicative costs, and attorney's fees. Such an action may be commenced against any responsible party or (subject to section 2716 of this title) guarantor, or against any other person who is liable, pursuant to any law, to the compensated claimant or to the Fund, for the cost or damages for which the compensation was paid. Such an action shall be commenced against the responsible foreign government or other responsible party to recover any removal costs or damages paid from the Fund as the result of the discharge, or substantial threat of discharge, of oil from a foreign offshore unit.

(d) Authority to settle

The head of any department or agency responsible for recovering amounts for which a person is liable under this subchapter may consider, compromise, and settle a claim for such amounts, including such costs paid from the Fund, if the claim has not been referred to the Attorney General. In any case in which the total amount to be recovered may exceed $500,000 (excluding interest), a claim may be compromised and settled under the preceding sentence only with the prior written approval of the Attorney General.

(Pub. L. 101–380, title I, § 1015, Aug. 18, 1990, 104 Stat. 502; Pub. L. 104–324, title XI, § 1142(d), Oct. 19, 1996, 110 Stat. 3991; Pub. L. 108–293, title VII, § 706, Aug. 9, 2004, 118 Stat. 1076.)

REFERENCES IN TEXT

This Act, referred to in text, is Pub. L. 101–380, Aug. 18, 1990, 104 Stat. 484, as amended, known as the Oil Pollution Act of 1990, which is classified principally to this chapter. For complete classification of this Act to the Code, see Short Title note set out under section 2701 of this title and Tables.

AMENDMENTS

2004—Subsec. (d). Pub. L. 108–293 added subsec. (d).

1996—Subsecs. (b), (c). Pub. L. 104–324 added subsec. (b) and redesignated former subsec. (b) as (c).

§ 2716. Financial responsibility

(a) Requirement

The responsible party for—

(1) any vessel over 300 gross tons (except a non-self-propelled vessel that does not carry oil as cargo or fuel) using any place subject to the jurisdiction of the United States; or

(2) any vessel using the waters of the exclusive economic zone to transship or lighter oil destined for a place subject to the jurisdiction of the United States;

shall establish and maintain, in accordance with regulations promulgated by the Secretary, evidence of financial responsibility sufficient to meet the maximum amount of liability to which the responsible party could be subjected under section 2704(a) or (d) of this title, in a case where the responsible party would be entitled to limit liability under that section. If the responsible party owns or operates more than one vessel, evidence of financial responsibility need be established only to meet the amount of the maximum liability applicable to the vessel having the greatest maximum liability.

(b) Sanctions

(1) Withholding clearance

The Secretary of the Treasury shall withhold or revoke the clearance required by section 60105 of title 46 of any vessel subject to this section that does not have the evidence of financial responsibility required for the vessel under this section.

(2) Denying entry to or detaining vessels

The Secretary may—

(A) deny entry to any vessel to any place in the United States, or to the navigable waters, or

(B) detain at the place,

any vessel that, upon request, does not produce the evidence of financial responsibility required for the vessel under this section.

(3) Seizure of vessel

Any vessel subject to the requirements of this section which is found in the navigable waters without the necessary evidence of financial responsibility for the vessel shall be subject to seizure by and forfeiture to the United States.

(c) Offshore facilities

(1) In general

(A) Evidence of financial responsibility required

Except as provided in paragraph (2), a responsible party with respect to an offshore facility that—

(i)(I) is located seaward of the line of ordinary low water along that portion of the coast that is in direct contact with the open sea and the line marking the seaward limit of inland waters; or

(II) is located in coastal inland waters, such as bays or estuaries, seaward of the line of ordinary low water along that portion of the coast that is not in direct contact with the open sea;

(ii) is used for exploring for, drilling for, producing, or transporting oil from facilities engaged in oil exploration, drilling, or production; and

(iii) has a worst-case oil spill discharge potential of more than 1,000 barrels of oil (or a lesser amount if the President determines that the risks posed by such facility justify it),

shall establish and maintain evidence of financial responsibility in the amount required under subparagraph (B) or (C), as applicable.

(B) Amount required generally

Except as provided in subparagraph (C), the amount of financial responsibility for offshore facilities that meet the criteria of subparagraph (A) is—

(i) $35,000,000 for an offshore facility located seaward of the seaward boundary of a State; or

(ii) $10,000,000 for an offshore facility located landward of the seaward boundary of a State.

(C) Greater amount

If the President determines that an amount of financial responsibility for a responsible party greater than the amount required by subparagraph (B) is justified based on the relative operational, environmental, human health, and other risks posed by the quantity or quality of oil that is explored for, drilled for, produced, or transported by the responsible party, the evidence of financial responsibility required shall be for an amount determined by the President not exceeding $150,000,000.

(D) Multiple facilities

In a case in which a person is a responsible party for more than one facility subject to this subsection, evidence of financial responsibility need be established only to meet the amount applicable to the facility having the greatest financial responsibility requirement under this subsection.

(E) Definition

For the purpose of this paragraph, the seaward boundary of a State shall be determined in accordance with section 1301(b) of title 43.

(2) Deepwater ports

Each responsible party with respect to a deepwater port shall establish and maintain evidence of financial responsibility sufficient to meet the maximum amount of liability to which the responsible party could be subjected under section 2704(a) of this title in a case where the responsible party would be entitled to limit liability under that section. If the Secretary exercises the authority under section 2704(d)(2) of this title to lower the limit of liability for deepwater ports, the responsible party shall establish and maintain evidence of financial responsibility sufficient to meet the maximum amount of liability so established. In a case in which a person is the responsible party for more than one deepwater port, evidence of financial responsibility need be established only to meet the maximum liability applicable to the deepwater port having the greatest maximum liability.

(e)[1] Methods of financial responsibility

Financial responsibility under this section may be established by any one, or by any combination, of the following methods which the Secretary (in the case of a vessel) or the President (in the case of a facility) determines to be acceptable: evidence of insurance, surety bond, guarantee, letter of credit, qualification as a self-insurer, or other evidence of financial responsibility. Any bond filed shall be issued by a bonding company authorized to do business in the United States. In promulgating requirements under this section, the Secretary or the President, as appropriate, may specify policy or other contractual terms, conditions, or defenses which are necessary, or which are unacceptable, in establishing evidence of financial responsibility to effectuate the purposes of this Act.

(f) Claims against guarantor

(1) In general

Subject to paragraph (2), a claim for which liability may be established under section 2702 of this title may be asserted directly against any guarantor providing evidence of financial responsibility for a responsible party liable under that section for removal costs and damages to which the claim pertains. In defending against such a claim, the guarantor may invoke—

(A) all rights and defenses which would be available to the responsible party under this Act;

(B) any defense authorized under subsection (e) of this section; and

(C) the defense that the incident was caused by the willful misconduct of the responsible party.

The guarantor may not invoke any other defense that might be available in proceedings brought by the responsible party against the guarantor.

(2) Further requirement

A claim may be asserted pursuant to paragraph (1) directly against a guarantor providing evidence of financial responsibility under subsection (c)(1) of this section with respect to an offshore facility only if—

(A) the responsible party for whom evidence of financial responsibility has been provided has denied or failed to pay a claim under this Act on the basis of being insolvent, as defined under section 101(32) of title 11, and applying generally accepted accounting principles;

(B) the responsible party for whom evidence of financial responsibility has been provided has filed a petition for bankruptcy under title 11; or

(C) the claim is asserted by the United States for removal costs and damages or for compensation paid by the Fund under this Act, including costs incurred by the Fund for processing compensation claims.

(3) Rulemaking authority

Not later than 1 year after October 19, 1996, the President shall promulgate regulations to establish a process for implementing paragraph (2) in a manner that will allow for the orderly and expeditious presentation and resolution of claims and effectuate the purposes of this Act.

(g) Limitation on guarantor's liability

Nothing in this Act shall impose liability with respect to an incident on any guarantor for damages or removal costs which exceed, in the aggregate, the amount of financial responsibility which that guarantor has provided for a responsible party pursuant to this section. The total liability of the guarantor on direct action for claims brought under this Act with respect to an incident shall be limited to that amount.

(h) Continuation of regulations

Any regulation relating to financial responsibility, which has been issued pursuant to any provision of law repealed or superseded by this Act, and which is in effect on the date immediately preceding the effective date of this Act, is deemed and shall be construed to be a regulation issued pursuant to this section. Such a regulation shall remain in full force and effect unless and until superseded by a new regulation issued under this section.

(i) Unified certificate

The Secretary may issue a single unified certificate of financial responsibility for purposes of this Act and any other law.

(Pub. L. 101–380, title I, §1016, Aug. 18, 1990, 104 Stat. 502; Pub. L. 104–55, §2(d)(2), Nov. 20, 1995, 109 Stat. 547; Pub. L. 104–324, title XI, §1125(a), Oct. 19, 1996, 110 Stat. 3981.)

REFERENCES IN TEXT

This Act, referred to in subsecs. (e), (f), (g), (h), and (i), is Pub. L. 101–380, Aug. 18, 1990, 104 Stat. 484, as

[1] So in original. No subsec. (d) has been enacted.

amended, known as the Oil Pollution Act of 1990, which is classified principally to this chapter. For complete classification of this Act to the Code, see Short Title note set out under section 2701 of this title and Tables.

The effective date of this Act, referred to in subsec. (h), is the effective date of Pub. L. 101–380 which is applicable to incidents occurring after Aug. 18, 1990, see section 1020 of Pub. L. 101–380, set out as an Effective Date note under section 2701 of this title.

CODIFICATION

In subsec. (b)(1), "section 60105 of title 46" substituted for "section 4197 of the Revised Statutes of the United States" on authority of Pub. L. 109–304, § 18(c), Oct. 6, 2006, 120 Stat. 1709, which Act enacted section 60105 of Title 46, Shipping.

AMENDMENTS

1996—Subsec. (c)(1). Pub. L. 104–324, § 1125(a)(1), reenacted heading without change and amended text generally. Prior to amendment, text read as follows: "Except as provided in paragraph (2), each responsible party with respect to an offshore facility shall establish and maintain evidence of financial responsibility of $150,000,000 to meet the amount of liability to which the responsible party could be subjected under section 2704(a) of this title in a case in which the responsible party would be entitled to limit liability under that section. In a case in which a person is the responsible party for more than one facility subject to this subsection, evidence of financial responsibility need be established only to meet the maximum liability applicable to the facility having the greatest maximum liability."

Subsec. (f). Pub. L. 104–324, § 1125(a)(2), reenacted heading without change and amended text generally. Prior to amendment, text read as follows: "Any claim for which liability may be established under section 2702 of this title may be asserted directly against any guarantor providing evidence of financial responsibility for a responsible party liable under that section for removal costs and damages to which the claim pertains. In defending against such a claim, the guarantor may invoke (1) all rights and defenses which would be available to the responsible party under this Act, (2) any defense authorized under subsection (e) of this section, and (3) the defense that the incident was caused by the willful misconduct of the responsible party. The guarantor may not invoke any other defense that might be available in proceedings brought by the responsible party against the guarantor."

Subsec. (g). Pub. L. 104–324, § 1125(a)(3), reenacted heading without change and amended text generally. Prior to amendment, text read as follows: "Nothing in this Act shall impose liability with respect to an incident on any guarantor for damages or removal costs which exceed, in the aggregate, the amount of financial responsibility required under this Act which that guarantor has provided for a responsible party."

1995—Subsec. (a). Pub. L. 104–55 substituted "the responsible party could be subjected under section 2704(a) or (d) of this title" for ", in the case of a tank vessel, the responsible party could be subject under section 2704(a)(1) or (d) of this title, or to which, in the case of any other vessel, the responsible party could be subjected under section 2704(a)(2) or (d) of this title".

EFFECTIVE DATE OF 1996 AMENDMENT

Section 1125(b) of Pub. L. 104–324 provided that: "The amendment made by subsection (a)(2) [amending this section] shall not apply to any final rule issued before the date of enactment of this section [Oct. 19, 1996]."

DELEGATION OF FUNCTIONS

Specific functions of President under subsec. (e) of this section delegated to Secretary of the Interior and Secretary of the Department in which the Coast Guard is operating by section 5(a) of Ex. Ord. No. 12777, Oct. 18, 1991, 56 F.R. 54764, as amended, set out as a note under section 1321 of this title.

§ 2716a. Financial responsibility civil penalties

(a) Administrative

Any person who, after notice and an opportunity for a hearing, is found to have failed to comply with the requirements of section 2716 of this title or the regulations issued under that section, or with a denial or detention order issued under subsection (c)(2) of that section, shall be liable to the United States for a civil penalty, not to exceed $25,000 per day of violation. The amount of the civil penalty shall be assessed by the President by written notice. In determining the amount of the penalty, the President shall take into account the nature, circumstances, extent, and gravity of the violation, the degree of culpability, any history of prior violation, ability to pay, and such other matters as justice may require. The President may compromise, modify, or remit, with or without conditions, any civil penalty which is subject to imposition or which had been imposed under this paragraph. If any person fails to pay an assessed civil penalty after it has become final, the President may refer the matter to the Attorney General for collection.

(b) Judicial

In addition to, or in lieu of, assessing a penalty under subsection (a) of this section, the President may request the Attorney General to secure such relief as necessary to compel compliance with this[1] section 2716 of this title, including a judicial order terminating operations. The district courts of the United States shall have jurisdiction to grant any relief as the public interest and the equities of the case may require.

(Pub. L. 101–380, title IV, § 4303, Aug. 18, 1990, 104 Stat. 539.)

CODIFICATION

Section was not enacted as part of title I of Pub. L. 101–380 which comprises this subchapter.

DELEGATION OF FUNCTIONS

Specific functions of President under this section delegated to Secretary of Department in which Coast Guard is operating and Secretary of the Interior by section 5(b) of Ex. Ord. No. 12777, Oct. 18, 1991, 56 F.R. 54765, as amended, set out as a note under section 1321 of this title.

§ 2717. Litigation, jurisdiction, and venue

(a) Review of regulations

Review of any regulation promulgated under this Act may be had upon application by any interested person only in the Circuit Court of Appeals of the United States for the District of Columbia. Any such application shall be made within 90 days from the date of promulgation of such regulations. Any matter with respect to which review could have been obtained under this subsection shall not be subject to judicial review in any civil or criminal proceeding for enforcement or to obtain damages or recovery of response costs.

(b) Jurisdiction

Except as provided in subsections (a) and (c) of this section, the United States district courts

[1] So in original. The word "this" probably should not appear.

shall have exclusive original jurisdiction over all controversies arising under this Act, without regard to the citizenship of the parties or the amount in controversy. Venue shall lie in any district in which the discharge or injury or damages occurred, or in which the defendant resides, may be found, has its principal office, or has appointed an agent for service of process. For the purposes of this section, the Fund shall reside in the District of Columbia.

(c) State court jurisdiction

A State trial court of competent jurisdiction over claims for removal costs or damages, as defined under this Act, may consider claims under this Act or State law and any final judgment of such court (when no longer subject to ordinary forms of review) shall be recognized, valid, and enforceable for all purposes of this Act.

(d) Assessment and collection of tax

The provisions of subsections (a), (b), and (c) of this section shall not apply to any controversy or other matter resulting from the assessment or collection of any tax, or to the review of any regulation promulgated under title 26.

(e) Savings provision

Nothing in this subchapter shall apply to any cause of action or right of recovery arising from any incident which occurred prior to August 18, 1990. Such claims shall be adjudicated pursuant to the law applicable on the date of the incident.

(f) Period of limitations

(1) Damages

Except as provided in paragraphs (3) and (4), an action for damages under this Act shall be barred unless the action is brought within 3 years after—

(A) the date on which the loss and the connection of the loss with the discharge in question are reasonably discoverable with the exercise of due care, or

(B) in the case of natural resource damages under section 2702(b)(2)(A) of this title, the date of completion of the natural resources damage assessment under section 2706(c) of this title.

(2) Removal costs

An action for recovery of removal costs referred to in section 2702(b)(1) of this title must be commenced within 3 years after completion of the removal action. In any such action described in this subsection, the court shall enter a declaratory judgment on liability for removal costs or damages that will be binding on any subsequent action or actions to recover further removal costs or damages. Except as otherwise provided in this paragraph, an action may be commenced under this subchapter for recovery of removal costs at any time after such costs have been incurred.

(3) Contribution

No action for contribution for any removal costs or damages may be commenced more than 3 years after—

(A) the date of judgment in any action under this Act for recovery of such costs or damages, or

(B) the date of entry of a judicially approved settlement with respect to such costs or damages.

(4) Subrogation

No action based on rights subrogated pursuant to this Act by reason of payment of a claim may be commenced under this Act more than 3 years after the date of payment of such claim.

(5) Commencement

The time limitations contained herein shall not begin to run—

(A) against a minor until the earlier of the date when such minor reaches 18 years of age or the date on which a legal representative is duly appointed for such minor, or

(B) against an incompetent person until the earlier of the date on which such incompetent's incompetency ends or the date on which a legal representative is duly appointed for such incompetent.

(Pub. L. 101–380, title I, § 1017, Aug. 18, 1990, 104 Stat. 504.)

REFERENCES IN TEXT

This Act, referred to in subsecs. (a), (b), (c), and (f), is Pub. L. 101–380, Aug. 18, 1990, 104 Stat. 484, as amended, known as the Oil Pollution Act of 1990, which is classified principally to this chapter. For complete classification of this Act to the Code, see Short Title note set out under section 2701 of this title and Tables.

§ 2718. Relationship to other law

(a) Preservation of State authorities; Solid Waste Disposal Act

Nothing in this Act or the Act of March 3, 1851 shall—

(1) affect, or be construed or interpreted as preempting, the authority of any State or political subdivision thereof from imposing any additional liability or requirements with respect to—

(A) the discharge of oil or other pollution by oil within such State; or

(B) any removal activities in connection with such a discharge; or

(2) affect, or be construed or interpreted to affect or modify in any way the obligations or liabilities of any person under the Solid Waste Disposal Act (42 U.S.C. 6901 et seq.) or State law, including common law.

(b) Preservation of State funds

Nothing in this Act or in section 9509 of title 26 shall in any way affect, or be construed to affect, the authority of any State—

(1) to establish, or to continue in effect, a fund any purpose of which is to pay for costs or damages arising out of, or directly resulting from, oil pollution or the substantial threat of oil pollution; or

(2) to require any person to contribute to such a fund.

(c) Additional requirements and liabilities; penalties

Nothing in this Act, the Act of March 3, 1851 (46 U.S.C. 183 et seq.),[1] or section 9509 of title 26,

[1] See References in Text note below.

shall in any way affect, or be construed to affect, the authority of the United States or any State or political subdivision thereof—

(1) to impose additional liability or additional requirements; or

(2) to impose, or to determine the amount of, any fine or penalty (whether criminal or civil in nature) for any violation of law;

relating to the discharge, or substantial threat of a discharge, of oil.

(d) Federal employee liability

For purposes of section 2679(b)(2)(B) of title 28, nothing in this Act shall be construed to authorize or create a cause of action against a Federal officer or employee in the officer's or employee's personal or individual capacity for any act or omission while acting within the scope of the officer's or employee's office or employment.

(Pub. L. 101–380, title I, §1018, Aug. 18, 1990, 104 Stat. 505.)

REFERENCES IN TEXT

This Act, referred to in text, is Pub. L. 101–380, Aug. 18, 1990, 104 Stat. 484, as amended, known as the Oil Pollution Act of 1990, which is classified principally to this chapter. For complete classification of this Act to the Code, see Short Title note set out under section 2701 of this title and Tables.

Act of March 3, 1851, referred to in subsecs. (a) and (c), is act Mar. 3, 1851, ch. 43, 9 Stat. 635, which was incorporated into the Revised Statutes as R.S. §§4282, 4283, 4284 to 4287 and 4289, and was classified to sections 182, 183, and 184 to 188 of Title 46, Appendix, Shipping, prior to being repealed and restated in chapter 305 of Title 46, Shipping, by Pub. L. 109–304, §§6(c), 19, Oct. 6, 2006, 120 Stat. 1509, 1710. For disposition of sections of the former Appendix to Title 46, see Disposition Table preceding section 101 of Title 46.

The Solid Waste Disposal Act, referred to in subsec. (a)(2), is title II of Pub. L. 89–272, Oct. 20, 1965, 79 Stat. 997, as amended generally by Pub. L. 94–580, §2, Oct. 21, 1976, 90 Stat. 2795, which is classified generally to chapter 82 (§6901 et seq.) of Title 42, The Public Health and Welfare. For complete classification of this Act to the Code, see Short Title note set out under section 6901 of Title 42 and Tables.

REPORT ON VESSEL SAFETY AND ABILITY TO MEET LEGAL OBLIGATIONS

Pub. L. 102–241, §32, Dec. 19, 1991, 105 Stat. 2222, provided that: "Not later than one year after the date of enactment of this Act [Dec. 19, 1991], the Secretary of Transportation shall report to Congress on the effect of section 1018 of the Oil Pollution Act of 1990 (Public Law 101–380; 104 Stat. 484) [33 U.S.C. 2718] on the safety of vessels being used to transport oil and the capability of owners and operators to meet their legal obligations in the event of an oil spill."

§2719. State financial responsibility

A State may enforce, on the navigable waters of the State, the requirements for evidence of financial responsibility under section 2716 of this title.

(Pub. L. 101–380, title I, §1019, Aug. 18, 1990, 104 Stat. 506.)

§2720. Differentiation among fats, oils, and greases

(a) In general

Except as provided in subsection (c) of this section, in issuing or enforcing any regulation or establishing any interpretation or guideline relating to the transportation, storage, discharge, release, emission, or disposal of a fat, oil, or grease under any Federal law, the head of that Federal agency shall—

(1) differentiate between and establish separate classes for—

(A) animal fats and oils and greases, and fish and marine mammal oils, within the meaning of paragraph (2) of section 61(a) of title 13, and oils of vegetable origin, including oils from the seeds, nuts, and kernels referred to in paragraph (1)(A) of that section; and

(B) other oils and greases, including petroleum; and

(2) apply standards to different classes of fats and oils based on considerations in subsection (b) of this section.

(b) Considerations

In differentiating between the class of fats, oils, and greases described in subsection (a)(1)(A) of this section and the class of oils and greases described in subsection (a)(1)(B) of this section, the head of the Federal agency shall consider differences in the physical, chemical, biological, and other properties, and in the environmental effects, of the classes.

(c) Exception

The requirements of this Act shall not apply to the Food and Drug Administration and the Food Safety and Inspection Service.

(Pub. L. 104–55, §2, Nov. 20, 1995, 109 Stat. 546.)

REFERENCES IN TEXT

This Act, referred to in subsec. (c), is Pub. L. 104–55, Nov. 20, 1995, 109 Stat. 546, which enacted this section and amended sections 2704 and 2716 of this title. For complete classification of this Act to the Code, see Short Title of 1995 Amendment note set out under section 2701 of this title and Tables.

CODIFICATION

Section was enacted as part of the Edible Oil Regulatory Reform Act, and not as part of title I of the Oil Pollution Act of 1990 which comprises this subchapter.

Section is comprised of section 2 of Pub. L. 104–55. Subsec. (d) of section 2 of Pub. L. 104–55 amended sections 2704 and 2716 of this title.

REGULATIONS

Pub. L. 105–277, div. A, §101(g) [title III, §343], Oct. 21, 1998, 112 Stat. 2681–439, 2681–473, provided that:

"(a) None of the funds made available by this Act or subsequent Acts may be used by the Coast Guard to issue, implement, or enforce a regulation or to establish an interpretation or guideline under the Edible Oil Regulatory Reform Act (Public Law 104–55) [see Short Title of 1995 Amendment note set out under section 2701 of this title], or the amendments made by that Act, that does not recognize and provide for, with respect to fats, oils, and greases (as described in that Act, or the amendments made by that Act) differences in—

"(1) physical, chemical, biological and other relevant properties; and

"(2) environmental effects.

"(b) Not later than March 31, 1999, the Secretary of Transportation shall issue regulations amending 33 CFR 154 to comply with the requirements of Public Law 104–55."

[For transfer of authorities, functions, personnel, and assets of the Coast Guard, including the authorities and functions of the Secretary of Transportation relating thereto, to the Department of Homeland Security, and for treatment of related references, see sections 468(b), 551(d), 552(d), and 557 of Title 6, Domestic Security, and the Department of Homeland Security Reorganization Plan of November 25, 2002, as modified, set out as a note under section 542 of Title 6.]

Pub. L. 105–276, title III, Oct. 21, 1998, 112 Stat. 2499, provided that: "Not later than March 31, 1999, the Administrator of the Environmental Protection Agency shall issue regulations amending 40 C.F.R. 112 to comply with the requirements of the Edible Oil Regulatory Reform Act (Public Law 104–55) [see Short Title of 1995 Amendment note set out under section 2701 of this title]. Such regulations shall differentiate between and establish separate classes for animal fats and oils and greases, and fish and marine mammal oils (as described in that Act), and other oils and greases, and shall apply standards to such different classes of fats and oils based on differences in the physical, chemical, biological, and other properties, and in the environmental effects, of the classes. None of the funds made available by this Act or in subsequent Acts may be used by the Environmental Protection Agency to issue or to establish an interpretation or guidance relating to fats, oils, and greases (as described in Public Law 104–55) that does not comply with the requirements of the Edible Oil Regulatory Reform Act."

SENSE OF CONGRESS ON IMPLEMENTATION OF REGULATIONS REGARDING ANIMAL FATS AND VEGETABLE OILS

Pub. L. 104–324, title XI, §1130, Oct. 19, 1996, 110 Stat. 3985, provided that:

"(a) SENSE OF CONGRESS.—It is the sense of Congress that, in an effort to reduce unnecessary regulatory burdens, a regulation issued or enforced and an interpretation or guideline established pursuant to Public Law 104–55 [see Short Title of 1995 Amendment note set out under section 2701 of this title] should in any manner possible recognize and provide for the differences in the physical, chemical, biological, and other properties, and in the environmental effects, of the classes of fats, oils, and greases described under that law.

"(b) REPORT.—Within 60 days after the date of enactment of this section [Oct. 19, 1996] and on January 1 of each year thereafter, the Secretary of Transportation shall submit a report to Congress on the extent to which the implementation by the United States Coast Guard of regulations issued or enforced, or interpretations or guidelines established, pursuant to Public Law 104–55, carry out the intent of Congress and recognize and provide for the differences in the physical, chemical, biological, and other properties, and in the environmental effects, of the classes of fats, oils, and greases described under that law."

[For transfer of authorities, functions, personnel, and assets of the Coast Guard, including the authorities and functions of the Secretary of Transportation relating thereto, to the Department of Homeland Security, and for treatment of related references, see sections 468(b), 551(d), 552(d), and 557 of Title 6, Domestic Security, and the Department of Homeland Security Reorganization Plan of November 25, 2002, as modified, set out as a note under section 542 of Title 6.]

SUBCHAPTER II—PRINCE WILLIAM SOUND PROVISIONS

§2731. Oil Spill Recovery Institute

(a) Establishment of Institute

The Secretary of Commerce shall provide for the establishment of a Prince William Sound Oil Spill Recovery Institute (hereinafter in this section referred to as the "Institute") through the Prince William Sound Science and Technology Institute located in Cordova, Alaska.

(b) Functions

The Institute shall conduct research and carry out educational and demonstration projects designed to—

(1) identify and develop the best available techniques, equipment, and materials for dealing with oil spills in the arctic and subarctic marine environment; and

(2) complement Federal and State damage assessment efforts and determine, document, assess, and understand the long-range effects of Arctic or Subarctic oil spills on the natural resources of Prince William Sound and its adjacent waters (as generally depicted on the map entitled "EXXON VALDEZ oil spill dated March 1990"), and the environment, the economy, and the lifestyle and well-being of the people who are dependent on them, except that the Institute shall not conduct studies or make recommendations on any matter which is not directly related to Arctic or Subarctic oil spills or the effects thereof.

(c) Advisory board

(1) In general

The policies of the Institute shall be determined by an advisory board, composed of 16 members appointed as follows:

(A) One representative appointed by each of the Commissioners of Fish and Game, Environmental Conservation, and Natural Resources of the State of Alaska, all of whom shall be State employees.

(B) One representative appointed by each of the Secretaries of Commerce and the Interior and the Commandant of the Coast Guard, who shall be Federal employees.

(C) Two representatives from the fishing industry appointed by the Governor of the State of Alaska from among residents of communities in Alaska that were affected by the EXXON VALDEZ oil spill, who shall serve terms of 2 years each. Interested organizations from within the fishing industry may submit the names of qualified individuals for consideration by the Governor.

(D) Two Alaska Natives who represent Native entities affected by the EXXON VALDEZ oil spill, at least one of whom represents an entity located in Prince William Sound, appointed by the Governor of Alaska from a list of 4 qualified individuals submitted by the Alaska Federation of Natives, who shall serve terms of 2 years each.

(E) Two representatives from the oil and gas industry to be appointed by the Governor of the State of Alaska who shall serve terms of 2 years each. Interested organizations from within the oil and gas industry may submit the names of qualified individuals for consideration by the Governor.

(F) Two at-large representatives from among residents of communities in Alaska that were affected by the EXXON VALDEZ oil spill who are knowledgeable about the marine environment and wildlife within Prince William Sound, and who shall serve terms of 2 years each, appointed by the remaining members of the Advisory Board. Interested parties may submit the names of qualified individuals for consideration by the Advisory Board.

(G) One nonvoting representative of the Institute of Marine Science.

(H) One nonvoting representative appointed by the Prince William Sound Science and Technology Institute.

(2) Chairman

The representative of the Secretary of Commerce shall serve as Chairman of the Advisory Board.

(3) Policies

Policies determined by the Advisory Board under this subsection shall include policies for the conduct and support, through contracts and grants awarded on a nationally competitive basis, of research, projects, and studies to be supported by the Institute in accordance with the purposes of this section.

(4) Scientific review

The Advisory Board may request a scientific review of the research program every five years by the National Academy of Sciences which shall perform the review, if requested, as part of its responsibilities under section 2761(b)(2) of this title.

(d) Scientific and technical committee

(1) In general

The Advisory Board shall establish a scientific and technical committee, composed of specialists in matters relating to oil spill containment and cleanup technology, arctic and subarctic marine ecology, and the living resources and socioeconomics of Prince William Sound and its adjacent waters, from the University of Alaska, the Institute of Marine Science, the Prince William Sound Science and Technology Institute, and elsewhere in the academic community.

(2) Functions

The Scientific and Technical Committee shall provide such advice to the Advisory Board as the Advisory Board shall request, including recommendations regarding the conduct and support of research, projects, and studies in accordance with the purposes of this section. The Advisory Board shall not request, and the Committee shall not provide, any advice which is not directly related to Arctic or Subarctic oil spills or the effects thereof.

(e) Director

The Institute shall be administered by a Director appointed by the Advisory Board. The Prince William Sound Science and Technology Institute and the Scientific and Technical Committee may each submit independent recommendations for the Advisory Board's consideration for appointment as Director. The Director may hire such staff and incur such expenses on behalf of the Institute as are authorized by the Advisory Board.

(f) Evaluation

The Secretary of Commerce may conduct an ongoing evaluation of the activities of the Institute to ensure that funds received by the Institute are used in a manner consistent with this section.

(g) Audit

The Comptroller General of the United States, and any of his or her duly authorized representatives, shall have access, for purposes of audit and examination, to any books, documents, papers, and records of the Institute and its administering agency that are pertinent to the funds received and expended by the Institute and its administering agency.

(h) Status of employees

Employees of the Institute shall not, by reason of such employment, be considered to be employees of the Federal Government for any purpose.

(i) Termination

The authorization in section 2736(b) of this title providing funding for the Institute shall terminate 1 year after the date on which the Secretary, in consultation with the Secretary of the Interior, determines that oil and gas exploration, development, and production in the State of Alaska have ceased.

(j) Use of funds

No funds made available to carry out this section may be used to initiate litigation. No funds made available to carry out this section may be used for the acquisition of real property (including buildings) or construction of any building. No more than 20 percent of funds made available to carry out this section may be used to lease necessary facilities and to administer the Institute. The Advisory Board may compensate its Federal representatives for their reasonable travel costs. None of the funds authorized by this section shall be used for any purpose other than the functions specified in subsection (b) of this section.

(k) Research

The Institute shall publish and make available to any person upon request the results of all research, educational, and demonstration projects conducted by the Institute. The Administrator shall provide a copy of all research, educational, and demonstration projects conducted by the Institute to the National Oceanic and Atmospheric Administration.

(*l*) "Prince William Sound and its adjacent waters" defined

In this section, the term "Prince William Sound and its adjacent waters" means such sound and waters as generally depicted on the map entitled "EXXON VALDEZ oil spill dated March 1990".

(Pub. L. 101–380, title V, §5001, Aug. 18, 1990, 104 Stat. 542; Pub. L. 104–324, title XI, §1102(a), Oct. 19, 1996, 110 Stat. 3964; Pub. L. 107–295, title IV, §427, Nov. 25, 2002, 116 Stat. 2127; Pub. L. 109–58, title III, §389(1), Aug. 8, 2005, 119 Stat. 747; Pub. L. 109–241, title IX, §902(*l*)(1), July 11, 2006, 120 Stat. 568.)

AMENDMENTS

2006—Subsec. (c)(1)(B). Pub. L. 109–241 substituted "Commerce and the Interior and the Commandant of the Coast Guard," for "Commerce, the Interior, and Transportation,".

2005—Subsec. (i). Pub. L. 109–58 substituted "1 year after the date on which the Secretary, in consultation with the Secretary of the Interior, determines that oil and gas exploration, development, and production in the State of Alaska have ceased" for "September 30, 2012".

2002—Subsec. (i). Pub. L. 107–295 substituted "September 30, 2012" for "10 years after October 19, 1996".

1996—Subsec. (a). Pub. L. 104–324, §1102(a)(1), (2), struck out "to be administered by the Secretary of Commerce" after "as the 'Institute')" and substituted "located" for "and located".

Subsec. (b)(2). Pub. L. 104–324, §1102(a)(3), substituted "Arctic or Subarctic oil spills" for "the EXXON VALDEZ oil spill" in two places.

Subsec. (c)(1). Pub. L. 104–324, §1102(a)(4), substituted "16" for "18" in introductory provisions.

Subsec. (c)(1)(A). Pub. L. 104–324, §1102(a)(5), substituted ", and Natural Resources" for ", Natural Resources, and Commerce and Economic Development".

Subsec. (c)(1)(B). Pub. L. 104–324, §1102(a)(6), (8), added subpar. (B) and struck out former subpar. (B) which read as follows: "One representative appointed by each of—

"(i) the Secretaries of Commerce, the Interior, Agriculture, Transportation, and the Navy; and

"(ii) the Administrator of the Environmental Protection Agency;

all of whom shall be Federal employees."

Subsec. (c)(1)(C). Pub. L. 104–324, §1102(a)(6), (8), added subpar. (C) and struck out former subpar. (C) which read as follows: "4 representatives appointed by the Secretary of Commerce from among residents of communities in Alaska that were affected by the EXXON VALDEZ oil spill who are knowledgeable about fisheries, other local industries, the marine environment, wildlife, public health, safety, or education. At least 2 of the representatives shall be appointed from among residents of communities located in Prince William Sound. The Secretary shall appoint residents to serve terms of 2 years each, from a list of 8 qualified individuals to be submitted by the Governor of the State of Alaska based on recommendations made by the governing body of each affected community. Each affected community may submit the names of 2 qualified individuals for the Governor's consideration. No more than 5 of the 8 qualified persons recommended by the Governor shall be members of the same political party."

Subsec. (c)(1)(D). Pub. L. 104–324, §1102(a)(6), (8), added subpar. (D) and struck out former subpar. (D) which read as follows: "3 Alaska Natives who represent Native entities affected by the EXXON VALDEZ oil spill, at least one of whom represents an entity located in Prince William Sound, to serve terms of 2 years each from a list of 6 qualified individuals submitted by the Alaska Federation of Natives."

Subsec. (c)(1)(E) to (H). Pub. L. 104–324, §1102(a)(7), (8), added subpars. (E) and (F) and redesignated former subpars. (E) and (F) as (G) and (H), respectively.

Subsec. (c)(4). Pub. L. 104–324, §1102(a)(9), added par. (4).

Subsec. (d)(2). Pub. L. 104–324, §1102(a)(10), substituted "Arctic or Subarctic oil spills" for "the EXXON VALDEZ oil spill".

Subsec. (e). Pub. L. 104–324, §1102(a)(11)–(13), substituted "appointed by the Advisory Board" for "appointed by the Secretary of Commerce", struck out ", the Advisory Board," after "Technology Institute", and substituted "Advisory Board's" for "Secretary's".

Subsec. (i). Pub. L. 104–324, §1102(a)(14), (15), inserted "authorization in section 2736(b) of this title providing funding for the" after "The" and substituted "October 19, 1996" for "August 18, 1990".

Subsec. (j). Pub. L. 104–324, §1102(a)(16), (17), struck out first sentence which read as follows: "All funds authorized for the Institute shall be provided through the National Oceanic and Atmospheric Administration.", and inserted "The Advisory Board may compensate its Federal representatives for their reasonable travel costs." after "Institute."

TERMINATION OF ADVISORY BOARDS

Advisory boards established after Jan. 5, 1973, to terminate not later than the expiration of the 2-year period beginning on the date of their establishment, unless, in the case of a board established by the President or an officer of the Federal Government, such board is renewed by appropriate action prior to the expiration of such 2-year period, or in the case of a board established by Congress, its duration is otherwise provided for by law. See sections 3(2) and 14 of Pub. L. 92–463, Oct. 6, 1972, 86 Stat. 770, 776, set out in the Appendix to Title 5, Government Organization and Employees.

§2732. Terminal and tanker oversight and monitoring

(a) Short title and findings

(1) Short title

This section may be cited as the "Oil Terminal and Oil Tanker Environmental Oversight and Monitoring Act of 1990".

(2) Findings

The Congress finds that—

(A) the March 24, 1989, grounding and rupture of the fully loaded oil tanker, the EXXON VALDEZ, spilled 11 million gallons of crude oil in Prince William Sound, an environmentally sensitive area;

(B) many people believe that complacency on the part of the industry and government personnel responsible for monitoring the operation of the Valdez terminal and vessel traffic in Prince William Sound was one of the contributing factors to the EXXON VALDEZ oil spill;

(C) one way to combat this complacency is to involve local citizens in the process of preparing, adopting, and revising oil spill contingency plans;

(D) a mechanism should be established which fosters the long-term partnership of industry, government, and local communities in overseeing compliance with environmental concerns in the operation of crude oil terminals;

(E) such a mechanism presently exists at the Sullom Voe terminal in the Shetland Islands and this terminal should serve as a model for others;

(F) because of the effective partnership that has developed at Sullom Voe, Sullom Voe is considered the safest terminal in Europe;

(G) the present system of regulation and oversight of crude oil terminals in the United States has degenerated into a process of continual mistrust and confrontation;

(H) only when local citizens are involved in the process will the trust develop that is necessary to change the present system from confrontation to consensus;

(I) a pilot program patterned after Sullom Voe should be established in Alaska to further refine the concepts and relationships involved; and

(J) similar programs should eventually be established in other major crude oil terminals in the United States because the recent oil spills in Texas, Delaware, and Rhode Island indicate that the safe transportation of crude oil is a national problem.

(b) Demonstration programs

(1) Establishment

There are established 2 Oil Terminal and Oil Tanker Environmental Oversight and Monitoring Demonstration Programs (hereinafter referred to as "Programs") to be carried out in the State of Alaska.

(2) Advisory function

The function of these Programs shall be advisory only.

(3) Purpose

The Prince William Sound Program shall be responsible for environmental monitoring of the terminal facilities in Prince William Sound and the crude oil tankers operating in Prince William Sound. The Cook Inlet Program shall be responsible for environmental monitoring of the terminal facilities and crude oil tankers operating in Cook Inlet located South of the latitude at Point Possession and North of the latitude at Amatuli Island, including offshore facilities in Cook Inlet.

(4) Suits barred

No program, association, council, committee or other organization created by this section may sue any person or entity, public or private, concerning any matter arising under this section except for the performance of contracts.

(c) Oil Terminal Facilities and Oil Tanker Operations Association

(1) Establishment

There is established an Oil Terminal Facilities and Oil Tanker Operations Association (hereinafter in this section referred to as the "Association") for each of the Programs established under subsection (b) of this section.

(2) Membership

Each Association shall be comprised of 4 individuals as follows:

(A) One individual shall be designated by the owners and operators of the terminal facilities and shall represent those owners and operators.

(B) One individual shall be designated by the owners and operators of the crude oil tankers calling at the terminal facilities and shall represent those owners and operators.

(C) One individual shall be an employee of the State of Alaska, shall be designated by the Governor of the State of Alaska, and shall represent the State government.

(D) One individual shall be an employee of the Federal Government, shall be designated by the President, and shall represent the Federal Government.

(3) Responsibilities

Each Association shall be responsible for reviewing policies relating to the operation and maintenance of the oil terminal facilities and crude oil tankers which affect or may affect the environment in the vicinity of their respective terminals. Each Association shall provide a forum among the owners and operators of the terminal facilities, the owners and operators of crude oil tankers calling at those facilities, the United States, and the State of Alaska to discuss and to make recommendations concerning all permits, plans, and site-specific regulations governing the activities and actions of the terminal facilities which affect or may affect the environment in the vicinity of the terminal facilities and of crude oil tankers calling at those facilities.

(4) Designation of existing organization

The Secretary may designate an existing nonprofit organization as an Association under this subsection if the organization is organized to meet the purposes of this section and consists of at least the individuals listed in paragraph (2).

(d) Regional Citizens' Advisory Councils

(1) Membership

There is established a Regional Citizens' Advisory Council (hereinafter in this section referred to as the "Council") for each of the programs established by subsection (b) of this section.

(2) Membership

Each Council shall be composed of voting members and nonvoting members, as follows:

(A) Voting members

Voting members shall be Alaska residents and, except as provided in clause (vii) of this paragraph, shall be appointed by the Governor of the State of Alaska from a list of nominees provided by each of the following interests, with one representative appointed to represent each of the following interests, taking into consideration the need for regional balance on the Council:

(i) Local commercial fishing industry organizations, the members of which depend on the fisheries resources of the waters in the vicinity of the terminal facilities.

(ii) Aquaculture associations in the vicinity of the terminal facilities.

(iii) Alaska Native Corporations and other Alaska Native organizations the members of which reside in the vicinity of the terminal facilities.

(iv) Environmental organizations the members of which reside in the vicinity of the terminal facilities.

(v) Recreational organizations the members of which reside in or use the vicinity of the terminal facilities.

(vi) The Alaska State Chamber of Commerce, to represent the locally based tourist industry.

(vii)(I) For the Prince William Sound Terminal Facilities Council, one representative selected by each of the following municipalities: Cordova, Whittier, Seward, Valdez, Kodiak, the Kodiak Island Borough, and the Kenai Peninsula Borough.

(II) For the Cook Inlet Terminal Facilities Council, one representative selected by each of the following municipalities: Homer, Seldovia, Anchorage, Kenai, Kodiak, the Kodiak Island Borough, and the Kenai Peninsula Borough.

(B) Nonvoting members

One ex-officio, nonvoting representative shall be designated by, and represent, each of the following:

(i) The Environmental Protection Agency.

(ii) The Coast Guard.

(iii) The National Oceanic and Atmospheric Administration.

(iv) The United States Forest Service.

(v) The Bureau of Land Management.

(vi) The Alaska Department of Environmental Conservation.

(vii) The Alaska Department of Fish and Game.

(viii) The Alaska Department of Natural Resources.

(ix) The Division of Emergency Services, Alaska Department of Military and Veterans Affairs.

(3) Terms

(A) Duration of Councils

The term of the Councils shall continue throughout the life of the operation of the Trans-Alaska Pipeline System and so long as oil is transported to or from Cook Inlet.

(B) Three years

The voting members of each Council shall be appointed for a term of 3 years except as provided for in subparagraph (C).

(C) Initial appointments

The terms of the first appointments shall be as follows:

(i) For the appointments by the Governor of the State of Alaska, one-third shall serve for 3 years, one-third shall serve for 2 years, and one-third shall serve for one year.

(ii) For the representatives of municipalities required by subsection (d)(2)(A)(vii) of this section, a drawing of lots among the appointees shall determine that one-third of that group serves for 3 years, one-third serves for 2 years, and the remainder serves for 1 year.

(4) Self-governing

Each Council shall elect its own chairperson, select its own staff, and make policies with regard to its internal operating procedures. After the initial organizational meeting called by the Secretary under subsection (i) of this section, each Council shall be self-governing.

(5) Dual membership and conflicts of interest prohibited

(A) No individual selected as a member of the Council shall serve on the Association.

(B) No individual selected as a voting member of the Council shall be engaged in any activity which might conflict with such individual carrying out his functions as a member thereof.

(6) Duties

Each Council shall—

(A) provide advice and recommendations to the Association on policies, permits, and site-specific regulations relating to the operation and maintenance of terminal facilities and crude oil tankers which affect or may affect the environment in the vicinity of the terminal facilities;

(B) monitor through the committee established under subsection (e) of this section, the environmental impacts of the operation of the terminal facilities and crude oil tankers;

(C) monitor those aspects of terminal facilities' and crude oil tankers' operations and maintenance which affect or may affect the environment in the vicinity of the terminal facilities;

(D) review through the committee established under subsection (f) of this section, the adequacy of oil spill prevention and contingency plans for the terminal facilities and the adequacy of oil spill prevention and contingency plans for crude oil tankers, operating in Prince William Sound or in Cook Inlet;

(E) provide advice and recommendations to the Association on port operations, policies and practices;

(F) recommend to the Association—

(i) standards and stipulations for permits and site-specific regulations intended to minimize the impact of the terminal facilities' and crude oil tankers' operations in the vicinity of the terminal facilities;

(ii) modifications of terminal facility operations and maintenance intended to minimize the risk and mitigate the impact of terminal facilities, operations in the vicinity of the terminal facilities and to minimize the risk of oil spills;

(iii) modifications of crude oil tanker operations and maintenance in Prince William Sound and Cook Inlet intended to minimize the risk and mitigate the impact of oil spills; and

(iv) modifications to the oil spill prevention and contingency plans for terminal facilities and for crude oil tankers in Prince William Sound and Cook Inlet intended to enhance the ability to prevent and respond to an oil spill; and

(G) create additional committees of the Council as necessary to carry out the above functions, including a scientific and technical advisory committee to the Prince William Sound Council.

(7) No estoppel

No Council shall be held liable under State or Federal law for costs or damages as a result of rendering advice under this section. Nor shall any advice given by a voting member of a Council, or program representative or agent, be grounds for estopping the interests represented by the voting Council members from seeking damages or other appropriate relief.

(8) Scientific work

In carrying out its research, development and monitoring functions, each Council is authorized to conduct its own scientific research and shall review the scientific work undertaken by or on behalf of the terminal operators or crude oil tanker operators as a result of a legal requirement to undertake that work. Each Council shall also review the relevant scientific work undertaken by or on behalf of any government entity relating to the terminal facilities or crude oil tankers. To the extent possible, to avoid unnecessary duplication, each Council shall coordinate its independent scientific work with the scientific work performed by or on behalf of the terminal operators and with the scientific work performed by or on behalf of the operators of the crude oil tankers.

(e) Committee for Terminal and Oil Tanker Operations and Environmental Monitoring

(1) Monitoring Committee

Each Council shall establish a standing Terminal and Oil Tanker Operations and Environmental Monitoring Committee (hereinafter in this section referred to as the "Monitoring Committee") to devise and manage a comprehensive program of monitoring the environmental impacts of the operations of terminal facilities and of crude oil tankers while operating in Prince William Sound and Cook Inlet. The membership of the Monitoring Committee shall be made up of members of the Council, citizens, and recognized scientific experts selected by the Council.

(2) Duties

In fulfilling its responsibilities, the Monitoring Committee shall—

(A) advise the Council on a monitoring strategy that will permit early detection of environmental impacts of terminal facility operations and crude oil tanker operations while in Prince William Sound and Cook Inlet;

(B) develop monitoring programs and make recommendations to the Council on the implementation of those programs;

(C) at its discretion, select and contract with universities and other scientific institutions to carry out specific monitoring projects authorized by the Council pursuant to an approved monitoring strategy;

(D) complete any other tasks assigned by the Council; and

(E) provide written reports to the Council which interpret and assess the results of all monitoring programs.

(f) Committee for Oil Spill Prevention, Safety, and Emergency Response

(1) Technical Oil Spill Committee

Each Council shall establish a standing technical committee (hereinafter referred to as "Oil Spill Committee") to review and assess measures designed to prevent oil spills and the planning and preparedness for responding to, containing, cleaning up, and mitigating impacts of oil spills. The membership of the Oil Spill Committee shall be made up of members of the Council, citizens, and recognized technical experts selected by the Council.

(2) Duties

In fulfilling its responsibilities, the Oil Spill Committee shall—

(A) periodically review the respective oil spill prevention and contingency plans for the terminal facilities and for the crude oil tankers while in Prince William Sound or Cook Inlet, in light of new technological developments and changed circumstances;

(B) monitor periodic drills and testing of the oil spill contingency plans for the terminal facilities and for crude oil tankers while in Prince William Sound and Cook Inlet;

(C) study wind and water currents and other environmental factors in the vicinity of the terminal facilities which may affect the ability to prevent, respond to, contain, and clean up an oil spill;

(D) identify highly sensitive areas which may require specific protective measures in the event of a spill in Prince William Sound or Cook Inlet;

(E) monitor developments in oil spill prevention, containment, response, and cleanup technology;

(F) periodically review port organization, operations, incidents, and the adequacy and maintenance of vessel traffic service systems designed to assure safe transit of crude oil tankers pertinent to terminal operations;

(G) periodically review the standards for tankers bound for, loading at, exiting from, or otherwise using the terminal facilities;

(H) complete any other tasks assigned by the Council; and

(I) provide written reports to the Council outlining its findings and recommendations.

(g) Agency cooperation

On and after the expiration of the 180-day period following August 18, 1990, each Federal department, agency, or other instrumentality shall, with respect to all permits, site-specific regulations, and other matters governing the activities and actions of the terminal facilities which affect or may affect the vicinity of the terminal facilities, consult with the appropriate Council prior to taking substantive action with respect to the permit, site-specific regulation, or other matter. This consultation shall be carried out with a view to enabling the appropriate Association and Council to review the permit, site-specific regulation, or other matters and make appropriate recommendations regarding operations, policy or agency actions. Prior consultation shall not be required if an authorized Federal agency representative reasonably believes that an emergency exists requiring action without delay.

(h) Recommendations of Council

In the event that the Association does not adopt, or significantly modifies before adoption, any recommendation of the Council made pursuant to the authority granted to the Council in subsection (d) of this section, the Association shall provide to the Council, in writing, within 5 days of its decision, notice of its decision and a written statement of reasons for its rejection or significant modification of the recommendation.

(i) Administrative actions

Appointments, designations, and selections of individuals to serve as members of the Associations and Councils under this section shall be submitted to the Secretary prior to the expiration of the 120-day period following August 18, 1990. On or before the expiration of the 180-day period following August 18, 1990, the Secretary shall call an initial meeting of each Association and Council for organizational purposes.

(j) Location and compensation

(1) Location

Each Association and Council established by this section shall be located in the State of Alaska.

(2) Compensation

No member of an Association or Council shall be compensated for the member's services as a member of the Association or Council, but shall be allowed travel expenses, including per diem in lieu of subsistence, at a rate established by the Association or Council not to exceed the rates authorized for employees of agencies under sections 5702 and 5703 of title 5. However, each Council may enter into contracts to provide compensation and expenses to members of the committees created under subsections (d), (e), and (f) of this section.

(k) Funding

(1) Requirement

Approval of the contingency plans required of owners and operators of the Cook Inlet and Prince William Sound terminal facilities and crude oil tankers while operating in Alaskan waters in commerce with those terminal facilities shall be effective only so long as the respective Association and Council for a facility are funded pursuant to paragraph (2).

(2) Prince William Sound Program

The owners or operators of terminal facilities or crude oil tankers operating in Prince William Sound shall provide, on an annual basis, an aggregate amount of not more than $2,000,000, as determined by the Secretary. Such amount—

(A) shall provide for the establishment and operation on the environmental oversight and monitoring program in Prince William Sound;

(B) shall be adjusted annually by the Anchorage Consumer Price Index; and

(C) may be adjusted periodically upon the mutual consent of the owners or operators of terminal facilities or crude oil tankers operating in Prince William Sound and the Prince William Sound terminal facilities Council.

(3) Cook Inlet Program

The owners or operators of terminal facilities, offshore facilities, or crude oil tankers operating in Cook Inlet shall provide, on an annual basis, an aggregate amount of not more than $1,000,000, as determined by the Secretary. Such amount—

(A) shall provide for the establishment and operation of the environmental oversight and monitoring program in Cook Inlet;

(B) shall be adjusted annually by the Anchorage Consumer Price Index; and

(C) may be adjusted periodically upon the mutual consent of the owners or operators of terminal facilities, offshore facilities, or crude oil tankers operating in Cook Inlet and the Cook Inlet Council.

(*l*) Reports

(1) Associations and Councils

Prior to the expiration of the 36-month period following August 18, 1990, each Association and Council established by this section shall report to the President and the Congress concerning its activities under this section, together with its recommendations.

(2) GAO

Prior to the expiration of the 36-month period following August 18, 1990, the General Accounting Office shall report to the President and the Congress as to the handling of funds, including donated funds, by the entities carrying out the programs under this section, and the effectiveness of the demonstration programs carried out under this section, together with its recommendations.

(m) Definitions

As used in this section, the term—

(1) "terminal facilities" means—

(A) in the case of the Prince William Sound Program, the entire oil terminal complex located in Valdez, Alaska, consisting of approximately 1,000 acres including all buildings, docks (except docks owned by the City of Valdez if those docks are not used for loading of crude oil), pipes, piping, roads, ponds, tanks, crude oil tankers only while at the terminal dock, tanker escorts owned or operated by the operator of the terminal, vehicles, and other facilities associated with, and necessary for, assisting tanker movement of crude oil into and out of the oil terminal complex; and

(B) in the case of the Cook Inlet Program, the entire oil terminal complex including all buildings, docks, pipes, piping, roads, ponds, tanks, vessels, vehicles, crude oil tankers only while at the terminal dock, tanker escorts owned or operated by the operator of the terminal, emergency spill response vessels owned or operated by the operator of the terminal, and other facilities associated with, and necessary for, assisting tanker movement of crude oil into and out of the oil terminal complex;

(2) "crude oil tanker" means a tanker (as that term is defined under section 2101 of title 46)—

(A) in the case of the Prince William Sound Program, calling at the terminal facilities for the purpose of receiving and transporting oil to refineries, operating north of Middleston Island and bound for or exiting from Prince William Sound; and

(B) in the case of the Cook Inlet Program, calling at the terminal facilities for the purpose of receiving and transporting oil to refineries and operating in Cook Inlet and the Gulf of Alaska north of Amatuli Island, including tankers transiting to Cook Inlet from Prince William Sound;

(3) "vicinity of the terminal facilities" means that geographical area surrounding the environment of terminal facilities which is directly affected or may be directly affected by the operation of the terminal facilities; and

(4) "Secretary" means the Secretary of the department in which the Coast Guard is operating.

(n) Savings clause

(1) Regulatory authority

Nothing in this section shall be construed as modifying, repealing, superseding, or preempting any municipal, State or Federal law or regulation, or in any way affecting litigation arising from oil spills or the rights and responsibilities of the United States or the State of Alaska, or municipalities thereof, to preserve and protect the environment through regulation of land, air, and water uses, of safety, and of related development. The monitoring provided for by this section shall be designed to help assure compliance with applicable laws and regulations and shall only extend to activities—

(A) that would affect or have the potential to affect the vicinity of the terminal facilities and the area of crude oil tanker operations included in the Programs; and

(B) are subject to the United States or State of Alaska, or municipality thereof, law, regulation, or other legal requirement.

(2) Recommendations

This subsection is not intended to prevent the Association or Council from recommending to appropriate authorities that existing legal requirements should be modified or that new legal requirements should be adopted.

(*o*) Alternative voluntary advisory group in lieu of Council

The requirements of subsections (c) through (*l*) of this section, as such subsections apply respectively to the Prince William Sound Program and the Cook Inlet Program, are deemed to have been satisfied so long as the following conditions are met:

(1) Prince William Sound

With respect to the Prince William Sound Program, the Alyeska Pipeline Service Company or any of its owner companies enters into a contract for the duration of the operation of the Trans-Alaska Pipeline System with the Alyeska Citizens Advisory Committee in existence on August 18, 1990, or a successor organization, to fund that Committee or organization on an annual basis in the amount provided for by subsection (k)(2)(A) of this section and the President annually certifies that the Committee or organization fosters the general goals and purposes of this section and is broadly representative of the communities and interests in the vicinity of the terminal facilities and Prince William Sound.

(2) Cook Inlet

With respect to the Cook Inlet Program, the terminal facilities, offshore facilities, or crude oil tanker owners and operators enter into a contract with a voluntary advisory organization to fund that organization on an annual basis and the President annually certifies that the organization fosters the general goals and purposes of this section and is broadly representative of the communities and interests in the vicinity of the terminal facilities and Cook Inlet.

(Pub. L. 101–380, title V, § 5002, Aug. 18, 1990, 104 Stat. 544; Pub. L. 109–241, title IX, § 902(*l*)(2), July 11, 2006, 120 Stat. 568.)

AMENDMENTS

2006—Subsec. (m)(4). Pub. L. 109–241 substituted "of the department in which the Coast Guard is operating." for "of Transportation."

CHANGE OF NAME

General Accounting Office redesignated Government Accountability Office by section 8 of Pub. L. 108–271, set out as a note under section 702 of Title 31, Money and Finance.

DELEGATION OF FUNCTIONS

Functions of President under subsecs. (c)(2)(D) and (*o*) of this section delegated to Secretary of the Department in which the Coast Guard is operating by section 8(f), (g) of Ex. Ord. No. 12777, Oct. 18, 1991, 56 F.R. 54769, as amended, set out as a note under section 1321 of this title.

PRINCE WILLIAM SOUND REGIONAL CITIZENS ADVISORY COMMITTEE

Certification of President of the United States, Mar. 21, 1991, 56 F.R. 12439, provided:

By the authority vested in me as President by the Constitution and the laws of the United States of America, including section 5002(*o*)(1) of the Oil Pollution Act of 1990 (Public Law 101–380, 104 Stat. 552) [33 U.S.C. 2732(*o*)(1)], I hereby certify for the year 1991 the following:

(1) that the Prince William Sound Regional Citizens Advisory Committee fosters the general goals and purposes of section 5002 of the Oil Pollution Act of 1990 for the year 1991; and

(2) that the Prince William Sound Regional Citizens Advisory Committee is broadly representative of the communities and interests in the vicinity of the terminal facilities and Prince William Sound.

This certification shall be published in the Federal Register.

GEORGE BUSH.

COOK INLET REGIONAL CITIZENS ADVISORY COUNCIL

Certification of President of the United States, Aug. 6, 1991, 56 F.R. 37819, provided:

By the authority vested in me as President by the Constitution and the laws of the United States of America, including section 5002(*o*)(2) of the Oil Pollution Act of 1990 [33 U.S.C. 2732(*o*)(2)], I hereby certify for the year 1991 the following:

(1) that the Cook Inlet Regional Citizens Advisory Council has met the general goals and purposes of section 5002 of the Oil Pollution Act of 1990 for the year 1991; and

(2) that the Cook Inlet Regional Citizens Advisory Council is broadly representative of the communities and interests in the vicinity of the terminal facilities and offshore facilities in Cook Inlet.

This certification shall be published in the Federal Register.

GEORGE BUSH.

§ 2733. Bligh Reef light

The Secretary of Transportation shall within one year after August 18, 1990, install and ensure operation of an automated navigation light on or adjacent to Bligh Reef in Prince William Sound, Alaska, of sufficient power and height to provide long-range warning of the location of Bligh Reef.

(Pub. L. 101–380, title V, § 5003, Aug. 18, 1990, 104 Stat. 553.)

§ 2734. Vessel traffic service system

The Secretary of Transportation shall within one year after August 18, 1990—

(1) acquire, install, and operate such additional equipment (which may consist of radar, closed circuit television, satellite tracking systems, or other shipboard dependent surveillance), train and locate such personnel, and issue such final regulations as are necessary to increase the range of the existing VTS system in the Port of Valdez, Alaska, sufficiently to track the locations and movements of tank vessels carrying oil from the Trans-Alaska Pipeline when such vessels are transiting Prince William Sound, Alaska, and to sound an audible alarm when such tankers depart from designated navigation routes; and

(2) submit to the Committee on Commerce, Science, and Transportation of the Senate and the Committee on Transportation and Infrastructure of the House of Representatives a report on the feasibility and desirability of instituting positive control of tank vessel movements in Prince William Sound by Coast Guard personnel using the Port of Valdez, Alaska, VTS system, as modified pursuant to paragraph (1).

(Pub. L. 101–380, title V, § 5004, Aug. 18, 1990, 104 Stat. 553; Pub. L. 107–295, title IV, § 408(b)(2), Nov. 25, 2002, 116 Stat. 2117.)

AMENDMENTS

2002—Par. (2). Pub. L. 107–295 substituted "Transportation and Infrastructure" for "Merchant Marine and Fisheries".

TRANSFER OF FUNCTIONS

For transfer of authorities, functions, personnel, and assets of the Coast Guard, including the authorities and functions of the Secretary of Transportation relating thereto, to the Department of Homeland Security, and for treatment of related references, see sections 468(b), 551(d), 552(d), and 557 of Title 6, Domestic Security, and the Department of Homeland Security Reorganization Plan of November 25, 2002, as modified, set out as a note under section 542 of Title 6.

§ 2735. Equipment and personnel requirements under tank vessel and facility response plans

(a) In general

In addition to the requirements for response plans for vessels established by section 1321(j) of this title, a response plan for a tanker loading cargo at a facility permitted under the Trans-Alaska Pipeline Authorization Act (43 U.S.C. 1651 et seq.), and a response plan for such a facility, shall provide for—

(1) prepositioned oil spill containment and removal equipment in communities and other strategic locations within the geographic boundaries of Prince William Sound, including escort vessels with skimming capability; barges to receive recovered oil; heavy duty sea boom, pumping, transferring, and lightering equipment; and other appropriate removal equipment for the protection of the environment, including fish hatcheries;

(2) the establishment of an oil spill removal organization at appropriate locations in Prince William Sound, consisting of trained personnel in sufficient numbers to immediately remove, to the maximum extent practicable, a worst case discharge or a discharge of 200,000 barrels of oil, whichever is greater;

(3) training in oil removal techniques for local residents and individuals engaged in the cultivation or production of fish or fish products in Prince William Sound;

(4) practice exercises not less than 2 times per year which test the capacity of the equipment and personnel required under this paragraph; and

(5) periodic testing and certification of equipment required under this paragraph, as required by the Secretary.

(b) Definitions

In this section—

(1) the term "Prince William Sound" means all State and Federal waters within Prince William Sound, Alaska, including the approach to Hinchenbrook Entrance out to and encompassing Seal Rocks; and

(2) the term "worst case discharge" means—

(A) in the case of a vessel, a discharge in adverse weather conditions of its entire cargo; and

(B) in the case of a facility, the largest foreseeable discharge in adverse weather conditions.

(Pub. L. 101–380, title V, § 5005, Aug. 18, 1990, 104 Stat. 553; Pub. L. 102–388, title III, § 354, Oct. 6, 1992, 106 Stat. 1555.)

REFERENCES IN TEXT

The Trans-Alaska Pipeline Authorization Act, referred to in subsec. (a), is title II of Pub. L. 93–153, Nov. 16, 1973, 87 Stat. 584, which is classified generally to chapter 34 (§ 1651 et seq.) of Title 43, Public Lands. For complete classification of this Act to the Code, see Short Title note set out under section 1651 of Title 43 and Tables.

AMENDMENTS

1992—Subsec. (a). Pub. L. 102–388 substituted "tanker loading cargo at" for "tank vessel operating on Prince William Sound, or" and directed the insertion of "and a response plan for such a facility," after "(43 U.S.C. 1651 et seq.).", which was executed by making the insertion after "(43 U.S.C. 1651 et seq.)," to reflect the probable intent of Congress.

§ 2736. Funding

(a) Sections 2731, 2733, and 2734

Amounts in the Fund shall be available, without further appropriations and without fiscal year limitation, to carry out section 2731 of this title in the amount as determined in subsection (b) of this section, and to carry out sections 2733 and 2734 of this title, in an amount not to exceed $5,000,000.

(b) Use of interest only

The amount of funding to be made available annually to carry out section 2731 of this title shall be the interest produced by the Fund's investment of the $22,500,000 remaining funding authorized for the Prince William Sound Oil Spill Recovery Institute and currently deposited in the Fund and invested by the Secretary of the Treasury in income producing securities along with other funds comprising the Fund. The National Pollution Funds Center shall transfer all such accrued interest, including the interest earned from the date funds in the Trans-Alaska Liability Pipeline Fund were transferred into the Oil Spill Liability Trust Fund pursuant to section 8102(a)(2)(B)(ii), to the Prince William Sound Oil Spill Recovery Institute annually, beginning 60 days after October 19, 1996.

(c) Use for section 2712

Beginning 1 year after the date on which the Secretary, in consultation with the Secretary of the Interior, determines that oil and gas exploration, development, and production in the State of Alaska have ceased, the funding authorized for the Prince William Sound Oil Spill Recovery Institute and deposited in the Fund shall thereafter be made available for purposes of section 2712 of this title in Alaska.

(d) Section 2738

Amounts in the Fund shall be available, without further appropriation and without fiscal year limitation, to carry out section 2738(b) of this title, in an annual amount not to exceed $5,000,000 of which up to $3,000,000 may be used for the lease payment to the Alaska SeaLife Center under section 2738(b)(2) of this title: *Provided*, That the entire amount is designated by the Congress as an emergency requirement pursuant to section 251(b)(2)(A) of the Balanced Budget and Emergency Deficit Control Act of 1985, as amended [2 U.S.C. 901(b)(2)(A)]: *Provided further*, That the entire amount shall be available only to the extent an official budget request that includes designation of the entire amount of the request as an emergency requirement as defined in the Balanced Budget and Emergency Deficit Control Act of 1985, as amended, is transmitted by the President to the Congress.

(Pub. L. 101–380, title V, § 5006, Aug. 18, 1990, 104 Stat. 554; Pub. L. 104–324, title XI, § 1102(b), Oct. 19, 1996, 110 Stat. 3965; Pub. L. 106–246, div. B, title II, § 2204(2), July 13, 2000, 114 Stat. 547; Pub. L. 106–554, § 1(a)(4) [div. B, title I, § 144(c)(1)(C)], Dec. 21, 2000, 114 Stat. 2763, 2763A–239; Pub. L. 108–293, title VII, § 704, Aug. 9, 2004, 118 Stat. 1075; Pub. L. 109–58, title III, § 389(2), Aug. 8, 2005, 119 Stat. 747; Pub. L. 109–59, title IV, § 4413, Aug. 10, 2005, 119 Stat. 1779; Pub. L. 109–241, title IX, § 901(j), July 11, 2006, 120 Stat. 564.)

REFERENCES IN TEXT

Section 8102(a)(2)(B)(ii), referred to in subsec. (b), is section 8102(a)(2)(B)(ii) of Pub. L. 101–380, title VIII, Aug. 18, 1990, 104 Stat. 565, which is set out as a note under section 1653 of Title 43, Public Lands.

The Balanced Budget and Emergency Deficit Control Act of 1985, referred to in subsec. (d), is title II of Pub. L. 99–177, Dec. 12, 1985, 99 Stat. 1038, as amended, which enacted chapter 20 (§ 900 et seq.) and sections 654 to 656 of Title 2, The Congress, amended sections 602, 622, 631 to 642, and 651 to 653 of Title 2, sections 1104 to 1106, and 1109 of Title 31, Money and Finance, and section 911 of Title 42, The Public Health and Welfare, repealed section 661 of Title 2, enacted provisions set out as notes under section 900 of Title 2 and section 911 of Title 42, and amended provisions set out as a note under section 621 of Title 2. For complete classification of this Act to the Code, see Short Title note set out under section 900 of Title 2 and Tables.

AMENDMENTS

2006—Subsec. (c). Pub. L. 109–241, which directed the insertion of a comma after "October 1, 2012", could not be executed because "October 1, 2012" did not appear subsequent to amendment by Pub. L. 109–58. See 2005 Amendment note below.

2005—Subsec. (c). Pub. L. 109–58 substituted "1 year after the date on which the Secretary, in consultation with the Secretary of the Interior, determines that oil and gas exploration, development, and production in the State of Alaska have ceased," for "October 1, 2012".

Subsec. (d). Pub. L. 109–59, which directed insertion of "annual" before "amount", was executed by making the insertion before "amount not to exceed", to reflect the probable intent of Congress.

2004—Subsecs. (c), (d). Pub. L. 108–293 in subsec. (c) relating to section 2712, substituted "October 1, 2012" for "with the eleventh year following October 19, 1996," and redesignated subsec. (c) relating to section 2738 as (d).

2000—Subsec. (c). Pub. L. 106–554 inserted "of which up to $3,000,000 may be used for the lease payment to the Alaska SeaLife Center under section 2738(b)(2) of this title" after "$5,000,000" in subsec. (c) relating to section 2738.

Pub. L. 106–246 added subsec. (c) relating to section 2738.

1996—Subsec. (a). Pub. L. 104–324, § 1102(b)(1)–(3), redesignated subsec. (b) as (a), substituted "2731, 2733," for "2733" in heading, inserted "to carry out section 2731 of this title in the amount as determined in subsection (b) of this section, and" after "limitation,", and struck out heading and text of former subsec. (a). Text read as follows: "Amounts in the Fund shall be available, subject to appropriations, and shall remain available until expended, to carry out section 2731 of this title as follows:

"(1) $5,000,000 shall be available for the first fiscal year beginning after August 18, 1990.

"(2) $2,000,000 shall be available for each of the 9 fiscal years following the fiscal year described in paragraph (1)."

Subsecs. (b), (c). Pub. L. 104–324, § 1102(b)(4), added subsecs. (b) and (c). Former subsec. (b) redesignated (a).

§ 2737. Limitation

Notwithstanding any other law, tank vessels that have spilled more than 1,000,000 gallons of oil into the marine environment after March 22, 1989, are prohibited from operating on the navigable waters of Prince William Sound, Alaska.

(Pub. L. 101–380, title V, § 5007, Aug. 18, 1990, 104 Stat. 554.)

§ 2738. North Pacific Marine Research Institute

(a) Institute established

The Secretary of Commerce shall establish a North Pacific Marine Research Institute (hereafter in this section referred to as the "Institute") to be administered at the Alaska SeaLife Center by the North Pacific Research Board.

(b) Functions

The Institute shall—

(1) conduct research and carry out education and demonstration projects on or relating to the North Pacific marine ecosystem with particular emphasis on marine mammal, sea bird, fish, and shellfish populations in the Bering Sea and Gulf of Alaska including populations located in or near Kenai Fjords National Park and the Alaska Maritime National Wildlife Refuge; and

(2) lease, maintain, operate, and upgrade the necessary research equipment and related facilities necessary to conduct such research at the Alaska SeaLife Center.

(c) Evaluation and audit

The Secretary of Commerce may periodically evaluate the activities of the Institute to ensure that funds received by the Institute are used in a manner consistent with this section. The Federal Advisory Committee Act [5 U.S.C. App.] shall not apply to the Institute.

(d) Status of employees

Employees of the Institute shall not, by reason of such employment, be considered to be employees of the Federal Government for any purpose.

(e) Use of funds

No funds made available to carry out this section may be used to initiate litigation, or for the acquisition of real property (other than facilities leased at the Alaska SeaLife Center). No more than 10 percent of the funds made available to carry out subsection (b)(1) of this section may be used to administer the Institute. The administrative funds of the Institute and the administrative funds of the North Pacific Research Board created under Public Law 105–83 may be used to jointly administer such programs at the discretion of the North Pacific Research Board.

(f) Availability of research

The Institute shall publish and make available to any person on request the results of all research, educational, and demonstration projects conducted by the Institute. The Institute shall provide a copy of all research, educational, and demonstration projects conducted by the Institute to the National Park Service, the United States Fish and Wildlife Service, and the National Oceanic and Atmospheric Administration.

(Pub. L. 101–380, title V, §5008, as added Pub. L. 106–246, div. B, title II, §2204(1), July 13, 2000, 114 Stat. 546; amended Pub. L. 106–554, §1(a)(4) [div. B, title I, §144(c)(1)(A), (B)], Dec. 21, 2000, 114 Stat. 2763, 2763A–238, 2763A–239.)

REFERENCES IN TEXT

The Federal Advisory Committee Act, referred to in subsec. (c), is Pub. L. 92–463, Oct. 6, 1972, 86 Stat. 770, as amended, which is set out in the Appendix to Title 5, Government Organization and Employees.

Public Law 105–83, referred to in subsec. (e), is Pub. L. 105–83, Nov. 14, 1997, 111 Stat. 1543, as amended, known as the Department of the Interior and Related Agencies Appropriations Act, 1998. For complete classification of this Act to the Code, see Tables.

AMENDMENTS

2000—Subsec. (c). Pub. L. 106–554, §1(a)(4) [div. B, title I, §144(c)(1)(A)], inserted second sentence and struck out former second sentence which read as follows: "The Comptroller General of the United States, and any of his or her duly authorized representatives, shall have access, for purposes of audit and examination, to any books, documents, papers, and records of the Institute that are pertinent to the funds received and expended by the Institute."

Subsec. (e). Pub. L. 106–554, §1(a)(4) [div. B, title I, §144(c)(1)(B)], inserted at end "The administrative funds of the Institute and the administrative funds of the North Pacific Research Board created under Public Law 105–83 may be used to jointly administer such programs at the discretion of the North Pacific Research Board."

SUBCHAPTER III—MISCELLANEOUS

§2751. Savings provision

(a) Cross-references

A reference to a law replaced by this Act, including a reference in a regulation, order, or other law, is deemed to refer to the corresponding provision of this Act.

(b) Continuation of regulations

An order, rule, or regulation in effect under a law replaced by this Act continues in effect under the corresponding provision of this Act until repealed, amended, or superseded.

(c) Rule of construction

An inference of legislative construction shall not be drawn by reason of the caption or catch line of a provision enacted by this Act.

(d) Actions and rights

Nothing in this Act shall apply to any rights and duties that matured, penalties that were incurred, and proceedings that were begun before August 18, 1990, except as provided by this section, and shall be adjudicated pursuant to the law applicable on the date prior to August 18, 1990.

(e) Admiralty and maritime law

Except as otherwise provided in this Act, this Act does not affect—

(1) admiralty and maritime law; or

(2) the jurisdiction of the district courts of the United States with respect to civil actions under admiralty and maritime jurisdiction, saving to suitors in all cases all other remedies to which they are otherwise entitled.

(Pub. L. 101–380, title VI, §6001, Aug. 18, 1990, 104 Stat. 554.)

REFERENCES IN TEXT

This Act, referred to in text, is Pub. L. 101–380, Aug. 18, 1990, 104 Stat. 484, as amended, known as the Oil Pollution Act of 1990, which is classified principally to this chapter. For complete classification of this Act to the Code, see Short Title note set out under section 2701 of this title and Tables.

§2752. Annual appropriations

(a) Required

Except as provided in subsection (b) of this section, amounts in the Fund shall be available only as provided in annual appropriation Acts.

(b) Exceptions

Subsection (a) of this section shall not apply to sections[1] 2706(f), 2712(a)(4), or 2736 of this title, and shall not apply to an amount not to exceed $50,000,000 in any fiscal year which the President may make available from the Fund to carry out section 1321(c) of this title and to initiate the assessment of natural resources damages required under section 2706 of this title. To the extent that such amount is not adequate, the Coast Guard may obtain an advance from the Fund of such sums as may be necessary, up to a maximum of $100,000,000, and within 30 days shall notify Congress of the amount advanced and the facts and circumstances necessitating the advance. Amounts advanced shall be repaid to the Fund when, and to the extent that, removal costs are recovered by the Coast Guard from responsible parties for the discharge or substantial threat of discharge. Sums to which

[1] So in original. Probably should be "section".

this subsection applies shall remain available until expended.

(Pub. L. 101–380, title VI, § 6002, Aug. 18, 1990, 104 Stat. 555; Pub. L. 104–324, title XI, § 1102(c)(1), Oct. 19, 1996, 110 Stat. 3966; Pub. L. 107–295, title III, § 323, Nov. 25, 2002, 116 Stat. 2104.)

AMENDMENTS

2002—Subsec. (b). Pub. L. 107–295 inserted after first sentence "To the extent that such amount is not adequate, the Coast Guard may obtain an advance from the Fund of such sums as may be necessary, up to a maximum of $100,000,000, and within 30 days shall notify Congress of the amount advanced and the facts and circumstances necessitating the advance. Amounts advanced shall be repaid to the Fund when, and to the extent that, removal costs are recovered by the Coast Guard from responsible parties for the discharge or substantial threat of discharge."

1996—Subsec. (b). Pub. L. 104–324 substituted "2736" for "2736(b)".

TRANSFER OF FUNCTIONS

For transfer of authorities, functions, personnel, and assets of the Coast Guard, including the authorities and functions of the Secretary of Transportation relating thereto, to the Department of Homeland Security, and for treatment of related references, see sections 468(b), 551(d), 552(d), and 557 of Title 6, Domestic Security, and the Department of Homeland Security Reorganization Plan of November 25, 2002, as modified, set out as a note under section 542 of Title 6.

DELEGATION OF FUNCTIONS

Functions of President under subsec. (b) of this section delegated to Secretary of Department in which Coast Guard is operating by section 7(a)(1)(B) of Ex. Ord. No. 12777, Oct. 18, 1991, 56 F.R. 54766, set out as a note under section 1321 of this title.

§ 2753. Repealed. Pub. L. 104–134, title I, § 101(c) [title I, § 109], Apr. 26, 1996, 110 Stat. 1321–156, 1321–177; renumbered title I, Pub. L. 104–140, § 1(a), May 2, 1996, 110 Stat. 1327

Section, Pub. L. 101–380, title VI, § 6003, Aug. 18, 1990, 104 Stat. 555, related to protection of the Outer Banks of North Carolina.

SUBCHAPTER IV—OIL POLLUTION RESEARCH AND DEVELOPMENT PROGRAM

§ 2761. Oil pollution research and development program

(a) Interagency Coordinating Committee on Oil Pollution Research

(1) Establishment

There is established an Interagency Coordinating Committee on Oil Pollution Research (hereinafter in this section referred to as the "Interagency Committee").

(2) Purposes

The Interagency Committee shall coordinate a comprehensive program of oil pollution research, technology development, and demonstration among the Federal agencies, in cooperation and coordination with industry, universities, research institutions, State governments, and other nations, as appropriate, and shall foster cost-effective research mechanisms, including the joint funding of research.

(3) Membership

The Interagency Committee shall include representatives from the Coast Guard, the Department of Commerce (including the National Oceanic and Atmospheric Administration and the National Institute of Standards and Technology), the Department of Energy, the Department of the Interior (including the Minerals Management Service and the United States Fish and Wildlife Service), the Department of Transportation (including the Maritime Administration and the Pipeline and Hazardous Materials Safety Administration), the Department of Defense (including the Army Corps of Engineers and the Navy), the Department of Homeland Security (including the United States Fire Administration in the Federal Emergency Management Agency), the Environmental Protection Agency, the National Aeronautics and Space Administration, and such other Federal agencies the President may designate.

(4) Chairman

A representative of the Coast Guard shall serve as Chairman.

(b) Oil pollution research and technology plan

(1) Implementation plan

Within 180 days after August 18, 1990, the Interagency Committee shall submit to Congress a plan for the implementation of the oil pollution research, development, and demonstration program established pursuant to subsection (c) of this section. The research plan shall—

(A) identify agency roles and responsibilities;

(B) assess the current status of knowledge on oil pollution prevention, response, and mitigation technologies and effects of oil pollution on the environment;

(C) identify significant oil pollution research gaps including an assessment of major technological deficiencies in responses to past oil discharges;

(D) establish research priorities and goals for oil pollution technology development related to prevention, response, mitigation, and environmental effects;

(E) estimate the resources needed to conduct the oil pollution research and development program established pursuant to subsection (c) of this section, and timetables for completing research tasks; and

(F) identify, in consultation with the States, regional oil pollution research needs and priorities for a coordinated, multidisciplinary program of research at the regional level.

(2) Advice and guidance

The Chairman, through the Department of Transportation, shall contract with the National Academy of Sciences to—

(A) provide advice and guidance in the preparation and development of the research plan; and

(B) assess the adequacy of the plan as submitted, and submit a report to Congress on the conclusions of such assessment.

The National Institute of Standards and Technology shall provide the Interagency Committee with advice and guidance on issues relating to quality assurance and standards measurements relating to its activities under this section.

(c) Oil pollution research and development program

(1) Establishment

The Interagency Committee shall coordinate the establishment, by the agencies represented on the Interagency Committee, of a program for conducting oil pollution research and development, as provided in this subsection.

(2) Innovative oil pollution technology

The program established under this subsection shall provide for research, development, and demonstration of new or improved technologies which are effective in preventing or mitigating oil discharges and which protect the environment, including—

(A) development of improved designs for vessels and facilities, and improved operational practices;

(B) research, development, and demonstration of improved technologies to measure the ullage of a vessel tank, prevent discharges from tank vents, prevent discharges during lightering and bunkering operations, contain discharges on the deck of a vessel, prevent discharges through the use of vacuums in tanks, and otherwise contain discharges of oil from vessels and facilities;

(C) research, development, and demonstration of new or improved systems of mechanical, chemical, biological, and other methods (including the use of dispersants, solvents, and bioremediation) for the recovery, removal, and disposal of oil, including evaluation of the environmental effects of the use of such systems;

(D) research and training, in consultation with the National Response Team, to improve industry's and Government's ability to quickly and effectively remove an oil discharge, including the long-term use, as appropriate, of the National Spill Control School in Corpus Christi, Texas, and the Center for Marine Training and Safety in Galveston, Texas;

(E) research to improve information systems for decisionmaking, including the use of data from coastal mapping, baseline data, and other data related to the environmental effects of oil discharges, and cleanup technologies;

(F) development of technologies and methods to protect public health and safety from oil discharges, including the population directly exposed to an oil discharge;

(G) development of technologies, methods, and standards for protecting removal personnel, including training, adequate supervision, protective equipment, maximum exposure limits, and decontamination procedures;

(H) research and development of methods to restore and rehabilitate natural resources damaged by oil discharges;

(I) research to evaluate the relative effectiveness and environmental impacts of bioremediation technologies; and

(J) the demonstration of a satellite-based, dependent surveillance vessel traffic system in Narragansett Bay to evaluate the utility of such system in reducing the risk of oil discharges from vessel collisions and groundings in confined waters.

(3) Oil pollution technology evaluation

The program established under this subsection shall provide for oil pollution prevention and mitigation technology evaluation including—

(A) the evaluation and testing of technologies developed independently of the research and development program established under this subsection;

(B) the establishment, where appropriate, of standards and testing protocols traceable to national standards to measure the performance of oil pollution prevention or mitigation technologies; and

(C) the use, where appropriate, of controlled field testing to evaluate real-world application of oil discharge prevention or mitigation technologies.

(4) Oil pollution effects research

(A) The Committee shall establish a research program to monitor and evaluate the environmental effects of oil discharges. Such program shall include the following elements:

(i) The development of improved models and capabilities for predicting the environmental fate, transport, and effects of oil discharges.

(ii) The development of methods, including economic methods, to assess damages to natural resources resulting from oil discharges.

(iii) The identification of types of ecologically sensitive areas at particular risk to oil discharges and the preparation of scientific monitoring and evaluation plans, one for each of several types of ecological conditions, to be implemented in the event of major oil discharges in such areas.

(iv) The collection of environmental baseline data in ecologically sensitive areas at particular risk to oil discharges where such data are insufficient.

(B) The Department of Commerce in consultation with the Environmental Protection Agency shall monitor and scientifically evaluate the long-term environmental effects of oil discharges if—

(i) the amount of oil discharged exceeds 250,000 gallons;

(ii) the oil discharge has occurred on or after January 1, 1989; and

(iii) the Interagency Committee determines that a study of the long-term environmental effects of the discharge would be of significant scientific value, especially for preventing or responding to future oil discharges.

Areas for study may include the following sites where oil discharges have occurred: the New York/New Jersey Harbor area, where oil was discharged by an Exxon underwater pipeline, the T/B CIBRO SAVANNAH, and the M/V BT NAUTILUS; Narragansett Bay where oil was discharged by the WORLD PRODIGY; the Houston Ship Channel where oil was discharged by the RACHEL B; the Delaware River, where oil was discharged by the PRESIDENTE RIVERA and the T/V ATHOS I, and Huntington Beach, California, where oil was discharged by the AMERICAN TRADER.

(C) Research conducted under this paragraph by, or through, the United States Fish and Wildlife Service shall be directed and coordinated by the National Wetland Research Center.

(5) Marine simulation research

The program established under this subsection shall include research on the greater use and application of geographic and vessel response simulation models, including the development of additional data bases and updating of existing data bases using, among others, the resources of the National Maritime Research Center. It shall include research and vessel simulations for—

(A) contingency plan evaluation and amendment;

(B) removal and strike team training;

(C) tank vessel personnel training; and

(D) those geographic areas where there is a significant likelihood of a major oil discharge.

(6) Demonstration projects

The United States Coast Guard, in conjunction with such agencies as the President may designate, shall conduct 4 port oil pollution minimization demonstration projects, one each with (A) the Port Authority of New York and New Jersey, (B) the Ports of Los Angeles and Long Beach, California, (C) the Port of New Orleans, Louisiana, and (D) ports on the Great Lakes, for the purpose of developing and demonstrating integrated port oil pollution prevention and cleanup systems which utilize the information and implement the improved practices and technologies developed from the research, development, and demonstration program established in this section. Such systems shall utilize improved technologies and management practices for reducing the risk of oil discharges, including, as appropriate, improved data access, computerized tracking of oil shipments, improved vessel tracking and navigation systems, advanced technology to monitor pipeline and tank conditions, improved oil spill response capability, improved capability to predict the flow and effects of oil discharges in both the inner and outer harbor areas for the purposes of making infrastructure decisions, and such other activities necessary to achieve the purposes of this section.

(7) Simulated environmental testing

Agencies represented on the Interagency Committee shall ensure the long-term use and operation of the Oil and Hazardous Materials Simulated Environmental Test Tank (OHMSETT) Research Center in New Jersey for oil pollution technology testing and evaluations.

(8) Regional research program

(A) Consistent with the research plan in subsection (b) of this section, the Interagency Committee shall coordinate a program of competitive grants to universities or other research institutions, or groups of universities or research institutions, for the purposes of conducting a coordinated research program related to the regional aspects of oil pollution, such as prevention, removal, mitigation, and the effects of discharged oil on regional environments. For the purposes of this paragraph, a region means a Coast Guard district as set out in part 3 of title 33, Code of Federal Regulations (1989).

(B) The Interagency Committee shall coordinate the publication by the agencies represented on the Interagency Committee of a solicitation for grants under this subsection. The application shall be in such form and contain such information as may be required in the published solicitation. The applications shall be reviewed by the Interagency Committee, which shall make recommendations to the appropriate granting agency represented on the Interagency Committee for awarding the grant. The granting agency shall award the grants recommended by the Interagency Committee unless the agency decides not to award the grant due to budgetary or other compelling considerations and publishes its reasons for such a determination in the Federal Register. No grants may be made by any agency from any funds authorized for this paragraph unless such grant award has first been recommended by the Interagency Committee.

(C) Any university or other research institution, or group of universities or research institutions, may apply for a grant for the regional research program established by this paragraph. The applicant must be located in the region, or in a State a part of which is in the region, for which the project is proposed as part of the regional research program. With respect to a group application, the entity or entities which will carry out the substantial portion of the proposed research must be located in the region, or in a State a part of which is in the region, for which the project is proposed as part of the regional research program.

(D) The Interagency Committee shall make recommendations on grants in such a manner as to ensure an appropriate balance within a region among the various aspects of oil pollution research, including prevention, removal, mitigation, and the effects of discharged oil on regional environments. In addition, the Interagency Committee shall make recommendations for grants based on the following criteria:

(i) There is available to the applicant for carrying out this paragraph demonstrated research resources.

(ii) The applicant demonstrates the capability of making a significant contribution to regional research needs.

(iii) The projects which the applicant proposes to carry out under the grant are consistent with the research plan under subsection (b)(1)(F) of this section and would further the objectives of the research and development program established in this section.

(E) Grants provided under this paragraph shall be for a period up to 3 years, subject to annual review by the granting agency, and provide not more than 80 percent of the costs of the research activities carried out in connection with the grant.

(F) No funds made available to carry out this subsection may be used for the acquisition of real property (including buildings) or construction of any building.

(G) Nothing in this paragraph is intended to alter or abridge the authority under existing law of any Federal agency to make grants, or enter into contracts or cooperative agreements, using funds other than those authorized in this Act for the purposes of carrying out this paragraph.

(9) Funding

For each of the fiscal years 1991, 1992, 1993, 1994, and 1995, $6,000,000 of amounts in the Fund shall be available to carry out the regional research program in paragraph (8), such amounts to be available in equal amounts for the regional research program in each region; except that if the agencies represented on the Interagency Committee determine that regional research needs exist which cannot be addressed within such funding limits, such agencies may use their authority under paragraph (10) to make additional grants to meet such needs. For the purposes of this paragraph, the research program carried out by the Prince William Sound Oil Spill Recovery Institute established under section 2731 of this title, shall not be eligible to receive grants under this paragraph until the authorization for funding under section 2736(b) of this title expires.

(10) Grants

In carrying out the research and development program established under this subsection, the agencies represented on the Interagency Committee may enter into contracts and cooperative agreements and make grants to universities, research institutions, and other persons. Such contracts, cooperative agreements, and grants shall address research and technology priorities set forth in the oil pollution research plan under subsection (b) of this section.

(11) Utilization of resources

In carrying out research under this section, the Department of Transportation shall continue to utilize the resources of the Pipeline and Hazardous Materials Safety Administration of the Department of Transportation, to the maximum extent practicable.

(d) International cooperation

In accordance with the research plan submitted under subsection (b) of this section, the Interagency Committee shall coordinate and cooperate with other nations and foreign research entities in conducting oil pollution research, development, and demonstration activities, including controlled field tests of oil discharges.

(e) Biennial reports

The Chairman of the Interagency Committee shall submit to Congress every 2 years on October 30 a report on the activities carried out under this section in the preceding 2 fiscal years, and on activities proposed to be carried out under this section in the current 2 fiscal year period.

(f) Funding

Not to exceed $22,000,000 of amounts in the Fund shall be available annually to carry out this section except for subsection (c)(8) of this section. Of such sums—

(1) funds authorized to be appropriated to carry out the activities under subsection (c)(4) of this section shall not exceed $5,000,000 for fiscal year 1991 or $3,500,000 for any subsequent fiscal year; and

(2) not less than $3,000,000 shall be available for carrying out the activities in subsection (c)(6) of this section for fiscal years 1992, 1993, 1994, and 1995.

All activities authorized in this section, including subsection (c)(8) of this section, are subject to appropriations.

(Pub. L. 101–380, title VII, §7001, Aug. 18, 1990, 104 Stat. 559; Pub. L. 101–537, title II, §2002, Nov. 8, 1990, 104 Stat. 2375; Pub. L. 101–646, title IV, §4002, Nov. 29, 1990, 104 Stat. 4788; Pub. L. 104–324, title XI, §§1102(c)(2), 1108, Oct. 19, 1996, 110 Stat. 3966, 3968; Pub. L. 104–332, §2(h)(1), (2), Oct. 26, 1996, 110 Stat. 4091; Pub. L. 108–426, §2(c)(5), Nov. 30, 2004, 118 Stat. 2424; Pub. L. 109–241, title VI, §605(a)(1), title IX, §902(*l*)(3), (4), July 11, 2006, 120 Stat. 555, 568.)

REFERENCES IN TEXT

This Act, referred to in subsec. (c)(8)(G), is Pub. L. 101–380, Aug. 18, 1990, 104 Stat. 484, as amended, known as the Oil Pollution Act of 1990, which is classified principally to this chapter. For complete classification of this Act to the Code, see Short Title note set out under section 2701 of this title and Tables.

AMENDMENTS

2006—Subsec. (a). Pub. L. 109–241, §902(*l*)(3), added pars. (3) and (4) and struck out former par. (3) and concluding provisions which read as follows:

"MEMBERSHIP.—The Interagency Committee shall include representatives from the Department of Commerce (including the National Oceanic and Atmospheric Administration and the National Institute of Standards and Technology), the Department of Energy, the Department of the Interior (including the Minerals Management Service and the United States Fish and Wildlife Service), the Department of Transportation (including the United States Coast Guard, the Maritime Administration, and the Pipeline and Hazardous Materials Safety Administration), the Department of Defense (including the Army Corps of Engineers and the Navy), the Environmental Protection Agency, the National Aeronautics and Space Administration, and the United States Fire Administration in the Federal Emergency Management Agency, as well as such other Federal agencies as the President may designate.

A representative of the Department of Transportation shall serve as Chairman."

Subsec. (c)(4)(B). Pub. L. 109–241, §605(a)(1), substituted "RIVERA and the T/V ATHOS I," for "RIVERA,".

Subsec. (c)(6). Pub. L. 109–241, §902(*l*)(4), substituted "such agencies as the President may designate," for "other such agencies in the Department of Transportation as the Secretary of Transportation may designate,".

2004—Subsec. (a)(3). Pub. L. 108–426, §2(c)(5)(A), substituted "Pipeline and Hazardous Materials Safety Administration'' for ''Research and Special Projects Administration''.

Subsec. (c)(11). Pub. L. 108–426, § 2(c)(5)(B), substituted ''Pipeline and Hazardous Materials Safety Administration'' for ''Research and Special Programs Administration''.

1996—Subsec. (c)(2)(D). Pub. L. 104–324, § 1108, inserted '', and the Center for Marine Training and Safety in Galveston, Texas'' before semicolon at end.

Subsec. (c)(6). Pub. L. 104–332, § 2(h)(1), made technical amendment to Pub. L. 101–646, § 4002(1). See 1990 Amendment note below.

Subsec. (c)(9). Pub. L. 104–324, § 1102(c)(2), inserted ''until the authorization for funding under section 2736(b) of this title expires'' before period at end.

Subsec. (f). Pub. L. 104–332 made technical amendment to Pub. L. 101–646, § 4002(2). See 1990 Amendment note below.

1990—Subsec. (c)(6). Pub. L. 101–537, § 2002(1), and Pub. L. 101–646, § 4002(1), as amended by Pub. L. 104–332, § 2(h)(1), made substantially identical amendments, substituting ''4'' for ''3'' and inserting cl. (D).

Subsec. (f). Pub. L. 101–537, § 2002(2), and Pub. L. 101–646, § 4002(2), as amended by Pub. L. 104–332, amended subsec. (f) identically, substituting ''$22,000,000'' for ''$21,250,000'' in introductory provisions and ''$3,000,000'' for ''$2,250,000'' in par. (2).

TRANSFER OF FUNCTIONS

For transfer of all functions, personnel, assets, components, authorities, grant programs, and liabilities of the Federal Emergency Management Agency, including the functions of the Under Secretary for Federal Emergency Management relating thereto, to the Federal Emergency Management Agency, see section 315(a)(1) of Title 6, Domestic Security.

DELEGATION OF FUNCTIONS

Functions of President under subsec. (a)(3) of this section delegated to Secretary of the Department in which the Coast Guard is operating by section 8(h) of Ex. Ord. No. 12777, Oct. 18, 1991, 56 F.R. 54769, as amended, set out as a note under section 1321 of this title.

§ 2762. Submerged oil program

(a) Program

(1) Establishment

The Under Secretary of Commerce for Oceans and Atmosphere, in conjunction with the Commandant of the Coast Guard, shall establish a program to detect, monitor, and evaluate the environmental effects of submerged oil in the Delaware River and Bay region. The program shall include the following elements:

(A) The development of methods to remove, disperse, or otherwise diminish the persistence of submerged oil.

(B) The development of improved models and capacities for predicting the environmental fate, transport, and effects of submerged oil.

(C) The development of techniques to detect and monitor submerged oil.

(2) Report

Not later than 3 years after July 11, 2006, the Secretary of Commerce shall submit to the Committee on Commerce, Science, and Transportation of the Senate and the Committee on Transportation and Infrastructure of the House of Representatives a report on the activities carried out under this subsection and activities proposed to be carried out under this subsection.

(b) Demonstration project

(1) Removal of submerged oil

The Commandant of the Coast Guard, in conjunction with the Under Secretary of Commerce for Oceans and Atmosphere, shall conduct a demonstration project for the purpose of developing and demonstrating technologies and management practices to remove submerged oil from the Delaware River and other navigable waters.

(2) Funding

There is authorized to be appropriated to the Commandant of the Coast Guard $2,000,000 for each of fiscal years 2006 through 2010 to carry out this subsection.

(Pub. L. 101–380, title VII, § 7002, as added Pub. L. 109–241, title VI, § 605(a)(2), July 11, 2006, 120 Stat. 555.)

CHAPTER 41—NATIONAL COASTAL MONITORING

§ 2801. Purposes

The purposes of this chapter are to—

(1) establish a comprehensive national program for consistent monitoring of the Nation's coastal ecosystems;

(2) establish long-term water quality assessment and monitoring programs for high priority coastal waters that will enhance the ability of Federal, State, and local authorities to develop and implement effective remedial programs for those waters;

(3) establish a system for reviewing and evaluating the scientific, analytical, and technological means that are available for monitoring the environmental quality of coastal ecosystems;

(4) establish methods for identifying uniform indicators of coastal ecosystem quality;

(5) provide for periodic, comprehensive reports to Congress concerning the quality of the Nation's coastal ecosystems;

(6) establish a coastal environment information program to distribute coastal monitoring information;

(7) provide state[1] programs authorized under the Coastal Zone Management Act of 1972 (16 U.S.C. 1451 et seq.) with information necessary to design land use plans and coastal zone regulations that will contribute to the protection of coastal ecosystems; and

(8) provide certain water pollution control programs authorized under the Federal Water Pollution Control Act (33 U.S.C. 1251 et seq.) with information necessary to design and implement effective coastal water pollution controls.

(Pub. L. 92–532, title V, § 501, as added Pub. L. 102–567, title V, § 501, Oct. 29, 1992, 106 Stat. 4293.)

[1] So in original. Probably should be capitalized.

REFERENCES IN TEXT

The Coastal Zone Management Act of 1972, referred to in par. (7), is title III of Pub. L. 89–454 as added by Pub. L. 92–583, Oct. 27, 1972, 86 Stat. 1280, as amended, which is classified generally to chapter 33 (§1451 et seq.) of Title 16, Conservation. For complete classification of this Act to the Code, see Short Title note set out under section 1451 of Title 16 and Tables.

The Federal Water Pollution Control Act, referred to in par. (8), is act June 30, 1948, ch. 758, as amended generally by Pub. L. 92–500, §2, Oct. 18, 1972, 86 Stat. 816, which is classified generally to chapter 26 (§1251 et seq.) of this title. For complete classification of this Act to the Code, see Short Title note set out under section 1251 of this title and Tables.

SHORT TITLE

Title V of Pub. L. 92–532, which comprises this chapter, is popularly known as the "National Coastal Monitoring Act".

§2802. Definitions

For the purposes of this chapter, the term—

(1) "Administrator" means the Administrator of the Environmental Protection Agency;

(2) "coastal ecosystem" means a system of interacting biological, chemical, and physical components throughout the water column, water surface, and benthic environment of coastal waters;

(3) "coastal water quality" means the physical, chemical and biological parameters that relate to the health and integrity of coastal ecosystems;

(4) "coastal water quality monitoring" means a continuing program of measurement, analysis, and synthesis to identify and quantify coastal water quality conditions and trends to provide a technical basis for decisionmaking;

(5) "coastal waters" means waters of the Great Lakes, including their connecting waters and those portions of rivers, streams, and other bodies of water having unimpaired connection with the open sea up to the head of tidal influence, including wetlands, intertidal areas, bays, harbors, and lagoons, including waters of the territorial sea of the United States and the contiguous zone";[1] and

(6) "Under Secretary" means Under Secretary of Commerce for Oceans and Atmosphere.

(Pub. L. 92–532, title V, §502, as added Pub. L. 102–567, title V, §501, Oct. 29, 1992, 106 Stat. 4294.)

TERRITORIAL SEA AND CONTIGUOUS ZONE OF UNITED STATES

For extension of territorial sea and contiguous zone of United States, see Proc. No. 5928 and Proc. No. 7219, respectively, set out as notes under section 1331 of Title 43, Public Lands.

[1] So in original. The closing quotation marks preceding the semicolon probably should not appear.

§2803. Comprehensive Coastal Water Quality Monitoring Program

(a) Authority; joint implementation

(1) The Administrator and the Under Secretary, in conjunction with other Federal, State, and local authorities, shall jointly develop and implement a program for the long-term collection, assimilation, and analysis of scientific data designed to measure the environmental quality of the Nation's coastal ecosystems pursuant to this section. Monitoring conducted pursuant to this section shall be coordinated with relevant monitoring programs conducted by the Administrator, Under Secretary, and other Federal, State, and local authorities.

(2) Primary leadership for the monitoring program activities conducted by the Environmental Protection Agency pursuant to this section shall be located at the Environmental Research Laboratory in Narragansett, Rhode Island.

(b) Program elements

The Comprehensive Coastal Water Quality Monitoring Program shall include, but not be limited to—

(1) identification and analysis of the status of environmental quality in the Nation's coastal ecosystems, including but not limited to, assessment of—

(A) ambient water quality, including contaminant levels in relation to criteria and standards issued pursuant to title III or[1] the Federal Water Pollution Control Act (33 U.S.C. 1311 et seq.);

(B) benthic environmental quality, including analysis of contaminant levels in sediments in relation to criteria and standards issued pursuant to title III of the Federal Water Pollution Control Act (33 U.S.C. 1311 et seq.); and

(C) health and quality of living resources.[2]

(2) identification of sources of environmental degradation affecting the Nation's coastal ecosystems;

(3) assessment of the impact of governmental programs and management strategies and measures designed to abate or prevent the environmental degradation of the Nation's coastal ecosystems;

(4) assessment of the accumulation of floatables along coastal shorelines;

(5) analysis of expected short-term and long-term trends in the environmental quality of the Nation's coastal ecosystems; and

(6) the development and implementation of intensive coastal water quality monitoring programs in accordance with subsection (d) of this section.

(c) Monitoring guidelines and protocols

(1) Guidelines

Not later than 18 months after October 29, 1992, the Administrator and the Under Secretary shall jointly issue coastal water quality monitoring guidelines to assist in the development and implementation of coastal water quality monitoring programs. The guidelines shall—

(A) provide an appropriate degree of uniformity among the coastal water quality monitoring methods and data while preserving the flexibility of monitoring programs to address specific needs;

(B) establish scientifically valid monitoring methods that will—

[1] So in original. Probably should be "of".

[2] So in original. The period probably should be a semicolon.

(i) provide simplified methods to survey and assess the water quality and ecological health of coastal waters;

(ii) identify and quantify through more intensive efforts the severity of existing or anticipated problems in selected coastal waters;

(iii) identify and quantify sources of pollution that cause or contribute to those problems, including point and nonpoint sources; and

(iv) evaluate over time the effectiveness of efforts to reduce or eliminate pollution from those sources;

(C) provide for data compatibility to enable data to be efficiently stored and shared by various users; and

(D) identify appropriate physical, chemical, and biological indicators of the health and quality of coastal ecosystems.

(2) Technical protocols

Guidelines issued under paragraph (1) shall include protocols for—

(A) designing statistically valid coastal water quality monitoring networks and monitoring surveys, including assessment of the accumulation of floatables.[2]

(B) sampling and analysis, including appropriate physical and chemical parameters, living resource parameters, and sediment analysis techniques; and

(C) quality control, quality assessment, and data consistency and management.

(3) Periodic review

The Administrator and the Under Secretary shall periodically review the guidelines and protocols issued under this subsection to evaluate their effectiveness, the degree to which they continue to answer program objectives and provide an appropriate degree of uniformity while taking local conditions into account, and any need to modify or supplement them with new guidelines and protocols, as needed.

(4) Discharge permit data

The Administrator or a State permitting authority shall ensure that compliance monitoring conducted pursuant to section 402(a)(2) of the Federal Water Pollution Control Act (33 U.S.C. 1342(a)(2)) for permits for discharges to coastal waters is consistent with the guidelines issued under this subsection. Any modifications of discharge permits necessary to implement this subsection shall be deemed to be minor modifications of such permit. Nothing in this subsection requires dischargers to conduct monitoring other than compliance monitoring pursuant to permits under section 402(a)(2) of the Federal Water Pollution Control Act (33 U.S.C. 1342(a)(2)).

(d) Intensive coastal water quality monitoring programs

(1) In general

The Comprehensive Coastal Water Quality Monitoring Program established pursuant to this section shall include intensive coastal water quality monitoring programs developed under this subsection.

(2) Designation of intensive monitoring areas

Not later than 24 months after October 29, 1992, and periodically thereafter, the Administrator and the Under Secretary shall, based on recommendations by the National Research Council, jointly designate coastal areas to be intensively monitored.

(3) Identification of suitable coastal areas

(A) The Administrator and the Under Secretary shall contract with the National Research Council to conduct a study to identify coastal areas suitable for the establishment of intensive coastal monitoring programs. In identifying these coastal areas, the National Research Council shall consider areas that—

(i) are representatives of coastal ecosystems throughout the United States;

(ii) will provide information to assess the status and trends of coastal water quality nation-wide; and

(iii) would benefit from intensive water quality monitoring because of local management needs.

(B) In making recommendations under this paragraph, the National Research Council shall consult with Regional Research Boards established pursuant to title IV of this Act [16 U.S.C. 1447 et seq.].

(C) The National Research Council shall, within 18 months of October 29, 1992, submit a report to the Administrator and the Under Secretary listing areas suitable for intensive monitoring.

(D) The Administrator and the Under Secretary, in conjunction with other Federal, State, and local authorities, shall develop and implement multi-year programs of intensive monitoring for Massachusetts and Cape Cod Bays, the Gulf of Maine, the Chesapeake Bay, the Hudson-Raritan Estuary, and each area jointly designated by the Administrator and the Under Secretary pursuant to paragraph (2).

(4) Intensive coastal water quality monitoring programs

Each intensive coastal water quality monitoring program developed pursuant to this subsection shall—

(A) identify water quality conditions and problems and provide information to assist in improving coastal water quality;

(B) clearly state the goals and objectives of the monitoring program and their relationship to the water quality objectives for coastal waters covered by the program;

(C) identify the water quality and biological parameters of the monitoring program and their relationship to these goals and objectives;

(D) describe the types of monitoring networks, surveys and other activities to be used to achieve these goals and objectives, using where appropriate the guidelines issued under subsection (c) of this section;

(E) survey existing Federal, State, and local coastal monitoring activities and private compliance monitoring activities in or on the coastal waters covered by the program, describe the relationship of the program to those other monitoring activities, and integrate them, as appropriate, into the intensive monitoring program;

(F) describe the data management and quality control components of the program;

(G) specify the implementation requirements for the program, including—

(i) the lead Federal, State, or regional authority that will administer the program;

(ii) the public and private parties that will implement the program;

(iii) a detailed schedule for program implementation;

(iv) all Federal and State responsibilities for implementing the program; and

(v) the changes in Federal, State, and local monitoring programs necessary to implement the program;

(H) estimate the costs to Federal and State governments, and other participants, of implementing the monitoring program; and

(I) describe the methods to assess periodically the success of the monitoring program in meeting its goals and objectives, and the manner in which the program may be modified from time-to-time.

(5) Criteria for monitoring Massachusetts and Cape Cod Bays

In addition to the criteria listed in paragraph (4), the intensive monitoring program for Massachusetts and Cape Cod Bays shall establish baseline data on environmental phenomena (such as quantity of bacteria and quality of indigenous species, and swimmability) and determine the ecological impacts resulting from major point source discharges.

(6) Memorandum of Understanding

Prior to implementing any intensive coastal water quality monitoring program under this subsection, the Administrator and the Under Secretary shall enter into a Memorandum of Understanding to implement the intensive coastal water quality monitoring programs and may extend the memorandum[3] of Understanding to include other appropriate Federal agencies. The Memorandum of Understanding shall identify the monitoring and reporting responsibilities of each agency and shall encourage the coordination of monitoring activities.

(7) Implementation

(A) The Administrator, the Under Secretary, and the Governor of each State having waters subject to an intensive coastal water quality monitoring program developed pursuant to this subsection shall ensure compliance with that program.

(B) The Administrator and the Under Secretary are authorized to enter into cooperative agreements to provide financial assistance to non-Federal agencies and institutions to support implementation of intensive monitoring programs under this subsection. Federal financial assistance may only be provided on the condition that not less than fifty percent of the costs of the monitoring to be conducted by a non-Federal agency or institution is provided from non-Federal funds.

(e) Comprehensive Implementation Strategy

(1) In general

Within 1 year after October 29, 1992, the Administrator and the Under Secretary shall jointly submit to Congress a Comprehensive Implementation Strategy identifying the current and planned activities to implement the Comprehensive Coastal Monitoring Program pursuant to this section.

(2) Consultation

The Administrator and the Under Secretary shall consult with the National Academy of Sciences, the Director of the United States Fish and Wildlife Service, the Director of the Minerals Management Service, the Commandant of the Coast Guard, the Secretary of the Navy, the Secretary of Agriculture, the heads of any other relevant Federal or regional agencies, and the Governors of coastal States in developing the Strategy.

(3) Public comment

Not less than 3 months before submitting the Strategy to Congress, the Administrator and the Under Secretary shall jointly publish a draft version of the Strategy in the Federal Register and shall solicit public comments regarding the Strategy.

(4) Memorandum of Understanding

Within 1 year after submission of the Strategy under paragraph (1), the Administrator and the Under Secretary shall enter into a Memorandum of Understanding with appropriate Federal agencies necessary to effect the coordination of Federal coastal monitoring programs. The Memorandum of Understanding shall identify the monitoring and reporting responsibilities of each agency and shall encourage the coordination of monitoring activities where possible.

(Pub. L. 92–532, title V, §503, as added Pub. L. 102–567, title V, §501, Oct. 29, 1992, 106 Stat. 4294.)

REFERENCES IN TEXT

The Federal Water Pollution Control Act, referred to in subsec. (b)(1), is act June 30, 1948, ch. 758, as amended generally by Pub. L. 92–500, §2, Oct. 18, 1972, 86 Stat. 816. Title III of the Act is classified generally to subchapter III (§1311 et seq.) of chapter 26 of this title. For complete classification of this Act to the Code, see Short Title note set out under section 1251 of this title and Tables.

Title IV of this Act, referred to in subsec. (d)(3)(B), is title IV of Pub. L. 92–532 which is classified generally to chapter 32A (§1447 et seq.) of Title 16, Conservation.

TRANSFER OF FUNCTIONS

For transfer of authorities, functions, personnel, and assets of the Coast Guard, including the authorities and functions of the Secretary of Transportation relating thereto, to the Department of Homeland Security, and for treatment of related references, see sections 468(b), 551(d), 552(d), and 557 of Title 6, Domestic Security, and the Department of Homeland Security Reorganization Plan of November 25, 2002, as modified, set out as a note under section 542 of Title 6.

§2804. Report to Congress

On September 30 of each other year beginning in 1993, the Administrator and the Under Sec-

[3] So in original. Probably should be capitalized.

retary shall jointly submit to the Committee on Commerce, Science, and Transportation and the Committee on Environment and Public Works of the Senate and the Committee on Merchant Marine and Fisheries and the Committee on Public Works and Transportation of the House of Representatives a report describing the condition of the Nation's coastal ecosystems, including the following:

(1) an assessment of the status and health of the Nation's coastal ecosystems;

(2) an evaluation of environmental trends in coastal ecosystems;

(3) identification of sources of enironmental[1] degradation affecting coastal ecosystems;

(4) an assessment of the extent to which floatables degrade coastal ecosystems, including trends in the accumulation of floatables and the threat posed by floatables to aquatic life;

(5) an assessment of the impact of government programs designed to abate the degradation of coastal ecosystems:[2]

(6) an evaluation of the adequacy of monitoring programs and identification of any additional program elements which may be needed; and

(7) a summary of monitoring results in areas monitored under subsection[3] 2803(d) of this title.

(Pub. L. 92–532, title V, § 504, as added Pub. L. 102–567, title V, § 501, Oct. 29, 1992, 106 Stat. 4299.)

CHANGE OF NAME

Committee on Public Works and Transportation of House of Representatives treated as referring to Committee on Transportation and Infrastructure of House of Representatives by section 1(a) of Pub. L. 104–14, set out as a note preceding section 21 of Title 2, The Congress.

ABOLITION OF HOUSE COMMITTEE ON MERCHANT MARINE AND FISHERIES

Committee on Merchant Marine and Fisheries of House of Representatives abolished and its jurisdiction transferred by House Resolution No. 6, One Hundred Fourth Congress, Jan. 4, 1995. For treatment of references to Committee on Merchant Marine and Fisheries, see section 1(b)(3) of Pub. L. 104–14, set out as a note preceding section 21 of Title 2, The Congress.

§ 2805. Authorization of appropriations

(a) NOAA authorization

For development and implementation of programs under this chapter, including financial assistance to non-Federal agencies and institutions to support implementation of intensive monitoring programs under section 2803(d) of this title, there is authorized to be appropriated to the Under Secretary amounts not to exceed $5,000,000 for fiscal year 1993, $8,000,000 for fiscal year 1994, $10,000,000 for fiscal year 1995, and $12,000,000 for fiscal year 1996.

(b) EPA authorization

For development and implementation of programs under this chapter, including financial assistance to non-Federal agencies and institutions to support implementation of intensive monitoring programs under section 2803(d) of this title, there is authorized to be appropriated to the Administrator amounts not to exceed $5,000,000 for fiscal year 1993, $8,000,000 for fiscal year 1994, and $10,000,000 for fiscal year 1995, and $12,000,000 for fiscal year 1996.

(Pub. L. 92–532, title V, § 505, as added Pub. L. 102–567, title V, § 501, Oct. 29, 1992, 106 Stat. 4299.)

CHAPTER 42—ESTUARY RESTORATION

§ 2901. Purposes

The purposes of this chapter are—

(1) to promote the restoration of estuary habitat by implementing a coordinated Federal approach to estuary habitat restoration activities, including the use of common monitoring standards and a common system for tracking restoration acreage;

(2) to develop and implement a national estuary habitat restoration strategy for creating and maintaining effective estuary habitat restoration partnerships among public agencies at all levels of government and to establish new partnerships between the public and private sectors;

(3) to provide Federal assistance for estuary habitat restoration projects through cooperative agreements and to promote efficient financing of such projects; and

(4) to develop and enhance monitoring and research capabilities through the use of the environmental technology innovation program associated with the National Estuarine Research Reserve System established by section 1461 of title 16 to ensure that estuary habitat restoration efforts are based on sound scientific understanding and innovative technologies.

(Pub. L. 106–457, title I, § 102, Nov. 7, 2000, 114 Stat. 1958; Pub. L. 110–114, title V, § 5017(a), Nov. 8, 2007, 121 Stat. 1197.)

AMENDMENTS

2007—Par. (1). Pub. L. 110–114, § 5017(a)(1), inserted "by implementing a coordinated Federal approach to estuary habitat restoration activities, including the use of common monitoring standards and a common system for tracking restoration acreage" before semicolon at end.

Par. (2). Pub. L. 110–114, § 5017(a)(2), inserted "and implement" after "to develop".

Par. (3). Pub. L. 110–114, § 5017(a)(3), inserted "through cooperative agreements" after "restoration projects".

SHORT TITLE

Pub. L. 106–457, § 1(a), Nov. 7, 2000, 114 Stat. 1957, provided that: "This Act [enacting this chapter, sections 1273 and 1300 of this title, and sections 277d–43 to 277d–46

[1] So in original. Probably should be "environmental".
[2] So in original. Probably should be a semicolon.
[3] So in original. Probably should be "section".

of Title 22, Foreign Relations and Intercourse, amending sections 1263a, 1267, 1269, 1324, and 1330 of this title, and enacting provisions set out as notes under this section, sections 1251 and 1267 of this title, and section 277d–43 of Title 22] may be cited as the 'Estuaries and Clean Waters Act of 2000'."

Pub. L. 106–457, title I, §101, Nov. 7, 2000, 114 Stat. 1958, provided that: "This title [enacting this chapter] may be cited as the 'Estuary Restoration Act of 2000'."

PURCHASE OF AMERICAN-MADE EQUIPMENT AND PRODUCTS

Pub. L. 106–457, title IX, §901, Nov. 7, 2000, 114 Stat. 1981, provided that:

"(a) IN GENERAL.—It is the sense of Congress that, to the extent practicable, all equipment and products purchased with funds made available under this Act [see Short Title note above] should be American made.

"(b) NOTICE TO RECIPIENTS OF ASSISTANCE.—The head of each Federal Agency [sic] providing financial assistance under this Act, to the extent practicable, shall provide to each recipient of the assistance a notice describing the statement made in subsection (a)."

LONG-TERM ESTUARY ASSESSMENT

Pub. L. 106–457, title IX, §902, Nov. 7, 2000, 114 Stat. 1981, provided that:

"(a) IN GENERAL.—The Secretary of Commerce (acting through the Under Secretary for Oceans and Atmosphere) and the Secretary of the Interior (acting through the Director of the Geological Survey) may carry out a long-term estuary assessment project (in this section referred to as the 'project') in accordance with the requirements of this section.

"(b) PURPOSE.—The purpose of the project shall be to establish a network of strategic environmental assessment and monitoring projects for the Mississippi River south of Vicksburg, Mississippi, and the Gulf of Mexico, in order to develop advanced long-term assessment and monitoring systems and models relating to the Mississippi River and other aquatic ecosystems, including developing equipment and techniques necessary to implement the project.

"(c) MANAGEMENT AGREEMENT.—To establish, operate, and implement the project, the Secretary of Commerce and the Secretary of the Interior may enter into a management agreement with a university-based consortium.

"(d) AUTHORIZATION OF APPROPRIATIONS.—There is authorized to be appropriated—

"(1) $1,000,000 for fiscal year 2001 to develop the management agreement under subsection (c); and

"(2) $4,000,000 for each of fiscal years 2002, 2003, 2004, and 2005 to carry out the project.

Such sums shall remain available until expended."

§ 2902. Definitions

In this chapter, the following definitions apply:

(1) Council

The term "Council" means the Estuary Habitat Restoration Council established by section 2904 of this title.

(2) Estuary

The term "estuary" means a part of a river or stream or other body of water that has an unimpaired connection with the open sea and where the sea water is measurably diluted with fresh water derived from land drainage. The term also includes near coastal waters and wetlands of the Great Lakes that are similar in form and function to estuaries, including the area located in the Great Lakes biogeographic region and designated as a National Estuarine Research Reserve under the Coastal Zone Management Act of 1972 (16 U.S.C. 1451 et seq.) as of November 7, 2000.

(3) Estuary habitat

The term "estuary habitat" means the physical, biological, and chemical elements associated with an estuary, including the complex of physical and hydrologic features and living organisms within the estuary and associated ecosystems.

(4) Estuary habitat restoration activity

(A) In general

The term "estuary habitat restoration activity" means an activity that results in improving degraded estuaries or estuary habitat or creating estuary habitat (including both physical and functional restoration), with the goal of attaining a self-sustaining system integrated into the surrounding landscape.

(B) Included activities

The term "estuary habitat restoration activity" includes—

(i) the reestablishment of chemical, physical, hydrologic, and biological features and components associated with an estuary;

(ii) except as provided in subparagraph (C), the cleanup of pollution for the benefit of estuary habitat;

(iii) the control of nonnative and invasive species in the estuary;

(iv) the reintroduction of species native to the estuary, including through such means as planting or promoting natural succession;

(v) the construction of reefs to promote fish and shellfish production and to provide estuary habitat for living resources; and

(vi) other activities that improve estuary habitat.

(C) Excluded activities

The term "estuary habitat restoration activity" does not include an activity that—

(i) constitutes mitigation required under any Federal or State law for the adverse effects of an activity regulated or otherwise governed by Federal or State law; or

(ii) constitutes restoration for natural resource damages required under any Federal or State law.

(5) Estuary habitat restoration project

The term "estuary habitat restoration project" means a project to carry out an estuary habitat restoration activity.

(6) Estuary habitat restoration plan

(A) In general

The term "estuary habitat restoration plan" means any Federal, State, or regional plan for restoration of degraded estuary habitat that was developed with the substantial participation of appropriate public and private stakeholders.

(B) Included plans and programs

The term "estuary habitat restoration plan" includes estuary habitat restoration components of—

(i) a comprehensive conservation and management plan approved under section 1330 of this title;

(ii) a lakewide management plan or remedial action plan developed under section 1268 of this title;

(iii) a management plan approved under the Coastal Zone Management Act of 1972 (16 U.S.C. 1451 et seq.); and

(iv) the interstate management plan developed pursuant to the Chesapeake Bay program under section 1267 of this title.

(7) Indian tribe

The term "Indian tribe" has the meaning given such term by section 450b of title 25.

(8) Non-Federal interest

The term "non-Federal interest" means a State, a political subdivision of a State, an Indian tribe, a regional or interstate agency, or, as provided in section 2903(f)(2) of this title, a nongovernmental organization.

(9) Secretary

The term "Secretary" means the Secretary of the Army.

(10) State

The term "State" means the States of Alabama, Alaska, California, Connecticut, Delaware, Florida, Georgia, Hawaii, Illinois, Indiana, Louisiana, Maine, Maryland, Massachusetts, Michigan, Minnesota, Mississippi, New Hampshire, New Jersey, New York, North Carolina, Ohio, Oregon, Pennsylvania, Rhode Island, South Carolina, Texas, Virginia, Washington, and Wisconsin, the District of Columbia, the Commonwealth of Puerto Rico, the Commonwealth of the Northern Mariana Islands, the United States Virgin Islands, American Samoa, and Guam.

(Pub. L. 106–457, title I, §103, Nov. 7, 2000, 114 Stat. 1958; Pub. L. 110–114, title V, §5017(b), Nov. 8, 2007, 121 Stat. 1197.)

REFERENCES IN TEXT

The Coastal Zone Management Act of 1972, referred to in pars. (2) and (6)(B)(iii), is title III of Pub. L. 89–454 as added by Pub. L. 92–583, Oct. 27, 1972, 86 Stat. 1280, as amended, which is classified generally to chapter 33 (§1451 et seq.) of Title 16, Conservation. For complete classification of this Act to the Code, see Short Title note set out under section 1451 of Title 16 and Tables.

AMENDMENTS

2007—Par. (6)(A). Pub. L. 110–114 substituted "Federal, State, or regional" for "Federal or State".

§2903. Estuary habitat restoration program

(a) Establishment

There is established an estuary habitat restoration program under which the Secretary may carry out estuary habitat restoration projects and provide technical assistance through the award of contracts and cooperative agreements in accordance with the requirements of this chapter.

(b) Origin of projects

A proposed estuary habitat restoration project shall originate from a non-Federal interest consistent with State or local laws.

(c) Selection of projects

(1) In general

The Secretary shall select estuary habitat restoration projects from a list of project proposals submitted by the Estuary Habitat Restoration Council under section 2904(b) of this title.

(2) Required elements

Each estuary habitat restoration project selected by the Secretary must—

(A) address restoration needs identified in an estuary habitat restoration plan;

(B) be consistent with the estuary habitat restoration strategy developed under section 2905 of this title;

(C) include a monitoring plan that is consistent with standards for monitoring developed under section 2906 of this title to ensure that short-term and long-term restoration goals are achieved; and

(D) include satisfactory assurance from the non-Federal interests proposing the project that the non-Federal interests will have adequate personnel, funding, and authority to carry out items of local cooperation and properly maintain the project.

(3) Factors for selection of projects

In selecting an estuary habitat restoration project, the Secretary shall consider the following factors:

(A) Whether the project is part of an approved Federal or State estuary management or habitat restoration plan.

(B) The technical feasibility of the project.

(C) The scientific merit of the project.

(D) Whether the project will encourage increased coordination and cooperation among Federal, State, and local government agencies.

(E) Whether the project fosters public-private partnerships and uses Federal resources to encourage increased private sector involvement, including consideration of the amount of private funds or in-kind contributions for an estuary habitat restoration activity.

(F) Whether the project is cost-effective.

(G) Whether the State in which the non-Federal interest is proposing the project has a dedicated source of funding to acquire or restore estuary habitat, natural areas, and open spaces for the benefit of estuary habitat restoration or protection.

(H) Other factors that the Secretary determines to be reasonable and necessary for consideration.

(4) Priority

In selecting estuary habitat restoration projects to be carried out under this chapter, the Secretary shall give priority consideration to a project if, in addition to meriting selection based on the factors under paragraph (3)—

(A) the project occurs within a watershed in which there is a program being carried out that addresses sources of pollution and other activities that otherwise would re-impair the restored habitat; or

(B) the project includes pilot testing of or a demonstration of an innovative technology or approach having the potential for improved cost-effectiveness in estuary habitat restoration.

(d) Cost sharing

(1) Federal share

(A) In general

Except as provided in paragraph (2) and subsection (e)(2) of this section, the Federal share of the cost of an estuary habitat restoration project (other than the cost of operation and maintenance of the project) carried out under this chapter shall not exceed 65 percent of such cost.

(B) Monitoring

(i) Costs

The costs of monitoring an estuary habitat restoration project funded under this chapter may be included in the total cost of the estuary habitat restoration project.

(ii) Goals

The goals of the monitoring shall be—

(I) to measure the effectiveness of the restoration project; and

(II) to allow adaptive management to ensure project success.

(2) Innovative technology costs

The Federal share of the incremental additional cost of including in a project pilot testing of or a demonstration of an innovative technology or approach described in subsection (c)(4)(B) of this section shall be 85 percent.

(3) Non-Federal share

The non-Federal share of the cost of an estuary habitat restoration project carried out under this chapter shall include lands, easements, rights-of-way, and relocations and may include services (including monitoring), or any other form of in-kind contribution determined by the Secretary to be an appropriate contribution equivalent to the monetary amount required for the non-Federal share of the activity.

(4) Operation and maintenance

The non-Federal interests shall be responsible for all costs associated with operating, maintaining, replacing, repairing, and rehabilitating all projects carried out under this section.

(e) Interim actions

(1) In general

Pending completion of the estuary habitat restoration strategy to be developed under section 2905 of this title, the Secretary may take interim actions to carry out an estuary habitat restoration activity.

(2) Federal share

The Federal share of the cost of an estuary habitat restoration activity before the completion of the estuary habitat restoration strategy shall not exceed 25 percent of such cost.

(f) Cooperation of non-Federal interests

(1) In general

The Secretary may not carry out an estuary habitat restoration project until a non-Federal interest has entered into a written agreement with the Secretary in which the non-Federal interest agrees to—

(A) provide all lands, easements, rights-of-way, and relocations and any other elements the Secretary determines appropriate under subsection (d)(3) of this section; and

(B) provide for long-term maintenance and monitoring of the project.

(2) Nongovernmental organizations

Notwithstanding section 1962d–5b(b) of title 42, for any project to be undertaken under this chapter, the Secretary, in consultation and coordination with appropriate State and local governmental agencies and Indian tribes, may allow a nongovernmental organization to serve as the non-Federal interest for the project.

(g) Delegation of project implementation

(1) In general

In carrying out this chapter, the Secretary may delegate project implementation to another Federal department or agency on a reimbursable basis if the Secretary, upon the recommendation of the Council, determines such delegation is appropriate.

(2) Small projects

(A) Small project defined

In this paragraph, the term "small project" means a project carried out under this chapter with an estimated Federal cost of less than $1,000,000.

(B) Delegation of project implementation

In carrying out this section, the Secretary, on recommendation of the Council, may delegate implementation of a small project to—

(i) the Secretary of the Interior (acting through the Director of the United States Fish and Wildlife Service);

(ii) the Under Secretary for Oceans and Atmosphere of the Department of Commerce;

(iii) the Administrator of the Environmental Protection Agency; or

(iv) the Secretary of Agriculture.

(C) Funding

A small project delegated to the head of a Federal department or agency under this paragraph may be carried out using funds appropriated to the department or agency under section 2908(a)(1) of this title or other funds available to the department or agency.

(D) Agreements

The head of a Federal department or agency to which a small project is delegated under this paragraph shall enter into an agreement with the non-Federal interest for the project generally in conformance with the criteria in subsections (d) and (e). Cooperative agreements may be used for any delegated project to allow the non-Federal interest to carry out the project on behalf of the Federal agency.

(Pub. L. 106–457, title I, §104, Nov. 7, 2000, 114 Stat. 1960; Pub. L. 110–114, title V, §5017(c), Nov. 8, 2007, 121 Stat. 1197.)

AMENDMENTS

2007—Subsec. (a). Pub. L. 110–114, § 5017(c)(1), inserted "through the award of contracts and cooperative agreements" after "assistance".

Subsec. (c)(3)(A). Pub. L. 110–114, § 5017(c)(2)(A), inserted "or State" after "Federal".

Subsec. (c)(4)(B). Pub. L. 110–114, § 5017(c)(2)(B), inserted "or approach" after "technology".

Subsec. (d)(1). Pub. L. 110–114, § 5017(c)(3)(A), designated existing provisions as subpar. (A), inserted heading, and added subpar. (B).

Subsec. (d)(2). Pub. L. 110–114, § 5017(c)(3)(B), inserted "or approach" after "technology".

Subsec. (d)(3). Pub. L. 110–114, § 5017(c)(3)(C), inserted "(including monitoring)" after "services".

Subsec. (f)(1)(B). Pub. L. 110–114, § 5017(c)(4), inserted "long-term" before "maintenance".

Subsec. (g). Pub. L. 110–114, § 5017(c)(5), designated existing provisions as par. (1), inserted heading, and added par. (2).

§ 2904. Establishment of Estuary Habitat Restoration Council

(a) Council

There is established a council to be known as the "Estuary Habitat Restoration Council".

(b) Duties

The Council shall be responsible for—

(1) soliciting, reviewing, and evaluating project proposals and developing recommendations concerning such proposals based on the factors specified in section 2903(c)(3) of this title;

(2) submitting to the Secretary a list of recommended projects, including a recommended priority order and any recommendation as to whether a project should be carried out by the Secretary or by another Federal department or agency under section 2903(g) of this title;

(3) developing and transmitting to Congress a national strategy for restoration of estuary habitat;

(4) periodically reviewing the effectiveness of the national strategy in meeting the purposes of this chapter and, as necessary, updating the national strategy;

(5) providing advice on the development of the database, monitoring standards, and report required under sections 2906 and 2907 of this title;

(6) cooperating in the implementation of the strategy developed under section 2905 of this title;

(7) recommending standards for monitoring for restoration projects and contribution of project information to the database developed under section 2906 of this title; and

(8) otherwise using the respective authorities of the Council members to carry out this chapter.

(c) Membership

The Council shall be composed of the following members:

(1) The Secretary (or the Secretary's designee).

(2) The Under Secretary for Oceans and Atmosphere of the Department of Commerce (or the Under Secretary's designee).

(3) The Administrator of the Environmental Protection Agency (or the Administrator's designee).

(4) The Secretary of the Interior, acting through the Director of the United States Fish and Wildlife Service (or such Secretary's designee).

(5) The Secretary of Agriculture (or such Secretary's designee).

(6) The head of any other Federal agency designated by the President to serve as an ex officio member of the Council.

(d) Prohibition of compensation

Members of the Council may not receive compensation for their service as members of the Council.

(e) Chairperson

The chairperson shall be elected by the Council from among its members for a 3-year term, except that the first elected chairperson may serve a term of fewer than 3 years.

(f) Convening of Council

(1) First meeting

The Secretary shall convene the first meeting of the Council not later than 60 days after November 7, 2000, for the purpose of electing a chairperson.

(2) Additional meetings

The chairperson shall convene additional meetings of the Council as often as appropriate to ensure that this chapter is fully carried out, but not less often than annually.

(g) Council procedures

The Council shall establish procedures for voting, the conduct of meetings, and other matters, as necessary.

(h) Public participation

Meetings of the Council shall be open to the public. The Council shall provide notice to the public of such meetings.

(i) Advice

The Council shall consult with persons with recognized scientific expertise in estuary or estuary habitat restoration, representatives of State agencies, local or regional government agencies, and nongovernmental organizations with expertise in estuary or estuary habitat restoration, and representatives of Indian tribes, agricultural interests, fishing interests, and other estuary users—

(1) to assist the Council in the development of the estuary habitat restoration strategy to be developed under section 2905 of this title; and

(2) to provide advice and recommendations to the Council on proposed estuary habitat restoration projects, including advice on the scientific merit, technical merit, and feasibility of a project.

(Pub. L. 106–457, title I, § 105, Nov. 7, 2000, 114 Stat. 1962; Pub. L. 110–114, title V, § 5017(d), Nov. 8, 2007, 121 Stat. 1198.)

AMENDMENTS

2007—Subsec. (b)(6) to (8). Pub. L. 110–114 added pars. (6) to (8).

§2905. Estuary habitat restoration strategy

(a) In general

Not later than 1 year after November 7, 2000, the Council,[1] shall develop an estuary habitat restoration strategy designed to ensure a comprehensive approach to maximize benefits derived from estuary habitat restoration projects and to foster the coordination of Federal and non-Federal activities related to restoration of estuary habitat.

(b) Goal

The goal of the strategy shall be the restoration of 1,000,000 acres of estuary habitat by the year 2010.

(c) Integration of estuary habitat restoration plans, programs, and partnerships

In developing the estuary habitat restoration strategy, the Council shall—

(1) conduct a review of estuary management or habitat restoration plans and Federal programs established under other laws that authorize funding for estuary habitat restoration activities; and

(2) ensure that the estuary habitat restoration strategy is developed in a manner that is consistent with the estuary management or habitat restoration plans.

(d) Elements of the strategy

The estuary habitat restoration strategy shall include proposals, methods, and guidance on—

(1) maximizing the incentives for the creation of new public-private partnerships to carry out estuary habitat restoration projects and the use of Federal resources to encourage increased private sector involvement in estuary habitat restoration activities;

(2) ensuring that the estuary habitat restoration strategy will be implemented in a manner that is consistent with the estuary management or habitat restoration plans;

(3) promoting estuary habitat restoration projects to—

(A) provide healthy ecosystems in order to support—

(i) wildlife, including endangered and threatened species, migratory birds, and resident species of an estuary watershed; and

(ii) fish and shellfish, including commercial and recreational fisheries;

(B) improve surface and ground water quality and quantity, and flood control;

(C) provide outdoor recreation; and

(D) address other areas of concern that the Council determines to be appropriate for consideration;

(4) addressing the estimated historic losses, estimated current rate of loss, and extent of the threat of future loss or degradation of each type of estuary habitat;

(5) measuring the rate of change for each type of estuary habitat;

(6) selecting a balance of smaller and larger estuary habitat restoration projects; and

(7) ensuring equitable geographic distribution of projects funded under this chapter.

(e) Public review and comment

Before the Council adopts a final or revised estuary habitat restoration strategy, the Secretary shall publish in the Federal Register a draft of the estuary habitat restoration strategy and provide an opportunity for public review and comment.

(f) Periodic revision

Using data and information developed through project monitoring and management, and other relevant information, the Council may periodically review and update, as necessary, the estuary habitat restoration strategy.

(Pub. L. 106–457, title I, §106, Nov. 7, 2000, 114 Stat. 1963.)

§2906. Monitoring of estuary habitat restoration projects

(a) Under Secretary

In this section, the term "Under Secretary" means the Under Secretary for Oceans and Atmosphere of the Department of Commerce.

(b) Database of restoration project information

The Under Secretary, in consultation with the Council, shall develop and maintain an appropriate database of information concerning estuary habitat restoration projects carried out under this chapter, including information on project techniques, project completion, monitoring data, and other relevant information.

(c) Monitoring data standards

The Under Secretary, in consultation with the Council, shall develop standard data formats for monitoring projects, along with requirements for types of data collected and frequency of monitoring.

(d) Coordination of data

The Under Secretary shall have general data compilation, coordination, and analysis responsibilities to carry out this chapter and in support of the strategy developed under this section, including compilation of information that pertains to estuary habitat restoration projects from other Federal, State, and local sources and that meets the quality control requirements and data standards established under this section.

(e) Use of existing programs

The Under Secretary shall use existing programs within the National Oceanic and Atmospheric Administration to create and maintain the database required under this section.

(f) Public availability

The Under Secretary shall make the information collected and maintained under this section available to the public.

(Pub. L. 106–457, title I, §107, Nov. 7, 2000, 114 Stat. 1964; Pub. L. 110–114, title V, §5017(e), Nov. 8, 2007, 121 Stat. 1198.)

AMENDMENTS

2007—Subsec. (d). Pub. L. 110–114 substituted "have general data compilation, coordination, and analysis responsibilities to carry out this chapter and in support of the strategy developed under this section, including compilation of" for "compile".

[1] So in original. The comma probably should not appear.

§ 2907. Reporting

(a) In general

Not later than September 30, 2008, and every 2 years thereafter, the Secretary, after considering the advice and recommendations of the Council, shall transmit to Congress a report on the results of activities carried out under this chapter.

(b) Contents of report

A report under subsection (a) of this section shall include—

(1) data on the number of acres of estuary habitat restored under this chapter, including descriptions of, and partners involved with, projects selected, in progress, and completed under this chapter that comprise those acres;

(2) information from the database established under section 2906(b) of this title related to ongoing monitoring of projects to ensure that short-term and long-term restoration goals are achieved;

(3) an estimate of the long-term success of varying restoration techniques used in carrying out estuary habitat restoration projects;

(4) a review of how the information described in paragraphs (1) through (3) has been incorporated in the selection and implementation of estuary habitat restoration projects;

(5) a review of efforts made to maintain an appropriate database of restoration projects carried out under this chapter; and

(6) a review of the measures taken to provide the information described in paragraphs (1) through (3) to persons with responsibility for assisting in the restoration of estuary habitat.

(Pub. L. 106–457, title I, § 108, Nov. 7, 2000, 114 Stat. 1965; Pub. L. 110–114, title V, § 5017(f), Nov. 8, 2007, 121 Stat. 1198.)

AMENDMENTS

2007—Subsec. (a). Pub. L. 110–114 substituted "Not later than September 30, 2008, and every 2 years thereafter" for "At the end of the third and fifth fiscal years following November 7, 2000".

§ 2908. Funding

(a) Authorization of appropriations

(1) Estuary habitat restoration projects

There is authorized to be appropriated for carrying out and providing technical assistance for estuary habitat restoration projects—

(A) to the Secretary, $25,000,000 for each of fiscal years 2008 through 2012;

(B) to the Secretary of the Interior (acting through the Director of the United States Fish and Wildlife Service), $2,500,000 for each of fiscal years 2008 through 2012;

(C) to the Under Secretary for Oceans and Atmosphere of the Department of Commerce, $2,500,000 for each of fiscal years 2008 through 2012;

(D) to the Administrator of the Environmental Protection Agency, $2,500,000 for each of fiscal years 2008 through 2012; and

(E) to the Secretary of Agriculture, $2,500,000 for each of fiscal years 2008 through 2012.

Such sums shall remain available until expended.

(2) Monitoring

There is authorized to be appropriated to the Under Secretary for Oceans and Atmosphere of the Department of Commerce for the acquisition, maintenance, and management of monitoring data on restoration projects carried out under this chapter and other information compiled under section 2906 of this title, $1,500,000 for each of fiscal years 2001 through 2012. Such sums shall remain available until expended.

(b) Set-aside for administrative expenses of the Council

Not to exceed 3 percent of the amounts appropriated for a fiscal year under subsection (a)(1) of this section or $1,500,000, whichever is greater, may be used by the Secretary for administration and operation of the Council.

(Pub. L. 106–457, title I, § 109, Nov. 7, 2000, 114 Stat. 1965; Pub. L. 110–114, title V, § 5017(g), Nov. 8, 2007, 121 Stat. 1198.)

AMENDMENTS

2007—Subsec. (a)(1). Pub. L. 110–114, § 5017(g)(1), struck out "to the Secretary" after "appropriated" in introductory provisions, added subpars. (A) to (E), and struck out former subpars. (A) to (D) which read as follows:

"(A) $40,000,000 for fiscal year 2001;

"(B) $50,000,000 for each of fiscal years 2002 and 2003;

"(C) $60,000,000 for fiscal year 2004; and

"(D) $75,000,000 for fiscal year 2005."

Subsec. (a)(2). Pub. L. 110–114, § 5017(g)(2), inserted "and other information compiled under section 2906 of this title" after "this chapter" and substituted "2012" for "2005".

§ 2909. General provisions

(a) Agency consultation and coordination

In carrying out this chapter, the Secretary shall, as necessary, consult with, cooperate with, and coordinate its activities with the activities of other Federal departments and agencies.

(b) Cooperative agreements; memoranda of understanding

In carrying out this chapter, the Secretary may—

(1) enter into cooperative agreements or contracts with Federal, State, and local government agencies, nongovernmental organizations, and other entities; and

(2) execute such memoranda of understanding as are necessary to reflect the agreements.

(c) Federal agency facilities and personnel

Federal agencies may cooperate in carrying out scientific and other programs necessary to carry out this chapter, and may provide facilities and personnel, for the purpose of assisting the Council in carrying out its duties under this chapter.

(Pub. L. 106–457, title I, § 110, Nov. 7, 2000, 114 Stat. 1966; Pub. L. 110–114, title V, § 5017(h), Nov. 8, 2007, 121 Stat. 1199.)

AMENDMENTS

2007—Subsec. (b)(1). Pub. L. 110–114, § 5017(h)(1), inserted "or contracts" after "agreements" and ", nongovernmental organizations," after "agencies".

Subsecs. (d), (e). Pub. L. 110–114, § 5017(h)(2), struck out subsecs. (d) and (e) which related to identification and mapping of dredged material disposal sites and study of bioremediation technology, respectively.

CHAPTER 43—NATIONAL OCEANIC AND ATMOSPHERIC ADMINISTRATION COMMISSIONED OFFICER CORPS

SUBCHAPTER I—GENERAL PROVISIONS

SUBCHAPTER I—GENERAL PROVISIONS

§ 3001. Commissioned officer corps

There shall be in the National Oceanic and Atmospheric Administration a commissioned officer corps.

(Pub. L. 107–372, title II, § 211, Dec. 19, 2002, 116 Stat. 3082.)

SHORT TITLE

Pub. L. 107–372, title II, § 201, Dec. 19, 2002, 116 Stat. 3082, provided that: "This title [enacting this chapter, amending section 1406 of Title 10, Armed Services, and section 2396 of Title 22, Foreign Relations and Intercourse, repealing sections 853a to 853*l*, 853*o*, 853p to 853r, 853t to 854, 855, 856 to 857–5, 858, 864, and 874 of this title, amending provisions set out as a note under section 1293 of Title 10, and repealing provisions set out as notes under sections 853a and 857–1 of this title and section 101 of Title 38, Veterans' Benefits] may be cited as the 'National Oceanic and Atmospheric Administration Commissioned Officer Corps Act of 2002'."

§ 3002. Definitions

(a) Applicability of definitions in title 10

Except as provided in subsection (b) of this section, the definitions provided in section 101 of title 10 apply to the provisions of this chapter.

(b) Additional definitions

In this chapter:

(1) Active duty

The term "active duty" means full-time duty in the active service of a uniformed service.

(2) Grade

The term "grade" means a step or degree, in a graduated scale of office or rank, that is established and designated as a grade by law or regulation.

(3) Officer

The term "officer" means an officer of the commissioned corps.

(4) Flag officer

The term "flag officer" means an officer serving in, or having the grade of, vice admiral, rear admiral, or rear admiral (lower half).

(5) Secretary

The term "Secretary" means the Secretary of Commerce.

(6) Administration

The term "Administration" means the National Oceanic and Atmospheric Administration.

(Pub. L. 107–372, title II, § 212, Dec. 19, 2002, 116 Stat. 3082.)

REFERENCES IN TEXT

This chapter, referred to in text, was in the original "this title", meaning title II of Pub. L. 107–372, Dec. 19, 2002, 116 Stat. 3082, which is classified principally to this chapter. For complete classification of this title to the Code, see Short Title note set out under section 3001 of this title and Tables.

PRIOR PROVISIONS

Provisions similar to those in this section were contained in section 857–1 of this title prior to repeal by Pub. L. 107–372.

§3003. Authorized number on the active list

(a) Annual strength on active list

The annual strength of the commissioned corps in officers on the lineal list of active duty officers of the corps shall be prescribed by law.

(b) Lineal list

The Secretary shall maintain a list, known as the "lineal list", of officers on active duty. Officers shall be carried on the lineal list by grade and, within grade, by seniority in grade.

(Pub. L. 107–372, title II, §213, Dec. 19, 2002, 116 Stat. 3083.)

§3004. Strength and distribution in grade

(a) Relative rank; proportion

Of the total authorized number of officers on the lineal list of the commissioned corps, there are authorized numbers in permanent grade, in relative rank with officers of the Navy, in proportions as follows:

(1) 8 in the grade of captain.
(2) 14 in the grade of commander.
(3) 19 in the grade of lieutenant commander.
(4) 23 in the grade of lieutenant.
(5) 18 in the grade of lieutenant (junior grade).
(6) 18 in the grade of ensign.

(b) Computation of number in grade

(1) In general

Subject to paragraph (2), whenever a final fraction occurs in computing the authorized number of officers in a grade, the nearest whole number shall be taken, and if the fraction is one-half the next higher whole number shall be taken.

(2) Limitation on increase in total number

The total number of officers on the lineal list authorized by law may not be increased as the result of the computations prescribed in this section, and if necessary the number of officers in the lowest grade shall be reduced accordingly.

(c) Preservation of grade and pay, etc.

No officer may be reduced in grade or pay or separated from the commissioned corps as the result of a computation made to determine the authorized number of officers in the various grades.

(d) Filling of vacancies; additional numbers

Nothing in this section may be construed as requiring the filling of any vacancy or as prohibiting additional numbers in any grade to compensate for vacancies existing in higher grades.

(e) Temporary increase in numbers

The total number of officers authorized by law to be on the lineal list during a fiscal year may be temporarily exceeded so long as the average number on that list during that fiscal year does not exceed the authorized number.

(Pub. L. 107–372, title II, §214, Dec. 19, 2002, 116 Stat. 3083.)

PRIOR PROVISIONS

Provisions similar to those in this section were contained in section 853a of this title prior to repeal by Pub. L. 107–372.

§3005. Number of authorized commissioned officers

Effective October 1, 2009, the total number of authorized commissioned officers on the lineal list of the commissioned corps of the National Oceanic and Atmospheric Administration shall be increased from 321 to 379 if—

(1) the Secretary has submitted to the Congress—

(A) the Administration's ship recapitalization plan for fiscal years 2010 through 2024;
(B) the Administration's aircraft remodernization plan; and
(C) supporting workforce management plans;

(2) appropriated funding is available; and
(3) the Secretary has justified organizational needs for the commissioned corps for each such fiscal year.

(Pub. L. 107–372, title II, §215, Dec. 19, 2002, 116 Stat. 3084; Pub. L. 110–386, §6, Oct. 10, 2008, 122 Stat. 4108.)

PRIOR PROVISIONS

Provisions similar to those in this section were contained in section 853a of this title prior to repeal by Pub. L. 107–372.

AMENDMENTS

2008—Pub. L. 110–386 amended section generally. Prior to amendment, section read as follows: "There are authorized to be on the lineal list of the commissioned corps of the National Oceanic and Atmospheric Administration—

"(1) 270 officers for fiscal year 2003;
"(2) 285 officers for fiscal year 2004; and
"(3) 299 officers for fiscal year 2005."

SUBCHAPTER II—APPOINTMENT AND PROMOTION OF OFFICERS

§3021. Original appointments

(a) In general

(1) Grades

Original appointments may be made in the grades of ensign, lieutenant (junior grade), and lieutenant.

(2) Qualifications

Under regulations prescribed by the Secretary, such an appointment may be given only to a person who—

(A) meets the qualification requirements specified in paragraphs (1) through (4) of section 532(a) of title 10; and
(B) has such other special qualifications as the Secretary may prescribe by regulation.

(3) Examination

A person may be given such an appointment only after passage of a mental and physical examination given in accordance with regulations prescribed by the Secretary.

(4) Revocation of commission of officers found not qualified

The President may revoke the commission of any officer appointed under this section during the officer's first three years of service if the officer is found not qualified for the service. Any such revocation shall be made under regulations prescribed by the President.

(b) Lineal list

Each person appointed under this section shall be placed on the lineal list in a position commensurate with that person's age, education, and experience, in accordance with regulations prescribed by the Secretary.

(c) Service credit upon original appointment in grade above ensign

(1) In general

For the purposes of basic pay, a person appointed under this section in the grade of lieutenant shall be credited as having, on the date of that appointment, three years of service, and a person appointed under this section in the grade of lieutenant (junior grade) shall be credited as having, as of the date of that appointment, 1½ years of service.

(2) Higher credit under other law

If a person appointed under this section is entitled to credit for the purpose of basic pay under any other provision of law that would exceed the amount of credit authorized by paragraph (1), that person shall be credited with that amount of service in lieu of the credit authorized by paragraph (1).

(Pub. L. 107–372, title II, §221, Dec. 19, 2002, 116 Stat. 3084.)

PRIOR PROVISIONS

Provisions similar to those in this section were contained in section 853t of this title prior to repeal by Pub. L. 107–372.

DELEGATION OF FUNCTIONS

Functions of President under subsec. (a)(4) of this section delegated to Secretary of Commerce by section 1(g) of Ex. Ord. No. 11023, May 28, 1962, 27 F.R. 5131, as amended, set out as a note under section 301 of Title 3, The President.

§3022. Personnel boards

(a) Convening

At least once a year and at such other times as the Secretary determines necessary, the Secretary shall convene a personnel board. A personnel board shall consist of not less than five officers on the lineal list in the permanent grade of commander or above.

(b) Duties

Each personnel board shall—

(1) recommend to the Secretary such changes in the lineal list as the board may determine; and

(2) make selections and recommendations to the Secretary and President for the appointment, promotion, separation, continuation, and retirement of officers as prescribed in this subchapter and subchapter III of this chapter.

(c) Action on recommendations not acceptable

In a case in which any recommendation by a board convened under subsection (a) of this section is not accepted by the Secretary or the President, the board shall make such further recommendations as are acceptable.

(Pub. L. 107–372, title II, §222, Dec. 19, 2002, 116 Stat. 3085.)

PRIOR PROVISIONS

Provisions similar to those in this section were contained in section 853r of this title prior to repeal by Pub. L. 107–372.

§3023. Promotion of ensigns to grade of lieutenant (junior grade)

(a) In general

An officer in the permanent grade of ensign shall be promoted to and appointed in the grade of lieutenant (junior grade) upon completion of three years of service. The authorized number of officers in the grade of lieutenant (junior grade) shall be temporarily increased as necessary to authorize such appointment.

(b) Separation of ensigns found not fully qualified

If an officer in the permanent grade of ensign is at any time found not fully qualified, the officer's commission shall be revoked and the officer shall be separated from the commissioned service.

(Pub. L. 107–372, title II, §223, Dec. 19, 2002, 116 Stat. 3085.)

PRIOR PROVISIONS

Provisions similar to those in this section were contained in section 853e of this title prior to repeal by Pub. L. 107–372.

DELEGATION OF FUNCTIONS

Functions of President under subsec. (b) of this section delegated to Secretary of Commerce by section 1(a) of Ex. Ord. No. 11023, May 28, 1962, 27 F.R. 5131, as amended, set out as a note under section 301 of Title 3, The President.

§3024. Promotion by selection to permanent grades above lieutenant (junior grade)

Promotion to fill vacancies in each permanent grade above the grade of lieutenant (junior grade) shall be made by selection from the next lower grade upon recommendation of the personnel board.

(Pub. L. 107–372, title II, §224, Dec. 19, 2002, 116 Stat. 3085.)

PRIOR PROVISIONS

Provisions similar to those in this section were contained in section 853b of this title prior to repeal by Pub. L. 107–372.

§3025. Length of service for promotion purposes

(a) General rule

Each officer shall be assumed to have, for promotion purposes, at least the same length of service as any other officer below that officer on the lineal list.

(b) Exception

Notwithstanding subsection (a) of this section, an officer who has lost numbers shall be assumed to have, for promotion purposes, no greater service than the officer next above such officer in such officer's new position on the lineal list.

(Pub. L. 107–372, title II, §225, Dec. 19, 2002, 116 Stat. 3085.)

PRIOR PROVISIONS

Provisions similar to those in this section were contained in section 853f of this title prior to repeal by Pub. L. 107–372.

§ 3026. Appointments and promotions to permanent grades

Appointments in and promotions to all permanent grades shall be made by the President, by and with the advice and consent of the Senate.

(Pub. L. 107–372, title II, § 226, Dec. 19, 2002, 116 Stat. 3085.)

PRIOR PROVISIONS

Provisions similar to those in this section were contained in section 853i(a) of this title prior to repeal by Pub. L. 107–372.

§ 3027. General qualification of officers for promotion to higher permanent grade

No officer may be promoted to a higher permanent grade on the active list until the officer has passed a satisfactory mental and physical examination in accordance with regulations prescribed by the Secretary.

(Pub. L. 107–372, title II, § 227, Dec. 19, 2002, 116 Stat. 3085.)

PRIOR PROVISIONS

Provisions similar to those in this section were contained in section 854 of this title prior to repeal by Pub. L. 107–372.

§ 3028. Positions of importance and responsibility

(a) Designation of positions

The Secretary may designate positions in the Administration as being positions of importance and responsibility for which it is appropriate that officers of the Administration, if serving in those positions, serve in the grade of vice admiral, rear admiral, or rear admiral (lower half), as designated by the Secretary for each position.

(b) Assignment of officers to designated positions

The Secretary may assign officers to positions designated under subsection (a) of this section.

(c) Director of NOAA Corps and Office of Marine and Aviation Operations

The Secretary shall designate one position under this section as responsible for oversight of the vessel and aircraft fleets and for the administration of the commissioned officer corps. That position shall be filled by an officer on the lineal list serving in or above the grade of rear admiral (lower half). For the specific purpose of administering the commissioned officer corps, that position shall carry the title of Director of the National Oceanic and Atmospheric Administration Commissioned Officer Corps. For the specific purpose of administering the vessel and aircraft fleets, that position shall carry the title of Director of the Office of Marine and Aviation Operations.

(d) Grade

(1) Temporary appointment to grade designated for position

An officer assigned to a position under this section while so serving has the grade designated for that position, if appointed to that grade by the President, by and with the advice and consent of the Senate.

(2) Reversion to permanent grade

An officer who has served in a grade above captain, upon termination of the officer's assignment to the position for which that appointment was made, shall, unless appointed or assigned to another position for which a higher grade is designated, revert to the grade and number the officer would have occupied but for serving in a grade above that of captain. In such a case, the officer shall be an extra number in that grade.

(e) Number of officers appointed

(1) Overall limit

The total number of officers serving on active duty at any one time in the grade of rear admiral (lower half) or above may not exceed four.

(2) Limit by grade

The number of officers serving on active duty under appointments under this section may not exceed—

(A) one in the grade of vice admiral;

(B) two in the grade of rear admiral; and

(C) two in the grade of rear admiral (lower half).

(f) Pay and allowances

An officer appointed to a grade under this section, while serving in that grade, shall have the pay and allowances of the grade to which appointed.

(g) Effect of appointment

An appointment of an officer under this section—

(1) does not vacate the permanent grade held by the officer; and

(2) creates a vacancy on the active list.

(Pub. L. 107–372, title II, § 228, Dec. 19, 2002, 116 Stat. 3086.)

PRIOR PROVISIONS

Provisions similar to those in this section were contained in section 853u of this title prior to repeal by Pub. L. 107–372.

APPOINTMENT OF COMMISSIONED OFFICERS

Pub. L. 98–498, title III, § 320(c)(2), Oct. 19, 1984, 98 Stat. 2309, provided that: "After the date of the enactment of this Act [Oct. 19, 1984], no appointment of a commissioned officer may be made under section 2(d) or 2(f) of Reorganization Plan Numbered 4 of 1970 (84 Stat. 2090, 5 U.S.C. App.)."

§ 3029. Temporary appointments and promotions generally

(a) Ensign

Temporary appointments in the grade of ensign may be made by the President alone. Each such temporary appointment terminates at the close of the next regular session of the Congress unless the Senate sooner gives its advice and consent to the appointment.

(b) Lieutenant (junior grade)

Officers in the permanent grade of ensign may be temporarily promoted to and appointed in the grade of lieutenant (junior grade) by the President alone whenever vacancies exist in higher grades.

(c) Any one grade

When determined by the Secretary to be in the best interest of the service, officers in any permanent grade may be temporarily promoted one grade by the President alone. Any such temporary promotion terminates upon the transfer of the officer to a new assignment.

(Pub. L. 107–372, title II, §229, Dec. 19, 2002, 116 Stat. 3087.)

PRIOR PROVISIONS

Provisions similar to those in this section were contained in section 853j–1 of this title prior to repeal by Pub. L. 107–372.

DELEGATION OF FUNCTIONS

Functions of President under this section delegated to Secretary of Commerce by section 1(b)–(d) of Ex. Ord. No. 11023, May 28, 1962, 27 F.R. 5131, as amended, set out as a note under section 301 of Title 3, The President.

§3030. Temporary appointment or advancement of commissioned officers in time of war or national emergency

(a) In general

Officers of the Administration shall be subject in like manner and to the same extent as personnel of the Navy to all laws authorizing temporary appointment or advancement of commissioned officers in time of war or national emergency.

(b) Limitations

Subsection (a) of this section shall be applied subject to the following limitations:

(1) A commissioned officer in the service of a military department under section 3061 of this title may, upon the recommendation of the Secretary of the military department concerned, be temporarily promoted to a higher rank or grade.

(2) A commissioned officer in the service of the Administration may be temporarily promoted to fill vacancies in ranks and grades caused by the transfer of commissioned officers to the service and jurisdiction of a military department under section 3061 of this title.

(3) Temporary appointments may be made in all grades to which original appointments in the Administration are authorized, except that the number of officers holding temporary appointments may not exceed the number of officers transferred to a military department under section 3061 of this title.

(Pub. L. 107–372, title II, §230, Dec. 19, 2002, 116 Stat. 3087.)

CODIFICATION

Provisions similar to this section are contained in section 854a–1 of this title.

DELEGATION OF FUNCTIONS

Functions of President under subsec. (b) of this section delegated to Secretary of Commerce by section 1(h)–(j) of Ex. Ord. No. 11023, May 28, 1962, 27 F.R. 5131, as amended, set out as a note under section 301 of Title 3, The President.

§3031. Pay and allowances; date of acceptance of promotion

(a) Acceptance and date of promotion

An officer of the commissioned corps who is promoted to a higher grade—

(1) is deemed for all purposes to have accepted the promotion upon the date the promotion is made by the President, unless the officer expressly declines the promotion; and

(2) shall receive the pay and allowances of the higher grade from that date unless the officer is entitled under another provision of law to receive the pay and allowances of the higher grade from an earlier date.

(b) Oath of office

An officer who subscribed to the oath of office required by section 3331 of title 5 shall not be required to renew such oath or to take a new oath upon promotion to a higher grade, if the service of the officer after the taking of such oath is continuous.

(Pub. L. 107–372, title II, §231, Dec. 19, 2002, 116 Stat. 3087.)

CODIFICATION

Provisions similar to this section are contained in section 854a–2 of this title.

§3032. Service credit as deck officer or junior engineer for promotion purposes

For purposes of promotion, there shall be counted in addition to active commissioned service, service as deck officer or junior engineer.

(Pub. L. 107–372, title II, §232, Dec. 19, 2002, 116 Stat. 3088.)

CODIFICATION

Provisions similar to this section are contained in section 854a of this title.

§3033. Suspension during war or emergency

In time of emergency declared by the President or by the Congress, and in time of war, the President is authorized, in the President's discretion, to suspend the operation of all or any part of the provisions of law pertaining to promotion of commissioned officers of the Administration.

(Pub. L. 107–372, title II, §233, Dec. 19, 2002, 116 Stat. 3088.)

PRIOR PROVISIONS

Provisions similar to those in this section were contained in section 853i(b) of this title prior to repeal by Pub. L. 107–372.

SUBCHAPTER III—SEPARATION AND RETIREMENT OF OFFICERS

§3041. Involuntary retirement or separation

(a) Transfer of officers to retired list; separation from service

As recommended by a personnel board convened under section 3022 of this title—

(1) an officer in the permanent grade of captain or commander may be transferred to the retired list; and

(2) an officer in the permanent grade of lieutenant commander, lieutenant, or lieutenant (junior grade) who is not qualified for retirement may be separated from the service.

(b) Computations

In any fiscal year, the total number of officers selected for retirement or separation under subsection (a) of this section plus the number of officers retired for age may not exceed the whole number nearest 4 percent of the total number of officers authorized to be on the active list, except as otherwise provided by law.

(c) Effective date of retirements and separations

A retirement or separation under subsection (a) of this section shall take effect on the first day of the sixth month beginning after the date on which the Secretary approves the retirement or separation, except that if the officer concerned requests an earlier retirement or separation date, the date shall be as determined by the Secretary.

(Pub. L. 107–372, title II, §241, Dec. 19, 2002, 116 Stat. 3088.)

PRIOR PROVISIONS

Provisions similar to those in this section were contained in section 853g of this title prior to repeal by Pub. L. 107–372.

§ 3042. Separation pay

(a) Authorization of payment

An officer who is separated under section 3041(a)(2) of this title and who has completed more than three years of continuous active service immediately before that separation is entitled to separation pay computed under subsection (b) of this section unless the Secretary determines that the conditions under which the officer is separated do not warrant payment of that pay.

(b) Amount of separation pay

(1) Six or more years

In the case of an officer who has completed six or more years of continuous active service immediately before that separation, the amount of separation pay to be paid to the officer under this section is 10 percent of the product of—

(A) the years of active service creditable to the officer; and

(B) 12 times the monthly basic pay to which the officer was entitled at the time of separation.

(2) Three to six years

In the case of an officer who has completed three or more but fewer than six years of continuous active service immediately before that separation, the amount of separation pay to be paid to the officer under this section is one-half of the amount computed under paragraph (1).

(c) Other conditions, requirements, and administrative provisions

The provisions of subsections (f), (g), and (h) of section 1174 of title 10 shall apply to separation pay under this section in the same manner as such provisions apply to separation pay under that section.

(Pub. L. 107–372, title II, §242, Dec. 19, 2002, 116 Stat. 3088.)

PRIOR PROVISIONS

Provisions similar to those in this section were contained in section 853h of this title prior to repeal by Pub. L. 107–372.

§ 3043. Mandatory retirement for age

(a) Officers below grade of rear admiral (lower half)

Unless retired or separated earlier, each officer on the lineal list of the commissioned corps who is serving in a grade below the grade of rear admiral (lower half) shall be retired on the first day of the month following the month in which the officer becomes 62 years of age.

(b) Flag officers

Notwithstanding subsection (a) of this section, the President may defer the retirement of an officer serving in a position that carries a grade above captain for such period as the President considers advisable, but such a deferment may not extend beyond the first day of the month following the month in which the officer becomes 64 years of age.

(Pub. L. 107–372, title II, §243, Dec. 19, 2002, 116 Stat. 3089.)

PRIOR PROVISIONS

Provisions similar to those in this section were contained in section 853k of this title prior to repeal by Pub. L. 107–372.

DELEGATION OF FUNCTIONS

Functions of President under subsec. (b) of this section delegated to Secretary of Commerce by section 1(e) of Ex. Ord. No. 11023, May 28, 1962, 27 F.R. 5131, as amended, set out as a note under section 301 of Title 3, The President.

§ 3044. Retirement for length of service

An officer who has completed 20 years of service, of which at least 10 years was service as a commissioned officer, may at any time thereafter, upon application by such officer and in the discretion of the President, be placed on the retired list.

(Pub. L. 107–372, title II, §244, Dec. 19, 2002, 116 Stat. 3089.)

PRIOR PROVISIONS

Provisions similar to those in this section were contained in section 853*l* of this title prior to repeal by Pub. L. 107–372.

DELEGATION OF FUNCTIONS

Functions of President under this section delegated to Secretary of Commerce by section 1(f) of Ex. Ord. No. 11023, May 28, 1962, 27 F.R. 5131, as amended, set out as a note under section 301 of Title 3, The President.

§ 3045. Computation of retired pay

(a) Officers first becoming members before September 8, 1980

Each officer on the retired list who first became a member of a uniformed service before September 8, 1980, shall receive retired pay at the rate determined by multiplying—

(1) the retired pay base determined under section 1406(g) of title 10; by

(2) 2½ percent of the number of years of service that may be credited to the officer under section 1405 of such title as if the officer's service were service as a member of the Armed Forces.

The retired pay so computed may not exceed 75 percent of the retired pay base.

(b) Officers first becoming members on or after September 8, 1980

Each officer on the retired list who first became a member of a uniformed service on or after September 8, 1980, shall receive retired pay at the rate determined by multiplying—

(1) the retired pay base determined under section 1407 of title 10; by

(2) the retired pay multiplier determined under section 1409 of such title for the number of years of service that may be credited to the officer under section 1405 of such title as if the officer's service were service as a member of the Armed Forces.

(c) Treatment of full and fractional parts of months in computing years of service

(1) In general

In computing the number of years of service of an officer for the purposes of subsection (a) of this section—

(A) each full month of service that is in addition to the number of full years of service creditable to the officer shall be credited as 1/12 of a year; and

(B) any remaining fractional part of a month shall be disregarded.

(2) Rounding

Retired pay computed under this section, if not a multiple of $1, shall be rounded to the next lower multiple of $1.

(Pub. L. 107–372, title II, §245, Dec. 19, 2002, 116 Stat. 3089.)

PRIOR PROVISIONS

Provisions similar to those in this section were contained in section 853*o* of this title prior to repeal by Pub. L. 107–372.

§3046. Retired grade and retired pay

Each officer retired pursuant to law shall be placed on the retired list with the highest grade satisfactorily held by that officer while on active duty including active duty pursuant to recall, under permanent or temporary appointment, and shall receive retired pay based on such highest grade, if—

(1) the officer's performance of duty in such highest grade has been satisfactory, as determined by the Secretary of the department or departments under whose jurisdiction the officer served; and

(2) unless retired for disability, the officer's length of service in such highest grade is no less than that required by the Secretary of officers retiring under permanent appointment in that grade.

(Pub. L. 107–372, title II, §246, Dec. 19, 2002, 116 Stat. 3090.)

PRIOR PROVISIONS

Provisions similar to those in this section were contained in sections 853p and 857–2 of this title prior to repeal by Pub. L. 107–372.

§3047. Retired rank and pay held pursuant to other laws unaffected

Nothing in this subchapter shall prevent an officer from being placed on the retired list with the highest rank and with the highest retired pay to which the officer is entitled under any other provision of law.

(Pub. L. 107–372, title II, §247, Dec. 19, 2002, 116 Stat. 3090.)

PRIOR PROVISIONS

Provisions similar to those in this section were contained in section 853q of this title prior to repeal by Pub. L. 107–372.

§3048. Continuation on active duty; deferral of retirement

The provisions of subchapter IV of chapter 36 of title 10 relating to continuation on active duty and deferral of retirement shall apply to commissioned officers of the Administration.

(Pub. L. 107–372, title II, §248, Dec. 19, 2002, 116 Stat. 3090.)

§3049. Recall to active duty

The provisions of chapter 39 of title 10 relating to recall of retired officers to active duty, including the limitations on such recalls, shall apply to commissioned officers of the Administration.

(Pub. L. 107–372, title II, §249, Dec. 19, 2002, 116 Stat. 3090.)

SUBCHAPTER IV—SERVICE OF OFFICERS WITH THE MILITARY DEPARTMENTS

§3061. Cooperation with and transfer to military departments

(a) Transfers of resources and officers during national emergency

(1) Transfers authorized

The President may, whenever in the judgment of the President a sufficient national emergency exists, transfer to the service and jurisdiction of a military department such vessels, equipment, stations, and officers of the Administration as the President considers to be in the best interest of the country.

(2) Responsibility for funding of transferred resources and officers

After any such transfer all expenses connected therewith shall be defrayed out of the appropriations for the department to which the transfer is made.

(3) Return of transferred resources and officers

Such transferred vessels, equipment, stations, and officers shall be returned to the Administration when the national emergency ceases, in the opinion of the President.

(4) Rule of construction

Nothing in this section shall be construed as transferring the Administration or any of its functions from the Department of Commerce except in time of national emergency and to the extent provided in this section.

(b) Limitation on transfer of officers

This section does not authorize the transfer of an officer of the Administration to a military department if the accession or retention of that officer in that military department is otherwise not authorized by law.

(c) Status of transferred officers

An officer of the Administration transferred under this section, shall, while under the jurisdiction of a military department, have proper military status and shall be subject to the laws, regulations, and orders for the government of the Army, Navy, or Air Force, as the case may be, insofar as the same may be applicable to persons whose retention permanently in the military service of the United States is not contemplated by law.

(Pub. L. 107–372, title II, §251, Dec. 19, 2002, 116 Stat. 3090.)

PRIOR PROVISIONS

Provisions similar to those in this section were contained in section 855 of this title prior to repeal by Pub. L. 107–372.

DELEGATION OF FUNCTIONS

Functions of President under this section delegated to Secretary of Commerce by section 1(k) of Ex. Ord. No. 11023, May 28, 1962, 27 F.R. 5131, as amended, set out as a note under section 301 of Title 3, The President.

§3062. Relative rank of officers when serving with Army, Navy, or Air Force

When serving with the Army, Navy, or Air Force, an officer of the Administration shall rank with and after officers of corresponding grade in the Army, Navy, or Air Force of the same length of service in grade. Nothing in this subchapter shall be construed to affect or alter an officer's rates of pay and allowances when not assigned to military duty.

(Pub. L. 107–372, title II, §252, Dec. 19, 2002, 116 Stat. 3091.)

PRIOR PROVISIONS

Provisions similar to those in this section were contained in section 856 of this title prior to repeal by Pub. L. 107–372.

§3063. Rules and regulations when cooperating with military departments

(a) Joint regulations

The Secretary of Defense and the Secretary of Commerce shall jointly prescribe regulations—

(1) governing the duties to be performed by the Administration in time of war; and

(2) providing for the cooperation of the Administration with the military departments in time of peace in preparation for its duties in time of war.

(b) Approval

Regulations under subsection (a) of this section shall not be effective unless approved by each of those Secretaries.

(c) Communications

Regulations under subsection (a) of this section may provide procedures for making reports and communications between a military department and the Administration.

(Pub. L. 107–372, title II, §253, Dec. 19, 2002, 116 Stat. 3091.)

PRIOR PROVISIONS

Provisions similar to those in this section were contained in section 858 of this title prior to repeal by Pub. L. 107–372.

SUBCHAPTER V—RIGHTS AND BENEFITS

§3071. Applicability of certain provisions of title 10

(a) Provisions made applicable to the corps

The rules of law that apply to the Armed Forces under the following provisions of title 10, as those provisions are in effect from time to time, apply also to the commissioned officer corps of the Administration:

(1) Chapter 40, relating to leave.

(2) Section 533(b), relating to constructive service.

(3) Section 716, relating to transfers between the armed forces and to and from National Oceanic and Atmospheric Administration.

(4) Section 1035, relating to deposits of savings.

(5) Section 1036, relating to transportation and travel allowances for escorts for dependents of members.

(6) Section 1052, relating to reimbursement for adoption expenses.

(7) Section 1174a, relating to special separation benefits (except that benefits under subsection (b)(2)(B) of such section are subject to the availability of appropriations for such purpose and are provided at the discretion of the Secretary of Commerce).

(8) Chapter 61, relating to retirement or separation for physical disability.

(9) Chapter 69, relating to retired grade, except sections 1370, 1375, and 1376.

(10) Chapter 71, relating to computation of retired pay.

(11) Chapter 73, relating to annuities based on retired or retainer pay.

(12) Subchapter II of chapter 75, relating to death benefits.

(13) Section 2634, relating to transportation of motor vehicles for members on permanent change of station.

(14) Sections 2731 and 2735, relating to property loss incident to service.

(15) Section 2771, relating to final settlement of accounts of deceased members.

(16) Such other provisions of subtitle A of that title as may be adopted for applicability to the commissioned officer corps of the National Oceanic and Atmospheric Administration by any other provision of law.

(b) References

The authority vested by title 10 in the "military departments", "the Secretary concerned", or "the Secretary of Defense" with respect to the provisions of law referred to in subsection (a) of this section shall be exercised, with respect to the commissioned officer corps of the Administration, by the Secretary of Commerce or the Secretary's designee.

(Pub. L. 107–372, title II, §261, Dec. 19, 2002, 116 Stat. 3091.)

PRIOR PROVISIONS

Provisions similar to those in this section were contained in section 857a of this title prior to repeal by Pub. L. 107–372.

§3072. Eligibility for veterans benefits and other rights, privileges, immunities, and benefits under certain provisions of law

(a) In general

Active service of officers of the Administration shall be deemed to be active military service for the purposes of all rights, privileges, immunities, and benefits under the following:

(1) Laws administered by the Secretary of Veterans Affairs.

(2) The Servicemembers Civil Relief Act [50 U.S.C. App. 501 et seq.].

(3) Section 410 of title 42, as in effect before September 1, 1950.

(b) Exercise of authority

In the administration of the laws and regulations referred to in subsection (a) of this section, with respect to the Administration, the authority vested in the Secretary of Defense and the Secretaries of the military departments and their respective departments shall be exercised by the Secretary of Commerce.

(Pub. L. 107–372, title II, §262, Dec. 19, 2002, 116 Stat. 3092; Pub. L. 108–189, §2(g), Dec. 19, 2003, 117 Stat. 2866.)

REFERENCES IN TEXT

The Servicemembers Civil Relief Act, referred to in subsec. (a)(2), is act Oct. 17, 1940, ch. 888, 54 Stat. 1178, as amended, which is classified to section 501 et seq. of Title 50, Appendix, War and National Defense. For complete classification of this Act to the Code, see section 501 of Title 50, Appendix, and Tables.

PRIOR PROVISIONS

Provisions similar to those in this section were contained in sections 857 and 857–3(a) of this title prior to repeal by Pub. L. 107–372.

AMENDMENTS

2003—Subsec. (a)(2). Pub. L. 108–189 amended par. (2) generally substituting "The Servicemembers Civil Relief Act" for "The Soldiers' and Sailors' Civil Relief Act of 1940 (50 App. U.S.C. 501 et seq.)".

§3073. Medical and dental care

The Secretary may provide medical and dental care, including care in private facilities, for personnel of the Administration entitled to that care by law or regulation.

(Pub. L. 107–372, title II, §263, Dec. 19, 2002, 116 Stat. 3093.)

PRIOR PROVISIONS

Provisions similar to those in this section were contained in section 857–3(b) of this title prior to repeal by Pub. L. 107–372.

§3074. Commissary privileges

(a) Extension of privilege

Commissioned officers, ships' officers, and members of crews of vessels of the Administration shall be permitted to purchase commissary and quartermaster supplies as far as available from the Armed Forces at the prices charged officers and enlisted members of the Armed Forces.

(b) Sales of rations, stores, uniforms, and related equipment

The Secretary may purchase ration supplies for messes, stores, uniforms, accouterments, and related equipment for sale aboard ship and shore stations of the Administration to members of the uniformed services and to personnel assigned to such ships or shore stations. Sales shall be in accordance with regulations prescribed by the Secretary, and proceeds therefrom shall, as far as is practicable, fully reimburse the appropriations charged without regard to fiscal year.

(c) Surviving spouses' rights

Rights extended to members of the uniformed services in this section are extended to their surviving spouses and to such others as are designated by the Secretary concerned.

(Pub. L. 107–372, title II, §264, Dec. 19, 2002, 116 Stat. 3093.)

PRIOR PROVISIONS

Provisions similar to those in this section were contained in section 857–4 of this title prior to repeal by Pub. L. 107–372.

§3075. Authority to use appropriated funds for transportation and reimbursement of certain items

(a) Transportation of effects of deceased officers

In the case of an officer who dies on active duty, the Secretary may provide, from appropriations made available to the Administration, transportation (including packing, unpacking, crating, and uncrating) of personal and household effects of that officer to the official residence of record of that officer. However, upon application by the dependents of such an officer, such transportation may be provided to such other location as may be determined by the Secretary.

(b) Reimbursement for supplies furnished by officers to distressed and shipwrecked persons

Under regulations prescribed by the Secretary, appropriations made available to the Administration may be used to reimburse an officer for food, clothing, medicines, and other supplies furnished by the officer—

(1) for the temporary relief of distressed persons in remote localities; or

(2) to shipwrecked persons who are temporarily provided for by the officer.

(Pub. L. 107–372, title II, §265, Dec. 19, 2002, 116 Stat. 3093.)

PRIOR PROVISIONS

Provisions similar to those in this section were contained in section 874 of this title prior to repeal by Pub. L. 107–372.

§3076. Presentation of United States flag upon retirement

(a) Presentation of flag upon retirement

Upon the release of a commissioned officer from active commissioned service for retirement, the Secretary shall present a United States flag to the officer.

(b) Multiple presentations not authorized

An officer is not eligible for presentation of a flag under subsection (a) of this section if the officer has previously been presented a flag under this section or any other provision of law providing for the presentation of a United States flag incident to release from active service for retirement.

(c) No cost to recipient

The presentation of a flag under this section shall be at no cost to the recipient.

(Pub. L. 107–372, title II, §266, Dec. 19, 2002, 116 Stat. 3093.)

PRIOR PROVISIONS

Provisions similar to those in this section were contained in section 853v of this title prior to repeal by Pub. L. 107–372.

CHAPTER 44—OCEANS AND HUMAN HEALTH

§3101. Interagency oceans and human health research program

(a) Coordination

The President, through the National Science and Technology Council, shall coordinate and support a national research program to improve understanding of the role of the oceans in human health.

(b) Implementation plan

Within 1 year after December 8, 2004, the National Science and Technology Council, through the Director of the Office of Science and Technology Policy shall develop and submit to the Congress a plan for coordinated Federal activities under the program. Nothing in this subsection is intended to duplicate or supersede the activities of the Inter-Agency Task Force on Harmful Algal Blooms and Hypoxia established under section 603 of the Harmful Algal Bloom and Hypoxia Research and Control Act of 1998 (16 U.S.C. 1451 note). In developing the plan, the Committee will consult with the Inter-Agency Task Force on Harmful Algal Blooms and Hypoxia. Such plan will build on and complement the ongoing activities of the National Oceanic and Atmospheric Administration, the National Science Foundation, and other departments and agencies and shall—

(1) establish, for the 10-year period beginning in the year it is submitted, the goals and priorities for Federal research which most effectively advance scientific understanding of the connections between the oceans and human health, provide usable information for the prediction of marine-related public health problems and use the biological potential of the oceans for development of new treatments of human diseases and a greater understanding of human biology;

(2) describe specific activities required to achieve such goals and priorities, including the funding of competitive research grants, ocean and coastal observations, training and support for scientists, and participation in international research efforts;

(3) identify and address, as appropriate, relevant programs and activities of the Federal agencies and departments that would contribute to the program;

(4) identify alternatives for preventive unnecessary duplication of effort among Federal agencies and departments with respect to the program;

(5) consider and use, as appropriate, reports and studies conducted by Federal agencies and departments, the National Research Council, the Ocean Research Advisory Panel, the Commission on Ocean Policy and other expert scientific bodies;

(6) make recommendations for the coordination of program activities with ocean and human health-related activities of other national and international organizations; and

(7) estimate Federal funding for research activities to be conducted under the program.

(c) Program scope

The program may include the following activities related to the role of oceans in human health:

(1) Interdisciplinary research among the ocean and medical sciences, and coordinated research and activities to improve understanding of processes within the ocean that may affect human health and to explore the potential contribution of marine organisms to medicine and research, including—

(A) vector- and water-borne diseases of humans and marine organisms, including marine mammals and fish;

(B) harmful algal blooms and hypoxia (through the Inter-Agency Task Force on Harmful Algal Blooms and Hypoxia);

(C) marine-derived pharmaceuticals;

(D) marine organisms as models for biomedical research and as indicators of marine environmental health;

(E) marine environmental microbiology;

(F) bioaccumulative and endocrine-disrupting chemical contaminants; and

(G) predictive models based on indicators of marine environmental health or public health threats.

(2) Coordination with the National Ocean Research Leadership Council (10 U.S.C. 7902(a)) to ensure that any integrated ocean and coastal observing system provides information necessary to monitor and reduce marine public health problems including health-related data on biological populations and detection of contaminants in marine waters and seafood.

(3) Development through partnerships among Federal agencies, States, academic institutions, or non-profit research organizations of new technologies and approaches for detecting and reducing hazards to human health from ocean sources and to strengthen understanding of the value of marine biodiversity to biomedicine, including—

(A) genomics and proteomics to develop genetic and immunological detection approaches and predictive tools and to discover new biomedical resources;

(B) biomaterials and bioengineering;

(C) in situ and remote sensors used to detect, quantify, and predict the presence and spread of contaminants in marine waters and organisms and to identify new genetic resources for biomedical purposes;

(D) techniques for supplying marine resources, including chemical synthesis, culturing and aquaculturing marine organisms, new fermentation methods and recombinant techniques; and

(E) adaptation of equipment and technologies from human health fields.

(4) Support for scholars, trainees and education opportunities that encourage an interdisciplinary and international approach to exploring the diversity of life in the oceans.

(d) Annual report

Beginning with the first year occurring more than 24 months after December 8, 2004, the National Science and Technology Council, through the Director of the Office of Science and Technology Policy shall prepare and submit to the President and the Congress not later than January 31st of each year an annual report on the activities conducted pursuant to this title during the preceding fiscal year, including—

(1) a summary of the achievements of Federal oceans and human health research, including Federally supported external research, during the preceding fiscal year;

(2) an analysis of the progress made toward achieving the goals and objectives of the plan developed under subsection (b), including identification of trends and emerging trends;

(3) a copy or summary of the plan and any changes made in the plan;

(4) a summary of agency budgets for oceans and human health activities for that preceding fiscal year; and

(5) any recommendations regarding additional action or legislation that may be required to assist in achieving the purposes of this chapter.

(Pub. L. 108–447, div. B, title IX, §902, Dec. 8, 2004, 118 Stat. 2930.)

REFERENCES IN TEXT

Section 603 of the Harmful Algal Bloom and Hypoxia Research and Control Act of 1998, referred to in subsec. (b), is section 603 of Pub. L. 105–383, which is set out in a note under section 1451 of Title 16, Conservation.

SHORT TITLE

Pub. L. 108–447, div. B, title IX, §901, Dec. 8, 2004, 118 Stat. 2930, provided that: "This title [enacting this chapter] may be cited as the 'Oceans and Human Health Act'."

§3102. National Oceanic and Atmospheric Administration Oceans and Human Health Initiative

(a) Establishment

As part of the interagency oceans and human health research program, the Secretary of Commerce is authorized to establish an Oceans and Human Health Initiative to coordinate and implement research and activities of the National Oceanic and Atmospheric Administration related to the role of the oceans, the coasts, and the Great Lakes in human health. In carrying out this section, the Secretary shall consult with other Federal agencies conducting integrated oceans and human health research and research in related areas, including the National Science Foundation. The Oceans and Human Health Initiative is authorized to provide support for—

(1) centralized program and research coordination;

(2) an advisory panel;

(3) one or more National Oceanic and Atmospheric Administration national centers of excellence;

(4) research grants; and

(5) distinguished scholars and traineeships.

(b) Advisory panel

The Secretary is authorized to establish an oceans and human health advisory panel to assist in the development and implementation of the Oceans and Human Health Initiative. Membership of the advisory group shall provide for balanced representation of individuals with multi-disciplinary expertise in the marine and biomedical sciences. The Federal Advisory Committee Act (5 U.S.C. App.) shall not apply to the oceans and human health advisory panel.

(c) National centers

(1) The Secretary is authorized to identify and provide financial support through a competitive process to develop, within the National Oceanic and Atmospheric Administration, for one or more centers of excellence that strengthen the capabilities of the National Oceanic and Atmospheric Administration to carry out its programs and activities related to the oceans' role in human health.

(2) The centers shall focus on areas related to agency missions, including use of marine organisms as indicators for marine environmental health, ocean pollutants, marine toxins and pathogens, harmful algal blooms, hypoxia, seafood testing, identification of potential marine products, and biology and pathobiology of marine mammals, and on disciplines including marine genomics, marine environmental microbiology, ecological chemistry and conservation medicine.

(3) In selecting centers for funding, the Secretary will give priority to proposals with strong interdisciplinary scientific merit that encourage educational opportunities and provide for effective partnerships among the Administration, other Federal entities, State, academic, non-profit research organizations, medical, and industry participants.

(d) Extramural research grants

(1) The Secretary is authorized to provide grants of financial assistance to the scientific community for critical research and projects that explore the relationship between the oceans and human health and that complement or strengthen programs and activities of the National Oceanic and Atmospheric Administration related to the ocean's[1] role in human health. Officers and employees of Federal agencies may

[1] So in original. Probably should be "oceans'".

collaborate with, and participate in, such research and projects to the extent requested by the grant recipient. The Secretary shall consult with the oceans and human health advisory panel established under subsection (b) and may work cooperatively with other agencies participating in the interagency program to establish joint criteria for such research and projects.

(2) Grants under this subsection shall be awarded through a competitive peer-reviewed, merit-based process that may be conducted jointly with other agencies participating in the interagency program.

(e) Traineeships

The Secretary of Commerce is authorized to establish a program to provide traineeships, training, and experience to pre-doctoral and post-doctoral students and to scientists at the beginning of their careers who are interested in the oceans in human health research conducted under the NOAA initiative.

(Pub. L. 108–447, div. B, title IX, § 903, Dec. 8, 2004, 118 Stat. 2933.)

REFERENCES IN TEXT

The Federal Advisory Committee Act, referred to in subsec. (b), is Pub. L. 92–463, Oct. 6, 1972, 86 Stat. 770, as amended, which is set out in the Appendix to Title 5, Government Organization and Employees.

§ 3103. Public information and outreach

(a) In general

The Secretary of Commerce, in consultation with other Federal agencies, and in cooperation with the National Sea Grant program, shall design and implement a program to disseminate information developed under the NOAA Oceans and Human Health Initiative, including research, assessments, and findings regarding the relationship between oceans and human health, on both a regional and national scale. The information, particularly with respect to potential health risks, shall be made available in a timely manner to appropriate Federal or State agencies, involved industries, and other interested persons through a variety of means, including through the Internet.

(b) Report

As part of this program, the Secretary shall submit to Congress an annual report reviewing the results of the research, assessments, and findings developed under the NOAA Oceans and Human Health Initiative, as well as recommendations for improving or expanding the program.

(Pub. L. 108–447, div. B, title IX, § 904, Dec. 8, 2004, 118 Stat. 2934.)

§ 3104. Authorization of appropriations

There are authorized to be appropriated to the Secretary of Commerce to carry out the National Oceanic and Atmospheric Administration Oceans and Human Health Initiative, $60,000,000 for fiscal years 2005 through 2008. Not less than 50 percent of the amounts appropriated to carry out the initiative shall be utilized in each fiscal year to support the extramural grant and traineeship programs of the Initiative.

(Pub. L. 108–447, div. B, title IX, § 905, Dec. 8, 2004, 118 Stat. 2934.)

CHAPTER 45—TSUNAMI WARNING AND EDUCATION

§ 3201. Definitions

In this chapter:

(1) The term "Administration" means the National Oceanic and Atmospheric Administration.

(2) The term "Administrator" means the Administrator of the National Oceanic and Atmospheric Administration.

(Pub. L. 109–424, § 2, Dec. 20, 2006, 120 Stat. 2902; Pub. L. 109–479, title VIII, § 802, Jan. 12, 2007, 120 Stat. 3653.)

CODIFICATION

Pub. L. 109–424 and title VIII of Pub. L. 109–479 enacted substantially identical sections. This section is based on the text of section 802 of Pub. L. 109–479.

SHORT TITLE

Pub. L. 109–479, title VIII, § 801, Jan. 12, 2007, 120 Stat. 3653, provided that: "This title [enacting this chapter] may be cited as the 'Tsunami Warning and Education Act'."

Pub. L. 109–424, § 1, Dec. 20, 2006, 120 Stat. 2902, provided that: "This Act [enacting this chapter] may be cited as the 'Tsunami Warning and Education Act'."

§ 3202. Purposes

The purposes of this chapter are—

(1) to improve tsunami detection, forecasting, warnings, notification, outreach, and mitigation to protect life and property in the United States;

(2) to enhance and modernize the existing Pacific Tsunami Warning System to increase coverage, reduce false alarms, and increase the accuracy of forecasts and warnings, and to expand detection and warning systems to include other vulnerable States and United States territories, including the Atlantic Ocean, Caribbean Sea, and Gulf of Mexico areas;

(3) to improve mapping, modeling, research, and assessment efforts to improve tsunami detection, forecasting, warnings, notification, outreach, mitigation, response, and recovery;

(4) to improve and increase education and outreach activities and ensure that those receiving tsunami warnings and the at-risk public know what to do when a tsunami is approaching;

(5) to provide technical and other assistance to speed international efforts to establish regional tsunami warning systems in vulnerable areas worldwide, including the Indian Ocean; and

(6) to improve Federal, State, and international coordination for detection, warnings,

and outreach for tsunami and other coastal impacts.

(Pub. L. 109–424, §3, Dec. 20, 2006, 120 Stat. 2902; Pub. L. 109–479, title VIII, §803, Jan. 12, 2007, 120 Stat. 3653.)

CODIFICATION

Pub. L. 109–424 and title VIII of Pub. L. 109–479 enacted substantially identical sections. This section is based on the text of section 803 of Pub. L. 109–479.

§3203. Tsunami forecasting and warning program

(a) In general

The Administrator, through the National Weather Service and in consultation with other relevant Administration offices, shall operate a program to provide tsunami detection, forecasting, and warnings for the Pacific and Arctic Ocean regions and for the Atlantic Ocean, Caribbean Sea, and Gulf of Mexico region.

(b) Components

The program under this section shall—

(1) include the tsunami warning centers established under subsection (d);

(2) utilize and maintain an array of robust tsunami detection technologies;

(3) maintain detection equipment in operational condition to fulfill the detection, forecasting, and warning requirements of this chapter;

(4) provide tsunami forecasting capability based on models and measurements, including tsunami inundation models and maps for use in increasing the preparedness of communities, including through the TsunamiReady program;

(5) maintain data quality and management systems to support the requirements of the program;

(6) include a cooperative effort among the Administration, the United States Geological Survey, and the National Science Foundation under which the Geological Survey and the National Science Foundation shall provide rapid and reliable seismic information to the Administration from international and domestic seismic networks;

(7) provide a capability for the dissemination of warnings to at-risk States and tsunami communities through rapid and reliable notification to government officials and the public, including utilization of and coordination with existing Federal warning systems, including the National Oceanic and Atmospheric Administration Weather Radio All Hazards Program;

(8) allow, as practicable, for integration of tsunami detection technologies with other environmental observing technologies; and

(9) include any technology the Administrator considers appropriate to fulfill the objectives of the program under this section.

(c) System areas

The program under this section shall operate—

(1) a Pacific tsunami warning system capable of forecasting tsunami anywhere in the Pacific and Arctic Ocean regions and providing adequate warnings; and

(2) an Atlantic Ocean, Caribbean Sea, and Gulf of Mexico tsunami warning system capable of forecasting tsunami and providing adequate warnings in areas of the Atlantic Ocean, Caribbean Sea, and Gulf of Mexico that are determined—

(A) to be geologically active, or to have significant potential for geological activity; and

(B) to pose significant risks of tsunami for States along the coastal areas of the Atlantic Ocean, Caribbean Sea, or Gulf of Mexico.

(d) Tsunami warning centers

(1) In general

The Administrator, through the National Weather Service, shall maintain or establish—

(A) a Pacific Tsunami Warning Center in Hawaii;

(B) a West Coast and Alaska Tsunami Warning Center in Alaska; and

(C) any additional forecast and warning centers determined by the National Weather Service to be necessary.

(2) Responsibilities

The responsibilities of each tsunami warning center shall include—

(A) continuously monitoring data from seismological, deep ocean, and tidal monitoring stations;

(B) evaluating earthquakes that have the potential to generate tsunami;

(C) evaluating deep ocean buoy data and tidal monitoring stations for indications of tsunami resulting from earthquakes and other sources;

(D) disseminating forecasts and tsunami warning bulletins to Federal, State, and local government officials and the public;

(E) coordinating with the tsunami hazard mitigation program described in section 3204 of this title to ensure ongoing sharing of information between forecasters and emergency management officials; and

(F) making data gathered under this chapter and post-warning analyses conducted by the National Weather Service or other relevant Administration offices available to researchers.

(e) Transfer of technology; maintenance and upgrades

(1) In general

In carrying out this section, the National Weather Service, in consultation with other relevant Administration offices, shall—

(A) develop requirements for the equipment used to forecast tsunami, which shall include provisions for multipurpose detection platforms, reliability and performance metrics, and to the maximum extent practicable how the equipment will be integrated with other United States and global ocean and coastal observation systems, the global earth observing system of systems, global seismic networks, and the Advanced National Seismic System;

(B) develop and execute a plan for the transfer of technology from ongoing research described in section 3205 of this title into the program under this section; and

(C) ensure that maintaining operational tsunami detection equipment is the highest priority within the program carried out under this chapter.

(2) Report to Congress

(A) Not later than 1 year after January 12, 2007, the National Weather Service, in consultation with other relevant Administration offices, shall transmit to Congress a report on how the tsunami forecast system under this section will be integrated with other United States and global ocean and coastal observation systems, the global earth observing system of systems, global seismic networks, and the Advanced National Seismic System.

(B) Not later than 3 years after January 12, 2007, the National Weather Service, in consultation with other relevant Administration offices, shall transmit a report to Congress on how technology developed under section 3205 of this title is being transferred into the program under this section.

(f) Federal cooperation

When deploying and maintaining tsunami detection technologies, the Administrator shall seek the assistance and assets of other appropriate Federal agencies.

(g) Annual equipment certification

At the same time Congress receives the budget justification documents in support of the President's annual budget request for each fiscal year, the Administrator shall transmit to the Committee on Commerce, Science, and Transportation of the Senate and the Committee on Science of the House of Representatives a certification that—

(1) identifies the tsunami detection equipment deployed pursuant to this chapter, as of December 31 of the preceding calendar year;

(2) certifies which equipment is operational as of December 31 of the preceding calendar year;

(3) in the case of any piece of such equipment that is not operational as of such date, identifies that equipment and describes the mitigation strategy that is in place—

(A) to repair or replace that piece of equipment within a reasonable period of time; or

(B) to otherwise ensure adequate tsunami detection coverage;

(4) identifies any equipment that is being developed or constructed to carry out this chapter but which has not yet been deployed, if the Administration has entered into a contract for that equipment prior to December 31 of the preceding calendar year, and provides a schedule for the deployment of that equipment; and

(5) certifies that the Administrator expects the equipment described in paragraph (4) to meet the requirements, cost, and schedule provided in that contract.

(h) Congressional notifications

The Administrator shall notify the Committee on Commerce, Science, and Transportation of the Senate and the Committee on Science of the House of Representatives within 30 days of—

(1) impaired regional forecasting capabilities due to equipment or system failures; and

(2) significant contractor failures or delays in completing work associated with the tsunami forecasting and warning system.

(i) Report

Not later than January 31, 2010, the Comptroller General of the United States shall transmit a report to the Committee on Commerce, Science, and Transportation of the Senate and the Committee on Science of the House of Representatives that—

(1) evaluates the current status of the tsunami detection, forecasting, and warning system and the tsunami hazard mitigation program established under this chapter, including progress toward tsunami inundation mapping of all coastal areas vulnerable to tsunami and whether there has been any degradation of services as a result of the expansion of the program;

(2) evaluates the National Weather Service's ability to achieve continued improvements in the delivery of tsunami detection, forecasting, and warning services by assessing policies and plans for the evolution of modernization systems, models, and computational abilities (including the adoption of new technologies); and

(3) lists the contributions of funding or other resources to the program by other Federal agencies, particularly agencies participating in the program.

(j) External review

The Administrator shall enter into an arrangement with the National Academy of Sciences to review the tsunami detection, forecast, and warning program established under this chapter to assess further modernization and coverage needs, as well as long-term operational reliability issues, taking into account measures implemented under this chapter. The review shall also include an assessment of how well the forecast equipment has been integrated into other United States and global ocean and coastal observation systems and the global earth observing system of systems. Not later than 2 years after January 12, 2007, the Administrator shall transmit a report containing the National Academy of Sciences' recommendations, the Administrator's responses to the recommendations, including those where the Administrator disagrees with the Academy, a timetable to implement the accepted recommendations, and the cost of implementing all the Academy's recommendations, to the Committee on Commerce, Science, and Transportation of the Senate and the Committee on Science of the House of Representatives.

(k) Report

Not later than 3 months after January 12, 2007, the Administrator shall establish a process for monitoring and certifying contractor performance in carrying out the requirements of any contract to construct or deploy tsunami detection equipment, including procedures and penalties to be imposed in cases of significant contractor failure or negligence.

(Pub. L. 109–424, §4, Dec. 20, 2006, 120 Stat. 2903; Pub. L. 109–479, title VIII, §804, Jan. 12, 2007, 120 Stat. 3654.)

CODIFICATION

Pub. L. 109–424 and title VIII of Pub. L. 109–479 enacted substantially identical sections. This section is based on the text of section 804 of Pub. L. 109–479.

CHANGE OF NAME

Committee on Science of House of Representatives changed to Committee on Science and Technology of House of Representatives by House Resolution No. 6, One Hundred Tenth Congress, Jan. 5, 2007.

§3204. National tsunami hazard mitigation program

(a) In general

The Administrator, through the National Weather Service and in consultation with other relevant Administration offices, shall conduct a community-based tsunami hazard mitigation program to improve tsunami preparedness of at-risk areas in the United States and its territories.

(b) Coordinating committee

In conducting the program under this section, the Administrator shall establish a coordinating committee comprising representatives of Federal, State, local, and tribal government officials. The Administrator may establish subcommittees to address region-specific issues. The committee shall—

(1) recommend how funds appropriated for carrying out the program under this section will be allocated;

(2) ensure that areas described in section 3203(c) of this title in the United States and its territories can have the opportunity to participate in the program;

(3) provide recommendations to the National Weather Service on how to improve the TsunamiReady program, particularly on ways to make communities more tsunami resilient through the use of inundation maps and other mitigation practices; and

(4) ensure that all components of the program are integrated with ongoing hazard warning and risk management activities, emergency response plans, and mitigation programs in affected areas, including integrating information to assist in tsunami evacuation route planning.

(c) Program components

The program under this section shall—

(1) use inundation models that meet a standard of accuracy defined by the Administration to improve the quality and extent of inundation mapping, including assessment of vulnerable inner coastal and nearshore areas, in a coordinated and standardized fashion to maximize resources and the utility of data collected;

(2) promote and improve community outreach and education networks and programs to ensure community readiness, including the development of comprehensive coastal risk and vulnerability assessment training and decision support tools, implementation of technical training and public education programs, and providing for certification of prepared communities;

(3) integrate tsunami preparedness and mitigation programs into ongoing hazard warning and risk management activities, emergency response plans, and mitigation programs in affected areas, including integrating information to assist in tsunami evacuation route planning;

(4) promote the adoption of tsunami warning and mitigation measures by Federal, State, tribal, and local governments and nongovernmental entities, including educational programs to discourage development in high-risk areas; and

(5) provide for periodic external review of the program.

(d) Savings clause

Nothing in this section shall be construed to require a change in the chair of any existing tsunami hazard mitigation program subcommittee.

(Pub. L. 109–424, §5, Dec. 20, 2006, 120 Stat. 2906; Pub. L. 109–479, title VIII, §805, Jan. 12, 2007, 120 Stat. 3657.)

CODIFICATION

Pub. L. 109–424 and title VIII of Pub. L. 109–479 enacted substantially identical sections. This section is based on the text of section 805 of Pub. L. 109–479.

§3205. Tsunami research program

The Administrator shall, in consultation with other agencies and academic institutions, and with the coordinating committee established under section 3204(b) of this title, establish or maintain a tsunami research program to develop detection, forecast, communication, and mitigation science and technology, including advanced sensing techniques, information and communication technology, data collection, analysis, and assessment for tsunami tracking and numerical forecast modeling. Such research program shall—

(1) consider other appropriate research to mitigate the impact of tsunami;

(2) coordinate with the National Weather Service on technology to be transferred to operations;

(3) include social science research to develop and assess community warning, education, and evacuation materials; and

(4) ensure that research and findings are available to the scientific community.

(Pub. L. 109–424, §6, Dec. 20, 2006, 120 Stat. 2907; Pub. L. 109–479, title VIII, §806, Jan. 12, 2007, 120 Stat. 3658.)

CODIFICATION

Pub. L. 109–424 and title VIII of Pub. L. 109–479 enacted substantially identical sections. This section is based on the text of section 806 of Pub. L. 109–479.

§3206. Global tsunami warning and mitigation network

(a) International Tsunami Warning System

The Administrator, through the National Weather Service and in consultation with other relevant Administration offices, in coordination with other members of the United States Interagency Committee of the National Tsunami Hazard Mitigation Program, shall provide technical assistance and training to the Intergovernmental Oceanographic Commission, the World Meteorological Organization, and other international entities, as part of international efforts to develop a fully functional global tsunami forecast and warning system comprising regional tsunami warning networks, modeled on the International Tsunami Warning System of the Pacific.

(b) International Tsunami Information Center

The Administrator, through the National Weather Service and in consultation with other relevant Administration offices, in cooperation with the Intergovernmental Oceanographic Commission, shall operate an International Tsunami Information Center to improve tsunami preparedness for all Pacific Ocean nations participating in the International Tsunami Warning System of the Pacific, and may also provide such assistance to other nations participating in a global tsunami warning system established through the Intergovernmental Oceanographic Commission. As part of its responsibilities around the world, the Center shall—

(1) monitor international tsunami warning activities around the world;

(2) assist member states in establishing national warning systems, and make information available on current technologies for tsunami warning systems;

(3) maintain a library of materials to promulgate knowledge about tsunami in general and for use by the scientific community; and

(4) disseminate information, including educational materials and research reports.

(c) Detection equipment; technical advice and training

In carrying out this section, the National Weather Service—

(1) shall give priority to assisting nations in identifying vulnerable coastal areas, creating inundation maps, obtaining or designing real-time detection and reporting equipment, and establishing communication and warning networks and contact points in each vulnerable nation;

(2) may establish a process for transfer of detection and communication technology to affected nations for the purposes of establishing the international tsunami warning system; and

(3) shall provide technical and other assistance to support international tsunami programs.

(d) Data-sharing requirement

The National Weather Service, when deciding to provide assistance under this section, may take into consideration the data sharing policies and practices of nations proposed to receive such assistance, with a goal to encourage all nations to support full and open exchange of data.

(Pub. L. 109–424, §7, Dec. 20, 2006, 120 Stat. 2907; Pub. L. 109–479, title VIII, §807, Jan. 12, 2007, 120 Stat. 3659.)

CODIFICATION

Pub. L. 109–424 and title VIII of Pub. L. 109–479 enacted substantially identical sections. This section is based on the text of section 807 of Pub. L. 109–479.

§ 3207. Authorization of appropriations

There are authorized to be appropriated to the Administrator to carry out this chapter—

(1) $25,000,000 for fiscal year 2008, of which—

(A) not less than 27 percent of the amount appropriated shall be for the tsunami hazard mitigation program under section 3204 of this title; and

(B) not less than 8 percent of the amount appropriated shall be for the tsunami research program under section 3205 of this title;

(2) $26,000,000 for fiscal year 2009, of which—

(A) not less than 27 percent of the amount appropriated shall be for the tsunami hazard mitigation program under section 3204 of this title; and

(B) not less than 8 percent of the amount appropriated shall be for the tsunami research program under section 3205 of this title;

(3) $27,000,000 for fiscal year 2010, of which—

(A) not less than 27 percent of the amount appropriated shall be for the tsunami hazard mitigation program under section 3204 of this title; and

(B) not less than 8 percent of the amount appropriated shall be for the tsunami research program under section 3205 of this title;

(4) $28,000,000 for fiscal year 2011, of which—

(A) not less than 27 percent of the amount appropriated shall be for the tsunami hazard mitigation program under section 3204 of this title; and

(B) not less than 8 percent of the amount appropriated shall be for the tsunami research program under section 3205 of this title; and

(5) $29,000,000 for fiscal year 2012, of which—

(A) not less than 27 percent of the amount appropriated shall be for the tsunami hazard mitigation program under section 3204 of this title; and

(B) not less than 8 percent of the amount appropriated shall be for the tsunami research program under section 3205 of this title.

(Pub. L. 109–424, §8, Dec. 20, 2006, 120 Stat. 2908; Pub. L. 109–479, title VIII, §808, Jan. 12, 2007, 120 Stat. 3660.)

CODIFICATION

Pub. L. 109–424 and title VIII of Pub. L. 109–479 enacted substantially identical sections. This section is based on the text of section 808 of Pub. L. 109–479.

CHAPTER 46—NATIONAL LEVEE SAFETY PROGRAM

§ 3301. Definitions

In this chapter, the following definitions apply:

(1) Committee

The term "committee" means the Committee on Levee Safety established by section 3302(a) of this title.

(2) Inspection

The term "inspection" means an actual inspection of a levee—

(A) to establish the global information system location of the levee;

(B) to determine the general condition of the levee; and

(C) to estimate the number of structures and population at risk and protected by the levee that would be adversely impacted if the levee fails or water levels exceed the height of the levee.

(3) Levee

(A) In general

The term "levee" means an embankment, including floodwalls—

(i) the primary purpose of which is to provide hurricane, storm, and flood protection relating to seasonal high water, storm surges, precipitation, and other weather events; and

(ii) that normally is subject to water loading for only a few days or weeks during a year.

(B) Inclusion

The term includes structures along canals that constrain water flows and are subject to more frequent water loadings but that do not constitute a barrier across a watercourse.

(4) State

The term "State" means—

(A) a State;

(B) the District of Columbia;

(C) the Commonwealth of Puerto Rico; and

(D) any other territory or possession of the United States.

(5) State levee safety agency

The term "State levee safety agency" means the agency of a State that has regulatory authority over the safety of any non-Federal levee in the State.

(6) United States

The term "United States", when used in a geographical sense, means all of the States.

(Pub. L. 110–114, title IX, §9002, Nov. 8, 2007, 121 Stat. 1288.)

SHORT TITLE

Pub. L. 110–114, title IX, §9001, Nov. 8, 2007, 121 Stat. 1288, provided that: "This title [enacting this chapter] may be cited as the 'National Levee Safety Act of 2007'."

§3302. Committee on Levee Safety

(a) Establishment

There is established a committee to be known as the "Committee on Levee Safety".

(b) Membership

The committee shall be composed of 16 members as follows:

(1) The Secretary (or the Secretary's designee), who shall serve as the chairperson of the Committee.[1]

(2) The Administrator of the Federal Emergency Management Agency (or the Administrator's designee).

(3) The following 14 members appointed by the Secretary:

(A) Eight representatives of State levee safety agencies, one from each of the eight civil works divisions of the Corps of Engineers.

(B) Two representatives of the private sector who have expertise in levee safety.

(C) Two representatives of local and regional governmental agencies who have expertise in levee safety.

(D) Two representatives of Indian tribes who have expertise in levee safety.

(c) Duties

(1) Development of recommendations for national levee safety program

The committee shall develop recomendations[2] for a national levee safety program, including a strategic plan for implementation of the program.

(2) Report

Not later than 180 days after November 8, 2007, the committee shall submit to the Secretary, the Committee on Transportation and Infrastructure of the House of Representatives, and the Committee on Environment and Public Works of the Senate a report containing the recommendations developed under paragraph (1).

(d) Purposes

In developing recommendations under subsection (c)(1), the committee shall ensure that the national levee safety program meets the following goals:

(1) Ensuring the protection of human life and property by levees through the development of technologically, economically, socially, and environmentally feasible programs and procedures for hazard reduction and mitigation relating to levees.

(2) Encouraging use of the best available engineering policies and procedures for levee site investigation, design, construction, operation and maintenance, and emergency preparedness.

(3) Encouraging the establishment and implementation of an effective national levee safety program that may be delegated to qualified States for implementation, including identification of incentives and disincentives for State levee safety programs.

(4) Ensuring that levees are operated and maintained in accordance with appropriate and protective standards by conducting an inventory and inspection of levees.

(5) Developing and supporting public education and awareness projects to increase public acceptance and support of State and national levee safety programs.

(6) Building public awareness of the residual risks associated with living in levee protected areas.

---

[1] So in original. Probably should not be capitalized.

[2] So in original.

(7) Developing technical assistance materials for State and national levee safety programs.

(8) Developing methods to provide technical assistance relating to levee safety to non-Federal entities.

(9) Developing technical assistance materials, seminars, and guidelines relating to the physical integrity of levees in the United States.

(e) Compensation of members

A member of the committee shall serve without compensation.

(f) Travel expenses

Subject to the availability of appropriations, the Secretary shall reimburse a member of the committee for travel expenses, including per diem in lieu of subsistence, at rates authorized for an employee of a Federal agency under subchapter I of chapter 57 of title 5, while away from the home or regular place of business of the member in performance of services for the committee.

(g) Applicability of Federal Advisory Committee Act

The Federal Advisory Committee Act (5 U.S.C. App.) shall not apply to the committee.

(Pub. L. 110–114, title IX, § 9003, Nov. 8, 2007, 121 Stat. 1288; Pub. L. 110–274, § 1, July 15, 2008, 122 Stat. 2493.)

REFERENCES IN TEXT

The Federal Advisory Committee Act, referred to in subsec. (g), is Pub. L. 92–463, Oct. 6, 1972, 86 Stat. 770, which is set out in the Appendix to Title 5, Government Organization and Employees.

AMENDMENTS

2008—Subsec. (f). Pub. L. 110–274 substituted "Subject to the availability of appropriations," for "To the extent amounts are made available in advance in appropriations Acts,".

"SECRETARY" DEFINED

Secretary means the Secretary of the Army, see section 2 of Pub. L. 110–114, set out as a note under section 2201 of this title.

§ 3303. Inventory and inspection of levees

(a) Levee database

(1) In general

Not later than one year after November 8, 2007, the Secretary shall establish and maintain a database with an inventory of the Nation's levees.

(2) Contents

The database shall include—

(A) location information of all Federal levees in the Nation (including global information system information) and, for non-Federal levees, such information on levee location as is provided to the Secretary by State and local governmental agencies;

(B) utilizing such information as is available, the general condition of each levee; and

(C) an estimate of the number of structures and population at risk and protected by each levee that would be adversely impacted if the levee fails or water levels exceed the height of the levee.

(3) Availability of information

(A) Availability to Federal, State, and local governmental agencies

The Secretary shall make all of the information in the database available to appropriate Federal, State, and local governmental agencies.

(B) Availability to the public

The Secretary shall make the information in the database described in paragraph (2)(A), and such other information in the database as the Secretary determines appropriate, available to the public.

(b) Inventory and inspection of levees

(1) Federal levees

The Secretary, at Federal expense, shall establish an inventory and conduct an inspection of all federally owned and operated levees.

(2) Federally constructed, nonfederally operated and maintained levees

The Secretary shall establish an inventory and conduct an inspection of all federally constructed, non-federally operated and maintained levees, at the original cost share for the project.

(3) Participating levees

For non-Federal levees the owners of which are participating in the emergency response to natural disasters program established under section 701n of this title, the Secretary shall establish an inventory and conduct an inspection of each such levee if the owner of the levee requests such inspection. The Federal share of the cost of an inspection under this paragraph shall be 65 percent.

(Pub. L. 110–114, title IX, § 9004, Nov. 8, 2007, 121 Stat. 1290.)

"SECRETARY" DEFINED

Secretary means the Secretary of the Army, see section 2 of Pub. L. 110–114, set out as a note under section 2201 of this title.

§ 3304. Limitations on statutory construction

Nothing in this chapter shall be construed as—

(1) creating any liability of the United States or its officers or employees for the recovery of damages caused by an action or failure to act; or

(2) relieving an owner or operator of a levee of a legal duty, obligation, or liability incident to the ownership or operation of a levee.

(Pub. L. 110–114, title IX, § 9005, Nov. 8, 2007, 121 Stat. 1290.)

§ 3305. Authorization of appropriations

There is authorized to be appropriated to the Secretary to carry out this chapter $20,000,000 for each of fiscal years 2008 through 2013.

(Pub. L. 110–114, title IX, § 9006, Nov. 8, 2007, 121 Stat. 1291.)

"SECRETARY" DEFINED

Secretary means the Secretary of the Army, see section 2 of Pub. L. 110–114, set out as a note under section 2201 of this title.

Made in the USA
Monee, IL
05 November 2026

67858279R00402